Contents

The MILEPOST®
All-The-North Travel Guide®

© Robin Brandt

© Ernest Manewal

Introduction

How to Use *The MILEPOST*® 5
Key to Highways Map 4
Welcome to the North Country 6
Travel Planning—Accommodations, Air Travel, Bus Lines, Calendar of Events, Camping, Cell Phones, Crossing the Border, Cruise Ships, Driving North, Ferry Travel, GPS, Hostels, Hunting & Fishing, Pets, Railroads, Rental Vehicles, Shipping, Tours, When to Go 10
Plan-A-Trip Map & Mileage Chart ... Pull-out

Major Attractions

Anchorage	317
Dawson City	266
Denali National Park and Preserve	399
Fairbanks	418
Glacier Bay National Park	686
Kenai Peninsula	504, 550
Kodiak Island	644
Prince William Sound	626
Southeastern Alaska/Inside Passage	651
Whitehorse	151
Wrangell-St. Elias National Park	475

Special Features

Cruising to Alaska this Summer	16
Denali Park's "Front Country"	389
Ice Roads of Northwest Territories	19
Paddling the Yukon River	164
Tracks through the Wilderness	29
Yukon's Interpretive Centres	129

Marine Access Routes

Ferry Travel	21
Alaska State Ferry Schedules	749
BC Ferries Schedules	25
Cruise Lines	16

Railroads

Alaska Railroad	28
White Pass & Yukon Route	29

Inside Passage

Haines	688	Prince of Wales Island	659
Juneau	676	Sitka	673
Ketchikan	652	Skagway	695
Petersburg	669	Wrangell	666

Major Highways

Alaska Highway	Dawson Creek, BC, to Delta Junction, AK	92
Alaska Highway via East Access Route	Great Falls, MT, to Dawson Creek, BC	33
Alaska Highway via West Access Route	Seattle, WA, to Dawson Creek, BC	61
Campbell Highway	Watson Lake to Carmacks, YT	715
Canol Road	Alaska Highway, YT, to NWT Border	720
Cassiar Highway	Yellowhead Highway, BC, to Alaska Highway, YT	238
Dalton Highway	Elliott Highway to Deadhorse, AK	493
Dempster Highway	Klondike Highway, YT, to Inuvik, NWT	724
Denali Highway	Paxson to Cantwell, AK	477
Edgerton Highway/McCarthy Road	Richardson Highway to McCarthy, AK	470
Elliott Highway	Fox to Manley Hot Springs, AK	488
Glenn Highway/Tok Cutoff	Tok to Anchorage, AK	284
Haines Highway	Haines, AK, to Haines Junction, YT	702
Klondike Loop	Whitehorse, YT, to Taylor Highway, AK	253
Liard Highway	Alaska Highway, BC, to Mackenzie Highway, NWT	732
Mackenzie Route	Valleyview, AB, to Yellowknife, NWT	736
Parks Highway	Anchorage to Fairbanks, AK	357
Richardson Highway	Valdez to Fairbanks, AK	452
Seward Highway	Anchorage to Seward, AK	504
South Klondike Highway	Skagway, AK, to Alaska Highway, YT	706
Steese Highway	Fairbanks to Circle, AK	482
Sterling Highway	Seward Highway to Homer, AK	550
Taylor Highway	Tetlin Junction to Eagle, AK	276
Yellowhead Highway 16	Edmonton, AB, to Prince Rupert, BC	206

Other Routes

Alyeska Highway	511	Kalifornsky Beach Road	590
Atlin Road	711	Kenai Spur Highway	582
Bighorn Route	213	Knik Road	366
Canadian Badlands	41	Lake Louise Road	297
Chena Hot Springs Road	446	Nabesna Road	288
Chilcotin Highway	73	Old Glenn Highway	308
Copper Center Loop	458	Petersville Road	383
Copper River Highway	642	Silver Trail	261
Devon Bypass	43	Stewart-Hyder Road	242
Exit Glacier Road	528	Tagish Road	714
Hatcher Pass Road	305	Talkeetna Spur Road	375
Historic Athabasca Route	48	Telegraph Creek Road	248
Hope Highway	521	Top of the World Hwy.	274
Hudson's Hope Loop	90	Whittier/Portage Road	517

www.themilepost.com — 2003 ■ The MILEPOST® ■ 1

The MILEPOST®

PUBLISHER
William S. Morris III

Editor, Kris Valencia Graef
Art Director/Production Mgr., David L. Ranta
Production Coordinator, Sheryl Granger
Production Asst., Katie Marshall
Asst. Art Director, Mishelle Kennedy
Associate Editor, Carol A. Phillips
Editorial Asst., Leah Burke
Page Design, Pam Smith
Field Editors and Advertising Representatives, Earl L. Brown, Blake Hanna, Marion Nelson, Lynn Owen, Nyla Simmons, Fatima Mulholland
General Manager, David C. Foster
Advertising Sales Director, Lea Cockerham
Marketing Specialist, Marcela Clinton
Advertising Administrator, Elisabeth Putnam
Circulation Director, Gail Weaverling
Circulation Fulfillment, Fran Jarriel
Fulfillment Asst., Karen Johnston
Controller, Scott Ferguson

To order *The MILEPOST®* and related products, phone 1-800-726-4707; email books@themilepost.com; or visit our book catalog at www.themilepost.com.

The MILEPOST® is an annual publication of Morris Communications Company LLC, 735 Broad Street, Augusta, GA 30901.

EDITORIAL AND ADVERTISING SALES OFFICES:
301 Arctic Slope Ave., Suite 300
Anchorage, AK 99518
Phone (907) 272-6070
Fax (907) 275-2117

Copyright © 2003 Morris Communications Company LLC. (First published 1949.) All rights reserved. No part of this book may be reproduced or transmitted in any form or by any means electronic or mechanical, including photocopying, recording, on-line reproduction or by any information storage and retrieval system, without written permission of the publisher.

ISSN 0361-1361 ISBN 1-892154-11-0
Key title: The Milepost   Printed in U.S.A.

Photography credits:
Cover— Barbara Willard.
Column insets not credited: Deborah M. Bernard, page 503; Gladys Blyth, page 228; Earl L. Brown, pages 55, 60, 64, 88, 90, 98, 106-107, 114, 123-124, 129, 134, 141, 146, 151, 161, 171, 174-175, 178-179, 249, 252, 255-258, 265, 272-275, 710, 712, 722, 726; Blake Hanna, pages 39, 42-44, 46, 51, 53, 67-70, 74, 81, 84, 214, 218, 220, 223, 226, 228, 244, 250-251, 671-672; Kris Graef, pages 61, 92, 99, 182-183, 189, 197, 279-281, 283, 288, 306, 311, 316, 366-367, 369, 374, 383-385, 3969-397, 439, 447, 457, 459, 460, 462-463, 468-471, 473, 475, 480, 484-484, 487, 491-492, 496, 498, 510, 515-516, 520, 523-525, 546, 562-563, 567, 581, 583, 587, 593, 605-606, 617, 533, 652, 656-658, 662, 664-665, 704; Lynn Owen, pages 492, 484; Judy Parkin, page 66; Rollo Pool, page 263.

Photo submissions: Photo submission guidelines *must* be requested before submitting photos. Send request and postpaid return envelope to the Editor. *The MILEPOST®* assumes no responsibility for unsolicited materials.

Advertising and Editorial Policy: *The MILEPOST®* does not endorse or guarantee any advertised service or facility. A sincere effort is made to give complete, accurate and annually up-to-date travel information for this immense segment of North America. However, between the time of our field surveys and the time of the readers' trip, many things may change. In all such cases, the publisher will not be held responsible.

 A PUBLICATION OF THE MAGAZINE DIVISION OF MORRIS COMMUNICATIONS COMPANY LLC

THE MILEPOST® FAMILY OF BOOKS!

THE ALASKA WILDERNESS GUIDE
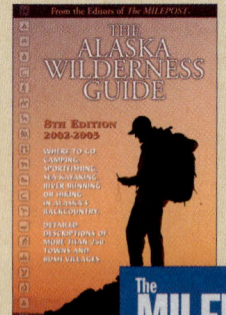
The MILEPOST® of backcountry Alaska! Includes tips on visiting Native villages, an adventure travel directory, descriptions of bush villages, park lands, fishing, hiking, river running and public use cabins. 8th edition. $19.95 U.S.

THE MILEPOST® SOUVENIR LOGBOOK
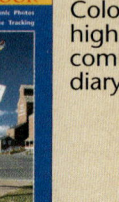
Color photos of Alaska highlight this 88-page commemorative travel diary. $12.95 U.S.

ALASKA ROADHOUSE RECIPES

Features recipes from roadhouses, lodges, bed and breakfasts, cafés, restaurants and campgrounds along the highways and byways of Alaska and Canada. $16.95 U.S.

ALASKA A TO Z
Fun and informative reference on Alaska with 200 pages of history, culture, geography, flora and fauna. $10.95 U.S.

TO ORDER CALL TODAY! TOLL FREE 1-800-726-4707
Morris Communications Corp. • P.O. Box 1668, Augusta GA 30903
(706) 823-3558 • Fax (706) 828-3846 • www.themilepost.com • e-mail: books@themilepost.com

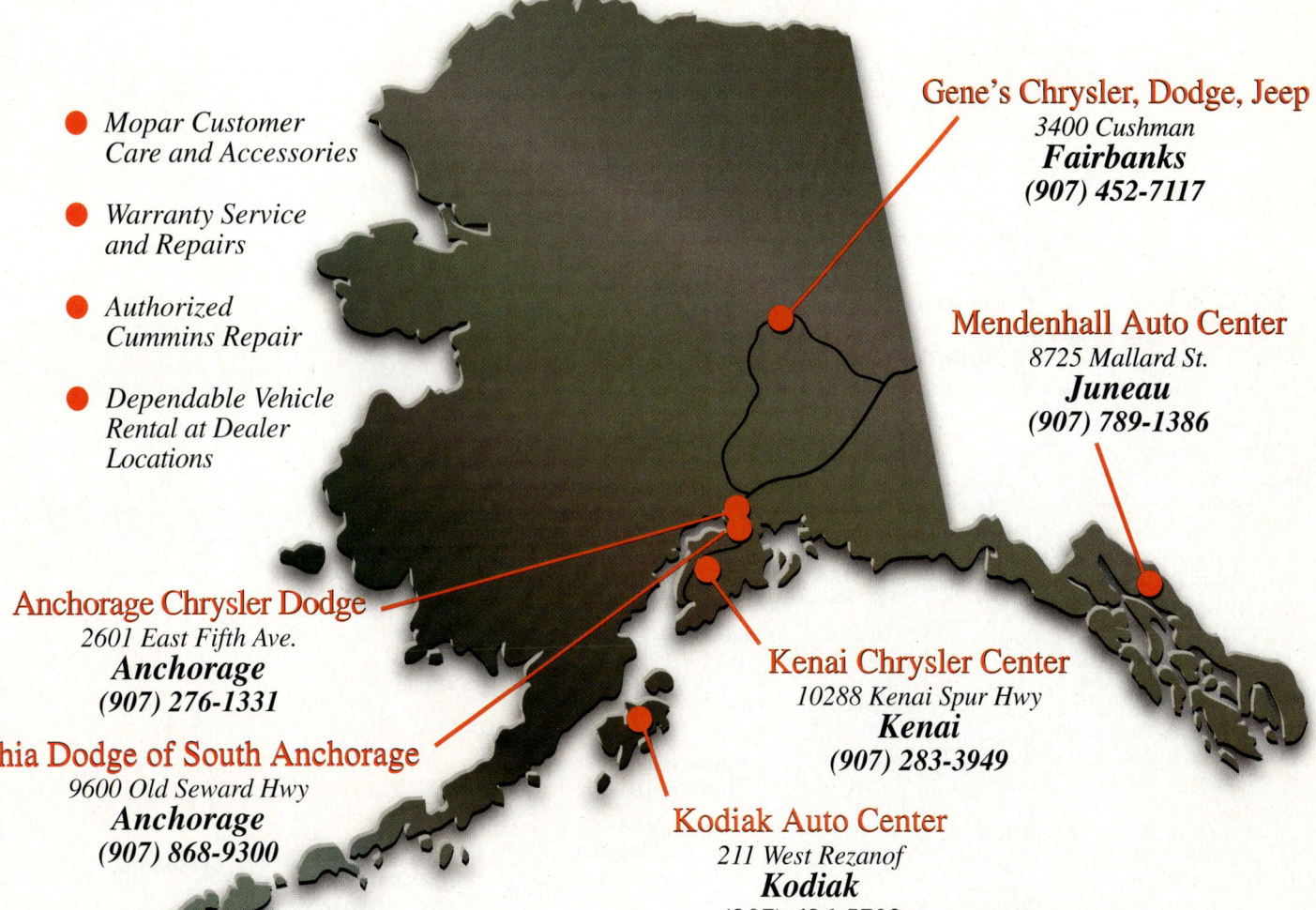

How to Use The MILEPOST®

The MILEPOST® provides mile-by-mile descriptions of all major highways and roads in Alaska and northwestern Canada; detailed information on all major destinations (cities, communities, national parks and other attractions) in the North; and how-to help for various modes of transportation (air, ferry, railroads, etc.). Refer to the Contents page and Index for subjects and destinations.

The MILEPOST® will work for you regardless of how you plan to travel—whether by car, by plane, on a tour bus, or by bicycle. It will help you plan your trip, as well as acting as a valuable guide during your trip.

The backbone of *The MILEPOST®* is the highway logs. The Key to Highways map on the opposite page shows you what highways are covered in *The MILEPOST®*. In these mile-by-mile descriptions of the highways and byways of the North, you will find campgrounds; businesses offering food, lodging, gas and other services; attractions; fishing spots; road conditions; descriptions of the geography and history of the land and communities; and much more.

To the right is an abbreviated version of part of the Parks Highway log, keyed to help you understand how to read all highway logs in *The MILEPOST®*.

1. A boldface paragraph appears at the beginning of each highway log in *The MILEPOST®* that explains what beginning and ending destinations are used, and what boldface letters represent those destinations. In this log **A** represents **Anchorage**, **C** is **Cantwell** and **F** is **Fairbanks**.

2. The boldface numbers following the letters represent the distance in miles from the beginning and ending destinations. (In Canada, the metric equivalent in kilometres follows the boldface mileage.) In this example, the Denali National Park entrance is located at **A 237.4 C 27.4 F 124.6** or 237.4 miles from Anchorage, 27.4 miles from Cantwell and 124.6 miles from Fairbanks.

3. **Junctions** with other logged roads are indented and color-coded. And the cross-referenced section is always uppercased. In this example, the DENALI NATIONAL PARK section is referenced. (If a page number is not given, refer to the Contents page.)

4. "Log" advertisements are classified-type advertisements that appear in the text. These are identified by the boldface name of the business at the beginning of the entry and "[ADVERTISEMENT]" at the end. These log advertisements are written by the advertisers.

5. Display advertisements are keyed in the log by a boldface entry at their highway locations, followed by the words "See display ad." Their advertisement will appear near this entry or a page or section will be referenced.

It may also help you to know how our field editors log the highways. *The MILEPOST®* field editors drive each highway, taking notes on facilities, features and attractions along the way and noting the mile at which they appear. Mileages are measured from the beginning of the highway, which is generally at a junction or the city limits, to the end of the highway, also usually a junction or city limits. Most highways in *The MILEPOST®* are logged either south to north or east to west. If you are traveling the opposite direction of the log, you will read the log back to front.

To determine driving distance between 2 points, simply subtract the first mileage figures.

Look for these symbols throughout *The MILEPOST®*:

▲ Campground   ♿ Wheelchair accessible
➛ Fishing

Parks Highway Log

Distance from Anchorage (A) is followed by distance from Cantwell (C) and distance from Fairbanks (F). ❶

A 237 C 27 F 125 *Begin 40 mph speed zone northbound.*

A 237.3 C 27.3 F 124.7 Riley Creek bridge.

Distance marker southbound indicates Cantwell 27 miles, Wasilla 196 miles, Anchorage 237 miles.

❷ **A 237.4 C 27.6 F 124.6 Denali National Park and Preserve** entrance. The park visitor center is a half-mile west of the highway junction on the Park Road.

Junction with Park Road. See DENALI NATIONAL PARK section on page 399 for Park Road log and details on the park. ❸

DENALI PARK/McKINLEY PARK (pop. 169 in summer) refers to the business area that has developed along the Parks Highway from south of the Park entrance north to the Nenana River canyon. A variety of services are offered, including river running trip, gift shops, accommodations, restaurants and a gas station. Most are open in summer only. See "Denali's Front Country" this section.

A 238 C 28 F 124 Third bridge northbound over the Nenana River.

❹ **Nenana Raft Adventures.** Raft Denali with the first raft company in Alaska to outfit every client in a full drysuit. Day trips as well as multi-day expeditions on the Talkeetna River. Oar rafts and paddle rafting both available. Our riverfront office is directly next door to ERA Helicopters. Phone 1-800-789-RAFT; in Denali (907) 683-RAFT. [ADVERTISEMENT]

A 238.1 C 28.1 F 123.9 Public access to Nenana River.

A 238.2 C 28.2 F 123.8 Kingfisher Creek.

❺ **A 238.2 C 28.2 F 123.8 Alpenglow Restaurant.** See display ad in the DENALI NATIONAL PARK section.

The introduction to each highway logged in *The MILEPOST®* includes a chart of mileages between major points (see example).

Maps also accompany each highway logged in *The MILEPOST®*. Consult the map key for an explanation of abbreviations (see example at bottom). Mileage boxes at communities and junctions on the highway map reflect the rounded off mileage in the highway log at the corresponding point.

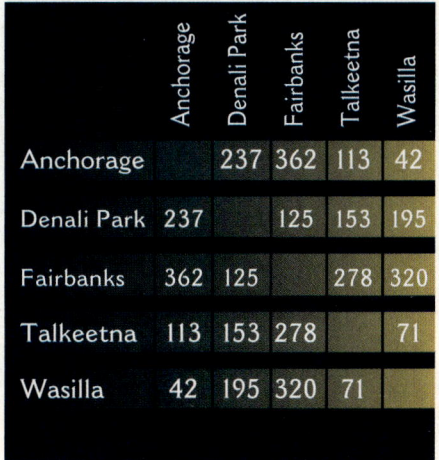

	Anchorage	Denali Park	Fairbanks	Talkeetna	Wasilla
Anchorage		237	362	113	42
Denali Park	237		125	153	195
Fairbanks	362	125		278	320
Talkeetna	113	153	278		71
Wasilla	42	195	320	71	

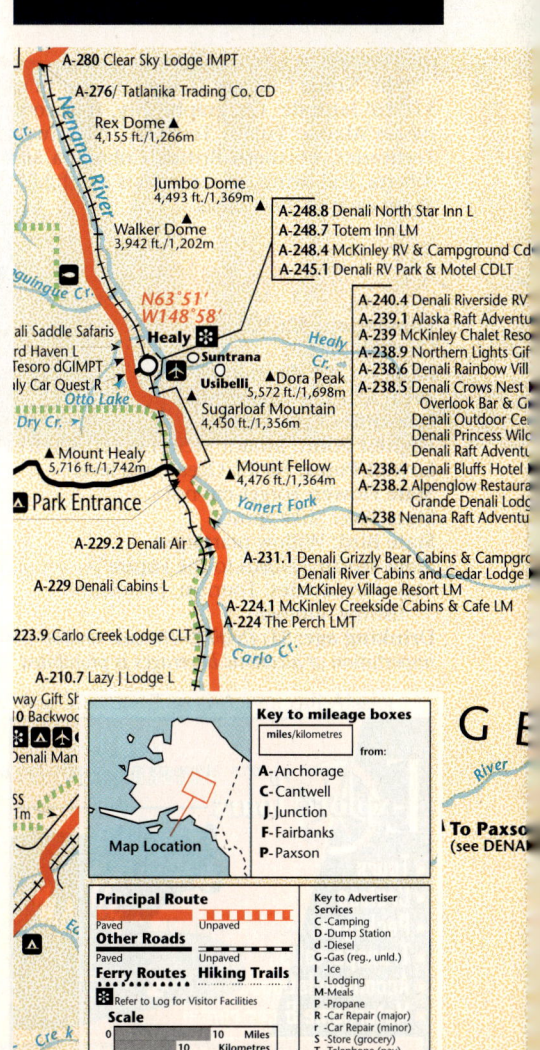

Muncho Lake is a favorite recreation area in British Columbia. (© Lyn Hancock)

Top Ten Attractions:
1. SS *Klondike*, Whitehorse
2. MacBride Museum, Whitehorse
3. Northern Lights Centre, Watson Lake
4. Diamond Tooth Gerties, Dawson City
5. Palace Grand Theatre, Dawson City
6. Beringia Interpretive Centre, Whitehorse
7. Dredge #4, Dawson City
8. Kluane National Park
9. Whitehorse Fish Ladder
10. Robert Service Cabin, Dawson City

Fish & Game: Fish & Wildlife, Yukon Government, Dept. of Environment Renewable Resources, Box 2703, Whitehorse, YT Y1A 2C6, phone (867) 667-5652; www.environmentyukon.gov.yk.ca
Visitor Information: Tourism Yukon, Box 2703, Whitehorse, YT Y1A 2C6; phone (867) 667-5340; email vacation@gov.yk.ca; www.touryukon.com

Shaped somewhat like a right triangle, Yukon Territory is bordered on the west by Alaska at 141° longitude; on the north by the Beaufort Sea/Arctic Ocean; on the south by British Columbia at latitude 60°; and on the east by the western Northwest Territories.

Yukon Territory is 3 times larger than all the New England states combined. Canada's highest peak, Mount Logan (elev. 19,545 feet/5,957m), is located in Yukon's St. Elias Mountains.

First Nations peoples of the Yukon belong to the Athabascan and Tlingit language families. These are Gwich'in, Han, Northern Tutchone, Southern Tutchone, Kaska, Tagish, Tlingit and Upper Tanana.

The Yukon was made a district of the Northwest Territories in 1895, and became a separate territory in June of 1898. The territory's first capital was Dawson City, site of the great Klondike gold rush, which brought thousands of gold seekers to the Yukon and Alaska in 1897–98. The Klondike gold rush began celebrating its centennial in 1996—marking the discovery of gold on Bonanza Creek on August 16, 1896—and continued the celebration through 1998.

At the height of the gold rush, an estimated 40,000 people lived in Dawson City. By 1903, as other gold stampedes drew off much of Dawson's population, the city's boom days were over, although mining continued to support the community for many years. On March 31, 1953, Whitehorse—on the railway and the highway, with a large airport—replaced Dawson City as capital.

Yukon Territory's parklands include Kluane National Park, a UNESCO World Heritage Site, accessible from the Haines and Alaska highways. The undeveloped Ivvavik and Vuntut national parks are in the remote northwestern corner of the territory. Klondike Gold Rush National Historical Park encompasses the Canadian portions of the Chilkoot and White Pass gold rush trails from Skagway.

Northwest Territories

Population: 41,403
Capital: Yellowknife
Largest City: Yellowknife
Area: 550,000 square miles/1.4 million square km
Highest Point: Cirque of the Unclimbables Mountain, 9,062 feet/2,762m
Lowest Point: Beaufort Sea, sea level

How to Use The MILEPOST®

The MILEPOST® provides mile-by-mile descriptions of all major highways and roads in Alaska and northwestern Canada; detailed information on all major destinations (cities, communities, national parks and other attractions) in the North; and how-to help for various modes of transportation (air, ferry, railroads, etc.). Refer to the Contents page and Index for subjects and destinations.

The MILEPOST® will work for you regardless of how you plan to travel—whether by car, by plane, on a tour bus, or by bicycle. It will help you plan your trip, as well as acting as a valuable guide during your trip.

The backbone of The MILEPOST® is the highway logs. The Key to Highways map on the opposite page shows you what highways are covered in The MILEPOST®. In these mile-by-mile descriptions of the highways and byways of the North, you will find campgrounds; businesses offering food, lodging, gas and other services; attractions; fishing spots; road conditions; descriptions of the geography and history of the land and communities; and much more.

To the right is an abbreviated version of part of the Parks Highway log, keyed to help you understand how to read all highway logs in The MILEPOST®.

1. A boldface paragraph appears at the beginning of each highway log in The MILEPOST® that explains what beginning and ending destinations are used, and what boldface letters represent those destinations. In this log **A** represents **Anchorage**, **C** is **Cantwell** and **F** is **Fairbanks**.

2. The boldface numbers following the letters represent the distance in miles from the beginning and ending destinations. (In Canada, the metric equivalent in kilometres follows the boldface mileage.) In this example, the Denali National Park entrance is located at **A 237.4 C 27.4 F 124.6** or 237.4 miles from Anchorage, 27.4 miles from Cantwell and 124.6 miles from Fairbanks.

3. **Junctions** with other logged roads are indented and color-coded. And the cross-referenced section is always uppercased. In this example, the DENALI NATIONAL PARK section is referenced. (If a page number is not given, refer to the Contents page.)

4. "Log" advertisements are classified-type advertisements that appear in the text. These are identified by the boldface name of the business at the beginning of the entry and "[ADVERTISEMENT]" at the end. These log advertisements are written by the advertisers.

5. Display advertisements are keyed in the log by a boldface entry at their highway locations, followed by the words "See display ad." Their advertisement will appear near this entry or a page or section will be referenced.

It may also help you to know how our field editors log the highways. The MILEPOST® field editors drive each highway, taking notes on facilities, features and attractions along the way and noting the mile at which they appear. Mileages are measured from the beginning of the highway, which is generally at a junction or the city limits, to the end of the highway, also usually a junction or city limits. Most highways in The MILEPOST® are logged either south to north or east to west. If you are traveling the opposite direction of the log, you will read the log back to front.

To determine driving distance between 2 points, simply subtract the first mileage figures.

Look for these symbols throughout The MILEPOST®:

▲ Campground   ♿ Wheelchair accessible
         ⌇ Fishing

Parks Highway Log

Distance from Anchorage (A) is followed by distance from Cantwell (C) and distance from Fairbanks (F). ❶

A 237 C 27 F 125 *Begin 40 mph speed zone northbound.*

A 237.3 C 27.3 F 124.7 Riley Creek bridge.
Distance marker southbound indicates Cantwell 27 miles, Wasilla 196 miles, Anchorage 237 miles.

❷ **A 237.4 C 27.6 F 124.6 Denali National Park and Preserve** entrance. The park visitor center is a half-mile west of the highway junction on the Park Road.

Junction with Park Road. See DENALI NATIONAL PARK section on page 399 for Park Road log and details on the park. ❸

DENALI PARK/McKINLEY PARK (pop. 169 in summer) refers to the business area that has developed along the Parks Highway from south of the Park entrance north to the Nenana River canyon. A variety of services are offered, including river running trip, gift shops, accommodations, restaurants and a gas station. Most are open in summer only. See "Denali's Front Country" this section.

A 238 C 28 F 124 Third bridge northbound over the Nenana River.

❹ **Nenana Raft Adventures.** Raft Denali with the first raft company in Alaska to outfit every client in a full drysuit. Day trips as well as multi-day expeditions on the Talkeetna River. Oar rafts and paddle rafting both available. Our riverfront office is directly next door to ERA Helicopters. Phone 1-800-789-RAFT; in Denali (907) 683-RAFT. [ADVERTISEMENT]

A 238.1 C 28.1 F 123.9 Public access to Nenana River.

A 238.2 C 28.2 F 123.8 Kingfisher Creek.

❺ **A 238.2 C 28.2 F 123.8 Alpenglow Restaurant.** See display ad in the DENALI NATIONAL PARK section.

The introduction to each highway logged in The MILEPOST® includes a chart of mileages between major points (see example). Maps also accompany each highway logged in The MILEPOST®. Consult the map key for an explanation of abbreviations (see example at bottom). Mileage boxes at communities and junctions on the highway map reflect the rounded off mileage in the highway log at the corresponding point.

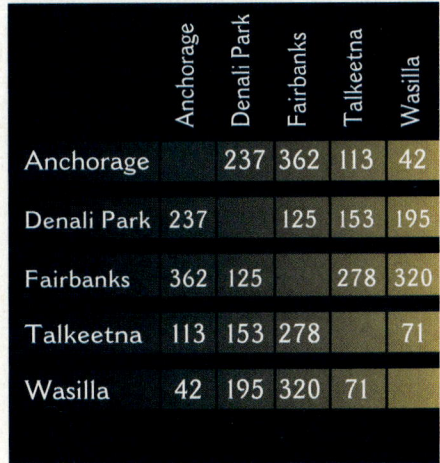

	Anchorage	Denali Park	Fairbanks	Talkeetna	Wasilla
Anchorage		237	362	113	42
Denali Park	237		125	153	195
Fairbanks	362	125		278	320
Talkeetna	113	153	278		71
Wasilla	42	195	320	71	

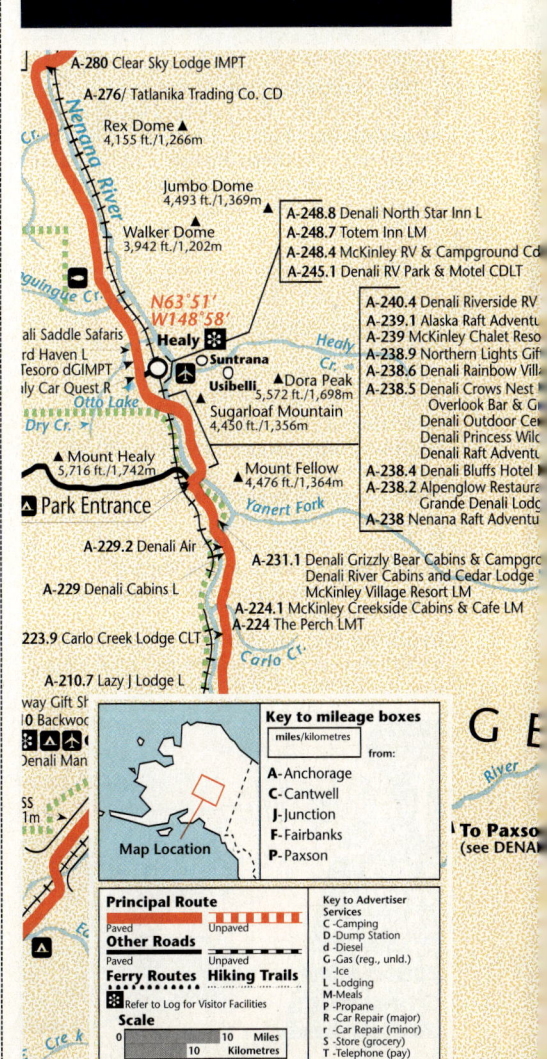

Welcome to the North Country

The north peak of Mount McKinley (19,470 feet) in Denali National Park.
(© Rich Reid, Colors of Nature)

The North Country is the land north of 51° 16' latitude. Geographically, it encompasses Alaska, Yukon Territory, Northwest Territories, northern British Columbia and Alberta. Following are some facts and figures about each of these areas.

Alaska

Population: 626,932
Capital: Juneau
Largest City: Anchorage
Area: 570,374 square miles
Coastline: 33,904 miles
Highest Point: Mount McKinley, 20,320 feet
Lowest Point: Pacific Ocean, sea level
State Flower: Forget-me-not
State Tree: Sitka spruce
State Bird: Willow ptarmigan
State Motto: "North to the Future"
Major Industries: Tourism, petroleum, fishing, lumber
Drinking age: 21. *(NOTE: The sale and/or importation of alcoholic beverages is prohibited in some bush communities.)*

Top Ten Attractions:
1. Glaciers
2. Inside Passage
3. Native Arts and Culture
4. Wildlife Viewing
5. Historic Mining Towns and Areas
6. Museums
7. Sportfishing
8. Trans-Alaska Pipeline
9. Russian Heritage
10. National Parks and Monuments

Fish & Game: Alaska Dept. of Fish and Game, Box 25526, Juneau, AK 99802-5526; phone (907) 465-4100; www.state.ak.us/adfg/adfghome.htm
Visitor Information: Alaska Division of Tourism, Box 110809, Juneau, AK 99811-0809; phone (907) 465-2017; www.dced.state.ak.us/tourism

Alaska was purchased by the U.S. from Russia in 1867. It became the 49th state on January 3, 1959. Alaska is the largest state in the union in area (twice the size of Texas), but ranks 48th in population, based on the 2000 census. (Only Vermont and Wyoming have fewer residents.) Approximately 15 percent of the population is Native: Eskimo, Aleut and Indian (Athabascan, Tlingit, Haida, Tsimshian).

Alaska has 17 of the 20 highest mountains in the United States, including the highest peak in North America—Mount McKinley (Denali). The state falls into 6 natural geographical regions: Southeastern, Southcentral, the Interior, Southwestern, Western and the Brooks Range/Arctic.

Southeastern Alaska is a moist, luxuriantly forested panhandle extending some 500 miles from Dixon Entrance south of Ketchikan to Icy Bay on the Gulf of Alaska coast. This narrow strip of coast, separated from the mainland and Canada by the Coast Mountains and the hundreds of islands of the Alexander Archipelago, form the Inside Passage water route used by ships and ferries. Cruise ships bring thousands of passengers through the Inside Passage each summer.

The Southcentral region of Alaska curves 650 miles north and west from the Gulf of Alaska coast to the Alaska Range. This region's tremendous geographic variety includes the Matanuska–Susitna river valleys, the Chugach and Wrangell–St. Elias mountain ranges, the Kenai Peninsula and the Prince William Sound glaciers. Anchorage, the state's largest city, is the hub of Southcentral.

Interior Alaska lies cradled between the Brooks Range to the north and the Alaska Range to the south, a vast area that drains the Yukon River and its tributaries. It is a climate of extremes, holding both the record high (100°F at Fort Yukon) and the record low (-80°F at Prospect Creek). Fairbanks is the hub of the Interior and a jump-off point for bush communities in both the Interior and Arctic.

Southwestern Alaska takes in Kodiak Island, the Alaska Peninsula and Aleutian Islands. Kodiak, less than an hour's flight from Anchorage and about 10 hours by ferry from Homer, is the largest island in Alaska. Kodiak was Russian Alaska's first capital city. Brown bear viewing is an attraction on Kodiak and at Katmai National Park and Preserve near King Salmon. The Southwest ferry system provides service from Kodiak to Unalaska/ Dutch Harbor.

Western Alaska stretches from the head of Bristol Bay north along the Bering Sea coast to the Seward Peninsula near the Arctic Circle. This region extends inland from the coast to encompass the Yukon–Kuskokwim Delta. Nome is one of the best known destinations in Western Alaska.

Arctic Alaska lies above the Arctic Circle (latitude 66°33'), between the Brooks Range to the south and the Arctic sea coast to the north, and from the Canadian border to the east westward to Kotzebue. Day and overnight trips to Kotzebue, Barrow and Prudhoe Bay are popular packages offered out of Anchorage and Fairbanks.

If you include the Marine Highway, all regions of Alaska are connected by highway with the exception of Western Alaska. And that region's hub cities—Bethel and Nome— are less than 2 hours from Anchorage by air.

Yukon Territory

Population: 31,305
Capital: Whitehorse
Largest City: Whitehorse
Area: 186,661 square miles/ 483,414 square km
Highest Point: Mount Logan, 19,545 feet/5,957m
Lowest Point: Beaufort Sea, sea level
Territorial Flower: Fireweed
Territorial Bird: Raven
Drinking age: 19. Packaged liquor, beer and wine are sold in government liquor stores.
Major Industries: Tourism, mining

Come enjoy our breathtaking sunsets.
Or lack thereof.

Better stock up on sunscreen. It's summertime in the Land of the Midnight Sun. And nobody covers Alaska like...well, Alaska. We offer daily service to 19 destinations in the Last Frontier. Go far off the beaten path with a complete vacation package to the Arctic or Katmai/King Salmon. Take a guided tundra walk. Or share a riverbank with a brown bear. Just see your Travel Agent, call Alaska Airlines Vacations at 1-800-468-2248, or plan and purchase your package at alaskaair.com. Because sunsets are so lower 48.

CELEBRATING 70 YEARS OF ALASKA SPIRIT.

Barrow day tours *from* $399

Kotzebue and Nome day tours *from* $369

King Salmon/Katmai National Park overnight tours *from* $683

Tour prices include round-trip airfare from Anchorage (Barrow is priced from Fairbanks), transfers, tours and admissions, and hotels where applicable. Tours operate daily: Barrow 5/18/03 to 9/18/03; Kotzebue/Nome 5/25/03 to 9/6/03; King Salmon/Katmai National Park 6/14/03 to 9/13/03. Based on double occupancy. All dates and prices apply to 2003. All terms of Alaska Airlines Vacations apply.

Muncho Lake is a favorite recreation area in British Columbia. (© Lyn Hancock)

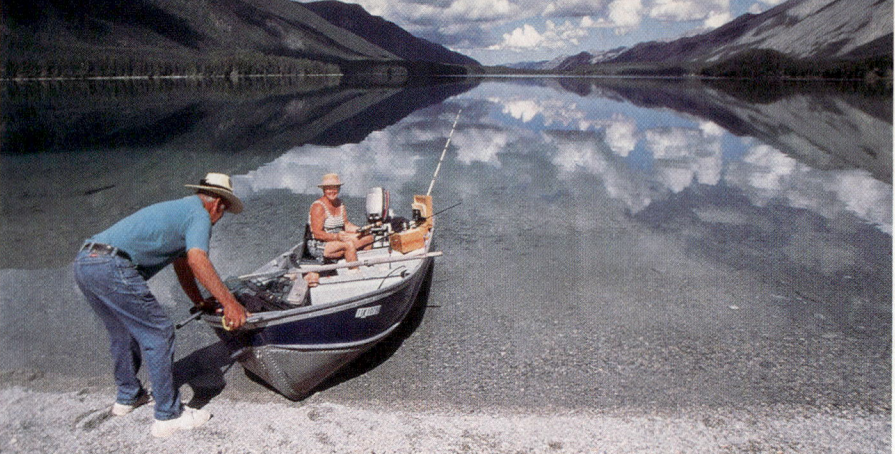

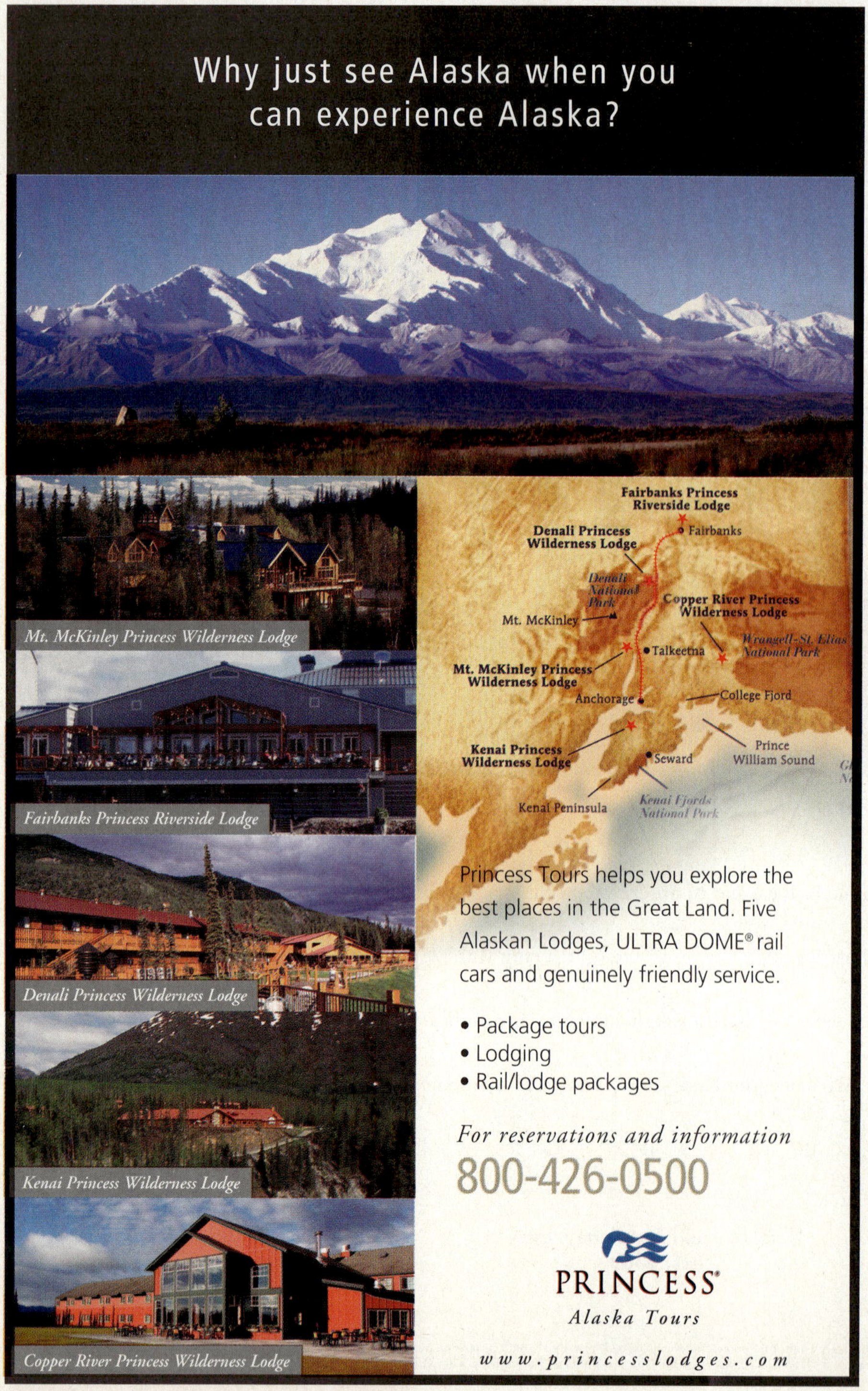
Why just see Alaska when you can experience Alaska?
Mt. McKinley Princess Wilderness Lodge
Fairbanks Princess Riverside Lodge
Denali Princess Wilderness Lodge
Kenai Princess Wilderness Lodge
Copper River Princess Wilderness Lodge
Fairbanks Princess Riverside Lodge
Fairbanks
Denali Princess Wilderness Lodge
Denali National Park
Copper River Princess Wilderness Lodge
Mt. McKinley
Talkeetna
Wrangell-St. Elias National Park
Mt. McKinley Princess Wilderness Lodge
Anchorage
College Fjord
Kenai Princess Wilderness Lodge
Seward
Prince William Sound
Kenai Peninsula
Kenai Fjords National Park
Princess Tours helps you explore the best places in the Great Land. Five Alaskan Lodges, ULTRA DOME® rail cars and genuinely friendly service.
• Package tours
• Lodging
• Rail/lodge packages
For reservations and information
800-426-0500
PRINCESS®
Alaska Tours
www.princesslodges.com

Top Ten Attractions:
1. SS *Klondike,* Whitehorse
2. MacBride Museum, Whitehorse
3. Northern Lights Centre, Watson Lake
4. Diamond Tooth Gerties, Dawson City
5. Palace Grand Theatre, Dawson City
6. Beringia Interpretive Centre, Whitehorse
7. Dredge #4, Dawson City
8. Kluane National Park
9. Whitehorse Fish Ladder
10. Robert Service Cabin, Dawson City

Fish & Game: Fish & Wildlife, Yukon Government, Dept. of Environment Renewable Resources, Box 2703, Whitehorse, YT Y1A 2C6, phone (867) 667-5652; www.environmentyukon.gov.yk.ca
Visitor Information: Tourism Yukon, Box 2703, Whitehorse, YT Y1A 2C6; phone (867) 667-5340; email vacation@gov.yk.ca; www.touryukon.com

Shaped somewhat like a right triangle, Yukon Territory is bordered on the west by Alaska at 141° longitude; on the north by the Beaufort Sea/Arctic Ocean; on the south by British Columbia at latitude 60°; and on the east by the western Northwest Territories.

Yukon Territory is 3 times larger than all the New England states combined. Canada's highest peak, Mount Logan (elev. 19,545 feet/5,957m), is located in Yukon's St. Elias Mountains.

First Nations peoples of the Yukon belong to the Athabascan and Tlingit language families. These are Gwich'in, Han, Northern Tutchone, Southern Tutchone, Kaska, Tagish, Tlingit and Upper Tanana.

The Yukon was made a district of the Northwest Territories in 1895, and became a separate territory in June of 1898. The territory's first capital was Dawson City, site of the great Klondike gold rush, which brought thousands of gold seekers to the Yukon and Alaska in 1897–98. The Klondike gold rush began celebrating its centennial in 1996—marking the discovery of gold on Bonanza Creek on August 16, 1896—and continued the celebration through 1998.

At the height of the gold rush, an estimated 40,000 people lived in Dawson City. By 1903, as other gold stampedes drew off much of Dawson's population, the city's boom days were over, although mining continued to support the community for many years. On March 31, 1953, Whitehorse—on the railway and the highway, with a large airport—replaced Dawson City as capital.

Yukon Territory's parklands include Kluane National Park, a UNESCO World Heritage Site, accessible from the Haines and Alaska highways. The undeveloped Ivvavik and Vuntut national parks are in the remote northwestern corner of the territory. Klondike Gold Rush National Historical Park encompasses the Canadian portions of the Chilkoot and White Pass gold rush trails from Skagway.

Northwest Territories

Population: 41,403
Capital: Yellowknife
Largest City: Yellowknife
Area: 550,000 square miles/1.4 million square km
Highest Point: Cirque of the Unclimbables Mountain, 9,062 feet/2,762m
Lowest Point: Beaufort Sea, sea level

Territorial Flower: Mountain aven
Drinking age: 19. Packaged liquor, beer and wine are sold in government liquor stores. Sale and possession of alcohol is prohibited in several communities.
Major Industries: Mining, manufacturing, fishing, tourism

Top Ten Attractions:
1. Nahanni National Park Reserve
2. Wood Buffalo National Park
3. Canol Heritage Trail Park Reserve
4. Dempster Highway
5. Pingos (cone-shaped hills) of the Tuktoyaktuk Peninsula
6. Roman Catholic "Igloo" Church, Inuvik
7. Twin Falls Gorge Territorial Park
8. Prince of Wales Northern Heritage Center, Yellowknife
9. Northwest Territories Legislative Assembly Building, Yellowknife
10. Old Town, Yellowknife

Fish & Game: Dept. of Resources, Wildlife & Economic, Tourism Development and Marketing, Box 1320, Yellowknife, NT X1A 2L9; www.nwtwildlife.rwed.gov.nt.ca
Visitor Information: Northwest Territories Tourism, Box 610, Yellowknife, NT X1A 2N5; (867) 873-7200 or toll-free within the U.S. and Canada at (800) 661-0788; email arctic@nwttravel.nt.ca; www.nwttravel.nt.ca

On April 1, 1999, Northwest Territories was divided into 2 territories. Passed by popular vote in 1982 and approved by the Canadian Parliament in 1993, this division created Nunavut and its capital, Iqaluit on Baffin Island, in what was the eastern half of the old Northwest Territories.

The new Northwest Territories comprises a sixth of Canada and is about the size of Alaska. Northwest Territories' Wood Buffalo National Park is the second largest national park in the world.

A majority of the population of Northwest Territories is Native. Aboriginal groups are the Dene, Inuvialuit, Inuit, Gwich'in, Dogrib and Metis.

Access to Northwest Territories is from Alberta via the Mackenzie Highway system, from British Columbia via the Liard Highway, and from Yukon Territory via the Dempster Highway. A major road-building project in the 1960s constructed most of the highway system in western Northwest Territories. Road improvement is ongoing, with most roads now paved.

British Columbia

Population: 4,095,900
Capital: Victoria
Largest City: Vancouver
Area: 365,900 square miles/947,796 square km
Highest Point: Mount Fairweather, 15,295 feet/4,662m
Lowest Point: Pacific Ocean, sea level
Provincial Flower: Pacific dogwood
Provincial Tree: Western red cedar
Provincial Bird: Steller's jay
Provincial Motto: *Splendor Sine Occasu* (Splendour Without Diminishment)
Major Industries: Forestry, mining and energy, tourism, agriculture, seafood products, food
Drinking age: 19. Packaged liquor, beer and wine are sold in government liquor stores.

Top Ten Attractions:
1. Royal BC Museum, Victoria
2. Butchart Gardens, Victoria
3. Vancouver Aquarium
4. Capilano Suspension Bridge, North Vancouver
5. Barkerville Historic Town
6. Fort Steele Heritage Town
7. Grist Mill and Gardens, Keremeos
8. Grouse Mountain, North Vancouver
9. Ksan Historical Indian Village Museum, Hazelton
10. UBC Museum of Anthropology, Vancouver

Fish & Game: Ministry of Agriculture, Food and Fisheries, Box 9058, Stn. Prov. Govt., Victoria, BC V8W 9E2; www.gov.bc.ca/agf
Visitor Information: Tourism British Columbia, Dept. TG, Box 9830, Stn. Prov. Govt., Victoria, B.C. V8W 9W5 Canada; phone 1-800-HELLOBC; www.hellobc.com

Canada's most westerly—and 3rd largest—province, British Columbia stretches 813 miles/1,300 km from its southern border with the United States to the northern boundary with Yukon Territory. It is bounded on the east by Alberta and on the west by the Pacific Ocean. The province encompasses the Queen Charlotte Islands and Vancouver Island, site of the capital city of Victoria. Approximately half the province's population resides in the Victoria–Vancouver area.

British Columbia entered the Dominion of Canada on July 20, 1871, as the 6th province. The region was important in early fur trade, and expansion of the province came with the 1860s Cariboo gold rush, followed by the completion of Canada's first transcontinental railway—the Canadian Pacific.

Vancouver and Victoria are popular tourist areas, as are Vancouver Island and the Gulf islands. The Sunshine Coast, along the shores of British Columbia facing Vancouver Island, is popular for its scenic drives, parks and beaches. The region's national parks, including Glacier, Mt. Revelstoke, Kootenay and Yoho, are among the most spectacular in North America.

Mile Zero of the Alaska Highway is located in Dawson Creek, BC (not to be confused with Dawson City, YT), in the northeastern part of the province.

Alberta

Population: 3,050,140
Capital: Edmonton
Largest City: Calgary
Area: 255,287 square miles/661,142 square km
Highest Point: Mount Columbia, 12,293 feet/3,747m
Lowest Point: Salt River at the border with Northwest Territories, 600 feet/183m
Major Industries: Petrochemicals, plastics, forest products, computer/business services, processed foods, electronics, tourism
Drinking age: 18. Liquor, beer and wine are sold in private liquor stores.

Top Ten Attractions:
1. West Edmonton Mall
2. Calgary Zoo
3. Glenbow Museum, Calgary
4. Heritage Park, Calgary
5. Alberta Legislature Building, Edmonton
6. Fort Edmonton Park, Edmonton

Bighorn sheep are common throughout the Canadian Rockies.
(© Rich Reid, Colors of Nature)

7. Muttart Conservatory, Edmonton
8. Provincial Museum of Alberta, Edmonton
9. Royal Tyrrell Museum of Palaeontology, Drumheller
10. Odyssium (Edmonton Space and Science Centre)

Fish & Game: Environmental Protection Branch, Information Centre, 9920 108 St., Edmonton, AB T5K 2M4; www.mb.ec.gc.ca
Visitor Information: Travel Alberta, 6th floor, Commerce Place, 10155 102 St., Edmonton, AB T5J 4G8 (P.O. Box 2500, T5J 2Z4); phone (800) 661-8888 toll-free in U.S. and Canada or (780) 427-4321; fax (780) 427-0867; travelinfo@travelalberta.com; www.travelalberta.com

The Province of Alberta is bounded to the west by British Columbia, to the south by Montana, to the east by Saskatchewan and to the north by the Northwest Territories. Among the dramatic features of this geographically fascinating area are a stretch of the Rocky Mountains and the Columbia Icefield—source of the Athabasca, Columbia and Saskatchewan glaciers—along the British Columbia border, and the bizarre rock formations of the badlands to the west along the Red Deer River.

Native inhabitants included Assiniboine, Blackfoot, Cree and Sarcee Indians. The first European settlers—fur traders—arrived in the mid-18th century. In 1875, Alberta became a province of Canada. Discoveries of oil and natural gas deposits in the 1930s caused economic growth, and in the 1970s and 1980s, these same deposits brought new industries and a resulting rise in population to the area.

Edmonton in central Alberta and Calgary to the south are popular areas. The national parks—Banff and Jasper along the British Columbia border, Waterton Lakes in the southwest corner and Wood Buffalo far in the north—are also major attractions.

Travel Planning

Motorcyclists stop off at a northern Canada lodge. (© Lyn Hancock)

Accommodations

Accommodations in the North—as anywhere else—can range from luxurious to utilitarian to downright funky. You'll find lodging in fine lodges and major-chain hotels/motels; in bed and breakfasts; in hostels; in rustic log cabins; and in mobile homes. Considering the remoteness of many communities and the seasonal nature of Northern travel, visitors are often surprised at the wide variety of lodging available.

The larger cities (Anchorage, Fairbanks, etc.) have more to choose from than the smaller, more remote communities. But in midsummer, even those locations with greater numbers of rooms available can fill up quickly. You should consider making reservations ahead of time during the busy summer season, whether your destination is a major city or a small highway community.

Some facilities along highways of the North may be a bit on the rustic side compared to what you're used to. This is, after all, the Last Frontier. You'll also find some first-class establishments in surprisingly remote locations. Sometimes, the frills of city travel may be missing, but the hospitality of the North more than makes up for it.

We do not rate accommodations. In our experience, you can have a 5-star experience in a 1-star hotel (or vice versa), and sometimes, the remote location and lack of choices in lodging make ratings moot anyway. Paid advertisements for accommodations appearing in *The MILEPOST*—whether display ads or "log ads" placed in the highway log—are written by the advertisers themselves. We do not endorse or guarantee any of these facilities or services, although we trust the advertisers will live up to their promises. If they don't, please write, phone or email us. We do not mediate disputes, but if we get enough complaints about a business not living up to its advertisement, we will ask the advertiser to do a reality check. Keep in mind that businesses may close, and ownership and rates may change.

Air Travel

Slightly more than half of all visitors to Alaska arrive by air. Air travel is also one of the most common forms of transportation in the North. You can fly just about anywhere. If there is no scheduled service, you can charter a plane. Aside from offering transportation from one place to another, many flying services also offer—or specialize in—flightseeing. For a fixed fee, you can fly around mountains or go looking for wildlife.

About 10 domestic airlines and 2 dozen small scheduled carriers provide scheduled passenger service within Alaska. There are more than 250 certified charter/air taxi operators in Alaska. Check the advertisements for scheduled and charter air service in the communities covered in *The MILEPOST*. There are many to choose from.

Air taxi rates may vary from carrier to carrier. Most operators charge an hourly rate either per plane load or per passenger; others may charge on a per-mile basis. Flightseeing trips to area attractions are often available at a fixed price per passenger.

Sample per-hour fares for charter planes with varied wheel, float and ski capabilities (luggage space limited and dependent on number of passengers): Piper Archer (3 passengers), $175; Piper Cherokee 6 (5 passengers), $250; Islander (9 passengers), $450; Chieftain (9 passengers), $650.

The MILEPOST highway logs include the location of most airstrips along the highways and in communities. *NOTE: The brief description of airstrips given in* The MILEPOST *is in no way intended as a guide.* Pilots should have a current copy of the *Alaska Supplement*.

Bus Lines

Transportation in this category ranges from no frills shuttle van service to narrated motorcoach tours. Most scheduled

LODGING • ACTIVITIES • TRANSPORTATION

Alaska Vacation Experts

ALASKA Tour & Travel / PARK CONNECTION Motorcoach

Specializing in custom vacations to Alaska's most spectacular destinations. We offer great value and quality products, contact us today!

www.alaskatravel.com
toll free 800-208-0200

bus service between or to cities in the North is seasonal (summer-only).

Alaska Direct Bus Line, P.O. Box 501, Anchorage, AK 99510. (907) 277-6652 or (800) 770-6652; www.tokalaska.com/dirctbus.shtml. Service from Anchorage to Fairbanks, Tok, Whitehorse, Dawson City and Skagway.

Alaska Sightseeing/Cruise West, 349 Wrangell St., Anchorage, AK 99501. (907) 276-1305; www.cruisewest.com. Package motorcoach tours from Anchorage to Denali and Fairbanks.

Alaska Park Connection Motorcoach/Alaska Tour & Travel, P.O. Box 22-1011, Anchoage, AK 99522. (907) 245-0200; toll-free (800) 266-8625; www.alaskacoach.com or www.alaskatravel.com. Daily coach service between Anchorage, Seward, Denali National Park and Talkeetna. Custom tour packages also available.

Alaska Trails/Parks Highway Express, Box 84278, Fairbanks, AK 99708; phone (907) 479-3065 or 1-888-600-6001; www.alaskashuttle.com. Two runs daily between Anchorage and Denali Park. Also service between Anchorage, Denali Park, Fairbanks, Valdez and Dawson City with connections to Seward.

Backcountry Connection, PO Box 65, Glennallen, AK 99588; (907) 822-5292 or 1-866-582-5292 (within Alaska); tourwithus@alaska.net; www.alaska–backcountry–tours.com. Tours and service to Kennicott/McCarthy.

Cruise Bus Alaska, Box 75, Seward, AK 99664. (907) 224-7239, or toll free (888) 371-7234; www.cruisebusalaska.com. Year-round charter service for preorganized groups and tours throughout Alaska.

Dalton Highway Express, P.O. Box 71665, Fairbanks, AK 99707. Phone/fax (907) 452-2031; info@daltonhighwayexpress.com; www.daltonhighwayexpress.com. One-day van service between Fairbanks and Deadhorse/Prudhoe Bay; drop-offs and pick-ups for bicyclists arranged.

Denali Overland Transportation Co. Box 330, Talkeetna, AK 99676. Phone (907) 733-2384; www.alaska.net/~denaliak/overland.html. Charter van service between Anchorage, Talkeetna and Denali National Park.

Gray Line of Alaska, 745 W. 4th Ave., Anchorage, AK 99501. (907) 277-5581 or (800) 478-6388; www.graylineofalaska.com. Sightseeing and package motorcoach tours throughout Alaska.

Greyhound Canada Transportation Corp., 2191 2nd Ave., Whitehorse, YT Y1A 3T8, phone (867) 667-2223, fax (867) 633-6858; www.greyhound.ca. Scheduled service to Whitehorse from all U.S.-Canada border crossings; also the Whitehorse depot has carriers to Dawson City and Alaska destinations. (Agents for Parks Highway Express.)

Homer Stage Line, P.O. Box 1912, Homer, AK 99603. (907) 235-7009 or (907) 399-1847; fax (907) 235-0565; hsl@xyz.net; http://homerstageline.com. Service between Anchorage, Seward and Homer.

Norline Coaches (Yukon) Ltd., 34 MacDonald Rd., Whitehorse, YT Y1A 4I2, phone (867) 633-3864; www.norlinecoaches.com. Tours and charters only.

Princess Tours®, 6441 Interstate Circle, Anchorage, AK 99518; phone 1-800-426-0500 or (907) 550-7711; www.princessalaskalodges.com. Motorcoach tours include Dawson City, YT, Anchorage, the Kenai Peninsula, Denali National Park, Fairbanks

Mount Drum rises 12,010 feet among the peaks of the Wrangell Mountains.
(© Carol P. Murdock)

TRAVEL PLANNING

A curious weasel checks out the terrain at Kluane National Park.
(© John Schweider Photography)

and Prudhoe Bay.

RC Shuttles, 1-877-479-0079; www.rcshuttles.com. Connects Haines, Fairbanks and all points in between. Winter service between Anchorage, Denali and Fairbanks.

Seward Bus Line, 1915 N. Seward Hwy.; Box 1338, Seward, AK 99664, phone (907) 224-3608 or (907) 563-0800; www.sewardbusline.com. Daily, year-round service between Anchorage and Seward.

Talkeetna Shuttle Service, P.O. Box 468, Talkeetna, AK 99676. (907) 733-1725 or 1-888-288-6008; tshuttle@alaska.net. Daily, round-trip service between Anchorage and Talkeetna.

Calendar of Events

Following are some of the major events and holidays by month. Also check the current Calendar of Events on www.themilepost.com.

January
Inuvik, NT—Sunrise Festival. **Seward**—Polar Bear Jump-Off Festival.

February
Anchorage—Fur Rendezvous. **Anchor Point**—Snow Rondi. **Cordova**—Iceworm Festival. **Fairbanks/Whitehorse, YT**—Yukon Quest Sled Dog Race; Yukon Sourdough Rendezvous. **Homer**—Winter Carnival. **Ketchikan**—Ketchikan Wearable Art & Runway Fashion Show. **Wasilla/Big Lake/Fairbanks/Nome**—Iron Dog Snowmobile race. **Whitehorse, YT**—Sourdough Rendezvous. **Willow**—Winter Carnival. **Wrangell**—Tent City Festival.

March
Anchorage—Iditarod Trail Sled Dog Race®. **Bethel**—Camai Native Dance Festival. **Dawson City, YT**—Thaw-Di-Graw Spring Carnival. **Fairbanks**—Winter Carnival; North American Sled Dog Championships. **Kodiak**—Pillar Mountain Golf Classic. **Nenana**—Tripod Raising. **Nome**—Bering Sea Ice Classic Golf Tournament; month of Iditarod events. **North Pole**—Winter Carnival. **Skagway**—Windfest; Buckwheat Ski Classic. **Valdez**—Winterfest.

April
Anchorage—Great Alaska Sportsman Show. **Cordova**—Copper Days Celebration. **Girdwood**—Alyeska Spring Carnival. **Juneau**—Alaska Folk Festival. **Skagway**—Mini Folk Festival. **Summit Lake (Richardson Highway)**—Arctic Man Ski and Snow Go Classic. **Valdez**—Extreme Skiing Championships; Mountain Man Snowmachine Hill Climb. **Whitehorse, YT**—Rotary Music Festival. **Wrangell**—Garnet Festival.

May
This month is a busy one for fishing derbies for halibut (Homer, Seldovia and Valdez) and salmon (Ketchikan, Petersburg, Seldovia and Sitka). **Cordova**—Copper River Delta Shorebird Festival. **Dawson City, YT**—International Gold Show. **Delta Junction**—Buffalo Wallow Square Dance Jamboree. **Haines**—Great Alaska Craft Beer & Homebrew Festival. **Haines Junction, YT**—Kluane Mountain Festival. **Homer**—Kachemak Bay Shorebird Festival. **Kodiak**—Crab Festival. **Nome**—Polar Bear Swim. **Petersburg**—Little Norway Festival.

June
Anchorage—Mayor's Midnight Sun Marathon. **Anchor Point**— Kids All-American Fishing Derby. **Cordova**—Annual Salmon & Seafood Festival. **Fairbanks**—Midnight Sun Baseball Game. **Fairbanks/Galena**—Yukon 800. **Haines Junction, YT**—Alsek Music Festival; Kluane Chilkat Bike Relay to **Haines, AK. Juneau**—Gold Rush Days. **Nome**—Midnight Sun Festival. **Palmer**—Colony Days. **Sitka**—Summer Music Festival. **Skagway**—"Golden Spike" Centennial; International Softball Tournament. **Whitehorse, YT**—Yukon International Storytelling Festival.

July
Anderson—Bluegrass Festival. **Chugiak/Eagle River**—Bear Paw Festival. **Dawson City, YT**—Canadian Airlines International Midnight Dome Race; Dawson City Music Festival; Yukon Gold Panning Championships. **Delta Junction**—Deltana Fair. **Fairbanks**—Golden Days; World Eskimo–Indian Olympics. **Girdwood**—Forest Fair. **Haines Junction, YT**—Canada Day celebration; Pine Lake Regatta. **Seward**—Mount Marathon Race®. **Skagway**—International Softball Tournament; Ducky Derby; Soapy Smith's Wake. **Soldotna**—Progress Days. **Stewart-Hyder**—International Rodeo. **Talkeetna**—Moose Dropping Festival. **Watson Lake, YT**—Watson Lake Rodeo.

August
Dawson City and Watson Lake, YT—Discovery Days. **Fairbanks**—Tanana Valley State Fair. **Haines**—Southeast Alaska State Fair; Bald Eagle Music Fest. **Ketchikan**—Blueberry Arts Festival. **Kodiak**—State Fair and Rodeo. **Ninilchik**—Kenai Peninsula State Fair. **Palmer**—Alaska State Fair. **Seward**—Silver Salmon Derby®. **Skagway**—Flower & Garden Show. **Talkeetna**—Bluegrass Festival. **Whitehorse/ Dawson City, YT**—Annual Sourdough Rendezvous Bathtub Race; Klondyke Harvest Fair.

September
Dawson City, YT—Great Klondike Outhouse Race and Bathroom Wall Limerick Contest. **Fairbanks**—Equinox Marathon. **Nome**—Great Bathtub Race. **Skagway/ Whitehorse**—Klondike Trail of '98 Road Relay.

October
Anchorage—Oktoberfest. **Kodiak**—Oktoberfest. **Sitka**—Alaska Day Festival.

November
Anchorage—Carrs/Safeway Great Alaska Shootout. **Fairbanks**—Athabascan Old-Time Fiddling Festival; Top of the World Classic. **Haines**—Bald Eagle Festival. **Ketchikan**—Winter Arts Fair.

December
Cordova—Community Tree Lighting. **Fairbanks**—Winter Solstice Festival. **North Pole**—Candle-lighting. **Talkeetna**—Winterfest.

Camping

Alaska and Canada have both government and private campgrounds. With few exceptions, government and private campgrounds are located along the road system, and most roadside campgrounds accommodate both tents and RVs. Wilderness camping is also available in most state, federal and provincial parklands. *The MILEPOST®* logs all public roadside campgrounds and includes facilities (water, firewood, etc.) and camping fees, length of vehicle or length of stay limits. *The MILEPOST®* highway logs also include private campgrounds. Keep in mind that government campgrounds generally do not offer hookups or other amenities, and often cannot accommodate large RVs and

Get Your ALASKA CAMPGROUND Map & Directory

For Information Call (907) 262-1272
Email: acoa@pobox.alaska.net
or visit us at
www.alaskacampgrounds.net

For A Full Color Alaska Map and Directory please send $2 U.S. postage and handling for requests to the U.S. Canada or Mexico. or $4 U.S. postage and handling for any other country to:

ACOA
P.O. Box 4291
Soldotna, AK 99669

5th-wheelers. Season dates for most campgrounds in the North depend on weather.

NOTE: Campers are urged to use established campgrounds. Overnighting in rest areas and turnouts may be unsafe and is illegal unless otherwise posted.

The MILEPOST® indicates both private and public campgrounds with ▲ tent symbols in the highway logs and on the strip maps.

Alaska

Federal agencies offering recreational campsites are the Bureau of Land Management (BLM), the National Park Service (NPS), the U.S. Forest Service (USFS) and the U.S. Fish and Wildlife Service (USF&WS). Alaska State Parks, the largest state park system in the United States, maintains more than 3,000 campsites within its 120-unit park system.

State Parks. Camping is available at 40 state recreation sites, 5 state parks (Chugach, Denali, Chilkat, Kachemak Bay and Wood-Tikchik), 14 state recreation areas and a state historic park. Reservations are not accepted at any state campgrounds. Camping fees (subject to change) range from $5 to $15. An annual pass, good for unlimited camping in a calendar year, is available for $100 for Alaska residents only. The pass is a windshield decal and is not transferable. There is a day-use parking fee of $3 to $5 per vehicle at state park picnic sites, trailheads and fishing access sites. A full-year (calendar year) parking pass can be purchased for $30. To obtain resident camping or parking passes, send check or money order payable to the State of Alaska. Mail to Alaska Camping Pass, 550 W. 7th Ave., Ste. 1260, Anchorage, AK 99501, or visit their web site at www.alaskastateparks.org.

BLM maintains about 12 campgrounds; fees are charged at some. Unless otherwise posted, all undeveloped BLM public lands are open to free camping, usually for a maximum of 14 days per stay. Contact the Bureau of Land Management, Alaska State Office at 222 W. 7th Avenue, #13, Anchorage, AK 99513-7599; phone (907) 271-5960. The BLM's Alaska State Office has a public information center, located on the first floor (Room 148) of the new Federal Bldg.—U.S. Courthouse in downtown Anchorage. Open 8 A.M. to 3:45 P.M. weekdays (closed holidays). In Fairbanks, stop by the BLM office at 1150 University Ave., phone (907) 474-2251. Online, visit www.ak.blm.gov.

The **National Park Service** maintains 6 campgrounds in Denali National Park and Preserve (see DENALI NATIONAL PARK section). There are established hike-in campgrounds at Glacier Bay and Katmai national parks and preserves, and wilderness camping in other national parks and preserves in Alaska. For more information, contact the parks directly, or access online information from the National Park Service at www.nps.gov.

U.S. Forest Service campgrounds are available in Alaska's 2 national forests: Tongass and Chugach. USFS campgrounds charge a fee of $9 to $15 per night depending on facilities. There is a 14-day limit at most campgrounds; this regulation is enforced. For more information and reservations, visit the National Recreation Reservation Service (NRRS) web site at www.reserveusa.com, or call toll-free 1-877-444-6777. The NRRS is open April 1–Labor Day 8 A.M. to midnight (EST) and from Labor Day–March 31 10 A.M. to 7 P.M. (EST). For more information on campgrounds and other National Forest programs and activities, visit www.fs.fed.us/r10/chugach, or www.fs.fed.us/r10/tongass.

U.S. Fish & Wildlife Service manages camping areas along Skilak Road and Swanson River/Swan Lake Roads within Kenai National Wildlife Refuge. Contact the Refuge Manager, Kenai National Wildlife Refuge, Box 2139, Soldotna, AK 99669, phone (907) 262-7021.

Alaska camping information can also be obtained through the Alaska Public Lands Information Centers; www.nps.gov/aplic.

Canada

Territorial campgrounds in Northwest Territories charge $12 or $15 per night, depending upon the site, in attended campgrounds and parks with facilities. Campground-use firewood is available for a fee.

Yukon Territory has about 45 government campgrounds located along its road system. These well-maintained campgrounds often have kitchen shelters (which may not be used as sleeping accommodations) and free firewood for use at the campground. There is a 14-day limit. A camping permit ($12/night) is required for nonresidents to camp in Yukon government campgrounds.

Self-registration has been reinstituted at all Yukon government campgrounds for the 2003 season. (Non-resident annual permits are *not* available.) Permits are no longer sold through highway vendors. Instructions for self-registration are available at all Yukon government campgrounds.

Provincial park campgrounds and private campgrounds are readily available along Alaska Highway connecting routes in British Columbia and Alberta. Provincial park camping fees range from $10 to $20 a night depending on facilities.

National park campgrounds in Canada generally have a per-night fee ranging from $8 for a tent site to $25 for a full-hookup site. A park motor-license sticker is required for motorists staying overnight in the national parks. Electrical service is standard 60 cycle. Wood for campfires is supplied free to all camping and picnicking grounds. Bring your own ax to split kindling. "Serviced" campgrounds have caretakers. For more information: BC Parks, http://wlapwww.gov.bc.ca/bcparks/.

A summer sunset at 1:30 A.M. on the Alaska Highway. (© Ernest Manewal)

Cell Phones

In the North, cell phone coverage is unpredictable and sporadic outside the cities. We've received and placed calls on our cell phones in the middle of the Alaska Range but have been unable to raise a signal just a few miles outside Fairbanks and even in some areas of Anchorage. Adding to the unpredictability is your cell phone provider's roaming agreements, which

A small plane is dwarfed against a backdrop of glacial ridges. (© Laurent Dick)

may black out certain areas. Cell phone coverage and reception is not as complete in the north as it is in the Lower 48. However, cellular service providers continue working to improve coverage by adding towers and testing equipment frequently.

Crossing the Border

The following provides general guidelines for traveling between the United States and Canada. Regulations and procedures change frequently. To make your trip across the borders easier, please contact U.S. and Canada customs agencies prior to traveling to obtain current customs regulations and information.

Travel between the United States and Canada is usually a fairly straightforward procedure. However, travelers are reminded that all persons and their vehicles are subject to search and possible seizure at the border, according to the laws of whichever country they are entering. Vehicles may be searched at the discretion of the customs officials, whether or not the traveler feels that he or she has complied with customs requirements.

Customs agents in both Canada and the U.S. are charged with enforcing a daunting number of regulations pertaining to agricultural products, commercial goods, alcohol, tobacco and firearms. Canada vigorously enforces its firearms importations laws, and border officials may—at their discretion—search any vehicle for handguns.

Certain items, mainly crafts and souvenirs made from parts of wild animals, have caused some problems for travelers to the North in recent years. An item which may be purchased legally in Alaska, for example carved ivory, can be brought back into the Lower 48 but may not be permitted transit through Canada without a permit. Some items which may be purchased legally in parts of Canada may not be allowed into the United States. For example, a seal-fur doll purchased in Inuvik, NT, would be confiscated by the U.S. Fish & Wildlife Service or U.S. customs because the import of seal products is prohibited except by special permit.

For information on Canadian customs, contact Canda Customs & Revenue Agency, Pacific Region, Main Floor, 333 Dunsmuir St., Vancouver, BC V6B 5R4; phone 1-800-461-9999 within Canada; (204) 983-3500 outside Canada for Automated Customs Information Service: www.ccra-adrc.gc.ca/customs.

For further U.S. customs information, contact the nearest U.S. customs office, or write to U.S. Customs Service, P.O. Box 7407, Washington, DC 20044. In Seattle, WA, phone (206) 553-4676. Also try the Internet at www.customs.gov.

Entry into Canada from the U.S. (non-residents)

Identification: Citizens or permanent residents of the United States do not require passports or visas to enter Canada. However, native-born U.S. citizens should carry some identifying paper that shows their citizenship, in case they are asked for it. This could include a driver's license and voter's registration (together), passport with photo or birth certificate. Social security cards or driver's licenses alone are not positive identification. Birth certificates of children are sometimes required. Proof of residency may also be required. Naturalized U.S. citizens should carry a naturalization certificate or some other evidence of citizenship. Permanent residents of the United States who are not U.S. citizens are advised to have their Resident Alien Card (U.S. Form 1-151 or Form 1-551).

Officials at Canadian Customs are concerned about child abductions. If you are traveling with children, remember to bring identification for them. A parent traveling with his or her young child, without the other parent, should be able to present a notarized statement of custody, a copy of divorce/custody papers or written authorization from the other parent. When traveling with children who are not your own, have proper identification and written permission from a parent or guardian. Persons under 18 years of age who are not accompanied by an adult should bring a letter with them from a parent or guardian giving them permission to travel into Canada. Proof of sufficient funds to travel within and back out of Canada may be required.

Motorists: U.S. motorists are advised to obtain a Canadian Non-resident Interprovincial Motor Vehicle Liability Insurance Card, which provides evidence of financial responsibility. This card is available only in the United States through U.S. insurance companies or their agents. All provinces in Canada require visiting motorists to produce evidence of financial responsibility should they be involved in an accident. Financial responsibility limits vary by province. All national driver's licenses are valid in Canada. (See also Driving Information this section.)

Entry by private boat or plane: Report to Canada Customs by phoning 1-888-226-7277. Provide the names, dates of birth and citizenships of all people on board and the purpose of the trip, and declare any firearms or other goods. You will then be given a reporting number for your records. Upon arriving at the designated customs reporting site, you must call Canada Customs a second time to be advised either to wait for a customs officer or to proceed with your travels.

Baggage: The necessary wearing apparel and personal effects in use by the visitor are admitted free of duty.

To simplify the customs process, carry 3 copies of the list of goods you are bringing with you into Canada. Also, pack consumable goods in containers that customs officers can tie and seal when you arrive at the border.

Up to 50 cigars, 200 cigarettes (1 carton) and 200 grams of manufactured tobacco, 200 tobacco sticks and up to 1.14 litres (40 ounces) of spirituous liquor or 1.5 litres of wine or 24 355 ml (12 ounce) cans or bottles (8.5 litres) of beer or ale may be allowed entry in this manner. Additional quantities of alcoholic beverages up to a maximum or 9.1 litres (2 gallons) may be imported into Canada (except the Northwest Territories) on payment of duty and taxes plus charges for a provincial permit at port of entry. To import tobacco products, a person must be 18 years of age or older, and to import alcoholic beverages, the importer must have reached the legal age established by authorities of the province into which the alcoholic beverages are being entered.

Under Canada's immigration law, foreign visitors with previous Driving Under the Influence (DUI) convictions may be refused entry into Canada or may be required to apply for admittance permits and pay fees of up to $1,500. Due to recent changes to this law, immigration agents will have the authority to admit foreign visitors to Canada with offenses committed more than 10 years ago, without paying the processing fee.

Gifts: Be prepared to provide receipts for gifts in case you are asked to show the dollar value. Gifts are duty- and tax-free when each gift is valued at $60 (Canadian) or less. You cannot claim alcoholic beverages, tobacco products or advertising matter as gifts. If the value of a gift exceeds $60, you may have to pay duties and taxes on the excess amount.

Firearms: Motorists traveling through Canada with hunting-type firearms must obtain an Alaskan Possession and Acquisition License (PAL). Firearms can be registered online at the Canadian Firearms Centre website at www.cfc-ccaf.gc.ca/en/default.asp, or call 1-800-731-4000 for more information. Other types of firearms may require different permits and registration or may be prohibited.

Firearms are classified as non-restricted, restricted or prohibited. Non-restricted firearms include: semi-automatic rifles and shotguns that have barrels at least 18.33 inches/470mm in length and do not otherwise fall into a restricted or prohibited category; and single shot or manual repeating rifles and shotguns of any length, as long as they are not designed or adapted to be fired when reduced to a length of less than 25.74 inches/660mm by folding, telescoping or other means. Prohibited firearms, weapons and devices include: handguns that do not fall into the restricted category; certain adapted rifles or shotguns; automatic weapons; switchblade knives; mace or pepper spray; blowguns; hand-held compact crossbows; silencers; replica firearms and certain cartridge magazines.

Visitors CANNOT, under any circumstances, import prohibited firearms. Contact the Canadian Firearms Centre for more details on firearm categories or for customs information on a specific firearm, weapon or device.

Non-residents can import 200 rounds of ammunition duty-free for hunting purposes, or up to 1,500 rounds duty-free for use at a recognized competition.

You must be at least 18 years of age to import a firearm into Canada. You are allowed to import non-restricted and restricted firearms with the proper documents. If you are importing restricted firearms, you need an Authorization to Transport from the Canadian Firearms Centre.

Non-restricted firearms may be imported only for sporting or hunting use; for use in competitions; for in-transit movement through Canada or for personal protection against wildlife in remote regions of Canada (excluding national parks) as long as the customs officer is satisfied that the circumstances warrant the importation of the firearm.

Non-restricted firearms being transported into Canada must be unloaded. If left unattended in your vehicle, the firearm must be locked in the trunk or a similar compartment of the vehicle or stored out of sight.

You must declare all firearms to the Canadian Customs officer and complete a Non-Resident Firearm Declaration Application Form ($50). The customs officer may check to ensure you have transported the firearm properly. If you have declared a non-restricted or restricted firearm but cannot meet the import requirements or do not have the proper documents, the officer may allow you to remove the firearm from Canada. Or the officer may hold the firearm until you can produce the correct documents. Prohibited firearms, weapons and devices will NOT be returned to you. *Anyone who fails to declare a firearm or illegally carries a firearm into Canada is subject to a number of penalties, including criminal charges and/or seizure of the weapon and the vehicle in which it is carried.*

Animals, plants and their products: To protect plants and animals from pests and disease, the Canadian Food Inspection Agency (CFIA) has controls, restrictions and prohibitions on the entry of plants, animals and their products, including food. To import some of these goods, you will need certificates or permits. Many goods do not need mandatory inspection by the CFIA, but if the goods you are importing need to be inspected, you may have to pay a fee. In some cases, customs officers collect fees for the CFIA.

If you plan to import agricultural, forestry or food items, contact one of the following CFIA Import Service Centres (ISCs) for information *before* you leave. ISC staff handle all enquiries about import requirements for all commodities regulated and inspected by the CFIA. There are three ISCs: Eastern, phone 1-877-493-0468 (in Canada and the U.S.) or (514) 493-0468; Central, phone 1-800-835-4486 (in Canada and the U.S.) or (905) 612-6285; Western, phone 1-888-732-6222 (in Canada and the U.S.) or (604) 666-7042.

Canada has complex requirements, restrictions and limitations that apply to importing meat, eggs, dairy products, fresh fruit and vegetables and other food from around the world. Some of these items can be imported from the United States, but there are limits on the quantity and dollar value of certain food products. To avoid any problems, contact the customs agencies for specific information on limits and restrictions, or do not bring questionable items into Canada.

Information on importing and exporting goods is also available from the CFIA at 1-888-732-6222 or at www.inspection.gc.ca.

Animals: Dogs and cats (over 3 months of age) from the United States must be accompanied by a certificate issued by a licensed veterinarian of Canada or the United States certifying that the animal has been vaccinated against rabies during the preceding 36 months (or 12 months if the certificate does not specify an expiration date); such a certificate shall describe the animal and date of vaccination and shall be initialed by inspectors and returned to the owner.

If you are bringing other kinds of animals from the United States or any animal from any other country, check with a Canadian Food Inspection Agency Import Services Centre before you bring them with you.

Tax rebates for visitors: The current duty rate under the U.S. Tariff treatment, when combined with GST and PST (for BC) is 14.5%. The current Provincial Tax for BC is 7.5%. Taxes in other provinces will be different.

When you leave, you may be eligible for a tax refund on goods you bought in Canada if you take them out of the country within 60 days. For more information, get a copy of the pamphlet called "Tax Refund for Visitors," or call 1-800-668-4748 for more information.

Re-entry into the U.S. (residents)

It is the responsibility of the traveler to satisfy U.S. immigration authorities of his right to re-enter the United States. Canadian immigration officers may caution persons entering from the United States if they may have difficulty in returning.

Re-entry to the United States can be simplified if you list all your purchases before you reach the border; have sales receipts and invoices; and pack purchases separately.

Within 48 hours: Residents of the U.S. visiting Canada for less than 48 hours may bring in for personal or household use merchandise to the fair retail value of $200, free of U.S. duty and tax. Any or all of the following may be included, as long as the total value does not exceed $200: 50 cigarettes, 10 cigars (non-Cuban in origin), 4 ounces/150 ml of alcoholic beverages or perfume.

If any article brought back is subject to

Cyclists encounter steep grades along the Glenn Highway near Caribou Creek.
(© Rich Reid, Colors of Nature)

duty or tax, or if the total value of all articles exceeds $200, no article may be exempted from duty or tax. Members of a family household are not permitted to combine the value of their purchases under this exception.

Persons crossing the international boundary at one point and re-entering the United States in order to travel to another part of Canada should inquire at U.S. customs regarding special exemption requirements.

After more than 48 hours: Residents may bring back, once every 30 days, merchandise for personal or household use to the value of $400 free of U.S. duty and tax. The exemption will be based on the fair retail value of the article acquired, and goods must accompany the resident upon arrival in the United States. Members of a family household traveling together may combine their personal exemptions—thus a family of 5 could be entitled to a total exemption of $2,000. Up to 100 cigars (non-Cuban in origin) per person may be imported into the United States by U.S. residents, and up to 200 cigarettes, and 1 liter of alcoholic beverages if the resident has reached the age of 21 years.

Animals: Your pets, including those taken out of the country and being returned, must have a valid veterinarian health certificate. Particularly, dogs must have proof of rabies vaccination. If you are traveling with pet birds, check with customs about specific requirements. Wildlife and fish are subject to certain import and export restrictions, prohibitions, permits or certificates and quarantine requirements. Endangered species of wildlife and products made from them are generally prohibited from being imported or exported.

Trademarked items: Foreign-made trademarked items may be limited as to the quantity which can be brought into the U.S. The types of items usually of interest to tourists are lenses, cameras, binoculars, optical goods, tape recorders, musical instruments,

TRAVEL PLANNING

Cruising to Alaska this Summer

It's fortunate that Alaska has more coastline than all the rest of the U.S. combined. Otherwise, Alaska-bound cruiseships might face a seaborne gridlock in 2003. But not to worry. At 6,640 miles of coast, there is plenty of room for all comers, even with a record-shattering 47 vessels scheduled to ply the Big State's sea lanes from late spring into fall.

The number and variety of ships has never been greater (see list following). Choices range from cruise yachts for 12 passengers to a megaliner carrying 2,600. Among all these vessels, there's a geniune sternwheel paddleboat, a floating condominium, even a modern ship styled like an early 1900s coastal steamer.

The ships come in 3 categories: large to mega liners carrying 1,000 passengers or more; mid-sized vessels with 300 to 1,000 guests; and the smaller members of the fleet carrying fewer than 300 passengers.

Most of the large and mid-sized ships are actually floating resorts. They come complete with swimming pools, theaters, Vegas-type stage shows, casinos, fitness centers, cocktail lounges and varied dining choices.

Guests aboard the smaller vessels forgo many resort amenities. In exchange, they get to explore small, remote wilderness inlets and crannies where all manner of sealife and wild critters reside.

Aboard all ships, large and small, the Alaska experience is further enhanced through on-board lectures and port programs.

While there is great number and variety to choose from among cruise ships, there are basically 4 choices when it comes to Alaska cruising routes. The most traditional route is the "Inside Passage" round trip from Vancouver or Seattle through the Southeast Alaska panhandle and return, with stops at various ports such as Ketchikan, Juneau, Sitka and Skagway.

Another favorite cruise route is the sail-one-way, fly-the-other "Gulf and Glaciers" option. This route provides a sailing between Vancouver and Seward via the Southeast Alaska panhandle, the Gulf of Alaska and Prince William Sound.

The third choice is a cruise route entirely within Alaska waters, with vessels exploring remote wilderness bays and channels. Some call at Native villages. Activities include whale watching, kayaking, Zodiac excursions and hikes on pristine island shores.

And finally there are expedition cruise routes, which may venture from Alaska ports across the Bering Sea to the Russian Far East and return.

Regardless of the cruise route, most Alaska voyages include time to view glaciers. Glacier Bay National Park and Preserve at the northern end of the Southeas panhandle and College Fjord in the southcentral region's Prince William Sound are the best known areas. Lesser known but just as spectacular are Hubbard Glacier in Russell Fjord and LeConte Glacier near Petersburg. Tracy Arm Fjord and twin Sawyer glaciers near Juneau provide other popular viewing areas.

Cruise ships make more than 500 port calls at Juneau during the summer.
(© David Job)

LARGE TO MEGA LINERS

Carnival Cruise Lines (1-800-CARNIVAL; www.carnival.com) will position its "Fun Ship" *Carnival Spirit* for a season of 7-night Gulf and Glaciers sailings between Vancouver and Seward and 7-night round trip Inside Passage voyages from Vancouver to Southeast Alaska. Fares from $799.

Celebrity Cruises (1-800-437-3111; www.celebrity.com) returns to Alaska with 3 vessels: *Infinity*, *Mercury* and *Summit*. The line will offer week-long round trip voyages from Vancouver to Southeast Alaska, 7-night 1-way itineraries between Vancouver and Seward and longer trips between San Diego, Southeast Alaska and Vancouver. Fares from $800.

Holland America Line (1-877-SAIL-HAL; www.hollandamerica.com) will dispatch 8 vessels to Alaska, ranging from A (for *Amsterdam*) to Z (for *Zaandam*) plus *Maasdam*, *Ryndam*, *Statendam*, *Veendam*, *Volendam* and recently acquired, mid-range *Prinsendam*. HAL will continue weekly Seattle- and Vancouver-based Inside Passage round trips to Southeast Alaska plus week-long journeys between Vancouver and Seward. *Prinsendam* will offer 2-week round trips from San Francisco. Fares from $889.

Norwegian Cruise Line (1-800-327-7030; www.ncl.com) will originate 7-night Inside Passage cruises from Seattle, this year with 2 ships: *Norwegian Sky* and *Norwegian Sun*. A third vessel, *Norwegian Wind*, will make weekly Inside Passage voyages from Vancouver. Fares from $849.

Princess Cruises (1-800-PRINCESS; www.princesscruises.com) also offers weekly Inside Passage sailings from Seattle aboard *Star Princess*, the largest ship (2,600 passengers) in the Alaska trade. *Pacific Princess* will make 11-night sailings between San Francisco and Southeast Alaska. Four other ships will sail weekly between Vancouver and Seward: *Coral Princess*, *Island Princess*, *Sun Princess* and *Dawn Princess*. Fares from $829.

Royal Caribbean International (1-800-327-6700; www.royalcaribbean.com) will send 3 ships to Alaska in 2003, offering 2 basic itineraries. *Vision of the Seas* and *Radiance of the Seas* will sail round trip from Vancouver in 7 nights (or, on one *Vision* trip, 5 nights) to and through Southeast Alaska. *Legend of the Sea* will sail between Vancouver and Seward, also in seven nights. Fares from $669.

MID-SIZED VESSELS

Crystal Cruises (1-800-820-6663; www.crystalcruises.com) returns the 6-star luxury liner *Crystal Harmony* to Alaska, offering round trips from San Francisco to Southeast Alaska (in 10 or 11 nights) and a 10-night option from Vancouver to Alaska with return to San Francisco. Fares from $2,520.

Radisson Seven Seas Cruises (1-800-285-1835; www.rssc.com) will dispatch its new all-suites, all balconies *Seven Seas Mariner* with a variety of choices. Among them: sailings between Vancouver and Seward in 7 nights; 8-night sailings from Los Angeles and San Francisco to Ketchikan then Vancouver; Vancouver to Vancouver via Southeast Alaska in 7 nights and an 11-night sailing from Vancouver to Southeast Alaska that disembarks in San Francisco. Fares from $2,515.

ResidenSea Ltd. (1-800-970-6601; www.residensea.com) brings *The World* to Alaska waters this year; it's a seagoing community of 110 privately-owned luxury apartments afloat, some available as rental condos. The vessel also offers 88 rental studios. the ship will arrive in Anchorage in July after a 2-week cruise from Japan. A 19-night voyage from Anchorage to Vancourver will call at Southcentral and Southeast ports. Alaska cruise fares from $7,650.

SMALLER SHIPS

American Safari Cruises (1-888-862-8881; www.americansafaricruises.com) is a line whose ships carry either 12 pampered passengers aboard the *Safari Escape* and *Safari Spirit* or 22 on the *Safari Quest*. The *Escape* and the *Spirit* will sail between Juneau and Prince Rupert, BC in 7 nights; the *Quest* will operate between Juneau and Sitka, also in 7 nights. Spring and fall positioning cruises will sail between Seattle and Juneau.

Fares from $3,695.

American West Steamboat Company (1-800-434-1232; www.empressofthenorth.com) brings a geniune sternwheel paddleboat to Alaska cruising. The U.S-built *Empress of the North* is brand new and will carry 236 passengers on an 11-night Inside Passage itinerary between Seattle and Juneau. Fares from $4,699.

Clipper Cruise Line (1-800-325-0010; www.clippercruise.com) offers 4 options aboard 2 vessels. *Yorktown Clipper* provides 11-night folklore and history sailings between Seattle and Juneau and 7-night Inside Passage panhandle trips between Juneau and Ketchikan. *Clipper Odyssey* offers a 13-night trip between Seward and Seattle and a 14-night expedition from Russia to Seward. Fares from $2,410.

Cruise West (1-800-888-9378; www.cruisewest.com) offers the most options of any cruise line in the Alaska trade. Company flagship *Spirit of Oceanus* will sail 13-night open-jaw voyages between Nome, Yanrakynnot in Russia and Anchorage. It also offers 12-night sailings between Vancouver and Anchorage. The line's vintage-style *Spirit of '98* will sail between Seattle and Juneau with an 8-night itinerary.

The other 5 ships of the fleet—*Spirit of Alaska, Spirit of Columbia, Spirit of Discovery, Spirit of Endeavor* and *Sheltered Seas*—offer additional options from 3 to 10 nights including cruises between Seattle and Juneau, trips within Southeast Alaska and Prince William Sound sailings from Whittier. Fares from $949.

Discovery Voyages (1-800-324-7602; www.discoveryvoyages.com) offers 4 Prince William Sound nature cruises aboard *Discovery*, a former missionary vessel. Choices vary from 4- and 5-night wilderness and whale viewing voyages to 5 days of cruising combined with 2 nights ashore with flightseeing and river rafting adventures. A fourth choice provides a 10-night birding/wildlife excursion. Fares from $2,750.

Glacier Bay Cruise Line (1-800-451-5952; www.glacierbaycruiseline.com) provides at least one full day in Glacier Bay National Park on each of its cruises. Vessels *Wilderness Discoverer, Wilderness Adventurer* and *Wilderness Explorer* provide varying degrees of adventure cruising that includes kayaking secluded inlets, hiking remote beaches, whale watching and calls at seldom-visited Native villages. Positioning trips to and from Seattle are also available. Fares from $1,780.

Lindblad Expeditions (1-800-EXPEDITION; www.expeditions.com) will dispatch twin vessels *Sea Lion* and *Sea Bird*, offering twin options for exploring the waters of the Inside Passage. One is a 7-night cruise between Juneau and Sitka. The other is a spring or fall 10-night sailing between Seattle and Juneau. Fares from $3,690.

Society Expeditions (1-800-548-8669; www.societyexpeditions.com) returns to the cruise line's elegant expedition-class *World Discoverer* to "far out" Alaska cruising, starting with a 3-week voyage from Japan to the Russian coast, then across the Bering Sea to Nome. Other 18- and 19-night expeditions explor the coast of Russia's Kamchatka Peninsula and even approach the edge of the Arctic ice pack. Fares from $7,749.

Juneau-based travel writer (and former Alaska legislator) Mike Miller has covered the North Country scene in newspapers, magazines and books since 1954.

MILEPOST® *field editor Earl Brown enjoys the view on Top of the World Highway.*
(© Earl L. Brown, staff)

jewelry, precious metal-ware, perfumes, watches and clocks. Returning residents are allowed an exemption, usually one article of a type bearing a protected trademark. The item must be for your personal use and not for sale.

Entry into the U.S. from Canada (non-residents)

Foreign visitors entering the U.S. for the first time are required to pay a land border user fee of $6 U.S. per person. This fee is payable in U.S. currency or U.S. travelers cheques only. Please have U.S. funds prior to arriving at the U.S. border. NOTE: This does not apply to citizens of Canada.

Exemptions: Non-residents of the U.S. may bring in for personal or household use merchandise to the fair retail value of $200, free of U.S. duty and tax. In addition to $200 in items, some articles may be brought in free of duty and tax. They must be for your personal use and not for others or for sale. These exemptions include personal effects (wearing apparel, articles of personal adornment, toilet articles, hunting, fishing and photographic equipment); one liter of alcoholic beverages (wine, beer or liquor) if you are an adult non-resident; 200 cigarettes, or 50 cigars, or 2 kilograms (4.4 lbs.) of smoking tobacco, or proportionate amounts of each; and vehicles for personal use if imported in connection with your arrival.

Gifts: Articles up to $100 in total value for use as bona fide gifts to other persons may be brought in free of duty and tax, if you will be in the U.S. for at least 72 hours and have not claimed this gift exemption in the past 6 months. This gift exemption may include up to 100 cigars.

Restricted or Prohibited Items: Some items must meet certain requirements, require a license or permit, or may be prohibited entry. Among these are: liquor-filled candy (prohibited); fruits, plants and endangered species of plants, vegetables and their products; firearms and ammunition, if not intended for legitimate hunting or lawful sporting purposes; hazardous articles (fireworks, dangerous toys, toxic or poisonous substances); lottery tickets; meats, poultry and products (sausage, pate); narcotics and dangerous drugs; pets (cats, dogs and birds); pornographic articles and publications; switchblade knives; trademarked items (certain cameras, watches, perfumes, musical instruments, jewelry and metal flatware); vehicles and motorcycles not equipped to comply with U.S. safety or clean air emission standards if your visit is for more than one year; wildlife (birds, fish, mammals, animals) and endangered species, including any part or product (pheasants, articles from reptile skins, whalebone or ivory, mounted specimens and trophies, feathers or skins of wild birds).

If you require medicine containing habit-forming drugs, carry only the quantity normally needed and properly identified, and have a prescription or written statement from your personal physician that the medicine is necessary for your physical well-being. Other pharmaceuticals and/or medicinal devices other than for the personal use of the traveler must be approved by the U.S. Food and Drug Administration.

Re-entry into Canada (residents)

When returning to Canada, residents must declare all of the goods they acquired abroad and are bringing back, as purchases, gifts, prizes or awards. Residents need to include goods still in their possession that they bought at a Canadian or foreign duty-free shop. They must also declare any repairs or modifications made to their vehicle, vessel or aircraft while they were out of the country. If unsure about whether an article is admissible or if it should be declared, residents should always declare it first and then ask a customs officer.

(NOTE: Residents of Canada should be aware that they may not import U.S. rental vehicles into Canada. These conveyances are not admissable under customs regulations for touring purposes or for other leisure activities, nor is any local use permitted. The only time a U.S. conveyance may be entered into Canada by a Canadian resident is if there is an emergency situation involving the Canadian resident, and he/she has no other means of getting back to Canada. If a U.S. vehicle is found in Canada and driven or rented by a Canadian resident, the vehicle is subject to customs seizure.)

Absence of 24 hours or more: Residents can claim goods worth up to $50 as a personal exemption. This does not apply to tobacco products and alcoholic beverages. Residents

TRAVEL PLANNING

Sukakpak Mountain is a landmark on the 414-mile Dalton Highway.
(© Rich Reid, Colors of Nature)

may have to make a written declaration. If the goods they bring in are worth more than $50, they cannot claim this exemption and must pay duties on the full value.

Absence of 48 hours or more: Residents can claim goods worth up to $200 in total. These goods can include tobacco products and alcoholic beverages. They may have to make written declaration.

After any trip of 48 hours or longer, you are entitled to a special duty rate on goods worth up to $300 more than your personal exemption. The current special duty rate under the United States Tariff treatment, when combined with GST, is 8 percent.

Absence of 7 days or more: Residents can claim goods up to $500 in total. These goods can include tobacco products and alcoholic beverages. Residents may have to make a written declaration.

To claim tobacco products and alcoholic beverages, residents must meet the age requirements set by the province or territory where they enter Canada. Tobacco products may include up to 200 cigarettes, 50 cigars or cigarillos, 200 tobacco sticks and 200 grams of manufactured tobacco. Alcoholic beverages may include up to 1.14 litres (40 ounces) of wine or liquor, or 24 355 ml (12-ounce) cans or bottles (8.5 liters) of beer or ale. If you bring in more than the free allowance, the cost may be high, since you will have to pay both customs and provincial or territorial assessments.

Gifts: Under certain conditions, residents may send gifts from outside Canada duty- and tax-free to friends in Canada. Each gift must be worth $60 or less and cannot be an alcoholic beverage, a tobacco product or advertising matter. If the gift is worth more than $60, the recipient will have to pay regular duties on the excess amount. It is always a good idea to include a gift card to avoid any misunderstanding. Gifts brought back with the resident do not qualify for the gift exemption.

In most cases, you have to pay regular duties on prizes and awards you receive outside Canada.

Driving North

Driving to the North is no longer the ordeal it was in the early days. Those old images of the Alaska Highway with vehicles stuck in mud up to their hubcaps are far removed from the asphalt-surfaced Alaska Highway of today.

Motorists can still expect road construction and some rough road. But have patience! Ongoing projects are helping to improve severely deteriorated sections of road.

Roads in the North range from multi-lane freeways to 1-lane dirt and gravel roads. The more remote roads are gravel. Motorists are much farther from assistance, and more preparation is required for these roads.

Major highways in Alaska are paved with the exception of the following highways that are at least partially gravel: Steese Highway (Alaska Route 6), Taylor Highway (Alaska Route 5), Elliott Highway (Alaska Route 2), Dalton Highway (Alaska Route 11) and Denali Highway (Alaska Route 8).

In Yukon Territory, the Alaska Highway, the Haines Highway and the Klondike Highway from Skagway to Dawson City are asphalt-surfaced. All other roads are gravel.

Major routes through Alberta and British Columbia are paved, with the exception of the Cassiar Highway (BC Highway 37), which has both paved and gravel sections.

Highways within western Northwest Territories are mostly gravel roads, although paving continues on many routes. Paving is almost completed on NWT Highway 3 to Yellowknife, and NWT Highway 1 is paved from its junction with Highway 3 to the Alberta border.

RV owners should be aware of the height of their vehicles in metric measurements, as bridge heights in Canada are noted in meters.

Know your vehicle and its limitations. Some Northern roads may not be suitable for a large motorhome or trailer, but most roads will present no problem to a motorist who allots adequate time and uses common sense.

Keep in mind the variable nature of road conditions. Some sections of road may be in poor condition because of current construction or recent bad weather. Other highways—particularly gravel roads closed in winter—may be very rough or very smooth, depending on when maintenance crews last worked on the road.

Asphalt surfacing for most Northern roads is Bituminous Surface Treatment (BST), an alternative to hot-mix pavement which involves application of aggregates and emulsified asphalt. Also known as "chip seal," recently applied or repaired BST is as smooth as any Lower 48 superhighway. However, weather and other factors can lead to failures in the surfacing which include potholes and loss of aggregate.

Also watch for "frost heaves" caused by subsidence of the ground under the road.

Many gravel roads in the North are treated with calcium chloride as a dust-control measure. This substance corrodes paint and metal; wash your vehicle as soon as possible. In heavy rains, calcium chloride and mud combine to make a very slippery road surface; drive carefully!

Safeguard against theft while at campgrounds, rest stops or in the cities. Always lock your vehicle, be sure valuables are out of sight in an unattended vehicle and report any thefts to the authorities.

NOTE: Driving with the headlights on at all times is the law in Yukon Territory and recommended on roads in Alaska.

Planning your trip

Depending on where you want to stop and how much time you have to spend, you can count on driving anywhere from 150 to 500 miles a day. On most roads in the North, you can figure on comfortably driving 250 to 300 miles a day.

In the individual highway sections, log mileages are keyed on the highway strip maps which accompany each highway section in *The MILEPOST*®. You may also use the mileage boxes on these maps to calculate mileages between points, or refer to the mileage box at the beginning of the highway as well. Also use the Mileage Chart on the back of the Plan-A-Trip Map.

Once you have figured the number of driving miles in your itinerary, you can calculate approximate gas cost using the Gas Price Averages chart on page 20. (Keep in mind that year 2003 prices will vary from 2002 summer averages.) U.S. motorists factor in the current exchange rate for Canadian prices using the conversion chart this section.

Normally, May through October is the best time to drive to Alaska. A severe winter or wet spring may affect road conditions, and there may be some rough road until road maintenance crews get out to upgrade and repair. Motels, hotels, gas stations and restaurants are open year-round in the cities and on many highways. On more remote routes, such as the Cassiar Highway, not all businesses are open year-round. Check ahead for accommodations and gas if traveling these roads in winter.

Road Condition Reports

General road conditions are noted in the introduction to each highway in *The MILEPOST*®. Specific areas of concern are also called out in the log. Current seasonal road conditions provided by government agencies may be obtained at www.themilepost.com. Or contact the following:

Alaska road conditions. Visit the home page of the Alaska Dept. of Transportation at www.dot.state.ak.us for both summer construction advisories and winter road conditions. The Department of Transportation has a new telephone and online system for obtaining road condition information. The new system is accessible by dialing 511 or by clicking on "Traveler Information" at www.dot.state.ak.us. The 511 Online Travel Information and the 511 telephone number provide current road conditions and hazards, and the online Road Weather Information

System provides current weather conditions from roads throughout the state. "Navigator" reports on road construction are available from visitor centers; also check local newspapers. For 24-hour recorded daily road construction advisories, phone (907) 273-6037 in Anchorage for Southcentral Alaska; phone (907) 456-7623 for Fairbanks, Tok and Valdez areas; or (907) 456-7623 for the Steese Highway. Or toll-free (in Alaska) 1-800-478-7675.

Yukon road conditions: For year-round daily recorded updates, phone (867) 456-7623; toll free in YT only 1-877-456-7623. Yukon Transportation Maintenance Daily Road Report on-line at www.gov.yk.ca/roadreport/.

British Columbia road conditions. General road information is available 24 hours-a-day at a charge of 75 cents per minute by phoning 1-900-565-4997 in Canada. For recorded road conditions on the Alaska Highway between Wonowon and the Yukon border, phone (250) 774-7447. Or go to www.gov.bc.ca/th and click on Road Reports (www.gov.th.gov.bc.ca/bchighways/roadreports/roadreports.htm).

Northwest Territories road conditions: For the South Mackenzie, phone 1-800-661-0751 in NWT; for the North Mackenzie, 1-800-661-0750 in NWT. For reports on condition of the Dempster Highway, call 1-800-661-0752 in NWT.

Alberta road conditions: Phone 1-800-642-3810 (in Alberta).

Speed Limits

A safe assumption when Alaska trip planning is to average 55 mph on paved highways. For more remote gravel roads, such as the Taylor Highway and Denali Highway, a safe average might be 40 to 45 mph.

Actual driving time may vary due to weather, road construction, current road conditions, amount of traffic, time of day, season, driver ability and rest stops, but 55 mph seems to be a reliable average for the main routes.

The MILEPOST® references speed limits on some sections of highways to give an idea of travel time, but on the whole, we do not include posted speed limits. Posted speed limits on paved highways in Alaska range from 65 mph on straightaways to 45 mph through communities to 35 mph on winding sections of road.

Vehicle Preparation

There are some simple preparations before your trip North that will make driving easier and more trouble-free. First, make sure your vehicle and tires are in good condition. An inexpensive and widely available item to include is a set of clear plastic headlight covers (or black metal matte screens). These protect your headlights from flying rocks and gravel. You might also consider a wire-mesh screen across the front of your vehicle to protect paint, grill and radiator from flying rocks. The finer the mesh, the more protection from flying gravel. For those hauling trailers, a piece of quarter-inch plywood fitted over the front of your trailer offers protection. There is no practical way to protect the windshield.

Crankcases are seldom damaged, but gas tanks can be harmed on rough gravel roads. Sometimes, rocks work their way in between the plate and gas tank, wearing a hole in the tank. However, drivers maintaining safe speeds should have no problems with punctured gas tanks. A high vehicle clearance is

Ice Roads of the Northwest Territories

I knelt on the glare ice in the middle lane of the Mackenzie River's East Channel and swept snow from the ice road with my gloved hands.

"Do you plan to clear the snow all the way to Tuk?" my northern tour guide Frank Pielack asked amusedly from his warm seat in the Bronco.

I was fascinated by a close-up look at the ice slabs we had been driving on since we'd set off from Inuvik for Tuktoyaktuk (Tuk). So many shapes and colours shone through the twinkling ice—not just whites but greens, blues and every shade in between. The ice slabs were over 6 feet thick but broken and streaked by fault lines, overflow cracks and air bubbles.

The ice was so shattered that I returned rather gingerly to the warm car. Why didn't we break through? Or why didn't we slither off the road despite our momentum? These questions along with the sounds of cracking ice haunted me all the way to Tuk.

I was cautious and a little nervous, but I was even more entranced by driving on the Kugmalit Bay sea ice closer to Tuk. Unlike the wide, flat river road, the ocean road was a narrow channel between high snowbanks and pressure ridges that evoked images of ice cream and meringue.

Despite the eminent dangers of the ice, Frank and I celebrated our safe arrival in Tuk at the Beluga Jamboree and enjoyed the local people, activities and natural wonders that can only be found in the spring by traveling the spectacular winter roads.

There are 2 types of these fascinating winter roads in the North: snow roads built over land and ice roads built over water. You can travel much farther on a winter road than a summer one in the Northwest Territories. In winter, ice bridges allow you to drive across the Liard River to Fort Simpson; the Mackenzie River to Fort Providence, Camsell Bend and Tsiigehtchic; and the Peel River to Fort McPherson.

Snow roads provide access to bush camps and communities and remote mining sites otherwise serviced by air. Usually open between mid-December and late March or early April, winter access roads connect: Inuvik to Tuk (114 miles/183 km) with a 53-mile/83-km spur to Aklavik; Mackenzie Highway to Trout Lake (78 miles/126 km); Wrigley to Fort Good Hope (300 miles/482 km) with spur roads to Colville Lakes (100 miles/161 km) and to Fort Franklin (65 miles/105 km); Yellowknife Highway to Rae Lakes (120 miles/194 km) with Wha Ti spur (94 miles/151 km); and the privately maintained Lupin gold mine road from the Ingraham Trail (380 miles/612 km).

Building an ice road in winter to have it disappear in spring is a challenge. Work starts when the ice on lakes and rivers is barely 18 inches/45cm thick. Scouts set off in lightweight, balloon-tired or tracked vehicles to select a route. Heavier tracked vehicles with snowplows scrape away the insulating snow to allow cold air to penetrate and thicken the ice. Compacted snowfill bridges or temporary single-lane steel bridges are put in place at some stream and river crossings.

Ice roads provide access during long Northern winters. (© Lyn Hancock)

The roadway is widened to 141 feet/40m in some areas, and holes are drilled to test the thickness of the ice and to determine allowable loads. Snow machines must have a minimum of 6 inches/15cm of ice and cars or light trucks at least 8 inches/20cm before they may travel the ice roadway. The ice is checked thoroughly for hazards before it is passable.

But even after precautions have been taken, winter road travel can be hazardous. Sudden drops in temperature, fluctuating water levels and overflows can cause cracks in the ice. Blowouts or popouts (sudden gaping holes caused by heavy vehicles creating waves under the ice that hit the shoreline, roll back and hit other oncoming waves) may be avoided by slowing down to about 12 mph/20 kmph, keeping safe distance between vehicles and meeting the shoreline at a 45-degree angle to decrease impact.

Cold temperatures made even colder by wind chill can freeze unprotected skin in less than a minute and cause vehicles to break down. Carry chains, extra gas and a portable gas heater, water, food, extra layers of warm clothing, a sleeping bag, a flashlight and flares and flags or reflectors. It is important to wear warm clothing and keep your hands and feet dry and your head, face and neck warm.

No services are available on winter roads, but signs are posted to indicate speed limits, distances between communities, maximum allowable weight, closures, and phone numbers for further information.

Despite the hazards, you'll really feel you're in the North if you travel a winter road—especially an ice road. From fall freezeup to spring breakup, you can drive to the Arctic Ocean and experience the Great White North as you always imagined it.

Author Lyn Hancock has traveled throughout the North—by car, by canoe, on foot, by airplane and probably by dog team. She has written several books and many articles and is also a photographer, lecturer and travel consultant.

best for some of the rougher gravel roads.

Also keep in mind the simple precautions that make driving easier. A visor or tinted glass helps when you're driving into the sun. Good windshield wipers and a full windshield washer (or a bottle of wash and a squeegee) make life easier. Many motorists also find bug screens to be a wise investment.

Dust and mud are generally not a major problem on northern roads, though you may run into both. Heavy rains combined with a gravel road or roadbed torn up for construction make mud. Mud flaps are suggested. Dust can seep into everything, and it's difficult if not impossible to keep it out. Remember to close the windows on your trailer or camper when on a dusty road. It also helps to keep clothes, food and bedding in sealed plastic bags. Also, check your air filter periodically.

Driving at slow, safe speeds not only keeps down the dust for drivers behind you, it also helps prevent you from spraying other vehicles with gravel (see Speed Limits this section).

Drive with your headlights on at all times. This allows you to be seen more easily, especially in dusty conditions or when approaching vehicles are driving into the sun. It is also the law in the Yukon and posted roads in Alaska.

NOTE: If driving on a paved surface, it is still necessary to observe "Loose Gravel" signs. Drive slowly.

Although auto shops in Northern communities are generally well-stocked with parts, carry the following for emergencies and on-the-spot repairs: flares; first-aid kit; trailer bearings; bumper jack with lug wrench; electrician's tape; assortment of nuts and bolts; fan belt; 1 or 2 spare tires (2 spares for remote roads); and a tool set including crescent wrenches, socket and/or open-end wrenches, hammer, screwdrivers, pliers, wire, and a prybar for changing the fan belt.

If you are driving a vehicle which may require parts not readily available up North, add whatever you think necessary. You may wish to carry a few extra gallons of gas, water, and fluid for brakes, power steering and automatic transmissions.

If your vehicle should break down on the highway, and tow truck service is needed, you will normally be able to flag down a passing motorist. Travelers in the North are generally helpful in such situations (traditionally, the etiquette of the country requires one to stop and provide assistance). If you are the only person traveling in the disabled vehicle, be sure to leave a note on your windshield indicating when you left the vehicle and in which direction you planned to travel.

Gasoline

Unleaded gas is widely available in Alaska and is the rule in Canada. Diesel fuel is also commonly available. Good advice for Northern travelers: gas up whenever possible.

In the North, as elsewhere, gas prices vary (see chart this section). Generally, gas prices are slightly higher in Canada and Alaska than the Lower 48, but this is not a hard and fast rule. You may find gas in Anchorage or elsewhere at the same price—or even lower—than at home. A general rule of thumb is the more remote the gas station, the higher the price. Gas prices may vary considerably from service station to service station within the same community.

It is a good idea to carry cash, since some gas stations in Alaska are independents and do not accept credit cards. Most Chevron, Shell/Texaco and Tesoro stations will accept VISA or MasterCard. Also watch for posted gas prices that are for *cash,* but not noted as such. Besides double-checking the posted price before filling up, also ask the attendant which pump is for unleaded, regular or diesel, depending on what you want.

Keep in mind that Canadian gas stations have converted to the metric system; quantity and price are based on liters (see Gas Cost in U.S. Funds Per Gallon chart this section). There are 3.785 liters per U.S. gallon, 4.5 liters per imperial gallon. See also Liters to U.S. Gallons conversion chart this section.

Insurance

Auto insurance is mandatory in Alaska and all Canadian provinces and territories. The minimum liability insurance requirement in Canada is $200,000 Canadian. Drivers should carry adequate car insurance before entering the country. Visiting motorists are required to produce evidence of financial responsibility should they be involved in an accident. There is an automatic fine if visitors are involved in an accident and found to be uninsured. Your car could be impounded for this. Your insurance company should be able to provide you with proof of insurance coverage (request a Canadian Nonresident Interprovincial Motor Vehicle Liability Insurance Card) that would be accepted as evidence of financial responsibility.

Tires

On gravel, the faster you drive, the faster your tires will wear out. So take it easy, and you should have no tire problems, provided you have the right size for your vehicle, with the right pressure, not overloaded, and not already overly worn. Belted bias or radial ply tires are recommended for gravel roads.

Carry 1 good spare. Consider 2 spares if you are traveling remote gravel roads such as the Dempster or Dalton highways. The space-saver (doughnut) spare tires found in some passenger cars are not adequate for travel on gravel roads.

LITERS TO U.S. GALLONS

Liters	Gallons	Liters	Gallons	Liters	Gallons
1	.3	21	5.5	41	10.8
2	.5	22	5.8	42	11.1
3	.8	23	6.1	43	11.4
4	1.1	24	6.3	44	11.6
5	1.3	25	6.6	45	11.9
6	1.6	26	6.9	46	12.2
7	1.8	27	7.1	47	12.4
8	2.1	28	7.4	48	12.7
9	2.4	29	7.7	49	12.9
10	2.6	30	7.9	50	13.2
11	2.9	31	8.2	51	13.5
12	3.2	32	8.5	52	13.7
13	3.4	33	8.7	53	14.0
14	3.7	34	9.0	54	14.3
15	4.0	35	9.2	55	14.5
16	4.2	36	9.5	56	14.8
17	4.5	37	9.8	57	15.0
18	4.8	38	10.0	58	15.3
19	5.0	39	10.3	59	15.6
20	5.3	40	10.6	60	15.9

For more precise conversion: 1 liter equals .2642 gallons; 1 gallon equals 3.785 liters.

GAS PRICE AVERAGES SUMMER 2002

Alaska Location	Per Gallon U.S. Funds	Canada Location	Per Liter Canadian Funds*
Anchorage	$1.49	Dawson Creek, BC	$.77
Coldfoot	2.34	Calgary, AB	.69
Denali Park	1.73	Fort Nelson, BC	.85
Fairbanks	1.48	Prince Rupert, BC	.74
Glennallen	1.77	Watson Lake, YT	.83
Valdez	1.85	Whitehorse, YT	.85

*See chart below for equivalent cost in U.S. funds for 1 gallon

GAS COST IN U.S. FUNDS PER GALLON

If the Canadian Exchange rate is: $1.00 U.S. equals Canadian funds:		40% $1.40	45% $1.45	50% $1.50	55% $1.55	60% $1.60
	.65	1.76	1.70	1.64	1.59	1.54
	.67	1.81	1.75	1.69	1.64	1.58
	.69	1.87	1.80	1.74	1.68	1.63
Canadian	.71	1.92	1.85	1.79	1.73	1.68
Price	.73	1.97	1.91	1.84	1.78	1.73
Per Liter	.75	2.03	1.96	1.89	1.83	1.77
	.77	2.08	2.01	1.94	1.88	1.82
	.79	2.14	2.06	1.99	1.93	1.87
	.81	2.19	2.11	2.04	1.98	1.92
	.83	2.24	2.17	2.09	2.03	1.96
	.85	2.30	2.22	2.14	2.08	2.01
	.87	2.35	2.27	2.20	2.12	2.06
	.89	2.41	2.32	2.25	2.17	2.11
	.91	2.46	2.38	2.30	2.22	2.15
	.93	2.51	2.43	2.35	2.27	2.20

For example: If gas costs $0.69 Canadian per liter and the current exchange rate is 40% ($1.00 U.S. equals $1.40 Canadian), using the above chart, the equivalent to 1 U.S. gallon of gas costs $1.87 U.S. Or cost per liter X 3.785 divided by exchange rate (1.40)=U.S. cost per gallon.

SOUTHCENTRAL/SOUTHWEST FERRY ROUTES

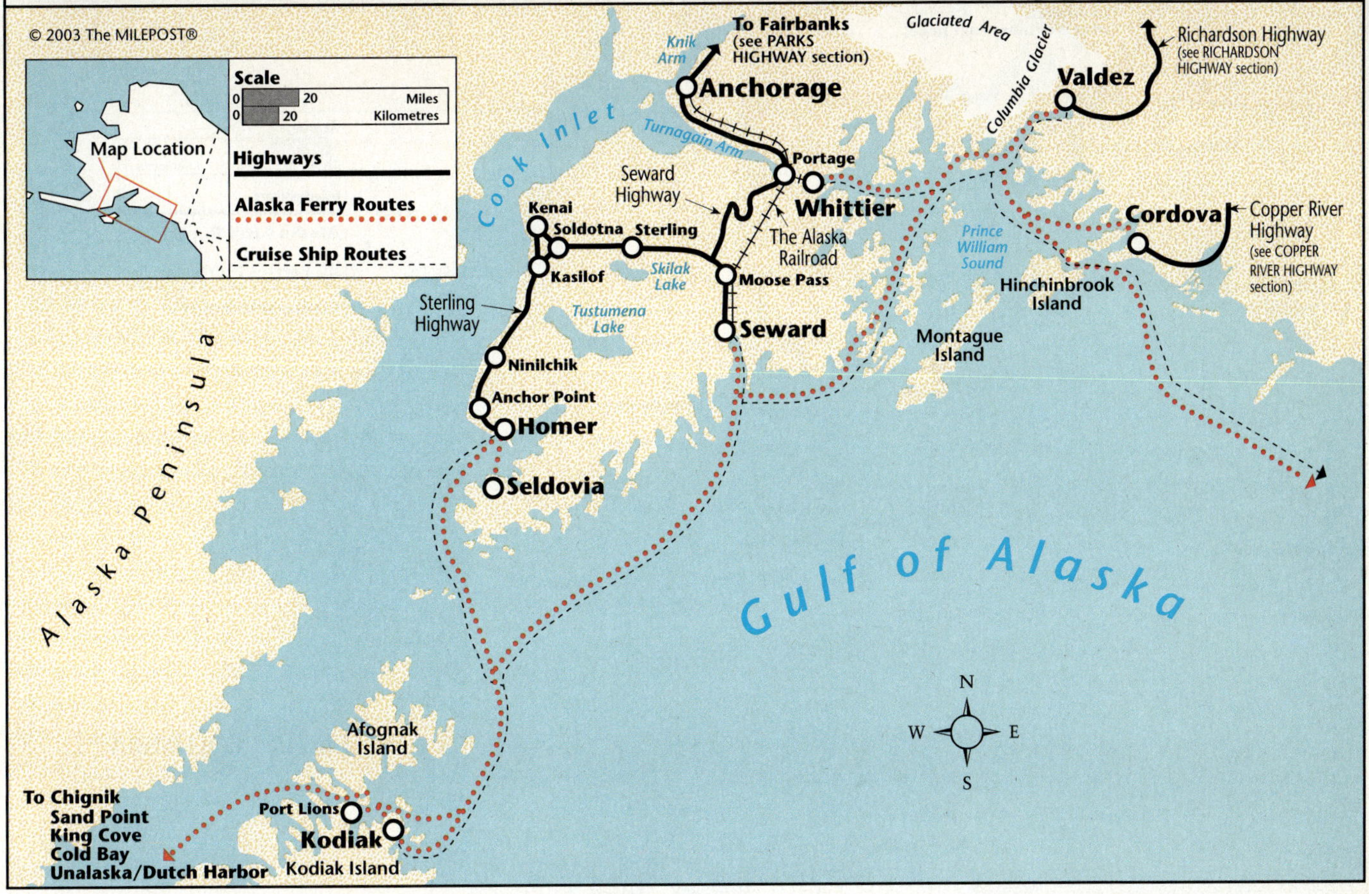

Winter Driving

In addition to the usual precautions taken when driving in winter, such as keeping the windshield clear of ice, checking antifreeze and reducing driving speeds on icy pavement, equip your vehicle with the following survival gear: traction material (ashes, kitty litter, wood chips); chains (even with snow tires); first-aid kit; shovel, ice scraper, flashlight, flares; fire extinguisher; extra warm clothing (including gloves, boots, hat and extra socks), blankets or sleeping bags; food; tools; and an extension cord to plug the car into a block heater. Other items which may be added to your survival gear are a tow rope or cable, ax, jumper cables and extra gas.

Extremely low temperatures occur in the North. A motorist may start out in -35° to -40°F weather and hit cold pockets along the road where temperatures drop to -60°F or more. If you do become stranded in weather like this, do not leave your vehicle; wait for aid. DO NOT attempt to drive unmaintained secondary roads or highways in winter (i.e. Denali Highway, Top of the World Highway), even if the roads look clear of snow.

Call ahead for road conditions and weather reports. See Road Condition Reports this section for more information.

Ferry Travel

Ferry travel to and within Alaska is provided by the Alaska Marine Highway, which is the name of the Alaska state ferry system and also refers to the water route the ferries follow from Bellingham, WA, up the Inside Passage to Skagway, AK. The Alaska Marine Highway was named a National Scenic Byway in 2002.

The Inside Passage is the route north along the coast of British Columbia and through southeastern Alaska that uses the protected waterways between the islands and the mainland. (Inside Passage is also commonly used to refer to Southeast Alaska and its communities.)

BC Ferries also serves the Inside Passage, providing marine transportation for passengers and vehicles between Port Hardy and Prince Rupert, BC. Port Hardy is located at the north end of Vancouver Island. Prince Rupert is the western terminus of Yellowhead Highway 16 and the southern port for a number of Alaska state ferries serving southeastern Alaska. Prince Rupert is also the farthest north of the 46 ports served by BC Ferries.

If traveling to Alaska by ferry, visitors may make their way up the Inside Passage to any Southeast Alaska community via the Inside Passage/Southeast ferry system. Motorists often use the Alaska Marine Highway northbound or southbound as an alternative to driving all of the Alaska Highway and its access routes. By using the Alaska Marine Highway System one way to transport themselves and their vehicles between Bellingham or Prince Rupert and Skagway or Haines, travelers can eliminate between 700 and 1,700 miles of highway driving (depending on their itinerary), avoid covering the same ground twice, and have the opportunity to take in the magnificent scenery and picturesque communities of the Inside Passage. The Southeast/Southwest Cross-Gulf Trips between Juneau, Valdez and Seward save additional highway mileage.

Details on the Alaska Marine Highway System and BC Ferries follow.

Alaska Marine Highway System

The main office of the Alaska Marine Highway is in Juneau. Write 6858 Glacier Highway, Juneau, AK 99801-7909; phone toll free 1-800-642-0066, TDD 1-800-764-3779; fax (907) 277-4829; email them at

(Continues on page 24)

ALASKA STATE FERRIES
Homer Ferry Terminal
Contract Agent • Alaska Marine Highway

Information, Reservations & Ticketing
1-800-382-9229

Open All Year • Major Credit Cards
(907) 235-8449 • Fax (907) 235-6907
www.akmhs.com

FERRY ROUTES
Washington and British Columbia from Puget Sound to Hecate Strait

(Continued from page 21)
ask_amhs@dot.state.ak.us, or visit their web site at www.alaska.gov/ferry. For summer schedules and fares and information on reservations, method of payment, deck passage, etc., see the ALASKA STATE FERRY SCHEDULES section beginning on page 749.

The Alaska ferry system has 2 seasons—May 1 to Sept. 30 (summer), when sailings are most frequent, and Oct. 1 to April 30 (fall/winter/spring). Summer schedules for 2003 appear in the ALASKA STATE FERRY SCHEDULES section.

Contact the Alaska Marine Highway office for fall/winter/spring schedules, fares and information. In winter, departures are somewhat less frequent on the Inside Passage/Southeast Alaska routes. On the Southcentral system, daily service in Prince William Sound ceases from mid-September through March, resuming sailings between Cordova and Valdez in April. The port of Whittier is not on the winter schedule, but service to Seldovia, Homer, Kodiak, Seward, Cordova and Valdez continues in winter.

The Alaska Marine Highway System is celebrating its 40th Anniversary in 2003. For more information on events commemorating the anniversary, call the main office, or visit www.alaska.gov/ferry.

The Alaska Marine Highway operates 2 ferry systems, one in Southeast Alaska and one in Southcentral/Southwest Alaska. The MV *Kennicott* connects the 2 systems with a once-a-month round-trip between Juneau, Valdez and Seward in summer. (See the MV *Kennicott* Southeast/Southwest Cross-Gulf Trips schedules beginning on page 750.)

The Alaska state ferries on the Southeast system depart from Bellingham, WA (85 miles north of Seattle on Interstate 5, Exit 250), or Prince Rupert, BC (450 miles/724 km west of Prince George, BC, or approximately 1,000 miles/1,609 km by highway from Seattle, WA) for Southeast Alaska communities.

Bellingham is accessible by Amtrak and bus. Fairhaven Station transportation center, next to the Bellingham Cruise Terminal at 401 Harris Avenue in south Bellingham, provides a central location for rail, bus, airporter, taxi and ferry services.

Motorists should keep in mind that only 2 major Southeast Alaska communities are connected to the Alaska Highway: Haines, via the Haines Highway; and Skagway, via South Klondike Highway. (See the HAINES HIGHWAY and SOUTH KLONDIKE HIGHWAY sections.) Driving distance from Skagway to Tok is 505 miles, to Anchorage 833 miles, to Fairbanks 711 miles. Driving distance from Haines to Tok is 447 miles, to Anchorage 775 miles, to Fairbanks 653 miles.

The Southeast state ferrry system includes feeder service between Ketchikan and Metlakatla, and between Juneau and Pelican. Ferry service between Ketchikan and Hollis is provided by the Inter-Island Ferry Authority aboard the M/V *Prince of Wales*. (See Inside Passage/Southeast Alaska schedules in the ALASKA STATE FERRY SCHEDULES section.)

The Southcentral/Southwest ferry system of the Alaska Marine Highway serves coastal communities from Prince William Sound to the Aleutian Islands. Southcentral communities on the ferry system that are also accessible by highway are Whittier, Valdez, Seward and Homer. Southcentral communities accessible only by ferry are Cordova, Seldovia and Kodiak. All communities on the Southwest system are accessible only by ferry or by air.

BC Ferries

BC Ferries provides year-round service on 25 routes throughout coastal British Columbia, with a fleet of 40 passenger- and vehicle-carrying ferries. For Alaska-bound travelers, BC Ferries' "Inside Passage" service between Port Hardy and Prince Rupert offers a convenient connection with the Alaska Marine Highway at Prince Rupert. The 2003 BC Ferries Northern Routes schedules—which includes Inside Passage, Discovery Coast and Queen Charlotte Islands service—appears on page 25.

Port Hardy is approximately 307 miles/494 km north of Victoria via Trans-Canada Highway 1 and BC Highway 19. From Nanaimo it is 236 miles/380 km—or about 5 hours' driving time—to Port Hardy. If you are driving from Victoria, allow about 7 hours (the route is almost all 4-lane highway between Victoria and Campbell River). The Port Hardy ferry terminal is located at Bear Cove, 4 miles/7 km south of downtown Port Hardy.

BC Ferries' Discovery Coast service from Port Hardy to Bella Coola connects with the WEST ACCESS ROUTE to the Alaska Highway logged in *The MILEPOST*®. See the "Chilcotin Highway" on pages 73-74.

Prince Rupert is located 450 miles/724 km west of Prince George via the Yellowhead Highway (see YELLOWHEAD HIGHWAY 16 section). The Queen Charlotte Islands are located west of Prince Rupert via BC Ferries' service to Skidegate on Graham Island. Attractions include Haida culture, and island flora and fauna.

Summer service (May 18 to Sept. 30, 2003) between Port Hardy and Prince Rupert is aboard the *Queen of the North*, which carries 750 passengers and 157 vehicles. The ferry has a cafeteria, buffet dining room, news/gift shop, elevator, reserved seating lounge, facilities for passengers with special needs, video arcade, licensed and view lounges, children's playroom, day cabins and staterooms (for round-trip use). Summer service on this route is during daylight hours to make the most of the scenery, so cabins are not necessary for the one-day trip. (Fall/winter/spring Inside Passage service is an overnight trip on the *Queen of Prince Rupert*.) Check-in time is 1 hour before sailing.

The *Queen of Prince Rupert* also serves the route between Prince Rupert and the Queen Charlotte Islands. Sailing times vary from 6 1/2 to 9 hours during the summer season (June 12 to Sept. 18, 2003).

A second travel option is the Discovery Coast Passage service—aboard the *Queen of Chilliwack*—between Port Hardy and Bella Coola. This summer-only service (June 10 to Sept. 8, 2003) connects Port Hardy on Vancouver Island with Bella Coola on the Chilcotin Highway (see pages 73-75 in the WEST ACCESS ROUTE section). The *Queen of Chilliwack* features a cafeteria, gift shop, licensed lounge, reclining seats and showers.

Fares: Inside Passage fares (1-way, in Canadian funds) are as follows: Adult passenger, $99; child (5 to 11 years), $49.50; car,

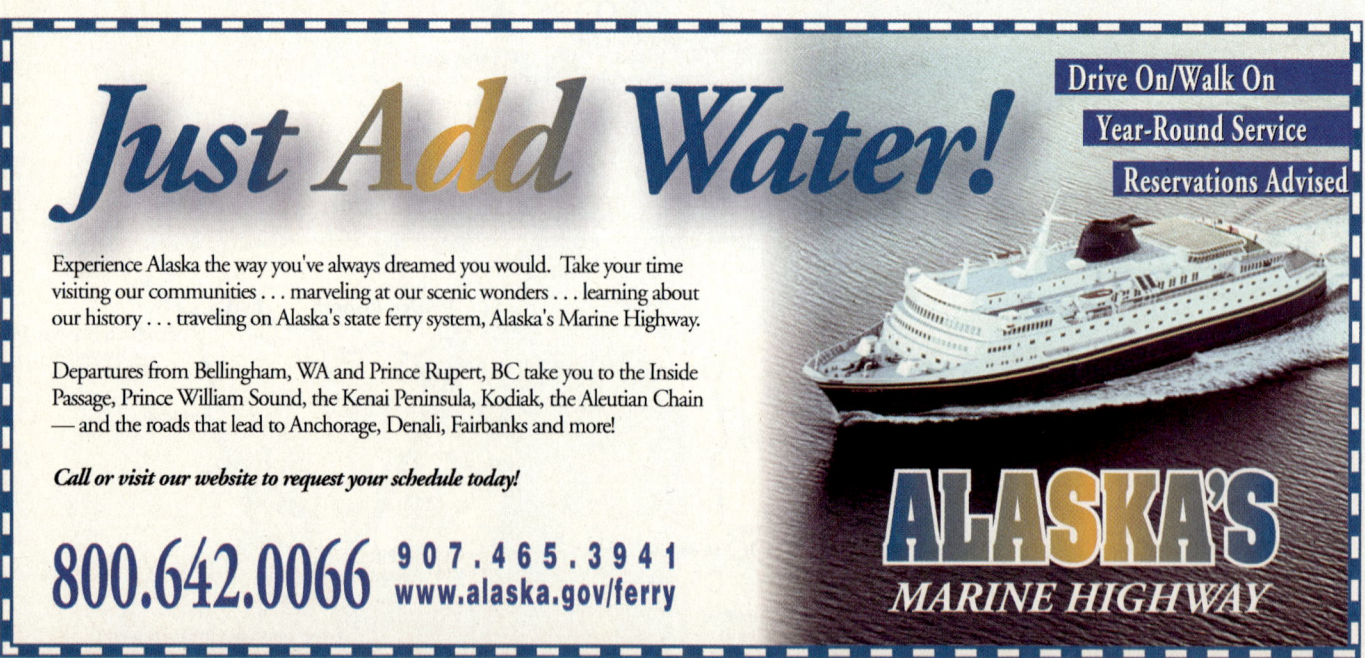

Just Add Water!

Drive On/Walk On
Year-Round Service
Reservations Advised

Experience Alaska the way you've always dreamed you would. Take your time visiting our communities... marveling at our scenic wonders... learning about our history... traveling on Alaska's state ferry system, Alaska's Marine Highway.

Departures from Bellingham, WA and Prince Rupert, BC take you to the Inside Passage, Prince William Sound, the Kenai Peninsula, Kodiak, the Aleutian Chain — and the roads that lead to Anchorage, Denali, Fairbanks and more!

Call or visit our website to request your schedule today!

800.642.0066   907.465.3941
www.alaska.gov/ferry

ALASKA'S MARINE HIGHWAY

BC FERRIES' NORTHERN ROUTES 2003 SCHEDULES

BC FERRIES Inside PASSAGE

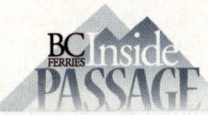

IN EFFECT SUNDAY, MAY 18 TO TUESDAY, SEPTEMBER 30

SOUTHBOUND SAILINGS

Leave Prince Rupert All Departures **7:30 am** Arrive Port Hardy Most Arrivals **10:30 pm***	**May**	19, 21, 23, 25, 27, 29, 31 only
	June	Even-numbered days
	July	Even-numbered days
	August	Odd-numbered days
	September	Even-numbered days

NORTHBOUND SAILINGS

Leave Port Hardy All Departures **7:30 am** Arrive Prince Rupert Most Arrivals **10:30 pm***	**May**	18, 20, 22, 24, 26, 28, 30 only
	June	Odd-numbered days
	July	Odd-numbered days
	August	Even-numbered days
	September	Odd-numbered days

*Some arrivals may be later. Check detailed schedules at www.bcferries.com, or call us for more information.

THE DISCOVERY COAST PASSAGE

IN EFFECT TUESDAY, JUNE 10 TO MONDAY, SEPTEMBER 8

SOUTHBOUND VOYAGES

	Depart	*Arrive*
MONDAYS	Bella Coola 8:00 am	Port Hardy 9:00 pm
WEDNESDAYS	Bella Coola 7:30 am Shearwater 4:30 pm McLoughlin Bay 7:45 pm	Shearwater 2:30 pm McLoughlin Bay 5:00 pm Port Hardy 7:45 am (Thurs)
FRIDAYS	Bella Coola 8:00 am Ocean Falls 5:00 pm Shearwater 9:30 pm McLoughlin Bay 11:00 pm	Ocean Falls 2:00 pm Shearwater 8:30 pm McLoughlin Bay 10:00 pm Port Hardy 9:00 am (Sat)

NORTHBOUND VOYAGES

	Depart	*Arrive*
TUESDAYS	Port Hardy 9:30 am McLoughlin Bay 9:15 pm Shearwater 11:00 pm	McLoughlin Bay 7:30 pm Shearwater 9:45 pm Bella Coola 6:30 am (Wed)
THURSDAYS	Port Hardy 9:30 am	Bella Coola 10:30 pm
SATURDAYS **SUNDAYS** **MONDAYS**	Port Hardy 9:30 pm (Sat) McLoughlin Bay 8:30 am (Sun) Shearwater 10:15 am (Sun) Klemtu 6:15 pm (Sun) Ocean Falls 2:00 am (Mon)	McLoughlin Bay 7:30 am (Sun) Shearwater 9:15 am (Sun) Klemtu 2:15 pm (Sun) Ocean Falls 1:00 am (Mon) Bella Coola 7:00 am (Mon)

The Queen Charlotte Islands

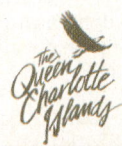

IN EFFECT THURSDAY, JUNE 12 TO THURSDAY, SEPTEMBER 18

WESTBOUND

Leave Prince Rupert		Arrive Skidegate	
Sunday	11:00 am	**Sunday**	5:30 pm
Monday	9:00 pm	**Tuesday**	6:00 am
Wednesday	● 1:00 pm	**Wednesday**	7:30 pm
Thursday	11:00 am	**Thursday**	5:30 pm
Friday	11:00 am	**Friday**	5:30 pm
Saturday	✳ 11:00 am	**Saturday**	5:30 pm

EASTBOUND

Leave Skidegate		Arrive Prince Rupert	
Monday	11:00 am	**Monday**	6:00 pm
Tuesday	11:00 am	**Tuesday**	6:00 pm
Wednesday	● 11:00 pm	**Thursday**	7:30 am
Thursday	11:00 pm	**Friday**	▲ 7:30 am
Friday	11:00 pm	**Saturday**	▲ 7:30 am
Saturday	✳ 11:00 pm	**Sunday**	7:30 am

● **Wednesdays** July 2, 9, 16, 23, 30 and August 6, 13, 20, 27. ✳**Saturdays** July 5, 12, 19, 26, August 2, 9, 16, 23, 30 and September 6, 13.

▲ **Connecting Service** To provide a connection Southbound with our Prince Rupert to Port Hardy route, arrival time in Prince Rupert will be 6:00 am: **Fridays** June 6, 20, July 4, 18, August 1, 15, 29, September 12. **Saturdays** June 14, 28, July 12, 26, August 9, 23, September 6.

RESERVATIONS REQUIRED ON OUR NORTHERN ROUTES. SCHEDULES SUBJECT TO CHANGE WITHOUT NOTICE.

BC FERRIES

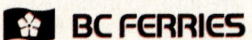

$233; camper/RV (up to 20 feet in length, over 6 feet 8 inches in height), $387; additional length, $19.35 per foot; motorcycle, $116.50; bicycle, $6.50. Service during the fall, winter and spring is less frequent and fares are reduced.

Schedules and fares are subject to change without notice.

Reservations: Strongly recommended for passengers and required for vehicles on the Inside Passage, Discovery Coast Passage and Queen Charlotte Islands routes. For reservations (7 A.M. to 10 P.M. daily) and recorded schedule information (24-hours) phone (250) 386-3431 in Victoria, or long distance from outside B.C.; or 1-888-223-3779 in British Columbia outside the Victoria dialing area. Reservations may also be made on-line at www.bcferries.com. Cancellations made less than 30 days prior to departure are subject to a cancellation fee.

Information: BC Ferries at 1112 Fort St., Victoria, BC V8V 4V2; www.bcferries.com.

GPS

GPS, global positioning system, is a satellite-based navigation system consisting of 24 orbiting satellites transmitting various data. GPS receivers translate this data into coordinates to help you determine your position. There are several manufacturers of GPS receivers, and each has many different models.

Latitudes and longitudes for most major communities have been included on the highway strip maps for GPS users. These coordinates were supplied by a variety of sources, including individual GPS receivers and the National Imagery and Mapping Agency's GEOnet Names Server (www.nima.mil).

Making The MILEPOST® user-friendly for GPS receivers is a pilot project for us. We would appreciate feedback from GPS users as to how best to serve your needs. Please contact the Editor at kris@themilepost.com with your comments.

Hostels

Hosteling, once known primarily as a province of young people seeking a budget-friendly way to see the world, appeals today to a much wider cross-section of travelers. Originating in Europe in the late 19th century, the hosteling movement was unknown in Alaska until the early 1950s. Today, there are 32 hostels scattered around the state, most of them independent operations, some affiliated with a national hosteling organization. Although the relaxed world of hosteling may not be for everyone, few other types of accommodations offer equal value. The adaptable traveler will be amply rewarded with easy sociability and low monetary impact at the Alaska and Canada hostels listed below. The MILEPOST® welcomes information about new hostels or changes in the listings given here.

Anchorage/Mat-Su & Area
Alyeska Home Hostel, P.O. Box 953, Girdwood, AK 99587; (907) 783-2099.
Anchorage Guest House, 2001 Hillcrest Dr., Anchorage, AK 99517; (907) 274-0408; email house@alaska.net; www.akhouse.com.
HI-Anchorage, 700 H St., Anchorage, AK 99501; (907) 276-3635.
International Backpackers Inn/Hostel, 3601 Peterkin Ave., Anchorage, AK 99508; (907) 274-3870; email ibhostel@alaska.net; www.internationalbackpackershostel.com.
Spenard Hostel International, 2845 W. 42nd Pl., Anchorage, AK 99517; phone/fax (907) 248-5036; email stay@alaskahostel.org; www.alaskahostel.org.
Wasilla Guest House B&B/Hostel, 3950 Carefree Dr., (Milepost A 39 Parks Hightway), Wasilla, AK 99654; (907) 357-3699; email info@wasillaguesthouse.com; www.wasillaguesthouse.com.

Denali Park & Area
Byers Creek Station, P.O. Box 13394, (Milepost A 144 Parks Highway), Trapper Creek, AK 99683; (907) 733-2990; www.byerscreek.com.
Denali Mountain Morning Hostel & Lodge, P.O. Box 208 (Milepost A 224 Parks Highway), Denali Park, AK 99755; (907) 683-7503; email akhostel@hotmail.com; www.hostelalaska.com.
Talkeetna Hostel International, P.O. Box 952, Talkeetna, AK 99676; (907) 733-4678; email hezim@gci.net; www.talkeetnahostel.com.

Fairbanks & Area
Arctic Circle Hot Springs Resort, P.O. Box 30069, Central, AK 99730; (907) 520-5113; http://php.indiana.edu/~kurichte/achshome.html.
Billie's Backpackers Hostel, 2895 Mack Rd., Fairbanks, AK 99709; (907) 479-2034 or 1-800-236-5350; www.alaskahostel.com.
Boyle's Hostel, 310 18th Ave., Fairbanks, AK 99701; (907) 456-4944.
Chandalar Ranch, 5804 Chena Hot Springs Rd. (Mile 18.6), P.O. Box 74877, Fairbanks, AK 99707; (907) 488-8402; email kckoontz@alaska.net; www.koontzalaska.com.
Fairbanks Shelter & Shower, 248 Madcap Lane, Fairbanks, AK 99709.
North Woods Lodge, Chena Hills Dr., P.O. Box 83615, Fairbanks, AK 99708; (907) 479-5300 or 1-800-478-5305.

Glenn Highway
HI-Tok, P.O. Box 532, Tok, AK 99780.
Sheep Mountain Lodge, Milepost A 113.5 Glenn Highway, HC 03 Box 8490, Palmer, AK 99645; (907) 745-5721; www.sheepmountain.com.
Huck Hobbit's Homestead Retreat & Campground, Mile 4 Nabesna Rd., Box 420, Slana, AK 99586; (907) 822-3196.

Kenai Peninsula
HI-Ninilchik, The Eagle Watch, Box 39083, Ninilchik, AK 99639; (907) 567-3905; email hitheeaglewatch@ak.net.
International Backpackers Hostel/Inn, 304 W. Pioneer Ave., Homer, AK 99603; (907) 235-1463; email 1hostel2@pobox.alaska.net; www.internationalbackpackershostel.com.
Jana House, Sterling, AK 99672; fax (907) 562-9982; email janamae@hotmail.com.
Moby Dick Hostel, P.O. Box 624, Seward, AK 99664; (907) 224-7072; email info@mobydickhostel.com; www.mobydickhostel.com.
Seaside Farms Hostel, 40904 Seaside Farm Dr., Homer, AK 99607; (907) 235-7850.
Snow River Hostel, 22634 Seward Hwy (Milepost S 16), Seward, AK 99664; (907) 440-1907.

Prince William Sound & Area
Kennicott River Lodge & Hostel, McCarthy, AK 99588; (907) 479-6822.

Southeast Alaska
Bear Creek Cabins & International Hostel, P.O. Box 908, Haines, AK 99827; (907) 766-2259.
Eagle View Hostel, 2303 5th Ave., Ketchikan, AK 99901; (907) 225-5461; email info@eagleviewhostel.com; www.eagleviewhostel.com.
HI-Ketchikan, 400 Main St., P.O. Box 8515, Ketchikan, AK 99901; (907) 225-3319.
HI-Sitka, P.O. Box 2645, Sitka, AK 99835; (907) 747-8661.
Juneau International Hostel, 614 Harris St., Juneau, AK 99801; (907) 586-9559; email juneauhostel@gci.net; www.juneauhostel.org.
Presbyterian Church Hostel, P.O. Box 439, Wrangell, AK 99929; (907) 874-3534.
Skagway Home Hostel, Box 231, Skagway, AK 99840; (907) 983-2131; email schave@aptalaska.net; www.skagwayhostel.com.

Western Canada
Dawson City River Hostel, Box 32, Dawson City, YT Canada Y0B 1G0; (867) 993-6823; email yukonhostels@yahoo.com; www.yukonhostels.com.

Hunting & Fishing

Hunting and fishing are popular sports in Alaska and a way of life for many residents. Both resident and nonresident sportfishermen and hunters in Alaska must be aware of rules and regulations before going out in the field. Regulation booklets are available from Alaska Dept. of Fish & Game offices and may be found at a variety of different outlets, from supermarkets to foodmarts. The intricacies of licenses, tags, reports, stamps, seals, and seasons, among other things, require advance study. Failure to comply with Fish & Game regulations can result in monetary fines and loss of trophies or property.

Hunting and fishing information is posted on the Alaska Dept. of Fish and Game home page at www.state.ak.us/adfg/adfghome.htm. Licenses are available from any designated licensing agent. Licenses may be obtained by mail from ADF&G, Licensing Section, P.O. Box 2-5525, Juneau, AK 99802-5525, phone (907) 465-2376. Online licensing is available as well.

Hunting
Nonresident hunters in Alaska must be accompanied by a registered guide or a close relative over 19 who is an Alaska resident when hunting brown bear, Dall sheep or mountain goats. A non-resident hunting license is $85; resident is $25.

There are 26 game management units in Alaska and a wide variation in both seasons and bag limits for various species. Check for special regulations in each unit.

Big game includes black and brown/grizzly bears, deer, elk, mountain goats, moose, wolves and wolverines, caribou, Dall sheep, musk-oxen and bison. Big game tags are required for residents hunting musk-ox and brown/grizzly bear and for nonresidents hunting any big game animal. These nonrefundable, nontransferable metal locking tags (valid for the calendar year) must be purchased prior to the taking of the animal. A tag may be used for any species for which the tag fee is of equal or lesser value.

Small game animals include grouse, ptarmigan and hares. Fur animals that may be hunted are the coyote, fox and lynx. Waterfowl are also abundant. There is no recreational hunting of polar bear, walrus or other marine animals.

The Alaska Department of Fish and Game

FOUL-WEATHER GEAR

RUGER ALL-WEATHER® RIFLES

It would be nice to be able to count on perfect conditions for every hunting trip, but you know that's not going to happen. Rain, snow, sleet, high humidity or salt spray can play havoc with your pampered blued steel and walnut-stocked hunting guns. That's why experienced, successful hunters prepare for such harsh conditions with the appropriate equipment. Ruger All-Weather models are specifically designed to function quite agreeably in environments that keep other guns indoors. These handsome firearms feature stainless steel actions and barrels combined with impervious, high-strength synthetic polymer stocks. You can count on their superb accuracy and reliability...performance that does not diminish with weather or hard use.

Whatever your shooting requirement, there is a Ruger All-Weather longarm that will more than satisfy it. The All-Weather M77 Mark II, All-Weather 77/44 bolt-action rifle, All-Weather 10/22 .22 autoloader, and All-Weather .223 Ranch Rifle (shown in this order top to bottom) are but four of the wide selection of Ruger All-Weather hunting arms. They're available in fourteen different models and sixteen calibers, at your local Ruger dealer.

STURM, RUGER & CO., INC.
Southport, CT 06890, U.S.A. • www.ruger.com

All Ruger firearms are designed and manufactured in our own factories in the United States of America.
FREE instruction manuals for all Ruger firearms available on request. Please specify model for which you require a manual.

RUGER
ARMS MAKERS FOR RESPONSIBLE CITIZENS

Northern rail lines traverse the vast wilderness of Alaska and Canada.
(© Earl L. Brown, staff)

brochure *"Planning Your Hunt"* (available online), lays out what hunters must do before, during and after their hunt.

Fishing

The biggest challenge for visiting fishermen is the sheer number and variety of fishing opportunities available. The Alaska Dept. of Fish and Game has hundreds of pamphlets on fishing regional waters, as well as online regional sport fishing updates. A nonresident fishing license is $100; resident is $15.

Visiting fishermen are advised to first identify whether they want to fish fresh water or salt water and their desired species. Salmon are the most popular sport fish in Alaska, with all 5 species of Pacific salmon found here: King (chinook), silver (coho), pink (humpy), chum (dog) and red (sockeye). Other sport fish include halibut, rainbow trout and steelhead, Dolly Varden and Arctic char, cutthroat and brook trout, northern pike, and lake trout.

Knowing the kind of fish and fishing you want may help plan your trip. For example, king salmon fishing in Southeast is restricted to salt water, but cutthroat are common on the mainland and every major island in Southeast. Alaska's Interior has the largest Arctic grayling fishery in North America. Northern pike is the most sought-after indigenous sport fish in Interior Alaska after the Arctic grayling. These popular game fish are the main sport fish species in the Tanana River drainage.

Although most fishing enthusiasts focus their trips between April and October, when the weather is generally more mild, the fish have something to say about timing. The Alaska Dept. of Fish and Game Sportfish Division gives a run timing for all fisheries by region. Also check local newspapers for ADF&G regional fishing updates.

Where to fish is probably the most difficult choice, with the number of fishing destinations available well beyond the capability of most anglers to visit. Throughout *The MILEPOST*® you will find this friendly little symbol. Wherever you see one, you will find a description of the fishing at that point. Fishing spots are also listed under Area Fishing in the Attractions section of each community covered in *The MILEPOST*®.

You can fish any body of water with fish in it, but local knowledge greatly increases chances for success. Many fishing guides and charter operators advertise in *The MILEPOST*®.

Pets

If you're mapping out a trip to Alaska and want to include Rover in your vacation plans, there are a few things to keep in mind.

Your pet must have a valid veterinarian health certificate to cross the border into Canada or Alaska. Dogs must be certified as having received a rabies vaccination during the 36 months preceding the trip, and the vaccination and certificate must be valid for the full extent of your trip. If you are traveling with pet birds (or other animals), check with customs about specific requirements. Refer to "Crossing the Border" this section, or visit the customs' web sites at www.inspection.gc.ca/english/anima/heasan/import/petse.shtml or www.customs.gov/travel/travel.htm.

Pet policies at hotels, motels, bed-and-breakfasts and campgrounds range from "no pets" to "pets okay" to it-depends-on-the-size-and-good-manners-of-your-dog. Check the advertisements in *The MILEPOST*® for pet policies at motels, bed and breakfasts, campgrounds and RV parks. If in doubt, call ahead.

Kennel accommodations are available in the larger cities like Anchorage and Fairbanks, and in some small communities near major attractions. Check with community information centers and local campgrounds and lodges for information on nearby kennel services.

Most communities in the North Country allow pets in parks and other outdoor public areas. However, you MUST clean up after your pets, and they must be kept on leashes in most areas. We recommend that you keep your dog on a leash whenever the dog is outside your vehicle. We have heard many horrific tales of pets lost during roadside stops along the highways, and very few have happy endings. We also recommend that you keep identification and contact information on your pet at all times, even if the pet has a microchip.

Dogs must be on leashes in National Forest and Alaska State Park campgrounds and on hiking trails. Dogs are not allowed on Denali National Park hiking trails or in the backcountry.

Be aware also that not all northern communities have resident veterinarians, so if your pet needs medical attention, it may be very far away (another reason to keep your pet on a leash or in your vehicle).

If you are traveling on the Alaska Marine Highway System with your pet, animals must be transported on the vehicle deck. Pets are not allowed in cabins or anywhere above deck, and you are only allowed to visit your pet during routine "car-deck calls."

Railroads

Although no railroads connect Alaska or the Yukon with the Lower 48, there are 2 railroads in the North: the Alaska Railroad and the White Pass & Yukon Route.

Two Canadian railways provide connections for travelers heading for Prince Rupert and on to Alaska. VIA Rail's "Skeena" goes from Jasper, Alberta to Prince George, where it overnights and then continues on to Prince Rupert for connection to the Alaska Marine Highway; phone 1-800-561-8630.

The Alaska Railroad

The Alaska Railroad operates year-round passenger and freight service between Anchorage and Fairbanks. In summer, service is available daily between Anchorage and Fairbanks via Talkeetna and Denali Park; between Anchorage and Whittier; and between Anchorage and Seward. For more information on the Alaska Railroad, write Passenger Services Dept., Box 107500, Anchorage 99510. Phone 1-800-544-0552 or (outside Anchorage) (907) 265-2494; fax 265-2323; email reservations@akrr.com; www.alaskarailroad.com/passenger.

Construction of the railroad began in 1915 under Pres. Woodrow Wilson. On July 15, 1923, Pres. Warren G. Harding drove the golden spike at Nenana, signifying completion of the railroad. The main line extends from Seward to Fairbanks, approximately 470 miles.

The Alaska Railroad accommodates visitors with disabilities. Wheelchair lifts are available at all scheduled stops. Coaches have provisions for occupied wheelchairs, and restrooms are accessible. With advance notice, sign language interpreters are available.

Following are services, schedules and fares available on Alaska Railroad routes. Keep in mind that schedules and fares are subject to change without notice.

Anchorage–Talkeetna–Denali–Fairbanks: Passenger service between Anchorage, Talkeetna, Denali Park and Fairbanks is offered daily on the *Denali Star* from May 16 to Sept. 14, 2003. The express service operates with full-service dining, a vista-dome for all passengers to share and coaches with comfortable reclining seats. Travel along the 350-mile/563-km route between Anchorage and Fairbanks at a leisurely pace with comfortable window seats and good views of the countryside. Packages including sightseeing tours, hotels, river rafting, hiking and flight-seeing are available in Talkeetna, Denali, Fairbanks and Anchorage from Alaska Railroad Scenic Tours.

Luxury railcars are available on the Anchorage–Denali Park–Fairbanks route through Gray Line of Alaska (Holland America Lines/Westours) and Princess Tours. These tour companies operate (respectively) the *McKinley Explorer* and *Midnight Sun Express*. These luxury railcars, which are coupled onto the end of the regular Alaska Railroad train, are glass-domed and offer gourmet cuisine along with other amenities. Tickets are priced higher than those for the regular Alaska Railroad cars, and are sold on a space-available basis. Packages with a Denali Park overnight are also available. Holland America is also beginning construction on additional luxury cars that feature full dining rooms and kitchens, lounges, viewing platforms and seating for 88 passengers. Phone Princess Tours at (800) 835-8907 (www.princesslodges.com/rail.htm), or Gray Line of Alaska at (800) 544-2206 for details.

During the summer, northbound express trains depart Anchorage at 8:15 A.M., arrive Talkeetna at 11:25 A.M., arrive Denali Park at 3:45 P.M., and arrive Fairbanks at 8:15 P.M. Southbound express trains depart Fairbanks at 8:15 A.M., arrive Denali Park at noon, and arrive Anchorage at 8:15 P.M.

One-way fares are as follows: Anchorage–Denali Park, $125; Anchorage–Talkeetna, $78; Fairbanks–Denali Park, $50; Anchorage–Fairbanks, $175. Children ages 2 through 11 ride for 50 percent of adult fare; under 2 ride free.

During fall, winter and spring, weekend-only rail service is provided between Anchorage and Fairbanks on the *Aurora*. The train travels from Anchorage to Fairbanks on Saturday and returns on Sunday. The *Aurora* is a "flag stop" train and will stop wherever people want to get on or off.

Reservations are recommended on all routes. Include the dates you plan to travel, points of departure and destination, the number of people in your party and your home phone number. Tickets may be purchased in advance by mail if you desire. Checks, Visa, MasterCard and Discover are accepted.

Each adult is allowed 2 pieces of luggage with a maximum combined weight of 100 lbs. Children are allowed 2 pieces of baggage with a maximum combined weight of 75 lbs. One carry-on is allowed per passenger. Excess baggage may be checked for a nominal fee. Bicycles are accepted for a charge of $20 per station, on a space-available basis on the day of travel. Keep in mind that baggage, including backpacks, must be checked before boarding, and it is not accessible during the trip. Canoes, motors, motorcycles, items weighing over 150 lbs., etc., are not accepted for transportation on passenger trains. These items are shipped via freight train.

Local Service: Local rural service between Talkeetna and Hurricane Gulch operates Thursday, Friday, Saturday and Sunday each week during the summer (May 15 to Sept. 14, 2003) and once a month in winter. This 1-day trip aboard the *Hurricane Turn* takes you past breathtaking views of Mount McKinley (weather permitting), into some remote areas and provides an opportunity to meet local residents who use the train for access. Local service uses self-propelled rail diesel cars and provides vending-machine snacks. The *Hurricane Turn* is a "flag stop" train and will stop wherever people want to get on or off.

Anchorage–Grandview: Rail passenger service aboard the *Glacier Discovery* between Anchorage and Grandview departs twice daily at 10 A.M. and 2 P.M. ($89). For $149, the route provides an optional 2-hour float trip down the Placer River from Spencer Glacier with professional guides.

Anchorage–Seward: Rail passenger service between Anchorage and Seward operates daily on the *Coastal Classic* May 10 and May 11 and daily from May 17 to Sept. 14, 2003. The 230-mile/370-km round-trip excursion follows Turnagain Arm south from Anchorage and passes through some of the most beautiful scenery to be found along the railroad. The train makes one stop in Girdwood before its final destination in Seward. Travel is aboard classic passenger coaches. Food service is available in the bar/deli car. Departs Anchorage at 6:45 A.M., arrives Girdwood at 8:05 A.M. and arrives Seward at 11:05 A.M. The return trip departs Seward at 6 P.M., arrives Girdwood at 8:55 P.M. and arrives Anchorage at 10:25 P.M. Reservations are recommended. The round-trip fare is $98 for adults; 50 percent fare for children 2 through 11. Overnight tours

Tracks through the Wilderness

"Breathtaking!" was the verdict of a fellow passenger as the Alaska Railroad train emerged from the tunnel, presenting a sweeping vista of mountain peaks and the shining paths of Bartlett and Trail glaciers. We were approaching the Grandview area on the Coastal Classic—a route which treats travelers to some of Alaska's most awe-inspiring scenery, traversing 114 miles from Anchorage to Seward on the Kenai Peninsula.

During another trip, this time heading north from Anchorage into Alaska's heartland, passengers stare down from a spidery trestle into 290-foot-deep Hurricane Gulch, the view of the gorge from the 384-foot-long deck-arch inspiring comments like, "Wow, I wouldn't want to fall down there!" Other dramatic scenes throughout the Alaska Range, including the coveted sight of Mount McKinley, are high points of the 12-hour, 356-mile Denali Star Anchorage-Fairbanks run.

Summer's arrival raises the railroad's level of activity to a high pitch as cruise ships, RVs, aircraft and automobiles deliver thousands of people eager to experience the attractions of the 49th state. The railroad offers a variety of tours that interact with cruise packages and recreational offerings. Cruise-ship companies piggyback their self-contained luxury rail cars on the Alaska Railroad, combining the amenities of shipboard life with the opportunity to see Alaska's scenic wonders as the trains amble on their leisurely treks north from Seward or south from Fairbanks. Mountains, rivers, glaciers stagger the senses. Odds are excellent for spotting wildlife. On one trip north we counted 7 moose, 2 caribou, numerous species of birds and waterfowl, and 2 young grizzlies relaxing just a few yards from the tracks near Denali National Park.

Independent travelers fill the summertime tour trains, enjoying comfortable seating, fine dining service and up-close views through the train's huge windows or from the vantage point of the dome cars. An undeniable asset of summer travel is the active presence on the rail cars of well-trained young guides who enliven the trips with anecdotes, creative skits and songs. Their energy, knowledge and good humor leave travelers with many positive memories.

In winter, the railroad offers special "ski trains" to Curry, north of Talkeetna. (For several decades, Grandview was the ski train destination, until curtailed winter maintenance on the southerly route changed the venue to Curry in 2003.)

Besides allowing summer visitors and winter skiers to revel in Alaska's scenery, the railroad also provides a valued service to residents. "This is our lifeline," one woman said at a hearing in 2002 to determine whether the railroad would discontinue the flag-stop train between Talkeetna and Hurricane. Other Bush dwellers added their comments, and fortunately for them and others who live along the roadless miles north of Talkeetna, railroad representatives paid attention to their testimonies. It was agreed that this last regular flag-stop run in the nation would continue, enabling residents of wilderness Alaska to pursue their preferred lifestyle. "Thank goodness!" was the relieved reaction.

"Thank goodness there's one place like this left in the world!"

Carol Phillips, associate editor of The MILEPOST®, left her desk last summer long enough to ride the rails and write this story.

which include hotel and Resurrection Bay boat excursions, Exit Glacier and Alaska SeaLife Center are available from the railroad ticket office.

Anchorage–Whittier: Rail passenger service between Anchorage and Whittier operates daily on the *Glacier Discovery* May 10 and May 11 and daily from May 17 to Sept. 14, 2003. The 50-mile/80-km excursion follows the Turnagain Arm of the Cook Inlet, stops briefly in Girdwood, arrives Girdwood at 11:20 A.M. and passes through 2 tunnels, and arrives in Whittier, located on the Prince William Sound. Food service is available in the bar/deli car. Departs Anchorage at 10 A.M., arrives Girdwood at 11:20 A.M. and arrives Whittier at 12:30 P.M. The return trip departs Whittier at 6:45 P.M., arrives Girdwood at 8 P.M. and arrives Anchorage at 9:30 P.M. Reservations are recommended. The round-trip fare is $55 for adults; children ages 2–11 are half-fare. Tours are available, including one-day connecting cruises of Prince William Sound and cruises offering overnight accommodations.

White Pass & Yukon Route

The White Pass & Yukon Route (WP&YR) is a narrow-gauge (36-inch) privately owned railroad built during the Klondike Gold

TRAVEL PLANNING

A fall hunting camp on the Nenana River along the Denali Highway.
(© Rich Reid, Colors of Nature)

Rush. From 1900 until 1982, the WP&YR provided passenger and freight service between Skagway, AK, and Whitehorse, YT.

The railroad offers daily train service (mid-May to mid-September) between Skagway and Fraser, BC; 3-hour round-trip train excursions between Skagway and the White Pass Summit; 8-hour steam excursions to Lake Bennett; Chilkoot Trail hiker service to and from Lake Bennett; and a combination train and bus trip between Skagway and Whitehorse, each direction.

You'll ride in comfort aboard an 1890s parlor car, viewing scenes of incredible beauty through wide panoramic windows. Cruise ship passengers will find ample space has been reserved for excursions on the WP&YR and should purchase excursion tickets on board their cruise vessel.

Construction of the WP&YR began in May 1898. The railroad reached White Pass in February 1899 and Whitehorse in July 1900. It was the first railroad in Alaska and at the time the most northern of any railroad in North America. The WP&YR has one of the steepest railroad grades in North America. From sea level at Skagway the railroad climbs to 2,885 feet/879m at White Pass in only 20 miles/32 km of track. In 1994, it was declared an International Historic Civil Engineering Landmark, one of only 34 in the world today.

The railroad follows the old White Pass trail. The upper section of the old "Dead Horse" trail near the summit (Mile 19 on the WP&YR railway) is visible beside the tracks. During the Klondike Gold Rush, thousands of men took the 40-mile/64-km White Pass trail from Skagway to Lake Bennett, where they built boats to float down the Yukon River to Dawson City and the goldfields.

Following are services, schedules and fares (U.S. funds) for White Pass & Yukon Route in 2003. All times indicated in schedules are local times (Skagway is on Alaska Time, which is 1 hour earlier than Whitehorse, which is on Pacific Time.) Children 3–12 ride for half fare when accompanied by an adult. Infants 2 and under ride free if not occupying a seat; half fare for separate seat. Reservations are required. (Tuesdays, Wednesday and Thursdays are especially busy days.) Contact the White Pass & Yukon Route, Box 435, Skagway, AK 99840. Phone toll free in the U.S. and Canada (800) 343-7373 or (907) 983-2217 in Skagway. Email: info@whitepass.net; www.whitepassrailroad.com.

Summit Excursion: This approximately 3-hour round-trip excursion features the most spectacular part of the WP&YR railway, including the steep climb (3000 feet in 20 miles) to White Pass Summit, Bridal Veil Falls, Inspiration Point and Dead Horse Gulch. Offered twice daily from mid-May to mid-September; the morning train departs Skagway at 8:30 A.M. and returns at 11:45 A.M.; the afternoon train departs Skagway at 1 P.M. and returns at 4:15 P.M. On Mondays, Tuesdays and Thursdays, another trip departs Skagway at 4:30 P.M. and returns at 7:30 P.M. Fares are $82 for adults and $41 for children 12 and under.

Skagway to Whitehorse: Through-service between Skagway, AK, and Whitehorse, YT, is offered daily from mid-May to mid-September. Through passengers travel 28 miles/45 km by train between Skagway, AK, and Fraser, BC, and then 87 miles/140 km by bus between Fraser and Whitehorse, YT. The train portion of this trip takes passengers over historic White Pass Summit. Northbound service departs Skagway at 8 A.M. Alaska time. Southbound service departs Whitehorse at 1:30 P.M. Yukon time. One-way fares are $95 for adults and $47.50 for children 12 and under.

Special Steam Excursions: Steam travel returns to the White Pass & Yukon Route with Saturday excursions to beautiful Lake Bennett. This 80-mile/128.7-km round-trip takes 8 hours and includes a layover at a restored 1903 station. Lunch is provided. Steam trips are scheduled for Saturdays in July and August, 2003. Departs Skagway at 8 A.M. Fares are $156 for adults and $78 for children 3-12; includes lunch. Diesel trips will operate June 14, 21 and 28, 2003. Fares for these trips are $128 for adults and $64 for children 3-12. Picture identification is required because this train crosses into Canada from Alaska.

Chilkoot Trail Hikers Service: Service between Bennett and Fraser, BC, offered Monday–Thursday and Saturday. Hikers who have completed the 33-mile/53 km Chilkoot Trail can be picked up at Lake Bennett and transported back to Skagway, or with bus connections on to Whitehorse. $30 to Fraser, BC; $65 to Skagway. Bring identification as this train crosses the border between Alaska and Canada. Advanced tickets are recommended.

Rental Vehicles

All cities and larger towns in Alaska, as well as some of the smaller communities, offer car rentals. RV rentals can be found in larger cities like Anchorage. Major rental car agencies are usually located at international airports.

As in other locations, rental policies vary from place to place in options available and prices charged. Unlimited mileage is allowed by most Alaska car rental agencies. Some companies prohibit use of their vehicles on unpaved roads, which precludes trips on certain roads, including the Denali, Steese, Taylor and Elliott highways and McCarthy Road. When renting from a company that does allow travel on unpaved roads, it is advisable to sign up for insurance to cover any damage. Other restrictions may apply, depending upon the particular agency. Inquiry should be made about restrictions and essential documentation if one's itinerary includes Canadian travel.

Rental of RVs, while initially expensive, offers worthwhile trade-off benefits for families and other groups, as the cost of overnight lodging is eliminated. Savings on food can also be realized if some meals are prepared in the RV rather than purchased in restaurants. Rental agencies throughout the North Country offer every type of rig, from modest tent trailers to top-of-the-line self-countained motorhomes. High gas prices are offset to some extent by the convenience and comfort of "taking your home with you" in one of today's luxurious recreational vehicles.

Whether renting a car or an RV, the "early bird gets the worm" adage applies here, so make reservations as soon as possible. That way, you get exactly the size and model you want.

Travel agencies may be able to provide

Alaska by RV

Great scenery...Useful information...

A professionally produced video for anyone planning a trip to Alaska. Forget the rumor mill... see for yourself...road conditions, campgrounds, wildlife and Alaska's natural beauty.

Join Bob & Judy Howen on a 67 day, 6,700 mile adventure up the Alaska Highway, through Alaska and down the Inside Passage by ferry. Order today...$19.95 plus $4.95 S/H.

Phone: 210 492-7100
Web: www.pvptravel.com

Pro Video Productions

promotional rates and special programs along with making all reservations for you.

Shipping

Whether you are moving to Alaska, or plan to ship your vehicle North rather than drive one or both ways, there is a shipper to accommodate your needs.

Vehicles: Carriers that will ship cars, campers, trailers and motorhomes from Anchorage to Seattle include: Alaska Railroad, Box 107500, Anchorage, AK 99510-7500, phone (907) 265-2485; 1-800-321-6518; www.alaskarailroad.com. Alaska Vehicle Transport, Inc., phone 1-800-422- 7925; CSX Lines, LLC, 1717 Tidewater Rd., Anchorage, AK 99501, phone (907) 263-5620 or 1-800-478-2671, www.csxlines.com; and Totem Ocean Trailer Express (TOTE), 2511 Tidewater, Anchorage, AK 99501, phone (907) 276-5868 or toll free 1-800-234-8683; www.totemocean.com.

In the Seattle, WA, area, contact A.A.D.A. Systems, Box 2323, Auburn 98071, phone (206) 762-7840 or 1-800-929-2773; Alaska Railroad, 2203 Airport Way S., Suite 215, Seattle, WA 98134, phone (206) 624-4234; CSX Lines, LLC, 1717 Tidewater Rd., Anchorage, AK 99501, phone (907) 263-5620 or 1-800-478-2671, www.csxlines.com; or Totem Ocean Trailer Express (TOTE), 500 Alexander Ave., Tacoma, WA 98421, phone (206) 628-9280 or 1-800-426-0074.

Vehicle shipment between southeastern Alaska and Seattle is provided by Alaska Marine Lines, 5615 W. Marginal Way SW, Seattle, WA 98106, phone (206) 763-4244 or toll free (800) 950-4AML or (800) 326-8346 (direct service to Ketchikan, Wrangell, Prince of Wales Island, Kake, Petersburg, Sitka, Juneau, Haines, Skagway, Yakutat, Excursion Inlet and Hawk Inlet). Boyer Alaska Barge Line, 7318 4th Ave. S., Seattle, WA 98108, phone (206) 763-8575 (serves Ketchikan, Metlakatla, Prince of Wales Island and Wrangell).

Persons shipping vehicles between Seattle/Tacoma and Anchorage are advised to shop around for the carrier that offers the services and rates most suited to the shipper's needs. Freight charges vary depending upon the carrier and the size of the vehicle. An approximate sample fare from Seattle/Tacoma to Anchorage to ship a 4-door sedan one-way is $1,100; for a truck, you might pay $1,400. From Anchorage to Seattle/Tacoma, it is approximately $750 for a vehicle and $950 to ship a truck.

Not all carriers accept rented moving trucks and trailers, and a few of those that do require authorization from the rental company to carry its equipment to Alaska. Check with the carrier and your rental company before booking service.

Book your reservation in advance and prepare to have the vehicle at the carrier's loading facility 2 days prior to sailing. Carriers differ on what non-vehicle items they allow to travel inside, from nothing at all to goods packaged and addressed separately. Regulations forbid the transport of vehicles holding more than $1/4$ tank of gas; so make sure your gas tank is under that requirement when you arrive. (It can take a surprisingly long time to drive off that extra gas, and the carriers don't make exceptions.) None of the carriers listed above allows owners to accompany their vehicles in transit. Remember to have fresh antifreeze installed in your car or truck prior to sailing!

Household Goods and Personal Effects: Most moving van lines have service to and from Alaska through their agency connections in most Alaska and Lower 48 cities. To initiate service contact the van line agents nearest your origin point.

Northbound goods are shipped to Seattle and transferred through a port agent to a water vessel for carriage to Alaska. Few shipments go over the road to Alaska. Southbound shipments are processed in a like manner through Alaska ports to Seattle, then on to destination.

U-Haul provides service into the North Country for those who prefer to move their goods themselves. There are 53 U-Haul dealerships in Alaska and northwestern Canada for over-the-road service. In Alaska, there are 8 dealerships in Anchorage, 6 in Fairbanks, 2 in Soldotna and Juneau and 1 in each of the following communities: Eagle River, Glennallen, Homer, Ketchikan, Delta Junction, Kenai, Palmer, Petersburg, Seward, Tok, Valdez, Wasilla, Sitka and North Pole. In Canada, there are dealerships and ready stations in Dawson City (summer only), Fort St. John, Fort Nelson, Whitehorse and at other locations along the Alaska Highway. There are also breakdown stations for service of U-Haul vehicles in Beaver Creek, Swift River and the Kluane Wilderness Area.

Tours

Packaged tours are multi-day itineraries which usually use several different vendors to provide transportation, accommodations

Dalton Highway tourists pose at a sign proving they've reached the Arctic Circle.
(© Rich Reid, Colors of Nature)

SOUTHBOUND RV RETURN
THE SHORTCUT HOME

Fly or cruise back to the Lower 48 while TOTE returns your RV on a drive-on, drive-off ferry cargo ship. TOTE's vessels conveniently depart Anchorage three times weekly. Total RV transit is five days. We do not take passengers.

For a free brochure or to book your vehicle, please call
1-800-234-8683, Ext. 235.

Visit our Web site at
www.totemocean.com

TOTEM OCEAN TRAILER EXPRESS, INC.
2511 Tidewater, Anchorage, AK 99501

Proudly serving Alaska for 25 years

A striking mask on display at the Tlingit Heritage Centre in Teslin, YT.
(© Bob Butterfield)

and sightseeing/activities. Costs vary and may or may not include all transportation, accommodations and sightseeing/activities, meals, tips, taxes, etc.

Generally speaking, these types of tours are not cheap, although for many travelers the expense of a packaged tour is offset by the convenience of reserved lodging and pre-arranged transportation and activities. Package tours often offer a number of options as to method of transportation (cruise; fly/cruise; cruise plus land tour by motorcoach, rail, etc.) and arrangement of the itinerary, and may be customized with optional add-ons, such as destinations and activities that are not part of the basic package.

Tour packages may be put together by a tour company, a travel agent, a travel wholesaler or you, the independent traveler. There is an incredible list of travel options to choose from in Alaska, as well as a huge geographical area. Your time, budget and interests will help narrow down the choices.

The larger tour companies in Alaska, such as Princess Tours and Holland America Westours, offer package tours using their own motorcoaches, cruiseships, railcars and motels. Other major Alaska tour companies, such as Alaska Sightseeing/Cruise West and Glacier Bay Cruise Line, use their own facilities (ships, motorcoaches, etc.) as well as other vendors to provide transportation, lodging, sightseeing and activities on their packaged tours.

If you are considering a package tour to Alaska from the Lower 49, start by reviewing the list of cruise lines offering all-inclusive cruise tours to Alaska this summer. Your travel agent or any of the travel agents in Alaska can also acquaint you with what package tours are available and their cost. Travelers who don't wish to join a large tour may customize their own package tour, either with the help of a travel agent or with the help of The MILEPOST®.

Read through the descriptions of major destinations in Alaska, such as Southeast/Inside Passage, Prince William Sound, Denali National Park, Kenai Peninsula, Anchorage, Fairbanks, etc. Everything from half-day motorcoach trips, sightseeing cruises or fly-in bear viewing to overnights on islands or on the North Slope, are covered in both the editorial and in the advertising.

As a travel agent or travel wholesaler would do, independent travelers can book any tour that might interest them, but they may also have to make arrangements for additional lodging and transportation. For example, a visitor might make independent arrangements for a flight to Anchorage and lodging for a night, then book a tour to Denali Park or Barrow or some other destination that would include transportation and lodging. The options are almost limitless. You can even purchase portions of the packaged tours (if space is available), such as the land tour portion of a cruise/tour.

When to go

One of the most often asked questions is, "When is the best time to travel?" The high season for travel in the North is June through August, usually the warmest months. But summer can also be the wettest months. Rain is heaviest in Anchorage in August and September; July and August in Fairbanks; and September and October in Juneau. Spring and fall weather almost anywhere in Alaska is beautiful—clear, sunny and mild.

But ultimately, the weather is as variable and unpredictable in the North as anywhere else. Go prepared for hot sunny days and cold rainy days. Waterproof footwear is always a good idea, as are a warm coat and rain gear. Generally, dress is casual. Comfortable shoes and easy-care clothes are best. There are stores in the North—just like at home—where you can buy whatever you forgot to bring along. There are laundromats (some with showers) in most communities and dry cleaners in the major cities and some smaller towns.

One advantage of summer travel to the North is the long hours of daylight. There are 19 hours and 21 minutes of daylight in Anchorage at summer solstice (June 21) and more than 21 hours of daylight in Fairbanks. Of course, if you are traveling in winter, the reverse is true: you'll have 3 hours and 42 minutes of daylight in Fairbanks at winter solstice (December 21) and about 5 1/2-hours in Anchorage. The farther north you go, the longer (or shorter) the days get. You can get sunrise and sunset times for any location, for any day or year, from the U.S. Naval Observatory website at www.usno.navy.mil (click on SunRise/Set under Popular Links).

Because most people travel in the summer, filling up hotels, motels, campgrounds and ferries, you might consider an early spring (April or May) or fall (late August into October) trip. There's usually more room at the lodges and campgrounds and on the ferries in these shoulder seasons. The weather can also be quite beautiful in early spring and in the fall. Keep in mind that some tours, attractions, lodges and other businesses operate seasonally. Check the advertisements in The MILEPOST® for details on months of operation or call ahead if in doubt.

The following numbers provide recorded weather information: Anchorage, phone (907) 936-2525; Fairbanks, phone (907) 452-3553; Alaska Highway in BC, phone (250) 774-6461; Alaska Highway in Yukon Territory, phone (867) 668-6061; Dawson Creek, BC, phone (250) 784-2244.

The Alaska region National Weather Service Internet address is www.arh.noaa.gov. To view weather conditions at various airports in Alaska, go to the FAA web site at http://akweathercams.faa.gov or visit http://climate.gi.alaska.edu or www.weather.com.

Cruise Passengers!

Combination shore excursion and transfer connecting to *all* Inside Passage cruises
Departs from Anchorage and Seward

Custom Itinerary Planning For groups and individuals

Alaska Cruise Transfers and Tours
In Alaska call toll free
(888) 275-8687

Web Site: www.alaskacruisetransfers.com

Boats-Sale or Lease/Purchase. Unique 3 pt. triangle locking loader. As low as $90.

When not car-topping E-Z TOTE boat use Hi-way approved Flip Up & Off Wheels.

Page: 888-861-1179
818-848-8590

WWW.EZTOTEBOATS.COM

Alaska Highway via
EAST ACCESS ROUTE

Connects: Great Falls, MT, to Dawson Creek, BC **Length:** 866 miles
Road Surface: Paved   **Season:** Open all year
Major Attractions: Canadian Rockies, Head-Smashed-In Buffalo Jump, Royal Tyrrell Museum, Fort Edmonton Park

(See maps, pages 34–35)

	Calgary	Dawson Creek	Edmonton	Great Falls	Lethbridge	Valleyview
Calgary		548	181	318	140	395
Dawson Creek	548		367	866	688	153
Edmonton	181	367		499	321	214
Great Falls	318	866	499		178	713
Lethbridge	140	688	321	178		535
Valleyview	395	153	214	713	535	

Whimsical ranch fence along Highway 2 in northern Alberta. *(© Blake Hanna, staff)*

The East Access Route is logged in *The MILEPOST* as one of the 2 major access routes (the other is the West Access Route) to the Alaska Highway. This driving log is divided into 3 sections: Great Falls to Sweetgrass, MT, at the Canadian border; Coutts, AB, at the Canadian border to Edmonton; and Edmonton to Dawson Creek, BC.

This was the only access route to Dawson Creek, BC, the start of the Alaska Highway, when the Alaska Highway opened to civilian traffic in 1948, although it differed from today's route. Instead of driving from Edmonton to Dawson Creek via Whitecourt and Valleyview via today's Highway 43 (completed in 1955), motorists had to drive north from Edmonton via Highway 2, then west to High Prairie, then south to Grande Prairie, AB, a route traced in the "Historic Athabasca Route" log starting on page 48.

All highways logged in this section are paved primary routes, with visitor services available along the way.

Total driving distance from Great Falls, MT, to Dawson Creek, BC, via Valleyview is 867 miles/1,394 km.

East Access Route Log

Distance from Great Falls (GF) followed by distance from Sweetgrass (SG).
Exit numbers and mileposts on Interstate 15 reflect distance from Idaho–Montana border.

INTERSTATE HIGHWAY 15 NORTH

GF 0 SG 117.5 (189 km) Exit 280 to **GREAT FALLS** (pop. 55,100; elev. 3,333 feet/1,016m), Montana's second largest city, located at the confluence of the Sun and Missouri rivers, Great Falls is home to the Charles M. Russell Museum. Giant Springs State Park on the north edge of the city has one of the largest springs in the world. The Roe River, which flows out of the springs, is 201 feet long and recognized by the Guinness Book of Records as the world's shortest river.

GF 10.5 (16.9 km) **SG 107** (172.2 km) Exit 290 west to U.S. Highway 89/Choteau.

GF 33.5 (53.9 km) **SG 84** (135.2 km) Junction with MT Highway 221 and exit 313 to Dutton; services.

GF 38.5 (61.9 km) **SG 79** (127.1 km) Rest areas near Teton River bridge.

GF 47 (75.6 km) **SG 70.5** (113.4 km) Exit 328 to Brady; services.

GF 54.5 (87.7 km) **SG 63** (101.4 km) Exit 335 to Midway Road.

GF 58.5 (94.1 km) **SG 59** (94.9 km) Exit 339 to **CONRAD** (pop. 3,074); 3 motels, 2 private campgrounds. ▲

GF 68.5 (110.2 km) **SG 49** (78.9 km) Exit 348 to **junction** with MT Highway 44 west to Valier and Lake Frances Recreation Area.

GF 73.5 (118.3 km) **SG 44** (70.8 km) Exit 352 to Bullhead Road and Marias River picnic area.

GF 81.5 (131.2 km) **SG 36** (57.9 km) Exit 363 to **SHELBY** (pop. 3,000); all visitor services available, including several private campgrounds. Marias Museum of History and Art located across from city park. ▲

Junction with U.S. Highway 2 to Cut Bank and Glacier National Park.

GF 83 (133.6 km) **SG 34.5** (55.5 km) Exit
(Continues on page 36)

Here's what you've been waiting for.

TravelAlberta.com

EAST ACCESS ROUTE
Great Falls, MT, to Edmonton, AB

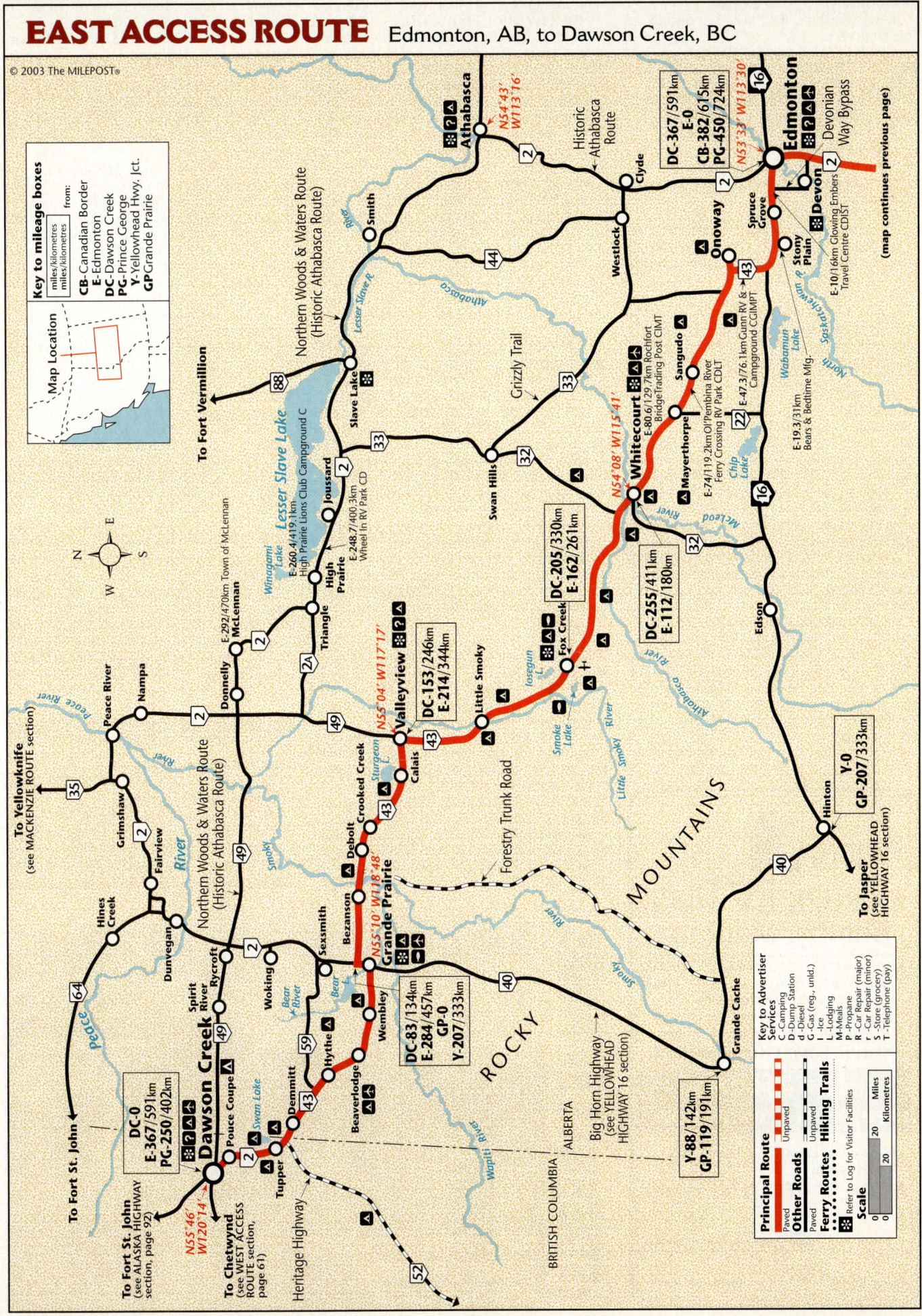

364 to Shelby; access to RV park.

Lewis & Clark RV Park. See display ad this section. ▲

GF 98.5 (158.5 km) **SG 19** (30.5 km) Exit 379 to Kevin/MT Highway 215 and Oilmont/MT Highway 343; services.

GF 109.5 (176.2 km) **SG 8** (12.9 km) Exit 389 to **SUNBURST** (pop. 520); all services.

GF 117.5 (189 km) **SG 0** Exit 397 to rest area at **SWEETGRASS, MT**, at U.S.–Canada border; food, gas and lodging. Duty-free shop. Customs and immigration open 24 hours a day.

ALBERTA HIGHWAY 4 NORTH

Distance from the Canadian border (CB) is followed by distance from Edmonton (E).

CB 0 E 382.2 (615 km) U.S.–Canada border crossing at **COUTTS, AB**; customs and immigration open 24 hours a day. Food, gas and lodging at border. Duty-free shop.

CB 7.4 (11.9 km) **E 374.7** (603.1 km) Private campground. ▲

CB 9.9 (15.9 km) **E 372.3** (599.1 km) **Junction** with Secondary Road 501, which leads west 67 miles/108 km to **CARDSTON** (pop. 3,502), located at the **junction** of Highways 2, 5 and 501. Established in 1887 by Mormon pioneers from Utah, Cardston's **Remington–Alberta Carriage Centre** features one of the world's foremost collections of horse-drawn vehicles.

Waterton Park, 25 miles/40.2 km west of Cardston, is the tourist centre for **Waterton Lakes National Park**. Known for its dramatic lake and mountain scenery, Waterton Lakes is actually one large lake broken into 3 sections—Lower, Middle and Upper Waterton lakes. Lower Waterton Lake extends down into Montana. Park adjoins Glacier National Park in Montana, and the 2 parks together are known as the Waterton–Glacier International Peace Park. Both parks are also noted for their grand old hotels. The Prince of Wales Hotel, just north of the townsite, was built in 1927 by the Great Northern Railway.

CB 11.9 (19.1 km) **E 370.3** (595.9 km) Milk River Travel Information and Interpretive Centre (wheelchair accessible); pay phone, picnic tables and dump station. The large dinosaur model on display here makes a good photo subject. Advanced bookings for Alberta adventures and attractions available here, open mid-May to Labour Day weekend for tickets. Open Victoria Day to Labour Day 9 A.M. to 7 P.M.; Labour Day to Canadian Thanksgiving 10 A.M. to 5 P.M.

CB 13 (21 km) **E 369.2** (594.1 km) **MILK RIVER** (pop. 926) has food, gas, stores and lodging. Public campground with 34 sites and 16 hookups. The 8 flags flying over the campground represent 7 countries and the Hudson's Bay Co., all of which once laid claim to the Milk River area. Grain elevators are on the west side of the highway, services are on the east side. ▲

CB 13.5 (21.7 km) **E 368.7** (593.3 km) **Junction** with Secondary Road 501 east to **Writing-on-Stone Provincial Park**, 26 miles/42 km; camping, Indian petroglyphs.

CB 23.6 (38 km) **E 358.6** (577.1 km) Road west to **WARNER** (pop. 434); store, gas, restaurant. Warner is the gateway to **Devil's Coulee Dinosaur Egg Site**, where dinosaur eggs, and fossilized fish and reptiles were discovered in 1987. Guided tours of Devil's Coulee are available through the Devil's Coulee Heritage Museum in Warner from mid-May to mid-September.

Junction with Highway 36 north to Taber, centre of Alberta's sugar beet industry.

CB 29 (46.8 km) **E 353.2** (576.8 km) Large turnouts with litter barrels both sides of highway.

CB 36.3 (58.5 km) **E 345.9** (556.6 km) Small community of New Dayton; camping and groceries. ▲

CB 41 (66 km) **E 341.2** (549.1 km) **Junction** at Craddock elevators with Highway 52 west to Raymond (10 miles/16 km), site of the annual Stampede and Heritage Days; Magrath (20 miles/32 km); Cardston (46 miles/74 km); and Waterton Lakes National Park (74 miles/119 km).

CB 44.4 (71.4 km) **E 337.8** (543.6 km) Small community of Stirling to west; municipal campground with 15 sites, some with power and water, dump station, showers and tennis court. Grain elevators and rail yards alongside highway. Stirling is the oldest, best-preserved Mormon settlement in Canada and a National Historic Site. ▲

CB 46.1 (74.2 km) **E 336.1** (540.9 km) **Junction** with Highway 61 east to Cypress Hills.

CB 57.1 (91.9 km) **E 325.1** (523.2 km) Turnout with information sign.

CB 62.1 (100 km) **E 320.1** (515.1 km) **Junction** with 43 Street truck route north to Highway 3.

CB 63 (101.4 km) **E 319.2** (513.7 km) **Junction** of Highways 4 and 5 at Lethbridge (description of city follows). Exit on Mayor Magrath Drive to north for access to motels, hotels and Henderson Lake campground. Continue northwest on Highway 4 (Scenic Drive) for access to Indian Battle Park/Fort Whoop-Up (via 3rd Avenue) and **junction** with Crowsnest Highway 3 West (log continues on page 38 for northbound travelers).

Highway 5 leads south to Cardston (48 miles/77 km) and Waterton Park (81 miles/131 km).

Lethbridge

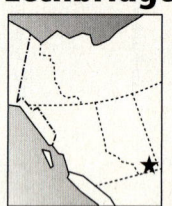

CB 63 (101.4 km) **E 319.2** (513.7 km) Located at the junction of Highways 3, 4 and 5. **Population:** 72,000. **Elevation:** 3,048 feet/929m. **Emergency Services:** Phone 911 for police, ambulance and fire department. **Hospital:** Lethbridge Regional Hospital, phone (403) 382-6111.

Visitor Information: Chinook Country Tourist Association, on the north side of the intersection of Highways 4, 5 and Mayor Magrath Drive; open year-round. RV parking, restrooms, picnic shelter, dump station and dumpster available. Phone (800) 661-1222 and ask for operator 48 (while in the

LETHBRIDGE ADVERTISERS

Best Western Heidelberg Inn..............................Ph. (800) 791-8488
Chinook Country Tourist Assoc.........................Ph. (800) 661-1222
Days Inn ....Ph. (403) 327-6000
Lethbridge R.V. Parks.......2 locations—see ad
Thriftlodge......................Ph. (403) 328-4436

area call 320-1222) for information on attractions and facilities in southwest Alberta. A tourist information centre is also located off Highway 3 at the Scenic Drive South entrance to the city, next to the Brewery Gardens; open March 1 to Oct. 31.
Newspaper: *Lethbridge Herald* (daily).

Private Aircraft: Airport 4 miles/6.4 km southeast; elev. 3,047 feet/929m; length 6,500 feet/1,981m; paved, fuel 100, jet. FSS.

The Lethbridge region was home to 3 Indian nations: the Sik-si-kah (Blackfoot), Kai'nah (Many Chiefs, now called Bloods), and Pi-ku'ni (Scabby Robes, now called Peigans). Collectively, they formed the Sow-ki'tapi (Prairie People). Because European fur traders along the North Saskatchewan River first came into contact with the Blackfoot, that tribal name came to be applied to the entire confederacy.

In 1869, the American Army decided to stop trade in alcohol with Indians on reservations across Montana. In December 1869, 2 American traders, John Jerome Healy and Alfred Baker Hamilton, built a trading post at the junction of the St. Mary and Belly (now Oldman) rivers, near the future site of Lethbridge. The post became known as Fort Whoop-Up, the most notorious of some 44 trading posts built in southern Alberta from 1869 to 1874. An important trade commodity was "whiskey," a concoction of 9 parts river water to 1 part pure alcohol, to which was added a plug of chewing tobacco for colour and a can of lye for more taste.

Alarmed by the activities of the whiskey traders, Prime Minister Sir John A. Macdonald formed the North West Mounted Police (NWMP), now the Royal Canadian Mounted Police, to bring law and order to the West. The NWMP reached Fort Whoop-Up on Oct. 9, 1874, and immediately put a stop to the whiskey trade.

Early development of Lethbridge commenced in 1874 with the arrival of Nicholas Sheran in search of gold. The gold turned out to be black gold—coal—and by the late 1870s a steady coal market and permanent settlement had developed.

The climax of the early development of Lethbridge came with the CPR construction in 1909 of the high level rail bridge that today carries freight shipments by rail west

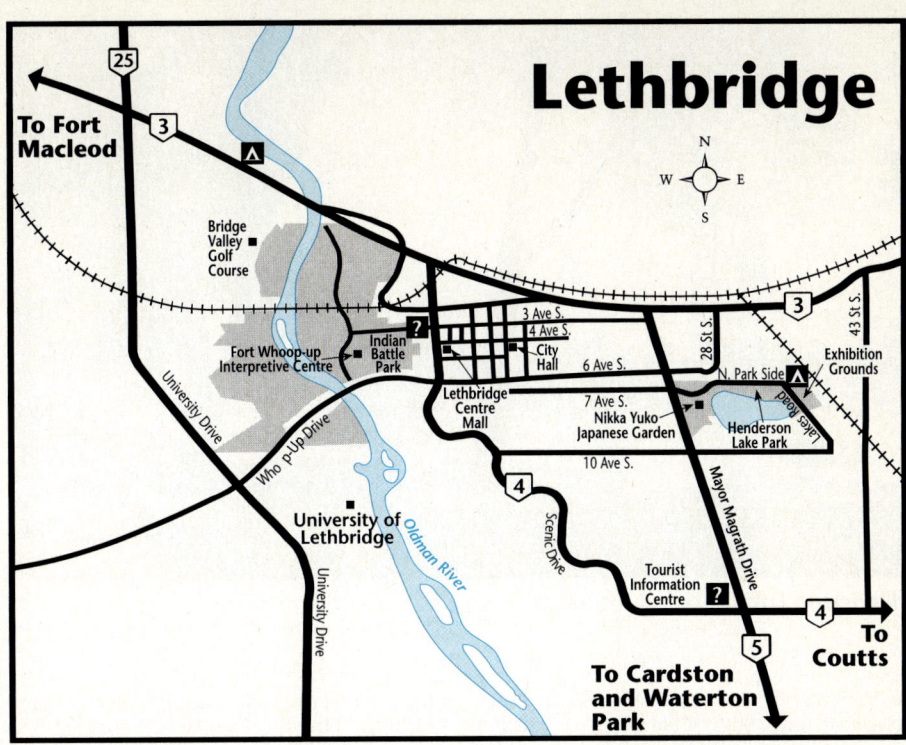

Welcome to LETHBRIDGE
ALBERTA'S CENTRE IN THE SOUTH

For special event details and more information call
1-800-661-1222
Operator #48

www.chinookcountry.com
info@chinookcountry.com

Offering you an incredible selection of attractions and services, Lethbridge is centrally located in southwest Alberta at the junction of highways 3, 4, and 5.

Experience the beauty in simplicity of the Nikka Yuko Japanese Garden, located in the heart of Henderson Lake Park. Recreational opportunities are many - swim in the pool, stroll through the rose garden, picnic in the park, enjoy the beauty of the lake at dusk... and more.

Discover Indian Battle Park in the beautiful Oldman river valley which showcases the Helen Schuler Coulee Centre, the Fort Whoop-Up Interpretive Centre, the Sir Alexander Galt Museum and the impressive High Level Bridge.

Golfers can choose from the championship Paradise Canyon Golf Resort, Henderson Lake Golf course, the family oriented Bridge Valley Par 3, or the executive length Evergreen Golf Centre.

Visit Lethbridge, where you'll find hospitality and service in Alberta's centre in the south.

Fort Whoop-Up, one of our attractions in Indian Battle Park offers educational family fun. Nearby, the Helen Schuler Coulee Centre offers insights into the river valley eco-system.

Henderson Lake Park offers diverse activities from fishing, boating and picnicking, to the Nikka Yuko Japanese Garden, a tranquil discovery of exceptional beauty. Henderson Pool and Henderson Ball Park are located nearby.

Henderson Lake Park in Lethbridge. (© Blake Hanna, staff)

to Vancouver. The "Bridge"—with a mile-long span and 300-foot elevation—is still the longest and highest bridge of its kind in the world.

Today, Lethbridge is Alberta's third largest city. It has a strong agricultural economy. In late June and early July, bright yellow fields of canola surround the highways leading into the city. Other fields produce wheat, sugar beets, potatoes, corn and a variety of other crops.

Lethbridge is southwest Alberta's service and shopping centre, with several malls and a variety of retail businesses. There is a wide choice of restaurants, hotel/motel accommodations, and bed and breakfasts.

Best Western Heidelberg Inn. Offering 66 immaculate rooms in modern 9-story building. On-site facilities include J.B.'s Restaurant, Hi Pub, sauna and fitness room. AAA Three Diamond rating. Frequency programs include: Gold Crown Club, Air Canada, Alaska, American, America West, Delta, Northwest and TWA. Top exchange on U.S. funds. 1303 Mayor Magrath Dr., Lethbridge, Alberta. Reservations 1-800-791-8488; fax (403) 328-8846. Email: info@heidelberginn.com; www.heidelberginn.com. [ADVERTISEMENT]

There are 2 campgrounds in the city: Henderson Lake and Bridgeview (see descriptions following).

Lethbridge R.V. Parks. Lethbridge has 2 beautiful RV parks. Bridgeview, on the banks of the Oldman River, has 175 serviced sites, 30–50 amp, lots of long pull-throughs and shade. Easy access from Highway 3. A 10,000-square-foot clubhouse which includes a registration office, large laundromat and bright, clean washrooms. Olympic-sized heated pool. Licensed restaurant and liquor store on site. Phone (403) 381-2357. Henderson Lake RV Park is centrally located in the city, has 100 sites, convenience store and laundromat. Close to shopping, restaurants, golf. Phone (403) 328-5452. www.holidaytrailsresorts.com. See display ad this section. [ADVERTISEMENT]

Henderson Lake Park also holds several of the city's attractions, including the **Nikka Yuko Japanese Garden**, a golf course, swimming pool, picnic area and rose gardens.

An extensive trail system leads to **Indian Battle Park** in the beautiful Oldman River valley. Indian Battle Park showcases a replica of **Fort Whoop-Up**, the Helen Schuler Coulee Centre, the Sir Alexander Galt Museum and the High Level Bridge.

Summer events include Whoop-Up Days and the Lethbridge International Airshow. Lethbridge hosts the Ag-Expo in March,

The Alberta Birds of Prey Centre, a 10-minute drive east of Lethbridge, is a 70-acre working conservation centre featuring hawks, falcons, eagles and owls from around the world. Live flying shows with hawks and falcons are presented, weather permitting. Open May 1 to early October, 9:30 A.M. to 5 P.M.; admission fee charged.

East Access Route Log
(continued)

CROWSNEST HIGHWAY 3 WEST

CB 66.6 (107.2 km) **E 315.6** (507.9 km) **Junction** with Crowsnest Highway 3. Tourist information centre beside Brewery Gardens.

CB 69.5 (111.8 km) **E 312.7** (503.2 km) **Junction** with Highway 25. Access to **Park Lake Provincial Park** (9 miles/14 km north); 40 campsites, swimming, boat launch, fishing, playground.

CB 71.9 (115.7 km) **E 310.3** (499.4 km) Rest area with litter barrels and historical information sign about Coalhurst.

CB 72.4 (116.5 km) **E 309.8** (498.6 km) Community of **COALHURST** just north of highway; gas station, dump station and campground.

CB 73.8 (118.9 km) **E 308.4** (496.3 km) CPR marshalling yards at Kipp. Large turnout southbound; litter barrels.

CB 75.8 (122.1 km) **E 306.4** (493.1 km) Turnout southbound with litter barrels.

CB 77.5 (124.7 km) **E 304.7** (490.3 km) Large turnout northbound with information sign and litter barrels.

CB 78.8 (126.8 km) **E 303.4** (488.3 km) **Junction** with Highway 23 north. Continue west on Highway 3 for Fort Macleod.

CB 81.5 (131.2 km) **E 300.7** (483.9 km) Westbound, the highway enters Oldman River valley. Good view west of the Rockies on a clear day.

CB 81.7 (131.5 km) **E 300.5** (483.6 km) Oldman River.

CB 82.9 (133.4 km) **E 299.3** (481.7 km) **Junction** with Highway 3A East and Highway 23 North.

CB 95.7 (154 km) **E 286.5** (461.1 km) **Junction** with Highway 2 south to Cardston and the U.S. border, with access to Waterton Lakes and Glacier national parks. Continue on Highway 3.

Fort Macleod

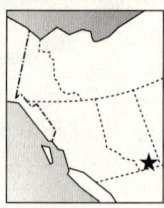

CB 96.1 (154.7 km) **E 286.1** (460.4 km) Turn south for tourist services and town centre. **Population:** 3,100. **Elevation:** 3,300 feet/1,006m. **Visitor Information:** The tourist office is located at the east entrance to town.

There are several hotels, motels, campgrounds, restaurants, shopping facilities and gas stations in Fort Macleod.

The town's **Main Street** is Alberta's only provincially designated historic area. Walking tours are available.

The main attraction in Fort Macleod is the **Fort Macleod Museum**, a replica of Fort Macleod, which features the history of the Mounted Police, local Native cultures and early pioneers, in a fort setting. The original fort, named for Colonel J.F. Macleod, was built in 1874 and was the first outpost of the North West Mounted Police (later the RCMP) in western Canada. Partial restoration of the 1884 NWMP Barracks site is under way as an Alberta Centennial Legacy project, with a

projected completion date in 2005.

During July and August, the museum features a local re-creation of the official RCMP Musical Ride: Youth in NWMP uniforms execute drills on horseback in a colorful display. The museum is open 9 A.M. to 5 P.M. daily from March 1 to December 24, with extended hours during July and August; closed Dec. 25 through February.

Town of Fort Macleod. See display ad this section.

The Sunset Motel, AAA/CAA approved. Winner of 12 Travel Alberta Housekeeping Awards. They emphasize clean, comfortable rooms, friendly service and reasonable prices. Air-conditioned 1-, 2-, and 3-bedroom units with in-room coffee, refrigerators, cable, free movies, free local calls, smoking and non-smoking. Park at your door. Laundromat, c-store, gas and fast food (and yes, breakfast) next door. Full U.S. exchange. At Fort Macleod's west entrance with easy access to Highways 2 and 3. Closest motel to Head-Smashed-In Buffalo Jump. Show *The MILEPOST®* to save 10 percent. Phone (403) 553-2784. Toll-free reservations 1-888-554-2784. Email: sunsetmo@telusplanet.net. [ADVERTISEMENT]

East Access Route Log
(continued)

CB 99 (159.4 km) **E 283.2** (455.8 km) **Junction** with Highway 2 north to Calgary and Edmonton; access to private campgrounds east and west of exit. ▲

Highway 3 (Crowsnest) continues 600 miles/966 km west to Hope, BC. The highway takes its name from Crowsnest Pass (elev. 4,534 feet/1,382m), one of the lowest passes in the Rockies, located 66 miles/106 km west of here.

ALBERTA HIGHWAY 2 NORTH

CB 100 (160.8 km) **E 282.2** (454.1 km) **Oldman River** bridge. Alberta government campground to southwest with 40 campsites, dump station, playground, fishing and swimming. North of the river is the largest turkey farm in Alberta. ◆▲

CB 100.4 (161.6 km) **E 281.8** (453.5 km) **Junction** with Highway 785, which leads 10 miles/16 km to **Head-Smashed-In Buffalo Jump**, a UNESCO World Heritage Site. The 1,000-foot/305-m-long cliff, where Plains peoples stampeded buffalo to their deaths for nearly 6,000 years, is one of the world's oldest, largest and best-preserved buffalo jumps. The site was named, according to legend, for a young brave whose skull was crushed when he tried to watch the stampede from under a protective ledge which gave way. An interpretive centre houses artifacts and displays describing the buffalo hunting culture. First Nations interpretive guides available on site. Guided walks available twice daily during July and August. Open daily year-round; 9 A.M. to 6 P.M., May 15 to Labour Day; 10 A.M. to 5 P.M., Labour Day to May; closed major holidays. Admission fee charged.

Head-Smashed-In Buffalo Jump. See display ad this section.

CB 102.1 (164.4 km) **E 280.1** (450.8 km) Turnout northbound with litter barrels.

CB 111.2 (179 km) **E 271** (436.1 km) **Junction** with Highway 519 east to small settlement of **GRANUM**. Private RV park with 27 campsites. Fuel, propane, dump station and groceries available. ▲

Granview RV Park. Easy access, 1/2 mile east on Highway 519. Large serviced sites,

pull-throughs, unserviced sites. Firepits, free showers, laundry, swimming, fishing lake within park. 2 minute walk to 9 hole par 3 golf course and driving range. Short drive to Head-Smashed-In Buffalo Jump and prime tourist attractions. Reservations 1-888-788-2222 or (403) 687-3830. [ADVERTISEMENT] ▲

CB 116.2 (187 km) **E 266** (428 km) Community of Woodhouse.

CB 121.8 (196 km) **E 260.4** (419.1 km) **CLARESHOLM** (pop. 3,427), a prosperous ranching centre with all visitor facilities. **Visitor Information:** The old railway station houses the tourist infocentre and a museum. Camping at Centennial Park; 17 sites, dump station, playground. ▲

Bluebird Motel. Winner of 9 Provincial Housekeeping awards. 23 meticulously clean, quiet units, each with its own unique charm. Choose between 1-, 2-, and 3-room suites, or pamper yourself in a heritage room decorated in antiques. Kitchenettes available. Large-screen cable TVs, free movie channels, fridges, in-room coffee, air-conditioning, laundry service. Pets welcome in certain rooms. Fair U.S. exchange, off-season rates. Don't be disappointed—call ahead. (403) 625-3395 or 1-800-661-4891; www.bluebirdmotel.ab.ca. [ADVERTISEMENT]

CB 125.5 (201.9 km) **E 256.7** (413.1 km) Turnout northbound with litter cans and historic sign.

CB 131.3 (211.3 km) **E 250.9** (403.8 km) Community of Stavely to the east.

CB 131.7 (212 km) **E 250.5** (403.1 km) Large turnout northbound with litter barrels and historic sign about Stavely.

CB 132.1 (212.6 km) **E 250.1** (402.5 km) Access west to **Willow Creek Provincial Park**; 40 campsites, swimming, fishing. ◆▲

CB 138.4 (222.8 km) **E 243.8** (392.3 km) Exit to small settlement of Parkland. Also access to Little Bow Provincial Park, 34 miles/54 km east, with camping, boat launch, beach and fishing. ◆▲

CB 146.8 (236.3 km) **E 235.4** (378.8 km) **NANTON** (pop. 1,841), about a 45-minute drive from Calgary, has all visitor facilities. Nanton's well preserved history is on display at the Antique and Art Walk of Alberta (open daily), and along Main Street, with its restored turn-of-the-century buildings.

Nanton is famous for its springwater, which is piped from Big Spring in the Porcupine Hills, 6 miles/10 km west of town, to a large tap located in town centre. Springwater tap operates mid-May to September.

The **Nanton Lancaster Society Air Museum**, located on Highway 2 South, houses an impressive display of WWII aircraft and artifacts. The centerpiece of the 26,000-square-foot museum is a 1945 Lancaster Bomber, one of the few in the world that is still intact. The museum is open daily from May to October; weekends the rest of the year.

CB 147.7 (237.8 km) **E 234.5** (377.4 km) Nanton campground (75 sites) at **junction** with Secondary Road 533; access to Nanton Golf Club 18-hole golf course. Chain Lakes Provincial Park is west on Sec-

Head-Smashed-In Buffalo Jump
UNESCO World Heritage Site
www.head-smashed-in.com
18 km north and west of Fort Macleod, Alberta, on Secondary Highway #785

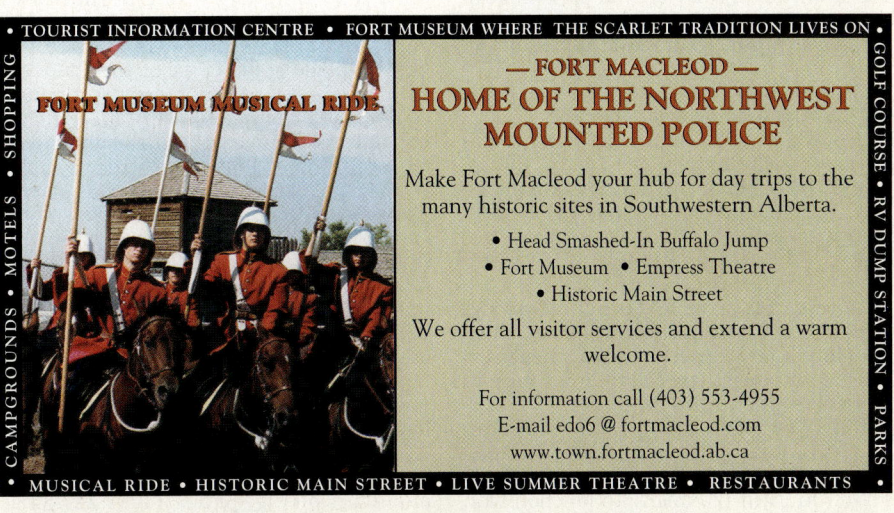

— FORT MACLEOD —
HOME OF THE NORTHWEST MOUNTED POLICE

Make Fort Macleod your hub for day trips to the many historic sites in Southwestern Alberta.

• Head Smashed-In Buffalo Jump
• Fort Museum • Empress Theatre
• Historic Main Street

We offer all visitor services and extend a warm welcome.

For information call (403) 553-4955
E-mail edo6 @ fortmacleod.com
www.town.fortmacleod.ab.ca

• TOURIST INFORMATION CENTRE • FORT MUSEUM WHERE THE SCARLET TRADITION LIVES ON • GOLF COURSE • RV DUMP STATION • PARKS • MUSICAL RIDE • HISTORIC MAIN STREET • LIVE SUMMER THEATRE • RESTAURANTS • CAMPGROUNDS • MOTELS • SHOPPING •

The Northwest Mounted Police (today's RCMP) were created in 1873 to police the Canadian west.

EAST ACCESS ROUTE • Calgary

The Okotoks Erratic, located west of Okotoks, is the largest known glacial erratic in the world. (© Brian Stein)

ondary Road 533.

CB 157.8 (254.1 km) **E 224.4** (361.1 km) **Junction** with Secondary Road 540, which leads west 21 miles/34 km to Bar U National Historic Site.

CB 162.8 (262 km) **E 219.4** (353.1 km) **Junction** with Highway 23 west to **HIGH RIVER** (pop. 6,893) located on Highway 2A. All visitor facilities. Once the centre of a harness-making industry, High River has elegant sandstone buildings and the Museum of the Highwood (open in summer).

CB 164 (264 km) **E 218.2** (351.1 km) Stop of interest commemorating Turner Valley oilfield.

CB 171.6 (276.1 km) **E 210.6** (338.9 km) **Junction** with Highways 2A and 7 to Okotoks, Black Diamond and Turner Valley (19 miles/30 km). Stop of interest commemorating the Turner Valley oil fields.

CB 172.6 (277.8 km) **E 209.6** (337.2 km) Sheep River Bridge.

CB 172.9 (278.3 km) **E 209.3** (336.7 km) Private campground. ▲

CB 179.3 (288.6 km) **E 202.9** (326.4 km) **Junction** with Highway 2A to **OKOTOKS** (5 miles/8 km west); all visitor services. Visitor information at "The Station," which also has a local history display and an art exhibit in summer. Open daily, May to Labour Day; Tuesdays through Saturdays, September to May.

The Okotoks Erratic, west of town, is the world's largest known glacial erratic.

CB 185.2 (298.1 km) **E 197** (317.1 km) Private campground. ▲

CB 186.6 (300.4 km) **E 195.6** (314.6 km) Exit 22X. Northbound exit for Highway 2 North (Deerfoot Trail). *NOTE: To bypass downtown Calgary, take exit 22X; keep right, follow Highway 2 (Deerfoot Trail) north.*

Access this exit to **Spruce Meadows Equestrian Centre**, a world famous show jumping facility. Spruce Meadows hosts several major equestrian events from June to September; phone (403) 974-4200.

CB 191.4 (308.1 km) **E 190.8** (306.9 km) Anderson Road West exit. Anderson Road West connects with Trans-Canada Highway 1 West to Banff (70 miles); to junction with Icefields Parkway (105 miles) and access to Jasper; and Vancouver, BC (640 miles).

Highway 2 becomes Macleod Trail northbound through Calgary.

Calgary

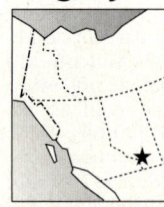

CB 200.8 (323.1 km) **E 181.4** (291.9 km) Located at the confluence of the Bow and Elbow rivers. **Population:** 904,987. **Elevation:** 3,440 feet/1,049m. **Emergency Services:** Phone 911 for emergency services. **Hospitals:** Alberta Children's Hospital, Richmond Rd. SW; Rockyview, 7007 14th St. SW; Peter Lougheed Center, 3500 26th Ave. NE; Foothills Hospital, 1403 29th St. NW.

Visitor Information: Downtown at Riley & McCormick Western Store, 220 8th Ave. SW, and at the Calgary Airport; both are open year-round. A visitor centre at Canada Olympic Park is open in summer only. Or call Tourism Calgary at (403) 263-8510 or (800) 661-1678 (toll-free in North America); or visit www.tourismcalgary.com.

Private Aircraft: Calgary International Airport, 10.5 miles/17 km northeast of downtown Calgary; elev. 3,557 feet/1,084m; 3 runways. See Canadian Flight Supplement.

This bustling city is one of Alberta's 2 major population and business centres. A great influx of homesteaders came to Calgary with the completion of the Canadian Pacific Railway in 1883. It grew as a trading centre for surrounding farms and ranches. Oil and gas discovered south of the city in 1914 contributed to more growth.

Calgary has large shopping malls, department stores, restaurants, and many hotels and motels. Most lodging is downtown, at the airport and on Highway 2 south (Macleod Trail), Trans-Canada Highway 1 north (16th Avenue) and Alternate 1A (Motel Village). There are several campgrounds in and around the city. ▲

Calgary has many major attractions. There are tours of **Canada Olympic Park**, located at 88 Canada Olympic Rd. SW, site of the 1988 XV Olympic Winter Games. Summer chairlift, bobsleigh rides and mountain biking; phone (403) 247-5452. **Calgary Science Centre**, 11th Street and 7th Avenue, is open year-round with hands-on exhibits, films and science demonstrations for the entire family. **Calgary Zoo, Botanical Garden and Prehistoric Park**, off Memorial Drive, has more than 1,200 live animals and a prehistoric park with life-sized replicas of dinosaurs. **Glenbow Museum**, at 130 9th Ave. SE, explores the heritage of the Canadian West; phone (403) 268-4100, www.glenbow.org. **Fort Calgary Historic Park**, at 750 9th Ave. SE, is an authentic reconstruction of the 1875 Fort, with interpretive centre, restaurant and activities; phone (403) 290-1875. **Heritage Park Historical Village**, on Heritage Drive SW, is Canada's largest living history park; phone (403) 259-1900, www.heritagepark.ab.ca.

Two 25-passenger high-speed elevators take you to the top of **Calgary Tower** in 62 seconds. Located on 9th Avenue SW, Calgary Tower's observation deck offers a panoramic view of the city.

The city's best-known event is the annual **Calgary Stampede**, which takes place at the Exhibition Grounds, July 4-13, 2003. The 10-day event includes a parade and daily rodeo. For Stampede information and tickets, phone (800) 661-1767 or (403) 269-9822. Tickets are also available online at www.calgarystampede.com.

East Access Route Log
(continued)

CB 211.3 (340 km) **E 170.9** (275 km) Calgary northern city limits.

Highway 2 from Calgary to Edmonton bypasses most communities. Except for a few service centres built especially for freeway traffic, motorists must exit the freeway for communities and gas, food or lodging.

CB 212.8 (342.6 km) **E 169.4** (272.6 km) Exit to community of **BALZAC**. Private RV park with dump station. ▲

CB 214.2 (344.8 km) **E 168** (270.4 km) Northbound vehicle inspection site; pay phone.

CB 216.9 (349.1 km) **E 165.3** (266 km) First of 3 exits northbound to **AIRDRIE** (pop. 14,506). **Emergency Services**; RCMP. Visitor facilities include hotels and motels, fuel and groceries.

CB 224.5 (361.4 km) **E 157.7** (253.8 km) Dickson–Stephensson Stopping House on Old Calgary Trail, a southbound-only rest area and tourist information on west side of highway.

CB 224.9 (361.9 km) **E 157.3** (253.1 km)

> **Junction** with Highway 72 east to Drumheller, 60 miles/97 km. See "Side Trip to the Canadian Badlands" on opposite page for log of this route.

CB 226.8 (365.1 km) **E 155.4** (250.1 km) Northbound-only access to gas, diesel and restaurant.

CB 231.2 (372 km) **E 151** (243 km) Exit to **CROSSFIELD**; gas, hotel, food.

CB 237 (381.5 km) **E 145.2** (233.7 km) Exit west for **CARSTAIRS** (pop. 2,254), a farm and service community with tourist information centre and campground. The campground has 28 sites, electric hookups, hot showers and dump station. Services here include groceries, liquor store, banks, a motel, propane and gas stations. ▲

CB 253.7 (408.3 km) **E 128.5** (206.8 km) **Junction** with Highway 27 west to **OLDS** (pop. 5,542); all visitor facilities, including a campground, museum and information booth. ▲

CB 258.2 (415.6 km) **E 124** (199.5 km)

Side Trip to the Canadian Badlands

Alberta Highways 72 and 9 lead 60 miles/97 km east to Drumheller in the Canadian Badlands—a region characterized by scanty vegetation and intricate erosional features. Besides its fantastic scenery, the Badlands is also famous for its dinosaurs. It is one of the best places in the world to recover the fossilized remains of dinosaurs, many of which are displayed at the world-famous Royal Tyrrell Museum in Drumheller.

Distance from Highway 2 junction (J) is shown.

ALBERTA HIGHWAY 72 EAST

J 0 Junction with Alberta Highway 2 at **Milepost CB 224.9** (approximately 25 miles/40 km north of Calgary).

J 7.5 (12.1 km) **Junction** with Highway 791, which leads to the Fairview Colony.

J 13.8 (22.2 km) Rosebud River.

J 14 (22.6 km) Beiseker Colony.

J 20.7 (33.4 km) **BEISEKER** (pop. 838); all services available. Small community campground. Highway 72 becomes Highway 9 eastbound.

ALBERTA HIGHWAY 9 EAST

J 33.2 (53.5 km) **Junction** with Highway 21 to Three Hills and Trans-Canada Highway 1.

J 37.3 (60.1 km) **Junction** with Highway 836. Food and gas available.

J 45.1 (72.6 km) **Junction** with Highway 840 to Rosebud and Standard.

J 50.6 (81.5 km) Horseshoe Canyon Viewpoint; restrooms and picnic tables.

J 60.1 (96.8 km) **DRUMHELLER** (pop. 7,833); all visitor facilities available, including bed and breakfasts, motels, campgrounds, restaurants and gas. **Visitor Information:** Drumheller Regional Chamber of Development and Tourism, Box 999, Alberta T0J 0Y0; phone (403) 823-8100; toll-free (866) 823-8100; web site www.canadianbadlands.com; email info@drcdt.com.

The first dinosaur fossil found in the badlands was an Albertosaurus (a slightly smaller version of the Tyrannosaurus), unearthed in 1884 by Joseph Burr Tyrrell pronounceds TEER-ell) just east of what is today Drumheller. The "Great Canadian Dinosaur Rush" followed, as famous fossil hunters Barnum Brown, Joseph Sternberg and others vied for trophies.

Today, the major attraction in Drumheller is the **Royal Tyrrell Museum**, located in Midland Provincial Park just outside the town limits. The museum boasts an outstanding fossil collection presented in stunning displays. More than 30 complete dinosaur skeletons, as well as flying reptiles, prehistoric mammals and marine invertebrates, are displayed in a huge walk-through diorama exhibit. A tropical plant conservatory with more than 100 species of plants simulates the botanical world of the dinosaurs. A viewing window in the main laboratory allows visitors to watch scientists at work. Park rangers lead visitors on 90-minute interpretive hikes into the badlands

View of Drumheller from the mouth of a Tyrannosaurus Rex. (© Blake Hanna, staff)

around the museum, and there are special programs for children. The museum has a restaurant and gift shop. Summer hours are 9 A.M. to 9 P.M. daily. Admission fee charged. For more information, contact the museum at Box 7500, Drumheller, AB T0J 0Y0; phone (403) 823-7707; www. tyrrellmuseum.com.

An annual event in Drumheller is the Canadian Badlands Passion Play, presented in a natural bowl amphitheatre each summer. Phone (403) 823-2001 for dates.

Dinosaur Trail RV Resort. Located in the scenic badlands only 3 kms from the Royal Tyrrell Museum on the North Dinosaur Trail. 200 full-service, partial and unserviced sites. Fully modern facilities made for big rigs, with heated pool, convenience store, clean washrooms and laundry, modem access and security gate. Close to all major attractions. Reservations recommended. Phone (403) 823-9333; Email: camping@dinosaurtrailrv.com; www.dinosaurtrailrv.com. [ADVERTISEMENT]

Return to Milepost CB 224.9 East Access Route

DRUMHELLER ADVERTISERS

Dinosaur Trail RV Resort..Ph. (403) 823-9333
Drumheller Regional Chamber of
  Development &
  Tourism.......................Ph. (403) 823-8100

EAST ACCESS ROUTE

Turnout northbound with litter barrels.

CB 263.6 (424.2 km) **E 118.6** (190.9 km) **Junction** with highway west to Bowden and Red Lodge Provincial Park (8.5 miles/14 km); 120 campsites, playground, swimming and fishing. **BOWDEN** (pop. 1,174) is the site of Alberta Nurseries and Seeds Ltd., a major employer. Most visitor services available. Heritage rest area with 24 campsites, dump station and tourist information booth at junction ▲

CB 266.1 (428.3 km) **E 116** (186.7 km) Exit for **RCMP Dog Training Centre**, the only one in Canada. Public tours at 1:30 P.M. Wednesdays, May to October; demonstration and video. Groups must book in advance; phone (403) 227-3346.

CB 271 (436.2km) **E 111.2** (179 km) **Junction** with Highway 54 west to **INNISFAIL** (pop. 6,064); all visitor facilities.

CB 273 (440.7 km) **E 109.2** (175.7 km) Turnouts with pay phones and litter cans both sides of highway.

CB 285.5 (459.5 km) **E 96.7** (155.6 km) First of 2 exits northbound with access to "Gasoline Alley" tourist service area with gas stations and restaurants.

CB 286.6 (461.3 km) **E 95.6** (153.8 km) **Junction** with Highway 2A (Gaetz Avenue) east to **RED DEER** (pop. 70,560). **Emergency Services:** Phone 911. **Visitor Information:** Red Deer Visitor Information Centre located at **Milepost CB 289.3**.

Attractions in Red Deer include **Fort Normandeau**; **Waskasoo Park**, an extensive system of trails and recreation areas throughout the city; **Heritage Square**, a collection of historic buildings in a park setting; and the award-winning and controversial architecture of **St. Mary's Church**, at 38th Street and Michell Avenue, designed by Douglas Cardinal. Historical walking tour brochures are available from the **Red Deer & District Museum**.

Red Deer has all visitor facilities, including major chain motels and retail outlets. Collicult Leisure Centre features a wave pool, waterslide, indoor tennis and other recreational facilities. Camping at Westerner Campground on Delburne Road (19th Street) and at Lions Municipal Campground on Riverside Drive. ▲

Westerner Campground. 19th Street (Delburne Road), Red Deer. 99 full-hookup sites, 30–50 amp, pull-throughs. Laundromat, showers. Walking distance to shopping and restaurants. Phone (403) 352-8801. Northbound on Highway 2 take Gaetz Avenue exit to 19th Street (Delburne Road). Southbound on Highway 2 take Delburne Road exit. Follow Delburne Road (19th Street) east to park entrance. [ADVERTISEMENT] ▲

CB 289.3 (465.6 km) **E 92.9** (149.5 km) **Red Deer Visitor and Convention Bureau** houses the visitor information centre and Alberta Sports Hall of Fame. The visitor centre is staffed and open daily year-round; restrooms, pay phone, picnic tables. Phone (800) 215-8946. Adjacent to the visitor centre is Heritage Ranch, which has trail rides, pony rides, a gift shop and snack bar. Ample parking and access to Waskasoo Park. Phone (403) 347-4977.

CB 291.6 (469.3 km) **E 90.6** (145.8 km) **Junction** with Highway 11 west to Sylvan Lake (10 miles/16 km), a popular watersports destination for Red Deer residents, with swimming beach and marina. **Sylvan Lake Provincial Park** has picnicking and swimming. Private campgrounds and waterslide nearby. ▲

Highway 11 leads 48 miles/78 km west to the town of Rocky Mountain House and to **Rocky Mountain House National Historic Park**. The park preserves the sites of 4 fur trading posts that operated between 1799 and 1875 near the confluence of the North Saskatchewan and Clearwater rivers. Interpretive trails and demonstrations, visitor centre with exhibits. Open daily, 10 A.M. to 6 P.M., May–Sept.; phone (403) 845-2412.

CB 304 (489.6 km) **E 78.2** (125.8 km) **Junction** with Highway 12. Exit east for **LACOMBE** (pop. 7,580); all visitor facilities. Camping at Michener Park; 57 sites. Site of the Federal Agricultural Research Station; open to the public weekdays, 8 A.M. to 4:30 P.M. Exit west on Highway 12 for **Aspen Beach Provincial Park** at Gull Lake (6 miles/10 km); camping, swimming. ▲

CB 321.3 (517.1 km) **E 60.9** (98 km) **Junction** with Highway 53 east to **PONOKA** (pop. 5,861); all visitor facilities. Camping at Ponoka Stampede Trailer Park, 134 sites; open May–Oct. Ponoka's Stampede is held June 29 to July 3 at Stampede Park. ▲

CB 325.4 (523.7 km) **E 56.8** (91.4 km) Turnout pay phone.

CB 336.7 (541.8 km) **E 455** (73.2 km) Northbound-only access to Wetaskiwin rest area; picnic tables, restrooms, gas, diesel, dump station, groceries, restaurant and camping. ▲

CB 340.5 (548 km) **E 41.7** (67.1 km) **Junction** of Highway 13 east to Highway 2A and comunity of **WETASKIWIN** (pop. 10,960). Visitor services include restaurants, hotels, motels and bed-and-breakfasts. Camping at Lions Campgrounds; 68 sites, hookups, showers and dump station. ▲

Wetaskiwin has more than a dozen restored turn-of-the-century buildings in its downtown area and a half-dozen antique and collectible stores.

Wetaskiwin is also the site of **Reynolds-Alberta Museum**, which celebrates the spirit of the machine in transportation, aviation, agriculture and industry. The transportation exhibit includes a 1929 Duesenberg Phaeton Royale as well as dozens of other antique

Call us for your free Travel Information Package with details on...
• Exciting Attractions
• Events & Festivals
• Recreational Activities
• Affordable Lodging, RVing & Camping and much more...

Travel AlbertaCentral
1-888-414-4139   www.travelalbertacentral.com

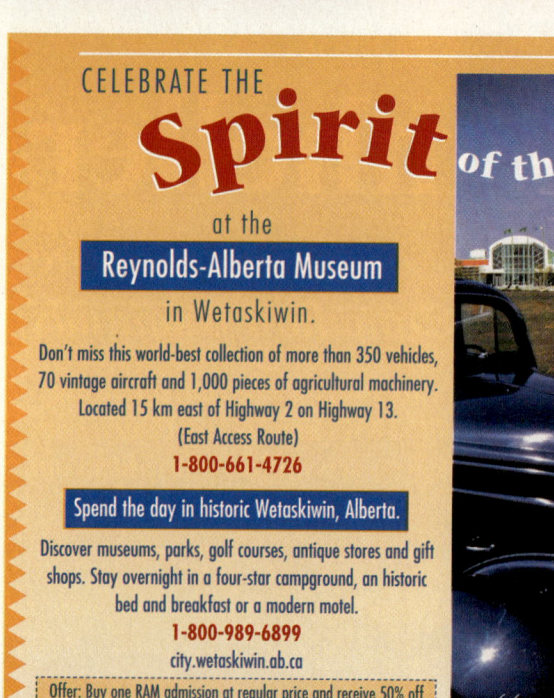

CELEBRATE THE **Spirit** at the **Reynolds-Alberta Museum** in Wetaskiwin.

Don't miss this world-best collection of more than 350 vehicles, 70 vintage aircraft and 1,000 pieces of agricultural machinery. Located 15 km east of Highway 2 on Highway 13. (East Access Route)
1-800-661-4726

Spend the day in historic Wetaskiwin, Alberta.
Discover museums, parks, golf courses, antique stores and gift shops. Stay overnight in a four-star campground, an historic bed and breakfast or a modern motel.
1-800-989-6899
city.wetaskiwin.ab.ca

Offer: Buy one RAM admission at regular price and receive 50% off a second admission of equal or lesser value. Not valid with other promotions or discounts. Expires December 31, 2003.

cars. The aviation exhibit includes Canada's Aviation Hall of Fame. Phone 1-800-661-4726 for more information.

Reynolds-Alberta Museum. See display ad this section.

CB 351.2 (565.2 km) **E 31** (49.9 km) Turnout to east with litter barrels and pay phone.

CB 362.4 (583.2 km) **E 19.8** (31.9 km) First of 3 exits northbound to **LEDUC** (pop. 14,117); all visitor facilities. Founded and named for the Leduc oil field. The 200-million barrel Leduc oil field was the first in a series of post-war oil and natural gas finds that changed the economy of Alberta.

CB 367.4 (591.3 km) **E 14.8** (23.8 km) Highway 19 Bypass; access west to Leduc No. 1 Well Historic Site. Secondary Road 625 east to Nisku; access to bed and breakfast.

Green Acres Bed & Breakfast. See display ad this section.

Highway 2 northbound becomes Calgary Trail; access to Edmonton Airport.

Junction with Highway 19 west and Edmonton Bypass route. See "Devonian Way Bypass" beginning on this page.

*NOTE: Northbound motorists wishing to avoid heavy traffic through Edmonton may exit west on Highway 19 (Devonian Way) for Devon Bypass route. Drive 8.2 miles/13.2 km west on Highway 19, then 14.5 miles/23.3 km north through Devon via Highway 60 to junction with Yellowhead Highway 16 ten miles/16 km west of Edmonton (see **Milepost E 10** on page 47 this section for continuation of East Access Route northbound log).*

CB 377.2 (607.1 km) **E 5** (8 km) Edmonton Tourism's Gateway Park Visitor Info Centre, open year-round; pay phones, restrooms, dump station.

CB 377.9 (608.2 km) **E 4.3** (6.9 km) Ellerslie Road exit.

CB 382.2 (615 km) **E 0 Junction** with Whitemud Drive/Highway 2.

IMPORTANT: Turn west on Whitemud Drive/Highway 2 (stay in middle lane) for campgrounds, Fort Edmonton Park, West Edmonton Mall and junction with Yellowhead Highways 16A and 16 West and Highway 2 North (Athabasca Route). Northbound travelers taking this turnoff will avoid Edmonton city centre traffic.

Devonian Way Bypass

This bypass route circles the southwest edge of Edmonton, connecting Highway 2 and Highway 16 via Secondary Highway 19 (Devonian Way) and Highway 60.
Distance from Highway 2 and Devonian Way junction (J) is shown.

J 0 Junction with Highway 19, Devonian Way, at **Milepost CB 367.4**. Follow Devonian Way west.

J 0.4 (0.7 km) Rest area to south.

J 2.1 (3.4 km) Budweiser Motorsports Park to south, Amerlea Meadows equestrian facility to north.

J 5.2 (8.3 km) Rabbit Hill Ski area to west.

J 8.2 (13.2 km) **Junction** with Highway 60 (Edmonton truck bypass). Turn north on Highway 60 for Devon and Yellowhead Highway; turn south at intersection and drive 0.6 mile/1 km for **Leduc No. 1 Well Historic Site** and Canadian Petroleum Interpretive Centre & Hall of Fame.

DEVON ADVERTISERS

Canadian Petroleum Interpretive Centre
 & Hall of Fame ....Ph. (780) 987-4323
Devon Golf & Country
 Club ....Ph. (780) 987-3569
Devon Lions Club
 Campground ....Ph. (780) 987-4777
Devonian Botanic
 Garden..........................Ph. (780) 987-3054
High Rigg Retrreat B&B...Ph. (780) 470-0462
Town of Devon ....Ph. (780) 987-8300

The Leduc Well was brought in on Feb. 13, 1947, before an invited asssembly of business people, government officials and reporters. It was the 134th try for Imperial Oil after drilling 133 dry wells, and it was wildly successful, making Edmonton the "Oil Capital of Canada." A 174-foot/53-m

EAST ACCESS ROUTE • Devon Bypass

2003 ■ The MILEPOST® ■ 43

EAST ACCESS ROUTE • Devon Bypass • Edmonton

derrick marks the site. Visitors may climb to the drilling floor to view drilling equipment and tools.

Canadian Petroleum Interpretive Centre. Over 50 years of oil field history. Equipment, models, murals, video, working drilling rig. Knowledgeable interpretive guides give you a memorable learning experience. Open April 15–Sept. 15. 10 A.M.–6 P.M. daily. Admission $4 adult, $2 child. RV campground. 1 mile south of Devon on Highway 60. Phone (780) 987-4323; www.cpic.org. [ADVERTISEMENT] ▲

J 9.2 (14.8 km) Dump station.

J 10.2 (16.4 km) Turn east on Athabasca Avenue for downtown **DEVON** (pop. 4,900). This small, relaxed community has all visitor services, including accommodations, restaurants, fast-food outlets, gas stations, grocery stores and an 18-hole golf course. It's an easy 20-minute drive from here to West Edmonton Mall.

Camping at **Devon Lions Club Campground**, 180 sites on North Saskatchewan River; follow signs for Patrick O'Brien Memorial Park. The campground is adjacent to Devon Golf & Country Club.

J 10.6 (17 km) Bridge over North Saskatchewan River.

J 11.9 (19.2 km) **High Rigg Retreat B&B**. Great views of the North Saskatchewan River valley and Blackhawk golf course. 4.9 miles or 7.9 kms east of Highway 60. Central to Devonian Botanic Garden and West Edmonton Mall. We offer cozy accommodations and warm hospitality. Pets welcome. See our website for more information: www.highriggretreat.com. Email: highrigg@oanet.com. Phone (780) 470-0462. [ADVERTISEMENT]

J 13.8 (22.2 km) **University of Alberta Devonian Botanic Garden**; alpine garden,

orchid house, 5-acre Kurimoto Japanese Garden, and other special collections gardens set in natural landscape. Live exotic butterfly showhouse with 30 species of butterflies. Open daily, 10 A.M. to 7 P.M. in summer, shorter hours rest of year. Fee charged.

J 16.9 (27.2 km) **Junction** with Secondary Highway 627; turn east for Edmonton.

J 22.7 (36.6 km) **Junction** with Yellowhead Highway 16; turn to **Milepost E 10**.

Return to Milepost E 10 or CB 367.4 East Access Route

Whitemud Drive/Highway 2 crosses the North Saskatchewan River; turns north to become 170th Street (access to West Edmonton Mall); then junctions with Highway 16A West and the continuation of East Access Route to the Alaska Highway for northbound travelers (log continues on page 47). Or follow Highway 2 North for Athabasca and the Northern Woods and Waters Route.

Rainbow Valley Campground. See display ad this section ▲

Shakers Acres. See display ad on page 46. ▲

See log of the "Historic Athabasca Route to Alaska Highway" beginning on page 48.

Edmonton

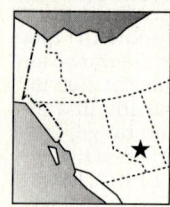

E 0 DC 367 (590.6 km) Capital of Alberta, 1,853 miles/2,982 km from Fairbanks, AK. **Population:** 666,104; area 937,845. **Emergency Services:** Phone 911 for all emergency services. **Hospitals:** Grey Nuns Community Health Centre, 3015–62 St., phone (780) 450-7000; Misericordia, 16940 87th Ave., phone (780) 930-5611; Royal Alexandra, 10240 Kingsway Ave., phone (780) 477-4111; University, 8440–112 St., phone (780) 407-8822.

Visitor Information: Edmonton Tourism operates visitor information centres downtown and on Highway 2 south. Or contact Edmonton Tourism, phone (780) 496-8400 or (800) 463-4667; email edeinfo@ede.org; web site www.tourism.ede.org.

Elevation: 2,182 feet/ 668m. **Climate:** Average temperatures in July range between 60–72°F/16–22°C. In January from 0 to 16°F/ -18 to -9°C. Average precipitation includes 13 inches of rain and 55 inches of snow. Edmonton is located on the 53rd latitutde and has 17 hours of daylight in midsummer. **Newspaper:** Edmonton Sun (daily), Edmonton Journal (daily), Edmonton Examiner (weekly).

Transportation: Air—Edmonton International Airport is located 17 miles/29 km south of city centre. Major airlines serving Edmonton include Air Canada, Northwest

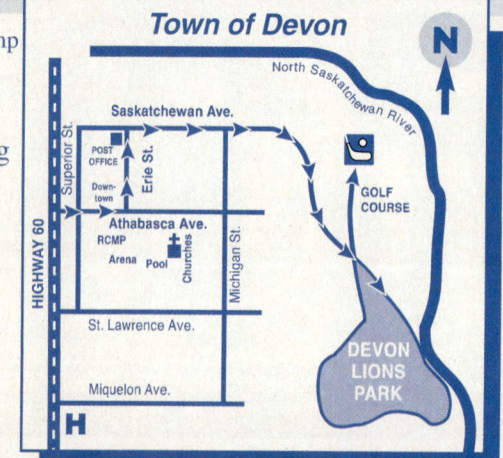

Giant boot captures Edmonton's western spirit.
(© Blake Hanna, staff)

EAST ACCESS ROUTE • Edmonton

Airlines, and United Airlines. Air North offers nonstop service to Whitehorse, YT. See also www.edmontonairports.com. **Bus**—Greyhound Canada scheduled service to most points in Canada and the U.S.; phone (403) 265-9111; www.greyhound.ca. Red Arrow to Calgary, Red Deer and Fort McMurray; phone (800) 232-1958; www.redarrow.pwt.ca. **Railroad**—Edmonton is on VIA Rail's "The Canadian," the transcontinental train connecting Toronto, ON, and Vancouver, BC. See www.viarail.ca. Edmonton station is at 12360 121st St. near the Yellowhead Highway.

Private Aircraft: Edmonton International Airport 14 miles/22.5 km southwest and Edmonton City Centre Airport north side of downtown. See Canadian Flight Supplement and www.edmontonairports.com.

There are 117 hotels and motels in Edmonton and some 2,000 restaurants. Within the Edmonton vicinity there is camping at Rainbow Campground and Shakers Acres on Whitemud Drive, and at Glowing Embers Travel Centre via the Devon Overpass.

Comfort Inn West. CAA/AAA 2.5 stars; Canada Select 3-Star Rating. 100 finely appointed rooms. Movie system, 1 km to West Edmonton Mall. Free parking, RV space. 100 percent satisfaction guarantee. On-site restaurant. Complete information, or make your own reservations on: www.choicehotels.ca/cn234. Toll-free reservation system 1-800-228-5150. Property reservations (780) 484-4415. Fax (780) 481-4034. Located on 100th Avenue and 176 Street. Choice Hotels Canada 2001 Gold Award Winning Inn. [ADVERTISEMENT]

The North Saskatchewan River winds through the centre of Edmonton, its banks lined with 22 public parks. It is the largest stretch of urban parkland in North America. Located along the river's parkland are Kinsmen Sports Centre, a top fitness and recreation facility, and Victoria Golf Course, the oldest (1907) municipal golf course in Canada. William **Hawrelak Park** on the

EDMONTON ADVERTISERS

Comfort Inn West	Ph. (800) 228-5150
Edmonton Queen Riverboat Cruise	Ph. (780) 424-2628
Glowing Embers Travel Centre & RV Park	Ph. (780) 962-8100
Rainbow Valley	Ph. (888) 434-3991
Shakers Acres	Ph. (877) 447-3565
West Harvest Inn	Ph. (800) 661-6993

Glass pyramids of Edmonton's Muttart Conservatory shelter plants from various climates. (© Blake Hanna, staff)

Welcome to Edmonton!
17803 Stony Plain Road N.W.
Edmonton, AB T5S 1B4 • 780-484-8000
2 Minutes From the WORLD'S LARGEST MALL
Budget Car & Truck Rental On Site.
Toll Free Reservations **1-800-661-6993**
Large, Quiet Rooms • Licensed Lounge & Restaurant • Bus Tour Specialists
Email: inn@westharvest.ab.ca • Website: www.westharvest.com
West Harvest inn AAA CAA

Shakers Acres
www.shakersacres.com
• 170 Sites • Pull-Thrus • Full Hook-ups
• Electric/Water • Laundry Facilities
• Also Sites with No Hookups
• Tenting • Washrooms • Hot Showers
• Sani-Dump • Fire Pits
• Convenience Store
• Superintendent on Site 24 Hrs a Day
• Open Year Round
21530 - 103rd Ave.
(NW Corner Winterburn Rd.)
Edmonton, Alta. T5S 2C4
RESERVATIONS
Phone: (780) 447-3564
Toll Free: 1-877-447-3565
Fax: (780) 447-3924
Take Winterburn Rd. (215 St.) turnoff to Shakers Acres.
From Calgary (Hwy. 2) follow Whitemud Drive west to 215 St. (Winterburn Drive).
21530 - 103 Ave. - NW Corner of Winterburn Rd.

Alberta was named in 1882 by the governor general of Canada for his wife.

river has the Heritage Amphitheatre, which hosts the River City Shakespeare Festival (June 26–July 20, 2003); the Heritage Festival (Aug. 2–4, 2003); and the Symphony Under the Sky (Aug. 28–Sept. 1, 2003).

Other major Edmonton festivals include: Jazz City International (June 20–29, 2003); International Street Performers (July 4–13, 2003); Klondike Days (July 17–26, 2003); Folk Music Festival (Aug. 7–10, 2003); and the International Fringe Theatre Festival (Aug. 14–24, 2003).

The 4 spectacular glass pyramids of **Muttart Conservatory** showcase plants from the temperate, tropical and arid climates of the world. Open daily. The conservatory has a cafe and gift shop. Located at 9626 96 A Street, phone (780) 496-8755; www.edmonton.ca/muttart.

Daily riverboat cruises along the North Saskatchewan River depart from Rafter's Landing across from Muttart Conservatory. The 170-foot *Edmonton Queen* offers scenic dining for 250 passengers. Phone (780) 424-2628 or visit www.edmontonqueen.com.

Top of the list of major attractions for visitors to Edmonton is the world's largest shopping mall—**West Edmonton Mall**. The mall features some 800 stores, services and restaurants, as well as a water park, ice skating rink, mini-golf, submarine rides, dolphin theatre and a spa. Also located in the mall are Palace Casino, Galaxyland Amusement Park, Sea Life Caverns and IMAX Theatre. Located on 87 Avenue at 170 Street, the shopping mall is open 7 days a week; www.westedmontonmall.com.

The **Odyssium**, formerly known as the Edmonton Space & Science Centre, has the largest planetarium dome in North America and an IMAX theatre. It is located at 11121–142 St.; phone (780) 451-3344; www.edmontonscience.com.

The architectural highlight of the city is the **Alberta Legislature Building** at 10800–97 Ave.; phone (780) 427-7362; www.assembly.ab.ca). The **Provincial Museum of Alberta**, at 12845–102 Avenue, features the Syncrude Gallery of Aboriginal Culture, the Natural History Gallery, the Bug Room and Wild Alberta. Also special exhibits, gift shop, cafe and a 400-seat theatre. Open daily; phone (780) 453-9100, or visit www.pma.edmonton.ab.ca.

Fort Edmonton Park is Canada's largest

living history park. Costumed interpreters recreate life as it was in 1846, 1885, 1905 and 1920. Period restaurants and retail shops are located in the park. The steam train and streetcar rides are included in the admission price. Open 10 A.M. daily, May to September. Located at Fox Drive and Whitemud Drive. For more information, phone (780) 496-8787 or visit www.edmonton.ca/fort.

East Access Route Log

(continued)
Distance from Edmonton (E) is followed by distance from Dawson Creek (DC).

HIGHWAY 16A WEST

E 0 DC 367 (590.6 km) Downtown Edmonton. Jasper Avenue westbound (becomes Yellowhead 16A).

E 10 (16 km) DC 357 (574.5 km) Junction of Highways 16A West and Highway 60 (Devon Overpass) to Devon. Access to Glowing Embers campground to the north. ▲

Glowing Embers Travel Center & RV Park. See display ad on page 45. ▲

NOTE: Southbound travelers may bypass Edmonton by taking Highway 60 south, then Highway 19 east to Highway 2.

> Junction with Highway 60 south to Highway 19 east and Edmonton Bypass route. See "Devonian Way Bypass" on pages 43–44 for log.

E 16 (26 km) DC 351 (564.9 km) SPRUCE GROVE (pop. 15,069). All visitor facilities including motels, restaurants, gas and service stations, grocery stores, farmer's market, shopping malls and all emergency services. Recreational facilities include a golf course, swimming pool, skating and curling rinks, parks, and extensive walking and cycling trails. The chamber of commerce tourist information booth, located on Highway 16A, is open year-round; phone (780) 962-2561.

E 19.3 (31 km) DC 347.7 (559.5 km) STONY PLAIN (pop. 9,000). All visitor facilities including hotels, restaurants, supermarkets, shopping mall, gas stations with major repair service, and RCMP and hospital. Turn north on South Park Drive for Lions RV Park and Campground; 47 sites, hookups, open year-round. ▲

Visitor Information: Housed in the Dog Rump Creek railway station at the Rotary Park rest area. Take Exit 779 and turn north on South Park Drive.

Recreation includes an outdoor swimming pool, tennis courts and 18-hole golf course. Attractions include 21 outdoor murals; Oppertshauser Art Gallery; and the Pioneer Museum at Exhibition Park. The Multicultural Heritage Centre here has historical archives, a craft shop and home-cooked meals.

Bears and Bedtime Mfg. The largest selection of bear-making supplies in Canada; Cherished Teddies; Boyd's Bearstones; Beanie Babies; handmade, limited edition collectible teddy bears and gift items. Hours: Monday–Friday 9 A.M.–5:30 P.M., Thursday 9 A.M.–8 P.M., Saturday 10 A.M.–5:30 P.M. Visit our web site at www.bearsandbedtime.com. Phone 1-800-461-BEAR(2327). 4812 50th Ave., Stony Plain, Alberta. [ADVERTISEMENT]

E 23.9 (38.5 km) DC 343.1 (552.1 km) Turnoff to south for Hasse Lake Parkland County day-use area (6 miles/10 km); picnicking, swimming and fishing. ▲

E 24.2 (39.4 km) DC 342.8 (551.7 km) Hubbles Lake turnoff to north; camping. ▲

E 25.5 (41.1 km) DC 341.5 (549.6 km) Restaurant, gas station and store to north.

E 29.8 (47.9 km) DC 337.2 (542.6 km)

> Junction of Yellowhead Highway 16 and Highway 43. If you are continuing west on Yellowhead Highway 16 for Prince George or Prince Rupert, BC, turn to **Milepost E 25** on page 211 in the YELLOWHEAD HIGHWAY section.

Turn north onto Highway 43 and continue with this log for Dawson Creek, BC.

HIGHWAY 43 NORTH

E 31.7 (51 km) DC 335.3 (539.6 km) Turnout to east with litter barrel and historical information sign about construction of the Alaska Highway.

E 33.7 (54.3 km) DC 333.3 (536.4 km) Gas station to east.

E 38 (61.1 km) DC 329 (529.5 km) Highway 633 west to Alberta Beach Recreation Area on Lac Ste. Anne. Facilities include a municipal campground (open May 15 to Sept. 15) with 115 sites. ▲

E 40.7 (65.5 km) DC 326.3 (525.1 km) ONOWAY (pop. 847) is located at the hub of Highways 16, 37 and 43. The village web site is at www.onoway.com.

Onoway has a post office, gas stations, banks and bank machines, grocery stores, a liquor store, laundromat, drugstore, medical clinic, dentist and veterinary clinics. Visitor services include restaurants, a motel, and car wash. Towing, propane and dump station available. Camping at Elks campground with 8 sites (no hookups). Recreation is provided by 7 area lakes and 7 golf courses. ▲

Onoway hosts the Lac Ste. Anne Pilgrimage. Held in late July, the annual event attracts some 40,000 aboriginal peoples.

E 46.8 (75.3 km) DC 320.2 (515.3 km) Junction of Highways 43 and 33 (Grizzly Trail). Continue on Highway 43.

Alberta government campground with dump station, water, toilets and stoves.

E 47.3 (76.1 km) DC 319.7 (514.5 km) Restaurant and gas station. Campground south on **Lac Ste. Anne**; fishing. ◆▲

Gunn RV & Campground. See display ad this section.

E 59.7 (96.1 km) DC 307.2 (494.5 km) Lessard Lake campground (County of Lac Ste. Anne), 1.9 miles/3 km; 53 sites, water, stoves, boat launch, fishing for pike and perch. ◆▲

E 72.7 (117 km) DC 294.3 (473.6 km) SANGUDO (pop. 377), located south of Highway 43 on the Pembina River. Restaurants, motel and hotel accommodations; gas station; grocery and liquor stores; banks, post office, pharmacy, laundromat and car wash.

Sportsgrounds along the Pembina River has a supervised campground with showers and dump station; shale baseball diamonds;

(Continues on page 53)

Gunn RV & Campground

1/2 mile south of Hwy 43 on the shore of Lac Ste Anne

*Hook ups (P/W) *Gas *Propane *Groceries
*Hardware *Liquor Store *Laundromat
*Car Wash *Shower
* "Very good" Western-style Restaurant
*Fishing Supplies *Fishing *Boat Launch

Phone (780) 967-1094

Explore the Edmonton River Valley like never before

EDMONTON QUEEN
THE RIVERBOAT CORPORATION
E-mail sales@edmontonqueen.com
Website www.edmontonqueen.com

Cruise by day or night through the heart of Alberta's capital. Enjoy delicious buffet style dining and dance to live entertainment in the evening.

9734 - 98 Avenue Edmonton, AB
Tel (780) 424-2628 • Fax (780) 466-0433

EAST ACCESS ROUTE • Athabasca Route

Historic Athabasca Route to Alaska Highway

"Field of Dreams" north of Athabasca is a private collection of antique farm equipment. (© Blake Hanna, staff)

When the Alaska Highway opened to civilian traffic in 1948, the original access route from Edmonton to Dawson Creek, BC, was north via Highway 2 to the historic fur-trading post of Athabasca; then west along what is today the Northern Woods & Waters Route to High Prairie; then south to Grande Prairie, AB. In late 1955, Highway 43 was completed connecting Edmonton and Valleyview via Whitecourt.

ALBERTA HIGHWAY 2 NORTH
Distance from Edmonton (E) is shown.

E 0 Junction with Whitemud Drive and Highway 2 at **Milepost CB 382.3**. Follow West Whitemud Drive/Highway 2 North.

E 6.5 (10.5 km) Follow 170th Street North. This is the easiest and most direct route to Highway 2.

E 13.7 (22 km) Entering community of **ST. ALBERT** (pop. 50,000). 170th Street becomes Gervais Road at Levasseur Road.

E 13.9 (22.4 km) St. Albert city limits. Continue on Gervais Road for Athabasca.

E 15.2 (24.5 km) Turn north (left) at **junction** of Gervais Road and St. Albert Road (Highway 2 North).

E 24.9 (40 km) **Junction** with Highway 37 west to Onoway and east to Fort Saskatchewan.

E 31.3 (50.3 km) Turnoff to east for Morinville and access to private campground. ▲

E 33.1 (53.3 km) Divided highway ends northbound. Canola fields alongside highway are a brilliant yellow in early summer.

E 42.6 (68.5 km) **Junction** with Highway 651; gas station and restaurant. Turnoff to east for town of Legal (1.8 miles/3 km).

E 57.5 (92.6 km) **Junction** with Highway 18 west to Highway 44.

E 58.2 (93.7 km) Gas station.

E 76.6 (123.3 km) Turnoff to east for Rochester (2.5 miles/4 km) and junction with Secondary Road 661.

E 94.8 (152.6 km) **Cross Lake Provincial Park** 27 miles/44 km; camping, boat launch, fishing, hiking, wildlife viewing and swimming. ▲

E 97.5 (157 km) Motel.

E 101.7 (163.7 km) Turnout to west.

E 105.6 (170 km) **ATHABASCA** (pop.

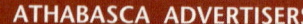

ATHABASCA ADVERTISERS
Athabasca Hillside Motel..Ph. (888) 675-8900
Best Western Athabasca Inn................Ph. (800) 567-5718
Blueberry Hill RV Park ......Ph. (800) 859-9452
Regional Tourism Committee of Athabasca County...Ph. (780) 675-2273
Super 8................Ph. (780) 675-8888

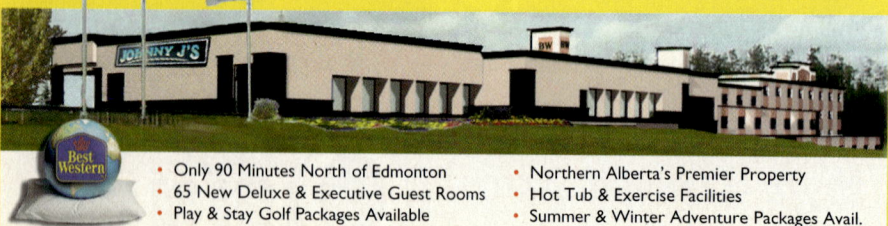

WORLD'S LARGEST HOTEL CHAIN
TRAVEL TO ALASKA VIA ATHABASCA

- Only 90 Minutes North of Edmonton
- 65 New Deluxe & Executive Guest Rooms
- Play & Stay Golf Packages Available
- Northern Alberta's Premier Property
- Hot Tub & Exercise Facilities
- Summer & Winter Adventure Packages Avail.

Best Western Athabasca Inn • 5211 - 41st Avenue, Athabasca, AB T9S 1A5
1-800-567-5718 • reservations@bestwesternathabascainn.com • www.bestwesternathabascainn.com

DISCOVER ATHABASCA COUNTRY...
Only 90 minutes North of Edmonton on Highway 2

The Town of Athabasca
Historical Gateway to the North
❖ Heritage Walkway ❖ Golf Course
❖ Canoe & Boat Launch ❖ Hiking & Skiing Trails
❖ Riverside Park & Campground
www.town.athabasca.ab.ca

The County of Athabasca
• Cottage Country • Bird Watching
• Northern Lights • Trans-Canada Trail
• Overland Route to the Klondike

ATHABASCA COUNTRY
Our Good Nature Beckons

For more information on Athabasca Country visit our website: www.athabascacountry.com
Email tourism@athabascacountry.com
Phone (780) 675-2273

2,313). **Visitor Information:** Tourist information booth along the Athabasca River in an old train caboose. Open during the summer months only.

Visitor facilities include 2 hotels, 3 motels, the full-service Blueberry Hill RV Park, a campground, restaurants, retail and grocery outlets, public library, hockey and curling rink, tennis courts and a swimming pool. An 18-hole golf course is 1.2 miles/2 km north on Highway 813. The course has a clubhouse, driving range and grass greens. ▲

Athabasca Landing was founded by the Hudson's Bay Co. in 1874, when the Athabasca Landing Trail was established and a trading post was constructed. In its early years, Athabasca was a busy transshipment point for freight movement in northwestern Canada. The Athabasca Landing Trail, running from Athabasca south 99 miles/160 km to Edmonton, became in 1880 the first registered highway in Alberta. The railroad arrived in Athabasca in 1912.

The Athabasca Landing Trail, a 76-mile/121-km corridor from Gibbons to Athabasca, runs roughly parallel to Highway 2 and served the Indians long before the arrival of the Europeans. It became the overland route connecting the Athabasca and North Saskatchewan rivers. The Hudson's Bay Co. developed the trail in 1875, and for the next 35 years it played a vital role in the development of the North. The first part of the old trail has been lost to the plough, and today the trail begins 24 miles/40 km north of Edmonton.

At a local park along the Athabasca River, a cairn commemorates the arrival of the first Ukranian pioneers to Canada in 1891, and honors those Ukranian pioneers who settled in the Athabasca area.

A major annual event in Athabasca is the Magnificent River Raft Festival, held on July 1st. This popular festival, featuring music and entertainment, attracts a very large attendance.

E **105.7** (170.1 km) Bridge over Muskeg Creek.

E **105.9** (170.4 km) University Drive.

E **106.9** (172.1 km) Turnout.

E **108.9** (175.3 km) **Field of Dreams**; a private collection of antique farm equipment.

E **113.7** (183 km) **Junction** with Highway 2 East and Secondary Road 812. Dawson Creek-bound traffic continue west on Highway 2 .

ALBERTA HIGHWAY 2 WEST

E **119** (191.5 km) Access road east 2.5 miles/4 km and then north 5 miles/8 km to Island Lake Recreation Campground, open mid-May to mid-September; 11 sites, water pump, fishing, boat launch, camping fee. Chain Lakes Provincial Recreation Area Campground, located another 7 miles/12 km north, has 20 sites, water pump, fishing, boat launch (electric motors only), camping fee.

Watch for Rocking Horse Ranch along the highway.

E **120.2** (193.5 km) Community of Island Lake South.

E **121** (194.9 km) North entrance east into Island Lake Recreation Area.

E **121.7** (196 km) **ISLAND LAKE** (pop. 126) store and gas station to east.

E **122.9** (197.8 km) Access road east 12 miles/20 km to Chain Lakes Provincial Recreation Area.

E **133.2** (214.4 km) **Lawrence Lake Provincial Recreation Area** to west; 27 campsites, picnic shelter, water pump, fishing, boat launch, camping fee.

E **145.5** (234.1 km) Secondary side road north 5.5 miles/9 km to Hondo.

E **149.5** (240.7 km) **Junction** with Alberta Highway 44 south 66 miles/105 km to Westlock and to Alberta Highway 18.

E **150** (241.6 km) Roadside turnout for large trucks on both sides of highway.

E **152** (244.8 km) **Junction** with Highway 2A north 1.8 miles/3 km to Hondo (no services) and 9 miles/15 km to **SMITH** (pop. 250). Smith has a hotel, restaurant, small store and service station with minor-repair facilities. A secondary road continues north and west out of Smith, along the Slave River, and rejoins the highway at **Milepost E 162.5**. Fawcett Lake, 20 miles/32 km northeast of Smith, has fishing and boating. Camping and boat launch at private resort and at provincial recreation area.

E **153.4** (246.9 km) Bridge over the Athabasca River.

E **154.8** (249.1 km) Evidence of 2001 forest fire next 7.5 miles/12 km westbound.

E **170** (260.6 km) Bridge over the Saulteaux River.

E **169.3** (272.5 km) Bridge over the Otauwau River.

E **185.2** (298.2 km) **Junction** with Alberta

Russian Orthodox churches along the Athabasca route reflect heritage of Ukranian pioneers. (© Blake Hanna, staff)

44 Large Sites (10 pull thru)
Coin Showers • Walking Trails
Laundry • Golf Course Next Door
Free Firewood

Alaska via Athabasca

Located 1.5 miles north of Athabasca Hwy 813 (underpass to Calling Lake)
P.O. Box 687, Athabasca, AB T9S 2A6

Reservations:
1-800-859-9452
Email: ssuther1@telusplanet.net

Historic Athabasca Route *(continued)*

Highway 88 (Bicentennial Highway), which leads north to Lesser Slave Lake Provincial Park (see description following); 105 miles/168 km to the community of Red Earth Creek; and 255 miles/410 km to Fort Vermilion. Highway 88 is paved to Red Earth Creek; the remainder of the road to Fort Vermilion is gravel and in poor condition.

Lesser Slave Lake Provincial Park, along the east shore of Lesser Slave Lake, is divided into 3 different recreational areas. Devonshire Beach day-use area is 3.6 miles/6 km north on Highway 88. Northshore day-use area, 7 miles/11 km north on Highway 88, has 14 picnic sites, shelter, water pump and a fish-cleaning stand. Marten River Campground, 18 miles/30 km north on Highway 88, has 113 sites, dump station, flush toilets, showers, playground, public phone, ski trails, hiking trails, swimming, fishing. ▲

E **186** (299.4 km) **SLAVE LAKE** (pop. 6,553) located on the southeast shore of Lesser Slave Lake. Visitor facilities include motels, restaurants and fast-food outlets, numerous stores, service stations with major-repair facilities and car washes.

Visitor Information: In a small building on the service road just off Highway 2, phone 849-4611. Open mid-May to mid-September. The town office is located at 328 2nd St. NE, phone 849-3606.

Originally known as Sawridge when it was founded in the 1880s, Slave Lake was an important jumping-off point for steamboat traffic that carried prospectors bound for the Yukon and the Klondike gold rushes. Early settlers included the Metis and Cree Indians. Today, their descendants contribute to the rich cultural heritage of this well-integrated community.

E **186.8** (300.7 km) Private campground to north. ▲

E **191.6** (308.4 km) Turnout with litter barrels to north.

E **197.5** (317.9 km) Access road north 0.6 mile/1 km to **WIDEWATER** (pop. 203).

E **199.5** (321.1 km) **CANYON CREEK** (pop. 164) to north has a hotel, gas station, dump station, pay phone and marina.

E **203.8** (328.1 km) Access road north 1.8 miles/3 km to Assineau (no services).

E **204.4** (329.1 km) Assineau River bridge.

SUPER 8 MOTEL
MOTEL & SUITES
Slave Lake
ALBERTA
101 - 14th St. SW, Slave Lake, AB
1-780-805-3100
Fax 1-780-805-3140
- **Swimming Pool & Slide**
- 58 Air-conditioned units
- Non-smoking rooms
- Cable TV
- Cardlock system
- Pet rooms available
- In-room coffee
- Free Continental Breakfast

Highway Motor INN *in Slave Lake, Alberta*
"Excellence at Affordable Prices!"
Queen & King Size Beds • Suites • Kitchenettes
Air Conditioned • Cable TV • Modem Jacks
Located 1 Block West of McDonalds - Adjacent to Highway #2
Toll Free 1-888-848-2400
Telephone 780-849-2400
Fax 780-849-5036

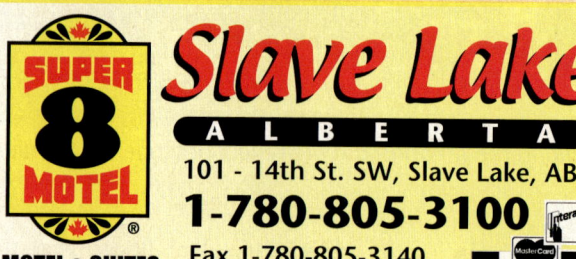

SLAVE LAKE ADVERTISERS

Big Lake Country Tourism........................Ph. (800) 267-4654
Highway Motor Inn..........Ph. (780) 849-2400
Super 8 Motel & Suites.....Ph. (780) 805-3100

Sawridge Hotel Slave Lake
Full Service
180 Room
3★ Hotel
- Indoor & Outdoor Jacuzzis
- Steam & Fitness Rooms
- VLTs & Gaming Room
- Basic & Jacuzzi Suites
- Ridge English Pub
- Bus Tours Welcome
- Sunrise Coffee Shop
- Room Service
- Cable Satellite • Gift Shop

Call us at
1-800-661-6657
Email us:
shslres@telusplanet.net
Visit our Website:
www.sawridge.com
WE OFFER ECO-TOURS

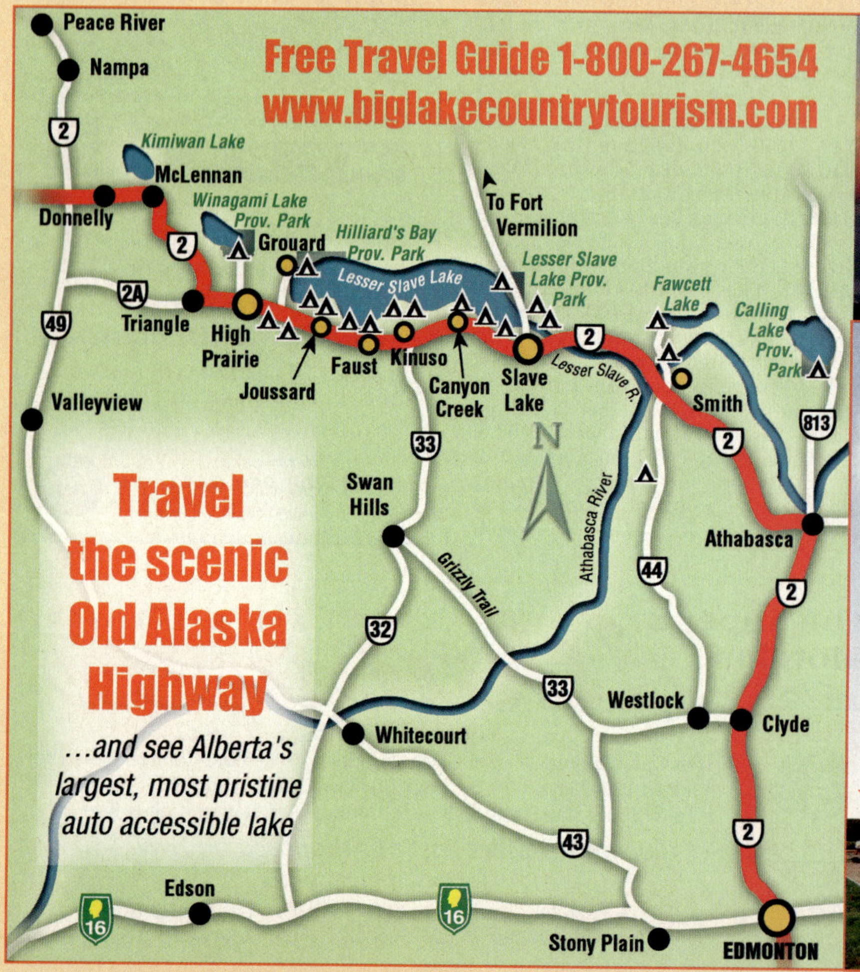

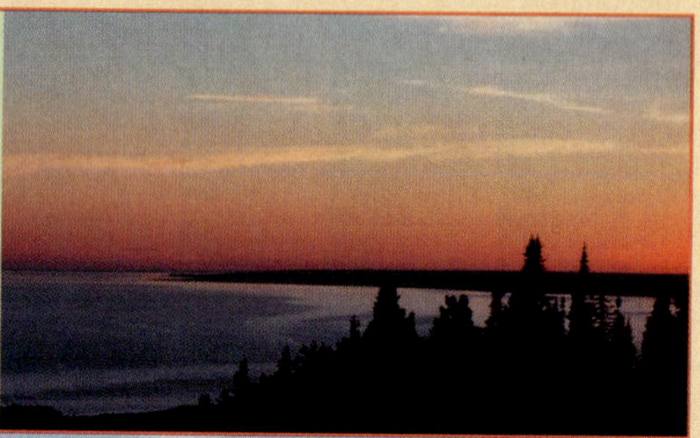

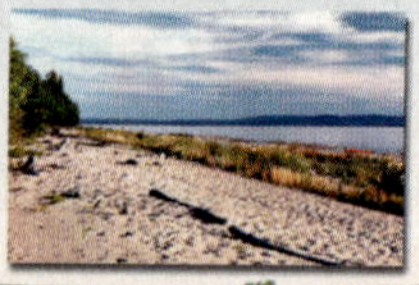

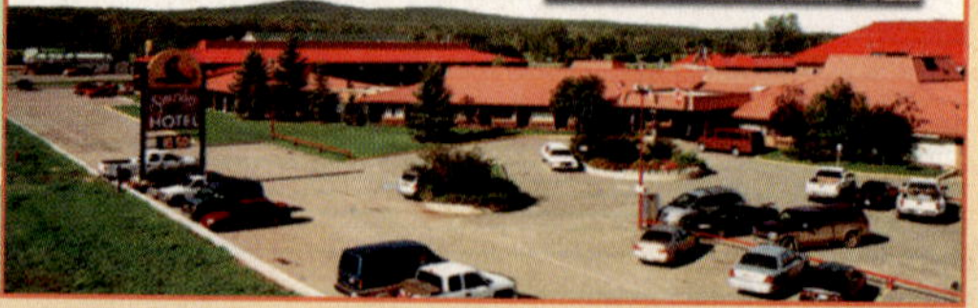

E 211.4 (340.3 km) **Junction** with Alberta Highway 33 (Grizzly Trail), which leads south to Swan Hills (45 miles/72 km) and Barrhead (108 miles/174 km) to junction with Alberta Highway 43 (136 miles/219 km).

E 213.6 (343.8 km) Bridge over the Swan River.

E 214 (344.4 km) **Junction** with side road north 1.2 miles/2 km to KINUSO (pop. 282); cafe and service station.

E 216.4 (348.4 km) Access road north 5 miles/9 km to Spruce Point Park Campground; 193 sites, hookups, dump station, water pump, showers, wheelchair-accessible washroom, shelter, store, public phone, beach, boat launch, 100-boat marina, boat rentals, fishing, fireplaces and firewood. Camping fee.

E 222 (357.2 km) FAUST (pop. 344); RCMP station, groceries, restaurant, gas station and camping.

E 229.2 (368.8 km) Bridge over the Driftpile River.

E 234 (376.6 km) Turnouts both sides of highway.

E 236 (379.7 km) JOUSSARD (pop. 269) to north has a store. Joussard Lakeshore Campground, located on the south shore of **Lesser Slave Lake**, has 23 sites, full hookups, dump station, tap water, showers, picnic tables, firewood, fishing and boat launch. Camping fee.

E 246.7 (397 km) Turnout to north with litter barrels and historical point of interest.

E 247.2 (397.8 km) **Junction** with Highway 750 northeast to Alberta Highway 88 (Bicentennial Highway), 103 miles/165 km. Highway 750 also provides access to GROUARD, 13 miles/21 km north, site of St. Bernard Mission Church and the Native Cultural Arts Museum.

Hilliard's Bay Provincial Park, 5 miles/8 km east of Grouard on Lesser Slave Lake, has 189 sites, tap water, hookups, dump station, showers, playground, phone, beach and fishing.

E 247.6 (398.6 km) Small store, gas and diesel to north.

E 248.2 (399.5 km) Small store and gas to north.

E 250.3 (402.8 km) ENILDA (pop. 128).

E 255.9 (411.9 km) East Prairie River.

E 260.4 (419.1 km) **High Prairie Lions Club Campground.** Open from May 1st to September 30th. 27 sites with power and water plus 5 unserviced sites. Day-use area with picnic tables and a camp kitchen. Wheelchair accessible showers and bathrooms. Laundry facilities. Firepits and free firewood. Horseshoe pits and playground. Toll-free 1-866-546-6724. [ADVERTISEMENT]

E 261.7 (421.4 km) HIGH PRAIRIE (pop. 2,932) has motels, restaurants, retail and grocery stores, and service stations with major-repair facilities. **Visitor Information:**

Tourist information centre in the centre of town on the north side of Highway 2. Open summer months only.

The High Prairie District Museum, part of the library complex located on Highway 2, features pioneer artifacts.

While the High Prairie area was being settled by homesteaders in the late 19th century, the arrival of the railroad in 1914 heralded the beginning of High Prairie as a town. A busy agricultural center, this picturesque community serves the surrounding forest and oil field industries.

E 261.9 (421.5 km) **Junction** with Highway 749. Highway 749 North from High Prairie becomes Highway 679, which leads west 18 miles/30 km to rejoin Highway 2. **Winagami Lake Provincial Park**, 20 miles/32 km northwest of High Prairie off Highway 679, has 63 campsites (one site for disabled use), day-use area, dump station, fishing, boat launch, wading pool, paved trails, bird-viewing platforms with scopes, fireplaces, firewood, shelter and tap water.

Heart River Dam Provincial Recreation Area, 24 miles/40 km northwest of High Prairie, is a day-use area with picnic tables, beach, fishing and boat launch.

E 262.4 (422.3 km) Bridge over the West Prairie River.

E 270.9 (436.1 km) **Junction** with Alberta Spur Highway 2A west to Highway 49 and Highway 2 north to McLennan. In the early days of Alaska Highway travel, this intersection was known as Triangle. From here, motorists either turned left on what was then Highway 34 (today's Highway 2A) and drove 100 miles to Grande Prairie via Valleyview, or turned right on Highway 2 to McLennan and Peace River.

Continue on Highway 2 North.

E 271.3 (436.6 km) **Pioneer Threshermen's Assoc. Antique Equipment Display and Museum.** Open free to the public from the end of May to the end of August. Special demonstration of all operational equipment held on Canada Day (July 1).

E 271.4 (436.8 km) Turnout with litter barrels to east.

E 283.8 (456.8 km) **Junction** with Highway 679 east 7 miles/11 km to **Winagami Lake** Provincial Park.

E 292 (470 km) MCLENNAN (pop. 1,100), "Bird Capital of Canada." **Visitor Information:** Phone (780) 324-3034 or (780) 324-3065. McLennan has all visitor facilities, including a hotel, motel, restaurants licensed dining room and lounge, grocery and retail stores, service stations with major-repair facilities, library, and a golf course. Local museum is housed in an old passenger rail car. Murals by artist Roger Noskiye can be found on various buildings throughout the town.

Camping at Kimiwan campground; 18 sites, firepits, firewood, electrical hookups, showers, dump station, camp kitchen, playground, fishing; attendant on site; groups welcome; phone (780) 324-2416. The golf

Boardwalk trails access Kimiwan Lake in McLennan for birdwatching.

(© Blake Hanna, staff)

course is located across from the campground.

The community is situated on the south shore of Kimiwan Lake, which is at the centre of 3 major migration flyways (Mississippi, Pacific and Central). Bird watching is excellent from mid-April to early November at the **Kimiwan Birdwalk and Interpretive Centre.** Tours, videos and reference books available. Phone (780) 324-2004 or 324-3010; email rlconsul@telusplanet.net.

The **NAR Golden Coach Museum** adjacent Kimiwan Birdwalk and Interpretive Centre, houses many Northern Alberta Railway and CR Rail artifacts, dating back to the days of steam engines. McLennan was founded in 1914 as a divisional point for the Edmonton, Dunvegan and British Columbia railway. The museum is open May 1 to Aug. 3; phone. (780) 324-3622.

McLennan is also the seat of the Roman Catholic Archdiocese of the Grouard–McLennan area. The Bishop's residence is adjacent **St. John the Baptist Cathedral.**

Recreational facilities here include a curling rink, tennis courts, ball diamonds and a 9-hole golf course.

Town of McLennan. See display ad this section.

E 292.7 (471 km) Kimiwan Lake visible to north.

E 292.8 (471.3 km) Smoky River Regional

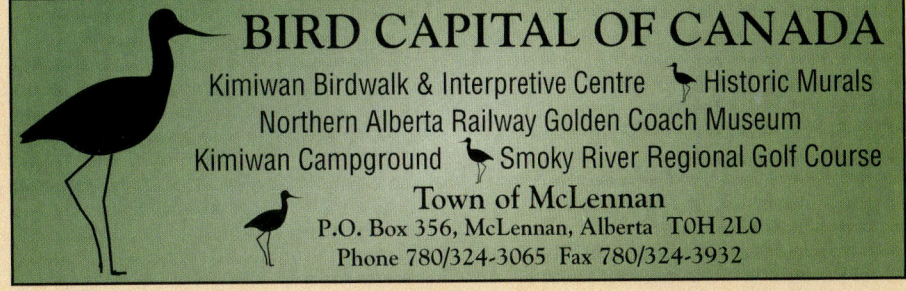

BIRD CAPITAL OF CANADA
Kimiwan Birdwalk & Interpretive Centre • Historic Murals
Northern Alberta Railway Golden Coach Museum
Kimiwan Campground • Smoky River Regional Golf Course
Town of McLennan
P.O. Box 356, McLennan, Alberta T0H 2L0
Phone 780/324-3065 Fax 780/324-3932

Historic Athabasca Route (continued)

The Athabasca route offers a number of lakeside campgrounds. (© Blake Hanna, staff)

Golf Course to south; 9 holes, pro shop, licensed dining and cart rental. Open April to October. Phone (780) 324-3661.

Historical point of interest to north about the Northern Woods & Waters Route.

E 299.8 (482.6 km) Donnelly to north, Smoky River Regional Airport to south. **DONNELLY** (pop. 450) has accommodations, a restaurant, post office and library. A historic site 3 miles/5 km south of town features a fully operational 1904 Case steam engine.

E 300.8 (484.2 km) **Junction** of Alberta Highway 49 west, Highway 43 south and Highway 2 north to Peace River and the Mackenzie Highway (see MACKENZIE ROUTE section). Gas station and store at junction.

The Northern Woods & Waters Route follows Alberta Highway 49 west to Dawson Creek, BC.

ALBERTA HIGHWAY 49 WEST

E 302.9 (487.5 km) Large alfalfa-dehydrating plant to the north.

E 303.3 (488.2 km) Falher Municipal Campground to north; 30 sites, full hookups, tap water, public phone. ▲

E 303.6 (488.6 km) Access road north 1 mile/1.6 km to **FALHER** (pop. 650), named after Father Constant Falher, who arrived in 1912. Falher is known as the "Honey Capital of Canada" and boasts the world's largest replica of a honey bee. The town has a strong agricultural base, with 5 grain elevators and 2 alfalfa-processing plants. Visitor facilities include a hotel, motel, stores, restaurants and service stations with major repair. Recreational facilities include an arena, an indoor swimming pool, tennis courts and ball diamonds.

E 308.8 (497.1 km) **Junction** with Highway 744 north 1.8 miles/3 km to **GIROUXVILLE** (pop. 367). Visitor facilities include a hotel, campground, family restaurant, service stations with repair facilities, grocery store, health food store and laundromat. Girouxville has one of the largest museums in Alberta. The museum features artifacts of Indian life, missionary works, pioneering and trapping, and early machinery and equipment. Open year-round. Small admission fee. ▲

E 320.8 (516.3 km) Bridge over the Smoky River.

E 321 (516.6 km) Turnout to north.

E 322.9 (519.8 km) **Junction** with Highway 740 north 34 miles/55 km to the Shaftsbury Crossing of Peace River and Tangent Park with 72 campsites and day-use area. ▲

E 330 (531.1 km) Access road south 0.6 mile/1 km to Lakeside Golf and Country Club; 9 holes and pro shop. Camping. ▲

E 330.8 (532.4 km) Store and gas station to north; propane.

E 331 (532.7 km) **Junction** with Highway 739 north 4 miles/6.4 km to community of **EAGLESHAM** (pop. 185); camping, restaurant, gas station, golf and curling rink. Kieyho Park, 10 miles/16 km north of town on the south shore of the Peace River, has picnic tables, hiking trails and boat launch.

E 350.7 (564.4 km) **Junction** with Highway 733 south to TeePee Creek (26 miles/42 km) and Alberta Highway 34 (35 miles/57 km). Access road north off Highway 49 leads 0.6 mile/1 km to **WANHAM** (pop. 250). Settled in 1914, today Wanham is a thriving community with a hotel, restaurant, service station with repair facilities, hockey and curling rink, and museum.

E 352.6 (567.6 km) Access road south 1.8 miles/3 km to **Dreamers Lake** Campground; 18 sites, water pump, picnic tables, public phone, boat launch, fishing and 9-hole golf course. Camping fee. No gas motors. ⊶▲

E 356.5 (573.8 km) Bridge over the Saddle River.

E 363.2 (584.5 km) **Junction** with Alberta Highway 2; gas station. Highway 2 North crosses the Peace River to connect with Alberta Highway 64 to Fort St. John or to Grimshaw, Mile Zero of the Mackenzie Highway (see MACKENZIE ROUTE section). Highway 2 South leads through the communities of Sexsmith and Grande Prairie on the EAST ACCESS ROUTE (see descriptions this section).

Continue west on Highway 49 for Dawson Creek.

E 363.3 (584.7 km) **RYCROFT** (pop. 534). Visitor facilities include a motel, restaurants, service stations with major-repair facilities, stores, bank, library, ball diamonds, ice arena and tennis courts.

E 364.2 (586.2 km) **Nardham Lake** Campground to north; 15 sites, hookups, picnic tables, water pump, canoeing, fishing. Camping fee. ⊶▲

E 366.3 (589.5 km) Access road south 2.4 miles/4 km to golf course; 9 holes, licensed dining, clubhouse, pro shop and carts for rent. Camping.

E 368.4 (592.9 km) Spirit River Airport entrance, visitor center and St. Elias Ukrainian Church to north. Small campground. ▲

E 368.5 (593.1 km) **SPIRIT RIVER** (pop. 1,150). Established as an agricultural centre in 1913, today Spirit River is a major trading centre for a large rural population. Visitor facilities include a hotel, motel, restaurants, retail and grocery stores, service stations, bank and library. A museum houses artifacts of the early days of Spirit River. Recreational facilities include an arena, curling rink, tennis courts, soccer field and ball diamond. Chepi Sepe Municipal Campground, located in town, has 12 sites (3 with hookups), tap water and public phone. Camping fee charged. ▲

E 369.4 (594.5 km) **Junction** with Highway 731 south 16 miles/26 km and east 3 miles/5 km to Woking, and then farther east 3 miles/5 km to Alberta Highway 2. Hilltop Recreation Area, located 11 miles/18 km south on Highway 731 and then west 7 miles/11 km on Highway 677, and then south 4 miles/6 km on Highway 724, has 9 sites, water pump and hiking trails. Camping fee.

Chinook Valley Golf Course, 12 miles/20 km south on Highway 741, has 9 holes, pro shop and licensed dining.

E 372.4 (599.4 km) **Junction** with Highway 727 north 6 miles/10 km to Devale.

E 384 (618.1 km) Ksituan River.

E 384.7 (619.2 km) Turnoff for **Jack Bird Pond** day-use area, 1.9 miles/3 km north; picnicking, wildlife viewing.

E 385.3 (620.2 km) **Junction** with Highway 725 north 4 miles/6 km to **Moonshine Lake Provincial Park**; 110 campsites (23 with power), tap water, dump station, public phone, canoeing, fishing, boat launch, shelter, firewood, ball diamond. Electric motors only. Camping fee. ♿⊶▲

E 398.4 (641.1 km) Gordendale to north (no services).

E 404.5 (651 km) Pillsworth Road to north leads 22 miles/35 km to Cotillion Park; 13 campsites, day-use area, tap water, picnic tables, shelter, firewood and boat launch. ▲

E 409.6 (659.2 km) **Junction** with Highway 719 north 5 miles/8 km to Bonanza; gas, food, pay phone.

E 412.5 (663.9 km) Baytree to north; gas, food, pay phone.

E 416.1 (669.7 km) Large roadside turnout with litter barrels to south. Truck weigh scales.

E 417.5 (671.9 km) Alberta–British Columbia border.

E 422.5 (680 km) Pouce Coupe River bridge.

E 424 (682.4 km) **Junction** with access road north 10 miles/16 km to Rolla and on to the crossing of the Peace River and Clayhurst. South from here, the road leads 3 miles/5 km to Pouce Coupe.

E 428 (688.9 km) Downtown Dawson Creek, BC. (See page 100 in the ALASKA HIGHWAY section for description.)

(Continued from page 47)
playground; and oval race car track with racing in summer. ▲

E 73.1 (117.7 km) **DC 293.9** (473 km) Pembina River bridge.

E 74 (119.2 km) **DC 293** (471.5. km) **Ol' Pembina River Ferry Crossing RV Park.** 1 km off Highway 43, turn south at RV park sign, flying 3 flags. Family operated. Spacious sites on 5 landscaped acres in the Pembina River Valley. Water and electric sites, pull-throughs, dry camping and tenting, showers and flush toilets, dump station, coin washer and dryer. Cozy motel unit. Telephone. Cookhouse. Private museum collection of antiques. Pioneer cabin with local artifacts. Vintage cars and trucks. Classsic cars. 50's Soda Shop. Restored tractors and machinery. Walking/history trails. Mystery Lane characters. Phone (780) 785-2379 with answering machine. Olpembina@yahoo.com. [ADVERTISEMENT] ▲

E 74.1 (119.3 km) **DC 292.9** (471.3 km) Gas station with diesel and restaurant to south.

E 78.3 (126 km) **DC 288.7** (464.6 km) Second longest wooden railway trestle in the world crosses highway and Paddle River. The C.N.R. Rochfort Bridge trestle is 2,414 feet/ 736m long and was originally built in 1914.

E 80.6 (129.7 km) **DC 286.4** (460.9 km) **ROCHFORT BRIDGE.** Trading post (open daily, year-round) with gift shop, restaurant and Lac Ste. Anne Pioneer Museum. Camping. ▲

Rochfort Bridge Trading Post. A must stop on the way. Do not miss lunch—homemade curly fries; fresh baked bread; rhubarb, sour-cream and raisin pies. Home of the Bridge Burger—biggest hamburger you will see to Alaska. Large gift shop featuring unique items for every family member. Buy donkey food for the petting zoo. A fun stop. See display ad this section. [ADVERTISEMENT]

E 83.1 (133.7 km) **DC 283.9** (456.1 km) Paved turnouts with litter barrels both sides of highway.

E 85 (136.8 km) **DC 282** (453.8 km) **MAYERTHORPE** (pop. 1,600). One mile/1.6 km from the highway on a paved access road. Hotel, motel, restaurant, grocery store, gas stations with repair service, car wash, hospital, laundromat, post office, RCMP and banks. A public campground with 30 sites (no hookups, pit toilets) and 9-hole golf course are located 1 mile/1.6 km south of town. Airstrip located 2 miles/3.2 km southwest of town; no services. (Most northbound air travelers use Whitecourt airport, which has fuel.) ▲

E 93.7 (150.8 km) **DC 273.3** (439.8 km) Turnout to south.

E 96.4 (155.1 km) **DC 270.6** (435.5 km) **Junction** with Highway 658 north to Goose Lake. Gas station, restaurant and groceries at junction.

E 108.2 (174.1 km) **DC 258.8** (416.5 km) Turnout (northbound-only) with litter barrel. ▲

E 109 (175.4 km) **DC 258** (415.2 km) Whitecourt & District **Forest Interpretive Centre and Heritage Park**. Access to **Lions Club Campground;** 74 sites, camping fee, flush toilets, showers, water, tables, dump station, firewood and firepits. ▲

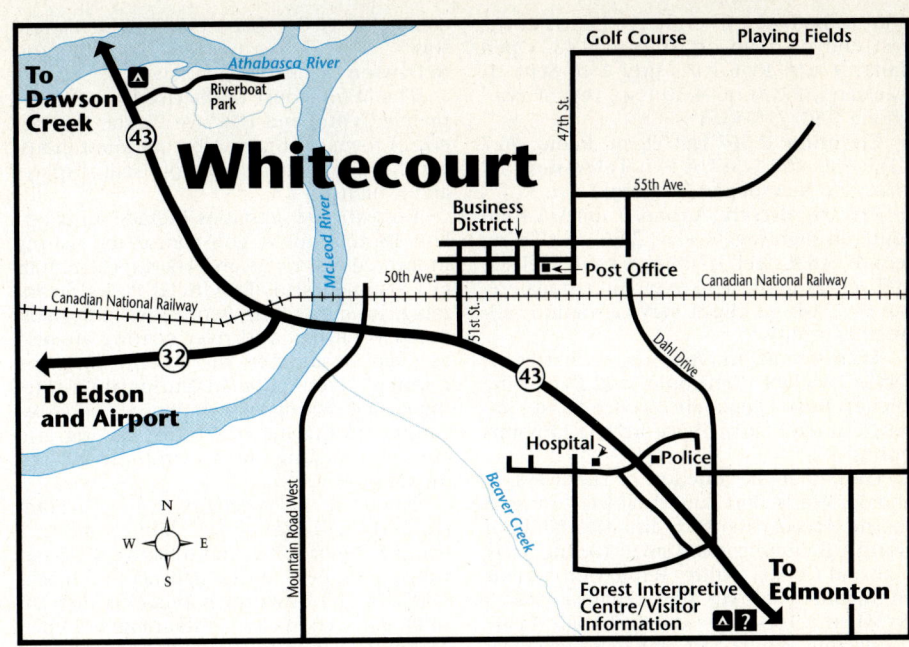

Whitecourt

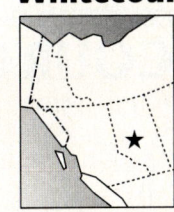

E 111.8 (179.9 km) **DC 255.2** (410.7 km). Located two hours from Edmonton. **Population:** 8,800. **Emergency Services:** For emergencies, phone 911. **Police**, phone (780) 778-5454. **Fire Department**, phone (780) 778-2311. **Hospital** located on Hilltop, phone (780) 778-2285. Ambulance service (780) 778-4911.

Visitor Information: Tourist informa-

WHITECOURT ADVERTISERS
Camp In Town RV Park.....Ph. (780) 706-5050
Forest Interpretive Centre & Heritage Park............Ph. (780) 778-2214
Glenview Motel ....Ph. (780) 778-2276
Quality Inn ....Ph. (800) 265-9660
Sagitawah RV Park............Ph. (780) 778-3734
Whitecourt Lions Club Campground ....Ph. (780) 778-6782

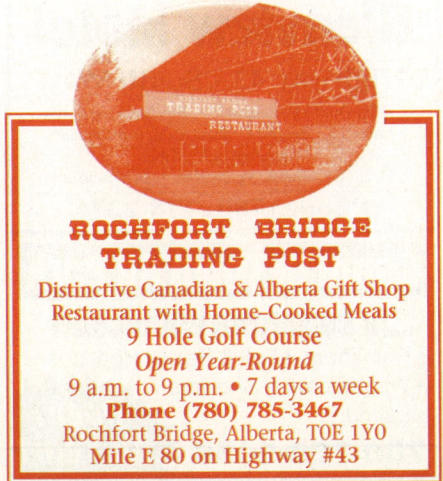

ROCHFORT BRIDGE TRADING POST
Distinctive Canadian & Alberta Gift Shop
Restaurant with Home–Cooked Meals
9 Hole Golf Course
Open Year-Round
9 a.m. to 9 p.m. • 7 days a week
Phone (780) 785-3467
Rochfort Bridge, Alberta, T0E 1Y0
Mile E 80 on Highway #43

Sagitawah RV Park — "Where the Rivers Meet"
Whitecourt's Premier RV Park
- Full 30 Amp Hook-ups ■ Free Hot Showers
- Large Grassed Pull-Through Lots ■ Firepits
- Laundry Facilities ■ Playground ■ Store
- Propane Sales ■ Jacuzzi Tub ■ Souvenirs
- RV Parts & Service ■ Modem Friendly
– SENIORS DISCOUNT –
Alberta Camping Select Recommended
North end of town on Hwy 43 & Boat Launch Rd.
P.O. Box 967, Whitecourt, Alberta T7S 1N9 ■ Telephone (780) 778-3734
Web: www.telusplanet.net/public/rvpark/index_html.html
Email: rvpark@telusplanet.net

tion in the Forest Interpretive Centre at the east end of town off Highway 43. Open daily, 9 A.M. to 6 P.M., July 1 to Sept. 1; weekdays, 9 A.M. to 4:30 P.M., rest of year. Phone (780) 778-5363

Elevation: 2,567 feet/782m. **Radio:** 96.7 CJYR-FM, 107.5 SKUA-FM. **Television:** 57 channels. **Newspaper:** *Whitecourt Star.*

Private Aircraft: Airport 4 miles/6.4 km south on Highway 32; elev. 2,567 feet/782m; length 5,800 feet/1,768m; paved; fuel 80, 100, jet (24-hour, self-serve). Aircraft maintenance, 24-hour flight service station, all-weather facility.

Transportation: **Air**—Local charter air service available; helicopter and fixed-wing aircraft. **Bus**—Greyhound service to Edmonton, Grande Prairie, Peace River and points north.

Located at the junction of Highways 43 and 32, Whitecourt dubs itself the "Gateway to the Alaska Highway and the fabulous North." Established as a small trading, trapping and forestry centre, Whitecourt became an important stop for Alaska Highway travelers when a 106-mile section of Highway 43 connecting Whitecourt and Valleyview was completed in October 1955. This new route was 72 miles shorter than the old Edmonton to Dawson Creek route via Slave Lake.

The Whitecourt & District Forest Interpretive Centre and Heritage Park at the east end of town celebrates Alberta's forest industry through artifacts, audio-visual displays and exhibits.

Recreational activities include an excellent 18-hole public golf course and fishing in area creeks, rivers and lakes (boat rentals at Carson–Pegasus Provincial Park). Swimming, in-line skating, tennis, walking trails, beach volleyball and river boating are also enjoyed in summer. In the fall, big game hunting is very popular. During the winter there is ice fishing, snowmobiling and cross-country skiing on area trails, skating and curling, bowling and swimming at the indoor pool.

There are 17 hotels/motels, 27 restaurants, 15 gas stations, 2 laundromats, 2 malls, 5 liquor stores and 6 banks. Most services are located on the highway or 2 blocks north in the downtown business district. Some gas stations and restaurants are open 24 hours. Camping available at downtown RV park and at Lion's Club Campground at the southeast end of town.

This full-service community also supports a library and 7 churches. Service clubs (Lions, Kinsmen) and community organizations (Masons, Knights of Columbus) welcome visitors.

A popular wilderness area nearby is **Carson–Pegasus Provincial Park**, located 14.6 miles/23.5 km west and north of town on Highway 32 (paved). The park has camping, a boat launch and boat rentals. There are 2 lakes at the park: McLeod (Carson) Lake, stocked with rainbow trout, has a speed limit of 12 kmph for boaters; Little McLeod (Pegasus) Lake has northern pike and whitefish; electric motors and canoes only.

East Access Route Log
(continued)

E 111.9 (180.1 km) **DC 255.1** (410.5 km) Beaver Creek bridge.

E 112.4 (180.9 km) **DC 254.6** (409.7 km) McLeod River.

E 112.6 (181.2 km) **DC 254.4** (409.4 km) **Junction** with Highway 32 South (paved). Highway 32 leads 42 miles/68 km to junction with Yellowhead Highway 16 at **Milepost E 97.5** (see the YELLOWHEAD HIGHWAY section).

E 112.7 (181.4 km) **DC 254.3** (409.2 km) Railroad crossing.

E 112.9 (181.7 km) **DC 254.1** (408.9 km) Gas stations both sides of highway.

E 113.2 (182.1 km) **DC 253.8** (408.5 km) Turnoff to north for **Sagitawah RV Park** (camping) and Riverboat Park (picnicking), both at the confluence of the McLeod and Athabasca rivers. Riverboat Park has a boat launch and toilets.

E 113.6 (182.8 km) **DC 253.4** (407.8 km) Athabasca River bridge.

E 115.6 (186 km) **DC 251.4** (404.6 km) Vehicle inspection station to north.

E 117.1 (188.4 km) **DC 249.9** (402.2 km) **Junction** with Highway 32 North (paved). Access to **Eric S. Huestis Demonstration Forest**, which has 4.3 miles/7 km of self-guided trails with information signs describing forest management techniques and the forest life-cycle.

Carson–Pegasus Provincial Park, 9.3 miles/15 km north, has 182 campsites, electrical hookups, tables, flush toilets, showers, water, dump station, firewood and play-

ground. Boat launch, boat rentals and rainbow trout fishing are available.

E 117.6 (189.2 km) DC 249.4 (401.4 km) Alberta Newsprint Co. to south.

E 122 (196.3 km) DC 245 (394.3 km) Turnout with litter barrel.

E 124.3 (200 km) DC 242.7 (390.6 km) Chickadee Creek.

E 131.8 (212.1 km) DC 235.2 (378.5 km) Turnouts with litter barrels both sides of highway.

E 142.5 (229.3 km) DC 224.5 (361.3 km) Turnout with litter barrel to south.

E 143 (230.1 km) DC 224 (360.5 km) Turnout with litter barrel to north.

E 159 (255.9 km) DC 208 (334.7 km) Fox Creek airport.

Fox Creek

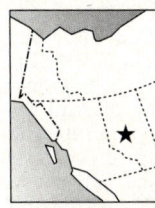

E 162 (260.7 km) DC 205 (329.9 km) **Population:** 2,600. **Elevation:** 2,800 feet/853m. **Emergency Services: RCMP,** phone (780) 622-3740. **Ambulance,** phone (780) 622-3000. **Hospital,** phone (780) 622-3545.

Visitor Information: Tourist Information Centre at the **Rig Earth Resource Park,** open in summer; gift shop, coffee area and selection of informational videos to view; phone (780) 622-2000. Off-season contact the Town Office at (780) 622-3896 for information. Across from the Information Centre is Fox Creek Museum.

Private Aircraft: Fox Creek airport, 3 miles/4.8 km south on Highway 43; elev. 2,840 feet/866m; length, 2,950 feet/899m; paved; no fuel. Unattended.

Fox Creek is in the centre of oil and gas exploration and production. (A Jomax 4, 150-foot/46m drilling rig is on display at Rig Earth Resource Park.) North America's largest known natural gas field is here.

All visitor facilities including 2 hotels, 3 motels, bed and breakfasts, and gas stations with repair service. Grocery store open daily

FOX CREEK ADVERTISERS

Alaskan Motel, The..........Ph. (780) 622-3073
Town of Fox Creek............Ph. (780) 622-3896

◼ The Alaskan Motel ◼
64 Modern Units • Colour TV
Air Conditioned
Direct Dial Phones
Free In-Room Coffee

Box 700 • Fox Creek, Alberta • T0H 1P0

PHONE (780) 622-3073
FAX (780) 622-2025

Boat rentals are available at Carson-Pegasus Provincial Park. (© Blake Hanna, staff)

until midnight. Convenience stores, pharmacy, laundromats, liquor stores, restaurants and banks.

Fox Creek R.V. Campground, located near the visitor information centre, is a municipal campground with 17 sites, full hookups, showers and dump station

Fox Creek is also a popular outdoor recreation area. Two local lakes popular with residents and visitors are **Iosegun** and **Smoke lakes,** which are located within 10 miles/16 km on either side of the townsite on good gravel road. Camping, boat launch and fishing for northern pike, perch and pickerel are favorites for this area.

The Alaskan Motel. See display ad this section.

Town of Fox Creek. See display ad this section.

East Access Route Log
(continued)

E 167 (268.7 km) DC 200 (321.9 km) Turnout with litter barrel.

E 169.5 (272.8 km) DC 197.5 (317.8 km) Turnouts with litter barrels both sides of highway.

E 182.1 (293 km) DC 184.9 (297.6 km) Turnout with litter barrel.

E 192 (309 km) DC 175 (281.6 km) LITTLE SMOKY (pop. about 34). Motel, RV park, antique shop, gift shop, pay phone, propane, grocery store, ice cream shop, service station and post office.

E 192.2 (309.3 km) DC 174.8 (281.3 km) Little Smoky River bridge.

E 193.5 (311.4 km) DC 173.5 (279.2 km) Waskahigan (House) River bridge at confluence with Smoky River. Alberta Government Recreation Area campground with 24 sites, pit toilets, tables and firepits.

E 197 (317 km) DC 170 (273.6 km) Turnout.

E 206.7 (332.6 km) DC 160.3 (258 km) Turnout with litter barrel.

E 208.5 (335.5 km) DC 158.5 (255.1 km) Peace pipeline storage tanks.

E 210.8 (339.2 km) DC 156.2 (251.4 km) Valleyview Riverside golf course.

E 213.2 (343.1 km) DC 153.8 (247.5 km) Valleyview & District Chamber of Commerce Visitor Information Centre (phone 780/524-2410) has local, regional, provincial and Canada-wide travel information; pay phone, postal service; souvenir gift shop with a good selection of books, including regional, Northern and local authors; picnic tables, water, flush toilets, dump station. Open daily in summer, 8 A.M. to 8 P.M.

E 213.4 (343.4 km) DC 153.6 (247.2 km) Valleyview airport to west.

Private Aircraft: Valleyview airport; elev. 2,434 feet/742m; length, 3,300 feet/1,006m; paved; no fuel. Unattended.

CAMPING IN FOX CREEK, ALBERTA

Fox Creek R.V. Campground
in town, with 18 fully serviced stalls, clean showers and dumping facilities. Near the Tourist Information Centre and shopping.

Iosegun Lake Campground
north of town, on the lake with 52 forested unserviced campsites with great fishing, boating and swimming.

Smoke Lake Campground
south of town, on the lake with 47 forested unserviced campsites with great fishing, boating and swimming.

Fox Creek, Alberta - Canada's Centennial Community
Incorporated July 9, 1967

For more information–Town of Fox Creek, Box 149, Fox Creek, Alberta T0H 1P0
Web: www.town.fox-creek.ab.ca

EAST ACCESS ROUTE • Valleyview

Sunset at Sturgeon Lake near Valleyview. *(© Earl L. Brown, staff)*

Valleyview

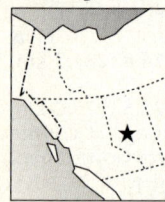

E 214.1 (344.4 km) DC 152.9 (246.1 km) Approximately 3 1/2 hour drive time from Edmonton. **Population:** 1,944. **Emergency Services:** Phone 911 for all emergency services. **RCMP,** phone (780) 524-3343. **Hospital,** Valleyview General, phone (780) 524-3356.

Visitor Information: Major tourist information centre and rest stop located 0.9 mile/1.5 km south of Valleyview on Highway 43. Open daily, 8 A.M. to 8 P.M. from May through Labour Day weekend; phone (780) 524-2410, fax (780) 524-2727, email at town office: valvadm@telusplanet.net. Postal service, souvenirs and refreshments, as well as regional and provincial travel and community events and services information. For information on small business opportunities, contact the Town Office at (780) 524-5150. Town information is available at www.vvw-teq.net/town/.

Elevation: 2247 feet/685m. **Newspaper:** *Valley Views* (weekly). **Transportation:** Air—Airport 0.7 mile/1.1 km south (see **Milepost E 213.4**). **Bus**—Greyhound.

Valleyview, known as the "Portal to the Peace Country" of northwestern Alberta, is located at the junction of Highways 43 and 49. From Valleyview, Highway 43 continues west to Grande Prairie and Dawson Creek. Highway 49 leads north to connect with Highway 2 east to Athabasca and north to Peace River. From Peace River, travelers may follow the Mackenzie Highway to Northwest Territories (see the MACKENZIE ROUTE section for details).

Originally called Red Willow Creek when it was homesteaded in 1916, Valleyview boomed with the discovery of oil and gas in the 1950s, and services grew along with the population. Today, Valleyview's economy has diversified to include the oil and gas industry, forestry, tourism, agriculture and government services. Farming consists mainly of grain, oilseed, beef cattle and forage production.

The community has a full range of services including banks, automatic teller machines, post office, a library, several churches and a veterinary clinic.

All visitor facilities available, including 5 motels and hotels, several restaurants, gas stations (many with major repair service, propane and diesel), laundromat, grocery, liquor store, clothing and hardware stores, gift shops and a golf course. Some gas stations and restaurants open 24 hours a day.

The area boasts many lakes and streams, abundant wildlife, and lush vegetation, including berries. Summer travelers can take advantage of the long summer days here by attending local rodeos, fairs and festivals; playing a round of golf on one of the local golf courses; visiting one of the provincial parks along Sturgeon Lake; taking a dip in

---

VALLEYVIEW ADVERTISERS

Horizon Motel & Humpty's
  Family Restaurant........Ph. (780) 524-3904
Olde Country Inn, The ....Main St.
Sherk's R.V. Park ....Ph. (780) 524-4949
Town of Valleyview ....Ph. (780) 524-5150
Valleyview Esso Service ....Ph. (780) 524-3504

HORIZON MOTEL

- Valleyview's newest hospitality centre
- 100 units with a good mix of family suites & kitchenettes. Non-smoking rooms available. Cable TV. Air conditioning
- 24-hour front desk & switchboard
- Bank rate of exchange paid on US funds.

PHONE: 780-524-3904 OR FAX: 780-524-4223
BOX 1590, VALLEYVIEW, AB T0H 3N0
RESERVATIONS: TOLL FREE 1-888-909-3908
E-mail: hmotelvv@telusplanet.net

Now Open

HUMPTY'S Family Restaurant
Breakfast Served All-Day-Long

THE OLDE COUNTRY INN

**Mom & Pop's Bakery
Deli & Tea Shop
Bed & Breakfast**

Daily Lunch Specials — Fully Licensed
Buffalo Steaks & Burgers
Everything Homemade
(Fresh Baked Goods Daily)

LOCAL CRAFTS • GIFTWARE
DEVELOPING MUSEUM • CURIOSITY SHOPPE

Your Hosts – Keith & Carole
Main Street, Valleyview

(780) 524-5020

SHERK'S R.V. PARK

OPEN MAY THROUGH SEPTEMBER

56 Full Hookup Sites (good gravel pads) including 14 Pull-throughs • All oversized sites — approximately 24' x 80'
Modem Access • 30-amp Services • Pay Phone • Laundry Facilities • Clean Modern Washrooms • Hot Showers
Firepits and Firewood • Ice • Enclosed Gazebo • Playground • Walking Trails • Good Sam Rated

Close to all Valleyview services including shopping, swimming pool and 9-hole golf course.

Your Host — Rose Sherk

PO Box 765, Valleyview, Alberta T0H 3N0 Canada • Phone (780) 524-4949 • FAX (780) 524-4346

Turn off Highway 43 West at Valleyview Esso & Turbo stations

the outdoor swimming pool in town; or exploring the wilderness by all-terrain vehicle, horse, canoe or hiking trail.

Horizon Motel & Humpty's Family Restaurant. At the Horizon, we have built our business on loyalty and customer satisfaction. Clean, well-appointed rooms, several nonsmoking and deluxe family suites available, reasonable rates. Enjoy great meals at our Humpty's Family Restaurant. Scrumptious sandwiches and salads, burgers and entrees, breakfast served all day long (try our bangers and eggs). Open daily 6 A.M. to 10:30 P.M. Tour buses welcome. Bank rate of exchange paid on U.S. funds. We take pride in our service; stop in and experience for yourself! Phone (780) 524-3904. Fax (780) 524-4223. [ADVERTISEMENT]

Camping at Sherk's RV Park; turn off Highway 43 West at Valleyview Esso and Turbo station.

East Access Route Log
(continued)

E 216 (347.6 km) DC 151 (243 km) Highways 49/2 lead north 86 miles/138.4 km to Peace River and **junction** with the Mackenzie Highway 12 miles/19 km west of Peace River. See the MACKENZIE ROUTE section for a description of Peace River and the log of the Mackenzie Highway to western Northwest Territories.

Continue on Highway 43 west for Dawson Creek.

E 222.6 (358.2 km) DC 144.4 (232.4 km) 24-hour convenience store and gas.

E 224.7 (361.6 km) DC 142.3 (229 km) Access north to **Sturgeon Lake**; fishing and camping. **Williamson Provincial Park** (1.2 miles/2 km); 60 campsites (some with electrical hookups), boat launch, dump station. Fishing for perch, pickerel, northern pike and whitefish.

E 227 (365.3 km) DC 140 (225.3 km) **CALAIS** (pop. about 550); post office and grocery store.

E 229 (368.5 km) DC 137.5 (221.3 km) Tea house, curio shoppe and bed and breakfast.

E 230 (370.1 km) DC 137 (220.5 km) Access to **Sturgeon Lake** (fishing) and to golf course.

E 232 (373.3 km) DC 135 (217.3 km) Sturgeon Heights. Turnoff for **Youngs Point Provincial Park**, 6 miles/10 km northeast; 97 campsites, boat launch, fishing in **Sturgeon Lake**.

E 235 (378.2 km) DC 132 (212.4 km) Turnouts both sides of highway at top of Clarkson Hill; historic marker. Access to Swan Lake, 4 miles west and 2.5 miles south. Day-use area, campground with 6 sites, toilets and boat launch (Canfor; phone 538-7736). Fishing for rainbow trout.

E 240 (386.2 km) DC 127 (204.4 km) **CROOKED CREEK** (pop. 10); gas station, grocery, ice cream store (with giant cones), post office and pay phone.

E 240.7 (387.3 km) DC 126.3 (203.2 km) Ridge Valley Road; access to bakery and bed-and-breakfast.

E 246 (395.9 km) DC 121 (194.7 km) **DeBOLT** (pop. 117), a small farming community north of highway with a general store and district museum.

E 246.6 (396.8 km) DC 120.4 (193.7 km) Watch for bison ranch to east.

E 253.8 (408.7 km) DC 113.2 (181.9 km) **Junction.** Forestry Trunk Road leads 632 miles/1,017 km south to Crowsnest Highway 3. The Forestry Trunk Road also junctions with Yellowhead Highway 16 and Trans-Canada Highway 1.

E 255.2 (410.7 km) DC 111.8 (179.9 km) Microwave towers to east.

E 259.5 (417.6 km) DC 107.5 (173 km) Smoky River bridge and government campground; 30 sites, shelter, firepits, firewood, tables, pit toilets, water pump and boat launch.

E 264 (424.9 km) DC 103 (165.7 km) **BEZANSON.** Post office, gas station with diesel, cafe, liquor store, grocery, general store, propane.

E 269 (432.9 km) DC 98 (157.7 km) Kleskun Hills Park to north 3 miles/5 km. The park features an ancient sea bottom with fossils of dinosaurs and marine life.

E 270.6 (435.5 km) DC 96.4 (155.1 km) Turnout to north with historical sign about the Kleskun Hills.

E 283.5 (456.2 km) DC 83.5 (134.4 km) Weigh scales to north.

E 283.8 (456.7 km) DC 83.2 (133.9 km) Railroad crossing.

E 284 (457 km) DC 83 (133.6 km) **Junction** with Highway 2. Dawson Creek-bound travelers continue on Highway 43. Access to Country Roads R.V. Park.

Turn north on Highway 2 for Sexsmith (8.5 miles/13.7 km) and Grimshaw (105 miles/169 km), Mile 0 of the Mackenzie Highway to Northwest Territories (see MACKENZIE ROUTE section).

To reach Grande Prairie city centre, keep straight ahead on Highway 43 (Clairmont Road) as it becomes 100th Street and follow it downtown. To skirt the downtown area, take the Highway 43 Bypass. Highway 43 becomes 100th Avenue (Richmond Avenue) on the west side of Grande Prairie.

To reach the Bighorn Highway, follow Wapiti Road (108th Street) south from Highway 43 on the west side of Grande Prairie. Bighorn Highway 40 (paved) connects Grande Prairie with Grande Cache (119 miles/191 km) and Yellowhead Highway 16 (207 miles/333 km). If you are headed south on the Big Horn Highway, fuel up in Grande Prairie, because there is no gas available southbound until Grande Cache. (See "Big Horn Highway Log" in the YELLOWHEAD HIGHWAY section.)

EAST ACCESS ROUTE • Valleyview

VALLEYVIEW ESSO SERVICE

24 Hour Service

Gas • Diesel
Propane • Confectionery • Ice
RESTAURANT

(780) 524-3504
Junction Hwy. 43 and Hwy. 49

Visa • MasterCard • American Express

PORTAL TO THE PEACE
Valleyview, Alberta

Located on scenic Highway 43 en route to the Alaska Highway, Valleyview offers many opportunities to tourists
*camping   *water sports
*regional parks   *fishing

*over 400 in-town and rural business services.

TOURIST INFORMATION CENTRE (open from May to September)
1-780-524-2410

Alberta, in all her majesty.
Canada
GAME COUNTRY

web: www.vvw-teq.net/town/
e-mail: valvadmn@telusplanet.net

Information about community amenities can be obtained year 'round by calling
1-780-524-5150

TOWN OF VALLEYVIEW

BOX 270, VALLEYVIEW, ALBERTA T0H 3N0 524-5150

EAST ACCESS ROUTE • Grande Prairie

106th Street. Plenty of visitor parking. The Visitor Information Centre is open 8:30 A.M. to 9 P.M., May to Labour Day; 8:30 A.M. to 4:30 P.M. in winter. phone (780) 539-7688. Chamber of Commerce office (11330-106 St., T8V 7X9) is open weekdays 8:30 A.M. to 4:30 P.M.

Private Aircraft: Airport 3 miles/4.8 km west; elev. 2,195 feet/669m; length 6,500 feet/1,981m; paved; fuel 80, 100, jet. 24-hour flight service station.

Elevation: 2,198 feet/670m. **Transportation: Air**—Scheduled air service to Vancouver, BC, Edmonton, Calgary, and points north. **Bus**—Greyhound.

Grande Prairie was first incorporated as a village in 1911, as a town in 1919, and as a city in 1958, by which time its population had reached nearly 8,000.

With a strong and diverse economy based on agriculture (cereal grains, fescue, honey, livestock), forestry (a bleached kraft pulp mill, sawmill and oriented strand board plant), and oil and gas, Grande Prairie is a regional centre for much of northwestern Alberta and northeastern British Columbia. The trumpeter swan is the symbol of Grande Prairie and is featured throughout the city.

A variety of shopping is available at a major mall, several strip malls and at large box stores around town. A well-developed downtown area offers boutique and specialty shopping. Entertainment includes theatres, nightclubs and a casino.

Visitor facilities include several restaurants, hotels, motels, and bed and breakfasts. Recreation facilities include 2 swimming pools, 3 18-hole golf courses, a par 3 golf course, ball diamonds, amusement park, tennis courts, public library, a public art gallery and 3 private galleries. Churches representing almost every denomination are located in Grande Prairie. There are several public schools and a regional college.

Camping within the city limits at Rotary Park public campground, located off the Highway 43 Bypass at the northwest edge of town near the college; Country Roads R.V. Park near the junction of Highway 43 and 2; and Camp Tamarack RV Park south on Highway 40. ▲

Camp Tamarack RV Park (Good Sam). When our family planned and constructed these new facilities, the needs and comfort of our guests were top priority, and our park was built with pride and attention to detail. From our guestbook: "Best campground yet!

GRANDE PRAIRIE ADVERTISERS

Best Western Hotel..........Ph. (866) 852-2378
Camp Tamarack RV Park ..Ph. (780) 532-9998
Country Roads R.V. Park...Ph. (780) 532-6323
Grande Prairie Museum
 and Gift Shop ....Ph. (780) 532-5482
GrapeVine Wine &
 Spirit Emporium ....Ph. (780) 538-3555
Igloo Inn ....Ph. (800) 665-0769
Lodge Motor Inn, The ......Ph. (780) 539-4700
Super 8 Motel ....Ph. (780) 532-8288

Grande Prairie

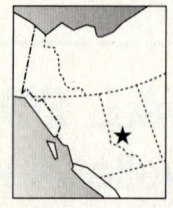

E 288 (463.5 km) DC 79 (127.1 km). Located at **junction** of Highways 43 and 40. **Population:** 38,000. **Emergency Services: RCMP**, phone (780) 538-5700. **Fire Department**, phone 911. **Ambulance**, phone (780) 532-9511. **Hospital**, Queen Elizabeth II, 10409 98th St., phone (780) 538-7100.

Visitor Information: In the Centre 2000 (look for the huge metal-clad sundial out in front), located off Highway 43 Bypass on

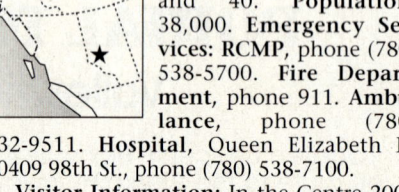

Alberta is on Mountain time.

Grande Prairie Hotel & Suites
Theme & Executive Suites - Indoor Pool & Jacuzzi - Deluxe Continental Breakfast - In-Room Movies & Gaming - Sorrentino's Italian Restaurant - Tony Roma's Famous for Ribs Restaurant on site - Airport Shuttle
Toll Free: 1.866.852.BEST (2378)
10745-117 Avenue - Across from Centre 2000 - Fax: (780) 402-8026

Muskoseepi Park offers walking and biking trails along Bear Creek.
(© Earl L. Brown, staff)

Weyerhaeuser offers tours of their pulp mill and sawmill in summer; phone (780) 539-8255. Canfor Lumber Mill also offers tours; phone (780) 538-7756. Tours should be booked at least a day in advance.

The area has prime hunting for both migratory birds and big game. Area lakes are the nesting sites of the trumpeter swan. Hiking, camping and fishing are popular outdoor activities.

Annual events include the Stompede, a major rodeo, held the first weekend in June; Canada Day celebrations on July 1; and the Bud Country Fever County Music Festival, held the first weekend in July. There are also several smaller rodeos; a Highland Games; pari-mutuel racing during July; Street Performers Festival (mid-July); Science Festival and Little Fringe Festival (both in early August); and an Art Walk in early September.

Contact the visitor information centre at gprtourism@southpeace.org for more information; or visit www.northernvisitor.com.

Grande Prairie Museum And Gift Shop. Dinosaurs once roamed the Grande Prairie area long before aboriginal tribes arrived some 8,000 years ago. Explorers, trappers and fur traders came, to be followed by missionaries and pioneer families. Grande Prairie Museum presents these fascinating stories and much, much more. Come see exciting new exhibits, as we expand at our original site and at the Centre 2000. Phone (780) 532-5482; fax (780) 831-7371; email gpmuseum@telusplanet.net; web page grandeprairiemuseum.com. [ADVERTISEMENT]

GrapeVine Wine & Spirit Emporium. We carry the largest selection of wine in Western Canada. Check out our "Fine Wine Room" with old vintages and large bottles of

Beautiful grounds, excellent facilities, wonderful service. Very clean and quiet. We'll be back!" We welcome you to come and discover for yourself. See our display ad for more information. Phone (780) 532-9998. [ADVERTISEMENT] ▲

Area attractions include **Muskoseepi Park**, which follows the Bear Creek corridor. The park includes 9 miles/15 km of paved walking and biking trails, a bird sanctuary at Crystal Lake, picnic areas, swimming pool, lawn bowling, mini-golf, stocked fishing pond for children, playground and canoe, paddleboat and bike rentals. Visitor services are available in the Pavilion. Nearby is the **Grande Prairie Museum & Pioneer Village** and the Regional College, a unique circular facility designed by Douglas Cardinal. Several of the downtown buildings have murals by local artists.

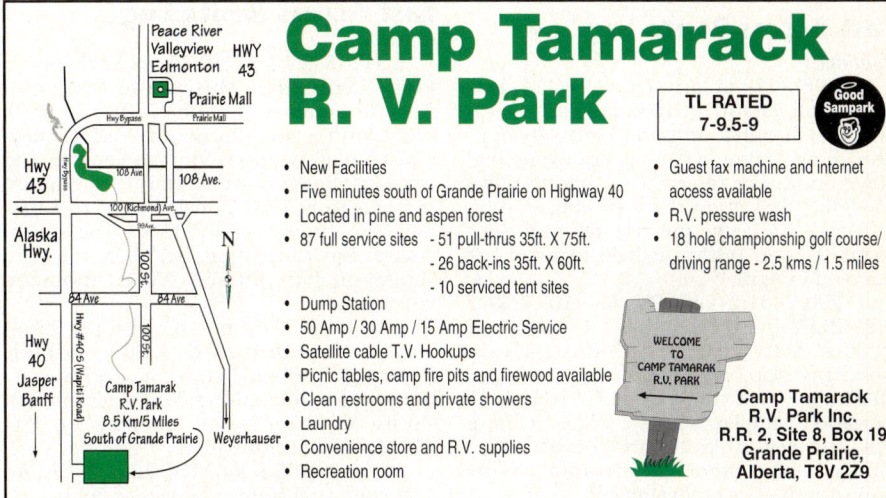

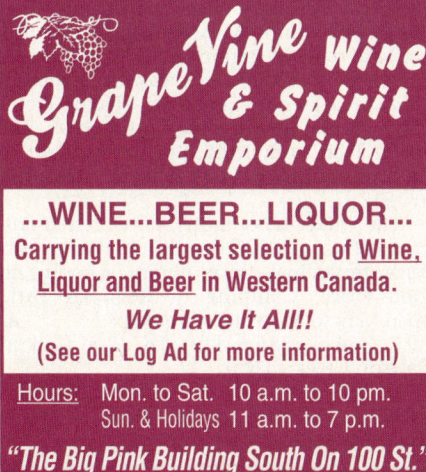

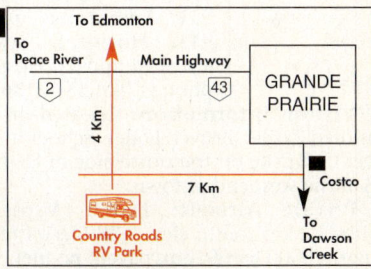

rare and hard to find wine. On the liquor side of our store, we carry over 60 different single-malt scotches. In the beer department, we specialize in small microbreweries and still have room for all your old favorites. The "GrapeVine" is a must stop in Grande Prairie. See us at 9506 100 Street. The big pink building south on 100 Street. (780) 538-3555. [ADVERTISEMENT]

East Access Route Log

(continued)

E 298 (479.6 km) DC 69 (111 km) **Saskatoon Island Provincial Park** is 1.9 miles/3 km north on park road; 96 campsites, dump station, boat launch, swimming, playground. For reservations phone (780) 766-3485. Saskatoon berry picking in July. This park is a game preserve for trumpeter swans. A Swan Festival is held here the last weekend in April. ▲

E 299 (481.2 km) DC 68 (109.4 km) **WEMBLEY** (pop. 1,523) has a hotel, liquor store (at hotel), bank, post office, grocery store, gas stop, car wash and restaurants. There are 3 area churches and 2 schools. A recreation complex houses a 3-sheet curling rink, hockey rink, tennis courts and a lounge. For more information, visit http://southpeace.org/wembley/.

Picnicking and camping at Sunset Lake Park in town (dump station). Camping May 1 to Oct. 15 at Pipestone Creek County Park, 9 miles/14.5 km south; 99 sites, showers, flush toilets, dump station, boat launch, firewood, fishing, playground, fossil display and an 18-hole golf course with grass greens nearby. Bird watching is good here for red-winged blackbirds and yellow-headed blackbirds. ◀▲

Beaverlodge

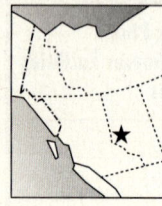

E 311 (500.5 km) DC 56 (90.1 km) **Population:** 2,110. **Elevation:** 2,419 feet/737m. **Emergency Services:** RCMP, phone 911. **Ambulance,** phone 911. **Hospital,** Beaverlodge Municipal Hospital, phone (780) 354-2136.

Visitor Information: Located in the restored Lower Beaver Lodge School at Pioneer Campsite on the north side of Highway 43 at the west end of town.

Private Aircraft: DeWit Airpark 2 miles/3.2 km south; elev. 2,289 feet/1,698m; length 3,000 feet/914m; paved; no fuel.

Beaverlodge is a service centre for the area with RCMP, hospital, medical and dental clinic. There are 9 churches, schools, a swimming pool and tennis courts.

Visitor services include 3 motels, 8 restaurants and gas stations. There are supermarkets, banks, a drugstore, car wash and sporting goods store. **Beaverlodge Area Cultural Centre,** at the south end of town, features local arts and crafts as well as a tea room. South Peace Centennial Museum is west of town (see **Milepost E 312**). Camping is available at **Pioneer Campsite,** a municipal campground with 19 sites, showers, dump station, electrical hookups, tourist information. The Beaverlodge Airpark, 2 miles/3.2 km south of town, is becoming a popular stopover on the flying route to Alaska. ▲

Beaverlodge is the gateway to Monkman Pass and Kinuseo Falls. Beaverlodge is also home to Canada's most northerly Agricultural Research Station (open to the public), and serves as regional centre for grain transportation, seed cleaning and seed production. Cereal grains, such as wheat, barley and oats, are the main crops in the area. The PRT Alberta Inc. reforestation nursery here, visible from the highway as you enter town, grows about 8 million seedlings a year. Tours are available; phone (780) 354-2288.

East Access Route Log

(continued)

E 312 (502.1 km) DC 55 (88.5 km) **South Peace Centennial Museum** to east, open daily in summer; phone (780) 354-8869. Well worth a stop, the South Peace Centennial Museum features vintage vehicles and working steam-powered farm equipment from the early 1900s. Open 10 A.M. to 8 P.M., mid-May through mid-October. The annual Pioneer Day celebration, held here the third Sunday in July, attracts several thousand visitors.

E 312.4 (502.7 km) DC 54.6 (87.9 km) Turnoff for Driftwood Ranch Wildlife Haven, 14.3 miles/23 km west, a private collection of exotic and endangered animals. Opens May 1 for season; phone (780) 356-3769 for more information.

E 314.3 (505.8 km) DC 52.6 (84.8 km) Golf course. This joint project of Hythe and Beaverlodge residents has a clubhouse that was once an NAR station. The 9-hole par 35 course has grass greens. Visitors are welcome; rentals available.

E 320 (515 km) DC 47 (75.6 km) **HYTHE** (pop. 623) is an agricultural service community and processing center for fruit and berry crops, especially Saskatoon berries. Canola is also a major crop. There's also bison ranching in this region; inquire locally for directions to Riverside Bison Ranch.

Visitor Information: Located between the highway and railroad tracks in an old 1910 tack shop, staffed by volunteers in summer. The town has a motel, a bed and breakfast, restaurant, laundromat, gas station, tire repair, car wash, outdoor covered heated swimming pool, complete shopping facilities and a hospital. Municipal campground in town with 17 sites, showers, dump station and playground. ▲

E 329 (529.4 km) DC 38 (61.1 km) **Junction** with Highway 59 east to Sexsmith.

E 337 (542.3 km) DC 30 (48.3 km) **DEMMITT,** an older settlement with postal service, cafe and gas.

E 340 (547.2 km) DC 27 (43.4 km) Railway crossing.

E 341 (548.8 km) DC 26 (41.8 km) Public campground to east; 15 sites, shelter, firewood, tables, pit toilets, pump water and playground. ▲

E 341.3 (549.2 km) DC 25.7 (41.3 km) Vehicle inspection station to west.

E 342 (550.4 km) DC 25 (40.2 km) Gas, diesel and convenience store.

E 343.3 (552.5 km) DC 23.7 (38.1 km) Alberta–British Columbia border. Turnout with litter barrels and pay phone.

TIME ZONE CHANGE: Alberta is on Mountain time; most of British Columbia is on Pacific time.

E 345.1 (555.4 km) DC 21.9 (35.2 km) **Junction** with Heritage Highway 52 (gravel surface) which leads 18.5 miles/30 km south to **One Island Lake Provincial Park** (30 campsites, $9 fee, open May–Oct., trout fishing) and 92 miles/148 km southwest from Highway 2 to Tumbler Ridge townsite, built in conjunction with the North East Coal development. Monkman Provincial Park, site of spectacular Kinuseo Falls, lies south of Tumbler Ridge. A campground with viewing platform of falls is accessible via a 25-mile/40-km road from Tumbler Ridge. Heritage Highway loops north 59.5 miles/96 km from Tumbler Ridge to join Highway 97 just west of Dawson Creek (see **Milepost PG 237.7** in the WEST ACCESS ROUTE section).

E 345.7 (556.3 km) DC 21.3 (34.3 km) Tupper Creek bridge.

E 347 (558.5 km) DC 20 (32.1 km) **TUPPER;** general store. **Swan Lake Provincial Park,** 1.2 miles/2 km north, open May–Oct.; 42 campsites, picnic area, playground and boat launch. ▲

E 347.9 (559.9 km) DC 19.1 (30.7 km) **Sudeten Provincial Park;** 14 campsites, $12 fee, picnic tables, open May–Oct. Plaque tells of immigration to this valley of displaced residents of Sudetenland in 1938–39. ▲

E 348.9 (561.5 km) DC 18.1 (29.1 km) Tate Creek bridge.

E 349.7 (562.7 km) DC 17.3 (27.8 km) Side road west to community of **Tomslake;** tea house, bakery and crafts shop in Tomslake.

E 356.3 (573.4 km) DC 10.7 (17.2 km) Turnout to east with litter barrel.

E 358 (576.1 km) DC 9 (14.5 km) Historic sign tells of Pouce Coupe Prairie.

E 359.4 (578.4 km) DC 7.6 (12.2 km) Railway crossing.

E 360 (579.3 km) DC 7 (11.2 km) Weigh scales to east.

E 360.4 (580 km) DC 6.6 (10.6 km) Bissett Creek bridge. Regional park located at south end of bridge.

E 361 (581 km) DC 6 (9.6 km) **POUCE COUPE** (pop. 904; elev. 2,118 feet/646m). **Visitor Information:** Tourist Bureau Office located in Pouce Coupe Museum, 5006 49th Ave. (1 block south of Highway 2). Open 8 A.M. to 5 P.M., May to August. Phone (250) 786-5555. Historical artifacts are displayed at the **Pouce Coupe Museum,** located in the old NAR railroad station.

The Pouce Coupe area was first settled in 1898 by a French Canadian, Hector Tremblay, who set up a trading post in 1908. The Edson Trail, completed in 1911, brought in the main influx of settlers from Edmonton in 1912.

The village has a motel, hotel, restaurant, post office, gas station, dump station, car wash, municipal office, library, schools and food store. Camping at Regional Park, open May to September; hookups. ▲

E 364.5 (586.6 km) DC 2.5 (4 km) Dawson Creek airport.

E 367 (590.6 km) DC 0 **DAWSON CREEK,** the beginning of the Alaska Highway.

Turn to the ALASKA HIGHWAY section, page 92, for description of Dawson Creek and log of the Alaska Highway.

Alaska Highway via
WEST ACCESS ROUTE

Connects: Seattle, WA, to Dawson Creek, BC   **Length:** 817 miles
Road Surface: Paved   **Season:** Open all year
Highest Summit: Pine Pass, 3,068 feet
Major Attractions: Fraser River Canyon/Hell's Gate, Barkerville

(See maps, pages 62–63)

	Cache Creek	Dawson Creek	Prince George	Seattle
Cache Creek		527	277	290
Dawson Creek	527		250	817
Prince George	277	250		567
Seattle	290	817	567	

Cattle cross the Chilcotin Highway west of Williams Lake. (© Blake Hanna, staff)

The West Access Route links Interstate 5, Trans-Canada Highway 1 and BC Highway 97 to form the most direct route to Dawson Creek, BC, for West Coast motorists. This has been the major western route to the start of the Alaska Highway since 1952, when the John Hart Highway connecting Prince George and Dawson Creek was completed.

Travelers may also continue on I-5 to the international border at Blaine (22 miles/35 km beyond Exit 256), the more direct route if you are bound for Vancouver, BC.

The West Access Route junctions with Yellowhead Highway 16 at Prince George. This east–west highway connects with the Alaska State Ferry System and BC Ferries at Prince Rupert, and with the East Access Route to the Alaska Highway at Edmonton. Turn to the YELLOWHEAD HIGHWAY 16 section for a complete log of that route.

Side trips and secondary routes detailed in this section include Highway 26 to Barkerville, a provincial historic town dating back to the 1860s; the scenic Chilcotin Highway to Bella Coola; and Highway 29, the Hudson's Hope Loop to the Alaska Highway.

Distances via this 817-mile route between Seattle, WA, and Dawson Creek, BC, are: Seattle to Abbotsford, 120 miles; Abbotsford to Cache Creek, 170 miles; Cache Creek to Prince George, 277 miles; and Prince George to Dawson Creek, 250 miles.

The West Access Route log is divided into 4 sections: Seattle to the Canadian border; Abbotsford to Cache Creek; Cache Creek to Prince George; and Prince George to Dawson Creek.

West Access Route Log

This section of the log shows distance from Seattle (S) followed by distance from the Canadian border (CB) at Sumas.

INTERSTATE HIGHWAY 5 NORTH

S 0 CB 116 Exit 165 northbound (165B southbound) to downtown **SEATTLE** (pop. 563,374).

S 12 CB 104 Exit 177 east to **Lake Forest Park** and west 4.5 miles to **Edmonds**. Food, gas, diesel east off exit.

S 14 CB 102 Exit 179 220th Street; gas west off exit.

S 17 CB 99 Exit 182 to Interstate 405 South.

S 24 CB 92 Exit 189 to Everett Mall.

S 27 CB 89 Exit 192 to Broadway Street and Everett city center.

S 28 CB 88 Exit 193 to **EVERETT** (pop. 91,488) city center; all services.

S 29 CB 87 Exit 194 to U.S. Highway 2 East.

S 30 CB 86 Exit 195 northbound to Port of Everett, Marine View Drive.

S 34 CB 82 Exit 199 to **Marysville**; food, gas and lodging either side of freeway.

S 41 CB 75 Exit 206; 24-hour gas, food and shopping east off exit.

S 42 CB 74 Rest area northbound.

S 56 CB 60 Exit 221 to **La Conner**, 11 miles northwest; gas station east off exit.

S 61 CB 55 Exit 226 to **MOUNT VERNON** (pop. 26,232) city center; all services.

S 62 CB 54 Exit 227 to College Way; easy access to food, gas, lodging and shopping just off exit.

S 65 CB 51 Exit 230 to **Burlington** to east, and **Anacortes** 16 miles west. Shopping, food, gas and lodging at exit.

S 66 CB 50 Exit 231 to Chuckanut Drive scenic route (Washington Highway 11 North).

S 67 CB 49 Exit 232 to diesel, 24-hour gas, food and camping.

S 73 CB 43 Milepost 238. Bow Hill Rest area.

S 76 CB 40 Exit 241; gas east off exit.

S 81 CB 35 Exit 246 to North Lake Samish and Lake Padden Recreation Area; diesel, gas and groceries west off exit.

S 85 CB 31 Exit 250 (Fairhaven Parkway)

to Bellingham waterfront and **Fairhaven Transportation Center** (follow signs).

(Continues on page 64)

Sumas R.V. Park & Campground

Rod & Lea Ann Fadden
(360) 988-8875
9600 Easterbrook
Sumas, WA 98295   *Private or Group Sites*

The mileposts start at Sumas R.V. Park.

80' Pull Throughs • 50 Amp Full Hookups
Cable • Laundry • 24 hr. Customs

Shortcut to ALASKA

WEST ACCESS ROUTE
Seattle, WA, to Lac La Hache, BC

© 2003 The MILEPOST®

Key to mileage boxes
miles/kilometres
miles/kilometres
from:
- **A** - Abbotsford
- **CC** - Cache Creek
- **PG** - Prince George
- **S** - Seattle
- **CB** - Canadian Border

Map Location

Principal Route
- Paved
- Unpaved

Other Roads
- Paved
- Unpaved

Ferry Routes
Hiking Trails

⬛ Refer to Log for Visitor Facilities

Scale
0 — 20 Miles
0 — 20 Kilometres

Key to Advertiser Services
- C - Camping
- D - Dump Station
- d - Diesel
- G - Gas (reg., unld.)
- I - Ice
- L - Lodging
- M - Meals
- P - Propane
- R - Car Repair (major)
- r - Car Repair (minor)
- S - Store (grocery)
- T - Telephone (pay)

PG-189/304km
CC-88/142km

(map continues next page)

To Tete Juane Cache

Lac La Hache
- CC-88/141.6km Lac La Hache Motel L
- CC-85/136.8km Lac La Hache KOA CDILST
- CC-78.2/125.8km 108 Resort CILMT
- N 51°38' W121°17' 100 Mile House
- CC-72/115.9km South Cariboo Visitor Info Centre

Canim Lake
Mahood Lake
Wells Gray Provincial Park

Cariboo Highway
Horse Lake
Green Lake
Bridge Lake
24
Little Fort

CC-51.8/83.4km Meadow Springs Ranch CLM
70 Mile House
Bonaparte R.
Bonaparte Lake
N 50°24' W121°17'
97

North Thompson River
5

PG-277/446km
CC-0
A-170/274km

Clinton
CC-24.5/39.4km Clinton Pines Campground CIT
CC-19.9/32km Willow Springs RV Park CD
CC-7/11.3km Historic Hat Creek Ranch
N 50°48' W121°19'

Loon Lake

Fraser River
99
Cariboo Wagon Road
Pavilion Lake
Cache Creek
97
Kamloops Lake
Kamloops

To Salmon Arm

Lillooet
12
Ashcroft
South Thompson River

A-168.2/270.7km Coyote Corner
A-141.2/227.2km Acacia Grove R.V. Park & Cabins CLS
Log Cabin Pub IMT
A-137/220.5km Big Horn, BC GT
Lytton
A-117.8/189.6km Lytton Chamber of Commerce

Logan Lake
Spences Bridge
Nicola R.
8
1
N 50°13' W121°34'
A-111.1/178.8km Siska Art Gallery & Museum
Merritt
5
5A

Coquihalla Highway

LILLOOET RANGE

Sea to Sky Highway
99

Garibaldi Provincial Park

Lillooet Lake

Fraser River

North Bend
Boston Bar
Hell's Gate
A-94/151.3km Canyon Alpine RV Park & Campground CT
N 49°51' W121°26'
5A

COAST MOUNTAINS

A-83.6/134.5km Hell's Gate Airtram
Harrison Lake

Yale
A-50.2/80.8km Telte Yet campsite C
Princeton
3
To Osoyoos

A-45.5/73.2km Hope Valley Campground CDS
Wild Rose Good Sampark CDIST

Coquihalla Highway

CC-120/193km
A-50/80km

Golden Ears Provincial Park
Harrison Hot Springs
Hope
N 49°22' W121°26'
3

BRITISH COLUMBIA
CANADA
UNITED STATES
WASHINGTON

Vancouver
7
Mission
Chilliwack
A-26.5/42.5km Minter Gardens M
A-23.2/37.4km Chilliwack RV Park CDIST

Alaska State Ferry
(see MARINE ACCESS ROUTES section)
99
Abbotsford
A-0 Super 8 Motel L

Manning Provincial Park

Vancouver Island
Blaine
Sumas
546
S-116 Sumas RV Park CD

PG-447/719km
CC-170/274km
A-0

Ferndale
539
S-91 Bellingham RV Park C

Bellingham
S-91/146km
CB-25/40km

S-116/187km
CB-0

To Okanogan

Victoria
20

Mount Vernon
North Cascades Highway

Strait of Juan de Fuca

CASCADE MOUNTAINS

5

Everett
2
To Wenatchee

S-0
CB-116/187km

Puget Sound
Seattle
5
90

N
W — E
S

To Ellensburg

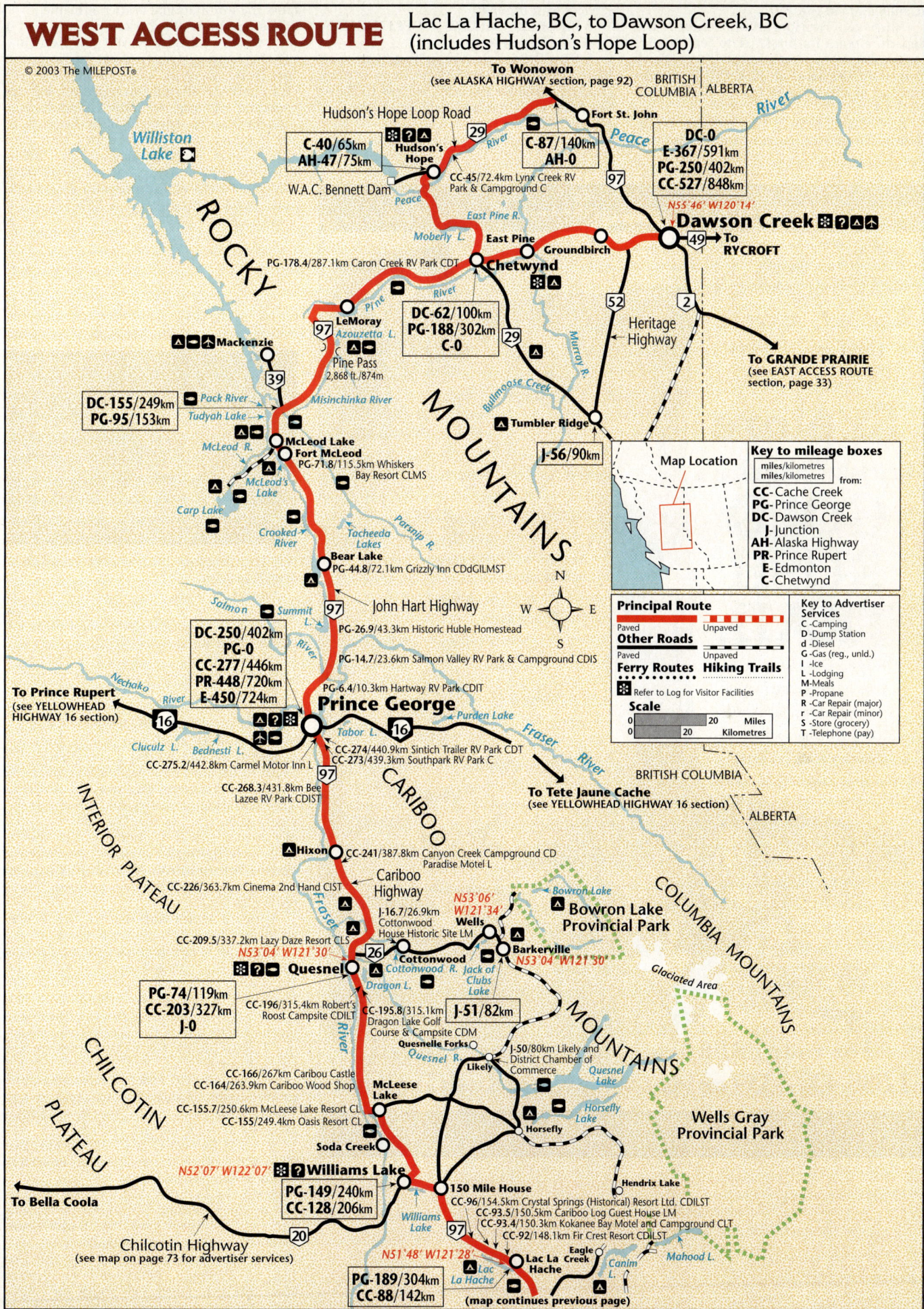

(Continued from page 61)

Fairhaven Transportation Center is the departure point for Alaska State Ferry service to Alaska from Washington (see "Ferry Travel" in the TRAVEL PLANNING section and the ALASKA STATE FERRY SCHEDULES section).

S 87 CB 29 Exit 252 to Western Washington University; access to food, gas and services west off exit.

S 88 CB 28 Exit 253 to **BELLINGHAM** (pop. 67,171); all services.

S 91 CB 25 Exit 256 to **junction** with Washington Highway 539 north to Lynden and the Canadian border; access to Bellis Fair Mall, food, gas and lodging at this exit. *The MILEPOST® log exits here to cross the border at Sumas.* (Continue north on I-5 to cross the international border at Blaine.)

Bellingham RV Park, I-5 Exit 258. 1 mile north of Highway 539 junction. Just off the freeway (west). Next to Hampton Inn Hotel. Easy in, easy out. Quiet, very clean park. 56 all pull-through sites. Big rigs welcome. 50-amp, 60 cable channels. Free modem hookup. Instant phone hookups to site ($3/day). Very clean laundry, restrooms and showers. Close to Alaskan ferry, Bellis-Fair shopping mall, Costco, Wal-Mart, Walgreen's, diesel and propane. Good Sam and AAA discounts. 1-888-372-1224. [ADVERTISEMENT] ▲

*Follow Highway 539 North 12 miles to **junction** with Highway 546. Continue on Highway 546 for 13 miles to **junction** with Highway 9.*

S 116 (186.7 km) **CB 0** U.S.–Canada border at **SUMAS** (pop. 978); accommodations and RV camping available. The Sumas, WA–Huntingdon, BC, border crossing is open 24 hours.

Sumas RV Park. See display ad on page 61. ▲

Follow BC Highway 11 north 4 miles/6.4 km to Abbotsford.

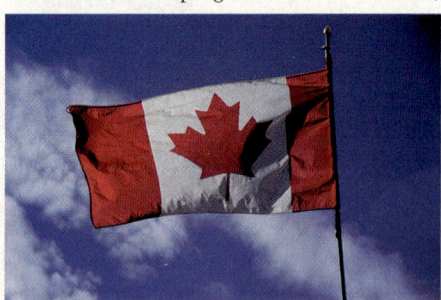

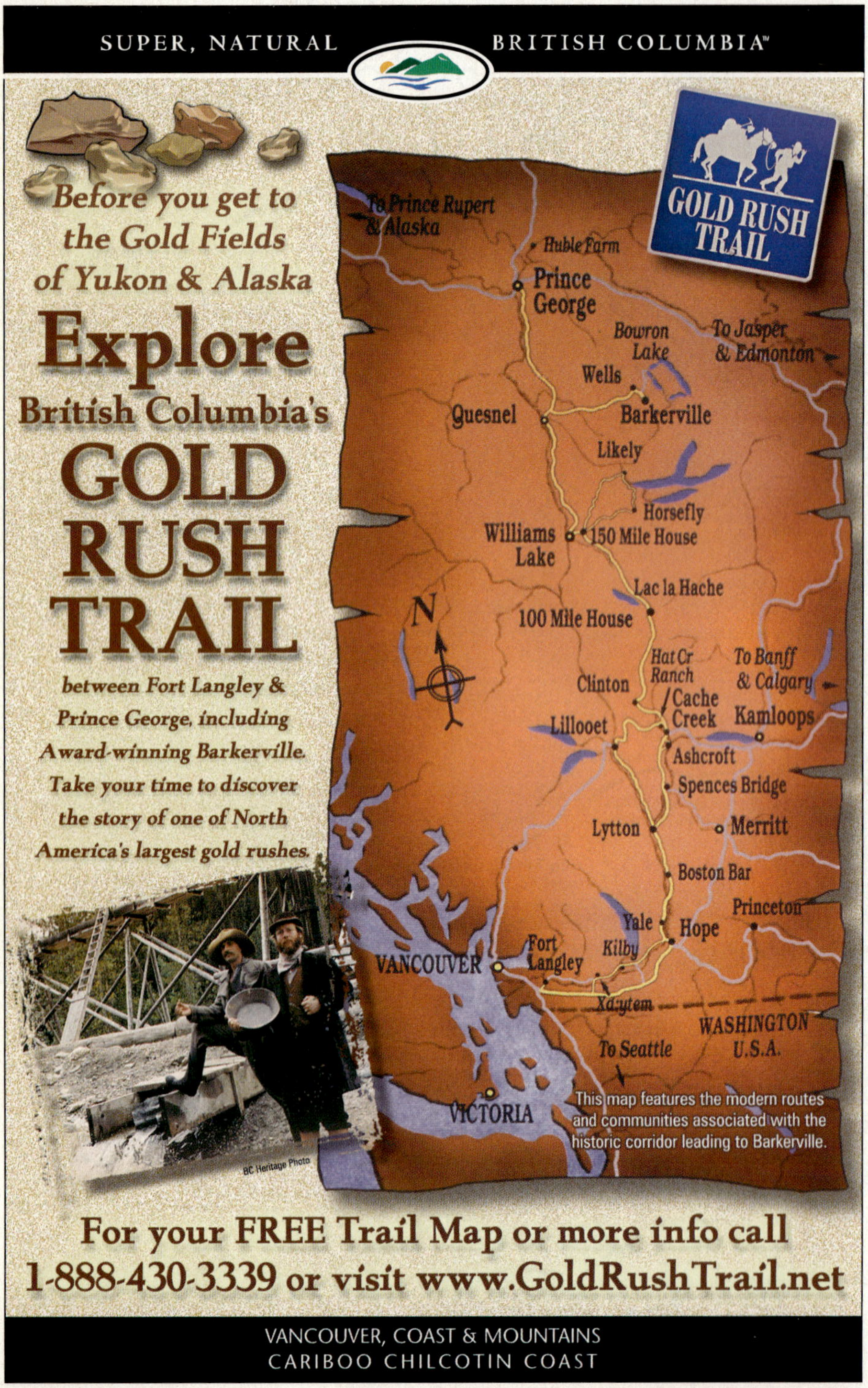

SUPER 8 MOTEL

Stay at the Abbotsford Super 8!

1881 Sumas Way (Hwy 11)
Abbotsford, BC V2S 4L5
Tel: 604-853-1141
Fax: 604-853-8967
www.super8.com • super8@telus.net

Air Conditioned • Kitchen Suites • Guest Laundry • Complimentary Local Calls
Complimentary Continental Breakfast • Non-Smoking & Pet Rooms Available
- EXIT 92 (1/2 BLOCK NORTH OF HWY #1) -
5 Minutes North of U.S. (Sumas/Huntington) Border
DIRECT TOLL FREE 1-800-663-9842
AAA Approved

This section of the log shows distance from Abbotsford (A) followed by distance from Cache Creek (CC).

TRANS-CANADA HIGHWAY 1 EAST

A 0 CC 170 (273.6 km) Exit 92. **Junction** of Trans-Canada Highway 1 and Highway 11 south to the international border crossing at Sumas–Huntingdon. Highway 11 north to **ABBOTSFORD** (pop. 105,403), all visitor services. Abbotsford is the "Raspberry Capital of Canada" and is the home of the Abbotsford International Airshow in August. **Visitor Information:** Abbotsford Chamber of Commerce, 2462 McCallum Road; phone (604) 859-9651.

Super 8 Motel Abbotsford. See display ad this section.

Highway 11 north crosses the bridge over the Fraser River to Mission (7.2 miles/11.9 km north), and connects with Highway 7 to Harrison Hot Springs (41 miles/66 km). This 2-lane highway traverses the rural farmland on the north side of the Fraser River, rejoining Trans-Canada Highway 1 at Hope (56 miles/90 km).

A 1.9 (3 km) **CC 168.1** (270.5 km) Exit 95 to Whatcom Road and westbound exit to Sumas River rest area. Access to Sumas Mountain Provincial Park; hiking.

A 5.3 (8.5 km) **CC 164.7** (265.1 km) Exit 99 to Sumas River rest area (eastbound only); tables, toilet, pay phones.

A 8.8 (14.2 km) **CC 161.2** (259.4 km) Exit 104 to small farming community of Yarrow and road to Cultus Lake. The Lower Fraser Valley is prime agricultural land.

A 15 (24.1 km) **CC 155** (249.4 km) Exit 116 to Lickman Road and Chilliwack (description follows); exit south for Chilliwack Visitor Information (open daily in

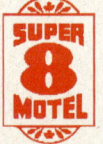

SAVE 35% FOR YOURSELF
AND KEEP ALASKA ALIVE ALL YEAR!

YES! Start my one-year subscription (10 issues) to Alaska magazine
FOR JUST $19.95—35% OFF THE COVER PRICE.

Name _____ (PLEASE PRINT) _____ Telephone _____

Address _____ E-Mail _____

City _____ State _____ Zip _____

Payment Method: ❑ VISA   ❑ MasterCard

Credit Card Number _____ Expiration date _____

BMP04

❑ Bill me later   ❑ Payment Enclosed

Alaska magazine is published ten times a year. *Regular cover price is $30.90. In Canada, add $10.00 and $20.00 for foreign subscriptions. All payments in U.S. funds. Please allow 6-8 weeks for delivery of your first issue.

SAVE 35% FOR A FRIEND
AND SHARE THE THRILL OF ALASKA!

YES! Send a one-year gift subscription (10 issues) to Alaska magazine
FOR JUST $19.95—35% OFF THE COVER PRICE.

TO:
Name _____ (PLEASE PRINT) _____ Telephone _____

Address _____ E-Mail _____

City _____ State _____ Zip _____

FROM:
Name _____ (PLEASE PRINT) _____ Telephone _____

Address _____ E-Mail _____

City _____ State _____ Zip _____

❑ Bill me later   ❑ Payment Enclosed

XMP04

Alaska magazine is published ten times a year. *Regular cover price is $30.90. In Canada, add $10.00 and $20.00 for foreign subscriptions. All payments in U.S. funds. Please allow 6-8 weeks for delivery of your first issue.

GIVE A COPY OF THE MILEPOST
TO A FRIEND AND PAY NO SHIPPING!

YES! I would like to order a copy of 2003's THE MILEPOST, including the original 1949 edition, for a friend at the low price of $25.95. Shipping is free!

TO:
Name _____ (PLEASE PRINT) _____ Telephone _____

Address _____ E-Mail _____

City _____ State _____ Zip _____

Payment Method: ❑ VISA   ❑ MasterCard

Credit Card Number _____ Expiration date _____

FROM:
Name _____ (PLEASE PRINT) _____ Telephone _____

Address _____ E-Mail _____

City _____ State _____ Zip _____

www.alaskamagazine.com

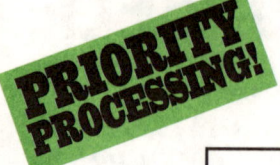

PRIORITY PROCESSING!

NO POSTAGE NECESSARY IF MAILED IN THE UNITED STATES

BUSINESS REPLY MAIL
FIRST-CLASS MAIL PERMIT NO. 512 MARION OH

POSTAGE WILL BE PAID BY ADDRESSEE

Alaska magazine
PO BOX 2036
MARION OH 43306-2136

PRIORITY PROCESSING!

NO POSTAGE NECESSARY IF MAILED IN THE UNITED STATES

BUSINESS REPLY MAIL
FIRST-CLASS MAIL PERMIT NO. 512 MARION OH

POSTAGE WILL BE PAID BY ADDRESSEE

Alaska magazine
PO BOX 2036
MARION OH 43306-2136

PRIORITY PROCESSING!

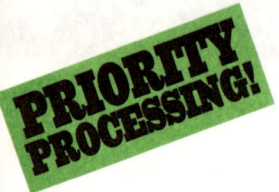

PLEASE PLACE POSTAGE HERE

The MILEPOST®
P.O. BOX 1668
AUGUSTA GA 30903

Vintage vehicles are on display at Chilliwack's Heritage Park. (© Blake Hanna, staff)

Lake resort area also offers water slides, go-carts and other activities.

A **17** (27.4 km) CC **153** (246.2 km) Exit 119B north to Chilliwack airport and downtown Chilliwack shopping and services (see description at **Milepost A 15**).

A **18** (29 km) CC **152** (244.6 km) Exit 123 Prest Road north to Rosedale, south to Ryder Lake.

A **23.2** (37.4 km) CC **146.8** (236.2 km) Exit 129 for Annis Road and Chilliwack RRV Park and Campground. ▲

Chilliwack RV Park & Campground. See display ad this setion. ▲

A **26.5** (42.5 km) CC **143.5** (230.9 km) Exit 135 to Highway 9 east to Harrison Hot Springs and alternate route Highway 7 to Hope and Vancouver. Westbound exit for **Bridal Veil Falls.** Also exit here for access to **Minter Garden**s, which rivals Victoria's famous Butchart Gardens for beauty.

summer) and Cottonwood Meadows RV park. ▲

CHILLIWACK (pop. 69,535), located in the fertile farmland of the Fraser River Valley, is surrounded by mountains and rivers. Chilliwack's agricultural heritage is evidenced throughout the community by the fresh farm products for sale. **Visitor Information:** Tourism Chilliwack Visitor InfoCentre, open year-round, 9 A.M. to 7 P.M. daily from June to August. Phone 1-800-567-9535; web site www.tourismchilliwack.com.

Chilliwack has motels, restaurants, shopping malls, banks, gas stations, RV parks and other services. There are a library, 2 movie theatres and an arts centre. **Chilliwack Heritage Park and Antique Powerland** are located behind the InfoCentre.

Area attractions include golf and the popular Cultus Lake Provincial Park area (see **Milepost A 16.8**) with water park, boat rentals, horseback riding, hiking, fishing and camping. For birdwatchers there is the **Great Blue Heron Nature Reserve**, a 130-hectares along the Vedder River that are home to more than 90 nesting great blue herons. Take Yale Road West exit to Sumas Prairie Road and drive south to parking area at road end.

Cottonwood Meadows RV Country Club. Exit 116. Highly rated, recommended by Good Sam, Woodalls, Tourism B.C. New, secure, clean, well-maintained, full service park. Easy access, electronic gates, well lit, well managed. Lazy stream, full hookups (15/30/50 amp), cable TV, wide level sites, paved roadways. Nicest washrooms, laundromat, clubhouse, Jacuzzi, pull-throughs, near all amenities, golf, fishing, shopping, watersports. Next to Chilliwack Heritage Park. Open year-round. Near U.S. border crossing. VISA, MasterCard. 44280 Luckakuck Way, Chilliwack, BC V2R 4A7. Phone (604) 824-PARK (7275). Email: camping@cottonwoodRVpark.com. Web site: www.cottonwoodRVpark.com. [ADVERTISEMENT] ▲

A **16.8** (27.1 km) CC **153.2** (246.5 km) Exit 119A south to **Sardis** (all services) and **Cultus Lake Provincial Park**. The Provincial Park has 300 campsites; water, flush and pit toilets, showers, firewood, water, boat launch, swimming, fishing, canoeing, kayaking, and hiking and walking trails. Cultus

CHILLIWACK ADVERTISERS

Cottonwood Mall	Luckakuck Way
Cottonwood Meadows RV Country Club	Ph. (604) 824-7275
Tourism Chilliwack	1-800-567-9535

share *the moments*

London Drugs, Sears, Sport Chek, Zellers
Plus 65 Shops & Services

Right at the Sardis Freeway Exit
Plenty of Free Parking

45585 Luckakuck Way, Chilliwack, BC

CHILLIWACK RV PARK & CAMPGROUND

- 48 full-service sites
- Some extra-long pull-throughs
- Some extra-wide pads
- 30 amp service • Hot showers
- Laundromat • Store

Scenic rural waterfall setting next to one of the best golf courses in B.C. — 7 miles east of Chilliwack on Hwy 1. Exit 129 Annis Road.

(604) 794-7800

Minter Gardens has 27 acres of floral displays featuring 11 themed gardens, 2 restaurants and a wine store. Open 9 A.M. daily, April to mid-October. Entertainment is scheduled Sundays and holidays, weather permitting. Internet: www.mintergardens.com.

Minter Gardens. See display ad this section.

Exit north for Cheam Lake Wetlands Regional Park. Once mined for its marl deposits, Cheam Lake is now a wildlife habitat; interpretive trails, good bird watching.

A **27.3** (43.9 km) CC **142.7** (229.6 km) Exit 138 to Popkum Road. Eastbound access to **Bridal Veil Falls Provincial Park** to south; picnicking, trail to base of falls. Also access to small community of Popkum and various roadside attractions, including water slide, Sandstone Gallery rock and gem museum, and prehistoric-themed amusement park. Food, gas and lodging.

A **34.5** (55.5 km) CC **135.5** (218.1 km) Exit 146 Herrling Island, a cottonwood tree farm (no access or services), visible from highway.

A **40.5** (65.2 km) CC **129.5** (208.4 km) Exit 153 to Laidlaw and access to Jones/Wahleach Lake (4WD gravel road to lake).

A **42.5** (68.4 km) CC **127.5** (205.2 km) Truck weigh scales; public phone.

A **44.7** (71.9 km) CC **125.3** (201.6 km) Exit 160 to Hunter Creek rest area; tables, toilet, pay phone, information kiosk.

A **45.5** (73.2 km) CC **124.5** (200.4 km) Exit 165 to Flood–Hope Road (eastbound); access to campgrounds. ▲

Hope Valley Campground. See display ad this section. ▲

Wild Rose Good Sampark. See display ad this section. ▲

A **48.5** (78.1 km) CC **121.5** (195.5 km) Exit 168 to Flood–Hope Road (westbound); access to Hope Valley Campground and Wild Rose Good Sampark (private campgrounds) and to Skagit Valley and Silver Lake provincial parks. ▲

A **48.7** (78.4 km) CC **121.3** (195.2 km) Silver Creek, Flood–Hope Road exit.

A **50** (80.5 km) CC **120** (193.1 km) **Junction** of Trans-Canada Highway 1, Highway 3 (Crowsnest Highway) and Highway 5 (Coquihalla Highway).

NOTE: Northbound travelers use Exit 170 for access to Hope and Trans-Canada Highway 1 East to Cache Creek. (Although you are driving north towards Cache Creek, highway directional signs indicate "East.")

Hope

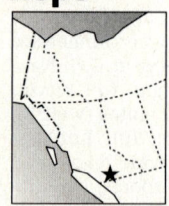

A **50.2** (80.8 km) CC **119.8** (192.8 km) Located on the Fraser River near Mount Hope (elev. 6,000 feet/1,289m). **Population:** 7,032. **Elevation:** 140feet/43m. **Emergency Services:** Phone 911. **Hospital,** 1275 7th Ave., phone (604) 869-5656.

Visitor Information: Visitor InfoCentre and museum building, corner of Hudson Bay Street and Water Avenue, on right northbound as you enter town on Trans-Canada Highway 1 East. Open 8 A.M. to 8 P.M. daily in July and August; 8 A.M. to 6 P.M. in May, June and September. Open 10 A.M. to 4 P.M weekdays rest of the year. Chamber web site: www.hopechamber.bc.ca.

Hope is a convenient stop with all services, including restaurants and about 30 area motels and resorts, as well as several private campgrounds. Hope is known as the "Chainsaw Carving Capital," with more than 20 large wood carvings in the downtown area. (A self-guided Art & Carving Walk starts at the InfoCentre.)

The major attraction in the Hope area is the Coquihalla Canyon Provincial Park, the focus of which is the Othello Quintette Tunnels. The 4 rock tunnels which cut through the tortuous canyon were part of the Kettle Valley Railway. This stretch of railway has been restored as a walking trail through the tunnels and across bridges. The tunnels are accessible from downtown Hope via Kawkawa Lake Road and Othello Road, about a 10-minute drive.

The Coquihalla Highway, completed in 1986, connects Hope with the Trans-Canada Highway just west of Kamloops, a distance of 118 miles/190 km. This is a 4-lane divided highway; toll charged.

Telte Yet Campsite. See display ad this section. ▲

West Access Route Log
(continued)

TRANS-CANADA HIGHWAY 1 EAST

A **50.7** (81.6 km) CC **119.3** (191.9 km) Bridge over Fraser River. Turnout at north end, access to pedestrian bridge across the Fraser.

A **51.5** (82.8 km) CC **118.5** (190.7 km) **Junction** with Highway 7, which leads west to Agassiz and access to Harrison Hot Springs via Highway 9 (23 miles/36 km) and on to Vancouver.

A **53.1** (85.5 km) CC **116.9** (188.1 km) Rest area (westbound access only) with picnic tables to west by Lake of the Woods.

A **60.8** (97.8 km) CC **109.2** (175.7 km) Easy-to-miss turnoff (watch for sign 1,320 feet/400m before turn) for Emory Creek Provincial Park east of highway; 34 level gravel sites in trees, water, fire rings, picnic tables, firewood, flush and pit toilets, and litter barrels. Camping fee April to October. Hiking and walking trails. Gold panning and fishing in **Fraser River.** ◆▲

Very much in evidence between Hope and Cache Creek are the tracks of the Canadian National and Canadian Pacific railways. Construction of the CPR—Canada's first transcontinental railway—played a significant role in the history of the Fraser and Thompson river valleys. Begun in 1880, the CPR line between Kamloops and Port Moody was contracted to Andrew Onderdonk.

A **64.8** (104.3 km) CC **105.2** (169.3 km) **YALE** (pop. 500; elev. 250 feet/76m). **Emergency Services:** Phone 911. **Visitor Information:** In the museum, phone (604) 863-2324; open May through September. Visitor facilities include motels, store, gas station and restaurant.

Yale is a popular starting point for river rafters on the Fraser River. Historically, Yale was the head of navigation for the Lower

Fraser River and the beginning of the overland gold rush trail to British Columbia's goldfields. The Anglican Church of Saint John the Divine here was built for the miners in 1859 and is the oldest church still on its original foundation in mainland British Columbia. Next to the church is Yale Museum and a bronze plaque honouring Chinese construction workers who helped build the Canadian Pacific Railway. Walking around town, look for the several plaques relating Yale's history. Daily guided walking tours of historic Yale are offered in summer; fee charged, includes admission to museum and church.

A **65.6** (105.5 km) CC **104.5** (168.2 km) Entering **Fraser Canyon** northbound. The Fraser River and canyon were named for Simon Fraser (1776–1862), the first white man to descend the river in 1808. This is the dry forest region of British Columbia, and it can be a hot drive in summer. The scenic Fraser Canyon travelers drive through today was a formidable obstacle for railroad engineers in 1881.

A **66** (106.2 km) CC **104** (167.4 km) Yale

Rugged Fraser Canyon was a formidable obstacle for railroad engineers in 1881.
(© Blake Hanna, staff)

Tunnel, first of 7 northbound through the Fraser Canyon.

A **67.3** (108.3 km) CC **102.7** (165.2 km) Turnout to east with plaque about the Cariboo Wagon Road, which connected Yale with the Cariboo goldfields near Barkerville. Built between 1861 and 1863 by the Royal Engineers, it replaced an earlier route to the goldfields—also called the Cariboo Wagon Road—which started from Lillooet.

A **68.4** (110.1 km) CC **101.6** (163.5 km) Saddle Rock Tunnel. This 480-foot-/146-m-long tunnel was constructed from 1957–58.

A **72.1** (116 km) CC **97.9** (157.5 km) Private campground. ▲

A **72.3** (116.3 km) CC **97.7** (157.2 km) Sailor Bar Tunnel, nearly 984 feet/300m long. There were dozens of bar claims along the Fraser River in the 1850s bearing colourful names such as Sailor Bar.

A **76.5** (123.1 km) CC **93.5** (150.5 km) Spuzzum (unincorporated).

A **77.1** (124.1 km) CC **92.9** (149.5 km) Stop of interest at south end of Alexandra Bridge, built in 1962, the second largest fixed arch span in the world at more than 1,640 feet/500m in length.

A **77.5** (124.8 km) CC **92.5** (148.9 km) **Alexandra Bridge Provincial Park**, picnic area on west side of highway. Hiking trail down to the old Alexandra Bridge, still intact. This suspension bridge was built in 1926, replacing the original built in 1863.

A **77.8** (125.2 km) CC **92.2** (148.4 km) Historic Alexandra Lodge (closed), is the last surviving original roadhouse on the Cariboo Wagon Road.

A **79.5** (128 km) CC **90.5** (145.6 km) Alexandra Tunnel.

A **80.5** (129.5 km) CC **89.5** (144 km) Turnout to east.

A **82.6** (133 km) CC **87.4** (140.7 km) Hell's Gate Tunnel (328 feet/100m long).

A **83.3** (134 km) CC **86.7** (139.5 km) Ferrabee Tunnel (328 feet/100m long).

A **83.6** (134.5 km) CC **86.4** (139 km) **Hell's Gate**, the narrowest point on the Fraser River and a popular attraction. (Northbound traffic park at lot immediately south of attraction on east side of road; southbound traffic park on west side of road at attraction.)

Two 25-passenger airtrams take visitors 500 feet down across the river to a restaurant and shop complex. Footbridge across river to view fishways through which millions of salmon pass each year. An education center details the life cycle of the salmon, the construction of the International Fishways and the history of Hell's Gate. From the footbridge, visitors may also see rafters running Hell's Gate. The trams operate daily, April 17 to Oct. 13, 2003. There is also a steep trail down to the suspension bridge; strenuous hike.

Hell's Gate was well named. It was by far the most difficult terrain for construction of both the highway and the railway. To haul supplies for the railway upstream of Hell's Gate, Andrew Onderdonk built the sternwheel steamer *Skuzzy*. The *Skuzzy* made its way upstream through Hell's Gate in 1882, hauled by ropes attached to the canyon walls by bolts.

Hell's Gate Airtram. See display ad this section.

A **83.8** (134.9 km) CC **86.2** (138.7 km) Hell's Gate turnaround for travelers who miss the Hell's Gate parking lot.

A **85.7** (137.9 km) CC **84.3** (135.7 km) China Bar Tunnel, built in 1960. It is almost 2,300 feet/700m long, one of the longest tunnels in North America. Point of interest sign at south end about Simon Fraser.

A **91** (146.5 km) CC **79** (127.1 km) **BOSTON BAR** (pop. 885; elev. 400 feet/122m). **Emergency Services:** Phone 911. Services include gas stations, cafes, grocery store, motels and private RV parks. Boston Bar was the southern landing for the steamer *Skuzzy*, which plied the Fraser River between here and Lytton during construction of the CPR.

North Bend, located across the river from Boston Bar, is a former railway community. Old cable cage from the aerial car ferry that once served North Bend is on display at the CN station in Boston Bar.

North Bend is the access point for the Nahatlatch River and lakes via a logging road. River rafting trips are available on the Nahatlatch River.

A **94** (151.3 km) CC **76** (122.3 km) **Canyon Alpine RV Park & Campground.** Still the best-kept secret in the Fraser Canyon, but quickly being discovered and

- pull thru parking
- full hookups
- adjacent to store/restaurant/laundromat
- hot showers
- cable t.v.
- tenting

3 mi (5 km) N of Boston Bar
50490 Trans Canada Hwy
Boston Bar, BC V0K 1C0
Tel/Fax (604) 867-9734
canyon_alpine@hotmail.com

EXPERIENCE THE EXCITEMENT! hell's gate airtram
Located in the Scenic Fraser Canyon on Trans Canada Hwy #1 between Cache Creek & Hope
- **Salmon House Restaurant** - 'world famous' salmon chowder & grilled salmon steaks
- **Gold Panner Gift Shop** -specializing in Canadian-made gifts & souvenirs
- **Fudge Factory** - over 30 flavours! • **Observation Deck** • **Suspension Bridge**
Phone (604) 867-9277 • Fax (604) 867-9279 • Website: www.hellsgateairtram.com • PO Box 129, Hope, BC Canada V0X 1L0

described as "...one of the nicest parks on the Alaskan route." Secure RV parking and tenting 3 miles north of Boston Bar. 31 level, pull-through sites, fully serviced with 30 amp, water, sewer and cable TV. Easy access and turnarounds for rigs over 35 feet. 14-foot entrance gate clearance. Away from traffic noise and railroads. Clean washrooms. Hot showers. Shaded sites. Fire rings. Firewood. 50 yards south of restaurant, store, laundromat and telephones. Pets on leash welcome. 10 minutes from world-famous Hell's Gate Airtram. Open April 1 to Oct. 31. 50490 Trans-Canada Highway. Toll free (800) 644-PARK. Your friendly hosts, Jay and Maggie. See display ad this section. [ADVERTISEMENT]

A **101** (162.5 km) CC **69** (111 km) Turnoff for Blue Lake, 0.6 mile/1 km gravel road; private campground.

A **111.1** (178.8 km) CC **58.9** (94.8 km) **Siska Art Gallery & Museum.** See display ad this section.

A **112.8** (181.5 km) CC **57.2** (92.1 km) Viewpoint to west overlooking the Fraser River.

A **113.6** (182.9 km) CC **56.4** (90.7 km) Canadian National and Canadian Pacific railways cross over the Fraser River at Siska. A favorite spot for photos. Gravel turnout to east.

A **114.6** (184.5 km) CC **55.4** (89.2 km) Skuppah rest area (northbound only); toilets, tables, litter barrels.

A **117.8** (189.6 km) CC **52.2** (84 km) **Junction** with Highway 12 to Lillooet (see description at **Milepost CC 7**). Turn west here for community of Lytton (description follows).

LYTTON (pop. 375; area pop. 2,500; elev. 561 feet/171m). **Emergency Services**: Phone 911. **Hospital**, St. Bartholomew's, phone (250) 455-2221. **Visitor Information**:

Visitor Infocentre, 400 Fraser St., phone (250) 455-2523.

Food, gas, lodging and other services available. Thanks to its location at the confluence of the Thompson and Fraser rivers, Lytton acts as headquarters for river raft trips. The community also boasts museums and art galleries. Historically, sand bars at Lytton yielded much gold, and river frontage has been set aside for recreational gold panning. Lytton has recorded the highest temperature in British Columbia, 111°F/44°C.

Lytton. Rafting capital of British Columbia. Whitewater on the Thompson, and Hell's Gate on the Fraser. Hiking is great in our interior dry climate, amid beautiful scenery. Enjoy the Stein Valley, Native and Gold Rush history in our museums. Sawmill tours arranged at the Visitor Infocentre, 400 Fraser St., phone (250) 455-2523, fax (250) 455-6669. [ADVERTISEMENT]

A **122.8** (197.6 km) CC **47.2** (76 km) **Skihist Provincial Park** to east; 56 campsites on east side of highway with water, flush and pit toilets, firewood and dump station. Picnic area on west side of highway (good place to watch the trains go by); wheelchair-accessible restrooms.

A **134.7** (216.8 km) CC **35.3** (56.8 km) **Goldpan Provincial Park** to west alongside river; 14 campsites, picnic area, water, firewood, canoeing, kayaking, fishing.

A **136** (218.9 km) CC **34** (54.7 km) In summer, watch for fruit stands selling locally grown produce along the highway. Watch for bighorn sheep on the hillsides in the fall.

A **137** (220.5 km) CC **33** (53.1 km) **Big Horn, BC.** Bring your binoculars! Depending on month and season, you may see eagles, osprey, bears, deer or bighorn sheep on our mountain face. Groceries; fishing tackle and licenses; fireworks, souvenirs and unique gifts. Large collection of Western hats, Bailey's, Eddy's and Outback's. Trading post. Fuel. 24-hour towing BCAA. Tire shop. (250) 458-2333. [ADVERTISEMENT]

A **140** (225.3 km) CC **30** (48.3 km) **Junction** with Highway 8 to Merritt and south access to Spences Bridge. Plaque here

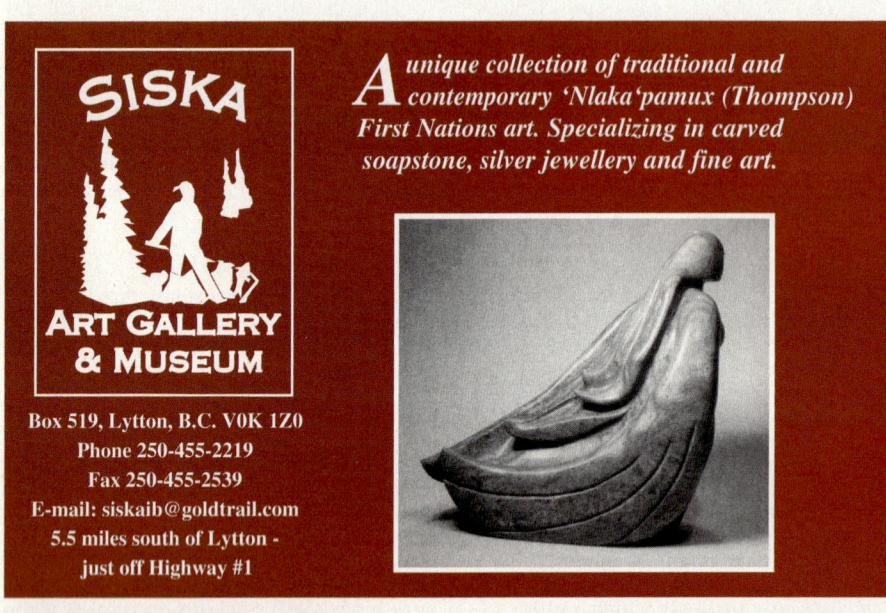

about the great landslide of 1905 reads:

"Suddenly on the afternoon of August 13, 1905, the lower side of the mountain slid away. Rumbling across the valley in seconds, the slide buried alive 5 Indians and dammed the Thompson River for over 4 hours. The trapped waters swept over the nearby Indian village drowning 13 persons."

A **141.2** (227.2 km) CC **28.8** (46.3 km) North access to **SPENCES BRIDGE** (pop. 300; elev. 760 feet/231m) located at the confluence of the Thompson and Nicola rivers. Services include lodging, gas station, camping, restaurant, pub and grocery with tackle and fishing licenses. A record 30-lb., 5-oz. steelhead was caught in the Thompson River in 1984. Look for an osprey nest atop the hydroelectric pole on the east side of the river.

Acacia Grove R.V. Park & Cabins. One block off Highway 1. RV park, cabins with kitchens, tenting. Lush setting overlooking the scenic Thompson River, famous for steelhead fishing and whitewater rafting. Visited by mountain sheep, August to May. Full hookups, pull-throughs, laundromat, free hot showers, flush toilets, small convenience/grocery store, pay phone/modem, game room, horseshoes, lawn bowling, volleyball and much more. Pets welcome (leashed). Your hosts Kim and Barry. VISA/MC/Amex/Interac. Phone/Fax (250) 458-2227. Email acaciagrove@goldtrail.com. 3814 Riverview Avenue E., Box 69, Spences Bridge, BC V0K 2L0. [ADVERTISEMENT]

Log Cabin Pub. You will appreciate this unique log structure. The logs were specially selected and prepared locally, some spanning 50 feet. This pub combines the rustic charm of a turn-of-the-century roadhouse with all the amenities of a neighborhood pub. Excellent food and hospitality by your hosts John and Laurie Kingston. [ADVERTISEMENT]

A **153.4** (246.9 km) CC **16.6** (26.7 km) Viewpoint overlooking Thompson River with plaque about the Canadian Northern Pacific (now the Canadian National Railway), Canada's third transcontinental railway, completed in 1915.

A **158.4** (255 km) CC **11.6** (18.7 km) Red Hill rest area to east; tables, toilets, litter barrels, pay phone.

A **164.3** (264.4 km) CC **5.7** (9.2 km) Stop of interest sign to east describes **Ashcroft Manor Historic Site**, British Columbia's oldest roadhouse, established in 1862. Ashcroft Manor & Tea House; food and lodging.

Summer temperatures in this dry and desert-like region typically reach the high 80s and 90s (26°C to 32°C). Fields under black plastic mesh tarps—which may be seen as the highway descends northbound—are ginseng, an Asian medicinal root crop. The world supply of North American ginseng, which takes 4 years to mature, is grown in the southern Cariboo region.

A **164.5** (264.7 km) CC **5.5** (8.9 km) **Junction** with road to **ASHCROFT**, a small village on the Thompson River with full tourist facilities just east of the highway. Historic Ashcroft supplanted Yale as gateway to the Cariboo with the arrival of the Canadian Pacific Railway in 1885. There are a number of original buildings with distinctive architectural details. Ashcroft Museum houses a fine collection of artifacts tracing the history of the region. Logan Lake, east of Ashcroft, is the site of what was the second largest open-pit copper mine in North America.

Also **junction** with Highway 97C to Logan Lake.

Visitor explores original log cabin at Ashcroft's open-air museum. (© Lyn Hancock)

A **168.2** (270.7 km) CC **1.8** (2.9 km) Second turnoff northbound for Ashcroft and **junction** with Highway 97C to Logan Lake.

Coyote Corner. Gold-trimmed ceramic pottery with a Southwestern flare created on site. Creamy fudge made fresh right here. Local soap, rope baskets, barbed wire art. Plush toys, Canadian mementos. Great selection of unusual and classy gift items. Friendly service. RV parking lot, easy in and out. Located 2 miles south of Cache Creek on Highway 1, across from Junction 97C. "Look for the big white coyote." Open daily. Phone (250) 457-6688. [ADVERTISEMENT]

Cache Creek

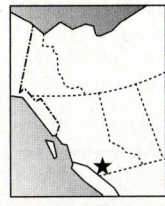

A **170** (273.6 km) PG **277** (445.8 km) Located at the junction of Trans-Canada Highway 1 and Highway 97. **Population:** 1,115. **Elevation:** 1,508 feet/460m. **Emergency Services: RCMP,** phone (250) 453-2216. **Ambulance,** phone (250)-374-5937. **Hospital,** phone (250) 453-5306.

Visitor Information: Write Box 460, Cache Creek, BC V0K 1H0; fax (250) 457-9669 or phone toll-free (877) 453-9467.

Cache Creek has ample facilities for the traveler (most located on or just off the main highways), including motels, restaurants, service stations and grocery store. A post office and bus depot are on Todd Road. Public park and swimming pool on the Bonaparte River, east off Highway 97 at the

CACHE CREEK ADVERTISERS

Bonaparte Motel	Ph. (888) 922-1333
Brookside Campsite	Ph. (250) 457-6633
Cariboo Jade Shoppe	Ph. (250) 457-9566
Desert Motel	Ph. (800) 663-0212
Tumbleweed Motel	Ph. (800) 667-1501
Wander Inn Restaurant	Ph. (250) 457-6511

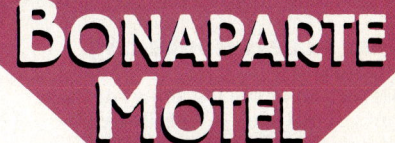

BONAPARTE MOTEL
CACHE CREEK

Queen Size Beds • Clean & Quiet
- All Rooms have Air Conditioners & Refrigerators
- Kitchenettes
- Remote Control 45 Channel Cable TV
- DD Phone/Fax & Auto Wake-Up Service
- Outdoor Pool Located in Central Courtyard
- Year-Round Indoor Sauna & Whirlpool
- Morning Coffee Service
- Near Restaurants and Golf Course

Halfway Point Between Vancouver & Prince George

TOLL FREE 1-888-922-1333

 Phone (250)457-9693
Fax (250)457-9697

LOCATED ON HIGHWAY 97 NORTH

TUMBLEWEED MOTEL
Cache Creek, B.C.

- Deluxe Rooms
- Reasonable Rates
- Air Conditioned
- Clean & Quiet
- Combination Bath
- Direct Dial Phones
- Remote Control TV
- 25 Channel Cable
- Non Smoking Units Available

On Hwy#1 at East Entrance to Cache Creek

For Reservations Call Toll Free 1-800-667-1501 or (250)457-6522

north edge of town. Private campground located east of Cache Creek on Trans-Canada Highway 1 (across from the golf course). ▲

Cariboo Jade Shoppe offers free stone-cutting demonstrations in summer. On display out front is a 2,850-lb. jade boulder.

The settlement grew up around the confluence of the creek and the Bonaparte River. The Hudson's Bay Co. opened a store here, and Cache Creek became a major supply point on the Cariboo Wagon Road. Today, hay and cattle ranching, ginseng farming, mining, logging and tourism support the community. Area soils are dry but fertile. Residents claim that with irrigation nearly anything can be grown here.

From the junction, Highway 97 leads north 277 miles/445.8 km to Prince George. Kamloops is 52 miles/84 km east via Trans-Canada Highway 1. Traveling north from Cache Creek the highway generally follows the historic route to the Cariboo goldfields.

Brookside Campsite. 1 km east of Cache Creek on Highway 1, full (30 amp) and partial hookups, pull-throughs, tent sites, super-clean heated wash and laundry rooms, free showers, sani-stations, store, playground, heated pool, golf course adjacent, pets on leash, pay phones. VISA, MasterCard. Cancellation policy 2 days. Box 737, Cache Creek, BC V0K 1H0. Phone/fax: (250) 457-6633. Email brooksidecampsite@hotmail.com; web site brooksidecampsite.com. [ADVERTISEMENT] ♿ ▲

West Access Route Log
(continued)
This section of the log shows distance from Cache Creek (CC) followed by distance from Prince George (PG).

**BC HIGHWAY 97 NORTH
CARIBOO HIGHWAY**

C 0 PG 277 (445.8 km) **Junction** of Trans-Canada Highway 1 and Highway 97 at Cache Creek. Southbound travelers follow Trans-Canada Highway 1 West. Northbound travelers follow Highway 97 North.

CC 1.1 (1.9 km) **PG 275.9** (443.9 km) Small southbound turnout with information signs.

CC 7 (11.3 km) **PG 270** (434.5 km) **Junction** with Highway 99 to Hat Creek Ranch (0.4 mile/0.7 km), Marble Canyon Provincial Park (18 miles/28 km), Lillooet (47 miles/75 km) and Seton Lake (53 miles/86 miles); descriptions follow.

Historic Hat Creek Ranch, just west on Highway 99, is a restored Cariboo Trail roadhouse and farm with reconstructed barn, working blacksmith shop, wagon and trail rides and tours. RV sites and tent rentals available. ▲

Historic Hat Creek Ranch. Take a break and come experience Historic Hat Creek Ranch. Interpretive tours of the 1860s Hat Creek Roadhouse and Shuswap Native Village will have you daydreaming. Trail rides and stagecoach adventures take you along the Cariboo Wagon Road and to the Shuswap Native Village. View our antique farm machinery. We welcome you in the air-conditioned information center, dining and gift shop area. For the outdoor enthusiast we offer camping, RV sites and tent rentals. Bus tours and caravans are always welcome. Open daily from 9 A.M. to 6 P.M., mid-May to September 30. For information call (250) 457-9722, toll free 1-800-782-0922. Email HHCR@goldtrail.com or visit us at www.hatcreekranch.com. [ADVERTISEMENT] ▲

Marble Canyon Provincial Park, about 20 minutes west on Highway 99, has 34 campsites, picnicking, swimming and hiking trails. ▲

LILLOOET (pop. 2,984), less than an hour's drive west from here, boasts high summer temperatures, rockhounding, gold panning and 15 historic points of interest from the gold rush days. **Seton Lake Reservoir Recreation Area**, 4 miles/6.4 km west of Lillooet, is a B.C. Hydro picnic site overlooking this beautiful jade-green lake.

Highway 99 between Lillooet and Pemberton was a logging road that was upgraded and paved and—along with what was formerly Highway 12 to Lilloett—designated the **"Sea to Sky Highway."** Completion of this route made it possible to drive to the Cariboo from Vancouver (209 miles/ 337 km from here) via Whistler (133 miles/215 km from here). This is a scenic route with stunning mountain scenery. But a note of caution: From west of Lilloett to Pemberton, motorists should be prepared for very long, very steep (to 15 percent) grades with hairpin turns. The section of road between Lilloett and Pemberton is not recommended for large RVs or trailers.

CC 10 (16 km) **PG 267** (430 km) Gravel turnout with plaque about the BX stagecoaches that once served Barkerville. Formally known as the BC Express Company, the BX served the Cariboo for 50 years.

CC 13.6 (21.9 km) **PG 263.4** (423.9 km) Paved road leads east to Loon Lake, rainbow fishing, boat launch. Camping at **Loon Lake Provincial Park** (16 miles/26 km); 14 sites, water, pit toilets, firewood. ⊶▲

CC 16.6 (26.7 km) **PG 260.4** (419.1 km) Carguile rest area.

CC 19.1 (30.8 km) **PG 257.9** (415 km) Large turnout beside small lake.

CC 19.9 (32 km) **PG 257.1** (413.8 km) **Willow Springs RV Park & Campground**. Easy on and off highway access. Relaxing and peaceful lakeshore RV parking. Pull-throughs. Hookups with 30- and 50-amp services. Clean and tested mountain water. Sani-station. Clean washrooms, Free showers. Laundry facilities. Firepits. Good trout fishing. Free boats and canoes. Lake swimming. Country Store and Bakery. Phone (250) 459-2744. Owners/operators David and Dianne Lee. Email daveanddi@goldtrail.com. Web www.willowspringsrvpark.com. [ADVERTISEMENT] ▲

CC 24.5 (39.4 km) **PG 252.5** (406.3 km) **Clinton Pines Campground.** Newer 20-acre facility. Easy access. Quiet and very relaxing. Large shady sites, pull-throughs. Full and partial hookups. Free hot showers. Immaculate washrooms. Laundromat. Walking distance to town. Open year-round. Beautiful scenery, nature trails, horseshoes. Internet access. Pets welcome. Credit cards/Interac accepted. Owner operated. Located south end of Clinton on east side of Highway 97. Phone (250) 459-0030; email clinton pines@goldcountry.bc.ca. [ADVERTISEMENT] ▲

CC 25 (40.2 km) **PG 252** (405.5 km) **Junction** with Pavilion Mountain Road west to Pavilion via Kelly Lake. Camping at **Downing Provincial Park** (11 miles/18 km); 25 sites, swimming, fishing. ⊶▲

CC 25.5 (41 km) **PG 251.5** (404.7 km) **CLINTON** (pop. 729, area 4,000; elev. 2,911 feet/887m). All visitor facilities are available, including 3 motels, campgrounds, gas stations, 24-hour towing and stores. Originally

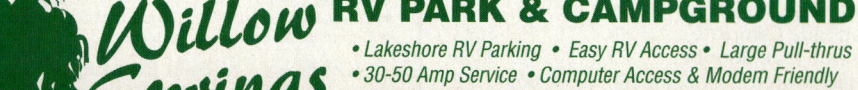

Big Bar rest area at Milepost CC 31. (© Blake Hanna, staff)

the site of 47 Mile Roadhouse, a gold-rush settlement on the Cariboo Wagon Road from Lillooet, today Clinton is called the "guest ranch capital of British Columbia." The museum, housed in a building of local, handmade red brick that once served as a courthouse, has fine displays of pioneer tools and items from the gold rush days, and a scale model of the Clinton Hotel. Clinton pioneer cemetery just north of town. Clinton boasts the oldest continuously held event in the province, the Clinton Ball (in May the weekend following Victoria Day), an annual event since 1868.

Clinton has its own sign forest. Visitors may sign a wooden slab (donated by the local sawmill) and add it to the sign forest.

CC 26 (41.9 km) **PG 250.9** (403.8 km) Small southbound turnout with information signs.

CC 31 (49.9 km) **PG 246** (395.9 km) Dirt and gravel road leads 21 miles/34 km west to **Big Bar Lake Provincial Park**; 33 campsites, water, pit toilets, firewood, swimming, fishing and boat launch.

Big Bar rest area to east just north of turnoff; large double-ended parking area, toilets, tables, litter barrels, good views from Clinton Lookout.

CC 35 (56.3 km) **PG 242** (389.5 km) Loop road leads east 3 miles/5 km to **Painted Chasm Provincial Park**; geological site, picnic area, hiking trails, great autumn colors. The geological site is a 1-mile/1.6-km-long bedrock box canyon that was cut by glacial meltwaters.

CC 45 (72.4 km) **PG 232** (373.4 km) 70 MILE HOUSE (unincorporated), originally a stage stop on the Cariboo Gold Rush Trail named for its distance from Lillooet (Mile 0). Motel and restaurant, general store, liquor store, post office, gas station and bus depot. Gymkana events held throughout the summer. Cariboo Country Night celebration on the second Saturdeay in September.

Junction with Bonaparte Road and access to Green Lake and Watch Lake. **Green Lake Provincial Park**, 7.5 miles/12 km east, has 121 campsites, water, toilets, firewood, dump station, good swimming and a boat launch. Rainbow and kokanee fishing at Green Lake. Paved road leads north to **Watch Lake**, east to **Bonaparte Lake**, and northeast to Lone Butte and Highway 24 return to Highway 97 at **Milepost CC 66**. The area offers a variety of lodging, dining, camping and shopping.

CC 51.8 (83.4 km) **PG 225.2** (362.4 km) **Meadow Springs Ranch.** Working ranch with comfortable 1-bedroom cabins. Family bunkhouse with kitchen and full bath. Meals available. Horseback riding, beginner to advanced. Ranch activities. RV sites, no hookups. Shower, outhouse. Secluded, wooded, natural meadows and springs. On-site pioneer museum. Group rates available. Pets. VISA/MasterCard; phone (250) 456-2425; fax (250) 456-2429; email msprings@bcinternet.net; www.meadowsprings.com. [ADVERTISEMENT]

CC 58.8 (94.7 km) **PG 218.2** (351.1 km) **83 MILE HOUSE**; site of the Historic 83 Mile Farm House Equipment Museum.

Turnoff for Green Lake, 7 miles/11 km east (see description at **Milepost CC 45**).

CC 60 (96 km) **PG 217** (347.2 km) Parking and picnic tables east side of highway at access to B.C. Forest Service **Lookout Tower**. Built in 1923 as part of a system to detect forest fires, the tower is open to visitors daily in summer from 8 A.M. to 5 P.M. Short interpretive hike to forestry tower atop Mount Begbie (elev. 4,186 feet/1,276m). Panoramic views of the South Cariboo.

CC 66 (106.2 km) **PG 211** (339.6 km) Junction with Highway 24 East to Little Fort (60 miles/97 km) on Yellowhead Highway 5. Highway 24, "the Fishing Highway," provides access to numerous resorts and camping facilities on area fishing lakes such as Fawn, Sheridan, Bridge, Deka, Hathaway, Sulphurous and Lac des Roches. **Bridge Lake Provincial Park**, 31 miles/50 km east, has 20 campsites.

100 Mile House

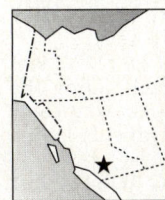

CC 72 (115.9 km) **PG 205** (329.9 km) **Population**: 2,000. **Elevation**: 3,050 feet/930m. **Emergency Services: Police**, phone (250) 395-2456. **Ambulance**, phone (250) 395-3288. **Hospital**, phone (250) 395-7600. **Fire**, phone (250) 395-2345.

Visitor Information: South Cariboo Visitor Info Centre located in the log cabin by 100 Mile House Marsh (a bird sanctuary at the centre of town); phone (250) 395-5353, fax 395-4085. Look for the 39-foot-/12-m-long skis! Or write Box 340, 100 Mile House, BC, V0K 2E0; phone (250) 395-5353 or toll free 1-877-511-5353; email visitors@100milehouse.com.

This bustling community is the service centre for the South Cariboo, an area stretching north from Clinton to 140 Mile House; west to the Fraser River; and east to Lac des Roches. 100 Mile House was once a stop for fur traders and later a post house on the Cariboo Wagon Road to the goldfields. In 1930, the Marquess of Exeter established the 15,000-acre Bridge Creek Ranch here. Today, 100 Mile House is the site of 2 lumber mills, an Oriented Strand Board (OSB) plant, and an extensive log home industry.

Visitor services include restaurants, motels, a campground, gas stations with repair service, stores, a post office, 2 golf courses, a theater, a government liquor store, 3 supermarkets, banks and ATMs. Shopping malls and the downtown area are located 1 block east of Highway 97.

Centennial Park in town has picnic sites, an elaborate playground for children, and a scenic walking trail to Bridge Creek Falls (10-minute hike).

From 100 Mile House, take Horse Lake Road east for **Horse Lake** (kokanee) and other fishing lakes of the high plateau.

South Cariboo Visitor Info Centre. See display ad this section.

West Access Route Log
(continued)

BC HIGHWAY 97 NORTH
CARIBOO HIGHWAY

CC 74 (119 km) **PG 203** (326.7 km) Junction with road east to **Ruth**, **Canim** and **Mahood** lakes; numerous lakeside fishing and camping resorts. **Canim Beach Provincial Park**, 27 miles/43 km, has 16 campsites, water, pit toilets, swimming. Also access to Mahood Lake Provincial Park and hiking trail to Deception Falls.

CC 78.2 (125.8 km) **PG 198.8** (319.9 km) **108 Mile Ranch**, once a cattle ranch, became a recreational community in the 1970s, and now has some 600 homes. Resort with lodging, camping, restaurant, golf and trail rides.

108 Resort. 1 mile off highway. Air-conditioned units with lake views. Some kitchenettes. Limited number of pet rooms. Cable TV, 15 RV/tenting sites (4 with power). Golf resort, tennis, biking, canoeing, trail rides. Pro shop. Heated pool, hot tub and saunas. Restaurant and lounge. Toll-free reservations 1-800-667-5233. Fax (250) 791-6537. Email 108rst@bcinternet.net. www.108resort.com. [ADVERTISEMENT]

CC 80.5 (129.5 km) **PG 196.5** (316.2 km) Rest area to west beside 108 Mile Lake; restrooms, picnic tables, walking and biking trails around lake. The rest area is adjacent the **108 Heritage Site**, which has some of the original log buildings from the old 108 Mile Ranch, as well as structures relocated from 105 Mile. Guided tours; open May to

WEST ACCESS ROUTE

early September.

CC 85 (136.8 km) **PG 192** (309 km) **Lac La Hache KOA.** Located on 60 acres of rolling ranchland 3 miles south of Lac La Hache on Highway 97. Heated swimming pool, free showers, store, laundromat, games room. Extra-long shady pull-throughs; shaded grassy tent sites; camping cabin. Full hookup facilities, sani-dump, phone. Pets welcome. VISA, MasterCard. (250) 396-4181. Box 68, Lac La Hache, BC V0K 1T0. [ADVERTISEMENT] ▲

CC 88 (141.6 km) **PG 189** (304.2 km) **LAC LA HACHE** (pop. 400; elev. 2,749 feet/838m), also known as the "longest town in the Cariboo" as the community stretches along some 11 miles of Highway 97. Visitor services include motels, gas station, general store (with liquor store agency), pub, restaurants, lakeside resorts and a museum.

The community holds a fishing derby in July and a winter carnival in mid-February. Lac La Hache is French for "Lake of the Ax." There are many stories of how the lake got its name, but local historian Molly Forbes says it was named by a French–Canadian *coureur de bois* (voyageur) "because of a small ax he found on its shores."

Lac La Hache Motel. See display ad this section. ▲

Lac La Hache, lake char, rainbow and kokanee; good fishing summer and winter (great ice fishing).

CC 92 (148.1 km) **PG 185** (297.7 km) **Fir Crest Resort.** Open all year. One of the most beautifully located RV parks on Highway 97. Parklike setting, very picturesque, on 1,700 feet of lakeshore, absolutely quiet, no highway noise! Lakeview/front from all 60 full hookups and pull-throughs (large and long units very welcome—up to 50-amp). Immaculate washrooms with laundry. Sandy beaches for good swimming and excellent fishing. Store, groceries, souvenirs, sani-dump, marina with boat rentals, soft adventure programs. 6 hours from the American border. 5 km north of the little town of Lac La Hache. Phone (250) 396-7337. Email: fircrestresort@bcinternet.net. Web page: www.fircrestresort.com. See display ad this section. [ADVERTISEMENT] ◆▲

CC 93.4 (150.3 km) **PG 183.6** (295.4 km) **Kokanee Bay Motel and Campground.** Relaxation at its finest right on the lakeshore. Fish for kokanee and char or take a refreshing dip. We have a modern, comfortable motel, cabins. Full trailer hookups, grassy tenting area, hot showers, laundromat. Aquabike, boat and canoe rentals. Fishing tackle and ice. Phone (250) 396-7345. Fax (250) 396-4990. [ADVERTISEMENT] ▲

CC 93.5 (150.5 km) **PG 183.5** (295.3 km) **Cariboo Log Guest House.** New, cozy log home in beautiful, quiet, peaceful lake setting. All rooms have private bath and lake view and sun deck. Full European breakfast included. Alpine-style dining room. Swiss-style dinner (advance dinner reservations required). Canadian and European restaurants nearby. Horseback riding, hiking, fishing, public beach. Championship golf course

Quesnelle Forks is a gold rush ghost town near Likely.
(© Blake Hanna, staff)

nearby. Single $65–$70; twin $75–$80. Phone (250) 396-4747; fax (250) 396-7400. Email ernst@cariboguesthouse.com; web site www.cariboguesthouse.com. [ADVERTISEMENT]

CC 96 (154.5 km) **PG 181** (291.3 km) **Crystal Springs (Historical) Resort Ltd.** Visit the Cariboo's best. We honour Good Sam, AAA and are a Good Neighbor Park. Ask about our senior rates. 8 miles north of Lac La Hache. Across from provincial park., Children free. Parklike setting. Last lakeshore camping northbound for 100 km. Showers, flush toilets, laundromat, full (20- and 30-amp pull-throughs) and partial hookups. Dry camping on lakefront. Tenting, boat rentals. Internet hookup. Chalets. Groceries, tackle, camping supplies, handicrafts. Playground, picnic shelter. Pets on leash. Fishing, public beach and boat launch available. Your hosts, Doug and Lorraine Whitesell. Phone (250) 396-4497. [ADVERTISEMENT] ♿▲

CC 96 (154.5 km) **PG 181** (291.3 km) **Lac La Hache Provincial Park** on east side of the highway with 83 campsites, water, flush and pit toilets, firewood, dump station and hiking trails; open May 15–Sept. 30. Lakeshore picnic area, boat launch, swimming and fishing on west side of highway; open May 15 to mid-October. ◆▲

CC 97 (156.1 km) **PG 180** (289.7 km) San Jose River parallels highway to west. Canadian artist A.Y. Jackson painted in this valley.

CC 102.4 (164.8 km) **PG 174.6** (280.9 km) Large turnout with litter barrels.

CC 104.4 (168 km) **PG 172.6** (277.7 km) Stop of interest sign commemorating the miners, traders and adventurers who came this way to the Cariboo goldfields in the 1860s.

CC 116.6 (187.6 km) **PG 160.4** (258.1 km) 148 Mile Ducks Unlimited conservation area. This is an important waterfowl breeding area in Canada and offers good bird watching for bald eagles, osprey, great horned owls, American kestrels and pileated woodpeckers.

CC 118.5 (190.7 km) **PG 158.5** (255.1 km) **150 MILE HOUSE**, so named because it was 150 miles from Lillooet on the old Cariboo Wagon Road. The post office, which serves about 1,200 people in the area, was established in 1871. Hotel, restaurant, pub, gas station with repair service and a store open daily. Hunting and fishing licenses available at the store.

CC 119.1 (191.7 km) **PG 157.9** (254.1 km) **Junction** with road to Quesnel and Horsefly lakes and to communities of Horsefly (35 miles/56 km) and to **LIKELY** (50 miles/80 km). **Quesnelle Forks**, a gold rush heritage site, is located near Likely. Travelers may also continue north from Likely to Barkerville, a historic gold rush park, via Matthew Valley Road (summer travel only). Main access to Barkerville is via Highway 26 from Quesnel (see log this section).

Cedar Point Provincial Park on Quesnel Lake is 3.7 miles/6 km from Likely; 20 campsites, boat launch, swimming, fishing and outdoor mining museum. **Horsefly Lake Provincial Park** (40 miles/65 km) has 22 campsites. Fishing for rainbow and lake trout. ◆▲

Likely. Drive the original 1859 BC Gold Rush Trail. Relax on Quesnel Lake, deepest fjord lake in North America. Fish trophy "Gerrard strain" rainbow trout. Explore hundreds of miles of pristine shoreline. Enjoy Quesnelle Forks ghost town; marvel at the 400-foot-deep Bullion Pit and Cedar Point Provincial Park gold rush mining equipment. Travel scenic (summer only) Matthew Valley Road to or from Barkerville. Likely Information, Box 29, Likely, BC V0L 1N0. Phone/fax (250) 790-2398. www.likely-bc.ca. Email: chamber@likely-bc.ca. [ADVERTISEMENT]

CC 122.5 (197.2 km) **PG 154.4** (248.6 km) Private campground, fuel and convenience store. ▲

CC 124.1 (199.8 km) **PG 152.8** (246 km) Large northbound turnout with litter barrels and information sign about Rick Hanson, who traveled 40,000 kms by wheelchair.

CC 124.8 (200.9 km) **PG 152.1** (244.9 km) Southbound turnout with litter barrel.

CC 128 (206 km) **PG 149** (239.8 km) **Junction** with BC Highway 20, the Chilcotin Highway, to Bella Coola.

Junction with BC Highway 20, which leads 279 miles/450 km west to Bella Coola. See "Chilcotin Highway" on pages 73-75 for log.

(Continues on page 76)

Lac La Hache MOTEL
"Relax on the Lake"
P.O. Box 152, Lac La Hache, B.C. V0K 1T0

NEXT TO RESTAURANTS & AMENITIES
Each room has a view and private access to the lake.
◆ Queen & King Beds ◆ Fridges ◆ Cable TV w/Movie Channel
◆ Kitchenette ◆ Soft Water ◆ BBQ ◆ Garden Chairs
RESERVATIONS 1-877-396-4423

Fir Crest Resort
RV-Park, Camping, Cabins
Lac La Hache - BC
Welcome to our panoramic lakeside resort. If you come for 1 night or for a vacation, relaxation is guaranteed. Enjoy our splendid location and our many offers...
By the way - no problems with mosquitoes!!!
Please read our log-ad for more details
Show this ad for 10% discount

Chilcotin Highway

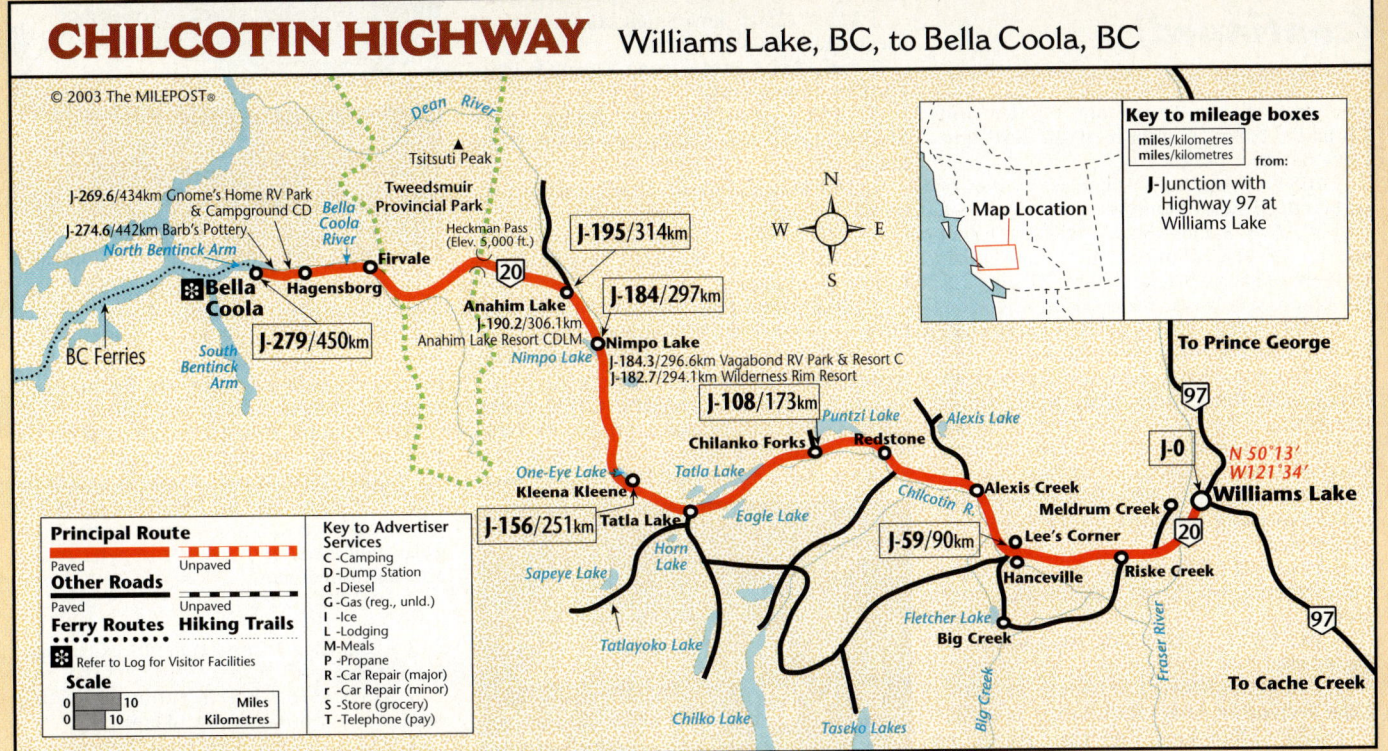

CHILCOTIN HIGHWAY
Williams Lake, BC, to Bella Coola, BC

WEST ACCESS ROUTE • Chilcotin Highway

The scenic Chilcotin Highway (BC Highway 20) leads 279.3 miles/449.5 km west from Williams Lake to Bella Coola. Food, gas and lodging are available along the way and in Bella Coola.

Called "Freedom Road" by residents, the highway was bulldozed across the mountains in the 1950s by local volunteers tired of waiting for the government to build a road.

Once a test of endurance, much of today's road is mostly paved and in good condition. There is still "The Hill," a narrow, 11.2-mile/18-km, gravel switchback descent from the top of Heckman Pass (elev. 5,000 feet/1,524m) into the Bella Coola Valley. Vehicles towing fifth wheels or travel trailers test your brakes before attempting The Hill.

The folks at Gnome's Home RV Park shared with us an RVers account of their first-time driving The Hill in a 1-ton Dodge 5-speed with a 3,000-plus lb. camper. These travelers used second gear going up the hill, and second and third gears going down. While they found The Hill less challenging than they had expected, they recognize that mountain driving is viewed quite differently by different drivers. Motorists should be aware that grades on The Hill reach 18 percent and there is one extremely narrow 1.1-mile section, with a bit of vertical overhang, that is essentially 1-lane. (NOTE: Major highway work was carried out on The Hill late last year, so motorists may expect some improved road in 2003.)

There are turnouts on The Hill and traffic is quite light. You'll pass everything from an occasional biker to 18-wheelers and the local bus that travels this route twice-weekly between Williams Lake and Bella Coola.

Distance from junction (J) with Highway 97 at Williams Lake is shown.

J 0 Junction with Highway 97 **Milepost** CC 128 at Williams Lake.

J 1.5 (2.5 km) Road south to Alkali Lake, and Dog Creek. Road closure sign nearby warns if Heckman Pass is closed.

Westbound, Highway 20 climbs to plateau, then drops down a 5 percent grade to the Fraser River.

J 12.3 (19.8 km) Turnout.

J 15 (24 km) Viewpoint at east end of Sheep Creek bridge over Fraser River. *Begin 6 percent grade westbound.*

J 17.4 (28 km) Small turnout with map of Chilcotin wildlife viewing areas and information on the Chilcotin grasslands.

J 20.3 (32.7 km) Turnout with toilets and litter barrels. Begin steep downgrade eastbound; watch for logging trucks.

To the west is the great Fraser Plateau, with the snowcapped peaks of the Coast Range visible on the horizon. The country west of the Fraser is known as the Chilcotin, taking its name from the river that cuts through the plateau. The country is chiefly range land for cattle, though forestry is also important.

J 21.5 (34.7 km) Canadian Coast Guard Service Loran-C tower; phone (250) 659-5611 for tour information.

J 27.5 (44.4 km) Gravel road loops south and rejoins Highway 20 at Lee's Corner (50-mile/80-km drive). Follow this winding side road south 10 miles/16 km to spectacular **Farwell Canyon bridge** on the Chilcotin River.

J 28.7 (46.3 km) **Riske Creek**; food, general store, phone and camping. ▲

J 29.4 (47.3 km) Stack Valley Road to **Historic Chilcotin Lodge**, now a bed and breakfast. Camping. ▲

J 30.4 (48.9 km) Forest Service recreation area at Becher Dam; fishing for small rainbow, picnic tables.

J 35.6 (57.4 km) Riske Creek rodeo grounds. Stampede held in mid-June.

J 42.2 (68 km) Gravel road north to Forest Service recreation area on Raven and Palmer lakes; fishing; boat launch.

J 50.9 (81.9 km) **Hanceville Recreation Area** to south; rest area with toilet, litter barrel and historic marker about Norman Lee and ill-fated Yukon cattle drive of 1898. *Begin 9 percent downgrade westbound.*

J 56 (90.1) **Lee's Corner**, on site of Norman Lee's ranch house. Hanceville post office, gas, groceries and food in old-fashioned general store.

Turnoff south for old settlement of Hanceville, named for Tom Hance, the original settler. Gravel road continues south across Chilcotin River (a favorite with river rafters) to Fletcher Lake Forest Service Recreation Area; canoeing and fishing. Road loops back to the highway at Milepost J 27.5.

J 62.5 (100.6 km) Steepled church and houses of Anaham Village (TL'etinqox), on the largest of 6 Indian reserves in the Chilcotin. *NOTE: Speed limit 45 mph/70 kmph through reserve.*

J 69.5 (112 km) Turnout to north with information sign.

J 69.8 (112.3 km) **ALEXIS CREEK** (area pop. 1,200); gas, groceries, restaurant, motel, hotel, stores, RCMP and outpost hospital.

J 72.8 (117.3 km) *Steep downgrade westbound.* View of Chilcotin River and volcanic cliffs of Battle Mountain.

J 74.8 (120.5 km) **Bull Canyon Provincial Recreation Area**; picnic tables, outhouses, 20 campsites in aspen forest beside Chilcotin River. Kayaking, rafting and fishing are popular. ▲

J 90.2 (145.2 km) Chilcotin River bridge; Westbound, the Chilanko River is to the south of the highway.

J 103.3 (166.3 km) Native community of **Redstone**; general store, gas and diesel. Indi-

www.themilepost.com

Chilcotin Highway (continued)

ans west of the Fraser are Carrier and Chilcotin tribes, members of the northern Dene nation.

J 105 (169 km) Stunning views to west of snowcapped Coast Mountains.

J 107.6 (173.3 km) Small garage with fuel and repairs at **Chilanko Forks**. Road north to Puntzi Lake (4.5 miles/7 km); fishing for rainbow and kokanee, resorts, camping.

J 109 (175.5 km) Puntzi airport road leads to Chilanko Marsh Wildlife Area.

J 113.4 (182.5 km) Gravel road south to **Pyper Lake Recreation Area**; picnic tables and fishing.

J 115.7 (186.3 km) Gravel turnout with view of the long, deep valley of Tatla Lake.

J 130.5 (210 km) Rest area with picnic tables **Pollywog Marsh**, a wetlands conservation area.

J 131.6 (211.9 km) Road north to **Tatla Lake Recreation Area**; fishing and boat launch.

J 131.8 (212.2 km) Side road south to Eagle Lake.

J 133.1 (214.3 km) Road south to **Pinto Lake Recreation Area**; picnic tables, boating.

J 137 (220.6 km) Side road south to **Tatlayoko Lake** (21.5 miles/35 km), jumping-off point for expeditions to **Mount Waddington** (elev. 13,100 feet/3,994m), highest peak in the province, also known as Mystery Mountain.

J 137.9 (222 km) **Tatla Lake**; gas, store, restaurant, motel, post office and clinic.

J 146.1 (235.2 km) Bridge across Klinaklini River.

J 148.4 (238.9 km) Large turnout to north.

J 152.5 (245.5 km) Road north to **One Eye Lake Recreation Area**; fishing and boating.

J 155.7 (250.7 km) Small community of **Kleena Kleene**; no services.

J 156 (251.1 km) Kleena Kleene bridge. Turnout at west end.

J 162.5 (261.5 km) Bridge over McClinchie Creek, a tributary of the Dean River. *CAUTION: Cattle at large.*

J 163.8 (263.7 km) Small turnout to south.

J 177.7 (286.1 km) Road south to Charlotte Lake (12 miles/20 km); rainbow fishing and lodging.

J 180.8 (291.1 km) Turnout to north with information sign about Nimpo Lake.

J 182.7 (294.1 km) **Wilderness Rim Resort**. See display ad this section.

J 184.3 (296.6 km) **NIMPO LAKE**; motel, general store, gas, propane, phone, RV park, restaurant, fishing resorts. The 7.5-mile-/12-km-long lake contains rainbow trout.

Vagabond RV Park & Resort. See display ad this section.

Westbound, Highway 20 follows the upper reaches of the Dean River, famous for its fishing.

J 187.4 (301.6 km) Dean River bridge. Forest Service recreation site turnout; canoeing and fishing.

J 190.2 (306.1 km) **Anahim Lake Resort**. See display ad this section.

J 195.2 (314.2 km) ANAHIM LAKE, largest community in the Chilcotin. Full tourist services; daily 1-hour flights to/from Vancouver. Anahim Lake is a centre for guided wilderness hiking and fishing trips. Annual stampede held in mid-July.

The Anahim area is a major stop on the Pacific Interior Flyway. Good bird watching on **Eagle's Nest Marsh Trail** on southwest side of Anahim Lake for American white pelicans, eagles and osprey, great horned and great grey owls, goshawks, trumpeter swans, and sandhill cranes.

J 196 (315.5 km) *Pavement ends, gravel begins, westbound.*

J 212.5 (342.1 km) Louie Creek; turnout at west end.

J 215.1 (346.2 km) Turnout with information sign on the West Chilcotin.

J 217.1 (349.5 km) East entrance to **Tweedsmuir Provincial Park**, the largest park in British Columbia, which stretches along Highway 20 for the next 34 miles/54 km westbound. View to north of Rainbow Mountains.

J 221 (355.7 km) Trailhead and picnic site with outhouse and information sign.

J 221.5 (356.4 km) Summit of **Heckman Pass** (elev. 5,000 feet/1,524m). The pass is kept open year-round.

J 221.9 (357.1 km) Brake check area and road closure gate. *CAUTION: Highway begins steep 2-part descent westbound; 18 percent grade, narrow road, few guardrails, rock slides, hairpin bends. Use low gear. Use turnouts*

J 225.2 (362.4 km) Bridge over Young Creek; turnout at east end.

J 232.7 (374.5 km) *Begin steep climb eastbound to Heckman Pass.*

J 233.3 (375.5 km) Hunden Falls/Turner Lakes trailhead.

J 233.6 (376 km) Turnout with litter barrels and information signs.

J 234.1 (376.8 km) **Atnarko River Campground**; 28 campsites, sani-station, camping fee, fishing.

J 234.5 (377.4 km) Tweedsmuir Provin-

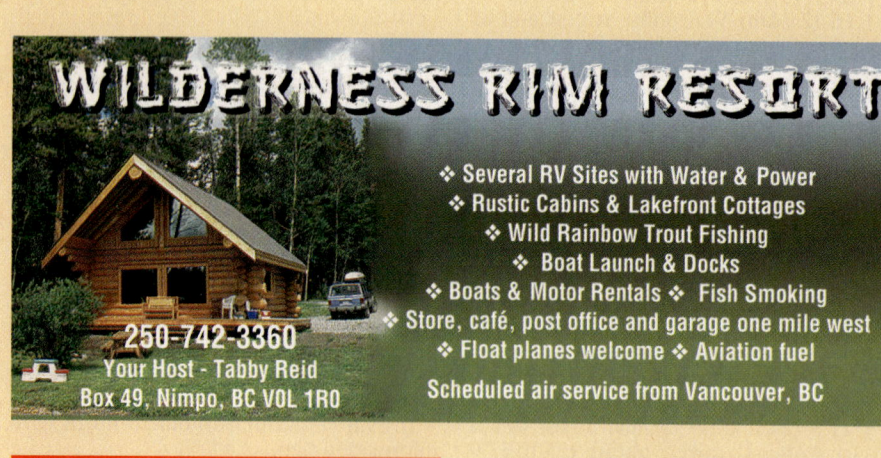

VAGABOND RV PARK & RESORT
Nimpo Lake, BC
Easy RV Access - Pull Thrus - Full Hookups
Bathrooms - Showers - Laundry
30 Amp Service - Sani-Station
Lake view cabins - Lake Fishing - Boat Rental
Dock - Adjacent to Public Boat Launch
250-742-3347

cial Park headquarters. Dump station.

J 236.5 (380.6 km) **Tweedsmuir Trailhead** on Mosher Creek.

J 241.1 (388.1 km) **Big Rock Picnic Area** and Kettle Pond trailhead (1-hour loop).

J 243.3 (391.6 km) **Tweedsmuir Lodge**.

J 243.8 (392.4 km) **Fisheries Pool Campground**; 14 campsites, fee, boat launch and picnic area beside Atnarko River. Salmon spawning channels and viewing pool.

J 246.8 (397.2 km) Boat launch.

J 247 (397.6 km) Horsetail Falls Creek.

J 249.7 (402 km) Heritage MacKenzie/Grease trailhead and picnic area; water, litter barrels. Valley View loop trail (1 to 1-1/2 hours) along a portion of the Grease Trail leads to a good viewpoint of the river and Stupendous Mountain (elev. 8,800 feet/2,700 m).

J 249.9 (402.2 km) Burnt Bridge. West boundary of Tweedsmuir Provincial Park.

J 254.4 (409.4 km) Settlement of **Firvale**.

J 259.1 (417 km) Bridge across Bella Coola River.

J 268.4 (432 km) **HAGENSBORG** (pop. 600), food, gas, lodging. Settled in 1894 by Norwegians from Minnesota, who found the country similar to the fjords of their home land. Notable here are the Augsburg Church and restored Sons of Norway heritage house.

J 269.6 (434 km) **Gnome's Home RV Park & Campground**. See display ad this section.

J 271.2 (436.5 km) Turnoff to Bella Coola airport.

J 272.4 (438 km) Snootli Creek Fish Hatchery.

J 274.6 (442 km) **Barb's Pottery**. Housed in a historic log cabin and surrounded by beautiful gardens. The studio and shop feature wheel-thrown stoneware, Raku and porcelain pottery. Choose from a fine collection of selected giftware created by British Columbia artists. Stone carvings, selected wood crafts, hand-blown glass, weavings, paintings and more. Phone (250) 799-5380.
[ADVERTISEMENT]

J 276.2 (444.5 km) Road south up Thorsen Creek leads to a large and important Indian petroglyph site with more than 100 glyphs. Inquire locally for directions.

J 277 (446 km) Acwsalcta, School of the Nuxalk Nation, constructed of cedar with Indian graphic designs and carvings; well worth a stop.

Bella Coola

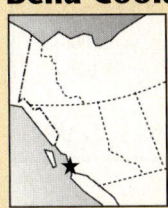

J 279.3 (449.5 km) Entering Bella Coola via Highway 20. Paved road continues around the tidewater flats at the head of the inlet for 1.2 miles/2 km to the fishing harbor and B.C. Ferries dock.

Transportation: B.C. Ferries vessels link Bella Coola and other coastal communities with Port Hardy on the north tip of Vancouver Island. The ferries carry autos, so Highway 20 travelers have the option of taking the ferry rather than driving back out. See Discovery Coast route in B.C. FERRIES

BELLA COOLA ADVERTISERS	
Bella Coola Valley Inn	Ph. (250) 799-5316
B.C. Ferries	Ph. (888) 223-3779
Kopas Store	Ph. (250) 799-5553

SCHEDULES section. Or visit their web site at www.bcferries.com.

The Hudson's Bay Co. established a trading post here in 1869 (the factor's house by the river still remains). The museum displays Hudson's Bay Co. relics and items brought by Norwegian settlers, as well as a good photo display of building "The Freedom Road."

Bella Coola has all visitor services. The town is home to the Bella Coola Band of the Nuxalk Nation; look for totems outside the band office and the traditional house replica next to the church. Alexander Mackenzie was the first white man to visit this settlement at the head of North Bentinck Arm in 1793. Attractions here include boat trips to Alexander Mackenzie Historic Park in Dean Channel, where the explorer left a record of his momentous journey: "From Canada by Land, 22nd July, 1793" inscribed on a rock.

The Bella Coola rodeo, held in July, take place at Walker Island regional park.

Kopas Store. Established in 1937, the store offers fine Native jewelry and artwork. Wide range of souvenirs and gift items. Fishing and hunting licences. Books, photo supplies sporting goods, maps and marine charts. Clothing and footwear. Open 6 days a week, 8:30 A.M. to 5:30 P.M. Extended hours Friday evenings. Sundays (June to September) 3 P.M. to 5 P.M. (250) 799-5553. [ADVERTISEMENT]

First Nations carver with mask in Bella Coola. (© Blake Hanna, staff)

YOU will COME BACK CHANGED.

Come to a land where porpoises, whales and eagles move in harmony with nature. Sail BC Ferries' Discovery Coast Passage between Port Hardy and Bella Coola, with fascinating stops at McLoughlin Bay, Shearwater, Klemtu and Ocean Falls.

From Bella Coola you can travel Highway 20 and make your exploration part of a circle tour including Vancouver Island and the Coast-Chilcotin-Cariboo.

THE DISCOVERY COAST PASSAGE

(250) 386-3431 Toll-free in B.C. 1-888-BC FERRY 1112 Fort Street, Victoria, B.C. Canada V8V 4V2
www.bcferries.com

 BC FERRIES

Bella Coola Valley Inn
• Canada Select 3 1/2 Stars
1-250-799-5316
• Located in Downtown Bella Coola
Call Toll Free 1-888-799-5316 • Web: www.bellacoolavalleyinn.com

(Continued from page 72)

Williams Lake

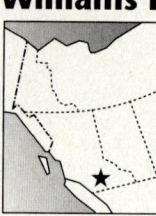

CC 128 (206 km) PG 149 (239.8 km) Located on the shore of Williams Lake, at the junction of Highways 97 and 20. **Population:** 12,000. **Elevation:** 1,922 feet/586m. **Emergency Services: Police,** phone (250) 392-6211. **Hospital,** phone (250) 392-4411. **Ambulance,** phone (250) 392-5402.

Visitor Information: Visitor Infocentre located on east side of highway just south of the junction of Highways 97 and 20, open year-round; phone (250) 392-5025, fax (250) 392-4214. Write the Williams Lake Chamber of Commerce, 1148 S. Broadway, Williams Lake, BC V2G 1A2; email wldcc@stardate.bc.ca. Or contact the Cariboo Chilcotin Coast Tourism Assoc., 118 A North 1st Ave., Williams Lake, BC V2G 1Y8; phone toll free (800) 663-5885.

Williams Lake is the name of both the town and body of water. (© Blake Hanna, staff)

WILLIAMS LAKE ADVERTISERS	
Jamboree Motel	Ph. (250) 398-8208
Super 8 Motel	Ph. (800) 800-8000
Tamlaght Stone Antiques and The Painted Door	Ph. (250) 392-1921
Williams Lake Visitor InfoCentre	Ph. (250) 392-5025

Williams Lake was named for Shuswap Indian Chief Willyum. The town grew rapidly with the advent of the Pacific Great Eastern Railway (now B.C. Railway) in 1919, to become a major cattle marketing and shipping centre for the Cariboo–Chilcotin.

Williams Lake has complete services, including hotels/motels, restaurants, an 18-hole golf course and par-3 golf course, a twin sheet arena and pool complex. Highway 97 northbound bypasses the business and shopping districts of downtown Williams Lake, which are situated to the west of the highway. Motels, gas stations and fast-food restaurants are located on frontage roads paralleling Highway 97 on the south side of town.

The famous **Williams Lake Stampede,** British Columbia's premier rodeo, is held here annually on the July 1 holiday. The 4-

SUPER 8 MOTEL — WILLIAMS LAKE

- Air Conditioned
- Smoking Rooms & Non-Smoking Rooms
- Remote Cable TV
- Superchannel
- Jacuzzis • Laundry
- Complimentary Breakfast

Toll Free Reservations
1-800-800-8000

1712 Broadway Ave. South
Williams Lake, B.C.
Phone (250)398-8884
Fax (250)398-8270

The Cariboo's ultimate destination for Antiques, Gifts & Home Decor

The Painted Door
635 Oliver Street,
Williams Lake, B.C.
(250) 392-1921

Tamlaght Stone Antiques
1-888-521-7792

CARIBOO CHILCOTIN COAST
SUPER, NATURAL BRITISH COLUMBIA

WILLIAMS LAKE ...A Great Place to Be!

WILLIAMS LAKE...offers many fine amenities, including golfing, fine dining, recreational parks, close proximity to many recreational lakes, scenic circle tours for cyclists and/or motorists alike.

TREAT...yourself at the Cariboo Memorial Complex, a recreational complex complete with a six-lane pool, fitness centre, hot tub, sauna and suntan beds for your enjoyment.

EXPERIENCE...the True West at the world famous Williams Lake Stampede. The 2003 Williams Lake Stampede will be held Friday, June 27 thru Monday, June 30. Come and enjoy the many events held throughout the fun packed weekend. For more information call 1-800-71-RODEO or 250-392-6585. Visit our web site at www.williamslakestampede.com or email office@williamslakestampede.com.

CAMP...at our fully serviced Stampede Campground and RV Park. The campground is located at 850 Mackenzie Ave. Pets are welcome and we are open from May thru October. For reservations call 250-398-6718.

EXPLORE...our Williams Lake River Valley through a scenic, 14km hike down a meandering, groomed trail to the shore of the Fraser River.

FOR MORE INFO...visit the Williams Lake Visitor Info Centre's friendly staff and they will assist you with your holiday needs.

For more info: 250-392-5025 OR
wldcc@stardate.bc.ca OR
www.bcadventure.com/wlcc/index.htm

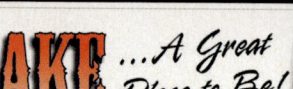
WILLIAMS LAKE STAMPEDE

CITY OF WILLIAMS LAKE

FOR TRAVEL INFORMATION CALL THE CARIBOO CHILCOTIN TOURISM ASSOCIATION
1-800-663-5885 OR VISIT **www.landwithoutlimits.com**

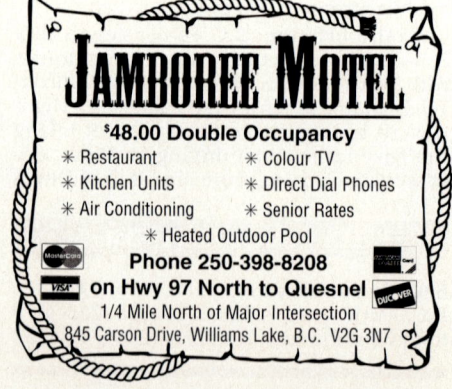

JAMBOREE MOTEL

$48.00 Double Occupancy

- Restaurant
- Kitchen Units
- Air Conditioning
- Colour TV
- Direct Dial Phones
- Senior Rates
- Heated Outdoor Pool

Phone 250-398-8208
on Hwy 97 North to Quesnel
1/4 Mile North of Major Intersection
845 Carson Drive, Williams Lake, B.C. V2G 3N7

day event draws contestants from all over Canada and the United States. The rodeo grounds are located in the city. The city campground/RV park is located at the stampede grounds.

At the north end of Williams Lake is Scout Island Nature Center. This island is reached by a causeway, with boardwalks providing access to the marshes. A nature house is open May to August.

Tamlaght Stone Antiques and The Painted Door. A definite "stopping house" for travelers visiting the Cariboo. We have an amazing array of home decor, gifts and antiques from around the world. Over 4,000 square feet of collectibles, gifts, antique furniture and fine china. Stop by and say hello. We are located in Williams Lake just past the Mall on Oliver Street across from Denny's. 635 Oliver Street. (250) 392-1921.
[ADVERTISEMENT]

West Access Route Log
(continued)

**BC HIGHWAY 97 NORTH
CARIBOO HIGHWAY**

C 136.4 (219.5 km) **PG 140.6** (226.3 km) Gas station, store, campground.

C 141.3 (227.3 km) **PG 135.7** (218.4 km) Turnout with litter barrel.

CC 142.2 (228.8 km) **PG 134.8** (216.9 km) Store with gas.

CC 145.3 (233.9 km) **PG 131.7** (211.9 km) Large turnout with litter barrel.

CC 147.8 (237.9 km) **PG 129.2** (207.9 km) Replica of a turn-of-the-century roadhouse (current status of services unknown) at junction with side road which leads west 2.5 miles/4.5km to the tiny settlement of **SODA CREEK**. The original wagon road to the goldfields ended here and miners went the rest of the way to Quesnel by river steamboats. Soda Creek became an important transfer point for men and supplies until the railway went through in 1920. Soda Creek was so named because the creek bed is carbonate of lime and the water bubbles like soda water.

CC 155 (249.4 km) **PG 122** (196.4 km) **McLEESE LAKE**, small community with gas stations, cafe, post office, store, pub, private campground and motel on McLeese Lake. The lake was named for a Fraser River steamboat skipper. **McLeese Lake**, rainbow to 2 lbs., troll using a flasher, worms or flatfish lure.

Oasis Resort. Lakefront resort overlooking beautiful McLeese Lake. Kitchenettes and sleeping units. Covered patio deck with tables and chairs. Double occupancy from $50. Serviced RV parking and camping on lakeshore. Firepits, washrooms, coin showers. Boat launch and rentals. Private dock. 6557 Highway 97, McLeese Lake, BC. Phone (250) 297-6447; fax (250) 297-6279; email henger@midbc.com; www.quesnellinks.com/oasisresort.html. [ADVERTISEMENT]

Junction with road to Beaver Lake and to community of **LIKELY**, 53 miles/85 km (see description of Likely at Milepost CC 119.1). Also access to historic Quesnelle Forks, **Bullion Pit**, Keithley Creek and Cedar Point Provincial Park on Quesnel Lake (camping, fishing). Travelers may continue north from Likely to Barkerville via Matthew Valley Road (summer travel only) and rejoin Highway 97 at Quesnel via Highway 26 (see log this section)

CC 155.5 (250.2 km) **PG 121.5** (195.5 km) Rest area with restrooms to west overlooking McLeese Lake.

Likely on Quesnel Lake is one of the Cariboo's many lakeside communities.
(© Blake Hanna, staff)

CC 155.7 (250.6 km) **PG 121.3** (195.2 km) **McLeese Lake Resort.** Camping on the lake! Lakefront sleeping and housekeeping units. Cabins. Canada Select 2 1/2 stars. Satellite TV. 20 lakeshore and 35 secluded off-highway RV sites. Full hookup and pull-through, 30- and 50-amp, group sites. Lakeside camping. Laundromat, showers, firepits, large lawns, horseshoes, table tennis, swimming, fishing, boat rental/launch, ice, major credit cards, pets, Internet access. Rex and Maj Sutherland. Phone (250) 297-6525. Fax (250) 297-6531. Email McleeseLakeResort@telus.net. www.McLeeseLake.com. [ADVERTISEMENT]

CC 160 (257.5 km) **PG 117** (188.3 km) Turnout with litter barrel to west with plaque about Fraser River paddle-wheelers.

CC 164 (263.9 km) **PG 113** (181.8 km) **Cariboo Wood Shop.** A gift shop you must stop at. We specialize in Canadian-made gifts and souvenirs. Our woodshop produces quality furniture and accessories. We have plush animals, pottery, art calendars, intarsia, easy listening music on tapes and CDs— to name a few of the great gifts we have. Best of all our famous homemade fudge. 20 flavors to choose from: Maple nut, Amaretto, Heavenly Goo and many more! Ask for a free taste. 16 flavors of sugar-free candy. Come in for a visit and treat yourself to a relaxing atmosphere and friendly staff. Easy access drive-through loop for every size of RV. Open 7 days a week 9:30 A.M.–5:30 P.M. Groups welcome. Phone (800) 986-WOOD.
[ADVERTISEMENT]

CC 166 (267 km) **PG 111** (178.6 km) Glass sculpture museum and rock shop. **Caribou Castle.** See display ad this section.

CC 166.5 (267.9 km) **PG 110.5** (177.8 km) Marguerite rest area. View upriver to **Marguerite reaction cable ferry** across the Fraser River.

CC 168.5 (271.2 km) **PG 108.5** (174.6 km) Basalt columns to east create a formation known as the Devil's Palisades. Cliff swallows nest in the columns.

CC 169.8 (273.2 km) **PG 107.2** (172.5 km) Stone cairn commemorates **Fort Alexandria**, the last North West Co. fur-trading post established west of the Rockies, built in 1821. The actual site of the fort is across the river. Cairn also marks the approximate farthest point reached by Alexander Mackenzie in his descent of the Fraser in 1793.

CC 180 (289.7 km) **PG 97** (156.1 km) Australian rest area to west with toilets, tables and litter barrels. Private campground to east.

CC 188.5 (303.4 km) **PG 88.5** (142.4 km) Kersley (unincorporated), gas and food.

CC 188.6 (303.6 km) **PG 88.4** (142.3 km) Restaurant, gas and private campground.

CC 193.2 (310.9 km) **PG 83.8** (134.9 km) Antique machinery museum to east.

CC 195.8 (315.1 km) **PG 81.2** (130.6 km) **Dragon Lake Golf Course & Campsite.** Situated on edge of Dragon Lake. RV and campsites at $10 per night. Flush toilets, showers, sani-dump, wharf, trout fishing. Located off Hwy 97 just 10 minutes south of city centre. 9-hole golf course with driving range. Snack bar, lounge. Campers register at golf club pro shop. Phone (250) 747-1358. 1692 Flint Avenue, Quesnel, BC, V2J 4R8.
[ADVERTISEMENT]

CC 196 (315.4 km) **PG 81** (130.4 km) South end of loop road east to **Dragon Lake**, a small, shallow lake popular with Quesnel families. Camping and fishing for rainbow.

CC 196 (315.4 km) **PG 81** (130.4 km) **Robert's Roost Campsite** located 6 km south of Quesnel and 2 km east of Highway 97 in a parklike setting on beautiful Dragon Lake. Partial and fully serviced. 15- and 30-amp service. Sani-dump, fishing, boat rental, swimming, horseshoes, playground, showers, flush toilets and laundromat. Email

CARIBOU CASTLE

FREE! Bigfoot Exhibit
"WORLD FAMOUS"
Local Gold Nugget Jewellery
Rock Shop, Unique Gift Shop
Easy RV Access & Parking
U.S. Dollars = $1.50

§1-800-567-9096

Hwy 97 • Marguerite, BC

access. Can accommodate any length unit. Limited accommodation. Approved by Tourism BC. Wetland birding. Close to golfing. Hosts: Bob and Vivian Wurm, 3121 Gook Road, Quesnel, BC V2J 4K7. Phone (250) 747-2015 or (888) 227-8877; Roberts Roost@bcadventure.com. [ADVERTISEMENT]

Quesnel

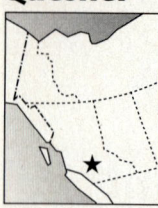

CC 203 (326.7 km) PG 74 (119.1 km). Located at the confluence of the Fraser and Quesnel rivers. **Population:** 11,114. **Elevation:** 1,789 feet/545m. **Emergency Services:** Emergency only, phone 911. **RCMP,** phone (250) 992-9211. **Ambulance,** phone (250) 992-3211. **Hospital,** phone (250) 992-0600.

Visitor Information: Located on the west side of the highway just north of Quesnel River bridge, in LeBourdais Park. Open year-round. Write Quesnel Visitor Information Centre, 703 Carson Ave., Quesnel, BC, V2J 2B6; phone (250) 992-8716, or toll free (800) 992-4922. For information on the Cariboo Tourist Region, contact the Cariboo Tourist Assoc., P.O. Box 4900, Williams Lake, BC V2G 2V8; phone toll free (800) 663-5885.

Quesnel (kwe NEL) began as a supply town for the miners in the gold rush of the 1860s. The city was named after the Quesnel River, which in turn was named after fur trader Jules Maurice Quesnel, a member of Simon Fraser's 1808 expedition down the Fraser River and later a political figure in Quebec. Today, forestry is the dominant economic force in Quesnel, with 2 pulp mills, a plywood plant, and 5 sawmills, planer mills and an MDF plant. Check with the Visitor Information Centre about tours.

Cottonwood House Historic Site is located 17 miles east of Quesnel on Highway 26. (© Blake Hanna, staff)

Accommodations include 5 hotels, 11 motels, 7 bed and breakfasts and 7 campgrounds. There are gas stations (with diesel and propane), 2 shopping malls and 45 restaurants offering everything from fast food to fine dining. Golf and a recreation centre with pool are available.

Visitors can take a walking tour of the city along the **Riverfront Park** trail system. The 3.1-mile/5-km north Quesnel trail starts at Ceal Tingley Park at the confluence of the Fraser and Quesnel rivers. The west Quesnel trail is a 2.7-mile/4.3-km walk through a residential area. Trail information is available at the Visitor Information Centre.

The 260-mile/420-km trail blazed by explorer Alexander Mackenzie from Quesnel has been retraced and restored in a joint federal, provincial and regional project. The land trail terminates near Burnt Creek bridge (**Milepost J 249.9** on the Chilcotin Highway). Mackenzie, the first white man to cross the North American continent, left Lake Athabaska in 1793 to find a trade route to the Pacific. His journey took 72-days through 1,200 miles/2,000 km of unmapped territory. .

There are some interesting hoodoo formations and scenic canyon views at nearby **Pinnacles Provincial Park**, 5 miles/8 km west of Highway 97; picnicking. It is a 1.1-mile/1.8-km walk round-trip from the parking area to the pinnacle viewpoints.

Quesnel offers gold panning tours, guided hiking tours and jet boating and river rafting on the Fraser River. Boat tours are also available on other area rivers. Contact the Visitor Information Centre for more information.

A worthwhile side trip is Highway 26, which intersects Highway 97 at **Milepost CC 206** (see log this section). This paved highway leads to Wells, Bowron Lake and **Barkerville Provincial Historic Park,** a reconstructed and restored Cariboo gold rush town. Local charters offer tours of Barkerville and area from Quesnel.

Billy Barker Days, a 4-day event held the third full weekend in July, commemorates the discovery of gold at Barkerville in 1862. Held in conjunction with the Quesnel Rodeo, Billy Barker Days is the third largest outdoor family festival in the province. For more information, write Box 4441, Quesnel, BC V2J 3J4.

Quesnel & District Museum and Archives. The best-kept secret in the Cariboo. Exhibits from farming, logging and mining. Artifacts used by our pioneers in their homes. Coins from all over the world; 1911 White car; a famous Centennial quilt. First Nations exhibit and a collection of

QUESNEL'S OUTSTANDING VALUE

- Affordable Rates
- Queen-size Beds
- Refrigerator & In-room coffee
- Children 12 & Under Free
- Remote Control Cable TV

Pinocchio Family Restaurant
- Large Menu - Kids Menu
- Fully Licensed
- Senior's Discount

1-888-843-8922

Phone (250) 747-1111 Fax (250) 747-4322
2010 Valhalla Rd., Quesnel, BC V2J 4C1

REST EASY IN QUESNEL AT...

- Quiet, Modern, Central Location
- Pools & Whirlpool
- Air Conditioned
- Kitchenettes
- Queen & King Beds
- Business Suites
- FREE Continental Breakfast

Toll Free 1-800-663-1581 or 250-992-5575

383 St. Laurent Avenue, Quesnel, B.C.

RAMADA LIMITED

River Rock PUB & STEAKHOUSE
Follow the Signs to West Quesnel!
Family Dining in Historic Log House
Overlooking the Fraser & Quesnel Rivers
Pub: 11:30am to 12pm
Steakhouse: 12am to 2pm & 5pm to 10pm
290 Hoy Street, Quesnel, BC
RESERVATIONS 1-250-991-0100

Talisman Inn
753 Front Street, Quesnel B.C.
- Direct Dial Telephones
- Extra Long Queen Size Beds
- Fully Air-conditioned Units
- 29" Colour TV with Cable
- All Rooms with Refrigerators
- Modern Kitchen Units • Business Suites
- Executive Suites with Jacuzzi Tubs

For Reservations call Toll Free
1-800-663-8090
www.talismaninn.bc.ca
Phone 250-992-7247 or Fax 250-992-3126

QUESNEL ADVERTISERS

Best Western Tower Inn....Ph. (800) 663-2009
Billy Barker Casino Hotel...Ph. (888) 992-4255
Country Haven Family
 Restaurant ....Ph. (250) 992-9654
Econo Lodge ....Ph. (800) 663-1585
North Cariboo Tourism .....Ph. (800) 992-4922
Quesnel & District Museum
 and Archives ....Adjacent Infocentre
Quesnel Farmers Market ....Kinchant & Carson
Ramada Limited................Ph. (800) 663-1581
River Rock Pub &
 Steakhouse ....Ph. (250) 991-0100
Super 8............................Ph. (888) 843-8922
Talisman Inn ....Ph. (250) 992-7247

Visit the North Cariboo!

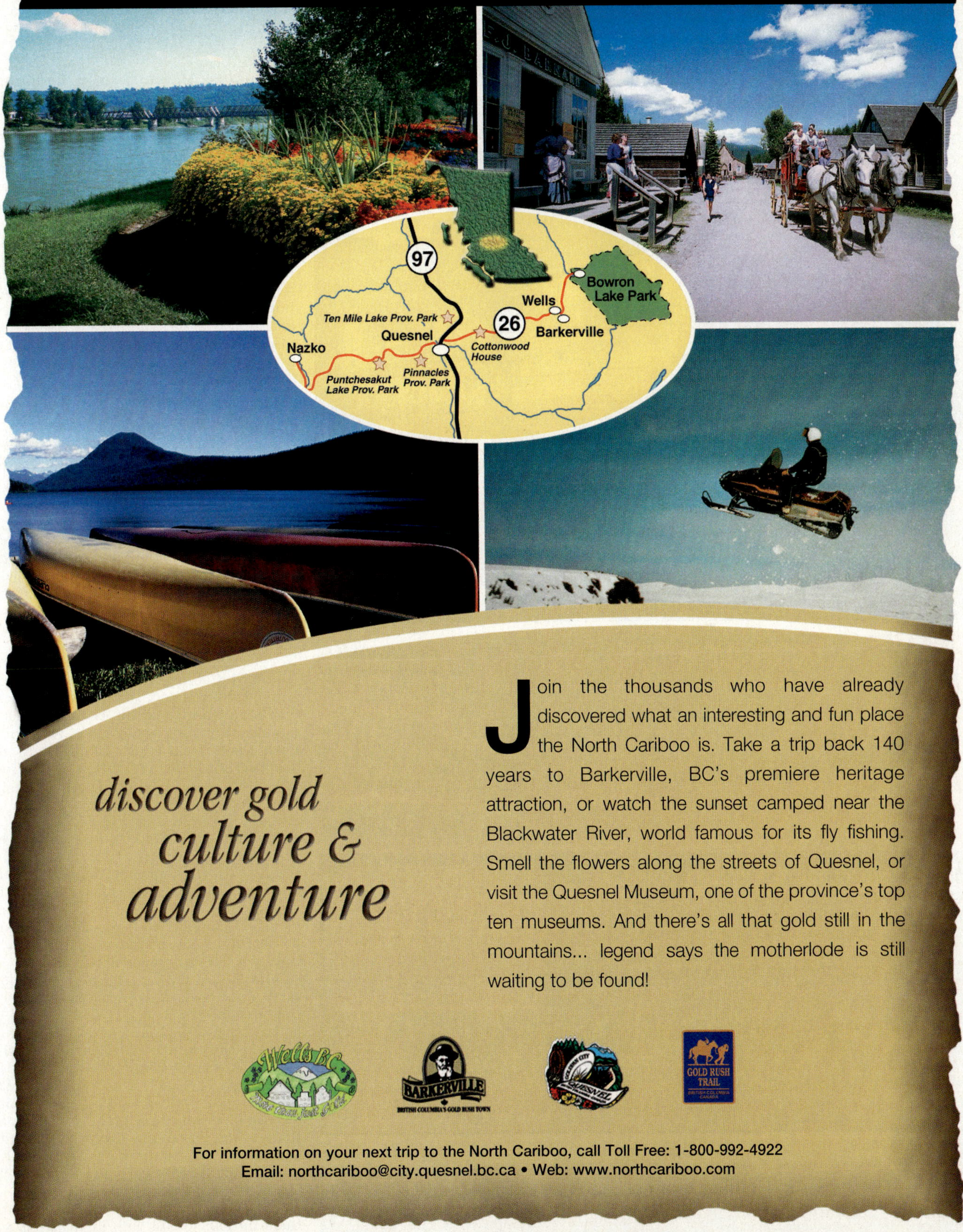

discover gold culture & adventure

Join the thousands who have already discovered what an interesting and fun place the North Cariboo is. Take a trip back 140 years to Barkerville, BC's premiere heritage attraction, or watch the sunset camped near the Blackwater River, world famous for its fly fishing. Smell the flowers along the streets of Quesnel, or visit the Quesnel Museum, one of the province's top ten museums. And there's all that gold still in the mountains... legend says the motherlode is still waiting to be found!

For information on your next trip to the North Cariboo, call Toll Free: 1-800-992-4922
Email: northcariboo@city.quesnel.bc.ca • Web: www.northcariboo.com

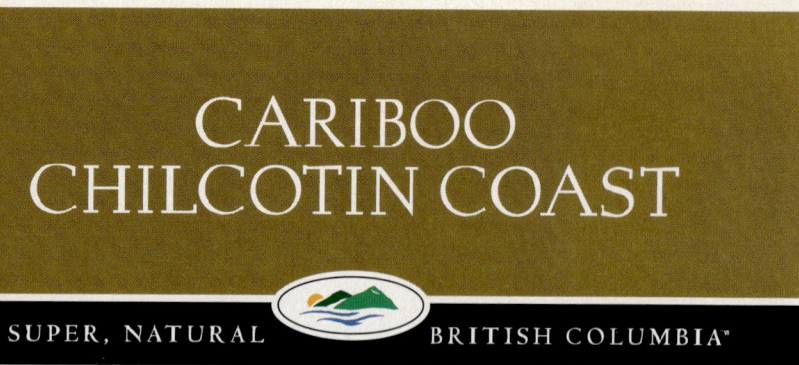
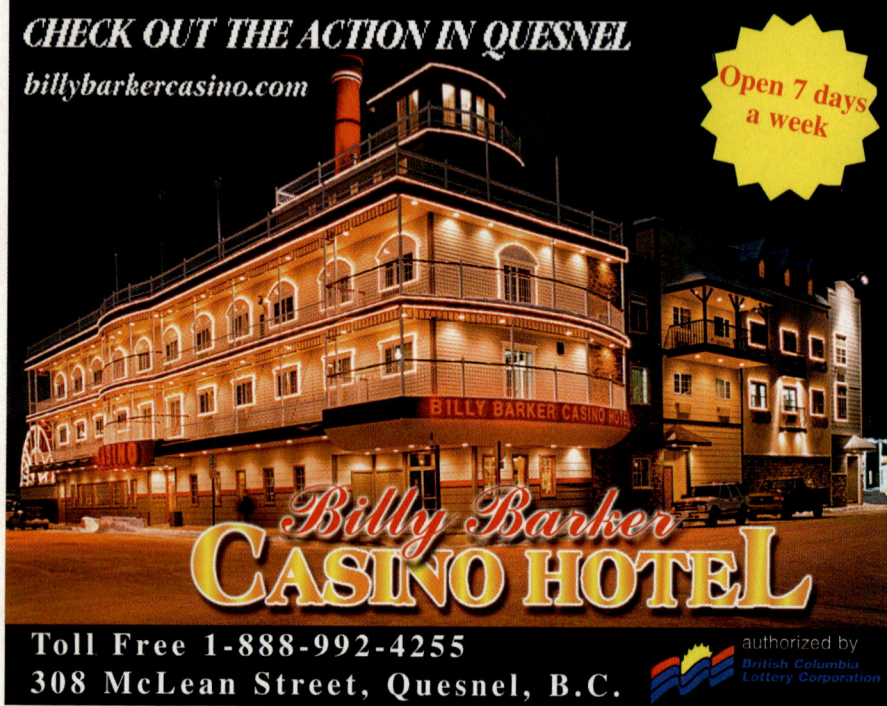

some of the rarest Chinese artifacts found in western Canada. Mystery surrounds our museum with Mandy, our "haunted doll," and for a chuckle and a smile see the 80-year-old prophylactic. Considered one of the top 10 British Columbia museums! Admission fee $3 per person; 12 and under free. A historical walking tour brochure of downtown Quesnel is available at the museum. Located across from BC Rail amongst the famous rose garden and adjacent to the Tourist Information Centre on Highway 97. Open year-round. Phone 1-250-992-9580. [ADVERTISEMENT]

Country Haven Family Restaurant. Home-style cooking. Breakfast served all day. Fully licensed. Located 1/2-block from Quesnel Tourist Information Center on Highway 97 North (490 Carson Ave.). Open year-round. Summer hours Monday–Saturday 6:30 A.M.–9 P.M.; Sundays and holidays 8 A.M.–8 P.M. Tour groups welcome. Please phone ahead. (250) 992-9654. [ADVERTISEMENT]

Quesnel Farmers Markets. Runs Saturdays, May to October, on the corner of Kinchant and Carson. 20 to 30 vendors selling the freshest veggies, fruits, flowers, honey, bedding plants, woodwork, herbs and much more. Homemade; everything made, baked or grown in the Cariboo. Stop by between 8:30 A.M. and 1 P.M. every Saturday. [ADVERTISEMENT]

West Access Route Log
(continued)

**BC HIGHWAY 97 NORTH
CARIBOO HIGHWAY**

CC 206 (331.5 km) PG 71 (114.3 km) Quesnel airport.

Junction with Highway 26 to Barkerville. See "Highway 26 to Barkerville" log on opposite page.

CC 209.5 (337.2 km) PG 67.5 (108.6 km) **Lazy Daze Resort.** New owners. Year-round accommodation, 3 minutes off Highway 97 North. RV sites, 30-amp service, pull-throughs. Cabins, tenting, hot showers, laundry, convenience store, play area, picnic gazebo. Swimming dock, boat dock. Rainbow trout fishing, boat rentals, ice fishing, cross-country ski trails. Hosts Doug and Sharon Thompson. 714 Ritchie Road, Quesnel, BC V2J 6X2. Phone (250) 992-6700. Email: lazy_daze@telus.net. [ADVERTISEMENT]

CC 210 (338 km) PG 67 (107.8 km) Paved side road leads 0.6 mile/1 km **10 Mile Lake Provincial Park**; 141 sites, tables, firepits, showers, playground, hiking and bike trails, interpretive programs. Fishing for rainbow to 3 lbs.

CC 214.2 (344.7 km) PG 62.8 (101.1 km) Cottonwood River bridge. Turnout with litter barrels at north end of bridge.

CC 218.7 (352 km) PG 58.3 (93.8 km) Hush Lake rest area to west; toilets, tables, litter barrels.

CC 226 (363.7 km) PG 51 (82 km) **Cinema 2nd Hand.** General store, groceries. Fireworks, movie rentals, souvenirs. Local artwork, circle drive. 9 A.M.–9 P.M. every day. Free camping, picnic tables, firepits and wood, toilet, some long pull-throughs, some shady sites, phone. Welcome to friendly Cinema, BC. Vic and Theresa Olson, RR 1 Box 1, Site 10, Hixon, BC V0K 1S0. (250) 998-4774. [ADVERTISEMENT]

CC 235 (378.5 km) PG 42 (67.2 km) Large turnout to east with litter barrels and toilet.

CC 241 (387.8 km) **PG 36** (58 km) **HIXON** (pop. 500) has a post office, 2 motels, gas stations, grocery stores, 2 restaurants (1 with licensed premises), a pub and Canyon Creek Campground. Hixon is the Cariboo's most northerly community. Extensive placer mining began here in the early 1900s, and is still under way today.

Southbound motorists watch for roadside display on points of interest in the Cariboo region located just north of Hixon. ▲

Canyon Creek Campground. See display ad this section.

Paradise Motel. Sleeping and kitchenette units. Combination baths. Satellite TV. Quiet creekside setting. Near stores and food services. Singles from $40; doubles from $48. Ask about our senior and off-season rates. Major credit cards. Pets welcome. Phone (250) 998-4685. 270 Colgrove Road, Box 456, Hixon, BC V0K 1S0. [ADVERTISEMENT]

CC 247.6 (398.5 km) **PG 29.4** (47.3 km) Woodpecker rest area to west; toilets, tables, litter barrels.

CC 257.7 (414.7 km) **PG 19.3** (31 km) Stone Creek (unincorporated), no services.

CC 258.3 (415.7 km) **PG 18.7** (30.1 km) Private campground. ▲

CC 261.8 (421.3 km) **PG 15.2** (24.5 km) Red Rock (unincorporated); pay phone.

CC 268.3 (431.8 km) **PG 8.7** (14 km) **Bee Lazee RV Park, Campground.** See display ad this section.

CC 270.6 (435.5 km) **PG 6.4** (10.3 km) **Junction** with bypass road to Yellowhead 16 East. Keep left for Prince George; continue straight ahead for Jasper and Edmonton.

If you are headed east on Yellowhead

Highway 26 to Barkerville

This 51-mile/82-km paved road leads to Barkerville Historic Town in the Cariboo gold fields. The Barkerville gold strike was made in 1861. Highway 26 follows the route of the original Cariboo Wagon Road built to serve the boom towns. Gas is available in Wells.

Distance from Highway 97 junction (J) is shown.

J 0 Junction with Highway 97 at **Milepost CC 206.**

J 13 (21 km) Rest area and interpretive trails to south.

J 15.2 (24.5 km) Cottonwood River bridge.

J 16.7 (26.9 km) **Cottonwood House Historic Site.** This magnificent roadhouse complex built in 1864 is a monument to all

the miners, stagecoach passengers and other weary travelers who journeyed along the Cariboo Wagon Road. Guided house tours, wagon rides, barns, animals and much more. Meals and gift shop. Overnight accommodation available in rustic cabins. Washroom and hot showers included. Phone (250) 992-2071; fax (250) 992-6830; www.cottonwoodhouse.ca. [ADVERTISEMENT]

J 20.1 (32.4 km) Swift River Forest Road leads 0.2 mile/0.3 km to Lightning Creek Forest Service recreation site (first turn on left); free camping, 14-day limit. *Active logging road, drive with headlights on.* ▲

J 21.4 (34.5 km) Lover's Leap viewpoint and Mexican Hill Summit, one of the steepest grades on the original Cariboo Wagon Road, to the south.

J 27.1 (43.6 km) Historical stop of interest marker for **Blessing's Grave.** Charles Morgan Blessing was murdered in 1866 while on his way to Barkerville. His killer, James Barry, was caught when he gave Blessing's keepsake gold nugget stickpin, in the shape of a skull, to a Barkerville dance-hall girl. James Barry was the only white man hanged in the Cariboo during the gold rush.

J 37.3 (60.1 km) **Junction** with Stanley Road (1.9-mile/3-km loop) to gold-rush ghost towns of Stanley and Van Winkle. Sites include the old **Lightning Hotel** and gold rush-era gravesites. A worthwhile sidetrip.

J 38.6 (62.2 km) Stanley (Loop) Road, Chisholm Creek.

J 40.2 (64.7 km) Devil's Canyon paved turnout to south. This was the highest point on the Cariboo Wagon Road.

J 42.9 (69 km) Slough Creek, site of much hydraulic mining activity after Joe Shaw discovered gold here in 1870.

J 44.9 (72.2 km) Paved turnout to litter barrel to south. Jack o' Clubs Lake; fishing for rainbows, lake trout and Dolly Varden.

J 45.2 (72.7 km) Rest area on peninsula to south with picnic tables, information signs, pit toilets and boat launch.

J 45.7 (73.6 km) Large paved turnout with litter barrels to south.

J 46.1 (74.2 km) Double-ended lakeshore turnout with information sign.

J 46.7 (75.2 km) **WELLS** (pop. 300, elevation 4,200 feet/1280m) was built in the 1930s when the Cariboo Gold Quartz Mine, promoted and developed by Fred Wells, brought hundreds of workers to this valley. The mine closed in 1967, but the town has continued as a service centre and attraction for tourists, with art galleries, gift shops, food, gas, lodging and camping.

J 47.6 (76.1 km) Turnout with litter barrels, interpretive signs and map.

J 49.6 (79.8 km) Barkerville Provincial Park. Camping at Forest Rose, Lowhee and Government Hill. Dump station. ▲

J 50 (80.5 km) Gravel road leads north 18 miles/29 km to **Bowron Lakes Provincial Park,** noted for its 72-mile/116-km canoe circuit which takes from 7 to 10 days to complete. Visitor information available at registration centre next to main parking lot where canoeists must register and pay circuit fees. Reservations recommended in July and August (required for groups); phone 1-800-435-5622.

There are 2 private lodges at the north end of the lake with restaurants, camping, a general store and canoe rentals. Provincial park campground has 25 sites, water, pit toilets, firewood and a boat launch. Swimming, fishing, canoeing, kayaking and hiking. ◂▲

J 51 (82.1 km) **BARKERVILLE.** A provincial historic town; admission fee charged. Barkerville is open year-round, although it is best to visit between mid-May and September, when all exhibits are open. **Visitor information**: At the Reception Centre; phone (250) 994-3302.

Barkerville was named for miner Billy Barker, who struck gold on Williams Creek. The resulting gold rush in 1862 created Barkerville. Virtually a ghost town when the provincial government began restoration in 1958, today Barkerville's buildings and boardwalks are faithful restorations or reconstructions from the town's heyday, with costumed interpreters conducting tours and staging daily dramas in summer. Visitors can pan for gold, shop at the old-time general store, watch a blacksmith at work, or take in a show at the Theatre Royal. The hour-long show plays daily except Fridays in summer at 1 P.M. and 4 P.M. Admission is charged. Restaurants and food service available.

Travelers may continue south from Barkerville via Matthew Valley Road (summer travel only) to community of Likely and return to Highway 97.

Return to Milepost CC 206
West Access Route

WEST ACCESS ROUTE • Prince George

Highway 16 for Jasper or Edmonton, turn to **Milepost E 450** in the YELLOWHEAD HIGHWAY 16 section and read the log back to front.

CC 273 (439.3 km) **PG 4** (6.4 km) **Southpark RV Park.** See display ad this section. ▲

CC 273.4 (440 km) **PG 3.6** (5.8 km) Access to Prince George airport to east.

CC 274 (440.9 km) **PG 3** (4.8 km) **Sintich Trailer RV Park.** See display ad this section. ▲

CC 275.2 (442.8 km) **PG 1.8** (2.8 km) Bridge over the Fraser River. Turn right at north end of bridge then left at stop sign for city centre via Queensway. This is the easiest access for Fort George Park; follow Queensway to 20th Avenue and turn east.

Continue straight ahead for Highway 16 entrance to city.

Carmel Motor Inn. Trip AAA approved. Air-conditioned, kitchenettes, cable TV, movie channels. Restaurants, RV parking, gift shop. Smoking accommodation available. Ample parking. Major credit cards, debit cards. No pets. Adjacent Esso store with diesel, gas and car wash. Located just north of bridge. Phone toll free 1-800-665-4484 or (250) 564-6339. Email carmel@mag–net.com. [ADVERTISEMENT]

CC 276 (444.1 km) **PG 1** (1.6 km) **Junction** of Highway 97 with Yellowhead 16 West. Description of Prince George follows.

If you are headed west on Yellowhead Highway 16 for Prince Rupert, turn to **Milepost PG 0** on page 218 in the YELLOWHEAD HIGHWAY 16 section. Prince Rupert is port of call for Alaska state ferries and BC Ferries.

Dramatic architecture of Two Rivers Gallery reflects Prince George's landscape.
(© Blake Hanna, staff)

Prince George

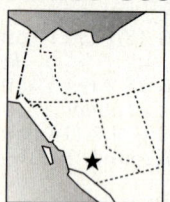

CC 277 (445.8 km) **Population:** 80,000, area 160,000. **Emergency Services:** Phone 911. RCMP, phone (250) 562-3371. **Poison Control Centre,** phone (250) 565-2442. **Hospital,** Prince George Regional, phone (250) 565-2000.

Visitor Information: Tourism Prince George & Area, 1198 Victoria St., phone (250) 562-3700 or fax 563-3584, or toll free (800) 668-7646. Open year-round, 8:30 A.M.

PRINCE GEORGE ADVERTISERS

Aberdeen Glen..................Ph. (250) 563-8901
Blue Spruce RV Park &
 Campground ....Ph. (250) 964-7272
Connaught Motor Inn ......Ph. (800) 663-6620
Downtown Motel ....Ph. (250) 563-9241
Econo Lodge ....Ph. (250) 563-7106
Esther's Inn ....Ph. (250) 562-4131
Exploration Place, The......Ph. (250) 562-1612
Grama's Inn ....Ph. (877) 563-7174
Historic Huble
 Homestead ....Ph. (250) 564-7033
Moose Springs Resort ......Ph. (250) 964-3137
Pine Centre Mall ....Ph. (250) 563-3681
P.G. Hi-Way Motel ....Ph. (888) 557-4557
Railway & Forestry
 Museum ....Ph. (250) 563-7351
Ricky's Pancake & Family
 Restaurant ....Ph. (250) 564-8114
Travelodge ....Ph. (250) 563-0666
Two Rivers Gallery ....Ph. (250) 614-7800

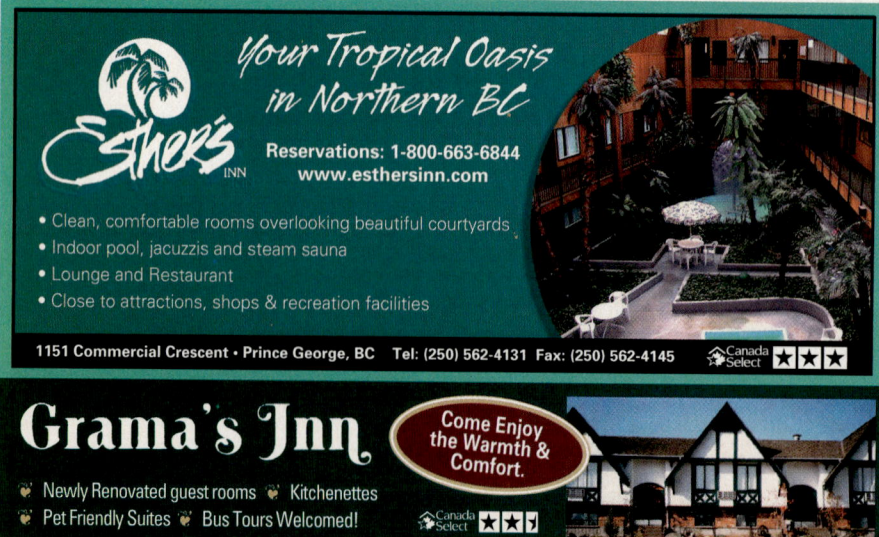

to 5 P.M. weekdays Monday through Saturday. Visitor centre, junction Yellowhead 16 and Highway 97; open daily late-May to Labour Day; www.tourismpg.bc.ca.

Elevation: 1,868 feet/569m. **Climate:** The inland location is tempered by the protection of mountains. The average annual frost-free period is 85 days, with 1,793 hours of bright sunshine. Dry in summer; chinooks off and on during winter which, accompanied by a western flow of air, break up the cold weather. Summer temperatures average 72°F/22°C with lows to 46°F/8°C. **Radio:** CKPG 550, CJCI 620, 94X-FM, CBC-FM 91.5, Hits 101.3. **Television:** 36 channels via cable. **Newspaper:** *The Citizen* (daily except Sunday); *Prince George This Week* (Sunday and Thursday); *Free Press* (Thursday and Sunday).

Prince George is British Columbia's 4th largest city. Located at the confluence of the Nechako and Fraser rivers, near the geographical centre of the province, it is a hub of trade and travel routes in the region. Prince George is located at the junction of Yellowhead Highway 16—linking Prince Rupert on the west coast with the Interior of Canada—and Highway 97, which runs south to Vancouver and north to Dawson Creek.

In the early 1800s, Simon Fraser of the North West Trading Co. erected a post here which he named Fort George in honour of the reigning English monarch. In 1906, survey parties for the transcontinental Grand Trunk Pacific Railway (later Canadian National Railways) passed through the area, and with the building of the railroad a great

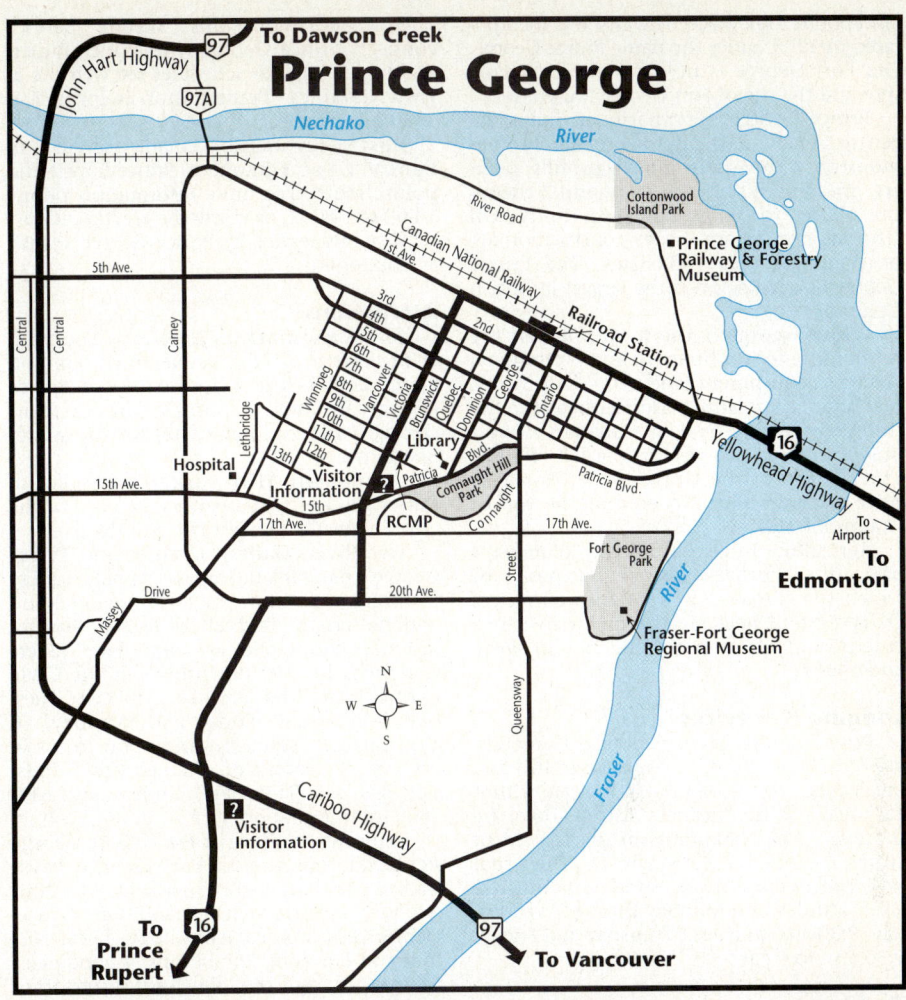

WEST ACCESS ROUTE • Prince George

P.G. HI·WAY MOTEL
45 Comfortable Budget & Deluxe Units
1 Mile N.E. of Highways 97/16

❈ 31 Brand New, Well Appointed Rooms
❈ 12 Full Size Kitchens • Air-Conditioning
❈ Barrier-Free Suite • Quiet Location
❈ Close to Laundromat and Shopping Mall
❈ Restaurants Nearby • Cable TV
❈ Direct Dial Phones • Major Credit Cards

1737 - 20th Avenue, Prince George, BC
Telephone (250) 564-6869 • FAX (250) 562-5687
Toll Free Reservations: 1-888-557-4557
www.princegeorge.com/pghiway/

DELUXE FAMILY FACILITIES
Blue Spruce R.V. Park and Campground
Prince George, B.C.
Owners & Hosts: Ted & Reina McAfee

Store • Ice • Heated Pool • Mini Golf
128 Sites • Long Pull-Throughs
Full Hook-ups • Sani-Dump
Camping Cabins • Grassy Tenting
Laundromat • Free Showers
Pay Phones • Modem Friendly
Postal Services • 24-Hour Security
52 Channel Cable TV Available

3 Miles West of Highway 97 on
Highway 16 West Yellowhead
Route to Prince Rupert

TOLL FREE 1-877-964-7272
E-MAIL: bluesprucervpark@shaw.ca
(250) 964-7272

www.themilepost.com

While in PRINCE GEORGE stay at...
Connaught Motor INN

◆ 98 Units w/Fridges ◆ Indoor Pool, Sauna, Swirl ◆ Cable TV
◆ Downtown Location ◆ Licensed Restaurant ◆ Air Conditioned

1550 Victoria St., Prince George, BC V2L 2L3 • Tel/Fax: (250)562-4441
TOLL FREE RESERVATIONS: 1-800-663-6620 AAA Approved

Travelodge®
While in Prince George Be Our Guest
Downtown Location

1458 - 7th Ave., Prince George, BC V2L 3P2
Phone: 250-563-0666
Reservations 1-800-663-8239
www.goldcapinn.com • info@goldcapinn.com

Moose Springs Resort

Inn • RV Park & Campground • Country Store
Restaurant & Pub • ATV/Snowmobile Trails
Hiking/Biking Trails Baseball Fields • Horseshoe Pits
30 Minutes from Prince George!

34000 Blackwater Rd., Prince George, BC
Website: www.moosespringsresort.com

Pub & Restaurant	General Store	Resort
964-3136	964-0766	964-3137

You Can Go Anywhere in the World Or Come Here and Get Away From It.

Complete Public Golf Facility • Prince George

"Where Service Exceeds Expectations" • Easy RV Access

Proshop - Driving Range 1-250-563-8901
Eagles Nest Grill - Residential Sales 1-250-563-8982

Web: www.aberdeenglen.ca • 1010 Clubhouse Dr., Prince George

Aberdeen Glen

British Columbia became the 6th province of Canada on July 20, 1871.

land boom took place. The city was incorporated in 1915 under the name Prince George. Old Fort George is now a park and picnic spot and the site of Fort George Museum.

Prince George is primarily an industrial centre, fairly dependent on the lumber industry, with 3 pulp mills, sawmills, planers, dry kilns, a plywood plant and 2 chemical plants to serve the pulp mills. Oil refining, mining and heavy construction are other major area industries. The Prince George Forest Region is the largest in British Columbia.

Prince George is the focal point of the central Interior for financial and professional services, equipment and wholesale firms, machine shops and many services for the timber industry. One of Canada's newest universities opened here in the fall of 1994. The campus of the University of Northern British Columbia is located at the top of Cranbrook Hill.

Agriculture in central British Columbia is basically a forage-livestock business, for which the climate and soils are well suited. Dairying and beef are the major livestock enterprises, with minor production in sheep and poultry.

Lodging & Services

Prince George offers 5 hotels, 17 motels, 9 RV parks, and more than 3 dozen bed and breakfasts. Most accommodations are within easy reach of the business district. There are more than 80 restaurants in the city. Most stores are open 7 days a week. The usual hours of operation are: Sunday, noon to 5 P.M.; Saturday and Monday through Wednesday, 9:30 A.M. to 6 P.M.; Thursday and Friday, 9:30 A.M. to 9 P.M.

Transportation

Air: Prince George airport is 6.8 miles/11 km southeast of the city centre, serviced by Air Canada Regional, Central Mountain Air, West Jet and Peace Air. Limousine and taxi service to and from the airport.

Railroad: VIA Rail's "Skeena" service connects Prince George with Prince Rupert and Jasper, AB. For schedules see web site at www.viarail.ca. Train station is located at 1300 1st Avenue.

Bus: Greyhound Canada service to Dawson Creek, Edmonton, Prince Rupert and points south. For more information phone 1-800-661-8747, or visit www.greyhound.ca.

City bus service by Prince George Transit & Charter Ltd.

Attractions

City Landmarks: Centennial Fountain at the corner of 7th Avenue and Dominion Street depicts the early history of Prince George in mosaic tile. A cairn at Fort George Park commemorates Sir Alexander Mackenzie.

Connaught Hill Park offers colorful flower gardens and a panoramic view of the city. Follow Connaught Drive to the park.

Two Rivers Gallery, modeled after Prince George's natural landscape, is a public gallery featuring exhibitions by local, regional and national artists. Shop at the Gallery features unique, handmade artwork. Two Rivers Gallery is located downtown in the Civic Centre Plaza. Hours are 10 A.M. to 5 P.M. Tuesday, Wednesday, Friday and Saturday; 10 A.M. to 9 P.M. Thursday; and noon to 5 P.M. on Sunday. Admission charged (free admission 3–9 p.m. Thursdays). Phone (250) 614-7800 for information.

Exploration Place at **Fraser-Fort George Regional Museum** in **Fort George Park**. Located in Fort George Park at 333 20th Avenue. Galleries include Hands On Science, Demonstrations, Palaeontology, Local History and Traveling Exhibitions. A good place to learn about the Northern Interior of British Columbia. Friendly staff, atrium with food service and gift shop. Fort George Park has miles of paved walking trails along the Fraser and Nechako rivers; picnic tables, barbecue facilities; playgrounds; spray park; and train rides. The Fort George Railway operates on weekends and holidays at the park from a railway building patterned after the original Grand Trunk Pacific stations. Open daily year-round. Free parking for cars and RVs. Wheelchair accessible. Admission fee charged. For more information phone (250) 562-1612.

City Parks. Over 3,706 acres/1,500 hectares of parks and open space are found in Prince George. There are 120 parks and playgrounds, 7 nature parks, 7 athletic parks, 97 sports fields, 73 tennis courts and 66 miles/106 km of trails. **Forest of the World** park, minutes from downtown, has more than 9 miles/15 km of trails through various habitats; self-guided nature walks, hiking, biking and picnics. The upper lookout at Shane Lake has a great view of the city. For park information and trail maps, phone (250) 561-7600.

Prince George Railway and Forestry Museum features a dozen original railway buildings, including 2 stations. Among the 50 pieces of rolling stock are 5 locomotives, a 1903 snow plow, a 1913 100-ton steam wrecking crane and a 90-foot 100-ton turntable. Items from 8 past and present rail-

way companies are displayed. There is also a small collection of forestry, mining and agricultural machinery. Located at 850 River Road next to Cottonwood Island Nature Park on the Nechako River. Open daily May to September from 10 A.M. to 5 P.M. For more information phone (250) 563-7351.

Swimming. Four Seasons Swimming Pool at the corner of 7th Avenue and Dominion Street has a pool, water slide, diving tank and fitness centre. Open to the public afternoons and evenings. Or check out the new Aquatic Centre at 1770 Munroe Street. It's equipped with a leisure-style wave pool and a 10-metre diving tower.

Tennis Courts. A total of 20 courts currently available to the public at 3 places: 20th Avenue near the entrance to Fort George Park; at Massey Drive in Carrie Jane Gray Park; and on Ospika Boulevard in the Lakewood Secondary School complex.

Golf Courses. Aberdeen Glen Golf Club was nominated BCPGA facility of the year. It is located just north of Prince George, 0.6 mile/1 km off Highway 97 North. Aspen Grove Golf Club is on Highway 97 South. Links of Maggie May Golf Course is located 4 miles/6.5 km from the junction of Shelley Road and Yellowhead Highway 16 East. Pine Valley Golf Club and Prince George Golf and Curling Club are on Yellowhead

WEST ACCESS ROUTE • Prince George

RAILWAY & FORESTRY MUSEUM
PRINCE GEORGE & REGION
850 River Road
Open Mid May to Mid October
www.pgrfm.bc.ca
(250) 563-7351

Historic
Huble Homestead & Giscome Portage
40km North of Prince George, off Highway 97 on Mitchell Rd.
Open May 17th to Labour Day
www.rdffg.bc.ca/parks/Giscome.html
(250) 564-7033

THE EXPLORATION PLACE
At the end of 20th Ave in Fort George Park
Open Year Round
www.theexplorationplace.com
(250) 562-1612

two rivers gallery
prince george and region
725 Civic Plaza
Open Year Round
www.tworiversartgallery.com
(250) 614-7800

Inspire Your Imagination, **Discover** Our History, **Explore** Our Culture
Prince George, British Columbia, Canada

SUPPORTED BY **REGIONAL DISTRICT** of Fraser-Fort George

www.themilepost.com   2003 ■ The MILEPOST® ■ 85

Colorful flower display at Prince George's Connaught Hill Park.
(© Earl L. Brown, staff)

Highway 16 West.

Industrial Tours. Tours through the pulp and wood products divisions of Canfor are available during the summer by contacting Tourism Prince George at (250) 562-3700. Availability and times/dates vary; reservations are required.

Tours of the Pacific Western Brewery are available; reservations required. Phone (250) 562-2424 or (800) 663-8002, Monday through Friday.

Rockhounding. The hills and river valleys in the area provide abundant caches of Omineca agate and Schmoos. For more information, contact Prince George Rock and Gem Club, phone (250) 562-4526; or Spruce City Rock and Gem Club, phone (250) 562-1013.

Special Events: Elks May Day celebration; Forest Expo in May (even years); Canada Day (July 1); Annual Sandblast Skiing, Summerfest and Prince George Fringe Festival in August; Oktoberfest and Harvest Festival in October; Studio Fair and Festival of Trees in November; Mardi Gras Winter Festival, Cercle des Canadiens Francais Winter Festival in February. Details on these and other events are availabie from Tourism Prince George, phone (250) 562-3700.

Side Trips: Prince George is the starting point for some of the finest holiday country in the province. There are numerous lakes and resorts nearby, among them: Bednesti Lake, 30 miles/48 km west of Prince George; Cluculz Lake, 44 miles/71 km west; Purden Lake, 42 miles/68 km east; and Tabor Lake, 6 miles/10 km east; and Moose Springs Resort, located 17 miles/27 km west of Prince George via Yellowhead Highway 16 and Blackwater Road.

Huble Homestead, next to the scenic Fraser River and the Giscome Portage Regional Park, dates from 1912. These original and reconstructed buildings are surrounded by grazing land and forest. Picnic tables and snackbar. Guided interpretive tours during peak season; admission free. Located north of Prince George on Highway 97; turn east off the highway at **Milepost PG 26.9** and drive 3.7 miles/6 km.

AREA FISHING: Highways 16 and 97 are the ideal routes for the sportsman, with year-round fishing and easy access to lakes and rivers. Hunters and fishermen stop over in Prince George as the jumping-off place for some of North America's finest big game hunting and fishing. For more information contact Fish & Wildlife at (250) 565-6145, or Tourism Prince George & Area, phone (250) 562-3700.

West Access Route Log
(continued)

BC HIGHWAY 97/HART HIGHWAY

The John Hart Highway, completed in 1952, was named for the former B.C. premier who sponsored its construction. The highway is a 2-lane paved highway with both straight stretches and winding stretches.

This section of the log shows distance from Prince George (PG) followed by distance from Dawson Creek (DC).

PG 0 DC 250 (402.3 km) John Hart Bridge over the Nechako River. The 4-lane highway extends 6.5 miles/10.5 km northbound through the commercial and residential suburbs of Prince George.

PG 1.5 (2.4 km) **DC 248.5** (399.9 km) Truck weigh scales. 24-hour gas station with diesel and propane; lube and oil service.

PG 1.7 (2.8 km) **DC 248.3** (399.5 km) Turnoff on Northwood Road East for Aberdeen Glen Golf Club.

PG 6.4 (10.3 km) **DC 243.6** (392 km) **Hartway RV Park.** Shaded, fully-serviced, extra long sites. Free hot showers, laundromat, 30-amp, free cable TV. Modem friendly.

Groceries nearby. Phone. On-site antique, gift and fabric shop. Approximately 6 miles/10 km north of Nechako Bridges. Next left after MacDonalds, then right on South Kelly Road. 7729 South Kelly Rd., Prince George, BC V2K 2H5. Phone (250) 962-8848; email tony_smith@mindlink.bc.ca. [ADVERTISEMENT]

PG 6.5 (10.5 km) **DC 243.5** (391.9 km) Two-lane highway (with passing lanes) begins abruptly northbound.

PG 14.6 (23.5 km) **DC 235.4** (378.8 km) Salmon River bridge. Litter barrel and river access to west at north end of bridge.

PG 14.7 (23.6 km) **DC 235.3** (378.7 km) **Salmon Valley RV Park and Campground** and convenience store, on over 27 acres along the scenic Salmon River. All facilities are wheelchair accessible, including showers.

50 treed sites, 12 pull-throughs, all with firerings, tables, laundry. Limited water and power 20–30 amp. Swimming and camping on the Salmon that's second to none. Fair fishing for rainbows, grayling and spring salmon. "Home of the Happy Camper." Phone (250) 971-2212. Fax (250) 971-2212. Good Sam discounts. [ADVERTISEMENT]

PG 16.4 (26.4 km) **DC 233.6** (375.9 km) Highway overpass crosses railroad tracks.

PG 19.3 (31.1 km) **DC 230.7** (371.3 km) Turnoff for **Goodsir Nature Park**; 1.5 miles/2.4 km west via Old Summit Lake Road (gravel). This 160-acre park features 160 kinds of trees, shrubs and wildflowers; 6 miles/10 km of nature trails; and an interpretive center. Open May to October, 8 A.M. to dusk; admission by donation.

PG 22 (35.4 km) **DC 228** (366.9 km) Gravel turnouts both sides of highway.

PG 26.5 (42.6 km) **DC 223.5** (359.7 km) Paved turnout to east with litter barrels and point-of-interest sign about Crooked River Forest Recreation Area.

PG 26.9 (43.3 km) **DC 223.1** (359 km) Access east 3.7 miles/6 km to Giscome Portage regional park via Mitchell Road. Site of historic Huble Homestead; guided tours, picnicking. Donations accepted.

Historic Huble Homestead. Northern BC Pioneer Homestead and Fraser River Trading Post. Scenic riverfront location. Original furnished log buildings, including the Huble House—oldest home in the region. Guided interpretive tours. farm animals, picnic areas, general store. Admission by donation. Just 6 km east of Highway 97. Phone (250) 564-7033. [ADVERTISEMENT]

PG 28.2 (45.4 km) **DC 221.8** (356.9 km) Turnoff to west for **Summit Lake**, a resort area popular with Prince George residents; lake char and rainbow fishing spring and fall.

PG 29.3 (47.2 km) **DC 220.7** (355.2 km) Westcoast Energy compressor station.

PG 30.7 (49.4 km) **DC 219.3** (352.9 km) Second turnoff to west for Summit Lake.

PG 36.6 (58.9 km) **DC 213.4** (343.4 km) Cottonwood Creek.

PG 38.8 (62.4 km) **DC 211.2** (339.9 km) Paved turnout with litter barrel.

PG 40.6 (65.3 km) **DC 209.4** (337 km) Railroad crossing.

PG 42 (67.6 km) **DC 208** (334.7 km) Slow down for sharp turn across railroad tracks.

PG 43.9 (70.6 km) **DC 206.1** (331.7 km) Turnoff to west for **Crooked River Provincial Park**; 90 campsites, picnic area, picnic shelter, flush toilets, tables, firepits, dump station. Camping fee charged. Also horseshoe pits, volleyball, playground, trails and swimming. Powerboats prohibited. Crooked River and area lakes have fair fishing for rainbow, Dolly Varden, grayling and whitefish.

Highway 97 follows the Crooked River north to McLeod Lake.

PG 44.8 (72.1 km) **DC 205.2** (330.1 km) **BEAR LAKE** (pop. 300); unincorporated. Gas, diesel, propane, grocery, restaurant, motel, RV park, gift shop, post office and ambulance station. Highway maintenance camp.

The 2 lumber mills in town are the main industry of the area, employing approximately two-thirds of the community. Inquire locally about area fly fishing for rainbow. Information on area fishing, hiking, hunting and swimming may also be obtained from the Bear Lake Community Commission; phone (250) 972-4488, or write general delivery, Bear Lake, BC V0J 3G0.

Grizzly Inn, Restaurant, Motel & RV Park. See display ad this section. ▲

PG 50.7 (81.6 km) DC 199.3 (320.7 km) Angusmac Creek.

PG 54.2 (87.2 km) DC 195.8 (315.1 km) Tumbler Ridge branch line British Columbia Railway connects Tumbler Ridge with the B.C. Railway and Canadian National Railway, allowing for shipments of coal from Tumbler Ridge to Ridley Island near Prince Rupert.

PG 55.6 (89.5 km) DC 194.4 (312.8 km) Large gravel turnout with litter barrel to west.

PG 56.1 (90.3 km) DC 193.9 (312 km) Large gravel turnout with litter barrel to west.

PG 57 (91.7 km) DC 193 (310.6 km) Large gravel turnout with litter barrel to west.

PG 60.8 (97.8 km) DC 189.2 (304.5 km) Turnout with litter barrel to east.

PG 62.4 (100.4 km) DC 187.6 (301.9 km) Large gravel turnout with litter barrel to east.

PG 65.2 (104.9 km) DC 184.8 (297.4 km) Lomas Creek.

PG 67.9 (109.3 km) DC 182.1 (293 km) Large, double-ended, paved rest area to west beside small lake; litter barrels, picnic tables and pit toilets.

PG 68.8 (110.7 km) DC 181.2 (291.6 km) 42 Mile Creek.

PG 71.8 (115.5 km) DC 178.2 (286.8 km) **Whiskers Bay Resort** has beautiful lakeside camping spots on a quiet bay, some with electricity and water. Hot showers. Cabins with showers, fridges and cooking facilities. Fishing is right off our dock or in the many surrounding lakes. Sunsets are sensational and hummingbirds are bountiful. The cafe offers breakfast, lunch, wonderful burgers, homemade pies, soups, the best coffee on the highway and real northern hospitality. Come visit us! [ADVERTISEMENT]

PG 76.6 (123.3 km) DC 173.4 (279.1 km) First view northbound of McLeod Lake and view of Whisker's Point.

PG 77.7 (125 km) DC 172.3 (277.3 km) **Whisker's Point Provincial Park** to west on McLeod Lake; paved loop road, 69 level gravel sites, tap water, flush toilets, boat ramp, fire rings, firewood and picnic tables. Also horseshoe pits, volleyball, playground and picnic shelter. Camping fee charged. Boat launch, swimming and sandy beach. McLeod Lake has fair fishing for rainbow, lake char and Dolly Varden, spring and fall, trolling is best. ▲

PG 84 (135.2 km) DC 166 (267.1 km) Food, gas, camping and lodging. ▲

PG 84.5 (136 km) DC 165.5 (266.3 km) **FORT McLEOD** (unincorporated) has a grocery. A monument here commemorates the founding of Fort McLeod, oldest permanent settlement west of the Rockies and west of San Francisco. Founded in 1805 by Simon Fraser as a trading post for the North West Trading Co., the post was named by Fraser for Archie McLeod.

PG 84.7 (136.3 km) DC 165.3 (266 km) **McLEOD LAKE** (unincorporated), post office, store and liquor store.

PG 85 (136.8 km) DC 165 (265.5 km) Turnoff for **Carp Lake Provincial Park**, 20 miles/32 km west via gravel road; 105 campsites on Carp and War lakes, limited island camping, picnic tables, firepits, boat launch, fishing and swimming. Also tap water, dump station, horseshoe pits, playground and picnic shelter. Ten-minute walk to scenic War Falls. Camping fee charged. Park access road follows McLeod River to Carp Lake. Carp Lake, rainbow June through September; special restrictions in effect, check current posted information. **McLeod River**, rainbow from July, fly-fishing only. ▲

PG 85.6 (137.8 km) DC 164.4 (264.6 km) Paved turnout with litter barrel to west.

PG 87.6 (141 km) DC 162.4 (261.4 km) Westcoast Energy compressor station and McLeod Lake school.

PG 89.8 (144.5 km) DC 160.2 (257.8 km) Turnoff to west for **Tudyah Lake Provincial Park**; 36 campsites, picnic tables, fire rings, firewood, pit toilets, drinking water. Also swimming, boat ramp, fishing. Camping fee charged. ▲

Tudyah Lake, shore access, rainbow, Dolly Varden and some grayling in summer and late fall. **Pack River** (flows into Tudyah Lake), fishing for grayling (catch-and-release only), June 1 to July 1; rainbow, June 10 to November; large Dolly Varden, Sept. 15 to Oct. 10, spinning. ▲

PG 89.9 (144.7 km) DC 160.1 (257.6 km) Bear Creek bridge.

PG 93.9 (151.1 km) DC 156.1 (251.2 km) Gas, food and lodging (open year-round).

PG 94.7 (152.4 km) DC 155.3 (249.9 km) Parsnip River bridge. This is the Rocky Mountain Trench, marking the western boundary of the Rocky Mountains. Northbound motorists begin gradual climb through the Misinchinka then Hart ranges of the Rocky Mountains.

Parsnip River, good fishing for grayling and Dolly Varden, some rainbow, best from August to October; a boat is necessary. ▲

PG 95.2 (153.2 km) DC 154.8 (249.1 km) **Junction** with Highway 39 (paved), which leads 18 miles/29 km to the community of Mackenzie (description follows); food, gas, lodging and camping. **Tourist information caboose** at junction; picnic tables, toilets.

MACKENZIE (pop. 5,206) lies at the south end of Williston Lake, one of the largest man-made reservoirs on the continent. Mackenzie was built in 1965, its construction sparked by the Peace River Dam project. The first residents moved here in July 1966. Today, industry includes mining and forestry. On display in Mackenzie is the "world's largest tree crusher": The 56-foot-long electrically powered Le Tourneau G175 tree crusher was used in clearing land at the Peace River Power Project in the mid-1960s. Mackenzie has all visitor facilities, including motels, restaurants, shopping malls, gas stations and a municipal campground. Attractions include swimming, waterskiing, fishing and boating at Morfee Lake. ▲

PG 95.5 (153.7 km) DC 154.5 (248.6 km) Highway crosses railroad tracks.

PG 98.9 (158.2 km) DC 151.1 (243.2 km) Gravel turnout with litter barrel to east.

PG 106 (170.6 km) DC 144 (231.7 km) Turnout with litter barrel to east.

PG 108.4 (174.4 km) DC 141.6 (227.9 km) Highway maintenance yard.

PG 108.5 (174.6 km) DC 141.5 (227.7 km) Bridge over Honeymoon Creek.

Improved road northbound to Dawson Creek.

PG 109.6 (176.4 km) DC 140.4 (225.9 km) Powerlines crossing highway carry electricity south from hydro dams in the Hudson's Hope area (see **Milepost PG 187.9**).

PG 110.5 (177.8 km) DC 139.5 (224.5 km) Slow down for sharp curve across railroad tracks.

PG 112.3 (180.7 km) DC 137.7 (221.6 km) Bridge over Rolston Creek; dirt turnout by small falls to west.

PG 115.3 (185.6 km) DC 134.7 (216.8 km) **Bijoux Falls Provincial Park**; parking area, picnic tables, toilets (wheelchair accessible). A pleasant stop on the west side of highway to view the falls and spot Steller's jays. Good photo opportunities.

Misinchinka River, southeast of the highway; fishing for grayling, whitefish and Dolly Varden. ▲

WEST ACCESS ROUTE

Popular rest stop for motorists is Bijoux Falls Provincial Park at Milepost PG 115.3. (© Earl L. Brown, staff)

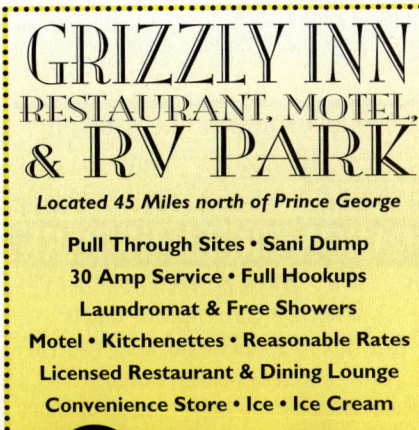

GRIZZLY INN
RESTAURANT, MOTEL, & RV PARK

Located 45 Miles north of Prince George

Pull Through Sites • Sani Dump
30 Amp Service • Full Hookups
Laundromat & Free Showers
Motel • Kitchenettes • Reasonable Rates
Licensed Restaurant & Dining Lounge
Convenience Store • Ice • Ice Cream

• Regular
• Supreme
• Diesel

250-972-4333
Box 1802, Bear Lake, BC V0J 3G0

WEST ACCESS ROUTE • Chetwynd

PG 116.3 (187.2 km) DC 133.7 (215.2 km) Highway crosses under railroad.

PG 119.3 (191.8 km) DC 130.8 (210.5 km) Crossing **Pine Pass** (elev. 2,868 feet/874m), the highest point on the John Hart–Peace River Highway, and the lowest pass breaching the Rocky Mountains in Canada. Beautiful view of the Rockies to the northeast. Good highway over pass; steep grade southbound.

PG 119.4 (192.2 km) DC 130.6 (210.2 km) Turnoff to Powder King Ski Village. Skiing November to late April; chalet with ski shop, cafeteria, restaurant and lounge, hostel-style hotel. This area receives an annual average snowfall of 495 inches.

PG 121.4 (195.4 km) DC 128.6 (207 km) Paved viewpoint to east with point-of-interest sign about Pine Pass and view of Azouzetta Lake. Pit toilet and litter barrels.

PG 122.4 (197 km) DC 127.6 (205.3 km) Access to Azouzetta Lake Lodge on **Azouzetta Lake**; food, lodging and camping (closed in 2002; current status unknown). Very scenic spot. Spectacular hiking on

Murray Mountain Trail. Fishing for rainbow (stocked lake) to 1½ lbs., flies or lures, July to October. Boat launch.

PG 125.5 (202 km) DC 124.5 (200.3 km) Microwave station and receiving dish to west.

PG 125.7 (202.3 km) DC 124.3 (200 km) Duke Energy compressor station.

PG 128.7 (207.1 km) DC 121.3 (195.2 km) Power lines cross highway.

PG 131.1 (211 km) DC 118.9 (191.3 km) Turnout with litter barrel. Watch for moose northbound.

PG 140.6 (226.3 km) DC 109.4 (176.1 km) Bridge over Link Creek.

PG 141.4 (227.5 km) DC 108.6 (174.8 km) Gravel turnout with litter barrels.

PG 142.3 (229 km) DC 107.7 (173.3 km) Bridge over West Pine River.

PG 142.8 (229.8 km) DC 107.2 (172.5 km) Bridge over West Pine River.

PG 143 (230.1 km) DC 107 (172.2 km) Large, double-ended paved rest area with picnic tables, litter barrels and pit toilets beside Pine River. Across the road is **Heart Lake** Forestry campground with toilets, picnic tables, firepits and garbage containers; fishing for stocked trout.

PG 143.4 (230.8 km) DC 106.6 (171.6 km) Bridge over West Pine River, B.C. Railway overpass. Private RV park.

PG 144.3 (232.2 km) DC 105.7 (170.1 km) Silver Sands Lodge; food, gas, lodging and camping.

PG 146.1 (235.1 km) DC 103.9 (167.2 km) Cairns Creek.

PG 146.9 (236.4 km) DC 103.1 (165.9 km) Gravel access road to Pine River to south.

PG 148.2 (238.5 km) DC 101.8 (163.8 km) LeMoray (unincorporated). Highway maintenance camp.

PG 148.3 (238.7 km) DC 101.7 (163.7 km) Gravel turnout to south.

PG 148.8 (239.5 km) DC 101.2 (162.9 km) Lillico Creek.

PG 149.7 (240.9 km) DC 100.3 (161.4 km) Marten Creek.

PG 150.4 (242 km) DC 99.6 (160.3 km) Big Boulder Creek.

PG 156.2 (251.4 km) DC 93.8 (151 km) Fisher Creek.

PG 156.9 (252.5 km) DC 93.1 (149.8 km) Large gravel turnout with litter barrel to south beside Pine River.

PG 159.9 (257.3 km) DC 90.1 (145 km) Crassier Creek. Watch for moose and deer in area, especially at dusk and night.

PG 161.7 (260.2 km) DC 88.3 (142.1 km) Duke Energy compressor station.

PG 163.6 (263.3 km) DC 86.4 (139 km) Pull-off to south.

PG 169.5 (272.8 km) DC 80.5 (129.5 km) Turnout with picnic tables, pit toilets and litter barrel to south at Jack Pine Point overlooking the beautiful Pine River valley. Chetwynd area map.

PG 172.4 (277.4 km) DC 77.6 (124.9 km) Duke Energy (natural gas), Pine River plant. View of the Rocky Mountain foothills to the south and west.

PG 177.4 (285.5 km) DC 72.6 (116.8 km) Turnout with litter barrel.

PG 178.4 (287.1 km) DC 71.6 (115.2 km) **Caron Creek RV Park.** See display ad this section.

PG 181.9 (292.7 km) DC 68.1 (109.6 km) Bissett Creek.

PG 183.6 (295.5 km) DC 66.4 (106.9 km) Turnout with litter barrels at Wildmare Creek.

PG 184.1 (296.3 km) DC 65.9 (106 km) Truck stop; gas, diesel, food and lodging.

PG 187 (300.9 km) DC 63 (101.4 km) Trailhead for 50-mile/80-km Chetwynd area hiking and biking trail system.

PG 187.2 (301.3 km) DC 62.8 (101.1 km) **Little Prairie Heritage Museum.** Features the region's pioneer days, and is well worth a visit. The museum is open from the first Tuesday in July to the last Saturday in August. Phone (250) 788-3358.

Chetwynd

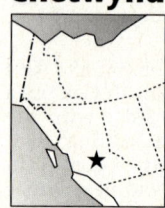

PG 187.6 (301.9 km) DC 62.4 (100.4 km) Located on Highway 97 at the junction with Highway 29 north to the Alaska Highway via Hudson's Hope, and south to Tumbler Ridge. **Population:** 3,119; area 9,000. **Emergency Services:** Phone 911.

Visitor Information: Open 9 A.M. to 5 P.M. in summer, 9 A.M. to 4 P.M. weekdays rest of year. Write District of Chetwynd, Box 357, Chetwynd V0C 1J0, or phone (250) 401-4100; fax (250) 401-4101.

Elevation: 2,017 feet/615m. **Radio:** CISN-FM 103.9, CJDC 890, CKNL 560, CBC-FM 93.5, CHET-FM 94.5. **Television:** 7 channels (includes CBC, BCTV, ABC, CBS, CHETTV and NBC) plus pay cable.

The town, formerly known as Little Prairie, is a division point on the British Columbia Railway. The name was changed to honour the late British Columbia Minister of Railways, Ralph Chetwynd, who was instrumental in the northward extension of the province-owned railway.

In recent years, Chetwynd's collection of chain saw sculptures has earned it the title, "Chain Saw Sculpture Capital of the World." The Infocentre has a map showing locations of the more than 45 sculptures in town.

Forestry, mining, natural gas processing, ranching and farming are the main industries in Chetwynd. Louisiana Pacific has a modern non-polluting pulp mill here.

CHETWYND ADVERTISERS

District of Chetwynd ....Ph. (250) 401-4100
Pine Cone Motor Inn ....Ph. (250) 788-3311
The Swiss Inn Restaurant .Ph. (250) 788-2566
Westwind RV Park ....Ph. (250) 788-2190

---

10 miles west of Chetwynd on Highway 97 South
170 miles North East of Prince George

CARON CREEK RV PARK

JUNK & STUFF
ANTIQUES • COLLECTABLES • CRAFTS

P.O. Box 551, Chetwynd, B.C. V0C 1J0
Grass & Gravel Pull Through
Full Service Sites-30 amp power • Pay Phone
Clean washrooms with FREE HOT SHOWERS

DISCOUNTS FOR SENIORS AND ALL TRAVEL CLUB MEMBERS

SET IN THE BEAUTIFUL ROCKY MOUNTAIN FOOTHILLS
ALLEN & LORRIE KINKEAD-HOSTS   phone-250-788-2522
                                 fax   -250-788-2208

WESTWIND R.V. PARK

Newly Opened Summer '96 ❋ Chetwynd, B.C.

Located on 53rd Ave. 2 km past lights on Hwy 97 North Towards Dawson Creek

50 Large Pull Thru Sites with Full Hookups
New Restrooms, Showers & Laundry Facility with Handicap Access
30 Amps ❋ Town Water ❋ Grassy Sites ❋ R.V. Wash ❋ Hot Showers
Picnic Area ❋ Playground ❋ Firepits ❋ Sani-Station ❋ T.V. – 10 Channels
Modem Friendly ❋ Public Phone ❋ Owner On Site for Supervision & Security

Groups Welcome!

Your Hosts David & Laurie Gayse
Box 2157 Chetwynd, B.C. V0C 1J0

Phone (250) 788-2190 • Fax (250) 788-2086
e-mail: wwrvpark@pris.bc.ca

Chetwynd has an extensive collection of chainsaw sculptures displayed around town. (© Earl L. Brown, staff)

Chetwynd lies at the northern end of the North East Coal resource, one of the largest known coal deposits on earth. Quintette Mine near Tumbler Ridge (56 miles/90 km south of Chetwynd) was the world's largest computerized open pit coal mine until is shut down in 2000.

Chetwynd has several large motels, fast-food outlets, restaurants, banks and bank machines, post office, 3 laundromats, gas stations, supermarkets and 2 9-hole golf courses. Good traveler's stop with easy access to all services. (Heavy commercial and industrial traffic often fill up local motels and campgrounds; reserve ahead.) Free Internet access available for travelers at the Infocentre, the library and Northern Lights College.

Recreation includes a hockey arena, curling rink, soccer fields and ball diamonds. Chetwynd & District Leisure Pool has a wave machine, whirlpool, sauna and weight room; open daily, visitors welcome.

There is a Farmer's Market every Friday in summer at the Elks Hall.

There is a dump station at the 51st Avenue car/truck wash. There are private RV parks in town and on Highway 97. **Moberly Lake Provincial Park** is 12 miles/19.3 km north of Chetwynd via Highway 29 north (see "Highway 29/Hudson's Hope Loop" log this section). The park has 109 campsites, beach, picnic area, playground, nature trail, boat launch and a private marina next door with RV sites, boat rental and concession. Good swimming at Moberly Lake on a warm summer day. Worth the drive. ▲

Westwind RV Park. Good Sam. Area's newest and most modern. On Highway 97 North towards Dawson Creek. 50 large pull-through sites with full hookups. New, immaculate restrooms and showers. Laundry facility. Wheelchair access. Walking distance to leisure pool and hiking trails. Your perfect stopping point for your Northern travels ... ask about our area attractions. Your hosts, David and Laurie Gayse. Phone (250) 788-2190, fax (250) 788-2086. See our display ad for more. [ADVERTISEMENT] ▲

West Access Route Log
(continued)

PG 187.8 (302.2 km) DC 62.2 (100.1 km) Highway crosses railroad tracks.

PG 187.9 (302.4 km) DC 62.1 (99.9 km)

Junction with Highway 29 north to Moberly Lake, Peace River Provincial Recreation Area and Peace Canyon Dam and Hudson's Hope. Highway 29 north connects with the Alaska Highway 53.7 miles/86.4 km north of Dawson Creek. See "Hudson's Hope Loop/Highway 29" on pages 90-91.

Highway climbs next 12 miles/19 km for Dawson Creek-bound motorists.

PG 189.4 (304.8 km) DC 60.6 (97.5 km) **Junction** with Highway 29 (paved) south to Gwillim Lake and Tumbler Ridge. Travelers can make a loop trip by taking Highway 29 (paved) south 56 miles/90 km to Tumbler Ridge, then driving Highway 52 (the Heritage Highway) 60 miles/96 km back to junction with Highway 97 just west of Dawson Creek at **Milepost PG 237.7**. Highway 52 is paved with many rolling hills, some 8 percent grades and several S curves.

Major attraction on this side trip is the spectacular 225-foot/69-m **Kinuseo Falls** in Monkman Provincial Park. The falls are accessible by riverboat tour, or drive 37miles/60 km south from Tumbler Ridge via a gravel road to a 42-site campground; viewing platform of falls is a short walk from the campground.

TUMBLER RIDGE (pop. 3,775) has all visitor facilities. Tumbler Ridge is the site of some important recent dinosaur fossil finds.

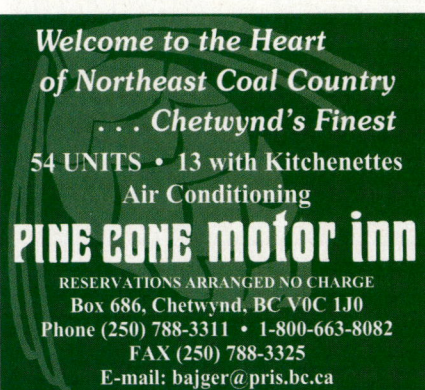

Call District of Chetwynd
Box 357, Chetwynd, BC, V0C 1J0,
Phone: 250-401-4100
d-chet@gochetwynd.com
http://www.gochetwynd.com

The Super Natural Beauty of Chetwynd is sure to impress EVERYONE!

Chetwynd has on–site carving demonstrations. Contact the visitor information centre for a free chainsaw tour map and demonstration times.

OTHER ATTRACTIONS INCLUDE:

WAVE pool, curling, snowmobiling, boating, cross country skiing, downhill skiing, fishing, industrial tours, camping, hunting, golf, hiking trails, airport, shopping, friendly people, wilderness .....

Hudson's Hope Loop/Highway 29

WEST ACCESS ROUTE • Hudson's Hope Loop

The Hudson's Hope Loop links the John Hart Highway (Highway 97) with the Alaska Highway (also Highway 97) via BC Highway 29 north from Chetwynd or east from the Alaska Highway north of Fort St. John. This 86.9-mile/139.8-km paved loop road provides year-round access to the town of Hudson's Hope, W.A.C. Bennett Dam, Peace Canyon Dam and Moberly Lake. As a shortcut bypassing Dawson Creek, the Hudson's Hope Loop saves about 29 miles/47 km.

Highway 29 is a good, scenic 2-lane road with a few steep and winding sections.

Distance from Chetwynd (C) is followed by distance from Alaska Highway junction (AH).

C 0 AH 86.9 (139.8 km) Junction of Highways 29 and 97 at Chetwynd.

C 0.5 (0.8 km) AH 86.4 (139 km) Truck weigh scales to west. Highway climbs next 4.3 miles/7 km westbound.

C 2.3 (3.7 km) AH 84.6 (136.1 km) Jackfish Road to east.

C 5 (8 km) AH 81.9 (131.9 km) Turnout with litter barrel to west.

C 12 (19.3 km) AH 74.9 (120.5 km) Gravel access road leads 2 miles/3.2 km west to **Moberly Lake Provincial Park** on south shore; 109 campsites, swimming, waterskiing, picnicking, drinking water, dump station, boat launch, $12 camping fee. This beautiful 9-mile/14.5-km-long lake drains at its east end into Moberly River, which in turn runs into the Peace River. Fishing for lake trout, Dolly Varden and whitefish.

C 12.2 (19.6 km) AH 74.7 (120.2 km) Moberly River bridge; parking area with litter barrel at south end.

C 15.9 (25.6 km) AH 71 (114.3 km) Highway cairn is memorial to John Moberly, fur trader and explorer who first landed here in 1865.

C 16.4 (26.4 km) AH 70.5 (113.5 km) Spencer Tuck Regional Park; picnic tables, swimming, fishing and boat launch.

C 17.4 (28 km) AH 69.5 (111.8 km) Camping resort.

C 18.3 (29.5 km) AH 68.6 (110.4 km) MOBERLY LAKE. Post office, cafe, store and pay phone.

C 18.5 (29.8 km) AH 68.4 (110.1 km) Moberly Lake and District Golf Club, 0.7 mile/1.1 km from highway; 9 holes, grass greens, rentals, clubhouse, licensed lounge. Open May to September.

C 25.4 (40.9 km) AH 61.5 (99 km) Cameron Lake Campground; tables, water, toilets, firewood, playground, horseshoe pits, boat launch (no motorboats) and swimming. Camping fee $7/night. Open May to September.

C 30.7 (49.4 km) AH 56.2 (90.4 km) Gravel turnout with litter barrel to east. Highway descends northbound to Hudson's Hope.

C 35.9 (57.8 km) AH 51 (82.1 km) Suspension bridge over Peace River; paved turnouts at both ends of bridge with concrete totem pole sculptures. View of Peace Canyon Dam.

C 36.5 (58.7 km) AH 50.4 (81.1 km) Turnoff to west for Dinosaur Lake Campground and B.C. Hydro **Peace Canyon Dam Visitor Centre** (0.6 mile/1 km) adjacent the Powerhouse. The dam's visitor centre is open from 8 A.M. to 4 P.M. daily from late May through Labour Day; weekdays the rest of the year (closed holidays). Self-guided tour includes a full-scale model of duck-billed dinosaurs and a tableau portraying Alexander Mackenzie's discovery of the Peace River canyon. A pictorial display traces the construction of the Peace Canyon Dam. No admission charge. Tour guides on duty from May to September. For more information, phone (250) 783-5000; or www.bchydro.com/recreation.

Dinosaur Lake Campground, on Dinosaur Lake, has 50 campsites, firepits, water pump, toilets and tables. Boat launch and swimming area. Camping fee of $7/night. Open May to September.

C 38.3 (61.6 km) AH 48.6 (78.2 km) Alwin Holland Memorial Park (0.5 mile/0.8 km east of highway) is named for the first teacher in Hudson's Hope, who willed his property, known locally as The Glen, to be used as a public park. There are 17 campsites, picnic grounds, barbecues and water. Camping fee of $7/night.

C 39 (62.8 km) AH 47.9 (77.1 km) King Gething Park; small campground with 15 grassy sites, picnic tables, cookhouse, flush toilets, showers and dump station east side of highway. Camping fee of $7/night.

Hudson's Hope

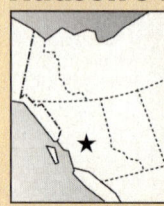

C 40.4 (65 km) AH 46.5 (74.8 km). Population: 1,122. **Emergency Services:** Phone 911. **Visitor Information:** Tourist information booth at Beattie Park is open daily in May and June from 8:30 A.M. to 5:30 P.M., and in July and August from 8:30 A.M. to 9 P.M. Info hotline, phone (250) 783-9901; web site http://dist.hudsons-hope.bc.ca.

Elevation: 1,707 feet/520m. **Climate:** Summer temperatures range from 60°F/16°C to 90°F/32°C, with an average of 135 frost-free days annually. **Radio:** CBC, CKNL 560, CJDC 870. **Television:** Channels 2, 5, 8, 11 and cable.

HUDSON'S HOPE ADVERTISERS

District of Hudson's
  Hope ....Ph. (250) 783-5194
Hudson's Hope Museum ...Ph. (250) 783-5735

VISIT THE LAND OF DINOSAURS AND DAMS
HUDSON'S HOPE, BC

While in Hudson's Hope & Area, Visit:
• Hudson's Hope Museum
• Dunlevy Wildlife Area
• W.A.C. Bennett Dam
• Peace Canyon Dam
• Trappers Cabin
• Municipal Campgrounds

Phone (250) 783-5194 • FAX (250) 783-5598
Box 330, Hudson's Hope, BC V0C 1V0
website: http://dist.hudsons-hope.bc.ca e-mail: info@dist.hudsons-hope.bc.ca

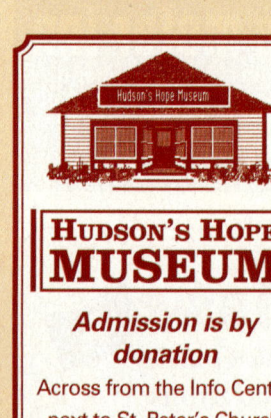

HUDSON'S HOPE MUSEUM
DISPLAYS
Fossil
Dinosaur
Pioneer
Aboriginal

Worth a stop!

Admission is by donation
Across from the Info Center next to St. Peter's Church

Summer Hours
9:30-5:30 Daily

GIFT SHOP Large variety of gifts, books and souvenirs
Great ideas for all occasions

(250) 783-5735
e-mail: hhmuseum@pris.ca

Private Aircraft: Hudson's Hope airstrip, 3.7 miles/6 km west; elev. 2,200 feet/671m; length 5,200 feet/1,585m; asphalt.

Visitor services in Hudson's Hope include 2 hotels, 2 bed and breakfasts, 3 restaurants, 2 service stations, a laundromat, bank, post office, supermarket, bakery, and convenience and hardware stores. Camping at private RV park on the Peace River. ▲

The Hudson's Hope area was first visited in 1793 by Alexander Mackenzie. In 1805, a Hudson's Bay trading post was established here by Simon Fraser. In 1916, after the fur-trading days were over, a major influx of settlers arrived in the area. It was the head of navigation for steamboats on the lower Peace River until 1936, the year of the last scheduled steamboat run. Area coal mines supplied Alaska Highway maintenance camps during the 1940s.

Modern development of Hudson's Hope was spurred by construction of the Peace Power project in the 1960s. Today the area's principal claim to fame is the 600-foot-/183-m-high **W.A.C. Bennett Dam** at the upper end of the Peace River canyon, 15 miles/24 km west of Hudson's Hope. The 100-million-ton dam is one of the largest earth-fill structures in the world, and Williston Lake, behind it, is the largest body of fresh water in British Columbia. The dam provides 30 percent of British Columbia's hydroelectricity.

Free, guided, 1-hour bus tours of the powerhouse are available from the **W.A.C. Bennett Dam Visitor Centre** overlooking Williston Lake Reservoir. The visitor centre also has exhibits, an audio-visual theatre and a deli-style cafe. The visitor centre is open daily from 10 A.M. to 6 P.M., Victoria Day weekend (mid-May) to September (end of Labour Day weekend). Bus tours depart on the half-hour between 10:30 A.M. and 4:30 P.M. Large groups please phone ahead, (250) 783-5048 or 1-888-333-6667. Of-season tours weekdays by appointment only; phone (250) 783-5000.

Also of interest is the **Hudson's Hope Museum** on Highway 29 in town. The Museum, housed in the former Hudson's Bay Post store, has an extensive fossil and prehistory collection. Exhibits include pioneer displays in on-site buildings and an arrowhead/projectile point collection Inquire about dinosaur/paleontology activities. The Museum shop offers a large selection of books, souvenirs and gift items. Admission by donation; phone (250) 783-5735. The historic log **St. Peter's Anglican United Church** is next door to the museum.

Hudson's Hope Loop Log

(continued)
C 41.2 (66.3 km) AH 45.7 (73.5 km) Turnout to north with Hudson's Hope visitor map.
CAUTION: Watch for deer between here and the Alaska Highway, especially at dusk and at night.
C 44 (70.8 km) AH 42.9 (69 km) Lynx Creek bridge.
C 45 (72.4 km) AH 41.9 (67.4 km) **Lynx Creek RV Park & Campground.** See display ad this section. ▲
C 48.4 (77.9 km) AH 38.5 (62 km) Turnout to south for view of the Peace River.
C 50.9 (81.9 km) AH 36 (57.9 km) Farrell Creek bridge.
C 56.6 (91.1 km) AH 30.3 (48.8 km) Pull-through turnout with litter barrels. View of Peace River valley.
C 57.1 (91.9 km) AH 29.8 (48 km) Turnout to south with litter barrels and view of Peace River valley.
C 59.3 (95.4 km) AH 27.6 (44.4 km) Turnout to south with litter barrels.
C 64.7 (104.1 km) AH 22.2 (35.7 km) Halfway River.
C 67.2 (108.1 km) AH 19.7 (31.7 km) Rest area to south with point of interest sign, litter barrel and toilet. A slide occurred here on May 26, 1973, involving an estimated 10 million to 15 million cubic yards of overburden. Slide debris completely blocked the river channel for some 12 hours, backing up the river an estimated 24 feet/7.3m above normal level.
C 71.1 (114.4 km) AH 15.8 (25.4 km) Turnout to north.
C 73.5 (118.3 km) AH 13.4 (21.6 km) Beaver dam to north.
C 74.6 (120.1 km) AH 12.3 (19.8 km) Cache Creek 1-lane bridge. Turnout to north at east end of bridge for picnic area with litter barrels.
C 76.6 (123.3 km) AH 10.3 (16.6 km) Turnout with litter barrel to north overlooking Bear Flat in the Peace River valley. Highway begins climb eastbound. *CAUTION: Switchbacks.*
C 78.1 (125.7 km) AH 8.8 (14.2 km) Highest point on Highway 29 (2,750 feet/838m) overlooking Peace River Plateau. Highway descends on a 10 percent grade westbound. *CAUTION: Switchbacks.*
C 86.9 (139.8 km) AH 0 Junction with the Alaska Highway, 6.7 miles/10.8 km north of Fort St. John. Truck stop at junction with gas, diesel, propane, tire repair, restaurant and convenience store.

Return to Milepost PG 187.6 West Access Route or Milepost DC 53.7 Alaska Highway

For more information on the area, phone (250) 242-3123; or visit their web site at www.tumblerridge.ca.
PG 199.3 (320.7 km) DC 50.7 (81.6 km) Gravel turnouts with litter barrels both sides of highway.
PG 201.2 (323.8 km) DC 48.8 (78.5 km) Slow down for sharp curve across railroad tracks.
PG 204.3 (328.8km) DC 45.7 (73.5km) Access to Louisiana Pacific Pulp Mill to north.
PG 205.6 (330.9 km) DC 44.4 (71.5 km) Turnout with litter barrel and view of the East Pine River valley to the south.
PG 206.5 (332.3 km) DC 43.5 (70 km) Sharp curves approximately next 2 miles/3.2 km as highway descends toward Dawson Creek. View of Table Mountain.
PG 207.9 (334.6 km) DC 42.1 (67.7 km) Highway crosses under railroad.
PG 208.1 (334.9 km) DC 41.9 (67.4 km) East Pine River bridge.

Sharp turn to south at west end of bridge for **East Pine Provincial Park** (0.5 mile on gravel road); boat launch on Pine River. Turnout with litter barrel at park entrance.

From East Pine Provincial Park, canoeists may make a 2-day canoe trip down the Pine River to the Peace River; take-out at Taylor Landing Provincial Park (at **Milepost DC 34** on the Alaska Highway).
PG 208.2 (335.1 km) DC 41.8 (67.3 km) Bridge across East Pine River. Railroad also crosses river here.
PG 208.3 (335.5 km) DC 41.7 (67.1 km) Turnout with litter barrel to south.
PG 209.8 (337.6 km) DC 40.2 (64.7 km) East Pine (unincorporated) has a store and gas station.

Watch for good views of East Pine River bridges next mile northbound.
PG 211.7 (340.7 km) DC 38.3 (61.6 km) Turnout with litter barrel to north. West-bound brake-check area.
PG 221.5 (356.5 km) DC 28.5 (45.9 km) Turnouts with litter barrels both sides of highway.
PG 222 (357.3 km) DC 28 (45 km) **Groundbirch** (unincorporated); store, liquor outlet, gas, propane, diesel and post office.
PG 237.7 (382.5 km) DC 12.3 (19.8 km) **Junction** with Heritage Highway (Highway 52), which leads 59.6 miles/96 km south to the community of Tumbler Ridge. From Tumbler Ridge, the Heritage Highway continues 92 miles/148 km east and north to connect with Highway 2 southeast of Dawson Creek. Inquire locally about road conditions.
PG 238 (383 km) DC 12 (19.3 km) Kiskatinaw River bridge.
PG 240.7 (387.6 km) DC 9.3 (15 km) Arras (unincorporated), cafe and gas station.
PG 247.9 (398.9 km) DC 2.1 (3.4 km) Small turnout with litter barrel and point of interest sign to south.
PG 248 (399.1 km) DC 2 (3.2 km) Northern Lights RV Park. ▲
PG 249.9 (402.2 km) DC 0.1 (0.2 km) Entering Dawson Creek. Tubby's RV Park on south side of highway; **Rotary Lake Park** and camping on north side of highway. ▲
PG 250 (402.3 km) DC 0 **Junction** of the Hart Highway and Alaska Highway; turn right for downtown Dawson Creek, Mile Zero of the Alaska Highway.

Turn to the ALASKA HIGHWAY section on page 92 for description of Dawson Creek and log of the Alaska Highway.

On the Banks of the Mighty Peace River — NEW
LYNX CREEK RV PARK
Highway 29, 6 km north of Hudson's Hope
- Large Level Pull Thrus
- RV Sites - 50 ft. Wide by 80 ft. long
- Free RV Wash
- 30 & 50 Amp Service
- Spotless washrooms/Showers
- Sani-dump
- Fishing
- Great Wildlife Viewing

Owner on site: Kip & Julie Howard • Ph/Fax (250) 783-5333
Box 149, Hudson's Hope, BC V0C 1V0

ALASKA HIGHWAY

	Dawson Cr.	Delta Jct.	Fairbanks	Ft. Nelson	Haines Jct.	Tok	Watson Lk.	Whitehorse
Dawson Cr.		1390	1488	283	985	1282	613	895
Delta Jct.	1390		98	1107	405	108	777	495
Fairbanks	1488	98		1205	503	206	875	603
Ft. Nelson	283	1107	1205		702	999	330	612
Haines Jct.	985	405	503	702		297	372	100
Tok	1282	108	206	999	297		669	387
Watson Lk.	613	777	875	330	372	669		282
Whitehorse	895	495	603	612	100	387	282	

Connects: Dawson Creek, BC, to Delta Junction, AK **Length:** 1,390 miles
Road Surface: Paved **Season:** Open all year
Highest Summit: Summit Lake 4,250 feet
Major Attractions: Muncho Lake, Liard Hotsprings, Watson Lake Signforest, SS *Klondike*, Kluane Lake, Trans-Alaska Pipeline Crossing

(See maps, pages 93–97)

The Alaska Highway just south of Summit Pass, elev. 4,250 feet/1,295m, highest point on the highway. (© Earl L. Brown, staff)

For many people, the Alaska Highway is a great adventure. For others, it's a long drive. But whether you fall into the first group or the second, the vastness of wilderness this pioneer road crosses can't fail to impress you. It is truly a marvelous journey across a great expanse of North America. If you can, take the time to stop and meet the people and see the sights.

Following are some facts about the Alaska Highway and answers to common questions about driving the highway. (Also see the accompanying feature on the history of the highway.) But for the experience, you'll have to drive it yourself!

Alaska Highway facts
The Alaska Highway was built in 1942 (see "History of the Alaska Highway" this section). Quite a few people still refer to the Alaska Highway as the "Alcan" Highway. ALCAN was the military's name for the pioneer road at its completion in 1942, an acronym for Alaska-Canada military highway. But it was not a popular name with many Alaskans, who were unhappy with restrictions placed on civilian traffic on the highway during the war years. The pioneer road was officially renamed the Alaska Highway in March 1943.

It begins at **Mile 0** in Dawson Creek, BC. The first 613 miles/987 km of the Alaska Highway are in British Columbia, where it is designated BC Highway 97. The highway travels in a northwesterly direction to the Yukon Territory border near Watson Lake, YT (**Historical Mile 635**). From there it con-

tinues as Yukon Highway 1, crossing 577 miles/929 km of Yukon Territory to Port Alcan on the Alaska border. The Alaska Highway crosses into Alaska at **Historical**

Mile 1221.8, where it becomes Alaska Route 2. From this international border, it is 200 miles/322 km to Delta Junction, AK (**Historical Mile 1422**), the official end of the Alaska Highway, and 298 miles to Fairbanks, the unofficial end of the highway, at **Historical Mile 1520**.

The 98-mile stretch of highway between Delta Junction and Fairbanks is part of the Richardson Highway from Valdez, although it is designated Alaska Route 2 and often treated as a natural extension of the Alaska Highway. The Richardson Highway (Alaska Route 4) was originally known as the Richardson Trail and predates construction of the Alaska Highway by some 50 years. (Turn to the RICHARDSON HIGHWAY section for the highway log between Delta Junction and Fairbanks.)

The Historical Miles reflect historical driving distances along the Alaska Highway. The highway is shorter today than it was in the 1940s. Reconstruction and rerouting have shaved 30 to 40 miles off the length of the highway, and it continues to get shorter. (Refer to "Mileposts and Kilometreposts" this section for more on the subject.)

Is the Alaska Highway paved?
All of the Alaska Highway is paved, although highway improvement projects—such as the Shakwak Project between Haines Junction and the AK–YT border—often mean motorists have to drive miles of gravel road through construction areas, bringing into question whether that statement is altogether accurate.

But the Alaska Highway is much
(Continues on page 98)

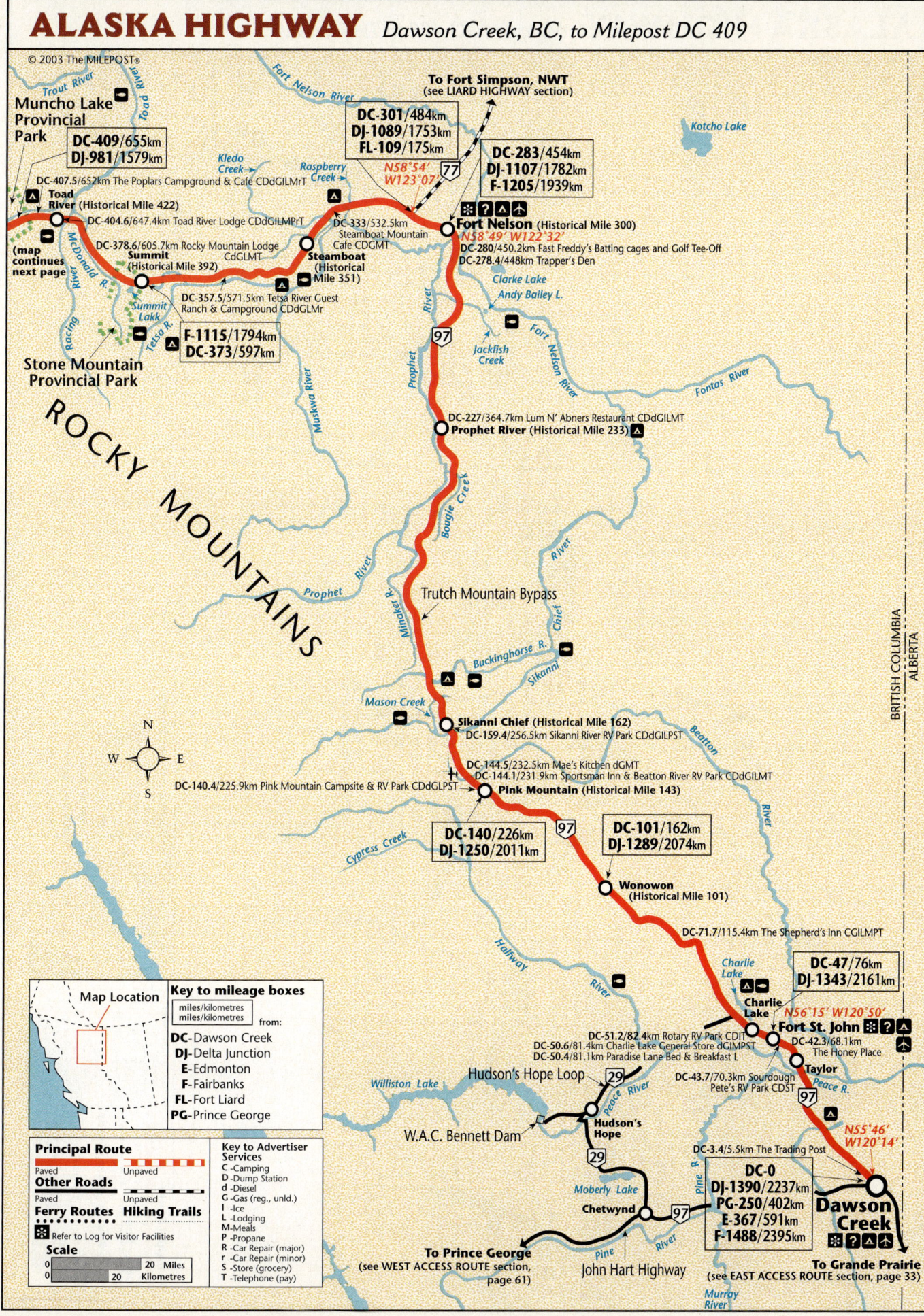

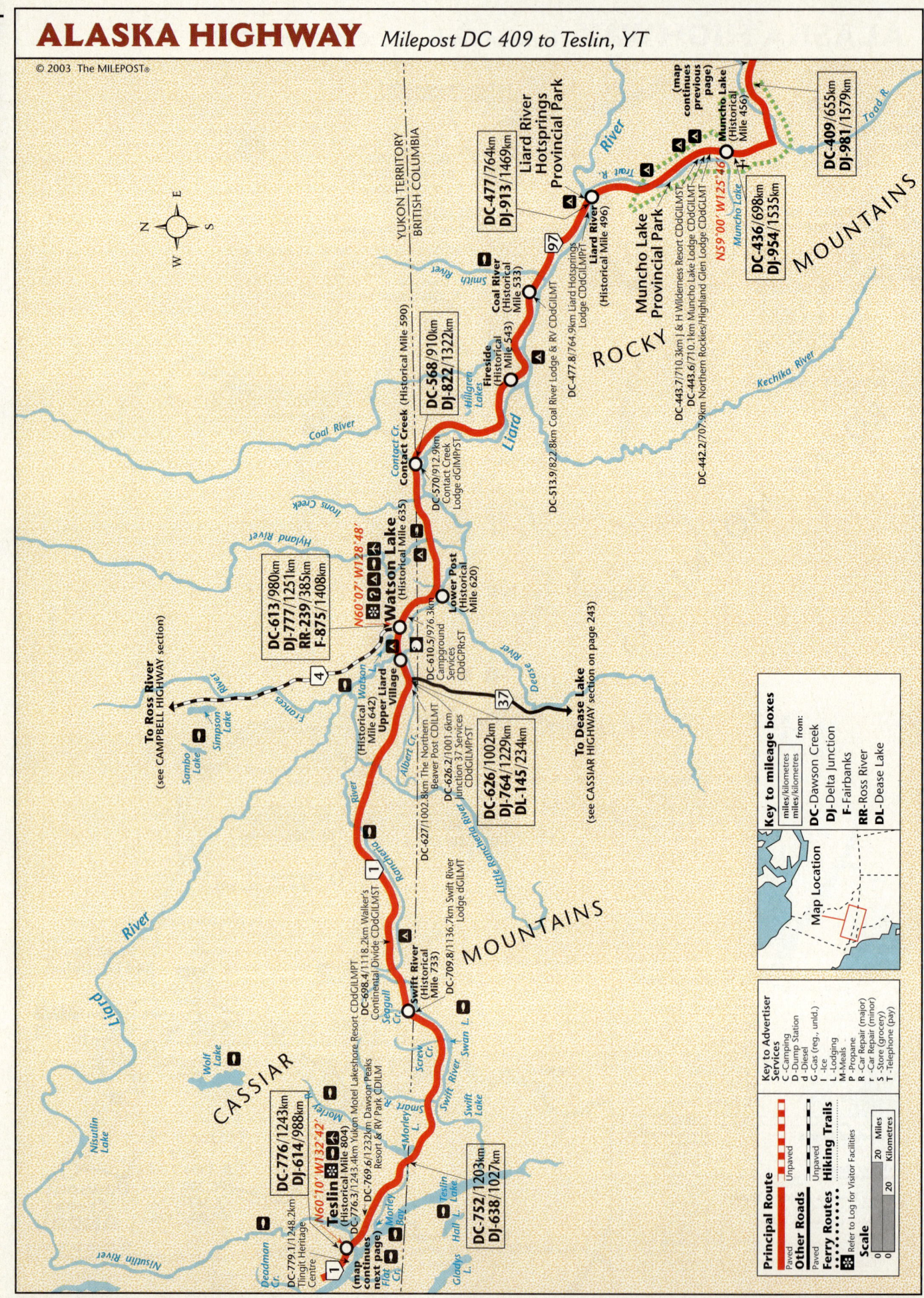

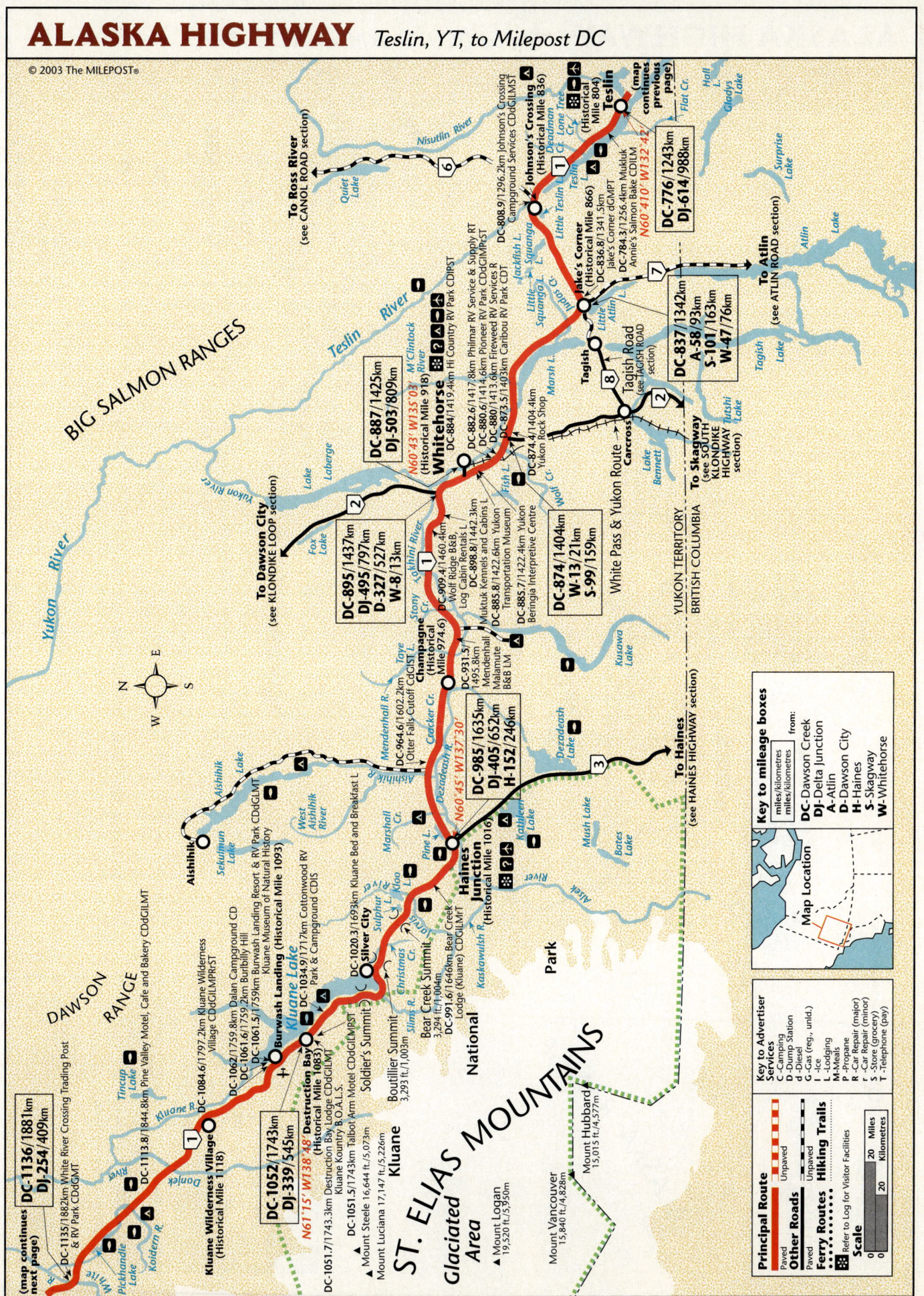

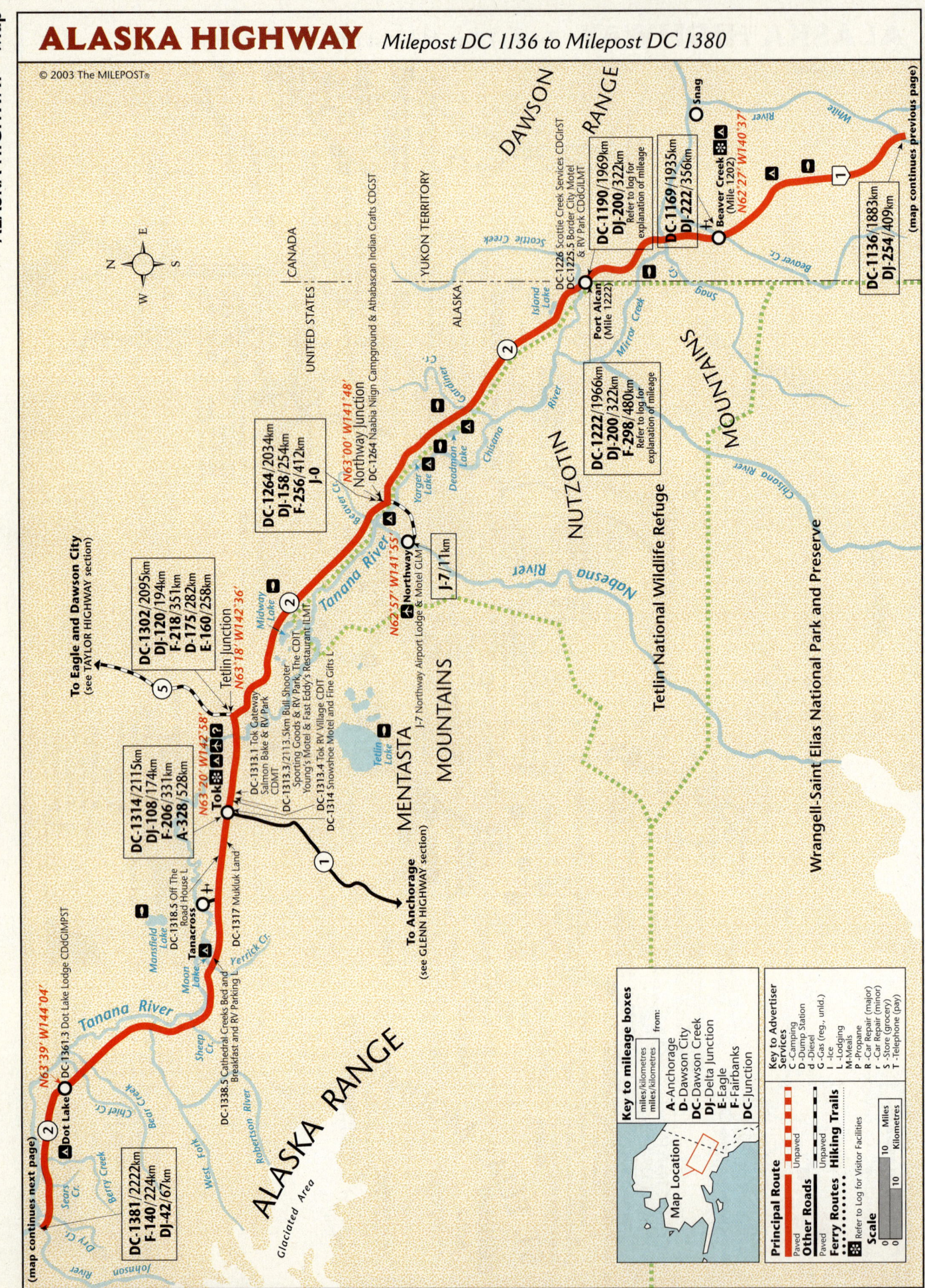

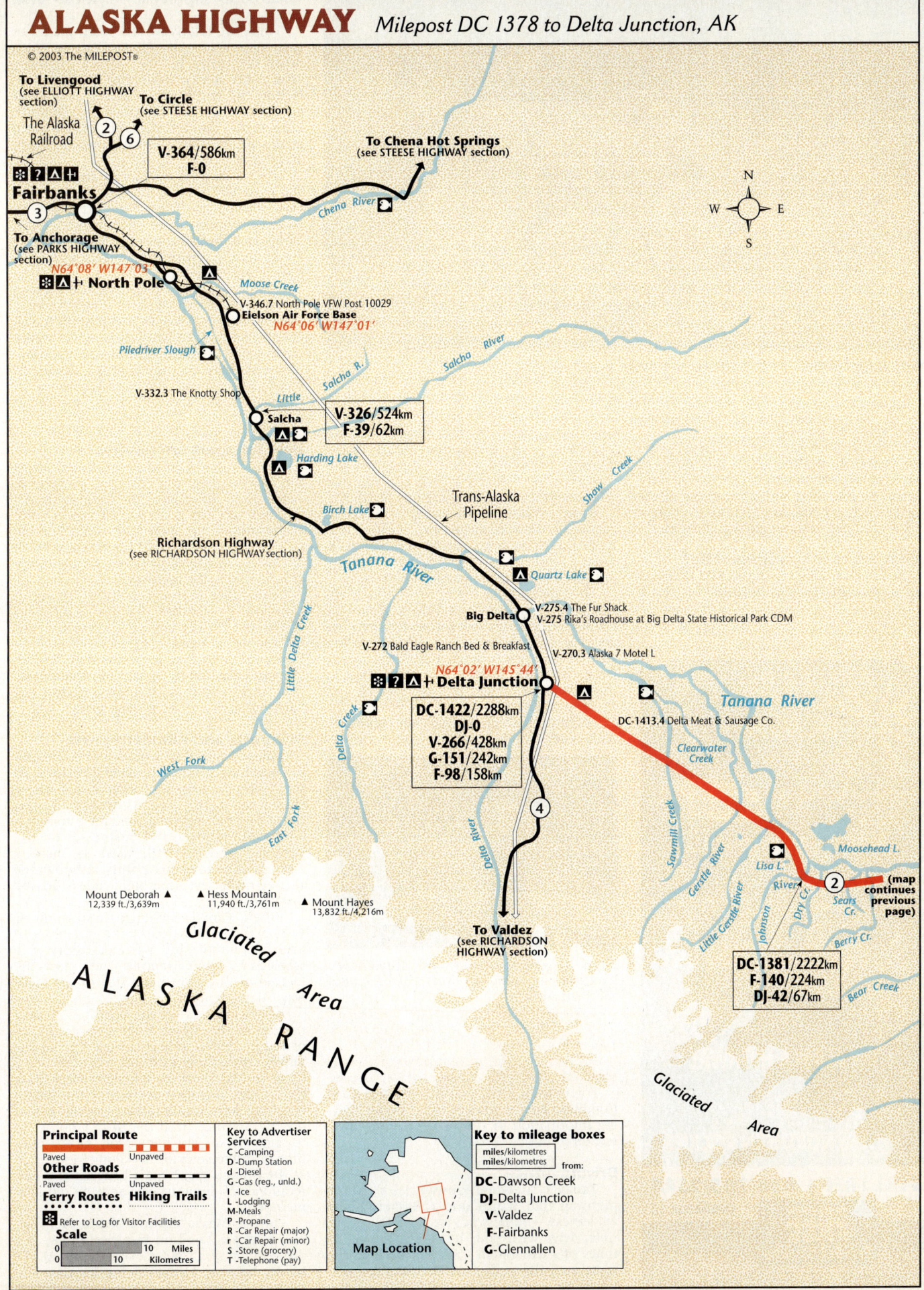

Watch for caribou on the Alaska Highway. (© Earl L. Brown, staff)

(Continued from page 92)
improved from what is was even 20 years ago. It was during the 1980s that many of the rerouting and paving projects were completed. By 1992, the 50th anniversary of the Alaska Highway, the last section of original gravel road had been rerouted and paved.

What are road conditions like?
Road conditions on the Alaska Highway are not unlike road conditions on many secondary roads in the Lower 48 and Canada. It is the tremendous length of the highway, combined with its remoteness and the extremes of the Northern climate, that often result in surprises along this highway.

Road conditions are always subject to change on the Alaska Highway. Weather and traffic can cause deterioration of newer pavement, while construction can quickly improve previously damaged sections.

The asphalt surfacing of the Alaska Highway ranges from poor to excellent. Relatively few stretches of road fall into the 'poor' category, i.e. chuckholes, gravel breaks, hardtop with loose gravel, deteriorated shoulders, bumps and frost heaves (a rippling effect in the pavement caused by the freezing and thawing of the ground).

Much of the highway is in fair condition, with older patched pavement and a mini-

mum of gravel breaks and chuckholes. Recently upgraded sections of road offer excellent surfacing.

CAUTION: Loose gravel patches are common on the Alaska Highway and are often signed. Slow down for loose gravel patches and for gravel road in construction areas. Excessive speeds can lead to loss of control of your vehicle.

For current road conditions, see Road Condition Report sources listed under Driving Information in the TRAVEL PLANNING section of this book.

Driving advice
Today's Alaska Highway is a 2-lane highway that winds and rolls across the wilderness. The best advice is to take your time; drive with your headlights on at all times (it's the law in Canada); keep to the right on hills and corners; use turnouts; watch for wildlife on the road; and—as you would on any highway anywhere else—drive defensively.

There are relatively few steep grades or high summits on the Alaska Highway, with most occurring as the Alaska Highway crosses the Rocky Mountains between Fort Nelson, BC, and Watson Lake, YT. The highest summit on the highway is at Summit Lake, elev. 4,250 feet/1,295m. The few steep grades are generally short stretches from 6 to 10 percent.

Always be alert for bumps and holes in the road and for abrupt changes in highway surfacing. There are stretches of narrow, winding road without shoulders. Also watch for soft shoulders. Dust and mud are generally a problem only in construction areas.

Always watch for construction crews along the Alaska Highway. Extensive road construction may require a detour, or travelers may be delayed while waiting for a pilot car to guide them through the construction. Motorists may encounter rough driving at construction areas, and muddy roadway if there are heavy rains while the roadbed is torn up.

How far apart are services?
Gas, food and lodging are found along the Alaska Highway on an average of every 20 to 50 miles. (The longest stretch without services is about 100 miles.) Not all businesses are open year-round, nor are most services available 24 hours a day. There are dozens of government and private campgrounds along the highway.

Remember that you will be driving in 2 different countries that use 2 different currencies: For the best rate, exchange your money at a bank. There are banks in Dawson Creek, Fort St. John, Fort Nelson, Watson Lake, Whitehorse, Tok, Delta Junction and Fairbanks. Haines Junction has banking service at the general store.

Mileposts and Kilometreposts
Mileposts were first put up at communities and lodges along the Alaska Highway in the 1940s to help motorists know where they were in this vast wilderness. Today, those original mileposts remain a tradition with communities and businesses on the highway and are still used as mailing addresses and reference points, although the figures no longer accurately reflect driving distance.

When Canada switched to the metric system in the mid-1970s, the mileposts in British Columbia and Yukon Territory were replaced by kilometreposts. These posts are located on the right-hand side of the highway (Alaska-bound).

Kilometreposts on the British Columbia portion of the Alaska Highway were recalibrated in 1990 to reflect current driving distances rather than historical mileposts.

In the fall of 2002, kilometreposts along the Yukon Territory portion of the Alaska Highway were recalibrated to reflect actual driving distance from the BC–YT border to the new bypass at Champagne. At our press time, a discrepancy of 56 kilometres existed at the Champagne bypass between the new recalibrated kilometreposts and the old kilometreposts.

On the Alaska portion of the highway, mileposts are based on historical miles, so a discrepancy of 32 miles exists at the AK–YT border between actual driving distance and physical milepost.

History of the Alaska Highway

Alaska Highway motorists are reminded to slow down for safety.

(© Earl L. Brown, staff)

In addition to the kilometreposts in Canada, the governments of British Columbia and Yukon installed commemorative mileposts as part of the 50th anniversary celebration of the Alaska Highway in 1992.

Many of these historic markers are accompanied by signs and interpretive panels. These mileposts reflect the original or traditional mileage and do not reflect actual driving distance.

Kilometreposts and mileposts may be missing altogether in some sections along the Alaska Highway, due to road construction, vandalism or because they have succumbed to the elements.

How do I read the Alaska Highway log?

The MILEPOST® log of the Alaska Highway takes into account physical mileposts and kilometreposts, historical mileposts and actual driving distance.

On the Canadian portion of the highway, The MILEPOST® log gives distance to the AK–YT border from Dawson Creek (**DC**) as actual driving distance in miles followed by kilometre distance based on the kilometreposts (*not necessarily a metric conversion of the first figure*). Use our mileage figure from Dawson Creek to figure correct distance between points on the Alaska Highway within Canada. Use our kilometre figure from Dawson Creek to pinpoint location in reference to physical kilometreposts on the Alaska Highway in Canada.

Traditional milepost figures in Canada are indicated in the text as **Historical Mile**.

On the Alaska portion of the highway,

The MILEPOST® log gives distance from Dawson Creek (**DC**) based on the physical mileposts up along the highway. The mileposts in Alaska reflect historical mileages—not actual driving distance—from Dawson Creek. Thus when you reach the AK–YT border at **Historical Mile 1221.8**, it is **Milepost DC 1189.8** in Canada (the actual driving distance from Dawson Creek) and **Milepost DC 1221.8** in Alaska, reflecting the physical mileposts.

It is not as confusing as it may seem at first glance. The driving distances between points within each country are correct. For driving distances between a destination in Alaska and a starting point in Canada, refer to the Mileage Box at the beginning of this section.

When driving the highway and reading the log, it helps to pay attention to all landmarks, not just the mileposts and kilometreposts. If the highway log indicates a campground is 2 miles north of a certain river crossing, then it will be 2 miles north of that river regardless of the presence of a milepost or kilometrepost.

Weather information

Since the weather frequently influences

Construction of the Alaska Highway officially began on March 9, 1942, and ended 8 months and 12 days later on Oct. 25, 1942. But an overland link between Alaska and the Lower 48 had been studied as early as 1930 under President Herbert Hoover's authorization. It was not until the bombing of Pearl Harbor in December 1941 that construction of the highway was deemed a military necessity. Alaska was considered vulnerable to a Japanese invasion. On Feb. 6, 1942, approval for the Alaska Highway was given by the Chief of Staff, U.S. Army. On Feb. 11, President Roosevelt authorized construction of the pioneer road.

The general route of the highway, determined by the War Department, was along a line of existing airfields from Edmonton, AB, to Fairbanks, AK. This chain of airfields was known as the Northwest Staging Route, and was used to ferry more than 8,000 war planes from Great Falls, MT, to Ladd Air Force Base in Fairbanks, AK, as part of the Russian–American Lend Lease Program. The planes were flown from Fairbanks to Nome, then on to Russia.

In March 1942, rights-of-way through Canada were secured by formal agreement between the 2 countries. The Americans agreed to pay for construction and turn over the Canadian portion of the highway to the Canadian government after the war ended. Canada furnished the right-of-way, waived import duties, sales taxes, income taxes and immigration regulations, and provided construction materials along the route.

A massive mobilization of men and equipment began. Regiments of the U.S. Army Corps of Engineers were moved north to work on the highway. By June, more than 10,000 American troops had poured into the Canadian North. The Public Roads Administration tackled the task of organizing civilian engineers and equipment. Trucks, road-building equipment, office furniture, food, tents and other supplies all had to be located and then shipped north.

Road work began in April, with crews working out of the 2 largest construction camps, Whitehorse and Fort St. John. The highway followed existing winter roads, old Indian trails, rivers and, on occasion, "sight" engineering.

For the soldiers and civilian workers, it was a hard life. Working 7 days a week, they endured mosquitoes and black flies in summer, and below zero temperatures in winter. Weeks would pass with no communication between headquarters and field parties. According to one senior officer with the Public Roads Administration, "Equipment was always a critical problem. There never was enough."

In June 1942, the Japanese invaded Attu and Kiska islands in the Aleutians, adding a new sense of urgency to completion of the road. Crews working from east and west connected at Contact Creek on Sept. 25. By October, it was possible for vehicles to travel the entire length of the highway. The official opening of the Alaska Highway was a ribbon-cutting ceremony held Nov. 20, 1942, on Soldier's Summit at Kluane Lake. (A rededication ceremony was held Nov. 20, 1992, as part of the 50th anniversary celebration of the Alaska Highway.) The Alaska Highway was named an International Historical Engineering Landmark in 1996.

road conditions along the Alaska Highway, weather forecasts may be crucial to a trip up the highway. Detailed weather information for the Canadian portion of the Alaska Highway is available from Atmospheric Environment Service of Environment Canada.

For 24-hour recorded weather information between Dawson Creek and Sikanni Chief, phone (250) 784-2244 or (250) 785-7669; for detailed weather information, phone the weather office at (250) 785-4304 between 6:15 A.M. and 4:45 P.M.; or for weather broadcasts, tune to 580 AM.

Between Sikanni Chief and the BC–YT border, phone (250) 774-6461 for 24-hour recorded message; for detailed weather information phone (250) 774-2302 between 3 A.M. and 6:15 P.M.; or tune your radio to 102.3 FM for weather broadcasts.

Between the BC–YT border and the YT–AK border, phone (867) 668-6061 for 24-hour recorded message; for detailed weather information phone (867) 667-8464 (24 hours a day); or tune your radio to CBC Yukon (570 AM) for weather broadcasts.

Regional weather forecasts are also supplied to local visitor information centres, local hotels and motels, and lodges along the highway.

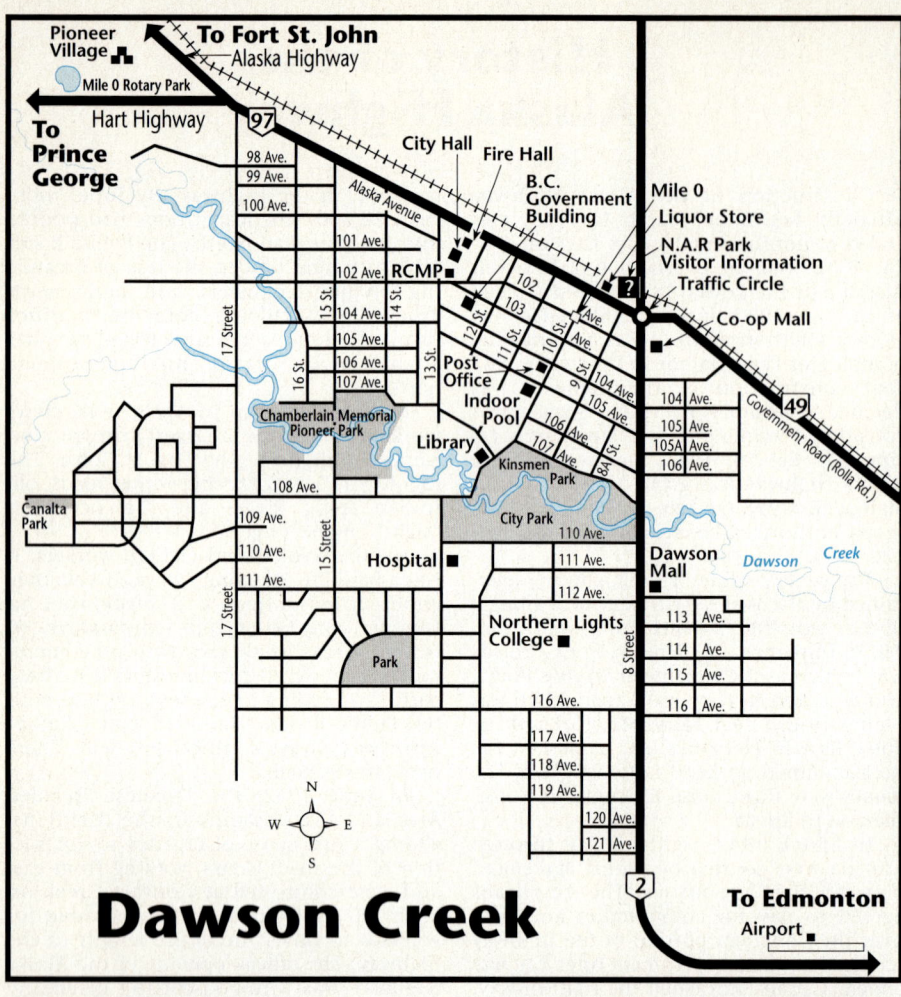

Dawson Creek

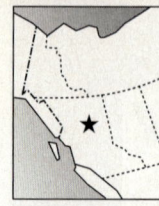

Milepost 0 of the Alaska Highway; 367 miles/591 km northwest of Edmonton, AB; 250 miles/402 km northeast of Prince George, BC. **Population:** 12,800, area 27,000. **Emergency Services: RCMP,** phone (250) 782-5211. **Fire Department,** phone (250) 782-5000. **Ambulance,** phone (250) 782-2211. **Hospital and Poison Centre,** Dawson Creek and District Hospital, 11000 13th St., phone (250) 782-8501.

Visitor Information: At NAR (Northern Alberta Railway) Park on Alaska Avenue at 10th Street (one block west of the traffic circle), in the building behind the railway car. Open year-round, 8 A.M. to 7 P.M. daily in

DAWSON CREEK ADVERTISERS

Alahart RV Park	Ph. (250) 782-4702
Alaska Hotel, Cafe & Diner's Pub	Ph. (250) 782-7040
Dawson Creek Coin Laundry Ltd.	Ph. (250) 782-9389
Dawson Creek Visitor Information Bureau	Ph. (866) 645-3022
Joy Propane	Ph. (888) 782-6008
King Koin Laundromat	Ph. (250) 782-2395
Lodge Motor Inn & Cafe, The	Ph. (250) 782-4837
Mile 0 Gifts	Ph. (250) 782-8538
Mile "0" RV Park & Campground	Ph. (250) 782-2590
Northern Lights RV Park Ltd.	Ph. (250) 782-9433
Northern Treasures Gift Shop	Ph. (250) 782-2601
Northwinds Lodge	Ph. 1-800-665-1759
Peace Villa Motel	Ph. (250) 782-8175
Ramada Limited	Ph. (250) 782-8595
Rowland House Bed & Breakfast	Ph. (250) 782-5654
Shirley's RV Park	Ph. (250) 782-4143
Super 8 Motel	Ph. (250) 782-8899
Tubby's RV Park	Ph. (250) 782-2584
Under the Willow Tea Room and Antiques	901A–103 Ave.
United Spring & Brake Ltd.	Ph. (250) 782-1136

DAWSON CREEK ART GALLERY

Northern Treasures Gift Shop

N.A.R. Park - Next to Visitors Centre

Featuring the works of local artists and craftsmen.

Visit Our Alaska Highway Photo Exhibit

(250) 782-2601

www.pris.bc.ca/artgallery
dcagchin@pris.bc.ca

summer, 10 A.M. to 4 P.M. Tuesday through Saturday in winter. Phone (250) 782-9595, or e-mail dctourin@pris.bc.ca. Trained visitor-information counselors can answer questions about weather and road conditions, local events and attractions. Plenty of public parking in front of the refurbished grain elevator that houses the Dawson Creek Art Gallery and Museum.

Elevation: 2,186 feet/666m. **Climate:** Average temperature in January is 0°F/-18°C; in July it is 60°F/15°C. The average annual snowfall is 72 inches with the average depth of snow in midwinter at 19.7 inches. Frost-free days total 97, with the first frost of the year occurring about the first week of September. **Radio:** CJDC 890. **Television:** 13 channels via cable including pay TV. **Newspapers:** *Peace River Block News* (daily); *The Mirror* (weekly).

Private Aircraft: Dawson Creek airport, 2 SE; elev. 2,148 feet/655m; length 5,000 feet/1,524m and 2,300 feet/701m; asphalt; fuel 100, jet. Floatplane base parallels runway.

Dawson Creek (like Dawson City in the Yukon Territory) was named for George Mercer Dawson of the Geological Survey of Canada, whose geodetic surveys of this region in 1879 helped lead to its development as an agricultural settlement. The open, level townsite is surrounded by rolling farmland, part of the government-designated Peace River Block.

The Peace River Block consists of 3.5 million acres of arable land in northeastern British Columbia, which the province gave to the Dominion Government in 1883 in return for financial aid toward construction of the Canadian Pacific Railway. (While a

View down 8th Street in Dawson Creek, BC. (© Earl L. Brown, staff)

The Alaska
Hotel, Cafe & Diner's Pub
55 paces south of the Mile '0' Post, Dawson Creek, B.C.

DEW DROP INN!
P.O. Box 246
Dawson Creek, B.C. V1G 4G7

Reservations:
Cafe (250) 782-7040
Hotel (250) 782-7998 (24 hrs)
FAX (250) 782-6277

e-mail: alaskahotel@telus.net
Internet: http://www.alaskahotel.com

"READ ABOUT US IN THE ACCOMMODATION SECTION"

Peace Country Cuisine.
Heritage Rooms at Affordable Rates.
Pets Welcome.
Featured in "Where to Eat in Canada"

Private Dining & Meeting Room Groups, Reunions, Caravans.

The Lodge
MOTOR INN & CAFE

24 Hour Lobby • Cafe 5 a.m.-Midnight
(Newly Renovated)

• D.D. Phones - Free Local Calls
• 40 Air Conditioned Rooms
• Non-Smoking Rooms Available
• Cable Color TV • Super Channel
• Private Shower & Bath
• Non Sodium Soft Water
• **Central Location**
• Clean - Quiet - Comfortable
• Complimentary Coffee
• Fridges in Every Room

1317-Alaska Ave.
Dawson Creek, BC V1G 1Z4
Phone 250-782-4837
Fax 250-782-3003
Toll Free 1-800-935-3336

www.lodgemotorinn.com
e-mail: info@lodgemotorinn.com

Dawson Creek

NEWEST MOTEL IN TOWN

★★★ *2001 Clean & Friendly Award Winner* ★★★

48 Clean, Comfortable Air Conditioned Rooms • SuperSTART® Breakfast • Smoking Rooms Available • 24-Hour Desk • Free Local Calls & Newspaper • All Queen or King Beds • Full Cable TV • VCR, Nintendo and Microwaves Available • In-room Refrigerator, Hairdryer, Iron/Ironing Board and Coffee/Tea • High Speed Internet & Free Email Service Available • Fax and Copy Service • Work Stations • PC Hookups • Handicap Room • Pet Rooms Available • Guest Laundry • Large Vehicle Parking • Outside Outlets • Discounts at Adjacent Restaurant • 2 for 1 Fitness and Golf Passes • AAA/CAA Approved

SUPER 8 MOTEL

1440 Alaska Avenue • Dawson Creek, BC V1G 1Z5 • (250) 782-8899
Toll-Free Reservations 1-888-482-8884 or 1-800-800-8000
www.super8.com • E-mail: super8dawsoncreek@telus.net

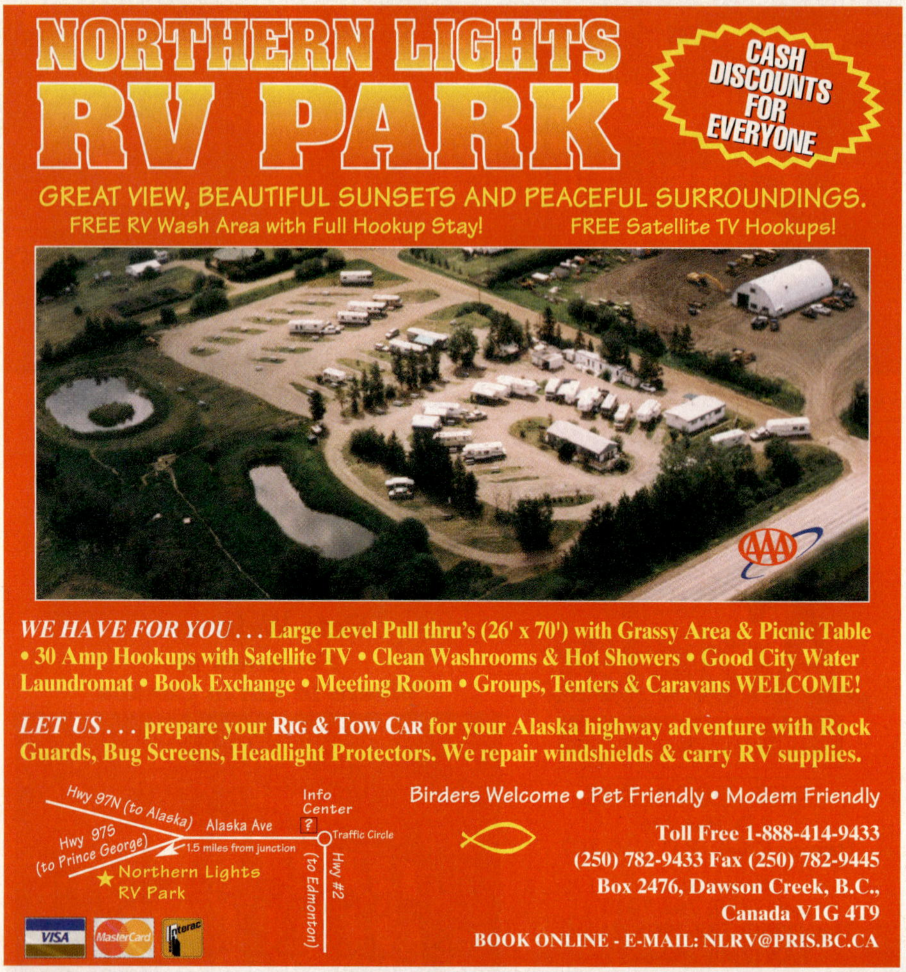

route through the Peace River country was surveyed by CPR in 1878, the railroad was eventually routed west from Calgary through Kicking Horse Pass.) The Peace River Block was held in reserve by the Dominion Government until 1920, when some of the land was opened for homesteading. The federal government restored the Peace River Block to the province of British Columbia in 1930.

Today, agriculture is an important part of this area's economy. The fields of bright yellow flowers (in season) in the area are canola, a hybrid of rapeseed that was developed as a low cholesterol oil seed. Raw seed is processed in Alberta and Japan. The Peace River region also produces most of the province's cereal grain, along with fodder, cattle and dairy cattle. Other industries include the production of honey, hogs, eggs and poultry. Some potato and vegetable farming is also done here.

On the British Columbia Railway line and the western terminus of the Northern Alberta Railway (now Canadian National Railway), Dawson Creek is also the hub of four major highways: the John Hart Highway (Highway 97 South) to Prince George; the Alaska Highway (Highway 97 North); Highway 2, which leads east to Grande Prairie, AB; and Highway 49, which leads east to Spirit River and Donnelly.

The Northern Alberta Railway reached Dawson Creek in 1931. As a railhead, Dawson Creek was an important funnel for supplies and equipment during construction of the Alaska Highway in 1942. Some 600 carloads arrived by rail within a period of five weeks in preparation for the construction program, according to a report by the

Flowering traffic circle by Alaska Highway monument in Dawson Creek, BC. (© Earl L. Brown)

Public Roads Administration in 1942. A "rutted provincial road" linked Dawson Creek with Fort St. John, affording the only approach to the southern base of operations. Field headquarters were established at Fort St. John and Whitehorse. Meanwhile, men and machines continued to arrive at Dawson Creek. By May of 1942, 4,720 carloads of equipment had arrived by rail at Dawson Creek for dispersion to troops and civilian engineers to the north.

With the completion of the Alaska Highway in 1942 (and opening to the public in 1948) and the John Hart Highway in 1952, Dawson Creek expanded both as a distribution centre and tourist destination. Dawson Creek was incorporated as a city in 1958.

The development of oil and natural gas exploration in northeastern British Columbia, and related industries such as pipeline construction and oil storage, contributed to the economic expansion of Dawson Creek. (The city was also one of the major supply centres for the massive development of North East Coal, located southwest of Dawson Creek via the Hintage Highway to Tumbler Ridge.)

Provincial government offices and social services for the South Peace region are located in Dawson Creek. City Hall is located on Ben Heppner Way, a street recently renamed in honor of the famous opera tenor, who comes from this area.

The city has a modern 100-bed hospital, a public library and a college (Northern Lights, associated with the University of Northern BC in Prince George).

There are numerous churches in Dawson Creek. (Check at the Visitor Infocentre for location and hours of worship.) There are 2 skating arenas, an indoor swimming pool, a curling rink, bowling alley, golf course, art gallery, museum, tennis and racquetball courts. Downhill skiing, and snowmobile and cross-country ski trails are available in winter.

Lodging & Services

There are 15 hotels/motels, several bed and breakfasts, and dozens of restaurants; department stores, banks, grocery, an organic bakery, drug and hardware stores, antique shop and other specialty shops. Shopping is downtown and in the 2 shopping centres, Co-op Mall and Dawson Mall. Visitors will also find laundromats, car washes, gas stations and automotive repair shops. The liquor store is adjacent the NAR Visitor Infocentre on Alaska Avenue.

The Alaska Hotel, Cafe & Diner's Pub extends a red carpet welcome and combines the spirit of Northern Adventure with Old World charm. Where to Eat in Canada,

JOY PROPANE LTD
www.joypropane.com

Toll Free 1-888-782-6008

DAWSON CREEK
Main Loc: 724-114 Ave.
West Loc: 1901 Hart Hwy.
(250) 782-6000

TUMBLER RIDGE
#139 Commercial Park
(250) 242-4400

FORT ST. JOHN
10304 Alaska Rd.
(250) 785-5000

CHETWYND
4805 S. Access Rd.
(250) 788-9333

FAIRVIEW, AB
9809-102 Ave.
(780) 835-5557

Our Service Includes:
- Bulk/Auto Propane • Cylinder Refills
- Propane Conversions • Tune Ups
- 24 Hour Cardlock Refuelling
- **ArmorThane** Spray-On Box Liners

RAMADA LIMITED

DAWSON CREEK
Mile 1 Alaska Highway
On six acres
only 7 blocks to downtown
41 Rooms

FEATURES
AM/FM Radio Clock
Air Conditioning / Heating
25" TV with 60 Channels
Premium / Movie Channels
DD Telephone, Data Port
Refrigerator, Coffee Maker
Voice Mail, Hairdryer,
Iron & Ironing Board,
Electronic Key Card.
Room with Jacuzzi, Fireplace,
King Size Bed.

SERVICES
Free Newspaper
Free local Phone Calls
Free 5 Course Deluxe
Continental Breakfast
Non-Smoking Rooms
2 Pet Rooms
(contact property direct)

CONTACT US
1748 Alaska Avenue
Dawson Creek, BC
Canda, V1G 1P4
Telephone: 250.782.8595
Facsimile: 250.782.9657
Toll Free: 800-2-RAMADA

TUBBY'S RV PARK

*. . . on Hwy. 97 South (Hart Hwy.) toward Prince George
1 1/2 blocks from the junction with Alaska Highway*

CARAVANS & TOUR GROUPS WELCOME!
97 FULL HOOKUPS

30 Amp Service • Easy Entry • Level Sites • Pull-Throughs
Security Fence • Picnic Tables • Ice • Free Hot Showers
Large Laundromat • Clean, Modern Restrooms
3 Bay Car & RV Wash • Dump Station
24 Hour E-mail / Internet Access.

Adjacent to Swimming Pool and The Pioneer Village
Walking Distance to Restaurants on City Bus Route

1913 - 96 Ave., Dawson Creek, BC V1G 1M2
Your Hosts: George & Florence Streeper
• **PHONE & FAX (250) 782-2584** •

which lists the 500 top restaurants, suggests, "It is a good idea to start out on the Alaska Highway with a good meal under your belt, and there's no better place than the Alaska Cafe." The cafe holds membership in World Famous Restaurants International and received the 2002 CAA/AAA Diamond rating. Be sure to take home a piece of the Alaska experience with you from our gift selections—T-shirts, aprons, mugs, spoons, and Luv & Luk line of apparel. The pub features live entertainment nightly, a hot spot in town. The building, having 15 themed period rooms, provides a perfect backdrop for the Kux-Kardos collection of antiques and works of art (tours available by special appointment). At the Alaska, our philosophy is Deluxe Evolutionary ... "Always changing for the better." Phone (250) 782-7998 to reserve. Pets welcome. Located 55 paces south of the mile "0" post. A definite must to experience. [ADVERTISEMENT]

Camping

There are 5 campgrounds in Dawson Creek: 2 located on either side of the Hart Highway at its junction with the Alaska Highway; 2 located on Alaska Avenue; and one on Highway 2 at the southeast entrance to the city. There is a private campground west of the city on the Hart Highway, 2

MILE "0" PARK
PIONEER VILLAGE
ROTARY LAKE & GARDENS NORTH
RV PARK & CAMPRGOUND

- BEAUTIFUL TREED SITES
- LARGE PULL THRU SITES 30' X 80'
- ELECTRICAL/WATER HOOKUPS – 20/30 AMP
- FREE HOT SHOWERS
- LAUNDRY • SANI DUMP • PAY PHONE
- PHONE LINE SERVICE FOR E-MAIL

Relax at the Rotary Lake *(with poolside concession)* at Walter Wright Pioneer Village.
Be sure to *visit* The Gardens North, Harpers Store, Mile 1 Cafe, The Antler Carver, the many heritage displays . . . and more!

Located at Mile 1½ on the Alaska Highway

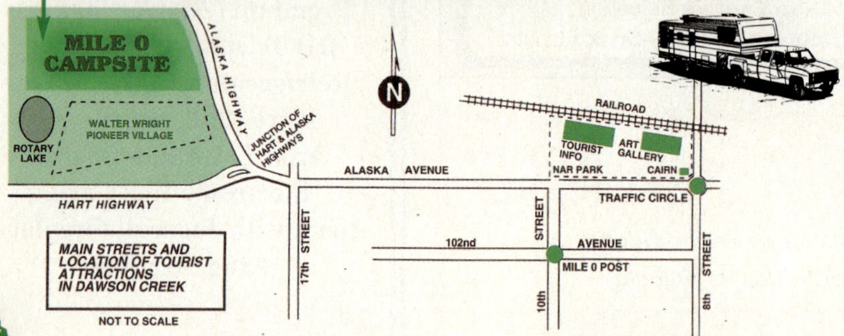

Mailing Address
P.O. Box 2383
Dawson Creek B.C.
V1G 4T9

Phone:
(250) 782-2590
FAX:
(250) 782-2597

Your Hosts: Garry & Lois Lutz
e-mail: mile0campground@aol.com
Web: www.citydirect.ca/mile0

PEACE VILLA MOTEL

1641 ALASKA AVENUE
DAWSON CREEK, B.C.
V1G 1Z9

Phone: (250) 782-8175
Fax: (250) 782-4030
Toll Free: 1-877-782-8175
E-mail: peacevilla@pris.bc.ca

East of Junction #97 & Alaska Highways

- 46 Clean, Quiet Air Conditioned Units
- 2 New Suites • Non-Smoking Rooms Available
- Full Baths • Fridge/Coffee Pot in Every Room
- Sauna • DD Phones (free local)
- Laundromat • Fax & Photocopy Service
- Data Ports • Voicemail • Get Together Rooms
- Remote Colour TV • Movie Channel

- Interac & major credit cards
- Corporate • Seniors • Crews • Military Discounts
- Close to Golf Course, Pioneer Village, Restaurants

"Experience Northern Hospitality"

Alahart RV Park

A Fair Exchange on US Currency

(250) 782-4702
Fax (250) 782-7302

at the junction of the Alaska and Hart Highways
Full Hookups and Tent sites - Pull throughs
Free showers - Laundromat - Dump station
Free Ice to Guests - Cable TV
Website: www.pris.bc.ca/alahart
E-mail: alahart@pris.bc.ca

Open Year Round

Closest Full Service RV Park to Downtown

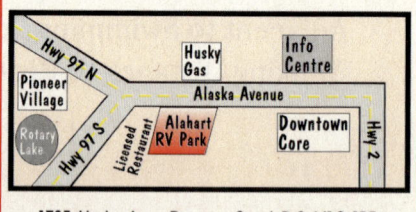

1725 Alaska Ave. Dawson Creek B.C. V1G 1P5

DAWSON CREEK COIN LAUNDRY LTD.

SOFT WATER • OPEN 7 DAYS A WEEK 8 A.M. TO 10 P.M. • **SHOWERS**
ATTENDANT ON DUTY • AIR CONDITIONED • AMPLE PARKING AREA
800 - 106th Ave. • 782-9389 • (Five blocks south of the Traffic Circle)

miles/3.2 km from the Alaska Highway junction. There are also campgrounds (both private and provincial) north of Dawson Creek on the Alaska Highway. ▲

Northern Lights RV Park welcomes you! Enjoy peaceful surroundings just 1.5 miles from Dawson Creek. Sit back and relax while we pamper you and your rig to prepare you for your Alaska Highway adventure! Birders welcome. Your hosts—the Ferguson Family. Phone (250) 782-9433. Modem friendly park. Email nlrv@pris.bc.ca; www.pris.bc.ca\rvpark\. [ADVERTISEMENT] ▲

Transportation

Air: Scheduled service from Dawson Creek airport to Prince George, Vancouver, Edmonton, Grande Prairie and Calgary via Air BC. The airport is located 2 miles/3.2 km south of the Alaska Avenue traffic circle via 8th Street/Highway 2; there is a small terminal at the airport. There is also a floatplane base and restaurant service available.

Railroad: Canadian National Railroad and British Columbia Railway provide freight service only. B.C. Railway provides passenger service from Vancouver to Prince George.

Bus: Greyhound service to Prince George and Vancouver, BC; Edmonton, AB; and Whitehorse, YT. Dawson Creek also has a city bus transit system.

Attractions

NAR Park, on Alaska Avenue at 10th Street (near the traffic circle), is the site of the Visitor Infocentre, which is housed in a restored railway station; phone (250) 782-9595. The Visitor Infocentre offers a self-guided historical walking tour with descriptions of Dawson Creek in the early 1940s during construction of the Alaska Highway.

Also at the station is the **Dawson Creek Station Museum**, operated by the South Peace Historical Society, which contains pioneer artifacts and wildlife displays, including a collection of more than 50 birds' eggs from this area. Be sure to leave enough time to view the hour-long video about the building of the Alaska Highway. Museum admission is $1/person, $2/family. Souvenirs and restrooms at the museum. In front of the station is a 1903 railway car, called "The Blue Goose Caboose."

Adjacent to the station is a huge wooden grain elevator. The last of Dawson Creek's old elevators, it was bought and moved to its present location through the efforts of community organizations and has been refurbished to house the **Dawson Creek Art Gallery**. Art exhibitions, held here throughout the summer, feature local and regional artists. This building also has an impressive display of historical Alaska Highway construction photos. Admission is by donation; restroom, gift shop.

Saturdays in summer there is an outdoor farmer's market at NAR Park with flowers, produce, baked goods and crafts for sale.

Inquire at the Visitor Infocentre for the location of Bear Mountain Community Forest. This Ministry of Forests recreation area features interpretive trails on the flora and fauna of the area. It is located 6 miles/10 km south of the city.

Under the Willow Tea Room and Antiques. Welcome to Dawson Creek's only tea room, featuring healthy and hearty homemade soups and luncheon menu. Afternoon high tea. Famous carrot cake. Local musicians showcased 11:30 A.M.–3 P.M. Saturdays. Antiques and collectables, jewelry, junk, local crafts and willow furniture. Estate pieces. Something for everybody. Open 10 A.M.–6 P.M. Tuesday–Saturday. 901A–103 Ave., Dawson Creek, BC. (250) 782-8811. [ADVERTISEMENT]

Recreational facilities in Dawson Creek include a bowling alley, miniature golf, indoor pool, 2 ice arenas, curling rink, 18-

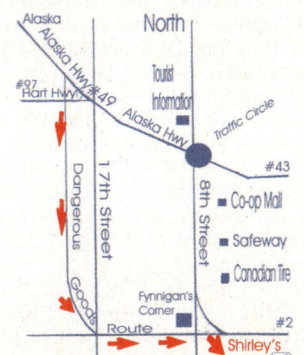

WELCOME TO SHIRLEY'S R.V. PARK
NEW
THE NEWEST RV PARK IN DAWSON CREEK

- LARGE FULLY SERVICED PULL-THROUGHS • ACCOMMODATE BIG RIGS
- 30 & 50 AMP SERVICE • SECURITY FENCED • CLEAN HOT SHOWERS
- PAYPHONES • PICNIC TABLES * NON-SERVICED SITES AVAILABLE * GRASSY TENT SITES

MINUTES TO DOWNTOWN ATTRACTIONS AND SHOPPING

PHONE/FAX: 250-782-4143
EMAIL: shirleysrvpark@shaw.ca
WEB: www.shirleysrvpark.com

MAILING ADDRESS
#307 1200 ADAMS RD.
DAWSON CREEK, BC
V1G 4L2

"YOU SHIRLEY DON'T WANT TO MISS IT"

ALASKA HIGHWAY T-SHIRTS
IN FULL COLOUR AND BEAUTIFUL WILDLIFE DESIGNS

We have a large selection of souvenirs. Eskimo soapstone carvings and totem poles. B.C. Jade, Indian and Eskimo dolls, moccasins, gold nugget jewelry and Alaska Black Diamond jewelry and carvings. You'll also enjoy our beautiful gifts, which we import from many countries. Come in & browse; you'll like our low prices.

10109 • 10th Street
Dawson Creek, BC
Located between tourist information and the Mile "0" Post

MILE "0" GIFTS

Phone (250) 782-8538

UNITED SPRING & BRAKE LTD.
"THE SPECIALISTS"

Largest R.V. Running Gear & Chassis Parts in the North

CERTIFIED MECHANICS

Brakes • Suspensions • Axels • Hitches
Wheel Alignment Service

COMPLETE SHOP FACILITIES

All Chassis Repairs — Including the Largest Motorhomes

Toll Free Phone Number 1-800-283-5040
11634 - 7th Street, Dawson Creek, BC
Phone (250) 782-1136 • FAX (250) 782-7888
e-mail: usb@pris.bc.ca   web: www.pris.bc.ca/usb

www.themilepost.com

hole golf course, tennis courts and an outdoor pool at Rotary Lake Park.

Walter Wright Pioneer Village and Mile 0 Rotary Park. The entrance to the village is highlighted by Gardens North. Follow the path through the front garden to the gift shop, where the staff will guide you into the village. Gardens North consists of 9 separate gardens, including a memorial rose garden. Bring a camera to capture the amazing variety of perennials and annuals that grow in the North. The pioneer village contains an impressive collection of local pioneer buildings as well as recently built replicas like the fire hall and telegraph office. There are also collectible shops and a cafe (open daily for breakfast, lunch and dinner featuring homemade pie). Admission to the village is by donation.

Adjacent to the village is the **Sudeten Hall**, which holds occasional dinner theatre and other entertainments. Also located here is **Rotary Lake**, an outdoor man-made swimming facility with restrooms and picnic areas. No lifeguard on duty; supervise children. For information on the village phone (250) 782-7144. The village is open daily 9 A.M. to 8 P.M., late May to early September.

Dawson Creek Walking Path, a community project to restore the creek, provides a peaceful path for travelers to stretch their legs and take in some local scenery. When complete, the path will connect Rotary Park with Kinsmen Park on 8th Street. Ask at the Visitor Infocentre for directions.

Alaska Highway Log

BC HIGHWAY 97 NORTH

Distance from Dawson Creek (DC)* is followed by distance from Delta Junction (DJ). Historical mileposts are indicated in the text as Historical Mile.

*In the Canada portion of *The MILEPOST®* Alaska Highway log, mileages from Dawson Creek are based on actual driving distance and kilometres are based on physical kilometreposts. (Mileages from Delta Junction are based on actual driving distance, followed by the metric conversion.) See "Mileposts and Kilometreposts" in the introduction beginning on page 98 for more details.

BC HIGHWAY 97 NORTH

DC 0 DJ 1390 (2236.9 km) **Mile 0** marker of the Alaska Highway on 10th Street in downtown Dawson Creek.

Northbound: Good pavement approximately next 284 miles/457 km (through Fort Nelson). Watch for road construction and surface changes from Pink Mountain north.

DC 1.2 (1.9 km) **DJ 1388.8** (2235 km) Junction of the Alaska Highway and John Hart Highway.

> Prince George-bound travelers turn to the end of the WEST ACCESS ROUTE section on page 91 and read log back to front. Alaska-bound travelers continue with this log.

DC 1.5 (2.4 km) **DJ 1388.5** (2234.5 km) Mile 0 Rotary Park (picnicking and swimming), Walter Wright Pioneer Village and Mile 0 RV Park & Campground to west. ▲

DC 1.7 (2.7 km) **DJ 1388.3** (2234.2 km) Historic Milepost 2. Sign about Cantel Repeater Station. Cantel telephone–teletype lines stretched from Alberta to Fairbanks, AK, making it one of the world's longest open-wire toll circuits at the time.

DC 2 (3.2 km) **DJ 1388** (2233.7 km) Recreation centre and golf course to west. Louisiana Pacific waferboard plant to east.

DC 2.7 (4.3 km) **DJ 1387.3** (2232.6 km) Truck scales and public phone to east. Truck stop to west; gas, cafe.

DC 2.9 (4.7 km) **DJ 1387.1** (2232.3 km) Northern Alberta Railway (NAR) tracks.

DC 3.3 (5.3 km) **DC 1386.7** (2231.6 km) Turnout with litter barrel to east. Historic Milepost 3; historic sign marks Curan & Briggs Ltd. Construction Camp, U.S. Army Traffic Control Centre.

DC 3.4 (5.5 km) **DJ 1386.6** (2231.4 km) Historical Mile 3. The Trading Post to east.

The Trading Post. You'll want to stop in and check out our selection of handmade mukluks and moccasins, Native handicrafts and moose hair tuftings, fish scale art, jade carvings and jewelry, Alaska black diamond and more. Craft supplies, collectables and medicine spirit stones. We look forward to seeing you! (250) 782-4974. [ADVERTISEMENT]

DC 9.5 (15.3 km) **DJ 1380.5** (2221.6 km) Golf course, driving range and RV park. ▲

DC 11.2 (18 km) **DJ 1378.8** (2218.9 km) Turnout with litter barrels to west.

DC 11.5 (18.5 km) **DJ 1378.5** (2218.4 km) Turnout with litter barrels to east.

DC 14.8 (24 km) **DJ 1375.2** (2213.1 km) Farmington (unincorporated).

DC 15.8 (25.4 km) **DJ 1374.2** (2211.5 km) Farmington store to west; gas, groceries, phone.

DC 17.3 (27.8 km) **DJ 1372.7** (2209.1 km) Exit east for loop road to **Kiskatinaw Provincial Park**. Follow 2-lane paved road (old Alaska Highway) 2.5 miles/4 km for provincial park; 28 campsites, drinking water, firewood, picnic tables, fire rings, outhouses and garbage containers. Camping fee $12. ▲

This interesting side road gives travelers the opportunity to drive the original old Alaska Highway and to cross the historic curved wooden **Kiskatinaw River Bridge**. A sign at the bridge notes that this 531-foot/162-m-long structure is the only original timber bridge built along the Alaska Highway that is still in use today.

DC 17.5 (28.2 km) **DJ 1372.5** (2208.8 km) Distance marker indicates Fort St. John 29 miles/47 km.

CAUTION: *Watch for deer.*

DC 19.4 (31.2 km) **DJ 1370.6** (2205.7 km) Large turnout to east.

DC 19.8 (31.9 km) **DJ 1370.2** (2205.1 km) Highway descends northbound to Kiskatinaw River.

DC 20.9 (33.6 km) **DJ 1369.1** (2203.3 km) Kiskatinaw River bridge.

CAUTION: *Strong crosswinds on bridge.*

Turnout with litter barrel and picnic tables to east at north end of bridge. View of unique bridge support.

DC 21.6 (34.5 km) **DJ 1368.4** (2202.2 km) Loop road to Kiskatinaw Provincial Park and Kiskatinaw River bridge (see **Milepost DC 17.3**).

DC 25.4 (41 km) **DJ 1364.6** (2196.1 km) NorthwesTel microwave tower to east. Alaska Highway travelers will be seeing many of these towers as they drive north. The Northwest Communications System was constructed by the U.S. Army in 1942–43. This land line was replaced in 1963 with the construction of 42 microwave relay stations by Canadian National Telecommunications (Cantel, now NorthwesTel) between Grande Prairie, AB, and the YT–AK border.

DC 30.5 (49.1 km) **DJ 1359.5** (2187.8 km) Turnout to east with litter barrels. Turnout to west with litter barrels, pit toilet and historical marker about explorer Alexander Mackenzie.

Highway begins steep winding descent northbound to the Peace River bridge. Good views to northeast of Peace River valley and industrial community of Taylor. Some wide gravel shoulder next 4 miles/6.4 km for northbound traffic to pull off.

CAUTION: *Trucks check your brakes.*

DC 32.1 (51.6 km) **DJ 1357.9** (2185.3 km) Large turnout with litter barrels.

DC 33.8 (54.4 km) **DJ 1356.2** (2182.5 km) Pingle Creek.

DC 34 (54.7 km) **DJ 1356** (2182.2 km) Access to **Taylor Landing Provincial Park**; boat launch, parking and fishing. Jet boat outfitter. Also access to **Peace Island Park**, 0.5 mile/0.8 km west of the highway, situated on an island in the Peace River connected to the south shore by a causeway. Peace Island Park has 35 shaded campsites with gravel pads, firewood, fire rings, picnic tables, picnic shelter, toilets, potable water, playground and horseshoe pits. There are also 4 large picnic areas and a tenting area. Camping fee. Open Memorial Day to Labour

Day. Nature trail, good bird watching and good fishing in clear water. Boaters should use caution on the Peace River since both parks are downstream from the W.A.C. Bennett and Peace Canyon dams and water levels may fluctuate rapidly.

The Honey Place at Milepost DC 42.3 Alaska Highway, seen from the air.
(© Earl L. Brown, staff)

DC 34.4 (55.4 km) **DJ 1355.6** (2181.6 km) **Peace River Bridge**. Bridging the Peace was one of the first goals of Alaska Highway engineers in 1942. Traffic moving north from Dawson Creek was limited by the Peace River crossing, where 2 ferries with a capacity of 10 trucks per hour were operating in May. Three different pile trestles were constructed across the Peace River, only to be washed out by high water. Work on the permanent 2,130-foot suspension bridge began in December 1942 and was completed in July 1943. One of 2 suspension bridges on the Alaska Highway, the Peace River bridge collapsed in 1957 after erosion undermined the north anchor block of the bridge. The cantilever and truss-type bridge that crosses the Peace River today was completed in 1960.

Gas pipeline bridge visible to east.

DC 35 (56.3 km) **DJ 1355** (2180.6 km) **Historic Milepost 35** at TAYLOR (pop. 1,300; elev. 1,804 feet/550m), located on the north bank of the Peace River. **Visitor Information**: Infocentre, on left northbound (10114 100 St.), open May to September; phone (250) 789-9015. Inquire here about industrial tours.

Taylor is an industrial community clustered around a Duke Energy Inc. gas-processing plant and a lumber mill. Established in 1955 with the discovery and development of a natural gas field in the area, Taylor is the site of Fibreco pulp mill and plants that handle sulfur processing, gas compressing, high-octane aviation gas production and other byproducts of natural gas. The Duke Energy natural gas pipeline reaches from here to Vancouver, BC, with a branch to western Washington.

The fertile Taylor Flats area has several market gardens and roadside stands in summer. A hotel, motels, cafes, grocery store, private RV park, gas station and post office are located here. Free municipal dump station and potable water located behind the North Taylor Inn.

Recreation facilities include the 18-hole, par 72 Lone Wolf golf course (home of the world's largest golf ball); tennis courts; a motorcross track; and a recreation complex with swimming pool, curling rink and district ice centre for skating (open year-round). The World's Invitational Gold Panning Championships are held at Peace Island Park on the first weekend in August.

DC 36.3 (58.4 km) **DJ 1353.7** (2178.5 km) Railroad tracks.

DC 40 (64.5 km) **DJ 1350** (2172.6 km) **Historical Mile 41**. Post office.

DC 40.3 (64.9 km) **DJ 1349.7** (2172.1 km) Exit east for Fort St. John airport.

DC 40.4 (65 km) **DJ 1349.6** (2171.9 km) B.C. Railway overhead tracks.

DC 40.9 (65.8 km) **DJ 1349.1** (2171.1 km) **Historic Milepost 42** Access Road to Fort St. John Airport.

DC 42.3 (68.1 km) **DJ 1347.7** (2168.9 km) World's largest glass beehive at the Honey Place to west. Well worth a visit. The Peace Country produces several tons of high quality honey annually.

The Honey Place. See display ad this section.

DC 43.7 (70.3 km) **DJ 1346.3** (2166.6 km) **Historical Mile 44. Sourdough Pete's RV Park**. See display ad this section. ▲

DC 44.6 (71.7 km) **DJ 1345.4** (2165.2 km) Access to Fort St. John via 86th Street.

DC 45.7 (73.5 km) **DJ 1344.3** (2163.4 km) **Historic Milepost 47**, Fort St. John/ "Camp Alcan" sign. In 1942, Fort St. John "exploded." What had been home to 200

the HONEY PLACE

SEE THE WORLD'S LARGEST GLASS BEEHIVE
OPEN 9:00 A.M. to 5:30 P.M.
CLOSED SUNDAY AND HOLIDAYS

HONEY, POLLEN, LEATHERCRAFT

VISA MasterCard

Mile DC 42.3, KM 66.5 Alaska Highway • R.R. 1, Fort St. John, BC V1J 4M6 • 785-4808

SOURDOUGH PETE'S RV PARK

Good Sampark

RV Park
64 Long Pull-thru's, Tenting Area, 80 Complete Hookups, 15 & 30 amp, Showers, Laundry, Store. Fenced. Manager on site. Minutes from downtown Fort St. John. Modem Friendly Pay Phone.

Phone (250) 785-9255 ☎ Toll free 1-800-227-8388 ☎ Fax (250) 785-9287
rfurman@pris.bc.ca • Mile 44 Alaska Hwy. • RR1, Site 1, Comp 25, Fort St. John, BC Canada V1J 4M6

ALASKA HIGHWAY • Fort St. John

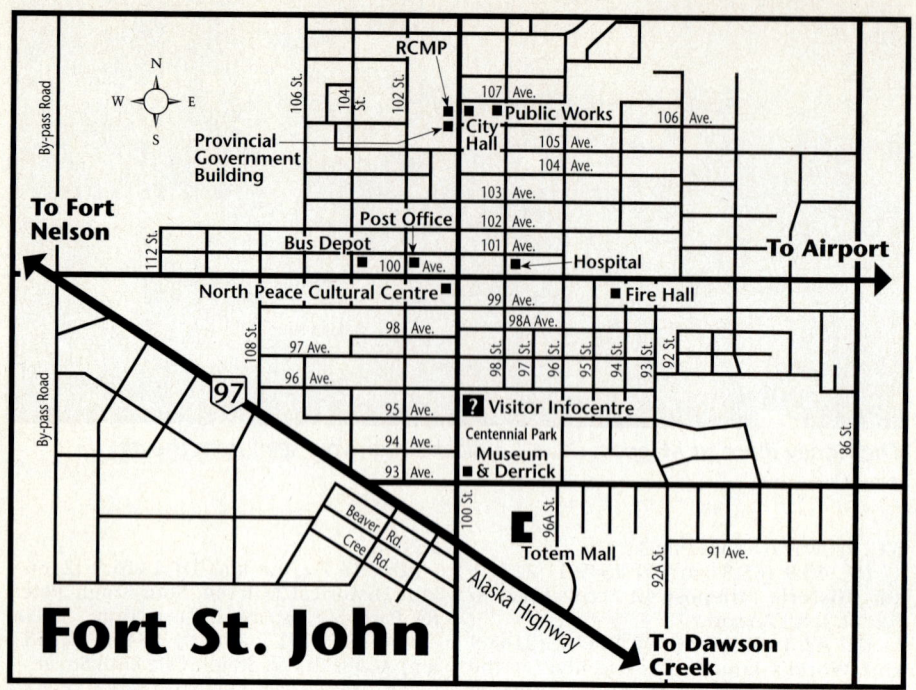

Fort St. John

Fort St. John

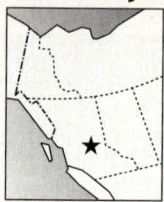

DC 47 (75.6 km) **DJ 1343** (2161.3 km) Dubbed the "Energetic City," it is located approximately 236 miles/ 380 km south of Fort Nelson. **Population:** 17,000; area 55,000. **Emergency Services:** For all emergency service phone 911. **RCMP**, phone (250) 787-8100. **Hospital**, on 100th Avenue and 96th Street, phone (250) 785-6611.

Visitor Information: Visitor Information Centre is located at 9923–96th Ave., corner of 100th St. and 96th Ave.; phone (250) 785-3033. It is in the same building as the Chamber of Commerce and the Northern Rockies Alaska Highway Tourism Assoc. Open year-round; regular hours are 9 A.M. to 5 P.M.; extended hours in summer. Write Chamber of Commerce, 9923 96th Ave., Fort St. John, BC V1J 4K9; phone (250) 785-6037, fax (250) 785-7181, email fsjchofcom@awink.com; web site www.fortstjohnchamber.com.

Visitors may also contact the following agencies for information on wilderness hiking and camping opportunities: BC Parks (Ministry of Water, Land and Air Protection), Peace Region, #150, 10003–110th Ave., Fort St. John, BC V1J 6M7, phone (250) 787-3411; and Ministry of Forests, 8808–72nd St., Fort St. John, BC V1J 6M2, phone (250) 787-5600.

Direct hunting and fishing queries to the Ministry of Environment, #400, 10003–110th Ave., Fort St. John, BC V1J 6M7; phone (250) 787-3411.

became a temporary base for more than 6,000, as U.S. Army troops and civilian engineers arrived to begin work on construction of the Alaska Highway.

DC 45.8 (73.7 km) **DJ 1344.2** (2163.2 km) Traffic light. South access to Fort St. John via 100th Street. Exit east for Visitor Infocentre and downtown Fort St. John.

DC 47 (75.6 km) **DJ 1343** (2161.3 km) **Historical Mile 48**. North access to Fort St. John via 100th Avenue to downtown. Husky Car and Truck Wash; 24-hour gas (unleaded, diesel), across from McDonald's.

Best Western Coachman Inn

* 70 Deluxe Smoking & Non-Smoking Rooms
* Ample Parking • Cable TV • Air Conditioning
* Refrigerators In Each Room
* Sauna, Jacuzzi & Fitness Room
* In Room Coffee • Limited Pet Room
* Restaurant & Lounge • Handicap Accessible
* Direct Dial Phones • Irons & Ironing Boards

* 24 Hr Front Desk Service

Reservations:
1-888-388-9408
Phone: 250-787-0651, Fax: 250-787-5266
On the Alaska Highway
Fort St. John, B.C.

Canada is on the metric system.

The right location for an oil change and lube ... 1500 miles up and 1500 miles back

Summer Hours 7 am - 7 pm (Sun Noon - 5 pm)
11204-100th Ave., Fort St. John, BC • 250-785-2191

- Complete Lube & Oil Service – Major Brands of Oil
- Drive Through *(unhitching not required)* ...No Appointment Necessary
- Custom Car Care
- RV and Car Wash
- 50 ft. Bays - 12' x 14' Doors

Fort St. John's Newest Hotel

RAMADA LIMITED

At Ramada you'll find attractive and clean accomodations at outstanding value.

- 73 Deluxe Guest Rooms
- Executive / Whirlpool Suites
- Kitchenettes

Fogg n' Suds Restaurant & Taps on site

- Fitness Centre, Whirlpool, Guest Laundry
- Complimentary Executive Continental Breakfast
- In-room Refrigerators, Microwaves, Hair Dryers
- In-room Coffee Makers, Complimentary Coffee/Tea
- 25" Color TV's with Cable, Movie Channel
- Direct Dial Phones, Data Ports, Voice Mail
- High Speed Internet Access
- Ample Free Parking, Winter Plug-ins
- Business Services, Meeting Rooms, Airport Shuttle

Phone: (250) 787-0779 • Fax: (250) 787-0709
Hotel Direct Reservations: **1-888-346-7711**
10103-98th Avenue, Fort St. John, BC V1J 1P8

Elevation: 2,275 feet/693m. **Climate:** Average high temperature in July, 73°F/23°C, average low 50°F/10°C. In January, average high is 12°F/-11°C; low is -2°F/-19°C. **Radio:** CKNL 560, CHRX Energy 98.5 FM, CBC 88.3. **Television:** Cable. **Newspaper:** *Alaska Highway News* (daily), *The Northerner* (weekly).

Private Aircraft: Fort St. John airport, 3.8 E; elev. 2,280 feet/695m; length 6,900 feet/2,103m and 6,700 feet/2,042m; asphalt; fuel 100, Jet. Charlie Lake airstrip, 6.7 NW; elev. 2,680 feet/817m; length 1,800 feet/549m; gravel; fuel 100.

Fort St. John is set in the low, rolling hills of the Peace River Valley. The original Fort St. John was established as Rocky Mountain Fort in 1794, making Fort St. John the oldest white settlement in mainland British Columbia.

The Peace region was homesteaded in the early 1900s. The town's early commercial development centered around a store established by settler C.M. Finch. His stepson, Clement Brooks, carried on Finch's entrepreneurship, starting several businesses in Fort St. John after WWII.

In 1942, Fort St. John became field headquarters for U.S. Army troops and civilian engineers working on construction of the

Fort St. John's 100th Street is a main thoroughfare. (© Earl L. Brown, staff)

FORT ST. JOHN ADVERTISERS

Best Western Coachman
 Inn..............................Ph. 1-888-388-9408
City of Fort St. John..........Ph. (250) 785-3033
Fort St. John–North Peace
 Museum.....................Ph. (250) 787-0430
Husky Car and Truck
 Wash..........................Ph. (250) 785-3121
North Peace Cultural
 Centre............................10015–100th Ave.
Petro Canada Truck Stop.Ph. (250) 787-6066
Ramada Limited..............Ph. (250) 787-0779
Rapid Lube & Wash............11204–100th Ave.
Tirecraft..........................Ph. (250) 785-2411

PETRO-CANADA TRUCK STOP
OPEN 24 HOURS

On The Alaska Highway
(North End of Town)

* **Convenience Store** *

- Subs & Sandwiches
- Cold Drinks
- Ice Cream
- Novelties
- Bank Machine
- Lotto Centre
- Ice

PROPANE
OILS • REGULAR &
PREMIUM GAS - DIESEL
FREE SANI DUMP WITH FILLUP

Restaurant Adjacent

(250) 787-6066
11724 Alaska Highway
Fort St. John, B.C.

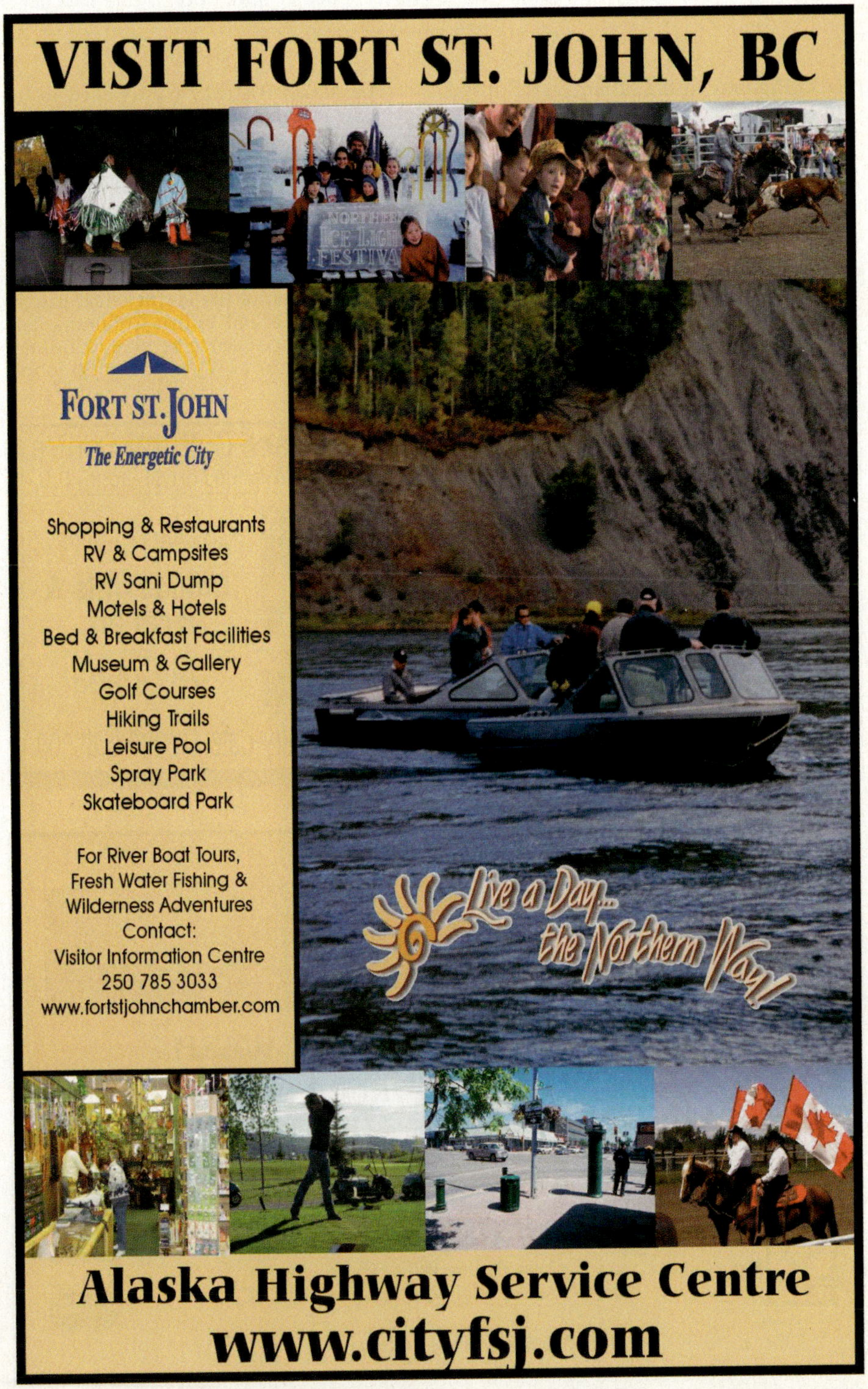

VISIT FORT ST. JOHN, BC

FORT ST. JOHN
The Energetic City

Shopping & Restaurants
RV & Campsites
RV Sani Dump
Motels & Hotels
Bed & Breakfast Facilities
Museum & Gallery
Golf Courses
Hiking Trails
Leisure Pool
Spray Park
Skateboard Park

For River Boat Tours,
Fresh Water Fishing &
Wilderness Adventures
Contact:
Visitor Information Centre
250 785 3033
www.fortstjohnchamber.com

Live a Day... the Northern Way!

Alaska Highway Service Centre
www.cityfsj.com

Kids enjoy Rotary Spray Park adjacent to North Peace Leisure Pool. (© Earl L. Brown, staff)

Alaska Highway in the eastern sector. It was the largest camp, along with Whitehorse (headquarters for the western sector), of the dozen or so construction camps along the highway. Much of the field housing, road building equipment and even office supplies were scrounged from old Civilian Conservation Corps camps and the Work Projects Administration.

The Alaska Highway was opened to the traveling public in 1948, attracting vacationers and homesteaders. An immense natural oil and gas field discovered in 1955 made Fort St. John the oil capital of British Columbia. "Energetic City," referring to the natural energy resources and the city's potential for positive growth, became the slogan for the region.

An extension of the Pacific Great Eastern Railway, now called British Columbia Railway, from Prince George in 1958 (continued to Fort Nelson in 1971), gave Fort St. John a link with the rail yards and docks at North Vancouver.

Today, Fort St. John's economy is based primarily on oil and gas exploration, forestry and agriculture, tourism, hydro-electric power generation, and consumer and public services. It is home of northeastern BC's largest shopping mall and a variety of unique stores.

Transportation

Air: Served by Air Canada, Peace Air and Central Mountain Air. Connecting flights to Fort Nelson, Whitehorse, Vancouver, Grande Prairie, Edmonton and Prince George. **Bus:** Coachways service to Prince George, Vancouver, Edmonton and Whitehorse; depot at 10355 101st Ave., phone (250) 785-6695.

Lodging & Services

Visitor services are located just off the Alaska Highway and in the city centre, several blocks north of the highway.

More than a dozen motels/hotels and a few bed-and-breakfasts provide accommodations. Restaurants, fast-food outlets and full-service gas stations are located on the Alaska Highway and in town. Shopping malls include Totem Mall, MacKenzie Inn Mall, Co-op Mall, Northgate Mall, the IGA complex and Overwaitea complex.

Fort St. John has a movie theatre, the Lido; 5 supermarkets; laundromats; several banks (automatic teller machines at Totem Mall and downtown at Charter Banks); car washes; and 2 bowling alleys.

North Peace Recreation Centre, located on 96 Avenue in Centennial park, has a skateboard park, golf driving range and a summer indoor tennis court and winter ice skating rink. A Farmer's Market is held in the lobby on Saturdays, 9 A.M. to 4 P.M., from May through December. The North Peace Leisure Pool, on the other side of the recreation centre, has a waterslide, wave pool, lap pool, diving boards, a sauna and steam room; phone (250) 787-8178. The outdoor spray park is located beside the pool.

Camping

A private campground (Sourdough Pete's RV Park) is located south of town at **Milepost DC 43.7**. North of town at Charlie Lake is Rotary R.V. Park, **Milepost DC 51.2**.

Camping at Beatton Provincial Park, 5 miles east of **Milepost DC 49.5**, and at Charlie Lake Provincial Park, **Milepost DC 53.7**.

Fresh water fill-up and dump station located at the northwest corner of 86th Street and the Alaska Highway.

Attractions

Centennial Park, located on 100th Street, is home to the Visitor Information Centre, Fort St. John–North Peace Museum and North Peace Recreation Centre and Leisure Pool. The park offers a curling rink, tennis courts, volleyball court, splash park, skateboard park, horseshoe pits and grassy picnic area. **Fort St. John–North Peace Museum** features more than 6,000 artifacts from the region, including items from Finch's Store, an 1806 Fort St. John post, a trapper's cabin and early-day schoolroom. The museum gift shop offers a good selection of local and Northwest books, videos on the construction of the Alaska Highway, and many souvenir items. The museum is open year-round; phone (250) 787-0430.

Outside the museum is a 136-foot-high oil derrick, presented to the North Peace Historical Society and the people of Fort St. John.

A granite monument in Centennial Park commemorates Sir Alexander Mackenzie's stop here on his journey west to the Pacific Ocean in 1793.

North Peace Cultural Centre, at 10015 100th Ave., houses Fort St. John Public Library (250) 785-3731; a 413-seat theatre; an art gallery (Peace Gallery North); and a cafe and gift shop. Phone (250) 785-1992.

Play golf. Fort St. John's only in-town golf course is Links Golf Course, just off the Bypass Road at 86 Street; 9 holes, pro shop and lounge; phone (250) 785-9995. The Lakepoint Golf Course, on Golf Course Road at Charlie Lake, has 18 holes, pro shop, lounge and restaurant; phone (250) 785-5566. And there is also Lone Wolf Golf Course (18 holes, par 72) in Taylor.

Industry and agriculture of the area are showcased for the public at various places; check with the Infocentre. Canada Forest Products (Canfor) offers 1-hour tours booked 1-day in advance. Phone (250) 787-3621 for more information. (No open-toe or high-heeled shoes.)

The Honey Place, just south of town on the Alaska Highway, offers guided tours, fresh honey for sale, and the world's largest glass beehive for viewing year-round. Phone (250) 785-4808 for more information.

Visitors can see and feed llamas at East Yoke Llama Farm, located at the junction of the Alaska Highway and Beatton Provincial Park Road. Phone (250) 785-1168 for tour information.

Fish Creek Community Forest, adjacent to Northern Lights College, has 3 interpretive trails to view forest management activities and learn more about the forest. Cross-country ski trails in winter. From the Alaska Highway follow 100th Street north 1.2 miles/2 km and turn right on the Bypass Road just before the railway tracks. Take the first left and park behind Northern Lights College.

W.A.C. Bennett Dam is a major attraction in the area. For an interesting sidetrip, drive north from Fort St. John on the Alaska Highway to **Milepost DC 53.7** and take Highway 29 west 46.5 miles/74.8 km to Hudson's Hope. Highway 29 follows the original Canadian government telegraph trail of 1918. Hudson's Hope, formerly a pioneer community established in 1805 by explorer Simon Fraser, grew with construction of the W.A.C. Bennett Dam, which is located 13.5 miles/21.7 km west of town. B.C. Hydro's Peace Canyon dam is located approximately 4 miles/6.4 km south of Hudson's Hope. See "Hudson's Hope Loop" log on pages 90-91.

Easy Yoke Llama Farm is a local attraction in Fort St. John. (© Earl L. Brown, staff)

Alaska Highway Log
(continued)

BC HIGHWAY 97 NORTH

Distance from Dawson Creek (DC)* is followed by distance from Delta Junction (DJ). Original mileposts are indicated in the text as Historical Mile.

*In the Canada portion of *The MILEPOST®* Alaska Highway log, mileages from Dawson Creek are based on actual driving distance and kilometres are based on physical kilometreposts. (Mileages from Delta Junction are based on actual driving distance, followed by the metric conversion.) See "Mileposts and Kilometreposts" in the introduction beginning on page 98 for more details.

DC 45.8 (73.7 km) **DJ 1344.2** (2163.2 km) South access to Fort St. John via 100th Street.

DC 47 (75.6 km) **DJ 1343** (2161.3 km) **Historical Mile 48**. Traffic light. North access to Fort St. John via 100th Avenue.

DC 48.6 (78.2 km) **DJ 1341.4** (2157.3 km) **Historic Milepost 49** commemorates "Camp Alcan."

DC 49.5 (79.6 km) **DJ 1340.5** (2157.3 km) **Exit for Easy Yoke Llama Farm** and **Beatton Provincial Park** (5 miles/8 km east via paved road; 37 campsites, picnic shelter, horseshoe pits, playground, baseball field, sandy beach swimming and boat launch. Camping fee $12. Fishing for northern pike, walleye (July best) and yellow perch in **Charlie Lake**.

DC 50.4 (81.1 km) **DJ 1339.6** (2155.8 km) **Paradise Lane Bed & Breakfast**. See display ad this section.

DC 50.6 (81.4 km) **DJ 1339.4** (2155.5 km) **CHARLIE LAKE** (unincorporated), gas, diesel and propane, grocery, pub, post office, bed and breakfast, private RV parks and Ministry of Energy, Mines and Petroleum. Access to lakeshore east side of highway; boat launch, no parking. At one time during construction of the Alaska Highway, Charlie Lake was designated Mile 0, as there was already a road between the railhead at Dawson Creek and Fort St. John, the eastern sector headquarters for troops and engineers.

Charlie Lake General Store. See display ad this section.

PARADISE LANE
BED & BREAKFAST

- Lakefront Log Home
- Clean, Quiet Lakeview Rooms
- Quality Comfortable Beds
- Delicious Homemade Breakfast
- Complimentary Coffee/Tea in Rooms

NO PETS PLEASE

Adult Oriented • Smoke Free Home

"Truly a Piece of Paradise"

Just 10 Minutes from Fort St. John

Your Friendly Host: Faye Reeves
Box 207, Charlie Lake, BC V0C 1H0
Phone (250) 785-7477
E-mail: paradiseln_bb@awink.com

CHARLIE LAKE GENERAL STORE

Gas • Diesel • Propane **TEMPO**
Groceries • Confectionary
Books • Ice • ATM Machine

Famous Take Out Food
Country Fried Chicken & Ribs

GREAT FISHING!
- Boat Rentals
- Bait & Tackle
- Fishing & Hunting Licenses
- Sporting Goods

MILE 50.6 ALASKA HIGHWAY
250-787-0655

VISA • MasterCard

DC 51.2 (82.4 km) **DJ 1338.8** (2154.5 km) **Historic Milepost 52** Turnoff for Rotary Park (day-use only) on Charlie Lake, Rotary R.V. Park (camping), restaurant and pub. Rotary Park day-use area has 2 public boat launches, boat dock, toilet, nature trails and parking. Fishing off dock for walleye and northern pike. No parking on dike (strictly enforced).

Rotary R.V. Park. See display ad this section.

Historical Mile 52 was Charlie Lake Mile 0 of the Army Tote Road during construction of the Alaska Highway. It was also the site of a major distribution camp for workers and supplies heading north. 12 American soldiers drowned here in 1942 while crossing the lake aboard pontoon barges.

DC 52 (83.7 km) **DJ 1338** (2153.2 km) Exit east on Charlie Lake Road for lakeshore picnicking.

DC 53.6 (86.3 km) **DJ 1336.4** (2150.7 km) Truck weigh scales east side of highway.

DC 53.7 (86.4 km) **DJ 1336.3** (2150.5 km) Highway 29 **junction**; truck stop.

Junction with Highway 29, which leads west 47 miles/76 km to Hudson's Hope and the W.A.C. Bennett Dam, then south to connect with the Hart Highway at Chetwynd. See "Hudson's Hope Loop" log on pages 90-91.

Sawmill lumberjack is dressed for the season at Milepost DC 62.4.
(© Earl L. Brown, staff)

Turn east for **Charlie Lake Provincial Park**, just off highway; paved loop road (with speed bumps) leads through campground. There are 58 shaded sites, picnic tables, kitchen shelter with wood stove, firepits, firewood, outhouses, dump station, water and garbage containers. Level gravel sites, some will accommodate 2 large RVs. Camping fee $12. Playfield, playground, horseshoe pits, volleyball net and a 1.2-mile/2-km hiking trail down to lake. Watch for wildflowers. Because of the wide variety of plants here, including some that may not be seen elsewhere along the Alaska Highway, Verna E. Pratt's *Wildflowers Along the Alaska Highway* includes a special list of species for this park. Fishing in Charlie Lake for walleye, northern pike and yellow perch. Access to the lake for vehicles and boats is from the Alaska Highway just east of the park entrance. Boat launch and picnic area at lake.

DC 62.4 (100.4 km) **DJ 1327.6** (2136.5 km) A 30-foot/9-m statue of a lumberjack marks Clarke Sawmill to west. (The statue wears a Santa suit at Christmas.)

DC 63.6 (102 km) **DJ 1326.4** (2134.6 km) Microwave tower to east.

DC 65.4 (105 km) **DJ 1324.6** (2131.7 km) Turnout with litter barrel to west.

DC 71.7 (115.4 km) **DJ 1318.3** (2121.5 km) Historical Mile 72. Food, gas, camping, lodging and crafts store.

The Shepherd's Inn. We specialize in making folks at home, offering regular and breakfast specials, complete lunch and dinner menu. Low-fat buffalo burgers. Our specialties: homemade soups, home-baked sweet rolls, cinnamon rolls, blueberry and bran muffins, bread, biscuits and trappers bannock. Delicious desserts, rhubarb-strawberry, Dutch apple and chocolate dream pie, cherry and strawberry cheesecake. Hard ice cream. Refreshing fruit drinks from local fruits: blueberry and raspberry coolers.

ROTARY R.V. PARK
On Beautiful Charlie Lake • "A Friendly Place To Stay"

- A **Secured** Park Bordering on a Nature Reserve.
- Full service Pull-Through sites to • Tenting sites
- **Super clean restrooms and showers** • Modem Friendly Telephone
- Laundry room • Sani dump • 30 Amp service • Fire pits & firewood

The Best Walleye Fishing in B.C.

Public boat launch and fishing dock • Nature Trails • Swimming complex • Museum • Shopping

(250) 785-1700
www.rvparkcanada.com
e-mail: office@rvparkcanada.com
Next to Country Pub & Restaurant

Your Hosts: Jim & Pam Haslett - P.O. Box 6306 Fort St. John, B.C., V1J 4H8

The Shepherd's Inn

MILE 72 Alaska Highway

7 am - 9 pm Mon.-Sat.
Closed Sunday

LOCAL CRAFTS AND GIFTS

Your Hosts:
Don and Dorothy Rutherford

"An Oasis on the Alaska Highway"

RESTAURANT and DINING ROOM ... *A Dining Treat*

Employees Food Safety Certified • Fine Home Cooking • Delicious Fresh-Baked Goods
Clean Air Concept – No Smoking Please

Here on the Alaska Highway it's Husky

23 CLEAN, MODERN ROOMS • TV • Ideal for Families • Motel Open 24 Hours
Reasonable Rates • **FULL RV PULL-THROUGH HOOKUPS** • In-house Showers

We Welcome Bus Tours & R.V. Caravans

GAS and PROPANE
Free Shower with Fillup

Phone (250) 827-3676 • FAX (250) 827-3135
Box 6425, Fort St. John, BC V1J 4H8, Canada

Attention caravaners and bus tours ... a convenient and delightful stop on your Alaska Highway adventure! You may reserve your stop–break with us. Full RV hookups, motel service 24 hours. NOTE: Highway 29 traffic from Hudson's Hope northbound entering Alaska Highway ... your first motel stop. Southbound ... your last motel selection. Quality Husky products. Your "Husky Buck" is a great traveling idea. Phone (250) 827-3676. An oasis on the Alcan at Mile 72.

[ADVERTISEMENT]

DC 72.7 (117 km) **DJ 1317.3** (2119.9 km) Cafe and private campground. ▲

DC 72.8 (117.1 km) **DJ 1317.2** (2119.8 km) **Historic Milepost 73** commemorates Beatton River Flight Strip, 1 of 4 gravel airstrips built for American military aircraft during WWII. Road to Prespetu and Buick Creek.

DC 79.1 (127.3 km) **DJ 1310.9** (2109.6 km) **Historical Mile 80** paved rest area to west with litter barrels, picnic tables, water and flush toilets.

DC 91.4 (147.1 km) **DJ 1298.6** (2089.8 km) **Historical Mile 92.** Duke Energy compressor station to west.

DC 94.6 (152.2 km) **DJ 1295.4** (2084.7 km) Oil pump east of highway behind trees.

DC 95 (152.9 km) **DJ 1295** (2084 km) Access west to Crystal Springs Ranch (32 miles/52 km).

DC 101 (161.7 km) **DJ 1289** (2074.4 km) **Historic Milepost 101. WONOWON** (pop. 150), unincorporated, has 3 gas stations (gas, diesel, propane), 2 restaurants, 2 motels, camping, a food store, pub and post office. Formerly known as Blueberry, Wonowon was the site of an official traffic control gate during WWII. Wonowon Horse Club holds an annual race meet and gymkhana at the track beside the highway, where the community club holds its annual snowmobile rally in February. ▲

The historic sign and interpretive panel here commemorate Blueberry Control Station, "site of the Blueberry Control Gate, a 24-hour military checkpoint operated by U.S. Army personnel through the war years."

The Alaska Highway follows the Blueberry and Prophet river drainages north to Fort Nelson. The Blueberry River, not visible from the highway, lies a few miles east of Wonowon.

DC 101.5 (163.3 km) **DJ 1288.5** (2073.6 km) Food, diesel, gas, camping and lodging to east; open year-round. ▲

DC 103.5 (166.5 km) **DJ 1244** (2002 km) **Historic Milepost 104** marks start of Adolphson, Huseth, Layer & Welch contract during Alaska Highway construction.

DC 114 (183.2 km) **DJ 1276** (2053.5 km) Paved turnout with litter barrel to east.

DC 122.9 (197.8 km) **DJ 1267.1** (2039.1 km) Townsend Creek.

DC 124.1 (199.7 km) **DJ 1265.9** (2037.2 km) Turnout to east with dumpster.

DC 124.3 (200 km) **DJ 1265.7** (2036.9 km) **The Cut** (highway goes through a small rock cut). Relatively few rock cuts were necessary during construction of the Alaska Highway in 1942–43. However, rock excavation was often made outside of the roadway to obtain gravel fill for the new roadbed.

DC 135.3 (217.7 km) **DJ 1254.7** (2019.2 km) Gravel turnout to east.

CAUTION: Northbound travelers watch for moose next 15 miles/24 km, especially at dusk and at night.

DC 140.4 (225.9 km) **DJ 1249.6** (2011

km) **Historical Mile 143. PINK MOUNTAIN** (pop. 99, area 300; elev. 3,600 feet/1,097m). Post office, grocery, motels, restaurant, campgrounds, gas stations (gas, diesel, propane) with minor repair service. Pink Mountain is home to Darryl Mills, Canadian champion bullrider. ▲

According to local resident Ron Tyerman, Pink Mountain gets its name from the local fall foliage, when red-barked willows give the mountain a pink colour in the morning sun. Another source attributes the pink colour of the mountain—and thus the name—to concentrations of feldspar.

Pink Mountain Campsite & R.V. Park, on the left northbound. Take it easy folks, you've arrived at one of the nicest campgrounds on the highway ... coffee's always on. Unleaded gas, diesel, metered propane for RVs and auto. Fuel discount for overnight guests. Post office, general store, liquor store, fishing and hunting licenses. Souvenirs—you'll like our prices. Shaded

campsites, picnic tables, firepits and free firewood. Tents and RVs welcome. Full hookups, power hookups, water and sanidump. Pull-throughs. Something for everyone. Laundromat and clean free showers. Open year-round. Your hosts: Korey and Lory. VISA and MasterCard. Phone and fax (250) 772-5133. [ADVERTISEMENT] ▲

DC 144.1 (231.9 km) **DJ 1245.9** (2005 km) **Historical Mile 147.** Sportsman Inn; motel, restaurant, gas and diesel, RV park, cabins.

Sportsman Inn & Beatton River RV Park. See display ad this section. ▲

PINK MOUNTAIN CAMPSITE AND R.V. PARK

MILE 143 ALASKA HIGHWAY

Gas • Propane • Diesel • Groceries • Liquor Store • Post Office
Gifts & Souvenirs • Fishing Licenses • Showers • Laundromat
Shaded Campsite • Full Service Sites • Internet & E-mail Access Available
• Pull-Throughs • **(250) 772-5133** • Power Hookups

BOX 26, PINK MOUNTAIN, BC V0C 2B0

VISA   MasterCard

SPORTSMAN INN
MOTEL, RESTAURANT, GAS & DIESEL

BEATTON RIVER RV PARK
• Full Hookups

CABIN with Kitchen Unit.
HUNTING & FISHING

MILE 147, ALASKA HIGHWAY, BC • PINKMOUNTAIN, BC V0C 2B0
Phone/Fax (250) 772-3220   Your Hosts: Cheryl & Vern Myers

VISA MasterCard

South to Fort St John — Pink Mntn Campsite / Pink Mntn Motor Inn — 4km — ★ SPORTSMAN INN & BEATTON RIVER RV PARK — Mae's Kitchen — 223km — North to Fort Nelson

DC 144.5 (232.5 km) **DJ 1245.5** (2004.4 km) **Historical Mile 147.** Mae's Kitchen restaurant, motel, gas and diesel; open year-round, closed Sundays.

Mae's Kitchen. See display ad this section.

DC 144.7 (232.9 km) **DJ 1245.3** (2004. km) **Historic Milepost 148** commemorates **Suicide Hill**, one of the most treacherous hills on the original highway, noted for its ominous greeting: "Prepare to meet thy maker."

Beatton River bridge. The Beatton River was named for Frank Beatton, a Hudson's Bay Co. employee. The Beatton River flows east and then south into the Peace River system.

DC 146 (234 km) **DJ 1244** (2002 km) **Private Aircraft:** Sikanni Chief flight strip to east; elev. 3,258 feet/993m; length, 6,000 feet/1,829m; gravel, current status unknown. Well-known local pilot Jimmy "Midnight" Anderson used the Sikanni Chief airstrip, which was the southernmost airfield in the Northwest Staging Route used during WWII.

DC 150.3 (241.9 km) **DJ 1239.7** (1995

Sikanni River bridge at Milepost DC 159.2. (© Earl L. Brown, staff)

km) **CAUTION:** *Southbound travelers watch for moose next 15 miles/24 km, especially at dusk and at night.*

DC 155.6 (250.4 km) **DJ 1234.4** (1986.5 km) Large double-ended, gravel turnout with litter barrels. **CAUTION:** *Slow down! Watch for loose gravel.*

DC 156.6 (252 km) **DJ 1233.4** (1984.9km) Sikanni Hill. **CAUTION:** *Slow down for hill. Watch for falling rocks!*

DC 159.2 (256.2 km) **DJ 1230.8** (1980.9 km) Sikanni Chief River bridge (elev. 2,662 feet/811m). To the west you may see steel stanchions, all that remains of the historic wooden Sikanni bridge, which was destroyed by arson July 10, 1992. The original timber

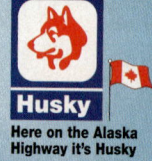

truss bridge built across the Sikanni Chief River in the spring of 1943 was the first permanent structure completed on the Alaska Highway. Highway construction crews rerouted much of the pioneer road built in 1942 and replaced temporary bridges with permanent structures in 1943. The Sikanni Chief River flows east and then north into the Fort Nelson River, which flows into the Liard River and on to the Mackenzie River, which empties into the Arctic Ocean. Check at the lodge for information on Sikanni Chief Falls (see **Milepost DC 168.5**).

Sikanni Chief River, fair fishing at mouth of tributaries in summer for pike; grayling to 2½ lbs.; whitefish to 2 lbs.

DC 159.4 (256.5 km) **DJ 1230.6** (1980.4 km) **Historical Mile 162. SIKANNI CHIEF.** Food, gas, diesel, propane, lodging and camping.

Sikanni River RV Park. See display ad this section.

One of the largest ichthyosaur specimens ever found was discovered on the banks of

---

Mae's Kitchen
Div. of Headwaters Ranch Ltd.

❖ **BUS TOURS WELCOME** ❖
(Please call ahead)

❖ **RESTAURANT** ❖
Well prepared foods served with fresh baked breads and pastries.

❖ **LOCAL CRAFTS** ❖
Postcards and T-Shirts

Mile 147, Alaska Hwy.
Pink Mountain, BC V0C 2B0

Phone (250) 772-3215
Fax (250) 772-5147

OPEN YEAR-ROUND
7 a.m. to 9 p.m. Mon.-Fri.
7 a.m. to 6 p.m. Saturday
Closed on Sunday

Husky — Here on the Alaska Highway it's Husky
ONE CUP OF COFFEE FREE WITH FILL-UP

UNLEADED GAS AND DIESEL

Sikanni River RV Park
MILE 162, ALASKA HIGHWAY

FULL SERVICE R.V. PARK & CAMPGROUND
LONG PULL THRU SITES • FULL HOOKUPS • 20 AMP • TENTING SITES • LAUNDRY
ICE • PUBLIC PHONE • CONFECTIONARY ITEMS • SOUVENIRS • FIREWOOD • CABINS
FREE: HOT SHOWERS • **FREE:** VIDEO RENTALS
TOP QUALITY GAS • DIESEL • PROPANE
Phone/Fax (250) 772-5400

the Sikanni Chief River. The 75-foot/23-m marine reptile was excavated by the Royal Tyrrell Museum of Alberta. Ichthyosaurs looked a little bit like large, ugly dolphins.

DC 160 (257.5 km) **DJ 1230** (1979.4 km) "Drunken Forest" on hillside to west is shallow-rooted black spruce trees growing in unstable clay-based soil that is subject to slide activity in wet weather.

DC 160.4 (258.1 km) **DJ 1229.6** (1978.8 km) Section of the old Alaska Highway is visible to east; no access.

DC 168.5 (271.2 km) **DJ 1221.5** (1965.7 km) Gravel road west to **Sikanni Chief Falls Protected Area**. Drive in 10.5 miles/16.9 km to parking area at trailhead for 0.9-mile/1.5-km hike on well-marked trail to view the 98-foot/30-m falls. Gravel access road has some steep hills and a single-lane bridge. CAUTION: Do not travel this road in wet weather. Not recommended for vehicles with trailers.

IMPORTANT: Watch for moose on highway northbound to **Milepost DC 200**, especially at dusk. Drive carefully!

DC 172.5 (277.6 km) **DJ 1217.5** (1959.3 km) Polka Dot Creek.

DC 173.1 (278.6 km) **DJ 1216.9** (1958.3 km) Buckinghorse River bridge; access to river at north end of bridge.

DC 173.2 (278.7 km) **DJ 1216.8** (1958.2 km) Turnoff to east for **Buckinghorse River Wayside Provincial Park**. Follow the narrow gravel road past the gravel pit 0.7 mile/1.1 km along river to camping and picnic area. The park has 30 picnic tables, side-by-side camper parking, fire rings, water pump, outhouses and garbage containers; user-maintained, $9 camping fee.

Fishing for grayling in **Buckinghorse River**. Swimming in downstream pools.

DC 173.4 (279 km) **DJ 1216.6** (1957.9 km) **Historical Mile 175**. Buckinghorse River Lodge, on left northbound; food, gas, diesel, lodging and tent camping. Open year-round. Bus stop.

DC 176 (283.2 km) **DJ 1214** (1953.7 km) South end of 27-mile/43-km **Trutch Mountain Bypass**. Completed in 1987, this section of road rerouted the Alaska Highway around Trutch Mountain, eliminating the steep, winding climb to Trutch Summit (and the views). Named for Joseph W. Trutch, civil engineer and first governor of British Columbia, Trutch Mountain was the second highest summit on the Alaska Highway, with an elevation of 4,134 feet/1,260m. The new roadbed cuts a wide swath through the flat Minnaker River valley. The river, not visible to motorists, is west of the highway; and was named for local trapper George Minnaker. Trutch Mountain is to the east of the highway. Motorists can see part of the old highway on Trutch Mountain.

DC 182.8 (294.2 km) **DJ 1207.2** (1942.7 km) Large gravel turnout to west with dumpster.

DC 199.1 (320 km) **DJ 1190.9** (1916.5 km) Large gravel turnout with litter barrels.

DC 202.5 (325.5 km) **DJ 1187.5** (1911 km) Turnout with dumpster at north end of Trutch Mountain bypass (see **Milepost DC 176**).

CAUTION: Southbound travelers watch for moose on highway, especially at dusk, to Sikanni Chief. Drive carefully!

DC 204.2 (328 km) **DJ 1185.8** (1908.3 km) **Beaver Creek**; fishing for grayling to 2½ lbs.

DC 217.2 (349.3 km) **DJ 1172.8** (1887.4 km) Turnoff to west for former Prophet River Wayside Provincial Park. Drive in 0.4 mile/0.6 km via gravel road; no facilities. The park access road crosses an airstrip (originally an emergency airstrip on the Northwest Air Staging Route) and part of the old Alaska Highway (the Alcan). Trembling aspen stands and mature white spruce.

The Alaska Highway roughly parallels the Prophet River from here north to the Muskwa River south of Fort Nelson.

Private Aircraft: Prophet River emergency airstrip; elev. 1,954 feet/596m; length 6,000 feet/1,829m; gravel; no services.

DC 218.2 (350.7 km) **DJ 1171.8** (1885.8 km) View of Prophet River to west.

DC 222.3 (357.2 km) **DJ 1167.7** (1879.2 km) Bougie Creek bridge; turnout with litter barrel beside creek at south end of bridge. Note the typical climax white spruce stand and trees of a variety of ages.

CAUTION: Watch for rough road approaching Bougie Creek bridge from either direction.

DC 224.8 (360.6 km) **DJ 1165.2** (1875.2 km) Microwave tower to east.

DC 226.2 (363.4 km) **DJ 1163.8** (1872.9 km) Prophet River Indian Reserve to east.

DC 226.5 (363.9 km) **DJ 1163.5** (1872.4 km) St. Paul's Roman Catholic Church to east.

DC 227 (364.7 km) **DJ 1163** (1871.6 km) **Historical Mile 233. PROPHET RIVER**, gas, diesel, propane, food, camping and lodging.

Lum N' Abners Restaurant. See display ad this section.

Southbound travelers note: Next service 68 miles/109 km.

DC 227.6 (366.3 km) **DJ 1162.4** (1870.6 km) Historic Milepost 234, Adsett Creek Highway Realignment. This major rerouting eliminated 132 curves on the stretch of highway that originally ran between Miles 234 and 275. Double-ended turnout with dumpster.

DC 227.7 (366.4 km) **DJ 1162.3** (1870.5 km) Adsett Creek.

DC 230.7 (371.3 km) **DJ 1159.3** (1865.7 km) Natural gas pipeline crosses beneath highway.

DC 232.9 (374.8 km) **DJ 1157.1** (1862.1 km) Turnout to west with dumpster.

DC 235.5 (378.4 km) **DJ 1154.5** (1857.9 km) Mesa-like topography to the east is Mount Yakatchie.

DC 241.5 (388 km) **DJ 1148.5** (1848.3 km) Parker Creek.

DC 242.6 (390 km) **DJ 1147.4** (1846.5 km) Little Beaver Creek.

DC 245.9 (395.7 km) **DJ 1144.1** (1841.2 km) Gravel turnout with dumpster.

DC 248.5 (400 km) **DJ 1141.5** (1837 km) Big Beaver Creek.

Watch for black bears—which may also be brown or cinnamon-colored—along the Alaska Highway in British Columbia. (© Earl L. Brown, staff)

Lum N' Abners Restaurant | **HISTORICAL SITE**

On the Left for Northbound Travellers

RV PARKING WITH HOOKUPS
Tenting • Rooms
Homestyle Cooking
Gas & Diesel

MILEPOST 233
Mel & Pat Pydde

Bus Tours Welcome
(Please call ahead)

(250) 773-6366
Fax (250) 773-6367

DC 261.1 (420.2 km) **DJ 1128.9** (1816.7 km) Turnout to east with dumpster.

DC 264.6 (425.2 km) **DJ 1125.4** (1811.1 km) Jackfish Creek bridge. Note the variety of trembling aspen stands and the white spruce seedlings under them.

DC 265.5 (426.5 km) **DJ 1124.5** (18.09.6 km) Turnoff to east for **Andy Bailey Regional Park** via 6.8-mile/11-km dirt and gravel access road. (Large RVs and trailers note: only turnaround space on access road is approximately halfway in.) The park is located on Andy Bailey Lake (formerly Jackfish Lake); 6 campsites, picnic sites, picnic tables, fire rings, firewood, water, outhouses, garbage containers, boat launch (no powerboats), swimming and fair fishing for northern pike. Bring insect repellent!

DC 270.8 (435.1 km) **DJ 1119.2** (1801.1 km) Sulphur gas pipeline crosses highway overhead.

DC 271 (435.4 km) **DJ 1119** (1800.8 km) Duke Energy gas processing plant to east. Sulfur pelletizing to west.

DC 276.2 (443.8 km) **DJ 1113.8** (1792.4 km) Rodeo grounds to west. The rodeo is held in August.

DC 276.7 (444.6 km) **DJ 1113.3** (1791.6 km) Railroad tracks. Microwave tower.

DC 277.5 (446.2 km) **DJ 1112.5** (1790.3 km) **Muskwa Heights** (unincorporated), an industrial area with rail yard, plywood plant, sawmill and bulk fuel outlet.

DC 277.9 (447.2 km) **DJ 1112.1** (1789.7 km) RV park; gas station with 24-hour gas, diesel; propane.

DC 278.1 (447.5 km) **DJ 1111.9** (1789.4 km) Truck scales to west.

DC 278.4 (448 km) **DJ 1111.6** (1788.9 km) **Trapper's Den. Historic Mile 293.** Owned and operated by a local trapping family. Moose antlers and antler carvings, diamond willow, Northern books. Fur hats, headbands, earmuffs, and Teddy bears. Local

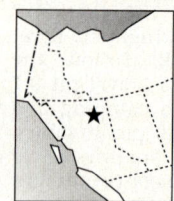

Native crafts. Birchbark baskets, moose-hair tuftings, mukluks, moccasins and mitts. Wild furs and leather. See our "Muskwa River Pearls." Photographers welcome. Solar Products and Deep Cycle Batteries. Alaskans shop here! Located across highway from weigh scales, 6 miles south of Fort Nelson. Open 10 A.M.–6 P.M. Monday through Saturday. Closed Sundays. Box 1164, Fort Nelson, BC V0C 1R0. (250) 774-3400; www.trappersden.ca. Recommended.

DC 279 (448.6 km) **DJ 1111** (1787.9 km) Site of oriented strand board plant processing aspen and balsam poplar. This 400,000-square-foot building is the largest industrial building of its kind in the province.

DC 280 (450.2km) **DJ 1110** (1786.3 km) **Fast Freddy's Batting Cages and Golf Tee-Off.** Test your skill (settings from slo-pitch softball to 102 MPH softball). Bats and helmets provided, golf clubs and balls supplied. Drop in—no appointment necessary, lots of parking. Refreshments. Authentic Native crafts and souvenirs. Open sunrise to sunset. (250) 774-3720.
[ADVERTISEMENT]

The Alaska Highway swings west at Fort Nelson above the Muskwa River, winding through the Canadian Rockies.

DC 283 (454.3 km) **DJ 1107** (1781.5 km) Entering Fort Nelson northbound. Fort Nelson's central business district extends along the highway from the private campground at the east end of the town to the private campground at the west end. Businesses and services are located both north and south of the highway.

Fort Nelson

DC 283 (454.3 km) **DJ 1107** (1781.5 km) **Historical Mile 300.** Population: 4,401; area 5,720. **Emergency Services: RCMP,** phone (250) 774-2777. **Fire Department,** phone (250) 774-2222. **Hospital,** 35 beds, phone (250) 774-8100. **Ambulance,** phone (250) 774-2344. Medical, dental and optometric clinics; resident physiotherapist and veterinarian; visiting chiropractors.

Visitor Information: Visitor Info Centre located in the Recreation Centre at the west end of town; open 8 A.M. to 8 P.M., mid-May to September. Inquire here about local attractions, industrial tours, the new guide to local hiking trails, and information about the Liard Highway. Fort Nelson Heritage Museum across the highway from the Infocentre. Contact the Town of Fort Nelson by writing Bag Service 399M, Fort Nelson, BC V0C 1R0; phone (250) 774-6400 or (250)

FORT NELSON ADVERTISERS

Autumn Images	Ph. (250) 774-3488
Bluebell Inn, The	Ph. 1-800-663-5267
Capp A Lu's Espresso Cafe	Ph. (250) 774-7222
Dixie Lee	Ph. (250) 774-6226
Fabric Fun	#17 Landmark Plaza
Fort Nelson Heritage Museum	Ph. (250) 774-3536
Fort Nelson Hotel	Ph. (250) 774-6971
Fort Nelson Husky	Ph. (250) 774-2376
Kacee's Koin Laundromat	Downtown on Main St.
Mini-Price Inn	1 blk. behind CIBC Banking Centre
Northern Deli	Landmark Plaza
Northern Vision Health Foods	Landmark Plaza
Pioneer Motel	Ph. (250) 774-6459
Ramada Limited	Downtown
Subway, The	Ph. (250) 774-7827
Town of Fort Nelson	Ph. (250) 774-2541
Westend R.V. Campground	West end of town
Woodlands Inn	Ph. (250) 774-6669

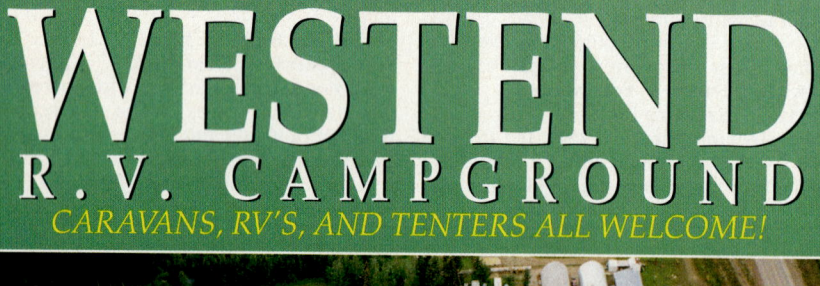

WESTEND
R.V. CAMPGROUND
CARAVANS, RV'S, AND TENTERS ALL WELCOME!

• **Open April 1 - November 1** •

Over 160 Sites • Pull-throughs • Grassy Tent Sites • Full Hookups
All Sites with 30 Amp Service, Cable TV + Some Dry Sites Available
Picnic Tables • Native Crafts • Laundromat • Ice • Dump Station
Hot Showers • Pay Phones • E-mail Modem Access • Convenience Store
Oil Changes • Pressure RV Wash • RV Supplies • Gifts and Souvenirs • Chip Repairs
Central Meeting Place and BBQ Pit • Wildlife Display

Your hosts: The Brown's
Box 398, Fort Nelson, BC V0C 1R0
Phone (250) 774-2340 • FAX (250) 774-2840
www.fnbc.net/campground

On the Alaska Highway In Town, Next to Museum, Easy Walking to Downtown

774-2541, ext. 240; ecdev@northernrockies.org; www.northernrockies.org.

Elevation: 1,383 feet/422m. **Climate:** Winters are cold with short days. Summers are hot and the days are long. In mid-June (summer solstice), twilight continues throughout the night. The average number of frost-free days annually is 116. Last frost occurs about May 11, and the first frost Sept. 21. Average annual precipitation of 17.7 inches. **Radio:** CBC 88.3-FM, Energy 102.3-FM. **Television:** Channels 8 and cable. **Newspaper:** *Fort Nelson News* (weekly).

Transportation: Air—Scheduled service to Edmonton, Calgary, Grande Prairie, and Vancouver via Air Canada and Peace Air. Charter service available. **Bus**—Greyhound service. **Railroad**—B.C. Railway (freight service only).

Private Aircraft: Fort Nelson airport, 3.8 ENE; elev. 1,253 feet/382m; length 6,400 feet/1,950m; asphalt; fuel 100, Jet.

Fort Nelson is located in the lee of the Rocky Mountains, surrounded by the Muskwa, Fort Nelson and Prophet rivers. The area is heavily forested with white spruce, poplar and aspen. Geographically, the town is located about 59° north latitude and 122° west longitude.

Flowing east and north, the Muskwa, Prophet and Sikanni Chief rivers converge to form the Fort Nelson River, which flows into the Liard River, then on to the Mackenzie River, which empties into the Arctic Ocean. Rivers provided the only means of transportation in both summer and winter in this isolated region until 1922, when the Godsell Trail opened, connecting Fort Nelson with Fort St. John. The Alaska Highway linked Fort Nelson with the Outside in 1942.

In the spring, the Muskwa River frequently floods the low country around Fort Nelson and can rise more than 20 feet/6m. At an elevation of 1,000 feet/305m, the Muskwa (which means "bear") is the lowest point on the Alaska Highway. There was a danger of the Muskwa River bridge washing out every June during spring runoff until 1970, when a higher bridge—with piers arranged to prevent log jams—was built.

Fort Nelson's existence was originally based on the fur trade. In the 1920s, trapping was the main business in this isolated pioneer community populated with fewer than 200 Indians and a few white men. Trappers still harvest beaver, wolverine, weasel, wolf, fox, lynx, mink, muskrat and marten. Other area wildlife includes black bear, which are plentiful, some deer, caribou

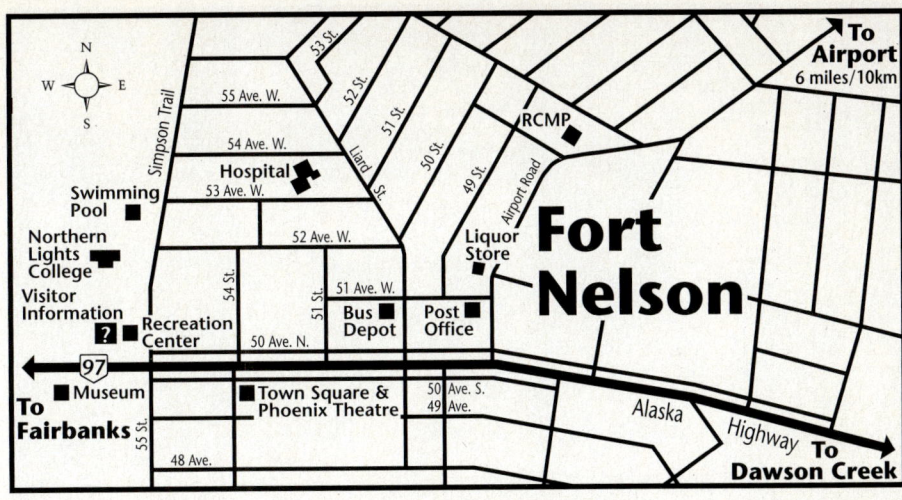

ALASKA HIGHWAY • Fort Nelson

Aerial view of Fort Nelson, BC, at Historical Mile 300 on the Alaska Highway.
(© Earl L. Brown, staff)

and a few grizzly bears. Moose remains an important food source for the Indians.

Fort Nelson aboriginal people are mostly Dene, who arrived here about 1775 from the Great Slave Lake area. The Dene speak an Athabascan dialect.

Fort Nelson was first established in 1805 by the North West Fur Trading Co. The post, believed to have been located about 80 miles/129 km south of Nelson Forks, was named for Lord Horatio Nelson, the English admiral who won the Battle of Trafalgar.

A second Fort Nelson was later located south of the first fort, but was destroyed by fire in 1813 after Indians massacred its 8 residents. A third Fort Nelson was established in 1865 on the Fort Nelson River's west bank (1 mile from the present Fort Nelson airport) by W. Cornwallis King, a Hudson's Bay Co. clerk. This trading post was built to keep out the free traders who were filtering in from the Mackenzie River and Fort St. John areas. The free traders' higher fur prices were a threat to the Hudson's Bay Co., which in 1821 had absorbed the rival North West Fur

FORT NELSON HOTEL
(Bus Tour Specialists)

135 modern rooms, some with kitchenettes - all with private baths. Cable colour TV and phones in every room. Ample hard surface parking. Licensed dining rooms and cocktail lounge. Air conditioned. Courtesy airport limousine.

**Deluxe Units • Indoor Pool • Saunas
Cable Colour TV • Telephones • Coffee Shop
Nightly Entertainment and Dancing
For Reservations (250) 774-6971 • 1-800-663-5225
Fax (250) 774-6711**

FORT NELSON HOTEL, BOX 240, FORT NELSON V0C 1R0

NORTHERN DELI
We will help make your trip a happier one.

- Subs & Sandwiches Party Trays • Deep Fryer Menu
- Salads and much, much more • Ice

LUNCHES TO GO FOR TOUR BUSES & CARAVANS

- COLD SOFTDRINKS
- SLUSH PUPPIE MACHINE
- 39 FLAVOURS OF SOFT ICE CREAM AND MILKSHAKES
- SEVERAL VARIETIES OF HARD ICE CREAM

Open 7 Days a Week 6 a.m. to 10 p.m.
Phone (250) 774-3311 • FAX (250) 774-2710

Fort Nelson, BC
Downtown – In the Landmark Plaza

PIONEER MOTEL
"The Travellers Friend"

Centrally Located • Clean
Reasonable Rates

12 Units – Kitchenettes Available
Cozy Cabins
Direct Dial Phones
Air Conditioning
Cable TV • Movie Channel
Pets Welcome
RV Stalls • Full Hook-Up
Cable • Shower/Washrooms
Coin-op Laundry Facilities

Your Hosts — John & Estrella Godfrey

Box 1643, Fort Nelson B.C.
(250) 774-5800
FAX (250) 774-6253
pioneermotel@yt.sympatico.ca

FULL ESPRESSO CAFE
CAPP * A * LU'S
~ A WARM AND FRIENDLY PLACE TO VISIT ~

FEATURING: GREAT COFFEE, COOL DRINKS, SOUP & SANDWICH LUNCH SPECIALS, FRESH BAKING DAILY, GOURMET DESSERTS & SWEETS, OUTSIDE TABLES, COFFEE BEAN SALES, GIFT BASKETS, A UNIQUE EXPERIENCE WITH FRIENDLY SERVICE.

OPEN: MON TO SAT
4916 - 50 AVE. N., MAIN ST. LOCATION.

capp-a-lu@yt.sympatico.ca
INTERNET ACCESS
FORT NELSON BC
774-7222

Trading Co. and gained a monopoly on the fur trade in Canada.

This Hudson's Bay Co. trading post was destroyed by a flood in 1890 and a fourth Fort Nelson was established on higher ground upstream and across the river, which is now known as Old Fort Nelson. The present town of Fort Nelson is the fifth site.

Fort Nelson saw its first mail service in 1936. Scheduled air service to Fort Nelson—by ski- and floatplane—also was begun in the 1930s by Yukon Southern Air (which was later absorbed by CPAir, now Air Canada). The Canadian government began construction of an airport in 1941 as part of the Northwest Air Staging Route, and this was followed by perhaps the biggest boom to Fort Nelson—the construction of the Alaska Highway in 1942. About 2,000 soldiers were bivouacked in Fort Nelson, which they referred to as Zero, as it was the beginning of a road to Whitehorse and another road to Fort Simpson. Later Dawson Creek became Mile 0 and Fort Nelson Mile 300.

Fort Nelson expanded in the 1940s and 1950s as people came here to work for the government or to start their own small businesses: trucking, barging, aviation, construction, garages, stores, cafes, motels and sawmills. It is surprising to consider that as recently as the 1950s Fort Nelson was still a pioneer community without power, phones, running water, refrigerators or doctors.

Fort Nelson was an unorganized territory until 1957 when it was declared an Improvement District. Fort Nelson took on village status in 1971 and town status in 1987.

Forestry is a major industry here with a veneer plant, plywood plant, oriented strand board plant and sawmill complex. Check with the Infocentre about scheduled industrial tours.

Forestry products are shipped south by truck and rail. Fort Nelson became a railhead in 1971 with the completion of a 250-mile extension of the Pacific Great Eastern Railway (now British Columbia Railway) from Fort St. John.

Agriculture is under development here

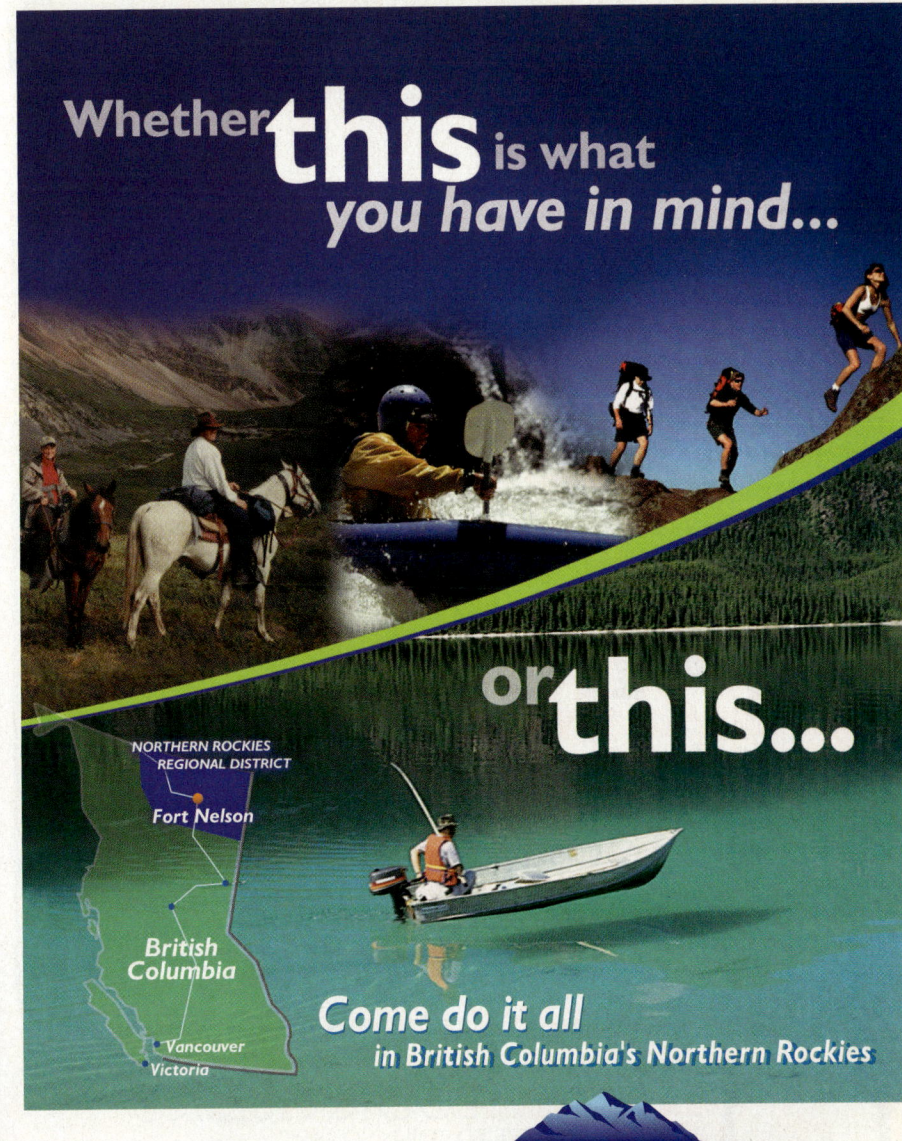

ALASKA HIGHWAY • Fort Nelson

Fort Nelson Heritage Museum preserves antique vehicles and pioneer artifacts.
(© Earl L. Brown, staff)

with the establishment of the 55,000-acre McConachie Creek agricultural subdivision.

Northeastern British Columbia is the only sedimentary area in the province currently producing oil and gas. Oil seeps in the Fort Nelson area were noted by early residents. Major gas discoveries were made in the 1960s when the Clarke Lake, Yoyo/Kotcho, Beaver River and Pointed Mountain gas reserves were developed. The Westcoast Energy natural gas processing plant at Fort Nelson, the largest in North America, was constructed in 1964. This plant purifies the gas before sending it south through the 800-mile-long pipeline that connects the Fort Nelson area with the British Columbia lower mainland. Sulfur, a byproduct of natural gas processing, is processed in a recovery plant and shipped to outside markets in pellet form.

In 1997, the BC government set aside more than 4.4 million hectares of Northern Rockies wilderness near Fort Nelson. Known as the "Serengeti of the North," the Muskwa-Kechika (MK) Managements Area is one of the largest predator-prey systems in North America. It is the largest intact, unroaded wilderness area south of the 60th parallel. The Muskwa–Kechika area preserves critical wildlife habitat while allowing logging, mining, oil and gas exploration, and is designed to balance resource management with conservation. For more information contact the Muskwa-Kechika Program Manager, phone (250) 787-3534, or visit www.muskwa-kechika.com.

Lodging & Services

Fort Nelson's 11 hotels/motels and a few bed and breakfasts provide accommodations.

Most stores and services are located just off the Alaska Highway. There are gas stations; restaurants; grocery and and health food outlets; laundromats; auto supply stores, and department stores. The post office and liquor store are on Airport Drive. There are 2 banks, both with ATMs, on the business frontage road north of the highway.

Internet access is available at Capp A Lu's on main street, at the Downtown Internet Cafe and at the library.

Fresh water fill-up and free municipal dump station adjacent to the pink chalet near the museum. Inquire at the Infocentre for location of local churches and their hours of worship.

Camping

Fort Nelson has 2 campgrounds: one is located at the north (or west) end of town near the museum; the other is at Muskwa Heights south of Fort Nelson. ▲

Westend RV Campground welcomes RVs, caravans and tenters. Located in town next to the Museum, only a few minutes from stores and downtown. Over 160 sites, lots of shade, full hookups, pull-throughs,

Eat in — Take out
Dixie Lee
CHICKEN — FISH N' CHIPS
MOUTHWATERING HAMBURGERS
SOFT ICE CREAM
MILKSHAKES & TREATS
"Pressure Prepared Chicken Using Only The Best Vegetable Oils!"
Downtown Fort Nelson
(250) 774-6226 VISA

Fabric Fun
▶ Sewing & Home Decorating Fabrics
▶ Bridal & Special Occasions
▶ Notions, Laces, Ribbons
▶ Heritage Sewing
▶ Quilting Supplies & Fabric Crafts
▶ Ribbon Embroidery / DMC Floss

Janome Sewing Machines
JANOME
The Power Behind The Stitch®

Browsers Welcome
Phone (250) 774-6468
FAX (250) 774-6288

#17-New Landmark Plaza   Laura Stankiewicz
Box 857, Fort Nelson V0C 1R0   Darleen Dixon
4903 · 51 Ave. W.   e-mail: fab_fun@pris.ca

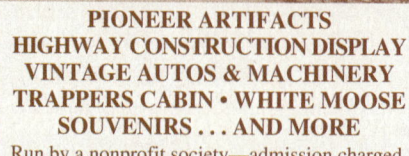

Fort Nelson Heritage Museum

**PIONEER ARTIFACTS
HIGHWAY CONSTRUCTION DISPLAY
VINTAGE AUTOS & MACHINERY
TRAPPERS CABIN • WHITE MOOSE
SOUVENIRS... AND MORE**

Run by a nonprofit society—admission charged.

*See our life size
"Chadwick Ram" sculpture*

Fort Nelson Historical Society
Box 716, Fort Nelson, BC, V0C 1R0
Phone/Fax **(250) 774-3536**

Husky
Here in Canada it's Husky

FORT NELSON HUSKY
DOWNTOWN NEXT TO TOWN SQUARE

UNLEADED * PREMIUM * DIESEL * PROPANE * ICE * ATM * AIR
BOTTLED PROPANE * PUBLIC PHONE * MAGAZINES * FOOD STORE
SNACKS & BAKERY ITEMS * ICE CREAM * LOTTERY SALES
PHONE CARDS * NEWSPAPERS * HOT & COLD FOOD

 Save at least $1.00 on every fill-up May-Sept.

OPEN YEAR ROUND! • 5AM to 10 PM

SEE YOU THERE! • (250) 774-2376

CAA Members - save up to 3% off the value of your purchases towards your next membership renewal! Check for details!

cable TV, email modem access. Town water, coin-op showers, laundry. Pressure RV wash and firewood. Wildlife display, convenience store, crafts. Open April 1–Nov. 1. The Browns welcome you to enjoy their Northern hospitality. Phone (250) 774-2340; fax (250) 774-5218. [ADVERTISEMENT] ▲

Attractions

Fort Nelson offers travelers a free "Welcome Visitor Program" in June and July, Monday through Thursday evenings at 6:45 P.M. in the Phoenix Theatre. These interesting and entertaining presentations are put on by local residents and range from slide shows to talks on items of local interest. Check with the Visitor Infocentre or at the Town Square for details.

The **Fort Nelson Heritage Museum**, across the highway from the Travel Infocentre, has excellent displays of pioneer artifacts, Alaska Highway history, wildlife (including a white moose), a spruce bark canoe, and souvenirs and books for sale. Outside the museum is the Chadwick Ram, a bronze sculpture by Rick Taylor. The statue commemorates the world-record stone sheep taken in the Muskwa Valley area in 1936. This nonprofit museum charges a modest admission fee. Native crafts are displayed at the Fort Nelson–Liard Native Friendship Centre, located on 49th Avenue.

The **Fort Nelson Recreation Centre**, across from the museum, has tennis courts; hockey and curling arena for winter sports. Swimming pool, swirl pool, sauna and gym located in the Aqua Centre on Simpson Trail.

Fort Nelson's **Skateboard Park** is a popular attraction. It is located next to the Recreation Centre on Simpson Trail.

For golfers, the **Poplar Hills Golf and Country Club**, just north of town on the Old Alaska Highway, has grass greens; open daily.

A community demonstration forest is open to the public. There is a forest trail (0.6 mile/1 km, half-hour walk), a silviculture trail (1.9 miles/3 km, 45-minute walk) and a Native trail. Located off the Simpson Trail via Mountainview Drive; check at the Infocentre for trail guide.

Fort Nelson hosts a number of annual benefits, dances, tournaments and exhibits. Check locally for details and dates on all events. Summer events include the Canada Day celebration, various ball and golf tournaments, and a rodeo in August. Winter events include a big cash prize curling bonspiel in February and the Canadian Open Sled Dog Races in December (with local racers from the well-known Streeper Kennels). Terry Streeper is a four-time World Champion (Anchorage) and also an Open North American Champion (Fairbanks) sled dog racer, has won more than 30 major races in 6 countries during the 1990s. Streeper Kennels is located on Radar Road.

The Northern Rockies Quilter's Guild meets on the first Monday of every month. Travelling quilters are welcome to drop in. For more information, contact the visitor infocentre. The Guild's "Millennium Quilt" is on display in the Town Square offices.

The Northern Rockies Toastmasters Club meets at Town Square every second Thursday (check with the Visitor Infocentre). Travelling Toastmasters are welcome to join the meeting, according to Earl Brown, *The MILEPOST* field editor and past president of the local club.

Alaska Highway Log
(continued)

BC HIGHWAY 97 WEST
Distance from Dawson Creek (DC)* is followed by distance from Delta Junction (DJ). Original mileposts are indicated in the text as Historical Mile.

*In the Canada portion of *The MILEPOST* Alaska Highway log, mileages from Dawson Creek are based on actual driving distance and kilometres are based on physical kilometreposts. (Mileages from Delta Junction are based on actual driving distance, followed by the metric conversion.) See "Mileposts and Kilometreposts" in the introduction beginning on page 98 for more details.

DC 284 (456.4 km) **DJ 1106** (1779.9 km) **Historic Milepost 300**, historic sign and interpretive panel at west end of Fort Nelson. Visitor information in the Recreation Centre north side of highway, log museum south side of highway. Private campground adjacent museum. ▲

Northbound: Watch for sections of rough, narrow, winding road and breaks in surfacing between Fort Nelson and the BC–YT border (approximately next 321 miles/516.5 km).

Southbound: Good pavement, wider road, next 284 miles/457 km (to Dawson Creek).

DC 284.5 (457.5 km) **DJ 1105.5** (1779.1 km) Fort Nelson Forest District Office to north.

Leaving Fort Nelson, the highway veers to the west and winds through the northern Canadian Rockies for the next 200 miles. In this densely forested region, there are many scenic vistas, where rivers meander through the wilderness to disappear in the haze of horizons 100 miles distant. Opportunities for many fine photos are offered by the beautiful scenery along this part of the highway, and fortunate travelers occasionally see moose, bear, caribou and stone sheep.

DC 284.7 (458.2 km) **DJ 1105.3** (1778.8 km) **Junction** with south end of Old Alaska Highway (**Mile 301–308**). The Muskwa Valley bypass between Mile 301 and 308 opened in 1992.

DC 287.9 (462.6 km) **DJ 1102.1** (1773.6 km) Access to Poplar Hills Golf and Country Club, located on Old Alaska Highway; 9-hole golf course, driving range, grass greens, clubhouse (licensed), golf club rentals. Open 8 A.M. to dusk, May to October.

DC 288.7 (463.9 km) **DJ 1101.3** (1772.3 km) Watch for bison ranches to north.

DC 291 (467.6 km) **DJ 1099** (1768.6 km) Parker Lake Road. **Junction** with north end

of Old Alaska Highway (**Mile 308–301**).

DC 292 (469.9 km) **DJ 1098** (1767 km) Private airstrip alongside highway; status unknown.

DC 301 (483.5 km) **DJ 1089** (1752.5 km)

Junction with Liard Highway (BC Highway 77) north to Fort Liard, Fort Simpson and other Northwest Territories destinations. See LIARD HIGHWAY section.

DC 304.1 (489.4 km) **DJ 1085.9** (1747.4 km) **Historic Milepost 320.** Sign marks start

STEAMBOAT mountain café

CHECK OUT OUR HISTORIC ALASKA HIGHWAY PHOTOS

GAS • CAFE - BREAKFAST
FRESH BAKING • CONFECTIONARY

(250) 774-3388

Picnic & Tenting Area
Pull-Through RV Sites
FULL HOOKUPS
Public Phone • Souvenirs

TETSA RIVER GUEST RANCH & CAMPGROUND

JUST 11 MILES BEYOND TETSA RIVER PROVINCIAL PARK

• CINNAMON BUN CENTER OF THE GALACTIC CLUSTER
• HOMEMADE BREAD AND BAKING
• CAMPING – HOOKUPS
• CABINS • WILDLIFE DISPLAY
• GUIDED FISHING TRIPS
• TRAIL RIDES: DAILY - WEEKLY *INTO WOKKAPASH LAKE AND NORTHERN ROCKY MOUNTAIN WILDERNESS PARKS BY SADDLE & PACK HORSE*
• UNLEADED GAS • DIESEL
• MINOR REPAIRS • TIRE REPAIR
• WELDING

HISTORICAL MILE 375 ALASKA HIGHWAY

YOUR HOSTS: CLIFF & LORI ANDREWS

(250) 774-1005

SEE OUR LOG AD FOR MORE

View of landmark Indian Head Mountain at Milepost DC 341.
(© Earl L. Brown, staff)

of Reese & Olson contract during construction of the Alaska Highway.

DC 308.2 (495.3 km) **DJ 1081.8** (1740.9 km) Raspberry Creek. Turnout with dumpster to south.

DC 316.6 (506.2 km) **DJ 1073.4** (1727.6 km) Turnout with dumpster to south.

DC 318.4 (509.1 km) **DJ 1071.6** (1724.5 km) Kledo Creek bridge. The Kledo River is a tributary of the Muskwa River. This is a popular hunting area in the fall.

DC 318.7 (509.5 km) **DJ 1071.3** (1724 km) Kledo Creek wayside rest area to north with dumpster.

DC 322.7 (516 km) **DJ 1067.3** (1717.6 km) Steamboat Creek bridge. *NOTE: Improved highway begins climb westbound up Steamboat Mountain; winding road, some 10 percent grades.*

DC 329 (526.1 km) **DJ 1061** (1707.5 km) Pull-through turnout with dumpster to south.

DC 332.4 (531.6 km) **DJ 1057.6** (1702 km) **Historic Milepost 351.** STEAMBOAT (unincorporated), lodge with food, gas and camping to south. Historical sign marks start of Curran & Briggs Ltd. contract during construction of the Alaska Highway. ▲

Steamboat Mountain Cafe. See display ad this section. ▲

DC 333.7 (533.5 km) **DJ 1056.3** (1699.9 km) Winding road ascends Steamboat Mountain westbound. Views of the **Muskwa River Valley** and Rocky Mountains to the southwest from summit of 3,500-foot/1,067-m Steamboat Mountain, named because of its resemblance to a steamship.

DC 334.8 (535.3 km) **DJ 1055.2** (1698.1 km) Turnout to south with view of Muskwa River Valley; dumpster.

DC 336.5 (536.8 km) **DJ 1054.3** (1696.7 km) Large turnouts both sides of highway with dumpsters, calling card phones and toilets.

Highway descends for westbound travelers. *NOTE: Road reconstruction has improved and shortened the highway in this area. Kilometreposts and driving distances have not been recalibrated.*

DC 341 (545.4 km) **DJ 1049** (1688.2 km) Turnout with dumpster and point of interest sign to south. *IMPORTANT: Do not feed bears!* View of **Indian Head Mountain**, a high crag resembling the classic Indian profile.

DC 343.2 (548.9 km) **DJ 1046.8** (1684.6 km) **Teetering Rock** viewpoint with dumpster and outhouses to north. (Westbound travelers note: this turnout is poorly marked and easy to miss.) Teetering Rock is in the distance on the horizon.

Fort Nelson Forest District (phone 250/774-5511) has developed a hiking guide which includes the 7.6-mile/12.3-km trail to Teetering Rock. Steep climbs; stay on marked trail; keep pets on leash.

DC 344 (550.2 km) **DJ 1046** (1683.3 km) Welcome to Muskwa Ketchica (sign).

DC 344.6 (551.2 km) **DJ 1045.4** (1682.4 km) Mill Creek, which flows into the Tetsa River. The highway follows the Tetsa River westbound. The Tetsa heads near Summit Lake in the northern Canadian Rockies.

Tetsa River, good fishing for grayling to 4 lbs., average 1$\frac{1}{2}$ lbs., flies or spin cast with lures; Dolly Varden to 7 lbs., average 3 lbs., spin cast or flies; whitefish, small but plentiful, use flies or eggs, summer.

DC 344.7 (551.4 km) **DJ 1045.3** (1682.2 km) Turnoff to south for **Tetsa River Regional Park**, 1.2 miles/1.9 km via gravel road. Grass tenting area, 25 level gravel sites in trees, picnic tables, fire rings, firewood, outhouses, water and garbage containers. Camping fee $12. ▲

DC 345.5 (552.7 km) **DJ 1044.5** (1680.9 km) Road narrows north bound.

DC 357.5 (571.5 km) **DJ 1032.5** (1661.6 km) **Historical Mile 375.** Tetsa River Guest Ranch and Campground; gas, store, cabins and private campground. ▲

Tetsa River Guest Ranch and Campground. A favorite stopping spot along the highway. Fresh bread and baking daily. Treed and open camping sites, some pull-throughs, water and power hookups, dump station. Showers, store. Rustic log cabins with kitchenettes. Bed and breakfast. Great fishing! Licenses and local information. Horse boarding. Guided fishing trips. Local arts and handiwork. Experience Rocky Mountain wilderness by horseback. (Reservations recommended.) Phone (250) 774-1005. [ADVERTISEMENT] ▲

DC 358.6 (573.3 km) **DJ 1031.4** (1659.8 km) Highway follows Tetsa River westbound. Turnouts along river to south next 0.2 mile/0.3 km westbound.

DC 360.2 (575.94 km) **DJ 1029.8** (1657.2 km) Turnout with dumpster, picnic site. Note the aspen-dominated slopes on the north side of the Tetsa River and the white spruce on the south side.

DC 364.4 (582.6 km) **DJ 1025.6** (1650.5 km) Gravel turnout to south.

DC 365.6 (584.6 km) **DJ 1024.4** (1648.6 km) Tetsa River bridge No. 1, clearance 17 feet/5.2m.

DC 366 (585.4 km) **DJ 1024** (1647.9 km) Pull-through turnout with dumpster to north.

DC 366.1 (585.6 km) **DJ 1023.9** (1647.7 km) Beaver dam to north.

DC 367.3 (587.3 km) **DJ 1022.7** (1645.8 km) Tetsa River bridge No. 2.

The high bare peaks of the central Canadian Rockies are visible ahead westbound.

DC 371.5 (594.2 km) **DJ 1018.5** (1639.1 km) East boundary of **Stone Mountain Provincial Park**. Stone Mountain Park encompasses the Summit Pass area and extends south to include Wokkpash Protected Area. Access is via MacDonald Creek hiking trail and by 4-wheel drive from 113 Creek (see **Milepost DC 382.2**) to Wokkpash Creek trail. Contact BC Parks District Office in Fort St. John; phone (250) 787-3407.

Stone sheep are frequently sighted in this area. *PLEASE REDUCE YOUR SPEED.*

Stone sheep are indigenous to the mountains of northern British Columbia and southern Yukon Territory. They are darker and somewhat slighter than the bighorn sheep found in the Rocky Mountains. Dall or white sheep are found in the mountains of Yukon, Alaska and Northwest Territories.

CAUTION: Northbound, watch for caribou and Stone sheep along the highway. DO NOT FEED WILDLIFE. DO NOT STOP VEHICLES ON THE HIGHWAY TO TAKE PHOTOS; use shoulders or turnouts. You are now in bear country ... a fed bear is a dead bear—don't feed bears!

DC 372.2 (595.2 km) **DJ 1017.8** (1637.9 km) **Historical Mile 390**. North Tetsa River flows under road through large culverts.

DC 372.7 (596 km) **DJ 1017.3** (1637.1 km) Pull-through turnout with dumpster to north. Steep access to Tetsa River canyon.

DC 373.3 (597 km) **DJ 1016.7** (1636.2 km) **Historical Mile 392. SUMMIT LAKE** (unincorporated). Summit Lake Lodge (closed in 2002, current status unknown).

The peak behind Summit Lake is Mount St. George (elev. 7,419 feet/2,261m) in the Stone Mountain range. The Summit area is known for dramatic and sudden weather changes.

DC 373.5 (597.4 km) **DJ 1016.5** (1635.9 km) Rough gravel side road leads 1.5 miles/2.5 km to Flower Springs Lake trailhead, 4.3 miles/7 km to microwave tower viewpoint.

DC 373.6 (597.6 km) **DJ 1016.4** (1635.7 km) **Historic Milepost 392 Summit Pass** (elev. 4,250 feet/1,295m); gravel turnout, sign and interpretive panel at the highest summit on the Alaska Highway. A very beautiful area of bare rocky peaks (which can be snow-covered any time of the year).

Summit Lake Provincial Campground to south at east end of lake; 28 level gravel sites; camping fee $12; picnic tables; water and garbage containers; information shelter; boat launch. Hiking trails to Flower Springs Lake and Summit Peak. Fair fishing for lake trout, whitefish and rainbows. ▲

DC 375.6 (600.8 km) **DJ 1014.4** (1632.5 km) Turnout to north.

DC 375.9 (601.3 km) **DJ 1014.1** (1632 km) Picnic site to south with tables and dumpster on Rocky Crest Lake. Nice spot for photos; good reflections in lake when calm.

DC 376 (601.5 km) **DJ 1014** (1631.8 km) Erosion pillars (hoodoos) north of highway (0.6-mile/1-km hike north). Northbound, the highway winds through a rocky limestone gorge before descending into the wide and picturesque MacDonald River valley. Watch for caribou.

Turnouts next 2.5 miles/4 km northbound with views of the valley. Watch for Stone sheep along the rock cut; they are frequently sighted along this stretch of road.

DC 378.2 (605.1 km) **DJ 1011.8** (1628.3 km) Baba Canyon to north. Popular with hikers (strenuous).

DC 378.6 (605.7 km) **DJ 1011.4** (1627.6 km) **Historical Mile 397**. Rocky Mountain Lodge to south; food, gas, lodging and camping. Outdoor map display shows Wokkpash hiking trails. ▲

Rocky Mountain Lodge. See display ad this section. ▲

DC 379.7 (607.4 km) **DJ 1010.3** (1625.9 km) Large turnout to south.

DC 380.7 (609 km) **DJ 1009.3** (1624.3 km) West boundary of **Stone Mountain Provincial Park** (see description at the east boundary of the park at Milepost **DC 371.5**).

CAUTION: Southbound, watch for wildlife alongside and on the road. DO NOT FEED WILDLIFE.

DC 381.2 (611.2 km) **DJ 1008.8** (1623.5 km) Highway winds along above the wide rocky valley of MacDonald Creek. MacDonald Creek and river were named for Charlie MacDonald, a Cree Indian credited with helping Alaska Highway survey crews locate the best route for the pioneer road.

DC 382.2 (612.8 km) **DJ 1007.8** (1621.8km) Trail access via abandoned Churchill Copper Mine Road (4-wheel drive only beyond river) to **Wokkpash Protected Area**, located 12 miles/20 km south of the highway, which adjoins the southwest boundary of Stone Mountain Provincial Park. This remote area features extensive hoodoos (erosion pillars) in Wokkpash Gorge, and the scenic Forlorn Gorge and Stepped Lakes. Excellent hiking opportunities. Wokkpash Creek hiking trail follows Wokkpash Creek to Wokkpash Lake: 9 miles/15 km. Contact BC Parks District Office in Fort St. John before venturing into this area; phone (250) 787-3407.

DC 383.3 (614.6 km) **DJ 1006.7** (1620.1 km) 113 Creek. The creek was named during construction of the Alaska Highway for its distance from Mile 0 at Fort Nelson. While Dawson Creek was to become Mile 0 on the completed pioneer road, clearing crews began their work at Fort Nelson, since a rough winter road already existed between Dawson Creek and Fort Nelson. Stone Range to the northeast and Muskwa Ranges of the Rocky Mountains to the west.

DC 384.2 (615.4 km) **DJ 1005.8** (1618.6 km) Access to 115 Creek and **MacDonald Creek**. User maintained parking area (former provincial campground); informal camping. Beaver dams nearby. Fishing for grayling and Dolly Varden. ◆▲

DC 385.4 (616.6 km) **DJ 1004.6** (1616.7 km) 115 Creek bridge. Turnout to south at east end of bridge with tables and dumpster. Like 113 Creek, 115 Creek was named during construction of the Alaska Highway for its distance from Fort Nelson, Mile 0 for clearing crews.

DC 390.5 (624.8 km) **DJ 999.5** (1608.5 km) **Historical Mile 408**. MacDonald River Services (closed for many years).

DC 392.5 (627.8 km) **DJ 997.5** (1605.3 km) MacDonald River bridge, clearance 17 feet/5.2m. Highway winds through narrow valley.

MacDonald River, fair fishing from May to July for Dolly Varden and grayling. ◆

DC 394.8 (631.8 km) **DJ 995.2** (1601.6 km) Turnout with litter barrel to east.

DC 396.1 (633.8 km) **DJ 993.9** (1599.5 km) Folding rock formations on mountain face to west. The Racing River forms the boundary between the Sentinel Range and the Stone Range, both of which are composed of folded and sedimentary rock.

DC 399.1 (638.6 km) **DJ 990.9** (1594.7 km) Stringer Creek.

DC 400.7 (641.1 km) **DJ 989.3** (1592.1 km) Racing River bridge, clearance 17 feet/5.2m, posted speed limit 50 Kmph on bridge. River access to north at east end of bridge.

Note the open south-facing slopes on the north side of the river that are used as winter range by Stone sheep, elk and deer. Periodic controlled burns encourage the growth of forage grasses and shrubs, and also allow chinook winds to clear snow from grazing grounds in winter. *CAUTION: Watch for horses.*

Erosion pillars at Milepost DC 376 are a short walk from the highway.

(© Earl L. Brown, staff)

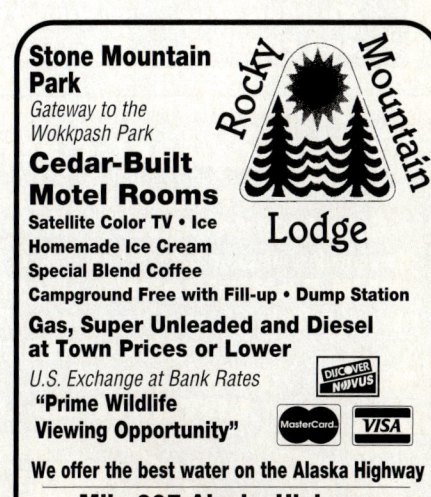

Stone Mountain Park
Gateway to the Wokkpash Park
Cedar-Built Motel Rooms
Satellite Color TV • Ice
Homemade Ice Cream
Special Blend Coffee
Campground Free with Fill-up • Dump Station
Gas, Super Unleaded and Diesel at Town Prices or Lower
U.S. Exchange at Bank Rates
"Prime Wildlife Viewing Opportunity"
We offer the best water on the Alaska Highway
Mile 397 Alaska Highway
Phone and FAX (250) 232-7000
British Columbia, Canada

TOAD RIVER LODGE

Open Year Round

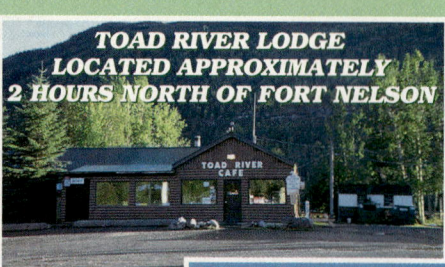

Hang your hat where it's at!

Mile 422
Alaska Highway, BC V0C 2X0
Phone (250) 232-5401
FAX (250) 232-5215

SEE OUR WORLD FAMOUS HAT COLLECTION
WWW.TOADRIVERLODGE.COM

Modern Motel and Cabins with Satellite TV & Kitchenetts

RESTAURANT • Home Cooked Meals
FRESH BAKING DAILY

Post Office and Ambulance Station
Public Phones • Bus Depot
Gift Shop • Soft Ice Cream and Souvenirs
Camping • Ice • Dump Station

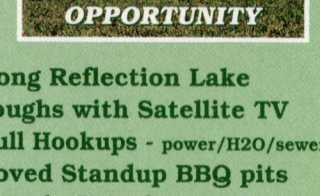

RV Sites along Reflection Lake
Level Pull-throughs with Satellite TV
30-amp Power • Full Hookups - power/H2O/sewer
Forestry Approved Standup BBQ pits
Free Firewood • Laundromat
Complementary Hot Showers

SERVICE STATION
Husky & Affiliates Honoured
GAS, DIESEL, PROPANE
Tires & Tire Repairs
24 Hour Towing Service
Airstrip

Your Hosts:
Darrel Stevens,
Matthew Roy
and Families

The Poplars Campground & Cafe

4 Miles Northbound Past Toad River

GOOD FOOD & FRIENDLY SERVICE • Home of the Foot Long Hotdog!
Homemade Cinnamon Buns & Fresh Baking • Fresh Fruit Frozen Yogurt • Ice Cream • Ice
NEW CAMPGROUND with 40 Large Treed Level Pull Through Sites
Full & Partial Hook-ups • 30 Amp Service • Hot Showers
GAS • DIESEL • WELDING
NEW CABINS with Double or Queen Beds
GIFT SHOP with Unique Northern Gifts

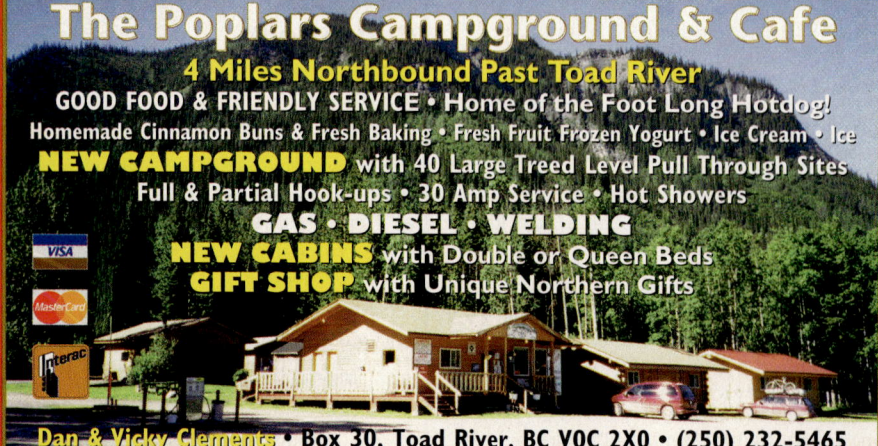

Dan & Vicky Clements • Box 30, Toad River, BC V0C 2X0 • (250) 232-5465

Racing River, grayling to 16 inches; Dolly Varden to 2 lbs., use flies, July through September.

DC 404.1 (646.6 km) **DJ 985.9** (1586.6 km) Welcome to Toad River (sign).

DC 404.6 (647.4 km) **DJ 985.4** (1585.8 km) **Historical Mile 422. TOAD RIVER** (unincorporated), situated in a picturesque valley. Popular artist Trish Croal makes her home here. Highway maintenance camp, school and private residences on north side of highway.

Toad River Lodge. See display ad this section.

Toad River Lodge on south side of highway with cafe, gas, tire repair, propane, camping and lodging. Open year-round. The lodge is known for its collection of hats, which numbered 6,098 in fall 2002. Inquire at the lodge about nearby wildlife viewing and whitewater rafting.

Private Aircraft: Toad River airstrip; elev. 2,400 feet/732m; length 3,000 feet/914m. Unattended; no fuel; prior permission to land required.

DC 405.5 (648.8 km) **DJ 984.5** (1584.4 km) Turnout to south with **Historic Milepost 422**. Sign and interpretive panel commemorate Toad River/Camp 138 Jupp Construction.

DC 406.3 (650.1 km) **DJ 983.7** (1583.1 km) Turnout with dumpster.

DC 406.4 (650.3 km) **DJ 983.6** (1582.9 km) Wood Creek.

DC 406.9 (651.1 km) **DJ 983.1** (1582.1 km) 141 Creek.

DC 407.5 (652 km) **DJ 982.5** (1581.1 km) **Historical Mile 426**. Poplars Campground and Cafe; food, gas, lodging and camping south side of highway.

The Poplars Campground & Cafe. See display ad this section.

DC 409.2 (654.6 km) **DJ 980.8** (1578.4 km) South boundary of **Muncho Lake Provincial Park**. (The north boundary is at Milepost DC 460.7 on the highway.) Muncho Lake Park straddles the Alaska Highway, encompassing the alpine peaks and valleys surrounding Muncho Lake. There are no signed trails. Guides and outfitters offers trips into the backcountry.

DC 410.2 (656.4 km) **DJ 979.8** (1576.8 km) Turnoff for lodge with bed and breakfast accommodations (3 miles/4.8 km north).

DC 410.6 (656.8 km) **DJ 979.4** (1576.1 km) Turnout with information panel on area geology. Impressive rock folding formation on mountain face, known as Folded Mountain.

DC 411 (657.4 km) **DJ 979** (1575.5 km) Beautiful turquoise-coloured Toad River to north. The highway now follows the Toad River westbound. Whitewater raft trips available.

Toad River, grayling to 16 inches; Dolly Varden to 10 lbs., use flies, July through September.

DC 415.5 (664.7 km) **DJ 974.5** (1568.3

km) **150 Creek** bridge. Creek access to south at east end of bridge.

DC 416.9 (667.1 km) DJ 973.1 (1566 km) 151 Creek culvert.

DC 417.6 (668.2 km) DJ 972.4 (1564.9 km) Centennial Falls to south. (Waterfall dries up in summer, unless it is raining.)

DC 419.8 (671.7 km) DJ 970.2 (1561.3 km) **Toad River** bridge. Turnout with dumpster to south at west end of bridge; fishing.

DC 422.6 (676.2 km) DJ 967.4 (1556.8 km) Watch for moose in pond to north; morning or evening best.

DC 423 (676.8 km) DJ 967 (1556.2 km) Double-ended turnout with dumpster to north. Excellent wildlife viewing area; watch for Stone sheep, caribou, bear and moose.

CAUTION: Watch for Stone sheep along the highway (or standing in the middle of the highway). DO NOT FEED WILDLIFE. Do not stop vehicles on the highway to take photos; use shoulders or turnouts.

DC 423.1 (677 km) DJ 966.9 (1556 km) The highway swings north for Alaska-bound travelers. Highway climbs next 6 miles/10 km northbound. For Dawson Creek-bound travelers, the highway follows an easterly direction.

DC 424.1 (678.7 km) DJ 965.9 (1554.4 km) **Historic Milepost 443** at Peterson Creek No. 1 bridge. The creek was named for local trapper Pete Peterson, who helped Alaska Highway construction crews select a route through this area. Historic sign marks start of Campbell Construction Co. Ltd. contract during construction of the Alaska Highway.

DC 424.3 (679 km) DJ 965.7 (1554.1 km) The Village (closed).

DC 429.5 (688.9 km) DJ 960.5 (1545.7 km) Viewpoint to east with information shelter and dumpster. Information panel on geology of "Sawtooth Mountains."

DC 434.5 (695.3 km) DJ 955.5 (1537.7 km) Muncho Creek.

DC 436.5 (698.5 km) DJ 953.5 (1534.5 km) **Historic Milepost 456.** Entering **MUNCHO LAKE** (pop. 29; elev. 2,700 feet/823m). Muncho Lake businesses extend from here north along the east shore of Muncho Lake to approximately **Milepost DC 443.7.** Businesses in Muncho Lake include 4 lodges, gas stations with repair, restaurants, cafes and campgrounds. The post office is located at Double G Service; open year-round. ▲

A historic sign and interpretive panel mark Muncho Lake/Refueling Stop, Checkpoint during Alaska Highway construction. The road around the lake was a particular challenge. Workers had to cut their way through the lake's rocky banks. Horses were used to haul away the rock.

The Muncho Lake area offers hiking in the summer and cross-country skiing in the winter. Flightseeing and fly-in fishing service available at Northern Rockies Lodge with Liard Air Ltd. For rafting trips on the Trout River inquire at J&H Wilderness Resort. Drive up to the microwave tower for stunning mountain views.

CAUTION: Watch for Stone sheep and caribou on the highway north of here. Please DO NOT FEED WILDLIFE. Please do not stop on the highway to take photos; use shoulders or turnouts.

DC 436.6 (698.7 km) DJ 953.4 (1534.3 km) Double G Service; post office, gas, diesel, food and lodging.

DC 436.9 (699.2 km) DJ 953.1 (1533.8 km) Gravel airstrip to west; length 1,200 feet/366m. View of Muncho Lake ahead

Highland Glen Lodge Ltd., d.b.a.
NORTHERN ROCKIES LODGE
Hotel & Licensed Dining Room • RV Park

TOLL FREE RESERVATION LINE 1-800-663-5269
PHONE (250) 776-3481 FAX (250) 776-3482
www.northern-rockies-lodge.com

➤ New Hotel open year-round, featuring satellite TV. Lakeshore Chalets and Motel Rooms, Licensed Dining Room, Lakeshore RV Park, Children's Playground. Reservations recommended. Owned and operated by "bush pilot" Urs and wife Marianne.

➤ Newest and largest Lodge on Muncho Lake, featuring a 45 ft. high fire place, in a vaulted ceiling log dining room. European trained chefs.

➤ 30 Spacious new Lakeshore and Pull-through RV Sites with 20 amp electric service.

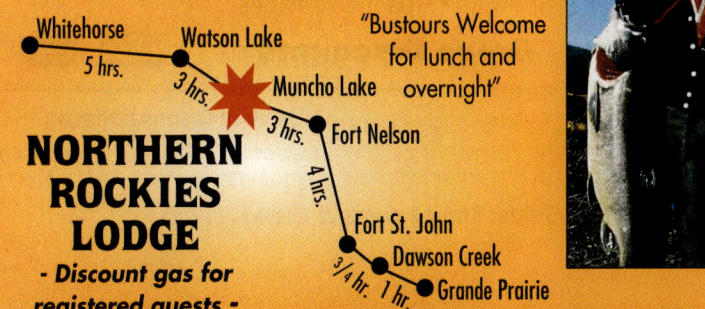

NORTHERN ROCKIES LODGE
- Discount gas for registered guests -

"Bustours Welcome for lunch and overnight"

LIARD AIR LTD.
– Outpost cabins on remote mountain lakes
– Fly-in fishing and Northern Rockies Sightseeing Tours
– Nahanni National Park excursions
– Air Taxi Service

Mile 462 Alaska Highway • Box 8-M, Muncho Lake, B.C. V0C 1Z0

ALASKA HIGHWAY • British Columbia

Flightseeing beautiful Muncho Lake with Liard Air. (© Earl L. Brown, staff)

northbound. The highway along Muncho Lake required considerable rock excavation by the Army in 1942. The original route went along the top of the cliffs, which proved particularly hazardous. (Portions of this hair-raising road can be seen high above the lake; local residents use it for mountain biking.) The Army relocated the road by benching into the cliffs a few feet above lake level.

Muncho Lake, known for its beautiful deep green and blue waters, is 7 miles/11 km in length, and 1 mile/1.6 km in width; elevation of the lake is 2,680 feet/817m. The colours are attributed to copper oxide leaching into the lake. Deepest point has been reported to be 730 feet/223m, although government tests have not located any point deeper than 400 feet/122m. The lake drains the Sentinel Range to the east and the Terminal Range to the west, feeding the raging Trout River in its 1,000-foot/305-m drop to the mighty Liard River. The mountains surrounding the lake are approximately 7,000 feet/2,134m high.

For fishermen, Muncho Lake offers Dolly Varden; some grayling; rainbow trout; whitefish to 12 inches; and lake trout. The lake trout quota is 3 trout per person, minimum size 15¾ inches; use spoons, spinners, diving plug or weighted spoons; June and July best. A 40-lb. lake trout was landed here in summer 1999; record is 50 lbs. Make sure you have a current British Columbia fishing license and a copy of the current regulations.

DC 437.7 (700.5 km) **DJ 952.3** (1532.5 km) Strawberry Flats Campground, Muncho Lake Provincial Park; 15 sites on rocky lakeshore, picnic tables, outhouses, garbage containers. Camping fee $12. ▲
CAUTION: Watch for bears in area.

DC 440.1 (704.4 km) **DJ 949.9** (1528.7 km) Large turnout with information panels.

DC 442.2 (707.9 km) **DJ 947.8** (1525.3 km) Historical Mile 462. Northern Rockies/Highland Glen Lodge (open year-round) with lodging, restaurant, gas and camping west side of highway. Flying service for sightseeing and fly-in fishing. ▲

Northern Rockies/Highland Glen Lodge, Mile 462, Muncho Lake, BC. Toll-free reservation line: (800) 663-5269. Phone (250) 776-3481, fax (250) 776-3482. New hotel open year-round, lakeshore chalets and motel rooms. The newest and largest log building on the Alaska Highway. Featuring a 45-foot-high fireplace in vaulted ceiling dining room. European-trained chef. Spacious lakeshore and pull-through RV sites, power and water hookups, dump station for guests. Children's playground. Fly-in fishing trips for arctic grayling, Dolly Varden, rainbow trout, lake trout, northern pike and walleye. Outpost fishing cabins. Air taxi service, glacier and Northern Rocky Mountain local sightseeing flights. www.northern–rockies–lodge.com. See Display ad on page 125. [ADVERTISEMENT] ▲

DC 442.9 (709 km) **DJ 947.1** (1524.2 km) Turnoff to west for MacDonald campground, Muncho Lake Provincial Park; 15 level gravel sites, firewood, picnic tables, outhouses, boat launch, information shelter, pump water, on Muncho Lake. Camping fee $12. *CAUTION: Watch for bears in area.* ▲

DC 443.6 (710.1 km) **DJ 946.4** (1523 km) Historical Mile 463. Muncho Lake Lodge; gas, food, camping and lodging. ▲

Muncho Lake Lodge. See display ad this section. ▲

Historical Mile 463.1. J&H Wilderness Resort; food, gas, lodging, camping, store, boat rentals, tackle, flightseeing and rafting trips available. Muncho Lake businesses extend south to **Milepost DC 436.5.** ▲

DC 443.7 (710.3 km) **DJ 946.3** (1522.9 km) **J&H Wilderness Resort.** See display ad this section. ▲

DC 444.9 (712.2 km) **DJ 945.1** (1520.9 km) Muncho Lake viewpoint to west with information panel and memorial to highway worker Ernie Birkbeck; large parking area, picnic tables, dumpster and outhouses. View of Peterson Mountain at south end of lake. The island you see is Honeymoon Island.
CAUTION: Watch for Stone sheep on highway next 10 miles/16 km northbound.

DC 445.1 (712.5 km) **DJ 944.9** (1520.6 km) Launch point for raft trips.

DC 453.3 (725.6 km) **DJ 936.7** (1507.4 km) Turnout with dumpster to east.

DC 454 (726.7 km) **DJ 936** (1506.3 km) Mineral lick; watch for Stone sheep. There is a trailhead 0.2 mile/0.3 km off the highway; a 5- to 10-minute loop hike takes you to viewpoints overlooking the Trout River valley and the steep mineral-laden banks frequented by sheep, goats, caribou and elk. Good photo opportunities, early morning best. *CAUTION: Steep banks, slippery when wet. Bring insect repellent.*

DC 455.5 (729.2 km) **DJ 934.5** (1503.9 km) Turnout with dumpster and message board to west.

HISTORIC
MUNCHO LAKE LODGE

GAS FOR LESS DIESEL

Mile 463 Caravans Welcome

Hotel Accommodations – Modern Cabins with Kitchenettes
Licensed Restaurant

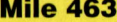
Featuring Home Cooking and Baking

50 Pull-Through Sites

Showers • Resonable Rates

 **Group Discounts**

- **10% Discount to Senior Citizens on Motel or Trailer Park**
- Sanitary Disposal Station
- Over 25 Additional Camp Sites

Your Hosts: Mary Tauers & David Nishio

Open May to October

Phone: (250) 776-3456   FAX: (250) 776-3457
Box 10, Muncho Lake, BC   V0C 1Z0

Visit with Mary . . . celebrating over 30 years at Muncho Lake Lodge

Alaska Highway winds along Trout River in the Canadian Rockies.
(© Earl L. Brown, staff)

J & H WILDERNESS RESORT
ON BEAUTIFUL MUNCHO LAKE

COME CHECK OUT OUR GREAT FUEL PRICES

Open May–September • MILE 463.3 Alaska Highway

GAS • DIESEL • ICE • CAFE • MODERN MOTEL UNITS
CONVENIENCE STORE AND GIFT SHOP

BC Tourism Approved Accommodation
Comfortable Motel Units
Reservations Recommended
Including Complimentary
Continental Breakfast
served to you in our cafe.

J&H WILDERNESS RESORT
MILE 463 ALASKA HIGHWAY
MUNCHO LAKE, B.C.

*"FOR SERVICE, HOSPITALITY AND REASONABLE RATES...
VISIT US, THE LAST RESORT NORTHBOUND ALONG MUNCHO LAKE"*

Activities From Our Great Location
- White Water Rafting
- Fishing Packages
- Muncho Lake Boat Tours
- Wilderness Adventures & More

— Fishing Tackle & Licenses —
Inquire About Air Charters & Wilderness Flightseeing Tours

RV CARAVAN SPECIALISTS

Pull-through RV Hookups • 73 Level Serviced Sites by the Lake
Dump Station • Free Showers • Laundromat
Group Activity Centre • Fire Pits and Firewood • Horseshoe Pits

P.O. Box 38,
Muncho Lake, BC V0C 1Z0

(250) 776-3453
FAX (250) 776-3454

**Winter Reservations:
(250) 315-2255**

*Your Hosts:
Dennis and Joey Froese*

ALASKA HIGHWAY • British Columbia

DC 457.7 (732.7 km) DJ 932.3 (1500.4 km) Trout River bridge. The Trout River drains into the Liard River. The Trout River offers rafting: Grade II from Muncho Lake to the bridge here; Grade III to Liard River. Inquire locally for river conditions.

The highway follows the Trout River north for several miles.

Trout River, grayling to 18 inches; whitefish to 12 inches, flies, spinners, May, June and August best.

DC 458.9 (734.6 km) DJ 931.1 (1498.4 km) Gravel turnout to east.

DC 460.7 (737.4 km) DJ 929.3 (1495.5 km) Prochniak Creek bridge. The creek was named for a member of Company A, 648th Engineers Topographic Battalion, during construction of the Alaska Highway. North boundary of Muncho Lake Provincial Park.

DC 463.3 (741.6 km) DJ 926.7 (1491.3 km) Watch for curves next 0.6 mile/1 km northbound.

DC 465.6 (745.3 km) DJ 924.4 (1487.6 km) Turnout with dumpster to east.

DC 466.3 (746.3 km) DJ 923.7 (1486.5 km) CAUTION: Dangerous curves next 3 miles/5 km northbound. Watch for road improvement between Kilometreposts 750 and 762.

DC 468.9 (749.5 km) DJ 921.1 (1482.3 km) Pull-through turnout with dumpster to east. A fire in 1959 swept across the valley bottom here. Lodgepole pine, trembling aspen and paper birch are the dominant species that re-established this area.

DC 471 (754.1 km) DJ 919 (1478.9 km) First glimpse of the mighty Liard River for northbound travelers. Named by French-Canadian voyageurs for the poplar ("liard") that line the banks of the lower river. The Alaska Highway parallels the Liard River from here north to Watson Lake. The river offered engineers a natural line to follow during routing and construction of the

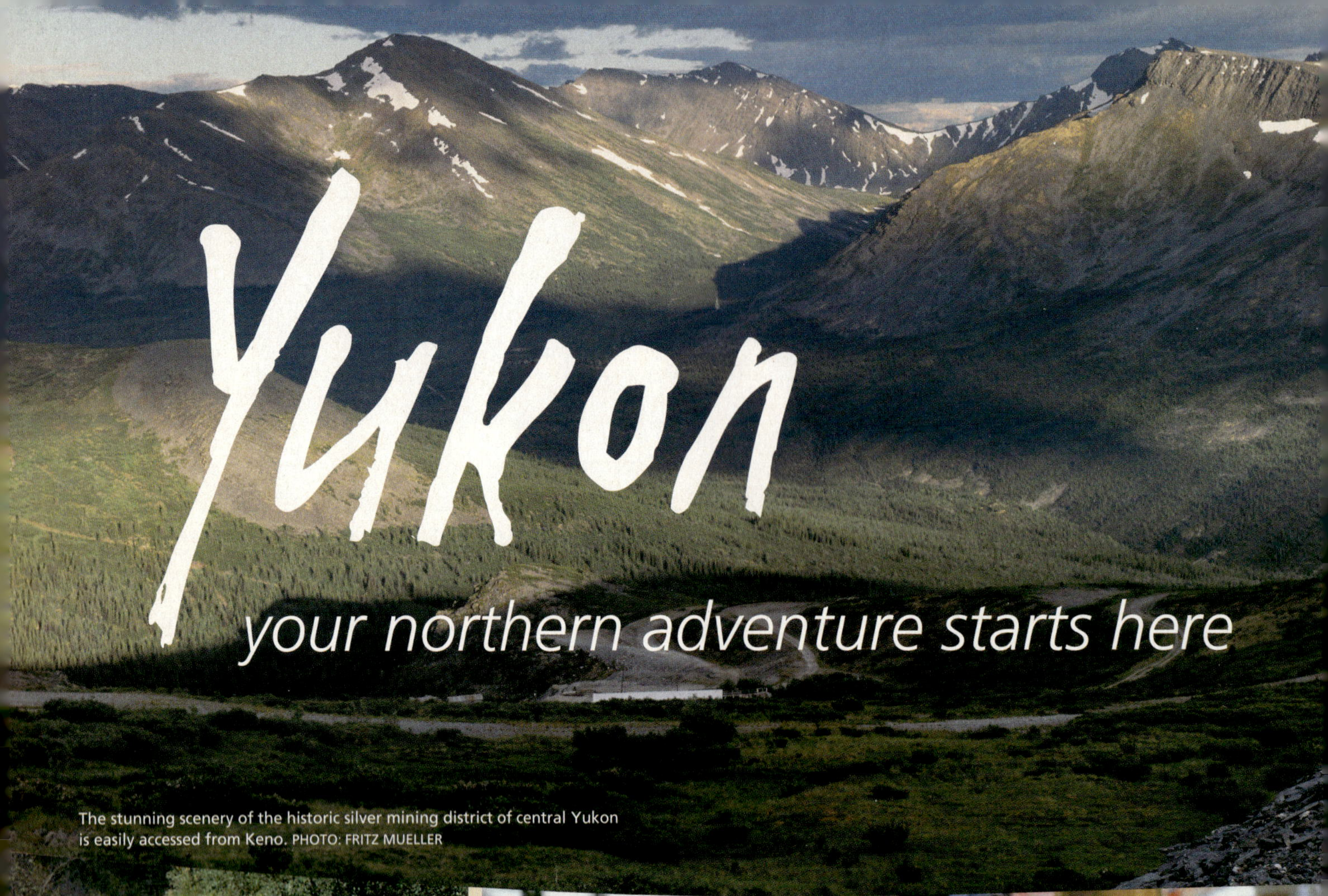

Yukon
your northern adventure starts here

The stunning scenery of the historic silver mining district of central Yukon is easily accessed from Keno. PHOTO: FRITZ MUELLER

There's still gold to be found in the streams of the Klondike, near the historic gold rush town of Dawson City.

Dall Sheep are often seen from viewing stations at Sheep Mountain in Kluane National Park.

Colourful First Nation's heritage and pageantry are on display at celebrations like the *Gathering of Traditions* in Whitehorse.

Be sure to plan your Yukon adventure with these free guides. They include the official Yukon Road Map, information on accommodations, campgrounds and R.V. parks. Also included is a calendar of events and detailed regional information about activities and attractions available in the Yukon. Fill in the reply card or visit **www.milepost.touryukon.com** to get your free guides. When you arrive stop at any of the six Visitor Reception Centres in the Yukon.

enter to win
one of 20 Yukon Attraction Packages
(approx. package value $100)
Visit www.milepost.touryukon.com

Let us help your friends plan their Yukon adventure.
We'll send them the following **guides for FREE!**

Fill in the card or visit www.milepost.touryukon.com

☐ FREE **Yukon Vacation Guide**
includes official Yukon Road Map, Campgrounds, RV Parks, Calendar of Events and Accommodations

☐ FREE **Places to Go** *On Yukon Time*
includes detailed regional information on activities and attractions available in the Yukon

MILEPOST 2604C

Numerous well-marked hiking trails lead visitors high up into the pristine areas of Kluane National Park.

Let us help you plan your Yukon adventure.
We'll send you the following **guides for FREE!**

Fill in the card or visit www.milepost.touryukon.com

☐ FREE **Yukon Vacation Guide**
includes official Yukon Road Map, Campgrounds, RV Parks, Calendar of Events and Accommodations

☐ FREE **Places to Go** *On Yukon Time*
includes detailed regional information on activities and attractions available in the Yukon

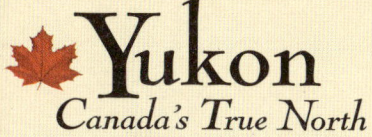

Yukon
Canada's True North

Talk to our travel counselor
at 1-867-667-5340 or
e-mail: vacation@gov.yk.ca

MILEPOST 2606C

Whitehorse

Historic Dawson City

Yukon Visitor Reception Centre in Whitehorse

on Yukon time

enter to win
one of 20 Yukon Attraction Packages (approx. package value $100)
Visit **www.milepost.touryukon.com**

Tourism Yukon
P.O. Box 2745
Whitehorse, Yukon Canada
Y1A 5B9

Tourism Yukon
P.O. Box 2745
Whitehorse, Yukon Canada
Y1A 5B9

things to do

Yukon International Story Telling Festival
MAY/JUNE, WHITEHORSE

Kluane Chilkat International Bike Relay
JUNE, HAINES JUNCTION

Yukon River Quest Canoe and Kayak Race
JUNE, WHITEHORSE

Yukon Gold Panning Championships
JULY, DAWSON CITY

Dawson City Music Festival
JULY, DAWSON CITY

Discovery Days Festival
AUGUST, DAWSON CITY

Farrago Music Festival
AUGUST, FARO

Klondike Trail of '98 International Road Relay
SEPTEMBER, WHITEHORSE

places to go

Signpost Forest
WATSON LAKE

Northern Lights Centre
WATSON LAKE

Teslin Tlingit Heritage Centre
TESLIN

Beringia Interpretive Centre
WHITEHORSE

SS Klondike National Historical Site
WHITEHORSE

Kluane Museum of Natural History
BURWASH LANDING

Kluane National Park
HAINES JUNCTION

Tage Cho Hudan Interpretive Centre
CARMACKS

Keno City Mining Museum
KENO CITY

Klondike Goldfields
DAWSON CITY

Robert Service Cabin
DAWSON CITY

Arctic Circle Crossing
DEMPSTER HIGHWAY

Alaska Highway in 1942.
   DC 472.2 (756 km) **DJ 917.8** (1477 km) Washout Creek.
   DC 474.3 (759.5 km) **DJ 915.7** (1473.6 km) Turnout with dumpster to west.

DC 476.7 (763 km) **DJ 913.3** (1469.8 km) Lower Liard River bridge (elev. 1,400 feet/427m). This is the only remaining suspension bridge on the Alaska Highway. The 1,143-foot suspension bridge was built by the American Bridge Co. and McNamara Construction Co. of Toronto in 1943.

The **Liard River** flows eastward toward the Fort Nelson River and parallels the Alaska Highway from the Lower Liard River bridge to the BC-YT border. The scenic Grand Canyon of the Liard is to the east and not visible from the highway. Many early fur traders lost their lives negotiating the wild waters of the Liard. The river offers good fishing for Dolly Varden, grayling, northern pike and whitefish.

DC 477.1 (763.8 km) **DJ 912.9** (1469.1 km) **Historical Mile 496. LIARD RIVER** (unincorporated); lodge.

DC 477.7 (764.7 km) **DJ 912.3** (1468.2 km) Historic Milepost 496. Turnoff to north for **Liard River Hotsprings Provincial Park**, long a favorite stop for Alaska Highway travelers.

The park has become so popular in recent years that the campground fills up very early each day in summer. Overflow day-parking area across highway from park entrance. The park is open year-round. This well-developed provincial park has 53 large, shaded, level gravel sites (some will accommodate 2 RVs), picnic tables, picnic shelter, water pump, garbage containers, firewood, fire rings, playground and restrooms at the hot springs with wheelchair-accessible toilet. Camping fee $15 from May 1 to Aug. 30; $9 Sept. 1 to April 31.. There is no fee to use the hot springs. Pay phone at park entrance. Park gate closes at 11 P.M. and opens at 6 A.M.

Excellent interpretive programs and nature walks in summer; check schedule posted at park entrance and at information shelter near trailhead. Emergency phone at park headquarters. *CAUTION: BEWARE OF BEARS!*

A short walk leads to the pools. The boardwalk trail crosses a wetlands environment that supports more than 250 boreal forest plants, including 14 orchid species

Yukon's Interpretive Centres— A Must Stop

For those visitors who wish to enrich their travels by learning more about the history and geography of the North, the Yukon offers many popular and accessible interpretive sites. These sites range from small museums to historic city blocks, and focus on everything from woolly mammoths and Yukon wildlife to the Gold Rush days and First Nations (aboriginal) heritage.

Interpretive displays are also found at many of Tourism Yukon's Visitor Reception Centres. Designed to give travelers current information on activities, accommodations and attractions in Yukon, many of these visitor centres also offer audio-visual programs and natural history exhibits.

A stop at one of Yukon's interpretive centres will enhance your trip, whether your interest is glaciers, gold or highway history. Descriptions of some of Yukon's interpretive sites follow. (See highway logs and community descriptions in this book for more on these sites and others.)

Alaska Highway Interpretive Centre, Watson Lake. Located behind the Signpost Forest, this Tourism Yukon visitor reception centre focuses on the history of the construction of the Alaska Highway. Open daily 8 A.M. to 8 P.M., mid-May to mid-September.

Northern Lights Centre, Watson Lake. This space and science center focuses on the aurora borealis (northern lights) as well as the Canadian space program. Laser show, star projection, photographs, models and interactive exhibits designed by the National Museum of Science and Technology. Open daily year-round.

George Johnston Museum, Teslin. Features photographs early Tlingit life recorded by George Johnston (1884–1972). Exhibits include Tlinigt ceremonial robes and trade goods, and an ice-highway car. Open daily in summer.

Teslin Tlingit Heritage Centre, Teslin. Located about 2.5 miles/4 km north of Teslin on the Alaska Highway, this interpretive centre showcases 200 years of Inland Tlingit history and culture.

Yukon Beringia Interpretive Centre, Whitehorse. Located near Whitehorse International Airport on the Alaska Highway, this major interpretive centre traces the Ice Age in Yukon through dioramas, interactive displays and displays of prehistoric skeletons. Beringia is open daily in summer, from 9 A.M. to 6 P.M. in May and September, 8:30 A.M. to 7 P.M. June–August.

Yukon Transportation Museum, Whitehorse. Located on the Alaska Highway adjacent Whitehorse International Airport. All forms of transportation in the North are on display, from dogsleds to vintage vehicles and railway rolling stock. Open daily from mid-May to mid-September.

SS *Klondike* National Historic Site, Whitehorse. One of the most popular attractions in Whitehorse, this old stern-wheeler sits on the bank of the Yukon River and has an adjacent interpretive centre with more than 7,000 artifacts on display. Guided tours of the SS *Klondike* begin with a 20-minute film on the history of riverboats. The interpretive centre is open and tours are given from mid-May to mid-September.

MacBride Museum, Whitehorse. Located at 1st Avenue and Wood Street, the museum focuses on mining and gold rush history, First Nations, wildlife and the history of Whitehorse. Exhibits include a large gold collection, a 1900 telegraph office and Sam McGee's cabin. Open daily in summer.

Kluane National Park Visitor Centre, Haines Junction. This Parks Canada interpretive centre focuses on the natural history and geography of Kluane National Park. Interpretive programs daily from June through August.

Sheep Mountain Visitor Information Centre, Milepost DC 1028.8 Alaska Highway. Located north of Haines Junction, this is a popular spot for viewing sheep (late May to early June and late August and September). Viewing telescopes available. Interpretive programs in summer.

Kluane Museum of Natural History, Burwash Landing. Highly recommended local museum featuring displays of wildlife, minerals and First Nations artifacts.

Tage Cho Hudan Interpretive Centre, Carmacks, YT. Located in Carmacks on the North Klondike Highway, the centre showcases the traditional lifestyles of the Little Salmon/Carmacks First Nation (Northern Tutchone).

Fort Selkirk, Minto. Accessible by riverboat tour from Minto Resorts, this site has about 40 buildings dating from 1892 to 1940. Gives travelers a glimpse of what early-day life was like for fur traders, missionaries and the RCMP. Government preservation and interpretation staff are available on site.

Dawson Historical Complex/National Historic Site, Dawson City. Much of Dawson City is an interpretive site, with exhibits ranging from the stern-wheeler SS *Keno* to restored commerical and residential buildings such as the Commissioner's Residence and Palace Grand Theatre. The Dawson City Visitor Reception Centre, operated by Tourism Yukon and Parks Canada, has Klondike history exhibits and displays as well as information on guided walking tours around the city.

Tr'ondek Hwech'in Cultural Centre, Dawson City. Highlights the history and culture of the Han people through displays, photos, dioramas, artifacts, art and audio-visual presentations. Open June–September.

Binet House Interpretive Centre, Mayo. Exhibits include flower and mineral displays, silver and galena samples, and information panels on mining and geology. Open daily in summer.

Keno City Museum, Keno. Well worth a visit. this off-the-beaten-path interpretive site has photographs and tools illustrating the mining history of the area. Open 10 A.M. to 6 P.M. in summer.

and 14 plants that survive at this latitude because of the hot springs. Watch for moose feeding in the wetlands. There are 2 hot springs pools with water temperatures ranging from 108° to 126°F/42° to 52°C. Nearer is the Alpha pool with a children's wading area. Beyond the Alpha pool is Beta pool, which is larger and deeper. Both have changing rooms. Beta pool is about a 0.4-mile/0.6-km walk. Plenty of parking at trailhead. *NOTE: No pets on boardwalk trail.*

DC 477.8 (764.9 km) DJ 912.2 (1468 km) **Historical Mile 497.** Liard Hotsprings Lodge (open year-round) with food, gas, lodging and camping. Inquire about fishing and sightseeing charter trips.

Liard Hotsprings Lodge. See display ad this section.

CAUTION: Highway narrows westbound. Watch for bison next 73 miles/117 km westbound. Use extreme caution at night and in fog or other poor driving conditions.

DC 480 (768.3 km) DJ 910 (1464.5 km) Mould Creek.

DC 482.8 (772.9 km) DJ 907.2 (1460 km) Teeter Creek. A footpath leads upstream; 10-minute walk to falls. Grayling fishing.

DC 485.4 (777 km) DJ 904.6 (1455.8 km) Small turnout overlooking the Liard River.

DC 489 (783.6 km) DJ 901 (1450 km) **Private Aircraft:** Liard River airstrip; elev. 1,400 feet/427m; length 4,000 feet/1,219m; gravel; no fuel.

DC 495 (792.3 km) DJ 895 (1440.3 km) **Historic Milepost 514.** Smith River bridge, clearance 17 feet/5.2m.

Access to **Smith River Falls** via 1.6-mile/2.6-km gravel road; not recommended for large RVs or trailers or in wet weather. There is a hiking trail down to 2-tiered Smith River Falls from the parking area. Grayling fishing.

Historic sign here commemorates **Smith River Airport**, part of the Northwest Staging Route, located about 25 miles/40 km from the highway (accessible by 4-wheel drive only). In the early days of the Northwest Staging Route—the system of airfields used to ferry supplies and aircraft to Alaska and on to Russia during WWII—there were no aeronautical maps to guide pilots flying between Edmonton and Whitehorse. The young and relatively inexperienced pilots were given hand-drawn maps showing rivers and lakes and sent on their way with a cheery "you can't miss it!", according to the book, *Wings Over the Alaska Highway: A Photographic History of Aviation on the Alaska Highway*. This kind of navigation led to some misadventures. In January 1942, three B-26 Martin Marauder bombers, lost and out of fuel in a storm, crash-landed in the Million Dollar Valley west of here. All crew members survived, the bombers were salvaged, and the incident became one of the more popular stories from that time.

DC 509.4 (815.6 km) DJ 880.6 (1417.1 km) Large turnout with dumpster to east.

DC 513.9 (822.8 km) DJ 876.1 (1409.9 km) **Historical Mile 533. COAL RIVER.** Lodge with food, gas, diesel, lodging and camping.

Coal River Lodge & RV. See display ad this section.

DC 514.2 (823.2 km) DJ 875.8 (1409.4 km) **Historical Mile 533.2.** Coal River bridge. The Coal River flows into the Liard River south of the bridge.

DC 519.5 (831.4 km) DJ 870.5 (1400.9 km) Sharp, easy-to-miss turnoff to west for undeveloped "do-it-yourself campsite" (watch for sign). Small gravel parking area with outhouse, dumpster, and beautiful view of the Liard River (not visible from the highway). Although signed "Whirlpool Canyon," this scenic stretch of the Liard River has been identified by one astute reader as **Mountain Portage Rapids**, with Whirlpool Canyon being located farther downriver.

DC 524.2 (839.2 km) DJ 865.8 (1393 km) **Historical Mile 543. FIRESIDE** (unincorporated). This community was partially destroyed by fire in the summer of 1982. Evidence of the fire can still be seen from south of Fireside north to Lower Post. The 1982 burn, known as the Eg fire, was the second largest fire in British Columbia history, destroying more than 400,000 acres.

Highway maintenance camp. Truck stop with food, gas, lodging and camping.

DC 524.7 (840 km) DJ 865.3 (1392.5 km) Good view of Liard River and Cranberry Rapids to west.

DC 530 (848.7 km) DJ 860 (1384 km) Gravel turnout with dumpster to south.

DC 540.4 (865.3 km) DJ 849.6 (1367.3 km) North end of rerouting of Alaska Highway (see **Milepost DC 527.7**).

DC 545.9 (874.2 km) DJ 844.1 (1358.4 km) Turnout with litter barrel to west overlooking the Liard River.

DC 550.9 (882.2 km) DJ 839.1 (1350.4 km) **Historical Mile 570, Allen's Lookout.** Very large pull-through turnout with picnic tables, firepits, outhouse and dumpster to

---

NORTHBOUND?...
PLAN TO STOP AT
BABY NUGGET R.V. PARK
30/50 AMP   100ft PULL THROUGHS
NORTHERN BEAVER POST
4 STAR CABINS
WITH SATELLITE TV & JACUZZI SUITES
GIFT SHOP • RESTAURANT • GOLD PANNING
MILE 650 ALASKA HIGHWAY
20 MINUTES WEST OF WATSON LAKE
PHONE: 867.536.2307

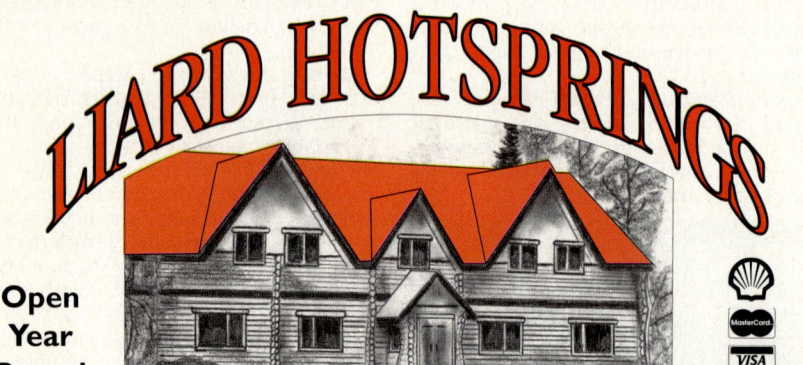

LIARD HOTSPRINGS

Open Year Round

LODGE
12 Comfortable Guest Rooms with Private Baths • Handicap Suite Available
You'll like our feature "Diamond Willow Staircase"

CAFE: Home Baking • Ice Cream • Ice • Souvenirs • Snacks

Unleaded • Diesel • Propane • Tire Repair • Sani-Dump

CAMPING: Pull-Through RV Sites • Tent Sites • Showers

Phone/Fax (250) 776-7349 • Across from Liard River Hotsprings

Mile 497, Alaska Highway, BC V1G 4J8

COAL RIVER LODGE & RV
(Open May thru September)

MILE 533

- **Licensed Restaurant** with "Home Cooking"

Be Sure to Try our Buffalo Burgers & Steaks

Hard Ice Cream and Ice Cream Treats

(Bus Tours Welcome – Please call ahead)

- **Motel** • Camping • Pay Phone
- Full Service **Pull Thru RV**
- Laundromat • Showers

VISIT OUR BUFFALO GIFT SHOP
GAS & DIESEL
Free Ice With Fill-Up

Your hosts: Brent & Donna Rogers

(250) 776-7306
e-mail: drogers@pris.bc.ca

Home of "Berry Delightful"
Wild Berry Jams, Jellies & Chocolates!

west overlooking the Liard River. Goat Mountain to west.

Legend has it that a band of outlaws took advantage of this sweeping view of the Liard River to attack and rob riverboats. A cairn near the picnic area is dedicated to the surveyors of the Alaska Highway. It shows the elevation and latitude and longitude of Allen's Lookout (N59°52′34″, W 127°24′21″)

CAUTION: Watch for buffalo next 73 miles/117 km eastbound to Liard Hotsprings. Use extreme caution at night and in fog or other poor driving conditions.

DC 555 (888.8 km) **DJ 835** (1343.8 km) Good berry picking in July among roadside raspberry bushes; watch for bears.

DC 556 (890.4 km) **DJ 834** (1342.2 km) Highway swings west for Alaska-bound travelers.

DC 562.5 (900.8 km) **DJ 827.5** (1331.7 km) Large gravel turnout with dumpster.

DC 565.8 (906 km) **DJ 824.2** (1326.4 km) Large turnout and cairn at first of 7 crossings northbound of the BC–YT border.

DC 567.9 (909.4 km) **DJ 822.1** (1323 km) **Historic Milepost 588, Contact Creek.** (Contact Creek Bridge was replaced by a culvert in 1999.) Turnout with historic sign and interpretive panel. Contact Creek was named by soldiers of the 35th Regiment from the south and the 340th Regiment from the north who met here Sept. 24, 1942, completing the southern sector of the Alaska Highway. A personal reminiscence about the work of A Company 35th Combat Engineers is found in Chester Russell's "Tales of a Catskinner."

DC 568.3 (910.2 km) **DJ 821.7** (1322.4 km) Large gravel turnout to north. Point of interest sign (missing in 2002):

"The Yukon Territory takes its name from the Indian word *Youcon*, meaning 'big river.' It was first explored in the 1840s by the Hudson's Bay Co., which established several trading posts. The territory, which was then considered a district of the Northwest Territories, remained largely untouched until the Klondike Gold Rush, when thousands of people flooded into the country and communities sprang up almost overnight. This sudden expansion led to the official formation of the Yukon Territory on June 13, 1898."

DC 570 (912.9 km) **DJ 820** (1319.6 km) **Historical Mile 590. CONTACT CREEK.** Contact Creek Lodge is open year-round; snacks, gas, diesel, car repair, 24-hour towing and pay phone.

Contact Creek Lodge. See display ad this section.

DC 573.9 (918.9 km) **DJ 816.1** (1313.3 km) Highway crosses Iron Creek. A temporary single-lane bridge replaced the Iron Creek culvert here after it collapsed in June 2001. The culvert, which had been installed in 1998, was one of the largest culverts in the world at 25 feet high, 135 feet long and 62 feet wide. The culvert failure closed the Alaska Highway for 2 days.

According to local sources, Iron Creek was named during construction of the Alaska Highway for the trucks that stopped here to put on tire irons (chains) in order to make it up the hill.

DC 575.9 (922 km) **DJ 814.1** (1310.1 km) **Historical Mile 596.** Iron Creek Lodge (closed in 2002, current status unknown).

DC 582 (931.8 km) **DJ 808** (1300.3 km) NorthwesTel microwave tower.

DC 585 (937 km) **DJ 805** (1295.5 km) **Hyland River** bridge; good fishing for rainbow, Dolly Varden and grayling.

DC 585.3 (937.2 km) **DJ 804.7** (1295 km) **Historical Mile 605.9.** Hyland River bridge.

Flaggers are a familiar sight at road construction areas along the Alaska Highway. (© Earl L. Brown, staff)

The Hyland River is a tributary of the Liard River. The river was named for Frank Hyland, an early-day trader at Telegraph Creek on the Stikine River. Hyland operated trading posts throughout northern British Columbia, competing successfully with the Hudson's Bay Co., and at one time printing his own currency.

DC 595 (951.5 km) **DC 795** (1279.4 km) *CAUTION: Watch for horses.*

DC 598.4 (957 km) **DJ 791.6** (1273.9 km) Mayfield Creek.

DC 598.7 (957.5 km) **DJ 791.3** (1273.4 km) Access to Lower Post (unincorporated), at **Historical Mile 620**, via short gravel road.

DC 599.5 (964.9 km) **DJ 790.5** (1272.2 km) Little Beaver Trail.

DC 605 (967.8 km) **DJ 784.9** (1263.1 km) **Historic Milepost 627** marks official BC–YT border. Double-ended turnout with litter barrels. The Alaska Highway (Yukon Highway 1) dips back into British Columbia several times before making its final crossing into the Yukon Territory near Morley Lake (**Milepost DC 751.5**).

Northbound: Good paved highway with wide shoulders next 380 miles/612 km to Haines Junction, with the exception of some short sections of narrow road and occasional gravel breaks.

Southbound: Good sections of reconstructed road. Watch for more construction and rough, narrow, winding road and breaks in surfacing between border and Fort Nelson (approximately 321 miles/517 km).

DC 606.8 (970.5 km) **DJ 783.2** (1260 km) Turnoff to south for **Lucky Lake** picnic area and **Liard Canyon Overlook**; waterslide, ball diamond and 1.4-mile/2.2-km hiking trail through mature pine and spruce forest down to observation platform overlooking the Liard River. Information panels on natural features of the area. Allow at least an hour for hike. Watch for gray jays, Northern flickers and black-capped and boreal chickadees.

Lucky Lake is a popular local swimming hole for Watson Lake residents. Relatively shallow, the lake warms up quickly in summer, making it one of the few area lakes where swimming is possible. Stocked with rainbow trout.

According to R. Coutts in *Yukon Places & Names*, Lucky Lake was named by American Army Engineer troops working on construction of the Alaska Highway in 1942: "A young woman set up a tent business and clients there referred to transactions as 'a change of luck.'"

ALASKA HIGHWAY • Yukon Territory

First stop in the Yukon . . .
MILE 590, ALASKA HIGHWAY

Contact Creek Lodge

Open Year-Round
Budget Friendly Gas Prices - Stop and Check Us Out

Gas • Diesel • Propane • Minor Repairs • Welding

WRECKER SERVICE (24 HOURS)
Wheel Lifts For Damage Free Towing
SOFT ICE CREAM • COFFEE SHOP • Groceries • Spring Water
Ice • Pay Phone • Souvenirs • BC and Yukon Fishing Licenses

Bus Tours Welcome   **Phone & Fax (867) 536-2262**

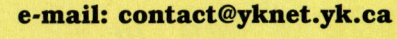

e-mail: contact@yknet.yk.ca

Your Hosts: Richard and Dennie Hair

Great Northern Oil Inc.

Petroleum Marketing for Northern Canada

When you are visiting the north, you are always welcomed at anyone of our Fas Gas and Race Trac Gas Facilities

"RV'ers" Specials at FasGas Locations

ALASKA HIGHWAY	MILE	KM
Watson Lake – FasGas	635	1021
Walkers Continental Divide – Race Trac	721	1162
Carcross Corner – Race Trac	905	1455
Whitehorse – FasGas	917	1474
Whitehorse KopperKing – FasGas	919	1477
Haines Junction – FasGas	1016	1635
Source Motors – Race Trac	1017	1637
Kluane Wilderness Village – Race Trac	1118	1797
Beaver Creek Westmark – Race Trac	1201	1934
HAINES HIGHWAY		
Kathleen Lake Lodge – Race Trac	143	231
TAGISH ROAD		
Tagish Service – Race Trac	13	21
KLONDIKE HIGHWAY		
Pelly Crossing - Selkirk – Race Trac	289	465
Dempster Corner – FasGas	307	494
DEMPSTER HIGHWAY		
Dempster Corner – FasGas	0	0
Inuvik – FasGas	456	733
CASSIAR HIGHWAY		
Good Hope Lake – Race Trac	385	625

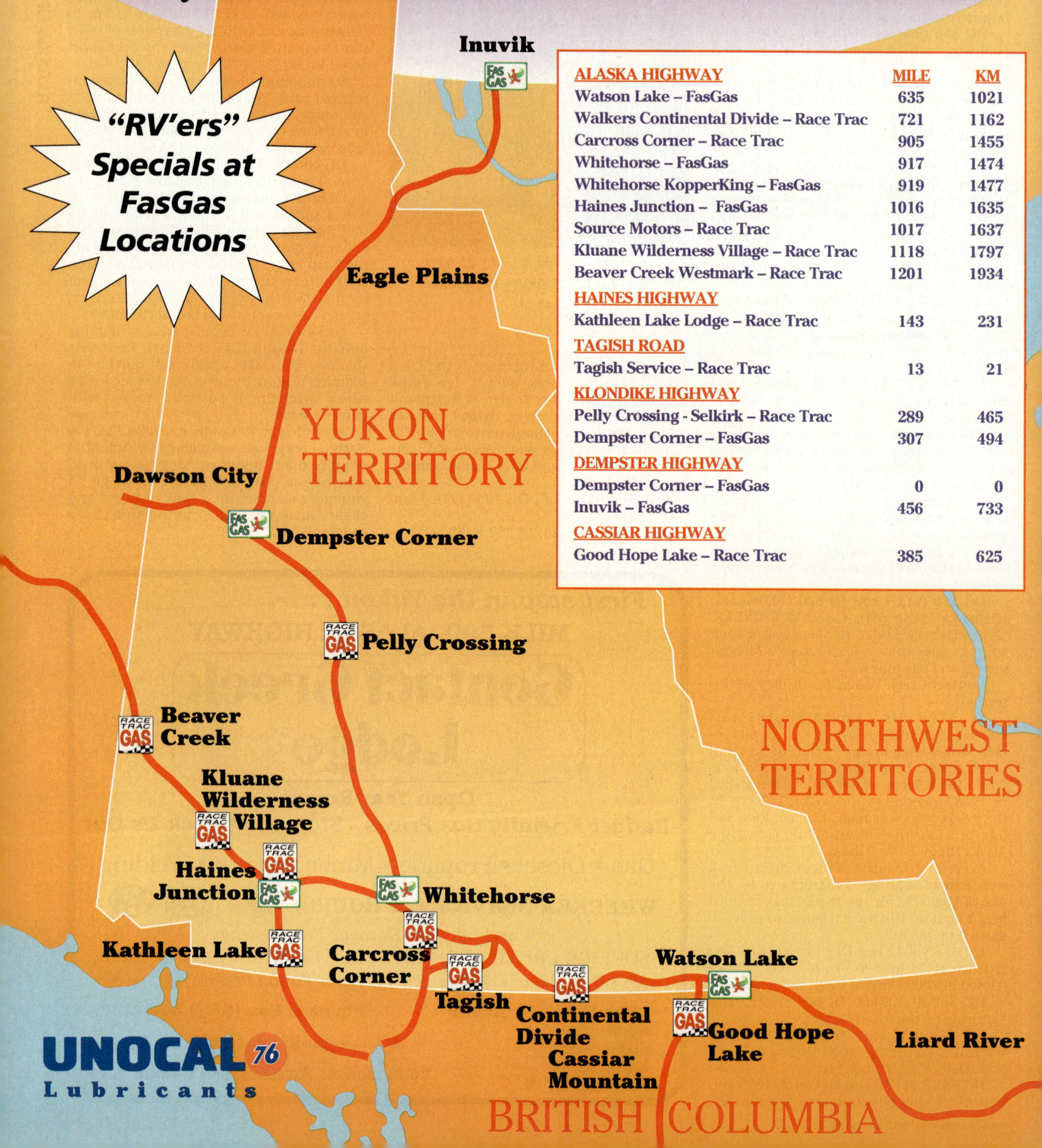

UNOCAL 76 Lubricants

Inuvik · Eagle Plains · YUKON TERRITORY · Dawson City · Dempster Corner · Pelly Crossing · Beaver Creek · Kluane Wilderness Village · Haines Junction · Whitehorse · Kathleen Lake · Carcross Corner · Tagish · Continental Divide Cassiar Mountain · Watson Lake · Good Hope Lake · Liard River · NORTHWEST TERRITORIES · BRITISH COLUMBIA

DC 606.9 (970.7 km) **DJ 783.1** (1260.2 km) Large double-ended turnout to north with Welcome to Yukon sign.
DC 609.2 (974.1 km) **DJ 780.8** (1256.5 km) Paved drive-through rest area to north with litter barrel, outhouses and Watson Lake community map.
DC 610.4 (976.1 km) **DJ 779.6** (1254.6 km) Weigh station.
DC 610.5 (976.3 km) **DJ 779.5** (1254.4 km) **Historical Mile 632.5.** Private campground.
Campground Services at Mile 632.5 is the largest and best equipped RV park in Watson Lake, the gateway to the Yukon. The park features 140 full or partial hookups

and pull-throughs, tent sites, playground, firepits and a screened kitchen. Coin-op showers, laundry and car wash. A food market stocks groceries, fresh produce, bakery and convenience items. Gasoline and diesel and propane are available at the self-serve pumps. A licensed mechanic is available for repairs, alignments, tire changes, etc. Open for business year-round, serving the traveler's needs for over 30 years! Phone (867) 536-7448. [ADVERTISEMENT] ▲

Watson Lake

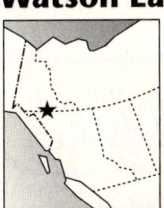

DC 612.9 (980 km) **DJ 777.1** (1250.6 km) **Historic Milepost 635.** "Gateway to the Yukon," located 330 miles/531 km from Fort Nelson, 275 miles/443 km from Whitehorse. Population: 1,794. **Emergency Services:** RCMP, phone (867) 536-5555 (if no answer call 867/667-5555). **Fire Department,** phone (867) 536-2222. **Ambulance,** phone (867) 536-4444. **Hospital,** phone (867) 536-4444.

WATSON LAKE ADVERTISERS

Air Force Lodge ....Ph. (867) 536-2890
Bee Jay's Cafe....................Ph. (867) 536-2335
Bee Jay's Services ....Ph. (867) 536-2335
Belvedere Motor Hotel......Ph. (867) 536-7712
Big Horn Hotel ....Ph. (867) 536-2020
Blue Moose Crafts and
    Souvenirs ....Adjacent Signpost Forest
Campground Services .....Ph. (867) 536-7448
Cedar Lodge Motel...........Ph. (867) 536-7406
Cozy Nest B&B..................Ph. (867) 536-2204
C.P. Collision Services.......Ph. (867) 536-2345
Downtown R.V. Park ....Ph. (867) 536-2646
Gateway Motor Inn ....Ph. (867) 536-7744
Green Valley RV Park........Ph. (867) 536-2276
Hadwens Airport B&B ....303 Airport Road
Hougen's Department
    Store ....Downtown
Napa Auto Parts ....Ph. (867) 536-2521
Northern Lights Centre ....Ph. (867) 536-7827
Rudy's Towing ....Ph. (867) 536-2123
Town of Watson Lake.......Ph. (867) 536-7827
Watson Lake Hotel ....Ph. (867) 536-7781
Watson Lake
    Motors ....Across from Signpost Forest

Watson Lake Signpost Forest is a must-stop for Alaska Highway travelers.
(© Earl L Brown, staff)

Visitor Information: Located in the Alaska Highway Interpretive Centre behind the Signpost Forest, north of the Alaska Highway; access to the centre is from the Campbell Highway. Open 8 A.M. to 8 P.M. daily, mid-May to September. Phone (867) 536-7469; fax (867) 536-2003. Pay phone with data port. Pick up a copy of the *Watson Lake Walking Tour* brochure here.
Inquire here about Yukon Government campground permits. One permit ($12) pays for one night of camping. These permits are sold at visitor centres, lodges, stores and other vendors and may also be purchased from campground attendants. Permits are transferable.
Elevation: 2,265 feet/690m. **Climate:** Average temperature in January is -16°F/-27°C, in July 59°F/15°C. Record high temperature 93°F/34°C in June 1950, record low -74°F/-59°C in January 1947. Annual snowfall is 90.6 inches. Driest month is April, wettest month is September. Average date of last spring frost is June 2; average date of first fall frost is Sept. 14. **Radio:** CBC 990. **Television:** Channel 8 and cable.
Private Aircraft: Watson Lake airport, 8 miles/12.9 km north on Campbell Highway; elev. 2,262 feet/689m; length 5,500 feet/1,676m and 3,530 feet/1,076m; asphalt; fuel 100, jet. Heliport and floatplane bases also located here. A major port of entry for aircraft, Watson Lake airport has camping

---

NORTHBOUND?...
PLAN TO STOP AT
BABY NUGGET R.V. PARK
30/50 AMP   100ft PULL THROUGHS
NORTHERN BEAVER POST
4 STAR CABINS
WITH SATELLITE TV & JACUZZI SUITES
GIFT SHOP • RESTAURANT • GOLD PANNING
MILE 650 ALASKA HIGHWAY
20 MINUTES WEST OF WATSON LAKE
PHONE: 867.536.2307

CEDAR LODGE MOTEL

• 12 Rooms with Complete Baths
• Kitchenettes & Suites Available
• Complimentary Coffee & Tea in Rooms

Box 844, Watson Lake, Yukon Y0A 1C0
Phone (867) 536-7406
www.cedarlodge.yk.net

Peter and Terri Skerget

BIG HORN HOTEL

(Built 1993 - Watson Lake's newest travellers accommodation)

• *Comfort + Value* •
Quality at a reasonable price

• Quiet - Spacious - Clean
• Queen size beds
• Colour cable T.V.
• Full bath & shower
• Direct dial phones
• Complimentary coffee
• Full wheelchair accessible suite
• Jacuzzi suites

Reservations Recommended
P.O.Box 157 • Watson Lake, Yukon • Y0A 1C0
Phone • (867) 536-2020
FAX • (867) 536-2021
e-mail: bighorn@yknet.yk.ca

for locations of local churches. Dennis Ball Memorial Swimming Pool is open weekdays in summer. Watson Lake has a Skateboard Park.

Air Force Lodge welcomes you to Watson Lake and invites you to stay at our historic

1942 pilots quarters, lovingly and completely restored (2001). Check out our photo displays and period artifact exhibits. Rooms equipped with custom-made extra long beds. (Value priced—cheaper per day the longer you stay.) From our guestbook: "We enjoyed a lovely and quiet sleep. Everything was so clean and comfortable." P.O. Bag 4700, Watson Lake, YT Y0A 1C0; Phone/fax (867) 536-2890. [ADVERTISEMENT]

Belvedere Motor Hotel, located in the centre of town, is Watson Lake's newest and finest full-service hotel. It offers such luxuries as Jacuzzi tubs in the rooms, Internet access, in-room coffee, cable TV, and all at competitive prices. Dining is excellent, whether you decide to try the superb dining room menu or the coffee shop menu. Phone (867) 536-7712, fax (867) 536-7563. [ADVERTISEMENT]

Big Horn Hotel. New in 1993. 29 beautiful rooms. Centrally located on the Alaska Highway in downtown Watson Lake, YT. Our rooms are quiet, spacious, clean and they boast queen-size beds and complimentary coffee. You get quality at a reasonable price. Available to you are king-size motionless waterbeds, Jacuzzi rooms, kitchenette suites. We know you'll enjoy staying with us. Book ahead. Phone (867) 536-2020, fax (867) 536-2021. [ADVERTISEMENT]

Cozy Nest B&B. Open year-round. Clean, quiet and cozy rooms. Continental breakfast. Lake activities at or nearby. Your hosts, Gord and Cindy, invite you to join us in the sauna or just sit and relax looking over the lake and rock gardens. Box 335 Watson Lake, Yukon Y0A 1C0; phone (867) 536-2204; email cozynest@yknet.yk.ca; www.cozynestbb.com. [ADVERTISEMENT]

Hadwens Airport Bed & Breakfast. Our home was originally built in 1943 on this site as the first Roman Catholic mission. We have completely renovated the 1,100 square-feet of space upstairs into a comfortable living area featuring 3 bedrooms, large living room, kitchenette, satellite TV and Internet. Includes an ample continental breakfast. Your hosts are Rob and Deb Hadwen. Please call (867) 536-7055 or (867) 536-2886; email hadwensbb@hotmail.com. [ADVERTISEMENT]

Watson Lake Hotel. The historic Watson Lake Hotel. We're right in the heart of Watson Lake's historical Signpost Forest. Enjoy northern hospitality at its finest. Ample parking on our 6 acres of property. (For construction 2002, new sheltered secure motorcycle parking.) Quiet outside modern units, boardwalk gift shops. Senior, government, military and corporate discounts. Phone for reservations (867) 536-7781; fax (867) 536-2724. [ADVERTISEMENT]

Camping

Camping in Watson Lake at Downtown R.V. Park. Camping at south entrance to town at Campground Services, 2.4 miles/3.9 km east of the Signpost Forest on the Alaska Highway (see **Milepost DC 610.5**). Camping north of town at Green Valley RV Park, 6.7 miles/10.8 km west of the Signpost Forest (see **Milepost DC 619.6**). Watson Lake Yukon Recreation Park campground is 2.4 miles/3.9 km west of the Signpost Forest (see **Milepost DC 615.3**). ▲

Downtown R.V. Park (Good Sam), situated in the centre of town. 71 full-hookup stalls, 19 with pull-through parking; showers; laundromat. Town water. Free truck/trailer, motorhome wash with overnight stay. Modem access. Easy walking distance to stores, garages, hotels, restaurants, liquor store, banking, churches, information centre and the world-famous Signpost Forest. Just across the street from Wye Lake Park. Excellent hiking trails. Phone (867) 536-2646 in summer. [ADVERTISEMENT] ▲

Transportation

Air: No scheduled service. Helicopter charters available from Trans North Helicopters.
Bus: Scheduled service to Edmonton and Whitehorse via Greyhound.
Taxi and **Car Rental:** Available.

Attractions

The **Alaska Highway Interpretive Centre**, operated by Tourism Yukon, is well worth a visit. Located behind the Signpost Forest, north of the Alaska Highway, the centre offers a video on Yukon history and the Alaska Highway. Excellent slide presentation and displays, including photographs taken in the mid-1940s showing the construction of the Alaska Highway in this area. The centre is open daily, May to mid-September. Free admission. Phone (867) 536-7469.

© Lyn Hancock

Northern Lights Centre. The only planetarium in North America featuring the myth and science of the northern lights. Using advanced video and laser technology, the centre offers presentations on the aurora borealis inside a 100-seat "Electric Sky" theatre environment. A 15-minute Yukon Wildlife presentation and interactive displays are also offered. Afternoon and evening showings daily from May to September. Admission charged (check with the Infocentre for coupon savings on admission fee). Located across from the Signpost Forest. Get your Yukon Explorer's Passport stamped here. Phone (867) 536-7827; Internet www.northernlightscentre.ca.

The Watson Lake Signpost Forest, seen at the north end of town at the junction of the Alaska and Robert Campbell highways, was started by Carl K. Lindley (1919–2002) of Danville, IL, a U.S. Army soldier in Company D, 341st Engineers, working on the construction of the Alaska Highway in 1942. Travelers are still adding signs to the collection, which numbered more than 49,800 in September 2002. Visitors are encouraged to add a sign to the Signpost Forest. **Historic Milepost 635** is located at the Signpost Forest.

Blue Moose Crafts and Souvenirs, snuggled in adjacent the Signpost Forest. Locally made handcrafts, quilted collectables, distinctive Yukon attire, Northern books, postcards and souvenirs. Something for nearly everyone. Forgot to bring your own hometown sign? ... Great news—make your own sign here! So, why are we called "Blue Moose?" Stop by and find out from Deb. We'll be waiting for you! (867) 536-2934.
[ADVERTISEMENT]

Special Events. The annual Watson Lake Rodeo (NRA-approved) is held in July. A parade, 8 main events and junior events are featured.

Wye Lake Park offers a picnic area, a bandshell, kitchen shelter and wheelchair-accessible restrooms. A 1-mile/1.5-km trail winds around First Wye Lake. Interpretive panels along the trail present information

NAPA AUTO PARTS
NEHRING AUTO & INDUSTRIAL

Cars • Trucks • RV's • Parts and Accessories

Call (867) 536-2521 • Fax (867) 536-2520 • tnehring@yknet.ca
Or write Box 861, Watson Lake, Yukon Y0A 1C0
After hours number (867) 536-7636

See Alaska's Inside Passage!

FJORD EXPRESS TO Juneau

**Day Cruise Package
From Skagway $129, Haines $119**
Price includes roundtrip wildlife cruise; continental breakfast and dinner; sightseeing bus tour of Juneau and Mendenhall Glacier; free time downtown Juneau for lunch, shopping and sightseeing.

ALASKA FJORDLINES • P.O. BOX 246 • HAINES, AK 99827
toll free 1-800-320-0146   www.alaskafjordlines.com

Whitehorse replaced Dawson City as capital of the Yukon Territory on March 3, 1953.

on Yukon wildflowers and local birds. The lake attracts both migrating birds (spring and fall) and resident species, such as nesting red-necked grebes. Also watch for tree swallows, violet-green swallows, mountain bluebirds and white-throated sparrows. The development of this park was initiated by a local citizens group.

St. John the Baptist Anglican Church has a memorial stained-glass window designed by Yukon artist Kathy Spalding. Titled "Our Land of Plenty," the window features a scene just north of Watson Lake off the Campbell Highway.

Lucky Lake, a few miles east of town on the Alaska Highway, is a popular local swimming hole for Watson Lake residents. There is a waterslide at the lake; it is open on weekends in summer from 1–4 P.M.

Watson Lake Community Library offers public access to the Internet, email, photocopying and fax service. The library is open 10 A.M. to 8 P.M. Tuesday through Friday and noon to 6 P.M. on Saturday in summer. (Stop by and see the community quilt on display here.) Phone (867) 536-7517 for more information.

Drive the Campbell Highway. This good gravel road offers an excellent wilderness highway experience. Motorists can travel the entire 373 miles/600 km of the Campbell Highway, stopping at Ross River and Faro en route, to junction with the Klondike Highway at Carmacks. Or drive north 52 miles/83 km from Watson Lake to Simpson Lake for picnicking, fishing and camping. (See CAMPBELL HIGHWAY section for details.)

Play golf at Greenway's Greens outside Upper Liard Village at **Milepost DC 620.3** Alaska Highway. The 9-hole, par-35 course has grass greens and is open daily May through September. Phone (867) 536-2477.

Explore the area. Take time to fish, canoe a lake, take a wilderness trek or sightsee by helicopter. Outfitters in the area offer guided fishing trips to area lakes. Trips can be arranged by the day or by the week.

Check with the visitor information centre.

AREA FISHING: Watson Lake has grayling, trout and pike. **McKinnon Lake** (walk-in only), 20 miles/32 km west of Watson Lake, pike 5 to 10 lbs. **Toobally Lake**, string of lakes 14 miles/23 km long, 90 air miles/145 km east, lake trout 8 to 10 lbs.; pike 5 to 10 lbs.; grayling 1 to 3 lbs. **Stewart Lake**, 45 air miles/72 km north northeast; lake trout, grayling.

Alaska Highway Log
(continued)

Distance from Dawson Creek (DC)* is followed by distance from Delta Junction (DJ). Original mileposts are indicated in the text as Historical Mile.

*In the Canada portion of *The MILEPOST®* Alaska Highway log, mileages from Dawson Creek are based on actual driving distance and kilometres are based on physical kilometreposts. (Mileages from Delta Junction are based on actual driving distance, followed by the metric conversion.) See "Mileposts and Kilometreposts" in the introduction beginning on page 98 for more details.

YUKON HIGHWAY 1 WEST

DC 612.9 (980.6 km) DJ 777.1 (1250.6 km) Watson Lake Signpost Forest at the **junction** of the Campbell Highway (Yukon Route 4) and Alaska Highway. The first 6 miles/9.7 km of the Campbell Highway is known locally as Airport Road; turn here for access to visitor information (in the Alaska Highway Interpretive Centre), airport, hospital and ski hill.

> The Campbell Highway leads north to Ross River and Faro, and junctions with the Klondike Highway to Dawson City just north of Carmacks. Turn to the CAMPBELL HIGHWAY section for log.

DC 615.3 (984 km) DJ 774.7 (1246.7 km) Turnoff to north for **Watson Lake Recreation Park**. Drive in 1 mile/1.5 km for campground; 55 gravel sites, most level, some pull-through, drinking water, kitchen shelters, outhouses, firepits, firewood and litter barrels. Camping permit ($12/night). There is a separate group camping area and also a day-use area (boat launch, swimming, picnicking at Watson Lake). Follow signs at fork in access road. Trails connect all areas.

DC 617.1 (986.9 km) DJ 772.9 (1243.8 km) Watson Lake city limits.

DC 618.5 (989 km) DJ 771.5 (1241.6 km) Watch for livestock.

DC 619.6 (990.9 km) DJ 770.4 (1239.8 km) Green Valley RV Park. See display ad this section.

DC 620 (991.3 km) DJ 770 (1239.2 km) Upper Liard River bridge. The Liard River heads in the St. Cyr Range in southcentral Yukon Territory and flows southeast into British Columbia, then turns east and north to join the Mackenzie River at Fort Simpson, NWT.

Liard River, grayling, lake trout, whitefish and northern pike.

DC 620.2 (991.7 km) DJ 769.8 (1238.8 km) Historical Mile 642. UPPER LIARD VILLAGE, site of **Our Lady of the Yukon Church**. Food, lodging and camping.

DC 620.3 (992.3 km) DJ 769.7 (1238.7 km) Greenway's Greens golf course to south with 9 holes, par 35, grass greens, clubhouse, club rentals, putting green, pro shop, power and pull carts. Open daily in summer.

DC 620.8 (993 km) DJ 769.2 (1237.9 km) Albert Creek bridge. Turnout with litter barrel to north at east end of bridge. A sign near here marks the first tree planting project in the Yukon. Approximately 200,000 white spruce seedlings were planted in the Albert Creek area in 1993.

White spruce is the most common conifer in the Yukon, and the most widely distributed. Mature trees are 23 to 66 feet tall. An average mature spruce can produce 8,000 cones in a good year. Each cone has 140 seeds. The seed cones are about 2 inches/5 cm long and slender in shape. The pollen cones are small and pale red in colour.

DC 625.5 (1001.1 km) DJ 764.5 (1230.5 km) Ratlin Lake access road.

DC 626.2 (1001.6 km) DJ 763.8 (1229.2 km) Historic Milepost 649. Services here include gas, store with souvenirs, propane, car repair, car wash, laundromat, cafe, camping and lodging.

Junction 37 Services. See display ad this section.

> **Junction** with the Cassiar Highway, which leads south to Yellowhead Highway 16. See CASSIAR HIGHWAY section on page 238.

DC 627 (1002.8 km) DJ 763 (1227.9 km) Historical Mile 650. Nugget City: Northern Beaver Post, Wolf It Down Restaurant and Baby Nugget RV Park.

Nugget City. Open every day. Beaver Post—Gifts and souvenirs galore! Buy Canadian. Specializing in gold, jewelry, mukluks, moccasins, Native crafts and jade. Regular priced Tees 10 percent discount. Save $5 on family's gold mine book with free nugget. Four star cabins, Jacuzzis, satellite TV. Wolf It Down Restaurant and Bakery, full course home cooked meals. Buffalo burgers and steaks. Ice cream. Liquor. Baby Nugget RV Park—pull-throughs, laundromat, RV wash, goldpanning. (867) 536-2307. (Off season 250/494-0131). See display ad this section.

[ADVERTISEMENT]

JUNCTION 37 SERVICES

Tel. (867) 536-2794 • Fax (867) 536-7902

Regular • Unleaded • Diesel
Propane • Welding
Car Wash • Ice • Free RV Dumping • Fishing Licenses
Cafe • Campground With Full Hookups • 30 Amp Service
Motel • Laundromat • Store With Groceries & Souvenirs
Showers • Beer Offsales • Licensed Dining and Bar

Mile 649 Km 1043 Alaska Highway

Come see what NUGGET CITY has to offer...

ONLY AVAILABLE HERE

Northern Beaver Post Gift Shop & Cabins
Wolf It Down Restaurant & Bakery
Baby Nugget RV Park

Save $5.00 on Bear with $50.00 Purchase

- FULL MENU • LICENSED DECK
- LICENSED DINING ROOM
- BUFFALO STEAKS/BURGERS
- ESPRESSO • CAPPUCCINO
- LIQUOR TO GO • ICE CREAM
- BAKERY • FRESH FRUIT PIES
- FRIENDLY • NON-SMOKING

- 4-STAR CABINS
- JACUZZIS AVAILABLE
- SATELLITE TV
- COFFEE MAKERS
- REFRIGERATORS
- PRIVATE WASHROOMS
- SPARKLING FRESH & CLEAN

- GOLD NUGGETS
- GOLD NUGGET JEWELRY
- MUKLUKS & FURS
- MOCCASINS
- BOOKS & TAPES
- JADE CARVINGS & JEWELRY
- NATIVE CRAFTS

- 100 FOOT PULL THROUGHS
- 15/30/50 AMP TREED SITES
- LAUNDROMAT
- RV WASH
- NATURE TRAILS
- FISHING & WILDLIFE VIEWING
- CARAVAN MEETING BUILDING

GOLD PANNING LESSONS

HISTORIC MILE 650, ACTUAL MILE 627 ALASKA HWY (20 MIN WEST OF WATSON LAKE) – 1003 km – (4 1/2 HOURS EAST OF WHITEHORSE) – 1/2 MILE WEST OF HWY #37

e-mail: nuggetcity@telus.net • website: www.nuggetcity.com

(867) 536-2307 fax (867) 536-7667 • winter (250) 494-0131 fax (250) 494-9001

Bison are a driving hazard to watch for along some sections of the Alaska Highway. (© Earl L. Brown, staff)

DC 627.3 (1003.4 km) DJ 762.7 (1227.4 km) Large double-ended gravel turnout and rest area with litter barrels, pit toilets and Watson Lake community map.

DC 630 (1009.7 km) DJ 760 (1223.1 km) Several hundred rock messages are spelled out along the highway here. The rock messages were started in summer 1990 by a Fort Nelson swim team.

DC 633 (1014.5 km) DJ 757 (1218.2 km) Gravel turnout to north.

DC 637.8 (1020.5 km) DJ 752.2 (1210.5 km) Microwave tower access road.

DC 639.8 (1023.7 km) DJ 750.2 (1207.3 km) NOTE: Hill and sharp curve.

DC 647.2 (1035.4 km) DJ 742.8 (1195.4 km) Turnout with litter barrel on Little Rancheria Creek to north.

DC 647.4 (1035.9 km) DJ 742.6 (1195.1 km) Little Rancheria Creek bridge. Northbound winter travelers put on chains here.

DC 650.6 (1041.3 km) DJ 739.4 (1189.9 km) Highway descends westbound to Big Creek.

DC 651.1 (1042.1 km) DJ 738.9 (1189.1 km) Big Creek bridge, clearance 17.7 feet/5.4m. Turnout at east end of bridge.

DC 651.2 (1042.3 km) DJ 738.8 (1189 km) Turnoff to north for Big Creek Yukon government campground, adjacent highway on Big Creek; 15 sites on gravel loop road, outhouses, firewood, kitchen shelter, litter barrels, picnic tables, water pump. Camping permit ($12/night). ▲

DC 652.5 (1044.6 km) DJ 737.5 (1186.8 km) Sign reads: "Northbound winter travelers chains may be removed."

DC 662.3 (1058.8 km) DJ 727.7 (1171.1 km) NorthwesTel microwave tower road to north.

DC 664.1 (1062.7 km) DJ 725.9 (1168.2 km) Double-ended turnout to north to Lower Rancheria River.

DC 664.3 (1063.1 km) DJ 725.7 (1167.9 km) Bridge over Lower Rancheria River. For northbound travelers, the highway closely follows the Rancheria River west from here to the Swift River. Northern bush pilot Les Cook was credited with helping find the best route for the Alaska Highway between Watson Lake and Whitehorse. Cook's Rancheria River route saved engineers hundreds of miles of highway construction.

Rancheria River, fishing for Dolly Varden and grayling.

DC 665.1 (1067 km) DJ 724.9 (1166.6 km) Scenic viewpoint.

DC 667.2 (1070.3 km) DJ 722.8 (1163.2 km) Turnout to south.

DC 667.6 (1070.9 km) DJ 722.4 (1162.5 km) Large double-ended turnout with litter barrel to south.

DC 671.9 (1075.3 km) DJ 718.1 (1155.6 km) Spencer Creek.

DC 673.4 (1077.7 km) DJ 716.6 (1153.2 km) Improved highway and view of Cassiar Mountains westbound.

DC 677 (1083.7 km) DJ 713 (1147.4 km) Turnout with litter barrel to south overlooking the Rancheria River. Trail down to river.

According to R.C. Coutts, author of *Yukon: Places & Names*, the Rancheria River was named by Cassiar miners working Sayyea Creek in 1875, site of a minor gold rush at the time. Rancheria is an old Californian or Mexican miners' term from the Spanish, meaning a native village or settlement. It is pronounced Ran-che-RI-ah.

DC 678.5 (1085.8 km) DJ 711.5 (1145 km) George's Gorge, culvert.

DC 683.2 (1093 km) DJ 706.8 (1137.4 km) NorthwesTel microwave tower to south.

DC 684 (1094.4 km) DJ 706 (1136.2 km) Turnout with litter barrel overlooking Rancheria River. CAUTION: Watch for livestock on or near highway in this area.

DC 687.2 (1099.8 km) DJ 702.8 (1131 km) **Historic Milepost 710.** Rancheria Hotel–Motel to south; gas, food, camping and lodging. Historic sign and interpretive panel on highway lodges. ▲

DC 687.4 (1100 km) DJ 702.6 (1130.7 km) Turnoff to south for private campground (formerly Rancheria Yukon government campground) adjacent highway overlooking Rancheria River. The Rancheria is a tributary of the Liard River. ▲

DC 689.2 (1103 km) DJ 700.8 (1127.8 km) Canyon Creek.

DC 690 (1104.4 km) DJ 700 (1126.5 km) Highway follows the Rancheria River.

DC 692.5 (1109 km) DJ 697.5 (1122.5 km) Young Creek. Named after Major Richard Henry Young of the Royal Canadian Engineers, Northwest Highway Systems.

DC 694.2 (1111.3 km) DJ 695.8 (1119.7 km) **Historical Mile 717.5.** Abandoned building.

DC 695.2 (1112.5 km) DJ 694.8 (1118.1 km) **Rancheria Falls Recreation Site** has a good gravel and boardwalk trail through boreal forest to the picturesque falls; easy 10-minute walk. Large parking area with toilets and litter barrels at trailhead.

DC 696 (1112.8 km) DJ 694 (1116.8 km) Porcupine Creek.

DC 697.4 (1116.6 km) DJ 692.6 (1114.6 km) Beautiful view of the Cassiar Mountains.

DC 698.4 (1118.2 km) DJ 691.6 (1113 km) **Historical Mile 721.** Walker's Continental Divide; gas, diesel, food, camping and lodging. ▲

Walker's Continental Divide. Fresh baking daily, mouth-watering cinnamon rolls, rhubarb pie, muffins and tarts. Breakfast served all day—try our sourdough pancakes. Gift shop, hard ice cream. Gas and diesel at always competitive prices. New motel, clean, comfortable, cozy rooms (non-smoking rooms available). RV park with water and power hookups, pull-throughs, showers and trailer dump. Clean wash-

---

WALKER'S CONTINENTAL DIVIDE

RACE TRAC GAS

MILE 721

Gas • Diesel • Cafe • Pub

Fresh Home Baking
Sourdough Bread • Gift Shop
RV Parking • Hookups
Pull-throughs
• Large Wooded Sites
New Motel • Cabins
Telephone

Bus Tours Welcome – Phone Ahead

Phone/Fax
VISA **(867) 851-6451** MasterCard

MILE 721. SWIFT RIVER. YUKON Y0A 1B0

"Jesus Is Lord"
Only 100 Miles To
MUKLUK ANNIE'S SALMON BAKE

At KM 1306
Just 9 Miles Northbound From Teslin

• Great Food!
• Ask About How to Get Our Free Houseboat Ride

rooms. Hospitality spoken here, free of charge. Phone/fax (867) 851-6451. See display ad this section. [ADVERTISEMENT] ▲

DC 698.7 (1118.6 km) **DJ 691.3** (1112.5 km) Upper Rancheria River bridge, clearance 17.7 feet/5.4m. For northbound travelers, the highway leaves the Rancheria River.

DC 699.3 (1119.6 km) **DJ 690.7** (1111.5 km) **Historic Milepost 722. Private Aircraft:** Pine Lake airstrip 3 miles/4.8 km north; deserted WWII emergency airstrip; elev. 3,250 feet/991m; length 6,000 feet/1,829m; gravel, status unknown.

DC 699.4 (1119.8 km) **DJ 690.6** (1111.4 km) Large gravel turnout to north; outhouses, litter barrels. Point of interest signs on the **Continental Divide**, which divides 2 of the largest drainage systems in North America—the Yukon River and Mackenzie River watersheds. Water draining west from this point forms the Swift River. This river drains into the Yukon River and continues a northwest journey of 3,680 kilometres (2,300 miles) to the Bering Sea (Pacific Ocean). Water that drains to the east forms the Rancheria River which flows into the Liard River then the Mackenzie River. These waters flow northward and empty into the Beaufort Sea (Arctic Ocean) after a journey of 4,200 kilometres (2,650 miles). Sign reads:

"There is a distinct difference in traditional land use patterns corresponding with this separation of river drainages. Pacific salmon migrate up the Yukon River watershed providing a reliable and relatively abundant food resource. This resource could generally support a larger and less transient human population than lands to the east."

All rivers crossed by the Alaska Highway between here and Fairbanks, AK, drain into the Yukon River system.

DC 702.2 (1124.3 km) **DJ 687.8** (1106.9 km) Swift River culvert. For northbound travelers, the highway now follows the Swift River west to the Morley River.

DC 706.2 (1130.7 km) **DJ 683.8** (1100.4 km) *Steep hill for westbound travelers.*

DC 709.5 (1136.2 km) **DJ 680.5** (1095.1 km) Seagull Creek.

DC 709.8 (1136.7 km) **DJ 680.2** (1094.6 km) **Historic Milepost 733, SWIFT RIVER.** Lodge with food, gas, diesel, lodging, pay phone and highway maintenance camp. Open year-round.

Swift River Lodge. Friendly haven in a beautiful mountain valley. Tasty cooking with a plentiful supply of coffee. Mouthwatering homemade pies and pastries fresh daily. Wrecker service and minor repairs. Reasonable rates. Gas and diesel at some of the best prices on the highway. Gifts—gold nugget jewelery, jade and Native crafts. See display ad this section. [ADVERTISEMENT]

DC 710.3 (1137.4 km) **DJ 679.7** (1093.8 km) **Historical Mile 733.5.** The highway re-enters British Columbia for approximately 42 miles/68 km northbound.

DC 712.7 (1140.9 km) **DJ 677.3** (1090 km) Partridge Creek.

DC 716 (1146.2 km) **DJ 674** (1084.7 km) Gravel turnout with litter barrels.

DC 718.5 (1151.1 km) **DJ 671.5** (1080.6 km) Screw Creek.

DC 719.6 (1152.9 km) **DJ 670.4** (1078.9 km) **Historical Mile 743.** Turnout with outhouse and litter barrel to south on **Swan Lake.** Fishing for trout and whitefish. The pyramid-shaped mountain to south is Simpson Peak. 🐟

DC 723.5 (1159 km) **DJ 666.5** (1072.8 km) Access to Swan Lake Ranch, a fishing and hunting camp.

DC 727.9 (1165 km) **DJ 662.1** (1065.5 km) Logjam Creek.

DC 735.8 (1177.4 km) **DJ 654.2** (1052.8 km) Smart River bridge. The **Smart River** flows south into the Cassiar Mountains in British Columbia. The river was originally called Smarch, after the Tlingit family of that name who lived and trapped in this area. The Smarch family currently includes well-known artist Keith Wolfe Smarch, whose carvings are found in collections around the world.

DC 741.4 (1186.8 km) **DJ 648.6** (1043.8 km) Microwave tower access road to north.

DC 744.1 (1190.9 km) **DJ 645.9** (1039.4 km) Upper Hazel Creek.

DC 745.2 (1192.9 km) **DJ 644.8** (1037.7 km) Lower Hazel Creek.

DC 745.7 (1193.7 km) **DJ 644.3** (1036.9 km) Short access road to lake.

DC 746.9 (1195.7 km) **DJ 643.1** (1034.9 km) Turnouts both sides of highway; litter barrel at south turnout.

DC 749 (1199.1 km) **DJ 641** (1031.5 km) Andrew Creek.

DC 751.5 (1202.6 km) **DJ 638.5** (1027.5 km) Morley Lake to north. The Alaska Highway re-enters the Yukon Territory northbound. This is the last of 7 crossings of the YT-BC border.

DC 752 (1204 km) **DJ 638** (1026.7 km) Sharp turnoff to north for **Morley River** Yukon government day-use area; large gravel parking area, picnic tables, kitchen shelter, water, litter barrels and outhouses. Fishing. 🐟

DC 752.3 (1204.4 km) **DJ 637.7** (1026.2 km) Morley River bridge; turnout with litter barrel to north at east end of bridge. Morley River flows into the southeast corner of Teslin Lake. The river, lake and Morley Bay (on Teslin Lake) were named for W. Morley Ogilvie, assistant to Arthur St. Cyr on the 1897 survey of the Telegraph Creek–Teslin Lake route.

Morley Bay and **River**, good fishing near mouth of river for northern pike 6 to 8 lbs., best June to August, use small Red Devils; grayling 3 to 5 lbs., in May and August, use small spinner; lake trout 6 to 8 lbs., June to August, use large spoon.

DC 752.9 (1205.5 km) **DJ 637.1** (1025.3 km) **Historic Milepost 777.7.** Morley River Lodge; food, gas, camping and lodging. ▲

DC 754.8 (1209.5 km) **DJ 635.2** (1022.2 km) CAUTION: Watch for livestock on highway.

DC 757.9 (1214.5 km) **DJ 632.1** (1017.2 km) Small marker (missing in 2002) to south read: "In memory of Max Richardson 39163467, Corporal Co. F 340th Eng. Army of the United States; born Oct. 10, 1918, died Oct. 17, 1942. Faith is the victory."

DC 761.5 (1218.2 km) **DJ 628.5** (1011.4 km) Strawberry Creek.

SWIFT RIVER LODGE
Mile 733 Alaska Highway
Swift River, Yukon Y0A 1C0

Motel • Licensed Restaurant • Gold Nugget Jewelry, Jade, Moccasins and Mukluks • Local and Native Crafts • Rock Shop • Wrecker Service

Gas • Diesel • Off Sales – Cold Beer & Liquor

Need R.V. Water? Tire Repair? Rest Rooms? ... or just a break?

Stop with us for home cooking and Northern Hospitality!

OPEN YEAR ROUND
Reasonable Prices

FREE R.V. PARKING

(867) 851-6401 • FAX (867) 851-6400

Nisutlin Bay Bridge at Teslin is the longest water span on the Alaska Highway. (© Earl L. Brown, staff)

DC 764.1 (1223.2 km) **DJ 625.9** (1007.3 km) Hayes Creek.

DC 769.6 (1232 km) **DJ 620.4** (998.4 km) **Historical Mile 797.** Dawson Peaks Resort; food, lodging and camping. ▲

Dawson Peaks Resort & RV Park. Slow down folks! No need to drive any farther. Fishing's good, coffee's on, camping is easy and the rhubarb pie can't be beat. Couple that with our renowned Yukon hospitality and you'll have one of the best experiences on your trip. We're looking forward to seeing you this summer. See display ad this section. [ADVERTISEMENT] ▲

DC 769.9 (1232.5 km) **DJ 620.1** (997.9 km) Gas bar (closed in 2002; current status unknown).

DC 776 (1242.8 km) **DJ 614** (988.1 km) **Nisutlin Bay Bridge**, longest water span on the Alaska Highway at 1,917 feet/584m. *NOTE: Posted speed limit on bridge is 50 kmph/30 mph.* The Nisutlin River forms the "bay" as it flows into Teslin Lake here. Put-in for canoeing the Nisutlin River is at Mile 42 on the South Canol Road.

Good view northbound of the village of Teslin and Teslin Lake. **Teslin Lake** straddles the BC–YT border; it is 86 miles/138 km long, averages 2 miles/3.2 km across, and has an average depth of 194 feet/59m. The name is taken from the Indian name for the lake—Teslintoo ("long, narrow water").

Turnout with litter barrel and point of interest sign at south end of bridge, east side of highway.

Historic Milepost 804 at the north end of the bridge, west side of the highway; historic sign and interpretive panel, parking area, marina and day-use area with picnic tables and boat ramp. Turn west on side road here for access to Teslin village (description follows).

The Nisutlin Delta National Wildlife Area is an important waterfowl migration stopover for trumpeter and tundra swans, Canada and white-fronted geese, Northern pintail and Barrow's goldeneye.

DC 776.3 (1243.4 km) **DJ 613.7** (987.6 km) Entering Teslin (**Historic Milepost 804**) at north end of bridge. Yukon Motel Lakeshore Resort; food, gas, camping, lodging and Northern wildlife gallery.

Yukon Motel Lakeshore Resort, just right (northbound) on the north side of Nisutlin Bridge. An excellent stop for a fresh lake trout dinner (or full menu), accompanied by good and friendly service topped off with a piece of fantastic rhubarb and strawberry pie (lots of fresh baking). Ice cream. New in 1998 ... visit our Yukon wildlife display. Five satellite TV channels. Open year-round, summer hours 6 A.M.–11 P.M. New lakeshore RV park (mosquito control area), 70 sites, full and partial hookups, 40 pull-throughs. "Good Sam Park"—washhouse rated TL 9.5. A real home away from home on the shore of beautiful Nisutlin Bay. Phone (867) 390-2575. See display ad this section. [ADVERTISEMENT] ▲

Teslin

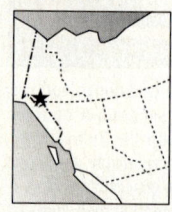

Historic Milepost 804. Teslin is located west of the Alaska Highway, accessible via a short side road from the north end of Nisutlin Bay bridge. Teslin is 111 miles/179 km southeast of Whitehorse, and 163 miles/263 km northwest of Watson Lake. **Population:** 482. **Emergency Services:** RCMP, phone (867) 390-5555 (if no answer call 867/667-5555). **Fire Department**, phone (867) 390-2222. **Nurse**, phone (867) 390-4444.

Elevation: 2,239 feet/682.4m. **Climate:** Average temperature in January, -7°F/-22°C, in July 57°F/14°C. Annual snowfall 66.2 inches/168.2 cm. Driest month April, wettest month July. Average date of last spring frost is June 19; first fall frost Aug. 19. **Radio:** CBC 940; CHONFM 90.5; CKRW 98.7. **Television:** Channel 13.

Situated at the confluence of the Nisutlin River and Teslin Lake, Teslin began as a trading post in 1903. Today the community consists of a trading post, Catholic church, health centre and post office. There is a 3-sheet regulation curling rink and a skating

TESLIN ADVERTISERS

George Johnston
  Museum ....Ph. (867) 390-2550
Nisutlin Trading Post ....Ph. (867) 390-2521
Tlingit Heritage Centre
  ....Milepost DC 779.1 Alaska Hwy.
Totem Pole ....Ph. (867) 390-2752
Yukon Motel Lakeshore
  Resort ....Ph. (867) 390-2575

7 miles south of Teslin at Km 1232

DAWSON PEAKS RESORT & RV PARK

"...one of the best restaurants on the Alaska Highway."
— Alaska Yukon Handbook

"...stands out as one of the better places to stay."
— Alaskan Camping

Licensed Lakeview Dining
Daily Lunch & Dinner Specials
Prize Winning Rhubarb Pie
Grilled Catch of the Day
New York Steak, Beer & Wine

A Beautiful Campground In A Natural Setting
30/20 amp, Pull Throughs, Tentsites, Water, Sani Dump, Hot Showers, Firepits,

Accommodations
Luxurious Lakefront Cabins With Private Baths & Satellite TV, Motel Rooms, Affordable Camping Cabins

Recreational Activities
Chartered Fishing, Boat & Canoe Rental, Boat Launch, Expediting Services

Gift Shop
Souvenirs, Sweats & T's, Hand Knit Sweaters, Northern Bookstore, Cuban Cigars

EXTRA! SUE HENRY'S mystery novel "DEAD NORTH" ends at Dawson Peaks and features Dave & Carolyn as characters. **GET YOUR COPY HERE!**

Bus Tours and Caravans Welcome - Please Call Ahead
Your Hosts: David Hett and Carolyn Allen • Box 80, Teslin, Yukon, Y0A 1B0
Mobile 2M3169 Teslin Channel • Phone/Fax (867) 390-2244
www.yukonweb.com/tourism/dawsonpeaks/ • e-mail: dpeaks@hotmail.com

rink. Teslin has one of the largest Native populations in Yukon Territory and much of the community's livelihood revolves around traditional hunting, trapping and fishing. In addition, some Tlingit (Klink-it) residents are involved in the development of Native woodworking crafts (canoes, snowshoes and sleds); traditional sewn art and craft items (moccasins, mitts, moose hair tufting, gun cases); and the tanning of moose hides.

Groceries and general merchandise available at Nisutlin Trading Post in the village. Gas, diesel and propane, car repair, gift shop, restaurants and motels are found along the Alaska Highway. The Yukon Motel has an impressive display of Yukon wildlife. The Teslin area has boat rentals, houseboat tours and an air charter service. Canoeists can fly into Wolf Lake for a 5- to 6-day trip down the Wolf River and Nisutlin River to Teslin Lake.

Nisutlin Trading Post, on short loop road, left northbound in Teslin Village. A pioneer store established in 1928, and located on the shore of Nisutlin Bay, an

Tlingit Heritage Centre displays 200 years of Inland Tlingit history and culture.
(© Earl L. Brown, staff)

ALASKA HIGHWAY • Teslin

YUKON MOTEL
LAKESHORE RESORT

...on the shore of Beautiful Nisutlin Bay

Visit Our Northern Wildlife Gallery
"... the finest the Yukon has to offer."
SOUVENIR SHOP
Licensed Restaurant & Lounge • Liquor & Beer Off-Sales.
Motel Rooms - Satellite TV
Shell Supreme -Regular-Diesel-Propane
Lakeshore R.V. Park
40 Pull-throughs - Full Hookups - 20/30 Amps • R.V. Wash - Fishing Charters
Good Sam RV Park (w/h Rated TL9.5)

email: yukonmotel@yknet.yk.ca
website: www.yukonmotel.com

Reservations/Restaurant (867) 390-2575   Office (867) 390-2443   Fax (867) 390-2003
Km 1293/Mile 804 Alaska Highway Teslin, Box 187 • Yukon Territory, Canada Y0A 1B0

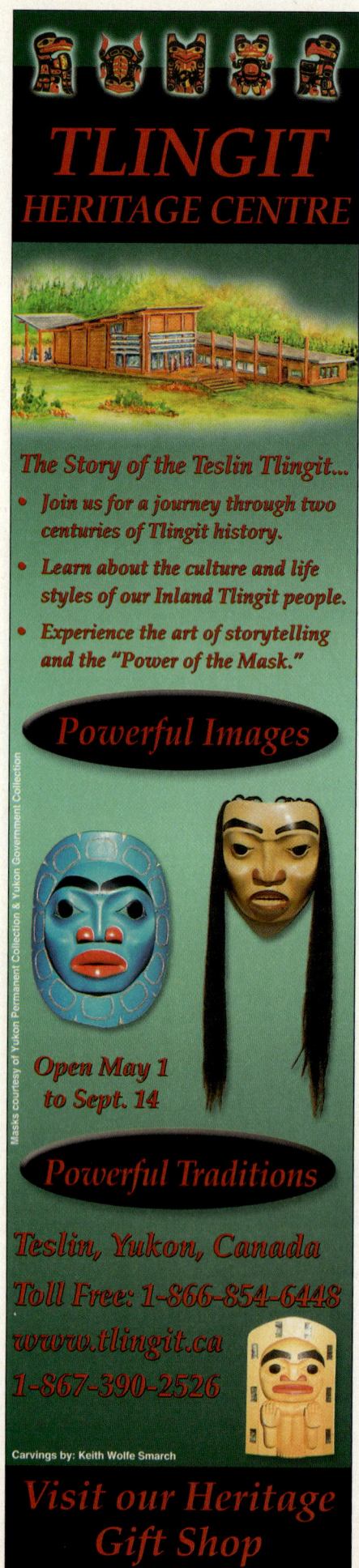

"arm" of Teslin Lake. This store handles a complete line of groceries, general merchandise including clothing, hardware, fishing tackle and licenses. Lottery tickets. ATM. Open all year 9 A.M. to 5:30 P.M. Closed Sunday. Founded by the late R. McCleery, Teslin pioneer, the trading post is now operated by Mr. and Mrs. Bob Hassard. Phone (867) 390-2521, fax 390-2103.
[ADVERTISEMENT]

George Johnston Museum is located on the left side of the Alaska Highway heading north. The museum, operated by the Teslin Historical Museum Society (phone 867/390-2550), is open daily, 9 A.M. to 5:30 P.M. in summer; admission fee charged, wheelchair accessible. Get your Yukon Explorer's Passport stamped here. The museum displays Tlingit ceremonial robes and trade goods, a photo gallery of early Tlingit life, George Johnston's reconstructed general store and ice-highway car, and life-size subsistence trapping and hunting dioramas. Website: www.yukonweb.com/community/teslin/museum.

A Tlingit Indian, George Johnston (1884–1972) was an innovative individual, known for his trapping as well as his photography. With his camera he captured the life of the inland Tlingit people of Teslin and Atlin between 1910 and 1940. Johnston also brought the first car to Teslin, a 1928 Chevrolet. Since the Alaska Highway had not been built yet, George built a 3-mile road for his "Teslin taxi." In winter, he put chains on the car and drove it on frozen Teslin Lake. The '28 Chevy has been restored and is now on permanent display at the museum.

For more information on Tlingit history and culture, a highly recommended stop is the **Tlingit Heritage Centre** just north of town at **Milepost DC 779.1**. The centre's displays feature 200 years of Inland Tlingit history and culture. Narrated tours available.

AREA FISHING: Guides and boats are available at Nisutlin Bay Marina. **Teslin Lake's Nisutlin Bay** (at the confluence of the Nisutlin River and Teslin Lake), troll the mud line in May and June for lake trout up to 25 lbs.; **Eagle Bay**, casting close to shore for northern pike to 15 lbs.; **Morley Bay**, excellent fishing for lake trout at south end of the bay's mouth, good fishing at the bay's shallow east side for northern pike to 10 lbs. **Morley River**, excellent fly fishing for grayling to 4 lbs. near river mouth and upriver several miles (by boat), fish deep water.

Alaska Highway Log
(continued)

Distance from Dawson Creek (DC)* is followed by distance from Delta Junction (DJ). Original mileposts are indicated in the text as Historical Mile.

*In the Canada portion of *The MILEPOST®* Alaska Highway log, mileages from Dawson Creek are based on actual driving distance and kilometres are based on physical kilometreposts. (Mileages from Delta Junction are based on actual driving distance, followed by the metric conversion.) See "Mileposts and Kilometreposts" in the introduction beginning on page 98 for more details.

YUKON HIGHWAY 1 WEST

DC 777 (1245.7 km) DJ 613 (986.5 km) **Historic Milepost 805. Private Aircraft:** Teslin airstrip to east; elev. 2,313 feet/705m; length 5,500 feet/1,676m; gravel; fuel 100, jet. Runway may be unusable during spring breakup.

DC 778 (1247 km) DJ 612 (984.9 km) Teslin Lake Viewing Platform at **Historic Milepost 806**, west side of highway, overlooks Teslin Lake. Interpretive panels, outhouses and parking.

DC 779.1 (1248.2 km) DJ 610.9 (983.1 km) Turnoff to south for **Tlingit Heritage Centre** (not visible from highway), a highly recommended stop. The centre highlights the last 200 years of Inland Tlingit history and includes displays on the lifestyles of the Tlingit people and "power of the mask." Includes Great Hall meeting place and gift shop.

The 5 outdoor totems, carved by Keith Wolfe Smarch, represent the Wolf, Eagle, Frog, Beaver and Raven clans.

Tlingit Heritage Centre. See display ad this section.

DC 779.5 (1248.7 km) DJ 610.5 (982.5 km) Fox Creek.

DC 784.3 (1256.4 km) DJ 605.7 (974.7 km) **Historical Mile 812**. Mukluk Annie's; food, lodging and camping.

TESLIN ◆ YUKON

George Johnston Museum

Open late May - early September.
Tlinget Indian Artifacts and History.

Teslin Historical Museum Society
Box 146, Teslin, Yukon,
Canada Y0A 1B0
(867) 390-2550

TOTEM POLE
Ice Cream & Confections
Slushies • Grocery Items
Cards • Gifts • Souvenirs
Fishing Licenses & Tackle
Campground Permits
FREE RV Parking
(867) 390-2752
Box 235, Teslin, Yukon Y0A 1B0

Welcome to the North Country!

Third longest water span of the Alaska Highway is the Teslin River Bridge. (© Earl L. Brown, staff)

Mukluk Annie's Salmon Bake. See display ad this section.

DC 785.2 (1257.9 km) DJ 604.8 (973.3 km) **Historical Mile 813.** Teslin Lake Yukon government campground to west; 27 sites (some level) in trees on **Teslin Lake**, water pump, litter barrels, kitchen shelter, firewood, firepits, picnic tables. Camping permit ($12/night). Fishing. Boat launch 0.3 mile/0.5 km north of campground.

DC 785.3 (1258 km) DJ 604.7 (973.1 km) Tenmile Creek.

DC 788.9 (1264.1 km) DJ 601.1 (967.3 km) Lone Tree Creek.

DC 794.6 (1273.2 km) DJ 595.4 (958.2 km) Deadman's Creek.

DC 797.5 (1277.9 km) DJ 592.5 (953.5 km) Timber Point.

DC 800.8 (1283.5 km) DJ 589.2 (948.2 km) Robertson Creek.

DC 801.6 (1284.5 km) DJ 588.4 (946.9 km) **Historic Milepost 829.** Brooks' Brook. According to R.C. Coutts in *Yukon: Places & Names*, this stream was named by black Army engineers, who completed this section of road in 1942, for their company officer, Lieutenant Brooks.

DC 808.2 (1295 km) DJ 581.8 (936.3 km)

Junction with the Canol Road (Yukon Highway 6) which leads northeast to the Campbell Highway. See the CANOL ROAD section for details.

Historic sign and interpretive panel about the Canol Project at junction. The Canol (Canadian Oil) Road was built in 1942–44 to provide access to oil fields at Norman Wells, NWT. Conceived by the U.S. War Dept., the $134 million project was abandoned soon after the war ended in 1945. Canol truck "graveyard" nearby.

DC 808.6 (1295.6 km) DJ 581.4 (935.6 km) **Teslin River Bridge**, third longest water span on the highway (1,770 feet/539m), was constructed with a very high clearance above the river to permit steamers of the British Yukon Navigation Co. to pass under it en route from Whitehorse to Teslin. River steamers ceased operation on the Teslin River in 1942. Before the construction of the Alaska Highway, all freight and supplies for Teslin traveled this water route from Whitehorse.

DC 808.9 (1296.2 km) DJ 581.11 (935.2 km) **Historic Milepost 836.** JOHNSON'S CROSSING to east at north end of bridge; store, food, lodging and camping. One of the original lodges on the Alaska Highway, this business has been advertising in *The*

"JESUS IS LORD"

JUST 9 MILES NORTHBOUND FROM TESLIN

Free RV Parking • Free Camping • Free Water
Free Dump Station
for All At . . .

MUKLUK ANNIE'S

Featuring:
- **Pacific Salmon**
- **Bar-B-Que Ribs, Bar-B-Que Steaks and Bar-B-Que Pork Chops**
- **All-you-can-eat Salad Bar**

SALMON BAKE

SALMON BAKE SERVING FROM 11 a.m. to 9 p.m. DAILY
Free R.V. Wash and Free nightly houseboat rides to all salmon bake customers on our 35-passenger houseboat

CAFE • Open from 7 a.m. to 10 p.m. (short order menu available)
Now featuring Mukluk Chuck's Unique Yukon Breakfast
Serving from 7 a.m. to 11 a.m.
All-you-can-eat Blueberry Pancakes with Scrambled Eggs,
Bacon & Sausage and Coffee or Tea

Caravans & Bus Tours – Call
Collect For Special Rates & Information
Inside seating for 116

Motel with Low Rates	Gift Shop	Tenting Area
Smoked Salmon	26 Power / Water	Hot Showers
Ice	Hookups	Laundromat

Our Motto is "You can't leave 'till you're full"

VISA **Phone (867) 390-2600** **MasterCard**

Mile 812 Alaska Highway – KM 1306 Alaska Highway
Box 101, Teslin, YT Y0A 1B0

MILEPOST® every year since the first edition in 1949. The history of Johnson's Crossing is related in Ellen Davignon's *The Cinnamon Mine*. Ellen also writes a regular column, "Lives of Quiet Desperation," that may be viewed at www.yukonbooks.com.

Access to Teslin River; boat launch, no camping on riverbank. The bridge is home to a large colony of cliff swallows. ▲

Johnson's Crossing Campground Services (Good Sam). Located across the Teslin River bridge, home of the "world famous cinnamon buns," including a small store with a full array of mouth-watering baked goods, souvenirs and groceries. Deli-type meals ... chicken, ribs, salads. Full-service RV campground facilities include treed pull-throughs, complete laundry and washhouse facilities, Shell gasoline products, cold beer and ice, and great fishing. Great view from our new facilities and motel units. Treat yourselves to the historically scenic Km 1346 (Mile 836) Alaska Highway, YT Y1A 9Z0. Phone (867) 390-2607. See display ad this section. [ADVERTISEMENT]

Teslin River, excellent grayling fishing from spring to late fall, 10 to 15 inches, use spinner or red-and-white spoons for spinning or black gnat for fly-fishing. King salmon in August.

Canoeists report that the Teslin River is wide and slow, but with gravel, rocks and weeds. Adequate camping sites on numerous sand bars; boil drinking water. Abundant wildlife—muskrat, porcupine, moose, eagles and wolves—also bugs and rain. Watch for bear. The Teslin enters the Yukon River at Hootalinqua, an old steamboat landing and supply point (under restoration). Roaring Bull rapids: choppy water. Pullout at Carmacks. Inquire locally about river conditions before setting out.

DC 809.1 (1296.4 km) **DJ 580.9** (934.8 km) Access road east to the Teslin River. The Big Salmon Range, also to the east, parallels the Teslin. For Alaska-bound travelers, the highway now swings west.

DC 812.8 (1302.4 km) **DJ 577.2** (928.9 km) Little Teslin Lake on south side of highway.

DC 814.5 (1305.2 km) **DJ 575.5** (926.2 km) **Historic Milepost 843** and sign about Squanga Lake flightstrip. A pair of osprey make their nest on top of a nearby tower. Osprey feed on fish and may be observed perched on top of the poles along the highway here.

Private Aircraft: Squanga Lake airstrip, 1 N; elev. 2,630 feet/802m; length 6,000 feet/965m; gravel, summer only, current status unknown; no services.

DC 816.8 (1308.9 km) **DJ 573.2** (922.4 km) In mid-June, the roadside is a profusion of purple Jacob's ladder and yellow dandelions.

DC 820 (1314.2 km) **DJ 570** (917.3 km) Access to Salmo Lake.

DC 820.4 (1314.8 km) **DJ 569.6** (916.6 km) Seaforth Creek bridge.

DC 820.8 (1315.6 km) **DJ 569.2** (916 km) Squanga Lake to northwest. The Tagish name for Squanga Lake is Desgwaage Mene, "whitefish lake", referring to the rare Squanga Pygmy whitefish found in these waters.

DC 821 (1315.9 km) **DJ 569** (915.7 km) Turnoff to northwest for **Squanga Lake** Yukon government campground: 16 sites, kitchen shelter, drinking water, camping permit ($12/night). Small boat launch. Fishing for northern pike, grayling, whitefish, rainbow and burbot. ◄▲

DC 827.5 (1326.5 km) **DJ 562.5** (905.2 km) White Mountain, to the southeast, was named by William Ogilvie during his 1887 survey, for Thomas White, then Minister of the Interior. The Yukon government introduced mountain goats to this area in 1981.

DC 828.7 (1328.5 km) **DJ 561.3** (903.3 km) Rest area with litter barrels and outhouses.

DC 836.8 (1341.5 km) **DJ 553.2** (890.3 km) **Junction** with Atlin Road. **Historic Milepost 866, JAKE'S CORNER**; food, showers, gas, diesel and propane. Open year-round. Information panels.

Jake's Corner. See display ad this section.

> **Junction** with Yukon Highway 7 south to Atlin, a very scenic spot that is well worth a side trip. See ATLIN ROAD section. This turnoff also provides access to Yukon Highway 8 (Tagish Road) to Carcross and South Klondike Highway to Skagway, AK (see TAGISH ROAD and SOUTH KLONDIKE HIGHWAY sections for details).

There are 2 versions of how Jake's Corner got its name. In 1942, the U.S. Army Corps of Engineers set up a construction camp here to build this section of the Alcan Highway and the Tagish Road cutoff to Carcross for the Canol pipeline. (The highway south to Atlin, BC, was not constructed until 1949–50.) The camp was under the command of Captain Jacobson, thus Jake's Corner. However, another version that predates the Alcan con-

Atlin Side Trip

The village of Atlin is located in a spectacular setting overlooking 90-mile/145-km-long Atlin Lake and surrounded by mountains. This historic gold rush community is accessible from the Alaska Highway by turning south at Jake's Corner and driving about a mile to junction with the 58-mile/93-km Atlin Road (see ATLIN ROAD section for detailed log).

Well-known sights in Atlin include the MV *Tarahne* (pictured above), a gas-driven boat that once carried passengers across Atlin Lake; the Atlin Historical Museum, with mining artifacts from the Atlin gold rush; and The Grotto on Warm Bay Road.

Mile 836 **KM 1346**

Alaska Highway, Yukon
Phone/FAX (867) 390-2607

SCRUMPTIOUS HOME BAKING
"WORLD FAMOUS CINNAMON BUNS"

Johnson's Crossing Campground Services

HOT TABLE - CHICKEN - RIBS - SALADS

FULL SERVICE RV PARK
(Treed Camping Sites)

NEW FACILITIES AND MOTEL
LEVEL PULL-THROUGHS
RV DUMP STATION  Good Sampark

SERVICE STATION • LAUNDROMAT
GROCERIES • OFF-SALES BEER
ICE • HOT SHOWERS
GIFTS AND SOUVENIRS

SUPER FISHING! – BRING YOUR CAMERA
OPEN YEAR ROUND

JAKE'S CORNER

GAS • DIESEL • PROPANE
24 Hour VISA/MC Fuel Service
Daytime Attendant
"Check Out Our Low Fuel Prices"
• RESTAURANT •
Home-style Cooking and Baked Goodies
Chinese and Western Cuisine
• SHOWERS •
Mile 866, Alaska Highway
Yukon Territory Y1A 4S8
(867) 399-2727
"Come on in and meet Jake the Bear"

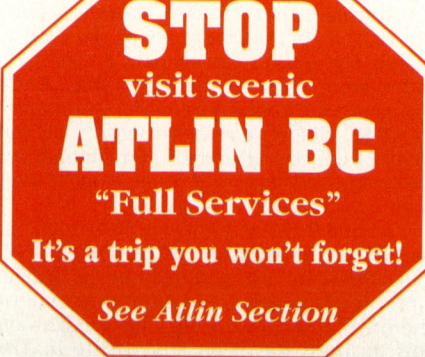

STOP
visit scenic
ATLIN BC
"Full Services"
It's a trip you won't forget!
See Atlin Section

struction is that Jake's Corner was named for Jake Jackson, a Teslin Indian who camped in this area on his way to Carcross. Roman "Jake" Chaykowsky (1900–1995) operated Jake's Corner Service here for many years. It was known locally as The Crystal Palace, after the first lodge Chaykowsky had owned at Judas Creek, just up the road.

Cliff swallows nest on the specially designed bird houses outside the service station. This is also the only known location in the Yukon of the black arctic ground squirrel.

DC 837.5 (1342.7 km) **DJ 552.5** (889.1 km) Entering 911 service response area northbound.

DC 843.2 (1351.8 km) **DJ 546.8** (880 km) Judas Creek bridge.

DC 847.7 (1359.5 km) **DJ 542.3** (872.7 km) Turnoff for Judas Creek subdivision.

DC 850 (1362.5 km) **DJ 540** (869 km) Turnoff for Marsh Lake resort; boating and excellent fishing for grayling and northern pike.

DC 851.6 (1365 km) **DJ 538.4** (866.4 km) Several access roads along here which lead to summer cottages. Marsh Lake is a popular recreation area for Whitehorse residents.

DC 852.7 (1366.8 km) **DJ 537.3** (864.7 km) Good view of **Marsh Lake** to west. The highway parallels this beautiful lake for several miles. Marsh Lake (elev. 2,152 feet/656m) is part of the Yukon River system. It is approximately 20 miles/32 km long and was named in 1883 by Lt. Frederick Schwatka, U.S. Army, for Yale professor Othniel Charles Marsh.

DC 854.4 (1370 km) **DJ 535.6** (861.9 km) **Historic Milepost 883,** Marsh Lake Camp historic sign. Boat ramp turnoff to west.

DC 854.8 (1370.2km) **DJ 535.2** (861.3 km) Caribou Road leads northwest to Airplane Lake; hiking trail, good skiing and snowmachining in winter. This road was bulldozed out to get men and equipment into a small lake where an airplane had made an emergency landing.

DC 859.9 (1379 km) **DJ 530.1** (853.1 km) **Historical Mile 890.** Turnoff to west for Marsh Lake Yukon government campground via 0.4-mile/0.6-km gravel loop road: 41 sites, most level, some pull-through; outhouses, firewood, firepits, litter barrels, picnic tables, kitchen shelter, water pump. Camping permit ($12).

For group camping and day-use area, follow signs near campground entrance. Day-use area includes sandy beach, change house, picnic area, playground, kitchen shelter and boat launch.

DC 861.1 (1381.4 km) **DJ 528.9** (851.2 km) M'Clintock River bridge. Turnout to west at north end of bridge has boat ramp access, litter barrels and outhouse.

This boat launch is a popular put-in spot for canoe trips down the M'Clintock River to **M'Clintock Bay**, at the north end of Marsh Lake, where the river flows into the lake. Put-in here for a 1-day 8-mile/12-km canoe paddle across M'Clintock Bay to Lewes River Marsh (see **Milepost DC 867.3**). M'Clintock Bay is a critical habitat for migrating waterfowl in spring. Good bird watching (Northern pintail, canvasback, American wigeon, common goldeneye, common merganser, American kestrels and bald eagles); best place to see mule deer in the Yukon; look for beaver lodges in sloughs. Fishing for grayling, jackfish and some trout.

The M'Clintock River is narrow, winding and silty with thick brush along the shoreline. However, it is a good river for boat trips, especially in late fall.

The river was named by Lieutenant Schwatka for Arctic explorer Sir Francis M'Clintock.

DC 861.3 (1381.8 km) **DJ 528.7** (850.8 km) **Swan Haven Interpretive Centre** (2 miles/3.2 km from highway via good gravel road) overlooks M'Clintock Bay and is staffed from early April to mid-May, when thousands of migrating tundra and trumpeter swans stop over here. The annual Celebration of Swans is held at the centre the third week of April.

NOTE: Watch for highway improvement next 3.7 miles/6 km northbound in summer 2003.

DC 864.3 (1388.1 km) **DJ 525.7** (846 km) Bridge over Kettley's Canyon.

DC 867.3 (1393 km) **DJ 522.7** (841.2 km) **Historic Milepost 897. Yukon River Bridge** (elev. 2,150 feet/645m). Turnout to north for day-use area and boat launch on Yukon River at Marsh Lake bridge near Northern Canada Power Commission (NCPC) control gate. Point of interest sign and litter barrels. Interpretive trail with information panels about area history and wildlife. Viewing platform on hillside overlooks the beginning of the Yukon River (locally known as **Lewes River Marsh**).

From here, the Yukon River flows 1,980 miles/3,186 km to the Bering Sea.

Improved highway next 6 miles/10 km northbound.

DC 873.5 (1403 km) **DJ 516.5** (831.2 km) **Historical Mile 904.** The Caribou RV Park.▲

The Caribou RV Park, 15 minutes from downtown. Good Sam. We are the little ones in town, your privacy and relaxation are important to us! Pets are welcome. Treed sites, walking trails, dump station, laundromat, car wash. Spacious pull-through sites (15/30-amp power and good drinking water) and the famous clean, private washrooms. From a guest: "From East to West, just the best!" (J. Thomson, WY). See it for yourself! Phone (867) 668-2961. See display ad this section. [ADVERTISEMENT] ▲

DC 874.4 (1404.4 km) **DJ 515.6** (829.7 km) **Historical Mile 905. Junction** with South Klondike Highway (Yukon Highway 2 south). Restaurant, convenience store, gas, diesel, propane, car repair and rock shop at junction.

Yukon Rock Shop. See display ad this section.

> **Junction** with South Klondike Highway (Carcross Road) which leads south to Carcross and Skagway. See SOUTH KLONDIKE HIGHWAY section.

DC 874.6 (1405.2 km) **DJ 515.4** (829.4 km) Whitehorse city limits. Incorporated June 1, 1950, Whitehorse expanded in 1974 from its original 3 square miles/8 square km to 162 square miles/420 square km.

DC 875.9 (1406.7 km) **DJ 514.1** (827.3 km) Cowley Creek.

DC 876.8 (1408.2 km) **DJ 513.2** (825.9 km) **Historical Mile 906.** Wolf Creek Yukon Government Campground to east. An 0.8-mile/1.3-km gravel loop road leads through this campground: 40 sites, most level, some pull-through; kitchen shelters, water pumps, picnic tables, firepits, firewood, outhouses, litter barrels, playground; camping permit ($12). A 1.2-mile/2-km nature loop trail winds through boreal forest to an overlook of the Yukon River and returns along Wolf Creek. Interpretive brochure at trailhead and information panels at campground entrance. Fishing in Wolf Creek for grayling.

DC 879.4 (1412.3 km) **DJ 510.6** (821.7 km) Highway crosses abandoned railroad tracks of the White Pass & Yukon Route

Emerald Lake on the South Klondike Highway ia a 25-mile/41-km drive from the Alaska Highway. (© Earl L. Brown, staff)

Just out of City limits, 1 mile off the turnoff to Skagway!
The Caribou RV Park
(aka Sourdough Country Campsite)
No Sewer-Sites, but...
all the amenities you might possibly need, incl. Dump Station and the best showers in town! We are the small ones with the big heart for your pets! Drop in and see, why so many RV-ers and tenters keep coming back!
new for 2003: Wolf's Den Restaurant
Spring Special: 20% Discount on overnight stays in May!
(not valid with other Discount, cash only!)
We are the ones who care!
VISA www.sourdough.yk.ca MasterCard
Golden Host awarded: 1998/1999/2001
Mile 904, AK Hwy, Box 10346, Whitehorse Y1A 7A1
Tel/Fax: (867) 688-2961, northof60@polarcom.com

YUKON ROCK SHOP
MINING AND MINERAL DISPLAY
Operated by The Wrays . . . Open 7 days a week
Souvenirs — Gifts — Gold Pans
Open Evenings — No G.S.T.
VISA accepted . . . Bank rate on U.S. funds
(867) 668-2772
Box 10035, STN MAIN
Whitehorse, Yukon Y1A 7A1
"Check here for rock collecting information"
Mile 905, Alaska Highway at Junction
of Klondike Highway (Carcross Road)

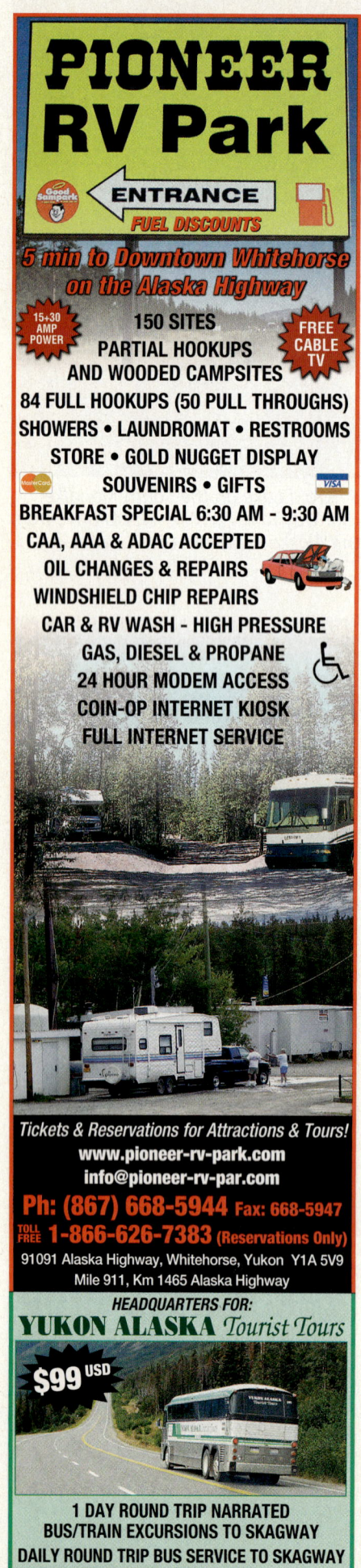

Scenic Miles Canyon is accessible by car from Milepost DC 881.7. (© Earl L. Brown, staff)

(WP&YR) narrow-gauge railroad. Although the WP&YR no longer serves Whitehorse by rail, it does offer scenic rail trips in summer out of Skagway, AK, to White Pass Summit and Lake Bennett. (See Railroads in the TRAVEL PLANNING section for details. See also SOUTH KLONDIKE HIGHWAY section for map of rail route.)

Construction of the WP&YR began in May 1898 at the height of the Klondike Gold Rush. Completion of the railway in 1900 linked the port of Skagway, AK, with Whitehorse, YT, providing passenger and freight service for thousands of gold seekers. The WP&YR ceased operation in 1982. In 1988, WP&YR started their sightseeing rail trips between Skagway and Fraser.

DC 879.6 (1412.9 km) **DJ 510.4** (821.4 km) Point of interest sign about 135th meridian to east; small turnout. Gas station.

DC 879.8 (1413.3 km) **DJ 510.2** (821.1 km) **Historic Milepost 910.** Historic sign reads: "McCrae originated in 1900 as a flag stop on the newly-constructed White Pass & Yukon Railway. During WWII, this area served as a major service and supply depot, a major construction camp and a recreation centre." McCrae truck stop to east.

DC 880 (1413.6 km) **DJ 510** (820.7 km) Historical Mile 910.5.

Fireweed R.V. Services Ltd. See display ad this section.

DC 880.4 (1414.2 km) **DJ 509.6** (820.1 km) Turnoff to west for Whitehorse Copper Mines (closed). Road to east leads to Yukon River.

DC 880.6 (1414.6 km) **DJ 509.4** (819.7 km) **Historic Milepost 911.** Site of Utah Construction Co. Camp. Pioneer R.V. Park to east.

Pioneer R.V. Park. See display ad this section. ▲

DC 881.3 (1415.7 km) **DJ 508.7** (818.6 km) White Pass & Yukon Route's Utah siding to east. This was also the site of an Army camp where thousands of soldiers were stationed during construction of the Alaska Highway.

DC 881.7 (1416.3 km) **DJ 508.3** (818 km) Sharp turnoff to east (watch for camera viewpoint sign) to see **Miles Canyon**. Drive down side road 0.3 mile/0.5 km to fork. The right fork leads to Miles Canyon parking lot. From the parking area it is a short walk to the Miles Canyon bridge; good photo spot. Cross bridge for easy hiking trails overlooking Yukon River.

Wildlife to watch for include least chipmunks and arctic ground squirrels along south-facing slopes; violet-green, cliff and bank swallows; belted kingfishers; and Townsend's solitaires in the forest on the far side of the bridge.

A 1.1-mile/1.7-km hiking trail from the bridge leads to the historic site of **Canyon City**, a gold rush settlement that existed from 1897 to 1900 as a portage point around Miles Canyon and Whitehorse Rapids. Two tramways, each several miles long, transported goods along the east and west sides of the river. Completion of the White Pass & Yukon Route in 1900 made the trams obsolete, and the settlement was abandoned. YCS conducts free interpretive walks to Canyon City twice daily during July and August. Contact the Yukon Conservation Society (867/668-5678) for more information.

The left fork on this side road leads to Schwatka Lake Road, which follows the lake and intersects the South Access Road into Whitehorse. Turnouts along road overlook Miles Canyon.

DC 881.9 (1416.7 km) **DJ 508.1** (817.7 km) Riding stable with daily trail rides in summer.

DC 882.6 (1417.8 km) **DJ 507.4** (816.5 km) **Philmar RV Service and Supply**. See display ad this section.

DC 882.9 (1418.2 km) **DJ 507.1** (816 km) **Historical Mile 912**. Motel and RV park. ▲

DC 883.7 (1419 km) **DJ 506.3** (814.8 km) Turnout to east with litter barrel, outhouses and information sign.

DC 884 (1419.4 km) **DJ 506** (814.3 km) **Hi Country R.V. Park**. Good Sam. First-class facilities to serve the traveler. Large wooded sites, full hookups, 30-amp power, cable TV,

and firepits, gift shop. 24-hour e-mail/Internet access. Conveniently located on the highway at the south access to Whitehorse. Just 2 minutes by vehicle to Miles Canyon, the Beringia Centre and the Transportation Museum. Mile 913.4 Alaska Highway. Mail 91374 Alaska Hwy., Whitehorse, YT Y1A 6E4; phone (867) 667-7445, fax (867) 668-6342. Toll-free reservations 1-877-458-3806. See display ad this section. [ADVERTISEMENT] ▲

DC 884 (1419.4 km) **DJ 506** (814.3 km). *First exit northbound for Whitehorse.* Exit east for Robert Service Way (also known as South Access Road) to Whitehorse via 4th Avenue and 2nd Avenue. *RVers NOTE: Watch for signed RV route through Whitehorse and signed RV parking areas in town.*

At Mile 1.4/2.3 km on this access road is the side road to Miles Canyon and Schwatka Lake; at Mile 1.6/2.6 km is Robert Service Campground (tent camping only) with a picnic area for day use; at Mile 2.6/4.2 km is the SS *Klondike* National Historic Site, turn left for downtown Whitehorse. ▲

DC 884.5 (1420.2 km) **DJ 505.5** (813.5 km) Government weigh scale and vehicle inspection station to west.

DC 885.3 (1422.1 km) **DJ 504.7** (812.2 km) Entrance to Yukon Beringia Centre (see description next milepost).

DC 885.7 (1422.4 km) **DJ 504.3** (811.6 km) **Historical Mile 915**. Yukon Beringia Interpretive Centre traces the Ice Age in Yukon, which, unlike the rest of Canada, was ice-free. The Blue Fish Caves near Old Crow reputedly hold the earliest evidence of humans in the New World. Displays at the centre trace the science and myth of an Ice Age subcontinent inhabited by great woolly mammoths, giant short-faced bears, lions, scimitar cats, camels and Jefferson's Ground Sloth. Ice Age artifacts include a cast of the largest woolly mammoth skeleton ever recov-

PHILMAR RV SERVICE AND SUPPLY

COMPLETE RV REPAIRS PARTS AND WELDING

Mile 912, KM 1468 Alaska Highway

(867) 668-6129

FAX (867) 668-4927

HOURS Monday — Saturday
8:30 a.m. – 5 p.m.

Mary-Anne Phillips & Staff
Whitehorse, YT

E-Mail: philmarrv@yukon.net

HI COUNTRY R.V. PARK
Country Charm - Convenient City Access
- Full Hookups • 30 Amp Power • Cable TV • Pull-Through Sites
- Hot Clean Showers • Pay Phone • Laundromat • Dump Station • Picnic Tables
- Fire Pits • Shaded Sites • Ticket Sales for Local Shows and Attractions
- 24 Hour Internet Access • Coin-op Pressurized Vehicle Wash

GIFT SHOP WITH YUKON WILDLIFE DISPLAY

Good Sam Club

YOUR HOSTS - WAYNE & LYNETTE KING
FOR RESERVATIONS CALL TOLL FREE 1-877-458-3806
91374 Alaska Highway, Whitehorse, Yukon Y1A 6E4
(867) 667-7445 • FAX (867) 668-6342
e-mail: hicountryrv@polarcom.com

Located 5 minutes from downtown
At Mile 913.4 Alaska Highway
at the south access to Whitehorse

www.themilepost.com

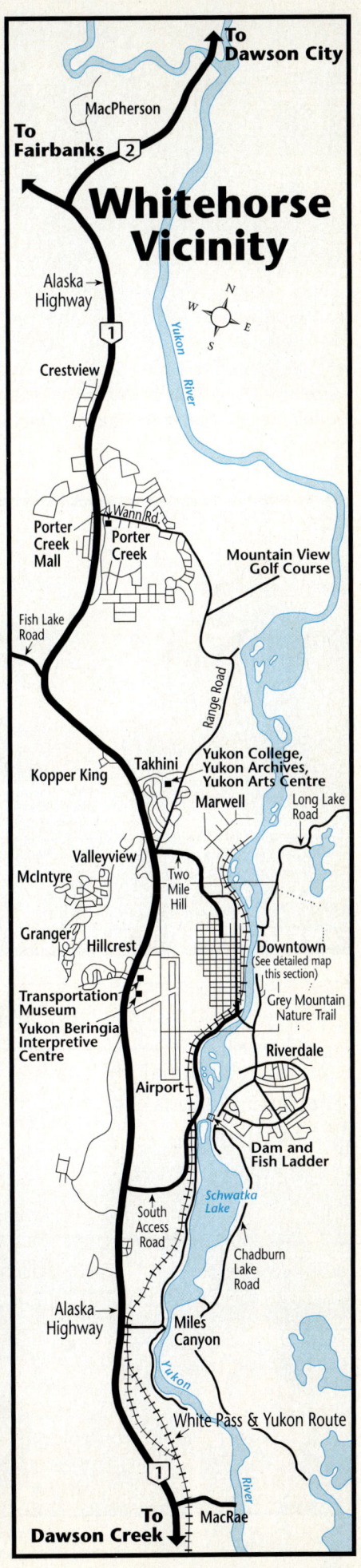

Whitehorse Vicinity

ALASKA HIGHWAY • Yukon Territory

Exhibits at the Yukon Beringia Interpretive Centre feature ice-age predators.
(© Earl L. Brown, staff)

ered. Open daily, mid-May to late September. Hours are 9 A.M. to 6 P.M. in May and September; 8:30 A.M. to 7 P.M., June through August. Open Sundays 1–5 P.M. or by appointment in winter. Phone (867) 667-8855; fax (867) 667-8844; email beringia@gov.yk.ca; www.beringia.com. Admission charged.

Yukon Beringia Interpretive Centre. See display ad this section.

DC 885.8 (1422.6 km) DJ 504.2 (811.4 km) Yukon Transportation Museum features exhibits about all forms of transportation in the North (see Attractions in following description of Whitehorse for more details). A mural on the front of the museum depicts the methods of transportation used in construction of the Alaska Highway in 1942. The 16-by-60-foot/5-by-8-m mural was painted by members of the Yukon Art Society. Open 10 A.M. to 6 P.M., mid-May to mid-September. Admission charged.

Cairns in front of the museum commemorate 18 years of service on the Alaska Highway (1946–64) by the Corps of Royal Canadian Engineers. Near this site, the U.S. Army officially handed over the Alaska Highway to the Canadian Army on April 1, 1946.

Yukon Transportation Museum. See display ad this section.

DC 886.2 (1423 km) DJ 503.8 (810.7 km) Turnoff to east for Whitehorse International Airport. Built for and used by both U.S. and Canadian forces during WWII.

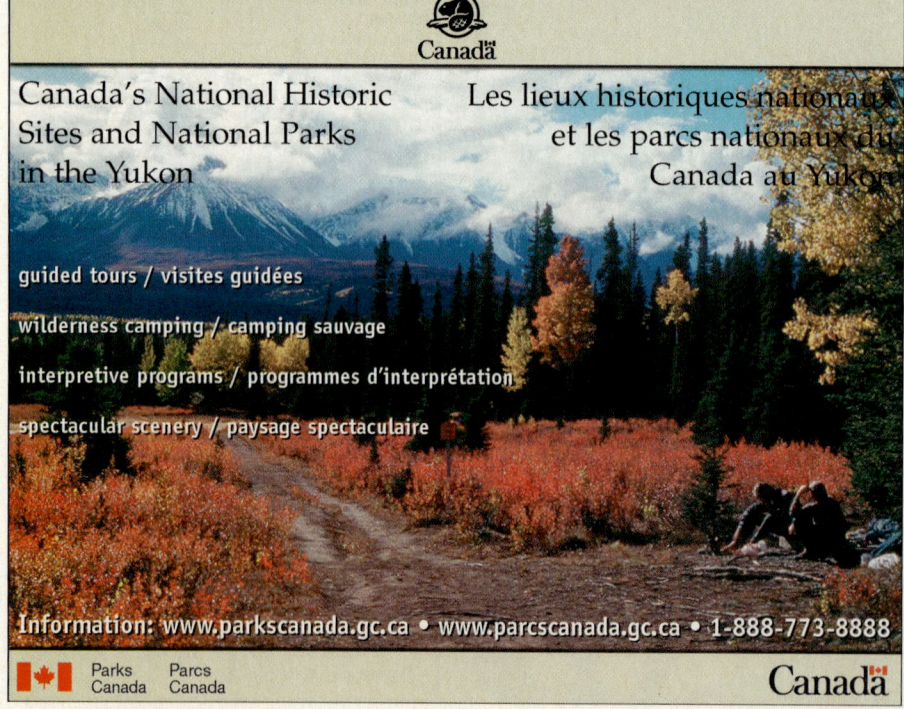

Watch for the DC–3 weathervane (see Attractions in description of Whitehorse following for more details).

DC 886.4 (1423.3 km) DJ 503.6 (810.4 km) Airport Chalet.

DC 887.4 (1425.3 km) DJ 502.6 (808.8 km) Stoplight at second (and last) exit northbound for Whitehorse. North access road to Whitehorse (exit east) is via Two-Mile Hill and 4th Avenue. At Mile 1.2/1.9 km on this access road is Qwanlin Mall.

Alaska Highway log continues on page 166.

Whitehorse

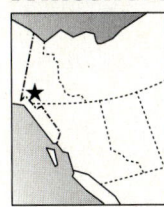

Historic Milepost 918. Located on the upper reaches of the Yukon River in Canada's subarctic at latitude 61°N. Whitehorse is 100 miles/160 km from Haines Junction; 109 miles/175 km from Skagway, AK; 250 miles/241 km from Haines, AK; and 396 miles/637 km from Tok, AK. **Population:** 22,526. **Emergency Services:** RCMP, Fire Department, Ambulance, Hospital, phone 911.

Visitor Information: Yukon Visitor Reception Centre is located next to the Yukon Territorial Government Building on 2nd Avenue. Visitor guides and touch-screen terminals are available; 15-minute film on the Yukon; daily updated information on accommodations, weather and road

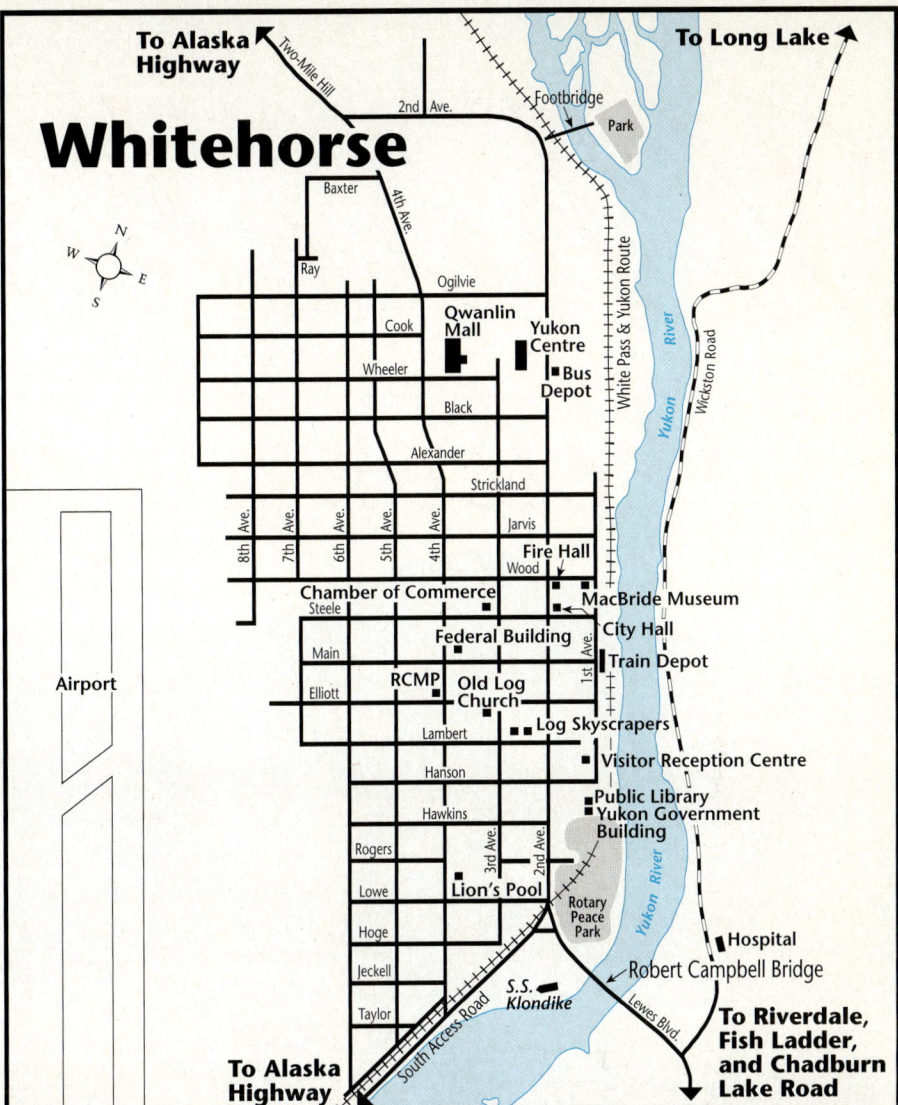

MacKenzie's RV PARK

79 Large Full-Service Sites
20 & 30 AMP Available
22 Camping Sites
Reasonable Rates

Good Sampark

• **FREE GOLD PANNING** •

Horseshoe Pit
HOT CLEAN SHOWERS • PLAYGROUND
LAUNDROMAT • STORE • CABLE TV

— modem access —

City Bus Stops Here
Handicap Accessible

— R.V./CAR WASH —

Phone (867) 633-2337
FAX (867) 667-6797
e-mail: tdmacken@yknet.yk.ca
**18 Azure Road
Whitehorse, Yukon Y1A 6E1**

Just 6 miles north of City Centre
Jct. Azure Rd. & Alaska Hwy

FAMILY HOTEL
A FULL SERVICE HOTEL IN DOWNTOWN WHITEHORSE
• 44 New Rooms • Sauna • Restaurant • Barber Shop •
• Elevators • Air Conditioned • PUBLIC LAUNDRY
"REASONABLE RATES"
email: famhotel@polarcom.com
314 Ray St., Whitehorse, Yukon Y1A 5R3 • Phone (867) 668-5558 • Fax (867) 668-5568

AIRPORT CHALET

• Easy access hotel rooms or deluxe motel units including coffee maker and refrigerator.
• Guest laundry
• Friendly lounge with aviation pictorial display
• Family priced • Pets welcome

• Licensed family restaurant
• Liquor & beer offsales
• Located across the Alaska Highway from Whitehorse Airport, Beringia Interpretive Center and Yukon Transportation Museums.

91634 Alaska Highway, Whitehorse, Yukon Territory Y1A 3E4
Phone: (867) 668-2166 / Fax: (867) 668-2173

Whitehorse Welcomes you!

This is your year to visit the Yukon!

Summer Events

May 2 - 4
Yukon Trade Show.

June to August
"Summer Arts in the Park" LePage Park.

June
Peter Gzowksi Golf Tournament.

June 21
National Aboriginal Day.

June 21
Kluane Chilkat International Bike Relay.

June 21
Midnight Sun Golf Tournament.

June 21-22
Hoof n' Woof Horse Show.

June 24
St-Jean Baptiste Day.

June 26
Yukon River Quest Canoe Race.

July 1
Canada Day Celebrations.

July 3 - 6
Yukon International Storytelling Festival.

July 11-13
Whitehorse Rodeo.

July 17 -20
Dustball International Slowpitch Tournament.

July 19-20
Annual Horse Show.

July 26
Coca Cola Classic Golf Tournament.

August 14-18
Yukon River Bathtub Race.

August 23 -24
Klondike Harvest Fair.

August 23-24
Open Golf Championships.

August 29
Corn Roast

September 5-6
Klondike Trail of '98 International Road Relay.

Whitehorse welcomes visitors travelling the Alaska Highway. Take time to stay in the Capital of Yukon and enjoy some of our warm Yukon hospitality. There is lots to see and do in Whitehorse and the surrounding areas: great Fishing, beautiful Hotsprings, trips on the historic Yukon River, a walking tour of our downtown, great shopping, exciting entertainment from Vaudeville to Bach, an interpreted River Walk, Golf under the midnight sun, wildlife viewing, restaurants both casual and chic, tons of summer events and a gorgeous new Visitor Reception Centre with easy access RV Parking.

Whitehorse provides RV Parking, throughout the city core. We have some of the best RV Campgrounds surrounding us, with the nicest hosts you would wish to meet. Please take your time to enjoy us for a few days. Stop in at the City Hall for more information, sign our guest book and collect your city pin.

Call or write ahead to:
**Tourism,
City of Whitehorse,
2121, 2nd Avenue
Whitehorse, Yukon Y1A 1C2
Ph(867)668-8687
F(867)668-8384
www.city.whitehorse.yk.ca**

Places to see

Waterfront Trolly
SS Klondike Sternwheeler
MacBride Museum
Yukon Transportation Museum
Yukon Arts Centre Gallery
Yukon Berengia Interpretive Centre
Miles Canyon
Canyon City
Whitehorse Fishway
Old Log Church
LePage Park, Heritage walking tour
The Visitor Reception Centre and film
The Yukon River by boat
All the great nightly entertainment and fabulous shopping.

Day Trips

Skagway and the White Pass and Yukon Route Railway, Kookatsoon Lake, the Hot Springs, Ibex Valley, Marsh Lake and Swan Haven wildlife viewing, Atlin, Fox Lake, Carcross and the smallest desert in the world.

World's largest weathervane—a vintage Douglas DC-3 at the Whitehorse International Airport. (© Earl L. Brown, staff)

conditions; printout information on attractions, restaurants or events in Whitehorse. The centre is open mid-May to mid-September daily 8 A.M. to 8 P.M.; phone (867) 667-3084. Or contact Tourism Yukon, Box 2703, Whitehorse, YT Y1A 2C6; phone (867) 667-5340; fax (867) 667-3546; Internet www.touryukon.com.

The city of Whitehorse offers year-round visitor information through their Tourism

WHITEHORSE ADVERTISERS

Airport Chalet ....Ph. (867) 668-2166	Pot O' Gold ....4129 4th Ave.
Canadream Campers.......Ph. (867) 668-3610	Qwanlin Mall ....4th Ave. & Ogilvie St.
Caribou RV Park ....Ph. (867) 668-2961	River View Hotel..............Ph. (867) 667-7801
City of Whitehorse...........Ph. (867) 668-8687	S'igedi Gifts & Things ....101-100 Main St.
Coffee • Tea & Spice ....Qwanlin Mall	Sandor's............................Ph. (867) 667-6171
Edgewater Hotel, The................101 Main St.	Select Reservations ....Ph. (867) 667-2161
Fireweed R.V. Services ....Ph. (867) 668-5082	Stop In Family Hotel.......Ph. (867) 668-5558
Fountain Tire ....Ph. (867) 668-6171	Superior Lube & RV
Frantic Follies ....Ph. (867) 668-2042	Services ....115 Jasper Rd.
Glass Magnum Mobile	Takhini Hot Springs ....Ph. (867) 633-2706
Repair Inc. ....Ph. (867) 668-2484	Three Beans Natural
Goldpanner Gift Shop ....Ph. (867) 668-6842	Foods.................................308 Wood St.
Happy Daze R.V. Center ......110 Industrial Rd.	Troyer's Mobile RV
Hawkins House Bed &	Services ....Ph. (867) 667-4175
Breakfast ....Ph. (867) 668-7638	Tutchone Air.....................Ph. (867) 667-2488
Hi Country R.V. Park ....Ph. (867) 667-7445	Unique Tailors ....2 locations—see ad
High Country Inn ....4051 4th Ave.	Westmark Klondike
Klondike Rib & Salmon	Inn...................................Ph. (867) 668-4747
BBQ ....2116 2nd Ave.	Westmark Whitehorse
MacBride Museum ....1st. Ave. & Wood St.	Hotel............................Ph. (867) 393-9700
MacKenzie's RV Park..........Ph. (867) 633-2337	Wharf On Fourth, The ....Ph. (867) 667-7473
Mac's Fireweed Books................203 Main St.	White Pass & Yukon
Main Man, The ....Ph. (867) 633-6139	Route ....Ph. (800) 343-7373
Midnight Sun	Whitehorse General
Bed & Breakfast ....Ph. (867) 667-2255	Store ....205 Main St.
Midnight Sun Gallery	Yukon Beringia Intrepetive
& Gifts ....205C Main St.	Centre ....Ph. (867) 667-8855
Muktuk Adventures..........Ph. (867) 668-3647	Yukon Brewing Co. ....Ph. (867) 668-4183
Murdoch's ....207 Main St.	Yukon Game Farm
North End Gallery ....Ph. (867) 393-3590	Wildlife Preserve ....Ph. (867) 633-2922
Paradise Alley.....................206B Main St.	Yukon River Cruises ....Ph. (867) 668-4716
Parks Canada ....Ph. 1-888-773-8888	Yukon Rock Shop ....Ph. (867) 668-2772
Philmar RV Service &	Yukon Tire Centre ....Ph. (867) 667-6102
Supply ....Ph. (867) 668-6129	Yukon Transportation
Pioneer RV Park...............Ph. (867) 668-5944	Museum ....Ph. (867) 668-4792

Coordinator; phone (867) 668-8687 for information or write: Tourism Coordinator, City of Whitehorse, 2121 Second Avenue, Whitehorse, YT Y1A 1C2. Access up-to-date information on events, accommodations and attractions on the City of Whitehorse Internet web page at www.city.whitehorse.yk.ca. Visitors are invited to stop by City Hall and pick up a free 3-day parking pass and free city pin.

Elevation: 2,305 feet/703m. **Climate:** Wide variations are the theme here with no two winters alike. The lowest recorded temperature is -62°F/-52°C and the warmest 94°F/35°C. Mean temperature for month of January is -6°F/-21°C and for July 57°F/14°C. Annual precipitation is 10.3 inches, equal parts snow and rain. On June 21 Whitehorse enjoys 19 hours, 11 minutes of daylight and on Dec. 21 only 5 hours, 37 minutes. **Radio:** CFWH 570, CBC network with repeaters throughout territory; CBC Montreal; CKRW 610, local; CHON-FM 98.1; CFET-FM 106.7. **Television:** CBC–TV live, colour via ANIK satellite, Canadian network; WHTV, NADR (First Nation issues), local cable; CanCom stations via satellite, many channels. **Newspapers:** *Whitehorse Star* (weekdays); *Yukon News* (3 times a week).

Private Aircraft: Whitehorse International Airport, 3 runways; has approach over city and an abrupt escarpment; elev. 2,305 feet/703m; main runway length 9,000 feet/2,743m; surfaced; fuel 80, 100, jet fuel available. Customs clearance available.

Floatplane base on Schwatka Lake above Whitehorse Dam (take the South Access Road from Alaska Highway and turn on Robert Service Way by the railroad tracks).

Description

Whitehorse has been the capital of Yukon Territory since 1953, and serves as the centre for transportation, communications and supplies for Yukon Territory and

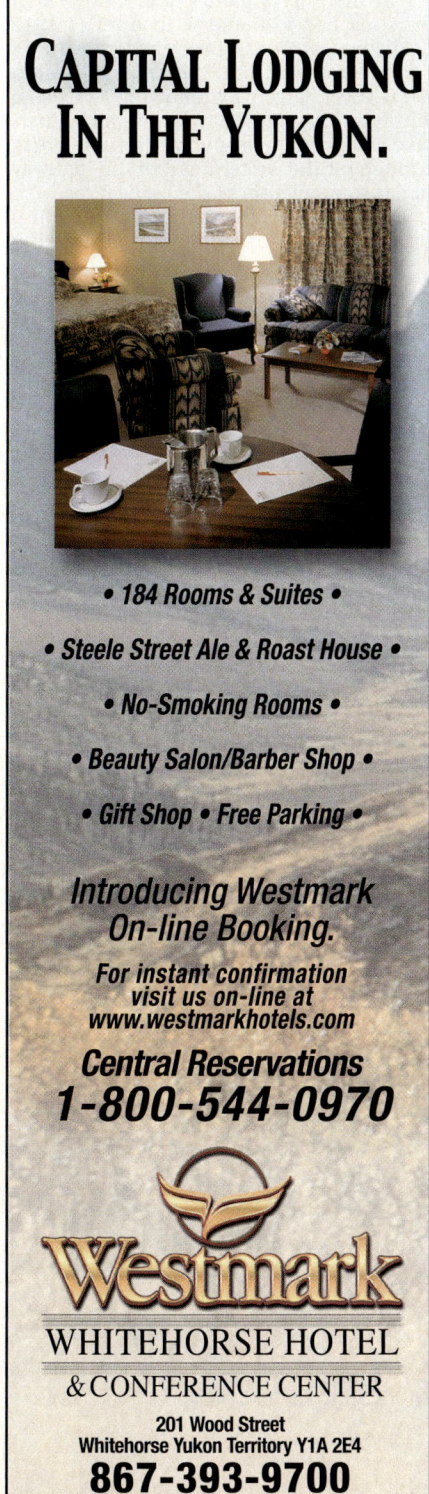

the Northwest Territories.

The downtown business section of Whitehorse lies on the west bank of the Yukon River. The Riverdale subdivision is on the east side. The low mountains rising behind Riverdale are dominated by Canyon Mountain, known locally as Grey Mountain. Wolf Creek, Hillcrest and Granger subdivisions lie south of the city; McIntyre subdivision is to the west; and Porter Creek, Takhini and Crestview subdivisions are north of the city. The Takhini area is the location of the Yukon College campus.

Downtown Whitehorse is flat and marked at its western limit by a rising escarpment dominated by the Whitehorse International Airport. Originally a woodcutter's lot, the airstrip was first cleared in 1920 to accommodate 4 U.S. Army planes on a test flight from New York to Nome. Access to the city is by Two-Mile Hill from the north and by Robert Service Way (South Access Road) from the south; both connect with the Alaska Highway.

In 1974, the city limits of Whitehorse were expanded from the original 2.7 square miles/6.9 square kilometres to 162 square miles/421 square kilometres, making Whitehorse at one time the largest metropolitan area in Canada. More than two-thirds of the population of Yukon Territory live in the city. Whitehorse is the hub of a network of about 2,664 miles/4,287 km of all-weather roads serving Yukon Territory.

History & Economy

When the White Pass & Yukon Route railway was completed in July 1900, connecting Skagway with the Yukon River, Whitehorse came into being as the northern terminus. Here the famed river steamers connected the railhead to Dawson City, and some of these boats made the trip all the way to St. Michael, a small outfitting point on Alaska's Bering Sea coast.

Klondike stampeders landed at Whitehorse to dry out and repack their supplies after running the famous Whitehorse Rapids. (The name Whitehorse was in common use by the late 1800s; it is believed that the first miners in the area thought that the foaming rapids resembled white horses' manes and so named the river rapids.) The rapids are no longer visible since construction of the Yukon Energy Corporation's hydroelectric dam on the river. This dam created man-made Schwatka Lake, named in honour of U.S. Army Lt. Frederick Schwatka, who named many of the points along the Yukon River during his 1883 exploration of the region.

The gold rush brought stampeders and the railroad. The community grew as a transportation centre and transshipment point for freight from the Skagway–Whitehorse railroad and the stern-wheelers plying the Yukon River to Dawson City. The river was the only highway until WWII, when military expediency built the Alaska Highway in 1942.

Whitehorse was headquarters for the western sector during construction of the Alaska Highway. Fort St. John was headquarters for the eastern sector. Both were the largest construction camps on the highway.

The first survey parties of U.S. Army engineers reached Whitehorse in April of 1942. By the end of August, they had constructed a pioneer road from Whitehorse west to White River, largely by following an existing winter trail between Whitehorse and Kluane Lake. November brought the final breakthrough on the western end of the highway, marking completion of the pioneer road.

During the height of the construction of the Alaska Highway, thousands of American

The Yukon's Premier Hotel

- Executive and Jacuzzi suites.
- Delightful 'country inn' atmosphere.
- Enjoy a barbeque on the deck of the 'world famous' Yukon Mining Company.
- Great views, guest laundry, free parking.
- Full kitchens and kitchenettes.

Toll free
1-800-554-4471

4051 4th Ave, Whitehorse, Yukon, Canada Y1A 1H1
867.667.4471   F 867.667.6457
e-mail: info@highcountryinn.yk.ca or check our
website: www.highcountryinn.yk.ca

High Country Inn

military and civilian workers were employed in the Canadian North. It was the second boom period for Whitehorse.

There was an economic lull following the war, but the new highway was then opened to civilian travel, encouraging new development. Mineral exploration and the development of new mines had a profound effect on the economy of the region, as did the steady growth of tourism. The Whitehorse Copper Mine, located a few miles south of the city in the historic Whitehorse copper belt, is now closed. The Grum Mine site north of Faro produced lead, silver and zinc concentrates for Cyprus–Anvil (1969–1982), Curragh Resources (1986–1992) and Anvil Range Mining Corp. (1994–1998). Stop by the Yukon Chamber of Mines office at 3rd and Strickland for information on mining and rockhounding in Yukon Territory. There is an excellent Yukon mineral display at the entrance to the Visitor Reception Centre downtown.

Because of its accessibility, Whitehorse became capital of the Yukon Territory (replacing Dawson City in that role) on March 31, 1953.

Lodging & Services

Whitehorse offers 22 hotels and motels for a total of about 840 rooms. Several hotels

Fireweed is Yukon Territory's official floral emblem.

include conference facilities; most have cocktail lounges, licensed dining rooms and taverns. Bed-and-breakfast accommodations and 2 hostels are also available.

The city has 31 restaurants downtown and in surrounding residential subdivisions that serve meals ranging from French and German cuisine to fast food.

Whitehorse has a downtown shopping district stretching along Main Street. The Qwanlin Mall at 4th Avenue and Ogilvie has a supermarket and a variety of shops. The Yukon Centre Mall on 2nd Avenue has a restaurant, supermarket, shops and a liquor store. Whitehorse also has a Wal-Mart.

In addition to numerous supermarkets, garages and service stations, there are churches, movie houses, beauty salons and a covered swimming pool. Whitehorse also has several banks with ATMs. (Many businesses in Whitehorse participate in the Fair Exchange Program, which guarantees an exchange rate within 4 percent of the bank rate set once a week on Mondays. Participating businesses display the Fair Exchange logo.)

NOTE: There is no central post office in Whitehorse. Postal services are available in Qwanlin Mall at Coffee • Tea & Spice; The Hougen Centre on Main Street (lower floor below Shoppers Drugs); and in Riverdale and Porter Creek subdivisions. Stamps are available at several locations.

Specialty stores include gold nugget and ivory shops where distinctive jewellery is manufactured, and Indian craft shops spe-

Aerial view of Whitehorse photographed on a flightseeing trip with Tutchone Air.
(© Earl L. Brown, staff)

cializing in moose hide jackets, parkas, vests, moccasins, slippers, mukluks and gauntlets. Inuit and Indian handicrafts from Canada's Arctic regions are featured in some stores. Whitehorse area maps are available at Mac's Fireweed Bookstore at 203 Main Street; phone (867) 668-2434.

Hawkins House Bed & Breakfast. Enjoy the Yukon's most luxurious accommodations in our Victorian home in downtown Whitehorse. Turn-of-the-century charm includes a grand foyer, guest parlor, high ceilings, balconies, hardwood floors, and historical and cultural themes. 5 star rating Canada Select. Rates $100–$175. Phone (867) 668-7638, fax (867) 668-7632, or write 303 Hawkins St., Whitehorse, YT, Canada Y1A 1X5. www.hawkinshouse.yk.ca. [ADVERTISEMENT]

High Country Inn. During your stay in Whitehorse, relax and enjoy "Country Inn" atmosphere and great Northern hospitality. We offer 100 rooms from executive and Jacuzzi suites to deluxe double rooms. Located downtown, great views, elevators, guest laundry, exercise room, colour TV, coffee maker, etc. AAA approved (Canada select 4 stars, reservations recommended). Phone (800) 554-4471 or (867) 667-4471, fax (867) 667-6457. See our display ad.
[ADVERTISEMENT]

Camping

Tent camping only is available at Robert Service Park on Robert Service Way (South Access Road). There are several private RV campgrounds south of Whitehorse on the Alaska Highway (see **Mileposts DC 873.5, 881, 882.9** and **884** in the highway log), and 1 private campground 6 miles/9.6 km north of the city on the highway (see **Milepost DC 891.9**). Wolf Creek Yukon government campground is 7 miles/11 km south of Whitehorse at **Milepost DC 876.8** on the Alaska Highway. A private campground and Yukon government campground are located at Marsh Lake. Takhini Hot Springs on the Klondike Loop is also a popular camping spot (1/2-hour drive from Whitehorse). ▲

Transportation

Air: Service by Air Canada to major cities and Yukon communities. Air North to Dawson City, Old Crow, Edmonton, Calgary, Vancouver, Juneau and Fairbanks, AK. Also fixed-wing charter and flightseeing trips from the airport. Whitehorse International Airport is reached from the Alaska Highway.

Seaplane dock on Schwatka Lake just above the Whitehorse Dam (take Robert Service Way from Alaska Highway and turn right on road by the railroad tracks to reach the base). Flightseeing tours available.

Trans North Air offers helicopter sightseeing tours from the airport.

Bus: Whitehorse Transit offers downtown and rural service. See also Bus Lines in the TRAVEL PLANNING section.

Railroad: Arrangements for White Pass & Yukon Route rail trips may be made by phoning WP&YR in Skagway at (800) 343-7373, or contacting local travel agencies.

Car, Truck, Motorhome and **Camper Rentals:** Several local and national agencies are located in Whitehorse.

Attractions

The SS *Klondike* National Historic Site is hard to miss. This grand old stern-wheeler sits beside the Yukon River near the Robert Campbell bridge.

The SS *Klondike* was built in 1929 by the British Yukon Navigation Company (BYNC). The vessel was the largest on the Yukon, had a cargo capacity 50 percent greater than previous boats, and could carry over 300 tons. She ran aground in 1936 at the confluence of the Teslin and Yukon rivers. Salvaged parts were used to construct a new ship—the second SS *Klondike*—that was almost identical to the first.

The *Klondike* carried mail, general supplies, passengers and silver lead ore along the 460-mile route between Whitehorse and Dawson City until 1955, when she was retired. Donated to the Canadian government, the SS *Klondike* now rests on the west bank of the Yukon near the Robert Campbell Bridge in Whitehorse, where she is undergoing a 7-year, $1.2 million renovation.

The renovation work will be part of the summer tours on the SS *Klondike* until the work is completed. Visitors will relive history as the great stern-wheeler is rebuilt and returned to her original state. Visitors will have the opportunity to witness the skill and effort that goes into building a riverboat: Shipbuilders on the project are using techniques and tools from the early 1900s to reconstruct the ship.

There is an interpretive centre, a gift shop and public parking at the SS *Klondike* National Historic Site. There are more than 7,000 artifacts on display, and the centre offers guided tours of the SS *Klondike* on the half-hour. The tours begin with a 20-minute film on the history of riverboats, shown in the tent theatre adjacent to the vessel. The interpretive centre is open and tours are given from mid-May to mid-September.

Admission fees (subject to change) to the SS *Klondike* National Historic Site are: $5 for adults, $4.50 for seniors, $2.75 child, $12

Unique Tailors
- Local First Nation Crafts
- Custom Made Northern Parkas & Anoraks
- Fabrics & Gifts
- Alterations

TWO LOCATIONS:
4101-4th Ave
Ph 867.633.5818
Fax 867.668.6410

Yukon Inn Plaza
L4230-4th Ave
Whitehorse Y1A 1K1
Ph 867.633.6088

family pass. Large groups should book tours ahead of time with Parks Canada; phone (867) 667-3910, toll free (800) 661-0486, fax (867) 393-6701.

Special Events. The Yukon International Storytelling Festival, held May 30–June 2, 2003, features storytellers, musicians and theatre groups from around the world. Other events in June include the Yukon River Quest Canoe Race, June 26, 2003, and Kids Day in the Park. July 1st is Canada Day, and it's celebrated with events and entertainment for the whole family.

The Annual Yukon River Bathtub Race from Whitehorse to Dawson City is scheduled for Aug. 14–18, 2003. Participants set off from Rotary Peace Park in 5-foot-by-3-foot bathtubs. Half-way point is Minto Landing, where the "tubbers" take a mandatory overnight rest before setting off for Dawson City the next morning. Prizes and drinks at Dawson's Downtown Hotel await the finishers of this grueling 480-mile race.

The Klondike International Road Relay, Sept. 5–6, 2003, is the 21st annual running of the road relay from Skagway, AK, to Whitehorse, YT.

Live Shows. The long-running vaudeville stage show, **Frantic Follies**, is held nightly mid-May through mid-September at the Westmark Whitehorse Hotel. 2003 marks the 34th season for this popular 1½-hour show,

A striking monument at the Yukon Arts Centre Gallery. (© Earl L. Brown, staff)

which features a chorus line, rousing music and hilarious skits from Robert W. Service ballads. Visitors are advised to get tickets in advance; available at the box office in the Westmark or phone (867) 668-2042. Tickets are also available at most area RV parks.

Picnic at a Park. Central to downtown and a popular picnic spot, **Rotary Peace Park** is the site of several Whitehorse special events. Visitors may also board the vintage **Waterfront Trolley** in front of the visitor centre for a scenic ride along the Yukon River ($1 charge).

Live entertainment featuring local artists takes place daily in summer during the lunch hour at **Lepage Park**.

North End Gallery features art created in Canada's "North End." Original works, Inuit sculpture and made-in-Yukon crafts such as First Nation masks, moosehair tufting, pottery, baskets, art glass and burl woodwork, are a specialty. Klondike jewellery—gold nugget, mastodon ivory, trade bead—is available, as is a wide selection of illustrated children's books of the North. We ship worldwide! Located on First Avenue across from the MacBride Museum, at the north end of Horwood's Mall. See display ad this section. [ADVERTISEMENT]

Pot O'Gold
Where Service & Quality Really Count!

Designers and manufacturers of natural gold nugget jewellery.

Natural gold nugget rings, earrings, necklaces, bracelets and watch bands.

Quality made Yukon Crafts.

E-mail: potogold@klondiker.com
4129-4th Avenue
Corner of 4th & Wood St
668-2058
Fax: 668-4941
21 Years of Serving Satisfied Customers

Superior Lube and RV Services
* Oil Changes * Hoists to Handle the Big Rigs
* Licensed Mechanics * General Repairs
* Welding * Machining * Springs & Brakes
* Diesel Engines

115 Jasper Rd.
Whitehorse, Yukon Y1A 2Z8
Wayne Lerner - Owner
(867) 633-6327
Fax (867) 633-4921
"Ask About Our MILEPOST Special"

S'igèdí Gifts & Things
- Souvenirs.
- All occasion gifts.
- Large selection of t-shirts, sweatshirts & fleece.
- Native crafts - including tuftings, slippers, jewellery, soapstone & dolls.
- Crystal, jewellery, and lots more…

Horwood's Mall
Unit 101-100 Main St.
Whitehorse, Y.T. Y1A 2A8
Phone: (867) 456-4157
Fax: (867) 456-4158
E-mail: sigedi@polarcom.com

HAPPY DAZE R.V. CENTER
FULL R.V. PARTS & SERVICE
Repairs to Propane Appliances,
Electrical & Plumbing Systems.
Welding & Trailer Hitches
Spring, Axle & Brake Repairs

110 INDUSTRIAL ROAD
WHITEHORSE, YUKON
(Just off the Two Mile Hill)
(867) 667-7069

Yukon Arts Centre Gallery, at 300 College Drive, is the Yukon's only public art museum. The Arts Centre has new shows every 6 to 10 weeks featuring international, national and regional artists. Phone (867) 667-8578 for hours; admission by donation.

The MacBride Museum is located on 1st Avenue and Wood Street. Indoor exhibits include a large gold collection, mining and stampede history, First Nations, Mounties, Yukon wildlife and minerals, and the history of Whitehorse. Outdoor exhibits feature transportation and mining artifacts, a 1900 telegraph office and Sam McGee's Cabin. Admission charged. Open daily in summer, 10 A.M. to 6 P.M.; Wednesday–Saturday in winter, noon to 5 P.M. Tours and educational programs available on request. Gift shop. For more information phone (867) 667-2709; fax 633-6607; or email info@macbridemuseum.com.

Old Log Church Museum, 1 block off Main on Elliott at 3rd. Built in 1900 by Rev. R.J. Bowen for the Church of England, this recently restored log church and rectory have been declared the first territorial historic sites in the Yukon. The museum, located in the log church, displays artifacts of the northern missions, Inuit and First Nation people, whaling history and an audio recording of "The Bishop Who Ate His Boots," as well as an interactive computer station on Herschel Island. Museum shop. Open to the public June to September; admission fee charged.

Historical walking tours of Whitehorse are conducted by the Yukon Historical & Museums Association. Tour guides wear period costumes for these walks that take in the city's heritage buildings. Meet at the Donnenworth House, 3126 3rd Ave.; phone 667-4704. A $2 fee is charged. There are tours Monday through Saturday from June to the end of August. For self-guided tours, *Exploring Old Whitehorse* is available from local stores or from the Yukon Historical and Museums Assoc., 3126–3rd Avenue, Whitehorse, YT Y1A 1E7.

Tour the Yukon's only brewery. A popular stop in Whitehorse is the Yukon

Brewing Company, located at 102A Copper Road. Yukon's only brewery offers an informative daily "tour and taste." Morning and afternoon tour times. For more information, phone (867) 668-4183.

Yukon Government Building, 2nd Avenue and Hawkins, open 9 A.M. to 5 P.M. Administrative and Legislative headquarters of Yukon Territory, the building contains some notable artworks. On the main floor mall is an acrylic resin mural, 120 feet/37m long, which portrays the historical evolution of the Yukon. The 24 panels, each measuring 4 by 5 feet/1.2 by 1.5m, highlight events such as the arrival of Sir John Franklin at Herschel Island in 1825, the Klondike Gold Rush, and the coming of the automobile. The mural was created by Vancouver, BC, artist David MacLagen.

In the Legislative Chamber, an 18-by-12-

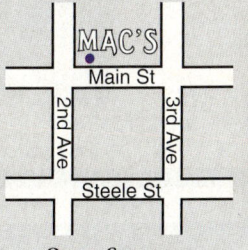

MAC'S FIREWEED BOOKS

Pick up a Yukon memory... pick up a book from Mac's

Long after the vacation is over, the North will live on in your bookshelves. The finest selection of Northern books, magazines & newspapers North of 60°.

Open Summer 8:00 am - Midnight
Winter 8:00 am - 9:00 pm
E-mail: macsbook@yknet.yk.ca
www.yukonbooks.com

Topo Maps
Nautical Charts
Antiquarian Books

Phone (867) 668-2434 • 203 Main Street, Whitehorse, YT Y1A 2B2

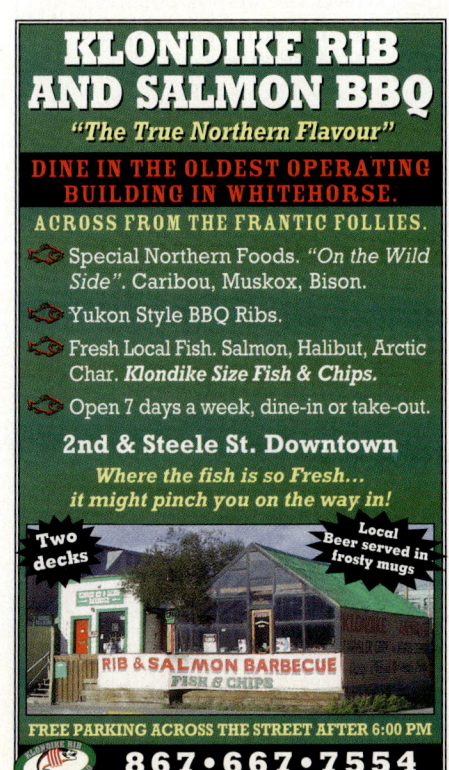

KLONDIKE RIB AND SALMON BBQ
"The True Northern Flavour"

DINE IN THE OLDEST OPERATING BUILDING IN WHITEHORSE.
ACROSS FROM THE FRANTIC FOLLIES.

- Special Northern Foods. *"On the Wild Side"*. Caribou, Muskox, Bison.
- Yukon Style BBQ Ribs.
- Fresh Local Fish. Salmon, Halibut, Arctic Char. **Klondike Size Fish & Chips.**
- Open 7 days a week, dine-in or take-out.

2nd & Steele St. Downtown
Where the fish is so Fresh... it might pinch you on the way in!

Two decks • Local Beer served in frosty mugs

FREE PARKING ACROSS THE STREET AFTER 6:00 PM
867•667•7554
www.themilepost.com

PARADISE ALLEY

- Framed Wildlife Art
- Fine Gifts & Collectibles
- Art Cards & Matted Prints
- Yukon Apparel & Souvenirs
- Jade & Soapstone Sculptures
- Sterling & Semi-Precious Jewellery
- Handmade Belgian Chocolates

Don't miss the Yukon's largest Saltwater Reef Aquarium and our Antique Player Piano

206 Main Street • Phone: (867) 456-4228

foot/5-by-4m tapestry is an abstraction of the fireweed plant, Yukon's floral emblem. The Yukon Women's Tapestry, 5 panels each 7-by-13-feet/2-by-4m, hangs in the legislative library lounge. The wool panels portray the role of women in the development of the territory, depicting the 5 seasons of the North; spring, summer, autumn, winter and "survival," the cold gray season between winter and spring and fall and winter. Begun by the Whitehorse Branch of the Canadian Federation of Business and Professional Women in 1976 to mark International Women's Year, the wall hangings were stitched by some 2,500 Yukoners.

Tutchone Air, based at the Whitehorse Airport, operates a flight school and air charter service. We produce some excellent air photos suitable for framing and offer custom sightseeing flights around the Whitehorse area. Or travel further and experience the spectacular glaciers of Kluane or Atlin. (867)667-2488; www.tutchoneair.com.

[ADVERTISEMENT]

World's largest weathervane. Located in front of the Whitehorse International Airport is the world's largest weathervane—a Douglas DC-3. This vintage plane (registration number CF–CPY) flew for several Yukon airlines from 1946 until 1970, when it blew an engine during takeoff. The plane was restored by Joe Muff with the help of the Yukon Flying Club and the Whitehorse community. It is now owned and managed by the Yukon Transportation Museum. The restored plane was mounted on a rotating pedestal in 1981 and now acts as a weathervane, pointing its nose into the wind.

Whitehorse Rapids Fishway. Located at the end of Nisutlin Drive in the Riverdale suburb. The fish ladder was built in 1959 to provide access for chinook (king) salmon and other species above the Yukon Energy Corporation hydroelectric dam. It is the longest wooden fish ladder in the world. The fish ladder is flowing from mid-July to early September during salmon-spawning season. Interpretive displays and viewing decks; open daily.

Take a hike. In July and August, the Yukon Conservation Society (YCS) offers free guided nature walks, ranging in difficulty from easy to strenuous. Trips are 2 to 6 hours in length and informative guides explain the local flora, fauna, geology and history along the trails. The YCS also conducts free interpretive walks to Canyon City (see **Milepost DC 881.7**) twice daily, 7 days a week during July and August. For a schedule of hikes, contact the Yukon Conservation Society at 302 Hawkins St.; phone (867) 668-5678.

The Boreal Worlds Trail starts at the end of the student parking lot at Yukon College. The trail leads through an aspen grove, past

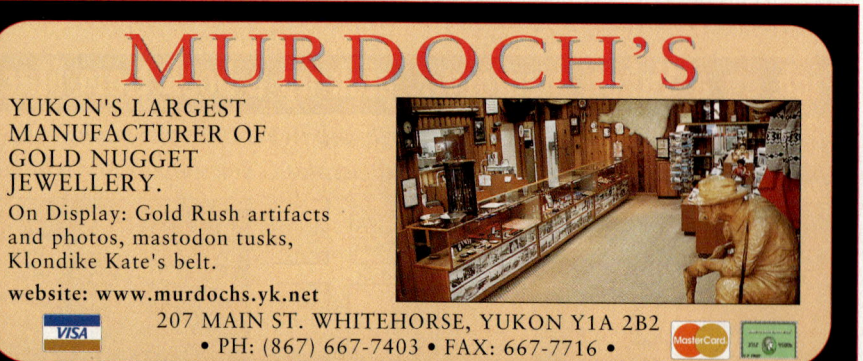

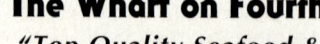

All types of northern transport are featured in exhibits at the Yukon Transportation Museum. (© Earl L. Brown, staff)

5867, Whitehorse, YT Y1A 5L6 or phone (867) 668-4792, fax 633-5547.

Play Golf. Mountain View Public Golf Course is accessible via the Porter Creek exit off the Alaska Highway or from Range Road; 18 holes, grass greens; green fees. Meadow Lakes Golf and Country Club, 5 minutes south of Whitehorse at **Milepost DC 878**, has a 9-hole par 36 course, clubhouse, cart and club rentals; phone (867) 668-4653.

Whitehorse Public Library, part of the Yukon Government Building on 2nd Avenue, has a room with art displays and books about the Yukon and the gold rush. It features a large stone and copper double fireplace, comfortable chairs, tables and helpful staff. Open 10 A.M. to 9 P.M. weekdays, 10 A.M. to 6 P.M. Saturday, 1 to 9 P.M. Sunday; closed holidays. Phone (867) 667-5239.

Yukon Archives is located adjacent Yukon College at Yukon Place. The archives were established in 1972 to acquire, preserve and make available the documented history of the Yukon. The holdings, dating from 1845, include government records, private manuscripts, corporate records, photographs, maps, newspapers (most are on microfilm), sound recordings, university theses, books, pamphlets and periodicals. Visitors are welcome. Phone (867) 667-5321 for hours, or write Box 2703, Whitehorse, YT Y1A 2C6, for more information.

a beaver pond, and through an area dense with lichen. Free interpretive brochure available at the bookstore.

Grey Mountain Nature Trail, east of downtown and the Riverdale subdivision, offers views of the Upper Yukon River valley.

Yukon Beringia Interpretive Centre traces the Ice Age in Yukon, which, unlike the rest of Canada, was ice-free. The Blue Fish Caves near Old Crow reputedly hold the earliest evidence of humans in the New World. Displays at the centre trace the science and myth of an Ice Age subcontinent inhabited by great woolly mammoths, giant short-faced bears, lions, scimitar cats, camels and Jefferson's Ground Sloth. Ice Age artifacts include a cast of the largest woolly mammoth skeleton ever recovered. Open daily, mid-May to late September. Phone (867) 667-8855; fax (867) 667-8844; email beringia@gov.yk.ca; www.beringia.com. Admission fee charged. (Inquire about special combined ticket prices available for the Beringia Centre and Transportation Museum.)

The Yukon Transportation Museum, located on the Alaska Highway adjacent to the Whitehorse Airport (see **Milepost DC 885.8**), features exhibits of all forms of transportation in the North. Displays inside include the full-size replica of the *Queen of the Yukon* Ryan monoplane, sister ship to Lindbergh's *Spirit of St. Louis;* railway rolling stock; Alaska Highway vintage vehicles, dogsleds and stagecoaches. Also featured are the Chilkoot Trail, the Canol Highway and bush pilots of the North. The museum includes video theatres and a gift shop with a selection of Northern books. Plenty of parking. Admission fee charged. (Special combined ticket prices available for the Beringia Centre and Transportation Museum.) Open daily, 10 A.M. to 6 P.M., mid-May to mid-September. Write P.O. Box

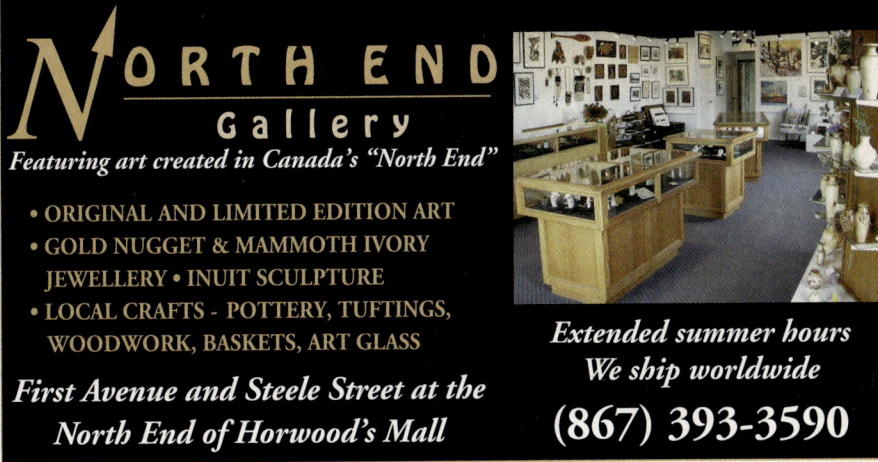

Paddling the Yukon River from Whitehorse to Dawson City

I have paddled the Yukon River twice.

The first time was in 1973 when on a whim, I left my parents on the riverbank in Whitehorse and joined the Yukon's 75th Anniversary Canoe Pageant—a flotilla of five 25-foot fiberglass canoes, a speedboat and a Canadian Armed Forces support team. I met my parents for community celebrations in Carmacks, Minto and Dawson City—the only places where the river and road came together.

My second trip was in 1998. The Yukon was celebrating its 100th anniversary, and 8 of us paddled in one voyageur and one tandem canoe on a 9-day, 250-mile trip from Carmacks to Dawson City guided by Nahanni River Adventures, a company headquartered in Whitehorse.

Despite its immensity and hazards such as constantly changing weather, channels, islands, sweepers and sand and gravel bars, the Yukon River is generally shallow and slow moving, and paddling is relaxing.

And aside from the quirks of individual paddlers, I recommend that ultimate relaxation is paddling with a group and leaving everything to the experts. Although our guides kept reminding us we had a schedule to keep, we often tied our canoes together, lay back on the gear, passed the peanuts and drifted with the current.

Travelers from all over the world paddle the Yukon River, and like us, most were there to relax. One German couple let their canoe drift while they lounged in deck chairs. Two Japanese men cooked on a hibachi while they floated. A Swiss adventurer paddled while his partner read a book. An Englishman, oblivious to rocks and whirlpools, stretched out in the bottom of his canoe and, using his gear as a pillow, closed his eyes. He wasn't at all concerned about when he might reach Dawson City. "I'll get there when I get there," he said calmly as we paddled past.

The Yukon was much more hectic in 1898-99, when 50,000 people and more than 7,000 boats hustled along this same waterway bound for Dawson City with dreams of making it rich in the gold-bearing creeks of the Klondike.

And the river was still busy the first half of the 20th century, when some 250 sternwheelers carried mail, freight and passengers to Dawson City, then the capital of the Yukon. Trading posts, roadhouses, stables, wood-cutting camps and tiny communities proliferated along the banks of this busy marine highway.

But by the 1950s, roads had become the preferred routes for travel through the Yukon. Log cabins collapsed, boats were wrecked or buried in silt, the Bush closed in and the river reverted to its peaceful pre-Gold Rush condition. Today, you have to search to find many of the abandoned places noted on Yukon River maps. At Yukon Crossing, for example, the log barn, stables and roadhouse were partly collapsed but still standing. At Merrice Creek, the roof of one cabin had caved in, but the moss, grass and fir trees growing from the remains were picturesque.

One place on the river where paddlers can still experience the Yukon's history is

Travelers from all over the world paddle the Yukon River. (© Lyn Hancock)

Fort Selkirk, at the confluence of the Yukon and the Pelly rivers. The fort site dates back to Robert Campbell, but the last residents left in 1950, with the exception of Danny and Abby Roberts. One of the highlights of my trip was chatting with Danny Roberts at Fort Selkirk. Born there in 1924, Danny had worked as a hunter, trapper, deckhand and woodcutter for the paddlewheel boats. I also visited the colorful grave sites of past settlers (where a grizzly bear with cubs had terrorized tourists just days before).

Ancient Voices Wilderness Camp, 4 hours upstream from Dawson City, was another highlight on my trip. An aboriginal flag on an island in the river intrigued us. I sprinted up the bank to find a grassy clearing, moose meat hanging over a smoking fire, a couple of moss- and grass-roofed log cabins and a warm welcome from one of the 4 people who run the camp. She told me the retreat teaches people to live in harmony with each other and the earth. What better place to learn these skills than on the Yukon River, where travelers experience wilderness and the simple romance of the past?

And paddling the river is the best way to relive this romantic history.

For more information, contact Nahanni River Adventures, P.O. Box 31203 Whitehorse, YT Y1A 5P7; phone (867) 668-3180; info@nahanni.com; www.nahanni.com.

For information on heritage sites along the river, contact the Yukon government Heritage Branch in Whitehorse at 1-800-661-0408.

A writer, photographer, lecturer and travel consultant, Lyn Hancock has lived and traveled throughout the North. She is the author of several books, including "There's a Seal in My Sleeping Bag."

Yukon Game Farm Wildlife Preserve. Take the opportunity to view and photograph North American wildlife species in a natural setting. See Dall sheep, Stone sheep, bighorn sheep, mountain goats, musk-oxen, wood bison, moose, caribou, elk and mule deer, as well as numerous species of birds. Located at Mile 5 (Km 8) Takhini Hot Springs Road. Guided tours only. Phone (867) 633-2922; Fax (867) 633-2425; email gamefarm@polarcom.com; web site www.yukongamefarm.com. Tours departing daily at location. For downtown departures, contact Grayline of Yukon in the Westmark Hotel; phone (867) 668-3225. [ADVERTISEMENT]

North West Mounted Police Patrol Cabin. This re-creation of an early NWMP Patrol Cabin was built in 1995 as part of the 100th anniversary of the RCMP. It is located next to the RCMP building at 4th Avenue and Elliott. Whitehorse became the territorial headquarters of the NWMP in 1900. The NWMP were bestowed the title "Royal" in 1904, and in 1920 became the Royal Canadian Mounted Police. The Patrol Cabin is dedicated each year to a famous figure in NWMP history. The NWMP Patrol Cabin Society sponsors the Red Serge Student program and Horse & Rider program in Whitehorse. The distinctive red serge of the RCMP is now worn only at formal occasions or for special programs. The red cloth tunic was first worn by the NWMP in 1897.

Day trips from Whitehorse. Marsh Lake, 24 miles/39 km south of Whitehorse on the Alaska Highway, and Takhini Hot Springs Road, 17 miles/27 km north of town via the Alaska and Klondike highways, are within easy driving distance of Whitehorse.

Drive south on the Alaska Highway to turnoff for Marsh Lake Yukon Government Recreation Site, a scenic 30-minute drive

from Whitehorse city centre. The recreation area offers an excellent day-use area and campground at Army Beach on Marsh Lake. In the winter, trails originating from this recreation site are used for cross-country skiing and snowmobiling. In spring, this is a popular swan migration viewing area. Swan Haven Interpretive Centre (turnoff at **Milepost DC 861.3**), overlooking M'Clintock Bay, is staffed from early April to mid-May, when thousands of migrating tundra and trumpeter swans stop over here. The annual Celebration of Swans is held at the centre the third week of April.

Go north on the Alaska Highway to **Milepost DC 894.8** and turn off onto Klondike Highway 2 (the road to Dawson City) and drive just 3.8 miles/6.1 km from the junction to reach Takhini Hot Springs Road and access to both Takhini Hot Springs Resort (swimming, horseback riding, camping) and Yukon game Farm, a wildlife preserve. See the KLONDIKE LOOP section for more information on attractions along the North Klondike Highway.

Longer trips (which you may want to extend to an overnight) are to Atlin, about 2½ hours by car, and Skagway, 3 hours by car. Skagway is an old gold rush town and port of call for both the Alaska state ferries and cruise ships. Skagway is also home to the famed White Pass & Yukon Route Railway, said to be the most scenic railway in the world as it climbs through beautiful mountain terrain to White Pass summit. Book ahead for the trip. Complete your Skagway visit with a trip to Dyea, a short drive from downtown, to see the start of the Chilkoot Trail and a gold rush graveyard.

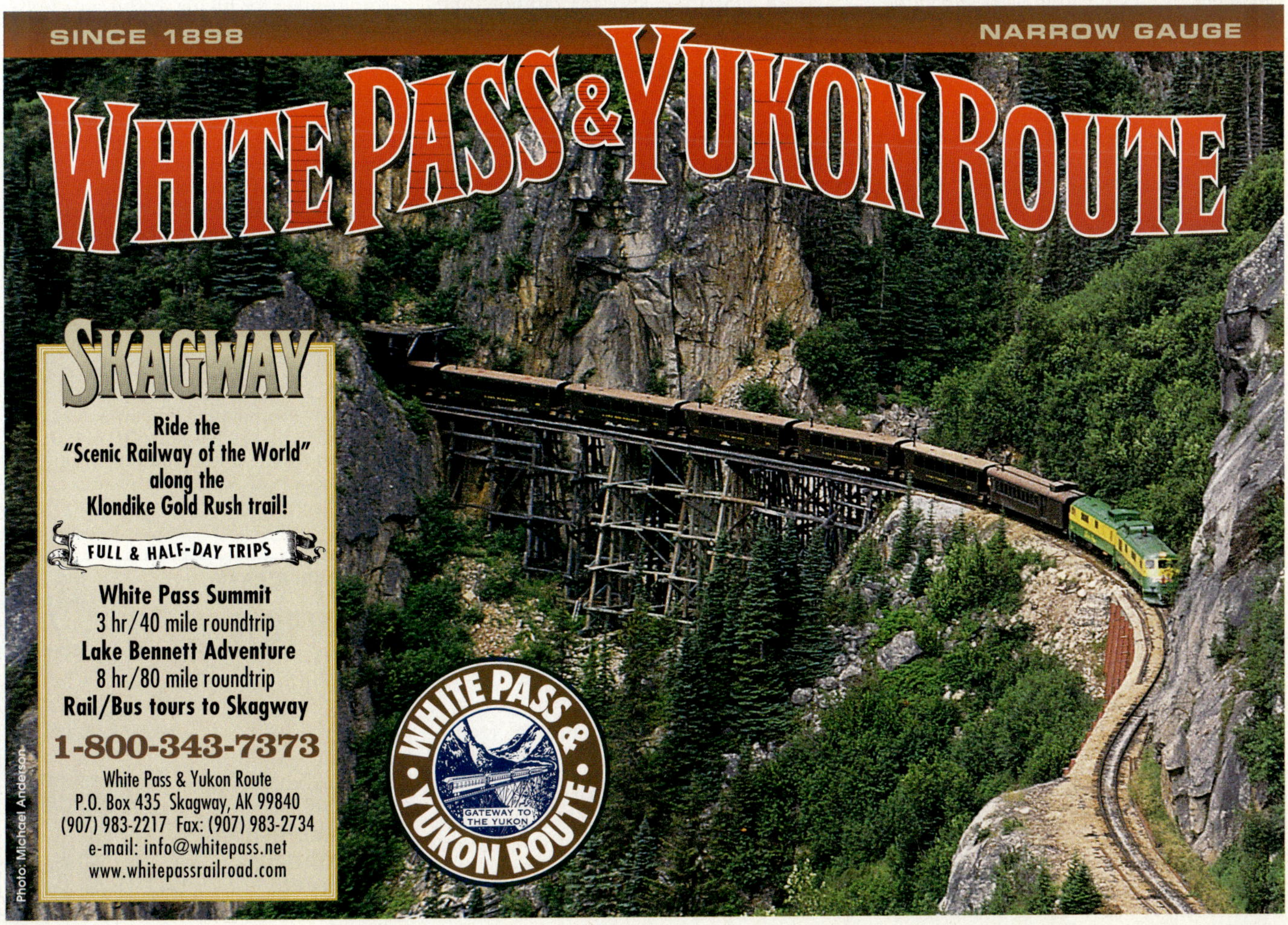

Atlin, which also dates from 1898, is known for its spectacular scenery. Visitors heading for Skagway should call ahead for accommodations if they expect to overnight. You may make a circle tour, driving down to Skagway then turning off onto the Tagish Road on your way back and continuing on to Atlin via the Atlin Road (see SOUTH KLONDIKE, ATLIN ROAD and TAGISH ROAD sections for logs).

Chadburn Lake Recreation Area is accessed via a gravel side road just before reaching the Whitehorse Rapids and Fish Ladder at the end of Nisutlin Drive. Several small lakes with trails, picnic sites and boat launches make up the recreation area. Bird watching for yellow warblers, ruby-crowned kinglets, Northern waterthrush and Swainson's thrush.

Rockhounding and Mining. A wide variety of minerals can be found in the Whitehorse area. Sources of information for rock hounds and gold panners include the Yukon Rock Shop, at the junction of the Alaska Highway and Klondike Highway 2 (Carcross Road), which has mineral samples, gold pans and nuggets, and Murdoch's gem shop on Main Street, which displays gold nugget jewellery and gold rush artifacts and photos.

The following rockhounding location was suggested by the late Fred Dorward of the Whitehorse Gem & Mineral Club. Drive north on the Alaska Highway to the Fish Lake Road turnoff (**Milepost DC 889.4**), located 2 miles/3.2 km from the north entrance to Whitehorse. About 0.5 mile/0.8 km in on Fish Lake Road, park and walk across McIntyre Creek to the old Copper King mine workings. Excellent but small specimens of brown garnet, also serpentine. IMPORTANT: Rock hounds should exercise extreme caution when exploring. Do not enter old mine workings. Please respect No Trespassing signs.

Canoe, Raft or Boat the Yukon River. Boat tours are offered of the Yukon River and scenic Miles Canyon. Inquire locally for tour operators. Miles Canyon is accessible by road: take Schwatka Lake Road off Robert Service Way (South Access Road) into Whitehorse, or turn off the Alaska Highway (see **Milepost DC 881.7**); follow signs.

Canoe rentals by the day, week or month, and guide services are available in Whitehorse. From Whitehorse to Dawson City it is 467 miles/752 km by river and can take from 14 to 21 days to travel. There is a boat launch at Rotary Peace Park, behind the Yukon Government Bldg. You may also launch at Deep Creek Campground on Lake Laberge. See also "Paddling the Yukon River from Whitehorse to Dawson City" feature this section.

Hike the Chilkoot Trail. The 33-mile/53-km trail begins near Skagway, AK, and climbs Chilkoot Pass (elev. 3,739 feet/1,140m) to Lake Bennett, following the historic route of the gold seekers of 1897–98. Check with Parks Canada, in the Federal Building at 4th and Main, for information on permits, fees, customs, regulations and reservations. Or phone (867) 667-3910 or 1-800-661-0486. On the Internet, visit www.nps.gov/klgo/chilkoot.htm; you may link to the Parks Canada web site from this site for current Chilkoot Trail fees and permit information on the Canadian portion of the trail.

Sportsmen can obtain complete information on fishing and hunting in the Whitehorse area by writing Tourism Yukon, Box 2703, Whitehorse, YT Y1A 2C6. They will provide lists of guides and advise what licenses are required.

AREA FISHING: Fish for rainbow and coho salmon in the following lakes: **Hidden, Scout, Long, Jackson** and **McLean**. Inquire locally for directions. Nearby fly-in fishing lakes are accessible by charter plane; see advertisements in this section. **Yukon River**, fish for grayling below the dam and bridge. Fishing below the dam prohibited in August during the salmon run.

Sled-dog adventures are a highlight at Frank Turner's Muktuk Kennels on the Takhini River. (© Earl L. Brown, staff)

Alaska Highway Log
(continued from page 152)
Distance from Dawson Creek (DC)* is followed by distance from Delta Junction (DJ). Original mileposts are indicated in the text as Historical Mile.
*In the Canada portion of *The MILEPOST*® Alaska Highway log, mileages from Dawson Creek are based on actual driving distance and kilometres are based on physical kilometreposts. (Mileages from Delta Junction are based on actual driving distance, followed by the metric conversion.) See "Mileposts and Kilometreposts" in the introduction beginning on page 98 for more details.

YUKON HIGHWAY 1 WEST
DC 887.4 (1425.3 km) DJ 502.6 (808.8 km) First exit southbound for Whitehorse. North access road to Whitehorse (exit east) is via Two-Mile Hill and 4th Avenue.

DC 888.5 (1426.9 km) DJ 501.5 (807.1 km) **Historical Mile 918.3**. Gas, store, food.

DC 889.1 (1428 km) DJ 500.7 (805.8 km) McIntyre Creek.

DC 889.4 (1428.2 km) DJ 500.6 (805.6 km) Fish Lake Road to west. Located only 9.3 miles/15 km from Whitehorse, Fish Lake and adjacent Bonneville Lakes were the site of a Kwanlin Dun First Nations archaeology project documenting the long history of habitation in this area.

DC 890.1 (1429.3 km) DJ 499.9 (804.5 km) Rabbit's Foot Canyon.

DC 890.5 (1430 km) DJ 499.5 (803.8 km) Turnoff to Porter Creek to east.

DC 891 (1430.7 km) DJ 499 (803 km) Porter Creek grocery.

DC 891.3 (1431.3 km) DJ 498.7 (802.6 km) **Historical Mile 921**, laundromat, gas and other businesses.

DC 891.5 (1431.6 km) DJ 498.5 (802.2 km) Porter Creek Centre to east on Clyde Wann Road; convenience store. Access to Porter Creek subdivision, a residential suburb of Whitehorse. Also access to Range Road and Mountain View golf course (18 holes).

DC 891.6 (1431.8 km) DJ 498.4 (802 km) **Historical Mile 922**. Truck stop with food, gas, diesel and lodging.

DC 891.9 (1432.5 km) DJ 498.1 (801.6 km) **Historical Mile 922.5**. Azure Road. Access to **MacKenzie's RV Park**. ▲

DC 894.3 (1434.9 km) DJ 495.7 (797.7 km) Turnoff east to Cousins dirt airstrip.

DC 894.5 (1436.5 km) DJ 495.5 (797.4 km) Rest area to west with litter barrels, outhouses, information sign and pay phone.

DC 894.8 (1437.1 km) DJ 495.2 (796.9 km) For Alaska-bound travelers, the highway now swings west. Turn off to north on Klondike Highway 2 for Takhini Hot Springs (swimming, camping) and Yukon Game Farm, 3.8 miles/6.1 km north. ▲

Junction with Klondike Highway 2 to Dawson City. See KLONDIKE LOOP section page 253 for log of that route.

DC 895.5 (1438.2 km) DJ 494.5 (795.8 km) Turnoff to south for Haeckel Hill. Not recommended for hiking as this area is used for target practice.

DC 897.7 (1440.9 km) DJ 510.3 (821.2 km) Whitehorse city limits.

DC 898.8 (1442.3 km) DJ 491.2 (790.5 km) Yukon Quest dog musher Frank Turner's kennels; tours. Cabin accommodations.

Muktuk Kennels and Cabins. For an authentic adventure with champion huskies, visit Frank Turner, 1995 Yukon Quest Champion, the only musher to enter all 20 Yukon Quests. Cabins open all year. Summer kennel tours, fall training runs, winter adventure tours with sled dogs. Great camping, hiking, swimming and canoeing in summer. Share our lifestyle at our beautiful ranch on the Takhini River. Phone (867) 668-DOGS(3647); fax (867) 633-4200. Email: arabbit@knet.ca. Web site: www.muktuk.com. [ADVERTISEMENT]

DC 899.1 (1443.4 km) DJ 490.9 (790 km) Turnoff for 3-mile/4.8-km loop drive on old section of Alaska Highway. Access to stocked lake.

DC 901.6 (1447.3 km) DJ 488.4 (786 km) Turnoff to north to sled dog track.

DC 905.4 (1454.1 km) DJ 484.6 (779.9 km) **Historic Milepost 937.** Camera viewpoint turnout to north with point of interest sign about the old Dawson Trail. There were at least 50 stopping places along the old Dawson Trail winter stagecoach route between Whitehorse and Dawson City, and from 1 to 3 roadhouses at each stop. At this point, the stagecoach route crossed the Takhini River. This route was discontinued in 1950 when the Mayo–Dawson Road (now Klondike Highway 2) was constructed.

DC 908.7 (1459.3 km) DJ 481.3 (774.5 km) Private farm and windmill; good example of Yukon agriculture. Facilities for overnighting large livestock.

DC 909.4 (1460.4 km) DJ 480.6 (773.4 km) **Historical Mile 941. Wolf Ridge B&B Log Cabin Rentals.** Relax and enjoy Northern hospitality in our cozy log cabins! A 30-minute drive from Whitehorse brings you to our peaceful, scenic property. You have your

Aerial view of the Alaska Highway and Takhini River north of Whitehorse.
(© Earl L. Brown, staff)

choice of a delicious prepared breakfast in our lodge or fix your own meals in the equipped cabins. Showers available. We are open year-round. Phone (867) 456-4101; email info@wolfridge-cabins.com; web site www.wolf-ridge.com. P.O. Box 20729, Whitehorse, YT Y1A 7A2. [ADVERTISEMENT]

DC 914 (1467.9 km) DJ 476 (766 km) **Takhini Salt Flats**, a series of bowl-shaped depressions where salts form on the surface as water brought up from underground springs evaporates. Although alkaline flats are not uncommon in the Yukon, this one is notable for the size of its salt crystals as well as the variety of salt-loving plants that thrive here, such as the distinctive red sea asparagus.

DC 914.7 (1468.9 km) DJ 475.3 (764.9 km) **Takhini River** bridge. According to R. Coutts in *Yukon: Places & Names*, the name Takhini derives from the Tagish Indian *tahk*, meaning mosquito, and *heena*, meaning river.

DC 922.7 (1479 km) DJ 467.3 (752 km) *CAUTION: Watch for horses and other livestock grazing on open range near highway.*

DC 923.9 (1481 km) DJ 466.1 (750 km) Annie Ned Creek.

DC 924.5 (1484.9 km) DJ 465.5 (749.1 km) Stoney Creek.

DC 924.7 (1485.2 km) DJ 465.3 (748.8 km) View of Mount Bratnober, elev. 6,313 feet/1,924m. According to R. Coutts in *Yukon: Places & Names*, the mountain was named in 1897 by J.J. McArthur, Canadian government surveyor, for Henry Bratnober, who along with Jack Dalton was assisting in a cursory survey of the Dalton Trail.

DC 926 (1487 km) DJ 464 (746.7 km) **Takhini River Valley Viewpoint.** Turnout to south with litter barrels and viewing platform with information panels on wildlife found in the Takhini River Valley. Point of interest sign about 1958 Takhini Burn. More than 1.5 million acres/629,058 hectares of Yukon forest lands were burned in 1958. Campfires were responsible for most of these fires.

Watch for free-ranging elk often seen near the highway here. Introduced in 1951–1954 from Elk Island National Park, the elk moved into this area following the 1958 burn. The elk population numbers around 60 animals (1999 count).

DC 927.3 (1489.2 km) DJ 462.7 (744.6 km) Turnoff to south for **Kusawa Lake** access road, a narrow, winding gravel side road that leads 15 miles;/24 km to the lake. The road is slippery when wet and not recommended for large RVs or trailers. At Mile 1.9/3 km on Kusawa Lake Road there is a viewpoint at Mendenhall Landing, which was a freight transfer point in the early 1900s for goods shipped up the Yukon and Takhini rivers. From the landing, goods were loaded onto wagons headed for Kluane mining operations. At Mile 9/15 km on the side road is Takhini River Yukon government campground, with 13 sites. Kusawa Lake Yukon government campground at end of road at north end of lake has 48 sites, kitchen shelter, firepits and drinking water. Camping permit ($12). Fishing for lake trout to 20 lbs., good to excellent; also grayling and pike.

Kusawa Lake (formerly Arkell Lake), located in the Coast Mountains, is 45 miles/72 km long and averages 2 miles/3.2 km wide, with a shoreline perimeter of 125 miles/200 km. An access road to the lake was first constructed by the U.S. Army in 1945 to obtain bridge timbers for Alaska Highway construction.

DC 931.5 (1495.8 km) DJ 458.5 (737.8 km) **Mendenhall Malamute Bed & Breakfast.** Open year-round. A rustic but comfortable atmosphere that offers you unique hospitality. Cabins, teepee, or walltent accommodations with central shower facilities in a wilderness setting. In addition there is hiking, biking, canoeing and spectacular view. Full gourmet breakfast prepared by a Swiss chef, other great meals by arrangements. Reservations welcome. Phone (867) 668-7275 (leave message); P.O. Box 20623, Whitehorse, Yukon Y1A 7A2; Email: malamute@yknet.ca; http://myhome.yknet.ca/malamutebandb. [ADVERTISEMENT]

DC 935.9 (1502.2 km) DJ 454.1 (730.8 km) End of 911 access area northbound.

DC 936.8 (1503.7 km) DJ 453.2 (729.3 km) Mendenhall River culvert. A tributary of the Takhini River, the Mendenhall River—like the Mendenhall Glacier outside Juneau, AK—was named for Thomas Corwin Mendenhall (1841–1924), superintendent of the U.S. Coast & Geodetic Survey.

DC 937.2 (1504.4 km) DJ 452.8 (728.7 km) *NOTE: Begin new (2002) Champagne Bypass route northbound.* Completion of this 8.6-mile/13.9-km stretch of new highway in 2002 reroutes the Alaska Highway around **CHAMPAGNE, Historical Mile 974** on the Alaska Highway.

Originally a camping spot on the Dalton Trail to Dawson City, established by Jack Dalton in the late 1800s, a roadhouse and trading post were built at Champagne in 1902 by Harlow "Shorty" Chambers. It became a supply centre for first the Bullion Creek rush and later the Burwash Creek gold rush in 1904. The origin of the name is uncertain, although one account is that Dalton's men—after successfully negotiating a herd of cattle through the first part of the trail—celebrated here with a bottle of French champagne. Today, it is home to members of the Champagne–Aishihik Indian Band.

DC 945.8 (1518.3 km) DJ 444.2 (714.8 km) *SOUTHBOUND TRAVELERS NOTE: Begin new (2002) Champagne Bypass route next 8.6 miles/13.9 km. Begin recalibrated kilometreposts south to YT–BC border.*

NORTHBOUND TRAVELERS NOTE: Recalibrated kilometreposts end with Kmpost 1518. The next kilometrepost northbound is Kmpost 1576, 1.5 miles/2.4 kms from Kmpost 1518, resulting in a 56 kilometre discrepancy in the signage.

DC 955.8 (1588 km) DJ 434.2 (698.7 km) First glimpse northbound of Kluane Range.

DC 957 (1590 km) DJ 433 (696.8 km) **Historic Milepost 987.** Cracker Creek. Former roadhouse site on old stagecoach trail. Watch for **Old Man Mountain** on right northbound (the rocky crags look like a face, particularly in evening light).

DC 964.6 (1602.2 km) DJ 425.4 (684.6

Otter Falls, once pictured on the Canadian $5 bill, is at Mile 17.6 Aishihik Road. (© Earl L. Brown, staff)

km) **Historical Mile 995. Otter Falls Cutoff, junction** with Aishihik Road. Gas station, store, motel and campground with dump station to south, Bird-watching trails. Aishihik Road turnoff to north (description follows). ▲

Otter Falls Cutoff. See display ad this section. ▲

Aishihik Road leads north 26.1 miles/ 42.2 km to Aishihik Lake campground and 84 miles/135 km to the old Indian village of Aishihik (AYSH-ee-ak, means high place). This is a narrow, winding gravel road, maintained for summer travel only to the government campground at the lake. There are some steep hills and single-lane bridges. Aishihik Road is not recommended for large RVs and trailers. It is a scenic drive, and visitors have a good chance of seeing bison.

CAUTION: Watch for bison. Bears in area.

At Mile 17.6/28.4 km is the **Otter Falls** viewpoint and day-use area with outhouse and information panels. Otter Falls was once pictured on the back of the Canadian $5 bill, but in 1975 the Aishihik Power Plant diverted water from the falls. The 32-megawatt dam was built by Northern Canada Power Commission to supply power principally to the mining industry. Some water is still released over the falls during the summer. Flow hours for Otter Falls are given at the start of Aishihik Road. An interpretive sign here describes the reintroduction of the wood bison.

At Mile 26.1/42.2 km is the turnoff for Aishihik Lake Yukon government campground, located at the south end of the lake; 13 sites, drinking water, picnic tables, firepits, kitchen shelter, boat launch and playground. Camping permit ($12). ▲

Aishihik Lake, fishing for lake trout and grayling. As with most large Yukon lakes, ice is not out until late June. Low water levels may make boat launching difficult. *WARNING: Winds can come up suddenly on this lake.*
Pole Cat Lake, just before the Aishihik weather station; fishing for pike.

DC 965.6 (1603.8 km) DJ 424.4 (683 km) **Historic Milepost 996.** Turnoff to north at east end of Aishihik River for **Canyon Creek Bridge** viewpoint; outhouses.

The original bridge was built about 1920 by the Jacquot brothers to move freight and passengers across the Aishihik River to Silver City on Kluane Lake, and from there by boat to Burwash Landing. The bridge was reconstructed in 1942 by Army Corps of Engineers during construction of the Alaska Highway. It was rebuilt again in 1987 by the Yukon government.

DC 965.7 (1604 km) DJ 424.3 (682.8 km) Aishihik River bridge.

DC 966.3 (1605 km) DJ 423.7 (618.9 km) View of impressive Kluane Range ice fields straight ahead northbound between Kilometreposts 1604 and 1616.

DC 974.9 (1619 km) DJ 415.1 (668 km) Turnout to south on Marshall Creek.

DC 977.1 (1622.4 km) DJ 421.9 (664.5 km) The rugged snowcapped peaks of the Kluane Icefield Ranges and the outer portion of the St. Elias Mountains are visible to the west, straight ahead northbound.

The Kluane National Park Icefield Ranges are Canada's highest and the world's largest nonpolar alpine ice field, forming the interior wilderness of the park. In clear weather, Mount Kennedy and Mount Hubbard, 2 peaks that are twice as high as the front ranges seen before you, are visible from here.

DC 979.3 (1626 km) DJ 410.7 (660.9 km) Between Kilometreposts 1626 and 1628, look for the NorthwesTel microwave repeater station on top of Paint Mountain. The station was installed with the aid of helicopters and supplied by the tramline also visible from here.

DC 980.8 (1628.4 km) DJ 409.2 (658.5 km) Turnoff to north for Yukon government **Pine Lake Recreation Park.** Day-use area with sandy beach, boat launch and dock, group firepits, drinking water and 7 tent sites near beach. The campground, adjacent Pine Lake with a view of the St. Elias Mountains, has 42 sites, outhouses, firewood, litter barrels, kitchen shelter, playground and drinking water. Camping permit ($12). Fishing is good for lake trout, northern pike and grayling. *CAUTION: Bears in area.* ▲

A short nature trail winds through the boreal forest from the beach to the campground. Panels along the trail interpret the lake's aquatic habitats and marl formations. The white sediment marl is a form of calcium carbonate, and the marl beds intensify the blue and green reflections of the lake on a sunny day. Forest dwellers to watch for on the trail include: gray jays, ruby-crowned kinglets, boreal chickadees and red squirrels.

A 3.5-mile/6-km walking and biking trail begins at the campground entrance and ends at Haines Junction.

DC 980.9 (1628.5 km) DJ 409.1 (658.4 km) Access road to floatplane dock.

DC 982.2 (1630.8 km) DJ 407.8 (656.3 km) Turnoff to north for Haines Junction airport. Flightseeing tours of glaciers, fly-in fishing and air charters available; fixed-wing aircraft or helicopters.

Private Aircraft: Haines Junction airstrip; elev. 2,150 feet/655m; length 5,500 feet/ 1,676m; gravel; fuel (100L).

Highway swings to south for last few miles into Haines Junction, offering a panoramic, close-up view of the Auriol Range straight ahead.

DC 982.3 (1631 km) DJ 407.7 (656.1 km) Turnout with information kiosk.

DC 984.1 (1633.9 km) DJ 405.9 (653.2 km) Welcome to Haines Junction sign northbound.

DC 984.8 (1635 km) DJ 405.2 (652.1 km) Northbound travelers turn right (southbound travelers turn left) on Kluane Street for Kluane National Park Visitor Centre.

DC 985 (1635.3 km) DJ 405 (651.8 km) **Historic Milepost 1016.** *IMPORTANT: THIS JUNCTION CAN BE CONFUSING; CHOOSE YOUR ROUTE CAREFULLY! Fairbanks- and Anchorage-bound travelers TURN NORTH at this junction for continuation of Alaska Highway (Yukon 1). Alaska Highway log continues on page 174.* (Haines-bound motorists note: It is a good idea fill up with gas in Haines Junction.)

Junction of Alaska Highway and Haines Highway (Haines Road). Head west on the Haines Highway (Yukon Highway 3) for port of Haines, AK. See HAINES HIGHWAY section.

OTTER FALLS CUTOFF
LOCATED 20 MILES EAST OF HAINES JCT AT KM 1602

FREE WILDLIFE MUSEUM

RV PARK • HOOKUPS
PULL THROUGHS • CARAVAN DISCOUNT

TENT SITES • LAUNDROMAT • SHOWERS • MOTEL
MODEM HOOKUP • PAY PHONE • DUMP STATION

GAS STATION • UNLEADED • DIESEL
CHEAPEST GAS FROM HERE TO ALASKA

CONVENIENCE STORE • GIFT SHOP • SOUVENIRS

WALKING TRAIL – A BIRDERS DELIGHT
GUIDED TRIPS TO OTTER FALLS

BOX 5450 HAINES JCT. YUKON Y0B1L0
TEL. 867-634-2812   FAX 867-634-2133

bbeecher@yknet.yk.ca

Haines Junction

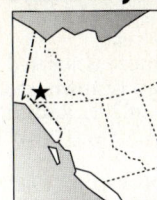

DC 985 (1635.3 km) DJ 405 (651.8 km) **Historic Milepost 1016**, at the **junction** of the Alaska Highway (Yukon Highway 1) and the Haines Highway (Yukon Highway 3, also known as the Haines Road). Driving distance to Whitehorse, 100 miles/161 km; YT–AK border, 205 miles/330 km; Tok, 296 miles/476 km; and Haines, 150.5 miles/242 km. **Population:** 811. **Elevation:** 1,956 feet/596m. **Emergency Services: RCMP**, phone (867) 634-5555 or (867) 667-5555 **Fire Department**, phone (867) 634-2222. **Nursing Centre**, phone (867) 634-4444.

Visitor Information: At the Yukon Government and **Kluane National Park Visitor Information Centre**, 0.2 mile/0.3 km east of the junction just off the Alaska Highway. Phone (867) 634-2345. Interpretive exhibits, displays and a 27-minute video presentation on Kluane National Park. No fee charged.

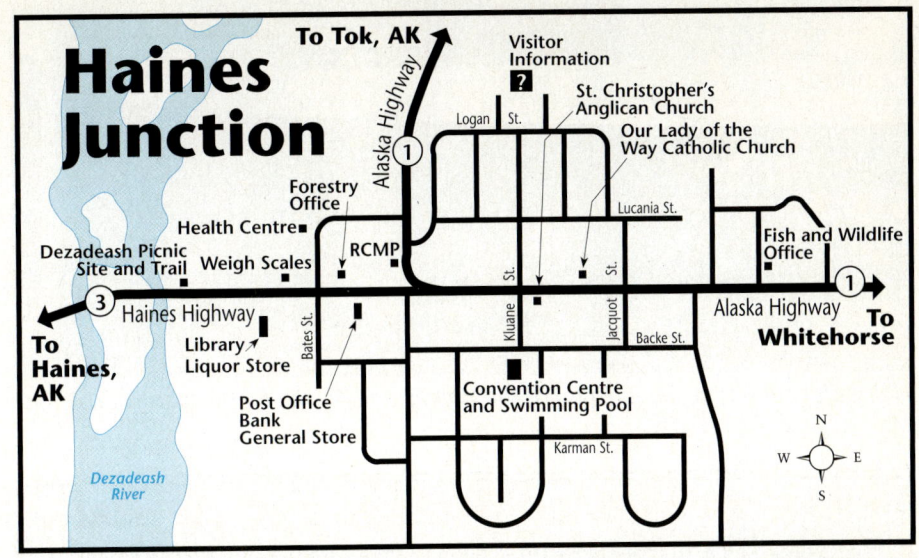

The Haines Road was built in 1943, connecting the Alaska Highway to tidewater.

Alcan Motor Inn
Newest Motel in Haines Junction

Panoramic view of the Majestic St. Elias Mountains in Kluane National Park.
At the junction of the Alaska & Haines Highways

- 19 Deluxe rooms with air conditioning
- 1 suite, 2 kitchenettes and Jacuzzi Room
- All rooms with private baths & shower
- Continental breakfast (seasonal)
- Fridges, hair dryers, microwaves, irons & in room coffee
- Satellite TV on 27" TV, 70+ channels
- Direct dial phones, multiple jacks w/data port
- Handicap accessible • Non-smoking rooms
- Pets welcome • Reasonable rates
- Laundromat • Sports Lounge • Conference Room
- Rooms available 24 hours, year round.   Winter plug ins

email: alcan@yknet.yk.ca
www.yukonweb.com/tourism/alcan

Box 5460 Haines Junction, Yukon Y0B 1L0

Toll Free Reservation 1-888-265-1018
(867) 634-2371   fax (867) 634-2833

Haines Junction is at the junction of the Haines and Alaska highways. (© Kris Graef, staff)

The centre is open 8 A.M. to 8 P.M. daily from May to September; 10 A.M. to 4 P.M., Monday through Friday, the rest of the year.

Private Aircraft: The airport is located on the Alaska Highway just east of town; see description at **Milepost DC 982.2. Radio:** CBC North at 106.1 FM; 103.5 FM; CKRW 98.7 FM; CHON 90.5 FM.

Haines Junction was established in 1942 during construction of the Alaska Highway. The first buildings here were Army barracks for the U.S. Army Corps of Engineers. The engineers were to build a new branch road connecting the Alaska Highway with the port of Haines on Lynn Canal. The branch road—today's Haines Highway— was completed in 1943.

Haines Junction is still an important stop for travelers on the Alaska and Haines highways. Services are located along both highways, and clustered around Village

HAINES JUNCTION ADVERTISERS

Alcan Motor Inn	Ph. (867) 634-2371
Fas Gas Service Station and RV Park	Ph. (867) 634-2505
Frosty Freeze	Ph. (867) 634-2674
Kluane Park Inn	Ph. (867) 634-2261
Kluane R.V. Kampground	Ph. (867) 634-2709
Madley's General Store	Ph. (867) 634-2200
Raven, The	Ph. (867) 634-2500
Source Motors Ltd.	Ph. (867) 634-2268
Stardust Motel	Ph. (867) 634-2591
Village Bakery	Ph. (867) 634-2867
Village of Haines Junction	Ph. (867) 634-7100

enjoy your visit to VILLAGE OF HAINES JUNCTION
"GATEWAY TO KLUANE"

World Class Adventure & Spectacular Scenery

KLUANE NATIONAL PARK VISITOR INFORMATION CENTRE

HIKING * FISHING * RAFTING * FLIGHTSEEING
CYCLING * GUIDED WALKS * MUSIC FESTIVAL
...AND MORE!

Bring your camera for the wildlife & wildflowers

Travel the scenic Alaska & Haines highways

A FULL SERVICE COMMUNITY
WITH GREAT PLACES TO STAY AND DINE
CAMPGROUNDS * HOTELS * MOTELS * BAKERY
BED & BREAKFASTS * CONVENTION CENTRE

VILLAGE OF HAINES JUNCTION
Box 5339, Haines Junction, Y0B 1L0   ph. 867.634.7100   fax. 867.634.2008
email: vhj@yknet.ca   website: www.hainesjunctionyukon.com

EXPERIENCE NATURE AT ITS BEST

Square at the junction, where the 24-foot **Village Monument** depicts area wildlife.

Haines Junction is on the eastern boundary of Kluane (pronounced kloo-WA-nee) National Park and Reserve. The park was first suggested in 1942, and in 1943 land was set aside and designated the Kluane Game Sanctuary. A formal park region was established in 1972 and the national park and reserve boundaries were official in 1976. In 1980, Kluane National Park Reserve, along with Wrangell–St. Elias National Park in Alaska, became a joint UNESCO World Heritage Site. Kluane National Park and Reserve encompasses extensive ice fields, mountains and wilderness, and has become a world-class wilderness destination among outdoor recreation enthusiasts.

Lodging & Services

Haines Junction offers an excellent range of accommodations and also has a convention centre. Visitor services include motels, 2 bed and breakfasts, restaurants, gas stations, garage services, groceries, souvenirs and a bakery. Gourmet dining at The Raven. There is a full-facility indoor heated swimming pool with showers available; open daily from May to late-August, fee charged. Also here are a RCMP office, Lands and Forest District Office and health centre. The post office and bank are located in Madley's General Store. (Banking service weekday afternoons; extended hours on Fridays.) Internet access

available at Village Bakery.

The St. Elias Convention Center houses a 3,000-square-foot Grand Hall and offers a food service area. The Commissioner James Smith Administration Building, at Kilometre 255.6 Haines Road, 0.2 mile/0.3 km south from the Alaska Highway junction, contains the government liquor store and public library.

Camping

RV camping available at several campgrounds in and near town; see advertisements this section. Dump stations and water are also available at local service station and campgrounds. Yukon government campground located 4.2 miles/6.7 km east of junction on the Alaska Highway at Pine Lake. Kluane National Park has one campground, Kathleen Lake, located 16 miles/27 km south of town on the Haines Highway.

Attractions

Kluane National Park Visitor Centre, open 8 A.M. to 8 P.M. daily in summer, has information on the park and natural history exhibits. Video presentations include the 50-minute feature "Staying Safe in Bear Country." Check at the centre for details on the park's numerous hiking trails and for a schedule of guided hikes, walks and campfire talks. (Hikers note: There is mandatory registration for overnight trips into the park. Nightly or annual wilderness permits may be purchased. Bear resistant food canisters are mandatory on some overnight hikes; a $150 deposit is required.) Interpretive programs are available daily from the third week in June through August; fee charged. Contact Kluane National Park at Box 5495, Haines Junction, YT Y0B 1L0, or phone (867) 634-7207, fax (867) 634-7208.

Flightseeing Kluane National Park by fixed-wing aircraft or helicopter from Haines Junction is a popular way to see the spectacular mountain scenery. Check with charter services at the airport.

Tatshenshini–Alsek Wilderness Park. Created in 1993, the park protects the magnificent Tatshenshini and Alsek rivers area in Canada, where the 2 rivers join and flow (as the Alsek) to the Gulf of Alaska at Dry Bay. Known to river runners as "the Tat," the Tatshenshini is famous for its whitewater rafting, stunning scenery and wildlife. Due to a dramatic increase in river traffic in recent years, permits are required

Our Lady of the Way Catholic Mission was built in 1954. (© Kris Graef, staff)

from the park agencies (the National Park Service in Alaska and B.C. Parks in Canada). For more information about the park, contact BC Parks, Tatshenshini Office, Box 5544, Haines Junction, YT Y0B 1L0; phone (867) 634-7043, fax (867) 634-7208.

The **Dezadeash River** offers a relaxed rafting experience. Picnicking and hiking trail are available at a day-use area on the river at the west edge of town on the Haines Highway.

Our Lady of the Way Catholic Mission

FROSTY FREEZE
PIZZA • BURGERS • FRIES
SOFT ICE CREAM
PICK-UP (867) 634-2674 **TAKE-OUT**
BED & BREAKFAST
PHONE/FAX
(867) 634-2850
Box 5472, Haines Junction, Yukon Y0B 1L0

ALASKA HIGHWAY • Haines Junction

Haines Junction, Yukon
"Gateway to Kluane"

Haines Junction is the ideal base for adventure travel in Kluane National Park & Tatshenshini-Alsek Park. You can go flightseeing, river rafting, mountain biking, horseback riding, llama trekking, hiking, fishing and hunting! Or bring your business and social gatherings to the new St. Elias Convention Centre, overlooking spectacular mountains and glaciers. There is something for everyone in Haines Junction. Join us for these special events in 2003:

June 13, 14, 15   Alsek Music Festival
A showcase of Northern Talent, Under the St. Elias Mountains.   634-2520

Saturday, June 21   Kluane to Chilkat International Bike Relay
On a team of eight, four, or two, cycle one of the most scenic mountain passes in the world. In 2000 over 1100 riders participated!   633-2579

Late June - August   Kluane National Park Interpretive Programs Begin
Join the experienced park staff for campfire talks and guided hikes.
634-7207

Tuesday, July 1   Canada Day
Celebrate Canada's 136th Birthday Haines Junction Style   634-7100

For more information about **Haines Junction** *contact: Village of Haines Junction, Box 5339, Haines Junction, YT Y0B 1L0*
867-634-7100 or Fax 867-634-2008
Email: vhj@yknet.ca
www.hainesjunctionyukon.com

Canada is on the metric system.

MADLEY'S GENERAL STORE
We've got it all!

- GROCERIES
- FRESH MEAT
- PRODUCE & DAIRY
- CUBE AND BLOCK ICE
- HARDWARE & FISHING TACKLE
- CAMPING AND RV SUPPLIES
- FULL IN STORE BAKERY

MADLEY'S DELI & TAKE OUT
Enjoy our terrific deli sandwiches, or Chester Fried Chicken at our deli counter, or step outside and enjoy our picnic area with the best view in Haines Junction

Home of Madley's World Famous Smoked Salmon

POST OFFICE AND BANKING SERVICES   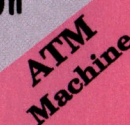 ATM Machine

BOX 5371, HAINES JCT, YUKON (867) 634-2200 Fax 634-2725

ALASKA
YOU'RE ONLY 208 MILES AWAY
BORDER CITY MOTEL & RV PARK
LOW U.S. PRICES   CURRENCY EXCHANGE   LOW U.S. PRICES
RV SITES (25 FT. BY 100 FT., WATER, ELECTRIC, SEWER DUMP, CABLE TV)
MOTEL (CLEAN, SPACIOUS, PRIVATE BATHROOMS, CABLE TV)
FACTORY OUTLET (T-SHIRTS, SWEATSHIRTS, DENIMS, JACKET, CAPS, GIFTS)
STOP, SHOP, SLEEP, EAT AND FUEL UP
AT THE FRIENDLIEST STOP ON THE ALASKA HIGHWAY
MOTEL & RV RESERVATIONS CALL (907) 774-2205

Kluane to Chilkat International Bike Relay participants on the Haines Highway.
(© Kris Graef, staff)

is a local landmark and visitor attraction. It was built in 1954, using parts from an old Army hut left from highway construction days.

Special events in Haines Junction include the Alsek Music Festival held June 13-15, 2003, and Canada Day (the anniversary of Canada's confederation), celebrated on July 1st with parades, barbecue and flags.

The Kluane to Chilkat International Bike Relay is scheduled for June 21, 2003. This event draws more than a thousand participants: *Watch for cyclists on the highway!*

Alaska Highway Log
(continued from page 168)

YUKON HIGHWAY 1 NORTH

Distance from Dawson Creek (DC)* is followed by distance from Delta Junction (DJ). Original mileposts are indicated in the text as Historical Mile.

*In the Canada portion of *The MILEPOST®* Alaska Highway log, mileages from Dawson Creek are based on actual driving distance and kilometres are based on physical kilometreposts. (Mileages from Delta Junction are based on actual driving distance, followed by the metric conversion.) See "Mileposts and Kilometreposts" in the introduction beginning on page 98 for more details.

DC 985 (1635.3 km) **F 503** (809.5 km) **Junction** of the Alaska Highway (Yukon Highway 1) and the Haines Highway (Yukon Highway 3).

NOTE: *This junction can be confusing; choose your route carefully!* Whitehorse-bound travelers turn east at junction for continuation of Alaska Highway (Yukon Highway 1). Turn west for the Haines Highway (Yukon Highway 3) to the port of Haines, AK, 152 miles/246 km from here.

See the HAINES HIGHWAY section for log of that route. (Haines-bound motorists note: It is a good idea to fill up with gas in Haines Junction.)

Northbound: From Haines Junction to the YT–AK border, the Alaska Highway is in fair to good condition. *Watch for road construction.* Distance marker indicates Destruction Bay 67 miles/108 km, Beaver Creek 186 miles/299 km.

Southbound: Good paved highway with wide shoulders next 380 miles/612 km (from here to Watson Lake) with the exception of some short sections of narrow road and occasional gravel breaks.

DC 985.3 (1635.9 km) **DJ 404.7** (651.3 km) **Kluane RV Kampground**; RV and tent

camping, gas, diesel, dump station, pay phone.

DC 985.8 (1636.5 km) **DJ 404.2** (650.2 km) **Historical Mile 1017. Source Motors**; gas, diesel, propane, auto repair, towing, snowmachine, ATV and watercraft rentals

---

SOURCE
MOTORS, LTD.

Haines Junction
Mile 1017

* Free Coffee *

GAS • DIESEL • PROPANE
AUTO & TIRE REPAIR
WELDING • TOWING
ROADSIDE REPAIR
SERVICE

Free Water Fill-up
Free Overnight Parking With Fill-Up

Snowmachine, Watercraft & A.T.V.
Sales, Rentals & Repairs

Thomas & Lynn Eckervogt
Box 5377
Haines Junction, Yukon
Y0B 1L0

Phone (867) 634-2268
FAX (867) 634-2338

"Wir Sprechen Deutsch"

LOCATED NEXT TO THE KLUANE VISITOR CENTRE
(Turn at Raven Hotel)

FRESH "SCRATCH" BAKING DAILY • BREAD-PASTRY-MUFFINS
SOURDOUGH PIZZA • DELI SANDWICHES & SOUP • REFRESHMENTS •
ICE CREAM • ESPRESSO • ICE • SPANAKOPITA...& MORE!
HOT & COLD SMOKED SALMON FRESH DAILY
OUTDOOR SEATING & COZY FIREPLACE HEATED SHELTER
LICENSED FOR BEER & WINE
PUBLIC WASHROOMS • PAY PHONE • OPEN 7:00 AM-9:00 PM

SOURDOUGH IS OUR SPECIALTY!
ASK ABOUT OUR SALMON BBQ AND LIVE MUSIC NIGHTS.

PHONE (867) 634-BUNS

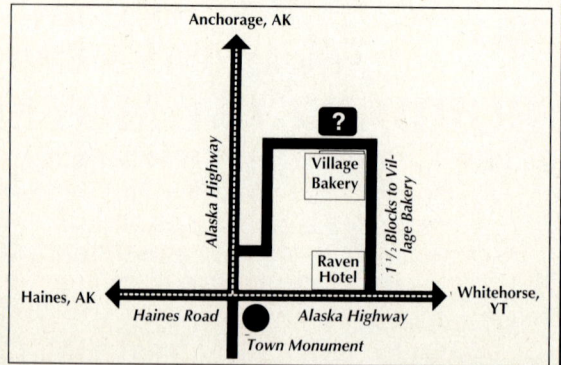

and repairs. Open daily, year-round.

DC 985.9 (1636.7 km) DJ 404.1 (650.3 km) **Stardust Motel** and service station.

DC 986.6 (1637.8 km) DJ 403.4 (649.2 km) Highway follows the Kluane Ranges which are to the west.

DC 987.8 (1639.8 km) DJ 402.2 (647.3 km) **Historical Mile 1019.** Kluane National Park warden headquarters. (Visitor information in Haines Junction at the visitor centre.)

DC 988.3 (1640.6 km) DJ 401.7 (646.4 km) Rest area to west with pit toilets.

DC 991.4 (1645.6 km) DJ 398.6 (641.5 km) Highway climbs next 9 miles/14.5 km northbound to Bear Creek Summit.

DC 991.6 (1646 km) DJ 398.4 (641.1 km) **Historic Milepost 1022**, Mackintosh Trading Post historic sign. **Bear Creek Lodge** to east; food, gas, lodging and camping. Corral for overnighting horses. Trailhead to west for Alsek Pass trail; 18 miles/29 km long, suitable for shorter day hikes, mountain bikes permitted. ▲

Bear Creek Lodge (Kluane). Welcome to our full service restaurant, offering great food and fast friendly service. (Coaches—please call ahead.) Off-sales available at our

Bears Den Lounge. Clean and comfortable motel rooms at reasonable rates. RV park with full and partial hookups, pull-through sites, tent sites, showers. Caravans welcome. Unleaded gas. Phone (867) 634-2301.
[ADVERTISEMENT]

DC 999 (1653.2 km) DJ 391 (629.2 km) Turnout with 1-mile/1.7-km **Spruce Beetle Interpretive Trail.** This easy loop interpretive trail examines the life of the spruce bark beetle and its effect on the forests of the area. Allow 35 to 45 minutes for walk. (The spruce beetle has also infested areas of Alaska, particularly around Anchorage and on the Kenai Peninsula.)

DC 1000.1 (1660 km) DJ 389.9 (627.5 km) **Bear Creek Summit** (elev. 3,294 feet/1,004m), highest point on the Alaska Highway between Whitehorse and Fairbanks.

Glimpse of Kloo Lake to north of highway between Kilometreposts 1660 and 1662.

DC 1003.5 (1665.4 km) DJ 386.5 (622 km) Jarvis River.

DC 1003.6 (1665.6 km) DJ 386.4 (621.8 km) **Historic Milepost 1035.** Turnout to west just north of crossing Jarvis River. Pretty spot for a picnic. Poor to fair fishing for grayling 8 to 16 inches all summer; Dolly Varden 8 to 10 inches, early summer. ◀

NOTE: Watch for road construction northbound between Kilometreposts 1674 and 1684 in summer 2003.

DC 1006 (1671 km) DJ 384 (238.6 km) Turnout to north at **Sulphur Lake**; canoeing, birdwatching. Thousands of birds use the lake, mostly in late summer, for moulting. Look for 2 bald eagle nests along shore. Wolf pack in area.

DC 1013.6 (1682 km) DJ 376.4 (605.7 km) Beautiful view to west of the snow-covered **Kluane Ranges**. The Alaska Highway parallels the Kluane Ranges from Haines Junction to Koidern, presenting a nearly unbroken chain of mountains to 8,000 feet/2,438m interrupted by only a few large valleys cut by glacier-fed rivers and streams. West of the Kluane Ranges is the Duke Depression, a narrow trough separating the Kluane Ranges from the St. Elias Mountains. Major peaks in the St. Elias (not visible from the highway) are: Mount Logan, Canada's highest peak, at 19,545 feet/5,959m; Mount St. Elias, 18,008 feet/5,489m; Mount Lucania, 17,147 feet/5,226m; King Peak, 16,971 feet/5,173m; and Mounts Wood, Vancouver, Hubbard and Steele, all over 15,000 feet/4,572m. Mount Steele (16,664 feet/5,079m) was named for Superintendent Sam Steele of the North West Mounted Police. As commanding officer of the NWMP in the Yukon in 1898, Steele established permanent detachments at the summits of the White and Chilkoot passes to ensure not only that gold stampeders obeyed Canadian laws, but also had sufficient supplies to carry them through to the gold fields.

DC 1016.5 (1686.7 km) DJ 373.5 (601.1 km) Large gravel turnout to west with view of Kluane Ranges.

DC 1017.2 (1687.8 km) DJ 372.8 (599.9 km) Christmas Creek.

DC 1019 (1689 km) DJ 371 (597 km) Highway climbs northbound.

DC 1019.8 (1692 km) DJ 370.2 (595.7 km) First glimpse of Kluane Lake for northbound travelers at **Boutillier Summit** (elev. 3,293 feet/1,003m), second highest point on the highway between Whitehorse and Fairbanks.

DC 1020 (1692.5 km) DJ 370 (595.4 km) Double-ended photo viewpoint to east with information plaques on area history and geography.

DC 1020.5 (1693.3 km) DJ 369.5 (595 km) **Historic Milepost 1053.** Historic sign and interpretive panel at turnoff for **Silver City**. Kluane Bed and Breakfast. Follow dirt and gravel road east 3.1 miles/5 km to ruins of Silver City. Silver City was the site of a trading post, roadhouse and North West Mounted Police barracks. It served traffic traveling the wagon road from Whitehorse to the placer goldfields of the Kluane Lake district from 1904 to 1924. Silver City's picturesque old buildings offer good photo opportunities. Kluane Bed and Breakfast offers ATV tours.

Kluane Bed and Breakfast. Just 3 miles off the highway at historical Silver City on the shore of Kluane Lake. Private, heated, A-frame cabins on lakeshore with mountain view, cooking and shower facilities, full family-style breakfast. Mountain bike rentals, high-country Alpine Argo (8-wheel ATV) trips. Your hosts—The Sias Family, a sixth generation Yukon family. Contact mobile operator (area code 867), Destruction Bay channel 2M 3924. Reservations recommended. Mailing address: c/o Box 5459, Haines Junction, YT Y0B 1L0. See display ad this section. [ADVERTISEMENT]

Picturesque old buildings at Silver City, Milepost DC 1020.5.
(© Earl L. Brown, staff)

DC 1020.9 (1694 km) DJ 369.1 (594 km) Silver Creek.

DC 1022.5 (1696.5 km) DJ 367.5 (591.4 km) Turnoff to east for Kluane Lake Research Station and airstrip, 0.9 mile/1.4 km via a straight gravel road. The research station, sponsored by the Arctic Institute of North America/University of Calgary, has an interpretive room with information on area expeditions and research. Visitors welcome.

Private Aircraft: Silver City airstrip; elev. 2,570 feet/783m; length 3,000 feet/914m; gravel; no services.

Highway follows west shore of Kluane Lake next 39 miles/63 km northbound to Burwash Landing.

DC 1023.7 (1698.5 km) DJ 366.3 (589.5 km) **Historical Mile 1056 (Historical milepost 1055).** Kluane Camp commemorative plaque. Kluane Lake Lodge (closed).

KLUANE
BED & BREAKFAST

Km 1693 - Mile 1055
"3 miles off Alaska Highway at Historic Silver City on the shore of Kluane Lake"

- Private Heated A-Frame Cabins
- Full Family Style Breakfast
- Cooking and Shower Facilities
- Mountain Bike Rentals
- Alpine Argo Trips

Reservations Recommended
Phone Mobile Operator (867)
Destruction Bay
Channel 2M 3924

Mailing Address
c/o Box 5459
Haines Junction
Yukon Y0B 1L0

ALASKA HIGHWAY • Yukon Territory

Kluane Lake reflects snow-dusted mountains in October. *(© Earl L. Brown, staff)*

COTTONWOOD RV PARK

On the shores of beautiful Kluane Lake

Mile 1067 KM 1717 16 Miles South of Destruction Bay

Pull Throughs • Hookups • Dump Station • Clean Restrooms • Cabin Rental
Unmetered Hot Showers • Laundromat • Campstore • Horseshoe Pits
Hot Tub Rental • Fishing Tackle • Licenses • Mini Golf

"Between Sonoma CA and Fairbanks AK, this was the most Picturesque and friendly camp spot we visited in a month of travel." Steve Snyder Sonoma CA

"We have travelled 16,000 miles and Cottonwood is the most beautiful setting of any RV park" Walter Lenz - Eau Claire, WI

Phone Mobile Operator 2M3972 Destruction Bay Channel

DESTRUCTION BAY LODGE

STOP HERE FOR GAS LAUNDRY RV HOOK UPS CAFE

- Fishing Charters for Trophy Lake Trout
- Low Fuel Prices
- Private BBQ's
- 40 Pull Through Sites
- Very Friendly Service
- Caravan Specialists
- The most unique Bowls, Burls & Diamond Willow crafted by "Dubie"

10th Anniversary

* NEW FOR 2002 *
30 AMP SERVICE

Good Sam Rating 8.5

Mile 1083 Destruction Bay
Yukon, Y0B 1H0
Phone/Fax 867-841-5332

DISCOVER MasterCard VISA

DC 1024.6 (1700 km) DJ 365.4 (588 km) Informal gravel turnout on Kluane Lake; access to beach.

DC 1026.8 (1703.4 km) DJ 363.2 (584.5 km) Slim's River East trail turnoff (2-mile/3.3-km access road, not recommended for motorhomes); parking at trailhead. This 12.4-mile/20-km trail is rated "easy" by the *Kluane Hiking Guide*. NOTE: Hikers must register for overnight hikes in Kluane National Park at either the Sheep Mountain or Haines Junction visitor centres.

DC 1027.8 (1705 km) DJ 362.2 (582.9 km) Slim's River bridge (clearance 17.7 feet/5.4m). Slim's River, which flows into Kluane Lake, was named for a packhorse that drowned here during the 1903 Kluane gold rush. Sheep Mountain is directly ahead for northbound travelers. The highway winds along Kluane Lake: Drive carefully!

DC 1028.8 (1706.6 km) DJ 361.2 (581.3 km) Sheep Mountain Visitor Information Centre. Excellent interpretive programs, laser disc information videos, parking and outhouses are available. Open mid-May to early September. Hours are 9 A.M. to 5 P.M. Stop here for information on Kluane National Park's flora and fauna. A viewing telescope is set up to look for sheep on Sheep Mountain. This is the sheep's winter range; best chance to see them is late August and September, good chance in late May to early June. Register at the Sheep Mountain Centre for hiking in the park. The face of Sheep Mountain has been designated a special preservation zone. Check with the centre for designated hiking areas, trail conditions and bear activity.

DC 1029 (1706.9 km) DJ 361 (581 km) Slim's River West trail; trailhead adjacent visitor information centre.

The small white cross on the side of Sheep Mountain marks the grave of Alexander Clark Fisher, a prospector who came into this area about 1906.

DC 1030.7 (1709.5 km) DJ 359.3 (578.2 km) Historic Milepost 1061. Large gravel turnouts both sides of highway at **Soldier's Summit**. The Alaska Canada Military Highway was officially opened with a ribbon-cutting ceremony here on blizzardy Nov. 20, 1942. A rededication ceremony was held Nov. 20, 1992, commemorating the 50th anniversary of the highway. A trail leads up to the original dedication site from the parking area.

Several turnouts overlooking **Kluane Lake** next mile northbound. This beautiful lake is the largest in Yukon Territory, covering approximately 154 square miles/400 square km. The Ruby Range lies on the east side of the lake. Boat rentals are available at Destruction Bay and Burwash Landing. Excellent fishing for lake trout, northern pike and grayling.

DC 1034.5 (1715.8 km) DJ 355.5 (572.1 km) Williscroft Creek. Named for Walt Williscroft, Superintendent of Highway maintenance for the southern part of the Alaska Highway from 1950 to 1970.

DC 1034.9 (1717 km) DJ 355.1 (571.5 km) Historical Mile 1067. Cottonwood RV Park and Campground. Welcome to our "Wilderness Paradise." Park your RV by the lake or pitch a tent on the shore. Relax in our hot tub on the deck. Play mini-golf, horseshoes or volleyball. View Dall sheep from your campsite or fish for trout and grayling. Hiking trails nearby. Spectacular scenery! Just 4 hours from Whitehorse, 6 hours from Tok. "A place where people stop for a day and stay another." See display ad this section. ▲

DC 1039.9 (1725 km) **DJ 350.1** (563.4 km) Historical Mile 1072. Turnoff to east for **Congdon Creek** Yukon government campground on Kluane Lake. Drive in 0.4 mile/0.6 km via gravel loop road; tenting area, 81 level sites (some pull-through), outhouses, kitchen shelters, water pump, firewood, firepits, picnic tables, sandy beach, interpretive talks, playground, boat launch. Short, self-guiding interpretive trail follows shoreline of Kluane Lake. Camping permit ($12).▲

DC 1040.4 (1725.6 km) **DJ 349.6** (562.6 km) Congdon Creek. According to R. Coutts, *Yukon: Places & Names*, Congdon Creek is believed to have been named by a miner after Frederick Tennyson Congdon. A lawyer from Nova Scotia, Congdon came to the Yukon in 1898 and held various political posts until 1911.

DC 1040.6 (1726 km) **DJ 349.4** (562.3 km) NOTE: Hills next 1.2 miles/2 km northbound; winding 2-lane road, no shoulders, informal gravel turnouts.

DC 1046.9 (1735.3 km) **DJ 343.1** (552.1 km) Nines Creek. Turnout to east.

DC 1047.3 (1736.2 km) **DJ 342.7** (551.5 km) Mines Creek.

NOTE: Expect improved highway northbound through Destruction Bay in summer 2003.

DC 1048.9 (1739 km) **DJ 341.1** (548.9 km) Bock's Brook.

Destruction Bay

DC 1051.5 (1743 km) **DJ 338.5** (544.7 km) At **Historic Milepost 1083**. **Population:** 100. **Emergency Services: Health clinic,** phone (867) 841-4444; **Ambulance,** phone (867) 841-3333; **Fire Department,** phone (867) 841-3331.

Located on the shore of Kluane Lake, Destruction Bay is one of several towns that grew out of the building of the Alaska Highway. It earned its name when a storm destroyed buildings and materials here. Destruction Bay was one of the many relay stations spaced at 100-mile intervals to give truck drivers a break and a chance to repair their vehicles. Historic sign adjacent historic milepost. A highway maintenance camp is located here.

Food, gas, camping and lodging available at Talbot Arm Motel and at Destruction Bay Lodge. ▲

Destruction Bay has camping, boat launch, boat rentals and guided fishing tours. The Kluane Lake Fishing Derby is held in July.

Kluane Kountry "B.O.A.L.S."* is located in Destruction Bay at historic Destruction Bay Lodge. *"Bump On A Log Shapes" are unique, authentic spruce, cottonwood and poplar burl shapes, hand-crafted into bowls, candleholders and more. Cobra-flare diamond willow walkin' sticks and canes are a specialty. Visit the "B.O.A.L.S."* shop, and chat with Dubie while we whittle a willow or two. See you when I do. Remember, the "Joy is in the journey." Dubie. See display ad this section. [ADVERTISEMENT]

Alaska Highway Log
(continued)

DC 1051.7 (1743.3 km) **DJ 338.3** (544.4 km) **Destruction Bay Lodge** celebrates 50 years of service and 10 years as an RV lodge with a Good Sam rating of 8.5. Better service, better value, better stop! Come and see "Dubie" make bowls and stuff. Stay a night or two and enjoy the beauty of Kluane and our new highway. (867) 841-5332. See display ad opposite page. [ADVERTISEMENT] ▲

Kluane Country "B.O.A.L.S." See display ad this section.

DC 1051.9 (1743.6 km) **DJ 338.1** (544.1 km) Rest area with litter barrels and toilet.

Don't miss...
Kluane Kountry "B.O.A.L.S."*
by Dubie
AT DESTRUCTION BAY LODGE
*BUMP ON A LOG SHAPES

111 BURL PLACE
Destruction Bay, Yukon
Y0B 1H0
867.841.4809

Welcome to the North Country!

TALBOT ARM MOTEL

Ready to Serve All Alaska highway Travellers Year-Round

WITH

- **32 MODERN SPACIOUS CLEAN ROOMS**
  Complimented with Satellite TV and Laundromat
- **90-SEAT CAFETERIA**
  Good Food Already Prepared for Tour Groups and Others
- **FULL SERVE DINING ROOM**
  Friendly, Efficient Waitered Service for Families, Truckers, and Small Groups
- **INTIMATE LOUNGE**

- **SHELL SERVICE STATION**
  Gasoline, Diesel, Oils and Propane.
- **GENERAL STORE**
  Local and Canadian-made Souvenirs, T-Shirts, Sunglasses, Fresh, Frozen and Canned Goods, Cigarettes, *Film*, Toiletries and Some Drug Store Remedies.
- **CAMPER and MOTORHOMES • RV PARK**
  Propane, Dump Station, Electric Hookups, Drinking Water, Store, Showers, Laundromat, Large Clean Restrooms • ICE

FAX: (867) 841-4804
— **FOR RESERVATIONS** — CALL: **(867) 841-4461**
WRITE: Box M, Destruction Bay, Yukon, Y0B 1H0

DEDICATED SERVICE TO TRAVELLERS SINCE 1967
The Van Der Veens, Your Hosts

DESTRUCTION BAY ADVERTISERS

Destruction Bay Lodge .....Ph. (867) 841-5332
Kluane Kountry
  "B.O.A.L.S." ....Ph. (867) 841-4809
Talbot Arm Motel ....Ph. (867) 841-4461

ALASKA HIGHWAY • Burwash Landing

Watch for grizzly bears along the Alaska Highway near Kluane National Park.
(© Earl L. Brown, staff)

The **Kluane Museum of Natural History** houses world-class wildlife exhibits with animals, birds and fish in dioramic settings depicting their natural habitats. Included are displays of Native clothing, tools and weapons and of Yukon minerals. The theatre plays videos of life, history and animals of the North and is included in the reasonable admission charge. The gift shop has many locally made crafts including beaded, fur trimmed moccasins made of moose hide as well as a good selection of books dealing with the North, the Alaska Highway and the Gold Rush. A large parking lot with 2 entrances makes pull-through access easy for vehicles up to transport truck length. Watch for the World's Largest Gold Pan! Phone (867) 841-5561. [ADVERTISEMENT]

Burls are either "green," harvested from live trees in the spring, or they are "dry burls," taken from dead burl trees. Burls are peeled of their bark and used in their natural form as fenceposts, for example, or they may be shaped and finished into a variety of objects, such as bowls. Check out Burlbilly Hill at **Milepost DC 1061.6**.

DC 1054.5 (1747.8 km) **DJ 335.5** (539.9 km) Evidence of June 1999 fire from here north to **Milepost DC 1066.2**. The human-caused fire closed the Alaska Highway and destroyed 5 homes in Burwash Landing (the town was evacuated). Some 8,000 acres were burned before fire crews were able to contain the fire. Fireweed, as its name implies, is one of the first plants to reestablish itself in burn areas.

DC 1055.1 (1748.8 km) **DJ 334.9** (539 km) Lewes Creek.

DC 1058.3 (1753.9 km) **DJ 331.7** (533.8 km) Halfbreed (Copper Joe) Creek trailhead.

DC 1061.3 (1758.7 km) **DJ 328.7** (529 km) Store.

Burwash Landing

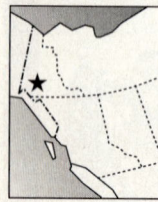

DC 1061.5 (1759 km) **DJ 328.5** (528.6 km) Historic Milepost 1093. Located on Kluane Lake. **Population:** 84. **Emergency Services: Ambulance,** phone (867) 841-333; **Fire Department,** phone (867) 841-2221. **Visitor Information:** Check at the Kluane Museum of Natural History, located on the east side of the Alaska Highway at the turnoff to Burwash Landing; Open 9 A.M. to 9 P.M. in summer; phone (867) 841-5561. Also ask at the museum about the self-guided walking trail.

Burwash Landing has a post office, community hall, and church. Visitor services include gas, food, camping and lodging. Flightseeing trips of Kluane National Park are also available out of Burwash Landing.

Burwash Landing Resort & RV Park. See display ad this section. ▲

Boat rentals and guided fishing trips are available locally. Canoeists may make a 1-day float trip down the Kluane River to Kluane Wilderness Village (25 miles/40 km) from Burwash Landing. Paddle 6 miles/10 km on Kluane Lake to mouth of Kluane River. *CAUTION: Beware of high winds on Kluane Lake.* Wildlife on the Kluane River includes bears, wolves and eagles. The Kluane River is rated Class I. ●▲

Burwash Landing is known for its black spruce burl bowls. Burls start as an irritation in the spruce. The tree sends extra sap as healant, which creates a growth or burl.

Burwash Landing was settled in 1904 by the Jacquot brothers, Louis and Eugene, as a supply centre for local miners. The log Our Lady of the Holy Rosary Mission was built in 1944. Sign reads:

"This was the first church northwest of Whitehorse on the new Alcan Highway. Father Morrisset, then auxiliary chaplain to the U.S. Army at the road construction camps, was asked by the local residents to start a mission and day school. Land was donated by Eugene Jacquot, trading post owner. Building materials came from the Duke River camp site and included an unfinished U.S. Army mess hall and a log cabin, which form the 2 arms

---

Overlooking Beautiful Kluane Lake
BURWASH LANDING RESORT & RV PARK

Be sure to visit Burlbilly Hill Unique Wood Bowls, Burls & Diamond Willow

25 Units • 24-hour Accommodations
135-seat Licensed Dining Room And Lounge

BUS TOURS WELCOME
YOUR PLACE- *Self-serve Cafeteria for 250*
Fishing Trips * Lakeshore RV Parking * Tenting
Hiking * Camping * Airport * Museum

Mile 1093 / Km 1759 ALASKA HIGHWAY
Open 6:30 am to Midnight
Phone (867) 841-4441 Fax (867) 841-4040
NORGAS FULL SERVICE STATION
UNLEADED • DIESEL

The Shakwak Project is reconstructing the Alaska Highway between Haines Junction and the Alaska border. (© Earl L. Brown, staff)

of the complex. The day school closed in 1952. The church opened with Christmas eve mass in 1944 and is still in use today."

Alaska Highway Log
(continued)

DC 1061.6 (1759.2 km) **DJ 328.4** (528.5 km) **Burlbilly Hill.** The most unique stop at Mile 1093 is "Burlbilly Hill," 200 feet north of the museum. The visitor will see rows of "burly logs" on the hill. Another

surprise is a small woodshop with its variety of finely finished burl products, "burl bowls" and "diamond willow canes." Come and watch Obie and Karin at work. Wir sprechen deutsch! Phone (867) 841-4607. [ADVERTISEMENT]

DC 1062 (1759.8 km) **DJ 328** (527.8 km) Dalan Campground to north. ▲

Dalan Campground. Turn off north, to Dalan Campground, 1 km off the Alaska Highway on the shores of beautiful Kluane Lake, "largest lake in the Yukon." Owned and operated by Kluane First Nation, this campground offers 25 individual private campsites, RVs welcome! Firewood, water, picnic tables, covered common area and dump station are available. Visit the Dalan crafts shop. Cultural programs and campfire talks available. For additional information, view our web site at www.yukonweb.com/tourism/dalan. See display ad this section. [ADVERTISEMENT] ▲

DC 1062.7 (1761 km) **DJ 327.3** (526.7 km) Historic Milepost 1094. **Private Aircraft:** Burwash Yukon government airstrip to north; elev. 2,643 feet/806m; length 6,000 feet/1,829m; gravel, no fuel.

DC 1066.2 (1767.5 km) **DJ 323.8** (521.1 km) First evidence southbound of June 1999 Burwash Landing fire (see **Milepost DC 1054.5**).

DC 1067 (1768.8 km) **DJ 323** (519.8 km) **Duke River** bridge (clearance 17.7 feet/5.4m). The Duke River flows into Kluane Lake; named for George Duke, an early prospector.

NOTE: Northbound watch for road construction and resurfacing (BST) next 12.4 miles/20 km from Kilometrepost 1768 to 1788, in summer 2003.

DC 1071.9 (1776.5 km) **DJ 318.1** (511.9 km) Turnout to north. Burwash Creek, named for Lachlin Taylor Burwash, a mining recorder at Silver City in 1903.

DC 1076.7 (1784.1 km) **DJ 313.3** (504.2 km) Sakiw Creek.

DC 1077.3 (1785.1 km) **DJ 312.7** (503.2 km) **Kluane River Overlook.** Rest area with information panels and observation platform overlooking Kluane River. Interpretive panels describe the life cycle of the chum salmon that come to spawn in this river in August and September. Watch for grizzly bears and bald eagles feeding on salmon.

DC 1078.5 (1787 km) **DJ 311.5** (501.3 km) Buildings to west belong to Hudson Bay Mining and Smelting Co.'s Wellgreen Nickel Mines, named for Wellington Bridgeman Green, the prospector who discovered the mineral showing in 1952. During the mine's operation, from May 1972 to July 1973, three shiploads of concentrates (averaging 13,000 tons each) were trucked to Haines, AK. The material proved to be too insufficient to be economical. No facilities or services.

DC 1079.4 (1788.5 km) **DJ 310.6** (499.8 km) Quill Creek.

NOTE: Watch for road construction and resurfacing (BST) next 12.4 miles/20 km southbound from Kilometrepost 1788 to 1768, in summer 2003.

DC 1080.9 (1791 km) **DJ 309.1** (497.4 km) Glacier Creek. Kluane River to east of highway.

DC 1084.6 (1797.2 km) **DJ 305.4** (491.5 km) **Historical Mile 1118, Kluane Wilderness Village** (unincorporated). Lodge complex with gas, restaurant, bar; camping and lodging. Open year-round. Scully, "Burl King of the North," resides here. His work can be seen across the highway from Kluane Wilderness Village, as well as in the saloon (which has a burl bar). Viewing platform of Mount Kennedy, Mount Logan and Mount Lucania. Halfway mark between Whitehorse and Tok. ▲

DALAN CAMPGROUND
Owned/Operated By: Kluane First Nation

- **• 25 Private Sites •**
- **Wood • Water**
- **Dump Station**

Quiet scenic view, located 1km off the Alaska Hwy on the shores of beautiful Kluane Lake.

Historic Mile 1093 (DC 1062) - Box 20, Burwash Landing, YT Y0B 1V0

www.yukonweb.com/tourism/dalan

The 3 panels of colour in Yukon's flag represent rivers and lakes (blue); the forest (green); and snow (white).

ALASKA HIGHWAY • Yukon Territory

Alaska Highway cyclists take a break—and plug The MILEPOST—at Kluane Wilderness Village. (© Earl L. Brown, staff)

Kluane Wilderness Village offers all amenities to modern day travelers. 24-hour service station (summer). Full-menu restaurant, "Scully's Saloon" and comfortable accommodation. Our Good Sam R.V. Park (with direct Satellite TV) is the ideal resting location halfway between Whitehorse and Tok, nestled in the beautiful Kluane Mountains. See our display ad below for more. Phone/fax (867) 841-4141. See display ad this section. [ADVERTISEMENT] ▲

DC 1086.6 (1799.5 km) DJ 303.4 (488.3 km) Swede Johnson Creek. Turnout to east.

DC 1095 (1814 km) DJ 295 (474.7 km) NorthwesTel microwave tower visible ahead northbound.

DC 1095.4 (1814.6 km) DJ 294.6 (474.1 km) Abandoned Mountain View Lodge. View of Donjek River Valley.

Alaska Highway workers faced one of their toughest construction jobs during completion of the Alaska Highway in 1943 from the Donjek River to the Alaska border. Swampy ground underlain by permafrost, numerous creeks, lakes and rivers, plus a

Kluane Wilderness Village & RV Park
MILE 1118
200 MILES FROM WHITEHORSE AND TOK

"Celebrating over 30 Years Serving the Travellers"

The Most Reasons To $top, Year-Around

MOTOR COACH STOP
- Self-serve Dining Room — Seats 150
- Lunch, overnight
- **We cater to overnight buses**

RESTAURANT
- Full Service
- Complete Menu Service

"SCULLY'S SALOON"
- See the world-famous "Burl Bar"
- Packaged Beer & Liquor

SOUVENIRS
- Unique BURL Crafts — See Scully at work

SERVICE STATION
- Towing • Tires
- Welding • Repairs
- Gas • Diesel
- Propane
- U-Haul Repair Depot
- **Good Sam Emergency Road Service**

ACCOMMODATIONS
- 25 Log Cabins (May - October) Each with electric heat and bath
- 6 Motel Units Year-Around
- Direct Satellite TV
- Fax Service

All beds with Beautyrest Mattresses

RVs & CAMPERS
- Full-service and Pull-through Hook-ups
- Campsites
- BBQ Pit • Cookhouse
- Showers • Bag Ice • Propane
- Laundromat • **3 Public Phone**

Good Sampark — Good Sam Emergency Road Service

CONVENIENCE STORE
- Ice Cream • Souvenirs
- T-Shirts • Sweats

NOW HAVE DIRECT SATELITE TV IN RV PARK

YOUR HOSTS LIZ AND JOHN TROUT
Phone ahead for reservations — Year-Around: PH/FAX (867) 841-4141
Or Write: Mile 1118 Alaska Highway, Yukon Territory Y0B 1H0

thick insulating ground cover, made this section particularly difficult for road builders.

In recent years, this same section of highway has been the object of a massive, ongoing reconstruction known as the Shakwak Highway project.

DC 1096.3 (1816 km) **DJ 293.7** (472.6 km) Turnout to west with view of **Donjek River Valley** and the Icefield Ranges of the St. Elias Mountains. Interpretive display.

DC 1099.7 (1819.5 km) **DJ 290.3** (467.2 km) **Historic Milepost 1130.** Turnout with interpretive panel on the Donjek River bridge. Sign reads: "Glacial rivers, like the Donjek, posed a unique problem for the builders of the Alaska Highway. These braided mountain streams would flood after a heavy rainfall or rapid glacial melt, altering the waters' course and often leaving bridges crossing dry ground."

DC 1100 (1820 km) **DJ 290** (466.7 km) **Donjek River** bridge (clearance 17.4 feet/5.3m). Access to river at north end of bridge on west side of highway. This wide silty river is a major tributary of the White River. According to R. Coutts, *Yukon: Places & Names*, the Donjek is believed to have been named by Charles Willard Hayes in 1891 from the Indian word for a peavine that grows in the area.

DC 1108.7 (1834 km) **DJ 381.3** (613.6 km) NOTE: *Northbound travelers watch for sections of highway with loose gravel, bumps, frost heaves, patched pavement, narrow road, no shoulders, road construction and improved highway.*

DC 1113.5 (1844.4 km) **DJ 276.5** (445 km) **Edith Creek** bridge, turnout to west. Try your hand at gold panning here; "colours" have been found. Grayling fishing, June through September.

DC 1113.8 (1844.8 km) **DJ 276.2** (444.5 km) **Historical Mile 1147. Pine Valley Motel, Cafe and Bakery.** Hi! Thanks to all our customers for your patronage from your host Carmen and our staff. Open 6 A.M. to midnight. We have unleaded and diesel available (seniors gas discount). RV park and treed campground located out back ... away from the highway traffic. Pull-throughs,

power, picnic tables, free showers and coffee included with any overnight stay. Good fishing nearby. Rooms, cabins with TV, bath, showers. Lounge and cafe with full menu. Hearty soups, homemade breads, pies, pastries—all made here. Caravans welcome. Enjoy a scenic view while our friendly morning cook prepares you up a mean breakfast, or sink your teeth into Carmen's wonderful sweet rolls. (Carmen also known as Buckshot Betty.) We have cold beer and spirits for take-out, or sit and relax in our lounge. Pay phone, cubed ice, fishing licenses, souvenirs. Book exchange. Corral for over-nighting horses. VISA/MasterCard accepted. Interac direct payment. Enjoy your drive through Kluane National Park and keep it clean and green. Thanks! If you liked us at Pine Valley, catch us at Buckshot Betty's in Beaver Creek. Phone/fax (867) 862-7407. [ADVERTISEMENT]

DC 1118.3 (1852.2 km) **DJ 271.7** (437.2 km) Koidern River bridge No. 1.

DC 1118.8 (1853 km) **DJ 271.2** (436.4 km) **Historical Mile 1152. Lake Creek** Yukon government campground just west of highway; 27 large level sites (6 pull-through), water pump, litter barrels, firewood, firepits, picnic tables, kitchen shelter and outhouses. Camping permit ($12).

DC 1122.7 (1859.5 km) **DJ 267.3** (430.2 km) **Historical Mile 1156.** Longs Creek.

DC 1125 (1863.5 km) **DJ 265** (426.5 km) Turnout to east with litter barrel.

DC 1125.7 (1864.7 km) **DJ 264.3** (425.3 km) **Pickhandle Lake** to west; interpretive panels on Native trading routes, pond life and muskrats. Good fishing from boat for northern pike all summer; also grayling, whitefish and lingcod.

DC 1128 (1868.4 km) **DJ 262** (421.6 km) Aptly named Reflection Lake to west mirrors the Kluane Range. The highway parallels this range between Koidern and Haines Junction.

DC 1130.6 (1872.6 km) **DJ 259.4** (417.4 km) **Historical Mile 1164.** Lodge.

DC 1130.7 (1872.8 km) **DJ 259.3** (417.3 km) Koidern River bridge No. 2.

DC 1133.7 (1877.6 km) **DJ 256.3** (412.5 km) **Historic Milepost 1167.** Bear Flats Lodge (closed in 2002; current status unknown).

DC 1135 (1882 km) **DJ 255** (410.4 km) **Historical Mile 1169.** White River Crossing; trading post, RV park, food, gas, diesel, dump station and camping.

White River Crossing Trading Post & RV Park. Great news folks, Bob and Caulene are back to take care of the travellers. Yes we have ice cream. Hungry? You'll want to take in our new Salmon Bake and Buffalo BBQ outside under the big top afternoons and evenings. (Free parking with your supper.) Our RV park has shaded pull-through sites, full RV hookups, 30 amp power and great water. Interested in "old stuff"? Check out our antiques and collectables. Unbranded gas and diesel at one of the lowest prices on this end of the highway. We look forward to making your White River visit a memorable one. See display ad this section. [ADVERTISEMENT]

DC 1135.6 (1881 km) **DJ 254.4** (409.4 km) **White River** bridge. The White River, a major tributary of the Yukon River, was named by Hudson's Bay Co. explorer Robert Campbell for its white colour, caused by the volcanic ash in the water. *NOTE: This river is considered very dangerous; not recommended for boating.*

DC 1141.5 (1890.5 km) **DJ 248.5** (399.9 km) **Moose Lake** to west, grayling to 18 inches, use dry flies and small spinners, mid-summer. Boat needed for lake.

DC 1144.3 (1895 km) **DJ 245.7** (395.4 km) **Sanpete Creek**, named by an early prospector after Sanpete County in Utah.

DC 1147.5 (1900.3 km) **DJ 242.5** (390.2 km) Dry Creek No. 1.

DC 1150.3 (1904.5 km) **DJ 239.7** (385.7 km) Dry Creek No. 2.

DC 1155.2 (1913 km) **234.8** (377.9 km) **Historical Mile 1188.** Turnoff for **Snag Junction** Yukon government campground, 0.4 mile/0.6 km in on gravel loop road. There are 15 tent and vehicle sites (some level), a kitchen shelter, outhouses, picnic tables, firewood, firepits and litter barrels. Camping permit ($12). Small-boat launch.

ALASKA HIGHWAY • Beaver Creek

WE'VE GOT YOU COVERED AT THE BORDER.

- 174 Rooms •
- Dining Room & Lounge •
- Northern Wonders Gift Shop •
- Guest Laundry • Wildlife Display •
- R.V. Park • Grocery Store •
- Gas Station •

Introducing Westmark On-line Booking.
For instant confirmation visit us on-line at www.westmarkhotels.com

Central Reservations
1-800-544-0970

BEAVER CREEK RENDEZVOUS

Dinner Theatre
Spice up your travels with the Beaver Creek Rendezvous, a light hearted dinner show about the history of life on the Alaska highway featuring a family style barbeque dinner with all the fixings. Fun, music, romance, history and plenty of food – a great addition to include among your northern adventurers.

Westmark INN
BEAVER CREEK
MP 1202 Alaska Highway
Beaver Creek, Yukon Territory Y0B 1A0
867-862-7501

Swimming in Small Lake. ▲
A dirt road (status unknown) connects the Alaska Highway here with the abandoned airfield and Indian village at **Snag** to the northeast. Snag's claim to fame is the lowest recorded temperature in Canada: -83° F/-63° C on Feb. 3, 1947.

DC 1162.1 (1924.5 km) DJ 227.9 (366.7 km) Enger Creek.

DC 1165.7 (1930 km) DJ 224.3 (361 km) View of Nutzotin Mountains to northwest, Kluane Ranges to southwest. On a clear day you should be able to see the snow-clad Wrangell Mountains in the distance to the west.

DC 1167.2 (1932.4 km) DJ 222.8 (358.5 km) Beaver Creek plank bridge, clearance 17.1 feet/5.2m.

Beaver Creek

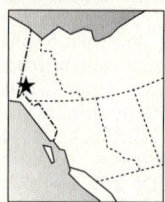

DC 1168.5 (1934.5 km) DJ 221.5 (356.4 km) **Historic Milepost 1202.** Driving distance to Haines Junction, 184 miles/295 km; to Tok, 113 miles/182 km; to Haines, 334 miles/ 538. km. **Population:** 112. **Emergency Services:** RCMP, phone (867) 862-5555. Ambulance, phone (867) 862-3333. **Nursing Station:** (867) 862-4444.

Visitor Information: Yukon government Visitor Reception Centre in the log building pictured above, is open daily late May through September. Phone (867) 862-7321.

The visitor centre has a book on display of dried Yukon wildflowers for those interested in the flora of the territory. The centre also has an Alaska Highway scrapbook with historical photos of lodges and life along the north Alaska Highway.

Private Aircraft: Beaver Creek Yukon government airstrip 1 NW; see description at **Milepost DC 1170.3. Radio:** CBC North at 93.3 FM, CHON 90.5 FM.

Site of the old Canadian customs station. Local residents were pleased to see customs relocated north of town in 1983, having long endured the flashing lights and screaming sirens set off whenever a tourist forgot to stop.

Beaver Creek is 1 of 2 sites where Alaska Highway construction crews working from opposite directions connected the highway. In October 1942, Alaska Highway construction operations were being rushed to conclusion as winter set in. Eastern and western sector construction crews (the 97th and 18th Engineers) pushed through to meet at a junction on Beaver Creek on Oct. 28., thus making it possible for the first time for vehicles to travel the entire length of the highway. East–west crews had connected at Contact Creek on Sept. 24, 1942.

Motels, cabins, gas stations with repair service, mini-mart and licensed restaurants are located here. (Beaver Creek is an overnight stop for bus travelers.) There is a post office; a bank, open 2 days a week, located in the post office building; ATMs; community library; and public swimming pool beside the community club. Showers available at Buckshot Betty's. RV campground with hookups at the Westmark. ▲

BEAVER CREEK ADVERTISERS

Buckshot Betty's	Ph. (867) 862-7111
Ida's Motel & Restaurant	Ph. (867) 862-7223
1202 Motor Inn	Ph. (867) 862-7600
Westmark Inn	Ph. (867) 862-7501

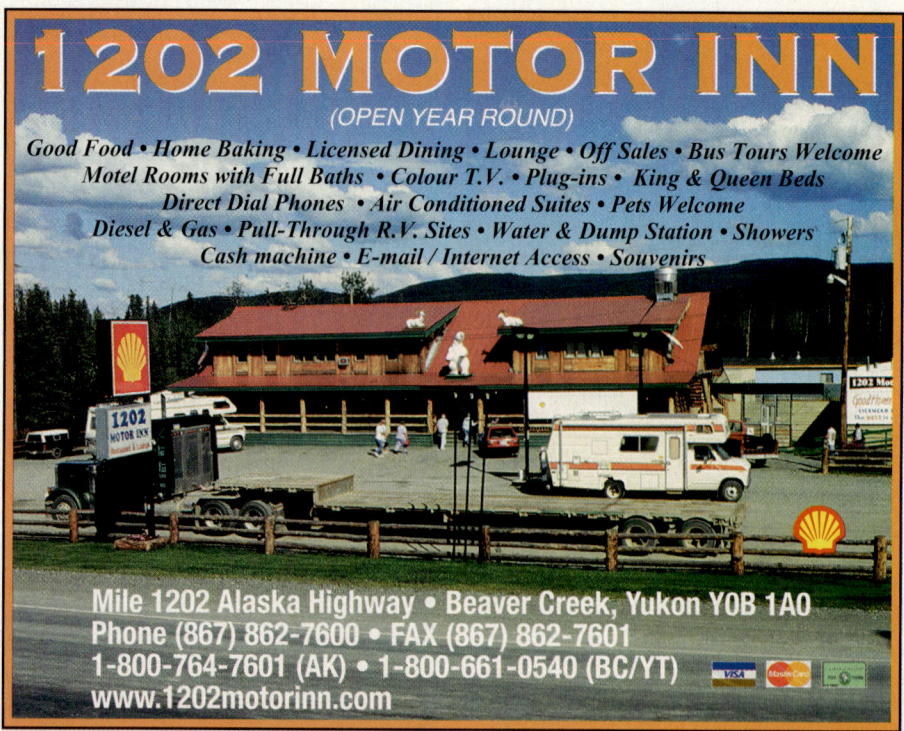

The interesting looking church here is **Our Lady of Grace mission.** Built in 1961 from a salvaged quonset hut left over from highway construction days, it is 1 of 3 Catholic missions on the north Alaska Highway (the others are in Burwash Landing and Haines Junction). St. Columba's Anglican Church in Beaver Creek was prefabricated in Whitehorse and constructed in one week in 1975.

Stretch your legs on 1 of 2 walking paths (both 1.2 miles/2 km in length) at either end of town. One goes east to the Beaver Creek bridge; the other west to Canada Customs.

Yukon Centennial Gold Rush figurines and displays are located just west of How Far West Plaza (celebrating Beaver Creek's status as most westerly Canadian community) at town centre. The plaza features information panels on wildlife and a map of Beaver Creek.

Check with the information centre about the live stage show at the Westmark Inn, evenings in summer; admission charged. The Westmark also has a wildlife display and mini-golf.

Buckshot Betty's. Check us out, we're new! A hearty welcome to all our customers from your host Buckshot Betty and her hired hands. Open 24 hours, 7 days a week, all year. Bakery, licensed restaurant with full menu, gift shop, books, ATM, showers, truck stop, gas and diesel. Our breads, pastries and pies are all made here. Diabetic baked goods available. Ice cream and pizzas. Campground permits and fishing licenses. Cozy new cabins, satellite TV. Pay phones. Phone (867) 862-7111; fax (867) 862-7112. Interac, VISA/MasterCard. Enjoy your stay. See display ad this section. [ADVERTISEMENT] ▲

Alaska Highway Log
(continued)

DC 1169.7 (1936.3 km) DJ 220.3 (354.5 km) Rest area to west with litter barrels, picnic tables and outhouses.

DC 1170.3 (1937.3 km) DJ 219.7 (353.6km) **Private Aircraft:** Beaver Creek Yukon government airstrip; elev. 2,129 feet/649m; length 3,740 feet/1,140m; gravel; no fuel. Airport of entry for Canada customs.

DC 1170.5 (1937.6 km) DJ 219.5 (353.2 km) **Beaver Creek Canada Customs** station; phone (867) 862-7230. Open 24 hours a day year-round. All traffic entering Canada must stop here for clearance. Expect vigorous enforcement of customs requirements (see "Crossing the Border" in the Travel Planning section for more details).

DC 1175.4 (1945.5 km) DJ 214.8 (345.7 km) Snag Creek plank bridge. *CAUTION: Slippery when wet.*

DC 1176.3 (1946.9 km) DJ 213.7 (343.9 km) Mirror Creek.

DC 1177 (1950 km) DJ 213 (342.8 km) **Swan Lake**, east side of highway, is home to a nesting pair of trumpeter swans. Also look for shorebirds and migratory waterfowl.

DC 1178.3 (1952 km) DJ 211.7 (340.7 km) Lake to east, turnout to west.

DC 1186 (1963 km) DJ 204 (328.3 km) Little Scottie Creek.

DC 1189.5 (1967.5 km) DJ 200.5 (322.7 km) **Historic Milepost 1221. Canada–U.S. International Border.** Parking and rest area to south with interpretive panels on the 141st Meridian and the challenges of Northern road construction.

From the viewing decks, note the narrow clearing marking the border. This is part of the 20-foot-/6-m-wide swath cut by surveyors from 1904 to 1920 along the 141st meridian (from Demarcation Point on the Arctic Ocean south 600 miles/966 km to Mount St. Elias in the Wrangell Mountains) to mark the Alaska–Canada border. This swath continues south to mark the boundary between southeastern Alaska and Canada. Portions of the swath are cleared periodically by the International Boundary Commission.

The boundary line between Alaska and Yukon was originally described in an 1825 treaty between Russia and England. The U.S. accepted this version of the boundary with its purchase of Alaska from Russia in 1867. But after gold was discovered in the Klondike in 1896, a dispute arose between the U.S. and Canada, with both claiming the seaports at the head of Lynn Canal. An international tribunal decided in favor of the U.S. in 1903.

TIME ZONE CHANGE: Alaska observes Alaska time; Yukon Territory observes Pacific time. Alaska time is 1 hour earlier than Pacific time.

Welcome to Alaska and Welcome to Yukon signs for northbound and southbound travelers respectively.

DC 1189.8 (1968 km) DJ 200.2 (322.2 km) **Historical Mile 1221.8.** U.S. customs border station.

IMPORTANT: The MILEPOST® log now switches to physical mileposts for northbound travelers. For southbound travelers, the log is

BUCKSHOT BETTY'S
BEAVER CREEK, YUKON
OPEN 24/7 YEAR ROUND

- RESTAURANT
- CABINS
- FRESH BAKING DAILY
- GAS & DIESEL

(SEE OUR LOG AD FOR MORE)

THANKS FOR BEING PART OF OUR DAY!

Ida's MOTEL & RESTAURANT
ALL DAY CARIBOU SAUSAGE BREAKFAST
BISON BURGERS • DRIP DECAFFEINATED COFFEE
MILE 1202 KM 1934.4
20 BRAND NEW MOTEL UNITS • King & Queen Size Beds
Rooms with Private Baths, TV and phone
Licensed *DINING & COCKTAIL LOUNGE*
Homestyle Cooking • *Homey Atmosphere* • Liquor
Cold Beer to Go • Caribou Stew • Bannock
DIESEL • UNLEADED GAS • "SOUVENIRS"
Pay Telephone • Winter Plug-ins • MASTERCARD, VISA ACCEPTED
BUS TOURS WELCOME (RESERVATIONS PLEASE)

Beaver Creek, Yukon Y0B 1A0	OFF SEASON
Phone (867) 862-7223	Phone 867-668-5558
Fax (867) 862-7221	fax 867-668-5568

email: famhotel@polarcom.com

ALASKA
YOU'RE ONLY 23 MILES AWAY
BORDER CITY MOTEL & RV PARK
LOW U.S. PRICES   ALL PULL THROUGH SITES   LOW U.S. PRICES
RV SITES (25 FT. BY 100 FT., WATER, ELECTRIC, SEWER DUMP, CABLE TV)
MOTEL (CLEAN, SPACIOUS, PRIVATE BATHROOMS, CABLE TV)
FACTORY OUTLET (T-SHIRTS, SWEATSHIRTS, DENIMS, JACKET, CAPS, GIFTS)
STOP, SHOP, SLEEP, EAT AND FUEL UP
AT THE FRIENDLIEST STOP ON THE ALASKA HIGHWAY
MOTEL & RV RESERVATIONS CALL (907) 774-2205

BORDER CITY MOTEL & RV PARK

$ $ $ CURRENCY EXCHANGE $ $ $

Mile 1225.5 Alaska Highway
3-1/2 miles north of U.S. Customs

TAX FREE   OPEN LONG HOURS

**First & Last Stop In Alaska
Perfect Place For All Your Travel Needs**

**LOW FUEL PRICES
RV WASH**

RV PARK
* ALL GRASS SITES *
* TV *
(HBO, CMAX, SHOWTIME, CNN, ETC)
* ALL SITES 25 FT. BY 100 FT. *
* DUMP STATION *
* WATER & ELECTRIC *
* 55 PULL THRU SITES *
(ALL 30 AMPS)
* PRIVATE SHOWERS *
* CLEAN RESTROOMS *
ALL THIS FOR $15.00

FACTORY OUTLET
* Apparel * Caps * Gifts *
(Denim Shirts, T-Shirts, Jackets, Sweaters)
3500 SQ FEET GIFT STORE

MOTEL ROOMS
* CABLE TV *
(HBO, CMAX, SHOWTIME, CNN, ETC)
* CLEAN & SPACIOUS *
AS LOW AS $49.95

CAFE
* Breakfast * Lunch * Dinner * Ice Cream *

**RESERVATIONS
(907) 774-2205**

Email: BorderCityLodge@att.net

**STOP, SHOP, SLEEP, EAT, FUEL UP
AND GOLF AT THE FRIENDLIEST STOP
ON THE ALASKA HIGHWAY**

---

based on actual driving distance. The Alaska Highway is approximately 32 miles/51 km shorter than the traditional figure of 1,221.8 miles between Dawson Creek and the YT–AK border. Please read the information on Mileposts and Kilometreposts in the introduction to the Alaska Highway.

Northbound: Fair to good pavement to Fairbanks. Watch for patches of rough road, loose gravel and patched pavement.

Southbound: Expect improved highway, road construction and unimproved highway (narrow winding road) to Haines Junction. *CAUTION: Slow down for loose gravel!*

ALASKA ROUTE 2
Distance from Dawson Creek (DC)* is followed by distance from Delta Junction (DJ) and distance from Fairbanks (F).
*Mileages from Dawson Creek, Delta Junction and Fairbanks are based on physical mileposts in Alaska.

DC 1221.8 DJ 200.2 F 298.2 Port Alcan U.S. Customs and Immigration Service border station, open 24 hours a day year-round; pay phone (credit card and collect calls only) and restrooms. All traffic entering Alaska must stop for clearance. Phone (907) 774-2242; emergencies, (907) 774-2252.

Border Branch U.S. post office is located here (ZIP 99764); ask for directions at the customs office.

DC 1222.5 DJ 199.5 F 297.5 Tetlin National Wildlife Refuge boundary sign to west. Established in 1980, the 730,000-acre refuge stretches south from the Alaska Highway and west from the Canadian border. The major physical features include rolling hills, hundreds of small lakes and 2 glacial rivers (the Nabesna and Chisana), which combine to form the Tanana River. The complex association of lakes, ponds, marshes, streams, and rivers provide variety of habitat favorable to numerous species of waterfowl. As a migration stop for all types of birds, the refuge provides habitat for 143 nesting species and 47 migrants. Other wildlife includes moose, black and grizzly bear, wolf, coyote, beaver, red fox, lynx and caribou.

Activities allowed on the refuge include wildlife observation, hunting, fishing, trapping, camping, photography and canoeing. For more detailed information, contact the Refuge Manager, Tetlin National Wildlife Refuge, Box 779, Tok, AK 99780; phone (907) 883-5312; fax (907) 883-5747. Or stop by refuge headquarters in Tok at **Milepost DC 1314** Alaska Highway. Information on the refuge is available seasonally at the Tetlin National Wildlife Refuge Visitor Center at **Milepost DC 1229** on the Alaska Highway.

DC 1223.4 DJ 198.6 F 296.6 Scottie Creek bridge. Old cabins to west.

DC 1224.6 DJ 197.4 F 295.4 Double-ended gravel turnout to southwest at Highway Lake with interpretive sign on wetlands; beaver lodges.

DC 1225.4 DJ 196.6 F 294.6 Parking area and canoe launch (not signed) for Despert Creek and access to Tetlin NWR.

DC 1225.5 DJ 196.5 F 294.5 Border City Motel & RV Park west side of highway.

Border City Motel & RV Park. See display ad this section. ▲

DC 1226 DJ 196 F 294 Scottie Creek Services and RV Park east side of highway.

Cache and viewing deck at Tetlin NWR Visitor Center at Milepost DC 1229.
(© Kris Graef, staff)

Scottie Creek Services & RV Park. See display ad this section.

The old cabin adjacent Scottie Creek Services was identified in summer 1999 as the "Original Historic Canadian Customs Log Cabin (1946–1952)." It was built by Pete Ecklund and Bill Blair of Beaver Creek, YT. Originally it stood at Milepost 1220, but it was purchased by an unknown party in the early 1960s and moved to its present location. The cabin is being restored.

DC 1227.8 DJ 194.2 F 292.2 Large double-ended paved parking area to west with interpretive sign; see excerpts following. Good view to south of lakes in Chisana (SHOE-shanna) River valley. The Nutzotin Mountains are to the west.

"Flyways for the World: Alaska's habitat is critical for summer nesting and rearing of young birds in preparation for the fall migration southward. The Tetlin National Wildlife Refuge is one of many such units in Alaska located along major flyways where hundreds of thousands of avian species such as ducks, geese, swans, sandhill cranes, songbirds and raptors rest and feed before continuing their long migration.

"Rivers for the Yukon: In the distant past the stream before you flowed eastward into Canada's White River before entering the Yukon River. With the help of geologic forces, its headwaters have been 'captured' and its passage redirected. Today, the stream flows westward into the Chisana River, the Tanana River and finally into the mighty Yukon River hundreds of miles downstream for its prehistoric confluence point. Such rivers and floodplains are important wildlife habitat for Alaska's diversity and abundance of fish, mammals and birds."

DC 1229 DJ 193 F 291 Tetlin National Wildlife Refuge Visitor Center west side of highway. Viewing deck with telescopes, displays on wildlife and other subjects. Interpretive programs and demonstrations on traditional Native culture presented daily in summer. Nature videos shown on request. Free audio tour tape available for travelers headed towards Tok (return tape to Public Lands Information Center in Tok). Restrooms (wheelchair accessible). Public phone available. Fresh-water faucet located beneath cache. The visitor center is open 8 A.M. to 4:30 P.M. May 15 to September 15. (The center extends its hours to 6:30 P.M. on most weekdays.) Current highway conditions and fishing information posted on outside message boards.

DC 1230.7 DJ 200.3 F 289.3 View of Island Lake.

DC 1231 DJ 200 F 289 Long double-ended dirt and gravel turnout to northeast.

DC 1233.3 DJ 188.7 F 286.7 Long, narrow, double-ended paved parking area to northeast on old alignment.

DC 1238 DJ 184 F 282 Watch for moose.

DC 1240 DJ 182 F 280 Gravel parking area to southwest is public access to **Hidden Lake** (1 mile hike); stocked with rainbow trout; use spinners, wobbling spoons, or flies (streamers and bucktails with black and red in their patterns). Interpretive signs on rainbow trout and permafrost (see excerpts following).

"Rainbows do not naturally occur in this area, and will not reproduce in landlocked lakes like Hidden Lake. These trout will live 5 years. After the first year, they will reach 5 or 6 inches in length. In 3 years, they will measure 9 to 12 inches. Eighteen inches is as big as they can get here in Hidden Lake.

"Permafrost forms when the average soil temperature is 27°F (–3°C). Ice slowly forms in poorly drained soils. One sign of existing permafrost is a black spruce bog. Black spruce are small, scraggly trees that can survive in the few inches of soil that thaws out above the permafrost. A tree of only 2 inches in diameter is often 100 years old. In a black spruce bog, a thick mat of mosses and other small plants covers the ground. This mat acts as a sponge that holds moisture, and serves as insulation keeping the permafrost from melting. Be prepared to get your feet wet!"

DC 1240.3 DJ 181.7 F 279.7 Waist-high vertical corrugated metal culverts topped with cone-shaped "hats" seen on either side of highway are an experiment to keep ground from thawing and thus prevent frost heaves.

DC 1241.9 DJ 180.1 F 278.1 Tetlin NWR boundary marker southbound.

DC 1243 DJ 179 F 277 Good examples of sand dune road cut and rock graffiti typical along this stretch of highway. Westbound, the highway cuts through several of these sand dunes stabilized by aspen and spruce trees. (See interpretive sign on sand dunes at **Milepost DC 1243.7.**)

DC 1243.7 DJ 178.3 F 276.3 Scenic viewpoint to south on loop road has interpretive signs on fire management and changing landscape (see excerpts following).

"Fire can be an effective habitat management tool. On most of Tetlin NWR, fire is the only feasible means of habitat manipulation. Under natural conditions, about every 200 years a forest fire sets spruce climax forests back into earlier and more productive sequences of plant succession.

"The majority of wildland fires occurring in Interior Alaska are lightning-caused, with the fire season running from late May to early August. As many as 100 fire starts have been known to occur in a single day.

"During the Ice Age, tremendous amounts of glacial sediments were carried downstream from the Wrangell Mountains and dumped along the edge of the ice-free river basins. The hills around you are stabilized sand dunes blown into this vicinity from ancient glacial outwash plains and stream deposits located on the far side of the river basin.

"In time, vegetation will stabilize old sand dunes, although the steep, unstable front slope of the dune continues to resist total domination. These easily disturbed edges attract broadleaf tree species such as aspen, poplar and birch. The long and gently sloping back portion of the dune allows a climax spruce forest to eventually dominate that zone."

DC 1246.6 DJ 175.4 F 273.4 Gardiner Creek bridge; dirt turnout to west. Grayling fishing.

DC 1247.6 DJ 174.4 F 272.4 Paved double-ended viewpoint to north.

DC 1249.3 DJ 172.7 F 270.7 Historic Milepost 1254. Sharp turn southwest for **Deadman Lake Campground** (Tetlin NWR), 1.2 miles in on narrow dirt and gravel access road. No fee campground with 16 sites in spruce forest along a half-mile loop road; firepits, toilets, picnic tables, no drinking water, boat ramp, interpretive signs information board and self-guided nature trail. Maximum 14-day stay within a 28-day period. Evening naturalist programs offered Monday through Friday at 7:30 P.M. during the summer season. Wheelchair accessible. Scenic spot. Swimming and fishing. Northern pike average 2 feet, but skinny (local residents call them "snakes"); use steel leader with wobbling lures or spinners.

DC 1250.2 DJ 171.8 F 269.8 Rest area to south is a double-ended paved parking area with picnic tables and concrete fireplaces. No water or toilets.

DC 1252.2 DJ 169.8 F 267.8 Double-ended scenic viewpoint on hill to southwest with interpretive signs on sunbowls and cranes (see text excerpts following).

"Sunbowls or solar basins are the summer expression for the warm landform depressions which have fewer cloudy days, less wind, and less precipitation than the surrounding highlands. The sun's radiation at the earth's surface varies greatly with the angle of the topography. The northwestern portion of the Tetlin Refuge is within one of these solar basins. This area becomes snow and ice-free earlier in the spring than do other areas.

"The number of trumpeter swans nesting on the Tetlin Refuge is rapidly expanding from when they first pioneered into the valley in the early 1980s. In addition, several thousand trumpeter and tundra swans rest and stage here during their migrations.

"As many as 150,000 sandhill cranes migrate through the Tetlin Refuge in the spring and fall. Utilizing high winds aloft, the cranes can be seen circling upward until they catch a current of air to take them onward to their next destination."

DC 1254 DJ 168 F 266 Distance marker westbound shows Northway Junction 10 miles, Tok 60 miles.

Views of lakes and muskeg in Chisana River valley.

DC 1256.3 DJ 165.7 F 263.7 Northway Station (state highway maintenance) to south; no services.

DC 1256.7 DJ 165.3 F 263.3 Turnoff to south for **Lakeview Campground** (Tetlin NWR), 0.2 mile from highway via a narrow, bumpy access road. There are 8 sites on a small loop next to beautiful Yarger Lake; tables, toilets, firepits, firewood, garbage container, no drinking water. No camping fee. Wheelchair accessible. Interpretive signs.

NOTE: *Not recommended for trailers, 5th wheels or RVs over 30 feet.* ♿▲

This is a good place to view ducks and loons. Look for the Nutzotin Mountains to the south and Mentasta Mountains to the west. These 2 mountain masses form the eastern end of the Alaska Range.

DC 1261 DJ 161 F 259 Old Wrangell View to south (closed). Beautiful view westbound on a clear day of Wrangell Mountains.

DC 1263.5 DJ 158.5 F 265.5 Chisana River parallels the highway to the southwest. This is the land of a thousand ponds, most unnamed. Good trapping country. In early June, travelers may note numerous cottony white seeds blowing in the wind; these seeds are from willow and poplars.

DC 1264 DJ 158 F 256 Northway Junction. Campground, gas, laundromat, store, and Native arts and crafts shop located at junction. Alaska State Troopers east side of highway. ▲

Naabia Niign Campground & Athabascan Indian Crafts. See display ad this section. ▲

Junction with 9-mile-long Northway Road (paved), which leads south across the Chisana River bridge to Northway Airport and village (see description opposite page).

DC 1264.5 DJ 157.5 F 255.5 Distance marker westbound shows Tok 50 miles, Delta Junction 158 miles, Fairbanks 254 miles, Anchorage 371 miles.

DC 1267.3 DJ 154.7 F 252.7 Wonderful view of the Tanana River at Beaver Slide.

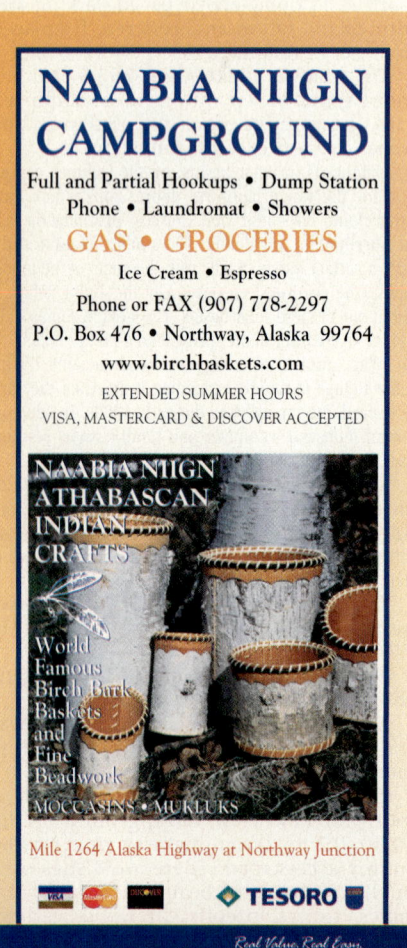

NAABIA NIIGN CAMPGROUND

Full and Partial Hookups • Dump Station
Phone • Laundromat • Showers

GAS • GROCERIES

Ice Cream • Espresso

Phone or FAX (907) 778-2297
P.O. Box 476 • Northway, Alaska 99764
www.birchbaskets.com

EXTENDED SUMMER HOURS
VISA, MASTERCARD & DISCOVER ACCEPTED

NAABIA NIIGN ATHABASCAN INDIAN CRAFTS

World Famous Birch Bark Baskets and Fine Beadwork

MOCCASINS • MUKLUKS

Mile 1264 Alaska Highway at Northway Junction

TESORO

Scenic viewpoints with interpretive signs are located along the Alaska Highway.
(© Kris Graef, staff)

There is a tower at the top of Beaver Slide. The Tanana River is the largest tributary of the Yukon River.

DC 1268 DJ 154 F 252 Beaver Creek bridge. The tea-colored water flowing in the creek is the result of tannins absorbed by the water as it flows through muskeg. This phenomenon may be observed in other northern creeks.

DC 1269 DJ 153 F 251 Historic Milepost 1271. Scenic viewpoint. Double-ended gravel turnout to south has a litter barrel and Gold Rush Centennial sign about the short-lived Chisana Gold Rush. The 1913 gold discovery on the north side of the Wrangell Mountains triggered the last major rush of the Gold Rush era. Some 2,000 stampeders reached the Chisana diggings, but most left disappointed: only a few creeks had gold and the area was remote and expensive to supply. The boom lasted little more than a year.

DC 1269.2 DJ 152.8 F 250.8 CAUTION: *Slow for loose gravel and rough road.*

DC 1272.7 DJ 149.3 F 247.3 Scenic viewpoint to south is a double-ended paved turnout with interpretive sign on pond ecology and mosquitoes.

To the northwest the Tanana River flows near the highway; beyond, the Kalukna River snakes its way through plain and marshland. Mentasta Mountains are visible to the southwest.

DC 1274 DJ 148 F 246 Paved parking area to south.

DC 1275 DJ 147 F 245 Slide areas next mile westbound.

DC 1276 DJ 146 F 244 Slide areas next mile eastbound.

DC 1284 DJ 138 F 236 Distance marker westbound shows Tok 30 miles, Fairbanks 235 miles.

DC 1284.6 DJ 137.4 F 235.4) Long double-ended paved turnout to north.

DC 1286 DJ 136 F 234 View westbound of 3.4-mile-long Midway Lake.

DC 1289 DJ 133 F 231 Long double-ended dirt turnout (unmaintained) to south.

DC 1289.5 DJ 132.5 F 230.5 Historic Milepost 1292. *Sharp turn to gravel uphill* for paved parking area to north with view of Midway Lake and Wrangell Mountains. Interpretive signs on Wrangell–St. Elias National Park, subsistence and Native claims (see excerpts following).

Wrangell-St. Elias: "The mountains visible to the south are part of Wrangell-St. Elias National Park and Preserve. Encompassing nearly 13.2 million acres, Wrangell-St. Elias is the largest national park unit in the U.S. In 1980, Wrangell-St. Elias National Park and Preserve and adjoining Kluane National Park in Canada were commemorated as a World Heritage Site by the United Nations. Together these parks are recognized by the UNESCO World Heritage Convention as a superlative mountain wilderness area of worldwide significance. Despite the rugged wilderness character of Wrangell-St. Elias, it is one of only 3 road accessible national parks in Alaska. The Glenn and Richardson highways skirt the northern and western boundaries of the park, while the Nabesna and McCarthy roads provide nearly 100 miles of road travel within the park and preserve."

The Land, The People: "Alaskan native cultures have always been closely tied to the land and its resources. The fish and wildlife resources of a given area provided the basics of survival—food, shelter and clothing. In a traditional sense, the wildlife of an area defined the lifestyloe of the native people found there. Today, subsistence has become a more complicated issue. The concept of 'living off the land' is still very important in rural Alaska, but new weapons, means of access and more people have changed the way subsistence activities occur. Defining who qualifies as a subsistence user has been one of the most complicated issues. The Alaska National Interest Lands Conservation Act that established the Tetlin National Wildlife Refuge and many other conservation units around the state recognized the importance of subsistence in rural Alaska. This act mandated that subsistence priority be given to wildlife resources on these public lands to ensure the preservation of the subsistence lifestyle into the future.

"In 1971 the U.S. Congress found and declared: 'There is an immediate need for a fair and just settlement of all claims by natives and native groups of Alaska, based on aboriginal land claims.' The resulting legislation, known as the Alaska Native Claims Settlement Act, was a comprehensive and complete law involving cash and land settlements and the establishment of regional and village corporations. Forty-four million acres and nearly a billion dollars were involved in the settlement. The intent of the 'corporate' structuring was to create a revenue producing entity that would assure a financial future for all Alaskan Natives.

"In additional to the (12) regional corporations the Alaska Native Claims Settlement Act created a system of local village corporations. These smaller organizations were awarded lands in the immediate vicinity of the village. The population of the village (according to the 1970 census) determined the amount of land the village was entitled to. The Northway Native corporation lies within the exterior boundary of the Tetlin National Wildlife Refuge and the Tetlin Indian Reserve lies just to the west."

DC 1290 DJ 132 F 230 Beautiful view of Midway Lake eastbound.

DC 1291 DJ 131 F 229 Burn area from 1998 fire visible westbound.

DC 1292.4 DJ 129.6 F 227.6 Paved parking to south.

DC 1293.7 DJ 128.3 F 226.3 Paved parking to south.

DC 1294 DJ 128 F 226 Distance marker westbound shows Tok 20 miles, Fairbanks 225 miles, Anchorage 355 miles.

DC 1301.7 DJ 120.3 F 218.3 Historic Milepost 1306 Tetlin Junction.

Junction of the Alaska Highway with the Taylor Highway (Alaska Route 5), which leads northeast 160 miles to Eagle on the Yukon River (see TAYLOR HIGHWAY section page 276). The Taylor Highway junctions with Yukon Highway 9 (Top of the World Highway) to Dawson City. See KLONDIKE LOOP section page 253 for log of Yukon Highway 9 (Top of the World Highway) and description of Dawson City.

NOTE: If you are traveling to Dawson City, keep in mind that both the Canada and U.S. customs stations are closed at night; you CANNOT cross the border unless customs stations are open. Customs hours in summer have been 8 A.M. to 8 P.M. Alaska time, 9 A.M. to 9 P.M. Pacific time on the Canadian side. Travelers are advised to check for current information at Alaska Public Lands Information Center in Tok.

DC 1301.8 DJ 120.2 F218.2 Distance marker westbound shows Tok 12 miles, Fairbanks 217 miles, Anchorage 347 miles.

DC 1302.7 DJ 119.3 F 219.3 Scenic viewpoint to southwest is a paved parking area with Gold Rush Centennial signs on Alaska's Gold Rush era and the gold strike on the Fortymile River in 1886.

DC 1303.4 DJ 118.6 F 216.6 Tanana River bridge (clearance 15' 14"). Tanana (TAN-uh-naw), an Indian name, was first reported by the Western Union Telegraph Expedition of 1886. According to William Henry Dall, chief scientist of the expedition, the name means "mountain river."

Northbound, the highway parallels the Tanana River to Fairbanks. The Alaska Range is to the northwest.

DC 1303.6 DJ 118.4 F216.6 Turnoff to northeast for side road to informal parking area and boat launch on Tanana River.

DC 1304.6 DJ 117.4 F 215.4 Evidence of burn from here north to Tok. The Tok River fire occurred in July of 1990 and burned more than 100,000 acres. The fire closed the Alaska Highway and Tok Cutoff. Tok was evacuated as firefighters' efforts to stop the fire appeared to be in vain. A "miracle wind" diverted the fire from town at the last minute.

STOP FOR DAWSON CITY 2003
TAKE TAYLOR HIGHWAY "TOP OF THE WORLD" HIGHWAY FROM TOK

www.themilepost.com

View of Midway Lake from scenic viewpoint at Milepost DC 1289.5. (© Kris Graef, staff)

ALASKA HIGHWAY • Northway

Northway

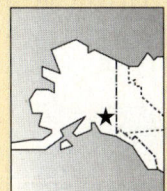

Located 9 miles south of the Alaska Highway on Northway Road; 59 miles from Tok. **Population:** 351 (area). **Emergency Services: Alaska State Troopers,** phone (907) 778-2245. **EMS,** phone (907) 778-2211. **Clinic,** phone (907) 778-2283.

Elevation: 1,710 feet. **Climate:** Mean monthly temperature in July, 58.5°F; average high, 69°F. Mean monthly temperature in January, -21°F; average low -27°F. Record high 91°F in June 1969; record low-72°F in January 1952. Average annual precipitation, 10 inches; snowfall 30 inches.

Private Aircraft: Northway airport, adjacent south; elev. 1,716 feet; length 5,130 feet; asphalt; fuel 100LL, Jet, MOGAS; customs available. Floatplanes use Yarger Lake 8 nm E.

Northway consists of 3 dispersed settlements: Northway Junction at **Milepost DC 1264** on the Alaska Highway; Northway at the airport, 6.5 miles south of Northway Junction on Northway Road; and the Native Village of Northway, 2 miles beyond the airport on the spur road. Northway has a community hall, post office, school, FAA station and customs office. Visitor services include a motel, cafe and bar at the airport.

Northway is the aviation entry point into Alaska for most private planes. According to customs agent Thomas Teasdale, some 700 planes clear customs each year here, most arriving between May and September.

Northway's airport was built in the 1940s as part of the Northwest Staging Route. This cooperative project of the United States and Canada was a chain of air bases from Edmonton, AB, through Whitehorse, YT, to Fairbanks. This chain of air bases helped build up and supply Alaska defense during WWII and also was used during construction of the Alcan and the Canol project. Lend-lease aircraft bound for Russia were flown up this route to Ladd Field (now Fort Wainwright) in Fairbanks. A propeller from one of these lend-lease planes (a P-39 Bell Aerocobra) that crashed in a nearby marsh in 1944 is on display outside the Northwest Airport Lodge.

Historically occupied by Athabascan Indians, Northway was named to honor the village chief who adopted the name of a riverboat captain in the early 1900s. (Chief Walter Northway died in 1993. He was thought to be 117 years old.) The rich Athabascan traditions of dancing, crafts, and hunting and trapping continue today in Northway Village. Local Athabascan handicrafts available for purchase include birch-bark baskets, beadwork accessories, and moose hide and fur items such as moccasins, mukluks, mittens and hats.

Confluence of Moose Creek and Chisana River, about 0.8 mile/1.3 km downstream from Chisana River bridge on Northway Road, south side of river, northern pike to 15 lbs., use red-and-white spoon, spring or fall. Look for rivers on the Chisana River. **Chisana River,** downstream from bridge, lingcod (burbot) to 8 lbs., use chunks of liver or meat, spring. **Nabesna Slough,** south end of runway, grayling to 3 lbs., use spinner or gold flies, late May.

Northway Airport Lodge & Motel. See display ad this section.

NORTHWAY AIRPORT LODGE & MOTEL

10 MODERN ROOMS WITH BATH & TV
Restaurant ♦ Package Store ♦ Cold Beer ♦ Lounge
Auto & AV Gas   Picnic Area ♦ Information

P.O. Box 400, Northway, AK 99764   Jim & Rose Moody (907) 778-2266

*Turn off Alaska Highway at MILEPOST 1264
7 miles to Northway Airport*

DC 1308.4 DJ 113.6 F 211.6 Weigh station to south; phone.

DC 1308.5 DJ 113.5 F 211.5 Turnoff to north for U.S. Coast Guard Loran-C station and signal towers. This loran (Long Range Aids to Navigation) station is 1 of 7 in Alaska. It was constructed by the U.S. Coast Guard in 1976. A series of four 700-foot towers suspends a multi-element wire antenna used to transmit navigation signals. These signals may be used by air, land and sea navigators as an aid in determining their position. This station is located here as necessary for good geometry with 2 Gulf of Alaska loran transmitting stations.

DC 1308.8 DJ 113.2 F 211.2 Wide paved shoulder to south.

DC 1309.2 DJ 112.8 F 210.8 Turnoff to north for **Tok River State Recreation Site**; 43 campsites (maximum vehicle length 60 feet) located along a good loop road beside the Tok River; campground host, tables, firepits, toilets (wheelchair accessible), litter barrels, nature trail, boat launch and pay phone. Check bulletin board for schedule of interpretive programs. Camping fee $10/night. *CAUTION: Swift water.*

DC 1309.4 DJ 112.6 F 210.6 Tok River bridge.

DC 1312.6 DJ 109.4 F 207.4 Tok community limits.

DC 1312.8 DJ 109.2 F 207.2 Tok Dog Mushers Assoc. track and buildings. Paved bike trail from Tok ends here.

DC 1313 DJ 109 F 207.1 Tok Junction airstrip. See Private Aircraft information in Tok section. Entering Tok (northbound), description follows.

Southbound travelers: Driving distance from Tok to Beaver Creek is 113 miles/182 km; Haines Junction 296 miles/476 km; Haines (departure point for Alaska state ferries) 446 miles/718 km; and Whitehorse 396 miles/637 km.

CAUTION: Watch for and slow down for sections of rough road with loose gravel and road construction southbound to border.

DC 1313.1 DJ 108.9 F 206.9 Tok Gateway Salmon Bake and RV Park. Rated, *Alaska's Best Places*, Tok's Gateway Salmon Bake, features outdoor flame-grilled Alaska wild salmon, halibut, ribs and reindeer sausage. Buffalo burgers. Chowder. Good food, friendly people; casual dining at its best. Open 11 A.M. to 9 P.M., except Sunday 4 P.M. to 9 P.M. Wooded RV and tent sites with tables, clean restrooms, dump station and water. Showers available. P.O. Box 482, Tok, AK 99780; fax (907) 883-5023; email edyoung@aptalaska.net. [ADVERTISEMENT]

DC 1313.2 DJ 108.8 F 206.8 Young's Motel and Fast Eddy's Restaurant. A touch of Alaskana in a modern setting. Affordable, clean and spacious. We cater to the independent highway traveler. Open year-round with all the amenities: telephones, private baths, satellite TV, ample parking. Nonsmoking rooms available. Check in at Fast Eddy's

full-service restaurant, open 6 A.M. to 11 P.M. Reserve early! P.O. Box 482, Tok, AK 99780. (907) 883-4411; fax (907) 883-5023; email edyoung@aptalaska.net. [ADVERTISEMENT]

DC 1313.3 DJ 108.7 F 206.7 **The Bull Shooter Sporting Goods & RV Park.** Fishing and hunting licenses and supplies. Stay at the Bull Shooter's RV park. 30 spaces, 24 pull-throughs. Full or partial hookups, 30-amp electric, dump station. Non-metered showers, ice, phone. VISA, MasterCard. On the left coming into Tok. P.O. Box 553, Tok, AK 99780. Reservations: (907) 883-5625. See display ad in Tok section. [ADVERTISEMENT] ▲

DC 1313.4 DJ 108.6 F 206.6 **Tok RV Village.** See display ad this section. ▲

DC 1314 DJ 108 F 206 **Snowshoe Motel and Fine Gifts** invites you to come in and browse our selection of fine Alaskan arts and gifts. If you are staying the night with us, you will enjoy the spacious 2-room accommodations with a private bath, perfect for a family or couples traveling together. We offer satellite TV, phone and data port in every room. Don't forget our free continental breakfast for our guests, served from 6:30 A.M. to 10 A.M., summer only. Phone (907) 883-4511. [ADVERTISEMENT]

DC 1314.2 DJ 107.8 F 205.8 **Tok Junction.** Tok Mainstreet Visitor Center and Tok Memorial Park (picnicking) to east at intersection with Alaska Route 1.

Junction of the Alaska Highway (Alaska Route 2) and the Tok Cutoff to the Glenn Highway (Alaska Route 1). It is 328 miles from Tok to Anchorage via Alaska Route 1. Turn to the GLENN HIGHWAY section on page 284 for log of that route.

Tok

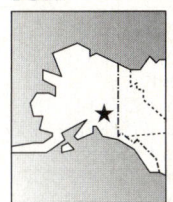

Milepost 1314 Alaska Highway, at the junction with the Tok Cutoff (Glenn Highway). Tok is 328 driving miles from Anchorage, 254 miles from Valdez and 206 miles from Fairbanks. **Population:** 1,393. **Emergency Services:** Phone 911 for emergency services. **Alaska State Troopers,** phone (907) 883-5111. **Fire Department,** phone (907) 883-5831. **Ambulance,** phone (907) 883-5111. EMT squad and air medivac available. **Community Clinic,** across from the fire hall on the Tok Cutoff, phone (907) 883-5855 during business hours. **Public Health Clinic,** next to the Alaska State Troopers at **Milepost 1314.1,** phone (907) 883-4101.

Visitor Information: The **Alaska Public Lands Information Center** (APLIC), located in the Troopers Building just east of the junction, offers state ferry information for the Alaska Marine Highway System, and information on state and national parks and

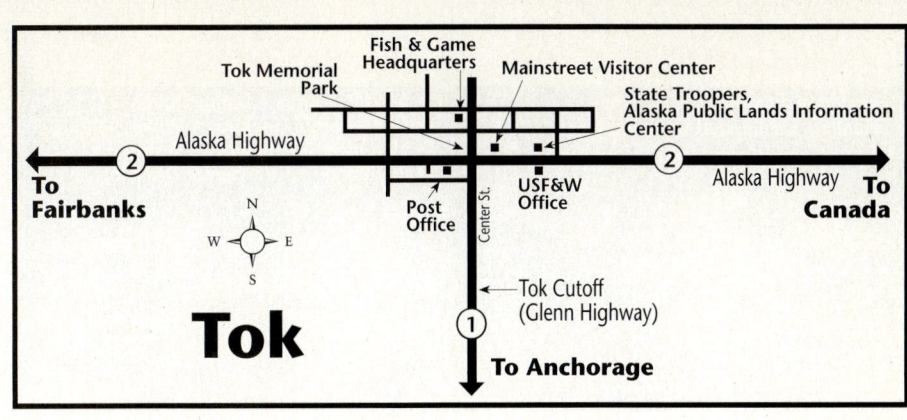

THE BULL SHOOTER Sporting Goods
- One Stop Shopping for All Your Hunting, Fishing and Camping Needs
- Fishing and Hunting Licenses and Tags

THE BULL SHOOTER RV Park
- Level Pull-thrus • Dump Station
- Full & Partial Hookups • Water
- Non-metered Showers • Restrooms
- Pay Phone • Ice • Senior Discounts

P.O. Box 553, Tok, Alaska 99780 • (907) 883-5625
www.aptalaska.net/~thebull/index.htm e-mail: thebull@aptalaska.net
On your left coming into Tok • See log ad Mile 1313.3 Alaska Highway

Not accepted for hunting & fishing licenses

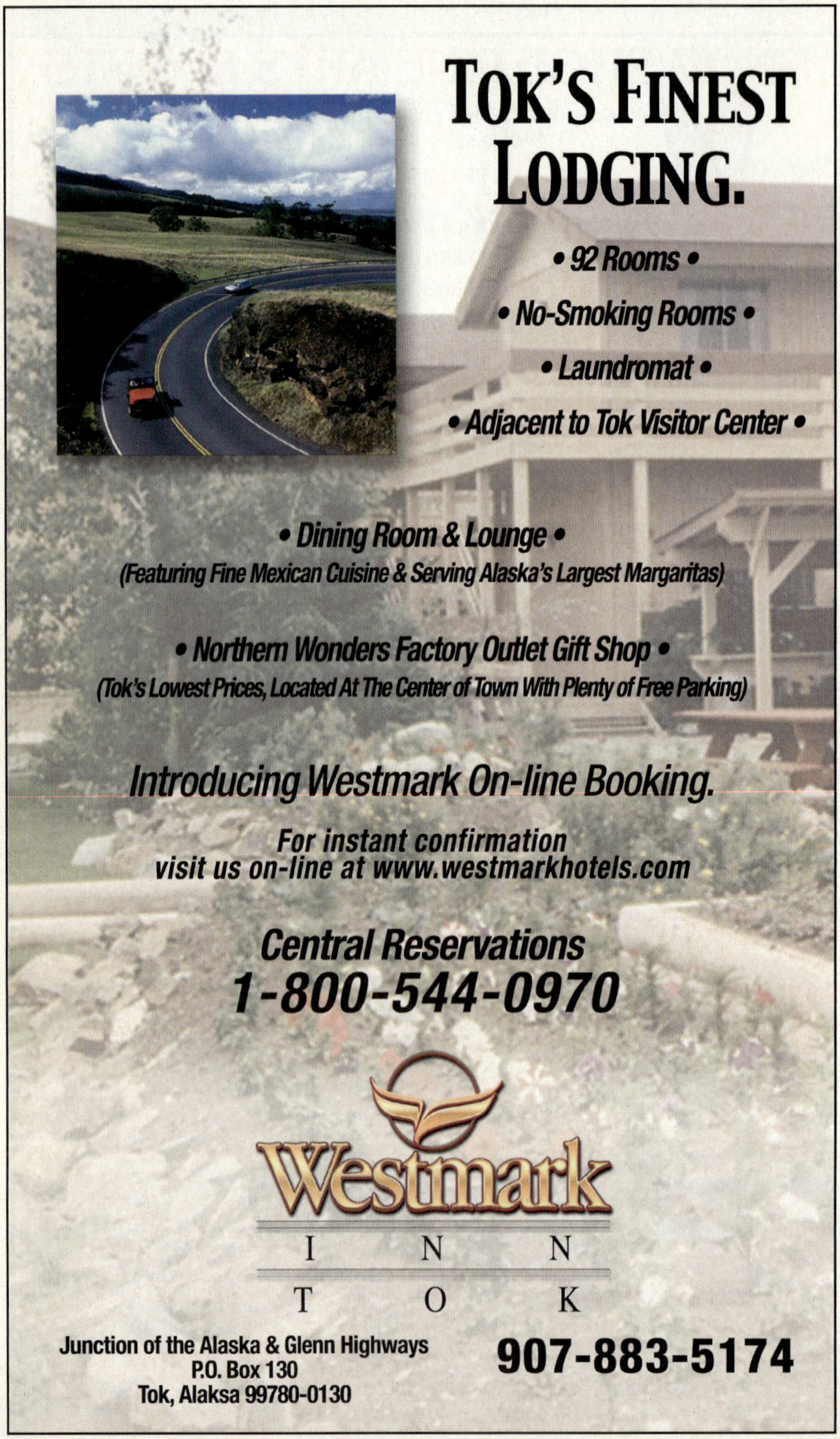

TOK'S FINEST LODGING.

- 92 Rooms •
- No-Smoking Rooms •
- Laundromat •
- Adjacent to Tok Visitor Center •

• Dining Room & Lounge •
(Featuring Fine Mexican Cuisine & Serving Alaska's Largest Margaritas)

• Northern Wonders Factory Outlet Gift Shop •
(Tok's Lowest Prices, Located At The Center of Town With Plenty of Free Parking)

Introducing Westmark On-line Booking.

For instant confirmation
visit us on-line at www.westmarkhotels.com

Central Reservations
1-800-544-0970

Westmark INN TOK

Junction of the Alaska & Glenn Highways
P.O. Box 130
Tok, Alaksa 99780-0130

907-883-5174

---

campgrounds. Write P.O. Box 359, Tok, Alaska 99780; phone (907) 883-5666.

At the Tok "Mainstreet Alaska" Visitors Center, located at the junction of the Alaska Highway and Tok Cutoff; open May through September. This beautiful log building houses the Tok Chamber of Commerce (fax 907/883-3682) and the Tok Library. The visitor center offers trip planning help and complete travel information on the Alaska Highway, travel in and around Alaska, statewide brochures to most destinations and attractions, displays from communities around the state, as well as local information on private campgrounds, RV parks, hotel/motel/B & B's, restaurants, things to do and see in Tok, art exhibits, and films. The center also offers public telephones, restrooms, current road conditions and a message board. Their friendly staff will gladly answer any questions you may have. Write P.O. Box 389, Tok, AK 99780; phone (907) 883-5775. Internet www.tok

TOK ADVERTISERS

All Alaska Gifts & Crafts	Ph. (907) 883-5081
Bull Shooter Sporting Goods, The	Ph. (907) 883-5625
Bull Shooter RV Park, The	Mile 1313.3 Alaska Hwy.
Burnt Paw Gift Shop, Cabins, Outback B&B	Ph. (907) 883-4121
Canoe Alaska, Inc.	Mile 0.6 Scoby Way
Cleft of the Rock B&B	Ph. (800) 478-5646
Community After-School Programs	Ph. (907) 883-5151
Cozy Brs+Cabins+Hostel	Ph. (907) 883-3602
Denali State Bank	Ph. (907) 883-2265
Discovery Inn Bed & Breakfast	Ph. (907) 883-5559
Fast Eddy's Restaurant	Ph. (907) 883-4411
40 Mile Air	Ph. (907) 883-5191
Golden Bear Motel, Restaurant, RV Park	Ph. (907) 883-2561
Jack Wade Gold Co.	Ph. (907) 883-5887
Mainstreet Visitors Center	Ph. (907) 883-5775
Mukluk Land	Ph. (907) 883-2571
Northern Energy	Ph. (907) 883-4251
Off the Road House	Ph. (907) 883-5600
Shamrock Hardware	Ph. (907) 883-2161
Snowshoe Fine Arts and Gifts	Ph. (907) 883-4181
Snowshoe Motel	Ph. (907) 883-4511
Sourdough Campground	Ph. (907) 883-5543
Sourdough Campground's Pancake Breakfast	Mile 1.7 Tok Cutoff
Tok Chamber of Commerce	Ph. (907) 883-5775
Tok Gateway Salmon Bake	Ph. (907) 883-4411
Tok Line Camp B&B	Ph. (907) 883-5506
Tok Lodge	Ph. (907) 883-2851
Tok RV Village	Ph. (907) 883-5877
Toklat Auto Parts	Ph. (800) 906-5858
Towing by James Enterprises	Ph. (907) 883-5346
Tundra Lodge & RV Park	Ph. (907) 883-7875
Westmark Inn Tok	Ph. (907) 883-5174
Young's Cafe	Ph. (907) 883-2233
Young's Chevron	Ph. (907) 883-2821
Young's Motel	Ph. (907) 883-4411

Please support our MILEPOST® advertisers!

Tok Chamber of Commerce Welcomes You to Alaska

Partial Membership Sponsors:

Mainstreet Visitor Center
Trip planning, travel information.
Wildlife displays, gifts. 8am–7pm daily.
http://www.TokAlaskaInfo.com
info@tokalaskainfo.com
907-883-5775

Cleft of the Rock B&B
Cabins & rooms. Hearty, hot breakfast, free videos, phones, TV/VCR's, private baths.
www.cleftoftherock.net
info@cleftoftherock.net
1-800-478-5646

Northern Energy
One-Stop TLC for your RV
Discounts • Gas • Diesel • Tires
Propane • Free use of car wash & dump
with fill-up • Mile 1315 Ak Hwy
907-883-4251

Toklat Auto Parts
For All Your Automotive Needs
RV Supplies 907-883-5858
1-800-906-5858
Mile 1314 Alaska Highway, Tok

Tok Line Camp B&B
Quiet, Modern Cabins
Horse Rides - Hour, Day, Trip
jbzinc@aptalaska.net
Fax 907-883-5500
907-883-5506

Westmark Tok Hotel
Factory Outlet Gift Shop (great low prices)
92 modern rooms, satellite TV, Full service restaurant, lounge, and laundromat. Offering AAA, Corporate, and Government Rates.
Located at the center of town.
907-883-5174
Reservations
1-800-544-0970
www.Westmarkhotels.com

Golden Bear
Motel–Restaurant–RV Park
Gift & Cappuccino Shops, Large rooms,
King & Queen beds available
1-866-883-2561
907-883-2561 Fax 907-883-5950

Sourdough Campground
Full hook-ups, wooded sites,
Sourdough breakfast daily 7am-11am.
June 1–Aug 31.
1 1/2 Mile South on Tok Cutoff
907-883-5543
Fax 907-883-3332

Tok RV Village
Full & partial pull thrus, showers included, modem service, laundry, vehicle wash,
907-883-5877
TokRV@aptalaska.net

Discovery Inn Bed & Breakfast
New log home with private balconies.
alaskawillow75@yahoo.com
www.discoveryinnalaska.com
907-883-5559

All Alaska Gifts & Crafts
Quality T-shirts, Jewelry, Native crafts,
Eskimo dolls, Homemade Fudge.
You'll like our prices.
At the main intersection in Tok.
907-883-5081

Burnt Paw Gift Shop Cabins Outback B&B
All log with sod roofs. All conveniences inside.
Gifts, quality apparel, Native Crafts
907-883-4121
www.burntpawcabins.com
nrthland@yahoo.com

Tundra Lodge & RV Park
78 Large shade sites, 30-50 Amp. service,
tent sites, RV wash, laundromat, modem
hookup, cocktail lounge.
907-883-7875
tundrarv@aptalaska.net

Community After-School Programs
Learning is FUN for everyone!
GAP (Gateway After-school Programs) provides academic, enrichment and recreational programs for students, parents and community members
Year-round. Contact LeAnn Young at
(907) 883-5151 EXT 110

Denali State Bank
Full Service Bank
Travelers checks, Canadian Exchange.
Located inside Three Bears Grocery
907-883-2265

Jack Wade Gold Co.
Mining Museum–Antique display.
Alaska gold nugget jewelry made in store.
Year-round, 8am–8pm.
jwgold@aptalaska.net
jackwadegold.com
907-883-5887

Snowshoe Gifts
Souvenirs, fine art, carvings, prints
jewelry, Alaska made gifts.
Adjacent to Snowshoe Motel.
907-883-4181

Snowshoe Motel
24 Modern units TV, phones, & data ports.
Year-round Summer: Continental breakfast.
Reservations:
907-883-4511
1-800-478-4511
FAX: 907-883-4512
Snowshoe@aptalaska.net
P.O. Box 559, Tok, AK 99780
Hosts: Geneva Smith & Candy Troupe

Off the Road House
International Friendship House Bed & Breakfast and Gallery. Mile 1318.5 Alaska Highway. **Wir sprechen Deutsch!**
907-883-5600
rdhouse@aptalaska.net

Cozy BRs Cabins HOSTEL
Big breakfast $25/Night & Up
$10 tent/RV parking picnic tables
BBQ Info eve FREE movie/eats
Box 277 1313.5 Ak Hwy (907)-883-3602
Year round we're blessed to serve YOU!

40 Mile Air
Flight seeing, fishing & hunting trips,
just need a ride to Fairbanks?
907-883-5191

ALASKA HIGHWAY • Tok

There are no traffic lights or stop signs on the Alaska Highway in Tok. *(© Kris Graef, staff)*

Description

Tok had its beginnings as a construction camp on the Alcan Highway in 1942. Highway engineer C.G. Polk was sent to Fairbanks in May of 1942 to take charge of Alaskan construction and start work on the road between Tok Junction and Big Delta. Work was also under way on the Gulkana–Slana–Tok Junction road (now the Tok Cutoff on the Glenn Highway to Anchorage). But on June 7, 1942, a Japanese task force invaded Attu and Kiska islands in the Aleutians, and the Alcan took priority over the Slana cutoff.

The name Tok (rhymes with poke) was long believed to be derived from Tokyo Camp, a road construction camp sprung up in 1943 as part of the straightening and improvement projects on the Alcan Highway. During WWII, Tokyo Camp was patriotically shortened to "Tok." After much research and documentation, according to local author and historian, Donna Blasor-Bernhardt in "Tok, The Real Story" (1996), Tok was actually named after a husky pup on August 15, 1942 when the U.S. Army's Corp (the 97th engineers—an all black corps) were breaking trail north from Slana on what is now the Tok Cutoff. They were working their way to the point where they would intersect with and begin breaking trail southeast on what would become the Alaska Highway. Their job consisted of not only building the road, but naming points along the way. The young pup, named Tok, was their beloved mascot, and upon their arrival at where Tok now is, it was unanimously decided to name the junction after the pup.

Because Tok is the major overland point

alaska.info.com; email: info@tokalaska info.com.

Fishing and hunting regulations are available at the Alaska Dept. of Fish and Game office located on Center Street, across from Tok Mainstreet Visitor Center at **Milepost DC 1314.2**. Contact ADF&G, Box 355, Tok, AK 99780; Phone (907) 883-2971; fax (907) 883-2970. Fishing licenses are available at local dealers.

The U.S. Fish & Wildlife Service office is located at **Milepost DC 1314.1** next to the grocery store, directly across the highway from the State Troopers. Visitors are welcome. Stop in for information regarding Tetlin National Wildlife Refuge and wildlife import/export permits. Office hours are 7:30 A.M. to 5 P.M., weekdays. Or write U.S. Fish & Wildlife Service, Box 155, Tok, AK 99780; phone (907) 883-5312.

Elevation: 1,635 feet. **Climate:** Mean monthly temperature in January is -19° F; average low is -32°F. Mean monthly temperature in July is 59°F; average high is 72°F. Record low was -71°F (January 1965); record high, 99°F. **Radio:** FM stations are 90.5, 91.1 (KUAC-FM, University of Alaska Fairbanks) and 101.5. **Television:** Satellite channel 13. **Newspaper:** *Mukluk News* (twice monthly).

Private Aircraft: Tok Junction, 1 E; elev. 1,630 feet; length 2,510 feet; asphalt; fuel 100LL; unattended. Tok airstrip, on Tok Cutoff, 2 S; elev. 1,670 feet; length 3,000 feet; gravel; no fuel, unattended.

GOLDEN BEAR
RESTAURANT   MOTEL   RV PARK

60 Modern Rooms   Private Baths   Daily Lunch   Dinner Specials
Laundry Facilities   Bath and Shower in Room   Gift Shop

1-866-883-2561
www.tokalaska.com/901   gldnbear@aptalaska.net

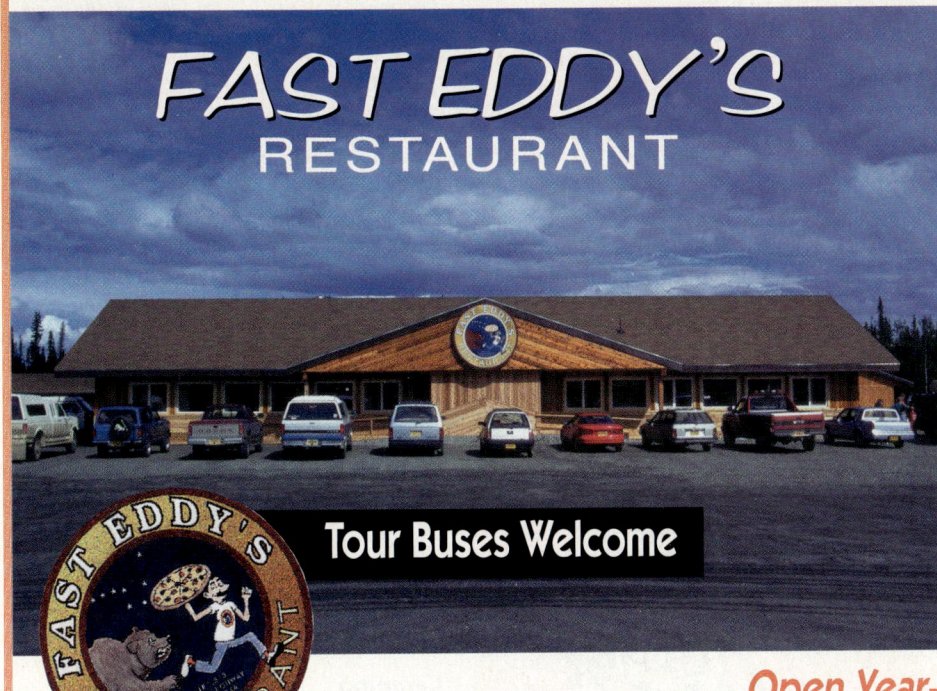

FAST EDDY'S RESTAURANT

(907) 883-4411

Breakfast • Lunch • Dinner
Steaks • Seafood
Pasta • Burgers
• Sandwiches •
Fresh Salad Bar
Pies • Ice Cream
Milk Shakes

Entire Menu Available To Go

Open Year-Round • 6am to 11pm

Tour Buses Welcome

YOUNG'S MOTEL

(907) 883-4411

43 Large,
Clean, Modern Rooms
Non-Smoking Rooms
Private Baths
with Tubs & Showers
Satellite TV • Private,
In-Room Telephones

Ample Parking

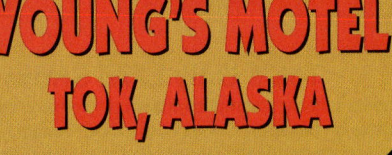
YOUNG'S MOTEL TOK, ALASKA

When You Visit Tok, Enjoy the Comfort!

Office and Motel Check-In Inside Fast Eddy's Restaurant

(907) 883-4411 • fax (907) 883-5023
e-mail: edyoung@aptalaska.net
Box 482, Tok, Alaska 99780
See our log ad at Mile 1313.3 Alaska Highway • 3/4 mile from the Junction

of entry to Alaska, it is primarily a trade and service center for all types of transportation, especially for summer travelers coming up the Alaska Highway. A stopover here is a good opportunity to meet other travelers and swap experiences. Tok is the only town in Alaska that the highway traveler must pass through twice—once when arriving in the state and again on leaving the state. The governor proclaimed Tok "Mainstreet Alaska" in 1991. Townspeople are proud of this designation and work hard to make visitors happy.

Tok's central business district is at the junction of the Alaska Highway and Tok Cutoff. From the junction, homes and businesses spread out along both highways on flat terrain dotted with densely timbered stands of black spruce.

Tok has 13 churches, a public library, an elementary school, a 4-year accredited high school and a University of Alaska extension program. Local clubs include the Lions, Disabled American Veterans, Veterans of Foreign Wars and Chamber of Commerce.

Tok has become known as the "Sled Dog Capital of Alaska," because so many of its residents have been involved in some way with dogs and dog mushing, Alaska's official state sport. Sled dogs may be any registered breed or crossbreed, since mushers look for conformation, attitude and speed when putting together a working team rather than pedigrees.

Lodging & Services

There are 8 hotels/motels/bed and breakfast, a youth hostel, restaurants and gas stations in the Tok area, located along both the Alaska Highway and Tok Cutoff. Tok AYH youth hostel is located on Pringle Road, 0.8 miles south of **Milepost DC 1322.6**; phone (907) 883-3745.

Tok Lodge, located 1 block south of junction. Full-service restaurant, gift shop and cocktail lounge. 36 new motel rooms. Common comments are "nicest rooms on the highway" and "best meal since leaving home." Mini-Mart and liquor store located on the premises. Internet: www.alaskan.com/toklodge/. Email: toklodge@aptalaska.net. See display ad this section. [ADVERTISEMENT]

The post office is located on the Alaska Highway just northwest of its junction with the Tok Cutoff, between the Westmark and Burnt Paw gift shop. Grocery, hardware and sporting goods stores, beauty shop, gift shops, liquor stores, auto repair and auto parts stores, wrecker services and laundromats are available. Tok has ATMs and one bank, Denali State Bank, which is located inside the Three Bears Grocery.

Parking, playground and picnic shelters are available at Tok Memorial Park, across from the Tok Mainstreet Visitor Center.

Visitors are welcome at the senior citizens center.

Camping

There are several full-service private RV parks in Tok (see ads this section), located

TOUR BUSES WELCOME

MOTEL
DINING ROOM
COCKTAILS

1-800-883-3007
(907) 883-2851
(907) 883-4452 fax
Box 135-M, Tok AK 99780

TOK LODGE

ALASKA HIGHWAY • Tok

TUNDRA
LODGE AND RV PARK

78 SPACIOUS NATURALLY FORESTED SITES

★ Full partial Hookups
★ Tent (dry) Sites
★ Pull Throughs
★ Showers Included in Price
★ Dump Station
★ Picnic Tables
★ Fire Rings - Wood
★ E-mail Access

★ 20/30/50 Amp Power
★ Laundromat
★ Vehicle Wash
★ Pay Phone
★ Ice
★ Cocktail Lounge
★ Meeting Room

PO Box 760, Tok, Alaska 99780 • Mile 1315 Alaska Highway

(907) 883-7875

Fax (907) 883-7876
e-mail: tundrarv@aptalaska.net

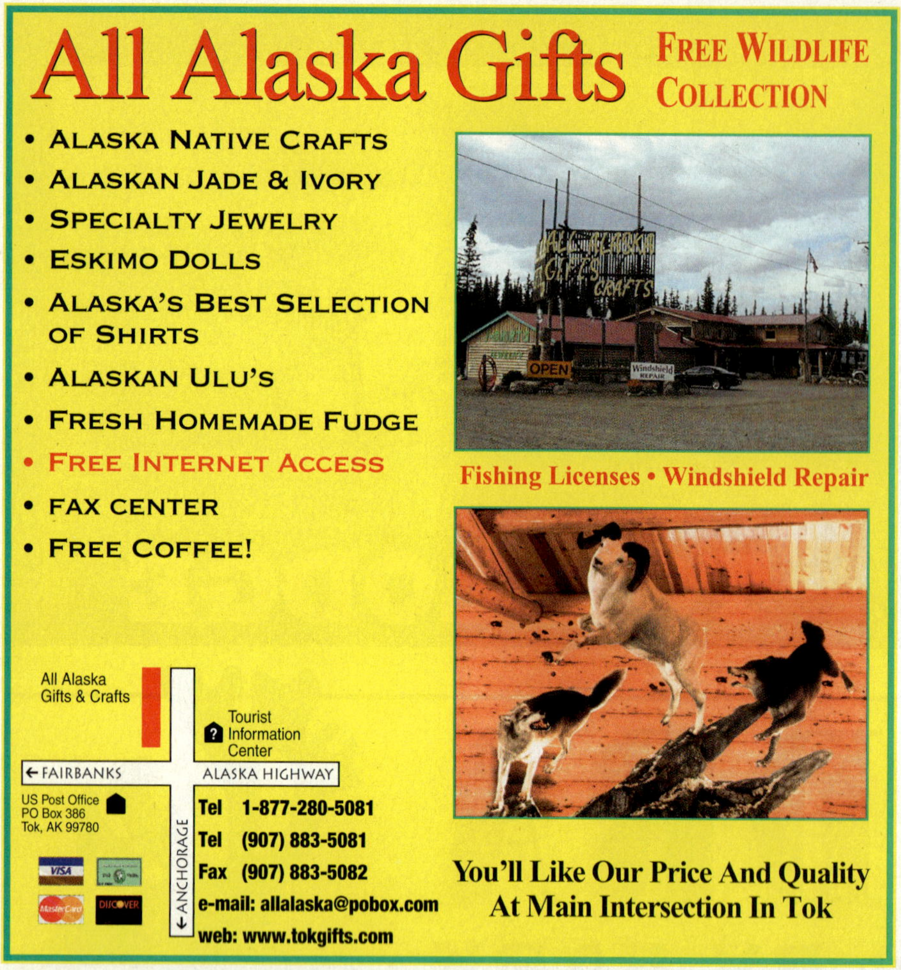
All Alaska Gifts
Free Wildlife Collection
• Alaska Native Crafts
• Alaskan Jade & Ivory
• Specialty Jewelry
• Eskimo Dolls
• Alaska's Best Selection of Shirts
• Alaskan Ulu's
• Fresh Homemade Fudge
• Free Internet Access
• Fax Center
• Free Coffee!
OPEN
Fishing Licenses • Windshield Repair
All Alaska Gifts & Crafts
Tourist Information Center
← FAIRBANKS
ALASKA HIGHWAY
US Post Office PO Box 386 Tok, AK 99780
← ANCHORAGE
Tel 1-877-280-5081
Tel (907) 883-5081
Fax (907) 883-5082
e-mail: allalaska@pobox.com
web: www.tokgifts.com
You'll Like Our Price And Quality At Main Intersection In Tok

along the Alaska Highway and Tok Cutoff.

Nearby state campgrounds include: Tok River State Recreation Site, 5 miles south of Tok on the Alaska Highway at **Milepost DC 1309.2**; Moon Lake State Recreation Site, 17.7 miles north of Tok at **Milepost DC 1331.9** Alaska Highway; and Eagle Trail State Recreation Site, 16 miles west of Tok at **Milepost GJ 109.3** Tok Cutoff. ▲

Sourdough Campground's Pancake Breakfast, served 7–11 A.M. (June, July, August). Genuine "Sourdough!" Full and partial RV hookups. Dry campsites. Showers included. Guaranteed clean restrooms. High-pressure car wash. Open-air museum with gold rush memorabilia. Free evening video program. Located 1.7 miles from the junction toward Anchorage on Tok Cutoff (Glenn Highway). See display ad this section. [ADVERTISEMENT] ▲

Tundra Lodge & RV Park. Spacious, naturally forested camping sites. Full and partial hookups; 20-, 30-, 50-amp power. Tent sites. Pull-throughs. Clean restrooms and showers included in price. Picnic tables, fire rings and wood. Dump station. Laundromat. Vehicle wash. Pay phone. Ice. Cocktail lounge and meeting room. E-mail access: tundrarv@aptalaska.net. See display ad **Milepost 1315** Alaska Highway. [ADVERTISEMENT] ▲

Transportation

Air: Charter air service available; inquire at Tok state airstrip (**Milepost DC 1313**). Charter flightseeing and fly-in fishing trips available. Scheduled passenger and freight service between Tok, Delta Junction and Fairbanks 4 days a week via 40-Mile Air.

Bus: Alaska Direct Busline.

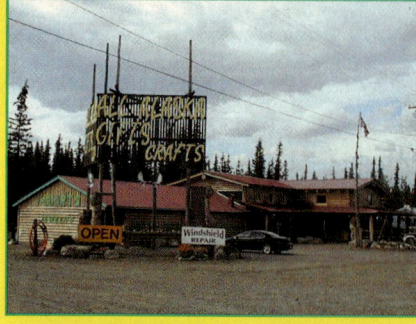

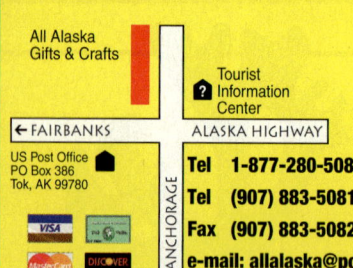

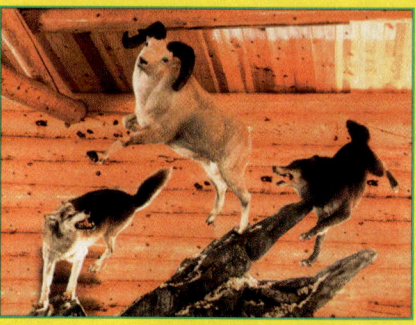

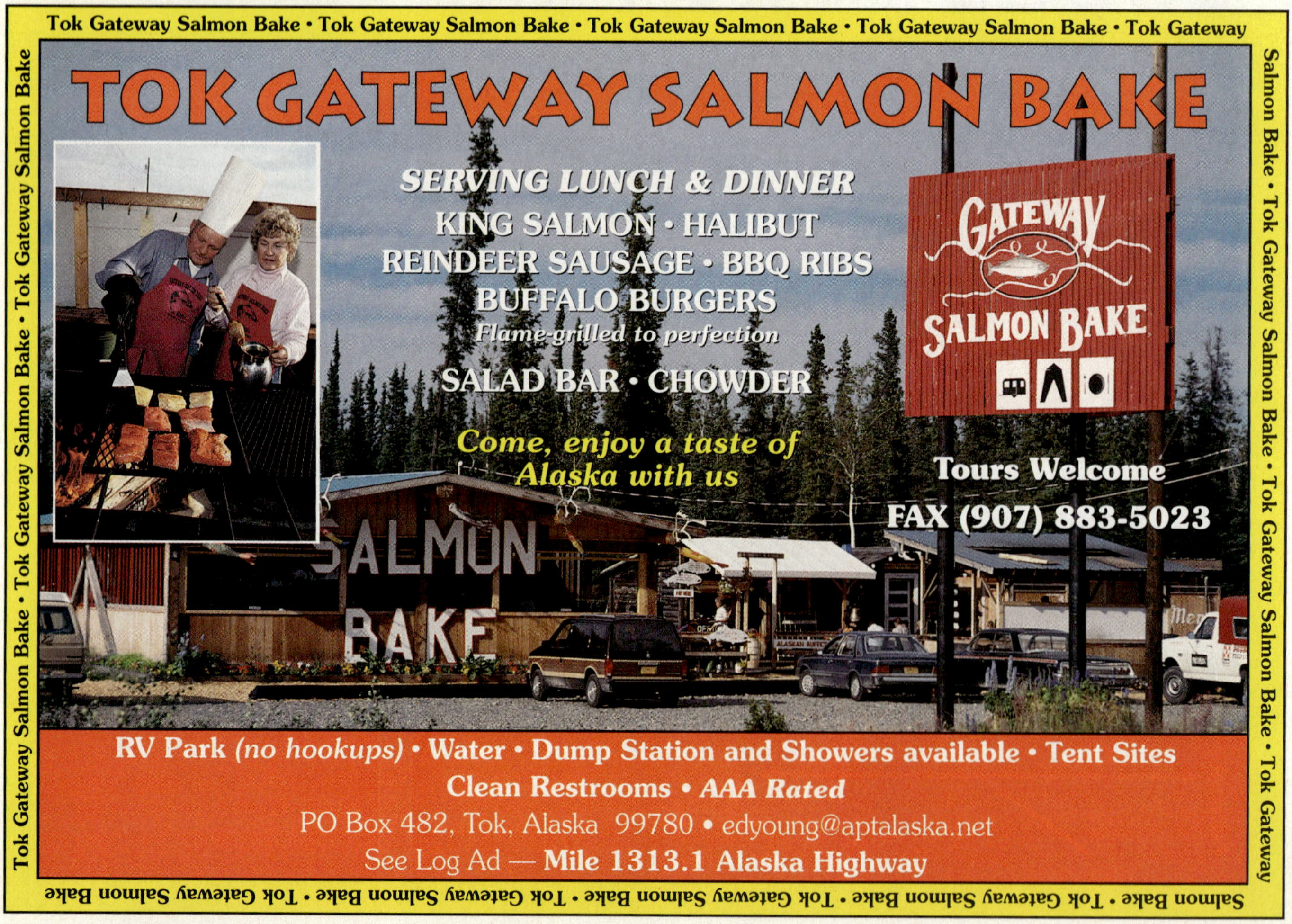
Tok Gateway Salmon Bake • Tok Gateway Salmon Bake • Tok Gateway Salmon Bake • Tok Gateway Salmon Bake • Tok Gateway
TOK GATEWAY SALMON BAKE
SERVING LUNCH & DINNER
KING SALMON • HALIBUT
REINDEER SAUSAGE • BBQ RIBS
BUFFALO BURGERS
Flame-grilled to perfection
SALAD BAR • CHOWDER
Come, enjoy a taste of Alaska with us
GATEWAY SALMON BAKE
Tours Welcome
FAX (907) 883-5023
SALMON BAKE
RV Park (no hookups) • Water • Dump Station and Showers available • Tent Sites
Clean Restrooms • AAA Rated
PO Box 482, Tok, Alaska 99780 • edyoung@aptalaska.net
See Log Ad — Mile 1313.1 Alaska Highway

Attractions

Tok Mainstreet Visitors Center. Located at the junction of the Alaska Highway and Tok Cutoff, this 7,000-square-foot building houses the Tok Mainstreet Visitor Center and the Tok Community Public Library. Huge natural white spruce logs brought in locally, support an open-beamed, cathedral ceiling. Large picture windows frame the Alaska Range. Displays include: rock, gems and fossils; the gold rush; Alaska wildlife and waterfowl; and Alaska Highway memorabilia.

Tok Mainstreet Visitors Center has wildlife displays and brochures. *(© Kris Graef, staff)*

Tok Memorial Park, at the Alaska Highway and Tok Cutoff intersection (across from Tok Mainstreet Visitors Center), has day parking, a picnic shelter and playground.

Canoe Alaska, Inc. Learn proper paddling techniques with American Canoe Association certified instructors. Join us for an interpretive paddle in a 16-person, 34-foot Voyageur canoe, or embark on a guided wilderness river adventure. Local rentals available to qualified paddlers. Phone (907) 883-2628 or info@canoealaska.net. www.canoealaska.net. [ADVERTISEMENT]

Biking: A wide paved bike trail parallels the Alaska Highway and extends from Tok southeast to the Dog Mushers Assoc. track, and northwest to Tanacross Junction. Approximate length is 13 miles. There is also a 2.4-mile bike trail along the Tok-Cutoff west from Tok. Travelers may park their vehicles in and around Tok and find a bike trail nearby leading into or out of Tok.

Native Crafts: Tok is a trade center for the Athabascan Native villages of Tanacross, Northway, Tetlin, Mentasta, Dot Lake and Eagle. Several of the Native women make birch baskets, beaded moccasins, boots and beaded necklaces. Examples of Native work may be seen at the Native-operated gift shop at Northway junction and at several gift shops and other outlets in Tok.

The state of Alaska has a crafts identification program which authenticates Alaskan Native and Alaskan Craftsmen products.

Birch baskets were once used in the Native camps and villages. Traditionally they had folded corners, which held water, and were even used for cooking by dropping heated stones into the liquid in the baskets. The baskets are made by peeling the bark from the birch trees, usually in the early summer months. The bark is easiest to work with when moist and pliable. It is cut into shape and sewn together with strips of spruce root dug out of the ground and split. If the root is too dry it is soaked until it is manageable. Holes are put in the birch bark with a punch or screwdriver, and the spruce root is laced in and out. Native women dye the spruce root with food coloring, watercolors or berry juice. A few Natives also make model birch canoes and birch baby carriers.

Many of the moccasins and mukluks for sale in Tok are made with moose hide that

Young's Chevron Service
VOLUME FUEL DISCOUNTS

OPEN 24 HOURS

Gas • Diesel • Propane • Tires • Ice • Foodmart
ATM • Espresso

COMPLETE AUTO SERVICE CENTER
Tune-ups, Electrical, Brakes, Alignments

TIRE SALES & SERVICE
Complete line of auto, R.V., and trailer tires

SPECIALIZING IN R.V. & AUTO FAST LUBE, OIL & FILTER

R.V. & CAR WASH • *FREE* R.V. parking, dump & water with fill-up

Located at the Junction in Tok, across from Visitor Center

(907) 883-2821

Young's Cafe
Homemade Pies & Goodies (907) 883-2233

Full Menu • Sourdough Hotcakes • Steaks, Salmon & Salad Bar
BBQ Ribs & Chicken • Daily Specials • Beer & Wine • Friendly Staff
At the Junction, next to Young's Chevron

has the "Native tan." This means moose hide tanned by the Native. First the excess fat and meat is scraped off the hide, then it is soaked in a soap solution (some use a mixture of brains and ashes). After soaking, all the moisture is taken out by constant scraping with a dull knife or scraper. The hide is then scraped again and rubbed together to soften it. Next it is often smoke-cured in rotted spruce wood smoke. The tanning process takes from a few days to a week.

Beading can be a slow and tedious process. Most women say if they work steadily all day they can put the beading on one moccasin, but usually they do their beadwork over a period of several days, alternating it with other activities.

Sled Dog Trails and Races: Tok boasts a well-known and long-established dog mushing trail, which draws many world-class and recreational mushers. The 20.5-mile/33-km trail begins at the rustic log Tok Dog Mushers Assoc. building at **Milepost DC 1312.8** on the Alaska Highway. The trail is a favorite with spectators because it affords many miles of viewing from along the Alaska Highway.

Racing begins in late November and extends through the end of March. Junior mushers include 1-, 2-, 3- and 5-dog classes; junior adult mushers include 5- and 8-dog classes. Open (unlimited) classes can run as many as 16 dogs.

The biggest race of the season in Tok is the Race of Champions, held in late March, which also has the largest entry of any sprint race in Alaska. Begun in 1954 as a bet between 2 roadhouse proprietors, today the Race of Champions includes over 100 teams in 3 classes competing for prize money and trophies. It is considered to be the third leg of sled dog racing's "triple crown," following the Fur Rendezvous in Anchorage and the Fairbanks North American Championship. Visitors are also welcome to attend the Tok Native Assoc.'s potlatch, held the same weekend as the race, in the Tok school gym.

AREA FISHING: Fly-in fishing to area lakes for northern pike, grayling and lake trout; inquire at Tok state airstrip. There are 43 lakes in the Delta–Tok area that are stocked by the Alaska Dept. of Fish and Game. Lakes are stocked primarily with rainbow trout; other stocked species include arctic grayling, lake trout, arctic char and king salmon. Most of these lakes are located close to the road system, but there are walk-in lakes available as well. Most easily accessible are **North Twin**, **South Twin** and **Mark lakes.** There is a trailhead 0.5 mile/0.8 km east of the Gerstle River bridge for **Big Donna Lake** (3.5-mile/5.6-km hike) and **Little Donna Lake** (4.5 miles/7.2 km). **Quartz Lake**, north of Delta Junction, is a popular spot for rainbow trout and silver salmon. Consult ADF&G offices in Tok or Delta Junction for other locations; phone (907) 883-2971.

Alaska Highway Log
(continued)

ALASKA ROUTE 2 WEST
Distance from Dawson Creek (DC)* is followed by distance from Delta Junction (DJ) and distance from Fairbanks (F).
*Mileages from Dawson Creek, Delta Junction and Fairbanks are based on physical mileposts in Alaska.

DC 1314.8 DJ 107.2 F 205.2 Gas, diesel,

tire repair and car wash.
Northern Energy Corp. See display ad this section.

DC 1315 DJ 107 F 205 Tundra Lodge and RV Park. ▲

DC 1316.6 DJ 105.4 F 203.4 Scoby Road, Sundog Trail. Access to Cleft of the Rock B&B.

DC 1317 DJ 105 F 203 Mukluk Land; gold panning, activities for kids, videos, educational displays.

Mukluk Land. See display ad this section.

DC 1317.7 DJ 104.3 F 202.3 Tok community limits.

DC 1318.5 DJ 103.5 F 201.5 Bed and breakfast and gallery.

Off The Road House. See display ad this section.

DC 1322.6 DJ 99.4 F 197.4 Pringle Road. Tok youth hostel, housed in a wall tent, is located 0.8 mile/1.3 km south; 10 beds, tent space available.

DC 1324.6 DJ 97.4 F 195.4 Alaska Dept. of Natural Resources (DNR) **Tanacross Air Tanker Base**. Gravel access road (Old Tanacross Road) leads 1.6 miles northeast to Tanacross airstrip. The airfield was built in the 1930s, with assistance from local Tanacross Natives, and was used by the U.S. Army in WWII as part of the Russia–America Lend Lease Program. (The Lend Lease Program sent war planes to Russia, a U.S. ally, to use in fighting Nazi Germany.) After WWII, the airfield was used for specialized arctic operations and maneuvers. The Tanacross Airfield was the sixth largest city in Alaska in 1962, housing more than 8,000 troops for "Operation Great Bear." In 1970, the Bureau of Land Management acquired the property because of the strategic location of its paved runway for refueling air tankers fighting forest fires. Alaska DNR now controls the air tanker operations at the airfield.

Private Aircraft: Tanacross airstrip; elev. 1,549 feet; 2 runways, length 5,000 feet and 5,100 feet; asphalt; unattended. *CAUTION: Forest fire aviation support may be in progress.*

DC 1324.8 DJ 97.6 F 195.2 Distance marker westbound shows Dot Lake 37 miles, Delta Junction 99 miles, Fairbanks 195 miles.

DC 1325.6 DJ 96.4 F 194.4 Historic Milepost 1328.

DC 1325.7 DJ 96.3 F 194.3 End of paved bike trail from Tok. **Junction** with Tanacross Road, the main access road north to Tanacross. Drive 1.2 miles on gravel road to "Y" intersection; turn right for airstrip (see **Milepost DC 1324.6**), turn left for loop road through Native village of **TANACROSS** (pop. 140), home of the once numerous Denn daey, Athabascan Indians.

DC 1327.3 DJ 94.6 F 192.7 Informal turnout by small lake to southwest.

DC 1330.1 DJ 91.9 F 189.9 Scenic viewpoint to north is a paved turnout.

DC 1331.9 DJ 90.1 F 188.1 Moon Lake State Recreation Site, 0.2 mile off highway; 17 campsites, picnic area, toilets, tables, water, firepits, boat launch, sandy beach, swimming (watch for floatplanes). Camping fee $10/night. ▲

DC 1333.6 DJ 88.4 F 186.4 Historic Milepost 1339. Yerrick Creek bridge.

DC 1338.2 DJ 83.8 F 181.8 Highway crosses Cathedral Creek 3 times between here and **Milepost DC 1339**.

DC 1338.3 DJ 83.5 F 181.5 Cathedral Creek Bed and Breakfast and RV Parking. Beautifully nestled between mountains and creeks, we offer breathtaking views, hiking, fishing, swimming at nearby Moon Lake,

Johnson River bridge crosses a tributary of the Tanana River. (© Bob Butterfield)

playground, firepit, boat/bicycle rentals. Clean, inviting accommodations, home-cooked breakfasts on sundeck and choice of room or private cabin with kitchenette. Shared bath only. $65 double occupancy. RVs $8. Weekly rates; group discounts. Wir Sprechen Deutsch! Phone (907) 883-4455. www.cathedralcreeks.com; email contact@catehdralcreeks.com. [ADVERTISEMENT]

DC 1342.2 DJ 79.8 F 177.8 Sheep Creek culvert.

DC 1344.5 DJ 77.5 F 175.5 Historic Milepost 1352. Paved parking area to north. Interpretive panel on the "father of the international highway," Donald MacDonald. Alaska Range to the south. Good photo stop.

DC 1347.2 DJ 74.8 F 172.8 Forest Lake trailhead; 6-mile ATV trail (not easy access) to lake stocked with rainbow trout.

DC 1347.3 DJ 74.7 F 172.7 Entering Game Management Unit 20D westbound, Unit 12 eastbound.

DC 1347.5 DJ 74.5 F 172.5 Robertson River bridge. The river was named by Lt. Henry T. Allen for a member of his 1885 expedition.

The Robertson River heads at the terminus of Robertson Glacier in the Alaska Range and flows 33 miles northeast to the Tanana River.

DC 1348 DJ 74 F 172) *CAUTION: Watch for loose gravel northbound.*

DC 1348.1 DJ 73.9 F 171.9 Side road west to public fishing access; parking. Hike in 0.3 mile for **Robertson No. 2 Lake**; rainbow fishing (stocked by ADF&G).

DC 1350.5 DJ 71.5 F 169.5 Double-ended paved turnout to west. *Rough road next 1.5 miles westbound.*

DC 1353.6 DJ 68.4 F 166.4 Jan Lake Road to south; public fishing access. Drive in 0.5 mile/0.8 km to parking area with boat launch and toilets. No overnight camping, carry out garbage. **Jan Lake** is stocked by

TOK, MILE 1318.5 AK HIGHWAY
OFF THE ROAD · HOUSE ·
INTERNATIONAL FRIENDSHIP HOUSE
BED & BREAKFAST AND GALLERY
Where people can get in touch with nature and art.
Helga Wagenleiter PO Box 264 Tok, AK 99780
Ph: (907) 883-5600   E-mail: rdhouse@aptalaska.net
WIR SPRECHEN DEUTSCH

A Trip Highlight for Every Age!
═══ MUKLUK LAND ═══
Mile 1317 AK. HWY., 3 miles west of Tok Junction
(907) 883-2571 • e-mail: mukluk@aptalaska.net
www.tokalaska.com/mukluk.shtml

Alaska Garden, Pipeline Video and Display, "Bush" Golf, Indoor-Outdoor Museum, Northern Lights Video, Tent-in-Tok, Large Mosquito, Skee Ball, Heater Heaven, Igloo, Santa's Rocket Ship, Doll House . . . & More — All FREE with Admission
Adults $5, Senior Citizens $4.50, Kids $2 — Open 2-8 Daily, June 1 - August 31
GOLD PANNING — *Gold Guaranteed* **— $5/ Pan with admission**

Alaska's state flower is the forget-me-not. The willow ptarmigan is the state bird.

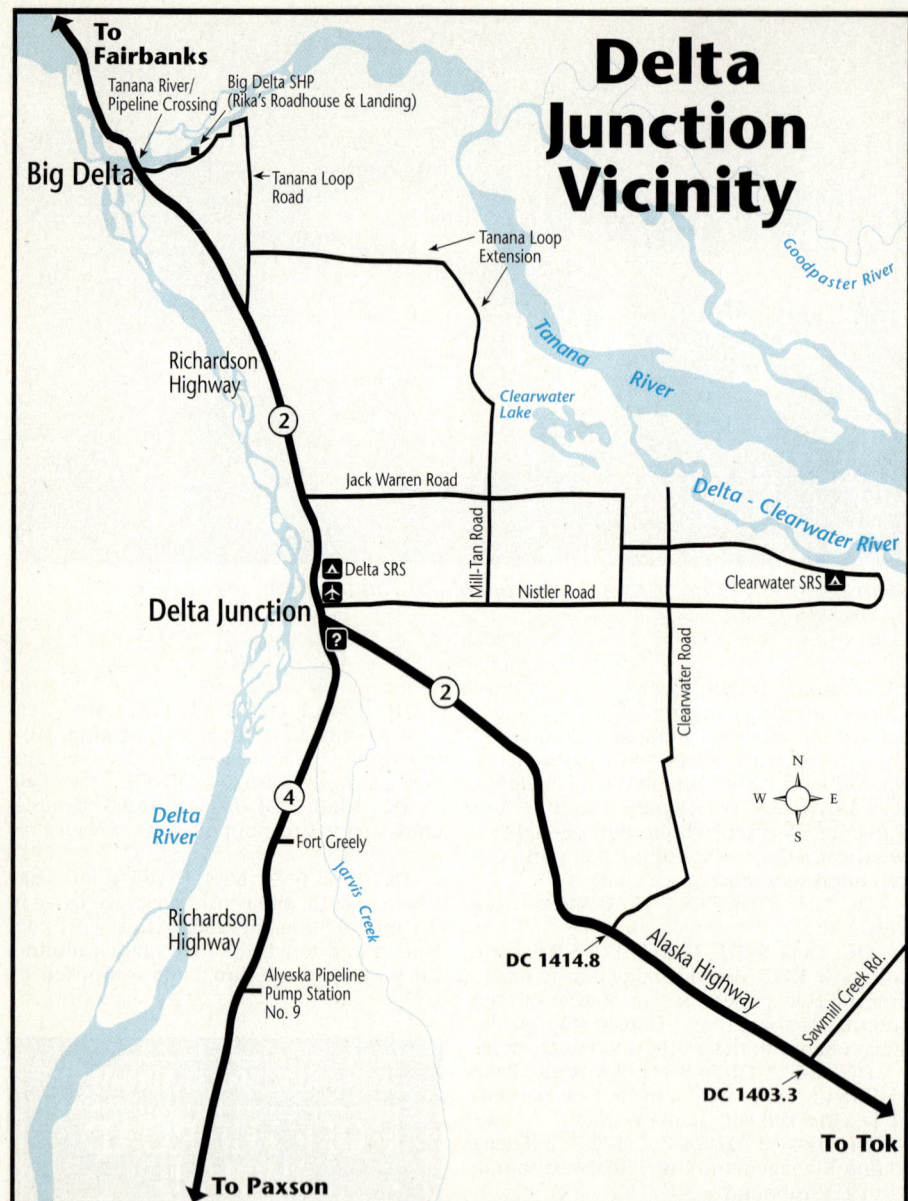

Delta Junction Vicinity

DOT LAKE LODGE
HOME OF THE ALASKAN BIGGER BURGER
AND HOME STYLE COOKING WITH A TOUCH OF HEALTH
SERVING THE HEART OF ALASKA SINCE THE 40'S
WITH STILL A TINGE OF THE PAST.

WHEELCHAIR ACCESSIBLE CAFE -
OPEN YEAR-ROUND BUT
CLOSED EVERY SUNDAY -
NATIVE & OTHER ARTS & CRAFTS -
SMALL CONVENIENCE STORE.

YOU WILL PROBABLY
REMEMBER YOUR STOP AT DOT LAKE -
FOR OUR MOSQUITO REPELLENT TEA OR FOR
OUR INDIAN FREINDS THAT LIVE NEAR BY - OR
PERHAPS OUR THOUGHTFULNESS.

MILEPOST 1361.3 ALASKA HWY.
PHONE (907) 882-2691
SERVICES:
LAKE BACKWATERS CAMPING - GAS - PROPANE -
DIESEL- MEALS STORE - TELEPHONE - POST OFFICE
SEE YOU LATER!

Drive with headlights on at all times.

ADF&G with rainbow; use spinners, flies, or salmon eggs with bobber. Dot Lake Native Corp. land, limited public access.

DC 1357.3 DJ 64.7 F 162.7 Bear Creek bridge. Paved parking area to south at west end of bridge.

DC 1358.7 DJ 63.3 F 161.3 Chief Creek bridge. Paved parking area to south at west end of bridge.

DC 1361 DJ 61 F 159 Dot Lake School.

DC 1361.3 DJ 60.7 F 158.7 DOT LAKE (pop. 61). Pioneer lodge with gas, groceries, restaurant, car wash, motel, camping and post office recalls early days of Alaska Highway travel. Headquarters for the Dot Lake Native Corp. Dot Lake was once an Athabascan hunting camp and a spot on an Indian freight trail to the Yukon River. During construction of the Alaska Highway in 1942 and 1943 it was a work camp called Sears City. Dot Lake was homesteaded in the 1940s. Dot Lake's historic chapel was built in 1949.

Dot Lake Lodge. See display ad this section.

DC 1361.5 DJ 60.5 F 158.5 Historic Milepost 1368. *CAUTION: Rough road westbound; watch for gravel breaks.*

DC 1370.2 DJ 51.8 F 149.8 Double-ended paved scenic viewpoint to north.

DC 1370.8 DJ 51.2 F 149.2 Entering **Tanana Valley State Forest** westbound. Established as the first unit of Alaska's state forest system in 1983, Tanana Valley State Forest encompasses 1.81 million acres and lies almost entirely within the Tanana River Basin. The forest extends 265 miles from near the Canadian border to Manley Hot Springs. Almost 90 percent of the state forest is forested. Principal tree species are paper birch, quaking aspen, balsam poplar, black spruce, white spruce and tamarack. Almost 7 percent of the forest is shrubland, chiefly willow. The forest is managed by the Dept. of Natural Resources.

DC 1371.5 DJ 50.5 F 148.5 Berry Creek bridge. Parking area to south at west end of bridge.

DC 1374.3 DJ 47.7 F 145.5 Sears Creek bridge. Parking area to south at west end of bridge.

DC 1376.5 DJ 45.5 F 143.5 Entering Tanana Valley State Forest eastbound.

DC 1378 DJ 44 F 142 Bridge over Dry Creek.

DC 1379 DJ 43 F 141 Double-ended paved parking area with mountain views to south. Pay phone.

DC 1380.5 DJ 41.5 F 139.5 Johnson River bridge (clearance 15' 6"). A tributary of the Tanana River, the Johnson River was named by Lt. Henry T. Allen in 1887 for Peder Johnson, a Swedish miner and member of his party.

Moose hunters: Antler restriction area.

DC 1381.1 DJ 40.9 F 138.9 Paved parking area to south. Hiking trail to **Lisa Lake** (stocked).

DC 1382.6 DJ 39.4 F 137.4 Sign: $1,000 fine for littering.

DC 1383.8 DJ 38.2 F 136.2 **Craig Lake** access west side of highway via 0.5-mile trail; rainbow trout fishing.

DC 1385 DJ 37 F 135 Paved parking area to north with Gold Rush Centennial sign about the effect of the Gold Rush era on Tanana Valley Natives. Access to Tanana River.

DC 1386 DJ 36 F 134 *Improved wide road westbound to* **Milepost DC 1398.**

DC 1388.4 DJ 33.6 F 131.6 Parking area to south.

DC 1388.5 DJ 33.5 F 131.5 Little Gerstle River bridge.

DC 1391.9 DJ 30.1 F 128.1 Parking area to south; public fishing access. **Big Donna Lake**, 3.5 miles, and **Little Donna Lake**, 4.5 miles; stocked with rainbow.

DC 1392.7 DJ 29.3 F 127.3 Gerstle River Black Veterans Memorial bridge. The Gerstle River Bridge, built in 1944, is 1 of 4 "steel through truss-style" bridge constructions on the Alaska Highway. It was renamed Black Veterans Memorial Bridge in 1993, to commemorate the 3,695 black soldiers of the 93rd, 94th, 95th, 97th and 388th U.S. Army Corps of Engineers for their contribution in constructing the Alcan Highway.

The Gerstle River was named for Lewis Gerstle, president of the Alaska Commercial Co., by Lt. Henry T. Allen, whose 1885 expedition explored the Copper, Tanana and Koyukuk river regions for the U.S. Army.

DC 1393 DJ 29 F 127 Rest area to south at west end of bridge.

DC 1398 DJ 24 F 122 *Improved highway eastbound to* **Milepost DC 1386.**

DC 1400.9 DJ 21.1 F 119.1 Double-ended paved parking area to northeast.

DC 1403.3 DJ 18.7 F 116.7 Sawmill

Creek Road to northeast goes through the heart of the Delta barley fields. A sign just off the highway explains the barley project. Visiting farmers are welcome to talk with local farmers along the road, except during planting (May) and harvesting (August or September) when they are too busy.

DC 1403.6 DJ 18.4 F116.4 Sawmill Creek.

DC 1404.3 DJ 17.7 F 115.7 Watch for buffalo sign. On the southwest side of the Alaska Highway approaching Delta Junction is the Bison Sanctuary. This range provides the bison herd with autumn and winter grazing on over 3,000 acres of grassland. It was developed to reduce agricultural crop depredation by bison.

DC 1408 DJ 14 F 112 Knight Lane. Access to University of Alaska Agricultural and Forestry Experiment Station. Major research at this facility concentrates on agricultural cropping, fertilization and tillage management.

DC 1410 DJ 12 F 110 Spruce Road. Access road north to Delta barley project.

DC 1411.7 DJ 10.3 F 108.3 Paved double-ended scenic viewpoint of Alaska Range to south.

DC 1413.3 DJ 8.7 F 106.7 Grain storage facility to south.

DC 1413.4 DJ 8.6 F 106.6 Delta Meat & Sausage Co. to south.

Delta Meat & Sausage Co. See display ad this section.

DC 1414.8 DJ 7.2 F 105.2 Junction with Clearwater Road, which leads north past farmlands to **Clearwater State Recreation Site** campground and junctions with Remington Road. Stay on pavement leading to Jack Warren Road, which goes west to the Richardson Highway at **Milepost V 268.3**. Good opportunity to see area agriculture; see Delta Vicinity map this page.

To reach the state campground, follow Clearwater Road 5.2 miles north to junction with Remington Road; turn right and drive 2.8 miles east for Clearwater state campground, situated on the bank of Clearwater Creek. There are 15 campsites, toilets, tables, firepits, water and boat ramp. Camping fee $8/night. ▲

Delta–Clearwater River (local reference; stream is actually Clearwater Creek, which flows northwest to the Tanana River), boat needed for best fishing; beautiful spring-fed stream; grayling and whitefish; silver salmon spawn here in October. **Goodpaster River**, accessible by boat via Delta–Clearwater and Tanana rivers; excellent grayling fishing.

DC 1415.4 DJ 6.6 F 104.6 Dorshorst Road.

DC 1420.7 DJ 1.3 F 99.3 Alaska State Troopers and veterinarian to south.

DC 1422 DJ 0 V 266 F 98 Milepost 1422 in the Alaska Highway from Dawson Creek, B.C. **Milepost V 266** on the Richardson Highway from Valdez. End of the Alaska highway at Delta Junction (description follows); visitor center.

Junction of the Alaska Highway (Alaska Route 2) and the Richardson Highway (Alaska Route 4). Turn to **Milepost V 266** in the RICHARDSON HIGHWAY section for log of the highway north to Fairbanks 98 miles (read log front to back), or south to Paxson 81 miles and Valdez 266 miles (read log back to front).

Delta Junction

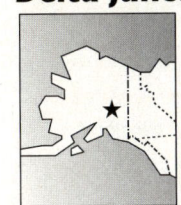

Junction of the Alaska and Richardson highways: **Milepost DC 1422** Alaska Highway, **Milepost V 266** Richardson Highway. **Population:** 840. **Emergency Services:** Phone 911 for all emergency services. **Alaska State Troopers**, in the Jarvis Office Center at **Milepost DC 1420.7**, phone (907) 895-4800. **Fire Department** and **Ambulance**, Delta Rescue Squad/EMS at **Milepost V 265.2** Richardson Highway, phone (907) 895-4656. **Clinic**, Family Medical Center (1 doctor); 2 dentists in private practice.

Visitor Information: Visitor Center at junction of Alaska and Richardson highways, open daily 8 A.M. to 8 P.M., May to mid-September; phone (907) 895-5068, fax (907) 895-5141. The visitor center has historical and wildflower displays and a pay phone. Highway information, phone (907) 451-2207. Dept. of Fish and Game at north

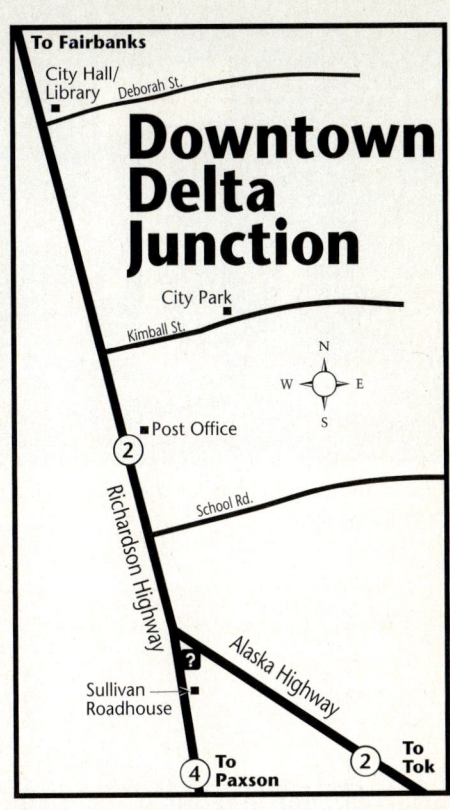

VISITOR INFORMATION
ALASKA HIGHWAY
ALASKA HIGHWAY

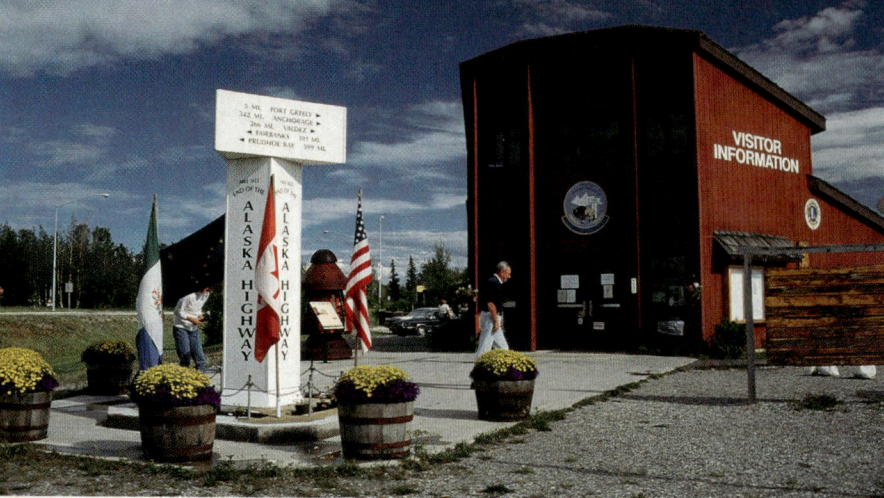

Visitor Center and End of the Alaska Highway display in Delta Junction.
(© Earl L. Brown, staff)

edge of town; phone (907) 895-4484.

The Delta Junction Community Library and City Hall, located at **Milepost V 266.5**, are also good sources of information. The Library/City Hall building has a pay phone, public restrooms, local maps, and an Alaska Highway historical map display. A small conference room is available to the public for meetings. Check with City Hall for reservations. City employees welcome all visitors, and are well versed in giving directions to local businesses and attractions in both Delta and along the Richardson and Alaska Highways. A free paperback and magazine exchange is a favorite among locals and visitors alike. Internet access at the Library is

DELTA JUNCTION ADVERTISERS

Alaska 7 Motel .... Ph. (907) 895-4848
Delta Chamber of Commerce .... Ph. (907) 895-5068
Delta Meat & Sausage Co. .... Ph. (907) 895-4006
Delta Texaco .... Ph. (907) 895-4067
Golden Eagle Outfitters .... Ph. (907) 895-4139
Granite View Sports .... Ph. (907) 895-4990
Kelly's Alaska Country Inn .... Ph. (907) 895-4667
Pizza Bella Family Restaurant .... Ph. (907) 895-4841
Rika's Roadhouse and Landing .... Ph. (907) 895-4201
Smith's Green Acres RV Park & Campground .... Ph. (800) 895-4369
True North B&B .... Ph. (907) 895-4963

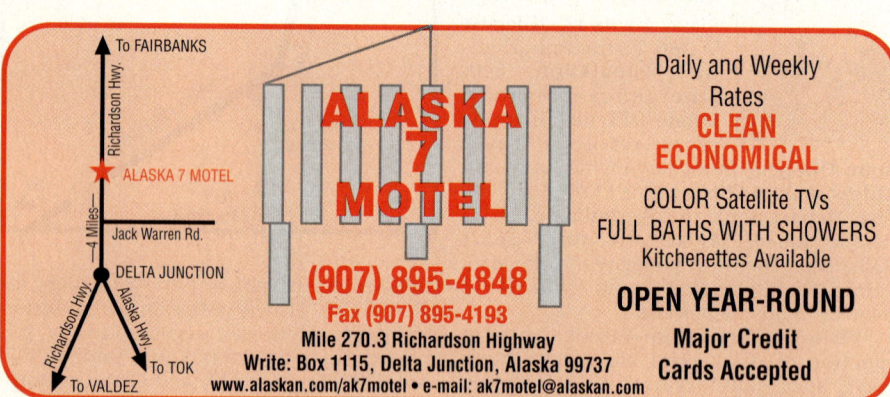

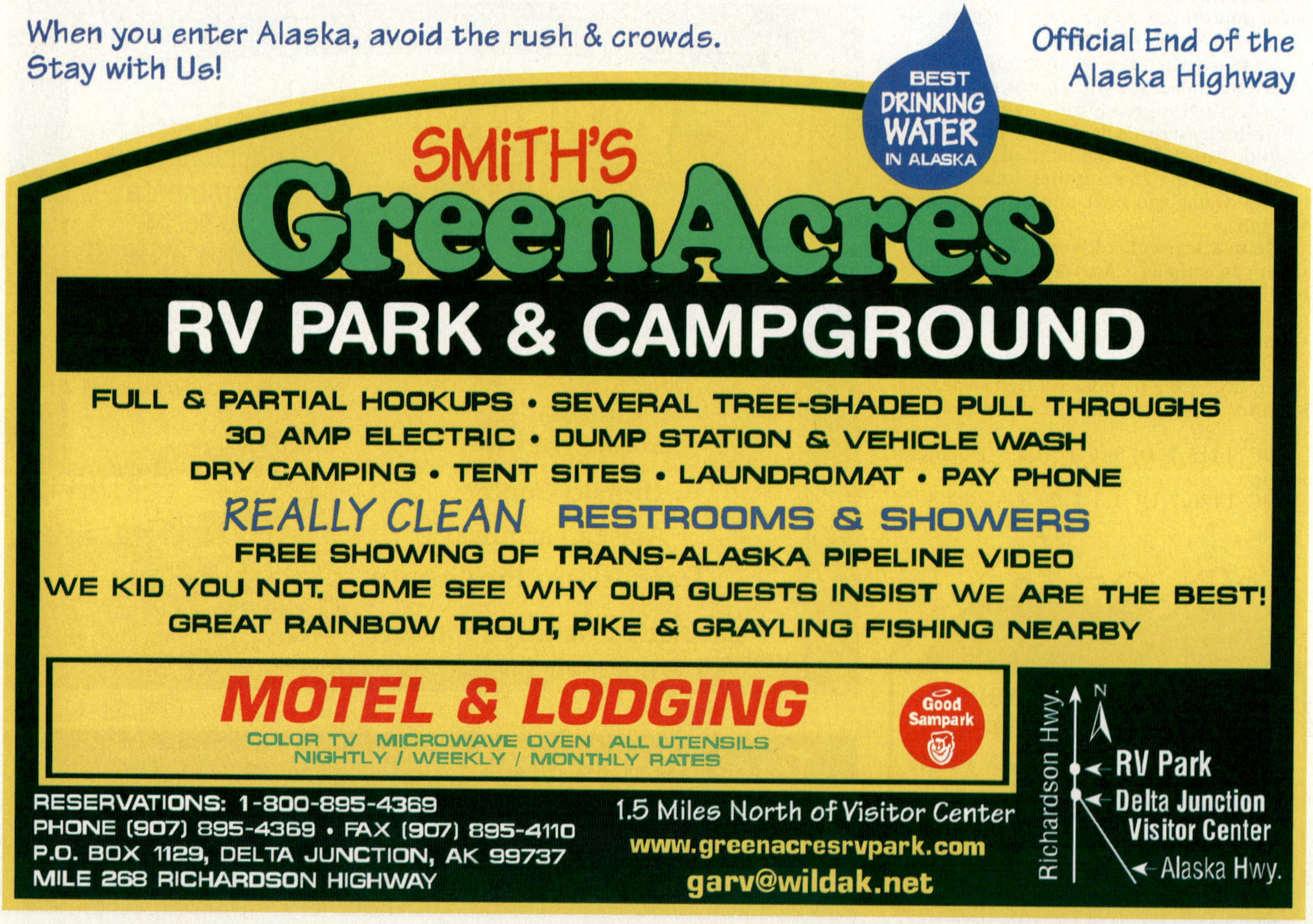

To FAIRBANKS
Richardson Hwy.
ALASKA 7 MOTEL
~4 Miles~
Jack Warren Rd.
DELTA JUNCTION
Richardson Hwy.
Alaska Hwy.
To TOK
To VALDEZ
ALASKA 7 MOTEL
(907) 895-4848
Fax (907) 895-4193
Mile 270.3 Richardson Highway
Write: Box 1115, Delta Junction, Alaska 99737
www.alaskan.com/ak7motel • e-mail: ak7motel@alaskan.com
Daily and Weekly Rates
CLEAN
ECONOMICAL
COLOR Satellite TVs
FULL BATHS WITH SHOWERS
Kitchenettes Available
OPEN YEAR-ROUND
Major Credit Cards Accepted

When you enter Alaska, avoid the rush & crowds.
Stay with Us!
Official End of the Alaska Highway
BEST DRINKING WATER IN ALASKA
SMiTH'S
GreenAcres
RV PARK & CAMPGROUND
FULL & PARTIAL HOOKUPS • SEVERAL TREE-SHADED PULL THROUGHS
30 AMP ELECTRIC • DUMP STATION & VEHICLE WASH
DRY CAMPING • TENT SITES • LAUNDROMAT • PAY PHONE
REALLY CLEAN RESTROOMS & SHOWERS
FREE SHOWING OF TRANS-ALASKA PIPELINE VIDEO
WE KID YOU NOT. COME SEE WHY OUR GUESTS INSIST WE ARE THE BEST!
GREAT RAINBOW TROUT, PIKE & GRAYLING FISHING NEARBY
MOTEL & LODGING
COLOR TV MICROWAVE OVEN ALL UTENSILS
NIGHTLY / WEEKLY / MONTHLY RATES
Good Sampark
RESERVATIONS: 1-800-895-4369
PHONE (907) 895-4369 • FAX (907) 895-4110
P.O. BOX 1129, DELTA JUNCTION, AK 99737
MILE 268 RICHARDSON HIGHWAY
1.5 Miles North of Visitor Center
www.greenacresrvpark.com
garv@wildak.net
Richardson Hwy.
N
RV Park
Delta Junction Visitor Center
Alaska Hwy.

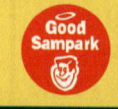

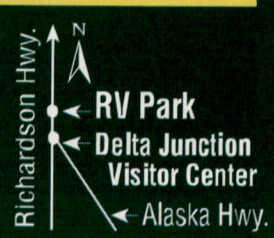

free and available in 30-minute sessions. Sign up at the front desk. A fax and copier are available for a nominal charge. The Library also offers free Alaska videos (and a sympathetic ear) to any traveler who needs to pass the time waiting for vehicle repairs in Delta Junction. Phone 895-4102 for walking directions to the Library from any repair shop or downtown location. City Hall, open 9 A.M. to 5 P.M. weekdays, and offers Notary Public service at no charge, and copies for 25 cents each. Summer hours at the Delta Community Library are 10 A.M. to 6 P.M. Monday to Thursday, and 10 A.M. to 4 P.M. Friday and Saturday.

Elevation: 1,180 feet. **Climate:** Mean monthly temperature in January, -15° F; in July 58°F. Record low was -66°F in January 1989; record high was 88°F in August 1990. Mean monthly precipitation in July, 2.57 inches. **Radio:** KUAC-FM 91.7 (University of Alaska, Fairbanks). **Television:** 3 Fairbanks channels.

Private Aircraft: Delta Junction (former BLM) airstrip, 1 mile north; elev. 1,150 feet; length 2,400 feet, gravel; length 1,600 feet, dirt; no fuel; unattended.

Delta Junction is the end of the Alaska Highway. From here, the Richardson Highway leads to Fairbanks. The Richardson Highway, connecting Valdez at tidewater with Fairbanks in the Interior, predates the Alaska Highway by 20 years. The Richardson was already a wagon road in 1910, and was updated to automobile standards in the 1920s by the Alaska Road Commission (ARC).

Named after the nearby Delta River, Delta Junction began as a construction camp on the Richardson Highway in 1919. (It was first known as Buffalo Center because of the American bison that were transplanted here in the 1920s.)

Since the late 1970s, the state has encouraged development of the agricultural industry in the Delta area by disposing of more than 112,000 acres of local land for farming purposes. Farms range in size from 20 acres to 3,000 acres, with the average being around 500 acres.

Barley is the major feed grain grown in Delta. Other crops include oats, wheat, forage, pasture, grass seed, canola, potatoes and field peas. There are also small-scale vegetable farms; dairies; beef producers; swine producers; bison, elk, reindeer, yak and musk-ox ranches; and several commercial greenhouses.

Also contributing to Delta Junction's economy are the military and the trans-Alaska pipeline. Fort Greely is located 5 miles south of town on the Richardson Highway. Although deactivited in 2000, Fort Greely is a proposed national missile defense test site. Alyeska Pipeline's Pump Station No. 9 is located 7 miles south of Delta Junction on the Richardson Highway.

Lodging & Services

Delta Junction has 3 motels, several bed and breakfasts, restaurants, gas stations, a coin-operated car wash, a shopping center, post office, gift shops, RV parks, bank with ATM and other businesses. There are several churches. Delta Community Park, on Kimball Street one block off the highway, has softball and soccer fields and playground.

Camping

A private RV park, Smith's Green Acres, is just north of town. There are 3 public campgrounds in the area: Delta state campground, 1.1 miles north at **Milepost V 267.1** Richardson Highway; Quartz Lake Recreation Area, 10.7 miles north via the Richardson Highway to **Milepost V 277.7** and 2.5 miles east on a side road; and Clearwater state campground on Remington Road, accessible from **Milepost DC 1414.9** Alaska Highway or **V 268.3** Richardson Highway (see Delta Vicinity map on page 204). ▲

Transportation

Air: Scheduled service via 40-Mile Air from Tok to Fairbanks; Delta stop on request. Local air service available.

Attractions

Delta Junction Visitor Center. Have your picture taken with the monument in front of the visitor center that marks the highway's end. The chamber of commerce visitor center also has free brochures describing area businesses and attractions, and displays of Alaska wildflowers, mounted animals and furs to touch. Travelers may also purchase certificates here, certifying that they have reached the end of the Alaska Highway. There is also an interesting display of pipe used in 3 Alaska pipeline projects outside the visitor center.

Rika's Roadhouse. Located north of town about 8 miles/12.9 km at **Milepost V 275** Richardson Highway at Big Delta State Historical Park, this roadhouse was built in 1910 by John Hajdukovich. In 1923, Hajdukovich sold it to Rika Wallen, a Swedish immigrant who had managed the roadhouse since 1917. Rika ran the roadhouse into the late 1940s and lived there until her death in 1969. Rika's Roadhouse is now part

---

When you're in Delta Junction...
STAY WITH US
AT THE END OF THE ALASKA HIGHWAY!

- Clean Rooms
- Private Baths
- Telephones/TV
- Kitchens
- Open All Year

KELLY'S ALASKA COUNTRY INN

Tel (907) 895-4667   Fax (907) 895-4481

Visit us at www.kellysalaskacountryinn.com/milepost • Email us at mp@kellysalaskacountryinn.com

1616 Richardson Hwy. • Box 849MP • Delta Junction, AK 99737
View the magnificent Alaska Range!
MasterCard • VISA • American Express • Discover

NEW, SPACIOUS COMFORTABLE DINING ROOM • QUICK TABLE SERVICE

PIZZA BELLA FAMILY RESTAURANT

FULL MENU • ITALIAN & AMERICAN CUISINE
Homemade Soups • Salads • Pizza • Hot Sandwiches
Steaks • Prime Rib • Seafood • Orders To Go
Wines and Cold Beer • Satisfaction Guaranteed

TOUR BUSES WELCOME
Reservations Appreciated *(not required)*

Open 7 Days 10 a.m. to 10 p.m.

In Delta Junction Across from Visitor Information Center - (907) 895-4841 or 895-4524.
Also in Fairbanks at 1694 Airport Way, Across from movie theater,
1 block from Alaskaland - (907) 456-5657.

GRANITE VIEW SPORTS & GIFTS

Full Line of Hunting & Fishing Supplies & Licenses

Large Selection of Alaska Gifts & Fine Clothing

Across from the Visitors Center

907-895-4990

OPEN 7 DAYS A WEEK 9AM – 7PM

Trans-Alaska pipeline spans the Tanana River north of Delta Junction.
(© Ron Niebrugge)

spring and fall migrations of sandhill cranes, geese and other waterfowl.

AREA FISHING: Delta–Clearwater River (local name for Clearwater Creek), grayling and whitefish; silver salmon spawn here in October. Access via Clearwater Road or Jack Warren Road (see map). **Goodpaster River**, accessible by boat via Delta–Clearwater and Tanana rivers; excellent grayling fishing.

There are 43 lakes in the Delta–Tok area that are stocked by the ADF&G. Lakes are stocked primarily with rainbow trout, and also with arctic grayling, lake trout, arctic char and king salmon. Lakes are located along the road or reached by trail. **Quartz Lake**, at **Milepost V 277.7** north of Delta Junction, one of the most popular fishing lakes in the Delta area, is also the largest and most easily accessed of area lakes; angler success is excellent. Consult ADF&G offices in Delta or Tok for other locations.

Junction of the Alaska Highway (Alaska Route 2) and the Richardson Highway (Alaska Route 4). Turn to **Milepost V 266** in the RICHARDSON HIGHWAY section for log of the highway north to Fairbanks 98 miles (read log front to back), or south to Paxson 81 miles and Valdez 266 miles (read log back to front).

of **Big Delta State Historical Park**. Drive in on gravel access road to large parking area; it is a short walk through trees to Rika's Roadhouse complex. The parking area also accommodates overnight RV parking; camping fee is $8/vehicle, dump station ($3). Open daily in summer. There are a number of other historic outbuildings, a gift shop, restaurant, telephone and toilets.

Buffalo Herd. American bison were transplanted into the Delta Junction area in the 1920s. Because the bison have become costly pests to many farmers in the Delta area, the 90,000-acre Delta Bison Sanctuary was created south of the Alaska Highway in 1980. However, keeping the bison on their refuge and out of the barley fields is a continuing problem. Summer visitors who wish to look at the bison are advised to visit the viewpoint at **Milepost V 241.3** on the Richardson Highway; use binoculars. The herd contained 482 bison in 1992 when the last census was taken by the ADF&G.

See the Pipeline Crossing. Delta Junction is the first view of the trans-Alaska pipeline for travelers coming up the Alaska Highway from Canada. A good spot to see and photograph the pipeline is at **Milepost V 275.4** Richardson Highway, 9.5 miles north of town, where the pipeline crosses the Tanana River.

Special Events: The Deltana Fair is held in late July. The fair includes a barbecue, Lions' pancake breakfast, local handicrafts, horse show, livestock display and show, games, concessions, contests and a parade. A highlight of the fair is the Great Alaska Outhouse Race, held on Sunday, in which 4 pushers and 1 sitter compete for the coveted "Golden Throne" award.

The Festival of Lights is held in February. Check with the Chamber of Commerce for dates; phone (907) 895-5068.

Sullivan Roadhouse, relocated across from the visitor center, was originally built in 1906. It is one of the last remaining roadhouses from the Valdez to Fairbanks Trail. Open daily in summer.

Tour the agriculture of the area by driving Sawmill Creek Road (turn off at **Milepost DC 1403.6** Alaska Highway) and Clearwater Road (see **Milepost DC 1414.9**). Sawmill Creek Road goes through the heart of the grain-producing Delta Ag Project.

Along Clearwater and Remington roads you may view the older farms, which produce forage crops and livestock. Tanana Loop Road (**Milepost V 271.7**), Tanana Loop Extension and Milltan Road also go past many farms.

The University of Alaska, Cooperative Extension Service and the Alaska Farm Bureau–Delta Chapter host an annual farm tour in the Delta area scheduled for the second Wednesday in August. The tour alternates visiting the Tanana Loop area, the Clearwater area, or the Sawmill Creek area each year. This is an all-day bus tour that includes an Alaska Grown Luncheon prepared and served by members of the Alaska Farm Bureau. For information and cost, contact the Cooperative Extension, P.O. Box 349, Delta Junction, AK 99737; phone (907) 895-4215; or email: fnpnk@uaf.edu.

Bird Watching. Delta's barley fields are a popular migration stop for 150,000 to 200,000 sandhill cranes. In 1998, a common crane was sighted among a flock of lesser sandhill cranes. It was only the sixth sighting of a common crane—classified as a Eurasian species—in North America. Delta–Clearwater Creek is a good place to see

www.themilepost.com

YELLOWHEAD HIGHWAY 16

	Edmonton	Jasper	Prince George	Prince Rupert	Terrace
Edmonton		216	450	898	807
Jasper	216		234	682	591
Prince George	450	234		448	357
Prince Rupert	898	682	448		91
Terrace	807	591	357	91	

Connects: Edmonton, AB, to Prince Rupert, BC **Length:** 898 miles
Road Surface: Paved **Season:** Open all year
Highest Summit: Obed Summit, 3,819 feet
Major Attractions: Canadian Rockies/Jasper National Park, Mt. Robson, Fort St. James, 'Ksan, North Pacific Cannery

(See maps, pages 207–209)

Centuries-old Gitksan Village is replicated at 'Ksan Historical Village & Museum.
(© Four Corners Imaging, Ralph Barrett & Leonor Barrett)

Yellowhead Highway 16 is a paved trans-Canada highway that extends from Winnipeg, MB, through Saskatchewan, Alberta, and British Columbia to the coastal city of Prince Rupert. (The highway connecting Masset and Queen Charlotte on Graham Island has also been designated as part of Yellowhead Highway 16.) *The MILEPOST®* logs Yellowhead Highway 16 from Edmonton, AB, to Prince Rupert, BC, which is a distance of 898 miles/1,444 km.

Yellowhead Highway 16 terminates at Prince Rupert, BC, where you may connect with the Alaska Marine Highway System to southeastern Alaska cities, and the British Columbia ferry system to Port Hardy on Vancouver Island and Skidegate in the Queen Charlotte Islands.

This is a major east–west route, providing access to a number of attractions in Alberta and British Columbia. Yellowhead Highway 16 is also a very scenic highway, passing through mountains, forest and farmland. Visitor services are readily available in towns along the way, and campsites may be found in towns and along the highway at both private and provincial park campgrounds. (It is unsafe and illegal to overnight in rest areas.)

Yellowhead Highway 16 Log

This section of the log shows distance from Edmonton (E) followed by distance from Prince George (PG).
The Yellowhead Highway log is divided into 2 sections: Edmonton to Prince George, and Prince George to Prince Rupert.
Kilometreposts on Yellowhead reflect distances within highway maintenance districts; The MILEPOST® does not use these physical posts as reference points.

HIGHWAY 16

E 0 PG 450 (724.2 km) **EDMONTON** city limit. See page 44 in the EAST ACCESS ROUTE section for description of city.

E 4 (6.4 km) **PG 446** (717.8 km) **Junction** of Highways 16 West and 60 (Devon Overpass); access to Glowing Embers Travel Centre campground (273 sites) via Devon exit.

E 12 (19.3 km) **PG 438** (704.9 km) **SPRUCE GROVE** (pop. 15,632). All visitor facilities including motels, restaurants, gas and service stations, grocery stores, farmer's market, shopping malls and all emergency services.

Visitor Information: The chamber of commerce tourist information booth, located on Highway 16A, is open year-round; phone (780) 962-2561.

(Continues on page 211)

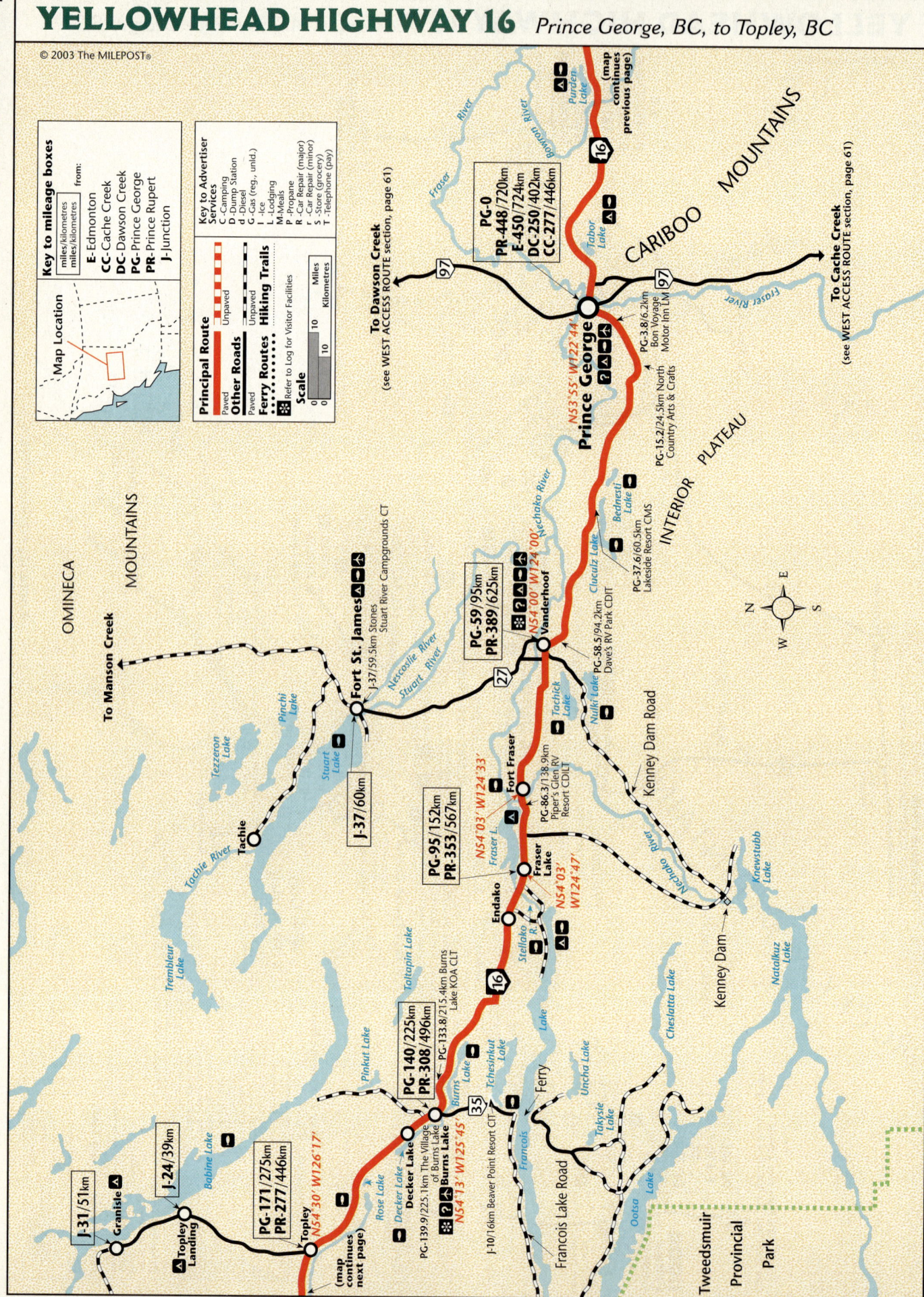

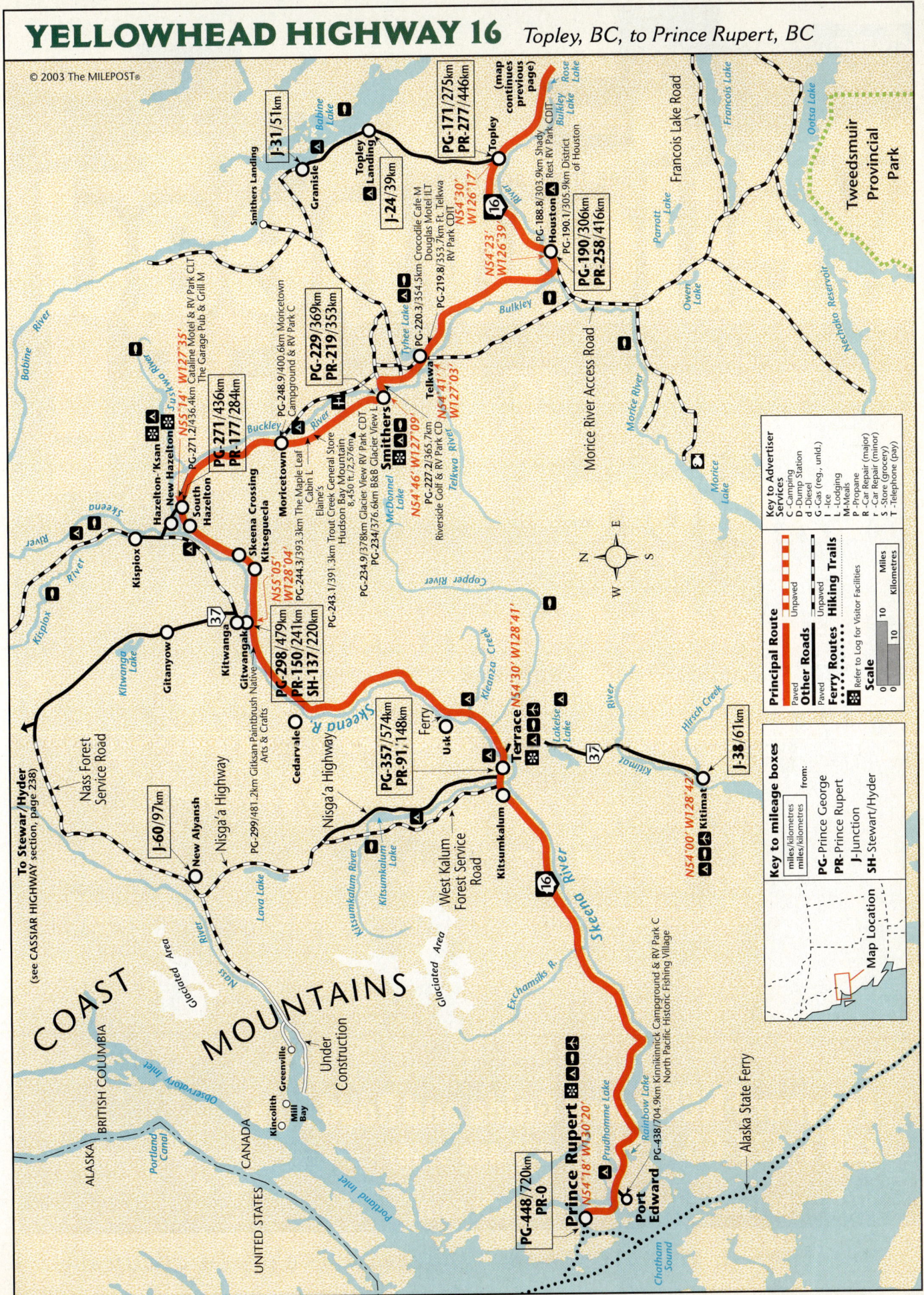

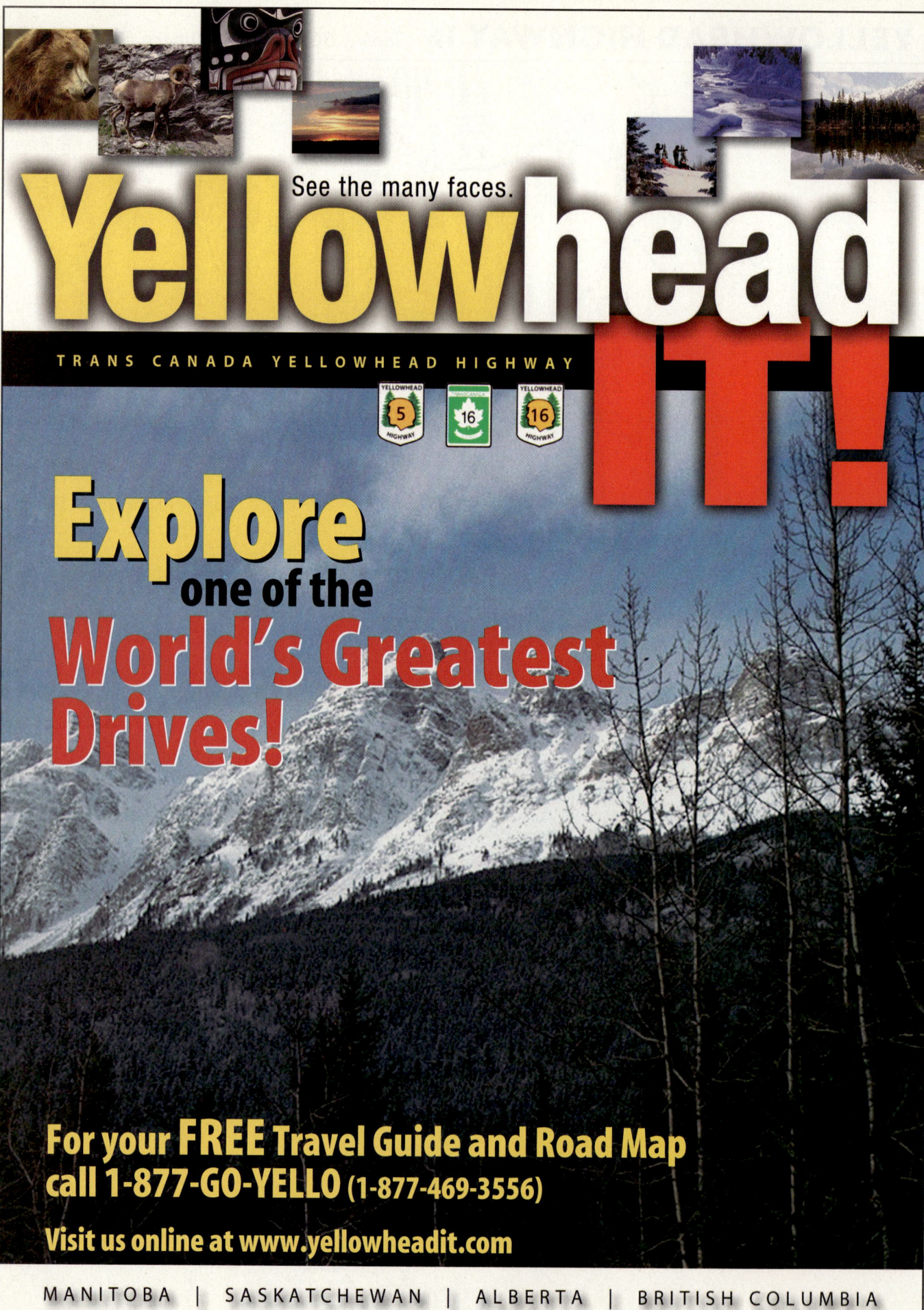

(Continued from page 206)

Spruce Grove has a skateboard park, 18-hole golf course and 350-seat performing arts venue. The Trans Alta Tri Leisure Centre features an indoor running track, aquatic centre, family fitness centre, ice arenas and soccer field.

E 18.1 (29.1 km) **PG 431.9** (695.1 km) **STONY PLAIN** (pop. 9,000). All visitor facilities including major-chain motels, restaurants, supermarkets, shopping mall and gas stations with major repair service; RCMP and hospital; outdoor swimming pool and 18-hole golf course. Turn north on South Park Drive for camping at Lions RV Park and Campground; 47 sites, hookups. ▲

Visitor Information: Take Exit 779 to the Rotary Park rest area. The infocentre is housed in the Dog Rump Creek railway station.

The **Multicultural Heritage Centre** (use Exit 779) has historical archives, gift shops and home-cooked meals. Other attractions include 22 outdoor murals; a farmer's market; a teahouse; Oppertshauser House; Parkland County Demonstration Farm; and the Pioneer Museum at Exhibition Park. Bears & Bedtime Unique Collectible Teddy Bears is located in Stony Plain (off Exit 779).

E 19.6 (31.5 km) **PG 430.4** (692.7 km) Turnoff to south for Hasse Lake Parkland County day-use area (6 miles/10 km); picnicking, swimming and fishing.

E 20.1 (32.3 km) **PG 429.9** (691.9 km) Hubbles Lake turnoff to north; camping. ▲

E 21.2 (34.1 km) **PG 428.8** (690.1 km) Restaurant, gas station and store to north.

E 25 (40.2 km) **PG 425** (684 km) **Junction** with Highway 43 to Dawson Creek, BC (337 miles/543 km). Continue west for Prince George.

> Turn to Milepost E 29.8 on page 47 in the EAST ACCESS ROUTE section for log of Highway 43, which also accesses the Mackenzie Highway to Northwest Territories.

E 30.3 (48.8 km) **PG 419.7** (675.4 km) Gas and groceries south side of road.

E 33 (53.1 km) **PG 417** (671.1 km) **Wabamun Lake Provincial Park**, 1 mile/1.6 km south on access road; 287 campsites, fishing, boating and swimming. ▲

E 34.7 (55.9 km) **PG 415.3** (668.3 km) Village of **WABAMUN** with gas, convenience store, car wash, laundromat, dump station, hotel and post office. Park with shelter, tables, litter barrels, washroom and flush toilets. Also located here is Trans Alta Utilities generating station, which generates electricity from coal.

E 38.5 (61.9 km) **PG 411.5** (662.3 km) Propane, fuel, groceries and pay phone.

E 39.3 (63.3 km) **PG 410.7** (660.9 km) Watch for evidence of strip mining for coal along the highway.

E 42.5 (68.4 km) **PG 407.5** (655.8 km) **FALLIS** (pop. 190); no services.

E 48.7 (78.3 km) **PG 401.3** (645.9 km) **GAINFORD** (pop. 205). Cafe, hotel and post office. Free public campground at west end of town with 8 sites, firewood, tables, pit toilets and water. ▲

E 56.6 (91.1 km) **PG 393.4** (633.1 km) **ENTWISTLE** (pop. 477). Restaurants, gas station, 2 motels, post office, swimming pool and grocery store. **Pembina River Provincial Park**, 1.9 miles/3.1 km north; 132 campsites, tables, showers, flush toilets, water and dump station. Open all year; camping fee

Bighorn sheep on the highway near Jasper National Park. (© Blake Hanna, staff)

$15 to $17. Fishing, swimming, playground and phone. ▲

E 66.2 (106.5 km) **PG 383.8** (617.7 km) **WILDWOOD** (pop. 375), the "Bingo Capital of Canada." Post office, hotel, gas station, restaurants and shops. Campground at **Chip Lake** with 14 sites, tables, firewood, pit toilets, water, fishing, swimming and boat launch. ▲

E 68.7 (110.6 km) **PG 381.3** (613.6 km) View of Chip Lake to north.

E 81.5 (131.1 km) **PG 368.5** (593.1 km) **NOJACK** (pop. 250); grocery, post office, restaurant and gas station with towing, diesel and major repair service.

E 82 (132 km) **PG 368** (592.2 km) Turnoff for Mackay.

E 83 (133.6 km) **PG 367** (590.6 km) Nojack Recreation Area and campground. ▲

E 84.6 (136.1 km) **PG 365.4** (588.1 km) Private campground to north. ▲

E 89.5 (144 km) **PG 360.5** (580.2 km) **NITON JUNCTION.** Hamlet has 2 gas stations with tires and parts, diesel, propane, car wash, pay phone, groceries, post office, 2 restaurants, lounge, motel. Private campground with full hookups. ▲

E 93.7 (150.8 km) **PG 356.3** (573.4 km) **CARROT CREEK.** Post office, grocery store, gas station, propane, car wash and phone.

E 97.5 (157 km) **PG 352.5** (567.2 km) **Junction** with Highway 32 which leads 42 miles/67.6 km north to Whitecourt and Highway 43.

E 99.4 (160 km) **PG 350.5** (564.2 km) Westbound access to weigh scale and litter barrel.

E 100.9 (162.4 km) **PG 349.1** (561.5 km) Turnout with litter barrels.

E 102.1 (164.4 km) **PG 347.9** (559.8 km) Wolf Lake public campground, 33 miles/53 km south on gravel road; 32 sites, pit toilets, boat launch, water pumps, tables, litter barrels. ▲

E 105 (169 km) **PG 345** (555.2 km) Edson rest area to south with handicap-accessible flush toilets, water, tables, shelter, phone and sani-dump.

E 106 (170.6 km) **PG 344** (553.6 km) Rosevear Road; eastbound access to Edson rest area.

E 110 (177.1 km) **PG 340** (547.1 km) Private campground. ▲

E 113.1 (182 km) **PG 336.9** (542.2 km) McLeod River bridge.

E 114.9 (185 km) **PG 335.1** (539.2 km) **EDSON** (pop. 7,400). **Emergency Services: Hospital** and RCMP post **Visitor Information:** South on 55th Street. Edson's economy is based on coal mining, forestry, oil, natural gas and manufacturing. Edson is a large highway community with 16 motels, many restaurants and gas stations; 18-hole golf course and driving range; and an indoor pool.

Private campground, located at the east end of Edson, south of Highway 16 on the road to the golf course. The nearest public campgrounds are Lions Park Campground east of town and Willmore Recreation Park south of town. ▲

E 123.2 (198.3 km) **PG 326.8** (525.9 km) Food, gas, lodging and phone.

E 128 (206 km) **PG 322** (518.2 km) Hornbeck Creek government campground to north adjacent to highway; 33 sites, picnic area, firewood, water pump, stream fishing. ▲

E 133 (214 km) **PG 317** (510.2 km) Small community of Marlboro to north. First view of Canadian Rockies westbound.

E 140.8 (226.6 km) **PG 309.2** (497.6 km) Westbound-only turnout with picnic tables, pit toilets and litter barrels; generous, paved parking area.

E 142.7 (229.6 km) **PG 307.3** (494.6 km) Eastbound-only turnout with litter barrels.

E 148.1 (238.3 km) **PG 301.9** (485.9 km) **Obed Lake** government campground to north; 7 sites, picnic area, firewood, pit toilets, boat launch, beach area. Fishing for rainbows, brown and eastern brook trout, and yellow perch. ▲

E 156.4 (251.8 km) **PG 293.6** (472.4 km) **Obed Summit**, highest elevation on the Yellowhead Highway at 3,819 feet/1,164m.

E 157.7 (253.9 km) **PG 292.3** (470.3 km) Treed roadside turnout; generous parking area, picnic tables, toilets and litter barrels. Good view of the Rockies from here.

YELLOWHEAD HIGHWAY • Hinton

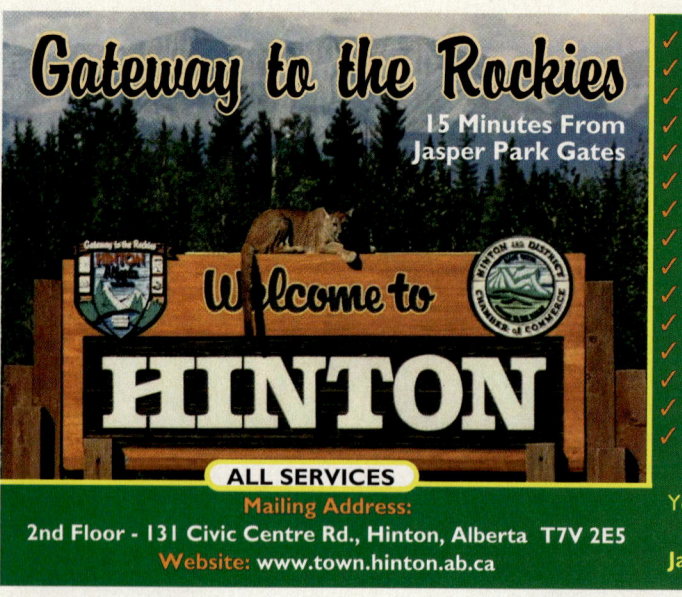

Gateway to the Rockies
15 Minutes From Jasper Park Gates

✓ Fishing
✓ Hiking Trails
✓ Mountain Biking
✓ Boating
✓ Canoeing
✓ Swimming
✓ Golf
✓ Wildlife Observation
✓ RV Parks
✓ Camping
✓ Accommodations
✓ Restaurants
✓ Shopping
✓ Mine & Mill Tours
✓ ATV Rentals & Tours

Hinton is located on Yellowhead Highway 16 only 18 miles east of Jasper National Park

Welcome to HINTON — ALL SERVICES
Mailing Address: 2nd Floor - 131 Civic Centre Rd., Hinton, Alberta T7V 2E5
Website: www.town.hinton.ab.ca

Fishing on a tranquil lake on the Yellowhead Highway. (© Blake Hanna, staff)

DAYS INN HINTON — HINTON, ALBERTA
• Smoking & Non-Smoking Rooms
• Kitchenettes • Exercise Room
• Hot Tub • Continental Breakfast
Web: www.the.daysinn.com/hinton14345
AAA AAA Fax: 780-865-4064
Phone: 780-817-1960
HIGHWAY 16 WEST
1-800-DAYS-INN

CRESTWOOD HOTEL
Located Across from Hinton's 18 Hole Golf Course on Hwy 16
★★★ 97 Well-appointed A/C Rooms • Fine Licensed Dining • Heated Indoor Pool & Sauna
Complimentary In-room Coffee & Tea • In-room Modem • Corporate, AAA/CAA, Senior & Group Rates
E-mail: reservations@crestwoodhotel.com
Web: www.crestwoodhotel.com
678 Carmichael Lane
Hinton, Alberta T7V 1S9
Toll Free: 1-800-661-7288

HINTON Pines MOTEL — 15 Minutes to Jasper Park Gates
Non-Smoking Rooms • Regular & 2 Bedroom Units • Cable TV
Competitive Rates • Fridges, Microwaves & In-Room Coffee
Mountainview • 8 Time Housekeeping Award Winner
Hwy. 16 Next to Golf Course in Hinton
1-780-865-2624 • www.pines-motel.com • Email: pines.motel@shaw.ca

Hinton

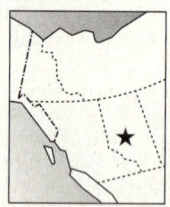

E 166.7 (268.3 km) PG 283.3 (455.9 km) Located about a 3-hour's drive from Edmonton. **Population:** 10,000. **Emergency services:** Hospital, dentist and RCMP post.

Visitor information: Travel Alberta Information Centre, phone 1-800-661-8888 or (780) 427-4321; fax (780) 427-0687. Open Victoria Day to Canadian Thanksgiving 9 A.M. to 7:30 P.M.; Canadian Thanksgiving to Victoria Day, Monday–Friday 9 A.M. to 4:30 P.M. Closed Saturday and Sunday. On the Internet, visit www.town.hinton.ab.ca.

A major service stop on Yellowhead Highway 16, Hinton has all visitor facilities, including hotels and motels; gas stations; shopping centres and shopping mall; bowling alley, curling rink, golf course and recreation complex with indoor pool. Hinton is only 18 miles/28 km east of Jasper National Park gate.

There are 3 campgrounds in town. Nearby William A. Switzer Provincial Park on Highway 40 encompasses 4 campgrounds and offers fishing. ▲

Hinton is the site of Weldwood of Canada Ltd. pulp mill; tours of the mill complex may be arranged. Hinton began in the 1900s as a construction camp for rail-

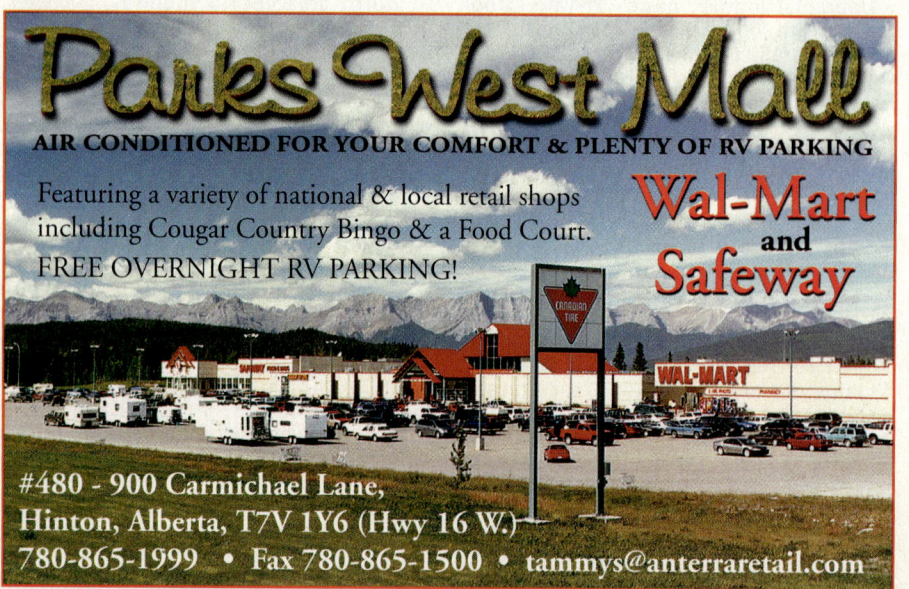

Parks West Mall
AIR CONDITIONED FOR YOUR COMFORT & PLENTY OF RV PARKING
Featuring a variety of national & local retail shops including Cougar Country Bingo & a Food Court.
FREE OVERNIGHT RV PARKING!
Wal-Mart and Safeway
#480 - 900 Carmichael Lane,
Hinton, Alberta, T7V 1Y6 (Hwy 16 W.)
780-865-1999 • Fax 780-865-1500 • tammys@anterraretail.com

HINTON ADVERTISERS

Crestwood Hotel.............Ph. 1-800-661-7288
Days Inn Hinton...............Ph. (780) 817-1960
Parks West Mall ....Ph. (780) 865-1999
Pines Motel ....Ph. (780) 865-2624
Town of Hinton ....Hwy. 16 West

road, coal mining and logging crews. The commmunity grew dramatically after construction of the pulp mill in 1955. The subsequent addition of 3 major coal mining operations and a sawmill further increased the population.

Yellowhead Highway 16 Log
(continued)

E 171 (275.3 km) **PG 279** (448.9 km) South **junction** with Bighorn Highway 40.

E 172.2 (277.1 km) **PG 277.8** (447.1 km) Bighorn Highway leads north 16.8 miles/27 km to **William A. Switzer Provincial Park**; camping, picnicking, fishing. Bighorn Highway also leads north 88 miles/142 km to Grande Cache then another 117 miles/188 km to Grande Prairie. ▲

Junction with Bighorn Highway 40 (paved) to Grande Cache and Grande Prairie. See "Bighorn Route" log beginning on this page.

E 176.8 (284.5 km) **PG 273.2** (439.7 km) Maskuta Creek. Private campground. ▲

E 177.8 (286.2 km) **PG 272.2** (438 km) Weigh scales and pay phone.

E 179 (288.1 km) **PG 271** (436.1 km) Public campground 3.1 miles/5 km north. ▲

E 180.9 (291.1 km) **PG 269.1** (433.1 km) Private campground, cabins, pay phone. ▲

E 181.8 (292.6 km) **PG 268.2** (431.6 km) Turnout to north with litter barrels and point of interest sign about Yellowhead/Tete Jaune.

E 182.4 (293.5 km) **PG 267.6** (430.7 km) **Overlander Mountain Lodge.** Open year-round. Enjoy a fabulous view overlooking Jasper National Park from this lodge, nestled in the foothills of the Rocky Mountains. Fine dining restaurant. Chalets, lodge and Miette rooms or seasonal cabins. Selected rooms have jetted tubs and modem jacks available. Phone (780) 866-2330; email overland@telusplanet.net. Web www.overlandermountainlodge.com. [ADVERTISEMENT]

E 184.2 (296.5 km) **PG 265.8** (427.7 km) **Jasper National Park, East Entrance.** Park fees are charged on a per-person basis and must be paid by all visitors using facilities in Rocky Mountain national parks. Public phones.

Alberta's Jasper National Park is part of the Canadian Rocky Mountains World Heritage Site. It is the largest of Canada's Rocky Mountain parks, covering 4,200 square miles/20,878 square kms. It adjoins Banff National Park to the south. Most visitors sightsee Jasper's (and Banff's) spectacular mountain scenery from Highway 93 (Icefields Parkway).

E 185.6 (298.8 km) **PG 264.4** (425.4 km) Fiddle River bridge.

E 189 (304.2 km) **PG 261** (420 km) **POCAHONTAS** has a motel with cabins, swimming pool and restaurant; and grocery.

Junction with Miette Hot Springs Road. Self-guiding interpretive trail 0.2 mile/0.3 km south on Miette Road; Park Service campground (140 sites) 0.6 mile/1 km south; and **Miette Hot Springs** resort 11 miles/18 km south. The resort has a motel and cafe; 2 thermal pools and one cool pool (towels and bathing suits for rent, admission fee). Beautiful setting, look for mountain sheep and black bear. ▲

E 192 (309 km) **PG 258** (415.2 km) Turnout with cairn to south. Mineral lick here is frequented by goats and sheep. Watch for wildlife, especially at dawn and dusk.

Bighorn Route

Victor Lake on the Bighorn Route is popular with canoeists and fishermen.
(© Blake Hanna, staff)

This 207-mile/333.2-km paved highway connects Yellowhead Highway 16 and Highway 43, and the communities of Hinton, Grande Cache and Grande Prairie.

ALBERTA HIGHWAY 40

Distance from Yellowhead Highway 16 junction (Y) is followed by the distance from Grande Prairie (GP).

Y 0 GP 207 (333.2 km) **Junction** with Yellowhead Highway 16 at **Milepost E 172.2**.

Y 2.1 (3.4 km) **GP 204.9** (329.8 km) Community of **ENTRANCE** (pop. 79) to west.

Y 3 (4.8 km) **GP 204** (328.4 km) Athabasca River bridge.

Y 3.7 (5.9 km) **GP 203.3** (327.3 km) Access road to west leads 10 miles/16 km to the community of **Brule** (pop. 161), which has a guest ranch with trail riding, fishing and cross-country skiing in winter. 🐟

Y 8.5 (13.6 km) **GP 198.5** (319.6 km) Access road leads west 4 miles/7 km to Athabasca Lookout Nordic Centre; cross-country and biathlon skiing, hiking trails and day lodge.

Y 8.9 (14.3 km) **GP 198.1** (318.9 km) Turnout to east with litter barrels and information sign about William A. Switzer Provincial Park.

Y 9.8 (15.8 km) **GP 197.2** (317.4 km) Access road leads east to **Jarvis Lake** day-use area; pump water, public phone, beach and boat launch.

Y 12.8 (20.5 km) **GP 194.2** (312.7 km) **Kelley's Bathtub** day-use area to west; large easy-access parking area with toilets, public phone, swimming and hiking trail.

Y 15.2 (24.5 km) **GP 191.8** (308.7 km) Winter Creek.

Y 15.3 (24.7 km) **GP 191.7** (308.5 km) Side road to east leads 1.2 miles/2 km to Cache Lake and 2.4 miles/4 km to Graveyard Lake. **Cache Lake Campground** has 14 sites, sewer hookups, water pump, picnic tables, shelter, children's playground, camping fee $9. **Graveyard Campground** has 16 sites, sewer hookups, water available at Cache Lake campground, camping fee. ▲

Y 16.8 (27 km) **GP 190.3** (306.2 km) Access road to east leads to **Gregg Lake** day-use area and campground; 164 sites, sewer hookups, tap water, picnic tables, shelter, playground, fish-cleaning stand, beach, hiking trails, boat launch, dock, public phone. Camping fee. ◀▲

Y 17.6 (28.4 km) **GP 189.4** (304.8 km) Turnout to west with litter barrels and information sign about William A. Switzer Provincial Park for southbound travelers.

Y 22.9 (36.9 km) **GP 184.1** (296.3 km) Wild Hay River bridge.

Y 25.6 (41.2 km) **GP 181.4** (292 km) Side road to west leads 20 miles/32 km to **Rock Lake Campground** on Rock Lake; 96 sites, sewer hookups, water pump, picnic tables, shelter, hiking trails, boat launch, camping fee. ▲

Y 28.9 (46.5 km) **GP 178.1** (286.7 km) Entering Grande Cache ranger district northbound.

Y 30.6 (49.3 km) **GP 176.4** (283.9 km) Fred Creek.

Y 36.3 (58.5 km) **GP 170.7** (274.7 km) Pinto Creek.

Y 40.5 (65.2 km) **GP 166.5** (268 km) Bridge over the Little Berland River.

Y 43.2 (69.6 km) **GP 163.8** (263.6 km) Fox Creek.

Y 48.4 (77.9 km) **GP 158.6** (255.3 km) Bridge over the Big Berland River. **Big Berland River Campground** at north end of bridge to west has 12 sites, sewer hookups, water pump, picnic tables, shelter, camping fee. ▲

Y 52.9 (85.2 km) **GP 154.1** (248 km) Hendrickson Creek.

Y 56.4 (90.7 km) **GP 150.6** (242.5 km) Access road to east leads 1.8 miles/3 km to Hucklebury Tower.

Y 57.4 (92.3 km) **GP 149.6** (240.9 km) Shand Creek.

Y 61.3 (98.6 km) **GP 145.7** (234.6 km) Burleigh Creek.

Y 65.2 (105 km) **GP 141.8** (228.2 km) **Pierre Grey's Lakes Provincial Recreation Area** to east; 83 campsites, sewer hookups, pump water, picnic tables, shelter, fireplaces, firewood (for sale), hiking trails, boat launch, camping fee. ▲

Y 66.1 (106.4 km) **GP 140.9** (226.8 km) Entering **MUSKEG RIVER** (pop. 22) northbound; pay phone.

Y 67.9 (109.3 km) **GP 139.1** (223.9 km) **Junction** with Highway 734 (Forestry Trunk Road, gravel) which leads north 116

www.themilepost.com

Big Horn Motor Inn & Family Restaurant

Clean • Quiet • Comfortable • Friendly

37 Rooms w/Fridges • Cable TV • 3 Movie Channels
Coin Laundry • Kitchenettes • Senior Discounts
Non-Smoking Rooms • Fax/Modem Ready Phones
– SPORTS LOUNGE WITH VLT'S –

Phone 780-827-3744
Toll Free Reservation Line
1-888-880-2444 (in Canada)

PO Box 689, Grande Cache, Alberta T0E 0Y0
http://www.yahoo.com Keyword: Grande Cache

Acorn Motel
Clean & Quiet

51 very modern rooms including:
- Suites with fully equipped kitchenettes
- Non-smoking available
- Business Suites • Colour TV with remote
- Guest Laundry on Site • Pet Friendly
- Complimentary Coffee/Tea

Toll Free 1-888-827-7202
Phone 780-827-2412 • Fax 780-827-2447
Email: acorn1@telusplanet.net

Alpine Lodge
MOTEL & RESTAURANT

34 Renovated Rooms • Kitchenettes • Cable TV
Movie Channel • Senior rates • Non-Smoking Rooms
Complimentary Coffee in All Rooms

**Restaurant Open Daily
5:30am to 11pm**
Check our daily specials! • Licensed
• Smoke Free Solarium

Phone 780-827-2450 • Fax 780-827-2666
Toll Free 1-888-HI LODGE
Email: grcache@telusplanet.net

INN ON THE VALLEY
Grande Cache

- Friendly, knowledgable staff
- Clean comfortable rooms
- Restaurants near by • Cable TV
- Kitchenettes • Non-smoking rooms
- Complimentary coffee
- Major credit cards accepted

Welcome! Spend a Night; Not a Fortune

Phone 780-827-2453
Fax: 780-827-2455
Email: bjpaton@hotmail.com

Bighorn Route (continued)

miles/187 km to Highway 34. There are no services along the highway.

Y 69.4 (111.7 km) **GP 137.6** (221.5 km) Turnout to south.

Y 70 (112.6 km) **GP 137** (220.6 km) Veronique Creek.

Y 74.1 (119.3 km) **GP 132.9** (213.9 km) Muskeg River bridge.

Y 74.9 (120.6 km) **GP 132.1** (212.6 km) Mason Creek day-use area; picnic facilities and hiking trail to the Muskeg River.

Y 75.1 (120.8 km) **GP 131.9** (212.3 km) Mason Creek.

Y 75.7 (121.8 km) **GP 131.3** (211.4 km) Access road to Grande Cache airport.

Y 80.8 (130.1 km) **GP 126.2** (203.1 km) Susa Creek.

Y 82 (132 km) **GP 125** (201.2 km) Washy Creek.

Y 84.1 (135.3 km) **GP 122.9** (197.9 km) Carconte Creek.

Y 84.5 (136 km) **GP 122.5** (197.2 km) **Grande Cache Lake** to south; picnic area, swimming, boat launch. Easy access for RVs.

Y 85.3 (137.3 km) **GP 121.7** (195.9 km) Allen Creek.

Y 86.7 (139.5 km) **GP 120.3** (193.7 km) **Victor Lake** to south; canoeing, fishing. ◆

Y 88.1 (141.7 km) **GP 118.9** (191.5 km) Entering Grande Cache northbound. Visitor information and interpretive centre to east. Wildlife displays, rest area, the Bighorn Gallery and souvenirs.

Grande Cache

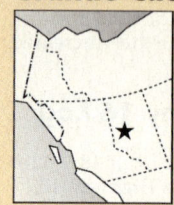

Y 88.2 (142 km) **GP 118.8** (191.2 km) Located 130 miles/214 km northwest of Jasper National Park in the Canadian Rocky Mountains and 118.8 miles/191.2 km south of Grande Prairie. **Population:** 4,200. **Emergency services:** Hospital, phone (780) 827-3701, RCMP, Ambulance, Fire department, 911.

Visitor information: Tourist information centre is located on 100th Street (Highway 40) at the south entrance into town, open 9 A.M. to 7 P.M. daily, May–September; 9 A.M. to 5 P.M. Monday–Friday the rest of the year. Phone (888) 827-3790; www.grandecache.ca.

Elevation: 4,200 feet/1,280m. **Private Aircraft:** Grande Cache airport, 12 miles/19 km east on Highway 40; elev. 4,117 feet/1,255m; length 5,000 feet/1,524m; asphalt; no fuel available.

Grande Cache was established in 1969 in conjunction with resource development by McIntyre Porcupine Coal Ltd. In 1980 a sawmill was constructed by British Columbia Forest Products Ltd. and in 1984 a medium security correctional centre was built.

Historically, the location was used as a staging area for fur trappers and Natives prior to their departure to trap lines in the valleys and mountain ranges now known as Willmore Wilderness Park. Upon their return, they stored large caches of furs while waiting for transportation opportunities to

General Information: Grande Cache Tourism & Interpretive Centre
toll free: 1.888.827.3790 website: www.grandecache.ca
Central Reservations: toll free: 1.866.EXPLORR (397.5677)
website: www.visitgrandecache.com

ATV & Snowmobiles: H&R Rentals
Golfing: Grande Cache Golf & Country Club
Heli Tours: Pacific Western Helicopters
Hiking: Taste of Wilderness Tours
Jet Boat: Avalanche Jet Boat Tours
Photos: Photoscapes by Margaret
Trail Riding: U Bar Trail Rides
White Water Rafting: Wild Blue Yonder Tours

Accommodations
Bed & Breakfast: EJ's Roost B&B
Hotel: Grande Cache Hotel
Vacation Suites: Misty Mountain Suites
Cabins: Sheep Creek Back Country Lodge
Campgrounds:
Marv Moore Municipal Campground
North 40 Wilderness Campgrounds

THIS AD SPONSORED BY THE GRANDE CACHE TOURISM OPERATORS ASSOCIATION, THE TOWN OF GRANDE CACHE AND TRAVEL ALBERTA

Baseball diamond in Canadian Rockies setting at Grande Cache. (© Blake Hanna, staff)

trading posts.

Visitor facilities include hotel, bed and breakfast, 4 motels, 2 banks, restaurants, laundromats, service stations with repair facilities, car washes and a library. Shopping facilities include several small shopping centres, 2 supermarkets, a bakery, sporting goods store and department store.

Recreational facilities include a recreation centre which houses a curling rink, swimming pool, skating rink, fitness rooms and saunas. Grande Cache Golf and Country Club, located in the northeast part of town, has 9 holes, grass greens, clubhouse and pro shop.

Camping at Marv Moore Municipal Campground at the north end of town, next to the golf course; 77 serviced sites, full hookups, washroom facilities, showers, public phone, laundromat, open May–Oct. North 40 Wilderness Campgrounds along Highway 40 north of Grande Cache are Smokey River South, Sulphur Gates, Southview and Kakwa River. ▲

Bighorn Route Log
(continued)

Y 91.3 (146.9 km) GP 115.7 (186.3 km) **Smoky River South Campground** to south has 22 sites, water pump, firewood, firepits, tables, pit toilets, boat launch. Camping fee. ▲

Y 91.5 (147.2 km) GP 115.5 (186 km) **Smoky River** bridge, fishing for arctic grayling, Dolly Varden and whitefish.

Y 92.3 (148.6 km) GP 114.7 (184.6 km) Turnoff to south for **Sulphur Gates Provincial Recreation Area** (4 miles/6.4 km south); 14 sites, camping fee $10. Trail access to Willmore Wilderness Park. Horse staging area for entering Willmore Wilderness Park. ▲

Y 93.4 (150.4 km) GP 113.6 (182.8 km) Turnout with litter barrels.

Y 96.3 (155 km) GP 110.7 (178.2 km) Grande Cache gun range to east. Northbound, the highway parallels the Northern Alberta Resource Railroad and the Smoky River.

Y 100.8 (162.2 km) GP 106.2 (171 km) Turnout to east overlooks Smoky River Coal Ltd. and H.R. Milner Generating Station.

Y 106.7 (171.7 km) GP 100.3 (161.5 km) Turnoff to east for **Sheep Creek Recreation Area** to east; 9 campsites, camping fee, shaded picnic tables, water pump, firepits, firewood, litter barrels, outhouses and gravel parking areas. Boat launch on the Smoky River. ▲

Y 107.1 (172.4 km) GP 99.9 (160.8 km) Ship Creek.

Y 110.1 (177.2 km) GP 96.9 (156 km) Wayandie Road. NOTE: Highway ascends steep hill northbound, some 7 percent grades.

Y 115.5 (185.9 km) GP 91.5 (147.3 km) Turnout with litter barrel.

Y 125.1 (201.3 km) GP 81.9 (131.9 km) **Southview Recreation Area** to east; gravel parking area, 8 campsites, picnic tables, litter barrels, outhouses, highbush cranberries in season. Camping fee.

Y 128.5 (206.8 km) GP 78.5 (126.4 km) CAUTION: Logging trucks next 36 miles/60 km northbound.

Y 130.4 (209.8 km) GP 76.6 (123.4 km) 16th base line sign marks north–south hunting boundary.

Y 145.6 (234.3 km) GP 61.4 (98.9 km) Kakwa River bridge.

Y 145.9 (234.8 km) GP 61.1 (98.4 km) Turnoff for **Kakwa River Recreation Area**; 14 campsites, picnic tables, firewood, firepits, water pump, litter barrels, outhouses, gravel parking area. Camping fee. Open April to October. Fishing for arctic grayling. ▲

Y 159.1 (256.1 km) GP 47.9 (77.1 km) Access road eads east 3.6 miles/6 km to **Musreau Lake Campground** and day-use area; 50 picnic sites, 69 campsites, picnic tables, firewood, firepits, water pump, litter barrels, outhouses, equestrian trails, boat launch and fishing. ▲

Y 161.8 (260.4 km) GP 45.2 (72.8 km) Steep Creek.

Y 164.1 (264.2 km) GP 42.8 (69 km) Turnout and information sign.

Y 164.3 (264.4 km) GP 42.7 (68.8 km) Cutbank River bridge. River access at north end of bridge.

Y 165.6 (266.5 km) GP 41.4 (66.7 km) Elk Creek.

Y 165.8 (266.8 km) GP 41.2 (66.4 km) CAUTION: Logging trucks next 36 miles/60 km southbound.

Y 180.9 (291.1 km) GP 26.1 (42.1 km) Big Mountain Creek.

Y 182.8 (294.1 km) GP 24.2 (39.1 km) Bald Mountain Creek.

Y 191.1 (307.5 km) GP 15.7 (25.7 km) Bent Pipe Creek.

Y 194.1 (312.4 km) GP 12.9 (20.8 km) Ainsworth O.S.B. Plant.

Y 199.7 (321.3 km) GP 7.3 (11.8 km) Junction with Highway 666 which leads southwest to **O'Brien Provincial Park** and day-use area; water pump, firewood, playground, hiking trails. Also access to Nitehawk ski resort. ▲

Y 199.8 (321.5 km) GP 7.2 (11.6 km) Wapiti River bridge.

Y 201.6 (324.4 km) GP 5.4 (8.7 km) Turnoff for Camp Tamarack RV Park. Also access to Dunes golf and winter club (15 miles/25 km east); 18 holes, grass greens, driving range, pro shop. ▲

Y 207 (333.2 km) GP 0 Entering Grande Prairie northbound. Turn east on 100th Avenue for **Grande Prairie Museum**.

**Return to Milepost E 284
East Access Route or Milepost E 172.2
Yellowhead Highway**

Highway 16 has restricted speed zones where wildlife sightings are frequent. Drive carefully and watch out for moose, elk, white-tailed and mule deer, mountain goats, bighorn sheep, and black and grizzly bears. NOTE: It is illegal to feed, touch, disturb or hunt wildlife in the national park. All plants and natural objects are also protected and may not be removed or destroyed.

Many turnouts next 25 miles/40 km westbound.

E 193 (310.6 km) PG 257 (413.6 km) First Rocky River bridge westbound.

E 194.3 (312.7 km) PG 255.7 (411.5 km) Second Rocky River bridge westbound.

E 203 (326.7 km) PG 247 (397.5 km) Two bridges spanning the Athabasca River. Raft trips down the Athabasca may be arranged in Jasper. Watch for elk and bighorn sheep.

E 205.1 (330.1 km) PG 244.9 (394.1 km) Snaring River bridge.

E 206.7 (332.7 km) PG 243.3 (391.5 km) Jasper airfield to south.

E 208.1 (335 km) PG 241.9 (389.2 km) Snaring overflow camping south. ▲

E 208.4 (335.4 km) PG 241.6 (388.8 km) Snaring rest area to south.

E 208.5 (336 km) PG 241.2 (388.2 km) Palisades picnic area.

E 212.9 (342.6 km) PG 237.1 (381.6 km) Access road to Jasper Park Lodge (lodging, restaurant, golf, etc.), Maligne Canyon and **Maligne Lake**. Glacier-fed Maligne Lake (35 miles/56 km south) is one of Jasper's premier attractions; scheduled boat tours.

E 215.8 (347.3 km) PG 234.2 (376.9 km) **Junction** with Highway 93A. Lodging and restaurant to south.

E 216.6 (348.6 km) PG 233.4 (375.6 km) Access to **JASPER** (pop. 4,800), townsite for Jasper National Park. **Visitor Information:** At park headquarters in town. All visitor services available downtown along Connaught Blvd.

Junction with Highway 93, the scenic Icefields Parkway, south to junction with Trans-Canada Highway 1 (140 miles/225 km), providing access to Columbia Icefield, Lake Louise and Banff.

NOTE: No fuel next 63 miles/101 km westbound on Highway 16.

E 217.1 (349.5 km) PG 232.9 (374.7 km) Miette River.

E 222.2 (357.6 km) PG 227.8 (366.6 km) Paved turnout to north with outhouses, litter barrels and interpretive sign about Yellowhead Pass. Many turnouts next 25 miles/40 km eastbound.

E 223.2 (359.3 km) PG 226.8 (364.9 km) Meadow Creek.

E 223.4 (359.5 km) PG 226.6 (364.7 km) Trailhead for Virl Lake, Dorothy Lake and Christine Lake.

E 226.1 (363.9 km) PG 223.9 (360.3 km) Clairvaux Creek.

E 229.4 (369.3 km) PG 220.6 (354.9 km) **Jasper National Park, West Entrance.** Park fee must be paid by all visitors using facilities in Rocky Mountain national parks.

E 231.6 (372.7 km) PG 218.4 (351.5 km) **Yellowhead Pass** (elev. 3,760 feet/1,146m), Alberta–British Columbia border. Named for an Iroquois trapper and guide who worked for the Hudson's Bay Co. in the early 1800s. His light-colored hair earned him the name Tete Jaune ("yellow head") from the French voyageurs.

Mount Robson Provincial Park, East Entrance. Portal Lake picnic area with tables, toilets, information board and hiking trail.

YELLOWHEAD HIGHWAY

Mount Robson, highest peak in the Canadian Rockies, viewed from Milepost E 268.8. (© Blake Hanna, staff)

TIME ZONE CHANGE: Alberta observes Mountain standard time. Most of British Columbia observes Pacific standard time. Both observe daylight saving time.

E 235.2 (378.5 km) **PG 214.8** (345.7 km) Large turnout with toilet, interpretive sign and plaque on Japanese internment camps of WWII.

E 235.8 (379.6 km) **PG 214.2** (344.6 km) Rockingham Creek.

E 236.2 (380.1 km) **PG 213.8** (344.1 km) **Yellowhead Lake**; picnic tables, viewpoint, boat launch and fishing.

E 238 (383 km) **PG 212** (341.2 km) Lucerne Campground; 32 sites, picnic tables, drinking water, firewood and swimming; camping fee charged.

E 239.3 (385.2 km) **PG 210.7** (339 km) Fraser Crossing rest area to south; litter barrels and toilets.

E 239.4 (385.3 km) **PG 210.6** (338.9 km) Fraser River bridge No. 1.

E 242.4 (390.1 km) **PG 207.6** (334.1 km) Fraser River bridge No. 2.

E 246.2 (396.2 km) **PG 203.8** (328 km) Grant Brook Creek.

E 249 (400.8 km) **PG 201** (323.4 km) Moose Creek bridge.

E 251.1 (404.2 km) **PG 198.9** (320 km) Turnout at east end of Moose Lake; information kiosk, litter barrels, toilet and boat launch.

E 255.5 (411.2 km) **PG 194.5** (313 km) Turnout with litter barrels.

E 263.7 (424.4 km) **PG 186.3** (299.8 km) Paved turnout with litter barrels.

E 268 (431.3 km) **PG 182** (292.9 km) **Overlander Falls** rest area to south; pit toilets, litter barrels. Hiking trail to Overlander Falls, about 30 minutes round-trip.

E 268.8 (432.7 km) **PG 181.2** (291.4 km) Viewpoint of **Mount Robson** (elev. 12,972 feet/3,954m), highest peak in the Canadian Rockies, and Visitor Infocentre. Parking, picnic tables, restrooms, litter barrels, gas and restaurant. Berg Lake trailhead; hike-in campgrounds. Private campground north of highway. Robson Meadows government campground south of highway with 125 sites, dump station, showers, pay phone, interpretive programs, tables, firewood, flush toilets, water and horseshoe pits; group camping; camping fee charged.

E 269.4 (433.6 km) **PG 180.6** (290.6 km) Robson River government campground to north with 19 sites (some wheelchair-accessible), tables, firewood, pit toilets, showers, water and horseshoe pits; camping fee charged.

E 269.9 (434.4 km) **PG 180.1** (289.8 km) Robson River bridge. Look for Indian paintbrush June through August. The bracts are orange-red while the petals are green.

E 270.3 (435.1 km) **PG 179.7** (289.1 km) West entrance to Mount Robson Provincial Park. Turnout with litter barrels and statue.

E 270.5 (435.3 km) **PG 179.5** (288.9 km) Paved turnout to south.

E 271.4 (436.8 km) **PG 178.6** (287.4 km) Swift Current Creek.

E 273.4 (440.1 km) **PG 176.5** (284.1 km) Private campground.

E 274.4 (441.7 km) **PG 175.6** (282.5 km) **Mount Terry Fox Provincial Park** picnic area with tables, restrooms and viewing telescope. The information board here points out the location of Mount Terry Fox in the Selwyn Range of the Rocky Mountains. The peak was named in 1981 to honour cancer victim Terry Fox, who, before his death from the disease, raised some $25 million for cancer research during his attempt to run across Canada.

E 276.3 (444.7 km) **PG 173.7** (280.5 km) Gravel turnout to north with Yellowhead Highway information sign.

E 276.4 (444.9 km) **PG 173.6** (280.3 km) **Rearguard Falls Provincial Park** picnic area. Easy half-hour round-trip to falls viewpoint. Upper limit of 800-mile/1,300-km migration of Pacific salmon; look for chinook in late summer.

E 277.8 (447.1 km) **PG 172.2** (277.1 km) Gravel turnout with litter barrels to south overlooking Fraser River.

E 278.2 (447.8 km) **PG 171.8** (276.4 km) Weigh scales.

E 278.7 (448.6 km) **PG 171.3** (275.6 km) Tete Jaune Cache rest area with tables, litter barrels and toilets.

E 279 (449.1 km) **PG 171** (275.1 km) **Junction** with Yellowhead Highway 5 at **Tete Jaune Cache**.

Yellowhead Highway 5 leads south 12 miles/20 km to **VALEMOUNT** (pop. 1,200; tourist information office and all visitor facilities. Yellowhead Highway 5 junctions with Trans Canada Highway 1 at Kamloops, 208 miles/335 km south of here.

Irvin's Park & Campground. See display ad this section.

E 279.6 (450.1 km) **PG 170.4** (274.1 km) Private lodging, restaurants, gas, camping.

NOTE: No fuel eastbound until Jasper, 63 miles/101 km.

Tete Jaune Lodge. A hidden treasure you'll add to your list of highlights. Stay and dine by the Fraser River. Licensed dining with patio. Peaceful riverfront property, spacious clean rooms, cabins available. Friendly staff. Riverside tenting spots. RV sites with hookups. Showers. Fishing, hiking, picnic spots, gas, diesel, confectionery, gifts. (250) 566-9815; toll-free 1-866-566-9815; www.tetejaunelodge.com. [ADVERTISEMENT]

E 283.1 (455.7 km) **PG 166.9** (268.5 km) Spittal Creek Interpretive Forest; hiking trails, tables, litter barrels and toilets.

E 288.2 (463.8 km) **PG 161.8** (260.4 km) Private resort. Lodging, restaurant.

E 289.1 (465.3 km) **PG 160.9** (258.9 km) Small River rest area by stream with tables, toilets and litter barrels.

E 293.6 (472.5 km) **PG 156.4** (251.7 km) Horsey Creek.

E 300 (482.9 km) **PG 150** (241.3 km) Turnoff to south for settlement of Dunster; gas and general store.

E 305.2 (491.2 km) **PG 144.8** (233 km) Baker Creek rest area with tables, litter barrels and toilets.

E 308.9 (497.2 km) **PG 141.1** (227 km) Nevin Creek.

E 309.5 (498.1 km) **PG 140.5** (226.1 km) **Deer Meadows Golf and RV Resort.** See display ad this section.

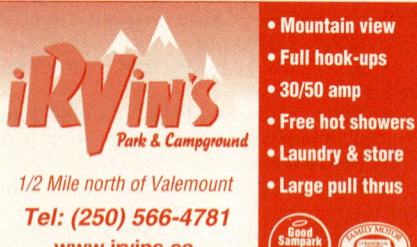

iRVin's Park & Campground
- Mountain view
- Full hook-ups
- 30/50 amp
- Free hot showers
- Laundry & store
- Large pull thrus

1/2 Mile north of Valemount
Tel: (250) 566-4781
www.irvins.ca
irvins@valemount.com

MCBRIDE, BRITISH COLUMBIA
Deer Meadows GOLF & RV RESORT
- Public Golf Course with Rentals
- LICENSED CAFE
- Easy access w/RV turnaround
- Camping
- FREE hot showers, laundry, flush toilets
- All sites pull-throughs, 15/30 amp, water & sani-dump

Phone 250-569-0191 Fax 250-569-3383 www.mcbridebc.net\deermeadows\

Yellowhead Highway 16 extends from Winnipeg, MB, to Prince Rupert, BC.

E 312 (502.1 km) PG 138 (222.1 km) Turnouts at both ends of Holmes River bridge.

E 317.4 (510.8 km) PG 132.6 (213.4 km) **Beaverview Campsite.** See display ad this section. ▲

E 317.9 (511.6 km) PG 132.1 (212.6 km) Fraser River bridge.

E 318.2 (512.1 km) PG 131.8 (212.1 km) Turnout to north with litter barrels.

E 318.8 (513.1 km) PG 131.2 (211.1 km) **McBRIDE** (pop. 700; elev. 2,369 feet/722.1m), located in the Robson Valley by the Fraser River. The Park Ranges of the Rocky Mountains are to the northeast and the Cariboo Mountains are to the southeast. A road leads to Teare Mountain lookout for a spectacular view of countryside. The village of McBride was established in 1913 as a divisional point on the railroad and was named for Richard McBride, then premier of British Columbia. Forest products are a major industry here today.

Visitor Information: In the historic train station at the end of Main Street in town, or McBride Village Office; open 9 A.M. to 5 P.M.

McBride has all visitor facilities, including 5 hotels/motels, 2 bed and breakfasts, 2 supermarkets, 2 convenience/video stores, clothing stores, restaurants, pharmacy, hospital and gas stations. A library, museum and neighborhood pub are 1.9 miles/3 km from town. Full-service private campground just east of town. A dump station is located at the gas station in town. ▲

While in McBride, watch wood ducks, scoters, teals and more at the Horseshoe Lake Bird Watch. In late summer, see the salmon run in the Holmes River. In winter, go cross-country skiing on developed trails and snowmobiling in the backcountry. Helicopter service available for fly-in skiing and hiking.

North Country Lodge. See display ad this section.

McBride Chevron. See display ad this section.

NOTE: Next gas westbound is 91 miles/146 km from here (Purden Lake).

E 319.5 (514.2 km) PG 130.5 (210 km) Turnout with litter barrel.

E 321.9 (518.1 km) PG 128.1 (206.1 km) Dore River bridge.

E 326.7 (525.8 km) PG 123.3 (198.4 km) Macintosh Creek.

E 328.8 (529.2 km) PG 121.2 (195 km) Clyde Creek.

E 336.9 (542.3 km) PG 113.1 (181.9 km) West Twin Creek bridge.

E 343.6 (553.1 km) PG 106.4 (171.1 km) Goat River bridge. Paved rest area to north with tables, toilets and litter barrels.

E 346.7 (558 km) PG 103.3 (166.2 km) Little LaSalle Recreation Area and BC Forest Service site. Small lake, small wharf, toilet.

E 351.2 (565.2 km) PG 98.8 (159 km) Snowshoe Creek.

E 354.9 (571.2 km) PG 95.1 (153 km) Catfish Creek.

E 360.7 (580.6 km) PG 89.3 (143.6 km) Ptarmigan Creek bridge.

E 363.8 (585.6 km) PG 86.2 (138.6 km) Turnout with litter barrels to north.

E 369.2 (594.1 km) PG 80.8 (130.1 km) Dome Creek.

E 371.5 (597.9 km) PG 78.5 (126.3 km) Cafe.

E 373.3 (600.8 km) PG 76.7 (123.4 km) Slim Creek paved rest area to south with information kiosk, tables, playground, litter barrels and wheelchair-accessible toilets. Watch for bears. ♿

E 373.4 (601 km) PG 76.6 (123.2 km) Ministry of Highways camp.

E 374.1 (602.1 km) PG 75.9 (122.1 km) Slim Creek bridge.

E 385.6 (620.7 km) PG 64.4 (103.5 km) Driscol Creek.

E 386.4 (621.9 km) PG 63.6 (102.3 km) Forests in this area have been destroyed by the hemlock looper, an insect which has killed or damaged over 45.9 million cubic feet/1.3 million cubic metres of wood in British Columbia.

E 387.6 (623.9 km) PG 62.4 (100.3 km) Gravel turnout with litter barrel to north.

E 388.9 (626 km) PG 61.1 (98.2 km) Lunate Creek.

E 391.8 (630.6 km) PG 58.2 (93.6 km) Grizzly hiking trail to south.

E 392 (630.9 km) PG 58 (93.3 km) Hungary Creek. Watch for Ministry of Forests signs indicating the year in which a logged area was replanted. Wildflowers include fireweed, mid-July through August.

E 395.8 (637 km) PG 54.2 (87.2 km) Sugarbowl Creek.

E 400.5 (644.6 km) PG 49.5 (79.6 km) Paved turnout with litter barrel to north.

E 408.2 (657 km) PG 41.8 (67.2 km) Kenneth Creek.

E 408.4 (657.4 km) PG 41.6 (66.8 km) Purden Mountain ski resort.

E 409.7 (659.1 km) PG 40.5 (65.1 km) **Purden Lake Resort** with cafe, gas, phone, lodging and camping. ▲

Purden Lake and Ski Resorts. Campground with lakefront camping; full hookups; sani-dump; hot showers. Cabin rentals, boat rentals, boat launch. Good rainbow trout fishing. Cafe, gas station (propane, diesel, unleaded). Ski area has 23 runs, 2 double chairlifts, T-bar, day lodge, equipment rentals, lessons, cafeteria. P.O. Box 1239, Prince George, BC V2L 4V3. (250) 565-7777, www.purden.com. [ADVERTISEMENT]

NOTE: Next gas eastbound is 91 miles/146 km from here (McBride).

E 411.2 (661.9 km) PG 38.8 (62.3 km) **Purden Lake Provincial Park,** 1.9 miles/3 km from highway; 78 campsites, 48 picnic tables, water, dump station, firewood, playground and horseshoe pits. This recreation area offers a sandy beach, change houses, swimming, walking trails, waterskiing and

Pastoral scene along the Yellowhead Highway near McBride. (© Bob Butterfield)

Beaverview Campsite (250) 569-2513

Laundry • Sani-Station
FREE HOT SHOWERS
Grassed Pull-thru • Hookups

Yellowhead Highway East, McBride, BC

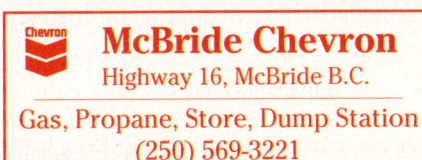

McBride Chevron
Highway 16, McBride B.C.

Gas, Propane, Store, Dump Station
(250) 569-3221
OPEN 24 HOURS

NORTH COUNTRY LODGE — McBRIDE, B.C., CANADA

www.northcountrylodge.ca

– TOUR GROUPS WELCOME –
• 48 spacious rooms w/queen size beds
• Remote control TV with complimentary movie channels
• Whirlpool
• Two bedroom suites equipped with full size kitchens
• Restaurant (Licensed, open 6AM to 10PM)
• AM coffee • Direct dial phones • A/C

Just 1hr. 30 min. to or from Jasper on Yellowhead #16.
Phone (250)569-0001 or Fax (250)569-0002

Lakeside Resort attracts serious sportsmen to fish-rich Cluculz Lake. (© Blake Hanna, staff)

boat launch. Good rainbow fishing to 4 lbs. Camping fee charged.

E 412.6 (664.1 km) **PG 37.4** (60.1 km) Bowron River bridge. Paved rest area to north beside river, on west side of bridge; toilets, tables and litter barrels. Entrance on curve; use care. Turnaround space.

E 421 (677.6 km) **PG 29** (46.6 km) Vama Vama Creek.

E 424 (682.4 km) **PG 26** (41.8 km) Wansa Creek.

E 427.1 (687.4 km) **PG 22.9** (36.8 km) Willow River bridge. Rest area at west end of bridge beside river; tables, litter barrels, toilets and nature trail. The 1.2-mile-/1.9-km-long Willow River Forest Interpretation Trail is an easy 45-minute walk.

E 429.5 (691.3 km) **PG 20.5** (32.9 km) Bowes Creek.

E 429.7 (691.6 km) **PG 20.3** (32.6 km) Turnout to north with litter barrels and information board on 1961 forest fire and moose habitat. Circle trail to moose observation site.

E 435.2 (700.5 km) **PG 14.8** (23.7 km) Tabor Mountain ski hill.

E 435.4 (700.8 km) **PG 14.6** (23.4 km) Paved turnout to north with litter barrels.

E 437.6 (704.3 km) **PG 12.4** (19.9 km) Access to **Tabor Lake**; good fishing for rainbow in spring.

E 444.8 (715.9 km) **PG 5.2** (8.3 km) **Junction** of Highway 16B with Highway 97 south bypass. Turn to page 82 in the WEST ACCESS ROUTE section for log of Highway 97 South to Cache Creek.

E 450 (724.2 km) **PG 0 PRINCE GEORGE** (see description on pages 82–86). Continue west on Yellowhead Highway 16 for Prince Rupert (log follows).

Junction with Highway 97 north to Dawson Creek and the beginning of the Alaska Highway. Turn to page 86 in the WEST ACCESS ROUTE section for the log of Highway 97 North.

This section of the log shows distance from Prince George (PG) followed by distance from Prince Rupert (PR).

NOTE: Physical kilometreposts west from here are up along Highway 16 about every 5 km and reflect distance from Prince Rupert. Because the posts do not always accurately reflect driving distance, mileages from Prince Rupert are based on actual driving distance while the kilometre conversion is based on physical kilometreposts as they occurred in summer 2002.

PG 0 PR 447.7 (720 km) **Junction** of Highways 16 and 97 (Central Avenue/Cariboo Highway) in Prince George. **Visitor Information:** Visitor centre at southeast corner of intersection (look for Mr. P.G. mascot); open daily in summer.

From Prince George to Prince Rupert, Highway 16 is a 2-lane highway with 3-lane passing stretches. Fairly straight, with no high summits, the highway follows the valleys of the Nechako, Bulkley and Skeena rivers, paralleling the Canadian National Railway route. There are few services between towns.

PG 0.2 (0.4 km) **PR 447.5** (719.6 km) Prince George Golf and Curling Club.

PG 0.6 (1 km) **PR 447.1** (719 km) Ferry Avenue.

PG 1.2 (1.9 km) **PR 446.5** (718.1 km) Tyner/Domano Blvd.; access to the University of Northern B.C.

PG 3.8 (6.2 km) **PR 443.9** (714.4 km) **Bon Voyage Motor Inn.** New 1998. Air-conditioning, kitchenettes, cable TV. Gift shop. Restaurant. RV parking. Seniors' discount. Smoking accommodation available. Adjacent Esso and Plaza offers diesel, gas, propane, RV and car wash, laundromat, dry cleaners, fishing/hunting supplies, hair salon, etc. Major credit cards, debits cards. 1-888-611-3872 or (250) 964-2333. Email: bvoyage@mag-net.com. [ADVERTISEMENT]

PG 5.7 (9.2 km) **PR 442** (711.3 km) Blackwater Road. Access to Moose Springs Resort with camping, restaurant, pub and country store.

West Lake Provincial Park 8 miles/12.9 km south; day-use area with picnic shelter, swimming, fishing and boat launch.

PG 7.3 (11.8 km) **PR 440.4** (708.7 km) Western Road.

PG 12.5 (20.2 km) **PR 435.2** (700.4 km) Chilko River.

PG 15.2 (24.5 km) **PR 432.5** (696 km) **North Country Arts & Crafts.** See display ad this section.

PG 25.8 (41.5 km) **PR 421.8** (678.8 km) Berman Lake Regional Park to south.

PG 28.2 (45.4 km) **PR 419.5** (675.1 km) Tamarac Lake to south.

PG 30.6 (49.3 km) **PR 417.1** (671.2 km) Bednesti Lake Resort.

PG 37.6 (60.5 km) **PR 410.1** (660 km) **Lakeside Resort.** See display ad this section.

Access to lakeside resort and fishing at **Cluculz Lake** (not visible from highway). Rainbow to 3¾ lbs. by trolling, use snell hook and worms; kokanee to 1½ lbs., troll with snell hook and worms in spring; char to 57 lbs., use large flatfish, spoons, plugs and weights, early spring and late fall; whitefish to 5 lbs., year-round. Very good fishing in spring; ice goes out about the first week of May. Good ice fishing December to March. In September kokanee are at their peak. *Lake gets rough when windy.*

PG 38.7 (62.4 km) **PR 409** (658.2 km) Cluculz rest area to south with flush toilets (summer only), picnic tables and litter barrels.

PG 58.5 (94.2 km) **PR 389** (626 km) Derksen Road; access to RV Park.

Dave's R.V. Park. 2 miles east of Vanderhoof, 1/2 mile down Derksen Road. Clean, quiet, relaxing setting. 55 sites, 31 long pull-throughs, full hookups (30 amps). Partial hookups or no hookups. Regular sites, tenting. Sani-dump. Limited groceries, RV supplies and souvenir shop. Grass putting course. Phone (250) 567-3161; fax (250) 567-5461. See display ad this section. [ADVERTISEMENT]

PG 58.6 (94.4 km) **PR 389.1** (626.2 km) Pullout to west; litter barrels, picnic tables, map.

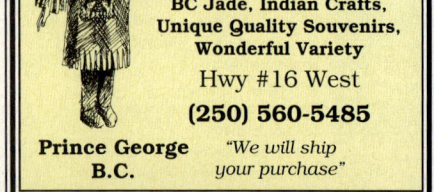

NORTH COUNTRY ARTS & CRAFTS
BC Jade, Indian Crafts, Unique Quality Souvenirs, Wonderful Variety
Hwy #16 West
(250) 560-5485
Prince George B.C. *"We will ship your purchase"*

Vanderhoof

PG 58.7 (94.5 km) PR 389 (624.8 km). Stoplight at junction with Highway 27; turnoff to downtown Vanderhoof. **Population:** 4,500; area 12,000. **Emergency Services: Police,** phone (250) 567-2222. **Fire Department,** phone (250) 567-2345. **Ambulance,** phone (800) 461-9911. **Hospital,** St. John's, Northside District, phone (250) 567-2211.

Visitor Information: Visitor Infocentre downtown on Burrard Avenue, 1 block off Highway 16. Write Vanderhoof & District Chamber of Commerce, Box 126-MP, Vanderhoof, BC V0J 3A0; phone (250) 567-2124.

Elevation: 2,225 feet/667.5m. **Radio:** CJCI 620, CFPR-FM 96.7, CKPG 550, CIVH 1340, CIRX-FM 95.9. **Television:** Channels 2, 4, 5, 6, 8. **Newspapers:** *Omineca Express–Bugle* (weekly). **Transportation: Air**—Vanderhoof airport, 2 miles/3.2 km from intersection of Highways 16 and 27; 5,000-foot/1,524-m paved runway. Seaplane landings on Nechako River at corner of View Street and Boundary Avenue. **Railroad**—VIA Rail. **Bus**—Greyhound.

Vanderhoof is the geographical centre of British Columbia. The city was named for Chicago publisher Herbert Vanderhoof, who founded the village in 1914 when he was associated with the Grand Trunk Development Co. Today, Vanderhoof is the supply and distribution centre for a large agricultural, lumbering and mining area.

The community's history is preserved at **Vanderhoof Heritage Village Museum,** on Highway 16 west. Relocated pioneer structures furnished with period artifacts recall the early days of the Nechako Valley.

Located on the Nechako River, Vanderhoof is a stopping place in April and September for thousands of migrating waterfowl. The river flats upstream of the bridge are a bird sanctuary. Pelicans have been spotted feeding at Tachick Lake south of town.

There are 7 hotels and motels, 2 bed and breakfasts, and 17 restaurants in the town. All shopping facilities and several gas stations. There are 4 fishing and camping resorts. An 18-hole golf course is located 1.9 miles/3.1 km north of town. Dump station at Dave's R.V. Park at **Milepost PG 58.5** and at Riverside Campsite (municipal campground) on Burrard Avenue. ▲

Riverside Campsite. Overlooking Nechako River with bird-watching tower and groomed walking trails. Private sites, some with 30-/50-amp service; some with hook-ups. Firepits and firewood. Flush toilets and free hot showers for guests. Public phone. Sani-dump. Pets welcome. Attendant on duty 24 hours. Gates open 7 A.M. to 10 P.M. 3100 Burrard Avenue, P.O. Box 380, Vanderhoof, BC V0J 3A0. Phone (250) 567-4710. ▲
[ADVERTISEMENT]

Yellowhead Highway 16 Log

(continued)

PG 58.7 (94.5 km) PR 389 (624.8 km) **Junction** with Highway 27 north 37 miles/60 km to Fort St. James. See description on page 220.

PG 59.2 (95.2 km) PR 388.5 (624.1 km) Vanderhoof Heritage Museum to south.

PG 63.2 (101.7 km) PR 384.5 (617.6 km) Second **junction** westbound with Highway 27 (see description at Milepost PG 58.7). This route skirts Vanderhoof. Truck weigh scales to north.

PG 72.3 (116.3 km) PR 375.4 (602.9 km) Plateau Division Sawmill to south.

PG 81.5 (131.1 km) PR 366.2 (588 km) Turnout to south with view of Nechako River. The Grand Trunk Pacific Railway was completed near this site in 1914. The railroad (later the Canadian National) linked Prince Rupert, a deep-water port, with interior British Columbia. Entering Lakes District. This high country has over 300 freshwater lakes.

PG 81.8 (131.6 km) PR 365.9 (587.5 km) FORT FRASER (pop. 600). **Radio:** CBC-FM 102.9. Small community with food, gas, propane, lodging and first-aid station. Gas station with hot showers, convenience store and restaurant. Named for Simon Fraser, who established a trading post here in 1806. Now a supply centre for surrounding farms and sawmills. The last spike of the Grand Trunk Railway was driven here on April 7, 1914.

PG 82.6 (133 km) PR 365.1 (586.1 km) Nechako River bridge. Turnout to south with parking, litter barrels and access to **Nechako River;** fishing for rainbow and Dolly Varden, June to fall. At the east end of Fraser Lake, the Nautley River—less than a mile long—drains into the Nechako River. 🐟

Relocated structures preserve pioneer history at Vanderhoof Heritage Village Museum. (© Blake Hanna, staff)

VANDERHOOF ADVERTISERS

Dave's R.V. Park .... Ph. (250) 567-3161
Finger Lake Wilderness
  Resort .... Ph. 1-866-334-6437
Riverside Campsite .... Ph. (250) 567-4710
Siesta Inn .... Ph. (250) 567-2365

"GETAWAY, Relax & Unwind"
FingerLakeResort.com

Wildlife viewing — Cozy Log Cabins
Motor Boats, ATVs — RV Sites, power
Pristine Wilderness — Drive Thrus.

Finger Lake Wilderness Resort
Toll Free: 1-866-334-6437
1-250-563-1883 @ Beep 4125
1 hr South of Vanderhoof • 2 hrs SW of Prince George
British Columbia, Canada

Dave's RV Park
2 Miles East of Vanderhoof
CLEAN • QUIET • RELAXING
31 Full Hookup 30 AMP Pullthroughs
50 AMP $ - Cable TV $
Regular Lots - Partial or No Hookups
Excellent Tent Sites
Clean - Modern - Washrooms
Showers - Laundry
Free Hot Showers for Guests
See DAVE'S RV PARK - Log Section

Box 1512
Vanderhoof, BC V0J 3A0
Ph: 250-567-3161 • Fax: 250-567-5461

Siesta INN
1-800-914-3388
All New Beds
Recently Renovated In & Out. Kitchen & Sleeping Units
On Hwy 16, just 1 hour west of Prince George.
Friendly service, affordably priced.
Tanya & Ivan Lobelle, Box 582, Vanderhoof, B.C. V0J 3A0
www.hwy16.com/~siesta   Ph: (250) 567-2365   Fax: (250)567-2393
Movie Central - Cable TV - Data Compatible Phones - 24 Hour Switchboard
Close to Downtown - Winter Plug-ins - All Major Credit Cards Accepted

Fort St. James

Fort St. James

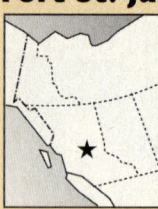

Located 37 miles/59.5 km north of Vanderhoof on Highway 27. **Population:** 2,146. **Emergency Services: Police,** phone (250) 996-8269. **Ambulance:** phone 1-562-7241. **Elevation:** 2,208 feet/ 673m. **Radio:** CKPG 550, CJCI 1480; CBC-FM 107.0. **Visitor Information:** At the Visitor Infocentre.

Fort St. James is located on Stuart Lake. Named for John Stuart, the man who succeeded Simon Fraser as head of the New Caledonia district, the 59-mile-/95-km-long lake is the southernmost in a 3-lake chain which provides hundreds of miles of boating and fishing. Fort St. James also boasts the Nation Lakes, a chain of 4 lakes (Tsayta, Indata, Tchentlo and Chuchi) connected by the Nation River.

Fort St. James has several hotel/motels, restaurants, gas stations, private campgrounds, dump stations and 2 shopping centres. Picnicking and swimming at Cottonwood Park on Stuart Lake. A 9-hole golf course overlooks Stuart Lake; rentals available. ▲

Stuart River Campgrounds. Treed sites, tenting to full hookups, showers and laundry, firepits and firewood, pay phone. Playgrounds, horseshoe pits; marina with launching ramp and moorage space. Great fishing! River and lake charters. Your hosts, George and Heather Malbeuf, Box 306, Fort St. James, BC V0J 1P0. (250) 996-8690, fax (250) 996-7832. [ADVERTISEMENT]

Camping is also available at **Paarens Beach Provincial Park,** located 6.8 miles/ 10.9 km off Highway 27 on Sowchea Bay Road; 36 campsites, picnic shelter, picnic tables, toilets, water, firepits, firewood, boat launch and swimming; camping fee. **Sowchea Bay Provincial Park,** located 10.6 miles/17.1 km off Highway 27 on Sowchea Bay Road, has 30 campsites, camping fee, picnic tables, toilets, water, firepits, firewood, boat launch and swimming. ▲

Attractions include the Our Lady of Good Hope Catholic Church and the Chief Kwah burial site. The church is one of the oldest in British Columbia. Chief Kwah, one of the first Carrier Indian chiefs to confront early white explorers, is buried on the Nak'azdli Indian Reserve at the mouth of the Stuart River. At Cottonwood Park on the shore of Lake Stuart, look for a model of a Junkers airplane, which depicts the Fort's major role in early bush flying in Northern British Columbia.

Stones. The most beautiful little store north of Vancouver is a must see when visiting Fort St. James. Stones is full of truly fabulous things for the home and garden. Stones also has a wonderful selection of wedding shower and baby gifts. Stones is located at 169 West Stuart Drive in Fort St. James. Stones hours are Monday–Saturday 10 A.M. to 5:30 P.M. Phone (250) 996-2255. [ADVERTISEMENT]

Fort St. James is the home of **Fort St. James National Historic Site.** Established in 1806 by Simon Fraser as a fur trading post for the Northwest Co., Fort St. James served throughout the 19th century as headquarters for the Hudson's Bay Co.'s New Caledonia fur trade district. The fur warehouse, fish cache, men's house, the Murray House and trade store have been restored in 1896-style. The site is open from mid-May to September. Admission is charged.

Good fishing in **Stuart Lake** for rainbow and char (to trophy size), kokanee and Dolly Varden.

**Return to Milepost PG 58.7 or PG 63.2
Yellowhead Highway 16**

Fort St. James features restored 19th century buildings of the New Caledonia fur district. (© Blake hanna, staff)

PG 84.1 (135.4 km) **PR 363.6** (583.7 km) Nautley Road. **Beaumont Provincial Park,** on beautiful **Fraser Lake,** north side of highway; site of original Fort Fraser. Boat launch, swimming, hiking, fishing, 49 campsites, picnic tables, firewood, flush toilets, water, playground, horseshoe pits, dump station. Fishing for rainbow and lake trout, burbot, sturgeon and Dolly Varden.

PG 85.9 (138.3 km) **PR 361.8** (580.8 km) View of Fraser Lake to north.

PG 86.3 (138.9 km) **PR 361.7** (580.5 km) Access to private campground on Fraser Lake; chainsaw sculpture.

Pipers Glen RV Resort. See display ad this section. ▲

PG 88 (141.6 km) **PR 359.7** (578.7 km) Dry William Lake rest area to south with picnic tables, toilets and litter barrels.

PG 89.7 (144.4 km) **PR 358** (575 km) View of Mouse Mountain to northwest.

PG 90.9 (146.3 km) **PR 356.8** (573 km) Fraser Lake sawmill to north.

PG 91.3 (147 km) **PR 356.4** (572.3 km) Gas and diesel.

PG 94.5 (152.1 km) **PR 353.2** (567.2 km) **FRASER LAKE** (pop. 1,400; elev. 2,580 feet/786m). **Visitor Information:** Fraser Lake Museum and Visitor Infocentre in log building. **Radio:** CJCI 1450. Small community with all facilities. Created by Endako Mines Ltd. in 1964 on an older townsite; named after the explorer Simon Fraser. Endako Mines Ltd. began operating in 1965 and was Canada's largest molybdenum mine until production slowed in 1982. Mining resumed in 1986. Also located here is Fraser Lake Sawmills, the town's largest employer.

PG 96.9 (156 km) **PR 350.8** (563.3 km) **Junction** with main access road south to scenic Francois Lake; also accessible via roads from Burns Lake to Houston. Francois Lake Road (chip seal surfacing) leads south 7 miles/11 km to the east end of Francois Lake (where the Stellako River flows from the lake) and back to Highway 16 at Endako. (It does *not* link up to the Francois Lake Ferry, south of Burns Lake.) Golf course and several resorts with camping, cabins and boats are located on this scenic rural road along the lake through the Glenannan area. ▲

Francois Lake, good fishing for rainbow to 5 lbs., May to October; kokanee to ¾ lb.,

Pipers Glen RV RESORT
☆ Hookups, Some 30 Amps
☆ Sani-dump ☆ Some Pull-throughs
☆ Boat Rentals ☆ Good Fishing
☆ Hot Showers ☆ Cabins
☆ Tenters Welcome

(250) 690-7565
P.O. Box 35,
Fort Fraser, B.C. V0J 1N0

use flashers, willow leaf, flashers with worms, flatfish or spinners, August and September; char to 30 lbs., use large flatfish or spoon, June and July. **Stellako River** is considered one of British Columbia's better fly-fishing streams with rainbow over 2 lbs., all summer; whitefish averaging 1 lb., year-round.

PG 97.6 (157.1 km) **PR 350.1** (562.2 km) Bridge over Stellako River. Highway passes through the Stellako Indian Reserve. Slenyah Indian village to north.

PG 102.5 (164.9 km) **PR 345.2** (554.3 km) Endako Road; access to Francois Lake Road and private campgrounds in the Glenannan area.

PG 103 (165.8 km) **PR 344.7** (553.4 km) ENDAKO, a small highway community. A log home construction company is located here.

PG 103.8 (167.1 km) **PR 343.9** (552 km) CNR Bunkhouse.

Watch for moose next 10 miles/16 km westbound.

PG 105.5 (169.8 km) **PR 342.2** (549.3 km) Endako River bridge.

PG 109.1 (175.6 km) **PR 338.6** (543.5 km) Savory Rest Area is a large double-ended turnout with picnic tables and litter barrels to north beside Watskin Creek.

PG 112 (180.3 km) **PR 335.7** (538.8 km) Ross Creek.

PG 112.9 (181.7 km) **PR 334.8** (537.4 km) Tschinkut Creek and moose flats.

PG 120.4 (193.8 km) **PR 327.3** (525.2 km) Moose meadow to south.

PG 121 (194.7 km) **PR 326.6** (524.3 km) Large, double-ended paved turnout to south with litter barrel.

PG 125 (201.1 km) **PR 322.7** (517.8 km) Babine Forest Products sawmill to south.

PG 128.3 (206.4 km) **PR 319.4** (512.5 km) View of Burns Lake to south.

PG 130.1 (209.4 km) **PR 317.6** (509.5 km) Tintagel Creek.

PG 130.2 (209.6 km) **PR 317.5** (509.3 km) Rest area to south is a large double-ended turnout with toilet, tables, litter barrels and Tintagel Cairn point of interest.

PG 133.8 (215.4 km) **PR 313.8** (503.4 km) **Burns Lake K.O.A.**, a day's drive from Prince Rupert ferry. Cabins, tenting to full hookups, store, heated showers, laundromat, game room, playground. Lake swimming. Open May 1 to Sept. 30. Pay phone. Your host, Ed Brown, Box 491, Burns Lake, BC V0J 1E0. Phone (250) 692-3105, (800) 562-0905. [ADVERTISEMENT]

PG 137.5 (221.3 km) **PR 310.2** (497.5 km) Welcome to Burns Lake sign.

Junction with scenic Highway 35 (paved) south 18 miles/29 km past **Tchesinkut Lake** to **Francois Lake Ferry** landing. A free 36-car ferry departs from the south shore on the hour, from the north shore on the half-hour. From the south shore of Francois Lake, Highway 35 continues to **Takysie Lake** and **Ootsa Lake**, with access to a number of other fishing lakes. Another of the Yellowhead's popular fishing areas with a variety of family-owned camping and cabin resorts. Gas stations, stores and food service are also available.

Beaver Point Resort. Open May 15–Sept. 15. Located on Tchesinkut Lake, 10 miles south of Burns Lake on Highway 35. Good fishing. Lake sites within 50 feet of lakeshore. Full and partial hookups. Tenting. Picnic tables, fire rings, firewood, coin showers. Sani-dump. Cabins and cottages. Boat launch, docks. Boat rentals. Your hosts, Jake and Brenda Hiebert. Phone (250) 695-6519. Off-season (250) 698-7665. Email: beaverpoint@fourwinds.ca. [ADVERTISEMENT]

Burns Lake is in the heart of the Lakes District, known for "3000 miles of fishing."
(© Judy Parkin)

Burns Lake

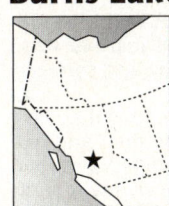

PG 139.9 (225.1 km) **PR 307.8** (496.3 km) **Junction** with road to Babine Lake. **Population:** 2,523; area 10,000. **Visitor Information:** At 540 W. Highway 16 in the **Burns Lake Heritage Centre**, the former Old Forestry Home, built in 1919. The Heritage Centre also houses the Lakes District Museum and an art gallery. Contact the Village of Burns Lake, Box 570, Burns Lake, BC V0J 1E0; phone (250) 692-7587; fax (250) 692-3059; email village@burnslake.org; www.burnslake.org.

Elevation: 2,300 feet/707m. **Radio:** CFLD 760, CJFW-FM 92.9 or 105.5, CBC-FM 99.1. **Transportation:** Greyhound Bus, VIA Rail.

The village of Burns Lake had its modest beginnings in 1911, as the site of railway construction. Forestry is the mainstay of the economy, along with ranching and tourism.

Burns Lake has 5 motels, a hotel, almost a dozen bed and breakfasts, 16 restaurants, 3 shopping centres and a golf course.

Camping is available at the municipal campground at Radley Beach, 2 blocks off Highway 16 on Highway 35; washrooms, playground, picnic tables and swimming area. Skateboard park and playground nearby. Private lakeside campgrounds are located east and south of town.

Burns Lake is situated in the heart of the Lakes District, which boasts "3000 miles of fishing." Species include kokanee, rainbow trout, char (lake trout) and salmon. Small family-owned campgrounds and fishing resorts, offering lodging, camping and boat rentals, are tucked along these lakes.

From Burns Lake, a side road leads north to Babine Lake, the longest natural lake in the province. One of British Columbia's most important salmon producing lakes, Babine Lake drains into the Skeena River. Excellent fishing for char and trout in summer. Tours of Pinkut Fish Hatchery available. Look for pictographs on cliffs across from hatchery. Pendleton Bay Provincial Park on Babine Lake, 28 miles/45 km from Burns Lake, offers camping, fishing, swimming and a boat launch; open May to October.

The Village of Burns Lake. See display ad this section.

Yellowhead Highway 16 Log
(continued)

PG 140.3 (225.3 km) **PR 307.4** (494.7 km) Turnout with map and information sign to south.

PG 143.9 (231.5 km) **PR 303.8** (489.9 km) Small community of DECKER LAKE.

Decker Lake, good char and trout fishing; fly-fishing in **Endako River**, which joins Decker and Burns lakes.

PG 149.3 (240.3 km) **PR 298.4** (481.2 km) Golf course.

PG 150.9 (242.8 km) **PR 296.8** (478.7 km) Palling Rest Area is a large double-ended turnout with picnic tables, toilets, litter barrels and a map.

PG 153.2 (246.5 km) **PR 294.5** (475 km) Baker Lake airstrip to south is used by fire-fighting tankers. Weather station. Emergency telephone.

PG 158 (254.2 km) **PR 289.7** (467.3 km) Rose Lake to south.

PG 161.7 (260.3 km) **PR 286** (461.2 km) **Broman Lake** (natives call it Duncan Lake), rainbow and char to 4 lbs., use white-winged flies, spring and summer. Duncan Lake Indian band. Duncan Lake Gas.

The fish fountain at Steelhead Park in Houston, BC. (© Blake Hanna, staff)

PG 164.7 (265.1 km) **PR 283** (456.4 km) Six Mile Summit (elev. 4,669 feet/1,423m) to west. China Nose Mountain, with steep west-facing cliff, is visible to the south.

PG 165 (265.5 km) **PR 282.7** (456 km) Turnout to north with brake check, toilet and litter barrel. Turnout to south with litter barrel.

PG 166.3 (267.7 km) **PR 281.4** (453.7 km) Turnout to south with litter barrel.

PG 171 (275.3 km) **PR 276.7** (446.1 km) Large turnout to north with information sign on Lakes District. Entering **TOPLEY** (pop. 300) westbound; grocery, post office, cafe, motel and gas station.

Access to Babine Lake Recreation Area via paved side road north to Topley Landing and Granisle on Babine Lake. From its junction with the highway at Topley, mileages on this side road are as follows: Mile 24.4/39.3 km, turnoff to village of Topley Landing; Mile 28.8/46.3 km, Fulton River spawning channel (sockeye run in August and September); Mile 28/45.1 km, Red Bluff Provincial Park with camping, picnicking, boat launch, swimming and fishing; Mile 30.6/49 km, Lions Beach Park with camping, picnicking, boat launch, swimming and fishing; Mile 31.4/50.5 km, **GRANISLE** (pop. 400); food, gas, lodging and marina. Road continues to Smithers Landing and connects with back road to Smithers. ▲

Babine Lake, rainbow 6 to 8 lbs.; lake trout to 40 lbs., use spoons, flashers and red-and-white spoons, May through November. When fishing early in the year, use a short troll.

PG 172.3 (277.3 km) **PR 275.4** (444 km) Large rest area with map of Babine Lake, toilets and litter barrels.

PG 176.9 (284.7 km) **PR 270.8** (437.8 km) Byman Creek.

PG 180.1 (289.9 km) **PR 267.6** (432.5 km) Turnout to north with litter barrels.

PG 185.6 (298.7 km) **PR 262.2** (422 km) Golf course to south.

PG 188.4 (303.2 km) **PR 259.3** (417.3 km) Golf course to south.

PG 188.8 (303.9 km) **PR 258.9** (418.4 km) **Shady Rest RV Park**. 1 km east of Houston. Level and easy access. Long pull-through sites. Up to 65 feet. Full hookups. 15- and 30-amp service. Free clean hot showers. Free sani-dump. Laundromat. Mini-golf. Public telephone. Internet access. Great bird watching. VISA/MasterCard. Ask about discounts. 1-800-343-3777 Canada only. Phone/fax (250) 845-2314. [ADVERTISEMENT] ▲

Houston

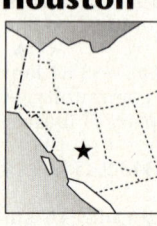

PG 190.1 (305.9 km) **PR 257.6** (416.4 km) Houston Infocentre. **Population:** 4,000. **Emergency Services: Police,** phone (250) 845-2204. **Ambulance,** phone (250) 845-2900. **Visitor Information:** Visitor Infocentre in log building on Highway 16 across from the mall and next to Steelhead Park (look for the fish fountain); open year-round. Write Houston Visitor Infocentre, Box 396, Houston, BC V0J 1Z0, or phone (250) 845-7640.

The World's Largest Fly Fishing Rod is on display at the Visitor Infocentre. The 60-foot-long anodized aluminum fly rod was designed by a local avid fly fisherman and built by local volunteers. (The 21-inch fly is a fluorescent "Skykomish Sunrise.")

Elevation: 1,926 feet/587m. **Climate:** Average temperature in summer, 71°F/21°C; in winter, 19°F/-7°C. **Radio:** CFBV 1450, CFPR-FM 102.1, CJFW-FM 105.5. **Newspaper:** *The Houston Today.* **Transportation:** Greyhound bus, VIA Rail.

Houston has all visitor facilities, including motels, campgrounds, restaurants, gas stations, a shopping centre and golf courses. ▲

Established in the early 1900s, Houston was a tie-cutting centre during construction of the Grand Trunk Pacific Railway in 1912. It was named for Prince Rupert newspaperman John Houston, the former mayor of Nelson, BC. Logging continued to support the local economy with the rapid growth of mills and planer mills in the 1940s and 1950s. Houston was incorporated as a village in 1957.

The main industry in Houston today is still forest products. There are 2 large sawmills here, Houston Forest Products and Canadian Forest Products Ltd. Inquire at the Visitor Infocentre about forestry-awareness tours.

Mining is also an industry here. The Equity Silver Mine operated from 1980 to 1994. The Huckleberry Copper Mine, southwest of Houston, went into production in 1997. This open pit mine has an estimated life of 16 to 25 years, extracting copper as well as molybdenum, silver and gold.

Hunting, canoeing, snowmobiling and sportfishing are major attractions here. Special events include Pleasant Valley Days in May and Canada Day celebrations in July.

District of Houston. See display ad this section.

Yellowhead Highway 16 Log
(continued)

PG 192.6 (310 km) **PR 255.1** (412.2 km) **Junction** with the Morice River access road which extends 52 miles/84 km south to Morice Lake. Approximately 20 miles/32 km along the Morice River Road you can turn east on a gravel road which leads past Owen

---

HOUSTON
Where the welcome is warm... and the wilderness beckons.

For More Information:
Houston & District Chamber of Commerce
P.O. Box 396, Houston, B.C.
V0J 1Z0
(250) 845-7640
Fax (250) 845-3682

District of Houston
P.O. Box 370, Houston, B.C.
V0J 1Z0
(250) 845-2238
Fax (250) 845-3429

Home of the World's Largest Fly Fishing Rod: 18 meters long and 383 kilograms

Fishing: Home of the World Famous Bulkley & Morice River systems for steelhead, spring & coho salmon. Numerous great producing lakes with trout & char.

Pleasant Valley Days - May: Rodeo activities and ball tournament.

Kid's Triathlon - June

Mill & Forestry Tours - Weekdays - July & August: Enjoy a free six-hour tour of Houston's Forest Area or take a free 1.5 hour tour of a modern high-tech lumber mill.

Bulkley Valley Cruisers - Drag Races - August: Drag racing at the Houston Airport

Discover Houston Trade Show - September: Business, Home, & Recreation Show

Morice Mountain Cross-Country Ski Trails: 35 km. of skiing - from gentle to alpine groomed & natural trails, two cabins, night skiing

Soft Adventure Tours: Wildlife viewing, rockhounding

Full Facilities for the Traveller: Motels & restaurants; RV parks; Excellent Camping; Two nine hole Golf Courses

---

Babine Lake is British Columbia's longest natural lake.

Lake and Nadina River Road to Francois Lake. From Francois Lake ferry landing Highway 35 leads north to Burns Lake.

The 2 famous salmon and steelhead streams, **Morice** and **Bulkley**, unite near Houston, and it is possible to fish scores of pools all along the Morice River. Fishing for resident rainbow, cutthroat and Dolly Varden; steelhead and salmon (chinook, coho) in season. *NOTE: Special requirements apply to fishing these streams; check with Fish and Game office.*

PG 193 (310.7 km) PR 254.7 (411.5 km) Bulkley River bridge and rest area; tables, litter barrel and toilets.

PG 196.7 (316.5 km) PR 251 (405.7 km) Barrett Station Airport. View of Barrett's Hat northbound.

PG 200.5 (322.6 km) PR 247.2 (399.6 km) **Hungry Hill Summit** (elev. 2,769 feet/844m). To the north are the snow-capped peaks of the Babine Mountains, to the west is the Hudson Bay Range.

PG 203.3 (327.2 km) PR 244.4 (394.9 km) Bulkley View Rest Area is a large paved parking area (easy access westbound) with picnic tables, toilets and litter barrels.

PG 208.1 (334.9 km) PR 239.6 (387 km) Deep Creek.

PG 210.4 (338.7 km) PR 237.6 (383.2 km) Quick Road East. Original telegraph cabin.

PG 211.4 (340.2 km) PR 236.3 (381.7 km) Garage.

PG 213.3 (343.3 km) PR 234.4 (378.6 km) Quick Road West.

PG 216.8 (348.9 km) PR 230.9 (373 km) Private campground.

PG 217.1 (349.4 km) PR 230.6 (372.5 km) Large double-ended rest area to south with toilets and litter barrels overlooking the Bulkley River.

PG 219.8 (353.7 km) PR 227.9 (368.1 km) **Ft. Telkwa R.V. Park.** See display ad this section.

PG 220.3 (354.5 km) PR 227.4 (367.3 km) **TELKWA** (pop. 1,250). A pleasant village at the confluence of the Telkwa and Bulkley rivers (you can fish from Riverside Street or the riverbanks). Visitor Infocentre at the village office and museum. Facilities include a grocery, post office, gas station with auto repair, and unique shops. Lodging at Douglas Motel, dining at Crocodile Cafe and area restaurants.

Fishing and hunting information, licenses and supplies available at the general store. Kinsmen Barbecue is held over Labour Day weekend; games, contests and demolition derby. Eddy Park, on the western edge of town beside the Bulkley River, is a good spot for picnicking (look for the wishing

well). St. Stephen's Anglican Church was built in 1911 and the bell and English gate added in 1921. Other Heritage buildings date back to 1908.

Crocodile Cafe. See display ad this section.

Early 20th century telegraph line cabin at Milepost PG 210.4 is a reminder of a bygone era. (© Judy Parkin)

Douglas Motel. Resort on Bulkley River rapids; all riverview units, family suites with balconies and fireplaces; 1 and 2 bedroom log cabins with fireplaces, queen beds, full kitchens with microwaves; patios, barbecues, complimentary coffee, cablevision, summer fans, sauna whirlpool complex, recreational games, picnic areas, fishing. Near lake, store, restaurants, fast food. VISA and MasterCard. Phone (250) 846-5679; fax (250) 846-5656; web: www.monday.com/douglasmotel. [ADVERTISEMENT]

PG 220.7 (355.3 km) PR 227 (366.5 km) Turnoff to north for **Tyhee Lake Provincial Park**; 55 campsites, 20 picnic tables, dump station, hiking trails, fishing, swimming, boat launch. Seaplane base at lake; charter fly-in fishing.

Also turnoff here on the Telkwa High Road, which intersects with Babine Lake access road (gravel), which leads 46 miles/74 km north to Smithers Landing on Babine Lake and 56 miles/90 km to Granisle.

Tyhee Lake, rainbow and lake trout to 2 lbs., June through August; Kamloops trout to 2 lbs. **Babine River**, steelhead to 40 lbs., late fall. **Telkwa River**, spring and coho salmon to 24 lbs., summer to fall.

PG 221.1 (355.9 km) PR 226.6 (365.9 km) Gas station with diesel.

PG 225.5 (362.9 km) PR 222.2 (358.8 km) Second turnoff westbound for Babine Lake.

PG 227.2 (365.7 km) PR 220.5 (356 km) **Riverside Golf & RV Park**. Pull-throughs, some full service, 15 and 30 amp. Tenting sites. Restrooms, free hot showers, sani-dump. Security, public phone w/ modem. River and fishing, nature trails. Discount for RVers on our 18-hole golf course and driving range. Open April 1–October 31. Walking distance to Smithers. (250) 847-3229. [ADVERTISEMENT]

PG 227.5 (366.1 km) PR 220.2 (355.7 km) Turnoff to north on gravel road for **Driftwood Canyon Provincial Park**; picnic area and toilets. Fossil beds in shale outcroppings along creekbank. *(Please do not remove fossils.)* This gravel side road continues north to Smithers Landing.

PG 227.7 (366.4 km) PR 220 (355.3 km) Bridge over Bulkley River.

"BEST ROUTE TO ALASKA"
JUST EAST OF TELKWA ON HWY. 16
FT. TELKWA R.V. PARK
"MODEM FRIENDLY"
DELUXE ADULT FACILITIES
RIVERFRONT SITES • GLACIER VIEW
FULL HOOKUPS • LAUNDRY
FREE PRIVATE DELUXE SHOWER ROOMS
CABLE TV • SAUNA
FREE RV HIGH-PRESSURE WASH

RESERVATIONS
(250) 846-5012
FAX 846-5016
GROUPS ARE WELCOME

CROCODILE CAFE
Daily Lunch & Dinner Specials
Open 7 Days a Week - 8AM to 9PM
15% OFF for Seniors • RV Parking Back of Cafe
LOCATED ON HWY 16 IN TELKWA, BC
EVERYTHING HOMEMADE
from Soups, Sauces, Mustards & Breads to Desserts

British Columbia became Canada's sixth province on July 20, 1871.

Smithers

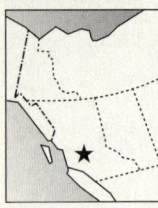

PG 229.2 (368.8 km) PR 218.5 (352.6 km). Smithers infocentre. **Population:** 6,000; area 30,000. **Emergency Services:** Police, phone (250)847-3233. **Hospital and Poison Centre**, 3950 8th Ave., phone (250) 847-2611. **Ambulance**, phone 1-562-7241.

Visitor Information: Visitor Infocentre and Chamber of Commerce are located adjacent to the Central Park Bldg., which houses the museum and art gallery; open year-round. Detailed maps of the area showing all hiking trails are available at the Infocentre. Contact P.O. Box 2379, Smithers, BC V0J 2N0; phone (800) 542-6673; www. TourismSmithers.com; email info@tourismsmithers.com.

Elevation: 1,621 feet/494m. **Climate:** Relatively warmer and drier than mountainous areas to the west; average temperature in July is 58°F/14°C, in January 14°F/-10°C; annual precipitation, 13 inches. **Radio:** CFBV 870, CJFW-FM 92.9 or 105.5, CBC-FM 97.5. **Television:** Channels 5, 13 and cable. **Newspaper:** *Interior News* (weekly).

Transportation: Air—Scheduled service via Air Canada, Hawk Air and Central Mountain Air. **Railroad**—VIA Rail. **Bus**—Greyhound. **Car Rentals**—Available.

Sitting amidst rugged mountains, the town is enhanced by alpine-themed storefronts that have been added to many of the buildings. Murals on buildings add character and make for a unique walk. Reconstructed in 1979, Main Street offers many shops and restaurants. Incorporated as a village in 1921, Smithers officially became a town in Canada's centennial year, 1967. The original site was chosen in 1913 by construction crews working on the Grand Trunk Pacific Railway (the town was named for one-time chairman of the railway A.W. Smithers). Today it is a distribution and supply centre for farms, mills and mines in the area.

Smithers is the largest town in the Bulkley Valley and the site of Hudson Bay Mountain, a popular ski area in winter (skiing from November to mid-April); hiking and climbing in summer.

SMITHERS ADVERTISERS

Aspen Motor Inn	Ph. (250) 847-4551
Canadian Tire	Ph. 1-866-847-3117
Capri Family Restaurant & Steakhouse	Ph. (250) 847-4412
Capri Motor Inn	Ph. (250) 847-4226
Hudson Bay Lodge	Ph. (250) 847-4581
Old School House B&B, The	Ph. (250) 846-5939
Riverside Park Municipal Campsite	Ph. (250) 847-1600
Smithers Visitor Info Centre	Ph. (250) 847-5072
Stork Nest Inn	Ph. (250) 847-3831

Statue of an alpenhorn player at Smithers reflects the alpine flavour of the town. (© Lyn Hancock)

Smithers has several motels, bed and breakfasts, gas stations, restaurants, laundromat/car wash and good shopping. Government liquor store located on Queen Street at Broadway Avenue. There are 2 18-hole golf courses, both with rentals and clubhouses.

There is a municipal campground with security, firewood, no hookups, pit-toilets, potable water and picnic area at Riverside Park on the Bulkley River; turn north at the museum across from Main Street and drive up the hill about a mile and watch for sign. There are private campgrounds located east and west of town; see highway log. ▲

Special events include the Bulkley Valley Fall Fair, held on the last weekend in August each year, one of the largest agricultural exhibitions in the province. The Midsummer Music Festival in June features local, regional and national artists.

Smithers offers a number of scenic drives. Hudson Bay Mountain (elev. 8,700 feet/ 2,652m) is a 14-mile/23-km drive from Highway 16; the plateau above timberline at the ski area is a good spot for summer hikes. In the winter months, Smithers boasts one of the largest ski hills in northern British Columbia. A 6,000-foot/1,829-m triple chair and 2 T-bars climb the 1,750-foot/533-m vertical, offering skiers 18 different runs.

Fossil enthusiasts should drive to Driftwood Canyon Provincial Park; turn off Highway 16 just east of the Bulkley River bridge (travelers are advised to stop first at the Visitor Infocentre in town for a map and directions). A display at the park illustrates the fossils, such as metasequoia, a type of redwood which occurs in the shale formation. BC Parks ask visitors to refrain from removing any fossils.

A beautiful spot not to be missed is Twin Falls and Glacier Gulch. Take the 4-mile/6.4-km-long gravel road (steep in places) from Highway 16 on the western edge of town.

An extensive list of lake and river fishing spots in the area, with information on boat launches and boat rentals, is available from the Smithers District Chamber of Commerce, Box 2379, Smithers, BC V0J 2N0; phone (250) 847-5092; or ask at the Visitor Infocentre.

Yellowhead Highway 16 Log
(continued)

PG 230.6 (371.1 km) PR 217.1 (350.1 km) Smithers golf club.

PG 231.7 (372.8 km) PR 216 (348.4 km) Paved access road to Lake Kathlyn. There is a municipal park with small beach and boat launch located here. Powerboats not permitted. Closed to waterfowl hunting. Side road continues 4 miles/6.4 km (gravel) to Twin Falls and Glacier Gulch.

PG 232.7 (374.5 km) PR 215 (346.7 km) Road to north leads to Smithers airport.

PG 234 (376.6 km) PR 213.7 (344.6 km) Lake Kathlyn Road to west; access to B&B Glacier View.

B&B Glacier View. Take Lake Kathlyn Road to 8335 Kroeker Road, just 5 minutes off Highway 16. Quiet, cozy, modern log home. Open year-round. All rooms offer a million dollar view of Kathlyn Glacier, Hudson Bay Mountain and Twin Falls. We specialize in organizing unique outdoor activities. Wir Sprechen Deutsch. Reservations: www.bbcanada.com/glacierview, or call (250) 847-6045. [ADVERTISEMENT]

PG 234.9 (378 km) PR 212.8 (343.6 km) **Glacier View RV Park.** Panoramic view of Hudson Bay Glacier. New shower house facilities. 15/30-amp electric and water hookup; serviced and dry pull-throughs; gravel and grass sites; free showers; laundromat, private handicap-accessible shower; dishwashing station, sani-station, coin vacuum, cement picnic tables, firepits, flower gardens, horseshoe pits, pay phone. (250) 847-3961. www.glacierviewrvpark.com. [ADVERTISEMENT] ▲

PG 235.4 (378.8 km) PR 212.3 (342.4 km) Hudson Bay rest area to west with picnic tables, toilets and litter barrels. Beautiful view of Hudson Bay Mountain.

PG 238.4 (383.6 km) PR 209.3 (337.6 km) Tobaggan Creek Fish Hatchery. Tours available upon arrival. Open 8 A.M. to 4 P.M. daily.

PG 243.1 (391.3 km) PR 204.6 (329.8 km) Trout Creek bridge. Groceries, post

CANADIAN TIRE • SMITHERS
• RV Repairs & Supplies • Fishing, Hunting & Camping Supplies
FREE Sani-dump • **FREE** Fresh Water • **FREE** Overnight RV Parking
Located on Hwy 16 ▼ Toll Free 1-866-847-3117 ▼ Email: cantire631@telus.net

Tourism Smithers
A town for all seasons...

Call Toll Free 1-800-542-6673 • www.TourismSmithers.com • infomp@TourismSmithers.com

YELLOWHEAD HIGHWAY • Smithers

Hudson Bay Lodge
SMITHERS, BC

Discover the Difference

3251E Highway 16, Smithers
- Affordable Luxury • Air-conditioned rooms
- Remote control TV • Pet friendly

The Alpine Cafe • Fireside Pub
Pepper Jack's Grill

Canada Select ★★★

Reservations Call Toll Free **1-800-663-5040** • 250-847-4581
Fax: 250-847-4878 • Email: reservations@hblodge.com • www.hblodge.com

Riverside Park
MUNICIPAL CAMPSITE
"Overlooking the Bulkley River"

Pull-thrus • Electric & water hookups • Fire pits
Dry toilets • Free firewood • Pay phone
Pets on leash • River fishing

OPEN MAY – OCTOBER
Access from Hwy 16
Follow Main St. North
to 19th Ave.

CONTACT
1-250-847-1600

CAPRI — A Cut Above the Rest!
FAMILY RESTAURANT & STEAKHOUSE

Centrally Located • Fully Licensed • Air Conditioned
Steak, Schnitzels, Pasta & MORE!
Open from 6:00am to 10:00pm

Hwy 16 Smithers **(250) 847-4412**

Capri MOTOR INN
- 62 Modern, Air Conditioned Rooms
- Movie & Sports Channels

Within walking distance of downtown businesses and shopping

(250) 847-4226 • Fax (250) 847-3731

TOLL FREE IN BC 1-800-663-3120

P.O. Box 3418, Smithers BC V0J 2N0
Email: caprismithers@bulkley.net • www.hiway16.com/capri

Stork Nest Inn
Free Full Menu Breakfast
1485 Main St. (1 block off Hwy 16)
Next to Museum & Tourism Info Centre

Call 1-250-847-3831
Fax 1-250-847-3852 • www.storknestinn.com

The Old School House B&B

"Self Contained, Self Catering"
Heritage Home Overlooking
the Bulkley River
1617 Riverside, Telkwa, BC
1-250-846-5939

www.highway16.com/schoolhouse/

ASPEN Motor Inn & Family Restaurant

60 FULL FACILITY ROOMS
- Indoor swimming pool • Hot tub
- Non-smoking rooms available

We're please to offer smoke-free dining in the restaurant!

– RESERVATIONS –
250-847-4551

BC & ALTA TOLL FREE **1-800-663-7676**
Fax: 1-250-847-4492
Email: ed@bulkley.net

4268 Highway 16 West
Smithers, BC V0J 2N0
Web: hiway16.com/aspen

Moricetown Canyon, for centuries a First Nation's fishing spot on the Bulkley River. (© Blake Hanna, staff)

office and phone; fishing licenses available.

Trout Creek General Store. Quaint, beautiful setting. Known for its renowned steelhead and coho salmon fishing. Some RV sites, electric hookup only. Boat launch, camping, picnicking. Store offers necessities and unique products. Liquor agency. Fishing licenses, tackle, fireworks. Karen's collectables, local crafts and much more. Takeout foods. (250) 847-3440. [ADVERTISEMENT] ▲

PG 244.3 (393.3 km) PR 203.4 (327.3 km) **Elaine's**. Exotic home decor and unique treasures. Elaine's is a showcase of wonderful discoveries. Eclectic one-of-a-kind decorative ware. Beautiful selection of linens, candles, basketware, fine antiques, silver jewelry, area rugs, tapestries, bed and bath and much more. Easy RV access with large turnaround. Showroom open daily. Summer hours 9 A.M. to 7 P.M. (250) 847-9940. See display ad this section. [ADVERTISEMENT]

The Maple Leaf Cabins unique cozy cedar log cabins located on the banks of the Bulkley River. World class salmon and steelhead fishing. Cabin is fully contained. Complete with fridge, stove, three-piece bathroom, two queen-sized beds and wood heater. Quiet location one minute off Highway 16. Contact Randy or Elaine at Elaine's, (250) 847-9940; email mapleleaf@mail.bulkley.net. [ADVERTISEMENT]

PG 248.5 (400 km) PR 199.2 (320.6 km) Pullout with historic sign on Moricetown Canyon; litter barrels.

PG 248.7 (400.3 km) PR 199 (320.7 km) Turnout to north with picnic tables and view of Bulkley River and Moricetown Canyon; good photo stop.

PG 248.9 (400.6 km) PR 198.8 (320.4 km) Telkwa High Road is a short side road on the north side of the highway leading to **Moricetown Canyon and Falls** on the Bulkley River and Moricetown Campground and RV Park, for centuries a famous First Nation's fishing spot. Aboriginal people may still be seen here netting salmon in July and August. A worthwhile stop. ▲

Moricetown Campground and RV Park. See display ad this section. ▲

PG 249.2 (401.1 km) PR 198.5 (319.9 km) **MORICETOWN** (pop. 680; elev. 1,341 feet/409m). **Radio:** CBC-FM 96.5. Moricetown has a gas station with minor repair service and diesel fuel. There is a handicraft store. A campground is located in Moricetown Canyon (turnoff at Milepost PG 255.7). Moricetown is a First Nations reserve and village, the oldest settlement in the Bulkley Valley. Traditionally, the Native people (Wet'su-wet'en) took advantage of the narrow canyon to trap salmon. The centuries-old settlement ('Kyah Wiget) is now named after Father A.G. Morice, a Roman Catholic missionary. Born in France, Father Morice came to British Columbia in 1880 and worked with the aboriginals of northern British Columbia from 1885 to 1904. He achieved world recognition for his writings in anthropology, ethnology and history.

PG 253.8 (408.5 km) PR 193.9 (312.4 km) Chicken Creek.

PG 255.9 (411.9 km) PR 191.8 (306.6 km) East Boulder Creek.

PG 258.1 (415.3 km) PR 189.6 (305.6 km) Large paved turnout to north.

PG 258.9 (416.6 km) PR 188.8 (304.3 km) Paved turnout with litter barrel.

PG 260.7 (419.5 km) PR 187 (301.4 km) Viewpoint with picnic tables and litter barrels.

PG 260.9 (419.9 km) PR 186.8 (300.9 km) View of Bulkley River.

PG 261.5 (420.9 km) PR 186.2 (299.9 km) Long paved turnout.

PG 269.1 (433.1 km) PR 178.6 (287.6 km) Turnoff to north for **Ross Lake Provincial Park**; 25 picnic sites, boat launch (no powerboats), swimming. Fishing for rainbow to 4 lbs. 🐟

PG 270.5 (435.3 km) PR 177.2 (285.4 km) Turnout with historic information sign.

Entering New Hazelton, the first of 3 communities westbound sharing the name Hazelton (the others are Hazelton and South Hazelton), known collectively as The Hazeltons; description follows.

New Hazelton

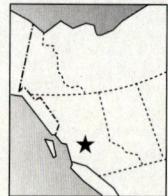

PG 271.1 (436.3 km) PR 176.6 (284.4 km) **Junction** of Highway 16 with Highway 62 to Hazelton, 'Ksan and Kispiox (descriptions follow). The turnoff for Highway 62 is located just west of the railway overpass in New Hazelton. The turn is on the north side (right for westbound travelers) of Highway 16 between the overpass and the Visitor Infocentre at the base of the hill. **Population:** area 6,500. **Emergency Services: Police**, phone (250) 842-5244.

Visitor Information: Visitor Infocentre in 2-story log building at the junction;

Grimacing totem at Hazelton, known as "totem pole capital of the world."
(© Earl L. Brown, staff)

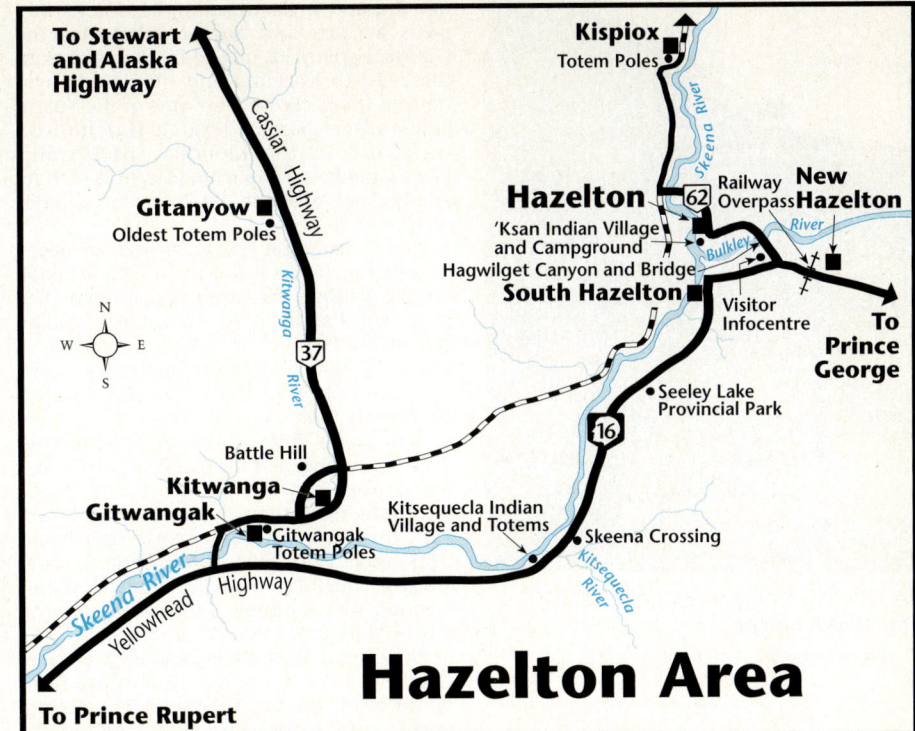

Hazelton Area

museum, local artisan display, restrooms, free sani-dump, potable water, picnic tables. Look for the 3 statues representing the gold rush packer Cataline, the Northwest miner, and the Upper Skeena logger.

Elevation: 1,150 feet/351m. **Radio:** CBC 1170. **Transportation:** VIA Rail. Greyhound bus and regional transit system.

This small highway community has gas stations, major auto repair, restaurants, cafes, post office, general store, a hotel and a motel. Laundromat, propane, sporting goods, and hunting and fishing licenses available in town. ATMs located at the Chevron station in New Hazelton and at Bulkley Valley Credit Union in the mall on Highway 16.

Attractions here include historic Hazelton, the Indian village of 'Ksan and sportfishing the Bulkley and Kispiox rivers (descriptions follow). Mount Rocher Deboule, elev. 8,000 feet/2,438m, towers behind the town.

Northern ATVentures. Experience a trip of a lifetime on one of our quiet 4-wheel-drive, fully automatic ATVs. Let our experienced guide take you on a breathtaking mountain alpine excursion to the treeline at

HAZELTON AREA ADVERTISERS
Hazeltons Travel Info Centre ....Hwy. 16
'Ksan Campground..........Ph. (250) 842-5297
'Ksan Historic Village & Museum ....Ph. (877) 842-5518
Northern ATVentures......Ph. (250) 842-6816
Robbers Roost Motel.......Ph. (877) 305-2233
Skeena Eco-Expeditions...Ph. (250) 842-7057
Steelhead Rest B&B ....Ph. (250) 842-0402
Suu Dee's Wild & Free Studio ....Ph. (250) 842-6855
28 Inn ....Ph. (250) 842-6006

The Hazeltons
Historic Heartland of Northern British Columbia

☐ Totem Pole Capital of the World
☐ Trophy Salmon & Steelhead
☐ 'Ksan Historic Indian Village & Museum
☐ Historic "Old Town" Hazelton
☐ Full Visitor Services

For a free brochure write:
Hazeltons Travel Info Centre
Box 340Z, New Hazelton
BC, Canada V0J 2J0

Distinctive fenceposts at Hazelton's municipal offices.
(© Blake Hanna, staff)

4,800 feet, or choose one of our riverside tours. Suitable for all ages. Fantastic photo opportunities, wildlife viewing, mountain vistas and more. We supply everything from safety equipment to delicious deli lunches. Contact Doug or Kristin Spooner at (250) 842-6816; email northernatventures@hotmail.com; wwwgeocities.com/atv_tours/. [ADVERTISEMENT]

The **Hagwilget Canyon** of the Bulkley River is one of the most photographed places in Canada. A 1-lane bridge spans the canyon on the road to Hazelton.

HAZELTON. Situated at the confluence of the Skeena and Bulkley rivers, Hazelton grew up at "The Forks" as a transshipping point at the head of navigation on the Skeena and a wintering place for miners and prospectors from the rigorous Interior. Thomas Hankin established a Hudson's Bay Co. trading post here in 1868. The name Hazelton comes from the numerous hazelnut bushes growing on the flats.

Cataline, famous pioneer packer and traveler, is buried near here in an unmarked grave at Pioneer Cemetery. Jean Caux (his real name) was a Basque who, from 1852 to 1912, with loaded mules, supplied mining and construction camps from Yale and Ashcroft northward through Hazelton, where he often wintered.

For some years, before the arrival of the railroad and highways, supplies for trading posts at Bear and Babine lakes and the Omineca goldfields moved by riverboat from the coast to Hazelton and from there over trails to the backcountry. Some of the Yukon gold rushers passed through Hazelton on their way to the Klondike, pack trains having made the trip from Hazelton to Telegraph Creek over the old Telegraph Trail as early as 1874.

"Old" Hazelton has been reconstructed to look much like it did in the 1890s. Look for the antique machinery downtown. The history of the Hazelton area can be traced by car on the Hand of History tour. Pick up a brochure from the Visitor Infocentre showing the location of the 19 historic sites on the driving tour.

Suu Dee's Wild and Free Studio. Specializing in First Nation (Gitxsan) art. Original artwork and carvings. Button blankets, wall hangings, vests, moose tufting, birchbark biting, bentwood boxes. Fine beadwork, moccasins, pine needle baskets, silver jewelry. Custom cards, homemade soaps, wooden toys. Summer hours 9 A.M.–6 P.M. Phone (250) 842-6855. [ADVERTISEMENT]

Steelhead Rest B&B. Secluded 86-acre riverfront retreat, located 10 minutes norh of Hazelton on the Skeena River. Hiking, rafting and world-class river angling for steelhead and salmon right out the front door. One could fish the Bulkley, Kispiox and Skeena in a single day. Enjoy our rock fireplace or view the rapids in armchair comfort through cathedral windows. We've seen bears, eagles and deer from the couch. Amenities include riverfront cedar hot tub and deck with BBQ. www.steelheadrest.com. Phone (250) 842-0402. [ADVERTISEMENT]

'KSAN HISTORICAL VILLAGE and Museum, a replica Gitksan Indian village, is 4.5 miles/7.2 km from Highway 16. It is a reconstruction of the traditional Gitksan Village, which has stood at this site for centuries. It is located at the confluence of the Bulkley and Skeena rivers by the 'Ksan Assoc. There are 7 communal houses, totem poles and dugout canoes. At the carving shed, carvers produce First Nation's arts and crafts which can be purchased. Food service is available on site.

For a nominal charge from May to September, you can join a guided tour of the communal houses. Performances of traditional song and dance are presented every Friday evening during July and August in the Wolf House. Admission to grounds is $2, children under 6 are free. Guided tours of the grounds run $10 for adults, $8.50 for students and seniors. The site is open year-round, hours vary. Open daily April 15–Oct. 15. Tours are available mid-April to late September. Phone (250) 842-5544.

A well-maintained full-service trailer park and campground on the banks of the Skeena and Bulkley rivers is operated by the Gitanmaax Band.

KISPIOX (pop. 825) Indian village and 3 fishing resorts are 20 miles/32 km north on a good paved road at the confluence of the Skeena and Kispiox rivers. Kispiox is noted for its stand of totems close to the river. There is a market garden (fresh vegetables) located approximately 7 miles/11 km north on the Kispiox Road (about 2 miles/ 3.2 km before the Kispiox totem poles). Camping, cabins and fishing at lodges and campgrounds in the valley. Valley residents host the Kispiox Rodeo, which has run annually since 1952, the first weekend of June. An annual music festival is held the last weekend in July

Skeena Eco-Expeditions. Cultural and outdoor adventures. We offer a variety of exciting outdoor opportunities. Totem pole interpretive tours, river drifting, river rafting, fishing, canoe rentals, guided hiking trips with an experienced Native guide, area bus tours. Cultural information centre. Supervised campground. Tenting and dry sites. Quiet and scenic. Firewood, water, shower and outhouses. Contact us for cross-country skiing, snowshoeing and winter hiking. Book your trip at the Cultural Information Centre, Monday to Friday from 8 A.M. to 4 P.M., or call us at (250) 842-7057 or toll free at 1-877-842-5911. Visit our web site at www.kispioxadventures.com. [ADVERTISEMENT]

Bulkley River, Dolly Varden to 5 lbs.; spring salmon, mid-July to mid-August; coho salmon 4 to 12 lbs., Aug. 15 through September, flies, spoons and spinners; steelhead to 20 lbs., July through November, flies, Kitamats, weighted spoons and soft bobbers. **Kispiox River** is famous for its trophy-sized steelhead. Check on regulations and obtain a fishing license before your arrival. Fishing is done with single-hook only, with catch-release for steelhead between Aug. 15 and Sept. 30. Season is July 1 to Nov. 30 for salmon, trout and steelhead. Excellent fly-fishing waters: spring salmon, July to early August; coho salmon, late August to early September; steelhead from September until freezeup. Sizable Dolly Vardens and cutthroat. Steelhead average 20 lbs., with some catches over 30 lbs.

Yellowhead Highway 16 Log
(continued)

PG 271.2 (436.4 km) PR 174.5 (280.8 km) Turnoff to north for Cataline Motel and RV Park and Garage Pub & Grill restaurant and. Side road continues through residential area of **SOUTH HAZELTON** and loops back to the highway.

The Garage Pub & Grill. Two blocks off Highway 16 on South Hazelton Loop. Easy RV parking. Uniquely renovated pre-1950 Shell garage decorated with period memora-

bilia, antiques and curios. Comfortable, friendly atmosphere. Extensive menu of high-quality pub-sized portions. Daily specials. Super clean. No minors. Open 7 days a week at 11 A.M. (250) 842-5488. www.bulkley.net/~garagepub. [ADVERTISEMENT]

Cataline Motel and RV Park. Near easterly turnoff. Low rates year-round. Northern hospitality/information. Kitchen and sleeping rooms with cable TV, phones, full bath. Some pull-throughs; 15-, 20- and 30-amp full service grassed sites; seasonal tenting, toilets, pay showers, barbecue. Public phone, laundromat, beverages, snacks, book exchange, personal amenities. Reservations, phone (250) 842-5271. [ADVERTISEMENT] ▲

PG 275 (442.6 km) PR 172.7 (277.9 km) Seeley Lake Provincial Park; 20 campsites, drinking water, pit toilets, firewood, sanidump, day-use area with picnic tables, swimming, fishing.

PG 282.4 (454.5 km) PR 165.3 (266.1 km) Carnaby Sawmill; beehive burner.

PG 286.6 (461.2 km) PR 161.1 (259.3 km) KITSEGUECLA, First Nation's village. Totem poles throughout village are classic examples, still in original locations. Historical plaque about Skeena Crossing.

PG 287.4 (462.5 km) PR 160.3 (258 km) Skeena Crossing. Historic Canadian National Railways bridge (see plaque at Kitseguecla).

PG 287.7 (463 km) PR 160 (257.6 km) Sheep's Rapids.

PG 292.5 (470.7 km) PR 155.2 (250 km) Road winds along edge of river.

CAUTION: Watch for falling rock next 32 miles/51.5 km.

PG 295.4 (475.4 km) PR 152.3 (245.1 km) Gravel turnout with litter barrel.

PG 297.7 (479.1 km) PR 150 (241.4 km) Gas station and cafe at Cassiar Highway turnoff. GITWANGAK, 0.2 mile/0.4 km north, has many fine old totems and St. Paul's church and bell tower.

Junction with Cassiar Highway (BC Highway 37). Bridge across Skeena River to Kitwanga and Cassiar Highway to Stewart, Hyder, AK, and Alaska Highway. See CASSIAR HIGHWAY section on page 238.

Westbound, the Yellowhead Highway passes Seven Sisters peaks; the highest is 9,140 feet/2,786m.

PG 299 (481.2 km) PR 148.7 (239.4 km) **Gitksan Paintbrush Native Arts & Crafts.** Silver and gold jewelry: rings, earrings, bracelets. BC jade. Limited edition prints and originals. Smoked moosehide moccasins, beaded leatherwork. Wood carvings, cedar baskets. Clothing and souvenirs. Quality merchandise, most from local artists. Excellent prices. Easy access. Summer hours 9 A.M.–7 P.M. P.O. Box 97, Kitwanga, BC V0J 2A0. Phone or fax (250) 849-5085; gitksanpaintbrush.bc.ca. [ADVERTISEMENT]

PG 302 (486 km) PR 145.7 (234.6 km) Paved double-ended turnout to south with litter barrel. Good view of Seven Sisters Mountains on a clear day.

PG 303.4 (488.2 km) PR 144.3 (232.4 km) Boulder Creek Rest Area is a double-ended turnout with parking for large vehicle,; toilets, litter barrels and picnic tables.

PG 306.6 (493.6 km) PR 141.1 (227.3 km) Whiskey Creek.

PG 307.6 (495 km) PR 140.1 (225.8 km) Paved turnout to north with litter barrel.

PG 308 (495.6 km) PR 139.7 (225.2 km) Gull Creek.

Innovative decor at the Garage Pub & Grill on South Hazelton Loop. (© Blake Hanna, staff)

PG 309.2 (497.6 km) PR 138.5 (223.2 km) Hand of History sign about "Holy City." Watch for bears fishing the river for salmon in late July and early August.

PG 312.5 (502.9 km) PR 135.2 (218 km) Paved turnout to north.

PG 313.6 (504.6 km) PR 134.1 (216.4 km) Watch for fallen rock on this stretch of highway.

PG 315.3 (507.4 km) PR 132.4 (213.6 km) Flint Creek.

PG 318.5 (512.6 km) PR 129.2 (208.5 km) Large turnout along river with historical plaque about Skeena River Boats: "From 1889, stern-wheelers and smaller craft fought their way through the Coast Mountains, churning past such awesome places as 'The Devil's Elbow' and 'The Hornet's Nest.' Men and supplies were freighted upstream, furs and gold downstream. A quarter century of colour and excitement began to fade in 1912, as the Grand Trunk Pacific neared completion."

PG 322.4 (518.8 km) PR 125.2 (202.4 km) Paved turnout to north with litter barrel.

PG 332 (534.3 km) PR 115.7 (187.3 km) Legate Creek.

PG 335.7 (540.2 km) PR 112 (181.5 km) Large rest area on river with easy access; water pump, picnic tables, toilets and litter barrels.

PG 336 (540.7 km) PR 111.7 (181 km) Skeena Cellulose bridge (private) crosses Skeena River to access tree farms on north side.

PG 336.9 (542.1 km) PR 110.8 (179.6 km) St. Croix Creek.

PG 340.3 (547.7 km) PR 107.4 (173.9 km) Chindemash Creek.

PG 342.8 (551.6 km) PR 104.9 (170 km) Tiny chapel to south serves small community of USK. The nondenominational chapel is a replica of the pioneer church that stood in Usk until 1936, when the Skeena River flooded, sweeping away the village and the church. The only item from the church to survive was the Bible, which was found floating atop a small pine table.

PG 345 (555.2 km) PR 102.7 (166.4 km) Entrance to Kitselas Canyon (1 mile/1.6 km).

PG 345.2 (555.6 km) PR 102.4 (166 km) Side road leads 0.5 mile/0.8 km south to Kleanza Creek Provincial Park; 21 campsites, 25 picnic sites, fishing, drinking water, toilets, firewood, wheelchair access. Short trail to remains from Cassiar Hydraulic Mining Co. gold-sluicing operations here (1911–14).

PG 345.4 (555.9 km) PR 102.3 (165.7 km) Kleanza Bridge.

PG 346.9 (558.3 km) PR 100.8 (163.3 km) Gravel turnout to north.

PG 349.7 (562.8 km) PR 98 (158.7 km) Fishing lodge.

PG 350.5 (564.1 km) PR 97.2 (157.4 km) **Copper (Zymoetz) River**, can be fished from Highway 16 or follow local maps. Coho salmon to 10 lbs., use tee-spinners in July; steelhead to 20 lbs., check locally for season and restrictions.

PG 352 (566.5 km) PR 95.7 (155 km) Double-ended turnout to north with tourist information sign and area map.

PG 352.2 (566.8 km) PR 95.5 (154.7 km) Motel.

PG 352.9 (568 km) PR 94.8 (153.5 km) Motel.

PG 354.3 (570.2 km) PR 93.4 (151.3 km) Old Lakelse Lake Road; access to Terrace golf course.

PG 354.7 (570.8 km) PR 93 (150.7 km) **Junction** with Highway 37 South. Turn north for downtown Terrace. Turn south for Lakelse Lake Provincial Park (8.7 miles/14 km) and KITIMAT (pop. 11,500), 37 miles/60 km south via Highway 37. Kitimat is a major port and home to several industries.

PG 354.9 (571.1 km) PR 92.8 (150.4 km) First bridge westbound over **Skeena River**. "Skeena" means "River of the mist" in First Nation's language.

PG 355.2 (571.7 km) PR 92.5 (149.8 km) Ferry Island municipal campground; 68 sites, some electrical hookups. Covered picnic shelters, barbecues, walking trails and a fishing bar are also available.

PG 355.3 (571.8 km) PR 92.4 (149.7 km) Second westbound Skeena River Bridge.

PG 355.7 (572.4 km) PR 92 (149.1 km) Terrace Chamber of Commerce Visitor Infocentre to south.

PG 356.6 (573.8 km) PR 91.1 (147.7 km) Stoplight; west access to Terrace. Turn north at intersection for downtown. Continue through intersection on High-

YELLOWHEAD HIGHWAY • Terrace

RED FISH. WHITE BEARS.
TERRACE. THINGS ARE A LITTLE *DIFFERENT* UP HERE.

The Coast Inn of the West

The Coast Inn of the West is Terrace's finest, with a location that is second to none. All our recently renovated guest rooms are deluxe and air-conditioned. We offer business traveller services and more facilities than any other hotel in town.

4620 Lakelse Ave., Terrace, BC V8G 1R1
(250) 638-8141
Toll Free within BC 1-800-549-3939
Central Reservations 1-800-663-1144

DON DIEGO'S RESTAURANT
Mon-Sat. 11:30 AM - 9:00 PM
Reservation recommended
Phone: 250-635-2307
3212 Kalum Street, Terrace
Homemade fresh food
Menu changes twice daily

Bear Country INN
FAMILY RESTAURANT
Licensed. Open 7 days a week.
• Jacuzzi suites • Non-smoking rooms • Fridges
• Air-conditioning • In-room coffee
• Relaxed family atmosphere

For reservations call
1-888-226-6222
4702 Lakelse Ave., Terrace, B.C.
(250) 635-6302
www.innbc.com

NORTHERN MOTOR INN
Where Terrace comes for country hospitality
3086 Yellowhead Highway 16 Terrace, B.C.
Toll Free Reservations:
1-800-663-3390

Full Service Liquor Store w/Cold Beer & Wine
George's Pub • 3 Great Places to Eat
Live Country Entertainment
A/C • Quality Mattresses
Reasonable rates • Giant Parking Lot

(250) 635-6375
www.innbc.com

CANADIAN TIRE Terrace
Your "one stop shop" for fishing, hunting, camping or R.V. needs and repair.

(There's more to Canadian Tire than just tires)
5100 Highway 16 West, Terrace, BC, Canada V8G 5S5
Store (250) 635-7178 Mail Order 1-888-317-8473

Authentic Indian Arts & Crafts
Three miles west of Terrace on Highway 16. See the 40' totem poles erected next to the building in 1987.
▼ Jewellery ▼ Prints ▼ Books ▼ Carvings
▼ Moccasins
House of Sim-oi-ghets
P.O. Box 544, Terrace, B.C. V8G 4B5
Office (250) 638-1629 www.kitsumkalum.bc.ca

Join us to CELEBRATE TERRACE 1928-2003
1-800-499-1637
www.terracetourism.bc.ca

---

way 16 westbound for Prince Rupert, eastbound for Prince George.

Terrace

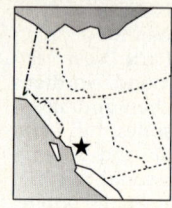

Located on the Skeena River. City centre is located north of Highway 16: Exit at **PG 356.6** or at Highway 37 junction (**PG 354.7**). **Population:** 13,000; area 21,500. **Emergency Services:** Police, fire and ambulance located at intersection of Eby Street and Highway 16. **Police,** phone (250) 635-4911. **Fire Department,** phone (250) 638-8121. **Ambulance,** phone (250) 638-1102. **Hospital,** phone (250) 635-2211.

Visitor Information: Visitor Infocentre located in the chamber of commerce log building at **Milepost PG 355.7** Open daily in summer, 9 A.M. to 6 P.M.; weekdays in winter, 8:30 A.M. to 4:30 P.M. Write 4511 Keith Ave, Terrace, BC V8G 1K1; phone (250) 635-2063; 1-800-499-1637; www.terracetourism.bc.ca.

Elevation: 220 feet/67m. **Climate:** Average summer temperature is 69°F/21°C; average annual rainfall 44 inches/112 cm, snowfall 129 inches/327 cm. **Radio:** CFTK 590; CFPR-FM 95.3, CFNR 92.1. **Television:** local television CFTK-TV and cable (50 channels). **Newspaper:** *Terrace Standard* (weekly).

Transportation: Air—Air Canada and Hawk Air from Terrace-Kitimat airport on Highway 37 South. **Railroad**—VIA Rail, 4531 Railway Ave. **Bus**—Farwest Bus Lines, Greyhound and Seaport Limousine with connection between Terrace and Stewart/Hyder. **Car and Motorhome Rentals**—Available.

Terrace was once a port of call for Skeena River stern-wheelers. The first farmer in the area, George Little, gave land to the community that became a port of call and post office in 1905. Originally it was known as Little Town, and later was named Terrace because of the natural terraces cut by the river. The village site was laid out in 1910 and the Grand Trunk Pacific Railway reached Terrace in 1914. The municipality was incorporated in 1927.

There are 17 motels/hotels, 35 restaurants and 2 shopping centres. The government liquor store is at 3250 Eby St. There are 3 cold beer and wine outlets and 5 laundromats. The community has a library and art gallery, indoor swimming pool, tennis courts, a golf course, bingo parlor, bowling alley, theatre and billiards.

Terrace has private campgrounds (see advertisements this section) and a public campground located at Ferry Island (see **Milepost PG 355.2**). Lakelse Lake Provincial Park at Furlong Bay, 11.4 miles/18.3 km south of Highway 16 on Highway 37, offers

TERRACE ADVERTISERS

Bear Country Inn	Ph. (250) 635-6302
Canadian Tire	Ph. (250) 635-7178
Coast Inn of the West, The	Ph. (250) 638-8141
Don Diego's Restaurant	Ph. (250) 635-2307
House of Sim-oi-Ghets	Ph. (250) 638-1629
Northern Motor Inn	Ph. 1-800-663-3390
Terrace Tourism	Ph. 1-800-499-1637
Wild Duck Motel & RV Park	Ph. (250) 638-1511

Log buildings at Heritage Park represent Terrace's pioneer tradition. (© Blake Hanna, staff)

campsites and day-use facilities, restrooms, changing rooms, showers, boat launch, sandy beaches, swimming, nature trails and interpretive forestry programs. Kleanza Creek Provincial Park Campground is located on Highway 16 West. ▲

Wild Duck Motel & RV Park. 5504 Hwy. 16 West, Terrace, BC (3 km west of town). RV Park: Treed, level sites, 30-amp electric, cable, water/sewer, laundromat, showers, picnic tables, tenting, fish cleaning/freezing facilities. Motel: Sparkling clean rooms, coffee, DD phones, cable, kitchen/sleeping units. Open all year. Toll-free 1-866-638-1511; phone/fax (250) 638-1511; wildduckmotelrvp@hotmail.com or www.mapchannel.com/wildduck. [ADVERTISEMENT] ▲

Major attractions in Terrace include **Heritage Park**, a collection of original log buildings from this region. Chosen to represent both the different aspects of pioneer life as well as various log building techniques, the structures include a trapper's cabin, miner's cabin and lineman's cabin. The 9 structures also house artifacts from the period. Guided tours available in summer, admission charged.

Recreation includes hiking, biking, rock-climbing, canoeing, kayaking and snowmobiling. Hiking trails in the Terrace area range from easy to moderate. Terrace Mountain Nature Trail is a 3.2-mile/5.1-km uphill hike which offers good views of the area; it begins at Halliwell and Anderson streets. Ferry Island hiking trail and municipal campground features approximately 70 face carvings in the cottonwood trees. The Grand Trunk Pathway offers beautiful trees and paved walking trails; it is located along Highway 16. The Howe Creek Trail System, off Sparks Street, offers scenic hiking with many bridges. Check with the Visitor Infocentre for details on other area trails.

Special events in Terrace include the Skeena Valley Fall Fair, Labour Day weekend; River Boat Days, B.C. Day weekend; and the Terrace Trade Show in late April.

Nisga'a Lava Memorial Park lava beds are 42 miles/67 km north of Terrace via the Nisga'a Highway (see description at **Milepost PG 357.5**). Limited picnic spots; limited camping; interesting hikes. Canada's youngest volcano last erupted approximately 250 years ago, burying 2 Indian villages.

Terrace is ideally situated for sportfishing, with easy access to the **Skeena**, **Copper**, **Kalum**, **Kitimat** and **Lakelse rivers**. Cutthroat, Dolly Varden and rainbow are found in all lakes and streams; salmon (king and coho) from May to late autumn. Kings average 40 to 70 lbs.; coho 14 to 20 lbs. Check locally for season and restrictions on steelhead. Information and fishing licenses are available from B.C. Government Access Centre, 3220 Eby St., Terrace (phone 250/638-6515), and at most sporting goods stores.

Yellowhead Highway 16 Log
(continued)

PG 356.6 (573.8 km) **PR 91.1** (147.7 km) Stoplight; west access to Terrace. Turn north at intersection for downtown. Continue through intersection eastbound for Prince George, westbound for Prince Rupert.

PG 357.5 (575.4 km) **PR 90.2** (146.1 km) Junction with Nisga'a Highway (Kalum Lake Road). The **Nisga'a Highway/Nass Forest Service Road** travels north to New Aiyansh and then east to join the Cassiar Highway. Total driving distance is 99 miles/159 km and the first 39 miles/63 km are paved; the remainder is gravel. Beyond the Nass Road junction, the Nisga'a Highway is narrow and used by logging trucks. Services along this route are limited.

The southern boundary of **Nisga'a Memorial Lava Bed Park** is at Mile 42.2/67.9 km on the Nisga'a Highway. This lava flow is thought to be the most recent volcanic eruption in Canada (approximately 250 years ago). It covers an area approximately 6.3 miles/10 km long and 1.8 miles/3 km wide and was created by a volcano less than 361 feet/100m high. The eruption produced little ash or cinder, but large quantities of basalt. The eruption destroyed 2 villages and killed more than 2,000 people.

Principal access to the Cassiar Highway is from Kitwanga at **Milepost PG 306.6** Yellowhead Highway.

PG 357.9 (576 km) **PR 89.8** (145.5 km) Skeena Sawmill.

PG 358.7 (577.4 km) **PR 89.5** (144.1 km) Fishermen's Memorial Park and Boat Launch.

PG 359 (377.8 km) **PR 88.7** (143.7 km) Kalum Bridge.

PG 359.2 (578 km) **PR 88.5** (143.5 km) Private boat launch and campground. ▲

PG 359.3 (578.2 km) **PR 88.4** (143.3 km) KITSUMKALUM. Grocery store and Native craft centre. House of Sim-oi-Ghets handles only authentic arts and crafts such as totem poles, leather goods and local carvings.

This is also the **junction** with West Kalum Forest Service Road, which leads north to **Kitsumkalum Provincial Park** (15 miles/24 km), with 20 campsites, and to Red Sand Demonstration Forest, with 14 campsites. West Kalum Road junctions with the Nisga'a Highway. ▲

Westbound, Highway 16 is in good condition westbound although the few straightaways are interrupted by some amazing 70-degree zigzags as the highway crosses the railroad tracks. The highway along the Skeena River is spectacular, with waterfalls cascading down the steep rock faces.

PG 359.7 (578.8 km) **PR 88** (142.7 km) Large turnout to south.

PG 363.1 (584.4 km) **PR 84.6** (137 km) Zimacord Bridge.

PG 366.1 (589.2 km) **PR 81.6** (132.1 km) Turnout to south.

PG 368.7 (589.2 km) **PR 79** (127.9 km) Delta Creek.

PG 371.3 (597.5 km) **PR 76.4** (123.7 km) Shames River.

PG 371.4 (597.7 km) **PR 76.3** (123.5 km) Shames Mountain Ski Area.

PG 377.2 (607.1 km) **PR 70.5** (113.8 km) Double-ended turnout to south is a rest area with picnic tables, toilets and water pump.

PG 378 (607.7 km) **PR 69.7** (112.3 km) Exstew River.

PG 378.2 (608.7 km) **PR 69.5** (112.4 km) Boat launch.

PG 381.7 (613.7 km) **PR 66** (106.3 km) Boat launch (not signed).

PG 383 (616.4 km) **PR 64.7** (104.9 km) *CAUTION! Highway turns sharply across railroad tracks.*

PG 385.3 (620.1 km) **PR 62.4** (100.9 km) *CAUTION: Carwash Rock overhangs highway. Water cascades down mountain and onto highway during heavy rains.*

PG 385.8 (620.8 km) **PR 61.9** (100.2 km) Sharp curves and falling rocks approximately next mile westbound. *CAUTION: Slow down for sharp curve and steep grade.*

PG 389.6 (627 km) **PR 58.1** (94 km) **Exchamsiks River Provincial Park**, day-use only; has 20 picnic sites among old-growth Sitka spruce. Open May to October, camping fee, water and pit toilets. Good salmon fishing in Exchamsiks River. Access to Gitnadoix River canoeing area across Skeena River. ᗢ

PG 389.8 (627.3 km) **PR 57.9** (93.7 km) Very pleasant rest area north side of road at west end of Exchamsiks bridge; boat launch on Exchamsiks River. Toilets, tables and litter barrels.

PG 390 (627.7 km) **PR 57.7** (93.3 km) Boat launch.

PG 390.2 (628 km) **PR 57.5** (93 km) *CAUTION: Very narrow road next to railway.*

PG 391.3 (629.7 km) **PR 56.4** (91.3 km) Conspicuous example of Sitka spruce on north side of highway. Aboriginal people ate its inner bark fresh or dried in cakes, served with berries. As you travel west, the vegetation becomes increasingly influenced by the maritime climate.

PG 394.1 (634.2 km) **PR 53.6** (86.8 km) Kasiks River and view of mountains.

PG 394.8 (635.3 km) **PR 52.9** (85.7 km) Kasiks River; boat launch.

PG 394.9 (635.5 km) **PR 52.8** (85.5 km) River access at east end of bridge.

PG 396 (637.3 km) **PR 51.7** (83.7 km) Bridal Falls.

PG 399.9 (643.5 km) **PR 47.8** (77.4 km)

YELLOWHEAD HIGHWAY • Prince Rupert

During springtime and salmon season, seals and sea lions may be seen in the Skeena River. (© Blake Hanna, staff)

Boat launch.

PG 401.1 (645.6 km) **PR 46.6** (75.3 km) Hanging Valley and Blackwater Creek.

PG 404.8 (651.4 km) **PR 42.9** (69.5 km) Kwinitsa River bridge and boat launch. No public moorage.

PG 409.3 (658.7 km) **PR 38.4** (62.1 km) Telegraph Point Rest Area to south on bank of Skeena River is a paved, double-ended turnout with outhouses, picnic tables, litter barrels and water pump. Watch for seals and sea lions in spring and during salmon season.

PG 413.3 (665.1 km) **PR 34.4** (55.7 km) Paved turnout with litter barrel.

PG 415.5 (668.7 km) **PR 32.2** (52.1 km) Basalt Creek rest area to south with picnic tables.

PG 416.3 (669.9 km) **PR 31.4** (50.8 km) Khyex River bridge. Remains of old sawmill visible at west end of bridge to south.

PG 420.2 (676.2 km) **PR 27.5** (44.5 km) Turnout to south.

PG 421.1 (673.9 km) **PR 26.6** (42.1 km) The old highway alignment passed through the base of the hydro-electric tower. *Caution: narrow road.*

PG 422.5 (680 km) **PR 25.2** (39.8 km) Watch for pictograph, visible from the road for eastbound traffic only, possibly a boundary marker for Chief Legaic over 150 years ago. It was rediscovered in the early 1950s by Dan Lippett of Prince Rupert. There is no turnout here.

PG 423.7 (681.8 km) **PR 24** (38 km) **Skeena River Viewpoint** to south with litter barrels, historical plaque about the Skeena River and information sign on Port Edward. *NOTE: You can park here and walk back along the highway to see the pictograph described at Milepost PG 422.5. Watch for traffic.*

Highway leaves Skeena River westbound. Abandoned townsite of Port Essington visible on opposite side of river.

PG 424.3 (682.3 km) **PR 23.4** (37.7 km) Green River Forest Service road.

PG 424.6 (683.3 km) **PR 23.1** (37.4 km) Large turnout.

PG 427.5 (688 km) **PR 20.2** (32.7 km) **Rainbow Summit**, elev. 528 feet/161m.

PG 429.1 (690.1 km) **PR 18.6** (29.9 km) Large paved turnout.

PG 430 (692 km) **PR 17.7** (28.7 km) Side road south to Rainbow Lake Reservoir; boat launch. The reservoir water is used by the pulp mill on Watson Island.

PG 432.5 (695.9 km) **PR 15.2** (24.7 km) **Prudhomme Lake Provincial Park**; 24 campsites, well water, toilets, firewood, fishing, camping fee.

PG 432.9 (696.6 km) **PR 14.8** (24 km) Paved turnout to north with litter barrel.

PG 433.4 (697.5 km) **PR 14.3** (23.1 km) Turnoff for **Diana Lake Provincial Park**, 1.5 miles/2.4 km south via single-lane gravel road (use turnouts). Day-use facility. Very pleasant grassy picnic area on lakeshore with 50 picnic tables, kitchen shelter, firewood, grills, wheelchair access, outhouses, water pump and garbage cans. Parking for 229 vehicles. The only freshwater swimming beach in the Prince Rupert area. Fish viewing at Diana Creek on the way into the lake; 2 hiking trails.

PG 438 (704.9 km) **PR 9.7** (15.6 km) **Junction**. Turnoff for **PORT EDWARD**, pulp mill and historic cannery. The **North Pacific Historic Fishing Village** at Port Edward is open daily in summer. Built in 1889, this is the oldest cannery village on the north coast. Phone (250) 628-3538 for more information.

Kinnikinnick Campground and RV Park. Directions: Take Port Edward turnoff (6 miles before Prince Rupert on Highway 16) and travel 2 miles to campground. Beautiful treed sites; great fishing, minutes to boat launch and museum. Serviced sites and tenting. Hot showers, toilets, laundry. Packages available. Phone (250) 628-9449; rvpark@citytel.net; www.geocities.com/kinnikca. Box 1107 Port Edward, BC, V0V 1G0.
[ADVERTISEMENT]

North Pacific Historic Fishing Village. Don't miss Canada's premiere northcoast attraction. A National Historic Site of Canada, featured on TV, newspapers and magazines. Laugh and learn through entertaining live shows, tours and exhibits, all housed in the world's oldest remaining cannery village. Dine in the old mess house. Visit local artisans in MacGregor Studio. Guaranteed to please families, seniors and all photobugs. Open daily. Admission charged. (250) 628-3538 or www.northpacific.org.
[ADVERTISEMENT]

PG 438.3 (705.3 km) **PR 9.4** (15.2 km) Galloway Rapids rest area to south with litter barrels, picnic tables and visitor information sign. View of Watson Island pulp mill.

PG 439.5 (707.3 km) **PR 8.2** (13.2 km) Ridley Island access road. Ridley Island is the site of terminals used for the transfer of coal and grain from, respectively, the North East Coal resource near Dawson Creek and Canada's prairies, to ships

PG 440.2 (708.5 km) **PR 7.5** (12 km) Oliver Lake rest area to south just off highway; picnic tables, grills, firewood. Point of interest sign about bogs.

PG 441.2 (710 km) **PR 6.5** (10.5 km) Shoe Tree or Tree of Lost Soles to east. Tongue-in-cheek local attraction which has grown over years. Worn-out footwear is hung from trees in this local shrine to shoes.

PG 442.3 (711.8 km) **PR 5.4** (8.7 km) **Butze Rapids** viewpoint and trail. The current flowing over these rapids changes direction with the tide. The phenomenon is called a reversing tidal rapid, and the effect is most dramatic an hour after low tide. Easy, fairly level hiking on well-maintained, chip-covered trail.

PG 442.7 (712.4 km) **PR 5** (8.1 km) Prince Rupert industrial park on the outskirts of Prince Rupert. Yellowhead Highway 16 becomes McBride Street as you enter the city centre.

PG 443.4 (713.7 km) **PR 4.2** (6.8 km) Frederick Street junction.

PG 447 (719.3 km) **PR 0.7** (1.2 km) Park Avenue campground.

PG 447.7 (720 km) **PR 0** Ferry terminal for B.C. Ferries and Alaska state ferries. Airport ferry terminal. End of Highway 16.

Prince Rupert

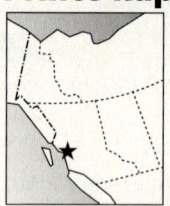

Located on Kaien Island near the mouth of the Skeena River, 90 miles/145 km by air or water (6-hour ferry ride) south of Ketchikan, AK. **Population:** 14,500; area 21,000. **Emergency Services:** Phone 911 for **Police**, **Ambulance** and **Fire Department.** RCMP, 6th Avenue and McBride Street, non-emergency phone (250) 627-0700. Hospital, Prince Rupert Regional, phone (250) 624-2171.

Visitor Information: Visitor Infocentre at 215 Cow Bay Road, Suite 100; open daily in summer, 7:30 A.M. to 9 P.M. The Park Avenue Campground; open daily in summer, 9 A.M. to 9 P.M., and until midnight for B.C. Ferry arrivals. Write the Prince Rupert Visitor Information Centre, 215 Cow Bay Road, Suite 100, Prince Rupert, BC V8J 1A2, phone (800) 667-1994 and (250) 624-5637, fax (250) 627-0992; email prtravel@citytel.net; web site at www.tourismprincerupert.com. Also check with the Visitor Infocentre about guided tours, or pick up a brochure for a self-guided tour.

Elevation: Sea level. **Climate:** Temperate

PRINCE RUPERT ADVERTISERS

Adventure Tours & Water Taxi	Ph. 1-800-201-8377
Anchor Inn	Ph. 1-800-627-8522
Car-To-Go Rentals	Ph. (250) 627-1525
Coast Prince Rupert Hotel, The	Ph. (250) 624-6711
Cow Bay Cafe	Ph. (250) 627-1212
Crest Hotel	Ph. 1-800-663-8150
Eagle Bluff Bed & Breakfast	Ph. 1-800-833-1550
Harbour Air Ltd.	Ph. 1-800-689-4234
Highliner Inn	Ph. (250) 624-9060
Inn on the Harbour	Ph. 1-800-663-8155
Moby Dick Inn	Ph. 1-800-663-0822
Museum of Northern British Columbia	Ph. (250) 624-3207
North Pacific Historic Fishing Village	Ph. (250) 628-3538
Pacific Inn	Ph. 1-888-663-1999
Park Avenue Campground	Ph. (250) 624-5861
Parkside Resort Motel	Ph. 1-888-575-2288
Pike Island Guided Tours (Laxspa'aws)	Ph. (250) 628-3201
Prince Rupert Info Centre	Ph. (250) 624-5637
Rupert Square Shopping Centre	Ph. (250) 624-5163
Totem Lodge Motel	Ph. 1-800-550-0178
Tourism Prince Rupert	Ph. 1-800-667-1994

Prince Rupert
Your BC Coast Adventure Centre

Spend a day whalewatching, sea kayaking and grizzly bear viewing. Hire a fishing charter and catch one of our famed barn-door size halibut or wild Skeena River salmon. Take your camera flight-seeing or on a first nations tour. Visit our Museum of Northern B.C. or relive days of old at the North Pacific Cannery. And to top it all off… dig into a plateful of world-class seafood! Slow down and relax...Canadian style. Plan a couple days to discover the people, history and spirit of Canada's northern rainforest. You'll find some of the best Humpback Whale & Grizzly Bear Viewing on the West Coast, World-Class Saltwater Fishing, Ocean Kayaking, Great Attractions and so much more...all affordably priced in Canadian dollars.

A walk through history

Join our First Nations interpretive guides on the groomed trails of Pike Island. See 1800 year old village sites. Examine petroglyphs in the intertidal zone and learn how Our People used the cedar tree and plants of the area.

Laxspa'aws

Metlakatla Development Corporation
Phone (250) 628-3201   Fax (250) 628-9259
www.pikeisland.ca
Email: metdevco@citytel.net

Inn on the Harbour

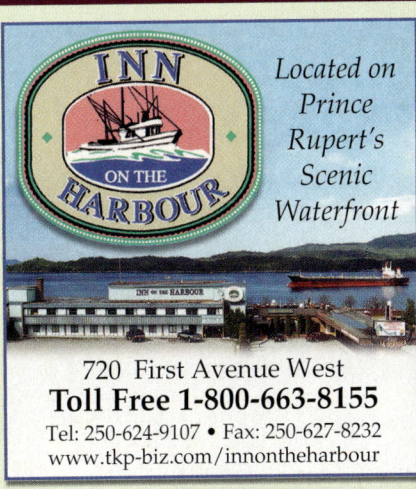

Located on Prince Rupert's Scenic Waterfront

720 First Avenue West
Toll Free 1-800-663-8155
Tel: 250-624-9107 • Fax: 250-627-8232
www.tkp-biz.com/innontheharbour

Totem Lodge Motel

Toll Free 1-800-550-0178
Tel: 250-624-6761 • Fax: 250-624-3831
Web: tkp-biz.com/totemlodgemotel

Closest Motel to Via Rail Station and BC and Alaska Ferry Terminals

Excellent location with spectacular views!

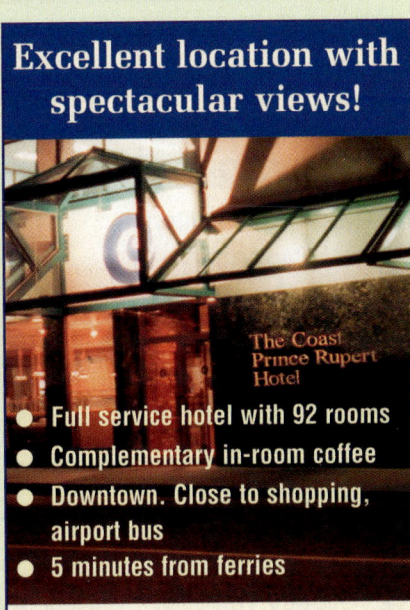

The Coast Prince Rupert Hotel

- Full service hotel with 92 rooms
- Complementary in-room coffee
- Downtown. Close to shopping, airport bus
- 5 minutes from ferries

The Coast Prince Rupert Hotel

Canada Select ★★★½

118 - 6th St., Prince Rupert, B.C. V8J 3L7
Phone (250)624-6711 Fax (250)624-3288
Email: coastprh@citytel.net

CENTRAL RESERVATIONS
1-800-663-1144

Prince Rupert ...where there's so much more to enjoy!
Call 1-800-667-1994 now for your FREE Adventure Travel Guide

NATURALLY PRINCE RUPERT

Park Avenue Campground

- 1/2 Mile from Ferries
- 77 Full Service Sites

1750 Park Ave., PO Box 612
Prince Rupert, BC V8J 3R5

**Call Toll Free
1-800-667-1994**

Ph 250-624-5861
Fax 250-622-2619

ANCHOR INN
PRINCE • RUPERT

- 45 spacious rooms
- Closest hotel to Alaska and BC Ferries
- Free parking plus motorcoach space
- Portside Restaurant & Pub and Grill
- Satellite TV with movie channels

Toll Free: 1-888-627-8522

Phone: (250) 627-8522   FAX: (250) 624-8137
Email: info@anchor-inn.com
Website: www.anchor-inn.com

Howard Johnson Plaza Hotel / HIGHLINER PRINCE RUPERT

A better quality of life on the road.

Howard Johnson SUPERMILES
AIR CANADA Aeroplan
PETRO POINTS

- Extra large guest rooms with balconies
- Located in the heart of downtown
- Complimentary in-room coffee
- Restaurant & Pub
- Full meeting and banquet facilities

815 First Avenue West,
Prince Rupert, British Columbia
Canada V8J 1B3

Toll Free 1-800-668-3115
Tel: (250) 624-9060   Fax: (250) 627-7759
www.hojoprincerupert.com

Let Us Plan Your Adventure!

▲ Prince Rupert Panoramas
▲ Khutzeymateen - Valley of the Grizzly Bear
▲ North to Ketchikan, Alaska
▲ Queen Charlotte Islands/Haida Gwaii Day Trip

VISA   MasterCard

**1-800-689-4234
(250) 627-1341**

Seal Cove Seaplane Base
Box 99, Prince Rupert, B.C.
V8J 3P4 Canada

HARBOUR AIR LTD.

PACIFIC INN

Convenient, Affordable, Downtown

COVERED PARKING

909-3rd Ave. W., Prince Rupert V8J 1MP
Toll Free 1-888-663-1999
250-627-1711 • Fax: 250-627-4212

A Royal Canadian Welcome

...is waiting for you at the

Prince Rupert Visitor Info Centre

at the new Atlin Cruise Ship Terminal just a few blocks away in Cow Bay!

100-215 Cow Bay Rd.
Phone 250-624-5637
Email: prtravel@citytel.net
www.TourismPrinceRupert.com

NATURALLY PRINCE RUPERT

Prince Rupert...where there's so much more to enjoy!

Call 1-800-667-1994 now for your FREE Adventure Travel Guide

Cow Bay Cafe
A waterfront Experience
Seafood entrées, gourmet lunches and dinners, plus sinfully delicious desserts – all homemade!
(250) 627•1212

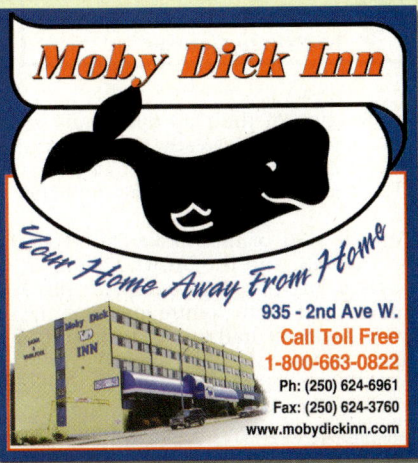

Moby Dick Inn
Your Home Away From Home
935 - 2nd Ave W.
Call Toll Free
1-800-663-0822
Ph: (250) 624-6961
Fax: (250) 624-3760
www.mobydickinn.com

Outstanding accommodation is only the beginning…

Prince Rupert's
Crest HOTEL

Toll Free
1-800-663-8150
(CANADA/USA)

222 First Avenue West P.O. Box 277, Prince Rupert, B.C., Canada V8J 3P6
Tel (250) 624-6771 Fax (250) 627-7666
Email: info@cresthotel.bc.ca Web site: www.cresthotel.bc.ca

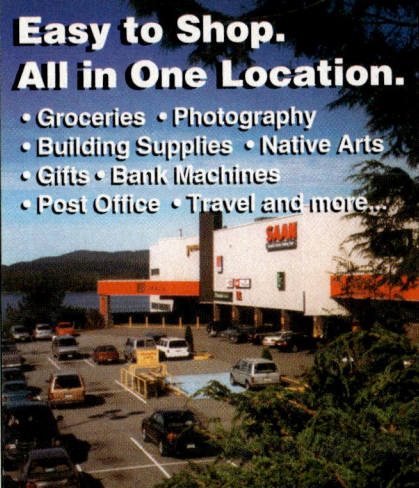

Easy to Shop. All in One Location.
• Groceries • Photography
• Building Supplies • Native Arts
• Gifts • Bank Machines
• Post Office • Travel and more...

Rupert Square Shopping Centre

HOURS OF OPERATION
9:30 AM - 6:00 PM
Mon., Tues., Wed., Sat.

9:30 AM - 9:00 PM
Thursday & Friday

10:00 AM - 5:00 PM
Sundays & Holidays

Ph: 250/624-5163 Fx: 624-4596
500 Second Avenue West
rsquare@citytel.net

PRINCE RUPERT ADVENTURE TOURS & WATER TAXI
■ Whale Watching
■ Kaien Island Circle Tours
■ Grizzly Bear Tours & More!

Toll Free 1-800-201-8377
Email: mail@westcoastlaunch.com
Web: westcoastlaunch.com
Telephone: 250-627-9166

A Great Place to Stay
❧ Suites ❧ Kitchenettes ❧ Cable TV
❧ Continental B'fast ❧ Internet Service
❧ Weekly Rates ❧ Car Storage
❧ Trailer & Camper Hook-Ups

PARKSIDE RESORT MOTEL
101-11th Ave. E.
Prince Rupert,
B.C. V8J 2W2

1-888-575-2288
Phone: (250) 624-9131 Fax: (250) 627-8547
www.parksideresortmotel.com
Email: parkside@citytel.net

Photo by V. Kimmet.

North Pacific Historic Fishing Village
"A NATIONAL HISTORIC SITE"

LIVE THEATRE - GUIDED TOURS
RESIDENT ARTISTS - SHOPS
LICENSED DINING - ACCOMMODATION

Located in Port Edward -
20 minutes from Prince Rupert

Open daily May through September

www.cannery.ca
Phone: (250) 628-3538
Fax: (250) 628-3540

NATURALLY PRINCE RUPERT

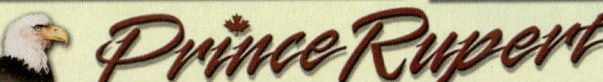

Prince Rupert *...where there's so much more to enjoy!*
Call 1-800-667-1994 now for your FREE Adventure Travel Guide

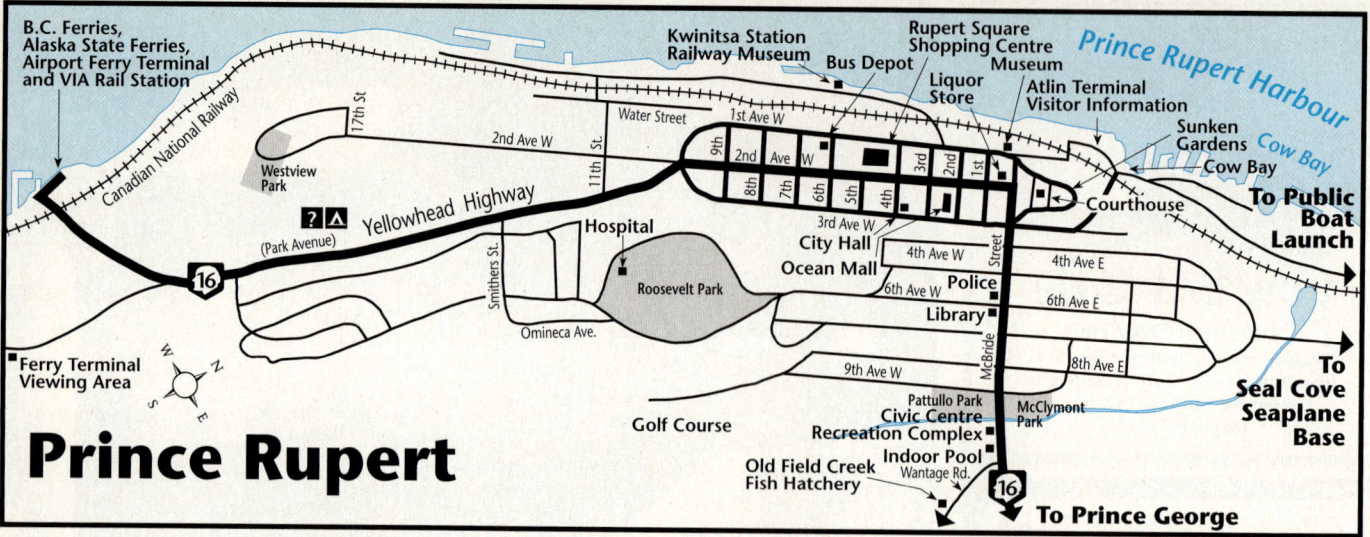

with mild winters. Annual precipitation 95.4 inches. **Radio:** CHTK 560, CBC 860; CJFW-FM 101.9. **Television:** 31 channels, cable. **Newspaper:** *The Prince Rupert Daily News.*

Prince Rupert, "Gateway to Alaska," was surveyed prior to 1905 by the Grand Trunk Pacific Railway (later Canadian National Railways) as the terminus for Canada's second transcontinental railroad.

Twelve thousand miles/19,300 km of survey lines were studied before a final route along the Skeena River was chosen. Some 833 miles/1,340 km had to be blasted from solid rock, 50 men drowned and costs rose to $105,000 a mile (the final cost of $300 million was comparable to Panama Canal construction) before the last spike was driven near Fraser Lake on April 7, 1914. Financial problems continued to plague the company, forcing it to amalgamate to become part of the Canadian National Railways system in 1923.

Charles M. Hays, president of the company, was an enthusiastic promoter of the new terminus, which was named by competition from 12,000 entries. While "Port Rupert" had been submitted by two contestants, "Prince Rupert" (from Miss Eleanor M. Macdonald of Winnipeg) called to mind the dashing soldier–explorer, cousin to Charles II of England and first governor of the Hudson's Bay Co., who had traded on the coast rivers for years. Three first prizes of $250 were awarded and Prince Rupert was officially named in 1906.

Prince Rupert's proposed port and adjacent waters were surveyed by G. Blanchard Dodge of the Hydrographic branch of the Marine Dept. in 1906, and in May the little steamer *Constance* carried settlers from the village of Metlakatla to clear the first ground on Kaien Island. Its post office opened Nov. 23, 1906, and Prince Rupert, with a tent-town population of 200, began an association with communities on the Queen Charlotte Islands, with Stewart served by Union steamships and Canadian Pacific Railways boats, and with Hazelton 200 miles/322 km up the Skeena River on which the stern-wheelers of the Grand Trunk Pacific and the Hudson's Bay Co. traveled.

Incorporated as a city March 10, 1910, Prince Rupert attracted settlers responding to the enthusiasm of Hays, with his dreams of a population of 50,000 and world markets supplied by his railroad. Both the city and the railway suffered a great loss when Charles M. Hays went down with the *Titanic* in April 1912. Even so, work went ahead on the Grand Trunk Pacific. Two years later the first train arrived at Prince Rupert, linking the western port with the rest of Canada. Since then, the city has progressed through 2 world wars and economic ups and downs to its present period of growth and expansion, not only as a busy port but as a visitor centre.

During WWII, more than a million tons of freight and 73,000 people, both military and civilian, passed through Prince Rupert on their way to military operations in Alaska and the South Pacific.

Construction of the pulp operations on Watson Island in 1951 greatly increased the economic and industrial potential of the area. The operations include a pulp mill and a kraft mill.

With the start of the Alaska State Ferry System in 1963, and the British Columbia Ferry System in 1966, Prince Rupert's place as an important visitor centre and terminal point for highway, rail and marine transportation was assured.

Prince Rupert is the second major deep-sea port on Canada's west coast, exporting grain, pulp, lumber and other resources to Europe and Asia. Prince Rupert has also become a major coal and grain port with facilities on Ridley Island. Other industries include fishing and fish processing, and the manufacture of forest products.

Prince Rupert is underlaid by muskeg over solid rock. Some of the older buildings have sagged slightly as a result of unstable foundations.

Lodging & Services

More than a dozen hotels and motels accommodate the influx of ferry passengers each summer. Many restaurants feature fresh local seafood in season.

Modern supermarkets and shopping centres are available. Government liquor store is at the corner of 2nd Avenue and Highway 16. There are 5 main banks and 2 laundromats.

The Civic Centre Recreation Complex, located on McBride Street, has a fitness gym, squash, basketball and volleyball; ice skating and roller skating rinks; phone (250) 624-6707 for more information. Earl Mah Aquatic Centre next door has an indoor swimming pool, tot pool, weight room, saunas, showers, whirlpool, slides and diving boards. Access for persons with disabilities. Phone (250) 627-7946. Admission charged.

The golf course includes 18-hole course, resident pro, equipment rental, clubhouse and restaurant. Entrance on 9th Avenue W.

Eagle Bluff Bed & Breakfast. Experience Prince Rupert's waterfront in historic Cow Bay. Located on the Wharf next to Visitor Information Centre and nearby restaurants. Open year-round. Panoramic view of the harbour and soaring eagles. Full breakfast. Families welcome. MasterCard/VISA accepted. 1-800-833-1550. 201 Cow Bay Road, Prince

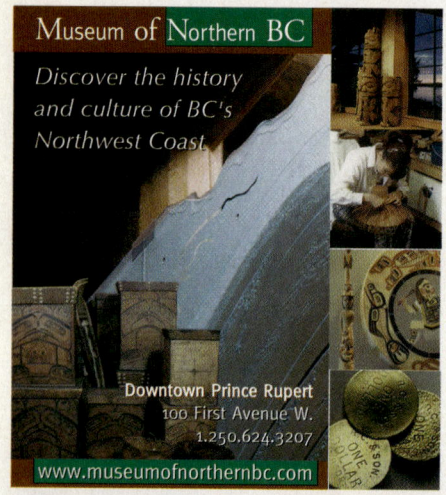

Rupert, BC. Email eaglebed@citytel.net; www.citytel.net/eaglebluff. [ADVERTISEMENT]

Camping

Park Avenue Campground on Highway 16 in the city has 87 campsites with hookups, unserviced sites, restrooms with hot showers, coin-operated laundry facilities, children's play area and picnic shelters. A private RV park on McBride Street offers camper and trailer parking. Kinnikinnick Campground and RV Park is located east of the city at Port Edward, **Milepost PG 438** Yellowhead Highway. There are 24 campsites at Prudhomme Lake Provincial Park, 12.5 miles/20.1 km east at **Milepost PG 432.5** Yellowhead Highway 16. ▲

Transportation

Air: Harbour Air and Inland Air Charter to outlying villages and Queen Charlotte Islands; Air Canada and Hawk Air offer daily jet service to Vancouver.

Prince Rupert airport is located on Digby Island, which is connected by city-operated ferry to Prince Rupert. There is a small terminal at the airport. The airport ferry leaves from the Fairview dock, next to the Alaska state ferry dock; fare is charged for the 20-minute ride. Bus service to airport from the Atlin Terminal.

There is a seaplane base at Seal Cove with airline and helicopter charter services.

Ferries: British Columbia Ferry System, Fairview dock, phone (250) 624-9627, provides automobile and passenger service from Prince Rupert to Port Hardy, and between Prince Rupert and Skidegate in the Queen Charlotte Islands.

Alaska Marine Highway System, Fairview dock, phone (250) 627-1744 or (800) 642-0066, provides automobile and passenger service to southeastern Alaska.

NOTE: Vehicle storage is available; inquire at the Information Centre.

Car Rentals: Car-To-Go, phone (250) 627-1525; National Car Rental, phone (250) 624-5318.

Taxi: Available. Prince Rupert taxi cabs are powered by LNG (liquefied natural gas); phone (250) 624-2185.

Railroad: VIA Rail "Skeena" service to Prince George and Jasper. VIA Rail station is located at the BC Ferries terminal. In British Columbia, phone (800) 561-8630; in the U.S. phone (800) 561-3949; or www.viarail.ca.

Bus: PR Transit System, phone (250) 624-3343. Greyhound, phone (250) 624-5090; www.greyhound.ca. Farwest Bus Lines, phone (250) 624-6400. Charter sightseeing tours available.

Attractions

Totem Pole Tour. Scattered throughout the city are 18 large cedar totem poles, each with its own story. Most are reproductions by Native craftsmen of the original Tsimshian (SHIM shian) poles from the mainland and the Haida (HI duh) carvings from the Queen Charlotte Islands. The originals are now in the British Columbia Provincial Museum in Victoria. Several totem poles may be seen at Totem Park near the hospital. Maps are available at the Visitor Infocentre, and guidebooks are available at the Museum of Northern British Columbia.

City Parks. Mariner's Park, overlooking the harbour, has memorials to those who have been lost at sea. Roosevelt Park honours Prince Rupert's wartime history. Service

A store in the Cow Bay area, where a bovine theme prevails at many businesses. (© Blake Hanna, staff)

Park overlooks downtown Prince Rupert. And Kinsmen's Linear Park takes you from one end of town to the other via a system of trails. Sunken Gardens, located behind the Provincial Courthouse, is a public garden planted in the excavations for an earlier court building. Maps are available at the Visitor Infocentre.

New Museum of Northern British Columbia/Ruth Harvey Art Gallery, situated in an award-winning Chatham Village Longhouse, displays an outstanding collection of artifacts depicting the settlement history of British Columbia's north coast. Traveling art collections are displayed in the gallery, and works by local artists are available for purchase. Centrally located at 1st Avenue and McBride Street. Summer hours 9 A.M. to 8 P.M. Monday through Saturday; 9 A.M. to 5 P.M. Sunday. Winter hours 9 A.M. to 5 P.M. Monday through Saturday. Phone (250) 624-3207. Admission charged.

Pike Island Guided Tours. Knowledgeable First Nation's guides conduct excursions of Pike Island, site of 3 ancient Tsimshian village sites. Pike Island is accessible by 40-minute water taxi from Prince Rupert Harbour. The walking tour also explores the natural history of this tiny island. Tour tickets may be purchased at the museum, which is also the departure point for the tours. Daily departures at 12:30 P.M. in summer. The 3-1/2-hour tour includes transportation, snacks and guide services.

Kwinitsa Station Railway Museum. Built in 1911, Kwinitsa Station is one of the few surviving stations of the nearly 400 built along the Grand Trunk Pacific Railway line. In 1985 the station was moved to the Prince Rupert waterfront park. Restored rooms, exhibits and videos tell the story of early Prince Rupert and the role the railroad played in the city's development. Open daily in summer.

Performing Arts Centre offers both professional and amateur theatre, with productions for children, and classical and contemporary plays presented. The 700-seat facility may be toured in summer; phone (250) 627-8888.

Special Events. Seafest is a 4-day celebration, held the second weekend in June, which includes a parade and water-jousting competition. Indian Culture Days, a 2-day event held during Seafest, features Native food, traditional dance, and arts and crafts. The All Native Basketball Tournament, held in February, is the largest event of its kind in Canada.

Watch the Seaplanes. From McBride Street, head north on 6th Avenue E. (watch for signs to seaplane base); drive a few miles to Solly's Pub, then turn right to Seal Cove seaplane base. Visitors can spend a fascinating hour here watching seaplanes loading, taking off and landing. Helicopter and seaplane tours of the area are available at Seal Cove.

Cow Bay. Located along the waterfront northeast of downtown, this revitalized area boasts numerous boutiques, cafes, a popular pub and 2 bed-and-breakfasts. The ambience is historic (antique phone booths, old-fashioned lampposts), but the theme is bovine, with businesses and buildings bearing cow names (like Cowpuccinos, a coffee house) or cow colors (black and white pattern).

North Pacific Village Museum at Port Edward, located east of Prince Rupert on the Yellowhead Highway ((turnoff at **Milepost PG 438**), was built in 1889. This restored heritage site has dozens of displays on this once-major regional industry. A live performance highlights the history of the cannery. Open daily in summer; admission charged. Phone (250) 628-3538.

Butze Rapids. This reversing tidal rapid, most dramatic about an hour after low tide, can be seen from a viewpoint 5.4 miles/8.7 km east from the ferry terminal in Prince Rupert at **Milepost PG 442.3** Yellowhead Highway. From the parking area, an easy trail takes you past Grassy Bay to the rapids.

Swim at Diana Lake. This provincial park, about 13 miles/21 km from downtown on Highway 16, offers the only freshwater swimming in the Prince Rupert area. Picnic tables, kitchen shelter, parking and beach.

Visit the Queen Charlotte Islands. Ferry service is available between Prince Rupert and Skidegate on Graham Island, largest of the 150 islands and islets that form the Queen Charlotte Islands. Located west of Prince Rupert—a 6- to 8-hour ferry ride—Graham Island's paved road system connects Skidegate with Masset, the largest town in the Queen Charlottes. Scheduled flights from Prince Rupert to Sandspit and Masset are available. Island attractions include wild beaches, Haida culture, flora and fauna. For more information, contact the Visitor Infocentre in Queen Charlotte; phone (250) 559-8316.

Go Fishing. Numerous freshwater fishing areas are available near Prince Rupert. For information on bait, locations, regulations and licensing, contact local sporting goods stores or the Visitor Infocentre. This area abounds in all species of salmon, steelhead, crab and shrimp. Public boat launch facility is located at Rushbrook Public Floats at the north end of the waterfront. Public floats are also available at Fairview, past the Alaska state ferry terminal near the breakwater.

Harbour Tours and Fishing Charters are available. For more information, contact the Prince Rupert Infocentre; phone (800) 667-1994.

CASSIAR HIGHWAY

	Alaska Hwy.	Dease Lake	Iskut	Stewart/Hyder	Yellowhead Hwy.	Watson Lake
Alaska Hwy.		145	196	390	446	14
Dease Lake	145		51	245	301	159
Iskut	196	51		194	250	210
Stewart/Hyder	390	245	194		136	404
Yellowhead Hwy.	446	301	250	136		460
Watson Lake	14	159	210	404	460	

Connects: Yellowhead Hwy. 16 to Alaska Hwy.   **Length:** 446 miles
Road Surface: 80% paved, 20% gravel   **Season:** Open all year
Highest Summit: Gnat Pass 4,072 feet
Major Attractions: Bear and Salmon glaciers, Stikine River

(See map, page 239)

Provincial rest area at Hodder Lake, Milepost J 152.1. (© Bob Butterfield)

The Cassiar Highway junctions with Yellowhead Highway 16 at the Skeena River bridge (**Milepost PG 297.7** in the YELLOWHEAD HIGHWAY 16 section) and travels north to junction with the Alaska Highway 13.3 miles/21.4 km west of Watson Lake, YT (**Milepost DC 626.2** in the ALASKA HIGHWAY section). Total driving distance is 446.1 miles/ 718 km.

The Cassiar also provides access to Hyder, AK, and Stewart, BC, via a 38-mile/61-km side road from Meziadin Junction at **Milepost J 96.2**, and to Telegraph Creek via a 70-mile/113-km side road from Dease Lake junction at **Milepost J 300.9**. See detailed road logs and community descriptions this section.

The Cassiar offers outstanding scenery and good wildlife viewing. Watch for bears with cubs along the highway (especially in spring); caribou at Gnat Pass (spring and fall); and Dall sheep south of Good Hope.

Travelers driving between Prince George and the junction of the Alaska and Cassiar highways will save 132 miles/213 km by taking the Cassiar Highway. (Yellowhead–Cassiar route is 744 miles/1,197 km; Alaska Highway route is 876 miles/1,410 km.) The Cassiar Highway, which was completed in 1972, is a somewhat rougher road than the Alaska Highway, and has fewer (but sufficient) fuel and service stops along the way.

Although much of the highway is asphalt-surfaced, keep in mind that seal coat is subject to deterioration from weather and traffic. Also, a few bridges are still single lane. Watch for potholes at bridge ends and slippery bridge decks. There are several 8 percent grades. Drive with your headlights on at all times. On gravel stretches of highway watch for washboard and potholes. Gravel road may be dusty in dry weather and muddy in wet weather. The calcium chloride, which is used for dust control and to stabilize the road base, results in the road surface becoming muddy and rough in wet weather. (Wash calcium chloride off your vehicle as soon as possible.)

Watch for logging and freight trucks on the highway. *WARNING: Exercise extreme caution when passing or being passed by these trucks; reduce speed and allow trucks adequate clearance.*

Food, gas and lodging are available along the Cassiar Highway, but check the highway log for distances between services. Be sure your vehicle is mechanically sound with good tires and carry a spare. It is a good idea to carry extra fuel in the off-season. In case of emergency, motorists are advised to flag down trucks to radio for help. *NOTE: It is unlawful to camp overnight in turnouts and rest areas unless otherwise posted.* Camp at private campgrounds or in the provincial park campgrounds.

According to the Ministry of Highways, litter barrels on the Cassiar Highway are often moved to areas which are being used more frequently. Litter barrels may not be in the same location from season to season. Also, the presence of litter barrels and other rest stop facilities is dependent upon sufficient highway funding.

Cassiar Highway Log

Distance from junction with the Yellowhead Highway (J) is followed by distance from Alaska Highway (AH).

BC HIGHWAY 37 NORTH

J 0 AH 446.1 (718 km) Bridge across Skeena River from Yellowhead Highway 16 to start of Cassiar Highway.

Junction with Yellowhead Highway 16 (see **Milepost PG 297.7** on page 229 in the YELLOWHEAD HIGHWAY 16 section).

J 0.2 (0.3 km) **AH 445.9** (717.6 km) Turn east on Bridge Road to view totem poles of **GITWANGAK**. The Native reserve of Git-

CASSIAR HIGHWAY

wangak was renamed after sharing the name Kitwanga with the adjacent white settlement. Gitwangak has some of the finest authentic totem poles in the area. Also here is St. Paul's Anglican Church (the bell tower standing beside the church houses the original bell from the 1893 bell tower).

J 2.5 (4 km) **AH 443.6** (714 km) Kitwanga post office and Cassiar RV Park. ▲

Cassiar RV Park. See display ad this section. ▲

J 2.6 (4.2 km) **AH 443.5** (713.8 km) South end of 1.6-mile/2.5-km loop access road which leads to **KITWANGA** (pop. 1,200). **Radio:** CBC 630 AM. **Emergency Services:** Ambulance. Gas station, towing, car wash and a general store. There is a free public campground across from the gas station. (Donations for campground upkeep gratefully accepted at the Kitwanga Tempo service station.) ▲

Kitwanga is at the crossroads of the old upper Skeena "grease trail" trade. The "grease" was eulachon (candlefish) oil, which was a trading staple among tribes of the Coast and Interior. The grease trails are believed to have extended north to the Bering Sea.

A paved turnout with litter barrel and sign on the Kitwanga access road mark **Kitwanga Fort National Historic Site**, where a wooden fortress and palisade once crowned the large rounded hill here. Seven interpretive panels along the trail up Battle Hill explain the history of the site. Kitwanga Fort was the first major western Canadian Native site commemorated by Parks Canada.

Kitwanga Auto Service. See display ad this section.

J 4 (6.4 km) **AH 442.1** (711.5 km) North end of 1.6-mile/2.6-km loop access road (Kitwanga North Road) to Kitwanga; see description preceding milepost. Also **junction** with alternate access route (signed Hazelton–Kitwanga Road) from Hazelton to the Cassiar Highway via the north side of the Skeena River.

J 5 (8 km) **AH 441.1** (710 km) The mountain chain of Seven Sisters is visible to southwest (weather permitting) next 4 miles/6.4 km northbound.

J 12.5 (20.2 km) **AH 433.6** (697.9 km) Turnout with litter barrels to west.

J 12.6 (20.3 km) **AH 433.5** (697.7 km)

Indian village of Gitanyow has one of BC's most extensive display of totem poles. (© Bob Butterfield)

Highway follows Kitwanga River and former grease trail route.

J 13 (21 km) **AH 433.1** (697.1 km) South access to **GITANYOW**, formerly Kitwancool (2 miles/3.3 km from highway), is a small Indian village; gas available. Gitanyow has one of the largest concentrations of standing totem poles in northwestern British Columbia. Guided tours of the totem poles may be available. A museum, interpretive trail and information kiosk are under development in this community as part of the Historic Village Project.

J 16.1 (25.9 km) **AH 430** (692.1 km) North access to Gitanyow.

J 18.8 (30.2 km) **AH 427.3** (687.8 km) Bridge over Moonlit Creek.

J 18.9 (30.4 km) **AH 427.2** (687.5 km) Rest area north of creek, east of road, with tables, toilets, litter barrels and information sign. Road west is the old highway and access to **Kitwanga Lake**. Fishing, camping and boat launch spots on lake. Old highway may be in poor condition; drive carefully. It rejoins the main highway at Mile 24.1. Access to the lake is strictly from the old highway. ◀▲

J 38.4 (61.8 km) **AH 407.7** (656.1 km) **Cranberry River** bridge No. 1. A favorite salmon stream in summer; consult fishing regulations.

J 46.4 (74.7 km) **AH 399.7** (643.2 km) **Junction** with the Nass Forest Service Road/Nisga'a Highway to New Aiyansh (38 miles/62 km) and Terrace (99 miles/159 km).

J 46.7 (75.2 km) **AH 399.4** (642.8 km) Cranberry River bridge No. 2. Turnout with toilets, tables and litter barrels.

J 49.8 (80.2 km) **AH 396.3** (637.8 km) Paved turnout to west.

J 52.2 (84 km) **AH 393.9** (933.9 km) Donus Lake Recreation Site, BC Forest Service.

J 53.1 (85.4 km) **AH 393** (632.6 km) BC Hydro power line crosses and parallels highway. Completed in 1990, this line links Stewart to the BC Hydro power grid. Previously, Stewart's power was generated by diesel fuel.

Entering Kalum Forest District northbound. Watch for signs telling dates of logging activity, and observe patterns of regrowth.

J 64.1 (103.1 km) **AH 382** (614.9 km) Paved turnout.

J 66.4 (106.8 km) **AH 379.7** (611.1 km) Views northbound (weather permitting) of the Coast Mountains to the west. Cambrian ice field to west.

J 69.9 (112.6 km) **AH 376.2** (605.4 km) Paved turnout with litter barrel to west.

J 76.6 (123.4 km) **AH 369.5** (594.6 km) Paved turnout.

J 85 (136.7 km) **AH 361.1** (581.2 km) Paved turnout with litter barrels to west.

J 85.7 (137.9 km) **AH 360.4** (580.1 km) Elsworth logging camp and Meziadin Lake General Store (VanDyke Camp Services); fuel, groceries, accommodation, hunting and fishing licenses, emergency phone.

J 87.9 (141.4 km) **AH 358.2** (576.6 km) *CAUTION: 1-lane bridge over Nass River*. Paved rest area with picnic tables, toilets and litter barrel to east at south end of bridge. A

CASSIAR RV PARK
Oasis of the North

- Spacious Full-Service Sites
- Long 30 Amp Pull Throughs
- Free Hot Showers

Laundry • RV Supplies • RV Pressure Wash
Public Phone • Hiking Trails • Book Exchange

In Season Phone/fax: (250) 849-5799 - May-Sept.
e-mail: cassiarrv@navigata.net
OFF SEASON PHONE: 250-849-5525
P.O. Box 301, Kitwanga, B.C. V0J 2A0
Newest, Shortest Route to Alaska

KITWANGA AUTO SERVICE

Access on Through Road at J 2.7 Or J 4.2

AUTOMOTIVE and RV SERVICE & REPAIRS

Gas • Diesel • Auto Propane • Pressure Car Washing

Ph: (250) 849-5521

Fair U.S. Exchange

plaque at the north end commemorates bridge opening in 1972 that joined roads to form Highway 37. The gorge is almost 400 feet/122m wide; main span of bridge is 1feet/57m. Bridge decking is 130 feet/40m above the riverbed.

J 89.4 (143.8 km) AH 356.7 (574.1 km) Tintina Logging Road.

J 93.1 (149.8 km) AH 353 (568.1 km) Tintina Creek. Along with Hanna Creek, this stream produces 40 percent of the sockeye salmon spawning in the Meziadin Lake watershed.

J 94.3 (151.7 km) AH 351.8 (566.3 km) Large gravel turnout to west with litter barrels.

J 94.4 (151.9 km) AH 351.7 (566 km) Bridge over Hanna Creek South. Sockeye salmon spawn here in autumn and can be observed from creek banks and bridge deck. It is illegal to fish for or harass these fish. *CAUTION: Watch for bears.*

J 95.6 (153.8 km) AH 350.5 (564.2 km) **Meziadin** (Mezy-AD-in) **Lake Provincial Park**; 46 campsites (many on lake), drinking water, toilets, wheelchair access, swimming, firewood, bear-proof garbage containers, boat launch. The lake has a significant fish population, including rainbow trout, mountain whitefish and Dolly Varden. Fishing is especially good at the mouths of small streams draining into Meziadin Lake.

Four species of salmon spawn in the lake. This is one of only 3 areas in the province where salmon spawn in the bays and inlets of a lake. *CAUTION: Watch for bears. The hills around the lake are prime bear habitat.*

J 96.2 (154.8 km) AH 349.9 (563.1 km) **Meziadin Junction**; turnoff for spur road to Stewart, BC, and Hyder, AK. Food, gas, camping and minor car repair at junction. *NOTE: This junction can be confusing. Choose your route carefully.* ▲

Meziadin Junction Esso. See display ad this section. ▲

> **Junction** with BC Highway 37A West to Stewart, BC, and Hyder, AK. See "Stewart, BC–Hyder, AK, Access Road" log beginning on page 242.

J 100.8 (162.2 km) AH 345.3 (555.8 km) Hanna Creek North river and bridge. Gravel turnout to west at north end of bridge.

J 104.5 (168.2 km) AH 341.6 (549.7 km) Large turnout to west with litter barrels and brake check.

J 116 (186.6 km) AH 330.1 (531.3 km) **Bell I Crossing** of Bell-Irving River. Double-ended paved turnout at north end of bridge to rest area with picnic tables, pit toilets and litter barrels.

J 118.2 (190.2 km) AH 327.9 (527.7 km) Spruce Creek bridge.

J 122.8 (197.6 km) AH 323.3 (520.3 km) Bell–Irving River parallels highway.

J 125.1 (201.3 km) AH 321 (516.7 km) Cousins Creek.

There are numerous small pullouts along the highway from here north to Dease Lake.

J 127 (204.5 km) AH 319.1 (513.5 km) Ritchie Creek bridge. *NOTE: Wood-decked bridge is slippery when wet.*

J 130.8 (210.5 km) AH 315.3 (507.4 km) Taft Creek bridge. *NOTE: Wood-decked bridge is slippery when wet.*

J 136.1 (219 km) AH 310 (499 km) Deltaic Creek.

J 141.5 (227.7 km) AH 304.6 (490.3 km) Glacier Creek.

J 143.6 (231 km) AH 302.5 (486.8 km) Skowill Creek Bridge.

J 148.1 (238.3 km) AH 298 (479.7 km) Oweegee Creek.

J 152.1 (244.7 km) AH 294 (473.2 km) Provincial rest area by **Hodder Lake**; information kiosk, tables, litter barrels, pit toilets, cartop boat launch. Fly or troll for small rainbows.

J 153.6 (247 km) AH 292.5 (470.7 km) **Bell II Crossing**; food, lodging, camping, propane, gas, diesel, pay phone and lodging just south of second crossing (northbound) of Bell-Irving River.

Bell II Lodge. Beautiful new resort offering 22 guest rooms in log chalets with separate entrance and en-suite bathrooms. Full RV hookups (15 amp power) with pull-through access and overflow parking. Tenting/camping facilities. Gas, diesel, propane, telephone, Internet access, coffee shop and minor tire repairs. Clean, licensed restaurant serving a variety of home-style cooking. We accept all major credit cards. Open year-round. For reservations and information call toll-free 1-877-617-2288 or visit www.bell2lodge.com. Bell II Lodge is the home of Last Frontier Heliskiing in the winter months. We offer guided fly fishing packages for steelhead in September and October. See display ad this section. ▲
[ADVERTISEMENT]

J 153.8 (247.5 km) AH 292.3 (470.5 km) Bridge crosses Bell-Irving River.

NOTE: Watch for road repair and seal coating under way northbound to Iskut in summer 2003.

J 159.2 (256.2 km) AH 286.9 (461.7 km) Snowbank Creek.

J 161.2 (259.4 km) AH 284.9 (458.6 km) Double-ended turnout with picnic tables, handicap toilets and signs about avalanche *(Continues on page 245)*

Popular campground at Meziadin Lake. (© Carol P. Murdock)

MEZIADIN JUNCTION Esso

Gas • Diesel • Tire Repair
Home Cooked Meals at Cafe
RV Sites
Friendly Tourist Information

– Caravan Discount –
for Fuel

Open 7:00AM to 9:00PM
Summer Hours 6:00AM to 10:00PM

250-636-9240

Highway 37's Most Unique All Service Lodge — bell II LODGE
Gas/Diesel/Propane • Restaurant • RV & Tent Sites • Log Style Chalets • All Services
Tel (604) 881-8530 • Toll Free 1-877-617-2288 • Website www.bell2lodge.com

Stewart–Hyder Access Road

This paved spur road junctions with the Cassiar Highway at **Milepost J 96.2** and leads west 38.1 miles/61.4 km to Stewart, BC, and Hyder, AK. All visitor services are available at the 2 communities. Major area attractions include Bear Glacier (along the access road), Salmon Glacier and Fish Creek bear viewing area.

Distance is measured from Meziadin Lake Junction (M).

HIGHWAY 37A WEST

M 0 Junction with Cassiar Highway at Milepost J 96.2. Visitor information cabin.

M 7.6 (12.2 km) Surprise Creek bridge.

M 7.9 (12.7 km) Turnout.

M 10 (16.1 km) Turnout to north with view of hanging glaciers.

M 10.3 (16.6 km) Turnout to south with view of hanging glaciers.

M 11.4 (18.4 km) Windy Point bridge.

M 12 (19.4 km) Entrance bridge.

M 12.7 (20.5 km) Cornice Creek bridge.

M 13.3 (21.5 km) Strohn Creek bridge.

M 15 (24.2 km) Turnouts along lake into which **Bear Glacier** calves its icebergs. Watch for falling rock from slopes above road in spring. Morning light is best for photographing spectacular Bear Glacier. At one time the glacier reached this side of the valley; the old highway can be seen hundreds of feet above the present road.

M 18 (29.1 km) Cullen River bridge.

M 18.6 (30 km) Huge delta of accumulated avalanche snow. No shoulder, no stopping.

M 21.2 (34.1 km) Argyle Creek.

M 22.6 (36.4 km) Narrow, steep-walled Bear River canyon. Watch for rocks on road.

M 24.2 (39 km) Turnout with litter barrel to north.

M 29.2 (47 km) Turnout with litter barrel to southeast.

M 29.8 (48.1 km) Bitter Creek bridge.

M 32.1 (51.7 km) Wards Pass cemetery. The straight stretch of road along here is the former railbed from Stewart.

M 36.4 (58.7 km) Bear River bridge and welcome portal to Stewart.

M 36.7 (59.1 km) **Bear River RV Park**. See display ad this section.

M 38.1 (61.4 km) Highway joins main street of Stewart (description follows).

M 40.5 (65.2 km) **U.S.–Canada Border**. Hyder (description follows). TIME ZONE CHANGE: Stewart observes Pacific time, Hyder observes Alaska time.

Stewart, BC–Hyder, AK

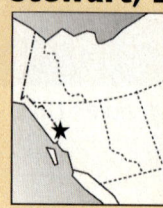

Stewart is at the head of Portland Canal on the AK–BC border. **Hyder** is 2.3 miles/3.7 km beyond Stewart. **Population: Stewart** 500; **Hyder** 102. **Emergency Services:** In Stewart, RCMP, phone (250) 636-2233. EMS personnel and Medivac helicopter. **Fire Department,** phone (250) 636-2345. **Hospital** and **Ambulance,** Stewart Health Care Facility (10 beds), phone (250) 636-2221. Canadian Customs at Hyder–Stewart Border Crossing. Open 24 hours a day, 7 days a week. No U.S. Customs

Visitor Information: Stewart Visitor Infocentre (Box 306, Stewart, BC V0T 1W0), located in Chamber of Commerce/ Infocentre Building on 5th Avenue; phone (250) 636-9224, toll-free 1-888-366-5999, fax (250) 636-2199, www.stewartbchyderak.home stead.com/homepage.html. Limited off-season hours.

Bicycles for local touring are free of charge at Stewart's Visitor Infocentre.
(© Blake Hanna, staff)

Elevation: Sea level. **Climate:** Maritime, with warm winters and cool rainy summers. Summer temperatures range from 50°F/11°C to 68°F/20°C; winter temperatures range from 25°F/-4°C to 43°F/6°C. Average temperature in January is 27°F/-3°C; in July, 67°F/19°C. Reported record high 89°F/32°C, record low -18°F/-28°C. Slightly less summer rain than other Northwest communities, but heavy snowfall in winter. **Radio:** CBC 1415. **Television:** Cable, 15 channels.

Private Aircraft: Stewart airport, on 5th Street; elev. 10 feet/3m; length 3,900 feet/ 1,189m; asphalt; fuel 80, 100.

STEWART ADVERTISERS

Bitter Creek Cafe ....Ph. (250) 636-2166
King Edward Hotel/
 Motel ....Ph. (250) 636-2244
Rainey Creek Municipal Campground
 & RV Park....................Ph. (250) 636-2537
Ripley Creek Inn...............Ph. (250) 636-2344
Stewart Cassiar Tourism
 Council.......................Ph. (250) 636-2518

Hyder's motto is "The Friendliest Little Ghost Town in Alaska." (© Rich Reid, Colors of Nature)

CASSIAR HIGHWAY • Stewart • Hyder

Description

Stewart and Hyder are on a spur of the Cassiar Highway, at the head of Portland Canal, a narrow saltwater fjord approximately 90 miles/145 km long. The fjord forms a natural boundary between Alaska and Canada. Stewart has a deep harbour and boasts of being Canada's most northerly ice-free port.

Prior to the coming of the white man, Nass River Indians knew the head of Portland Canal as *Skam-A-Kounst,* meaning safe place, probably referring to the place as a retreat from the harassment of the coastal Haidas. The Nass came here annually to hunt birds and pick berries. Little evidence of their presence remains.

In 1896, Captain D.D. Gaillard (after whom the Gaillard Cut in the Panama Canal was later named) explored Portland Canal for the U.S. Army Corps of Engineers. Two years after Gaillard's visit, the first prospectors and settlers arrived. Among them was D.J. Raine, for whom a creek and mountain in the area were named. The Stewart brothers arrived in 1902 and in 1905 Robert M. Stewart, the first postmaster, named the town Stewart. Hyder was first called Portland City. It was then renamed Hyder, after Canadian mining engineer Frederick B. Hyder, when the U.S. Postal Authority told residents there were already too many cities named Portland.

Gold and silver mining dominated the early economy. Hyder boomed with the discovery of rich silver veins in the upper Salmon River basin in 1917–18. Hundreds of pilings, which supported structures during this boom period, are visible on the tidal flats at Hyder.

Hyder became an access and supply point for the mines, while Stewart served as the centre for Canadian mining activity. Mining ceased in 1956, with the exception of the Granduc copper mine, which operated until 1984. Today the economy is driven by forestry, mining and tourism.

Lodging & Services

Stewart: 2 hotels/motels, 5 restaurants, 2 grocery stores, 4 churches, service stations, laundromat, pharmacy available at hospital, post office, a bank (open Monday, Wednesday and Friday), ATM, liquor store, visitor information, museum 2 gift shops and other shops. Camping at Bear River RV Park and Rainey Creek Muncipal Campground. ▲

Ripley Creek Inn. Fine, affordable accommodation overlooking estuary with fantastic mountain vistas. Located in lane behind 306–5th Avenue office. 18 unique rooms in lodge and adjoining historic buildings. Suites furnished with antiques; spacious, quiet and private. Decks, common areas and sauna. Additional units available in our 1928 brothel and in historic Bayview Hotel, also home of renowned Bitter Creek Cafe. Pets on approval. Phone (250) 636-2344; fax (250) 636-2623; email kamermans@yahoo.com; www.ripleycreekinn.homestead.com. [ADVERTISEMENT]

Hyder: 5 gift shops, a post office, 2 cafes, 2 motels and 2 bars, laundromat, museum and a Baptist church. There is no bank in Hyder. There is an ATM in Stewart.

Kathy's Korner Bed & Breakfast. Located on Main Street in central Hyder, AK, with all village amenities within walking distance. Only 3 miles from the world famous Fish Creek Bear Viewing Area. Three nonsmoking bedrooms. Two shared full bathrooms. Phone (250) 636-2393; fax (250) 636-2343; email kathys_korner@hotmail.com. ADVERTISEMENT]

Transportation

Bus: Limousine service to Terrace with connections to Greyhound and airlines.

Private Boats: Public dock and boat launch available.

Attractions

Historic Buildings: In Stewart, the former fire hall at 6th and Columbia streets built in 1910, which now houses the Historical Society Museum; the Empress Hotel on 4th Street; and St. Mark's Church (built in 1910) on 9th Street at Columbia. On the

---

RAINEY CREEK MUNICIPAL CAMPGROUND & RV PARK

Operated by: Stewart/Hyder International Chamber of Commerce

- 98 shaded, gravelled sites, each with picnic table.
- 65 sites with electrical hookup.
- Flush toilets, coin shower for registered guests only, public phone, horseshoe pits, tennis courts and nature walk.
- Five minute walk from downtown.

Reservations:
May - Sept. call (250) 636-2537
Off Season call 1-888-366-5999
P.O. Box 306-MP, Stewart, BC V0T 1W0
Fax (250) 636-2668
E-mail: stewhydcofc@hotmail.com
www.raineycreekcampground.homestead.com

YOUR HOME AWAY FROM HOME! ...in STEWART, B.C.

- Kitchenettes Available
- All Units Air Conditioned
- Licensed Dining Room
- Coffee Shop
- Lounge
- Pets Welcome
- Seafood is Our Specialty
- Fair Exchange on U.S. Currency

The KING EDWARD HOTEL MOTEL

Box 86 - 5th Avenue, Stewart, B.C. V0T 1W0   Toll Free 1-800-663-3126
Fax 250-636-9160   •   Phone 250-636-2244   •   www.kingedwardhotel.com

---

The RIPLEY CREEK INN

...for a memorable stay in quiet, affordable luxury. 17 unique rooms furnished with antiques. Carefully detailed woodwork and great views.
PH: (250) 636-2344   FAX: 636-2623
www.ripleycreekinn.homestead.com
kamermans@yahoo.com

BITTER CREEK CAFÉ

Since opening in 1994 the café has maintained a reputation for the finest quality seafood dinners and a menu that is always fresh, innovative ...and still 'Homemade'.
PHONE (250) 636-2166   FAX 636-2623
www.bittercreek.homestead.com

EAT WELL.   STAY WELL.
See log ad this section

CASSIAR HIGHWAY • Stewart • Hyder

Stewart–Hyder Access Road (continued)

Spectacular Bear Glacier calves icebergs into this lake at Milepost 15 of Highway 37A West. (© Blake Hanna, staff)

border at Eagle Point is the stone storehouse built by Captain D.D. Gaillard of the U.S. Army Corps of Engineers in 1896. This is the oldest masonry building in Alaska. Originally 4 of these buildings were built to hold exploration supplies. This one was subse-

quently used as a cobbler shop and jail. Storehouses Nos. 3 and 4 are included on the (U.S.) National Register of Historic Places.

Stewart Historical Society Museum, in the fire hall, has a wildlife exhibit on the main floor and an exhibit of historical items on the top floor. Included is a display on movies filmed here: "Bear Island" (1978), John Carpenter's "The Thing" (1981), "The Ice Man" (1982) and "Leaving Normal."

Toaster Museum. This unique private museum is located in the Ripley Creek Inn's registration office. More than 500 different toasters are on display.

Boundary Gallery & Gifts. Specializing in beautiful hand-made beads. Representing over a dozen local artists, featuring fine art, cards, candles, glass sun catchers, paw print castings, and walking sticks. Try our "Fresh Fudge," from traditional Chocolate to exotic Pina Colada. Passports stamped; copy and fax service available. Located on the border in Hyder. http://boundarygalleryandgifts.homestead.com.
[ADVERTISEMENT]

HYDER ADVERTISERS

Boundary Gallery & Gifts	Ph. (250) 636-2658
Grand View Inn, The	Ph. (250) 636-9174
Kathy's Korner Bed & Breakfast	Ph. (250) 636-2393
Sealaska Inn	Ph. (250) 636-2486
Wildflour Coffee Shop	Ph. (250) 636-2875

Hyder's night life is well-known, and has helped Hyder earn the reputation and town motto of "The Friendliest Little Ghost Town in Alaska."

Salmon Glacier. Take a self-guided or guided sightseeing tour out Salmon Glacier Road to see spectacular **Salmon Glacier**. The toe of Salmon Glacier is seen at Mile 17.2/27.7 km Salmon Glacier Road. Summit Viewpoint at Mile 22.9/37 km provides a spectacular view of the glacier.

Built to connect Stewart with mining interests to the north, Salmon Glacier Road is narrow and winding.

Fish Creek Wildlife Viewing Area, located 3 mile /4.8 km north of Hyder on Salmon Glacier Road, is a day-use recreation area operated by the U.S. Forest Service. Both brown (grizzly) and black bears can be easily observed and photographed here as they fish for chum and pink salmon in the shallow waters of Fish Creek and Marx Creek from mid-July through early September.

Viewing is from a boardwalk viewing area. Site rules are posted on the Tongass National Forest web site (www.fs.fed.us/r10/tongass/recreation).

International Days. Fourth of July begins July 1 as Stewart and Hyder celebrate Canada Day and Independence Day. Parade and fireworks.

International Rodeo. The Stewart–Hyder International Rodeo is held the second weekend in June.

Charter trips by small boat on Portland Canal and vicinity available for sightseeing and fishing. Flightseeing air tours available.

AREA FISHING: Portland Canal, salmon to 50 lbs., use herring, spring and late fall; coho to 12 lbs. in fall, fly-fishing. (NOTE: Alaska or British Columbia fishing license required, depending on whether you fish U.S. or Canadian waters in Portland Canal.) Excellent fishing for salmon and Dolly Varden at mouth of **Salmon River**. Up the Salmon River road from Hyder, Fish Creek has Dolly Varden 2 to 3 lbs., use salmon eggs and lures, best in summer. **Fish Creek** is a spawning ground for some of the world's largest chum salmon, mid-summer to fall; it is illegal to kill chum in fresh water in British Columbia. It is legal to harvest chum from both salt and fresh water in Alaska.

Return to Milepost J 96.2 on the Cassiar Highway

STAY IN ALASKA
HYDER
CAMP-RUN-A-MUCK FULL SERVICE RV PARK
30 Amp Drive Thrus • Phone • Showers
TV - LAUNDROMATS
Phone 250-636-9006

SEALASKA INN
Hotel	Bar	Restaurant
Lowest Rates	A Fun Saloon	Halibut to Pizza

Toll Free RV Park & Inn: 1-888-393-1199
Fax (250) 636-9003 • Phone (250) 636-2486
www.sealaskainn.com

The GRAND VIEW INN
Hyder's Best Accommodations
Daily and Weekly Rates
TV ❖ Kitchenettes ❖ Bus Tours Welcome
For reservations Call (250) 636-9174
Fax: (250) 636-2673 or (360) 983-3391
E-mail: grandviewhyder@yahoo.com
Visit our website at www.grandviewinn.net
Mail: Box 49, Hyder, AK 99923

WILDFLOUR COFFEE SHOP — HOMEMADE — Cinnamon Rolls & Muffins BREAKFAST EVERY DAY — FRESHLY GROUND COFFEE — HYDER, ALASKA
Open June to September - "Baking Daily"
Phone 250-636-2875 • Groups with Prior Notice

(Continued from page 241) control programs. Memorial plaque is dedicated to highway avalanche technicians killed in a slide here. The avalanche chutes are clearly visible on mountain slopes to the west in summer.

CAUTION: Avalanche area northbound to Ningunsaw Pass; no stopping in winter or spring.

J 161.6 (260 km) **AH 284.5** (457.9 km) Redflat Creek.

J 164.1 (264 km) **AH 282** (453.8 km) Revision Creek.

J 165.1 (265.6 km) **AH 281** (452.2 km) Fan Creek.

J 168.7 (271.4 km) **AH 277.4** (446.5 km) Turnout with litter barrels to east overlooking large moose pasture, beaver lodge.

J 169.6 (272.9 km) **AH 276.5** (445 km) **Ningunsaw Pass** (elev. 1,530 feet/466m). Nass–Stikine water divide; turnout with litter barrels to west beside **Ningunsaw River**. Mountain whitefish and Dolly Varden. The highway parallels the Ningunsaw northbound. Watch for fallen rock on road through the canyon. The Ningunsaw is a tributary of the Stikine watershed.

J 169.9 (273.4 km) **AH 276.2** (444.5 km) Beaverpond Creek Bridge.

J 170.3 (274 km) **AH 275.8** (443.9 km) Liz Creek Bridge.

J 172.7 (277.9 km) **AH 273.4** (440 km) Alger Creek. The massive piles of logs and debris in this creek are from a 1989 avalanche. Avalanche chutes visible to west.

J 174.8 (281.3 km) **AH 271.3** (436.7 km) Bend Creek.

J 175.6 (282.5 km) **AH 270.5** (435.4 km) Gamma Creek.

J 176.9 (284.1 km) **AH 269.2** (433.2 km) Ogilvie Creek. Pullout beside river.

J 177.8 (286.1 km) **AH 268.3** (431.9 km) Point of interest sign about Yukon Telegraph line: "Born of the Klondike Gold Rush of 1898, the 1,900-mile Dominion Telegraph Line linked Dawson City with Vancouver via the CPR wires through Ashcroft. Built in 1899–1901, the line blazed a route across the vast northern section of the Province but gave way to radio communications in the 1930s. Today, some of the trail and cabins used by the isolated telegraphers still serve wilderness travellers."

J 178 (286.4 km) **AH 268.1** (431.5 km) Echo Lake. Flooded telegraph cabins are visible in the lake below. Good view of Coast Mountains to west. Spectacular cliffs seen to the east are part of the Skeena Mountains (Bowser Basin).

J 181 (291.2 km) **AH 265.1** (426.6 km) Bob Quinn Forest Service Road, under construction as the Iskut Mining Road, will provide year-round access to goldfields west of the Ningunsaw River. The road will follow the Iskut River Valley toward the Stikine River, with a side branch to Eskay Creek gold deposit. CAUTION: Watch for turning trucks.

J 181.5 (292 km) **AH 264.6** (425.9 km) **Little Bob Quinn Lake**, rainbow and Dolly Varden, summer and fall. Access to Bob Quinn Lake at **Milepost J 183.3**.

J 182.2 (293.2 km) **AH 263.9** (424.7 km) Bob Quinn flight airstrip. This is a staging site for supplies headed for the Stikine/Iskut goldfields. Paved rest area with litter barrels, picnic tables and toilet.

J 183.3 (295 km) **AH 262.8** (423 km) Bob Quinn highway maintenance camp; helicopter base. Emergency assistance. Access to Bob Quinn Lake; toilet, picnic table, cartop boat launch.

J 187 (300.9 km) **AH 259.1** (417 km) Gravel turnout with litter barrels on both sides of road.

J 190.2 (306.1 km) **AH 255.9** (411.8 km) Devil Creek Canyon bridge.

J 191.1 (307.5 km) **AH 255** (410.5 km) Gravel turnout with litter barrel to west.

J 191.6 (308.3 km) **AH 254.5** (409.6 km) Devil Creek Forest Service Road.

J 193.6 (311.5 km) **AH 252.5** (406.4 km) Thomas Creek.

Highway passes through Iskut burn, where fire destroyed 78,000 acres in 1958. This is also British Columbia's largest huckleberry patch.

Northbound, the vegetation begins to change to northern boreal white and black spruce. This zone has cold, long winters and low forest productivity. Look for trembling aspen and lodgepole pine.

Southbound, the vegetation changes to become part of the interior cedar–hemlock zone. Cool wet winters and long dry summers produce a variety of tree species including western hemlock and red cedar, hybrid white spruce and subalpine fir.

CAUTION: Watch for turning trucks.

J 196.3 (315.9 km) **AH 249.8** (402 km) Large gravel turnout to west.

J 197.3 (317.5 km) **AH 248.8** (400.5 km) Slate Creek.

J 199 (320.2 km) **AH 247.1** (397.7 km) Brake-check pullout.

J 199.7 (321.3 km) **AH 246.4** (396.6 km) Durham Creek.

J 205.1 (330.1 km) **AH 241** (387.9 km) **Burrage River** Bridge. Note rock pinnacle upstream to east.

J 205.5 (330.7 km) **AH 240.6** (387.2 km) Iskut River to west. Small pull-out.

J 206.8 (332.8 km) **AH 239.3** (385.2 km) Gravel turnout to west.

J 207.8 (334.4 km) **AH 238.3** (383.6 km) Turnout with litter barrels. Former emergency airstrip crosses road.

J 213 (342.7 km) **AH 233.1** (375.1 km) Rest area by Eastman Creek; picnic tables, outhouses, litter barrels, and information sign with map and list of services in Iskut Lakes Recreation Area. The creek was named for George Eastman (of Eastman Kodak fame), who hunted big game in this area before the highway was built.

J 216 (347.6 km) **AH 230.1** (370.3 km) Slow down for narrow 2-lane bridge across Rescue Creek.

J 217.9 (350.6 km) **AH 228.2** (367.2 km) Narrow 2-lane bridge over Willow Creek.

J 218.3 (351.3 km) **AH 227.8** (366.6 km) Willow Creek Forest Service Road.

J 220.6 (355 km) **AH 225.5** (362.9 km) Natadesleen Lake trailhead to west; toilets and litter barrel. Hike 0.6 mile/1 km west to lake.

J 225.1 (362.2 km) **AH 221** (355.7 km) Entrance to **Kinaskan Provincial Park** campground with 50 sites, outhouses, firewood, picnic and day-use area, wheelchair access, swimming, 2 hiking trails, drinking water and boat launch on Kinaskan Lake; rainbow fishing, July and August. Start of 15-mile/24.1-km hiking trail to Mowdade Lake in Mount Edziza Provincial Park.

J 230.1 (370.3 km) **AH 216** (347.6 km) Turnout to west.

J 231.1 (371.9 km) **AH 215** (346.1 km) Pullout with litter barrel at small lake to east.

J 233.1 (375.1 km) **AH 213** (342.8 km) Gravel turnout.

J 233.4 (375.6 km) **AH 212.7** (342.3 km) Todagin Creek 1-lane bridge, northbound traffic yields.

J 240.7 (387.4 km) **AH 205.4** (330.6 km) Resort with gas, diesel, food, lodging, camping and air charter service.

Harbour Air Ltd. See display ad this section.

Looking south toward snowcapped mountains along the Cassiar.
(© Bob Butterfield)

HARBOUR AIR LTD

Flightseeing Adventures
Fly-in Fishing & Hunting
Hiking & Sightseeing

Float Plane Base at
Tatogga Lake Resort Mile J240.7

(250) 234-3526
Write P.O. Box 59, Iskut, B.C. V0J 2K0

Total driving distance on the Cassiar is 446.1 miles/718 km.

Tatogga Lake Resort. See display ad this section.

J 241.3 (388.3 km) **AH 204.8** (329.7 km) Coyote Creek.

J 244.5 (393.4 km) **AH 201.6** (324.5 km) Boat launch and picnic table.

J 244.6 (393.6 km) **AH 201.5** (324.3 km) Turnout beside **Eddontenajon Lake** (Ed-don-TEN-ajon); picnic tables, litter barrels and toilets. It is unlawful to camp overnight at turnouts. People drink from the lake; be careful not to contaminate it. Use dump stations. Spatsizi trailhead to east. Lake breaks up in late May; freezeup is early November. Rainbow fishing July and August.

J 248.2 (399.4 km) **AH 197.9** (318.6 km) Food, lodging, camping, propane and tire repair at Tenajon Motel and Restaurant and Red Goat Lodge (descriptions follow).

Red Goat Lodge. Lovely treed lakeshore setting with power, water for RVs and sani-dump. Coin showers, laundry, phone. Bed and Breakfast with unparalleled reputation. Modern cabins. Canoe rentals. Fishing is excellent from shore. Choose Red Goat for a special vacation experience. AAA approved and undoubtedly one of the finest facilities on Highway 37. Open year-round. Your hosts, Jacquie and Mitch. Phone/fax (250) 234-3261. Email redgoatlodge@aol.com. [ADVERTISEMENT]

Tenajon Motel & Restaurant. Open year-round. Restaurant offers home-style cooking and fresh home baking. Friendly atmosphere. Clean, affordable rooms. Close to fantastic rainbow trout fishing and good hunting. Minor tire and mechanical repairs. Propane bottle filling. Phone (250) 234-3141; fax (250) 234-3603. Your hosts, Joe and Chelan Benoit. P.O. Box 120, Iskut, BC V0J 1K0. [ADVERTISEMENT]

J 250 (402.3 km) **AH 196.1** (315.6 km) Zetu Creek. B.C. Hydro generating plant, supplies power for Iskut area.

J 250.2 (402.6 km) **AH 195.9** (315.3 km) **ISKUT** (pop. 300). **Clinic:** Phone (250) 234-3511. Small Tahltan Native community with post office in the Kluachon Centre on the highway, grocery store, public phone, motel and gas station. Quality leather goods available locally. Camping and cabins available at local lodges and guest ranches. Horse trips, canoe rentals and river rafting may be available; inquire at local lodges and resorts.

Kluachon Centre. See display ad this section.

Private Aircraft: Eddontenajon airstrip, 0.6 mile/1 km north of Iskut; elev. 3,100 feet/945m; length 3,000 feet/914m; gravel; fuel available.

NOTE: Watch for road repair and seal coating under way southbound to Iskut in summer 2003.

J 251.8 (405.2 km) **AH 194.3** (312.7 km) **Mountain Shadow RV Park & Campground.** Only 1/3 mile off highway. Quiet, secluded, park-like setting with spectacular mountain vistas and lake views. Short nature walk to Kluachon Lake with excellent fishing. Wilderness trails, bird and wildlife viewing. A unique and breathtaking wilderness setting. [ADVERTISEMENT]

J 255.2 (410.7 km) **AH 190.9** (307.2 km) **Bear Paw Resort.** See display ad this section.

J 256 (412 km) **AH 190.1** (306 km) **Trapper's Souvenirs.** See display ad this

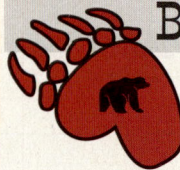

Tatooga Lake at Milepost J 240.7. (© Bob Butterfield)

section.

J 257.6 (414.5 km) **AH 188.5** (303.4 km) Tsaybahe Creek. Watch for beaver lodges which are visible from the highway.

J 260.6 (419.3 km) **AH 185.5** (298.5 km) Rest area, toilets, picnic tables. Turnout with litter barrels to west. From here the dormant volcano of **Mount Edziza** (elev. 9,143 feet/2,787m) and its adjunct cinder cone can be seen to the southwest. The park, not accessible by road, is a rugged wilderness with a glacier, cinder cones, craters and lava flows. Panoramic view of Skeena and Cassiar mountains for next several miles northbound. Information signs.

J 261.8 (421.3 km) **AH 184.3** (296.6 km) Turnoff to Morchuea Lake B.C. Forest Service campsite. Rustic, some tables, rock fire rings (bring firewood), no fee. ▲

J 264 (424.8 km) **AH 182.1** (293.1 km) Entering Stikine River Recreation Area.

J 264.7 (426 km) **AH 181.4** (291.9 km) Pullout with litter barrel; brake check area. *NOTE: Steep (8 percent) grade northbound.*

J 266.3 (428.5 km) **AH 179.8** (289.4 km) *Winding road next 1.2 miles/2 km northbound.*

J 267.2 (430 km) **AH 178.9** (287.9 km) *Hairpin turn: Keep to right. Highway descends to Stikine River in switchbacks.*

J 269 (432.9 km) **AH 177.1** (285 km) Turnout with litter barrels and toilets to south. Tourist map and services directory for area located here.

J 269.5 (433.7 km) **AH 176.6** (284.3 km) Stikine River bridge. Turnout at north end of bridge.

J 271.3 (436.6 km) **AH 174.8** (281.4 km) Turnout to east.

J 273.4 (440 km) **AH 172.7** (278 km) Leaving Stikine River Recreation Area northbound. Brake check pullout with litter barrel.

J 279 (449 km) **AH 167.1** (268.9 km) Large gravel turnout with litter barrel to east at Tees Creek.

J 282 (453..8 km) **AH 164.1** (264.1 km) Gravel turnout with litter barrel to east.

J 283.9 (456.8 km) **AH 162.2** (261.1 km) Gravel turnout to east.

J 284.2 (457.3 km) **AH 161.9** (260.5 km) **Upper Gnat Lake Rest Area**; litter barrels. Long scar across Gnat Pass valley to east is grading preparation for B.C. Railway's proposed Dease Lake extension from Prince George. Construction was halted in 1977. Grade is visible for several miles northbound.

J 285.8 (459.9 km) **AH 160.3** (258 km) Turnout overlooking **Lower Gnat Lake**, abundant rainbow; litter barrel. ⚓

J 287.9 (463.3 km) **AH 158.2** (254.7 km) Turnout with litter barrel.

J 290.6 (467.6 km) **AH 155.5** (250.2 km) **Gnat Pass Summit**, elev. 4,072 feet/1,241m. Watch for caribou in spring.

J 291.7 (469.4 km) **AH 154.4** (248.5 km) *Steep 6 percent downgrade northbound.*

J 295.2 (475 km) **AH 150.9** (242.8 km) **Tanzilla River** bridge. Pleasant rest area with picnic tables and outhouses at north end of bridge beside river. Fishing for grayling to 16 inches, June and July; use flies. ⚓

Dease Lake Lions Tanzilla River Campground. 16 natural wooded RV sites plus tenting on Tanzilla River, adjacent to Highway 37. Facilities: Picnic tables, firepits, overnight or day-use, no hookups, non-flush toilets. Fees: $7 per night, $3 per bundle for firewood. Voluntary donation for day-use. ▲
[ADVERTISEMENT]

J 296.5 (477.1 km) **AH 149.6** (240.7 km) Dalby Creek.

J 298.2 (479.9 km) **AH 147.9** (238 km) Turnout with litter barrel to west.

J 300.1 (483 km) **AH 146** (235 km) Divide (elev. 2,690 feet/820m) between Pacific and Arctic ocean watersheds.

J 300.4 (483.4 km) **AH 145.7** (234.6 km) Chamber of Commerce pullout to west; 2 handicap accessible toilets, change tables, information signs for area; litter barrels.

J 300.5 (483.6 km) **AH 145.6** (234.3 km) **Dease Lake R.V. Park**. See display ad this section. ▲

J 300.7 (483.9 km) **AH 165.4** (266.2 km) Turnout with information sign.

J 300.9 (484.2 km) **AH 145.2** (233.7 km) **Dease Lake Junction**. Access west to Dease Lake (description follows) and Telegraph Creek.

Junction with Telegraph Creek Road. See "Telegraph Creek Road" log beginning on page 248.

Dease Lake

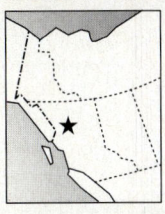

Located just west of the Cassiar Highway. **Emergency Services:** RCMP detachment. **Private Aircraft:** Dease Lake airstrip, 1.5 miles/2.4 km south; elev. 2,600 feet/792m; length 6,000 feet/1,829m; asphalt; fuel JP4, 100. Vis-

DEASE LAKE ADVERTISERS

Arctic Divide Inn and
  Motel ....Ph. (250) 771-3119
Dease Lake RV Park ....Ph. (250) 771-4666
Dease Lake Service
  Station ....Ph. (250) 771-5329
Northway Motor Inn
  & Restaurant................Ph. (250) 771-5341
Trapper's Den Gift
  Shoppe, The ....Ph. (250) 771-3224

DEASE LAKE R.V. PARK

◆ Level Pull-Throughs
◆ Full and Partial Hook-ups
◆ 30 Amp Service

Hosts Bill & Margaret

P.O. Box 129, Dease Lake, BC V0C 1L0

Phone (250) 771-4666
Fax (250) 771-4667

NORTHWAY MOTOR INN & RESTAURANT
AN "OASIS" ON HIGHWAY 37   **TOLL FREE: 1-866-888-2588**

• 46 Modern Rooms
• TV • Kitchenettes
• Licensed Restaurant
• Winter Plug-ins

Motel Phone: (250) 771-5341
Motel Fax: (250) 771-5342

Restaurant Phone:
(250) 771-4114

P.O. Box 158
Dease Lake, BC V0C 1L0

RESTAURANT located on main highway, open May - October.
MOTEL located on side street, open year round.

Telegraph Creek Road

The Grand Canyon of the Stikine River en route to Telegraph Creek. (© Blake Hanna, staff)

Built in 1922, this was the first road in the Cassiar area of northern British Columbia. The scenery is remarkable and the town of Telegraph Creek is a picture from the turn of the century. Many of the original buildings remain from the gold rush days.

CAUTION: Telegraph Creek Road has some steep narrow sections and several sets of steep switchbacks; it is not recommended for trailers or large RVs. Car and camper drivers who are familiar with mountain driving should have no difficulty, although some motorists consider it a challenging drive even for the experienced. DRIVE CAREFULLY! Use caution when road is wet or icy. Watch for rocks and mud. There are no visitor facilities en route. Allow a minimum of 2 hours driving time with good conditions. Check road conditions at highway maintenance camp or RCMP office in Dease Lake before starting the 70.1 miles/112.8 km to Telegraph Creek. Phone the Stikine River-Song Cafe (250) 235-3196 for weather and road conditions.

Distance from Dease Lake junction (D) on the Cassiar Highway is shown.

D 0 **Dease Lake junction**, Milepost J 300.9 Cassiar Highway.

D 0.9 (1.4 km) **Junction** with road to Dease Lake. Turn left for Telegraph Creek.

D 1.4 (2.3 km) Entrance to airport.

D 3.1 (5 km) *Pavement ends, gravel begins westbound.*

D 5 (8 km) Entering Tanzilla Plateau.

D 7.2 (11.6 km) Tatsho Creek (Eightmile).

D 15.7 (25.3 km) 16 Mile Creek.

D 16.9 (27.2 km) Augustchilde Creek, 1-lane bridge.

D 18.6 (30 km) 19 Mile Creek.

D 18.7 (30.1 km) Turnout to east with litter barrel.

D 20 (32.3 km) 22 Mile Creek. Turnout with litter barrels south.

D 21.7 (35 km) Kilmetrepost 35.

D 22.2 (35.8 km) Tanzilla River to south.

D 24.3 (39.2 km) Turnout with litter barrel.

D 27.9 (45 km) Kilmetreost 45.

D 31.9 (51.3 km) Moose Horn swamp.

D 36.6 (59 km) Entering **Stikine River Recreation Area**. Turnout with toilet. Short walk uphill for good views and photographs.

D 37.7 (60.7 km) Approximate halfway point to Telegraph Creek from Dease Lake. Turnout with litter barrels to north. Excellent view of Mount Edziza on clear days.

D 42.1 (67.8 km) CAUTION: *Begin 18 percent grade as road descends canyon; steep and narrow with switchbacks.*

D 46.1 (74.2 km) Turnout with litter barrels to south.

D 47.3 (76.1 km) Tuya River bridge. Turnout with litter barrel.

D 49 (79 km) Y–intersection. Old road to left; keep right for newer section westbound.

D 50.2 (80.8 km) Old road rejoins newer road.

D 50.8 (81.7 km) Golden Bear Mine access road. Private.

D 51.5 (82.9 km) CAUTION: *20 percent downhill grade for approximately 0.6 mile/ 1 km.* Day's Ranch on left.

D 51.8 (83.4 km) Small turnout with litter barrels; excellent viewpoint.

D 54.6 (87.9 km) Rest area with table, toilet and litter barrel; overlooks river gorge.

D 56.1 (90.3 km) Road runs through lava beds, on narrow promontory about 150 feet/51m wide, dropping 400 feet/122m on each side to Tahltan and Stikine rivers. Excellent views of the **Grand Canyon of the Stikine** and Tahltan Canyon can be seen by walking a short distance across lava beds to promontory point. Best views of the river canyon are by flightseeing trip. The Stikine River canyon is only 8 feet/2.4m wide at its narrowest point.

D 56.4 (90.9 km) CAUTION: *Sudden 180-degree right turn begins 18 percent downhill grade to Tahltan River and Indian fishing camps.*

D 56.8 (91.5 km) **Tahltan River** bridge. Turnout with litter barrel south, on north side of bridge. Traditional communal Indian smokehouses adjacent to road at bridge. Smokehouse on north side of bridge is operated by a commercial fisherman; fresh and smoked salmon sold. There is a commercial inland fishery on the Stikine River, one of only a few such licensed operations in Canada.

D 57.2 (92.1 km) CAUTION: Begin section of very narrow road on ledge rising steeply up the wall of the Stikine Canyon next 3 miles/4.8 km, rising to 400 feet/122m above the river.

D 60.4 (97.3 km) Ninemile Creek.

D 60.5 (97.4 km) Old **Tahltan** Indian community above road. *Private property: No trespassing!* Former home of Tahltan bear dogs. The Tahltan bear dog, believed to be extinct, was only about a foot high and weighed about 15 lbs. Short-haired, with oversize ears and shaving-brush tail, the breed was recognized by the Canadian Kennel Club. First seen by explorer Samuel Black in 1824, the dogs were used to hunt bears.

D 62.1 (100 km) Eightmile Creek. Spectacular falls into canyon on left below. There is a trailhead and parking on the west side of the creek opposite the old gravel pit at the top of the hill.

D 63.4 (102.1 km) Turnout with litter barrel. Good photo ops of Stikine Canyon.

D 68.9 (111 km) Indian community. Road follows steep winding descent into old town, crossing a deep narrow canyon via a short bridge. Excellent picture spot 0.2

mile/0.3 km from bridge.

D 69.5 (111.9 km) **Glenora Road junction**; 12-mile/19.3-km road leads west to Glenora, site of attempted railroad route to the Yukon and limit of larger riverboat navigation. There are 2 primitive B.C. Forest Service campsites on the road to Glenora. Several spur roads lead to the Stikine River and to Native fish camps. ▲

D 70 (112.7 km) **TELEGRAPH CREEK** (pop. 300; elev. 1,100 feet/335m). Former head of navigation on the Stikine and once a telegraph communication terminal. During the gold rush, an estimated 5,000 stampeders set off from Telegraph Creek to attempt the Stikine–Teslin Trail to the goldfields in Atlin and the Klondike.

There are a cafe, lodge, general store, post office, and a public school and nursing station here. Gas, minor auto and tire repair are available. Anglican church services held weekly; Roman Catholic services held every other week.

Stikine RiverSong. Located on the bank of "The Great River," the RiverSong offers nostalgic accommodations in a renovated historic (1898) Hudson's Bay Post. Great food, including fresh homemade bread, soups, pies and sockeye salmon. Comfortable rooms include shared bath, sitting room and kitchens. Tour the historic Stikine River route to the Klondike. Jet boat tours into the Grand Canyon; 1-1/2 hour, half-day and day trips. Reservations recommended. Free public Internet access. Phone/fax (250) 235-3196; email info@stikineriversong.com; or visit www.stikineriversong.com. See display ad this section. [ADVERTISEMENT]

Residents make their living fishing commercially for salmon, doing local construction work and guiding visitors on hunting, fishing and river trips. Telegraph Creek is becoming a jumping-off point for wilderness hikers headed for Mount Edziza Provincial Park.

The scenic view along the main street bordering the river has scarcely changed since gold rush days. The 1898 Hudson's Bay Co. post, which now houses the RiverSong Cafe, is a recognized Heritage Building. Historic St. Aidan's Church (Anglican) and several other buildings pre-dating 1930 are also located here.

Canoeing, kayaking and rafting the lower 130 miles of the Stikine River from Telegraph Creek to Wrangell, AK, is a popular wilderness adventure. The Class I and II river trip takes about 4 days. Stikine River boating etiquette and information on public recreation cabins within the Stikine–LeConte Wilderness are available on the Tongass National Forest web site (www.fs.fed.us/r10/tongass/recreation/). Guided Stikine River trips and charter flights are available locally.

Return to Milepost J 300.9
Cassiar Highway

www.themilepost.com

A black bear poses among the flowers along a British Columbia highway.
(© Carol P. Murdock)

itor Information: Write Dease Lake and Tahltan District Chamber of Commerce, Box 338, Dease Lake, BC V0C 1L0; phone (250) 771-3900.

Dease Lake has motels, RV park, gas stations (with regular, unleaded, diesel, propane and minor repairs), food stores, restaurant, a post office, hardware/sporting goods, highway maintenance centre and government offices. Information kiosks at south entrance to town. ▲

The Trapper's Den Gift Shoppe. Quality Canadian and British Columbian gift items ranging from local jade to Native moccasins and cottage crafts. Probably the most reasonable jade prices around. Located near southwest corner of Petro Canada gas station, 500 feet off Highway 37. Look for the old log trapper's cabin. VISA/MasterCard accepted. (250) 771-3224. [ADVERTISEMENT]

A Hudson's Bay Co. post was established by Robert Campbell at Dease Lake in 1838, but abandoned a year later. The lake was named in 1834 by John McLeod of the Hudson's Bay Co. for Chief Factor Peter Warren Dease. Laketon, on the west side of the lake (see **Milepost J 327.7**), was a centre for boat building during the Cassiar gold rush of 1872–80. In 1874, William Moore, following an old Indian trail, cut a trail from Telegraph Creek on the Stikine River to the gold rush settlement on Dease Lake. This trail became Telegraph Creek Road, which was used in 1941 to haul supplies for Alaska Highway construction and Watson Lake Airport to Dease Lake. The supplies were then ferried down the Dease River.

Today, Dease Lake is a government centre and supply point for the district. Northern Lights College (University of Northern British Columbia) has a campus here. The community has dubbed itself the "jade capital of the world." It is also a popular point from which to fly-in, hike-in, or pack-in to Mount Edziza and Spatsizi wilderness parks.

Arctic Divide Inn and Motel. Centrally located on Highway 37. Inn is log construction, nonsmoking, with complimentary continental breakfast, common kitchenette, fitness room. Motel has drive-up rooms, smoking and pet rooms, 2 kitchenettes. All rooms clean, comfortable, spacious with ensuites, satellite TV, DD phones, outside plug-ins. Open year-round. Accept VISA, AMEX, MasterCard. Box 219, Dease Lake, BC V0C 1L0. Phone (250) 771-3119; fax (250) 771-3903; arcticdivide@stikine.net. [ADVERTISEMENT]

Cassiar Highway Log
(continued)

J 300.9 (484.2 km) **AH 145.2** (233.7 km) **Dease Lake Junction.** Access west to Dease Lake and Telegraph Creek.

> Junction with Telegraph Creek Road. See "Telegraph Creek Road" beginning on opposite page.

J 301.7 (485.5 km) **AH 144.4** (232.4 km) Hotel Creek.

J 308.8 (496.9 km) **AH 137.3** (220.9 km) Turnout with litter barrel to west.

J 309.6 (498.2 km) **AH 136.5** (219.7 km)

CASSIAR HIGHWAY

Simmons Lake at Milepost J 363.1 offers fishing for lake trout. (© Blake Hanna, staff)

Serpentine Creek.

J 313.5 (504.5 km) AH 132.6 (213.5 km) Gravel turnout to west.

J 315.7 (508 km) AH 130.4 (209.9 km) Gravel turnout to west with litter barrel and view.

J 316.3 (509 km) AH 129.8 (208.9 km) Halfmoon Creek.

J 318.8 (513 km) AH 127.3 (204.9 km) **Rabid Grizzly Rest Area** with picnic tables, travel information signs, litter barrels and handicap accessible toilets. View of Dease Lake.

J 322.2 (518.5 km) AH 123.9 (199.4 km) Gravel turnout to west; litter barrel.

J 324.2 (521.7 km) AH 121.9 (196.2 km) Black Creek.

J 326.3 (525.1 km) AH 119.8 (192.8 km) Turnoff (poorly marked) for **Sawmill Point Recreation Site** to west. Side road leads to **Dease Lake** for fishing; lake trout to 30 lbs., use spoons, plugs, spinners, June–Oct., deep trolling in summer, spin casting in fall.

J 327.2 (526.5 km) AH 118.9 (191.4 km) Dorothy Creek.

J 327.7 (527.3 km) AH 118.4 (190.5 km) The site of the ghost town **Laketon** lies across the lake. Laketon was the administrative centre for the district during the Cassiar gold rush (1872–80). Boat building was a major activity along the lake during the gold rush years, with miners heading up various creeks and rivers off the lake in search of gold. Today's miners ford the lake when the water is low to reach claims on the northwest side.

J 330.2 (531.3 km) AH 115.9 (186.5 km) Beady Creek. Entering the Cassiar Mountains northbound.

J 332.5 (535.1 km) AH 113.6 (182.9 km) Turnout to west with litter barrels. **Dease River** parallels the highway. Grayling to 17 inches; Dolly Varden and lake trout to 15 lbs.; northern pike 8 to 10 lbs., May through September.

Marshy areas to west; good moose pasture. Watch for wildlife, especially at dawn and dusk.

J 334.2 (537.8 km) AH 112.3 (180.7 km) Large turnout to west with litter barrels.

J 334.4 (538.1 km) AH 111.7 (179.7 km) Packer Tom Creek, named for a well-known Indian who lived in this area.

J 336.1 (540.8 km) AH 110 (177 km) Elbow Lake.

J 342 (550.3 km) AH 104.1 (167.5 km) Pyramid Creek.

J 342.4 (551 km) AH 103.7 (166.9 km) Dease River 2-lane concrete bridge.

Dease River Crossing RV & Campground. A beautiful stop along the Dease River. Easy RV access for large rigs. Pull-throughs. Lakefront RV parking. Excellent fishing. Canoe rentals and trips. Easy lake access. Cabins, hostel rooms. Sani-dump, new showers and laundry. Veterans welcome. See display ad this section. [ADVERTISEMENT] ▲

J 343.9 (553.5 km) AH 102.2 (164.5 km) Beale Creek.

J 347.2 (558.7 km) AH 98.9 (159.2 km) Turnout with litter barrel.

J 347.9 (559.8 km) AH 98.3 (158.2 km) Turnout beside **Pine Tree Lake**. Good

grayling and lake char fishing.

J 352.8 (567.7 km) AH 93.3 (150.2 km) **Moose Meadows**. Quiet, tranquil setting on Cotton Lake and Dease River. Log cabins and many sites right on the lake. Enjoy the scenery and the evening cry of the loons. Potential wildlife may include beaver, moose, mountain goats and a variety of birds. Dry sites. Hot showers. Drinking water. Pit toilets. Extra-long level pull-throughs. Covered tenting sites. Group sites. RV wash. Sani-dump. Tenters cabin. Boat launch. Fishing. Canoe rentals and shuttles. Canoe trips from 6 to 180 miles. Emergency phone. Reasonable rates. C–8, Jade City, BC V0C 1E0. Radio phone (250) N416219. Chicken Neck Channel. Voice call Whitehorse operator. See display ad this section. [ADVERTISEMENT] ▲

J 353.7 (569.2 km) AH 92.4 (148.7 km) Gravel turnout with litter barrels to east. Views of **Needlenose Mountain** southbound.

J 357.9 (575.9 km) AH 88.2 (141.9 km) **Cottonwood River** bridge; rest area 0.4 mile/0.6 km west on old highway on south side of river. Fishing for grayling and whitefish. Early summer runs of Dolly Varden.

J 358.7 (577.2 km) AH 87.4 (140.7 km) Cottonwood River rest area No. 2 is 0.5 mile/0.8 km west on old highway on north side of river.

J 363.6 (585.1 km) AH 82.5 (132.8 km) Large turnout to west beside **Simmons Lake**; information kiosk, picnic shelter and small beach. Fishing for lake trout.

J 365.2 (587.7 km) AH 80.9 (130.2 km) Small turnout to west.

J 365.3 (587.8 km) AH 80.8 (130 km) Road runs on causeway between Twin Lakes.

J 365.8 (588.6 km) AH 80.3 (129.2 km)

Dease River Crossing RV & Campground
Lakefront RV sites • Large pull-throughs • Easy RV access
Fire pits • Cabins • Fishing • Canoe rentals
VETERANS WELCOME

Moose Meadows
RV PARK • CAMPGROUND • RESORT
Quiet lake front location - Easy RV access
Extra long pull throughs - Hot showers - Free firewood
Potable drinking water - RV wash - Sani-dump
Log cabins - Canoe rentals & shuttles
FOR MORE INFORMATION SEE LOG AD THIS SECTION

British Columbia is Canada's most westerly and 3rd largest province.

Core samples on view at Jade City. (© Gladys Blyth)

Vines Lake (unsigned), named for bush pilot Lionel Vines; fishing for lake trout.
   J 366.9 (590.4 km) AH 79.2 (127.4 km) Limestone Creek.
   J 367.3 (591.1 km) AH 78.8 (126.8 km) Lang Lake and creek. Needlepoint Mountain visible straight ahead southbound.
   J 370.9 (596.8 km) AH 75.2 (121 km) Trout Line Creek.
   J 371 (597 km) AH 75.1 (120.9 km) JADE CITY (pop. 10) was named for the jade deposits found to the east of the highway community. The huge jade boulders

that visitors can see being cut here are from the Princess Jade Mine, one of the largest jade claims in the world. The Cassiar Mountain Range supplies about 75 percent of the world jade supply.

   Cassiar Mountain Jade Store. Direct from our mine to you. By the pound or by the ton. We mine it, we cut it, we sell it to you. The hard rock jade boulder in the Guiness Book of Records is on site. Owners of the Princess Jade Mine. Gold panning. Local, hand-crafted items. Custom cut jade and rhodonite, semi-precious stones, local gold nugget and jade jewelry. Largest personally designed collection of jade and rhodonite carvings and jewelry. Outdoor interactive mining museum specializing in jade, gold and Cassiar asbestos mining equipment. Come and see our jade cutting and polishing process. See our historic photo gallery of local mining operations from 1890s to present day. Friendly, knowledgeable staff. German speaking staff member. Hot, fresh and free coffee and tea. Caravan and bus tours welcome. Full indoor bathroom facilities. Wheelchair accessible. Free overnight parking. Grocery and confections. Minor repairs. VISA, Mastercard, American Express. Cassiar Mountain Jade Store is here to serve you. Phone (403) 997-3374. email cassiarmountain@yahoo.ca; www.cassiarmountainjadestoreandmine.com. See display ad this section. [ADVERTISEMENT]

   Jade City Jade Store & Gift Shop. Southbound traffic turn left to jade store; northbound traffic turn right. World famous jade capital. Extensive selection of raw jade, jade jewelery and carvings crafted from local Cassiar polar and kutcho jade. Best jade and jewelery prices in the North. Rock hounds will appreciate the extensive selection of raw Canadian gemstones and jewelry. Don't miss our large selection of jade boulders featuring Cassiar Jade. Large selection of Canadian gift items and more. Caravans and bus tours welcome. Friendly staff, family owned and operated. Jesus is Lord. See display ad this section. [ADVERTISEMENT]

   J 372.5 (599.4 km) AH 73.6 (118.5 km) **Cassiar junction.** Cassiar Road to west leads 9.7 miles/15.6 km to the former Cassiar townsite and Cassiar Asbestos Mine. Continue straight ahead for Alaska Highway.

   CASSIAR (pop. 25) was the company town of Cassiar Mining Corp. Much of the

www.themilepost.com   2003 ■ The MILEPOST® ■ 251

CASSIAR HIGHWAY

Along the northern section of the Cassiar. (© Blake Hanna, staff)

world's high-grade chrysotile asbestos came from Cassiar. The mine closed in March 1992, and the site is closed to visitors. It is now the site of a B.C. Chrysotile Corp. reclamation project. No services available.

J 372.7 (599.7 km) AH 73.4 (118.2 km) Snow Creek. Turnout to west with litter barrel.

J 372.8 (599.8 km) AH 73.3 (117.9 km) Gravel turnout with litter barrel to east.

J 373.6 (601.2 km) AH 72.5 (116.8 km) McDame Creek.

J 377.4 (607.3 km) AH 68.7 (110.6 km) No. 3 North Fork Creek.

J 378.4 (609 km) AH 67.7 (108.9 km) No. 2 North Fork Creek. Small gold mining operations may be visible to east.

J 378.6 (609.3 km) AH 67.5 (108.6 km) Turnout with litter barrel.

J 379.5 (610.7 km) AH 66.6 (107.2 km) Turnout with litter barrel overlooking mining site.

J 381 (613.1 km) AH 65.1 (104.7 km) Historic plaque about Cassiar gold; litter barrels.

CENTREVILLE (pop. 2; elev. 2,600 feet/792m), a former gold rush town of 3,000. The only evidence of Centreville along the highway today is the town name painted on an old piece of mining equipment parked on the east side of the road. Centreville was founded and named by miners for its central location between Sylvester's Landing (later McDame Post) at the junction of McDame Creek with the Dease River, and Quartzrock Creek, the upstream limit of pay gravel on McDame Creek. A miner named Alfred Freeman washed out the biggest all-gold (no quartz) nugget ever found in British Columbia on a claim near Centreville in 1877; it weighed 72 ounces. Active mining in area.

J 381.1 (613.3 km) AH 65 (104.6 km) No. 1 North Fork Creek.

J 383 (616.3 km) AH 63.1 (101.5 km) Watch for Dall sheep in this area.

J 385.2 (619.9 km) AH 60.9 (98 km) GOOD HOPE LAKE (pop. 100); fuel, groceries and phone.

J 386.9 (622.6 km) AH 59.2 (95.3 km) Turnout to east alongside Aeroplane Lake.

J 387.7 (623.9 km) AH 58.4 (94 km) Dry Creek; pullout.

J 389.2 (626.3 km) AH 56.9 (91.6 km) Mud Lake to east.

J 393.6 (633.4 km) AH 52.5 (84.5 km) Boya Lake Provincial Park. The park is 1.6 miles/2.6 km east of highway; 45 campsites, picnic area on lakeshore, boat launch, toilets, wheelchair access, walking trails, drinking water, firewood and swimming. Fishing for lake char, whitefish and burbot. Attendant on duty during summer.

J 393.7 (633.6 km) AH 52.4 (84.4 km) Turnout with litter barrel.

Horseranch Range may be seen on the eastern horizon northbound. These mountains date back to the Cambrian period, or earlier, and are the oldest in northern British Columbia. According to the Canadian Geological Survey, this area contains numerous permatites with crystals of tourmaline, garnet, feldspar, quartz and beryl. Road crosses Baking Powder Creek and then follows Dease River.

J 397.9 (640.3 km) AH 48.2 (77.6 km) Camp Creek.

J 399.4 (642.8 km) AH 46.7 (75.1 km) Beaver Dam Creek.

J 400.3 (644.2 km) AH 45.8 (73.7 km) Beaver Dam rest area with visitor information sign to west. Picnic tables, litter barrels.

J 400.6 (644.7 km) AH 45.5 (73.3 km) Leaving Cassiar Mountains, entering Yukon Plateau, northbound.

J 402.5 (647.7 km) AH 43.6 (70.2 km) Baking Powder Creek.

J 410.9 (661.3 km) AH 35.2 (56.7 km) Gravel access road to French Creek B.C. Forest Service campsite 0.6 miles/1 km from highway. Rustic. Tables, rock fire ring (bring firewood), small boat launch into Dease River, no fee.

J 411.2 (661.7 km) AH 34.9 (56.1 km) French Creek 2-lane concrete bridge.

J 417.5 (671.8 km) AH 28.6 (46.1 km) Twentyeight Mile Creek. Cassiar Mountains rise to south.

J 420.2 (676.2 km) AH 25.9 (41.6 km) Wheeler Lake to west.

J 422.9 (680.6 km) AH 23.2 (37.3 km) Blue River Forest Service Road to east.

J 426.3 (686 km) AH 19.8 (31.9 km) Blue River 2-lane concrete bridge.

J 429.7 (691.5 km) AH 16.4 (26.4 km) Turnout at Blue Lakes; litter barrels, picnic tables and fishing for pike and grayling.

J 431.5 (694.4 km) AH 14.6 (23.5 km) Mud Hill Creek.

J 436 (701.6 km) AH 10.1 (16.2 km) Old Faddy Forest Service Road.

J 440.1 (708.2 km) AH 6 (9.6 km) Turnout with litter barrels beside Cormier Creek.

J 443 (713 km) AH 3.1 (5 km) High Lake to east.

J 444 (714.5 km) AH 2.1 (3.4 km) Turnout to west at BC–YT Border, 60th parallel. Information sign.

Yukon Territory's flag consists of 3 vertical panels of colour: blue, representing the rivers and lakes; green symbolizing forests; and white signifying snow. The Yukon coat of arms appears on the central panel, framed by 2 stems of fireweed, the territory's floral emblem. The flag was chosen from a design competition sponsored in 1967. Yukon Territory was made a district of Northwest Territories in 1895 and became a separate territory in June 1898, at the height of the Klondike Gold Rush.

NOTE: Drive with headlights on at all times in Yukon Territory.

J 445.3 (716.6 km) AH 0.8 (1.2 km) Albert Creek. Good grayling fishing. Yukon Territory fishing license required.

J 446.1 (718 km) AH 0 Junction of Cassiar Highway with Alaska Highway. Gas, store, campground and RV park, cafe, souvenirs, laundromat, camp-style motel, saloon, propane, towing and car repair at junction. Turn left for Whitehorse, right for Watson Lake, 13.3 miles/21.4 km southeast. Watson Lake is the nearest major community.

Junction 37 Services. See display ad this section.

Turn to Milepost DC 626.2 on page 138 in the ALASKA HIGHWAY section for log of Alaska Highway from this junction.Creek.

J 37 JUNCTION 37 SERVICES
Mile 649 Alaska Hwy.   Phone (867) 536-2794

— GAS — DIESEL — PROPANE —
MOTEL • CAFE
STORE with Groceries & Souvenirs

RV PARK • 30 amp • Full Hookups • FREE RV Dumping
Camping • Showers • Laundromat • Car Wash • Ice

Fishing Licenses For Sale

FAX (867) 536-7902

Mailing Address: Box 845, Watson Lake, Yukon Y0A 1C0
See Our Full Color Ad on the Alaska Highway Section

Drive with headlights on!

KLONDIKE LOOP

	Alaska Hwy. Jct.	Carmacks	Dawson City	Taylor Hwy Jct.	Whitehorse
Alaska Hwy Jct.		102	323	402	10
Carmacks	102		221	300	112
Dawson City	323	221		79	333
Taylor Hwy Jct.	402	300	79		412
Whitehorse	10	112	333	412	

Connects: Alaska Hwy. in Yukon to Alaska Hwy. in Alaska
Length: 498 miles
Road Surface: Pavement, seal coat and gravel
Season: Hwy. 2 open all year, Hwys. 9 and 5 closed in winter
Major Attraction: Dawson City, Klondike Gold Fields, Silver Trail

(See maps, pages 254–255)

A fish wheel at Ancient Voices Wilderness Camp on the Yukon River, 27 miles from Dawson City. (© Earl L. Brown, staff)

The "Klondike Loop" refers to the 323-mile/520-km-long stretch of Yukon Highway 2 (the North Klondike Highway, also sometimes called the "Mayo Road"), from its junction with the Alaska Highway north of Whitehorse to Dawson City; the 79-mile/127-km Top of the World Highway (Yukon Highway 9); and the 96 miles/154 kms of the Taylor Highway (Alaska Route 5) that connect with the Alaska Highway near Tok.

The North Klondike Highway and Top of the World Highway are logged in this section. An abbreviated southbound log of the Taylor Highway from Jack Wade Junction is included as well. For a more detailed log of the Taylor Highway, see the TAYLOR HIGHWAY section starting on page 276.

Alaska-bound motorists turn off the Alaska Highway north of Whitehorse (**Milepost DC 894.8**); follow the Klondike Highway to Dawson City; ferry from there across the Yukon River; drive west via the Top of the World Highway into Alaska; then take the Taylor Highway south back to the Alaska Highway near Tok (**Milepost DC 1301.7**). Total driving distance is 498 miles/801 km. (Driving distance from Whitehorse to Tok via the Alaska Highway is approximately 396 miles/637 km.)

All of the Klondike Highway between the Alaska Highway junction and Dawson City is asphalt-surfaced. The Top of the World Highway—a truly scenic route—is seal-coated on the Canadian portion with some hills. It is gravel on the U.S. side with some steep grades and winding sections that can be slippery in wet weather. Check with the Dawson City Visitor Centre for current road and weather conditions; phone (867) 993-5566.

The Taylor Highway is narrow gravel road with some steep, winding sections and washboard south to Chicken. From Chicken south to the Alaska Highway the highway is chip seal and pavement.

Both the Taylor and Top of the World highways are not maintained from mid-October to April and the arrival of snow effectively closes the roads for winter. Yukon Highway 2 is open year-round. *Drive with your headlights on at all times.*

Travelers should be aware that the Top of the World Highway (reached by ferry from Dawson City) may not open until late spring. In heavy traffic, there may be a wait as long as 3 hours for the Yukon River ferry at Dawson City during peak hours. Customs stations are open in summer only, 12 hours a day: 9 A.M. to 9 P.M. (Pacific time), 8 A.M. to 8 P.M. (Alaska time). There are no restrooms, services or currency exchanges available at the border.

The highway between Skagway and the Alaska Highway, referred to as the South Klondike, is also designated Klondike Highway 2 (see SOUTH KLONDIKE HIGHWAY section for log of that road).

The route from Whitehorse to Dawson City began as a trail, used first by Natives, trappers and prospectors, and then by stampeders during the Klondike Gold Rush of 1897–98. Steamships also provided passenger service between Whitehorse and Dawson City. A road was built connecting the Alaska Highway with the United Keno Hill Mine at Mayo in 1950. By 1955, the Mayo Road had been upgraded for automobile traffic and extended to Dawson City. In 1960, the last of 3 steel bridges, crossing the Yukon, Pelly and Stewart rivers, was completed. The only ferry crossing remaining is the Yukon River crossing at Dawson City. Mayo Road (Yukon Highway 11) from Stewart Crossing to Mayo, Elsa and Keno was redesignated the Silver Trail in 1985 (see "Silver Trail" road log beginning on page 261 this section).

Emergency Medical Services: On Yukon Highway 2 from **Milepost J 0** to **J 55.2** (Whitehorse to Braeburn Lodge), phone Whitehorse Ambulance toll free 1-667-3333 or RCMP 1-667-3333. From **Milepost J 55.2** to **J 167.7** (Braeburn Lodge to Pelly Crossing), phone Carmacks Medical Emergency (867) 863-4444 or RCMP (867) 863-5555. From **Milepost J 167.7** to **J 240** (Pelly Crossing to McQuesten River Lodge), phone Mayo Medical Emergency (867) 996-4444 or RCMP (867) 996-5555. From **Milepost J 240** to **J 323.4** and on Yukon Highway 9 from **Milepost D 0** to **D 66.1** (McQuesten River Lodge

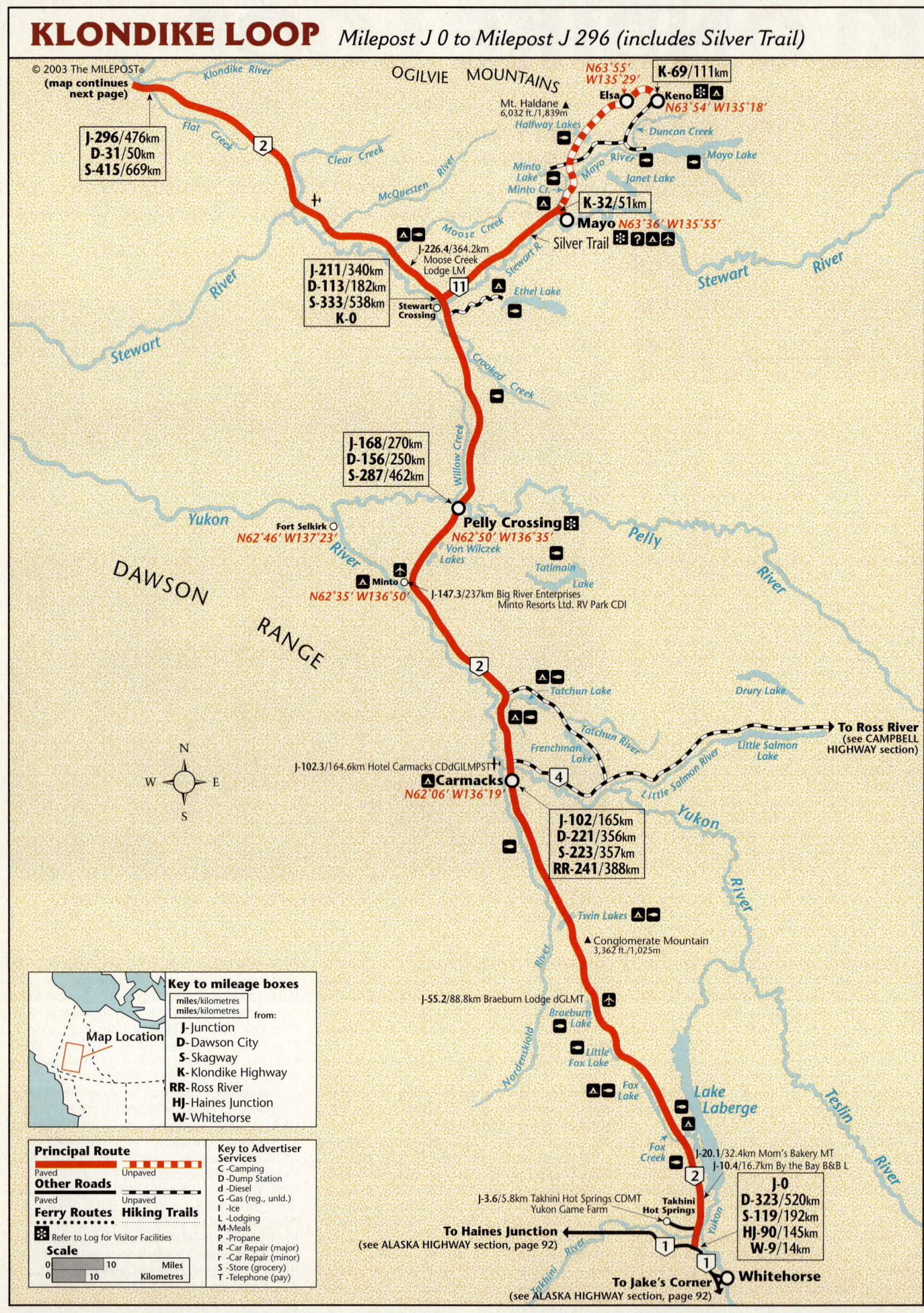

KLONDIKE LOOP
Milepost J 296 to Tetlin Junction, Alaska Highway (includes Taylor Highway)

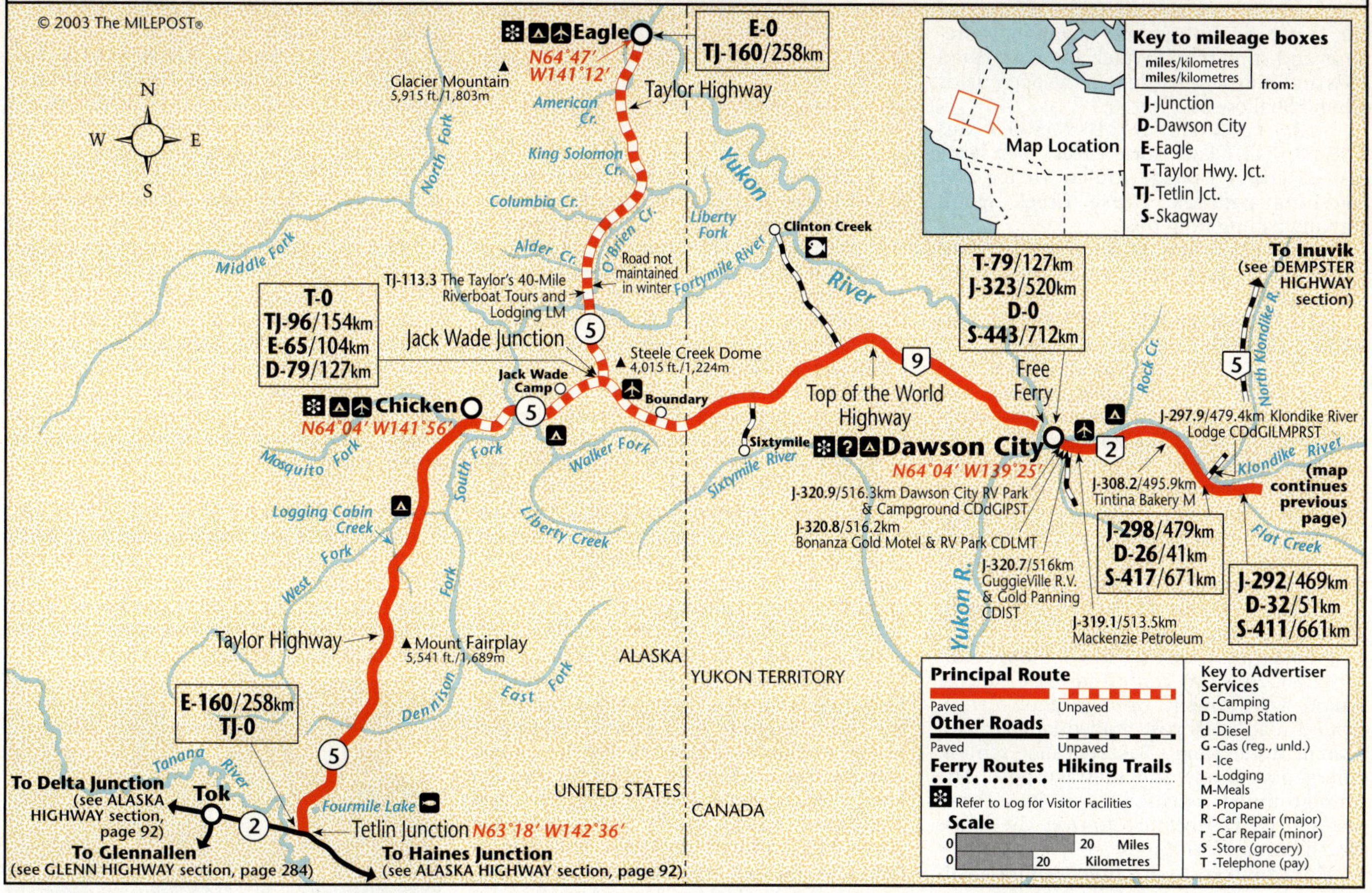

to Dawson City to Alaska border), phone Dawson City Medical Emergency (867) 993-4444 or RCMP (867) 993-5555. From **Milepost D 66.1** to **D 78.8** (Alaska border to Taylor Highway), phone Tok Area EMS at 911 or (907) 883-5111.

Klondike Loop Log

This section of the log shows distance from junction with the Alaska Highway (J) followed by distance from Dawson City (D) and distance from Skagway (S). Physical kilometreposts show distance from Skagway.

YUKON HIGHWAY 2
J 0 D 323.4 (520.3 km) S 119.3 (192 km)

Junction with the Alaska Highway at **Milepost DC 894.8**; see log of the ALASKA HIGHWAY on page 166.

J 0.6 (1 km) **D 322.8** (519.5 km) **S 119.9** (193 km) McPherson subdivision.

J 1 (1.6 km) **D 322.4** (518.8 km) **S 120.3** (193 km) Ranches, farms and livestock next 20 miles/32 km northbound.

J 2.2 (3.5 km) **D 321.2** (516.9 km) **S 121.5** (195.5 km) Takhini River bridge. The Takhini flows into the Yukon River. The name is Tagish Indian, *takh* meaning mosquito and *heena* meaning river, according to R. Coutts in *Yukon: Places & Names*.

J 3.6 (5.8 km) **D 319.8** (514.6 km) **S 122.9** (197.8 km) Gas bar and convenience store at **junction** with Takhini Hot Springs Road. Drive west 5 miles/8 km for **Yukon Game Farm Wildlife Preserve** and 6 miles/9.7 km via paved road for **Takhini Hot Springs** (open year-round, hot springs pool, camping, cafe, trail rides, winter ski trails).

Yukon Game Farm Wildlife Preserve. Take the opportunity to view and photograph North American wildlife species in a natural setting. See Dall sheep, Stone sheep, bighorn sheep, mountain goats, musk-oxen, wood bison, moose, caribou, elk and mule deer, as well as numerous species of birds. Located at Mile 5 (Km 8) Takhini Hot Springs Road. Guided tours only. Phone (867) 633-2922; Fax (867) 633-2425; email gamefarm@polarcom.com; web site www.yukongamefarm.com. Tours departing daily at location. For downtown departures, contact Grayline of Yukon in the Westmark Hotel; phone (867) 668-3225. [ADVERTISEMENT]

Trappers and Indians used Takhini hot springs around the turn of the century, arriving by way of the Takhini River or the old Dawson Trail. During construction of the Alaska Highway in the early 1940s, the U.S. Army maintained greenhouses in the area and reported remarkable growth regardless of the season.

The source of the springs maintains a constant 117°F/47°C temperature and flows at 86 gallons a minute. The hot springs pool averages 100°F/38°C year-round. The water contains no sulfur. The chief minerals present are calcium, magnesium and iron. ▲

Takhini Hot Springs. After a long drive there is nothing like a long hot soak in the springs. Our licensed restaurant offers a full menu and delicious daily specials. Hiking, trail rides and sleigh rides. Sites for tents, campers and RVs, with pull-throughs, power, water and dump station. Open year-round, call regarding winter hours. Phone (867) 633-2706. [ADVERTISEMENT] ▲

J 6.8 (10.9 km) **D 316.6** (509.5 km) **S 126.1** (202.9 km) Whitehorse rodeo grounds to west.

J 10.4 (16.7 km) **D 313** (503.7 km) **S 129** (208.7 km) Shallow Bay Road; access to bed and breakfast.

By The Bay Bed and Breakfast. Shallow Bay Road, first driveway to the left. Enjoy all of the best the area has to offer! Comfortable 22x22-foot scribe log cabin with kitchen facilities on Shallow Bay, south end of lake Laberge. Excellent birdwatching. Water access and canoes. Your hosts, Peter and Mary Beattie. (867) 633-5995. [ADVERTISEMENT]

According to Yukon's Renewable Resources Wildlife Viewing Program, there is a trail on the east side of the highway 300 feet/100m north of the junction with Shallow Bay Road. The trail leads to a good waterfowl viewing site at Shallow Bay on Lake Laberge. Northern pintail, Barrow's goldeneye, and tundra and trumpeter swans stage here by the thousands in spring and fall. It is also a hot spot for migrating shorebirds and song birds. Watch for short-eared owls and northern harriers in the open fields around Shallow Bay.

J 12.5 (20.1 km) D 310.9 (500.3 km) S 131.8 (212.1 km) Horse Creek Road leads east to Lower Laberge Indian village and lakeshore cottages. **Horse Creek**; good grayling fishing from road.

J 15.7 (25.2 km) D 307.7 (495.2 km) S 135 (217.2 km) Northwestel microwave tower access.

J 16.7 (26.8 km) D 306.7 (493.6 km) S 136 (218.8 km) Large turnout to west.

J 17.2 (27.7 km) D 306.2 (492.8 km) S 136.5 (219.7 km) Lake Laberge to east. The Yukon River widens to form this 40-mile-/64-km-long lake. **Lake Laberge** was made famous by Robert W. Service with the lines: "The Northern Lights have seen queer sights. But the queerest they ever did see, was that night on the marge of Lake Lebarge I cremated Sam McGee," (from his poem "The Cremation of Sam McGee").

J 19.9 (32 km) D 303.5 (488.4 km) S 139.2 (224 km) Deep Creek.

J 20.1 (32.4 km) D 303.3 (488.1 km) S 139.4 (224.4 km) Turnoff for Lake Laberge Yukon government campground. Campground road leads past residential area with a small store, Mom's Bakery, canoe rentals, emergency phone and message post. The campground is situated 1.8 miles/2.9 km east on Lake Laberge next to Deep Creek (see description following).

Mom's Bakery, a favourite spot for locals and visitors, home of tummy-pleasing sourdough bread baked in our European-style outdoor oven, pancakes, giant cinnamon buns and pastries. Relax on the patio amidst a Northern garden. Fishing licenses, ice, telephone. Long-time Yukon host, Tracie Harris. Box 21036, Whitehorse, YT Y1A 6P6. Phone (867) 456-4010 email: momsbakery30@hotmail.com. [ADVERTISEMENT]

Lake Laberge Yukon government campground has 16 sites, camping permit ($12), resident campground host, group camping area, kitchen shelter, water, boat launch, and fishing for lake trout, grayling and northern pike. Interpretive panels located lakeside at the campground highlight the 30-mile Heritage River.

According to Yukon Renewable Resources, Lake Laberge is the only place in the Yukon where cormorants are seen. Loons and other water birds are commonly seen here.

CAUTION: Storms can blow up quickly and without warning on Lake Laberge, as on other northern lakes. Canoes and small craft stay to the west side of the lake, where the shoreline offers safe refuges. The east side of the lake is lined with high rocky bluffs, and there are few places to pull out. Small craft should not navigate the middle of the lake.

J 21.2 (34.1 km) D 302.2 (486.3 km) S 140.4 (226 km) Northbound the highway enters the Miners Range, plateau country of the Yukon, an immense wilderness of forested dome-shaped mountains and high ridges, dotted with lakes and traversed by tributaries of the Yukon River. To the west, Pilot Mountain in the Miners Range (elev. 6,739 feet/2,054m) is visible.

J 22.6 (36.3 km) D 300.8 (484.1 km) S 142 (228.3 km) **Fox Creek** bridge; grayling, excellent in June and July.

J 28.4 (46.6 km) D 295 (474.7 km) S 148 (238 km) Highway now follows the east shoreline of **Fox Lake** northbound. Fox Lake is a waterfowl stop during spring migration. Muskrats also feed here: muskrat "push-ups" can be seen dotting the frozen surface of the lake in the winter and spring.

J 29 (46.6 km) D 294.4 (473.8 km) S 148.3 (238.6 km) Turnout to west on Fox Lake. Sign reads: "In 1883, U.S. Army Lt. Frederick Schwatka completed a survey of the entire length of the Yukon River. One of many geographical features that he named was Fox Lake, which he called Richthofen Lake, after geographer Freiherr Von Richthofen. Known locally as Fox Lake, the name was adopted in 1957. The Miners Range to the west was named by geologist/explorer George Mercer Dawson in 1887 'for the miners met by us along the river.'"

J 34.6 (55.7 km) D 288.8 (464.8 km) S 154 (247.7 km) Turnoff west for **Fox Lake** Yukon government campground; 30 RV and 3 tent-only sites, camping permit ($12 kitchen shelter, drinking water and boat launch. Good fishing for lake trout and burbot from the shore at the campground; excellent grayling year-round. ◆▲

J 35 (56.3 km) D 288.4 (464.1 km) S 154.3 (248.3 km) Turnout with view of Fox Lake. Good photo spot.

J 38.3 (61.7 km) D 285.1 (458.8 km) S 157.6 (253.7 km) Lake Burn northbound. There was a major forest fire in this area in summer 1998.

J 41.7 (67.1 km) D 281.7 (453.3 km) S 161 (259 km) **Little Fox Lake** to west; lake trout 3 to 8 lbs., fish the islands.

J 43.5 (70 km) D 279.9 (450.4 km) S 162.8 (262 km) Double-ended turnout with litter barrel to west beside Little Fox Lake. Small boat launch.

J 47 (75.6 km) D 276.4 (444.8 km) S 166.6 (267 km) **Boreal Fire Interpretive Site** turnout with outhouses, litter barrels and interpretive panels (missing in 2002) on fire and the boreal forest ecosystem.

J 49.2 (79.2 km) D 274.2 (441.3 km) S 168.5 (271.1 km) Large turnout to west.

J 52.2 (84 km) D 271.2 (436.4 km) S 171.5 (276 km) Gravel pit turnout to east. According to Renewable Resources Wildlife Viewing Program, about 50 elk live here year-round. They are most commonly seen in winter and spring. Look for their distinctive white rumps on the exposed south-facing slopes. Elk are a protected species in the Yukon. Grizzly bears feed on roadside vegetation (and also elk) in this area in spring and summer.

CAUTION: Watch for elk along highway.

J 55.2 (88.8 km) D 268.2 (431.6 km) S 174.5 (280.8 km) Braeburn Lodge to west; food, gas, lodging and minor car repairs. One Braeburn Lodge cinnamon bun will feed 4 people. The lodge is also home of the 200-mile/320-km "Cinnamon Bun" Dog Sled Race, held the first weekend in February.

Braeburn Lodge. See display ad this section. &

J 55.5 (89.4 km) D 267.9 (431.1 km) S 174.9 (281.4 km) **Private Aircraft:** Braeburn airstrip to east, dubbed Cinnamon Bun Strip; elev. 2,350 feet/716m; length 3,000 feet/914m; dirt strip; wind sock.

J 65.9 (106 km) D 257.5 (414.4 km) S 185.2 (298 km) Photo stop; pull-through turnout on east side of highway with information sign about **Conglomerate Mountain** (elev. 3,361 feet/1,024m). Sign reads: "The Laberge Series was formed at the leading edge of volcanic mud flows some 185 million years ago (Early Jurassic). These flows solidified into sheets several kilometres long and about 1 km wide and 100m thick. This particular series of sheets stretches from Atlin, BC, to north of Carmacks, a distance of about 350 km. Other conglomerates of this series form Five Finger Rapids."

Several outcroppings of conglomerate may be found in the immediate area. Conglomerate, also called "Puddingstone" because of its appearance, consists of pebbles welded into solid masses of varying size by a natural cement. Composition of the cementing material varies, as does the size and composition of the pebbles.

J 71.4 (114.9 km) D 252 (405.5 km) S 190.8 (307 km) Turnouts on both sides of highway between Twin Lakes. These 2 small lakes, 1 on either side of the road, are known for their beauty and colour.

J 72.1 (116 km) D 251.3 (404.4 km) S 191.4 (308 km) Turnoff to west for **Twin Lakes** Yukon government campground; 18

sites, camping permit ($12), drinking water, boat launch. Lake is stocked. Large parking area with informational panels on the Nordenskiold River. Enjoyable fishing for lake trout, grayling and pike. Good swimming for the *hardy*! 🐟▲

J 81 (130.4 km) **D 242.4** (390.1 km) **S 200.3** (322.4 km) Large turnout with litter barrel to east at remains of **Montague House**, a typical early-day roadhouse which offered lodging and meals on the stagecoach route between Whitehorse and Dawson City. A total of 52 stopping places along this route were listed in the Jan. 16, 1901, edition of the *Whitehorse Star* under "On the Winter Trail between White Horse and Dawson Good Accommodations for Travellers." Montague House was listed at Mile 99. Good photo stop.

J 88.8 (142.9 km) **D 234.6** (377.5 km) **S 208.1** (334.9 km) Rook Bluff to east.

J 93.3 (150.1 km) **D 230.1** (370.3 km) **S 213.2** (343 km) Plume Trail Agate Road to east, information sign about agate deposits.

Hill northbound overlooking Nordenskoild River. The Nodenskiold was named by Lt. Frederick Schwatka, U.S. Army, for Swedish arctic explorer Erik Nordenskiold. This river, which parallels the highway for several miles, flows into the Yukon River at Carmacks. Good grayling and pike fishing all summer.

J 99.1 (159.5 km) **D 224.3** (361 km) **S 218.4** (351.5 km) Wetlands to west are part of the **Nordenskiold River** system. Waterfowl stage here during spring and fall migrations. Watch for trumpeter swans and ruddy ducks. Other area wildlife include beaver, muskrat, moose, mink and fox.

J 101.2 (162.9 km) **D 222.2** (357.6 km) **S 220.2** (354.4 km) Pull-through rest area to east with litter barrels and outhouses.

The Welcome to Carmacks loon mosaic seen here was designed by artists Chris Schearbarth, Brian Tom and Clarence Washpan and constructed by members of Little Salmon First Natives.

Carmacks

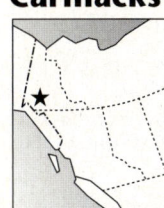

J 102.3 (164.6 km) **D 221.1** (355.8 km) **S 221.9** (357.1 km). Located on the banks of the Yukon River, Carmacks is the only highway crossing of the Yukon River between Whitehorse and Dawson City. **Population:** 489. **Emergency Services:** RCMP, phone (867) 863-5555. **Fire Department**, phone (867) 863-2222. **Nurse**, phone (867) 863-4444. **Ambulance**, phone (867) 863-4444. **Forest Fire Control**, phone (867) 863-5271.

Visitor Information: Located in the Old Telegraph Office. Write Village of Carmacks, P.O. 113, Carmacks, YT Y0B 1C0; phone (867) 863-6271, fax (867) 883-6606. Open 8:30 A.M. to 5 P.M. Monday through Friday.

Private Aircraft: Carmacks airstrip; elev. 1,770 feet/539m; length 5,200 feet/1,585m; gravel; no fuel.

Carmacks was once an important stop for Yukon River steamers traveling between Dawson City and Whitehorse, and it continues as a supply point today for modern river travelers. Carmacks has survived—while other river ports have not—as a service centre for highway traffic and mining interests. Carmacks was also a major stopping point on the old Whitehorse to Dawson Trail.

Carmacks was named for George Carmack, who established a trading post here in the 1890s. Carmack had come North in 1885, hoping to strike it rich. He spent the next 10 years prospecting without success. In 1896, when the trading post went bankrupt, Carmack moved his family to Fortymile, where he could fish to eat and cut timber to sell. That summer, Carmack's remarkable persistence paid off—he unearthed a 5-dollar pan of coarse gold, during a time when a 10-cent pan was considered a good find. That same winter, he extracted more than a ton of gold from the creek, which he renamed Bonanza Creek, and its tributary, Eldorado. When word of Carmack's discovery reached the outside world the following spring, it set off the Klondike Gold Rush.

Traveler facilities include a hotel/motel, campground and RV parking with hookups, restaurant, gas (unleaded, diesel), grocery and convenience stores, laundromat and showers, and post office and bank (both with limited hours). There are also churches, a school, recreation centre, swimming pool and library. ▲

A 1.2-mile/2-km interpretive boardwalk makes it possible to enjoy a stroll along the Yukon River; beautiful view of countryside and Tantalus Butte, gazebo and park at end of trail. Wheelchair accessible. ♿

The Northern Tutchone First Nations Tage Cho Hudan Interpretive Centre features archaeological displays on Native life in a series of indoor and outdoor exhibits, and marked interpretive trails. The centre also features a mammoth snare diorama and has an arts and crafts store.

Restored pioneer structures here include the Carmacks Roadhouse and the Hazel Brown cabin.

For rock hounds, there are 5 agate trails in the area, which can double as good, short hiking trails. Abundant fishing in area rivers and lakes: salmon, grayling, northern pike, lake and rainbow trout and whitefish. 🐟

Hotel Carmacks. See display ad this section.

A loon mosaic constructed by Little Salmon First Natives welcomes Carmacks visitors. (© Earl L. Brown, staff)

STOP — **DISCOVER FRIENDLY FARO and the CAMPBELL HIGHWAY**

www.faro.yk.net

(See our full-colour info in the Campbell Highway section)

Hotel Carmacks

Gas • Oil • Diesel **ESSO**

THE KLONDIKE HIGHWAY STOPPING PLACE

Hotel and Motel Units
Gold Panner Restaurant • Gold Dust Lounge
FIVE FINGER RAPID BOAT TOURS

Tatchun Centre General Store
Groceries • In-store Bakery • Gifts • Ice
Souvenirs • Magazines • Camping Supplies
Laundromat • Showers
Fishing and Hunting Licenses
Fishing Tackle • Hardware

Riverfront RV Sites
15 Fully Serviced Sites • 30 & 50 Amp Power
Some Pull-Thrus • Water • Sewer
Phone • Dump Station

 Canada Select

Box 160, Carmacks, Yukon Y0B 1C0
Phone (867) 863-5221 • FAX (867) 863-5605
hotelcarmacks@yt.sympatico.ca

 Good Sampark

Colourful picket fence surrounds aboriginal cemetery at Fort Selkirk.
(© Lyn Hancock)

Klondike Loop Log
(continued)

J 102.8 (165.4 km) **D 220.6** (355 km)
S 222.4 (357.9 km) Yukon River bridge. Turnout and parking area at south end of bridge; 2.3-mile-/3.7-km-long trail to Coal Mine Lake.

J 103.2 (166 km) **D 220.2** (354.4 km)
S 222.5 (358 km) Northern Tutchone Trading Post with store and post office at north end of Yukon River bridge. Fishing tackle and licenses available. Tage Cho Hudan Interpretive Centre.

J 103.9 (167.1 km) **D 219.5** (353.2 km)
S 223.1 (359.1 km) Turnoff to east for Campbell Highway, also known as Watson Lake–Carmacks Road, which leads south to Faro (107 miles/173 km), Ross River (141 miles/226 km) and Watson Lake (373 miles/600 km). Private campground at junction. ▲

Junction with Campbell Highway (Yukon Highway 4). Turn to end of CAMPBELL HIGHWAY section and read log back to front.

J 104.4 (168 km) **D 219** (352.4 km)
S 223.7 (360 km) Side road east to Tantalus Butte Coal Mine; the coal was used in Cyprus Anvil Mine's mill near Faro for drying concentrates. The butte was named by Lt. Frederick Schwatka because it is seen many times before it is actually reached.

J 104.7 (168.5 km) **D 218.7** (352 km)
S 223.5 (359.8 km) Turnout to west with litter barrels, information sign, view of Yukon River Valley.

J 107.4 (172.8 km) **D 218.7** (352 km)
S 223.5 (359.8 km) Side road west to agate site for rock hounds.

J 116.8 (188 km) **D 206.6** (332.5 km)
S 236.1 (380 km) Large double-ended rest area to west with toilets, litter barrels and viewing platform for **Five Finger Rapids**. Information sign here reads: "Five Finger Rapids named by early miners for the 5 channels, or fingers, formed by the rock pillars. They are a navigational hazard. The safest passage is through the nearest, or east, passage." Stairs (219 steps) and a trail lead down to rapids. Flora includes prairie crocus, kinnikinnick, common juniper and sage. Watch for white-crowned sparrows and American tree sparrows. Interpretive panels.

J 118.1 (190 km) **D 205.3** (330.4 km)
S 237.41 (382 km) Tatchun Creek bridge.

J 117.6 (189.3 km) **D 205.8** (331.2 km)
S 236.9 (381.3 km) First turnoff (northbound) to east for **Tatchun Creek** Yukon government campground; 12 sites, camping permit ($12), kitchen shelter and drinking water. Good fishing for grayling, June through September; salmon, July through August. ◄▲

J 118.3 (190.3 km) **D 205.1** (330.1 km)
S 237.5 (382.3 km) Side road leads east to **Tatchun Lake**. Follow side road 4.3 miles/6.9 km east to boat launch and pit toilets. Continue past boat launch 1.1 miles/1.8 km for Tatchun Lake Yukon government campground with 20 sites, camping permit ($12), pit toilets, firewood, litter barrels and picnic tables. Fishing for northern pike, best in spring or fall. ◄▲

This maintained side road continues east past Tatchun Lake to Frenchman Lake, then loops south to the Campbell Highway, approximately 25 miles/40 km distance. The main access to Frenchman Lake is from the Campbell Highway.

J 126 (202.7 km) **D 197.4** (317.7 km)
S 245.3 (394.8 km) Yukon crossing viewpoint; large turnout overlooking Yukon River. Good photo stop.

J 128.5 (206.7 km) **D 194.9** (313.6 km)
S 247.8 (398.9 km) Top of hill; highway descends hill, northbound. Watch for falling rocks.

J 131.4 (211.4 km) **D 192** (309 km)
S 250.7 (403.4 km) McGregor Creek.

J 135.2 (217.5 km) **D 188.2** (302.9 km)
S 254.4 (409.5 km) Northbound, first evidence of 1995 burn. The fire consumed 325,000 acres of forest. Dramatic summer fireweed displays here in recent years.

J 136 (218.8 km) **D 187.4** (301.6 km)
S 255.3 (410.8 km) Good representation of White River ash layer for approximately one mile northbound. About 1,250 years ago a layer of white volcanic ash coated a third of the southern Yukon, or some 125,000 square miles/323,725 square km, and it is easily visible along many roadcuts. This distinct line conveniently provides a division used by archaeologists for dating artifacts: Materials found below this major stratigraphic marker are considered to have been deposited before A.D. 700, while those found above the ash layer are postdated A.D. 700. The small amount of data available does not support volcanic activity in the White River area during the same period. One theory is that the ash could have spewn forth from a single violent volcanic eruption. The source may be buried under the Klutlan Glacier in the St. Elias Mountains in eastern Alaska.

J 143.3 (230.5 km) **D 180.1** (289.8 km)
S 262.5 (422.5 km) McCabe Creek.

J 147.3 (237 km) **D 176.1** (283.4 km)
S 266.6 (429 km) **Big River Enterprises**. See display ad this section.

Minto Resorts Ltd. R.V. Park. 1,400-foot Yukon River frontage. Halfway between Whitehorse and Dawson City on the Old Stage Road, Minto was once a steamboat landing and trading post. 27 sites, wide easy access, picnic tables, firepits, ice, snacks, pop, ice cream. Coin-op showers and laundry, clean restrooms, dump station and water. Bus tour buffet, reservation only. Caravans welcome. Wildlife viewing opportunities. Try fishing the river. Owned and operated by Yukoners. Come and visit us!

BOAT TOURS
Explore the Yukon River through unspoiled wilderness to Historic Fort Selkirk

MOST OFTEN HEARD COMMENT:
"The highlight of our Yukon trip!"

6 Hour Trip leaving MINTO RESORT
10 a.m. Daily • 2 HR. Evening Trip

OPERATED BY EXPERIENCED LOCAL RIVERMEN

$70 - incl. GST • $50 - U.S.
BRING A LUNCH

FOR BOOKINGS CALL
SELECT RESERVATIONS AT
PHONE (867) 393-2420
FAX (867) 667-2171
TOLL FREE 1-877-735-3281

EMAIL jeano@yknet.yk.ca
(SORRY, NO CREDIT CARDS)

BIG RIVER ENTERPRISES

Midway between Whitehorse & Dawson City

MINTO RESORT

Campground • Laundry • Showers
Pull-throughs • Dumping • Fresh Water
Fire Pits • Over 20 RV Sites
Group Tenting Sites • Dry Camping
Tour bus facilities

Tour Bus Lunch by Reservation Only
Radio Phone: 2M-8419 Minto Channel
PO Box 9211, Whitehorse Y1A 4A2
Ph: (867) 633-5537 (Sept - May)

Five Finger Rapids, a navigational hazard on the Yukon, are formed by these rock pillars. (© David Job)

See display ad this section. [ADVERTISEMENT] ▲

J 147.9 (238 km) **D** 175.5 (282.4 km) **S** 267.2 (430 km) Minto Road, a short loop road, leads west to location of the former riverboat landing and trading post of **MINTO**. Check with Big River Enterprises about river tours to Sheep Mountain and Fort Selkirk leaving daily from Minto Resorts.

FORT SELKIRK, 25 river miles/40 km from here, was established by Robert Campbell in 1848 for the Hudson's Bay Co. In 1852, the fort was destroyed by Chilkat Indians, who had dominated the fur trade of central Yukon—trading here with the Northern Tutchone people (Selkirk First Nation), who used the area as a seasonal home and exchanged furs for the Chilkats' coastal goods—until the arrival of the Hudson's Bay Co. The site was occupied sporadically by traders, missionaries and the RCMP until the 1950s. About 40 buildings—dating from 1892 to 1940—still stand in good repair. A river trip to Fort Selkirk lets travelers see the fort virtually unchanged since the turn of the century. A highly recommended side trip, if time permits. Government preservation and interpretation staff are available on site.

Private Aircraft: Minto airstrip; elev. 1,550 feet/472m; length 5,000 feet/1,524m; gravel.

J 158.5 (255.1 km) **D** 166.9 (268.6 km) **S** 279.5 (450.5 km) Side road east to **L'hutsaw Wetlands (Von Wilczek Lakes)**, now a protected area; an important wetlands for duck staging, nesting and moulting.

J 161.7 (260.1 km) **D** 161.7 (260.2 km) **S** 280.9 (452.1 km) **Tthi Ndu Mun Lake (Rock Island Lake)** to east. Water lilies and other seldom seen aquatic wildflowers bloom in the shallow areas of the lake. American coots, rarely seen in the Yukon, nest in the area.

J 162.5 (261.5 km) **D** 160.9 (258.9 km) **S** 281.8 (453.5 km) Turnout by **Meadow Lake** to west. This shallow lake is an athalassic or inland salt lake. Note the white salts deposted on old stumps along the lakeshore. Look for American coots and horned grebes.

Pelly Crossing

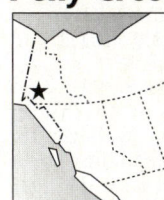

J 167.7 (269.8 km) **D** 155.7 (250.6 km) **S** 287 (461.8 km) Located on the banks of the Pelly River. **Population:** 350. **Emergency Services:** RCMP, phone (867) 537-5555; Nurse, phone (867) 537-4444. **Radio:** CBC North 106.1 FM. **Private Aircraft:** Pelly Airstrip, elev. 1,870 feet/570m; length 3,000 feet/914m; gravel; no services.

Traveler facilities include a motel, take-out food, grocery store, gas and diesel (24-hour access with MasterCard or Visa), minor vehicle repairs, campground, post office and a bank. There is a school, curling rink, baseball field, swimming pool, church and craft shop. ▲

Pelly Crossing became a settlement when the Klondike Highway was put through in 1950. A ferry transported people and vehicles across the Pelly River, where the road eventually continued to Dawson City. Most inhabitants of Pelly Crossing came from historic Fort Selkirk. Today, the restored Fort Selkirk can be visited by boat from Pelly Crossing.

This Selkirk Indian community attracted residents from Minto when the highway to Dawson City was built. School, mission and sawmill located near the big bridge. The local economy is based on hunting, trapping, fishing and guiding. The Selkirk Indian Band has erected signs near the bridge on the history and culture of the Selkirk people.

The Selkirk Heritage Centre, located adjacent to the Selkirk Gas Bar, is a replica of the Big Jonathon House at Fort Selkirk. The centre offers self-guided tours of First Nation heritage.

Penny's Place. A unique and cozy oasis in the middle of Yukon's vast wilderness, a "must" visit on your travels North. Stop by for your favourite ice cream, a delicious burger, an espresso while enjoying this quaint spot. Unique gifts. So who is Penny? Drop by and see for yourself. Phone (867) 537-3115. [ADVERTISEMENT]

Klondike Loop Log
(continued)

J 168 (270.3 km) **D** 155.4 (250.1 km) **S** 287.3 (462.3 km) Pelly River bridge.

J 168.6 (271.2 km) **D** 154.8 (249.1 km)

PELLY CROSSING ADVERTISERS

Penny's Place ....Ph. (867) 537-3115
Selkirk Centre ....Ph. (867) 537-3031

KLONDIKE LOOP

Yukon tourists arrive at Moose Creek Lodge at Milepost J 226.4. (© Earl L. Brown, staff)

S 287.8 (463.2 km) Turnout with litter barrel to east. View of Pelly Crossing and river valley. A historical marker here honours the Canadian Centennial (1867–1967). The Pelly River was named in 1840 by explorer Robert Campbell for Sir John Henry Pelly, governor of the Hudson's Bay Co. The Pelly heads near the Northwest Territories border and flows approximately 375 miles/603 km to the Yukon River.

J 169.7 (273 km) D 153.7 (247.3 km) S 288.9 (465 km) **Private Aircraft:** Airstrip to east; elev. 1,870 feet/570m; length 3,000 feet/914m; gravel. No services.

J 184.2 (296.4 km) D 139.2 (224 km) S 301.1 (484.6 km) Large turnout to west. Bridge over Willow Creek.

J 194 (312.1 km) D 129.4 (208.2 km) S 313.2 (504.1 km) Access road west to **Wrong Lake** (stocked); fishing.

J 195 (313.8 km) D 128.4 (206.6 km) S 314.3 (505.8 km) Turnout with litter barrel to west. Winding descent begins for northbound traffic.

J 203.4 (327.3 km) D 120 (193.1 km) S 322.7 (519.3 km) Bridge over **Crooked Creek.** Southern boundary of Ddhaw Gro Special Management Area (formerly McArthur Wildlife Sanctuary). Pike; grayling, use flies, summer best.

Grey Hunter Peak and surrounding hillsides support many species of wildlife, including Fannin sheep.

J 204.7 (329.4 km) D 118.7 (191 km) S 324 (521.4 km) Pull-through turnout with litter barrel to east at turnoff for **Ethel Lake** Yukon government campground. Drive in 16.6 miles/26.7 km on narrow and winding side road (not recommended for large RVs) for campground; 12 sites, boat launch, fishing. Camping permit ($12).

J 211.3 (340 km) D 112.1 (180.2 km) S 330.7 (532.2 km) Stewart Crossing government maintenance camp to east.

J 211.4 (340.2 km) D 113.3 (182.3 km) S 333.1 (537.5 km) Stewart Crossing; gas station, RV camping available. Turnout with information sign west side of highway; Silver Trail information booth.

In 1886 **STEWART CROSSING** was the site of a trading post established by Arthur Harper, Alfred Mayo and Jack McQuesten to support gold mining in the area. Later a roadhouse was built here as part of the Whitehorse to Dawson overland stage route. Stewart Crossing also functioned as a fuel stop for the riverboats and during the 1930s was a transfer point for the silver ore barges from Mayo. Harper, Mayo and McQuesten are 3 prominent names in Yukon history. Harper, an Irish immigrant, was one of the first white men to prospect in the Yukon, although he never struck it rich. He died in 1898 in Arizona. (His son, Walter Harper, was on the first complete ascent of Mount McKinley in 1913. Walter died in 1918 in the SS *Princess Sophia* disaster off Juneau.)

Mayo, a native of Maine, explored, prospected and traded in the Yukon until his death in 1924.

McQuesten, like Harper, worked his way north from the California goldfields. Often referred to as the "Father of the Yukon" and a founding member of the Yukon order of Pioneers, Jack Leroy Napoleon McQuesten ended his trading and prospecting days in 1898 when he moved to California. He died in 1909 while in Seattle for the Alaska–Yukon–Pacific Exposition.

J 211.7 (340.7 km) D 111.7 (179.7 km) S 331 (532.7 km) Stewart River bridge. The Stewart River flows into the Yukon River upstream from Dawson City.

J 211.8 (340.8 km) D 111.6 (179.5 km) S 331.1 (532.8 km) Turnoff for Mayo, Elsa and Keno.

Junction with the Silver Trail (Yukon Highway 11) to Mayo, Elsa and Keno. See the "Silver Trail" log beginning on the opposite page.

J 212.2 (341.4 km) D 111.2 (179 km) S 331.4 (533.4 km) View to west of Stewart River and mountains as highway climbs northbound.

J 218.2 (351.1 km) D 105.2 (169.3 km) S 337.5 (543.1 km) Dry Creek.

J 221.7 (356.7 km) D 101.7 (163.7 km) S 341 (548.7 km) Stewart River viewpoint to west. A major tributary of the Yukon River, the Stewart River was named for James G. Stewart, who discovered it in 1849. Stewart was assistant to Robert Campbell of the Hudson's Bay Co.

J 226.4 (364.2 km) D 97 (156.1 km) S 345.6 (556.2 km) **Moose Creek Lodge.** A must for Yukon travelers! An authentic trapper's cabin and a large selection of Northern books, souvenirs and crafts. In our cozy cafe, enjoy a hearty breakfast, our scrumptious cinnamon buns and home-baked bread. We feature daily homemade soups, delicious belt-bustin' sandwiches and burgers, and mouth-watering home-baked pies. Meet Max the Mosquito and Murray the Moose! Cozy log cabins. For reservations call operator, ask for JL 39570 Stewart Crossing Channel; fax (867) 996-2048; or write Bag 1, Mayo, YT Y0B 1M0. Moose Creek is also serving group tours in their beautiful open-air gazebo, reservations a must. VISA. Your hosts, Andre and Maja Gigon. [ADVERTISEMENT]

J 226.5 (364.5 km) D 96.9 (155.9 km) S 345.8 (556.5 km) Moose Creek bridge.

J 226.8 (364.9 km) D 96.6 (155.4 km) S 346.1 (556.9 km) Turnout to west at turnoff for Moose Creek Yukon government campground adjacent to **Moose Creek** and Stewart River; good picnic spot. There are 30 RV sites, 6 tent-only sites, kitchen shelter, playground and playfield. Camping permit ($12). Good fishing for grayling, 1 to 1¼ lbs. Short trail to Stewart River is a 30-minute walk through boreal forest along Moose Creek. Note the change of habitat from dry spruce forest to floodplain willow. Listen for Northern waterthrush, Wilson's warbler and common yellowthroat.

J 239.8 (385.9 km) D 83.6 (134.5 km) S 359.1 (577.9 km) Bridge over McQuesten River, a tributary of the Stewart River, named for Jack (Leroy Napoleon) McQuesten.

J 244.4 (393.3 km) D 79 (127.1 km) S 364.3 (586.3 km) Partridge Creek Farm.

J 246.2 (396.2 km) D 77.2 (124.2 km) S 365.5 (588.2 km) **Private Aircraft:** McQuesten airstrip 1.2 miles/1.9 km west; elev. 1,500 feet/457m; length 5,000 feet/1,524m; gravel and turf. No services.

J 248.2 (399.4 km) D 75.2 (127.1 km) S 367.5 (591.4 km) Clear Creek, access via side road west.

J 260.5 (419.2 km) D 63.5 (102.2 km) S 382.9 (617.2 km) Beaver Dam Creek.

J 262.8 (422.9 km) D 62.9 (101.2 km) S 379.8 (611.2 km) Willow Creek.

J 265.9 (427.9 km) D 57.5 (92.5 km) S 385.2 (619.9 km) Turnout to east at **Gravel Lake,** an important wetland for migratory birds in spring and fall. Just north of the turnout a dirt road leads to the lake. Because of its location on the Tintina Trench corridor, unusual birds are sometimes seen here, including ruddy ducks, black scoters and the most northerly sightings of American coots. (See also **Milepost J 286.1.**)

J 268.9 (432.7 km) D 54.5 (87.7 km) S 388.2 (624.7 km) Meadow Creek.

J 269.2 (433.2 km) D 54.2 (87.2 km) S 388.5 (625.2 km) Rest area with litter barrel to south.

J 273.1 (439.5 km) D 50.3 (80.9 km) S 392.4 (631.5 km) French Creek.

J 276.1 (444.7 km) D 47 (75.6 km) S 396.9 (638.7 km) Stone Boat Creek.

J 285.5 (459.3 km) D 37.9 (61 km) S 404.7 (651.3 km) Rest area.

J 286.1 (460.3 km) D 37.3 (60 km) S 405.3 (652.3 km) **Tintina Trench Viewpoint.** Large gravel turnout to east overlooking Tintina Trench. This geologic feature, which extends hundreds of miles across

(Continues on page 264)

Silver Trail

The Silver Trail leads northeast from **Milepost J 211.8** Klondike Highway to Mayo, Elsa and Keno City. It is approximately 140 miles/225 km round-trip to Keno City and an easy day trip for motorists. If you have a Yukon Explorer's Passport, the Binet House and the Keno Mining Museum in Keno are considered the 2 most exclusive passport stamps.

The road is asphalt-surfaced to Mayo, and well-maintained gravel from Mayo to Keno City. Gas is available only at Stewart Crossing and Mayo.

The Silver Trail to Mayo follows the Stewart River through what has been one of the richest silver mining regions in Canada. The Silver Trail region encompasses the traditional lands of the Na Cho N'y'ak Dun First Nations.

YUKON HIGHWAY 11
Distance is measured from the junction with the Klondike Highway (K).

K 0 Silver Trail (Stewart Crossing). The Silver Trail leads northeast from **Milepost J 211.8** on the Klondike Highway.

K 0.2 (0.3 km) Distance marker shows Mayo 51 km, Elsa 97 km, Keno 110 km.

K 1.2 (2 km) Stewart River to the south.

K 3 (4.8 km) CAUTION: Slow for curve. Turnout to south.

K 9.6 (15.4 km) Large gravel pit turnout to south.

K 12 (19.2 km) Large double-ended turnout with litter barrels overlooking the Stewart River.

K 27.4 (44.1 km) Pull-through rest area; outhouses, litter barrel, picnic tables.

K 30.7 (49.5 km) Winding descent for northeast-bound traffic; good view of valley.

K 31.2 (50.2 km) McIntyre Park picnic area to south on banks of the Mayo River; 9 picnic sites and a shelter.

K 31.3 (50.3 km) Mayo River bridge. Good fishing from bridge for grayling.

K 31.9 (51.3 km) Junction with access road to Mayo (description follows). Turn right (south) for Mayo, keep left (north) for road to Elsa and Keno City.

Interpretive panels at this viewing deck provide information about the Mayo–Keno area. (© Earl L. Brown, staff)

Silver Trail Tourism Assn

Box 268
Mayo, Yukon
Y0B 1M0

The Heart of the Yukon
Where History Beats Strong!

Phone: (867) 996-2050
Fax: (867) 996-2728
email: ronaghan@yknet.yk.ca

• History • Canoeing • Fishing • Wildlife • Biking • Hiking • Photography • Gold-Panning • Snowshoeing • Snowmobiling • Horseback Riding • Cross Country Skiing

The Yukon's Best Kept Secret!

Km 76, Silver Trail Hwy
Halfway Lakes
Mayo, Yukon
Y0B 1M0

The Largest Log Lodge in the Yukon
Beautiful Lakeside View
Cozy Atmosphere
Spacious Accomodations
Home Cooking - Fresh Baking
Daily Specials
Open Daily - Year Round

(403) 997-0542
Fax or Voice Message: (867) 996-2118
Sorry, We are Unable to Accept Debit or Credit Cards

North Star Motel
Bernard & Silvia Menelon
Kitchen Units & Color T.V. Winter Plug-ins

Box 340
Mayo, Yukon
Y0B 1M0

Phone: (867) 996-2231
Fax: (867) 996-2936
northstar@yknet.yk.ca

Heartland Services
Full Service Gas & Diesel
Auto and Bottled Propane
Towing Services
Convenience Store
Video Rentals
Visitor Information
Phone Cards
Fishing Licenses
Free Coffee with Fill-up
OPEN 7 DAYS A WEEK 8AM - 8PM

Phone: (867) 996-2329
Fax: (867) 996-2503
YEAR ROUND

Mayo Petroleum Sales, Cafe & Cabins
P.O. Box 219, Yukon, YT Y0B 1M0
Tel: (867) 996-2530, Fax: (867) 996-2022

Located at the Mayo junction on the Silver Trail Hwy.
Gas and Diesel. Oil and lube. Full service.
Cafe, home cooking and fresh baking.
Clean washrooms & pay phone. OPEN DAILY

Keno City, Yukon
Art Cards, Prints, Watercolours,
Acrylics and Workshops
LOPONEN ARTS NORTH
June 1st - Aug 15th, 10AM - 6PM & Group Requests
www.loponenartsnorth.com

Crooked Creek Wilderness Tours
Come visit pristine wilderness in the Heart of the Yukon
Your Interactive Wilderness Adventures

Fishing Photography Wildlife Viewing
email: crookedcreekwildtours@yahoo.com Ph/Fx (867) 996-2721
www.crookedcreekwildtours.com Dan & Dorothy McDiarmid

Duncan Creek Gold Dusters
Operating Placer Mine
Family Operation
Unlimited Gold Panning
Souvenir Shop Guided Tours
Call Operator and ask for Radio Phone
JJ3-6558, Elsa Channel

Bedrock Motel
12 modern Rooms Full serviced grassed RV Park
Propane Sale Laundry Satelite TV
Open Year Round
www.bedrockmotel.yt.ca Phone: (867) 996-2290
email: bedrockmotel@yt.sympatico.ca Fax: (867) 996-2728

Silver Trail (continued)

Mayo

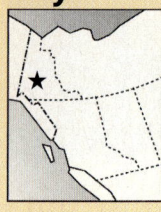

Located on the bank of the Stewart River near its confluence with the Mayo River. **Population:** 470. **Emergency Services: RCMP,** phone (867) 996-5555. **Fire Dept.,** phone (867) 996-2222. **Nursing Station,** phone (867) 996-4444.

Visitor Information: At Binet House Interpretive Centre, open 10 A.M. to 6 P.M. daily from late June through first week in September; phone (867) 996-2926. Web site: www.yukonweb.com/community/mayo. Exhibits at the interpretive centre include floral and mineral displays, silver and galena samples, and information panels on mining and geology. Get your Yukon Explorer's Passport stamped here.

Elevation: 1,650 feet/503m. **Climate:** Residents claim it's the coldest and hottest spot in Yukon. Record low, -80°F/-62.2°C (February 1947); record high, 97°F/36.1°C (June 1969). **Radio:** CBC 1230, CHON-FM 98.5, CKRN 98-FM. **Television:** CBC Anik, Channel 7, BCTV, TVNC, ITV, WDIV. **Transportation:** Charter floatplane and helicopter service available. Scheduled bus service.

Private Aircraft: Mayo airstrip, 4 miles/6.5 km north; elev. 1,653 feet/504m; length 4,850 feet/1,478m; gravel; fuel 100, Jet B.

Mayo began as a river settlement and port in 1902–03 after gold was discovered in the area. It was also known as Mayo Landing. River traffic increased with silver ore shipments from Keno Hill silver mines to Whitehorse. Today, Mayo is a service centre for mineral exploration in the area. Yukon Electrical Co. Ltd. operates a hydroelectric project here.

Mayo has most traveler facilities including 2 motels and bed and breakfasts; food service at Bedrock Motel, Chinese restaurant and a cafe; laundromat; 2 gas stations (diesel); fishing licenses and snack bar; hardware, grocery and variety stores (closed Sunday). Tire repair and minor vehicle repair are available. Post office, liquor store and library located in the Territorial Building. Bank service available.

Bedrock Motel. Located 1 mile north of Mayo on the Silver Trail. New facility containing 12 spacious rooms. Full baths, continental breakfast, laundry facilities, air conditioning, wheelchair-accessible suite. Major credit cards accepted. Rates from $85 up. Automotive and bottle propane available, dump station, shower, camping, grassed RV sites, full hookups available. Darren and Joyce Ronaghan, Box 69, Mayo, YT Y0B 1M0. Phone (867) 996-2290, fax (867) 996-2728 or email bedrock@yt.sympatico.ca. www.silvertrail.net/bedrock. [ADVERTISEMENT] ▲

A walking tour brochure of Mayo's historic sites is available. There is a viewing deck with interpretive signs overlooking the Stewart River. Canoeists can put in at Mayo on the Stewart River for a paddle to Stewart Crossing or Dawson City.

The Mayo Midnight Marathon takes

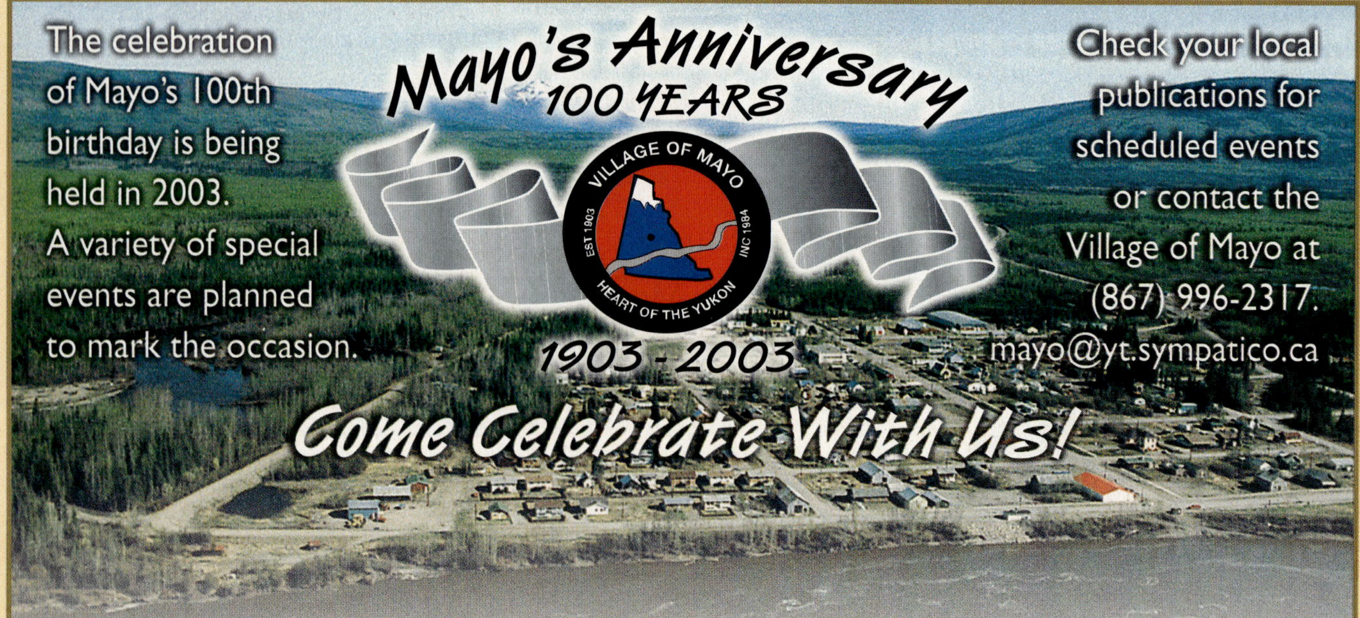

Be sure to get your Yukon Explorer's Passport stamped at the Binet House in Mayo.
(© Earl L. Brown, staff)

KENO CITY

A charming frontier community of 25 with great back country. Ideal for outdoor activities; (hiking, fishing, rock-hunting, gold panning, photography, skiing, etc.) Also an ideal refuge for people with artistic interests- quiet and unhurried. A place for people who would like to experience the wilderness while still enjoying the comforts of civilization.

place in June. The race includes a half marathon, half marathon walk and 10K races. Phone (867) 996-2368 for details.

Village of Mayo. See display ad this section.

Silver Trail Log
(continued)

K 32.8 (52.8 km) Mayo airport, built in 1928 by the Treadwell Mining Co.

K 34.9 (56.2 km) Side road to Mayo hydro dam, built in 1951 and completed in 1952.

K 35.8 (57.6 km) Turnoff to west for **Five Mile Lake** Yukon government campground; 20 sites, picnic tables, firepits, swimming and boat launch.

K 36.1 (58.1 km) Five Mile Lake day-use area. *Pavement ends, gravel begins, northbound.*

K 37.6 (60.5 km) Wareham Lake to east, created by the Mayo River power project.

K 38.2 (61.4 km) Survival shelter to east.

K 42.9 (69 km) **Junction** of Yukon Highway 11 with Minto Lake Road and Duncan Creek Road. Continue on Yukon Highway 11 for Keno City.

For **Minto Lake** drive 12 miles/19 km west on Minto Lake Road; good fishing for lake trout and grayling. Also access to Highet Creek.

The 25-mile/40-km Duncan Creek Road to east was the original Silver Trail used by Treadwell-Yukon during the 1930s to haul silver ore from Keno into Mayo. It is now a back road into Keno City. Inquire in Keno City about road conditions on this side road.

K 47.1 (77 km) Watch for turnoff for Mount Haldane trail; follow gravel road 2 miles/3.2 km to trailhead. This 4-mile-/6.4-km-long walking trail leads to the summit of **Mount Haldane**, elev. 6,023 feet/1,836m, and offers sweeping views of the McQuesten River valley and the towns of Elsa and Mayo. A brochure on the trail suggests anyone in average physical condition can make the round-trip in 6 hours (including an hour for lunch at the top). But a couple of MILEPOST® readers said they found the trail was poorly marked and a *strenuous* 6-hour (minimum) hike, with slippery sections and a huge scree at the end. Inquire locally for current conditions. The switch-backed trail is visible on the south face of Mount Haldane. The trail was cut by a mining company in the 1970s.

K 48 (77.2 km) **Halfway Lakes**; fishing for northern pike. Silver Trail Inn; food and lodging in summer.

K 49 (78.8 km) Mount Haldane Lions survival shelter.

K 54.9 (88.3 km) South McQuesten River Road.

K 60.3 (97 km) **ELSA** (pop. 10); information sign here reads: "In 1924, prospector Charlie Brefalt staked a silver claim here on Galena Hill and named it after his sister, Elsa. It proved to be a major discovery and eventually produced millions of ounces of silver. Other properties in the area, such as the Silver King and Calumet, also developed into major mines. By the 1930s, the town of Elsa had taken shape and it gradually became the major community serving the mines. Since, 1948, Elsa has been home to United Keno Hill Mines, which at one time was the world's fourth largest producer of silver concentrates."

A plaque here commemorates American engineer Livingston Wernecke, who came to the Keno Hill area in 1919 to investigate the silver–lead ore discoveries for Treadwell–Yukon Mining Co.

The Mining Museum at Keno—another highly valued stamp on the Yukon Explorer's Passport. (© Earl L. Brown, staff)

K 63.8 (102.6 km) Side road leads north to Hanson Lakes and McQuesten Lake. Galena Mountains to east. An information sign marks the Wind River trail, a former winter road to oil and mining exploration sites, which leads 300 miles/483 km north to the Bell River. The twin towers are abandoned telephone relays.

Keno City

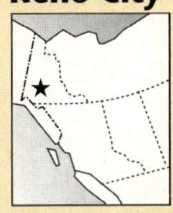

K 69.1 (111.2 km) Historic frontier town nestled in the mountains at the end of the Silver Trail. **Population: 20. Visitor Information:** At the Keno Mining Museum; or visit www.kenocity.yk.ca. Originally called Sheep Hill by the early miners, Keno City was renamed Keno—a gambling game—after the Keno mining claim that was staked by Louis Bouvette in July 1919. Enormously rich discoveries of silver made Keno City a boom town in the 1920s. Today it is home to an eclectic mix of oldtimers, miners, and artists.

Visitor services in Keno City include accommodations at Keno Cabins B&B; food at Keno Cafe, Mooseberry Bakery and the Keno City Hotel snack bar; and gift shops and galleries. Washers, dryers and showers are available for public use at the recreation hall. Keno City Campground, in town next to Lightning Creek, has 17 secluded sites, water, firewood and firepits.

The Keno Mining Museum is well worth a visit. Unique and informative displays capture the area's rich gold and silver mining history. Displays include tools and equipment used in the early days of mining; a large photograph collection; and artifacts associated with everyday life in the Yukon's isolated mining communities. Museum hours are 10 A.M. to 6 P.M. in summer. Have your Yukon Passport stamped here. Phone (867) 995-2792.

A network of good hiking and biking trails criss-cross the area, leading to historic mine sites. scenic valleys and alpine meadows. The trails vary in distance from a half-mile/1 km to 12 miles/20 kms, and range from easy to strenuous. There is also fishing and canoeing on area lakes.

A popular side trip is walking or driving the winding Keno Hill Road 6.5 miles/10.5 km to the signpost monument on top of **Keno Hill**, elev. 6,065 feet/1,849m. Panoramic views of the valley and mountains ranges from the summer.

NOTE: Inquire locally about road conditions before driving Keno Hill Road to the summit, or Duncan Creek Road back to Mayo.

**Return to Milepost J 211.8
Klondike Loop**

KENO CITY ADVERTISERS

Insa Design Studio
 Gallery..........................www.kenocity.info
Keno Cabins B&B..............Ph. (867) 995-2829
Keno Campground......Beside Lightning Creek
Keno Mining Museum......Ph. (867) 995-2729

KLONDIKE LOOP

(Continued from page 260)
Yukon and Alaska, is the largest fault in North America and 1 of 2 major bird migration corridors in the Yukon (the other is the Shakwak Trench).

J 291.6 (469.2 km) **D 31.8** (51.2 km) **S 410.9** (661.2 km) Flat Creek bridge.

J 294 (473 km) **D 29.4** (47.3 km) **S 413.2** (665 km) Large turnout to east with historic sign about Klondike River and information sign on Dempster Highway.

J 297.9 (479.4 km) **D 25.5** (41 km) **S 417.2** (671.4 km) **Dempster Corner**; Klondike River Lodge east side of highway just north of the junction; open year-round, food, lodging, camping, gas, diesel and propane. ▲

Klondike River Lodge. See display ad this section.

Junction of Klondike Highway and the Dempster Highway (Yukon Highway 5), which leads northeast to Inuvik, NWT. See DEMPSTER HIGHWAY section for log of that road.

NOTE: The Dempster Highway and Northwest Territories Information Centre is located in the B.Y.N. Building on Front Street in Dawson

Information panel at Milepost J 0.1 of the Dempster Highway outlines history, culture and wildlife. (© Earl L. Brown, staff)

City; it is open 9 A.M. to 8 P.M., June to September. Phone (867) 993-6167, fax 993-6334.

J 303.7 (488.7 km) **D 19.97** (31.7 km) **S 423** (680.7 km) Goring Creek.

J 308.2 (495.9) **D 15.2** (24.5 km) **S 427.4** (687.9 km) **Tintina Bakery.** Great news, folks, you've arrived at the favourite little bakery in the Klondike. A worthy destination, or a marvelous stop en route! Homemade pastries made with real butter; Danishes with wild berry filling; savory snacks featuring fresh, homegrown herbs; and a renowned selection of handcrafted bread, including authentic sourdough. Cappuccino. Home of Tombstone Gallery: a celebration of our talented artists, and a view of the North through their eyes. Unique art cards available. 2 minutes from the highway. Ample RV turnaround area. Open daily from 8 A.M. to 6 P.M. Phone (867) 993-5558. [ADVERTISEMENT]

J 311.5 (501.2 km) **D 11.9** (19.2 km) **S 430.7** (693.2 km) Turnoff to north for **Klondike River** Yukon government campground, located on Rock Creek near the Klondike River; 38 sites, kitchen shelter, drinking water, playground. Camping permit ($12). A nature trail leads to the river. Flora includes Labrador tea, highbush cranberry, prickly rose, Arctic bearberry and horsetails. ▲

J 312 (502 km) **D 11.4** (18.3 km) **S 431.2** (694 km) Dawson City airport to south. Pay phone in airport terminal.

Private Aircraft: Runway 02-20; elev. 1,211 feet/369m; length 5,000 feet/1,524m; gravel; fuel 80 (in drums at Dawson City), 100, JP4. Flightseeing trips and air charters available.

J 313.6 (504.6 km) **D 9.8** (15.8 km) **S 433** (696.8 km) Hunker Creek Road to south. Hunker Creek Road (gravel) connects with Upper Bonanza Creek Road and loops back to the Klondike Highway via Bonanza Creek Road.

J 314.5 (506.2 km) **D 8.9** (14.3 km) **S 433.9** (7698.2 km) Turnout to south with point of interest sign about Hunker Creek. Albert Hunker staked the first claim on Hunker Creek Sept. 11, 1896. George Carmack made the big discovery on Bonanza Creek on Aug. 17, 1896. Hunker Creek is 16 miles/26 km long, of which 13 miles/21 km was dredged between 1906 and 1966.

J 315.2 (507.2 km) **D 8.2** (13.2 km) **S 434.5** (699.2 km) Bear Creek Road leads to subdivision.

J 315.8 (508.2 km) **D 7.6** (12.2 km) **S 435.1** (700.2 km) Turnout with historic sign about the Yukon Ditch and tailings to north. To the south is **Bear Creek Historical Site**, operated by Parks Canada. This 62-acre compound of the Yukon Consolidated Gold Corp. features blacksmith and machinery shops and Gold Room. Tours daily from the end of May to early September. Admission charged.

J 319.1 (513.5 km) **D 4.3** (6.9 km) **S 438.4** (705.5 km) Callison industrial area; Mackenzie Petroleum Ltd. (diesel, unleaded), charter helicopter service, ministorage, bulk fuel plant and heavy equipment repairs. Access to Ridge Road Heritage Trail lower trailhead (see Attractions in Dawson City).

Mackenzie Petroleum Ltd. See display ad this section.

J 320.7 (516 km) **D 2.7** (4.3 km) **S 439.9** (708 km) Commercial RV park and gold panning at **junction** with **Bonanza Creek Road**; access to Dredge No. 4 (7.8 miles/12.3 km) and Discovery Claim (9.3 miles/14.8 km). Bonanza Creek Road is maintained for 11 miles/18 km. It connects with Upper

---

25 Miles South of Dawson City At Dempster Corner

Klondike River Lodge

MILE 0 DEMPSTER HIGHWAY

Phone/FAX (867) 993-6892
OPEN ALL YEAR
WINTER HOURS 7:30 a.m. to 8:30 p.m.
SUMMER HOURS 7:00 a.m. to 10:30 p.m.
Extended Summer Hours
"YUKON HOSPITALITY"
Restaurant • Motel • Grocery Store
Ice • Lounge & Off Sales

Gas & Diesel • Propane VISA
 Towing • Tires & Repairs MasterCard
Licensed Mechanic

RV Park With Hookups
Dump Station • Car Wash
Pay Phone • Laundromat & Showers

"Stop Here For Dempster Highway Information"

MACKENZIE PETROLEUM LTD.

(CALLISON INDUSTRIAL AREA – ENTERING DAWSON CITY)

PLAN TO FILL UP HERE FOR THE LOWEST PRICE GAS & DIESEL IN DAWSON AND AREA

VISA • DIESEL • UNLEADED • OILS & LUBES Interac

867-995-5130 - OPEN 8AM - 6PM (MON - SAT)

Klondike Loop traverses the heart of the legendary Klondike gold fields.

Bonanza Creek Road (gravel), which provides access to Ridge Road Heritage Trail and loops back to the Klondike Highway via Hunker Creek Road.

GuggieVille R.V. & Gold Panning. Good Sam. This clean, attractive campground is built on dredge tailings at the former site of the Guggenheim's mining camp. 70 RV sites with water and electricity (15- and 30-amp), 15 pull-throughs, 20 unserviced sites, public

Gold panners at Dawson City hope for more than just a "flash in the pan."
(© David Job)

showers ($2 each). RV wash, dump station and laundromat. Email access. Gold panning discount for those staying at GuggieVille. Gasoline discount coupons available. Phone (867) 993-5008. Fax (867) 993-5006. Reservations recommended. Email: guggieville@dawson.net. www.yukoninfo.com/guggieville. [ADVERTISEMENT] ▲

Dredge No. 4 is the largest wooden hull dredge in North America. (See "Gold Dredges" on page 277 in the TAYLOR HIGHWAY section.) Interpretive centre at dredge site; scheduled tours and a 10-minute video on the restoration of this historic site are offered daily, end of May through August. Admission: $5 adults, $2.50 youth, $12.50 family, or Parks Pass.

Marked by a plaque, **Discovery Claim** was the first gold claim on Bonanza Creek and the one that started the Klondike Stampede of 1898. Visitors are welcome to try gold panning for free at Klondike Visitor Association's **Claim No. 6**, located above Discovery at Mile 9/Km 14 Bonanza Creek Road. Bring your own gold pan.

J 320.8 (516.2 km) D 2.6 (4.2 km) S 440 (708.2 km) **Bonanza Gold Motel & R.V. Park**. See display ad this section. ▲

J 320.9 (516.3 km) D 2.5 (4 km) S 440.1 (708.3 km) RV Park and gas station.

Dawson City R.V. Park & Campground. See display ad this section. ▲

J 321.1 (516.6 km) D 2.3 (3.7 km) S 440.3 (708.6 km) Klondike River bridge.

J 321.8 (517.8 km) D 1.6 (2.6 km) S 441.1 (709.8 km) Dome Road (chip-sealed) to north leads 4.5 miles/7.2 km to **Dome Mountain** (elev. 2,911 feet/887m),

KLONDIKE LOOP

DAWSON CITY R.V. PARK & CAMPGROUND

ON BONANZA CREEK, 5 MINUTES TO DOWNTOWN, FULL FACILITIES, 15 @ 30 AMP SERVICE, SPACIOUS PULL THROUGHS, PICNIC TABLES, TENTING, LAUNDROMAT, SHOWERS, CAR WASH, PROPANE, STORE, RESTAURANT, PAY PHONES, FAX AND INTERNET ACCESS.

Box 750, Dawson City, Yukon Y0B 1G0 • Phone/FAX (867) 993-5142

BONANZA GOLD

MOTEL
New, Clean & Comfortable
45 Rooms • Queen/Standard
Jacuzzi Suites • Handicap Suite
Non-Smoking Rooms
Direct Dial Phones • Cable TV
High Speed Internet Access
Laundromat • Car Wash
"In Window" Fans or Air Conditioners

RV PARK
*Dawson's Only–
Full 'on-site' Hookups*
15/30/50 Amps • Cable TV
Telephone & High Speed Internet Access
Spacious Sites • RV Wash • Ice
Restaurant On Site • Laundromat • Public
Showers • Phone Cards • Post Cards
Northern Books • ON–Site Manager
All Day Goldpanning!

TOLL FREE: 1-888-993-6789 • E-MAIL: bonanzagold@dawson.net • www.bonanzagold.ca
BAG 5000 DAWSON CITY, YUKON Y0B 1G0

which offers views of Dawson City, the Yukon and Klondike rivers, Bonanza Creek and the Ogilvie Mountains.

Rock face on right northbound is known locally as **Crocus Bluff**. Short (0.3 mile/0.4 km) interpretive foot trail leads to viewpoint overlooking Klondike River and Dawson City; interpretive panels. Trailhead is located near the cemetery on Dome Road.

J 322.1 (518.3 km) D 1.3 (2.1 km) S 441.4 (710.3 km) Fifth Avenue. Turnout with sign about the Klondike River to south: "With headwaters in the Ogilvie Mountains, the Klondike River and its tributaries gave birth to the world's greatest gold rush—the Klondike Gold Rush of '98."

J 323.4 (520.3 km) D 0 S 442.6 (712.3 km) Dawson City, ferry at Yukon River. *Description of Dawson City follows. Log of Klondike Loop continues on page 274.*

Dawson City

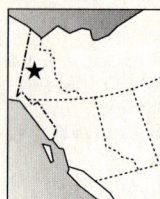

J 323.4 (520.3 km) D 0 S 442.6 (712.3km) Located 165 miles/266 km south of the Arctic Circle on the Yukon River at its junction with the Klondike River. **Population:** 2,019. **Emergency Services: RCMP**, 1st Avenue S., phone (867) 993-5555. **Fire Department**, phone (867) 993-2222. **Nursing station**, phone (867) 993-4444. **Ambulance**, phone (867) 993-4444.

Visitor Information: Visitor Reception Centre, operated by Tourism Yukon and Parks Canada, at Front and King streets, is housed in a replica of the 1897 Alaska Commercial Co. store. Accommodation information, schedule of daily events and a Dawson City street map are available. Three continuous films/videos on Dawson history. Walking tours are part of the daily schedule (fee charged). Open daily, 8 A.M. to 8 P.M. mid-May to mid-September, phone (867) 993-5566, fax (867) 993-6449; web site www.dawsoncity.org. Dawson City has lots to do and see. If you want to take it all in, plan for 3 days to cover most of the attractions. Ask about a Parks Pass, which entitles you to admission to 5 Parks Canada sites for one price.

The Dempster Highway and Northwest Territories Information Centre is located in the B.Y.N. (British Yukon Navigation) Building on Front Street, across from the Yukon visitor centre; open 9 A.M. to 8 P.M., June to September. Information on Northwest Territories and the Dempster Highway. Phone (867) 993-6167, fax 993-6334.

Elevation: 1,050 feet/320m. **Climate:** There are 20.9 hours of daylight June 21, 3.8 hours of daylight on Dec. 21. Mean high in July, 72°F/22.2°C. Mean low in January, -30.5°F/ -34.7°C. First fall frost end of August, last spring frost end of May. Annual snowfall 59.8 inches. **Radio:** CBC 560 AM and 104.9 FM. **Television:** Cable. **Newspaper:** *Klondike Sun* (semi-monthly).

Private Aircraft: Dawson City airport located 11.5 miles/18.5 km southeast (see **Milepost J 315.7**). Customs available.

View of Dawson City from the Top of the World Highway. (© Earl L. Brown, staff)

Description

Dawson City sits at the confluence of the Klondike and Yukon rivers, at what was once a summer fish camp of the Han people. With the discovery of gold on a Klondike River tributary (Rabbit Creek, renamed Bonanza Creek) in 1896, the Han were soon displaced by the influx of whites and the boom town built to serve them.

Most of the prospectors who staked claims on Klondike creeks were already in the North before the big strike, many working claims in the Fortymile area. The men coming North in the great gold rush the following year found most of the gold-bearing streams already staked.

Dawson City was Yukon's first capital, when the Yukon became a separate territory in 1898. But by 1953, Whitehorse—on the railway and the highway, and with a large airport—was so much the hub of activity that the federal government moved the capital from Dawson City, along with 800 civil servants, and years of tradition and pride. Some recompense was offered in the form of a road linking Whitehorse with the mining at Mayo and Dawson City. With its completion, White Pass trucks replaced White Pass river steamers.

New government buildings were built in Dawson, including a fire hall. In 1962 the federal government reconstructed the Palace Grand Theatre for a gold rush festival that featured the Broadway musical *Foxy*, with Bert Lahr, who played the cowardly lion in the classic *Wizard of Oz*. A museum was established in the Administration Building and tours and entertainments were begun.

Dawson City was declared a national historic site in the early 1960s. Parks Canada is currently involved with 35 properties in Dawson City. Many buildings have been restored, some reconstructed and others stabilized. Parks Canada offers an interpretive program each summer for visitors to this historic city.

Lodging & Services

Accustomed to a summer influx of visitors, Dawson has modern hotels and motels (rates average $75 and up) and several bed and breakfasts. The community has a bank, ATM (cash advances on MasterCard and VISA are also available at Diamond Tooth Gertie's Casino), restaurants, 4 laundromats (with showers), a grocery store with bakery, a deli/grocery store, general stores, souvenir

---

DAWSON CITY ADVERTISERS

Amica's Ristorante	Ph. (867) 993-6800
Ancient Voices Wilderness Camp	Ph. (867) 993-5605
Bombay Peggy's Victorian Inn & Lounge	2nd Ave. & Princess St.
Bonanza Gold Motel	Ph. (867) 993-6789
Bonanza Gold R.V. Park	1 mi. from city centre
Claim No. 6	Bonanza Creek Rd.
Cruise the Yukon River	Ph. (867) 993-5599
Dancing Moose Gifts	2nd Ave.
Danoja Zho	Ph. (867) 993-6768
Dawson City Museum	5th Ave. & Church St.
Dawson City RV Park & Campground	Ph. (867) 993-5142
Diamond Tooth Gerties	Ph. (867) 993-5566
Downtown Hotel	Ph. (867) 993-5346
Eldorado Hotel, The	Ph. (867) 993-5451
5th Avenue Bed and Breakfast	Ph. (867) 993-5941
Fortymile Gold Workshop/ Studio	Ph. (867) 993-5690
Gaslight Follies	Palace Grand Theatre
Gold City Tours	Ph. (867) 993-5175
Gold Rush Campground RV Park	5th Ave. & York St.
Guggieville R.V. & Gold Panning	Ph. (867) 993-5008
Hair Cabaret	Ph. (867) 993-5222
Jack London Cabin & Interpretive Centre	Ph. (867) 993-5575
Klondike Kate's Cabins and Restaurant	Ph. (867) 993-6527
Klondike Nugget & Ivory Shop	Ph. (867) 993-5432
Klondike Visitor's Association	Ph. (867) 993-5575
Mackenzie Petroleum Ltd.	Ph. (867) 995-5130
Maximilian's Gold Rush Emporium	Ph. (867) 993-5486
Peabody's Photo Parlour	Ph. (867) 993-5209
PR Service Ltd.	Ph. (867) 667-4144
River of Culture River Cruise & Salmon Bake	Front St.
Select Reservations	Ph. 1-877-735-3281
Top Of The World Golf Course	Ph. (867) 993-5888
Triple J Hotel	Ph. (867) 993-5323
Tr'ondek Hwech'in Cultural Centre	Ph. (867) 993-6768
Westmark Hotels	Ph. (867) 993-5542
Whitehouse Motel	Ph. (867) 993-5576
Yukon Queen II	Ph. (867) 993-5599

shops, churches, art gallery, post office, government offices, government liquor store, nursing station and doctor services, information centre, hostel, swimming pool, tennis, basketball and plenty of entertainment. Many Dawson City merchants abide by the Fair Exchange Policy, offering travelers an exchange rate within 4 percent of the banks'. Dawson City's hotels and motels fill up early, especially at times of special events. Reservations are a must from June through August.

Bombay Peggy's Victorian Inn & Lounge. Centrally located heritage house boasting a past as a house of ill-fame. Victorian-style rooms with private baths and modern amenities for the discerning traveler. Open year-round. 2nd Ave. and Princess Street. Box 411, Dawson City, YT Y0B 1G0. Phone (867) 993-6969; fax 993-6199. [ADVERTISEMENT]

Bonanza Gold Motel. Dawson City's newest accommodation. Located at the south entrance to Dawson, 1 mile from city

centre at the entrance to Bonanza Creek Road. Queen rooms, standard rooms, Jacuzzi suites with private decks, handicap rooms, non-smoking rooms available. Cable TV, direct dial phones, in-window fans or air conditioners. Fax and high speed Internet service. Hungry? Restaurant on site. Full RV facilities at Bonanza Gold RV Park (Good Sam). Our guarantee: if there is a room in Dawson, we'll find it for you. Phone (867) 993-6789, toll-free 1-888-993-6789. Fax (867) 993-6777. Bag 5000, Dawson City, Yukon Y0B 1G0. E-mail: bonanzagold.net; web site www.bonanzagold.ca. [ADVERTISEMENT]

5th Avenue Bed and Breakfast. Located adjacent to the museum overlooking Victory Gardens. A modern air-conditioned home with a historic finish, serving a hot and

hearty, all-you-can-eat breakfast. We guarantee comfort, cleanliness and courteous service along with the most convenient location in town. VISA, MasterCard. Call Tracy and Steve Nordick at phone/fax (867) 993-5941; toll-free 1-866-631-5237. Email: 5thave@5thavebandb.com; www.5thavebandb.com. Box 722, Dawson City, YT Y0B 1G0. [ADVERTISEMENT]

Klondike Kate's Cabins and Restaurant. All new 15 log cabins with private bath, cable TV, telephone and Internet hookup. Canada Select 3 1/2 stars; CAA–AAA 2 diamonds. CAA–AAA recommended restau-

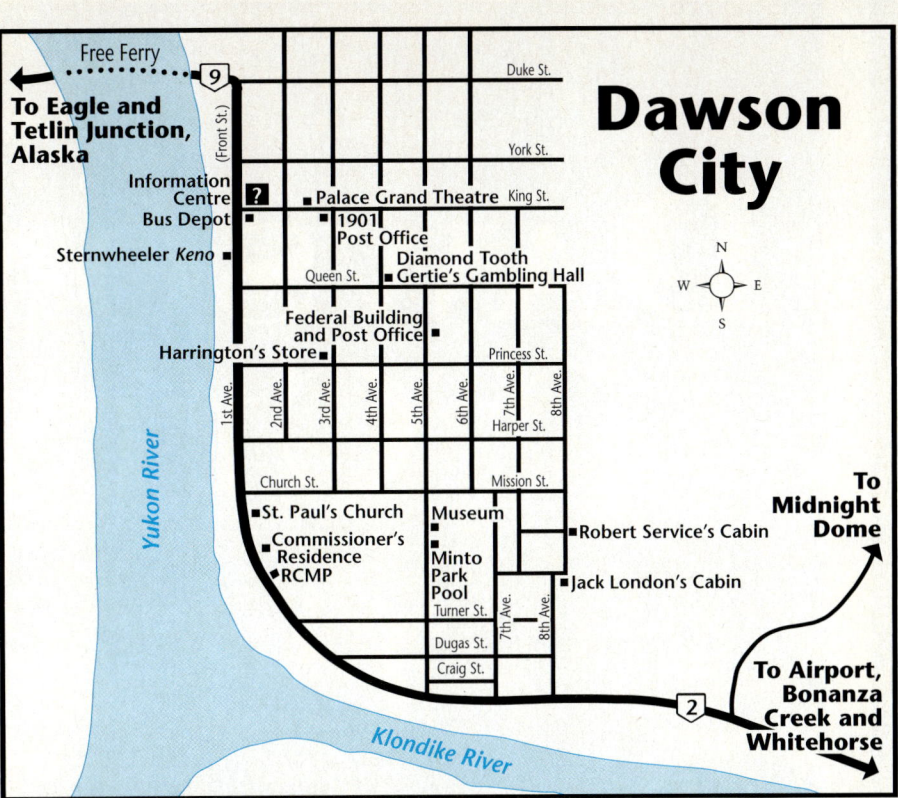

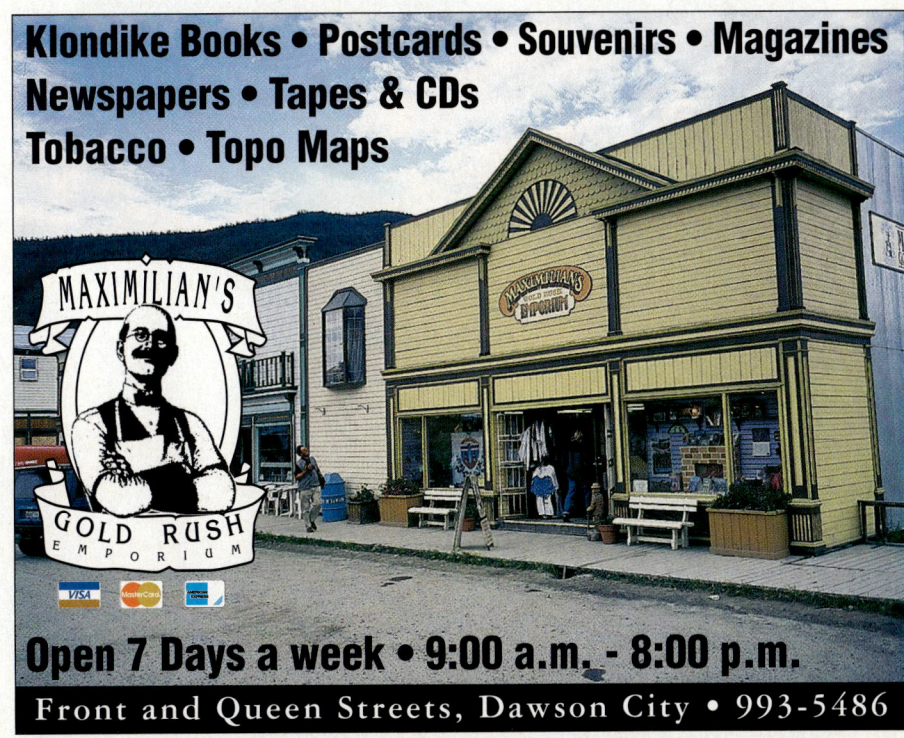

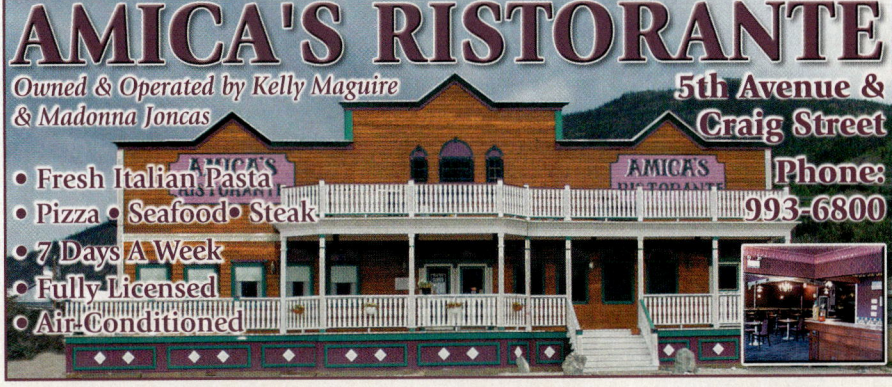

Come for the History...
DAWSON CITY
Stay for the Adventure!

Send for your Dawson City information package today!

Klondike Visitors Association

P.O. Box 389M
Dawson City, Yukon,
Canada Y0B 1G0

tel: (867) 993-5575
fax: (867) 993-6415
e-mail: kva@dawson.net

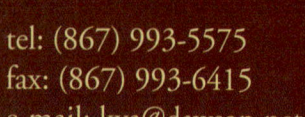
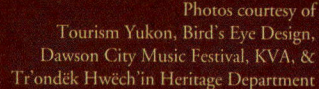

Photos courtesy of Tourism Yukon, Bird's Eye Design, Dawson City Music Festival, KVA, & Tr'ondëk Hwëch'in Heritage Department

www.dawsoncity.ca

DIAMOND TOOTH GERTIES
LIVE ENTERTAINMENT & CASINO
Visit the Yukon's #1 attraction...
Open 7 days a week,
mid-may to mid-september.

GASLIGHT FOLLIES
The magnificent Palace Grand Theatre presents a classical musical comedy.
Mid May - Mid September

JACK LONDON CABIN & INTERPRETIVE CENTRE
Historic Home of the Famous Author
Interpretive Centre & Displays
Daily Presentations

GOLD PANNING
Free Gold Panning!
Claim #6 situated on historic Bonanza Creek.

ACCOMMODATIONS • ATTRACTIONS

Dänojà Zho
long time ago house

Tr'ondëk Hwëch'in Cultural Center, Dawson City, Yukon

Gallery Tours   Photographic Exhibits   AudioVisual Presentations   Interpretive Programs

Open June - Sept   www.trondek.com   867-993-6768
across the street from the Visitor Center   fee for admission

---

THE ELDORADO HOTEL
1-800-764-ELDO (3536)

Bonanza Dining Room
Featuring northern specialties
Pleasant surroundings, excellent service

Sluice Box Lounge
Air Conditioned

Open Year-Round • All Modern Rooms • Suites • Kitchenettes • Phones
Color TV • Laundry • Winter Plug-Ins • All Major Credit Cards Accepted

We are northern hospitality!

3rd Avenue & Princess Street P.O. Box 338 Dawson City, Yukon Y0B 1G0
FOR RESERVATIONS CALL (867) 993-5451 • Fax 993-5256
e-mail: eldorado@yknet.yk.ca • www.eldoradohotel.ca

DAWSON CITY
TRIPLE J HOTEL

- Hotel Rooms • Executive Suite
- Cabins with Kitchenettes/Full Baths
- Air-Conditioned Lounge & Restaurant
- Licensed Outdoor Patio
- Coin Laundry, Cable TV
- Complimentary Airport Shuttle Service

www.triplejhotel.com

Toll Free Reservations 1-800-764-3555 • E-mail: triplej@yknet.ca

5th AVE & QUEEN, BOX 359, DAWSON CITY, Y0B 1G0 • PH: (867) 993-5323 • FAX: (867) 993-5030

WESTMARK HOTELS & INNS

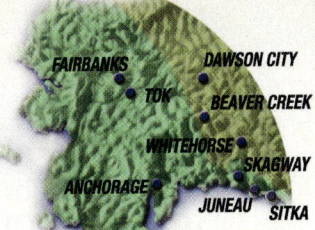

Your Comfort Zone Throughout The Yukon & Alaska.

Nobody knows the Yukon and Alaska like Westmark Hotels. We've got the locations you need, the quality you desire and the service you expect. Comfortable rooms and warm northern hospitality are yours at every Westmark Hotel.

- Full Service Locations
- Restaurants & Lounges
- Convenient Locations
- Northern Wonders Gift Shops
- Alaska Airlines Miles
- Aeroplan Miles

Call us today for information about locations, rates and room availability.

Westmark HOTELS
YUKON / ALASKA
A Holland America Westours Company

Central Reservations
1-800-544-0970
www.westmarkhotels.com

DAWSON CITY:
Fifth & Harper Streets
P.O. Box 420
Dawson City, Yukon Territory Y0B 1G0

867-993-5542

THE YUKON & ALASKA

DAWSON CITY

www.dawsoncity.ca

ACCOMMODATIONS • ATTRACTIONS

DAWSON CITY

WHY STAY ANYWHERE BUT DOWNTOWN AT THE DOWNTOWN!
RESERVATIONS ONLY TOLL FREE: 1-800-661-0514
Ph: (867) 993-5346 Fax: (867) 993-5076 www.downtownhotel.ca
Sourdough Saloon - Home of the SourToe Cocktail

GuggieVille
GOLD GOLD GOLD GOLD GOLD GOLD GOLD GOLD GOLD GOLD GOLD
CLEAN AND QUIET CAMPGROUND ON FAMOUS BONANZA CREEK
RV & GOLD PANNING
Guggieville Campers receive 1 free gold panning per site with this coupon! Toll Free 1-866-860-6535
Box 311, Dawson City, YT Y0B 1G0 • Phone (867) 993-5008 • www.yukoninfo.com/guggieville

river of culture
First Nation Owned & Operated

Beautiful Scenic Tour on the Yukon River
Learn About First Nation History
Daily Cruises Available

YUKON RIVER CRUISE & SMOKED SALMON BBQ

Little Birch Cabin on Front Street
Bag 7070, Dawson City, Yukon Y0B 1G0
E-mail: rivercii@yknet.yk.ca
Phone: (867) 993-5482 • Winter: (867) 993-5384

GOLD RUSH CAMPGROUND RV PARK

DAWSON CITY'S ONLY DOWNTOWN RV PARK
Full Facilities- 30 & 15 Amp Power
Clean & Modern- Internet Access Available
EASY WALKING TO MOST ATTRACTIONS
5th Avenue & York Street Dawson City
E-mail: goldrush@cityofdawson.ca
Phone: (867) 993-5247
Fax (867) 993-6047

YUKON QUEEN II

The beautiful Yukon Queen II was introduced into service in 1999 and offers daily excursions from Dawson City to Eagle, Alaska and return. Let the Captain and crew take you on a river cruise that you will remember fondly as being one of the best excursions you have ever taken.

Visit our office on Front Street in Dawson City or call (867) 993-5599
For advance reservations,
call (867) 668-3225 or
e-mail yukonqueen@dawson.net

KLONDIKE KATE'S RESTAURANT & CABINS
EST. 1990

Historic 3rd Ave. & King St.
• 15 New Beautiful Log Cabins
• All private bath, cable TV, telephone & internet access.
• Open Daily 6:30 am - 11 pm
• $4.99 Breakfast Special
• Canadian & Ethnic Food
• Fully Licensed Dining
• Espresso Coffee
• Dine In or On Our Covered Heated Outdoor Patio

Box 417
Dawson City YT Y0B 1G0
www.klondikekates.ca
ph. 867.993.6527
fx. 867.993.6044

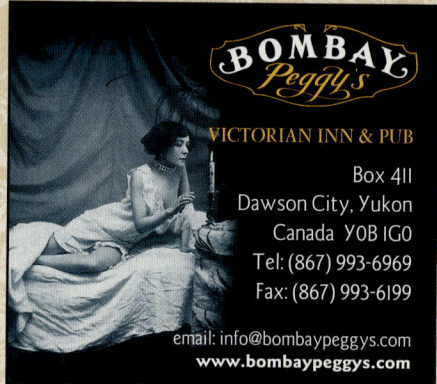

BOMBAY Peggy's
VICTORIAN INN & PUB
Box 411
Dawson City, Yukon
Canada Y0B 1G0
Tel: (867) 993-6969
Fax: (867) 993-6199
email: info@bombaypeggys.com
www.bombaypeggys.com

Need a bed? Call ahead!
Toll Free: **1-877-735-3281**

Select Reservations & Tours

Central reservations and trip planning for individuals, families and groups. Covering BC, Yukon, NWT and Alaska – Tickets, Car Rentals, Alaska State Ferries.
867-393-2420 or E-mail: jeano@yknet.ca
Summer Hours: 8am–8pm (Pacific) 7 days/wk
May 15–Aug 31 **Winter Hours:** 9am–6pm

www.selectrez.com

ATTRACTIONS • SHOPPING

DAWSON CITY

Dancing Moose Gifts

- Features Yukon Made Arts and Crafts
- Fireweed Pottery
- Prints From Local Artists
- Aroma Borealis Products
- Great Souvenir Clothing
- Silver Jewellery

Check us out on 2nd Ave beside Dawson Hardware
Ph: (867) 993-5549 • E-mail: dancingmoose@seewolf.ca

GOLD CITY TOURS

Sightseeing Tours
- Klondike Goldfields
- Dawson City
- Midnight Dome
- Dempster Highway

- Agents for Air North
- Van & bus charters
- Airport shuttles
- Open year-round
- Locally owned & operated

www.goldcitytours.info • (867) 993-5175 • goldcitytours@cityofdawson.ca

P.O. Box 960, Dawson City, Yukon Y0B 1G0 • FAX 993-5261
Located on Front Street, Across from the Steamship "Keno"

Top Of The World Golf Course
Free Overnight RV Parking
www.topoftheworldgolf.com
(867) 993-5888 (on season)
(867) 993-6933 (off season)

Fortymile Gold
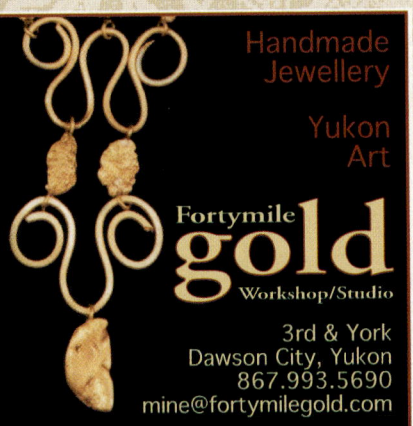
Handmade Jewellery
Yukon Art
Workshop/Studio
3rd & York
Dawson City, Yukon
867.993.5690
mine@fortymilegold.com

KLONDIKE Nugget and Ivory Shop Ltd.
ESTABLISHED 1904
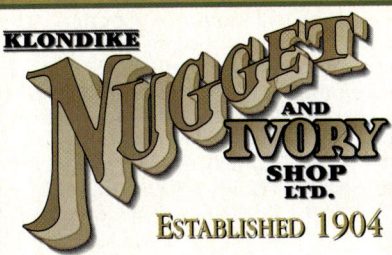

Dawson City's Largest Manufacturer of Gold Nugget Jewellery • OPEN YEAR-ROUND

- Gold Nugget Specimens, Pendants, Jewellery
- Mammoth Ivory Jewellery & Carvings.
- Gold Nugget Display From Over 50 Creeks

Phone: 867•993•5432
E-mail: nuggetshop@dawson.net
Corner of Front & Queen St.
Box 250, Dawson City, Yukon, Y0B 1G0

HAIR Cabaret

Complete Hair Styling • Tanning Salon
Cuts • Colours • Perms
Contact Info:
Maria Fras Hair Stylist
867.993.5222

Massage REGISTERED **THERAPIST**
Sandy McClintock R.M.T

Dawson City Museum

When in town visit the...
DAWSON CITY MUSEUM
Open 10 a.m. - 6 p.m.
Victoria Day - Labour Day
Otherwise by Appointment

The Gold Fields & City Life Galleries
First Nations Collection - Visible Storage
Movies - Demonstrations - Tours
"Meet a Klondike Character"
Gift and Coffee Shop
Klondike History Library
Historic Steam Locomotives

Located on 5th Avenue in the Old Territorial Administration Building
Ph: (867) 993-5291 • FAX: (867) 993-5839 • email: dcmuseum@yknet.yk.ca
P.O. Box 303, Dawson City, Yukon Y0B 1G0

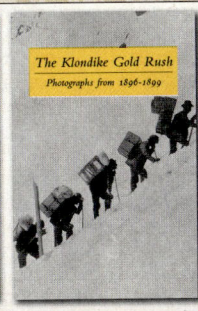
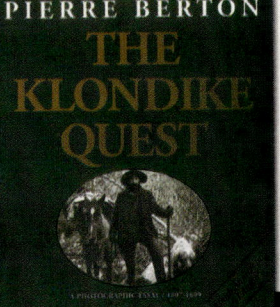
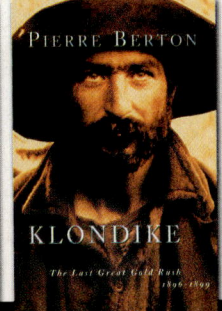
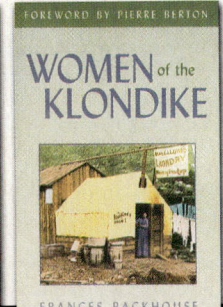

AVAILABLE EVERYWHERE! Distributed by PR Services Ltd. Ph: (867) 667-4144

KLONDIKE LOOP • Dawson City

Gold rush exhibits, locomotives, lectures and demonstrations are featured at the Dawson City Museum. (© Earl L. Brown, staff)

rant. Located near all major attractions. Enjoy the friendly atmosphere of our restaurant, set in a 1904 historic building. Dine inside or on our heated, covered outdoor patio. Full-service, fully licensed restaurant with Canadian and ethnic foods. Espresso coffees. Special $4.99 breakfast. Box 417, Dawson City, YT Y0B 1G0. Phone (867) 993-6527. Fax (867) 993-6044. www.klondikekates.ca. [ADVERTISEMENT]

Whitehouse Motel. Enjoy comfortable and clean accommodations overlooking the Yukon River! Our turn-of-the-century buildings offer quaint and affordable units with kitchenettes, cable TV, private bath, balconies, barbecue and sitting areas. Guest comments: "What a great stay! Quiet spot, excellent view, comfortable room, friendly people. We'd love to come back!" and "The cleanest, friendliest place from Ketchikan to Dawson." A quiet and rustic setting within walking distance from town. Located at the north end of Front Street (just past the ferry landing). Bag 2020, Dawson City, YT Y0B 1G0; phone (867) 993-5576. Email: dcotter@yknet.ca. [ADVERTISEMENT]

Camping

There are 2 Yukon government (YTG) campgrounds in the Dawson area. Yukon River YTG campground is across the Yukon River (by ferry) from town, adjacent to the west-side ferry approach (see **Milepost D 0.2** on Top of the World Highway log, following Dawson City section). Klondike River YTG campground is southeast of town near the airport (see **Milepost J 311.5**). Private RV parks in the Dawson area include Gold Rush Campground, downtown at 5th and York; GuggieVille, east of town at **Milepost J 320.7**; Bonanza Gold RV Park at **Milepost J 320.8**; and Dawson City R.V. Park and Campground at **Milepost J 320.9**. ▲

Transportation

Air: Dawson City airport is 11.5 miles/18.5 km southeast of the city. Air North connects Dawson City with Whitehorse (daily service, except Saturday, in summer); with Inuvik, NWT, Old Crow and Juneau (3 times weekly in summer); and Fairbanks (4 times weekly in summer). Charter service from Alkan Air. Charter and flightseeing tours available.

Ferry: The Yukon government operates a free ferry, the *George Black,* across the Yukon from about the third week in May to mid-October (depending upon breakup and freezeup). The ferry operates 24 hours a day (except for Wednesdays, 5–7 A.M. when it is shut down for servicing), and departs Dawson City on demand. It carries vehicles and passengers across to the public campground and is the only connection to the Top of the World Highway (Yukon Highway 9). Be prepared to wait as long as 3 hours during peak traffic periods (7–11 A.M. and 4–7 P.M. daily). Shut off all propane appliances and follow directions from ferry personnel when loading/unloading. Tour bus traffic has priority 6–9 A.M. and 5–9 P.M.; fuel truck traffic has priority 7 P.M. to 6 A.M. Phone (867) 993-5441 or 993-5344 for more information.

Bus: Service between Whitehorse and Dawson City by Dawson City Courier, 6 days a week year-round; phone (867) 993-6688 (reservations recommended). Service between Inuvik, NWT and Dawson City available by charter only, contact Gold City Tours. Service from Whitehorse via Dawson City to Tok, AK by Alaska Direct Buslines; weekly. Phone (800) 770-6652. Service between Fairbanks and Dawson City by Parks Highway Express, phone 1-888-600-6001.

Taxi: Airport taxi service available from downtown hotels and bed and breakfasts. Scheduled and charter limo service available from Gold City Tours.

Rental Car: Budget Rent-A-Car is located on Craig Street. Car and truck rentals also at Norcan, located 7 miles/11 kms south of town at Fisherville.

Attractions

Take a Walking Tour. Town-core tours leave the Visitor Reception Centre daily in summer. The 1 1/2-hour guided walk highlights the history and charters of Dawson City. Audio tapes also available. Fee charged.

The Commissioner's Residence on Front Street was once the residence of Hon. George Black, M.P., Speaker of the House of Commons, and his famous wife, Martha Louise, who walked to Dawson City via the Trail of '98 and stayed to become the First Lady of the Yukon. A 1-hour tour is given twice daily in summer. Admission is $5 adult, $2.50 youth, $12.50 family.

Take a Bus Tour. Motorcoach and van tours of Klondike creeks, goldfields and Dawson City are available; inquire at Gold City Tours (ask about step-on guide service, too). For a panoramic view of Dawson City, the Klondike River, Bonanza Creek and Yukon River, take the bus or drive the 5 miles/8 km to the top of Dome Mountain (elev. 2,911 feet/887m).

Take a River Tour. The *Yukon Queen II* operates on the Yukon River between Dawson City and Eagle, AK; check with their office on Front Street. River of Culture is a daily cruise on the Yukon River specializing in First Nation history. Check with the Little Birch Cabin on Front Street. Ancient Voices Wilderness Camp transports their guests via *River Dancer* boat to their camp on the Yukon River. Canoe rentals available from Dawson Trading Post and at the hostel across the river.

Ancient Voices Wilderness Camp is your answer if you're looking for a true remote wilderness experience, a place where you can be one-on-one with the beauty of the wilderness and the solitude of nature. Custom design your own experience as this camp offers rustic cabins, wall tents, meals, transportation and a chance to get away from it all! Located 27 miles from Dawson City on the banks of the famous Yukon River. Summer and winter packages from 2 days to 2 weeks. Specialty visits to our renowned Salmon BBQs or Tea & Bannock Outings are available for advanced group bookings. Contact avwcamp@dawson.net or phone (867) 993-5605. www.ancientvoices.ca. [ADVERTISEMENT]

Cruise the Yukon River. Cruise from Dawson City down the famous Yukon River to Eagle, Alaska, aboard the MV *Yukon Queen II.* Retrace the old stern-wheeler route of this historic Gold Rush area as you cruise past abandoned settlements among the forested hills. A hearty prospector's meal is included. Daily departures. One-way fare is $87 U.S. per person. Prices subject to change. Phone (867) 993-5599. [ADVERTISEMENT]

River of Culture River Cruise & Salmon Bake. Enjoy a 2-hour Yukon River cruise aboard the *Luk Chö.* The tour is highlighted with a salmon bake dinner at Little Moosehide Island. Tours depart daily. Located at the "Little Birch Cabin" on Front Street, Dawson City, Yukon. (867) 993-5482. Email: rivercii@yknet.ca. Or visit our web site at www.riverofculture.com. [ADVERTISEMENT]

Diamond Tooth Gertie's Casino, open daily 7 P.M. to 2 A.M. mid-May to mid-September, with 3 shows nightly. Admission charged. No minors. The casino has Klondike gambling tables (specially licensed in Yukon), 56 "Vegas-style" slot machines, bar service and floor shows nightly. You may have a soft drink if you prefer, and still see the cancan girls present their floor show. Persons under 19 not admitted. Gertie's hosts Yukon Talent Night in September.

Dawson City Museum is located in the Old Territorial Administration Building, now a National Historic Site, on 5th Avenue. The museum is open daily from 10 A.M. to 6 P.M., mid-May through early September; by appointment year-round. Admission fees: $7 adults, $5 senior or youth, $16 family, $5/person in pre-booked groups.

Featured are the Kings of the Klondike and City Life Galleries, First Nation and pre-gold rush exhibits, audiovisual and dramatic presentations, and the museum's collection of narrow-gauge locomotives, including a Vauclain-type Baldwin engine, the last one in existence in Canada. Weekly lecture series during summer; check for schedule. The films "City of Gold" and "The Yukoner" are shown daily. Participate in rocker box, gold panning and gold pouring demonstrations.

The museum has a gift shop, wheelchair

Stern-wheelers on the Yukon

During their heyday, there were some 250 stern-wheelers on the Yukon River and other major rivers in the North. Defined as a paddle-wheel steamer having a stern wheel instead of side wheels, these massive wooden vessels plied Northern rivers for almost 100 years, hauling supplies, equipment, ore and passengers.

Stern-wheelers were first introduced to the Yukon River in 1866. Paddle wheels churning, boilers chugging, they moved up and down the river, from after breakup until just before the river froze for the winter.

Yukon stern-wheelers were patterned after the stately Missouri River boats, with flat hulls to keep up speed and "hog posts" on the upper decks to prevent twisting and to haul the ships over shallow points along the river. Because the boats were often lost to snags, rocks, sandbars, ice floes, rapids and other river hazards, they had to be economical to build and repair, so they were constructed from native Douglas fir, cedar and pine.

The typical vessels were about 170 feet long, 35 feet wide and could carry up to 250 tons of cargo. They were run by locomotive-type boiler engines, which cost $1 to $2 per mile to operate, burning about 120 cords of wood on a trip from Whitehorse to Dawson. Wood camps sprang up along the river to provide fuel for the stern-wheelers during their journey.

Airplanes and all-weather roads eventually ended the stern-wheeler's supremacy. Bridges built along the highway to Dawson City were too low to accommodate the old river steamers, and by 1955 all steamers had been beached.

Today, only 2 of these grand old river-

The SS Keno, the last steamer to run the Yukon, rests at Dawson City's riverbank.
(© Earl L. Brown, staff)

boats survive in the Yukon and both are Parks Canada National Historic Sites: the SS *Klondike* in Whitehorse, and the SS *Keno* in Dawson City. The hundreds of others have been lost. Some were sold and moved out of the North. Others were wrecked on the river. One of the worst steamboat disasters on the Yukon River occurred on Sept. 25, 1906, when the paddle-wheeler *Columbia* blew up and burned, killing 6 men on board, after a crew member accidentally fired a shot into a cargo of gunpowder. The SS *Tutshi* (too-shy) survived to become a historic site in Carcross, until she burned to the ground in July 1990.

The SS *Keno* was the last steamer to run the Yukon River. In 1960, she sailed from Whitehorse to her final resting place on the riverbank in Dawson City. The 130-foot SS *Keno* was built in Whitehorse in 1922 by the British Yukon Navigation Company (BYNC). She was used to transport silver, lead and zinc ore from the Mayo District to Stewart.

---

ramp, resource library, genealogy service and an extensive photograph collection. For more information write the museum at Box 303, Dawson City, YT Y0B 1G0; phone (867) 993-5291, fax 993-5839; or email: dcmuseum@yknet.yk.ca.

Visit the Palace Grand Theatre. This magnificently reconstructed theatre, now a national historic site, is home to the "**Gaslight Follies**," a turn-of-the-century entertainment. Performances nightly from mid-May to mid-September. Arizona Charlie Meadows opened the Palace Grand in 1899, and today's visitors, sitting in the curtained boxes around the balcony, will succumb to the charm of this beautiful theatre. Tours of the building are offered daily by Parks Canada, from the end of May through early September. Admission charged or Parks Pass. Reservations and information (867) 993-6217.

Peabody's Photo Parlour. Capture summer memories with a unique Klondike photo in 1900s costumes. Same-day film processing (ask about our 1-hour service), film and camera supplies. Northern artwork, a great selection of postcards, Yukon souvenirs. VISA, MasterCard. Located on 2nd Avenue at Princess. Phone (867) 993-5209.
[ADVERTISEMENT]

SS *Keno* National Historic Site, on the riverbank next to the bank, has tours and an interpretive display. See "Stern-Wheelers on the Yukon" this page for more about this historic Yukon River steamer.

Visit Robert Service's Cabin. On the hillside on 8th Avenue, the author–bank clerk's cabin has been restored by Parks Canada. Visitors come from every part of the world to sign the guest book on the rickety desk where Service wrote his famous poems, including "The Shooting of Dan McGrew" and "The Cremation of Sam McGee." Open daily. Admission fee charged.

Visit the Historic Post Office, where you may buy stamps; all first-class mail sent from here receives the old hand-cancellation stamp. Open daily.

Visit the Jack London Interpretive Centre at the corner of 8th Avenue and First Street. The centre features a log cabin built with some of the original logs from the cabin where London stayed in 1897. (Original logs were also used to build a second replica cabin located in Jack London Square in Oakland, CA.) Also at the site are a cache and a museum with a collection of photos tracing London's journey to the Klondike during the Gold Rush. Interpretations daily mid-May to September. Jack London was the author of *The Call of the Wild* and *White Fang*.

Tr'ondëk Hwëch'in (Han) Cultural Centre, at Front and York streets overlooking the Yukon River, presents the culture and history of the Han First Nation people. The centre has a theatre, arts and crafts shop, art exhibit area and barbecue and picnic facilities. www.trondek.com.

Pierre Berton Residence, located on 8th Avenue, was once home of the famous Canadian author. Now used as a writers' retreat, tours of the home are not available, but you may visit the grounds and read the interpretive signs placed outside by the Klondike Visitors Association.

Special Events. Dawson City hosts a number of unique celebrations during the year. May 16–17, 2003, it's the annual Dawson City International Gold Show, North America's largest consumer trade show for the placer mining industry.

On June 14, 2003, there's Commissioner's Day and the Commissioner's Tea, held at the Commissioner's Residence. The Aboriginal Day Celebration is scheduled for June 21, 2003. And the Midnight Sun Golf Tournament take place June 14, 20–21 and 28, 2003.

KLONDIKE LOOP

The Yukon Gold Panning Championship is held July 1 each year in Dawson City, along with a celebration of Canada Day. The Annual Dawson City Music Festival, July 18–20, 2003, features entertainers and artists from Canada and around the world. July 19, 2003, is the International Dome Race, with participants running or walking to Midnight Dome.

If you are in Dawson City Aug. 15–18, 2003, be sure to join the Discovery Days Festival fun when Yukon Order of Pioneers stages its annual parade. This event is a Yukon holiday commemorating the Klondike gold discovery of Aug. 17, 1896.

The Great Klondike International Outhouse Race, held Aug. 31, 2003, is a race of decorated outhouses on wheels over a 3-km course through the streets of Dawson City. The Mixed Slo-Pitch Tournament, August 29 to September 1, 2003, draws teams from the Yukon and Alaska. And at Yukon Talent Night, Sept. 19, 2003, local stars and visitors take to the stage at Diamond Tooth Gertie's Casino to perform songs, skits and comedy.

Klondike Nugget & Ivory Shop features a unique display of gold nuggets from over 50 Klondike creeks. We are Dawson City's

largest jewellery manufacturer and specialize in gold nugget jewellery, natural gold nuggets and mammoth ivory. Don't miss the 9-foot mammoth tusk also on exhibit! Located at the corner of Front and Queen streets. Phone (867) 993-5432. E-mail: nuggetshop@dawson.net. [ADVERTISEMENT]

Fire Fighters Museum, located at the fire hall on Front Street, features some rare turn-of-the-century firefighting equipment. The museum is open Monday to Saturday, 12:30 P.M. to 5:30 P.M. Admission by donation.

Pan for Gold. The chief attraction for many visitors is panning for gold. There are several mining operations set up to permit you to actually pan for your own "colours" under friendly guidance. The Klondike Visitors Assoc. sponsors a public panning area at No. 6 above Discovery, 13 miles/21 km from Dawson City on Bonanza Creek Road. Check with the Visitor Reception Centre for more information.

Bear Creek Camp, (see Milepost J 315.8 on the Klondike Highway), was operated by Yukon Consolidated Gold Corp. until 1966. Tours are conducted by Parks Canada interpreters; check with the Visitor Reception Centre for current tour schedule. The compound features the Gold Room, where the gold was melted and poured into bricks, complete blacksmith and machinery shops, and other well-preserved structures. Open 9:30 A.M. to 5 P.M. from mid-June to late August. Admission charged, or Parks Pass.

Dredge No. 4. Built in 1912 for the Canadian Klondike Mining Co.'s claim on Bonanza Creek, this historic dredge is the largest wooden hull bucket-line dredge in North America. Scheduled 1-hour tours several times daily June through August. Admission charged, or Parks Pass. To reach the dredge, take Bonanza Creek Road from **Milepost J 320.7** 7.8 miles/12.3 km up famous Bonanza Creek, to Dredge No. 4. Continue up Bonanza Creek Road for Discovery Claim and to see miles of gravel tailings worked over 2 and 3 times in the continuing search for gold.

See the Midnight Sun: If you are in Dawson City on June 21, be sure to make it to the top of the Dome by midnight, when the sun barely dips behind the 6,000-foot/1,829-m Ogilvie Mountains to the north—the picture of a lifetime. There's quite a local celebration on the Dome on June 21, so for those who don't like crowds, a visit before or after summer solstice will also afford fine views and photos. Turnoff for Dome Mountain is at **Milepost J 321.8**; it's about a 5-mile/8-km drive.

Ridge Road Heritage Trail. Originally built in 1899 to move mining supplies along Bonanza Creek, the Ridge Road was abandoned by 1902. The road was reopened in 1996 as a 20-mile/32-km heritage trail. Travel time is 1½ to 2 days by foot (or 4–6 hours by mountain bike). Interpretive signs and building remnants are along the route, which winds along the high ground between Bonanza and Hunker creeks. Short walks possible from the Upper Trailhead (outhouses) on Upper Bonanza Road to Soda Station on the abandoned Klondike Mines Railway line, and from Jackson Gulch (Lower) Trailhead behind Callison subdivision to the Yukon Ditch (Trail Gulch diversion). There are 2 tent campgrounds on the trail: 11-Mile at Mile 7/11.3 km, and 15-Mile at Mile 12.2/19.2; outhouses, firepits and water pump.

Klondike Loop Log

(continued from page 266)
The **Top of the World Highway** (Yukon Highway 9) connects Dawson City with the Taylor Highway (Alaska Route 5). The Alaska Highway is 175 miles/281 km from here via Highways 9 and 5. Yukon Highway 9 and the Alaska Route 5 are not maintained from mid-October to April, and the arrival of snow effectively closes the roads for winter. *CAUTION: Allow plenty of time for this drive; average speed for this road is 25 to 40 mph/40 to 64 kmph. DRIVE WITH YOUR HEADLIGHTS ON! The Canadian portion of the Highway 9 is seal coated; the Alaska side is gravel. Check with the Dawson City Visitor Reception Centre for current road and weather conditions; phone (867)993-5566.*

This section of the log shows distance from Dawson City (D) followed by distance from junction with the Taylor Highway (T) at Jack Wade Junction. Physical kilometreposts show distance from Dawson City.

TOP OF THE WORLD HIGHWAY
YUKON HIGHWAY 9

D 0 T 78.8 (126.8 km) **DAWSON CITY.** A free ferry carries passengers and vehicles from Dawson City across the Yukon River to the beginning of the Top of the World Highway in summer. *NOTE: The ferry wait in heavy traffic may be as long as 3 hours during peak times.*

D 0.2 (0.3 km) **T 78.6** (126.5 km) **Yukon River** government campground on riverbank opposite Dawson City; 74 RV sites, 24 tent-only sites, 2 kitchen shelters, playground and drinking water. Camping permit ($12). Within walking distance of sternwheeler graveyard. Put in and takeout spot for Yukon River travelers. Deck overlooks the Yukon River. A family of peregrine falcons nests in the cliffs across the river during the summer.

D 2.7 (4.4 km) **T 76.1** (122.5 km) Access to 9-hole golf course via 3.2-mile/5.1-km gravel road; rentals.

D 2.9 (4.6 km) **T 75.9** (122.1 km) Turnout for viewpoint overlooking Dawson City and the Yukon and Klondike rivers.

D 3.2 (5 km) **T 75.6** (121.7 km) Turnout with good view of Yukon River and river valley farms.

D 9 (12.4 km) **T 69.8** (112.3 km) Large rest area with toilets, picnic tables, litter barrels. A short trail leads to a deck overlooking the Yukon River valley. Interpretive displays about the Fortymile caribou herd and the history of the people of this area. Welcome to Dawson City information kiosk.

D 11 (15.6 km) **T 67.8** (109.1 km) "Top of the world" view as highway climbs above tree line.

D 16.4 (26.2 km) **T 62.4** (100.4 km) Snow fence along highway next 8 miles/13 km westbound.

D 18.4 (29.4 km) **T 60.4** (97.2 km) Turnout to south.

D 29.2 (47 km) **T 49.6** (79.8 km) Evidence of 1989 burn.

D 32.1 (51.2 km) **T 46.7** (75.2 km) First outcropping (westbound) of Castle Rock. Turnout to south with view of countryside.

D 33.1 (52.8 km) **T 45.7** (73.5 km) Distance marker shows customs 52 km, Dawson City 53 km.

D 35.2 (56 km) **T 43.6** (70.2 km) Main outcropping of Castle Rock; lesser formations are also found along this stretch. Centuries of erosion have created these formations. Turnout to south.

D 37.4 (59 km) **T 41.4** (66.6 km) Unmaintained road leads 25 miles/40 km to the former settlement of Clinton Creek, which served the Cassiar Asbestos Mine from 1967–79. There are no facilities or services available there. Distance marker shows U.S. border 43 km.

The confluence of the Yukon and Fortymile rivers is 3 miles/4.8 km below the former townsite of Clinton Creek. Clinton Creek bridge is an access point on the Fortymile River National Wild and Scenic River system, managed by the Bureau of Land Management. The Fortymile River offers intermediate and advanced canoeists over 100 miles/160 km of challenging water.

Yukon River, near Clinton Creek, grayling to 3 lbs. in April; chum salmon to 12 lbs. in August; king salmon to 40 lbs., July and August. **Fortymile River**, near Clinton Creek, grayling to 3 lbs. during spring breakup and fall freezeup; inconnu (sheefish) to 10 lbs. in July and August. ◆

D 54 (85.6 km) **T 24.8** (39.9 km) Rest stop with outhouses near adjacent old sod-roofed cabin to north. This was originally a supply and stopping place for the McCormick Transportation Co.

D 54.3 (86.1 km) **T 24.5** (39.4 km) Road forks south to old mine workings at Sixtymile, which have been reactivated by Cogasa Mining Co. Keep to right for Alaska. The road winds above timberline for many miles. The lack of fuel for warmth and shelter made this a perilous trip for the early sourdoughs.

D 64.1 (101.9 km) T 14.7 (23.7 km) Large gravel turnout. Information sign about Top of the World Highway viewpoint.

D 65.2 (103.7 km) T 13.6 (21.9 km) Pull-through rest area with toilet and litter barrels; good viewpoint. Just across the highway, short hike to cairn, excellent viewpoint. Highest point on Top of the World Highway (elev. 4,515 feet/1,376 m).

D 66.1 (105.1 km) T 12.7 (20.4 km) U.S.–Canada Border (elev. 4,127 feet/1,258m). **U.S. and Canada Customs and Immigration Station.** All traffic entering Alaska or Canada must stop here. A short hike up the hill behind the border station provides good viewpoint.

IMPORTANT: U.S. and Canada customs are open from about May 15 to Sept. 15. In summer 2002, customs was open 7 days a week, 9 A.M. to 9 P.M. (Pacific time) on the Canadian side; 8 A.M. to 8 P.M. (Alaska time) on the U.S. side. Customs hours of operation subject to change. Check with the RCMP or Visitor Reception Centre in Dawson City to make certain the border crossing will be open. Serious fines are levied for crossing the border without clearing customs! There are no services or currency exchanges available here.

TIME ZONE CHANGE: Alaska observes Alaska time; Yukon Territory observes Pacific time.

BOUNDARY SPUR ROAD

D 67.1 (108 km) T 11.7 (18.8 km) Large double-ended turnout to north with viewing platform, toilet, litter barrel. Welcome to Alaska and Fortymile River interpretive signs.

D 69.2 (111.4 km) T 9.6 (15.4 km) **BOUNDARY.** Boundary Lodge was one of the first roadhouses in Alaska; food, gas, lodging, diesel, tire repair, emergency phone.

Watch your gas supply. Between here and Tetlin Junction on the Alaska Highway, gas is available again only at Chicken, **Milepost TJ 66.5.** From here to Eagle, gas may be available at O'Brien Creek Lodge, **Milepost TJ 125.4.** Gas is available in Eagle.

Private Aircraft: Boundary airstrip; elev. 2,940 feet/896m; length 2,100 feet/640m;

earth and gravel; fuel 80; unattended.

D 78 (125.6 km) T 0.8 (1.3 km) Viewpoint.

D 78.8 (126.9 km) T 0 **Jack Wade Junction.** Junction with the Taylor Highway (Alaska Route 5), which leads north 64.6 miles/104 km to Eagle, AK, or south 95.7 miles/154 km to Tetlin Junction, just east of Tok, on the Alaska Highway. *CAUTION: Watch for cross traffic at this intersection.*

TAYLOR HIGHWAY
ALASKA ROUTE 5 SOUTH

Distance from Tetlin Junction (TJ) is followed by distance from Dawson City (D).

For a detailed log of the Taylor Highway (logged from the Alaska Highway to Eagle), see the TAYLOR HIGHWAY section on page 276.

TJ 95.7 D 78.8 Jack Wade Junction. Turn to **Milepost TJ 95.7** on page 281 in the TAYLOR HIGHWAY section for log of highway north to Eagle.

CAUTION: Sections of rough road, hairpin curves, steep grades and narrow road south to Chicken.

TJ 86.1 D 88.4 Old **Jack Wade No. 1 Dredge** in creek next to road. Turnout to east. This is actually the Butte Creek Dredge, installed in 1934 below the mouth of Butte Creek and eventually moved to Wade Creek. This was one of the first bucketline dredges used in the area, according to the BLM. Please keep off the dredge and obey safety signs.

TJ 82.1 D 92.4 **Walker Fork BLM Campground** to west; 21 level sites on loop road with tables, garbage container, outhouses; $8 camping fee. Picnic area. Old road grader on display at campground entrance. ▲

TJ 81.9 D 92.6 Walker Fork bridge.

TJ 76.8 D 97.7 Turnout to west. View of oxbow lakes in South Fork valley.

TJ 75.3 D 99.2 South Fork Fortymile River bridge. **BLM South Fork Wayside and River Access** to west at south end of bridge; day-use area with picnic tables, cooking grill, outhouse, garbage container and information brochures. Access point for the Fortymile River National Wild and Scenic River system.

The muddy, bumpy road leading into the brush is used by miners.

TJ 74.5 D 100 South Fork DOT/PF state highway maintenance station.

TJ 68.9 D 105.6 Lost Chicken Creek. Site of Lost Chicken Hill Mine, established in 1895. Mining was under way in this area several years before the Klondike Gold Rush of 1897–98. The first major placer gold strike was in 1886 at Franklin Gulch, a tributary of the Fortymile. Hydraulic mining operations in the creek.

TJ 68.2 D 106.3 BLM Chicken field station to west; information and emergency communications. Trailhead for **Mosquito Fork Dredge Hiking Trail** to east; park at turnout on west side of road.

This well-marked trail leads to a bench overlooking the old Mosquito Fork Dredge. It is about a 20-minute walk to the overlook; moderate downhill climb with a short, steep stepped section near the end. Allow more time for uphill return. Well-maintained trail, but trees roots make for uneven walking surface. If you are short on time (or energy), it is only a 5-minute walk from the highway to a bench and a great view of the Chicken Creek area.

TJ 66.6 D 107.9 Chicken Creek bridge. Private access to "Old" Chicken across from

turnoff to "Chicken Center"; The Goldpanner offers gas, diesel, propane, RV camping, gold panning and gift shop.

Chicken Center. See display ad on page 280 in the TAYLOR HIGHWAY section. ▲

TJ 66.4 D 108.1 Chicken Airport Road to east provides access to Beautiful Downtown Chicken (0.2 mile), a combination store, restaurant, bar and gas station; to the Original Chicken Gold Camp/Chicken Creek Outpost (0.3 mile), which offers RV camping, tours of Pedro Dredge, gold panning, espresso and gift shop; and to the airport (0.8 mile). ▲

Beautiful Downtown Chicken Mercantile Emporium, Chicken Creek Cafe, Saloon and Gas. See display ad on pages 278-279 in the TAYLOR HIGHWAY section. ▲

The Original Chicken Gold Camp/ Chicken Creek Outpost. See display ad on page 278 in the TAYLOR HIGHWAY section. ▲

TJ 66.3 D 108.2 **CHICKEN** post office to west. See description of Chicken on pages 278-280 in the TAYLOR HIGHWAY section.

Improved highway southbound to Alaska Highway junction.

TJ 64.3 D 110.2 Bridge over Mosquito Fork of the Fortymile River. **BLM Mosquito Fork Wayside** to west at north end of bridge; day-use area with parking, picnic table, outhouse and information brochures. A nice picnic spot overlooking the river.

TJ 50.5 D 124 Taylor Creek bridge.

TJ 49.3 D 125.2 Bridge over **West Fork of the Dennison Fork of the Fortymile River.** Access point for Fortymile River National Wild and Scenic River system. Fishing for grayling. 🐟

TJ 49 D 125.5 Turnoff to west for **West Fork Campground** (Forty Mile River BLM Recreation Management). Side road forks: right fork leads to open informal camping area; left fork leads to individual campsites on loop road. Take left fork for campground host, 25 level, back-in sites (in trees), many overlooking a scenic small lake (watch for trumpeter swans). Some pull-through sites; garbarge container, outhouses, drinking water; tables, firepits; free firewood, camping fee $8. ▲

TJ 43 D 131.5 **Logging Cabin Creek** bridge. Side road west to creek at south end of bridge.

TJ 35.1 D 139.4 **Mount Fairplay Wayside.** Large double-ended turnout to east near summit of Mount Fairplay (elev. 5,541 feet). Interpretive signs (Taylor Highway, Fortymile River, caribou and boreal forest), viewing platform, outhouse, wheelchair accessible. ♿

NOTE: Road descends next 25 miles southbound with long, winding 5 to 7 percent uphill and downhill grades.

TJ 22.1 D 152.4 Double-ended parking area to east. Information panels on Fortymile region and caribou herd.

TJ 12.1 D 162.4 Entering Tok Management Area, Tanana State Forest, southbound.

TJ 9.3 D 165.2 Entering Game Management Unit 12 southbound, 20E northbound. Caribou hunting by permit only.

TJ 0 D 174.5 **Tetlin Junction.** Old 40 Mile Roadhouse (closed).

Junction with the Alaska Highway. Turn to **Milepost DC 1301.7** on page 187 in the ALASKA HIGHWAY section for log of that route.

TAYLOR HIGHWAY

Connects: Alaska Hwy. (Tetlin Jct.) to Eagle, AK
Length: 160 miles   **Road Surface:** 60% gravel, 40% paved
Season: Closed in winter   **Steepest Grade:** 9 percent
Major Attraction: Fort Egbert National Historic Landmark, Eagle Historic District

(See map, page 255)

	Chicken	Dawson City	Eagle	Tok
Chicken		108	94	77
Dawson City	108		143	185
Eagle	94	143		171
Tok	77	185	171	

The Taylor Highway is a beautiful "top of the world" drive. (© Earl L. Brown, staff)

The 160.3-mile Taylor Highway (Alaska Route 5) begins at Tetlin Junction on the Alaska Highway, approximately 11 miles southeast of Tok, and ends at the small town of Eagle on the Yukon River. The Taylor Highway also forms part of the Klondike Loop for traffic coming from (or going to) Canada via the Top of the World Highway (Yukon Highway 9). The Taylor Highway splits at **Milepost TJ 95.7** (Jack Wade Junction) with one fork going east towards the border and the other north to Eagle.

This is a beautiful "top of the world" drive, and Eagle is well worth a visit. Construction of the Taylor Highway began in 1946, and was completed to Eagle in late 1953, providing access to the historic Fortymile Mining District.

Gas is available in Chicken (**Milepost TJ 66**) and in Eagle. En route to Canada via the Top of the World Highway, gas is available at Boundary (**Milepost D 69.2**).

Between Chicken and the Alaska Highway junction, the Taylor Highway is mostly paved with some winding sections and hills. Between Chicken and Eagle, the Taylor Highway is a narrow, winding, gravel road with many steep hills and some hairpin curves. Watch for pilot cars accompanying tour buses between Chicken and Eagle.

The first 61 miles of the Taylor Highway are paved. The gravel portion of highway has sporadic soft spots during breakup or after heavy rains. Road surface ranges from good to poor depending on maintenance. Rough spots are often flagged. Shoulders are generally narrow and may be unstable.

The Taylor Highway is not maintained from mid-October to April. The arrival of snow effectively closes the road to vehicle traffic for the winter, although it is open to snowmobiles. (In February, there's an organized snowmobile ride from Tok to Dawson City called the Trek Over The Top. This adventure for the hardy attracts about 850 participants.)

The highway provides river runners with access to the Fortymile River National Wild and Scenic River system. A brochure on access points and float times is available from the Bureau of Land Management, P.O. Box 309, Tok AK 99780; phone (907) 883-5121.

The Taylor is the shortest route to Dawson City, YT, from Alaska. Drive 95.7 miles/154 km north on the Taylor Highway (Scenic Byway) to Jack Wade Junction, and turn east on the Boundary Spur Road for the Top of the World Highway (Yukon Highway 9) for Dawson City. (See page 2274 in the KLONDIKE LOOP section for log of Yukon Highway 9.)

Dawson City-bound travelers keep in mind that the U.S. and Canadian customs offices at the border are open from about mid-May to mid-September. Customs hours for summer 2002 were 8 A.M. to 8 P.M. Alaska time; 9 A.M. to 9 P.M. Pacific time on the Canadian side. Check for current information with Alaska Public Lands Information Center in Tok; phone (907) 883-5667. There are no services or currency exchanges available at the border.

IMPORTANT: You cannot cross the border unless the customs office for the country you are entering is open. Severe fines are levied for crossing without clearing customs. Officials at Canadian customs are concerned about child abductions. If you are traveling with children, remember to bring identification for them.

NOTE: All gold-bearing ground in area is claimed. Do not pan in streams.

Emergency medical services: Between Tetlin Junction and O'Brien Creek bridge at **Milepost TJ 113.2**, phone the Tok Area EMS at 911 or (907) 883-5111. Between O'Brien Creek bridge and Eagle, phone the Eagle EMS at (907) 547-2300 or (907) 547-2211. Use CB channel 21.

Taylor Highway Log

Distance from Tetlin Junction (TJ) is followed by distance from Eagle (E).

ALASKA ROUTE 5

TJ 0 E 160.3 Tetlin Junction. Old 40 Mile Roadhouse (closed).
Highway begins long, winding climb (up and down grades, 5 to 7 percent) out of the Tanana River valley.

Distance marker shows Chicken 66 miles, Boundary 104 miles, Eagle 160 miles.

Junction with the Alaska Highway. Turn to **Milepost DC 1301.7** on page 187 in the ALASKA HIGHWAY section for log of that route.

Note stabilized sand dunes (and rock graffiti) first 5 miles.

TJ 0.9 E 159.4 Double-ended gravel parking area to east.

TJ 2.7 E 157.6 Double-ended gravel parking area to west; watch for soft spots.

TJ 4.4 E 155.9 Large double-ended gravel turnout to east. A 0.7-mile/ trail leads to **Four Mile Lake**; rainbow trout, sheefish.

TJ 5.7 E 154.6 Entering Tok Management

Area, **Tanana Valley State Forest**, northbound. Established as the first unit of Alaska's state forest system in 1983, Tanana Valley State Forest encompasses 1.81 million acres and lies almost entirely within the Tanana River Basin. The forest extends 265 miles from near the Canadian border to Manley Hot Springs. Almost 90 percent of the state forest is forested. Principal tree species are paper birch, quaking aspen, balsam poplar, black spruce, white spruce and tamarack. Almost 7 percent of the forest is shrubland, chiefly willow. The forest is managed by the Dept. of Natural Resources.

Evidence of 1990 forest fire known as the Porcupine burn.

TJ 6 E 154.3 Gravel turnout to east.

TJ 9.3 E 151 Entering Game Management Unit 20E northbound; entering GMU 12 southbound. Caribou hunting by permit only.

Road begins gradual climb of Mount Fairplay for northbound travelers.

TJ 10.1 E 150.2 Parking area to east.

TJ 10.7 E 149.6 Parking at gravel stockpile area to west.

TJ 12.1 E 148.2 Entering Tok Management Area, Tanana State Forest, southbound.

TJ 12.4 E 147.9 Turnout to east.

TJ 15.6 E 144.7 Turnout to east.

TJ 16.2 E 144.1 Small turnout to east. Views ahead northbound of highway climbing up Mount Fairplay.

TJ 21.2 E 139.1 Long descent (7 percent grade) northbound from true summit of Mount Fairplay.

TJ 21.4 E 138.9 Turnout to west.

TJ 22.1 E 138.2 Double-ended parking area to east. Information panels on Fortymile region and caribou herd. The Fortymile area is home range for the Fortymile caribou herd. Once a massive herd of 500,000 animals, the herd declined to a low of 6,000 in the mid-1970s. A 4-year recovery effort by the ADF&G using wolf control saw the herd grow from 22,500 to nearly 35,000. The herd moves east across the highway in late fall for the winter, and returns again in spring for calving. During the summer, small bands of caribou can sometimes be seen in the high country above timberline.

TJ 28.4 E 131.9 Turnout with view of mountains to west. Scenic views; Alaska Range visible to west on clear days.

TJ 30.2 E 130.1 Informal turnout to west; watch for soft spots.

TJ 34.3 E 126 Large double-ended turnout with view to west.

TJ 35.1 E 125.2 **Mount Fairplay Wayside.** Large double-ended turnout to east near summit of Mount Fairplay (elev. 5,541 feet). Interpretive signs (Taylor Highway, Fortymile River, caribou and boreal forest), viewing platform, outhouse, wheelchair accessible. ♿

NOTE: Begin 9 percent downgrade northbound. Southbound, the road descends for the next 25 miles from Mount Fairplay's summit, with long, winding 5 to 7 percent uphill and downhill grades through forested terrain. Panoramic views of the Fortymile River forks' valleys. Views of the Alaska Range to the southwest.

Entering **Fortymile Mining District** northbound. The second-oldest mining district in Alaska, it first yielded gold in 1886. Claims were filed in both Canada and Alaska due to boundary uncertainties.

This is the south end of the Fortymile River National Wild and Scenic River corridor managed by BLM.

Gold Dredges

Jack Wade No. 1 Dredge at Milepost TJ 86.1 Taylor Highway. (© Kris Graef, staff)

Mining dredges were used in Yukon and Alaska from the turn-of-the-century on into the 1950s to extract gold from the land. Several of these old dredges still litter the landscape of the North, one of the most visible reminders of the glory days of the Klondike Gold Rush.

The first gold dredge appeared in the Yukon in the fall of 1899. There were eventually some 2 dozen dredges working the Klondike area. The machines allowed miners to work large amounts of ground, extracting as much gold as possible from the dwindling supply in a relatively short amount of time. But the arrival of the dredges also signaled the end of an era. Big companies who could afford to mechanize gold mining by using dredges quickly replaced the colorful stampeders with their shovels and sluice boxes that characterized the early days of the Klondike Gold Rush.

Gold dredges were used as early as 1900 on the Seward Peninsula in Alaska, but it wasn't until 1908 that gold dredging became a financially viable option. By 1910, there were 18 dredges in Alaska. In 1914, 42 were operating throughout the state.

The mining dredges were land-locked floating machines, digged the ponds that allowed them to float—and thus move—across the area to be mined. The floating dredge most commonly operated in the North was the California-type, also known as the bucket-line dredge. This type of dredge used a continuous line of buckets (called the "digging ladder") to scrape the bottom and edge of the pond. The buckets carried the mud and rock to a screening area, where the heavier metal particles were separated from the rest of the material. After the metal was captured, the waste rock—"tailings"— would be deposited out the back.

The dredges, which operated 24 hours a day, were efficient and economical. The operating season averaged 200 days, starting in late April or early May and ending in November.

It is startling to come across one of these old dredges, like some mechanical behemoth sitting silently alongside a dusty road. There are 3 good examples of gold dredges on the Taylor Highway: Jack Wade No. 1 Dredge, the Mosquito Fork Dredge and the Pedro Dredge.

Two of these gold dredges are in the Chicken area. **Pedro Dredge**, which now sits on the property of The Original Chicken Gold Camp/Chicken Creek Outpost, was purchased by owner Mike Busby and moved a mile down Chicken Creek to its present location in 1998 as a visitor attraction. The Pedro Dredge operated on Chicken Creek between 1959 and 1967. Prior to 1959, the dredge had been located on Pedro Creek outside Fairbanks. Visible from the highway, turn on Chicken Airport Road at **Milepost TJ 66.4** and drive 0.3 mile to The Original Chicken Gold Camp/Chicken Creek Outpost to tour the Pedro Dredge.

A little more than a mile past Chicken, the **Mosquito Fork Dredge** can be seen from an overlook 20 minutes by trail from **Milepost TJ 68.2** on the Taylor Highway (across from the BLM Chicken field station). The well-marked path is a moderate downhill climb with a short, steep, stepped section near the end. The Mosquito Fork Dredge is on property owned by The Goldpanner, which is located at **Milepost TJ 66.6** in Chicken at the Chicken Creek bridge.

Jack Wade No. 1 Dredge, located at **Milepost TJ 86.1** on the Taylor Highway, was one of the first bucketline dredges used in the area. Originally called the Butte Creek Dredge, it was installed in 1934 below the mouth of Butte Creek and eventually moved to its present location on Wade Creek.

Another fine example of these early gold dredges is **Gold Dredge No. 4**, located just outside Dawson City, about a 100-mile drive from Chicken via the Taylor and Top of the World highways. A Canadian National Historic Site, Dredge No. 4 is one of some 2 dozen dredges that once worked the Klondike gold fields. Today Dredge No. 4 rests alongside Bonanza Creek on Claim No. 17 (below Discovery claim), where it ceased operations in 1960.

Designed by the Marion Steam Shovel Company and built in 1912, Dredge No. 4 was the largest wooden hull, bucket-line dredge in North America. It operated from 1913 until 1959 in the Klondike and Bonanza Creek valleys. There's an interpretive centre at the dredge site, and scheduled tours are offered daily from the end of May through August. (Admission fee charged.)

Hunters use ATVs to travel the Fortymile country along the Taylor Highway.
(© Kris Graef, staff)

TJ 35.2 E 125.1 Federal Subsistence Hunting Area boundary. These areas allow local residents earlier hunting seasons for subsistence hunting of moose and caribou. There are several of these signs along the Taylor Highway.

TJ 36.2 E 124.1 Unmaintained turnout to east.

TJ 41.2 E 119.1 Informal gravel turnout to east.

TJ 43 E 117.3 **Logging Cabin Creek** bridge. Side road west to creek at south end of bridge.

TJ 43.4 E 116.9 Access to a gravel pit to east.

TJ 44.5 E 115.8 Federal Subsistence Hunting Area boundary.

TJ 48.3 E 112 Federal Subsistence Hunting Area boundary.

TJ 49 E 111.3 Turnoff to west for **West Fork Campground** (Forty Mile River BLM Recreation Management). Side road forks: right fork leads to open informal camping area; left fork leads to individual campsites on loop road. Take left fork for campground host, 25 level, back-in sites (in trees), many overlooking a scenic small lake (watch for trumpeter swans). Some pull-through sites; garbarge container, outhouses, drinking water; tables, firepits; free firewood, camping fee $8.

TJ 49.3 E 111 Bridge over **West Fork of the Dennison Fork of the Fortymile River**. Access point for Fortymile River National Wild and Scenic River system. Fishing for grayling.

TJ 50.5 E 109.8 Taylor Creek bridge. All-terrain vehicle trail to Taylor and Kechumstuk mountains; heavily used in hunting season.

TJ 55 E 105.3 Large turnout to east.

TJ 56.7 E 103.6 South end of long double-ended gravel turnout to east.

TJ 58.9 E 101.4 Scenic viewpoint turnout to east.

TJ 61 E 99.3 *Pavement ends, gravel begins, northbound. Watch for continued road construction northbound in summer 2003.*

TJ 62.5 E 97.8 Large turnout to west. Begin downhill grade northbound.

TJ 63.2 E 97.1 View of Chicken northbound.

TJ 63.7 E 96.6 Federal Subsistence Hunting Area boundary.

TJ 64.1 E 96.2 Well-traveled road leads east to private buildings, not into Chicken.

TJ 64.3 E 96 Bridge over Mosquito Fork of the Fortymile River. **BLM Mosquito Fork Wayside** to west; day-use area with parking, picnic table, outhouse and information brochures to west at north end of bridge. A nice picnic spot overlooking the river.

TJ 65.1 E 95.2 Federal Subsistance Hunting Area boundary.

TJ 65.9 E 94.4 Welcome to Chicken sign.

TJ 66 E 94.3 *Driving distance between Mileposts TJ 66 and 67 is 0.7 mile.*

TJ 66.3 E 94 Chicken post office (ZIP code 99732), located up hill to west of road, was established in 1903 along with the mining camp.

Chicken

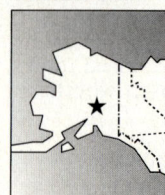

TJ 66.4 E 93.9 Located 80 miles from Tok, AK, and 108 miles/174 km from Dawson City, YT. **Population:** 37. **Private Aircraft:** Chicken airstrip, 0.8 mile east of highway (N 64° 04′ W 141° 56′); elev. 1,640 feet; length 2,500 feet; gravel; maintained year-round.

CHICKEN ADVERTISERS

**Beautiful Downtown
 Chicken, Alaska** .... Chicken Airport Rd.
**Chicken Center/The
 Goldpanner** .... Milepost 66.6 Taylor Hwy.
**Original Chicken Gold Camp/Chicken
 Creek Outpost, The** ...... Chicken Airport Rd.

Chicken post office was established in 1903. *(© Kris Graef, staff)*

Commercial Chicken consists of 3 businesses: Beautiful Downtown Chicken and Chicken Gold Camp/Chicken Creek Outpost (turn on Chicken Airport Road) and Chicken Center/The Goldpanner (on the highway). Camping, gas, gifts, meals, snacks, and gold panning are available in Chicken. There is no phone service; cell phone service is sporadic.

Although remote, Chicken is getting more and more traffic each year as the Klondike Loop grows in popularity with motorists driving to and from Alaska. It's not unusual to see quite a diverse group of travelers enjoying this scenic little spot on the highway.

Chicken was supposedly named by early miners who wanted to name their camp ptarmigan, but were unable to spell it and settled instead for chicken, the common name in the North for ptarmigan. Chicken is perhaps best known as the home of the late Ann Purdy, whose book *Tisha* was based on her experiences as a young schoolteacher in the Bush.

Tisha's schoolhouse is one of the dozen or so old structures dating back to the early 1900s that comprise **Historic Chicken Gold Camp**. This historic area—on the National Register of Historic Places—is located on

private property; inquire at The Goldpanner for information on guided tours. The tin roofs of Historic Chicken townsite may be seen from the road.

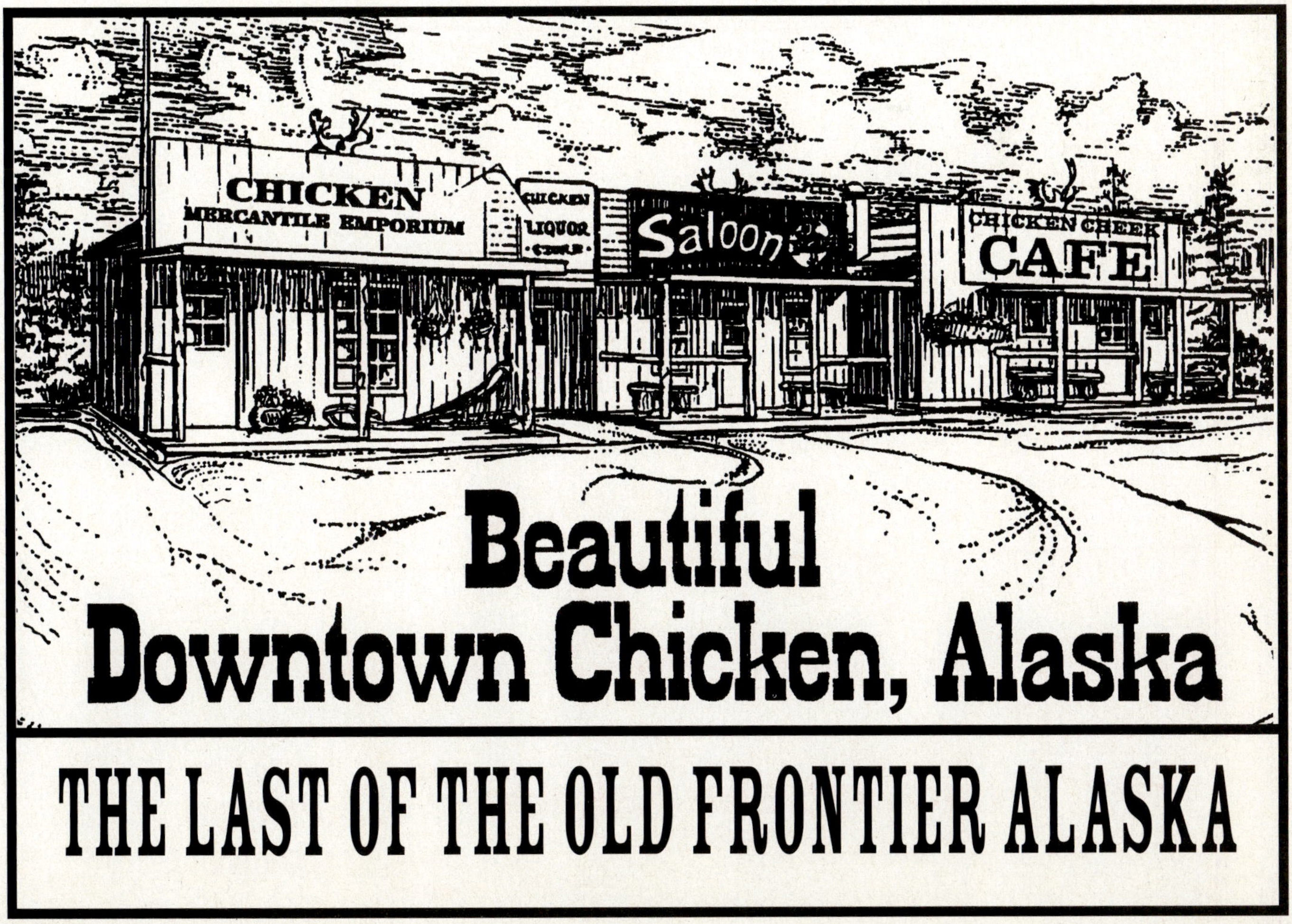

Beautiful Downtown Chicken, Alaska

THE LAST OF THE OLD FRONTIER ALASKA

Another reminder of the past in Chicken is the **Pedro Dredge No. 4**, located at Chicken Gold Camp/Chicken Creek Outpost. This dredge operated on Chicken Creek

between 1959 and 1967. (Prior to 1959, the dredge worked Pedro Creek outside Fairbanks, hence its name.) Mike Busby and Bernie Karl moved the dredge down to Chicken in 1998 as a tourist attraction.

Another old gold dredge, the Mosquito Fork Dredge, can be seen from the BLM hiking trail just north of town. (See description of trail at **Milepost TJ 68.2**.)

Downtown Chicken Mercantile Emporium, Chicken Creek Cafe, Saloon and Gas. Unfortunately, as too often happens, the main road bypasses the most interesting part of Chicken. If it's modern facilities you are looking for, original Chicken is not for you. The Chicken Creek Saloon and Cafe are some of the last remnants of the old frontier Alaska. It is a trading post where local mniners (some straight out of Jack London and Robert Service) trade gold for supplies and drink. A wealth of gifts abound in the Chicken Mercantile, many designed by owner Susan Wiren. The cafe is famous throughout Alaska for its surprisingly good, real homemade food, including hot homemade pies, cookies and cinnamon rolls voted "Best" by many bus drivers. The Chicken Creek Salmon Bake, featuring wild Alaskan salmon and barbecued chicken, is open 4 P.M. to 8 P.M. daily. Chicken Creek Saloon, Cafe and Mercantile Emporium are a rare treat for those with the courage to stray just a few hundred yards from the beaten path. Major credit cards are accepted. Note: The Goldpanner, located on the main road, is not the same as "Beautiful Downtown Chicken, Alaska." [ADVERTISEMENT]

The Original Chicken Gold Camp/Chicken Creek Outpost. Escape the highway noise and dust in a quaint, relaxing

atmosphere. Learn about modern mining techniques, visit the Pedro Dredge, and try panning for gold. Picnic tables, firepits, video viewing, espresso drinks, handicap friendly, walking distance to local attractions, "cleanest outhouse around," consistent friendly service, easy access. VISA/Mastercard. [ADVERTISEMENT] ▲

Taylor Highway Log
(continued)

TJ 66.6 E 93.7 Chicken Creek bridge. *Highway climbs northbound.*

TJ 68.2 E 92.1 BLM Chicken field station to west; information and emergency communications. Trailhead for **Mosquito Fork Dredge Hiking Trail** to east; park at turnout on west side of road.

The Fortymile caribou herd ranges from Alaska into Canada. (© Ralph & Leonor Barrett)

This well-marked trail leads to a bench overlooking the old Mosquito Fork Dredge. It's about a 20-minute walk to the overlook; moderate downhill climb with a short, steep stepped section near the end. Allow more time for uphill return. Well-maintained trail, but trees roots make for uneven walking surface. If you are short on time (or energy), it is only a 5-minute walk from the road to a bench and a great view of the Chicken Creek area.

TJ 68.9 E 91.4 Lost Chicken Creek. Site of Lost Chicken Hill Mine, established in 1895. Mining was under way in this area several years before the Klondike Gold Rush of 1897–98. The first major placer gold strike was in 1886 at Franklin Gulch, a tributary of the Fortymile. Hydraulic mining operations in the creek.

TJ 70 E 90.3 *CAUTION: Road narrows, road surface deteriorates northbound. Watch for hairpin curves.*

TJ 72 E 88.3 *NOTE: Slow for steep descent northbound as road switchbacks down to South Fork.* Good views northbound of South Fork Fortymile River.

TJ 74.4 E 85.9 South Fork River access.

TJ 74.5 E 85.8 South Fork DOT/PF state highway maintenance station.

TJ 75.3 E 85 South Fork Fortymile River bridge. **BLM South Fork Wayside and River Access** to west at south end of bridge; day-use area with picnic tables, cooking grill, outhouse, garbage container and information brochures. Access point for the Fortymile River National Wild and Scenic River system.

The muddy, bumpy road leading into the brush is used by miners.

TJ 76.8 E 83.5 Turnout to west. View of oxbow lakes in South Fork valley.

TJ 77.2 E 83.1 *CAUTION: Slow for sharp turns and watch for rough road northbound.*

TJ 78.5 E 81.8 Views of Fortymile River valley to west northbound between **Mileposts TJ 78** and **82**.

TJ 78.8 E 81.5 Steep descent northbound.

TJ 81.9 E 78.4 Walker Fork bridge.

TJ 82.1 E 78.2 Walker Fork BLM Campground to west; 21 level sites on loop road with tables, garbage container, outhouses; $8 camping fee. Picnic area. Old road grader on display at campground entrance. ▲

TJ 86.1 E 74.2 Old **Jack Wade No. 1 Dredge** in creek next to road. Turnout to east. This is actually the Butte Creek Dredge, installed in 1934 below the mouth of Butte Creek and eventually moved to Wade Creek. This was one of the first bucketline dredges used in the area, according to the BLM. Please keep off the dredge and obey safety signs.

TJ 88.3 E 72 Mining claims and active mining under way next 4 miles northbound. *Do not trespass on mining claims.*

NOTE: Road width varies from here to Eagle. Large vehicles use turnouts when meeting oncoming vehicles.

TJ 90 E 70.3 Jack Wade, an old mining camp that operated until 1940, to west.

TJ 91.9 E 68.4 Rough turnout to east; primitive campsite by stream.

TJ 93 E 67.3 *Slow down for hairpin curves. Steep climb northbound as highway ascends Jack Wade Hill.*

TJ 94.1 E 66.2 Turnout to west.

TJ 95.7 E 64.6 Jack Wade Junction. Northbound travelers turn left (north) for Eagle; keep right for Canadian border to east. *CAUTION: Watch for oncoming traffic when turning here.*

Junction with Boundary Spur Road east to the Alaska–Canada border and Top of the World Highway (Yukon Highway 9) to Dawson City, YT (78.8 miles from here). Turn to page 275 in the KLONDIKE LOOP section and read log back to front.

TJ 96.2 E 64.1 Large turnout to west. Fireweed displays. Lupine and chiming bells bloom in June. Views northbound of Canada's Ogilvie Mountains in the distance to the north-northeast.

TJ 99.5 E 60.8 Road winds around the summit of Steele Creek Dome (elev. 4,015 feet) visible directly above the road to the east. *CAUTION: Rough road, slippery when wet.*

TJ 105.5 E 54.8 Turnout to east. Scenic views of mountains on horizon as road descends next 7 miles northbound to the valley of the Fortymile River, so named because its mouth was 40 miles below Fort Reliance, an old trading post near the confluence of the Yukon and Klondike rivers.

TJ 108 E 52.3 *CAUTION: Steep, narrow, winding road northbound. Slippery when wet. Slow down for hairpin curves.*

Frequent small turnouts and breathtaking views to north and west. Watch for arctic poppies and lupine along the highway in June.

TJ 112.5 E 47.8 Fortymile River bridge; parking area at south end of bridge, toilet, canoe launch. No camping. Active mining in area. Nearly vertical beds of white marble can be seen on the northeast side of the river. Access to the Fortymile River National Wild and Scenic River system.

TJ 112.7 E 47.6 Private log home to west.

TJ 113.1 E 47.2 O'Brien Creek DOT/PF state highway maintenance camp located here.

TJ 113.2 E 47.1 O'Brien Creek bridge. *CAUTION: Watch for small aircraft using road as runway.*

TJ 113.3 E 47 Sign and flags mark entrance to Larry and June Taylor's residence; riverboat tours.

The Taylor's 40-Mile Riverboat Tours and Lodging. Let us take you back in time. See the historic 40-Mile River gold rush country seen only by riverboat! We offer hourly or full-package adventurous, safe, riverboat tours. Thrilling and exciting Hovercraft rapids shootover; ride on a cushion of air. Enjoy the peaceful and beautiful wilderness from one of our 4 comfortable cabins with a private creek at your front door. Rejuvenate in a luxurious, relaxing Alaska-style sauna nightly. Only the best coffee, tea and

homemade breads for our lodging guests. While visiting, take time to stroll about our beautiful vegetable and flower gardens and tour the greenhouse. Something for everyone. We often have moose strolling about who enjoy having their picture taken. Many varieties of birds make their summer home here. Special interests for rockhounds; interesting geology; and the Largest Golden Nugget for pictures. Free gold panning. You're guaranteed to find gold in every pan! Free brochures about the area and information on road and river conditions. This is a fun place to see and visit. Stop in! We are located 3/4 mile past the 40-Mile River bridge on the left towards Eagle. Email: boattours@starband.net. [ADVERTISEMENT]

TJ 114.4 E 45.9 *Road narrows to 1-lane northbound. Watch for falling rock next 1.5 miles northbound.* Highway parallels O'Brien

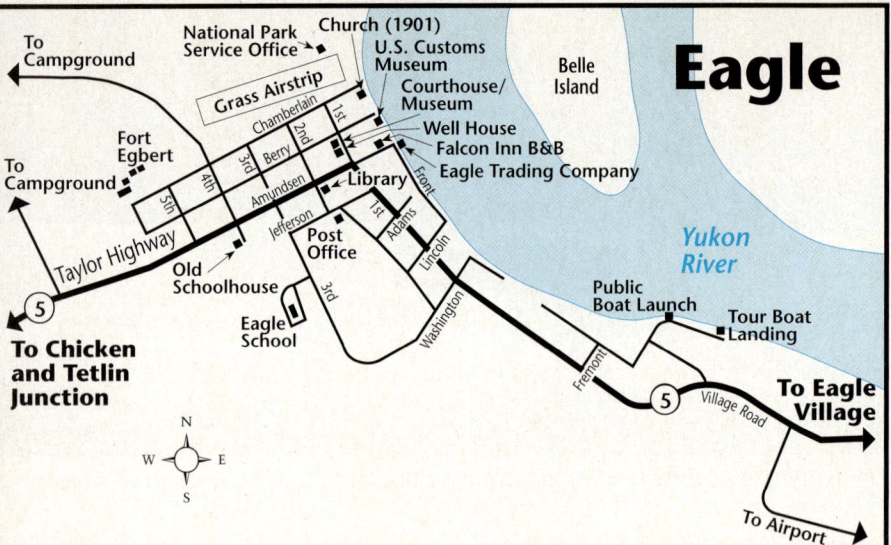

Creek to Liberty Fork; several turnouts.

TJ 117.2 E 43.1 Alder Creek bridge.

TJ 119.2 E 41.1 "Slide area" sign, watch for rocks northbound.

TJ 119.7 E 40.6 "End slide area" sign northbound. Turnout to east.

TJ 121.1 E 39.2 Large turnout at gravel pit to west.

TJ 122.4 E 37.9 CAUTION: Slow down for hairpin curves northbound.

TJ 123.2 E 37.1 Turnout to east.

TJ 124.6 E 35.7 Columbia Creek bridge.

TJ 125.4 E 34.9 O'Brien Creek Lodge (closed in 2002, current status unknown).

TJ 126.3 E 34 Small turnout to east.

TJ 128 E 32.3 Small turnout to east.

TJ 130.5 E 29.8 Turnout to east.

TJ 131.5 E 28.8 Turnout. Federal subsistence land boundary.

TJ 131.6 E 28.7 King Solomon Creek bridge. (The creek has a tributary named Queen of Sheba.) Private homestead to east at north end of bridge.

TJ 133.6 E 26.7 Turnout to a rock pit to east.

TJ 134.6 E 25.7 Turnout to west.

TJ 135.8 E 24.5 North Fork Solomon Creek bridge. Road narrows northbound.

TJ 141 E 19.3 Glacier Mountain management area; walk-in hunting only. Top of the world views to west.

TJ 142.5 E 17.8 American Summit liquor store.

TJ 143.2 E 17.1 Turnout on American Summit. Top of the world views. Road begins winding descent northbound to Yukon River.

TJ 148 E 12.3 Two small turnouts.

TJ 149.1 E 11.2 Bridge over Discovery Fork Creek.

TJ 150.7 E 9.6 Old cabin by creek to west is a local landmark. Private property.

TJ 151.8 E 8.5 American Fork Creek bridge No. 1. Turnout to east at north end of bridge. Narrow winding road through American Creek Canyon. Outcroppings of asbestos, greenish or gray with white, and serpentine along roadcut. Doyon Ltd. claims ownership of surface and mineral estates on these lands; do not trespass.

TJ 152.5 E 7.8 Bridge No. 2 over American Creek. Turnout to west at north end of bridge.

TJ 153.2 E 7.1 Small turnout. Springwater piped to road.

TJ 153.6 E 6.7 Small turnout. Springwater piped to road.

TJ 159.3 E 1 Telegraph Hill Services; gas and tire repair. Telegraph Hill is visible from the road.

TJ 159.4 E 0.9 Access to Eagle BLM campground.

TJ 159.7 E 0.6 Historical sign about the settlement of Eagle.

TJ 160.3 E 0 Taylor Highway becomes Amundsen Avenue as it enters Eagle (description follows). Eagle school to east. Turn west on 4th Avenue for Fort Egbert and Eagle BLM campground. ▲

Eagle

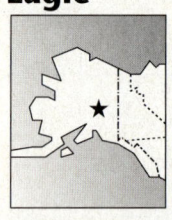

Population: 152. **Emergency Services:** Eagle EMS/Ambulance, phone (907) 547-2256; Eagle Village Health Clinic, phone (907) 547-2243. **Visitor Information:** Contact the Eagle Historical Society and Museums, Box 23, Eagle, AK 99738; phone 907/547-2325; fax 907/547-2232; www.eagleak.org.

The National Park Service visitor center in Eagle, headquarters for Yukon–Charley Rivers National Preserve, is located along the Yukon River at the end of the grass airstrip. Informal talks and interpretive programs available; reference library; maps and books for sale; video on the preserve shown on request. Visitor center hours are 8 A.M. to 5 P.M. daily in summer (Memorial Day weekend through Labor Day weekend). Write Box 167, Eagle, AK 99738, or phone (907) 547-2233.

Elevation: 820 feet. **Climate:** Mean monthly temperature in July 59°F/15°C; in January -13°F/-25°C. Record low -71°F/-57°C in January 1952; record high 95°F/35°C in July 1925. July also has the greatest mean number of days (21) with temperatures above 70°F/21°C. Mean precipitation in July, 1.94 inches; in December, 10.1 inches. Record snow depth 42 inches in April 1948.

Transportation: By road via the Taylor Highway (closed by snow October to April); air taxi, scheduled air service; dog team and snow machine in winter. Eagle is also accessible via the Yukon River. U.S. customs available for persons entering Alaska via the Yukon River or by air.

Private Aircraft: Eagle airstrip, 1.2 miles east on First Avenue, then 0.3 miles on airport access road; elev. 880 feet; length 4,500 feet; gravel; unattended. Floatplanes land on the Yukon River.

Visitor services in Eagle include 2 gas stations, a cafe, grocery store, gift shops, museum store, post office, shower, laundromat and mechanic shop with tire repair. Overnight accommodations and hookups at the motel, rental cabins and bed and breakfast. Camping at Eagle BLM campground just outside town (take 4th Avenue to Fort Egbert and follow signs). The BLM campground has 16 sites, outhouses, campground host, $8 camping fee. ▲

This small community was once the supply and transportation center for miners working the upper Yukon and its tributaries. Francois Mercier established his Belle Isle

---

EAGLE TRADING CO.
END OF THE TAYLOR HIGHWAY ON THE BANKS OF THE YUKON

- Groceries • Cafe • Lodging
- Ice • Propane • Tire Repair
- Gas • Diesel • AV Gas
- Coin-op Laundry • Gifts
- RV Hookups • Public Showers
- Hunting & Fishing Licenses
- Airport Shuttle

AV Gas 10¢ per gallon discount with motel stay.

MOTEL
CLEAN MODERN ROOMS
Queen Size Beds • Private Bath
Telephone • View of the Yukon

STARTING AT: **$60.00**

Information & Motel Reservations
Contact Eagle Trading 122.8
Box 36, Eagle, AK 99738

(907) 547-2220 • (907) 547-2326 Fax
www.eagletrading.com

EAGLE ADVERTISERS

Eagle Canoe Rentals	Ph. (907) 547-2203
Eagle Historical Society & Museums	Ph. (907) 547-2325
Eagle Trading Co. Motel	Ph. (907) 547-2220
Falcon Inn Bed & Breakfast	Ph. (907) 547-2254

trading post here in 1874. Eagle City was founded in 1897 and became the commercial, military and judicial center for the Upper Yukon. By 1898, Eagle's population was 1,700.

Fort Egbert was established in 1899 adjacent to the city, and became a key communications center for Alaska when the 1,506-mile-long Washington-Alaska Military Cable and Telelgraph System (WAMCATS) was completed in June 1903.

On July 15, 1900, Judge James Wickersham arrived to establish the first federal court in the Interior of Alaska. In 1901, Eagle became the first incorporated city in the Interior of Alaska. But by 1910, the population had dwindled to 178, as gold strikes in Fairbanks and Nome lured away many of Eagle's residents. With the conversion of telegraph communication to the wireless, the U.S. Army left Fort Egbert in 1911.

Eagle is perched on the south bank of the Yukon River below Eagle Bluff (elev. 1000 feet/305m). It remains relatively untouched, with many of the town's original structures still standing.

Daily walking tours of **Eagle Historic District** are offered from Memorial Day through mid-September by the historical society. Two of Eagle's best known sites are the Wickersham Courthouse, built in 1901 for Judge James Wickersham, and the windmill and wellhouse (hand-dug in 1903). The well still provides water for over half the town's population. Other original structures include the church (1901), the Waterfront Customs House (1900), and the schoolhouse (1903).

Museum tours are available daily at 9 A.M. from Memorial Day to mid-September. Fee is $5 for adults; children and museum members free. Archives and photo collection available to public. Special tours may be arranged. For more information, contact the Eagle Historical Society and Museums, Box 23, Eagle, AK 99738; phone (907) 547-2325. Books, videos, crafts, and gold items are available in museum store.

Fort Egbert, a National Historic Landmark, is comprised of 5 of the 46 original structures which were stabilized and restored by the BLM between 1974 and 1979. The BLM and Eagle Historical Society and Museums manage the Fort Egbert National Historic Landmark, which includes the Quartermaster Storehouse (1899), the Mule Barn (1900) pictured here, the Water Wagon Shed, the Granary (1903), and the NCO quarters (1900). The Granary has an interpretive exhibit and photo display showing the stages of reconstruction.

Historically an important riverboat landing, today Eagle is a popular jumping-off point for Yukon River travelers. Breakup on the Yukon is in May; freezeup in October.

Riverrunners float the 154 miles of the Yukon River between Eagle and Circle through **Yukon-Charley Rivers National**

National Park Service visitor center in Eagle. (© Kris Graef, staff)

Preserve. Suitable for canoes, kayaks or rafts, the Yukon River float trip takes from 5 to 10 days. For details on weather, gear and precautions, stop by the National Park Service visitor center in Eagle or visit www.nps.gov/yuch/.

Commercial boat trips are also available on the Yukon. The *Yukon Queen* makes round trips daily between Eagle and Dawson City, YT.

Eagle Canoe Rentals. Canoe and raft rentals on the Yukon River between Dawson City, Yukon Territory; Eagle City, Alaska; and Circle City. For information and reservations: Eagle Canoe Rentals, Mike Sager, Box 4, Eagle, AK 99738; Phone/fax (907) 547-2203 (all year); www.aptalaska.net/~paddleak. Dawson City River Hostel, Box 32, Dawson City, YT Y0B 1G0; phone (867) 993-6823 (May through October). [ADVERTISEMENT]

Special events in Eagle include a Memorial Day Service and an old-fashioned 4th of July celebration.

EAGLE VILLAGE (pop. 32) a traditional Han Kutchin Indian settlement, is located 3 miles east of Eagle (follow First Avenue out of town) overlooking the Yukon River. Some village residents have relocated to housing near the road end at Mile 7.8 due to erosion and seasonal flooding on the Yukon River. There are no visitor facilities at Eagle Village.

FALCON INN BED & BREAKFAST

Unique log get-away on the banks of the Yukon River

Pilots welcome, we'll pick you up – call 122.75 frequency

- Rooms $60 and up – Includes Homecooked Hot Breakfast and Complimentary Tea/Coffee
- Suite Available • TV & VCR Available
- Private Baths • Queen or Twin Beds
- Come & Watch the Yukon River Break-up on our Deck
- Decks & Observation Tower
- Excellent Spring & Fall Lights Viewing
- Personal Checks Accepted – No Credit Cards
- Shuttle Service From Boat or Airport
- Located One Block From Museum & Downtown

For Information & Reservations Call (907) 547-2254 Or email: falconin@aptalaska.net
Charlie & Marlys House, 220 Front Street, PO Box 136, Eagle, Alaska 99738
www.aptalaska.net/~falconin

GLENN HIGHWAY/ TOK CUTOFF

Connects: Tok to Anchorage, AK **Length:** 328 miles
Road Surface: Paved **Season:** Open all year
Highest Summit: Eureka Summit 3,322 feet
Major Attractions: Matanuska Glacier, Palmer State Fair
(See maps, pages 285–286)

	Anchorage	Glennallen	Palmer	Tok	Valdez
Anchorage		189	42	328	304
Glennallen	189		147	139	115
Palmer	42	147		286	262
Tok	328	139	286		254
Valdez	304	115	262	254	

Fall color along the Glenn Highway near Tahneta Pass. (© Carol P. Murdock)

The Glenn Highway/Tok Cutoff (Alaska Route 1) is the principal access route from the Alaska Highway west to Anchorage, a distance of 328 miles. This paved all-weather route includes the 125-mile Tok Cutoff, between Tok and the Richardson Highway junction; a 14-mile link via the Richardson Highway; and the 189-mile Glenn Highway, between the Richardson Highway and Anchorage. In 2002, the 130-mile stretch of the Glenn Highway between Anchorage and Eureka Summit was declared a National Scenic Byway.

It is a full day's drive between Tok and Anchorage, although there are enough attractions along the way to recommend making this a 2- or 3-day drive. There is some spectacular scenery along the Glenn Highway with mountain peaks to the north and south. Road conditions are generally good. The highway between Tok and Glennallen has a few very narrow sections with no shoulders. There is also winding road without shoulders between Matanuska Glacier and Palmer.

Five side roads are logged in this section: the Nabesna Road, which also provides access to Wrangell–St. Elias National Park and Preserve; Lake Louise Road to Lake Louise Recreation Area; the Hatcher Pass Road, connecting the Glenn and Parks highways to Independence Mine State Historical Park; the Palmer-Wasilla Highway; and the Old Glenn Highway, an alternate route between Palmer and Anchorage.

Emergency medical services: Between Tok and Duffy's Roadhouse at **Milepost GJ 63**, phone the Alaska State Troopers at 911 or (907) 883-5111. Between Duffy's and Gakona Junction, phone the Copper River EMS at Glennallen at (907) 822-3203 or 911. From Gakona Junction to Anchorage phone 911. CB channel 9 between **Milepost A 30.8** and Anchorage.

Tok Cutoff Log

Distance from junction with the Richardson Highway at Gakona Junction (GJ) is followed by distance from Anchorage (A) and distance from Tok (T).

Physical mileposts (located on the southeast side of the highway) read from Milepost 125 at Tok to Milepost 0 at Gakona Junction, the north junction with the Richardson Highway, located 16 miles from Glennallen and 129 miles from Valdez.

ALASKA ROUTE 1
GJ 125 A 328 T 0 TOK.

Junction of the Glenn Highway/Alaska Route 1, at **Milepost GJ 125**, and the Alaska Highway/Alaska Route 2, at **Milepost DC 1314.2**, in Tok. Turn to page 189 in the ALASKA HIGHWAY section for description of Tok and log of the Alaska Highway southeast to the Canadian border or northwest to Delta Junction.

GJ 124.7 A 327.7 T 0.3 Golden Bear Motel. Quiet location, 62 deluxe units, RV park with wooded pull-through sites, heated bathhouse, laundry; fine restaurant. Open 6 A.M. to 11 P.M. Our gift shop carries an extensive selection of Alaskana, jewelry, T-shirts and souvenirs. The friendly atmosphere you came to Alaska to find! Phone (888) 252-2123. Internet: www.tokalaska.com/gol. See display ad in Tok in the ALASKA HIGHWAY section. [ADVERTISEMENT] ▲

GJ 123.5 A 326.5 T 1.5 *CAUTION: Road narrows westbound; no shoulders. Road widens eastbound.*

GJ 122.8 A 325.8 T 2.2 Sourdough Campground to northwest; camping, pancake breakfast. ▲

GJ 122.6 A 325.6 T 2.4 Paved bike trail from Tok ends here.

Private Aircraft: Tok airstrip to southeast; elev. 1,670 feet; length 1,700 feet; gravel; unattended. No services. Private airfield across the highway.

GJ 116.6 A 319.6 T 8.4 Entering Tok Management Area, **Tanana Valley State Forest**, westbound. Established as the first unit of Alaska's state forest system in 1983, Tanana Valley State Forest encompasses 1.81 million acres and lies almost entirely within the Tanana River Basin. The forest extends 265 miles from near the Canadian border to Manley Hot Springs. Almost 90 percent of the state forest is forested. Principal tree species are paper birch, quaking aspen, balsam poplar, black spruce, white spruce

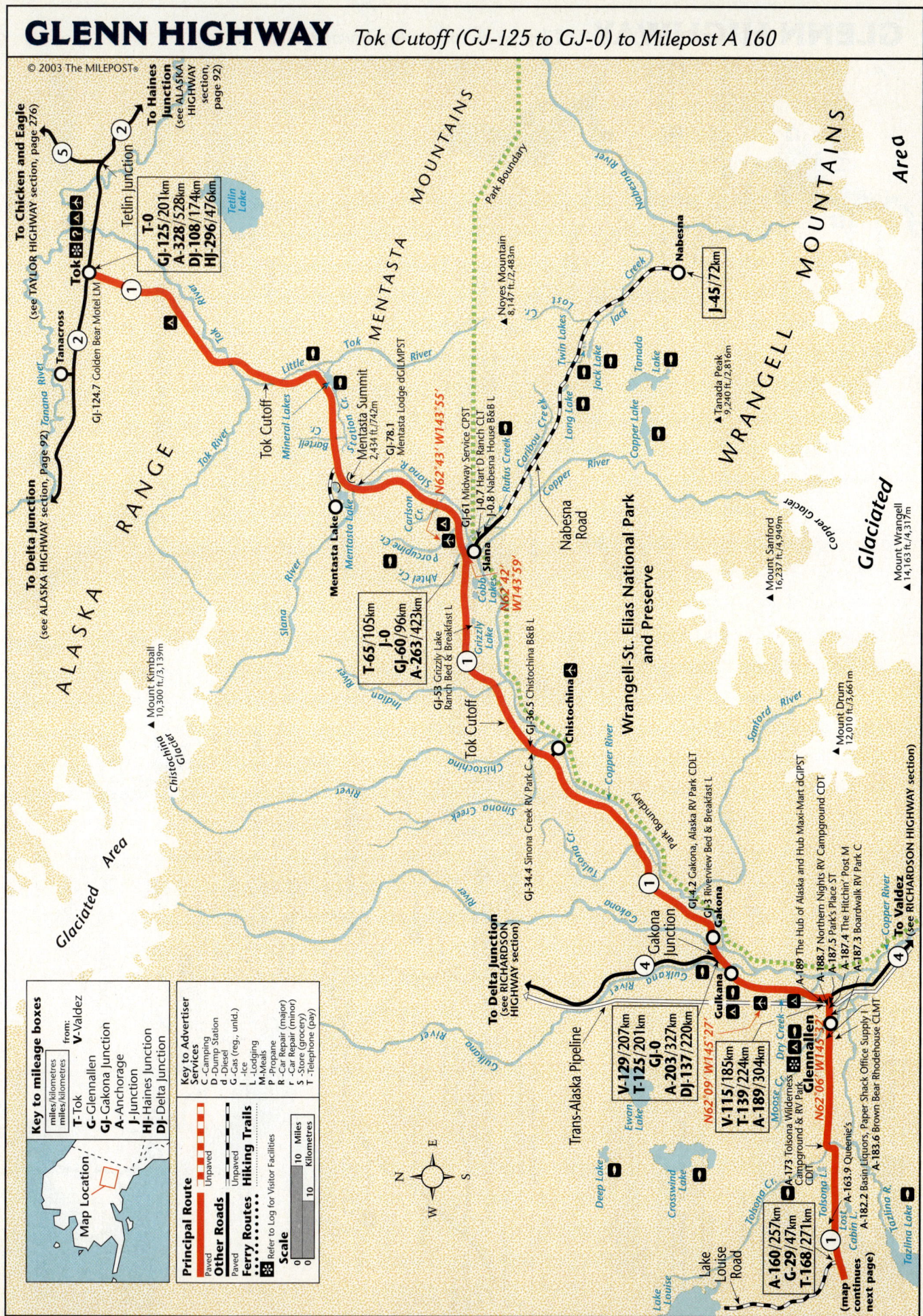

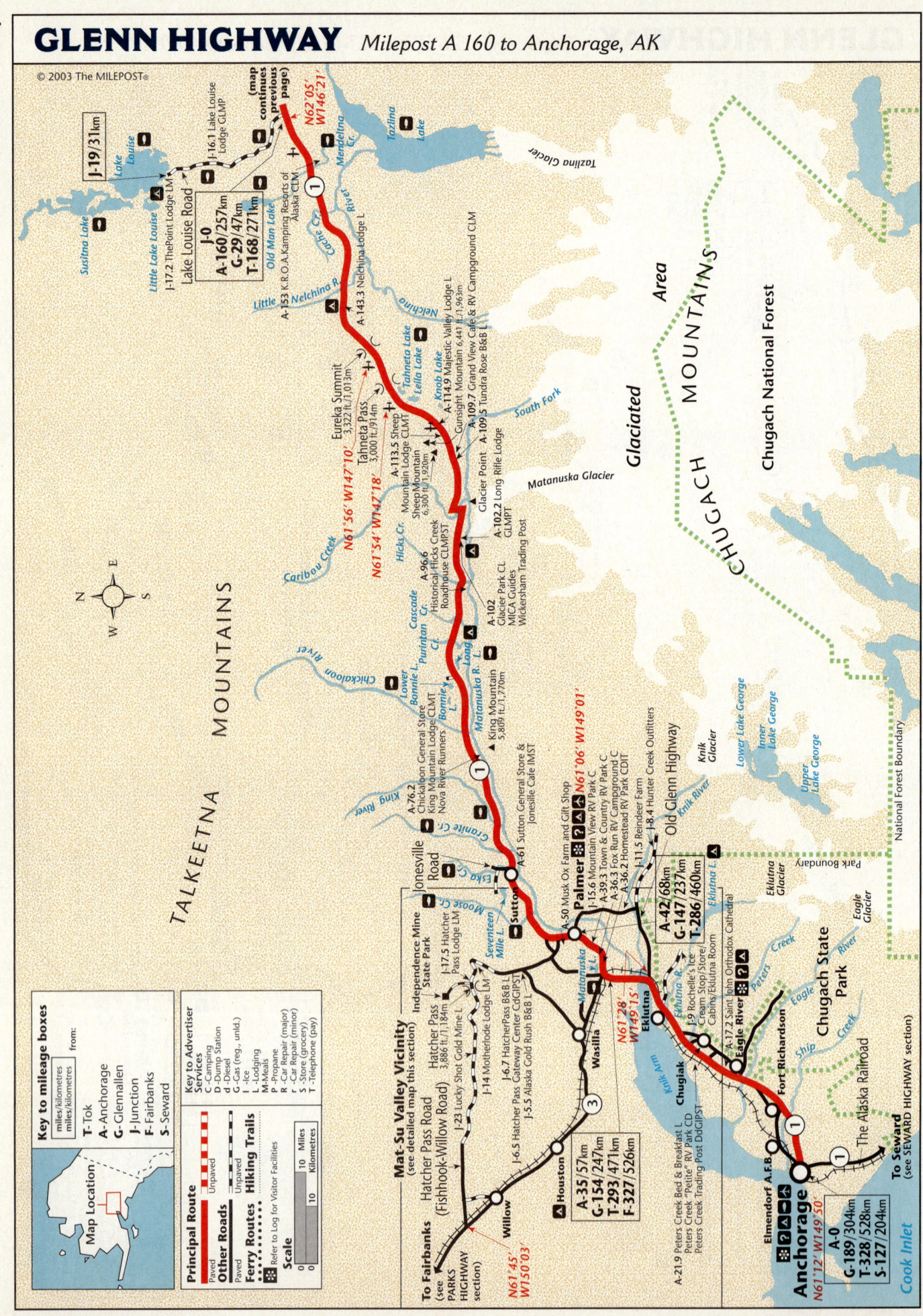

and tamarack. Almost 7 percent of the forest is shrubland, chiefly willow. The forest is managed by the Dept. of Natural Resources.

GJ 114 A 317 T 11 Distance marker eastbound shows Tok 10 miles, Canada Border 100 miles.

GJ 111 A 314 T 14 Distance marker westbound shows Nabesna Junction 53 miles, Glennallen 128 miles, Anchorage 315 miles.

GJ 110 A 313 T 15 Flashing lights to north are from U.S. Coast Guard loran station at **Milepost DC 1308.5** on the Alaska Highway.

GJ 109.4 A 312.4 T 15.6 Eagle Trail State Recreation Site to north; 35 campsites, 15-day limit, 4 picnic sites, water, toilets, firepits, pay phone, picnic pavilion, Clearwater Creek. Camping fee $10/night or resident pass. The access road is designed with several loops to aid larger vehicles. Valdez to Eagle Trail (Old Slana Highway and WAMCATS); 1 mile nature rail or 2.5 mile trail to overview of Tok River Valley. ▲

NOTE: Highway widens westbound; watch for dips. Road narrows eastbound; no shoulders.

GJ 106 A 309 T 19 Mountain views westbound as the highway passes through the Alaska Range. The Mentasta Mountains are to the southeast.

GJ 104.5 A 307.5 T 20.5 Extra wide shoulders to north for pulling off highway. **Little Tok River** overflow runs under highway in culvert; fishing for grayling and Dolly Varden.

GJ 103.7 A 306.7 T 21.3 Bridge over **Tok River**, side road north to riverbank and boat launch. The Tok River heads at Tok Glacier in the Alaska Range and flows northeast 60 miles to the Tanana River. Tok-bound travelers are in the Tok River Valley, although the river is out of sight to the southeast most of the time.

GJ 103.5 A 306.5 T 21.5 Paved turnout to north. **Little Tok River** overflow; fishing for grayling and Dolly Varden.

GJ 102.4 A 305.4 T 22.6 Entering Tok Management Area, Tanana Valley State Forest, eastbound. (See **Milepost GJ 116.7**.)

GJ 99.3 A 302.3 T 25.7 Rest area; narrow, paved, double-ended turnout to north. Cranberries may be found in late summer.

GJ 98.2 A 301.2 T 26.8 Bridge over **Little Tok River**, which parallels highway. The Little Tok River heads at a glacier terminus in the Mentasta Mountains and flows north 32 miles to the Tok River.

GJ 95.7 A 298.7 T 29.3 Paved rest area to southeast; very scenic setting.

GJ 95.2 A 298.2 T 29.8 Gravel turnout with view to south.

GJ 91 A 294 T 34 Side road south to **Little Tok River** bridge (weight limit 20 tons); good fishing for grayling, 12 to 14 inches, use small spinner.

Distance marker westbound shows Slana 34 miles, Glennallen 109 miles.

GJ 90 A 293 T 35 Paved turnout to south.

GJ 89.5 A 292.5 T 35.5 Watch for moose and birds in ponds along the highway to the southeast between **Mileposts A 89.5** and 86. These are sloughs of the Little Tok River and provide both moose habitat and a breeding place for waterfowl. Good fishing for northern pike and grayling.

GJ 89 A 292 T 36 Turnout to south.

GJ 85.7 A 288.7 T 39.3 Turnout to north.

GJ 83.2 A 286.2 T 41.8 Bridge over Bartell Creek. Just beyond is the divide between the drainage of the Tanana River, tributary of the Yukon River system flowing into the Bering Sea, and the Copper River system, emptying into the North Pacific near Cordova.

GJ 82.3 A 285.3 T 42.7 Distance marker eastbound shows Tok 40 miles, Canada Border 136 miles.

GJ 81 A 284 T 44 Access road leads north 7 miles to **MENTASTA LAKE** (pop. 142), a primarily Athabascan community, unincorporated.

The Mentasta area was particularly hard hit by the Nov. 3, 2002, earthquake and its aftershocks. The 7.9 earthquake struck at 1:12 p.m.. It was the strongest quake ever recorded along the Denali Fault. (See interpretive viewpoint about the Denali Fault at **Milepost V 262.5** Richardson Highway.)

GJ 79.4 A 282.4 T 45.6 Mentasta Summit (elev. 2,434 feet). The U.S. Army Signal Corps established a telegraph station here in 1902. The Mentasta Mountains rise to about 6,000 feet on either side of the highway. The 40-mile-long, 25-mile-wide Mentasta Range is bounded on the north by the Alaska Range. Watch for Dall sheep on mountainsides.

Boundary between Game Management Units 12 and 13C and Sportfish Management Units 8 and 2.

GJ 78.1 A 281.1 T 46.9 Mentasta Lodge to southeast with cafe, motel, gas, diesel, laundromat, showers, bar and liquor store.

Mentasta Lodge. See display this section.

GJ 78 A 281 T 47 View for westbound traffic of snow-covered Mount Sanford (elev. 16,237 feet). Mount Sanford, in the Wrangell Mountains, is 1 of Alaska's 10 highest peaks.

GJ 77.9 A 280.9 T 47.1 Paved turnout to north by Slana Slough; salmon spawning area in August. Watch for beavers.

GJ 76.3 A 279.3 T 48.7 Bridge over Mable Creek. Mastodon flowers (marsh fleabane) in late July; very large (to 4 feet) with showy seed heads.

CAUTION: Watch for gravel breaks westbound.

GJ 75.8 A 278.8 T 49.2 Bridge over Slana Slough.

GJ 75.5 A 278.5 T 49.5 Bridge over **Slana River**. This river flows from its source glaciers some 55 miles to the Copper River.

Rest area to south just west of bridge.

GJ 74 A 277 T 51 Large gravel turnout to south is scenic viewpoint overlooking Slana River.

GJ 72.3 A 275.3 T 52.7 Distance marker westbound shows Nabesna Junction 13 miles, Glennallen 88 miles.

GJ 70.7 A 273.7 T 54.3 Good views of Mount Sanford westbound, weather permitting.

GJ 69.1 A 272.1 T 55.9 Large gravel turnout to north. View of Mount Sanford ahead westbound. Mount Drum is to the right of Sanford.

GJ 67.9 A 270.9 T 57.1 Carlson Creek bridge.

GJ 65.5 A 268.5 T 59.5 Paved turnout to south by mail boxes is scenic viewpoint. Magnificent views (weather permitting) of the Wrangell mountains. Dominant peak is **Mount Sanford**, elev. 16,237 feet.

GJ 64.3 A 267.3 T 60.7 Sharp turn to north at east end of Porcupine Creek bridge for **Porcupine Creek State Recreation Site** 0.2 mile from highway; 12 forested campsites on loop road, 15-day limit, $10 nightly fee or resident pass, water pump, firepits, outhouses, picnic tables and fishing. Hiking trails up Porcupine Creek to Carlson Lake and Bear Valley (trails are poorly marked, carry topo map). Lowbush cranberries in fall. CAUTION: Watch for bears. ▲

Moose browse on willow, birch, aspen, sedges, grasses and pond weeds.
(© Robin Brandt)

GJ 64.2 A 267.4 T 60.8 Bridge over Porcupine Creek.

GJ 63 A 266 T 62 Scenic viewpoint to southeast with view of Wrangell Mountains. The dominant peak to the southwest is Mount Sanford, a dormant volcano; the pinnacles of Capital Mountain can be seen against its lower slopes. Mount Jarvis (elev. 13,421 feet) is visible to the south behind Mount Sanford; Tanada Peak (elev. 9,240 feet) is more to the south. (Tanada Peak is sometimes mistaken for Noyes Mountain.)

Walk up the gravel hill to view Noyes Mountain (elev. 8,147 feet), named for U.S. Army Brig. Gen. John Rutherford Noyes, a one-time commissioner of roads in the territory of Alaska. Appointed adjutant general of the Alaska National Guard in 1953, he died in 1956 from injuries and frostbite after his plane crashed near Nome.

GJ 62.7 A 265.7 T 62.3 Duffy's Roadhouse to southeast; gas, cafe, bar, airstrip.

GJ 61.8 A 264.8 T 63.2 NOTE: 7 percent downhill grade westbound.

GJ 61 A 264 T 64 Midway Service to northwest; groceries, showers, fishing/hunting licenses, laundromat and campground. ▲

Midway Service. See display ad on page 289.

MENTASTA LODGE
MILE 78 TOK CUTOFF
OPEN YEAR ROUND
(907) 291-2324
CAFE * GAS * DIESEL * PROPANE * BAR
ICE * ATM * LAUNDROMAT * MOTEL
SHOWERS * LIQUOR STORE
OVERNIGHT PARKING*
HC01 BOX 585, GAKONA, ALASKA 99586
mentastalodge@att.net

Nabesna Road

Nabesna Road offers beautiful mountain views. (© Kris Graef, staff)

Nabesna Road leads 45 miles southeast from **Milepost GJ 59.8** on the Tok Cutoff to the old Nabesna Mine. The road crosses the northwest corner of Wrangell–St. Elias National Park and Preserve. Stop at the ranger station at **Milepost J 0.2** for current road conditions and information on back-country travel in the park.

There are no formal public campgrounds on this side road, but there are plenty of spots to camp and a private campground at Mile 0.7. The area offers good fishing and several hiking trails. Horses are permitted on all trails. Off-road vehicles must have permits from the National Park Service.

The first 4 miles of road are paved. The remainder is gravel, in fair condition to **Milepost J 30.8** (Lost Creek crossing). Beyond the road becomes rough and crosses several creeks which may be difficult to ford. Vehicles are not recommended beyond Mile 42, where state road maintainence ends. Distance is measured from the junction with the Tok Cutoff (J).

There are few physical mileposts along the road. Distance is based on actual driving distance.

J 0 Junction with the Tok Cutoff.

J 0.2 Turnoff to right southbound for access to **Slana Ranger Station**. Information on road conditions and on Wrangell–St. Elias National Park and Preserve. The ranger

station also has ATV permits available, back-country trip planning assistance; bear-proof containers for rent; hunting information and subsistence hunting permits available. USGS maps and natural history books for sale. Open 8 A.M. to 5 P.M. daily, Memorial Day through September; weekdays in May and October; by appointment remainder of the year. Phone (907) 882-5238.

Also access to Slana DOT Maintenance Station.

J 0.7 Slana post office and pay phone station at entrance to Hart D Ranch; lodging (year-round) and RV campground. This picturesque ranch is the home and studio of sculptor Mary Frances DeHart. DeHart also raises Affenpinscher dogs.

Hart D Ranch. See display ad this section.

J 0.8 Nabesna House B&B. This spacious log home offers room to relax after a day of

exploring the beautiful nearby Wrangell St. Elias National Park. Fishing, hiking, flight-seeing, gold panning all available locally. Long-time Alaskan residents, your hosts are Gary and Maraley McMichael. Box 970, Slana, AK 99586. Email nabesna@pobox.alaska.net. (907) 822-4284. [ADVERTISEMENT]

J 1 Slana elementary school. **SLANA** (pop. 55; unincorporated), once an Indian village on the north bank of the Slana River, now refers to this general area, much of which was homesteaded in the 1980s. Besides the Indian settlement, Slana boasted a popular roadhouse, now a private home.

J 1.5 Slana River Bridge. Boundary between Game Management Units 11 and 13C.

J 3.8 Entering Wrangell–St. Elias National Park and Preserve.

J 4 Four Mile Creek Road. Hostel: Huck Hobbit's Homestead Retreat & Campground.
Pavement ends, gravel begins, southbound.

J 7 Road crosses **Rufus Creek** culvert. Private homes. Fishing in creek for Dolly Varden to 8 inches, June to October. Watch for bears, especially during berry season.

J 11.1 Gravel pit parking area to west. Walk back to **Suslota Lake trailhead** on east side of road.

J 12.2 Turnout to east; picnic table, primitive campsite. **Copper Lake trailhead**; fishing for lake trout, grayling and burbot.

J 16.6 Primitive campsite with picnic table to west.

J 16.7 Physical milepost 17.

Beautiful views of Kettle Lake, Mount Sanford, Capital Mountain, Mount Wrangell, Mount Zanetti and Tanada Peak in the Wrangell Mountains to the southwest.

J 17.8 Dead Dog Hill Rest Area; picnic table, outhouse, garbage container, aluminum recyle. Camping. View of Noyes Mountain (elev. 8,235 feet) in the highly mineralized Mentasta Mountains to the north.

J 18.3 Caribou Creek culvert.

J 18.5 Milepost 19.

J 18.8 Gravel pit parking area to east.

J 19.2 Caribou Creek trailhead, multi-use trail first 3 miles. Park at **Milepost J 18.8**.

J 19.7 Parking areas both sides of road.

Alaska's Hart D Ranch est 1960

Wrangell Roost Lodge • Private Baths
Post Office • RV Park • Showers • Cabin
Tent Camping • Affenpinscher Kennel
Studio & Fine Art Gallery of Bronze
Sculptor: Mary Frances DeHart

dehart@hartd.com
LODGE OPEN ALL YEAR

0.5 mile Nabesna Road at Slana
(59.8 GLENN HIGHWAY/TOK CUTOFF)

"A Unique Touch of Elegance"

on the northern edge of
WRANGELL ST. ELIAS NATIONAL PARK

••HART D RANCH • SLANA AK 99586 • PH 907.822.3973 • WWW.HARTD.COM••

J 20.5 Milepost 21.
J 20.6 Parking area.
J 21.8 **Rock Lake Rest Area**; picnic table, outhouse, garbage container, aluminum recycle. Camping.
J 22.9 **Long Lake**; grayling fishing.
J 23.7 Turnout.
J 24 **Tanada Lake trailhead**; parking to west. Multi-use trail. Fishing for grayling and lake trout.
J 24.7 Watershed divide (elev. 3,320 feet) between streams draining into the Copper River watershed and into the Gulf of Alaska, and those entering the Yukon River watershed which drains into the Bering Sea. Boundary between Sportfish Areas C and K, and Game Management Areas 11 and 12.
J 24.8 Lodge. Glimpse of Tanada Lake beneath Tanada Peak to the south.
J 25.2 Little Jack Creek.
J 27.5 Turnout.
J 27.6 Horse crossing.
J 27.8 **Twin Lakes** rest area and camping; picnic table, outhouse, garbage container, aluminum recycle. Good place to observe waterfowl. Fishing for grayling 10 to 18 inches, mid-May to October, flies or small spinner. Wildflowers in June include Lapland rosebay, lupine and 8-petalled mountain avens.
J 27.9 Sportsmen Paradise Lodge.
J 29 Trail Creek crossing and trailhead. Changing water levels possible in spring or during periods of rain, requiring high clearance or 4-wheel-drive vehicle to cross creek.
J 30.7 Lost Creek crossing. Changing water levels possible in spring or during periods of rain, requiring high clearance or 4-wheel-drive vehicle to cross creek.
J 31 **Lost Creek trailhead**, a multi-use trail with access to Big Grayling Lake, Soda Creek, Platinum Creek, Mineral Springs and Soda Lake.
J 31.5 Chalk Creek bridge.
J 35.3 **Jack Creek** bridge and rest area; camping, picnic tables, outhouse, garbage container, aluminum recycle. Grayling fishing.
The road deteriorates beyond this point and you may have to ford several more creeks beyond here. Inquire at Slana Ranger Station about road conditions.
J 36.2 Skookum Volcano trail (hiking only).
J 40.2 Reeve's Field trailhead. This trail was constructed during WWII to connect Nabesna Road with a large airstrip near the Nabesna River. The airstrip and trail were named for aviation pioneer Bob Reeve.
J 42 State-maintained road ends. Hiking recommended beyond this point. Lodge (private property) charges for parking here.
J 45 **Nabesna Gold Mine**; no visitor services. The mine, on the National Register of Historic Sites, operated from 1923 until the lates 1940s, mining primarily for gold. The buildings, mill and mine adits are privately owned. Some of the tailings are on national park land. Visitors are reminded not to pick up historic artifacts on either private property or park lands.

Return to Milepost GJ 59.8 Tok Cutoff

Drive with headlights on at all times.

J 61 A 264 T 64 **Midway Service**. See display ad this section.
NOTE: 7 percent uphill grade eastbound.
GJ 60.8 A 263.8 T 64.2 Bridge over **Ahtell Creek**; grayling. Gravel parking area to south at east end of bridge across from midway service. This stream drains a mountain area of igneous rock, where several gold and silver-lead claims are located.
GJ 60 A 263 T 65 Distance marker eastbound shows Tok 66 miles, Tetlin Junction 78 miles, Canada Border 158 miles.
GJ 59.8 A 262.8 T 65.2 Turnoff to south for post office, pay phone, private camping and lodging (open year-round), and Wrangell-St. Elias National Park rangerstation.

Junction with Nabesna Road. See "Nabesna Road" log beginning on opposite page.

Long 6 percent uphill grade westbound.
GJ 59.4 A 262.4 T 65.6 Distance marker westbound shows Glennallen 76 miles; Valdez 189 miles; Anchorage 263 miles.
GJ 58.5 A 261.5 T 66.5 *Long 6 percent downgrade eastbound.*
GJ 56.5 A 259.5 T 68.5 Double-ended turnout to south is a scenic viewpoint overlooking Cobb Lakes. View to the south and southwest of Tanada Peak (9,240 feet); Mount Sanford ((16,237 feet), center; Mount Blackburn (16,390 feet); and Mount Drum (12,010 feet). The Mentasta Mountains are to the east. Gold Rush Centennial sign:
In 1885, Lieutenant Henry T. Allen led one of America's epic journeys of exploration. In 5 months, his expedition crossed 1,500 miles of largely unexplored territory including this valley. Ordered to investigate the unmapped Copper and Tanana river valleys, Allen started up the Copper River in March 1885 and passed this point 2 months later, reaching the headwaters of the Copper River and entering the Tanana Valley. Allen descended the Tanana River and trekked from the Yukon to the headwaters of the Koyukuk River.
GJ 55.2 A 258.2 T 69.8 Tanada Peak viewpoint; narrow double-ended gravel turnout to south.
CAUTION: Watch for horses on road.
GJ 53 A 256 T 72 Grizzly Lake; lodging, camping, trail rides.
Grizzly Lake Ranch Bed & Breakfast. See display ad this section.
GJ 47 A 250 T 78 Indian Creek trailhead to north; parking.
GJ 46 A 249 T 79 Wesbound, Mount Drum is directly ahead; Mount Sanford is to the left of Mount Drum.
GJ 44.6 A 247.6 T 80.4 Long double-ended parking area to north. Eagle Trail access (sign).
GJ 43.8 A 246.8 T 81.2 Bridge over Indian River. Watch for salmon spawning in late-June through July. *(This river is closed to chinook salmon fishing.)*
GJ 43.7 A 246.7 T 81.3 Rest area to southwest of bridge.
GJ 43.3 A 246.3 T 81.7 Turnout to south.
GJ 43 A 246 T 82 *CAUTION: Slow for dips westbound.*
GJ 40.1 A 243.1 T 84.9 Gravel turnout to south.
GJ 39 A 242 T 86 Views of the Copper River valley and Wrangell Mountains. Looking south, peak on left is Mount Sanford and on right is Mount Drum (elev. 12,010 feet).
GJ 38.7 A 241.7 T 86.3 Turnout to northwest.
GJ 38 A 241 T 87 *NOTE: Road narrows westbound. Road widens eastbound.*
GJ 37.1 A 240.1 T 87.9 Chistochina (sign westbound).
GJ 36.5 A 239.5 T 88.5 **Chistochina Bed and Breakfast** to northwest. See display ad this section.

MIDWAY SERVICE
The Only Full Line Grocery Store within 60 miles • Easy on-off ramp

Groceries • Sporting Goods • Hardware
Auto Supplies • Two Entrances
Fishing & Hunting • Licenses & Supplies
Cabin Rentals • Free Tent Camping
Showers & Laundromat
Propane • Ample Parking
Free Coffee • Public Phone & Fax
Major Credit Cards Accepted

Open Year Round
Summers: 8 a.m. to 8 p.m.
7 Days a Week
(907) 822-5877
Jay & Debbie Capps
1 Mile North of Nabesna Road
Entrance to Wrangell-St. Elias Park
Mile 61 Tok Cut-Off

Grizzly Lake Ranch
Bed & Breakfast
RV & Tent Camping
Trail Rides or Horse & Buggy
Rides by Appointment
Kitchennettes, Showers

"Doc" & Phoebe Taylor
Jim & Cathy Knighten
(907) 822-5214 • (907) 822-3239
P.O. Box 340, Gakona, AK 99586
Mile 53 Tok Cutoff

CHISTOCHINA B&B
• OPEN ALL YEAR • SMOKE FREE
PO Box 288 Mile 36.5 Tok Cut Off
Chistochina, AK 99586
PHONE/FAX 907-822-3989
Relax in the "Bear's Den"

chistobb@alaska.net

GJ 35.9 A 238.9 T 89.1 Gravel turnout to north.

GJ 35.6 A 238.6 T 89.4 Chistochina River Bridge No. 2. Mount Sanford is first large mountain to the southeast, then Mount Drum.

GJ 35.4 A 238.4 T 89.6 Chistochina River Bridge No. 1; parking at west end. Chistochina River trailhead on north side of highway. This trail allows access to approximately 40 miles of trail in hills north of the highway, according to the BLM. Used during hunting season by ATV and large track vehicles; may be muddy in wet weather.

The Chistochina River heads in the Chistochina Glacier on Mount Kimball (elev. 10,300 feet) in the Alaska Range and flows south 48 miles to the Copper River, which is just south of the highway here. The Tok Cutoff parallels the Copper River from here southeast to the Richardson Highway. Chistochina is thought to mean marmot creek.

GJ 34.7 A 237.7 T 90.3 Posty's Sinona Creek Trading Post (current status unknown).

GJ 34.6 A 237.6 T 90.4 Bridge over Sinona Creek. Sinona is said to mean place of the many burls, and there are indeed many burls on area spruce trees.

GJ 34.4 A 237.4 T 90.6 Sinona Creek RV Park. See display ad this section. ▲

GJ 32.9 A 235.9 T 92.1 Chistochina school. Road access to **CHISTOCHINA** (pop. 93, unincorporated), a traditional Copper River Athabascan Indian village.

GJ 32.8 A 235.8 T 92.2 Chistochina Lodge to southeast, a National Historic Site, burned to the ground in November 1999. Built in the early 1900s, the original roadhouse served foot and sled traffic on the Valdez to Eagle Trail (later the Valdez to Fairbanks Trail). The owners plan to rebuild.

Private Aircraft: Chistochina airstrip, adjacent south; elev. 1,850 feet; length 2,060 feet; turf and gravel; autogas.

GJ 31 A 234 T 94 Chistochina (sign eastbound).

NOTE: Begin 40 mph speed zone eastbound.

GJ 30.2 A 233.2 T 94.8 NOTE: Road narrows eastbound; no shoulders. Road widens westbound.

GJ 28.1 A 231.1 T 96.9 Double-ended paved parking area to south with a marker on the Alaska Road Commission. The ARC was established in 1905, the same year the first automobile arrived in Alaska at Skagway. The ARC operated for 51 years, building roads, airfields, trails and other transportation facilities. It was replaced by the Bureau of Public Roads (referred to by some Alaskans at the time as the Bureau of Parallel Ruts) in 1956. In 1960 the Bureau of Public Roads was replaced by the Dept. of Public Works.

GJ 24.4 A 227.4 T 100.6 Large rest area to south with paved double-ended parking area, toilets, picnic tables and firepits. Gold Rush Centennial sign on Discovering Gold on the Chistochina. During the Klondike Gold Rush of 1898, a few stampeders heard of a gold discovery in the upper Copper River and actually found gold in the headwaters of the Chistochina River north of here.

Paths from parking area lead to the **Copper River**. The Copper River heads on the north side of the Wrangell Mountains and flows 250 miles to the Gulf of Alaska. The river parallels Nabesna Road then the Tok Cutoff and finally the Richardson Highway.

GJ 21.7 A 224.7 T 103.3 Highway climbs long grade westbound. Views to southeast of the Wrangell Moutains: Mount Sanford on the left, Mount Drum on the right.

GJ 19 A 222 T 106 CAUTION: Slow for dips and bumps westbound.

GJ 17.5 A 220.5 T 107.5 Tulsona Creek bridge. Good grayling fishing.

GJ 14.2 A 217.2 T 110.8 Highway descends long grade eastbound. Views of mountains.

Snowshoe hare are pure white in winter, shades of gray and brown in summer. (© Craig Brandt)

GJ 13 A 216 T 112 Turnout to north.

GJ 12.2 A 215.2 T 112.8 Distance marker westbound shows Glennallen 28 miles, Anchorage 215 miles.

GJ 11.7 A 214.7 T 113.3 Wide shoulder for parking to southeast. Yellow pond lily (*Nuphar polysepalum*) in ponds north of highway.

GJ 11.3 A 214.3 T 113.7 HAARP (High frequency Active Auroral Research Program) to north of highway. This is a major Dept. of Defense Arctic facility for upper atmospheric and solar-terrestrial research. Principal elements include a high-power, high-frequency phased array radio transmitter—known as the Ionospheric Research Instrument (IRI)—and an ultra-high frequency incoherent scatter radar (IST). An annual open house is held in August.

GJ 6 A 209 T 119 View opens up westbound as highway descends to Gakona River.

GJ 4.7 A 207.7 T 120.3 Highway climbs uphill grade next mile eastbound.

GJ 4.2 A 207.2 T 120.8 Gakona Alaska R.V. Park to south. See display ad this section. ▲

GJ 3 A 206 T 122 Riverview Bed & Breakfast to south. See display ad this section.

GJ 2.7 A 205.7 T 122.3 Post office to south serves **GAKONA** (pop. 215). Originally a Native wood and fish camp., and then a permanent village of the Ahtna Indians, Gakona is located at the confluence of the Gakona and Copper rivers. (Gakona is

---

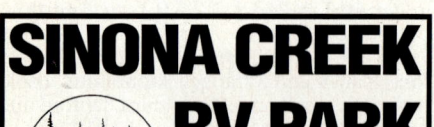

SINONA CREEK RV PARK

Offering the traveler:
- Full RV Service
- Pull-Through Spaces
- Clean Wooded Spaces
- Tent Sites • Showers
- Local Native Arts and Crafts Gift Store

For reservations call or write:
SINONA CREEK RV PARK
SR 224 Mile 34.4 Tok Cut-Off
Chistochina, Alaska 99586
Tel (907) 822-3914
Fax (907) 822-3886

GAKONA ALASKA RV PARK

MILE 4.2 TOK CUTOFF

48 SPACES • 24 PULL-THROUGHS
IGLOO CABINS • TENTS WELCOME
FULL & PARTIAL HOOKUPS – 50, 30, 20 AMPS
DUMP STATION • SHOWERS • PHONE HOOKUPS
LAUNDRY • CONCESSIONS • PROPANE
ALASKAN ADVENTURES

COPPER RIVER ACCESS & CAMPING
Large Recreational Area
Wrangell Mountain Views
Close to a fine restaurant,
excellent fishing, rafting, and hiking opportunities.

Watch & photograph working Indian-made fish wheels.

Information & Reservations:
(907) 822-3550
P.O. Box 229, Gakona, Alaska 99586

Riverview Bed & Breakfast

**Log Home on Copper River • Alaska Decor
Full Breakfast • Quiet Area • Smoke Free
New Rooms w/ Private Baths**

PO Box 261, Gakona, AK 99586 • Mile 3 Tok Cutoff

Phone/Fax (907) 822-3321

e-mail: riverv@alaska.net • website: www.alaska.net/~riverv

Athabascan for rabbit.) The community has a commercial district, a non-Native residential area, and a Native village.

GJ 2 A 205 T 123 Gakona Lodge, entered on the National Register of Historic Places in 1977, was built in 1929. It replaced an earlier roadhouse built in 1904 known as Doyle's. Located at the junction of the Valdez to Eagle and Valdez to Fairbanks trails, this was an essential stopping point for travelers.

GJ 1.8 A 204.8 T 123.2 Bridge over **Gakona River** bridge (15' clearance). The river flows 64 miles south from Gakona Glacier in the Alaska Range to join the Copper River here.

Entering Game Management Unit 13B westbound and 13C eastbound.

NOTE: Highway climbs westbound. Watch for gravel breaks.

GJ 1 A 204 T 124 Paved viewpoint to south overlooks the valley of the Gakona and Copper rivers; picnic table. Fine view of the many channels where the Gakona and Copper rivers join. View of Mount Drum and Mount Sanford. Good photo stop. Gold Rush Centennial sign about Alaska's first telegraph.

Known as the Washington-Alaska Military Cable and Telegraph System (WAMCATS), the line was built to assist communication between U.S. Army posts during the Gold Rush. Crews completed the 1,506-mile line in 1903. Although a military line, WAMCATS carried more civilian than military messages, as it assisted commerce and safe travel between gold camps and brought in news of the outside world. By the late 1920s, radio technology made WAMCATS obsolete.

GJ 0.2 A 203.2 T 124.8 Gakona (sign eastbound); see description at **Milepost GJ 2.7.**

GJ 0.1 A 203.1 T 124.9 Distance markers eastbound shows Tok 125 miles; Tetlin Junction 137 miles; Canadian border 210 miles.

GJ 0 A 203 T 125 Gakona Junction; gas station. Stop sign westbound at **junction** of Tok Cutoff (Alaska Route 1) and Richardson Highway (Alaska Route 4). The 2 roads share a common alignment for the next 14 miles westbound. Turn north here for Delta Junction. Turn south for Anchorage or Valdez. *NOTE: This junction can be confusing. Choose your route carefully.*

Paxson- or Delta Junction-bound travelers turn to **Milepost V 128.6** in the RICHARDSON HIGHWAY section for log of Alaska Route 4 North.

Distance from Anchorage (A) is followed by distance from Tok (T) and distance from Valdez (V).

Physical mileposts for the next 14 miles southbound give distance from Valdez.

ALASKA ROUTE 4

A 203 T 125 V 128.6 Gakona Junction (see description above). Improved highway southbound.

Distance marker southbound shows Glennallen 16 miles, Valdez 129 miles, Anchorage 196 miles.

Distance marker northbound shows Paxson 56 miles, Delta Junction 137 miles; Fairbanks 235 miles.

A 201 T 127 V 126.9 Access road east to village of **GULKANA** (pop. 88) on the east bank of the Gulkana River at its confluence with the Copper River. Established as a telegraph station in 1903 and named "Kulkana" after the river. Most of the Gulkana River frontage in this area is owned by Gulkana village and managed by Ahtna, Inc. Ahtna lands are closed to the public for hunting, fishing and trapping. The sale, importation and possession of alcohol are prohibited.

A 200.9 T 127.1 V 126.8 Gulkana River Bridge. Public access to river from gravel parking area east side of highway just south of bridge. *(NOTE: No public access at north end of bridge.)* Very popular fishing spot in season. Watch for pedestrians. Grayling fishing and good king and sockeye salmon fishing (June and July) in the Gulkana River; check current fishing regulations. The Gulkana River flows 60 miles from Gulkana Glacier in the Alaska Range to the Copper River.

Entering Game Management Unit 13B eastbound, 13A westbound.

A 200.3 T 127.7 V 126.2 The Fiddler's Green on Bear Creek bed and breakfast.

A 200.1 T 127.9 V 126 Paved double-ended turnout to west.

A 197.3 T 130.7 V 123.2 Large paved turnout to east.

A 192.1 T 135.9 V 118.1 Private Aircraft: Gulkana airstrip to east; elev. 1,579 feet; length 5,000 feet; asphalt; fuel 100LL.

A 192 T 136 V 118 Dry Creek State Recreation Site to west. *NOTE: This campground was closed during summer 2002. For current status, phone (907) 269-8400 or go to www.dnr.state.ak.us/parks/.* ▲

A 189.2 T 138.8 V 115.2 Distance marker northbound shows Paxson 71 miles, Tok 139 miles, Fairbanks 251 miles, Canada Border 256 miles.

Improved highway northbound.

A 189 T 139 V 115 Junction of Glenn

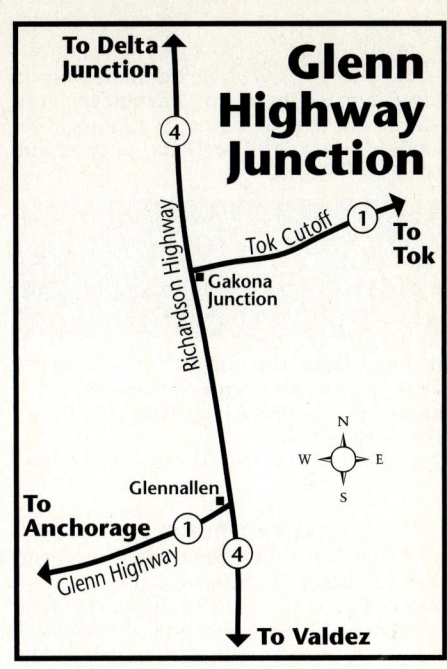

and Richardson highways; The Hub and visitor center at northwest corner; 24-hour gas, diesel, and convenience grocery. **Copper River Valley Visitor Information Center** is open daily in summer.

The Hub of Alaska and **Hub Maxi-Mart.** See display ad this section.

Alaska Court System and Dept. of Public Safety (Alaska State Troopers) located in the Ahtna Building on east side of Richardson

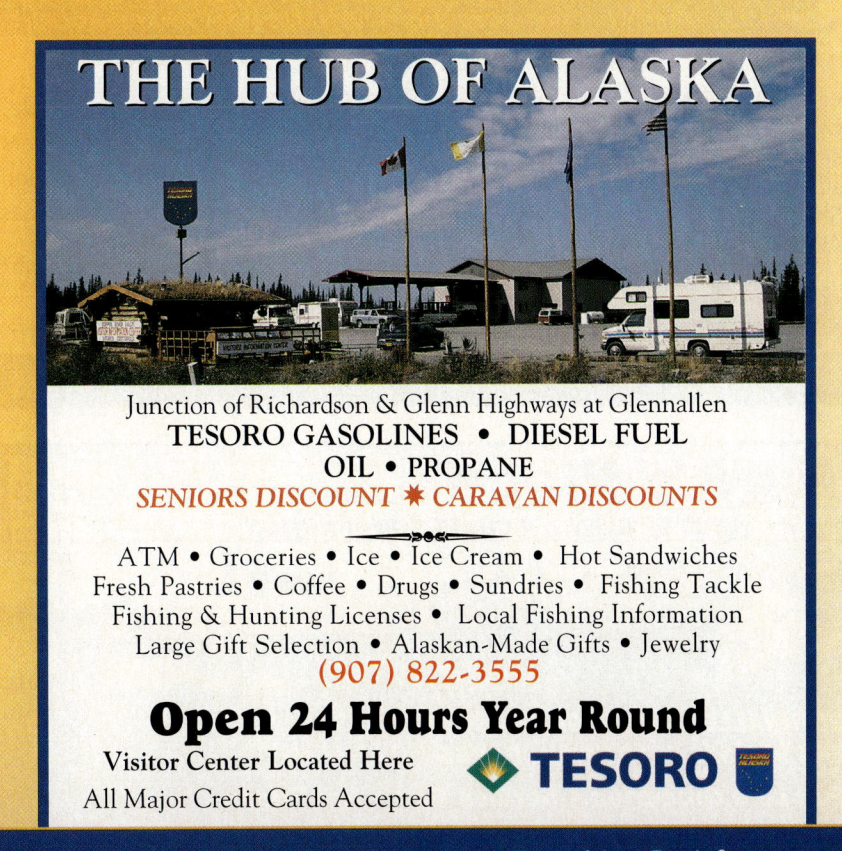

GLENN HIGHWAY • Glennallen

Highway.

NOTE: *This junction can be confusing. Choose your route carefully.* Continue west on the Glenn Highway for Anchorage. Turn south on the Richardson Highway for Valdez. Turn north for Delta Junction and Tok Cutoff to Tok.

Junction of the Richardson Highway (Alaska Route 4) and Glenn Highway (Alaska Route 1). Turn to **Milepost V 115** in the RICHARDSON HIGHWAY section for log of highway south to Valdez.

Distance from Anchorage (A) is followed by distance from Glenn–Richardson highways junction (G) and distance from Tok (T). *Physical mileposts between Glennallen and Anchorage show distance from Anchorage.*

ALASKA ROUTE 1

A 189 G 0 T 139 Junction of the Glenn and Richardson Highways.

A 188.9 G 0.5 T 139.1 Sign westbound for "Bruce A. Heck Memorial Corridor." A plaque also memorializes this slain Alaska State Trooper at **Milepost A 120.2**.

Glennallen is a busy crossroads at the junction of the Glenn and Richardson highways. (© Carol P. Murdock)

A 188.7 G 0.3 T 139.3 Northern Nights RV Campground. See display ad this section. ▲

A 187.5 G 1.5 T 140.5 Park's Place grocery complex southside of highway.

Park's Place. See display ad this section.

A 187.4 G 1.6 T 140.6 The Hitchin' Post. Good food fast! Juicy handmade burgers, great sub sandwiches, soups and soft ice cream treats. $3.99 breakfast special! Very nice Alaskan gift shop: nice selection, low prices, many Alaskan books. Lots of books-on-tape, all at half price, and used books at $2 each. Original oil paintings. Red and white building on the right as you come down the hill, across from the RV park and car wash. (907) 424-3338. [ADVERTISEMENT]

A 187.3 G 1.7 T 140.7 Boardwalk RV Park. See display ad this section. ▲

Glennallen

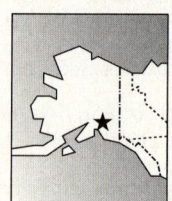

A 187 G 2 T 141 Located west of the junction of the Glenn and Richardson highways; 117 miles from Valdez. **Population:** 554. **Emergency Services: Alaska State Troopers,** Milepost A 189, phone (907) 822-3263. **Fire Department,** phone 911. **Ambulance,** Copper River EMS, phone (907) 822-3203 or 911. **Clinic,** Cross Road Medical Center at Milepost A 186.6, phone (907) 822-3203.

Visitor Information: The Copper River

BOARDWALK RV PARK
FULL HOOKUPS
LARGE PULL THROUGHS
NEXT TO STORE * LAUNDRY
CAFÉ * CARWASH
LOWEST RATES
907-822-4420   MILE 187.3 GLENN HWY

NORTHERN NIGHTS RV CAMPGROUND
HALF WAY BETWEEN ANCHORAGE-VALDEZ-FAIRBANKS & TOK • MAY 1 TO OCT. 1

IN THE **HEART** OF TOWN AT **188.7 GLENN HWY**

Large "SPRUCE TREE" lined pull-thru sites with electric (30 amp), water & sewer dump station. Some sites have sewer at site. Shaded tent sites with pads. All sites have tables & firerings.

FREE Guest amenities include:
Always Hot Showers
Flush Toilets • Firewood
E-mail/Internet Access

"DESSERT NITES"
(Mon. & Fri.—mid-June—mid-Aug.)

GLENNALLEN, AK   907.822.3199   nnites@yahoo.com
http://www.alaska-rv-campground-glennallen-northernnights.net

---

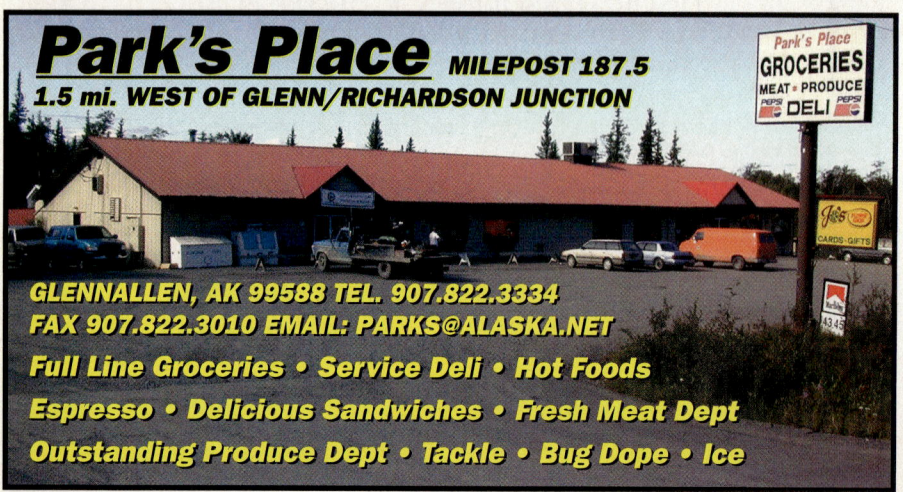

Park's Place MILEPOST 187.5
1.5 mi. WEST OF GLENN/RICHARDSON JUNCTION

GLENNALLEN, AK 99588 TEL. 907.822.3334
FAX 907.822.3010 EMAIL: PARKS@ALASKA.NET

Full Line Groceries • Service Deli • Hot Foods
Espresso • Delicious Sandwiches • Fresh Meat Dept
Outstanding Produce Dept • Tackle • Bug Dope • Ice

THE SPORTS PAGE
CABINS ON THE GLENN

MILE 187 GLENN HWY
GLENNALLEN, ALASKA

907-822-5833

TENT CAMPING • CABIN RENTALS
RESTAURANT • INFORMATION
22 RV SPOTS WITH FULL HOOK-UPS
SPORTING GOODS • LAUNDRY
CLOTHING • HOT SHOWERS

ALORA'S QUILT SHOP
THE LARGEST QUILT SHOP IN INTERIOR ALASKA

Valley Visitor Information Center is located at the junction of the Glenn and Richardson highways, **Milepost A 189**; open 8 A.M. to 7 P.M. daily in summer, phone (907) 822-5555 or write Box 469MP, Glennallen, AK 99588. The Alaska Dept. of Fish and Game office is located at **Milepost A 186.3** on the Glenn Highway, open weekdays 8 A.M. to 5 P.M.; phone (907) 822-3309.

Elevation: 1,460 feet. **Climate:** Mean monthly temperature in January, -10°F; in July, 56°F. Record low was -61°F in January 1975; record high, 90°F in June 1969. Mean precipitation in July, 1.53 inches. Mean precipitation (snow/sleet) in December, 11.4 inches. **Radio:** KCAM 790, KOOL 107.1, KUAC-FM 92.1. **Television:** KYUK (Bethel) and Wrangell Mountain TV Club via satellite; Public Broadcasting System.

Private Aircraft: Gulkana airstrip, northeast of Glennallen at **Milepost A 192.1**; elev. 1,579 feet; length 5,000 feet; asphalt; fuel 100LL. Parking with tie downs.

The name Glennallen is derived from the combined last names of Capt. Edwin F. Glenn and Lt. Henry T. Allen, both leaders in the early exploration of the Copper River region.

Glennallen lies at the western edge of the huge Wrangell–St. Elias National Park and Preserve. It is a gateway to the Wrangell Mountains and the service center for the Copper River basin. Glennallen is also a fly-in base for several guides and outfitters.

Four prominent peaks of the majestic Wrangell Mountains are to the east; from left they are Mounts Sanford, Drum, Wrangell and Blackburn. The best views are on crisp winter days at sunset. The rest of the countryside is relatively flat.

Towering above the town is an AT&T

GLENNALLEN ADVERTISERS

Ahtna Inc.	Ph. (907) 822-3476
Backcountry Connection	Ph. (907) 822-5292
Basin Liquors, Paper Shack, Office Supply	Ph. (907) 822-3319
Boardwalk RV Park	Ph. (907) 822-4420
Brown Bear Rhodehouse	Ph. (907) 822-3663
Cross Road Medical Center	Ph. (907) 822-3203
Glennallen Chevron	Ph. (907) 822-3303
Hitchin' Post, The	Ph. (907) 822-3338
KCAM Radio	Ph. (907) 822-5226
New Caribou Hotel, Gift Shop and Restaurant	Ph. (907) 822-3302
Northern Nights RV Campground	Ph. (907) 822-3199
Park's Place	Ph. (907) 822-3334
Sports Page, The	Ph. (907) 822-5833
Tolsona Wilderness Campground	Ph. (907) 822-3865

BROWN BEAR RHODEHOUSE

Alaskan Hospitality Year Around

-80° to +90°

4 Miles from Glennallen toward Anchorage

Campground • Camping Cabins • Restaurant • Bar

HOME OF THE BROWN BEAR MUSIC FESTIVAL

Unique Alaskan Gifts

Steaks • Fresh Seafood • Pizza

BROASTED CHICKEN BY THE BUCKET

Phone (907) **822-FOOD**

RV Parking • Picnic Sites

Caravan and Bus Tours Please Call Ahead

Unbelievable Grizzly/Brown Bear Photo Collection

Mile 183.6 Glenn Highway • Your Hosts: Doug & Cindy Rhodes
P.O. Box 110, Glennallen, Alaska 99588 • (907) 822-3663

THE NEW CARIBOU HOTEL
Glennallen, Alaska

FAMILY RESTAURANT
- FULLY REMODELED
- PROFESSIONAL CHEFS
- DAILY SPECIALS
- HOMEMADE SOUPS, PIES, PASTRIES

GIFT SHOP & CONVENIENT GLENNALLEN CHEVRON COMPLEX
- CHEVRON QUALITY PRODUCTS
- PROPANE • COOPER TIRES
- MECHANIC ON DUTY MON. - FRI.

HOT TUBS, SUITES, BANQUET ROOM, BUSES WELCOME

HOTEL RESERVATIONS 800.478.3302 • RESTAURANT RESERVATIONS 907.822.3149

SERVICE STATION 907.822.3303 • email: chotel@alaska.net

P.O. BOX 329 • GLENNALLEN, ALASKA 99588

Gulkana Airport on the Richardson Highway serves Glennallen. (© Kris Graef, staff)

Alascom microwave tower. AT&T Alascom owns and operates 180 communications towers throughout the state of Alaska. The towers are also located along the Alaska, Parks, Richardson, Dalton and Sterling highways, as well as on mountaintops in Southeast Alaska and in remote locations such as Nome. With heights ranging from 100 to over 300 feet, they are often used as landmarks, but their primary purpose is to carry digital or analog microwave signals for the transmission of long-distance voice and data messages and, in some cases, 2-way radio communications.

Glennallen businesses are located for several miles along the Glenn Highway west from the junction of the Glenn and Richardson highways. About two-thirds of the area's residents are employed by trade/service firms; the balance hold various government positions. Offices for the Bureau of Land Management, the Alaska State Troopers and Dept. of Fish and Game are located here. There are several small farms in the area. There is a substantial Native population in the area, and the Native-owned Ahtna Corp. has its headquarters in Glennallen at the junction of the Glenn and Richardson highways.

Also headquartered here is KCAM radio (www.kcam.org), which broadcasts on station 790. KCAM broadcasts area road condition reports daily and also airs the popular "Caribou Clatters," which broadcasts personal messages. Radio messages are still a popular form of communication in Alaska and a necessary one in the Bush. Caribou Clatters are received and read by KCAM announcers during the KCAM news reports, airing at about 7:30 A.M., 12:30 P.M. and 5:30 P.M. and between 9 and 9:15 P.M. Each Clatter is read at 3 consecutive newscasts. To leave a Clatter, phone (907) 822-3306; fax (907) 822-3761; email caribouclatters@yahoo.com.

Lodging & Services

Because of its strategic location, most traveler services are available. During summer months reservations are advised for visitor accommodations. Glennallen has several RV campgrounds, motels and restaurants. Auto parts, groceries, gift shops, clothing, propane, sporting goods and other supplies are available at local stores. Services include a Wells Fargo Bank with ATM, a dentist, several churches, a chiropractic center, a laundromat, gas stations and major auto repair.

New Caribou Hotel, Restaurant, Gift Shop & Glennallen Chevron Complex. Caribou Hotel with 55 new rooms, whirlpool bath and suites available. Alaska decor, satellite TV, fax lines. Also Pipeline man Camp economy rooms. Caribou Restaurants is totally remodeled with professional chefs, seats 135 with private dining room for tour buses. Daily specials, homemade soups, pies and pastries. Caribou Gift Shop in a quaint Alaska log cabin full of gifts, souvenirs, hand-made items, jewelry, furs, knives, T-shirts and sweat shirts. Glennallen Chevron Service Station carries Chevron quality products, diesel, Cooper tires and propane. Mechanic on duty Monday–Friday. Ask about our B&B accommodations. New

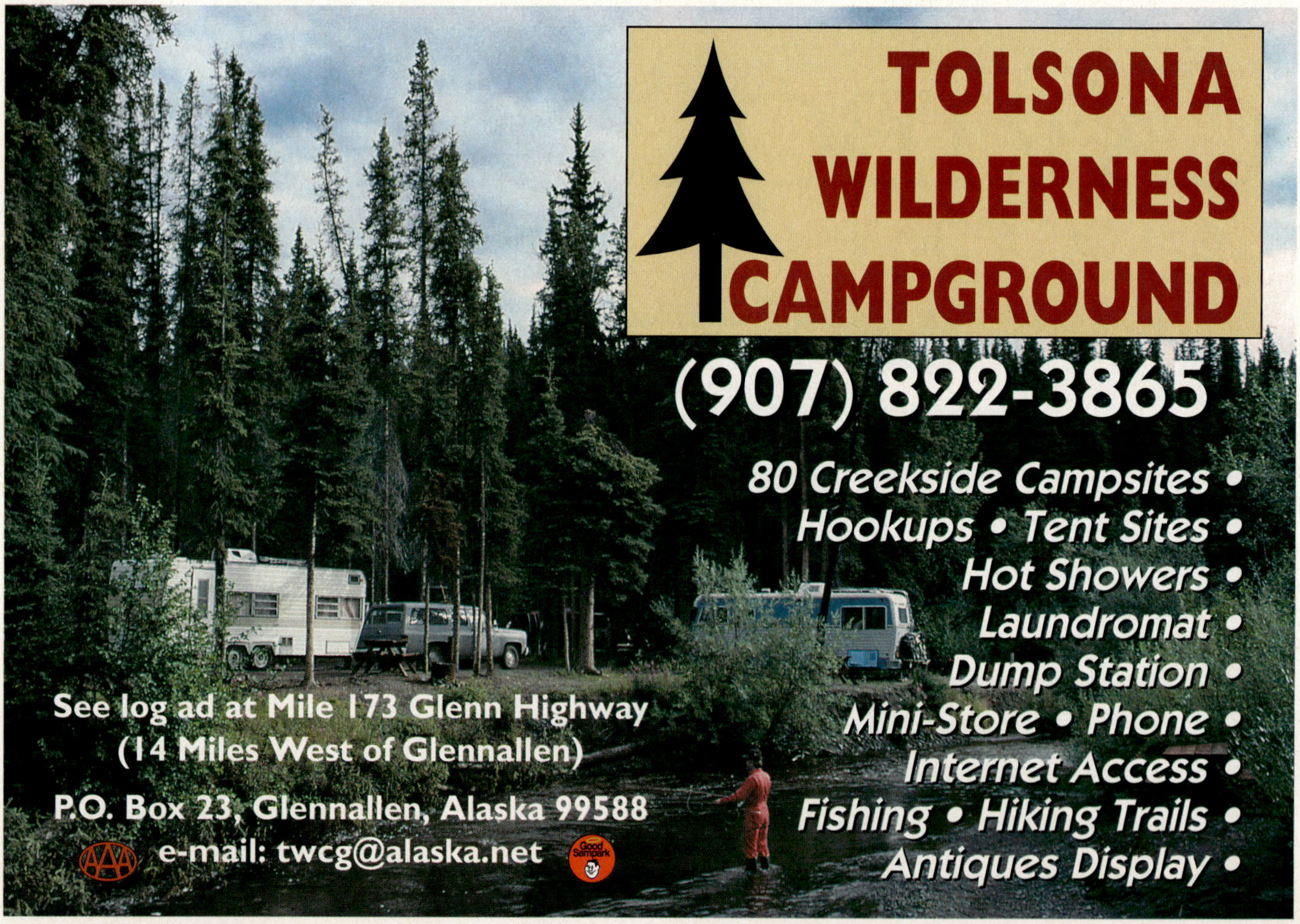

TOLSONA WILDERNESS CAMPGROUND

(907) 822-3865

- 80 Creekside Campsites
- Hookups • Tent Sites
- Hot Showers
- Laundromat
- Dump Station
- Mini-Store • Phone
- Internet Access
- Fishing • Hiking Trails
- Antiques Display

See log ad at Mile 173 Glenn Highway
(14 Miles West of Glennallen)

P.O. Box 23, Glennallen, Alaska 99588

e-mail: twcg@alaska.net

Caribou Hotel, Restaurant, Gift Shop & Glennallen Chevron Complex, P.O. Box 329, Glennallen, AK 99588. Mile 189.6 Glenn Highway. Hotel reservations (800) 478-3302. Restaurant reservations (907) 822-3149. Service Station (907) 822-3303. www.alaskan.com/caribouhotel; email chotel@alaska.net. See display ad this section.
[ADVERTISEMENT]

Camping

There are several RV campgrounds in the Glennallen area. Northern Nights RV Campground is near the Glenn–Rich Highway junction at **Milepost A 188.7**. Boardwalk RV Park is at **Milepost A 187.3**. The Sports Page is in town at **Milepost A 187**. Campgrounds west of town include Brown Bear Rhodehouse at and Tolsona Wilderness Campground and RV Park. Contact Alaska State Parks at (907) 269-8400 for current status of campsites at Dry Creek and Lake Louise. ▲

Northern Nights RV Campground. A very well-maintained, beautifully landscaped RV campground offering large, level, spruce tree-lined pull-through sites. "Ultimate Tow" vehicles with triple slide rigs will have no problem parking here. The friendly and knowledgeable owner/operators, who reside on site, enjoy making their guests' stay relaxing and fun. A new, always hot, private, individual showers facility with flush toilets—and even a jet tub—is available to help guests unwind after a long day of sightseeing and fishing. Free "Dessert Nights" are offered to guests on Monday and Friday nights from mid-June through August. Located only 600 yards from the Richardson and Glenn Highway junction on the Glenn Highway. This park is open from May 1 to October 1. [ADVERTISEMENT]

The Sports Page. A nicely landscaped, full service RV park. Newly constructed authentic log cabins with refrigerators, microwaves and coffee makers. Hot showers available. Full service sporting goods store, gift shop and Interior Alaska's largest quilt and fabric store with over 2,000 bolts of material in stock. Custom screen printing, embroidery and lots of information. (907) 822-5833. Mile 187 Glenn Highway. See display ad this section.
[ADVERTISEMENT] ▲

Transportation

Bus: Scheduled service between Anchorage and Whitehorse via Glennallen. Bus service between Glennallen and McCarthy via Copper Center and Chitina in summer via Backcountry Connection.

Backcountry Connection, LLC provides daily shuttle service into Wrangell-St. Elias National Park & Preserve to McCarthy and Kennicott. One-way and round trips avail-

Welcomes you to the Ahtna Region.

We own and manage 1.5 million acres of land throughout the Copper River Basin and Cantwell. Much of our land encompasses some of the most spectacular scenery in the world and possesses abundant fish and wildlife resources. We believe in being good stewards of the land. Ahtna has closed its land to hunting to protect the subsistence rights of our people. Ahtna, Inc. has opened portions of its land to access with a Limited Use Permit. These permits allow you to use Ahtna land for fishing and camping at designated sites along the Gulkana and Klutina Rivers. If you desire access across Ahtna land, permits are available on the Klutina Lake Trail Mile 100.8 of the Richardson Hwy., Sailor's Pit Camp Mile 129.5 of the Richardson Hwy and at our main office at the junction of the Glenn and Richardson Highways.

able. Photo stops. Gravel road atop old Copper River & Northwestern Railway. Save your tires and ride with us. Great option for hikers accessing Dixie Pass. (907) 822-5292; (866) 582-5292; email bakcntry@alaska.net; web site www.alaska-backcountry-tours.com.
[ADVERTISEMENT]

Attractions

Fourth of July weekend is a major event in Glennallen. Activities include the Ahtna Arts and Crafts Fair, a music festival, raft race, parade and salmon bake.

Recreational opportunities in the Glennallen area include hiking, flightseeing, hunting, river running, bird watching and fishing. According to the ADF&G, 28 lakes in the Glennallen area are stocked with grayling, rainbow trout and coho salmon. A complete list of lakes, locations and species is available at the Copper River Valley Visitor Center at **Milepost A 189**, or from the ADF&G office at **Milepost A 186.3**. Locally, there is good grayling fishing in **Moose Creek**; **Tulsona Creek** to the east at **Milepost GJ 17.5**; west on the Glenn Highway at **Tolsona Creek, Milepost A 173**. **Lake Louise**, approximately 27 miles west and 16 miles north from Glennallen, offers excellent grayling and lake trout fishing.

Many fly-in lakes are located in the Copper River basin and Chugach Mountains near Glennallen. **Crosswind Lake**, large lake trout, whitefish and grayling, early June to early July. **Deep Lake**, all summer for lake trout to 30 inches. **High Lake**, lake trout to 22 inches, June and early July with small spoons; fly-fishing; cabin, boat and motor rental. **Tebay Lakes**, excellent rainbow fishing, 12 to 15 inches, all summer, small spinners; cabin, boat and motor rental. **Jan Lake**, 12- to 14-inch silver salmon, June, spinners; also rainbow. **Hanagita Lake**, excellent grayling fishing all summer. **Minnesota Lake**, lake trout to 30 inches, all summer; boat only, no cabins.

Glenn Highway Log
(continued)

Distance from Anchorage (A) is followed by distance from Glenn–Richardson highways junction (G) and distance from Tok (T).

A 186.6 G 2.4 T 141.4 Cross Road Medical Center clinic (EMS, 24-hour emergency room). Alaska Bible College, the state's only accredited resident 4-year Bible college, is located behind the clinic.

A 186.4 G 2.6 T 141.6 Bureau of Land Management Glennallen Field Office; phone (907) 822-3217.

A 186.3 G 2.7 T 141.7 Alaska State Dept. of Fish and Game; phone (907) 822-3309.

A 186 G 3 T 142 Moose Creek culvert. Copper Valley library.

A 185.4 G 3.6 T 142.6 NOTE: Begin 40 mph speed zone eastbound. Improved highway, 55 mph, westbound.

A 183.6 G 5.4 T 144.4 Lodge restaurant to north.

Brown Bear Rhodehouse. Because of the excellent food, reasonable prices and Alaskan hospitality, this famous old lodge is a favorite eating and gathering place for local people and travelers alike. If eating in the Glennallen area, we recommend stopping here, and if coming from south it is well worth the extra few minutes' wait. Superb steaks and seafood are the specialties, along with broasted chicken and the widest sandwich selection in the area. Your hosts, Doug and Cindy Rhodes, have managed to take one of the largest grizzly brown bear photograph collections anywhere. So, if not dining, you will enjoy just stopping and looking at the many photographs that cover the walls. This is the only place in the area where you have a campground, camping cabins, restaurant and bar at one stop. This is also the only place on the highway to get a bucket of golden brown broasted chicken to go. Phone (907) 822-3663. See display ad this section. [ADVERTISEMENT] ▲

A 182.2 G 6.8 T 145.8 Liquor and office supply store to south has some interesting topiary done in native shrubs like willow and birch.

Basin Liquors, Paper Shack Office Supply. Liquor store opens 8 A.M., 7 days a week, 365 days a year. Liquor, snacks, ice,

cigarettes. We invite you to take a break; walk around in one of the most beautiful yards on the Glenn Highway and check out our book exchange. [ADVERTISEMENT]

A 177 G 12 T 151 Distance marker westbound shows Palmer 129 miles, Anchorage 177 miles.

A 176.6 G 12.4 T 151.4 Paved historical viewpoint to south with interpretive sign about the Wrangell Mountains and view southeast across the Copper River valley to Mount Drum. Northeast of Mount Drum is Mount Sanford and southeast is Mount Wrangell (elev. 14,163 feet), a semiactive volcano. Mount Wrangell last erupted in 1912 when lava flowed to its base and ash fell as far west as this point.

Wildflowers growing along the roadside include lupine, cinquefoil, oxytrope, Jacob's ladder and sweet pea.

A 176.4 G 12.6 T 151.6 Distance marker eastbound shows Glennallen 10 miles, Tok 152 miles.

A 174.4 G 14.6 T 153.6 Double-ended paved turnout to south.

Great views (on clear days) of Mount Sanford directly ahead for eastbound travelers.

A 173 G 16 T 155 Turnoff to north for Tolsona Wilderness Campground and RV Park with dump station and laundromat.

Tolsona Wilderness Campground & RV Park. AAA approved, Good Sam Park. This beautiful campground, located three-quarter mile north of the highway, is surrounded on 3 sides by untouched wilderness. All 80 campsites are situated beside sparkling Tolsona Creek and are complete with table, litter barrel and fireplace. It is a full-service campground with tent sites, restrooms, dump station, hot showers, laundromat, water and electric hookups for RVs. Internet access available. Browse through the extensive turn-of-the-century antique display. Hiking trail and public phone. Open from May 20 through Sept. 10. Phone (907) 822-3865. Email: twcg@alaska.net. See display ad in Glennallen section. [ADVERTISEMENT] ▲

A 172.9 G 16.1 T 155.1 Ranch House Lodge.

A 172.8 G 16.2 T 155.2 Turnout to south at east end of **Tolsona Creek** bridge; parking for walk-in use (no overnight camping), phone (907) 745-3975 for information. Fishing for grayling to 16 inches, use mosquito flies in still, clear pools behind obstructions, June, July and August. Best fishing 1.5 miles upstream from highway.

A 170.5 G 18.5 T 157.5 Tolsona Lake Road to north. **Tolsona** and **Moose lakes**, rainbow trout, burbot, grayling to 16 inches, all summer; good ice fishing for burbot in winter.

A 169.3 G 19.7 T 158.7 Paved double-ended parking area to south. Long narrow **Mae West Lake**, fed by Little Woods Creek, is a little less than 1 mile away. Grayling fishing.

A 168 G 21 T 160 Soup Lake to north. Trumpeter swans can sometimes be seen in lakes and ponds along this section of highway. Watch for moose. In June and July look for wildflowers such as sweet pea, fireweed, lupine, cinquefoil, oxytrope, Jacob's ladder and milk-vetch.

A 167 G 22 T 161 Distance marker eastbound shows Glennallen 20 miles, Tok 162 miles.

A 166.9 G 22.1 T 161.1 Distance marker westbound shows Sutton 106 miles, Palmer 119 miles.

A 166.1 G 22.9 T 161.9 **Atlasta House**, a local landmark, was named by the homesteader who was happy to have a real house at last.

A 165.9 G 23.1 T 162.1 Paved double-ended turnout to south and 2-mile hiking trail to **Lost Cabin Lake**; grayling fishing.

Tolsona Mountain (elev. 2,974 feet), a prominent ridge just north of highway, is a landmark for miles in both directions. This area is popular with berry-pickers in late summer and early fall. Varieties of wild berries include blueberries, lowbush cranberries and raspberries.

A 164 G 25 T 164 First glimpse westbound of Tazlina Glacier and lake to south. Half-way point between Tok and Anchorage.

A 163.9 G 25.1 T 164.1 Crafts and gift shop to north.

Queenies. See display ad this section.

A 162.3 G 26.7 T 165.7 Paved turnout to south.

A 162 G 27 T 166 Turnout to north; access to **Tex Smith Lake** to north; stocked with rainbow.

NOTE: Watch for horses.

A 160 G 29 T 168 TOLSONA (sign).

A 159.8 G 29.2 T 168.2 Turnoff to north for Lake Louise Road.

Junction with 19.3-mile Lake Louise Road (gravel) to Lake Louise State Recreation Area. See "Lake Louise Road" log on opposite page.

Lake Louise Road

This road leads north 19.3 miles from **Milepost A 159.8** Glenn Highway to Lake Louise State Recreation Area. The road is state-maintained and open year-round. Lake Louise is known for its lake trout and grayling fishing; lodges, dining, boat rentals and fishing charters at lake. Views of Tazlina Glacier and Lake; berry picking for wild strawberries and blueberries (July and August), and cranberries (September). Excellent cross-country skiing and snowmobiling in winter.

Distance is measured from the junction with the Glenn Highway (J).

J 0 **Junction** with Glenn Highway at **Milepost A 159.8.**

J 0.2 **Junction Lake** to east; grayling fishing.

J 1.1 Turnout.

J 1.2 Double-ended turnout to west with view of Tazlina Glacier.

Just north is the road west to **Little Crater Lake** and **Carter Lake**, stocked with rainbow trout by ADF&G.

J 5.2 **Old Road Lake** and **Round Lake** to east (1/4 mile); rainbow fishing.

J 6.7 **Mendeltna Creek** to west 5 miles via rough road (4-wheel-drive access only). Arctic grayling fishing.

J 7 **Forgotten Lake** to east (0.1 mile); grayling fishing.

J 9.4 Parking area to west with view of pothole lakes. First view of Lake Louise northbound.

J 10.5 Hill; use low-gear. Good view on clear days of the Alaska Range and Susitna River valley.

J 11.5 Road west to **Caribou Lake**; grayling fishing. Turnout to east by **Elbow Lake**; grayling fishing.

J 11.6 Parking.

J 14 Boundary of Matanuska–Susitna Borough.

J 15.4 Gas.

J 15.8 Parking area to east.

J 16 **North and South Jans Lakes** to east (7 miles); fishing.

J 16.1 Turnoff for Lake Louise Lodge (0.9 miles).

Lake Louise Lodge. See display ad this section.

J 16.5 Turnoff for Wolverine Lodge (0.3 miles).

J 16.8 **Conner Lake** public access; grayling fishing.

J 17.2 Side road leads northeast to The Point Lodge (0.9 miles) and **Lake Louise State Recreation Area**. Drive 0.4 miles to "T"; turn left for The Point Lodge (0.5 mile) and Lake Louise Campground (0.3 mile); turn right for Army Point Campground (0.7 mile). Army Point and Lake Louise campgrounds have 52 campsites on loop roads, firepits, water pumps, toilets (wheelchair accessible), covered picnic tables, picnic shelter, walking trail and a boat launch. Camping fee $10/night or resident pass. Swimming in Lake Louise. Winter ski trail access. *These campgrounds were closed in summer 2002. For current status, phone (907) 269-8400 or go to www.dnr.state.ak.us/parks/.*

The Point Lodge. See display ad this section.

J 19.3 Road ends. Parking and boat launch to west on **Dinty Lake**. Side road east to Lake Louise rest area; picnic tables, fireplaces, toilets.

Lake Louise, grayling and lake trout fishing good year-round, best spring through July, then again in the fall; early season use herring or whitefish bait, cast from boat; later (warmer water) troll with #16 red-and-white spoon, silver Alaskan plug or large silver flatfish; for grayling, casting flies or small spinners, June, July and August; in winter jig for lake trout. Check ADF&G regulations for Lake Louise area.

Susitna Lake can be reached by boat across Lake Louise (narrow channel; watch for signs); burbot, lake trout and grayling fishing. *Both lakes can be rough; under-powered boats not recommended.* **Dinty Lake**, launch from public launch at Mile 19.3; grayling and lake trout fishing.

Return to Milepost A 159.8 Glenn Highway

Calm waters of Lake Louise reflect the skies on a fine summer day.
(© Alan D. Musy/ADM PhotoGraphics)

GLENN HIGHWAY

Ice still clogs this lake along the Glenn Highway in mid-May. (© Kris Graef, staff)

A 159.6 G 29.4 T 168.4 **Little Junction Lake** public fishing access, 0.5-mile hike south; grayling.

A 157 G 32 T 171 Public fishing access trails to south to **DJ Lake** 0.5 mile (rainbow fishing) and **Sucker Lake** 4 miles (grayling and burbot).

Distance marker westbound shows Palmer 109 miles, Anchorage 157 miles. Distance marker eastbound shows Glennallen 31 miles, Tok 173 miles.

A 156.4 G 32.6 T 171.6 Good view (weather permitting) of **Tazlina Glacier** to the south. The glacier feeds into 20-mile-long **Tazlina Lake** at its foot.

A 156.3 G 32.7 T 171.7 **Buffalo Lake** public fishing access to north; stocked with rainbow.

A 156.2 G 32.8 T 171.8 Tazlina Glacier Lodge.

A 156 G 33 T 172 Tazlina airstrip to south; elev. 2,450 feet; length 1,200 feet; gravel. Not recommended for use.

A 155.8 G 33.2 T 172.2 **Arizona Lake** public fishing access to south; stocked with arctic grayling.

A 155.6 G 33.4 T 172.4 Paved turnout to south.

A 155.2 G 33.8 T 172.8 **Gergie Lake** public fishing access to south (1 1/4 mile); fishing for grayling and rainbow.

A 154 G 35 T 174 MENDELTNA (pop. 63) sign westbound. This unincorporated community includes the large RV campground (K.R.O.A.), the state highway maintenance station and general store at Nelchina, and Eureka Lodge. The area was originally a stop used by Natives traveling from Lake Tyone to Tazlina Lake. Gold brought prospectors into the area in the 1800s.

A 153.5 G 35.5 T 174.5 Mendeltna Community chapel to south.

A 153 G 36 T 175 K.R.O.A. campground and lodge-style restaurant, bar, liquor store, cabins and gas to south.

K.R.O.A. Kamping Resorts of Alaska. See display ad this section.

A 152.7 G 36.3 T 175.3 **Mendeltna Creek** bridge. Watch for spawning salmon in August. Fishing for grayling and whitefish, May to November, use spinners and flies. This creek is closed to all salmon fishing. Good fishing north to Old Man Lake; watch for bears.

A 152.6 G 36.6 T 175.4 Paved double-ended turnout to north.

A 151.4 G 37.6 T 176.6 Mendeltna (sign eastbound); see description at **Milepost A 154**.

A 150.9 G 38.1 T 177.1 Distance marker eastbound shows Glennallen 37 miles, Tok 179 miles.

A 150.4 G 38.6 T 177.6 NELCHINA (sign). Census figures for this area show a population of 71.

A 150 G 39 T 178 Distance marker westbound shows Sutton 89 miles, Palmer 103 miles. Eastbound view of Mount Sanford and Mount Drum straight ahead.

A 149.1 G 39.9 T 178.9 **Ryan Lake** public fishing access; grayling and rainbow.

A 149 G 40 T 179 Food, lodging and towing service on south side of highway.

A 144.9 G 44.1 T 183.1 Lottie Sparks (Nelchina) Elementary School to north.

A 143.3 G 45.7 T 184.7 Nelchina Lodge. See display ad this section.

A 142.6 G 46.4 T 185.4 Distance marker eastbound shows Lake Louise Junction 17 miles, Glennallen 47 miles, Tok 189 miles.

A 141.2 G 47.8 T 186.8 Nelchina state highway maintenance station.

Slide Mountain trailhead. DOT Trails Inventory says this is a 13-mile-long trail around Slide Mountain described by the BLM as a "tractor trail."

A 138.5 G 50.5 T 189.5 NELCHINA (sign).

A 137.6 G 51.4 T 190.4 **Little Nelchina State Recreation Site** 0.3 mile north from highway; 11 campsites, 15-day limit, no camping fee, no drinking water, tables, firepits, toilet, boat launch. Watch for moose and bear. Fishing for Arctic grayling.

A 137.5 G 51.5 T 190.5 Little Nelchina River bridge.

NOTE: Eastbound, highway curves uphill from bridge. Westbound to summit it is good paved straightaway with passing lanes.

A 137.4 G 51.6 T 190.6 Boundary of Matanuska–Susitna Borough (sign).

A 135.9 G 53.1 T 192.1 Paved turnout to north; gravel road continues north.

A 135.1 G 53.9 T 192.9 Slide Mountain Cabins to north.

MENDELTNA LODGE
KAMPING RESORTS OF ALASKA

SHOWERS, LAUNDROMAT, GAS, FISHING, CABINS, RV PARKING, FULL HOOK-UPS

MILE 153 GLENN HIGHWAY 35 MILES SW OF GLENNALLEN
HALFWAY BETWEEN ANCHORAGE-VALDEZ & TOK-ANCHORAGE
RESTAURANT, HOMEMADE PIZZA AND GIANT CINNAMON BUNS
ARE AN ALASKAN TRADITION AT MENDELTNA
MUSEUM OF ALASKA'S DRUNKEN FOREST – FREE
HCI BOX 2560 GLENNALLEN AK 99588 907.822.3346

NELCHINA LODGE
MILE 143.3 GLENN HWY.

Log Cabins from $50

Open Year Around
Snowmachine & ATV Trails
Fossil Hunting On Slide Mtn.
Close To Eureka & Lake Louise

(907) 822-3605
email: shj@alaska.net
HC 1 Box 2425, Glennallen, AK 99588

A 134.1 G 54.9 T 193.9 Truck lane begins westbound.

A 133.9 G 55.1 T 194.1 Gravel parking to south.

A 133.8 G 55.2 T 194.2 Gravel parking to south.

A 133.2 G 55.8 T 194.8 John Lake trail (signed) north side of highway.

A 133 G 56 T 195 Double-ended paved turnout to north.

Truck lane ends westbound. Highway descends eastbound.

A 132 G 57 T 196 Great views to southwest of Nelchina Glacier. View of snow-covered Mount Sanford eastbound.

A 130.5 G 58.5 T 197.5 Large gravel parking area to north used by hunters, ATVers and hikers. Old Man Creek trailhead (Old Man Creek 2 miles; Crooked Creek 9 miles; Nelchina Town 14.5 miles). Established trails west from here to Palmer are part of the Chickaloon–Knik–Nelchina trail system.

A 129.5 G 59.5 T 198.5 Eureka Summit (elev. 3,322 feet), highest point on the Glenn Highway. Turnout to south with unobstructed views of the Chugach Mountains. Snow poles along roadside guide snow plows in winter. Truck lane ends westbound.

Gold Rush Centennial sign about Captain Edwin F. Glenn, who passed near here on his way from Cook Inlet to the Tanana River in 1898. Glenn led one of 3 teams, the Cook Inlet Exploring Expedition. His orders were to locate the most practical route from Prince William Sound through Cook Inlet to the Tanana River. The Glenn Highway is named in his honor.

The Nelchina Glacier winds downward through a cleft in the mountains. To the northwest are the peaks of the Talkeetnas, and to the west the highway descends through river valleys which separate these 2 mountain ranges. This is the divide of 3 big river systems: Susitna, Matanuska and Copper.

A 128.5 G 60.5 T 199.5 Distance marker eastbound shows Glennallen 58 miles, Valdez 179 miles, Tok 198 miles.

A 128.3 G 60.7 T 199.7 Food, gas, diesel, lodging, bar and liquor store at the Eureka Lodge. The first lodge on the Glenn Highway, it was opened in 1937 by Paul Waverly and has operated continuously ever since. The original log building (Eureka Roadhouse) is next to Eureka Lodge.

Private Aircraft: Eureka (Skelton) airstrip, one of the highest in the state; elev. 3,289 feet; length 2,400 feet; gravel; fuel autogas; unattended. Runway narrows to 15 feet.

A 128 G 61 T 200 Bruce A. Heck Memorial Corridor (sign); see **Milepost A 120.2.**

A 127 G 62 T 201 CAUTION: Watch for caribou. Caribou crossing. The Nelchina caribou herd travels through here October through November.

A 126.4 G 62.6 T 201.6 Watch for turnoff to south to Chickaloon-Knik-Nelchina Trail System. (Eureka Creek 1.5 miles, Goober Lake 8 miles, Nelchina River 9 miles), trailhead parking.

A 125 G 63 T 203 Gunsight Mountain (elev. 6,441 feet) is visible to the west for the next few miles to those approaching from Glennallen.The notch or "gunsight" is plain if one looks closely. Eastbound views of snow-covered Mount Sanford (weather permitting), Mount Drum, Mount Wrangell and Mount Blackburn.

A 123.4 G 65.6 T 204.6 Belanger Pass

Snow poles line the Glenn Highway at Eureka Summit. (© Kris Graef, staff)

trailhead to north via Marten Road; parking by lake at highway. Marten Road (rutted dirt) leads north 1.5 miles through private homesteads and then forks: keep to left at fork for Belanger Pass trail. According to the DOT, this 8-mile trail terminates at Caribou Creek Trail. It is part of a network of ATV trails and mining roads around Syncline Mountain in the Talkeetna Mountains to the north.

A 123.1 G 65.9 T 204.9 Remains of old Tahneta Inn to south.

A 123 G66 T 205 Old Gunsight Mountain Lodge to north (closed; posted private property, no trespassing).

A 122.7 G 66.3 T 205.3 Tahneta Lake to south.

A 122.1 G 66.9 T 205.9 Double-ended gravel turnout to north on old highway alignment.

A 122 G 67 T 206 Tahneta Pass (elev. 3,000 feet).

A 121.4 G 76.6 T 206.6 Signed trailhead to north; small parking area. According to DOT, this 1-mile-long trail loops around a small lake north of Leila Lake. **Leila Lake;** grayling 8 to 14 inches abundant through summer, best fishing June and July. Burbot, success spotty for 12 to 18 inches in fall and winter.

NOTE: Improved highway westbound to Milepost A 109.

A 120.8 G 68.2 T 207.2 Boundary of Sportfish Management Area 2 and Sheep Mountain Closed Area.

A 120.2 G 68.8 T 207.8 Scenic viewpoint to south (double-ended paved turnout). The largest lake is Leila Lake; in the distance is Tahneta Lake. A monument here honoring Trooper Bruce A. Heck reads:

"On a cold winter night, on January 10, 1997, Alaska State Trooper Bruce Heck gave his life in the line of duty near this location. While on duty in the area of Mile 157.9 of the Glenn Highway, Trooper Heck attempted to arrest a suspect who had run into the woods after wrecking a stolen taxicab. In sub-zero temperatures and deep snow, a struggle ensued where the suspect overpowered Trooper Heck and took his life. The suspect, who was arrested by other officers who arrived on scene shortly thereafter, was convicted and sentenced to life in prison. In 1999, the Alaska State Legislature designated the Glenn Highway from Mile 128 to Mile 189 as the Trooper Bruce A. Heck Memorial Corridor so that his sacrifice will not be forgotten. This monument is placed in remembrance of Trooper Heck's selfless act of giving his life while protecting the citizens of Alaska."

A 119 G 70 T 209 Double-ended turnout to south with beautiful view of Chugach Mountains and lakes (weather permitting). **Knob Lake;** stocked with rainbow trout. The landmark "knob" (elev. 3,000 feet, topped by microwave tower, marks entrance to Chickaloon Pass for small planes.

This turnout is a popular birder gathering spot in the spring, when various raptors pass through on their way to western Alaska nesting sites. The migration of golden eagles, gyrfalcons, kestrels, hawks and other raptors usually takes place during a 2- to 4-week window beginning in early April. The Anchorage Audubon Society holds an annual Raptor Tailgate Party and Census during April.

A 118.5 G 70.5 T 209.5 Trailhead Road to north leads to large parking area with outhouses, picnic tables, viewing telescope and Gold Rush Centennial signs. Nice stop, good views.

Access to 4-mile section of Old Glenn Highway from parking area (abandoned road; ditches across road). See also **Milepost A 115.** Trailhead for the Chickaloon-Knik-Nelchina Trail System.

A 118.4 G 70.6 T 209.6 Alascom Road leads 3.3 miles south to microwave tower visible on hill. This gravel road is narrow and rutted with no turnarounds for large vehicles. Small turnouts along the road used as informal campsites. Road up to tower is steep and narrow (single-vehicle only) with small turnaround at stop; signed No Trespassing.

A 118.3 G 70.7 T 209.7 Trail Creek.

A 118 G 71 T 210 Truck lane ends eastbound and begins westbound.

A 117.4 G 71.6 T 210.6 Truck lane begins eastbound.

A 117.2 G 71.8 T 210.8 Paved double-ended turnout to south with view of Chugach Mountains. Signed Camp Creek Trail Trailhead.

A 117.1 G 71.9 T 210.9 Camp Creek.

A 116.9 G 72.1 T 211.1 Truck lane ends eastbound.

A 116 G 73 T 212 Truck lane begins eastbound.

A 115.5 G 73.5 T 212.5 Large paved double-ended turnout to south with view of Chugach Mountains.

Slow for rough road westbound.

A 115 G 74 T 213 Double-ended paved turnout to north. Access to 4-mile section of Old Glenn Highway alignment (abandoned road; ditches across road). See also **Milepost**

GLENN HIGHWAY

A 118.5.

A 114.9 G 74.1 T 213.1 Majestic Valley Lodge to south. Watch for sheep on mountainside.

Majestic Valley Lodge is a hand-crafted log lodge with all modern conveniences. In the 3,000-foot Tahneta Pass area, enjoy hiking treks, Dall sheep and other wildlife, blueberry picking, glacier walks, cross-country skiing and snowmobiling. Gourmet meals (advance reservation required). Sauna and the spectacular view top off a day in the mountains. Rooms and cabins include private baths and use of the large viewing lounge and Alaskan library. Phone (907) 746-2930; fax (907) 746-2931; Web site: www.majesticvalleylodge.com. See display ad this section. [ADVERTISEMENT]

A 114.8 G 74.2 T 213.2 *Truck lane ends eastbound*.

For Anchorage-bound travelers a vista of incomparable beauty as the road descends in a long straightaway toward Glacier Point, also known as the **Lion Head**, an oddly formed rocky dome.

A 114.5 G 74.5 T 213.5 Glacial Fan Creek.

A 113.6 G 75.4 T 214.4 *Truck lane begins eastbound*.

A 113.5 G 75.5 T 214.5 Sheep Mountain Lodge on north side of highway; restaurant, lodging, pay phone. Wonderful views to north of **Sheep Mountain** (elev. 6,300 feet). Sheep are often seen high up these slopes. The area surrounding Sheep Mountain is closed to the taking of mountain sheep.

View of Lion Head westbound on the Glenn Highway.
(© Kris Graef, staff)

Sheep Mountain Lodge. Our charming log lodge, established in 1946, has been serving travelers for half a century. We're famous for our wholesome homemade food, fresh baked breads, pastries and desserts. Our comfortable guest cabins, all with private bathrooms, boast spectacular mountain views. We also have RV hookups, full bar, liquor store and Alaskan gifts. You can watch Dall Sheep through our telescope and relax in the hot tub or sauna after a day of traveling or hiking. Toll free (877) 645-5121. Phone (907) 745-5121; fax (907) 745-5120. E-mail: sheepmtl@alaska.net. Internet: www.sheepmountain.com. See display ad this section. [ADVERTISEMENT] ▲

As the highway descends westbound into the valley of the Matanuska River, there is a view of the great glacier which is the main headwater source and gives the water its milky color.

A 113 G 76 T 215 Turnoff for Sheep Mountain airstrip to north. **Private Aircraft:**

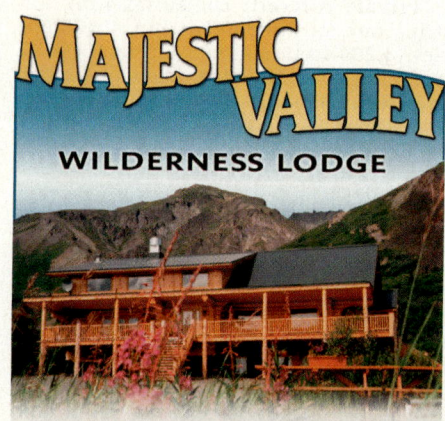

Sheep Mountain airstrip; elev. 2,750 feet; length 2,300 feet; gravel/dirt; unattended.

A 112.8 G 76.2 T 215.2 Large paved turnout to south with picnic table; good camera viewpoint for Sheep Mountain to north and Chugach Mountains to south. Interpretive signs on Sheep Mountain gypsum and Dall sheep (excerpt):

"Current theories indicate Dall sheep use licks each spring to replenish depleted supplies of calcium and magnesium. In this area, the Dall sheep may be getting calcium by eating gypsum (a form of calcium sulfate).

"Gypsum is a clear to white mineral, but here it is stained with small amounts of iron oxide. The same hydrothermal system that created the gypsum also oxidized (rusted) the iron underground, by exposing it to hot water and sulfuric acid."

A 112.6 G 76.4 T 215.4 *Truck lane ends eastbound.*

A 112.2 G 76.8 T 215.8 Gypsum Creek (sign).

A 111.6 G 77.4 T 216.4 *Truck lane begins eastbound.*

A 111.2 G 77.8 T 216.8 Bug Lake (signed). Bug Lake is on the north side of the highway, not visible from the road.

A 111.1 G 77.9 T 216.9 Informal gravel turnout to north, just west of Bug Lake sign.

A 111 G 78 T 217 *Truck lane ends eastbound.*

A 110.9 G 78.1 T 217.1 Distance marker eastbound shows Glennallen 77 miles, Valdez 194 miles, Tok 218 miles.

A 110.5 G 78.5 T 217.5 *Truck lane begins eastbound.*

A 109.7 G 79.3 T 218.3 Grand View Cafe and Campground to south. Good views westbound of Matanuska Glacier. ▲

Grand View Cafe & RV Campground. We invite you to relax in our handcrafted log lodge, featuring meals, desserts and espresso. Enjoy spectacular mountain scenery while viewing Dall sheep or an occasional black bear or moose in their natural habitat. The Grand View's virtually mosquito-free environment is just minutes to the Matanuska Glacier. RV sites with easy on/off pull-throughs can accommodate your big rig. We offer sewer; 30/50 amp electric; delicious well water; shower and laundry facilities. Caravans welcome. Excellent halfway stop while traveling to or from the Kenai Peninsula or Valdez. The Dietrich Family invites you to stop by and experience their friendly atmosphere! (907) 746-4480. See display ad this section. [ADVERTISEMENT] ⚒▲

A 109.5 G 79.5 T 218.5 Access to bed and breakfast.

Tundra Rose Bed & Breakfast. "Alaska Hideaway with a Glacier View," writes the *San Francisco Examiner*. Quiet, relaxed setting. Private log cottage or 2-bedroom suite offers kitchenettes, private baths and spectacular views of Matanuska Glacier and surrounding mountains. View Dall sheep from our yard. Continental breakfast. (907) 745-5865. www.tundrarosebnb.com. See display ad this section. [ADVERTISEMENT]

A 109.4 G 79.6 T 218.6 *NOTE: Watch for road construction westbound to* **Milepost A 100** *in summer 2003.*

Begin improved highway eastbound.

A 108 G 81 T 220 Shoulder parking to south with good view of Matanuska Glacier. End slide area eastbound.

A 107.8 G 81.2 T 220.2 Slide area. Exceptional views westbound of Glacier Point (Lion Head) and Matanuska Glacier.

A 107.7 G 81.3 T 220.3 Watch for Dall sheep in avalanche chute on north side of highway.

Snow-covered Chugach Range in late spring from viewpoint at Milepost A 112.8.
(© Kris Graef, staff)

A 107.5 G 81.5 T 220.5 Wide gravel shoulder to south along highway with views of Matanuska Glacier to southwest.

A 107 G 82 T 221 Sheep Mountain Closed Area (ADF&G sign): "Closed to the taking of Dall sheep and mountain goats." Turnout.

Road climbs eastbound.

A 106.8 G 82.2 T 221.2 *Highway makes a steep, winding descent down to Caribou Creek Bridge (bridge replacement scheduled for summer 2003).* NOTE: Public access to creek is from **Milepost A 106** via Caribou Creek Recreational Gold Mining Area.

Fortress Ridge (elev. 5,000 feet) above the highway to the north. Sheep Mountain reserve boundary.

A 106 G 83 T 222 Large gravel parking area for **Caribou Creek Recreational Gold Mining Area** (Dept. of Natural Resources); outhouse. Steep trail leads from parking area down to creek (pedestrians only, no ATVs). Recreational gold panning, mineral prospecting or mining using light portable field equipment (e.g. hand-operated pick, backpack power drill, etc.) allowed in designated recreational mining area on state lands without mining claims below the ordinary high water mark of Caribou Creek, its tributaries and the Matanuska River. Suction dredging requires a permit from the ADF&G. Contact Dept. of Natural Resources Public Information Center in Anchorage for more information; phone (907) 269-8400.

Grand View Cafe & RV Campground

Meals, Desserts and Espresso
Spectacular Mountain Scenery • Dall Sheep Viewing
Pull Thru Sites with Full Hookups • Laundry & Showers

Phone 907-746-4480 • Fax 907-745-5854 • www.grandviewrv.com

Open Memorial Day thru mid September
SEE LOG AD 109.7 GLENN HWY

Tundra Rose Bed & Breakfast
Matanuska Glacier View & Dall Sheep Viewing
Log Cottage or Two Bedroom Suite w/Kitchenettes
& Private Baths

Milepost 109.5 Glenn Hwy   907-745-5865
www.tundrarosebnb.com

GLENN HIGHWAY

Matanuska Glacier view from the state recreation site at Milepost A 101.
(© Kris Graef, staff)

A 105.5 G 83.5 T 222.5 Small turnout to south. Great views of Matanuska Glacier from the highway westbound.

From here west to Palmer is a very scenic stretch of the Glenn Highway, but also one of the slowest, thanks to winding road and few truck lanes. *Narrow, winding road westbound; slow for 30- to 40-mph curves. End slide area westbound.*

Begin slide area eastbound as highway makes winding descent to Caribou Creek Bridge.

A 104 G 85 T 224 Access to Glacier View School, which overlooks Matanuska Glacier.

A 102.8 G 86.2 T 225.2 Turnout to south with view through trees of Matanuska Glacier.

A 102.2 G 86.8 T 225.8 Long Rifle Lodge to south; food, gas and lodging.

Long Rifle Lodge. Welcome to Alaska's most fabulous dining view of the Matanuska Glacier. We offer a complete breakfast, lunch and dinner menu, specializing in home-cooked meals. Twenty-five wildlife mounts make our lodge a "must see" for all ages. Numerous hiking, cross-country skiing and snowmobile trails surround the area. In addition, we have motel rooms, gasoline, 24-hour wrecker service, gift shop and a full-service lounge. Phone (907) 745-5151. www.longriflelodge.com. Email: lrl@matnet.com. See display ad this section. [ADVERTISEMENT]

A 102 G 87 T 226 Access to foot of Matanuska Glacier via Glacier Park to south (admission charged).

Wickersham Trading Post. See display ad this section.

MICA Guides. See display ad this section.

Glacier Access at Glacier Park. Join us for a fun-filled day exploring the Matanuska Glacier. "The largest glacier accessible by car in Alaska." 15-20-minute hike from parking area to the white ice. A real Alaskan adventure. Group and per person rates. Camping with glacier access. Off-season reservations required. Gift shop, film, snacks. Access at Mile 102 Glenn Highway. HC03 Box 8449, Palmer, AK 99645; 1-888-253-4480. See display ad this section. [ADVERTISEMENT] ▲

A 101.7 G 87.3 T 226.3 Scenic viewpoint to south with good view of **Matanuska Glacier**, which heads in the Chugach Mountains and trends northwest 27 miles. Some 18,000 years ago the glacier reached all the way to the Palmer area. The glacier's average width is 2 miles; at its terminus it is 4 miles wide. The glacier has remained fairly stable the past 400 years. At the glacier terminus meltwater drains into a stream which flows into the Matanuska River.

A 101 G 88 T 227 Matanuska Glacier State Recreation Site to south; camping and rest area with scenic viewpoint. There are 12 campsites on a gravel loop drive; 15-day limit, $10 nightly fee or resident pass, wheelchair accessible, water pump, toilets. Paved parking area and scenic viewpoint has spotting scopes, interpretive shelter, dumpster, toilets. Excellent views of the glacier from scenic overlook. *NOTE: The campground and the rest area toilets were closed in summer 2002. For current status, phone (907) 269-8400 or go to www.dnr.state.ak.us/parks/.*

Stop and stretch your legs on the Edge Nature Trail, a fairly easy trail (20-minute walk) through boreal forest to glacier viewing platforms with interpretive signs. Trail has moderate inclines and uneven walking surface due to tree roots. ♿▲

Distance marker westbound shows Chickaloon 23 miles, Sutton 42 miles, Palmer 53 miles, Anchorage 94 miles.

A 100 G 89 T 228 *Improved highway widens westbound. Highway narrows eastbound. Watch for road construction eastbound to* **Milepost A 109** *in summer 2003.*

A 99.8 G 89.2 T 228.2 Pinochle Lane.

A 99.7 G 89.3 T 228.3 Scenic viewpoint to north with view of Matanuska Glacier.

LONG RIFLE LODGE
OVERLOOKING MATANUSKA GLACIER
Restaurant - Rooms - Gift Shop - Gas
MILE 102.2 GLENN HWY OPEN YEAR ROUND
907.745.5151   www.longriflelodge.com

Wickersham Trading Post
Mile 102 Glenn Hwy.
Open 10 a.m. - 5 p.m. June-August

Family-owned unique Alaska gift shop, with Alaskan made crafts, products and gold jewelry. Enjoy snack items while viewing the beautiful Matanuska Glacier

Phone 907-745-5159
HC03 Box 8443-D, Palmer, AK 99645

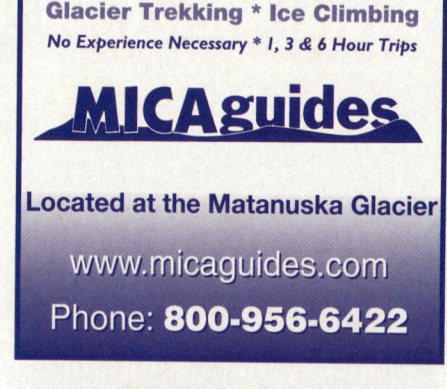

Glacier Trekking * Ice Climbing
No Experience Necessary * 1, 3 & 6 Hour Trips
MICAguides
Located at the Matanuska Glacier
www.micaguides.com
Phone: 800-956-6422

A Real Alaskan Adventure
GLACIER ACCESS at GLACIER PARK
888.253.4480 • MP 102 GLENN HWY

HYSTERICAL
HICKS CREEK ROADHOUSE

HORSEBACK TRAIL RIDING
Homestyle Cooking & Baking ● Ice Cream
RV Hook-ups ● Creekside Camping
Cabins ● Pay Phone ● Tire Service
Laundry & Shower House

Hosts: Arnie, Carol & Dustin Hrncir
hickscreek@hotmail.com

(907) 745-8213
Fax: (907) 745-8214
HC 3 Box 8410, Palmer, AK 99645
MILE 96.6 GLENN HIGHWAY

A 99 G 90 T 229 *Truck lane begins westbound.*
A 98.9 G 90.1 T 229.1 *Truck lane ends eastbound.*
CAUTION: Watch for moose.
A 98.6 G 90.4 T 229.4 Scenic viewpoint to south on wide paved shoulder; view of Matanuska Glacier.
A 98.4 G 90.6 T 229.6 *Truck lane ends westbound.*
A 97.5 G 91.5 T 230.5 Pinochle Hill Road. Distance marker eastbound shows Glennallen 90 miles, Valdez 207 miles, Tok 226 miles.
A 97.1 G 91.9 T 230.9 *Truck lane begins eastbound. Begin improved highway eastbound.*
A 96.6 G 92.4 T 231.4 Historical Hicks Creek Roadhouse; food, espresso, lodging, camping and trail rides.
Hicks Creek Roadhouse. See display ad this section. ▲

Hicks Creek was named by Captain Glenn in 1898 for H.H. Hicks, the guide of his expedition. A highway construction camp was set up here in the early 1940s, as the rough, narrow Glenn Highway was pushed through to connect with the Tok Cutoff, connecting it to the Alaska Highway in 1945.
A 96.5 G 92.5 T 231.5 Bridge over Hicks Creek. Anthracite Ridge to the north.
Winding road westbound with 7 percent grades; slow for 35 mph curves.
A 95 G 94 T 233 Beautiful views westbound to south of Matanuska River and peaks and glaciers in the Chugach Range. The **Chugach Mountains** arc 250 miles from Bering Glacier on the Gulf of Alaska to the east to Turnagain Arm south of Anchorage. They are bounded on the north by the Matanuska, Copper and Chitina Rivers, and on the south by the gulf and Prince William Sound.
Hill and winding descent eastbound; trucks use low gear.
A 94.6 G 94.4 T 233.4 Victory Road. Spring Creek Country Store.
A 93.2 G 95.8 T 234.8 Cascade state highway (DOT) maintenance station to north.
A 91.4 G 97.6 T 236.6 Highway descends long hill eastbound.
A 90.8 G 98.2 T 237.2 Purinton Creek Trailhead (sign); large gravel turnout to north.
A 89 G 100 T 239 Puritan (sign) Creek bridge; small turnout to north at west end of bridge. The stream (actually Purinton Creek) heads on Anthracite Ridge and flows into the Matanuska River.
CAUTION: Watch for moose.

A 87.4 G 101.6 T 240.6 Weiner Lake (stocked) to south; public access. Fishing for rainbow and grayling. ◆
A 87.1 G 101.9 T 240.9 End slide area eastbound. Begin slide area westbound.
CAUTION: Winding road; gravel shoulder to south with steep dropoffs and no guardrails.
A 85.5 G 103.5 T 242.5 Begin slide area eastbound.

Long Lake at Milepost A 85.4 is a popular fishing spot.
(© Carol P. Murdock)

A 85.4 G 103.6 T 242.6 **Long Lake State Recreation Site**; 9 campsites, 15-day limit, no camping fee, no water, no garbage; tables, firepits and toilets. Long Lake is a favorite fishing spot for Anchorage residents. Stocked with rainbow and Arctic char. Fair for grayling to 18 inches, spring through fall; fish deeper as the water warms in summer. Good ice fishing in winter for burbot, average 12 inches. ◆▲
A 84.6 G 104.4 T 243.4 *Highway descends hill next 0.8 mile eastbound.*
A 84.4 G 104.6 T 243.6 End slide area westbound. Begin slide area eastbound.
A 84.1 G 104.9 T 243.9 Large gravel turnout to southeast. Great views of Matanuska River and Chugach Mountains to south as highway descends eastbound.
A 83.2 G 105.8 T 244.8 Narrow gravel road (unsigned) leads north to Ravine and Lower Bonnie lakes. Drive in 0.8 mile on side road to reach **Ravine Lake**; fishing from shore for rainbow. Lower Bonnie Lake is a 2-mile drive from the highway; ADF&G public access. NOTE: *This steep and winding side road is signed as unsafe and closed to motorhomes, large vehicles or trailers. All travel is at owner's risk. During rainy season this side road is not recommended for any vehicle.* ◆
A 82 G 107 T 246 View westbound of distinctive pyramid shape of **King Mountain** (elev. 5,809 feet) to the southeast.

A 80.8 G 108.2 T 247.2 Eastern boundary of Matanuska Valley Moose Range. Gravel turnout to south.
CAUTION: Watch for moose.
A 80.5 G 108.5 T 247.5 Distance marker eastbound shows Glennallen 107 miles, Tok 224 miles, Valdez 243 miles.
A 78.3 G 110.7 T 249.7 Gravel pull-out to south with view of King Mountain and Matanuska River.
A 77.9 G 111.1 T 250.1 *Highway climbs steeply eastbound.*
A 77.7 G 111.3 T 250.3 Chickaloon River bridge. Gravel turnout to south at east end of bridge. Boundary between Game Management Units 13 and 14.
At west end of bridge is turnoff to north for **Chickaloon River Road** (gravel; state road maintenance ends 1.2 miles from highway). No trespassing and private property signs are posted along this road.
A 77.5 G 111.5 T 250.5 Gravel turnout to south. Highway closely parallels the **Matanuska River** westbound to Palmer. Nova River Runners in Chickaloon offers scenic floats and whitewater trips on the river. The Matanuska River is formed by its East and South forks and flows southwest 75 miles to the Knik Arm of Cook Inlet.
A 76.5 G 112.5 T 251.5 Wide gravel turnouts to south along Matanuska River.
A 76.2 G 112.8 T 251.8 **CHICKALOON** (pop. 213); post office, lodge, cafe, cabins, camping, general store and river rafting office. Chickaloon was established around 1916 as the terminus of an Alaska Railroad spur. ▲

Chickaloon General Store. Historic Chickaloon, "Where the River meets the Road" coal mining community. Breathtaking views of King Mountain and Castle Mountain. Fishing, rafting and wildlife viewing. Snow machine trails. Local Alaskan gifts. Good jumping off place for fishing, hunting and flightseeing. P.O. Box 1229, Chickaloon, AK 99674. (907) 746-1801. [ADVERTISEMENT]

Nova River Runners. See display ad this section.

King Mountain Lodge, established 1947, oldest continuously operated lodge on the Glenn Highway, with its own resident ghost. Authentic Alaskan atmosphere in the plank-floor bar ("Chickaloon Performing Arts Center") dates from coal mining days. Stay in a real miner's cabin or camp free along the Matanuska River. All cooking from scratch. Famous sausage gravy, musk ox or buffalo burgers. Home of the King Mountain Burger,

Rafting & Glacier Hikes
Scenic floats - Matanuska & Glacier Run - 4 hrs.
Class IV Whitewater - Lion Head - 4 hrs.
Glacier Hikes - Matanuska Glacier - 4 & 6 hrs.
800-746-5753
Mile 76 & 96 Glenn Hwy.
nova Since 1975
novalaska.com

KING MOUNTAIN LODGE
Authentic Alaskan Atmosphere
Motel • Cabins • Bar • Package Store
Burgers • Pizza
Cafe with Home Cooking
Camping & RV Parking
on the Matanuska River
Est. 1947   Your Host: Judy Nix and Darryl Dean
(907) 745-4280   MILE 76.2 Glenn Highway

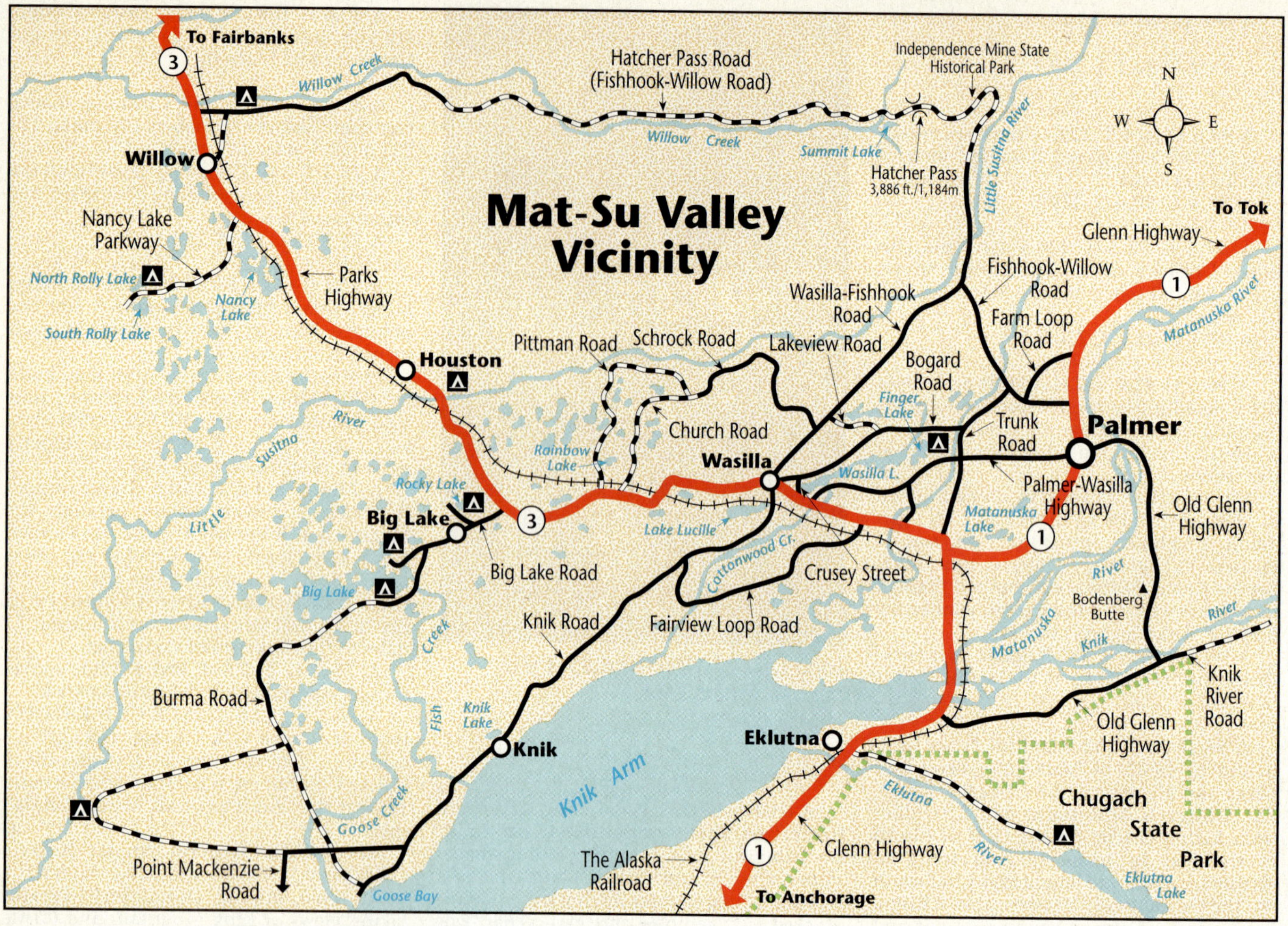

GLENN HIGHWAY

Mat-Su Valley Vicinity

the most bodacious burger of all. See display ad this section. [ADVERTISEMENT] ▲

A 76.1 G 112.9 T 251.9 King Mountain State Recreation Site. Pleasant campground on the banks of the Matanuska River *(Danger: Swift current)*; 22 campsites, picnic shelter, campground host, fireplaces, picnic tables, water, toilets. Camping fee $10/night or resident pass; 15-day limit. NOTE: This campground was closed in summer 2002. For current status, phone (907) 269-8400 or go to www.dnr.state.ak.us/parks/.

View of King Mountain to the southeast.

A 75.8 G 113.2 T 252.2 Distance marker westbound shows Palmer 29 miles, Anchorage 70 miles.

End slide area eastbound.

A 73.7 G 115.3 T 254.3 *"Hill"; winding descent eastbound.*

A 72.9 G 116.1 A 255.1 Fish Lake Road leads north 3 miles through rural residential area; views of Castle Mountain. Public fishing access to Thirtymile Lake via Gronvold Drive (0.1 mile north from highway), then left on Ida and Oline. No gas-powered boats allowed; steep walk down to lake.

A 72.8 G 116.2 T 255.2 Ida Lake.

A 70.6 G 118.4 T 257.4 Access to Matanuska River to south.

A 68 G 121 T 260 Begin slide area eastbound. Watch for gravel turnouts to south eastbound as highway winds along bank of the Matanuska River.

Pinnacle Mountain (elev. 4,541 feet) rises directly southeast of the highway—easy to identify by its unusual top. Cottonwoods and aspen along the highway. Talkeetna Mountains to the north.

A 66.6 G 122.4 T 261.4 Rough turnout slopes down to Matanuska River to south.

A 66.4 G 122.6 T 261.6 King River bridge. Gravel turnout to north and access to river at east end of bridge. Fishing for trout, early summer best, use eggs.

A 66.3 G 122.7 T 261.7 Turnoff to north just west of **King River** bridge for paved access road to river (no turnaround) and access to **King River Trail** (multi-use public access; ATVs 15 mph) with parking in loop road.

Turnoff to south for improved gravel access road to King River at confluence with Matanuska River; informal camping.

A 66 G 123 T 262 *Begin truck lane and improved highway westbound.*

A 65.4 G 123.6 T 262.6 *End truck lane eastbound.*

A 64.3 G 124.7 T 263.7 Distance marker eastbound shows Glennallen 123 miles, Valdez 240 miles, Tok 259 miles.

A 64.1 G 124.9 T 263.9 *End truck lane westbound. Begin truck lane eastbound.*

A 62.8 G 126.2 T 265.2 Large gravel turnout with interpretive sign to south along Matanuska River. Dwarf fireweed and sweet pea in June.

A 62.4 G 126.6 T 265.6 Granite Creek bridge; beautiful stream. Fishing for small Dolly Varden and trout, spring or early summer, use flies or single eggs.

Paved bike path begins westbound on the north side of the highway and extends to Sutton.

A 61.6 G 127.4 T 266.4 Turnoff on Chickaloon Way to north for Sutton post office (Zip 99674) and entrance to **Alpine Historical Park**, an open-air museum featuring the concrete ruins of the Sutton Coal Washery (1920–22). Donations accepted.

A 61 G 128 T 267 SUTTON (pop. 470) at junction with Jonesville Road; fire station with emergency phone to south; general store and cafe to north. Sutton, a small highway community, was established as a railroad siding in about 1918 for the once-flourishing coal industry (Jonesville Mine). The Sutton General Store has photos and antiques from the old mine.

Sutton General Store and Jonesville Cafe. Full line menu, good food, homemade pies, orders to go. We supply all your camping, fishing and cooking needs. Groceries, snacks, ice cream, ice, general merchandise.

Clean restrooms, shower, dryers, phone and propane. Tour buses welcome. Stop by and see us! (907) 746-7461 and (907) 746-7561. [ADVERTISEMENT]

Jonesville Road leads north to Sutton residential area; access to Sutton library. Pavement ends at Mile 1.3. Access to **Slipper Lake** west from Mile 1.5 (physical milepost 2). State maintenance ends and road deteriorates at Mile 1.9. Road (in *very poor condition*) continues to Coyote Lake and Granite Peak; not recommended for pas-

Hatcher Pass Road

Independence Mine State Historical Park on Hatcher Pass Road. (© Kris Graef, staff)

A highly recommended side trip to scenic alpine country and the historic Independence Mine, Hatcher Pass Road is both an old-time Alaska road—narrow, bumpy, dirt and gravel—and a newer paved side road, complete with scenic turnouts for the tourists. The 49-mile-long road loops over Hatcher Pass (elev. 3,886 feet) between the Glenn Highway and the Parks Highway (see Mat-Su Valley Vicinity map this section). It is improved paved road to **Milepost P 13.8** from the Palmer side, and for the first 10 miles from the Willow side. The gravel stretch in-between is undergoing improvement, but be prepared for steep, narrow, switch-backed road and potholed and washboard surface.

Hatcher Pass Road from the Palmer side to the historical park and Hatcher Pass Lodge is maintained in winter. Hatcher Pass is a popular winter sports area for snowmobiling and cross-country skiing. However, the 3-mile stretch of Hatcher Pass Road from **Milepost P 17.5** to **P 20.5** is not maintained in winter and may be closed and gated from October to June, depending on snow.

Distance from junction with the Glenn Highway at Palmer (P) is followed by distance from junction with the Parks Highway at Willow (W).

P 0 W 49.1 Junction of Hatcher Pass Road (signed Palmer-Fishhook Road) with the Glenn Highway at **Milepost A 49.5**.

P 1.4 W 47.7 Junction with Farm Loop Road.

P 2.4 W 46.7 Junction with Trunk Road.

P 3.2 W 45.9 Wasilla Creek.

P 5.5 W 43.6 Alaska Gold Rush B&B Inn. See display ad in Palmer section.

P 6.5 W 42.5 Tesoro gas station with diesel, propane, grocery, ice, liquor store, laundromat and showers; overnight RV parking.

Hatcher Pass Gateway Center. See display ad this section.

P 6.7 W 42.4 Access to bed and breakfast.

Hatcher Pass Bed & Breakfast. Experience our authentic Alaskan log cabins and chalets located at the base of beautiful Hatcher Pass. Comfortable, sparkling clean, private, and equipped with all the modern conveniences. Breakfast is included in the privacy of your own cabin. Come enjoy a peaceful getaway! Phone (907) 745-6788, fax (907) 745-6787. Web site www.hatcherpassbb.com. [ADVERTISEMENT]

P 6.8 W 42.3 Junction with Wasilla–Fishhook Road (Wasilla 11 miles).

P 7.8 W 41.3 Hatcher Pass Public Use Area boundary northbound. Recreational activities allowed within this public use area include (unless posted as prohibited): hiking, picnicking, berry picking, camping, skiing, snow machining, snow boarding, fishing, grazing, hunting and trapping. ATVs and dirt bikes are prohibited on roadway. No discharge of weapons within 1/4 mile of roadway. *No flower picking or plant removal without a permit.*

Recreational mining is allowed within the boundaries of the public use area except on land with valid active mining claims. The Dept. of Natural Resources suggests recreational miners use the parking areas along the Little Susitna River or the Gold Mint Trail, which runs north along the Little Susitna River from the trailhead parking lot. Gold panning is also allowed in the Independence Mine State Historical Park, but consult with park personnel before panning.

P 8.5 W 40.6 Little Susitna River bridge. Large double-ended paved turnout at north end of bridge. Road parallels river northbound. This scenic mountain stream heads at Mint Glacier in the Talkeetna Mountains and flows 110 miles to Cook Inlet. This is a gold-bearing stream.

P 9 W 40.1 Parking on loop turnout.

P 9.2 W 39.9 Parking along Little Susitna River.

P 9.4 W 39.7 Parking area.

P 11.2 W 37.9 Parking area.

P 12.7 W 36.4 Parking area.

P 13 W 36.1 Parking area.

P 13.8 W 35.3 Milepost 14. Motherlode Lodge. Retreat to rustic elegance in a historic mountain bed and breakfast lodge on the banks of the Little Susitna River, surrounded by the unparalleled majestic gold country of Hatcher Pass. Our banquet room seats 165. We have 11 guestrooms, a comfortable lounge and a wood burning sauna. Our chef is a graduate of the Culinary Institute of America. Hiking trails, gold panning, snow sports, wildlife. Easy access year-round. Private use available. [ADVERTISEMENT]

Gold Mint Trailhead parking area; restrooms. Very popular hiking area. Naturalist programs here in summer; phone (907) 745-2827 or (907) 745-3975 for information.

*NOTE: Pavement ends, improved gravel begins westbound as Hatcher Pass Road makes a sharp turn and begins climb to Hatcher Pass via a series of switchbacks. Watch for road construction westbound to **Milepost P 17.5** in summer 2003.*

Gravel ends, pavement begins, eastbound.

P 14.6 W 34.5 Parking area and junction with Archangel Road (very rough road) which leads 4 miles up Archangel Valley and ends at Fern Mine (private property, do not trespass). Access to Reed Lakes Trail from this side road.

P 16.4 W 32.7 Fishhook Trailhead parking area; outhouse. Hiking in summer; snowmobiling in winter, on this trail.

Gateway to Hatcher Pass
HATCHER PASS GATEWAY CENTER
Gas • Diesel • Propane • Grocery • Ice
Liquor Store • ATM • Laundromat • Showers
Restrooms • Air • Phone • Water
FREE Overnight RV Parking with Fill-up (no hookups)
(907) 745-6161 • Mile 6.5 Hatcher Pass Road

Real Value. Real Easy.

Hatcher Pass Road (continued)

P 17 W 32.1 Hatcher Pass Road makes a sharp turn; turn on side road for access to Independence Mine State Historical Park (drive in 1.2 miles). Hatcher Pass Lodge (restaurant, lodging) is located at this junction.

Hatcher Pass Lodge. See display ad this section.

The 271-acre **Independence Mine and State Historical Park** includes several buildings and old mining machinery. Park visitor center (wheelchair accessible) is housed in what was originally the mine manager's home, built in 1939. Alaska Pacific Consolidated Mine Co., one of the largest gold producers in the Willow Creek mining district, operated here from 1938 through 1941. The Gold Cord Mine buildings (private property) are visible on the hill above and to the north of Independence Mine. For season dates and operating hours, phone (907) 745-2827.

Snowmobiling is prohibited in the park in winter. Watch for parasailers in summer.

P 17.5 W 31.6 Gates. Winter road closure for westbound traffic from October to July.

Watch for road construction eastbound to Milepost P 13.8.

P 18.5 W 30.6 Summit Lake State Recreation Site boundary westbound; no camping or ground fires permitted.

P 18.9 W 30.2 Hatcher Pass Summit (elev. 3,886 feet); parking area, hiking trails.

P 19.3 W 29.8 Parking area at **Summit Lake State Recreation Site**; no facilities. Summit Lake is the headwaters of Willow Creek. Visitors can walk around lake or up to bluff for scenic views to west. Good view to northeast of "Nixon's Nose," a launch point for parasailers.

Westbound, the road descends following Willow Creek from here to the Parks Highway. *CAUTION: Steep, narrow, winding road westbound as highway descends.*

View of Summit Lake SRS parking area and "Nixon's Nose" at Milepost P 19.3.
(© Kris Graef, staff)

P 20.5 W 28.6 Summit Lake State Recreation Site boundary eastbound; no camping or ground fires permitted.

Gates. Winter road closure for eastbound traffic from October to July.

P 20.6 W 28.5 Junction with Upper Willow Creek Valley Road (road deadends).

P 23 W 26.1 Lucky Shot Mine Tours, open 10 A.M. to 8 P.M., June 15 to September 15. Mining exhibit, espresso and 20-minute tour of mill available on site. Or arrange in advance for guided underground tours of area mines by phoning (907) 746-0511.

P 23.8 W 25.3 Craigie Creek Road (rough) leads to old mine sites. Remains of historic Lucky Shot (on left) and War Baby (on right) mines visible on hillside to north.

P 26.2 W 22.9 *NOTE: Road narrows and begins more steep grades eastbound; watch for potholes and rough road.*

P 27.2 W 21.9 Small turnout; good view of beaver ponds and terraced beaver dams. Watch for more beaver dams and lodges along here.

P 27.8 W 21.3 Distance marker eastbound shows Independence Mine 12 miles.

P 28.2 W 20.9 Pullout above creek.

P 30.3 W 18.8 Leaving Hatcher Pass public-use area westbound.

P 30.5 W 18.6 Pullout by river.

P 31.9 W 17.2 Dave Churchill Memorial Trail.

P 32.4 W 16.7 No winter maintenance beyond this point (eastbound sign).

P 34.2 W 14.9 Little Willow Creek bridge; large parking area.

P 34.5 W 14.6 Turnout to north with view of Willow Creek.

P 35.7 W 13.4 Twelvemile Lake.

P 36.4 W 12.6 North Star Bible Camp.

P 38.9 P 10.2 *Gravel ends, pavement begins, westbound.*

Pavement ends, narrow gravel road begins eastbound. Watch for potholes.

P 39.2 W 9.9 Public Safety Building to north; *Emergency Phone 911*.

P 41.7 W 7.4 Coyote Gardens (private). The gardens at this private home are open one weekend a year in July as a fund-raiser for the Willow Garden Club and the Alaska Botanical Garden in Anchorage. Phone (907) 770-3692 for more information.

P 47.7 W 1.4 Deception Creek public fishing access.

P 47.8 W 1.3 Deception Creek bridge; turnout at east end.

P 47.9 W 1.2 Junction with Willow Station Road (gravel); leads south to Willow to rejoin the Parks Highway at **Milepost A 69.6**.

P 48.5 W 0.6 Road crosses railroad tracks. Turnoff to south for North Country RV Park.

J 49.1 P 0 Junction of Fishhook-Willow Road (Hatcher Pass Road) with the Parks Highway at **Milepost A 71.2**. (Turn to the PARKS HIGHWAY section.)

Return to
Milepost A 49.5 Glenn Highway
or Milepost A 71.2 Parks Highway

Two-hour drive north of Anchorage, four hours to Denali over scenic Hatcher Pass. Modern cabins, gorgeous views and gourmet dining.

☎ 907 745-5897
fax 907 745-1200
P.O. Box 763
Palmer, AK 99645

info@hatcherpasslodge.com
Visit our website at: www.hatcherpasslodge.com

Lucky Shot Gold Mine

Located Mile 23 Hatcher Pass Road

**Bed & Breakfast • Gold Mill Tours
Underground Gold Mine Tours
Espresso • Snacks • Drinks
Restrooms**

For Reservations and Information:
P.O. Box 2832 Palmer, AK 99645
(907) 746-0511
www.luckyshotgoldmine.com
e-mail: luckyshotgoldmine@gci.net

Drive with headlights on at all times.

GLENN HIGHWAY

senger vehicles
A 60.8 G 128.2 T 267.2 Eska Creek bridge.
A 60.7 G 128.3 T 267.3 Distance marker westbound shows Palmer 13 miles, Anchorage 54 miles.
A 60.5 G 128.5 T 267.5 *Begin 45 mph speed zone eastbound.*
Begin truck lane westbound.
A 60.4 G 128.6 T 267.6 Long double-ended turnout to south.
A 60.1 G 128.9 T 267.9 Long double-ended turnout to south.
A 59.6 G 129.4 T 268.4 Gas station to south.
A 58.6 G 130.4 T 269.4 Scenic viewpoint to south with view of Matanuska River.
A 58.2 G 130.8 T 269.8 *Truck lane ends eastbound.*
A 58 G 131 T 270 58–Mile Road leads north 1 mile to Palmer Correctional Center. Also access to **Seventeenmile Lake**. Drive 0.5 mile north and turn east; continue 2.4 miles through rural residential area, keeping to right at forks, to reach lake. Seventeenmile Lake day-use area provides parking (no camping) for boaters and public-access to lake. Private property in area. Fishing for small grayling, early spring, use flies or spinners; trout, early spring, use eggs.
A 57.8 G 131.2 T 270.2 *Truck lane ends westbound.*
A 56.8 G 132.2 T 271.2 Western boundary of Matanuska Valley Moose Range.
A 55.8 G 133.2 T 272.2 *Truck lane begins eastbound. Begin improved highway eastbound to* **Milepost A 66.**
A 54.6 G 134.4 T 273.4 Bridge over **Moose Creek**. Fishing for trout and Dolly Varden, summer, use eggs.
A 54.5 G 134.5 T 273.5 Turnout to north and 0.3-mile gravel loop through former campground (no facilities).
A 54 G 135 T 274 *Truck lane begins westbound.*
A 53.4 G 135.6 T 274.6 *Truck lane ends westbound.*
A 53 G 136 T 275 **Buffalo Mine Road** to north. Access to Wishbone Lake 4-wheel-drive trail.
A 52 G 137 T 276 Wolf Country U.S.A.

A 50.9 G 138.1 T 277.1 Harold Stephan Fire Station.
A 50.7 G 138.3 T 277.3 Farm Loop Road, a 3-mile loop road connecting with Fishhook–Willow Road.
A 50.3 G 138.7 T 277.7 Distance marker eastbound shows Glennallen 137 miles, Valdez 254 miles, Tok 273 miles.
A 50.1 G 138.9 T 277.9 Sharp turn north (watch for signs) for the Musk-Ox Farm.
Musk Ox Farm and Gift Shop. The world's only domestic musk-oxen farm. The animals are combed for the precious qiviut, which is then hand-knit by Eskimos in isolated villages, aiding the Arctic economy. During the farm tours in the summer, you can see these shaggy ice age survivors romping in beautiful pastures with Pioneer Peak as a backdrop. Open May to September. Phone (907) 745-4151. P.O. Box 587, Palmer, AK 99645. See display ad this section. [ADVERTISEMENT]
Begin 4-lane highway westbound.
Begin 2-lane highway eastbound.
A 50 G 139 T 278 Double-ended turnout to south is a Matanuska River viewpoint. A short pedestrian walkway leads up to a fenced viewing area CAUTION: *Steep, eroding cliffs.* Good photo op. Gold Rush interpretive sign about Hatcher Pass.
A 49.5 G 139.5 T 278.5 Turnoff for Hatcher Pass Road to Independence Mine State Historical Park (17 miles).

Twin baby musk-oxen at Palmer's Musk Ox Farm. (© Barbara Willard)

© Linda Lockhart

Junction with Hatcher Pass (Fishhook–Willow) Road which follows the Little Susitna River to Hatcher Pass and connects with the Parks Highway at **Milepost A 71.2** north of Willow. See "Hatcher Pass Road" beginning on page 305.

www.themilepost.com   2003 ■ The MILEPOST® ■ 307

Old Glenn Highway

This 18.6-mile paved road (2 lanes, 45 mph curves) is a scenic alternate route between Palmer and Anchorage, exiting the Glenn Highway at **Milepost A 29.6** and rejoining the Glenn Highway at **Milepost A 42.1**. The Old Glenn Highway goes through the heart of the original Matanuska Colony agricultural lands.

Distance from south junction with the Glenn Highway (J) is followed by distance from Palmer (P).

J 0 P 18.6 Exit from Glenn Highway at Milepost A 29.6.

J 4 P 14.6 Eklutna Power Plant (Alaska Power Administration) uses water from Eklutna Lake to provide power to Anchorage and the Mat-Su Valley.

J 6 P 12.6 Goat Creek Bridge.

J 7.4 P 11.2 Small turnout to west with view of Bodenburg Butte across Knik River.

J 8.5 P 10.1 Junction with **Knik River Road.** Road dead-ends 11.2 miles east of here. Knik River Road is a mostly flat road that is bordered by private property (do not trespass). The first 9.8 miles are paved. The only public access to the Knik River is at Mile 1.4. Of interest: **Pioneer Falls** (a waterfall) at Mile 1.2 *(CAUTION: Black bears)*; Pioneer Ridge-Knik River trailhead at Mile 3.8; and a view of Knik Glacier at about Mile 7. The glacier is best viewed from the river. Hunter Creek Outfitters at Mile 8.4 offers airboat trips to the glacier face. Shuttle bus service available.

Hunter Creek Outfitters, Mile 8.4 Knik River Road. Log cabin surrounded by breathtaking scenery. Inside has photos and historic video of the area's largest glacier. Park has RV and tent sites. Hiking trails with glacier views. Airboat tours depart daily to our wilderness camp at the face of this spectacular glacier. Camping equipment and kayak rentals. Reservations phone (907) 745-1577. Web: www.huntercreekoutfitters.com.
[ADVERTISEMENT]

J 8.8 P 9.8 Knik River bridge. Entering Game Management Subunit 14A northbound. Pedestrian bridge adjacent highway bridge.

J 9 P 9.6 Access to river and pedestrian bridge at east end of Knik River bridge.

J 10 P 8.6 Bar.
Pioneer Peak dominates the skyline for southbound travelers.

J 10.5 P 8.1 Turnoff for Alaska Raceway Park (0.8 mile).

J 11.5 P 7.1 Gas station/grocery at **junction** of Bodenburg Loop Road and Plumley Road.
The 5.8-mile Bodenburg Butte Road rejoins the Old Glenn Highway opposite Dack Acres Road (**Milepost J 12.5**). From this junction it is 0.6 mile to **Bodenburg Butte** trailhead and 0.7 mile to reindeer farm (visitors welcome, fee charged) and trail rides. The Bodenburg Butte area has original Matanuska Colony farms.

Reindeer Farm. Bodenburg Loop Road 0.8 mile off Old Glenn Highway (turn at Mile J 11.5 at the flashing light). Hand feed

reindeer. View moose, black-tailed deer and elk. Bring camera. Hours 10 A.M.–6 P.M. daily. Fee charged. Guided horseback trail rides by appointment. (907) 745-4000. Email: reindeer@corecom.net. [ADVERTISEMENT]

J 11.8 P 6.8 BUTTE (pop. 2,561); fire and ambulance service station #21; emergency phone 911. Fire permits May 1 to Sept. 30.

Young hikers take a break atop Bodenburg Butte.
(© Lilly Graef)

J 12 P 6.6 Store, gas and post office. Junction with Marilyn Road.

J 12.6 P 6 Junction with Back Acres Road, north end of Bodenburg Butte Loop Road (see **Milepost J 11.5**).

J 15.6 P 3 Junction with Smith Road. Access to private campground (0.8 mile). Turn east on Smith Road and drive 1.5 miles for Matanuska Peak trailhead.

Mountain View RV Park. See display ad this section. ▲

J 16.1 P 2.5 Clark–Wolverine Road; access to several garden nurseries and to **Lazy Mountain Recreation Area.** For recreation area, drive east 0.8 mile to "T"; turn right on Huntley Road at T and drive 0.9 mile; then take right fork downhill 0.2 mile to trailhead parking for popular 2.5-mile hike to summit of Lazy Mountain (elev. 3,720 feet); steep and strenuous. Outhouse at trailhead.

J 16.6 P 2 Paved loop road down to Matanuska River photo viewpoint.

J 17 P 1.6 George Palmer Memorial Bridge crosses the Matanuska River. Photo viewpoint to east at north end of bridge on old alignment; access to pedestrian bridge.

J 17.4 P 1.2 Turnoff for **Matanuska River Park** (Mat-Su Borough Parks & Recreation) camping and day-use areas; 80 level tent/RV sites with picnic tables on gravel loop road. Day-use area has playground and picnic pavilions. Facilities include some pull-through sites, water, fireplaces, dump station, flush toilets, hot showers, softball fields and hiking trails. Camping, shower and dump station fees charged. Phone (907) 745-9631 for more information. ▲

J 17.6 P 1 Palmer municipal airport.
Begin 35 mph speed zone northbound.

J 18.4 P 0.2 South Valley Way west to Palmer city center.

J 18.5 P 0.1 South Alaska Street west to Palmer city center.

J 18.6 P 0 Junction of Old Glenn Highway (West Arctic Avenue) at Palmer, **Milepost A 42.1** Glenn Highway. Gas station.

Return to Milepost A 42.1 or A 29.6 Glenn Highway

A 49.1 G 139.9 T 278.9 Cedar Hills subdivision to north. Entering Palmer, which extends to **Milepost A 41.** *(Actual driving distance between Milepost 49 and 42 is 1 mile.)* Good view westbound of the farms and homes of one of Alaska's major agricultural areas.

NOTE: Begin 45 mph speed zone westbound.

A 42.1 G 146.9 T 285.9 **Junction** with West Arctic Avenue and Old Glenn Highway. Access to Palmer High School to north at this junction. Turn south for downtown Palmer and for the **Old Glenn Highway**, a scenic alternate route to Anchorage that rejoins the Glenn Highway at **Milepost A 29.6.** Highlights along the old Glenn Highway include the original Matanuska Colony Farms and a reindeer farm.

Turn to "Old Glenn Highway" log on opposite page for log. and read log back to front from this junction

Palmer

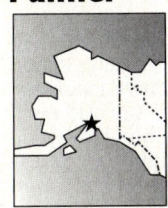

A 42 G 147 T 286 In the Matanuska Valley northeast of Anchorage. **Population:** 4,533. **Emergency Services:** Phone 911. **Alaska State Troopers,** phone (907) 745-2131. **City Police,** phone (907) 745-4811. **Fire Department and Ambulance,** phone (907) 745-3271. **Valley Hospital,** Valley Hospital, 515 E. Dahlia, phone (907) 745-4813.

Visitor Information: Visitor center in log cabin across the railroad tracks on South

PALMER ADVERTISERS

Alaska Gold Rush B&B Inn	Ph. (907) 746-5312
Colony Inn	Ph. (907) 745-3330
Gold Miner's Hotel	Ph. 1-800-7ALASKA
Mail Boxes Etc.	Ph. (907) 746-6245
Mountain View RV Park	Ph. (907) 745-5747
Musk Ox Farm & Gift Shop	Mile 50 Glenn Hwy.
Pioneer Motel & Apt.	Ph. (907) 745-3425
Tara Dells Bed & Breakfast	Ph. (907) 745-0407
Valley Hotel	606 South Alaska St.

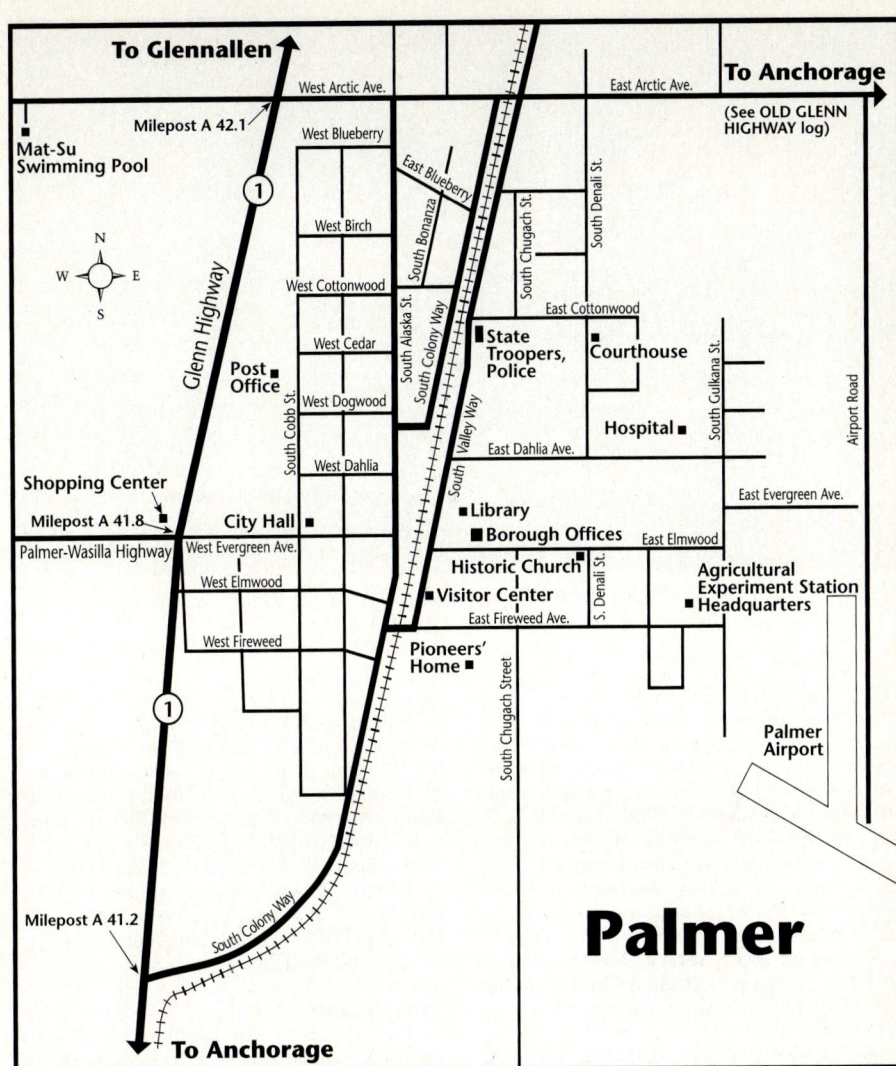

• HISTORIC TEACHER'S DORM •
COLONY INN
CHARMING ROOMS • GREAT VIEWS
INN CAFE • NON-SMOKING • TV
FOR RESERVATIONS CALL:
907-745-3330
325 EAST ELMWOOD • PALMER, AK

Valley Hotel

Historic, Clean & Affordable

* Laundry * Cable TV * Phones * Downtown Palmer *

Cafe Open 24 Hours, 365 Days

We specialize in Homemade Pies, Great Breakfast, Lunch & Dinners.
From Breakfast to Salads, Burgers, Chicken, Halibut, Steaks & Pizza.

Caboose Lounge & Liquor Store

Contact us: www.valleyhotelalaska.com   ph.# (907) 745-3330
Valley Hotel 606 S. Alaska St. Palmer, AK 99645

See Alaska's Famous and Beautiful MATANUSKA VALLEY
28 Units, Cable TV, Apartments – daily or weekly
PIONEER MOTEL & APT.
124 W. Arctic
Palmer, AK 99645
Turn off the Glenn Highway toward Palmer at the Tesoro Station (Arctic Avenue) Across from Arctic Qwik Mart
videosal@alaska.net
(907) 745-3425
Fax (907) 746-0777

Agriculture is a major industry in Palmer and the Mat-Su Valley. (© Barbara Willard)

Valley Way at East Fireweed Avenue. Pick up a brochure and map of downtown Palmer's historic buildings. Open daily 8 A.M. to 7 P.M. May to Sept. 15; weekdays 9 A.M. to 4 P.M. mid-September to May. Pay phone. Small museum in basement; Alaskan-made gifts may be for sale on main floor. Mailing address: Chamber of Commerce, P.O. Box 45, Palmer, AK 99645. Matanuska Valley Agricultural Showcase adjacent visitor center features flower and vegetable gardens.

Excellent local library, located at 655 S. Valley Way; open Monday through Saturday. Paperback and magazine exchange. Wheelchair accessible.

Elevation: 240 feet. **Climate:** Temperatures range from 4° to 21°F in January and December, with a mean monthly snowfall of 8 to 10 inches. Record low was -40°F in January 1975. Temperatures range from 44° to 68°F in June and July, with a mean monthly precipitation of 2 inches. Record high was 89°F in June 1969. Mean annual rainfall is 15.5 inches, with 50.7 inches of snow. **Radio:** Anchorage stations; KMBQ (Wasilla). **Television:** Anchorage channels and cable. **Newspaper:** *The Frontiersman* (twice weekly). **Private Aircraft:** Palmer Municipal Airport, 1 nm SE; elev. 232 feet; length 6,000 feet and 3,616 feet; asphalt; fuel 100LL, Jet. FSS and full services.

Description

This appealing community is both a bit of pioneer Alaska as well as a modern-day commercial center for the Matanuska and Susitna valleys (collectively referred to as the Mat–Su valleys). Take time to explore the small downtown area off the highway.

Palmer was established about 1916 as a railway station on the Matanuska branch of the Alaska Railroad.

In 1935, Palmer became the site of one of the most unusual experiments in American history: the Matanuska Valley Colony. The Federal Emergency Relief Administration, one of the many New Deal relief agencies created during Franklin Roosevelt's first year in office, planned an agricultural colony in Alaska to utilize the great agricultural potential in the Matanuska–Susitna valleys, and to get some American farm families—struck by first the dust bowl, then the Great Depression—off the dole. Social workers picked 203 families, mostly from the northern counties of Michigan, Wisconsin and Minnesota, to join the colony, because it was thought that the many hardy farmers of Scandinavian descent in those 3 states would have a natural advantage over other ethnic groups. The colonists arrived in Palmer in the early summer of 1935, and though the failure rate was high, many of their descendants still live in the Matanuska Valley. Palmer gradually became the unofficial capital of the Matanuska Valley, acting as headquarters for a farmers' cooperative marketing organization and as the business and social center for the state's most productive farming region.

Palmer is Alaska's only community that developed primarily from an agricultural economy. (Real estate now takes a close second to agriculture.) The growing season averages 80 to 110 days a year, with long hours of sunshine. Fresh vegetables from Valley farms are popular with Anchorage residents, many of whom drive out to pick up "Valley peas" and other favorites in season. Local produce is available at roadside stands and is marketed in local stores.

The University of Alaska–Fairbanks has an Agricultural and Forestry Experiment Station Office and a district Cooperative Extension Service Office here. The university also operates its Matanuska Research Farm, located on Trunk Road off the Parks Highway, about a 7-mile drive from Palmer. The university farm conducts research in agronomy, horticulture, soil science and animal science.

The community has a hospital, the Mat–Su College (University of Alaska), a library, banks, the Mat–Su Borough offices, borough school district, and several other state and federal agency offices. Palmer has churches representing most denominations. The United Protestant Church in Palmer, the

Church of a Thousand Logs, dates from Matanuska Colony days and is one of the oldest churches in Alaska still holding services. It is included in the National Register of Historic Places.

Lodging & Services

Palmer has all visitor facilities including 3 hotels, 2 motels, bed and breakfasts, gas stations, grocery stores, laundromat, auto repair and parts, and shopping. The Matanuska Valley region has several lake resorts offering boat rentals, golf, fly-in fishing, hunting and horseback riding.

Alaska Gold Rush B&B Inn, HC 05, Box 6914P, Palmer, AK 99645; phone

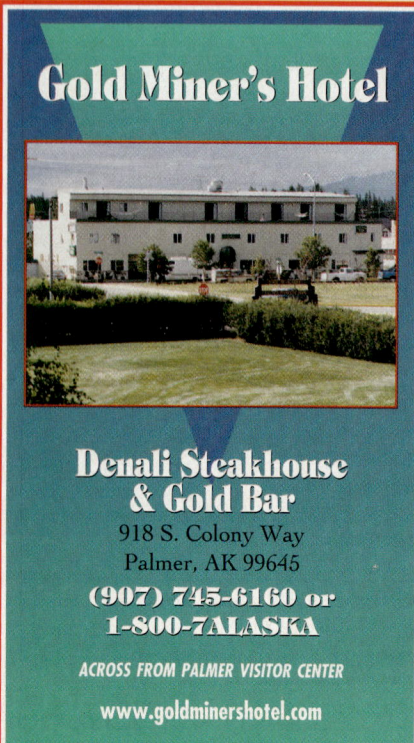

(877) 745-5312. Voted "Best B&B in Alaska" 2003. www.alaskagoldrush.com. Mile 5.5 Hatcher Pass Road. [ADVERTISEMENT]

Mail Boxes Etc. Let the experts pack and ship your "Alaska catch" frozen fish and other great souvenirs. And while you're here, check your email, purchase stamps, mail postcards and look around at the many other services we provide. At Mail Boxes Etc. "we'll take it from here." See display ad this section. [ADVERTISEMENT]

Camping

There is a private RV park on Smith Road off the Old Glenn Highway. There are also private campgrounds on the Glenn Highway a few miles west of Palmer. The Mat-Su Borough operates **Matanuska River Park**, located 1.1 miles south of town at Mile 17.5 Old Glenn Highway; 80 campsites for tents or RVs, picnic area, water, dump station (fee charged), firewood for sale, flush toilets, hot showers, camping fee. **Finger Lake State Recreation Site** (see "Palmer-Wasilla Highway" log this section), has 69 campsites, 7-day limit, toilets, water, boating and fishing; camping fee $10/night. ▲

Mountain View RV Park offers breathtaking views of the Matanuska mountains. Watch wildlife from your door. Full hookups, hot showers included. New bathrooms and laundromat, dump station. Good Sam Park. Half-day scenic airboat tours on Knik River. Call (907) 745-5747 for reservations. Mail forwarding. Write P.O. Box 2521,

Palmer, AK 99745. From Mile A 42.1 Glenn Highway (Arctic), follow Old Glenn Highway 2.8 miles. Turn east on Smith Road, drive 0.6 mile, turn right (0.3 mile). We're 3.7 miles from the Glenn Highway. www.matnet.com/~mtviewrv/; email: str@matnet.com See display ad this section. [ADVERTISEMENT]

Transportation

Air: No scheduled service, but the local airport has a number of charter operators.

Bus: Mat-Su Community Transit connects Palmer, Wasilla, Eagle River and Anchorage.

Attractions

Go Swimming: The 80-foot swimming pool is open to the public weekdays (closed weekends). Fees are: $4.25 for adults, $3 youth and seniors. Showers available. The pool is located at Palmer High School on West Arctic Avenue; phone (907) 745-5091.

Get Acquainted: Stop at the visitor information center, a log building just off the "main drag" (across the railroad tracks at the intersection of East Fireweed Avenue and South Valley Way). The center includes a museum, artifacts, a gift shop and agricultural showcase garden.

Visit the Musk Ox Farm. Located east of Palmer on the Glenn Highway at **Milepost 50.1**, the Musk Ox Farm is the only place in the world where these exotic animals are raised domestically. Hunted to near extinction in Alaska in 1865, the species was reintroduced in the 1930s. The farm is open May to September; admission is charged.

Visit a Reindeer Farm, located 8.1 miles south of Palmer via the Old Glenn Highway to Bodenburg Loop Road. This commercial reindeer farm is open daily in summer; admission is charged.

Play Golf in the spectacular Matanuska Valley. The Palmer Golf Course has 18 holes (par 72, USGA rated), rental carts and clubs, driving range, pro shop, practice green and snack bar. Phone (907) 745-4653.

Enjoy Water Sports. Fishing, boating, waterskiing and other water sports are popular in summer at Finger Lake west of Palmer. Kepler–Bradley Lakes State Recreation Area on Matanuska Lake has canoe rentals; turn off the Glenn Highway at Milepost A 36.4.

Special events include **Colony Days** (June 13–14, 2003), the **Palmer Pride Picnic** (July 25, 2003) and the **Alaska State Fair** (Aug. 22–Sept. 1, 2003). The 11-day state fair, ending on Labor Day, has agricultural exhibits from farms throughout Alaska. There are also food booths, games, pony rides and midway rides. This is a very popular event, and fairgoers from Anchorage can tie up traffic. But it's worth the drive just to see the huge vegetables. Phone (907) 745-4827.

Palmer–Wasilla Highway

This 10-mile road connects Palmer on the Glenn Highway with Wasilla on the Parks Highway. The Palmer-Wasilla Highway accesses several business parks and residential subdivisions, and acts as a shortcut between the 2 communities for local traffic. A very busy road. Posted speed limit is 45- to 55-mph. There is a bike path along this highway.

Distance from Palmer (P) is followed by distance from Wasilla (W).

P 0 W 10 Junction with Glenn Highway at **Milepost A 41.8** in Palmer; Carrs Mall (24-hour supermarket) and McDonalds.

P 0.4 W 9.6 NOAA Tsunami Warning Center; informative tours of the facility are offered on Fridays at 1, 2 and 3 P.M.; no reservations required. Phone (907) 745-4212 for more information.

P 2 W 8 Loma Prieta Drive. Access to **Crevasse–Moraine Trail.** Drive 0.8 mile west on Loma Prieta Drive to end of pavement, then proceed downhill to trailhead parking area. This loop trail system is used for cross-country skiing in winter and hiking, mountain biking and horseback riding in summer.

P 2.3 W 7.7 Trinity Barn Plaza; coffee.

P 2.8 W 7.2 Stoplight at **junction** with North 49th/State Street. Car wash.

P 3.3 W 6.7 Midtown Community Business Park; pizza.

P 4 W 6 Four Corners junction. Tesoro gas station and grocery at **junction** with North Trunk Road. Turn north for access to Bogard Road and **Finger Lake State Recreation Site**; go north on Trunk Road 1 mile

to Bogard Road; turn west and drive 0.7 mile to park entrance; drive in 0.3 mile on gravel road. A scenic spot with 41 campsites, wheelchair-accessible toilets, picnic tables, water, hiking trails and boat launch, $10 camping fee, 7-day limit. Use the life jackets provided! Finger Lake is on the 7-**Mile Canoe Trail.** Public access to canoe trail also from Wasilla and Cottonwood lakes. ▲

P 4.2 W 5.8 Wasilla Creek.
P 6 W 4 North Hyer Road.
P 6.2 W 3.8 The Frontiersman newspaper.
P 6.7 W 3.3 Fort Green gift shop and fur museum east side of highway.

Fort Green. Charming Alaskan gift shop, museum, large rustic log cabin on the Palmer-Wasilla Highway. Easy access, RV parking, buses. Beautiful view, Chugach Mountains, Knik Glacier. Largest Alaskan basket selection, 500. Wildlife display. Moose, caribou antlers sold. Northern Trappers, Fur Industry Museum; interesting, educational. Displaying art, posters, calendars, bear traps, trapping artifacts from 1700s to present. Truly an Alaskan experience! Phone (907) 376-5873. [ADVERTISEMENT]

P 7 W 3 Brentwood Plaza.
P 7.1 W 2.9 Hatcherview Center; Valley Center.
P 7.5 W 2.5 Landscape Supply.
P 7.6 W 2.4 Schwabenhof's, a popular German restaurant.
P 8.2 W 1.8 Junction with North Seward Meridian Parkway; Tesoro gas station/Subway. Cottonwood Public Safety Building.
P 8.6 W 1.4 Post office.
P 9.1 W 0.9 Diversified Tire. See display ad on page 362..
P 9.2 W 0.8 Kwik Kard gas station to west.
P 9.4 W 0.6 Cottonwood Creek.
P 9.6 W 0.4 Gas station.
P 10 W 0 Junction with Parks Highway at **Milepost A 41** Fred Meyer store and Cottonwood Creek Mall.

Return to Milepost A 41.8 Glenn Highway or Milepost A 41 Parks Highway

Visit Scenic Hatcher Pass. From Milepost A 49.5 near Palmer, Hatcher Pass Road provides access to the beautiful Hatcher Pass Recreation Area and Independence Mine State Historical Park. Well worth the 20-mile drive. (See "Hatcher Pass Road" log this section.)

See the Matanuska Glacier: Drive 60 miles east on the Glenn Highway from Palmer to visit this spectacular 27-mile-long glacier, one of the few you can drive to and explore on foot. Access to the foot of the glacier is through a private campground at **Milepost A 102**; admission charged. If you're not interested in getting close, there are several vantage points along the highway and from trails at Matanuska Glacier Campground, **Milepost A 101**.

The annual Alaska State Fair takes place at the fairgrounds in Palmer.
(© Barbara Willard)

Glenn Highway Log
(continued)

A 41.8 G 147.2 T 286.2 **Junction** with Palmer–Wasilla Highway and West Evergreen Avenue. Gas station, fast food and Carrs Pioneer Square shopping mall (24-hour supermarket) north side of highway. Access to downtown Palmer to south. A bronze sculpture by Jacques and Mary Regat dedicated to the Matanuska Valley pioneers is located at the mall.

Junction with Palmer–Wasilla Highway which leads northwest 10 miles to the Parks Highway at Wasilla. See the "Palmer–Wasilla Highway" log on page 311.

A 41.6 G 147.4 T 286.4 Gas station and fast-food south side of highway.

A 41.2 G 147.8 T 286.8 First access eastbound to Palmer business district via South Colony Way.

A 41.1 G 147.9 T 286.9 Commercial Avenue.

A 40.2 G 148.8 T 287.8 Main entrance to fairgrounds (site of **Alaska State Fair**) and Herman Field (home of the Mat–Su Miners baseball team). Alaska State Fair is held the end of August through the first week in September (heavy traffic during the fair; drive carefully!).

A 39.6 G 149.4 T 288.4 Inner Springer Loop.

A 39.3 G 149.7 T 288.7 **Town & Country RV Park Bed & Breakfast.** See display ad this section. ▲

A 39.2 G 149.8 T 288.8 Outer Springer Loop. Gift shop. Short, steep trail to **Meier Lake**; grayling fishing.

A 37.4 G 151.6 T 290.6 Kepler Drive; access to private campground and lake. ▲

A 37.2 G 151.8 T 290.8 **Echo Lake** public parking and fishing access to south; 4-vehicle parking and short trail to lake (visible from parking area). Fishing for land-locked salmon and rainbow (stocked).

A 37 G 152 T 291 Echo Lake Road.

A 36.4 G 152.6 T 291.6 Entrance to **Kepler–Bradley Lakes State Recreation Area.** Turnoff to north for day-use area on Matanuska Lake; water, toilets, parking, picnic tables, hiking trails and fishing. ADF&G stocks lakes with rainbow trout, grayling and silver salmon. Wheelchair-accessible trail to lake. The lakes are Kepler, Bradley, Matanuska, Canoe, Irene, Long, Claire and Victor.

A 36.3 G 152.7 T 291.7 Fox Run RV Campground sits on Matanuska Lake with a fantastic view of the Chugach Mountains. We offer full hookups, pull-throughs,

---

OPEN YEAR ROUND
Town & Country RV Park
Mile 39.5 Glenn Hwy
1/4 mile south of Alaska State Fairgrounds

- Full Hookups • Large Pull-Thrus
- Laundry Facilities • Showers
- Dump Station
- Excellent Location For Day Excursions
- Golf Course 1.5 Miles Away
- Close to Stocked Lakes
- Super Views • Friendly Staff

Daily, Weekly and Monthly Rates

(907) 746-6642

Coming in 2003
Bed & Breakfast
Cabin Rentals

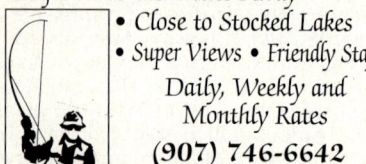

FOX RUN RV CAMPGROUND
On the shores of Matanuska Lake at Mile 36.3 Glenn Hwy

PALMER, ALASKA
Reservations (AK only): 1.877.745.6120

- Full Hookups
- Pull-Thrus
- Wide gravelled sites
- 30 & 50 Amp service
- Laundry
- Clean Restrooms & Showers
- Boat Rentals
- Phone
- Fishing
- Hiking

Email: foxrun@alaska.net
URL: www.foxrun.freeservers.com
Tel: 907-745-6120
PO Box 4174 Palmer, AK 99645

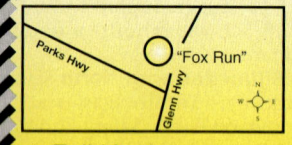
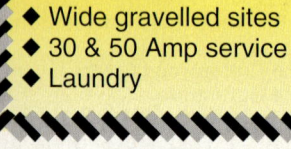

THE HOMESTEAD RV PARK
At the "Crossroads of Alaska"...
1-800-478-3570 In Alaska

5 miles south of Palmer on Glenn Highway • Commuting distance to Anchorage

WATER & ELECTRIC HOOKUPS • TENT SITES
DUMP STATION • SHOWERS • LAUNDRY

P.O. Box 2415, Palmer, AK 99645 • (907) 745-6005
http:\\homesteadrvpark.com • e-mail: homesteadrvpark@att.net

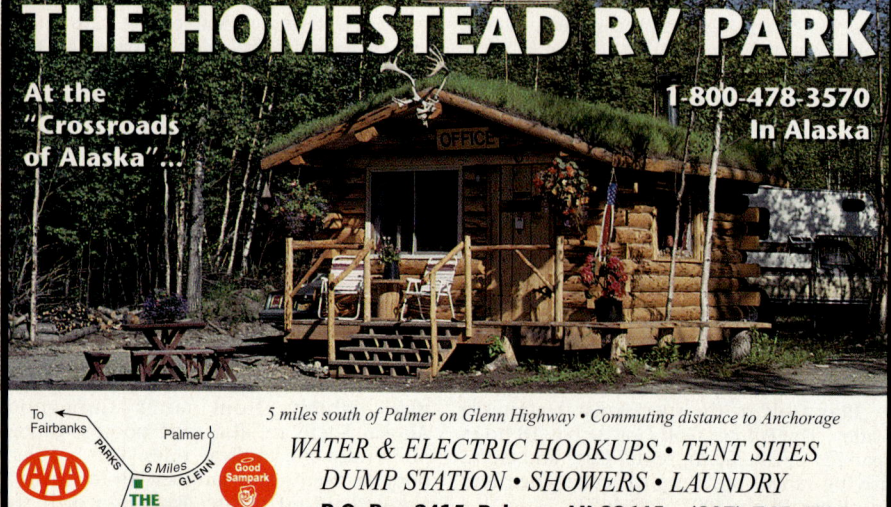

tents sites, clean restrooms and showers, laundry, e-mail, phone. Hiking, fishing, swimming and boating. Open May 1–September 15. E-mail: foxrun@alaska.net. Web site: www. foxrun.freeservers.com. Phone (907) 745-6120; 877-745-6120. See display ad this section. [ADVERTISEMENT]

A 36.2 G 152.8 T 291.8 **The Homestead RV Park.** Beautiful, wooded setting overlooking the scenic Matanuska Valley. Good Sam, AAA, 63 sites, pull-throughs to 70 feet. Very clean restrooms and showers. Electric and water hookups; dump station; also on-site portable dumping and laundry. Picnic tables, pay phone. Enclosed pavilion, square dancing Thursday nights. Walking and jogging trails, trout fishing nearby; modem friendly. Handicap access. Commuting distance to Anchorage. Caravans welcome. Phone (907) 745-6005. Toll free in Alaska (800) 478-3570. See display ad this section. [ADVERTISEMENT]

A 35.3 G 153.7 T 292.7 Junction of the Glenn Highway with the Parks Highway. NOTE: Construction of a new Glenn–Parks Interchange underway in 2003. Watch for lane closures and traffic changes.

Matanuska-Susitna Convention and Visitors Bureau. See display ad this section.

Junction of the Glenn Highway (Alaska Route 1) with the Parks Highway (Alaska Route 3) to Denali Park and Fairbanks. See the PARKS HIGHWAY section on page 357 for log.

A 34.8 G 154.2 T 293.2 Drive-thru espresso service on west side of highway. Follow gravel road south from espresso stop 0.7 mile (paralleling the highway) for **Rabbit Slough Access** to **Palmer Hay Flats State Game Refuge.** Rabbit Slough (Wasilla Creek) is a tributary of the Matanuska River. The refuge is closed to all ORV use from April to mid-August. According to the ADF&G, Palmer Hay Flats is the most heavily utilized waterfowl hunting area in Alaska. The refuge is also accessible from Knik Road and from Fairview Loop Road, both off the Parks Highway. Moose winter in this area, and the cows and calves may be seen early in the morning and in the evening as late as early July.

CAUTION: Watch for moose.

A 31.5 G 157.5 T 296.5 Bridge over the Matanuska River, which is fed by the Matanuska Glacier.

A 30.8 G 158.2 T 297.5 Sgt. James Bondsteel Bridge of Honor crosses Knik River. The **Knik River** comes down from the Knik Glacier to the east and splits into several branches as it approaches Knik Arm. Knik Arm is a 3-mile-wide estuary that extends 40 miles southeast to Cook Inlet.

Game Management Unit 14C boundary. Also boundary of Matanuska–Susitna Borough.

A 30.6 G 158.4 T 297.4 Knik River Access; exits both sides of highway lead west to parking area next to Knik River via short potholed road. NOTE: Knik River Access is subject to seasonal closure Nov. 1–April 30.

A 30.3 G 158.7 T 297.7 Knik River bridge. Entering Game Management Unit 15A northbound.

A 29.6 G 159.4 T 298.4 Exit to the Old Glenn Highway (Palmer Alternate).

Junction with Old Glenn Highway. See "Old Glenn Highway" log on page 308.

A 27.3 G 161.7 T 300.7 The highway

Gravel bars provide access to the Knik River on the Old Glenn Highway.
(© Kris Graef, staff)

crosses a swampy area known locally as Eklutna Flats. These flats are a protected wildflower area (picking flowers is strictly prohibited). Look for wild iris, shooting star, chocolate lily and wild rose in early June.

A 26.3 G 162.7 T 301.7 Eklutna exit. Exit east for Eklutna Lake Road and Eklutna Historical Park (descriptions follow). This exit is also the southbound access to Thunderbird Falls (see **Milepost A 25.2** for description).

Exit west for **EKLUTNA** (pop. 46), a residential community and Athabascan village, and for **Eklutna Historical Park**. The small historical park, just west of the highway, preserves the heritage and traditions of the Athabascan Alaska Natives in the Eklutna Heritage Museum; the historic St. Nicholas Russian Orthodox Church; a hand-built Siberian prayer chapel; and traditional spirit houses or grave houses. Admission fee charged. Open daily mid-May to mid-September.

From the overpass, follow signs east for Eklutna Lake Road and Thunderbird Falls. Eklutna Lake Road leads 10 miles to **Eklutna Lake Recreation Area** in Chugach State

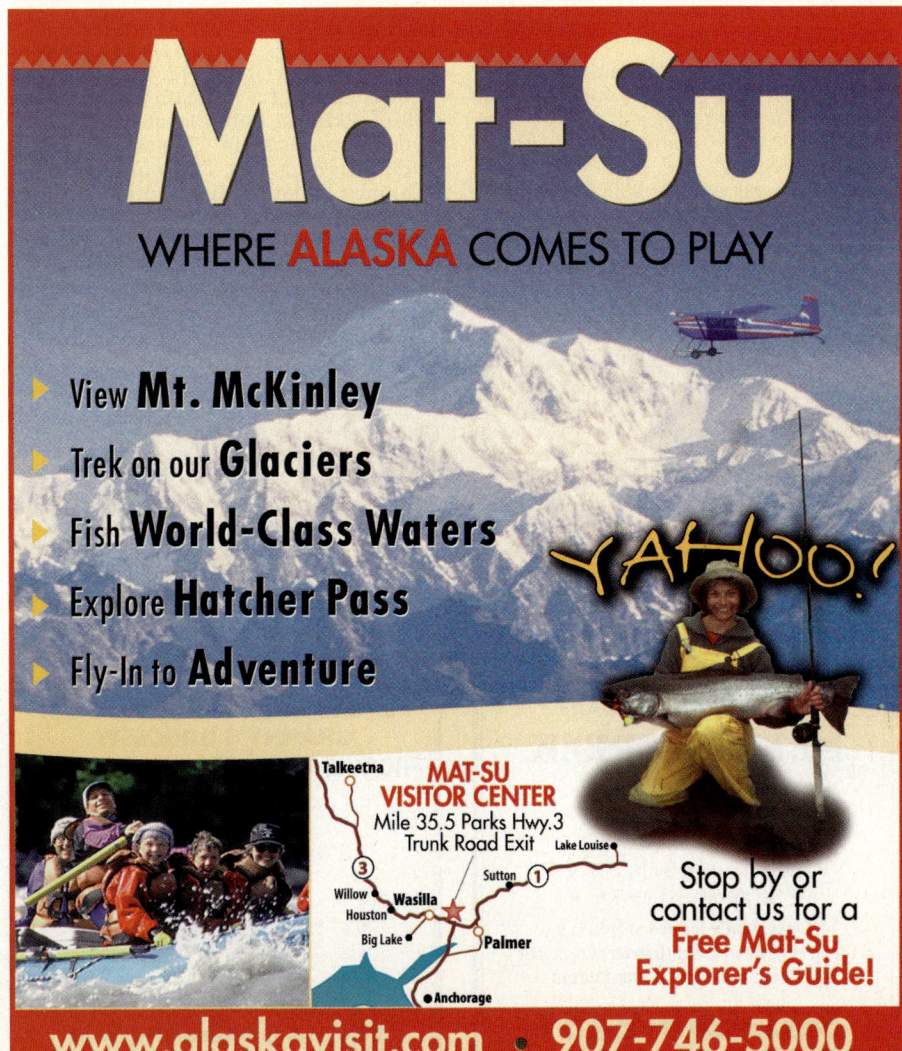

Eagle River Road

Eagle River Road leads 12.5 miles east from downtown Eagle River through a rural residential area to Eagle River Nature Center in Chugach State Park. It is a good paved 2-lane road, with older patched pavement beginning about Mile 6. Speed limits are 40 mph on curves, 55 mph on straightaways. *Note: Watch for driveway traffic, school bus stops, pedestrians and moose.*

Distance from junction (J) with Old Glenn Highway is shown.

J 0 **Junction** with Old Glenn Highway (Artillery Road).

J 0.3 Fire station.

J 1.5 **Junction** with Eagle River Loop Road.

J 1.6 Wal-Mart.

J 2.3 End bike route from Eagle River.

J 3.2 P & M Garden Services (a nursery).

J 4.8 AT&T Alaskacom.

J 7.8 **Mile 7.4 North Fork Put-In.** Short, bumpy, gravel road south to **North Fork Eagle River** access for kayaks, rafts and canoes; large gravel parking area, outhouse. Day-use area only, no camping. No fires; carry out trash. Hiking trail from parking area to main stem of river. The Eagle River offers class II, III and IV float trips. Fishing for rainbow trout, Dolly Varden and a limited king salmon fishery. Cross-country skiing and snow machining in winter. Check with Chugach State Park ranger (345-5014) for information on river conditions.

J 8.9 **Mile 9 Moose Pond Put-In**; small gravel parking area at boat access for Eagle River floats.

J 10.5 Chugach State Park (sign).

J 11.6 Rough gravel turnout to south; abrupt pavement edge.

J 12.5 **Eagle River Nature Center**; pay phone, restrooms. Natural history displays, viewing telescope, self-guiding nature trails, guided nature hikes offered daily in summer, year-round nature programs. Operated by the non-profit Friends of Eagle River Nature Center to provide educational and interpretive opportunities for Chugach State Park visitors. Beautiful views of the Chugach Mountains. Also the trailhead for the **Old Iditarod–Crow Pass Trail.** Public-use yurt and cabin available for rent; reserve in advance with the Nature Center. The center is open daily in summer from 10 A.M. to 5 P.M.; $5 parking fee. (Overnight hikers use designated parking space; $5 for 3 nights.) Phone (907) 694-2108 for activities schedule, cabin reservations and winter hours; (907) 694-6391 recorded message; (907) 345-5014 Chugach State Park ranger.

Return to Milepost A 13.4 Glenn Highway

Thunderbird Falls trail is an easy 2-mile walk round trip.
(© Kris Graef, staff)

Park. The access road is paved to Mile 1.8, and then dirt and gravel to road end. *(No turnarounds on gravel portion of the road. Also, watch for bicyclists on road. Posted speed is 35mph.)* Rochelle's Ice Cream Stop and Cheely's General Store at Mile 9. The recreation area has 50 campsites in the trees; 23 picnic sites, also in the trees; water pumps, picnic tables, firepits, outhouses; campground host in residence; ranger station; overflow camping area; and hiking trails. Camping fee $10/night or resident pass; 15-day limit. A public use cabin is available for rent at $40/night. Reservations may be made in person or via mail. Call the Dept. of Natural Resources Public Information Center at (907) 269-8400 for more information. The trailhead parking lot offers easy access to the lake and will accommodate 80 cars. It also acts as a boat launch for hand-carried boats. Three trails branch off the trailhead: Twin Peaks, Lakeside and Bold Ridge. The Lakeside trail—popular with hikers and bicyclists—follows Eklutna Lake shoreline and gives access to Eklutna Glacier (12.7 miles).

Rochelle's Ice Cream Stop/Store/Cabins/Eklutna Room located 1 1/4 mile from Eklutna Lake in Chugach State Park wildlife viewing area. Best milkshakes, old fashioned banana splits, espresso, fishing licenses, ice, groceries, picnic supplies, Eklutna Lake posters/postcards. Shower/laundry available. Phone (907) 688-6201, 1-800-764-6201; web site: goalaskan.com. [ADVERTISEMENT]

Eklutna Lake is the largest lake in Chugach State Park, measuring approximately 7 miles long by a mile wide. The lake is used to generate power at the Eklutna Plant, and is also a water source for Anchorage. Fed by Eklutna Glacier, Eklutna Lake offers fair fishing for Dolly Varden. *CAUTION: High winds can make this lake dangerous for boaters.* Interpretive displays on wildlife and a viewing telescope are located at the trailhead.

A 25.2 G 163.8 T 302.8 **Thunderbird Falls** exit (eastbound traffic only) and eastbound access to Eklutna Road (see **Milepost A 26.3** for description). From exit drive 0.3 mile (follow signs) to trailhead parking lot just before Eklutna River bridge. (Return to Glenn Highway is 0.7 mile from parking lot via Ekutna exit at **Milepost A 26.3**.) Thunderbird Falls is a 2-mile round-trip hike from the trailhead. This easy family walk is along a wide, scenic trail, but supervise children because there are steep cliffs just off the trail. The trail forks, with the right fork leading to a viewing platform, and the left fork leading down a steep path to Thunderbird Creek. The falls are just upstream. CAUTION: *Do NOT venture beyond the end of the trail to climb the steep cliffs overhanging the falls!*

A 24.5 G 164.5 T 303.5 Southbound-only exit to Edmonds Lake residential area and **Mirror Lake Park** Municipality of Anchorage); picnic shelters, outhouses, volleyball court, play field, beach and swings. The shallow 73-acre **Mirror Lake**, located at the foot of Mount Eklutna, is stocked with rainbow.

A 23.6 G 165.4 T 304.4 Northbound-only exit to **Mirror Lake Park** (see description above), located just off exit. Also access to Edmonds Lake.

A 23 G 166 T 305 Exit to North Peters Creek Business Loop (use next exit at **Milepost A 21.9** for more direct access to services).

A 21.9 G 167.1 T 306.1 Westbound off ramp to South Peters Creek exit (see description of businesses next milepost).

A 21.5 G 167.5 T 306.5 PETERS CREEK. Eastbound off-ramp to South Peters Creek exit; take Voyles to Old Glenn Highway/Bill Stephens Drive. Access to Oberg Road and ball fields. Services this exit include gas stations, grocery, body repair shop and restaurant.

Peters Creek Bed & Breakfast. Located on the north shore of Peters Creek only 0.8 mile from exit. Wheelchair accessible; open year-round. Rooms have private baths, cable TV, VCR, refrigerator; full Alaskan breakfast. Lovely new home, wooded setting, smoke-free environment, major credit cards accepted. Phone (888) 688-3465, (907) 688-3465, fax (907) 688-3466. [ADVERTISEMENT]

Peters Creek "Petite" RV Park. See display ad this section.

Peters Creek Trading Post. See display ad this section.

A 20.9 G 168.1 T 306.9 North Birchwood Loop Road exits both sides of highway. Turn east for community of **CHUGIAK** (pop. 10,000), Chugiak post office, senior center, convenience store with gas, diesel, showers and laundromat on Old Glenn Highway.

A 17.2 G 171.8 T 310.8 South Birchwood Loop Road exits both sides of highway. Access west to Chugiak High School and **Beach Lake Municipal Park** (0.8 mile west, turn left and follow winding gravel road 2 miles). Fishing and canoeing at Beach Lake. Exit east for to St. John Orthodox Cathedral; follow Birchwood Loop 0.6 mile east; turn right on Old Glenn Highway and drive 0.2 mile; turn on Monastery Drive and drive 0.3 mile.

Saint John Orthodox Cathedral. Take a peaceful break from your travels. Visit this unique, geodesic-dome cathedral with birch

ceiling and beautiful icons. Or hike to Sergius Chapel. Visitors are welcome at our services: Saturday Vespers, 7:15 P.M.; Sunday Divine Liturgy, 10 A.M. Bookstore. Monastery Drive off Old Glenn. (907) 696-2002. [ADVERTISEMENT]

A 15.3 G 173.7 T 312.7 Exit to North Eagle River, Terrace Lane. Access to Eagle River Car Wash and Duck Pond at Mile 15.5 Old Glenn Highway.

A 13.4 G 175.6 T 314.6 Eagle River exit east to community of Eagle River via Artillery Road; all visitor services (description follows). Also access to Eagle River Road to Eagle River Nature Center in Chugach State Park (see Eagle River Road description this page).

Eagle River

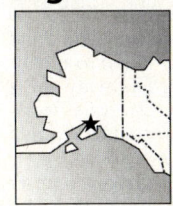

A 13.4 G 175.6 T 314.6 **Population:** Area 21,000. **Emergency Services: Police,** Anchorage Police Dept., phone (907) 786-8500. **Alaska State Troopers,** phone (907) 269-5711. **Ambulance,** phone 911. **Fire Department,** phone 911 **Visitor Information:** Contact the Chugiak–Eagle River Chamber of Commerce, P.O. Box 770353, Eagle River, AK 99577; phone (907) 694-4702. You can also visit the Chamber office at 11401 Old Glenn Highway, #105, in the Eagle River Shopping Center. **Radio:** KAXX 1020.

EAGLE RIVER ADVERTISERS

Chugiak–Eagle River Chamber of Commerce .... Ph. (907) 694-4702
Eagle River Car Wash & Duck Pond .... Mile 15.5 Old Glenn Hwy.
Eagle River Motel Ph.1-866-AKMOTEL
Mail Boxes Etc. .... Ph. (907) 694-7447

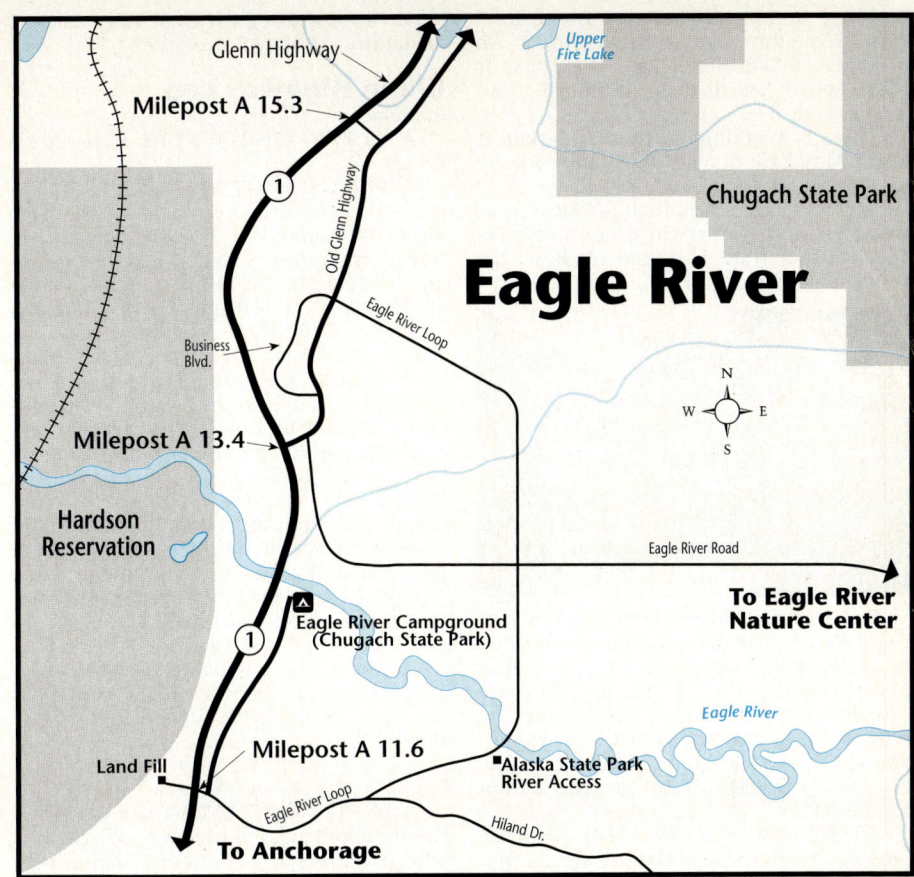

The Chugiak–Eagle River area was homesteaded after WWII when the new Glenn Highway opened this rural area northeast of Anchorage. Today, Eagle River is a fast-growing residential area with a full range of businesses, most located along the Old Glenn Highway east off the Glenn Highway.

Visitor services include fast-food restaurants, supermarkets, banks, laundromat, post office, gas stations and shopping centers. Eagle River has a movie theatre. Ice skating, hockey and speed skating at the Harry J. McDonald Memorial Center located just north of Spenard Builders Supply on the Old Glenn Highway. The nearest public campground is Eagle River Campground, at **Milepost A 11.6**. Take Hiland exit, then follow signs on frontage road.

Eagle River Car Wash and Duck Pond. Facilities available for washing cars, campers, trucks, boats and travel homes. Vacuums available. A duck pond on the premises is open to the public and features cedar viewing decks for observing some of the natural wild Alaskan waterfowl in their natural habitat. Mile 15.5 Old Glenn Highway. Turn off at North Eagle River access for car wash. See display ad this section. [ADVERTISEMENT]

Mail Boxes Etc. Let the experts at Mail Boxes Etc. pack and ship your "Alaskan catch" frozen fish and other great souvenirs. And while you're here, check your email,

CHUGIAK-EAGLE RIVER CHAMBER OF COMMERCE
VISITOR INFORMATION
11401 OLD GLENN HIGHWAY, STE 105
P.O. BOX 770353, EAGLE RIVER, ALASKA 99577
www.cer.org   e-mail: info@cer.org
(907) 694-4702
July 3 – Fireworks and Festivities at Lions Park
July 4 – Chugiak Community Parade
July 9-13 – Bear Paw Festival and Parade

EAGLE RIVER MOTEL
Clean • Quiet • Comfortable
20 Minutes to Downtown Anchorage
• Suites • Kitchenettes • Cable Television • Pets Accepted
1-866-AKMOTEL
fax (907) 694-1713
www.eaglerivermotel.com
Just off Eagle River Exit
11111 Old Eagle River Road, Eagle River

Why pay Anchorage prices?

purchase stamps, mail postcards and look around at the many other services we provide. At Mail Boxes Etc. "We'll take it from here." See display ad this section.

[ADVERTISEMENT]

There is a summer **Farmer's Market** at Chief Alex Park downtown; inquire locally for days and hours.

Special events include the Alaskan Scottish Highland Games (in June); fireworks and a parade (July 3–4); and the Bear Paw Festival and parade (July 13, 2003).

Eagle River Nature Center at Mile 12.5 Eagle River Road has natural history displays, viewing telescope and self-guiding nature trails. Guided nature hikes are offered daily in summer and there are nature programs scheduled year-round. Phone (907) 694-2108 for activities information. See "Eagle River Road" log this section for directions.

The 4.5 mile **Eagle River Loop** (see map) provides access to Eagle River residential and business areas. Eagle Pointe (follow signs from Hiland Road intersection) is a good example of one of Anchorage's newer suburban subdivisions. Alaska State Parks maintains a day-use area and river access at Mile 1.5 Eagle River Loop (eastbound access only). Boaters are advised that a permit is required for boating the Eagle River on Fort Richardson Military Reservation.

Glenn Highway Log
(continued)

A 12.8 G 176.2 T 315.2 Eagle River Bridge.

A 11.6 G 177.4 T 316.4 Exit to Hiland Drive/Eagle River Loop; access to Anchorage Municipal Landfill (343-6298); state correctional center (follow signs); and state campground (description follows). The 4.5-mile Eagle River Loop/Eagle River Veterans Memorial Highway provides access to Alaska State Parks River Access (1.5 miles, eastbound access only); Eagle River Road (2.5 miles); and downtown Eagle River. Also access this exit for Eagle Pointe subdivision.

For **Eagle River Campground** (Chugach State Park) follow signs 1.4 miles from the highway; 58 campsites, walk-in tent camping, 4-day camping limit, picnic shelter (may be reserved in advance), dump station, pay phones, flush toilets and drinking water. Camping fee is $15/night. Day-use fee $5. Dump station $5. Operated by concessionaire; phone (907) 694-7982.

Canoe/kayak staging area for the lower Eagle River. A permit (fee charged) is required to float the lower Eagle River through Fork Richardson. ▲

Highway narrows from 3 to 2 northbound lanes.

A 10.6 G 178.4 T 317.4 Truck weigh stations on both sides of highway; pay phones. Trooper Hans Roelle Memorial Station eastbound only.

The last 9 miles of the Glenn Highway into Anchorage has been designated the **Veterans' Memorial Parkway**.

A 7.5 G 181.5 T 320.5 Exit west for main gate to **FORT RICHARDSON**, home of "America's Arctic Warriors." Exit east for southbound access to **Arctic Valley Road** (see description next milepost).

NOTE: A driver's license, proof of insurance and vehicle registration or rental agreement are required for civilians visiting the base. Other restrictions may apply; check with gate personnel.

There is a National Cemetery at Fort Richardson. Ask for directions to the cemetery at the gate.

CAUTION: Watch for moose next 7 miles northbound.

A 6.1 G 182.9 T 321.9 Northbound only exit to Arctic Valley Road (description follows) and access to Fort Richardson Army base (1 mile; follow signs). Follow Arctic Valley Road 1 mile for **Moose Run Military Golf Course**; 36-holes (2 courses), driving range, rental carts and clubs, clubhouse. Public welcome. Open May to October (season depends on snow), 7 A.M.–9 P.M. Phone (907) 428-0056.

Arctic Valley Road leads 7 miles to Arctic Valley ski area; hiking, alpine wildflowers and berry picking in summer. Pavement ends at Mile 1.6. Good wide gravel road to end; some steep grades; posted 25 to 30 mph. Views of Fort Richardson and Anchorage from turnouts at Mile 3.1 and Mile 4.1. Arctic Valley trailhead (Chugach State Park) at Mile 6.3. Fee parking, toilets and summer hiking at Arctic Valley ski area, Mile 7. Trailhead for Rendezvous Peak Trail: "The hike to the saddle (elev. 3,468 feet) is a relatively gentle climb, and the added push to Rendezvous Peak (elev. 4,050 feet), is well worth the spectacular scenery that awaits." Allow 2 to 5 hours for the 3.5-mile round trip hike up Rendezvous Peak.

In winter, the Anchorage Ski Club operates Alpenglow ski area at Arctic Valley. The weekend ski area offers a T-bar and a chairlift.

A 5.1 G 183.9 T 322.9 *CAUTION: Watch for moose.*

A 4.4 G 184.6 T 323.6 Muldoon Road overpass. Exit north for **Alaska Native Heritage Center**, a 26-acre site featuring 5 traditional village sites along a walking path around a 2-acre lake. Cultural presentations, food and crafts in the dramatic Welcoming House. Admission fee charged. U.S. Air Force Hospital and Bartlett High School also to the north.

Exit south for **Centennial Park** municipal campground (follow signs), and to connect with Seward Highway via Muldoon and Tudor roads bypass. ▲

There is a bicycle trail from Muldoon Road to Mirror Lake, **Milepost A 23.6**.

A 3.7 G 185.3 T 324.3 Turpin Road (eastbound exit only).

A 3.5 G 185.5 T 324.5 Distance marker eastbound shows Eagle River 10 miles, Palmer 38 miles, Wasilla 39 miles.

A 3 G 186 T 325 Boniface Parkway. Exit south for businesses and Russian Jack Springs city campground on Boniface Parkway just north of DeBarr.

Exit north and drive 0.5 mile for Boniface Gate **ELMENDORF AFB**, 3rd Wing. *NOTE: Visitor and vehicle passes required to get on base. Visitors must have current vehicle registration or rental car agreement; current driver's license; name, location and phone number of sponsor on base. Other restrictions may apply; check with gate personnel.*

A 1.9 G 187.1 T 326.1 Bragaw Street. Veterans Memorial Parkway (sign). The first 9 miles of the Glenn Highway is designated as the Veterans Memorial Parkway.

A 1.2 G 187.8 T 326.8 Welcome to Anchorage sign. Airport Heights Drive to south; access to Northway Mall, Merrill Field and hospital. Mountain View Drive to north.

A 0 T 328 G 189 Glenn Highway forks and becomes 5th Avenue (one-way westbound) to downtown Anchorage, 6th Avenue (one-way eastbound) from downtown.

A **Blue Star Memorial Highway** marker is located at the Glenn Highway 'Y.' The bronze marker "A tribute to the Armed Forces that have defended the United States of America" sits in a small triangular park. The Anchorage Garden Club is responsible for the annual flower display surrounding the base of the memorial.

The Blue Star Memorial Highway program began in 1945 in cooperation with the National Council of State Garden Clubs as a way to honor the armed forces of the United States. Blue Star Memorials are found on highways in every state, each marker sponsored and maintained by a local garden club.

Turn south at Gambell Street (one-way southbound) for the Seward Highway to the Kenai Peninsula (see SEWARD HIGHWAY section). See ANCHORAGE section following for description of city.

Visit the Eagle River Nature Center.

ANCHORAGE

(See maps, pages 323, 324 and 330)

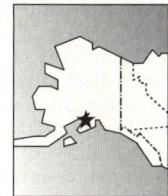

Anchorage, Alaska's largest city, is in the heart of the state's southcentral gulf coast. Located on the upper shores of Cook Inlet, at 61° north latitude and 150° west longitude, the Anchorage bowl is on a low-lying alluvial plain bordered by mountains, water and dense forests of spruce, birch and aspen. Cook Inlet's Turnagain Arm and Knik Arm define the broad peninsula that is the city's home, and the rugged Chugach Mountains form a striking backdrop. Of Alaska's 634,892 citizens, nearly 42 percent live in Anchorage and the Matanuska region. Anchorage is situated 358 miles south of Fairbanks via the Parks Highway; 328 miles from Tok; 304 miles from Valdez, southern terminus of the trans-Alaska pipeline, via the Glenn and Richardson highways; 2,459 driving miles via the West Access Route, Alaska Highway and Glenn Highway/Tok Cutoff from Seattle; 1,644 nautical miles, and approximately 3 hours flying time from Seattle. Prior to the opening of Russia's Far East to air traffic and refueling, Anchorage was considered the "Air Crossroads of the World," and today is still the major air logistics center and cargo carrier for Asia, Europe and North America. In terms of nonstop air mileages, Anchorage is the following distance from each of these cities: Amsterdam, 4,475; Chicago, 2,839; Copenhagen, 4,313; Hamburg, 4,430; Honolulu, 2,780; London, 4,487; Paris, 4,683; San Francisco, 2,015; Seattle, 1,445; Tokyo, 3,460.

Population: Anchorage Municipality, 260,283. **Emergency Services: Police, Fire Department, Ambulance** and **Search & Rescue,** phone 911, CB Channel 9. **Police,** phone (907) 786-8500. **Alaska State Troopers,** phone (907) 269-5511. **Alaska Department of Public Safety,** web site: www.dps.state.ak.us. **Hospitals:** Alaska Regional Hospital, phone (907) 276-1131; Alaska Native Medical Center, phone (907) 563-2662; Providence Alaska Medical Center, phone (907) 562-2211; Elmendorf Air Force Base emergency room, phone (907) 580-5555. **Dental Emergencies,** phone (907) 279-9144 (24-hour service). **Emergency Management,** phone 1-800-478-8999. **Suicide Intervention,** phone (907) 563-3200 (24-hour service). **Rape & Assault,** phone (907) 276-7273 (24-hour service). **Battered Women,** phone (907) 272-0100. **Pet Emergency,** phone (907) 274-5636. **Poison Control,** phone (907) 261-3193. **Road Conditions,** statewide, phone (800) 478-7675 or (907) 273-6037.

Visitor Information: The Anchorage Convention & Visitors Bureau (ACVB) operates the **Log Cabin Visitor Information Center,** located at 4th Avenue and F Street. The cabin is open daily, year-round. Hours are 7:30 A.M. to 7 P.M. June through August; 8 A.M. to 6 P.M. in May and September; and 9 A.M. to 4 P.M. the remainder of the year; closed only on Thanksgiving, Christmas and New Year's Day. The cabin offers a wide assortment of free brochures and maps.

The ACVB produces several publications including an annual visitor guide. The web site also lists current and upcoming events. Write 524 W. 4th Ave., Anchorage 99501; phone (907) 274-3531; web site www.anchorage.net. Email info@anchorage.net.

Visitor information centers are also located at Ted Stevens Anchorage International Airport, one in the South Terminal baggage claim area for domestic flights; one in the customs-secured area of the North Terminal (international concourse); and a third in the lobby of the international terminal.

A visitor information center kiosk is located in The Mall at Sears at Northern Lights Blvd. and the Seward Highway; open daily. And the North Anchorage Visitor Information Center, a self-serve information site, is located in the Parkgate Building, 11723 Old Glenn Highway, Eagle River.

The **Alaska Visitors Center and Activities,** at 4619 Spenard Road (near the airport), offers a wide assortment of brochures, books and maps, as well as assistance with trip planning. Visitors may also purchase tickets and make reservations here for various attractions in the state; phone (907) 929-2822.

The **Alaska Public Lands Information Center,** 605 W. 4th, in the historic Old Federal Building, has extensive displays and information on outdoor recreation lands in Alaska; phone (907) 271-2737. (See detailed description under Attractions, this section.)

The **Bureau of Land Management's Public Information Center** is located on the first floor of the New Federal Bldg.–U.S. Courthouse at 8th Avenue and A Street. Open weekdays, 8 a.m. to 3:45 p.m.; phone (907) 271-5960. The office carries brochures and informational booklets on public lands as well as mining information.

Elevation: 38 to 120 feet. **Climate:** Anchorage has a climate resembling that of the Rocky Mountains area, tempered by proximity to the Pacific Ocean. Shielded from excess ocean moisture by the Kenai Mountains to the south, the city has an annual average of only 16.1 inches of precipitation. Winter snowfall averages about 70 inches per year, with snow on the ground typically from October to April. On March 16 and 17, 2002, Anchorage received record snowfalls of 28.6 inches in 26 hours.

Anchorage is in a transition zone between the moderating influence of the Pacific and the extreme temperatures of interior Alaska. The average temperature in January (coldest

The Anchorage skyline against the backdrop of the Chugach Mountains.
(© Bill Sherwonit)

The Log Cabin Visitor Information Center in downtown Anchorage. (© Barb Willard)

month) is 16°F; in July (warmest month), 65°F. A record 40 days of 70°F temperatures or higher was set in 1936, according to the National Weather Service. The record high was 85°F in June of 1969. The record low was -34°F in January 1975. Anchorage and surrounding areas set daily record highs in spring and summer 2002, as several days reached temperatures into the 70s and 80s.

The growing season of 100 to 120 days typically extends from late May to early September. Anchorage has a daily maximum of 19 hours, 21 minutes of daylight in summer, and 5 hours, 28 minutes in winter. Prevailing wind direction is north.

Radio: AM stations: KTZN 550 (Sports Radio); KHAR 590 (Easy Listening); KENI 650 (News, Talk, Sports); KBYR 700 (News, Talk, Sports); KFQD 750 (News, Talk); KAXX 1020 (Sports Radio); KUDO 1080 (Business/financial news, talk, BBC); FM stations: KZND 87.7 (The End- Alternative); KRUA 88.1 (University of Alaska station); KAKL 88.5 (Contemporary Christian); KATB 89.3 (Christian radio); KNBA 90.3 (Public Radio, Native-owned); KSKA 91.1 (National Public Radio); KAFC 93.7 (Christian radio); KQEZ 92.1 (Easy Favorites); KFAT 92.9 (R&B, Rap); KADX 94.7 (Talk, Sports); KRPM 96.3 (Pure Retro- 80s rock); KEAG 97.3 (Oldies); KLEF 98.1 (Classical Music); KYMG 98.9 (Adult Contemporary); KBFX 100.5 (The Fox - Pure Rock); KGOT 101.3 (Top 40); KDBZ 102.1 (Classic Rock); KMXS 103.1 (Contemporary); KBRJ 104.1 (Country Favorites); KNIK 105.7 (The Breeze - Smooth Jazz); KWHL 106.5 (Modern Rock); KASH 107.5 (New Country). **Television:** KTUU (NBC), Channel 2; KTBY (Fox), Channel 4; KYES (Independent), Channel 5; KAKM (PBS), Channel 7; KTVA (CBS), Channel 11; KIMO (ABC), Channel 13; KCFT TV UHF 20 (Christian Family); KDMD TV PAXX33 (Home Shopping Network); other UHF channels, satellite and pay cable television are also available. **Newspapers:** *Anchorage Daily News* (daily); *Arctic Sounder* (weekly); *Anchorage Chronicle* (weekly); *Alaska Journal of Commerce*; *Anchorage Press* (weekly); *Alaska Military Weekly* (weekly); *Alaska Star* (semi-weekly).

Private Aircraft: Anchorage airports provide facilities and services to accommodate all types of aircraft. Consult the *Alaska Supplement*, the *Anchorage VFR Terminal Area Chart* and *Terminal Alaska Book* for the following airports: Ted Stevens Anchorage International, Merrill Field and Lake Hood seaplane and strip.

History & Economy

In 1914 Congress authorized the building of a railroad linking an ocean port with the interior river shipping routes. The anchorage at the mouth of Ship Creek became the construction camp and headquarters for the Alaskan Engineering Commission. By the summer of 1915 the population, housed mainly in tents, had grown to about 2,000.

Among the names suggested for the settlement were Ship Creek, Spenard, Woodrow and Knik Anchorage, and the name Anchorage was selected by the federal government when the first post office opened in May 1915. Later that year the bluff south of Ship Creek was cleared and surveyed, and 655 lots, on 347 acres, were auctioned off by the General Land Office for $148,000. The center of the business district was the 4th Avenue and C Street intersection. Anchorage prospered and was incorporated in 1920.

Anchorage's growth has been in spurts, spurred by: (1) construction of the Alaska Railroad and the transfer of its headquarters from Seward to Anchorage in 1917; (2) colonization of the Matanuska Valley, a farming region 45 miles to the north, in 1935; (3) construction of Fort Richardson and Elmendorf Field (now Elmendorf Air Force Base) in 1940; (4) discovery of oil in Cook Inlet between 1957 and 1961; and (5) the development of North Slope/Prudhoe Bay oil fields and the construction of the trans-Alaska pipeline—all since 1968.

The current population of 260,283 includes diverse racial and cultural groups, with about 72 percent white, 10.4 percent Native Alaskan, and between 6 and 7 percent African-American, Asian-Pacific Islander and Hispanic groups. Government jobs, including the military, account for about one-quarter of the employment picture; service industries for another quarter. The oil, gas and mining industries employ roughly 3 percent. Other fields of work are similar to those in other American cities of this size (in the classified section of the Anchorage phone directory, 78 pages are devoted to attorneys and law firms).

The Good Friday earthquake of March 27, 1964, the most powerful quake (8.6 on the Richter scale, Mw 9.2) ever recorded in North America, caused more than $300 million in damage throughout southcentral Alaska. In Anchorage most losses resulted from landslides caused by changes in the composition of the clay underlying much of the city. Government Hill, downtown neighborhoods, and the Turnagain area now known as Earthquake Park suffered the most extensive damage, losing many homes and other buildings. Considering the severity of the disaster, the number of casualties (131) was miraculously low. Relief funds in the form of federal Small Business Administration loans helped many rebuild, and from the devastation a distinctly new Anchorage emerged.

In the 1970s and 1980s, Anchorage experienced a population and construction boom related to oil production. Major oil companies set up corporate headquarters, and Anchorage's first 20-story buildings punctuated the skyline. Declining oil prices in the 1980s and 1990s triggered a slowdown in the economic climate, but business prospects are upbeat today, and the number of new building starts is high. The advent of several national retail chains during the past decade has resulted in the closure of many smaller, family-owned businesses. Mergers, malls and megastores are the order of the day here as in the Lower 48. With its strategic location and modern facilities, Anchorage's key role as the center of commerce and distribution for the rest of Alaska is assured.

Description

Covering 1,961 square miles (1,697 square miles of land and 264 of water), Anchorage lies between the Chugach Mountains on the east and Knik Arm of Cook Inlet on the west. The surrounding mountain ranges—the Chugach, the Kenais, the Talkeetnas, the icy peaks of the Tordrillo Mountains across Cook Inlet, and the dramatic peaks of the Alaska Range (with Mount McKinley visible on the northern horizon, weather permitting)—encompass the city in a setting of scenic splendor.

Perched on the edge of Alaska's vast, varied expanse of forests, mountains, rivers, taiga and tundra, Anchorage has sometimes been described as "half an hour from Alaska." Its similarities to other medium-sized American cities increase steadily, but, although it is true that a half-hour trip in any direction from the city offers an abundance of wilderness experiences, this modern metropolis still possesses many features that mark it as uniquely Alaskan. Combining cosmopolitan amenities with the creative enthusiasm of a young, progressive state has made Anchorage a spirited city and an exciting destination.

Among the many buildings erected during Project 80s, the largest construction program in the city's history, funded by millions of dollars allocated by the legislature, is the **Alaska Center for the Performing Arts** on 5th Avenue and F Street. During its 15 years the center has hosted a wide range of productions, from Broadway shows, world-renowned performers and Anchorage's own symphony orchestra to local productions of choral, theatrical and dance groups. Fences were added on the center's steep-pitched roof to prevent snow from sliding off onto

The extras aren't extra.^{SM}

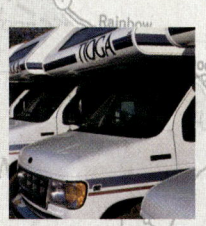

Great Alaskan Holidays has been providing unmatched value and service in motorhome rentals in Alaska for over two decades.

Compare us to the competition and discover why we say the "extras aren't extra" at Great Alaskan Holidays.

Included in Rental:

- Power Generator, Roof Air & Microwave.
- Color TV/DVD, Lawn Chairs & BBQ.
- A 2002 or newer motorhome, guaranteed!*
- Housekeeping and linen package.
- Cleaning of motorhome.
- FREE camping at Alaska State Parks, a savings of up to $15 per night!
- Insurance coverage.
- No provisioning, dump or housekeeping fees.
- Located at Anchorage International Airport.

Begin planning your Great Alaskan Holiday by calling for a free brochure.

Great Alaskan Holidays, Inc.™

1-888-2-ALASKA
1-888-225-2752
www.greatalaskanholidays.com

*2003 season

3901 W. International Airport Rd. • Anchorage, AK 99502 • tel (907) 248-7777 • fax (907) 248-7878

ANCHORAGE

Colorful programs are featured at the Alaska Native Heritage Center. (© Barb Willard)

unsuspecting pedestrians below. Other completed projects include the George M. Sullivan Sports Arena, William A. Egan Civic and Convention Center, Z.J. Loussac Public Library, and a major expansion and renovation of the Anchorage Museum of History and Art.

In June 2002, Anchorage was voted an All-American City for the fourth time. Sponsored by the National Civic League and awarded to only 10 cities in 2002, the award recognizes the cities' citizens, governments, businesses and non-profit organizations and their ability to successfully address local issues and produce positive results. Winning the award for the first time in 1956, Anchorage is one of only 7 cities to have won the award four or more times.

With its distinctive mixture of old frontier and jet age, Anchorage is a truly unique city. It is noted for the profusion of flowers and hanging baskets that decorate homes and businesses during summer months: parks, street medians and lamp posts are vibrant with the colors of millions of flowers. As shadows lengthen with winter's approach in October, residents are encouraged to follow the lead of municipal agencies in displaying strings of miniature white lights on homes, trees and office buildings, brightening the entire city "until the last Iditarod racer makes it to Nome" in March. The summertime City of Flowers becomes the wintertime City of Lights.

Anchorage is also the City of Moose, sharing its streets and yards with these largest members of the deer family, especially when winter's deep snows drive the moose toward easier browsing in settled areas where cultivated trees and shrubs

ANCHORAGE ADVERTISERS

Accommodations
A Rabbit Creek B&B 325
Alaska Private Lodgings 322
Alaska Sunset Inn Bed & Breakfast 327
Ask Alaska Travel & Tours 325
Alaska Tundra Inn, The 326
Alaskan Frontier Gardens
  Bed and Breakfast 325
Alaska's Tudor Motel 326
Anchor Arms Motel 326
Anchorage Guest House 325
Anchorage Suite Lodge 328
Apartment Blue Book 322
Arctic Fox Bed & Breakfast Inn 325
Arctic Inn Motel 322
Aspen Hotels 327
Aurora Winds Resort, The 325
Bed & Breakfast On the Park 326
Caribou Inn 327
Diana's Downtown
  Bed & Breakfast 328
Duke's 8th Avenue Hotel 328
Fernbrook Bed & Breakfast 326
Hawthorn Suites Ltd. 321
Inlet Tower Hotel & Suites 322
John's Motel 328
Long House Alaskan Hotel 322
Merrill Field Inn 326
Moose Gardens Bed & Breakfast 326
New Puffin Inn, The 327
Parkwood Inn 328
Puffin Place Studios & Suites 327
Sourdough Visitors Lodge 322
Teddy Bear House
  Bed & Breakfast, The 327
Walkabout Town
  Bed & Breakfast 328

Attractions & Entertainment
Alaska Aviation Heritage Museum 329
Alaska Botanical Gardens 329
Alaska Native Heritage Center 329
Alaska State Trooper Museum 333
Anchorage Museum Association 333
H2-Oasis Waterpark 335

Auto & RV Rentals
ABC Motorhome & Car Rentals 337
Affordable New Car Rental 339
Alaska Economy RVs 340
Alaska Motor Home Rentals 338
Alaska Panorama RV Rentals 336
Alaska Vacation Motorhome
  Rentals 340
Alexander's RV Rental 340
Beauty Vans of Alaska 340
Clippership Motorhome Rentals 339
Great Alaskan Holidays 319
High Country Car & Truck Rental 339
Murphy's R.V. Inc. 340
Sweet Retreat Motorhome Rentals 338

Auto & RV Sales, Service, Supplies
Alaska Performance RV & Marine 343
American Tire 341
Dean's Automotive & RV
  Service Center 343
Garrett's Tesoro 341
Jiffy Lube 344
John's RV & Auto Consignment 348
Johnson RV Center 344
Karen's RV Service Center 343
Mobile Trailer Supply, Inc. 343
Mountain View Car Wash, Inc. 341
Suburban Propane 341

Campgrounds
Anchorage RV Park 346, 328
Centennial Camper Park 346
Midtown Camper Park 348
Golden Nugget Camper Park 345
Hillside on Gambell
  Motel & R.V. Park 324
John's RV Park 348
Ship Creek Landings
  Downtown RV Park 347

Churches
First Baptist Church of Anchorage 350

Dining
Denny's 350

Healthcare
Providence Alaska Medical Center 350

Recreation
Municipality of Anchorage Parks
  & Recreation 350

Shopping & Services
Alaska Fur Exchange 351
Alaska Mint 334
Alaska Unique 352
Cleaning World I & II 351
Cook Inlet Book Co. 332
David Green Master Furrier 333
Downtown Saturday
  Market 331
Great Northern Guns 351
Knitting Frenzy Store 335
Laura Wright Alaskan Parkys 333
Mail Boxes Etc. 352, 327
Mall at Sears, The 352
Oomingmak, Musk Ox Producers
  Co-op 333
Quilt Tree, The 351
Seams Like Home Quilt Shoppe 351
Stewart's Photo Shop 333
10th & M Seafoods 351
Title Wave Books 351
Ulu Factory, The 332
Wild Furs Ltd. 331

Tours & Transportation
Alaska Air Taxi 356
Alaska ATV Adventures 356
Alaska Railroad Corp. 356, 340
Kenai Fjords Tours Ltd. 353, 340
Major Marine Tours 355, 340
People Mover 356
Phillips' Cruises & Tours 321
Portage Glacier Cruise 341
Renown Charters & Tours 356, 341
Train to Denali 341
Thunderbird Air, Inc. 335
26 Glacier Cruise 341

Visitor Information
Anchorage Convention &
  Visitors Bureau 331
Southcentral Navigator
  (Alaska Dept. of
  Transportation) 354

abound. Frequent summertime sightings attest to the steady increase of the moose population.

CAUTION: Do not attempt to approach or intercept moose at any time, whether for purposes of photography or to satisfy curiosity. Unpredictable and aggressive, moose are huge wild animals that can be extremely dangerous. This applies also to bears that occasionally wander into the city.

In profile, Anchorage has:
- About 92 schools, including special education and alternative public programs, a number of privately operated schools, both secular and parochial; also the University of Alaska, Alaska Pacific University and Charter College, a computer-oriented, "career-building" technical school; also rehabilitation/ training centers for the blind and the deaf.
- More than 200 churches and temples.
- Z.J. Loussac Public Library, plus 5 branch libraries, and the Alaska Resources Library and Information Services (ARLIS), which comprises 9 natural and cultural resource libraries; the Wells Fargo Heritage Library Museum, Alaska State Library Services for the Blind and the University of Alaska and Alaska Pacific University Consortium Library.
- Municipal bus service, 4 major taxi companies and various shuttle bus services.
- In the arts—**Dance:** Alaska Center for the Performing Arts; Alaska Dance Theatre; Anchorage Concert Assoc.; Anchorage Opera; Ballet Alaska. **Music:** Alaska Airlines Autumn Classics; Anchorage Concert Chorus; Anchorage Opera; Anchorage Community Concert Band; Anchorage Concert Assoc.; Anchorage Children's Choir; Anchorage Symphony Orchestra; Anchorage Festival of Music; Anchorage Folk Music Festival; Irish Music Festival (Galway Days on G St.); Sweet Adelines (Sourdough, Cheechako and Top of the World choruses); University of Alaska Anchorage Singers; Alaska Chamber Singers; Young People's Concerts. **Theater:** Alaska Community Theatre; Alaska Festival Theatre; Alaska Junior Theater; Alaska Stage Company; Alaska Theatre of Youth; Cyrano's Off Center Playhouse; Out North Theater Company; UAA Theatre; Valley Performing Arts. **Art:** About 25 art galleries.

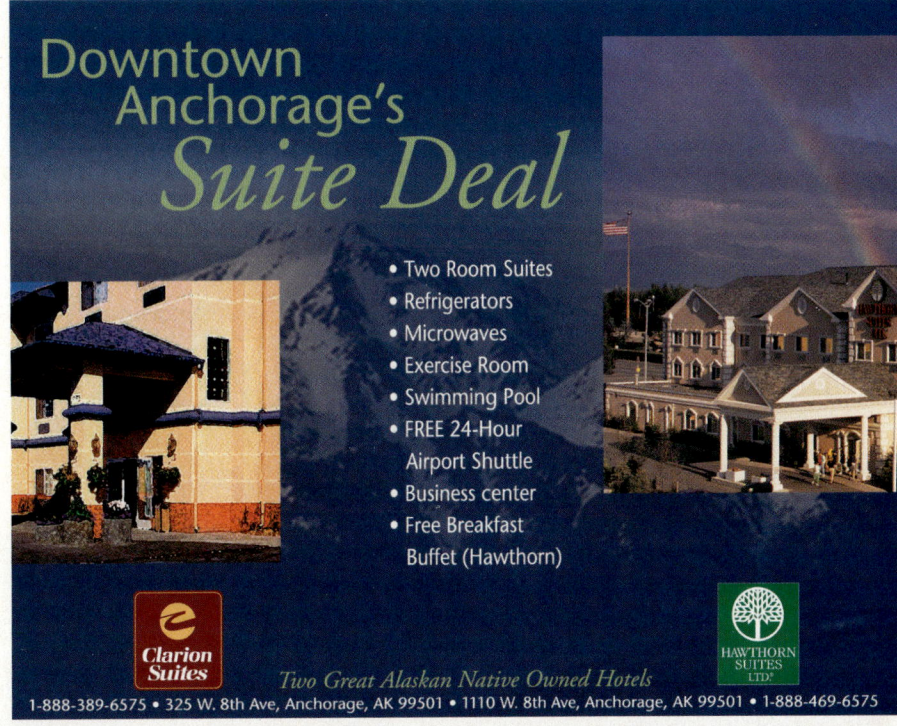

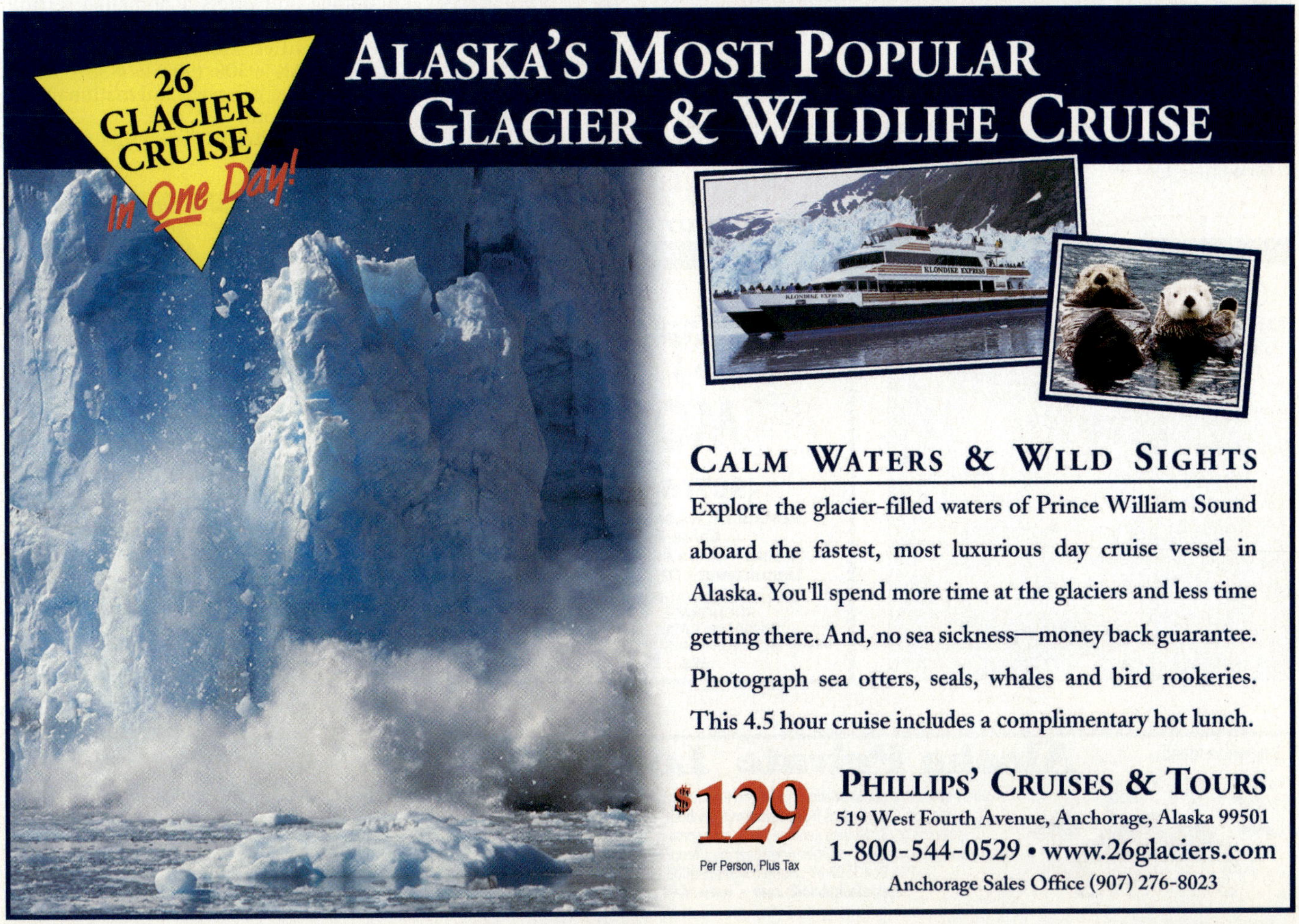

- A total of 300 miles of urban and wilderness trails for hiking, biking, jogging, skiing and dog mushing, including 120 miles of paved trails and about 105 miles of maintained ski trails.

Lodging & Services

There are more than 70 motels and hotels in the Anchorage area with prices for a double room ranging from $50 to $150 and up. Reservations are a must. Bed-and-breakfast accommodations are also available in more than 250 private residences; prices range from $60–$100.

Comfortable, low-cost accommodations are available for hostellers and other budget-conscious travelers:

Anchorage Guest House welcomes hostellers. Located at 2001 Hillcrest Drive, Anchorage, AK 99517, phone (907) 274-0408.

Hosteling International–Anchorage is located at 700 H St., 1 block from the People Mover Transit Center in downtown Anchorage. The hostel office is open 8:00 A.M. to noon and 5 P.M. to 11 P.M. with a 1 A.M. curfew. Common areas open all day. Cost for members: $16 per night, nonmembers: $19. AYH cards available at hostel or by mail. Dormitory rooms with bunkbeds, kitchen facilities, common rooms, laundry room and TV room. Additional, private accommodations available in the Amundsen House, an historic house near the hostel. For information or reservations no less than 1 day in advance with VISA or MasterCard, phone (907) 276-3635. 700 H St., Anchorage, AK 99501; email hianch@alaska.net; www.alaska.net/~hianch.

International Backpackers Hostel is located in the Mountain View section of Anchorage and offers a homelike setting, kitchen and laundry facilities, cable TV, and other amenities. 3601 Peterkin Avenue, Anchorage, AK 99508; (907) 274-3870; email ibhostel@alaska.net; www.internationalbackpackershostel.com.

Spenard Hostel International is a non-

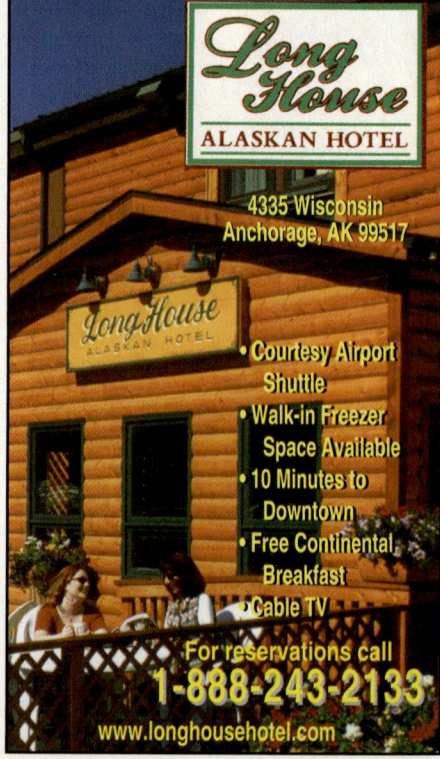

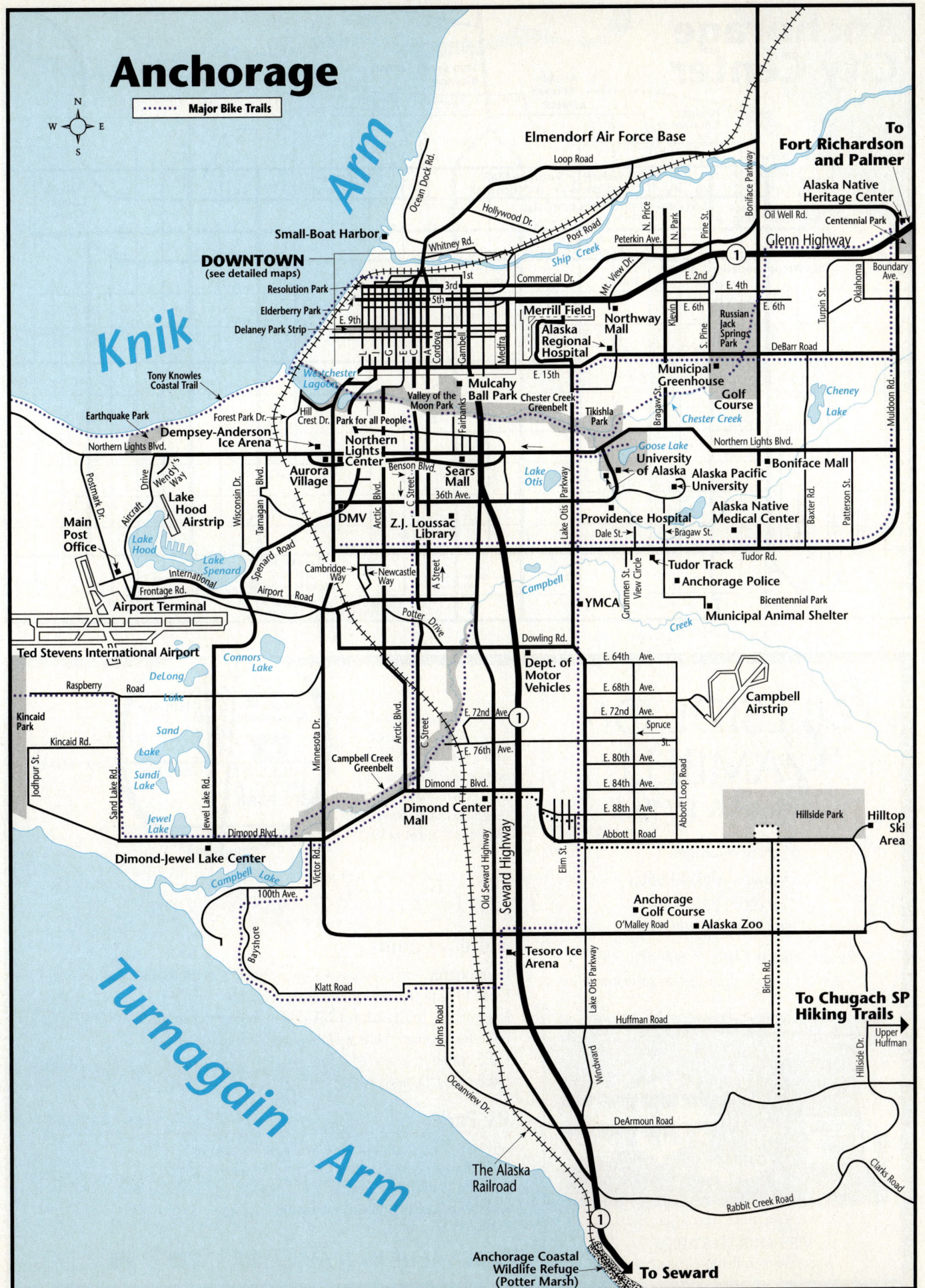

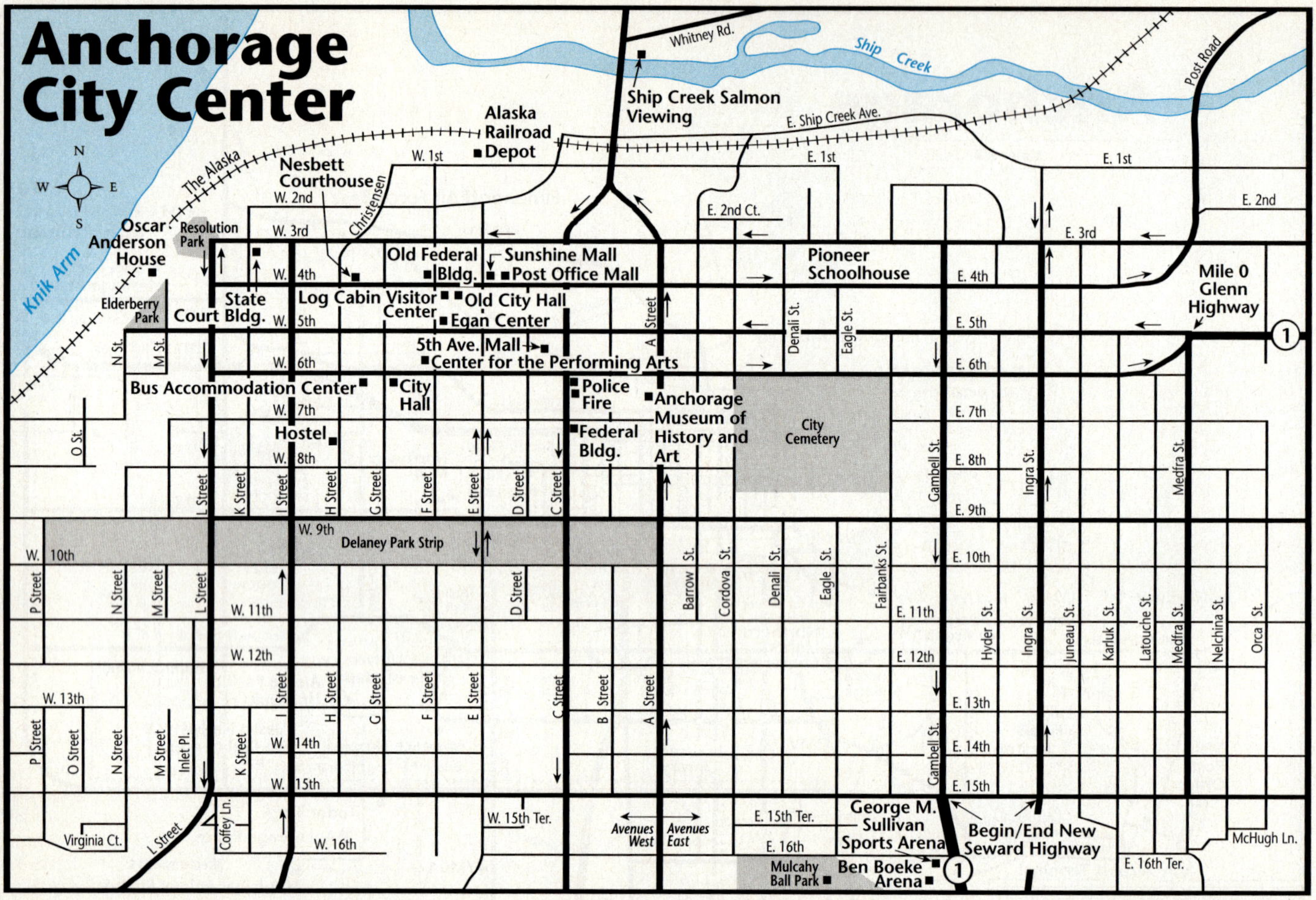

Anchorage City Center

Connects to map above

HILLSIDE ON GAMBELL
Motel & RV Park

2150 Gambell
Anchorage, Alaska 99503
Tel: (907) 258-6006
Fax: (907) 279-8972

Reservations Only: 1-800-478-6008
e-mail: info@hillside-alaska.com

Next to beautiful walking and bike paths, Sears mall, restaurants, grocery stores and theatres. In mid-town, minutes from every place in Anchorage you might want to visit.

A Warm and Happy Welcome!

Motel - Cabins

Comfortable, clean rooms • Queen beds in each room
Large fully equipped kitchenettes available
Microwave, refrigerator, FREE coffee, hairdryers in all rooms
FREE local phone calls • Data ports for internet access
FREE coffee in lobby 24 hours
FREE cable TV with HBO

RV Park

68 spaces • 58 full hookups • Cable TV available
FREE showers for RV guests • Fish freezer available
Laundry Facility • Propane
Deliciously pure artesian well water
Daily/weekly rates

VISIT OUR WEBSITE AT:
http://www.hillside-alaska.com

BEST VALUE IN TOWN

affiliated hostel on the bus line at 2845 W. 42nd Place, Anchorage, AK. For reservations, phone/fax (907) 248-5036; email stay@alaskahostel.org; www.alaskahostel.org.

Restaurants number more than 600, with many major fast-food chains, formal dining rooms and specialty establishments including Italian, Japanese, Korean, Chinese (Cantonese and Mandarin), Mexican, Polynesian, Greek, German, Sicilian, Thai, soul food, seafood, smorgasbord and vegetarian.

Alaskan Frontier Gardens Bed and Breakfast. Elegant Alaska hillside estate on peaceful scenic 3 acres by Chugach State Park, 20 minutes from downtown. Spacious luxury suites with big Jacuzzi, sauna, king bed and fireplace. Getaway for honeymooners. Gourmet breakfast, museum-like environment with Alaskan hospitality and exceptional comfort. Truly Alaska's finest. Year-round service. Credit cards accepted. P.O. Box 241881, Anchorage, AK 99524-1881. (907) 345-6556. Fax (907) 348-0253. Web site: www.alaskafrontiergarden.com. [ADVERTISEMENT]

Anchorage Guest House. 2001 Hillcrest Drive, Anchorage, AK 99517. Phone/fax (907) 274-0408; Email: house@alaska.net; web page: www.akhouse.com. Large friendly house on Coastal Trail, close to downtown and Westchester Lagoon. Single beds and private rooms for low rates. Continental breakfast served. Groups up to 6 persons. Internet, laundry, bike rentals. Open year-round. [ADVERTISEMENT]

A Rabbit Creek B&B. Peaceful & dramatic view. Recognized in Arrington's B&B Journal as "Best in Alaska" and one of the top 15 B&B's in 2003 Book of Lists. 1.5 miles off Seward Hwy on prestigious "Hillside." Bedrooms on separate floors, king beds, private baths, telephone, Internet, refrigerator, TV, VCR. Honeymoon suite. Antiques, Alaskana. Open all year. 4540 Rabbit Creek Rd. Anchorage, AK 99516 (907) 345-0733 www.arabbitcreekbandb.com. [ADVERTISEMENT]

Arctic Fox Bed & Breakfast Inn. 326 E. 2nd Ct., Anchorage, AK 99501. Phone (907) 272-4818, fax 272-4819. Quiet downtown location with some inlet views. Tastefully decorated rooms and suites with moderate summer rates, low winter rates. Near downtown hotels, restaurants, museum, bike trail, train and Ship Creek. Laundry. Private baths, TV and phone in room. [ADVERTISEMENT]

The Aurora Winds Resort. Anchorage's exceptional Bed and Breakfast sits within 2 acres of beautifully landscaped gardens. With over 12,000 square feet of living space this home features 5-suites, with private bath. TV, VCR, phone, data ports, hair dryer, bathrobes

Playing hide-and-seek in front of the Anchorage Museum of History and Art.
(© Carol A. Phillips, staff)

Ask Alaska
Travel & Tours
Reservations and Free Itinerary Planning Service

- Rate Inspect and Guarantee Over 300 Bed & Breakfast and All Our Adventures
- Flightseeing • Glacier Cruises
- Kayaking/Rafting
- Bear Viewing
- City Tours • Bus Tour
- Denali • Dog Sled • Fishing

And So Much More! Talk to Alaskans about Alaska.

**Call Today Toll Free
1-888-655-4723
Local (907) 277-4676
www.see-alaska.com**

24-Hour Hotline to Bed & Breakfasts, Cabins and Lodge Accommodations – Over 300 Properties Throughout Alaska

ANCHORAGE

ACCOMMODATIONS

Alaska Tundra Inn Bed & Breakfast

HOSTED BY: ROY & TINA BRILEY

Enjoy your stay in Anchorage, Alaska at the Tundra Inn Bed & Breakfast. Located in a beautiful neighborhood setting within walking distance to Jewel lake. Also close to the airport, downtown, Mulcahey Stadium and other major area attractions.

- Beautiful 6,000 sq. ft. Alaskan B&B
- Elegant Clean Smoke-free Rooms • Private Deck w/BBQ
- Spacious Rooms w/ Private Baths
- Family & Apartment Suite *(pictured below)* available

For additional information, visit our web site at:
www.alaskatundrainn.com

9431 Emerald St., Anchorage, AK 99502 • (907) 248-7176

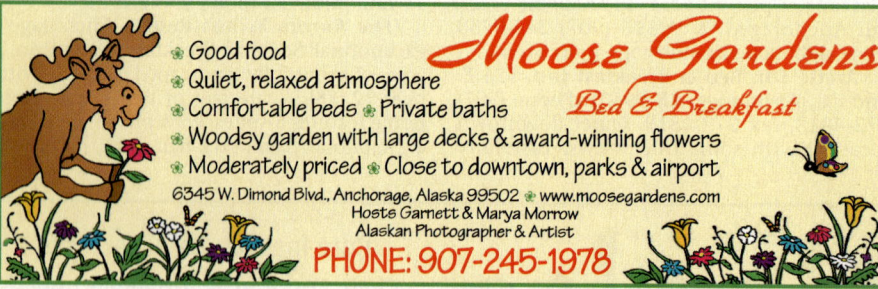

Moose Gardens Bed & Breakfast

- Good food
- Quiet, relaxed atmosphere
- Comfortable beds • Private baths
- Woodsy garden with large decks & award-winning flowers
- Moderately priced • Close to downtown, parks & airport

6345 W. Dimond Blvd., Anchorage, Alaska 99502 • www.moosegardens.com
Hosts Garnett & Marya Morrow
Alaskan Photographer & Artist

PHONE: 907-245-1978

Former Log Cabin Church

All the comforts of home in downtown Anchorage

Call (907) 277-0878
Toll free: 800-353-0878
Fax: (907) 277-8905

Bed & Breakfast On the Park

bedandbreakfastonthepark.com
Charming Rooms • Private Baths • Full Breakfast
For Reservations Call Helen or Stella
602 West 10th Ave. Anchorage, AK 99501

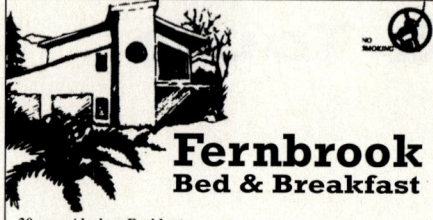

Fernbrook Bed & Breakfast

30 year Alaskan Resident offers friendly accommodation in the Chugach Mountains, minutes from Chugach State Park. Relax, pet an Alaskan Sled Dog, and enjoy sourdough pancakes in this country setting.

★ Reasonable Rates ★

8120 Rabbit Creek Road
Anchorage, Alaska 99516
(907) 345-1954

Best Motel Value in Anchorage . . . spend a night not a fortune!

ALASKA'S TUDOR MOTEL

(907) 561-2234 • Fax (907) 561-8914 • 1-800-550-2234
www.AKTudorMotel.com • info@AkTudorMotel.com

- One bedroom apartments with 380 sq.ft.
- Color TV with Multi-Visions • Direct dial phones
- Full kitchen with utensils • Laundry nearby
- Military and senior citizen discounts
- CONVENIENT TO DOWNTOWN AIRPORTS

4423 Lake Otis Parkway, Anchorage Alaska 99507

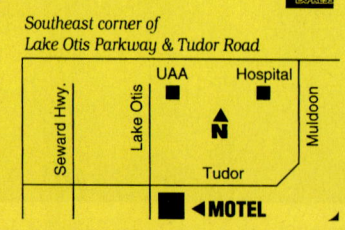

Southeast corner of Lake Otis Parkway & Tudor Road

Anchor Arms Hotel

$49 and up

DOWNTOWN 1 BEDROOM SUITES

- FREE AIRPORT PICKUP - 7 AM TO 10 PM
- FULLY FURNISHED KITCHENS
- COMPLETE 1 & 2 BEDROOMS SUITES
- DAILY / WEEKLY / MONTHLY
- ONSITE LAUNDRY
- ALL CREDIT CARDS ACCEPTED
- OPEN 24 HOURS

Walk to Everything!!

(907) 272-9619
RESERVATIONS

433 EAGLE ST., ANCHORAGE, AK 99501
Price does not include tax.

MERRILL FIELD INN
HOSPITALITY AND CONVENIENCE

420 SITKA STREET • ANCHORAGE, AK 99501
(907) 276-4547 • Fax (907) 276-5064
1-800-898-4547

- 2 RESTAURANTS ON PREMESIS
- KITCHENETTES AVAILABLE
- QUEEN & KING BEDS
- FREE CONTINENTAL BREAKFAST
- FREE AIRPORT SHUTTLE
- COIN-OP LAUNDRY
- HONEYMOON SUITE WITH LARGE JACUZZI

ALL ROOMS HAVE HAIRDRYERS, CABLE TV & HBO, REFRIGERATORS AND MICROWAVE OVENS
AAA APPROVED

Phone 844 for local time and temperature in Anchorage.

Fountains and colorful flowers at the Town Square. (© Carol A. Phillips, staff)

We cover your creature comforts in Anchorage.

The Aspen Hotel in downtown Anchorage is perfect for travelers ready to enjoy the area's urban delights and outdoor sites. Our amenities and stylish, comfortable rooms will make you feel right at home.

- 89 spacious rooms
- Complimentary continental breakfast
- Guest laundry
- Swimming pool, spa and exercise room
- VCR, speaker phone and data port
- Coffee maker, refrigerator, microwave, iron and hair dryer in room
- Family and extended stay suites

108 E. 8TH AVENUE, ANCHORAGE, AK 99501 »
1-866-GUEST4U »
WWW.ASPENHOTELSAK.COM

and all the amenities expected by today's discriminating traveler. Enjoy quiet elegance, contemporary with an Alaskan home-style atmosphere where breakfast is a gourmet delight and the staff strives to satisfy your every need. Be sure to stay long enough to take advantage of the full gym, theater room, billiard room, library, 10-person outdoor hot tub or the indoor pool. Our recommendation for Anchorage's best B&B, the Aurora Winds Resort. For reservations call (907) 346-2533, e-mail: awbnb@alaska.net web site www.aurorawinds.com. [ADVERTISEMENT]

Caribou Inn. 501 L Street, Anchorage, AK 99501. Clean, comfortable rooms in an excellent downtown Anchorage location. Shared or private bath, some with kitchenettes. Major credit cards accepted. Free shuttle to airport and train station. (907) 272-0444 or fax (907) 274-4828. Toll free (800) 272-5878. Email: caribou@alaska.net. Web site: http://www.alaska.net/~caribou. [ADVERTISEMENT]

The New Puffin Inn. Grand opening! Showcasing the New Puffin Inn is a spectacular semi-circular lobby with slate floors, picturesque windows and a warm fireplace. There is something for everyone. You can choose from economy, moderate and deluxe rooms. Our friendly Alaskan hospitality includes coffee, tea, muffins and a newspaper daily. Courtesy 24-hour airport shuttle; freezer space for fish and game; fitness room; business center; and much more. Handicap accessible. 4400 Spenard Rd., Anchorage, AK, 99517. Phone (907) 243-4044. Fax (907) 248-6853. (800) 4-PUFFIN; www.puffininn.net. [ADVERTISEMENT]

Puffin Place Studios & Suites. Relax and enjoy 1 of our 38 attractively furnished studios and 1-bedroom suites featuring fully equipped kitchens with microwaves. Within walking distance of restaurants, shopping and Tony Knowles Coastal Trail. Our amenities include: courtesy airport shuttle, nonsmoking rooms, laundry facility, freezer space, cable TV. Weekly and monthly rates offered October–May. 1058 W. 27th, Anchorage, AK 99503, (907) 279-1058. Fax (907) 257-9595. (800) 71-PLACE; www.puffininn.net. [ADVERTISEMENT]

The Teddy Bear House Bed & Breakfast. Experience a traditional home stay in our uniquely decorated home in a quiet south Anchorage neighborhood, 15 minutes from airport and downtown. Close to Anchorage Zoo and shopping. Twin or queen beds. Private and shared bath. Continental or traditional breakfast. Large deck for your relaxation. Open year-round. No smoking. P.O. Box 190265, Anchorage, AK 99519; (907) 344-3111, email: tbearbb@alaska.net; www.teddybearbnb.com. [ADVERTISEMENT]

Mail Boxes Etc. Let the experts at Mail Boxes Etc. pack and ship your "Alaskan catch" frozen fish and other great souvenirs. And while you're here check your email, purchase stamps, mail postcards and look around at the many other services we provide. At Mail Boxes Etc. "We'll take it from here." [ADVERTISEMENT]

Camping

Anchorage has several private campgrounds; see ads this section.

Anchorage has 2 public campgrounds: Centennial Park, open from May through September, and Lions Camper Park, open July and part of August on an as-needed basis. Fees are $13 for non-Alaskans and $11 for Alaska residents. To reach Centennial Park, take the Muldoon Road exit south off the Glenn Highway, take the first left onto Boundary, take the next left and follow the signs. Lions Camper Park is located at 5800 Boniface Parkway, half a mile south of the Glenn Highway. Centennial, recommended for large RVs, has 90 RV sites and 40 tent sites. Lions has 50 gravel tent sites. Both feature barracks-type showers, flush toilets, pay phones, water and dump stations and no hookups. Between May and September, phone (907) 333-9711 for details on either park. In the off-season, phone (907) 343-6397.

Chugach State Park has campgrounds located near Anchorage at Bird Creek (Seward Highway), and at Eagle River and Eklutna Lake (Glenn Highway). Nightly fees range from $5 to $15, or residents may purchase a $100 annual camping pass.

There are also many public lands campgrounds around the Anchorage area and throughout the state. These campgrounds are maintained by the U.S. Forest Service, U.S. Fish & Wildlife Service, BLM and the

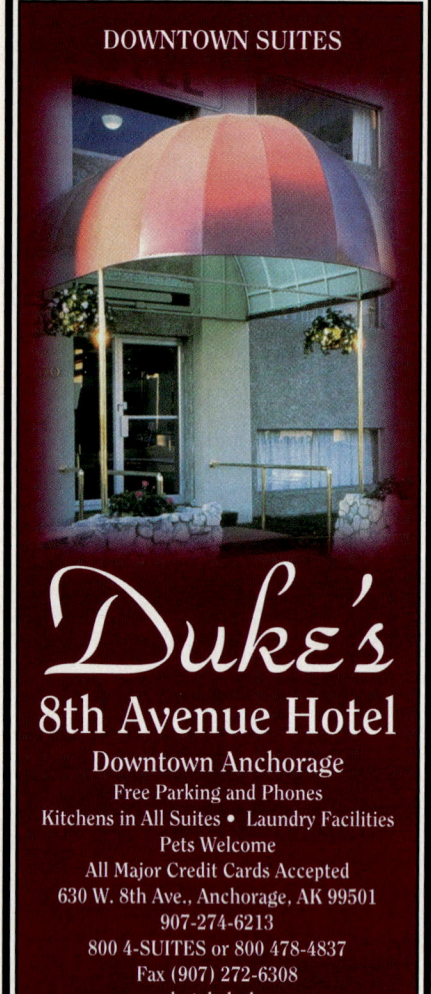

Walkabout Town Bed & Breakfast
Anchorage Downtown Convenience
(907) 279-7808 • *Free Bicycles*
e-mail: tstimson@compuserve.com
website: www.travelguides.com/bb/walkabout/

JOHN'S MOTEL
3543 Mountain View Drive
Anchorage, Alaska 99508
907-277-4332
800-478-4332
• Single • Doubles • Kitchenettes
Affordable Rates
Daily & Weekly
• Combination Tub and Showers
• Individual Heat Control
• Cable TV
• Headbolt Heater Plug-Ins
• FREE LOCAL CALLS
NON SMOKING ROOMS AVAILABLE
www.johnsmotel.com

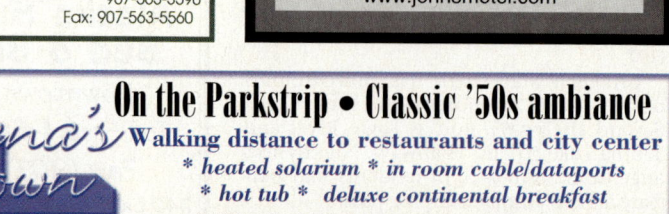

Sunset is at 11:43 P.M. on June 21, 2003 (summer solstice) in Anchorage.

National Park Service. A map of these campgrounds is available from the Alaska Public Lands Information Center; phone (907) 271-2737.

Chugach National Forest offers 42 public recreation cabins in the Kenai Peninsula and Prince William Sound area. The cabins are located along trails, lakes, streams and saltwater beaches and are accessible by plane, boat, trail or road. Fees range from $25 to $45 per night. For reservations, call 1-877-444-6777, or visit www.reserveusa.com.

Anchorage RV Park. Experience Alaska's premier RV park located in a secluded wooded setting just 10 minutes from downtown Anchorage and just across from the new Alaska Native Heritage Center. Fully equipped with all the essentials plus much more including: cable TV connections, laundry, showers, and work station with modem port in our comfortable main lodge. The park has 195 spaces with 78 pull-throughs and access to a network of bike trails. Open mid-May through mid-Sept. Enjoy Alaska's premier RV park. Call today for reservations 800-400-7275 or (907) 338-7275. GPS: N61° 13.81' W149° 44.46'. 1200 N. Muldoon Rd., Anchorage, AK 99506. See display ad this section. [ADVERTISEMENT]

Transportation

Air: More than 20 international and domestic air carriers and numerous intrastate airlines serve Ted Stevens Anchorage International Airport, located 6 miles from downtown. More than 255 flights arrive daily.

Ferry: The nearest ferry port to Anchorage is Whittier on Prince William Sound, served by Alaska state ferry from Cordova and Valdez. Whittier is accessible from Anchorage via the Seward Highway and Whittier Access Road. See the Southcentral/Southwest Alaska–M/V *Bartlett* Schedule in the ALASKA STATE FERRY SCHEDULES section.

Railroad: The Alaska Railroad offers daily passenger service in summer from Anchorage to Seward and to Fairbanks via Denali National Park. Reduced service in winter. Summer passenger service is also available between Anchorage and Whittier, with optional connections to Prince William Sound cruises. Contact Passenger Services Dept., Box 107500, Anchorage 99510-7500; phone (800) 544-0552 or (907) 265-2494, fax 265-2323; www.alaskarailroad.com or www.akrr.com.

The **Alaska Railroad Depot** is located on 1st Avenue, within easy walking distance of downtown.

Bus: Local service via People Mover, serving most of the Anchorage bowl from Peters Creek to Oceanview. Fares are $1.25 for adults, 75¢ for youth 5 to 18, 25¢ for senior citizens and disabled citizens with transit identification. Monthly passes are sold at the Transit Center (6th Avenue and H Street), the Dimond Transit Center, municipal libraries and Cook Inlet Book Co. on 5th Ave. downtown; monthly adult commuter pass $36. Day passes are also available for $2.50 for day of purchase only at the Transit Center, Dimond Transit Center and Tesoro 2 Go stores. For bus route information, phone the Rideline at (907) 343-6543.

The municipality also provides Share-A-Ride carpool and vanpool service, AnchorRIDES for senior citizens and people with disabilities and the Ship Creek Shuttle. For more information, visit www.muni.org/transit1/index.cfm.

Taxi: There are 4 major taxi companies, as well as various shuttle services. Consult the yellow pages under Taxicabs.

Car and Camper Rentals: There are dozens of car rental agencies located at the airport and downtown, as well as several RV rental agencies (see advertisements this section).

RV Parking: The Anchorage Parking Authority offers a lot with spaces for oversized vehicles (motorcoaches, campers, large trucks) at 3rd Avenue, north of the Holiday Inn, between A and C streets. Parking is $5 per space, per day. For more information, phone (907) 276-PARK or (800) 770-ACAR.

Highway: Anchorage can be reached via the Glenn Highway and the Seward Highway. See GLENN HIGHWAY and SEWARD HIGHWAY sections for details.

Attractions

(See also Downtown section beginning on page 330.)

Sea Services Veterans Memorial Park, at the mouth of Ship Creek, is a good place to see the Anchorage waterfront, with its huge cargo cranes off-loading supplies from container ships. The park is dedicated to veterans of the Navy, Marine Corps, Coast Guard and Merchant Marine. The monument consists of a huge anchor and chain weighing 22,500 pounds upon a raised mound. Inscription reads: "This anchor presented to the Municipality of Anchorage by the USS *Anchorage* (LSD36) on June 10, 1992, is a place in memory of Jeremiah Cornelius 'Jerry' Harrington, Damage Control, Master Chief US Navy, retired. A shipmate to all and a dedicated force in the Anchorage community." The park also offers good whale watching when belugas are in the inlet. From downtown, take E Street and West 2nd down the hill to merge with North C Street. Continue across the second set of railroad tracks and turn left. The access road follows Ship Creek out to the small-boat dry dock harbor and the park.

Enjoy the Parks: Anchorage is rich in parks, and the parks are rich in the range of activities they offer. More than 200 designated parks and 10 large reserves have something for everyone's taste, from small "pocket parks" perfect for relaxing or picnicking to vast tracts set aside for skiing,

(Continues on page 335)

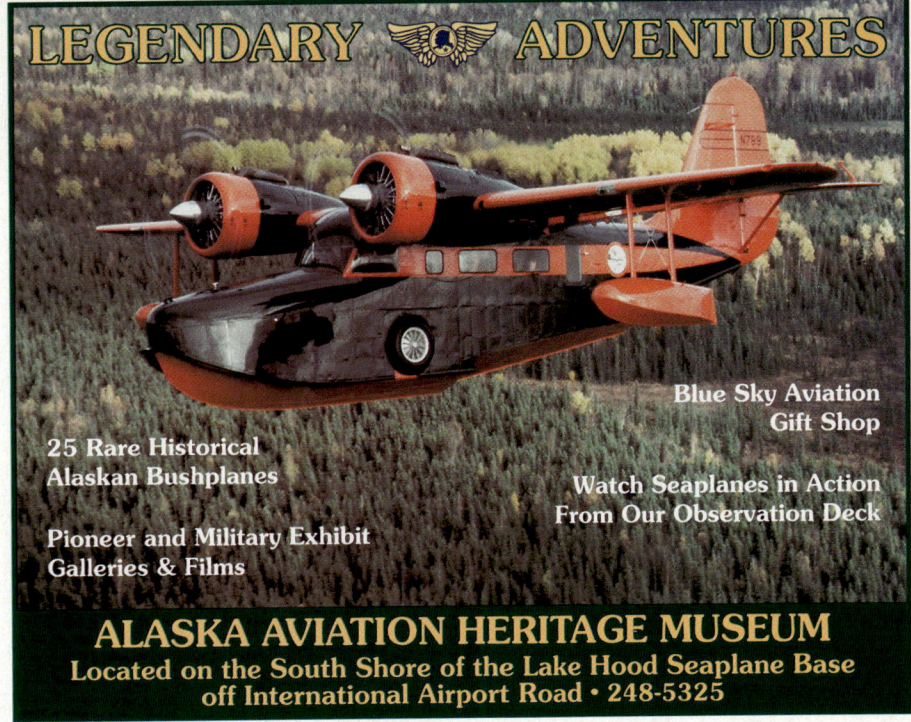

LEGENDARY ADVENTURES

- 25 Rare Historical Alaskan Bushplanes
- Pioneer and Military Exhibit Galleries & Films
- Blue Sky Aviation Gift Shop
- Watch Seaplanes in Action From Our Observation Deck

ALASKA AVIATION HERITAGE MUSEUM
Located on the South Shore of the Lake Hood Seaplane Base off International Airport Road • 248-5325

Come to the Garden

Alaska Botanical Garden

Visit the Perennial Flower Gardens, Herb Garden, Rock Garden, and the Native Wildflower Walk. Experience the "Wilds of Alaska" on the self-guided, 1.1 mile, Lowenfels Family Nature Trail in the foothills of the Chugach Mountains.

Many events throughout the summer
Call 907-770-3692 for more information
Open daily 9 a.m. to 9 p.m.
Suggested Donation $5 Individual • $10 Family
Free Parking

Tudor Road East (toward the mountains)
Right at Campbell Airstrip Road
Left at ABG sign, park at the school

Alaska Botanical Garden P.O. Box 202202 Anchorage, Alaska 99520

Sunrise is at 4:20 A.M. on June 21, 2003 (summer solstice) in Anchorage.

ALASKA NATIVE HERITAGE CENTER

800.315.6608
907.330.8000

8800 Heritage Center Drive
*Ten minutes from downtown Anchorage.
Shuttle available.*

Come face-to-face with Alaska's first people.

Anchorage's Premier Cultural Experience

- INTERPRETIVE EXHIBITS
- DANCE PERFORMANCES
- STORYTELLERS
- FILM PRESENTATIONS
- DEMONSTRATING ARTISANS
- FIVE LAKESIDE VILLAGE SITES

www.alaskanative.net

downtown ANCHORAGE

Downtown Advertisers

1. Anchorage Convention & Visitors Bureau
2. Anchorage Museum of History & Art
3. Alaska State Troopers Museum
4. Alaska Mint
5. David Green Master Furrier
6. Downtown Saturday Market
7. Cook Inlet Book Company
8. Oomingmak, Musk Ox Producers
9. Stewart's Photo Shop
10. The Ulu Factory
11. Adam Glazer Wild Furs

The best way to begin your exploration of downtown Anchorage is with a stop at the **Log Cabin Visitor Information Center**, located on 4th Avenue and F Street. The Anchorage Convention & Visitors Bureau's *Anchorage Visitors Guide* suggests an excellent downtown walking tour. The visitor center is open 7:30 A.M. to 7 P.M. June through August; 8 A.M. to 6 P.M. in May and September; and 9 A.M. to 4 P.M. the remainder of the year; phone (907) 274-3531; web site www.anchorage.net.

Following are attractions and shopping opportunities found in the downtown area. (For more attractions and shopping in Anchorage, see the Attractions starting on page 329.)

Downtown Anchorage parks include **Delaney Park Strip**, from A to P streets between 9th and 10th avenues, which has ball fields, tennis courts and **Engine No. 556** at 9th and E Street, a real locomotive for children to explore. **Elderberry Park**, at the foot of 5th Avenue, faces Knik Arm. And **Resolution Park**, at 3rd Avenue and L Street (no vehicle access to this park), where the statue of Capt. James Cook overlooks Knik Arm of the inlet which bears his name. The statue was dedicated in 1976 as a bicentennial project.

The city park at 4th Avenue and E Street hosts a **Music in the Park** series in summer. The concerts, featuring local groups playing everything from jazz to country, are scheduled at least once weekly during the afternoons. Check locally for a current schedule. Next door to the park is the **Historic City Hall**, which now houses the corporate offices of the Anchorage Convention & Visitors Bureau.

Alaska Statehood Monument. Located at the corner of 2nd Avenue and E Street (just a block down from the Hilton), a plaque and bronze bust of President Eisenhower commemorates the Alaska Statehood Act making Alaska the 49th state on January 3, 1959.

Enjoy the Flowers. Numerous hanging baskets transform the core area of downtown Anchorage, and thematic arrangements highlight the well-maintained flower beds lining the city's walkways. The Centennial Rose Garden is the centerpiece of the Delaney Park Strip at 9th and N streets, and the downtown area at the **Town Square** municipal park, located between 5th and 6th avenues along E Street, next door to the **Performing Arts Center**, offers the city's most spectacular flower displays in summer.

Across E Street from Town Square on the west wall of the J.C. Penney store is the **"Whaling Wall,"** a 400-foot-long airbrushed mural of beluga whales, bowhead whales and seals by artist Wyland.

Located at the west end of 5th Avenue, at 420 M Street, in the north corner of Elderberry Park, is the **Oscar Anderson House Museum**, one of the city's first wood-frame houses. Built in 1915, it was home to Oscar Anderson, a Swedish immigrant and early Anchorage pioneer and businessman. Now on the National Register of Historic Places, it has been beautifully restored and is well worth a visit. Open mid-May through mid-September for guided tours. Hours are 11 A.M. to 4 P.M., Tuesday through Saturday. Swedish Christmas tours, first 2 weekends in December. Adults, $3; seniors, $2; children 5 to 12, $1. Group tours (maximum 10 participants per group) must be arranged in advance. Phone (907) 274-2336 or 274-3600; fax (907) 274-3610; www.themilepost.com

Adam Glazer
WILD FURS LTD.
"From Head To Toe We've Got You Covered"

FUR & LEATHER
Coats • Jackets • Hats
Largest Selection of Fur Boots In Alaska

277-9453

"Anchorage's Most Recommended Furrier"   411 WEST 4TH AVE. (SUNSHINE PLAZA)

FREE Admission & FREE Entertainment!
- Fresh Alaskan Produce & Fish
- Wide Variety of Food to eat on site
- Alaska Made Gifts Clothing, Souvenirs and MUCH MORE!

for information call **907-272-5634**
www.anchoragemarkets.com

Northway Mall Wednesday Market
June 11th thru August 20th
3101 Penland ParkWay

Downtown Saturday Market
May 17th thru Sept. 13th
3rd Ave. Between C & E St.

CREATURE
(bear, moose, fish, eagles, whales)

COMFORTS
(hotels, restaurants, shopping, tours)

Come to **Anchorage** & experience it ALL!

anchorage.net
ANCHORAGE CONVENTION & VISITORS BUREAU

Alaska became the 49th state on Jan. 3, 1959, under Pres. Dwight D. Eisenhower.

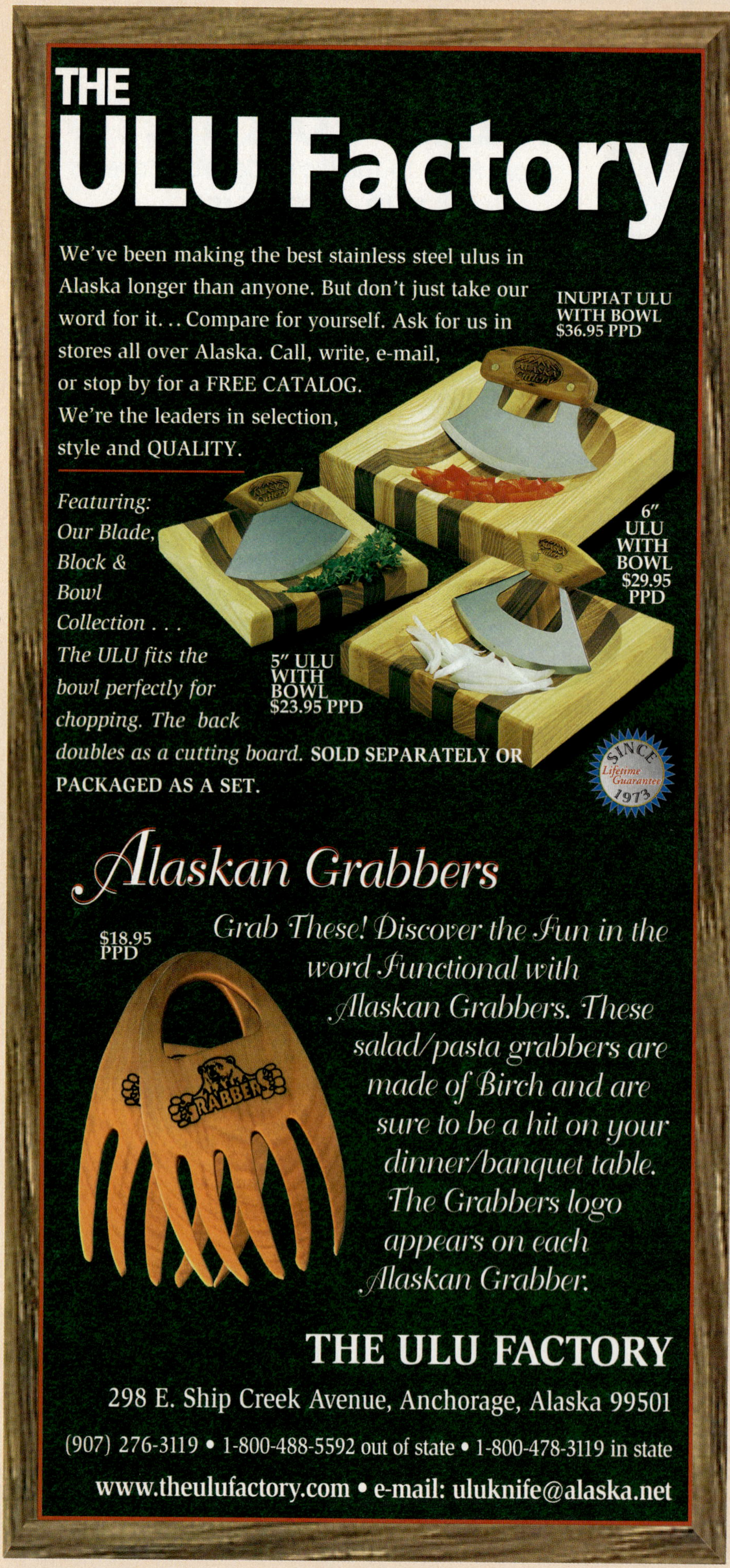
THE
ULU Factory
We've been making the best stainless steel ulus in Alaska longer than anyone. But don't just take our word for it... Compare for yourself. Ask for us in stores all over Alaska. Call, write, e-mail, or stop by for a FREE CATALOG. We're the leaders in selection, style and QUALITY.
INUPIAT ULU WITH BOWL $36.95 PPD
6" ULU WITH BOWL $29.95 PPD
5" ULU WITH BOWL $23.95 PPD
Featuring: Our Blade, Block & Bowl Collection . . . The ULU fits the bowl perfectly for chopping. The back doubles as a cutting board. SOLD SEPARATELY OR PACKAGED AS A SET.
SINCE Lifetime Guarantee 1973
Alaskan Grabbers
$18.95 PPD
Grab These! Discover the Fun in the word Functional with Alaskan Grabbers. These salad/pasta grabbers are made of Birch and are sure to be a hit on your dinner/banquet table. The Grabbers logo appears on each Alaskan Grabber.
GRABBER
THE ULU FACTORY
298 E. Ship Creek Avenue, Anchorage, Alaska 99501
(907) 276-3119 • 1-800-488-5592 out of state • 1-800-478-3119 in state
www.theulufactory.com • e-mail: uluknife@alaska.net

www.anchoragehistoricproperties.org.

Exercise Your Imagination: Visit The Imaginarium Science Discovery Center, 737 W. 5th Ave., Suite G (across from the Westmark Hotel, use Glacier Brewhouse entrance), a hands-on science discovery center offering unique insights into the wonders of nature, science and technology. The Imaginarium offers hourly demonstrations, interactive displays and exhibits (live marine touch tanks, giant bubble lab, arctic ecology, reptiles and insects, planetarium and others) and special events. Open daily year-round Monday through Saturday 10 A.M. to 6 P.M., Sunday noon to 5 P.M., closed on major holidays. Adults, $5; seniors, $4.50; children 2 to 12, $4.50. Wheelchair accessible. Phone (907) 276-3179; email info@imaginarium.org; www.imaginarium.org. ♿

The Alaska Public Lands Information Center, located in the historic Old Federal Building on 4th Avenue and F Street, offers a wide variety of exhibits, movies, special programs and information on all of Alaska's state and federal parks, forests and wildlife refuges. Natural history exhibits, cultural exhibits, a GIS computer and self-help trip-planning area provide an enjoyable way to obtain knowledge and information necessary for a safe and exhilarating Alaskan adventure whether you are a cruise passenger or an avid hiker. Expert staff provide additional assistance and supply maps, brochures and other aids. Federal passports (Golden Age, Eagle and National Park Pass) and state park passes are available. Rangers, authors and experts present programs at 2 A.M. daily. Live animal demonstrations occur every Thursday and Saturday at 2 P.M. in the

Cook Inlet Book Company
Alaska's Premier Bookstore
WORLD'S LARGEST SELECTION OF BOOKS ON ALASKA.
GOLD RUSH WOMEN
A CHILD'S ALASKA
ALASKA'S WILDLIFE
AURORA
A Tale of the Northern Lights
Baked Alaska
We offer you the best variety of books and magazines from around the world.
We're open 7 days a week.
258-4544 • 1-800-240-4148
www.cookinlet.com • info@cookinlet.com
415 WEST 5TH AVENUE • ANCHORAGE
LOCATED IN DOWNTOWN ANCHORAGE ACROSS FROM JC PENNEY

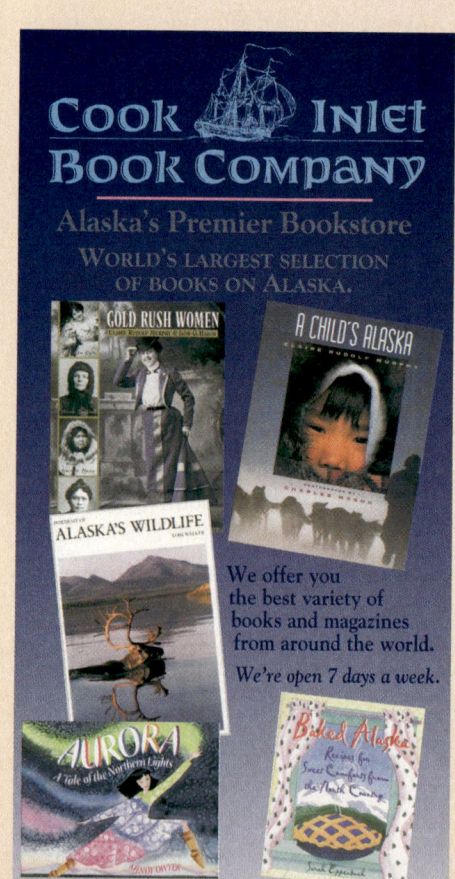

summer. Call for current schedule. Museum scavenger hunts are a popular activity enjoyed by young and old alike. The center is open year-round. Summer hours (Memorial Day to Labor Day) are 9 A.M. to 6 P.M. daily; winter hours are 10 A.M. to 6 P.M. Monday through Friday; closed weekends and holidays. Hours may change; please call for changes. Phone (907) 271-2737, write the center at 605 W. 4th Ave., Suite 105, Anchorage, AK 99501, or visit the web at www.nps.gov/aplic for more information.

Laura Wright Alaskan Parkys. Known worldwide for beautiful Eskimo-style summer and winter parkas. Off the rack or custom-made. Started by Laura Wright in Fairbanks in 1947; continuing the tradition is granddaughter Sheila Ezelle. Purchase "Wearable Alaskan Art" at: Moose Hollow, 720 D St. Suite A, Anchorage, AK 99501 and Alaska Native Heritage Center, Anchorage. Phone (907) 274-4215. Mail and phone orders accepted. We airmail worldwide; www.alaskan.com/parkys. [ADVERTISEMENT]

Oomingmak, Musk Ox Producers' Co-operative, is a Native-owned co-operative specializing in knitted masterpieces. Using

Qiviut, the soft and rare fiber from the arctic Musk Oxen, our 250 Native Alaskan knitters create hats and scarves in a variety of traditional patterns from their culture. Since 1969, this co-operative organization has provided the opportunity for Native women to earn a supplementary income while still pursuing their subsistence lifestyle. For over 25 years, the exquisite items the co-op members make on their knitting needles have been worn with pride and enjoyment by satisfied customers from around the world. We invite you to visit us in downtown Anchorage at the little brown house with the Musk Ox mural on the corner of 6th and H streets. (907) 272-9225, 604 H Street, Anchorage, AK 99501. [ADVERTISEMENT]

The Anchorage Museum of History and

DAVID GREEN
Alaska's Master Furrier
"If you don't know furs, know your furrier"

Visit us and explore the warmth and beauty of natural fur from Alaska's premier furrier, David Green. Since 1922.

Factory Direct Prices. Whether you visit our store or shop by mail, you'll enjoy the largest selection, complete service, and of course…factory direct prices which make David Green Furs an excellent value.

www.davidgreenfurs.com

Alaska's Most Recommended Furrier (907) 277-9595 130 West 4th Avenue (Between 'A' and 'B' Streets)

STEWART'S PHOTO SHOP
ACROSS FROM THE TOURIST LOG CABIN
531 West Fourth Ave. • Anchorage • Phone 272-8581
ALASKA'S LARGEST PHOTO SHOP   Open 9-9 Mon.-Sat., 10-6 Sun.
Photograph our live reindeer!
Over 60 years' collection of Alaska color slides, movies, photos, and postcards.
Alaskan jade for sale by the pound or ton!

Alaska State Trooper Museum

245 W. 5th Avenue
Anchorage, Alaska

907-344-5673   800-770-5050

Please support our MILEPOST® advertisers.

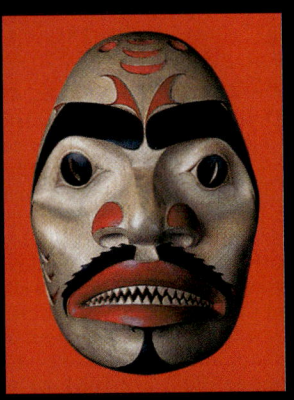

Experience Alaska's cultural treasures

One of the 10 most visited attractions in Alaska, there's no better way to fully appreciate Alaska's history, art and culture. Explore 10,000 years of history in the Alaska Gallery, an entire floor devoted to Alaska's history and cultures.

Anchorage Museum
OF HISTORY AND ART

Downtown Anchorage, Corner of 7th and A
907.343.4326
www.anchoragemuseum.org

Tour Alaska Mint

The Official Mint for:
- State of Alaska
- Iditarod
- Alaska Railroad and more...

Largest selection of Natural Gold Nugget and Gold-n-Quartz Jewelry

Downtown Anchorage
Corner of 4th & E
429 W. 4th Ave.
Anchorage, Alaska 99501
800.770.6468
www.alaskamint.com

Relaxing on a bench near the dam at Ship Creek Salmon viewing area.
(© Kris Graef, staff)

Art, located at 121 W. 7th Ave., is a must stop. One of the most visited attractions in Anchorage, this world-class museum features permanent displays of Alaska's cultural heritage and artifacts from its history.

The 15,000-square-foot Alaska Gallery on the second floor is the museum's showcase, presenting Alaska Native cultures—Aleut, Eskimo and Indian—and displays about the Russians, New England whalers, the gold rush, WWII, statehood and Alaska today. Displays include full-scale dwellings and detailed miniature dioramas. The gallery contains some 300 photographs, more than 1,000 artifacts, 33 maps, and specially made ship and aircraft models.

The main floor of the museum consists of 6 connecting galleries displaying Alaska art, such as works by Sydney Laurence. Also on the 1st floor are a Children's Gallery and 3 temporary exhibition galleries. The museum has a reference library and archives, a free film series and public tours (daily in summer). The Museum Shop features art, crafts, jewelry, books and other items inspired by the museum's collection, and the cafe in the atrium serves lunch and snacks by the reflective pool.

Admission is $6.50 for adults, $6 for seniors, under 18 free. Open 9 A.M. to 6 P.M. daily in summer. Mid-September to mid-May, open 10 A.M. to 6 P.M. Tuesday through Saturday, and 1–5 P.M. Sunday (closed Mondays and on Thanksgiving, Christmas and New Year's Day). Phone (907) 343-6173 for recorded information about special shows, or (907) 343-4326 during business hours for more information. www.anchoragemuseum.org. The museum is wheelchair accessible.

Ship Creek Salmon Viewing. From downtown, either walk down the hill from the Hilton towards the train station, or stroll down Christensen Street (with its fish fence and fine views of the inlet) past the train station, to reach Ship Creek. Visitors can watch the salmon—as well as the fishermen—from spots along either bank, from the viewing platform or from the dam. Watch for kings from early June until mid-July, silvers in August.

Alaska State Troopers Museum. This unique little museum presents the history of law enforcement in the Territory and State of Alaska, with displays of photos and exhibits of historic police equipment. Gifts and memorabilia are available. Admission free. Hours are 10 A.M. to 5 P.M. weekdays and noon to 4 P.M. Saturdays. 6th Avenue near C Street. Phone (907) 279-5050; email foast@alaska.net; www.alaska.net/~foast.

4th Avenue Theatre. Built in 1947 by Alaska millionaire "Cap" Lathrop, this Anchorage landmark has been refurbished and now includes a gift shop, city trolley tours, cafe, museum exhibit and special events center. Much of the original art-deco design has been preserved, and the trademarks of the theater have been restored, including the bas-relief gold leaf murals and the ceiling lights marking the Big Dipper. There is no admission fee to the theater. The 4th Avenue Theatre is located a half block from the visitor center. Open year-round 8 A.M.–10 P.M. summers, 10 A.M.–6 P.M. Tuesdays to Saturdays winters. For more information phone (907) 257-5635.

Visit the Downtown Saturday Market. This popular outdoor market operates each Saturday May 17 through September 13, 10 A.M. to 6 P.M. The festivities are held in the parking lot at 3rd Avenue between C and E streets. There is no admission fee. More than 300 booths sell a variety of Alaska-made and Alaska-grown products as well as handmade and imported home and novelty items of all types. Local entertainment and community groups add to the fun. For more information phone (907) 272-5634, or visit www.anchoragemarkets.com.

See an Old Schoolhouse: The Pioneer Schoolhouse at 3rd Avenue and Eagle Street is a 2-story memorial to the late Ben Crawford, an Anchorage banker. This was the first school in Anchorage. The interior is not open to the public.

(Continued from page 329)

hiking and bicycling. Many municipal parks are ideal for family picnics and outings. To make group reservations to use municipal park picnic facilities, phone (907) 343-4474. Parks & Recreation publishes a complete listing of all parks and trails, available for $2. Also see the Municipality's web site at www.ci.anchorage.ak.us or www.muni.org.

It is not unusual to run into a moose or see a bear at 1,400-acre **Kincaid Park**. Located southwest of the airport, this park's rugged trails are popular with mountain bikers and runners in summer and cross-country skiers in winter. Kincaid was picked by "Runners World" magazine as one of the country's top 50 running trails. To reach Kincaid, follow Raspberry Road west from Minnesota Drive to the park entrance. The park road winds uphill (past trailheads) to end at a large parking area in front of the park's chalet, which houses an information desk, tables, restrooms and vending machines. Kincaid is accessible via the Tony Knowles Coastal Trail (see description under "Tour Anchorage by Bicycle").

The best park pick for bikers and joggers looking for a pleasant ride or run through the trees is **Chester Creek Greenbelt**, which stretches from Westchester Lagoon, at 15th Avenue and U Street, to Russian Jack Springs Park. The 6.5-mile trail traverses the heart of Anchorage, following Chester Creek past Goose Lake, a favorite summer swimming beach (accessible from E. Northern Lights Blvd.) to Westchester Lagoon. The greenbelt has a paved bike trail that runs its length, passing through several small parks along the way. The greenbelt's bike trail is accessible from all of these parks, including Tikishla (in the Airport Heights area), Valley of the Moon Park (from Arctic Blvd./E Street) and Westchester Lagoon, where the Lanie Fleischer Chester Creek bike trail junctions with the Coastal bike trail. (Street access to Westchester Lagoon from midtown Anchorage is via Spenard Road; from downtown Anchorage take L Street and exit west at 15th.)

Campbell Creek Greenbelt also has a paved trail system and begins at Dimond Boulevard between Minnesota Drive and Jewel Lake Road and continues along Campbell Creek to the Old Seward Highway and International Airport Road.

The best park for parents with children looking for a playground to keep them entertained is **Valley of the Moon Park**, located on Arctic Blvd./E Street in the Chester Creek Greenbelt. This park also has plenty of parking, restrooms, a large grassy area and picnic tables.

The best park views of Cook Inlet (Knik Arm) and the Alaska Range are at Earthquake Park and Point Woronzof. From the New Seward Highway, drive west (towards the water) on Northern Lights Blvd. for 3.5 miles to reach **Earthquake Park**. Set aside to commemorate the 1964 Good Friday Earthquake, evidence of the 9.2 earthquake has been obscured by time. But Earthquake Park offers great views, as well as interpretive displays about the quake. A paved path leads from the parking lot to the earthquake exhibit and Knik Arm overlook; picnic tables, benches, interpretive sign.

Continue driving west on Northern Lights Blvd., which becomes Point Woronzof Road at Postmark Drive. (Postmark Drive leads 1-mile south to Anchorage's 24-hour airport post office). A gravel parking area near this intersection also offers good inlet views. Follow Point Woronzof Road 1 mile to **Point Woronzof**. (A gate and security checkpoint are located near the intersection.) This park offers fine views of the inlet and mountains from the parking lot. Point Woronzof can also be reached via the Tony Knowles Coastal Trail (see description under "Tour Anchorage by Bicycle" following).

Tour Anchorage by Bicycle: The municipality has about 120 miles of paved bike trails (including trails in Eagle River and Girdwood) paralleling many major traffic arteries and passing through some of the city's beautiful greenbelt areas. Maps of the trail system are available at Anchorage Parks & Recreation, 120 South Bragaw St. Bicycle rentals are available locally.

Offering an especially unique experience is the 11-mile **Tony Knowles Coastal Trail**, which begins at the west end of 2nd Avenue and Christensen Drive, and follows the coast around Point Woronzof to Point Campbell and Kincaid Park. This is one of the most popular trails in the city with bicyclists, joggers and walkers, who are treated to close-up views of area wildlife, Knik Arm (watch for beluga whales) and on clear days a beautiful view of the Alaska Range. The trail is open year-round and is groomed for cross-country skiing in the winter.

The Knitting Frenzy Store. Best source for yarn, fiber, books, patterns, supplies for use in knitting, crochet, tatting, cross stitch and needlepoint. Largest Alaskan inventory. Choose a project for the road! Open Monday through Saturday 10-6. Day phone (907) 563-2717 or toll free (800) 478-8322. 4240 Old Seward Hwy. #18, corner of Old Seward and Tudor. Fax (907) 563-1081. Email: frenzy@alaska.net. [ADVERTISEMENT]

Z.J. Loussac Public Library, located at 36th Avenue and Denali Street (3600 Denali St.), is headquarters for the Anchorage library system. Its unique architecture also makes it a local landmark. The library hosts various events throughout the year, from brown bag slide shows to summer reading

Lunch hour crowds enjoy summer concerts in the park at 4th and E streets.
(© Lynn Owen, staff)

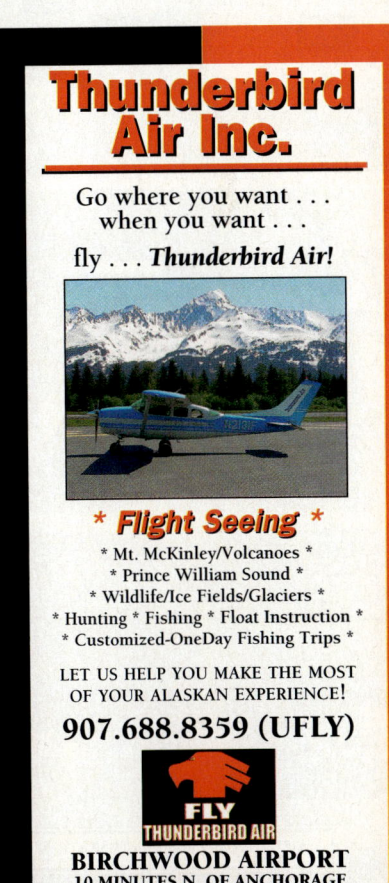

ANCHORAGE

programs for kids. The Loussac also has an extensive collection of books related to Alaska. For information and hours of operation, phone (907) 343-2975.

Visit the Alaska Native Heritage Center: Located just 10 minutes east of downtown, the Heritage Center allows visitors the opportunity to view all of Alaska's Native cultures in one facility. Located on 26 wooded acres on Heritage Center Drive (take the Muldoon Road exit off the Glenn Highway), the center includes the 26,000-square-foot Welcome House, 5 traditional village settings, a 2-acre lake and walking trails.

Many of the programs and exhibits celebrating Alaska Native culture take place indoors in the Welcome House. A 95-seat theater offers a film introduction to Native history and culture. Native dancers, singers and storytellers perform on the Gathering Place stage. In the Hall of Cultures, visitors can see Native artists at work; listen to audiotapes of Natives speaking in their own languages; and read first-person accounts of tanning a moose hide, subsistence fishing and other aspects of Native life. Heritage Gifts provides an outlet for Native arts and crafts.

An outdoor walk around Tiulana Lake takes visitors to 5 different habitats, each representing one of Alaska's 5 Native cultures: Athabascan, Yup'ik, Inupiaq, Aleut/Alutiiq and Tlingit/Haida/Eyak/Tsimshian. Demonstrations of traditional techniques for fishing, hunting, building kayaks and constructing dwellings take place in summer.

Heritage Center hours are from 9 A.M. to 6 P.M. daily mid-May through September; noon to 5 P.M. Saturdays only in winter. Summer rates: adults, $20.95; children (7-16), $15.95; seniors (62 or older), $18.90. Phone (907) 330-8000; toll free 1-800-315-6608; www.alaskanative.net.

Other Native art displays and gift shops are located at the Alaska Native Medical Center and the Anchorage Museum of History and Art.

Stroll through Alaska Botanical Garden. The garden is located off Campbell Airstrip Road across from the Benny Benson School in East Anchorage. (Go east—towards the mountains—on Tudor Road 3.2 miles; turn right on Campbell Airstrip Road; go 0.2 mile then turn left into Benny Benson School; garden entrance is adjacent school.) The garden is a total of 110 acres, but only 10 acres are used for the beds and nursery. The Alaska Botanical Garden showcases perennials hardy to southcentral Alaska (including a blue poppy) in 21 large display gardens. There is also an herb garden. Interpretive signs guide visitors and identify plants. Paths provide easy walking through a native spruce and birch forest with wildflowers adding seasonal interest. A 1.1-mile nature trail offers views of Campbell Creek, the Chugach Mountains and a natural wetland. Many of the garden beds and trails are maintained by volunteers. Open daily, year-round, 9 A.M. to 9 P.M. Call for recorded information on hours, special events and guided tours; phone (907) 770-3692; email garden@alaskabg.org; www.alaskabg.org. Free parking. Admission by donation.

See Alaska Wildlife: Fort Richardson Alaskan Fish and Wildlife Center has been closed for extensive renovation, and its reopening date is indefinite. The operator at

RENT ALASKA'S LEADER

Rest Assured. Whether you are renting, or driving your own R.V. to Alaska, you can rely on Alaska Panorama in Anchorage. We've been renting motorhomes for perfect Alaskan vacations since 1981. Let us help make yours unforgettable! We offer late model, completely self-contained motorhomes of all sizes, free pickup from the airport or your hotel, and everything you need to know about motorhome travel in the Last Frontier.

Call or write for our brochure!

ALASKA PANORAMA
712 W. Potter Drive, Anchorage, AK 99518
Toll Free 1-800-478-1401
Tel 907-562-1401 Fax 907-561-8762
email: akpanorama@cs.com
website: http://www.alaskapanorama.com

AUTHORIZED WARRANTY STATION
FLEETWOOD · ALLEGRO · Gulf Stream Coach, Inc.

Jayco

Anchorage Convention & Visitors Bureau · AVA

ASTA · BBB

Simply The Best.

MotorHOME is where the heart is...

Now put your heart into exploring Alaska at YOUR OWN PACE.
Relax. Take it easy. Enjoy any season.
View breathtaking scenery, sights & wildlife from your mobile living room.

Only ABC offers you simplicity, convenience and reasonable rates
for motorhomes and other vehicle rentals.

OUR RATES INCLUDE:
- ☑ Convenient airport location
- ☑ 2001 and newer models
- ☑ Unlimited mileage!
- ☑ Fully stocked bedding
- ☑ Fully stocked kitchen & bath
- ☑ No cleaning charges
- ☑ Complete orientation
- ☑ Full coverage insurance
- ☑ 24-hour customer assistance
- ☑ Alaska owned and operated

ABC MOTORHOMES
3875 Old Int'l Airport Road
Anchorage, Alaska 99502

rvakaska.net (email)
800-421-7456 (toll free)
907-279-2000 (phone)
907-243-6363 (fax)

1•800•421•7456
abcmotorhome.com

EXPERIENCE THE MAJESTY OF ALASKA AT YOUR OWN PACE.

Welcome to Alaska. Sweet Retreat is a family-owned and operated business serving Alaskan visitors since 1983. We take personal pride in our motorhomes and thoroughly detail and mechanically maintian each one because *your safety and comfort is our number one concern!* Price includes complete insurance coverage.

RENT A FULLY EQUIPPED MOTORHOME

- ❖ Several sizes ❖ Fully self-contained including microwave & generator
- ❖ Trip planning and fishing gear available ❖ Free airport & hotel transfers
- ❖ No cleanup fees ❖ New model motorhomes
- ❖ Unlimited mileage available ❖ Linens & dishes stocked at no fee

SWEET RETREAT INC.
MOTORHOME RENTALS

Call or write for a free brochure: 1-800-759-4861
6820 Arctic Blvd. Anchorage, AK 99518 • (907) 344-9155 Fax (907) 344-8279
Home Page: http://www.sweetretreat.com • E-mail- sweetretreat@customcpu.com

---

Choice Motorhomes For Rent
Alaska's Leader in Quality Motorhome Vacations.

- Alaska's Newest Fleet of Class C Motorhomes
- Meticulously Maintained Company-owned Vehicles
- Locations in Anchorage, Fairbanks, Skagway & Seattle
- One-way Rentals Available • AAA/AARP Discounts
- Toll-free Roadside Assistance • Discount Camping in Anchorage, Denali and Skagway.

CALL FOR A FREE BROCHURE

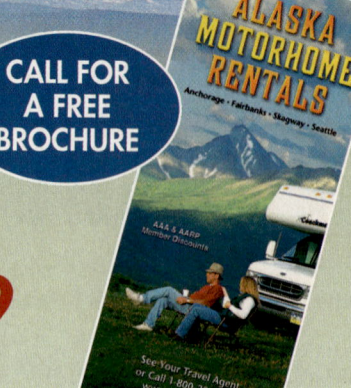

1-800-254-9929
www.alaskarv.com

ALASKA MOTORHOME RENTALS
A division of Alaska Travel Adventures, Inc.

9085 Glacier Hwy, Suite 301, Juneau, AK 99801 • Fax 425-882-2479 • Email: alaskarv@aol.com

the base can provide information for those interested in visiting this exhibit of approximately 250 mounts and trophies of Alaska sport fish, birds and mammals, located in Building 600 on the military reservation. Call (907) 384-1110. Elmendorf Air Force Base Wildlife Museum is open year-round Monday–Thursday 3 P.M.–4:45 P.M.; Friday noon–5 P.M.; Saturday 3 P.M.–4:45 P.M.; and closed on Sunday. Displays include more than 200 native Alaska species, from big game to small birds and fish, displayed in groupings of forest, tundra, wetlands, mountains and coastal habitat. Wheelchair access but not to restroom. Enter the base from the intersection of Boniface Parkway and the Glenn Highway. Ask guards for directions to Building 4-803. Phone (907) 552-2282 for details.

Heritage Library Museum, at Wells Fargo Bank, Northern Lights Boulevard and C Street, has an excellent collection of historical artifacts, Native tools, clothing and weapons, paintings by Alaskan artists and a research library. Free admission and parking. Open weekdays noon to 5 P.M. between Memorial Day and Labor Day, noon to 4 P.M. at other times of the year. Phone (907) 265-2834; Fax (907) 265-2860.

Charter a Plane: Dozens of air taxi operators are based in Anchorage. Fixed-wheel planes or floatplanes (skis in winter) may be chartered for flightseeing trips to Mount McKinley and Prince William Sound, for fly-in hunting and fishing or just for transportation. Scheduled flightseeing trips by helicopter are also available. See advertisements in this section and inquire locally. Weather is a factor when traveling by aircraft in Alaska. Be prepared to change plans if the weather is bad. Check the FAA web site at www.alaska.faa.gov.

Watch Small Planes: Drive out to Merrill Field, Lake Hood or Lake Spenard for an afternoon of airplane watching. Lake Hood is the world's largest and busiest seaplane base, with more than 800 takeoffs and landings on a peak summer day. Easy access to lakes Hood and Spenard off International Airport Road (follow signs).

Merrill Field, named for early Alaska aviator, Russell Hyde Merrill, ranked 104th busiest light-plane airport in the nation in 2001, with 188,254 takeoffs and landings. Follow 15th Street East to light at Lake Otis Parkway, and turn north on Merrill Field Drive. This route takes you under the approach to one of the runways. Merrill Field is also accessible off the Glenn Highway and from Airport Heights Drive (across from Northway Mall).

Alaska Aviation Heritage Museum, 4721 Aircraft Dr. on the south shore of Lake Hood, preserves the colorful history of Alaska's pioneer bush pilots. Rare historical films and extensive photo exhibit. The museum features a collection of 26 Alaska bush planes. RV parking. Open year-round, 9 A.M. to 6 P.M. daily in summer; Friday and Saturday 10 A.M. to 4 P.M. and Sunday noon to 4 P.M. in winter; or by special arrangements. Phone (907) 248-5325; fax (907) 248-6391. Adults $7.00, seniors and active military, $5.00, children 7 to 12, $2.75, children under 7 free. Handicap-accessible.

Elmendorf Air Force Base. Visitor and vehicles passes and an on-base sponsor are usually required to visit Elmendorf, except during their annual **Air Show and Open House**, held one weekend each summer. This 2-day event features aerial shows, air-

---

Affordable NEW CAR RENTAL

- **Courtesy Pick Up & Delivery**
- **One Way Rentals To Fairbanks**
- **4 x 4's • Vans • Wagons • Cars**
- **10% Discount With This Ad***
- **All Major Credit Cards Accepted**

*Certain Restrictions Apply. See Agent for Details.

SEE ALASKA THE AFFORDABLE WAY

249 Alta Way
Fairbanks 99701
(907) 452-7341 or 1-800-471-3101
Email: nissan@polarnet.com

4707 Spenard Rd.
Anchorage 99517
(907) 243-3370 or 1-800-248-3765
Email: ancr@alaska.net

NEW MODEL AUTOMOBILES
TRUCKS • VANS
Shuttle Service Available
Airport and Anchorage Area
Vehicles Available 7 Days a Week
(907) 562-8078 or (888) 685-1155
FAX (907) 562-1156

10% OFF WITH COUPON

HIGH COUNTRY CAR & TRUCK RENTAL
Anchorage International Airport
3609 Spenard Road • Anchorage, AK 99503
email: kiskaak@alaska.net • Visit our website at: www.kiska.com

---

CLIPPERSHIP MOTORHOME RENTALS

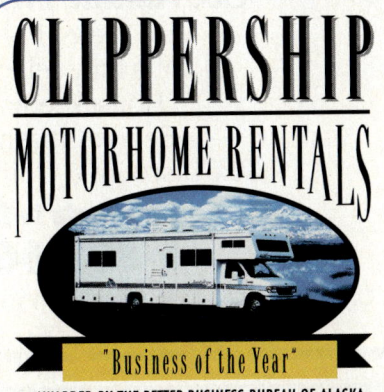

"Business of the Year"
AWARDED BY THE BETTER BUSINESS BUREAU OF ALASKA

MAKE RESERVATIONS EARLY!

1-800-421-3456

5401 Old Seward Highway Anchorage, AK 99518
phone: (907) 562-7051 fax: (907) 562-7053
e-mail: clippership@customcpu.com
website: www.clippershiprv.com

We offer an **unlimited mileage** option; self-contained units with heat, air-condition, range, refrigerator, freezer, **bath with shower;** free linen package; free utensils and cookware; insurance coverage (included in rates); complimentary airport or motel/hotel pickup; no preparation or cleaning fees; full maintenance and safety inspections by Ford factory-trained mechanics.

All motorhomes are 20' to 29' late model Fleetwood coaches on Ford chassis with **power steering** and **cruise control.**

craft displays, ground demonstrations, booths and more. Phone (907) 552-SHOW (7469) for dates and details, or visit their web site at www.elmendorf.af.mil.

Elmendorf Air Force Base is reached via the Boniface Gate off the Glenn Highway, the Post Road Gate and Government Hill Gate.

Take a Tour: Several tour operators offer local and area sightseeing tours. These range from a 1-hour narrated trolley tour of Anchorage to full-day tours of area attractions such as Portage Glacier and Alyeska Resort. Two-day or longer excursions by motorcoach, rail, ferry and air to nearby attractions such as Prince William Sound or remote areas are also available. Inquire at your hotel, see ads this section, or contact a travel agent.

Kenai Fjords Tours. Don't miss Kenai Fjords National Park with its abundant wildlife and glaciers. "Alaska's #1 Wildlife and Glacier Cruise" departs daily from Seward and has a convenient reservation office in downtown Anchorage. Located at 513 W. 4th Ave. Phone (970) 276-6249 or (800) 468-8068. Convenient one-day transportation packages are available from Anchorage aboard our Wildlife Express private dome car. This is the original Kenai Fjords National Park cruise you've been looking for. [ADVERTISEMENT]

A dog handler at the Iditarod start in downtown Anchorage.
(© Kris Graef, staff)

Major Marine Glacier Tours. Half-day ($69) and full-day ($109) cruises to Kenai Fjords National Park (only cruises hosted by National Park Rangers) from Seward; 5-hour glacier cruise ($99) in Prince William Sound from Whittier. Add all-you-can-eat salmon and prime rib meal, $12. Daily May-September. Call 800-764-7300 or 907-274-7300 for

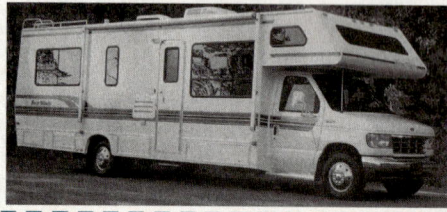

ALEXANDER'S RV
- RENTALS
- SALES
- SERVICE

See Alaska Through Our Windows
New 21' – 32' Class C & A's
All units fully self contained with generators
Housekeeping & Linen Packages
Senior Citizen & Military Discount
30% Discount & Unlimited miles Sept. thru May

Call Early to Reserve Your's Today!
1-888-660-5115 (toll free)
Office (907) 563-5115 • Fax (907) 563-5154 • P.O. Box 221805, Anchorage, AK 99502
website: alaska-RV.com   e-mail: rvman@alaska-RV.com

reservations or free brochure. Major Marine Tours, 411 W. 4th A, Anchorage, AK 99501. www.majormarine.com. [ADVERTISEMENT]

26 Glacier Cruise. Cruise the calm, protected waters of Prince William Sound and come face to face with tidewater glaciers plus an amazing array of wildlife on the fastest, largest and most luxurious high-speed catamaran in Alaska. Departs daily from Whittier. See our ad in the Anchorage section. Phillips Cruises year-round sales office is located at 519 W. 4th Ave., Anchorage, AK 99501. Toll free from USA and Canada 1-800-544-0529, (907) 276-8023 or bswanberg@26glaciers.com. [ADVERTISEMENT]

Portage Glacier Cruise. See Alaska's most popular attraction, up close from the deck of the MV *Ptarmigan*. This Gray Line of Alaska cruise takes you right to the face of imposing 10-story-high Portage Glacier. An incredible experience. Tours depart Anchorage twice daily or you may drive to Portage Glacier and board the MV *Ptarmigan* for the cruise-only portion. Tour price is $60 per person; cruise-only price is $25 per person. Prices subject to change. Phone (907) 277-5581. [ADVERTISEMENT]

Renown Charters & Tours. Our mission statement is "Providing quality cruises at affordable prices." We are Alaska's only year round cruise company. Heated cabins, walk around decks, healthy lunches along with a safe, experienced and knowledgeable crew. Since we are a smaller company and can afford to pass along more affordable rates, it is easy to see why we are the customer's favorite. Cruises starting at $39.99. (800) 655-3806 or (907) 272-1961. www.renowncharters.com. See display ad this section. [ADVERTISEMENT]

Train to Denali. Ride the luxurious private, domed railcars of the *McKinley Explorer* to Denali National Park from either Anchorage or Fairbanks. Overnight packages in Denali with round-trip train service available from $425-$535 ppdo. for 3 days/2 nights, overnight in Anchorage or Fairbanks included. Prices subject to change. Phone Gray Line of Alaska at (907) 277-5581 for train and package tour options. [ADVERTISEMENT]

Tour a Campus: Two colleges are located in Anchorage: the University of Alaska Anchorage at 3211 Providence Dr. and Alaska Pacific (formerly Alaska Methodist) University at 4101 University Dr.

Alaska Pacific University was dedicated June 29, 1959, the same year that Alaska became the 49th state, and is now the state's largest private 4-year university. APU's first students were enrolled in the fall of 1960. The university offers liberal arts-based educational programs for all ages, including an annual Elderhostel. The APU campus is located on 170 forested acres, featuring the 3-tiered Atwood Fountain, Waldron Carillon Bell Tower and the Jim Mahaffey Trail System for skiers, runners, hikers and mountain bikers. Phone (907) 564-8248 or (800) 252-7528 for tours or information about university programs, or access the university on the Internet at www.alaskapacific.edu.

The University of Alaska Anchorage is 1 of 3 regional institutions in the state's university system (the others are in Fairbanks and Southeast Alaska). For information on tours of the UA campus in Anchorage, phone (907) 786-1529; www.uaa.alaska.edu.

Go to the Zoo: The Alaska Zoo, home of Ahpun and Oreo (the polar bear and grizzly bear that were raised together from cubs), is located on 20 acres of wooded land in South

Garrett's Tesoro
Open 24 Hours

GAS • DIESEL (Volume Truck Rates)
PROPANE • WATER • AIR

2 LOCATIONS

Northern Lights & Seward Highway
(907) 277-6025

Arctic & International
(907) 561-2581

TESORO

Credit Cards Accepted

Real Value. Real Easy.

Mountain View Car Wash, Inc.
3433 Commercial Drive • (907) 279-4819

Large Stalls — COIN OPERATED — Foam & Brush
Vacuums — **OPEN** — Hot Wax
RV Dump — **24** — Degreaser
High Pressure — **HOURS** — Tar Remover
Rug & Upholstery — FULLTIME ATTENDANT — Power Dryer
Armorall Dispenser — Glenn Highway Westbound, Turn Right at Bragaw Then Turn left for Three Blocks on Mt. View Drive — Fragrance Centers

---

AMERICAN TIRE & AUTO
"Statewide Since 1974"

WE FEATURE
GOODYEAR – COOPER
BRIDGESTONE • MICHELIN
AMERICAN RACING WHEELS

AUTO SERVICE CENTERS
Brakes • Shocks • Alignment
Motorhome Servicing

219 3rd Ave. • FAIRBANKS
(907) 452-5145

832 E. 4th Ave. • ANCHORAGE
(907) 276-7878

7835 Old Seward Hwy. • ANCHORAGE
(907) 336-7878

Moose are a common sight in Anchorage neighborhoods and along Anchorage streets. *Drive carefully!*

Winter Attractions

Winter Events

Anchorage Fur Rendezvous: The major event of the winter season in Anchorage. Billed as the "Mardi Gras of the North," this elaborate winter festival attracts thousands of celebrants each February.

The 10-day-long celebration dates from 1936 when it began primarily as a fur auction where trappers could bring their pelts to town and sell them to buyers from around the world. Trappers still bring the pelts, and the fur auction still attracts many buyers.

Alaskans shake off cabin fever during "Rondy" (the local term for the Fur Rendezvous) as they enjoy arts and crafts exhibits, a parade, the Miners' and Trappers' Ball, a carnival, an ice and snow sculpturing contest and a home-brew competition. There are more than 120 events.

Highlights of the Fur Rendezvous include the Annual World Championship Dog Weight Pulling Contest and the World Championship Sled Dog Race. The race attracts dozens of mushers from Alaska, Canada and the Lower 48. Spectators line the 25-mile race course, which begins and ends on 4th Avenue in downtown Anchorage. The women's and junior world championship sled dog races are held at Tozier Track the first weekend of the Fur Rendezvous. For more information, phone (907) 274-1177; www.furrondy.net.

The Iditarod Trail Sled Dog Race begins on 4th Avenue in downtown Anchorage on the first Saturday in March. Mushers can be seen on the trail along the Glenn Highway to Eagle River. The racers then pack up and head to Wasilla for the restart of the race the following day, an event which also draws crowds. For more information, visit www.iditarod.com.

Winter Basketball. Anchorage hosts 2 major collegiate basketball events. Carrs/Safeway Great Alaska Shootout, held Thanksgiving weekend, features 8 major college basketball teams in this well-known invitational tournament. The women's version of the Shootout, formerly known as the Northern Lights Invitational, is also held Thanksgiving weekend and showcases women's collegiate basketball with 8 teams in a 3-day playoff. For more information, visit www.goseawolves.com.

The Slush Cup. This spring skiing event is well worth the drive to Girdwood. Participants dress up in costumes then ski downhill and attempt to cross a pool of icy water at the bottom. Points are awarded for costumes and style, as well as for successfully crossing the pool.

Downhill Skiing

Alyeska Resort. Located in the community of Girdwood, Alyeska Resort is a 45-mile drive south from Anchorage along scenic Turnagain Arm via the Seward Highway. Judged by *Conde Nast Traveler* as having the "best view" of any U.S. ski resort, Alyeska Resort is Alaska's largest ski resort, with snow typically from early November to the middle of April. Night skiing is available during holiday periods in December and on Fridays and Saturdays from January through March. Ski facilities include a high-speed detachable bubble quad, 2 fixed grip quads, 3 double chair lifts and 2 pony tows. A 60-passenger aerial tram takes sightseers and skiers from the mountain's base at 250 feet to a mountaintop facility at the 2,300-foot level. This facility, open year-round and handicap-accessible, features a large viewing deck, a cafeteria-style restaurant and a fine dining restaurant and lounge. Centerpiece for the resort is the 307-room, chateau-style Alyeska Prince Hotel. For more information, phone (907) 754-2111 or (800) 880-3880, or go to www.alyeskaresort.com.

Alpenglow at Arctic Valley. East of Anchorage in the Chugach Mountains, Alpenglow Ski Area has a T-bar platter lift combination and 2 chairlifts on 320 acres of terrain, covering almost 2,000 vertical feet. The ski area also has a day lodge with a full cafeteria. Cross-country skiing available, but trails are not maintained. The ski area operates from about Thanksgiving to early May. Take the Glenn Highway to Arctic Valley Road exit and follow the road 7 miles to the ski area. For more information, phone (907) 428-1208, or go to www.skialpenglow.com.

Hilltop Ski Area: Located 15 minutes from downtown Anchorage, 4 miles east of the Seward Highway off Abbott Road, Hilltop has 2 miles of lighted slopes classified as beginner to intermediate. Ski facilities include a triple chair lift; a platter lift; a beginner rope tow; 15m, 40m and 60m lighted jumps; and certified snowboard halfpipe. New lodge, ski rentals (Alpine and snowboards), ski school, gift shop and snack bar. Open daily with complete night lighting, 3–8 P.M. weekdays and 9 A.M. to 9 P.M. weekends and holidays. For more information, phone (907) 346-2167 or 346-1446; www.hilltopskiarea.org.

Russian Jack Springs has a beginner ski slope and rope tow. Open daily, with night lighting, in winter. Phone (907) 343-6992 or (907) 343-4474 for hours and fees.

Cross-Country Skiing

Chugach State Park: Although the entire park is open to cross-country skiers, most maintained ski trails are found in the Hillside Trail System/Campbell Creek area, accessible via Upper Huffman Road and Upper O'Malley Road. Skiers are encouraged to use established trails as most of Chugach State Park is prime avalanche country. Skijoring on Anchorage trails and throughout the area is also popular.

The Glen Alps trailhead has a $5 parking fee.

Ski trail maps are available at the trailheads or from the park office, phone (907) 269-8400.

The Municipality of Anchorage maintains ski trails throughout the city park system. Several are lighted for evening use. City parks or city-maintained trails include: Russian Jack Springs, DeBarr Road and Boniface Parkway; Far North Bicentennial/Hillside Parks, access via Hilltop Ski Area on Abbott Road; Tony Knowles Coastal Trail; Campbell Creek Green Belt; Centennial Park, located near Glenn Highway and Muldoon Road.; Chester Creek Green Belt, located in the heart of Anchorage; Kincaid Park, access is from the west end of Raspberry Road. Ski trail maps are available at Anchorage Parks & Recreation, phone (907) 343-4474; or Kincaid Park, phone (907) 343-6397.

There are many skiing events in and around Anchorage, including the annual Ski for Women and the Tour of Anchorage.

Ice Skating & Hockey

There are 3 municipal indoor ice facilities (with a total of 4 rinks): Ben Boeke Ice Arena (334 E. 16th Ave.), Harry J. McDonald Center (Mile 2.2 Old Glenn Highway, Eagle River), and Dempsey-Anderson Ice Arena (1741 W. Northern Lights).

City-maintained outdoor ice-skating lakes include Cheney Lake, Goose Lake and Jewel Lake. Delong Lake is hot-mopped in winter. Westchester Lagoon's ice-skating area is enhanced with warming barrels and nearly 1/2 mile of ice trails. The municipality also maintains outdoor areas for both skating and hockey at Tikishla Park, Chester Creek Sports Complex, Delaney Park Strip and Wendler Jr. High.

Private facilities include Dimond Ice Chalet in the Dimond Mall; Bonnie Cusack Rink on Abbott Loop and the Tesoro Sports Center on O'Malley Centre Drive.

Hockey is a very popular sport in Anchorage. Visitors can support this local pastime and the local teams by taking in a game or tournament. Watch the Anchorage Aces or the University of Alaska Anchorage Seawolves in regular season games, or partake in the annual October Hockey Tournament.

Sledding & Snowshoeing

Popular sledding hills with beginning to advanced slopes are at Balto Seppala Park, Centennial Park, Conifer Park, Conners Lake, Kincaid Park, Nunaka Valley Park, Oceanview Park, Sitka Street Park, Sunset Park, Service High School, Windsong Park and Alaska Pacific University. Contact Anchorage Parks & Recreation for more information.

Muldoon Park, Far North Bicentennial Park and Campbell Creek Green Belt are used for snowshoeing, as are backcountry areas of Chugach National Forest and Chugach State Park.

Snowmobiling

Chugach State Park: Five major areas in the park are open to snowmobiling when snow levels are deep enough: Eklutna Lake Valley, reached from the Glenn Highway via Eklutna Road; Eagle River Valley, also accessible from the Glenn Highway; Bird Creek, **Milepost S 101.2** Seward Highway; Peters Creek Valley and Little Peters Creek, accessible from the Glenn Highway; and portions of the Hillside/Campbell Creek area, accessible from Upper Huffman Road. Snowmobiling information is available from the park office; There is a $5 parking fee at the Glen Alps trailhead; phone (907) 345-5014. Snow machines must be registered to use the park.

Turnagain Pass: On the Seward Highway, about 59 miles south of downtown Anchorage. Turnagain Pass (elev. 988 feet) is a popular winter recreation area in the Chugach National Forest. The west side of the pass is open to snowmobiling as soon as snow cover permits; the east side is reserved for skiers. Snow depths in this pass often exceed 12 feet.

Please use caution when snowmobiling in these areas as there is avalanche danger. Contact the Department of Natural Resources at (907) 269-8400 for avalanche reports.

Anchorage. The zoo has more than 85 animals and more than 40 species of Arctic wildlife, including glacier bears, polar bears, brown (grizzly) and black bears, reindeer, moose, Dall sheep, otters, wolves, foxes, musk-oxen and wolverines, as well as non-Alaskan species such as Bactrian camels, Siberian tigers and an elephant. Be sure to stop in for Bactrian camel hair mittens at the gift shop, located on your right as you enter. In September 2002, the zoo opened a new snow leopard exhibit with a male and a female leopard, and the facility is now approved as a breeding facility. The zoo is open 9 A.M. to 6 P.M. daily from May 1 to Labor Day weekend with extended hours on Tuesdays; 10 A.M. to 5 P.M. (or until dark) the remainder of the year. Drive south from the downtown area on the Seward Highway to **Milepost S 120.8**. Take O'Malley exit, turn east (towards the mountains) on O'Malley Road and drive 2 miles to the zoo, which will be on your left. Admission is $8 for adults, $7 for seniors, $5 for students 12-17 and $4 for children 3 to 11. Family passes $50. Free admission for children under 3. Handicap parking, wheelchair accessible. Phone (907) 346-3242 for details.

Visit the Greenhouses: The municipality maintains the extensive Mann Leiser greenhouses at Russian Jack Park, 5200 DeBarr Road, where myriad plantings supply local parks—like downtown's Town Square—with flowers. Visitors enjoy the displays of tropical plants, the fish pond and the aviary where finches, cockatiels and tropical birds enliven an attractive area popular for small weddings and school tours. Open year-round, 8 A.M. to 3 P.M., the greenhouses are closed only on a few specific holidays. Phone (907) 343-4717 for additional information.

Watch the Tide Come In: With frequent tidal ranges of 30 feet within 6 hours, and many approaching 40 feet, one of Anchorage's best nature shows is the action of the tides in both the Knik and Turnagain arms of upper Cook Inlet. Vantage points along Knik Arm are Earthquake Park, Elderberry Park (west end of 5th Avenue), Resolution Park (near corner of 3rd Avenue and L Street) and the Anchorage small-boat harbor.

Turnagain Arm has the second highest tides in North America, rising to a maximum high of 42 feet, exceeded only by the Bay of

Alaska Performance RV & Marine
522-8965
www.alaskaperformancerv.com

FULL SERVICE RV CENTER
FACTORY TRAINED AND CERTIFIED TECHNICIANS
Body Work
Metal & Fiberglass/Insurance Repairs
Structural Rebuilding • Welding
Interior Remodeling • Appliance Repair
Service • Parts • Accessories

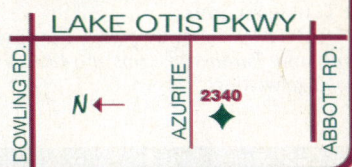

KAREN'S RV SERVICE CENTER
(907) 336-2055 • 1850 Viking Drive • Anchorage, AK 99501

Authorized warranty for most major brands of Motorhomes, Travel Trailers, Appliances, Awnings, Body Repair, Painting, Plumbing, and Electrical.

Karen's Specializing in R.V. Service Repair
(907) 336-2055

MOBILE TRAILER SUPPLY, INC.

COMPLETE PARTS, SERVICE, ACCESSORIES & INSTALLATIONS
FOR: CAMPERS, MOTOR HOMES, 5TH WHEELS & TRAVEL TRAILERS

RV Storage
277-1811

SERVING ANCHORAGE SINCE 1969 • OPEN MON. - SAT.
300 La Touche St. - Anchorage

DEAN'S
AUTOMOTIVE & RV SERVICE CENTER
FEATURING THE LATEST EQUIPMENT

COOLING SYSTEM SPECIALISTS
TIRE DEALER — All Major Brands

276-5731
1131 E. 7TH AVE., ANCHORAGE
OPEN MON-FRI 8-6 SAT 8-5

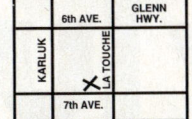
10% Discount on Parts

- Electric tune-ups
- Starters
- Shocks
- Brakes
- Alternators
- Engines
- Electrical
- Automatic Transmissions
- Auto Air Conditioning
- Wheel Alignment

Fundy in eastern Canada. A good overlook for Turnagain tides is Bird Creek State Recreation Site south of Anchorage at **Milepost S 101.2** on the Seward Highway. With careful timing you might see a tidal bore, an interesting phenomenon rarely seen elsewhere. A bore tide is a foaming wall of tidal water, up to 6 feet in height, formed by a flood tide surging into constricted inlets such as Knik or Turnagain arms.

CAUTION: In many places, the mud flats of Knik and Turnagain arms are like quicksand. Don't go wading!

Play Golf: The golf season lasts from 3 to 5 months in Alaska. The Municipality of Anchorage maintains a 9-hole golf course at Russian Jack Springs Park, Debarr Road and Boniface Parkway, featuring artificial turf greens. It is open from mid-May through September; phone (907) 343-6992 or 343-4474 off-season (October–April). Tanglewood Lakes Golf Club also has maintains a 18-hole course at 11701 Brayton Drive; phone (907) 345-4600. Alyeska Resort maintains the Anchorage Golf Course, 3651 O'Malley Road, an all-grass, 18-hole course open from mid-May through mid-September; phone (907) 522-3363 for more information. Two military courses are open to civilians. Eagleglen Golf Course, an 18-hole par-72 course, is located on Elmendorf Air Force Base, near the Post Road gate. Open mid-May through September. Phone (907) 552-2773 or 552-3821 for tee times; rentals available. Fort Richardson's Moose Run Golf Course is the oldest golf course in Alaska and the world's northernmost 36-hole course. The course is accessible from Arctic Valley Road (**Milepost A 6.1** on the Glenn Highway) and is open May through September. Rentals available. Phone (907) 428-0056 for tee times. All golf course hours depend on the weather and amount of sunlight. Greens fees vary.

There are many charity golf tournaments throughout the season, as well as Alaska Golf Association tournaments, including the State Amateur, State Senior Amateur, the Mayor's Cup, Spring Scramble and Fall tournaments. For more information, phone (907) 349-GOLF, or visit www.agagolf.org.

Play Disc Golf: Disc golf or "folf" is similar to golf but played with a rubber flying disc instead of clubs and a ball. On an established course, players throw their discs into the "holes" or disc entrapment devices (metal poles with baskets on top).

Anchorage has 3 disc golf courses. The Municipality maintains a 9-hole, grass course at the Russian Jack Springs Golf Course. The fee is $10, and the area offers camping and restrooms and is handicap-accessible; phone (907) 343-6992. There is also a free course at Westchester Lagoon. This is a 9-hole, par-3 course that begins near the parking lot (maps of course provided). The University of Alaska Anchorage has a free 18-hole course called Seawolf Streams.

For more information on disc golf and courses and events around the world, visit the Professional Disc Golf Association's web site at www.pdga.com.

Play Tennis: The Municipality of Anchorage maintains more than 55 tennis courts, including those in Eagle River and Girdwood. In addition, private clubs offer year-round indoor courts. Parks & Recreation offers tennis lessons in June and July; phone (907) 343-4474 for details.

Run: Few summer weeks pass in Anchorage without at least one scheduled race for every cause, interest and level of ability imaginable. Parks & Recreation, phone (907) 343-4474, publishes the "Alaska Runners Calendar," a complete schedule of these events, from 5k runs/walks to marathons and triathlons. Great for spectators and participants alike.

Summer Solstice. Alaskans celebrate the longest day of the year with a variety of special events. In Anchorage, there's the Abused Women's Aid in Crisis (AWAIC) Summer Solstice Festival, the annual Mayor's Midnight Sun Marathon, a 26-mile, 385-yard run through the city, as well as two other runs: a half-marathon and a 5-miler. These events are usually scheduled on the Saturday nearest summer solstice (June 20 or 21).

Watch Birds: Excellent bird-watching opportunities are abundant within the city limits. Lakes Hood and Spenard, for example, are teeming with seaplanes but also, during the summer, are nesting areas for grebes and arctic loons. Also seen are widgeons, arctic terns, mew gulls, green-winged teals and sandpipers.

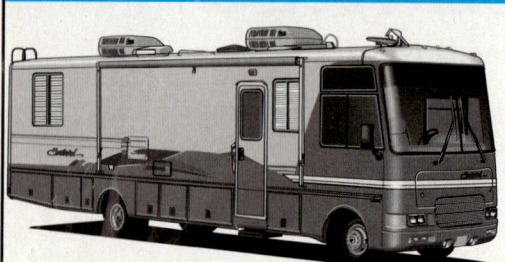

RV SERVICE CENTER

- Factory Trained Technicians
- Parts & Accessory Showroom
- Rental Cars
- Servicing All Makes & Models
- Winnebago & Fleetwood Dealer
- Complete Body Shop
- Quick Service "While You Wait"

JOHNSON RV CENTER

907-646-0660
4551 Fairbanks St., Suite D
Anchorage

Seattle 2,435
Great Falls 2,473

IF EVER THERE WAS A TIME

After driving the Highway, you'll want to make us your first stop in Anchorage. We'll do everything from changing your oil to topping off most vital fluids – all in a matter of minutes.

We service motor homes.

jiffy lube®

360 W. Dimond Blvd.	3429 E. Tudor Rd.	1221 S. Bragaw St.
(directly in front of Costco)	(across from dog sled track)	(directly in front of Costco)
522-3800	562-0900	337-1248

Golden Nugget Camper Park

Anchorage, Alaska — Open Year-Round — 215 Spaces

Corner of DeBarr Rd. & Hoyt St.

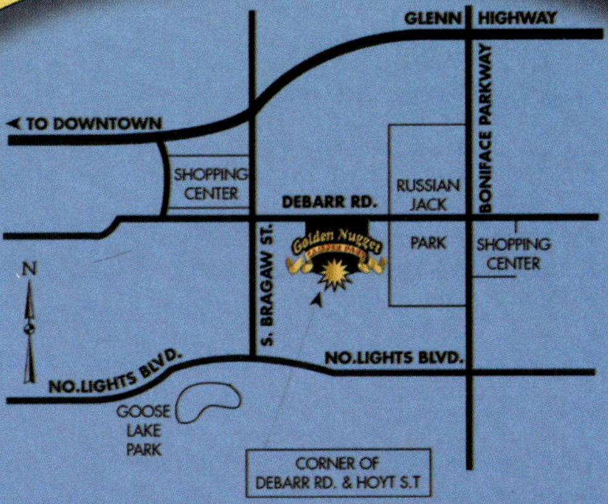

Back Packers Welcome

Picnic Tables At All Sites

Souvenir Shop

~ Friendly Service ~
~ Full Hookups ~
~ Free Hot Showers ~
~ Laundromat ~

Convenient to:
Shopping Centers • Restaurants
Service & Gas Stations
Beauty Salon • Propane
Churches • Price Costco

Ask For Reservation to:
Flightseeing
Cruise Tours
Guided Fishing Trips
Railroad Travel

215 Spaces

Clean Restrooms

You're Always Welcome at the Golden Nugget!

4100 DeBarr Road • Anchorage, Alaska • 907-333-5311 • 1-800-449-2012

MasterCard / VISA

CENTENNIAL CAMPER PARK

CAMPING
Just 5 miles from downtown Anchorage
Close to stores, gas stations and bus stop

90 Spaces
Showers • Dump Station
Picnic Tables • 40 Tent Spaces
50-meter Pool 1/2 mile away

Turn south off Glenn Highway onto Muldoon Road, then turn east on Boundary Avenue.

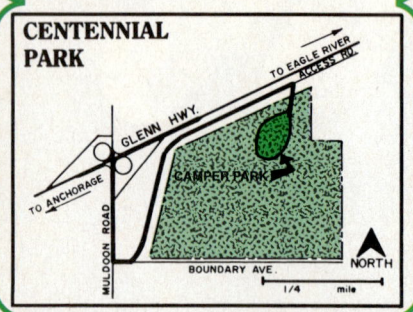

WATCH FOR THE SIGNS!
Parks are open May-September
Phone: 343-6986
"MUNICIPALITY OF ANCHORAGE"

The Alaska Zoo houses both native and exotic animal species. (© Kris Graef, staff)

Huge flocks of Canada geese nest and raise their young during the summer. It is not unusual to see traffic at a standstill as a pair of geese, followed by a tandem procession of goslings, cross the city's highways.

Another great spot is the **Potter Point (Potter Marsh) State Game Refuge** (also known as the Anchorage Coastal Wildlife Refuge), south of downtown on the Seward Highway at **Milepost S 117.4**. Early July evenings are best, according to local bird watchers. Forests surrounding Anchorage also are good for warblers, juncos, robins, white-crowned sparrows, varied thrushes and other species.

At the Park for All People on W. 19th Avenue and Spenard Road in the Chester Creek Greenbelt, a nature trail winds through a bird-nesting area.

See a Baseball Game: Some fine semi-pro baseball is played in Anchorage. Every summer some of the nation's top

ALASKA'S PREMIER RV PARK

Anchorage RV Park

An Alaska Heritage Tours Company

A secluded wooded setting just outside the city.

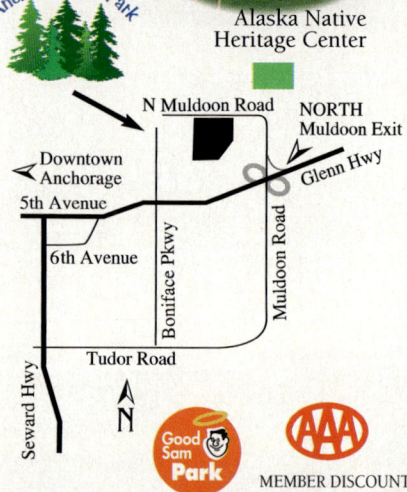

- Main Lodge
- Laundry and Shower Facilities
- Dump Station
- Cable TV Connections
- BBQ Pavilion
- 195 Full Hookups
- Ice, Groceries, RV Supplies & Gifts
- Work Station With Modem Port
- Reservations Recommended

907-338-7275
1200 N. Muldoon
Anchorage, AK 99506
www.anchrvpark.com

Anchorage RV Park is off Highway #1 at the intersection of Glenn Highway and Muldoon Road. Take the Muldoon exit NORTH.
GPS: N61° 13.81' W 149° 44.46'

800-400-7275 (PARK)

college players (among past notables are Tom Seaver and 1998 home-run king Mark McGwire) play for the Anchorage Glacier Pilots and Anchorage Bucs, the Peninsula Oilers, the Mat–Su Miners and the Fairbanks Goldpanners. Anchorage games are played at Mulcahy Ball Park, Cordova Street and E. 16th Avenue. Check local newspapers for schedules or phone the Anchorage Bucs, (907) 561-2827, or the Glacier Pilots, (907) 344-5444.

Go for a Hike. Hiking trails in the Anchorage area are found in Chugach State Park and in Municipality of Anchorage parks. Popular hikes in Chugach State Park that are easily accessible from downtown include Flattop, Powerline, Williwaw Lakes and Wolverine Peak. (See "Chugach State Park" on page 354 for details.)

Hilltop Ski Area, 3.8 miles east of the New Seward Highway on Abbott Road (use Dimond exit), is the trailhead for summer hiking, biking and horseback riding trails in Bicentennial and Hillside municipal parks. The trails range in length from an easy mile walk to a strenuous 16-mile hike. For more information phone Hilltop Ski Area at (907) 346-1446.

Other Anchorage parks offering hiking, jogging or biking include Kincaid Park, Russian Jack Springs Park and Far North Bicentennial Park. For more information phone Anchorage Parks and Recreation at (907) 343-4474.

Chugach National Forest also offers many maintained hiking and biking trails outside of Anchorage.

Go Berry Picking. There are nearly 50 types of berries (most of which are edible) found all over Alaska. These berries and other native fruit have been a major source of food for Native peoples for centuries.

Berries in the Anchorage area include blueberries, mossberries, crowberries and cranberries, and there are numerous places to pick berries around the area. The most popular spots include Mt. Alyeska off the Seward Highway in Girdwood, along the Flattop Mountain Trail, Rendevous Peak Trail adjacent to Alpenglow Ski Area, South Fork Valley Trail off the Glenn Highway, Peters Creek Trail on Mt. Eklutna and Bear Mountain and Eklutna Lakeside Trail off Eklutna Lake Road.

Watch Salmon: King, coho, pink and a few chum salmon swim up Ship Creek and can be seen at the Ship Creek Viewing Area (see description in Downtown Anchorage attractions) and near the Alaska Department of Fish and Game Elmendorf Hatchery at Reeve Blvd. Watch for kings from early June until mid-July and for other species from mid-August until September. Salmon can also be viewed in Campbell Creek, which runs through the middle of Anchorage. Watch for coho in late July and August from the boardwalks at Folker Street off Tudor Road. Another excellent viewing spot is the Potter Marsh Nature Trail, June through August.

Watch an Equestrian Event. The William Clark Chamberlin Equestrian Center in 530-acre Ruth Arcand Park (1.8 miles east of Dimond exit off the New Seward Highway on Abbott Road) hosts a variety of equestrian events every weekend from late-May through August. This public facility is open from 11 A.M. to 9 P.M. Phone (907) 522-1552. The Eaton Equestrian Center at 5801 Moose Meadow on the Hillside offers riding lessons and special events.

Phone (907) 346-3745 for more information.

Kayaking, Canoeing, Rafting: All are available in or near Anchorage. Guided tours from 1-14 days run on several rivers within 100 miles of Anchorage, including the Chulitna, Susitna, Little Susitna, Matanuska and Kenai rivers. Information on guided raft and canoe trips is available through travel agencies, local sporting goods stores and in the free *Visitors Guide* available from the Log Cabin Visitor Information Center.

Several flying services provide unguided float trips. The service flies customers to a remote river, then picks them up at a predetermined time and place downriver.

Several area streams offer excellent canoeing and kayaking. Information on the Swanson River and Swan Lake canoe trails on the Kenai Peninsula is available from the Kenai National Wildlife Refuge Manager, Box 2139, Soldotna, AK 99669-2139; phone (907) 262-7021. Nancy Lake State Recreation Area, 67 miles north of Anchorage, offers a popular canoe trail system. Contact the Alaska State Parks, Mat–Su/Valdez–Copper River Area, H.C. 32, Box 6706, Wasilla, AK 99654-9719; phone (907) 745-3975.

Sailing in the Anchorage area is limited to freshwater lakes and lagoons (usually ice free by May).

Mirror Lake, 24.5 miles north of Anchorage on the Glenn Highway, and Big Lake, 52.3 miles north of Anchorage on the Parks Highway, are popular spots for small sailboats.

Motorboating: Big Lake and Lake Lucille along the Parks Highway offer motorboating. Several rivers, including the Susitna, offer riverboating, but the shallowness and silty, shifting beds of most Alaska rivers require jet-equipped, flat-bottomed boards for maximum safety.

Cruises on larger boats are available from Whittier into Prince William Sound, from Homer Spit into Kachemak Bay and Cook Inlet, and from Seward into Resurrection Bay and Kenai Fjords National Park. Venturing into those areas in small boats without a knowledgeable local guide is dangerous and should not be attempted.

Cook Inlet waters around Anchorage are only for the experienced because of powerful bore tides, unpredictable weather, dangerous mud flats and icy, silty waters. Turnagain Arm is strictly off-limits for any boat, and Knik Arm and most of the north end of Cook Inlet is the domain of large ships and experienced skiff and dory operators.

Swimming: Anchorage has an indoor waterpark, H2Oasis, located east off the O'Malley exit on the New Seward Highway. The YMCA, 5353 Lake Otis Parkway has a swimming pool; phone (907) 563-3211.

The following pools, operated by Parks & Recreation, are open to the public: Service High School pool, 5577 Abbott Road, phone (907) 346-3040; Bartlett High School pool, 25-500 Muldoon Road, phone (907) 343-6981; West High School pool (with a water slide), 1700 Hillcrest Dr., phone (907) 274-5161; East High School pool, 4025 E. 24th Ave., phone (907) 278-9761; Dimond High

Day Trips From Anchorage

Anchorage is the hub for Southcentral Alaska: You can get anywhere in the state from here, traveling by car, plane or train. Here are just a few driving trips you can make, ranging from a few hours to all day.

Eklutna Lake/Thunderbird Falls

Drive out the Glenn Highway to the Eklutna exit at **Milepost A 26.3** for **Eklutna Lake Recreation Area**, located 10 miles from the highway via a gravel road. Located within Chugach State Park, Eklutna Lake offers camping, picnicking and hiking. The 13-mile Lakeside trail, especially popular with local hikers and mountain bikers, follows the Eklutna Lake shoreline.

Another hiking trail accessible from this exit is the **Thunderbird Falls** trail. This easy family trail is only about 2 miles round trip from the parking lot to the viewing platform of the falls. This trail is also accessible via the Thunderbird Falls exit for eastbound traffic.

Eklutna Lake is an easy 72-mile round-trip drive from downtown Anchorage. (See pages 313–314 in the GLENN HIGHWAY section.)

Alyeska

Drive south on the Seward Highway to **Milepost S 90** (37 miles from Anchorage) and turn off on the Alyeska Highway. About 2 miles up this road is the small town of Girdwood, where the **Girdwood Forest Fair** takes place in July. Drive another 2 miles up the Alyeska Highway to reach the Alyeska Prince Hotel. Located at the base of Mt. Alyeska, Alyeska Resort is Alaska's largest ski resort. The 60-passenger **Alyeska Aerial Tramway** carries summer sightseers (and winter skiers) from the hotel to a mountaintop complex featuring the Seven Glaciers and Glacier Express restaurants. The tram ride offers wonderful views of Turnagain Arm. This is an 82-mile round-trip drive from downtown Anchorage. (See "Alyeska Highway" in the SEWARD HIGHWAY section.)

Hatcher Pass

Drive out the Glenn Highway from Anchorage through Palmer to **Milepost A 49.5** and turn on to Palmer–Fishhook Road for Hatcher Pass. Hatcher Pass Road is paved from the Palmer end up to the Motherlode Lodge at Mile 14, then improved gravel up to the Independence Mine State Historical Park turnoff at Mile 17. This is a beautiful drive up the Little Susitna River into the Hatcher Pass area. Great views and the old mine ruins are well worth the drive. Continue on Hatcher Pass Road a couple of miles to Summit Lake and then on to the Lucky Shot Mine tour at Mile 23 before returning to Anchorage the way you came for a total of 145 driving miles.

If you are prepared to drive an old-time Alaska road—narrow, winding dirt and gravel—continue on Hatcher Pass Road to Willow and return to Anchorage via the Parks and Glenn highways (215 miles).

See pages 305–306 in the GLENN HIGHWAY section.

Whittier Tunnel/Portage Glacier

Drive south on the Seward Highway to **Milepost S 78.9** (48.1 miles from Anchorage) to junction with the access road east to Portage Glacier (5.4 miles from the highway) and Whittier (11.4 miles from the highway). Total driving miles round-trip from downtown Anchorage is 119.

At Portage Glacier, the Begich, Boggs Visitor Center offers interactive interpretive displays, films and other programs on the natural history of this area, regular showings of films of interest and Forest Service naturalists available to answer your questions.

Continue on the side road for Whittier. At Mile 7, traffic enters the Anton Anderson Memorial Tunnel, at 13,200 feet the longest highway tunnel in North America. It takes a vehicle 6.5 minutes to travel through this tunnel which was formerly dedicated to train travel. There is a toll charged and vehicles must wait in the staging area before entering the tunnel.

Returning to the Seward Highway for the drive back to Anchorage, stop by **Big Game Alaska Wildlife Center**, just north of the junction (on the west side of the road) at **Milepost S 79**, for a drive-through tour of this wild animal park. Big Game Alaska is home to moose, bears, caribou, bison, elk, Sitka black tailed deer and other wildlife. (See "Whittier/Portage Glacier Road" in the SEWARD HIGHWAY section.)

Hope

From downtown Anchorage, take the Seward Highway south to the Hope Cutoff at **Milepost S 56.3**, then drive 16.5 miles northwest to the town of Hope. Hope's historic district, just off the paved Hope Highway, includes the 1896 store (now a cafe) and the 1902 log Social Hall, which still hosts community events. The popular 5-mile Gull Rock Trail is located at the end of the Hope Highway. A relatively flat trail, it ends at Gull Rock overlooking Turnagain Arm. Another popular hiking trail accessible from the Hope Highway is the 38-mile-long Resurrection Pass Trail.

The historic little town of Hope on the south shore of Turnagain Arm.
(© Kris Graef, staff)

This is a 177-mile round-trip drive from downtown Anchorage, offering many fine views of Turnagain Arm. There are outfitters located on the Hope Highway offering rafting trips on Sixmile Creek. For those wishing to make this a 2-day trip, Hope offers both food and accommodations. (See "Hope Highway" in the SEWARD HIGHWAY section.)

Mat-Su Valley

Wasilla and Palmer are the portals to Alaska's famous Mat-Su Valley. For a daylong circle tour of this area, drive out the Glenn Highway to **Milepost A 29.6** and take the Old Glenn Highway to downtown Palmer for lunch and shopping. Depart Palmer for Wasilla via the Palmer–Wasilla Highway. Located at Mile 6.7 on this busy local highway is Fort Green gift shop and museum, featuring the history of the fur industry in Alaska.

Local history is featured at Wasilla's Dorothy Page Museum and Historical Townsite in downtown Wasilla. Follow Main Street across the Parks Highway to Knik Road and drive west 2.2 miles for the **Iditarod Trail Sled Dog Race Headquarters and Visitor Center**. The center has displays of race memorabilia, films on dog mushing and Iditarod souvenirs. Continue on Knik Road to Mile 13.9 for the **Knik Museum Mushers' Hall of Fame** for more Iditarod Race history.

This itinerary is approximately 130 miles round-trip from Anchorage. Other Mat-Su attractions that may be added include the **Museum of Alaska Transportation and Industry**, just north of downtown Wasilla at **Milepost A 47** Parks Highway, and the **Musk Ox Farm**, just east of Palmer at **Milepost A 50.1** Glenn Highway. (See pages 361-369 in the PARKS HIGHWAY section and pages 307–311 in the GLENN HIGHWAY section.)

ANCHORAGE

First Baptist Church of Anchorage

Warmth, Encouragement, Acceptance

Sunday Bible Study .... 9:45 AM
Sunday Worship ...... 11:00 AM & 6:00 PM
Wednesday .... 6:00 PM

Preschool, Children, Youth, Singles, Senior Adult, Family Activities & Music Ministries

1100 West 10th Avenue
907-279-8481
http://www.firstbaptistanchorage.org
firstbaptistanchorage@alaska.com

Denny's
ALWAYS OPEN
Three locations in ANCHORAGE
- DeBarr & Bragaw
- Benson & Denali St.
- Dimond Blvd. & New Seward Hwy.

FAIRBANKS - Airport Road
Children's Menu   No Smoking Section

SOMETHING FOR EVERYONE

★ Racquetball ★ Aerobics ★
★ Weightroom ★ Dance ★ Ceramics ★
★ Badminton ★ Martial Arts ★ *Room Rentals* ★
★ Kitchen Facilities ★ Showers ★

& MUCH MUCH MORE!

We invite you to visit your 2 Community Recreation Centers or call to see which center offers the program for you.

- **Fairview Community Rec. Ctr.**
  1121 E. 10th Ave., 343-4130

- **Spenard Community Rec. Ctr.**
  2020 W. 48th, 343-4160

 Municipality of Anchorage
Parks & Recreation

June sunset at 11:50 P.M. over Potter Marsh, just south of Anchorage. (© Franklin Durr)

School pool, 2909 W. 88th Ave., phone (907) 249-0355; general information phone (907) 343-4476.

Chugiak High School pool, operated by Eagle River Parks & Recreation, is located off South Birchwood Loop Road, off the Glenn Highway north of Anchorage, phone (907) 696-2010. The University of Alaska pool is located on Providence Drive; phone (907) 786-1233.

Anchorage Parks & Recreation can answer questions about aquatics; phone (907) 343-4476.

Goose Lake is open daily, June through August; bathhouse and picnic area. **Goose Lake** is located on UAA Drive, 2 miles east of the New Seward Highway via Benson Blvd./Northern Lights Blvd.

Jewel Lake, 6.5 miles from downtown Anchorage on W. 88th Avenue off Jewel Lake Road, is open daily June through August; lifeguards, restrooms and covered

... helping you live life to the fullest.

For a century we've had the privilege of helping Alaskans, and those visiting our state, through life's journey. In times of need we're here, providing the highest level of care — quality, compassionate care, that people travel across the country to receive — and you'll find it right here in Alaska.

Providence Alaska Medical Center
Anchorage
(907) 562-2211

Providence Seward Medical Center
Seward
(907) 224-5205

Providence Kodiak Island Medical Center
Kodiak
(907) 486-3281

Nurse Advice and Physician Referral Service
Anchorage
(907) 261-4900

Providence | Health System
Alaska Region

3200 Providence Drive • Anchorage, Alaska 99508 • (907) 562-2211 • www.providence.org/alaska

THE QUILT TREE

We invite you to visit Alaska's Quilting source.
- One of the largest selections of quality 100% cotton fabric
- Unique Alaskan patterns
- Full line of current Books, Notions & Supplies
- Classes • Classes • Classes
- Experienced helpful staff

• (907) 561-4115
341 East Benson Blvd., Ste #5
www.quilttree.com

CLEANING WORLD I & II

- Full Service Coin-op Laundry
- Drop Off Laundry
- Professional Dry Cleaning
- Alterations

Cleaning World I
1120 Huffman Rd.
(in Huffman Sq)
Old Seward & Huffman
345-2311

All Sizes Coin-op Machines To Do Comforters, Sleeping Bags, Rugs, Etc

Cleaning World II
Lake Otis & Tudor
Across from AK Korral
561-7406

OPEN 7 DAYS • 8: AM TO 9: P.M.
Off Seward Hwy on way to Kenai
NON SMOKING VERY CLEAN W/FULL TIME ATTENDANT

Seams Like Home Quilt Shoppe

A Sophisticated Quilt Shoppe with Friendly Knowledgeable Staff

- Quality Quilting & Alaskan Fabrics
- Books, Notions, Kits, Patterns
- Silk Ribbon Supplies
- Classes for All Skill Levels

1041 E. 76th Avenue • www.seamslikehome.net

EASY ACCESS FROM NEW OR OLD SEWARD HIGHWAY AT THE 76TH EXIT
(907) 677-8790 • 1-866-677-8790

Fresh Alaskan Seafood

Retail • Custom • Travel Packs • Express Shipping

10th and M Seafoods is Alaska's premiere retail seafood store. Choose from our excellent variety of fresh and frozen seafood from Alaska and around the world. We can express ship seafood almost anywhere or create special packaging for hand-carrying your purchase. Custom game and fish processing and fish smoking available.

1020 M Street
(907) 272-FISH
8 - 6 Mon.- Fri.
9 - 6 Sat.
Closed Sun.

301 Muldoon Road
(907) 337-8831
11 - 7 Tues.- Sat.
12 - 6 Sun.
Closed Mon.

www.10thandMseafoods.com

Serving Alaskans since 1943

The annual Iditarod race to Nome starts in downtown Anchorage on March 1, 2003.

ALASKA FUR EXCHANGE

Not Just Furs, but a Truly Alaskan Store

Alaska's Finest selection of Authentic Alaskan Gifts.

We Ship Anywhere

(907) 563-3877
SE Corner of Old Seward Hwy & Tudor - Midtown
4417 Old Seward Hwy
Anchorage, AK 99503

GREAT NORTHERN GUNS
THE LARGEST SPECIALTY GUN SHOP IN ALASKA

- CUSTOM SPORTING ARMS
- ENGLISH DOUBLE RIFLES
- GERMAN & AUSTRIAN GUNS
- PRE '64 WINCHESTERS
- COLT COLLECTABLES
- TRAP & SKEET ACCESSORIES
- AMERICAN & EUROPEAN OPTICS
- FINE SPORTING SHOTGUNS
- FIREARMS APPRAISER
- ANTIQUE ARMS
- COLLECTIONS PURCHASED
- TRADES CONSIDERED
- HUNTING & FISHING LICENSES

Buy Sell Trade
Visa/MC Discover/AMEX

(907) 563-3006
2920 E. Tudor Road, Anchorage, AK 99507
(behind Williams Express)

Title Wave Books
TRULY ALASKAN • TRULY INDEPENDENT

Used, New, Collectible & Bargain Books
¼ Million books! We Ship Everywhere
Voted Anchorage's Best Book Store
Internet Cafe
OPEN 7 DAYS A WEEK, EVENINGS, TOO!

1360 NORTHERN LIGHTS BLVD.
www.wavebooks.com • 907-278-9283
IN THE NORTHERN LIGHTS CENTER NEAR REI

Denise's ALASKA UNIQUE
Ivory • Carvings • Art • Jewelry

Huge inventory for great selection of the finest Alaskan art available featuring ivory, whale bone, soapstone, walrus bone, jade, gold nugget, fine art & much more.

Shipping Available
All major credit cards accepted

email: info@alaskaunique.com
website: www.alaskaunique.com

(907) 561-9498
3601 Minnesota Dr. • Anchorage, AK 99503

One Stop Shopping in Anchorage

at Sears

offers a wide selection of unique, local and national stores.

- 59-minute photo processing
- Beauty and barber shops
- Groceries
- Extended-hour pharmacy (Carrs)
- Shoe, clothing and jewelry stores
- Specialty gift shops
- Wells Fargo, Alaska
- Anchorage Convention and Visitor's Bureau Information Kiosk

Located at the Southwest corner of Northern Lights and the New Seward Highway
Frequent Service on Bus Routes 3, 4 & 60

**Easy Access Off Both Benson and Northern Lights Blvds.
Free Parking**

Weekdays 10 AM - 9 PM
Saturdays 10 AM - 7 PM
Sundays Noon - 6 PM

---

picnic area.

Call (907) 343-4476 for lifeguarding hours.

Swimming is also offered at Taku Lake and at private clubs.

CAUTION: Do not even consider swimming in Cook Inlet! Soft mud, swift tides and icy water make these waters extremely dangerous!

Saltwater Charter Boats: Sightseeing and fishing charters are available at Whittier, Seward, Soldotna, Deep Creek and Homer. Peak times for saltwater fishing for salmon and halibut are June and July. May and August can also be excellent fishing, depending on the weather.

Freshwater Charter Boats: There is a wide variety of river and lake fishing charters available throughout Southcentral, from Cantwell to Homer. River seasons run from the May king salmon fishery through the September silver salmon fishery. Some lake charters run year-round for ice fishing.

Fishing: The Alaska Dept. of Fish and Game annually stocks about 22 lakes and 3 streams in the Anchorage area with rainbow trout, landlocked and anadromous chinook (king) salmon, anadromous coho salmon, grayling and arctic char. All stocked lakes are open to the public. In addition, salmon-viewing areas and limited salmon fishing are available in the immediate Anchorage area. For specific information, check the Alaska fishing regulations book; contact the agency at (907) 267-2218; 333 Raspberry Road, Anchorage, AK 99518. Urban salmon fisheries have been developed by the Alaska Dept. of Fish and Game in 4 Anchorage-area streams. King and coho (silver) salmon can be caught in **Ship Creek** in downtown Anchorage through July as well as in **Eagle River** just north of town. Coho salmon fisheries are found in **Campbell Creek** in Anchorage and at **Bird Creek** just north of Girdwood on the Seward Highway.

Several derbies are held throughout the summer in and around Anchorage. The Ship Creek King Salmon Derby takes place in early June. Ship Creek is also a popular fishing spot in early August for the Silver Salmon Derby.

In winter, lakes in the Anchorage and the Matanuska–Susitna Valley offer excellent ice fishing. Ice fishing is especially good in the early winter in Southcentral.

Several excellent fishing spots are within a day's drive of Anchorage. The Kenai Peninsula offers streams where king, red, silver, pink and chum salmon may be caught during the summer. Dolly Varden and steelhead also run in peninsula streams. Several lakes contain trout and landlocked salmon.

(Continues on page 356)

A snowball fight in June along Flattop trail. (© Shane Ohms)

EVERYTHING YOU NEED FOR TRAVEL UNDER ONE ROOF.

Postal Services • Packing & Shipping • Document Services • Office Supplies • Fax Sending & Receiving

How convenient, 13 Mail Boxes Etc. locations in South Central Alaska. We're your one stop support center with dozens of ways to make your life easier.
So, how can we help you?

www.mbe.com

MAIL BOXES ETC. We'll take it from here.

MBE Centers are owned and operated by licensed franchisees of Mail Boxes Etc. USA, Inc in the USA. Services and hours of operation may vary by location. ©1999 Mail Boxes Etc. USA, Inc

ANCHORAGE
5432 E. Northern Lights Blvd.
Anchorage, AK 99508
(907) 338-3003

205 E. Dimond Blvd.
Anchorage, AK 99515
(907) 344-1211

1120 E. Huffman Rd.
Anchorage, AK 99515
(907) 345-7311

200 W. 34th Ave.
Anchorage, AK 99503
(907) 561-4410

2440 E. Tudor Rd.
Anchorage, AK 99507
(907) 563-2281

645 G. St. Ste. 100
Anchorage, AK 99501
(907) 276-7888

104 Muldoon Rd.
Anchorage, AK 99504
(907) 337-3322

5800 Westover (Elmendorf)
Anchorage, AK 99506
(907) 753-4477

EAGLE RIVER
12110 Business Blvd. Ste. A06
Eagle River, AK 99577
(907) 694-7447

PALMER
1150 S. Colony Way Ste. 3
Palmer, AK 99645
(907) 746-6245

SOLDOTNA
35555 Spur Hwy.
Soldotna, AK 99669
(907) 262-8774

WASILLA
1830 E. Parks Hwy. Ste. A113
Wasilla, AK 99654
(907) 376-6245

7362 W. Parks Hwy
Wasilla, AK 99654
(907) 373-6245

ALL ABOARD!

Alaska's #1 Wildlife and Glacier Cruise!

Travel the scenic railway between Anchorage and Seward aboard Kenai Fjords Tours Wildlife Express private railcar. Watch for Dall sheep, moose and Beluga whales. Then join Alaska's #1 Wildlife and Glacier Cruise as we explore the waters around Kenai Fjords National Park. You'll see abundant marine wildlife, colorful seabirds, and spectacular glaciers calving - up close! Both tours are fully narrated and meals are included at no additional charge. **Call Today!**

The m/v Coastal Explorer at Holgate Glacier in Kenai Fjords National Park.

In Anchorage
513 W. 4th Avenue
907-276-6249

In Seward
The Seward Small Boat Harbor
907-224-8068

KENAI FJORDS TOURS
An Alaska Heritage Tours Company

Toll-Free 800-478-8068
www.kenaifjords.com

Spend extra time viewing marine wildlife including Steller sea lions.

Enjoy a spectacular wilderness setting while watching for orcas.

Chugach State Park

This 495,000-acre park, flanking Anchorage to the north, east and south, offers wilderness opportunities for all seasons: hiking, wildlife viewing, camping, berry picking, skiing and snowmobiling.

Stop by the Alaska Public Lands Information Center on 4th Avenue in downtown Anchorage for help planning a day hike or back-country trip. Information and trail maps for Chugach State Park are also available from park headquarters, located in Potter Section House on the Seward Highway, 11.8 miles south of downtown Anchorage. Phone (907) 345-5014, or write Chugach State Park, H.C. 52, Box 8999, Indian, AK 99540. Park information is also available from the Department of Natural Resources, phone (907) 269-8400; or online at www.alaskastateparks.org.

There are numerous hiking opportunities in Anchorage thanks to the park's Hillside trail system, accessed from either the Glen Alps or Prospect Heights trailheads.

Glen Alps trailhead accesses several trails, including the most popular hiking trail in the state, **Flattop**. To reach the Glen Alps trailhead, take the New Seward Highway south to the O'Malley exit and go east on O'Malley 3.7 miles to Hillside Drive; take a right on Hillside, go 1 mile to Upper Huffman; turn left on Upper Huffman and go 0.7 mile to Toilsome Hill Road; follow Toilsome Hill Road, which becomes Glen Alps Road, 1.9 miles to parking lot (last 1.3 miles is gravel road). Parking fee is $5.

The hike up Flattop Mountain has an elevation gain of 1,550 feet in 3.5 miles; hiking time 3–5 hours. Also accessible from Glen Alps is the Powerline trail; total length 11 miles, elevation gain 1,300 feet. Williwaw Lakes trail branches off Powerline trail to several small alpine lakes; round-trip is 13 miles with a 742-foot elevation gain.

The **Prospect Heights Trailhead** accesses Near Point, Wolverine Peak and the Middlefork trail to Williwaw Lakes. To reach the Prospect Heights Trailhead, take the O'Malley exit from the New Seward Highway, and go east on O'Malley 3.7 miles to Hillside Drive, but keep to the left; continue 0.1 mile, and turn onto Upper O'Malley Road. Follow Upper O'Malley for 0.6 mile; turn left on Prospect (Trail's End Road is to right), and continue 1.1 miles to the trailhead entrance. Large gravel parking area (pay $5 at fee station) and toilets.

Backpackers on the Crow Pass trail in Chugach State Park.
(© Rich Reid, Colors of Nature)

Chugach State Park also offers great mountain biking opportunities in and around the Anchorage area. Old logging roads, maintained trails and service roads are all part of the Chugach State Park trail system. This trail system includes Bird Creek Logging Roads (trailhead 1 mile off Seward Highway, **Milepost S 100**), Eklutna Lakeside Trail (13.5 miles, trailhead at Eklutna Lake Campground), Gasline Service Road (13.5 miles, from Prospect Heights Trailhead to Indian), Glen Alps (0.3 mile, parking lot to Powerline Trail), Middle Fork Loop Trail (0.75 mile, from intersection of Near Point Trail to south end of Homestead roadbed), Near Point Trail (3 miles, Prospect Heights Trailhead to overlook at north end of Homestead roadbed), Peters Creek Trail (5 miles, trailhead at Malcolm Drive) and Powerline Trail (13 miles, Prospect Heights Trailhead to Indian.) Trails are moderate to steep and offer excellent views of Anchorage and the surrounding mountains.

There are several access points to Chugach State Park attractions from the Glenn Highway. Take the Eklutna Road exit (**Milepost A 26.3**), and drive in 10 miles to reach **Eklutna Lake Recreation Area**. Eklutna Lake is the largest lake in Chugach State Park. The recreation area has a campground, picnic area and hiking trails.

From the Eagle River exit off the Glenn Highway (**Milepost A 13.4**) follow Eagle River Road 12.7 miles to reach **Eagle River Nature Center**, a beautiful spot with views of the Chugach Mountains. Excellent wildlife displays, a nature trail and a year-round program of naturalist-led hikes and talks make this a worthwhile stop. Phone (907) 694-2108 for more information.

Arctic Valley is another park area easily accessible from the Glenn Highway via Arctic Valley Road exit at **Milepost A 6.1**. Drive in 7.5 miles for spectacular views of Anchorage and Cook Inlet. Good berry picking and hiking in summer; downhill and cross-country skiing in winter.

There are $5 parking fees at Chugach State Park access sites, or a parking pass can be purchased for $30 per calendar year from the park office.

The Seward Highway south from Anchorage also gives access to several Chugach State Park hiking trails. See the SEWARD HIGHWAY section for details.

Summer Construction Advisories for Southcentral Alaska
Anchorage, Kenai Peninsula, Mat-Su Valley

24-HOUR RECORDED CONSTRUCTION HOTLINES ARE 273-6037 in Anchorage, 1-800-478-7675 TOLL FREE, or WWW.DOT.STATE.AK.US/NAVIGATOR on the Information Super-Highway

To assist you with your travel planning in the Southcentral area, please refer to the NAVIGATOR construction advisory and detailed maps that appear each week in the Friday editions of the *Anchorage Daily News*, *Peninsula Clarion* and the *Frontiersman* newspapers. The NAVIGATOR provides additional telephone numbers and up-to-date information on construction sites, delays, and lane and road closures during our construction season from about mid-April to mid-October.

STATE of ALASKA DEPARTMENT of TRANSPORTATION and PUBLIC FACILITIES
Central Region, Highway Construction, 4111 Aviation Avenue, P.O. Box 196900, Anchorage, AK 99519-6900, 1-907-269-0450

CELEBRATING THE 40TH ANNIVERSARY OF THE ALASKA MARINE HIGHWAY SYSTEM, 1963-2003

Three Exceptional Reasons to Cruise with Major Marine Tours

1. Reserved table seating for every guest 
2. Hosted by a National Park Ranger* 
3. All-you-can-eat salmon & prime rib meal–$12

Kenai Fjords National Park
- Half-day and full-day cruises
- Puffins, sea lions, otters, whales, bird colonies and more
- Spectacular alpine, piedmont and tidewater glaciers
- Educational Junior Ranger program for kids
- Departs daily from Seward at 11:45 am, 12:45 pm and 6:00 pm**

STARTING AT $54

Prince William Sound Glaciers
- Relaxing 5-hour cruise in calm, protected waters
- Prince William Sound's best glacier viewing. We spend more time at the glaciers to see more calving
- Wildlife, towering waterfalls and more
- Daily departures from Whittier
- Rail/Cruise packages available from Seward and Whittier

$99

Reservations/Information
800-764-7300
907-274-7300

Book Online!
www.majormarine.com

World-Class Wildlife and Glacier Cruises
411 West 4th • Anchorage
Seward Small Boat Harbor
Whittier Boat Harbor

*Kenai Fjords cruises only. **The 6:00 pm cruise commences mid-June.
Children 11 and under are half-price for both the cruise and the meal. Prices and departure times subject to change.

ANCHORAGE

TOURS & TRANSPORTATION

Visiting Anchorage? Not sure where to go? Let People Mover take you there!

Anchorage Public Transportation can take you to RV parks, campgrounds and thousands of other places in Anchorage and Eagle River. If you would like a packet of information before you arrive, send us your request by mail or check our website: www.peoplemover.org

(907)343-6543
People Mover
Attn: Marketing
3650-A E. Tudor
Anchorage, AK
99507-1252

Open Year Round - Kenai Fjords Nat'l Park

Whales, Wildlife & Glacier Cruises

Cruises starting at $39.99

RENOWN
Charters & Tours

In Anchorage (907) 272-1961
Outside Anchorage 1-800-655-3806

e-mail: renown@alaska.com
www.renowncharters.com

A boy and his dog, fishing.
(© Emanuel Canady)

(Continued from page 352)
In-season saltwater fishing for halibut, rockfish and several species of salmon is excellent at many spots along the peninsula and out of Whittier, Homer and Seward. For specific fishing spots both north and south of Anchorage, see the Seward, Sterling, Glenn and Parks highways sections. Because of the importance of fishing to Alaska both commercially and for sport, regulations are strictly enforced. Regulations are updated yearly by the state, often after *The MILEPOST®* deadline, so it is wise to obtain a current regulations book. Check the ADF&G Sport Fish Division home page at www.state.ak.us/adfg/adfghome.htm.

EXPLORE
Alaska's Scenic Backcountry on our fully guided, safe, easy to operate Honda four wheelers.

Combination Tours on Request
Four Wheelers & Kayak
Four Wheelers & Fishing
No experience necessary, transportation can be arranged, instruction and gear provided.

www.alaskaatvadventures.com
e-mail: tim@alaskaatvadventures.com

**FOR RESERVATIONS CALL
(907) 694-4BY4
(907) 694-4294**

PARKS HIGHWAY

Connects: Anchorage to Fairbanks, AK **Length:** 362 miles
Road Surface: Paved   **Season:** Open all year
Highest Summit: Broad Pass 2,400 feet
Major Attraction: Denali National Park

(See maps, pages 358–359)

	Anchorage	Denali Park	Fairbanks	Talkeetna	Wasilla
Anchorage		237	362	113	42
Denali Park	237		125	153	195
Fairbanks	362	125		278	320
Talkeetna	113	153	278		71
Wasilla	42	195	320	71	

Fall colors along the Parks Highway lure photographers. (© Rich Reid, Colors of Nature)

The Parks Highway was called the Anchorage–Fairbanks Highway after its completion in 1971, and renamed the George Parks Highway in July 1975 in honor of George A. Parks (1883–1984), the territorial governor from 1925 to 1933. Abbreviated to the "Parks" Highway over the years, it is designated Alaska Route 3. The Parks Highway junctions with the Glenn Highway (Alaska Route 1) 35 miles from Anchorage and leads 327 miles north to Fairbanks. Together, these highways connect Alaska's largest population centers.

The entire route runs 362 miles through some of the grandest scenery that Alaska has to offer. Highest summit on the Parks Highway is at Broad Pass (see **Milepost A 195**), at approximately 2,400 feet. Motorists can see current weather conditions at Broad Pass by checking the FAA videocam at Summit airport at www.akweathercams.com.

The Parks Highway junctions with the Denali Highway (Alaska Route 8) at Cantwell at **Milepost A 210**. The entrance to Denali National Park is located at **Milepost A 237.4** on the Parks Highway, approximately 27 miles north of Cantwell and 125 miles south of Fairbanks.

The Parks Highway is a good 2-lane paved road, with passing lanes on improved sections. Several sections of moderate S-curves and heavy foliage reduce sight distance: Pass with care. *CAUTION: Drive with headlights on at all times. Watch for moose. Watch for local cross traffic.* Motorists who plan to drive the highway during the winter should check highway conditions before proceeding.

The Parks Highway provides the most direct highway access to Denali National Park and Preserve (formerly Mount McKinley National Park) from either Anchorage or Fairbanks. Mount McKinley—also called Denali—(elev. 20,320 feet) is visible from the highway, weather permitting. Best formal viewpoints along the highway are Denali Viewpoint South, **Milepost A 135.2**; Denali Viewpoint North, **Milepost A 162.4**, and Denali View North Campground at **Milepost A 162.7**. There is also a Denali viewpoint on the Talkeetna Spur Road, 12.8 miles from **Milepost A 98.7**. For details on Denali National Park, read through the DENALI NATIONAL PARK section. See also "Denali Park's Front Country" feature on page 389.

Emergency medical services: Between the Glenn Highway junction and **Milepost A 202.1**, phone 911. Between **Milepost A 174** at Hurricane Gulch bridge and **Milepost A 224** at Carlo Creek bridge, phone the Cantwell ambulance at 768-2982 or the state troopers at 768-2202. Between **Milepost A 224** and Fairbanks, phone 911.

Parks Highway Log

Distance from Anchorage (A) is followed by distance from Cantwell (C) and distance from Fairbanks (F).
Mileposts along the Parks Highway indicate distance from Anchorage.

(Continues on page 360)

PARKS HIGHWAY
Milepost A 169 to Fairbanks, AK

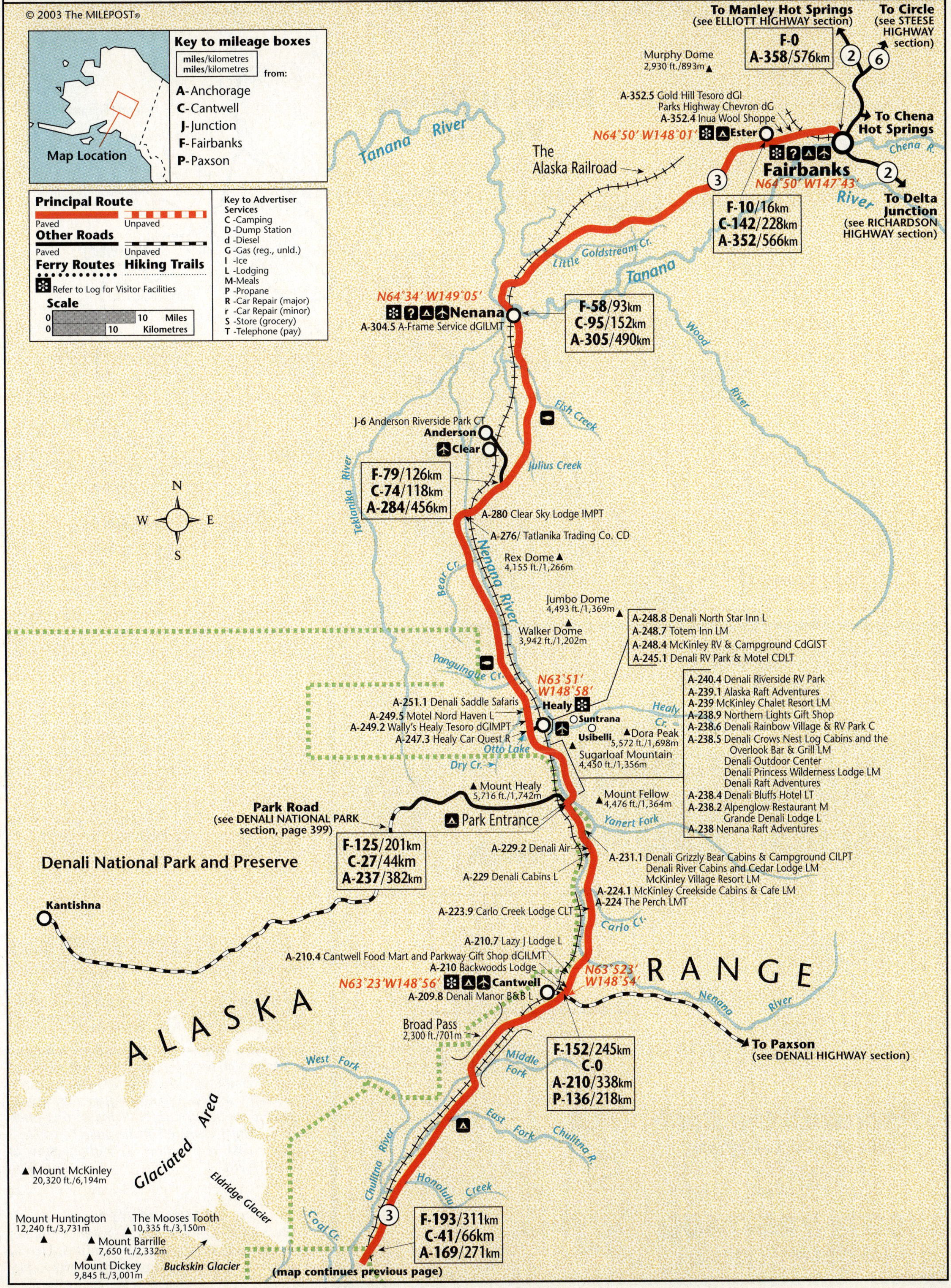

© 2003 The MILEPOST®

Key to mileage boxes

miles/kilometres
miles/kilometres from:
- **A**-Anchorage
- **C**-Cantwell
- **J**-Junction
- **F**-Fairbanks
- **P**-Paxson

Map Location

Principal Route
- Paved
- Unpaved

Other Roads
- Paved
- Unpaved

Ferry Routes   **Hiking Trails**

Refer to Log for Visitor Facilities

Key to Advertiser Services
- C -Camping
- D -Dump Station
- d -Diesel
- G -Gas (reg., unld.)
- I -Ice
- L -Lodging
- M -Meals
- P -Propane
- R -Car Repair (major)
- r -Car Repair (minor)
- S -Store (grocery)
- T -Telephone (pay)

Scale
0 — 10 Miles
0 — 10 Kilometres

To Manley Hot Springs (see ELLIOTT HIGHWAY section)
To Circle (see STEESE HIGHWAY section)

Murphy Dome 2,930 ft./893m

F-0
A-358/576km

A-352.5 Gold Hill Tesoro dGI
Parks Highway Chevron dG
A-352.4 Inua Wool Shoppe

N64°50' W148°01' Ester

To Chena Hot Springs

Fairbanks
N64°50' W147°43'

F-10/16km
C-142/228km
A-352/566km

To Delta Junction (see RICHARDSON HIGHWAY section)

Tanana River
The Alaska Railroad
Little Goldstream Cr.
Tanana River
Wood River
Chena R.

N64°34' W149°05'
Nenana
A-304.5 A-Frame Service dGILMT

F-58/93km
C-95/152km
A-305/490km

Fish Creek

J-6 Anderson Riverside Park CT
Anderson
Clear

F-79/126km
C-74/118km
A-284/456km

A-280 Clear Sky Lodge IMPT
A-276/ Tatlanika Trading Co. CD

Teklanika River
Julius Creek
Nenana River
Bear Cr.

Rex Dome 4,155 ft./1,266m

Jumbo Dome 4,493 ft./1,369m

A-248.8 Denali North Star Inn L
A-248.7 Totem Inn LM
A-248.4 McKinley RV & Campground CdGIST
A-245.1 Denali RV Park & Motel CDLT

Walker Dome 3,942 ft./1,202m

Panguingue Cr.

N63°51' W148°58'
Healy
Suntrana
Usibelli

Dora Peak 5,572 ft./1,698m

Healy Cr.

A-251.1 Denali Saddle Safaris
A-249.5 Motel Nord Haven L
A-249.2 Wally's Healy Tesoro dGIMPT
A-247.3 Healy Car Quest R

Otto Lake
Dry Cr.

Sugarloaf Mountain 4,450 ft./1,356m

A-240.4 Denali Riverside RV Park
A-239.1 Alaska Raft Adventures
A-239 McKinley Chalet Resort LM
A-238.9 Northern Lights Gift Shop
A-238.6 Denali Rainbow Village & RV Park C
A-238.5 Denali Crows Nest Log Cabins and the Overlook Bar & Grill LM
Denali Outdoor Center
Denali Princess Wilderness Lodge LM
Denali Raft Adventures
A-238.4 Denali Bluffs Hotel LT
A-238.2 Alpenglow Restaurant M
Grande Denali Lodge L
A-238 Nenana Raft Adventures

Mount Healy 5,716 ft./1,742m
Mount Fellow 4,476 ft./1,364m

Park Road (see DENALI NATIONAL PARK section, page 399)

Park Entrance

F-125/201km
C-27/44km
A-237/382km

A-229.2 Denali Air
A-229 Denali Cabins L

Yanert Fork

A-231.1 Denali Grizzly Bear Cabins & Campground CILPT
Denali River Cabins and Cedar Lodge LM
McKinley Village Resort LM
A-224.1 McKinley Creekside Cabins & Cafe LM
A-224 The Perch LMT

Denali National Park and Preserve

Kantishna

A-223.9 Carlo Creek Lodge CLT
Carlo Cr.
A-210.7 Lazy J Lodge L
A-210.4 Cantwell Food Mart and Parkway Gift Shop dGIMPT
A-210 Backwoods Lodge

N63°23' W148°56'
Cantwell
N63°23' W148°54'

A-209.8 Denali Manor B&B L

Broad Pass 2,300 ft./701m

ALASKA RANGE

Nenana River

To Paxson (see DENALI HIGHWAY section)

F-152/245km
C-0
A-210/338km
P-136/218km

West Fork
Middle Fork
East Fork Chulitna R.

Mount McKinley 20,320 ft./6,194m
Mount Huntington 12,240 ft./3,731m
The Mooses Tooth 10,335 ft./3,150m
Mount Barrille 7,650 ft./2,332m
Mount Dickey 9,845 ft./3,001m

Glaciated Area
Eldridge Glacier
Buckskin Glacier
Coal Cr.
Honolulu Creek
Chulitna River

F-193/311km
C-41/66km
A-169/271km

(map continues previous page)

www.themilepost.com

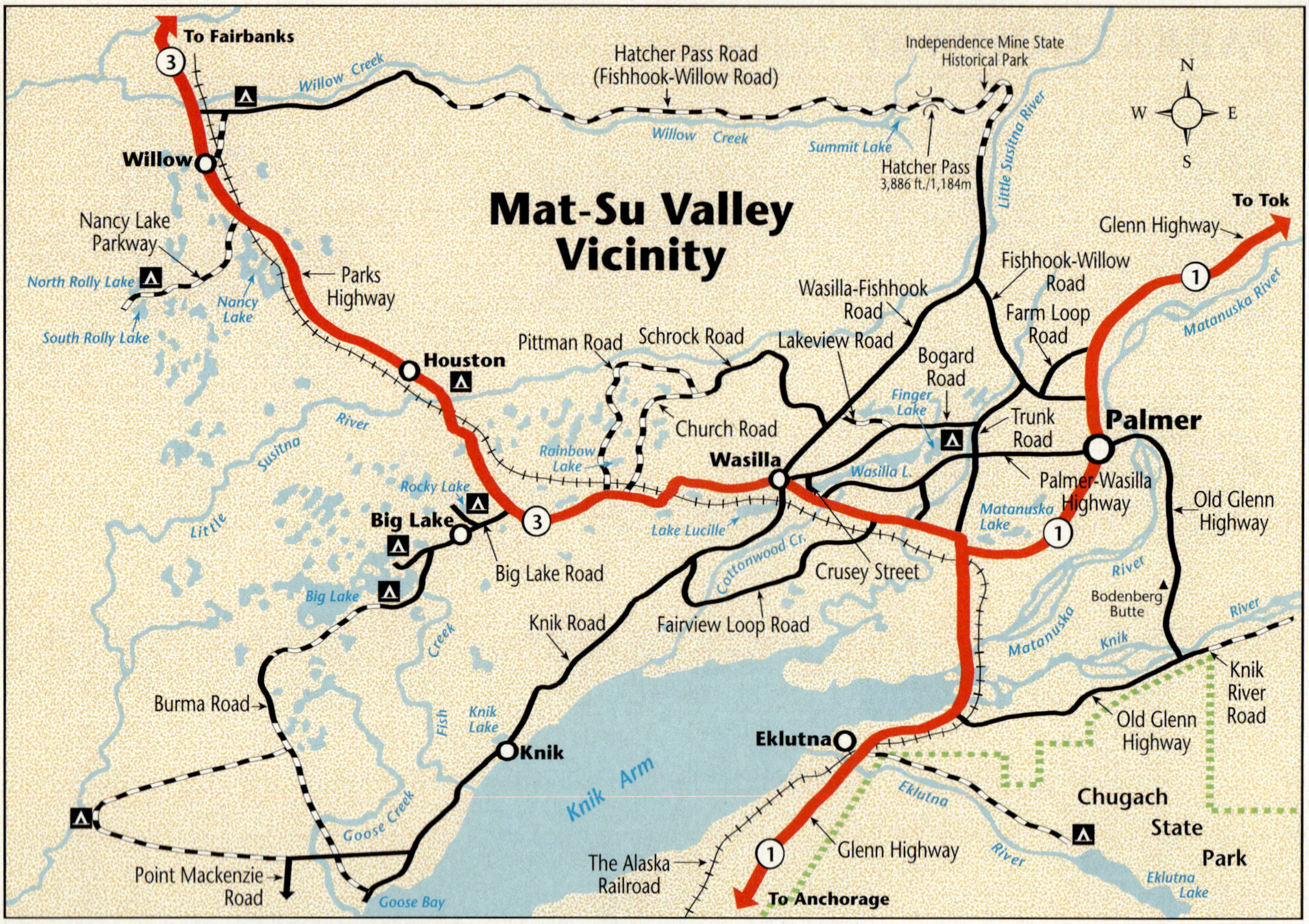

PARKS HIGHWAY

Mat-Su Valley Vicinity

LOCATED AT THE GATEWAY TO THE MAT-SU VALLEY

Best View RV PARK

Good Sampark

- 63 LARGE VIEW SPACES
- FULL HOOKUPS
- DRIVE-THRUS
- DUMP STATION
- HOT SHOWERS INCLUDED
- TENT CAMPERS
- PICNIC TABLES • FIREPITS
- LAUNDRY

Park with the Best
Mile 35.5 Parks Highway
Best View
P.O. Box 872001, Wasilla, AK 99687

(907) 745-7400
1-800-478-6600 (Toll Free in Alaska)

(Continued from page 357)

ALASKA ROUTE 1
A 0 C 210 F 362 **ANCHORAGE**. Follow the Glenn Highway (Alaska Route 1) north 35 miles to junction with the Parks Highway. (Turn to the end of the GLENN HIGHWAY section on page 316 and read log back to front from Anchorage to junction with the Parks Highway.)

A 35.3 C 174.7 F 326.7 **Glenn–Parks Interchange**. Parks Highway travelers turn north here. *NOTE: Construction of a new Glenn–Parks Interchange underway in 2003. Watch for lane closures and traffic changes. Distance and directions may vary from log due to construction detours.*

Junction of the Parks Highway (Alaska Route 3) and the Glenn Highway (Alaska Route 1). Turn to Milepost A 35.3 on page 313 in the GLENN HIGHWAY section for log.

The new Glenn–Parks Interchange, scheduled for completion in November 2004, will provide 2 lanes of continuous flow traffic in either direction, with a new Wasilla-Palmer off ramp, replacing the former traffic lights at this intersection. Major elements of the project include 5 bridges and more than 3 million tons of embankment. *NOTE: Traffic fines double in construction areas. Obey posted speed limits.*

ALASKA ROUTE 3
A 35.4 C 174.6 F 326.6 Distance marker northbound shows Wasilla 7 miles, Denali National Park 201 miles, Fairbanks 319 miles.

360 ■ The MILEPOST® ■ 2003   www.themilepost.com

A 35.5 C 174.5 F 326.5 Best View RV Park and Mat-Su Visitor Center are visible from the highway on hill to east (use Trunk Road exit).

Best View RV Park. See display ad this section. ▲

Matanuska–Susitna Convention & Visitors Bureau. See display ad this section.

A 35.8 C 174.2 F 326.2 Northbound exit to **Trunk Road**; access to Mat-Su Visitor Center and Best View RV Park and North Star Speedway Nascar racing (follow signs) .

Trunk Road leads northeast 0.7 mile to University of Alaska Fairbanks' Matanuska agricultural research farm; no tours, but you can walk through the display gardens. Also access via Trunk Road to Mat-Su College (1.8 miles); Palmer-Wasilla Highway (3.1 miles); Bogard Road (4.2 miles); and Palmer-Fishhook Road (6.5 miles).

Mat–Su Visitor Center is open May 15 to Sept. 15, 8 A.M. to 6 P.M. daily. This large center offers a wide variety of displays and information on the Mat–Su Valley; pay phone, gift shop. The visitor center operates a booking and reservation service; phone (907) 746-5000; or visit their web site at www.alaskavisit.com..

Adjacent to the Visitors Center is a **Veterans Monument and the Wall of Honor**. The Veterans Monument, a 20-ton granite boulder with a bronze plaque and inscription, honors all veterans of the U.S. armed forces. The Veterans Wall of Honor consists of black granite panels, each 36 inches wide and 72 inches high, inscribed with the names of veterans, living or deceased, who have either received an honorable discharge or are presently serving in the military. The Wall is intended to resemble the Vietnam Wall in Washington D.C. Mt. POW/MIA, a peak in the nearby Chugach Range, is visible from the site. Named in 1999, a small plaque commemorating the Nov. 11, 1999 dedication reads "Climbed and named by a Marine vet who cared." The names of the only 2 Alaskan MIAs (missing in action) from the Vietnam War appear on the Wasilla Wall of Honor, in view of Mt. POW/MIA: They are Marine E4 Thomas E. Anderson and Navy E3 Howard M. Koslosky.

North Star Speedway. See display ad this section.

A 36.4 C 173.6 F 325.6 Southbound exit to Trunk Road; see description at **Milepost A 35.8**.

A 37.6 C 172.4 F 324.4 Northbound exit to Fairview Loop and Hyer Road Access to Palmer Hay Flats State Game Refuge from Fairview Loop (see description at **Milepost J 4.1** Knik–Goose Bay Road log on page 366). Gas station/foodmart west of turnoff.

A 38.2 C 171.8 F 323.8 Southbound exit to Fairview Loop and Hyer Road.

A 38.8 C 171.2 F 323.2 *Begin 2-lane traffic northbound. Begin 4-lane divided highway southbound.*

NOTE: Construction of a divided 4-lane highway next 3 miles northbound (to Crusey Street) underway in summer 2003. Expect reduced speed limits, lane restrictions, detours and minor delays. Distance and directions may vary from log due to road construction.

A 39.3 C 170.7 F 322.7 **Junction** with Seward Meridian Road; Meridian Center Mall and Wal-Mart store to west, Sears to east.

A 39.5 C 170.5 F 322.5 Wasilla city limits (sign).

A 40 C 170 F 322 Alaskan View Motel. See display ad this section.

www.themilepost.com

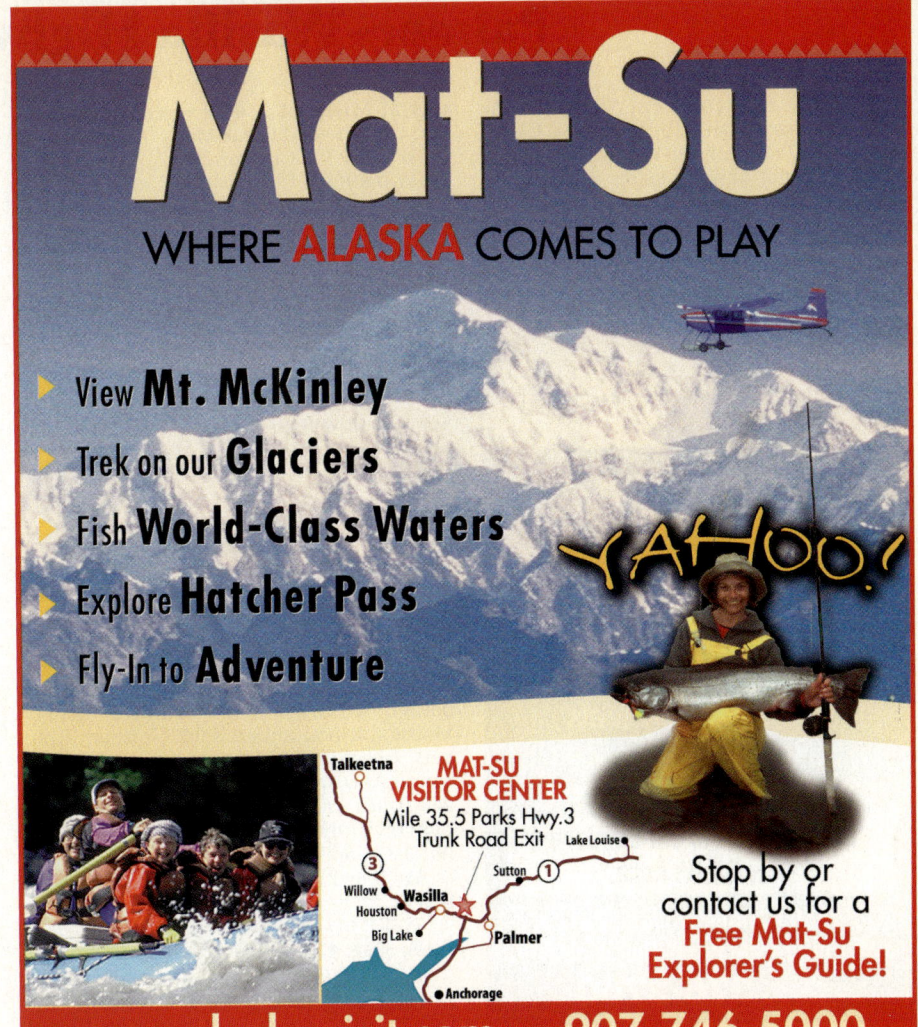

Exercise caution in road construction areas in 2003.

Palmer–Wasilla Highway

This 10-mile road connects Wasilla on the Parks Highway with Palmer on the Glenn Highway. The Palmer-Wasilla Highway accesses several business parks and residential subdivisions, and acts as a shortcut between the 2 communities for local traffic. A very busy road. Posted speed limit is 45- to 55-mph. There is a bike path along this highway.

Distance from Wasilla (W) is followed by distance from Palmer (P).

W 0 P 10.1 Junction with Parks Highway at **Milepost A 41.1**; Fred Meyer store and Cottonwood Creek Mall.

W 0.4 P 9.6 Gas station.

W 0.6 P 9.4 Cottonwood Creek.

W 0.8 P 9.2 Kwik Kard gas station to west.

W 0.9 P 9.1 Diversified Tire. See display ad this section.

W 1.8 P 8.2 W 1.8 Junction with North Seward Meridian Parkway; Tesoro gas station/Subway. Cottonwood Public Safety Building.

W 2.4 P 7.6 Schwabenhof's, a popular German restaurant.

W 2.5 P 7.5 Landscape Supply.

W 2.9 P 7.1 Hatcherview Center; Valley Center.

W 3 P 7 Brentwood Plaza.

W 3.3 P 6.7 Fort Green gift shop and fur museum east side of highway.

Fort Green. Charming Alaskan gift shop, museum, large rustic log cabin on the Palmer-Wasilla Highway. Easy access, RV parking, buses. Beautiful view, Chugach Mountains, Knik Glacier. Largest Alaskan basket selection, 500. Wildlife display. Moose, caribou antlers sold. Northern Trappers, Fur Industry Museum; interesting, educational. Displaying art, posters, calendars, bear traps, trapping artifacts from 1700s to present. Truly an Alaskan experience! Phone (907) 376-5873. [ADVERTISEMENT]

W 3.8 P 6.2 The Frontiersman newspaper.

W 4 P 6 North Hyer Road.

W 5.8 P 4.2 Wasilla Creek.

W 6 P 4 Four Corners junction. Tesoro gas station and grocery at **junction** with North Trunk Road. Turn north for Bogard Road and **Finger Lake State Recreation Site**; go north on Trunk Road 1 mile to Bogard Road; turn west and drive 0.7 mile to park entrance; drive in 0.3 mile on gravel road. A scenic spot with 41 campsites, wheelchair-accessible toilets, picnic tables, water, hiking trails and boat launch, $10 camping fee, 7-day limit. Use the life jackets provided! Finger Lake is on the **7-Mile Canoe Trail**. Public access to the canoe trail is also from Wasilla Lake and Cottonwood Lake.

W 6.7 P 3.3 Midtown Community Business Park; pizza.

W 7.2 P 2.8 Stoplight at **junction** with North 49th/State Street. Car wash.

W 7.7 P 2.3 Trinity Barn Plaza; coffee.

W 8 P 2 Loma Prieta Drive. Access to **Crevasse–Moraine Trail.** Drive 0.8 mile west on Loma Prieta Drive to end of pavement, then proceed downhill to trailhead parking area. This loop trail system is used for cross-country skiing in winter and hiking, mountain biking and horseback riding in summer.

W 9.3 P 0.7 Hemmer Road to Palmer High School.

W 9.6 P 0.4 NOAA Tsunami Warning Center; informative tours of the facility are offered on Fridays at 1, 2 and 3 P.M.; no reservations required. Phone (907) 745-4212 for more information.

W 10 P 0 Junction with Glenn Highway at **Milepost A 41.8** in Palmer; Carrs Mall (24-hour supermarket) and McDonalds.

**Return to Milepost A 41
Parks Highway or A 41.8
Glenn Highway**

A 40 C 170 F 322 Northern Recreation. See display ad this section.

A 40.1 C 169.9 F 321.9 **Evangelo's Restaurant.** See display ad this section.

A 40.5 C 169.5 F 321.5 Access to the Windbreak (cafe/hotel/bar) on the east side of the highway, and Pilgrims Baptist church on the west side of the highway.

Pilgrims Baptist Church. See display ad this section.

The Windbreak. See display ad this section.

A 40.9 C 169.1 F 321.1 Cottonwood Creek Mall east side of highway. Wasilla Police Dept. west side of highway. Also access to medical clinic to west (behind Arby's).

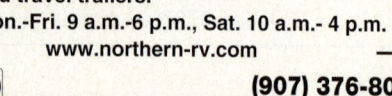

Begin 4-lane divided highway northbound. End 4-lane divided highway southbound. NOTE: Watch for construction next 3 miles southbound in summer 2003.

A 41 C 169 F 321 Access to Cottonwood Creek Mall and Fred Meyer to east via Palmer–Wasilla Highway. Tesoro gas station. Palmer-Wasilla Highway extension to west connects with Glenwood Avenue to Knik–Goose Bay Road.

Junction with Palmer–Wasilla Highway, which leads east 10 miles to the Glenn Highway at Palmer. See "Palmer–Wasilla Highway" log on opposite page.

A 41.7 C 168.3 F 320.3 Northbound access to **Newcomb Wasilla Lake Park**; limited parking, picnic shelter, restrooms, playground and swimming beach, rainbow trout fishing. Monument to George Parks.

A 41.8 C 168.2 F 320.2 Crusey Street intersection; McDonald's. Southbound access to Wasilla Lake.

Turn east on Crusey Street for Bogard Road and access to **Mat-Su Resort** (1.3 miles) and Finger Lake State Recreation Site (6.6 miles).

Mat-Su Resort. See display ad this section.

A 42 C 168 F 320 Carr's Mall to east; supermarket.

A 42.1 C 167.9 F 319.9 Old Town Square shopping to east. Welcome to Wasilla, home of the Iditarod Re-Start (sign and summer floral display) to west.

A 42.2 C 167.8 F 319.8 Junction with Knik–Goose Bay Road to west, Main Street to east. Historic Alaska Railroad Depot on west side of highway (see description in Wasilla Attractions). Main Street leads 1 block east to the visitor center and museum and 2 blocks to the post office (ZIP code 99687). Description of Wasilla follows.

Junction with Knik–Goose Bay Road and access to Lake Lucille park, Iditarod Trail Sled Dog Race Headquarters and other attractions. See "Knik–Goose Bay Road" log on page 366.

Main Street becomes Wasilla–Fishhook Road, which leads northeast about 10 miles to junction with the Hatcher Pass (Fishhook–Willow) Road to Independence Mine State Historical Park; see the map on page 360. (The Hatcher Pass Road is logged on pages 305-306 in the GLENN HIGHWAY section.)

Wasilla

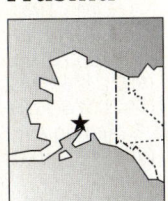

A 42.2 C 167.8 F 319.8 Located between Wasilla and Lucille lakes in the Susitna Valley, about an hour's drive from Anchorage. **Population:** 5,213. **Emergency Services: Police**, phone (907) 745-2131, emergency only phone 911. **Fire Department** and **Ambulance**, phone 911. **Hospital**, in Palmer.

Visitor Information: At the Dorothy Page Museum and Historical Townsite on Main Street just off the Parks Highway, phone (907) 373-9071, fax 373-9072. Or contact Greater Wasilla Chamber of Commerce, Box 871826, Wasilla 99687, phone (907) 376-1299. Exit at Trunk Road and

Boating and camping are popular at Finger Lake State Recreation Site.
(© Kris Graef, staff)

THE WINDBREAK
BEST SMALL CAFE/HOTEL/BAR IN THE STATE

LOCATION:
Mile 40.5 Parks Highway - Downtown Wasilla
40 Miles North of Anchorage.

CAFE:
Open at 6:00 A.M. to 11:00 P.M.
PRICES: Breakfast............$3.75 and up
Lunch..................$3.98 and up

HOTEL RATES:
$65 to $75 per night - 10 Rooms
Includes: Cable TV, telephones, private bath & continental breakfast

FOOD:
Our Motto is: "We feed you, We don't fool you"
(Daily Breakfast, Lunch and Dinner Specials)
Dinner ....$15.95 Prime Rib

BEST FOOD IN THE STATE
A wide variety of fresh garden salads!

FISHING:
Trout fishermen from all over the world stop here for information and advice. Cafe is decorated with fish mounts from all over the state.

CAFE (907) 376-4484
HOTEL (907) 376-4209
2201 E. PARKS HWY. • WASILLA, ALASKA 99687
windcafe@corecom.net

- Deluxe rooms with lake & mountain views, cable TV, telephone and kitchenette
- Floatplane dock & 60 passenger paddle wheeler ♦ 45 minutes from Anchorage
- Restaurant and lounge open daily for Breakfast, Lunch and Dinner
- Sunday brunch ♦ Banquet and meeting rooms

Mat-Su Resort
907-376-3228 ♦ Fax: 907-376-7781
1850 Bogard Road   Wasilla, Alaska 99654
www.matsuresort.com

Alaska's Lake Lucille Bed & Breakfast

Affordable 1st class lakeside accommodations in the heart of Wasilla, in the Mat-Su Valley, CLOSE TO EVERYTHING!

Toll Free: 888-353-0352 • Fax: 907-357-0353

Visit us at
www.alaskaslakelucillebnb.com
or email us at
stay@alaskaslakelucillebnb.com
...you'll be glad you did!

CHECK YOUR EMAIL
www.meadscoffeehouse.com

Mead's Coffeehouse
A Gathering Place
405 E Herning Ave
Wasilla

357-5633

Fresh soups, salads, sandwiches, and breads
An Old time store with a few modern twists

Downtown Wasilla

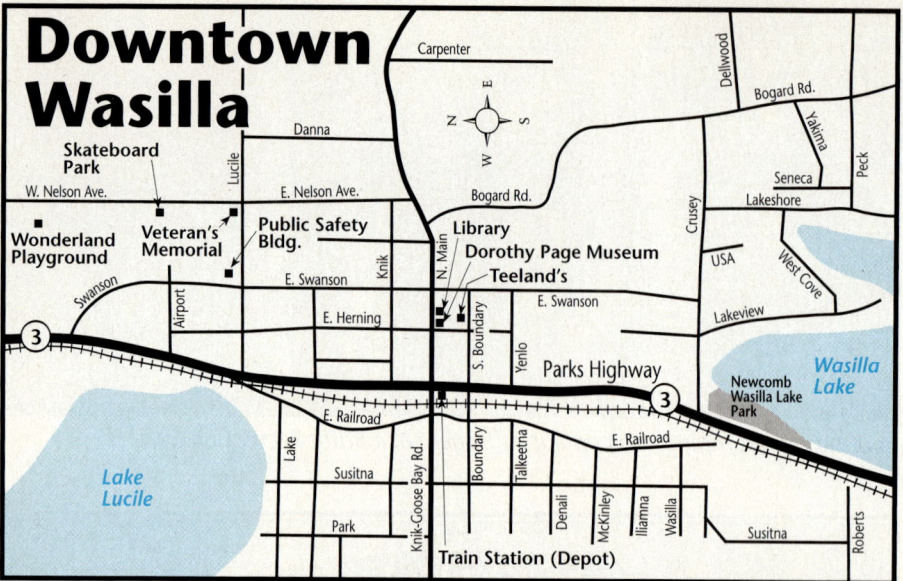

Alaska KOZEY CABINS

- 1 Mile from Town (Wasilla)
- All Heated Cabins Fully Furnished with Kitchens and Baths
- Rent by Day, Week or Monthly
- Overnighters Welcome

Call Ahead for Reservations
351 E. Spruce Avenue, Wasilla, AK 99654
website: www.kozeycabins.com
e-mail: akc@kozeycabins.com
(907) 376-3190

Lake Lucille Inn — THE WORLD'S LARGEST HOTEL CHAIN
Superb location on beautiful Lake Lucille
Breathtaking views of the Chugach Mountains
Full service hotel – restaurant, lounge, convention facilities, watercraft rentals & fitness room with hot tub and sauna.
Conveniently located 45 miles from Anchorage.
1300 W. Lake Lucille Dr., Wasilla, AK 99654
907-373-1776 • Fax: 907-376-6199 • www.bestwestern.com/lakelucilleinn

---

follow signs to Mat-Su Visitors Center. Write Mat-Su Convention & Visitors Bureau, HC 01, Box 6166J21-MP, Palmer, AK 99645; phone (907) 746-5000.

Radio and **Television** via Anchorage stations; KMBQ 99.7. **Newspapers:** *The Valley Sun* (weekly); *The Frontiersman* (triweekly). **Transportation: Air**—Charter service available. **Railroad**—Alaska Railroad. **Bus**—Mat-Su Community Transit, service between Mat-Su locations and Anchorage; phone (907) 376-5000.

Private Aircraft: Wasilla municipal airport, 4.8 miles north on Neuser Drive; elev. 348 feet; length 3,700 feet; asphalt; unattended. Wasilla Lake seaplane base, 0.9 mile east; elev. 330 feet. Numerous private airstrips and lakes in vicinity.

One of the Matanuska–Susitna Valley's pioneer communities, Wasilla began as a station on the Alaska Railroad about 1916. With the railroad, and a government land auction bringing in new settlement, Wasilla became a supply staging point for gold mines in the Willow Creek Mining District.

With the advent of a farm-based economy in the 1930s and 40s—precipitated by the Matanuska Valley Colony project—Palmer replaced Wasilla as the regional service and supply center. Palmer remained the commercial hub of the Mat-Su Valley until the 1970s, when the new Glenn Highway bypassed downtown Palmer, and the Anchorage–Fairbanks Highway (now Parks Highway) was completed. The new highway, coupled with the pipeline boom, brought both people and traffic to Wasilla.

Today, major chain retail stores, small businesses, fast-food outlets and auto dealerships line the Parks Highway in Wasilla. New residential subdivisions have sprung up along the Wasilla's back roads in this fastest-growing area in the state.

Lodging & Services

All visitor facilities are available here, including banks, post office, gas stations, major-chain retail stores, supermarkets, tire

WASILLA ADVERTISERS

Alaska Kozey Cabins
 & RV Rental ....Ph. (907) 376-3190
Alaska's Lake Lucille Bed
 & Breakfast ....Ph. (888) 353-0352
Annabel's Used Books ......Ph. (907) 373-7273
Best Western Lake
 Lucille Inn ....Ph. (907) 373-1776
Cis' Unique Antiques ....Ph. (907) 376-7870
Dorothy Page Museum &
 Historical Townsite............323 Main Street
Fort Green.........................Ph. (907) 376-5873
Hall's Auto Rental 1-877-611-HALL
Iditarod Trail Headquarters Mile 2.2 Knik Rd.
Knik Knack Mud Shack..........Mile 10 Knik Rd.
Mail Boxes Etc..................Ph. (907) 376-6245
Mat-Su Resort ....Ph. (907) 376-3228
Mead's Coffeehouse..........405 E. Herring Ave.
Mr. Lube ....Ph. (907) 373-4645
Museum of Alaska
 Transportation.............Ph. (907) 376-1211
Point Mackenzie General Store
 & Cafe ....Ph. (907) 373-0931
Suburban Propane............Ph. (800) 880-7581
Town Square Art Gallery ..Ph. (907) 376-0123
Trail Masters Gifts................Mile 2.2 Knik Rd.
Valley River Charters ....Ph. (877) 376-6583
Veterans of Foreign
 Wars Post #9365 ....Mile 0.2 Knik Rd.

and RV repair, laundromats and other services.

Wasilla Skateboard Park and adjacent Wonderland Playground, located on Nelson Avenue, make great stops for families traveling with active children. The Brett Memorial Ice Arena, at Bogard Road and Crusey Street, has ice skating and fitness court.

Alaska Kozey Cabins & RV Rental. Modern, hand-crafted log cabins set in the state's No. 1 recreation area. Cabins feature queen and full beds, fully equipped kitchens, bath and living rooms. Cross-country skiing, snow machining, hiking, fishing, and hunting abound. Near the official Iditarod restart. Open year-round. Phone (907) 376-3190. See display ad this section. [ADVERTISEMENT]

Point Mackenzie General Store & Cafe. Mile 7 Mackenzie Road, 4 miles from Little Susitna campground and boat launch. Cabin rentals, laundry, showers, fishing/hunting licenses. Storage. Fuels. Beer, wine. Turn

Along the boardwalk at Lake Lucille Park in Wasilla. (© Kris Graef, staff)

right off Knik-Goose Bay Road at Mile 17, then 7 miles to this unique and highly gratifying experience. Open year-round. (907) 373-0931. [ADVERTISEMENT]

Mail Boxes Etc. Let the experts at Mail Boxes Etc. pack and ship your "Alaskan catch" frozen fish and other great souvenirs. And while you're here, check your email, purchase stamps, mail postcards and look around at the many other services we provide. At Mail Boxes Etc. "We'll take it from here." [ADVERTISEMENT]

Camping

Public campgrounds in the Wasilla area include Lake Lucille Park on Knik Road; Little Susitna River Public-use Site off Point Mackenzie Road; and Finger Lake SRS on Bogard Road (descriptions follow). There are several RV parks on the Parks Highway south and north of Wasilla. The nearest of these are Best View RV Park, **Milepost A 35.5**, accessible from the Trunk Road exit, and Ice Worm RV Park & Country Store at **Milepost A 50.2**.

For **Lake Lucille Park** (Mat–Su Borough), take Knik Road 2.3 miles southwest and turn on Endeavor Street (just beyond Iditarod headquarters parking lot), then drive 0.6 mile on a gravel access road. There are 64 campsites in a heavily wooded area on a gravel loop road; picnic pavilions; campground host; firewood, firepits, restrooms. Camping fee charged. See Mile J 2.3 "Knik–Goose Bay Road" log this section.

Little Susitna River campground is located off Point Mackenzie Road, 29.8 miles from the Parks Highway. There are 83

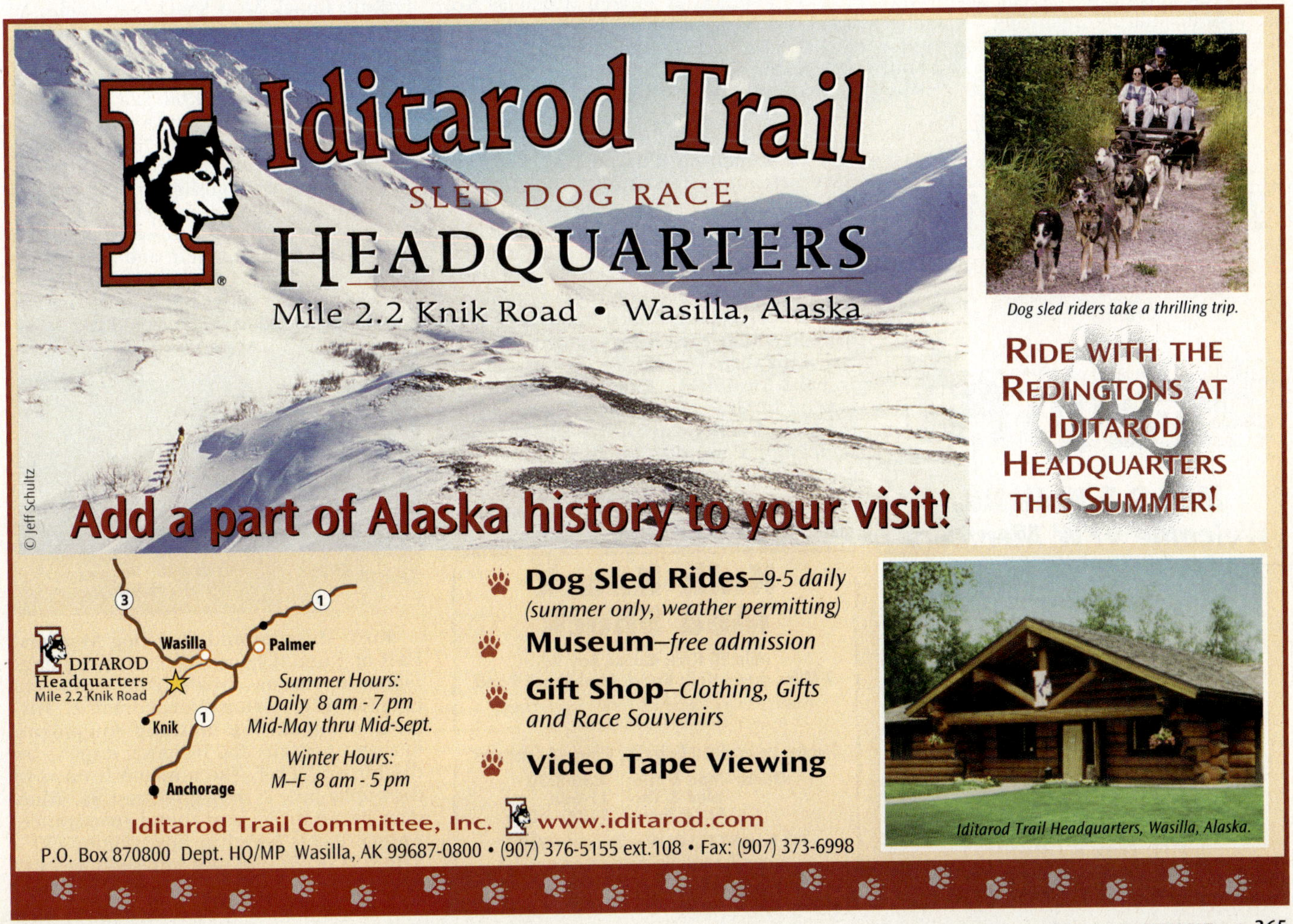

Knik–Goose Bay Road

Colorful headquarters of the Iditarod Trail Sled Dog Race®. (© Kris Graef, staff)

Knik Road-Goose Bay Road leads 20.6 miles southwest from Wasilla. It provides access to Goose Bay State Game Refuge and Point Mackenzie Road access to the popular Little Susitna River Public-use Site at Susitna Flats State Game Refuge.

The first 15 miles of Knik Road have been designated the Joe Redington Sr. Memorial Trail, in memory of the Alaskan musher who was instrumental in organizing the annual Iditarod Trail Sled Dog Race. (Stop by the Iditarod Trail headquarters at Mile J 2.2 Knik Road for more on the history of this major Alaskan sporting event.)

KNIK-GOOSE BAY ROAD
Distance from the junction (J) with Parks Highway.

J 0 Junction with Parks Highway at Milepost A 42.2, Main Street, Wasilla.
J 0.1 *CAUTION: Road crosses railroad tracks.*
J 0.2 Veterans of Foreign Wars Post No. 9365. See display ad this section.
J 0.7 Traffic light at Glenwood Avenue, which connects with the Palmer-Wasilla Highway at **Milepost A 41** Parks Highway.
J 1.4 Gas station.
J 1.9 Smith ball fields.
J 2.2 Turnoff for **Iditarod Trail Sled Dog Race® Headquarters** and visitor center. The center has historical displays and films on sled dog racing and mushers, as well as a souvenir shop with Iditarod memorabilia. Dog sled rides are often available, and there are usually some sled dog puppies running around (or sleeping). Open 8 A.M. to 7 P.M., daily in summer, weekdays until 5 P.M. the rest of the year.
J 2.3 Turnoff on Endeavor Street (just beyond Iditarod headquarters parking lot) for **Lake Lucille Park** (Mat–Su Borough) campground and day-use area, located 0.6 mile north via gravel road. There are 64 campsites in a heavily wooded area on a gravel loop road; picnic pavilions; campground host; water; firewood, firepits, restrooms. Camping fee charged. Fishing for landlocked silver salmon. Short boardwalk walking trail to lake.
J 4.1 Tesoro gas station and grocery at **junction** with Fairview Loop Road, which leads 11 miles to junction with the Parks Highway at **Milepost A 38**.
Palmer Hay Flats State Game Refuge is accessed via Fairview Loop. From this junction, drive 1.9 miles on Fairview Loop to where the road makes a 90-degree turn and intersects with a gravel side road. Instead of turning the corner to continue on Fairview Loop, follow the gravel side road 1.3 miles to the signed turnoff for Palmer Hay Flats. Steep, rough access road from signed turnoff 0.6 mile to observation deck. No motorized access beyond this point; foot and canoe access to marsh along Cottonwood Creek.
J 6.8 Junction with Vine Road, which leads 3.4 miles to the Parks Highway. Vine Road also junctions with Hollywood Road, which leads 6.5 miles to connect with Big Lake Road.
J 7 Central Station No. 629; *emergency phone*.
J 8 Settlers Bay residential area; post office. Access to 18-hole Settlers Bay golf course (follow signs).
J 10.1 Turnoff for **Homestead Museum**, with a large collection of early Alaskan memorabilia, and gift shop.
Knik Knack Mud Shack. See display ad this section.
J 13 KNIK (pop. 483); bar, pay phone, liquor store, gas station and private campground on Knik Lake. Knik is a checkpoint on the Iditarod Trail Sled Dog Race® route and has been called the "Dog Mushing Center of the World" in reference to the many Alaskan dog mushers that have lived in this area.
J 13.9 Turnoff to northwest (watch for "Old Knik" sign); museum and public fishing access to **Knik Lake** (stocked with rainbow; 5hp motors only). Short, steep, narrow gravel access road to museum and lake.

Knik Museum and Sled Dog Mushers' Hall of Fame is housed in 1 of 2 buildings remaining from Knik's gold rush era (1897–1917). Regional memorabilia, artifacts, archives, dog mushing equipment, mushers' portraits and historical displays on the Iditarod Trail. The museum is open to the public June 1 through August 31. Tours may be arranged year-round in advance. Annual Picnic Social in July. Phone (907) 376-7755 or 376-2005 for admission fees and hours.

A traditional Athabascan graveyard with

Veterans of Foreign Wars Post #9365

Mile 0.2 Knik Rd.
Welcome VFW Members

PICNIC FACILITIES AVAILABLE

R.V. SPACES FREE TO MEMBERS

(907) 376-5820
P.O. Box 872000
Wasilla, Alaska 99687

Knik Knack Mud Shack
Mile 10 Knik-Goose Bay Rd
2 Miles down Knik Knack Mud Shack Road
Alaska's Largest Ceramic & Pottery Supply House
Visit our Gift Shop & Showroom
Featuring Alaska's Finest Native Clay Giftware & Collectables
Open: Mon & Tues   4:30-8:30
       Wed & Thur   11-6:00
       Sat & Sun   11:00-3:00
PO Box 877550, Wasilla, AK 99687
e-mail: ceramic@mtaonline.net
(907) 376-5793

fenced graves and spirit houses is located behind the museum. The graveyard is on sacred ground; visitors may view it from a section of the Iditarod Trail.

J 16.1 Fish Creek bridge.

J 17.2 Point Mackenzie Road junction; turn here for access to Little Susitna River Public-Use Site (see Point Mackenzie Road log following).

J 18.5 Tag Bar (367-5978); liquor store, ATM, camping, cabin and snow machine rentals.

Pavement ends, gravel begins, westbound.

J 19.5 "Y" junction at Goose Bay Airport Road. Keep to right at this intersection and keep to left at next "Y" for Goose Bay access.

J 20.6 Steep, rough, winding access road to boat launch; recommended for 4WD only. **Goose Bay State Game Refuge** is a 10,880-acre refuge encompassing Goose Bay wetlands complex drained by Goose Creek. The refuge offers good waterfowl hunting in the fall; no developed public-use facilities.

POINT MACKENZIE ROAD

Distance is measured from junction with Knik-Goose Bay Road at Mile J 17.2 (K) followed by distance from junction of Knik Road with Parks Highway (J).

K 0 J 17.2 Junction with Knik Road.

K 2.4 J 19.6 Goose Creek.

K 3.4 J 20.6 Central Mat-Su EMS; *emergency phone*.

K 7 J 24.2 Point Mackenzie General Store & Cafe. Cabin rentals, laundry, showers, fishing/hunting licenses; beer and wine.

K 7.4 J 24.6 'T' junction: turn left for Point Mackenzie, 13.5 miles to end of road (gated); turn right for Susitna Flats State Game Refuge, 5.2 miles (continue with this road log).

Pavement ends, gravel begins.

K 7.6 J 24.8 Junction with Burma Road, which leads 8.5 miles to Big Lake Road.

K 9.5 J 26.7 Guernsey Road; access to Point Mackenzie Rehabilitation Farm (0.6 mile), Farmer and Barley lakes.

K 10.2 J 27.4 Road forks; keep to right for Little Susitna.

K 12.6 J 29.8 Fee station for **Little Susitna River Public-use Site** at Susitna Flats State Game Refuge; 83 parking spaces, 65 campsites, campsite host, boat ramps, dump station, water, tables, toilets. Daily parking $5; boat launch, $10 (includes parking); overnight camping, $10. Popular boat launch site for fishermen after salmon on the Little Susitna. For more information phone (907) 745-3975. ▲▼

Return to Milepost A 42.2
Parks Highway

Wasilla's railway depot dates from 1917.

parking spaces, 65 campsites, campsite host, boat ramps, dump station, water, tables, toilets. Daily parking $5; boat launch, $10 (includes parking); overnight camping, $10. See Mile K 12.6 "Knik–Goose Bay Road" log this section.

Finger Lake State Recreation Site is located at Mile 6.6 Bogard Road from the Crusey Street intersection on the Parks Highway. A scenic spot with 41 campsites, wheelchair-accessible toilets, picnic tables, water, hiking trails and boat launch, $10 camping fee, 7-day limit. (Bogard Road is also accessible from the Trunk Road off the Palmer–Wasilla Highway.)

Attractions

Dorothy Page Museum and Historical Townsite are adjacent the library and post office on Main Street. The historical park—behind the museum—has 7 renovated buildings from before, during and after Wasilla's pioneer days, including Wasilla's first schoolhouse (built in 1917). The museum and historical townsite are open Tuesdays to Saturdays in summer, 9 A.M. to 5 P.M.. Closed in winter (October through March). Admission fees are $3 adults, $2.50 senior citizens; 12 and under are free. Picnic tables and museum shop on site.

"Teelands," which now houses Mead's Coffeehouse, is the restored Herning/Teeland Country Store. Teelands, located on Herning Avenue adjacent the historical park, is on the National Register of Historic Sites.

Wasilla's 1917 Alaska Railroad Depot is also on the National Register of Historic Places. Restored by the local Lions Clubs and the Wasilla Chamber of Commerce, the depot is located on the east side of the Parks Highway at Main Street. A sign there reads: "Construction of the depot began 1916 as part of a national goal for the Alaska Railroad to open access to the interior of Alaska. This site marks the R.R. junction with the important Carle Trail (now known as Knik Rd./Main St./Fishhook Rd.) that was the main supply route between the tidewater trade center of Knik and the gold mines of the Willow Creek (Hatcher Pass) area. By drastically improving the lines of supply to miners and settlers in this region, this junction both created the new town of Wasilla and hastened the demise of Knik. For

Mining relics and summer flowers at Wasilla's Dorothy Page Museum in downtown Wasilla. (© Kris Graef, staff)

"WASILLA...
Home of the Iditarod and Iron Dog"

Dorothy Page Museum & Historical Townsite

Summer Hours: April 1 to Sept. 30
Tuesday - Saturday 9am - 5pm

Farmers Market - 12-6 Wednesdays
Admission: Adults $3 • Under 12 Free • Senior $2.50
323 Main Street, Wasilla, Alaska 99654
Phone (907) 373-9071 • Fax (907) 373-9072

FORT GREEN

Alaskan Gift Shop - Native Arts & Crafts
500+ Baskets - Moose & Caribou Antlers
Northern Trappers & Fur Industry Museum
Restroom - Ample Parking
907-376-5873 Email: nelchina@matnet.com
5401 East Mayflower Lane, Wasilla, AK 99654

PARKS HIGHWAY • Wasilla

Wasilla's public library on North Main Street. (© Kris Graef, staff)

may years this depot was the major 'Outside' communication point for the surrounding district, via trains, the telegraph, and later one railroad system telephone. (On a regional basis, electricity did not become available to local farms and homes until 1942, and telephone until 1957.)"

Iditarod Trail Sled Dog Race® Headquarters is located just west of the Parks Highway in Wasilla at Mile 2.2 Knik Road. The internationally known 1,150-mile Iditarod Trail Sled Dog Race® between Anchorage and Nome takes place in March. The visitor center has historical displays on the Iditarod, videos, an Iditarod musher and dog team, and a gift shop with unique souvenirs. Open daily in summer, weekdays in winter. Large tours are welcome, phone (907) 376-5155 in advance. Circular drive for buses and motorhomes. No fee for museum or film. Fee charged for rides on wheeled dogsled.

Historical displays on Alaskan mushers and sled-dog trails can be found at the **Knik Museum** at Mile 13.9 Knik Road.

See "Knik–Goose Bay Road" log this section for more details on both attractions.

Cis' Unique Antiques. Owned and operated by Jim and Cis Durham. Large inventory of Depression glass, carnival, fire king, pottery, jewelry—costume and gold nugget. Also many miscellaneous smalls, Alaskana and furniture. Located 6 1/2 miles north of Wasilla, RV turnaround. Open daily by chance or by appointment. Call for directions (907) 376-7870. [ADVERTISEMENT]

Town Square Art Gallery. Representing the best of Alaskan and national artists—prints and originals distinctively custom framed. Local jewelry, pottery, unique

RUMELY OIL-PULL TRACTOR

Summer: May 1 Through September 30
9 AM - 6 PM Daily
Winter: LIMITED HOURS
ADMISSION CHARGE

Mile 47 Parks Highway
Neuser Drive
(FOLLOW SIGNS – 3/4 mile)
P.O. Box 870646, WASILLA, AK 99687
(907) 376-1211

Historical displays are featured at Iditarod Headquarters on Knik–Goose Bay Road.

MAIL BOXES ETC.
We'll take it from here.

7362 W. Parks Hwy
Wasilla, AK 99654
(907) 373-6245

1830 E. Parks Hwy. Ste. A113
Wasilla, AK 99654
(907) 376-6245

*See our ad in the Anchorage services section

gifts, porcelain collectibles, plates, books, cards. Open Monday–Friday 10 A.M.–6 P.M., Saturday 10 A.M.–5 P.M. We pack and ship. We welcome credit cards. Carrs Mall. 591 E Parks Highway, #406. Phone (907) 376-0123. [ADVERTISEMENT]

Annabel's Used Books. Trade in your books for some of ours! We offer Alaskana, history, science fiction, Westerns, religious, nonfiction and more. Monday–Saturday, 10 A.M.–6 P.M.. Located kitty-corner from Carr's under the Clock Tower in the Meta Rose Square. 290 N. Yenlo Street, Wasilla. (907) 373-7273. [ADVERTISEMENT]

Special Events. Check with the Wasilla Chamber of Commerce for details on summer and winter events. A Farmer's Market is held at the Historical Townsite on Wednesdays in summer. Iditarod Days is held in conjunction with the Iditarod Race in March.

Area Fishing. Check the ADF&G web site for sport fishing updates for Mat-Su Valley (Northern Cook Inlet) lakes and streams at www.sf.adfg.state.ak.us/Region2/html/r2weekly.stm. Also check with local fishing guides.

Mat-Su valley lakes are stocked with either rainbow trout, landlocked salmon, Arctic grayling, lake trout, or Arctic char, or some combination of these fish. A list of stocked lakes is available from ADF&G.

King salmon begin to move into the clear water streams of the Susitna River drainage in early June. Highest catch rates in early June are usually from Alexander Creek, Deshka River and the Little Susitna River. The **Little Susitna River** produces fair to good catches of king salmon through June, with most of the fishing occurring from the Little Susitna Public-Use Facility (see "Knik–Goose Bay Road" log this section) upstream to the Parks Highway. By late June, fishing is good near the Parks Highway bridge.

As June wears on, king fishing improves in the Parks Highway streams. Willow Creek and the other Parks Highway roadside streams are open to king fishing from Jan. 1 through June 18, and then the following 2 weekends. When fishing is open, it is allowed 24-hours-per-day. A weekend is Saturday, Sunday, and Monday. NOTE: Check the regulations carefully for seasons, bait and tackle restrictions, stream closures, etc.

Parks Highway Log
(continued)

A 42.5 C 167.5 F 319.5 View of Lake Lucille to west.

A 42.7 C 167.3 F 319.3 Frontier Mall to east.

A 42.8 C 167.2 F 319.2 Wasilla Shopping Center to east.

A 43.2 C 166.8 F 318.8 Westside Center.

A 43.5 C 166.5 F 318.5 Lucas Road; Hallea Lane access to Lake Lucille; access to Best Western Lake Lucille Inn to west.

Best Western Lake Lucille Inn. See display ad this section.

Bike route begins northbound.

A 44 C 166 F 318 *Begin 2-lane highway northbound.*
Begin 4-lane highway southbound.

A 44.5 C 165.5 F 317.5 Church Road. Access to Bumpus ball fields.

CAUTION: Moose Danger Zone. Watch for moose next 12.7 miles northbound.

A 45.2 C 164.8 F 316.8 Distance marker northbound shows Cantwell 164 miles, Denali National Park 192 miles, Fairbanks 309 miles.

A 45.4 C 164.6 F 316.6 Wasilla city limits.

A 47 C 163 F 315 Neuser Drive. Turnoff to west for Wasilla municipal airport and the **Museum of Alaska Transportation and Industry**. The 20-acre museum features historic aircraft, railroad equipment, old farm machinery and heavy equipment. Admission charged. RV parking and turnaround. Open daily, May through September. Group tours by arrangement.

A 47.3 C 162.7 F 314.7 Distance marker northbound shows Big Lake Junction 5 miles, Houston 10 miles.

A 47.7 C 162.3 F 314.3 Kwik Kard gas station to west.

A 48.8 C 161.2 F 313.2 Stoplight at **junction** with Sylvan Road and Pittman Road to Rainbow Lake. Tesoro/7-Eleven and cafe to west at intersection. Also access to BJ Center.

A 49 C 161 F 313 Williams Express gas station/Subway to east; BJ Center to west.

Lonestar Laundry. See display ad this section.

Turnoff for Meadow Lakes Road to east; access to Seymour, Lalen Visnaw lakes.

A 49.5 C 160.5 F 312.5 **The Roadside Cafe.** See display ad this section.

A 50.1 C 159.9 F 311.9 Sheele Road.

A 50.2 C 159.8 F 311.8 Ice Worm RV Park. See display ad this section. ▲

A 51 C 159 F 311 Veterinary hospital.

A 51.5 C 158.5 F 310.5 Tesoro gas station with diesel to west.

A 52.2 C 157.8 F 309.8 Southbound distance marker indicates Wasilla 10 miles, Anchorage 52 miles.

A 52.3 C 157.7 F 309.7 Junction. Meadowood shopping mall at Big Lake turnoff to west. State troopers office in mall, *emergency phone* on outside of building.

Junction with Big Lake Road. See "Big Lake Road" log page 370.

Houston city limits. There are several fireworks outlets around Big Lake Road junction. Fireworks are illegal in Anchorage.

Houston is the only place in the Mat-Su Borough where it is legal to sell fireworks.

Begin bike route southbound.
Passing lane southbound.

A 52.5 C 157.3 F 309.3 Distance marker northbound indicates Cantwell 157 miles,

---

TRAIL MASTERS GIFTS AND THE ALASKA BIRCH SYRUP COMPANY

We sell a variety of unique Alaska made gifts and make pure, organic, birch syrup in our log cabin sugar house located on the IDITAROD trail. Mile 2.2 Knik Goosebay Rd. Next to IDITAROD Headquarters and near the Lake Lucille Campground.

HC 30 2150 S. Endeavor Rd., Wasilla, AK 99654
http://www.birchforests.com
Tel (907) 357-4889 Fax (907) 376-9424

Please support our MILEPOST® advertisers.

HALL'S AUTO RENTAL INC
QUALITY LATE MODEL CARS, PICK-UPS & 4X4s

CHECK OUT OUR **AFFORDABLE RATES**
* daily * special weekly & monthly discounts

PICK UP & DELIVERY AVAILABLE

CALL: 746-HALL
TOLL FREE 877-611-HALL
AFTER HOURS 232-2991
MI. 4.4 Palmer - Wasilla Highway

★ **LONESTAR LAUNDRY** ★
CLEAN ★ NON-SMOKING ★ SHOWERS
MILE 49 PARKS HWY.
OPEN DAILY 8-8
B&J RAINBOW CTR. ★ WASILLA, AK
907-357-1028

The Roadside Café
Mile 49.5 Parks Hwy.

"We are where you want to be!"
• Home Cooked Meals & Desserts.
• Full Bar on site.
• Close to Shopping, Fishing, Service Stations, Package Stores.

Summer Hours: 6 A.M. – 10 P.M.
Sunday: 8 A.M. – 9 P.M.

Free RV Parking throughout the year.

(907) 357-7240

ICEWORM RV Park
(907) 892-8200
1-888-484-9088

20 - Full Hook-Ups
15 - Pull Throughs
5 - Back in Spaces
4 - Tent Spaces

Gifts • Food • Ice
Dump Station • Showers
Laundry • Modem Friendly

Mile 50.2 Parks Hwy
Wasilla, Alaska
www.icewormrvp.com

Big Lake

Big Lake has been a resort destination for Alaskans since the 1940s. Summer recreation includes swimming, camping, boating, fishing and jet skiing. Winter sports include snow machining, cross-country skiing and ice fishing. There is a bike trail along Big Lake Road.

Distance is measured from the junction (J) with the Parks Highway.

J 0 Junction with Parks Highway.

J 0.1 Meadowood Mall. **Alaska State Troopers** office inside mall; office hours 8 A.M.–4:30 P.M. weekdays. If you require assistance and there is no trooper available, phone (907) 745-2131. *Emergency phone* on outside of building at east end of mall.

J 1.3 Turnoff to north for Houston High School and senior center.

Evidence of the June 1996 Miller's Reach wildfire, which destroyed some 37,500 acres and 433 buildings and homes, is visible along Big Lake Road. Willow, birch and aspen trees are growing among the charred spruce killed by the fire. New ground cover includes Labrador tea, moss and yarrow.

J 3.3 Beaver Lake Road turnoff. Turn north and drive 0.5 mile (follow signs) for **Rocky Lake State Recreation Site**; 10 campsites on bumpy loop road through birch trees, outhouses, firepits, water pump and boat launch. Rocky Lake is closed to jet skis, jet boats and airboats. *NOTE: This campground was closed in summer 2002. For current status, phone (907) 269-8400 or go to www.dnr.state.ak.us/parks/.*

J 3.4 Tesoro 24-hour gas station, store, ATM. Welcome to Alaska's Year-Round Playground sign here has map of Big Lake.

Big Lake is connected with smaller lakes by dredged waterways. It is possible to boat

Big Lake offers a wide range of recreation an easy drive north of Anchorage.
(© Barb Willard)

for several miles. Fish in Big Lake include lake trout, Dolly Varden, rainbow, red and coho salmon, and burbot.

J 3.6 Fisher's Y; junction with North Shore Drive. **BIG LAKE** (pop. 2,162) post office at 'Y' (ZIP code 99652); liquor store, laundromat.

Take North Shore Drive to end (1.4 miles) at **Big Lake North State Recreation Site**; 60 overnight parking spaces, walk-in tent sites, campground host, pay phone, picnicking, shelters, water, outhouses, dumpsters. Located on the lake; good views of Alaska Range (Mount McKinley/Denali). *NOTE: This campground was closed in summer 2002. For current status, phone (907) 269-8400 or go to www.dnr.state.ak.us/parks/.*

J 3.8 Edward "Bud" Beech Firehall. *Emergency phone*.

J 3.9 Big Lake Library to north.

J 4 East Lake Mall; grocery store, pizza, liquor store, espresso and other businesses.

J 4.4 Elementary school.

J 4.5 Aero drive to Big Lake airport. Big Lake is a 15-minute flight from Anchorage.

Private Aircraft: 1 mile southeast; elev. 150 feet; length 2,400 feet; gravel; fuel 100LL.

J 4.8 Big Lake Motel. See display ad this section.

J 4.9 Fish Creek Park (Mat-Su Borough), a day-use area with access to Fish Creek, salmon spawning observation deck, picnic area, pavilion, restroom, playground, parking and open lawn area. End bike lane.

Bridge over Fish Creek.

J 5 Big Lake Community Church. Lakeview Drive

J 5.1 Big Lake South State Recreation Site; day-use area with parking, outhouses, water, dumpsters, boat ramp. *NOTE: This day-use area was unmaintained by Alaska State Parks in summer 2002. For current status, phone (907) 269-8400 or go to www.dnr.state.ak.us/parks/.*

J 5.4 Turnoff for South Port Marina; food, phone, snowmachine, ATV, watercraftrentals and repair service; boat launch, gas, propane.

J 8 State road maintenance ends (sign); turnout.

J 8.4 Informal turnout, good view of lake.

J 9 Stop sign at intersection of South Big Lake Road and Marion and Susitna Streets. *Pavement ends, gravel begins.*

Continue straight ahead for Burma Road (winding gravel), which leads 8.5 miles south to junction with Point Mackenzie Road.

Return to Milepost A 52.3 Parks Highway

BIG LAKE MOTEL
THE HANGER

Lg. Comfortable Rooms - Dining & Cocktails
Located in the heart of Big Lake
Across from Airport, Mile 1.5
So. Big Lake Rd.
Park Adjacent

Owners:
Mark & Cindy Riley

(907) 892-7976
FAX (907) 892-9229

MAJOR CREDIT CARDS ACCEPTED

Denali National Park 184 miles, Fairbanks 302 miles.

A 53.2 C 156.8 F 308.8 Turnoff for Houston High School and Wasilla Senior Center.

A 54 C 156 F 308 *Begin passing lane northbound.*

A 54.8 C 155.2 F 307.2 *Begin bike route northbound.*

A 55.3 C 154.7 F 306.7 *End passing lane northbound.*

A 56.1 C 153.9 F 305.7 Miller's Reach Road. Alaska's most destructive wildfire began here in June 1996. The Big Lake wildfire burned some 37,500 acres and 433 buildings and homes.

A 56.3 C 153.7 F 305.7 Alaska Railroad overpass.

A 56.6 C 153.4 F 305.4 King Arthur Drive; public access to Bear Paw, Prator and Loon lakes to east (no camping).

Views of Pioneer Peak southbound.

A 56.8 C 153.2 F 305.2 Parking areas both sides of highway and pedestrian access to Little Susitna River. Bike route ends northbound.

CAUTION: Moose Danger Zone. Watch for moose next 12.7 miles southbound.

Improved highway northbound.

A 57 C 153 F 305 Bridge over the Little Susitna River; a very popular fishing and camping area. Pedestrian bridge.

The **Little Susitna River** has a tremendous king salmon run and one of the largest silver salmon runs in southcentral Alaska. Kings to 30 lbs. enter the river in late May and June; use large red spinners or salmon eggs. Silvers to 15 lbs. come in late July and August, with the biggest run in August; use small weighted spoons or fresh salmon roe. Artificials are required during the early weeks of the fishery in the first part of August. Also red salmon to 10 lbs.; in mid-July, use coho flies or salmon eggs. Charter boats nearby. This river heads at Mint Glacier in the Talkeetna Mountains to the northeast and flows 110 miles/177 km into Upper Cook Inlet.

A 57.3 C 152.7 F 304.7 Turnoff to east

for Houston City Hall, William A. Philo Public Safety Bldg. (*emergency phone*) and city-operated campground.

The **Little Susitna River Campground** (follow signs) is a large, well-maintained campground with 86 sites (many wide, level gravel sites); picnic tables, firepits; restrooms, water pump, playground, large picnic pavilion; 10-day limit, $10 camping fee charged. Off-road parking lot near river with access to river. Follow signs to camping and river. Day-use area with water and toilets west side of highway. ▲

A 57.4 C 152.6 F 304.6 HOUSTON (pop. 1,202) has a grocery store, restaurant (open daily), laundromat, gift shop, inn with food, lodging and pay phone, a campground and gas station. Post office located in the grocery store.

Houston Lodge. See display ad this section.

Houston is a popular fishing center for anglers on the Little Susitna River. Fishing charter operators and marine service are located here. Emergency phone at Houston fire station. Originally Houston siding on the Alaska Railroad, the area was homesteaded in the 1950s and incorporated as a city in 1966. A Founder's Day celebration is held in August. This annual event features a barbecue dinner, fireworks and entertainment. ▲

A 57.5 C 152.5 F 304.5 **Miller's Place.** Don't miss this stop! Groceries, post office, laundry, RV parking, cabin rentals, tenting on riverbank. Gift shop, fishing tackle and licenses, fresh salmon eggs. Ice, sporting goods sales and rental, pay phone. Fishing charters available; full day only $45. Probably the best soft ice cream and hamburgers in Alaska. Clean restrooms. Visitor information experts. Family-run Christian business. Gary and Debbie Miller. (907) 892-6129. [ADVERTISEMENT] ▲

A 57.7 C 152.3 F 304.3 **Riverside Camper Park.** Good Sam RV Park on the Little Susitna River. 56 full-service hookups (water, sewer and electric on each site). Showers, laundromat and public phone, modem hookup in office. Kings, silvers and sockeye charters and drop-offs available. Center lawn with pavilion for group activities. (907) 892-9020. P.O. Box 940087, Houston, AK 99694. Email:aksalmon@mtaonline.net. [ADVERTISEMENT]

A 57.8 C 152.2 F 304.2 **Fisherman's Choice Charters.** See display ad this section.

A 58.3 C 151.7 F 303.7 *Begin passsing lane northbound.*

A 60.3 C 149.7 F 301.7 Good view northbound of Sleeping Lady to west.

A 60.6 C 149.4 F 301.4 *End passing lane northbound.*

A 61 C 149 F 301 *End passing lane southbound.*

A 61.2 C 148.8 F 300.8 Willow (sign).

A 61.5 C 148.5 F 300.5 Family Health Clinic to west.

A 62.2 C 147.8 F 299.8 *Begin passing lane southbound.*

A 62.3 C 147.7 F 299.7 *Begin passing lane northbound.*

A 63.7 C 146.3 F 298.3 *End passing lane northbound.*

A 64.5 C 145.5 F 297.5 Turnoff to west for Nancy Lake Resort.

A 66.3 C 143.7 F 295.7 New (2002) highway bridge crosses Alaska Railroad tracks. **White's Crossing** on old highway alignment to east.

A 66.5 C 143.5 F 295.5 Turnoff to west for **Nancy Lake State Recreation Site**; then

Even the huskies enjoy boating on the Little Sustina River.
(© Barb Willard)

turn left (south) on Buckingham Palace road and drive 0.3 mile; 30 campsites, 30 picnic sites, toilets, boat launch, horseshoe pits, camping fee $10/night or resident pass. Also access to bed and breakfast this exit. ▲

Alaskan Host B&B. See display ad this section.

A 67 C 143 F 295 Catholic church.

A 67.3 C 142.7 F 294.7 Turnoff to west on Nancy Lake Parkway for **Nancy Lake State Recreation Area** (South Rolly Campground; canoe trails, public-use cabins, picnicking and camping.

State Park Ranger at Mile 1.3 Nancy Lake Parkway; Tanaina Lake canoe trail at Mile 4.6; Rhein Lake trailhead at Mile 5; South Rolly Lake picnic area at Mile 6.1. Public road ends 6.5 miles west at **South Rolly Lake Campground**; 106 campsites, firepits, toilets, water, canoe rental and boat launch; firewood is sometimes provided. Camping fee $10/night or resident pass. South Rolly Lake has a small population of rainbow, 12 to 14 inches.

NOTE: Watch for road construction under way northbound to **Milepost A 72** *in summer 2003. Expect reduced speed limits, lane restrictions and delays.*

Begin bike path southbound on west side of highway.

A 67.6 C 142.4 F 294.4 United Methodist Church to west.

A 68.6 C 141.4 F 293.4 Entering Willow, northbound. *Begin 45 mph speed zone northbound.*

Begin 55 mph speed limit southbound.

A 68.8 C 141.2 F 293.2 Newman's Hilltop Tesoro west side of highway; gas, diesel, coffee and ice cream.

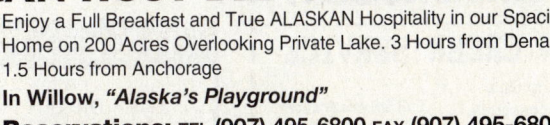

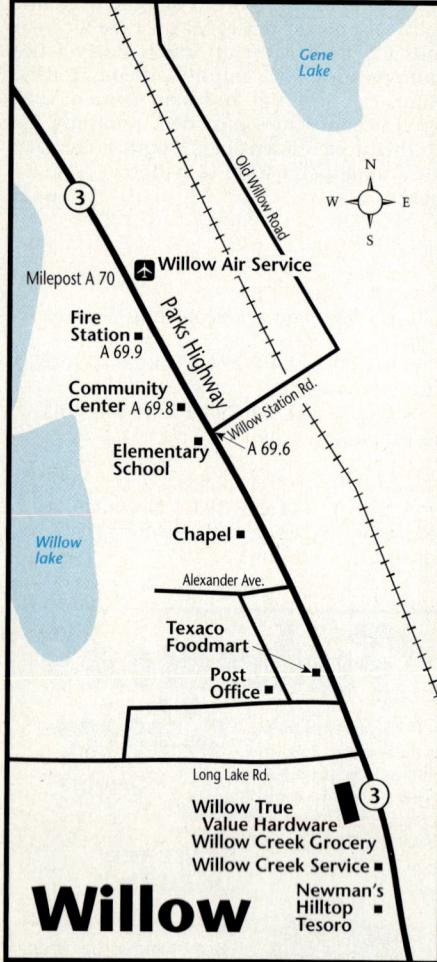

Fishing is great at numerous roadside streams along the Parks Highway.
(© Barb Willard)

Newman's Hilltop Tesoro. See display ad this section.

A 69 C 141 F 293 Gas station, grocery and hardware store to west side of highway. Willow extends about 2.5 miles north along the Parks Highway.

Willow True Value Hardware, Willow Creek Grocery and **Willow Creek Service.** See display ad this section.

A 69.2 C 140.8 F 292.8 Long Lake Road.

A 69.5 C 140.5 F 292.5 Texaco gas station (diesel) with foodmart, restaurant, pay phone to west. Alexander Avenue; access west to Willow Post Office.

Texaco Foodmart. See display ad this section.

WILLOW (pop. 507), had its start about 1897, when gold was discovered in the area. In the early 1940s, mining in the nearby Talkeetna Mountains slacked off, leaving Willow a virtual ghost town. The community made a comeback upon completion of the Parks Highway in 1972. In 1976, Alaska voters selected the Willow area for their new capital site. However, funding for the capital move from Juneau to Willow was defeated in the November 1982 election.

The community is also a stop on the Alaska Railroad. The Willow civic organization sponsors an annual Winter Carnival in January.

A 69.6 C 140.4 F 292.4 Willow elementary school to west. Willow Station Road to east to Alaska Railroad Depot and 0.4 mile to Willow Trading Post (food service) on Old Willow Road.

A 69.8 C 140.2 F 292.2 Access road west to Willow Library and Willow Community Center; visitor information. The community center is open daily and has a large parking area, commercial kitchen, showers, covered picnic pavilion, grills, ball court, boat launch and pay phone. (Available for rent to groups, 500-person capacity; phone 907/495-6633).

A 69.9 C 140.1 F 292.1 Fire station to west. **Emergency phone.**

A 70 C 140 F 292 Access to flying services.

Willow Air Service. See display ad this section.

A 70.1 C 139.9 F 291.9 *Begin 45 mph speed zone southbound.*

A 70.3 C 139.7 F 291.7 Willow Airport Road to east. **Private Aircraft:** Willow airport; elev. 220 feet; length 4,400 feet; gravel; fuel 100LL. Unattended.

A 70.8 C 139.2 F 291.2 Willow Creek Parkway (Susitna River access road) is a wide, straight, gravel road (watch for soft spots and soft shoulders) that leads west 3.7 miles to entrance to **Willow Creek State Recreation Area**; fee station, camping $10/night, parking $5/day. Large gravel parking area with picnic tables, litter barrels, water, toilets. Campground hosts, gravel paths with interpretive displays. A popular fishing spot; walk to creek. Fishing for silvers, pinks, chum and king salmon (gets busy during king season).

Access to **Deshka Landing** boat launch facility off Willow Creek Parkway; turn on Crystal Lake Road and drive about 4 miles. This concessionaire-operated facility is open daily 5 A.M. to midnight in summer; call for winter hours. Fees charged for boat launch and parking; season pass available. Fishing for king and silver salmon, rainbow trout.

The Susitna River heads at Susitna Glacier in the Alaska Range to the northeast and flows west then south for 260 miles to Cook Inlet. The Deshka River, a tributary of the Susitna River about 6 miles downstream from Deshka Landing, is one of Southcentral Alaska's best king salmon fisheries. According to the ADF&G, peak fishing at the mouth of the Deshka River is usually between June 8 and 15. After that, fish are still available if you are willing to travel upstream. The Deshka River is open to the retention of king salmon for the first 19 miles, which is indicated by a marker at Chijuk Creek.

A 71.2 C 138.8 F 290.8 **Junction** with Fishhook–Willow (Hatcher Pass) Road; private RV park 0.6 mile east.

Fishhook-Willow Road leads east to cross Hatcher Pass, before descending to junction with the Glenn Highway near Palmer. This 49-mile side road is logged on pages 305-306 in the GLENN HIGHWAY section.

A 71.4 C 138.6 F 290.6 Pioneer Lodge to west on south side of **Willow Creek** bridge; Food, camping, lodging. Excellent king salmon fishing; also silvers, rainbow. Inquire at either lodge or resort for information.

Pioneer Lodge. See display ad this

packages. These trips are all 5 star and offer incredible wildlife viewing and excellent fishing from beginner to expert. 1-800-353-2677. See display ad. [ADVERTISEMENT]

Fishing. The **Susitna River** basin offers many top fishing streams and lakes, either accessible by road, plane or riverboat.

Doug Geeting's Peak Dodger Flight Tours. Take flight with world renowned Doug Geeting Aviation. Look up at 14,000-foot rock and ice walls and land on a glacier—an Alaskan adventure highlight that will astound even the most experienced world traveler! We hold an NPS concession for Mount McKinley glacier landings, available only from the Talkeetna State Airport. Planes are intercom equipped. Group rates

Fishing for salmon at Clear Creek on the Talkeetna River. (© Rich Reid, Colors of Nature)

available. Overnight accommodations available. For prices and reservations: Doug Geeting Aviation, P.O. Box 42MP, Talkeetna, AK 99676; (800) 770-2366. Fax (907) 733-1000. E-mail: alaskaairtours.com. Web: alaskaairtours.com. See display ad this section. [ADVERTISEMENT]

Talkeetna Air Taxi. View Denali's most spectacular peaks and glaciers. Circle McKinley and land on a glacier, starting at $99. Anchorage–Denali Park–Talkeetna packages: Fly-Rail-Bus. Leave the logistics to us. Since 1947. Call 1-800-533-2219 or (907) 733-2218. www.talkeetnaair.com. See display ad. [ADVERTISEMENT]

ERA Helicopters Flightseeing Tours. Offering fully-narrated tours of Denali Park and Mount McKinley. Experience the Talkeetna backcountry on a personally guided heli-hiking adventure, or land on and explore a glacier with your pilot on our glacier expedition tour. Tours also available from Milepost 134, Denali,. Anchorage, Juneau and Valdez. Located at Talkeetna Airport. Tours operate May–September. Local phone (907) 733-2575 or (800) 843-1947. 6160 Carl Brady Dr., Anchorage, AK 99502; www.eraaviation.com; fltsg@eraaviation.com. [ADVERTISEMENT]

Winterfest is an annual month-long event in December featuring various special events and competition, of which the best known are the Wilderness Women's Contest and the Bachelor Auction. Wilderness Women competitors haul water and wood and shoot (bird balloons). The **Talkeetna Bachelor Auction** raises funds for a local charity by auctioning off bachelors for cash. Winning bidders get a drink and a dance with the bachelor. Bidding gets quite frenzied, fueled both by the liquid refreshments and the pectorals of the bachelor.

Return to Milepost A 98.7
Parks Highway

A prime fishing spot on Peters Creek on the Petersville Road. (© Kris Graef, staff)

(Continued from page 375)

A 104.6 C 105.4 F 257.4 Rabideux Creek access; parking, 0.3 mile trail to mouth of creek. Watch for seasonal flooding.

A 104.8 C 105.2 F 257.2 Large dirt and gravel turnout to west.

A 105.7 C 104.3 F 256.3 Rabideux Creek.

A 107.6 C 102.4 F 254.4 View of Mount McKinley (weather permitting) for northbound travelers.

A 108 C 102 F 254 CAUTION: Watch for moose.

A 109.9 C 100.1 F 252.1 Distance marker northbound indicates Trapper Creek 5 miles.

A 114 C 96 F 248 NOTE: Slow for 55 mph speed zone northbound.

A 114.4 C 95.6 F 247.6 Trapper Creek (northbound sign).

A 114.8 C 95.2 F 247.2 TRAPPER CREEK (pop. 344); post office to east, library and emergency phone to west. Emergency services: Ambulance, phone 911.

Miners built the Petersville Road in the 1920s, and federal homesteading began here in 1948. Today, a cluster of businesses around the junction with Petersville Road serve highway travelers. Accommodations are also available along Petersville Road.

The Other Place. See display ad this section.

Trapper Creek Inn & General Store. Gateway to Denali visitors information center. Tesoro gas, diesel, comfortable lodging with Mount McKinley view, large RV campground, full hookups, dump station, large barbecue/picnic pavilion, ATM, propane, showers, restrooms, laundry, pay phone, deli, espresso, groceries, coffee, ice, etc. Fishing and hunting licenses, supplies and charters. Flightseeing Mount McKinley. Major credit cards accepted. Phone (907) 733-2302. Fax (907) 733-1002. Email: innmaster@matnet.com; www.trappercreekinn.com. Tour buses welcome. See large display ad this section. [ADVERTISEMENT] ▲

A 114.9 C 95.1 F 247.1 Petersville Road turnoff; access to several bed and breakfasts. Historic Trapper Creek post office (ZIP code 99683) is located on the north side of this junction on the east side of the Parks Highway.

Junction with Petersville Road, which leads west 18.7 miles. See "Petersville Road" log on opposite page.

The Other Place

Stop by to see us at Mile 114.8 Parks Hwy., in Trapper Creek, Alaska, or call (907) 733-3513.

Open all year, Tue.–Sat., 11am to 5pm

Although we are the local DMV, we also have crafts, gifts, greeting cards, fax, notary, copies, and cyber cafe available to the public.

North Country B&B

PRIVATE BATHS • PRIVATE ENTRIES
Mile 2.7 Petersville Rd. • (907) 733-3981
See log ad Mile J 2.7 Petersville Road
www.alaskan.com/northcountrybnb

Petersville Road

Petersville Road leads west and north from Trapper Creek on the Parks Highway through a homestead area notable for its mountain views and its number of bed and breakfasts. Built as a mining road (see **Milepost 0.7**), today the road is very popular with 4-wheelers in summer and snow machines in winter.

The MILEPOST® logs the first 18.7 miles of Petersville Road to the historic Forks Roadhouse. Beyond Forks, the road continues 17.8 miles, providing access to Petersville Recreational Mining Area in Peters Creek canyon (see description in log). The former mining camp of Petersville, which now consists of 4 buildings, is located approximately 11 miles beyond Forks Roadhouse.

The first 9.4 miles of Petersville Road are paved, the remainder is gravel. In summer 2002, the gravel portion of the road was in good condition with poor to fair surfacing from Milepost 13 to Forks Roadhouse. Inquire at Forks Roadhouse for current road conditions beyond Forks. *Please respect private property.*

Distance from junction with the Parks Highway (J) is shown.

J 0 Junction with Parks Highway at Milepost A 114.9.

J 0.3 Trapper Creek Bed & Breakfast. Enjoy the best nature has to offer while still keeping modern day luxuries, including a complete home-cooked breakfast. All rooms

are spotlessly clean with their own Alaskan theme. Reasonably priced and open year-round. Your hosts, Jim and Susan Henderson. trappercreekbnb@gci.net. Phone (907) 733-2234; www.trappercreekbedandbreakfast.com. [ADVERTISEMENT]

J 0.7 Trapper Creek Museum and gift shop to south, housed in historic Donaldson 59er Cabin. Gold Rush Centennial sign *Packing to the Creeks* reads:

"In 1906, prospectors ascended the Susitna River and discovered gold in several creeks in the Cache Creek–Dutch Hills area. News of the discoveries set off a rush the following year. Miners later developed an easier route to their claims that included travel by boat from Cook Inlet up the Susitna and Yentna rivers to a supply point called McDougall. Hiking and using packhorses, they continued up the McDougall Trail crossing rushing streams, swampy bogs and rugged mountains. In winter, travel was easier over firm, frozen ground with the use of dog and hand sleds.

"Miners improved the 50-mile McDougall Trail, but in places it was hard to follow. In 1917, packer Richard Feltham lost his way in the swamps near Hungryman Camp. After 6 days, a search party found him near his horse. 'Evidences of the struggle of the man to find his way went pitiful to see,' according to one of his rescuers. Feltham had blazed marks on trees in a futile effort to find what other miners considered 'a most obscure trail.' Feltham died several hours after he was found.

"Miners in the area petitioned the government for help in the construction of a 'dirt road that will guarantee us home in safety ... and won't leave us some-

where to perish, as it did Dick Feltham.' After crews started building a railroad through the area, miner Henry Bamburg blazed a trail from the mines to the new railstop called Talkeetna. In 1918, the Alaska Road Commission began improving the trail, which is now the Petersville Road that passes in front of the Trapper Creek Museum."

J 2 Denali View Chalets. Private, secluded, modern chalets with spectacular views of Mount McKinley and the Alaska

Range. Open year-round with access by paved road. Each chalet is furnished with a kitchenette, microwave, coffee pot, TV/VCR, double bed, 2 twin beds, linens, pots and pans and dishes. The wilderness is at your doorstep. Email address: roxie@alaska.net. Homepage address: denaliviewchalets.com. P.O. Box 13330, Trapper Creek, AK 99683. Phone (907) 733-1333. [ADVERTISEMENT]

J 2.6 Trapper Creek elementary school to south.

J 2.7 North Country Bed and Breakfast to north.

North Country Bed and Breakfast. Nestled on a lake with a spectacular view of Mount McKinley. Five first-class rooms with private bathrooms and private entries. Mount McKinley flightseeing trips available at the lake by appointment. Bird watching, wildlife, paddleboating and horseshoes available. Open year-round. Your hosts—Mike and Sheryl Uher. Phone (907) 733-3981. See display ad this section. [ADVERTISEMENT]

J 6.2 Dog Team Crossing (sign).

J 6.3 Oilwell Road.

J 7 Moose Creek; private campground and homes.

J 9.4 *Pavement ends, gravel begins, westbound.*

J 10.5 Gate Creek Cabins. Beautifully decorated "family size" log cabins. Year-round access. Located Mile 10.5 Historic Petersville Road. Completely furnished, full

kitchen, private baths, TV, VCR, barbecue grill, community sauna. Views of Mount McKinley overlooking small lakes, canoes and mountain bikes provided. Hiking, biking, fishing, photography. ATV and snowmachine rentals. $125 first couple, $45 for each additional person; children 7 through

12 $25 each; 6 and under free. Weekly rate, 7th night free. Friendly dogs welcome; $15 per visit. Reservations (907) 733-1393 or email gatecreek@worldnet.att.net. Web page www.gatecreekcabins.com. [ADVERTISEMENT]

J 13.7 Large gravel parking area (snowplow turnaround in winter). No winter maintenance beyond this point October 15–June 1.

J 13.9 Kroto Creek. *Road narrows and climbs westbound. Slow for rough road (washboard and potholes).*

J 17.2 McKinley Foothills B&B/Cabins. Off Mile 17.2 Petersville Road. Furnished, rustic log cabins, kitchenettes. Full breakfast. Great food, Alaskan hospitality. Mount McKinley views. Summer: gold panning tours, fishing, birding, hiking, mountain biking. Winter: skiing, snow machining, dog mushing tours. Major credit cards. Homepage: www.matnet.com/~mckinley. Email: mckinley@matnet.com. Phone/fax (907) 733-1454. P.O. Box 13089, Trapper Creek, AK 99683. [ADVERTISEMENT]

J 18.7 (30.1 km) Petersville Road forks at historic **Forks Roadhouse**: Right fork is continuation of Petersville Road (description below). Left fork leads 0.2 mile to informal camping (no facilities) on Mat-Su Borough public land at **Peters Creek**. Beautiful spot. Fishing for salmon and trout; bridge across Peters Creek is Dollar Creek Trailhead: ORVs only, no cars on bridge or trail.

Forks Roadhouse was established in 1900, to serve the thousands of miners living in area tent cities. The roadhouse continues to provide rooms, food and drink to travelers year-round.

Petersville Road continues beyond Forks Roadhouse to the former mining camp of Petersville and the downstream boundary of **Petersville Recreational Mining Area** (about 11 miles). Peters Creek must be forded to reach the upper end of the Recreational Mining Area. *High clearance 4-wheel drive vehicles only beyond Forks Roadhouse.* Petersville Road ends about 18 miles beyond the Forks. This stretch of road is usually not passable until late June. Check at Forks Roadhouse for road conditions. Recreational gold panning, mineral prospecting or mining using light portable field equipment, such as pick and shovel, pan, earth auger or a backpack power drill or auger, are allowed without any permit. (To use a small suction dredge, obtain a permit from the Alaska Dept. of Fish and Game.) For more information, contact Dept. of Natural Resources in Anchorage by phoning (907) 269-8400; online at www.dnr.state.ak.us/mlw/index.htm.

Return to Milepost A 114.9 Parks Highway

Riders head out with D&S Alaskan Trail Rides near Mt. McKinley Princess Lodge.
(© Kris Graef, staff)

A 115.4 C 94.6 F 246.6 Distance marker northbound indicates Cantwell 94 miles, Denali National Park 122 miles, Fairbanks 239 miles.

A 115.5 C 94.5 F 246.5 Trapper Creek Trading Post east side of highway; cafe, gas, diesel, grocery, cabins, campground. ▲

A 115.6 C 94.4 F 246.4 Highway crosses Trapper Creek.

Excellent views of Mount McKinley (weather permitting) northbound.

A 115.9 C 94.1 F 246.1 Trapper Creek Pizza Pub–Angela's Heaven Enjoy delicious homemade pizza, fresh salads, great sandwiches (hot and cold) in a friendly atmosphere. If you like tasty, dark bread, call 1 day ahead to order a loaf or two of Angela's famous German Beer Bread—made according to a very old family recipe. By the way: We also speak German! Phone (907) 733-3344. [ADVERTISEMENT]

A 116.5 C 93.5 F 245.5 *Begin 55 mph speed zone southbound.*

A 119.6 C 90.4 F 242.4 Distance marker southbound shows Trapper Creek 5 miles, Wasilla 78 miles, Anchorage 120 miles.

A 121.1 C 88.9 F 240.9 Chulitna highway maintenance camp to west.

A 121.5 C 88.5 F 240.5 Large paved double-ended rest area to east with tables, firepits, drinking water, toilet and interpretive bulletin board. Shade trees; cow parsnip grows lush here.

A 123.8 C 86.2 F 238.2 Large gravel turnout to west.

A 126.5 C 83.5 F 235.4 Large paved parking area to east.

A 127.1 C 82.9 F 234.9 Large gravel turnout to west.

A 132.2 C 77.8 F 229.8 Denali State Park entrance sign northbound. This 325,460-acre state park has 48 miles of hiking trails. Camping at Troublesome Creek (**Milepost A 137.3**), Byers Lake (**Milepost A 147**) and Denali View North (**Milepost A 162.7**). Hunting is permitted in the park, but discharge of firearms is prohibited within 0.3 mile of highway, 0.5 mile of a developed facility or 0.5 mile of trail around Byers Lake (this is between **Milepost A 132 to A 170**). ▲

A 132.8 C 77.2 F 229.2 Middle of the **Chulitna River** bridge. Fishing for grayling, rainbow. ⌒

Entering Game Management Subunit 13E, leaving unit 16A, northbound.

Slow for 45mph curve, turning traffic.

A 132.9 C 77.1 F 229.1 Intersection with **Mt. McKinley Princess Drive** at north end of bridge. Turn east uphill and follow paved road 0.4 mile for turnout with view and 1 mile for Mt. McKinley Princess Lodge. Turn off for D & S Trail Rides at top of hill, 0.7 mile from highway (before entrance to lodge), and follow signs 0.6 mile to stable.

D & S Alaskan Trail Rides. Open mid-May through mid-September, offers 1 ½- to 8-hour adventurous trail rides with majestic views of Mount McKinley. Ride into the wilderness to experience the beauty of Alaska and all that nature has to offer. Outback coats, cowboy hats and helmets are provided. Summer phone (907) 733-2205; winter (907) 733-2207; email akrides@mtaonlinenet.com; www.alaskantrailrides.com. [ADVERTISEMENT]

A 134.3 C 75.7 F 227.7 Helicopter sightseeing service; private airstrip.

From here northbound for many miles there are views of glaciers on the southern slopes of the Alaska Range to the west. Ruth, Buckskin and Eldridge glaciers are the most conspicuous. Ruth Glacier trends southeast through the Great Gorge for 31 miles. The glacier was named in 1903 by F.A. Cook for his daughter. The Great Gorge was named by mountain climbers in the late 1940s. Peaks on either side of the gorge tower up to 5,000 feet above Ruth Glacier. The gorge, nicknamed the Grand Canyon of Alaska, opens into Don Sheldon Amphitheater at the head of Ruth Glacier, where the Don Sheldon mountain house sits. Donald E. Sheldon (1921–75) was a well-known bush pilot who helped map, patrol, and aid search and rescue efforts in this area.

Flightseeing trips can be arranged that take you close to Mount McKinley, into the Don Sheldon Amphitheater, through the Great Gorge and beneath the peak of the Mooses Tooth. Inquire with flightseeing operators along the Parks Highway and in the national park.

A 134.5 C 75.5 F 227.5 Mary's McKinley View Lodge. Located on Mary Carey's original homestead. Spectacular view of McKinley from every room, especially the glass-walled restaurant. Mary, famous for Alaskan books, homesteaded before the state park was created. She fought for highway completion to share her magnificent view with travelers. Now a movie is being filmed about her life. Enjoy dining, browse the gift shop, get a personally autographed childrens' book from Mary's daughter, Jean Richardson, or spend a pleasant night in the modern rooms. Call (907) 733-1555. See display ad this section. [ADVERTISEMENT]

A 135.2 C 74.8 F 226.8 Denali Viewpoint South, Ruth Glacier Vista (Denali State Park) is a large paved turnout overlooking the Chulitna River; toilet. *CAUTION: Congested traffic area, drive carefully.*

A display board here points out peaks. View of 20,320-foot Mount McKinley on a clear day. Peaks to be sighted, south to north, along the next 20 miles to the west are: Mount Hunter (elev. 14,573 feet); Mount Huntington (12,240 feet); Mount Barrille (7,650 feet); and Mount Dickey (9,845 feet).

A 135.5 C 74.5 F 226.5 Distance marker northbound shows Cantwell 75 miles, Denali National Park 102 miles, Fairbanks 220 miles.

A 137.3 C 72.7 F 224.7 Lower Trouble-

MARY'S McKINLEY VIEW LODGE

For the Best View of the Nation's Tallest Peak While Dining in Glassed-in Comfort, Stop at MARY'S MCKINLEY VIEW LODGE Mile 134.5 Parks Highway

Pleasant rooms, private baths, reasonable rates, good food with the closest and most spectacular view of Mount McKinley from any lodge in Alaska.

Historic homestead of Mary Carey. Meet Mary and get a special autograph on one of her many books about Alaska. Watch for a movie adapted from her book, *My Three Lives In Headlines*, coming to the big screen soon.

Meet Mary's daughter, Jean Carey Richardson, a children's author with five series of books, including her latest, the *Grumpy Granny Series*. Personal autographs are our specialty.

For reservations or book orders call Mary's McKinley View Lodge (907) 733-1555 or (907) 355-6939 or write to P.O. Box 13314 Trapper Creek, Alaska 99683

Denali Park's "Front Country"

Many traveler-related businesses are located in Denali Park's "front country."
(© Kris Graef, staff)

The "front country" of Denali National Park is a 40-mile stretch of the Parks Highway between Cantwell and Healy where thousands of park visitors end up eating and sleeping, thanks to the limited services available inside the park's boundaries. It is also where a majority of the park's outfitters are headquartered, those seasonal businesses offering river trips, hiking, horseback riding, and other outdoor adventures in Denali National Park.

Here's a sampling of the traveler-related businesses for Denali Park visitors that are found along the Parks Highway, starting from Cantwell at the south end of Denali's "front country."

Cantwell sits at the junction of the Parks and Denali highways (**Milepost A 210**). Until the completion of the George Parks Highway in 1972, the Denali Highway was the primary access route to Denali National Park (then Mount McKinley National Park). On a clear day you may be treated to a view of Mount McKinley (Denali) from this intersection.

At the junction is **Denali Manor Bed & Breakfast**, the first of many Cantwell area businesses catering to Denali Park visitors. Just east of the junction is the secluded **Backwoods Lodge**, open year-round, with 11 units and all amenities. West of the intersection is **Cantwell RV Park**, one of the many private camper parks available to Denali Park visitors. Continue west 2 miles from the highway for **Cantwell Lodge** (motel and campsites) and **Atkins Guiding/Flying Service**, located at the Cantwell townsite.

Back on the Parks Highway, stop at the **Cantwell Food Mart & Parkway Gift Shop** at **Milepost A 210.4** for gifts, good supplies and Chevron gas and services. Just up the highway at **Milepost A 210.7**, the full-service **Lazy J Lodge** features private baths, cable TV and T-bone steak dinners.

North of Cantwell, a cluster of businesses borders picturesque Carlo Creek at **Milepost A 223.9**. On the south bank of the creek, on the west side of the highway, **Carlo Creek Lodge** offers comfortable log cabins and camping. Across the highway from them is **The Perch**, with a deli/bakery at roadside, numerous cabins throughout wooded land in back, and, "perched" high on a hill, a popular restaurant. On the north bank of Carlo Creek, west side of the highway, the rustic buildings of **Denali Mountain Morning Hostel & Lodge** provide a variety of budget-friendly accommodations as well as raft trips. Across the highway, **McKinley Creekside Cabins & Café** offers cabins and a casual dining atmosphere.

Continuing north, the cedar buildings at **Milepost A 229** belong to **Denali Cabins**, which offering lodging, outdoor hot tubs and free shuttles to area restaurants. Nearby is **Denali Air** flightseeing service, whose 1-hour tour of the park is a prime attraction.

Rounding the long hill to the Nenana River at **Milepost A 231**, several large developments fill the view. Farthest to the east is the 150-room **McKinley Village Resort**, the first business to settle at this riverside location nearly 40 years ago. Like many of these highway lodges, McKinley Village Resort also has a restaurant and tour booking service as well as overnight accommodations. Beside this resort are the numerous buildings of **Denali River Cabins and Cedars Lodge**, which feature sundecks, a tour desk and a Finnish-style sauna for guests. To the west, **Denali Grizzly Bear Cabins & Campground** provides attractive cabins, a store and an AAA-approved campground.

Continuing north, the Parks Highway junctions with the road into Denali National Park at **Milepost A 237.4**. The park offers camping and a visitor center, but food, gas and lodging are found in the "front country" along the Parks Highway.

The center of Denali Park's front country is just north of the park entrance around **Milepost A 238.5**, in an area known as "Glitter Gulch." Here, crowded into a mile-long strip of highway, are hotels, lodges, restaurants, gift shops, river rafting outfitters, flightseeing operators, a gas station/convenience store, RV parks and other businesses serving the traveler.

Accommodations abound at Glitter Gulch, from motels to cabins to lodges to large hotels. Find your preference among the **McKinley Chalet Resort, Denali Bluffs Hotel, Grande Denali Lodge, Denali Wilderness Princess Lodge, Denali Crow's Nest Cabins** and **Westmark's Sourdough Cabins**.

Motels and local outfitters offer information on booking park activities such as fly-in fishing trips, bus trips through the park, dog sled demonstrations, guided hiking or backpacking and horseback trips. Flightseeing is also a popular way to see Denali National Park, and several operators have booking offices at Glitter Gulch.

But river rafters rule in this area, which borders the Nenana River, with **Denali Raft Adventures, Denali Outdoor Center, Alaska Raft Adventures** and **Nenana Raft Adventures** offering whitewater or scenic floats on the Nenana River.

Indoor entertainment at Glitter Gulch includes the **Cabin Nite Dinner Theatre** at McKinley Chalet Resort; the mountain-climbing highlights of the **Peak Experience Theatre** at Grande Denali Lodge, and the vicarious thrill of viewing the aurora borealis at the **Northern Lights Theatre**, next to their fine gift shop.

Appetites can be appeased at local restaurants such as the **Alpenglow** at Grande Denali Lodge, the **Overlook** at the Denali Crow's Nest, and the Cabin Nite Dinner Theatre at McKinley Chalet Resort. Dining facilities are found at other hotels as well, and continental breakfasts are provided at most lodgings.

Denali Rainbow Village and **Denali Riverside Park** welcome RV campers.

North from the heavy concentration of businesses at Glitter Gulch, the Parks Highway winds through the Nenana River Canyon to the Healy area, where many businesses also cater to Denali National Park visitors.

West of **Milepost A 247**, just south of Healy on Otto Lake Road, you'll find the new **Denali Park Hotel**, which offers 48 rooms. Nearby is **Park's Edge**, with comfortable log cabin accommodations, and farther down the road the beautifully situated **Denali Lakeview Inn**. Other types of lodgings are available at motels, inns and lodges such as the **Totem Inn, Denali North Star Inn, Denali Suites, White Moose Lodge** and **Motel Nord Haven**. RVers will find all appropriate services at **Denali RV Park & Motel** or **McKinley RV & Campground**. If your vehicle demands attention, a stop at **Wally's Tesoro** or **Healy Car Quest** will undoubtedly solve any problems.

At **Milepost A 251.1** a detour to the west leads to the unspoiled environment of Stampede Road, which traverses the highland country north of Denali National Park, and is the north end of Denali Park's "front country." Horse lovers will want to check out **Denali Saddle Safaris**, Mile 3.9 Stampede Road, and for an overnight stay along this wilderness road **Earth Song Lodge** at Mile 4.1 offers comfortable log cabins, dog sled rides and demonstrations, and a coffeehouse named after a sled dog named Henry.

Dall sheep are often seen in the Denali National Park area. (© Craig Brandt)

discounts given for last-minute bookings if space is available. www.denalilodge.com. Phone (800) 841-0692. See display ad this section. [ADVERTISEMENT]

A 229.2 C 19.2 F 132.8 Turnoff to east for private airstrip and Denali Air.

Denali Air, Inc. Fly closer to Denali's beauty on our 1-hour aerial tour of Mount McKinley/Denali National Park. Our private airstrip is the closest to Denali Park hotels

and the Alaska Range, offering the best tour and value. A pioneer service with the most experienced pilots. 2 person minimum. Reservations: (907) 683-2261. See display ad in the DENALI NATIONAL PARK section. [ADVERTISEMENT]

A 229.8 C 19.8 F 132.2 Double-ended paved turnout to west.

A 230.5 C 20.5 F 131.5 *Highway descends 6 percent grade northbound.*

A 231.1 C 21.1 F 130.9 Crabb's Crossing (sign)

McKinley Village Resort in Denali is nestled in the trees on the banks of the Nenana River at Milepost 231.3 and boasts 150 comfortable rooms, rustic lobby and fireplace,

casual dining room, lounge, shopping and full-service tour and activities desk. Call 1-800-276-7234. In Anchorage (907) 276-7234. Or visit www.denalinationalpark.com. [ADVERTISEMENT]

Denali Grizzly Bear Cabins & Campground. South boundary Denali National Park. Denali's only AAA-approved campground. Drive directly to your individual kitchen, sleeping or tent cabin with its old-time Alaskan atmosphere overlooking scenic Nenana River. Two conveniently located buildings with toilets, sinks, coin-operated hot showers. Advance reservations suggested. Tenting and RV campsite available in peaceful wooded areas. Hookups. Propane, laundromat. Caravans welcome! Coffee and rolls, ice cream, snacks, groceries, ice, liquor store, Alaskan gifts, tour desk. VISA, MasterCard, Discover accepted. Owned and operated by pioneer Alaskan family. Reservations phone (907) 683-2696 summer; (907) 683-1337 winter; Internet www.denaligrizzlybear.com. See display ad this section and in the DENALI NATIONAL PARK section. [ADVERTISEMENT]

Denali River Cabins and Cedars Lodge. Located on the banks of the Nenana River near the entrance to Denali National Park We offer your choice of comfy, cedar cabins or modern hotel accommodations. All rooms have private baths, televisions, telephones and easy access to our full-service restaurant and bar, riverside sun decks, and our Finnish-style sauna. Attend our on-site interpretive programs, then let our staff assist you in reserving all of your activities at our full-service tour desk. This property is the point of origin for the only private excursion into the park. Kantishna Wilderness Trails boards daily and takes our guests on a fully supported excursion deep into Denali National Park. Phone us at 1-800-230-7275 to make your reservations. Email us at drcriver@mtaonline.net. Visit our web site at www.denalirivercabins.com. See display ad in the DENALI NATIONAL PARK section. [ADVERTISEMENT]

A 231.3 C 21.3 F 130.7 Crabb's Crossing, second bridge northbound over the Nenana River.

A 231.4 C 21.4 F 130.6 Boundary of Denali National Park and Preserve. From here north for 6.8 miles the Parks Highway is within the boundaries of the park and travelers must abide by park rules. No discharge of firearms permitted.

A 233.1 C 23 F 128.9 Gravel turnout to east. Posted no overnight camping.

A 234.1 C 24.1 F 127.9 Double-ended scenic viewpoint up hill to east; litter barrels, no camping. Mount Fellows (elev. 4,476 feet), to the east, makes an excellent camera subject with its constantly changing shadows. Exceptionally beautiful in the evening. To the southeast stands Pyramid Peak (elev. 5,201 feet).

Travel information tune to 1610 radio (sign).

A 235.1 C 25.1 F 126.9 CAUTION: Railroad crossing. Solar panels and wind generators provide power for crossing signals.

A 236 C 26 F 126 *Begin 55 mph speed zone northbound.*

A 236.5 C 26.5 F 125.5 *Highway begins 6 percent downgrade northbound.*

A 236.7 C 26.7 F 125.3 Alaska Railroad crosses over highway.

A 237 C 27 F 125 *Begin 40 mph speed zone northbound.*

A 237.3 C 27.3 F 124.7 Riley Creek bridge.

Distance marker southbound indicates Cantwell 27 miles, Wasilla 196 miles, Anchorage 237 miles.

A 237.4 C 27.6 F 124.6 Denali National Park and Preserve entrance. The park visitor center is a half-mile west of the highway junction on the Park Road.

Junction with Park Road. See DENALI NATIONAL PARK section on page 399 for Park Road log and details on the park.

DENALI PARK/McKINLEY PARK (pop. 169 in summer) refers to the business area that has developed along the Parks Highway from south of the Park entrance north to the Nenana River canyon. A variety of services are offered, including river running trips, gift shops, accommodations, restaurants and a gas station. Most are open in summer only. See "Denali National Park's Front Country" this section.

A 238 C 28 F 124 Third bridge northbound over the Nenana River. Staging area for Nenana Raft Adventures raft trips on the Nenana River.

Nenana Raft Adventures. Raft Denali with the first raft company in Alaska to outfit

every client in a full drysuit. Day trips as well as multi-day expeditions on the Talkeetna River. Oar rafts and paddle rafting both available. Our riverfront office is directly next door to ERA Helicopters. Phone 1-800-789-RAFT; in Denali (907) 683-RAFT. [ADVERTISEMENT]

Dall sheep are regularly sighted in the early and late summer months on Sugarloaf Mountain (elev. 4,450 feet), to the east (closed to hunting). Mount Healy (elev. 5,716 feet) is to the west.

Southbound for 6.8 miles the Parks Highway is within Denali National Park and Preserve and travelers must abide by park rules. No discharge of firearms.

A 238.1 C 28.1 F 123.9 Public access to Nenana River.

Distance marker northbound indicates Healy 11 miles, Nenana 67 miles, Fairbanks 117 miles.

A 238.2 C 28.2 F 123.8 Kingfisher Creek.

A 238.2 C 28.2 F 123.8 Alpenglow Restaurant. A truly unique dining experience with unparalleled views of the Alaska Range. The restaurant offers a variety of menu choices to tantalize your taste buds. Enjoy your favorite beverage from the full-service lounge. View the vast expanse of the Alaska Range, smell the wildflowers and trees; listen to and feel the clean mountain breeze and let the spirit of Alaska surround you. Open mid-May through mid-September. Wheelchair accessible. Credit cards accepted. Phone (907) 683-5150. Fax (907) 683-5101. Email: info@denalialaska.com. Web page: www.denalialaska.com. See display ad in the DENALI NATIONAL PARK section. [ADVERTISEMENT]

Grande Denali Lodge. A peak lodge experience. Spectacular panoramic views from high above the hustle and bustle of the highway corridor. Take in views of Mt. Healy, the Nenana River or Mt. Sugarloaf. Each room features 2 queen beds, TV, telephone, coffee maker, hair dryer, AC and private bath. Lodge offers large seating areas, gift shop, coin-operated laundry and the Peak Experience Theater. Also 6 deluxe family cabins with private deck—will sleep 5. Open mid-May through mid-September. Credit cards accepted. P.O. Box 72460, Fairbanks, AK 99707. Phone (866) 683-8500. Fax (907) 683-8599. Email: info@denalialaska.com. Web page: www.denalialaska.com. See display ad in the DENALI NATIONAL PARK section. [ADVERTISEMENT]

A 238.4 C 28.4 F 123.6 Denali Bluffs Hotel. AAA approved. Conveniently located 1 mile from the Denali National Park entrance, the hotel offers great views of the Alaska Range. 112 rooms; each room features double beds, TVs, phones, refrigerators, coffee makers and private bath. The lodge features a large stone fireplace with comfortable sitting areas to relax after a long day. Or sit outside on the large deck to enjoy the panoramic views. Gift shop, coin-operated laundry, tour desk and shuttle. Wheelchair accessible. Open mid-May through mid-September. Credit cards accepted. P.O. Box 72460, Fairbanks, AK 99707. Phone (866) 683-8500. Fax (907) 683-8599. Email: info@denalialaska.com. Web page: www.denalialaska.com. See display ad in the DENALI NATIONAL PARK section. [ADVERTISEMENT]

A 238.5 C 28.5 F 123.5 Turnoff to east (uphill) for Denali Crow's Nest. Tesoro gas station to east. River rafting outfitters. Alaska flag display in front of Denali Princess Lodge (west side of highway) features a 10-by-15-foot state flag and plaques detailing history of flag design and song.

CAUTION: Congested area! Slow for pedestrians and turning traffic.

Denali Crow's Nest Log Cabins and The Overlook Bar & Grill. Open mid-May to mid-September, offering spectacular views of the Park entrance area. One mile north of Park entrance road. Authentic Alaska log cabins with hotel comforts; all rooms with private bath. Courtesy transportation. Hot tub, tour bookings. Dine on steaks, seafood, burgers, salmon and halibut indoors or on the deck at The Overlook Bar & Grill. 66 varieties of beer, 9 draft beers; meals 11 A.M. to 11 P.M. Bar open till midnight. For restaurant's courtesy shuttle from all local hotels, call (907) 683-2723; fax (907) 683-2323; Toll-free reservations (888) 917-8130. See display ad in DENALI NATIONAL PARK section. [ADVERTISEMENT]

Denali Princess Wilderness Lodge. Riverside lodging near the entrance to Denali National Park featuring spectacular park and Nenana River views, several dining options including dinner theatre, tour desk, gift shop, complimentary shuttle to rail depot and park activities. Open mid-May through mid-September. Reservations (800) 426-0500 year-round. [ADVERTISEMENT]

Denali Raft Adventures. Come with the original Nenana River rafters! Paddleboats too! Age 5 or older welcome. 7 departures

daily. Whitewater or scenic floats. Get away to untouched wilderness! 2-hour, 4-hour and full-day trips are available. See display ad in DENALI NATIONAL PARK section. Phone (907) 683-2234. Internet: www.denaliraft.com. Email: denraft@mtaonline.net. VISA, Mastercard accepted. [ADVERTISEMENT]

Denali Outdoor Center. Denali's most diversified river outfitter! Oar rafts, paddle rafts, inflatable kayak tours and mountain bike rentals. 2-hour, 4-hour, and 1/2-day

guided whitewater and scenic wilderness river trips. Custom "drysuits," professional guides and exceptional equipment provided. Ages 5 and up. Call for reservations (888) 303-1925 or (907) 683-1925. Major credit cards accepted. See display ad in DENALI NATIONAL PARK section. [ADVERTISEMENT]

A 238.6 C 28.6 F 123.4 Denali Rainbow Village & RV Park. The closest full-service RV park to Denali Park. Just one mile north of Park entrance. 77 full and partial hookup sites surrounded by all services and activities. Denali's premier campground. Reasonable prices. 25 percent off 3rd night. For the best vacation yet call (907) 683-7777. See display ad in the DENALI NATIONAL PARK section. [ADVERTISEMENT] ▲

A 238.9 C 28.9 F 123.1 Northern Lights Gift Shop. See the Northern Lights in all their sweeping beauty and mystery. It's the film everyone is talking about. Come and experience Denali's other spectacle. Six shows daily. Call or stop by for show times and tickets. Free shuttle pick up from many area hotels. Also, don't miss Denali's finest gift shop housed in a beautiful natural log building. Located one mile north of the park entrance. [ADVERTISEMENT]

A 239 C 29 F 123 McKinley Chalet Resort in Denali features 345 comfortable rooms and mini-suites and provides the most convenient access to Denali Park Tours, river rafting and walking trails. Home of the famous Alaska Cabin Nite Dinner Theater and featuring the Chalet Center Cafe and Nenana View Restaurant with private deck overlooking the river. Special weekend rates. Call 1-800-276-7234. In Anchorage (907) 276-7234. Or visit www.denalinationalpark.com. [ADVERTISEMENT]

A 239.1 C 29.1 F 122.9 Entering Nenana Canyon northbound. Begin slide area northbound.

Alaska Raft Adventures in Denali offers river rafting with experienced guides. Float through a glacial valley along the Park boundary on the Wilderness Run, or take on exciting whitewater on the Canyon Run. Free transportation available between area hotels and train depot. Visit the tour desks at McKinley Chalet or McKinley Village resorts. (907)276-7234. [ADVERTISEMENT]

A 239.8 C 29.8 F 122.2 End slide area northbound.

A 239.9 C 29.9 F 122 Bridge over Iceworm Gulch.

CAUTION: Sharp curves, rock slide area, northbound. Do not park along the highway. Use the many parking areas provided. High winds in the Nenana Canyon can make this stretch of road dangerous for campers.

A 240.1 C 30.1 F 121.9 Hornet Creek.

A 240.3 C 30.3 F 121.7 Double-ended parking area to west.

A 240.4 C 30.4 F 121.6 Entrance to Denali Riverside RV Park to west. ▲

Denali Riverside RV Park. Two miles from park entrance. 100 sites, 20 to 50 amp, pull-throughs, dry and tent camping. Shoulder season discount. Handicapped-accessible restrooms, pay showers, laundry, propane, gift shop, tours. Caravans and groups welcome. Reservations: P.O. Box 158, Denali National Park, AK 99755; phone (888) 778-8800; alaskarv@aol.com; www.alaskarv.com. [ADVERTISEMENT] ▲

A 240.7 C 30.7 F 121.3 Double-ended turnout to west.

A 241.6 C 31.6 F 120.4 Large gravel parking area to west. No camping.

A 242.2 C 32.2 F 119.8 Paved double-ended turnout to west.

A 242.3 C 32.3 F 119.7 Dragonfly Creek.

A 242.7 C 32.7 F 119.3 Paved double-ended turnout to west.

A 242.8 C 32.8 F 119.2 Moody Bridge across Nenana River. *CAUTION: Windy area next mile northbound.* Wind sock mid-span. This 4th bridge northbound over the Nenana River measures 174 feet from its deck to the bottom of the canyon. Dall sheep can be spotted from the bridge. Entering Game Management Unit 20A northbound, 20C southbound.

A 243.5 C 33.5 F 114.5 Bridge over Bison Gulch. Sharp turn at north end to east for paved viewpoint.

A 244 C 34 F 114 Large gravel turnout to east.

NOTE: Watch for bumpy, patched pavement and frost heaves northbound.

Healy

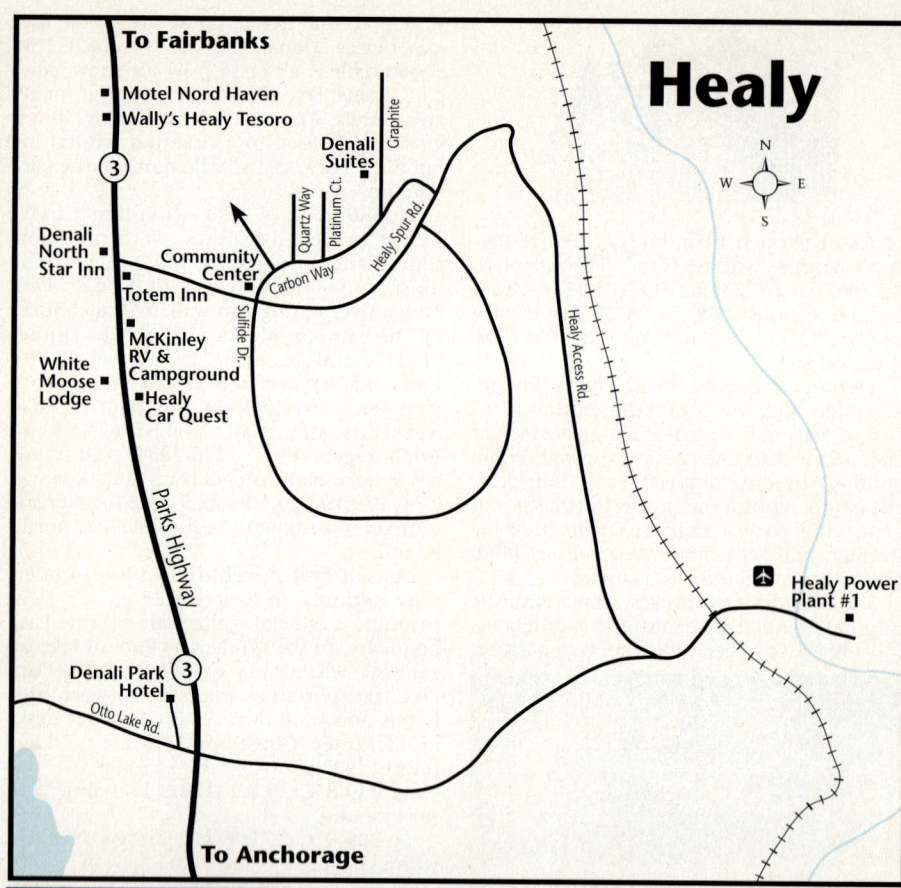

A 244.5 C 34.5 F 113.5 Bridge over Antler Creek.

A 245.1 C 35.1 F 116.9 **Denali RV Park & Motel.** 90 full and partial RV hookups, cable TV, 30-amp electric, pull-throughs, level sites, easy access. RV rates $15–$28. Caravans welcome! Private restrooms with pay showers, dump station. 14 motel rooms. Double with bath $74; family units with full kitchen and TV $119. Laundry, pay phones, outdoor cooking area, covered meeting area. Gift shop, tour booking, information. Beautiful panoramic mountain views, hiking trails. Email access line available. VISA/Mastercard/Discover. Web address: www.denaliRV-park.com. Email: stay@denaliRVpark.com. Located 8 miles north of park entrance. Box 155, Denali National Park, AK 99755. (800) 478-1501, (907) 683-1500. See dislay ad in the DENALI NATIONAL PARK section. [ADVERTISEMENT] ▲

A 246.9 C 36.9 F 115.1 Paved turnout to east. *End passing lane southbound.*

A 247 C 37 F 115 **Junction** with **Otto Lake Road**, which leads west to **Denali Park Hotel** turnoff (0.1 mile); Lion's Club Park day-use area on **Otto Lake** (0.7 mile); Black Diamond Golf Course and Park's Edge log cabins (0.9 mile); **Denali Lakeview Inn** (1.1 mile); and road end (1.4 mile).

Highway descends long downhill grade to Healy northbound.

A 247.3 C 37.3 F 114.7 Auto and truck repair and parts.

Healy Car Quest. See display ad this section.

A 247.8 C 37.8 F 114.2 *Begin truck lane southbound.*

A 248 C 38 F 114 **White Moose Lodge.** See display ad in DENALI NATIONAL PARK section.

A 248.1 C 38.1 F 113.9 *Begin 45 mph speed zone northbound.*

A 248.4 C 38.4 F 113.6 Gas station. McKinley RV Campground to east.

McKinley RV & Campground. See display ad this section. ▲

A 248.6 C 38.6 F 113.4 Paved turnout to east.

A 248.7 C 38.7 F 113.5 **Junction** with Healy Road to Healy (description follows). Totem Inn on south side of Healy Road interesection; Denali North Star Inn on north side of Healy Road intersection (see **Milepost A 248.8**). Homes and businesses of Healy are dispersed along Healy Road, as well as along the Parks Highway between Otto Lake Road and Stampede Road.

Totem Inn. Full-service facility year-round. Deluxe, economy rooms, restaurant, lounge and gift shop. Satellite TV and laundry facilities for guests. 24-hour access to pay telephones. Good food, reasonable rates, Alaskan hospitality. MasterCard/VISA/Discover. Restaurant (907) 683-2420. Motel (907) 683-2384. Fax (907) 683-2432. [ADVERTISEMENT]

Healy

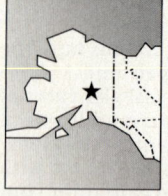

Located along the Parks Highway at Healy Road. **Population:** 889. **Emergency Services: Alaska State Troopers,** phone (907) 683-2232. **Fire Department,** Tri–Valley Volunteer Fire Dept., phone 911 or (907) 683-2223. **Clinic,** Healy Clinic, located on 2nd floor of Tri–Valley Community Center at Mile 0.5 Healy Road, phone (907) 683-2211 or 911 (open 24 hours).

CARQUEST
HEALY CAR QUEST
AUTO PARTS & SERVICE
Tire Repair
(907) 683-2374
Open 8:00 a.m. – 6:00 p.m.
Monday–Friday
Saturday 9:00 a.m. – 5:00 p.m.
Milepost 247.3

McKinley RV & Campground

Grocery • Laundry • Private Showers • Ice • Pay Phone
Full Hookups • Tent Sites • Picnic Tables • Firepits
Alaska Gifts • Quiet, Hidden Sites • Propane Service
Gas & Diesel • ATM • Deli

1-800-478-2562, (907) 683-2379, FAX (907) 683-2281
Box 340-MP, Healy, AK 99743
MILE 248.4 George Parks Highway

Forests and mountains near Healy, just north of Denali National Park.
(© Laurent Dick)

test) removing the soil, or overburden, to expose the coal seams. This 4,275,000-lb. machine, erected in 1978, moves an average of 24,000 cubic yards each 24 hours. Private vehicles are not allowed into the mining area and no tours are available.

Denali Suites. Located 15 minutes north of entrance to Denali National Park on Healy Spur Road. Units include 2 or 3 bedrooms, kitchen and dining area, living room with queen-sized hide-a-bed, TV and VCR, and private baths. Coin-operated laundry facilities. Clean, comfortable, affordable. Each unit accommodates up to 6 people, one accommodates 8, with 2 private baths; families welcome. VISA, MasterCard, Discover. Open all year. Call (907) 683-2848 or write Box 393, Healy, AK 99743. Email: denalisuites@usibelli.com. Internet: www.alaskaone.com/densuites. See display ad in the DENALI NATIONAL PARK section.
[ADVERTISEMENT]

Parks Highway Log
(continued)

A 248.8 C 38.8 F 113.2 North side of Healy Road intersection.

Denali North Star Inn is a full-service year-round hotel located in Healy, 10 miles north of Denali National Park at Milepost 248.8 George Parks Highway (Route 3). Amenities offered to our guests include comfortable, reasonably priced rooms; finest food and cocktail lounge in the Denali Park area. Alaskan gifts, self-service laundry, hair salon, and recreation and exercise areas with

Visitor Information: Available at the Greater Healy/Denali Chamber of Commerce log building at Mile 0.4 Healy Spur Road from 9 A.M. to 5 P.M. in summer. Phone (907) 683-4636; www.denalichamber.com.

Elevation: 1,294 feet. **Radio:** KUAC-FM 101.7. **Private Aircraft:** Healy River airstrip 2.1 miles east of Parks Highway via Healy Road; length 2,800 feet; paved; unattended. 8 tie-downs available. A commercial air taxi operates here in summer.

Healy Power Plant, located 3.3 miles east of the Parks Highway at the end of Healy Road, has the distinction of being the largest coal-fired steam plant in Alaska, as well as the only mine-mouth power plant. This plant is part of the Golden Valley Electric Assoc., which furnishes electric power for Fairbanks and vicinity. The Fairbanks–Tanana Valley area uses primarily coal and also oil to meet its electrical needs.

Across the Nenana River lie the abandoned and historic mining settlements of Suntrana and Usibelli. Dry Creek, Healy and Nenana river valleys comprise the area referred to as Tri–Valley. Coal mining began here in 1918 and has grown to become Alaska's largest coal mining operation. Usibelli Coal Mine, the state's only commercial coal mine, mines just under a million tons of coal a year to supply the University of Alaska, the military and Aurora Energy utilities. Free tours may be available with limited seating in summer. Phone (907) 683-2226 for information.

From the highway, you may see a 33-cubic-yard walking dragline (named Ace in the Hole by local schoolchildren in a con-

HEALY AREA ADVERTISERS	
Denali North Star Inn	Mile 248.8 Parks Hwy.
Denali Saddle Safaris	Ph. (907) 683-1200
Denali Suites	Ph. (907) 683-2848
Healy Car Quest	Ph. (907) 683-2374
McKinley RV & Campground	Ph. (907) 683-2379
Motel Nord Haven	Ph. (907) 683-4500
Totem Inn	Ph. (907) 683-2384
Wally's Healy Tesoro	Ph. (907) 683-2408

www.themilepost.com

WALLY'S HEALY TESORO

Open 24 Hours (907) 683-2408

GAS • DIESEL • PROPANE
Essential Groceries • Deli • Ice
Pay Phone • ATM
Major Credit Cards

Mile 249.2 Parks Highway

North
Fairbanks — 109 Miles
Nenana — 55 Miles

★ **Wally's Healy Tesoro** ★

South
Denali National Park Entrance — 12 Miles
Cantwell — 40 Miles
Anchorage — 249 Miles

Real Value. Real Easy.

tanning beds and saunas. Information and reservations for Denali Park tours and other activities; courtesy shuttle service. (800) 684-1560 www.denalinorthstarinn.com.
[ADVERTISEMENT]

A 249 C 39 F 113 Suntrana Road to east; post office and Tri–Valley School.

A 249.2 C 39.2 F 112.8 Wally's Healy Tesoro gas station to east; 24-hour fuel.

Wally's Healy Tesoro. See display ad this section.

A 249.3 C 39.3 F 112.7 Dry Creek Bridge No. 1.

A 249.5 C 39.5 F 112.5 Motel Nord Haven to west.

Motel Nord Haven. Meticulously kept family-owned inn. 28 large rooms, all non-smoking, feature queen beds, TVs, telephones, private baths, and Alaskan art. Let us pack your lunch for your Denali Park visit! Peaceful location away from the crowds and only a 15-minute drive from park entrance. Open year-round. Phone 1-800-683-4501. Fax (907) 683-4503. Email: info@motelnordhaven.com. Web site: www.motelnordhaven.com.
[ADVERTISEMENT]

A 249.8 C 39.8 F 112.2 Dry Creek Bridge No. 2. Good berry picking area first part of August.

Speed zone begins 45 mph southbound.

A 251.1 C 41.1 F 110.9 **Junction** with **Stampede Road** (to west). Stampede Road accesses some beautiful highland country on the north side of Denali. At Mile 2.1 Stampede Road is a "Welcome to Panguingue Creek" community sign; camping, hunting and shooting prohibited. *Please drive slowly.* At Mile 2.9 is a bed-and-breakfast/restaurant. At Mile 3.9 is Denali Saddle Safaris. At Mile 4.1 is Earth Song Lodge and Henry's Coffeehouse (named after a sled dog). The road ends about 8 miles from the Parks Highway.

Denali Saddle Safaris. See display ad this section.

If you've read *Into the Wild* and want to visit the memorial at the bus, locals advise it is a long hike in from the end of Stampede Road and you have to cross the Savage and Teklanika Rivers. Inquire locally for more information.

A 251.2 C 41.2 F 110.8 Paved turnout to west. Coal seams visible in bluff to east.

A 252.4 C 42.4 F 109.6 Gravel turnout to west.

A 252.5 C 42.5 F 109.5 Bridge over **Panguingue Creek**. Moderate success fishing for grayling. This stream, which flows 8 miles to the Nenana River, was named for a Philippine card game.

A 259.4 C 49.4 F 102.6 Large paved turnout to east. Views of Rex Dome to the northeast. Walker and Jumbo domes to the east. Liberty Bell mining area lies between the peaks and highway.

A 260.7 C 50.7 F 101.3 Slide area next 0.3 mile northbound.

A 262.7 C 52.7 F 99.3 Large gravel turnout to east.

A 264.5 C 54.5 F 97.5 Paved turnout to west.

A 265 C 55 F 97 Extra-wide gravel shoulder for emergency parking.

A 269 C 59 F 93 June Creek rest area and picnic spot to east; large gravel parking area, outhouse. Follow wooden stairs and path up to picnic sites in trees with view of Nenana River. There are picnic tables, fireplaces, toilets, a litter bin and a sheltered table. Cut wood may be available. Gravel road leads downhill to parking place with table on June Creek (trailers and large RVs check turnaround space before driving down).

A 269.2 C 59.2 F 92.8 Gravel turnout to east.

A 269.5 C 59.5 F 92.5 Bridge over Bear Creek.

A 270 C 60 F 92 Extra-wide gravel shoulders for emergency parking northbound to Milepost A 285.

Distance marker northbound indicates Nenana 34 miles, Fairbanks 89 miles.

A 271.4 C 61.4 F 90.6 Paved turnout to west.

A 275.7 C 65.7 F 86.3 Entering Game Management Unit 20A northbound, 20C southbound.

A 275.8 C 65.8 F 86.2 Rex Bridge over Nenana River. Scenic spot.

A 276 C 66 F 86 **Tatlanika Trading Co.** Located in a beautiful pristine wilderness setting. Tent sites and RV parking with electricity, water, dump station, showers. 39 miles from Denali National Park on the Nenana River. Our gift shop features a gathering of handmade art/crafts/artifacts from various villages. See the rare Samson fox, along with relics and antiques from Alaska's colorful past in a museum atmosphere. Many historical and educational displays. Visitor information. Coffee, pop, juice, snacks. Clean restrooms. This is a must stop. Also a must see: Our huge world-class polar bear. See display ad this section.
[ADVERTISEMENT] ▲

A 276.3 C 66.3 F 85.7 *CAUTION: Railroad crossing.*

A 280 C 70 F 82 Clear Sky Lodge with dining to west.

Clear Sky Lodge. See display ad this section.

A 282.3 C 72.3 F 79.7 Denali Borough Landfill.

CAUTION: Moose Danger Zone next 22 miles northbound. Watch for moose!

A 283.5 C 73.5 F 78.5 **Junction** with paved access road west to **Clear Air Force Station** gate (1.9 miles) and to the community of Anderson (6 miles); description follows. Clear is a military installation (ballistic missile early warning site); sign at turnoff states it is unlawful to enter without permission. However, you can drive into Anderson without permission. The turnoff for Anderson is 1.2 miles west of the Parks Highway before you get to Clear AFS.

ANDERSON (pop. 517), named for homesteader Arthur Anderson, was settled in the late 1950s and was incorporated in 1962. **Visitor information:** Contact the city office at (907) 582-2500. **Emergency services:** Anderson Fire Dept./EMS Ambulance, phone 911. Anderson has a city campground with 40 sites on the Nenana River. The community also has a medical clinic, city hall/post office, store, churches, a restaurant, softball fields and shooting range. Anderson hosts an annual Bluegrass Festival the last weekend in July. ▲

Anderson Riverside Park. Come enjoy our city's 616 beautiful acres located along the bank of the Nenana River! Featuring restrooms, showers, RV dump station, electrical hookups. River campsites, rustic campsites with barbecue pits, picnic area with

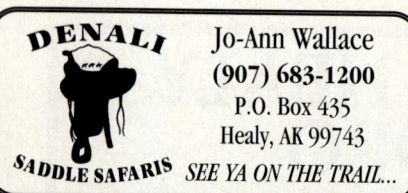

Jo-Ann Wallace
(907) 683-1200
P.O. Box 435
Healy, AK 99743
SEE YA ON THE TRAIL...

Not just another *Gift Shop*...
...but an EXPERIENCE!
TATLANIKA TRADING CO.

• MOOSE ANTLER JEWELRY AND HANDMADE ULUS
• HANDMADE BEADED JEWELRY AND DREAMCATCHERS
• MUSEUM ATMOSPHERE, HISTORICAL & EDUCATIONAL DISPLAYS
• MORE THAN 70 ALASKAN ARTISTS & CRAFTSMEN REPRESENTED
• HANDCRAFTED TOTEMS, FUR SLIPPERS AND MASKS
• BIRCH BARK BASKETS AND RAW DIAMOND WILLOW

SEE OUR LOG AD AT MI. 276

CLEAN RESTROOMS, PICNIC TABLES, VISITOR INFORMATION, RV PARKING AND HOOKUPS!

THE GIFTSHOP YOUR HUSBAND WILL LOVE!

39 MILES NORTH OF DENALI NATIONAL PARK AT MILE 276 PARKS HWY

OPEN 9AM TO 6PM

Phone (907) 582-2341
P.O. Box 40179
Clear, Alaska 99704

Jay Reeder, owner

COME IN AND MEET GEORGE!

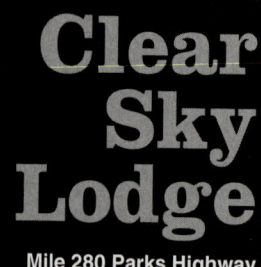

Clear Sky Lodge
Mile 280 Parks Highway

• Cocktail Lounge • Steak Dinners
• Great Burgers • Propane
• Liquor Store • Ice • Phone

Open Year-Round
Serving Lunch and Dinner 11 A.M. - 11 P.M.
Phone (907) 582-2251 Clear, Alaska 99704

covered pavilion, fireplace. New this year: multi-purpose recreational trails. Shooting range, bandstand, telephone. Home of the annual Anderson Bluegrass Festival, held the last weekend in July. City of Anderson, P.O. Box 3100, Anderson, AK 99744. Phone (907) 582-2500; fax (907) 582-2496. [ADVERTISEMENT]▲

Private Aircraft: Clear Airport, 2.5 miles from Parks Highway; elev. 552 feet; length 4,000 feet; asphalt; unattended.

A 283.6 C 73.6 F 78.4 Distance marker northbound indicates Nenana 20 miles, Fairbanks 78 miles.

A 284.2 C 74.2 F 77.8 AT&T/Alascom tower to west.

A 285 C 75 F 77 Extra-wide gravel shoulders for emergency parking south to **Milepost A 270**.

A 285.7 C 75.5 F 76.3 Julius Creek bridge.

A 286.3 C 76.3 F 75.7 View of Mount McKinley southbound.

A 286.6 C 76.6 F 75.4 Large double-ended paved parking area to east.

A 288.3 C 78.3 F 73.7 Denali Borough boundary.

A 288.7 C 78.7 F 73.3 Fireweed 288 Roadhouse.

A 296.7 C 86.7 F 65.3 Bridge over **Fish Creek**. Small gravel turnout with litter barrels by creek. Access to creek at south end of bridge; moderate success fishing for grayling.

A 298 C 88 F 64 Tamarack Inn. *Emergency phone.*

A 301.5 C 91.5 F 60.6 Nenana city limits.

A 303 C 93 F 55 *Begin 55 mph speed zone northbound.*

A 303.7 C 93.7 F 58.3 Nenana Airport Road.

A 304.3 C 94.3 F 57.7 ADF&G Boat Launch Facility to west; parking area, toilets, interpretive signs.

Begin 45 mph speed zone northbound.

A 304.5 C 94.5 F 57.5 Chevron gas station, diesel, food mart to west.

A Frame Service. See display ad this section.

CAUTION: Moose Danger Zone next 22 miles southbound. Watch for moose!

Nenana

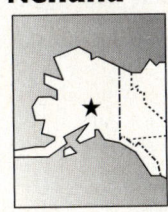

A 304.5 C 94.5 F 57.5 Located at the confluence of the Tanana and Nenana rivers. **Population:** 435. **Emergency Services:** Emergency only (fire, police, ambulance), phone 911. **Fire Department/ EMT,** phone (907) 832-5632.

Visitor Information: In the sod-roofed log cabin at the junction of the highway and A Street. Open 8 A.M. to 6 P.M., 7 days a week, Memorial Day to Labor Day; phone (907) 832-9953. Pay phone. Ice Classic tickets may be purchased here. Picnic tables and restrooms are beside the restored *Taku Chief*,

NENANA ADVERTISERS

A Frame Service	Ph. (907) 832-5823
Coghill's General Merchandise	Ph. (907) 832-5422
Nenana Visitor Center	Ph. (907) 832-9953
Roughwoods Inn and Cafe	Ph. (907) 832-5299
Tripod Motel & RV Park	Ph. (907) 832-5590

www.themilepost.com

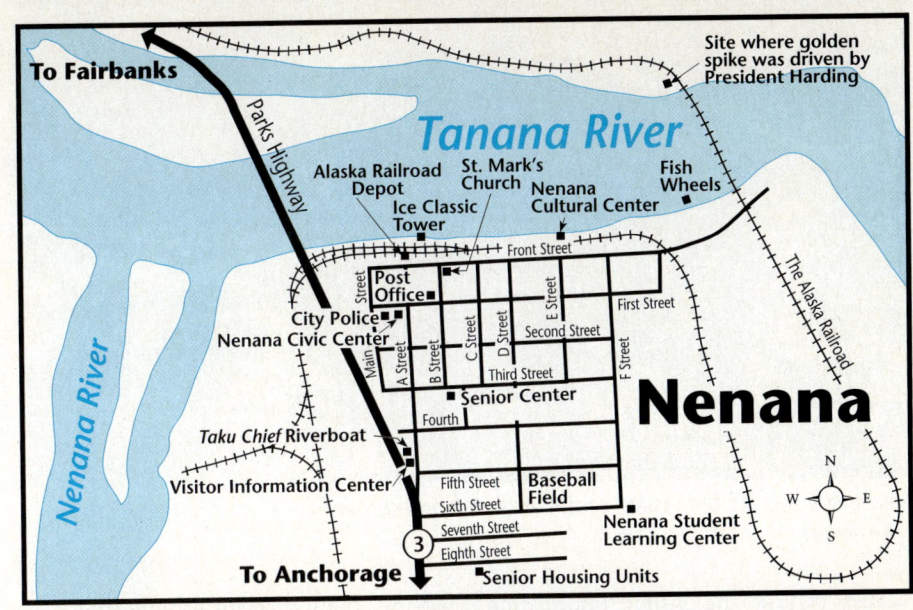

NEAR THE 'Y' AT NENANA MI A 304.5 PARKS HWY.

- Chevron Gas • Diesel • Chevron Products
- Kerosene • Cafe • Sandwiches
- Ice • Essential Groceries • Pay Phone • ATM

**Hours: 6 a.m.-12 a.m.
(907) 832-5823**

Tripod Motel & R.V. Park

Single Rooms ~ Family Suites ~ Tent Sites ~ Showers ~ Picnic Tables
"Winter Rates All Summer Long"
***** Guided Scenic Tours & Treks Available *****
ALSO Visit Our
ALASKAN CRAFTS WOODWORKING SHOP
Diamond Willow / Burls / Canes & Walking Sticks / Rustic Furniture
Personalized Signs Made/ Chainsaw Art / Items Made To Order

 P.O. Box 250, Nenana, AK 99760 907-832-5590
Email: tripodmotel_rvpark@hotmail.com

ROUGHWOODS INN AND CAFE
Quality Dining - Rustic Decor - Clean Quiet Rooms
2nd and A Street Nenana, Alaska **907-832-5299**
email: roughwoods1@juno.com

Nenana is known as the town "where rail and river meet."

Nenana's sod-roofed visitor center has welcomed travelers since the early 1970s.
(© Ron Niebrugge)

located behind the visitor information center. This proud little tugboat plied the waters of the Tanana, Yukon and Koyukuk rivers for many years.

Elevation: 400 feet. **Radio:** KIAM 630, KUAC-FM 91.1. **Transportation: Air—** Nenana maintains an FAA-approved airport. **Railroad—**The Alaska Railroad.

Private Aircraft: Nenana Municipal Airport, 0.9 mile south; elev. 362 feet; length 5,000 feet; asphalt; fuel 100, Jet B. Floatplane and skiplane strip.

Nenana has an auto repair shop, radio station, several churches, a library, restaurants, a cultural center, a laundromat, a seniors' social center and senior housing units, gift shops, and Coghill's, a grocery/general store that has served the community for more than 80 years. Accommodations are available at a motel, inn and bed and breakfast. RV park with hookups.

The town was first known as Tortella, a white man's interpretation of the Athabascan word *Toghottele*. A 1902 map indicates a village spelled Tortilli on the north bank of the Tanana River, on the side of the hill still known as Tortella. In the same year Jim Duke built a roadhouse and trading post, supplying river travelers with goods and lodging. The settlement became known as Nenana, an Athabascan word meaning, "a good place to camp between the rivers." The town thrived as a trading center for Natives of the region and travelers on the vast network of interior rivers.

Nenana boomed during the early 1920s as a construction base for the Alaska Railroad. On July 15, 1923, Pres. Warren G. Harding drove the golden spike at Nenana signifying the completion of the railroad. The depot, located at the end of Main Street,

is on the National Register of Historic Places. Built in 1923 and renovated in 1988, the depot houses the state's **Alaska Railroad Museum**, open 9 A.M. to 6 P.M. daily.

One block from the railroad depot is **St. Mark's Mission Church.** This little log building, sometimes open to the public, is graced with hand-hewn pews and a raised altar decorated with Native beaded moosehide frontal and dossal hangings.

Today, Nenana is the hub for the tug boat /barge shipping industry that traverses the rivers of the Interior, providing goods to numerous villages. Tons of fuel, freight and supplies move from the docks at Nenana from late May through September each year. Because the rivers are shallow and silt-laden, the barges move about 12 mph downstream and 5 mph upstream. The dock area is to the right of the highway northbound.

Nenana is perhaps best known for the **Nenana Ice Classic**, an annual event that awards cash prizes to the lucky winners who guess the exact minute of the ice breakup on the Tanana River. The contest has been a spring highlight throughout the state since 1917.

Ice Classic festivities begin the last weekend in February with the Tripod Raising Festival and culminate at breakup time in late April or May. When the surging ice on the Tanana River dislodges the tripod, a line attached to the tripod trips a clock located in a tower atop the Ice Classic office, thus recording the official breakup time. Summer visitors can see the clock tower and this year's winning time at the Ice Classic office on Front Street. The tripod for the next Ice Classic is displayed next to the office during River Daze, held the first weekend in June.

Parks Highway Log
(continued)

A 305 C 95 F 57 **Alaska Native Veterans' Honor Bridge** across the Tanana River. This steel through-truss style bridge was built in 1966-67. It was dedicated on August 5, 2000, to commemorate Alaska Natives who have served in U.S. Armed Forces. The bridge spans the Tanana River just upstream of the confluence of the Nenana River. There is no other bridge downstream of this one all the way to the mouth of the Yukon River in Norton Sound.

A 305.4 C 95.4 F 56.6 Large paved turnout to west at north end of bridge. The Tanana is formed by the joining of the Chisana and the Nabesna rivers near Northway and flows 440 miles westward to the Yukon River. From the bridge, watch for freight-laden river barges bound for the Yukon River. North of this bridge, fish wheels may sometimes be seen in action and occasionally fish may be purchased from the owners of the wheels. Entering Game Management Unit 20B northbound, 20A southbound.

A 305.8 C 95.8 F 56.2 Double-ended gravel turnout to east.

A 306 C 96 F 56 *Begin 55 mph speed zone southbound.*

Begin 65 mph speed limit northbound.

A 308.8 C 98.8 F 53.2 CAUTION: *Railroad crossing.*

Monderosa restaurant to east.

A 312 C 102 F 52 Distance marker northbound indicates Ester 39 miles, Fairbanks 49 miles.

Highway begins a series of long winding grades with intermittent passing lanes next 38 miles northbound.

A 313.7 C 107.7 E 44.3 Towing service.

A 314.6 C 104.6 F 47.4 Paved double-ended turnout to west.

A 314.8 C 104.8 F 47.2 Bridge over Little Goldstream Creek.

A 318.7 C 108.7 F 43.3 Paved double-ended scenic viewpoint to west. Beautiful view of lowland country, mostly bogs, small lakes, and creeks with names like Hard Luck and Fortune.

Southbound travelers will see the Tanana River on both sides of the highway. It follows a horseshoe-shaped course, the top of the closed end being the bridge at Nenana.

COGHILL'S
GENERAL MERCHANDISE

1ST & A STREET NENANA
(907) 832-5422

GROCERIES • HARDWARE • FISHING & HUNTING LICENSES, SUPPLIES
9-6 MONDAY-SATURDAY • DOWNTOWN NENANA

NENANA VISITOR CENTER

Open daily Memorial Day to Labor Day
(907) 832-9953
Sponsored by Nenana Ice Classic
Alaska's Biggest Guessing Game Since 1917
AVERAGE ANNUAL PAYOFF OVER $300,000

*Tickets May Be Purchased At The
Visitors Information Center In Nenana (No mail orders)*

Ester

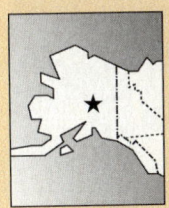

Located 0.6 mile west of highway. **Population:** 240. **Emergency Services:** Emergency only, phone 911. **Fire Department,** phone (907) 479-6858. Ester has a hotel, RV camping, 2 saloons, 3 gift shops and a post office. A village sign on Main Street locates these services.

Ester was a raucous mining camp in 1906, with a population of some 5,000 miners. In 1936, the Fairbanks Exploration Company built Ester Camp to support a large-scale gold dredge operation. After 20 years of operation, the camp was closed. It opened again in 1958, but this time as a summer visitor attraction.

Ester's heydays are relived in music, song and dance at the Malemute Saloon. The

Ester Gold Camp complex also includes the historic bunkhouse building, which houses a buffet restaurant and hotel. Overnight RV parking is available. An aurora borealis show is presented nightly adjacent the Malemute Saloon.

Several artists make their home in Ester. Judie Gumm's studio is open to visitors. Active gold mining is still under way in the area.

Judie Gumm Designs. Noted for her sculptural interpretations of northern images, her work has been featured in many national publications. Priced moderately; easy to pack—her jewelry makes a perfect remembrance of your adventure North. Follow the signs in Ester. Weekdays 10-6; Saturdays 12-5. Catalog available. P.O. Box 169, Ester, AK 99725. Phone (907)479-4568. See display ad this section. [ADVERTISEMENT]

Return to Milepost A 351.7 Parks Highway

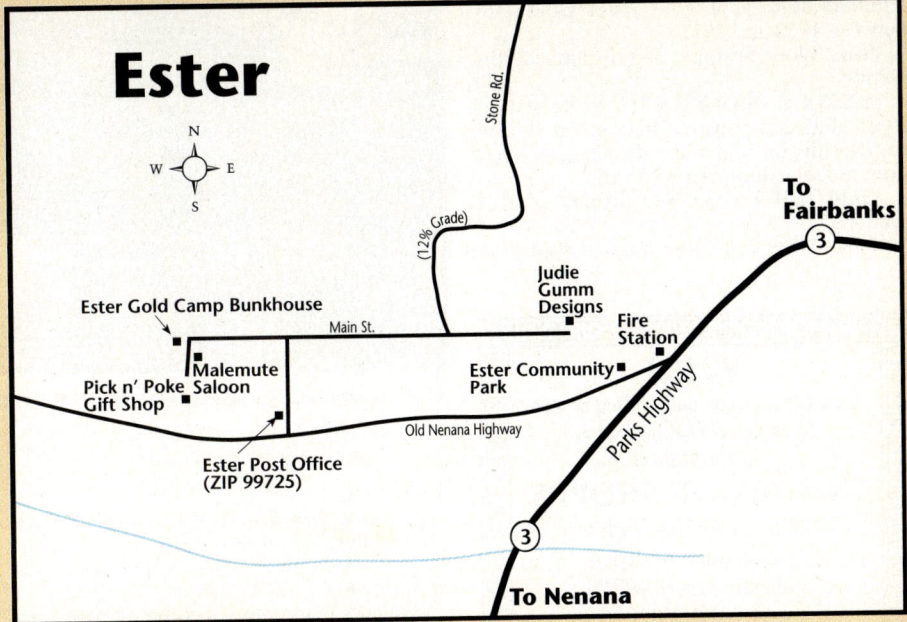

A 324.4 C 114.4 F 37.6 South end of 0.3-mile-long gravel turnout (**Purvis Lookout**) to east along an on old highway alignment. North end at **Milepost A 324.7.**

A 325.6 C 115.6 F 36.4 Entering Fairbanks North Star Borough northbound.

A 328 C 118 F 34 Skinny Dick's Halfway Inn.

A 328.3 C 118.3 F 33.7 Emergency parking west side of highway.

A 338.5 C 128.5 F 23.5 Expansive views to southeast of Tanana River. To west, look for Murphy Dome (elev. 2,930 feet), with white communication installations on summit.

This stretch of highway is often called Skyline Drive; views to west.

A 339.9 C 129.9 F 22.1 Turnoff (unmarked) for Bonanza Experimental Forest via 1-mile loop road east; scenic viewpoint.

A 341 C 131 F 21 South end of long double-ended gravel turnout to west. North end at **Milepost A 341.2.**

A 342.4 C 132.4 F 19.6 Old Nenana Highway to west.

A 344.2 C 134.2 F 17.8 Viewpoint to east with view of Tanana River; good photo opportunity. Monument in honor of George Alexander Parks (1883-1984) the territorial governor of Alaska from 1925 to 1933, for whom the Parks Highway is named. Also here is a Blue Star Memorial highway plaque honoring the armed forces.

A 349 C 139 F 13 Cripple Creek Road to south, Park Ridge Road to north.

A 350 C 140 F 12 Alder Creek.

A 350.1 C 140.1 F 11.9 Welcome to Fairbanks North Star Borough sign.

A 350.6 C 140.6 F 11.3 *Begin 55 mph speed zone northbound.*

Highway begins a series of long winding grades with intermittent passing lanes next 38 miles southbound.

A 351.7 C 141.7 F 10.3 Turnoff for Ester; fire station.

Junction with side road west to Ester; see "Ester" description this page.

A 351.8 C 141.8 F 10.2 Weigh stations.

A 352.4 C 142.4 F 9.5 Gold Hill Road. Access to Inua Wool Shoppe. The U.S. Smelting, Refining and Mining Co. mined some 126,000 ounces of gold from Gold Hill between 1953 and 1957.

Inua Wool Shoppe. See display ad this section.

A 353.4 C 143.4 F 8.6 Tesoro gas station north side of highway, Chevron gas station south side of highway; diesel, groceries, liquor. Public dumpster to north.

Gold Hill Tesoro. See display ad this section.

Parks Highway Chevron. See display ad this section.

A 354 C 144 F 8 **Troy L. Pewe Climate Change Permafrost Reserve** to north (gated). To gain access, phone the Geophysical Institute at UAF (907) 474-7291 or 474-7292. This site commemorates the work of University of Alaska professor Troy L. Pewe, head of the geology department from 1958 to 1965. This permanent scientific research site records geological and climatic history to about 3 million years ago.

A 355.8 C 145.8 F 6.2 Sheep Creek Road and Tanana Drive. Road to Murphy Dome (a restricted military site).

A 356 C 146 F 6 *Begin 4-lane divided highway eastbound.*

Begin 2-lane highway westbound.

A 356.3 C 146.3 F 5.7 Welcome to Fairbanks (sign).

A 356.8 C 146.8 F 5.2 Geist Road/Chena Pump Road Exit. Access to University of Alaska Museum (2.5 miles north from highway via Geist Road and Fairbanks Street).

A 357.6 C 147.6 F 4.4 Bridge over Chena River.

A 357.7 C 147.7 F 4 West Airport Way exit to Fairbanks International Airport and access to *Discovery* sternwheeler.

A 358 C 148 F 4 East Airport Way exit to River's Edge RV Park and University Avenue to Chena River State Recreation Site; access to Johansen Expressway. Parks Highway (Alaska Route 3) continues through Fairbanks as the Mitchell Expressway.

A 359 C 149 F 3 Stoplight at University Avenue.

A 359.9 C 149.9 F 2.1 Peger Road South exit for eastbound traffic.

A 360.3 C 150.3 F 1.7 Stoplight at intersection with Peger Road; access to North Peger Road. Turn north for access to Pioneer Park.

A 361.2 C 151.2 F 0.8 Stoplight at Lathrop Street intersection.

A 362 C 152 F 0 First visible milepost westbound, last post eastbound. Exit to Cushman Street to Fairbanks City Centre. See FAIRBANKS section beginning on page 418 for description of city.

The Parks Highway divides eastbound about 0.3 mile from here, merging with the Steese Expressway (Alaska Route 2 North) and the Richardson Highway (Alaska Route 2 South).

Junction with Richardson Highway (Alaska Route 2 South) and Steese Highway (Alaska Route 2 North). Turn to the end of the RICHARDSON HIGHWAY section on page 469 and read log back to front for log of Alaska Route 2 South. Turn to the STEESE HIGHWAY section on page 482 for log of Alaska Route 2 North

The historic stern-wheeler SS Nenana is a highlight at Pioneer Park in Fairbanks.
(© Kris Graef, staff)

YARN
A complete and unique knitting shoppe featuring QIVIUQ and other fine wool yarns
INUA WOOL SHOPPE
Mile 352.5 Parks Highway
202 Henderson Road
Fairbanks, AK 99709
907-479-5830
(In Alaska 800-478-9848)

GOLD HILL
Mile 352.5 Parks Highway

Gas * Diesel * Water * Ice
Essential Groceries * Liquor * Beer * Wine

(907) 479-2333

24 Hour Fuel Available

TESORO

Real Value. Real Easy.

PARKS HIGHWAY CHEVRON SERVICE

Chevron

Mile 352.5 Parks Highway

CASH SALES 8am to 10pm • 907-479-3312

EASY ACCESS FOR RVS & TRUCKS
LOTS OF PARKING!

• 24 HR Refuel
• Diesel
• Propane
• Restrooms
• Sewer Dump Available
• Food Mart
• ATM
• Ice

DENALI NATIONAL PARK

Includes log of Park Road

(See map on page 400)

Denali National Park and Preserve was established in 1917 as Mount McKinley National Park. It was designated a park and preserve—and renamed Denali—in 1980. The park lies on the north flank of the Alaska Range, 250 miles south of the Arctic Circle. The park entrance is 237 highway miles north of Anchorage and 124 miles south of Fairbanks via the Parks Highway.

The park is open all year, although visitor access varies with the change of seasons. From May to September, the public can travel the park road via the Visitor Transportation System (i.e. shuttle buses and tour buses). From October through April, the park road is maintained only to Milepost 3. Beyond Milepost 3 the road is left unplowed and access to the park is by skis, snowshoes or dog sleds depending on snow cover.

Most campgrounds, as well as food and shuttle bus service within the park, are available only from late May to early September. Opening dates for facilities and activities for the summer season are announced in the spring by the Park Service and depend mainly on snow conditons in May. Closing dates for facilities and activities are announced in the fall.

Most rules and regulations affecting visitors are mentioned here. For specific regulations governing the use of aircraft, firearms, snow machines and motorboats in the park additions and in the natonal preserve units, and for all other questions, contact the park.

For detailed information about the park, write Denali National Park and Preserve, P.O. Box 9, Denali Park, AK 99755; phone (907)683-2294, web site: www.nps.gov/dena.

The crown jewel of the park is Mount McKinley, North America's highest mountain at 20,320 feet. On a clear day, Mount McKinley is visible from Anchorage and many points along the Parks Highway; however, summer's often overcast or rainy weather frequently obscures the mountain, allowing summertime visitors only about a 30–40 percent chance of seeing it.

First mention of "the mountain" was in 1794, when English explorer Capt. George Vancouver spotted "a stupendous snow mountain" from Cook Inlet. Early Russian explorers and traders called the peak *Bolshaia Gora,* or "Big Mountain." The Athabascan Indians of the region called it Denali, "the High One." In 1896 a prospector, William A. Dickey, named the mountain for presidential nominee William McKinley of Ohio, although McKinley had no connection with Alaska. Protests that the mountain be returned to its original name, Denali, ensued almost at once. But it was not until the Alaska National Interest Lands Conservation Act of 1980 changed the park's status and name that the Alaska Board of Geo-

Park visitors enjoy a superb view of Denali (Mount McKinley) from Stony Dome.
(© Ron Niebrugge)

graphic Names changed the mountain's name back to Denali. (The U.S. Board of Geographic Names, however, still shows the mountain as McKinley.) The 1980 legislation also enlarged the park from 3.2 million acres to its present 6 million acres to protect Mount McKinley on all sides and to preserve the habitat of area wildlife.

The history of climbs on McKinley is as intriguing as its names. In 1903, Judge James Wickersham and party climbed to an estimated 8,000 feet, while the Dr. Frederick A. Cook party reached the 11,000-foot level in 1906. Cook returned to the mountain and made 2 attempts at the summit–the first unsuccessful, the second (according to Cook) successful. Cook's vague description of his ascent route and a questionable summit photo led many to doubt his claim. The exhaustive research of McKinley expert Bradford Washburn has proven the exaggeration of Cook's claim. Tom Lloyd, of the 1910 Sourdough Party, which included Charles McGonagall, Pete Anderson and Billy Taylor, claimed they had reached both summits (north and south peaks), but could not provide any photographic evidence. The first complete and well documented ascent of the true summit of Mount McKinley was made in June 1913 by the Rev. Hudson Stuck, Episcopal archdeacon of the Yukon, accompanied by Walter Harper, Harry Karstens and Robert Tatum. Harper, a Native Athabascan, was the first person to set foot on the higher south peak. The story of their achievement was colorfully recorded in Stuck's book, *The Ascent of Denali.* Out of respect for the Native people among whom he lived and worked, Stuck refused to refer to the mountain as McKinley.

Today, more than a thousand people attempt to climb McKinley each year between April and June, most flying in to base camp at 7,200 feet on Kahiltna Glacier. In the 2002 climbing season, 642 climbers achieved the summit of Denali—52 percent of the 1,232 who attempted it.

The first airplane landing on the mountain was flown in 1932 by Joe Crosson. Geographic features of McKinley and its sister peaks bear the names of early explorers: Eldridge and Muldrow glaciers, after George Eldridge and Robert Muldrow of the U.S. Geographic Service who determined the peak's altitude in 1898; Wickersham Wall; Karsten's Ridge; Harper Icefall; and Mount Carpe and Mount Koven, named for Allen Carpe and Theodore Koven, both killed in a 1932 climb.

Climate and Landscape: Typical summer weather in the park is cool, wet and windy. Visitors should bring clothing for temperatures that range from 40°F to 80°F. Rain gear, a light coat, sturdy walking shoes or boots and insect repellent are essential. Winter weather is cold and clear, with

DENALI NATIONAL PARK AND PRESERVE

temperatures sometimes dropping to -50°F at park headquarters. In the lowlands, snow seldom accumulates to more than 3 feet.

In June 2002, as part of a joint project between the U.S. and Japan, a new weather instrument was installed near the summit of Mt. McKinley. The instrument was originally a weather station set up to honor a group of 4 Japanese climbers, including the famed Naomi Uemura, who disappeared near the spot in separate attempts to reach the summit. The new instrument takes extreme altitude measurements of temperature and wind speed and direction and transmits them via the satellite TIROS to the International Arctic Research Center at the University of Alaska Fairbanks. The information collected by the station is available from the Geophysical Institute on the Internet at www.denali.gi.alaska.edu.

Timberline in the park is at 2,700 feet. Below timberline are vast areas of taiga, a term of Russian origin that describes scant tree growth. Together with the subarctic tundra, the landscape of Denali National Park and Preserve supports more than 450 species of trees, shrubs, herbs and flowering plants. Major species of the taiga are white spruce in dry areas; dry tundra covers the upper ridges and rocky slopes above the tree line from about 3,500 to 7,500 feet. In the wet tundra black spruce is common, intermingled with aspen, paper birch and balsam poplar. Wet tundra features willow and dwarf birch, often with horsetails, sedges and grasses along pothole ponds.

Denali's subarctic ecosystem helped it gain International Biosphere Reserve status in 1976. Outstanding features of the park include the Outer Range, Savage River Canyon, Wonder Lake, Sanctuary River, Muldrow Glacier and the Kantishna Hills. The Outer Range, located just north of the central Alaska Range, is composed of some of Alaska's oldest rocks, called Bison Gulch schist, which can be clearly seen in the Savage River Canyon.

Caribou calving grounds are located near the headwaters of the Sanctuary River,

A bull caribou, antlers in velvet, seen near the western end of the Park Road.
(© John Schwieder Photography)

DENALI MOUNTAIN MORNING HOSTEL AND LODGE
Wake to mountain peaks and the sound of Carlo Creek! Starting at $23 + tax
Beautiful log cabins, great atmosphere • Rooms and cabins sleep 3-7: private or shared • Tour desk
Cook your own meals, buy food basics here • $3 Park area shuttles • Outdoor gear rentals/sales
Raft Trips
CALL US AT (907) 683-7503
Mile 224 Parks Hwy. • P.O. Box 208 Denali Parks, AK 99755   hostelalaska.com   SEE LOG AD

DENALI RV PARK & MOTEL

Full & Partial RV Hookups • 30-Amp Electric • Easy Access • Level Sites
Pull-Throughs • Dump Station • Private Showers • Pay Phones
RV Sites $15-$28 (Best Value in the Denali Area)
Double Room with Bath $74 • Full Kitchen Units $119
Gift Shop • Laundry • Tour Booking • email Access
Hiking Trails • Beautiful Mountain Views • Reasonable Rates
Cable TV

1-800-478-1501   (907) 683-1500

245.1 Geo.Parks Hwy
DENALI RV PARK & MOTEL

VISA MasterCard DISCOVER

Box 155, Denali Park, AK 99755 • *See log ad under visitor services*
Mile 245.1 Parks Highway • 8 Miles North of Park Entrance
website: www.denalirvpark.com   email: stay@denalirvpark.com

DENALI NATIONAL PARK

When Cabin Fever Is Good.
Mile 238.8 Parks Highway
One Mile North of Denali Park Entrance

Sourdough Cabins are Alaskan operated to provide you the best "Alaskan Experience" possible. Charming individual cabins nestled in a peaceful spruce forest. Conveniently located within walking distance of all services and activities.

- Flightseeing
- National Park Tours
- Rafting • Dinner Theatre
- Horseback Riding

**Central Reservations
1-800-544-0970**
www.westmarkhotels.com

P.O. Box 118
Denali National Park, Alaska 99755

907-683-2773

ABOVE THE REST™
DENALI NATIONAL PARK

Crow's Nest

Lodging Restaurant and Bar
(888) 917-8130
e-mail: crowsnet@mtaonline.net
www.denalicrowsnest.com
(see narrative listing)

Cooking shelter and food storage area at Wonder Lake campground.
(© John Schwieder Photography)

which passes through the Outer Range between Mount Wright and Primrose Ridge. Muldrow Glacier, the largest glacier on the north side of the Alaska Range, is 32 miles long and descends 16,000 feet from near Denali's summit. Wonder Lake, 2.6 miles long and 280 feet deep, is a summer home for loons, grebes and many migrating species, and offers a peerless reflection of Denali's massif.

The Kantishna Hills were first mined in 1908 when the town of Eureka boomed with gold seekers. In 1980 the Kantishna area was included in the park. From the main entrance of the park at Milepost 237.3 of the Parks Highway, the 92-mile Park Road traverses the national park to private land holdings in Kantishna.

Visitor Information

Visitor Centers: The park currently has 2 visitors centers, one near the park entrance, and Eielson Visitor Center at Mile 66 of the park road.

The visitor center located at Mile 1 park road is the most accessible and the best single resource for on-site information about activities, camping, backcountry travel and the Visitor Transportation System (VTS). It is open from about mid-April to September 30.

DENALI PARK AREA ADVERTISERS

Accommodations
Backwoods Lodge 407
Camp Denali 408, 410
Carlo Creek Lodge.............................408
Denali Backcountry Lodge 409, 410
Denali Bluffs Hotel 405
Denali Cabins 407
Denali Crow's Nest Cabins................402
Denali Grizzly Bear Cabins &
  Campground 407
Denali Lakeview Inn 408
Denali Mountain Morning
  Hostel & Lodge 401, 409
Denali Park Hotel 406, 409
Denali Princess Wilderness Lodge 409, 417
Denali River Cabins and
  Cedars Lodge 404
Denali RV Park & Motel 401, 415
Denali Suites 406
Denali Wilderness Lodge 409, 411
Earth Song Lodge 408
Grande Denali 405, 412
Healy Heights Family Cabins...........407
Kantishna Roadhouse 409, 412
Lazy J Cabins 407
McKinley Creekside Cabins..............404
Motel Nord Haven 408
Mt. McKinley Princess
  Wilderness Lodge 412, 417
North Face Lodge 410, 412
Park's Edge 408
Perch, The 412
Totem Inn 408
Westmark Hotel/Sourdough Cabins........402
White Moose Lodge............................405

Attractions & Activities
Denali Outdoor Center 413
Denali Raft Adventures 414
Kantishna Wilderness Trails...........412
Nenana Raft Adventures 413
Peak Experience Theatre................405

Campgrounds
Cantwell RV Park.............................412
Denali Rainbow Village & RV Park.....403
Denali Riverside RV Park.................412
Denali RV Park & Motel 401, 415
McKinley RV & Campground 415

Dining & Entertainment
Alpenglow Restaurant.....................405
Creekside Cafe................................404
Perch, The 412

Tours & Transportation
Alpenglow Tours.............................417
Denali Air.......................................415
Denali Sightseeing Safaris 414
Doug Geeting Aviation 416
Era Helicopters
  Flightseeing Tours 413, 414
K2 Aviation 415
Midnight Sun Express® 413, 417
Princess Tours 417
Talkeetna Aero Services 416
Talkeetna Air Taxi 413

DENALI RAINBOW VILLAGE & RV PARK

DENALI NATIONAL PARK

PHONE 907.683.7777 FAX 907.683.7275
MILE 238.6 PARKS HIGHWAY
BOX 777 DENALI PARK AK 99755
Email: stayatdenalirainbowrvpark@gci.net
Web: denalirvrvpark.com

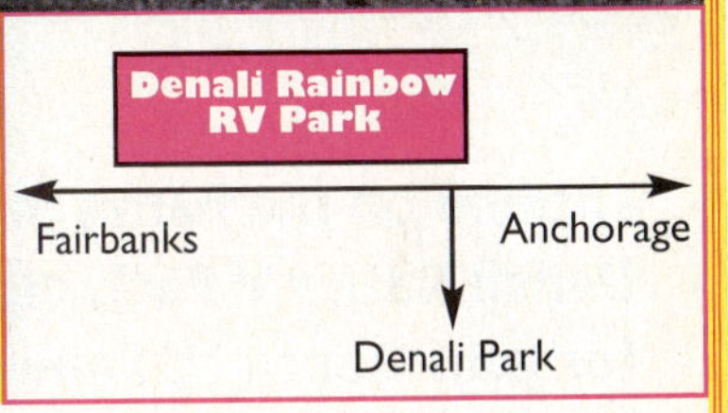

Denali Rainbow RV Park — Fairbanks ← → Anchorage ↓ Denali Park

RV PARK

- The closest full service **RV Park** to Denali National Park • Just one mile north of Park Entrance
- 77 full and partial sites surrounded by all services and activities • Walk to stores and restaurants
- 20, 30, 50 amp electric • Pull thru sites • Water and dump stations
- Picnic tables, fire rings, firewood, propane and ice
- Video rentals • Pay phones • Email and fax service • Laundry, showers, clean bathrooms
- Local tour bookings • Beautiful mountain view • Visitor information • Easy hwy access
- Friendly staff • Night security • RV supplies, gas, groceries and Post Office nearby
- Credit cards accepted • RV's, caravans and tents welcome • Fun for the whole family
- Reasonable prices, group discount • Reservations suggested
- **25% off 3rd night with this ad**

OPEN MAY THROUGH SEPTEMBER

Enjoy shopping through our Country Mall Shops on the boardwalk. You will find Alaskan gifts and souvenirs, gold jewelry, ivory and antler carvings, Alaska paintings, film and photo developing, espresso, handmade gifts, art gallery, restaurants.

BOOK A LOCAL ACTIVITY: flightseeing, horseback riding, river rafting, gold panning or golfing.

COME AND SEE FOR YOURSELF WHY TRAVELERS KEEP COMING BACK!!

SHOPPING MALL

www.themilepost.com

McKinley Creekside Cabins
& Creekside Cafe
Casual Dining at its finest.
Offering the Best Steaks & Fish,
Breakfast 'till Noon, Homemade Soups
& a Full Espresso Bar.
Affordable Family Suites & Kitchenettes
Tour Information & Reservations Available
Located on Carlo Creek
13 miles south of the
Park entrance at mile 224
AAA Approved
Denali's
Best Value
1-888-5DENALI
www.mckinleycabins.com

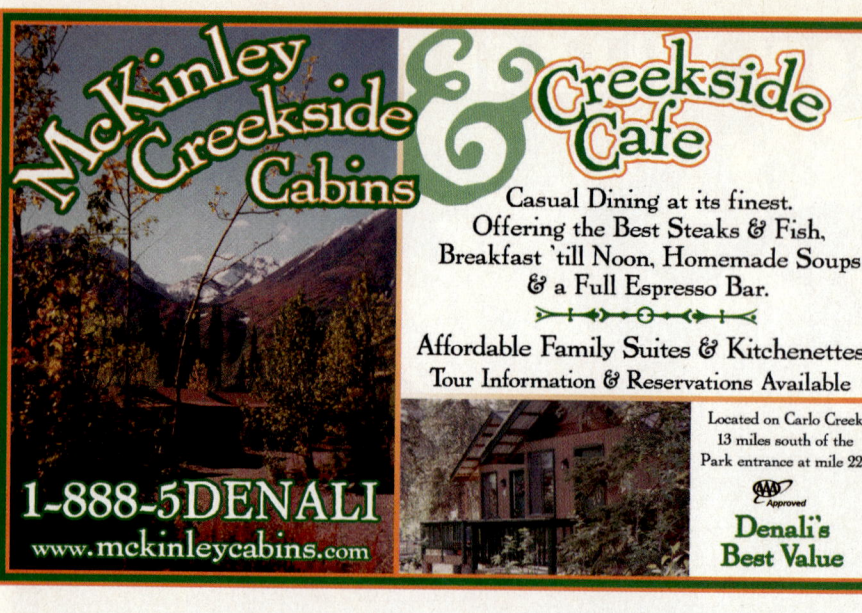

April and September hours are from 10 A.M. to 4 P.M. Starting in mid-May, hours are extended to about 7 A.M. to 8 P.M. Parking space is limited at the visitor center, but day parking is available at Riley Creek Campground, with shuttle bus service to the visitor center.

At the center, a visitor can make reservations for shuttle or bus tours, campgrounds and backcountry camping, view an interpretive slide show, browse in the bookstore operated by the Alaska Natural History Association, chat with a Denali Park ranger, and obtain information about the daily ranger-led hikes, walks and programs, the locations of all these activities and the buses that will take visitors where they want to go.

NOTE: Construction of new facilities in the entrance area of the park will be in progress during the summer of 2003. A new visitor center and a science and learning center are expected to be completed in summer of 2004.

Eielson Visitor Center, located at Mile 66 on the Park Road, is accessible via the park's shuttle bus system. Eielson is an excellent Mount McKinley viewpoint. On clear days the north and south peaks of Mount McKin-

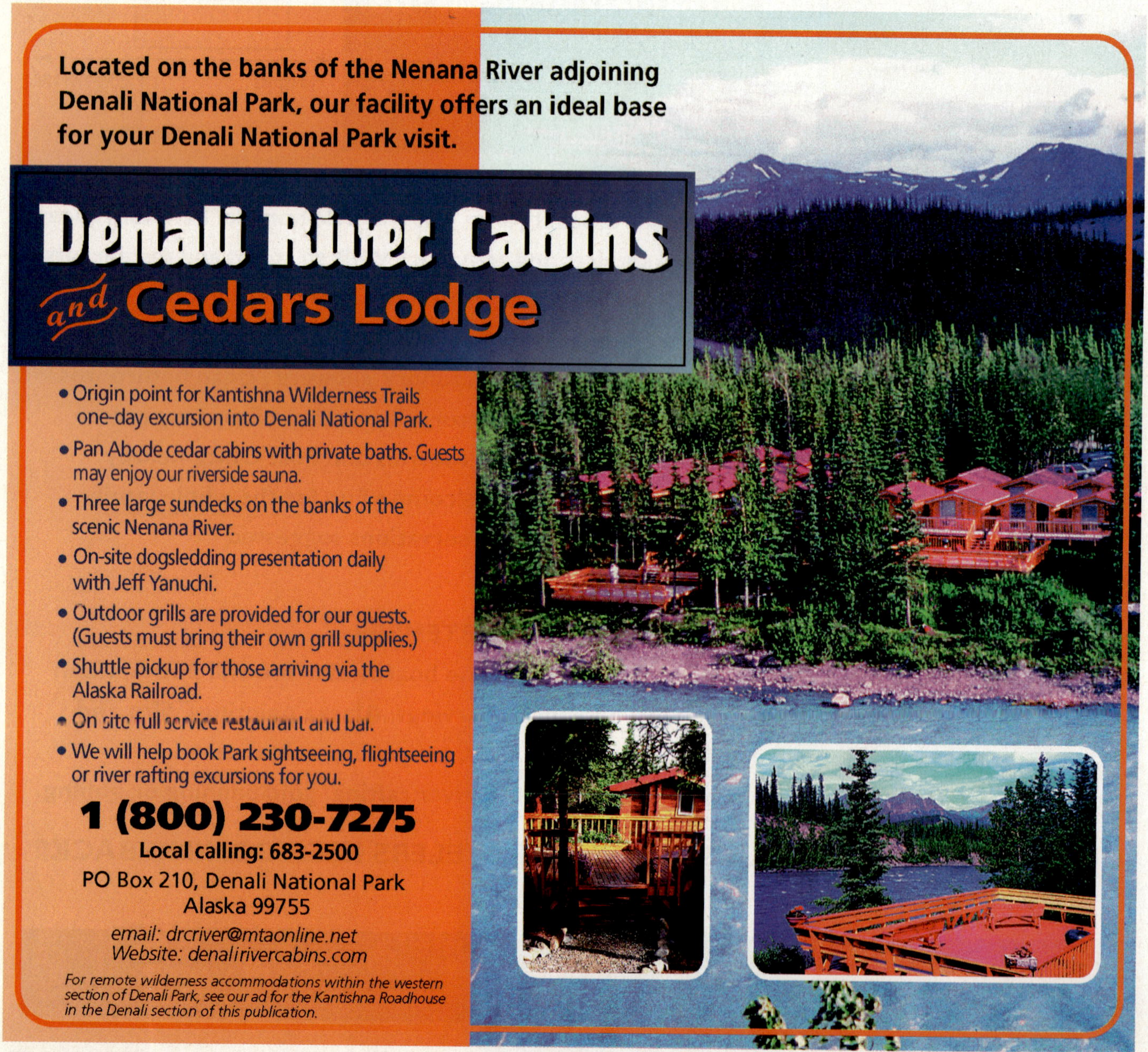
Located on the banks of the Nenana River adjoining Denali National Park, our facility offers an ideal base for your Denali National Park visit.
Denali River Cabins
and Cedars Lodge
• Origin point for Kantishna Wilderness Trails one-day excursion into Denali National Park.
• Pan Abode cedar cabins with private baths. Guests may enjoy our riverside sauna.
• Three large sundecks on the banks of the scenic Nenana River.
• On-site dogsledding presentation daily with Jeff Yanuchi.
• Outdoor grills are provided for our guests. (Guests must bring their own grill supplies.)
• Shuttle pickup for those arriving via the Alaska Railroad.
• On site full service restaurant and bar.
• We will help book Park sightseeing, flightseeing or river rafting excursions for you.
1 (800) 230-7275
Local calling: 683-2500
PO Box 210, Denali National Park
Alaska 99755
email: drcriver@mtaonline.net
Website: denalirivercabins.com
For remote wilderness accommodations within the western section of Denali Park, see our ad for the Kantishna Roadhouse in the Denali section of this publication.

ley are visible to the southwest. Ranger-led hikes, nature programs, displays, restrooms and drinking water are located at Eielson. Film, maps and natural history publications for sale. The Eielson Visitor Center will be remodeled in 2005.

For more information, contact Denali National Park and Preserve, P.O. Box 9, Denali Park, AK 99755; phone (907) 683-2294, web site: www.nps.gov/dena.

Entrance Fees: Visitors camping in the park or riding a shuttle bus (green bus) or tour bus (tan bus) will pay a park entrance fee of $5 per adult (17-62) or $10 per family/vehicle (up to 8 people). The National Parks Pass, the Golden Eagle Pass and the Golden Age Pass can be applied to the fee, and information about these passes may be obtained at the visitor center. In addition to entrance and camping fees, there is a nonrefundable $4 processing fee for each campground reservation.

Reservations: Park shuttle bus tickets and park campsites may be reserved. Reservation information and forms are available on the park's web site (www.nps.gov/dena). Reservations can be made by fax, phone or in person at any time from when the reservation systems open (see dates below) up to 2 days in advance of your visit. Mail-in reservations must be received 30 days in advance.

For reservations by phone, call 1-800-622-7275 (nationwide); 1-907-272-7275 (international); or (907) 272-7275 (in Anchorage). Phone reservation service began February 25, 2002, and extends to September 12, 2002. Fax and mail-in reservations began December 1, 2002. The fax number is (907)

White Moose Lodge

800-481-1232

Wilderness Mountain View
Reasonable Rates
11 Miles North of Denali Park
Mile 248 Parks Highway

Convenient Location
Private Wooded Area
Deck with Grill & Picnic Table
Clean Quiet Comfortable Rooms
Complimentary Continental Breakfast

907 683-1231
Fax: 907 683-1232

info@whitemooselodge.com
WhiteMooseLodge.com

DENALI LODGING
The Peak Experience

Grande Denali Lodge
The newest hotel in Denali

Denali Bluffs Hotel
The closest to the Park entrance

Alpenglow Restaurant
Fine dining with a spectacular view

Peak Experience Theater
Experience Denali with a seasoned mountaineer

Denali Lodging is your best bet for the best in Denali National Park. Lodging, Fine Dining, Entertainment, Outdoor Activities. We've got it all, including the best views in the Park.

Toll Free
1-866-683-8500

(907) 683-8500 (local calls)
fax: (907) 683-8599

PO Box 72460, Fairbanks, AK 99707

info@denalialaska.com
www.denalialaska.com

Owned & operated by Alaskans, let us show you *our* Alaska.

Approved

Denali park ranger with a sled dog pup from the park's kennels.
(© Rich Reid, Colors of Nature)

264-4684. Address mail-in requests to: Denali Park Resorts VTS, 241 West Ship Creek Ave., Anchorage, AK 99501. Both fax and mail-in requests are processed in the order received.

When faxing or mailing reservation requests, include names and ages of each passenger, as youth discounts do apply. It is helpful to include alternative dates of travel. Include credit card numbers (VISA, Mastercard or Discover), and their expiration dates. Other payment options are personal check (received 10 working days in advance) or money order. Cancellation fees ($6 for each seat or campsite) apply.

Sixty-five percent of the park's shuttle bus seats, and 100 percent of Riley, Savage, Teklanika and Wonder Lake campsites, are available for advance reservations.

Prepaid, reserved shuttle bus tickets may be picked up at the visitor center shuttle desk. Any unclaimed, prepaid tickets for buses departing before 7 A.M. will be in the possession of the bus driver; however, the drivers do not sell tickets.

Backcountry Permits: Backpackers must obtain a free backcountry permit and Bear-Resistant Food Containers (BRFCs). BRFCs are available for use at the visitor center or park headquarters, and must be returned at the end of your trip. These containers can also be purchased at the visitor center bookstore.

Backcountry permits are available at the visitor center in summer, and at park headquarters in the winter. Backcountry permits are issued 1 day in advance and reservations are not accepted. Day hikers do not need a special permit. Before obtaining permits, backpackers must: 1) Watch the Backcountry Simulator program, available at the Backcountry Desk, with its information on bear safety, minimum-impact camping, river crossing tips, wildlife and safety emergencies; 2) Check the Quota Board at the Backcountry Desk for unit availability. Denali's backcountry consists of 43 units, in which a limited number of visitors are allowed per night. Backpackers must confirm that their desired unit is not closed. *NOTE: Large groups may be divided if units are too full.* 3) Read Backcountry Description Guides available from the Backcountry Desk or the visitor center bookstore; 4) Consult topographic maps to plan your trip and routes through the park; 5) Consult the backcountry gear checklist provided by the Park Service.

Camping gear should include a gasoline or propane stove, rain gear and a tent or waterproof shelter. Water should be boiled or treated. Pets are not allowed in the backcountry. A camper bus pass ($15.50) must be purchased in order to reach most backcountry camping units.

Mountaineering: Whether you call it McKinley or Denali, climbing "the moun-

Denali Park Hotel
Toll Free 866-683-1800 • 907-683-1800 • Mile Post 247 Parks Highway

Located 10 miles North of the Denali National Park entrance

Lobby located in historic railroad car

Near Golf Course, Horseback Riding, Rafting and Flightseeing.

Accommodations:
King Size or
Two Extra Long Full Beds,
Telephone, Satellite TV,
and Private Bath.

www.denaliparkhotel.com

DENALI SUITES
OPEN ALL YEAR
2-Bedroom Suites
Kitchen with Dining Area
Living Rooms with Queen-Size
Hide-a-Beds
TV and VCR • Telephone
Coin-Operated Laundry
Newly Remodeled • Families Welcome

(907) 683-2848
e-mail: denalisuites@usibelli.com
www.alaskaone.com/densuites

PO Box 393, Healy, AK 99743
Mile 248.8 Parks Highway
15 minutes north of Denali National Park

Lazy J Cabins
CAFE & LOUNGE
FOR YOUR ALASKAN EXPERIENCE!

Mile 210 Parks Highway - Just 20 minutes from the Denali National Park Entrance and only 1 mile from the beginning of Denali Hwy!

ROOMS WITH PRIVATE BATHS and several **COZY LOG CABINS** *available*. All cabins are surrounded by a beautiful view of Alaska's mountains and **WILDLIFE** plus a spectacular view of the Northern Lights during winter.

OPEN: FEB - OCT

TEL: (907) 768-2414 • FAX: (907) 768-2415

DENALI NATIONAL PARK

MILE 231.1

Denali Grizzly Bear® Cabins & Campground

Mile 231.1 Parks Highway, South Boundary Denali National Park, on Nenana River

Cabins • RV and Tent Sites • Hookups • Tent Cabins • Hot Showers
Alaskan Gifts • Beer • Liquor • Ice • Hot and Cold Snacks
Laundromat • Propane • Phone • Tour Desk

Bookings for Local Activities
Kitchen or Sleeping Cabins
Most with Private Baths

Reservations Suggested
Deposit Required
www.denaligrizzlybear.com

Summer:
Denali Grizzly Bear, Box 7
Denali National Park, Alaska 99755
(907) 683-2696

Winter:
Denali Grizzly Bear
910 Senate Loop
Fairbanks, Alaska 99712
(907) 683-1337

AFFORDABLE LODGING
DENALI CABINS - DENALI NATIONAL PARK ALASKA

Clean, comfortable cedar cabins
2 outdoor hot tubs
Activities desk
Courtesy shuttle

Where your Denali Adventures begin!

888-560-2489
www.denali-cabins.com

SAVE $5 WITH THIS AD!

HEALY HEIGHTS FAMILY CABINS

12 MILES FROM DENALI NATIONAL PARK
OPEN MAY TO SEPTEMBER

- New, heated cedar cabins with private bath, coffee maker, refrigerator, and microwave oven. Some kitchens. Quaint, comfortable, & spotless.
- Spectacular rural setting away from the crowds, with mountain views & outside decks on 12 wooded acres. Family owned & operated.
- Nonsmoking. No Pets. Children welcome.
- Visa/MC/Discover Accepted.

<u>Free Brochure</u>: PO Box 277, Healy, AK 99743
Turn at Milepost 247, George Parks Hwy.

Phone: (907)683-2639
Fax: (907) 683-2640
E-mail: johnson@healycabins.com

In 2002, 642 climbers reached the summit of Denali (Mount McKinley)

BACKWOODS LODGE
OPEN YEAR ROUND

"You have a great inn with very comfortable rooms and warm hospitality. Thanks for taking care of our railroaders."
- Pat Gamble, President & CEO - Alaska Railroad Corporation

"The cleanliness was only surpassed by the hospitality."
- Henery & Ellen Stanley

"This was the best place we booked for our 10 day trip to Alaska! This place was so roomy & decorated so nice!"
- Judy Dedricks

Denali Highway
.2 BACKWOODS LODGE
MP 210 • Parks Highway

"... it is exceptionally clean & well cared for – and large enough to move around in – and TV channels that actually come in! And a good mattress." – Jeanne Caverly

E-mail: backwoodslodge@hotmail.com

.2 mile from the intersection of the Parks and Denali Highways. Cantwell, AK

Reservations 1.800.292.2232
Fax 1.907.768.2472

DENALI NATIONAL PARK

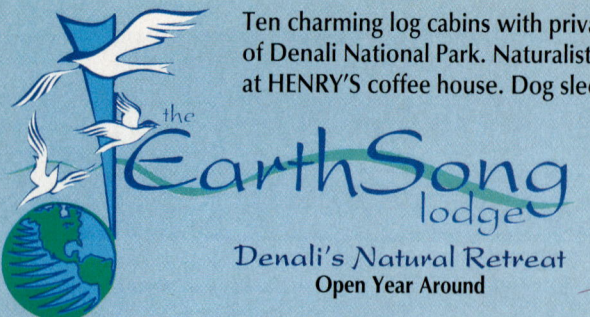

The EarthSong Lodge
Denali's Natural Retreat
Open Year Around

Ten charming log cabins with private bath. Located just north of Denali National Park. Naturalist on staff, Evening programs at HENRY'S coffee house. Dog sled demos and rides.

P.O. Box 89 Healy, Alaska 99743
Jon & Karin Nierenberg, Proprietors
Phone 907-683-2863 Fax 907-683-2868
e-mail: koala@mtaonline.net
Internet: www.earthsonglodge.com
HENRY'S - 907-683-2865

MOTEL • Open 24 Hours Year-round • CAFE
Deluxe & Economy Rooms
FULL MENU • COCKTAIL LOUNGE
TOTEM INN
Cafe: (907) 683-2420
Motel: (907) 683-2384
Fax: (907) 683-2432
Mile 248.7 PARKS HWY

Park's Edge
Log Cabin Accomodations

- Located off of Milepost 247 on the Parks Highway
- 15 minutes from Denali National Park
- Adjacent to the Black Diamond Golf course
- Comfortable, Private cabins
- Sleep up to six people

DENALI LAKEVIEW INN
"Just what you are looking for when you come to Alaska"
Spectacular Lake & Mountain Views
Private Entrances and Baths - Jacuzzi Tubs Available
King & Queen Beds - No Smoking on Property
Open Year Round - 10 minutes to Denali Park Tranquil Surroundings

(907) 683-4035
MILE 247 PARKS HIGHWAY
AAA Approved
www.DenaliLakeviewInn.com
e-mail: info@DenaliLakeviewInn.com

Cozy Creekside
Log Cabins with own
Bathroom Showers • RV Park
Dump Station • Potable Water
Clean Bathroom • Laundry
8 Showers • Dishwashing Facility
Individual Sheltered Tent sites each with Picnic Table and Firepit.
Unique Gift Shop
Information • Pay Phone

You won't be disappointed
It's a beautiful place to be!

Carlo Creek Lodge
HC 2 Box 1530, Healy, AK 99743
Lodge Phone (907) 683-2576 Home Phone (907) 683-2573

---

tain" requires extensive planning. Registration is mandatory for all climbs on McKinley and Foraker. Mountaineering expeditions are required to acquire a permit and pay a $150 fee before climbing McKinley or Foraker. Permit applications must be received at least 60 days prior to the start of the expedition.

The National Park Service maintains a ranger station in Talkeetna that is staffed full-time year-round. Rangers there can provide all necessary information on climbing McKinley, Foraker and other peaks of the Alaska Range. Contact the Talkeetna Ranger Station at P.O. Box 588, Talkeetna, AK 99676; phone (907) 733-2231; or see www.nps.gov/dena/home/mountaineering/home.html.

Special Permits: Each year the park issues permits to a limited number of individuals, selected by lottery, to drive their vehicles through the park on assigned days in early September. It is not unusual for these late-season visitors to have their tour curtailed by early snows within the park. Road lottery applications are accepted by mail during the month of July; phone (907) 683-2294 for details.

Log on to the park website at www.nps.gov/dena for information concerning special permits for the Professional Photographer Program, the Artist Program and Commercial Filming.

Fishing Licenses: Not required in the wilderness area; state law is applicable on all other lands. Specified limits for each person per day should be carefully observed. Fishing is poor because most rivers are silty and ponds are shallow.

Emergency Services: Call 911, or contact state troopers in Healy, (907) 683-2232, or in Cantwell, (907) 768-2202.

Lodging & Services

There are 4 wilderness lodges in the Kantishna area at the far western side of the park. North of the park entrance about a mile on the Parks Highway is a commercial district with numerous hotels, restaurants, RV parks, a gas station with convenience store, assorted shops and commercial outfitters. Lodges, cabins, campgrounds and restaurants are also found along the Parks Highway south and north of the park entrance, from Cantwell to Healy. See pages 386–394 in the PARKS HIGHWAY section. (See also "Denali's Front Country" on page 389 and "Denali's Backcountry Lodges" on pages 409–411.)

The Riley Creek Mercantile at Riley Creek Campground is stocked with a limited selection of groceries. Showers are available at a minimum cost, and there are laundry facilities. No food/drink service is available in the park past Mile 0.5.

Camp Denali. Unparalleled views of

MOTEL NORD HAVEN

QUALITY LODGING * QUEEN BEDS * NON-SMOKING
1.800.683.4501
Mile 249.5 Parks Highway

Denali Park's Backcountry Lodges

Backcountry hikers take time out to enjoy the view of Denali. (© John Schwieder Photography)

Mount McKinley beckon active learning adventurers to Alaska's premier wilderness lodge. Situated in the remote heart of Denali National Park, its rustic ambience blends historic log cabins with naturalist-guided backcountry hiking, wildlife observation, canoeing, biking, and a special emphasis lecture and workshop series. 3-, 4-, and 7-night stays include lodging, all meals and activities, and round-trip transportation from the park entrance. Brochure: P.O. Box 67, Denali National Park, AK 99755. 907-683-2290. Email: info@campdenali.com. Web site: www.campdenali.com. [ADVERTISEMENT]

Denali Backcountry Lodge. Escape the park's crowded entrance and immerse yourself deep within Denali National Park for a few days. Located at the end of the 95-mile Park Road, Denali Backcountry Lodge features comfortable cedar cabins with private baths, dining room, and lounge. 2- to 4-night stays include Denali wildlife drive to the end of the Denali Park Road on our private bus, all meals and lodging, guided hikes, wildlife viewing, bicycling, photography, and natural history programs. Credit cards accepted and discounts given for last-minute bookings if space is available. www.denalilodge.com/mp. Phone (800) 841-0692. See display ad this section. [ADVERTISEMENT]

Denali Mountain Morning Hostel and Lodge. Every budget traveler's dream come true! A creek, a campfire, a cabin in the mountains. Your choice: a private cabin, a private room, a bunk or even a beautiful tent site. Buy or rent outdoor gear here! Raft trips now available. Take a hot shower, modern kitchen, Internet. Park area shuttles. P.O. Box 208 Denali Park, AK 99755. www.hostelalaska.com. Toll free instate 1-866-D-HOSTEL or (907) 683-7503. [ADVERTISEMENT]

Denali Park Hotel's 48 rooms offer King sized or two Full sized extra-long beds, easy one-level access, 27" Satellite TV's, data-port telephones, private baths, and great views. Away from noisy high-density multi-level hotels, our 8-acre site sometimes hosts moose and other Alaskan wildlife. Convenient to Golf Course, Horseback Riding, Rafting, and Flightseeing. Delicatessen and Bakery. 1-866-683-1800 www.denaliparkhotel.com. [ADVERTISEMENT]

Denali Wilderness Lodge is Alaska's classic fly-in adventure lodge. Located in the pristine Wood River valley, it's accessible only by a spectacular bush-plane flight. Itineraries can be tailored to your needs. Delicious meals, comfortable rooms with private baths. Naturalist programs, flightseeing, horseback riding, nature/photo hikes, gold panning, and 24 log buildings, hand-hewn over decades, offer an enticing glimpse into Alaska's trapping, hunting and gold mining history. One to 4-night stays. Call 800-541-9779 for brochure, or visit: www.denaliwildernesslodge.com. See display ad this section. [ADVERTISEMENT]

Grande Denali Lodge. A peak lodge experience. Spectacular panoramic views from high above the hustle and bustle of the highway corridor. Take in views of Mt. Healy, the Nenana River or Mt. Sugarloaf. Each room features 2 queen beds, TV, telephone, coffee maker, hair dryer, AC and private bath. Lodge offers large seating areas, gift shop, coin-operated laundry and the Peak Experience Theater. Also 6 deluxe family cabins with private deck—will sleep 5. Open mid-May through mid-September. Credit cards accepted. P.O. Box 72460, Fair-

(Continues on page 412)

For visitors who prefer to experience the remote backcountry of Denali National Park and Preserve, there are several destinations with high appeal. The legendary Kantishna mining district, located within the park at the far western end of the park road, offers several choices, and there is at least 1 fly-in lodge in wilderness lands surrounding the park.

These backcountry destinations are for

DENALI BACKCOUNTRY LODGE

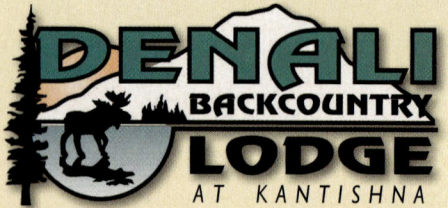
AT KANTISHNA

A Complete Wilderness Lodge Package for Denali National Park Visitors

Wildlife, guided activities & comfortable cabins

Come join us deep within Denali National Park, away from the crowded park entrance. The lodge, located at the very end of the 95-mile park road, offers a complete Denali Park vacation experience — and surprising comfort.

Photographic splendors abound.

- Full service wilderness lodge, cozy cabins, dining room, lounge, and natural history library
- Guided hikes, wildlife viewing, bicycling, photography, gold panning, and natural history programs
- Wildlife drive along the entire 95-mile restricted Denali National Park road
- Exclusive Kantishna location deep within Denali National Park

800-841-0692
e-mail: info@denalilodge.com

SEE LOG NARRATIVE

www.denalilodge.com

Denali Park's Backcountry Lodges (continued)

visitors who crave a more nature-oriented vacation, away from the crowds and traffic that are unavoidable in Denali's "front country" along the Parks Highway on the eastern boundary of the park. The backcountry experience can be more expensive, but owners and personnel of remote-site lodges are careful that the accommodations, amenities and personal attention provide unique experiences and enduring memories which often result in return visits by satisfied clients.

The Kantishna area features 4 outstanding lodges that offer a variety of accommodations, cuisine and activities. All 4 possess views or accessibility to views (weather permitting) of the north side of the park's centerpiece, 20,320-foot Mount McKinley (Denali). From the lodges' locations near Wonder Lake and Reflection Pond, visitors may see the largest of the glaciers on the north side of the Alaska Range, Muldrow Glacier, 32 miles long and descending 16,000 feet from near Denali's summit.

Camp Denali, starting its 51st year of operation in 2002, emphasizes environmental elements through naturalist programs, naturalist-guided hikes, biking, canoeing and wildlife observation. Accommodations are comfortable and adequate, although rustic compared to some other lodges. Three-, 4- and 7-night visits include lodging, meals, activities and the round-trip bus ride through the park. Camp Denali attracts "ecotourists," dedicated nature lovers who appreciate a basic approach to experiencing the park's distinctive features. **North Face Lodge**, under the same ownership as Camp Denali, offers the same range of activities at its small, comfortable inn just down the hill from Camp Denali. Both these lodges are situated within full view of the massif of Mount McKinley.

Farther along the road, the **Kantishna Roadhouse Resort**, situated on the banks of Moose Creek in the heart of the historic Kantishna mining district, presents comfortable cabins with private baths, guided hiking, gold-panning, horseback trail rides, exploring, photography, wildlife viewing

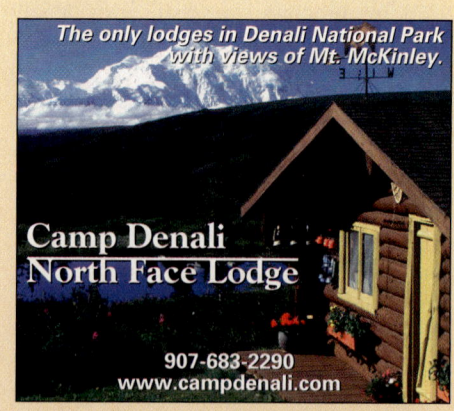

A backcountry hiker scans the terrain for Denali wildlife.
(© Lynn Ledbetter)

and varied evening programs. Gourmets endorse the excellent cuisine and full-service bar. All visitors enjoy the cheerful warmth of the wood stove in the relaxing area off the lobby, and reading or viewing Alaskana books and videos in the second-floor meeting room/library.

Kantishna Wilderness Trails is a Kantishna Roadhouse tour which brings in visitors by bus across the park for luncheon at the Roadhouse and participation in gold-panning or an interpretive program before returning by bus to the park entrance. This full-day excursion is recommended for those with limited time at the park, as it guarantees a round trip across the full length of the park road, with many opportunities to view wildlife and experience the grandeur of this remote wilderness, with a tasty meal and choice of activities to re-energize visitors before the return trip.

At the end of the 92-mile-long Park Road, **Denali Backcountry Lodge** features a full-service wilderness experience. Well-appointed cabins, fine dining and activities including photography, bicycling, guided hikes and natural history programs enhance this highly rated lodge.

A different setting awaits visitors at **Denali Wilderness Lodge**, located in the Wood River valley, a 30-minute bush-plane flight east of Denali Park. The resort's cabins surround a large log lodge. Horseback trail rides are a paramount feature of this fly-in getaway, as well as naturalist-led hikes, fishing and gold-panning.

Per night costs vary, as do amenities included in the package price. At both Kantishna Roadhouse and Denali Backcountry Lodge, for example, the round trip by bus across the park is included in the cost.

These backcountry retreats all provide fulfilling experiences for visitors who are seeking the unspoiled reality of Alaska's vast wilderness.

Carol Phillips, associate editor of The MILEPOST®, is a frequent backcountry visitor to Denali and author of this feature.

800·541·9779

DENALI WILDERNESS LODGE

Alaska's Classic Fly-In Adventure Lodge

DENALI NATIONAL PARK

- A scenic 30 minute flight leaves Denali park crowds behind
- Warm comfort in historic Alaskan bush style
- Cozy cabins surrounding a beautiful log lodge
- Trail rides on horseback with experienced wranglers
- Naturalist-led hikes
- Hearty Alaskan dining & relaxing lounge

"The lodge is such a tremendous getaway. Everything was excellent! This has been our best vacation yet!" -Marci A. & Darren C

Call about Shoulder Season Discounts

www.denaliwildernesslodge.com

DENALI NATIONAL PARK

BEST of ALASKA RV PARKS

DENALI RIVERSIDE RV PARK

Our scenic RV sites are located just two miles from Denali Park entrance and overlook the Nenana River.

From $14 Night

1978 — 25th — 2003 ALASKA TRAVEL ADVENTURES

Denali's Newest Full-Service Campground

Water & Electric, Dry & Pull-Through Sites • Propane & Firewood • Gift & Sundries Shop
Showers & Restrooms (handicap access) • Laundry Facilities • Picnic Tables & Fire Pits
Local Tour Reservations • Group & Caravan Rates • Dump Station

For reservations or a free brochure call toll-free:
1-888-778-7700
www.alaskarv.com

LOCATED AT MILEPOST 240, GEORGE PARKS HIGHWAY

MAJOR CREDIT CARDS ACCEPTED

See our ads for Anchorage Ship Creek Landings RV Park and Skagway Mountain View RV Park

Flightseeing offers rewarding up-close views of the Alaska Range.
(© W. Wright-Diamond Photo)

CANTWELL RV PARK VISA MasterCard

Mile 209.9 Parks Highway, 27 miles south of Denali Park Entrance
Go west 3/10 mile at the intersection of the Parks and Denali Highways

- Long, level pull-through sites
- Dump & water fill stations
- Clean restrooms, showers, laundry
- Free modem hook-up
- 20/30 amp electric
- Tour arrangements available
- Walking distance to fishing
- Water & electric sites

1-800-940-2210 • Open May 15-Sept. 15 • (907) 768-2210

Internet: www.alaskaone.com/cantwellrv • e-mail: cantwellrvpark@ak.net
Write: P.O. Box 210, Cantwell, AK 99729 Fax: **(907) 262-5149**

The PERCH
Bar, Restaurant & Cabins

Fine Dining in a Spectacular Setting

BREAKFAST, LUNCH & DINNER DAILY, SUMMERS • WEEKENDS ONLY, WINTER
Home Made Bread & Cinnamon Rolls Baked Fresh Daily
Steaks • Seafood • Full Bar • Bakery
Open Year Round • 10 New Cabins
Private Bath or Economy Cabins for Rent
See log ad at mile 224 Parks Highway • (907) 683-2523

The first successful ascent of Denali was accomplished in June 1913 by the Hudson Stuck expedition.

(Continued from page 409)
banks, AK 99707. Phone (907) 683-8599 or 1-866-683-8500. Email: info@denalialaska.com. Web page: www.denalialaska.com. See display ad in this section. [ADVERTISEMENT]

Kantishna Roadhouse. Premier wilderness lodge located at the west end of the only road in Denali National Park. Enjoy opportunities to view wildlife, take photographs and explore the park. Packages include comfortable log cabins with private baths, guided hiking, gold panning, interpretive programs, fishing and fine meals along with our famous Alaskan hospitality. Phone us at (800) 942-7420 to reserve your stay. P.O. Box 81670, Fairbanks, AK 99708. Email us at kantshna@ptialaska.net. Visit our web site at www.kantishnaroadhouse.com. [ADVERTISEMENT]

Kantishna Wilderness Trails. The ultimate excursion through Denali National Park. 95 miles each way with breathtaking mountain vistas and the likelihood of seeing some of Denali's wildlife en route. Arrive at Kantishna Roadhouse in time for lunch in the dining room, followed by gold panning or an interpretive program. For reservations phone (800) 230-7275; email: drcriver@mtaonline.net. Visit our web site at www.denaliwildlifetour.com. [ADVERTISEMENT]

Mt. McKinley Princess Wilderness Lodge. Borders south side of Denali Park and features spectacular views of McKinley and the Alaska Range. Daily rail packages aboard Princess' Midnight Sun Express from Anchorage or Fairbanks. Open mid-May through mid-September. Lodge often runs special summer rates. Call 800-426-0500 for reservations and information. www.princesslodges.com. [ADVERTISEMENT]

North Face Lodge. Spectacular views of Mount McKinley grace this small, well-appointed inn in the remote heart of Denali National Park. Active learning adventures feature guided backcountry hiking, wildlife observation, canoeing, and biking. 3-, 4-, and 7-night stays include lodging, all meals and activities, and round-trip transportation from the park entrance. Brochure: P.O. Box 67, Denali National Park, AK 99755. (907) 683-2290. Email: info@campdenali.com. Web site: www.northfacelodge.com. See display ad this section. [ADVERTISEMENT]

Transportation

Highway: Access via the Parks Highway from Anchorage or Fairbanks.

Air: Charter flights are available from many nearby locations, and flightseeing tours are offered by operators from the park area or out of Talkeetna, Anchorage or Fairbanks. A round-trip air tour of the park from Anchorage takes 3-4 hours.

Era Helicopter Flightseeing Tours. Offering fully narrated tours of Denali National Park and Mt. McKinley. Experience the pristine backcountry on a personally guided Heli-Hiking Adventure, or land on and explore a glacier with your pilot on our Glacier Expedition Tour. Free transportation from local hotels. Tours operate May–September. Located at Milepost 238. Local Phone: 907-683-2574 or 800-843-1947. 6160 Carl Brady Drive, Anchorage, AK 99502. www.eraaviation.com; fltsg@eraaviation.com. [ADVERTISEMENT]

Railroad: The Alaska Railroad offers daily northbound and southbound trains between Anchorage and Fairbanks, with stops at Denali Park, during the summer season. For reservations, phone (800) 544-0552.

Midnight Sun Express®. ULTRA DOMES® feature glass-domed ceilings, meals freshly prepared by on-board chefs, and exclusive outdoor viewing platforms. Daily service between Anchorage, Talkeetna, Denali National Park and Fairbanks. Rail packages include overnights at Mt. McKinley Princess Lodge® and/or Denali Princess Lodge®, May through September. Phone (800) 835-8907. [ADVERTISEMENT]

Talkeetna Air Taxi. See Mt. McKinley up close! Enter an ice age world of sculptured peaks and blue glaciers. Alaska's #1 rated

tour. Also, Natural History Walking Tours and Glacier Trekking. Located in Talkeetna. Call for free brochure: 1-800-533-2219 or (907) 733-2218, Web site: info@talkeetnaair.com. [ADVERTISEMENT]

Bus: Daily bus service to the park is available from Anchorage and Fairbanks. There are 2 formal bus tours offered by concessionaires within the park. Both the Tundra Wildlife Tour and the Denali Natural History Tour include an interpretive program and lunch or snack.

Park Shuttle Bus System: The Park Service provides shuttle bus service for visitors within the park, with designated buses serving specific destinations. Some buses operate exclusively in the entrance area, shuttling visitors between the visitor center, Riley Creek Campground, the railroad depot, the sled dog demonstrations and out to the Savage River area at Mile 15. Other buses

Camping, hiking, rafting and flightseeing are favorite recreational activities at Denali National Park & Preserve.

DENALI NATIONAL PARK

A lone hiker pauses above Sanctuary River bridge at Mile 22 on the Park Road.
(© John Schwieger Photography)

travel farther out into the park, beyond the vehicle check station at Mile 15, providing service to Teklanika River and Wonder Lake campgrounds and Eielson Visitor Center. Wheelchair-accessible buses are available. A round-trip between the visitor center and Eielson Visitor Center takes appoximately 8 hours.

Buses run daily from mid-May to mid-September (specific dates depend on weather).

Bicycles: There is no policy restricting bicycle access on the Park Road, although bicyclists must stay on the road. Bicyclists wishing to camp in the park must either camp in one of the campgrounds or, if they are camping in the backcountry, must park their bikes in one of the campgrounds.

Camping

Denali National Park has 6 campgrounds. Visitors may camp a total of 14 days per year. Riley Creek Campground, largest in the park, is open year-round. All campsites at Riley Creek, Savage River, Teklanika River and Wonder Lake may be reserved in advance. Campgrounds along the paved portion of the road (Riley and Savage River) are accessible by personal vehicle at any time. Those visitors planning to camp at Sanctuary campground must register for sites at the visitor center.

Teklanika Campground is accessible by camper bus or by car for those wishing to drive their vehicles to the campground for a minimum 3-night stay. (Teklanika campers are not permitted to drive their vehicles back and forth between the campground and the front-country area, except when

Campground	Spaces	Tent	Trailer	Pit toilets	Flush toilets	Tap water	Fee
Riley Creek	142	•	•		•	•	$12
Savage River	33	•	•		•	•	$12
Sanctuary River	7	•		•		•	$6
Teklanika River	50	•	•		•	•	$12
Igloo Creek	7	•		•		•	$6
Wonder Lake	28	•			•	•	$12

they are checking out). The Teklanika (Tek) Shuttle Pass is for campers headed for Teklanika Campground and ensures a bus seat farther into the park. On the first complete day of a visitor's stay, the Tek Pass is good for a confirmed space on any available shuttle (green) bus. During the remainder of the stay, the pass allows space available seating on any shuttle bus.

There are no RV hookups in park campgrounds. Several private campgrounds are located outside the park along the Parks Highway. See display ads this section.

Denali RV Park and Motel. 90 full and partial RV hookups, cable TV, 30-amp electric. Pull-throughs, level sites, easy access. RV rates $15-$28. Caravans welcome! Private rest-rooms with pay showers, dump station. 14 motel rooms. Double with bath $74; family units with full kitchen and TV $119. Laundry, pay phones, outdoor cooking area, covered meeting area. Gift shop, tour booking, information. Beautiful panoramic mountain views, hiking trails. Email access line available. VISA/Mastercard/Discover. Web address: denaliRVpark.com. E-mail: stay@denaliRVpark.com. Located 8 miles north of park entrance. (245.1 George Parks Highway) Box 155, Denali National Park, AK 99755. (800) 478-1501, (907) 683-1500. See display ad this section. [ADVERTISEMENT]

McKinley RV & Campground. One of the nicest campgrounds around; 89 sites and utilities available. We book area activities. We offer dump station, wooded landscape, fax service, propant, gas and diesel.

Caravans/groups welcome. Reservations recommended. Write Box 340, Healy, AK 99743. Phone (907) 683-2379. Fax: (907) 683-2281. National (800) 478-2561. See display ad in the PARKS HIGHWAY section. [ADVERTISEMENT]

Attractions

Mountaineering, wildlife viewing and photography, hiking and camping are the major wilderness activities in the park. For visitors staying near the visitor center or in campgrounds, there are ranger-led nature walks, slide programs, sled dog demonstrations and bus and flightseeing tours.

Wildlife viewing is probably second only to mountain viewing as a major pastime in Denali. The park is home to 37 species of mammals, including caribou, grizzly bear, wolf, wolverine, moose, Dall sheep, red fox, lynx, ground squirrel, snowshoe hare and vole. About 155 species of birds inhabit the park. Year-round residents include the great horned owl, raven and white-tailed, rock and willow ptarmigan. The majority of species, however, visit the park only during summer. Some of these are sandhill cranes, oldsquaws, sandpipers, plovers, gulls, buffleheads and goldeneyes. Golden eagles are a common sight throughout the park. Feeding of any wildlife is prohibited. Wild animals need wild food, and your food is of no benefit to them.

Hiking in Denali National Park is cross-country: there are no established trails in the backcountry. For the day-hiker or the visitor with only a short amount of time, however, there are 7 trails in the front-country from Mile 1 to Mile 15 (Savage River) that are accessible by car, Savage River shuttle, on foot or bike. These trails range from easy to strenuous and provide opportunities to experience the wildlife and grandeur of Denali.

If you have half a day, see the dog demonstration; hike a front-country trail or join a ranger-guided walk; watch the orientation slide program at the visitor center; ride the Savage River shuttle bus to Mile 15; you can get off the bus at any location, do a day hike, then reboard, all for $2. At Mile 9, Mount McKinley is visible in the distance, weather permitting.

If you have a full day, take a bus out into the park; get off and hike or just sit and enjoy the wilderness; join a ranger for Discovery Hike or Guided Walk (schedules and locations at visitor center); plan your own hike (topo maps, guide books and knowledgeable staff can assist you with trip planning).

If you have a few days, visit Wonder Lake and hike the McKinley Bar Trail or do another Discovery Hike; attend a ranger-led program; investigate activities outside the park such as river-rafting, flightseeing and horseback riding.

DENALI NATIONAL PARK

During Denali summers when there are between 18 and 21 hours of daylight, recreational opportunities such as hiking, gold panning and other activities extend into late evening hours. Evenings are ideal for flightseeing adventures or for an easy hike around Horseshoe Lake. Visitors staying in the commercial area just north of the park entrance will enjoy unique entertainment at the Cabin Nite Dinner Theatre, with two shows presented nightly at McKinley Chalet Resort. At the Grande Denali, high above the Parks Highway, the Peak Experience Theatre enthralls visitors with the challenges of mountaineering on Mount McKinley. And although the fabled aurora borealis of the north country is rarely visible during the long, light summer nights, this phenomenon can be experienced vicariously at the Northern Lights Theatre, which offers 6 shows daily and a free shuttle pick-up from local hotels.

The park is accessible in winter beyond Mile 3.1 Park Road by skis, snowshoes, skijor or dog sled. Winter attractions include observing wildlife, viewing the aurora borealis and seeing the park's impressive wintertime landscape.

The annual Winterfest Celebration (Feb. 21–23, 2003) is a 3-day celebration offering ski and skijoring events, avalanche safety awareness clinics, stargazing, winter ecology programs and more. Information available at park headquarters, phone (907) 683-2294.

Park Road Log

Distance from the junction (J) with Parks Highway is shown.

J 0 Junction. Turn west off the Parks Highway (Alaska Route 3) at **Milepost A 237.4** onto the Park Road. The Park Road is paved to the Savage River bridge.
NOTE: The park was designed for scenic enjoyment, not for high speed. Maximum speed is 35 mph except where lower limits are posted.

J 0.2 Turnoff for **Riley Creek Campground** and overflow parking area. Make sure you get all necessary supplies before proceeding to campgrounds west of Mile 15, Savage River. Riley Creek Mercantile, in the Riley Creek campground area, has showers, laundry facilities and some convenience foods.

© Robin Brandt

J 0.5 Visitor Center has information on all visitor activities as well as shuttle bus tickets and camping and overnight hiking permits. A park orientation program is available in the theater. The center is open daily. This is also the shuttle bus departure point.

J 1.2 Alaska Railroad crossing. Horseshoe Lake trailhead; length, 1.5 miles round trip, allow about 1 hour..

J 1.5 Taiga Loop Trail begins and ends here; length 1.3 miles, allow 1-hour round trip.

J 1.6 Denali Park Station (elev. 1,730 feet), where visitors can make train connections to Anchorage and Fairbanks; daily service during the summer.
NOTE: No commercial traffic allowed without permit beyond this point.
Private Aircraft: McKinley Park airstrip; elev. 1,720 feet; length 3,000 feet; gravel; unattended.

J 3.5 Park Headquarters. This is the administration area for Denali National Park and Preserve. In winter, information on all visitor activities can be obtained here. Report accidents and emergencies to the rangers; or call 911; or contact state troopers at Healy, (907) 683-2232, or at Cantwell, (907) 768-2202. *NOTE: There are no public phones west of this point.*

J 5.5 Paved viewpoint with litter barrel. There are numerous small turnouts along the Park Road. Mount McKinley/Denali is first visible about Mile 9.

J 12.8 Savage River Campground (elev. 2,780 feet); 3 group tent sites (9 to 20 people each); 33 sites (8 people each); advance reservations required. ▲

J 14.7 Bridge over the Savage River. Blacktop pavement ends. Access to river, toilet and picnic tables at east end of bridge.

J 14.8 Savage River check station. *Permit or shuttle bus ticket required beyond this point.* Road travel permits for access to the Kantishna area are issued at park headquarters only under special conditions. In early May and late September, the road may be open to all vehicles to Mile 30 (weather permitting).

J 17.3 Viewpoint of the Alaska Range and tundra.

J 21.3 Hogan Creek bridge.

J 22 Sanctuary River bridge, ranger station and **Sanctuary River Campground** (tents only). Sanctuary available by shuttle bus only. ▲

J 29.1 Teklanika River Campground, elev. 2,580 feet; 3-night minimum stay. No towed vehicles except for 5th wheels. Look for grizzly bears on gravel bars nearby. ▲

J 30.7 Rest area with chemical toilets.

J 31.3 Bridge over Teklanika River. Habitat closure at bridge.

J 34.1 Igloo Creek Campground (tents only); currently closed. ▲

J 37 Igloo Creek bridge. Toklat grizzlies are often seen in the area.

SUMMIT McKINLEY!

- Mt. McKinley Scenic Flights
- Denali Park Day Trips
- Twin Engine Aircraft
- Fly from Talkeetna or Denali Park

Talkeetna Aero Services
Box 433, Talkeetna, Alaska 99676

800-660-2688 • www.talkeetnaaero.com

Doug Geeting Aviation's
McKinley Flight Tours & Glacier Landings

- Denali National Park Glacier Landings
- *The Most* Spectacular Thing You Will Do In Alaska - We Guarantee It!
- 5 & 7 Passenger High Performance Aircraft On Skis
- Ask For Our Milepost Family Discount
- Located At Talkeetna Airport

Photo by Jim Balog

"...the gods of Denali have given Doug their blessing to be their courier for earthlings who wish to spend a few unforgettable moments in their Sacred Altitudes." — Jimmy Buffett

Write: Box 42MP, Talkeetna, AK 99676 • Phone: (907) 733-2366 1-800-770-2366
FAX us at: (907) 733-1000   alaskaairtours.com   airtours@alaska.net

*The grizzly bear (*Ursus arctos*) is frequently sighted in the Sable Pass area.* (© Craig Brandt)

NOTE: The area within 1 mile of each side of the Park Road from **Milepost J 38.3** to **J 42.9** is closed to all off-road foot travel as a special wildlife protection area.

J 39.1 Sable Pass (elev. 3,900 feet).

J 43.4 Bridge over East Fork Toklat River. Views of Polychrome Mountain, the Alaska Range and several glaciers are visible along the East Fork from open country south of the road.

J 45.9 Summit of **Polychrome Pass** (elev. 3,700 feet); rest stop with toilets. The broad valley of the Toklat River is visible below to the south. Good hiking in alpine tundra above the road.

J 53.1 Bridge over the Toklat River. The Toklat and all other streams crossed by the Park Road drain into the Tanana River, a tributary of the Yukon River.

J 53.7 Ranger station.

J 58.3 Summit of **Highway Pass** (elev. 3,980 feet). This is the highest point on the Park Road.

J 61 Stony Hill Overlook (elev. 4,508 feet). A good view of Mount McKinley and the Alaska Range on clear days.

J 62 Viewpoint.

J 64.5 Thorofare Pass (elev. 3,900 feet).

J 66 Eielson Visitor Center. Ranger-led hikes, nature programs, displays, restrooms and drinking water. Film, maps and natural history publications for sale. Report accidents and emergencies here.

Excellent Mount McKinley viewpoint. On clear days the north and south peaks of Mount McKinley are visible to the southwest. The impressive glacier, which drops from the mountain and spreads out over the valley floor at this point, is the Muldrow.

For several miles beyond the visitor center the road cut drops about 300 feet to the valley, paralleling the McKinley River.

J 84.6 Access road leads left, westbound, to **Wonder Lake Campground** (elev. 2,090 feet). Tents only; campground access by shuttle bus only. An excellent Mount McKinley viewpoint.

Road continues to Wonder Lake, where rafting and canoeing are permitted (no rental boats available).

J 85.6 Reflection Pond, a kettle lake formed by a glacier.

J 86.6 Wonder Lake ranger station.

J 87.7 Moose Creek bridge.

J 88 North Face Lodge.

J 88.2 Camp Denali.

J 91 KANTISHNA (pop. 135 in summer, 0 in winter; elev. 1,750 feet). Established in 1905 as a mining camp at the junction of Eureka and Moose creeks. Most of the area around Kantishna is private property and there may be active mining on area creeks in summer. Kantishna Roadhouse, consisting of a lodge, dining room and guest log cabins, comprises the townsite of Kantishna.

Private Aircraft: Kantishna airstrip, 1.3 miles northwest; elev. 1,575 feet; length 1,850 feet; gravel; unattended, no regular maintenance.

J 92 Denali Backcountry Lodge.

Venture far, far, far off the beaten path.

Because getting there should be half the fun, make sure you travel to Denali Park aboard Princess Tours® Midnight Sun Express.® Wrap-around glass ceilings and the largest viewing platform on rails ensure unobstructed views of Alaska's amazing scenery.

Combine the thrill of rail travel with the comfort of Princess' riverside lodges, both conveniently located along the route of the Midnight Sun Express. Stay with us at the Denali Princess Wilderness Lodge, located at the north entry to Denali National Park. Or, visit the south side of the Great One and stay at the Mt. McKinley Princess Wilderness Lodge.

Rail packages depart daily from Anchorage and Fairbanks and include one- and two-night stays at either Princess Lodge.

Call your travel agent or
800-426-0500
for reservations and information.

PRINCESS®
Alaska Lodges
www.princesslodges.com

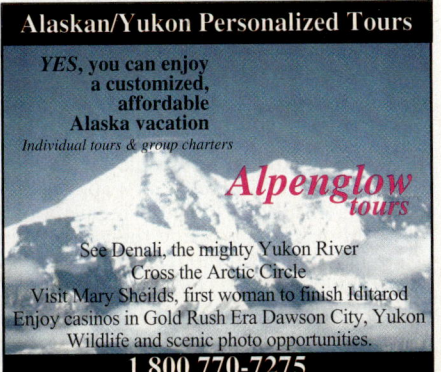

Alaskan/Yukon Personalized Tours

YES, you can enjoy a customized, affordable Alaska vacation
Individual tours & group charters

Alpenglow *tours*

See Denali, the mighty Yukon River
Cross the Arctic Circle
Visit Mary Sheilds, first woman to finish Iditarod
Enjoy casinos in Gold Rush Era Dawson City, Yukon
Wildlife and scenic photo opportunities.

1 800 770-7275

FAIRBANKS

(See maps, page 424)

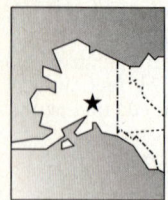

Located in the heart of Alaska's Great Interior country. By highway, it is approximately 1,488 miles north of Dawson Creek, BC, the start of the Alaska Highway (traditional milepost distance is 1,523 miles); 98 miles from Delta Junction (official end of the Alaska Highway); 358 miles from Anchorage via the Parks Highway; and 2,305 miles from Seattle.

Population: Fairbanks city, 30,224; Fairbanks–North Star Borough, 83,694. **Emergency Services: Alaska State Troopers,** 1979 Peger Road, emergency phone 911; for nonemergencies, (907) 451-5100, and for TTY service, (907) 451-5344. phone **Fairbanks Police,** 656 7th Ave., phone 911 or, for nonemergencies, phone (907) 459-6500. **Fire Department** and **Ambulance Service,** phone 911. **Hospitals,** Fairbanks Memorial, 1650 Cowles St., phone (907) 452-8181; Bassett Army Hospital, Fort Wainwright, phone (907) 353-5172; Emergency room (907) 353-5143; Eielson Clinic, Eielson AFB, phone (907) 377-1847. **Interior Alaska Center for Non-Violent Living,** phone (907) 452-2293. **Emergency Management,** phone (907) 459-1481 or (907) 474-7721 (24-hour line). **Borough Information,** phone (907) 459-1000.

Visitor Information: Fairbanks Log Cabin Visitor Information Center at 550 1st Ave. (at Cushman Street, where a riverside marker reads "Mile 1523, Official End of the Alaska Highway"); phone (907) 456-5774 or 1-800-327-5774. Public parking across the bridge by the church. Open daily in summer, weekdays only in winter. Phone (907) 456-4636 or email info@explorefairbanks.com for current events and activities, or visit www.explorefairbanks.com.

Visitor information is also available at Fairbanks International Airport in the baggage claim area and at the Alaska Railroad depot.

For information on Alaska's state parks, national parks, national forests, wildlife refuges and other outdoor recreational sites, visit the **Alaska Public Lands Information Center** downstairs in historic Courthouse Square at 250 N. Cushman St. The center offers free trip-planning assistance and is a free museum featuring films on Alaska, interpretive programs, lectures, exhibits, artifacts, photographs and short video programs on each region in the state. The exhibit area and information desk are open 7 days a week in summer, 9 A.M. to 6 P.M.; Tuesday through Saturday in winter, 10 A.M. to 6 P.M. Phone (907) 456-0527. For recorded information on Denali National Park, phone (907) 456-0510. TDD information line is (907) 456-0532. www.nps.gov/aplic.

Elevation: 434 feet at Fairbanks International Airport. **Climate:** January temperatures range from -2°F to -19°F. The lowest temperature ever recorded was -66°F on January 14, 1934. July temperatures average 62°F, with a record high of 99°F in July 1919. In June and early July daylight lasts 21 hours—and the nights are really only twilight. Annual precipitation is 10.4 inches, with an annual average snowfall of 65.5 inches. The record for snowfall is 147.3 inches, set the winter of 1990–91. **Radio:** KSUA-FM, KFAR, KCBF, KAKQ, KYSC, KKED, KUWL-FM, KXLR-FM, KWLF-FM, KIAK, KIAK-FM, KJNP-AM and FM (North Pole), KUAC-FM 104.7. **Television:** Channels 2, 4, 7, 9, 11, 13 and cable. **Newspapers:** *Fairbanks Daily News–Miner.*

Private Aircraft: Consult the *Alaska Supplement* for information on Eielson AFB, Fairbanks International, Fairbanks International Seaplane, Chena Marina Air Field and Fort Wainwright. Or phone the Fairbanks Flight Service Station at (907) 474-0137. For information on restricted military airspace, phone 1-800-758-8723.

History

In 1901, Captain E.T. Barnette set out from St. Michael on the stern-wheeler *Lavelle Young,* traveling up the Yukon River with supplies for his trading post, which he proposed to set up at Tanana Crossing (Tanacross), the halfway point on the Valdez–Eagle trail. But the stern-wheeler could not navigate the fast-moving, shallow Tanana River beyond the mouth of the Chena River. The stern-wheeler's captain dropped off Barnette on the Chena near the present site of 1st Avenue and Cushman Street. A year later, Felix Pedro, an Italian prospector, discovered gold about 16 miles north of Barnette's temporary trading post. The opportunistic Barnette quickly abandoned his original plan to continue on to Tanana Crossing.

In September 1902, Barnette convinced the 25 or so miners in the area to use the name "Fairbanks" for the town that he expected would grow up around his trading post. The name had been suggested that summer by Court District Judge James Wickersham, who admired Charles W. Fairbanks, the senior senator from Indiana. The senator later became vice president of the United States under Theodore Roosevelt.

The town grew, largely due to Barnette's promotion of gold prospects and discoveries in the area, and in 1903 Judge Wickersham moved the headquarters of his Third Judicial District Court (a district which encompassed 300,000 square miles) from Eagle to Fairbanks.

Thanks to Wickersham, the town gained government offices and a jail. Thanks to Barnette, it gained a post office and a branch of the Northern Commercial Company, a large Alaska trading firm based in San Francisco. In addition, after Barnette became the first mayor of Fairbanks in 1903, the town acquired telephone service, set up fire protection, passed sanitation ordinances and contracted for electric light and steam heat. In 1904, Barnette started a bank.

The town of "Fairbanks" first appeared in the U.S. Census in 1910 with a population of 3,541. Miners living beside their claims on creeks north of town brought the area population figure to about 11,000.

Barnette stayed in Fairbanks until late 1910, when he resigned the presidency of the Washington–Alaska Bank and moved to California. When the bank collapsed early in

Fall colors of the Interior surround the campus of the University of Alaska Fairbanks. (© Laurent Dick)

FAIRBANKS' PREMIER ATTRACTIONS

• Riverboat Discovery •
Call Toll Free 1-866-479-6673

Join the Binkley family aboard the authentic sternwheeler Riverboat Discovery

- Rated the #1 boat tour in North America
- Operating since 1950
- Cruise the Chena and Tanana Rivers with third and fourth generation Alaskan captains
- Experience Alaskan Native cultural traditions
- Take a guided walking tour of the Chena Indian Village
- See Susan Butcher's Iditarod champion sled dogs in action
- View a bush pilot demonstration
- Enjoy our complimentary fresh baked donuts and coffee
- Visit the Discovery Trading Post, Fairbanks' finest gift store

Experience Native culture

Visit Discovery Trading Post

Daily Sailing 8:45am & 2pm
www.riverboatdiscovery.com
reservations@riverboatdiscovery.com

3½ hour narrated tour. Sun deck and enclosed seating. Snack bar and restrooms
1975 Discovery Drive, Fairbanks, AK 99709

Call for reservations   **Local Calls 479-6673**

Riverboat Discovery • A most memorable adventure

The Riverboat Discovery is the one adventure you won't want to miss when you travel to Fairbanks. Owned and operated by the Binkley family, whose riverboating experience in Alaska spans four generations and more than 100 years, the Riverboat Discovery tour has been rated the top boating attraction in North America in *Travel Weekly Magazine*. Captain Jim Binkley and his crew of children, grandchildren and native Alaskans take you back to the heyday of sternwheelers, to an era when prospectors, fur traders and Native people of the Interior relied on rivers as their only link to the outside world.

Passengers relax in the comfort of glass-enclosed or open decks as the Discovery winds its way down the Chena and Tanana Rivers. Drawing on their knowledge of Alaskan history, the Binkley family entertains listeners with witty descriptions of Alaskan life during the 3½ hour narrated cruise. The Discovery makes a brief stop at the riverfront home of veteran Iditarod Dog Musher Susan Butcher, where visitors hear tales of Susan's Iditarod adventures and are introduced to her champion sled dogs.

One of the highlights of the trip is a stop ashore at the Old Chena Indian Village. Here passengers disembark for a guided tour. Alaskan Natives share their culture as they recount how their ancestors hunted, fished, sewed clothing and built shelters to survive for centuries in the harsh Alaskan wilderness. At the village guests will see Susan Butcher's Iditarod champion sled dogs in action during the sled dog demonstration.

The Discovery departs from Steamboat Landing, off Dale Road, daily at 8:45am and 2pm mid-May through mid-September. Call for reservations. For further information, call the toll free number of 1-866-479-6673; local callers may use 479-6673.

Before or after your cruise, step into the past at Steamboat Landing, one of the finest gift stores in Alaska. Stroll along the picturesque boardwalk beside the Chena River and enter any of the four turn-of-the century shops. Discovery Trading Post offers unique Alaskan gifts at great low prices. Susan's winning Iditarod dog sled and Iditarod trophies are conveniently located so you can take photos you'll always treasure. The Binkley and Barrington Gift Shop offers Alaskan made products, and the Pioneer Hotel is replica of Fairbanks' first luxury hotel. Be sure not to miss this cultural treat between Discovery departures—you'll find an impressive selection of gifts at some of the best prices in Alaska. Open 7 days a week. For more information, view www.discoverytradingpost.com

and pan for gold while enjoying El Dorado Gold Mine's famous Alaskan hospitality.

The two hour tour to a working gold mine begins when passengers board the Tanana Valley Railroad for a narrated trip through the original gold fields of the Interior that were once part of Alaska's richest mining district on record.

Passengers ride the narrow gauge rails through a permafrost tunnel where miners with head lamps and pick-axes seek out the rich gold veins, reminiscent of mining days gone by. Winding through the valley, the train comes to a halt as a prospector crouches down to dip his gold pan into the cold, clear waters of Fox Creek in search of a sparkle of gold.

At El Dorado Camp, local miners "Yukon Yonda" and her husband Dexter Clark are on hand to conduct a guided tour through a working gold mine. Visitors gather around to watch the operation of a modern day sluice box and enjoy stories about life in Alaskan mining camps.

A crash course in gold panning is followed by the real thing. Guests grab a poke filled with pay dirt right from the sluice box and try their hand at panning for gold. And when guests strike it rich, they keep the gold!

The next stop is the assay office where visitors, while enjoying complimentary homemade cookies and coffee, weigh their gold and assay its market value. The "all aboard" call gathers everyone onto the train for the short ride back to the station.

Daily tours (afternoon trips only Saturday & Monday) for the El Dorado Gold Mine depart from the old train station nine miles north of Fairbanks at 1.3 mile Elliott Highway/Highway #2, just past Fox, Alaska. Call toll free for reservations at 1-866-479-6673; local calls 479-6673.

El Dorado Gold Mine • Gold Mining History

Pan for gold, ride the train see a permafrost tunnel!

Pan for gold at the El Dorado Gold Mine. Join the Binkley family on another Alaskan experience that can't be missed! El Dorado Gold Mine is an exciting hands-on adventure for the whole family. Guests learn about the history of mining in Alaska, experience a modern day mining operation

Visit the web site:
www.riverboatdiscovery.com
www.eldoradogoldmine.com
reservations@riverboatdiscovery.com
reservations@eldoradogoldmine.com

FAIRBANKS' PREMIER ATTRACTIONS

•El Dorado Gold Mine•
Call Toll Free 1-866-479-6673

Join the Binkley family for an adventure into Fairbanks' gold mining history

- Pan for gold. Strike it rich. We guarantee it!
- Ride the Tanana Valley Railroad through a permafrost tunnel
- Featured nationally on NBC. Travel professionals call this "the best 2 hours you will spend in the state"
- Discover the history of Alaska's richest gold mining area
- Learn modern day placer mining methods
- Meet local miners Yukon Yonda & Dexter Clark
- Sample our complimentary fresh baked cookies and coffee
- Ask about our FREE shuttle service

Two-hour tour of an operating gold mine. Just 9 miles north of Fairbanks on the Elliott Highway/Highway #2. 1975 Discovery Drive, Fairbanks, AK 99709

Working gold mine

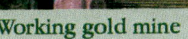

Conductor Earl Hughes

Permafrost tunnel

El Dorado Gold Mine

Daily Tours
www.eldoradogoldmine.com
reservations@eldoradogoldmine.com

Call for reservations **Local Calls 479-6673**

RIVER'S EDGE
RV PARK & CAMPGROUND

Located in the heart of Fairbanks

4140 Boat St, 99709 • (907) 474-0286

www.riversedge.net

"River's Edge is RV heaven!"
Dr. Helen Stover of Richmond, VA

Adventure guides on staff

NEW

Chena's Fine Dining & Deck
featuring Fresh Alaska Salmon

Full & Partial Hook-Ups • Gift Shop • Tour Sales
180 Sites • Pull Throughs • Car Wash • Laundry
Pay phones • Dry tent sites • Dump Station
Walking distance to major shopping & groceries

FREE Showers
FREE Shuttle to Riverboat & El Dorado Gold Mine

Tour bookings to the Arctic Circle, Pt. Barrow and local attractions.

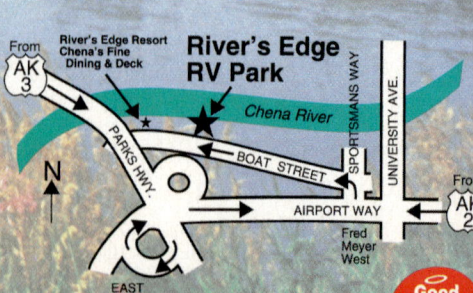

From Anchorage/Denali, AK3: take East Airport Way exit, left on Sportsmans Way, left on Boat Street.
From Tok/Richardson Hwy., AK2: left on Airport Way, cross University Ave., right on Sportsmans Way, left on Boat Street

Good Sampark

4140 Boat Street (off Airport Way),
Fairbanks, Alaska 99709 • 1-800-770-3343

BARROW

River's Edge Resort presents

Land of the Midnight Sun

1-Day or Overnight Tours from Fairbanks

Featuring Boeing 737 Jet service on Alaska Airlines and overnight accommodations with Top of the World Hotel.

Don't stop till you reach the top!

Inupiat Eskimo Village of Pt. Barrow
Arctic Ocean, Top of the World

One-Day Tour

River's Edge takes you to the airport in the early morning for your flight on **Alaska Airlines**. Receive a certificate after crossing the Arctic Circle.

Spend the day in Barrow with your own tour guide. Includes an extensive Native Culture Exhibition featuring a Blanket Toss and Inupiat Eskimo Traditional Dances.

Arrive that evening in Fairbanks. River's Edge picks you up.

Overnight Tour

All the excitement of the one-day tour *plus* for a few more dollars:

Stay overnight at the **Top of the World Hotel**.

Return to Fairbanks the next afternoon. River's Edge will meet you.

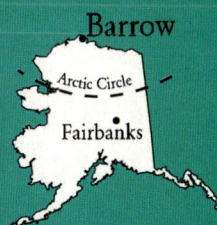

Barrow is only a 75 minute flight from Fairbanks.

Warm clothing is advised.

In-flight breakfast and dinner snack are provided.

1-800-770-3343
info@riversedge.net • www.riversedge.net

For reservations and information, call **River's Edge Resort**
1-800-770-3343

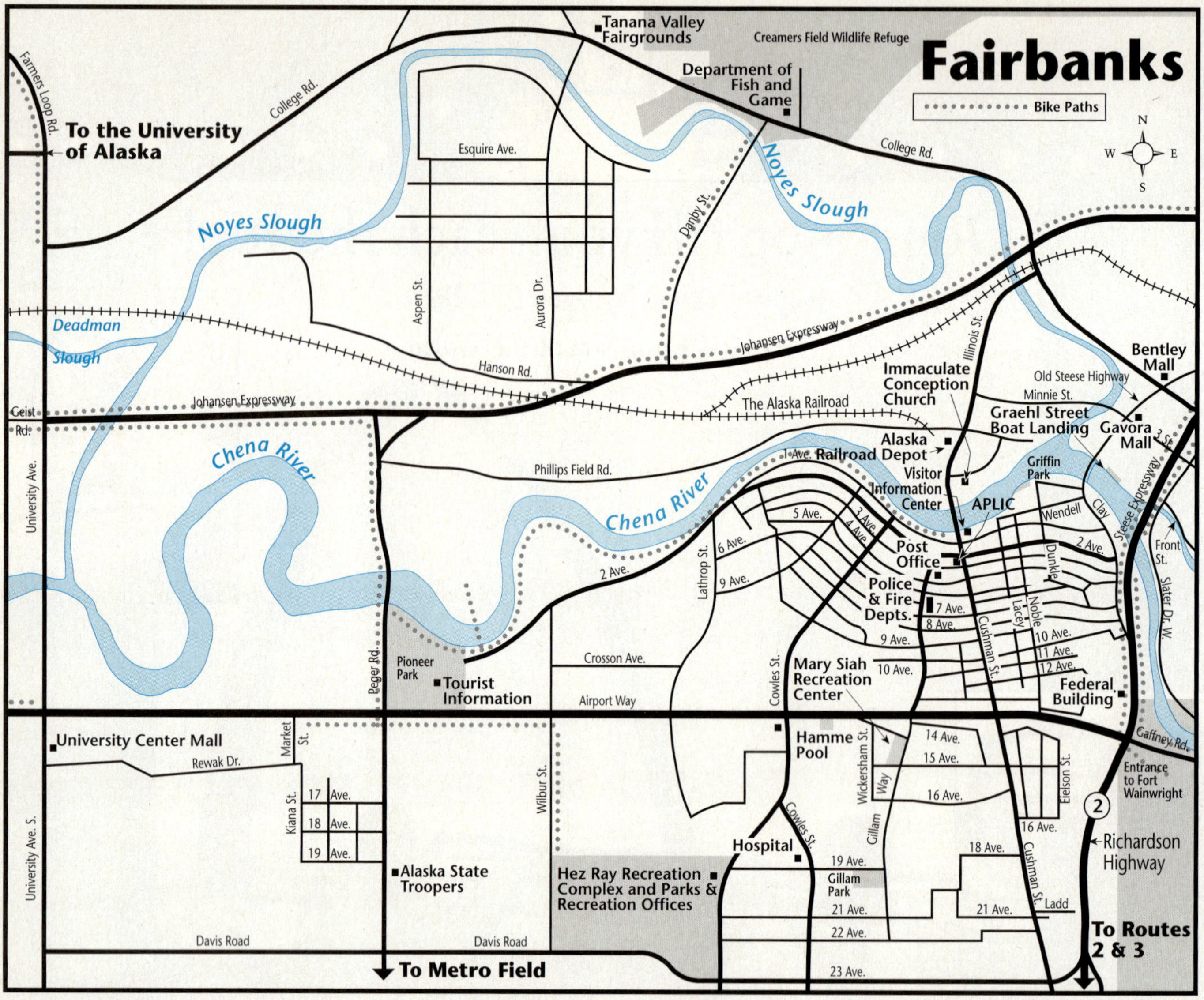

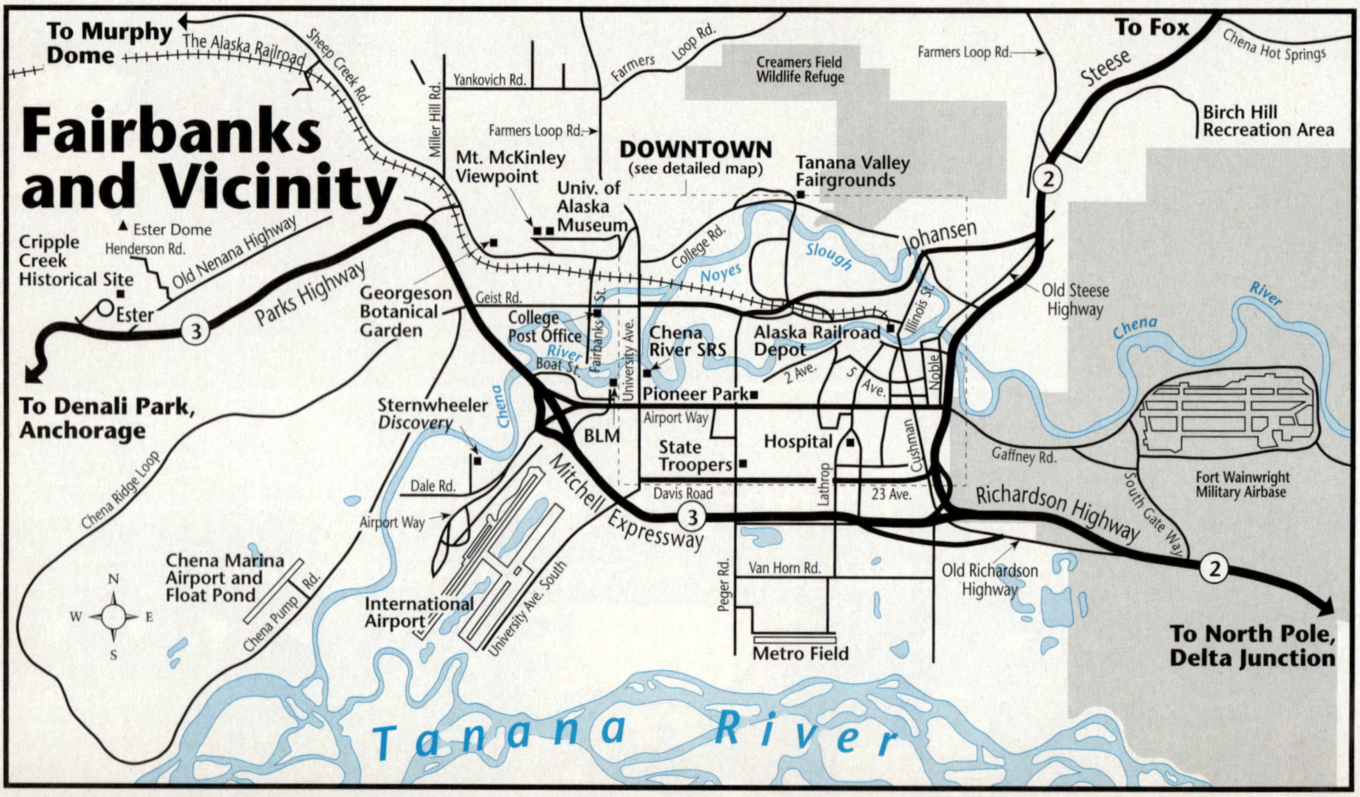

A brilliant aurora transforms the sky over Farmer's Loop Road.
(© Craig Brandt)

1911, the people of Fairbanks blamed Barnette. The tale of the "most hated man in Fairbanks" is told in *Crooked Past*.

Economy

The city's economy is linked to its role as a service and supply point for Interior and Arctic industrial activities. Fairbanks played a key role during construction of the trans-Alaska pipeline in the 1970s. The Dalton Highway (formerly the North Slope Haul Road) to Prudhoe Bay begins about 75 miles north of town. Extractive industries such as oil and mining continue to play a major role in the economy.

Government employment contributes significantly to the Fairbanks economy. Including military jobs, 50 percent of employment in Fairbanks is through the government. **Fort Wainwright** (formerly Ladd Field) was the first Army airfield in Alaska, established in 1938. The fort currently employs about 4,600 soldiers and 1,600 civilians, and it houses approximately 6,200 family members. Fort Wainwright also provides emergency services by assisting with search and rescue operations.

Eielson Air Force Base, located 25 miles southeast of Fairbanks on the Richardson Highway, also has a strong economic impact on the city. Eielson has about 2,700 military personnel and approximately 4,200 family members assigned, with about 1,200 military personnel and family members living off base.

Eielson Air Force Base was built in 1943. Originally a satellite base to Ladd Field (now Fort Wainwright) and called Mile 26, it served as a storage site for aircraft on their way to the Soviet Union under the WWII Lend–Lease program. Closed after WWII, the base was reactivated in 1946 and renamed Eielson AFB, after Carl Ben Eielson, the first man to fly from Alaska over the North Pole to Greenland. Eielson is the far-

FAIRBANKS

Sandhill cranes come by the thousands to Creamer's Field. (© John Schwieder Photography)

Description

Alaska's second largest city and the administrative capital of the Interior, Fairbanks lies on the flat valley floor of the Tanana River on the banks of the Chena River. Good views of the valley are available from Chena Ridge Road to the west and Farmers Loop Road to the north.

The city is a blend of old and new: Modern hotels and shopping strips stand beside log cabins and historic wooden buildings.

Fairbanks is bounded to the north, east and west by low rolling hills of birch and white spruce. To the south is the Alaska Range and Denali National Park, about a 2^1/$_2$-hour drive via the Parks Highway. The Steese and Elliott highways lead north to the White Mountains.

Lodging & Services

Fairbanks has more than 100 restaurants, about 2 dozen hotels and motels, 6 hostels and more than 100 bed and breakfasts. Many are open year-round. Rates vary widely, from a low of about $40 for a single to a high of $150 for a double (hostels are considerably cheaper). Reservations for all accommodations are suggested during the busy summer months.

AAA-7 Gables Inn & Suites. Central to major attractions, this renovated fraternity house is between the University campus thest-north fighter wing in the U.S. Air Force, and at 60,000 square miles of military training space, it has the largest aerial range in the country.

Also boosting the Fairbanks economy are the University of Alaska Fairbanks, and trade and service industries such as retail sales and tourism. The university and the tourism industry are critical components of the local economy.

FAIRBANKS ADVERTISERS

Accommodations
AAA-7 Gables Inn & Suites	426, 430
AAAA Care Bed & Breakfast	432
Ah, Rose Marie Downtown Bed & Breakfast	428
A-1 Yankovich Inn Bed & Breakfast	428
A N'ice Bed 'N Breakfast	432
Alaska Motel	428
Aspen Hotels/ Fairbanks	427
Beaver Point Lodge	427
Bridgewater Hotel	428, 429
Captain Bartlett Inn	429
Chena Hot Springs Resort	436, 447
Circle Hot Springs	432
College Inn	430
Eleanor's Northern Lights Bed & Breakfast	428
Ester Gold Camp Hotel	430
Fairbanks Bed and Breakfast	429
Fairbanks Golden Nugget Hotel	427
Fairbanks Hotel	429
Fairbanks Princess Riverside Lodge	429
Fountainhead Hotels	429
Golden North Motel	427
Gram's Cabin Bed & Breakfast	430
Klondike Inn	428
North Pole Cabins	430
Pike's Waterfront Lodge	430, 433
Regency Fairbanks	427
River's Edge Resort Cottages	425
Snowy River Bed & Breakfast	446
Sophie Station Hotel	429, 430
Super 8 Motel	432
Tamarac Inn Motel	430
3 Bears Bed & Breakfast	429
Towne House Motel & Apartments	428
Townsite Gardens Bed & Breakfast	430
Wedgewood Resort	429, 430

Attractions & Entertainment
Alaska Bird Observatory	442
Alaska Riverways	420
Alaskan Tails of the Trail	440
Chena Hot Springs Resort	436, 447
Creamer's Field Migratory Waterfowl Refuge	442
El Dorado Gold Mine	420-421, 445
Ester Gold Camp	430
Fort Knox Gold Mine	435, 438
Gold Rush Gold Camp	437
Greatland River Tours	440, 449
Historic Gold Dredge Number 8	445
Large Animal Research Station	434
North Star Golf Club	436
Pike's Riverboat Cruises	437, 441
Pioneer Air Museum	437
Pioneer Park	436
Riverboat *Discovery*	419, 420
University of Alaska Museum	434

Auto & RV Rentals, Services & Supplies
Affordable New Car Rental	441
American Tire & Auto	441
Arctic RV	439
Arctic Tire	438
Aurora Motors	441
Chevron Stations	438
Fairbanks RV Service Center	438
Gabe's Truck & Auto Repair	440
Gene's Chrysler	440
Harley-Davidson Motorcycles	448
Hill Top Truck Stop	441
Jiffy Lube	439
Sourdough Fuel, Texaco	440
University Avenue Car and Truck Wash	439

Campgrounds
Chena Marina RV Park	432, 442
Fairbanks RV Park & Campground	442
River's Edge RV Park & Campground	422, 432
Riverview RV Park	432, 443
Tanana Valley Campground	442

Dining
Alaska's Castle	444
Ester Gold Camp	430
Hot Licks Homemade Ice Cream	444
Klondike Lounge & Dining Hall	428
Turtle Club, The	444
Two Rivers Lodge	444

Shopping & Services
A Touch of Gold	448
Alaska Rag Co.	439
Alaska Raw Fur Co.	448
Alaskan Photographic Repair Service	448
Artworks, The	445
Beads & Things	447
Big Ray's All Weather Outfitters	448
Cushman Plaza Laundry, The	445
Expressions in Glass	449
First Alaskan Central Reservations	451
Great Alaska Bowl Co., The	445
Harley-Davidson Motorcycles	448
Plaza Cleaners & Laundry	448
Snow Goose Fibers & Quilting Company	449
Spinning Room, The	448
Tanana Valley Farmers Market	439
Valley Center Store	446

Tours & Transportation
Northern Alaska Tour Company	449-451
Barrow (River's Edge Resort)	423
Greatland River Tours	440, 449
Larry's Flying Service, Inc.	450
Marina Air, Inc.	451
Tanana Air Service	451
Train to Denali (Gray Line of Alaska)	432
Warbelow's Air Ventures, Inc.	450
Wilderness Enterprises	446

Visitor Information
Air Force	450
Fairbanks Convention & Visitors Bureau	431

Regency Fairbanks
Affordable Luxury

- Free airport & railroad shuttle
- Gourmet dining & room service
- Fully appointed kitchens
- Whirlpool rooms & suites
- Car & room packages
- Luxury limousine service
- Centrally located

1-800-348-1340
www.regencyfairbankshotel.com
95 Tenth Ave., Fairbanks, AK 99701 • (907) 452-3200

VALDEZ » SOLDOTNA » JUNEAU
FAIRBANKS » ANCHORAGE

We cover your creature comforts in Fairbanks.

The Aspen Hotel in the Golden Heart of Alaska delivers a delectable continental breakfast every morning, a relaxing pool and excercize room and a level of comfort beyond expectation.

- 97 spacious rooms
- Complimentary continental breakfast
- Guest laundry
- Swimming pool, spa and exercise room
- VCR, speaker phone and data port
- Coffee maker, refrigerator, microwave, iron and hair dryer in room
- Family and extended stay suites

4580 OLD AIRPORT ROAD,
FAIRBANKS, AK 99709 »
1-866-GUEST4U »
WWW.ASPENHOTELSAK.COM

FAIRBANKS
ACCOMMODATIONS

THE FAIRBANKS Golden Nugget Hotel
RESTAURANT & LOUNGE

- Non-smoking Rooms
- Free Local Calls
- Air Conditioned Rooms
- Spacious Suites
- Extra Large Rooms
- Color Cable T.V.
- Corporate & Government Rates Available
- Low Winter Rates, Weekly & Monthly

LOCALLY OWNED
IN DOWNTOWN FAIRBANKS

www.golden-nuggethotel.com
907-452-5141
Fax: 907-452-5458
900 Noble Street
Fairbanks, AK 99701
SENIORS DISCOUNT

Beaver Point Lodge

A year-round Alaskan wilderness retreat located on a remote lake nestled in the Dugan Hills, one hour's flight west of Fairbanks. Lodging, meals and recreation equipment provided. Air, water and ground transportation available. Please call for rates.

(907) 378-7565 or **(907) 388-7535**
beaverpoint@alaska.net

P.O. Box 72648 Fairbanks, AK 99707
www.alaska.net/~beaverpoint

---

www.goldennorthmotel.com   **FAIRBANKS, ALASKA**   sourdough@goldennorthmotel.com

GOLDEN NORTH MOTEL of Fairbanks, LLC

1-800-447-1910
(In Fairbanks call 907-479-6201)
4888 Old Airport Rd.
Fairbanks, Alaska 99709

- ✓ **Summer Rates Start at $69**
- ✓ **Near Major Tourist Attractions**
- ✓ Minutes from Downtown
- ✓ Cable TV
- ✓ Tub & Shower in Each Room
- ✓ Free Local Calls
- ✓ 62 Attractive Units
- ✓ Courtesy Van (Airport/RR)
- ✓ Fine Restaurant Nearby
- ✓ Open Year-Round
- ✓ Free Continental Breakfast
- ✓ Close to Shopping

All Major Credit Cards Welcome

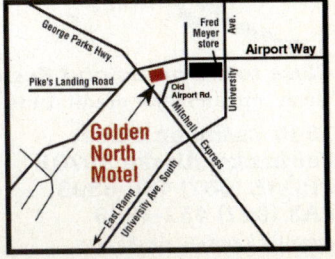

Take Airport Way or Mitchell Express to Old Airport Rd.

FAIRBANKS — ACCOMMODATIONS

When you're in Fairbanks — KLONDIKE INN

STAY WITH US!
☆ Minutes from the Airport
☆ Modern Kitchen Unit
☆ Cable T.V.
☆ On City Transit Route
☆ Park in Front of Your Unit
☆ Liquor Store

Reservations Only
1-888-966-6646
PHONE (907) 479-6241 • FAX (907) 479-6254

We're located between University Center & K-Mart!
University & Airport Way, 1316 Bedrock Street, Fairbanks, Alaska 99701

 **Klondike Lounge & Dining Hall**

Breakfast • Lunch • Dinner • Cocktails
Outdoor Seating
OPEN 7 DAYS A WEEK 6:00 a.m. • Sunday open at 10:00 a.m.
Next to Klondike Inn
(907) 479-2224

Relaxing in the sun at Chena Hot Springs resort, an hour's drive from Fairbanks. (© Julie Collins)

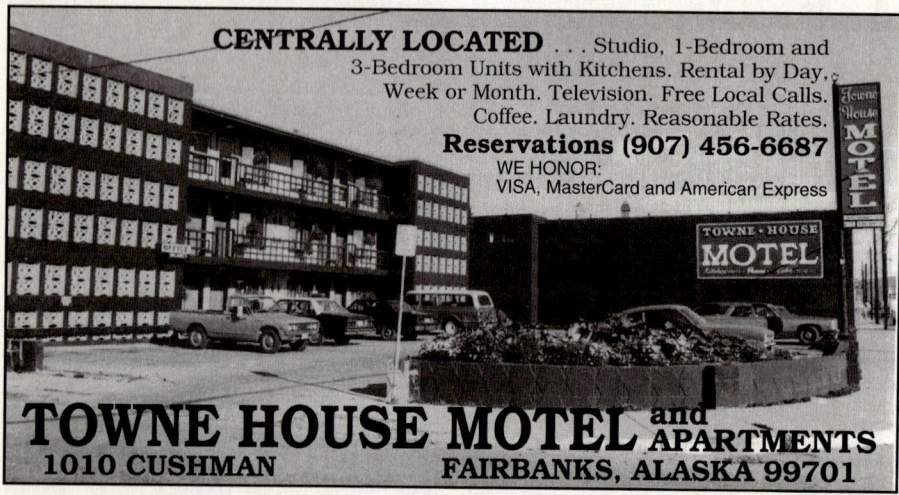

CENTRALLY LOCATED... Studio, 1-Bedroom and 3-Bedroom Units with Kitchens. Rental by Day, Week or Month. Television. Free Local Calls. Coffee. Laundry. Reasonable Rates.
Reservations **(907) 456-6687**
WE HONOR: VISA, MasterCard and American Express

TOWNE HOUSE MOTEL and APARTMENTS
1010 CUSHMAN, FAIRBANKS, ALASKA 99701

Alaska Motel

REASONABLE RATES!
Senior Citizens Discount • Weekly Rates
• Clean & Comfortable 36 Rooms
• Non-smoking Rooms Available
• Kitchenettes Available
• Laundry Facilities
• Cable TV
• Free Parking

Close to shopping and Restaurants
We accept all major credit cards
1546 Cushman Street
Fairbanks, Alaska 99701
PHONE (907) 456-6393
FAX (907) 452-4833
e-mail: akmotel@alaska.net
http://www.alaska.net/~akmotel

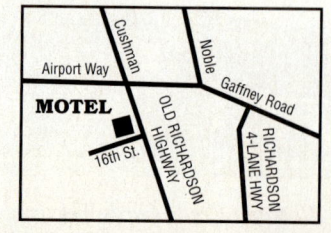

---

and the airport. The spacious Tudor-style house features a floral solarium, stained-glass foyer with indoor waterfall, cathedral ceilings, meeting room. Gourmet breakfast served daily. Cable TV/VCR, phones and data ports, laundry facilities. Complimentary canoes, bikes, car wash. Rates $60 and up; www.7gablesinn.com. Phone (907) 479-0751; fax (907) 479-2229. [ADVERTISEMENT]

Ah, Rose Marie Downtown Bed and Breakfast. Historic 1928 Fairbanks home. Very centrally located. Full hearty breakfasts. Friendly cat. Outdoor smoking areas. Singles, couples, triples, families welcomed. Open year-round. Extraordinary hospitality. Single $60 up, doubles $75 up. Wow! John E. Davis, 302 Cowles St., Fairbanks, AK 99701. Phone (907) 456-2040; fax (907) 456-6193; web site: www.akpub.com/akbbrv/ahrose.html [ADVERTISEMENT]

A-1 Yankovich Inn Bed & Breakfast. On a 2-acre estate bordering Muskox farm. Hiking/skiing trails, Aurora viewing. Dog sled rides available. Queen Beautyrest beds plus rollaway. $79 and up; this includes a full gourmet breakfast. 2268 Yankovich Road, Fairbanks, AK. Phone 1-888-801-2861 or (907) 479-2861. Email: yankovich@gci.net website: http://home.gci.net/~yankovich [ADVERTISEMENT]

Bridgewater Hotel. The Bridgewater is an absolutely charming hotel that sits in the heart of historic, downtown Fairbanks overlooking the Chena River. The 94-room hotel combines the quaint and personal feeling of a bed and breakfast with all of the generous amenities of a full service hotel, providing for a delightful, boutique-hotel type experience. 800-528-4916 or 907-452-6661. Write 723 First Ave., Fairbanks, AK 99701. www.fountainheadhotels.com. [ADVERTISEMENT]

Eleanor's Northern Lights Bed and Breakfast. Conveniently located, a 7-minute walk from downtown Fairbanks. Full, all-

you-can-eat "home-cooked breakfasts." (Free Internet use!) A selection of 6 clean rooms. Very reasonable rates: $65–$90. Energetic and bright hosts—Stella and Mike—have created a warm, cozy "home away from home." 360 State St. (corner of 4th Avenue and State Street), Fairbanks, AK 99701. Phone: (907) 452-2598, or 1-800-467-4167; fax: (907) 452-7247; email:nlightsb@eagle.ptialaska.net; web page: www.akpub.com/akbbrv/elean.html.
[ADVERTISEMENT]

Fairbanks Bed and Breakfast. Barbara Neubauer, hostess and 26-year resident, has many bear and gold mining tales. The quiet historical neighborhood is walking distance to town on bus route. Our home has many interesting ivory artifacts and Alaskan art. Private bath, large yard and deck. Deck smoking. Hearty breakfast and laundry facilities for fee plus ample parking. 902 Kellum Street. (907) 452-4967, fax (907) 451-6955.
[ADVERTISEMENT]

Fairbanks Princess Riverside Lodge. The remodeled 325 room lodge features scenic views of Chena River; gift shop; espresso bar; health club with steam rooms; business center and seasonal tour desk. Free airport shuttle. The hotel often has summer availability—call ahead. 4477 Pikes Landing Road, Fairbanks, AK 99709. Reservations 800-426-0500. www.princesslodges.com.
[ADVERTISEMENT]

Fountainhead Hotels. Fountainhead Hotels has been providing deluxe accommodations to Fairbanks visitors for more than 20 years. Being a small, locally owned company allows us to concentrate on special things that enhance your stay and provide for a more unique, personal experience,

FAIRBANKS HOTEL
Fairbanks' oldest hotel, newly restored
517 3RD AVENUE
Phone (907) 456-6411
Fax (907) 456-1792
(888) FBX-HOTL / (888) 329-4685
WWW.FBXHOTL.COM   INFO@FBXHOTL.COM
Since 1941

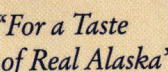

3 BEARS bed & breakfast
Enjoy the comfort of our cozy cabins nestled in the aspen and birch trees above Fairbanks. On 10 beautiful acres just minutes from downtown.
1068 Skiboot Hill Rd.
(907) 457-2449   Fax (907) 457-3349
e-mail: bb3bears@ptialaska.net

Fairbanks—The Golden Heart City.

The Captain Bartlett Inn
"For a Taste of Real Alaska"

Centrally located
Near Shopping & Major Attractions
Comfortable, Alaskan decor rooms

The Musher's Roadhouse Restaurant
Breakfast, Lunch, Dinner
Outdoor Dining

Dog Sled Saloon
Free Peanuts & Popcorn
World Renowned Alaskan Decor & Hospitality

1411 Airport Way, Fairbanks, AK 99701
1-800-544-7528 (outside Alaska)
1-800-478-7900 (inside Alaska)
cbi@ptialaska.net
www.captainbartlettinn.com

Good Night.
Fairbanks ◆ Alaska

Wedgewood Resort
212 Wedgewood Drive
Fairbanks, AK 99701
(907) 452-1442

Sophie Station
1717 University Avenue
Fairbanks, AK 99709
(907) 479-3650

Bridgewater Hotel
723 First Avenue
Fairbanks, AK 99701
(907) 452-6661

Enjoy the special, personal experience that can only be found in an Alaskan-owned hotel. Accommodating Alaska's visitors for more than 20 years, our hotels offer true Alaskan spirit and local flavor and feature elegant suites, spacious guest rooms and charming accommodations.

800-528-4916
1501 Queens Way ◆ Fairbanks, Alaska 99701
fhdhotels@mosquitonet.com ◆ www.fountainheadhotels.com
(907) 456-3642

Fountainhead Hotels
Your **First** Choice in the **Last** Frontier!

FAIRBANKS

ACCOMMODATIONS

7 Gables Inn & Suites
Fairbanks
Central location
Gourmet Breakfasts
Rooms, suites, efficiencies
Open year round
Laundry, canoes, Jacuzzis, bikes
Cable TV/VCR/DVD
Free computer use. High speed data ports.

Rates: $60 and up
www.7gablesinn.com
(907) 479-0751

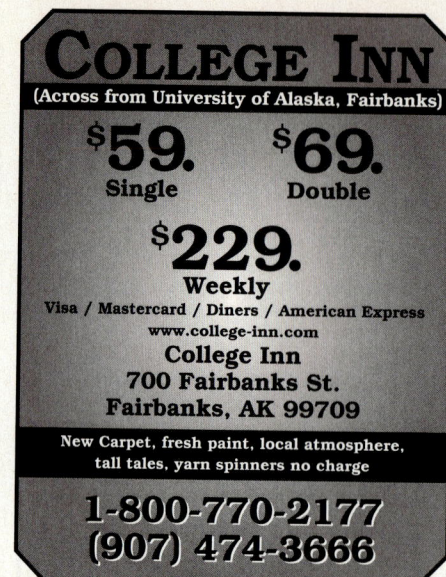

College Inn
(Across from University of Alaska, Fairbanks)

$59. Single   **$69.** Double

$229. Weekly

Visa / Mastercard / Diners / American Express
www.college-inn.com
College Inn
700 Fairbanks St.
Fairbanks, AK 99709

New Carpet, fresh paint, local atmosphere,
tall tales, yarn spinners no charge

1-800-770-2177
(907) 474-3666

TAMARAC INN MOTEL
Guest Laundry • Some Kitchens
Within Walking Distance to:
City Center • Train Station
Nearly Half the Shopping Malls

252 Minnie Street • Fairbanks
(907) 456-4606
tamaracinn@alaska.com
1-800-693-6406 • fax 907-456-7238

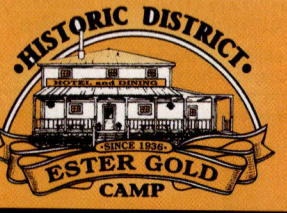

HISTORIC DISTRICT — ESTER GOLD CAMP (Est. 1938)

Home of The World Famous MALEMUTE SALOON
LIVE PERFORMANCES • SONGS • MUSIC • DANCE
STORIES • ROBERT SERVICE POETRY • DAILY
RESERVATIONS ADVISED

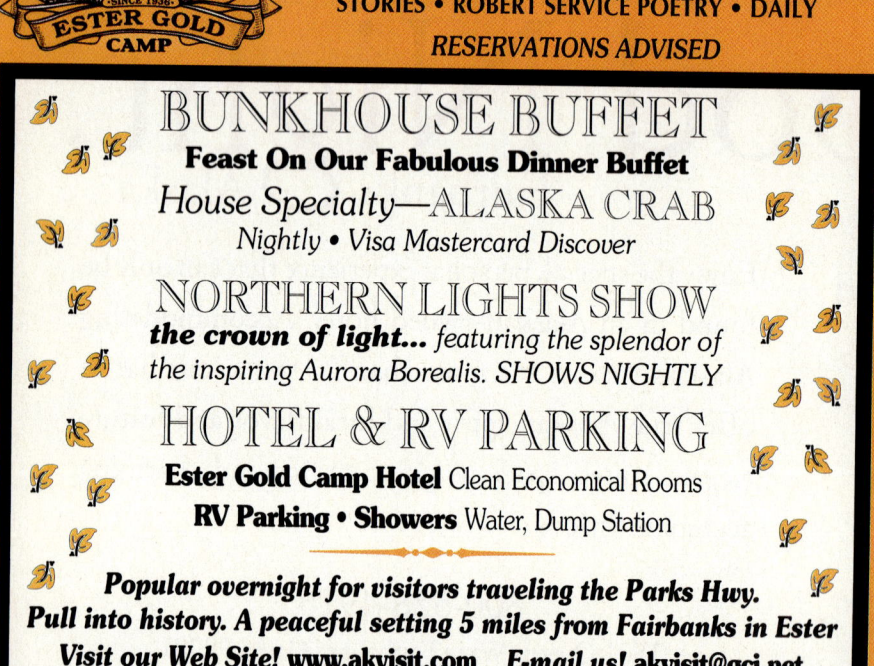

BUNKHOUSE BUFFET
Feast On Our Fabulous Dinner Buffet
House Specialty—ALASKA CRAB
Nightly • Visa Mastercard Discover

NORTHERN LIGHTS SHOW
the crown of light... featuring the splendor of
the inspiring Aurora Borealis. SHOWS NIGHTLY

HOTEL & RV PARKING
Ester Gold Camp Hotel Clean Economical Rooms
RV Parking • Showers Water, Dump Station

Popular overnight for visitors traveling the Parks Hwy.
Pull into history. A peaceful setting 5 miles from Fairbanks in Ester.
Visit our Web Site! www.akvisit.com E-mail us! akvisit@gci.net

QUALITY accents the experience. ECONOMY congratulates the budget!

ESTER GOLD CAMP
PO Box 109MP Ester Alaska 99725
800-676-6925 907-479-2500 Fax 474-1780

In June and early July, Fairbanks has about 21 hours of daylight each day.

---

while still providing all of the generous amenities that you expect from deluxe, full service hotels. For reservations at Sophie Station, Wedgewood Resort or the Bridgewater Hotel, phone 1-800-528-4916, (907) 456-3642; www.fountainheadhotels.com; 1501 Queens Way, Fairbanks, AK 99701. [ADVERTISEMENT]

Gram's Cabin Bed and Breakfast. Beautiful, partially-wooded site on 3 Chena riverfront acres. Two private cabins, each sleep up to 4. Full bathroom, kitchenette, private phone line. Continental breakfast fixings provided. Dogs on approval. Reasonable rates. P.O. Box 58034, Fairbanks, AK 99711; phone (907) 488-6513; Fax (907) 488-6593; email: mp@gramscabin.com; web site: www.gramscabin.com. [ADVERTISEMENT]

North Pole Cabins. Located one mile from Santa Claus House this lovely cabin retreat sets in quiet wooded waterfront privacy. Only 15 minutes from Fairbanks. Open year around. Private entrances. Private baths. Kitchenette. Queen beds. Therapeutic massage services available. www.northpolecabins.com, info@northpolecabins.com, P.O. Box 57194 North Pole, AK 99705. Phone (907) 490-6400. [ADVERTISEMENT]

Pike's Waterfront Lodge. A comfortable 180 room waterfront lodge on the Chena River, in Fairbanks, minutes from the airport, the Lodge features steam room, sauna, game room, coin operated laundry, Jacuzzi rooms, Aveda amenities and public rooms filled with original Alaskan art, slate floor and two story fireplace. Meeting rooms available. All rooms are air-conditioned and offer pay per view, cable and Nintendo. Mountain bike rental. The Lodge offers delicious dining at its own restaurant and lounges and at the famous Pike's Landing Restaurant next door. Free airport shuttle. Open year round. For rates www.pikeslodge.com and email; reservations 1-877-774-2400. [ADVERTISEMENT]

Sophie Station Hotel. Sophie Station is a striking all-suite hotel that offers exceptional guest service in a warm, upscale atmosphere. The hotel's beautifully appointed suites have been thoughtfully furnished with every conceivable comfort and feature art by Alaskan artists. Located just a mile from the airport, the hotel sits in the middle of one of Fairbanks' prime shopping corridors. Phone 1-800-528-4916 or (907) 479-3650. Write 1717 University Avenue, Fairbanks, AK 99709. www.fountainheadhotels.com. [ADVERTISEMENT]

Townsite Gardens B&B. Located downtown. Elegance, convenience, all rooms are new with private baths, phone, cable TV. One bedroom suite with full kitchen. Quiet neighborhood five minutes walk to downtown. Full breakfast. Open year-round rooms starting @ $85. 1003 8th Ave. Fairbanks, Alaska 99701 phone (907) 455-8288 Fax (907) 455-8295 e-mail townsite@mosquitonet.com www.mosquitonet.com/~townsite. [ADVERTISEMENT]

Wedgewood Resort. Wedgewood Resort offers deluxe accommodations including 1 and 2 bedroom suites, in a beautifully landscaped, naturally wooded, campus environment just a mile from downtown. Rich in natural beauty, the resort's private, park-like atmosphere features endless opportunity for enjoyment and exploration. Easy access to nature trails, wildlife preserve and the Alaska Bird Observatory. Phone 1-800-528-4916 or (907) 452-1442. Write: 212 Wedgewood Dr., Fairbanks, AK 99701. www.fountainheadhotels.com. [ADVERTISEMENT]

FAIRBANKS
the gateway to your authentic Alaskan adventure.

Pumphouse Restaurant

Alaska's Northernmost Oyster Bar
Fresh Seafood, Smoked Ribs, Riverside Dining
Proud Recipient of the DiRona Award
Located at 1.3 Mile Chena Pump Road

Phone: (907) 479-8452
Fax: (907) 479-8432
www.pumphouse.com
email: mail@pumphouse.com

FAIRBANKS
CONVENTION & VISITORS BUREAU

For your free 80-page Visitors Guide on Fairbanks and Interior Alaska contact
1-800-327-5774
www.explorefairbanks.com

Come by our Log Cabin Visitors Center for last-minute information.

Pick up your Alaska Highway Certificate.

550 First Ave. Fairbanks, AK 99701
(907) 456-5774
Open Daily in Summer

Fairbanks is the gateway to your authentic Alaskan adventure. Come be energized in summer's land of midnight sun. See award-winning exhibits on Alaska's cultural and natural history. Shop for exquisite Alaska Native crafts, both Athabascan and Eskimo. Celebrate our Fairbanks Centennial. Be enthralled by winter's unsurpassed display of northern lights. Go mushing with a dog team on a wooded trail. View the artistry of larger than life-sized ice sculptures. From our riverfront location, a tour transports you to the edge of the Last Frontier, Denali and the Arctic wilderness.

Camping

There are several private campgrounds in the Fairbanks area (see ads this section).

The only state campground in town is Chena River State Recreation Site, located on University Avenue by the Chena River Bridge. The Chena River SRS has 57 sites, tables, firepits, toilets, water and a dump station. The campground is operated seasonally by a contractor; fees and services subject to change. Phone the State Parks office at (907) 451-2695 for more information.

There is overnight camping at the Pioneer Park (formerly Alaskaland) parking lot for self-contained RVs only with a 4-night limit; $12 fee includes use of borough dump station on 2nd Avenue.

Public campgrounds are also located on Chena Hot Springs Road (see log this section.). ▲

Chena Marina RV Park guests speak: "Best little RV Park in Alaska."—Travel consultant. "Best restrooms in 10,000 miles."— New Zealand guest. "RV having fun yet? Yes, thanks to folks like you."—RVing women. Mile 3.1 Chena Pump Road, watch for signs. (907) 479-4653, 1145 Shypoke Dr., Fairbanks, AK 99709. See map in display ad for directions. Open April 15–Sept. 15 (dates approximate). [ADVERTISEMENT] ▲

River's Edge RV Park. Located in the Heart of Fairbanks! 15-acre wooded landscaped riverfront park. 180 sites. Full and partial hookups. Free showers, laundry, car wash, gift shop. Free local tour shuttles. Specialists in historical city tour, Point Barrow and Arctic Circle. Featuring "Chena's Fine Dining and Deck" serving Alaska's best fresh salmon and halibut. [ADVERTISEMENT] ▲

Riverview RV Park is one of the top-rated RV parks in Alaska. It is situated on 20 acres adjoining the beautiful Chena River. Total atmosphere and only 10 minutes from downtown Fairbanks. Cable TV and mail forwarding service. Call Riverview RV Park (888) 488-6392 or (907) 488-6281. Telephones and email. See display ad. [ADVERTISEMENT] ▲

Transportation

Air: Several international, interstate and intra-Alaska carriers serve Fairbanks International Airport, accessible via the West Airport Way exit off the Parks Highway (Alaska Route 3).

Fairbanks' Aurora Borealis monument is located on the road leaving Fairbanks International Airport. The *Solar Borealis* sculpture is faced with material which disperses sunlight into a rainbow of colors as you drive by.

Air charter services are available in Fairbanks for flightseeing; fly-in fishing, hunting and hiking, and trips to bush villages; see ads this section.

Railroad: Alaska Railroad passenger depot at 280 N. Cushman St. in the downtown area. Daily passenger service in summer between Fairbanks and Anchorage with stop-overs at Denali National Park; less frequent service in winter. For details, phone (800) 544-0552; www.alaskarailroad.com.

Train to Denali (Gray Line of Alaska). Ride the luxurious private-domed railcars of the *McKinley Explorer* to Denali National Park from either Anchorage or Fairbanks. Overnight packages in Denali with round-trip train service are available from $425 for 3 days/2 nights, ppdo. Pre-overnight in either Anchorage or Fairbanks is included. Prices subject to change. Call Gray Line of Alaska at (907) 451-6835 for train and package tour

Circle Hot Springs Resort
A Uniquely Alaskan Experience

Located a short 129 miles beyond the city of Fairbanks, Circle Hot Springs Resort will provide you with a uniquely Alaskan experience. You'll thrill at the scenic high country along the Steese Highway and be rewarded at the end of the journey as you soak in the mineral waters flowing from the mountain.

"Of all our Alaskan Adventures, this was the Best of the Best . . . and it's worth going out of the way to visit."

**Jerry Griswold
Los Angeles Times**

- Special Period Rooms
- Dining Facilities
- Private Guest Cabins
- Central's Oldest Saloon
- Olympic-sized Swimming Pool
- RV Parking (w/elec. hook-up)
- Hillside Campsites
- Complete Bathing Facilities
- Fishing & Flightseeing Trips
- 3,600' Lighted Airstrip

For More Information **Call (907) 520-5113**
Fax (907) 520-5116
or write to:
Circle Hot Springs Resort
Box 30069, Central Alaska 99730

AAAA CARE BED & BREAKFAST

Military Families Welcome on "TLA"

- Privacy of a hotel
- Hospitality of an Alaskan Log Home

Spacious rooms with private and shared baths, private living room, kitchen with beautiful decks for your personal use.
Privacy locks in each room.
Enjoy northern lights viewing. Conveniently located near airport, train depot and UAF.
OPEN YEAR ROUND

Your hosts Pat Obrist and Family
1-800-478-2705
(907) 479-2447 • Fax (907) 479-2484
557 Fairbanks Street (off Geist Rd.)
Fairbanks, Alaska 99709
e-mail: pat@aaaacare.com
www.aaaacare.com
Credit Cards Accepted

Private guest home available

A N'ICE Bed 'n Breakfast

Experience Real Alaskan Hospitality
Peaceful wooded setting
Near University & Chena River
Gourmet Breakfast, Open Year-Round

(907) 479-6054

4627 Stanford Dr., Fairbanks, AK 99709
e-mail: nicebnb@mosquitonet.com
web page: www.mosquitonet.com/~nicebnb

Check us out — Fairbanks Super 8 Motel

24-Hour Coffee – Guest Laundry
Near Alaskaland & Restaurants
Also visit Anchorage, Juneau & Ketchikan

1909 Airport Way – Fairbanks, AK 99701
907.451.8888, Fax 907.451.6690 1-800-800-8000 — www.super8.com

Fairbanks first appeared in the 1910 U.S. Census with a population of 3,541.

The Georgeson Botanical Gardens at the university attract summertime visitors.
(© Lynne Ledbetter)

options. [ADVERTISEMENT]

Bus: Local daily bus service is provided by the Metropolitan Area Commuter System (MACS). MACS service is available from Fairbanks to the University of Alaska, North Pole, Hamilton Acres, Davis Road and the International Airport daily Monday through Saturday (limited scheduled on Saturdays); no service on Sundays and 6 major holidays. Drivers do not carry change so exact change or tokens must be used. Fares: $1.50 or 1 token for adults; grade K-12, senior citizens or disabled, 75 cents. All-day passes are $3, purchased from the drivers. Tokens are available at Transit Park, UAF Wood Center, Fred Meyer West and North Pole Plaza. Information is available via the Transit Hotline at (907) 459-1011 or from MACS office at 3175 Peger Road, phone (907) 459-1002 or on the internet at www.co.fairbanks.ak.us/transportation. (See also Bus Lines in the TRAVEL PLANNING section.)

Tours: Local and area sightseeing tours are available from several companies; see ads in this section.

Taxi: More than 15 cab companies.

Car and Camper Rentals: Several companies rent cars, campers and trailers; see ads in this section.

Attractions

Get Acquainted: A good place to start is the Fairbanks Log Cabin Visitor Information Center at 550 1st Ave., where you'll find free brochures, maps and tips on what to see and how to get there. Phone (907) 456-5774 or 1-800-327-5774. For a recording of current daily events phone (907) 456-4636, email info@explorefairbanks.com or go to

Pike's Waterfront Lodge

On the Chena River
in Fairbanks, Alaska
(open year-round)

King and Queen size beds available

Comfortable lobby and lounge areas

info@pikeslodge.com **1-877-774-2400** www.pikeslodge.com

Memorial to Interior Alaska veterans on Cushman Street near 8th Avenue.
(© Kris Graef, staff)

UNIVERSITY OF ALASKA MUSEUM

"The Alaska tourist should start here"
Bob & Elsa Pendleton, Texas

Open Year-Round on the UAF campus

May 15 – September 15
9 am – 7 pm Daily

September 16 – May 14
9 am – 5 pm Weekdays
Noon – 5 pm Weekends

24-hour information
907.474.7505
www.uaf.edu/museum
Admission charged

Discover fascinating stories about **Alaska's people, places and wildlife**

See Alaska's largest public display of **gold**.

Meet **Blue Babe**, the world's only restored Ice Age steppe bison mummy.

Summer Programs
Enjoy daily lectures and presentations on the northern lights, bears, wolves and Alaska Native art and culture.

Listen to the Museum **Audio Guide** to bring Alaska alive with sound.

Shop for fine gifts, books and Native art in the **Museum Store**.

Voted "Best Museum in Alaska" in 2001

Come discover the finest tour in Fairbanks

View up-close the wondrous muskoxen, caribou, and reindeer that call the research station home. Learn about the natural history and biology of these unique arctic mammals. Tours available June thru September, call 907.474.7207 for more information. Gift shop available—including unique handmade qiviut items!

LARGE ANIMAL RESEARCH STATION
www.uaf.edu/lars

---

www.explorefairbanks.com.

Next to the Visitor Information Center log cabin is **Golden Heart Park**, site of the 18-foot bronze monument, "Unknown First Family." The statue, by sculptor Malcolm Alexander, and park were dedicated in July 1986 to celebrate Fairbanks' history and heritage.

Fairbanks has a number of public parks that make good stops for a picnic. **Graehl Park** has a boat launch and is a good place to watch river traffic.

Unless otherwise posted, pet owners may run their dogs in Fairbanks borough and city parks as long as the animals are on leashes and under control at all times. Owners are responsible also for cleaning up after their pets. A fenced park area where dogs can run freely is located at 27th and Rickert streets at the Allridge complex. The Fairbanks Borough Parks & Recreation office at (907) 459-1070 can provide directions and more information.

The Alaska Public Lands Information Center, located in the lower level of historic Courthouse Square on the corner of 3rd Avenue and Cushman Street, offers free information and trip planning assistance on recreational opportunities in the state. The center also offers films, interpretive programs, lectures, a book shop and free brochures and pamphlets on natural history, cultural artifacts and public lands in Alaska. The center is open 7 days a week in summer, 9 A.M. to 6 P.M.; Tuesday through Saturday in winter, 10 A.M. to 6 P.M. Phone (907) 456-0527. Web site: www.nps.gov/aplic.

Fairbanks Summer Arts Festival. July 13-27, 2003. "A Unique Festival in a Unique Setting" is the way many people describe this multi-discipline study-performance Festival in the Land of the Midnight Sun! Between 70-75 guest artists offer workshops and master classes in music, dance, theatre, opera theatre, figure skating and the visual arts. There are performance opportunities in orchestra, jazz band and choral groups as well as cabaret and jazz singing. UAF dorm housing available. (907) 474-8869, festival @ptialaska.net, www.fsaf.org.

The University of Alaska Museum is a "must-stop" for Fairbanks visitors. Located on the West Ridge of the UAF campus, the museum features cultural and natural history displays from Alaska's 5 geographical regions. The 5 galleries explore Alaska's history, Native culture, art, natural phenomena, wildlife, birds, geology and prehistoric past. Highlights include a 36,000-year-old Steppe bison mummy, the state's largest gold display, the trans-Alaska pipeline story, a special section on the northern lights and a new 80-minute audio guide which brings Alaska alive with whale calls, a Yup'ik language lesson and radio news reports from the Exxon Valdez oil spill. The museum grounds hold sculptures, totem poles, a Russian blockhouse and a nature trail with signs identifying local vegetation.

During summer, the museum offers presentations on wolves, bears, the northern lights and Alaska Native art and culture.

Construction on the museum's expansion will be under way in summer 2003. All work will be on the new wing, so the museum's galleries will remain open throughout the year, and summer visitor programs will continue with only minor adjustments. The grand opening for the expanded museum is planned for fall 2005. To find out more, visit www.uaf.edu/

museum/expand.

Museum hours: May 15–September 15: 9 A.M.–7 P.M. daily; September 16–May 14, 9 A.M.–5 P.M. Monday–Friday; noon to 5 P.M. Saturday–Sunday. Museum admission fees: adults, $5; seniors, $4.50; youth (7-17), $3; children under 6, free. Group rates are also available. For 24-hour information, call (907) 474-7505, or check our web site: www.uaf.edu/museum.

Tour the University of Alaska Fairbanks. Situated on a 2,250-acre ridge overlooking Fairbanks and the Alaska Range, UAF has the best view in town! With all the amenities of a small town, including a fire station, post office, radio and TV stations, medical clinic and a concert hall, it boasts a world-class faculty and a unique blend of students from around the world.

UAF is a Land, Sea and Space Grant Institution. It serves 170 communities statewide through distance delivery of instruction, public service and research activities. With an enrollment of over 8,000 students each year, it is America's only arctic university as well as an international arctic research center, playing center stage for researching global climate change and arctic phenomena.

A popular stop with visitors is the **Georgeson Botanical Garden.** These colorful gardens, open to the public free of charge, display many varieties of flowers and the gift shop and kiosk at the site offer information on horticulture in northern climes. A family fun day with outdoor and environmental education is scheduled for July 13, 2003, from noon to 3 P.M. at the botanical garden.

UAF offers special tours and programs from June through August. Free guided walking tours of campus are offered Monday through Friday at 10 A.M. Tours begin at the UA Museum and last about 2 hours. Several other summer tours are available, including a rocket range, international arctic research center and supercomputing center. Public tours of the university's Large Animal Research Station were suspended in 2001 but have now been resumed, and visitors can tour the station on Thursdays at 1:30 P.M. Call (907) 474-7581 or (907) 474-7207 for information on any tour; or visit www.uaf.edu/univrel/Tour. Guided tours of campus for prospective students can be arranged throughout the year by calling the Office of Admissions, (907) 474-7500 or (800) 478-1823.

Celebrate Summer Solstice: Fairbanks has several unique summer celebrations associated with summer solstice in June, when residents celebrate the longest day of the year (summer solstice is June 21). The Midnight Sun Baseball Game will be played at 10:30 P.M. on June 21, 2003, without artificial lights. For details, phone (907) 451-0095. The Midnight Sun 10K Fun Run on June 21, 2003; phone (907) 452-6046 for further information.

There are also many other races throughout the summer, including the Equinox Marathon on July 20, 2003. This trail run features views of Mount McKinley from the top of Ester Dome. The course is open for 10 hours, and runners and walkers of all abilities are invited to participate. Racers can run the entire marathon or participate in the 3-person "marathon relay." For more information, call (907) 452-8351, email runner49@ptialaska.net or visit www.active.com.

The World Eskimo and Indian

Visit Alaska's largest operating gold mine

Gold was first discovered here in 1901 and Fairbanks has been mining it ever since. Today you can visit an operating gold mine just 25 scenic miles north of Fairbanks. Watch modern-day gold miners as they work on a scale never imagined by the early prospectors.

Mine

Driving one of our 150-ton haul trucks would be like driving a 2-story house from a second story window. Every afternoon we blast new areas for removal.

Grind

Watch as the largest gold mill in North America grinds 40,000 tons of ore each day to extract the gold.

Pour

Over 1200 ounces of 90% pure gold is poured each day at over 2100°F.

Smile

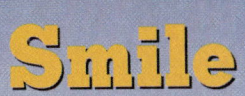

Every visitor has an opportunity to hold a real gold bar. Have your picture taken, no one will believe you!

FORT KNOX
Fairbanks Gold Mining, Inc.
Kinross Gold Corp.

Morning and afternoon tours by reservation only. For reservations call **(907) 488-GOLD, ext. 2800**
Tour includes walking and stairs. Dress comfortably.

PO Box 73726, Fairbanks, AK 99707
tours@fairbanksgold.com

FAIRBANKS

ATTRACTIONS & ENTERTAINMENT

CHENA Hot Springs

Finest year-round resort in Alaska!
Relax in the natural healing waters of pool, hot tubs or lake
440 acres of beautiful wilderness

Hiking, biking, fishing, rafting, massage, canoeing, horseback riding, flightseeing, x-c skiing, snow machining, ATVs, dog sled rides, sleigh rides, indoor golf

60 scenic miles from Fairbanks!

Reservations
(800) 478-4681
Locally call (907) 451-8104

chenahs@polarnet.com
www.chenahotsprings.com

GOLF in The Midnight Sun!
NORTH STAR GOLF CLUB
Fairbanks, Alaska

America's Northernmost 18 hole USGA course
$49 Visitor Special - everything you need plus logo ball, golf towel & certificate!
Cafe, proshop and unique gifts with logo.
North Star Golf Club 330 Golf Club Drive
907-457-4653   www.northstargolf.com

Olympics, with Native competition in such events as the high kick, greased pole walk, stick pull, fish cutting, parka contest and muktuk-eating contest will be held July 17-20, 2003. Phone (907) 452-6646.

Golden Days, when Fairbanksans turn out in turn-of-the-century dress and celebrate the gold rush, is July 16–20, 2003. Golden Days starts off with a Felix Pedro look-alike taking his gold to the bank and includes a parade and rededication of the Pedro Monument honoring the man who started it all when he discovered gold in the Tanana Hills. Other events include pancake breakfasts, a dance, canoe and raft races, and free outdoor concerts. For additional information, phone (907) 452-1105.

The Tanana Valley State Fair will be held Aug. 1–9, 2003. Alaska's oldest state fair, the Tanana Valley State Fair features agricultural exhibits, arts and crafts, food booths, a rodeo and other entertainment. Phone (907) 452-3750 for more information. Check with the Fairbanks Log Cabin Visitor Information Center for more information on all local events.

Besides these special events, summer visitors can take in a semipro baseball game at Growden Park where the Alaska Goldpanners take on other Alaska league teams.

Take a Day Trip to Chena Lakes Recreation Area, Eielson AFB and North Pole (50 miles round trip). Drive 17.3 miles southeast of Fairbanks on the Richardson Highway to the turnoff for Chena Lakes Recreation Area. Operated by the Fairbanks North Star Borough, this recreation area is built around the Chena Flood Project constructed by the Army Corps of Engineers.

PIONEER PARK

Spend a little time in the past

Alaska's only Pioneer Theme Park

• RV Parking • Gold Rush Town •
• Museums • Big Stampede Theater •
• Crooked Creek & Whiskey Island Railroad •
• Salmon Bake • Gold Panning •
• Picnic Areas • Art Gallery •
• Shops & Concessions •
• Sternwheeler Nenana •
• Folk Dancing • Harding Railroad Car •
• Mini-Golf • Canoe & Bike Rental •

Formerly Alaskaland

Free Park Admission

Airport Way & Peger
www.co.fairbanks.ak.us • (907) 459-1087

Drive 5.5 miles from the highway on the main road along Moose Creek Dike to the visitor kiosk below the dam site. You can also bike out to the dam on the 5-mile-long Moose Creek Dam Bikeway. From the Main Road, turn on Lake Park Road for 250-acre Chena Lakes. There's a swimming beach, play area, picnic tables, fishing dock and boat ramp. Chena Lakes Bike Trail begins at Chena Lakes swim beach and intersects with the Moose Creek Dam Bikeway. A per vehicle day-use fee is charged between Memorial Day and Labor Day.

Eielson Air Force Base, 26 miles southeast of Fairbanks on the Richardson Highway, offers free guided tours of the base 10:30 A.M. to noon every Friday between Memorial Day and Labor Day. The 90-minute tour briefly recalls the history of the base before turning to the current mission of the units assigned here. The tour includes a stop at the Lady of the Lake—an abandoned WB-29 airframe—and concludes with a photo stop at Heritage Park. The park features a 50 state flag display, an F-16 Fighting Falcon, an A-10 Thunderbolt II and an F-4 Phantom. Monuments at Heritage Park honor Carl Ben Eielson, Prisoners of War and MIAs, and Medal of Honor recipients. For more information, phone the 354th Fighter Wing public affairs office at (907) 377-2116.

On your way back to town, stop in North Pole to visit Santa Claus and get a head start on your Christmas shopping.

Visit a Gold Mine. Interested in gold mining and the gold rush? Head out the Steese Expressway to visit any of the 4 commercial gold mining/gold panning operations in the area. At **Milepost F 8.5** Steese Highway is **Gold Rush Gold Camp**, an operating underground gold mine offering tours and gold panning. Just past there, at **Milepost F 9.5**, turn on Goldstream Road to see the historic **Gold Dredge No. 8**, a 5-deck, 250-foot dredge built in 1928. Tours of the dredge and gold panning are available.

Continue up the Steese Expressway another 1.5 miles to its intersection with the Elliott Highway (Alaska Route 2) at Fox. Go straight through this intersection for 1.2

Miniature golf is a popular attraction at Pioneer Park. (© Kris Graef, staff)

PIONEER AIR MUSEUM
Pioneer Park

Rare Antique Aircraft & Stories of their Pilots
Displays from 1913 to present
Open Memorial Day - Labor Day
11 a.m. - 9 p.m. 7 days a week
P.O. Box 70437
Fairbanks, Alaska 99707-0437
(907) 451-0037
Internet http://www.akpub.com/akttt/aviat.html

Visit the museums at the university and Pioneer Park.

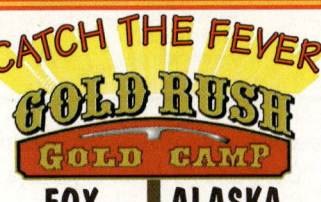

OPEN DAILY 7 AM 1 MAY TO 30 SEPT.

CATCH THE FEVER — GOLD RUSH GOLD CAMP — FOX, ALASKA

COME EARLY & PAN ALL DAY
7AM - 8PM

GOLD PANNING $12.00

TOUR INCLUDES GOLD PANNING $18.00

You are invited to
EXPERIENCE THE EXCITEMENT OF ALASKA GOLD MINING

Gold Rush Gold Camp is an operating underground **permafrost gold mine**. The actual mining is done only when the temperature is below 25° F (-4° C). During the summer months we run the dirt through a sluice box to wash out all the gold.

We shouldn't have all the fun.
NOW IT'S YOUR TURN.
What is permafrost?
What is a sluice box?
Can I go underground?
For the answers to these questions and more...
We look forward to seeing you.

Visit the Workshop and Watch First Hand as Professional Goldsmiths Create Unique Jewelry Designs Using Natural Alaskan Gold Nuggets.

1731 New Steese Highway
Fox, AK 99712
(907) 452-GOLD (4653)
Fax (907) 452-4617
goldrushgoldcamp.net

Hard hats are required during tours of Fort Knox, Alaska's largest working gold mine. (© Lynn Owen, staff)

miles on the Elliott Highway to reach the **El Dorado Gold Mine**, a commercial gold mine operation offering tours and gold panning.

Return to the intersection at Fox, turn up the Steese Highway (Alaska Route 6), and drive 10.5 miles to the scenic viewpoint at Cleary Summit (on a clear day there are excellent views of the Tanana Valley and Mount McKinley to the south and the White Mountains to the north.) Fairbanks Creek Road leads east from the summit to **Fort Knox Gold Mine**, Alaska's largest operating gold mine. Gold was first discovered here in 1901, and today, visitors can take hard-hat tours of this working gold mine, the largest in Alaska. Daily tours are by reservation only and offer visits to the excavation area where travelers can see the heavy equipment in action, the crusher and the gift shop, which features Fort Knox gold. The tour also includes a walking tour of the largest gold processing mill in North America and a chance to hold a real Fort Knox gold bar. Admission is charged. Visitors to the area can also see Fort Knox's restoration project, an 85-acre created wetland that will serve as a recreation area when completed. For reservations and more information, call (907) 488-GOLD, ext. 2800, or email tours@fairbanksgold.com.

After these stops, you can either return to Fairbanks to make this an easy 50-mile round trip, or extend your drive 100 miles to see a piece of gold mining history. From Cleary Summit/Fort Knox, drive out the Steese Highway another 37 miles to the **Davidson Ditch Historical Site** at Milepost F 57.3. This large pipe was built in 1925 by the Fairbanks Exploration Co. to carry water to float gold dredges. The 83-mile-long ditch begins at **Milepost F 44** Steese Highway and ends at Fox. If you are feeling adventurous, U.S. Creek Road (steep, gravel) winds up and over the hills from the Davidson Ditch site 7 miles to Nome Creek Gold Panning Area in the White Mountains National Recreation Area.

See the STEESE HIGHWAY section beginning on page 482 for more details.

See the Pipeline. For a good look at the trans-Alaska pipeline, and a taste of the Dalton Highway, consider this long day trip. Drive out the Steese Expressway from Fairbanks, stopping first at the Trans-Alaska Pipeline Viewpoint just outside Fairbanks at **Milepost F 8.4**. You can walk along a portion of the pipeline and see a real "pig"—a device used to collect data and clean the pipeline walls. Excellent opportunity for pipeline photos. Alyeska Pipeline Service Co. visitor center at the site is open daily from May to September. Free literature and information; phone (907) 450-5873.

Drive north a few more miles to the end of the Steese Expressway and then continue north on the Elliott Highway 73 miles to the

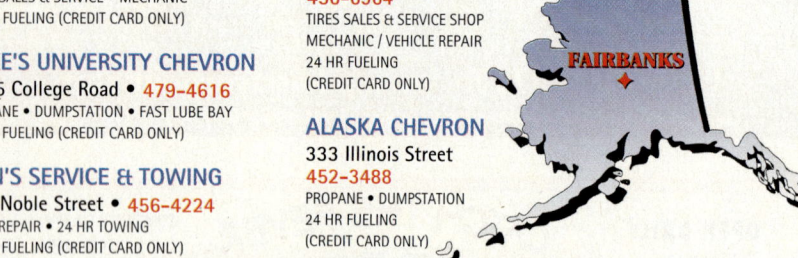

CHEVRON WELCOMES YOU TO INTERIOR ALASKA!

TOTEM CHEVRON
768 Gaffney Road • 456-4606
TIRES SALES & SERVICE • MECHANIC
24 HR FUELING (CREDIT CARD ONLY)

MIKE'S UNIVERSITY CHEVRON
3245 College Road • 479-4616
PROPANE • DUMPSTATION • FAST LUBE BAY
24 HR FUELING (CREDIT CARD ONLY)

RON'S SERVICE & TOWING
101 Noble Street • 456-4224
AUTO REPAIR • 24 HR TOWING
24 HR FUELING (CREDIT CARD ONLY)

GOLDPANNER SERVICE
809 Cushman Street
456-6964
TIRES SALES & SERVICE SHOP
MECHANIC / VEHICLE REPAIR
24 HR FUELING (CREDIT CARD ONLY)

ALASKA CHEVRON
333 Illinois Street
452-3488
PROPANE • DUMPSTATION
24 HR FUELING (CREDIT CARD ONLY)

"Largest In Interior Alaska"

RV SERVICE CENTER

- Factory Trained Technicians
- Parts & Accessory Showroom
- Servicing All Makes & Models
- Complete Body Shop
- Quick Service "While You Wait"

Factory Authorized Dealer for
ITASCA/WINNEBEGO/FLEETWOOD

249 Alta Way off S. Cushman, Fairbanks
(907) 452-4279

FAIRBANKS RV CENTER — Complete RV Parts & Service

ARCTIC TIRE
3200 S. Peger Rd.

✶ **MOTORHOME SERVICE** ✶
TIRES • ALIGNMENT
SHOCKS • BRAKES
BATTERIES

907/456-8622
1-888-319-0889

junction with the Dalton Highway. The Elliott Highway is paved to the Dalton Highway junction. Turn off onto the Dalton Highway and drive 55.6 miles north to the Yukon River bridge. The pipeline parallels the route much of the way, although there is no public access, so you'll get good views but no close-ups until you reach the BLM visitor center at Yukon River Crossing.

From the Yukon River Crossing it is another 60 miles to the **Arctic Circle BLM Wayside**, adding 120 miles to the already 280-mile trip. The Arctic Circle wayside has an interpretive display and picnic area, at N 66°33' W 150°48'. At this latitude, the sun does not set on summer solstice (June 20 or 21) and it does not rise on winter solstice (December 21 or 22).

See the ELLIOTT HIGHWAY section and the DALTON HIGHWAY section for more details on this trip.

Take a Day Trip to Chena Hot Springs (125 miles round trip). Drive north about 5 miles from Fairbanks via the Steese Expressway and exit west on Chena Hot Springs Road. This good all-weather paved road leads 57 miles east to Chena Hot Springs, a private resort (open daily year-round) offering an indoor hot springs pool, ATV rentals, trail rides and other activities.

Chena Hot Springs Road passes through the middle of Chena River State Recreation Area, a year-round recreation area with many places to stop and fish, picnic, camp and hike. See "Chena Hot Springs Road" on pages 446-447 for a detailed road log.

Tanana Valley Farmers Market. Visit Alaska's premier Farmers Market, located next to the Fairgrounds on College Road, open from mid-May to mid-September. Vendors offer a wide selection of locally grown vegetables; Alaskan meats, fish, honey, jams and syrups; made-in-Alaska handcrafts and baked goods; blue-ribbon florals; and lunch food vendors. Market hours are Wednesday 11 A.M. to 4 P.M. and Saturdays 9 A.M. to 4 P.M.; there's plenty of parking. Stop by the Market and enjoy Alaska made and grown products. "Meet You At the Market!" [ADVERTISEMENT]

The Alaska Rag Co. A must-see for Fairbanks travelers. This unique Alaskan gift shop manufactures beautiful handwoven rag rugs from 100 percent recycled clothing. The store also features works from 50-plus Alaskan artists. Items include jewelry, pottery, mittens, Polar fleece, jams and syrups, native dolls, cards and much more. Downtown Fairbanks at 603 Lacey Street. Phone (907) 451-4401. (Part of a non-profit vocational program) [ADVERTISEMENT]

Visit Historic Churches: St. Matthew's Episcopal Church, 1029 1st Ave., was originally built in 1904, but burned in 1947 and was rebuilt the following year. Of special interest is the church's intricately carved altar, made in 1906 of Interior Alaska birch and saved from the fire, and the church's 12

UNIVERSITY AVENUE CAR AND TRUCK WASH

Corner of University Avenue and Cameron

Large Bays for Motor Homes, Trailers and Big Trucks with catwalks to reach all areas.

OPEN 24 HOURS

ARCTIC RV Certified RV Technicians

The **ONLY** RV Parts & Accessories Showroom in Fairbanks

- DUO-THERM
- NORCOLD
- GENERAC
- SUBURBAN
- DOMETIC
- ATWOOD

SERVICE AND REPAIR AT A PRICE THAT'S FAIR.

(907) 451-8356 • www.arcticrv.com
3013 Peger Rd. • Fairbanks, AK 99709

Seattle 2,313
Great Falls 2,353

IF EVER THERE WAS A TIME

After driving the Highway, you'll want to make us your first stop in Fairbanks. We'll do everything from changing your oil to topping off most vital fluids – all in a matter of minutes.

We service motor homes.

jiffy lube®

54 College Rd.
(directly in front of Sam's Club)
456-8559

1780 Peger Rd.
(directly across from DMV)
479-5655

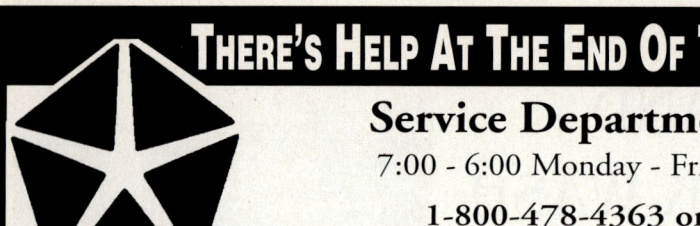

There's Help At The End Of The Road
Service Department
7:00 - 6:00 Monday - Friday
1-800-478-4363 or (907) 452-7117

GENE'S
• CHRYSLER • PLYMOUTH • DODGE
• DODGE TRUCK • JEEP

3400 CUSHMAN, FAIRBANKS, ALASKA 99701

GABE'S 24 HOUR TOWING
OVER 22 YEARS EXPERIENCE • LOCALLY OWNED AND OPERATED

TRUCK & AUTO REPAIR (907) 456-6156

YOUR ONE STOP CENTER FOR ALL YOUR REPAIR NEEDS!
CAR, TRUCKS AND RV'S!
COMPLETE REPAIR SERVICE • RECREATIONAL VEHICLES
DAMAGE FREE WHEEL LIFT
* LARGEST AUTO REPAIR FACILITY IN THE INTERIOR *

stained glass windows, 9 of which trace the historical events of the church and Fairbanks. **Immaculate Conception Church**, on the Chena River at Cushman Street bridge, was drawn by horses to its present location in the winter of 1911 from its original site at 1st Avenue and Dunkel Street.

Alaskan Tails of the Trail is a personal home visit with musher/author Mary Shields and her family of happy huskies. Learn about the dogs, wilderness travel, long-distance racing (Mary was the first woman to finish the Iditarod), and mushing in Siberia. Relax in Mary's sunny cabin. Her books and video are available. Phone (907) 455-6469; www.maryshields.com. [ADVERTISEMENT]

Take A River Cruise. Fairbanks is situated on the Chena River, near its confluence with the Tanana River, and several local businesses offer scenic river cruises.

The **Riverboat *Discovery*** departs daily at 8:45 A.M. and 2 P.M. in summer on a half-day cruise on the Chena and Tanana rivers. This is a popular cruise and reservations are required. The boat stops at Old Chena Indian Village, where passengers disembark for a tour with guides of Indian or Eskimo heritage, who explain past and present Native culture. For more information on the riverboat *Discovery*, contact Alaska Riverways, Inc., 1975 Discovery Dr., Fairbanks, AK 99709; phone (907) 479-6673, toll free 1-866-479-6673, fax (907) 479-4613. To reach the dock, drive out Airport Road, turn south at Dale Road and continue 0.5 mile on Dale to Discovery Drive.

Greatland River Tours. Join us aboard the sternwheeler *Tanana Chief* for a delicious Prime Rib dinner cruise while you take in the

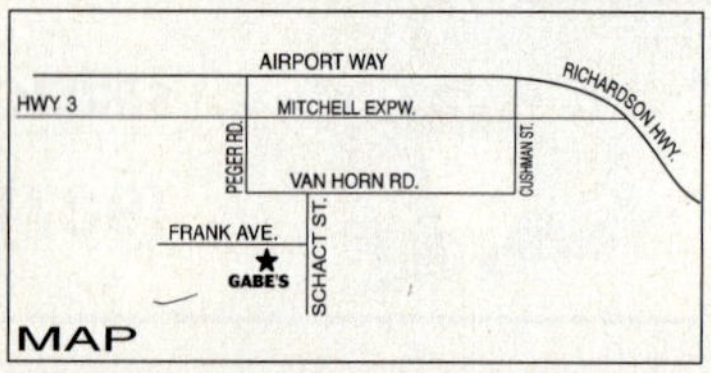

SOURDOUGH FUEL, FOODMARTS AND TEXACO WELCOME YOU TO ALASKA!

Look for the "Star of the American Road" all along your trip. It's your guarantee of quality fuel and service.

Sourdough fuel 456-7798

Locally Owned & Operated

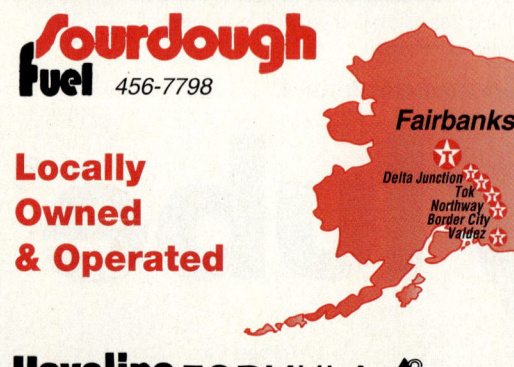

Havoline FORMULA 3 MOTOR OIL

FAIRBANKS
Farmer's Loop Market
Corner of Steese Hwy. & Farmer's Loop
• Great Meal Deals • 24 HR Food Mart
• Deli • Liquor • Propane Easy Exchange
• Gas & Diesel • Fleet One • ATM
(907) 457-4663

Airport Way Texaco
Airport & Lathrop
• Great Meal Deals • 24 HR Food Mart
• Propane Easy Exchange • Gas • Espresso
• Water • Dump Station
• Fleet One • ATM
(907) 452-2379

South Cushman Texaco
South of Airport Way on Cushman
• Always Low Fuel Prices
• Gas • Diesel • Propane Easy Exchange
• Delicious Snacks • Espresso
• 24 HR Pay at the Pump
• Fleet One • Water
(907) 452-8839

DELTA JUNCTION
Delta Texaco
1600 Richardson Hwy.
• Gas • Diesel • Propane
• Tire Service • Dump Station
• Food Mart • 24 HR Card Lock
(907) 895-4067

Everyday Great Taste And Value

Always Low Fuel Prices

Slalom race on the Chena River in downtown Fairbanks. (© Bob Butterfield)

Hilltop Truckstop

5.5 mile Elliot Hwy.
15 minutes from Fairbanks
Open Year Round
(907) 389-7600

24 Hour Gas
Diesel
Restaurant
ATM
Groceries
Ice
Propane
Discount Liquor
Phone
Showers
Ice Cream
Homemade Pie

Voted "Best Breakfast in Fairbanks- 2001"
by the UAF Sun Star Newspaper

sights along the historic Chena River. Departing nightly at 6:45 P.M. We are located where the Parks Highway crosses the Chena River. Phone (907) 452-8687 or toll free (866) 452-8687 for reservations. [ADVERTISEMENT]

Pike's Riverboat Cruise. Enjoy Fairbanks hospitality on the *Sam McGee* as Captain Jim Dunlap welcomes you aboard as you cruise the Chena and Tanana Rivers. It's a 31-passenger side paddle wheeler built for the Chena; you can watch historic Fairbanks drift by in our saloon or on the deck. Relaxing day and

Affordable NEW CAR RENTAL

STARTING AT
$33.95 per day
unlimited miles

- Courtesy Pick Up
- Vans, SUVs, Cars
- All Major Credit Cards Accepted

One Way Rentals to Anchorage

3101 S. Cushman; Fairbanks, Alaska 99701 **(907) 452-7341**
1-800-471-3101 SEE ALASKA THE AFFORDABLE WAY!

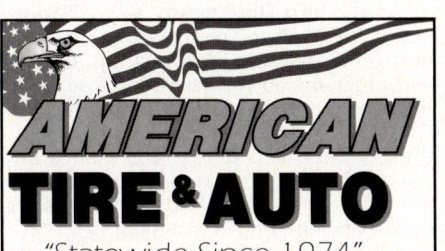

AMERICAN TIRE & AUTO
"Statewide Since 1974"

WE FEATURE
GOODYEAR - COOPER
BRIDGESTONE • MICHELIN
AMERICAN RACING WHEELS

AUTO SERVICE CENTERS
Brakes • Shocks • Alignment
Motorhome Servicing

219 3rd Ave. • FAIRBANKS
(907) 452-5145

832 E. 4th Ave. • ANCHORAGE
(907) 276-7878

7835 Old Seward Hwy. • ANCHORAGE
(907) 336-7878

THE BEST DEAL IN FAIRBANKS

Rental Vehicles
as low as $35.00 a day
Depending on availability

AURORA RENTALS
PONTIAC • BUICK • GMC • KIA

Corner of Johansen Expressway & Danby Street
www.auroramotors.com

Unlimited Miles
1-800-849-7033
1-907-459-7033
Fax: 1-907-459-7043

Golf enthusiasts play through at the 9-hole North Star Golf Club. (© Kris Graef, staff)

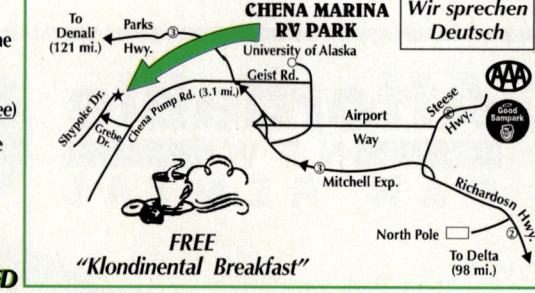

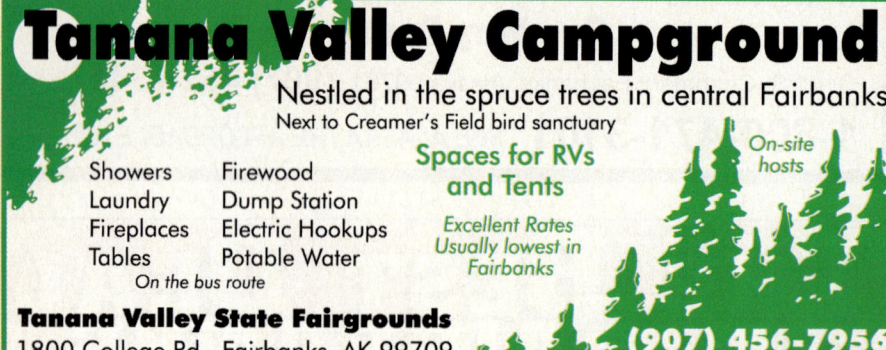

evening cruises from May to September; 1 877-750-4737 or (907) 457-BOAT or www.pikesriverboat.com. [ADVERTISEMENT]

Ride Bikes. Pick up a "Bikeways" map for Fairbanks and vicinity at the visitor center. The city is developing an extensive network of bike trails (multi-use paths). Best choices for day touring around Fairbanks include the bike trail from Pioneer Park to 1st Avenue downtown, and Airport Way/Boat Street west to Chena Pump Road or Geist Road. Farmer's Loop Road also has a bike trail.

Bicycle rentals and group tours are available from Pioneer Park in the summer and from the Fairbanks Hotel and Pike's Riverfront Lodge year-round. Rates and hours vary. For more information or for reservations, call (907) 457-BIKE (2453), or visit www.akbike.com.

Watch Birds. Follow the flocks of waterfowl to Creamer's Field Migratory Waterfowl Refuge. Located 1 mile from downtown Fairbanks, this 1,800-acre refuge managed by the Alaska Dept. of Fish and Game offers opportunities to observe large concentrations of ducks, swans, geese, shorebirds, cranes and other birds and wildlife in the spring and fall. Throughout the summer, thousands of sandhill cranes eat in the planted barley fields.

Explore the 2-mile self-guided nature trail and the renovated historic farmhouse that serves as a visitor center. Stop at 1300 College Road to find the trailhead, viewing areas and brochures on Creamer's Field. For more information, phone (907) 452-5162, or visit www.state.ak.us/adfg/wildlife/region3/refuge3/creamers.htm.

Creamer's Field Migratory Waterfowl Refuge—where nature is at its best. Summer visitor center hours, 10 A.M. to 5 P.M. Daily guided walks begin at Farmhouse Visitor Center, Tuesday and Thursday at 7 P.M.; Wednesday and Saturday at 9 A.M. Sandhill Crane Festival Aug. 23–Aug. 30, 2003. The refuge is always open and free of charge. Phone (907) 452-5162; www.creamersfield.org. [ADVERTISEMENT]

Alaska Bird Observatory at Wedgewood Resort (off College Road). Visit their education center featuring information, displays and programs on Alaska's birds. The center includes a nature store and trailhead to Creamer's Refuge. Bird-banding demonstrations at Creamer's Refuge and guided bird walks offered from May–September. Phone (907) 451-7159; email birds@alaskabird.org; www.alaskabird.org. [ADVERTISEMENT]

Visit Pioneer Park. Visitors will find a relaxed atmosphere at Pioneer Park, formerly known as Alaskaland. It makes a pleasant stop for visitors, especially those with children, with its historic buildings, small shops, food, entertainment, playgrounds and picnicking. The park—which has no admission fee—is open year-round, although most attractions within the park are open only from Memorial Day to Labor Day.

To drive to Pioneer Park (at Airport Way and Peger Road), take Airport Way to Wilbur, turn north onto Wilbur, then immediately west onto access road, which leads to Pioneer Park.

The 44-acre historic park was created in 1967 as the Alaska Centennial Park to commemorate the 100th anniversary of U.S. territorial status and provide a taste of Alaska history. Visitors may begin their visit at the information center, located just inside the park's main gate. Walk through Gold Rush Town, a narrow, winding street of authentic

old buildings that once graced downtown Fairbanks and now house gift shops. Here you will find the Kitty Hensley and Judge Wickersham houses, furnished with turn-of-the-century items; the First Presbyterian Church, constructed in 1904; and the Pioneers of Alaska Museum, dedicated to those who braved frontier life to establish Fairbanks. Free guided historical walking tours take place daily in summer.

The park is home to the renovated SS *Nenana*, a national landmark. The *Nenana* is the largest stern-wheeler ever built west of the Mississippi, and the second largest wooden vessel in existence. Also on display is a 300-foot diorama of life along the Tanana and Yukon rivers in the early 1900s.

The top level of the Alaska Centennial Center for the Arts houses an art gallery featuring rotating contemporary exhibits and paintings; open 11 A.M. to 9 P.M. daily, Memorial Day through Labor Day; noon to 8 P.M. daily, except Monday, during the rest of the year.

The Pioneer Air Museum, located behind the Alaska Centennial Center for the Arts, displays aircraft in Alaska from 1913 to 1948. Admission is charged.

At the rear of the park is Mining Valley, with displays of gold mining equipment. The popular Alaska Salmon Bake, with both outdoor and heated indoor seating areas, is also part of Mining Valley. The Alaska Salmon Bake is open daily for dinner, 5–9 P.M., from late May to mid-September. Salmon, barbecued ribs, halibut and porterhouse steaks are served, rain or shine.

The show season at Pioneer Park runs from mid-May through mid-September. The Palace Theatre & Saloon features the musical comedy review, "Golden Heart Revue," about life in Fairbanks. Performances daily at 8:15 P.M., with added shows at 6:30 P.M. depending on demand.

The Big Stampede show in Gold Rush Town is a theater in the round, presenting the paintings of Rusty Heurlin, depicting the trail of '98; narrative by Ruben Gaines.

The Crooked Creek & Whiskey Island Railroad, a narrow-gauge train, takes passengers for a 12-minute ride around the park. Admission fees: adults $2, children $1, seniors over 60, handicapped and children under 4 are free.

Fairbanks Summer Music Festival, June 14, 2003, is also held at Pioneer Park on the stage. The day-long festival features free live music provided by dozens of Alaska artists. Music of all types, including Folk, Bluegrass, Blues, Jazz and Celtic. For more information, call (907) 488-0556, or visit www.alaskafolkmusic.org.

Other recreational activities available at Pioneer Park include miniature golf, an antique carousel and picnicking in covered shelters. A public dock is located on the Chena River at the rear of the park, and visitors can rent canoes, kayaks and bicycles at Alaska Outdoor Rentals located near the boat dock..

Visitors are welcome to take part in square and round dances year-round at the Pioneer Park Dance Center. Phone (907) 452-5699 evenings for calendar of events. For more information about Pioneer Park, phone (907) 459-1087.

Ester Gold Camp. A raucous mining camp in 1906, with a population of some 5,000 miners, Ester today is a much quieter community just 7 miles west of Fairbanks. Ester's heydays are relived in music, song and dance at the Malemute Saloon, a popular stop with tourists in summer and always a good family show. The Northern Lights

first is the **World Ice Art Championships**, scheduled for March 5–16, 2003. This event hosts an international field of artists who come to carve art from ice. And not just any ice. The ice—harvested from a pond in Fairbanks—has been called "the purest ice in the world," so clear you can read through it. The competitors begin with blocks of ice up to 30 feet high, weighing almost 3,500 lbs. Their creations in past championships have ranged from life-sized reindeer and dragons to jousting knights on horseback and airplanes. Once completed, the colossal sculptures are exhibited at Ice Park and may be viewed during the day or at night, when each work is illuminated.

The second big winter event bringing visitors to Fairbanks is the opportunity to experience the **aurora borealis** or northern lights, described as "one of the most beautiful natural events that can be observed by man." The best time to see the northern lights is August 20 to September 20 and February to April during the new moon. In Fairbanks, the aurora is seen on at least 8 out of 10 clear, dark nights. Regular forecasts of auroral activity over Alaska are available on the Internet from the Geophysical Institute at UAF: go to www.gi.alaska.edu.

The third major winter attraction in Fairbanks is **sled dog racing**. The Alaska Dog Mushers' Assoc. (ADMA) hosts a series of sprint dog races from December to March, ending with the Open North American Championship (March 14–16, 2003), a 3-day event with 3 heats (of 20, 20 and 30 miles). The "Open" is considered by many to be the "granddaddy of dog races." It is the longest running sled dog race in the world (in terms of years). The ADMA has a Mushers Hall at 4 mile Farmers Loop Road where people can see dog teams train and race in the winter. For more information, visit

Alaska's Most Northern Stained Glass Store
Come visit our showroom!
• Gifts & handmade items
• Alaska patterns & supplies
M-F 10-6
Sat. 11-5

EXPRESSIONS in GLASS
3550 Airport Way, Suite 5 • 907-474-3923
Fairbanks, Alaska 99701

Snow Goose Fibers & Quilting Company
1875 South University Ave., Fairbanks, Alaska 99709

This is the quilting store you've been looking for, all the way up the Alaskan Highway!

Largest Selection of 100% Cotton Fabrics in the Interior. Alaskan patterns, Quilt Kits, Uniquely Alaskan Fabric, gifts and notions for the quilter! www.snogoose.com

Easy Access Off The Parks Highway on South University Ave. • **(907) 474-8118**

Dinner and Sightseeing Cruises departing daily on the
Sternwheeler Tanana Chief
1-866-452-TOUR (8687)
Local Phone: (907)452-8687
Fax: (907)455-8687
www.greatlandrivertours.com
Greatland River Tours 1020 Hoselton Rd., Fairbanks, AK 99709

ARCTIC CIRCLE AIR ADVENTURE®

Experience Alaska's Arctic By Air!

Fly north from Fairbanks and wonder at the story of the vast and remote land below as the flight traverses past and present goldfields, the remarkable Trans Alaska Pipeline, and the mighty Yukon River.

Thrill at the excitement of crossing the Arctic Circle. Experience the rugged and magnificent Brooks Mountain Range as the flight route passes just south of the Gates of the Arctic National Park.

Participate in a ceremonious Arctic Circle landing at a Brooks Range wilderness community along the Middle Fork Koyukuk River. Receive an official Arctic Circle Adventure Certificate.

Enjoy the long daylight hours of the Midnight Sun on the return flight to Fairbanks.

NORTHERN ALASKA TOUR COMPANY
1-800-474-1986, 907-474-8600 Fax 907-474-4767
PO Box 82991-MF, Fairbanks, AK 99708
www.northernalaska.com
adventure@northernalaska.com

Sled dog racing is Alaska's official state sport.

PRUDHOE BAY ADVENTURE™

A three day guided round trip journey to the shores of the Arctic Ocean.
Experience the breathtaking beauty and solitude of Alaska's Arctic, one of the world's last great wilderness regions •Travel the famed Dalton Highway •View the remarkable Trans Alaska Pipeline •Visit the Arctic Circle Trading Post •Experience the mighty Yukon River •Cross the Arctic Circle in ceremonious fashion •Overnight at rustic Coldfoot •Visit historic Wiseman •Pass through the majestic Brooks Mountain Range •Walk on the spongy arctic tundra of the vast Arctic Coastal Plain •Overnight at Prudhoe Bay •Tour Prudhoe Bay, site of North America's largest oil discovery •Complete your northward journey by dipping your toe in the frigid Arctic Ocean •Extend your journey with an optional overnight in the Inupiat Eskimo village of Barrow •Tour the community and participate in a cultural program •For further adventure continue your journey along the Arctic Coast to Kotzebue & Nome.

NORTHERN ALASKA TOUR COMPANY
1-800-474-1986, 907-474-8600 Fax 907-474-4767
www.northernalaska.com adventure@northernalaska.com PO Box 82991-MF, Fairbanks, AK 99708

FAIRBANKS

Amazing sculptures are carved at the World Ice Art Championships at Ice Park.
(© Laurent Dick)

www.sleddog.org.

Fairbanks also hosts the 1,000-mile Yukon Quest Sled Dog Race (distance race) between Fairbanks and Whitehorse, YT, with the start alternating between Fairbanks and Whitehorse each year. The 2003 race starts in Whitehorse on February 9. For more information, contact the Yukon Quest office at (907) 452-7954; www.yukonquest.com.

The area also hosts several races for junior mushers, including the Junior Yukon Quest for mushers age 14–17. This 120-mile run from Fairbanks to Twin Bears Camp and back is held one week prior to the Yukon Quest.

For lovers of mechanized dogs, the Tesoro Iron Dog, the world's longest snow machine race (2,000 miles), starts in Fairbanks on February 9, 2003, continues to Nome and ends in Wasilla. For more information, phone (907) 563-4414; irondog@ptialaska.net; www.irondog.org.

BARROW ADVENTURE™

Fly north across the Arctic Circle to the Inupiat Eskimo village of Barrow • Discover firsthand the lifestyles of Alaska's Arctic Coastal peoples with a tour of the village • Meet the Inupiat Eskimo people while enjoying a cultural program featuring ceremonial song and dance, traditional games, and demonstration of local crafts • Walk the shores of the Arctic Ocean near the northernmost point on the North American Continent • One day and overnight excursions available year-round.

NORTHERN ALASKA TOUR COMPANY
1-800-474-1986, 907-474-8600 Fax 907-474-4767
www.northernalaska.com adventure@northernalaska.com PO Box 82991-MF, Fairbanks, AK 99708

Warbelow's Air Ventures, Inc.

A UNIQUE ALASKAN EXPERIENCE
• Fly Bush Mail Routes - Above the Arctic Circle •
• Land at Rural Villages, accessible only by airplane •
• 14 Daily Departures •
• Guided Village Tours Available •

ARCTIC CIRCLE CERTIFICATES
www.warbelows.com
3758 University Avenue
East Ramp Fairbanks Int'l Airport
Fairbanks, AK 99709
(907) 474-0518 • (800) 478-0812
E-Mail: tours@warbelows.com

FLYING to ALASKA?

MILITARY OPERATION AREA SPECIAL USE AIRSPACE INFORMATION SERVICE (SUAIS)

IMPORTANT INFORMATION ON MILITARY AIRCRAFT OPERATIONS IN ALASKA FOR ALL PILOTS, RESIDENTS, AND VISITORS

DEPARTMENT OF THE AIR FORCE
11TH AIR FORCE
ELMENDORF AFB, ALASKA
1-800-758-8723
http://www.elmendorf.af.mil (Airspace & Ranges)

LARRY'S FLYING SERVICE
Fairbanks, Alaska
"Air Service to Alaska's Bush"

FLY BEYOND THE ARCTIC CIRCLE

- Fly an Alaskan Mail Route
- View the Alaskan Pipeline
- Tours to Fort Yukon
- Visit Anaktuvuk Pass
- View Mt. McKinley

Arctic Circle Certificates & Patches
**Scheduled Air Service
Call For Reservations**

SCHEDULED EVENING ARCTIC FLIGHTS

Phone: (907) 474-9169 Fax: 474-8815
Write: P.O. Box 72348, Fairbanks, AK 99707
E-Mail: larrys@larrysflying.com
www.larrysflying.com

TANANA Air Service

Scheduled or Charter Flights
Arctic Circle Flights
Flights Down The Yukon
Sightseeing At It's Best

MONDAY THRU FRIDAY
Ph. (907) 474-0301 • Fax (907) 474-9311
e-mail: tanana@polarnet.com
Fairbanks International - East Ramp
3730 S. UNIVERSITY AVE.

VISA / MasterCard

Some folks are satisfied to sit and wait for a bus... Some folks aren't.

800-770-7275

Some folks want to see Alaska at their pace, within their budget, away from crowds.

We understand. We're Alaskan.

See Alaska on your own.

Let us arrange your first class accommodations, interesting attractions, wildlife viewing, photo opportunities, & transportation at your pace, in your style, without the crowds, within your budget.

First Alaskan
Central Reservations
Let us design an Alaskan Adventure that is right for you.

KOTZEBUE NOME ADVENTURE

Experience Inupiat Eskimo culture above the Arctic Circle at the Chukchi Sea village of Kotzebue • Participate in a village tour highlighted by a cultural program at the Museum of the Arctic featuring demonstrations of Inupiat dance, song, and traditional skills • Enjoy a fascinating visit to the unique Culture Camp where village elders teach ancestral heritage to Kotzebue's youth • At Nome, relive the excitement of the Gold Rush • Pan for gold and keep what you find • Enjoy a dogsled demonstration on the famed Iditarod Trail • Excursions range from one to three days.

NORTHERN ALASKA TOUR COMPANY
1-800-474-1986, 907-474-8600 Fax 907-474-4767
PO Box 82991-MF, Fairbanks, AK 99708
www.northernalaska.com   adventure@northernalaska.com

ARCTIC CIRCLE ADVENTURE

Arctic Circle DRIVE
A one day guided round trip journey by land across the Arctic Circle.

Travel the famed Dalton Highway and view the remarkable Trans Alaska Pipeline.

Visit the Arctic Circle Trading Post situated in the rural community of Joy, Alaska.

Experience the mighty Yukon River.

Walk out on the amazing arctic tundra and feel the frozen ground beneath the surface.

Cross the Arctic Circle and receive an official Arctic Circle Adventure Certificate. Enjoy an evening riverside picnic meal on your return journey to Fairbanks.

Arctic Circle FLY / DRIVE
The one day Arctic Circle Fly/Drive Adventure includes all the highlights of the Drive Adventure plus:

Fly north from Fairbanks across the Arctic Circle and receive an aerial view of the vast Alaska wilderness.

Experience the mighty Yukon River. Enjoy a meal on your own on the banks of the Yukon River. Marvel at the majestic beauty of the northland's most famous waterway and learn of the river's storied past.

Travel the famed Dalton Highway under the Midnight Sun on the return journey to Fairbanks.

For further adventure extend your journey with an optional overnight stay in the Brooks Mountain Range.

Arctic Circle NATIVE CULTURE
The one day Arctic Circle Native Culture Adventure includes all the highlights of the Fly/Drive Adventure plus:

Fly the wilderness airways of the rugged and magnificent Brooks Mountain Range.

Visit the Nunamiut Eskimo village of Anaktuvuk Pass nestled in the pristine and scenic Gates of the Arctic National Park. Learn of the local Nunamiut culture and history.

The return flight to Fairbanks provides an aerial view of the vast Alaska wilderness.

NORTHERN ALASKA TOUR COMPANY
Sharing Alaska's Arctic With The World
1-800-474-1986, 907-474-8600 Fax 907-474-4767
PO Box 82991-MF, Fairbanks, AK 99708
www.northernalaska.com   adventure@northernalaska.com

FLY-IN FISHING

Starting at $150.00 each

MARINA AIR, INC.
Chena Marina Airport & Floatpond

Boat & Motor, Cabin or Tent Camp Provided

1195 Shypoke / Fairbanks, Alaska 99709 / Phone (907) 479-5684
http://www.akpikefishing.com

The aurora borealis, or northern lights, are most active from late August to late September and February to April.

FAIRBANKS — **TOURS & TRANSPORTATION**

RICHARDSON HIGHWAY

	Delta Jct.	Fairbanks	Glennallen	Paxson	Valdez
Delta Jct.		96	151	80	270
Fairbanks	96		247	177	366
Glennallen	151	247		71	119
Paxson	80	177	71		190
Valdez	270	366	119	190	

Connects: Valdez to Fairbanks, AK **Length:** 366 miles
Road Surface: Paved **Season:** Open all year
Highest Summit: Isabel Pass 3,280 feet
Major Attractions: Trans-Alaska Pipeline, Worthington Glacier
(See maps, pages 453–454)

A side-car motorcycle travels through scenic Thompson Pass northeast of Valdez.
(© Rich Reid, Colors of Nature)

The Richardson Highway extends 366 miles from Valdez on Prince William Sound to Fairbanks in the Interior of Alaska. The Richardson is a wide paved highway in good condition. It is also a scenic route, offering magnificent views of the Chugach Mountains and Alaska Range.

The Richardson Highway (Alaska Route 4) junctions with 7 other highways: the Edgerton Highway (Alaska Route 10) at **Milepost V 82.6**; the Glenn Highway (Alaska Route 1) at **Milepost V 115** at Glennallen; the Tok Cut-Off (Alaska Route 1) at **Milepost V 128.6** Gakona Junction; the Denali Highway (Alaska Route 8) at **Milepost V 185.5** at Paxson; the Alaska Highway (Alaska Route 2) at **Milepost V 266**, Delta Junction (where the Richardson Highway becomes Alaska Route 2 between Delta Junction and Fairbanks); and with the Parks Highway (Alaska Route 3) and the Steese Expressway/Steese Highway (Alaska Route 2/6) at its end in Fairbanks.

In Valdez, the Richardson Highway junctions with the Alaska Marine Highway's Southcentral ferry system. Ferry service to Cordova and Whittier is available from Valdez; see the ALASKA STATE FERRY SCHEDULES section.

The Richardson Highway also offers good views of the trans-Alaska pipeline. The trans-Alaska pipeline carries oil 800 miles from Prudhoe Bay on the Arctic Ocean to the pipeline terminus at Port Valdez. There are formal viewing points with interpretive signs at **Milepost V 64.7** (Pump Station 12), **Milepost V 216** (Denali Fault), **Milepost V 243.5**, and the Tanana River Pipeline Crossing at **Milepost V 275.4**.

The Richardson Highway was Alaska's first road, known to gold seekers in 1898 as the Valdez to Eagle trail. Gold stampeders started up the trail again in 1902, this time headed for Fairbanks, site of a big gold strike. The Valdez to Fairbanks trail became an important route to the Interior, and in 1910 the trail was upgraded to a wagon road under the direction of Gen. Wilds P. Richardson, first president of the Alaska Road Commission. The ARC updated the road to automobile standards in the 1920s. The Richardson Highway was hard-surfaced in 1957.

Although logged from south to north in this section, the Richardson is a popular corridor for southbound travelers from Anchorage and Fairbanks, headed either for the Copper River dip-net fishery near Chitina, or for the fishing at Valdez.

The Richardson Highway passes many fine salmon streams, such as the Gulkana and Klutina rivers, as well as other productive lakes and streams. Check the "Copper Basin Roadside Fishing Guide," available from Alaska Dept. of Fish and Game offices, for details. On the Internet, check weekly sport fishing updates for the Interior region (either Upper Copper/Upper Susitna Area or Arctic/Yukon management areas for the Richardson Highway) at www.sf.adfg.state.ak.us/statewide/html/sf_home.htm.

Emergency medical services: Phone 911 anywhere along the highway.

Richardson Highway Log

Distance from New Valdez (NV) is followed by distance from Old Valdez (OV).

Mileposts on the Richardson Highway were erected before the 1964 Good Friday earthquake and therefore begin 4 miles from present-day downtown Valdez near the Old Valdez townsite (destroyed during the earthquake).

ALASKA ROUTE 4

NV 0 OV 4 Intersection of Meals Avenue and the Richardson Highway.

NV 0.4 OV 3.6 Paved double-ended turnout to north with Valdez information kiosk, maps, brochures, pay phones.

NV 0.5 OV 3.5 DOT/PF district office.

Distance marker northbound indicates Glennallen 117 miles, Anchorage 306 miles, Fairbanks 355 miles.

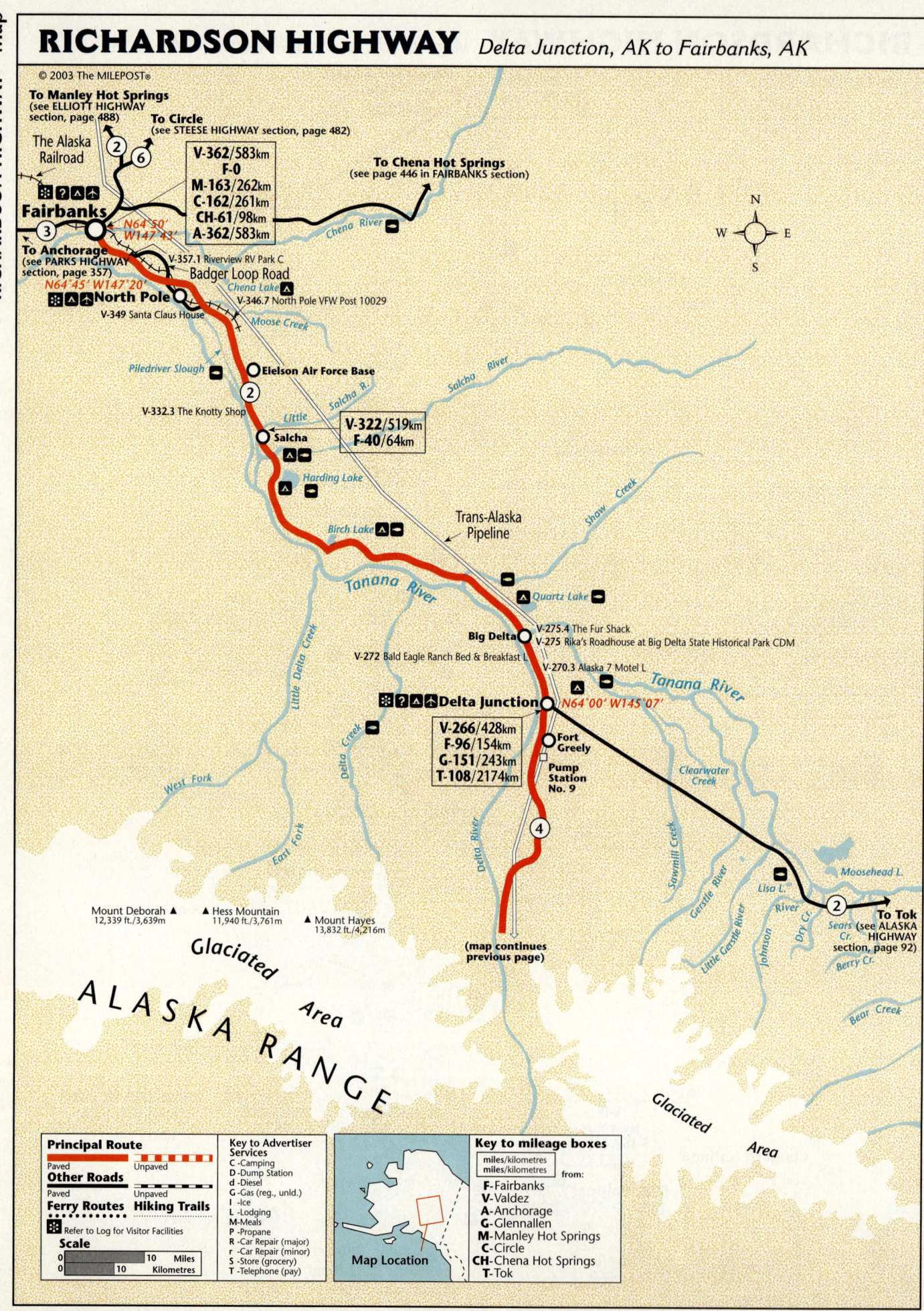

NV 0.6 OV 3.4 Valdez highway maintenance station.

NV 0.9 OV 3.1 Double-ended turnout to north at **Crooked Creek Salmon Spawning Viewing Area**. Viewing platform offers close-up look at spawning pink and chum salmon from mid-June to early September. Or for an underwater view of the fish, take a look at the Fish Cam inside the U.S. Forest Service information station. The information station, open Memorial Day to Labor Day, has informational exhibits and educational handouts.

Across the highway from the viewing area are intertidal wetlands known locally as "Duck Flats." Watch for migrating waterfowl here from late April to mid-May and in October. Nesting birds in summer. This is a game sanctuary; no shooting is allowed. Good spot for photos.

NV 1.7 OV 2.3 Paved turnout to south.

NV 2.1 OV 1.9 Mineral Creek Loop Road; access to Port of Valdez container terminal.

NV 3.4 OV 0.6 Junction with Airport Road; gas station, deli, market, liquor store and laundromat at intersection. Turn off to north for **Valdez Airport** (0.9 mile), Valdez Glacier campground (2.3 miles; see description below) and **Valdez Glacier** (3.9 miles; drive to end of pavement and take left fork). Parking area next to glacial moraine; good views of the glacier area are *not* available from this spot, nor is Valdez Glacier a very spectacular glacier.

Valdez Glacier Campground has 101 sites in wooded area with tables and grills, $10 camping fee, day-use area, tent camping, covered picnic area, litter barrels, water, toilets and fireplaces; 15-day limit, camping fee. *CAUTION: Beware of bears.*

NV 4 OV 0 Milepost 0 of the Richardson Highway (log continues).

Turnoff to south for **Original Valdez Townsite**; watch for memorial on your right, 0.4 mile south on side road. There are 2 plaques set in a foundation from "old" Valdez. One plaque lists the names of those residents of Valdez and Chenega who were killed in the Good Friday Earthquake on March 27, 1964, which destroyed the original townsite of Valdez. Also along here are Gold Rush Centennial signs about the stampeders, their perilous climb over Valdez Glacier, and the camp founded by gold stampeders in 1897 that became Valdez.

Side road continues (watch for deep ruts) to waterfront and views of pipeline marine terminal.

Distance from Old Valdez (V) is followed by distance from Fairbanks (F).

Physical mileposts begin northbound showing distance from Old Valdez. (Southbound travelers note: Physical mileposts end here; it is 4 miles to downtown Valdez.)

V 0 F 362 Milepost 0 of the Richardson Highway at access road to Original Valdez Townsite (see description at **Milepost NV 4**).

V 0.9 F 361.1 Valdez Glacier stream. The highway passes over the terminal moraine of the Valdez Glacier, bridging several channels and streams flowing from the melting ice.

V 1.4 F 360.6 Valdez Sportsmans Trap Club.

V 1.5 F 360.5 City of Valdez Goldfields Softball Complex.

V 2.9 F 359.1 Turnoff to south just west of weigh station for Dayville Road. This 5.7-mile paved road provides access to Solomon Gulch fish hatchery, camping and fishing at **Allison Point** (pink and silver salmon in season), and to **Alyeska Marine Terminal**, where supertankers load oil pumped from the North Slope facility via the trans-Alaska pipeline. *(NOTE: Public access to marine terminal by prearranged tour only.)*

At Mile 3.7 is Solomon Gulch Hydroelectric project (view of Solomon Gulch Falls) and **Solomon Gulch Hatchery**; visitor parking, self-guided tour. Trailhead for hike to Solomon Gulch is at Mile 4.7.

Signed day-use parking (fee charged) and overnight RV parking ($10 fee) located from approximately Mile 4.3 to Mile 5.3. Entrance to the pipeline marine terminal is at the end of the road at Mile 5.7. Bus tours of the terminal are available in Valdez; check with the visitor center there. A statue dedicated to the pipeline workers is located just outside the terminal entrance.

V 3 F 359 Weigh station.

V 3.4 F 358.6 Gravel road leads 0.5 mile north to floatplane base and Robe Lake Recreation Area (public welcome); sailing, jet skis. *Watch for bears!*

V 4.7 F 357.3 Turnout to east. Access to **Robe River**; Dolly Varden, red salmon (fly-fishing only, mid-May to mid-June).

V 9.7 F 352.3 Fire station.

V 11.6 F 350.4 Gravel turnout to southeast.

V 11.9 F 350.1 Turnoff to northwest on 0.8-mile loop road for access to Pack Trail of 1899. Follow narrow paved road 0.4 mile to trailhead; parking nearby.

V 12.8 F 349.2 Lowe River emerges from **Keystone Canyon**. The canyon was named by Captain William Ralph Abercrombie, presumably for Pennsylvania, the Keystone State. In 1884, Abercrombie had been selected to lead an exploring expedition up the Copper River to the Yukon River. Although unsuccessful in his attempt to ascend the Copper River, he did survey the Copper River Delta and a route to Port Valdez. He returned in 1898 and again in 1899, carrying out further explorations of the area (see **Milepost V 13.7**). The Lowe River is named for Lt. Percival Lowe, a member of his expedition. Glacier melt imparts the slate-gray color to the river.

V 13.4 F 348.6 Horsetail Falls; large paved turnout to west.

CAUTION: Watch for pedestrians.

V 13.8 F 348.2 Large paved turnout to west across from **Bridal Veil Falls**. Gold Rush Centennial interpretive sign at turnout.

This is also the trailhead for the **Valdez Goat Trail**; scenic overlook 1/4 mile, trail end 2 miles. This is a restored section of the Trans-Alaska Military Packtrain Trail through Keystone Canyon that led to the first glacier-free land route from Valdez to the Interior. The first gold rush trail led over the treacherous Valdez Glacier, then northeast to Eagle and the Yukon River route to the Klondike goldfields. Captain W.R. Abercrombie and the U.S. Army Copper River Exploring Expedition of 1899 rerouted the trail through Keystone Canyon and over Thompson Pass, thus avoiding the glacier. As the Klondike Gold Rush waned, the military kept the trail open to connect Fort Liscum in Valdez with Fort Egbert in Eagle. In 1903, the U.S. Army Signal Corps laid the trans-Alaska telegraph line along this route.

V 14.9 F 347.1 Lowe River Bridge No. 1 (first of 3 bridges northbound); turnout to east at north end of bridge. View of Huddleston Falls.

Bridal Veil Falls is a popular photo stop along Keystone Canyon.
(© Rich Reid, Colors of Nature)

V 15 F 347 Large paved turnout at **Old Railroad Tunnel** with sign that reads: "This tunnel was hand cut into the solid rock of Keystone Canyon and is all that is left of the railroad era when 9 companies fought to take advantage of the short route from the coast to the copper country. However, a feud interrupted progress. A gun battle was fought and the tunnel was never finished. *The Iron Trail* by Rex Beach describes these events and this area."

V 15.2 F 347.8 Turnout to east at south end of Lowe River Bridge No. 2. Horse and Sled Trail (sign) reads: "On the far side, just above the water, are the remains of the old sled trail used in the early days. It was cut out of the rock, just wide enough for 2 horses abreast. 200 feet above can be seen the old goat trail. This road was used until 1945."

V 15.4 F 346.6 Lowe River Bridge No. 2, built in 1980, replaced previous highway route through the long tunnel visible beside highway.

V 15.6 F 346.4 Informal gravel turnout to east.

V 15.9 F 346.1 Leaving Keystone Canyon northbound, entering Keystone Canyon southbound.

V 16 F 346 Turnout at rock quarry to east.

V 16.2 F 345.8 Avalanche gun emplacement; Alyeska pipeline acccess road.

V 16.3 F 345.7 Lowe River Bridge No. 3.

V 16.4 F 345.6 Rafting outfitter for Keystone Canyon river trips located here.

V 18.1 F 343.9 Large paved turnouts both sides of highway; *emergency phone* and trailhead at turnout to west. Good stop for northbound travelers before heading up the pass.

V 18.7 F 343.3 Sheep Creek bridge.

Truck lane begins northbound as highway climbs next 7.5 miles to Thompson Pass; few turnouts, steep grade. Snow poles along highway guide snow plows in winter.

This was one of the most difficult sec-

Worthington Glacier's accessibility makes this state recreation site a "must" stop.
(© Ernest Manewal)

tions of pipeline construction, requiring heavy blasting of solid rock for several miles. The pipeline runs underground beside the road.

V 23.6 F 338.4 Loop road past Thompson Lake to Blueberry Lake and state recreation site; see **Milepost V 24.1**.

V 24.1 F 337.9 Loop road to **Blueberry Lake State Recreation Site**; drive in 1 mile. Tucked into an alpine setting between tall mountain peaks, this is one of Alaska's most beautifully situated campgrounds; 10 campsites, 4 covered picnic tables, toilets, firepits and water. Camping fee $12/night or resident pass. ▲

Blueberry Lake and **Thompson Lake** (formerly Summit No. 1 Lake). Good grayling and rainbow fishing all summer.

V 24.4 F 337.6 Large paved turnout to west. Bare-bone peaks of the Chugach Mountains rise above the highway. Thompson Pass ahead; Marshall Pass is to the east.

During the winter of 1907, the A.J. Meals Co. freighted the 70-ton river steamer *Chitina* (or *Chittyna*) from Valdez over Marshall Pass and down the Tasnuna River to the Copper River. The ship was moved piece by piece on huge horse-drawn freight sleds and assembled at the mouth of the Tasnuna. The 110-foot-long ship navigated 170 miles of the Copper and Chitina rivers above Abercrombie Rapids, moving supplies for construction crews of the Copper River & Northwestern Railway. Much of the equipment for the Kennicott mill and tram was moved by this vessel.

V 25.5 F 336.5 Large paved turnout to west. Entering Game Management Unit 13D, leaving unit 6D, northbound.

V 25.7 F 336.3 Large paved turnout to west with view; Keystone Glacier to the south.

V 26 F 336 **Thompson Pass** (elev. 2,678 feet) at head of Ptarmigan Creek. Beautiful alpine area.

Truck lane ends northbound. Begin 7.5-mile steep descent southbound.

Thompson Pass, named by Captain Abercrombie in 1899, is comparatively low elevation but above timberline. Wildflower lovers will be well repaid for rambling over the rocks in this area: tiny alpine plants may be in bloom, such as Aleutian heather and mountain harebell.

The National Climatic Center credits snowfall extremes in Alaska to the Thompson Pass station, where record measurements are: 974.5 inches for season (1952–53); 298 inches for month (February 1953); and 62 inches for 24-hour period (December 1955). Snow poles along the highway mark the road edge for snow plows.

Private Aircraft: Thompson Pass airstrip; elev. 2,080 feet; length 2,500 feet; turf, gravel; unattended.

V 27 F 335 Thompson Pass highway maintenance station.

V 27.5 F 334.5 **Worthington Lake**; rainbow fishing.

V 27.7 F 334.3 Good viewpoint of 27 Mile Glacier.

V 28 F 334 Entering winter avalanche area southbound.

V 28.7 F 333.3 Paved turnout to west with interpretive signs at turnoff for **Worthington Glacier State Recreation Site**. Paved access road leads 0.4 mile up hill to large paved parking area (pull-through sites for large vehicles); shelter, viewing telescopes, interpretive displays, park host, restrooms. (Pay phone located near highway entrance.) No camping. Pets on leash.

According to state park rangers, this is the most visited site in the Copper River Basin. Views of Worthington Glacier, which heads on Girls Mountain (elev. 6,134 feet), from the parking area and from paved path which leads to glacier viewpoints with benches and interpretive signs. A National Natural Landmark, the glacier is also accessible for the more adventurous via the Ridge Trail (steep, primitive, difficult). *CAUTION: Walking on the glacier without proper equipment and training is dangerous because of crevasses.*

V 29 F 333 Paved parking area to west; good photo op of Worthington Glacier.

V 30.2 F 331.8 Large paved turnout. Excellent spot for photos of Worthington Glacier.

V 30.9 F 331.1 Avalanche gun emplacement.

V 32 F 330 Highway parallels Tsaina River northbound. Long climb up to Thompson Pass for southbound motorists; views of Worthington Glacier.

V 36.5 F 325.5 Pipeline runs under highway.

V 37 F 325 Entering BLM public lands northbound, leaving BLM public lands southbound.

V 37.3 F 324.7 Tsaina River bridge at scenic Devil's Elbow. Large paved turnout to east at south end of bridge.

V 39 F 323 Crest of hill; beautiful mountain views.

Highway descends next 1.7 miles northbound.

V 40.8 F 321.2 Large gravel turnout to west.

Highway climbs next 1.7 miles southbound.

V 42 F 320 Gravel turnout to west side. Spruce bark beetles have killed many of the trees in the forest here. View of waterbars (ridges on slope designed to slow runoff and control erosion).

V 43.3 F 318.7 Long double-ended turnout to west.

V 45 F 317 *Begin avalanche area southbound: Do not stop (in winter).*

V 45.6 F 316.4 Stuart Creek bridge.

V 45.8 F 316.2 Copper River Valley welcome sign. Watch for moose next 20 miles northbound.

V 46.9 F 315.1 **Tiekel River** bridge; small Dolly Varden. Small turnout to west at north end of bridge.

V 47.8 F 314.2 Views of Mount Billy Mitchell southbound. Large paved rest area to west in trees by Tiekel River; covered picnic sites, outhouses, no drinking water. Historical sign about **Mount Billy Mitchell**.

Lieutenant William "Billy" Mitchell was a member of the U.S. Army Signal Corps, which in 1903 was completing the trans-Alaska telegraph line (Washington–Alaska Military Cable and Telegraph System) to connect all the military posts in Alaska. The 2,000 miles/3,200 km of telegraph wire included the main line between Fort Egbert in Eagle and Fort Liscum at Valdez, and a branch line down the Tanana River to Fort Gibson and on to Fort St. Michael near the mouth of the Yukon and then to Nome. Mitchell was years later to become the "prophet of American military air power."

V 50.7 F 311.3 Bridge over Tiekel River. Dead spruce trees in this area were killed by beetles.

V 53.8 F 308.2 Squaw Creek culvert.

V 54.1 F 307.9 Large paved turnout to east. Look for lupine in June, dwarf fireweed along the Tiekel River in July.

V 54.5 F 307.5 Moose often seen here in the evenings.

CAUTION: Watch for moose.

V 55.1 F 306.9 Large paved turnout to east.

V 56 F 306 Tiekel River Lodge east side of highway; food, gas, lodging.

V 56.3 F 305.7 Large paved turnout to east alongside Tiekel River.

V 57 F 305 Old beaver lodge and dams in pond to east. Beaver may inhabit the same site for generations.

Tireless and skillful dam builders, beavers construct their houses in the pond created by the dam. Older beaver dams can reach 15 feet in height and may be hundreds of feet long. The largest rodent in North America, beavers range south from the Brooks Range. They eat a variety of vegetation, including aspen, willow, birch and poplar.

V 58.1 F 303.9 Wagon Point Creek culvert.

V 60 F 302 Large paved turnout to east. Highway parallels **Tiekel River**; fishing for small Dolly Varden.

V 62 F 300 Ernestine Station (DOT/PF highway maintenance) to west.

V 62.4 F 299.6 Boundary for Sport Fish Management areas. Entering Upper Susitna/Copper River Area N northbound, Prince William Sound southbound.

V 64.7 F 297.3 **Pump Station No. 12 Interpretive Viewpoint** to west, Pump Station 12 to east. Gravel drive leads west to parking area; short boardwalk trail to the viewpoint with interpretive signs about the station and the pipeline.

Begun in March 1975 and completed in 1977, pipeline construction employed some 30,000 workers at its peak and was the largest and most expensive privately funded construction project ever undertaken. These boom years, known as "pipeline days," also brought lasting changes to Alaska's landscape and economy.

Today, the pipeline is owned and operated by Alyeska Pipeline Service Company, a consortium of oil companies that includes BP, Phillips, Exxon/Mobil, Unocal, Williams and Amerada Hess.

The 48-inch-diameter pipeline winds through 3 major mountain ranges, with its highest point (4,739 feet) at Atigun Pass in the Brooks Range, 170 miles south of Prudhoe Bay. Along the Richardson Highway, the pipeline crests the Alaska Range at 3,420 foot at Isabel Pass, before descending into the Copper River basin. It crosses the Chugach Mountains at Thompson Pass and descends through the Keystone Canyon to Valdez, where it is fed by gravity into tanks or directly into waiting oil tankers at the marine terminal.

V 65 F 297 **Little Tonsina River**; fishing for Dolly Varden.

V 65.1 F 296.9 **Little Tonsina River State Recreation Site** to west on loop road; 10 campsites, firepits, water pump, litter barrels and toilets. Camping fee $10/night or resident pass. Dolly Varden fishing. Good berry picking in fall. *CAUTION: Beware of bears!*

V 71 F 291 Long double-ended paved turnout to east.

V 72 F 290 Double-ended paved turnout to west with view across valley of Trans-Alaska pipeline following base of mountains.

Leaving BLM public lands northbound, entering BLM public lands southbound.

V 74.4 F 287.6 Paved double-ended turnout to west.

V 78.6 F 283.4 Tonsina Controlled Use Area (sign); closed to vehicles and pack animals August and September.

V 79.2 F 282.8 Bridge over Tonsina River, which rises in Tonsina Lake to the southwest.

V 79.6 F 282.4 Bridge and **Squirrel Creek State Recreation Site**. Pleasant campsites on the bank of Squirrel Creek, some pull-through spaces; $10/ night or resident pass; dumpster, boat launch, water, outhouses and firepits. Fishing for rainbow and grayling at **Squirrel Creek Pit**.

V 79.7 F 282.3 Begin 1.3-mile truck lane northbound up Tonsina Hill. *CAUTION: Steep hill, watch for bumps; road can be slippery in winter.*

V 81 F 281 Gas station (diesel), coffee shop, gold nuggets.

CAUTION: Begin steep 8 percent downgrade southbound; watch for bumps.

V 82.6 F 279.4 Edgerton Highway junction.

Junction with the Edgerton Highway (Alaska Route 10) east to Chitina and McCarthy Road to McCarthy in Wrangell–St. Elias National Park and Preserve. See EDGERTON HIGHWAY section on page 470 for log of that route.

V 83 F 279 Paved turnout to west; public fishing access to **Pippin Lake**.

Highway descends hill next 3 miles northbound.

V 84.5 F 277.5 **The Knifeman** to west. See display ad this section.

V 87.7 F 274.3 Paved double-ended scenic viewpoint to east at **Willow Lake**. On a clear day this lake mirrors the Wrangell Mountains to the east, which lie within Wrangell–St. Elias National Park and Preserve. Gold Rush Centennial interpretive sign about copper mining on the Bonanza Ridge in the Wrangell Mountains.

V 88.5 F 273.5 APL pipeline access road leads west to **Pipeline Interpretive Viewpoint**, 1 of 3 Alyeska pipeline displays along the Richardson Highway. Gravel loop turnout; pedestrian access.

V 90.8 F 271.2 Large paved turnout to west by Willow Creek culvert; thick patches of diamond willow in woods off highway (and thick clouds of mosquitoes!).

V 100.2 F 261.8 South junction with Old Richardson Highway loop road through Copper Center; well worth a stop. Access to Klutina River charter services and food, gas and lodging in Copper Center.

See "Copper Center Loop" on page 458 for description of Copper Center and attractions along the Old Richardson Highway.

V 100.6 F 261.4 Gravel side road east to private RV park junctions with Old Richardson Highway. Also access to Klutina River charter service at Klutina River Bridge on Old Richardson Highway.

Grove's Klutina River King Salmon Charters. See display ad this section.

V 100.7 F 261.3 Klutina River bridges. Excellent fishing in the **Klutina River** for red (sockeye) and king (chinook) salmon. Also grayling and Dolly Varden. Kings to 50 lbs., average 30 lbs.; from June 15 to Aug. 10, peaking in mid-July. Reds' peak run is from late June to early August. Check current fishing regulations. *NOTE: Most riverfront property is privately owned. Inquire locally about river access.* Campgrounds and fishing charter services available in Copper Center.

Klutina Salmon Charters. See display ad this section.

V 101.5 F 260.5 Junction with Brenwick–Craig Road. Follow paved road 0.9 mile up hill to west for access to Copper River Princess Wilderness Lodge and Klutina Lake Road (descriptions follow). Turn east for 1.1-mile paved winding road through residential area that connects with the Old

---

The Knifeman
Alaska Handmade Knives - Hunting Knives, Fillet Knives, Ulu's— with Moose, Caribou, Sheep, and Fossil Ivory handles, Gold Nugget Jewelry.
Mile 84.5 Richardson Hwy. 1/4 mile West, on left, with RV turn around.
(907) 822-3938 ■ OPEN 8am - 10pm

GROVE'S KLUTINA RIVER KING SALMON CHARTERS
GREAT KING SALMON & RED SALMON FISHING
RV Parking • Electrical Hookups • Potable Water • Dump Station • Sleeping Rooms
LAUNDRY AND SHOWER FACILITIES FOR OUR GUESTS
Phone (907) 822-5822 • 1-800-770-5822 • Fax (907) 822-4028
website: www.alaskan.com/groves • e-mail: lgw@alaska.net
Mile 100.6 Old Richardson Highway (South Side of River)

FISHING FOOLS AND FIRST-TIMERS WELCOME

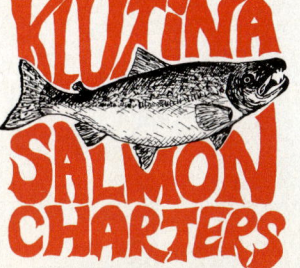

KLUTINA SALMON CHARTERS
GUIDED CHARTERS & CAMPGROUND

- U.S.C.G. Lic. Charters, Everything Furnished
- We'll Fillet, Freeze and Ship Your Catch
- Tackle: Rods, Reels, Licenses, Ice, Gifts
- RV Park: Electric Hookups, Water, Dump Station
- Alaska "Pot Luck" Friday, 7:30 p.m.

Call Shirleen May - Aug • Ph/Fax 907-822-3991
Aug - May Ph. 208-343-0277 • Fax 208-362-9635
email: shirleenB52@yahoo.com
OR
Captain Erick Nickell • Ph. 970-882-4023 Aug - May
nickell2@hubwest.com

Mile 101 Old Richardson (North side of Bridge)
P.O. Box 78, Copper Center, Alaska 99573
http://www.klutinacharters.com

Copper Center Loop

The Klutina River at Copper Center offers bountiful sockeye and king salmon fishing. (© Kris Graef, staff)

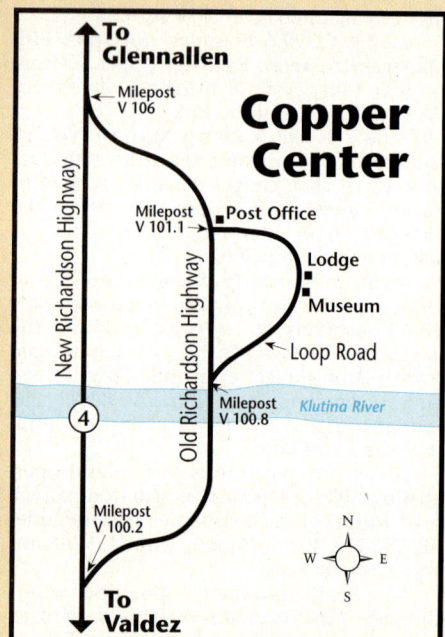

Copper Center

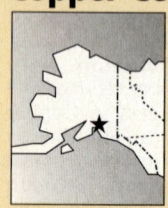

Located on the Old Richardson Highway; 105 miles north of Valdez via the Richardson Highway; 200 miles from Anchorage. **Population:** 362. **Emergency Services:** Phone 911. **Ambulance** in Glennallen, phone 911. **Elevation:** 1,000 feet.

Private Aircraft: Copper Center NR 2 airstrip, 1 S; elev. 1,150 feet; length 2,200 feet; gravel; unattended.

A historical marker at **Milepost V 101.9** Old Richardson Highway reads: "Founded in 1896 as a government agriculture experiment station, Copper Center was the first white settlement in this area. The Trail of '98 from Valdez over the glaciers came down from the mountains and joined here with the Eagle Trail to Forty Mile and Dawson. 300 miners, destitute and lonely, spent the winter here. Many suffered with scurvy and died. Soon after the turn of the century, the Washington–Alaska Military Cable and Telegraph System, known as WAMCATS, the forerunner of the Alaska communications system, operated telegraph service here between Valdez and Fairbanks."

A post office was established here in 1901, the same year as the telegraph station. Copper Center became the principal settlement and supply center in the Nelchina–Susitna region.

Lodging & Services

Facilities include lodging, private campgrounds, meals, groceries, liquor store, gas station, general store, post office, laundromat and gift shops. Fishing charters, tackle, riverboat services and guides available.

Copper Center Lodge. Beautifully rustic historic landmark, serving the public since 1898; 21 rooms, private or shared baths. Century-old sourdough starter hotcakes, homemade pies. Restaurant serving breakfast, lunch, dinner. Located near the base of the Wrangell–St. Elias National Park and next to the Copper and Klutina rivers. See display ad this section. [ADVERTISEMENT]

Attractions

The **Copper Center Lodge**, located on the inner loop road, selected by the Alaska Centennial Commission as a site of historic importance (a plaque is mounted to the right of the lodge's entrance), had its beginning as the Holman Hotel and was known as the Blix Roadhouse during the gold rush days of 1897–98. It was the first lodging place in the Copper River valley and was replaced by the Copper Center Lodge in 1932.

The **George I. Ashby Memorial Museum**, operated by the Copper Valley Historical Society, is housed in the bunkhouse annex at the Copper Center Lodge. It contains early Russian religious articles, Athabascan baskets, telegraph and mineral displays, copper and gold mining memorabilia, and trapping articles from early-day Copper Valley. Hours vary. Donations appreciated.

A visitor attraction in Copper Center is the log **Chapel on the Hill**, located at Milepost V 101 on the Old Richardson Highway. The chapel was built in 1942 by Rev. Vince Joy with the assistance of U.S. Army volunteers stationed in the area. The chapel is open daily and there is no admission charge. A short slide show on the Copper River area is usually shown to visitors in the chapel during the summer. A highway-level parking lot is connected by stairs to the Chapel on the Hill.

Copper Center is located on the Klutina River, 1 mile from its confluence with the Copper River. (The Copper River reportedly carries the highest sediment load of all Alaskan rivers.) The **Klutina River** is popular for its red (sockeye) salmon run from June to early August, and its king salmon run, which peaks in mid-July. Check current fishing regulations.

Richardson Highway at Copper Center.

Copper River Princess Wilderness Lodge. Overlooks America's largest national park, the Wrangell–St. Elias, this lodge features a true wilderness experience. Restaurant, lounge, espresso bar and tour desk. Reservations suggested. Lodge often runs special summer rates and packages on specific days. Open mid-May through mid-September. Call 800-426-0500 for reservations. www.princesslodges.com. [ADVERTISEMENT]

Klutina Lake Road starts just west of the Princess Lodge, 1.4 miles west of the Richardson Highway. A BLM sign warns that this 24-mile-long narrow dirt road has varying road conditions and is recommended for 4-wheel-drive vehicles only beyond Mile 10. On a May visit, we found the road deeply rutted beginning just past Mile 3 and unsuitable for low-clearance vehicles beyond that point. The casual visitor can park at the Princess Lodge and walk out along Klutina Lake Road for bird's eye views of the Klutina River. Visitors planning to drive Klutina Lake Road should contact the BLM office in Glennallen for more details, and inquire locally about road conditions, before starting out. In addition, permits are required for recreational use of Ahtna Inc. lands accessed off this road; contact Ahtna Inc. in Glennallen.

V 106 F 256 North junction with Old Richardson Highway loop road through Copper Center; well worth a stop. Access to Klutina River charter services and food, gas and lodging in Copper Center.

See "Copper Center Loop" on page 458 for description of Copper Center and attractions along the Old Richardson Highway.

V 106.5 F 255.5 Turnoff to east for 0.2 mile access road to **Wrangell-St. Elias National Park and Preserve Visitor Center**; parking, restrooms, visitor information on the park and the Copper River Valley region. Beautiful views of Wrangell mountains from a short interpretive trail at the center.

V 110 F 252 Dept. of Highways Tazlina station and Dept. of Natural Resources office. Report forest fires here or phone (907) 822-5533.

V 110.5 F 251.5 Tazlina River RV Park. ▲

V 110.6 F 251.4 Rest area to east on banks of Tazlina River; large paved surface, 2 covered picnic tables, water, toilets.

V 110.7 F 251.3 Tazlina River bridge. *Tazlina* is Indian for "swift water." The river flows east from Tazlina Glacier into the Copper River.

V 111 F 251 Tazlina River Trading Post to west; groceries and gas.

Tazlina River Trading Post & Western Auto. See display ad this section.

V 111.7 F 250.3 Copperville access road. Developed during pipeline construction, this area has a church and private homes. Glenn-

allen fire station.

V 112.3 F 249.7 Steep grade southbound from Tazlina River to the top of the Copper River bluffs.

V 112.6 F 249.4 Scenic viewpoint to east; paved parking area, with historical information sign on the development of transportation in Alaska. Short walk to good viewpoint on bluff with schematic diagram of Wrangell Mountains: Mount Sanford (elev. 16,237 feet); Mount Drum (12,010 feet); Mount Wrangell (14,163 feet); and Mount Blackburn (16,390 feet).

Sign at viewpoint reads: "Across the Copper River rise the peaks of the Wrangell Mountains. The 4 major peaks of the range can be seen from this point, with Mount Drum directly in front of you. The Wrangell Mountains, along with the St. Elias Mountains to the east, contain the most spectacular array of glaciers and ice fields outside polar regions. The Wrangell Mountains are part of Wrangell–St. Elias National Park and Preserve, the nation's largest national park. Together with Kluane National Park of Canada, the park has been designated a World Heritage site by the United Nations."

Visitor information for Wrangell–St. Elias National Park is available at **Milepost V 106.5** Richardson Highway.

V 114.1 F 247.9 Double-ended turnout down hill to west.

V 115 F 247 Junction of Richardson and Glenn highways at **GLENNALLEN** (see description on pages 292-296 in the GLENN HIGHWAY section). The town of Glennallen extends west along the Glenn Highway from here. **Alaska State Troopers** located in the Ahtna Building on east side of Richardson Highway.

The Hub of Alaska and visitor information are located at the northwest corner of the intersection; 24-hour gas and diesel, convenience grocery.

Junction of the Richardson Highway (Alaska Route 4) and the Glenn Highway (Alaska Route 1). Anchorage- or Tok-bound travelers turn to **Milepost A 189 on page 291** in the GLENN HIGHWAY section for log.

Valdez- or Fairbanks-bound travelers continue with this log. For the next 14 miles northbound the Richardson and Glenn highways share a common alignment. They separate at **Milepost V 128.6.**

Distance marker southbound indicates Copper Center 14 miles, Valdez 115 miles.

Improved highway northbound.

V 115.2 Distance marker northbound shows Paxson 71 miles, Tok 139 miles, Fairbanks 251 miles, Canada Border 256 miles.

V 115.5 F 246.5 Trailside Grill. Just what you're looking for: Delicious food in a genuine Alaskan atmosphere! Best burgers in town, homemade soups, chowder and chili. Alaskan halibut and Copper River salmon dinners. Gourmet Alaskan ice cream, fresh pies and huge cinnamon rolls. Nice Alaskan gift shop with good prices, T-shirts as low as $3 each! Named for the "Valdez to Fairbanks Trail," Alaska's first road, very early photos of the area are displayed. (907) 822-4448. [ADVERTISEMENT]

V 118 F 244 Dry Creek State Recreation Site to west. *NOTE: This campground was closed during summer 2002. For current status, phone (907) 269-8400 or go to www.dnr.state.ak.us/parks/.* ▲

V 118.1 F 243.9 Private Aircraft:

Sightseers on the interpretive trail at Wrangell-St. Elias National Park's visitor center. (© Kris Graef, staff)

Gulkana airport to east; elev. 1,579 feet; length 5,000 feet; asphalt; fuel 100LL.

V 123.2 F 238.8 Large paved turnout to east.

V 126 F 236 Paved double-ended turnout to west.

V 126.2 F 235.8 The Fiddler's Green on Bear Creek. See display ad this section.

V 126.8 F 235.2 Gulkana River Bridge. Public access to river from gravel parking area east side of highway just south of bridge. *(NOTE: No public access at north end of bridge.)* Very popular fishing spot in season. *Watch for pedestrians.* Grayling fishing and good king and sockeye salmon fishing (June and July) in the Gulkana River; check current fishing regulations. The Gulkana River flows 60 miles from Gulkana Glacier in the

Tazlina River Trading Post & TruValue Chevron Products
Groceries • Liquor • Ammunition
Fishing Tackle • Hunting & Fishing Licenses
9 a.m. to 9 p.m. • 10 a.m. to 6 p.m. Sunday
Don & Joyce Horrell   Mile 111.2
Box 364 • Glennallen, Alaska 99588

The Fiddler's Green on Bear Creek
A Bed & Breakfast
Spectacular view of the Wrangell Mountains • Close to outstanding fishing on the Gulkana River • Each room has it's own deck • Cabin on the Bluff with full bath and kitchen Families Welcome! • Open Year Round
907-822-5852   1-888-822-1178
LOCAL   TOLL FREE
UNIQUE ALASKAN EXPERIENCE   MILE 126.2 RICHARDSON HIGHWAY
DENISE & TAD KEHL - INNKEEPERS
e-mail fiddlers@bearcreekalaska.com

RICHARDSON HIGHWAY

Alaska Range to the Copper River.

Entering Game Management Unit 13B northbound, 13A southbound.

V 126.9 F 235.1 Access road east to village of **GULKANA** (pop. 88) on the east bank of the Gulkana River at its confluence with the Copper River. Established as a telegraph station in 1903 and named "Kulkana" after the river. Most of the Gulkana River frontage in this area is owned by Gulkana village and managed by Ahtna, Inc. Ahtna lands are closed to the public for hunting, fishing and trapping. The sale, importation and possession of alcohol are prohibited.

V 128.6 F 233.4 Gakona Junction; gas station. **Junction** of Richardson Highway (Alaska Route 4) and Tok Cutoff (Alaska Route 1). The 2 roads share a common alignment for the next 14 miles southbound. Turn east on Alaska Route 1 for Tok. Continue north on Alaska Route 4 for Paxson and Delta Junction. Continue south on Route 4 for Glennallen and junction with Alaska Route 1 West, and for Valdez.

Distance marker northbound shows Paxson 56 miles, Delta Junction 137 miles, Fairbanks 235 miles.

Distance marker southbound shows Glennallen 16 miles, Valdez 129 niles, Anchoage 196 miles.

Junction of the Richardson Highway and Tok Cutoff. Tok-bound travelers turn to **Milepost A 203** on page 291 in the GLENN HIGHWAY section for log.

Valdez- or Fairbanks-bound travelers continue with this log.

V 129 F 233 Sign: *$500 fine for littering.*

V 129.4 F 232.6 Turnoff to west for **Sailor's Pit** BLM public easement and Ahtna Inc. Gulkana River access. BLM trail at highway turnoff: access to public lands for foot traffic, dog sleds, animals, snowmobiles, 2 or 3 wheel vehicles, ATVs less than 3,000 lbs. GVW. Gated wide, gravel road leads 0.4 mile to Ahtna Inc. river access; $5/day-use, $20/camping, self-register using recreation fee permit envelopes. **Gulkana River**; fishing for rainbow trout, grayling, king and red salmon.

V 130 F 232 Parking area to west.
V 132.2 F 229.8 Parking area to west.
V 135.8 F 226.2 Paved parking to east.
V 136.4 F 227.6 Coleman Creek.
V 136.9 F 225.1 Gulkana River Trail.
V 138 F 224 Turnoff to west 0.3 mile on gravel side road for **Poplar Grove/ Gulkana River** Ahtna Inc. public fishing access (recreation permit fee charged) and BLM Gulkana River trail.

V 139 F 223 Distance marker southbound shows Glennallen 27 miles, Valdez 143 miles.

V 139.3 F 222.7 Paved parking to west.
V 140.6 F 221.4 Paved parking to east.
V 141.3 F 220.7 Paved double-ended scenic viewpoint to west. BLM trail (1-mile) to Gulkana River.

V 145 F 217 Distance marker northbound shows Paxson 40 miles, Delta Junction 120 miles.

V 147 F 215 Double-ended scenic viewpoint to west. Views of Alaska Range norhbound.

V 147.5 F 214.5 BLM **Sourdough Creek BLM Campground** to west; 60 level sites in gravel loop; tables, grills, outhouses; camping fee $6; campground host. Marked trail to Sourdough Creek.

Gulkana River Boat Launch. Large parking area, outhouse, picnic area. Guided fishing trips available. *Beware of bears.*

The Gulkana River is part of the National Wild and Scenic Rivers System managed by the BLM. A popular float trip for experienced canoeists begins at Paxson Lake and ends at Sourdough Campground. See description at Milepost V 175.

Gulkana River above Sourdough Creek, grayling 9 to 21 inches (same as Sourdough Creek below), rainbow 10 to 24 inches, spinners, June through September; red salmon 8 to 25 lbs. and king salmon up to 62 lbs., use streamer flies or spinners, mid-June through mid-July. **Sourdough Creek**, grayling 10 to 20 inches, use single yellow eggs or corn, fish deep early May through first week in June, use spinners or flies mid-June until freezeup.

V 147.6 F 214.4 Sourdough Creek.
V 147.7 F 214.3 Sourdough Roadhouse, established in 1903, destroyed by fire in 1992, reopened in 1994. Services: gasoline, propane, rustic cabins, showers, groceries, fishing tackle and licenses, raft rental, shuttles, RV plug-ins, salmon charters, restaurant with home cooking and baking, featuring our 1896 sourdough starter. (907) 822-7122 or (907) 488-8279; email: sourdoughlodge@yahoo.com; fax (907) 488-5981. [ADVERTISEMENT]

V 148.3 F 213.7 Sourdough Controlled Use Area.

V 148.5 F 213.5 *NOTE: Road narrows northbound; few turnouts, little or no shoulders. Drive with headlights on at all times. Pass with care.*

Improved highway southbound.

V 150.7 F 211.3 Gravel turnout to east. Entering Federal Land northbound.

V 154.4 F 207.6 Double-ended dirt and gravel turnout to east.

V 155.4 F 206.6 Gravel turnout to east by APL access road.

V 157 F 205.6 As the highway winds through the foothills of the Alaska Range, over a crest called Hogan Hill (elev. 2,647 feet), there are magnificent views of 3 mountain ranges (on a clear day): the Alaska Range through which the highway leads, the Wrangell Mountains to the southeast and the Chugach Mountains to the southwest.

Good views of pothole lakes to west. The headwaters of the Susitna River converge on the platform to the west. The Susitna empties into Cook Inlet west of Anchorage.

Good long-range viewpoints from highway. Moose and other game may be spotted from here (use binoculars).

V 160.7 F 201.3 Haggard Creek BLM trailhead to west; grayling fishing. Access to Gulkana River 7 miles to west.

V 160.9 F 201.5 Haggard Creek.

V 162.2 F 199.8 Long, narrow double-ended gravel turnout to east (muddy in wet weather).

V 166.5 F 195.5 June and **Nita Lakes** BLM trail; 1 mile to west. Fishing access 0.5 mile west.

V 168.1 F 193.9 Gillespie Lake BLM trailhead and parking to west. Walk up creek 0.5 mile to lake; grayling fishing.

V 169.3 F 192.7 Large gravel pit. Turnout to west.

V 169.4 F 192.6 Middle Fork BLM trail to **Meier's Lake** and Middle Fork Gulkana River at north corner of gravel pit turnout. Meier's Lake offers good grayling fishing.

V 170 F 192 Meier's Lake Roadhouse to west (open year-round); post office, gas (diesel), convenience store, food, lodging and camping. On display in the roadhouse restaurant is a 26 lb. 10 oz. lake trout caught in Paxson Lake.

V 171.2 F 190.8 Gravel turnout at north end of Meier's Lake (easier access for southbound traffic) is a good place to spot trumpeter swans, lesser scaups and other waterfowl in Meier's Lake. Birds are abundant in fall. Also watch for otters in the lake.

V 171.6 F 190.4 Gravel turnout to west.

V 172.9 F 189.1 Leaving Federal Hunting Area northbound.

V 173 F 189 Good view from highway across pothole lake of trans-Alaska oil pipeline to east.

V 173.3 F 188.7 Dick Lake to the east via narrow side road (easy to miss); *abrupt edge!*, no turnaround space. Good grayling fishing in summer. View of trans-Alaska oil pipeline across the lake. Good spot for photos.

V 175 F 187 BLM **Paxson Lake Campground** turnoff to west. Wide gravel access road (with great views of Paxson Lake) leads downhill 1.5 miles for access to camping and boat launch. The large camping area near the lakeshore has 50 campsites (some pull-throughs), outhouses, water, tables, firepits, and dump station. Camping fee $6 ($3 for walk-in campsites). Concrete boat launch and parking area for 80 vehicles. Bring mosquito repellent. Fishing in Paxson Lake for lake trout, grayling and red salmon. *CAUTION: Watch for bears.*

This is the launch site for floating the Gulkana River to Sourdough Campground at **Milepost V 147.6**. Total distance is about 50 miles and 4 days travel, according to the BLM, which manages this national wild river. While portions of the river are placid, the Gulkana does have Class II and III rapids, with a gradient of 38 feet/mile in one section. Canyon Rapids may be Class IV depending on water levels (there is a portage). Recommended for experienced boaters only. For further information on floating the Gulkana, contact the BLM at Box 147, Glennallen, AK 99588, or phone (907) 822-3217; www.glennallen.ak.blm.gov.

V 177 F 185 Gravel turnout to west.

V 180.1 F 181.9 Large double-ended gravel turnout to west.

V 180.2 F 181.8 Small gravel turnout to west beside Paxson Lake.

V 182.2 F 179.8 Gravel turnout. Southbound views of Paxson Lake.

Paxson Closed Area. This status dates from the 1950s, according to a local expert, when the Alaska Road Commission closed the area to the taking of all big game in order to assure the traveling public continued viewing access of large game along the road.

V 183 F 179 Small gravel turnout to west.

V 184 F 178 Good view of Gulkana River.

V 184.3 F 177.7 *Improved highway next 1.7 miles northbound; slow for dips.* Old highway alignment to east makes a good turnout for informal camping.

V 184.7 F 177.3 One Mile Creek bridge. Paxson Mountain to west; good example of a lateral moraine created by Gulkana Glacier (visible). Distance marker southbound.

V 185.5 F 176.5 PAXSON (pop. 43; elev. 2,650 feet), located at the junction of the Richardson Highway (Alaska Route 4) and the Denali Highway (Alaska Route 8). Paxson began in 1906 when Alvin Paxson established a roadhouse at Mile 192. He later built a larger roadhouse at Mile 191. Today, services in the Paxson area include lodging at Denali Highway Cabins and Paxson Inn & Lodge (with coffee shop). Wildlife viewing raft trips on the Gulkana River down to Paxson Lake are available in Paxson at Denali Highway Cabins.

Paxson Inn & Lodge. See display ad this section.

Private Aircraft: Paxson airstrip, adjacent south; elev. 2,653 feet; length 2,800 feet; gravel; emergency fuel; attended.

Junction with Denali Highway (Alaska Route 8) to Cantwell and the Parks Highway. See DENALI HIGHWAY section on page 477 for log.

V 185.7 F 176.3 Access west to Denali Highway Cabins; lodging, Gulkana River float trips.

Denali Highway Cabins offer what many visitors and natives call the state's finest road-accessible lodging. Oversized, very private riverside cabins boast mountain views, Serta Perfect Sleeper® mattresses, full baths, TV/VCR, smoking patios, barbecues and complimentary beverages. Each cabin's own water system ensures no getting scalded by another's shower! Join naturalist–host Dr. Audubon L. Bakewell IV, co-author of the *ABA Bird Finding Guide to Alaska*, on wildlife float trips through the Paxson Reserve, featuring up-close views of moose, beaver, salmon, grizzlies, lynx ... Join a wildflower or birdwatching tour of the spectacular Denali Highway tundra. Glacier hikes, bicycling, canoeing and much more make this a multi-day stop for all outdoor lovers. Phone (907) 822-5972; www.denalihwy.com. See display ad this section. [ADVERTISEMENT]

V 185.8 F 176.2 Ruins of old Paxson Roadhouse east side of highway. Paxson Station DOT highway maintenance station to west.

V 186.4 F 175.6 Leaving BLM public lands northbound, entering BLM public lands southbound.

V 188.3 F 173.7 South end of long paved double-ended rest area to east across from Gulkana River. Gold Rush Centennial interpretive sign about Alvin J. Paxson's Timberline Tent Roadhouse established near here in 1906. The Gulkana River flows south to the Copper River.

V 189.5 F 172.5 Long, narrow paved double-ended turnout to west.

A thirsty cow moose is reflected in a roadside pond. (© Rich Reid, Colors of Nature)

V 190.4 F 171.6 Paved parking area by Gulkana River to west with picnic table and interpretive sign about spawning red salmon. Fishing for salmon prohibited. Public fishing access to **Fish Lake** (2 miles) across highway from turnout; grayling fishing.

V 191.4 F 170.6 Summit Lake and Water's Edge Cottages to west.

Water's Edge Cottages on Summit Lake with a breathtaking view. Extra-nice cabins and rooms, some with cooking facilities. Tent and self-contained-only motorhome spaces, showers. Quiet setting, guided fishing, birding, berry picking. Lots of wildlife. Excellent winter snowmobiling. Hosts are long-time Alaskans. 3-week cancellation policy. Phone/fax (907) 822-4443; web site: www.summit-connection.com. [ADVERTISEMENT]

V 192.2 F 169.8 Gravel turnout with public access boat launch on **Summit Lake**; lake trout, grayling, burbot and red salmon. Summit Lake, 7 miles long, is named for its location near the water divide between the Delta and Gulkana rivers. The Gulkana River flows into the Copper River, which flows into Prince William Sound. The Delta River is part of the Yukon River drainage.

V 192.6 F 169.4 Large gravel turnout to west on Summit Lake. Highway winds along shore of Summit Lake northbound.

V 194.2 F 167.8 Hines Site 20/20 Bed and Breakfast overlooks Summit Lake. Five new beautifully decorated non-smoking view rooms with private baths. Queen-size bed. Full breakfast. Quiet, peaceful environment. Good fishing and snow machining. Open year around. Your host: "Boots" Hines, HC 72 Box 7195, Delta Junction, AK 99737. Just truck on in. [ADVERTISEMENT]

V 195 F 167 SUMMIT LAKE; elev. 3,210 feet. There are a number of homes and a bed and breakfast in this small settlement on the east side of Summit Lake..

Summit Lake hosts the 18th annual **Tesoro Arctic Man Ski & Snow–Go Classic** April 9–13, 2003. This event involves a downhill skier and a snowmachine and driver. The skiers start at 5,800 feet elevation and drop 1,700 feet in less than 2 miles to the bottom of a narrow canyon, where they must catch the tow rope from their partner on the snowmachine, who then tows them 2-1/4 miles uphill (at speeds up to 86 mph), before they separate and the skier finishes

---

PAXSON INN & LODGE

ROOMS WITH BATH
FULL RV HOOKUPS
RESTAURANT
COCKTAIL LOUNGE
PACKAGE LIQUOR
GAS • DIESEL
PROPANE • TOWING

(907) 822-3330

At Junction of Denali
& Richardson Highways

DENALI HIGHWAY CABINS
Luxurious Riverside Log Cabins with Mountain Views
Nightly Rentals • Full Bath • TV / VCR • Decks

Evening Wildlife Float Trips • Fishing • Rafting • Snow Machining
Sled Dog Tours • Hiking • Naturalist Led Birding & Tundra Tours
HC 72 Box 7292 / Paxson, AK 99737
(907) 822-5972 • Mile 0.2 Denali Highway
www.denalihwy.com
e-mail: paxtours@alaska.net

The trans-Alaska pipeline crosses Isabel Pass (elev. 3,280 feet). (© Laurent Dick)

the race by going over the side of a second mountain and dropping 1,200 feet to the finish line.

The Arctic Man draws more than 10,000 spectators, many of them camping at a specially cleared and organized parking area off the Richardson Highway. Details on parking as well as entry forms for the event are found at www.arcticman.com.

V 196.8 F 165.2 Gunn Creek bridge. View of Gulkana Glacier to the northeast. This glacier, perched on 8,000-foot Icefall Peak, feeds streams that drain into both Prince William Sound and the Yukon River.

V 197.5 F 164.5 Summit of **Isabel Pass** (elev. 3,280 feet). Large gravel turnout to east. Gold Rush Centennial interpretive sign about women in the gold rush, including Isabelle Barnette for whom Isabel Pass is named. This is a moose wintering area.

Memorial monument honoring Gen. Wilds P. Richardson, for whom the highway is named. Sign here reads: "Captain Wilds P. Richardson presented the need for roads to Congress in 1903. His familiarity with Alaska impressed Congress with his knowledge of the country and his ability as an engineer. When the Act of 1905 became a law, he was placed at the head of the Alaska Road Commission, a position he served for more than a decade. The Richardson Highway, from Valdez to Fairbanks, is a fitting monument to the first great road builder of Alaska."

Entering Sport Fish Management Area C southbound.

V 198.2 F 163.8 Rough gravel turnout to west.

V 198.5 F 163.5 Rough gravel parking area to west.

V 200.4 F 161.6 Gravel side road leads west 2 miles to **Fielding Lake State Campground.** Pleasant area above tree line; 7 campsites, no water, no camping fee, picnic tables, pit toilets, large parking areas and boat ramp. Look for marine fossils embedded in rock slides, approximately 200 yards up Rainbow Ridge. Good fishing for lake trout, grayling and burbot.

V 201 F 161 Snow poles along highway guide snowplows in winter.

V 201.4 F 160.6 Phelan Creek bridge. Phelan Creek heads near Gulkana Glacier and flows 16 miles to the Delta River.

V 202 F 160 Entering BLM public lands northbound, leaving BLM lands southbound.

V 202.4 F 159.6 McCallum Creek bridge, highway follows Phelan Creek northbound. This stream heads in Gulkana Glacier and flows northwest to the Delta River.

V 202.8 F 159.2 NOTE: Road construction was under way northbound to **Milepost V 207** in summer 2002.

V 207.1 F 154.9 Rock slide and avalanche begins northbound, ends southbound.

V 208.1 F 153.9 Turnout to west.

V 208 5 F 153.5 Large gravel parking area to west.

V 209 F 153 Gravel turnout to east. Watch for old beaver lodge east side of highway just north of here.

V 210 F 152 View of **Rainbow Ridge** and **Rainbow Mountain** southbound. This 6,000-foot-high ridge extends northwest 8 miles from McCallum Creek. The highest point on the ridge is 6,700-foot Rainbow Mountain. Popular photo subjects, the mountain and ridge were named for their vari-colored talus slopes. The reds and greens are volcanic rock; the yellows and pastels are siltstone and sandstone.

V 212 F 150 Wide gravel shoulders and turnouts to west beside Phelan Creek are found along the highway north and south of here.

Take-out point for Delta River float that begins at Tangle Lakes Campground on the Denali Highway is marked for river travelers along this stretch of the Richardson Highway. Take-out point changes due to river channeling.

V 213.6 F 148.4 Gravel turnout and road to gravel pit to east. Rock slide and avalanche area ends northbound, begins southbound.

V 214 F 148 Double-ended paved turnout to east. Highway follows Delta River northbound, Phelan Creek southbound.

V 215.1 F 146.9 Miller Creek bridge; access to creek to west south of bridge. Pipeline crosses creek next to bridge.

V 216 F 146 Large gravel parking area to west with interpretive sign is **Denali Fault/Pipeline Visitor Viewing Area;** good stop for pipeline photos. Interpretive signs at viewing area give pipeline history and facts, and detail design solutions used to make the pipeline earthquake proof. The zigzag pattern often seen in the above-ground sections allows for pipe expansion or contraction due to temperature changes or movement caused by other forces, such as earthquakes.

The pipeline has an earthquake detection system. Ground accelerometers at pump stations measure earth movement and computers identify critical supports, valves and other items to check after a quake.

The pipeline's design was tested in November 2002 by a 7.9 earthquake. For more on the earthquake and the Denali Fault, see **Milepost V 262.5.**

V 216.7 F 145.3 Lower Miller Creek bridge. Gravel turnout to west.

V 217.2 F 144.8 Castner Creek; parking at both ends of bridge, west side of road.

V 218.2 F 143.8 Trims Camp. Trims Station (DOT/PF highway maintenance).

V 218.8 F 143.2 Bridge over Trims Creek, parking. Wildflowers in the area include lupine, sweet pea and fireweed. Watch for caribou on slopes.

V 219.2 F 142.8 Access road west to Pump Station No. 10.

V 219.9 F 142.1 Michael Creek bridge; parking at both ends of bridge. Southbound drivers have a spectacular view of Pump Station No. 10 and the surrounding mountains.

V 220.9 F 141.1 Flood Creek bridge; parking.

V 223 F 139 Whistler Creek bridge.

V 223.8 F 138.2 Boulder Creek bridge.

V 224.5 F 137.5 Lower Suzy Q Creek bridge; parking.

V 224.7 F 137.3 Entering Federal Subsistence Lands southbound.

V 224.8 F 137.2 Upper Suzy Q Creek bridge.

V 225.2 F 136.8 Large gravel turnout to east. Watch for lush growths of cow parsnip along roadside in summer.

V 225.4 F 136.6 Double-ended scenic viewpoint with picnic table to west. Historical marker here identifies the terminal moraine of Black Rapids Glacier to the west. Currently a retreating glacier with little ice visible, this glacier was nicknamed the Galloping Glacier when it advanced more than 3 miles during the winter of 1936–37.

Rapids Lake Trail begins across from historical sign (0.3 mile to lake). Look for river beauty and wild sweet pea blooming in June.

V 226 F 136 Large gravel turnouts to west above Delta River. The Delta River heads at Tangle Lakes and flows 80 miles north to the Tanana River.

V 226.3 F 135.7 Falls Creek bridge. View of Black Rapids Glacier to west.

V 226.7 F 135.3 Black Rapids U.S. Army training site at Fall Creek. Boundary between Game Management Units 20D and 13.

V 227 F 135 Gunny Sack Creek. Wide gravel shoulder for parking to west at north end of bridge.

V 227.4 F 134.6 Black Rapids Road-

house, on the east side of the highway, was established about 1902 and is one of the last remaining roadhouses on the historic Valdez–Fairbank Trail (today's Richardson Highway).

Restoration efforts are underway on this old roadhouse. For more information phone (907) 455-6158 or visit www.blackrapids.org.

V 228.4 F 133.6 One Mile Creek bridge; large gravel parking areas.

V 229.8 F 132.2 Wide shoulder pull-offs west side of highway.

V 231 F 131 Darling Creek; gravel turnout to east at south end.

View of braided Delta River to west. The wind can really whip up the dust along the riverbed.

V 231.6 F 130.4 Large informal gravel turnout to west.

V 232.1 F 129.9 Gravel turnout to west.

V 233.3 F 128.7 Bear Creek bridge. Small gravel turnout with access to creek to west at south end of bridge. Wildflowers include pale oxytrope, yellow arnica, fireweed, wild rhubarb and cow parsnip.

V 234.2 F 127.8 Double-ended gravel turnout to east.

V 234.5 F 127.5 Paved turnout to west.

V 234.8 F 127.2 Ruby Creek bridge; parking to west at north end of bridge.

V 236 F 126 Distance marker southbound shows Paxson 51 miles, Glennallen 121 miles, Valdez 236 miles.

V 237.9 F 124.1 Distance marker southbound shows Paxson 53 miles, Glennallen 127 miles.

V 238 F 124 Narrow, gravel loop road (watch for potholes) to east through **Donnelly Creek State Recreation Site**, a scenic spot with mountain views, 12 treed campsites, tables, firepits, outhouses, water pump and garbage containers. Camping fee $10/night or resident pass. ▲

V 239 F 123 *Highway descends southbound: Winding road, little or no shoulders, next mile.*

V 239.1 F 122.9 Gravel turnout to east.

V 240 F 122 *Highway climbs northbound: winding road, little or no shoulders, next mile.*

V 241.3 F 120.7 Large paved turnout to west at top of hill with view of Delta River.

Highway makes long winding descent southbound.

V 242.1 F 119.9 Coal Mine Road (4-wheel-drive vehicles only) leads east to **Coalmine Road Lakes**, 8 small fishing lakes stocked with at least 2 species of fish. The ADF&G says: "A nice place to try on a bright sunny day with little or no wind, offering a beautiful vista of hanging glaciers and snow-capped mountains.

"Fishing from shore is tricky due to alders, but a float tube or small canoe or even just wading out from shore will increase your effectiveness. Try dry flies or mepps spinners (0 to 1) for best luck." Lakes include **Last Lake** (rainbow trout, arctic char) and **Brodie Lake** (arctic char).

V 243 F 119 Public fishing access to west for **Weasel Lake**; stocked with rainbow trout.

V 243.5 F 118.5 Pipeline Viewpoint to east with interpretive signs. Good photo stop. The trans-Alaska oil pipeline snakes along the ground and over the horizon.

Because of varying soil conditions along its route, the pipeline is both above and below ground. Where the warm oil would cause icy soil to thaw and erode, the pipeline goes above ground. Where the frozen ground is mostly well-drained gravel or solid rock, and thawing is not a problem, the line is underground.

V 243.9 F 118.1 Paved double-ended scenic viewpoint to east. A spectacular view (on a clear day) to the southwest of 3 of the highest peaks of the Alaska Range. From west to south they are: Mount Deborah (elev. 12,339 feet); Hess Mountain (11,940 feet), center foreground; and Mount Hayes (13,832 feet).

V 244 F 118 *CAUTION: Watch for moose.*

V 244.4 F 117.6 Public fishing access to east to **Donnelly Lake**; king and silver salmon; stocked with rainbow trout.

V 245.8 F 116.2 Distance marker northbound shows Delta Junction 20 miles, Fairbanks 118 miles.

V 246 F 116 Donnelly Dome immediately to the west (elev. 3,910 feet), was first named Delta Dome. For years the mountain has been used to predict the weather: "The first snow on the top of the Donnelly Dome means snow in Delta Junction within 2 weeks."

Great view southbound of peaks in the Alaska Range.

V 247.3 F 114.7 From here northbound the road extends straight as an arrow for 4.8 miles.

V 249.6 F 114.4 Distance marker southbound shows Paxson 65 miles, Glennallen 139 miles.

V 252.8 F 109.2 Paved, double-ended rest area to west with picnic tables and litter barrels.

V 256 F 106 Fort Greely Ridge Road to west.

V 256.3 F 105.7 Begin burn area northbound.

V 257.5 F 104.5 Entrance to U.S. Army Cold Regions Test Center at Fort Greely. Meadows Road; access to fishing lakes. Check regulations before entering military lands.

V 258.3 F 103.7 Alyeska Pipeline Pump Station No. 9 to east. *Public tours at the pump station were suspended in 2002 for security reasons.* This station is at Pipeline Mile 548.71, with the Prudhoe Bay station being Mile 0. The pipeline was designed with 12 pump stations, although Pump Station 11 was never built. Interpretive sign at pump station entrance reads:

"Construction of this facility was completed May 16, 1977. As oil was introduced into the line during a 39 day period in 1977, the oil front passed through this station at 10:37 A.M., July 20, 1977.

"The travel time of the oil from Prudhoe Bay to this site under normal operating conditons is 98.06 hours. Another 44.97 hours is required to move the oil to the Valdez Terminal. The oil travels at about 5.59 miles per hour.

"The mainline pumps at the station can move 22,000 gallons of oil a minute, which is 754.285 barrels a day. Hot gas provided by aircraft-type jet engines drives a turbine wheel to power each of the pumps. Each engine can produce 17,300 horsepower."

V 258.7 F 103.3 South boundary of Fort

Pump Station No. 10, with a backdrop of peaks of the Alaska Range.
(© Kris Graef, staff)

Greely.

V 260.9 F 101.1 Distance marker southbound shows Paxson 76 miles, Glennallen 150 miles.

V 261.1 F 100.9 FORT GREELY (restricted area) main gate to east. Fort Greely was established in 1941 by the Civil Aeronautics Administration as one of a chain of strategic defense airfields. It was an alternate landing field between 1942-45 for aircraft enroute to Russia during the Lend–Lease program. In 1948, Fort Greely was activated as a staging area for the U.S. Army's first post-WWII cold weather training maneuver—"Exercise Yukon"—which led to the establishment of the Northern Warfare Training Center here. Cold weather field tests of Army equipment began at Fort Greely's Cold Regions Test Center in 1949. The Fort Greely area has temperature extremes ranging from –69°F to 91°F. Fort Greely was named for A.W. Greely, arctic explorer and author of *Three Years of Arctic Service*. Scheduled for closure in 2001, Fort Greely was reactivated as a national missile defense site in 2002.

V 262.1 F 99.9 Short gravel road to west leads to parking area and viewpoint at Will Memorial Range. Interpretive signs on caribou, wildflowers, fish and birds of the Interior, as well as the history of Fort Greely.

V 262.5 F 99.5 Double-ended paved rest area to west with toilets, picnic tables, scenic view. Gold Rush Centennial sign about the Richardson Highway and interpretive sign on the Denali Fault.

"The Denali Fault runs in a great arc from Southeast Alaska through Canada, then re-enters Alaska, slicing Denali National Park in half. The great fault passes just south of here, allowing the spectacular Alaska Range to tower above its surroundings."

The Denali Fault became a little more real to Alaskans on November 3, 2002, when a 7.9 earthquake jolted the Interior and South-central regions. The quake struck at 1:12 P.M. and was centered about 80 miles south of

RICHARDSON HIGHWAY

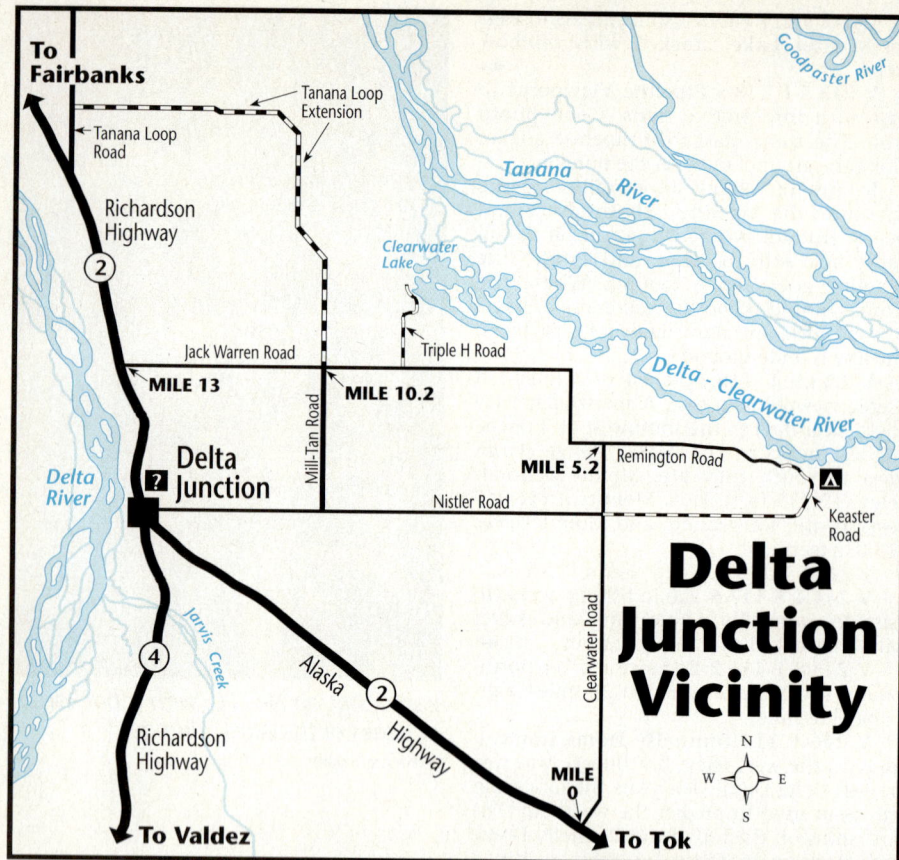

Delta Junction's visitor information center, at the official end of the Alaska Highway. (© Bob Butterfield)

Fairbanks. The Richardson Highway, Tok Cut-off and Glenn Highway all sustained damage.
Wind area northbound.
V 264.8 F 97.2 Jarvis Creek.
Leaving Fort Greely Military Reservation northbound, enering Fort Greely Military Reservation southbound.
V 265 F 97 Restaurant and motel.
V 265.1 F 96.9 "Welcome to Delta Junction" sign northbound.
CAUTION: Wind area southbound.
V 265.2 F 96.8 Delta Fire Department to east.

ALASKA ROUTE 2

V 266 F 96 Stop sign at intersection of the Richardson and Alaska highways in **DELTA JUNCTION** (see description on pages 201–205 in the ALASKA HIGHWAY section).
Delta Junction Visitor Information Center to east; End of Alaska Highway monument, pipeline display, water, brochures, restrooms.

Junction of the Richardson Highway (Alaska Route 4) and Alaska Highway (Alaska Route 2). Turn to **Milepost DC 1422** on page 201 in the ALASKA HIGHWAY section for log of that route to Tok and the Canadian border (read log back to front).

The Richardson Highway continues north to Fairbanks as Alaska Route 2, and south to Valdez as Alaska Route 4.
V 266.3 F 95.7 Delta Junction post office.
V 266.5 F 95.5 The Delta Junction Community Library and City Hall. The Library/City Hall building has a pay phone, public restrooms, local maps, and an Alaska Highway historical map display. A free paperback and magazine exchange is a favorite among locals and visitors alike. Free Internet access at the library.
V 266.7 F 95.3 *Begin 35 mph speed zone southbound.*
V 266.8 F 95.2 Alaska Dept. of Fish and Game office.
V 267 F 95 Airstrip.
V 267.1 F 94.9 **Delta state campground** to east; 24 sites, water, tables, shelter with covered tables, toilets, $8 nightly fee or resident pass. Large turnout at campground entrance. Turnout on west side of highway on bank of the Delta River offers excellent views of the Alaska Range. ▲
V 267.2 F 94.8 Alaska Division of Forestry office.
V 267.3 F 94.7 Medical clinic to east.
V 267.8 F 94.2 **True North B&B.** See display ad in the ALASKA HIGHWAY section.
V 268 F 94 **Smith's Green Acres RV Park.** See display ad in the ALASKA HIGHWAY section. ▲
V 268.3 F 93.7 Junction with Jack Warren Road (paved); see Delta Vicinity map this section. Turn here for access to **Clearwater State Campground** (10.5 miles). Clearwater campground has toilets, tables, water and boat launch; pleasant campsites on bank of river. Camping fee $8/night or resident pass. ▲
Driving this loop is a good opportunity to see local homesteads. Note that mileposts on these paved side roads run backward from Mile 13 at this junction to Mile 0 at the junction of Clearwater Road and the Alaska Highway.
V 270.3 F 91.7 Alaska 7 Motel on east side of highway.
Alaska 7 Motel, 16 large, clean, comfortable rooms with full bath and showers. Satellite TV and courtesy coffee in each room. Kitchenettes and phone available. Comfort at a comfortable price. Open year-round. Major credit cards accepted. **Milepost 270.3** Richardson Highway. Phone (907) 895-4848. Email: akmotel@alaskan.com. Internet: www.alaskan.com/ak7motel. See display ad on page 202 in the ALASKA HIGHWAY section. [ADVERTISEMENT]
V 270.6 F 91.4 Welcome to Delta Junction sign for southbound travelers.
V 271.7 F 90.3 Tanana Loop Road (gravel). Turn here to make a loop drive through Delta Junction farmlands. Follow Tanana Loop Road 1.3 miles east; turn south on Tanana Loop Extension and drive 7.8 miles to Jack Warren Road (unsigned). Go west on Jack Warren Road (paved) for 2.9 miles to junction with Alaska Highway north of Delta Junction (see Delta Vicinity map this section).
V 272 F 90 Turn off to west for Bald Eagle Ranch B&B.
Bald Eagle Ranch Bed and Breakfast. Open year-round! Lodging, cabins, RV parking, guided fishing, boat charters, wildlife tours, sightseeing, bird watching and horseback riding (all outdoor activities are weather permitting). Families and pets welcome. Your hosts offer warm Alaskan hospitality in a nonsmoking, nondrinking, family atmosphere. B&B has spacious rooms, king-size beds, private bathrooms, A/C, TVs, VCRs, mini-refrigerators, and a full breakfast of your choice. Located 6 miles north of Delta Junction. For reservations call toll-free 1-877-895-5270 or (907) 895-5270. Email: innkeeper@baldeagleranchbb.com. Web site: www.baldeagleranchbb.com. [ADVERTISEMENT]
V 272.1 F 89.9 Big D Fire station.
V 274.6 F 87.4 Distance marker eastbound shows Delta Junction 8 miles, Tok 117 miles.
V 275 F 87 Tanana Trading Post gas station on west side of highway, turnoff to east for Rika's Roadhouse (a worthwhile stop; see description following). Gold Rush Centennial interpretive sign about the beginnings of **BIG DELTA** (pop. 511). This unincorporated community at the junction of the

Delta and Tanana rivers was originally a stop on the Valdez to Fairbanks overland trail. It was first known as Bates Landing, then Rika's Landing, McCarty, and finally Big Delta. Big Delta was the site of a military telegraph station (part of WAMCATS), and it was also a work camp in 1919 during construction of the Richardson Highway.

Visitors can tour the grounds of **Rika's Roadhouse**, located just northeast of the highway and part of **Big Delta State Historical Park**. The complex offers a gift shop, restaurant and overnight parking The roadhouse was built in 1910 by John Hajdukovich, who sold it in 1923 to Rika Wallen, a Swedish immigrant who had managed the roadhouse since 1917. Rika ran the roadhouse into the late 1940s and lived there until her death in 1969. Drive in on gravel access road to large parking area; it is a short walk through trees to Rika's Roadhouse complex. The parking area also accommodates overnight RV parking; camping fee $8/vehicle, dump station ($3), toilets and phone. ▲

Rika's Roadhouse at Big Delta State Historical Park. Turn northeast at Rika's Road for Rika's Roadhouse and Landing on the banks of the Tanana River. Tour buses welcome. Parking areas with restrooms at both park entrances. The newly renovated Rika's Roadhouse offers worldwide postal service and gift shop specializing in furs, leather, gold and Alaska-made gifts. Meals served 9 A.M. to 5 P.M. in our Packhouse Restaurant which offers homemade soups, fresh salads and sandwiches. Guests love the

homemade baked goods of the Alaska Baking Co. Try our famous edible souvenir—the Bear Claw. We are also well-known for our pies: Strawberry-rhubarb, blueberry, pecan, coconut cream and chocolate truffle. Take a walk and visit the many historic buildings including the Roadhouse where you can also shop. After the dust of the highway, the green gardens of this 10-acre park are a welcome haven. Overnight parking and dump station. Brochure available. P.O. Box 1229, Delta Junction, AK 99737. Phone (907) 895-4201 or 895-4938 anytime. Free admission. Handicapped access. See display ad on page 203 in the ALASKA HIGHWAY section. [ADVERTISEMENT] ♿ ▲

V 275.4 F 86.6 Big Delta Bridge; **Tanana River/Pipeline Crossing.** Spectacular view of pipeline suspended across river. Slow down for parking area to east at south end of bridge; litter barrels, interpretive signs.

The Fur Shack. See display ad this section.

V 277.9 F 84.1 Turn off to east on Quartz Lake Road for **Quartz Lake Recreation Area.** Drive in 2.5 miles on gravel road to intersection: turn left for Lost Lake, continue straight ahead for Quartz Lake (another 0.3 mile). Lost Lake, 0.2 mile from intersection, has 8 campsites with picnic tables, toilet and a large parking area with tables and litter barrels. A shallow, picturesque lake with no fish. Quartz Lake has more developed campsites on good loop road, firepits, water, tables, toilet and 2 boat launches. Boat launch fee $3 or boat launch pass. Camping fees at both campgrounds: $8/night or resident pass. A trail connects Lost Lake and Quartz Lake camping areas. ▲

Private cabins are scattered along the northern and eastern shorelines of Quartz Lake. About half the land along the lake is undeveloped and there is no road access beyond the campground. The lake covers 1,500 acres, more than 80 percent of which are less than 15 feet deep. Maximum depth is 40 feet. Aquatic vegetation covers most of the lake surface, hampering swimmers and waterskiers. Boat and motor rentals available from Black Spruce Lodge. **Quartz Lake** offers excellent fishing for stocked rainbow and arctic char; use spinners, plugs and artificial flies. Ice fishing in winter. For more information phone the ADF&G office in Delta at (907) 895-4632. 🐟

V 280.3 F 81.7 Gravel turnout to east.

V 283.1 F 78.9 **81-Mile Pond** (stocked with rainbow trout); public fishing access to east.

V 284.2 F 77.8 Watch for moose in roadside ponds.

CAUTION: Watch for moose on highway.

V 286.6 F 75.4 Shaw Creek bridge.

V 286.7 F 75.3 Shaw Creek road. Good to excellent early spring and fall grayling fishing; subject to closure (check locally). 🐟

Good view northbound of Tanana River which parallels the highway.

V 288.2 F 73.8 Scenic viewpoint at parking area to west overlooking Tanana River with panoramic view (on clear days) to the south of 3 great peaks of the Alaska Range: Mount Hayes (elev. 13,832 feet) almost due south; Hess Mountain (11,940 feet) to the west or right of Mount Hayes; and Mount Deborah (12,339 feet) to the west or right of Hess Mountain. Mount Hayes is named for Charles Hayes, an early member of the U.S. Geological Survey. Mount Deborah was named in 1907 by the famous Alaskan Judge Wickersham for his wife.

V 289.7 F 72.3 South end of long paved double-ended parking area to east in trees.

V 291.8 F 70.2 *Begin truck lane northbound.*

V 292.8 F 69.2 *End truck lane northbound. End truck lane southbound.*

V 294 F 68 Paved double-ended turnout to west with Gold Rush Centennial interpretive signs on "Getting the Gold" (placer mining) and "Gold in the Tenderfoot" (excerpt follows):

"Two miners from the Fortymile District found gold flakes on Tenderfoot Creek in 1888. This site was too far from a supply camp, so they abandoned it. 17 years later, after gold was discovered near Fairbanks, prospector E.H. Luce found gold on Tenderfoot Creek. News of his discovery attracted about a thousand people to the area. Between 1905 and 1995, the Tenderfoot Mining District produced 120,770 ounces (3.77 tons) of placer gold. Its most productive years were 1905 to 1916."

V 294.2 F 67.8 *Begin truck lane southbound.*

V 294.9 F 67.1 Game Management Unit boundary between 20B and 20D. Fairbanks North Star Borough boundary.

V 295.4 F 66.6 Banner Creek bridge; historic placer gold stream.

V 295.6 F 66.4 Distance marker southbound shows Delta Junction 28 miles, Tok 136 miles, Valdez 300 miles.

V 296.4 F 65.6 Paved parking area to west; good view of Alaska Range and Tanana River to southwest.

CAUTION: Rough road, watch for frost heaves northbound.

V 297.7 F 64.3 Sharp turn downhill to southwest for scenic viewpoint overlooking the Tanana River.

The Tanana, Alaska's second largest river, meanders through a 500-mile-long Interior valley. (© Ron Niebrugge)

THE FUR SHACK
Home of "Ethel" and her World Famous Arctic Fur Bikini

Fur & Fur Products
Porcelain Dolls
Alaskan Clay

At the Tanana River/Pipeline Crossing
Mile 275.4
Richardson Highway

Steve & Kathy Fields
Alaskrafts®
P.O. Box 1013, Delta Junction, AK 99737-1013
(907) 895-1950

RICHARDSON HIGHWAY

Harding Lake is a favorite vacation and recreation site for Fairbanks residents.
(© Kris Graef, staff)

V 298.2 F 63.8 Parking area to west.
V 301.6 F 60.4 South end of long double-ended turnout east side of highway.
V 304.3 F 57.7 Parking area to east.
V 305 F 57 Distance marker southbound shows Delta Junction 38 miles, Tok 146 miles, Valdez 310 miles.
V 305.2 F 56.8 Turn off to northeast on Birch Lake Road for **Birch Lake State Recreation Site** (0.2 mile); lakeside picnic tables, firepits, toilets, garbage; overnight parking, campground host; parking for boat trailers; fee station; boat launch and fishing.
Just beyond the state recreation site is the entrance to Birch Lake Military Recreation Site (USAF Recreation Camp).
V 306 F 56 Large parking area east side of highway overlooks **Birch Lake**; unimproved gravel boat launch and beach; fish from shore in spring, from boat in summer. Stocked with chinook salmon, grayling and rainbow trout. Many Fairbanks residents have summer homes at Birch Lake.
V 307.2 F 54.8 Birch Lake highway maintenance station.
V 308 F 54 CAUTION: Watch for moose.

THE KNOTTY SHOP
An Alaskan Gift Shop and Mounted Wildlife Display

SeeMore, the Knotty Moose Invites You Inside to See More!
Antique Gun Collection
Big Ice Cream Cones
Alaska's Longest Burl Counter
and Unusual Burl Stools

Open Daily 8-8   Milepost 332.3
(907) 488-3014   www.alaskangifts.com

Improved highway next 3 miles northbound.
V 310 F 52 Large double-ended parking area to west.
V 313.1 F 48.9 Paved double-ended turnout to west on Tanana River. Gold Rush Centennial interpretive signs on "Alaska's Gold Rush Era" and "Tanana Valley Gold."
V 313.7 F 48.3 Double-ended dirt turnout to southwest.
V 315.6 F 46.4 Waste transfer site to east.
V 317.9 F 43.4 Double-ended gravel parking area to west.
V 319.8 F 42.2 Access road east to Harding Lake summer homes.
V 321.5 F 40.5 Turnoff to east for **Harding Lake State Recreation Area**; drive east 1.4 miles on paved road. Park headquarters, campground host, drinking water fill-up and dump station ($3) at entrance. Picnic tables on grassy area at lakeshore; boat ramp ($5 launch fee or boat launch pass), ball fields and about 80 campsites. Camping fee $8/night or resident pass. Fishing for lake trout, arctic char, burbot, northern pike and salmon. Lake is reported to be "hard to fish." Worth the drive! *Bring your insect repellent. You may need it!*
V 322.2 F 39.8 SALCHA (pop. 387, unincorporated) extends along the highway for several miles. Post office (ZIP code 99714) and Salcha River Lodge with food, gas and lodging on east side of highway. The village was first reported in 1898 as "Salchaket," meaning "mouth of the Salcha."
V 323.1 F 38.9 Access to **Salcha River State Recreation Site** to northeast, a popular boat launch with a large parking area (75 sites), boat ramp (launch fee or boat launch pass), picnic area, toilets and water. Camping fee $8/night per vehicle or resident pass. Fishing for king and chum salmon, grayling, sheefish, northern pike and burbot.
V 323.4 F 38.6 Salcha River bridge.
V 324.1 F 37.9 Clear Creek bridge.
V 324.6 F 37.4 Double-ended gravel turnout to northeast.
V 324.8 F 37.2 **Munsons Slough** bridge; fishing.
V 325.5 F 36.5 Salcha Elementary School to northeast.
V 326.8 F 35.2 Waste transfer site.
V 327.7 F 34.3 Little Salcha River bridge.

V 330 F 32 Tanana River flows next to highway.
V 330.1 F 31.9 Distance marker southbound shows Delta Junction 65 miles, Tok 173 miles.
V 330.5 F 31.5 Salcha Rescue; phone (907) 488-5274.
V 331.7 F 30.3 Salcha Fairgrounds. Salcha Fair is held in late June.
V 332.2 F 29.8 Access east to **31-Mile Pond**; stocked with arctic char and rainbow trout.
V 332.3 F 29.7 The Knotty Shop to west; gifts and wildlife museum.
The Knotty Shop. Stop and be impressed by a truly unique Alaskan gift shop and wildlife museum. Jim and Paula have attempted to maintain a genuine Alaskan flavor—from the unusual burl construction to the Alaskan wildlife displayed in a natural setting to the handcrafted Alaskan gifts. Don't miss the opportunity to stop and browse. Show us *The MILEPOST* advertisement for one free single scoop ice cream cone. See display ad this section. [ADVERTISEMENT]
V 334.8 F 27.2 Leaving Eielson AFB southbound.
V 335.1 F 26.9 Access east to **28-Mile Pond**; stocked with rainbow and arctic char.
V 338 F 24 View of Eielson AFB airstrip to northeast between Mileposts 338 and 339. Watch for various military aircraft taking off and landing to the east. Aircraft include Air Force F-16s, F-15s, KC-135s, C-130s, C-141s, OA-10s, Navy A-6s, F-14s and others.
V 340.5 F 21.5 *Begin divided 4-lane highway northbound.*
Begin 2 lane highway southbound.
CAUTION: Watch for heavy traffic southbound turning east into the base, 7–8 A.M., and merging northbound traffic, 3:45–5:30 P.M., weekdays.
V 341 F 21 Entrance to east to **EIELSON AIR FORCE BASE** (pop. 6,000). Eielson is the farthest north full-up fighter wing in the U.S. Air Force. The wing equips and trains 2 fighter squadrons that are ready to deploy around the world at a moment's notice. The 18th Figer Squadron flies the F-16 and the 355th Fighter Squadron flies the A-10 (tank killers). Eielson has more than 60,000 square miles of military training airspace—the largest aerial range in the country. Military units from around the U.S. and the world come to hone their skills in the skies of Alaska.
Built in 1943 as a satellite base to Ladd Field (now Fort Wainwright) in Fairbanks, and called Mile 26 because of its location 26 miles from Fairbanks, Eielson served as a storage site for aircraft enroute to the Soviet Union under the WWII Lend–Lease program. Closed after WWII, the base was reactivated in 1946 and renamed Eielson AFB, after Carl Ben Eielson, the first man to fly from Alaska over the North Pole to Greenland. For current information on public tours of the base, phone the public affairs office at (907) 377-2116.
Visitors with access to military installations may visit Eielson's Heritage Park, which features a 50 state flag display and monuments honoring Carl Ben Eielson, POWs and MIAs, as well as Medal of Honor recipients. The park also displays contemporary and historic military aircraft, inlcuding an F-16 Fighting Falcon, an A-10 Thunderbolt II, an F-4 Phantom, and an O-2 Skymaster.
Eielson also has a new (2002) military recreation site. The Bear Lake Family Camp

North Pole

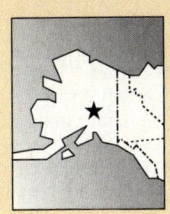

Located along the Richardson Highway, approximately 12 miles southeast of Fairbanks. **Population:** 1,616. **Emergency Services:** Emergencies only phone 911. **Police,** phone (907) 488-6902. **Alaska State Troopers,** phone (907) 452-2114. **Fire Dept./Ambulance,** phone (907) 488-0444.

Visitor Information: At Milepost V 348.7. Open daily 10 A.M. to 6 P.M. May 18 to Sept. 20, 2003. North Pole Chamber of Commerce, P.O. Box 55071, North Pole, AK 99705; phone (907) 488-2242, fax (907) 488-0366. Email: npccc@usa.net. Web site: www.fairnet.org/npcc/index.html.

Elevation: 500 feet. **Radio:** KJNP-AM 1170, KJNP-FM 100.3, TV Ch 4; also Fairbanks stations.

Private Aircraft: Bradley Sky Ranch, 1 NW; elev. 483 feet; length 4,100 feet; gravel;

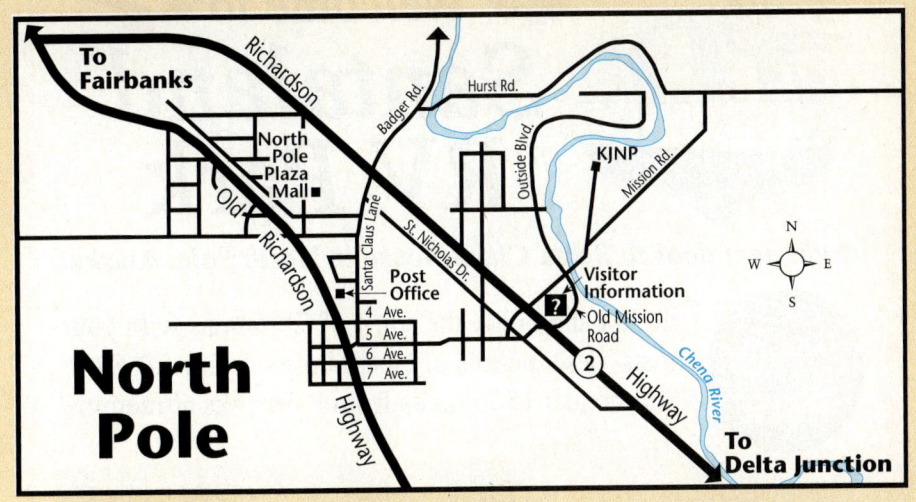

fuel 100.

North Pole has many services, including restaurants, a motel, bed and breakfasts, campgrounds, laundromats, car wash, grocery and gas stops, gift stores, barber and beauty shops, library, churches, a public park, pharmacy and supermarket. The post office is on Santa Claus Lane.

North Pole has an annual Winter Carnival with sled dog races, carnival games, food and craft booths and other activities. There's a big summer festival weekend celebration with carnival rides, food booths, arts and crafts booths, and a parade.

In 1944 Bon V. Davis homesteaded this area. Dahl and Gaske Development Co. bought the Davis homestead, subdivided it and named it North Pole, hoping to attract a toy manufacturer who could advertise products as being made in North Pole. Although the toy industry did not materialize, the city incorporated in 1953 and developed as a theme city; "Where the

NORTH POLE ADVERTISERS

Austin Enterprises RV
  Service .... 2828 Badger Rd.
Beaver Lake
  Resort Motel .... Ph. (970) 488-9600
KJNP .... Mission Rd.
North Pole Chamber of
  Commerce .... 2550 Mistletoe Dr.
North Pole VFW .... Ph. (907) 488-9184
North Pole Plaza Car, Truck
  & RV Wash .... North Pole Plaza
Riverview RV Park .... Ph. 1-888-488-6392
Santa Claus House .... 101 St. Nicholas Dr.
Santaland RV Park .... Ph. (907) 488-9123

Close to Fairbanks
On the Chena River
(907) 488-6392
See our ad in the Fairbanks section

BEAVER LAKE RESORT MOTEL
Quiet, beautiful setting next to lake
CORNER OF Mission Road & Richardson Hwy
ACROSS FROM Santa Claus House
2555 Mission Road #1103
North Pole, Alaska 99705
(907) 488-9600

North Pole, Alaska
"Where the Spirit of Christmas Lives All Year Long"

Stop by our center
Visitor Center Log Cabin
2550 Mistletoe Drive, Open Mid May through Mid Sept.
North Pole Community Chamber of Commerce
PO Box 55071, North Pole, Alaska 99705-0071
(907) 488-2242, (907) 488-8089 (fax)
www.northpolechamber.org e-mail: npccc@alaska.com

AM 1170 KJNP FM 100.3
RADIO
BOX 56359 NORTH POLE
All are welcome...
Log Cabins • Sod Roofs
The True Alaskan Motif
...to our community
KJHA - FM 88.7
Houston, Alaska
Channel 4 • TV
Bibles For Others
AM 50,000 W
FM 25,000 W
ALASKA 99705-1359

North Pole Plaza Car, Truck & RV Wash
OPEN 24 HOURS
6 Large Bays for Motorhomes, Vacuums • RV Parking
Mile 13 Richardson Highway in the North Pole Plaza

Welcome to Santaland RV Park

Right next door to Santa Claus House in North Pole, Alaska!

Relax and enjoy the spirit of Christmas with your hosts, descendents of North Pole's "original" Santa, and be just 15 minutes from Fairbanks attractions!

Tour Information & Reservations

We feature local attractions, fishing charters, Alaska Railroad and Arctic Circle tours.

- Full/Partial Hook-ups
- 30/50 Amp
- Laundry
- Very clean, unmetered, completely private showers & restrooms
- Spacious Pull-Thrus
- Free Cable TV
- E-mail hookup
- Pet-sitting service
- Dump station
- City water

Daily shuttle service to Fairbanks attractions.
Visit with Santa's reindeer!
Open All Year

888-488-9123 (907) 488-9123

125 St. Nicholas Dr. North Pole, AK 99705

info@SantalandRV.com   www.SantalandRV.com

Where Santa Spends His Summers!

Santa Claus House
Where It's Christmas Every Day!

- Alaska's Most Unique and Exciting Gift Shop
- Home of the "Original" Letter from Santa

800-588-4078 (907) 488-2200
101 St. Nicholas Dr. North Pole, AK 99705
www.SantaClausHouse.com

North Pole (continued)

spirit of Christmas lives year round." North Pole will celebrate its 50th anniversary in 2003 with a variety of special events throughout the year.

North Pole is the home of many Fairbanks commuters. It has an oil refinery that produces heating fuel, jet fuel and other products. Eielson and Wainwright military bases are nearby.

Radio station KJNP, operated by Calvary's Northern Lights Mission, broadcasts music and religious programs on 1170 AM and 100.3 FM. They also operate television station KJNP Channel 4. Visitors are welcome between 8 A.M. and 10 P.M.; tours may be arranged. KJNP is located on Mission Road about 0.6 mile northeast of the Alaska Highway. The missionary project includes a dozen hand-hewn, sod-roofed homes and other buildings constructed of spruce logs.

Santa Claus House is a North Pole landmark and favorite stp with travelers, who can shop for Christmas ornaments in July while their children tell Santa what they want for Christmas.

Full-service campgrounds at Santaland RV Park downtown, Road's End RV Park at **Milepost V 356.2** and Riverview RV Park at **Milepost V 357.1** Richardson Highway. North Pole Public Park, on 5th Avenue, has tent sites in the trees along a narrow dirt road; no camping fee. Dump station available at North Pole Plaza. ▲

AUSTIN ENTERPRISES RV SERVICE

907-490-6870

Fast Professional Service

Drive thru Lube Bay

2 Miles from Downtown

Rick & Denise Austin
2828 Badger Rd, North Pole, AK 99705

has 40 RV and 8 tent sites. Phone Eielson Outdoor Rec at (907) 377-1232 for more information.

V 342.1 F 19.9 North boundary of Eielson AFB.

V 343.5 F 18.5 Moose Creek Road and general store; diesel, gas, propane.

Piledriver Slough parallels the highway from here north, flowing into the Tanana River. It is stocked with rainbow trout. Check with general store for access and fishing information. **Bathing Beauty Pond**, stocked with rainbow, arctic char and grayling, is accessible via Eielson Farm Road off Moose Creek Road.

V 345.5 F 18.5 *CAUTION: Highway crosses Alaska Railroad tracks.*

V 346 F 15.9 Chena Flood Channel bridge. Upstream dam is part of flood control project initiated after the Chena River left its banks and flooded Fairbanks in 1967. A high water mark from this flood can be seen at the Pioneer Park (Alaskaland) train depot in Fairbanks.

V 346.7 F 15.3 Laurance Road; park-and-ride. Exit for VFW Post, Moose Creek Dam Bikeway and Chena Lake Recreation Area (descriptions follow).

North Pole VFW Post #10029. See display ad this section.

The 5-mile-long **Moose Creek Dam Bikeway** extends from the park-and-ride lot at Laurance and Nelson Roads (0.8 mile from the highway) to the damsite on the Chena River.

Entrance to **Chena Lake Recreation Area**, 2.5 miles from highway; day-use fee $3, RV/tent camping $10, bikes $1. It is 5.5 miles from the highway to the visitor kiosk below the damsite on the Chena River at the end of Main Road. Constructed by the Army Corps of Engineers and run by Fairbanks North Star Borough, the recreation area has 80 campsites, 92 picnic sites (some with wheelchair access), pump water, volleyball courts and a 250-acre lake with swimming beach. Chena Lake Bike Trail begins at Chena Lake swim beach and intersects with the Moose Creek Dam Bikeway. **Chena Lake** is stocked with silver salmon, arctic char, grayling and rainbow trout. Nonmotorized boats may be rented from a concessionaire. The **Chena River** flows through part of the recreation area and offers good grayling fishing and also northern pike, whitefish and burbot. Hiking and self-guiding nature trails. Open year-round. Fees are charged from Memorial Day to Labor Day.

V 347.7 F 14.3 Exit west for St. Nicholas Drive, east for Dawson Road.

V 348.7 F 13.3 Exit southwest for North Pole 5th Avenue businesses, RV park and Santa Claus House. Exit to northeast for **North Pole Visitor Information Center** (open daily, Memorial Day to mid-September) and for Mission Road to radio station KJNP.

These Gold Rush Centennial markers along Alaska's highways inform travelers of historic events. (© Ron Niebrugge)

North Pole 5th Avenue Exit. See description of "North Pole" on pages 467-468.

V 349 F 15 Santa Claus House is visible to southwest; description follows. Access to Santa Claus House is via Santa Claus Lane (next exit northbound).

Santa Claus House. In 1949, Con Miller began wearing a Santa Claus suit on business trips throughout the territory, bringing the spirit of St. Nicholas to hundreds of children for the first time. Here, the Miller family continues this tradition. Ask about ordering a letter. Mail your cards and letters here for authentic North Pole postmark. Enjoy the unique gift shop and exhibits. Open all year. Extended summer hours, Memorial Day through Labor Day. Visit with Santa Claus and his reindeer. Santa Claus House features exclusive gifts and souvenirs. See display ad this section. [ADVERTISEMENT]

V 349.5 F 12.5 Exits for North Pole Plaza/Santa Claus lane to southwest (fast food outlets, 24-hour gas/diesel, car and truck wash, supermarket) and Badger Road to the northeast (description follows).

North Pole/Badger Road Exit. See description of "North Pole" on pages 467-468.

From this exit, **Badger Road** loops northwest 11.1 miles and back to the Richardson Highway at **Milepost V 357.1**. Badger Road provides access to the following (distance from this junction shown): Nordale Road to Chena Hot Springs Road (4.6 mile); gas station and **Riverview RV Park** (8.4 miles); Fort Wainwright (10.1 miles); gas station (10.4 miles); and Old Richardson Highway (10.9 miles).

V 350.2 F 11.8 Peridot Street.

V 350.5 F 11.5 North Pole city limits.

V 350.6 F 11.4 *CAUTION: Highway crosses Alaska Railroad tracks.*

V 351.1 F 10.9 Old Richardson Highway/Twelvemile Village exit to south; airport

V 357.1 F 4.9 Traffic light at **junction** with **Badger Road** to north (eastbound traffic turnoff). This 11.1-mile road loops back to the Richardson Highway at **Milepost V349.5**, providing access to Old Richardson Highway (0.2 mile from this junction); gas station (0.7 mile); Fort Wainwright (1 mile); Riverview RV Park and gas station (2.7 miles); and Nordale Road to Chena Hot Springs Road (6.5 miles).

Riverview RV Park. See display ad on page 467.

V 357.6 F 4.4 *NOTE: Road construction/realignment was under way in this area in 2002.*

V 358.6 F 5.4 Entrance to U.S. Army Fort Wainwright via 3 Mile Gate Road.

V 359.1 F 2.9 Alaska Railroad tracks.

V 359.4 F 2.6 **Junction** with Old Richardson eastbound.

V 359.6 F 2.4 **Junction** with Old Richardson Highway westbound; access to Cushman Street Business Area.

V 360.6 F 1.4 Westbound exit from Richardson Highway to **junction** with Alaska Route 3 (Parks Highway) to Denali Park and Nenana.

Turn to end of PARKS HIGHWAY section on page 398 and read log back to front for log of that highway from Fairbanks south to Anchorage.

V 361 F 1 Entering Fairbanks City northbound.

V 361.2 F 0.8 Welcome to Fairbanks sign northbound.

V 362 F 0 **FAIRBANKS. Junction** with Airport Way and Steese Highway northbound; downtown Fairbanks to west; Fort Wainwright Main Gate (Gaffney Road) to east.

Turn to STEESE HIGHWAY section on page 482 for log of that highway north from end of Richardson Highway in Fairbanks to Circle.

North Pole VFW
Post 10029

RV Spaces
Available to
Veterans

We'd do anything for this country!

(907) 488-9184

Mile 346.7 Richardson Highway
Drive 1 mile West on Laurance Road.
Turn South on VFW Road, Drive 1/2 Mile.

EDGERTON HIGHWAY/ McCARTHY ROAD

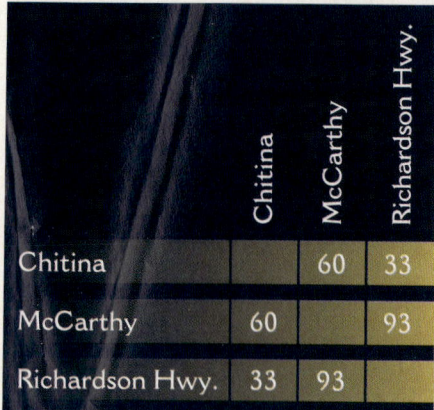

Connects: Richardson Highway Junction to McCarthy, AK
Length: 93 miles **Road Surface:** 40% paved, 60% gravel
Season: McCarthy Road not maintained in winter
Major Attraction: Wrangell–St. Elias National Park & Preserve

(10)

Fall colors along the McCarthy Road. (© Rich Reid, Colors of Nature)

The Edgerton Highway is a scenic paved road leading 33.5 miles east from its junction with the Richardson Highway to Chitina and the start of the McCarthy Road. The gravel McCarthy Road leads 59.5 miles east from Chitina and dead ends at the Kennicott River, about 1 mile west of the settlement of McCarthy. Total driving distance from the Richardson Highway turnoff to the end of the McCarthy Road is 93 miles.

There is no vehicle access across the Kennicott River from the McCarthy Road. The river is crossed by 2 pedestrian bridges. It is a 15-minute walk to McCarthy, where visitors can catch a shuttle to Kennicott.

The Edgerton Highway, known locally as the Edgerton Cutoff, is named for U.S. Army Maj. Glenn Edgerton of the Alaska Territorial Road Commission.

The McCarthy Road follows the right-of-way of the old Copper River & Northwestern Railway. Begun in 1907, the CR&NW (also referred to as the "can't run and never will") was built to carry copper ore from the Kennecott Mines to Cordova. It took 4 years to complete the railway. The railway and mine ceased operation in 1938.

The McCarthy Road is recommended for the adventurous traveler and only in the summer. Maximum speed is about 25 mph. Motorists with large vehicles or trailers should exercise caution, especially in wet weather. Watch for old railroad spikes in the roadbed. Unless recently graded, watch for potholes, soft spots and severe washboard.

Most land along the McCarthy Road is either privately or publicly held. Local residents have asked that visitors please help protect water sources from contamination.

The solitude and scenery of McCarthy, along with the historic Kennecott Mine and surrounding wilderness of Wrangell–St. Elias National Park and Preserve, have drawn increasing numbers of visitors to this area. It is a 126-mile drive from Glennallen to McCarthy, 315 miles from Anchorage.

The National Park Service ranger station in Chitina has information on current road conditions and also on backcountry travel in Wrangell–St. Elias National Park and Preserve.

Emergency medical services: Between the junction of the Richardson and Edgerton highways and McCarthy, contact the Copper River EMS in Glennallen, phone 911 or (907) 822-3203.

Edgerton Highway Log

Distance from junction with Richardson Highway (J) is followed by distance from Chitina (C).

ALASKA ROUTE 10 EAST
J 0 C 33.5 The Edgerton Highway leads east from the Richardson Highway.

Junction of the Edgerton Highway (Alaska Route 10) and the Richardson Highway (Alaska Route 4). Turn to **Milepost V 82.6** on page 458 in the RICHARDSON HIGHWAY section for log of Route 4.

Downgrade next 4 miles eastbound.
Excellent view of Mount Drum (to the northeast), a 12,010-foot peak of the Wrangell Mountains. Mount Wrangell (elev. 14,163 feet) and Mount Blackburn (elev. 16,390 feet) are visible straight ahead.

J 4.5 C 29 Begin bike path eastbound.
J 5.1 C 28.4 Kenny Lake Fire Station.
J 5.3 C 28.2 Kenny Lake School to the south.
J 7.2 C 26.3 Kenny Lake Mercantile & RV Park to north with grocery store, cafe, gas, laundromat, showers, camping and pay phone.

Kenny Lake RV Park & Mercantile. See display ad this section. ▲

J 7.3 C 26.2 Junction with Old Edgerton Loop Road (gravel), which leads 8 miles through homestead and farm country to the Richardson Highway at **Milepost V 91.1**.

End bike path eastbound. Begin bike path westbound.

J 7.5 C 26 Kenny Lake community hall and fairgrounds. **KENNY LAKE** (pop. 507) is an unincorporated agricultural commu-

EDGERTON HIGHWAY/McCARTHY ROAD

Richardson Highway to McCarthy, AK

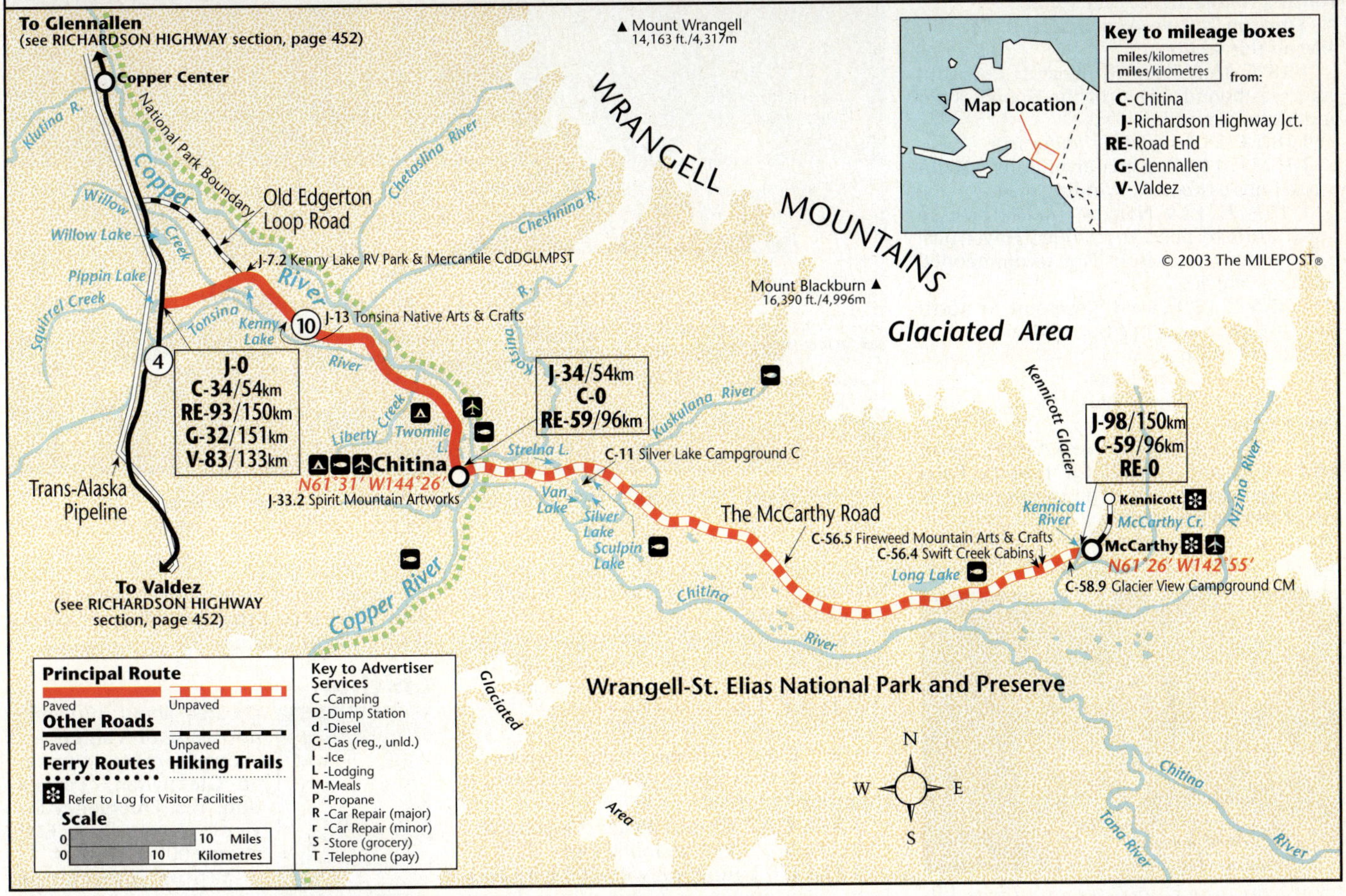

nity located along the Edgerton Highway between about Mile 1 and Mile 17.

The **Kenny Lake Fair**, held on a Friday evening and Saturday in August, is an enjoyable family event with games, food and crafts booths and local entertainment. The Kenny Lake Fair was first held in 1973 as part of the school carnival. It is sponsored by the Kenny Lake Community League.

J 7.7 C 25.8 Long double-ended paved rest area to south with picnic table on shore of Kenny Lake.

J 9 C 24.5 Kenny Lake Community Chapel to south.

J 9.5 C 24 Golden Spruce Cabins to north; lodging, snacks and gifts.

J 12.3 C 21.2 Paved parking area to south for **Tonsina River Trail**. Well-marked 2-mile BLM trail leads south through woods to a picnic site overlooking the Tonsina River. Rated easy. Private property borders trail.

J 12.5 C 21 Paved parking area to north for **Copper River Trail**. This BLM trail is 7 miles round trip and recommended as a good trail for bird watchers. The trail is fairly flat and marshy, winding through dense vegetation to end at the Copper River. Use

---

Open Year Around — Mile 7.2 Edgerton Highway
8 a.m.– 10 p.m. Monday - Saturday   9 a.m.– 9 p.m. Sunday

Kenny Lake RV Park & Mercantile

"OUR GUESTS CAN PICK THEIR OWN DIAMOND WILLOW STICKS"

Kenny Lake Hotel • Spectacular View of the Wrangells
New, Clean Rooms • Shared Baths • Tourist Information
GAS • PROPANE • GROCERIES • ICE • Fishing Licenses
10 Electric Sites • 10 Pull-Throughs (Dry) • Secluded RV & Tent Sites
Water • Dump Station • Laundromat • Showers
Pay Phone • Fax Service • Cafe

Secure RV Parking – Park at our place and take your towed vehicle to McCarthy or Valdez. Pick up point for scheduled van excursions to McCarthy & Kennicott. Ask about Alaska Trail Ventures 4 wheeler trips or Rather Rough It Float or Fishing Trips

Dick & Sue Winingham
(907) 822-3313
HC60 Box 230
Copper Center, AK 99573
knnylake@alaska.net
All Major Credit Cards Accepted

Gift Shop
Unique Local
Handcrafted Items

caution along the Copper River: it is very swift and cold.

J 13 C 20.5 Turnoff to south for access to Tonsina Native Arts & Crafts shop.

Tonsina Native Arts & Crafts. See display ad this section.

J 18 C 15.5 Steep (8 percent) downhill grade eastbound. Views of the Copper River and bluffs to north.

J 18.1 C 15.4 *Watch for falling rock.*

J 19.4 C 14.1 Tonsina River bridge. Highway climbs eastbound; winding road.

J 19.6 C 13.9 Narrow gravel track to north leads to pond (river-filled gravel pit); berry picking in season. Not recommended for large vehicles.

J 21.6 C 11.9 Paved viewpoint to north with sweeping view of Copper River.

J 21.9 C 11.6 *Begin long winding downhill (and uphill) grades eastbound.*

J 23.5 C 10 Liberty Falls Creek BLM trailhead to south.

J 23.7 C 9.8 Liberty Creek bridge (8-ton load limit) and turnoff for **Liberty Falls State Recreation Site**. The campground is just south of the highway on the banks of Liberty Creek, near the foot of the thundering falls. Very scenic spot; worth the stop.

Fish wheel on the Copper River during the salmon run. (© Ernest Manewal)

Loop road through campground (large RVs and trailers check road before driving in); 5 sites, no water, camping fee $12. Berry picking; watch for bears.

J 28.5 C 5 Side road north to Chitina DOT/PF maintenance station and Chitina Airport. ADF&G office (dip-net permits).

Private Aircraft: Chitina Airport; elev. 556 feet; length 2,800 feet; gravel; unattended.

J 29.5 C 4 Small gravel turnout by Three Mile Lake.

J 29.7 C 3.8 Paved turnout by **Three Mile Lake**; good grayling and rainbow trout fishing.

J 30.7 C 2.8 Large gravel parking area to south at east end of **Two Mile Lake** (stocked); good grayling and rainbow trout fishing.

J 31.8 C 1.7 One Mile Lake (also called First Lake). Access road to boat launch at east end of lake.

Entering "Uptown" Chitina; guest cabins. Chitina businesses are located along the Edgerton Highway and on Chitina Road.

J 31.9 C 1.6 NOTE: *Begin 30 mph speed zone eastbound.*

J 32.5 C 1 Raven Dance Pizza & Espresso.

J 33.1 C 0.4 Chitina Post office. Entering "Midtown" Chitina.

J 33.2 C 0.3 Chitina Road; "Downtown" Chitina (see description following).

J 33.4 C 0.1 Junction with O'Brien Creek Road (also known as Copper River Road/Copper River Highway). This road provides a state right-of-way access to popular fishing areas on large sandbars along the Copper River. Access to the Copper River is not permitted across private land. Access is permitted only at O'Brien Creek and Haley Creek and prohibited elsewhere unless official signs indicate access is allowed. Do not trespass, litter or disturb private lands in any way. O'Brien Creek river access and camping (litter barrels, outhouse) is 2.7 miles/4.3 km from Chitina (steep and narrow downhill to O'Brien Creek). A DOT travel advisory at warns of *"narrow road, rock slides, creek crossings, sharp curves and steep dropoffs."* Inquire locally for current road conditions.

J 33.5 C 0 Chitina Wayside; state-maintained paved parking area and public restrooms across from Trout/Town Lake.

McCarthy Road begins just beyond this point (see McCarthy Road Log following description of Chitina).

Chitina

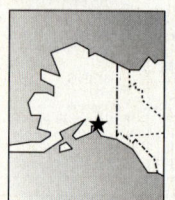

Located about 120 miles northeast of Valdez, and about 66 miles southeast of Glennallen. **Population:** 123. **Emergency Services:** Copper River EMS, phone (907) 822-3203.

Visitor Information: The Wrangell–St. Elias National Park and Preserve Chitina Ranger Station here is open daily in summer (June–August) from 10 A.M. to 6 P.M. Housed in the historic Ed S. Orr Cabin (1910), the ranger station has maps, books and brochures on the park and surrounding area. Backcountry hikers may sign-out here and obtain bear-proof containers. Information is available on road conditions as well as hiking trails and recreation within the park. A slide show on the McCarthy Road and video programs are available. Write Box 439, Copper Center, AK 99573, or phone (907) 822-5234 (park headquarters); Chitina ranger station, phone (907) 823-2205.

Chitina has a post office, grocery, gas, cafe, restaurant, overnight accommodations, and several tire repair services.

Chitina (pronounced CHIT-na) was established about 1908 as a railroad stop on the Copper River & Northwestern Railway and as a supply town for the Kennecott Copper Mines at McCarthy. A surveying engineer for the mines, Otto Adrian Nelson, owned much of the town in 1914, which consisted of 5 hotels, a general store, movie theater and several bars, restaurants and dance halls. When the mine and railroad were abandoned in 1938, Chitina became a ghost town. Pioneer bush pilot "Mudhole" Smith bought the Nelson estate in 1963 and sold off the townsite and buildings.

Today, few of the original buildings remain except for the tinsmith, now on the National Register of Historic Places, which houses Spirit Mountain Artworks.

Spirit Mountain Artworks. See display ad this section.

A big attraction here is the **Chitina**

Tonsina Native Arts & Crafts
Kenny Lake Area · Mile 13 Edgerton Hwy
Alaskan Native Crafts Made Here

May-Sept. Hours 10 a.m.-6 p.m. Closed Sunday
Dean & Ada Wilson-Owners

Main Street, (Box 22), Chitina, Alaska—(907) 823-2222

SPIRIT MOUNTAIN ARTWORKS
FINE ARTS & QUALITY CRAFTS FROM AROUND ALASKA

Art Koeninger, Custom Jeweler-National Historic Site

Dip-Net Fishery, coinciding with the seasonal salmon run (reds, kings or silvers) on the **Copper River**. The dip-net fishery for salmon runs June through September (depending on harvest levels). *This fishery is open to Alaska residents only.* Special regulations and permits apply; check with ADF&G. Call the state's recorded information line in Anchorage at (907) 267-2511; in Fairbanks at (907) 459-7382; and in the Glennallen area at (907) 822-5224.

McCarthy Road Log

Distance from Chitina (C) is followed by distance from road end (RE).

ALASKA ROUTE 10 EAST

C 0 RE 59.5 Chitina Wayside; state-maintained paved parking area and public

restrooms across from Trout/Town Lake.

C 0.1 RE 59.4 Pavement ends eastbound. No road maintenance east of here between Oct. 15 and May 15. Sign reads: "McCarthy Road: Road ends at Kennicott River—62 miles. Limited vehicle services. Drive at your own risk. Watch out for loose railroad spikes. Check locally for road conditions and services beyond this point."

Road passes through narrow rock cut.

C 0.2 RE 59.3 Turnout with view of the Copper River.

C 0.5 RE 59 Turnout with view of the Copper River bridge.

C 1.1 RE 58.4 Copper River bridge. This 1,378-foot steel span, designed for year-round use, cost $3.5 million. It reestablished access across the river into the McCarthy–Kennicott area when it was completed in 1971.

Entering Game Management Unit 11 eastbound, GMU 13D westbound.

C 1.5 RE 58 Turnoff to southeast for campground with treed sites with picnic tables, firepits and toilets. Turnoff to northwest for access to fishing and informal camping and vehicle parking on gravel bars along the **Copper River**; red and king salmon.

Sign on road reads: "Much of the land along the road is privately owned. For land ownership information, contact Chitina Village Corp. (907/823-2223), Ahtna Inc. (907/822-3476) or the National Park Service (907/822-5234)."

C 10 RE 49.5 Public fishing access via 0.3 mile trail north to **Strelna Lake**; rainbow trout and silver salmon. (Private property adjacent trail.)

C 11 RE 48.5 Turnout to north for parking and pedestrian public fishing access to **Silver Lake** and **Van Lake**; good rainbow trout fishing. Road access south to private campground on Silver Lake.

Silver Lake Campground. See display ad this section.

C 12.3 RE 47.2 Sculpin Lake public fishing access to south; pedestrian access only. Good rainbow trout fishing (stocked).

C 14.1 RE 45.4 Airstrip.

C 16.9 RE 42.6 Turnout with view of Kuskulana River and bridge; good photo op.

C 17 RE 42.5 Kuskulana Bridge. *NOTE: 1-lane bridge, yield to oncoming traffic.* This old railroad bridge (built in 1910) is approximately 525 feet long and 238 feet above the river. It is a narrow 3-span steel railway bridge with wood decking. Before it was rehabilitated in 1988 this bridge was referred to by motorists as "the biggest thrill on the road to McCarthy." Turnouts at east end of bridge.

C 18.3 RE 41.2 *CAUTION: Very narrow road next 0.5 mile eastbound; steep dropoff, no guardrail.*

C 24.7 RE 34.8 Turnouts both sides of road.

C 25 RE 34.5 Lou's Lake to north; silver salmon and grayling fishing.

C 25.8 RE 34.2 Turnout at end of lake.

C 26.6 RE 32.9 Private airstrip.

C 27 RE 32.5 Chokosna River bridge. Turnoff to north just east of bridge for "Parking, Camping, Outhouse" (signed in 2002), 0.1 mile north via rutted access road. Pleasant campsite in trees with picnic table, outhouse, garbage can; fee by donation.

C 29 RE 30.5 *Steep grades both directions down to river crossing.* Gilahina River bridge (1-lane); parking. A National Park Service foot path leads a short ways up the Gilahina River and under the old wooden railroad trestle.

C 35.5 RE 24 Access to lake to south.

C 44.2 RE 15.3 Lakina River bridge (1-lane); maximum height 13'2". Access to river at east end.

C 44.3 RE 15.2 Long Lake Wildlife Refuge sign; shooting prohibited (eastbound sign).

C 45.9 RE 13.6 Airstrip.

C 46 RE 13.5 Turnout on **Long Lake**; a beautiful spot. Fishing for lake trout, silver salmon, grayling, Dolly Varden, burbot.

C 56.4 RE 3.1 Swift Creek Cabins, located 3 miles from "the end of the road," offer a private, comfortable, scenic home away from home ... Alaska style. Spend time exploring the beautiful, historic McCarthy/Kennicott area and then relax and enjoy the private serenity of Swift Creek Cabins. Winter: (907) 235-5579. Summer: (907) 554 1234. SwiftCreekAlaska.com. Also visit

"The Potato," a unique eatery in downtown McCarthy offering breakfast, lunch and espresso. See display ad this section.
[ADVERTISEMENT]

C 56.5 RE 3 Fireweed Mountain Arts and Crafts in log building to north.

Fireweed Mountain Arts & Crafts. Experience Alaskan hospitality at our shop or stay in our handscribed log cabin. Stop and chat about log building or winter life with year-round McCarthy residents. Our private cabin contains a woodstove with breakfast provided. $50 double. Full service tire repair; used tires. Terry and Dee Frady. MasterCard, VISA. Phone (907) 554-4420.
[ADVERTISEMENT]

C 58.7 RE 0.8 Turnoff to north for National Park Service McCarthy Ranger Station, an information kiosk with personnel available according to posted hours (12:30–6 P.M. Sunday to Thursday, and 12:30–7:30 P.M. Friday and Saturday in summer 2002); outhouses. Airstrip to south.

C 58.9 RE 0.6 Glacier View Campground. Just ½ mile from the footbridge, our scenic and private campsites offer breath-taking views of the Root Glacier and surrounding Wrangell Mountains. Rent a mountain bike and hit the trails or just soak up the sun at our outdoor cafe featuring home-style barbecue cooking. At Glacier View we strive to make your ultimate road trip unforgettable. New cabin for rent. Phone (907) 554-4490 summer, (907) 345-7121 winter, e-mail glacierview@gci.net.
[ADVERTISEMENT]

C 59.3 RE 0.2 Welcome to Copperpoint, AK (sign).

C 59.5 RE 0 The road dead ends by the footbridge at the Kennicott River. Copperpoint wayside parking area (sign), a private parking lot, charges about $6/day to park a vehicle. Public pay phone by footbridge.

Two pedestrian-only footbridges cross the channels of the Kennicott River providing

SILVER LAKE Campground

Rainbow Trout Fishing
RV and Tent Camping on beautiful Silver Lake
Boat and Canoe Rental

MILEPOST 11   CHITINA
McCarthy Road   Alaska 99566

FOR SALE BY OWNER
TURNKEY OPERATION
http://angelfire.com/journal2/amerivoice/silverlk/

McCarthy Road speed limit is 25 mph.

access to the road on the other side of the river that leads to McCarthy and Kennicott. *There is no vehicle access across the river.* Visitors can easily walk the mile to McCarthy from here. Kennicott is about 5 miles: Use the shuttle service from McCarthy. Courtesy phone by parking lot has instructions for calling businesses in McCarthy and Kennicott. If you are staying at Kennicott Lodge, for example, they will pick you up on the other side of the bridge.

You can see the old hand-pulled, open-platform cable tram that travelers had to use to haul themselves across the river before the state constructed the footbridge across the Kennicott River in 1997.

CAUTION: Do not attempt to wade across this glacial river; strong currents and cold water make it extremely treacherous. ▲

McCarthy/Kennicott

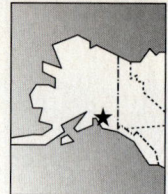

Located 315 miles from Anchorage. McCarthy is about 1 mile by road from the end of the McCarthy Road at the Kennicott River pedestrian bridge; Kennicott is about 5 miles by road from McCarthy. **Population:** 42.

Transportation: Air—Charter service to and from airstrip near McCarthy. **Van**—Scheduled service between Glennallen and McCarthy via Backcountry Connection; phone (907) 822-5292. Shuttle service between McCarthy and Kennicott via Wrangell Mountain Bus from Wrangell Mountain Air office; 1-way fare $5/adults, $2/dogs; phone (07) 554-4411.

Elevation: 1,531 feet. **Climate:** Temperature extremes from -58° F to 91° F; average snowfall 52 inches; annual precipitation 12 inches. **Radio:** KCAM (Glennallen), KSKO 870, KXKM 89.7.

Private Aircraft: McCarthy NR 2, 1 NE; elev. 1,531 feet; length 3,500 feet; gravel; unattended, unmaintained.

McCarthy has overnight accommodations, an espresso/cafe place (The Potato), a pizza place, flightseeing services and wilderness guide services. Kennicott has the Kennicott Glacier Lodge and a wilderness guide service. Businesses in both Kennicott and McCarthy can send and receive email and faxes, and cell phones work in both places as well. Neither place has a post office, school or television.

The Kennicott River flows by the west side of McCarthy and joins the Nizina River which flows into the Chitina River. The local McCarthy Museum, located in the railway depot, has historical artifacts and photos from the early mining days. Wrangell Mountains Center, a private non-profit educational organization for Wrangell-St. Elias National Park, is headquartered in the old Hardware Store in McCarthy (email wrangells@aol.com).

The old mining town of Kennicott is perched on the side of Bonanza Ridge next to Kennicott Glacier. Accommodations and services in Kennicott are limited. Businesses include the Kennicott Glacier Lodge (ask about daily meal specials), a bed and breakfast, flightseeing service and alpine/historic guide service.

Slides presentations and other summer programs presented by the National Park Service at the Jurick Building across from

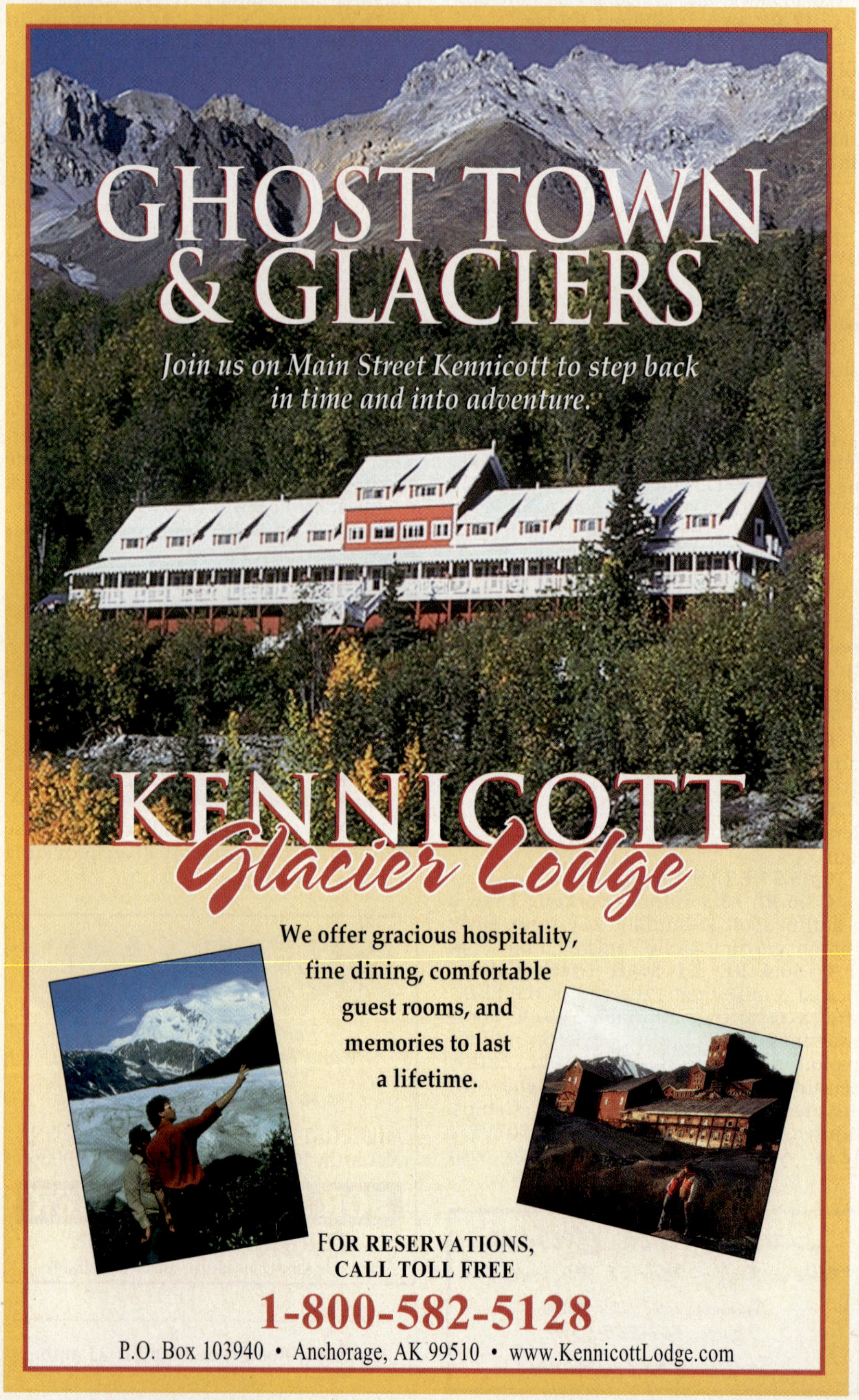

McCARTHY/KENNICOTT ADVERTISERS

Backcountry Connection ..Ph. (907) 822-5292
Kennicott Glacier
 Lodge...........................Ph. (800) 582-5128
Kennicott Wilderness
 Guides.......................Main Street Kennicott
McCarthy Lodge ....Ph. (907) 554-4402
Wrangell Mountain Air.....Ph. (800) 478-1160

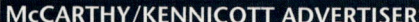

GHOST TOWN & GLACIERS

Join us on Main Street Kennicott to step back in time and into adventure.

KENNICOTT *Glacier Lodge*

We offer gracious hospitality, fine dining, comfortable guest rooms, and memories to last a lifetime.

FOR RESERVATIONS, CALL TOLL FREE

1-800-582-5128

P.O. Box 103940 • Anchorage, AK 99510 • www.KennicottLodge.com

---

BACKCOUNTRY CONNECTION LLC

Shuttle and charter service within Wrangell-St. Elias National Park to KENNICOTT & McCARTHY

See the beauty of Wrangell-St. Elias up close!

Avoid the spikes - save your tires!

(907) 822-5292

www.alaska-backcountry-tours.com

Drive with headlights on at all times.

Wrangell–St. Elias National Park and Preserve

Wrangell-St. Elias is the largest unit in the national park system, encompassing 13.2 million acres of wilderness. Formed by the Wrangell, St. Elias and Chugach mountain ranges, the park contains 9 of the 16 highest peaks in the United States, including Mount St. Elias (18,008 feet), the second tallest peak in the United States. Other major peaks in the park—all dormant volcanoes—are Mount Wrangell (14,163 feet), Mount Blackburn (16,390 feet), Mount Sanford (16,237 feet) and Mount Drum (12,010 feet).

The park also contains the largest concentration of glaciers on the continent. One of these, Malaspina Glacier, is North America's largest piedmont glacier, a type formed when 2 or more glaciers flow from confined valleys to form a broad fan- or lobe-shaped ice mass. Malaspina Glacier covers an area of about 1,500 square miles—larger than the state of Rhode Island. It has been designated a national natural landmark. Hubbard Glacier, which flows out of the St. Elias Mountains into Disenchantment Bay, is one of the largest and most active glaciers in North America.

Also located in the park are Chitistone and Nizina canyons. Both have been described as exceeding the scale of Yosemite Valley in California, with an even greater variety of geological wonders. There is a spectacular, 300-foot waterfall in upper Chitistone Canyon, and the lower canyon has sheer walls rising 4,000 feet above the river.

Although the scale of the park seems overwhelming, for motorists the choices of how to visit Wrangell-St. Elias are relatively few. Road access to the northern section of the park and preserve is from Slana on the Tok Cutoff via the 43-mile Nabesna Road. The major road access to the east side of Wrangell-St. Elias National Park is via the Edgerton Highway/McCarthy Road.

Guided tours of Kennicott Mill are available. (© Kris Graef, staff)

Park information is available on the Edgerton Highway/McCarthy Road access at the historic **Ed S. Orr Cabin** in Chitina, and at the McCarthy Ranger Station information kiosk at **Milepost C 58.7** McCarthy Road.

At the northern end of the park, information is available at the Slana ranger station at Mile 0.2 Nabesna Road off the Tok Cutoff.

The park's new (2002) Wrangell-St. Elias National Park and Preserve Visitor Center is located at **Milepost V 106.5** on the Richardson Highway.

The Kennicott area is one of the major centers of activity in the park, perhaps because it contains one of the park's best known attractions: the huge complex of barn-red buildings that make up the Kennicott mill, now a national historic landmark. The mill was built in 1907 by Kennecott Copper Corporation (an early day misspelling made the mining company Kennecott, while the glacier and river are Kennicott).

The National Park Service purchased many of the mill structures (although several are still privately owned) and work is under way to stabilize the site. Most of the buildings are locked for visitor safety. Narrated tours of the mill are available from Kennicott-McCarthy Wilderness Guides and St. Elias Alpine Guides. The National Park Service conducts summer interpretive programs and offers daily slide presentations in the Jurick Building in Kennicott.

The Kennecott mines, including 70 miles of subterranean tunnels, are up near the ridge top (behind present-day Kennicott Glacier Lodge), and were connected to the mill by aerial trams. Still known as the richest copper mine ever discovered, Kennecott processed more than 591,535 tons of copper ore valued at $200,000 and employed some 800 workers in its heyday between 1911-1938. The place was left as a ghost town after 1938 and was resettled in the 1970s.

While copper mining inspired some of the early prospectors to travel to the land that is now Wrangell-St. Elias National Park and Preserve, it was the discovery of gold in Chisana (pronounced Shooshana) that began the last great gold rush in Alaska. In 1913, thousands of stampeders made the treacherous journey through rugged country by whatever means possible to reach the newfound mining district. Chisana soon became known as "the largest log cabin town in the world." It was a short boom, lasting only a few years, but an important part of the history of this area.

Recreational opportunities in Wrangell-St. Elias include hunting, fishing, expedition mountaineering, backpacking/hiking, cross-country skiing, rafting/kayaking and wildlife observation. All hunting, fishing and trapping must be done in accordance with state laws and regulations.

Navigable rivers in the park include the Copper and Chitina rivers. It is also possible to float several other streams in the park, such as the Nabesna and Kennicott rivers. Several guides and outfitters offer a variety of trips in the park and preserve.

Hikes follow unimproved backcountry routes consisting of mining trails, historic routes, streambeds, shorelines, game trails and open country. For many hikers, hiring the services of a local guide will make the trip safer and more enjoyable. In general, the areas above treeline afford the easiest hiking and best views. These areas are often accessed by charter plane to one of the many "bush" landing strips in the park.

The Park Service cautions that visitors to the Wrangell-St. Elias backcountry must be self-sufficient; sources of assistance are frequently many miles away. Wilderness travel and survival skills are essential.

There are 10 cabins available for public use within Wrangell-St. Elias National Park and Preserve. The cabins are available on a first-come, first-served basis; the park does not have a cabin reservation system.

There are no designated campgrounds within the park/preserve; wilderness camping only. No permits are necessary for camping or backpacking although voluntary registration is requested.

For more detailed information, contact the park visitor center on the Richardson Highway or the ranger stations at Slana (907/822-5238), Chitina (907/823-2205) and in Yakutat (907/784-3295). Or write Wrangell St. Elias National Park and Preserve, Park Headquarters, P.O. Box 439, Copper Center, AK 99573; phone (907) 822-5234, fax (907) 822-7216. Or visit www.nps.gov/wrst/cabins.htm. Or email wrst_interpretation@nps.gov.

McCarthy offers food and lodging. (© Kris Graef, staff)

Kennicott Lodge. Narrated tours of the mill, guided mine hikes, glacier treks and fly-out hikes available locally from Kennicott-McCarthy Wilderness Guides.

A popular day hike from Kennicott is the **Root Glacier Trail**. The easy to moderate 3-mile round trip takes you from Kennicott townsite along the lateral moraine of the Kennicott and Root Glaciers to the toe of the glacier. Allow 2 to 4 hours to hike. Also makes a good mountain bike trip, according to the Park Service.

Kennicott Glacier Lodge, located in the ghost town of Kennicott, offers the area's finest accommodations and dining. Built in 1987, this new lodge has 25 clean, delightful guest rooms, 2 living rooms, a spacious dining room, and a 180-foot front porch with a spectacular panoramic view of the Wrangell Mountains, Chugach Mountains and Kennicott Glacier. The homemade food, served family-style, has been called "wilderness gourmet dining." Guest activities at this destination resort include glacier trekking, flightseeing, photography, alpine hiking, historical and nature tours, rafting. May 15 to Sept. 20. (800) 582-5128. See display ad this section. [ADVERTISEMENT]

McCarthy Lodge & Ma Johnson's Historic Hotel & Lancaster's Backpacker Accommodations. Surrounded by more mountains and glaciers than anywhere else in North America, McCarthy Lodge is one of Alaska's most famous buildings. Ma Johnson's 16-rooms are decorated with authentic McCarthy–Kennicott artifacts. Creatively utilizing local ingredients makes the McCarthy Lodge restaurant an essential part of your Alaskan experience. Hiking, rafting, flightseeing, guided adventures, photography, glacier exploration and historic ghost town magic await you. Our Nugget Deli-Bakery-General Store provides goodies for your backcountry hike. Mountain Arts features locally produced artwork, including area gems and minerals. No trip to McCarthy–Kennicott is complete without a visit to the Prohibition-days Golden Saloon! www.McCarthyLodge.com. (907) 554-4402. Locally owned, open year-round. [ADVERTISEMENT]

Wrangell Mountain Air provides twice daily, scheduled air service to McCarthy/Kennicott as a time saving alternative to driving the McCarthy Road. Park your car or RV in Chitina at the end of the paved road and enjoy a spectacular flight through the Wrangell–St. Elias Mountains. Affordable fly-in day trips to Kennicott are also available from Chitina. Wrangell Mountain Air specializes in world-class flightseeing, fly-in alpine hiking and river rafting. Aircraft are high wing for great viewing and equipped with intercom and headsets for each passenger. Phone free for reservations and information, (800) 478-1160 or (907) 554-4411. E-mail: info@wrangellmountainair.org. Internet: www.WrangellMountainAir.com. See display ad this section. [ADVERTISEMENT]

KENNICOTT WILDERNESS GUIDES
½ & full day Glacier Hikes!
Ice-Climbing & Backcountry Trips
- Alaskan Guides -
Main Street Kennicott, Alaska
1-800-ON-HIKES or (907)554-4444

DENALI HIGHWAY

	Cantwell	Delta Junction	Denali Park	Paxson
Cantwell		214	27	134
Delta Junction	214		241	80
Denali Park	27	241		161
Paxson	134	80	161	

Connects: Paxson to Cantwell, AK **Length:** 134 miles
Road Surface: 85% gravel, 15% paved **Season:** Closed in winter
Highest Summit: Maclaren Summit 4,086 feet
Major Attraction: Tangle Lakes–Delta River Canoe Trail
(See map, page 478)

View of Landmark Gap and Round Tangle Lake at Milepost P 22.
(© Rich Reid, Colors of Nature)

The 134-mile-long Denali Highway links Paxson at **Milepost V 185.5** on the Richardson Highway to Cantwell at **Milepost A 210** on the Parks Highway. Winter snow closes the highway to through traffic from about October to mid-May.

The first 21 miles of the Denali Highway from Paxson and the first 3 miles from Cantwell are paved. The remaining 110 miles are gravel. (Continued paving of the Denali Highway has been proposed.)

The condition of the gravel portion of the Denali Highway varies, depending on highway maintenance, weather and the opinion of the driver.

The Denali Highway was not maintained by the Dept. of Transportation in summer 2002, resulting in some rough road (potholes, washboard and washouts), particularly on the west end of the highway for about the first 20 or 30 miles out of Cantwell. Road surfacing on this highway normally ranges from good gravel to rough and rocky. Washboard can develop quickly. This can be a dusty drive for motorists—and a very dusty ride for bicyclists—in dry weather.

The highway becomes narrower and more winding west of Maclaren Summit (elev. 4,086 feet). This is the second highest highway pass in the state, and represents the only significant grade on the highway.

When the Denali Highway opened in 1957, it was the only road link to Denali National Park and Preserve (then Mount McKinley National Park) until the completion of the Parks Highway in 1972. (Prior to 1957, the national park had been accessible only by railroad.)

The Denali Highway has much to recommend it to today's travelers, including great scenery, ORV and mountain biking trails, fishing, hunting, good bird watching and interesting geography. Cross-country skiing, snowmachining and dog mushing are favorite winter sports at Tangle Lakes Lodge, **Milepost P 22**.

The Denali Highway provides access to the Delta River canoe trail at Tangle Lakes, headwaters of the Delta National Wild and Scenic River. For detailed information on ORV use on public lands or canoeing the Delta River, contact the Bureau of Land Management office in Glennallen, phone (907) 822-3217.

Birders will find Smith's Longspur, harlequin ducks, gyrfalcons, arctic warblers and more than 100 other species along the Denali Highway. Birders might want to stop in at Denali Highway Cabins (www.denalihwy.com) at **Milepost P 0.1** and talk to Dr. Audubon L. Bakewell IV, co-author of the *ABA Bird Finding Guide to Alaska*.

There are dozens of primitive campsites and turnouts along the highway which are heavily used by hunters during caribou and moose seasons. There are also many unmarked trails leading off into the Bush. Inquire locally and carry a good topographic map when hiking off the highway.

Emergency medical services: Between Paxson and **Milepost P 77.5** (Susitna Lodge), phone 911 or the state troopers at (907) 822-3263. Between **Milepost P 77.5** and Cantwell, phone the Cantwell ambulance at (907) 768-2982 or the state troopers at (907) 768-2202. NOTE: *We did not get cell phone service between Paxson and Cantwell when we traveled this road in summer 2002.*

Denali Highway Log

Distance from Paxson (P) is followed by distance from junction with the Parks Highway at Cantwell (C).
NOTE: There are relatively few physical mileposts along this highway.

ALASKA ROUTE 8

P 0 C 133.8 **PAXSON** (pop. 30; elev. 2,650 feet), at **Milepost V 185.5** on the Richardson highway, began in 1906 when Alvin Paxson established a roadhouse at Mile 192. He later built a larger roadhouse at Old Mile 191. The structure burned in the early 1970s; the ruins can be seen on the east side of the highway at **Milepost V 185.7** Richardson Highway. Today, businesses here include Paxson Inn and Lodge and Denali Highway Cabins.

Junction of the Richardson Highway (Alaska Route 4) with the Denali Highway (Alaska Route 8). Turn to **Milepost V 185.5** on page 461 in the RICHARDSON HIGHWAY section for log.

Private Aircraft: Paxson airstrip, adjacent south; elev. 2,653 feet; length 2,800 feet; gravel; emergency fuel; attended.

P 0.1 C 133.7 Side road north to **Denali Highway Cabins**; lodging. Naturalist-led river trips on the Gulkana River are available here.

P 0.2 C 133.6 Gulkana River bridge.

P 0.3 C 133.5 Gravel parking area at west end of bridge; informal camping. Spawning sockeye salmon in season. (This portion of the Gulkana River is closed to salmon fishing.) Look for "harleys" (harlequin ducks). Trail to Mud Lake; grayling fishing.

P 0.4 C 133.4 Entering Paxson Closed Area (sign) westbound. The area south of the Denali Highway and east of the Richardson Highway is closed to the taking of all big game.

There are several long upgrades and many

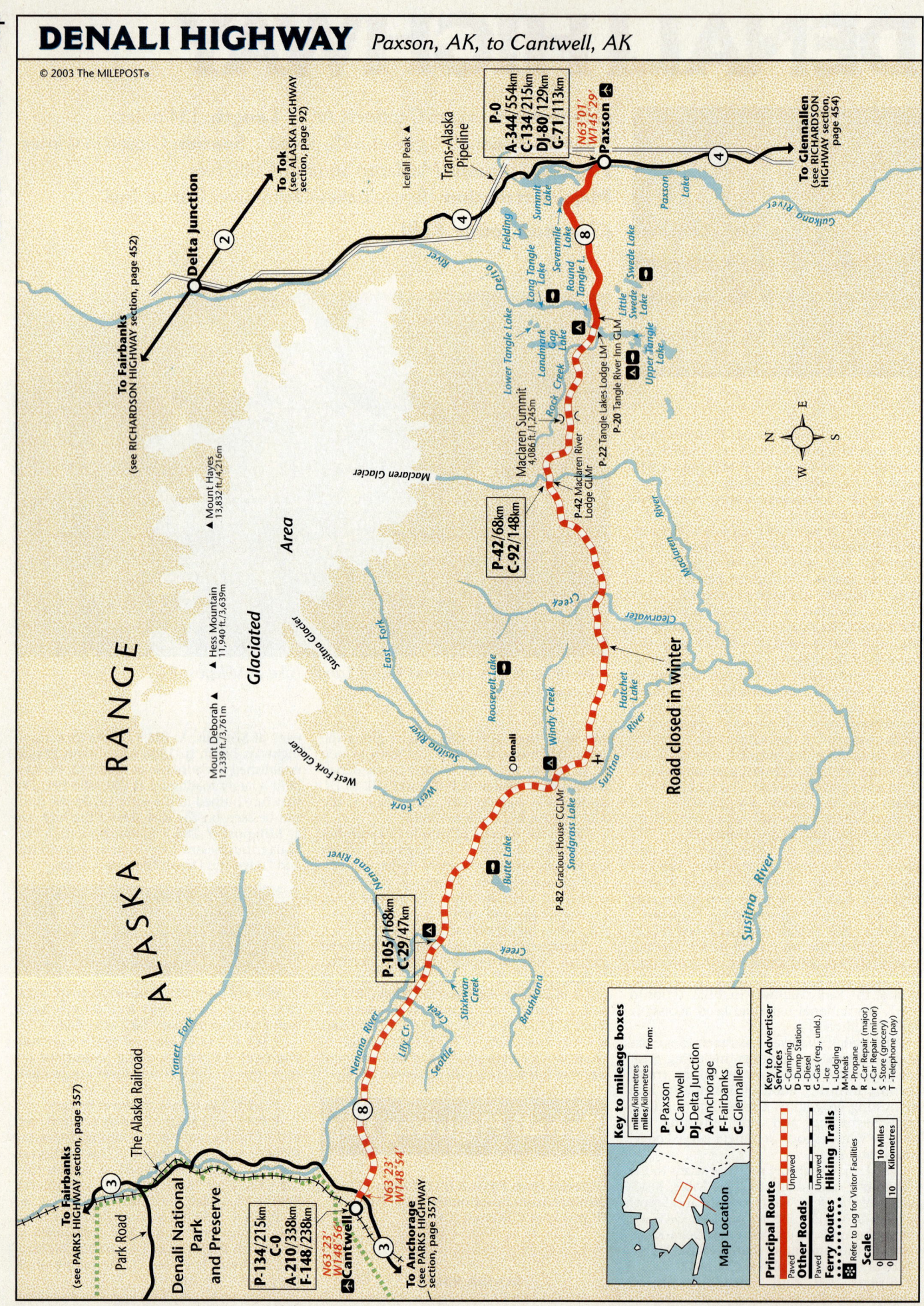

turnouts the next 21 miles westbound. Wildflowers carpet the tundra in the spring and summer. Watch for nesting swans.

P 0.7 C 133.1 Large paved turnout to south.

P 1.5 C 132.3 Large paved turnout to south.

P 2 C 131.8 Westbound travelers may note the change in vegetation from spruce forest to alpine tundra.

P 2.2 C 131.6 Large paved turnout to south.

P 3.6 C 130.2 Paved turnout to south. Several more turnouts next 3 miles westbound with views of Summit Lake to the north, Gakona Glacier to the northeast, Icefall Peak and Gulkana Glacier west of Icefall Peak, all in the **Alaska Range**. The 650-mile-long range, which extends across southcentral Alaska from the Canadian border southwest to Iliamna Lake, also contains Mount McKinley (Denali), the highest peak in North America.

P 4 C 129.8 Views to east next 3 miles westbound of Mounts Sanford, Wrangell and Drum in the Wrangell Mountains; see viewpoint at **Milepost P 13.1**.

P 4.1 C 129.7 Large paved turnout to north.

P 5.1 C 128.7 Larve paved turnout to north.

P 6.3 C 127.5 Large paved turnout to south.

P 6.8 C 127 Access to **Sevenmile Lake** 0.8 mile north; excellent fishing for lake trout in summer.

P 7.1 C 126.7 Paved turnout to south. Highway climbs westbound.

P 7.4 C 126.4 Large gravel turnout overlooking Sevenmile Lake. Two Bit Lake is the large lake to the north; Summit Lake is to the northeast.

P 7.6 C 126.2 Paved turnout to north overlooking Sevenmile Lake. Summit Lake visible to east.

P 9 C 124.8 Gravel turnout. Entering BLM public lands westbound.

P 10 C 123.8 Paved turnout to south overlooking **Ten Mile Lake**. Short hike downhill to outlet. Fishing for lake trout, grayling and burbot in summer.

P 10.4 C 123.4 Paved turnout overlooking **Teardrop Lake** to south. Short hike down steep hill to lake; lake trout, grayling and burbot in summer.

Views westbound of extensive glacial outwash plain dotted with kettle ponds; known locally as Hungry Hollow.

P 11.1 C 122.7 Paved turnout and trail to **Octopus Lake** 0.3 mile south; lake trout, grayling, whitefish.

P 11.7 C 122.1 Paved turnout to south.

P 12 C 121.8 Paved turnout to south.

P 12.6 C 121.2 Paved turnout to south.

P 13.1 C 120.7 Paved turnout to south is Wrangell Mountain viewpoint. The Wrangell Mountains are about 78 air miles southeast of here. The prominent peak on the left is Mount Sanford (16,237 feet); Mount Drum (12,010 feet) is on the right; and Mount Wrangell (14,163 feet) is in the center. Mount Wrangell is the northernmost active volcano on the Pacific Rim.

Lupine blooms alongside the road in late June.

P 14.6 C 119.2 Paved turnout; small lakes to north.

Highway begins descent westbound to Tangle Lakes area.

P 14.9 C 118.9 Turnout to south.

P 15.7 C 118.1 Paved turnout to south.

P 16.4 C 117.4 Swede Lake trail, 3 miles long, to south; **Little Swede Lake**, 2 miles. This trail connects with the Middle Fork Gulkana River branch trail (access to Dickey Lake and Meier Lake trail) and the Alphabet Hills trail. **Big Swede Lake** has excellent fishing for lake trout, grayling, whitefish and burbot. Little Swede Lake is excellent for lake trout. Inquire at Tangle River Inn for directions.

P 16.5 C 117.3 Entering BLM **Tangle Lakes Archaeological District** westbound. Within this 226,000-acre area, more than 400 archaeological sites chronicle man's seasonal exploitation of the local natural resources. For more than 10,000 years, hunter-gatherers have dug roots, picked berries, fished and hunted big game (primarily caribou) in this area. You may hike along the same high, gravel ridges once used by prehistoric people and used today by modern hunters, anglers and berry pickers.

P 16.8 C 117 Paved turnout to south by gravel pit. **16.8 Mile Lake** to north (walk up creek 200 yards); lake trout and grayling. **Rusty Lake**, 0.5 mile northwest of 16.8 Mile Lake; lake trout and grayling.

P 17.2 C 116.6 Paved turnout to north by **17 Mile Lake**; lake trout and grayling fishing.

P 17.8 C 116 Paved turnouts both sides of highway.

P 18.1 C 115.7 Paved turnouts by small lakes both sides of highway.

P 18.2 C 115.6 Paved turnout with lake access on both sides of highway.

P 18.5 C 115.3 ATV rentals may be available here.

P 18.7 C 115.1 Paved turnout to north.

P 19.6 C 114.2 Paved turnout to south.

P 20 C 113.8 Tangle River Inn to south; food, gas, lodging.

Tangle River Inn, known for our cleanliness and warm atmosphere. Restaurant with full menu featuring delicious home-style cooking. Karaoke bar, liquor store, game room. Cozy cabins, log cabin with 5 rooms, 10 beds and private bath—wonderful for groups or families. Great fishing, hunting, hiking, berry picking and bird watching. Jack and Naidine Johnson, original owners for over 30 years. Come, meet our friendly crew that's been here for years—a memorable experience. See display ad this section. [ADVERTISEMENT]

P 20.1 C 113.7 Large paved turnout to north overlooking **Round Tangle Lake**, one of a series of long, narrow lakes connected by the Tangle River and forming the headwaters of the Delta River. The name Tangle is a descriptive term for the maze of lakes and feeder streams contained in this drainage system Canoe rentals available at Tangle River Inn and Tangle Lakes Lodge.

P 20.6 C 113.2 Paved parking area with toilet to north.

P 21 C 112.8 The Nelchina caribou herd travels through this area, usually around the end of August or early in September.

P 21.3 C 112.5 *NOTE: Pavement ends, gravel begins westbound. Watch for potholes, washboard and washouts on highway west from here.*

P 21.4 C 112.4 One-lane bridge over Tangle River.

P 21.5 C 112.3 Turnoff to north for access to **Tangle Lakes BLM Campground**, 0.7 mile north from highway on Round Tangle Lake; 25 campsites on gravel loop road, toilets, tables, water pump, garbage cans, boat launch.

Easy access to boat launch for Delta River canoe trail, which goes north through Tangle Lakes to the Delta River. Self-register for river trips. The 2- to 3-day float to the takeout point on the Richardson Highway requires 1 portage. The Delta National Wild and Scenic River is managed by the BLM. For details on this river trail or the Gulkana River trail, contact the BLM, Box 147, Glennallen, AK 99588; phone (907) 822-3217.

Watershed divide. The Gulkana River joins the Copper River, which flows into Prince William Sound. The Delta River joins the Tanana River, which flows into the Yukon River. The Yukon flows into the Bering Sea.

P 21.7 C 113.8 **Delta National Wild and**

We're on the pavement - See log ad at Mile 20 Denali Highway

TANGLE RIVER INN

SUMMER:
(907) 822-3970
(907) 822-7304

CELL PHONE:
(907) 259-3970

WINTER:
(907) 895-4022

WRITE:
Mile 20, Denali Highway, Paxson, AK 99737

Interior Alaska's Finest Dining View Overlooking Tangle Lakes

- Restaurant
- Full Menu Homestyle Cooking
- Karaoke Bar
- Liquor Store
- Motel Rooms
- Cabins
- Canoe Rentals

Canoe down the lakes to see a variety of wildlife and spectacular scenery.

MasterCard VISA
http://www.tangleriverinn.com
e-mail: info@tangleriverinn.com

Lowest Gas Prices In 100 Miles

TESORO
Real Value. Real Easy.

Scenic River BLM Wayside and Boat Launch to south, day-use only; picnic tables, firepits, garbage cans, toilets, water pump, boat launch.

Launch point for Upper Tangle Lakes canoe trail, which goes south through Tangle Lakes (portages required) to Dickey Lake, then follows the Middle Fork to the main Gulkana River.

The Tangle Lakes system north and south of the highway (**Long Tangle, Round Tangle, Upper Tangle** and **Lower Tangle Lake**) offers good grayling and lake trout fishing. Fishing begins as soon as the ice goes out, usually in early June, and continues into September. Troll shelf edges for lake trout; use herring and flashers or large spoons. For grayling, use nymphs or small spinners.

P 22 C 111.8 Tangle Lakes Lodge. Located on the banks of a nationally designated "Wild and Scenic Waterway," Tangle Lakes Lodge lives up to this designation and offers the traveler a wonderful spot for an overnight stay and more. Log cabin rentals, canoe rentals, fine dining, cocktails and gift shop. Birding—arctic warblers on the property and Smith's longspur just down the road! World-class arctic grayling and trout fishing. Hiking trails and abundant photo opportunities. Snowmachining, cross-country skiing and dog mushing trails make Tangle Lakes Lodge your year-round destination. Phone or fax (907) 822-4202. Email tanglelakes@starband.net. P.O. Box 3006, Paxson, AK 99737. See display ad this section. [ADVERTISEMENT]

P 24.7 C 109.1 Double-ended turnout to south. **Landmark Gap**, the cut in the mountains to the north, is visible from the highway. It is used by caribou during migration.

Landmark Gap North ORV trail leads 4 miles north to south end of **Landmark Gap Lake**; grayling and lake trout fishing. According to the BLM, this trail is suitable for mountain bikes and hiking.

P 24.8 C 109 Rock Creek 1-lane bridge; turnout and informal camping to north at west end of bridge. Grayling fishing.

P 24.9 C 108.9 Landmark Gap South ORV trail provides access to Osar Lake area (11 miles) and to Tangle Lakes area (4 miles).

P 25 C 108.8 Gravel parking to south.
P 25.3 C 108.5 Informal campsite to south.
P 25.5 C 108.3 Informal campsite to south.
P 27.8 C 106 Rough turnout to north.
P 28.1 C 105.7 Very rough turnout and Downwind Lake north side of road.
P 28.9 C 104.9 Rough turnout to north.
P 29.3 C 104.5 Informal campsite beside small lake to south.
P 30.6 C 103.2 Glacier Lake ORV trail to north leads 3 miles to **Glacier Lake**; lake trout and grayling fishing. According to the BLM, this trail is not recommended for mountains bikes, and hikers should be prepared for exremely wet trail conditions.
P 30.8 C 103 Rough turnout to north.
P 32.1 C 101.7 Rough side road to turnout to north with dramatic view of Amphitheater Mountains above High Valley. Glacier Lake is visible in the gap in these mountains.
P 33.7 C 100.1 Rough doubled-ended parking area to south.
P 35.2 C 98.6 Turnout. Wildflowers here include: various heaths, frigid shooting star, dwarf fireweed.
P 35.7 C 98.1 Turnout to north.
P 36 C 97.8 36 Mile Lake 0.5-mile hike north; lake trout and grayling.
P 36.4 C 97.4 Entering ADSF&G controlled-use area westbound. Closed to motorized hunting. Small turnouts to north and south.
P 36.6 C 97.2 Osar Lake ORV trail leads 8 miles south to Osar Lake, originally named Asar Lake, the Scandinavian word for esker. (An esker is a ridge of sand and gravel marking the former stream channel of a glacier.) The BLM also recommends this trail for mountain biking and hiking. A profusion of black currant berries in season.
P 36.9 C 96.9 Maclaren Summit ORV trail leads 3 miles north to good view of Alaska Range; mountain biking.
P 37 C 96.8 Maclaren Summit (elev. 4,086 feet). Second highest highway pass in Alaska (after 4,800-foot Atigun Pass on the Dalton Highway). Turnout with view of Susitna River valley, Mount Hayes (13,382 feet) and the Alaska Range.
P 37.8 C 96 Leaving Tangle Lakes Archaeological District westbound (see description at Milepost P 16.5).
P 39.8 C 94 Sevenmile Lake ORV trail to north; 6.5 miles long, parallels Boulder Creek, crosses peat bog.
P 41.3 C 92.5 Double-ended turnout to south.
P 41.4 C 92.4 Turnout to north.
P 42 C 91.8 Maclaren River Bridge, a 364-foot multiple span crossing this tributary of the Susitna River. Parking and litter barrels. Maclaren River Lodge to south on west side of bridge; boat launch (pay fee at lodge). Look for cliff swallows nesting under bridge.

Maclaren River Lodge has breathtaking views of the Maclaren Glacier. Drop-off and guided wilderness fishing, rafting and sightseeing to alpine lakes and streams with limitless photographic opportunities. Glacier airboat trips. Trails for hiking, biking, off-road vehicles and winter snowmachining. Reservations: (888) 880-4264; lodge: (907) 882-7105; email: maclaren@starband.net; web site: www.maclarenriver.com. See display ad this section. [ADVERTISEMENT]

P 43.3 C 90.5 Maclaren River Road to north leads 12 miles to Maclaren Glacier; mountain biking. *NOTE: This side road may not be driveable beyond the river crossing at Mile 4.5.*

The Maclaren River rises in the glaciers surrounding Mount Hayes. For the next 60 miles westbound, the highest peaks of this portion of the mighty Alaska Range are visible, weather permitting, to the north. From east to west: Mount Hayes, Hess Mountain (11,940 feet) and Mount Deborah (12,339 feet). Mount Hayes, first climbed in August 1941, is named after Charles Hayes, an early member of the U.S. Geological Survey. Mount Deborah, first climbed in August 1954, was named in 1907 by Judge Wickersham after his wife.

P 44.1 C 89.7 Look for beaver lodge in pond to south.
P 44.6 C 89.2 Highway crosses **Crazy Notch**, a gap in the glacial moraine cut by a glacial stream.
P 46.9 C 86.9 Road north to **46.9 Mile Lake**; fishing for grayling in lake and outlet stream.
P 48 C 85.8 Excellent grayling fishing in **Crooked Creek**, which parallels the highway.
P 48.6 C 85.2 Informal campsite by small lake to south.
P 49 C 84.8 The road follows an esker between 4 lakes. Parts of the highway are built on eskers. Watch for ducks, geese, grebes and shorebirds in lakes, as well as bald eagles, moose, caribou, beaver and fox in the vicinity. Look for a pingo (earth-covered ice hill) at lakeshore.
P 49.6 C 84.2 Turnout to north.
P 49.7 C 84.1 Turnout to north overlooks **50 Mile Lake**. Interpretive plaque on glacial topography and wildlife. "Pools of Life: Hundreds of small lakes and ponds along the Denali Highway are reminders of ancient glaciers passing. As these glaciers receded they left behind blocks of slower melting ice that formed depressions called kettle holes or kettle lakes." The kettle lakes are home to beaver, loons, lesser yellowlegs, arctic terns and migrating trumpeter swans.
P 49.8 C 84 Road access north to 50 Mile Lake.
P 51.8 C 82 Private hunting camp to south. Trail to north.
P 55.6 C 78.2 Dirt track south to informal campsite.
P 56 C 77.8 Clearwater Creek 1-lane bridge. Rest area with toilet west side of bridge; informal camping, grayling fishing.
P 57.8 C 76 Clearwater Creek walk-in (no motorized vehicles) hunting area north of highway.
P 58.8 C 75 Road winds atop an esker flanked by kames and kettle lakes. Watch for moose.

Tangle Lakes Lodge
Discover The Real Alaska

Comfortable & Friendly Lodge
Fine Dining & Cocktails
Log Cabin & Canoe Rentals

(907) 822-4202

email: tanglelakes@starband.net

Mile 22 Denali Highway

The splendor of Alaska awaits you at...

MacLAREN RIVER LODGE

ROOMS, CABINS,
RESTAURANT, BAR
GAS & TIRE REPAIR

Lodge Reservations
907-822-7105

Email: maclaren@starband.net
Website: www.maclarenriver.com

mile 42 Denali Highway

P 59 C 74.8 Narrow turnout to north.
P 59.1 C 74.7 Long turnout to north.
P 62.5 C 71.3 Rough turnout to south.
P 63.8 C 70 Rough double-ended turnouts both sides of highway.
P 64 C 69.8 Road descends westbound into Susitna River valley. Highest elevation of mountains seen to north is 5,670 feet.
P 70 C 63.8 Great view of Susitna River valley as highway descends westbound.
P 73 C 60.8 Road widens westbound. Road narrows eastbound.
P 73.5 C 60.3 Access via dirt road north to informal campsite by lake.
P 74 C 59.8 Clearwater Mountains to north; watch for bears on slopes. View of Susitna River in valley below.
P 78.3 C 55.5 Narrow dirt track south to scenic viewpoint overlooking Susitna River.
P 78.8 C 55 Valdez Creek Road. Former mining camp of Denali, about 6 miles north of the highway, was first established in 1907 after the 1903 discovery of gold in the Clearwater Mountains. The Valdez Creek Mine operated at this site from 1990 to 1995, producing 495,000 ozs. of gold. Area mining equipment was donated to the Museum of Transportation and Industry (see **Milepost A 47** in the PARKS HIGHWAY section). Do not trespass on private mining claims.

Fair fishing reported in **Roosevelt Lake** and area creeks. Watch for bears.

P 79.3 C 54.5 **Susitna River Bridge** (1-lane), a combination multiple span and deck truss, 1,036 feet long. Butte Creek trailhead.

CAUTION: Bridge is slippery when wet. Rough road west of bridge.

The Susitna River heads at Susitna Glacier in the Alaska Range (between Mounts Hess and Hayes) and flows southwest 260 miles to Cook Inlet. Downstream through Devil's Canyon it is considered unfloatable. The river's Tanaina Indian name, said to mean "sandy river," first appeared in 1847 on a Russian chart.

Entering Game Management Unit 13E westbound, leaving unit 13B eastbound.

P 80 C 53.8 Gravel pit; parking.
P 80.3 C 53.5 Turnouts both sides of highway (used by hunters in season; watch for ATVs on road).
P 80.5 C 53.3 Double-ended turnout to south.
P 81 C 52.8 Gracious House campground on lake to north.
P 82 C 52.8 **Gracious House** to south. Centrally located on the shortest, most scenic route to Denali National Park. 27 modern units including a large den with adjoining rooms for groups, most with private baths. Bed and breakfast atmosphere. Bar and cafe featuring ice cream and home-baked pies. Tent sites, parking for self-contained RVs overlooking lake. Water, restrooms and showers available at lodge. Gas, towing, welding, mechanical repairs, tire service. Air taxi, for the most beautiful scenic flights in Alaska. Guide service available for hiking, biking, fishing, hunting and photography tours. Northern Lights viewing and winter snowmobiling. Same owners/operators for 45 years. Reasonable rates. For brochure on hunting and fishing trips, write to the Gracious Family. Summer address: P.O. Box 88, Cantwell, AK 99729. Winter address: P.O. Box 212549, Anchorage, AK 99521. Message phone/fax (907) 333-3148 or lodge phone/fax (907) 259-1111. Email: crhoa36683@aol.com/. Internet: www.alaskaone.com/gracious. [ADVERTISEMENT]

P 84 C 49.8 Stevenson's Lake 0.5 mile south; grayling fishing.

This old-style Alaskan cache is located at Gracious House.
(© Kris Graef, staff)

P 85.1 C 48.7 There are numerous informal campsites used by hunters the next 10 miles westbound.
P 90.5 C 43.3 Beaver lodge in pond to south. A major water drainage divide occurs near here. East of the divide, the tributary river system of the Susitna flows south to Cook Inlet. West of the divide, the Nenana River system flows north to the Yukon River, which empties into the Bering Sea.
P 93.8 C 40 **Butte Lake** ORV trail leads 5 miles south to lake. Best fishing June through September. Lake trout, troll with red-and-white spoons or grayling remains; grayling, small flies or spinners.
P 94.3 C 39.5 Short road north leads to parking area above pond. View of Monahan Flat and Alaska Range to the north. Interpretive plaque on earthquakes.
P 94.8 C 39 Bridge over Canyon Creek. Turnout to north at west end of bridge.
P 96.3 C 37.5 Rough access north leads to viewpoint of the West Fork Glacier. Looking north up the face of this glacier, Mount Deborah is to the left and Hess Mountain is in the center.
P 97 C 36.8 Looking at the Alaska Range to the north, Mount Deborah, Hess Mountain and Mount Hayes are the highest peaks to your right; to the left are the lower peaks of the Alaska Range and Nenana Mountain.
P 100 C 33.8 Residents of this area say it is a wonderful place for picking cranberries and blueberries in August.
P 103.2 C 30.6 Turnout to north.
Highway is built on an esker between kettle lakes.
P 104.6 C 29.2 **Brushkana River** Bridge. BLM campground to north at west end of bridge; 20 sites beside river, tables, firepits, toilets, litter barrels and water. Fishing for grayling. BLM Brushkana Creek trail (2 miles).
P 106.6 C 27.2 Canyon Creek, grayling fishing.
P 107.2 C 26.6 Turnout. **Stixkwan Creek** flows under highway in culvert. Grayling fishing.
P 110.5 C 23.3 *CAUTION: Steep downgrade westbound; trucks use low gear.*

P 111.2 C 22.6 **Seattle Creek** 1-lane bridge. Fishing for grayling and Dolly Varden.
P 111.5 C 22.3 Turnout to north with vista.
P 112 C 21.8 Matanuska–Susitna Borough boundary. Lily Creek.
P 113.2 C 20.6 View to east of the Alaska Range and extensive rolling hills grazed by caribou.
P 115.8 C 18 Informal turnout to north with beautiful view of the Nenana River area.
P 116 C 17.8 Turnout to north with BLM interpretive sign about the Denali Highway. The Denali Highway parallels the Nenana River westbound. The Nenana River heads in Nenana Glacier and flows into the Tanana River, a tributary of the Yukon River, which empties into the Bering Sea. The Nenana is popular with professional river rafters—particularly the stretch of river along the Parks Highway near the Denali Park entrance—but it is not good for fishing, due to heavy glacial silt.

Steep downgrade westbound.

P 117.2 C 16.6 Leaving BLM public lands westbound.
P 117.8 C 16 Turnout to north on Nenana River at **Mile 16 Put-In**. Sign reads: "Attention Nenana River Users: The Upper Nenana River float runs approximately 18 river miles from Mile 16 of the Denali Highway to take-out at Nenana River One Bridge at Parks Highway Mile 215.7. The river along this stretch is rated Class I to II. Warning: Below the Nenana River One Bridge the river rating changes to Class II, III and IV white-water. The Nenana River is about 45°F; an unprotected person will survive 6–10 minutes."
P 121 C 12.8 Turnout at gravel pit to north.
P 122.3 C 11.5 Views westbound of Mount McKinley/Denali (weather permitting).
P 125.7 C 8.1 **Joe Lake**, about 0.5 mile long (large enough for floatplane), is south of highway. **Jerry Lake** is about 0.2 mile north of the highway. Both lakes have grayling.
P 126 C 7.8 Turnout to south on Joe Lake.
P 128.2 C 5.6 Fish Creek. Access to creek and turnout to south at east end of bridge.

Beautiful view (weather permitting) of Talkeetna Mountains to the south.

P 131.1 C 2.7 *Gravel ends, pavement begins, westbound.*

Pavement ends, gravel begins, eastbound. Watch for potholes, washboard and washouts on highway east from here.

P 133.3 C 0.5 Cantwell Station DOT highway maintenance camp.
P 133.4 C 0.4 Alaska State Troopers to north.
P 133.8 C 0 **Cantwell** at intersection of Denali Highway (Alaska Route 8) and Parks Highway (Alaska Route 3); food, gas and lodging. Turn north on Parks Highway for Denali Park and Fairbanks. Turn south for Anchorage. See description of Cantwell on page 387 in the PARKS HIGHWAY section.

Junction of Denali Highway and Parks Highway at Cantwell. Turn to **Milepost A 210** on page 386 in the PARKS HIGHWAY section for log.

Travelers eastbound on the Denali Highway, read this log back to front.

STEESE HIGHWAY

Connects: Fairbanks to Circle, AK **Length:** 162 miles
Road Surface: 30% paved, 70% gravel **Season:** Open all year
Highest Summit: Eagle Summit, 3,624 feet
Major Attractions: Hot Springs, Gold Dredge No. 8, Pipeline Viewpoint, Davidson Ditch, Nome Creek Valley, Yukon River

	Central	Chena Hot Springs	Circle	Circle Hot Springs	Fairbanks
Central		180	35	8	128
Chena Hot Springs	180		214	188	61
Circle	35	214		43	162
Circle Hot Springs	8	188	43		136
Fairbanks	128	61	162	136	

Aerial view of old gold dredge and tailings along the Steese Highway. (© Laurent Dick)

The Steese Highway connects Fairbanks with Chena Hot Springs (61 miles) via Chena Hot Springs Road; the town of Central (128 miles); Circle Hot Springs (136 miles) via Circle Hot Springs Road; and with Circle, a small settlement 162 miles to the northeast on the Yukon River and 50 miles south of the Arctic Circle. The scenery alone makes this a worthwhile drive. It is especially colorful in late August and early September when the trees turn.

The first 44 miles of the Steese Highway are improved pavement. From pavement end at **Milepost F 44**, it is a wide gravel road into Central at **Milepost 127.5**, where there is a short stretch of paved road. From Central to Circle, the highway is a narrow, winding gravel road. Watch for paving under way in summer 2003 between **Mileposts F 44** and **F 66**.

The highway is open year-round; check with the Dept. of Transportation in Fairbanks regarding winter road conditions. The Steese Highway was completed in 1927 and named for Gen. James G. Steese, U.S. Army, former president of the Alaska Road Commission.

Among the attractions along the Steese are Eagle Summit, highest pass on the highway, where there is an unobstructed view of the midnight sun at summer solstice (June 21); the Chatanika River and Chena River recreation areas; and Chena and Circle Hot Springs.

The Steese Highway also provides access to the richest gold mining district in Alaska. Artifacts from the region's early mining days include dredges (at **Mileposts F 9.5** and **F 28.6**) and the Davidson Ditch (at **Milepost F 57.3**). Chatanika Gold Camp at **Milepost F 27.9** has a display of old mining equipment. Two operating gold mines offer tours: Fort Knox (phone 907/488-4653) and Gold Rush Gold Camp (907/452-4653). Gold Rush Camp and Gold Dredge No. 8 also offer gold panning. Recreational gold panning is allowed at Pedro Creek, across from the Pedro Monument at **Milepost F 16.6**, and at Nome Creek Valley, accessible from **Milepost F 57.3**. (For more information on Nome Creek, check with the Alaska Public Lands Information Center or go to http://aurora.ak.blm.gov/WhiteMtns/html/nomecr.html#goldpan.)

Emergency medical services: Between Fairbanks and Circle, phone the state troopers at 911 or (907) 452-1313. Use CB Channels 2, 19, 22.

Steese Highway Log

Distance from Fairbanks (F) is followed by distance from Circle (C).

ALASKA ROUTE 2

F 0 C 162 **Junction** with the Richardson Highway at Airport Way and Gaffney Road in Fairbanks. Begin 4-lane Steese Expressway northbound.

Turn to end of RICHARDSON HIGHWAY section on page 469 and read log back to front for log of that highway from Fairbanks south to Delta Junction, Paxson and Valdez.

F 0.4 C 161.6 Tenth Avenue exit.
F 0.6 C 161.4 Expressway crosses Chena River.
F 0.9 C 161.1 Third Street exit.
F 1 C 161 College Road exit to west and access to Bentley Mall; shopping, fast food, restaurants and other services.
F 1.4 C 160.6 Trainor Gate Road; access to Fort Wainright.
F 2 C 160 Johansen Expressway west to College Road, Peger Road and University Avenue. City Lights Blvd. to east.
F 2.2 C 159.8 Distance marker northbound shows Fox 8 miles, Livengood 76 miles, Circle 156 miles.
F 2.8 C 159.2 Gas station (diesel, unleaded) with foodmart at **junction** with Farmers Loop Road (to west) and Fairhill Road (to east).

Exit east for **Birch Hill Recreation Area**. Drive 1.8 miles to 'T' and turn right; continue 0.3 mile on gravel access road for this Fairbanks North Star Borough recreation area. Nordic skiing only (no dogs, sleds or foot traffic) Oct. 15–April 15.; chalet.

F 4.9 C 157.1 **Junction** with Chena Hot Springs Road northbound and southbound off ramps. Exit west for Curry's Corner (gas pump, grocery) and access to North Star Golf Club on Old Steese Highway (0.7 mile north from Curry's Corner). Exit east for Chena Hot Springs Road.

See "Chena Hot Springs Road" log on pages 446-447 in the FAIRBANKS section.

F 6.4 C 155.6 Steele Creek Road. Exit for

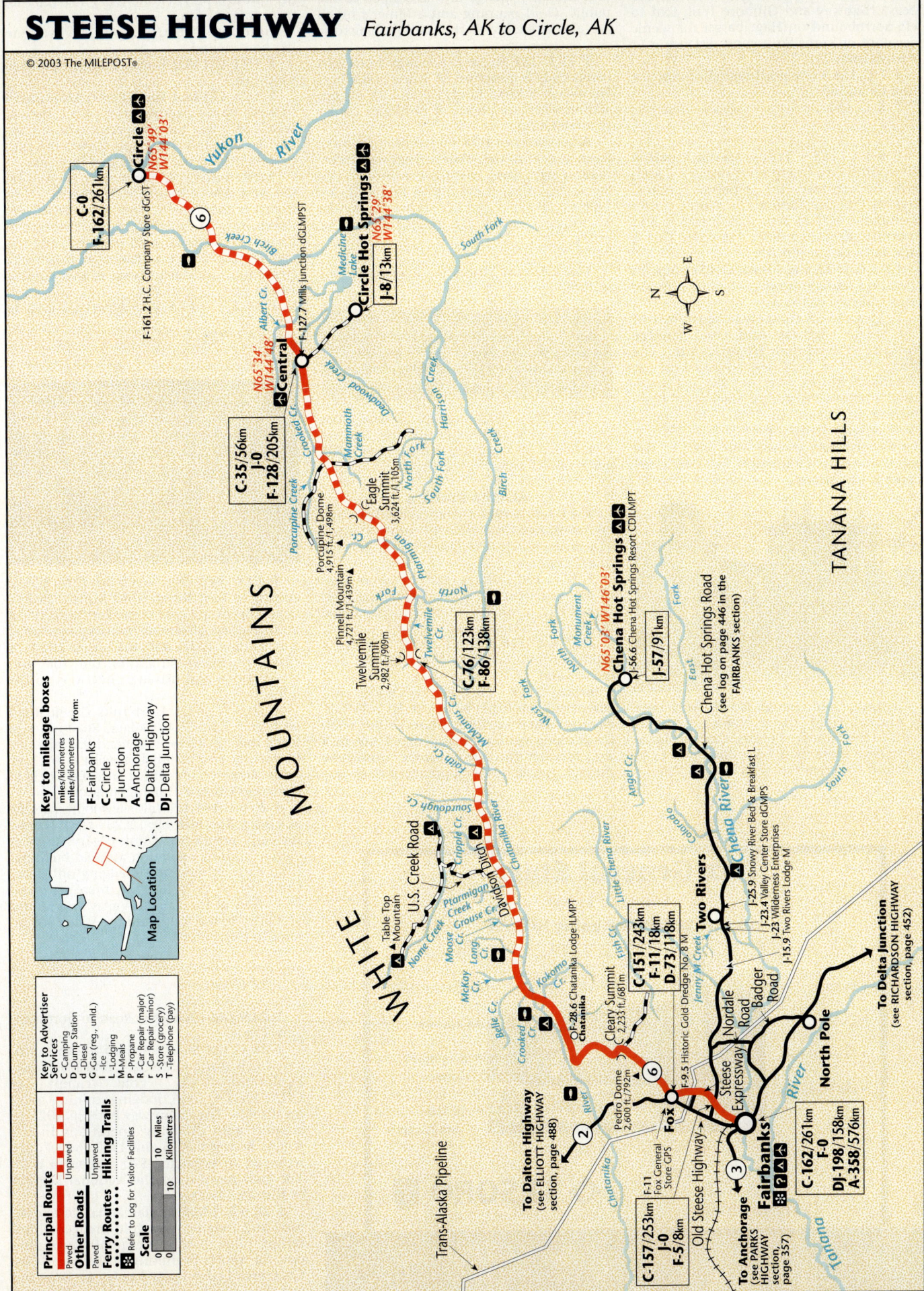

Bennett Road, Hagelbarger Avenue, Old Steese Highway and Gilmore Trail. Exit to left northbound on Hagelbarger for scenic viewpont of Fairbanks a short distance west of expressway.

F 7 C 155 View northbound of pipeline from top of hill.

F 8 C 154 *End 4-lane divided highway, begin 2 lanes, northbound.*
CAUTION: Watch for moose.

F 8.4 C 153.6 Trans–Alaska Pipeline Viewpoint with interpretive displays. Excellent opportunity for pipeline photos. Alyeska Pipeline Service Co. visitor center open daily, May to Sept. Free literature and information; phone (907) 456-9391. This is Mile 449.6 on the pipeline.

F 8.5 C 153.5 Gold Rush Gold Camp, an operating underground gold mine offering tours and gold panning.

F 9.5 C 152.5 Goldstream Road exit to Old Steese Highway and **Gold Dredge Number 8 National Historic Site**. The dredge, built in 1928, was added to the list of national historic sites in 1984 and designated a National Historical Mechanical Engineering Landmark in 1986. The 5-deck, 250-foot-long dredge operated until 1959; it is now privately owned and open to the public for tours (admission fee). McKersey Court to east; gravel.

Historic Gold Dredge No. 8 (Gray Line of Alaska). Gold Dredge No. 8 is a monument to the miners who used the machinery to produce more than 7.5 million ounces of gold and the engineers who built it. Visitors tour the only dredge in Alaska open to the public. Gold panning and a Miner's lunch are also available at this national historic site. [ADVERTISEMENT]

F 11 C 151 Steese Expressway from Fairbanks ends at **junction** of Steese and Elliott Highways (Alaska Routes 6 and 2). Weigh station with pay phone at northeast corner of intersection.

Access west to **FOX** (description follows); food, gas, groceries. Dalton Highway information sign. Turn east for continuation of Steese Highway, (now Alaska Route 6); log follows. Distance marker shows Chatanika 17 miles; Central 118 miles; Circle 152 miles. *NOTE: Next gas on Steese Highway is 117 miles from here.*

Fox General Store. See display ad this section.

Junction with Elliott Highway (Alaska Route 2) which continues northeast to the Dalton Highway and Manley Hot Springs See ELLIOTT HIGHWAY section on page 488 for log.

FOX (pop. 300), has Fox General Store and gas station and Fox Roadhouse. Fox was established as a mining camp before 1905 and named for nearby Fox Creek.

ALASKA ROUTE 6

F 11.1 C 149.9 Distance marker eastbound shows Chatanika 17 miles, Central 118 miles, Circle 152 miles. "Next gas 117 miles" (sign).

F 12 C 150 Tailings (gravel and boulders of dredged streambeds alongside highway) from early mining activity which yielded millions of dollars in gold.

F 13.6 C 148.4 Eisele Road; turnoff on right northbound for NOAA/NESDIS Command and Data Acquisition Station at Gilmore Creek. This facility tracks and commands multiple NOAA polar orbiting, environmental satellites. Tours of the satellite tracking station are available 9 A.M. to 4 P.M., Monday through Saturday, from June through August or by appointment September through May. Phone (907) 451-1200 for more information.

Junction with Old Steese Highway on left northbound.

F 16.1 C 145.9 Beaver lodge in pond to southeast.

F 16.6 C 145.4 Felix Pedro Monument to west; paved parking area, picnic shelter. Felix Pedro was the prospector who discovered gold in July 1902 and started the rush that resulted in the founding of Fairbanks.

Recreational gold panning is allowed on the west side of Pedro Creek, directly across from the monument. This is the Discovery Claim, owned by Igloo No. 4, Pioneers of Alaska. Recreational gold panning only (no mechanical devices). Pedro and Gilmore creeks join just downstream of the panning area to form Goldstream.

F 17.5 C 144.5 Paved parking area to east.

F 18 C 144 *Winding ascent (7 to 8 percent grades) northbound to Cleary Summit.*

F 20 C 142 Twin Creek Road (no public access) to **Fort Knox Gold Mine**, Alaska's largest operating gold mine. Fort Knox offers morning and afternoon tours *by reservation only*; phone (907) 488-4653, ext. 2800, or email tours@fairbanksgold.com for tour reservations and driving directions to the mine.

F 20.5 C 141.5 Fairbanks Creek Road leads east 0.2 mile to Skiland Road (ski area is 0.8 mile up access road) and 0.9 mile east to parking area at junction with Fish Creek Road. Access to residential area and Circle to Fairbanks Historic Trail (2.6 miles).

F 20.9 C 141.1 Scenic viewpoint, parking at **Cleary Summit** (elev. 2,233 feet). Named for early prospector Frank Cleary. View of current mining operation and old buildings from early mining and dredging on Cleary Creek below. On a clear day there are excellent views of the Tanana Valley and Mount McKinley to the south and the White Mountains to the north.

Highway descends steep winding 7 percent grade northbound.

F 22 C 140 *Improved highway to* **Milepost F 44**.

F 26.9 Old Chatanika Road to northeast; gravel trail.

F 28 C 134 Sharp turn up hill to southeast for historic Old F.E. Camp (Fairbanks Exploration Co. gold camp) at **CHATANIKA**; food, lodging, mining relics on display. The camp was built in 1925 to support gold dredging operations in the valley. Between 1926 and 1957 the F.E. Co. removed an estimated $70 million in gold. The gold camp is on the National Register of Historic Places.

F 28.6 C 133.4 Chatanika Lodge to east; food and lodging. Old gold dredge behind tailing piles to west. Originally a trading post for miners beginning in the late 1930s, Chatanika Lodge burned down in 1974 and was then rebuilt and expanded to offer food,

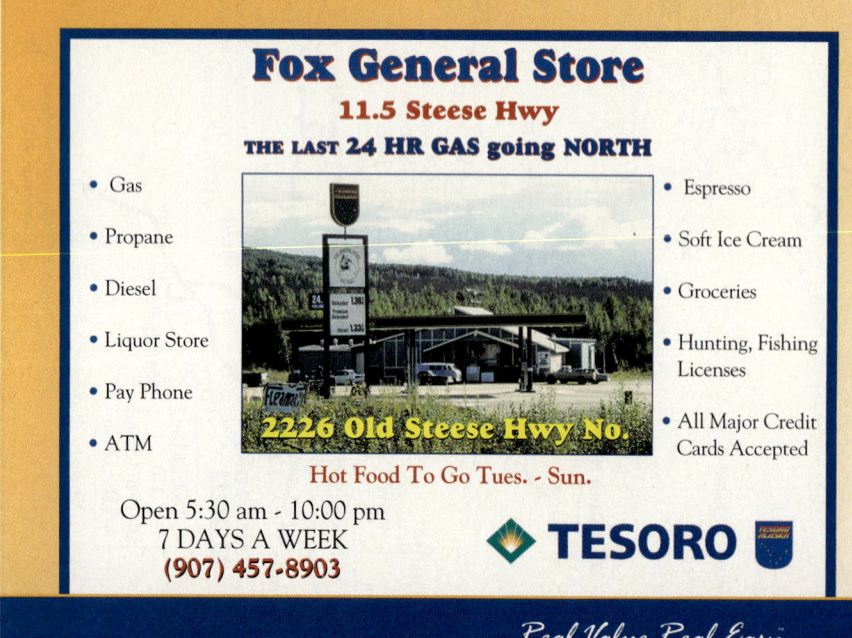

lodging and entertainment.

The dredge across the highway operated from the 1920s until 1962. It is the second largest stacker dredge in Alaska. *(Dredge is on private property; DO NOT TRESPASS)*

Chatanika Lodge. Cafe open 9 A.M. daily (year-round). Halibut/catfish fry Friday and Saturday, country-fried chicken on Sunday, served family-style, all you can eat. Diamond Willow Lounge. Rustic atmosphere, Alaska artifacts. Historic Alaska gold dredge across from lodge, plus aurora borealis videos on big-screen TV. Good grayling fishing. Great winter snow machining on groomed trails; snow machine rentals. Rooms available. See display ad this section.

[ADVERTISEMENT]

F 29.5 C 132.5 Junction east with Neal Brown Road. Access to **Poker Flat Rocket Facility**; off-limits except to authorized personnel and sponsored public tours. The Poker Flat Research Range, operated by the Geophysical Institute, University of Alaska Fairbanks—primarily under contract to NASA, Wallops Island Flight Facility—is dedicated to auroral and upper atmospheric research. It is the only university-owned sounding rocket range in the world and the only high latitude and auroral zone launch facility on U.S. soil. Poker Flat is also the home of NASA's Alaska Ground Station, providing 24/7 satellite data down-linking.

Tours of Poker Flat may be arranged through the Geophysical Institute Information office, phone (907) 474-7558. Web site: www.pfrr.alaska.edu.

F 31.3 C 130.7 Imaging Riometer Antenna Array is a joint 10-year study of polar middle and upper atmosphere by CRL of Japan and UAF's Geophysical Institute. "The Aurora Borealis makes the atmosphere opaque to radio noise from our galaxy at altitudes of 60–100 km, reducing the intensity of the noise received at the ground. The imaging riometer works like a camera, taking a picture of the radio noise once a second."

F 31.6 C 130.4 Public fishing access to **31.6 Mile Pond** to west; pond stocked with grayling.

F 32.3 C 129.7 Captain Creek bridge.

F 34.6 C 127.4 Mile 34.6 Pond public fishing access to east; stocked with rainbow.

F 34.7 C 127.3 Double-ended turnout to west.

F 35.8 C 126.2 Mile 35.8 Pond public fishing access to east.

F 36.6 C 125.4 Mile 36.6 Pond public fishing access to west; stocked with grayling.

F 37.3 C 124.7 Kokomo Creek bridge.

Chatanika Lodge was originally a trading post for area miners. (© Kris Graef, staff)

is usually available during the summer. Camping fee $10/night or resident pass. Campground host. Operated by concessionaire. Look for wild roses here in June. ▲

Boats can be launched on the gravel bars by the river. Bring your mosquito repellent and suntan lotion. This is an access point to the Chatanika River canoe trail. See **Milepost F 60** for more information on canoeing this river.

Chatanika River, grayling 8 to 20 inches, use flies or spinners, May to September.

F 39.3 C 122.7 Mile 39.3 Pond to west; stocked with grayling.

F 40.4 C 121.6 Bridge over Crooked Creek.

F 41.5 C 120.5 Bridge over Belle Creek.

F 42.5 C 119.5 Double-ended gravel turnout to west; sled dog unloading area. **McKay Creek Trailhead.** McKay Creek Trail is 17.5 miles long. It climbs steeply for 5.5 miles to ridgetop at boundary of White Mountains National Recreation Area. The first 8 miles are suitable for summer use, according to the BLM. Winter use from November to April. This trail intersects with the Lower Nome Creek Trail.

F 42.8 C 119.2 Bridge over McKay Creek.

F 43.9 C 118.1 Double-ended turnout to west.

F 44 C 118 *Pavement ends, gravel road begins, northbound. Watch for road construction and paving under way in summer 2003 to Milepost F 66.*

Highway parallels the Chatanika River for the next 10 miles northbound.

F 45.5 C 116.5 Long Creek bridge. Long Creek Trading Post to west at north end of bridge; gold panning equipment (and advice), groceries, liquor store, camping. Fishing (and gold panning) in **Long Creek**; grayling 8 to 14 inches, use spinners or flies, May to September.

F 48.5 C 113.5 Northbound views down Chatanika River valley to east.

F 50.8 C 111.2 Begin series of long, straight uphill and downhill grades (7 to 8 percent) northbound.

F 57.1 C 104.9 Entering **White Mountains National Recreation Area** (BLM) northbound. Access to this area's trails and cabins is from **Milepost F 57.3**.

F 57.3 C 104.7 Turnoff for the BLM's Nome Creek Valley Gold Panning Area via U.S. Creek Road to west (description follows). **Davidson Ditch Historical Site** immediately to the west on U.S. Creek. The large pipe was built in 1925 by the Fairbanks Exploration Co. to carry water to float gold dredges. The 83-mile-long ditch, designed and engineered by J.B. Lippincott,

F 39 C 123 Chatanika River bridge. **Upper Chatanika River State Recreation Site**, just north of the bridge, is a beautiful state campground with river access and rocky beach. There are 25 sites with fireplaces and a gravel parking area with toilets and a water pump at the entrance. Firewood

STEESE HIGHWAY

begins near **Milepost F 64** on the Steese Highway and ends near Fox. A system of ditches and inverted siphons, the pipeline was capable of carrying 56,100 gallons per minute. After the dredges closed, the water was used for power until 1967, when a flood destroyed a bridge and flattened almost 1,000 feet of pipe.

U.S. Creek Road (steep gravel) winds up and over the hills to the northwest 6.9 miles to the **Nome Creek Valley Gold Panning Area**; large gravel parking area, outhouse and signs about White Mountains National Recreation Area and the Nome Creek Gold Panning Area. *NOTE: Check with BLM in Fairbanks regarding status of U.S. Creek Road in wet weather.*

Recreational gold panning in Nome Creek Valley is limited to the designated area and non-motorized tools, such as gold pans, rocker boxes, sluice boxes, picks and shovels.

Nome Creek Road forks at the gold panning area. Follow Nome Creek Road to the upper end of Nome Creek Valley for Mt. Prindle Campground and Quartz Creek Trail (4 miles). Follow Nome Creek Road to the lower end of the valley for Ophir Creek Campground and Beaver Creek National Wild River put-in point (12 miles).

F 59 C 103 Double-ended dirt parking area to east.

F 60 C 102 **Cripple Creek BLM Campground** and river access to east; 7-day camping limit, 6 tent, 12 level trailer sites; water pumps, firepits, outhouses, bear-proof dumpsters, picnic tables, nature trail. Camping fee $6. Parking for walk-in campers. Firewood is usually available all summer. Recreational gold panning permitted. *Bring mosquito repellent!* ▲

Access to Cripple Creek BLM recreation cabin. Preregister and pay $10 fee at BLM office, 1150 University Ave., Fairbanks, AK 99709; phone (907) 474-2200.

Cripple Creek bridge is the uppermost access point to the Chatanika River canoe trail. Follow 0.2 mile side road near campground entrance to canoe launch site; parking area, outhouses. *CAUTION: This canoe trail may not be navigable at low water.* The Chatanika River is a clear-water Class II stream. The Steese Highway parallels the river for approximately 28 miles and there are many access points to the highway downstream from the Cripple Creek bridge. No major obstacles on this canoe trail, but watch for overhanging trees. Downstream pullout points are Perhaps Creek, Long Creek and Chatanika Campground.

F 62.3 C 99.7 Viewpoint to east overlooking Chatanika River.

F 63.3 C 98.7 View of historic Davidson Ditch pipeline to west (see **Milepost F 57.3**).

F 64.8 C 97.2 Side road east to scenic viewpoint. Large parking area.

F 65.4 C 96.6 Sourdough Creek bridge.

F 65.6 C 96.4 Davidson Ditch Road; trailhead.

F 69 C 93 Faith Creek bridge. Creek access to east at north end of bridge.

Highway climbs 7 percent grade northbound.

F 72 C 90 View ahead for northbound travelers of highway route along mountains, McManus Creek below.

F 79.1 C 82.9 Road widens for parking next 500 feet.

F 80.1 C 81.9 Montana Creek state highway maintenance station to west. Long double-ended turnout to east. Montana Creek runs under road and into McManus Creek to the east. McManus Dome (elev. 4,184 feet) to west.

F 81.2 C 80.8 Turnout to east. Spring water (untested) piped to roadside. *NOTE: Wide gravel highway begins ascent to Twelvemile Summit. Avalanche gates.*

F 83 C 79 *CAUTION: Slow down for 35 mph curve.*

F 85.5 C 76.5 Large parking area and viewpoint to east at **Twelvemile Summit Wayside**. Twelvemile Summit (elev. 3,190 feet) is on the divide of the Yukon and Tanana river drainages. Wildflowers carpet the alpine tundra slopes. Entering Game Management Unit 25C, leaving unit 20B, northbound. Fairbanks–North Star Borough limits. Circle to Fairbanks Historic Trail trailhead 0.4 mile. This is caribou country; from here to beyond Eagle Summit (**Milepost F 108**) migrating bands of caribou may be seen from late July through mid-September.

Access to Pinnell Mountain national recreation trail (Twelvemile Summit trailhead). The trail is also accessible from Eagle Summit at **Milepost F 107.1**. Named in honor of Robert Pinnell, who was fatally injured in 1952 while climbing nearby Porcupine Dome. This 27-mile-long hiking trail winds through alpine terrain, along mountain ridges and through high passes. Highest elevation point reached is 4,721 feet. The trail is marked by rock cairns. Shelter cabins at Mile 10.7 and Mile 17.7. Vantage points along the trail with views of the White Mountains, Tanana Hills, Brooks Range and Alaska Range. Watch for willow ptarmigan, hoary marmot, rock pika, moose, wolf and caribou. Mid-May through July is the prime time for wildflowers, with flowers peaking in mid-June. Carry drinking water and insect repellent at all times. Additional information on this trail is available from the Bureau of Land Management, 1150 University Ave., Fairbanks, AK 99708-3844; phone (907) 474-2350.

Distance marker northbound shows Central 40 miles, Circle 74 miles.

F 88.8 C 73.2 Bridge over Reed Creek.

F 90.6 C 71.4 Double-ended turnout to east.

F 93.4 C 68.6 Bridge over the North Fork Twelve Mile Creek. Nice picnic spot to west below bridge.

F 94 C 68 **Birch Creek Access.** Side road leads 0.2 mile down to north fork of Birch Creek; parking area and canoe launch for Birch Creek canoe trail. This is the main put-in point for canoeing Birch Creek, a Wild and Scenic River. Informal campsite by creek. Extensive mining in area. **Birch Creek**, grayling to 12 inches; use flies, June to October.

F 95.8 C 66.2 Bridge over Willow Creek.

F 97.6 C 64.4 Bridge over Bear Creek.

F 98 C 64 Watch for gold mining activity in streams along this part of the highway. These are private mining claims. *IMPORTANT: Do not trespass. Do not approach mining equipment without permission.*

F 99.7 C 62.3 Bridge over Fish Creek.

F 101.4 C 60.6 Remains of old 101 Lodge. Yukon Quest dog drop.

Avalanche gates. May be closed if road conditions are hazardous over the summit.

F 101.5 C 60.5 Bridge over Ptarmigan Creek (elev. 2,398 feet). Alpine meadows carpeted with wildflowers in spring and summer for next 9 miles.

F 103 C 59 Highway climbs to summit northbound. Good view to east of mining activity down in valleys. Scalloped waves of soil on hillsides to west are called solifluction lobes. These are formed when meltwater saturates the thawed surface soil, which then flows slowly downhill.

F 105 C 57 Snowpoles guide snowplows in winter.

F 107.1 C 54.9 Large parking area 0.2 mile west with wheelchair-accessible toilet, bear-proof litter container, emergency shelter, display. Hike to summit. Favorite spot for local residents to observe summer solstice (weather permitting) on June 21. Best wildflower viewing on Alaska highway system. Wildflowers found here include: dwarf forget-me-nots, alpine rhododendron or rosebay, rock jasmine, alpine azalea, arctic bell heather, mountain avens, Jacob's ladder, anemones, wallflowers, Labrador tea, lupine, oxytropes, gentians and louseworts. The museum in Central has a photographic display of Eagle Summit alpine flowers to help highway travelers identify the wildflowers of this area.

Pinnell Mountain Trail access (Eagle Summit trailhead); see description at **Milepost F 85.5**. Weather station. &

F 107.5 C 54.5 **Eagle Summit** (elev. 3,685 feet). This is the third and highest of 3 summits (including Cleary and Twelvemile) along the Steese Highway.

F 109.2 C 52.8 Large parking area to east; no guardrails. View down into Miller Creek far below.

Highway begins steep descent northbound.

F 111.4 C 50.6 Parking area to east.

F 114.2 C 47.8 Parking area to east looking down onto the Mastodon, Mammoth, Miller and Independence creeks area. The historic Miller House was located near here. Built in 1897, Miller House was originally a stopover on the sled trail between Circle City and Fairbanks. With the completion of the Steese Highway, it became a year-round roadhouse, offering meals, gas, groceries, a post office and rental cabins.

Avalanche gates.

F 116.2 C 45.8 Road east to Mammoth Creek.

F 116.4 C 45.6 Bridge over Mammoth Creek. Near here fossil remains of many species of preglacial Alaskan mammals have been excavated and may be seen at the University of Alaska museum in Fairbanks and at the museum in Central.

F 117 C 45 Highway crosses over Stack Pup Creek. From here the highway gradually descends to Central.

F 117.5 C 44.5 Parking area to west.

F 119.1 C 42.9 Bedrock Creek. Turnout. Access to creek.

F 120 C 42 View northbound through foliage of mining operations to west.

F 121 C 41 Bridge over Sawpit Creek.

F 122.5 C 39.5 Road west to parking space by pond.

F 125.4 C 36.6 Bridge over Boulder Creek.

F 126 C 36 Lupine and wild roses bloom along the road in June. *CAUTION: Road narrows, no shoulders; slow down for curves northbound.*

F 126.7 C 35.3 *Paved highway begins northbound. Begin 30 mph speed zone northbound.*

F 127.1 C 34.9 Central elementary school.

F 127.5 C 34.5 **CENTRAL** (pop. 134; elev. 965 feet). This small community has a post office (ZIP code 99730), airstrip and park with picnic area. Gas, bar and restaurant, laundry and showers, rooms and other services.

State-owned airstrip at **Milepost F 128.4**.

Circle Hot Springs Road

This wide, mostly flat gravel road, leads 8.2 miles from Central to Circle Hot Springs resort.

Distance is measured from junction (J) at Milepost F 127.8 Steese Highway.

J 0 Pavement extends first 0.3 mile of road.

J 0.3 Pavement ends.

J 0.8 Cemetery Road.

J 2.7 Bridge over Deadwood Creek.

J 4.7 Ketchem Creek Road (1-lane dirt and gravel) leads to private mining claims and rock formations (keep right at forks in road). Road deteriorates at about Mile 3.4.

J 5.8 Bridge over Ketchem Creek. Primitive camping at site of former Ketchem Creek BLM campground to south on west side of bridge. *Mosquitoes!*

J 8.2 Turnoff for **CIRCLE HOT SPRINGS** (pop. 35); this resort offers year-round swimming, lodging, restaurant, bar and self-contained RV parking. A popular spot with Alaskans.

The hot springs were used as a gathering place by area Athabascans before the gold rush. Local prospectors probably used the springs as early as the 1890s. Cassius Monohan homesteaded the site in 1905, selling out to Frank Leach in 1909. Leach built the airstrip, on which Noel Wien landed in 1924. (Wien pioneered many flight routes between Alaska communities.)

Private Aircraft: Circle Hot Springs state-maintained airstrip; elev. 956 feet; length 3,600 feet; gravel; lighted, unattended.

Return to Milepost F 127.8 Steese Highway

Formerly called Central House, Central is situated on Crooked Creek along the Steese Highway. Central is the central point in the huge Circle Mining District, one of the oldest and still one of the most active districts in the state. The annual Circle Mining District Picnic for local miners and their families is held in August.

The **Circle District Historical Society Museum** has displays covering the history of the Circle Mining District and its people. Also here are a photo display of wildflowers, fossilized remains of preglacial mammals, a minerals display, library and archives, gift shop and visitor information. Admission fee charged; members free. Open daily noon to 5 P.M., Memorial Day through Labor Day.

F 127.7 C 34.3 Mills Junction. New owners John and Shelly welcome you to Central with a host of roadhouse services—motel rooms, restaurants, bar, package store, convenience store, gas, diesel, propane, laundromat, public telephone. As an official checkpoint for the Yukon Quest, we are happy to answer questions on the race, Central and gold panning. Open year-round. Phone (907) 520-5599. [ADVERTISEMENT]

F 127.8 C 34.2 Turnoff for Circle Hot Springs.

Junction with Circle Hot Springs Road; see "Circle Hot Springs Road" log above.

F 127.9 C 34.1 Bridge over Crooked Creek. Site of Central House roadhouse on north side of bridge. Distance marker northbound shows Circle 33 miles.

F 128.1 C 33.9 Central DOT/PF highway maintenance station.

F 128.2 C 33.8 *Pavement ends, gravel begins, northbound.*

Watch for ptarmigan and snowshoe hares between Central and Circle.

F 128.4 C 33.6 Private Aircraft: Central state-maintained airstrip, adjacent north; elev. 932 feet; length 2,700 feet; gravel; unattended.

F 130.5 C 31.5 Pond frequented by a variety of ducks.

F 131.1 C 30.9 Albert Creek bridge.

F 138 C 24 *NOTE: Winding road to Circle. Road narrows northbound.*

F 140.5 C 21.5 Birch Creek Access, **Lower Birch Creek Wayside** (BLM) to east. *Slow for dips in access road!* Parking area with outhouse and garbage container.

F 147.2 C 14.8 One-lane bridge over Birch Creek; clearance 13 feet, 11 inches. Spur roads at south and north ends of bridge lead to turnouts on creek; primitive camping. Usual takeout point for the **Birch Creek Canoe Trail.**

F 147.5 C 14.5 Turnout to east.

F 148.5 C 13.5 Gravel pit to west.

F 156.7 C 5.3 Large turnout opposite gravel pit to east. Look for bank swallow nests in cliffs.

F 158.5 C 3.5 *Begin 25 mph speed zone northbound into Circle.*

F 159.5 C 2.5 Old Indian cemetery to east.

F 161 C 1 Circle post office (ZIP code 99733); airstrip (see **Private Aircraft** in Circle); school.

F 161.1 C 0.9 Private Aircraft: Circle City state-maintained airstrip, adjacent west; elev. 610 feet; length 3,000 feet; gravel; fuel 100LL.

F 161.2 C 0.8 H.C. Company Store. See display ad this section.

Circle

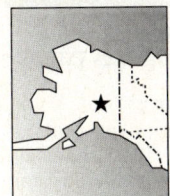

F 162 C 0 Located on the banks of the Yukon River, 50 miles south of the Arctic Circle. **Population:** 100. **Elevation:** 610 feet. **Climate:** Mean monthly temperature in July 61.4°F, in January -10.6°F. Record high 91°F July 1977, record low -69°F in February 1991. Snow from October (8 inches) through April (2 inches). Precipitation in the summer averages 1.45 inches a month.

Before the Klondike Gold Rush of 1898, Circle City was the largest gold mining town on the Yukon River. Prospectors discovered gold on Birch Creek in 1893, and the town of Circle City (so named because the early miners thought it was located on the Arctic Circle) grew up as the nearest supply point to the new diggings on the Yukon River.

Today, Circle serves a small local population and visitors coming in by highway or by river. There's a lot of summer river traffic here: canoeists put in and take out. Gas, groceries, snacks and sundries are available at the H.C. Company Store and Yukon Trading Post. A motel is located just beyond the trading post.

Scheduled air service is available 5 days a week. Inquire locally about guided river trips.

The old Pioneer Cemetery, with its markers dating back to the 1800s, is an interesting spot to visit. Walk a short way upriver (past the old machinery) on the gravel road to a barricade: You will have to cross through a private front yard (please be respectful of property) to get to the trail. Walk straight ahead on the short trail, which goes through dense underbrush (many mosquitoes), for about 10 minutes. Watch for a path on your left to the graves, which are scattered among the thick trees.

Free camping on the banks of the Yukon at the end of the road; tables, toilets, parking area. In 1989, when the Yukon flooded, water covered the bottom of the welcome sign at the campground entrance. From the campground you are looking at one channel of the mighty Yukon. The Yukon is Alaska's largest river. The 2,000-mile river heads in Canada and flows west into Norton Sound on the Bering Sea. ▲

FRIENDLY SERVICE at the END of the HIGHWAY

H.C. COMPANY STORE

• CIRCLE CITY •

Unleaded Gas • Diesel Fuel • AV Gas
Oil Products • Tire Repair

GROCERIES • SNACKS
COLD POP   **PHONE**
Gold Pans   Handcrafted Gifts

OPEN DAILY YEAR AROUND

Dick and Earla Hutchinson, Proprietors
Phone: (907) 773-1222 • Fax: (907) 773-1200
www2.polarnet.com/~hutch/aurora.html

Drive with headlights on at all times.

ELLIOTT HIGHWAY

Connects: Fox to Manley Hot Springs, AK **Length:** 152 miles
Road Surface: 50% paved, 50% gravel **Season:** Open all year
Major Attraction: Minto Lakes, Manley Hot Springs

	Dalton Hwy	Fairbanks	Manley	Minto
Dalton Hwy		84	79	48
Fairbanks	84		163	132
Manley	79	163		53
Minto	48	132	53	

Half of the Elliot Highway is still gravel and vehicles can get dusty. (© Kris Graef, staff)

The Elliott Highway leads 152 miles from its junction with the Steese Highway at Fox (11 miles north of Fairbanks) to Manley Hot Springs, a small settlement with a natural hot springs near the Tanana River. The Elliott Highway provides access to the Dalton Highway to Prudhoe Bay. The highway was named for Malcolm Elliott, president of the Alaska Road Commission from 1927 to 1932.

This is a great drive to a pocket of pioneer Alaska. The road travels the ridges and hills, providing a "top of the world" view of hundreds of square miles in all directions.

The first 73.1 miles of the Elliott Highway are paved to the Dalton Highway junction; the remaining 78.9 miles to Manley are mostly gravel, with a couple of sections of improved and/or chip-sealed road. Road conditions depend on weather and maintenance. The gravel portion of the highway is subject to potholes and ruts in wet weather. Gravel road may be treated with calcium chloride for dust control in dry weather; wash your vehicle after travel to prevent corrosion.

From Fox to the Dalton Highway junction, the Elliott Highway is a series of long upgrades and down grades, as the road winds through the White Mountains. From the Dalton Highway junction to Manley, the road is narrow and winding, with some steep grades and blind hills and curves.

Gas is available on the Elliott Highway at **Milepost F 5.5** (Hilltop, 24-hour), **F 66** (North Country Mercantile) and at Manley. If you are headed up the Dalton Highway, the first gas stop on that highway is at the Yukon River crossing, **Milepost J 56** (56 miles north of junction with the Elliott).

Watch for large trucks on the Elliott Highway between Fairbanks and the Dalton Highway junction. The Elliott Highway is open year-round.

The Elliott Highway also provides access to 4 trailheads in the White Mountains National Recreation Area. These trails (most are for winter use) lead to recreation cabins. For more information and cabin registration, stop by the BLM office at 1150 University Avenue in Fairbanks (phone 474-2350) or the Alaska Public Lands Information Center (APLIC), 250 N. Cushman (phone 456-0527).

Emergency medical services: Between Fox and Manley Hot Springs, phone the state troopers at 911 or (907) 452-1313. Use CB channels 9, 14, 19.

Elliott Highway Log

Distance from Fox (F) is followed by distance from Manley Hot Springs (M).

ALASKA ROUTE 2

F 0 M 152 Steese Expressway ends at **junction** of Alaska Routes 2 (Elliott Highway) and 6 (Steese Highway) at Fox (description follows), 11 miles north of Fairbanks; weigh station with pay phone at northeast intersection. Gas (24 hour fueling) and groceries at **Fox General Store** to west. Dalton Highway information sign. Turn east for Steese Highway; continue north for Elliott Highway.

Junction with Steese Highway (Alaska Route 6) to Circle. Turn to **Milepost F 11** in the STEESE HIGHWAY section on page 482 for log of that route.

FOX (pop. 332), has Fox General Store (gas, diesel, propane, groceries, liquor store, ATM) and Fox Roadhouse. Fox was established as a mining camp before 1905 and named for nearby Fox Creek.

F 0.4 M 151.6 Fox Spring picnic area; tables, spring water.

F 1.4 M 150.6 Turnoff for **El Dorado Gold Mine** to west, a commercial gold mine offering tours and gold panning to the public; admission charged.

F 3.4 M 148.6 Old Murphy Dome Road, very rough but passable, leads southwest around Murphy Dome to Murphy Dome Road.

F 5.5 M 146.8 Hilltop 24-hour gas and food mart; diesel, propane, phone and ATM.

F 7.5 M 144.5 Views to northeast of Pedro Dome and Dome Creek. Buildings of Dome and Eldorado camps are in the valley below to the east (best view is southbound).

F 8.6 M 143.4 Dome Creek Road to northeast.

F 9.2 M 142.8 Sign reads "Olnes City (pop. 1)." Olnes was a railroad station on the Tanana Valley Railroad and a mining camp. Old tailings and abandoned cabins.

F 10.6 M 141.4 Turnoff for **Olnes Pond**, 1 mile southwest of highway via wide gravel side road; fishing, informal camping (no facilities). Pond is stocked by the ADF&G. Access to Chatanika River.

F 11 M 141 Chatanika River bridge. Access to **Lower Chatanika River** to west at north end of bridge via former state campground road.

F 13.1 M 138.9 Willow Creek bridge.

F 18.3 M 133.7 Parking area to west. Watch for sign to southwest along highway (excerpt follows):

"Located here is an experimental trenching site that is part of a project studying the feasibility to construct a natural gas pipeline to transport gas from Alaska's North Slope to market. The technical trenching trials were con-

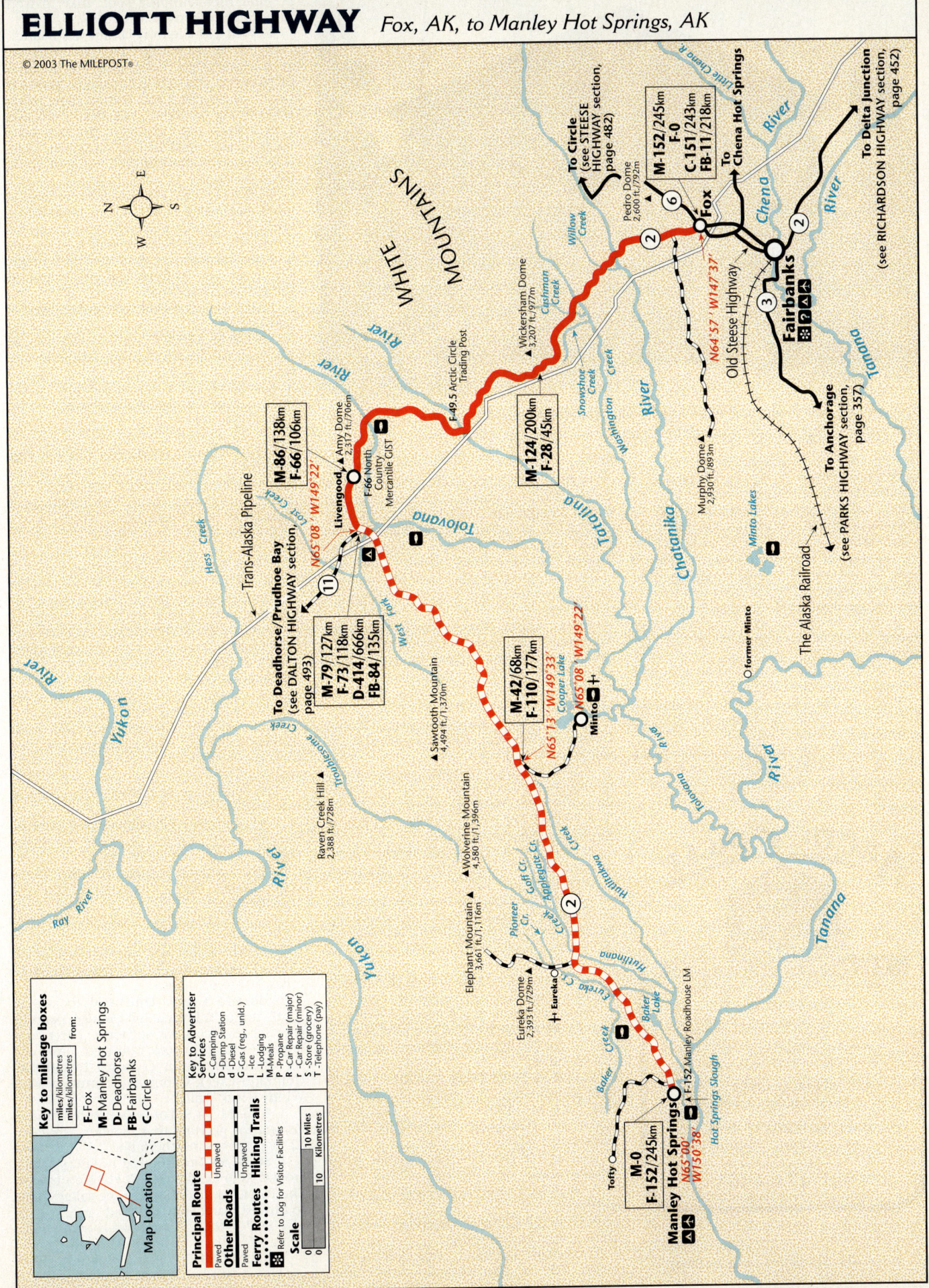

ELLIOTT HIGHWAY

The Arctic Circle Trading Post (formerly Wildwood General Store) offers free coffee and Dalton Highway road condition reports. (© Kris Graef, staff)

ducted here to determine the efficiency and economics of various methods of trenching in permafrost. This site, which is 1 of 3, was chosen because it is composed of discontinuous permafrost in silt. The other sites, which contain continuous permafrost, are located in the Prudhoe Bay area. The trenching trial was completed in spring 2002. The site will be monitored for 10 years to evaluate the amount of fill subsidence and to study the success of several methods of revegetation."

F 18.5 M 133.5 Washington Creek bridge. Access to creek to north at east end of bridge.

F 20.1 M 131.9 Paved double-ended parking area to northeast on curve.

F 23.5 M 128.5 Large double-ended parking area with view of forested valley to southwest.

F 24.2 M 127.8 Long double-ended turnout on Old Elliott Highway alignment to northeast at 40-mph curve.

ARCTIC CIRCLE TRADING POST
MILE 49, ELLIOTT HIGHWAY

The first stop on your journey to the Arctic Circle!

- **ARCTIC CIRCLE CERTIFICATES**
  Official Arctic Circle Registry
- **ARCTIC CIRCLE GIFTS**
  T-Shirts • Caps • Postcards • Pins
- **DALTON HIGHWAY INFO**
  Road Conditions, Safe Driving Tips

For general information:
907-474-4565
www.arcticcircletradingpost.com

Drive with headlights on at all times.

F 25 M 127 Long double-ended turnout on Old Elliott Highway alignment to northeast at 35 mph curve.

F 27.7 M 124.3 Large double-ended paved turnout to southwest. Highway winds around the base of Wickersham Dome (elev. 3,207 feet). Views of the White Mountains, a range of white limestone mountains (elev. 5,000 feet).

Wickersham Dome Trailhead (White Mountains National Recreation Area). The Wickersham Creek Trail (winter-use) is 20 miles long; ATVs are permitted. Summit Trail (year-round) is 20 miles long and accesses Borealis–LeFevre BLM cabin.

Entering Livengood/Tolovana Mining District northbound, Fairbanks Mining District southbound.

F 28.1 M 123.9 Distance marker northbound shows Livengood 44 miles, Yukon River 101 miles, Minto 94 miles.

F 29.2 M 122.8 Sled Dog Rocks on horizon for northbound travelers.

F 29.5 M 122.5 Long double-ended turnout on Old Elliott HIghway alignment to northeast.

F 29.7 M 122.3 Turnout to west. Spring water piped to road. (A sign here warns that the spring water is not tested for purity and it should be boiled or chemically disinfected before drinking.)

F 30.3 M 121.7 Large double-ended parking area to southwest; scenic view.

Fairbanks–North Star Borough boundary.

F 31 M 121 Long double-ended turnout on Old Elliott Highway alignment to northeast on curve.

F 31.8 M 120.2 Large turnout to southwest; scenic view.

F 32.6 M 119.4 *Long, steep downgrade northbound.* First good view northbound of trans-Alaska pipeline.

F 34 M 118 Good view of pipeline going underground.

F 36.4 M 115.6 Large parking area to northeast.

F 37 M 115 Globe Creek bridge. Access to creek at west end of bridge.

Grapefruit Rocks—2 large outcrops on either side of the highway—are visible ahead, northbound. Grapefruit Rocks is a popular rock-climbing spot; hike in from turnout at Milepost F 39 or 39.2.

F 38 M 114 Highway climbs westbound.

F 39 M 113 Side road to northeast at parking sign dead ends at a small turnaround. According to APLIC, access to Upper Grapefruit Rocks is from here; follow trail leading up above road. Beautiful views. Trail is steep and exposed to hot sun; bring water, insect repellent and sunscreen. Highway descends southbound. View of Globe Creek canyon.

F 39.3 M 112.7 Double-ended turnout to south. According to APLIC, Lower Grapefruit Rocks is accessible from this turnout by following the 4-wheel drive trail leading east from the turnout to a clearing with a firepit. Hike is an easy 1/4 mile. Trail can be muddy and mosquitoes are bad

F 40.5 M 111.5 Double-ended turnout to north.

F 41.2 M 110.8 Double-ended parking area on Old Elliott Highway alignment to north.

F 42.9 M 109.1 Pipeline pump station No. 7 to west (not visible from road).

F 43 M 109 *Begin long downgrade northbound.*

F 44.9 M 107.1 **Tatalina River** bridge (new bridge under construction in summer 2002). Walk to old bridge upstream from parking area beside river. The Tatalina is a tributary of the Chatanika.

F 46 M 106 *Highway begins long upgrade northbound to* **Milepost F 48**.

F 49.5 M 102.5 "Welcome to Joy, AK" (sign). Arctic Circle Trading post to east. (The sign still read Wildwood General Store last summer, but it's been Arctic Circle Trading Post since 1997.) The trading post has free coffee and Arctic Circle Crossing certificates, as well as gifts, snacks and other Arctic Circle memorabilia for sale. Posted by the door is a sign that reads: "Not a single mosquito at Joy ... they are all married with large families."

Arctic Circle Trading Post was built by the Carlsons, who homesteaded here with their 23 children (18 of whom were adopted).

The Arctic Circle Trading Post. See display ad this section.

F 51.8 M 100.2 Double-ended parking area to north on curve. View of White Mountains to northeast and the Elliott Highway descending slopes of Bridge Creek valley ahead. Bridge Creek flows into the Tolovana River.

Steep winding downgrades (signed) northbound to **Milepost F 54**.

F 57 M 95 Distance marker northbound shows Livengood 12 miles, Yukon River 72 miles, Minto 63 miles.

Colorado Creek Trailhead to east at south end of Tolovana River Bridge; parking, wheelchair-accessible outhouse, litter container. Colorado Creek trail (recommended for winter use) leads eastward 15 miles to Colorado Creek Cabin and connects with Windy Creek Trail.

F 57.1 M 94.9 Tolovana River bridge. Fishing for grayling to 11 inches; whitefish 12 to 18 inches; northern pike.

F 58 M 94 Northbound highway winds around Amy Dome (elev. 2,317 feet) to east. The Tolovana River flows in the valley to the southwest, paralleling the road.

F 59.7 M 92.3 Parking area to southwest. *Begin long upgrade northbound.*

F 62.3 M 89.7 Watch for narrow gravel road to northeast which winds uphill 0.3 mile to the **Fred Blixt BLM cabin** (pictured

here). Preregister to use the cabin with the BLM office in Fairbanks.

According to the BLM, the original cabin was built in 1935 by Fred Blixt, a Swedish trapper and prospector who built several such cabins in the Livengood area. The original cabin burned down in 1991 and was replaced in 1992. The cabin is 12-by-16 feet and constructed with 2-sided logs.

F 66 M 86 LIVENGOOD (pop. 29); general store.

North Country Mercantile. Groceries, liquor store, ice. Fish and Game vendor. Gas and tire store. Phone; coffee. Stop in for the latest road and travel information. Summer hours: Open May 1 to Oct. 1, 9 A.M. to midnight. Winter hours: Oct. 1 to "depends on business," 9 A.M. to 9 P.M. Closed Wednesday and Thursday. Phone (907) 295-6500. [ADVERTISEMENT]

Gold was discovered in this area in July 1914 by Nathaniel R. Hudson and Jay Livengood. A lively mining camp until 1920, it yielded some $9.5 million in gold. Large-scale mining was attempted in the late 1930s and again in the 1940s, but both operations were eventually shut down and Livengood became a ghost town. A mining corporation acquired much of the gold-rich Livengood Bench. *NO TRESPASSING* on mining claims.

F 68.5 M 83.5 *Long downgrade westbound; trucks use low gear.*

F 70.1 M 81.9 Livengood Creek bridge. Money Knob to northeast.

F 71 M 81 Double-ended turnout at **junction** with access road to Livengood state highway maintenance station. No visitor services.

F 71.1 M 80.9 Large double-ended turnout to south. Overnight parking allowed.

F 72.1 M 79.9 *Downgrade northbound; trucks use low gear.*

F 73 M 79 Distance marker shows Minto 48 miles, Manley 80 miles, Yukon River 56 miles.

F 73.1 M 78.9 TURN SOUTHWEST to continue on Elliott Highway to Minto and Manley Hot Springs.

Junction with the Dalton Highway (Alaska Route 11). See DALTON HIGHWAY section on page 493 for log.

Prickly rose blooms along the Elliott Highway in June. (© Kris Graef, staff)

NOTE: Pavement ends, gravel begins; road narrows (no shoulders) westbound.

F 74.3 M 77.7 Livengood pipeline camp to north.

F 74.7 M 77.3 River access and informal campsite to south at both ends of **Tolovana River** bridge; grayling to 15 inches, use spinners or flies.

Travelers may notice the abundance of dragonflies seen along the Elliott Highway: their main food is mosquitoes.

F 76.3 M 75.7 Cascaden Ridge (low hills to north).

F 78 M 74 Evidence of the Mile 78 Fire, which burned more than 115,000 acres in summer 2002. The fire started when the rear axle of a truck seized up and sent sparks into the grass.

F 82.5 M 69.5 *Slow for steep blind hill.*

F 86 M66 Road widens westbound for the next 2 miles.

F 86.7 M 65.3 Highway climbs westbound; no guard rails, 35-mph curve. Looking south toward the Tolovana River valley, travelers should be able to see Tolovana Hot Springs Dome (elev. 2,386 feet).

Tolovana Hot Springs itself is about 11 miles southeast of the highway. The hot springs has 2 wood tubs and 2 cabins. Phone (907) 455-6706 for reservations (required) and directions (necessary); www.mosquitonet.com/~tolovana/.

F 91.5 M 60.5 Distance marker westbound shows Minto 29 miles, Manley 61 miles.

F 92.5 M 59.5 Sweeping views to southeast and northwest as highway climbs westbound.

F 94.4 M 57.6 Double-ended turnout to south. Good vantage point to view Minto Flats, Tanana River and foothills of the Alaska Range to south. The White Mountains are to the northeast and Sawtooth Mountain is to the northwest.

F 96 M 56 Good view of Minto Lakes as highway climbs Ptarmigan Hill. Alaska cotton in June.

F 97 M 55 The mountains to the north are (from east to west): Sawtooth (elev. 4,494 feet); Wolverine (4,580 feet); and Elephant (3,661 feet). To the south are Tolovana River flats and Cooper Lake.

F 101.5 M 50.5 Gravel pit turnout.

F 106.8 M 45.2 Summit. Turnout with view of Sawtooth Mountains to north.

F 109.8 M 42.2 Junction with Minto Road (improved 2002) which leads south 11 miles to the Indian village of **MINTO** (pop. 258), located on the west bank of the Tolovana River. Food, gas, and lodging are available. Minto has a health clinic and one school. The sale or importation of alcohol is banned in the village.

Minto residents are mainly Tanana Athabascans. The Minto Band originally built permanent cabins at Old Minto on the Tanana River. The village was relocated to its present location, 40 miles north of the old site, in 1969 due to repeated flooding and erosion. The present site had been used as a fall and winter camp since the early 1900s. New housing and a new school were completed by 1971.

The climate here is extreme: the average daily maximum temperature during July is in the low 70s; the average daily minimum in January is well below zero, with extended periods of –40°F, and very strong wind chill factors common throughout the winter. Average annual precipitation is 12 inches, with 50 inches of snowfall.

Most of the year-round employment is with the school, clinic or village council. Many residents work during summers fire fighting for the BLM. Some residents trap or work in the arts and crafts center, making birch-bark baskets and beaded skin and fur items. Subsistence is an important part of the local economy. Salmon, whitefish, moose, bear, small game, waterfowl and berries are utilized. Several families have seasonal fishing/hunting camps and trapping areas on the Tanana River and Goldstream Creek.

Minto Flats is one of the most popular duck hunting spots in Alaska, according to the ADF&G. **Minto Lakes** refers to all lakes in this lowland area. Accessible only by plane or boat; best to fly in. Pike to 36 inches; use wobblers, bait, red-and-white spoons, good all summer. Also grayling, sheefish and whitefish.

Private Aircraft: Minto airstrip 1 mile east; elev. 460 feet; length 2,000 feet; gravel; unattended.

F 114.3 M 37.7 *CAUTION: Narrow, wind-*

Lush summer vegetation and pioneer artifacts characterize Manley Hot Springs.
(© Kris Graef, staff)

ing, roller-coaster road westbound for next 6 miles. Slow for blind hills and corners.

F 119.8 M 32.2 Summit. Eureka Dome (elev. 2,393 feet) to north.

F 120.4 M 31.6 Turnouts.

F 121 M 31 *Begin improved road surface westbound.*

F 123.5 M 28.5 Turnout; scenic view.

F 124 M 28 Highway descends Six Mile Hill westbound.

F 127.6 M 24.4 *End improved road surface westbound.*

F 129.3 M 22.7 Hutlinana Creek bridge. *CAUTION: Slow for one-lane bridge.*

F 130.7 M 21.3 *Begin improved road surface westbound.*

F 131.3 M 20.7 Junction with Eureka and Rampart Road (11.8 miles). Mining claims in area: *NO TRESPASSING*. Road is unmaintained beyond Mile 2.6. A trail leads to the former mining camp of Eureka, at the junction of Pioneer and Eureka creeks, 3 miles south of Eureka Dome.

F 132 M 20 Junction with Old Elliott Highway loop.

F 132.7 M 19.3 Junction with Old Elliott Highway loop.

F 137 M 15 Bridge over **Baker Creek**. Fishing for grayling 5 to 20 inches, use flies, black gnats, mosquitoes, May-Sept.

Watch for moose.

F 137.5 M 14.5 *End improved highway westbound. Narrow, winding road begins.*

F 150 M 2 Walter Woods Park to west.

F 150.4 M 1.6 Washeteria to north; laundromat, restrooms, showers and RV dump station.

F 151 M 1 "Welcome to Manley Hot Springs" sign. Community wellhouse to north (turn switch to activate water). Manley DOT Station to south.

F 151.2 M 0.8 Junction with Tofty Road, which leads 15 miles to gold mining area of Tofty, founded in 1908 by pioneer prospector A.F. Tofty. Active placer mining in area; do not trespass.

F 151.7 M 0.3 Turn uphill for private hot springs, which are contained in 3 concrete baths inside a greenhouse (use fee posted).

F 151.9 M 0.1 One-lane bridge over Hot Springs Slough.

Manley Hot Springs

F 152 M 0 Entering Manley Hot Springs; Manley Roadhouse on left. Road ends 3 miles from here at Tanana River. **Population:** 72. **Emergency Services:** Volunteer Rescue Squad (EMTs and ETTs). **Elevation:** 330 feet. **Climate:** Mean temperature in July is 59°F, in January -10.4°F. Record high 93°F in June 1969, record low -70°F in January 1934. Precipitation in summer averages 2.53 inches a month. Snow from October through April, with traces in September and May. Greatest mean monthly snowfall in January (11.1 inches). Record snowfall 49 inches in January 1937. **Transportation:** Air taxi service.

Private Aircraft: Manley Hot Springs civil airstrip (open year-round), adjacent southwest; elev. 270 feet; length 2,900 feet; gravel; fuel avgas.

A pocket of "Pioneer Alaska." J.F. Karshner homesteaded here in 1902, about the same time the U.S. Army Signal Corps established a telegraph station nearby. The location soon became known as Baker Hot Springs, after nearby Baker Creek, and later was known simply as Hot Springs. Frank Manley built the 4-story Resort Hotel here in 1907. The population peaked at 101 in 1910, as the village became a trading center for nearby Eureka and Tofty mining districts. In 1913, the hotel burned down. By 1950, the population was down to 29 as mining waned. The settlement's name was changed to Manley Hot Springs in 1957.

There is a big annual 4th of July celebration here, featuring a community feed and boat races on the slough. Manley Hot Springs hosts the Stanley Dayo Championship Sled Dog Race in winter.

Today, Manley Hot Springs is a quiet settlement with gardening, hunting and fishing helping to sustain many residents. Meals, a bar and overnight accommodations are available at the Manley Roadhouse. The post office, gas station and grocery are at the trading post.

Visitors can peek in the windows of the old **Northern Commercial Co.** store in Manley.

Picnic area, playground and tent camping at park on the slough across from Manley Roadhouse. Tent and vehicle camping and boat launch on slough west of bridge. Pay camping fee ($5) at Manley Roadhouse. Showers are available at the roadhouse for $3. The washeteria just outside town has showers and a laundry (see **Milepost F 150.4**).

Manley Roadhouse. Come visit one of Alaska's oldest original roadhouses from the gold rush era. See the many prehistoric and Alaskana artifacts on display. New rooms with private baths added 1997. Private cabins. The Manley Roadhouse is a great place to meet local miners, dog mushers, trappers or fishermen. We specialize in traditional Alaska home-style hospitality, fresh-baked pies, giant cinnamon rolls and good food. Largest liquor selection in Alaska. Stop by and see us. See display ad this section. [ADVERTISEMENT]

Hot Springs Slough flows into the Tanana River. Fishing for pike 18 to 36 inches, use spinning and trolling lures, May through September. Follow the dirt road from the old Northern Commercial Co. Store out of town for 2.5 miles to reach the **Tanana River**; king, silver and chum salmon from 7 to 40 lbs., June 15 to Sept. 30. Fish wheels and nets are used. Fishing charter services are available locally.

MANLEY ROADHOUSE
SERVING ALASKA SINCE 1906
Historic and Prehistoric Artifacts on display

ROOMS
CABINS
FOOD
BAR

Mile 152 Elliott Highway
Bob Lee, Innkeeper • Phone (907) 672-3161

Welcome to the North Country!

DALTON HIGHWAY

	Coldfoot	Deadhorse	Fairbanks
Coldfoot		239	259
Deadhorse	239		498
Fairbanks	259	498	

Connects: Elliott Hwy. to Deadhorse, AK **Length:** 414 miles
Road Surface: 75% gravel, 25% paved **Season:** Open all year
Steepest Grade: 12 percent
Highest Summit: Atigun Pass 4,800 feet
Major Attraction: Trans-Alaska Pipeline, Arctic Circle
(See map, page 494)   ⑪

An August snow storm on the North Slope turns the landscape white.
(© John Schwieder Photography)

The 414-mile Dalton Highway (often still referred to as the "Haul Road") begins at **Milepost F 73.1** on the Elliott Highway, 84 miles from Fairbanks, and ends—for the general public—at Deadhorse, a few miles from Prudhoe Bay and the Arctic Ocean. (Access to the Arctic Ocean is available only through commercial tour operators; private vehicles are not permitted on the oil field.)

The Dalton Highway is unique in its scenic beauty, wildlife and recreational opportunities, but it is also one of Alaska's most remote and challenging roads. The first 10 or 20 miles of the Dalton Highway will give you a pretty good idea of what to expect on the rest of the highway as far as road conditions.

Road conditions vary depending on weather, maintenance and time of year. On recently rehabilitated sections, you may find good paved road. On some sections of gravel road, the washboard can be so severe your teeth rattle. Calcium chloride is used only in limited areas on the road to control dust; it is corrosive to vehicles and slippery when wet. There are several steep (10 to 12 percent) grades. Drive with your headlights on at all times. Stop only at turnouts. *NOTE: Do not stop in the middle of the road to take pictures.*

Carry spare tires; flat tires are a common occurrence on this road. Keep in mind that towing fees by private wrecker service can be costly. DOT stations along the highway do not provide vehicles services or gas.

Watch for ruts, rocks, dust in dry weather, potholes in wet weather and trucks and road maintenance equipment at all times. The volume of truck traffic hauling materials between Fairbanks and Prudhoe Bay varies, but always give trucks the right-of-way. Slow down, and pull over to the side of the road when meeting oncoming trucks. *CAUTION: Soft shoulders and abrupt drop-offs from gravel roadway to tundra; pull over with care!*

Road construction projects will be under way in summer 2003. Check for current projects on the web at www.dot.state.ak.us (Summer Construction Advisories), or call the Alaska Department of Transportation's construction department at (907) 451-5466.

When planning your trip up the Dalton, keep in mind it is approximately 1,000 miles of driving round trip between Fairbanks and Deadhorse, much of it on gravel. For those who don't want to drive themselves, commercial tours are available (see advertisements this section).

Services along the Dalton Highway are limited. Shop for groceries before departing Fairbanks. There are no convenience stores or grocery stores along the Dalton Highway. Gas, food, phone and lodging are available at the Yukon River Crossing at **Milepost J 56**, the Hot Spot Cafe at **J 60.3** and at Coldfoot Camp at **J 175**. There is also lodging in Wiseman. Alyeska pump stations do not provide any public services. Although noted on the map, former pipeline camps have been removed.

The last dump station northbound until Deadhorse is at Coldfoot. *Please do NOT dump holding tanks along the road.*

The Bureau of Land Management (BLM), which manages 2.1 million acres of public land along the Dalton Highway, has 1 developed campground (Marion Creek, **Milepost J 179.7**) and 3 primitive campsites (Mile 60 Dump Station, **Milepost J 60.4**; Arctic Circle Wayside, **J 115.3**; and Galbraith Camp, **J 274.7**) along the highway. There is also a private campground in Coldfoot. In Deadhorse, there is overnight parking at the Tesoro station and Arctic Oilfield Hotel.

BLM is working with other state and federal agencies to construct additional visitor facilities along the Dalton Highway. Planned facilities over the next 15 years include additional dump stations, campgrounds, interpretive waysides, pullouts and a new visitor center. For information on BLM lands and traveling the Dalton Highway, contact the BLM's Northern Field Office at 1150 University Ave. in Fairbanks; phone (907) 474-2200, toll-free 1-800-437-7021; http://aurora.ak.blm.gov/dalton.

The highway is named for James William Dalton, an arctic engineer involved in early oil exploration efforts on the North Slope. It was built as a haul road between the Yukon River and Prudhoe Bay during construction of the trans-Alaska pipeline, and was origi-

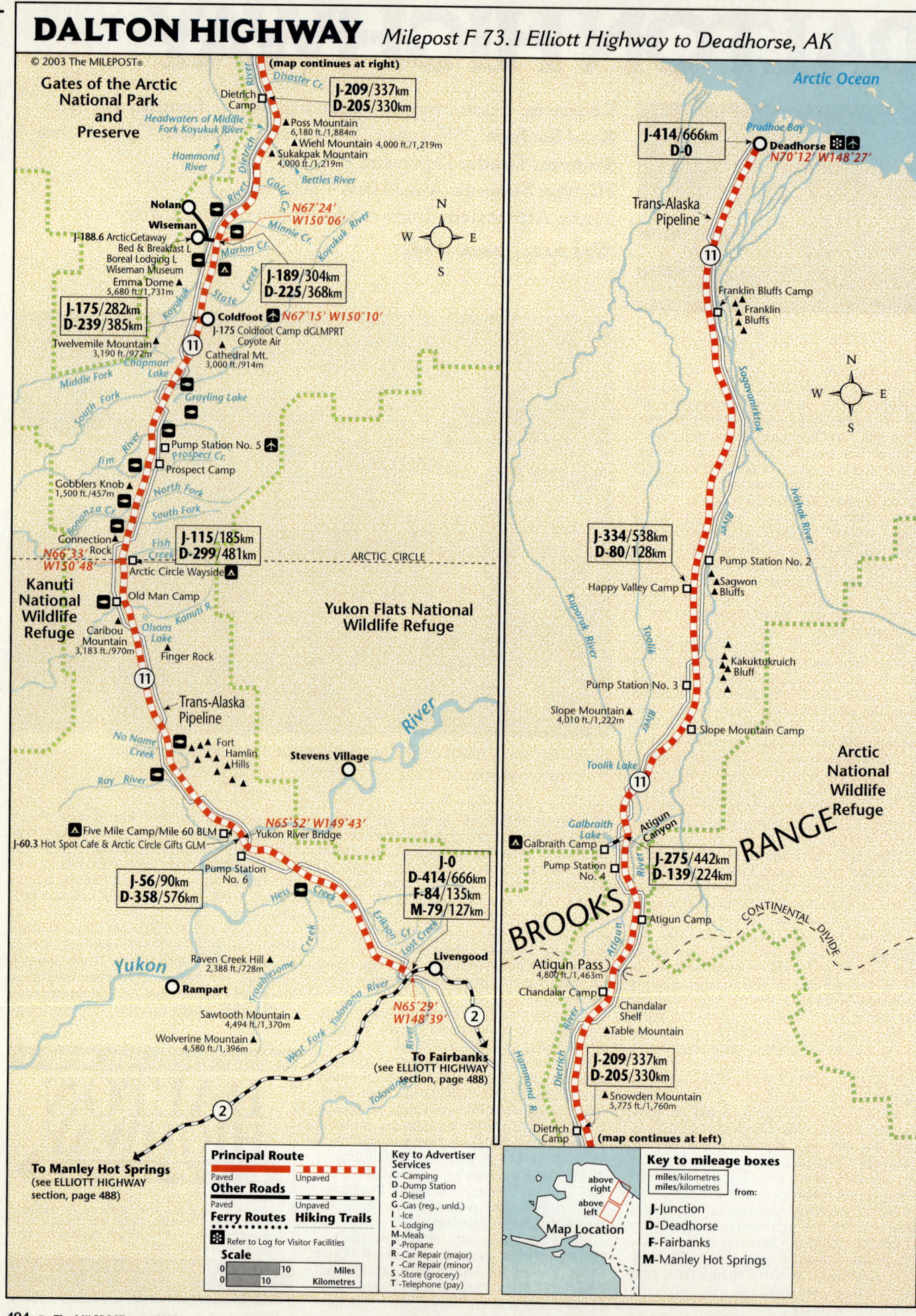

nally called the North Slope Haul Road. Construction of the road began April 29, 1974, and was completed 5 months later. The road is 28 feet wide with 3 to 6 feet of gravel surfacing. Some sections of road are underlain with plastic foam insulation to prevent thawing of the permafrost.

Construction of the 800-mile-long pipeline between Prudhoe Bay and Valdez took place between 1974 and 1977. The 48-inch-diameter pipeline, of which slightly more than half is above ground, has 7 operating pump stations. The control center is in Valdez. Design, construction and operation of the pipeline are managed by Alyeska Pipeline Service Company. For more information, contact Public Affairs Dept., Alyeska Pipeline Service Co., 1835 S. Bragaw St., Anchorage, AK 99512.

All waters between the Yukon River bridge and Dietrich River are part of the Yukon River system, and most are tributaries of the Koyukuk River. Fishing for arctic grayling is especially good in rivers accessible by foot from the highway. The large rivers also support burbot, salmon, pike and whitefish. Small Dolly Varden are at higher elevations in streams north of Coldfoot. Fishing for salmon is closed within the trans-Alaska pipeline corridor. According to the Dept. of Fish and Game, anglers should expect high, turbid water conditions throughout much of June as the snowpack melts in the Brooks Range, with the best fishing occurring during July and August.

Report wildlife violations to Fish & Wildlife or the State Troopers at Coldfoot.

Emergency services: Contact the Alaska State Troopers via CB radio, Channel 19, or contact any state highway maintenance camp along the highway. Department of Transportation maintenance camp personnel are not medically trained, but they will assist travelers in contacting the proper authorities to get medical attention. Highway maintenance camps can provide help in the event of an accident or medical emergency.

Bicyclists from Belguim take a break at Finger Mountain Wayside. (© Lynn Owen, staff)

Lost Creek flows into the West Fork Tolovana River. Pipeline is visible stretching across the ridge of the distant hill.

J 5.5 D 408.5 Turnout to west.

J 5.7 D 408.3 APL pipeline access road; no public admittance. There are many of these pipeline access roads along the highway; most are signed with the milepost on the pipeline. Because they are so numerous, most APL pipeline access roads are not included in *The MILEPOST* log unless they occur along with another feature. All these access roads are closed to the public for security and safety concerns. Do not block road access.

J 6.1 D 407.9 Turnout at gravel stockpile at top of grade.

J 7.7 D 406.3 Turnout.

J 8.4 D 405.6 Entering Game Management Unit 20F northbound.

J 9.2 D 404.8 CAUTION: Steep and winding downgrades next 3 miles northbound.

J 12 D 402 Turnout to west. Highway climbs northbound.

J 14.3 D 399.7 Highway climbs; steep grades next 3 miles northbound.

J 18.5 D 395.5 Highway curves past old alignment. Road widens northbound.

J 20.6 D 393.4 Distance marker southbound shows Fox 90 miles, Fairbanks

Dalton Highway Log

Distance from junction with Elliott Highway (J) is followed by distance from Deadhorse (D).

ALASKA ROUTE 11

J 0 D 414 Sign at start of Dalton Highway: "Heavy Industrial Traffic. All vehicles drive with headlights on. Speed 50 mph next 416 miles." CAUTION: Steep grades and narrow road northbound. Watch for trucks!

Junction with Elliott Highway to Fairbanks and Manley Hot Springs. Turn to Milepost F 73.1 on page 491 in the ELLIOTT HIGHWAY section for log of that route.

J 1 D 413 Distance marker northbound shows Yukon River 56 miles, Coldfoot 175 miles, Deadhorse 414 miles.

Distance marker southbound shows Fairbanks 81 miles, Minto 48 miles, Manley 80 miles.

J 2.9 D 411.1 Turnout to west.

J 4 D 410 Highway descends "Five Mile Hill" into the Lost Creek valley. This is a steep hill; there have been 2 truck accidents here.

ARCTIC CIRCLE ADVENTURE

Arctic Circle DRIVE

A one day guided round trip journey by land across the Arctic Circle.

Travel the famed Dalton Highway and view the remarkable Trans Alaska Pipeline.

Visit the Arctic Circle Trading Post situated in the rural community of Joy, Alaska.

Experience the mighty Yukon River.

Walk out on the amazing arctic tundra and feel the frozen ground beneath the surface.

Cross the Arctic Circle and receive an official Arctic Circle Adventure Certificate. Enjoy an evening riverside picnic meal on your return journey to Fairbanks.

Arctic Circle FLY / DRIVE

The one day Arctic Circle Fly/Drive Adventure includes all the highlights of the Drive Adventure plus:

Fly north from Fairbanks across the Arctic Circle and receive an aerial view of the vast Alaska wilderness.

Experience the mighty Yukon River. Enjoy a meal on your own on the banks of the Yukon River. Marvel at the majestic beauty of the northland's most famous waterway and learn of the river's storied past.

Travel the famed Dalton Highway under the Midnight Sun on the return journey to Fairbanks.

For further adventure extend your journey with an optional overnight stay in the Brooks Mountain Range.

Arctic Circle NATIVE CULTURE

The one day Arctic Circle Native Culture Adventure includes all the highlights of the Fly/Drive Adventure plus:

Fly the wilderness airways of the rugged and magnificent Brooks Mountain Range.

Visit the Nunamiut Eskimo village of Anaktuvuk Pass nestled in the pristine and scenic Gates of the Arctic National Park. Learn of the local Nunamiut culture and history.

The return flight to Fairbanks provides an aerial view of the vast Alaska wilderness.

NORTHERN ALASKA TOUR COMPANY
Sharing Alaska's Arctic With The World

1-800-474-1986, 907-474-8600 Fax 907-474-4767

PO Box 82991-MD, Fairbanks, AK 99708

www.northernalaska.com   adventure@northernalaska.com

BLM Yukon Crossing Visitor Contact Station at Milepost J 56. (© Kris Graef, staff)

100 miles.

J 20.8 D 393.2 Long parking area west side of road with sweeping view of mountains.

J 21.6 D 392.4 Turnout at gravel stockpile to east. Begin long (3 miles) descent northbound to Hess Creek.

J 21.8 D 392.2 Scenic viewpoint to west.

J 22.7 D 391.3 *Road narrows; rough road surface north to Milepost J 28.*

J 23.8 D 390.2 **Hess Creek** bridge. Dirt access road to west at north end of bridge to campsite in trees. Track can be muddy; an easy place to get stuck. Bring your mosquito repellent. Whitefish and grayling fishing. Hess Creek, known for its colorful mining history, is the largest stream between the junction and the Yukon River bridge.

J 23.9 D 390.1 Side road to west 0.2 mile to pond with parking space adequate for camping.

J 25 D 389 Double-ended rough turnout to east. Good view of pipeline and remote-operated valve site as the highway crosses Hess Creek and valley.

Highway climbs northbound; steep curve.

J 25.5 D 388.5 Small turnout at distance marker northbound: Yukon River 31 miles, Coldfoot 150 miles, Deadhorse 389 miles.

J 26.5 D 387.5 APL access (gated). Pipeline parallels highway about 250 feet away.

J 27 D 387 Evidence of lightning-caused forest fires.

J 28.2 D 385.8 Large turnout opposite APL access.

CAUTION: Downgrade northbound, slow for 35 mph curves next 1.5 miles.

J 32.7 D 381.3 Turnout to east.

J 33.7 D 380.3 Turnout at tributary of Hess Creek. Chiming bells bloom in June.

J 33.9 D 380.1 APL pipeline access road. Goalpost-like structures, called "**headache bars**," guard against vehicles large enough to run into and damage the pipeline.

J 35.5 D 378.5 Turnout to east.

J 38.1 D 375.9 Mile 38 Dalton Highway Crossing: pipeline goes under road. Good photo opportunity. APL access road.

J 38.5 D 375.5 *Steep uphill grades and 35 mph curves next 2 miles northbound.*

J 40.7 D 373.3 Double-ended turnout to east at crest of hill. Overview of Troublesome and Hess creeks area. Brush obscures sweeping views. Highway descends northbound.

J 42.2 D 371.8 Large turnout. Outcrop of dark gabbroic rock.

Begin steep downgrade with 30 to 35 mph curves northbound to Milepost J 43.

J 42.7 D 371.3 Turnout to east.

J 43.1 D 370.9 Isom Creek culvert.

J 44 D 370 *Steep upgrades northbound to Milepost J 47 with sections of 30 mph curves.*

J 44.6 D 369.4 Turnout to west.

J 47.3 D 366.7 Summit; sweeping view of mountains to west.

J 47.5 D 366.5 Side road east to Yukon radio repeater tower.

Highway begins descent to Yukon River northbound.

J 50.4 D 363.6 Turnout at pond to east.

J 51.1 D 362.9 Rough private side road leads east 5.4 miles to Yukon River. Closed to the public.

J 53 D 360.8 First view northbound of the Yukon River. As road drops, you can see the pipeline crossing the river. Fort Hamlin Hills are beyond the river.

J 53.8 D 360.2 **Pump Station No. 6** to west. Alyeska pump stations monitor the pipeline's oil flow on its journey from Prudhoe Bay to Valdez. No public facilities.

J 54.2 D 359.8 Highway passes over pipeline.

J 55.1 D 358.9 Distance marker northbound shows Arctic Circle 60 miles, Coldfoot 120 miles, Deadhorse 360 miles.

J 55.6 D 358.4 **Yukon River Bridge** (formally the E.L. Patton Bridge, named for the president of the Alyeska Pipeline Service Co. after his death in 1982). This wood-decked bridge, completed in 1975, is 2,290 feet long and has a 6 percent grade. The deck was replaced in 1999.

J 56 D 358 **Yukon River Crossing**; traveler services on west side of highway, BLM visitor center on east side of highway. This is the southern boundary of BLM-managed lands.

BLM Yukon Crossing Visitor Contact Station has outhouses, wooden observation deck, information plaques about the highway, pipeline and Yukon River; open daily in summer. Pick up BLM pamphlets on the Dalton Highway here.

Large parking area (no camping). Good close-up views of the pipeline. Short walking path to Yukon River viewpoint.

State law prohibits the use of motorized vehicles within 5 miles of either side of the Dalton Highway from the Yukon River north to Prudhoe Bay. Only persons with valid mining claims may use ORVs on certain trails to access their claims.

J 57 D 357 Note the change in vegetation as the highway passes through boreal forests, boggy lowlands and tundra. Tall, dense forests of white spruce and birch, like these, are found in well-drained soil without permafrost, usually on south-facing slopes.

J 60.3 D 353.7 Turnoff to west for loop road to Hot Spot Cafe (food, gifts, rooms, gas).

Hot Spot Cafe & Arctic Circle Gifts. Favorite stop for truckers and locals. Best BBQ in Alaska. Huge hamburgers, daily specials. The best coffee, ice cream and homemade pies and cakes. Rustic overnight rooms; (907) 451-7543. Arctic Circle Gifts—local Native crafts. 5 miles north of Yukon River bridge. We sell fuel! Lowest prices on

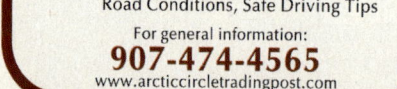

the road. Easy entrance and exit for motorhomes. See display ad this section.

[ADVERTISEMENT]

J 60.4 D 353.6 North end of loop road to Hot Spot Cafe (see **Milepost J 60.3**) provides direct access to **Mile 60 BLM Dump Station**; drive 0.3 mile west of highway past Alyeska pipeline water pump for the dump station. Overnight camping for self-contained RVs at former Five Mile pipeline construction camp. ▲

Next gas stop northbound at Coldfoot, 115 miles.

J 60.6 D 353.4 Highway crosses pipeline. Control gates. Entrance to Five Mile airstrip (length 3,500 feet); controlled by Alyeska Security.

J 61.3 D 352.7 Airstrip control tower.

J 61.5 D 352.5 Control gates.

J 61.8 D 352.2 Seven Mile Station DOT highway maintenance to east; no services. APL access road to west.

J 66.8 D 347.2 Long double-ended turnout to west at bottom of hill. Highway climbs northbound and southbound.

J 67.6 D 346.4 Turnouts both sides of road. *Highway descends steeply northbound with sharp curve at bottom of hill.*

J 69 D 345 Turnout to west.

J 70 D 344 Views of Ray River and Ray Mountains to the west.

J 72.5 D 341.5 Turnout to west. Fort Hamlin Hills Creek bridge. Rough tracks down to creek both ends of bridge.

J 73.5 D 340.5 *Begin steep 0.5-mile ascent of Sand Hill northbound.*

J 74.8 D 339.2 Turnouts both sides of highway.

Begin steep descent northbound followed by steep ascent; dubbed the "Roller Coaster."

J 75.8 D 338.2 *"Roller Coaster" begins southbound.*

J 77 D 337 Stunted, low-growing black spruce like those growing in this area indicate permafrost (permanently frozen soil) near the surface, or poorly drained soil.

J 79.1 D 334.9 **No Name Creek** bridge (narrow). Fishing for burbot, grayling and whitefish. ⟨fish⟩

Sign: Bow hunting only area.

J 81.6 D 332.4 Fort Hamlin Hills are visible to the southeast. Tree line on surrounding hills is about 2,000 feet.

J 86.5 D 327.5 Side road leads west 1 mile to scenic overlook. Access is steep with rough, rocky spots; no turnaround until you reach the top. Nice view of tors to northeast, Yukon Flats Wildlife Refuge to east and Fort Hamlin Hills to southeast. Tors are high, isolated pinnacles of jointed granite jutting up from the tundra and are a residual feature of erosion.

J 87.2 D 326.8 *Begin long, steep ascent of Mackey Hill next 1.5 miles northbound; slippery in wet weather.*

J 88.5 D 325.5 *Begin steep 0.5-mile descent of Mackey Hill northbound.*

Entering Game Management Unit 25D northbound, Unit 20F southbound.

J 90 D 324 *Improved paved highway northbound to Milepost J 175.*

J 90.2 D 323.8 Parking areas on both sides of highway at crest of hill. A good photo opportunity of the road and pipeline to the north. The zigzag design allows the pipeline to flex and accommodate temperature changes. The small green structure over the buried pipe is a radio-controlled valve, allowing the pipeline oil flow to be shut down when necessary.

Highway descends northbound to Dall

Travelers can stretch their legs at Finger Mountain Wayside.

(© Lynn Owen, staff)

Creek.

J 91.1 D 322.9 Dall Creek. Highway climbs steeply next mile northbound.

J 94.1 D 319.9 Turnout at former gravel pit road to west.

J 95 D 319 The vegetation changes noticeably northbound as the highway crosses an area of moist tundra and alpine tundra for about the next 5 miles. Lichens and white mountain avens dominate the well-drained rocky ridges, while the more saturated soils alongside the road are covered by dense stands of dwarf shrubs.

J 96 D 318 Good view northbound of **Finger Rock**, a tor, east of the road. Tors are visible for the next several miles northbound. Prehistoric hunting sites are also numerous in this region. Please do not collect or disturb artifacts.

J 97.9 D 316.1 Distance marker southbound shows Yukon River 42 miles, Fox 166 miles, Fairbanks 176 miles.

J 98.1 D 315.9 **Finger Mountain BLM Wayside** at crest of hill; outhouse, parking, interpretive trail. Good opportunities for photos, berry picking (blueberries, lowbush cranberries), wildflower viewing and hiking.

Caribou Mountain is in the distance to the northwest. Olsens Lake, Kanuti Flats, Kanuti River drainage and site of former Old Man Camp are visible ahead northbound as the road descends and passes through several miles of valley bottom. Excellent mountain views.

J 98.3 D 315.7 Turnout to east at crest of Finger Mountain.

Highway descends steeply next 1.7 miles northbound.

J 103.8 D 310.2 Turnout to east.

J 104.1 D 309.9 Distance marker northbound shows Coldfoot 71 miles, Deadhorse 311 miles.

J 105.8 D 308.2 Large parking area to east at south end of **Kanuti River** bridge; cement ramp to river, informal camping (no facilities), fishing for burbot and grayling. ⟨fish⟩

J 107 D 307 Site of Old Man Camp, a former pipeline construction camp; no structures remain.

J 109.8 D 304.2 Turnout at Beaver Slide. *Road descends 9 percent grade next 2 miles northbound. Watch for soft spots. Slippery when wet.*

J 112.2 D 301.8 Turnout at pipeline access road to east. Moose and bear frequent willow thickets here.

J 114 D 300 Turnouts at both ends of **Fish Creek** bridge. Bumpy, sandy access down to creek to west at north end of bridge; informal campsite in trees (no facilities). Fishing for grayling 12 to 18 inches. Nice spot. ⟨fish⟩

J 115.3 D 298.7 Distance marker northbound shows Coldfoot 60 miles, Deadhorse 300 miles.

Turnoff to east for loop road to **Arctic Circle BLM Wayside** with tables, grills, outhouses and interpretive display. Stop and have your picture taken with the sign showing you are at N 66°33′ W 150°48′. At this latitude, the sun does not set on summer solstice (June 20 or 21) and it does not rise on winter solstice (December 21 or 22). A third of Alaska lies within the Arctic Circle, the only true polar region in the state. Good photo point, with views to the south and to the west.

Follow road (tent sign) east from turnoff 0.6 mile for unmaintained camping area on dirt loop road on the hill behind the wayside. If you reach the Alyeska access gate you've gone too far. ▲

J 115.5 D 298.5 Long double-ended turnout to east at APL access road at Mile 294 on the pipeline.

Begin steep and winding descent northbound.

J 116.3 D 297.7 Turnout to east.

Highway climbs next 2 miles northbounbd.

J 120.8 D 293.2 Connection Rock (signed); north and south road-building crews linked up here.

Steep descent northbound (9 percent grade).

J 122.4 D 291.6 Long double-ended turnout at APL access road to east.

J 124.7 D 289.3 **South Fork Bonanza Creek**; burbot, grayling, whitefish. ⟨fish⟩

J 125.7 D 288.3 **North Fork Bonanza Creek** bridge (narrow). Access to creek to east at south end of bridge. Fishing for burbot, grayling, whitefish. ⟨fish⟩

J 126.5 D 287.5 *Steep uphill at curve northbound.* Highway climbs Paradise Hill. Blueberries and lowbush cranberries in season.

J 129 D 285 *Begin long, steep, ascent next 2 miles northbound.*

J 131.3 D 282.7 Solar-powered communications tower to west.

J 131.5 D 282.5 View of Pump Station No. 5 to north.

J 132 D 282 Large turnout with litter barrels and outhouse at **Gobblers Knob** (elev. 1,500 feet) overlooking the Jack White Range, Pope Creek Dome (the dominant peak to the northwest), Prospect Creek drainage, Pump Station No. 5, Jim River drainage, South Fork Koyukuk drainage and the Brooks Range on the northern horizon.

Begin long, steep descents northbound and southbound.

J 135.1 D 278.9 Narrow bridge over **Prospect Creek**; grayling, whitefish and pike. Active gold mining area. ⟨fish⟩

CAUTION: Steep uphill grade northbound; watch for trucks on blind hill.

J 135.7 D 278.3 Turnout. Old winter road

goes up creek to mines. Turn left for site of **PROSPECT CAMP**, which holds the record for lowest recorded temperature in Alaska (-80°F/-62°C, Jan. 23, 1971). Rough road leads 0.5 mile to Claja Pond; beaver, ducks. Undeveloped campsite on Jim River. Old winter road to Bettles crosses river here (this trail is not useable in summer). ▲

J 137.1 D 276.9 APL access road at Milepost 274.7 on the pipeline at **Pump Station No. 5** to east. Pump station No. 5 is not actually a pump station, but a "drain down" or pressure relief station to slow the gravity-fed flow of oil descending from Atigun Pass in the Brooks Range. Glacial moraine marks the southern boundary of Brooks Range glaciers during the most recent ice age.

Private Aircraft: Airstrip; length 5,000 feet; lighted runway. This airstrip is used as a BLM fire fighting staging area.

J 138.1 D 275.9 Jim River Station (DOT/PF highway maintenance) to west; no services.

J 140.1 D 273.9 Small turnout to east at south end of **Jim River No. 1** bridge; informal campsite. Fishing for burbot, chum and king salmon, grayling, pike, whitefish. *CAUTION: Bears here for fall salmon run.* ◂

J 141 D 273 Small turnout to west at south end of **Jim River No. 2** bridge; fishing. ◂

J 141.8 D 272.2 Douglas Creek crossing.

J 144.1 D 269.9 Large parking area at APL access road to east at south end of **Jim River No. 3** bridge crossing the river's main channel. Fishing.

J 145.6 D 268.4 Pipeline passes under road.

J 150.3 D 263.7 **Grayling Lake Wayside** to east; parking, outhouse and litter barrels overlooking lake.

J 150.8 D 263.2 Turnout to east.

J 155.2 D 258.8 Turnout to east.

J 156 D 258 Large parking area with outhouse and litter barrels to east at south end of **South Fork Koyukuk River** bridge. Self-contained RV camping in turnout. Fishing for grayling, whitefish, chum and king salmon. ◂▲

This large river flows past the villages of Bettles, Allakaket, Hughes and Huslia before draining into the Yukon River near Koyukuk.

The road is passing through the foothills of the Brooks Range. There is an active gold mining area behind the hills to the west. Many side roads off the Dalton Highway lead to private mining claims.

J 157.4 D 256.6 Turnout to east. *Steep uphill grade next 1.2 miles northbound.*

J 158.8 D 255.2 Turnout to east.

J 159.1 D 254.9 Bridge over pipeline; large-animal crossing over pipeline.

J 160 D 254 Good view of Chapman Lake west of road as highway descends steeply northbound. Old mine trail is visible from the road.

The 2 mountains visible to the north are Twelvemile Mountain (elev. 3,190 feet), left, and Cathedral Mountain (3,000 feet), on right.

J 161.1 D 252.9 Turnout to west.

J 164.3 D 249.7 Example of sag bend to east. This is a short section of buried pipeline that allows large animals to cross.

J 165.6 D 248.4 Turnout to west.

J 166.4 D 247.6 Pipeline goes under road.

J 168.5 D 245.5 Turnout to west.

J 169.8 D 244.2 Creek culvert.

J 170.7 D 243.3 Distance marker shows Deadhorse 244 miles.

J 172.6 D 241.4 Large turnout to west. Steep downgrade northbound.

J 173.8 D 240.2 Turnout to west.

J 174.8 D 239.2 First turnoff northbound for Coldfoot (to east via loop road); see description following.

J 175 D 239 Second turnoff northbound on loop road to east for **COLDFOOT**; food, gas, lodging, tire repair, visitor information, Troopers and Fish & Wildlife office.

A former mining camp at the mouth of Slate Creek on the east bank of the Middle Fork Koyukuk River, the name Coldfoot was first reported in 1933 by Robert Marshall, a forester who made a reconnaissance map of the northern Koyukuk Region. "As early as 1899 the town of Slate Creek was started at the mouth of the creek which bears that name. In the summer of 1900, one of the waves of green stampeders got as far up the Koyukuk as this point, then got cold feet, turned around, and departed. This incident was enough to change the first, unromantic appellation of the settlement to Coldfoot." A post office was established here in 1902, when Coldfoot consisted of "one gambling hole, 2 roadhouses, 2 stores and 7 saloons." Mining activity later moved upstream to Nolan and Wiseman Creeks. The post office was discontinued in 1912.

A construction camp during the pipeline boom, today Coldfoot Camp (phone 907/474-3400 or 1-866-474-3400) offers motel lodging and 24-hour restaurant. The "trucker's table" at the restaurant is a good place to get news on the highway. There is also a gift shop, general store, laundromat, fuel facility with gas, diesel and avgas; tire repair, minor vehicle repair; RV park with hookups and dump station; post office and phone. Area tours are available. Coldfoot is the jump-off point for flights into Gates of the Arctic National Park. ▲

There is a 3,500-foot runway to west, maintained by the state. An Alaska State Trooper is located at Coldfoot. A visitor center here, the Coldfoot Interagency Visitor Center, operated by the BLM, USF&WS and National Park Service, offers travel information and nightly slide presentations on the natural and cultural history of the Arctic. It is open from 10 A.M. to 10 P.M. daily, Memorial Day through Labor Day. Topographic maps for sale.

Coyote Air. Experience the vast wilderness beauty of the Brooks Range the only way possible, by aircraft with Coyote Air. We offer a full range of flightseeing trips throughout the Gates of the Arctic National Park and the Arctic National Wildlife Refuge, along with remote access to the wilderness of the Brooks Range. Coyote Air is located at the Coldfoot State Airport. When in Coldfoot phone 678-5995. For advanced reservations or information, please call 1-800-252-0603. See display ad this section. [ADVERTISEMENT]

Coldfoot Camp. See display ad this section. ▲

NOTE: Next services northbound are 244 miles from here.

J 175.1 D 238.9 Narrow bridge over Slate Creek.

Pavement ends, gravel begins, northbound. Asphalt surface treatment under way in summer 2003 between Milepost J 175 (Coldfoot) and Milepost J 209.

J 179.7 D 234.3 Turnoff to east for

COLDFOOT CAMP

Your base camp for exploring Alaska's Brooks Mountain Range!

Found 260 miles north of Fairbanks along the Dalton Highway, Coldfoot Camp is your base camp for exploring the Gates of the Arctic National Park and the Arctic National Wildlife Refuge.

Lodging • Food • Flightseeing • River Rafting • Tire Shop • Transportation

P.O. Box 81512
Fairbanks AK 99708

www.coldfootcamp.com

907-474-3400, 866-474-3400
Fax: 907-474-4767

Coyote Air Service

Gates of the Arctic National Park
Arctic Refuge – ANWR

1-800-252-0603

www.flycoyote.com

Marion Creek Campground (BLM); 28 sites on gravel loop road, $6 camping fee, tables, grills, firepits, firewood, water, toilets, bear-proof litter containers, resident campground host, information kiosk and 11 pull-through RV sites. ▲

Good berry picking (blueberries, low-brush cranberries) in season. Marion Creek trailhead.

J 179.8 D 234.2 Marion Creek bridge.

J 181 D 233 Entering BLM public Lands northbound.

J 184.3 D 229.7 Turnout to east.

J 186.1 D 227.9 Turnout to east.

J 186.7 D 227.3 Parking areas both sides of highway.

J 187.3 D 226.7 Parking area to west at south end of **Minnie Creek** bridge (narrow); fishing for burbot, grayling, whitefish.

J 188.3 D 225.7 Distance marker southbound shows Coldfoot 13 miles, Fairbanks 267 miles.

J 188.4 D 225.6 Distance marker northbound shows Wiseman 3 miles, Dietrich 22 miles, Deadhorse 227 miles.

J 188.5 D 225.5 **Middle Fork Koyukuk River No. 1** crossing (narrow bridge); turnout. Dolly Varden, grayling, whitefish.

J 188.6 D 225.4 Turnoff on improved access road which leads 1.6 miles south to **junction** with road to Nolan and 3 miles south to Wiseman (description follows). This side road also provides good views of the Koyukuk River and good photo opportunities of the pipeline as it goes under the river.

The road to **NOLAN** is narrow dirt and gravel, ranging from good to very poor, and leads 5.5 miles west to private mining claims.

WISEMAN (pop. 21), 3 miles south of the highway, is a historic mining town on the Koyukuk River established in 1908. The heyday of Wiseman came in about 1910, after gold seekers abandoned Coldfoot. This is still an active mining area.

Several interesting historic buildings are found in Wiseman. All the structures are privately owned and most are residences. Visitors can park by the the post office, located in an original log cabin, and walk over to the **Wiseman Historical Museum**, located in the historic Carl Frank Cabin. The museum contains old miner's journals, hotel registers and historical photos; limited gift items are for sale.

To reach the Arctic Getaway (housed in the Historic Pioneer Hall Igloo No. 8) and Boreal Lodging, continue on the access road past the post office and across the bridge and follow the road as it loops around to these accommodations. Also access to Wiseman Chapel and to the airstrip from this loop.

Arctic Getaway B&B. See display ad this section.

Boreal Lodging. See display ad this section.

Wiseman Museum. See display ad this section.

J 189 D 225 Spur (finger) dikes keep river away from highway and pipeline during high water.

J 190.2 D 223.8 Distance marker northbound shows Dietrich 20 miles, Deadhorse 225 miles.

J 190.5 D 223.5 Narrow bridge over Hammond River; gold mining area upstream.

J 190.8 D 223.2 **Middle Fork Koyukuk River No. 2** crossing (narrow bridge). "Guide banks," another example of river training structures.

J 192.8 D 221.2 Link Up (signed), where

Historic mining town of Wiseman on the Koyukuk River. (© Kris Graef, staff)

2 sections of road constructed by different crews were joined when the Dalton Highway was completed in 1974.

J 194 D 220 First view northbound of **Sukakpak Mountain** (elev. 4,000 feet) to north. Sukakpak Mountain is sometimes said to mark a traditional boundary between Eskimo and Athabascan Indian territories. Wiehl Mountain (4,000 feet) is east of Sukakpak.

J 195 D 219 Pipeline close to road is mounted on sliding shoes to allow flexing.

J 197 D 217 Gold Creek bridge (narrow).

J 197.2 D 216.8 Turnout to east.

J 197.3 D 216.7 Cat trail to gold mining area; motorized vehicle access restricted to holders of valid mining claims.

J 197.5 D 216.5 Linda Creek in culvert.

J 197.7 D 216.3 Turnout east and view of Wiehl Mountain.

J 200 D 214 View of the Middle Fork Koyukuk River, a typical braided river exhibiting frequent changes of the streambed during high water.

J 203.7 D 210.3 Parking area. The short mounds of earth between the road and Sukakpak Mountain are palsas, formed by ice beneath the soil pushing the vegetative mat and soil upward.

J 203.8 D 210.2 Turnouts next 0.6 mile northbound.

J 204 D 210 Parking to west.

J 204.3 D 209.7 **Middle Fork Koyukuk River No. 3** bridge. Large turnout to east at north end of bridge. Self-contained RV camping in turnout.

J 204.5 D 209.5 **Middle Fork Koyukuk River No. 4** crossing (narrow bridge).

J 205.3 D 208.7 Turnout to west. Good view of north side of Sukakpak Mountain.

J 206 D 208 View of Wiehl Mountain.

J 207 D 207 **Dietrich River** bridge. Halfway mark on the Dalton Highway. Turnout to west at south end of bridge. Access to river to west at north end. Fishing for burbot, grayling, whitefish and Dolly Varden.

J 208.6 D 205.4 $1,000 fine for littering (sign).

J 209 D 205 Road narrows northbound. *Asphalt surface treatment under way southbound in summer 2003 between* **Milepost J 209** *and* **Milepost J 175 (Coldfoot).**

J 209.1 D 204.9 Distance marker indicates Dietrich 1 mile (to west), Deadhorse 205 miles. Dietrich, to the west, is a former pipeline construction camp.

J 210.9 D 203.1 Large turnout with bear-proof litter container to east.

J 211 D 203 Disaster Creek.

J 216.2 D 197.8 Snowden Creek culvert. Panorama of Dietrich River valley and Brooks Range north and west of the road.

J 218 D 196 Rock spire to east is Snowden Mountain (elev. 5,775 feet). Cirque

BOREAL LODGING
Open Year Round in Wiseman Village
Cabin, Rooms, Shower, Kitchen, TV/Phone.
Great Winter Aurora & Scheduled Dogsled Trips.
Resv./Info: Ph/Fx (907) 678-4566
Email: boreallodge@juno.com

WISEMAN MUSEUM

180 miles above the Arctic Circle since 1908
Scenery, simplicity and history in Alaska's
Brooks Mountain Range

Visit Historic Wiseman. The Wiseman Museum is housed in the early 1900s Carl Frank cabin, 3 miles off the Dalton Highway in North Wiseman.
Wiseman Museum, Wiseman, Alaska 99790

Arctic Getaway
Cabin & Breakfast
In the historic Pioneer Hall **IGLOO No. 8**
Wiseman, AK 99790 * Berni & Uta Hicker
(907) 678-4456
arcticgetaway@mosquitonet.com

Drive with headlights on!

DALTON HIGHWAY

Dalton Highway and pipeline at Milepost J 239.9. (© John Schwieder Photography)

above highway was carved by a glacier; hike up to waterfall.

J 221.7 D 192.3 Quarry of black marble with white calcite veins to east.

J 222.5 D 191.5 Large gravel stockpile to west on the Dietrich River.

J 224 D 190 Turnout at gravel pit to east.

J 224.5 D 189.5 Winter trail access.

J 225.3 D 188.7 Parking area to east.

J 226 D 188 Pipeline remote valve just west of road. The arch-shaped concrete "saddle weights" keep pipeline buried in areas of possible flooding.

J 227.3 D 186.7 Narrow wooden bridge over an unnamed tributary to the Dietrich River.

J 228 D 186 Highway parallels Dietrich River.

J 229.5 D 184.5 Turnout to east next to stream in rock culvert.

J 230.9 D 183.1 Turnout to west overlooking river.

J 231.4 D 182.6 Small turnouts both sides of highway. Pipeline is buried under river.

J 232.8 D 181.2 Turnout to west.

J 234.4 D 179.6 View to east of pipeline emerging from under river.

J 234.8 D 179.2 Entering North Slope Borough—"the world's largest municipality"—northbound. North Slope Borough offices are located in Barrow.

J 235.3 D 178.7 Large turnouts with litter barrel at foot of Chandalar Shelf. Truck chain-up area. Last spruce tree northbound.

Begin 2-mile-long 10 percent grade northbound. Give trucks plenty of room. Do not stop on road. Dirt road surface can be slippery in wet weather. Watch for soft spots.

J 237.1 D 176.9 Turnout to west at top of Chandalar Shelf; spectacular views. Former checkpoint when travel on the highway north of here was restricted to permit holders.

Headwaters of the Chandalar River are to the east. Table Mountain (elev. 6,425 feet) is to the southeast. Dietrich River valley to south.

J 239 D 175 Airstrip.

J 239.2 D 174.8 Site of Chandalar Camp, a former pipeline construction camp.

J 239.4 D 174.6 Chandalar Station (DOT/PF highway maintenance) to west; no visitor services.

J 239.9 D 174.1 Distance marker shows Galbraith 34 miles, Deadhorse 173 miles.

J 240.7 D 173.3 Turnout to east.

J 242.1 D 171.9 Avalanche gun emplacement.

J 242.2 D 171.8 West Fork of the North Fork Chandalar River bridge.

Begin long, steep (12 percent), winding grade northbound to Atigun Pass. Winter avalanche area. Slide area next 5 miles northbound.

J 243.4 D 170.6 Turnout with spectacular view south of valley and pipeline.

J 244 D 170 Turnout. Look for Dall sheep on rocky slopes below.

J 244.7 D 169.3 Turnout at top of **Atigun Pass** (elev. 4,800 feet) in the Brooks Range, highest highway pass in Alaska; Continental Divide. A Wyoming Gauge to measure precipitation is located here. Nice example of a cirque, an amphitheater-shaped bowl or depression caused by glacier erosion, in mountain east of road. Endicott Mountains are to the west, Philip Smith Mountains to the east. James Dalton Mountain is to the left ahead northbound.

CAUTION: Watch for Dall sheep near or on the road.

J 245 D 169 Turnout. Many mountains in the area exceed 7,000 feet in elevation. The pipeline is in a buried, insulated concrete cribbing to the east to protect it from rock slides and avalanches, and to keep the ground frozen. Construction in this area was extremely complex, difficult and dangerous.

J 245.3 D 168.7 Large turnouts (no guardrails); avalanche gun emplacement. Look for Dall sheep alongside road.

Highway descends steeply next 3 miles northbound. Avalanche zone.

J 246.7 D 167.3 Turnout; avalanche gun emplacement.

J 248 D 166 Turnouts both sides of highway. Good spot to view Dall sheep.

J 249.8 D 164.2 Double-ended turnout to west. Highway construction camp to east at site of Atigun Camp, a former pipeline camp.

J 250 D 164 Bridge over Spike Camp Creek. Highway follows Atigun River.

J 250.2 D 163.8 Turnout to east.

J 251.5 D 162.5 Highway has wide shoulder for parking.

J 253.1 D 160.9 Atigun River Bridge No. 1.

J 256 D 158 Great photo opportunity of pipeline, mountains and highway.

J 257.5 D 156.5 Check valves on the pipeline keep oil from flowing backwards in the event of a leak.

J 258.5 D 155.5 Trevor Creek bridge.

J 258.7 D 155.3 Turnout to west. Good spot to park and hike up to rocks. *CAUTION: Grizzly bears in area.*

J 262 D 152 Good view of Pump Station No. 4 northbound; see description at **Milepost J 269.2**.

J 265 D 149 Roche Mountonee Creek bridge; turnout.

J 266.8 D 147.2 Small turnout to west.

J 267.4 D 146.6 Bridge over Holden Creek.

J 269.2 D 144.8 Entrance to **Pump Station No. 4**. This station has the highest elevation of all the pipeline stations (2,760 feet), and is also a launching and receiving station for special measuring and cleaning devices called "pigs." A scraper pig consists of spring-mounted scraper blades and/or brushes on a central body which moves through the pipe, cleaning accumulated wax from interior walls and monitoring conditions inside the pipe. There are "dumb" pigs and "smart" pigs. Dumb pigs clean out wax deposits in the line. Smart pigs scan the pipeline to check welds, wall thickness and other properties to help insure the integrity of the piping and identify maintenance needs.

J 269.4 D 144.6 Highway bridge passes over pipeline.

J 270.8 D 143.2 Large parking area to west.

J 270.9 D 143.1 Atigun River Bridge No. 2.

The Arctic National Wildlife Refuge boundary is located 3 miles east along the Atigun gorge. Galbraith Lake may be seen to the west. There are a large number of archaeological sites in this vicinity.

J 272 D 142 View of Galbraith Lake and Galbraith camp.

J 274.7 D 139.3 Side road leads southwest 1.5 miles to **GALBRAITH CAMP** airstrip and Alyeska buildings; 4 miles to old camp pad and camping area (outhouse, litter barrels). Nice wildflowers in season. ▲

J 276.5 D 137.5 Island Lake to west.

J 283 D 131 View of Toolik Field Station (see next milepost). Watch for caribou.

J 284.3 D 129.7 Side road west to Toolik Lake, a former construction camp, now the site of **Toolik Field Station**, run by the Institute of Arctic Biology of the University of Alaska Fairbanks. The field station conducts global warming studies and has no public facilities or services.

J 286.2 D 127.8 Turnout to east at high point in road. Excellent photo stop. View of Brooks Range south and east. Philip Smith Mountains to west. Panoramic views of incredible beauty.

J 288 D 126 Highway descends northbound to Kuparuk River bridge.

J 288.9 D 125.1 Kuparuk River bridge. Informal camping at turnout.

J 289.3 D 124.7 Pipeline crossing. Short buried section of pipeline to west is called a sag bend and allows for wildlife crossing. Watch for caribou northbound.

J 290.3 D 123.7 Turnout. Steep downgrade followed by long upgrade northbound.

J 290.6 D 123.4 Toolik Creek.

J 294.4 D 119.6 Sag bend in pipeline to west. *Watch for caribou crossing the highway.*

J 297 D 117 Pullout used by hunters in

Access to the Arctic Ocean is restricted. (© Ernest Manewal)

caribou season.

NOTE: *There are dozens of these single-vehicle pullouts along the highway from here to Deadhorse.*

J 297.8 D 116.2 Oksrukukuyik Creek culvert. Small turnout to east.

J 298.2 D 115.8 Turnout to west. First view northbound of Sagavanirktok ("the Sag") River valley.

J 301 D 113 APL access road. Slope Mountain (elev. 4,010 feet) to west. Watch for Dall sheep. This is the northern boundary of BLM-managed land. Land north of here is managed by the state.

J 303 D 111 *CAUTION: Steep up and down grades, blind hills and rough road northbound.*

J 305.7 D 108.3 Sag River Station DOT highway maintenance. Slope Mountain Camp, a former pipeline construction camp, 1 mile east.

J 309 D 105 Highway parallels Sagavanirktok River northbound.

J 311.8 D 102.2 Entrance to **Pump Station No. 3**; mobile construction camp facility.

J 313.7 D 100.3 Oksrukukuyik Creek in culvert.

J 319.8 D 94.2 Turnout to east at Oil Spill Hill.

J 320 D 94 The long range of hills east of the road is the Kakuktukruich Bluff. Nice views northbound of Sagavanirktok River.

J 325.3 D 88.7 Turnout to east at the bottom of a steep and rocky grade signed "Ice Cut."

J 327 D 87 Watch for grizzly bears digging for food around the pipeline supports.

J 330.7 D 83.3 Dan Creek bridge. Small turnout.

J 334.4 D 79.6 Happy Valley, a former pipeline construction camp, now used by road crews. Airstrip.

J 335 D 79 *Improved paved highway northbound to Milepost J 362.*

J 339.8 D 74.2 Distance marker northbound shows Deadhorse 74 miles.

J 344 D 70 Peregrine falcons, gyrfalcons and roughlegged hawks are often sighted here. They nest in the bluffs along the Sagavanirktok River.

J 350.5 D 63.5 View of Sagwon Bluffs to the east. Look for musk-ox on the horizon.

J 355 D 59 Turnout with litter barrel to east at crest of hill. Panoramic views, weather permitting, of Arctic coastal plain.

Porcupine and Central caribou herds migrate through this area on their way to and from their calving grounds.

Migratory birds from around the world nest and breed on the Arctic coastal plain. Bird watchers come to view the king eiders, spectacled eiders, Canada geese, snow geese, tundra swans, jaegers, snowy owls and a variety of other species..

Road widens as highway descends northbound.

J 358.8 D 55.2 Pump Station No. 2 to the east. Begin long, straight stretch northbound.

J 362 D 52 Snow poles mark highway for motorists. *CAUTION: The worst winter weather conditions on the Dalton Highway are experienced the next 38 miles northbound. Blowing snow may obscure visibility and block road.*

NOT:E Asphalt surface treatment under way in summer 2003 northbound to Deadhorse.

J 364 D 50 Low hills to the north are the Franklin Bluffs. East of the road, the Ivishak River empties into the Sagavanirktok River on its journey to the Arctic Ocean.

J 365.1 D 48.9 Turnout to west. Watch for nesting waterfowl in ponds along highway.

J 369.6 D 44.1 Distance marker northbound shows Deadhorse 44 miles. Southbound marker shows Coldfoot 186 miles, Fairbanks 450 miles.

J 376 D 38 The small hill that rises abruptly on the horizon about 5 miles west of the road is called a pingo. Pingos often form from the bed of a spring-fed lake that has been covered by vegetation. Freezing of the water can raise the surface several hundred feet above the surrounding terrain.

J 377.3 D 36.7 Large turnout to east at Franklin Bluffs, a former pipeline construction camp where winter equipment is stored in summer.

J 383 D 31 Franklin Bluffs to the east and a pingo to the west.

J 384 D 30 Dalton Highway snakes its way northbound across the flat coastal plain. Watch for golden eagles.

J 394.9 D 19.1 Distance marker northbound shows Deadhorse 20 miles. Southbound sign shows Coldfoot 20 miles, Fairbanks 474 miles.

J 403.4 D 10.6 Pullout to east; access to Sagavanirktok River.

J 413.7 D 0.3 Distance marker southbound shows Coldfoot 240 miles, Fairbanks 498 miles.

J 414 D 0 Northern end of Dalton Highway. Follow access road signs for visitor services (see map this section).

Deadhorse

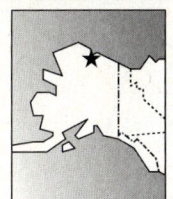

End of the Dalton Highway. **Population:** 25 permanent; 3,500 to 5,000 or more part-time depending on oil production. **Visitor Information:** Try the Prudhoe Bay General Store and the hotels. **Climate:** Arctic, with temperatures ranging from -56°F in winter to 78°F in summer. Precipitation averages 5 inches; snowfall 20 inches. **Radio:** KCDS 88.1 FM. **Transportation:** Scheduled jet service to

DEADHORSE ADVERTISERS

Arctic Caribou Inn .... Ph. 1-877-659-2368
Arctic Oilfield Hotel .... Ph. (907) 659-2614
Deadhorse–Prudhoe
  Bay Tesoro .... Ph. (907) 659-3198
Northern Alaska Tour Co. ... Ph. 1-800-474-1986
Prudhoe Bay General
  Store .... Ph. (907) 659-2412
Trans Arctic Circle Treks . Ph. 1-800-336-8735

BEST PRICES IN TOWN

Arctic Oilfield Hotel

Friendliest Staff

Delicious Buffet Style Meals

Rooms, showers and laundries available for travelers

— **RV Parking** —

Located on the corner of Sag River Road and Spine Rd. 1/2 mile north of the Tesoro

Other services include:

Tire Repair;

Heavy and Light duty repairs;

Towing; Body Shop; Welding;

Extensive Parts Inventory.

Hotel Reservations: 907-659-2614
Repairs: 907-659-3301

VECO

DALTON HIGHWAY • Deadhorse

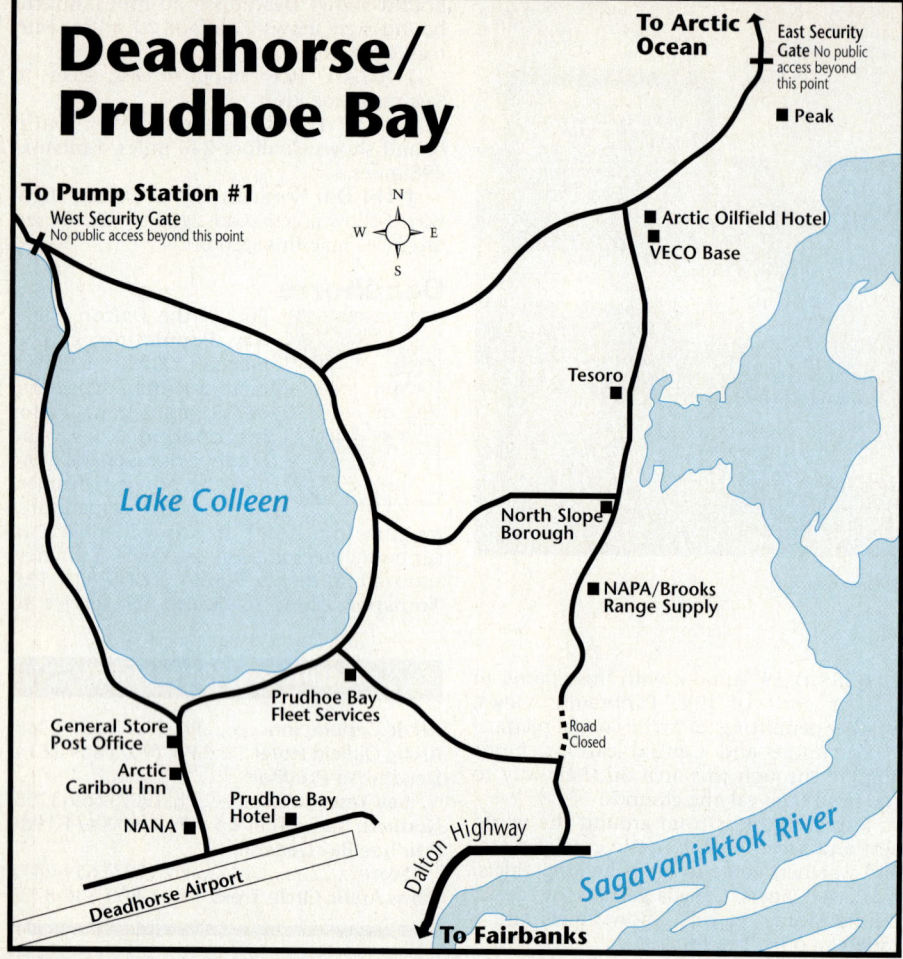

Snow dusts the ground and equipment in Deadhorse in late August.
(© Kris Graef, staff)

Deadhorse/Prudhoe Bay from Anchorage (flying time from Anchorage is 1 hour, 35 minutes), Fairbanks and Barrow. Packaged tours of the North Slope area are available from Anchorage and Fairbanks. Air taxi service is available at Deadhorse Airport.

Deadhorse is not a town in the traditional sense. It was established to support oil development in the surrounding area. A number of oil fields make up the Prudhoe Bay industrial area: Kuparuk, Milne Point, Point McIntyre, Prudhoe Bay, Niakuk, Endicott, Alpine Field and North Star Field.

Most buildings are modular, pre-fab-type construction, situated on gravel pads on tundra bog. Virtually all the businesses here are engaged in oil field or pipeline support activities, such as drilling, construction, maintenance, telecommunications, warehousing and transportation. Oil field employees work a rotation, such as 2 weeks on the job, then 2 weeks off. While on rotation, workers typically work 7 days a week, 10 to 12 hours each day. The largest employers are BP Exploration, Phillips and Alyeska Pipeline Services.

According to Deborah Bernard in an article in the *Prudhoe Bay Journal*, there is more than one version of how Deadhorse got its name, but basically it was named after Deadhorse Haulers, a company hired to do the gravel work at the Prudhoe Bay airstrip. (How the company came to be called Deadhorse Haulers is another story.) Everybody began calling the airstrip "Deadhorse" and the name stuck—too well for those who prefer the name Prudhoe Bay. Some people

Arctic Caribou Inn
Discover Prudhoe Bay

Tours Available June Thru August

**TWO HOUR
ARCTIC OCEAN
AND OIL FIELD TOUR:**
Guided tour through the Prudhoe Bay Oil Field and Deadhorse with a walk on the beach at the Arctic Ocean. Advanced reservations required for tour.

(VALID PICTURE ID IS REQUIRED FOR ALL ADULTS TAKING TOUR)

ARCTIC CARIBOU INN
Located near the Airport, Hotel and Restaurant, with 50 clean comfortable rooms & private bath, Visitors Center, and RV Parking.

FOR RESERVATIONS CALL:
Summer: (907) 659-2368
Toll Free: 1-877-659-2368
Fax: (907) 659-2692

Write: Arctic Caribou Inn/Tour Arctic
P.O. Box 340111
Prudhoe Bay, Alaska 99734

Email: info@arcticcaribouinn.com
http://www.arcticcaribouinn.com

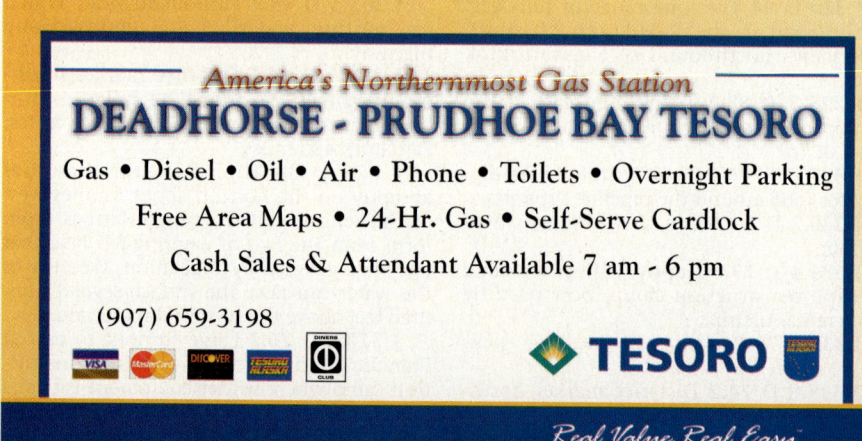

were surprised when Prudhoe Bay got its own ZIP code on June 3, 1982, and was listed as "Deadhorse AK 99734," not Prudhoe Bay. It was later changed to Prudhoe Bay, AK 99734.

It is a good idea to call ahead for lodging reservations and rates. Visitor accommodations are available at the Arctic Caribou Inn and Arctic Oilfield Hotel. Prudhoe Bay Hotel accommodates both oil field workers and visitors. Buffet-style meals are available at the hotel cafeterias, which generally serve breakfast 5:30–8 A.M., lunch noon–1 P.M., and dinner 5–8 P.M., with self-serve snacks available in-between.

Deadhorse at 10 P.M. in August under cloudy skies. *(© Kris Graef, staff)*

Prudhoe Bay General Store carries everything from postcards and snacks to Arctic survival gear. About the only exceptions are alcohol, ammunition and weapons, which are not available in Deadhorse. The store houses the post office and issues fishing and hunting licenses. (You can also get "Dalton Highway Survivor" certificates here.)

There is no bank and no ATM in Deadhorse. Credit cards and traveler's checks are generally accepted, but fish and game licenses and postage must be paid for in cash.

There is overnight RV parking with electrical hookups and water available at the Arctic Oilfield Hotel. Laundry and shower facilities at the hotel. Overnight parking and toilet available at Tesoro.

Regular unleaded gasoline and No. 1 diesel are available at NANA (Chevron) or the local Tesoro station. Tesoro is a 24-hour self-serve station; an attendant is available and cash accepted from 7 A.M. until 6 P.M. After hours, you can pump gas yourself as long as you have a credit card. Dump station at NANA Oilfield Services. Tire and vehicle repairs are available at Prudhoe Bay Fleet Service, Veco Base Fleet Services and NANA. Local auto parts and hardware store has an assortment of supplies.

Public access beyond Deadhorse is restricted. For security reasons, travel north of Deadhorse, including visits to the Arctic Ocean, is limited to commercial tours. Tour information is available at the hotels.

CAUTION: Beware of bears in the area. The Prudhoe Bay/Deadhorse area has been overrun with grizzly bears for the past few summers. Use caution when camping or walking around the entire area.

Arctic Caribou Inn invites you to tour Prudhoe Bay, June through August. Providing guided tours since 1975. Tour includes the town of Deadhorse and Prudhoe Bay oil field. See oil rigs and oil field visitor center, and oil field informative video presentation and exhibits. Walk on the beach at the Arctic Ocean. Clean comfortable rooms. Restaurant, shower facilities and RV parking. Summer phone (907) 659-2449; toll free 1-877-659-2368; fax (907) 659-2692. Mailing address: Arctic Caribou Inn/Arctic Tours, P.O. Box 340111, Prudhoe Bay, AK 99734. [ADVERTISEMENT]

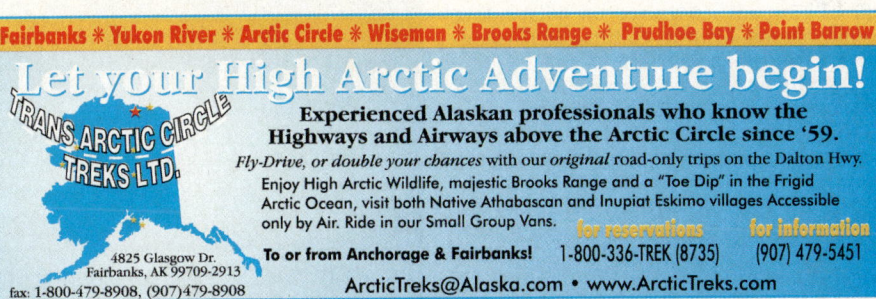

Kenai Peninsula
SEWARD HIGHWAY

	Alyeska	Anchorage	Hope	Seward	Whittier
Alyeska		42	56	95	28
Anchorage	42		88	127	60
Hope	56	88		75	52
Seward	95	127	75		91
Whittier	28	60	52	91	

Connects: Anchorage to Seward, AK **Length:** 127 miles
Road Surface: Paved **Season:** Open all year
Highest Summit: Turnagain Pass 988 feet
Major Attractions: Mount Alyeska; Portage Glacier; Kenai Fjords National Park

(See map, page 505)

Beautiful Upper Summit Lake on the Seward Highway. (© Laurent Dick)

The 127-mile-long Seward Highway connects Anchorage with the community of Seward on the east coast of the Kenai Peninsula. (Driving time is about 3 hours.) The Seward Highway has been called one of the most scenic highways in the country. It was designated a National Forest Scenic Byway in 1998, and an All-American Road in 2000, one of 15 roads recognized for outstanding scenic, natural, historic, cultural, archaeological and recreational qualities.

Leaving Anchorage, the Seward Highway follows the north shore of Turnagain Arm through Chugach State Park and Chugach National Forest, permitting a panoramic view of the south shore and the Kenai Mountains on the Kenai Peninsula. The Kenai Peninsula is just that—a peninsula, measuring 150 miles long and 70 miles wide, extending southwest from Turnagain Arm and Passage Canal. It is bounded to the east by the Gulf of Alaska, and to the west by Cook Inlet. The Seward Highway crosses the isthmus that separates the Kenai Peninsula from the rest of Southcentral Alaska at **Milepost S 75**, 52 miles south of Anchorage.

The Seward Highway provides access to Girdwood and Alyeska ski resort via the Alyeska Highway; to Hope via the Hope Highway; to Whittier and to Portage Glacier via the Whittier/Portage Road; and to Seward, gateway to Kenai Fjords National Park. The Seward Highway junctions with the Sterling Highway 90 miles south of Anchorage. The Sterling Highway leads to Soldotna, Kenai and Homer (see page 550).

The first 9 miles of the New Seward Highway are a major Anchorage thoroughfare (4-lane divided freeway), connecting South Anchorage with downtown. South of Anchorage, the Seward Highway is a paved, 2-lane highway with passing lanes. There are no gas stations on the Seward Highway between **Milepost S 90** (Girdwood turnoff) and **Milepost S 6.6**, just outside Seward.

The highway is open all year. Some sections of the highway are subject to avalanches in winter. Check locally for winter road conditions and avalanche road closures.

Bike trails along the Seward Highway include a 3-mile trail between Indian and Bird; a 6-mile trail between Girdwood and Bird Point; and an 8-mile bike trail (the Sixmile Trail) between the Hope Highway junction and the Johnson Pass Trailhead.

There are also a number of trailheads along the Seward Highway for both Chugach State Park and USFS hiking trails.

CAUTION: The Seward Highway from Anchorage to just past Girdwood statistically has one of the highest number of traffic accidents in the state. DRIVE CAREFULLY! Motorists must drive with headlights on at all times.

Delay of 5 vehicles or more is illegal; use slow vehicle turnouts. Pass with care!

Emergency medical services: Phone 911 or use CB channels 9, 11 or 19. Cellular phone service is available as far south as Girdwood and is also available in Seward. Emergency call boxes are located at Turnagain Pass (**Milepost S 68.5**), Hope Highway junction (**S 56.3**), Summit Lake Lodge (**S 45.8**) and at the Sterling Highway junction.

Seward Highway Log

Distance from Seward (S) is followed by distance from Anchorage (A).
Physical mileposts show distance from Seward. Many mileposts were missing in summer 2002.

ALASKA ROUTE 1

S 127 A 0 Gambell Street and 10th Avenue in Anchorage. The New Seward Highway (Gambell Street southbound, Ingra northbound)) connects with the Glenn Highway in Anchorage via 5th Avenue (westbound) and 6th Avenue (eastbound). (See map in the ANCHORAGE section.) Follow Gambell Street south.

S 126.7 A 0.3 15th Avenue.

S 126.6 A 0.4 16th Avenue; access to Sullivan sports arena, Ben Boeke ice rinks and baseball stadium. Begin divided 4-lane highway southbound.

S 126 A 1 Fireweed Lane. Shopping and services to west.

S 125.8 A 1.2 Northern Lights Boulevard (one-way westbound). Access west to **Sears Mall** from New Seward Highway. This was the first shopping mall in Anchorage. The Crab Pot Restaurant of Seward is located in Sears Mall. Shopping, services and 24-hour supermarket on Northern Lights Blvd. Fred Meyer shopping center east side

SEWARD HIGHWAY

Hikers run into Dall sheep on Flattop Mountain.
(© Bill Sherwonit)

of highway.

The Crab Pot Restaurant. See display ad this section.

S 125.7 A 1.3 Benson Boulevard (one-way eastbound).

S 125.4 A 1.6 Southbound access only to Old Seward Highway to 36th Ave.

S 125.3 A 1.7 36th Avenue; **Providence Hospital** approximately 2 miles east. Z.J. Loussac library and Midtown post office to west.

S 125.2 A 1.8 Freeway begins southbound.

S 124.7 A 2.3 Tudor Road overpass; exits both sides of highway for shopping and services.

S 124.2 A 2.8 Highway crosses Campbell Creek; Campbell Creek Greenbelt. Those are the Chugach Mountains to the east.

CAUTION: Watch for moose.

S 123.7 A 3.3 Dowling Road underpass; exits on both sides of highway to shopping and services. Access to Anchorage recycling center to west.

S 122.7 A 4.3 76th Avenue exit, southbound traffic only.

S 122.2 A 4.8 Dimond Boulevard overpass; exits on both sides of highway. Access west to **Dimond Mall**, gas stations, fast-food and major shopping area. Gas station to east.

S 120.8 A 6.2 O'Malley Road underpass; exits on both sides of highway. Turn east on O'Malley Road and drive 2 miles to reach the **Alaska Zoo.** Continue east on O'Malley for **Chugach State Park** Upper Hillside hiking trails (follow signs), which include the popular **Flattop Mountain trail.**

Turn west for access to Minnesota Drive to **Ted Stevens International Airport.**

S 119.7 A 7.3 Huffman Road underpass; exits on both sides of highway. Exit west for gas station, 24-hour supermarket and other services. Exit east for South Anchorage subdivisions.

S 118.5 A 8.5 DeArmoun Road overpass, southbound exit only. (Northbound access to DeArmoun is via Rabbit Creek exit, then north on Old Seward Highway.)

S 117.8 A 9.2 Overpass: Exits both sides of highway for Old Seward Highway (west); access to Rabbit Creek Road (east) to South

Relocation

The CRAB POT Restaurant

ANCHORAGE — Seward's Finest! — **ALASKA**

Seafood & Steak

- Prawns
- Scallops
- Halibut
- Salmon
- Clams
- Oysters

- Filet Mignon
- T-Bone
- Rib Eye
- New York
- Pasta

LIVE ALASKAN KING CRAB

(In Season) Extended Summer Hours

The Only Restaurant in the Anchorage Bowl & *beyond* to offer Live Crab

The largest, finest, freshest, expertly prepared selection of seafood and steaks available.
Find out why the locals dine *HERE*!

The Mall at Sears, Anchorage
Northern Lights & Seward Hwy.
(907) 929-5600

Anchorage subdivisions. The picturesque Chapel by the Sea overlooks Turnagain Arm. The church is often photographed because of its unique setting and its display of flowers.

View of Turnagain Arm and Mount Spurr southbound. Seward Highway Scenic Byway sign southbound.

S 117.4 A 9.6 Turnoff to west for **Rabbit Creek Rifle Range** (ADF&G); open to the public; summer and winter hours posted on gate or phone (907) 566-0130 for hours and fees. Covered firing positions on handgun and rifle ranges. Shotgun range (shot shells only).

Turnoff to east at Boardwalk Wildlife Viewing exit for **Potter Point State Game Refuge**. This is a very popular spot for bird watching. From the parking lot, an extensive boardwalk crosses Potter Marsh, a refuge and nesting area for waterfowl. The marsh was created when railroad construction dammed a small creek in the area. Today, the marsh is visited by arctic terns, Canada geese, trumpeter swans, many species of ducks and other water birds. Bring binoculars.

CAUTION: Highway narrows to 2 lanes southbound. Pass with care! Drive with headlights on at all times. Avalanche information phone 273-6037.

Distance marker southbound shows Girdwood 27 miles, Seward 115 miles, Homer 211 miles.

S 117.2 A 9.8 Potter Marsh pullout east side of highway.

S 115.4 A 11.6 Junction with Old Seward Highway; access to Potter Valley Road east to subdivision. Old Johnson trail begins 0.5 mile up Potter Valley Road; parking at trailhead. Only the first 10 miles of this state park trail are cleared. Moderate to difficult hike; watch for bears.

The natural gas pipeline from the Kenai Peninsula emerges from beneath Turnagain Arm here and follows the roadway to Anchorage.

WARNING: When the tide is out, the sand in Turnagain Arm might look inviting. DO NOT go out on it. Some of it is quicksand. You could become trapped in the mud and not be rescued before the tide comes in.

S 115.2 A 11.8 Entering Chugach State Park southbound. Turnoff to west for Chugach State Park Headquarters and the Kenai Peninsula Visitor Center; RV parking, public restrooms, visitor information, espresso and snacks.

A vintage snowplow train and interpretive panels on the railroad are on display on the grounds here.

Chugach State Park Headquarters is housed in the historic **Potter Section House**, once the home for a small crew of Alaska Railroad workers who maintained the tracks between Seward and Anchorage in the days of coal- and steam-powered locomotives. Maps and information on Chugach State Park, as well as park parking passes, are available in the headquarters building. Open Mon.–Fri. 10 A.M.–4:30 P.M. (closed for lunch 12–1 P.M.); phone (907) 345-5014.

Also at this location, housed in one of the old train cars, is the **Kenai Peninsula Visitor Center**, operated by the National Senior Service Corps in Alaska. The visitor center is open 8 A.M. to 5 P.M. daily in summer to assist visitors with Kenai Peninsula travel information as well as reservations for cruises, fishing, lodging and attractions. The visitor center also operates an espresso/snack stand. Phone (907) 336-3300 or visit www.kpvc.org for more information.

S 115.1 A 11.9 Turnoff to east for **Potter Creek Viewpoint and Trail** (Chugach State Park). Small parking area overlooking marsh with interpretive signs about wetlands and the railroad's role in creating these accidental marshes. Also an interpretive sign about the feeding habits of moose, who eat in marshes like these as well as in the backyards of Anchorage residents. Moose can eat the equivalent in twigs of a 50-lb. sack of dog food a day. Moose munch twigs and strip bark from willow, birch and aspen trees.

Drive up the hill via 2-lane paved road for large parking area, viewing platform with telescopes, interpretive signs and hiking trails. The 0.4-mile nature trail examines the natural history of the surrounding forest, a blending of 2 climates: the continental climate (the boreal forest of Interior Alaska) and the wetter coastal climate (Sitka spruce, hemlock).

This is the Potter Creek Trailhead for **Turnagain Arm Trail**. From here to McHugh Creek Picnic Area (at **Milepost S 111.9** on the Seward Highway) it is 3.3 miles, making it a good choice for a family hike. One-way walking time is about 1-1/2 hours. Turnagain Arm trail continues to Rainbow (7.5 miles) and to Windy Corner (9.4 miles) at **Milepost S 106.7** Seward Highway; see trail information signs. Turnagain Arm Trail parallels the Seward Highway and offers good views of Turnagain Arm. Rated as easy, with 250- to 700-foot elevation gains from the parking areas to the generally level trail on the hillside above the 4 trailheads.

S 114.7 A 12.3 Weigh station and pay phone to east.

S 114.5 A 12.5 Double-ended gravel turnout to east (posted no camping).

S 113.3 A 13.7 Slow vehicle turnout to west for southbound traffic. *Delay of 5 vehicles illegal; must use turnouts.*

S 113.1 A 13.9 The first of several informal gravel turnouts used by rock climbers on the east side of the highway. Watch for rock climbers practicing on rock walls alongside the highway for about the next 6 miles southbound.

S 113 A 14 Informal gravel turnout to east at McHugh boulder area. The cliffs are part of the base of McHugh Peak (elev. 4,298 feet).

S 111.9 A 15.1 Paved side road to east goes up hill to **McHugh Creek Picnic Area**.

The Seward Highway has several viewpoints with interpretive signs overlooking Turnagain Arm. (© Kris Graef, staff)

This state wayside on the flank of McHugh Peak has a multi-tiered parking area. Restrooms, paved pathways, boardwalk, picnic tables, viewing platform with telescopes and interpretive signs about wildlife are at second tier parking. Third tier parking for access to McHugh Creek trailhead. McHugh Creek Scenic Overlook offers views of Turnagain Arm. McHugh Creek trailhead to Turnagain Arm Trail.

S 111.6 A 15.4 Informal turnout to east used by rock climbers.

S 111.2 A 15.8 Rough gravel turnout to east.

S 110.9 A 16.1 Double-ended gravel turnout to east (posted no camping).

S 110.4 A 16.6 Beluga Point scenic viewpoint and photo stop to west is a large paved double-ended turnout with a commanding view of Turnagain Arm. A good place to see bore tides and beluga whales. (The only all-white whale, belugas are easy to identify.) Tables, benches, telescopes and interpretive signs on orcas, bore tides, mountain goats, Captain Cook, etc.

An easterly extension of Cook Inlet, **Turnagain Arm** was called Return by the Russians. Captain Cook, seeking the fabled Northwest Passage in 1778, called it Turnagain River, and Captain Vancouver, doing a more thorough job of surveying in 1794, gave it the present name of Turnagain Arm.

Turnagain Arm is known for having one of the world's remarkably high tides, with a diurnal range of more than 33 feet. A bore tide is an abrupt rise of tidal water just after low tide, moving rapidly landward, formed by a flood tide surging into a constricted inlet such as Turnagain Arm. This foaming wall of water may reach a height of 6 feet and is very dangerous to small craft. To see a bore tide, check the Anchorage-area tide tables for low tide, then add approximately 2 hours and 15 minutes to the Anchorage low tide for the bore to reach points between 32 miles and 37 miles south of Anchorage on the Seward Highway. Visitors should watch for bore tides from Beluga Point south to Girdwood.

WARNING: Do not go out on the mud flats at low tide. The glacial silt and water can create a dangerous quicksand.

S 110.2 A 16.8 Informal gravel turnout to east.

S 109.9 A 17.1 Turnout to west for parking.

S 109.2 A 17.8 Paved turnout to west.

Bird Creek fishing access is very popular with anglers during silver salmon runs.
(© Rich Reid, Colors of Nature)

S 109 A 18 Gravel turnout to east.

S 108.7 A 18.3 Paved double-ended viewpoint to west.

S 108.4 A 18.6 Rainbow trailhead (Turnagain Arm Trail) parking east side of highway; posted no camping.

S 108.3 A 18.7 Paved turnout to west.

S 107.9 A 19.1 Turnout to west with Gold Rush Centennial signs "Hope Survives Gold Fever" and "Stampeders Flood the Arm" (excerpt follows):

Alexander King discovered gold in about 1890 on Resurrection Creek, across the Arm from here. Prospectors set up camp at the mouth of the creek, where supply boats could land, and named it—legend has it—after Percy Hope, a 17 year-old stampeder. By spring of 1896, Hope City was overrun by 700 gold seekers. Hope was one of the largest towns in Alaska during its 1895-98 heyday. Many left Hope City for Sunrise City, the supply camp for prospectors working new gold discoveries at the mouth of Sixmile Creek, 8 miles east of Hope. While mining declined at Sunrise, commercial gold mining and new settlement kept Hope alive. Early residents like Robert Mathison and George Roll stayed after the stampede, making a life mining, hunting and subsistence gardening. Little mining is done around Hope these days, but the town's historic district retains the appearance and feel of its gold rush past.

S 106.9 A 20.1 Scenic viewpoint to west; double-ended paved turnout. Watch for Dall sheep near road. *NOTE: DO NOT FEED WILDLIFE.*

S 106.7 A 20.3 Windy Corner Trail trailhead to Turnagain Arm Trail east side of highway; parking.

S 106.6 A 20.4 Shoulder parking to west.

S 106.2 A 20.8 Slow vehicle turnout southbound.

S 105.9 A 21.1 Slow vehicle turnout southbound.

S 105.7 A 21.3 Falls Creek Trailhead and parking east side of highway. Moderate 1.5-mile hike along creek.

S 104.9 A 22.1 Single-vehicle turnout to east under rock overhang by small waterfall.

S 104.8 A 22.2 Distance marker northbound shows Anchorage 23 miles.

S 104.7 A 22.3 Single vehicle turnout to east.

S 104.4 A 22.6 Single vehicle turnout to east.

S 104.3 A 22.7 Slow vehicle turnout southbound.

S 104 A 23 Indian Valley Mine National Historic Site. See Peter Strougs' 1901 log cabin home, workshop and mine shaft along the shore of Turnagain Arm. Catch gold fever! We teach you to pan for gold here, then provide equipment and advice for excited gold seekers. Many areas are free and your prospects are good. Great family fun. Picnic tables. Museum. Gift shop. May 15–Sept. 15. 9 A.M. to 9 P.M. daily. Phone (907) 653-1120. [ADVERTISEMENT]

S 103.9 A 23.1 Indian Road to Indian Valley Meats.

Indian Valley Meats. Reindeer sausage and much more from this federally inspected processor of exotic game and fish. Fish boxes ready for shipping, gift packs with game jerky, smoked salmon and much more. Come visit our gift shop featuring our 20-plus flavor jerky bar. Great buys! In business 25 years. Please stop in, meet our pet reindeer and tour the stunning grounds, featuring flowers, rock walls, B&B, log conference hall and trophy animal mounts. Just 1/2 mile up Indian Road. See display ad this section. [ADVERTISEMENT]

S 103.6 A 23.4 INDIAN. Indian House.

S 103.1 A 23.9 Bore Tide Road, also called Ocean View Road. Access to Indian Valley trailhead (1.4 miles), a 6-mile moderately steep hike to Indian Pass. Turnagain House restaurant.

S 103 A 24 Bridge over **Indian Creek**. Rest area with interpretive signs and telescope to west at south end of bridge. Indian Creek is heavily fished for pink salmon, sea-run Dolly Varden, few coho (silver) salmon and rainbow.

Bar and liquor store to east; pay phone. Begin 3-mile-long Indian to Bird bike trail south to Bird Creek campground.

Brown Bear Saloon & Motel. See display ad this section.

S 102.1 A 24.9 Bird Ridge trailhead and parking east side of highway. This steep 2.5-mile hike (moderate dificulty) is the first snow-free spring hike in Chugach State Park, according to rangers. Hike offers good views of Turnagain Arm.

S 101.5 A 25.5 Bridge over **Bird Creek**; parking. This is a very popular fishing spot and it is *very* busy during salmon runs. Bird Creek has a tremendous silver salmon run in summer. Check current regulations for daily bag and possession limits and also for king salmon closures.

CAUTION: Watch for pedestrians next mile southbound. Anglers are urged not to trespass on private property or park illegally along the highway. Use Bird Ridge trailhead parking to north, or Bird Creek parking to south.

S 101.2 A 25.8 Bird Creek parking and fishing access to east; campground to west. Overflow paved camping to east above fishing access parking area. Interpretive signs, viewing area with telescope, picnic tables, toilet, firepits. Also acts as day-use parking area. 16 camping sites.

Bird Creek State Recreation Site campground west side of highway has 28 sites, firepits, pay phone, covered picnic tables, toilets and water. Firewood is sometimes available. Camping fee $10/night or resident pass. A pleasant campground densely wooded but cleared along the high banks of Turnagain Arm. Great spot for sunbathing. This campground is full most weekends in the summer. Campground also has additional walk-in tenting sites. Paved 3-mile Indian to Bird bike trail goes through campground.

WARNING: Do not go out on the mud flats at low tide. The glacial silt and water can create

---

INDIAN VALLEY MEATS

YOUR FISH
- Custom Smoking
- Lox
- Canned Fish
- Vacuum Packing

OUR FISH
- Smoked Salmon
- Fish Packs
- Fish & Game Packs
- Shipping in U.S.

Free Samples! Meet our pet Reindeer! Turn @ Milepost 103.9

Reindeer, Buffalo, Venison, Arctic Ox, Caribou, Salmon, Halibut

(907) 653-7511 visit our website: www.indianvalleymeats.com

"HALF THE PRICE OF HOTELS IN TOWN"
BROWN BEAR SALOON-HOTEL

BETWEEN THE MOUNTAINS & THE WATER

Rooms & Cabins • Private Baths • Full Kitchens in Cabins • Color TV • Super Deals on Weekly Rates
Salmon Fishing • Wildlife Viewing • Hiking • Pool Table

MILE 103 SEWARD HIGHWAY • INDIAN, AK • 20 MINS. FROM ANCHORAGE
(907) 653-7000 • www.brownbearmotel.com

a dangerous quicksand.

S 100.8 A 26.2 Gas station with diesel and grocery; cafe.

Essential Gas Station. See display ad this section.

S 100.7 A 26.3 Bird Ridge Motel, Cafe & Bakery. See display ad this section.

S 100.4 A 25.6 Distance marker southbound shows Girdwood 10 miles, Seward 98 miles, Homer 194 miles.

S 99.9 A 27.1 Paved turnout to west. Access to bike trail.

Southbound traffic entering "Avalanche alley," a 9-mile corridor from here south to the Girdwood turnoff that is prone to avalanches.

S 99.3 76 Gravel turnout to west.

View across Bird Flats on Turnagain Arm to the cut in the mountains where Sixmile Creek drains into the arm; the old mining settlement of Sunrise was located here. The town of Hope is to the southwest. The peak visible across Turnagain Arm between here and Girdwood is Mount Alpenglow in the Kenai mountain range. Avalanche gates.

S 99 A 28 Avalanche gun emplacement (motorists will notice several of these along the highway) and double-ended gravel turnout to west with plaque. The guns fire 105mm shells at Penguin Ridge above the highway south from Bird Hill to knock down potential slides and stabilize the slopes in winter. Plaque here memorializes Kerry Brookman:

"This monument is dedicated to Mr. Brookman and the men and women of the Alaska Railroad and Alaska Dept. of Transportation who work on the front line each winter keeping Alaska's railroad and highways safe for the traveling public. While working to clear 2 avalanches that had closed the railroad and highway east of this site, Mr. Brookman from the Alaska Railroad and 2 co-workers from the Dept. of Transportation were engulfed by a third avalanche. Mr. Brookman died on Feb. 1, 2000, from injuries sustained in this tragic incident. His co-workers survived."

S 98.8 A 28.2 *Begin 65 mph speed limit southbound. Begin 55 mph speed limit northbound.*

S 96.7 A 30.3 Improved highway begins southbound. The new "Bird to Gird" segment of the Seward Highway was completed in 1998, replacing the narrow, winding road over Bird Hill. The approximately 7 miles of new alignment lie on the water side of the railroad tracks along the shore of Turnagain Arm. The old Bird Hill road is now part of the Girdwood to Bird Point bike trail.

S 96.5 A 30.5 Turnoff for **Bird Point Scenic Overlook** (Chugach State Park); large paved parking area overlooking Turnagain Arm with walkway, wind shelter, information panels and restrooms. Access from overlook parking area to **Bird Point to Girdwood Trail**. This 6-mile bike trail goes over Bird Hill on the old Seward Highway alignment. The trail has information displays, viewpoints and telescopes along the way.

S 95.7 A 31.3 *Begin passing lane southbound. Watch for 2 directional passing lane.*

S 95.3 A 31.7 Double-ended scenic turnout to west overlooking Turnagain Arm. Gold Rush Centennial signs about Sunrise City, a gold rush camp established in 1895 at the mouth of Sixmile Creek, and the Crow Creek Boys, a partnership of stampeders formed in 1896 to mine gold on Crow Creek near present-day Girdwood. ("The boys" sold out to 2 Nome mining engineers in the early 1900s and Crow Creek mine went on to become one of the largest gold producing mines on Turnagain Arm.) Inter-

Bicyclists take advantage of the Seward Highway's bike trails.
(© David Foster)

pretive signs on Turnagain Arm (excerpts follow):

"The terrain surrounding Turnagain Arm varies widely, from flat-bottomed valleys to high, rocky peaks. Mountains around Turnagain Arm rise sharply from the shoreline to heights approaching 4,000 feet. Treeline occurs at about 1,500 feet here—much lower than in mountains of the Lower 48 states. Lying between Turnagain Arm's mountains are lowland valleys, like the one near Girdwood. Rivers and streams flow through these valleys and into the Arm. In the summer, most streams host spawning fish, providing a major food source for eagles and bears. The wetlands found in some valleys are important habitats for moose and ducks."

S 94.1 A 32.9 Scenic turnout to west with interpretive signs on belugas, hooligan and whales (excerpts follow):

"Five different populations of beluga whales live in Alaska. While 4 of these populations have overlapping ranges in the winter, the belugas living in Cook Inlet remain geographically separate and have grown genetically distinct." More than half of the Cook Inlet belugas disappeared in the 1990s, and they were declared "depleted" under the Marine Mammal Protection Act. Belugas have very low birthrates—one pregnancy every 2 to 3 years. The isolated Cook Inlet belugas must recover to about 60 percent of its optimum population in order to survive. "It is estimated this will take until at least 2025."

Belugas feed on hooligan and salmon. Hooligan—small, oily members of the smelt family—are the first fish species to appear in Turnagain Arm in the spring, usually in late April or early May. They are followed a few weeks later by salmon. The fish are gone by late October or early November. The belugas are believed to winter over in southern Cook Inlet.

S 93.6 A 33.4 *End passing lane southbound.*

S 93.3 A 33.7 Double-ended scenic turnout to west overlooking Turnagain Arm with interpretive signs on tides, mudflats and bore tides.

S 93 A 34 Vehicle turnout to east.

S 92.7 A 34.3 *End passing lane northbound.*

S 92.5 A 34.5 Double-ended scenic turnout to west overlooking Turnagain Arm with interpretive signs on the 1964 earthquake, Portage Pass and Trails, Rails and Blacktop.

S 92.4 A 34.6 Double-ended turnout to east. Watch for Dall sheep.

S 91.3 A 35.7 Double-ended scenic turnout to west overlooking Turnagain Arm with interpretive signs on glaciers (excerpt follows):

SEWARD HIGHWAY

"Look at the mountains surrounding Turnagain Arm and you can see V- and U-shaped valleys. These valleys are formed by streams and glaciers eroding away their banks and beds. The V-shaped valleys began with a mere trickle of water following an irregularity in the ground's surface. U-shaped valleys start as stream valleys but are carved into wide-bottom valleys by glaciers. Sometimes a V-shaped notch forms in the bottom of a U-shaped valley. This happens when a stream erodes a channel in the bottom of a glacier-carved valley after the glacier has receded."

S 90.5 A 36.5 Bridge crosses Tidewater Slough.

S 90.4 A 36.6 Single-vehicle turnout to east. Leaving Chugach State Park southbound.

Begin 55 mph speed zone southbound. Resume 65 mph speed limit northbound.

The 1964 Good Friday earthquake caused land to sink in the Turnagain Arm area, particularly apparent from here to **Milepost S 74**. As a result, many trees had their root systems invaded by salt water, as seen by the stands of dead spruce trees along here. Good bird watching, including bald eagles, arctic terns and sandhill cranes.

S 90.2 A 36.8 Girdwood highway maintenance station. End avalanche area southbound.

Begin passing lane northbound.

S 90 A 37 Girdwood Junction. This intersection of the Seward Highway and Alyeska Highway is "old" Girdwood. After the 1964 earthquake, Girdwood moved up the access road 2.1 miles (see "Alyeska Highway" log this section). Girdwood Station Mall here has a 24-hour gas station and convenience store; cafe, The Ice Cream Shop and Great Alaskan Tourist Trap.

Great Alaskan Tourist Trap. See display ad this section.

The Ice Cream Shop. See display ad this section.

Junction with 3-mile Alyeska Highway to Crow Creek mine, Girdwood and Alyeska Recreation Area. Worth the drive! See "Alyeska Highway" log beginning on page 511.

*NOTE: Next gas available southbound on the Seward Highway is at **Milepost S 6.6** (approximately 83 miles); next gas available northbound at **Milepost S 100.8** (10.8 miles from here); next gas available westbound on Sterling Highway is at **Milepost S 45**, Sunrise (approximately 60 miles);*

S 89.8 A 37.2 Glacier Creek bridge.

Resume 65 mph speed limit southbound. Begin 55 mph speed zone northbound.

S 89.2 A 37.8 Virgin Creek bridge. View of 3 glaciers to east.

S 88.8 A 38.2 Distance marker southbound shows Seward 87 miles, Homer 183 miles.

S 88.3 A 38.7 Abrupt turn to east for unmaintained narrow side road 0.3 mile to small turnaround; informal campsite.

S 87.4 A 39.6 Abrupt turn west for rough gravel turnout at **avalanche gun emplacement**.

Distance marker southbound shows Portage Glacier Road Junction 9 miles, Whittier 20 miles.

S 86.8 A 40.2 Sharp turn east (abrupt edge) for unsigned narrow, gravel side road; no turnaround, fords creek.

S 86.1 A 40.9 Small parking area with **Chugach National Forest** boundary sign.

Watch for belugas on incoming tides.

S 84.1 A 42.9 Peterson Creek. View of Blueberry Mountain. Watch for waterfalls on mountainsides east of the highway between Mileposts 84 and 83.

S 82 A 45 Good view of Spencer Glacier, directly ahead southbound.

S 81.1 A 45.9 *Begin 55 mph speed zone southbound. Slow for pedestrians and parked cars along this stretch of highway during hooligan fishing.*

S 81 A 46 Distance marker northbound shows Girdwood 9 miles, Anchorage 46 miles.

Turnoff to east for rough gravel side road leading 0.3 mile to dead end at Twentymile River between railroad and highway bridges.

S 80.7 A 46.3 Parking and boat launch to west at north end of **Twentymile River Bridge**. Watch for dip-netters in the spring fishing for hooligan (also known as eulachon or candlefish), a species of smelt.

The **Twentymile River** flows out of Twentymile Glacier and other glaciers through a long green valley. Twentymile Glacier can be seen at the end of the valley to the northeast. Twentymile River is a popular windsurfing area in summer. Good hooligan fishing in May. These smelt are taken with long-handled dip nets. Pink, red and silver (coho) salmon 4 to 10 lbs., use attraction lures, best in August. Dolly Varden 4 to 10 lbs., eggs best, good all summer in clearwater tributaries.

S 80.3 A 46.7 First turnoff southbound to Alaska Railroad parking area and visitor information center on east side of highway. Former Whittier shuttle vehicle loading area. Prior to the completion of the road to Whittier, the shuttle was the only means of
(Continues on page 515)

The Seward Highway was designated a National Forest Scenic Byway in 1998.

Alyeska Highway

The 3-mile Alyeska Highway provides access to Crow Creek Road, Girdwood, Mount Alyeska ski area and Alyeska Resort. There are many restaurants, gift shops and accommodations in the Girdwood/Alyeska area. Major attractions include the Alyeska Aerial Tramway and rainforest hiking trails. Well worth the drive.

There is a bike trail along this highway. **Distance is measured from junction with Seward Highway (J).**

J 0 Junction with Seward Highway at **Milepost S 90.** Girdwood Station Mall: 24-hour convenience store and gas station, Great Alaskan Tourist Trap; and The Ice Cream Shop.

Great Alaskan Tourist Trap. Getting caught in this "Trap" will be an experience you'll never forget! Not only is the "Trap" an upscale gift shop with a humorous twist, but a full on booking company as well. Connie and Twirl (yes, "Twirl") will point you in the right direction, at the right price, whether it be flightseeing, glacier cruises, whitewater rafting, dog sledding, B&B referrals and Glacier City Snowmobile Tours, led by Twirl himself! Grab an ice cream cone next door and come on into your one stop adventure shop. See ya at "The Trap!" Located in the mini-mall at the entrance to Girdwood. skiha@gci.net. (907) 783-5566. www.touristtrap.info. See display ad this section. [ADVERTISEMENT]

J 0.2 Bridge over Alaska Railroad tracks.

Paved bike trail to Alyeska Resort begins. This is also the south end of the Bird to Gird bike trail from Bird Point at **Milepost S 96.5** on the Seward Highway.

J 0.4 Forest Station Road. **Chugach National Forest Glacier Ranger District** office (P.O. Box 129, Girdwood, AK 99587; phone 907/783-3242). Open 7:30 A.M. to 5 P.M. weekdays in summer; closed holidays. Maps and information available here.

J 0.5 Alaska Candle Factory. One-half mile off Seward Highway on Alyeska Highway. Home of handcrafted candles made in

the form of Alaska wild animals. Hand-dipped tapers and molded candles made daily. All candles have unique individual designs. Open 7 days a week, 10 A.M. to 6 P.M., in summer until 7 P.M. Visitors welcome. dailey@chugach.net. (907) 783-2354. P.O. Box 786, Girdwood, AK 99587. [ADVERTISEMENT]

J 1.5 Bike rentals.

J 1.9 Junction with Crow Creek Road (1-lane dirt and gravel). **Crow Creek Mine National Historic Site** (description follows) at Mile 3.1; Crow Pass Trailhead at Mile 7. The road is not maintained past Mile 0.6 in winter.

Crow Creek Mine. Visit this historic 1898 mining camp located in the heart of Chugach National Forest. Drive 3 miles up Crow Creek Road (Old Iditarod Trail). Eight original buildings. Pan for gold. 1898 gold mining claims available for visitor prospect-

ing! Mining equipment available for the day. Small nuggets found on a regular basis. Visit our gift shop. Enjoy beautiful grounds, ponds, flowers, animals and friendly people. Call for special events schedule. This is the Girdwood area's only RV campground; $5 daily; no hookups. Open May 15 to September 15, 9 A.M. to 6 P.M. daily. Phone (907) 278-8060 (messages). www.crowcreekmine.com. [ADVERTISEMENT] ▲

The old **Iditarod Trail** winds through the hemlock forest from near Girdwood Elementary school along Crow Creek Road to end near Crow Creek Mine. Hikers can connect with the Winner Creek trail via the Four Corners tram across Glacier Creek (see Winner Creek/Girdwood Valley Loop description at **Milepost J 4.1** Alyeska Highway). The Crow Pass–Iditarod Trail trailhead is at Mile 7 Crow Creek Road. Crow Pass trail climbs steeply 3 miles to ruins of an old gold mine and a USFS public-use cabin at Crow Pass near Raven Glacier; hiking time approximately 2½ hours. The Old Iditarod trail extends 22.5 miles north from Crow Pass down Raven Creek drainage to the Chugach State Park Visitor Center on Eagle River Road. All of the hiking trail, from Crow Creek Road trailhead to the state park visitor center, is part of the Iditarod National Historic Trail used in the early 1900s. Trail is usually free of snow by mid-June. Closed to motorized vehicles; horses prohibited during early spring due to soft trail conditions.

J 2 California Creek bridge.

Girdwood

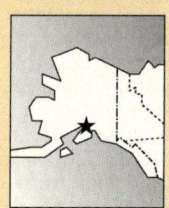

J 2.1 At the junction of Alyeska Highway and Hightower Road. **Population:** 1,935. **Emergency Services: Alaska State Troopers, EMS** and **Fire Department,** phone 911 or (907) 783-2704 (message only) or (907) 269-5711. **Medical Clinic:** Girdwood Clinic, adjacent post office, phone (907) 783-1355.

Visitor Information: The Girdwood Chamber of Commerce publishes a free map of local businesses and has a web site at www.girdwoodalaska.com. **Radio:** KEUL 88.9.

The town was named after Col. James Girdwood, who established a mining operation near here in 1901. Today, Girdwood has a substantial year-round community and a flourishing seasonal population, thanks to its appeal as both a winter and summer resort destination.

Lodging & Services

Girdwood has a variety of accommodations, several popular restaurants, a post

Mining relics adorn old buildings at historic Crow Creek Mine.
(© Rich Reid, Colors of Nature)

ONLY 35 MINUTES FROM ANCHORAGE AT BEAUTIFUL MT. ALYESKA

Alyeska Accommodations
Wide variety of quality lodging including cabins, condos, mountain chalets & executive homes.
Fully equipped kitchens and spectacular views.
907-783-2000
Email: vacation@girdwood.net   Website: www.alyeskaaccommodations.com
P.O. Box 1196 • Girdwood, AK 99587 • 800#: 888-783-2001 Fax: 907-783-2425

Alyeska Highway (continued)

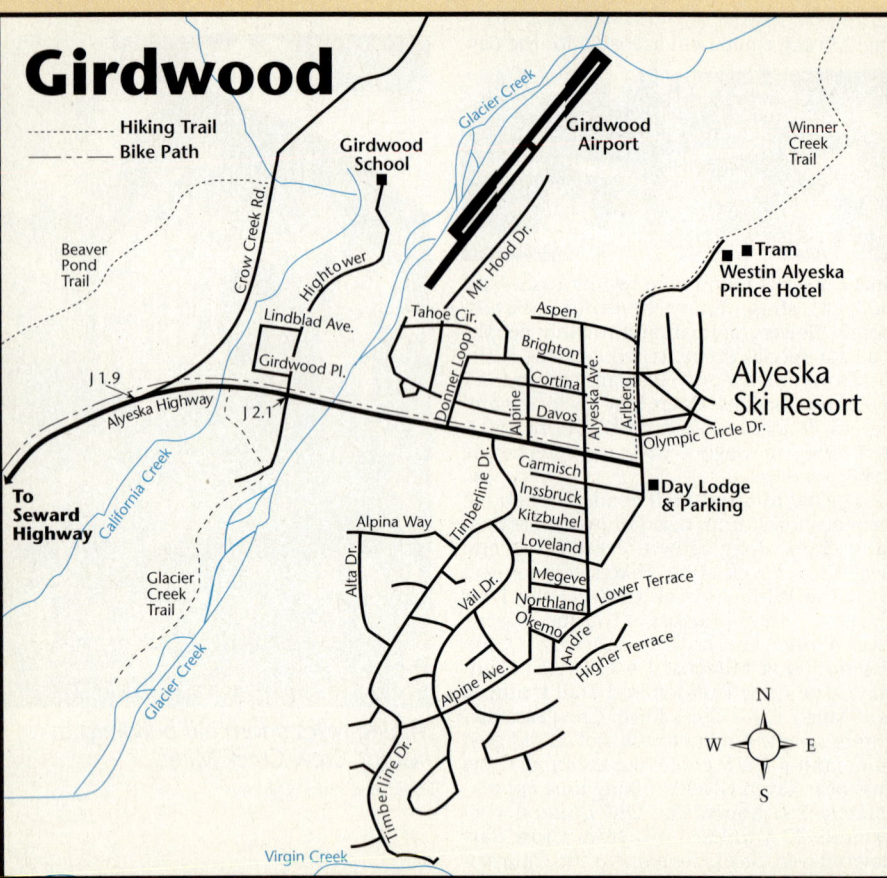

Girdwood's Forest Fair is a popular July event. (© David L. Ranta, staff)

office, vacation rental offices, grocery store with gas, a rafting business, small shops and fire hall. Flightseeing services located at Girdwood airport.

Alyeska East Studio. At base of Mount Alyeska, this condominium is perfect for use any time of year. Hike or ski in/out location affords unobstructed views of Girdwood valley and mountains. Sleeps 4-plus in upscale environment. Features full kitchen and bath, gas fireplace/stove, phone, TV/DVD/CD player. Laundry available. (907) 222-2614. asksp@gci.net. [ADVERTISEMENT]

Bud & Carol's Bed & Breakfast is a newly built home at the base of Mount Alyeska. Two beautiful guest rooms and fully equipped kitchen on ground level. No stairs! Each guest room has queen bed, cable TV/VCR, private bath, double vanities and jacuzzi. Mountain views! Families welcome. Non-smoking, no pets. Summer vacationers' paradise. Skiers/boarders winter dream home. Open year-round. Phone (907) 783-3182. Email info@budandcarols bandb.com. www.budandcarolsbandb.com. See display ad this section. [ADVERTISEMENT]

Chair Five Restaurant. A favorite of locals and travelers since 1983. This is a must stop, fun place to dine and drink. Daily offerings include fresh Alaskan halibut, salmon, and our famous gourmet burgers, ground fresh in Alaska at Mr. Prime Beef and Indian Valley Meats, or enjoy one of our homemade gourmet, fresh dough pizzas that get rave reviews. We offer one of the largest selections of single malt scotches in Alaska and over 60 microbrews on tap and in the bottle. So stop in, say hi to Spike, enjoy the jukebox and join us in the bar for a game of pool. Open daily 11 A.M.–11 P.M. AX/MC/Visa. Phone (907) 783-2500. www.chairfive.com. See display ad this section. [ADVERTISEMENT]

GIRDWOOD / ALYESKA ADVERTISERS

Alaska Candle
  Factory .... Mile 0.5 Alyeska Hwy.
Alaska Rider Tours .... Ph. (800) 756-1990
Alaskana Haus, The .... Ph. (907) 783-2481
Alpina Inn B&B .... Ph. (907) 783-2482
Alyeska Accommodations Ph. (907) 783-2000
Alyeska East Studio .... Ph. (907) 222-2614
Alyeska Resort .... Ph. 1-800-880-3880
Alyeska View Bed &
  Breakfast .... Ph. (907) 783-2747
Bake Shop, The .... Ph. (907) 783-2831
Bud & Carol's Bed &
  Breakfast .... Ph. (907) 783-3182
Chair 5 Restaurant .... Ph. (907) 783-2500
Class V Whitewater .... Ph. (907) 783-2004
Crow Creek Mine .... Mile 3.1 Crow Creek Rd.
Girdwood Bed &
  Breakfast Assoc. .... Ph. (907) 222-4858
Girdwood Center For
  Visual Arts .... Ph. (907) 783-3209
Girdwood Chamber of
  Commerce .... Ph. (907) 783-1135
Girdwood Clinic .... Ph. (907) 783-1355
Girdwood Guest House .... Ph. (907) 783-3488
Girdwood Rotary .... Ph. (907) 783-2128
Girdwood Ski & Cyclery .... Ph. (907) 783-2453
Great Alaskan Tourist Trap
  .... Ph. (907) 783-5566
Jack Sprat .... Ph. (907) 783-5225
Kobuk Valley Jade Co. .... Ph. (907) 783-2764
Northern Comfort
  Lodging .... Ph. (907) 783-3419

Alpina Inn Bed & Breakfast

TWO ROOM SUITE
Kitchen, Private Entrance
Non-smoking

CAROLE & PETER KUNG
P.O. Box 121 Girdwood, AK 99587
Phone/Fax **(907) 783-2482**
www.girdwood.net/alpina
kung@alaska.net

Alyeska View Bed & Breakfast

Enjoy a stay in a home with Austrian-Alaskan hospitality.
HOSTS: Heinrich and Emmy Gruber
P.O. Box 234, Girdwood, AK 99587 • Vail Drive
Tel/Fax **(907) 783-2747**
email: alyeska-view-bb@gci.net • website: www.alyeskaview.com

---

Girdwood Bed & Breakfast Association

FREE referrals to quality, licensed B&Bs in Girdwood, Alaska 99587
www.gbba.org
(907) 222-4858

Girdwood Clinic

— Providing health care in the Turnagain Arm Area —
Tues.-Sat. 10:30am-6:30pm   tel: 783-1355   fax: 783-1357
Located on Hightower Road in the New Girdwood Townsite
Kerry Dorius, FNP, Family Nurse Practitioner

Girdwood Guest House, Brighton Road, provides a lovely, completely private suite with private entrance, luxurious furnishings, sitting room, cable TV, full kitchen, full bath, washer/dryer, hearty breakfast. Guests say, "Wow, beautiful,

comfortable, yummy food, great laundry, so clean, fantastic view, restful, and minutes from Alyeska Resort!" www.girdwoodguesthouse.com; (907)783-3488; girdwoodguesthouse@gci.net. [ADVERTISEMENT]

Northern Comfort Lodging. "The thing I like the most is the atmosphere; it is quiet and fresh." "One of the most beautiful lodges that we visited during our holiday in your beautiful country!" ... comments from our guest book. Stay with us in a newly furnished one-bedroom suite with private entrance, steam/shower and stocked kitchenette. You'll be glad you did! Jane Barber (907) 783-3419. Fax (907) 783-2038. Email: jamaba0017@aol.com. www.northerncomfortlodging.com. (Location: Kitzbuhel Road; 3 blocks from ski mountain.) [ADVERTISEMENT]

Attractions

Girdwood Forest Fair, a popular summer crafts fair held in July at the com-

Alyeska Highway (continued)

munity park. This weekend event—which features crafts, food and entertainment—draws thousands of visitors.

Hiking trails in the area include Glacier Creek, Alyeska Basin, Iditarod, Beaver Pond and Winner Creek trails. The Winner Creek trail is a good one to experience Girdwood's rainforest. The trail starts near the Alyeska Aerial Tramway ticket office. Girdwood averages 67 inches of rainfall a year. Inquire at Ranger Station at **Milepost J 0.4** Alyeska Highway for more information on area hiking trails.

Class V Whitewater, Inc. offers daily the best whitewater rafting in Alaska and the closest to Anchorage. Pick from 3 different whitewater trips ranked class III, IV and V respectively (age limits apply), or 3 leisurely scenic floats. Company provides expert guides, gear and everything for a warm, comfortable trip. Advance reservations required. Stop by our office 12–5 P.M. or call (907) 783-2004; toll-free 1-877-783-2004. www.alaskanrafting.com. [ADVERTISEMENT]

Alyeska Highway
(continued)

J 2.3 Glacier Creek bridge.
J 2.5 Donner access to Girdwood airstrip (follow signs); flightseeing.
Private Aircraft: Girdwood airstrip; elev. 150 feet; length 2,100 feet; gravel; unattended.
J 2.6 Timberline Drive.
J 2.9 Alyeska Highway ends at **junction** with Arlberg Avenue, road forks; Welcome to Alyeska Resort sign. Turn west for Alyeska day lodge (ski school, rentals). Turn east for Alyeska Prince Hotel and tram. Bike and walking path continues to hotel.

Alyeska Resort, Alaska's largest ski area, is a popular year-round destination that includes the Alyeska Prince Hotel and the mountaintop Seven Glaciers restaurant, as well as the ski area and its facilities.

Ski season is generally from mid-Novem-

Alyeska Highway ends at the foot of Mount Alyeska. (© Laurent Dick)

ber through Memorial Day. Facilities include the 60-passenger aerial tramway, which operates year-round and departs from the Alyeska Prince Hotel (see description at **Milepost J 4.1**); a high-speed detachable bubble quad, 2 fixed-grip quads, 3 double chair lifts and 2 pony tows. Night skiing available during holiday periods in December, and Friday through Saturday from January through March. Ski school, ski rental shop and sports shops are available. Phone (907) 754-7669 for snow conditions and mountain information. Other winter activities include heli and snowcat skiing, Nordic skiing, dog sledding, snow-

---

✳ **The Bake Shop** ✳ At Alyeska Resort
Home of Alyeska Sourdough Bread
Open daily 7 a.m. – 7 p.m.
Saturdays 'til 8 p.m.
✳ Serving Breakfast –
Sourdough Pancakes, Sweet Rolls
Soup ✳ Pizza
✳ Hot & Cold Sandwiches
At Alyeska Ski Resort
(907) 783-2831
Michael & Stefanie Flynn
www.thebakeshop.com

Girdwood Ski & Cyclery (907) 783-BIKE (2453)
Great Repair Services & Rides from Our Shop!!
Bike Rentals $10 & Up
fun@girdwood.net
www.girdwood.net/fun
mi 1.5 Alyeska Hwy

.... **Alaska Rider Tours** ....
Explore the Last Frontier with a Dual-Purpose Motorcycle
Tours & Rentals Available for 2003 Season
800-756-1990
907-783-1990
www.akrider.com

Gifts of Jade
From North of the Arctic Circle

Jade Jewelry • Raw Jade
Jade and Ivory Carvings

- Located Near Alyeska Resort Day Lodge Mile 3 Alyeska Road.
- Open Daily. Winter: 10 a.m. to 5 pm. Summer: 9 a.m. to 6 pm.
We invite you to stop by and have a cup of coffee while you watch our jade being cut. You'll find our artifact collection interesting also.

Kobuk Valley Jade Company   907-783-2764
Box 516 • Phone (907) 783-2764 • Girdwood, Alaska 99587

GIRDWOOD CENTER FOR VISUAL ARTS
Visit This Delightful Gallery Featuring... Locally Created Fine Art & Craft Works
Open Daily — May 1 thru July 31
Winter: Open Most Weekends
• Year Round Events & Exhibits
Mi. 2.1 - 1 Block N. off Alyeska Hwy
(907) 783-3209
www.girdwood.org

GIRDWOOD ROTARY MEETS:
Thursday - 7pm
Alyeska Prince Hotel
Welcome Visiting Rotarians

For a spectacular view of Turnagain Arm, ride the aerial tramway at Mount Alyeska.

shoeing and snowmobiling.

Alyeska Resort hosts the Chevy Trucks U.S. Alpine Championships, March 16–25, 2003.

A popular skiing event at Alyeska in April is the **Spring Carnival and Slush Cup**, known as the "biggest beach party this side of Hawaii." Skiers in costume try to make it across a 100-foot-long pond of ice cold water.

Summer activities include sightseeing, hiking, bicycle rentals, tandem paragliding, berry picking and flightseeing. Summer events include the Alyeska 5-K Fun Run in July, held in conjunction with the Girdwood Forest Fair. The Alyeska Mountain Run is held in August, the final stop for the Alaska Mountain Runners Grand Prix series.

Alyeska Resort. See display ad this section.

J 3 Olympic Circle; Kobuk Valley Jade shop, The Bake Shop, Jack Sprat and other businesses.

Jack Sprat, located on Olympic Circle. This quaint A-frame is a comfortable dining oasis featuring fat and lean world cuisine. Wraps at lunch, off-the-menu brunch on the weekends, steak and creative vegetarian plates at dinner. Local favorites: Halibut burrito, Smoked Salmon Pasta and award-winning Pamela Anderson Cheesecake. Closed Tuesdays. (907) 783-JACK/5225. [ADVERTISEMENT]

The Bake Shop at Alyeska Resort is a MUST stop for food and flower lovers alike! Turn off the Seward Highway onto Alyeska Highway. Follow the road until you come to the "T" at Alyeska Resort. Turn left onto Arlberg and take the first right onto Olympic Circle. Don't be confused by a sign for another restaurant at the bottom of the road! Continue to drive to the very top of the gravel road, use the parking lot to your

right and walk up to the front of the condo building and the boardwalk. Here you'll find the annual display of summer flowers such as dazzling begonias, giant ferns and many all-time favorites. Then step inside the Bake Shop to enjoy the heartwarming aroma of freshly baked breads and buns. The Bake Shop creates these with the original sourdough starter which was once the "prized" possession of a fortune-seeking gold miner in this valley over 80 years ago. Now look at the large menu board and you will find a variety of egg dishes and pancakes for breakfast. For lunch choose between a great selection of sandwiches made with sourdough buns; pizzas and homemade soups. Don't forget to leave room for our "famous" sweet rolls. Bring your breakfast or lunch outside for a garden picnic, enjoy the beauty of the flowers and the valley and remember to take some of our bread and handcrafted preserves for the road! (907) 783-2831. www.thebakeshop.com. [ADVERTISEMENT]

J 3.2 Alyeska Field and Moose Meadow Park (Stumpy Faulkner Early Winter Trail).

J 3.9 Entrance to Alyeska Prince Hotel; follow signs for parking and shuttle bus to hotel and tram.

J 4.1 The Alyeska Prince Hotel and Aerial Tramway Glacier Terminal; no parking. The 307-room deluxe chateau-style hotel has a cafe, Japanese steakhouse, 2 lounges, 2 retail shops and a fitness center with indoor swimming pool, sauna, whirlpool and exercise room. For information phone (907) 754-1111 or (800) 880-3880; www.alyeskaresort.com.

The **Alyeska Aerial Tramway** transports visitors year-round to the 2,300-foot level of Mount Alyeska. (The mountain's summit is at 3,939 feet) and a mountaintop complex featuring fine dining at Seven Glaciers Restaurant and the Glacier Express cafeteria (check for food service hours before departing base). The Alyeska tram is a good sightseeing choice for anyone who has difficulty walking or negotiating stairs. You can drop off passengers right in front of the tram, and there's elevator access to the tram level at both the bottom of the mountain and at the top. The tram operates daily starting at 10:30 A.M. with seasonal closures for scheduled maintenance in October and May. Call the ticket office for operating times, (907) 754-2275. Tram cars depart about every 10 to 15 minutes. Purchase tickets at the ticket windows at the foot of the tram. Great views from the top.

Hikers can hike up the trail that starts at the base of Chair 7 behind the hotel and winds 2 miles up the mountain to the top of the Alyeska Tram. Hikers can ride the tram down for free.

Winner Creek Trail (foot travel only) trailhead by tram ticket office. Follow gravel path ¼ mile for easy walk through rainforest. Continue on 1.5 miles to Winner Creek and trailhead junction with the Gorge Trail and the Upper Winner Creek Basin trail. Access to Iditarod trail via Four Corners tram across Glacier Creek. Hikers can make the 7.5-mile Girdwood Valley Loop Trail by taking the Winner Creek Trail from the Alyeska Prince parking lot to the Four Corners tram across Glacier Creek to Crow Creek Mine, and then down the Old Iditarod trail along Crow Creek Road to the Alyeska Highway bike path back to the Alyeska parking lot. Check bulletin board at Winner Creek trailhead for bear alerts.

Return to Milepost S 90
Seward Highway

An Alaska Railroad train in the scenic Portage valley.

(© Rich Reid, Colors of Nature)

(Continued from page 510)
overland transportation to Whittier. Alaska Railroad currently offers day trips to Grandview from their Portage facility.

Kenai Peninsula Visitor Information Center. First turnoff southbound to gift shop and reservation service for lodging, tours and other activities. Open 7 days a week from 9 A.M. to 6 P.M., Memorial Day through Labor Day. From Portage, ride the Alaska Railroad to Grandview on the Glacier Discovery train for $69 per person. Explore rugged gorges, glacier-carved valleys and the towering peaks that border the Grandview Valley. Departs daily at 1:15 P.M. and 3:50 P.M. [ADVERTISEMENT]

S 80.1 A 46.9 Deteriorating buildings and rusting truck visible on the west side of the highway are all that remain of **PORTAGE**, once a flag stop on the Alaska Railroad. An estimated 50 to 100 residents of Portage were forced to move after the 1964 earthquake caused the land to drop between 6 and 12 feet along Turnagain Arm. High tides then flooded the area with salt water. (The dead trees you see along the highway here were killed by salt water.)

Leaving Game Management Unit 14C, entering unit 7, southbound.

S 80 A 47 Second turnoff southbound to former railroad loading area and Kenai Peninsula Visitor Information Center (reservation service for lodging, tours and other

SEWARD HIGHWAY

activities).

S 79.8 A 47.2 Third turnoff southbound, first turnoff northbound, to former railroad loading area and Kenai Peninsula Visitor Information Center (see **Milepost S 80.3**).

S 79.4 A 47.6 Portage Creek No. 2 bridge. Parking to west at south end of bridge. This gray-colored creek carries the silt-laden glacial meltwater from Portage Glacier and Portage Lake to Turnagain Arm. Mud flats in Turnagain Arm are created by silt from the creek settling close to shore.

S 79 A 48 Turnoff to west for **Big Game Alaska**, a drive-through animal park with a log lodge gift shop. The park features caribou, moose, musk-ox, bison, elk, Sitka black-tailed deer, eagles and owls. Besides offering visitors an opportunity to see wild animals, Big Game Alaska plays an important role in rescuing orphaned and injured wild animals. The park usually has an orphaned moose calf or bear cub with a story to tell.

Admission and gift store purchases at Big Game Alaska contribute to the animal care program. The center is dedicated to the rehabilitation of orphaned and injured animals and provides wildlife education to the public.

Big Game Alaska. See display ad this section.

Portage Creek No. 1 bridge.

S 78.9 A 48.1 Turnoff for Whittier and Portage Glacier. Large gravel turnout to east.

Junction with Whittier/Portage Glacier Access Road. See "Whittier/Portage Glacier Access Road" on pages 517-519.

The Whittier area offers hiking like this boardwalk trail to Horsetail Falls.
(© David L. Ranta, staff)

S 78.4 A 48.6 Placer River bridge; parking and access east side of highway at south end of bridge.

The Placer River has good hooligan fishing in May. These smelt are taken with long-handled dip nets. Silver salmon may be taken in August and September.

Between Placer River and Ingram Creek, there is an excellent view on clear days of Skookum Glacier to the northeast. To the north across Turnagain Arm is Twentymile Glacier. Arctic terns and waterfowl are often seen in the slough here.

S 77.9 A 49.1 Placer River overflow bridge. Paved turnout to east at south end of bridge.

S 77.8 A 49.2 Distance marker southbound shows Seward 76 miles, Homer 172 miles.

S 77 A 50 Boundary of Chugach National Forest.

S 75.5 A 51.5 Paved double-ended Scenic Byway turnouts both sides of highway.

Road access to **Ingram Creek** from east side turnout; fishing.

S 75.2 A 51.8 Bridge over Ingram Creek.

S 75 A 52 Paved turnout to west; Welcome to the Kenai Peninsula sign. The Seward Highway has now crossed the isthmus that separates the Kenai Peninsula from the rest of Southcentral Alaska.

Highway begins ascent to Turnagain Pass southbound.

S 74.9 A 52.1 *Passing lane begins southbound and extends 5.7 miles.*

S 74.5 A 52.5 Long paved double-ended turnout to east.

S 72.5 A 54.5 Double-ended paved turnout to east.

S 71.5 A 55.5 Long paved double-ended turnout to west.

S 71.2 A 55.8 Double-ended paved turnout to west.

S 71 A 56 Slow vehicle turnout for northbound traffic.

S 69.2 A 57.8 *Passing lane ends southbound.*

S 69 A 58 Slow vehicle turnout for northbound traffic.

S 68.9 A 58.1 Divided highway begins southbound, ends northbound.

S 68.5 A 58.5 Turnagain Pass Recreation Areaa (elev. 988 feet). Parking area west side of highway with restrooms and dumpster (southbound lane). *Emergency phone*. U-turn lane.

Turnagain Pass Recreation Area is a favorite winter recreation area for snowmobilers (west side of highway) and cross-country skiers (east side of highway). Snow depths here frequently exceed 12 feet. Patches of snow seen here into June.

S 68.1 A 58.9 Parking area east side of highway with restrooms and dumpster for northbound traffic. U-turn.

S 67.8 A 59.2 Bridge over Lyon Creek.

The highway traverses an area of mountain meadows and parklike stands of spruce, hemlock, birch and aspen interlaced with glacier-fed streams. The many flowers seen in surrounding alpine meadows here include lupine, wild geranium, yellow and purple

(Continues on page 520)

Whittier/Portage Glacier Access Road

The Whittier access road was the culmination of a 3-year project to connect Whittier to the road system. Opened in June 2000, the road branched off the already existing road to Portage Glacier. From the Seward Highway it is 5.4 miles to Portage Glacier and 11.4 miles to Whittier. Prior to construction of this access road, Whittier was accessible overland only by train.

A major project during construction of the Whittier access road was the modification of the 2.5-mile-long Anton Anderson Memorial Tunnel to handle both railroad and vehicle traffic. The Anton Anderson tunnel is 1-lane, and cars and trains take turns traveling through it. In summer, the tunnel is open daily 6 A.M. to 11 P.M., alternating directional use for vehicle traffic about every 1/2 hour, with short delays to accommodate scheduled passenger trains. Vehicles must wait in the staging areas on either end of the tunnel when the train is using the tunnel.

Tunnel tolls are charged according to vehicle class and are round-trip. Tolls in summer 2002 were as follows: Motorcycles and passenger vehicles not pulling trailers, $12; RVs to 28 feet or greater not pulling trailers, or less than 28 feet pulling a trailer, $20; RVs 28 feet or greater pulling a trailer, $35. Tolls are paid by eastbound motorists at the Bear Valley staging area. Tolls are not charged for vehicles traveling westbound from Whittier to Portage.

For current tolls and more tunnel information phone (907) 566-2244 from Anchorage; toll-free (877) 611-2586; or visit www.dot.state.ak.us/creg/whittiertunnel/index.htm. Schedule information is also broadcast on AM 530 radio in Whittier or AM 1610 in Portage.

Distance is measured from junction with the Seward Highway (J).

J 0 Junction with Seward Highway at Milepost S 78.9.
CAUTION: Alaska Railroad crossing.
J 1.2 Moose Flat day-use area. 2 toilets, picnic tables, parking, RV pull-throughs, garbage container. The "Wetland Walk" is a 1/4-mile gravel and boardwalk trail with interpretive displays.
J 1.4 Adler Pond access. Trout fishing.
J 2.4 Paved turnout. Explorer Glacier viewpoint on right.
J 3.1 Bridge. Beaver dam visible from road.
J 3.2 Tangle Pond access.
J 3.7 Black Bear USFS campground; 12 sites (2 will accommodate medium-sized trailers), toilets, water, firepits, dumpsters, tables, $10 fee. Pleasant wooded area.
J 3.8 Small gravel turnout to south.
J 4.1 Williwaw fish viewing observation deck. Spawning reds, pinks and dog salmon can be viewed from late July to mid-September. Parking.
J 4.3 Williwaw USFS campground, south of road below Middle Glacier; 60 campsites, toilets, dumpsters, water, firepits, tables, $12 single, $16 double (reservations available, phone 1-877-444-NRRS or visit www.reserveusa.com). Beautiful campground. View of Explorer Glacier. Campfire programs in the amphitheater; check bulletin board for schedule. Self-guided Williwaw nature trail off the campground loop road goes through moose and beaver habitat.
CAUTION: Unexploded artillery shells from avalanche mitigation may be found on parts of the mountain. If you find one, mark its location 10 feet away with a rock pile or bright cloth. Report it to the Glacier Ranger District in Girdwood; (907) 783-3242.
J 5.2 Road forks: right fork leads to Portage Glacier Lodge and 0.2 mile to Begich, Boggs Visitor Center at Portage Glacier and Lake (descriptions follow). Left fork leads to Whittier (continue with this log).

Portage Glacier Lodge, a family-owned day lodge, open daily from 9 A.M. to 7 P.M., year-round. Located in Chugach National Forest, across the street from Begich, Boggs Visitor Center. A great place for lunch! A wonderful place to shop! The cafeteria serves hearty soups, sandwiches and desserts. Espresso Bar! It's a must to sample the fudge, made daily on site. The gift shop is not a typical gift shop. You'll find an art gallery approach, presenting Alaskan Indian and Eskimo carvings, masks and jewelry. Friendly, knowledgeable local staff will answer any questions. You'll also find Limited Edition Collectibles, made in Alaska souvenirs, and a huge postcard and card display featuring Alaskan photographers. Mail orders welcome. We will ship your purchase anywhere. P.O. Box 469, Girdwood, AK 99587; (907) 783-3117; Fax (907) 783-3004. Email:portageldg@aol.com. See display ad this section. [ADVERTISEMENT]

Begich, Boggs Visitor Center at **Portage Glacier** and **Portage Lake**. Follow one-way loop around to lakefront parking lot and the visitor center, or turn right and go 1.2 miles for Byron Glacier trailhead or 1.5 miles for M/V *Ptarmigan* sightseeing boat cruise dock and passenger waiting area. Portage Glacier has retreated dramatically in recent years. In the 1970s, the glacier extended across the lake to within a mile of the visitor center, but in recent years it has retreated around the corner of Byron Peak's northeast ridge.

The Begich, Boggs Visitor Center focuses on Portage Valley and its resources. Main exhibit rooms are arranged so that the visitor has a sense of walking up Portage Valley, through Portage Pass and down into Prince William Sound. Visitors may also enter the "Alaskans and Their Stories" room, where they can read or listen to talks about real people who lived in this area. The "Wild Side" room focuses on animals that live in Portage Valley. Displays include a life-size moose and calf. The center originally opened in 1986. It was dedicated to congressmen Nick Begich of Alaska and Hale Boggs of Louisiana, who died in a plane crash in 1972.

The center is open 9 A.M. to 6 P.M. daily in summer. Phone the visitor center at (907) 783-2326 or the U.S. Forest Service district office at (907) 783-3242 for current schedule. Forest Service naturalists are available to answer questions.

J 5.3 Whittier Road enters 450-foot tunnel under Begich Peak.
J 6.4 Large paved parking area provides views of Portage Lake, Byron Glacier and part of the receding Portage Glacier.

There are several excellent spots in the

Low clouds don't obscure glacier views from turnout at Milepost J 6.4.
(© David L. Ranta, staff)

Whittier Access Road (continued)

View of Whittier harbor from hiking trail off Salmon Run Road. (© David L. Ranta, staff)

area to observe salmon spawning (August and September) in Portage Creek and its tributaries.

J 6.7 Toll booths and **Bear Valley staging area.** The 8-lane staging area controls vehicle traffic entering the **Anton Anderson Memorial Tunnel.** The tunnel uses a computerized traffic-control system that regulates both rail and highway traffic. Each vehicle class is metered into the tunnel at different time intervals, with commercial trucks entering the tunnel last. The speed limit in the tunnel is 25 mph. It takes 6.5 minutes for a vehicle to travel through the tunnel. The tunnel's ventilation system combines jet and portal fans. It is the longest highway tunnel in North America at 13,200 feet.

Driving the tunnel can be somewhat disorienting, as you can't see the beginning or end for much of its length. (You might also experience a dramatic change in weather as you pass between the Portage side and the Whittier side.) The Anton Anderson Memorial Tunnel was built in 1942–43 as part of the Whittier Cutoff, a 12.4-mile-long railway line constructed to safeguard the flow of military supplies from the port of Whittier. The tunnel was named in 1976 for the chief engineer of that project—Anton Anderson. The railway line includes a second tunnel between Bear Valley and Portage that is 4,910 feet long.

J 7.1 Entering Anton Anderson Memorial Tunnel eastbound.
J 9.6 Exiting Anton Anderson Memorial Tunnel eastbound.
J 10 Whittier staging area for westbound tunnel traffic.
J 10.1 Rest area with restrooms, pay phone and interpretive signs. No parking 11 P.M. to 4 A.M.
J 10.2 Shakespeare Creek.
J 11.1 Whittier Street. Access to paid parking lot, camping and Whittier businesses.

For area hiking trails, follow Whittier Street 0.5 mile to Eastern Avenue; cross Eastern and drive 0.3 mile up Blackstone Road, then turn right on Salmon Run Road just past the Buckner Building. Salmon Run Road (narrow, dirt) leads 0.4 mile to **Horsetail Falls Trail**, a 1-mile planked trail to a viewing platform overlooking Whittier and Passage canal. Or follow Salmon Run Road 0.2 mile and turn left on a second narrow dirt road for 0.4 mile to Smitty's Cove, Cove Creek picnic area and Salmon Run (Shotgun Cove) hiking trail along coastline.

J 11.2 Whittier Boat Harbor.
J 11.4 Alaska State Ferry terminal. The MV *Bartlett* serves Whittier. See the ALASKA STATE FERRY SCHEDULES section.

Whittier

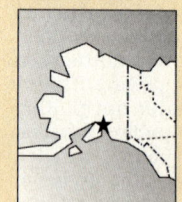

Located at the head of Passage Canal on Prince William Sound, 59.5 miles southeast of Anchorage. **Population:** 290. **Emergency Services: Police, Fire** and **Medical,** phone (907) 472-2340. **Visitor Information:** At Tunnel's End Stop Cafe & Espresso, as well as other local businesses.

Elevation: 30 feet. **Climate:** Normal daily temperature for July is 56°F; for January, 25°F. Maximum temperature is 84°F and minimum is -29°F. Mean annual precipitation is 174 inches, including 260 inches of snow. Winter winds can reach 60 mph.

Private Aircraft: Airstrip adjacent northwest; elev. 30 feet; length 1,100 feet; gravel; no fuel; unattended; emergency only.

Named after the poet John Greenleaf Whittier, the community of Whittier is nestled at the base of mountains that line Passage Canal, a fjord that extends eastward into Prince William Sound. Passage Canal, which leads to a portage between Prince William Sound and Cook Inlet, was named by Capt. Vancouver in 1794.

Whittier was created by the U.S. Army during WWII as a port and petroleum delivery center tied to bases farther north by the Alaska Railroad and later a pipeline. The railroad spur from Portage was completed in 1943, and Whittier became the primary

---

alaska sea kayakers • Honey Charters

Box 770 – Harbor Triangle
Whittier, AK 99693
(907) 472-2534
Toll Free **877-472-2534**
Kayak Rental • Guided Day Trips
Extended Trips • Custom Trips

Box 708 – Harbor Triangle
Whittier, AK 99693
(907) 472-2493
Toll Free **888-477-2493**
Water Transport for Kayakers
Custom Sightseeing Cruises

Professional Kayak Guiding, Rental, Transport Services in Prince William Sound
www.alaskaseakayakers.com • www.honeycharters.com

SEA MIST CHARTERS
Fishing Prince William Sound
Whittier — At Lisa's Ice Cream Parlor
1-877-688-2166
cgangestad@aol.com
P.O. Box 671201, Chugiak, AK 99567

WHITTIER ADVERTISERS

Alaska Outdoor
   Adventures ....Ph. (877) 408-2628
Alaska Sea Kayakers ....Ph. (877) 472-2534
Anchor Inn ....Ph. (907) 472-2351
Bread N' Butter Charters..Ph. (888) 472-2396
Honey Charters................Ph. (888) 477-2493
June's B&B Condo Suites..Ph. (888) 472-2396
Major Marine Tours..........Ph. (800) 764-7300
Sea Mist Charters ....Ph. (877) 688-2166
Soundview Getaway ....Ph. (907) 262-4958
Tunnel's End Stop Eatery &
   Espresso Log Cabin .....Ph. (907) 441-2248
26 Glacier Cruise...............Ph. (907) 276-8023
Varlys' Swiftwater
   Seafood Cafe ....Ph. (907) 472-2550

debarkation point for cargo, troops and dependents of the Alaska Command. Construction of the huge buildings that dominate Whittier began in 1948, and the Port of Whittier, strategically valuable for its ice-free deep-water port, remained activated until 1960, at which time the population was 1,200. The city of Whittier was incorporated in 1969. The government tank farm is still located here.

The 14-story Begich Towers, formerly the Hodge Building, houses more than half of Whittier's population. Now a condominium, the building was used by the U.S. Army for family housing and civilian bachelor quarters. The building was renamed in honor of U.S. Rep. Nick Begich of Alaska, who, along with Rep. Hale Boggs of Louisiana, disappeared in a small plane in this area in 1972 while on a campaign tour.

The Buckner Building, completed in 1953, once the largest building in Alaska, was called the "city under one roof." It is now privately owned and is to be renovated.

Whittier Manor was built in the early 1950s by private developers as rental units for civilian employees and soldiers who were ineligible for family housing elsewhere. In early 1964, the building was bought by another group of developers and became a condominium, which now houses the remainder of Whittier's population.

Since military and government activities ceased, the economy of Whittier rests largely on the fishing industry, the port and increasingly on tourism.

Annual events in Whittier include a Fourth of July parade, barbecue and fireworks; a Fish Derby, held Memorial Day weekend to Labor Day weekend; and Regatta, at the end of April or beginning of May, when residents boat to Valdez for Game Night and then bus or fly back to Whittier.

Whittier has limited accommodations, restaurants, 2 bars, gift shops, general stores, a gas station and post office. There is no bank in Whittier.

Whittier also has a harbor office, marine services and repairs, marine supply store, boat launch and lift, freight services, dry storage and self-storage units.

The 2-mile-long **Portage Pass Trail** leads from Whittier to Portage Pass, offering views of area glaciers. The trail ends at Divide Lake.

Alaska Outdoor Adventures. Half-day and full-day guided sea kayak tours in Prince William Sound. Get up close to abundant marine wildlife and spectacular coastal shorelines! All necessary gear and instruction is provided. Beginners and experienced paddlers are welcome. Sea kayak rentals, river rafting and horseback tours available. For reservations call (907) 276-2628 or (877) 408-2628 or www.akadventures.com. [ADVERTISEMENT]

Major Marine Tours. Relaxing 5-hour cruise to view active tidewater glaciers in Blackstone Bay. Boat stops for quiet viewing of glaciers; watch for glacier calving and wildlife (otters, eagles, seals and birds) from viewing decks or from assigned table seating inside heated cabins. Daily departures from Whittier mid-May to mid-September. Convenient rail and bus packages available from Anchoage. Cruise price $99; add freshly prepared, all-you-can-eat salmon and prime rib meal, $12. Call (800) 764-7300 or (907) 274-7300 for reservations or free brochure. Major Marine Tours, 411 W. 4th, Anchorage, AK 99501. www.majormarine.com. [ADVERTISEMENT]

26 Glacier Cruise. Cruise the calm, protected waters of Prince William Sound and

come face to face with tidewater glaciers plus an amazing array of wildlife on the fastest, largest and most luxurious high-speed catamaran in Alaska. Departs daily from Whittier. See our ad in the Anchorage section. Phillips Cruises year-round sales office is located at 519 West Fourth Avenue, Anchorage, AK 99501. Toll free from USA and Canada 1-800-544-0529, (907) 276-8023 or bswanberg@26glaciers.com. [ADVERTISEMENT]

Tunnel's End Eatery and Espresso Log Cabin. Feast on mouth-watering pristine oysters from Prince William Sound.

Wide variety of good meals; fresh seafoods, barbecue, box and picnic lunches. Excellent fresh espresso drinks; Chai, real hot chocolate, fresh baked goodies, daily specials. In a hurry? Check our fresh deli and dessert display. T-shirts. Relax, watch eagles nesting. Spectacular viewing of waterfalls and picturesque harbor. Free information on everything to do and see. History tidbits. Located by Whittier Creek, Shoreside Petro, across from railroad crossing. Clean, TLC, friendly. United we stand. Come ring my freedom bell. Call ahead for charter or picnic lunches. heckey2@excite.com. (907) 441-2248. [ADVERTISEMENT]

Return to Milepost S 78.9 Seward Highway

SEWARD HIGHWAY • Whittier/Portage Glacier Road

JUNE'S B&B CONDO SUITES - BREAD 'N BUTTER CHARTERS
One Call Does It ALL! 888-472-2396
- 10 Clean Beautiful **Condo B&B** Suites • Call for Best Dates!
- 6-Pak Custom **Fishing Charters** • Custom Sightseeing Tours
- Whale Watching & Glacier Tours In Beautiful **Whittier**, Alaska
- Heated Cabin • Private Head • Large Groups Welcome!

www.breadnbuttercharter.com
E-mail: junebbak@yahoo.com
Open Year Round

Soundview Getaway
WATERFRONT CONDOS
Full Kitchen • Private baths
1-800-515-2358
www.soundviewalaska.com
e-mail: soundviewgetaway@ak.net

Varly's Swiftwater Seafood Café
Whittier, Alaska
Fresh, Hand Battered Seafood From Prince William Sound
Open May-September
Featuring over 30 Specialty & Import Beers

"We've lived in Alaska for 42 years, and this is the best fried halibut we've ever had."
—Jamie Robinson, Anchorage

Don & Margaret Varlamos
(907) 472-2550
www.home.gci.net/~akvarly

ANCHOR INN
Satellite TV, Room Phones
Bar and Restaurant
Free Parking for Our Customers

WHY STAY IN ANCHORAGE?
Play & Stay in Whittier!
Save Drive Time and Money

Charters – Sightseeing
Mountain/Glacier Views

Grocery Store • Laundromat
Prince William Sound Tour & Fishing Information

GIFTS & SOUVENIRS!

Toll Free for Reservations: 877-870-8787 • Box 750, Whittier, AK 99693
email: anchjoe@aol.com • website: www.geocities.com/anchor_inn_2000

(Continued from page 516)
violets, mountain heliotrope, lousewort and paintbrush.

S 67.6 A 59.4 Divided highway ends southbound, begins northbound.

S 66.8 A 60.2 Paved double-ended turnout to east.

S 66 A 61 Large gravel turnout to east.

S 65.5 A 61.5 Bridge over Bertha Creek. Turnoff to west for **Bertha Creek USFS Campground**; 12 sites, water, toilets, firepits, table, garbage containers and $10 camping fee.

Near the entrance are 2 small bear-proof food lockers. These are 6-inch-diameter tubes, about 2 feet long, with twist-off caps. ▲

S 65.4 A 61.6 Paved parking area to west.

S 65.2 A 61.8 *Passing lane begins southbound.*

S 64.8 A 62.2 Spokane Creek.

S 64 A 63 Pete's Creek. *Passing lane ends southbound.*

S 63.7 A 63.3 Johnson Pass Trailhead. This is the north trailhead of the 23-mile-long Chugach National Forest trail. Rated easy, this is a good, fairly level, family trail which follows a portion of the Old Iditarod trail which went from Seward to Nome (see **Milepost S 32.6**). Johnson Pass trail leads to **Bench Lake**, which has arctic grayling, and **Johnson Lake**, which has rainbow trout. Both lakes are about halfway in on trail. ⌇

North end of **Sixmile Trail**, an 8-mile-long bike trail along Sixmile Creek's east fork to the Hope Highway Cutoff at **Milepost S 56.7**.

CAUTION: Watch for moose next 4 miles southbound.

S 63.3 A 63.7 Bridge over Granite Creek. Traditional halfway point on highway between Anchorage and Seward.

S 62.9 A 64.1 Granite Creek USFS Campground, 0.8 mile east of highway via good gravel road; 19 sites (some beside creek), water, toilets, dumpsters, tables, firepits,

campground host, $10 camping fee. Scenic setting (meadow and spruce forest) with mountains views. Fishing for small Dolly Varden. Interpretive sign explaining how beetles kill spruce trees. ⌇▲

Begin intermittent passing lanes next 2 miles southbound. End passing lanes northbound.

S 62.5 A 64.5 Bridge over East Fork Sixmile Creek.

S 62 A 65 Class V Whitewater, Inc. river guides depart from here. Pick from 3 different trips ranked class III, IV and V respectively; something for most everyone! All is provided for a warm, comfortable trip paddling the best whitewater runs in Alaska and the closest to Anchorage! Advance reservations required. Call (907) 783-2004, toll-free 1-877-783-2004. www.alaskanrafting.com.
[ADVERTISEMENT]

S 60.3 A 66.7 Silvertip Creek (sign).

S 60.2 A 66.8 Physical Milepost 61 was located here in 2002.

S 60 A 67 *Begin intermittent passing lanes*

Several outfitters offer whitewater trips on Sixmile Creek.
(© Ron Niebrugge)

next 2 miles northbound. End passing lanes southbound.

S 59 A 68 Paved parking area to west with interpretive sign about moose. Staging area for raft trips on **Sixmile Creek** to take-out near Sunrise on the Hope Highway. Excellent place to photograph this glacial stream. The Sixmile bike trail and walking path leads south to the Hope Highway junction and north to Johnson Pass trailhead.

Chugach Outdoor Center features Alaska's best whitewater rafting, with Class IV and V whitewater on Six Mile Creek. Scenic floats are also available. Whitewater drysuits for all guests and a hot tub for after the trip. Office and lodge located at Mile 7.5 Hope Highway. Phone (866) 277-7238 toll-free. Web: www.chugachoutdoorcenter.com. Email: info@chugachoutdoorcenter.com.
[ADVERTISEMENT]

S 58.5 A 68.5 Double-ended turnout on old highway alignment to west;

S 57.7 A 69.3 Scenic viewpoint; parking area. Steep climb down through trees overlooks Sixmile Creek canyon. Access to Sixmile Trail (bike trail).

S 56.8 A 70.2 Rest area (parking, toilets) and trailhead to east. Access to bike trail.

Distance marker southbound shows Seward 54 miles, Homer 150 miles.

Distance marker northbound shows Whittier 33 miles, Girdwood 33 miles, Anchorage 70 miles.

S 56.7 A 70.3 Canyon Creek Rest Area to west with large parking area and restrooms overlooks confluence of Canyon and Sixmile creeks; interpretive signs, access to Sixmile Trail (bike trail).

S 56.5 A 70.5 Canyon Creek bridge.

S 56.3 A 70.7 Hope Cutoff. Southbound turn lane for Hope Highway. Rest area and access to Sixmile Trail (bike trail) at Mile 0.1 Hope Highway. **Emergency phone** at Mile 0.2 Hope Highway.

Junction with Hope Highway to historic community of Hope. See "Hope Highway" log pages 521-523.

S 56.2 A 70.8 *Begin intermittent passing lanes southbound as highway climbs to Summit Lake.*

Distance marker southbound shows Seward 54 miles, Homer 150 miles.

S 55.3 A 71.7 Scenic viewpoint (shoulder parking) east side of highway.

S 54.8 A 72.2 Large paved parking area to east.

S 53.5 A 73.5 Parking area to east with Gold Rush Centennial signs about hydraulic mining and Wible's mining camp on Canyon Creek (excerpt follows):

"California engineer and banker Simon Wible had a relapse of gold fever and came to Alaska in 1898 when he was 67 years old. He introduced hydraulic mining in this area. His largest mine was just across Canyon Creek from this spot.

"Hydraulic mining used water under pressure to blast away entire hills and push gold-bearing gravel into sluice boxes that trapped the gold. The technology of hydraulics created an efficient but high impact method of mining."

S 52.7 A 74.3 Large parking area to east.

S 52.4 A 74.6 Slow vehicle turnout at parking area to east.

S 51.4 A 75.6 Scenic viewpoint to east.

S 50.5 A 76.5 Scenic viewpoint to east.

Begin 7 percent downgrade northbound.

S 50.2 A 76.8 *Begin 0.4 mile passing lane northbound.*

S 49.8 A 77.2 End avalanche area northbound.

S 48 A 79 Paved double-ended parking area to east.

S 47.7 A 79.3 Double-ended parking area to east at north end of Lower Summit Lake.

S 47.2 A 79.8 Slow vehicle turnout for northbound traffic at doubled-ended parking area to east at south end of Lower Summit Lake. A favorite photo stop. Extremely picturesque with lush growth of wildflowers in summer.

Upper and Lower Summit lakes, good spring and fall fishing for landlocked Dolly Varden (goldenfins). ⌇

S 46.7 A 80.3 Sign northbound reads: Delay of 5 vehicles illegal, must use turnouts.

S 46 A 81 Colorado Creek bridge. Turnoff to east at south end of bridge for **Tenderfoot Creek USFS Campground** 0.6 mile from highway via good gravel road. There are

27 sites (some pull-throughs) located along a loop road on the east side of Upper Summit Lake; campground host, water, toilets (wheelchair accessible), dumpsters, tables, firepits, boat launch, $10 camping fee. Scenic spot. Lake fishing for dollies and rainbow. ♿▲⌇

S 45.8 A 81.2 Summit Lake Lodge east side of highway; open year-round. Winter avalanche area begins southbound.

(Continues on page 524)

Hope Highway

The paved 17.8-mile Hope Highway leads northwest from **Milepost S 56.7** on the Seward Highway to the historic community of Hope on the south side of Turnagain Arm and provides access to the Resurrection Creek area. This is a good 2-lane road posted 50 mph speed limit with 35- to 40-mph curves.

There are a number of scenic highlights along this road, and Hope itself makes a good 1- or 2-day trip from Anchorage. There is a gas station at Mile 17.8 Hope Highway, but it is a good idea to fill up on the Seward Highway (nearest gas stop is at the Girdwood turnoff). **Distance is measured from junction with the Seward Highway (J).**

J 0 Junction with Seward Highway at **Milepost S 56.7**.

J 0.1 Rest area with outhouse, parking and access to Canyon Creek pedestrian bridge. This is the south end of the Sixmile Trail, an 8-mile-long bike trail along Sixmile Creek's east fork to the Johnson Pass trailhead at **Milepost S 63.7** Seward Highway.

J 0.2 Silvertip highway maintenance station. **Emergency phone.**

J 0.7 Double-ended turnout to east.

J 2.3 Turnout to east with mountain view.

J 3.4 Turnout to east. Narrow, bumpy, dirt track leads to informal campsite.

J 3.6 Dirt turnout to east.

J 3.9 Turnout to east.

J 5.8 Small dirt turnout to east.

J 7.5 Chugach Outdoor Center, Inc. See display ad this section.

J 8.1 Angle 45 Adventures. See display ad this section.

Mountain scenery surrounds the community of Hope at the end of the Hope Highway. (© Kris Graef, staff)

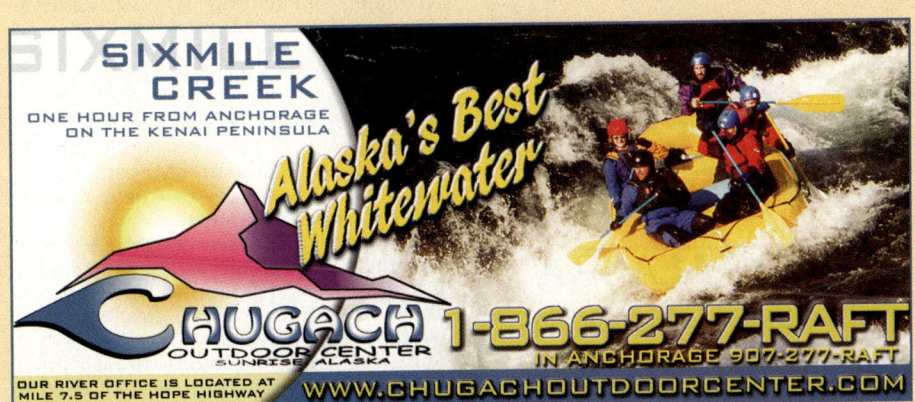

SEWARD HIGHWAY • Hope Highway

Hope Highway Log (continued)

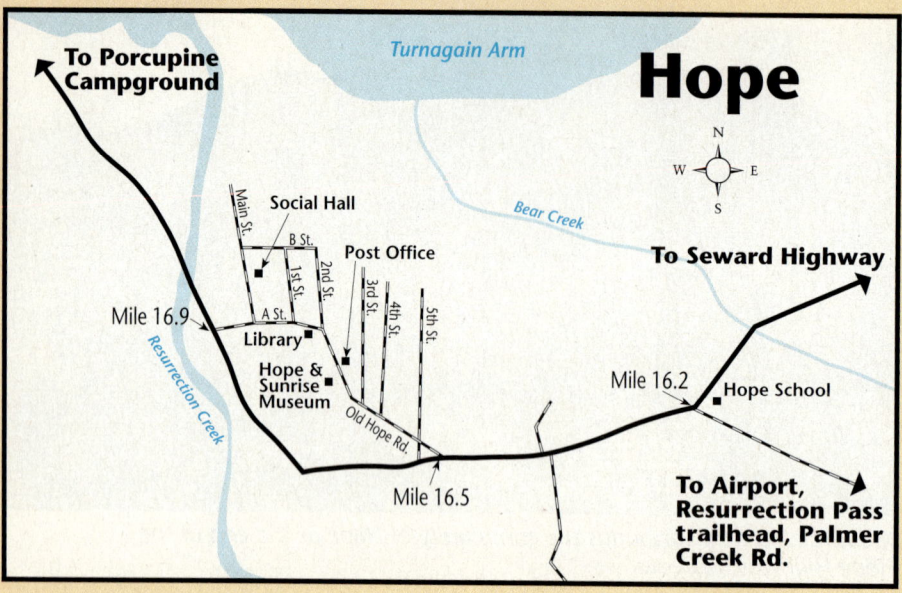

Gull Rock trailhead is located at Porcupine USFS Campground.
(© Kris Graef, staff)

J 10.2 Double-ended turnout to east with view of Turnagain Arm through trees.
J 11.3 Large paved turnout to east with view of Turnagain Arm.
J 11.9 Double-ended turnout to east overlooking Turnagain Arm.
J 13 Narrow dirt track loops down to scenic cove on Turnagain Arm; suitable for small cars.
J 15 *Begin 35 mph speed zone: Slow down for access to Hope businesses. Watch for pedestrians.*
J 15.8 Motel, campground and grocery.
Henry's One Stop. See display ad this section. ▲
J 15.9 Rental cabins and cafe.
Bear Creek Lodge and Cafe. See display ad this section.
J 16 Resurrection Creek.
J 16.2 Junction with Palmer Creek Road.

Turnoff to south for Hope School, Discovery Cabins (take first left on Nearhouse Lane, then right on Discovery Drive), Hope airport (1.7 miles from highway) and USFS Resurrection Pass trailhead (4 miles from highway). Descriptions follow.

Discovery Cabins. See display ad this section.

Palmer Creek Road becomes a winding gravel road (with narrow sections and soft shoulders) 0.6 mile south of the Hope Highway. It leads 6.4 miles to **Coeur d'Alene USFS Campground**; 6 tent sites, toilets, tables, firepits; no water, no garbage service, no camping fee. Palmer Creek Road continues past the campground to alpine country above 1,500 feet elevation; great views and wildflowers in summer (although snow can remain at higher elevations through June). The road past the campground is subject to closure. It is rough and narrow and recom-

522 ■ The MILEPOST® 2003

www.themilepost.com

mended for mountain bikes or ATVs only. ▲

For the **Resurrection Pass Trailhead**, drive 0.6 mile south from Hope Highway and turn on Resurrection Creek Road, then follow good gravel road 3.4 miles to the trailhead parking. This 38-mile-long trail climbs from an elevation of 400 feet at the trailhead to Resurrection Pass at 2,600 feet, then down to the south trailhead at **Milepost S 53.1** on the Sterling Highway. There are 8 public-use cabins along the trail.

J 16.5 First turnoff northbound for Hope via gravel loop road (description follows; also see map). Tito's cafe at turnoff.

Tito's Discovery Cafe. See display ad this section.

HOPE (pop. 130) has a post office, library and museum; cafes, lodging and camping here and along the highway starting at **Milepost J 15.9**. **Visitor Information:** Hope Chamber of Commerce, P.O. Box 89, Hope, AK 99605, www.advenalaska.com/hope.

Private aircraft: State-owned airstrip 1 SE; elev. 200 feet; length 2,000 feet; gravel.

This picturesque community at the end of the Hope Highway on Turnagain Arm was a frenzy of gold rush activity in 1896. Miners named their mining camp on Resurrection Creek Hope City, after 17-year-old prospector Percy Hope. But the gold rush here was short-lived. By 1899, many of the miners had joined the gold rush to the Klondike. Hope City persisted, and it is now the best preserved gold rush community in south-central Alaska. Hope's historic district, just off the paved highway, includes the 1896 store (now a cafe) and the 1902 log Social Hall, which still hosts community events.

Today, Hope is a quiet oasis popular with hikers, campers, bicyclists, fishermen, bird watchers and recreational gold miners.

Hope GoldRush B&B. Next right past post office. Enjoy delicious Alaska berry

pancakes along with the pioneer ambiance of this historic log cabin built by gold

Historic Hope Social Hall is still used to host local events. (© Kris Graef, staff)

prospector John Hirshey in 1916. The charming guest cabin provides a living room, full bath, sleeping accommodations. This is the Alaska you hoped to find. MasterCard/VISA accepted. P.O. Box 36, Hope, AK 99605. Phone (907) 782-3436. www.advenalaska.com/hope. Email: fayrene@alaska.net. [ADVERTISEMENT]

J 16.9 Second turnoff northbound for Hope via gravel loop road. Access to Seaview Cafe and campground.

Seaview Cafe and Bar. See display ad this section.

J 17 Resurrection Creek bridge.

J 17.8 Gas station. Hope Highway ends. An 0.8-mile loop road leads through **Porcupine USFS Campground** providing access to campsites, 2 overlooks with picnic tables, and 2 trailheads. This is a very pleasant campground set in lush vegetation with a few sites overlooking Turnagain Arm. There are 24 sites, tables, tent spaces, campground host, outhouses, firepits, dumpster, drinking water and $10 camping fee. Hope Point Trailhead is located near campground entrance. ▲

Trailhead parking for the 5-mile **Gull Rock Trail** is located about midway on the campground loop road. Rated easy, this is a relatively flat trail through lush vegetation that ends at Gull Rock overlooking Turnagain Arm. Allow 2- to 3-hours to hike one way. Trail has lots of tree roots and some muddy spots.

**Return to Milepost S 56.7
Seward Highway**

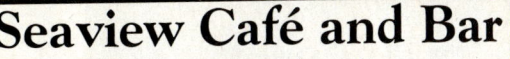

Seaview Café and Bar
RV Park • Campground • Cabins

Join us at the end of the road on Main Street in historic Hope. RV Park, campground, and cabins located where Resurrection Creek meets Turnagain Arm. Spectacular views. Enjoy excellent food and atmosphere in our century-old café and bar, or on our spacious sun deck. Fish for salmon and pan for gold!

website: www.home.gci.net/~hopeak
email: aussiealaska@hotmail.com
tel: 907-782-3300   fax: 907-782-3344
P.O. Box 110 Hope, Alaska 99605

Alexander King discovered gold in about 1890 on Resurrection Creek.

SEWARD HIGHWAY

(Continued from page 520)
Avalanche gates. **Emergency phone.**

Summit Lake Lodge. Genuine hospitality on the north shore of Summit Lake in Alaska's most beautiful log lodge. Located in the heart of Chugach National Forest, it is a

landmark for many. The view is spectacular and the food excellent. Complete menu from eye-opening omelettes to mouth-watering steaks. Enjoy our cozy motel and relaxing lounge. Open year-round. Fishing, hiking, photography, cross-country skiing, snowmobiling. It's a must stop for every visitor in the last frontier. Phone (907) 244-2031. See display ad this section. [ADVERTISEMENT]

S 45.5 A 81.5 Turnout to east overlooking Upper Summit Lake.

S 44.5 A 82.5 Large double-ended turnout with interpretive sign to east at end of Upper Summit Lake.

S 44 A 83 Gravel turnout to east. Avalanche gun emplacement.

S 43.8 A 83.2 Winter avalanche area begins northbound. Avalanche gates.

S 43.7 A 83.3 Paved double-ended turnout to east.

S 42.6 A 84.4 **Summit Creek.** Summit Creek trail to Resurrection Pass.
End passing lane northbound.

S 42.2 A 84.8 Quartz Creek (sign).

S 41.4 A 85.6 *Begin passing lane northbound.*

S 39.6 A 87.4 Avalanche gates. *Begin 55mph speed zone southbound.*

S 39.4 A 87.6 **Devils Pass Trail**; trailhead parking to west; toilets. This 10-mile USFS trail (rated more difficult) starts at an elevation of 1,000 feet and follows Devils Creek to Devils Pass (elev. 2,400 feet), continuing on to Devils Pass Lake and Resurrection Pass trail. Hiking time to Devils Pass is 5 to 6 hours.

S 39 A 88 *Begin 0.3 mile passing lane northbound.*

S 38.6 A 88.4 Small paved turnout overlooking Jerome Lake.

S 38.4 A 88.6 Paved double-ended Scenic Byway turnout to west adjacent **Jerome Lake**; interpretive signs and public fishing access. Lake is stocked; rainbow and Dolly Varden to 22 inches, use salmon egg clusters, year-round, still fish.

S 38.2 A 88.8 *Truck lane ends northbound.*

S 37.7 A 89.3 Southbound-only exit for Sterling Highway (Alaska Route 1) to west. Continue straight ahead on Alaska Route 9 for Seward.

First **junction** southbound with Sterling Highway to Soldotna, Homer and other Sterling Highway communities. Turn to **Milepost S 38.3** on page 550 in the STERLING HIGHWAY for log.

S 37.2 A 89.8 Paved double-ended turnout to west overlooks Tern Lake. Access to Tern Lake viewing platform is the Sterling Highway; use Tern Lake Junction turnoff (next turnoff southbound).

S 37 A 90 **Tern Lake Junction.** Turnoff to west (2-way traffic) on Sterling Highway for access to Tern Lake and **Tern Lake USFS Wildlife Viewing Platform.** Interpretive signs and ranger talks in summer. This is a good spot to see nesting birds, mountain goats, sheep and occasionally moose and bear. Continue around the lake to the Tern Lake picnic area; walk-in picnic sites with water, tables, toilets and fire grates. Salmon-spawning channel with a viewing platform and interpretive signs. Tern Lake is a prime bird-watching area in summer. ▲

Second turnoff southbound and first **junction** northbound of the Seward Highway with the Sterling Highway (Alaska Route 1) to Soldotna, Kenai and Homer. Turn to **Milepost S 37** on page 550 in the STERLING HIGHWAY section for log.

Seward-bound travelers continue straight ahead southbound on Alaska Route 9 for Seward (continue with this log).

ALASKA ROUTE 9

S 36.5 A 90.5 Distance marker southbound shows Moose Pass 7 miles, Seward 34 miles.

S 36.4 A 90.6 Avalanche gates.

S 35.8 A 91.2 Peak Anteak shop to west.

Peak Anteak. "Rejuvenated Teak and Hand-crafted Home Furnishings" is a quaint shop you won't want to miss on your travels to the Kenai Peninsula. Favored by visitors and locals alike, you'll find a wonderful selection of high quality merchandise from local artisans as well as craftsmen worldwide, that is seldom found elsewhere. The delightful, eye-catching designs are presented in a warm, welcoming way and customers soon find themselves charmed by the relaxing atmosphere, leaving behind the rush of the busy world around them. Peak Anteak is

proud to offer one-of-a-kind rustic, old-growth teak furniture that is imaginatively designed using teak wood ranging in age from 50 to approximately 1,400 years old (as seen on the Fox/Lifetime 7-episode television series: "Bachelorettes in Alaska," which aired in May of 2002). By using only recycled wood in the creations, the artist is helping to keep in our memory the beauy of the majestic, old-growth teak forests that once covered many mountain ranges throughout the world, but are now almost extinct. This pleasingly unique shop draws those seeking quality and authenticity and whose taste for the unusual surpasses their interest in the common souvenirs of Alaska. All major credit cards accepted. Your purchases graciously shipped worldwide. There is plenty of off-street parking for cars and motorhomes in this picturesque, park-like setting. Open year-round. Summer hours: 8 A.M.–9 P.M., 7 days a week. Fall hours, (which begin after Labor Day and continue until new Year's): 9 A.M.–8 P.M., Wednesday through Monday (closed Tuesday). Winter hours (January through March): 9 A.M.–5 P.M., Thursday through Monday (closed Tuesday and Wednesday). Peak Anteak is closed on Thanksgiving, Christmas and New Year's. Phone (907) 288-5644. Email: peakanteak@seward.net. Web site: www.peakanteak.com. Mailing address: P.O. Box 21, Moose Pass, AK 99631. See display ad this section. [ADVERTISEMENT]

S 33.1 A 93.9 Carter Lake USFS trailhead No. 4 to west; parking and toilets. Trail starts at an elevation of 500 feet and climbs 986 feet to **Carter Lake** (stocked with rainbow trout). Trail is 3.5 miles long, good, but steep; rated more difficult with a hiking time of 2 hours. Good access to sheep and mountain goat country. Excellent snowmobiling area in winter.

S 32.6 A 94.4 Johnson Pass USFS south trailhead with parking area, toilet. North trailhead at **Milepost S 63.7**.

S 32.5 A 94.5 Large paved double-ended turnout to west; USFS information sign on life cycle of salmon; short trail to observation deck on stream where spawning salmon may be seen in August.

S 32.4 A 94.6 Cook Inlet Aquaculture Association. **Trail Lake Fish Hatchery** on Moose Creek; display room. Open 8 A.M. to 5 P.M. daily; phone (907) 288-3688.

S 31.8 A 95.2 Paved double-ended rest area to east on Upper Trail Lake; toilets.

S 30.5 A 96.5 *Begin 45 mph speed zone southbound. Resume 55 mph speed limit northbound.*

S 29.9 A 97.1 *Begin 35 mph speed zone southbound. Begin 45 mph speed zone northbound.*

S 29.7 A 97.3 Seward Highway Scenic Byway turnout east side of highway with recreation map, view of Trail Lake.

Moose Pass Inn on west side of highway.

S 29.5 A 97.5 Moose Pass DOT Highway maintenance station. Avalanche phone 478-7675.

S 29.4 A 97.6 Estes Brothers Grocery and waterwheel west side of highway. Trail Lake Lodge (motel and restaurant) to east at turnoff to loop road which leads past Moose Pass school to post office. See "Moose Pass" description on this page.

Estes Brothers Grocery & Waterwheel. Drive slowly into our little town. Next to the highway is a unique country store where you can see and learn about Moose Pass history, and isn't this why you came to Alaska? Here is the original country store from "back

Moose Pass

Moose Pass (pop. 118) has food, lodging, camping, a general store, post office and

highway maintenance station. Pay phone located at Moose Pass Community Hall. *Emergency phone* at Alaska State Troopers.

This mountain village on Upper Trail Lake was a construction camp on the Alaska Railroad in 1912. Local resident Ed Estes attributed the name Moose Pass to a 1904 observation by Nate White of the first moose recorded in this area. Another version holds that "in 1903, a mail carrier driving a team of dogs had considerable trouble gaining the right-of-way from a giant moose." A post office was established in 1928 and first postmistress Leora (Estes) Roycroft officially named the town Moose Pass.

Moose Pass has a 1.3-mile-long paved bike trail which winds along Trail Lake from the Moose Pass ball diamond to the McFadden house on the south. Gravel turnout by lake.

MOOSE PASS ADVERTISERS

Crown Point Lodge...........Ph. (907) 288-3136
Estes Brothers Groceries &
   Water Wheel...............Ph. (907) 288-3151
Midnight Sun Log Cabins Ph. (907) 288-3627
Moose Pass RV Park &
   Campground ....Ph. (907) 288-5624
Trail Lake Lodge ....Ph. (907) 288-3101

The main street of town is the site of the Annual Moose Pass Summer Festival, a community-sponsored event which takes place the weekend nearest summer solstice (June 21). The festival features a triathlon, arts and crafts booths, a barbecue, auction and other events.

The large working waterwheel on the west side of the road was built by the late Ed Estes. It is a replica of the peltonwheel hydroelectric plant built by the Estes family in 1927 to power their sawmill. Rebuilt in 1976 by Ed Estes using an 18-inch pipeline from a lake up on the hillside, the peltonwheel generator still generates power to the grocery store in town. There is a parking area at the waterwheel replica and a sign which reads: "Moose Pass is a peaceful little town. If you have an ax to grind, do it here."

**Return to Milepost S 29.4
Seward Highway**

Midnight Sun Log Cabins
Each cabin is fully modern   Mile 28.9
and completely hand built.
Fridge, Microwave, Coffee, T.V.
Phone (907) 288-3627
P.O. Box 102, Moose Pass, AK 99631
www.midnightsunlogcabins.com

Estes Brothers Groceries & WaterWheel
THE SAME STORE THAT SUPPLIED THE MINERS DURING THE GOLD RUSH
Scooped Ice Cream • Snacks • Groceries • Souvenirs • Hunting, Fishing
Licenses • Espresso • Deli • Historic Photo Gallery • Visitor Information

Moose Pass is a peaceful town.
If you have an "ax to grind," do it here.

estesbros@seward.net • www.moosepass.net

288-3151

Birdhouse gable catches the eye in Moose Pass. (© Ralph & Leonor Barrett)

home," with groceries, espresso, ice cream, deli-sandwiches, souvenirs. Visit the information center, see historic photos and artifacts. The historic waterwheel is a duplicate of the one Ed Estes' stepfather, Frank Roycroft, built for him in 1928. It was refurbished in 2001 by Ed's family and friends ... so the big wheel keeps a-turnin'. It's a must stop. (907) 288-3151. www.moosepass.net. See display ad this section. [ADVERTISEMENT]

Trail Lake Lodge. AAA approved. Originally established in the late 1940s, the lodge now boasts a recently redecorated restaurant and bar, 22 rooms with private baths, floatplane dock and a reputation as "the place to stop." Easy access from the highway, plenty of parking space for big-rigs or fly-in by floatplane to our dock. The one-of-a-kind heated lakeside pavilion is a memory making site for your family or group event. Fabulous scenery surrounds you. Full service lounge and restaurant featuring their signature clam chowder, steaks, pasta, seafood and award-winning, homemade pies. Fjord tour bookings, river rafting excursions arranged on request. Fabulous flightseeing from Moose Pass and excellent hiking and cross-country skiing trails in immediate vicinity. Ideal snowmobile "base camp." Group rates. Open year-round. (907) 288-3101. www.traillakelodge.com. See display ad this section. [ADVERTISEMENT]

S 29.2 A 97.8 Turnoff for Moose Pass post office.

S 28.9 A 98.1 Midnight Sun Log Cabins. See display ad this section.

S 28.8 A 98.2 Moose Pass RV Park & Campground. 30 spaces, 8 pull-throughs. Electric hookups. Scenic, wooded, well-maintained, quiet, secure campground/RV park. Close to restaurant, post office, small store, telephone. Rural area in beautiful surroundings. Convenient to Seward, but away from the crowds. Just off main highway. Email access in office. (907) 288-5624, (907) 288 5682. Email: moosepassrvpark@yahoo.com. [ADVERTISEMENT]

S 28.5 A 98.5 *Begin 35 mph speed zone northbound. Begin 44 mph speed zone southbound.*

S 28.3 A 98.7 Moose Pass (sign) northbound.

S 27.4 A 99.6 *Begin 45 mph speed zone northbound. Resume 55 mph speed limit southbound.*

S 25.7 A 101.3 Gravel shoulder parking to west. Lower Trail Lake east side of highway. Timbered slopes of Madson Mountain (elev. 5,269 feet) to the west. Crescent Lake lies just west of Madson. Grant Lake lies just east of Lower Trail Lake.

S 25.4 A 101.6 Bridge over Trail River. Trail to Vagt Lake to east at south end of bridge.

S 25 A 102 Bridge over Falls Creek.

S 24.5 A 102.5 Trail River Gardens B&B to west.

S 24.2 A 102.8 Side road leads 1.2 miles to **Trail River USFS Campground**; 64 sites, picnic tables, firepits, dumpsters, toilets, and volleyball and horseshoe area. Group camping area (12 sites) with pavilion; reservations available. Group day-use picnic area. Spacious, wooded campsites in tall spruce on shore of Kenai Lake and Lower Trail River. Pull-through sites available. Fee $10 single, $18 double. Reservations available by phone (1-877-444-6777) or online (www.reserveusa.com). Campground host may be in residence during summer, providing fishing and hiking information. Good spot for mushrooming and berry picking in August.

Lower Trail River, lake trout, rainbow and Dolly Varden, July, August and September, small spinners. Access via Lower Trail River campground road. **Trail River**, Dolly Varden and rainbow. Closed to fishing mid-April to mid-June; use of bait prohibited year-round.

S 24.1 A 102.9 Crown Point Lodge. Special: All lodging includes full breakfast! Homemade breads, soups, desserts and more for breakfast, lunch and dinner. Ask for Jackie's fabulous French toast. Affordable packages for lodging, meals, charters. Clean comfortable rooms at moderate cost. Dormitory-style room sleeps 8. Circular drive, plenty of parking for big rigs. Phone (907) 288-3136. Fax (907) 288-3641. [ADVERTISEMENT]

S 23.4 A 103.6 CAUTION: Railroad crossing. USFS Kenai Lake work center (no information services available). Report forest fires here.

Private Aircraft: Lawing landing strip; elev. 475 feet; length 2,200 feet; gravel; unattended.

S 23.3 A 103.7 Ptarmigan Creek bridge and USFS picnic area and campground with 16 sites, water, toilets, tables, firepits and dumpsters, $10 fee (reservations phone 1-877-444-NRRS). Fair to good fishing in creek and in lake outlets at **Ptarmigan Lake** (hike in) for Dolly Varden. Watch for spawning salmon in Ptarmigan Creek in August.

Ptarmigan Creek USFS trail begins at campground (elev. 500 feet) and leads 3.5 miles to Ptarmigan Lake (elev. 755 feet). Trail is steep in spots; round-trip hiking time 5 hours. Good chance of seeing sheep, goats, moose and bears. Carry insect repellent. Trail is poor for winter use due to avalanche hazard.

S 22.6 A 104.4 Paved scenic viewpoint to west overlooking Kenai Lake. This lake (elev. 436 feet) extends 24 miles from the head of the Kenai River on the west to the mouth of Snow River on the east. A sign here explains how glacier meltwater gives the lake its distinctive color.

Winter avalanche area next 3 miles southbound.

S 22.4 A 104.6 Rough gravel double-ended turnout to east.

S 21.8 A 21.2 Gravel turnout to west with view of Kenai Lake.

S 21.4 A 105.6 Gravel turnout to west overlooking Kenai Lake.

S 19.5 A 107.5 Victor Creek bridge. Victor Creek USFS trail No. 23 on north side of bridge is a 2-mile hike with good view of mountains.

S 19.4 A 107.6 Renfro's Lakeside Retreat. Log cabins and RV spaces on Kenai Lake. Breath-taking scenery, surrounded by mountains and lake. Fully furnished with baths and kitchenettes. Comfortably sleeps 5. Pedal boats, playhouse, basketball goal, horseshoe pit! RV sites not on lake, but easy access. Each site has water, electricity. Toll free (877) 288-5059. www.sewardalaska.com/renfros. Email renfros@seward.net. [ADVERTISEMENT]

S 17.5 A 109.5 Bridge over center channel of Snow River. This river has 2 forks that flow into Kenai Lake.

Begin improved highway southbound.

S 17 A 110 Distance marker northbound shows Kenai 68 miles, Homer 151 miles, Anchorage 110 miles.

A 16.9 A 110.1 Primrose Spur Road. Turn west for **Primrose USFS Campground**, 1 mile from the highway. (Campground access road leads past private homes. Drive carefully!) The campground, overlooking Kenai Lake, has 10 sites, toilets, dumpsters, tables, firepits, boat ramp, water, $10 fee. Jet skis are permitted in limited areas of Kenai Lake. Primrose trail (6.5 miles) starts from the campground and connects with Lost Creek trail (7 miles). High alpine hike to **Lost Lake**, rainbow fishing (stocked); trail is posted.

Bridge over south channel of Snow River.

Begin passing lane southbound.

S 16.6 A 110.4 Distance marker southbound shows Seward 17 miles.

S 15.9 A 111.1 Snow River Hostel.

S 15.8 A 111.2 *End passing lane southbound.*

S 15.5 A 111.5 Large gravel turnout to east.

Lily Pad Lake at Milepost S 14.6 Seward Highway. (© Kris Graef, staff)

access to Winterset Guest House and Stoney Creek RV Park.

0.2 Winterset Guest House. First-class accommodations at $90/DO. Land's End down comforters on all our beds and quality mattresses for a good night's sleep. Hearty continental breakfast buffet. All rooms have private baths, cable TV. Laundry facilities, refrigerator, microwave, phone, coffee maker available to guests. Open year-round. (Discounted winter rates.) Smoke-free environment, wooded area with great mountain view. We will assist you with all your activity plans and book Fjord tours, fishing charters at discounted prices. Long-time Alaskan hosts. (907) 224-5185; www.wintersetguest house.com; email: winter set@seward.net. [ADVERTISEMENT]

S 14.6 A 112.4 Paved parking at boardwalk viewpoint overlooking **Lily Pad Lake** to east. Watch for moose in lake.

S 13.4 A 113.6 *Begin passing lane southbound.*

S 13.2 A 113.8 Large paved parking area to east.

Grayling Lake USFS trailhead parking to west; outhouse. Grayling Lake trail is rated easy. Allow 1 hour for the 2-mile hike. It connects with trails to Meridian and Leech lakes. Good spot for photos of Snow River valley. Watch for moose. **Grayling Lake,** 6- to 12-inch grayling, use flies, May to October.

S 12.3 A 114.7 Scenic viewpoint to east with interpretive signs on Chugach culture and the Native Claims Settlement Act.

S 12 A 115 *End passing lane northbound.*

S 11.6 A 115.4 Golden Fin Lake USFS trailhead parking to west; outhouse. This is a 0.6-mile hike on a very wet trail: wear rubber footwear. Fishing at Golden Fin Lake for Dolly Varden averaging 8 inches. Ski trails in winter.

S 10.8 A 116.2 Large paved turnout to east.

S 8.8 A 118.2 *Begin passing lane northbound.*

S 8.2 A 118.8 Turnout to east; leaving Chugach National Forest (sign) southbound.

S 8 A 119 Grouse Creek culvert (sign southbound).

End improved highway southbound. Watch for road construction next 8 miles southbound in summer 2003. Expect reduced speed limits, detours and minor delays during construction.

Begin improved highway northbound.

S 6.6 A 120.4 Bear Lake Road. Access to gas station and A Creekside RV Park at turnoff; 0.4 mile to Bear Creek RV Park; and 0.7 mile to state-operated fish weir.

A Creekside RV Park & Bear Creek Super Service Station. The only park in Seward to provide RV repair services at your site. Tire repair and sales, propane, refrigeration service, full service gas station, convenience store and drive-through espresso. 20-30-50-amp service. Partial hookups with free dump station for guests. Free showers for first 3 occupants. Look for the red and yellow sign at Bear Creek Road. Enjoy trout fishing and watch spawning salmon from the creek banks or arched footbridge. Check in at Bear Creek Super Service office cabin, on the right across the tracks. New owners Paul, Tammy and Cory invite you to experience old-fashioned hospitality. Email: bearcreeksuperservice@yahoo.com. 1-877-613-3647. See display ad this section.

Bear Creek RV Park, drive 1/2 mile on Bear Lake Road. Family-owned and operated Good Sam Park offers complimentary continental breakfast, full and partial hookups, dump station, private restrooms with showers, cable TV, travelers lounge, propane, laundry, convenience store, ice, video rentals. Pay phone inside. Excellent water. (907) 224-5725. Fax/e-mail service available. Free shuttle June–August when reservations are booked through our office for Kenai Fjords Tours. Fishing charter bookings available. RV and boat storage. Short walk to fish weir. Bear Creek RV Park is not to be mistaken for A Creekside RV Park or Bear Creek Super Service located at the gas station on the corner of the Seward Highway and Bear Lake Road. 1-877-924-5725; email hettick@ptialaska.net; www.bearcreekrv.com. See display ad this section. [ADVERTISEMENT] ▲

S 6.5 A 120.5 Bear Creek bridge. *Bridge widening scheduled for summer 2003.*

S 6.3 A 120.7 Stoney Creek Avenue;

Exit Glacier Road

Exit Glacier Salmon Bake & Cabins
Fresh Alaskan Salmon - Halibut - Steak - Burgers
• Full Service Restaurant
• Beer & Wine Pub • Fireplace
Hours: 12pm - 9pm • 1/4 Mile Exit Glacier Rd.
VISA **(907) 224-2204** MasterCard

CLEAR CREEK COTTAGE
.5 MILE OLD EXIT GLACIER ROAD
• FULL KITCHEN/BATH • 7 min. to HARBOR/DOWNTOWN
• PRIVATE • WOODED SETTING • 20 min. TO GLACIER
888-586-8420 • (907) 224-3968 • PO Box 241 Seward AK 99664
www.auroracharters.com • see log ad in seward lodging

First Class Fishing & Sightseeing Adventures
Fish for halibut, salmon, rockfish, shark and lingcod on our 34 ft. custom-built sportfisher.
5 Star USGS safety rating.
RESERVATIONS 907-227-3151
email: young@ptialaska.net
www.glaciersedge.net
PO Box 772442
Eagle River, AK 99577
GLACIER'S EDGE Sportfishing Charters, Inc

Box Canyon Cabins
Luxury Cabins
Sleeps up to 6
Private Baths * Phones * Kitchens
31515 Lois Way, Seward, AK 99664
(off of Old Exit Glacier Road)
Mailing: PO Box 1662, Seward, AK 99664
907-224-5046
www.boxcanyoncabin.com
Email: young@ptialaska.net • fax 694-5074

River Valley Cabins
6 Cabins with Private Bath, Phone, Fridge, Coffee
1 Large Family Cabin w/Kitchen, Sleeps 6
907-224-5740
www.ptialaska.net/~rvcswd
12672 Old Exit Glacier Road, Seward

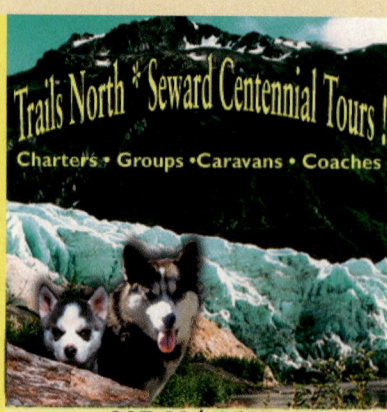

Trails North * Seward Centennial Tours!
Charters • Groups • Caravans • Coaches
907-224-3587
www.ptialaska.net/~tnorth
Email: tnorth@ptialaska.net

Alaska has 2 of North America's largest glaciers—Bering and Malaspina.

To drive out to Exit Glacier, turn west on Exit Glacier Road/Herman Leirer Road from **Milepost S 3.7** Seward Highway. This paved side road leads 8.4 miles to Exit Glacier in Kenai Fjords National Park. It is a worthwhile sidetrip to see this active glacier up close. Lodging and camping are located on Exit Glacier Road/Herman Leirer Road and on Old Exit Glacier Road, which loops off the main access road just west of the Seward Highway (logs for both there roads follow).

EXIT GLACIER ROAD/ HERMAN LEIRER ROAD

Distance from junction (J) with the Seward Highway is shown.

J 0 Junction with the Seward Highway at Milepost S 3.7.

J 0.1 Junction with Old Exit Glacier Road loop (see log following).

J 0.3 Exit Glacier Salmon Bake & Cabins. See display ad this section.

J 0.5 Seward Windsong Lodge.

J 0.7 Resurrection Roadhouse restaurant.

J 1 Fjords R.V. Park. Nestled in towering trees at Mile 1 of Herman Leirer Road, Gateway to Kenai Fjords National Park, on the

way to Exit Glacier. Seward's most beautiful RV park. Look for signs. Entrance is on the right. Large open sites with water and electric hookups. Easy access. www.fjordsrv.com. (907) 224-9134. [ADVERTISEMENT] ▲

J 1.2 Large parking area to south.

J 1.3 Junction with Old Exit Glacier Road loop (see log following).

J 1.4 Kenai Fjords National Park (sign). Winter gates; no maintenance beyond this point Nov. 1 to May 1. In winter, the road is closed to vehicle traffic beyond here for use by skiers, snow machines and mushers.

Entering the State of Alaska **Exit Glacier Road Special Use Area** westbound. Managed by the Dept. of Natural Resources, guidelines for this special use area allow recreational tent or RV camping for up to 8 days at designated pullouts the next 2.2 miles; pack out waste; use outhouses provided.

J 1.5 Informal campsite on gravel river bar.

J 3.2 Informal campsite at access to river.

J 3.6 Chugach National Forest (sign).

J 3.7 Large turnouts both sides of road.

J 3.8 J 6.5 First view from road of Exit Glacier.

J 4.5 Bridge.

J 4.6 Shoulder parking area.

J 5.8 Finger dikes visible on Resurrection River.

J 6.2 Shoulder parking; first view westbound from road of Exit Glacier.

J 6.7 Scenic viewpoint of Exit Glacier.

J 6.9 Trailhead parking for **Resurrection River Trail** (Chugach National Forest). The 16-mile trail ties in with the Russian Lakes trail. It is part of the 75-mile Hope-to-Seward route. *CAUTION: Black and brown bears also use this trail.*

J 7 Resurrection River bridge.

Visitors can walk up to Exit Glacier.
(© Rich Reid, Colors of Nature)

J 7.2 Welcome to Kenai Fjords National Park's Exit Glacier (sign).

J 8.1 Turnoff for walk-in tent campground with 12 sites (no fee, reservations). ▲

J 8.4 Toll booth for **Exit Glacier** (Kenai National Park) and entrance to paved parking areas for automobiles and RVs. Fees are $5 vehicle, $2 individual; $15 annual pass. From parking area, follow paths to handicap-accessible restrooms, picnic area, the ranger station and walking trails to Exit Glacier and Harding Icefield.

Visitor information at the ranger station (seasonal). Summer activities include daily ranger-led nature walks; phone (907) 224-3175. A public-use cabin is available in winter

From the parking lot, it is a flat, easy half-mile walk on a path through alder forest to the glacier's terminus. First 0.3 mile of path is paved and wheelchair accessible to the interpretive shelter. At the glacier's outwash plain, the longer half-mile Upper Loop trail offers excellent views of the glacier. The strenuous 3-mile-long Harding Icefield trail branches off this trail. Return to the parking lot by way of the easy 0.8 mile nature trail loop with its 10 interpretive signs on forest succession. *CAUTION: Falling ice at face of glacier; stay behind warning signs.*

Exit Glacier is 3 miles long and descends some 2,500 feet from the Harding Icefield. Watch for bears on surrounding hillsides.

OLD EXIT GLACIER ROAD

Distance is measured from the east junction (EJ) and west junction (WJ) with Exit Glacier Road.

EJ 0 WJ 1.6 Junction with Exit Glacier Road at Mile 0.1.

EJ 0.3 WJ 1.1 Clear Creek

EJ 0.5 WJ 0.9 Clear Creek Cottage. See display ad this section.

EJ 0.9 WJ 0.7 Turnoff for **Box Canyon Cabins.** See display ad this section.

Glacier's Edge Sportfishing Charters. See display ad this section.

EJ 1 WJ 0.6 River Valley Cabins. See display ad this section.

Trails North, Seward Centennial Tours. See display ad this section.

EJ 1.1 WJ 0.5 IdidaRide Sled Dog Tours.

EJ 1.5 WJ 0.1 Entering Glacier Road Special Use Area; 8-day camping limit.

EJ 1.6 WJ 0 Junction with Exit Glacier Road at Mile 1.3.

Return to Milepost S 3.7 Seward Highway

www.themilepost.com

Stoney Creek RV Park. Seward's newest RV park, built to accommodate travelers who enjoy cleanliness, friendliness, and full utility services at their individual sites, including water, power, sewer, cable TV. We also have clean, hot showers and laundry facilities. Phone, Internet access and shuttle to town available. Please see our display ad map for directions. (We hope to facilitate access with a direct bridge from Stoney Creek Avenue in 2003.) You may email us at info@stoneycreekrvpark.com. Phone (907) 224-4760. www.stoneycreekrvpark.com. See display ad this section. [ADVERTISEMENT] ▲

S 5.9 A 121.1 Salmon Creek bridge. *Bridge widening scheduled for summer 2003.* Good fishing in stream begins Aug. 1st for sea-run Dolly Varden averaging 10 inches; use of bait prohibited Sept. 16–Dec. 31. ◆

S 5.5 A 121.5 AutoTech west side of highway.

AutoTech. This family-owned and operated NAPA Autocare Center employs ASE-certified technicians. AutoTech performs full-service auto and RV repair including wheel alignment. It is an authorized dealer warranty center. Easy access off the Seward Highway for your RV. AutoTech is your best choice for friendly, competent vehicle service in Seward. Phone (907) 224-8667.
[ADVERTISEMENT]

S 5.2 A 122 Turnoff to west for Scout Lake subdivision and access to **Lost Lake USFS Trail.** For trailhead, drive west 0.2 mile and turn left on Heather Lee Lane; drive 0.2 mile and turn right on Hayden Berlin Road; rough and narrow road winds uphill and dead-ends at trailhead.

S 5.1 A 121.9 Bear Creek volunteer fire department. *Emergency phone.*

S 3.8 A 123.2 Clear Creek bridge. *Bridge widening scheduled for summer 2003.*

S 3.7 A 123.3 Turnoff to west for Exit Glacier in Kenai National Park, located 8.4 miles west via Herman Leirer Road. Lodging and attractions are located on Exit Glacier Road and Old Exit Glacier Road. A scenic drive.

> **Junction** with Exit Glacier Road/Herman Leirer Road. See "Exit Glacier" Road" beginning on opposite page.

A 3.5 A 123.5 Distance marker northbound shows Soldotna 91 miles, Anchorage 123 miles, Homer 165 miles.

S 3.2 A 123.8 Nash Road, access to bed and breakfasts. It is a scenic 5-mile drive out Nash Road to **Seward Marine Industrial Center** in the Fourth of July Creek valley. At Mile 2.1 is the trailhead for the Iditarod Trail, which begins at the ferry terminal in downtown Seward: Hike to Bear Lake; from north end of lake, trail continues to Mile 12 on the Seward Highway. Good views between Mile 3.2 and 3.8 on Nash Road of Resurrection Bay and the city of Seward.

The Alaska Native Claims Settlement Act of 1971 created 13 regional Native corporations.

THE FARM
Bed & Breakfast Inn

Choose our Main House, Cottages, Kitchenettes or Economy Bungalow

Continental Breakfast, Private Baths, Cable TV, Decks, BBQ, Laundry Facilities, Freezer Space

(907) 224-5691

Box 305 Seward, AK 99664-0305

www.alaskan.com/thefarm
e-mail: thefarm@ptialaska.net

SEE LOG AD - SEWARD LODGING

The Farm Bed & Breakfast Inn. See display ad this section.

Camelot Cottages. See display ad this section.

Mrs. Clock's B&B/Semaka Charters. See display ad this section.

Fjordland Inn. Nestled in a mountain panorama. Country charm, smoke free, mostly private baths. Private entrance to guest area. Families/groups welcome. Nine comfortable, uniquely decorated rooms. Alaskana originals–prints by owner/artist displayed. Phone (907) 224-3614 or 1-800-785-3614. Fax (907) 224-3615. www.fjordlandinn.com. Email fjordland@gci.net. Hosts Lee and Mary George. Mile 1.7 Nash Road. [ADVERTISEMENT]

S 3 A 124 Resurrection River bridge; first of 3 bridges southbound crossing 3 channels of the river. *(Replacement of these 3 bridges scheduled for summer 2003.)* This river flows from the Harding Icefield into Resurrection Bay just northeast of Seward.

Seward city limits.

S 2.9 A 124.1 Resurrection River bridge No. 2.

S 2.8 A 124.2 Resurrection River bridge No. 3.

S 2.7 A 124.3 Turnoff to east just south of bridge for Seward airport.

Godwin Glacier Dog Sled Tours. See display ad this section.

S 2.5 A 124.5 Hemlock Street. Access to bed and breakfast. Turnoff for municipal camping area just off highway; sites are on gravel loop road in trees, $10 camping fee, campground host, outhouse, no tables, 14-day limit. ▲

Harmony B&B, 3 charming, sparkling clean, cottage-style rooms. Private entrance, private decks and private baths. Fridge,

---

Mrs. Clock's B&B
- Private Baths • Clean As A Whistle
- Hearty Full Breakfast
- Wooded Setting/Salmon Stream ♥

SEMAKA CHARTERS
- Halibut - Cod - Rockfish - Salmon

1-877-224-3195

e-mail: clocksbb@ak.net

CAMELOT COTTAGES
Seward, Alaska

1-800-739-3039
(907)-224-3039

akcabins@alaska.net
www.camelotcottages.com

"Great place! Charming, clean as a whistle and very comfortable. You've thought of everything." —JM

"What a cute place—great flowers!" —HD

Private Cabins • Baths • Kitchens
Hot Tub • Laundry
Cable TV • Affordable Rates

Booking Sightseeing Trips & Fishing Charters on the World Famous Kenai Peninsula!

*see log ad in Seward Lodging

GODWIN GLACIER DOG SLED TOURS
a division of Ultimate Tours, LLC
Seward, Alaska • June-August
CHUGACH NATIONAL FOREST
Helicopter to a Glacier for a Dog Sled Ride!
(907) 224-8239 • (888) 989-8239 • www.alaskadogsled.com

Seward Resort • Alaska
56 Motel Rooms
12 Townhouses
Yurts • RV/Tent Sites
Log Cabin
Discount Tickets & Tours

A fun & affordable retreat for military, retirees, D.O.D. federal employees, their families and guests!

OPEN YEAR ROUND

Fish Charters
Glacier Cruises
Snow Machines
Playground

Reservations: (907) 224-2654/2659/5559
1-800-770-1858, http://www.usarak.army.mil/framwr/seward.htm

microwave, coffee, cable TV. Alaskan decor with handmade quilts. Nestled in quiet neighborhood with mountain views. Minutes from downtown and Small Boat Harbor activities. Freezer space available. Reasonable rates. Multi-night discounts. Open year-round,. Generous continental breakfast. Call Karen Ann for reservations: (907) 224-3661, (907) 491-1535. P.O. Box 3255, Seward, AK 99664. www.seward.net/~kevinc. See display ad in Seward section. [ADVERTISEMENT]

S 2.3 A 124.7 Sea Lion Drive. U.S. Air Force and U.S. Army Seward Recreation Area.

Seward Resort (Military). Hotel, townhouses, RV sites with cable TV, 50-amp electric and water, tent sites and yurts. Charter fishing, Holgate Glacier wildlife boat tour. Winter snowmachine rentals and discount tour and ticket sales. Open year-round. Authorized patrons: active duty military; retirees; National Guard and Reserves; DOD, federal employees families and guests. Phone (800) 770-1858; (907) 224-2659; (907) 224-2654. Internet: http://www.usarak.army.mil/framwr/seward.htm. See display ad this section. [ADVERTISEMENT] ▲

S 2 A 125 Turnoff to east for access to Seward train station. Seward Chamber of Commerce and Convention and Visitors Bureau visitor center west side of highway.

S 1.7 A 125.3 Eagle Center (grocery), Tesoro gas station west side of highway.

S 1.5 A 125.5 Access to ferry terminal via Resurrection Blvd.

S 1.4 A 125.6 Phoenix Road to west. Port Avenue to east, access to cruise ship and ferry dock. Train station to east (access is from **Milepost S 2**).

S 1.3 A 125.7 Dairy Hill Lane to west. Large parking area to west at **Benny Benson Memorial**. Benny Benson designed the Alaska state flag.

S 1.2 A 125.8 North Harbor Street; Texaco gas station.

S 1.1 A 125.9 South Harbor Street; Breeze Inn. Acccess to Seward Small Boat Harbor, Kenai Fjords National Park Visitor Center.

S 0.9 A 126.1 Van Buren Street.

S 0.6 A 126.4 Monroe Street.

S 0.4 A 126.6 Madison Street. Post office one block east. Hostel.

S 0.3 A 126.7 Jefferson Avenue. Information Cache railcar at intersection. Hospital 2 blocks west. Also access to Mount Marathon Trail.

S 0.2 A 126.8 Adams Street; historic downtown Seward.

S 0 A 127 Mile 0 of the Seward Highway (3rd Avenue) at Railway Avenue and Lowell Point Road. Seward Sealife Center. The new Kenai Fjords National park Visitor Center will be located near here.

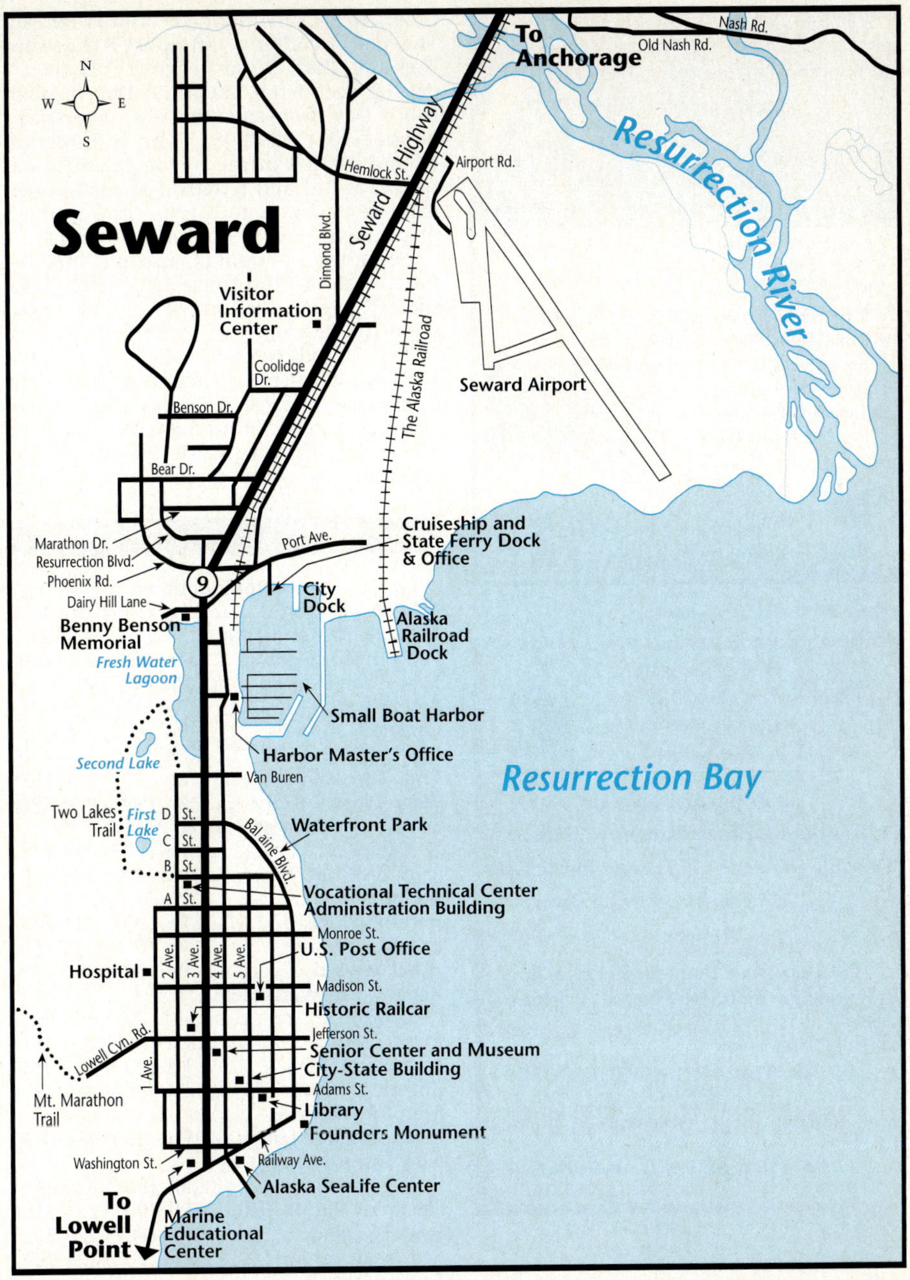

Seward

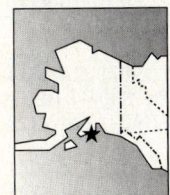

S 0 A 127 Located on Resurrection Bay, east coast of Kenai Peninsula; 127 miles south of Anchorage by road, or 35 minutes by air. **Population:** 3,010. **Emergency Services: Police, Fire Department** and **Ambulance,** emergency only, phone 911. **State Troopers,** phone (907) 224-3346. **Hospital,** Providence Seward Medical Center, 1st Avenue and Jefferson Street, phone (907) 224-5205. **Maritime Search and Rescue,** phone (800) 478-5555.

Visitor Information: Available at 2 locations, operated by the Seward Chamber of

Kenai Fjords Wilderness Lodge

Overnight on beautiful Fox Island, 14 miles south of Seward in Resurrection Bay.
Packages feature:
- Premiere wilderness destination on Fox Island.
- *Kenai Fjords Tours* wildlife & glacier cruise.
- Sea kayaking adventures.
- Delicious, hearty meals.
- Transportation provided by *Kenai Fjords Tours*.

P.O. Box 1889, Seward, AK 99664
In Anchorage 513 W. 4th Ave.
800-478-8068
www.kenaifjords.com

MARINA MOTEL

In-Room Refrigerator
In-Room Coffee • Phones in Rooms
Friendly Service • FREE Local Phone Calls
• FREE Cable TV • Private Baths

Located Near Train Station and The Departure Point for Tours of the Kenai Fjords and All Seward Activities.
ON THE RIGHT COMING INTO SEWARD

WWW.SEWARDMOTEL.COM
(907) 224-5518
BOX 1134, SEWARD AK 99664
EMAIL: donnactm@alaska.com

SEWARD, ALASKA
Free General Info Line
Call **800-844-2424**
in Seward call 224-2424
Free Lodging Res Line
Call **907-224-2323**
Discounted Tours for Customers using Free Lodging Res Service. Local Sewardite will help you find Reservations that fit YOUR needs. (Working with 100+ Lodgings.)
www.alaskasview.com
Alaska's Point of View Reservation Service

Seward is "Gateway to Kenai Fjords National Park."

Commerce–Convention & Visitors Bureau. The visitor center at **Milepost S 2** Seward Highway (2001 Seward Highway) is open 7 days a week from Memorial Day through Labor Day, weekdays the rest of the year; phone (907) 224-8051. The Information Cache, located in the historic railroad car *Seward* at 3rd and Jefferson Street, is open daily from 9 A.M. to 5 P.M., June through August; write Box 749, Seward, AK 99664.

Seward celebrates its Centennial in 2003. Inquire at the information centers about special events or online go to www.seward100th.com.

Kenai Fjords National Park Visitor Center, 1212 4th Ave. (in the Small Boat Harbor), is open 8 A.M. to 7 P.M. daily, Memorial Day to Labor Day; 8:30 A.M. to 5 P.M. weekdays the remainder of the year. Information on the park, slide show, interpretive programs and bookstore. Phone (907) 224-3175 or the Park Information Line (907) 224-2132. Or write P.O. Box 1727, Seward, AK 99664; web site: www.sewardak.org.

Chugach National Forest, Seward Ranger District office, is located at 334 4th Ave. USFS personnel can provide information on hiking, camping and fishing opportunities on national forest lands. Open weekdays, 8 A.M. to 5 P.M. Mailing address: P.O. Box 390, Seward, AK 99664. Phone (907) 224-3374.

Elevation: Sea level. **Climate:** Average daily maximum temperature in July, 62°F; average daily minimum in January, 18°F. Average annual precipitation, 67 inches; average snowfall, 80 inches. **Radio:** KSKA-FM 92, KWAVE 104.9, KPEN 102.3, KPFN 105.9, KSWD 950, KFSH 1240. **Television:** Several channels by cable. **Newspaper:** *Seward Phoenix Log* (weekly).

SEWARD ADVERTISERS

Accommodations
A Swan Nest Inn ....Ph. (907) 224-3080
Alaska Saltwater Lodge ....Ph. (907) 224-5271
Beach House, The ....Ph. (907) 224-7000
Bear's Den B&B ....Ph. (907) 224-3788
Breeze Inn ....Ph. (888) 224-5237
Camelot Cottages ....Ph. (800) 739-3039
Che'nai B&B ....Ph. (800) 726-4707
Crow's Nest Cottage ....Ph. (907) 224-3979
Clear Creek Cottage ....Ph. (907) 224-3968
Exit Glacier Salmon Bake &
  Cabins ....Ph. (907) 224-4752
Farm B&B Inn, The ....Ph. (907) 224-5691
Harborview Inn ....Ph. (907) 224-3217
Harmony B&B ....Ph. (907) 224-3661
Hotel Edgewater ....Ph. (888) 793-6800
Hotel Seward ....Ph. (888) 685-8574
Kenai Fjords Wilderness
  Lodge ....Ph. 1-800-478-8068
Marina Motel ....Ph. (907) 224-5518
Melody Inn B&B ....Ph. (907) 224-5356
Miller's Landing ....Ph. (907) 224-5739
Murphy's Motel &
  Long Shore Lodge ....Ph. (800) 686-8191
New Seward Hotel
  & Saloon ....Ph. (907) 224-8001
Northern Nights B&B ....Ph. (907) 224-5688
Ray's Lodging ....Ph. (907) 224-2323
Sea Treasures Inn ....Ph. (907) 224-7667
Seward Resort
  (Military) ....Ph. (907) 224-2659
Seward Waterfront
  Lodging ....Ph. (907) 224-5563
Seward Windsong Lodge..Ph.1-888-959-9590
Taroka Inn ....Ph. (907) 224-8975
Van Gilder Hotel, The ......Ph. 1-800-204-6835
Victorian Serenity By
  The Sea ....Ph. (877) 239-3637

Attractions
Alaska Sealife Center ....Ph. (800) 224-2525
Godwin Glacier
  Dog Sled Tours ....Ph. (888) 989-8239
IdidaRide Sled Dog Tours ..Ph. (907) 224-8607
Miller's Landing ....Ph. (907) 224-5739
Seward Centennial
  Celebration ....Ph. (907) 224-8051
Seward Museum ....Ph. (907) 224-3902

Auto & RV Rentals, Service & Supplies
Hertz Car Rental ....Ph. (907) 224-4378
Terry's Tire & Lube ....Ph. (907) 224-5505

Campgrounds
Bear Creek RV Park ....Ph. (907) 224-5725
Miller's Landing ....Ph. (907) 224-5739

Charters (Fishing & Sightseeing)
Alaska Fjord Charters........Ph. (907) 283-4199
Alaska Saltwater Lodge ...Ph. (907) 224-5271
Aurora Charters ....Ph. (907) 224-3968
Backlash Charters ....Ph. (800) 295-4396
Charter Option ....Ph. (800) 224-2026
Che'nai Charters ....Ph. (800) 726-4707
Discover Alaska Charters ..Ph. (907) 491-1363
Fish House, The................Ph. (907) 224-3674
Kenai Fjords Tours ....Ph. (800) 478-8068
Major Marine Tours..........Ph. (800) 764-7300
Mariah Tours ....Ph. (800) 478-8068
Puffin Fishing Charters .....Ph. (800) 978-3346
Renown Charters &
  Tours ....Ph. (800) 655-3806
Semaka Charters..............Ph. (877) 224-3195

Churches
Seward Church of Christ ....433 4th Ave.

Dining
Chinooks Waterfront
  Restaurant ....Ph. (907) 224-2207
Christo's Palace...............Ph. (907) 224-5255
Exit Glacier Salmon Bake
  & Cabins ....Ph. (907) 224-4752
Harbor Dinner Club ....Ph. (907) 224-3012
Ranting Raven, The ....Ph. (907) 224-2228
Ray's Waterfront..............Ph. (907) 224-5606

Healthcare
Providence/Seward Medical
  Care ....Ph. (907) 224-5205

Kayaking
Alaska Saltwater Lodge ....Ph. (907) 224-5271
Kayak & Custom Adventures
  Worldwide ....Ph. (907) 224-3960
Kayaker's Cove.................Ph. (907) 224-8662
Sunny Cove Sea
  Kayaking Co. ....Ph. (800) 770-9119

Shopping & Services
Brown & Hawkins ....Ph. (907) 224-3011
Helly Hansen.....................Ph. 800-41-HELLY
Ranting Raven, The ....Ph. (907) 224-2228
Resurrect Art Coffee
  House Gallery ....Ph. (907) 224-7161
Seward Laundry................Ph. (907) 224-5727
Sweet Darlings.................Ph. (907) 224-7313

Visitor Information
Seward Chamber of
  Commerce ....Ph. (907) 224-8051
Alaska's Point of View
  Reservation Service .....Ph. (800) 844-2424

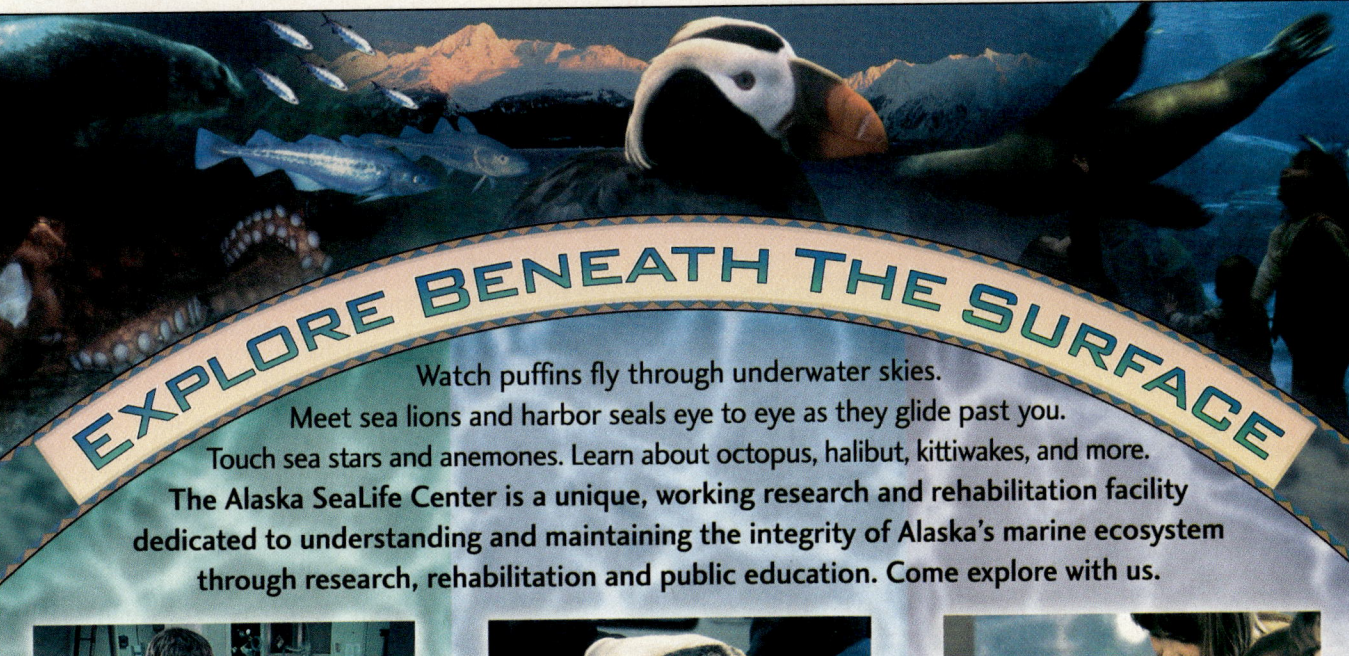

EXPLORE BENEATH THE SURFACE

Watch puffins fly through underwater skies.
Meet sea lions and harbor seals eye to eye as they glide past you.
Touch sea stars and anemones. Learn about octopus, halibut, kittiwakes, and more.
The Alaska SeaLife Center is a unique, working research and rehabilitation facility dedicated to understanding and maintaining the integrity of Alaska's marine ecosystem through research, rehabilitation and public education. Come explore with us.

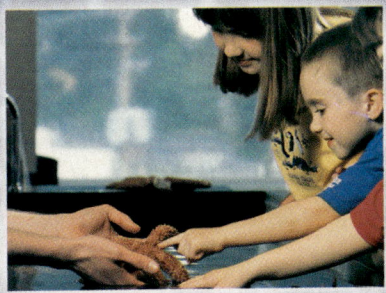

RESEARCH The Alaska SeaLife Center is a world-class marine science facility. Ongoing research projects at the Center provide vital information to help scientists discover reasons for Alaska's declining marine animal populations and other environmental changes throughout our ecosystem.

REHABILITATION The SeaLife Center is Alaska's only permanent facility designed to handle both injured marine mammals and birds, and is also the state's only marine mammal rehabilitation center. Our care for sick and injured animals also yields important information about wildlife populations.

EDUCATION We'll connect you with our current research and rehabilitation projects and provide wonderful viewing opportunities to marine wildlife. Our exhibits and presentations will expand your knowledge of Alaska's fragile marine ecosystem. Learning has never been more enjoyable!

Answers to the sea's mysteries are being unlocked daily by scientists, educators and visitors like you.

Join us in celebrating Seward's Centennial!

Alaska SeaLife Center

windows to the sea

Located in Seward at the edge of Resurrection Bay • Mile 0 of the Seward Highway
Open Year Round • Family & Group Discounts Available - Children 6 & Under Free

NEW EXHIBIT FOR 2003 - THE BERING SEA: ABUNDANCE & CHANGE

For up-to-date information visit our website at www.alaskasealife.org or call us in Seward at 800-224-2525

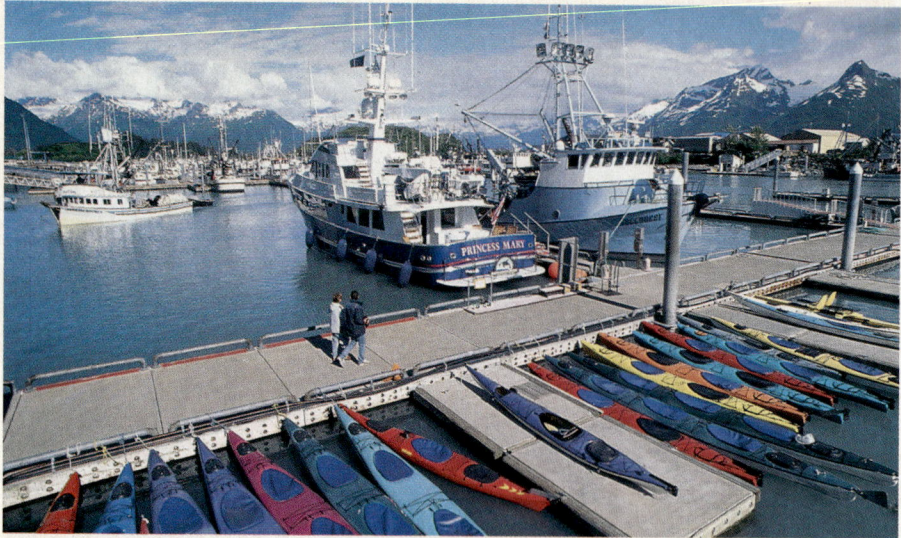

Seward's Small Boat Harbor is the place to be. (© Rich Reid, Colors of Nature)

FISHING & LODGING
SEWARD, ALASKA
Che'nai Charters
& Che'nai B&B
"Go With The Gusto"
VISA
907 224-8766
1-800-726-4707
www.chenai.com
MasterCard

Private Aircraft: Seward airport, 2 NE; elev. 22 feet; length 4,200 feet; asphalt; fuel 100LL, jet.

Seward—known as the "Gateway to Kenai Fjords National Park"—is a picturesque community nestled between high mountain ranges on a small rise stretching from Resurrection Bay to the foot of Mount Marathon. Thick groves of cottonwood and scattered spruce groves are found in the immediate vicinity of the city, with stands of spruce and alder growing on the surrounding mountainsides.

Downtown Seward (the main street is 4th Avenue) has a frontier-town atmosphere with some homes and buildings dating back to the early 1900s.

Historically, Seward was an important transportation hub for Alaska's mining, exploration, fishing and trapping industries. The town was established in 1903 by railroad surveyors as an ocean terminal and supply center. The Iditarod trail was surveyed in 1910 as a mail route between Seward and Nome. It was used until 1924, when it was replaced by the airplane. The 938-mile-long trail—now a National Historic Trail—is probably best known for the Iditarod Trail Sled Dog Race that is run each March between Anchorage and Nome, but the trail starts in Seward. Visitors may follow its marked course through town as a bike path. The trail continues for hikers from Mile 2.1 Nash Road (turnoff at **Milepost S 3.2** Seward Highway).

The 470-mile railway connecting Seward with Fairbanks in the Interior was completed in 1923.

The city was named for U.S. Secretary of

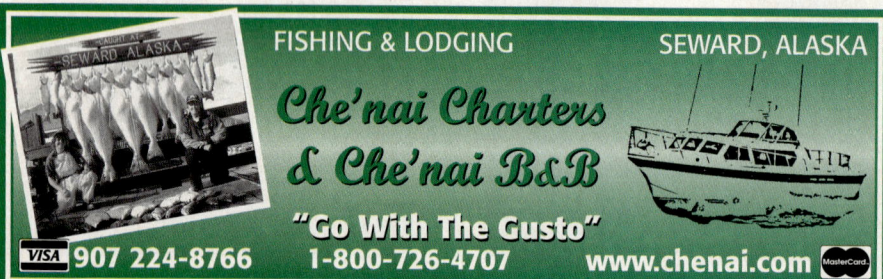

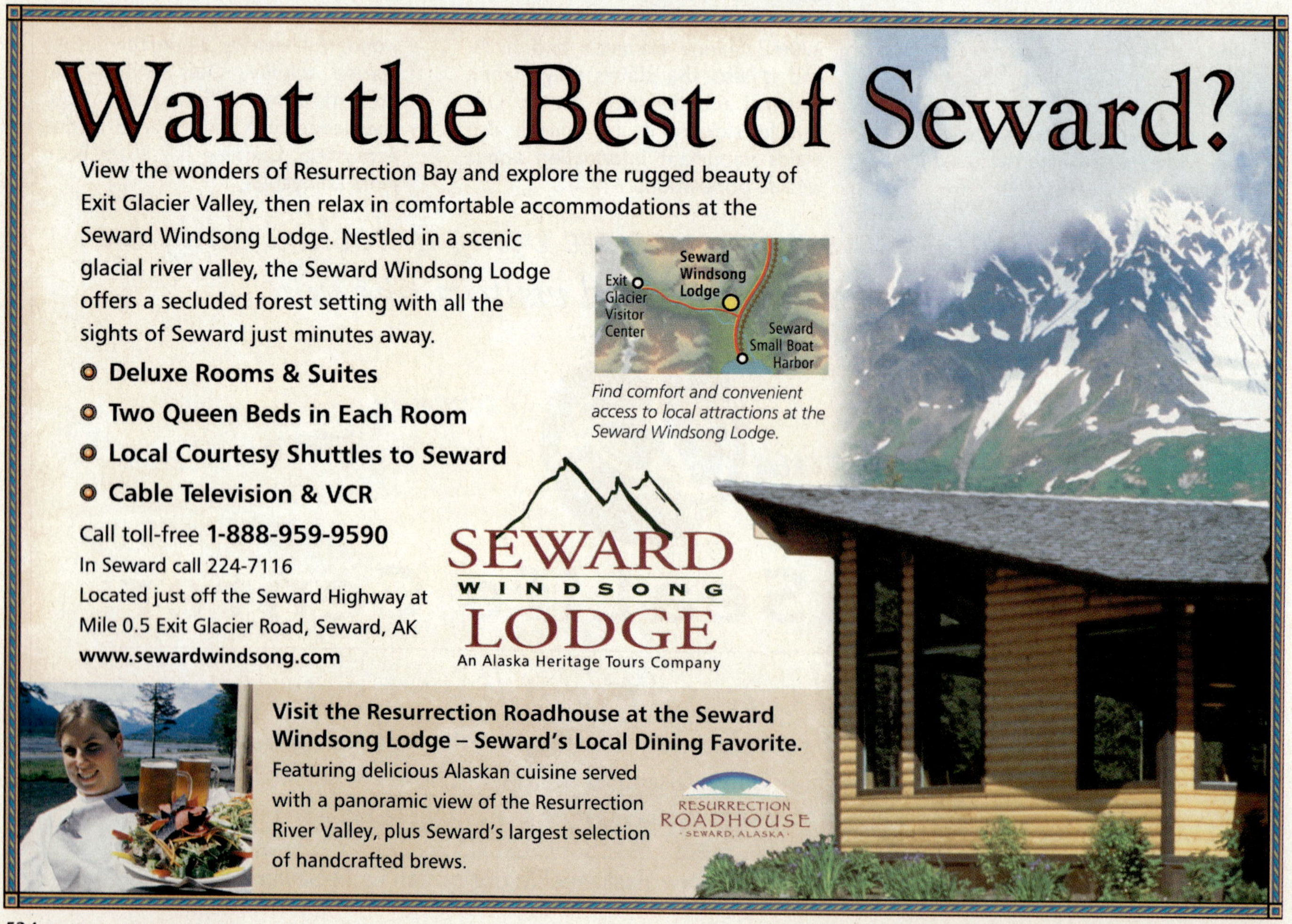
Want the Best of Seward?
View the wonders of Resurrection Bay and explore the rugged beauty of Exit Glacier Valley, then relax in comfortable accommodations at the Seward Windsong Lodge. Nestled in a scenic glacial river valley, the Seward Windsong Lodge offers a secluded forest setting with all the sights of Seward just minutes away.
Deluxe Rooms & Suites
Two Queen Beds in Each Room
Local Courtesy Shuttles to Seward
Cable Television & VCR
Call toll-free 1-888-959-9590
In Seward call 224-7116
Located just off the Seward Highway at Mile 0.5 Exit Glacier Road, Seward, AK
www.sewardwindsong.com
Exit Glacier Visitor Center
Seward Windsong Lodge
Seward Small Boat Harbor
Find comfort and convenient access to local attractions at the Seward Windsong Lodge.
SEWARD WINDSONG LODGE
An Alaska Heritage Tours Company
Visit the Resurrection Roadhouse at the Seward Windsong Lodge – Seward's Local Dining Favorite.
Featuring delicious Alaskan cuisine served with a panoramic view of the Resurrection River Valley, plus Seward's largest selection of handcrafted brews.
RESURRECTION ROADHOUSE
SEWARD, ALASKA

SEWARD
Centennial Celebration

1903 — 2003

"The place to be in 2003"

The City of Seward
Invites you and your family to join us in celebrating our first hundred years

Major Events
New Year's Cotillion—January 1
History Symposium—February 7-9
Seward's Day Pioneer Lunch—March 23
Seward Harbor Opening—May 17-18
4th of July / Mt. Marathon Race—July 4
Founders Days—August 28-30
Railroad Days—September 20-21
Old-Fashioned Christmas—December

Many more events...
Historic Exhibits, Art Shows, Publications, Reunions, and Fun Centennial Activities

For information contact:

Seward Chamber of Commerce
Mi. 2 Seward Hwy
907-224-8051
www.seward100th.com

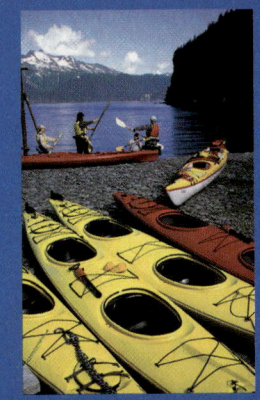

Seward Alaska 1903-2003 Centennial

SEWARD HIGHWAY • Seward

State William H. Seward, who was instrumental in arranging the purchase of Alaska from Russia in 1867.

Resurrection Bay, a year-round ice-free harbor, made Seward an important cargo and fishing port as well as a strategic military post during WWII.

Resurrection Bay was named in 1791 by Russian fur trader and explorer Alexander Baranof. While sailing from Kodiak to Yakutat he found unexpected shelter in this bay from a storm and named the bay Resurrection because it was the Russian Sunday of the Resurrection (Easter).

Seward's economic base includes tourism, a coal terminal, marine research, fisheries and government offices. The Alaska state ferry MV *Tustumena* calls at Seward. The Alaska Vocational Technical Center is located here. The Alaska SeaLife Center, a marine educational center, is located here (see Attractions this section for more details).

Lodging & Services

Seward has all visitor facilities, including hotels, motels, a hostel, bed and breakfasts, cafes and restaurants, post office, grocery store, drugstore, travel agencies, gift shops, gas stations, bars, laundromats, churches, bowling alley and theater.

The Harbormaster Building has public restrooms, pay showers, drinking water fill-up, mailbox and pay phones. Weather information is available here during the summer. Public restrooms and pay showers on Ballaine Boulevard along the ocean between the boat harbor and town. Dump station at the Small Boat Harbor at the end of 4th Avenue (see city map). There are picnic areas with covered tables along Ballaine Blvd., just south of the harbor, and at Adams Street.

Alaska Saltwater Lodge. Seward's only drive-to oceanfront lodge. Experience sea otters, sea lions, seals, eagles and whale viewing. Scenic mountain and glacier setting. Enjoy beachcombing and fishing, coastal nature trail, on-site kayaking, guided salt-water fishing and daily small group Kenai Fjords National Park wildlife and glacier tours. private baths. (907) 224-5271. www.alaskasaltwaterlodge.com. See display ad. [ADVERTISEMENT]

Breeze Inn, Restaurant, Motel, Lounge & Gift Shops. In the heart of the harbor. 86 deluxe rooms, including accessible units, Jacuzzi suites, smoking/nonsmoking rooms. All are exceptionally clean. In-room coffee makers. Free local calls. Friendly, courteous staff. The Breeze Inn Restaurant is open 6 A.M.–9 P.M. daily. Guests say: "The best breakfast in town." New lunch and dinner items. Delicious fresh halibut, salmon and choice-cut steak dinners. Box lunches to go. (907) 224-5238, (888) 224-5237. www.breezeinn.com. See display ad this section. [ADVERTISEMENT]

Brown and Hawkins. Alaska's oldest family-owned retail business; general merchandisers, outfitting Alaskans since 1900 with quality clothing and gear. Shop brand names—Patagonia, Filson, Carhartt, Levi, Nike, New Balance, Birkenstock. Hundreds of unique Alaskan-made gifts and souvenirs direct from the artists at Alaska's best prices for all Alaskans and their visitors, including

Cruise ships dock near Seward's Small Boat Harbor. (© David Foster)

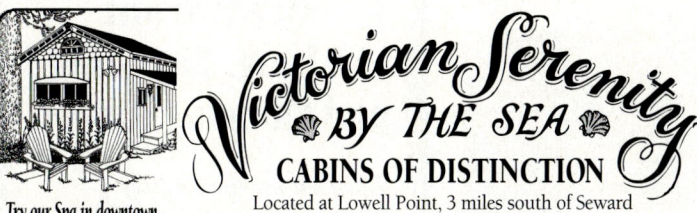

Harmony B&B

- Private Bath & Entrance
- Quiet & Minutes to Town & Boat Harbor

See log ad under Lodging

(907) 224-3661
www.seward.net/~kevinc

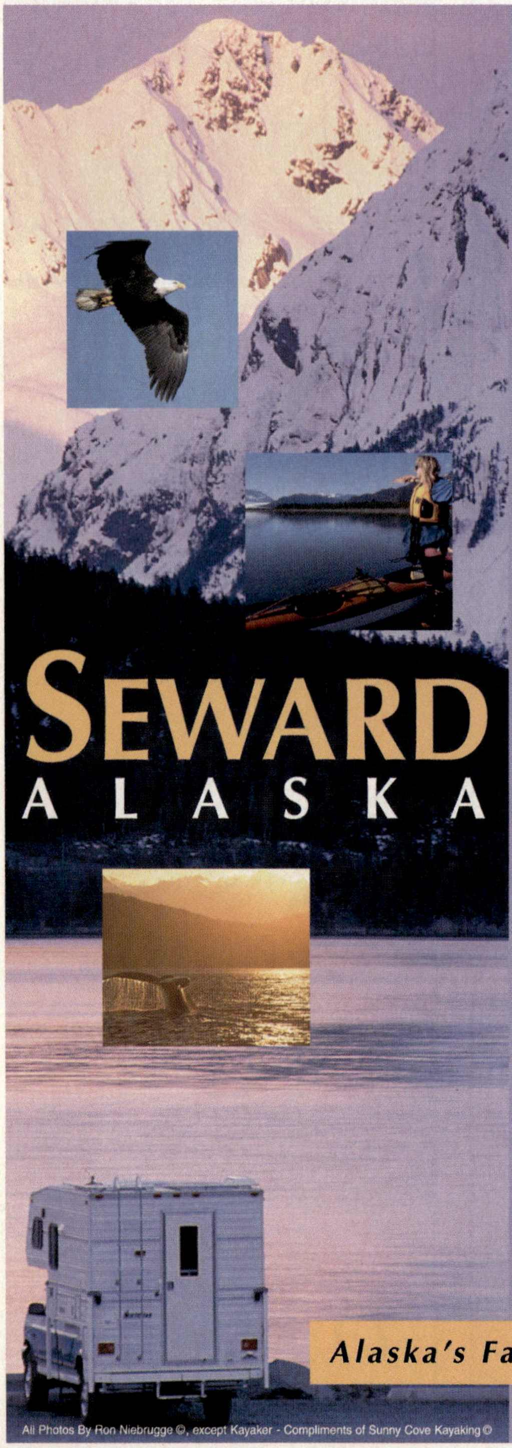

SEWARD ALASKA

Seward offers the best Alaskan adventure with the shortest drive time from Anchorage and is easily accessible via the Seward Scenic Byway, the Alaska Railroad, bus, air, ferry, or cruise ship.

Nestled off the Gulf of Alaska on Resurrection Bay, Seward offers a lifetime worth of adventure for all ages!

Seward welcomes you with it's unique small town charm and friendly atmosphere.

- World-class Fishing
- Kayaking
- Sailing
- Hiking
- Camping
- Dog Sledding
- Mountain Biking
- Wildlife & Glacier Viewing

For more info contact:
Seward Chamber of Commerce
P.O. Box 749
Seward, Alaska 99664
tel: 907.224.8051
fax: 907.224.5353

Alaska's Favorite Seaside Town!

www.SewardAk.org

All Photos By Ron Niebrugge ©, except Kayaker - Compliments of Sunny Cove Kayaking ©

Miller's Landing

Seward's Best
Oceanfront Fishing, Kayaking and Camping Resort!

Located on the Family Homestead on Beautiful Resurrection Bay!

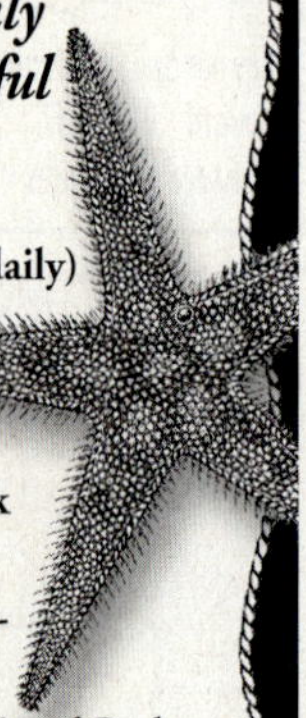

- Fishing Charters (8 boats daily)
- Sea Kayak Rentals
- Guided Kayaking Adventures
- Kenai Fjords National Park Wildlife/Glacier Tours
- Water Taxi Drop-Off/Pick-Up Services, Resurrection Bay and Kenai Fjords National Park
- Kayak Shuttle Services
- Boat and Motor Rentals
- Oceanfront and Wooded RV/Tent Camping
- Seaside Cabin Rentals
- Oceanfront Cabins and B&B Reservations
- Kayak Lessons
- State/National Park Cabin Drop-Off/Pick-Up Services
- Fishing Pole Rentals
- Oceanfront Country Store
- Laundry, Hot Showers, Flush Toilets

FREE COFFEE!

Fishing Advice
5¢
Guaranteed effective or your nickel back!

Captain Mike Miller & Captain Sherrie Miller
PO Box 81, Seward, Alaska 99664
Toll Free 1-866-541-5739
907-224-5739
millerslanding@alaska.com
www.millerslandingak.com

keepsakes, carvings, ivory, jade and gold. Custom designed T-shirts and sweatshirts. Come see the many turn-of-the-century antiques, including the old bank vault. It's a step back in time. Visit Sweet Darlings Candies! See candies being made: saltwater taffy, Alaska's finest fudge, barks and brittles. Gourmet candies are always a welcome gift and a visit to Sweet Darlings will long be remembered. The old-fashioned soda fountain is a great place to enjoy mouth-watering gourmet hot dogs, soup, sodas, scoop ice cream and sundaes. www.sweetdarlings.com. (907) 224-3011. See display ad this section. [ADVERTISEMENT]

Camelot Cottages. (800) 739-3039. Clean, cozy, affordable cabins in a natural woodland setting. Chalet available for families or groups. All units are furnished, heated, with private baths, fully equipped kitchens, linens and cable TV. Relax in our guest-only open air Hot-Tub. Laundry and fish freezer also available. Family-owned and operated by longtime Alaskans. We can also make your reservations for Kenai Fjords Park tours and fishing charters on the world-famous Kenai Peninsula. See display ad at Mile 3.2 Seward Highway. Phone (907) 224-3039 Seward; (907) 346-3039 Anchorage. akcabins@alaska.net and www.alaska.net/~akcabins. [ADVERTISEMENT]

Chinooks Waterfront Restaurant. Located at the north end of the Small Boat Harbor. Enjoy "the best view in town" from the two-story dining area. See wildlife from your table: sea otters, bald eagles, sea lions. Chinooks offers a complete lunch and dinner menu, including seafood, steaks, pasta. Ask about their halibut cheeks! ... and daily seafood specials. Complete wine list and a variety of Alaskan ales available. Summer season hours: 11 A.M.–10 P.M. MasterCard, Visa, American Express. Large private parties accommodated. (907) 224-2207. See our display ad. [ADVERTISEMENT]

Clear Creek Cottage. Fully furnished smoke-free 2-bedroom cabin, full kitchen. Sleeps up to 6. Clean, comfortable, affordable rates. Perfect hideaway for couples, families, small groups. On the banks of Clear Creek, on Old Exit Glacier Road, Mile 3.7 Seward Highway. 7 minutes to downtown Seward. (907) 224-3968. Fax (907) 224-7230. P.O. Box 241, Seward, AK 99664. See display ad in "Exit Glacier Road" log this section. [ADVERTISEMENT]

Exit Glacier Salmon Bake & Cabins. Come visit an authentic, rustic, comfortable, full-service Alaskan restaurant-pub in a delightful wooded setting on the way to Exit Glacier. "An unforgettable Alaskan experience." Fresh Alaskan salmon, halibut and other seafood, burgers, steaks and chicken. "You won't go away hungry!" The pub atmosphere includes tapped Alaskan microbrews

SEWARD WATERFRONT LODGING
(907) 224-5563
Next to Sea-life Center
Overlooking Resurrection Bay
Summer Breakfasts in Solarium
SEE LOG AD
www.alaskas-sewardwaterfrontlodging.com

The Beach House RENTALS
(907) 224-7000
2 Houses On Magical Lowell Pt.
www.beachhousealaska.com

Seward • Alaska

Get away to somewhere great!

Making your stay in Seward special.

Reservations:
1-888-793-6800

907-224-2700 • 907-224-2701 fax
e-mail: edgewater@seward.net
www.hoteledgewater.com

Seward's Waterfront Park offers camping, multi-use trails, interpretive signs and playgrounds. (© Ron Biebrugge)

and wines. Coffee is always free! The cabins are clean, comfortable, with private baths. Sleeps 3–5. Ask for Salmon Bake Cabins, (888) 227-2424. [ADVERTISEMENT]

The Farm Bed & Breakfast Inn. Turn off Seward Highway on to Nash Road, cross railroad tracks, turn left immediately on to Salmon Creek Road (watch for sign). Tranquil country setting on acres of trees and lawn. Families and senior citizens welcome. Continental breakfast. VISA, MasterCard, Discover, Amex. Box 305, Seward, AK 99664. (907) 224-5691. Fax (907) 224-5698. Email: thefarm@ptialaska.net. Internet: www.alaskan.com/thefarm/. See display ad at Mile 3.2 Seward Highway. [ADVERTISEMENT]

Harbor Dinner Club, downtown location next to Hotel Edgewater and Hotel Seward. Owned/operated by same family since 1958, serving huge, reasonably priced lunches, dinners. Burgers to filets to Alaska seafood plus super duper chowder. Dine in/outdoors on beautiful deck. Full bar, big-screen TV. Live music, dancing most weekends. Lions, Chamber, Rotary meet here. (907) 224-3012. See display ad this section. [ADVERTISEMENT]

Harborview Inn. AAA-approved. 804 Third Avenue. New: 38 rooms with private entrances, private baths, cable TV in room, telephone, fine art. Just 10-minute walk to tour boats, fishing charters, downtown and Alaska SeaLife Center. Also "Seaview," our 2 newly remodeled 2-bedroom apartments on the beachfront, breathtaking view of snow-capped mountains and bay. All nonsmoking. $129. Early reservations advised. Alaska Native hostess. Phone (907) 224-3217; 1-888-324-3217. P.O. Box 1305, Seward, AK 99664. Email: info@sewardhotel.com. Internet: www.sewardhotel.com. See display ad this section. [ADVERTISEMENT]

Hotel Edgewater features comfortable rooms, a conference center, a gift shop and espresso bar, exercise equipment, hot tub and sauna and a spacious atrium lobby and cozy fireplace lobby. Most rooms overlook Resurrection Bay or the Kenai Mountains. Amenities include coffee bar, TV and VCR, hair dryers. The hotel is one block from the Alaska SeaLife Center and offers tour booking services. In the summer, a complimentary continental breakfast is available as well as

free transportation to and from the Small Boat Harbor and railroad station. We book salmon and halibut charter fishing trips. 1-888-793-6800; www.hoteledgewater.com. Open year round. [ADVERTISEMENT]

Hotel Seward. Enjoy being in the center of activity, yet in a quiet setting overlooking Resurrection Bay. Our rooms include breathtaking views with new beds, in-room coffee and refrigerator. 2 floors all nonsmoking rooms. And check this out! For your in-room entertainment, all rooms include data ports, remote control TVs with cable vision and remote control VCRs with videotape rental. Complimentary scheduled shuttle bus service for our guests to boat harbor, train depot and airport. Half-block to the Alaska SeaLife Center. Credit cards accepted. Reservations (907) 224-2378 or (888) 639-9953 inside Alaska. Fax (907) 224-3112. www.alaskaone.com/hotelseward. See display ad this section. [ADVERTISEMENT]

Murphy's Motel & Long Shore Lodge. Economy to first-class accommodations. Murphy's offers private baths, cable TV, queen beds, free local calls, coffee maker, fridge, microwave, data ports, parking in front of rooms. Smoking/nonsmoking rooms. Murphy's Long Shore Lodge, 13 nonsmoking rooms. They provide all the amenities, lovely decor, plus a great view of Resurrection Bay, mountains and glaciers, from bay windows or second floor balconies. Ask about their handicapped accessibility, Jacuzzi bath, kitchenettes. Centrally located on Main Street, 2 blocks to Fjords Tour departures/fishing charters at the small boat harbor. Minutes to the SeaLife Center. Toll free (800) 686-8191; (907) 224-8090. murphys@seward.net; www.murphysmotel.com. See display ad. [ADVERTISEMENT]

New Seward Hotel & Saloon. Rooms $40–$96. Centrally located in downtown Seward, half-block to Alaska SeaLife Center, within walking distance of shops, beach, boat harbor; 35 rooms featuring cable TV and phones. Some kitchenettes. Salmon and halibut fishing charters or Kenai Fjords tours available. Year-round service. Credit cards accepted. (907) 224-8001. Fax (907) 224-3112. Two doors down: The happenin' place in Seward! DJ Dancing. [ADVERTISEMENT]

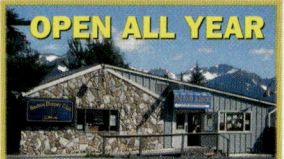

Harbor Dinner Club
Operated by the same family since 1958

OPEN ALL YEAR

- **Fresh Seafood** – Lobster, Shrimp, Halibut, Salmon, Scallops, Oysters
- **Huge, Reasonably Priced Lunches & Dinners** – From Burgers to Filets
- **Outdoor Dining** on the Beautiful Deck
- **Full Bar, Big Screen TV**, Pool, Ping-Pong, Foosball
- **Live Music & Dancing** Most Weekends

WHERE THE LOCALS EAT & PARTY • NEXT TO EDGEWATER & BEST WESTERN HOTELS
220 5TH AVE PO BOX 1169, SEWARD AK 99664 TEL (907) 224-3012 FAX (907) 224-2603

The Ranting Raven

• ESPRESSO • TEAS • DELICIOUS FRESH BREADS & PASTRIES

UNIQUE GIFTS
BAKERY

IN THE HEART OF DOWNTOWN SEWARD
DAILY LUNCH SPECIALS
(907) 224-2228

Come Stay With Us At
TRAIL RIVER GARDENS B&B

Mile 24.5 Seward Highway

Ray's LODGING

- Lovely, Spacious Two Bedroom Units
- Cable TV, Phone, Fully Equipped Kitchens, Full Baths
- Walk to Boat Harbor, No Parking Hassles
- Private Entry. Perfect for Groups, Families

(907) 224-2323   **www.rayslodging.com**

Ray's WATERFRONT

Spectacular Waterfront Setting
Overlooking Seward Boat Harbor
SEAFOOD is our specialty
Cocktails
Major Credit Cards Accepted
(907) 224-5606
Over 50 fish on display

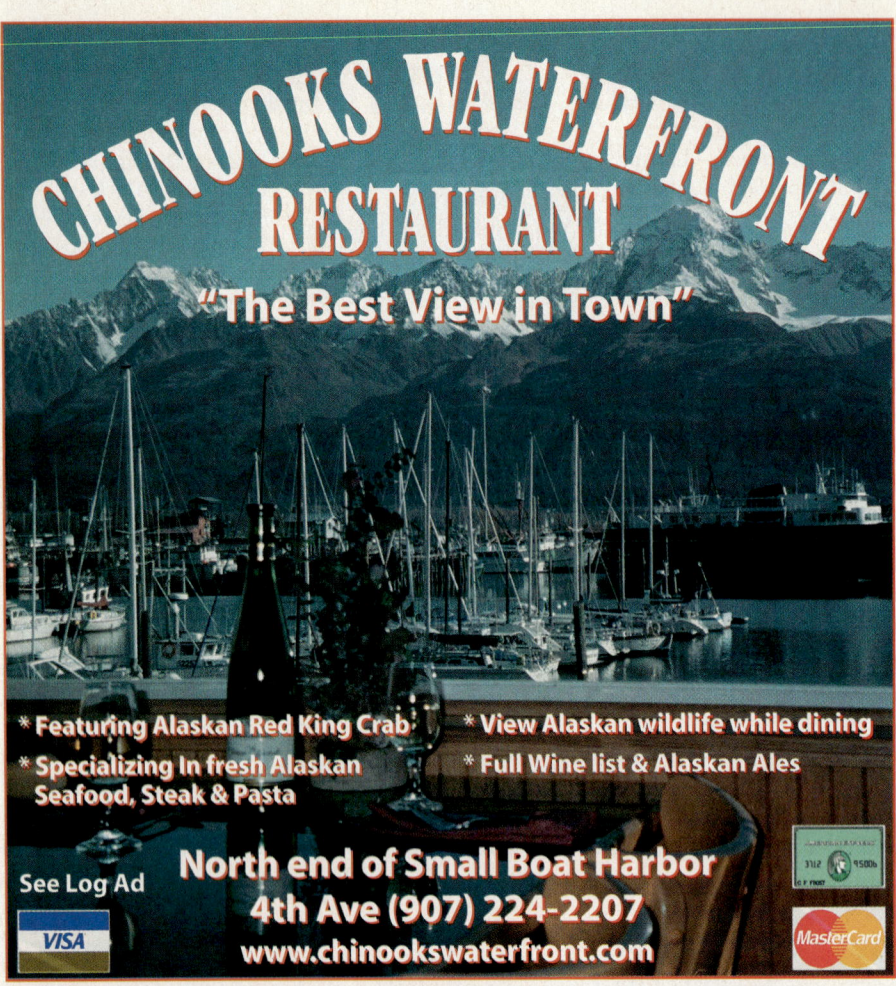

SEWARD CHURCH OF CHRIST

- Sunday Bible Study 10 am
- Sunday Worship 11am/6 pm
- Wednesday Bible Study 7 pm

Brad Holm ✝ Evangelist

Box 1215, Seward AK 99664 • (907) 224-3727

Ray's Waterfront. Innovative Alaskan cuisine in a spectacular waterfront setting featuring fresh local seafood, steaks and vegetarian selections. Specialties include macadamia nut crusted halibut with Thai curry sauce, cioppino, brandied pepper steak, oven-roasted Tuscan vegetables, king crab and daily specials. Serving lunch and dinner daily. Full bar service with excellent wine selections. Group reservations in advance are welcome. Gourmet box lunches available. Phone (907) 224-5606, fax (907) 224-5631. www.alaskaone.com/waterfront. See display ad this section. [ADVERTISEMENT]

Seward Waterfront Lodging. Enjoy healthy breakfasts served each summer's morning in our waterfront view solarium downtown overlooking Resurrection Bay. Adjacent to the Alaska SeaLife Center and just minutes away from Fjord Tour departures, restaurants and shops. Our lodging offers charming, cozy, clean, convenient rooms with cable TV and coffee service within. Decor features historic Alaskan artifacts and hosted by 37-year Alaskan resident. Perfect for small reunions, weddings, specialty groups and independent travelers. Handicapped access. Visa/MasterCard; (907) 224-5563 or www.alaskas–sewardwaterfront lodging.com. See display ad this section. [ADVERTISEMENT]

Seward Windsong Lodge. Conveniently located at Mile 0.5 Exit Glacier Road/Herman Leirer Road, just 2 miles north of the Seward Small Boat Harbor, the Seward Windsong Lodge offers 105 beautiful rooms in a forested setting. The on-site restaurant, Resurrection Roadhouse, serves delicious Alaskan cuisine offering guests a panoramic view of the Resurrection River Valley as they dine. For hiking or outdoor enthusiast, the lodge is located just 6 miles from Exit Glacier, the only glacier in Kenai Fjords National Park accessible by road. For reservations, call 888-959-9590; in Seward (907) 224-7116; or visit us on the web at www.sewardwindsong.com. [ADVERTISEMENT]

Taroka Inn. Clean, comfortable, convenient and affordable. Family-owned, operated and oriented. We offer kitchen units with private bathroom, cable TV, in-room phone, data ports. Couples traveling together have a little more privacy. One queen bed in the bedroom and another in the living room (not a fold-out). Our larger units accommodate up to 9 persons. Great for family on a budget! On the corner of 3rd and Adams. Two blocks from Alaska SeaLife Center. One block to restaurants, shops, museum. ³⁄₄ mile to Small Boat Harbor. Non-smoking available. Pets upon approval only. Phone (907) 224-8975. Email: taroka@arctic.net. Internet: www.alaskaone.com/taroka. See display ad this section. [ADVERTISEMENT]

Van Gilder Hotel. Registered National Historic Landmark Hotel, recently remodeled to original 1916 detail, with modern amenities. Historic downtown location near shops, museum, SeaLife Center and restaurants. 2-room suites with spectacular views.

SEWARD MUSEUM ★
The Place to Start Your Seward Visit!
2003 is SEWARD'S CENTENNIAL!
★ **(907) 224-3902** ★
336 3rd Ave. • Box 55 • Seward AK 99664

Participants scramble up Mount Marathon during 4th of July race.
(© Rich Reid, Colors of Nature)

Brass beds, historic photo gallery, player piano. Experience Alaskan history and hospitality at its best! Call 1-800-204-6835. P.O. Box 609, Seward, AK 99664. 308 Adams Street. www.vangilderhotel.com. See display ad this section. [ADVERTISEMENT]

Camping

Seward has made a good effort to provide overnight parking for self-contained RVs. There are designated tent and RV camping areas along the shore south of Van Buren; camping fee charged. Restrooms with coin-operated showers; water and electric hookups available at some sites. (RV caravans should contact the City Parks and Recreation Dept. for reservations, phone 907/224-4055.) Municipal campground is at **Milepost S 2.5** Seward Highway. Private RV parks at **Milepost S 6.6** (Bear Lake Road) and on Lowell Point Road; see ads this section. Walk-in tent camping is available at Exit Glacier (turnoff at **Milepost S 3.7** Seward Highway). ▲

Bear Creek RV Park. Good Sam Park, full and partial hookups, dump station, private restrooms with showers, cable TV, traveler's lounge, propane, laundry, convenience store, ice, video rentals, pay phone. Offers complimentary continental breakfast. Fax service available. Shuttle service available for Kenai Fjords Tour booking guests during June–August. Caravans and large groups welcome. Email: hettick@ptialaska.net. www.bearcreekrv.com. Phone (907) 224-5725. [ADVERTISEMENT] ▲

Miller's Landing. Oceanfront, wooded RV sites; electric, showers, laundry. Campground store. Mile-long beach, 5-mile coastal trail hiking. Beach fishing, kayaking,

www.themilepost.com

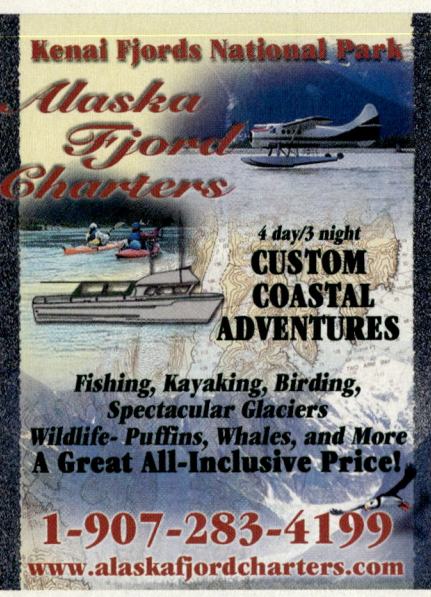

BACKLASH CHARTERS
1-800-295-4396
"WORLD CLASS SPORTFISHING AT ITS FINEST!"
WEBPAGE: fishingseward.com
EMAIL: backlash@seward.net

CROW'S NEST COTTAGE
(907) 224-3979
WALKING DISTANCE TO EVERYTHING!
PRIVATE COTTAGE FOR UP TO 6
WASHER/DRYER & FULL KITCHEN
WEBPAGE: www.seward-alaska.com/crowsnest/
EMAIL: crowsnestak@alaska.com

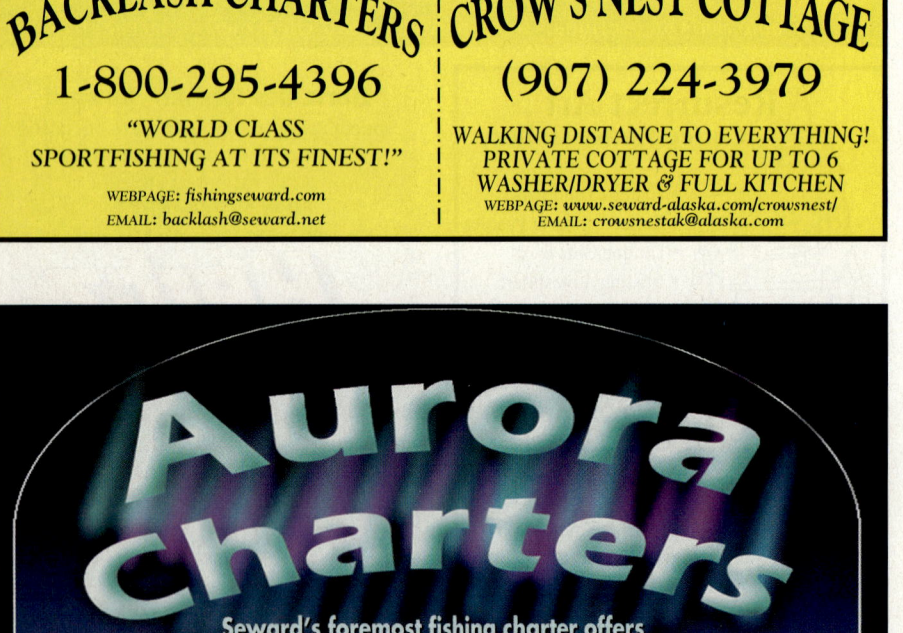

boat rentals, fishing charters, guided kayak trips/lessons; water taxi services; Kenai Fjords wildlife/glacier tours; kayak drop-offs; tractored boat launching; seaside cabin rentals; free coffee. Toll free 1-866-541-5739. www.millerslandingak.com. See display ad this section. [ADVERTISEMENT]

Transportation

Air: Seward airport is reached by turning east on Airport Road at **Milepost S 2.7** on the Seward Highway. Scheduled daily service to Anchorage; charters also available.

Ferry: Alaska Marine Highway office on Cruise Ship Dock; phone (907) 224-5485. The Alaska ferry MV *Tustumena* departs Seward for Kodiak and Valdez.

Railroad: Seward is Mile 0 of the Alaska Railroad. The Alaska Railroad connects Seward to Anchorage and Fairbanks.

Bus: Scheduled service to Anchorage.

Taxi: Service available.

Rental cars: Hertz, phone (907) 224-4378.

Highway: Seward is Mile 0 of the Seward Highway. The 127-mile Seward Highway (Alaska Routes 9 and 1) connects Seward with Anchorage.

Attractions

The Railcar *Seward* houses the chamber of commerce information center. Located at 3rd and Jefferson Street, this railcar was the Seward observation car on the Alaska Railroad from 1936 until the early 1960s. Information and detailed map of the city are available. Phone (907) 224-3094.

Walking Tour of Seward encompasses more than 30 attractions including homes and businesses that date back to the early 1900s; some are still being used, while others have been restored as historic sites. A brochure containing details on all the attractions of the tour is available at the railcar information center. The complete tour covers about 2 miles and takes about 1 to 2 hours, depending upon how much time you wish to spend browsing.

The **City of Seward** celebrates its first Centennial in 2003. Experience an early 1900s railroad port on Alaska's rugged coast by visiting renovated buildings, dedicated parks, colorful murals, the centennial quilt and other exhibits. Locate 9 sites on the National Register of Historic Places within the City of Seward. Shop for historic publications, games and postal cancellations. Join in special events throughout the year. Take this unique opportunity to learn about the resilient, innovative people of Seward and their role in the history of Alaska's transportation, shipping, education and government. Contact Seward Chamber of Commerce (907) 224-8051 for details. See display ad this section. [ADVERTISEMENT]

Alaska SeaLife Center. This 7-acre waterfront site combines research facilities with wildlife rehabilitation and public education. Construction of the SeaLife Center was funded by the Exxon Valdez Oil Spill Restoration fund and private donations.

The Center allows you to come face-to-face with Alaska's exciting marine wildlife, explore their undersea world and experience the wonder of nature in a one-of-a-kind marine science and visitor facility. This $50 million, 115,000-square-foot center opens windows to the sea—above and below the surface. Indoors, view the distinct habitats of marine birds, Steller sea lions, seals, fish and otters. Outdoors, step right to the edge of Resurrection Bay, teeming with Alaska marine wildlife. Open daily year-round. Admission fee charged. Web site: www.alaskasealife.org. Phone (907) 224-6300.

Visit the Small Boat Harbor. This municipal harbor, built after the 1964 earthquake, is home port to fishing boats, charter boats and sightseeing boats. The harbor is also home to sea otters—watch for them! Visitors may notice the great number of sailboats moored here: many are members of the William H. Seward Yacht Club, which sponsors an annual sailboat and yacht show.

Seward Museum, at Jefferson and 3rd Avenue, is operated by the Resurrection Bay Historical Society (Box 55, Seward 99664). The museum features artifacts and photographs from the 1964 earthquake, WWII, the founding days of Seward and other highlights of Seward's history. Also on display is a collection of Native baskets and ivory carvings. The museum is open daily, 9 A.M. to 5 P.M., May 1 to Sept. 30. Open reduced hours remainder of year; check locally, or phone (907) 224-3902. A modest

Catching his first fish in Seward delights this youngster. (© Tommy Krasnican)

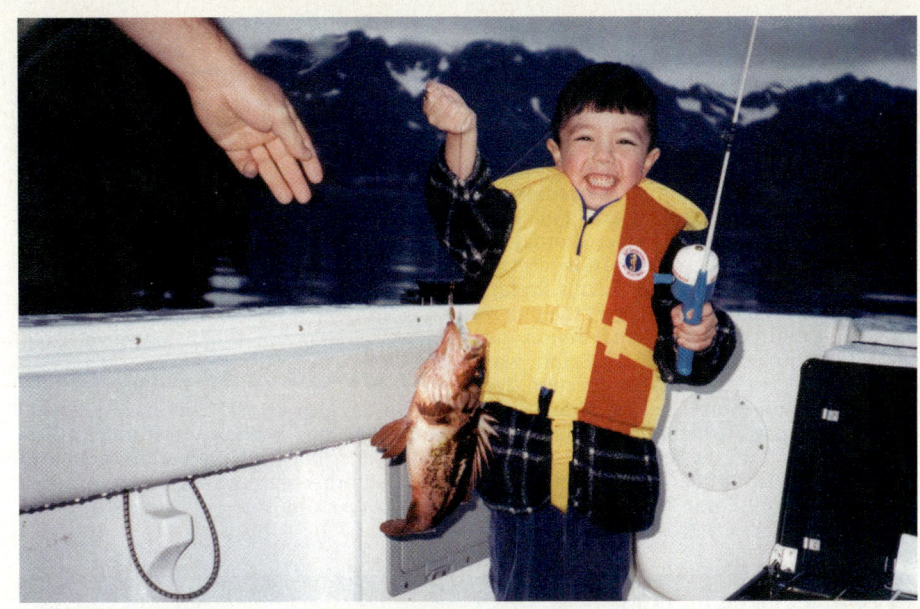

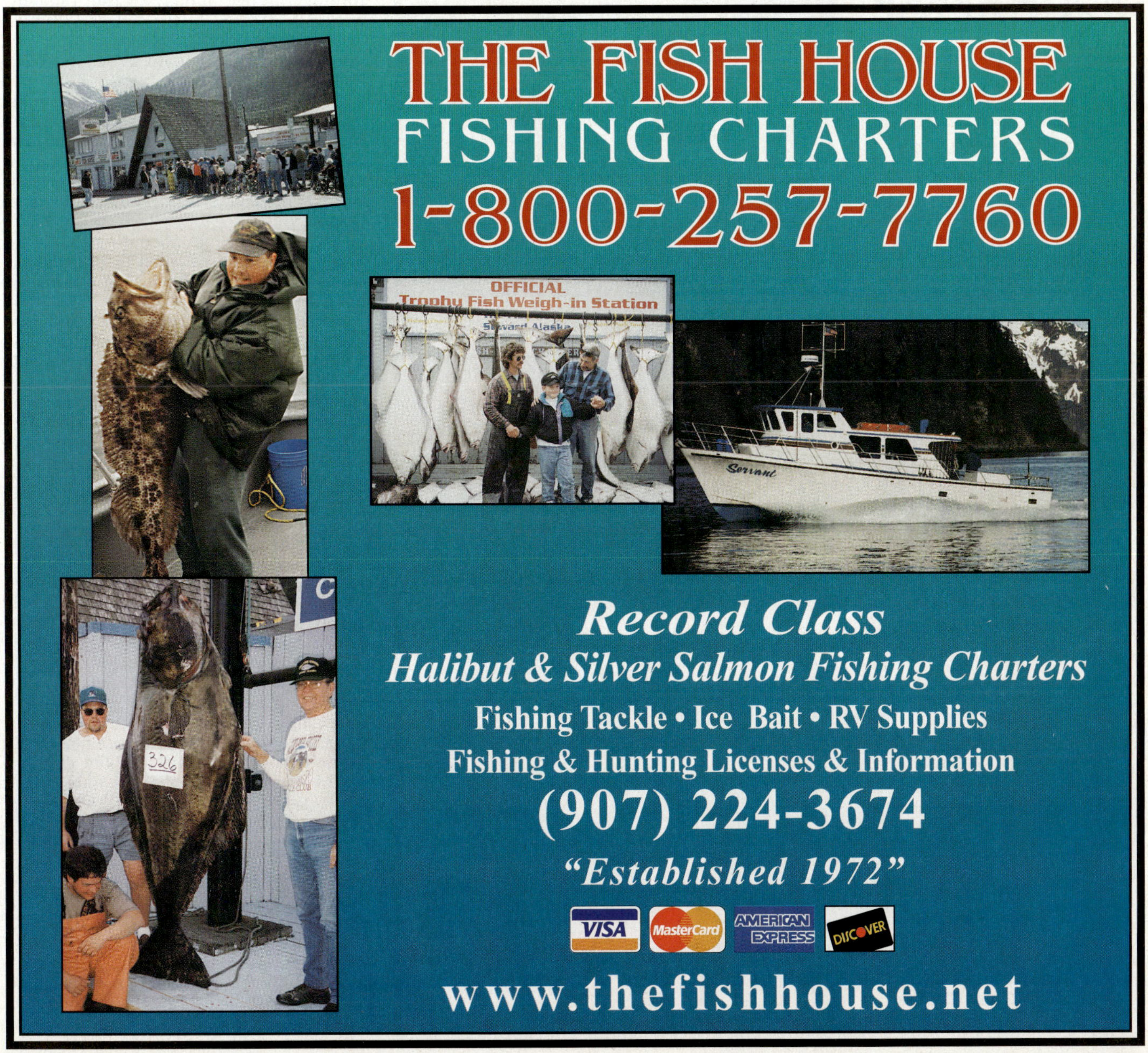
THE FISH HOUSE
FISHING CHARTERS
1-800-257-7760
OFFICIAL
Trophy Fish Weigh-in Station
Record Class
Halibut & Silver Salmon Fishing Charters
Fishing Tackle • Ice Bait • RV Supplies
Fishing & Hunting Licenses & Information
(907) 224-3674
"Established 1972"
VISA
MasterCard
AMERICAN EXPRESS
DISCOVER
www.thefishhouse.net

admission fee is charged.

Seward Community Library, across from the City–State Building, presents (on request) short slide/sound shows on a variety of subjects and has some informative displays. A program on the 1964 earthquake is shown daily at 2 P.M. (except Sunday) from June 15 through the first Saturday in September. Library hours are 1–8 P.M. Monday through Friday, 1–6 P.M. Saturday.

St. Peter's Episcopal Church, at the corner of 2nd Avenue and Adams Street, was built in 1906. It is considered the oldest Protestant church on the Kenai Peninsula. In 1925, Dutch artist Jan Van Emple was commissioned to paint the Resurrection, for which Alaskans were used as models and Resurrection Bay as the background. Obtain key to church from the Seward Museum.

Lowell Point State Recreation Area. Drive out Lowell Point Road 2.3 miles and turn on Martin Road for this day-use area (or drive 2.9 miles to end of Lowell Point Road and second junction with Martin Road).

The day-use area at the end of Lowell Point Road has parking, restrooms and a gravel path that leads to a short stretch of beach. Another trail connects this area with the upper parking area.

The upper parking lot on Martin Road has long term parking and is the trailhead for a hiking trail to Tonsina Point and Caines Head SRA. Caines Head is located 6 miles south of Seward. It is accessible by boat or via the 4.5-mile beach trail (low tide only). The Caines Head area has bunkers and gun emplacements that were used to guard the entrance to Resurrection Bay during WWII.

Mount Marathon Race, Seward's annual Fourth of July endurance race to the top of Mount Marathon (elev. 3,022 feet) and back down is a grueling test for athletes. The descent is so steep that it's part run, part jump and part slide. The race attracts competitors from all over, and thousands of spectators line the route each year. The race is said to have begun in 1909 with a wager between 2 sourdoughs as to how long it would take to run up and down Mount Marathon. The first year of the official race is uncertain: records indicate either 1912 or 1915. Fastest recorded time is 43 minutes, 23 seconds set in 1981 by Bill Spencer.

Annual Seward Silver Salmon Derby™ in August is one of the largest sporting events in Alaska. It is held over 9 days, starting the second Saturday in August and continuing through Sunday of the following weekend. 2003 will be the derby's 48th year. Record derby catch to date is a 20.59-lb. salmon caught off Twin Rocks by John Westlund of Anchorage.

There are more than $250,000 in prizes for the derby, including $10,000 in cash for the largest fish. Also part of the derby are the sought-after tagged silvers worth as much as $100,000. Prizes are sponsored by various merchants and the Chamber of Commerce.

The town fills up fast during the derby: Make reservations! For more information contact the Seward Chamber of Commerce; phone (907) 224-8051.

Charter Option. Come fishing and touring with us—full and half-day salmon and halibut charters. Our friendly staff will help you with everything you need to fish in Resurrection Bay. Our tours will show you the beautiful Resurrection Bay area through flight-seeing, kayaking, dogsledding and glacier viewing. Ask about our overnight packages with Hotel Edgewater! 1-800-224-2026; Email: edgewater@seward.net; www.hoteledgewater.com. [ADVERTISEMENT]

The Fish House. First and finest fishing charter service in Seward! Record-class halibut and silver salmon fishing charters available now. While fishing, enjoy the scenic beauty of the Kenai Fjords National Park— glaciers, mountains, puffins, whales, sea otters and seals. The Fish House also supplies a complete line of fishing tackle, bait, ice and RV supplies. Call now for reservations or information on fishing the scenic waters surrounding Seward. www.fishhouse.net. Email: fishhousecharters@gci.net. Halibut charters: April 1–Oct. 1. Salmon charters: June 1–Sept. 20. P.O. Box 1209, Seward, AK 99664. See display ad this section. [ADVERTISEMENT]

Godwin Glacier Dog Sled Tours, Princess Cruise Lines "tour of the year" award winner! A stunning helicopter flight takes you to the Godwin Glacier, where our experienced, longtime mushers and over 100 sled dogs wait to share this uniquely Alaskan adventure, dog mushing! See eagles, moose, mountain goats, bear and breathtaking deep, ice-blue crevasses from the safety and comfort of the best visibility/touring helicopter available. On the glacier, the

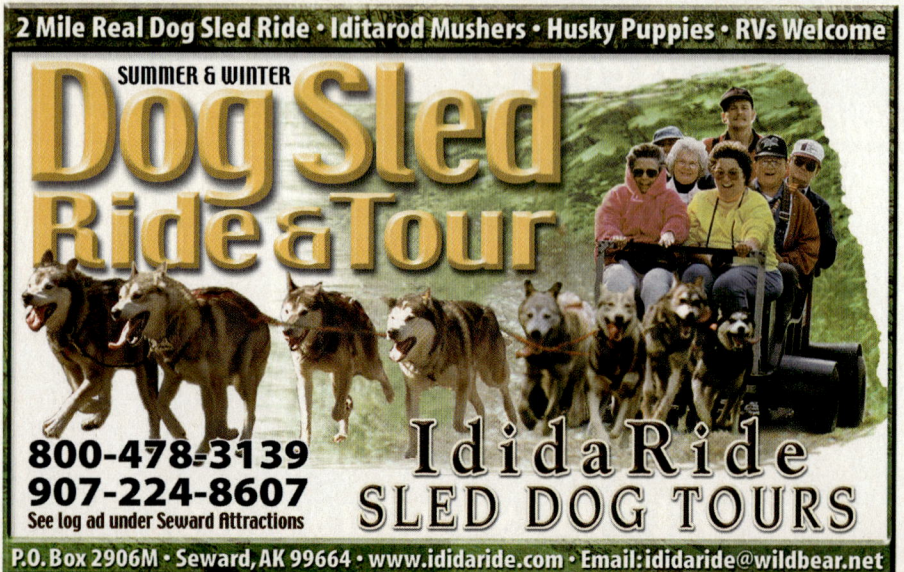

mushers share stories of their own experiences as anxious huskies are harnessed and wait to do what they love best, go mushing! A 2 mile trail takes you where it feels as if no person has been before; drive the team or simply enjoy this amazing moment that rekindles the excitement of days long past. Try on authentic gear; cuddle husky puppies ... this is the ultimate experience of a lifetime! Late May–early September. Groups welcome. Plenty of RV parking space. Handicap friendly. Call (888) 989-8239 or (907) 224-8239. www.alaskadogsled.com. See display ad this section. [ADVERTISEMENT]

IdidaRide Sled Dog Tours. Experience dog mushing, summer style, on a 2-mile wilderness dog sled ride guided by Iditarod mushers. Learn what it takes to compete in one of the most demanding races in the world while cuddling husky puppies and dressing up like a musher. 5 tours daily. Reservations recommended. Winter tours available. P.O. Box 2906, Seward, AK 99664. (907) 224-8607, fax (907) 224-8608. ididaride@wildbear.net. www.ididaride.com. Off Exit Glacier Road. See display ad this section. [ADVERTISEMENT]

Kayak & Custom Adventures Worldwide Sea Kayking with Alaska's most experienced outfitter. Day trips on the bay and wilderness expeditions into Kenai Fjords. Take home unforgettably wonderful memories that you can't find standing on the shore. Let us show you the real Alaska by sea kayak! Van-camping road trips also. Email: fun@KayakAK.com. Web site: www.KayakAK.com. Seward (907) 224-3960. Reservations: toll-free (800) 288-3134 or (907) 258-FUNN (3866). [ADVERTISEMENT]

Kenai Fjords Tours. The excitement begins the moment you pull away from the Seward boat harbor! You'll be greeted by playful sea otters, view boisterous Steller sea lions, look for whales and porpoises, photograph colorful puffins and bald eagles, and watch a calving glacier. Cruising since 1974,

Sunflower starfish on display at the Alaska Sealife Center. (© Hannah Peratta)

birds, and view spectacular glaciers. Large tour boats feature reserved table seating inside heated cabins and multiple outside decks for excellent viewing. Freshly prepared all-you-can-eat salmon and prime rib meal available on both cruises, $12. Daily departures from Seward, May to late September. Full-day cruise into Kenai Fjords National Park and Chiswell Islands National Wildlife Refuge to view wildlife and tidewater glacier departs 11:45 A.M., $109. Half-day wildlife cruise departing at 12:45 P.M., $69, and mid-June through mid-August 6 P.M., $54. Call (800) 764-7300 or (907) 274-7300

Kenai Fjords Tours is the original Kenai Fjords National Park tour and continues to be the most popular. Our new, custom sightseeing vessels have walk-around decks so you can easily watch and photograph the magnificent scenery. Our captains are experienced naturalists averaging more than 12 years in Kenai Fjords National Park, so you'll learn about this coastal wilderness from guides who really know the area. All cruises include a meal and many include a special stop at Fox Island for our delicious all-you-can-eat salmon bake at Kenai Fjords Wilderness Lodge. Don't miss it! Call today for reservations. Toll free (800) 478-8068 or (907) 224-8068. Located at the Seward Small Boat Harbor. See display ad this section. [ADVERTISEMENT]

Major Marine Tours. Cruise with National Park rangers. Watch for otters, sea lions, porpoises, whales (humpback, orca and others), eagles, puffins and other sea

SEMAKA CHARTERS

- Life long Alaskan Fisherman
- 6 year Charter Captain
- Fast, custom, 1st class boat / gear
- Fish with the best! (Slip H-41)

877-224-3195
www.semakacharters.com   semaka@ak.net

Big George Simagaa

SEA KAYAKING
Day Trips and Expeditions • Guided Instruction & Outfitting
Alaska's most experienced Sea Kayaking Outfitter
Reservations (907) 258-FUNN (3866) • (800) 288-3134 • Seward local phone (907) 224-3960
email: fun@KayakAK.com • www.KayakAK.com

Have you ever dreamed of fishing in Alaska?

This could be you!

PUFFIN FISHING CHARTERS

M/V Adventuress

1-800-978-3346 • www.puffincharters.com
Charter fishing out of Seward since 1982
Halibut, Salmon, Rockfish, and Combination Trips
New 36-foot vessel custom built for Alaskan waters

"I've been going out on charter boats from Mexico to Hawaii, and this is by far the most comfortable boat I've ever been on" - Tom from Florida

See Log Ad

10% discount for military, children 12 and younger, seniors 62 and older

Kenai Fjords National Park

The fjords of Kenai Fjords National Park were formed when glaciers flowed down to the sea from the ice field and then retreated, leaving behind the deep inlets that characterize the park's coastline and give it its name.

Substantial populations of marine mammals inhabit or migrate through the park's coastal waters, including sea otters, Steller sea lions, Dall porpoises and whales. Icebergs from calving glaciers provide ideal refuge for harbor seals, and the rugged coastline provides habitat for more than 100,000 nesting birds.

The park's scenic coastline and coastal wildlife is most commonly viewed by private tour and charter boats that depart from Seward's Small Boat Harbor daily in summer (see advertisements this section).

For independent wilderness travelers, 3 public-use cabins are located in the park at Holgate Arm, Aialik Bay and North Arm. The cabins are available for use in summer (May 22–Sept. 20) by reservation only. Reservations for public-use cabins are accepted by phone, mail or in person at the Kenai Fjords National Park Visitor Center. The Alaska Public Lands Information Center web site has good descriptions of the cabins and reservation process; go to www.nps.gov/aplic/nps_cabins.html.

Kayakers and boaters may camp on the beaches but must be aware ahead of time of land status. Some 42,000 acres of coastline are owned by Native corporations. Public camping is available by permit only from the Native corporations. For more information about Native lands and permits, phone (907) 284-2212. Maps indicating land ownership

Sightseeing Kenai Fjords National Park by tour boat.
(© Rich Reid, Colors of Nature)

are available from the park visitor center.
NOTE: Private boaters should consult with the Harbormaster in Seward for detailed information on boating conditions.

Another dominant feature of the 607,000-acre Kenai Fjords National Park is the Harding Icefield, a 300-square-mile vestige of the last ice age. Harding Icefield can be reached by a strenuous all-day hike (7 miles round trip) from the base of Exit Glacier or by a charter flightseeing trip out of Seward.

Exit Glacier is the most accessible of the park's glaciers. Turn at **Milepost S 3.7** on the Seward Highway and follow Exit Glacier Road to the visitor center parking area. There are several trails through the outwash plain of Exit Glacier that afford excellent views of the ice and surrounding mountains. A half-mile trail leads from the parking lot to the glacier. Ranger-led nature walks are available in summer at Exit Glacier, where there is a picnic area and walk-in campground. Visitor information is available at the Exit Glacier ranger station and visitor center; open summer only. Exit Glacier is accessible in winter by skis, dogsled or snow machine. One public-use cabin is available in winter by permit.

Slide programs, videos, exhibits and information on Kenai Fjords National Park and organized activities at the park are available at the park visitor center on 4th Avenue in the Small Boat Harbor area next to the Harbormaster's office. The center is open daily from Memorial Day to Labor Day; hours are 8 A.M. to 7 P.M. The remainder of the year hours are 8 A.M. to 5 P.M. (subject to change) weekdays. Contact the park superintendent, Box 1727, Seward, AK 99664. For more information, phone the park office at (907) 224-3175 or the Park Information Line at (907) 224-2132. On the Internet, visit www.nps.gov/kefj.

---

for reservations or free brochure. Major Marine Tours, 411 West 4th, Anchorage, AK 99501. www.majormarine.com. [ADVERTISEMENT]

Mariah Tours. Join us for a memorable day to the Chiswell Islands and Kenai Fjords National Park on the small ship alternative. You'll enjoy close-up viewing of whales, sea lions and seabirds. You'll appreciate the personalized attention on our 43-foot vessel, with a limit of only 16 passengers on board. Featuring tours to spectacular Northwestern Glacier via Granite Passage, the most scenic area within Kenai Fjords National Park. Popular exclusive tours for birding and naturalist groups. Operating mid-May–September. For reservations: (800) 478-8068. In Seward: (907) 224-8068. [ADVERTISEMENT]

Miller's Landing. Fishing charters; Kenai Fjords sightseeing/wildlife cruises; kayak rentals, lessons, guided trips; boat/motor rentals. Water-taxi dropoff services to Kenai Fjords National Park, state and national park cabins. Oceanfront RV/tent camping; seaside cabins; beach fishing; showers, laundry, store, gifts. 5 mile coastal hike. 1-866-541-5739. www.millerslandingak.com. See display ad this section. [ADVERTISEMENT]

Puffin Fishing Charters. Our new 36-foot custom-built vessel was designed for your comfort and safety. Its heated cabin features marine suspension seating and an enclosed head. *The Adventuress* provides plenty of deck space and travels at 30 knots: "Less time running means more time fishing." Reservations: 1-800-978-3346. Internet: www.puffincharters.com. Email: captainleslie@msn.com. See display ad this section. [ADVERTISEMENT]

Renown Charters & Tours. Our mission statement is: "Providing quality cruises at affordable prices." We are Alaska's only year-round cruise company. Heated cabins, walk-around decks, healthy lunches, along with a safe, experienced and knowledgeable crew. Since we are a smaller company and can afford to pass along more affordable rates, it is easy to see why we are the customer's favorite. Cruises starting at $39.99. (800) 655-3806 or (907) 272-1961. www.renowncharters.com. See display ad this section. [ADVERTISEMENT]

Sunny Cove Sea Kayaking Company. We are your Alaskan sea kayaking company. Offering the finest adventures in our backyard; Kenai Fjords National Park, Resurrection Bay and our exclusive location on remote Fox Island (kayak/wildlife cruise/salmon bake combo). Half-day to 10-day wilderness adventures for all experience levels. 1-800-770-9119 or direct 1-907-224-8810; www.sunnycove.com. [ADVERTISEMENT]

AREA FISHING: Resurrection Bay, coho (silver) salmon to 22 lbs., use herring, troll or cast, July to October; king salmon to 45 lbs., May to August; also bottom fish, flounder, halibut to 300 lbs. and cod, use weighted spoons and large red spinners by jigging, year-round. Charter and rental boats are available.

Experience Kenai Fjords National Park with "Alaska's #1 Wildlife & Glacier Cruise!"

Join Kenai Fjords Tours, the most knowledgeable and experienced guides to Kenai Fjords National Park. You'll cruise aboard our custom sightseeing vessels while spending extra time viewing marine wildlife and colorful seabirds, including Steller sea lions, otters, puffins, eagles, orcas and perhaps a giant humpback whale. On our National Park cruises you'll experience glaciers - up close. Kenai Fjords Tours has many options to choose from, including a stop at Fox Island for a grilled salmon buffet, kayaking and overnight packages. A visit to the Alaska SeaLife Center can be added to any of our cruises.
Daily departures from Seward, March - November.

The m/v Coastal Explorer at Holgate Glacier in Kenai Fjords National Park.

If you need transportation between Anchorage and Seward, we offer the only private rail car service via this scenic railway.

Visit us in Anchorage at 513 W. 4th Avenue or in Seward at the Seward Small Boat Harbor

Enjoy a grilled salmon buffet at Fox Island in beautiful Resurrection Bay.

Call today for reservations!
**In Anchorage 907-276-6249
In Seward 907-224-8068
Other areas 1-800-478-8068**

KENAI FJORDS
TOURS
An Alaska Heritage Tours Company

Spend extra time viewing marine wildlife including Steller sea lions.

www.kenaifjords.com

Kenai Peninsula
STERLING HIGHWAY

Connects: Seward Highway to Homer, AK **Length:** 143 miles
Road Surface: Paved **Season:** Open all year
Major Attractions: Kenai National Wildlife Refuge, Kenai River, Russian Orthodox Churches, Homer Spit

(See maps, pages 551-552)

	Anchorage	Homer	Kenai	Seward	Soldotna
Anchorage		233	158	127	147
Homer	233		96	180	85
Kenai	158	96		105	11
Seward	127	180	105		94
Soldotna	147	85	11	94	

Hikers enjoy the view of Skilak Lake in Kenai National Wildlife Refuge.
(© Rich Reid, Colors of Nature)

The Sterling Highway (Alaska Route 1) begins 90 miles south of Anchorage at its junction with the Seward Highway and travels 143 miles west and south to the community of Homer. Several major Kenai Peninsula side roads junction with the Sterling Highway, including Skilak Lake Loop Road, Swanson River Road, Kenai Spur Highway, Kalifornsky Beach Road, Cohoe Loop Road and Anchor River Beach Road.

From its junction with the Seward Highway at Tern Lake, the Sterling Highway passes through Chugach National Forest and Kenai National Wildlife Refuge. The Kenai Mountains are home to Dall sheep, mountain goats, black and brown bears, and caribou. The many lakes, rivers and streams of the Kenai Peninsula are famous for their sportfishing. The highway also provides access to the Resurrection Pass Trail System in Chugach National Forest.

From Soldotna south, the Sterling Highway follows the west coast of the peninsula along Cook Inlet. There are beautiful views of peaks on the Alaska Peninsula.

Physical mileposts on the Sterling Highway show distance from Seward. The Sterling Highway is a paved, mostly 2-lane highway, with few passing lanes and some short sections of 4-lane highway. The Sterling Highway is open year-round.

Emergency medical services: phone 911 or use CB channels 9, 11 or 19.

Sterling Highway Log

Distance from Seward (S) is followed by distance from Anchorage (A) and distance from Homer (H).
Physical mileposts show distance from Seward.

ALASKA ROUTE 1

S 37 A 90 H 142.5 Junction of the Seward and Sterling Highways. Turnout to south for Tern Lake Observation Site with interpretive boardwalk and viewing platforms. Information signs on area birds and wildlife.

Junction with Seward Highway (Alaska Route 9) to Seward and Anchorage. Turn to **Milepost S 37** on page 524 in the SEWARD HIGHWAY section for log.

Begin improved highway westbound with passing lanes, wide shoulders and turnouts.

S 37.4 A 90.4 H 142.1 Turnoff to south for USFS Tern Lake day-use picnic area; toilets, water, picnic tables. USFS spawning channel for king salmon on Daves Creek at outlet of Tern Lake. Short viewing trail with information signs illustrating use of log weirs and stream protection techniques. *Begin passing lane westbound.*

S 38 A 91 H 141.5 Distance marker westbound shows Soldotna 57 miles, Kenai 67 miles, Homer 131 miles.

S 39 A 92 H 140.5 *End passing lane westbound.*

S 39.7 A 92.7 H 139.8 Daves Creek. Protecting this scenic stream was a priority during the massive reconstruction of this section of the Sterling Highway in 1999-2000. Daves Creek flows west into Quartz Creek.

S 40 A 93 H 139.5 *Begin passing lane westbound.*

S 40.2 A 93.2 H 139.3 Turnout to north. Avalanche gates. *Emergency phone to south.*

S 40.7 A 93.7 H 138.8 *End passing lane westbound.*

S 40.8 A 93.8 H 138.7 Quartz Creek. This stream empties into Kenai Lake.

S 41.9 A 94.9 H 137.6 Small gravel turnout to south.

S 42.5 A 95.5 H 137 Large scenic viewpoint to south.

S 42.8 A 95.8 H 136.7 Turnout to south.

S 43 A 96 H 136.5 *Begin passing lane westbound.*

S 43.7 A 96.7 H 135.8 Small gravel turnouts to south.

S 44 A 97 H 135.5 *End passing lane westbound.*

S 44.6 A 97.6 H 134.9 *CAUTION: Watch for horses.*

S 44.9 A 97.9 H 134.6 Sunrise Inn (open year-round); food, gas, lodging, camping. Trail rides on Quartz Creek Road. ▲

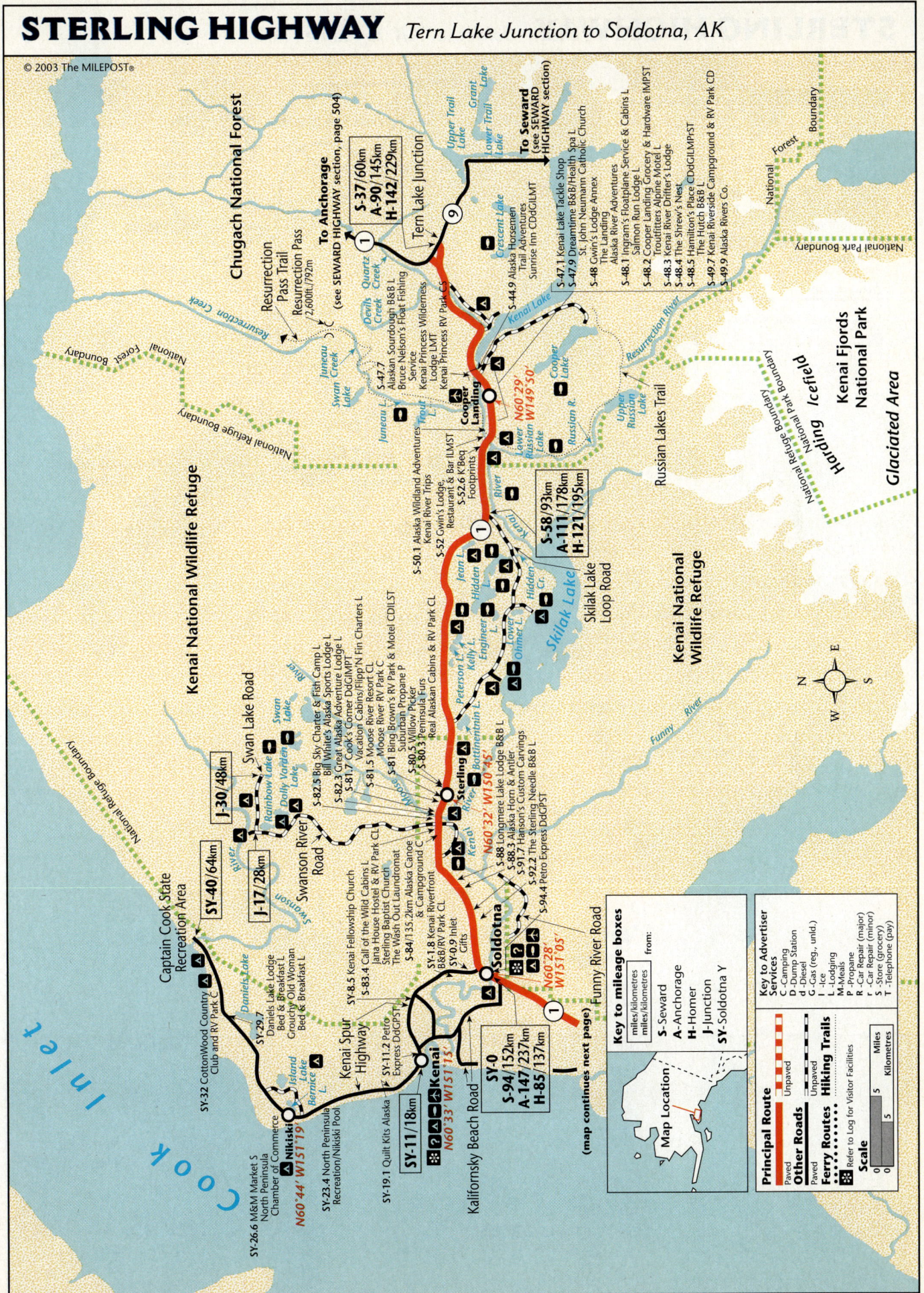

STERLING HIGHWAY *Soldotna, AK, to Homer, AK*

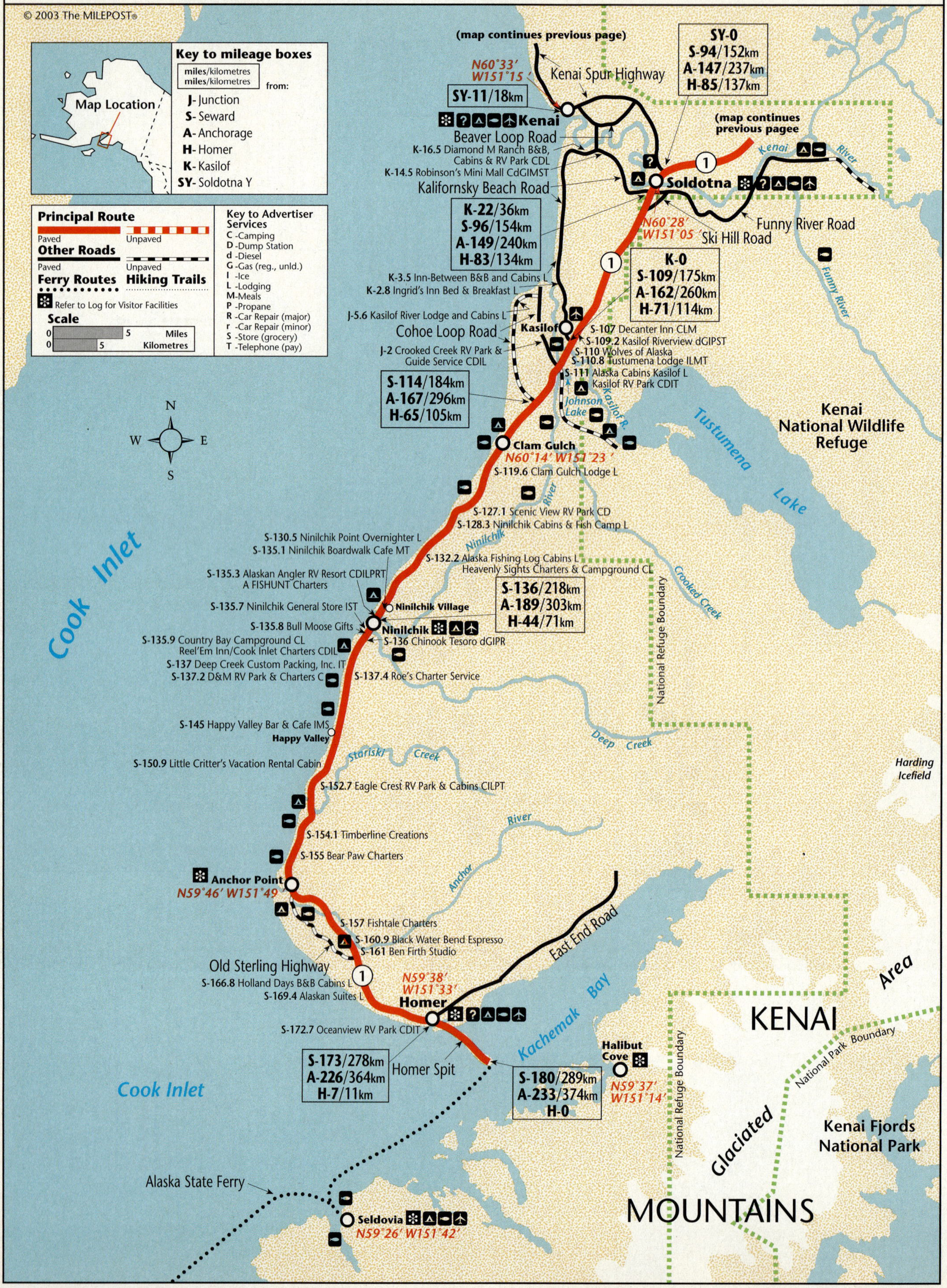

© 2003 The MILEPOST®
Map Location
Key to mileage boxes
miles/kilometres
miles/kilometres
from:
J- Junction
S- Seward
A- Anchorage
H- Homer
K- Kasilof
SY- Soldotna Y
Principal Route
Paved
Unpaved
Other Roads
Paved
Unpaved
Ferry Routes
Hiking Trails
Refer to Log for Visitor Facilities
Scale
0 5 Miles
0 5 Kilometres
Key to Advertiser Services
C -Camping
D -Dump Station
d -Diesel
G -Gas (reg., unld.)
I -Ice
L -Lodging
M -Meals
P -Propane
R -Car Repair (major)
r -Car Repair (minor)
S -Store (grocery)
T -Telephone (pay)
(map continues previous page)
N60°33' W151°15'
Kenai Spur Highway
SY-0
S-94/152km
A-147/237km
H-85/137km
SY-11/18km
Kenai
(map continues previous pagee)
Beaver Loop Road
K-16.5 Diamond M Ranch B&B, Cabins & RV Park CDL
K-14.5 Robinson's Mini Mall CdGIMST
Kalifornsky Beach Road
Soldotna
Kenai River
K-22/36km
S-96/154km
A-149/240km
H-83/134km
N60°28' W151°05'
Funny River Road
Ski Hill Road
K-0
S-109/175km
A-162/260km
H-71/114km
Funny River
K-3.5 Inn-Between B&B and Cabins L
K-2.8 Ingrid's Inn Bed & Breakfast L
J-5.6 Kasilof River Lodge and Cabins L
Cohoe Loop Road
Kasilof
S-107 Decanter Inn CLM
S-109.2 Kasilof Riverview dGIPST
S-110 Wolves of Alaska
S-110.8 Tustumena Lodge ILMT
S-111 Alaska Cabins Kasilof L
Kasilof RV Park CDIT
J-2 Crooked Creek RV Park & Guide Service CDIL
S-114/184km
A-167/296km
H-65/105km
Johnson Lake
Kasilof R.
Tustumena Lake
Kenai National Wildlife Refuge
N
W
E
S
Clam Gulch
N60°14' W151°23'
S-119.6 Clam Gulch Lodge L
S-127.1 Scenic View RV Park CD
S-128.3 Ninilchik Cabins & Fish Camp L
Ninilchik River
S-130.5 Ninilchik Point Overnighter L
S-135.1 Ninilchik Boardwalk Cafe MT
S-132.2 Alaska Fishing Log Cabins L
Heavenly Sights Charters & Campground CL
Cook Inlet
S-135.3 Alaskan Angler RV Resort CDILPRT
A FISHUNT Charters
S-136/218km
A-189/303km
H-44/71km
Crooked Creek
National Refuge Boundary
S-135.7 Ninilchik General Store IST
Ninilchik Village
S-135.8 Bull Moose Gifts
Ninilchik
S-136 Chinook Tesoro dGIPR
S-135.9 Country Bay Campground CL
Reel'Em Inn/Cook Inlet Charters CDIL
S-137 Deep Creek Custom Packing, Inc. IT
S-137.2 D&M RV Park & Charters C
S-137.4 Roe's Charter Service
S-145 Happy Valley Bar & Cafe IMS
Happy Valley
Deep Creek
Harding Icefield
Stariski Creek
S-150.9 Little Critter's Vacation Rental Cabin
S-152.7 Eagle Crest RV Park & Cabins CILPT
S-154.1 Timberline Creations
S-155 Bear Paw Charters
Anchor River
Anchor Point
N59°46' W151°49'
S-157 Fishtale Charters
S-160.9 Black Water Bend Espresso
S-161 Ben Firth Studio
East End Road
Old Sterling Highway
S-166.8 Holland Days B&B Cabins L
S-169.4 Alaskan Suites L
N59°38' W151°33'
Homer
Kachemak Bay
Area
S-172.7 Oceanview RV Park CDIT
KENAI
National Park Boundary
Halibut Cove
N59°37' W151°14'
S-173/278km
A-226/364km
H-7/11km
Homer Spit
S-180/289km
A-233/374km
H-0
Cook Inlet
National Refuge Boundary
Glaciated
Kenai Fjords National Park
Alaska State Ferry
MOUNTAINS
Seldovia
N59°26' W151°42'

Sunrise Inn Motel, Bar, Cafe & RV Park. See display ad this section.

Junction with Quartz Creek Road south to **Quartz Creek Recreation Area** (see "Quartz Creek Road" description this page).

S 45 A 98 H 134.5 Kenai Lake. Westbound travelers are entering one of Alaska's best-known lake and river fishing regions. Kenai Lake and tributaries are closed to salmon fishing.

NOTE: The diversity of fishing conditions and frequent regulation changes on all Kenai waters make it advisable to consult locally for fishing news and regulations.

See "Fishing the Kenai River", page 562 and pages 571–574 for more information.

S 46.3 A 99.3 H 133.2 Small gravel turnout to south.

S 47 A 100 H 132.5 Gravel turnout to south.

S 47.1 100.1 H 132.4 Kenai Lake Tackle Shop has a large selection of quality local fishing gear, flies, beads, rods, reels and rental equipment. We also book float-fish-

ing and fly-in trips to the local hot spots. Fisherman's cabins and hotel rooms for nightly rental at reasonable prices. Winter (907) 595-1802. Summer (907) 595-2248. klcabins@arctic.net. www.bnbweb.com/klcabins.html. [ADVERTISEMENT]

S 47.6 A 100.6 H 131.9 Restaurant, towing service and other businesses.

S 47.7 A 100.7 H 131.8 Turnoff to north on **Bean Creek Road** for access to Cooper Landing Community Center; Bruce Nelson's fishing guide service (0.3 mile), Alaskan Sourdough Bed and Breakfast (0.7 mile) and the Kenai Princess Lodge and RV Park on the Kenai River (2 miles).

Quartz Creek Road

Quartz Creek Road junctions with the Sterling Highway at **Milepost S 44.9**, next to the Sunrise Inn. This scenic side road leads south along Kenai Lake to Quartz and Crescent creeks and Chugach National Forest recreation facilities.

Distance from junction with the Sterling Highway (J) is shown.

J 0 Junction with Sterling HIghway at Milepost S 44.9 at Sunrise Inn.

J 0.1 Alaska Horsemen Trail Adventures. Family fun at our Alaskan outfit. Located on Quartz Creek Road behind Sunrise Inn. We offer a variety of trail ride adventures, carriage tours and gold panning. Planned for 2003, bunk-house lodging for adventure groups! Historical pioneer cabin

full of Alaskan gifts and furs. Many say our half-day trail ride is the finest horseback ride they have been on. Come visit our ranch, try your luck at gold panning from our local mine's "pay-dirt" and experience true Alaskan hospitality. www.alaskahorsemen.com. Email: horses@arctic.net. (907) 595-1806. [ADVERTISEMENT]

J 0.2 Turnoff for **Quartz Creek Day-use Area** and boat ramp on Kenai Lake; parking, picnic sites.

J 0.5 Entrance to **Quartz Creek Campground**; 45 sites on paved loop road, some pull-through sites, tables, firepits, flush toilets, campground host, camping fee $13 single, $20 double. Some campsites overlook Kenai Lake.

J 0.6 Pavement ends, gravel begins at 1-lane bridge over **Quartz Creek**; fishing for

Quartz Creek Road crosses Crescent Creek. (© Kris Graef, staff)

rainbow, midsummer; Dolly Varden to 25 inches, late May through June.

J 1.1 Road forks: Keep left for Crescent Creek Campground and Crescent Lake Trailhead (descriptions follow; continue with log).

For day-use area on Kenai Lake (parking only, no toilets or tables), keep right at this fork and drive 0.3 mile to second fork; keep right again and continue 0.2 mile through area of private homes to road end at Kenai Lake.

J 2.5 Crescent Creek 1-lane bridge.

J 2.6 Entrance to **Crescent Creek USFS Campground**; 9 level sites on gravel loop, toilet, firepits, tables, water pump, $10 camping fee.

J 3.2 Maintained road ends at **Crescent Creek Trailhead**; parking, toilets. Crescent Creek USFS Trail leads 6.2 miles through hemlock forest to subalpine **Crescent Lake**; stocked with grayling. *Watch for bears.* Public-use cabin at lake; permit required.

Return to Milepost S 44.9 Sterling Highway

STERLING HIGHWAY

MILE 45 STERLING HWY
AT THE QUARTZ CREEK ROAD INTERSECTION

SUNRISE INN

Cafe • Bar • Motel • Gas • RV with Electric
Gift Shop • Ice • Package Store

Information on local Rafting & Fishing
Music in the Bar Some Weekends
Daily Specials in the Café

Email: sunrise@arctic.net
www.alaskasunriseinn.com

OPEN YEAR ROUND
(907) 595-1222
PO Box 832 • Cooper Landing AK 99572

www.themilepost.com   2003 ■ The MILEPOST® ■ 553

STERLING HIGHWAY

Rafting the Upper Kenai River near Cooper Landing. (© Barbara Willard)

Deciding where you stay shouldn't be part of the adventure.

Perched above the turquoise beauty of the Kenai River, the Kenai Princess Wilderness Lodge is right on the edge of some of the most amazing scenery around—yet features all the comforts and amenities you've come to expect from Princess. Whether you seek the thrill of Alaska's wild side or the serenity of an out-of-the-way retreat, Kenai Princess Wilderness Lodge is the place.

The Kenai Princess Wilderness Lodge and RV Park overlook the upper Kenai River on Bean Creek Road in Cooper Landing.

Call your travel agent or
800-426-0500
for reservations and information.

PRINCESS
Alaska Lodges
www.princesslodges.com

Bruce Nelson's Float Fishing Service. See display ad this section.

Alaskan Sourdough B&B offers world-renowned Sourdough breakfast, our specialty. Clean rooms, beautiful peaceful area. Great rates. Centrally located on Peninsula. Russian and Kenai rivers, world-class fishing. We can reserve Kenai Fjords trips. Nearby guides, hiking, horseback rides. Wedding chapel, Eskimo minister. Phone/fax (907) 595-1541. Email: sourdoughbb@arctic.net. www.alaskansourdoughbb.com. Reserve early! Johnsons. [ADVERTISEMENT]

Kenai Princess Wilderness® Lodge. A wilderness retreat overlooking the salmon-rich Kenai River featuring cozy bungalow-style rooms with sun porches, wood stoves, televisions and telephones. Spacious view deck, fine restaurant, lounge, gift shop, tour desk, hot tubs, exercise room. Meeting facilities. Open year-round. Reservations (800) 426-0500. [ADVERTISEMENT]

Kenai Princess RV Park. At Cooper Landing on the salmon-rich Kenai River. Featuring 29 sites with water and power, general store, showers, laundry, septic. Use of facilities at adjacent Kenai Princess Lodge®. Open mid-May to mid-September. $27 per night. Phone (907) 595-1425 for reservations. [ADVERTISEMENT]

▲

S 47.8 A 100.8 H 131.7 Bridge over Kenai River at mouth of Kenai Lake. Kenai Lake serves as the headwaters of the Kenai River Special Management Area, established in 1984 to protect this unique resource. The 105-mile-long KRSMA stretches from Kenai Lake almost to the city of Kenai. The Kenai River flows directly alongside the highway for the next 10 miles westbound.

S 47.9 A 100.9 H 131.6 Snug Harbor Road. This side road leads 1 mile to picturesque St. John Neumann Catholic Church with a unique log shrine; named after one of the first American saints.

Also access to bed and breakfast (1 mile) and to Cooper Lake (12 miles) and trailheads for Rainbow Lake Trail (0.5 mile) and 23-mile USFS trail to Russian River Campground (see **Milepost S 52.6**).

St. John Neumann Catholic Church. See display ad this section.

Dreamtime B&B/Health Spa. Welcome to this lovely light-filled health spa on Kenai Lake. Modalities offered: eclectic massage, polarity therapy, reflexology, cranial sacral, essential oils and more! Personalized private healing baths. Food service for 4 or more upon request. Day visitor or groups by appointment. Create your own package or give a gift certificate of health to someone special. Located one mile off Sterling Hwy. Call Dreamtime (907) 595-1756. www.dreamtimealaska.com. [ADVERTISEMENT]

S 48 A 101 H 131.5 Turnoff to north for access road to **Cooper Landing State Recreation Site Boat Launch Facility**, adjacent to the Kenai River Bridge, and to **Cooper Landing Visitor Information Center**. The state boat launch facility has a concrete boat launch, day-use parking, restrooms, viewing decks, informational panels and telescopes. $5 launching fee or $5 parking fee for vehicles not launching boats.

The visitor center is open daily from May through September, 8 A.M. to 10 P.M., and has local and Kenai Peninsula information, maps, Cooper Landing Visitors Guide and brochures.

Upper Kenai River, from **Kenai Lake** to **Skilak Lake**, including Skilak Lake within a half mile of the Kenai River inlet, special regulations apply. For current recorded fishing forecast, phone (907) 267-2502. Silver salmon 5 to 15 lbs., August through October; pink salmon 3 to 7 lbs., July and August; red salmon 3 to 12 lbs., June 11 through mid-August; rainbow and Dolly Varden, June 11 through October. *IMPORTANT: Be familiar with current regulations and closures. Dates given here are subject to change!*

Gwin's Lodge Annex Clothing/Gift Shop and Tackle/Charter Booking Shop. Located adjacent to the Cooper Landing Visitor Information Center and the State Recreation Boat Launch Facility. Open daily June–September from 7 A.M.–10 P.M. The Clothing/Gift Shop features a cross-section of the Gwin's Lodge (at **Milepost 52**) main store's large array of exclusive embroidered clothing and gifts. The Tackle and Charter Booking Shop has fishing tackle, fishing gear/boot sales and rentals, snacks, beverages, sundries, and a charter booking service with trip selections encompassing the entire Kenai Peninsula. Charters booked include all types of guided fishing, remote fly-ins for fishing/bear-viewing combos, scenic or whitewater rafting, and horseback riding. (907) 595-1266 www.gwinslodge.com. See display ad this section. [ADVERTISEMENT]

The Landing. This unique 'Alaskan' style village, at the headwaters of the Upper Kenai River, is home to many of the outdoor adventure centers and guides' services for this area. Here you can hire some of the best local fishing and naturalist guides, visit the historic Visitor's Center, walk the river boardwalk, view Dall Sheep on the hills and watch local artists at work. Take the first right, after the Mile 48 bridge. [ADVERTISEMENT]

Alaska River Adventures. The most authentic way to explore this area is by river with a local naturalist guide. Alaska River Adventures offers a unique 14 mile journey along the river. We pass by historic gold miner's cabins and the Kenaitze Indian Site where we stop for a tour narrated by members of the tribe. After a riverside picnic, we head down river into the Kenai National Wildlife Refuge to see spawning salmon

Boaters approach the Cooper Landing boat launch facility at Milepost S 48.
(© Kris Graef, staff)

ST. JOHN NEUMANN CATHOLIC CHURCH

Mile 47.9 Sterling Highway
SNUG HARBOR RD. (1 MILE)

MAIL: PO BOX 686
COOPER LANDING, AK 99572
SUNDAY MASS: 12:30 PM

VISITORS WELCOME

QUIET SERENE SETTING
*Marian Shrine
Outdoor Stations
Pilgrimage Trail to the Cross*

Explore *from $49 per person* The Upper Kenai River

See it all from the river!
- Historic Cooper Landing Museum
- K-BEQ Kenaitze Indian Fish Camp
- Combat Fishing Zone
- Kenai National Wildlife Refuge
- Spawning Salmon

Alaska RIVER ADVENTURES
Mile 48 Sterling Highway • Cooper Landing
1-888-836-9027 www.UpperKenaiRiver.com

swarming upstream and the famous combat fishing zone. We often see wildlife along the river—bring your camera. Trips are safe for all ages. In our 25 year history, we have taken thousands down the river ... a few at a time. Come join us! (888) 836-9027. www.UpperKenaiRiver.com. See display ad this section. [ADVERTISEMENT]

S 48.1 A 101.1 H 131.4 Ingram's Sport Fishing Cabins on the Kenai River to north. Salmon Run Lodge to south. (Descriptions follow.)

Salmon Run Lodge. Very reasonably priced, large comfortable rooms with private

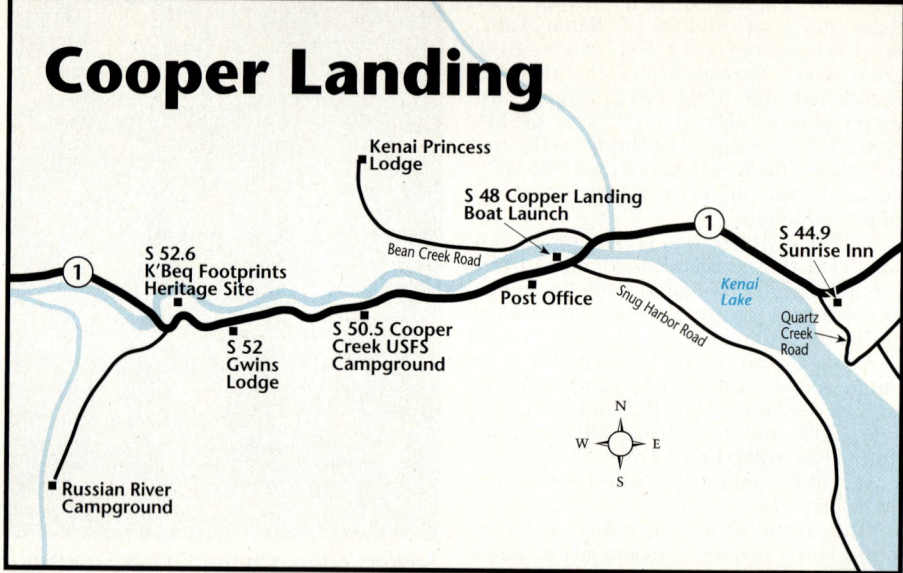

Cooper Landing

baths, sleep 2–6 people. Also, 4 backpacker cabins with beds. Shower house. Bring your own sleeping bags, save money! Short distance to grocery store, restaurants. Great views, watch moose, sheep, goats, bears. Located near the headwaters of the world famous Kenai River. Unbelievable salmon and trout fishing. Come fish with us for kings, sockeye, silvers or trout. Personalized service. Fishing/lodging packages. All gear included. Other activities include rafting, halibut charters, hiking, backpacking. Visa/MasterCard. Email: salmonrunlodge@yahoo.com. www.salmonrunlodge.com. Summer phone (907) 595-2197. Winter phone (907) 358-4397. [ADVERTISEMENT]

Ingram's Float Plane Service and Cabins. Bear viewing/lodging/fishing packages are right at your doorstep, with float plane fly-outs or river trips departing from Ingram's Kenai River dock and just a phone call/email away. Short flight to view bears fish for salmon, July through September. Bring your camera! Spectacular fly fishing for trout and grayling, along with fantastic salmon fishing. Enjoy all of the vacation fun the Kenai Peninsula has to offer along with personal service and attention to details. Early Season Discount! Book NOW for best dates. The charming, well spaced cabins feature private baths, furnished kitchens and breath-taking mountain and wildife views. One-person-cater-raft rentals are available for your fishing and floating fun. "Your satisfaction is our goal." Hosts, Diane and Steve Ingram. Toll-free 1-866-595-1213. www.kenairiverlodging.com. See display ad this section. [ADVERTISEMENT]

S 48.2 A 101.2 H 131.3 Troutfitter's Alpine Motel and Cooper Landing Grocery to south.

Troutfitters Alpine Motel. See display ad this section.

Cooper Landing Grocery & Hardware. See display ad this section.

S 48.3 A 101.3 H 131.2 Kenai River Drifter's Lodge to north.

Kenai River Drifter's Lodge. When life offers you the best, take it! On the bank of the Kenai River, enjoy comfortable first-class, tastefully furnished, new chalets, with awesome views. Each chalet includes a large private bath, fridge, stove and microwave. The 4-bedroom lodge, on the river, is also available. Join us in the morning for our complimentary Alaskan continental breakfast overlooking the river, and after a day of activities, enjoy the Alaskan tales around the evening campfire at river's edge. Guided fishing available. Chalets accommodate 6, or the entire property can host 50. Now open year-round. Reservations encouraged, all seasons. Toll-free: 1-866-595-5959. Great web site: www.drifterslodge.com. See display ad this section. [ADVERTISEMENT]

S 48.4 A 101.4 H 131.1 COOPER LANDING (pop. 285) stretches along several miles of the Sterling Highway at the west end of Kenai Lake. All visitor facilities available.

Emergency services: Cooper Landing ambulance, phone 911.

Private Aircraft: State-owned Quartz

Creek airstrip, 3 W; elev. 450 feet; length 2,200 feet; gravel; unattended. Floatplanes land at Cooper Lake.

Cooper Landing was named for Joseph Cooper, a miner who discovered gold here in 1894. A school and post office opened in the 1920s to serve the miners and their families living in the area. Cooper Landing was connected to Kenai by road in 1948, and to Anchorage in 1951. According to the Alaska Dept. of Community and Regional Affairs, the population of the area nearly doubles each summer to support tourism businesses and activities.

The Shrew's Nest to south. See display ad this section. ▲

S 48.5 A 101.5 H 131 Hamilton's Place to north; The Hutch bed and breakfast.

Hamilton's Place river resort, only complete stop on the upper Kenai River. Information center for the famous Russian River

STERLING HIGHWAY

and surrounding area. Centrally located for day trips to Seward, Soldotna/Kenai, Homer.

Make us your Kenai Peninsula headquarters. Tesoro services, 24-hour recovery and transport (flatbed) service, 24-hour locksmith, propane. All-emergency road service-providers. General store, groceries, licenses, tackle, ice, liquor store. Restaurant, lounge. RV hookups, modern cabins with cooking facilities, laundromat, phone. Fish freezing, storage, Federal Express shipping. Hamilton's Place, serving the public since 1952, hopes to make your stay enjoyable. Phone (907) 595-1260; fax (907) 595-1530. Email: hamspl@arctic.net. See display ad this section. [ADVERTISEMENT]

The Hutch B&B. 12 clean smoke-free rooms with private baths at very reasonable rates. Continental breakfast served until 10 A.M. Common area TV/VCR. View mountain goats, Dall sheep and Kenai River from our covered decks. Our parking area accommodates boat trailers and large vehicles. Also,

The Hutch B&B
- 12 Rooms • Cabins • Private Baths • Smoke Free
- Reasonable Rates • Large Parking Area • View Mountain Wildlife

hutch@arctic.net
www.arctic.net/~hutch
(907) 595-1270
See log ad at mile 48.5 Sterling Hwy   P.O. Box 823, Cooper Landing, AK 99572 • Look for the "Bunny Trail"

Wrangler and rider pose for a photo before taking off on a trail ride with Alaska Horsemen Trail Adventures.
(© Kris Graef, staff)

quiet, self-contained cabins with cooking facilities accommodate families/groups. Look for the "Bunny Trail" sign. Phone (907) 595-1270, fax (907) 595-1829. See display ad this section. [ADVERTISEMENT]

S 48.6 A 101.6 H 130.9 Cooper Landing post office, located in resort; open 9 A.M. to 5 P.M. weekdays and Saturday morning. Pay phone.

S 49.4 A 102.4 H 130.1 Large paved turnout to north by Kenai River. The highway winds along the Kenai River.

S 49.7 A 102.7 H 129.8 Kenai Riverside Campground and RV Park, located on the banks of the Kenai River. 25 open and wooded level RV-sites, full hookups, showers, dump station and riverside campsites. Discounts on fishing and rafting trips with every overnight stay. B&B rooms also available. Look for the sign! Visa/MasterCard; 1-888-KENAIRV (888-536-2478); fax: (907) 783-2130; www.kenairiversidecampground.com. info@kenairiversidecampground.com. [ADVERTISEMENT]

S 49.9 A 102.9 H 129.6 Alaska Rivers Co., right side westbound. Rafting daily on the beautiful Kenai River. Half-day scenic float, or full-day canyon trip with exhilarating rapids. Both trips include homemade picnic lunch, excellent viewing of wildlife, professional guides, all equipment provided.

KENAI EXPLORATION PACKAGE
THE BEST OF THE KENAI PENINSULA

All guided activities, lodging, meals, & transportation from Anchorage—Three, four, or five days—you choose!

- Guided Hiking
- Fjords Cruise
- Kenai River Rafting
- Scenic Alaska Railroad Ride
- Optional Fishing Add-on
- Family Friendly Staff, Activites and Meals

800-334-8730
www.alaskawildland.com/mp

ALASKA WILDLAND ADVENTURES
On the Kenai Since 1977

All ages welcome. Personalized guided drift boat fishing for all species of fish. Overnight accommodations available. Family-owned and operated by Cooper Landing residents. Gary Galbraith, owner. (907) 595-1226 for

Seward's Day, an Alaska state holiday, is celebrated on the last Monday in March.

reservations or just stop by. Email: lrg@arctic.net. www.alaskariverscompany.com. [ADVERTISEMENT]

S 50.1 A 103.1 H 129.4 Alaska Wildland Adventures. See display ad this section.

Kenai River Trips with Alaska Wildland Adventures. Don't miss out on one of the Kenai Peninsula's most exciting day trips! Join a rafting or fishing day-trip on the Kenai River. Enjoy a scenic natural history float or some premium fishing for rainbow trout and the Kenai's world famous salmon. Conveniently located on the upper Kenai in Cooper Landing, the heart of the Kenai Peninsula. Choose from 4 departures daily. This company is known for its friendly, professional guides, quality boats, and providing quality gear. On the Kenai since 1977! Alaska Wildland Adventures also offers Active Nature Safaris and Wilderness Lodge packages that allow you to experience the true character of Alaska by combining a variety of activities by day, with comfortable evenings in wilderness settings. Features include wildlife viewing opportunities, guided hiking, scenic Kenai River raft trips, marine wildlife and seacoast glacier cruises in Kenai Fjords National Park, all accommodations, delicious meals, and evenings in cozy cabins. For an additional cost, cast a line for some world-famous Kenai River salmon and rainbow trout. Please call (800) 478-4100 for information and reservations; or visit www.alaskarivertrips.com/mp. Watch for Alaska Wildland Adventures' blue sign at **Milepost S 50.1**! See display ad this section. [ADVERTISEMENT]

S 50.4 A 103.4 H 129.1 Juneau Creek, Dolly Varden and rainbow, mid-June through July.

S 50.5 A 103.5 H 129 Bridge over Cooper Creek.

Cooper Creek USFS Campground. Entrance to south for Loop B camping area: 23 large, level sites on good gravel road; tables, water, firepits, outhouses; campground host. Camping fee is $10 single, $18 double. (Campsites may be reserved, phone 1-877-444-NRRS or visit www.reserveusa.com). ▲

S 50.6 A 103.6 H 128.9 Turnoff to north for narrow 0.2-mile 1-way gravel road through Cooper Creek USFS Campground Loop A camping area; 7 small sites, tables, firepits, outhouse, $10 camping fee. ▲

S 50.9 A 103.9 H 128.6 Exit only for Cooper Creek Loop A campground road.

S 51 A 104 H 128.5 Begin 55 mph speed zone westbound; slow for curves. Reduce speed eastbound.

S 52 A 105 H 127.5 Gwin's Lodge to south; food, lodging, camping and fishing supplies (description follows).

Kenai Riverside
CAMPGROUND & RV PARK
Camp on the banks of the Kenai River—MP 49.7 Cooper Landing!
- ▲ 25 partial hookups + dumpsite
- ▲ Clean bathrooms & showers
- ▲ On-site fishing + licenses
- ▲ Groups welcome

Contact us at: **888-KENAIRV**
(888-536-2478)
www.kenairiversidecampground.com

KENAI RIVER TRIPS™

Trout & Salmon Fishing

Fish the Kenai - Fish for huge King Salmon and feisty silvers on the Lower river in power boats. Or quietly fish for trophy Rainbow Trout and Sockeye Salmon on the Upper river in drift boats. Top gear and professional guides. Full day $195 w/lunch, Half day $125 when available.

Scenic Raft Trips

Scenic Float - Take a 2-hour placid float and enjoy the snow-capped mountain scenery. Watch for moose, eagles, and salmon. Hear the stories behind the sights. Adults $45, Kids $29. Departs 9:30 am, 1:00 pm, & 5:00 pm.

Kenai Canyon Rafting - Explore the Kenai National Wildlife Refuge at the river's pace — by raft. This full day trip combines a scenic float, the mild whitewater of the Kenai Canyon, a glacier-carved lake cruise, and a picnic lunch. Adults $110, Kids $89. Departs 11:00 am.

ALASKA WILDLAND ADVENTURES

800-478-4100
www.alaska-river-trips.com/mp

MILEPOST 50.1 STERLING HWY in Cooper Landing

Save $5 with this ad

On the Kenai Since 1977

GWIN'S LODGE
ESTABLISHED 1952
MILEPOST 52 • STERLING HIGHWAY • COOPER LANDING • ALASKA

UPPER KENAI RAINBOW TROUT CHARTERS

PACIFIC HALIBUT CHARTERS

DOROTHY HOOK (ARTIST) - PRINTS, NOTECARDS & POSTCARDS AVAILABLE

LOWER KENAI KING & SILVER SALMON CHARTERS

KENAI FJORDS NATIONAL PARK CRUISES & DINNER CRUISES

WHITEWATER RAFTING

HELICOPTER FLY-INS TO SLED DOG MUSHING CAMP

REMOTE FLY-IN BEAR VIEWING & SALMON FISHING COMBOS

SCENIC & WILDLIFE VIEWING RAFT TRIPS

Your Kenai Peninsula Outdoor Recreation Headquarters

- World Renown Restaurant & Bar
- Package Liquor/Beer/Wine/Coolers
- Groceries/Snacks/Soda/Juices
- Espresso/Latte/Cappuccino
- Pizzeria/Ice Cream Shop

- Log Cabins, Chalets & Cottages
- Fishing Licenses/Tackle/Tips/Hotspot Info
- Pole/Reel/Hip Boot Rentals
- Ice/Firewood/Charcoal
- Charter Booking Service

- Exclusive "*Kenai River*" & "*Russian River*" Embroidered Hats, Shirts, Jackets & Polarfleece
- Alaska Gifts/Souvenirs/Cards
- "*Trapper's Creek Smoking Company*" Fish Processing/Smoking/Shipping Drop Site

DELUXE CHALET

DELUXE CHALET

STANDARD CHALET

LOG CABIN W/ LOFT & KITCHEN

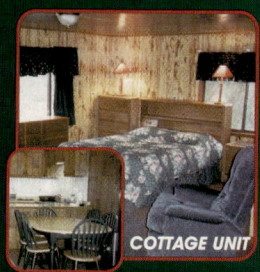
COTTAGE UNIT

COMFORTABLE LOG CABINS, CHALETS & COTTAGES W/ PRIVATE BATHS, NO PHONES OR TV

An Alaskan landmark log roadhouse lodge. Restaurant selected by USA Today in 2000 as a "Top 50 Plates in America" & by "Alaska Best Places" travel guide.

"The closest lodging & services to the Kenai & Russian Rivers Confluence, by far, the most productive Sockeye (Red) Salmon sportfishery on earth!!!"

The finest, most extensive line of embroidered outdoor recreation clothing on the Kenai Peninsula.

Extended Summer Hours:
OPEN 24 HOURS/DAY - 7 DAYS/WEEK
during Sockeye (Red) Salmon season (June 11-August 20)

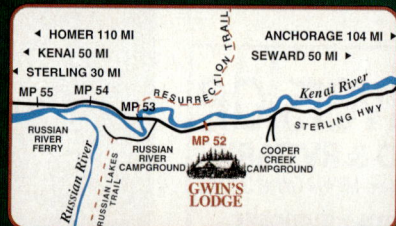

CHECK OUT OUR LOG AD!

PUBLIC PAY PHONES

PUBLIC USE RESTSTOP FACILITIES

MAILING ADDRESS:
14865 Sterling Highway
Cooper Landing, AK 99572

(907) 595-1266 • FAX (907) 595-1681 • www.gwinslodge.com • www.ool.com/gwins • gwins@arctic.net

HOMEMADE FOOD • "ALASKA" PORTIONS • PIONEER ROADHOUSE ATMOSPHERE

Gwin's Lodge, Restaurant and Bar, left side southbound. Nestled in the Kenai Mountains of the Chugach National Forest, Gwin's is the closest lodge and services to the Kenai and Russian Rivers confluence, the best sockeye salmon sportfishery on Earth and the finest road accessible rainbow trout fishery in Alaska. Restaurant/bar and store/tackle shop open 24 hours/day June 11–August 20. Gwin's celebrates over 50 years of service in 2003 as one of Alaska's few remaining historic, pioneer hand-built log roadhouses where Alaskans and visitors alike always stop for homemade "Alaska-sized" portions and fast, courteous service.

Fishermen of all ages enjoy fishing the Russian River. (© Susannah Clymer)

Selected in 2000 by "USA Today" newspaper as a Top 50 "America's Best Plates" restaurant. Selected by "Alaska Best Places" travel guide as the top restaurant on Northern Kenai Peninsula. Gwin's exclusive "around-the-clock" menu includes delicious, homemade chile, soups, award-winning chowders, quiches, pies, cheesecakes and giant cinnamon rolls as well as grilled steaks, salmon, halibut and our world-famous burger lineup. Accommodations include comfortable log cabins, chalets and cottages. All units include private baths/showers. Most units are new, well-appointed standard or deluxe sized chalets that include kitchen, dining, living and loft areas. Store/tackle shop features fishing gear/tackle/boots for sale/rental, licenses, groceries, gifts/cards, pizzeria, ice cream shop, fish freezing and "Trappers Creek Smoking Company" fish processing/smoking/shipping drop-off site. Gwin's large clothing showroom's exclusive line of embroidered outdoor recreation garments is the finest, most extensive selection on the Kenai Peninsula. Gwin's Charter Booking Service's wide array of excursions blankets the Kenai Peninsula. Trips include Upper Kenai River rainbow trout; Lower Kenai River king or silver salmon; Cook Inlet and Prince William Sound Pacific halibut; fly-ins to remote lakes and streams for spectacular, yet modestly priced bear viewing and salmon fishing combinations; fly-ins to remote rainbow trout or Arctic grayling; Upper Kenai River scenic and wildlife viewing rafting; helicopter flightseeing to "hands-on" sled dog mushing of Iditarod Race champions on a majestic glacier snowfield; whitewater rafting; horseback riding and flightseeing. VISA, MasterCard and Discover accepted. (907) 595-1266 (voice), (907) 595-1681 (fax); www.gwinslodge.com or www.ool.com/gwins; gwins@arctic.net. See display ad facing page. [ADVERTISEMENT]

S 52.6 A 105.6 H 126.9 Kenaitze Indian Tribe K'Beq Footprints Heritage Site north side of highway; USFS Russian River Campground to south (descriptions follow).

K'Beq Footprints. See display ad this section.

Interpretive tours of the **Kenaitze Footprints Heritage Site** are available Monday through Saturday 10 A.M. to 5:30 P.M., June 1 to August 31. Admission charged; children under 12 free. Parking for vehicles and RVs (no camping, parking fee charged), restrooms and picnic tables. The gift shop features Kenaitze Dena'ina arts and crafts.

Follow paved road south 2 miles for **Russian River USFS Campground,** parking areas and trailheads. Phones and overflow parking at exit to highway. Dump station at Mile 1.3 on the access road. Campground host at Mile 1.7. The Russian River Campground is often full during the summer, particularly during the Russian River red salmon runs. Arrive early! There are 84 sites, toilets, water, tables and firepits. Fish cleaning stations. Fees: $13 single RV occupancy, $20 double RV occupancy, $5 12-hour day-use parking, $6 dump station. Concessionaire-operated. (Campsites may be reserved, phone 1-877-444-NRRS or visit www. reserveusa.com).

CAUTION: Bears attracted by the salmon are frequent visitors to this campground.

Upper Russian Lake USFS trailhead parking at Mile 1 on campground road. Lower Russian Lake trailhead parking at Mile 2.6. Lower Russian Lakes Trail: elev. 500 feet; hiking time 1½ hours; good trail first 3 miles; spur trail to Russian River Falls viewing platform. A good place to view jumping salmon, and a nice family hike. Upper Russian Lake: elev. 690 feet, 12 miles. Trail continues to Cooper Lake at end of Snug Harbor Road (see **Milepost S 47.9**). Public-use cabins along trail. Winter use: good snowmobiling to lower lake only, avalanche danger beyond.

The **Russian River:** Closed to all fishing April 15 through June 10. Bait prohibited at all times in Russian River drainage. Check regulations for limits and other restrictions. Red (sockeye) salmon run starts mid-June. Second run begins July 20–25 and lasts about 3 weeks. Must use flies prior to Aug. 21. Silver (coho) salmon to 15 lbs., run begins mid-August. Catch-and-release only for rainbow trout in lower part of river at all times that season is open.

S 53 A 106 H 126.5 Bridge over Kenai

Fishing the Upper Kenai River

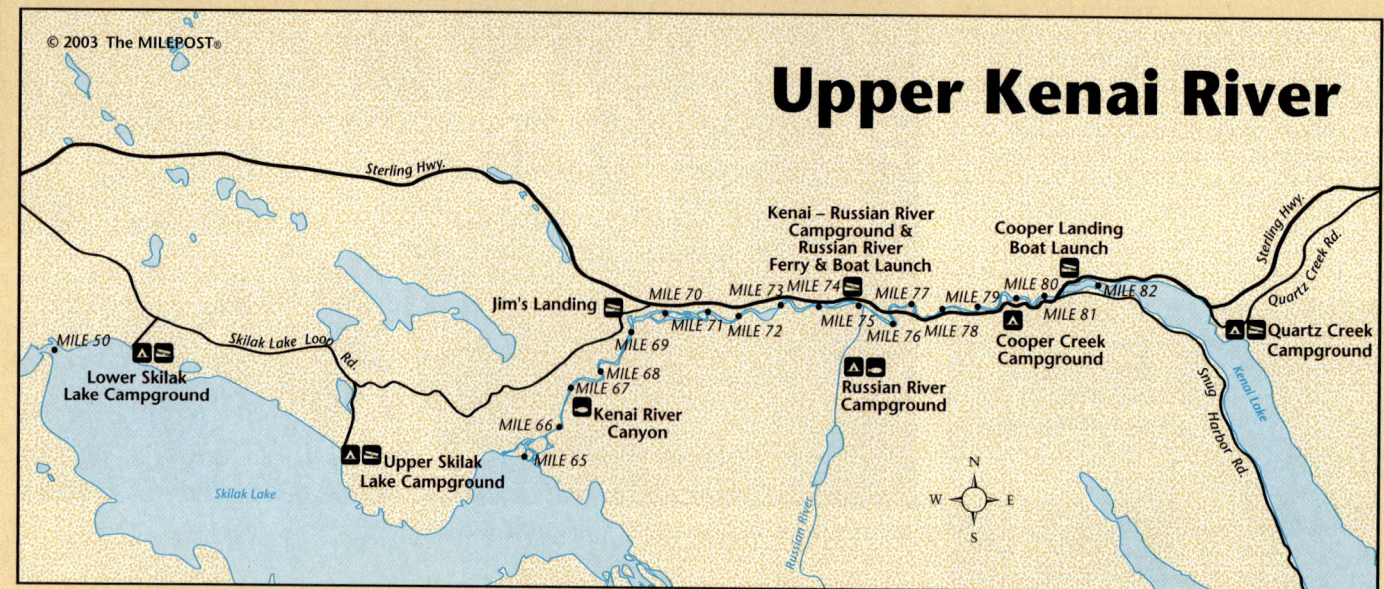

The Kenai River originates in Kenai Lake, about 100 road miles south of Anchorage, and flows 85 river miles west to Cook Inlet. For fishermen, the river divides itself into 2 rivers: the "upper" and the "lower" Kenai River. The first 17.3 miles of the river—from Kenai Lake to Skilak Lake—constitutes the Upper Kenai River.

Following is a log of campgrounds, recreation areas and river access points on the Upper Kenai River. See pages 571-574 for access points on the Lower Kenai River. If it is a road-accessible river access, the milepost and road are given first.

Upper Kenai River Access

Milepost 0.2 Quartz Creek Road/River Mile 85.5. Quartz Creek Recreation Area; boat launch, day-use area and campground on Kenai Lake, just south of Milepost 44.9 Sterling Highway.

Milepost 47.8 Sterling Highway/River Mile 82. Cooper Landing Boat Launch at Kenai Lake Outlet. This public access point is near the Kenai River Bridge. Concrete boat launch adjacent Kenai River Bridge; restrooms, day-use parking, viewing

decks, telescopes and informational panels. Fees charged for parking and boat launch.

Milepost 50.5 Sterling Highway/ River Mile 79.1. Cooper Creek Campground. The campground loop on the north side of the highway is on the south bank of the river.

Milepost 52.6 Sterling Highway/River Mile 75. Russian River Campground. Fish-cleaning stations and fishing access to Russian River. Good fishing for sockeye salmon. Popular during the salmon runs.

Milepost 55 Sterling Highway/River Mile 73.5. Russian River Ferry. The ferry crosses the Kenai River to the mouth of the Russian River. This recreation site is popular and heavily used during salmon runs.

Milepost 57 Sterling Highway/River Mile 71.1. Pullout. This is an unimproved site on the north bank of the Kenai River.

Milepost 0.3 Skilak Lake Loop Road/River Mile 70.4. Jim's Landing; accessed via a 0.2-mile road to the west bank of the river. Experienced boaters only.

Milepost 58 Sterling Highway/River Mile 69.9. Kenai National Wildlife Refuge Visitor Information Center.

River Mile 65 Skilak Lake Inlet. Hidden Creek Trail takes off at Milepost 4.6 Skilak Lake Loop Road and leads south to the lake. The Lower Kenai River Trail then leads upriver for about 2.5 miles. This trail provides fishing access to the Kenai River Canyon.

Milepost 8.5 Skilak Lake Loop Road/River Mile 58. Upper Skilak Lake Campground.

Milepost 13.8 Skilak Lake Loop Road/River Mile 51.1. Lower Skilak Lake Campground.

River Mile 50.2 Skilak Lake Outlet. Boat access only. Good fishing opportunities in this area.

River.

S 53.2 A 106.2 H 126.3 Wide shoulder parking to north. Turnoff to north for **Resurrection Pass Trailhead**; large parking area. This 38-mile-long USFS trail climbs to Resurrection Pass (elev. 2,600 feet) and descends to north trailhead near Hope on Turnagain Arm.

S 53.7 A 106.7 H 125.8 Kenaitze Indian Tribe Interpretive Site—Hchan'iynt "Beginnings"—to south. This is a 1,100-foot-long woodchip trail along the Kenai River. Established in 1992 to preserve, protect and interpret important cultural and natural resources in this area. Fishing, parking (no RVs or trailers).

S 53.8 A 106.8 H 125.7 Distance marker westbound shows Soldotna 41 miles, Kenai 57 miles, Homer 115 miles.

S 54.6 A 107.6 H 124.9 Gravel turnout at Chugach National Forest boundary sign.

Many turnouts with recreation access signs on the Kenai River between here and Milepost S 58.

S 54.8 A 107.8 H 124.7 Russian River Ferry entrance to southeast. 60-space outer parking lot, scenic overlook, boat launch, toilets and gatehouse. Tent sites available. During salmon season this recreation area is heavily used. Fees charged for boat launch, parking and camping.

Privately operated 28-person ferry crosses the Kenai River to opposite bank and to the mouth of the Russian River. Ferry fee is $5 adults round-trip, $2.50 children (3 to 11). Parking is $6 a day ($7 for vehicles over 20 feet). Boat launch $5.

S 55 A 108 H 124.5 Entering **Kenai National Wildlife Refuge** westbound, administered by the USF&WS; contains more than 1.97 million acres of land set aside to preserve the moose, bear, sheep and other wildlife found here.

Leaving Game Management Unit 7, entering Unit 15 westbound.

S 56.8 A 109.8 H 123.7 Double-ended turnout.

S 57.2 A 110.2 H 122.3 Fuller Lake trailhead (well marked); parking to north. **Lower Fuller Lake**, arctic grayling; **Upper Fuller Lake**, Dolly Varden.

S 57.8 A 110.8 H 121.7 Kenai National Wildlife Refuge visitor contact station to north. The information cabin is open Memorial Day through Labor Day; brochures and information on Kenai National Wildlife Refuge recreation opportunities. Large gravel parking area, water pump, toilets, trailer parking (no camping).

S 58 A 111 H 121.5 East junction with Skilak Lake Road to south. Actual driving distance between **Mileposts 58 and 59** is 1.2 miles.

Junction with Skilak Lake Loop Road. See "Skilak Lake Loop Road" log on this page.

CAUTION: Moose Danger Zone next 22 miles westbound. Watch for moose!

S 59 A 112 H 120.5 Actual driving distance between **Milepost 59** and **60** is 1.2 miles.

S 59.9 A 112.9 H 119.6 Large gravel turnout to north (*abrupt pavement edge!*). Easy-to-miss turnoff down hill to south

(no sign) leads to **Jean Lake Campground**; 3 sites, picnic area; boat launch, rainbow fishing.

S 60 A 113 H 119.5 Actual driving distance between **Milepost 60** and **61** is 1.4 miles.

S 60.6 A 113.6 H 118.9 Large gravel turnout to south.

S 60.9 A 113.9 H 118.6 Skyline Trail parking to south, trailhead to north. Skyline Trail leads north into the Mystery Hills, steep climb, good views. Double-ended gravel parking area to south.

S 62.3 A 115.3 H 117.2 Large gravel turnout to north. Hideout Hill to the south.

S 63.7 A 116.7 H 115.8 Mystery Creek Access Road (gated) to north. This road provides access to the Mystery Hills area. For seasonal opening of the road, contact Kenai NWR at (907) 262-7021.

S 64.4 A 117.4 H 115.1 Gravel turnout.

S 64.5 A 117.5 H 115 Highway straightens westbound and descends to transition zone of lowland marsh and spruce forest.

CAUTION: High speed traffic on straightaway westbound. Pass with care!
Narrow, winding road eastbound.

S 68.3 A 121.3 H 111.2 Turnoff to south for Peterson Lake (0.5 mile) and Kelly Lake (1 mile) public campgrounds. Both have tables and firepits for 3 camping parties, water and boat launch, and parking space for self-contained RVs. **Kelly** and **Peterson lakes** have rainbow population. Access to Seven Lakes trail.

S 68.8 A 121.8 H 110.7 Distance marker westbound shows Soldotna 25 miles, Kenai 35 miles and Homer 99 miles.

S 70.7 A 123.7 H 108.8 Egumen Lake gravel parking area to south. Half-mile marshy trail to **Egumen Lake** (lake not visible from highway); good rainbow population.

S 71.2 A 124.2 H 108.3 Parking area at entrance to Watson Lake public campground; 0.4-mile drive from highway to small campground with 3 sites, toilets, picnic tables, fire grates, water, dumpsters and steep boat launch (suitable for canoes or hand-carried boats). East Fork Moose River trailhead. **Watson Lake**, rainbow.

S 72.8 A 125.8 H 106.7 Paved double-ended turnout to south, lake to north.

S 75.3 A 128.3 H 104.2 West junction

Skilak Lake Loop Road Log

Originally part of the first Kenai Peninsula highway built in 1947, the 19.1-mile Skilak Lake Loop Road (good gravel) loops south through the Skilak Wildlife Recreation Area to campgrounds, trails and fishing spots. CAUTION: Do not leave valuables in unattended boats or vehicles.
Distance from east junction (EJ) with Sterling Highway at Milepost S 58 is followed by distance from west junction (WJ) with Sterling Highway at Milepost S 75.3.

EJ 0 WJ 19.1 Junction with Sterling Highway at **Milepost S 58**.

EJ 0.1 WJ 19 Jim's Landing day-use area on Kenai River, 0.2 mile from road; toilets, tables, firepits, water, boat launch, parking area.

NOTE: The Kenai River downstream from Jim's Landing is considered Class II and Class III white water and for experienced boaters only. Wear a personal flotation device. The Kenai River is non-motorized to Skilak Lake. Motors may be used on Skilak Lake to travel to Upper Skilak Lake Campground boat ramp. There is no road access to the Kenai River between Jim's Landing and Upper Skilak Lake Campground; be prepared to travel the entire distance by boat. Use caution when crosssing Skilak Lake, as winds from Skilak Glacier frequently create dangerous boating conditions. Be prepared to wait overnight at river mouth until winds abate.

Kenai River from Skilak Lake to Soldotna. Consult regulations for legal tackle, limits and seasons. King salmon 20 to 80 lbs., use spinners, excellent fishing June to August; red salmon 6 to 12 lbs., many, but hard to catch, use flies, best from July 15 to Aug. 10; pink salmon 4 to 8 lbs., abundant fish on even years Aug. 1 to Sept. 1, spoons; silver salmon 6 to 15 lbs., use spoons, Aug. 15 to Nov. 1; rainbow, Dolly Varden 15 to 20 inches, June through September, use spinners, winged bobber, small-weighted spoon.

EJ 0.6 WJ 18.5 East entrance parking area for Kenai River Trail; map and trail chart. Hike in 0.5 mile for scenic view of Kenai Canyon. Oversized vehicle parking.

EJ 2.3 WJ 16.8 West entrance parking area for Kenai River Trail. Hike in 0.3 mile to see regrowth from 1991 Pothole Lake Fire.

EJ 2.4 WJ 16.7 Pothole Lake Overlook; gravel parking area overlooks scene of Pothole Lake forest fire of 1991. Interpretive sign on fire.

EJ 3.6 WJ 15.5 Hidden Lake Campground 0.5 mile from road is an exceptionally nice lakeshore camping area with 44 sites on paved loop roads. It has picnic pavilions, a dump station, wheelchair-accessible toilets, tables, water, firepits and boat launch. Campfire programs Friday and Saturday evenings in summer at the amphitheater. Observation deck for viewing wildlife. Campground hosts in residence. Camping fee $10 for vehicles. Trailer parking area, interpretive exhibits and kitchen shelter with barbecue.

Hidden Lake, lake trout average 16 inches and kokanee 9 inches, year-round, best from May 15 to July 1, use spoon, red-and-white or weighted, by trolling, casting and jigging. This lake is a favorite among local ice fishermen from late December through March.

EJ 4.6 WJ 14.5 Parking area and information sign at Hidden Creek trailhead; 3 mile

View of Engineer Lake from Skilak Lake Loop Road. (© Kris Graef, staff)

round-trip hike to beach on Skilak Lake.

EJ 5.1 WJ 14 Scenic overlook with sweeping view of one arm of Skilak Lake. Evidence of 1996 Hidden Creek Fire is visible.

EJ 5.4 WJ 13.7 Parking area at Skilak Lookout trailhead; 5 mile round-trip hike.

EJ 6.4 WJ 12.7 Parking area at Bear Mountain trailhead; 2 mile round-trip hike (moderate, steep) to scenic view of Skilak Lake.

EJ 6.9 WJ 12.2 Scenic viewpoint of Skilak Lake.

EJ 8.5 WJ 10.6 Upper Skilak Lake Campground, drive 2 miles along Lower Ohmer Lake; 0.2-mile loop road through campground. There are 25 campsites (some sites on lakeshore), boat launch, toilets and tables; similar facilities to Hidden Lake Campground (Milepost EJ 3.6). Camping fee $10/vehicle, $5/tent site (walk-in).

Lower Ohmer Lake, rainbow 14 to 16 inches, year-round. **Skilak Lake** offers rainbow and Dolly Varden. Red (sockeye) salmon enter lake in mid-July.

EJ 8.6 WJ 10.5 Lower Ohmer Lake Campground via short side road to parking area on lake; 3 campsites, toilet, boat launch, firepits, tables.

EJ 9.4 WJ 9.7 Turnout overlooking Engineer Lake.

EJ 9.5 WJ 9.6 Short side road to **Engineer Lake** boat launch and Seven Lakes trailhead; turnaround and parking area with firepits at lake. Stocked silver salmon to 15 inches, best in July.

EJ 11.7 WJ 7.4 Dump station on paved double-ended turnout to east.

EJ 13.8 WJ 5.3 Well-marked 1-mile side road to **Lower Skilak Lake Campground**; 14 sites, tables, toilets, firepits, and boat launch for Skilak Lake and Kenai River fishing.

CAUTION: Skilak Lake is cold; winds are fierce and unpredictable. Wear life jackets!

EJ 14.2 WJ 4.9 Fire guard station.

EJ 18.7 WJ 0.4 Bottinintnin Lake; well-marked side road leads 0.3 mile to parking area on lakeshore. Shallow lake: No sport fish, but nice area for recreational canoeing. Watch for loons and grebes.

EJ 19.1 WJ 0 Junction with Sterling Highway at **Milepost S 75.3**.

Return to Milepost S 58 or S 75.3
Sterling Highway

with Skilak Lake Road.

See "Skilak Lake Loop Road" log on page 563.

S 76 A 129 H 103.5 Entering Kenai National Wildlife Refuge lands eastbound.

S 79.3 A 132.3 H 100.2 Tune radios to 920-AM for weather information.

S 79.5 A 132.5 H 100 Kenai Keys Road. *Begin 4-lane divided highway westbound. Begin 2-lane undivided highway eastbound. CAUTION: Moose Danger Zone next 22 miles eastbound.*

S 80.3 A 133.3 H 99.2 Turnoff for Peninsula Furs, Real Alaskan Cabins and RV Park, and Bing's Landing State Recreation Site.

Bing's Landing State Recreation Site has 36 RV and tent campsites, picnic area, water, boat launch, toilets (wheelchair accessible), dumpster; access to Kenai River; camping fee $10/night or resident pass; boat launch fee $5; day-use parking fee $5.

Peninsula Furs. See display ad this section.

Real Alaskan Cabins & RV Park. See display ad this section.

S 80.6 A 133.6 H 98.9 Large double-ended paved parking area to south. *Begin 45 mph speed zone westbound.*

S 80.5 A 133.5 H 99 Diamond Willow Picker. See display ad this section.

S 81 A 134 H 98.5 STERLING (pop. 6,138; elev. 150 feet). This unincorporated community, located on the Sterling Highway at the confluence of the Moose and Kenai rivers, serves the summer influx of sportfishermen, campers and others. The name was formalized in 1954 when a post office was established. Sterling has one school.

Traveler services include 2 gas stations, 2 motels, a hostel, several restaurants and cafes; gift, grocery, hardware, antique, fur and furniture stores, laundromat and several campgrounds. Post office at **Milepost S 81.6**. (Businesses with a Sterling mailing address extend west to **Milepost S 85**.) Nearby recreational opportunities include fishing and the extensive canoe trail system (see description at **Milepost S 82**). Moose River Raft Race and Sterling Days held in July.

Bing Brown's RV Park & Motel to north. See display ad this section. ▲

Suburban Propane. See display ad this section.

S 81.5 A 134.5 H 98.0 Moose River Resort & Hot Tub, Cabin & RV Sites. Take "Otter Trail" 1.3 miles, then left on "Moose Run Road" to this incredible river-front location on the peaceful Moose River, which feeds into the world famous Kenai River. This is an outlet for the Swanson River canoe trail system, and "next door" to the Kenai Moose Range. Large, fully outfitted, cabin

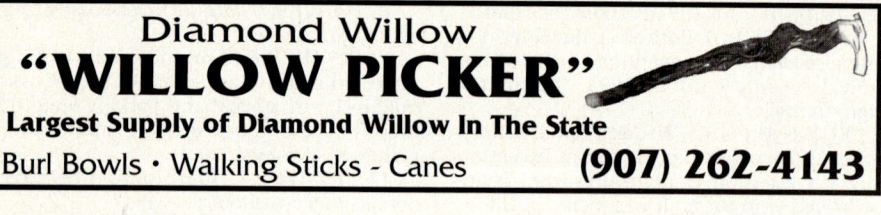

Alaska has 19 species of furbearers.—
ALASKA A to Z

with complete kitchen, private bath, laundry, Satellite-TV, phone. Sleeps up to 5 comfortably. Outdoor dining option in the gazebo. Lounge in the huge outdoor hot-tub. Also, 4 exclusive, secluded riverfront RV-sites with full hookups. First year discounts! Fish cleaning area, smoking, freezing facilities. Fire-pits, dry cut wood, BBQ and pavilion. Private boat-launch and dock for resort guests. See migratory swans and other wildlife. Perfect winter snow-machine running on this wide meandering river bed. This is a one-of-a-kind vacation location! Open year-round. Office (907) 262-9777 or Cell (907) 351-2441. www.mooseriverresort.com.

[ADVERTISEMENT]

Moose River RV Park, Cafe´ & Visitor Center. Located in the heart of Sterling. Less than 1/4-mile from the confluence of the Moose and Kenai rivers known for world-record king salmon. You'll love the convenience and location. Post office just across the street, a grocery/movie rental store a 1/2-mile away, gas, propane and snacks next door, a laundry facility 2 miles away. We serve awesome espresso drinks, soups and sandwiches here at the park. Hosts, Dennis and Anita Merkes, lifelong Alaska residents, have done their best to make Moose River RV Park a camping stop and a destination. We offer ongoing activities including: local slide shows, "Meet the Sourdough," potlucks, bonfires and numerous other activities. Ask Josh about the local fishing or let him take you there. Our brand new facility offers a landscaped treed setting, pull-thrus, full hookups, phone modem, DSL high speed Internet access, 100 channel satellite-TV, picnic tables, big fire-pit for pot-luck barbecues, shower facilities, laundry and clean restrooms. Whether it's fishing, hiking, sightseeing or just taking it easy, we can fix you up with the right people and businesses to assure you a great experience while on the Kenai Peninsula. Ask us about our "Fill-A-Seat" program. We can save you money, booking seats on a will-call basis. We've made it easy to come in and check us out with your big rigs, so stop by for coffee or just to say hello. Look for the signs. We pride ourselves on cleanliness and a friendly and hospitable atmosphere. We want your Alaskan vacation to be a memorable one. (907) 260-7829. Email: drmalaska1@gci.net. www.stayalaska.com. See display ad this section. [ADVERTISEMENT]

S 81.6 A 134.6 H 97.9 Sterling post office (ZIP code 99672) to south.

S 81.7 A 134.7 H 97.8 Tesoro gas station to north; cabins, seafood.

Cook's Corner. See display ad this section.

Vacation Cabins/Flipp'n Fin Charters. See display ad this section.

S 82 A 135 H 97.5 Pay phone on highway just before turnoff for **Izaak Walton State Recreation Site**, located at the confluence of the Kenai and Moose rivers. Paved access road, 25 campsites, parking, tables, toilets, water and dumpster. Camping fee $10/night or resident pass; day-use parking $5; boat launch $5 fee. Good access to Kenai River. Log cabin, totem pole and sign about Moose River archaeological site.

Bridge over **Moose River**; 0.3 mile of fishing down to confluence with Kenai River. *CAUTION: Drive carefully during fishing season when fishermen walk along bridge and highway.* Sockeyes here in June. Big summer run of reds follows into August; silvers into October. **Kenai** and **Moose rivers** (confluence), Dolly

(907) 260-7829
Mile 81.5
Sterling

www.stayalaska.com
See Log Ad

Moose River RV PARK

• Pull-thrus • Full Hookups • Phone / Modem
• **CLEAN** Restrooms • Visitor's Center • DSL High Speed Internet • Satellite TV • Coffee Café • Showers
• Laundry • Local Fishing • Easy Access for Big Rigs

STERLING HIGHWAY

Cook's Corner

Mile 81.7
Sterling Hwy.

One of the Lowest Gas and Diesel Prices Around

• Gas • Diesel
• Propane
• Water
• Free RV Dump with Fill-up

• Famous Cinnamon Rolls
• Deli • Bakery
• Soft Ice Cream
• Ice • Smoothies
• Espresso

ATM Machine
Pay Phone • Fishing Tackle • Gifts • (907) 262-6021

24 HR. GAS (Card Lock)
Extended Summer Hours
May 25 through Labor Day
7 Days A Week

Owned & Operated by the Cook Family, Old Time Alaskans

TESORO

Real Value. Real Easy.

VACATION CABINS
Kitchenettes • Private Baths
Fishing Lodging Packages
Antler Art

&

Flipp'n Fin CHARTERS

SALMON
HALIBUT
TROUT

www.flipnfincharters.com
e-mail: flipfin@ptialaska.net

Personalized Service Since 1989   Across from Cook's Tesoro
1-800-759-6679 or (907) 262-3732 • BOX 731, STERLING AK 99672 – MI 81.7

5 Pacific salmon species are found in Alaska waters: sockeye, king, pink, coho and chum.

Varden and rainbow trout, salmon (king, red, pink, silver). June 15 through October for trout; year-round for Dolly Varden. King salmon from May through July, pink salmon in August and silver salmon from August through October. This is a fly-fishing-only area from May 15 through Aug. 15; closed to fishing from boats, May 15 until the end of the king salmon season or July 31, whichever is later.

This is one terminus of the Swan Lake canoe trail (see "Swanson River Road" log this section).

S 82.3 A 135.3 H 97.2 Great Alaska Adventure Lodge. Charters, fly-ins, bear-viewing camp; 5 or 7 days. Canoe outfitting. Budget camp and fish trips; salmon, halibut and trout. Budget camping trips. We do it all! Phone (800) 544-2261; fax (907) 262-8797; web page: www.greatalaska.com; email: greatalaska@greatalaska.com. See display ad this section. [ADVERTISEMENT]

S 82.5 A 135.5 H 97 Greatland Street to Big Sky Charter & Fish Camp, 0.5 mile north.

Big Sky Charter & Fish Camp. See display ad this section.

Bill White's Alaska Sports Lodge. Where fishing, fun and comfort come together on the Kenai River with new chalets, rooms and the best guides on the Kenai Peninsula. This is where Alaskans come to play! Come play with us! Book today: (800) 662-9672 (use access code 00). In Alaska, (907) 260-8454, Mail: Bill White, P.O. Box 1201, Sterling, AK 99672. www.kenai-river.com. See display ad this section. [ADVERTISEMENT]

S 82.8 A 135.8 H 96.7 Truck weigh station; senior center to south.

Highway narrows to 2 lanes westbound.

Begin divided 4-lane highway eastbound.

S 83.4 A 136.4 H 96.1 Turnoff for **Swanson River Road** to north. Scout Lake Loop Road to south (see **Milepost S 84.9** for description).

Junction with Swanson River Road. See "Swanson River Road" on opposite page.

Call of the Wild Cabins. Six new deluxe fully furnished log cabins, complete kitchen and bath, deck with BBQ, sleeps 4–5. Private, secluded, non-smoking. Central location close to points of interest, world-class fishing, wildlife viewing, hiking, canoeing. Minutes from Kenai River and wildlife refuge canoe trails, freezer storage. Turn north on Swanson River Road, left on Robinson Loop, 1.6 miles to sign. Phone (907) 262-5325. Email: karen@alaska.net. See display ad this section. [ADVERTISEMENT]

Jana House Hostel & RV Park. New! Easy access for big rigs. Full-service 60 amp pull-through RV and tent sites. Fish cleaning station. Private/dorm-style rooms. Bathroom/shower/kitchen privileges. Satellite TV. Large parties welcome. Easy access to Moose and Kenai rivers. Turn north on Swanson River Road, Mile 83.4 Sterling Highway (0.4 mile in, off highway)). 38670 Swanson River Road. Reservations phone (907) 260-4151. Fax (907) 562-9982. Email janamae@hotmail.com. [ADVERTISEMENT]

Sterling Baptist Church. See display ad this section.

The Wash Out Laundromat. See display ad this section.

S 83.6 A 136.6 H 95.9 Sterling elementary school to north.

S 83.7 A 136.7 H 95.8 Central Emergency Services to north.

Swanson River Road

Swanson River Road is a fairly wide and level winding gravel road which leads north 17.9 miles to Swanson River Landing. It also junctions with Swan Lake Road, which leads east 12 miles and deadends at Paddle Lake. Both roads provide access to fishing, hiking trails and the 2 canoe trails in Kenai National Wildlife Refuge: the 60-mile Swan Lake route, connecting 30 lakes; and the 80-mile Swanson River route, linking 40 lakes. Portions of the canoe trail system may be traveled, taking anywhere from 1 to 4 days. Contact Kenai National Wildlife Refuge, Box 2139, Soldotna, AK 99669, for details.

CAUTION: *Do not leave valuables in vehicles at canoe trailheads.*

Distance from junction with the Sterling Highway (J) is shown.

J 0 Junction with Sterling Highway at **Milepost S 83.4.**

J 0.1 Gas station and grocery; laundromat.

J 0.7 Robinson Loop Road; rejoins Sterling Highway at **Milepost S 87.5.**

Pavement ends, gravel begins, northbound.

J 4.5 Entering Kenai National Wildlife Refuge.

J 7.9 Mosquito Lake, turnout; 0.5-mile trail to lake. Rainbow trout.

J 9.2 Silver Lake trailhead parking; 1-mile hike to lake. Rainbow trout and arctic char. Arctic char are most easily caught in spring when the surface water is still cool. Once summer temperatures warm the surface, the char descend to deeper waters and are much harder to catch.

J 10.7 Forest Lakes parking; 0.3-mile trail to lake. Rainbow trout; best fished from canoe or raft.

J 13 Small turnout by **Weed Lake**; rainbow trout.

J 13.3 Drake and **Skookum** lakes trailhead parking; 2-mile trail. Rainbow trout and arctic char (spring).

J 14 Parking and access to **Breeze Lake**.

J 14.2 Dolly Varden Lake Campground; 15 sites, water, toilets, boat launch. Large RVs and trailers note: 0.5-mile loop road to campground is narrow and very bumpy; check turnaround space before driving in. Some campsites overlook the lake. Fishing for Dolly Varden and rainbow; best in late August and September.

J 14.9 Continue straight ahead northbound for Swanson River Landing. Southbound stop sign at oil field access road to west (gated; closed to private vehicles). The Swanson River Road was originally built as an access road to the Swanson River oil field. Chevron operated the field from 1958 to 1986. It is currently operated by Unocal.

J 15.7 Rainbow Lake Campground; small 3-unit camping area on lakeshore with outhouse, water pump and boat launch. Pack out garbage. Fishing for Dolly Varden and rainbow trout. CAUTION: *Steep road; difficult turnaround. Large RVs check visually before driving in.*

J 17.4 Junction with **Swan Lake Road**, which leads east to: Fish Lake Campground, 3 miles; Canoe Lake (west entrance to Swan Lake Canoe Route), 4 miles; Merganser Lakes, 6 miles; Nest Lake, 8 miles; Portage Lake (east entrance to Swan Lake Canoe Route), 9.5 miles; and Paddle Lake (entrance to Swanson River Canoe Route), 12 miles.

J 17.9 Swanson River Landing at end of Swanson River Road; gravel parking area with picnic tables, firepits, water, outhouse, boat launch, fishing. This is the terminus of the Swanson River canoe route, which begins at Paddle Lake at the end of Swan Lake Road.

Return to Milepost S 83.4 Sterling Highway

S 84 A 137 H 95.5 Alaska Canoe & Campground. Full service, wooded setting, tent sites, RV-full hookups. Showers, laundry, outdoor supply store. Rental equipment (including bikes) for guided/self-guided trips. Book an outdoor experience on the Swanson River Canoe Lakes System or salmon fishing on the Kenai River or fish halibut in Cook Inlet. Also, rafting and kayak adventures. Shuttle service to put-in and take-out points. Single or multi-day trips. Look for canoes and signs. www.alaskacanoetrips.com, alaskacanoe@yahoo.com. (907) 262-2331. See display ad this section. [ADVERTISEMENT]

S 84.9 A 137.9 H 94.6 Scout Lake Loop (4.3-mile paved road) leads south. **Scout Lake State Recreation Site** (day-use only) is just south of the highway; parking ($5 fee), water, toilets and a covered picnic shelter.

Drive down Scout Lake Loop Road 1.5 miles and turn right on Lou Morgan Road (paved) and drive 2.4 miles for **Morgan's Landing State Recreation Area**; 42 campsites, 10 pull-through sites, some double sites in park-like setting; gravel paths down to Kenai River; toilets and water; $10 camping fee or resident pass, $5 day-use fee. Morgan's Landing is one of the few public areas offering good access to bank fishing on the **Kenai River**. Fishing for king salmon from mid-June through July, average 30 lbs. Red (sockeye) salmon average 8 lbs., use flies in July and August; silver (coho) salmon to 15 lbs., August and September, use lure; pink salmon average 4 lbs. with lure, best in July, even-numbered years only; rainbow and Dolly Varden, use lure, June through August.

Alaska State Parks area headquarters is located at Morgan's Landing. There are several private campgrounds located on Lou Morgan Road. Scout Lake Loop Road rejoins the Sterling Highway at **Milepost S 83.4.**

S 85.8 A 138.8 H 93.7 First turnoff westbound for Lakewood subdivision to south.

S 86 A 139 H 93.5 Second turnoff westbound for Lakewood subdivision.

S 87.5 A 140.5 H 92 Robinson Loop Road to northwest. Tustumena Loop Road to southeast.

S 88 A 141 H 91.5 St. Theresa Drive. Access to Longmere Lake Lodge B&B to south.

Longmere Lake Lodge B&B. AAA-approved. Look for blue highway sign. Follow St. Theresa's/Edgington to Ryan.

STERLING HIGHWAY • Soldotna

Fishing the Kenai River near Morgan's Landing. (© Kris Graef, staff)

ALASKA HORN & ANTLER

Specializing in Ram Horn Carvings
Also Moose, Caribou, and Scrimshaw on Fossil Mammoth and Walrus Ivory.
Alaskan Rocks and Minerals.
Custom orders welcome.
We ship anywhere in the USA
e-mail: alaskahornandantler@gci.net

Thomas W Cooper

Tom & Linda Cooper
38778 Sterling Highway
Soldotna, Alaska 99669

907-262-9759

Watch Tom and Linda carve.
8 - 6 Mon.-Sat.
Call for after hours appointment.

at Mile 88.3
Sterling Highway
Near Soldotna, Alaska
LARGE CIRCLE DRIVE

Available at Alaska's Finest Gift Shops

Beautiful lakeside setting. Comfortable, spacious accommodations. Large stone fireplace, Alaskan artifacts. Enjoy a hearty breakfast. Master bedrooms with full private baths, or large apartment with kitchen. Guided salmon, halibut, hiking, bird watching, flightseeing arranged. Longtime Alaskan hosts. P.O. Box 1707, Soldotna, AK 99669. Phone (907) 262-9799. www.longmerelakelodge.com. Email: bblodge@ptialaska.net. See display ad this section. [ADVERTISEMENT]

S 88.3 A 141.3 H 91.2 **Alaska Horn & Antler.** See display ad this section.

S 88.8 A 141.8 H 90.7 Tesoro gas station to north.

CAUTION: Moose Danger Zone next 6 miles westbound.

S 91.3 A 144.3 H 88.2 Tesoro gas station and grocery to south.

S 91.7 A 144.7 H 87.8 **Hanson's Custom Carvings.** FREE Admission! A photo-op-stop like no other. Ride the saddled king salmon. Even the Kenai River doesn't produce salmon this big! Get a giant bear "hug", sit or lie down on a really big bear's lap, or "Feel like a kid again," in the New Giant 10 foot chair. Big enough for group photos! Let us help you using your camera. What a Christmas card picture this will make! Meet Scott Hanson, Master chainsaw artist. Watch him work on his latest creations. Ask Scott about plans for the "Town of Living Trees." Shop the new gift shop with unique handcrafted items. Plenty of parking for big-rigs or entire RV-caravans. Watch for the sign, look for all the amazing bears and salmon. See display ad this section. P.O. Box 2254, Soldotna, AK 99669. (907) 260-5421. [ADVERTISEMENT]

S 91.8 A 144.8 H 87.7 Boundary Street.

S 92 A 145 H 87.5 Birch Ridge public golf course.

S 92.2 A 145.2 H 87.3 Car wash, laundry and showers to south. Access to bed and breakfast.

The Sterling Needle B&B. One mile from the "Y" in Soldotna, next to Birch Ridge golf course. Easy access off the highway; private, wooded area. 16x50 deck, birding, flower gardens all around, and friendly 30-year residents entertain you with lore and gore of the area! Custom breakfasts, quilt-covered beds, private baths. Creative, art-filled home. 355 Fairway Dr., Soldotna. (907) 262-3506; www.sterlingneedle.com; email sandrak@sterlingneedle.com. [ADVERTISEMENT]

S 92.4 A 145.4 H 87.1 State Division of Forest, Land and Water Management. Fire danger indicator sign. Veterinary hospital; phone (907) 260-7851.

S 92.7 A 145.7 H 86.8 Mackey Lake Road. Private lodging is available on this side road.

S 93.7 A 146.7 H 85.8 *Begin 4-lane highway and 35 mph speed zone westbound.*

S 94.1 A 147.1 H 85.4 Traffic light at East Redoubt Avenue; access to Swiftwater Park campground and Moose Range Meadows Fishing Access (descriptions follow). Fred Meyer to south; overnight RV parking permitted in parking lot. Access to fast food.

Follow East Redoubt 0.4 miles south to turnoff for **Swiftwater Park Municipal Campground**, then another 0.4 mile west to park entrance. This municipal campground has 42 campsites (some pull-throughs) along a loop road above the Kenai River; tables, firepits, firewood

($5.25), phone, dump station ($10.50), 2-week limit, litter barrels, toilets, boat launch ($7.35). Camping fee $9.45; day-use fee $5.25. No camping Sept. 30–May 1. Steep stairway down to Kenai River.

For **Moose Range Meadows Public Fishing Access**, continue on East Redoubt Avenue—which turns into Keystone Drive—3.7 miles to the fishing access on the north bank of the Kenai. This Kenai NWR Kenai River public fishing access is open July 1 to Sept. 30; gravel parking area, toilets, no camping. Fishing platforms and boardwalks along a 3-mile stretch of river in this area. Moose Range Meadows is subject to fishing closures.

East Redoubt Avenue/Keystone provides access to several Soldotna bed and breakfasts and lodges.

S 94.2 A 147.2 H 85.3 Soldotna Y. Turn right southbound on Kenai Spur Highway for more Soldotna businesses and for Kenai.

Junction with Kenai Spur Highway to city of Kenai. See the "Kenai Spur Highway" log beginning on page 582.

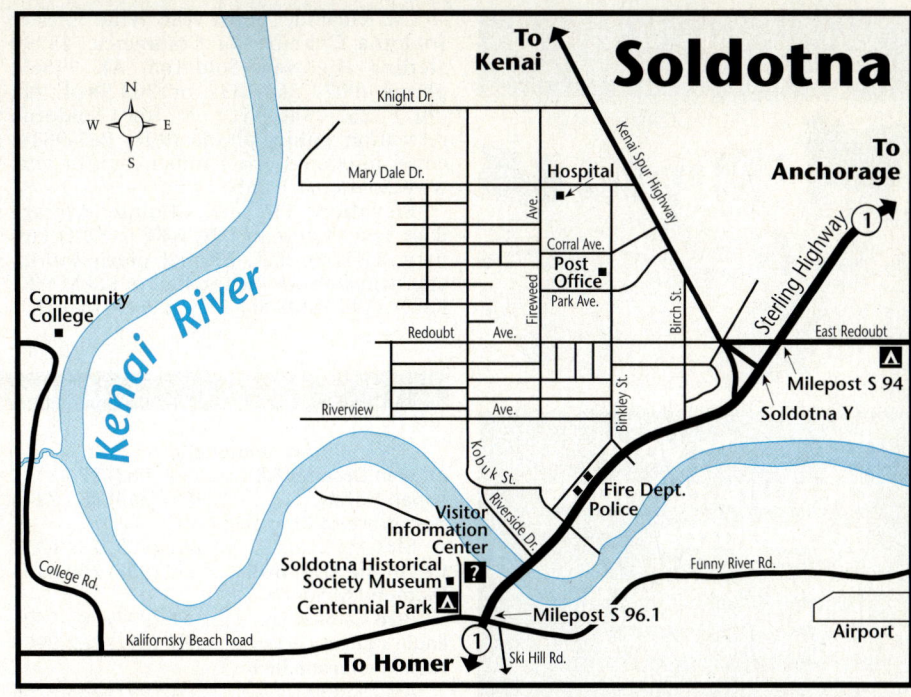

CAUTION: Moose Danger Zone next 6 miles eastbound.

S 94.4 A 147.4 H 85.1 Gas station. Access to **Soldotna Creek Park** (day use only); follow road behind Mexican restaurant. The park has a playground, picnic tables and restrooms. Follow trail down hill to fish walk along the Kenai River.

Petro Express. See display ad this section.

S 95.3 A 148.3 H 84.2 Binkley Street; access to fire station, police station and post office. Peninsula Center Mall, 24-hour supermarket. Soldotna city center. *See description of Soldotna beginning below.*

S 95.6 A 148.6 H 83.9 Kobuk Street; access to Soldotna High School.

S 95.9 A 148.9 H 83.6 Kenai River bridge.

S 96 A 149 H 83.5 Soldotna Visitor Center at south end of Kenai River bridge.

S 96.1 A 149.1 H 83.4 Intersection of Funny River Road and Kalifornsky Beach Road. *For description of Funny River Road, see page 581. For log of Kalifornsky Beach Road, see page 590. Sterling Highway log to Homer continues on page 591.*

Soldotna

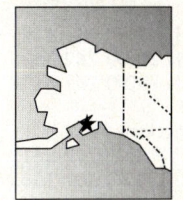

S 95.2 A 148.2 H 84.3 On the western Kenai Peninsula, the city stretches over a mile southwest along the Sterling Highway and northwest along the Kenai Spur Highway. **Population:** 3,759; Kenai Peninsula Borough 49,691. **Emergency Services:** Phone 911 for all emergency services. **Alaska State Troopers** at Mile 22 Kalifornsky Beach Road just off Sterling Highway, phone (907) 262-4453. **City Police**, phone (907) 262-4455. **Fire Department**, phone (907) 262-4792. **Ambulance**, phone (907) 262-4500. **Hospital**, Central Peninsula General on Marydale Drive, phone (907) 262-4404. **Veterinarian:** Soldotna Animal Hospital, **Milepost S 92.4** Sterling Highway, phone (907) 260-7851.

Visitor Information: The Soldotna Visitor Information Center is located in downtown Soldotna on the Sterling Highway south of the Kenai River bridge. Fishwalk access to Kenai River. The center is open daily, 9 A.M.–7 P.M. June–August, 9 A.M.–5 P.M. May and September; weekdays, 9 A.M.

–5 P.M. remainder of the year. Write: Greater Soldotna Chamber of Commerce, 44790 Sterling Highway, Soldotna, AK 99669; phone (907) 262-1337 or 262-9814, fax (907) 262-3566. For a free Soldotna recreation guide, phone (907) 262-9814; email info@soldotnachamber.com; or visit www.SoldotnaChamber.com.

Elevation: 115 feet. **Climate:** Average daily temperature in July, 63°F to 68°F; January, 19°F to 23°F. Annual precipitation, approximately 18 inches. **Radio:** KSRM 920, KSLD 1140, KKIS-FM 96.5, KPEN-FM 101.7.

Television: Channels 2, 4, 9, 12 and 13 via booster line from Anchorage, cable and KANG public education channel. **Newspapers:** *Peninsula Clarion* (daily), *Anchorage Daily News* (daily).

Private Aircraft: Soldotna airstrip 1 SE on Funny River Road; elev. 107 feet; length 5,000 feet; asphalt; fuel 100LL; unattended.

The town of Soldotna was established in the 1940s because of its strategic location at the Sterling–Kenai Spur Highway junction. (Visitors may see the homestead cabin, which became Soldotna's first post office in

VALDEZ » SOLDOTNA » JUNEAU FAIRBANKS » ANCHORAGE

We cover your creature comforts in Soldotna.

The Aspen Hotel in the heart of the Kenai Peninsula offers beautifully appointed rooms and exceptional added-value amenities in Alaska's outdoor paradise. We're your perfect catch in Soldotna.

- 63 spacious rooms
- Complimentary continental breakfast
- Guest laundry
- Swimming pool, spa and exercise room
- VCR, speaker phone and data port
- Coffee maker, refrigerator, microwave, iron and hair dryer in room
- Family and extended stay suites

ASPEN HOTELS

326 BINKLEY CIRCLE, SOLDOTNA, AK 99669 »
1-866-GUEST4U »
WWW.ASPENHOTELSAK.COM

Kenai Peninsula B&B Association
FREE Referrals
Licensed & Inspected
Quality Accommodations
(907) 283-2265
www.kenaipeninsulabba.com
Box 2992 • Kenai, AK 99611

Cook Inlet was named by the Earl of Sandwich for explorer Capt. James Cook.

SOLDOTNA ADVERTISERS

Accommodations
Alaskan Dream B&B..........Ph. (888) 326-3147
Aspen Hotels................Ph. (866) 483-7848
Best Western King Salmon
  Motel.....................Ph. (907) 262-5857
Call of the River B&B......Ph. (907) 260-6533
Diamond M Ranch
  B&B Cabins................Ph.(907) 283-9424
Eagle's Roost Lodge........Ph. (877) 262-9900
Kenai Peninsula B&B
  Association...............Ph. (907) 283-2265
Kenai River Lodge..........Ph. (907) 262-4292
Moose Hollow B&B...........Ph. (800) 262-7548
Poppy Ridge B&B
  Cabins....................Ph. (907) 262-4265
Posey's Kenai River
  Hideaway..................Ph. (907) 262-7430
Riverside House Hotel......Ph. (907) 262-0500
Russ's Cabins on the
  Kenai River...............Ph. (907) 252-4328
Soldotna Bed &
  Breakfast Lodge...........Ph. (907) 262-4779
Sterling Needle B&B........Ph. (907) 262-3506
Tom's Cabins...............Ph. (907) 262-3107

Activities & Attractions
Best Hikes.................Ph. (907) 252-5617
Go Kart Race Track.........Ph. (907) 262-1562

Auto & RV Rentals
Alaska Recreational
  Rentals...................Ph. (907) 262-2700

Campgrounds
Best Western King Salmon
  RV Park...................Ph. (907) 262-5857
Centennial Campground......Ph. (907) 262-5299
Diamond M Ranch
  RV Park...................Ph. (907) 283-9424
Edgewater RV Park..........Ph. (907) 262-7733
Kenai Riverbend Resort.....Ph. (800) 625-2324
River Quest RV Park........Ph. (907) 283-4991
River Terrace RV Park......Ph. (907) 262-5593
Riverside House RV Park....Ph. (907) 262-0500
Russ's Cabins on the
  Kenai River...............Ph. (907) 252-4328
Swiftwater Campground......Ph. (907) 262-3151

Churches
Christ Lutheran
  Church....................Ph. (907) 262-4757
First Baptist Church.......Ph. (907) 262-4304

Dining
Best Western King Salmon
  Restaurant................Ph. (907) 262-5857
Charlotte's Cafe...........Ph. (907) 262-6620
Gourmet Garden
  Market & Deli.............Ph. (907) 262-3232
Moose is Loose Bakery......Ph. (907) 260-3036
Mykel's Restaurant.........Ph. (907) 262-4305
Vintage Moose Tea Room.....Ph. (907) 260-7478

Fishing Guides & Charters
EZ Limit Guide Service.....Ph. (907) 262-6169
Harry Gaines Kenai River
  Fishing Guide.............Ph. (888) 262-5097
Jeff King's Budget
  Charters..................Ph. (907) 262-4564
Johnson Bros. Guides &
  Outfitters................Ph. (800) 918-7233
Kenai River Professional
  Guide Assoc. ....www.krpga.org
Kenai River Sportfishing
  Assoc.....................Ph. (907) 262-8588
Kenai Riverbend Resort.....Ph. (800) 625-2324
River Quest................Ph. (907) 283-4991
Riverside House Fishing
  Guide Service.............Ph. (907) 262-0500
Rod 'N Real Charters.......Ph. (907) 262-6064
Tom's Cabins &
  Guide Service.............Ph. (907) 262-3107

Shopping & Services
Alyeska Sales & Service....Ph. (907) 262-5068
Beemun's Variety...........Ph. (907) 262-5151
Birch Tree Gallery.........Ph. (907) 262-4048
Claudette's................Ph. (907) 262-9513
Craftsman Hobbies..........Ph. (907) 262-2839
Dan's Mobile RV Services...Ph. (907) 252-9029
Hooked On Fishing Gifts....Ph. (907) 260-3151
Inlet Gifts................Ph. (907) 262-7167
Mail Boxes Etc.............Ph. (907) 262-8774
River City Books...........Ph. (907) 260-7722
Robin Place Fabrics........Ph. (907) 262-5438
Soldotna Wash & Dry........Ph. (907) 262-9936
Sugar Magnolias............Ph. (907) 262-7004
Sweeney's Clothing.........Ph. (907) 262-5916
Tammy's Flowers & Gifts....Ph. (907) 260-5355

Visitor Information
City of Soldotna...........Ph. (907) 262-3151
Soldotna Chamber of
  Commerce..................Ph. (907) 262-9814
Soldotna Rotary............Ph. (907) 262-5916

The Sterling Needle B&B
Homestyle B&B • Homemade Quilts, Breakfasts, Bread
Private Baths • Creative Atmosphere
5 minutes to fish! • Near Golf Course
(907) 262-3506

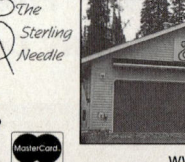

www.sterlingneedle.com

Fishing the Lower Kenai River

The Kenai River is one of Alaska's great treasures. Often referred to as the world's greatest sportfishing river, its turquoise waters have produced the world record king salmon (just over 97 lbs.). The Kenai offers sportfishermen 4 of the 5 types of Pacific salmon (king/chinook, red/sockeye, silver/coho, pink/humpy), as well as rainbow trout, Dolly Varden and lake trout.

The watershed of the Kenai covers approximately 2,200 square miles, or 1.4 million acres, across the central region of the Kenai Peninsula. Driving down from Anchorage, you'll enter the Kenai River Watershed at Summit Lake and remain in this vast drainage basin almost to Seward on the Seward Highway, and through Soldotna on the Sterling Highway.

Several groups have organized to help maintain the Kenai River. Two of the most active groups are the Kenai Watershed Forum and the Kenai River Sportfishing Association.

The Kenai Watershed Forum (KWF) sponsors the Kenai River Festival the second weekend in June each year. This annual event features live music, fishing demonstrations, arts and crafts and other festivities. The KWF is also dedicated to educating the public on ways to protect the Kenai River. See their web site at www.kenaiwatershed.org.

The Kenai River Sportfishing Association (KRSA) also dedicates itself to preserving the Kenai River, through habitat rehabilitation, fishery conservation and public aquatic education projects and programs. KRSA hosts the annual Kenai River Classic, an invitational fishing tournament that raises funds for the association's river preservation efforts. These efforts include the Classic Fishwalk, which provides anglers access to the river while protecting the streambank. Healthy streambank vegetation is critical for the health of the river's salmon population, since juvenile salmon spend 90 percent of their rearing time within 6 feet of the riverbank.

Many areas along the Kenai restrict boat fishing. Please check with Alaska Department of Fish and Game and Alaska State Parks for current closures and restrictions, and obtain the current fishing regulations before beginning your visit to the Kenai River.

Use extreme caution while fishing and boating on the Kenai River, as it is deep, swift, cold and presents many obstacles throughout its course. This area is also very heavily used, so be courteous of other visitors.

Following is a list of public access points along the lower Kenai River, beginning at Kenai Keys and ending at Cook Inlet.

Lower Kenai River Access

River Mile 44.5–46 Kenai Keys State Recreation Site, an undeveloped site accessible by boat on the north bank of the river. There are no facilities. There is sockeye fishing available on the gravel bars near the site.

Milepost 80.3 Sterling Highway/River Mile 39.5. Bing's Landing State Recreation Site is on the north side of the Kenai and has a boat launch.

Milepost 82 Sterling Highway/River Mile 36.5 Izaak Walton State Recreation Site, located at the confluence of the Kenai and Moose rivers. It is on the north bank of the Kenai and has a boat launch and good river access. Great salmon fishing but closed to boat fishing during king salmon runs. Also check for bank closures.

Milepost 84.9 Scout Lake Loop Road/River Mile 31. Morgan's Landing State Recreation Site offers good bank fishing in the Kenai River for trout and salmon throughout the summer. This is one of the few public parks with Kenai River bank fishing.

Mile 11.2 Funny River Road/River Mile 30.5. Funny River State Recreation Site, located on the south bank of the Kenai River, just upstream from the confluence of the Kenai and Funny rivers. Small site with short trail to Kenai River and fish walk. Fills up quickly mid-July when fishing season starts.

Milepost 94.1 Sterling Highway/River Miles 23 and 27. East Redoubt Avenue to **Swiftwater Park Municipal Campground** and **Moose Range Meadows Fishing Access.** Swiftwater Park has a fish walk and boat launch. Site also provides handicap access to riverbank.

For Moose Range Meadows, stay on East Redoubt Avenue until it turns into Keystone Drive; it is 3.7 miles to the fishing access on the north bank of the Kenai. Fishing platforms and boardwalks along a 3-mile stretch in this area. Moose Range Meadows is

Think Habitat: if we wait, it will be too late!

Welcome to the greatest sportfishing river in the world ... ...the Kenai!

We invite you to enjoy and help protect this unique resource!

- Fish from improved access sites.
- Don't pioneer trails or trample vegetation.
- Obey all fishing regulations.
- Be courteous to fellow anglers.
- Yield to anglers and boats with FISH ON!
- Reduce boat wake and travel in mid-channel.
- Respect the resource and practice careful catch & release.
- Have fun fishing and boating safely.

KENAI RIVER SPORTFISHING ASSOCIATION
Protecting Fish Habitat • Providing Education • Promoting Responsible Sportfishing

PO Box 1228
224 Kenai Avenue, Suite 102
Soldotna, AK 99669
(907) 262-8588
kenairiv@ptialaska.net
www.kenairiversportfishing.org

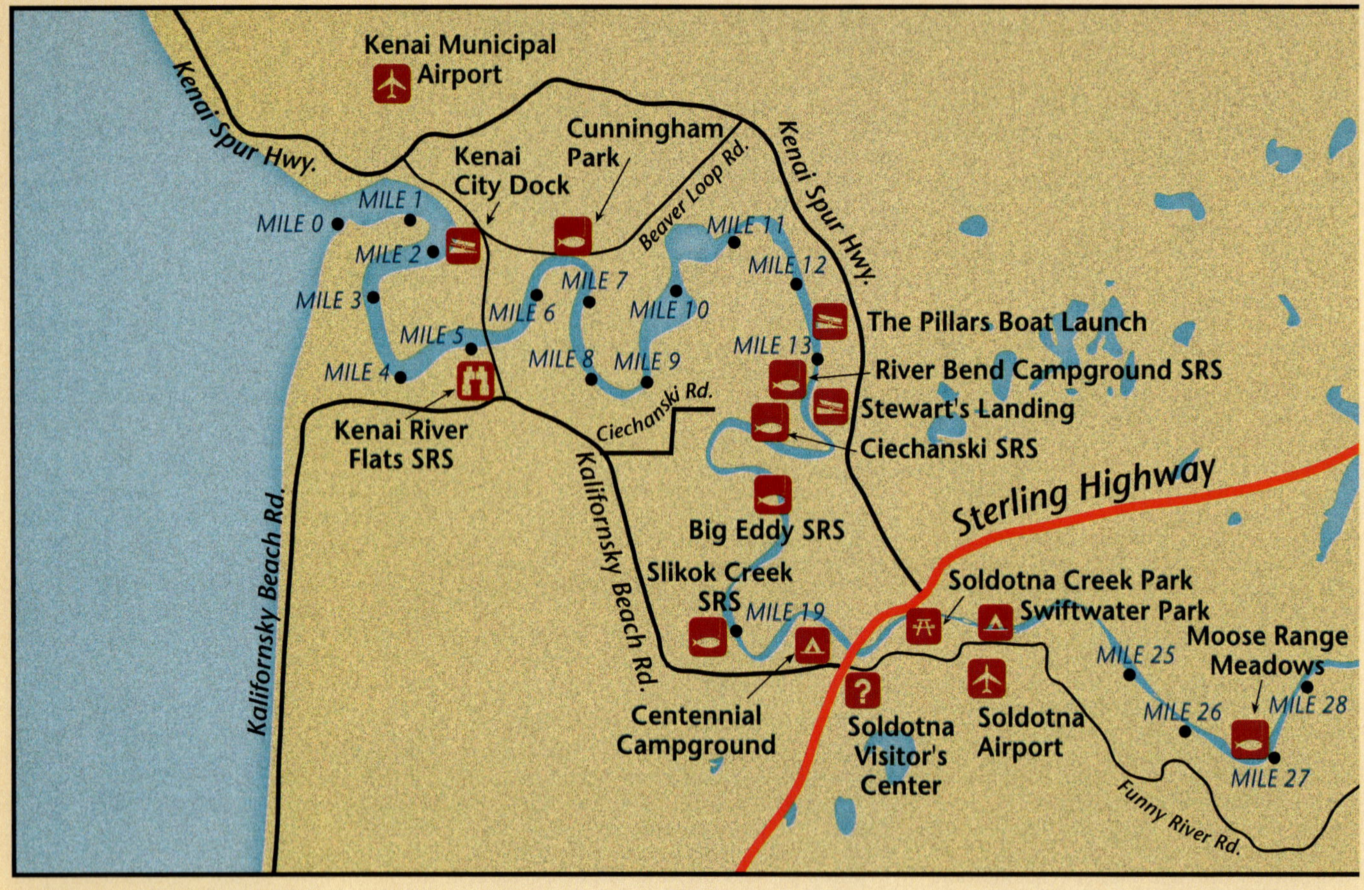

STERLING HIGHWAY • Soldotna

subject to fishing closures.

Milepost 94.4 Sterling Highway/River Mile 22. Soldotna Creek Park. Fish walk on the north bank of the Kenai River.

Milepost 96 Sterling Highway/River Mile 21. Soldotna Visitor Information Center. The visitor center is located just south of the Kenai River Bridge in Soldotna on the west side of the highway. Fish walk on the south bank of the Kenai River.

Milepost 96.1 Sterling Highway/River Mile 20.3. Centennial Park Municipal Campground, located off Kalifornsky Beach Road on the south bank of the Kenai River; popular bank fishing site. Area closed to boat fishing during king salmon runs.

Milepost 20.5 Kalifornsky Beach Road/River Mile 19. Slikok Creek State Recreation Site, accessible from College Loop Road to West Chugach Drive or from Endicott Drive. Slikok offers trail access to fishing access on both the north and south banks of Slikok Creek. Good sockeye fishing on south side of Slikok Creek.

Milepost 19.1 Kalifornsky Beach Road/River Mile 17. Follow Poppy Lane from K-Beach Road to **Pipeline State Recreation Site.** Located on the west side of the Kenai River, this site is not road accessible but can be reached by hiking down from Poppy Lane. The site offers picnic tables.

Milepost 17.5 Kalifornsky Beach Road/River Mile 15.3. From K-Beach Road, Ciechanski Road leads 2.4 miles to private RV parks and **Ciechanski State Recreation Site** on the Kenai River. This small state recreation site is easy to overlook, as it's tucked in the corner across from Kenai River Quest RV Park. Its primary purpose is to provide restroom access for boaters. There is 12-hour public parking (no camping), a picnic table, outhouse and dock walk (no fishing from dock). Kenai Riverbend Campground is 0.2 mile beyond the Ciechanski state recreation site.

Milepost 1.8 Kenai Spur Highway/River

Wilderness Setting in the City

250 FORESTED CAMPSITES ON THE BANKS OF THE KENAI RIVER

Enjoy some of the most beautiful campsites and Kenai River's best fishing access while camping in the City of Soldotna's Centennial or Swiftwater Campgrounds.

Protected boat launch lagoon, cleaning tables, fish walks, river access stairs, nature trails, ice, information booth, walking distance to city center

A RIVER CITY WITH EASY ACCESS TO ALL KENAI PENINSULA ACTIVITIES.

Swiftwater Directions: Turn left onto East Redoubt just past 1st light before Seekins Ford. Travel approx. 1 mile, turn right onto "Swiftwater Rd." Follow to pay booth and you're there.

Centennial Directions: Go through Soldotna and over Kenai River bridge. Turn right onto Kalibornsky Beach Rd. (4th light). Turn onto Centennial Rd. (100 yards). Follow to pay booth and you're there.

For Camping Information Sept. - May 15 call
907 262-3151

in the Summer
907 262-5299

Soldotna ALASKA

Views and maps at:  www.ci.soldotna.ak.us

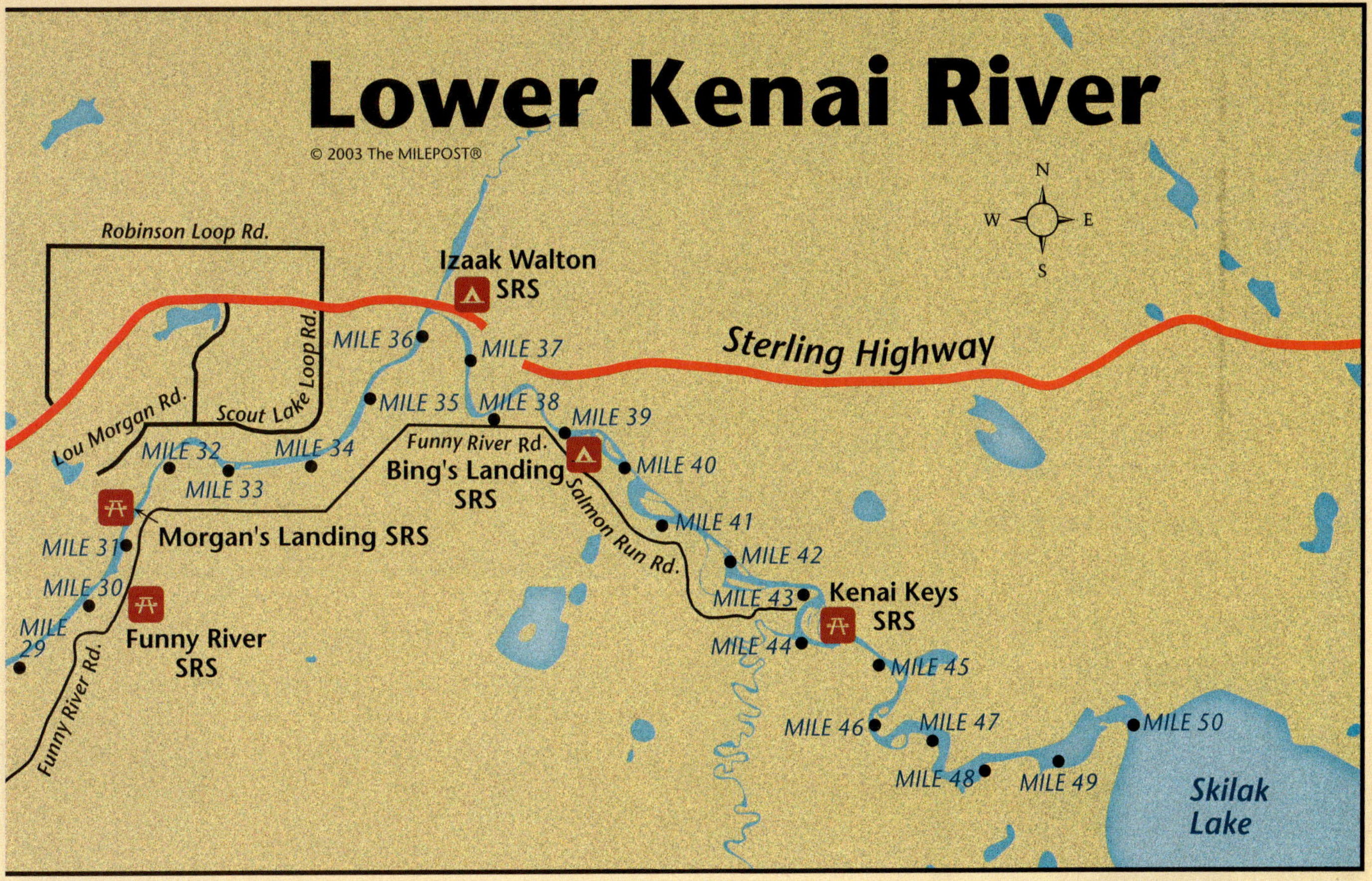
Lower Kenai River
© 2003 The MILEPOST®
N
W
E
S
Robinson Loop Rd.
Izaak Walton SRS
Sterling Highway
Scout Lake Loop Rd.
Lou Morgan Rd.
MILE 36
MILE 37
MILE 35
MILE 38
MILE 39
MILE 32
MILE 34
MILE 33
Funny River Rd.
Bing's Landing SRS
MILE 40
Salmon Run Rd.
MILE 41
MILE 31
Morgan's Landing SRS
MILE 42
MILE 30
MILE 29
Funny River SRS
Funny River Rd.
MILE 43
Kenai Keys SRS
MILE 44
MILE 45
MILE 46
MILE 47
MILE 50
MILE 48
MILE 49
Skilak Lake

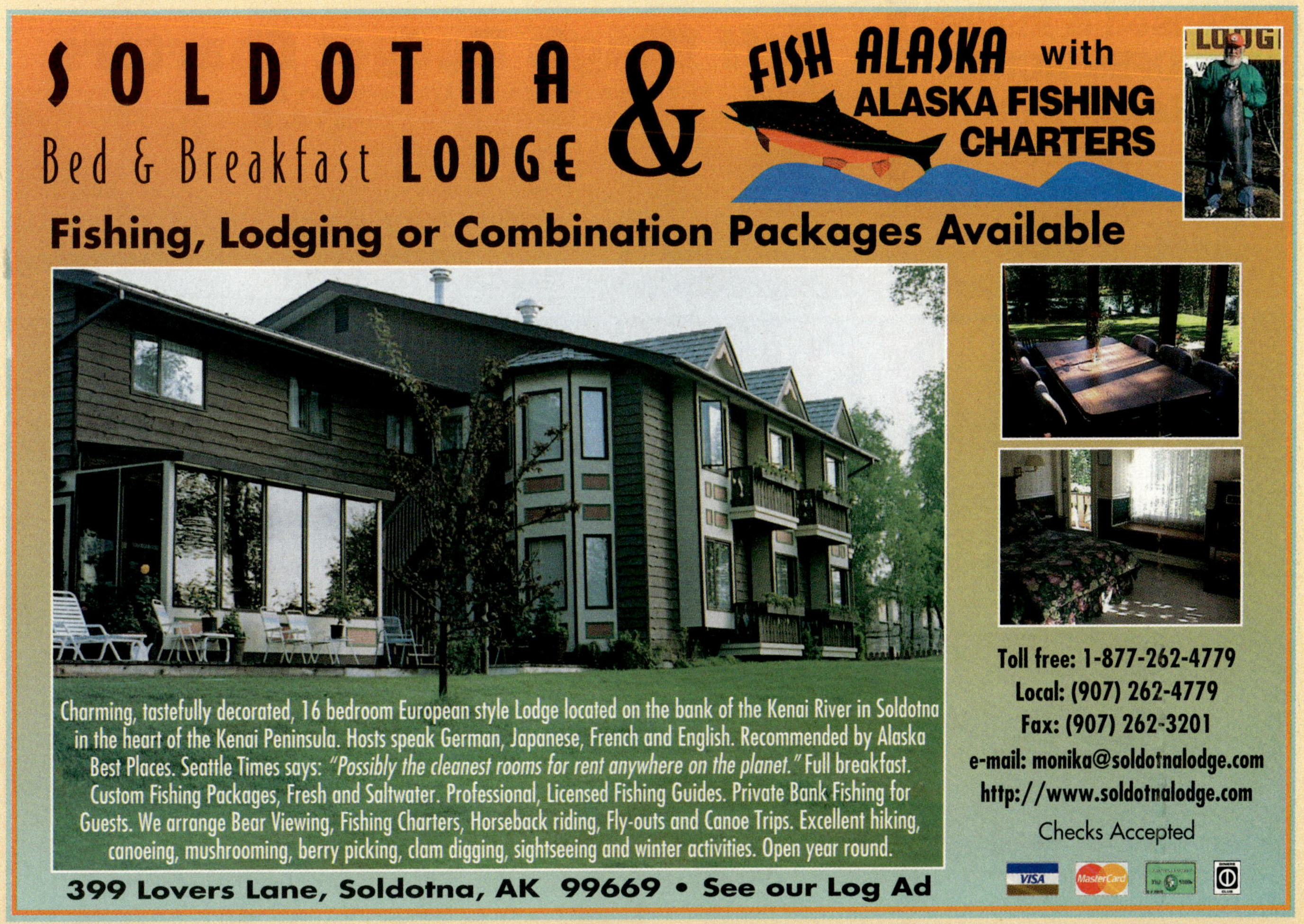
SOLDOTNA
Bed & Breakfast LODGE
&
FISH ALASKA with ALASKA FISHING CHARTERS
Fishing, Lodging or Combination Packages Available
Charming, tastefully decorated, 16 bedroom European style Lodge located on the bank of the Kenai River in Soldotna in the heart of the Kenai Peninsula. Hosts speak German, Japanese, French and English. Recommended by Alaska Best Places. Seattle Times says: "Possibly the cleanest rooms for rent anywhere on the planet." Full breakfast. Custom Fishing Packages, Fresh and Saltwater. Professional, Licensed Fishing Guides. Private Bank Fishing for Guests. We arrange Bear Viewing, Fishing Charters, Horseback riding, Fly-outs and Canoe Trips. Excellent hiking, canoeing, mushrooming, berry picking, clam digging, sightseeing and winter activities. Open year round.
Toll free: 1-877-262-4779
Local: (907) 262-4779
Fax: (907) 262-3201
e-mail: monika@soldotnalodge.com
http://www.soldotnalodge.com
Checks Accepted
VISA
399 Lovers Lane, Soldotna, AK 99669 • See our Log Ad

STERLING HIGHWAY • Soldotna

Mile 14. Big Eddy Road leads west to 12-hour public parking at Mile 1.4. Road ends at Mile 1.8 (end of Fish Trap Court); access to fishing guides and private boat launch, Big Eddy Jetty.

Milepost 4.2 Kenai Spur Highway/River Mile 12.4. Follow Silver Salmon Drive (paved and gravel) 0.5 mile west for **The Pillars Boat Launch** on the Kenai River. Open May 1. Bank fishing is prohibited.

Milepost 6.4 Kenai Spur Highway/River Mile 6.5. From Kenai Spur follow Beaver Loop Road 2.7 miles to **Cunningham Park** public access to Kenai River. The park, which has a trail, fishwalk and restrooms, is one of the more popular area bank fishing spots during peak salmon runs.

Milepost 11.5 Kenai Spur Highway/River Mile 1.6. Bridge Access Road leads west 1.6 miles to **City of Kenai public dock and boat ramp.** Boat launch fees start at $10.

MAY - SEPTEMBER

Fish with the Kenai River's oldest professional guide service - 30 years
Riverside Cabins • RV Parking

EVERYTHING FURNISHED
BIG TIME FUN GUARANTEED

Call or Write: Reuben Hanke, Box 624, Kenai, Alaska 99611
(888) 262-5097 - Fish Camp www.harrygaines.com

Jeff King's Budget Charters
—Expertly Guided Salmon Fishing on the Kenai River Since 1981—
PERSONABLE SERVICE • REASONABLE RATES
EMAIL: info@JeffKingFishing.com
www.JeffKingFishing.com
P. O. Box 2711 Soldotna, AK 99669
(907) 262-4564
Toll Free:
1-888-578-5333

Client RV Riverside Parking

RIVER QUEST RV PARK

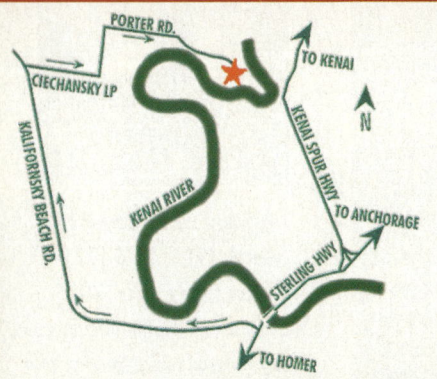

Centrally located on the Kenai Peninsula. The Kenai River's best spot for camping and fishing. R.V. Park has electric and water hook-ups, sewer pump hook-ups/service, pull-throughs and tent sites, clean laundry and shower facilities, boat moorage, boat launching, river bank fishing, fishing guide services (both halibut & salmon), convenience store, restaurant and cabins. Annual, seasonal, monthly, weekly and nightly rates available. Reservations recommended. CALL **(907) 283-4991**
WRITE PO Box 3457 Soldotna AK 99669 or visit us online **www.riverquestalaska.com**

1949, at its original location on the Kenai Spur Highway at Corral Street.)

Soldotna was incorporated as a first-class city in 1967. Kenai Peninsula Borough headquarters and state offices of the Departments of Highways, Public Safety, Fish and Game, and Forest, Land and Water Management are located here. Soldotna is also headquarters for the Kenai Peninsula Borough school district. There are 3 elementary schools, a junior high school and 2 high schools. University of Alaska–Kenai Peninsula College is also located in Soldotna.

The area affords a majestic view of volcanic mountains across Cook Inlet. Always snow-covered, they are Mount Spurr (elev. 11,100 feet), which erupted in 1992; Mount Iliamna (elev. 10,016 feet), which has 3 smaller peaks to the left of the larger one; and Mount Redoubt (elev. 10,197 feet), which was identified by its very regular cone shape until it erupted in December 1989.

Soldotna gets very busy during fishing season. Popular fishing rivers in the area include the Kasilof River and the Kenai River. For those fishermen who want a more remote fishing spot—or for visitors who want to see wildlife and glaciers— local outfitters offer fly-in fishing trips for rainbow, grayling, salmon and Dolly Varden, and flightseeing trips to see Tustumena Lake, the Harding Icefield and wildlife.

Lodging & Services

All facilities are available, including supermarkets, banks, hotels/motels, restaurants and drive-ins, medical and dental clinics, golf courses, veterinarians, and churches. The Joyce Carver Memorial Library offers internet service. Two shopping malls are located on the Sterling Highway near the center of town. There are also numerous area bed-and-breakfasts, cabin rentals and lodges.

Let the experts at **Mail Boxes Etc.** pack and ship your "Alaskan catch" frozen fish and other great souvenirs. And while you're here check your email, purchase stamps, mail postcards and look around at the many other services we provide. At Mail Boxes Etc. "We'll take it from here." [ADVERTISEMENT]

Alaskan Dream Bed and Breakfast. A unique property by the Kenai River (mile 24.25, Funny River side). Privacy? Located among 200 acres of undeveloped river habitat; frequently visited by Alaskan wildlife. However, we are only minutes from Soldotna shopping. Three rooms with river view, serving a full deluxe breakfast or boat brunches available for the fisher person. Enjoy over 500 feet of river frontage, 72 feet of fish walks; for fantastic sockeye, silver and pink salmon fishing July, August, and September. Experienced to assist you planning fishing charters, bear viewing, flight seeing, glacier viewing, and hiking adventures. Come savor Alaska at its best! July dates are frequently full; however, call. Book now for June king fishing, August and September silver salmon. (907) 260-3147. 1-888-326-3147. www.ptialaska.net/~akdream. Email: akdream@ptialaska.net. [ADVERTISEMENT]

Best Western King Salmon Motel, Restaurant and RV Park, downtown Soldotna on the Kenai Spur Highway. The most convenient, complete accommodation location on the Peninsula, with an easy access RV park; comfortable, clean motel; and full service, full menu restaurant. Large rooms, queen beds, some kitchenettes, cable

Diamond M Ranch
B&B • Cabins • RV Park

**Main Street Suites
Ranch House Bed and Breakfast
Cozy Rustic or Modern Cabins
Wooded RV Parking**

VIEW OF KENAI RIVER & ALASKA RANGE
B&B ASSOCIATION MEMBER

907-283-9424

MILE 16.5 K-BEACH ROAD
P.O. BOX 1776 • SOLDOTNA, AK 99669
EMAIL: martin@diamondmranch.com
www.diamondmranch.com

Moose Hollow Bed & Breakfast

Beautiful, Quiet, Relaxed Setting
Walk to Salmon Fishing On The Kenai River
Queen or Twin Bed • Bunkhouse for Groups
Non-smoking Rooms

Member Kenai Peninsula B&B Assn.

(907) 262-7526 • 1-800-262-7548

email: moosehol@alaska.net
http://www.AlaskaOne.com/moosehollow

35645 Brians Street
Mail: P.O. Box 2996, Soldotna, AK 99669

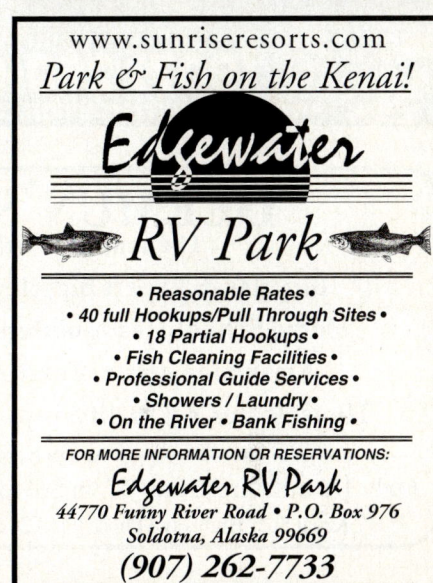

www.sunriseresorts.com
Park & Fish on the Kenai!

Edgewater RV Park

• Reasonable Rates •
• 40 full Hookups/Pull Through Sites •
• 18 Partial Hookups •
• Fish Cleaning Facilities •
• Professional Guide Services •
• Showers / Laundry •
• On the River • Bank Fishing •

FOR MORE INFORMATION OR RESERVATIONS:
Edgewater RV Park
44770 Funny River Road • P.O. Box 976
Soldotna, Alaska 99669
(907) 262-7733

BEST WESTERN KING SALMON
MOTEL, RV PARK & RESTAURANT

DOWNTOWN SOLDOTNA LOCATION
CLOSE TO FISHING, SHOPPING, SERVICES, ENTERTAINMENT
LARGE ROOMS • QUEEN BEDS • SOME KITCHENETTES • CABLE TV • PHONES • COFFEE
FULL SERVICE RESTAURANT, EARLY BREAKFASTS FOR FISHERMAN, STEAK, SEAFOOD, SALAD BAR, WINE & BEER SERVICE
39 WIDE SPACES • MOSTLY PULL-THRUS • FULL HOOK-UPS • RESTROOMS • SHOWERS LARGE LAUNDRY • BUSINESS CENTER
PLENTY OF ROOM FOR BIG RIG MANEUVERING

RESERVATIONS: 888.262.5857 • (907) 262-5857

ksalmon@alaska.com • www.bestwestern.com

STERLING HIGHWAY • Soldotna

KENAI RIVER LODGE
Soldotna, Alaska

MOTEL UNITS OVERLOOKING KENAI RIVER At the Bridge in Soldotna
GUIDED FISHING TRIPS • PRIVATE DOCKING FACILITIES
(888) 966-4292 • (907) 262-4292 • 393 Riverside Dr., Soldotna AK 99669
www.kenairiverlodge.com e-mail: Krlds@ptialaska.net

Call of the River B&B
"Sleep to the Sound of the River"

- On the Kenai River With Magnificent Scenery, Fishing & Accommodations
- Wonderful Hospitality & 4-Course Homemade Breakfasts!

(907) 260-6533
www.kenairiversalmon.com   See Log Ad

BEEMUN'S VARIETY®
The unusual as well as everyday needs

Bicycles & Expert Bicycle Repair! • Hallmark Cards
Home School Headquarters & Supplies • Arts & Crafts
Alaskana Gifts • Canning Supplies • Fax Service
Housewares • Quality Toys • Engraving • Free Popcorn!

www.beemuns.com

Only 1/2 mile From the "Y" in Soldotna   Open 9 - 6 Monday - Saturday
35277 Kenai Spur Highway • Phone (907) 262-1234 or (907) 262-5151 FAX (907) 262-3525

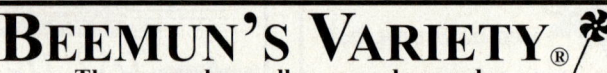

Sweeney's Clothing

Extended Summer Hours
Open 7 Days a Week
35081 Spur Highway • Soldotna
(907) 262-5916

The Place To Go For The Brands You Know!
WELCOME TO SOLDOTNA!

HEAD TO TOE OUTDOOR WEAR
Fleece Wear • Chest Waders • Rain Gear • Knee Boots

BIG WAREHOUSE CLEARANCE SALE JUNE-SEPTEMBER

Look for the Green & White Balloon!
We'll be happy to ship your purchase anywhere!

Poppy Ridge
B&B CABINS
- FULL KITCHENS
- PRIVATE BATHS
- 5 MINUTE HIKE TO KENAI RIVER FISHING

(907) 262-4265
P.O. Box 2773, Soldotna, AK 99669
e-mail: brentblume@gci.net
www.home.gci.net/~poppyridge

Christ Lutheran Church

Summer Schedule: 10 am & 6:30 pm Worship
Winter: 11 am & 6:30 pm Worship - 9:30 am Sunday School

Randy Parshall, Pastor
(907) 262-4757 • clchurch@gci.net

1 Block From Soldotna "Y" - Kenai Spur Highway

SUGAR MAGNOLIAS
"What a long strange trip it's been."

44224 Sterling Hwy -
LOCATED ABOVE
"LOG GIFT SHOP"

60s & 70s RETRO CLOTHING & MORE!

* INCENSE/OILS
* STICKERS * BEADS
* BODY JEWELRY
* IMPORTED CLOTHING

OPEN 10:30 AM - 7 PM
(907) 262-7004

ALASKA'S HOOKED ON FISHING GIFTS

Alaska's Premiere Source for Unique Jewelry & Gifts

Check Out our New Web Site
View our Beautiful Otolith Jewelry

Otoliths, ivory from fish "ears" - no two are alike

Gemstone Rosaries, Original Jewelry,
Dazzle Design Clothing

www.hookedonfishinggifts.com

907 260-3151
38470 Keystone Drive, Soldotna, Alaska
MADE IN ALASKA 4519/4520

Soldotna Rotary Welcomes Visiting Rotarians!

Thursdays, 12 noon
at Mykel's Restaurant
Next to Sweeney's Clothing

(907) 262-5916

This ad sponsored by Sweeney's Clothing

Boardwalk nature trail at Kenai National Wildlife Refuge Visitor Center.
(© Kris Graef, staff)

Soldotna WASH & DRY
We're Proud to Present
The Finest Coin-Op Laundromat on the Kenai Peninsula
EXTREMELY CLEAN • ATTENDANT ON DUTY • SHOWERS • TV

2 MODERN COIN-OP LAUNDROMATS • OPEN 7 DAYS A WEEK
Drop Off Laundry and Showers Available at Both Locations

Soldotna: 262-9936   Kenai: 283-9973
Open 24 Hours (summer)   Open 8 a.m. to 10 p.m.
SOLDOTNA at the "Y"   **DOWNTOWN KENAI**

TWO CONVENIENT KENAI SPUR ROAD LOCATIONS
Kenai WASH & DRY

Tammy's FLOWERS & GIFTS
New & Enlarged Shop! Same Wonderful Rustic Theme
- Moose, Fish & Bear Country!
- Unique & Charming Alaska Souvenirs
- Local Alaskan Hand-Crafted Gifts
- Gorgeous Flowers for Thank You & Goodbye Gifts

109 W. Riverview
Turn on Binkley, Located Across from Safeway
(907) 260-5355

TV, data ports, phones, fridge. Handicapped room. The RV park located behind the motel features 39 wide spaces with full hookups. Most are pull-throughs. Lots of room to maneuver big rigs. New laundry facility, coin-operated showers. Private restrooms. Large grassy park area. Caravans welcome. Email service for RV park guests. Restaurant serves early fisherman's breakfast, lunch, dinner. Steaks, seafood, salad bar. Daily specials. Beer and wine available. Phone (907) 262-5857; fax (907) 262-9441. www.bestwestern.com. See display ad this section. [ADVERTISEMENT]

Call of the River. Quiet, upscale B&B with a magnificent view, on the Kenai River. Relax and fish on our 126-foot walkway.

Robin Place Fabrics
"A Must Stop For Quilters"

- Original Alaskan Quilt Patterns & Kits
- Specialty Quilt Fabric, Notions & Books
- "Quilting On The Kenai" Summer Show 3rd Weekend in June

907 262-5438

Binkley to East Redoubt to 105 Robin Place • Soldotna, Alaska 99669 • Email: robinplacefabric@att.net

---

MAIL BOXES ETC.
35555 Spur Hwy.
Soldotna, AK 99669
(907) 262-8774
We'll take it from here.™
*See our ad in the Anchorage services section

MODEL TRAINS
HO and N Scale
Custom Alaska Railroad Models
CRAFTSMAN HOBBIES
Specializing in Trains
Quality • Shipping
35060 Spur Hwy • Soldotna
(907) 262-2839

Go Kart Race Track

262-1562

- Parties - Group Rentals
- Reasonable Rates
Sterling Hwy. & Funny River Rd. **(near SBS)**

Espresso & Ice Cream Shop
Hot Dogs • Pastries
drive thru or indoor seating

New Owners - New Equipment
Safe & Fun!

"Safety is our priority"

Sleep to the sound of the river. Three rooms with private baths and two rooms with a shared bath. Access to a beautifully decorated great room, fully equipped kitchen, laundry facilities and covered deck. Wonderful hospitality, great food (No Muffins!) and immaculate accommodations have given us a superb reputation. Perfect for small business retreats and executive facilities. Early and late season specials. Convenient Soldotna location. Phone (907) 260-6533. See web site: www.kenairiversalmon.com. See display ad this section. [ADVERTISEMENT]

Eagle's Roost Lodge on the Kenai River. Beautiful riverside lodge and cabins accommodating up to 40. Retreats, boat/gear rentals, salmon/halibut charters, flight-seeing/tour arranging. Campsites/dry RV parking. BBQs, wood-heated sauna, gift shop, kitchens. Reservations for the most powerful stress-relieving fishing on the Kenai River: (907) 262-8444, toll-free 1-877-262-9900. www.eaglesroostlodge.com. Email: fishing@eaglesroostlodge.com. [ADVERTISEMENT]

Riverside House Hotel, RV Park and Fishing Guide Service on the Kenai River in Soldotna. RV spaces with electricity and water $12. Recreational itineraries for fishing, sightseeing, etc., arranged. Walking distance to stores, churches, entertainment. Fine dining in the restaurant and lounge. Spacious rooms. 446111 Sterling Highway, Soldotna, AK 99669. Toll-free 1-877-262-0500. Internet: bob@riverside~house.com. [ADVERTISEMENT]

Russ's Cabins on the Kenai River. 30 minutes from Soldotna. Comfortable cabins overlooking the river, all with kitchens and bathrooms. Completely furnished. One cabin, handicap accessible with ramp and bathroom. RV camping sites, sauna, BBQs, bank fishing, local guides, charters for salmon and halibut. Boats for rent nearby. Book early for reservations. www.russcabinsonthekenai.com Call: (907) 262-1465. (907) 252-4328. [ADVERTISEMENT]

Tom's Cabins and Guide Service. Dock is close to cabins for "bed to boat" Kenai River fishing! 220 foot river frontage! Tom guides from power or drift boats for the best fishing. Bear viewing, salt/fresh water fishing, packages, newsletter specials. Beautiful cabins, sleep 4–5 comfortably, private baths. Outdoor BBQs, freezer space. (907) 262-3107. www.fishkenai.com. [ADVERTISEMENT]

Camping

There are several private campgrounds located in and near Soldotna; see ads this section. The Fred Meyer at the "Y" allows overnight RV parking (use signed areas).

There are 2 city campgrounds: Swiftwater and Centennial. Campsites for both tents and RVs (no hookups). These campgrounds are heavily used; check in early. For Swiftwater Campground, turn off the Sterling Highway on East Redoubt Street, between the Ford dealership and Williams gas station by the "Y" (**Milepost S 94.1** Sterling Highway), and drive 0.4 mile to campground turnoff; 42 campsites (some pull-throughs) along a loop road above the Kenai River; tables, firepits, firewood ($5.25), phone, dump station($10.50), 2-week limit, litter barrels, toilets, boat launch ($7.35). Camping fee $11.55; day-use fee $5.25. No camping Sept. 30–May 1. Steep stairway down to Kenai River.

Centennial Park Campground is 0.1 mile from the Sterling Highway just south of the Kenai River bridge on Kalifornsky Beach Road (turn west at **Milepost S 96.1**) on the banks of the Kenai River; 126 campsites (some on river), tables, firepits, firewood provided, water, restrooms, dump station, pay phone, 2-week limit. Register at entrance. Boat launch and favorite fishing site on fishwalk.

Edgewater RV Park on the banks of world famous Kenai River, across from Soldotna visitors' center. Full and partial hookups, laundry, showers, grassy sites, picnic tables, local guide service and fish cleaning facilities. Bank fishing. Walk to stores, restaurants. Reservations and information: (907) 262-7733. www.sunriseresorts.com. P.O. Box 976, Soldotna, AK 99669. [ADVERTISEMENT] ▲

River Terrace RV Park features a prime Kenai River location near the Soldotna bridge. Easy, comfortable, riverfront access

on the 1000-foot boardwalk with steps right into the river. Handicapped accessible with fishing platform. A great place to fish or view the exciting action. Large riverfront spaces, full hookups, 20-30-50 amp, heated restrooms, free showers, unlimited hot water, laundry. Fish processing available on premises. Local guides provide king and silver salmon charters. Early and late season dates are easier to get and very enjoyable. (907) 262-5593;. P.O. Box 322, Soldotna, AK 99669. [ADVERTISEMENT] ♿▲

Transportation

Air: Charters available. Soldotna airport is south of Soldotna at Mile 2 Funny River Road. Turn off the Sterling Highway at **Milepost S 96.1**, just after crossing Kenai River bridge.

Local: Taxi service, car rentals, vehicle leasing, boat rentals and charters.

Highway: Accessible via the Sterling Highway (Alaska Route 1), 148 miles from Anchorage.

Attractions

Fishwalks. Several public fishwalks have been constructed in the Soldotna area in order to make the popular Kenai River more accessible to the public. Although this beautiful stream cuts right through the center of town, public access is limited by private land ownership along the riverbank, as well as the river itself. The wide, swift Kenai River does not have an easily accessible, gently sloping riverbank. Try the fish-

---

First Baptist Church of Soldotna
Your Southern Baptist Convention Church on the Peninsula!
- Biblical, positive, contemporary preaching!
- Christ-centered, celebrative Worship!

Sundays: 9:30 SS, 11:00 Worship; Wed. 6:00 pm
Sunday Evening 6:00 pm
Please call for Information

159 Binkley Avenue   (907) 262-4304   www.fbcsoldotna.org
Near Safeway and McDonald's in the middle of town!

Inlet Gifts

- Quality Alaskan **T-shirts**
- **Sweatshirts**, Jackets, Caps
- Alaskan **Chocolates**, Jams, Jellies
- Gold & Silver **Alaska Mint** Coins
- **Toys & Souvenirs** Just for Children
- Charming Alaska **Decorating** Accessories
- **Ty Beanies** & **Boyds Bears** Collectibles
- **Huggable** plush **Moose, Bears** & More

A Most Unique Alaskan Gift Store

Inlet Gifts - 35462 Kenai Spur Hwy in Soldotna - **(907) 262-7167**

Alaska's 5 tallest volcanic peaks are Wrangell, Tobert, Spurr, Redoubt and Iliamna.

walks at the Soldotna Visitor Center, right below the Kenai River bridge, and at Soldotna Creek Park, located off the Sterling Highway in the center of town (access road is behind the Mexican restaurant).

Join in Local Celebrations. Soldotna's big summer event is the annual Progress Days, held during the 4th weekend of July. Started in 1960 to commemorate the completion of the natural gas line, Progress Days has grown into one of the peninsula's biggest annual attractions. The main event is the parade down Binkley Street, which begins 11 A.M. Saturday morning. Other activities include a rodeo, community barbecues, quilt displays, and other events.

In February, the Peninsula Winter Games take place in Soldotna. Activities include an ice sculpture contest, cross-country ski race, ice bowling, snow volleyball and the Alaska State Championship Sled Dog Races and Dog Weight Pull Contest. Games, booths, concessions and demonstrations are held throughout the weekend.

River City Books & Charlotte's Cafe is a charming bookstore in the heart of Soldotna. Listed in *Alaska's Best Places*, this cheerful oasis serves up a delightful concoction of mysteries, novels, adventures, nonfiction, children's books and a top-notch Alaska selection along with espresso drinks, fabulous quiches, salads, sandwiches and homemade desserts and breads made daily. On the left, at the second stoplight. 43977 Sterling Highway. (907) 260-7722. (907) 262-6620 for Cafe. [ADVERTISEMENT]

Birch Tree Gallery. You can feel the creativity when entering. Here's the place to find truly unique gifts for your hosts or "The List." Gallery emphasis is 2-fold; (1) A large selection of pottery, original art, jewelry, stained glass, baskets, note cards, and many other gift items by Alaskan artists. (2) Beautiful high quality yarn, luscious colors, clever patterns, (with finished samples) and knitting supplies. A yarn lover's paradise and Kathleen to help with that dropped stitch. Complimentary gift wrap and packaging for mailing. Birch Tree Gallery is located in wooded surroundings adjacent to Soldotna, 1/4 mile down Funny River Road from Sterling Highway intersection. www.alaska.net/~birchtre. (907) 262-4048. [ADVERTISEMENT]

Claudette's. On the left at the second stop

Let Soldotna Fill Your Senses

- See breathtaking vistas and wildlife.
- Taste fresh King Salmon, caught that day.
- Hear the rush of the river or the silence of a lake.
- Feel the exhilaration of our world class fishing.
- Smell the wildflowers that color the riverside.

Come visit us at the **Soldotna Visitors Center** in Soldotna, across the bridge and on the banks of the World Famous Kenai River or online at www.SoldotnaChamber.com

(907) 262-9814
44790 Sterling Hwy-MP
Soldotna, AK 99669
Fax: (907) 262-3566
Email: info@SoldotnaChamber.com

GREATER SOLDOTNA CHAMBER OF COMMERCE
Alaska's SOLDOTNA a river city

Dan's Mobile RV Service & Welding
RV
Kenai Peninsula
(907) 252-9029
cell – (907) 252-9030
Licensed • Dependable Service, Quality Parts

Alaska Recreational Rentals
Parts • Accessories • Repairs
Joe & Barbara Dilley - Owners
Box 592 • Soldotna, Alaska 99669
PHONE/FAX (907) 262-2700
www.akrecrentals.com
MILE 102 STERLING HIGHWAY

ALYESKA SALES & SERVICE

Full Mechanical Service Facility • All Sizes of RV Tires

We Welcome RV'ers and All Visitors

Goodyear, Continental & General Tires
Stay Trouble Free on the Road
Tune-ups • Brakes • Exhaust
Alignment • Shocks

 **Look for the Goodyear Sign** GOODYEAR

2 Locations to Serve You   1-800-858-4821
Soldotna: Spur Hwy - 262-5068   **Kenai:** 200 S. Willow St. - 283-4821
Mon-Fri 8-6 • Sat. 9-5   Mon-Fri 8-6 • Sat. 9-5

STERLING HIGHWAY • Soldotna

Soldotna Visitor Information Center is located just south of the Kenai River bridge.
(© Kris Graef, staff)

light. Old, new, handmade items by local artists. Willow tree angels, Illume candles, Clayworks, April Cornell clothing/linens. '50's hats, vintage jewelry. Find Depression Glass pieces! Tools, signs, stained glass, birch/splint baskets, pottery, silk arrangements. 1st Thursday of the month events! 43977 Sterling Highway, Suite B. Email: cbarber@alaska.net. (907) 262-9513. [ADVERTISEMENT]

Gourmet Garden Market & Deli features imported cheeses, olives, sausages, and fresh Europa bread. You will find a delectable selection of freshly prepared salads, desserts, sandwiches and a "Daily Dinner-To-Go" plus luscious organic fruits and vegetables. Located next to the bookstore in the red Cornerstone Market Place building at the second stoplight in Soldotna. 262-3232. [ADVERTISEMENT]

Inlet Gifts, a most unique Alaskan gift store, is housed in a spacious cedar building surrounded by gorgeous hanging baskets, colorful flowerbeds, Mugo pine trees and a manicured lawn. They offer an outstanding selection of Alaska T-shirts, sweatshirts, jackets and caps, plus many other appealing souvenirs and gifts for adults and children. Be sure to take your photo with Chocolate Charlie, their life-size, 8-foot tall plush moose. See display advertisement under Soldotna for more information. Inlet Gifts, 35462 Spur Highway in Soldotna. Phone (907) 262-7167. [ADVERTISEMENT]

Mykel's Restaurant. Featuring fantastic sauces and unique flavor combinations created from fresh local seafood and choice meats. A full page of special appetizers and entrees changes according to the freshest ingredients available and creative impulses. Try the Walnut Crusted Salmon with Raspberry Beurre Blanc! Exquisite food, comfortable atmosphere and friendly service will be sure to please you. A praiseworthy wine list,

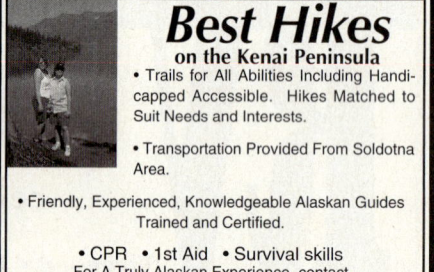

Please support The MILEPOST® advertisers.

Alaskan tap beers and premium well. Banquet facility available. Mykel's for a fabulous dining experience! 35041 Kenai Spur Highway; (907) 262-4305. [ADVERTISEMENT]

Soldotna Historical Society Museum, located on Centennial Park Road, features a wildlife museum and the Historic Homestead Village. The Slikok Valley School, the last of the Alaska Territory log schools, built in 1958, is one of the attractions at the museum's log village. Soldotna was settled in 1947. How the homesteaders lived is revealed in a collection of pioneer artifacts and photos in the former Soldotna Chamber of Commerce log tourist center. Damon Hall, a large building constructed for the Alaska Centennial, features an outstanding display of wildlife mounts with a background mural of these species' natural habitat. Open 10 A.M. to 4 P.M., Tuesday through Saturday; Sunday noon to 4 P.M.; closed Monday.

The Moose is Loose. Moosey into our full-line bakery featuring delicious donuts, pastry, eclairs, cookies, cakes, breads and

road-kill cinnamon rolls. Pick up a loaf of explosively delicious, Augustine Volcano bread! Friendly atmosphere to sit and enjoy an Espresso, cold drink, or with your own mug, free coffee. Double access drive, downtown on Sterling Highway. You moost stop. (907) 260-3036. (Open 6 A.M.) [ADVERTISEMENT]

The Vintage Moose Tea Room combines Victorian elegance with Alaskan charm to provide a unique dining experience. Specializing in premium teas, brewed by the pot,

accompanied by our wonderful homemade soups, scones, "Grizzly Wedge" stuffed sandwiches, baked potatoes, salads, crustless quiches and mouth-watering desserts. Orders to-go. Tea-related items for sale. 2.9 miles from Sterling Highway on Kalifornsky Beach Road. Visa/MC. tealadies@gci.net. (907) 260-7478 . [ADVERTISEMENT]

Joyce Carver Memorial Library offers temporary cards for visitors; Internet access, large sunlit reading areas for both adults and children; Alaska videos on summer Saturday afternoons at 2 P.M. Open 9 A.M. to 8 P.M. Monday through Thursday, noon to 6 P.M. Friday, and 9 A.M. to 6 P.M. Saturdays. 235 Binkley St., Soldotna, phone (907) 262-4227.

Fish the Kenai River. Soldotna is one of Alaska's best-known sportfishing headquarters. The early run of kings begins about May 15, with the peak of the run occurring between June 12 and 20. The late run enters the river about July 1, peaking between July 23 and 31; season closes July 31. The first run of red salmon enters the river during early June and is present in small numbers through the month; the second run enters about July 15 and is present through early August. In even years pink salmon are pre-

Funny River Road

Funny River Road branches east off the Sterling Highway at **Milepost S 96.1**, providing access to rural residential areas, lodges and a state recreation site. It is paved to Mile 17.

Distance from junction with the Sterling Highway is shown (J).

J 0 Junction with Sterling Highway. Access to Go Kart Race Track and espresso.

Junction with Ski Hill Road, which leads 0.8 mile to Kenai NWR visitor center.

J 0.1 Edgewater RV Park.

J 1.6 Kenai River Center; Soldotna Airport. On display at the entrance to the Soldotna Airport is a Starduster SA 100 single-engine, single seat, open cockpit biplane. Built by local residents in the early 1960s, the plane was used for aerobatics at Alaska air shows until the 1990s. It was retired to this spot in 2001 as a remembrance of early aviators from the Soldotna area.

Private Aircraft: Soldotna airstrip 1 SE on Funny River Road; elev. 107 feet; length 5,000 feet; asphalt; fuel 100LL; unattended.

J 2 Tom's Cabins.

J 2.9 Entering Kenai National Wildlife Refuge lands eastbound.

J 3.9 Small paved turnout to south. *Slow for 30 mph curves.*

J 6.5 Paved turnout to south.

J 6.7 Paved turnout to south; trailhead for horse trail.

J 8.7 Paved turnout to south.

J 9.3 Parking to north.

sent from early through mid-August. The early silver salmon run arrives in early August, peaks in mid-August, and is over by the end of the month. Late run silver salmon enter the Kenai in early September, peak in mid- to late September, and continue to enter the river through October. Dolly Varden and rainbow trout can be caught all summer.

Soldotna Sports Center, on Kalifornsky Beach (K-Beach) Road, has an Olympic-sized hockey rink, a jogging track, 2 racquetball/volleyball courts, a weight and exercise room, dressing rooms and showers. The Sports Center also has convention facilities and meeting rooms. Phone (907) 262-3150 for more information.

Kenai National Wildlife Refuge Visitor Center, located at the top of Ski Hill Road (turnoff at **Milepost S 97.9**) and also accessible from Funny River Road, hosts some 25,000 visitors annually. This modern center has dioramas containing lifelike mounts of area wildlife in simulated natural settings. Free wildlife films are shown on the hour daily from noon to 4 P.M., June to mid-August. Information available here on canoeing, hiking and camping. There is a 3/4-mile-long nature trail with an observation platform and spotting scope on Headquarters Lake. In winter, 8 miles of cross-country ski trails are available at the visitor center. The Alaska Natural History Assoc. has a sales outlet here with books, posters and videos. Pay phone located in center. Open weekdays 8 A.M. to 4:30 P.M year-round; weekends, 9 A.M. to 6 P.M. in summer, 10 A.M. to 5 P.M. rest of year. No admission fee.

The refuge was created in 1941 when President Franklin D. Roosevelt set aside

J 10.2 Scenic viewpoint to north; view of Kenai River.
J 10.8 Welcome to Funny River sign.
J 11 Funny River.

J 11.2 **Funny River State Recreation Site** to north; accommodates about 6 RVs, $10 camping fee, outhouse, tables, pack out trash; campground host. Open May–Sept., 7-day camping limit. Fills up quickly mid-July when fishing season starts. Short trail to **Kenai River** fish walk.

J 11.7 Isom's General Store.
J 12.5 Turnoff for Funny River Community Center.
J 13.3 Bend in the River subdivision.
J 15 Funny Moose Lodging.
J 16.9 Fire station (proposed).
J 17 Road forks; pavement ends, gravel begins.
J 21 Lou's Kenai River B&B Cabins.
J 21.5 Russ's Cabins on the Kenai River.

1,730,000 acres of land (then designated the Kenai National Moose Range) to assure that the large numbers of moose, Dall sheep and other wild game would remain for people to enjoy. With the passage of the Alaska National Interest Lands Conservation Act in 1980, the acreage was increased to 1.97 million acres and redesignated Kenai National Wildlife Refuge. The area is managed by the U.S. Dept. of the Interior's Fish and Wildlife Service. Write: Refuge Manager, Kenai National Wildlife Refuge, P.O. Box 2139, Soldotna, AK 99669-2139; phone (907) 262-7021.

Best Hikes on the Kenai Peninsula provides day-hikes with transportation from the Soldotna area. Trails for all abilities (including wheelchair accessible). Trails matched to interests. Easy lowland paths to lakeshores or mountain trails with views you'll never forget. Safety trained/gun-toting Alaskan leader. Contact Sheila: (907) 260-6986, cell (907) 252-5617. Email: sbest@kenai.net. See display ad this section. [ADVERTISEMENT]

Take a Canoe Trip on one of several routes available in the Kenai National Wildlife Refuge. Enjoyment of wildlife in their natural habitat, true wilderness scenery, camping, and fishing for trout and salmon are a few highlights of a canoe trip.

Established canoe trails include the Swanson River route (80 miles) and Swan Lake route (60 miles). Complete information on Kenai Peninsula canoe trails is available at the Kenai National Wildlife Refuge visitor contact station at Mile 58 Sterling Highway, the Kenai NWR visitor center in Soldotna and at chamber of commerce visitor centers in Kenai and Soldotna.

(Continues on page 591)

Kenai Spur Highway

The Kenai Spur Highway junctions with the Sterling Highway at the Soldotna Y and leads north through Soldotna 10 miles to the city of Kenai. It ends at Captain Cook State Recreation Area, 39 miles north of Soldotna. **Distance from Soldotna Y (SY) is shown.**

SY 0 Junction with Sterling Highway at Milepost S 94.2.
SY 0.6 Soldotna City Hall.
SY 0.7 Soldotna elementary school to east on E. Park Avenue; playground. Post office is on N. Binkley.
SY 0.9 Inlet Gifts. A most unique Alaskan gift store is housed in a spacious cedar building surrounded by gorgeous hanging baskets, colorful flowerbeds, Mugo pine trees, and a manicured lawn. Offering an outstanding selection of Alaska T-shirts, sweatshirts, jackets and caps, plus many other appealing souvenirs and gifts. 35462 Spur Highway. (907) 262-7167. [ADVERTISEMENT]

SY 1 Marydale Avenue. Central Peninsula General Hospital 0.4 mile west. 24-hour gas station east side of highway.
SY 1.8 Big Eddy Road to west; 12-hour public parking (1.4 miles); access to fishing guides, private camping and boat launches (1.8 miles).
Kenai Riverfront B&B/RV Park, 2-acre fishing and RV camping resort, on the banks of the Kenai River, features full service B&B suite and 10 RV sites with electric, shared water, level gravel sites, riverfront views, boat launch, superb bank fishing. Alaska family environment. www.kenairiverfront.com. Email fish@kenairiverfront.com. Or call (907) 227-1108. [ADVERTISEMENT]
SY 2.8 Distance marker northbound shows Kenai 8 miles, Nikiski 24 miles.
SY 3.3 Small chapel to east.
SY 3.7 Kenai city limits.
SY 4.2 Silver Salmon Drive (paved and gravel) leads 0.5 mile west to **The Pillars Boat Launch** (Alaska State Park) on the Kenai River; large gravel parking area, toilets, boat ramp, fee station. Bank angling is not permitted. Fees: $10/launch, $5/day-use.
SY 5.5 Gas station (diesel), grocery.
SY 6.2 Beaver Creek Park, a small neighborhood day-use park to west.
SY 6.4 Twin City Raceway to east. South junction with **Beaver Loop Road**: Drive 2.7 miles on Beaver Loop Road for **Cunningham Park** public access to Kenai River. The park, which has a trail, fishwalk and restrooms, is one of the more popular area bank fishing spots during peak salmon runs. From here it is 3.9 miles to the Bridge Access Road via Beaver Loop Road.
SY 8 *Begin divided 4-lane highway, 45 mph speed zone, northbound. Begin 2-lane highway southbound.* Paved bike trails both sides of highway north to Kenai.
SY 8.5 Kenai Fellowship, A Church of Christ. See display ad this section.
SY 9.4 Tinker Lane. Access to Peninsula Oilers baseball park, municipal golf course
SY 9.7 Kenai Central High School.
SY 9.9 Challenger Learning Center of Alaska; (907) 283-2000.
SY 10.1 Welcome to Kenai sign and turnoff for City of Kenai tent campground to east; $8 camping fee.
Begin 35 mph speed zone northbound.
SY 10.4 Junction with Airport Way and Walker Lane. Access to Kenai airport.
SY 10.5 Kenai Plaza shopping.
SY 10.8 Junction. Main Street Loop to east; Bridge Access Road to west.
SY 11 Leif Hansen Memorial Park; Merchant Marine Memorial. The memorial consists of an anchor, flagpole and a plaque dedicating the site to "American WWII Merchant Marine Veterans, all Mariners, present and future."
SY 11.2 Willow Street; access to Kenai airport. Petro Express Chevron station.
Petro Express. See display ad this section.
SY 11.5 Mainstreet; Kenai Visitors and Cultural Center.
The **Bridge Access Road** leads west to Port of Kenai (1 mile); junction with Beaver Loop Road (1.3 miles); City of Kenai public dock and boat ramp (1.6 miles); Kenai Flats boardwalk viewing telescope (2.2 miles); Warren Ames Bridge (2.8 miles); **Kenai Flats State Recreation Site** (3 miles); and junctions with Kalifornsky Road (3.4 miles; see Kalifornsky Road log on page 590).

Kenai

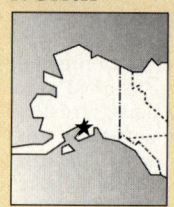

SY 11.5 Main Street; Kenai Visitors and Cultural Center. Kenai is 159 miles from Anchorage and 89 miles from Homer. **Population:** 7,058. **Emergency Services:** Phone 911 for all emergency services. **Alaska State Troopers** (in Soldotna), phone (907) 262-4453. **Kenai City Police,** phone (907) 283-7879. **Fire Department** and **Ambulance,** phone 911. Hospital

---

Kenai Fellowship
A Church of Christ   Mile 8.5 Spur Hwy.
SUMMER: Sunday Worship - 10:30am
Children's Church - 11am
Wednesday - 7pm
WINTER: Sunday Study - 10am
Sunday Worship - 11:15am
Wednesday - 7pm
(907) 283-7682
www.kenaifellowship.org

Chevron PETRO Express

Kenai's friendliest place for gas and convenience items.

- Easy Access
- Air and Water
- RV Dump
- Automated Brushless Car Wash
- Wand Wash
- Propane
- Highway Diesel

11152 Spur Hwy., Kenai (corner of Willow and Spur Hwy.)   1-907-283-8775

KENAI FABRIC CENTER
"A QUILTER'S HEAVEN"
Over 6,000 Bolts of Quality Cottons
115 N Willow St • Kenai, AK 99611 • 907-283-4595

Eldridge Haven
Bed & Breakfast

Relax in Comfortable
Christian Home
Near Beach & Kenai River
15 Min. to Kenai/Soldotna

★ REASONABLE RATES ★

(907) 283-7152
www.ptialaska.net/~lridgebb
See Log Ad.   Established 1987

(in Soldotna), phone (907) 262-4404. Maritime Search and Rescue, dial 0 for Zenith 5555, toll free.

Visitor Information: The **Kenai Visitors and Cultural Center**, located at Main Street and Kenai Spur Highway, provides brochures and other visitor information. Very nice restrooms. The center features an excellent cultural museum, wildlife displays, seasonal art shows and a museum store. May 1–Sept. 8, 2002, the center presents "Spirit of Alaska: The Inner Landscape," an art exhibition exploring the connection between Alaska and people. There is a $3 admission fee for

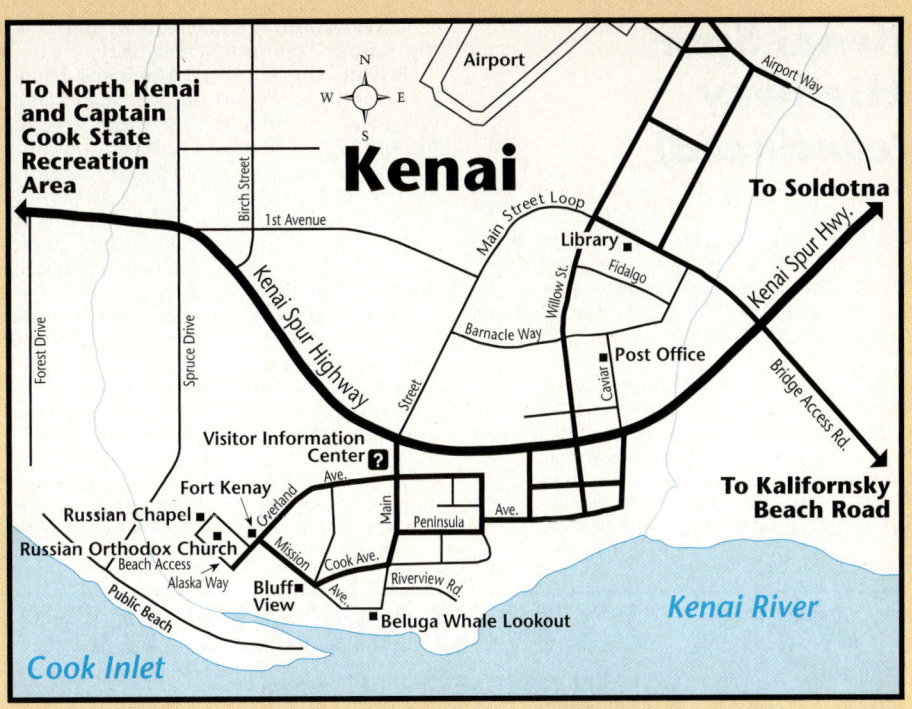

STERLING HIGHWAY • Kenai Spur Highway

KENAI ADVERTISERS

Alaskan Gift & Gallery ......Ph. (907) 283-3655
Already Read Books ....Ph. (907) 335-2665
Beluga Lookout RV Park ...Ph. (907) 283-5999
Burger Bus ....Ph. (907) 283-9611
Charlotte's Restaurant......Ph. (907) 283-2777
Eldridge Haven B&B ....Ph. (907) 283-7152
Fireweed Herb
   Garden & Gifts ....Ph. (907) 283-6107
Hertz ....Ph. (800) 478-7980
Katmai Hotel....................Ph. (800) 275-6101
Kenai Fabric Center ....Ph. (907) 283-4595
Kenai Merit Inn................Ph. (800) 227-6131
Kenai Municipal Airport ..Ph. (907) 283-7951
Kenai RV Park ....Ph. (907) 398-3382
Kenai Cultural & Visitors
   Bureau ....Ph. (907) 283-1991
McLennan House..............Ph. (907) 283-5939
Peninsula Art Guild..........Ph. (907) 283-7040
Petro Express
   Chevron.............Willow & Kenai Spur Hwy.
Tanglewood
   Bed & Breakfast...........Ph. (907) 283-6771
United Methodist Church of
   the New Convenant ....Ph. (907) 283-7868

— AT THE MOUTH OF THE KENAI RIVER —
BELUGA LOOKOUT R.V. PARK
HISTORIC OLD TOWN KENAI

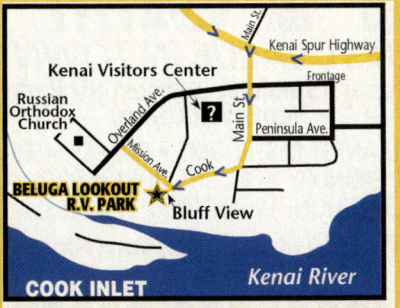

MAGNIFICENT VIEWS OF COOK INLET, KENAI RIVER
VOLCANOES • BELUGA WHALES • SEALS • FISHING • BEACH

75 Full RV Hookups • Pull Thrus • 20-30-50 Amp Power • Grills
Picnic Tables • Pavilion • Cable • Lodge Rooms • Clean Restrooms
Showers • Laundry • Fax • Internet Connection • Gift Shop • Bike Rentals

BOOK BEAR VIEWING & FISHING CHARTERS

929 Mission Avenue, Kenai, Alaska 99611
SEE LOG AD **(907) 283-5999 • 800-745-5999**
FAX (907) 283-4939 • www.belugalookout.com

Kenai Spur Highway (continued)

adults for the art show and museum. Write the Kenai Visitors and Cultural Center, 11471 Kenai Spur Highway, Kenai, AK 99611; phone (907) 283-1991, fax 283-2230. Email: kcvb@alaska.net. Web site: www.visitkenai.com.

Elevation: 93 feet. **Climate:** Average daily maximum temperature in July, 61°F; January temperatures range from 11° to -19°F. Lowest recorded temperature in Kenai was -48°F. Average annual precipitation, 19.9 inches (68.7 inches of snowfall). **Radio:** KDLL-FM 91.9, KWHQ-FM 100.1, KZXX 980, KDLL 91.9. **Television:** Several channels and cable. **Newspaper:** *Peninsula Clarion* (daily).

Private Aircraft: Kenai Municipal Airport is the principal airport on the Kenai Peninsula. It is accessible from Willow Street or Airport Way. There is a terminal building with ticket counter and baggage handling for commuter airlines, and a large parking lot. Elev. 92 feet; length 7,575 feet; asphalt; fuel 100LL; attended. A 2,000-foot gravel runway is also available. There is an adjacent 3,500-foot floatplane facility.

Kenai is situated on a low rise overlooking the mouth of the Kenai River where it empties into Cook Inlet. It is the largest city on the Kenai Peninsula. Prior to Russian Alaska, Kenai was a Dena'ina Native community. The Dena'ina people fished, hunted, trapped, farmed and traded with neighboring tribes here. In 1791 it became the second permanent settlement established by the Russians in Alaska, when a fortified post called Fort St. Nicholas, or St. Nicholas Redoubt, was built near here by Russian fur traders. In 1797, at the Battle of Kenai, the Dena'ina defeated the Russian settlement of 150 men. In subsequent years, the post remained a minor trading post. In 1848, the first Alaska gold discovery was made on the Russian River. In 1869 the U.S. Army established Fort Kenai (Kenay). The first fish canneries were established in the 1880s. A post office was authorized in 1899.

Oil exploration began in the mid-1950s, with the first major discovery in this area, the Swanson River oil reserves, 20 miles/32.2 km northeast of Kenai in 1957. Two years later, natural gas was discovered in the Kalifornsky Beach area 6 miles/9.6 km south of the city of Kenai. Extensive exploration offshore in upper Cook Inlet has established that Cook Inlet's middle-ground shoals contain one of the major oil and gas fields in the world.

The industrial complex on the North Kenai Road is the site of Agrium, which produces ammonia and urea for fertilizer. Phillips Alaska BP operates a gas to liquids technology. Tesoro has a refinery here.

Offshore in Cook Inlet are 15 drilling platforms, all with underwater pipelines bringing the oil to the shipping docks on both sides of Cook Inlet for loading onto tankers.

Federal and state agencies based in and around Kenai contribute to the local economy. Next to oil, tourism, fishing and fish processing are the leading industries.

Kenai is the home of the Kenai Peninsula Oilers, one of 3 teams that make up the Alaska Central Baseball League.

Kenai is also the home of Challenger Learning Center of Alaska, a science, math and technology space center for Alaskan youth, grades 4–12.

Lodging & Services

Kenai has all shopping facilities and conveniences. Medical and dental clinics, banks, laundromats, theaters, pharmacies, supermarkets, and numerous gift and specialty shops are located on and off the highway and in the shopping malls. Several motels and hotels and about a dozen restaurants and drive-ins are located in Kenai. Local artists are featured at the Kenai Fine Arts Center on Cook Street.

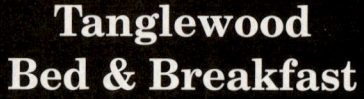

Get Hooked On Kenai

Old Town Kenai / Kenai Visitors and Cultural Center

One of Alaska's oldest cities, discover Kenai's beautiful views and rich history of Alaska Native, Russian and American heritage on a tour of Old Town Kenai.

At the Kenai Visitors and Cultural Center, attend free summer interpretive programs, watch Alaskan videos and pick-up travel information, maps and guides. Don't miss the major, international art show, *"Alaska 2003: A Celebration of Wildlife Art"* May 2002 through Labor Day, an exclusive exhibition of over 80 originals from such wildlife masters as Bateman, Coheleach, Machetanz and many others. Museum admission $3, students K-12 free.

City of Kenai - your vacation hub for the Kenai Peninsula

With its airport, accommodations, restaurants and many shops, the city of Kenai is your base camp for exploring Alaska's Playground!

- World-class Sportsfishing
- Canoe, River & Sea Kayaking
- Wildlife & Sightseeing Tours
- Arts & Culture
- Mountain-bike & Hiking Trails
- Miles of Sandy Beaches

Kenai Convention & Visitors Bureau

(Kenai Visitors & Cultural Center)
11471 Kenai Spur Highway
Kenai, AK 99611

www.visitkenai.com

the Kenai Peninsula's premiere travel website

Phone (907) 283-1991 • Fax (907) 283-2230 • email info@visitkenai.com

STERLING HIGHWAY • Kenai Spur Highway

Kenai Spur Highway (continued)

Kenai Recreation Center on Caviar Street has showers, sauna, weight room, racquetball courts and gym; phone (907) 283-3855 for hours. Indoor swimming and a waterslide are available at the Nikiski Pool (see **Mile SY 23.4** Kenai Spur Highway); phone (907) 776-8800. A multi-use facility at Rogers Road and the Spur Highway provides ice throughout the winter months and offers a variety of covered activities and events during the summer. For joggers there's the Bernie Huss Memorial Trail, a 0.5-mile jogging and exercise course located just off the Kenai Spur Highway on Main Street Loop. There's also a 1-mile jogging track at East End Park near the Peninsula Oilers Ballpark on Lawton Drive.

The Kenai Senior Center, located downtown, provides a wide variety of services to seniors. The Senior Center has a computer room, Internet access, arts and crafts classes, exercise program, quilting, sewing, no-host dinners and an active community outreach program. Visitors are welcome.

Charlotte's Restaurant. Everyone loves Charlotte and her contemporary home-style breakfasts and lunches. Fresh salads from her summer garden. Honey-oat bread baked daily and superb black-bottom coconut cream pie are 2 of Charlotte's many specialties. "A truly delightful atmosphere." Reservations for groups suggested 'cause everyone loves Charlotte's cooking! Special event catering. (907) 283-2777. Email: legg@ptialaska.net. [ADVERTISEMENT]

Eldridge Haven B&B. "Hospitality at its best" A Christian home in quiet wooded area near beach and Kenai River where breakfast is superb including low-fat and diabetic selections, beds draw raves, guests are pampered and children are cherished. Rooms have private/shared baths. Non-smoking. 2679 Bowpicker Lane, Kenai. (907) 283-7152, Email: lridgebb@ptialaska.net. www.ptialaska.net/~lridgebb. See display ad this section. [ADVERTISEMENT]

McLennan House. Distinction and comfort with the privacy and security of your own home defines this beautiful 3-bedroom, 2-bath ranch-style vacation retreat. Located

in the heart of Kenai, this home features a kitchen, great room, washer, dryer, 2 extra-long twins or a king-size bed in each bedroom, and a complete meeting facility for small groups. Come enjoy the solitude of expansive landscaped grounds, wilderness trails along a beautiful 10-acre beaver pond, and frequent visits by local wildlife. Open year-round. Reservations (907) 283-5939 or mclennanhouse.com. [ADVERTISEMENT]

Tanglewood Bed & Breakfast. Fish king salmon from our backyard, on lower Kenai River. View moose, caribou, bears, wolves, eagles, ducks, seals, beluga whales on regular basis. Rooms $75. Common room with fireplace. Fully equipped private suite with Jacuzzi, $125. Full breakfast. Laundry facilities. (907) 283-6771. Open year-round. Lifelong Alaskans. See display ad this section. [ADVERTISEMENT]

Camping

Arrangements for caravan camping may be made in advance through the Kenai Visitors and Cultural Center. Tent camping at **Milepost SY 10.1** Kenai Spur Highway. Private RV parks are available in Kenai; see ads this section or ask at the visitor center for directions. Public campgrounds are also available north of Kenai on the Kenai Spur Highway in Captain Cook State Recreation Area (see highway log).

Dump stations located at several local service stations and city dock.

Beluga Lookout RV Park, 2 blocks from Visitors Center in Historic Old Town Kenai. Overlooking bluff, spectacular views of Cook Inlet, Kenai River and beach, Mount Redoubt. Beluga whales, eagles, seals. Book bear viewing and fishing charters. Historic Russian Orthodox Church. Fort Kenay next door. Log lodge, office, gift shop, bike rentals. Hot showers, laundry. 75 full hookups, cable TV, picnic tables, pull-throughs, 20-30-50-amps. Private rooms

Fly TO KENAI!
Skip the Crowds, Skip the Drive!

Start your vacation in the very center of Alaska's Playground. Touchdown at the Kenai Municipal Airport!

- Frequent Scheduled Commuter Service - 20 min. Flight from Anch
- Check Luggage to "ENA"/Kenai
- 4 Major Car Rental Companies in Terminal
- Airport Courtesy Phone to Area Motels/B&Bs/Lodges
- Airport Lounge, Cafe, Local Transportation, Travel Agency
- Welcome Pilots! Float Plane Basin, Airplane Rental, Parking/Tie-Down Service Kenai Airport Manager Office: 283-7951

Kenai and the Kenai Peninsula — Alaska's Playground!

www.KenaiAirport.com

with kitchens and baths. Caravans welcome. Visa, MasterCard. Reservations: (907) 283-5999, (800) 745-5999. Fax (907) 283-4939. www.belugalookout.com. See display ad this section. [ADVERTISEMENT]

Kenai RV Park. Would you like a small park with grassy sites wide enough for sliders and awnings? Would you also like friendly, personalized service from on-site owners? How about burgers, lowest prices with showers included, and too many extras to list? Wrap this up in a convenient in-town location, and you have the Kenai RV Park, just one block from the Visitor Center. Motorcycles, bicycles and tents welcome. (907) 398-3382. See display ad this section. [ADVERTISEMENT]

Transportation

Air: Kenai Municipal Airport is served by Era Aviation (scheduled passenger service) as well as other charter services.

Local: Limousine and taxi service is available as well as car rentals, vehicle leasing, boat rentals and charters.

Highway: On the Kenai Spur Highway, 11 miles north of Soldotna.

Attractions

Get Acquainted. Kenai Visitors and Cultural Center has an abundance of brochures on attractions, activities and accommodations; a cultural and natural history museum; and features major summer art exhibitions.

Kenai River Festival. This annual event is held the second weekend in June on the park strip next to the City of Kenai ball fields on Main Street. The festival features activities for children and adults alike, from fish-hat making and puppet shows to how-to-fish demonstrations and educational exhibits on birds, commercial fishing and water conservation. A parade starts each festival day, led by the famous 29-foot Festival Salmon and the Kenaitze Tribal Drum group. Live music, food and crafts booths. For more information, phone (907) 260-5449.

Old Town Kenai self-guided walking tour takes in Fort Kenay, the Russian Parish House Rectory, Russian Orthodox church and chapel (see descriptions following). Pick up a walking tour brochure at Kenai Visitors and Cultural Center and walk down Overland Street toward Cook Inlet.

Kenai Community Library is centrally located at 163 Main Street Loop, adjacent the Fire Station and City Hall. The library has a large collection of Alaskana for history buffs, as well as books, periodicals, CDs, DVDs and video tapes. Popular with summer visitors are the library's books on tape. (A temporary library card is available to visitors and summer residents.) The library also boasts a garden featuring native plants; a magazine reading area with large picture windows; and free Internet access. Open 7 days a week. Phone (907) 283-4378; or go to www.kenailibrary.org.

Alaskan Gift & Gallery: Corner of Willow & Attla Way, next to the Kenai Merit Inn. Invest in unique work from Alaskan artists. Whalebone, ivory, & jade carvings, native baskets and original art. Shipping available. Free gift wrapping. Ask for a tour! Customers say "This is like a mini-museum!" www.alaskan-gift.com (907) 283-3655. See display ad this section. [ADVERTISEMENT]

Already Read Books. 100 Trading Bay, Kenai. Civic center area. Kitty-corner from the library and courthouse. Featuring a grand selection of already read books; paperback and hardcover. Find an escape from the splendor of Alaska in our melange of books. Use the exchange policy to replenish your books for the trip "home." (907) 335-2665. [ADVERTISEMENT]

Fireweed Herb Garden & Gifts. Take your picture by the colorful Boat Garden and the new 6 foot salmon topiary. See GIANT Alaskan veggies and huge tomatoes. Explore the gift shop packed with wildflower art, Alaska pottery and local crafts. Yes! We have Fireweed seeds and Giant Blue Poppies. Enjoy our specialty, "Moose Dropping Mocha." Susan and Porter would love to meet you! Mon–Sat 9–6, Sun 12–5. jordanpc@alaska.net. 202 N. Forest Drive, Kenai. Turn right, last traffic light headed North. 283-6107. See display ad this section. [ADVERTISEMENT]

Scenic viewpoint in Kenai overlooks Cook Inlet. (© Kris Graef, staff)

Fort Kenay was the first American military installation in the area, established in 1868. More than 100 men were stationed here in the 1½ years it officially served to protect American citizens in the area. A replica of the fort's barracks building was built as an Alaskan Purchase Centennial project by Kenai residents in 1967. This was the site of the original Russian schoolhouse which was torn down in 1956.

Parish House Rectory, constructed in 1881, directly east of Fort Kenay, is considered to be the oldest building on the Kenai Peninsula. Of the 4 rectories contracted by the Russian Orthodox Church in Alaska it is the only one still remaining. Restored in 1998–99, the rectory continues to be the residence of priests who serve the church. Hand-hewn logs, joined with square-notched corners, are covered by wood shingle siding and painted the original colors.

Holy Assumption of the Virgin Mary Russian Orthodox Church, across from the rectory, is one of the oldest Russian Orthodox churches in Alaska and the only National Historic Landmark on the Kenai Peninsula. The original church was founded in 1845 by a Russian monk, Father Nicholai. The present church was built with a $400 grant from the Russian Synod some 50 years after the original, and with its 3 onion-shaped domes is considered one of the finest examples of a Russian Orthodox church built on a vessel or quadrilateral floor plan. Icons from Russia and an 1847 Russian edition of the Holy Gospel—with enameled icons of Matthew, Mark, Luke and John on the cover—are displayed. Regular church services are held here. Tours are available during the summer from 11 A.M. to 4 P.M. daily except Sunday. Donations are welcomed.

United Methodist Church of the New Covenant

9:45 a.m. Discussion Group
11:00 a.m. Sunday Worship

Jon B. Walters, Pastor
Email: KenaiUMC@WebTv.net
http://community.webtv.net/KenaiUMC/KenaiAlaskaUnited

(907) 283-7868

607 Frontage Road, Kenai, AK 99611
The brown church across from Wells Fargo Bank

Kenai Fine Arts Center
Home of the Pottery Studio & The Peninsula Art Guild
Unique *Original* Artwork
Pottery, Paintings, Photography & More!
(907) 283-7040 • Mon – Sat 10 to 4

Kenai Spur Highway (continued)

Volcano and Whale Watching. The Kenai River beach at the west end of Spruce Street and Erick Hansen Scout Park at the end of Upland Street, offer good views of Kenai's fish-processing industry and volcanoes. Also look for beluga whales, the only all-white whale.

St. Nicholas Chapel was built in 1906 as a memorial to Father Nicholai and his helper, Makary Ivanov, on the site of the original church, which was inside the northwest corner of the Russian trading post of Fort St. Nicholas. The 2 men were honored for their distribution of the first smallpox vaccine in the territory.

Kenai River Flats is a must stop for birdwatchers. Great numbers of Siberian snow geese and other waterfowl stop to feed on this saltwater marsh in the spring. Kenai Flats State Recreation Site on the Bridge Access Road at the west end of Warren Ames Bridge; parking and interpretive signs. A boardwalk and viewing telescope for wildlife-watchers is located on the Bridge Access Road east of the Warren Ames Bridge.

Parks and Recreation. Most visitors driving through town will notice the Leif Hansen Memorial Park in downtown Kenai on the highway: it is perhaps the premier location in town for viewing flowers. The park also has a gazebo, water fountain, benches and drinking fountain. Erick Hansen Scout Park, at the end of Upland Street in Old Towne Kenai, features benches and a great view of Cook Inlet.

Don't miss the waterslide at the indoor Nikiski Pool, located 12 miles north of downtown Kenai at **Milepost SY 23.4** on the Kenai Spur Highway.

Kenai City Dock. Take the Bridge Access Road west from Kenai Spur Highway 1 mile then turnoff for the City of Kenai's boating facility. A busy and fascinating place in summer, the port has 2 boat launches, a 170-foot concrete dock with floats, 3 cranes, gas and diesel fuel, restrooms and parking. Trailered boats may be launched from May to September. Parking and launch fees charged.

Watch Baseball or Play Golf. Some fine semipro baseball is played at the Peninsula Oilers ball park on Tinker Lane. Golfers may try the 18-hole Kenai golf course on Lawton Drive.

Kenai Spur Highway Log
(Continued)

SY 11.7 Spruce Drive; access to beach, parking area; restrooms.

SY 11.9 Forest Drive. Municipal day-use park with playground, picnic tables and trails to west. Scenic viewpoint overlooking Cook Inlet 0.4 mile west on South Forest Drive is handicap accessible. Called **Handicapable Park**, it is a joint project of the City of Kenai and Kenai Lions; picnic table, firepits, covered overlook, restrooms.

End 4-lane highway, begin 2 lanes, northbound.

SY 12.2 C Plaza; shopping.

SY 12.3 Gas station.

SY 13 Mount Spurr is directly ahead northbound.

SY 15 Kenai city limits.

Holy Assumption of the Virgin Mary Russian Orthodox Church in Kenai.
(© Ralph & Leonor Barrett)

SY 16.1 Cafe.

SY 17.9 Nikiski Station No. 1; fire, paramedic.

SY 19 Views through trees of Mount Redoubt to west and Mount Spurr to north.

SY 19.1 South Miller Loop.

Quilt Kits Alaska. See display ad this section.

SY 20.4 Gas station.

SY 21 Agrium Kenai

SY 21.4 Phillips 66 LNG Plant.

SY 22.2 Tesoro Refinery.

SY 23.4 Dome-shaped building in trees near highway is the Nikiski recreational swimming pool, with lap lanes, kiddie swim area and a great indoor slide; hot tub; visitor observation area; weight room; racquetball courts; wheelchair access. Phone (907) 776-8800 for hours.

Nikiski Pool. See display ad this section.

SY 26.6 Shopping, restaurant, grocery, gas station and post office at **NIKISKI** (pop. 3,060). **Emergency Services**, phone 911 for fire and paramedics. **Radio:** KXBA 93.3.

Nikiski, also known as Port Nikiski and Nikishka, was homesteaded in the 1940s and grew with the discovery of oil on the Kenai Peninsula in 1957. By 1964, oil-related industries here included Unocal Chemical, Phillips LNG, Chevron and Tesoro. Oil docks serving offshore drilling platforms today include Rigtenders, Standard Oil, Phillips 66 and Unocal Chemical. Commercial fishing is still a source of income for some residents.

M&M Market. See display ad this section.

North Peninsula Chamber of Commerce. See display ad this section.

SY 26.7 Nikiski Fire Station No. 2 at turnoff for Nikiski Beach Road. Access west to Nikiski High School (0.3 mile) and OSK Heliport (0.5 mile). Drive to road end (0.8 mile, limited parking) for good view of Nikishka Bay and oil platforms in Cook Inlet; Arness Dock, built on a base of WWII Liberty ships (still visible); and scenic view of Mount Spurr and Alaska Range.

SY 29.7 Halbouty Road.

Daniels Lake Lodge Bed & Breakfast. See display ad this section.

Grouchy Old Woman B&B. See display ad this section.

SY 32 CottonWood Country Club and RV Park. Nestled peacefully on Suneva Lake with a breath taking view of the Alaska Range. 18-hole executive golf course with narrow, hilly fairways lined with giant cottonwoods. CottonWood Country Club also offers health resort, B&B, cabin rentals, fishing, canoeing, RV park with full hookups and tent camping. CottonWood Country Club, "Just a pleasant place to be!" (907) 776-7653 www.cottonwoodcountryclub.com. See display ad this section. [ADVERTISEMENT]

SY 32.4 Turnout west opposite Twin Lakes.

SY 35.1 Turnout to east.

SY 35.5 Entering **Captain Cook State Recreation Area.**

SY 35.9 Bishop Creek (Captain Cook SRA) to west; 15 tent campsites, parking, toilets, water, picnic area and trail to beach. Camping fee $8/night or resident pass. Watch for spawning red salmon in creek in July and August, silvers August to September. Closed to salmon fishing.

SY 36.5 Stormy Lake (Captain Cook SRA) day-use area located 0.5 mile east via gravel road (downhill grade); large parking area, swimming area (not much beach), change house, outhouse, water. Fishing for rainbow and arctic char.

SY 36.7 Stormy Lake Overlook, a large paved turnout to east, offers a panoramic view.

SY 36.9 Stormy Lake picnic area (not on lake); water, toilets, covered tables.

SY 37.9 Stormy Lake boat launch; water, toilets, parking.

SY 38.6 Swanson River canoe landing area; drive 0.6 mile east to parking and toilets, river access. End of the Swanson River canoe trail system.

SY 38.7 Clint Starnes Memorial Bridge crosses **Swanson River**; parking next to bridge. *Watch for fishermen on bridge.* View of Mount Spurr. Fishing for silver and red salmon, and rainbow.

SY 39 Highway ends. Turn left for **Discovery Campground** (0.4 mile) and picnic area (0.5 mile) via bumpy gravel access road. Campground has 53 campsites, Maggie Yurick Memorial hiking trail, water, scheduled fireside programs in season. Camping fee $10/night or resident pass.

Day-use picnic area (keep to right at second fork) has tables and toilets on bluff overlooking ocean. *CAUTION: Steep cliffs; supervise children and pets!*

Spur access road to beach (4-wheel drive vehicles only); signed as "unsafe due to high tides and loose sand." Parking area. ATVs are allowed in designated areas only.

Return to Milepost S 94.2
Sterling Highway

Captain Cook SRA parking area at end of Kenai Highway overlooks Cook Inlet.
(© Kris Graef, staff)

CottonWood
18 Hole Executive Golf Course
RV Park With Full Hookups
Cabins, Room Rentals
"Just a pleasant place to be."
(907) 776-7653
Box 7097, Nikiski, AK 99635
3 miles from Capt. Cook St. Park, Mile 32
www.cottoncountryclub.com

Welcome to the North Country!

Welcome to Nikiski...

...from the North Peninsula Chamber of Commerce and Nikiski Fire Department

* Magnificent Cook Inlet Sunsets and Sunrises
* Excellent Beach Combing
* Beautiful Captain Cook State Park and Campground
* Lakes for Fishing, Canoeing and Bird Watching
* Swanson River Canoe Trail-End

View the Impressive Oil Processing Facilities, The Economic Base of the Kenai Peninsula!
Visitor and Safety Information: (907) 776-3257

GROUCHY OLD WOMAN B&B
Beautiful Daniels Lake Location
Private/Shared Baths • Full Breakfast
Common Area with Phone, TV, Microwave
Alaska History, Flora & Fauna Abound
(907) 776-8775
gowoman@alaska.net
http://grouchyoldwoman.homestead.com

Daniels Lake Lodge Bed & Breakfast Est. 1984
Year-Round Wildlife Viewing, Rainbow Trout, Hiking
Log Cabins and Guest Rooms Secluded in a Relaxing Lake Cove
Boats & Canoes • Kitchens • Private Baths
Christian Hosts Jim & Karen Burris Welcome You
www.DanielsLakeLodge.com
Info: (907) 776-5578 • Reservations: 1-800-774-5578
Mile 29.7 Spur Hwy. • P.O. Box 1444, Kenai, Alaska 99611 • Email: info@danielslakelodge.com

Kalifornsky Beach Road

Also called K–Beach Road, Kalifornsky Beach Road is a paved 45 mph road which leads west from the Sterling Highway at Soldotna, following the shore of Cook Inlet south to Kasilof. K-Beach Road also provides access to Kenai via the Bridge Access Road. *Mileposts run south to north and reflect mileage from Kasilof.*

Distance from the Sterling Highway junction at Milepost S 96.1 at Soldotna (S) is followed by distance from Sterling Highway junction at Milepost S 108.8 at Kasilof (K).

S 0 K 22.2 Junction with Sterling Highway at **Milepost S 96.1.**

S 0.1 K 22.1 Centennial Park Municipal Campground, 0.1 mile west, on the banks of the Kenai River; 126 campsites (some on river), tables, firepits, firewood provided, water, restrooms, dump station, pay phone, 2-week limit. Register at entrance. Boat launch and fishwalk.

S 0.2 K 22 Alaska State Troopers.

S 0.3 K 21.9 Gehrke Field, rodeo grounds.

S 0.6 K 21.6 Soldotna Sports Center; hockey, ice skating, jogging track and other sports available; phone (907) 262-3150.

S 1.7 K 20.5 College Loop Road to Kenai Peninsula College (1.3 miles north).

S 2.9 K 19.3 K–Beach center. ADF&G office; stop in here for current sportfishing information.

S 3.1 K 19.1 East Poppy Lane intersection; Tesoro gas station.

Access to Kenai Peninsula College (0.9 mile north). Access to Slikok Creek State

Snow geese feed at Kenai River Flats. (© Bill Sherwonit)

Recreation Area at the college; Kenai River public fishing access.

S 3.5 K 18.7 Red Diamond shopping center, motel, restaurant and Texaco gas station. Coffee Roasters espresso is located in Red Diamond Center.

S 4.7 K 17.5 Ciechanski Road leads 2.4 miles to private RV parks and **Ciechanski State Recreation Site** on the Kenai River (River Mile 15.5). This small state recreation site is easy to overlook, as it's tucked in the corner across from Kenai River Quest RV Park. Its primary purpose is to provide restroom access for boaters. There is 12-hour public parking (no camping), a picnic table, outhouse and dock walk.

Kenai Riverbend Campground is 0.2 mile beyond the Ciechanski state recreation site. Road ends at private property; no public river access. a day-use only picnic area with tables, toilets, dumpster and Kenai River access. Also access to private campgrounds with RV hookups on the Kenai River.

S 5.7 K 16.5 Diamond M Ranch B&B, Cabins & RV Park. Hosts: Longtime Alaskans, JoAnne and Carrol Martin family. Nestled in the trees. Full hookups, laundromat, shower, dump station. Fish cleaning facility. Magnificent view of Kenai River, Alaska mountain range. Wildlife, hiking trails. Secluded, yet minutes from airport, shopping, restaurants, churches. Credit cards. (907) 283-9424. P.O. Box 1776, Soldotna, AK 99669. Internet: www.diamondmranch.com. See display ad in the Soldotna section.
[ADVERTISEMENT]

S 6 K 16.2 Junction. Turnoff for city of Kenai via Bridge Access Road. Access to **Kenai River Flats State Recreation Site** and boardwalk viewpoint via Bridge Access Road; good bird watching in season.

Bike route ends, road narrows, northbound.

S 7.5 K 14.5 Robinsons Mini Mall. See display ad this section.

S 8.8 K 13.4 K-Beach Fire Station.

S 17.4 K 4.8 Kasilof Beach Road; access to Cook Inlet Processing

S 18.7 K 3.5 Inn-Between B&B and Cabins. We welcome fishing fanatics, families, bird watchers, vacationing couch potatoes and you! Fabulous scenic location near

the beautiful Kasilof River and Cook Inlet, with mountain views. Fishing, hiking, biking or just relaxing in the sunroom. A comfortable friendly place to be. Go clamming with Barb and enjoy fried razor clams for breakfast. Full breakfast with fishing lunches on request. innbetween@alaska.net. (907) 335-2769. www.alaskainnbetween.com.
[ADVERTISEMENT]

S 18.8 K 3.4 Old Kasilof Road. Drive in ½ mile and turn on Alice Road; continue ½ mile for Old Kasilof Landing.

S 19.4 K 2.8 Ingrid's Inn Bed & Breakfast. See display ad this section.

S 20.1 K 2.1 Turnoff for Kasilof Airport (unsigned). **Private aircraft**; Kasilof airstrip, 2N; elev. 125 feet; length 2,100 feet; gravel; unattended.

S 22.1 K 0.1 Kasilof Post Office.

S 22.2 K 0 Junction with Sterling Highway at Kasilof, **Milepost S 108.8.**

Return to Milepost S 96.1 or S 108.8 Sterling Highway

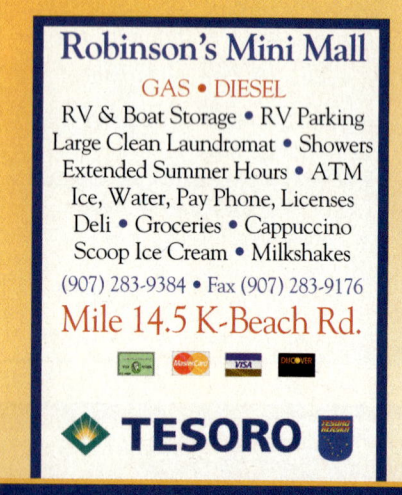

Sterling Highway Log
(continued from page 569)

S 95.9 A 148.9 H 83.6 Kenai River bridge.

S 96 A 149 H 83.5 **Soldotna Visitor Center** to west at south end of Kenai River bridge; visitor information, fish walk on Kenai River.

Entering Game Management Unit 15A northbound.

S 96.1 A 149.1 H 83.4 Funny River Road to east; access to Soldotna businesses, airport and state recreation site. Kalifornsky Beach Road to west; access to Centennial Park campground (description follows).

Junction with Kalifornsky Beach Road and with Funny River Road. See "Funny River Road" log on page 581; see "Kalifornsky Beach Road" log on opposite page.

Centennial Park Municipal Campground, 0.1 mile west, on the banks of the Kenai River; 126 campsites (some on river), tables, firepits, firewood provided, water, restrooms, dump station, pay phone, 2-week limit. Register at entrance. Boat launch and favorite fishing site on fishwalk.

S 97.9 A 150.9 H 81.6 Begin southbound turn lane for Skyview High School to west, and abrupt turnoff to east for Ski Hill Road and access to **Kenai National Wildlife Refuge Visitor Center** (description follows). Turnoff is easy to miss.

Skyview High School has the popular **Tsalteshi Trails System** (built by volunteers), with 7 miles of loop trails for walking, running and mountain biking in summer, and cross-country skiing in winter. Trails start behind the school.

Drive east 1 mile on Ski Hill Road for Kenai National Wildlife Refuge Visitor Center. This popular center has dioramas of area wildlife, free wildlife films, and rangers on hand to answer questions on canoeing, hiking and camping in the refuge. There is a nature trail down to an observation platform and spotting scope on Headquarters Lake. The center is open 8 A.M. to 4:30 P.M. on weekdays, 10 A.M. to 6 P.M. weekends.

Ski Hill Road loops back to Funny River Road.

S 98.5 A 151.5 H 85 CAUTION: Moose Danger Zone next 10 miles southbound.

S 107 A 160 H 68.9 **Decanter Inn Hotel, RV Park, Restaurant and Bar.** Established prior to statehood, the Decanter Inn has always been a gathering place where friends meet. Sitting on 60 beautifully wooded acres, we are now equipped for the modern traveler, with a 55-site RV park, with free dump station for our guests, 30 amp hookups, pull-thrus and pull-ins, with well-spaced sites. Adjacent to the RV Park is a 30-unit hotel with private baths, full-service restaurant and bar. For our guests, we provide free shuttle service to nearby fishing and clamming areas. There is a fish cleaning station and fire rings for your grilling or camping needs. The beautiful Roque Lake is stocked with salmon every other year for our guests' easy angling. This, coupled with the full-service Decanter Inn, makes this one of the finest destinations on the Kenai Peninsula. www.decanterinn.com (907) 262-5933. See display ad this page. [ADVERTISEMENT]

S 108.8 A 161.8 H 70.7 South junction with Kalifornsky Beach (K-Beach) Road. This loop road rejoins Sterling Highway at

Sign marks turnoff on Ski Hill Road for Kenai National Wildlife Refuge Visitor Center. (© Kris Graef, Staff)

Milepost S 96.1. Kasilof post office is just west of the highway on K-Beach Road.

Junction with Kalifornsky Beach Road. See "Kalifornsky Beach Road" log on opposite page.

S 109 A 162 H 70.5 Kasilof Mercantile. KASILOF was originally a settlement established in 1786 by the Russians as St. George. A Kenaitze Indian village grew up around the site, but no longer exists. The current population of Kasilof is 548 and is spread out over a general area. The area's income is derived from fishing and fish processing.

S 109.2 A 162.2 H 70.3 Tesoro gas station with diesel, groceries, liquor store, espresso and tackle to west at north end of Kasilof River bridge.

Kasilof Riverview. See display ad this section.

S 109.4 A 162.4 H 70.1 Bridge over Kasilof River, which drains Tustumena Lake, one of the largest lakes on the Kenai Penin-

Kasilof River and Crooked Creek

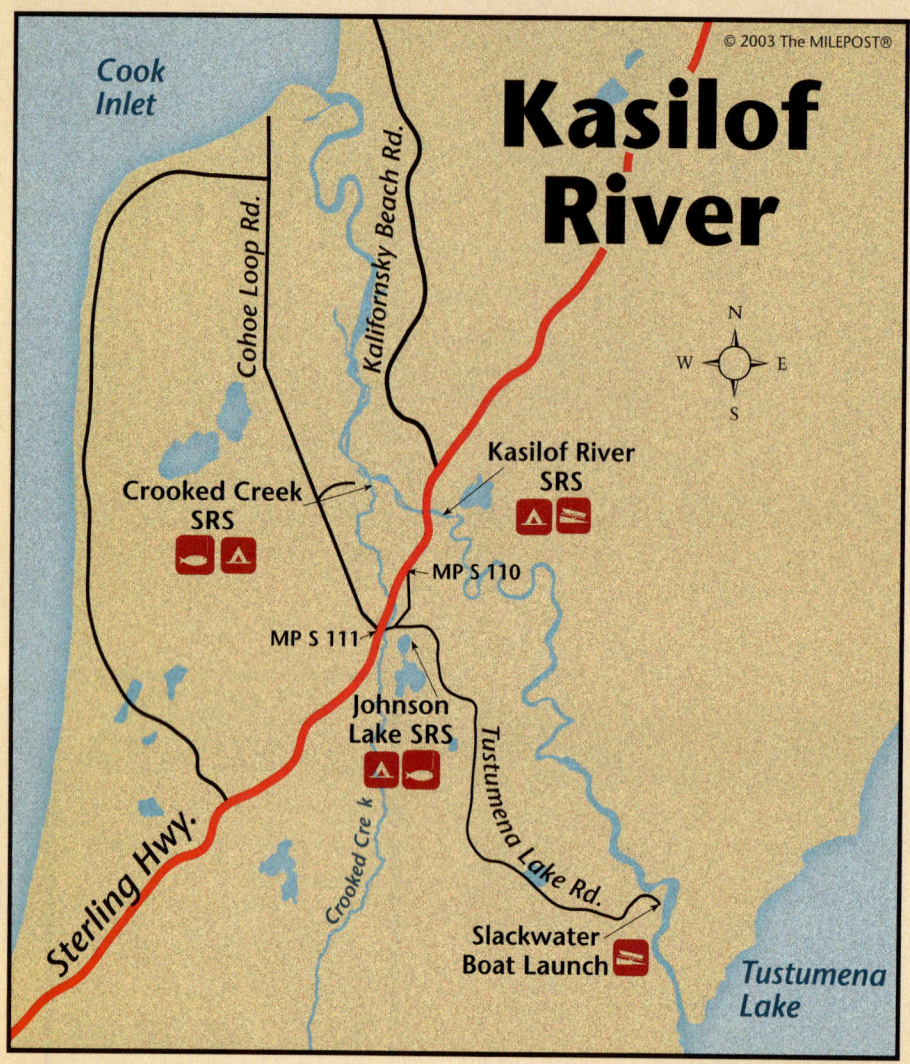

Kasilof River near Slackwater boat launch on Tustumena Lake Road.
(© Kris Graef, staff)

The Kasilof River is a powerful glacial lake-fed river draining Tustumena Lake, the Kenai Peninsula's largest lake. While most popular for its sportfishing opportunities, the Kasilof River is also popular for whitewater kayaking or canoeing and wildlife viewing.

The section of the Kasilof River between its outlet from Tustumena Lake downstream to the Sterling Highway bridge at **Milepost S 109.4** is the wildest and least used section of river. Several sections of Class II whitewater rapids make this section of river exciting for kayaking or canoeing by experienced boaters.

The most popular section for anglers fishing from drift boats is downstream from the Sterling Highway bridge, where the river is characterized by fewer rocks and obstacles. Most drift boats launch at the **Kasilof River State Recreation Site** at the Sterling Highway bridge to access the best fishing downstream.

Other anglers choose to access the popular king salmon bank fishing at the confluence of Crooked Creek and the Kasilof River at **Crooked Creek State Recreation Site** on Cohoe Loop Road. This is one of the most productive bank fishing spots on the Kenai Peninsula for king salmon fishing, and is also popular late in the season for silver salmon fishing. A large parking lot provides ample room for camping and day-use access at the state recreation site, located 1.8 miles west of **Milepost S 111** Sterling Highway via Cohoe Loop Road to Crooked Creek/Rilinda River. Crooked Creek SRS has 83 campsites, 36 day-use sites, toilets and water trails to Kasilof River for fishermen. Camping fee $10/ night or resident pass, day-use fee $5/vehicle.

Adjacent the state recreation site is the private Crooked Creek RV Park & Guide Service, which offers fishing charters, camping, tackle and snacks. Fishing access to Crooked Creek frontage above confluence is through this private RV park; a fee is charged.

One note of caution should be made for persons boating on the Kasilof River. This is a very cold and powerful river. Rocks are plentiful in this river. The silty nature of the glacial water makes it difficult to see underwater obstacles. During periods of low water, navigating the river in a power boat is nearly impossible due to the rocky, shallow conditions. During high water, the swift current makes boating conditions hazardous.

Recreational boaters should have moderate levels of experience with white water if boating this river. All boaters should plan for a safe trip by always wearing proper personal floatation devices and filing trip plans with friends or other responsible parties.

sula. Turnoff for **Kasilof River State Recreation Site** to east at south end of bridge; parking, $10 nightly camping fee or resident pass, $5 day-use fee, picnic tables, toilets and water. This is a popular boat launch for drift boaters fishing for king salmon late May to early July. Boat launch $5 fee.

Kasilof River. The red salmon dip-net fishery here is open by special announcement for Alaska residents only. Check with the ADF&G for current regulations.

Entering Game Management Subunit 15C southbound, 15B northbound.

S 110 A 163 H 69.5 Tustumena Elementary School and **junction** with north end of Johnson Lake Loop Road. Hybrid wolf viewing. See description and access to Johnson Lake at Milepost S 111.

Wolves of Alaska. See display ad this section.

S 110.1 A 163.1 H 69.4 Distance marker northbound shows Soldotna 14 miles, Kenai 25 miles, Anchorage 162 miles.

S 110.5 A 163.5 H 69 Double-ended paved parking to west by Crooked Creek.

S 110.8 A 163.8 H 68.7 Tustumena Lodge. Home of the Guinness World Record Hat Collection. Phone (907) 262-4216. Email: suzieq@ptialaska.net. Motel, cocktail lounge, outdoor patio, fishing guides. Clean affordable rooms at half the price of town. $45 single/double and $100, for 4 to 6 guests. Some kitchenettes. Friendly Alaskan atmosphere where a cold drink, and good fishing stories abound. Home of the $9 dinner: Monday and Wednesday, prime rib, Friday–New York steak. Soup and sandwich always available. See world's largest razor clam and look for a hat from your hometown among the over 24,000 hats on display! [ADVERTISEMENT]

S 111 A 164 H 68.5 *CAUTION: This is a busy intersection.* **Junction** with south end of Johnson Lake Loop Road to east and access to Kasilof RV Park and public campgrounds at Johnson and Tustumena lakes (descriptions follow).

Junction with the north end of 15.3-mile-long Cohoe Loop Road, which leads west to Crooked Creek State Recreation Site and Crooked Creek RV Park & Guide Service (see "Kasilof River and Crooked Creek" feature on opposite page).

Alaska Cabins Kasilof. Down Johnson Lake Road to Cabin Avenue Brand new! Cute, warm, comfortable cabins. Fully furnished, bedding, microwave, coffee included. Sleeps 2–4. Guest freezer, firepit and fish pro-

www.themilepost.com

Johnson Lake is just east of Milepost S 111. (© Kris Graef, Staff)

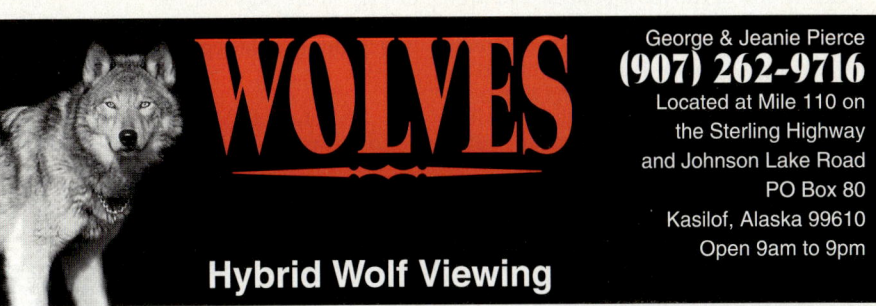

WOLVES
George & Jeanie Pierce
(907) 262-9716
Located at Mile 110 on
the Sterling Highway
and Johnson Lake Road
PO Box 80
Kasilof, Alaska 99610
Open 9am to 9pm

Hybrid Wolf Viewing

CROOKED CREEK RV PARK & GUIDE SERVICE
CONFLUENCE OF CROOKED CREEK AND KASILOF RIVER

KINGS • SILVERS • HALIBUT

➤ Largest Bank King Fishery On The Kenai Peninsula
➤ Open 7 Days A Week
➤ Fishing Charters—Kasilof & Kenai Rivers and Cook Inlet.

Tackle • Soft Drinks • Snacks

MORE OF WHAT YOU CAME TO ALASKA FOR!
➥ Large, Wooded Lots • Picnic Table & Barbecue
➥ Full Or Partial Hookups & Tent Sites
➥ Trailer Rentals (Fully Equipped)
➥ Good Water • Pay Showers • Dump Station

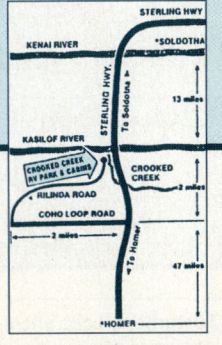

INFORMATION and RESERVATIONS
(907) 262-1299 • Open May–September
P.O. Box 601, Kasilof, Alaska 99610
Mile 111 Sterling Highway
1.8 Miles on Cohoe Loop Road

STERLING HIGHWAY

Cohoe Loop Road Log

The Cohoe Loop Road loops west and south 15.3 miles from **Milepost S 111** to **Milepost S 114.3** on the Sterling Highway. The popular Crooked Creek fishing and camping area is at the top or north end of the loop. **Distance from north junction with the Sterling Highway (NJ) at Milepost S 111** is followed by distance from south junction (SJ) at Milepost S 114.3.
Mileposts run south to north.

NJ 0 SJ 15.3 North junction with Sterling Highway at **Milepost S 111.**

NJ 1.8 SJ 13.5 Crooked Creek/Rilinda Drive; access to Crooked Creek RV Park & Guide Service and to **Crooked Creek State Recreation Site** at the confluence of Crooked Creek and the Kasilof River. The recreation site has 83 campsites, 36 day-use sites, toilets and water trails to Kasilof River for fishermen. Camping fee $10/ night or resident pass, day-use fee $5/vehicle. ▲

This is one of the most popular and productive sites in the area for bank angling for king salmon. Fishing in **Crooked Creek** closed to king salmon fishing and closed to all fishing near hatchery. Fishing access to confluence of Crooked Creek and Kasilof River is through the state recreation site.

NOTE: *Fishing access to Crooked Creek frontage above confluence is through a private RV park; fee charged.* Fishing in the **Kasilof River** for king salmon, 20–30 lbs., late May through early July, best in mid-June; coho salmon, mid-August to September, use salmon egg clusters, wet flies, assorted spoons and spinners. Steelhead available in late fall and early spring for catch-and-release.

NJ 2.4 SJ 12.9 Webb–Ramsell Road. Kasilof River access across private property, fee charged.

NJ 5.3 SJ 10 Cohoe Spur Road **junction.** A post office was established in 1950 at COHOE (area pop. 508), originally an agricultural settlement.

NJ 5.6 SJ 9.7 T intersection; go west 0.8 mile for beach and boat launch.

Cohoe Loop Road continues north and south. *Pavement begins northbound.* ▲

Kasilof River Lodge and Cabins. See display ad on page 592.

NJ 15.3 SJ 0 South junction with Sterling Highway at **Milepost S 114.3.**

Return to Milepost S 114.3
or Milepost S 111 Sterling Highway

cessing delivery. Families, groups and snow-machiners welcome. Tent space available. Bathhouse with with all the comforts of home, including towels, shampoo. Close to fishing, clamming and the Centennial Trail. Reasonable prices. Weekly rates! On-site host. Book now! bluebear@ptialaska.net. P.O. Box 451, Kasilof, AK 99610. Call Lucy (907) 262-2187. [ADVERTISEMENT]

Crooked Creek RV Park & Guide Service. See display ad this section. ▲

Kasilof River Lodge and Cabins, once an authentic Alaskan Fish Camp, now hosts avid sports fishermen and travelers drawn to Alaska's spectacular outdoors. Located only 5 miles down Cohoe Loop, fully equipped cabins perch on a bluff overlooking the Kasilof River and Cook Inlet. The lodge guides take you to select fishing spots and the lodge hosts arrange halibut charters, hunting excursions, and eco-tours. Walk on the beach, dig for clams, or simply enjoy the hot meals and Alaskan hospitality (262-6348, 398-6620) www.KasilofRiverLodge.com. See display ad this section. [ADVERTISEMENT]

Kasilof RV Park. Modern, clean facilities in a park-like setting make this one of the Kenai Peninsula's favorite RV parks. The traveler is offered a great alternative from the parking lot-style RV parks and a peaceful retreat from combat fishing campgrounds. The peaceful setting boasts wildflowers, beavers, moose, eagles and a variety of small birds. Enjoy walking, fishing for trout in Johnson Lake, salmon in nearby Kasilof and Kenai rivers, halibut in Cook Inlet, or clamming on Alaska's famous razor-clam beaches. Level gravel sites, picnic tables, full/partial hookups, spotless restrooms, free showers and friendly owners make for "two thumbs up." Open Memorial weekend to Labor Day. www.kasilofrvpark.com; Email: kasilofrv@ak.net. See display ad this section. [ADVERTISEMENT] ▲

Turnoff to east on Johnson Lake Loop Road for Crooked Creek (to Kasilof RV Park) and Tustumena Lake Road. **Johnson Lake State Recreation Area** (0.4 east, turn at T on Tustumena Road) has a large day-use area with parking, wheelchair accessible restrooms, water, dumpster, picnic tables and firepits in the trees next to the lake. Johnson Lake campground has 50 sites (some double and some pull-throughs), $10 nightly fee or resident pass, water, toilets, boat launch and firewood. Johnson Lake (non-motorized) is stocked with rainbow.

Tustumena Lake (Slackwater) boat launch on the Kasilof River is 5.8 miles beyond the entrance to Johnson Lake SRA via gravel road. This facility has a boat launch, parking and a few primitive campsites. Fishing for lake trout and salmon. Tustumena Lake is closed to king and sockeye salmon fishing. *CAUTION: Tustumena Lake is subject to severe winds.*

Tustumena Lake is 6 miles wide and 25 miles long, accounting for more than 60,000 acres of Kenai National Wildlife Refuge. Water temperatures in this lake rarely exceed 45°F. Strong winds coming off Tustumena Glacier and the Harding Icefield can change boating conditions from calm water to 3-foot waves without warning. Weather systems in Cook Inlet and the Gulf of Alaska can also bring high winds. Boaters not familiar with operating in these conditions should not venture out on this lake.

S 114.3 A 167.3 H 65.2 Junction with 15.3-mile Cohoe Loop Road which loops west and north back to the Sterling Highway

a peaceful escape...
Kasilof RV Park
Loon Serenades • Frequent Moose Visits
"Be still and know..."

PARK-LIKE SETTING — MODERN FACILITIES
- Full/Partial Hookups • Drive-Throughs
- Public Room • Laundry • Clean Restrooms
- Hot Showers • Dump Station • Small Gift Shop
- Clamming Equipment Rentals

Centrally located for your Kenai Peninsula vacation activities

1/2 mile off Highway • Mile Post 111
1-907-262-0418
in AK 1-800-264-0418
www.kasilofrvpark.com
kasilofrv@ak.net

ROAD SIGNS POSTED: Homer 60, Clam Gulch, Ninilchik 20, Kenai 20, Soldotna 15

Mile 111 — Crooked Creek Rd., Johnson Lake Rd.

Tustumena Lake encompasses more than 60,000 acres of Kenai National Wildlife Refuge.

at Milepost S 111.

S 117.4 A 170.4 H 62.1 Clam Gulch State Recreation Area, 0.5 mile from highway; picnic tables, picnic shelter, toilets, water, 116 campsites, $10 nightly fee or resident pass. $5 day-use fee. *CAUTION: High ocean bluffs are dangerous.* Short access road to beach (recommended for 4-wheel-drive vehicles only). ▲

Clam digging for razor clams on most of the sandy beaches of the western Kenai Peninsula from Kasilof to Anchor Point can be rewarding. Many thousands of clams are dug each year at Clam Gulch. You must have a sportfishing license to dig, and these are available at most sporting goods stores. The bag limit is 60 clams regardless of size (always check current regulations). There is no legally closed season, but quality of the clams varies with month; check locally. Good clamming and fewer people in March and April, although there may still be ice on the beach. Any tide lower than minus 1-foot is enough to dig clams; minus 4- to 5-foot tides are best.

The panoramic view of Mount Redoubt, Mount Iliamna and Mount Spurr across Cook Inlet and the expanse of beach are well worth the short side trip even during the off-season.

S 118.2 A 171.2 H 61.3 CLAM GULCH (pop. 173) post office (established in 1950).

S 119.6 A 172.6 H 59.9 Clam Gulch Lodge. Fishing, lodging packages. Guided Clam Trips on the best clam beach on the West Coast. Call for tides. Mountain/Inlet view from fireplace lounge. Country breakfast. Smoke-free environment. Large rooms, twin and king-size beds. Private/shared baths. 3 RV sites. Full hookups. Box 499, Clam Gulch, AK 99568. 1-800-700-9555. Phone/fax (907) 260-3778; www.clamgulch.com; email: kkatsion@yahoo.com. [ADVERTISEMENT] ▲

S 122.8 A 175.8 H 56.7 Paved, double-ended parking area to west (no view).

S 124.7 A 177.7 H 54.8 Paved, double-ended viewpoint to west.

S 126.8 A 179.8 H 52.7 Double-ended paved parking to west.

S 127.1 A 180.1 H 52.4 Double-ended paved scenic viewpoint to west. Private RV park to west.

Scenic View RV Park. Easy access off highway. 27 spaces. Full hookups, electric, water, dump station. Low monthly/weekly rates. Located between Soldotna and Homer overlooking Cook Inlet and Mt. Redoubt. Fish halibut and king salmon with Elby Charters, dig razor clams on nearby beaches. Email: scenicrv@yahoo.com. Phone (907) 567-3909. www.scenicviewrv.com. See display ad this section. [ADVERTISEMENT]

S 128.3 A 181.3 H 51.2 Ninilchik Cabins and Fish Camp. See display ad this section.

S 130.5 A 183.5 H 49 Ninilchik Point Overnighter. Spacious, very clean, comfortable, home-grown log cabins. Scenic getaway. Cook Inlet view. 2 cabins self-contained with kitchen. 3 cabins served by shower house. 2-burner electric units. Bedding, linens provided. Outdoor grill. RV spaces with electric. Open tenting area. Close to famous fishing, clam beaches. Local charters. www.ptialaska.net/~kathyj. (907) 567-3423. [ADVERTISEMENT]

S 132.2 A 185.2 H 47.3 Heavenly Sights Charters & Camping. See display ad this section. ▲

Alaska Fishing Log Cabins. New! Open year-round. Located in the heart of the Kenai Peninsula, Alaska's fishing and outdoor recreational playground. These custom-

built cabins provide guests with warm and nicely appointed sleeping accommodations. Private baths. Sleeps 1 to 4 and roll-away available. Winter rates for snowmobile

Old Ninilchik Village on the eastern shore of Cook Inlet. (© Laurent Dick)

enthusiasts. RV sites with water and electric hookups. Attn: Doc Blackard, 10704 Flagship Circle, Anchorage, AK 99515; (907) 567-3377, (907) 344-6988. Email: alaskafishing@chugach.net; www.alaskafishinglogcabins.com. [ADVERTISEMENT]

S 133.4 A 186.4 H 46.1 Distance marker northbound shows Soldotna 36 miles, Kenai 48 miles, Anchorage 184 miles.

S 134 A 187 H 45.5 *Begin 45 mph speed zone southbound.*

Begin 55 mph speed limit northbound.

S 134.6 A 187.6 H 44.9 Ninilchik River Scenic Overlook (Ninilchik SRA) to east. This is a 2-tiered parking area with walking trail (hike or to fish) above river; toilets, picnic tables, interpretive signs, barbecues, garbage, water pump; $10 camping fee or resident pass, $5 day-use fee.

S 134.7 A 187.7 H 44.8 Coal Street (unsigned); access west to Ninilchik's historic **Russian Orthodox Church** at top of hill; plenty of parking and turnaround space; scenic overlook.

S 134.8 A 187.8 H 44.7 *CAUTION: Slow for 35 mph curve.*

S 134.9 A 187.9 H 44.6 Ninilchik River Campground to east; 39 campsites in trees on gravel loops (upper and lower loops); campground host; picnic tables, grills, water, outhouses; $10 camping fee. Trail to Ninilchik River; fishing for king and silver salmon, steelhead and Dolly Varden.

S 135.1 A 188.1 H 44.4 Mission Avenue (beach access road); large gravel turnout just south of turnoff. Follow Mission Avenue 0.2 mile west to Y: right fork leads 0.3 mile to deadend at **NINILCHIK VILLAGE** at mouth of Ninilchik River; left fork leads 0.3 mile to deadend at beach and provides access to motel, RV park and state campground. Sea breezes here keep the beach free of mosquitoes. **Ninilchik Beach Campground** (Ninilchik SRA) has 35 campsites, toilets, water, $10 camping fee or resident pass. Popular beach for razor clamming. *CAUTION: Drownings have occurred here. Be aware of tide changes when clam digging. Incoming tides can quickly cut you off from the beach.* Access to the clamming beds adjacent to the campgrounds during minus tides.

Historic signs near beach and at village entrance tell about Ninilchik Village, which includes several old dovetailed log buildings. A walking tour brochure is available from businesses in the village and along the highway. Present-day Ninilchik is located at **Milepost S 135.5.**

The green and white **Holy Transfiguration of Our Lord Russian Orthodox Church** sits on a hill overlooking the sea above the historic old village. Trail leads up to it from the road into town (watch for sign just past the old village store). Built in 1901, the church is still in use. You are welcome to walk up to it, but use the well-defined path behind the store (please do not walk through private property), or drive up using the Coal Street access at **Milepost S 134.7.**

Ninilchik Boardwalk Café, built on Ninilchik Beach, with spectacular view of Cook Inlet volcanoes. Well known for delicious home-cooked meals, in a relaxed atmosphere. Local hand-breaded razor clams, halibut, salmon, crab, scallops, and delicious homemade clam chowder. Great burgers too. The Boardwalk is famous for homemade apple pie like Grandma used to make. Great food, great service indoors or on the deck. Don't miss this unique café. (907) 567-3388. [ADVERTISEMENT]

S 135.3 A 188.3 H 44.2 Kingsley Road leads east to junction with Oilwell Road; laundry, medical clinic. Ninilchik post office, Alaskan Angler RV Resort and charter services to east.

Alaskan Angler RV Resort and **Afishunt Charters.** Fishing charter discounts for campers. Newly remodeled park and cabins at great central Ninilchik location on the corner of Kingsley Road and highway. Walk to old village, downtown, clamming beaches, salmon fishing, post office. Fifty new 50-, 30, 20-amp full hookups; 10 partial; cable TV with HBO, telephone lines, tenting. One-, 2- and 3-bedroom furnished cabins. New public showers/ laundry. Propane in 2003. We specialize in local fishing and clamming, with licenses, cleaning tables, smoker, vacpak, freezing, shipping and tackle. Experience Alaska's best fishing for succulent halibut and king salmon with on-site AFISHUNT Charters, departing from the park. Our boats have heated cabins, marine head. Good Sam discounts. Owners on-site. Reservations (800) 347-4114, (907) 567-3393. Email: info@afishunt.com. www.afishunt.com. See display ad in Ninilchik section. [ADVERTISEMENT]

S 135.4 A 188.4 H 44.1 DOT/PF road maintenance station.

S 135.5 A 188.5 H 44 Inlet View (lodge) east side of highway, **Ninilchik View State Campground** west side of highway. State campground has 12 campsites on narrow gravel loop road, view of Ninilchik Village, tables, water, toilets, litter disposal, 2 dump stations ($5 fee), drinking water fill-up. Camping fee $10/night or resident pass. Foot trail from campground down to beach and village.

Ninilchik

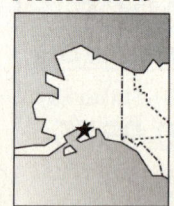

S 135.6 A 188.6 H 43.9 Ninilchik (pronounced Ni-NILL-chick) extends roughly from Ninilchik State Recreation Area on the north to Deep Creek on the south. **Population:** 772. **Emergency services:** Phone 911. **Visitor Information:** At Kiosk, **Milepost S 136.1.** Local businesses are also very helpful. **Private Air-**

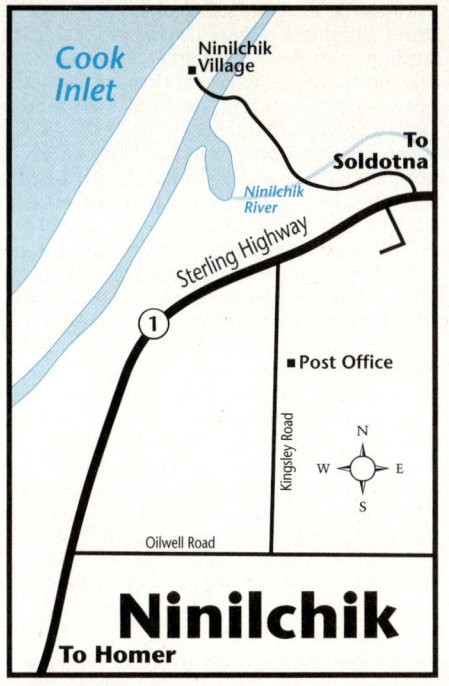

craft: Ninilchik airstrip, 3 SE; elev. 276 feet; length 2,400 feet; dirt and gravel; unattended.

Ninilchik has all services, including grocery stores, gas stations, lodging, dining, fishing charters and campgrounds. There is

NINILCHIK ADVERTISERS	
Afishunt Charters	Ph. (800) 347-4114
Alaskan Angler RV Resort	Ph. (800) 347-4114
Boardwalk Cafe	Ph. (907) 567-3388
Bull Moose Gifts	Ph. (907) 567-3415
Chihuly's	Ph. (907) 567-3374
Chinook Tesoro	Ph. (907) 567-3473
Deep Creek View Campground	Ph. (888) 425-4288
Deep Creek Custom Packing	Ph. (800) 764-0078
Inlet View Lodge	Ph. (907) 567-3330
Irish Lord Charters	Ph. (800) 515-2055
Ninilchik Chamber of Commerce	Ph. (907) 567-3571
Ninilchik Charters	Ph. (888) 290-3507
Ninilchik General Store	Ph. (907) 567-3378
Ninilchik Saltwater Charters & Lodge	Ph. (800) 382-3611
O'Fish'ial Charters	Ph. (907) 567-7314
Reel'em Inn and Cook Inlet Charters	Ph. (907) 567-7335
Roe's Charter Service	Ph. (888) 567-3496

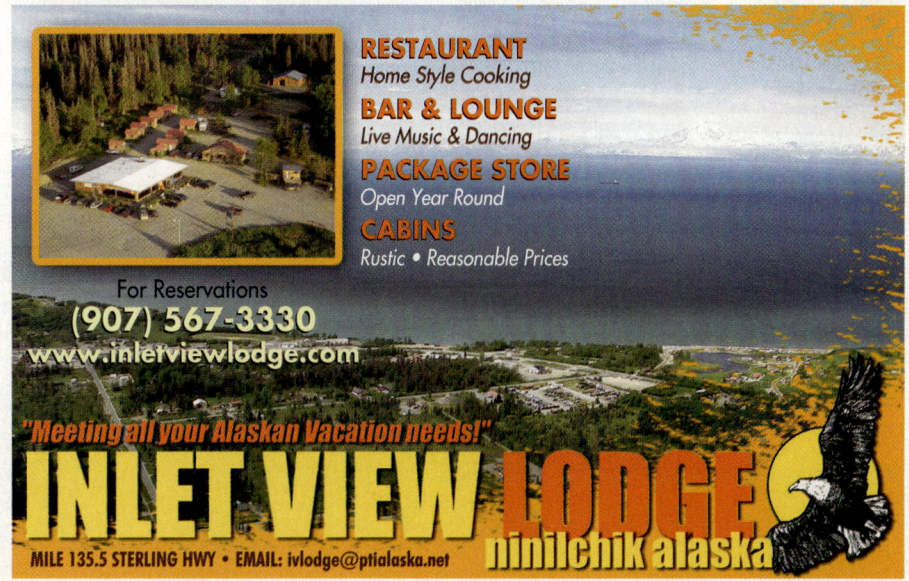

also a hostel located here (the Eagle Watch). There is an active senior center offering meals and events. Swimming pool at the high school.

The original village of Ninilchik (signed Ninilchik Village) is reached by a side road from **Milepost S 135.1**.

On Memorial Day weekend, Ninilchik is referred to as the third biggest city in Alaska, as thousands of Alaskans arrive for the fishing (see Area Fishing following).

The **Kenai Peninsula Fair** is held at Ninilchik the third weekend in August. Dubbed the "biggest little fair in Alaska," it features the Peninsula Rodeo, a parade, horse show, livestock competition and exhibits ranging from produce to arts and crafts. Pancake breakfasts, bingo and other events, such as the derby fish fry, are held at the fairgrounds throughout the year. The king salmon derby is held from May to June 15. A halibut derby, sponsored by the Ninilchik Chamber of Commerce, runs from Father's Day through Labor Day.

AREA FISHING: Well-known area for saltwater king salmon fishing and record halibut fishing. Charter services available. (Combination king salmon and halibut charters are available and popular.) Salt water south of the mouth of **Deep Creek** has produced top king salmon fishing in late May, June and July. Kings 50 lbs. and over are frequently caught. "Lunker" king salmon are available 1 mile south of Deep Creek in **Cook Inlet** from late May through July. Trolling a spinner or a spoon from a boat is the preferred method. Silver, red and pink salmon are available in salt water between Deep Creek and the Ninilchik River during July. A major halibut

Deep Creek View Campground
J&J Smart Charters

Ninilchik AK—Mile 136.2
Family Campground • Spectacular Views
Electric Hookups • Dump Station
Bathrooms & Showers
Halibut & Salmon Fishing - 28 Ft. Alumaweld Boats
Coast Guard Licensed Captains • Marine Head

www.smartcharters.com

1-888-HALIBUT (1-888-425-4288)
May - September - (907) 567-3320

NINILCHIK • DEEP CREEK • SEWARD

Choose Your Adventure
Fishing Discounts for our RV Customers

RV PARK, NINILCHIK
Big rigs welcome. 30/50 amp w/TV laundry/showers, fish processing.

DAY TRIPS OR PACKAGES
Multi-day fishing, lodging, transportation packages available.

LARGE CABINS
1, 2, or 3 bedroom fully furnished with kitchens and bathrooms.

TROPHY HALIBUT
Four 28' & 32' boats, bait, tackle, filleting included.

KING SALMON
Kasilof & Kenai River Charters. Halibut/King saltwater combinations.

SILVER SALMON
Seward saltwater or Kasilof River charters.

RAZOR CLAMS
Equipment rentals. Fish freeze, pack and ship.

FLY-IN
Floatplane trips for bear viewing or remote fishing.

ALASKAN ANGLER RV RESORT & CABINS
AFISHUNT CHARTERS

see log ad at mile 135.4 Sterling hwy, turn onto Kingsley rd.

Call Now!
800-347-4114
or visit online
www.afishunt.com

STERLING HIGHWAY • Ninilchik

BULL MOOSE GIFTS

Mile 135.8 Sterling Highway • 567-3415

"One of the Finest Gift Shops on the Kenai Peninsula"

- Alaskan Dolls • Framed Art Prints
- Native Arts & Crafts • Alaskan Gold Nuggets
- Russian Arts & Crafts • Postcards and Notecards
- Ivory Carvings and Scrimshaw
- Wide Selection of Jewelry • Over 50 Shirt Designs • Caps
- Jackets • Souvenirs • Books • Stuffed Animals

(907) 567-3415

Easy access for large RVs

Open 7 days a week

See log ad at Mile 135.8

P.O. Box 39434, Ninilchik, AK 99639

NINILCHIK GENERAL STORE

Mile 135.7 Sterling Highway • (907) 567-3378

See log ad at Mile 135.7

Hand-Dipped Ice Cream Cones

All your Fishing & Clamming needs

Licenses • Bait • Tackle • Public Phone • Groceries • Hardware
Sweatshirts • T-shirts • Caps • Jackets • Rain Gear
Gifts • Souvenirs • Postcards • Books • Film • Ice • Alaskan Gold Nuggets
Sandwiches • Hot Coffee • Espresso

Open Year-round – Easy access for large RVs – Extended Summer Hours

Fax Service Available – Fax 567-1091 • P.O. Box 39434, Ninilchik, AK 99639

fishery off Ninilchik has produced some of the largest trophy halibut found in Cook Inlet, including a 466-lb. unofficial world record sport-caught halibut.

Sterling Highway Log
(continued)

S 135.7 A 188.7 H 43.8 Ninilchik High School. Ninilchik Library, open 10 A.M. to 4 P.M. daily in the summer.

S 135.7 A 188.7 H 43.8 Ninilchik General Store. Open every day for all your travel needs. Offering groceries, bait, tackle, licenses, rain gear, ice, film, gifts, Beanie Babies, books, T-shirts, gold nugget jewelry, hardware and a snack bar with espresso and hand-dipped ice cream cones. Fresh popcorn! Stop in for free information packet on the Ninilchik area. You'll like our prices and service. Ask your friends who have met us. We compete for your business, we don't just wait for it to happen. See display ad this section. [ADVERTISEMENT]

S 135.8 A 188.8 H 43.7 Ninilchik Saltwater Charters & Lodge; Bull Moose Gifts.

Bull Moose Gifts. One of the nicest gift shops on the Kenai Peninsula, offering a wide selection of gifts, souvenirs and Beanie Babies. Alaskan and Russian arts and crafts, fine art prints, jewelry, including Alaskan gold nuggets, caps, postcards, notecards, and a large selection of T-shirts and Polarfleece. Easy access for large RVs, lots of parking and clean restroom. See display ad this section. [ADVERTISEMENT]

S 135.9 A 188.9 H 43.6 Junction with **Oilwell Road**; post office, airstrip, camping and charter services east on Oilwell Road; Tesoro gas station on Sterling Highway south side of junction. Oilwell Road provides access to Reel'Em Inn/Cook Inlet Charters and O'Fish'ial Charters.

Country Boy Campground. 3.1 miles down Oilwell Rd. Turn at Chinook Tesoro. 54 full hookups and 3 rental cabins fully furnished. Immaculate shower/laundry facilities. Fish cleaning tables, clam shovels available, fishing charters, and bear viewing. Potlucks every Sunday. Book and video library. Open all year-round. Bring your snow machines in the winter. If you miss us, you miss the party. At Country Boy Campground friends are family and family are friends. E-mail: countryboycamp@worldnet.att.net (907) 567-3396. [ADVERTISEMENT]

Reel'Em Inn/Cook Inlet Charters. East 1 mile on Oilwell Road from Chinook Tesoro. Owned, operated by Alaskan family with knowledge to show you how to experience the area's attractions. Full-service facility. Check us out, you will not be sorry! Reservations welcome. Phone (907) 567-7335. Email: lingmac@gci.net; www.cookinletcharters.com See display ad this section. [ADVERTISEMENT]

S 136 A 189 H 43.5 Chinook Tesoro. Ninilchik. 24-hour card lock. Open year-round. Self-serve Tesoro gasoline, propane, on-road and off-road diesel. We install quality NAPA Auto Parts. Auto/RV mechanics, tire sales and repair, water/air for RVs. Bait, ice, market items. Free tide books, visitor information on clamming and guided fishing. Tesoro, VISA, MasterCard, Discover, American Express. See display ad this section. [ADVERTISEMENT]

S 136.1 A 189.1 H 43.4 Chihuly's Charters, gift shop and cabins.

S 136.2 A 189.2 H 43.3 Deep Creek View Campground to west. **Peninsula Fairgrounds** to east, site of the Kenai Peninsula Fair (August) and 4th of July Rodeo. Ninilchik Chamber of Commerce Visitor Information Kiosk opposite the fairgrounds.

S 136.7 A 189.7 H 42.8 Bridge over Deep Creek. Developed recreation sites on both sides of creek: **Deep Creek North Scenic Overlook** and **Deep Creek South Scenic Overlook.** Deep Creek South offers camping May and June only, day-use only rest of summer. Both have restrooms, water, interpretive kiosks, tables and fireplaces. $10 camping fee or resident pass; $5 day-use fee.

Freshwater fishing in **Deep Creek** for king salmon up to 40 lbs., use spinners with red bead lures, Memorial Day weekend and the 3 weekends following; Dolly Varden in July and August; silver salmon to 15 lbs., August and September; steelhead to 15 lbs., late September through October. No bait fishing permitted after Aug. 31. Mouth of Deep Creek access from Deep Creek State Recreation Area turnoff at **Milepost S 137.3.**

S 137 A 190 H 42.5 Deep Creek Custom Packing to west.

Deep Creek Custom Packing, Inc. is an Alaska Seafood Processing facility that produces some of the world's finest smoked wild Alaskan salmon and halibut. This local family owned business sits next to the picturesque shores of Cook Inlet, overlooking the Deep Creek basin, Mount Redoubt and Mount Iliamna. We are easily accessible off a convenient double-ended highway access with plenty of parking for big rigs, RVs and trailers. Deep Creek prides itself on processing and offering the finest and freshest wild Alaskan seafood available anywhere, including salmon, halibut, rockfish, crab, scallops, clams, cod and much more. We invite you to stop by and try our free samples. Our great customer service, quality products are reasons sport fishermen choose to bring their catch to Deep Creek for custom processing, filleting, vacuum packing, freezing, canning and smoking. We offer Fed-Express overnight door-to-door shipping for your catch or seafood choices. Deep Creek's gourmet canned and smoked gift packs are a great holiday choice. World-class halibut and king fishing charters are available through our Sport Shop. Phone us at 1-800-764-0078 or (907) 567-3980. For general information and to shop our online retail store, check out our web site at www.deepcreekcustompacking.com; or email us at dccp@ptialaska.net. [ADVERTISEMENT]

S 137.2 A 190.2 H 42.3 D&M RV Park & Charters. Our park site on the bluff overlooking the beach at Deep Creek has a million dollar view. We have 38 sites, 24 with water and electric hookups. Dump stations, storage and fish cleaning facilities on site. Heated cabins available. Located near boat launch and access to salmon and halibut charters. For reservations, phone (800) 479-7357; (907) 567-4368; email aomn@gci.net. [ADVERTISEMENT]

S 137.3 A 190.3 H 42.2 Drive 0.5 mile west down paved road for **Deep Creek State Recreation Area** on the beach at the mouth of Deep Creek. Gravel parking area for 300 vehicles, overnight camping, water, tables,

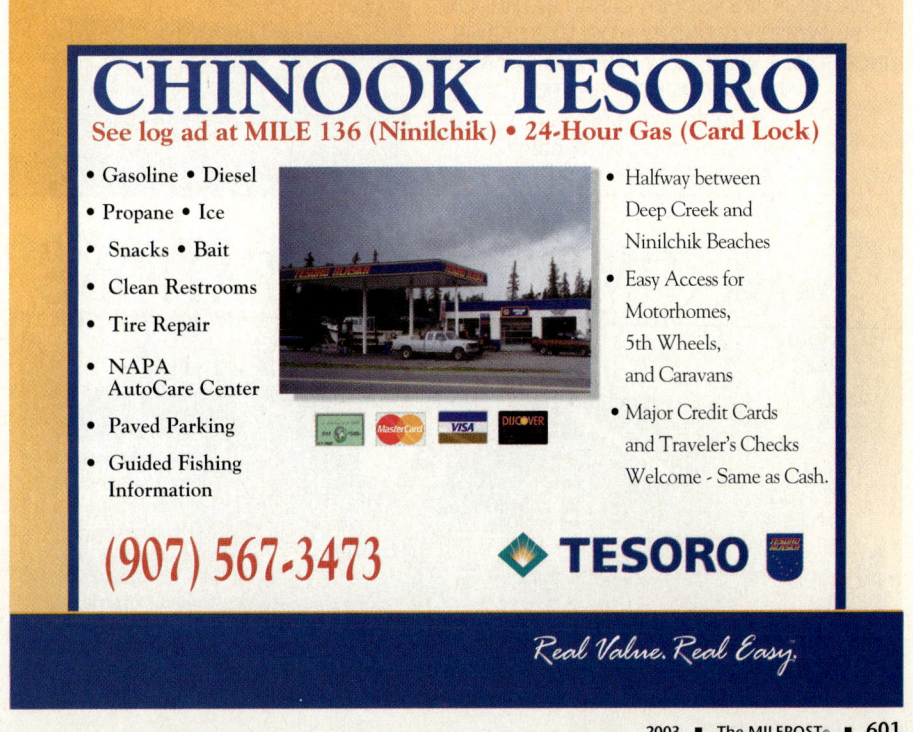

STERLING HIGHWAY

Cook Inlet clammer takes advantage of low tide and brisk clear day in early May.
(© Kris Graef, staff)

dumpsters, restrooms, pay phones and fireplaces. Camping fee $10/night per vehicle or resident pass, day-use fee $5, boat launch $5 fee. Anglers try to intercept king salmon in the saltwater before the salmon reach their spawning rivers. Private boat launch service here uses tractors to launch boats from beach into Cook Inlet. Seasonal checks by U.S. Coast Guard for personal flotation devices, boating safety. Good bird watching in wetlands behind beach; watch for eagles. Good clamming at low tide. The beaches here are lined with coal, which falls from the exposed seams of high cliffs. ◆▲

CAUTION: Extreme tides, cold water and bad weather can make boating here hazardous. Carry all required and recommended USCG safety equipment. Although the mouth of Deep Creek affords boaters good protection, low tides may prevent return; check tide tables.

S 137.4 A 190.4 H 42.1 Roe's Charter Service. Family owned, operated by year-round residents. Halibut, salmon combo charters, April–September. Friendly, personalized service at our quiet location. Circle drive for RV convenience. Fish from our custom-built 28- and 30-foot offshore boats, both with heated cabins and enclosed marine bathrooms. Comfortable seating, state-of-the-art electronics, custom made rods, top quality gear. Free filleting. Further processing, shipping services nearby. Lodging, etc. available. Phone (888) 567-3496, (907) 567-3496. Internet: www.alaskafishingcharter.com. Email: roe@alaskafishingcharter.com. See display ad this section. [ADVERTISEMENT]

S 137.5 A 190.5 H 42 *Begin 45 mph speed zone northbound.*

Begin 55 mph speed limit southbound.

S 142.5 A 195.5 H 37 Double-ended paved turnout with view of **Mount Iliamna** across the inlet. This is one of the best photo viewpoints, with a beanfield and fireweed in the foreground. Sign (missing in 2002) read:

"Looking westerly across Cook Inlet, Mt. Iliamna and Mt. Redoubt in the Chigmit Mountains of the Aleutian Range can be seen rising over 10,000 feet above sea level. This begins a chain of mountains and islands known as the Aleutian Chain extending west over 1,700 miles to Attu beyond the International Date Line to the Bering Sea, separating the Pacific and Arctic oceans. Mt. Redoubt on the right, and Iliamna on the left, were recorded as active volcanoes in the mid-18th century. Mt. Redoubt had a minor eruption in 1966."

Mount Redoubt had a major eruption in December 1989. The eruptions continued through April 1990, then subsided to steam plumes. Mount Redoubt is still considered active.

S 143.7 A 196.7 H 35.8 Highway crosses Happy Valley Creek. The area surrounding this creek is known locally as the Happy Valley community.

S 145 A 198 H 34.5 Happy Valley Bar & Cafe. See display ad this section.

S 148 A 201 H 31.5 Parking area to west at double-ended gravel turnout; good view.

S 150.9 A 203.9 H 28.6 Highway crosses Stariski Creek.

S 150.9 A 203.9 H 28.6 Little Critter's Vacation Rental Cabin, 970 square feet. Cozy log home with partial Inlet view. Alaskan authenticity with amenities. Non-smoking. Full kitchen, full bath, satellite-TV, stereo, phone. Gas barbecue. Sleeps 4–6. Complimentary Anchorage paper, coffee, Play-station. 2nd night half price, 7th night free! Call Donna, (907) 235-4381. Box 86, Anchor Point, AK 99556. donna@AlaskaLittleCritters.com. www.AlaskaLittleCritters.com. [ADVERTISEMENT]

S 151.9 A 204.9 H 27.6 Sharp turn west down steep access road to **Stariski State Recreation Site**; 16 campsites in trees on gravel loop road; $10 nightly fee or resident pass; toilets (wheel-chair accessible) and well water. This small campground has outstanding views across the inlet of Iliamna and Redoubt. No beach access. *CAUTION: Steep bluff.* ⛺▲

S 152.7 A 205.7 H 26.8 Eagle Crest RV Park & Cabins. See display ad this section. ▲

S 154.1 A 207.1 H 25.4 Timberline Creations Gift Shop specializes in unique antler, fossil ivory and scrimshaw gifts and jewelry created by the Lettis family in their workshop. They also sell Eskimo artifacts and mammoth fossils. Alaskan antiques decorate the log cabin shop. A must-stop for the traveler that enjoys quality craftsmanship. Call (907) 235-8288. Email: tcalaska@xyz.net. See display ad. [ADVERTISEMENT]

S 155 A 208 H 24.5 Bear Paw Charters.

Happy Valley BAR & CAFE
(907) 567-3357
Beer Garden • General Store w/ Videos
Prime Rib Every Friday & Saturday   Mile 145

EAGLE CREST RV PARK & CABINS
1-888-235-2905 • Mile 152.7 Sterling Hwy.
FULL HOOKUPS • SUPER CLEAN BATHROOMS
SHOWERS • LAUNDRY • DELUXE CABINS
INCREDIBLE INLET VIEW • FISHING CHARTERS
WEEKLY/MONTHLY RATES
(907) 235-6851
www.eaglecrestrvpark.com
e-mail: eagle@xyz.net

TIMBERLINE CREATIONS
MP 154.1 STERLING HWY.   LARGE CIRCLE DR
Antler & Fossil Ivory Gifts, Jewelry & Scrimshaw made in our workshop.
Alaskan Mammoth Fossils ~ Antiques
Eskimo Artifacts & More!
(907) 235-8288
Michael & Sandra Lettis
31685 Sterling Hwy., Anchor Point, AK 99556
Email: tcalaska@xyz.net
STOP IN FOR A FREE PIECE OF ANTLER OR MAMMOTH IVORY

BEAR PAW CABINS & CHARTERS
907/235-5399
Email: bearpaw@xyz.net
Milepost 155-PO Box 694, Anchor Point, AK 99556
www.BearPawCharters.com
ALSO HALIBUT & SALMON FISHING

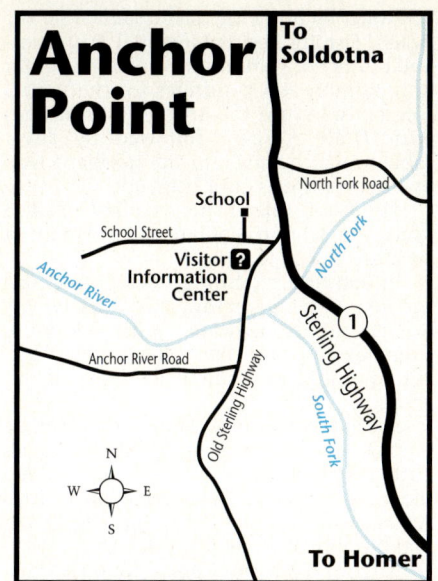

(907) 235-2600. Located in the small cabin at the "Y"; mini musuem.

Anchor Point is a full-service community with a post office and a variety of businesses. Lodging, restaurants, gas stations, fishing charters, tackle shops, seafood processors, RV parks, groceries, laundries and gift shops can be found along the highway and area roads. Churches, a library, senior citizen center and VFW are among the many organizations here.

Anchor Point was originally named "Laida" by Captain James Cook in the summer of 1778, when the *Resolution* and *Discovery* sailed into Cook Inlet looking for the Northwest Passage. It was later renamed Anchor Point by early homesteaders to commemorate the loss of an anchor off the point by Captain Cook. A post office was established here in 1949.

The Anchor Point area is noted for seasonal king and silver salmon, steelhead and rainbow fishing. There is bank fishing along the Anchor River, or fishermen can access

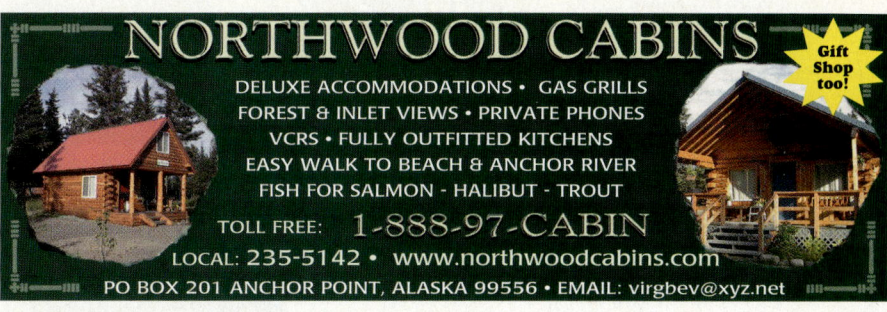

Private, unique log vacation rentals feature circular log staircase, wood inlaid mural, Alaska big game trophies. Sleeps 4–8. Rentals are 1,100 square feet. Fully outfitted down to the flannel sheets and cooking utensils. Large wrap-around decks, grills, fish cleaning facilities. These are so clean that dirt knows better than to try to cross the doorway. Minutes from trophy halibut, salmon fishing. (907) 235-5399. Email: bearpaw@xyz.net. Web site: www.bearpawcharters.com. See display ad this section. [ADVERTISEMENT]

S 155.7 A 208.7 H 23.8 Anchor Point welcome sign southbound.

Distance marker northbound shows Soldotna 58 miles, Kenai 69 miles, Anchorage 206 miles.

S 156 A 209 H 23.5 *Begin 45 mph speed zone southbound.*

Anchor Point

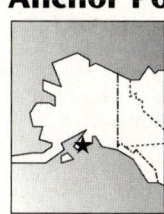

S 156 A 209 H 23.5 Junction of the Sterling Highway and Old Sterling Highway. **Population:** 1,845. **Emergency services:** Phone 911. **Visitor Information:** Anchor Point Chamber of Commerce, P.O. Box 610, Anchor Point, AK 99556; phone (907) 235-2600, fax

ANCHOR POINT ADVERTISERS

Anchor Point Chamber of
  Commerce ....Ph. (907) 235-2600
Anchor Point
  Lodging ....Ph. (907) 235-1236
Anchor Point Seafoods.....Ph. (800) 277-8885
Anchor River Inn ....Ph. (800) 435-8531
Anchor River Tesoro ....Ph. (907) 235-6005
Anchor's Away
  Cabin Rentals...............Ph. (907) 235-4996
Bear Paw Charters &
  Cabins ....Ph. (907) 235-5399
Blue Bus ....Ph. (907) 235-6285
Clive's Fishing Guide
  Service & Lodging ....Ph. (907) 235-1236
Fishtale Charters ....Ph. (907) 235-6944
Good Time Charters ....Ph. (907) 235-8579
Kyllonen's RV Park ....Ph. (907) 235-7762
Northwood Cabins ....Ph. (888) 972-2246
Sleepy Bear Cabins ....Ph. (866) 235-5630

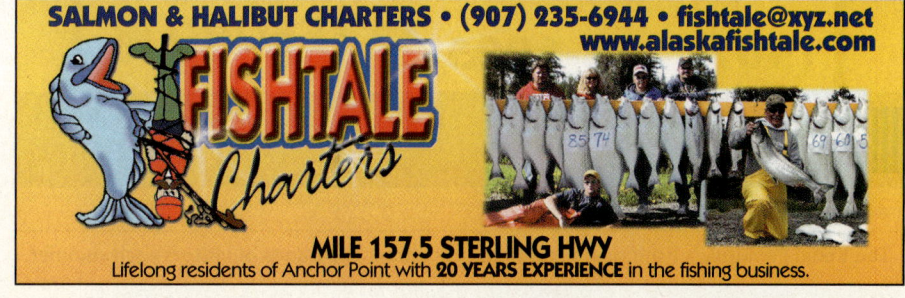

salt water by using the tractor launch on the beach. Fishing begins Memorial Day weekend in Anchor Point on the Anchor River for king salmon and continues for the next 3 weekends. In July, the Anchor River reopens with Dolly Varden, followed by silver salmon, which runs into the steelhead fishery that continues until freezeup.

The Cook Inlet fishery consist of all 5 species of salmon, halibut and a variety of rockfish.

In addition to fishing, local attractions include beachcombing and hiking. A Russian village is located just a few miles from downtown Anchor Point and has a picturesque Russian Church and several gift shops.

Special events in Anchor Point include Snow Rondi (last weekend in February); Calcutta Auction and Saltwater King Tournament (Mother's Day weekend); Kids All-American Fishing Derby (June 8, 2002); and the annual 4th of July celebration.

Anchor's Away Cabin Rentals, just minutes from the Anchor River's finest fishing, and the launching point for Cook Inlet charters. Ideal cabins for the Alaskan outdoor enthusiast or those wanting to escape for a quiet weekend getaway. The cabins are new, cute, comfortable and will sleep 4 comfortably. They include private bathrooms, fridges, microwaves, burners, coffee pots and BBQ's. Satellite-TV and hot beverages are also included. Groups, families welcome. Pets on approval. Call Kat or Dan now for best dates as they fill up fast! mumey@ptialaska.net. (907) 235-4996. [ADVERTISEMENT]

Anchor Point Lodging, Clive's Fishing Guide Service. Just off highway. Walking trails to river and beach. Large rooms with private bath. Central lounge with TV/VCR, coffee and phone. Combination salmon/halibut trips. All equipment furnished. Call (907) 235-1236; fax (907) 235-1905; www.puffin.ptialaska.net/~clives. Email: clives@ptialaska.net. Hosts: Clive and Marilyn Talkington, Box 497, Anchor Point, AK 99556. See display ad this section. [ADVERTISEMENT]

Anchor Point Seafoods. Quality and taste are the goal of our family-owned business. Our specialty is Smoking your fish! Bring your fresh catch to us and take home World-Class Alaska Smoked Fish. Or you can purchase some of our specialty products such as, Wild Alaskan Smoked Salmon (Cajun, Black Pepper or Traditional), Smoked Jerky, Hot Pepper Smoked Canned Salmon (Habanero Reds) or Regular Smoked Canned Salmon. Ask about our custom gift packs. We will ship any of our products (or yours) to anywhere in the United States. Visit us today for a FREE taste and tour. Located 3.2 miles out North Fork Rd. in Anchor Point. www.apseafoods.com. 1-800-277-8885. [ADVERTISEMENT]

Blue Bus—The best food in town. Ask the locals. Great taste, big portions. Priced right! Giant juicy burgers, chicken, shrimp. Real fruit milkshakes and malts. Mexican specialties with homemade salsa. Freshest halibut sandwiches, fish and chips. Free coffee! Great food to-go. Call ahead for faster service. (907) 235-6285. Open daily 11 A.M. to 7 P.M. [ADVERTISEMENT]

Sleepy Bear Cabins. New! Spacious, super clean, log cabins, located 1/8 mile North Fork Road. Look for our 10-foot-tall Sleepy Bear! 3 Cabins with lofts, 2 with skylights. Each is unique with full bathrooms, queen beds,

Anchor River (Beach) Road Log

Turn off the Sterling Highway at **Milepost S 156.9** on to the Old Sterling Highway and continue past the Anchor River Inn over the Anchor River. Just beyond the bridge, turn for Anchor River (Beach) Road, a 1.2-mile spur road providing access to the popular Anchor River Recreation Area for camping and fishing.

The Anchor River is open for all 4 weekends in June for king salmon. Dolly Varden begin to show up in the Anchor River by the end of June. By mid-July, pink salmon start to enter the Anchor River. Look for silver salmon by the end of July. Consult current sport fishing regulations prior to fishing the Anchor River.

Distance from junction (J) is shown.

J 0 Junction of Old Sterling Highway and Sterling Highway in Anchor Point at **Milepost S 156.9**.

J 0.1 School Road. Anchor Point visitor information center.

Anchor River Inn, overlooking beautiful Anchor River and in business for over 35 years, has the finest family restaurant on the peninsula, where you can see fish and wildlife exhibited and one of the largest displays of collectible plates in Alaska. Serving breakfast, lunch and dinner. Large cocktail lounge has a wide-screen TV, pool tables, dance floor and video games. 20 modern motel units with phones; 10 spacious units with color TV and 2 queen-sized beds, and 10 smaller units overlooking the river. Coin operated laundry and a fitness center for our guests. Our fully stocked liquor, grocery store and gift shop serve the Anchor Point area year-round. Write: Box 154, Anchor Point, AK 99556; phone 1-800-435-8531 in USA, or (907) 235-8531; fax (907) 235-2296. View the Anchor River live web cam and current weather at www.anchorriverinn.com; Your hosts: the Clutts family. See display ad this section. [ADVERTISEMENT]

J 0.3 Anchor River bridge, also known as "the erector set bridge."

J 0.4 Road forks: Old Sterling Highway continues south through rural residential area and rejoins Sterling Highway at **Milepost J 164.8**. Turn right for Anchor River (Beach) Road. Tackle shop at intersection across from **Silverking Campground** (Anchor River State Recreation Area); parking area, toilets, dumpster, $10 nightly fee or resident pass.

J 0.6 Coho Campground (Anchor River SRA); parking, toilets, $10 camping fee or resident pass.

J 0.8 Steelhead Campground (Anchor River SRA); day-use parking area, picnic tablers and toilets; $10 camping or resident pass.

J 1.1 Slidehole Campground (Anchor River SRA); 30 campsites on loop road, day-use parking area, $10 camping fee or resident pass, tables, water, special senior/wheelchair camping area, large day-use parking lot, trail access to river.

J 1.3 Kyllonen's RV Park, a few steps from famous Anchor River and picturesque Cook Inlet. Providing spring water, electricity and sewer. Additional amenities include fish cleaning station, BBQ pits, free firewood and picnic tables. Showers, restrooms and laundry. Gift shop and Espresso Bar. Fishing licenses. We book fishing charters. May through September. Year-round area information center, phone (907) 235-7762, fax (907) 235-6435. Email: susank@xyz.net. www.kyllonenrvpark.com. See display ad this section. [ADVERTISEMENT]

J 1.5 Halibut Campground (Anchor River SRA); day-use parking area and picnic sites, 20 campsites on gravel loop, toilets, water. $10 camping fee or resident pass; $5 day-use fee.

Access to beach. Beautiful view of Aleutian Range from parking area. Gold Rush Centennial sign here reads (excerpt):

"The first mining of gold on a commercial scale in Southcentral Alaska occurred along this beach. Miners sluiced gravel at the base of the bluff throughout the 1890s. They recovered small amounts of gold, but a bonanza eluded them."

J 1.6 Road deadends on shore of Cook Inlet; viewing deck, telescopes, beach access, 12-hour parking ($5 fee). Private tractor boat launch service. Tractor assistance has revolutionized sportfish access to Cook Inlet by allowing boats to launch at just about any tide, rather than having to wait for high tide. Sign here marks the most westerly point on the North American continent accessible by continuous road system. N 59°46′ W 151°52′. Display depicts outlines of Cook Inlet volcanoes.

Return to Milepost S 156.9 Sterling Highway

fridge, microwave, coffee, phone, satellite-TV, futons. Fish-cleaning station. Grills. Fishing, clamming, hiking trails nearby. Open year-round. Daily, weekly rates. Hosts, Marlene and Dan Rickard. Box 282, Anchor Point, AK 99556. (866) 235-5630; (907) 235-5625. Email: rickard@alaska.net. [ADVERTISEMENT]

Sterling Highway Log
(continued)

S 156.4 A 209.4 H 23.1 Anchor Point post office to east.

S 156.7 A 209.7 H 22.8 Junction with Milo Fritz Avenue to west and North Fork Road to east. Access to Anchor Point Senior Center and Anchor Point Seafoods (Mile 3.2) via North Fork Road. Library to west.

S 156.9 A 209.9 H 22.6 Anchor Point "Y" Junction. Old Sterling Highway access west to Anchor Point businesses (groceries, accommodations, dining), Visitor Information Center, Anchor River Inn and Anchor River (Beach) Road. Description of Anchor Point begins on page 603.

Blue Star Memorial Highway marker at turnoff. Gold Rush Centennial interpretive sign at **Milepost J 1.5** Anchor River Road.

> Junction with Old Sterling Highway and access to Anchor River (Beach) Road. See "Anchor River (Beach) Road" log on this page.

S 157 A 210 H 22.5 Fishtale Charters. A locally owned and family operated business, all lifetime residents of Anchor Point. Offering salmon and halibut trips on our 26 1/2 foot custom built boat with heated cabin and head, 6 person capacity. We supply all the gear and clean and fillet your fish at no extra charge. Fishing licenses available. (907) 235-6944. Email: fishtale@xyz.net/www.alaskafishtale.com. [ADVERTISEMENT]

S 157.1 A 210.1 H 22.4 Highway crosses Anchor River.

S 157.5 A 210.5 H 22 Welcome to Anchor Point (northbound) sign.

S 160.9 A 213.9 H 18.6 Black Water Bend Espresso. Not your average drip! Double entrances, easy access for big rigs to get your favorite coffee, latte, decaf, smoothie, tea, juice, sugar-free drink, bakery goodies. Something for everyone, fishing bait, treats for your dog! Look for big sign and red barn. Call ahead for faster service. ligenza@homernet.net; (907) 235-6884. See display ad this section. [ADVERTISEMENT]

S 161 A 214 H 18.5 Anchor River bridge.

S 161 A 214 H 18.5 Ben Firth Studio. Featuring sculpture in antler, wood, and bronze, works in pencil, watercolor and other media by Ben Firth; glass etching by Melanie Firth, and art work and handcrafts by the Firth children. Open 10–5 (often longer; look for the open sign) Monday–Saturday, mid-May through mid-September. [ADVERTISEMENT]

S 162.4 A 215.4 H 17.1 Gravel turnout to east by Anchor River.

S 164.3 A 217.3 H 15.2 North Fork (Loop) Road.

S 164.8 A 217.8 H 14.7 Junction with Old Sterling Highway which leads 9.4 miles northwest to connect with Anchor River (Beach) Road.

BLACK WATER BEND® ESPRESSO
Not Your Average Drip!
(907) 235-6884

Coffees, Decafs, Juices, Sugar-free Smoothies, Bakery Goodies & More!

See Log Ad Mile 161

STERLING HIGHWAY

S 166.8 A 219.8 H 12.7 Holland Days B&B Cabins. Guest comments: "Wonderful hospitality," "Great food," "Beautiful and peaceful surroundings." Guests enjoy a full breakfast in our spacious log home. Cabins are fully furnished. Guest rooms and cabins have private baths. Hosts are long time Alaska residents, in business for 11 years. Located 1/4 mile off Sterling Highway. Turn on Virginia Avenue. See display ad this section. 1-888-308-7604. [ADVERTISEMENT]

S 167.1 A 220.1 H 12.4 Diamond Ridge Road.

S 168.5 A 221.5 H 11 Alaska State Parks' South District ranger station is located on the bluff here. A small parking lot is adjacent to the log office where visitors may obtain information on Kachemak Bay state park, as well as other southern Kenai Peninsula state park lands.

S 169.2 A 222.2 H 10.3 Homer DOT/PF highway maintenance station to east. Distance marker northbound shows Soldotna 71 miles, Kenai 82 miles, Anchorage 219 miles.

Begin 4-lane highway southbound. Begin 2-lane highway northbound.

S 169.3 A 222.3 H 10.2 Gas station/food mart to west.

S 169.4 A 222.4 H 10.1 Alaskan Suites. See display ad this section.

S 169.6 A 222.6 H 9.9 Large viewpoint to west overlooking Kachemak Bay with view of Homer Spit. Good photo stop. Large parking area; toilets. Gold Rush Centennial interpretive signs (excerpt follows):

A party of 50 prospectors from Kings County (Brooklyn), New York, sailed to Alaska in 1898, bound for the Turnagain Arm gold fields. Their schooner reached Cook Inlet in late in the fall and encountered ice. The captain offloaded the stampeders at Kachemak Bay. The party, calling themselves the Kings County Mining Company, set off overland with their belongings in wheelbarrows. "The quantity and weight of their gear, not to mention the mode of transportation, was a serious impediment to traversing the rough terrain buried in deep snow. Add the penetrating cold of Alaska's winters and their journey quickly turned into an arduous trek. The exhausted party finally reached Skilak Lake and built a cabin.

"Discouraged by weather, sickness, squabbling and other hardships, the company disbanded the next spring." Most of the party returned to their home, although 3 stayed to search for gold. Some artifacts from this ill-fated expedition are displayed at Pratt Museum in Homer.

S 170 A 223 H 9.5 Bay View Inn.

S 171.9 A 224.9 H 7.6 West Hill Road; connects to Skyline Drive and East Hill Road for scenic drive along Homer Bluff.

S 172.2 A 225.2 H 7.3 West Homer Elementary School to east.

S 172.6 A 225.6 H 6.9 Homer Middle School to east.

S 172.7 A 225.7 H 6.8 USFWS Alaska Maritime National Wildlife Refuge Visitor Center. Good spot for birding information and free interpretive films. Open Memorial Day–Labor Day, daily from 9 A.M.–5 P.M.

Oceanview RV Park past Best Western Bidarka Inn on your right coming into Homer. Spectacular view of Kachemak Bay, beachfront setting. There are 85 large pull-through spaces in the terraced park. Full/partial hookups, heated restrooms, free showers, laundry, pay phone, cable TV, picnic area. Easy walking distance to downtown Homer. Special halibut charter rates for park guests. www.oceanview-RV.com. Email: camp4fun @xyz.net. Phone (907) 235-3951. Email service available. See display ad this section. [ADVERTISEMENT]

S 172.8 A 225.8 H 6.7 Pioneer Avenue; turn here for downtown **HOMER** (description follows). Drive 0.2 mile on Pioneer Avenue and turn left on Bartlett Avenue for the **Pratt Museum** (see Attractions in the

Homer section) and **Karen Hornaday Hillside Park** campground (see map). Pioneer Avenue connects with East Hill Road. ▲

S 173 A 226 H 6.5 Homer Chamber of Commerce Visitor Center on right side of highway going into Homer.

S 173.1 A 226.1 H 6.4 Turn up Main Street for Pioneer Avenue. Turn down Main Street (towards water), then left on E. Bunnell Avenue and right on Beluga Avenue for **Bishop's Beach Park**; public beach access, parking, picnic tables and Beluga Slough trailhead.

S 173.5 A 226.5 H 6 Eagle Quality Center; 24-hour supermarket.

S 173.7 A 226.7 H 5.8 Heath Street. Post office (ZIP code 99603).

S 173.9 A 226.9 H 5.6 Lake Street. Access to downtown Homer and Lakeside Center.

S 174 A 227 H 5.5 Beluga Lake; floatplane bases.

S 174.7 A 227.7 H 4.8 Alaska Dept. of Fish and Game office. Stop by for a current copy of the Kenai Peninsula–Cook Inlet Salt Water–Susitna–West Cook Inlet regulations.

S 174.8 A 227.8 H 4.7 Homer Tesoro. Airport (FAA) Road to Homer Airport terminal. **Beluga Wetlands Wildlife Observation deck** across from airport.

S 175 A 228 H 4.5 Sterling Highway crosses onto Homer Spit (see description in Homer Attractions). Parking for spit bike/walking trail. Kachemak Drive; access to air charter services.

S 178 A 231 H 1.5 Homer Spit Public Camping Fee Station; across from the Fishing Hole (Fishing Lagoon) and restroom.

S 178.1 A 231.1 H 1.4 Headquarters for the Homer Jackpot Halibut Derby; maps,

information, visitor assistance.

S 179.5 A 232.5 H 0 Sterling Highway ends at Land's End Resort at the tip of Homer Spit.

Homer

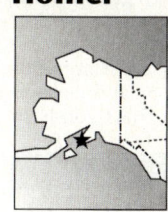

Located on the southwestern Kenai Peninsula on the north shore of Kachemak Bay at the easterly side of the mouth of Cook Inlet; 226 miles by highway or 40 minutes by jet aircraft from Anchorage. **Population:** 3,946. **Emergency Services:** Phone 911 for all emergency services. **City Police**, phone (907) 235-3150. **Alaska State Troopers**, in the Public Safety Bldg., phone (907) 235-8239. **Fire Department** and **Ambulance**, phone (907) 235-3155. **Animal Control**, phone (907) 235-3141. **Port/Harbor**, phone (907) 235-3160. **Coast Guard**, phone Zenith 5555. (Coast Guard Auxiliary, phone (907/235 7277.) **Hospital**, South Peninsula Hospital, phone (907) 235-8101. **Veterinary Clinic**, phone (907) 235-8960.

Visitor Information: Chamber of Commerce Visitor Center is located on the Sterling Highway (Homer Bypass) between Bartlett and Main Street as you drive into town. The center offers free maps, a phone for local calls, restrooms and information on activities and lodging. State park passes are also sold here. The visitor center also has a remote video camera that transmits live images from the McNeil River Brown Bear Sanctuary, located more than 100 miles away, across Cook Inlet.

Open year-round, 7 days a week in summer. Contact the Homer Chamber of Commerce, Box 541, Homer 99603; phone during business hours (907) 235-7740. Web site: www.homeralaska.org. To find out about local concerts, art shows and other arts events in Homer, phone the Homer Council of the Arts at (907) 235-4288. U.S. Fish & Wildlife Service, phone (907) 235-6961 (summer only).

The **Pratt Museum** is open daily 10 A.M. to 6 P.M. from mid-May to mid-September; open noon to 5 P.M. Tuesday through Sunday from mid-September to mid-May; closed in January. Contact the Pratt Museum, 3779 Bartlett St., Homer 99603. Phone (907) 235-8635; email info@prattmuseum.org; web site www.prattmuseum.org.

Elevation: Sea level to 800 feet. **Climate:** Winter temperatures occasionally fall below zero, but seldom colder. The Kenai Mountains north and east protect Homer from severe cold, and Cook Inlet provides warming air currents. The highest temperature recorded is 81°F. Average annual precipitation is 27.9 inches. Prevailing winds are from the northeast, averaging 6.5 mph/10.5 kmph. **Radio:** KGTL 620, KWVV 103.5/104.9/106.3, MBN-FM107.1/96.7/95.3, KBBI 890, KMJG 88.9; KPEN-FM 99.3/100.9/102.3, KWHQ-FM 98.3. **Television:** KTUU, KTBY, KTVA, KAKM, KIMO. **Newspaper:** *Homer News* (weekly), *Homer Tribune* (weekly).

Private Aircraft: Homer airport on Airport Road; elev. 78 feet; length 7,400 feet; asphalt; fuel 100LL, Jet A; attended. Terminal building.

In the late 1800s, a coal mine was operating at Homer's Bluff Point, and a railroad carried the coal out to the end of Homer Spit. (The railroad was abandoned in 1907.) Gold seekers debarked at Homer, bound for

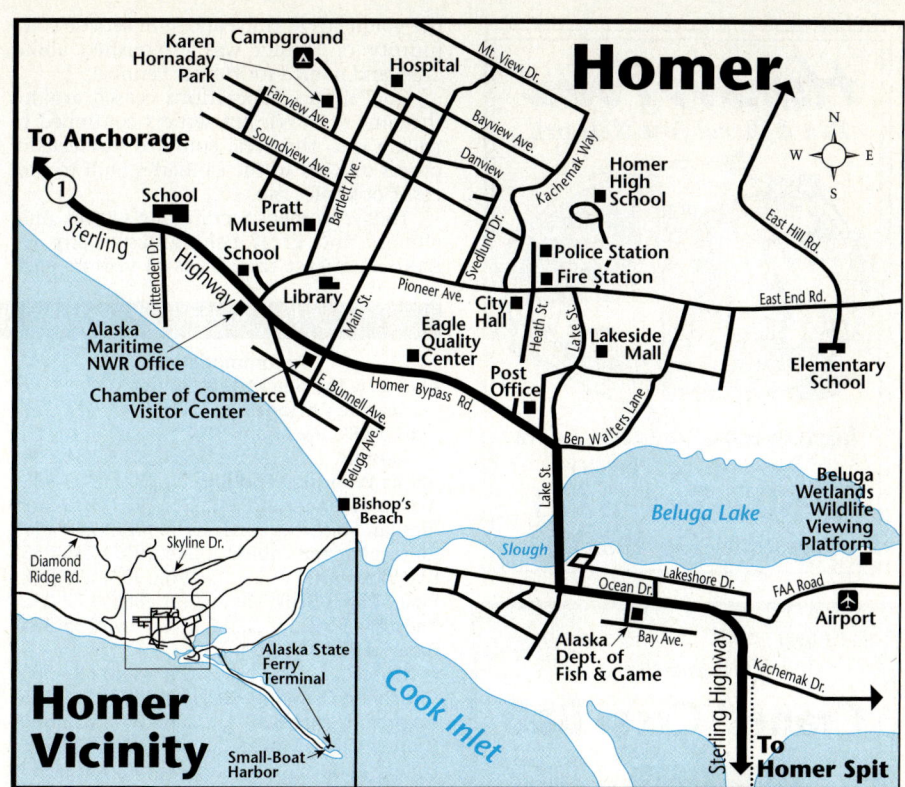

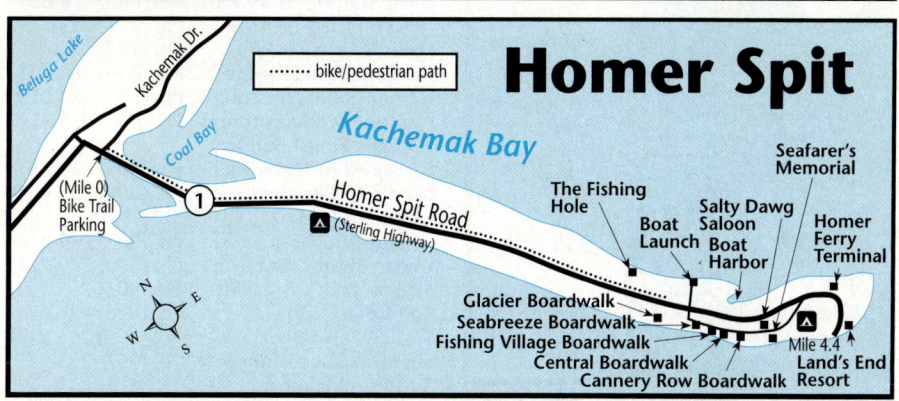

BAY VIEW INN
Charming Alaskan Ambiance
Rated by guests as "best view in Homer"
"beautifully clean and comfortable rooms"
Photos on Internet at www.bayviewalaska.com
Reservations 1-877-235-8485
More descriptive text under lodging

COPPER HELMET B&B
FINEST HOMER HOSPITALITY
• Full Country Buffet Breakfast
• Private Baths
• Outdoor Hot Tub
• Fantastic View
Hosted by Dwight & Lana Simpson • (907) 235-5608 • Email: copper@xyz.net • PO Box 2604, Homer, AK 99603
800-964-2991 • www.alaska-homer.com

the goldfields at Hope and Sunrise. The community of Homer was established about 1896 and named for Homer Pennock.

Coal mining operations ceased around the time of WWI, but settlers continued to trickle into the area, some to homestead, others to work in the canneries built to process Cook Inlet fish.

Today, Homer's picturesque setting, mild climate and great fishing (especially for halibut) attract thousands of visitors each year. In addition to its tourist industry and role as a trade center, Homer's commercial fishing industry is an important part of its economy. Homer calls itself the "Halibut Fishing Capital of the World." Manufacturing and seafood processing, government offices, trades and construction are other key industries.

Homer is host to a large artist community. Potters, sculptors, painters and jewelers practice their craft and sell their goods in

HOMER ADVERTISERS

Accommodations
Alaska by the Sea B&B & Homer
  Seaside Cottages ....Ph. (877) 374-2716
Alaska KR's Vacation
  Rentals ....Ph. (907) 235-6592
Alaska Woodside Lodging .Ph. (877) 909-8389
Alaska's Pioneer Inn..........Ph. (907) 235-5670
Alaskan Suites ....Ph. (888) 239-1972
Almost Homer Cabins........Ph. (907) 235-2553
Bay View Inn ....Ph. (907) 235-8485
Beary Patch B&B, The........Ph. (888) 977-2327
Beeson's B&B ....Ph. (907) 235-3757
Bidarka Best Western
  Hotel ....Ph. (866) 685-5000
Chocolate Drop Inn B&B ..Ph. (907) 235-3668
Copper Helmet B&B ....Ph. (907) 235-5608
Cranes' Crest B&B ....Ph. (800) 338-2969
Dandy Cabins.....................Ph. (907) 235-3839
Driftwood Inn & RV Park..Ph. (800) 478-8019
Halcyon Heights B&B ....Ph. (907) 235-2148
Halibut Cove Lodge ....Ph. (907) 235-6891
Heritage Hotel–Lodge ......Ph. (800) 380-7787
Homer Cabin Network .....Ph. (888) 364-0191
Homer Seaside Cottages ..Ph. (907) 235-2716
Homer's Finest Bed &
  Breakfast Network.......Ph. (800) 764-3211
Land's End Resort ....Ph. (907) 235-0400
Laughing Raven
  Guesthouse..................Ph. (907) 279-3264
Ocean Shores Motel ....Ph. (800) 770-7775
Skyline Bed & Breakfast....Ph. (907) 235-3832
Spit Road Lodge ....Ph. (888) 423-6764
Spruce Acres B&B ....Ph. (907) 235-8388
SunSpin Guest House ....Ph. (907) 235-6677
3 Moose Meadow
  Wilderness B&B ....Ph. (888) 777-0930
Wild Rose Cottages ....Ph. (907) 235-8780

Art Galleries
Art Shop Gallery ....Ph. (907) 235-7076
Bunnell Street Gallery ....Ph. (907) 235-2662
Fireweed Gallery ....Ph. (907) 235-3411
Jars of Clay ....Ph. (907) 235-8533
Homer Clay Works.............Ph. (907) 235-6118
Picture Alaska Art Gallery ..Ph. (907) 235-2300
Pratt Museum Gallery.......Ph. (907) 235-8635
Ptarmigan Arts...................Ph. (907) 235-5345
Sea Lion Gallery ....Ph. (907) 235-3400

Attractions & Entertainment
Kenai Peninsula
  Orchestra.....................Ph. (907) 235-6318
Pier One Theatre ....Ph. (907) 235-7333

Auto & RV Rentals, Gas, Services & Supplies
Hertz ....Ph. (800) 654-3131
Homer Jeep Rental............Ph. (907) 235-8640
Mobile RV Services ....Ph. (907) 399-7132
Petro Express ....Ph. (907) 235-3295

Campgrounds
Driftwood Inn & RV Park ..Ph. (800) 478-8019
Homer Spit Campground..Ph. (907) 235-8206
Homer's "Fishing Hole"
  RV Park ....Ph. (907) 235-8350

Oceanview RV Park...........Ph. (907) 235-3951

Churches
Faith Lutheran Church......Ph. (907) 235-7600
Homer United Methodist
  Church ....Ph. (907) 235-8528

Dining/Saloons/Breweries
Alice's Champagne Palace
  & The Palace Brewery ..Ph. (907) 235-7650
Land's End Resort ....Ph. (907) 235-0400

Fishing Charters
Bob's Trophy Charters.......Ph. (800) 770-6400
Cap'n George's
  Charters ....Ph. (907) 235-4801
Central Charters ....Ph. (800) 478-7847
Coastal Outfitters ....Ph. (888) 235-8492
Halibut Hunter
  Charters ....Ph. (907) 235-2739
Halibut King Charters........Ph. (800) 770-7303
Inlet Charters....................Ph. (800) 770-6126
North Country Halibut
  Charters ....Ph. (800) 770-7620
Silver Fox Charters............Ph. (800) 478-8792
Tacklebuster Charters.......Ph. (800) 789-5155

Guides & Outfitters
Bart The Guide ....Ph. (877) 909-8389
Coastal Outfitters ....Ph. (888) 235-8492
Glacier Kayaking &
  Hiking ....Ph. (888) 777-0930
Trails End Horse
  Adventures ....Ph. (907) 235-6393

Shopping and Services
Alaska Wild Berry
  Products.......................Ph. (907) 235-8858
Better Sweater, The.....................Homer Spit
Blackbeary Bog ....Ph. (907) 235-5668
Coal Point Seafood Co......Ph. (800) 325-3877
Homer Bookstore, The .....Ph. (907) 235-7496
Homer's Gold-Mine Gifts
  & Fine Jewelry.............Ph. (907) 235-6886
Main Street Mercantile.....Ph. (907) 235-9102
NOMAR ....Ph. (907) 235-8363
North Wind Home
  Collection ....Ph. (907) 235-0766
Old Inlet Book Shop, The .Ph. (907) 235-7984
Seams to Bee ....Ph. (907) 235-6555

Tours and Transportation
Bald Mountain Air
  Service ....Ph. (907) 235-7969
Coastal Outfitters ....Ph. (888) 235-8492
Emerald Air Service...........Ph. (907) 235-6993
Kachemak Bay Flying
  Service, Inc. ....Ph. (907) 235-8924
Trails End Horse
  Adventures ....Ph. (907) 235-6393

Visitor Information
Homer Chamber of
  Commerce ....Ph. (907) 235-7740

local shops and galleries. The local theater group provides live performances year-round. Homer has 8 schools, including the modern **Homer High School**, which has the complete skeleton of a sperm whale hanging from the ceiling of the school's lobby. A local fisherman found the dead whale washed up on Chugach Island (one of the Barren Islands) in 1998. It was recovered and the skeleton preserved through the efforts of the U.S. Coast Guard, the Pratt Museum and the high school students.

Rising behind the townsite are the gently sloping bluffs which level off at about 1,200 feet to form the southern rim of the western plateau of the Kenai. These green slopes are tinted in pastel shades by acres of wildflowers from June to September; fireweed predominates among scattered patches of geranium, paintbrush, lupine, rose and many other species. Two main roads (East Hill Road and West Hill Road) lead from the Homer business section to the "Skyline Drive" along the rim of the bluffs, and other roads connect with many homesteads on the "Hill."

The name *Kachemak* (in Aleut dialect said to mean "smoky bay") was supposedly derived from the smoke which once rose from the smoldering coal seams jutting from the clay bluffs of the upper north shore of Kachemak Bay and the cliffs near Anchor Point. In the early days many of the exposed coal seams were slowly burning from causes unknown. Today the erosion of these bluffs drops huge fragments of lignite and bituminous coal on the beaches, creating a plentiful supply of winter fuel for the residents. There are an estimated 400,000,000 tons of coal deposit in the immediate vicinity of Homer.

Kachemak is a magnificent deep-water bay that reaches inland from Cook Inlet for 30 miles, with an average width of 7 miles. The bay is rich in marine life. The wild timbered coastline of the south shore, across from Homer, is indented with many fjords and inlets, reaching far into the rugged glacier-capped peaks of the Kenai Mountains.

Jutting out for nearly 5 miles from the Homer shore is the Homer Spit, a long, narrow bar of gravel. The road along the backbone of the Spit is part of the Sterling Highway, which is the main road through Homer. The Spit has had quite a history, and it continues to be a center of activity for the town. In 1964, after the earthquake, the Spit sank 4 to 6 feet, requiring several buildings to be moved to higher ground. Today, the Spit is the site of a major dock facility for boat loading, unloading, servicing and refrigerating. The deep-water dock can accommodate 340-foot vessels and 30-foot drafts, making it accessible to cruise and cargo ships. It is also home port to the Alaska Marine Highway ferry MV *Tustumena*. Newly constructed in 2002 is the Pioneer Dock, which moors the MV *Tustumena* and the U.S. Coast Guard vessels Cutter *Sedge* and *Roanoke Island*. The dock can accommodate ships up to 800 feet. The small-boat harbor on the Spit has a 5-lane load/launch ramp. Also in the small-boat harbor area are the harbormaster's office, canneries, parking/camping areas, charter services, small shops, live theatre, galleries, restaurants, motels and bed and breakfasts.

Lodging & Services

Homer has hundreds of small businesses offering a wide variety of goods and services. There are many hotels, motels, bed and breakfasts; 2 hostels and private camp-

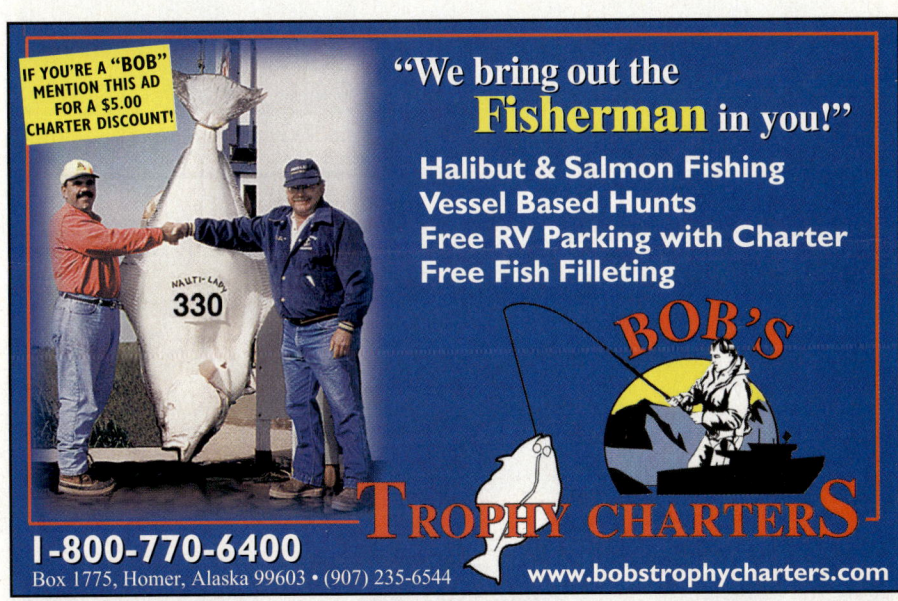

Kachemak Bay's name is derived from the Aleut dialect, meaning "smoky bay."

grounds (reservations advised in summer). Dozens of restaurants offer everything from fast food to fine dining.

Homer has a post office, library, museum, laundromats, gas stations with propane and dump stations, banks, a hospital and airport terminal. There are many fishing charter services, boat repair and storage facilities, marine fuel at Homer marina; bait, tackle and sporting goods stores; and also art galleries, gift shops and groceries.

Homer Spit has both long-term parking and camping. Camping and parking areas are well-marked.

Alaska by the Sea B&B & Homer Seaside Cottages. Charming private cottages, 1 beachfront, 3 one block from the ocean. 1 cottage handicap accessible. Full kitchens and 3/4 baths. Gallery, bakery, book store a few doors down and easy walk to downtown. B&B private rooms, shared bath, great rates. Marvelous view, helpful host. 877-374-2716 www.homerseasidecottages.com. See display ad this section. [ADVERTISEMENT]

Alaska Woodside Lodging. Offering 1–2 bedroom condos complete with full kitchens, cable TV, laundry facilities and barbecues. Lodging available by the night at very reasonable rates. Boasting a spectacular view of Kachemak Bay, we're centrally located and convenient to all shops, galleries and restaurants. Halibut fishing just 5 minutes away at the famous Homer Spit. King salmon charters available on site with "Bart the Guide." Phone toll free 1-877-909-8389. www.alaskawoodsidelodging.com. See display ad this section. [ADVERTISEMENT]

Alaska's Pioneer Inn. 244 Pioneer Ave., in downtown Homer. Spanky clean, comfortable 1-bedroom suites with private baths and furnished kitchens. Sleeps up to 4.

Complimentary coffee. Hotel-style guest rooms also available. Most rooms have views

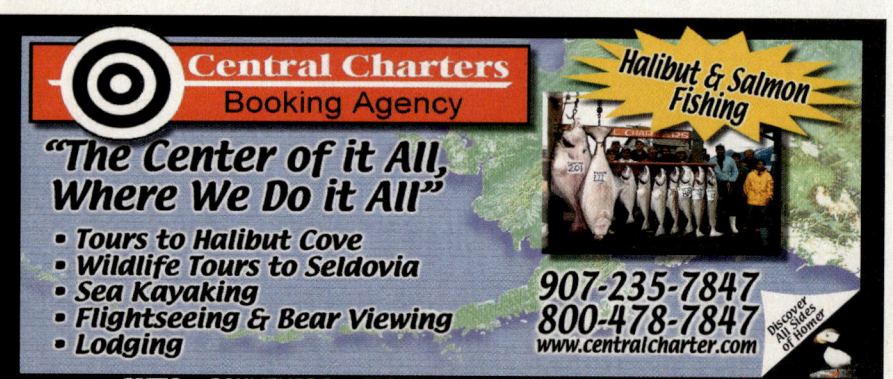

of bay and mountains. Year-round. Homer's best value. Credit cards accepted. Brochure: P.O. Box 1430, Homer, AK 99603. Phone (907) 235-5670; toll free 1-800-782-9655. Email abc@xyz.net. URL:www.xyz.net/~abc. [ADVERTISEMENT]

Alaskan Suites. Next door to the scenic pullout. Luxury cabins offer private lodging with a million dollar view for guests with discriminating taste. Kitchenette, satellite TV, VCR, DVD players. Surround-sound, gas grills. These are the cleanest, most accommodating rooms in town and your satisfaction is guaranteed. www.alaskansuites.com. Email: aksuites@alaska.net. Phone 1-888-239-1972. [ADVERTISEMENT]

Almost Homer Cabins and Sorry Charlie Charters. Panoramic view of the mountains and the bay. We offer cabins with complete kitchen, living room, bath and 2 bedrooms. Clean, comfortable, affordable and friendly!

Halibut fishing packages with hosts. Sorry Charlie Charters. Spacious boat with heated cabin and enclosed bathroom. For great fish pictures, see our website. Advance reservations recommended. Phone (907) 235-2553, fax (907) 235-0553. In Alaska: 1-800-478-2352; 1269 Upland Court, Homer, AK 99603. http://www.alaskaexcursion.com. Email: coates@xyz.net. [ADVERTISEMENT]

Bay View Inn. Spectacular panoramic view! Next to the scenic photographic viewpoint at the top of the hill entering Homer. From our breathtaking vantage point, every room overlooks Kachemak Bay, the Kenai Mountains, and lower Cook Inlet. Immaculately clean non-smoking rooms, firm comfortable beds, telephone, TV-HBO, private bathrooms, outside entrances, and freshly brewed morning coffee. Options include kitchenettes, suite with fireplace, and separate honeymoon cottage. Espresso bar, serene setting, picnic tables, and Adirondack chairs on the lawn. Friendly staff with local activity recommendations. Phone: (907) 235-8485, Fax (907) 235-8716. Reservations 1-877-235-8485. P.O. Box 804, Homer, AK 99603. Email: bayview@alaska.net See pictures at: www.bayviewalaska.com See display ad this section. [ADVERTISEMENT]

Bidarka Best Western Hotel. Located on the right coming into Homer. It is 1 block from the visitor center, 2 blocks from downtown shopping, museum and galleries and just a 15 minute drive out to the famous Homer Spit. The Bidarka offers 74 rooms including a limited number of view rooms and the two very special hot-tub suites. All rooms are equipped with queen or king beds and for your convenience; coffee maker, hair dryer, iron/board, micro/fridge,

cable TV, data-ports and free local calls. Visit the inviting, friendly Fireside Lounge where stories of the day's adventures are often heard and told. Big-screen TV's bring you the latest sporting events. Treat yourself to a spectacular view of glaciers and mountains at the Glacier View breakfast restaurant during the summer months. At the end of the day, enjoy the best steaks in town at the Otter Room Grill. Do you want to tour Homer's many wonderful sights, go on a memorable bear-viewing trip, watch whales, go halibut fishing, visit unique Halibut Cove or historic Seldovia? Book a trip right from the Bidarka's on-site tour desk. Guest's fish packaging, freezing and shipping available. Want to check your email? Use the business center's guest computer. New this year, the Bidarka Fitness Center! 575 Sterling Highway. Reservations 1-866-685-5000. Phone: 907-235-8148. Fax 907-235-8140. Email: info@bidarkainn.com. Internet: www.bidarkainn.com. See display ad this section. [ADVERTISEMENT]

Driftwood Inn and RV Park. Charming, historic beachfront inn with 20 rooms and full-hookup RV park. Both have spectacular view overlooking beautiful Kachemak Bay, mountains, glaciers. Quiet in-town location. Immaculately clean, charming rooms. Free coffee, tea, local information. Comfortable common areas with TV, fireplace, library, microwave, refrigerator, barbecue, shellfish cooker, fish cleaning area, freezer, picnic and laundry facilities. Continental breakfast available. We are a smoke-free facility. The RV park has 20-/30-/50-amp electric, water, sewer, clean and comfortable laundry and shower room for RV guests. Phone and cable available. Friendly, knowledgeable staff, specializing in helping make your stay in Homer the best possible. Reasonable, seasonal rates. Open year-round. Write, call for brochure. 135 W. Bunnell Ave., MP, Homer, AK 99603. (907) 235-8019. (800) 478-8019. Email: driftinn@xyz.net. Web site: www.thedriftwoodinn.com. See our display ad this section. [ADVERTISEMENT]

Halibut Cove Lodge is setting a new standard for adventure travel in Alaskan wilderness resorts. We offer world-class adventures coupled with first-class service, all in a striking wilderness setting. Whether you are looking for adventure or relaxation, enjoy the very best that Alaska has to offer at Hal-

ibut Cove Lodge. And, after enjoying a day of fishing, kayaking, or bear-viewing, it is time to relax with a soothing sauna, a soak in the hot-tub, and experience the gourmet dining, impeccable service and luxurious accommodations that set us apart! Open May–Sept. Twelve guest max. 2-, 4- and 6-day packages. www.halibutcovelodge.com (907) 235-6891. See display ad this section. [ADVERTISEMENT]

Heritage Hotel–Lodge. One of Alaska's finest log hotels, conveniently located in the heart of Homer. Specializing in small groups and fishing parties. Walking distance to beach, shops, museum. Accommodations: 36 rooms including suite with 2-person Jacuzzi. Reasonable rates. Cable TV, phones, free local calls. Courtesy coffee. Bakery and coffee shop adjacent. Alaskan hospitality. Open year-round. 147 E. Pioneer Ave., phone (907) 235-7787. Reservations 1-800-380-7787.Fax (907) 235-2804. heritage@xyz.net. www.alaskaheritagehotel.com See display ad this section. [ADVERTISEMENT]

Land's End Resort. Spectacular beachfront location, at the tip of the Homer Spit, on the shores of Kachemak Bay. Panoramic view of mountains and glaciers. See otters, whales and eagles from your private deck. Homer's favorite seafood restaurant and lounge. Spa and fitness center with outdoor hot tub. Tour desk to arrange activities. Walk to boat harbor. Call 1-800-478-0400. 4786 Homer Spit Rd., Homer, AK 99603. www.lands-end-resort.com. [ADVERTISEMENT]

Ocean Shores Motel. Modern seaside, spacious, spotless rooms located above our beautiful private beach. Each unit has a balcony and 7-foot picture window with spectacular views of the oean, mountains and glaciers. cable TV, phones, 5-star queen beds and handicap-accessible rooms. 2 blocks to downtown Homer, adjacent to restaurants, galleries and shopping. Quiet locale and reasonable rates, make this the best location in Homer. Minutes to the harbor, fishing charters, etc. 451, Sterling Highway #1, Homer, AK 99603. (800) 770-7775 or (907) 235-7775. www. oceanshoresalaska.com. See display ad this section. [ADVERTISEMENT]

Laughing Raven Guesthouse. Unhosted rental for independent travelers desiring fully furnished, luxurious, and spacious log vacation home with all amenities. Ideal for the entire family or multiple couples. You won't want to leave. Extraordinary views from 20 private acres close to all Homer activities. Year-round availability. Three private bedrooms and extra queen bed in loft. Winter and summer activities abound. Owners Mo Hillstrand and Jeff Foley. Website: www.alaska.net/~mojeff. Email: mojeff@alaska.net. Phone: (907) 279-3264. See display ad this section. [ADVERTISEMENT]

Spit Road Lodge/Charter, 1570 Spit Road is a Pan-Abode log lodge located at the base of the Homer Spit. Close to the airport, bike path and beach. Warm, friendly atmosphere. We treat you like family. Full home-cooked breakfasts, served in the dining room with a view. Immaculately clean rooms furnished with king, queen beds, cable, phones. Halibut and salmon charters on our 29 foot Almar boat. Heated cabin, marine head. All

The Pratt Museum on Bartlett Street is a must stop for visitors to Homer.
(© Kris Graef, staff)

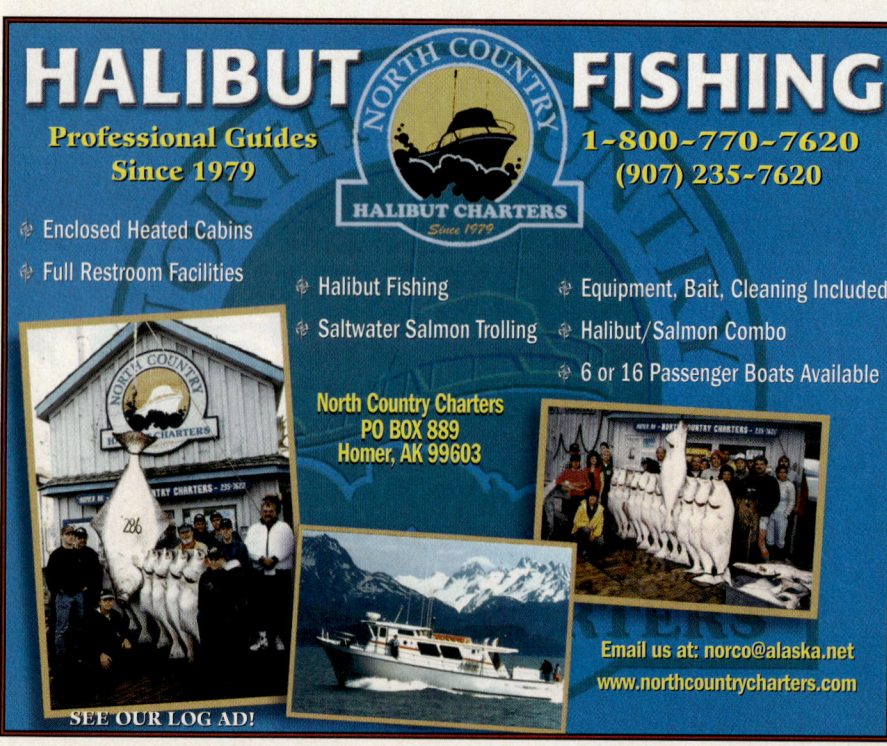

equipment, bait included. Free filleting. Fishing, lodging packages. www.spitroadlodge.com or email, stay@spitroadlodge.com. 1-888-423-6764 or (907) 235-6764. See display ad this section. [ADVERTISEMENT]

Wild Rose Cottages. Enjoy your own space in one of our 4 cozy cottages. Each different to accommodate your party. Charmingly furnished, bath with showers and well stocked kitchens. Slip into a complimentary pair of slippers and enjoy our breathtaking view while your catch of the day sizzles on the barbecue. Email: wildrose@xyz.net. www.alaskawildrose.com. P.O. Box 665, Homer, AK 99603. Phone (907) 235-8780. [ADVERTISEMENT]

Camping

The city campground is Karen Hornaday Hillside Park, accessed via Bartlett and Fairview avenues (follow signs). Located behind the ballfields, the park has 31 campsites, restrooms, water, picnic tables, firepits, dumpster and playground. Camping fee is $10/day for RVs, $6 for tents. No reservations, no hookups; only small RVs. Information available at visitor center.

Homer Spit camping fees are $10 per day for RVs and $6 per day for all other camping. There is a 14-day limit; restrooms, water and garbage available. Check in with the Fee Office across from the Fishing Hole; phone (907) 235-1583. No reservations; no hookups; pets on leash.

Homer Spit Campground. "Where the land ends and sea begins." Beachfront and ocean-view campsites surrounded by beautiful mountains and bay. Walk to harbor, restaurants and shops. Showers. Laundry. Dump station, electric, pull-throughs, overnight rentals, gifts. Bookings for halibut charters and all recreational needs. Satisfying visitors for 27 years. P.O. Box 1196, Homer, AK 99603. Phone (907) 235-8206. See display ad this section. [ADVERTISEMENT]

Homer's "Fishing Hole" RV Park. Opening summer of 2003. Homer's newest luxury RV park located on the Homer Spit adjacent to Homer's famous "Fishing Hole." 81 spacious RV sites with full hookups and 50 amp electrical service. Pull-thrus and drive-ins. On-site coin-op laundry and shower facility. Gift shop and Snack bar. Cable TV, phone and modem available at each site. Enjoy the adjacent Homer Spit pedestrian walkway and bike trail. Private beach access for clamming and beach-combing. Fishing charters, shopping and all Homer recreational opportunities within minutes of the Park. On-site host. Call (907) 235-8350 for information and reservations. See display ad this section. [ADVERTISEMENT]

Transportation

Air: Regularly scheduled air service to Anchorage. Several charter services also operate out of Homer.

Ferry: The Alaska State ferry *Tustumena* serves Seldovia, Kodiak, Seward, Port Lions, Valdez and Cordova from Homer with a limited schedule to Sand Point, King Cove and Dutch Harbor. Natural history programs offered on ferry in summer by Alaska Maritime National Wildlife Refuge naturalists. Contact the offices of the Alaska Marine Highway System at the Pioneer Dock, phone (907) 235-8449 for details. Tour boats offer passenger service to Seldovia and Halibut Cove.

Local: 4 rental car agencies and several taxi services.

 Mobile RV Services
(907) 399-7132

Furnaces, Fridges, Converters
Water Heaters, Electrical Systems & More

OPEN 7 DAYS
24 HOURS

Attractions

Pratt Museum, located at 3779 Bartlett St., features the natural and cultural history of southcentral Alaska. Exhibits range from artifacts of the area's first Native people, thousands of years ago, to those of homesteaders of the 1930s and 1940s. Excellent aquariums and a tide pool tank feature live Kachemak Bay sea creatures. Also exhibited are Alaskan birds and land and sea mammals, including the complete skeletons of a Bering Sea beaked whale and a beluga whale. Displays also feature local fish industry vessels and the restored Harrington homesteader cabin.

A popular attraction at the museum is the remote video camera, which transmits live images from the wildlife refuge at Gull Island, located 8 miles away in Kachemak Bay. Between May and September, visitors can observe live images of thousands of seabirds through this remote camera.

Summer visitors may take a self-guided tour through 3 outdoor exhibits, including a botanical garden, forest ecology trail and an original homesteader's cabin. The forest trail includes an art exhibit, "Facing the Elements," from mid-June through September. The museum also offers fish feedings Tuesdays and Fridays at 4 P.M. in the summer as well as other tours and exhibits.

The Museum Store features books, Alaskan gifts and jewelry, and Alaskan Native arts and crafts. On display around the museum are works by Alaskan artists in a variety of media.

The Pratt Museum is sponsored by the Homer Society of Natural History. All facilities are wheelchair accessible. $6 admission charged. Summer hours (mid-May to mid-September), 10 A.M. to 6 P.M. daily. Winter hours (mid-September to mid-May), noon to 5 P.M., Tuesday through Sunday. Closed January. Phone (907) 235-8635; fax (907) 235-2764; email info@prattmuseum.org; web site www.prattmuseum.org.

Homer Spit. Visitors and residents naturally gravitate toward this bustling strip of land jutting out into Kachemak Bay. Highlights include a 3-mile biking/walking trail from the parking area at Kachemak Drive out past the Fishing Hole. Watch for eagles

on the mud flats from the trail's viewing platforms.

Fishing charter services and a variety of shops are housed in the Spit's unique boardwalk structures.

The Homer Spit extends nearly 5 miles into Kachemak Bay. (© Laurent Dick)

A Spit landmark is the **Seafarer's Memorial**, dedicated to those who have lost their lives at sea. There is a parking area adjacent the memorial.

Bishop's Beach. is accessible from the Sterling Highway (Homer Bypass) at Main Street. It offers parking, public access to the beach, picnic tables and the trailhead for the award-winning Beluga Slough Pedestrian Trail. It is possible to walk several miles along the coastline in either direction from Bishop's Beach. *CAUTION: Check tide tables.*

Alaska Maritime National Wildlife Refuge, U.S. Fish and Wildlife Service, protects the habitats of seabirds and marine mammals on 3,500 islands and rocks along the coastline from Sitka to Barrow. The visitor center is open in summer from 9 A.M. to 5 P.M. daily. The center has displays focusing on the marine environment, videos and a small shop selling books and pamphlets. Wildlife programs include guided bird walks and beach walks and special slide presentations. Join the naturalists at the visitor center for an informative day. Naturalists are also on board the state ferry runs to Dutch Harbor and Kodiak. Information on the latest bird sightings can be obtained by calling the Bird Hotline at (907) 235-PEEP (7337). The visitor center is located at 451 Sterling Highway, Homer, AK 99603; phone (907) 235-6961 (summer only).

The Alaska Maritime National Wildlife Refuge, in partnership with the Kachemnak Bay Research Reserve, will be opening their Alaska Islands & Ocean Visitor Center in the fall of 2003. This new visitor center, research facility and administrative complex is dedicated to exploring and understanding the marine and estuarine habitats and wildlife of shoreline Alaska and its islands.

FAITH LUTHERAN CHURCH
On the Sterling Highway as you come into Homer
Summer Service Schedule
Saturday 7:00 pm • Sunday 9:30 am
faithlut@xyz.net • www.xyz.net/~faithlut
907-235-7600 • 3634 Soundview Ave. (at Sterling Hwy)

STERLING HIGHWAY • Homer

ALASKA'S FAVORITE VACATION SPOT!
HOMER

HOME OF THE BIGGEST CASH JACKPOT HALIBUT DERBY IN ALASKA! MAY 1 - LABOR DAY

Call (907) 235-7740
for your complete list of adventures!
www.homeralaska.org

Homer Chamber of Commerce
P.O. Box 541-MP
Homer, AK 99603-0541

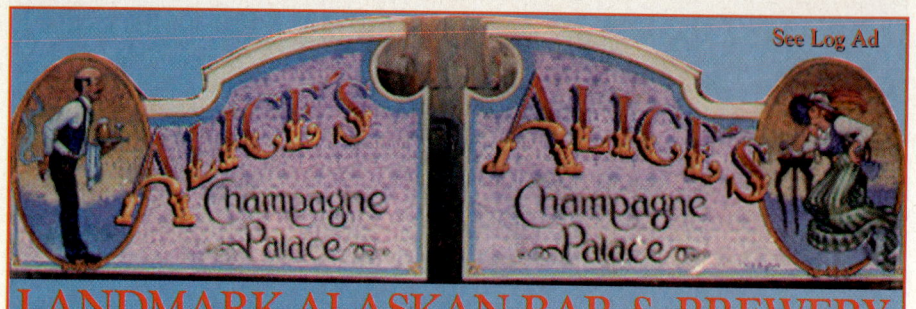

The visitor center occupies a 60-acre site overlooking Kachemak Bay.

The Kachemak Bay Shorebird Festival celebrates the arrival of 100,000 migrating shorebirds to the tidal flats of Kachemak Bay. The 11th annual festival is scheduled for May 9–12, 2003. The event promotes awareness of this critical shorebird habitat that provides a feeding and resting place for at least 20 species of shorebirds on the last leg of their journey from Central and South America to breeding grounds in western and northern Alaska. Festival highlights include guided bird walks, classes for beginning and advanced birders, children's activities and more. Sponsored by the Homer Chamber of Commerce and U.S. Fish & Wildlife Service; phone (907) 235-7740 for more details.

Taking place at the same time as the Shorebird Festival is the **Kachemak Bay Wooden Boat Festival**, which features boat building demonstrations, rowboat races and lots of boats.

Attend the Theatre. Homer's community theatre—Pier One Theatre—presents weekend performances of plays, dance concerts and a variety of other shows, from Memorial Day to Labor Day. Pier One, which started in 1973, is located in a converted city warehouse on Homer Spit. Phone (907) 235-7333.

Attend a Concert. The Kenai Peninsula Orchestra puts on its Summer String Festival in August. The festival features classical music concerts and a gala. Phone (907) 235-6318 for more information.

Fish the Homer Halibut Derby. The annual Jackpot Halibut Derby, sponsored by the Homer Chamber of Commerce, runs from May 1 through Labor Day. The state's largest cash halibut derby (over $100,000 in cash prizes) provides 4 monthly cash prizes, tagged fish and final jackpot prize. The derby also offers a $10,000 cash prize for the lucky angler releasing a fish over 80 pounds. Tickets are available at the Jackpot Halibut Derby headquarters on Homer Spit, at the visitor center or from local charter service offices and some lodging and tackle shops. Phone (907) 235-7740 for more information.

Charter Boats, operating out of the boat harbor on Homer Spit, offer sightseeing and halibut fishing trips. (Charter salmon fishing trips, clamming, crabbing, and sightseeing charters are also available.) These charter operators provide gear, bait and expert knowledge of the area. Homer is one of Alaska's largest charter fishing areas (most charters are for halibut fishing). Charter boats for halibut fishermen cost about $140 to $180 a day. Several sightseeing boats operate off the Homer Spit, taking visitors to view the bird rookery on Gull Island, to Halibut Cove and to Seldovia. (Most sightseeing trips are available Memorial Day to Labor Day). Watch for whales, puffins, sea otters, seals and other marine wildlife.

Take a Scenic Drive. A 13-mile drive out East Road offers beautiful views of Kachemak Bay. Or turn off East Road on to East Hill Road and drive up the bluffs to Skyline Drive; beautiful views of the bay and glaciers. Return to town via West Hill Road, which intersects the Sterling Highway at **Milepost S 167.1**.

The glaciers that spill down from the Harding Icefield straddling the Kenai Mountains across the bay create an ever-changing panorama visible from most points in Homer, particularly from the Skyline Drive. The most spectacular and largest of these

FUN IN HOMER!
AT ALASKA WILD BERRY PRODUCTS
jams, jellies & wild berry candies

No visit to Alaska Wild Berry would be complete without a pause at the taster's stand, where you can dip into savory, free samples of jams and jellies.

View the fascinating bits of Alaska's rich heritage collected over our 50 years as a Homer business.

VISIT US SOON!

Alaska Wild Berry Products is located in Homer on beautiful Kachemak Bay at the southern tip of the Kenai Peninsula. The drive south from Anchorage takes you through some of the most spectacular countryside in America. Once in Homer, turn left onto Pioneer Avenue and look for our log cabin store. We'll be waiting to greet you.

Take some time to browse through our unique gift shop, featuring Alaska Wild Berry jams, jellys and candies, fine jewelry, souvenirs and Alaska crafts.

Large parking lot. Picnic area. Open year round. Long summer hours: 7 days a week. For a free mail order catalog write Alaska Wild Berry Products, 5225 Juneau St., Anch. AK 99518. Also visit our Anchorage outlets at Fifth Avenue Mall and our main store and Wild Berry kitchens on International Airport Rd. and New Seward Hwy. (907) 562-8858

(907) 235-8858

glaciers is Grewingk Glacier in Kachemak Bay State Park, visible to the east directly across Kachemak Bay from Homer. The glacier was named by Alaska explorer William H. Dall in 1880 for Constantin Grewingk, a German geologist who had published a work on the geology and volcanism of Alaska. The Grewingk Glacier has a long gravel bar at its terminal moraine, behind which the water draining from the ice flows into the bay. This gravel bar, called Glacier Spit, is a popular excursion spot, and may be visited by charter plane or boat. (There are several charter plane operators and charter helicopter services in Homer.) Portlock and Dixon glaciers are also visible directly across from the Spit.

Kachemak Bay State Park is located on the south shore of the bay and accessible by float plane or private water taxis from Homer. It is one of Alaska's most popular parks for sea kayaking, hiking, fishing and beachcombing. The park's coves, bay, valleys and mountains provide a great variety of recreational opportunities, including: a 75-mile trail system with hiking from Glacier Spit to China Poot Peak; campsites at Glacier Spit, Halibut Cove Lagoon, China Poot Lake and additional backcountry locations; 5 public-use cabins; and excellent kayaking, clamming, tide pooling and beachcombing opportunities. For cabin reservations, phone (907) 262-5581. For more information, phone the district office at (907) 235-7024, stop by the state park office at Milepost S 168.5 Sterling Highway, or visit the Chamber of Commerce Visitor Center.

Visit Halibut Cove and Seldovia. These 2 communities on Kachemak Bay are accessible by ferry from Homer boat harbor. See descriptions of these charming destinations on pages 623-624.

McNeil River State Game Sanctuary/Katmai National Park. Homer is the main base for visitors flying across Cook Inlet to both locations, where the world's largest concentration of bears in a natural area this size is found. Brown bears congregate near the mouth of the McNeil River, where a falls slows down migrating salmon, making fishing easy for the bears. Visits to the game sanctuary are on a permit basis; a drawing for the limited number of permits is held in March each year. Permit applications are available from the Alaska Dept. of Fish and Game, Attn: McNeil River, 333 Raspberry Road, Anchorage 99518. Phone (907)267-2100.

Katmai National Park offers viewing platforms for close (and safe!) brown bear viewing. Several area outfitters provide service, including overnight stays and access to remote areas of the park.

Learn about the Natural History of the Area. The Center for Alaskan Coastal Studies is a Homer-based nonprofit organization that offers 2 summer educational programs. The guided natural history tours across Kachemak Bay include viewing the Gull Island seabird rookery, exploring the rich intertidal life (tide dependent) and hiking in the coastal forest. The Carl E. Wynn Nature Center located on East Skyline Drive overlooking

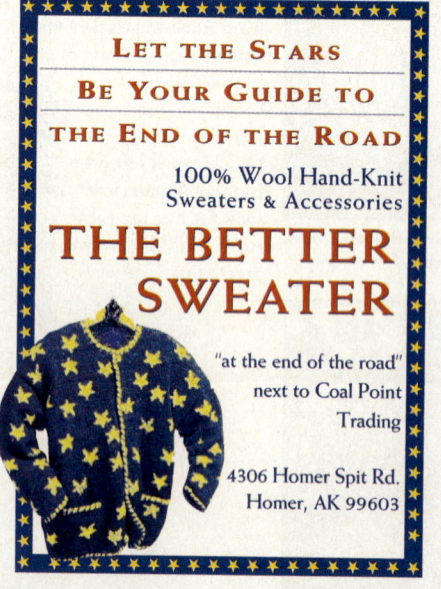

Homer offers guided walks through forest and wildflower meadows, plus free weekly children's programs. Box 2225-MP, Homer, AK 99603; phone (907) 235-6667; email cacs@xyz.net; www.akcoastalstudies.org.

Alaska Wild Berry Products, celebrating more than 50 years in downtown Homer, invites you to see our wild berry jams, jellies and chocolates handmade the old-fashioned way. Delicious free samples at our taster's stand. Gift shop. Picnic area. Open year-round, 528 East Pioneer Avenue. See display ad this section. [ADVERTISEMENT]

Alice's Champagne Palace and The Palace Brewery, located on Pioneer Avenue, undoubtedly qualifies as a Kenai Peninsula landmark. It has existed in various incarnations through the years, but has consistently kept its doors open to the great people of Homer. Fishermen, artists, hippies, business people and weary travelers congregate under one roof all year long and satiate their appetite for celebration. The Palace Brewery is a welcome addition to Alice's Champagne Palace and is now brewing and serving the finest of beers. Alice's currently borrows a little of the best from each of its former lives, hosting live music, concerts, karaoke, jam sessions and more for your pleasure. Alaska's "Official Balladeer," Hobo Jim, got his start here and continues to hit Alice's well-worn stage at full speed every Wednesday night through the summer. "Fat Rack" serves gourmet pizza, caesar salads and more. Alice's also features, without a doubt, the most attractive wait-staff this side of Clam Gulch! (Huge building with great fresh air circulation.) 195 E. Pioneer Avenue. (907) 235-7650, (907) 235-0630 office. See display ad this section. [ADVERTISEMENT]

Art Shop Gallery, where Homer shops for art. Open year-round. Original works, prints, posters by local, Alaskan and nationally recognized artists. Alaska Native art, jewelry, dolls, pottery, Christmas tree ornaments by Alaskan artists. Homer's premier gallery. A must. World-wide shipping. New location! 202 W. Pioneer Ave. (907) 235-7076 or 1-800-478-7076. artshopg@xyz.net. See display ad this section. [ADVERTISEMENT]

Bald Mountain Air. Extraordinary brown bear photo safaris to Kodiak/Katmai National Park. Departing from Homer daily, your Alaskan floatplane experience offers you the trip of a lifetime. Lifelong Alaskans Gary and Jeanne Porter will take you on a trip you'll never forget. P.O. Box 3134, Homer, AK 99603. (800) 478-7969. http://www.baldmountainair.com. Email: baldmt@ptialaska.net. See display ad this section. [ADVERTISEMENT]

Blackbeary Bog. Folded away somewhat, in Pioneer Square at 564 E. Pioneer Avenue, is a truly unique and magical store. A must see for visitors and locals. Come enter the world of the Blackbeary Bog, where the ambiance is deep, rich and thoroughly intoxicating to the senses. Owner, Shawnee Kinney has created a collection of collections. Cupboards and chests, corners and boxes filled with unusual treasures and intriguing finds. Leaded glass lamps, window panels, nautical, gorgeous furniture and fabric, spectacular orbs and lighted stars. Heirloom quality establishes the motif here, but there is truly something for everyone in every price range. Of all the shops you'll see and visit in Alaska, this is the one you don't want to miss, and the one you'll never forget. Open year-round. Shipping worldwide. Special orders welcome. (907) 235-5668. [ADVERTISEMENT]

Homer Spit offers camping, fishing and beachcombing. (© Carol P. Murdock)

Coastal Outfitters. Experience the best wilderness adventure and photographic opportunity for all that Alaska has to offer. Choose from the following custom marine tours aboard our 66-foot vessel. April, May and June—Thrill to the whale migration through the Gulf of Alaska, along with seeing glaciers, volcanoes, a multitude of seabirds and sea mammals. June through September—World-class bear viewing along the coast of Katmai National Park. Stay on our 66-foot vessel with all the comforts of home while watching the magnificent Alaskan brown bears. Unlimited opportunities for photography; often professional photographers on board for photo workshops. All tours include unparalleled opportunities for halibut fishing. See display ad. Phone (907) 235-8492; 1-888-235-8492; fax (907) 235-2967. Email: bear@xyz.net. Internet: www.alaska-vacations.com/Coastal. [ADVERTISEMENT]

Emerald Air Service. Ken and Chris Day love bears and it shows in the way they share them with their guests. What makes their trip unique? They *walk*-out across a landscape so large, it stretches your imagination. Theirs is a natural history trip revolving around the bears as seen in National Wildlife Federation's documentary "Bears" (showing at IMAX Theatres around the world). As preservationists, their commitment is sharing what they have learned over the years. Roaming with Ken and Chris through the bear's domain, you will take away more than good pictures, you'll gain a deep sense of "knowing the bears" and the country they live in. For those who want a

Homer United Methodist Church

Summer Worship Schedule
Worship 10am • Fellowship Hour 11am

Fall - Spring Worship Schedule
Worship 11am • Fellowship Hour 12pm

(907) 235-8528
email: humc@acsalaska.net
770 East End Road (Next to Homer H.S.)

Halibut Cove is a popular side trip from Homer. (© Laurent Dick)

bear viewing trip and more, this is *the* experience. Trips depart 7-days a week from late May through September. Groups are small so book as early as you can. P.O. Box 635, Homer, AK 99603. (907) 235-6993. www.emeraldairservice.com. Email: bears@emeraldairservice.com. [ADVERTISEMENT]

The Homer Bookstore located at 332 E. Pioneer Avenue in the middle of downtown Homer is often acclaimed to be "About the nicest bookstore in Alaska," It has been highly appreciated by locals and visitors alike for over 25 years. The newly remodeled location includes an espresso bar, one of the best Alaskana sections in the state, and one of the nicest card selections anywhere. It is a frequent destination for those wanting to browse as well as a great source of local information. Summer hours: 10–7, Monday–Saturday; 12–5 on Sunday. Phone: (907) 235-7496. Email: bookstor@alaska.net. [ADVERTISEMENT]

Kachemak Bay Flying Service, Inc. offers a unique opportunity to fly over the spectacular glaciers across Kachemak Bay with Bill deCreeft in his beautifully restored 1929 Travel Air S6000B floatplane "Limousine of the Air," with its large, mahogany-framed windows for each passenger. P.O. Box 1769, Homer, AK 99603. (907) 235-8924. Internet: www.alaskaseaplanes.com. [ADVERTISEMENT]

Main Street Mercantile sits proudly on the corner of Pioneer Avenue and Main Street and commands a wonderful view of Homer and Kachemak Bay. Come sit a spell on the big ol' front porch or inside by the pot-bellied stove. Enjoy the Good Old Days of Homer without having to get your hands dirty. In 1936, before electricity or a road into town, the Walli family opened "Homer Cash Store," Homer's finest grocery/dry goods store. It quickly became the center of town and remained so for many years. Now completely restored, this substantial, historic old building now owned by the Mitchell family, again *the* place to get "homesteading supplies," practical camping and outdoor gear, along with great and useful items reminiscent of the past. Don't miss this stop. Plenty of parking. Located next to NOMAR. Phone (907) 235-9102. 104 E. Pioneer, Homer, AK 99603. [ADVERTISEMENT]

NOMAR® (Northern Marine Canvas Products) began business the summer of 1978 in a yellow school bus! Today, visit our manufacturing facility and retail store at 104 E. Pioneer Ave., downtown Homer. NOMAR® manufactures a wide variety of products for our Alaskan lifestyles. Warm NOMAR® fleece clothing to keep you warm, no matter what the adventure. Soft-sided 'Laska Luggage that's stuffable and floatplane friendly. Watertight bags and camp gear for kayak tours or whitewater expeditions. Plus, well-made, Homer-made, packable, mailable, useful gifts, for everyone on the "list." Park in our spacious, paved parking lot and walk around our town, it's a nice stroll. We'll gladly ship your purchases for you. See display ad this section. [ADVERTISEMENT]

North Country Charters, on the Homer Spit. Sean and Gerri Martin, original owners since 1979. We have an excellent catch record with prize-winning derby fish, bringing in some of the largest halibut in Homer. Three 6-passenger and one 16-passenger boat for halibut fishing along with a salt-water salmon trolling boat. All vessels are Coast Guard equipped, heated cabins, full restrooms. 1-800-770-7620. Email: norco@alaska.net. www.northcountrycharters.com. See display ad this section. [ADVERTISEMENT]

North Wind Home Collection. "Shopping therapy for the outrageously eclectic." Where furniture is fashion and there is always something new and different in the way of furniture and fanciful accents for your home. North Wind has a grand selection of lamps, clocks, pillows, throws, rugs, dinnerware, glassware, serving pieces and much, much more. Made to order sofas and chairs are our specialty. Bridal and special occasion registry. Gift certificates and gift wrapping available. Suitcase too full? Shipping services available to ensure your North Wind treasures get home safely. Located on Pioneer Avenue in the heart of Homer. Plenty of parking, open year-round. 173 W. Pioneer Ave. (907) 235-0766. [ADVERTISEMENT]

The Old Inlet Bookshop. Family owned, third generation bookseller. Used rare and out-of-print books, original art. Located downstairs in The Old Inlet Trading Post, corner of Main and Bunnell. A treasure trove of books for your discovery, a block from beach. Coffee shop, gallery, nearby. Specializing in Alaskana, Polar Exploration, Nautical, Fine and Illustrated, and Contemporary Fiction. Box 382, Homer, Alaska 99603. (907) 235-7984. books@ptialaska.net. [ADVERTISEMENT]

Picture Alaska Art Gallery has something for everyone. Original fine art prints, native crafts, hand-carved decoys, burl bowls, vintage Alaskan photographs, plus jewelry, gifts...even art supplies for creating your own art. Located upstairs is The Upstairs Boutique, where fun in fashion begins, from outerwear to underwear. Fine lingerie, cozy sleepwear and accessories galore. Open year-round at 448 E. Pioneer Ave. (907) 235-2300. We ship anywhere. Phone orders: 800-770-2300. www.pcturealaska.com. [ADVERTISEMENT]

Seams to Bee, a fabric and Quilt shop, offering easy access and ample parking for RV's, right on your way to the Homer Spit. You'll find a wide selection of quilting fabric, including 'Alaskan' prints with moose, bears, eagles, wildflowers and more, plus, our specialty—flannel. Notions, patterns, books, quilt-kits, classes and gift items offer unlimited treats for the traveler. There's a lot of great stuff packed into this little shop. In-shop sewing machine rentals, and space for sewing. Bring your lunch and spend the day quilting (the ideal vacation) while he fishes. 10:00–5:30 Mon.–Sat., 1103 A Ocean Dr. (907) 235-6555. seams2bee@homernet.net. www.seamstobee.com. See display ad this section. [ADVERTISEMENT]

Trails End Horse Adventures. Horses and Alaska are my life. Join me in my 18th season offering trail rides in the Homer area. Featuring half-day rides and pack adventures to the head of Kachemak Bay. View mountains, glaciers, Fox River flats. Gentle Alaskan horses. Located at **Mile 11.2** East End Road. Write Mark Marette, 53435 East Rd., Homer, AK 99603. Phone (907) 235-6393. [ADVERTISEMENT]

AREA FISHING: The Kachemak Bay and Cook Inlet area is one of Alaska's most popular spots for halibut fishing, with catches often weighing 100 to 200 lbs. Guides and charters are available locally. Halibut up to 350 lbs. are fished from June through September; fish the bottom with herring. Year-round trolling for king salmon is popular; use small herring. King salmon may also be taken during late May and June in area streams. Pink salmon (4 to 5 lbs.) may be caught in July and August; use winged bobbers, small weighted spoons and spinners. Similar tackle or fresh roe will catch silver salmon weighing 6 to 8 lbs. in August and September. Dolly Varden are taken throughout the area April to October; try single eggs or wet flies. Steelhead/rainbow are available in local streams, but for conservation purposes must be immediately released unharmed.

Fishermen have had great success in recent years casting from the shore of Homer Spit for king salmon. **The Fishing Hole** (also referred to as the Fishing Lagoon or Spit Lagoon) on the Homer Spit supports a large run of hatchery-produced kings and silvers beginning in late May and continuing to September. Kings range from 20 to 40 lbs. The fishery is open 7 days a week in season.

Regulations vary depending on species and area fished, and anglers are cautioned to consult nearby tackle shops or Fish and Game before fishing.

Halibut Cove

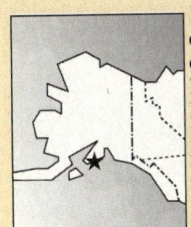

Located 7 miles southeast of Homer on the east shore of Kachemak Bay. **Population:** 35. **Emergency Services:** In Homer. **Elevation:** 10 feet. **Climate:** Summer temperatures from 45° to 65°F; winter temperatures from 14° to 27°F; average annual precipitation, 24 inches.

Visitor Information: Welcome and information shack at the top of the ramp at the main dock. www.halibutcove.com.

The community of Halibut Cove is nestled along a 3-mile-wide bay on the east shore of Kachemak Bay. The bay was named Halibut Cove by W.H. Dall of the U.S. Coast & Geodetic Survey in 1880.

Between 1911 and 1928, Halibut Cove had 42 herring salteries and a population of about 1,000. Today, the community of Halibut Cove is made up of self-employed artists, commercial fishermen and craftsmen. There are no state schools in the community.

Overnight guests in Halibut Cove can stay in cabins or bed and breakfasts (see ads this section). There is one restaurant (the Saltry). There is a post office. Banks, groceries and similar services are not available in Halibut Cove.

Cove Country Cabins. Charming, private, furnished cabins with kitchens; snuggled in the spruce or amazing views of the cove. Quality post-and-beam construction. Ask about writers and artists workshops throughout the year. Near restaurant. Kayaking, hiking, sightseeing. "Magical, full of history and wonder." "Thanks for being wonderful hosts." www.halibutcovealaska.com. 1-888-353-2683. (907) 235-6374. Email: ctjones@xyz.net. [ADVERTISEMENT]

Transportation: Air— Floatplane. Boat— The private Kachemak Bay Ferry, M/V *Danny J*, departs Homer at noon and 5 p.m. daily in summer; reservations and tickets through Central Charters. Group charters through Narrows Charters & Tours. Board at the bottom of Ramp A at Homer boat harbor. The 45-minute ferry ride includes Gull Island bird sanctuary.

HALIBUT COVE ADVERTISERS

Central Charters	Ph. (800) 478-7847
Cove Country Cabins	Ph. (888) 353-2683
Halibut Cove Cabins	Ph. (907) 296-2214
Halibut Cove Lodge	Ph. (907) 235-6891
The Cove Gallery	Ph. (907) 296-2207

Attractions

There are no roads in Halibut Cove, but some 12 blocks of boardwalk run along the water's edge and provide a scenic and relaxing way to explore this charming community. Stroll the boardwalks for spectacular views of Kachemak Bay, access to the Saltry restaurant and to galleries displaying the work of local artists. Well-known artist Diana Tillion, who is famous for her octopus ink and watercolor paintings, has a gallery here.

Visitors can also walk down to the floats to see several historic wooden boats.

Bird watching in the area is excellent and there are good hiking trails. Kachemak Bay State Park hiking trails are accessible from Halibut Cove. China Poot Lake Trail begins at Halibut Cove Lagoon. The Lagoon Trail winds along Halibut Cove to intersect with the China Poot Lake trail. The bay shoreline offers excellent kayaking, clamming, tide pooling and beach combing opportunities. Keep in mind that Kachemak Bay's tides are among the largest in the world and tidal currents can be substantial. A tide book is essential. Phone the district Alaska State Parks office at (907) 235-7024 for more information, or stop by the state park office outside Homer for more information on hiking Kachemak Bay State Park.

Walk to the end of the main boardwalk in Halibut Cove to reach the beach. Beachcomb, look at tide pools or have a picnic lunch at the tables provided. During salmon season, visitors may see seiners set out their nets.

Kachemak Bay is one of Alaska's most popular spots for halibut fishing, with catches often weighing 100 to 200 lbs. Halibut up to 350 lbs. are fished from June through September.

Seldovia

Visitor admires the beautiful coastline on Seldovia Bay. (© bill Sherwonit)

Located on the southwestern Kenai Peninsula on Seldovia Bay, an arm of Kachemak Bay, 16 miles southwest of Homer. **Population: 286. Emergency Services:** City Police, Ambulance, Fire and Rescue, emergency only, phone 911, monitor CB Channel 9. **Seldovia Medical Clinic**, phone (907) 234-7825. Seldovia has a resident doctor and visiting dentists.

Visitor Information: Seldovia Chamber of Commerce, Drawer F, Seldovia, AK 99663. Phone/Fax (970) 234-7612; email seldcity@xyz.net; web www.seldovia.com. Most Main Street businesses also provide visitor information.

Transportation: Air—Scheduled and charter service available. **Ferry**—Alaska's Southwestern Marine Highway system serves Seldovia, with connections to and from Homer, Port Lions, Kodiak, Valdez, Cordova and Seward. **Charter and Tour Boats**—Available for passenger service; inquire locally and in Homer.

Private Aircraft: Seldovia airport, 1 E; elev. 29 feet; length 1,845 feet; gravel; unattended.

Seldovia is a small community accessible by air (a 15-minute flight from Homer) or by ferry (it is connected to Homer by the Alaska Marine Highway's Southwest ferry system).

Because it is removed from Kenai Peninsula highways, Seldovia has retained much of its old Alaska charm and traditions (its historic boardwalk dates from 1931). *Alaska* magazine managing editor Tim Woody describes Seldovia: "Main Street—which carries about as many pedestrians and 4-wheelers as cars is only a few steps from the harbor, where a lone sea otter often swims among the small boats quietly moving in and out of their slips. Bald eagles soar overhead and rest in the trees that rim the harbor. The chatter of children is common as they happily roam the streets by foot and bicycle, unencumbered by close supervision.

"The relaxed atmosphere endears the town to its longtime residents as well as tourists, who sometimes fall so hard for Seldovia that they decide this is where they belong. For most, the town becomes a place where they can regularly escape for a couple of weeks, or maybe all summer."

The name Seldovia is derived from Russian *Seldevoy*, meaning "herring bay." Between 1869 and 1882, a trading station was located here. The St. Nicholas Russian Orthodox Church was built in 1891. It is now a national historic site. A post office was established in Nov. 1898.

The SOS (Seldovia Oil Spill) Response Team is located at 258 Seldovia Street. This one-of-a-kind community group, first organized after the *Exxon Valdez* oil spill, has the ability to respond to local emergencies in southern Cook Inlet and Kachemak Bay using local fishing boats and crews. SOS also serves as a community information center with phone, fax and e-mail access. Visitors are welcome, 8 A.M. to 5 P.M. weekdays.

Lodging & Services

Seldovia has most visitor facilities, including 2 hotels, several bed and breakfasts, a lodge, 2 general stores, grocery/deli, restaurants and a variety of shops. The post office is in the center of town. Public restrooms, showers and pay phone in front of the boat harbor near town center. Pay phones are also located at the ferry dock outside ferry office, at the airport, and library.

The Buzz Coffee House offers indoor and outdoor dining, overlooking Seldovia's harbor. This charming cafe's bakery features fresh, homemade gourmet breakfast, lunch, early dinner and snacks. Fresh roasted coffee, which includes the famous "Buzz Blend!" They specialize in all espresso drinks, hot or iced. Aromatherapy gifts. Phone (907) 234-7479. thebuzz@alaska.net www.thebuzzAK.webtv.net. [ADVERTISEMENT]

Alaska Dancing Eagles B&B and Cabin Rentals. Uniquely beautiful waterfront location on historic boardwalk; a healing place with lovely flowers, wildflower garden. Secluded, peaceful, panoramic view of boat

SELDOVIA ADVERTISERS

Alaska Dancing Eagles B&B
   and Cabin Rental.........Ph. (907) 234-7627
Alaska Tribal Cache..........Ph. (907) 234-7898
Buzz Coffee House, The ...Ph. (907) 234-7479
Mad Fish
   Restaurant, The ....Ph. (907) 234-7676
Seldovia Bayview Suites ...Ph. (800) 478-7898
Seldovia Boardwalk
   Hotel ....Ph. (800) 238-7862
Seldovia Chamber of
   Commerce ....Ph. (907) 234-7612

harbor, mountains, volcano, bay. Local activities: kayaking, mountain biking, hiking, fishing charters. Free airport pickup. Open May 15–September 15. (907) 234-7627; www.dancingeagles.com. See display ad this section. [ADVERTISEMENT]

Seldovia Boardwalk Hotel. Waterfront view. 14 lovely rooms with private baths. Large harbor-view deck. In-room phones. Near bike and kayak rentals and hiking trails. Close to restaurants. Free airport pickup. Friendly service. Romantic getaway. Package prices from Homer. Open year-round. P.O. Box 72, Seldovia, AK 99663. (907) 234-7816. Email: bbutler@alaska.net. [ADVERTISEMENT]

The Mad Fish Restaurant. Dine on fine gourmet cuisine by Chef Kate Fitzgerald-Haralson, as you overlook the picturesque Seldovia waterfront. We specialize in unique and delightful seafood specialties. "It's worth the trip just to eat here." Alaskan beers and fine wines available. Summer: 7 days a week. Winter: limited hours. Reservations recommended. VISA/MasterCard. (907) 234-7676. www.madfishalaska.com. Email: madfish@alaska.net. Recommended by Frommers Alaska Travel Guide. [ADVERTISEMENT]

Seldovia Bayview Suites. Newly remodeled, clean full-service grocery and liquor store. Convenience food and microwave for customer use. Bait, ice, fishing and hunting licenses, film, hot snack foods, video rentals. The Inn, located above the Market, is the best deal in town! Eight 1- to 4-bedroom apartment suites with complete kitchens, satellite TV and phones. Reasonable rates. Conference Suite available for small conventions, conferences, family reunions, retreats. Balcony overlooking harbor and Bay or Orthodox church view. We freeze fish for guests. www.alaskaadventurelodge.com; Email: snai@snai.com; phone (907) 234-7631; 800-478-7898. See display ad this section. [ADVERTISEMENT]

Kayakers paddle through Seldovia harbor. (© Bill Sherwonit)

Camping
RV camping at the city-owned Seldovia Wilderness Park located just outside the city. From downtown, drive 1 mile out via Anderson Way to fork in road; turn left and drive 0.9 mile to beach. ▲

Attractions
Visitors can learn about Seldovia's cultural and natural history from a series of interpretive signs placed about the town. Seldovia's sheltered bay is ideal for kayaking. The Otterbaun, a 1.2-mile hiking trail, is a popular way to get from town to Outside Beach, a beautiful spot with beachcombing, surf fishing and a view of Kachemak Bay and the volcanoes St. Augustine, Mount Iliamna and Mount Redoubt. The trailhead is behind the school. Check the tidal charts before you go; access to the Outside Beach is cut off at high tide.

Continue past the Outside Beach turnoff to hilly and unpaved Jakolof Bay Road, which offers panoramic views of Kachemak Bay, McDonald Spit, Jakolof Bay and Kasitsna Bay. At Mile 7.5, steps lead down to 1.5-mile-long McDonald Spit, a favorite spot for seabirds and marine life. Spend an afternoon exploring the spit, or continue out to Jakolof Bay, where the road offers many opportunities to get onto the beach. The road becomes impassable to vehicles at Mile 13.

Alaska Tribal Cache. Camai'! (Greetings from Seldovia Village Tribe!) We produce Alaska's finest jams, jellies and syrups using locally picked wild berries and Tribal recipes. We welcome you to visit our kitchen, gift shop and free museum. Free samples! In season, free permits available for picking berries on Tribal land. (907) 234-7898; www.alaskatribalcache.com; rhilts@tribalnet.org. [ADVERTISEMENT]

Special Events. Just about the whole town participates in Seldovia's old-fashioned Fourth of July celebration. The holiday includes food booths, parade, games and contests. Check with the chamber of commerce for details.

Fishing: Kachemak Bay, king salmon Jan.–Aug.; halibut May–Oct.; Dolly Varden June–Sept.; silver salmon in August and Sept.; red salmon July–Aug. **Seldovia Bay,** king, silver and red salmon, also halibut, May–Sept. Excellent bottom fishing. 🐟

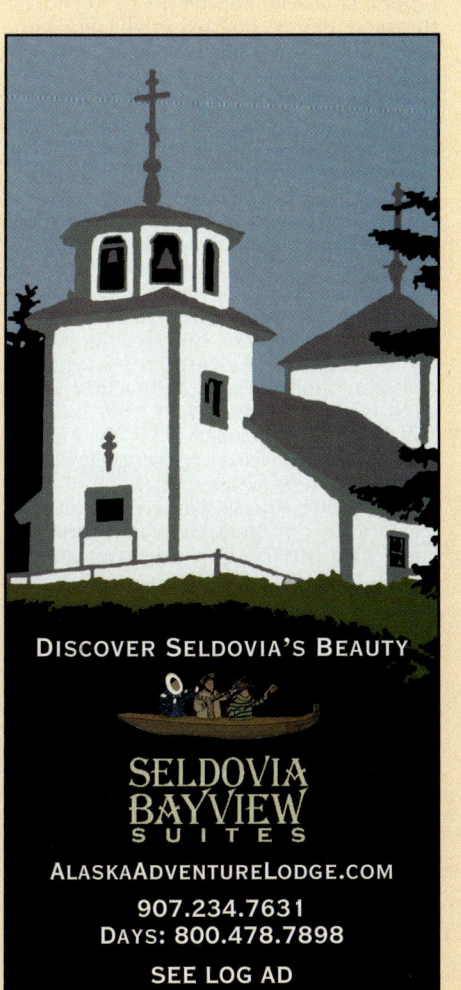

A photographer captures a giant 21-rayed sea star on Seldovia beach.
(© Greg Daniels, Lure of Alaska Images)

PRINCE WILLIAM SOUND

Includes communities of Valdez and Cordova and the Copper River Highway

Southcentral Alaska's Prince William Sound is an area famous for its scenery and its wildlife. Dotted with islands, this 70-mile-wide gulf extends 30 miles north and west from the Gulf of Alaska to the Kenai Peninsula. It is bounded to the southeast by Montague and Hinchinbrook islands, which form Hinchinbrook Entrance, the 10-mile-long water passage from the Gulf of Alaska to Prince William Sound. To the north: a rugged, glaciated coastline and the Chugach Mountains.

If you take the 7-hour-long ferry ride between Whittier, at the west end of the Sound, and Cordova, near the east end of the Sound, you will realize exactly how large this particular geographic area is. Hour after hour you'll chug along, surrounded by a spectacular pristine wilderness of snow-capped mountains, emerald isles and waters rich with whales, dolphins and other sealife.

The star attraction of Prince William Sound is Columbia Glacier, one of the largest and most magnificent of the tidewater glaciers along the Alaska coast. (The

Prince William Sound is a spectacular wilderness of mountains, glaciers and rich waters. (© Laurent Dick)

Hubbard Glacier is the largest tidewater glacier in Alaska.)

Columbia Glacier is also the world's fastest moving glacier, retreating at a speed of 80 to 115 feet per day. It has receded more than 6 miles since 1982. The glacier is currently 34 miles in length, 3 miles wide and more than 3,000 feet thick in some places. Visitors to Prince William Sound see its tidewater terminus 6 miles away. How close you get to the glacier's face depends on iceberg production: the more icebergs, the less chance boats have to get close.

The glacier was named by the Harriman Alaska expedition in 1899 for Columbia University in New York City. The glacier's source is Mount Einstein (elev. 11,552 feet) in the Chugach Mountains.

There are several ways to explore Prince William Sound. From Anchorage, drive south on the Seward Highway 47 miles and turn off on to the new Whittier Access Road.

It is approximately 11 miles from the main highway to the community of Whittier at the head of Passage Canal on Prince William Sound. (See detailed description of Whittier and the Whittier/Portage Glacier Access Road on pages 517–519 in the SEWARD HIGHWAY section.) From Whittier, you may catch the state ferry, MV *Bartlett*, for cross-sound service to Valdez and Cordova.

Or you may start your trip across Prince William Sound from Valdez, by driving 304 miles from Anchorage to Valdez via the Glenn and Richardson highways (see GLENN HIGHWAY and RICHARDSON HIGHWAY sections). From Valdez, the MV *Bartlett* serves both Cordova and Whittier. (See the Southcentral/Southwest Alaska MV *Bartlett* Schedule in the ALASKA MARINE HIGHWAY SCHEDULES section.)

From Whittier, Valdez or Cordova, you can board either the state ferry or one of the privately operated excursion boats to tour Prince William Sound. Flightseeing trips are also available. Depending on your itinerary and type of transportation, you may see Columbia Glacier and return to Anchorage the same day or stay overnight along the way. All-inclusive tours of Prince William Sound are available out of Anchorage.

Prince William Sound Cruises & Tours. Join Prince William Sound Cruises & Tours in Whittier–the Gateway to Prince William Sound. Explore glacier-carved fjords draped with cascading waterfalls and spectacular alpine glaciers. Watch for sea otters, sea lions, seals, porpoise, orcas and giant humpback whales, plus a wide variety of birds. Our experienced, knowledgeable captains and crew are your guides as you travel aboard our custom sightseeing vessels through spectacular Esther Passage. All cruises are fully narrated and include a delicious meal. Daily departures from Whittier. Toll free 800-468-8068 or (907) 277-2131, or visit us on the web at www.princewilliamsound.com. [ADVERTISEMENT]

26 Glacier Cruise. Cruise the calm, protected waters of Prince William Sound and come face to face with tidewater glaciers

plus an amazing array of wildlife on the fastest, largest and most luxurious high-speed catamaran in Alaska. Departs daily from Whittier. See our ad in the Anchorage section. Phillips Cruises' year-round sales office is located at 519 West 4th Avenue, Anchorage, AK 99501. Toll free from USA and Canada 1-800-544-0529, (907) 276-8023 or bswanberg@26glaciers.com. [ADVERTISEMENT]

Discover Prince William Sound From Whittier or Valdez!

Cruise the calm, sheltered waters of Prince William Sound. Our experienced captains and crew are your guides as you travel aboard our custom sightseeing vessels complete with oversized windows and outside viewing decks. Daily departures from Whittier and Valdez. Transportation available.

Prince William Sound Cruises & Tours
Operated by Stan Stephens
An Alaska Heritage Tours Company

Call Today for reservations! Toll-Free
800-992-1297
In Valdez 907-835-4731
In Anchorage 907-277-2131 • 513 W. 4th Avenue
www.princewilliamsound.com

See Beautiful Prince William Sound with HONEY CHARTERS

Personalized glacier viewing, whalewatching
Fast, beachable water transportation
Groups up to 30 – Reservations suggested

P.O. Box 708 • Whittier, AK 99693
1-888-477-2493
Email: honeycharters@hotmail.com
Website: www.honeycharters.com

VALDEZ

Population: 4,036

Mountains of the Chugach Range line the fjord at Port Valdez. (© Ralph & Leonor Barrett)

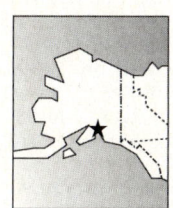

Located on Port Valdez (pronounced val-DEEZ), an estuary off Valdez Arm in Prince William Sound. Valdez is 115 air miles and 304 highway miles from Anchorage, 366 highway miles from Fairbanks. Valdez is the southern terminus of the Richardson Highway and the trans-Alaska pipeline.

Emergency Services: Alaska State Troopers, phone (907) 822-3263. **City Police, Fire Department** and **Ambulance,** emergency only phone 911. **Hospital,** Valdez Community, phone (907) 835-2249. **Maritime Search and Rescue,** dial 0 for Zenith 5555, toll free. Report oil spills to Dept. of Environmental Conservation, dial 0 and ask for Zenith 9300. **Fish and Wildlife Protection,** (907) 835-4307.

Visitor Information: The visitor information center is located at 200 Fairbanks Dr. (business office is at 200 Chenega St.). Write: Valdez Convention and Visitors Bureau, Box 1603-MP, Valdez 99686; or phone toll free 800-770-5954 or (907) 835-4636; fax (907) 835-4845; email info@valdezalaska.org; www.valdezalaska.org. Call for hours. Visitors may also check the community calendar at the Valdez Civic Center by phoning the hotline at (907) 835-3200.

Elevation: Sea level. **Climate:** Record high was 86°F in June 1997; record low -23°F in February 1968. Normal daily maximum in January, 27°F; daily minimum 17°F. Normal daily maximum in July, 62°F; daily minimum 48°F. Average snowfall in Valdez from October to May is 329.7 inches, or about 25 feet. (By comparison, Anchorage averages about 6 feet in that period.) New snowfall records were set in January 1990, with snowfall for one day at 47½ inches. Record monthly snowfall is 180 inches in February 1996. Windy (40 mph) in late fall. **Radio:** KCHU 770, AM, KVAK 1230 AM and KVAK 93.3 FM. **Television:** Many channels via cable and satellite. **Newspapers:** *Valdez Vanguard* (weekly) and *Valdez Star* (weekly).

Private Aircraft: Valdez, 3 miles east; elev. 120 feet; length 6,500 feet; asphalt; fuel 100LL, Jet B; attended. Valdez Airport is the site of the Alaska Cultural Center, home of the Jesse and Maxine Whitney Eskimo Museum. Magnificent collection of Alaskan trophy animal mounts, ivory carvings, Alaska Native artifacts, a film about the 1964 earthquake and much more. Small admission fee. Phone (907) 834-1690.

Situated in a majestic fjord, where the 5,000-foot-tall Chugach Mountains rise from Prince William Sound, Valdez is often called Alaska's "Little Switzerland." The city lies on the north shore of Port Valdez, an estuary named in 1790 by Spanish explorer Don Salvador Fidalgo for Antonio Valdes y Basan, a Spanish naval officer.

Valdez was established in 1897–98 as a port of entry for gold seekers bound for the Klondike goldfields. Thousands of stampeders arrived in Valdez to follow the All American Route to the Eagle mining district in Alaska's Interior, and from there up the Yukon River to Dawson City and the Klondike. The Valdez trail was an especially dangerous route, the first part of it leading over Valdez Glacier, where the early stampeders faced dangerous crevasses, snow-blindness and exhaustion.

Copper discoveries in the Wrangell Mountains north of Valdez in the early 1900s brought more development to Valdez, and conflict. A proposed railroad from tidewater to the rich Kennicott copper mines near McCarthy began a bitter rivalry between Valdez and Cordova for the railway line. The Copper River & Northwestern Railway eventually went to Cordova, but not before Valdez had started its own railroad

PRINCE WILLIAM SOUND • Valdez

Anna's Ptarmigan B&B

Huge Hot Breakfast
Super Clean Non-Smoking Rooms
Private & Semi-Private Baths
No Pets Please
Call or Write for brochure
Box 1104, Valdez, AK 99686
(907) 835-2202

Totem Inn
Hotel • Restaurant • Gift Shop

Hearty Alaskan Meals
Open at 5:00AM

Queen Beds

FISHING

Join Us During Your Alaskan Adventure

Alaskan Souvenirs
Gold Nuggets
Ivory Sculptures

Located Downtown Valdez on 144 East Egan
Call 907•835•4443
or write P.O. Box 648 • Valdez, Alaska 99686 • www.toteminn.com

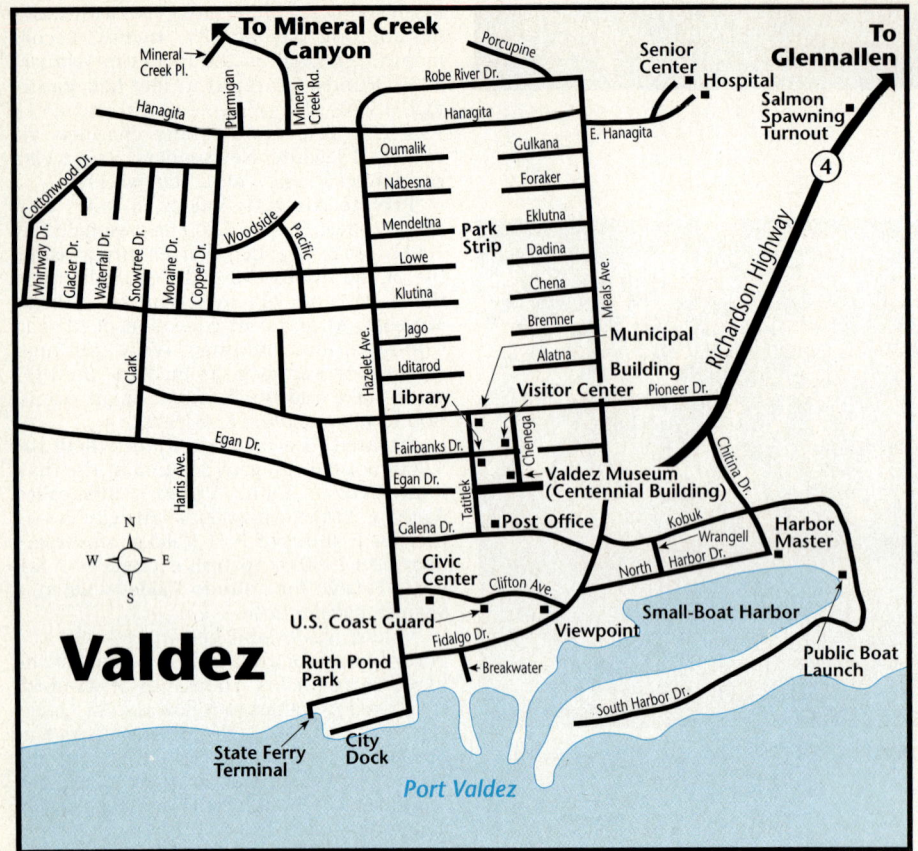

east of its present location, closer to the glacier. The 1964 Good Friday earthquake, the most destructive earthquake ever to hit southcentral Alaska, virtually destroyed Valdez. The quake measured 9.2 on the Richter scale and was centered in Prince William Sound. A series of local waves caused by massive underwater landslides swept over and engulfed the Valdez wharf, taking 33 people with it. Seismic action shook the downtown and residential areas with overwhelming power. Though much damage was sustained, only the waterfront was destroyed. After the quake the Army Corps of Engineers determined the town should be relocated as it was situated on unstable glacial remains. By late August 1964, reconstruction projects had been approved and relocation was under way. The last residents remaining at "old" Valdez moved to the new town in 1968.

Since its days as a port of entry for gold seekers, Valdez has been an important gateway to Interior Alaska. As the most northerly ice-free port in the Western Hemisphere, and connected by the Richardson Highway to the Alaska highway system, Valdez has evolved into a shipping center, offering the shortest link to much of interior Alaska for seaborne cargo.

Construction of the trans-Alaska pipeline began in 1974 and was completed in 1977. The 800-mile-long pipeline begins at Prudhoe Bay on the Arctic Ocean and ends at the marine terminal at Port Valdez, where it is fed by gravity into tanks or directly into waiting oil tankers. The first tanker load of oil shipped out of Valdez on Aug. 1, 1977. National attention was focused on Valdez and the pipeline when the oil tanker *Exxon Valdez* ran aground on Bligh Reef (some 30 miles from Valdez) in March 1989, causing an 11-million-gallon oil spill.

Valdez's economy depends on the oil industry, the Prince William Sound fishery, government and tourism. The city limits of Valdez comprise an area of 274 square miles and include all surrounding mountains to timberline. Valdez has long been known for its beautiful setting, with the Chugach Mountains rising behind the city and the

north. The Valdez railroad did not get very far: The only trace of its existence is an old hand-drilled railway tunnel at **Milepost V 14.9** on the Richardson Highway.

The old gold rush trail out of Valdez was developed into a sled and wagon road in the early 1900s. It was routed through Thompson Pass (rather than over the Valdez Glacier) by Captain Abercrombie of the U.S. Army, who was commissioned to connect Fort Liscum (a military post established in 1900 near the present-day location of the pipeline terminal) with Fort Egbert in Eagle. Colonel Wilds P. Richardson of the Alaska Road Commission further developed the wagon road, building the first automobile road from Valdez to Fairbanks which was completed in the early 1920s.

Old photos of Valdez show Valdez Glacier directly behind the town. This is because until 1964, Valdez was located about 4 miles

VALDEZ ADVERTISERS

ABC Liquors ....Ph. (907) 835-2579	Lakehouse B&B ....Ph. (907) 835-4752
Acres Kwick Trip ....Ph. (907) 835-3278	Lowe River Inn ....Ph. (907) 835-3695
Anadyr Adventures............Ph. (907) 835-2814	Lu-Lu Belle Glacier Wildlife
Anna's Ptarmigan B&B .....Ph. (907) 835-2202	Cruises ....Ph. (800) 411-0090
Aspen Hotels.....................Ph. (866) 483-7848	Majestic Tours....................Ph. (866) 282-2180
Bayside RV Park ....Ph. (888) 835-4425	One Call Does It All............Ph. (907) 835-4988
Bear Paw R.V. Park ....Ph. (907) 835-2530	Pangaea Adventures..........Ph. (800) 660-9637
Best of All B&B..................Ph. (907) 835-4524	Prince William Sound
Blessing House B&B..........Ph. (888) 853-5333	Community College ....Ph. (907) 834-8391
Brookside Inn ....Ph. (907) 835-9130	Prince William Sound
Calico Whale Quilt Shop....Ph. (907) 835-4263	Cruises & Tours............Ph. (800) 992-1297
Captain Jim's	Sea Otter RV Park ....Ph. (907) 835-2787
Campgrounds..............Ph. (907) 835-2282	Stan Stephens Glacier &
Chapel of the Sea ....See Ad	Wildlife Cruises............Ph. (866) 867-1297
Delsbrat Charters..............Ph. (907) 835-5935	Totem Inn ....Ph. (907) 835-4443
Downtown B&B Inn..........Ph. (800) 478-2791	Valdez Convention &
Eagle B&B ....Ph. (907) 835-3831	Visitors Bureau ....Ph. (800) 770-5954
Eagle's Rest RV Park..........Ph. (800) 553-7275	Valdez Drug & Photo ....Ph. (907) 835-4956
Era Helicopters..................Ph. (800) 843-1947	Valdez Heli-Camps............Ph. (907) 835-5898
Fu Kung ....Ph. (907) 835-5255	Valdez Museum ....Ph. (907) 835-2764
Harbor Landing	Valdez Prospector.............Ph. (907) 835-3858
General Store ....Ph. (907) 835-2331	Valdez Shuttle & Freight ...Ph. (907) 831-1105
Keystone Hotel ....Ph. (888) 835-0665	Valdez Tesoro ....Ph. (907) 835-5300
KVAK ....See Ad	Wild Roses By The Sea .....Ph. (907) 835-2930

small-boat harbor in front. The town has wide streets and open spaces, with the central residential district built around a park strip which runs from the business district almost to the base of the mountains behind the town.

Lodging & Services

Valdez has 8 motel/hotel facilities and numerous bed and breakfasts. You are advised to make reservations well in advance. Summer tourist season is also the peak work season, and accommodations fill up quickly. Services here include several restaurants and bars, grocery store, sporting goods stores, gift shops, gas stations, hardware, hair stylists, drugstore and pharmacy.

Best of All Bed and Breakfast. Downtown area, home with cathedral ceiling, Asian/Alaskan decor. Lots of windows provide view of mountains. Darkening blinds, TV/VCR in all rooms. Phone available in 2 suites with private baths. Queen/twin share bath. Full breakfast. Children welcome. Smoke-free. No pets. Open year-round. (907) 835-4524. www.akpub.com/best.com; email bestbb99686@yahoo.com. [ADVERTISEMENT]

Blessing House B & B near downtown Valdez, corner of 616 Meals/Dadina streets. "Your home away from home." Pet and smoke-free environment. Play piano or cook. Serve yourself continental. Single to king-sized beds. Rates $65–$85. Major credit cards. Reservations (907) 835-5333, 1-888-853-5333. www.blessinghouse.com/blessinghouse. Fax c/o (907) 835-4845 Attention: Blessing House. realhelp@alaska.net. [ADVERTISEMENT]

Downtown B & B Inn. Motel accommodations, 113 Galena Dr. Centrally located near small boat harbor, museum, ferry terminal, downtown shopping. View rooms, private and shared baths, coin-op laundry, TV and phones in rooms. Wheelchair accessible. Complimentary breakfast. Reasonable rates. Single, double, family rooms. Phone (800) 478-2791 or (907) 835-2791. E-mail: onen2rs@alaska.net. Internet: www.alaskaone.com/downinn/index.htm. See display ad this section. [ADVERTISEMENT]

Keystone Hotel. Located downtown (corner of Egan and Hazelet) within walking distance to ferry terminal and shops. 106 rooms with private baths, cable TV, phones, nonsmoking or smoking, wheelchair access, coin-op laundry. Complimentary continental breakfast. Enjoy our casual seafood grill for dinner. Comfortable, clean rooms at reasonable rates. (888) 835-0665. Email: keyston@alaska.net. [ADVERTISEMENT]

Totem Inn. Motel and restaurant. Open for breakfast at 5 A.M. Famous for chicken fried steak and reindeer sausage. Lunches include burgers, salad bar and more. Fresh seafood specialties and family favorite dinners affordably priced make our restaurant the "locals' choice." Remodeled rooms include private baths, queen beds, TV, phone, fridge and microwave, in-room coffee pots. Reservations suggested. Located downtown Valdez. Close to harbor where the Richardson meets Egan Drive. Open year round. RV parking available. Phone (907) 835-4443, fax (907) 834-4430. Email: toteminn@alaska.net. [ADVERTISEMENT]

Camping

There are 6 private RV parks with hook-ups near the small-boat harbor. Dump station and diesel at Valdez Tesoro and Capt'n Joe's Tesoro. Dump station at Bear Paw R.V. Park, Bayside RV Park and Eagle's Rest RV Park for registered guests.

The nearest public campground is **Valdez Glacier Campground**, located 3.4 miles east of downtown via the Richardson Highway, then 2.3 miles north via Airport Road. This city campground (operated by Captain Jim's) is situated in a wooded area; 101 sites suitable for any length RV or tent camping, day-use picnic areas, firepits, tables, litter barrels, water and toilets; 15-day limit, $10 fee charged.

There is also camping at **Allison Point.** Head out of town on the Richardson Highway and turn on Dayville Road at **Milepost V 2.9.** Signed day-use parking (fee charged) and overnight RV parking ($10 fee), located from approximately Mile 4.3 to Mile 5.3 on this public road, is operated by Captain

We cover your creature comforts in Valdez.

The Aspen Hotel in downtown Valdez is the natural choice for those looking for the perfect combination of outdoor adventure and creature comfort. We provide the finest lodging amenities, comfort and service along Prince William Sound.

- 104 spacious rooms
- Complimentary continental breakfast
- Exercise room
- Guest laundry
- Swimming pool
- Business center with internet access
- Free local calls
- VCR, coffee maker, refrigerator and microwave in room

100 MEALS AVE, VALDEZ, AK 99686 » 1-866-GUEST4U
WWW.ASPENHOTELSAK.COM

Wild Roses By The Sea
BED & BREAKFAST RETREAT

Ocean View • Private Baths • Jacuzzi • Close to Downtown & Ferry

By Reservation Only • (907) 835-2930 • P.O. Box 3396, Valdez, AK 99686
rose@ByTheSea.alaska.net • www.bytheseaalaskabb.com

DOWNTOWN B&B INN

Close to Small Boat Harbor, Ferry Terminal and Downtown Shopping

Motel Accommodations
Private and Shared Baths
View Rooms

Reasonable Rates • Families Welcome • Complimentary Breakfast
113 GALENA DR. • P.O. BOX 184, VALDEZ, AK 99686
See log ad under visitor services

(800) 478-2791 • (907) 835-2791 • Fax (907) 835-5406

PRINCE WILLIAM SOUND • Valdez

Jim's. Area has 75 sites, pay phone, wheelchair access and a free dump station. Dayville Road ends at the pipeline marine terminal at the end of the road (Mile 5.7). ▲

Bear Paw R.V. Park, centrally located on scenic North Harbor Drive overlooking the boat harbor, puts you within easy walking

distance of museum, shops, restaurants, entertainment, charter boats—no need to unhook and drive to grocery stores or points of interest. Full, partial or no hookups; immaculate private restrooms with hot, unmetered showers. Dump station and coin-operated launderette with irons and ironing boards available for guests. Also available, for adults only: waterfront full-hookup RV sites with cable TV, guest lounge, computer modem access line. Very nice, quiet wooded adult tent sites, some platforms, among the salmonberries on Porcupine Hill. Tables, fire pots and freezer available. Campfire wood for sale. Fuel discount coupons available. Let us book your glacier tour with Prince William Sound Cruises & Tours at the reservations desk in our spacious office lounge. We also book raft trips and flightseeing. Don't miss the Bear Paw Trading Post Gift Shop. Advance reservations recommended: (907) 835-2530.

(Bear Paw does fill up!) The coffee pot is always on at Bear Paw. Let us know if you're coming in on the evening ferry and we'll be there to help you get parked. Email: bpawcamp@alaska.net. Internet: www.bearpawvaldez.com. See our large display ad this section. [ADVERTISEMENT] ▲

Eagle's Rest RV Park, the friendliest RV park in downtown Valdez, offers you Good

Sam Park service with a smile. Let our help-

Eagle's Rest R.V. Park & Cabins

Valdez Alaska
P.O. Box 610 • 139 East Pioneer
Valdez, Alaska 99686
(907) 835-2373
Fax (907) 835-5267

ACOA • Good Sam Park • VISA • MasterCard

Toll Free 1-800-553-7275

Full Hookups • 50/30/20 AMP • Valet Parking
Pull Thrus • Tent Camping • E-Mail/Fax • Laundromat
Cabin Rentals • Hot/Unlimited Showers
Walk-in Freezer • Fish Cleaning Table • Hiking Trails
Ice Available • RV Dump Station

Friendly... Full Service RV Park

Complete Bookings For:
- Columbia/Mears Glacier Tours
- Helicopter Flightseeing
- Alyeska Pipeline Tours
- Rafting Adventures
- Fishing Charters
And Much More!

Capt'n Joe's Tesoro
Gas • Diesel • Propane
Located right in the park

1-800-553-7275
www.eaglesrestrv.com
rvpark@alaska.net

Eagle's Rest R.V. Park & Cabin Rentals
"Stay with us and leave feeling like part of the family!"

ful staff take care of all your bookings on cruises, tours and charters. Enjoy the beautiful panoramic view of our mountains and glaciers right off our front porch! We also can let you know where the hottest fishing spots are or the quietest walking trails! Fish-cleaning table and freezer available. Self-contained rental cabins available. Capt'n Joe's Tesoro next door offers gas, diesel, propane; potable water, sewer dump. Parking with us puts you within walking distance of our museum, gift shops, banks and even the largest grocery store on our same block. Shuttle service for glacier cruises. No charge to wash your RV at your-site. Phone us for reservations, 1-800-553-7275 or (907) 835-2373. Fax (907) 835-KAMP (835-5267). Email: rvpark@alaska.net. Internet: www.eaglerestrv.com. Stay with us and leave feeling like family. See display ad this section. [ADVERTISEMENT] ▲

Transportation

Air: Daily scheduled service via Alaska Airlines and Era Aviation. Air taxi and helicopter services available.

Ferry: Scheduled state ferry service to Cordova, Whittier and Seward. Phone (907) 835-4436. Reservations are a must!

Bus: Regularly scheduled service to Anchorage and Fairbanks, summer only.

Taxi: One local taxi service.

Car Rental: One company offers car rentals; available at airport terminal.

Highway: The Richardson Highway extends north from Valdez to the Glenn Highway and the Alaska Highway. See the RICHARDSON HIGHWAY section.

Attractions

Sightsee Valdez Boat Harbor. The waterfront in Valdez is very visitor friendly, with a promenade, picnic tables and public restrooms. Restaurants and shops line the other side of North Harbor Drive. There are canoe and kayak rentals available for those who want a close-up view of the harbor or sound. Dock Point Park, located at the east end of the boat harbor, has picnic tables, a restroom and a beautiful 1-mile hiking/walking trail with scenic overlooks of the Port of Valdez. The combination gravel and boardwalk trail provides easy access for people of all ability levels.

Visit Valdez Museum, located at 217 Egan Dr. On display outside the museum is an oil pipeline "pig" and a lifeboat. The

"pig" is used to clean wax deposits from inside pipeline walls (wax is a natural component/by-product of crude oil that collects on the pipeline walls and restricts flow).

Life Boat #4 is from the cruise ship MS *Prinsendam*, which caught fire in the Gulf of Alaska on Oct. 5, 1980. Most of the 329 passengers and 190 crew forced to abandon ship were transferred to the supertanker *Williamsburg* and ferried to Valdez (immediately increasing the city's population by 10 percent). The 80 passengers in Life Boat #4 were adrift for 12 hours in the Gulf before being rescued by the U.S. Coast Guard.

Inside the museum, exhibits depict lifestyles and workplaces from 1898 to present. Interpretive exhibits explain the impact of the gold rush, the 1964 earthquake, the construction of the trans-Alaska oil pipeline and the 1989 *Exxon Valdez* oil spill cleanup. Visitors can touch Columbia Glacier ice and feel the luxurious softness of a sea otter pelt. The museum's William A. Egan Commons provides a showcase setting for a restored 1907 Ahrens steam fire engine, models of antique aircraft, and the original Cape Hinchinbrook lighthouse lens. Valdez Museum is open year-round: 9 A.M. to 6 P.M. Monday–Saturday and 8 A.M. to 5 P.M. Sundays during summer months (May to September); Monday through Friday 1–5 P.M. and Saturday noon to 4 P.M. during off-season (October to April). Children free; $3 for adults (18 and older); $2.50 for seniors, $2 for youth 14-18. Phone (907) 835-2764 for more information, or visit www.alaska.net/~vldzmuse/index.html.

Valdez Museum Annex Warehouse. Open 9-4 daily June 1 through August 31. The centerpiece of the new facility is the Historic Old Town Model, a 1:20 scale model showing Valdez as it appeared in 1963, just prior to the earthquake. The model is surrounded by exhibits interpreting this period of time and an interactive Earthquake Exhibit. Admission $1.50 for adults over 18. Located at 436 South Hazelet Street, across from Ruth Pond.

Special Events. Valdez has several special events. In summer, there's Gold Rush Days (August 6–10, 2003), a celebration that includes a parade, contests, game night and town fish fry. During Gold Rush Days, cancan girls peruse local establishments and

---

One Call Does It All

Reservation Service
(907) 835-4988

- Lodging • Glacier Cruises
- Halibut & Salmon Charters
- Helicopter & Flightseeing
- Rafting • Kayaking
- Car Rentals

Also: Cordova, Kennicott and Denali National Park

Major Credit Cards Accepted
Fax: (907) 835-5865
P.O. Box 2197-MP, Valdez, Alaska 99686
e-mail: onecall@alaska.net

OUTFITTING THE ALASKAN LIFESTYLE

Complete lines of fishing tackle, camping & clothing.

"The Best Shopping Experience in Valdez"

Open Late
7 Days a Week

(907) 835-3858

141 Galena Street
behind the Valdez Post Office

HISTORIC MOMENTS
Valdez Museum
WHERE YOU CAN DISCOVER THE PAST

- Admire a fully operational 1886 Handpumped Fire Engine
- Check out a piece of the hull of the Exxon Valdez tanker
- Belly-up to the historic Pinzon Bar

907-835-2764 • vldzmuse@alaska.net
www.alaska.net/~vldzmuse/index.html

Valdez Museum Annex WAREHOUSE

Visit the Historic Old Town Model
And So MUCH MORE...

217 Egan Drive   Valdez, AK 99686

VALDEZ TESORO

Corner Of Meals & Egan, Downtown Valdez

- GAS, DIESEL, PROPANE
- 24 HR. CARD LOCK PUMPS

- Full line of Tires
- Tire repair
- ASE certified mechanics
- FREE dump station with fill-up

Phone (907) 835-5300

CAR WASH   **TESORO**

Real Value. Real Easy.

a jail is pulled through town by "deputies" who arrest citizens without beards.

Valdez also is known for its winter events. In March, there's the Ice Climbing & Film Festival (March 7–9, 2003), where spectators can watch world-class climbers make their way up Bridal Veil Falls, and there's the Mayor's Cup Cross-country Snowmachine Race (March 8, 2003), a 200-mile, cross-country race over a variety of terrain. In April, there's the King of the Hill international snowboard competition (April 1–11, 2003); the Chugach Mountain Festival & World Free Skiing Championship (April 4–20, 2003); and the Mountain Man Snowmobile Hill Climb Competition (April 4–6, 2003).

Contact the Valdez Convention and Visitors Bureau for more information and to confirm dates; phone (907) 835-4636. For more information on snowmobile events in the Valdez area, contact the Valdez Snowmobile Club, P.O. Box 3689, Valdez, AK 99686; www.valdezsnow.com.

See the Trans-Alaska Pipeline Terminal. The Alyeska Marine Terminal of the trans-Alaska oil pipeline is across the bay from the city of Valdez. While entry to the terminal is restricted, visitors can drive out to the entrance of the terminal, where there is a bronze sculpture commemorating the efforts of the men and women who built the pipeline. Dedicated in September 1980, the sculpture was created by Californian Malcolm Alexander. It is composed of 5 figures representing various crafts and skills employed in the construction project. The work is the focal point of a small park from which visitors can watch tankers loading Alaska crude oil at the terminal. A small parking lot accommodates about 30 cars, and a series of signs explains the pipeline and terminal operations.

From downtown Valdez, drive 6.9 miles out the Richardson Highway, turn south on Dayville Road, and drive 5.7 miles to the end of the road at the marine terminal.

Solomon Gulch Hatchery offers a self-guided tour and views of thousands of spawning salmon in season. Drive out the Richardson Highway 6.9 miles and turn south on Dayville Road; the hatchery is located at Mile 3.7. There are also views of Solomon Gulch Falls and the Solomon Gulch Hydroelectric project. (The trailhead for a hike to Solomon Gulch is at Mile 4.7 Dayville Road.)

Crooked Creek Salmon Spawning Viewing Area. Drive out the Richardson Highway about a mile from downtown to see salmon spawning in Crooked Creek. A viewing platform offers close-up look at spawning pink and chum salmon mid-June to early September. Or for an underwater view, take a look at the Fish Cam inside the U.S. Forest Service information station. The information station, open Memorial Day to Labor Day, has informational exhibits and educational handouts.

Across the highway from the viewing area are intertidal wetlands known locally as "Duck Flats." Watch for migrating waterfowl here from late April to mid-May and in October. Nesting birds in summer. This is a game sanctuary; no shooting is allowed. Good spot for photos.

Visit the Original Valdez Townsite, located 4 miles from downtown Valdez via the Richardson Highway. Watch for memorial on your right, 0.4 mile south of the highway on a side road. There are 2 plaques set in a foundation from "old" Valdez. One plaque lists the names of those residents of Valdez and Chenega who were killed in the Good Friday Earthquake on March 27, 1964, which destroyed the original townsite of Valdez.

See Waterfalls. From downtown Valdez, drive out the Richardson Highway 17.4 miles to see **Horsetail Falls.** A short distance beyond Horsetail Falls is **Bridal Veil Falls.** Both are favorite photo stops. There are also waterfalls visible from town.

Go flightseeing, and see Columbia Glacier, spectacular Prince William Sound and the surrounding Chugach Mountains from the air. There are 3 flightseeing charter services in Valdez: 1 fixed-wing, 1 floatplane, and 1 helicopter; see ads in this section.

Era Helicopters Flightseeing Tours. Offering one-hour fully narrated tours of Prince William Sound and the Columbia Glacier. Highlight your tour with a glacier landing. Local Phone: (907) 835-2595 or 1-800-843-1947. 6160 Carl Brady Drive, Anchorage, AK 99502. www.eraaviation.com. fltsg@eraaviation.com. [ADVERTISEMENT]

Valdez Consortium Library, located on Fairbanks Street, has an extensive Alaska Historical & Archive section, as well as many

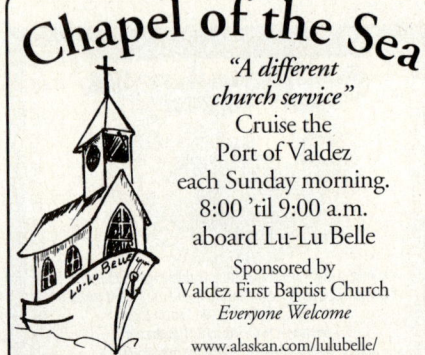

Alaska videos which can be viewed at the library. It also features a magazine and paperback exchange for travelers; a trade is appreciated but not required. The library has music listening booths, public computers, typewriters and a photocopier. Wheelchair accessible. Open Monday and Friday 10 A.M. to 6 P.M., Tuesday through Thursday 10 A.M. to 8 P.M., Saturday noon to 5 P.M. and Sunday 1–5 P.M. when school is in session.

Visit Prince William Sound Community College, located at 303 Lowe St. Two huge wooden carvings on campus (1 located in front of the dorms on Pioneer Street), by artist Peter Toth, are dedicated to the Indians of America. The College is home to an extensive display of Old Town Valdez and Gold Rush-era photographs. The 11th annual **Last Frontier Theatre Conference,** sponsored by the college, is scheduled for June 20–29, 2003, at the Valdez Convention and Civic Center. In attendance are Edward Albee, event founder, and visiting playwrights and directors. Past visiting playwrights at the nationally recognized conference have included Horton Foote, Arthur Miller and August Wilson. Events include daily play labs, panels, workshops, evening entertainment and a Saturday Night Gala. For more information, contact PWSCC, P.O. Box 97, Valdez, AK 99686; (907) 834-1612; vntc@uaa.alaska.edu; www.uaa.alaska.edu/pwscc.

See Boom Town, the historical comedy/musical review about Valdez. Performed in summer Tuesday–Saturday at 8 P.M. at 112 Egan Drive in the big tent next to the Pipeline Club. Tickets are available at Eagle's Rest RV Park. For more information: P.O. Box 2903, Valdez, AK 99686; phone (907) 835-3505; www.boomtowntheshow.com.

Drive Mineral Creek Road. A 5.5-mile drive behind town leading northwest through the breathtaking alpine scenery along Mineral Creek. *Drive carefully!* This is a narrow road; conditions depend on weather and how recently the road has been graded. Bears are frequently sighted here. To reach Mineral Creek Road drive to the end of Hazelet Street toward the mountains and turn left on Hanagita then right on Mineral Creek Road. Excellent view of the city from the water tower hill just to the right at the tart of Mineral Creek Road.

Take a boat tour to see Columbia Glacier, second largest tidewater glacier in North America, Shoup Glacier and other Prince William Sound attractions. Columbia Glacier, in Columbia Bay 28 miles southwest of Valdez, has become one of Alaska's best-known attractions. See ads in this section.

Stan Stephens Glacier & Wildlife Cruises. Explore the calm waters of Prince William Sound from Valdez. Cruise to Columbia and/or Meares glaciers. View our amazing wildlife—otters, sea lions, puffins, whales and more. Meals included. Come experience "our" Alaska. Box 1297, Valdez, AK 99686; toll-free (866) 867-1297; fax (907) 835-3765; www.stanstephenscruises.com. [ADVERTISEMENT]

Steller sea lions at a Prince William Sound rookery. (© Lynn Ledbetter)

Glacier Wildlife Cruises/Lu-Lu Belle. The motor yacht, *Lu-Lu Belle* is probably the cleanest, plushest tour vessel you will ever see! They cater to adult travelers. Unruly-unattended children will be sold to Pirates. When you come aboard and see all the teak, mahogany and oriental rugs, you will understand why Captain Fred Rodolf asks you to wipe your shoes before boarding. The *Lu-Lu Belle* has wide walk-around decks, thus assuring everyone ample opportunity for unobstructed viewing and photography, and is equipped with 110-volt outlets for your battery chargers. Captain Fred has logged over 3530 Columbia Glacier cruises since 1979. He will personally guide and narrate every cruise. The Columbia Glacier wildlife cruise of Prince William Sound is awesome! The wildlife that is seen on the cruises will vary, depending on the time of year and the time of day, as the *Lu-Lu Belle* cruises from Valdez to the Columbia Glacier on the calm, protected waters of the Sound. Boarding time is 1:45 P.M. each day from mid-May through Labor Day. This "5 hour" cruise may vary in duration as much as an hour because Captain Fred may run offshore in search of whales and other wildlife. Cost is $80 per person (with a cash discount price of $75). During the busier part of the season, an 8 A.M. cruise boarding at 7:45 is added each day except Sunday. The A.M. tour is $5 less because they cannot be as flexible with their time. On the cruise the crew prepares fresh-baked goods in the galley. Friendliness and gracious hospitality on a beautiful yacht with small intimate groups is the reason why people refer to the *Lu-Lu Belle* as the "limousine of Prince William Sound." On Sunday morning, the *Lu-Lu Belle* becomes the "Chapel of the Sea" from 8 to 9 A.M. Everyone is welcome. At the *Lu-Lu Belle* office there is also the *Little Lu-Lu* RV Park that can accommodate RVs up to 28 feet with full hookups. Our best advertisement is our happy guests. Join us for an extra-special day and find out why Captain Fred refers to Switzerland as the "Valdez of Europe" ! Phone 1-800-411-0090 or (907) 835-5141.

[ADVERTISEMENT]

Prince William Sound Cruises & Tours. Join Prince William Sound Cruises & Tours

as we explore the wonders of Prince William Sound. Experience many tidewater glaciers, including the famous Columbia Glacier, or the glaciers of Harriman Fjord. Explore glacier-carved fjords draped with cascading waterfalls and spectacular alpine glaciers. Wildlife abounds as you watch for sea otters, sea lions, seals, porpoise, orca and giant humpback whales, plus a wide variety of birds. Our experienced knowledgeable captains and crew are your guides as you travel aboard our custom sightseeing vessels complete with heated indoor seating, oversized windows, and wrap-around outside viewing decks. All cruises are fully narrated and include a delicious meal. Daily departures from Whittier and Valdez, call toll free 1-800-992-1297 or 907-835-4731. Visit us on the web at www.princewilliamsound.com.

[ADVERTISEMENT]

Sail, raft and kayak trips of Prince William Sound, Keystone Canyon and surrounding rivers are available. State marine parks in the Valdez area include Shoup Bay, Jack Bay and Sawmill Bay. Accessible mainly or only by water, these parks offer camping on tent platforms, fire rings and latrines. They are popular with fishermen and sea kayakers. For more information, contact the Dept. of Natural Resources, phone (907) 269-8400, or visit www.alaskastateparks.org.

Go Hiking. A popular short day hike is to Gold Creek, 3.5 miles from Valdez. Other area hikes include Keystone Canyon (2.6 miles), Dock Point Trail (1 mile) and Solomon Gulch Trail (3.8 miles). A 10-mile hike along Valdez Arm to Shoup Bay State Marine Park starts at the Mineral Creek trailhead in town. Public-use cabins are available at Shoup Bay, which is noted for its views of Shoup Glacier and its large kittiwake colony. Stop by the Visitor Information Center for maps and descriptions.

Fish a Derby. Valdez holds halibut (May–Sept.), silver salmon (August) and pink salmon (July) derbies every year, with cash prizes awarded to the first through third place winners for all 3 derbies daily, weekly and overall. For further information, contact the Valdez Chamber of Commerce at (907) 835-2330.

AREA FISHING: Valdez Arm supports the largest sport fishery in Prince William Sound. Important species include pink salmon, coho (silver) salmon, halibut, rockfish and Dolly Varden. Charter boats are available in Valdez. A hot fishing spot near Valdez and accessible by road is the **Allison Point** fishery created by the Solomon Gulch Hatchery, which produces major pink and silver salmon returns annually. Turn off the Richardson Highway at **Milepost V 2.9.** It is one of the largest pink salmon fisheries in the state. Pink salmon returns are best in odd years, but with hatchery production good pink runs are anticipated every year. Pinks average 3–5 lbs., from late June to early August; silvers from 6–10 lbs., late July into September.

Discover Prince William Sound From Whittier and Valdez!

Join Prince William Sound Cruises & Tours as we explore the wonders of Prince William Sound. Experience famous Columbia Glacier, the largest tidewater glacier in Southcentral Alaska. Explore glacier-carved fjords draped with cascading waterfalls and spectacular alpine glaciers. Watch for sea otters, sea lions, seals, porpoise, orca and giant humpback whales, plus a variety of birds. Our experienced, knowledgeable captains and crew are your guides as you travel aboard our modern vessels complete with heated indoor seating, oversized windows, and outside viewing decks. All cruises are fully narrated and include a delicious meal at no extra charge.

Call Today for reservations! Toll-Free
800-992-1297

In Valdez 907-835-4731
P.O. Box 1297
Valdez, AK 99686

In Anchorage 907-277-2131
513 W. 4th Avenue
Anchorage, AK 99501

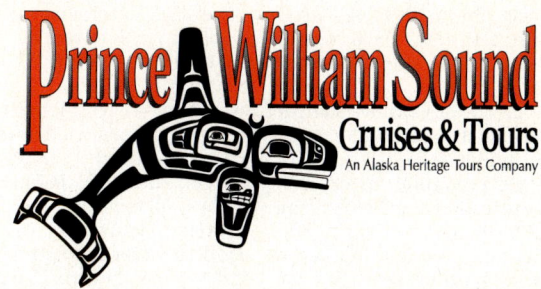

www.princewilliamsound.com

PRINCE WILLIAM SOUND • Cordova

CORDOVA

Population: 2,454

Hikers enjoy the view from Heney Ridge at Cordova. (© Rich Reid, Colors of Nature)

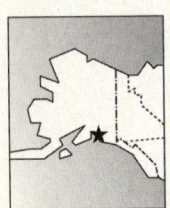

Located on the southeast shore of Orca Inlet on the east side of Prince William Sound. **Emergency Services: Alaska State Troopers,** phone (907) 424-7331, emergency phone 911. **Police, Fire Department, Ambulance,** emergency only phone 911; police department business calls, phone (907) 424-6100. **Hospital,** phone (907) 424-8000.

Visitor Information: Chamber of Commerce, 404 1st Street; phone (907) 424-7260 or write Box 99, Cordova, AK 99574. email: cchamber@ctcak.net. Web site: www.cordovachamber.com.

Chugach National Forest Cordova Ranger District office is located at 612 2nd Street in the original federal building for the town of Cordova, built in 1925. Natural history display in 2nd floor Interpretive Center. The USFS office is next to the old courtroom and jail. USFS personnel can provide information on trails, cabins and other activities on national forest lands. Open weekdays from 8 A.M. to 5 P.M. Write P.O. Box 280, Cordova, AK 99574, or phone (907) 424-7661; www.fs.fed.us/r10/chugach/cordova.

Elevation: Sea level to 400 feet. **Climate:** Average temperature in July is 65°F, in January 21°F. Average annual precipitation is 167 inches. During the winter of 1998-99, Cordova had almost 200 inches of snow, the largest amount since the record-breaking winter of 1971-72, when 275 inches fell. Prevailing winds are easterly at about 4 knots. **Radio:** KLAM-AM 1450 (country), KCHU-FM (National Public Radio), KCDV-FM 100.9 (The Eagle). **Television:** Cable. **Newspaper:** Cordova Times (weekly).

Private Aircraft: Merle K. "Mudhole" Smith Airport, Mile 12.1 Copper River Highway; elev. 42 feet; length 7,500 feet; asphalt; attended. Cordova Municipal (city airfield), 0.9 mile east; elev. 12 feet; length 1,900 feet; gravel; fuel 100, 100LL; unattended. Eyak Lake seaplane base, 0.9 mile east.

History: It was the Spanish explorer Don Salvador Fidalgo who named the adjacent water Puerto Cordoba in 1790. The town was named Cordova by Michael J. Heney, builder of the Copper River & Northwestern Railway. By 1889, the town had grown into a fish camp and cannery site. A post office was established in 1906. Cordova was incorporated in 1909.

The town was chosen as the railroad terminus and ocean shipping port for copper ore shipped by rail from the Kennecott mines. The railroad and town prospered until 1938 when the mine closed.

Commercial fishing in Cordova, source of the famous Copper River Red salmon, has now supplanted mining as the basis of the town's economy. The fishing fleet can be seen at Cordova harbor, home port of the MV *Bartlett* and the USCG cutter *Sycamore*.

The fishing and canning season for salmon runs from about May to September, with red, king and silver (coho) salmon taken from the Copper River area, chum, red and pink salmon from Prince William Sound. Black cod, crab and shrimp season runs during winter.

Lodging & Services

Accommodations at 2 motels, a hotel, several inns and bed and breakfasts, a condominium and 2 lodges (one on Whitshed Road and one located 2.2 miles from downtown on Orca Road). Cordova has several eating spots, a laundromat, a supermarket, a bookstore and other shops.

There are 2 banks in town: First National Bank of Anchorage and Wells Fargo. Local

CORDOVA ADVERTISERS

Alaska River Rafters	Ph. (800) 776-1864
Alaskan Hotel, Bar & Liquor Store	Ph. (907) 424-3299
Bear's Den Cabins	Ph. (907) 424-7168
Cordova Air Service, Inc.	Ph. (907) 424-3289
Cordova Auto Rentals	Ph. (907) 424-5982
Cordova Chamber of Commerce	Ph. (907) 424-7260
Cordova Coastal Outfitters	Ph. 800) 357-5145
Cordova Lighthouse Inn	Ph. (907) 424-7080
Cordova Outboard, Inc.	Ph. (907) 424-3220
Cordova Rose Lodge	Ph. (907) 424-7673
Cordova Telephone Co-op	611 2nd St.
Laura's	Ph. (907) 424-3144
Northern Lights Inn, The.	Ph. (907) 424-5356
Orca Adventure Lodge	Ph. (907) 424-7249
Orca Book & Sound	Ph. (907) 424-5305
Powder House Bar and Restaurant	Ph. (907) 424-3529
Prince William Motel	Ph. (888) 796-6835
Prince William Sound Science Center	Ph. (907) 424-5800
Reluctant Fisherman Inn	Ph. (907) 424-3272

merchants take cash and checks, but some do not take credit cards.

Short-term and long-term parking available in designated areas in the harbor area. For parking permits contact the Cordova Police Department, (907) 424-6100.

The small boat harbor has 850 slips available. Contact the Harbormaster for more information prior to arrival. The Harbormaster's office on Nicholoff has free tide books and other information. The office is open 8 A.M. to 5 P.M. weekdays; phone (907) 424-6400 or visit their website at www.ctcak.net/~cordovaharbor.

Cordova Library, located adjacent the museum in the Centennial Building on 1st Street, is open 10 A.M.–8 P.M. Tuesday through Friday, 1–5 P.M. Saturday; phone (907) 424-6667; www.cordovalibrary.org.

The Bidarki Recreation Center has a weight room, showers and exercise facility. It is located in the old city hall and jail at 2nd and Council. Phone (907) 424-7282.

Bob Korn Memorial Swimming Pool is located on Railroad Avenue, next to the police station at the head of Nicholoff. The indoor Olympic-sized pool offers lap swim, family swim, exercise classes and lessons. Open year-round (closed in May for maintenance). Phone (907) 424-7200 for pool hours and programs. Admission is $5/adults, $3/youth or senior, $12/family.

The historic Skater's Cabin on Eyak Lake is available for rent from the city. The rustic cabin has a woodstove and outhouse. The fee is $25 per night. Contact Bidarki Recreation Center, phone (907) 424-7282.

The U.S. Forest Service maintains 17 cabins in the Cordova district. Three are accessible by trail, the rest by boat or plane. For current fees, reservations and information, phone 1-877-444-6777, or visit www.reserveusa.com.

Camping

Cordova has one campground, Odiak Camper Park, operated by the city. The camper park, located on Whitshed Road next to the auto wrecking yard, is a flat gravel site with 24 RV spaces. Free shower tokens are available for paying campers. Contact Cordova's city hall; phone (907) 424-6200. ▲

Transportation

Cordova is accessible only by plane or boat.

Air: Scheduled service via Alaska Airlines and Era Aviation.

Ferry: The Alaska Marine Highway system ferries connect Cordova with Valdez, Whittier and Seward. Phone (907) 424-7333.

Taxi: Local service available.

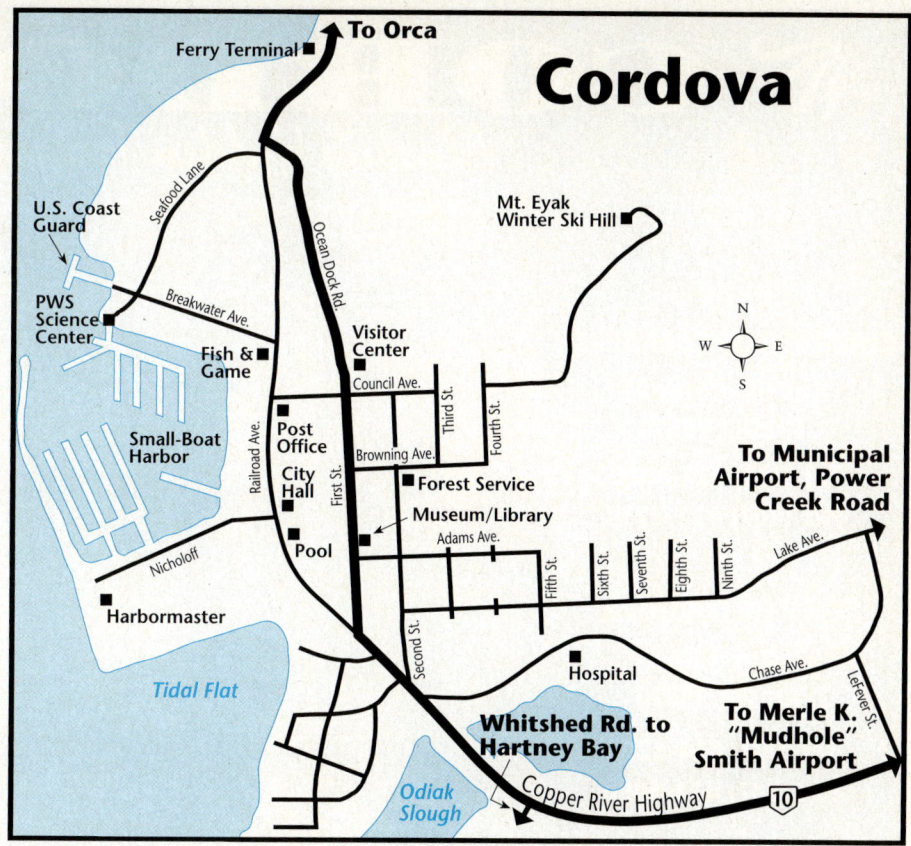

Car Rental: Available locally.

Highways: The Alaska state highway system does not connect to Cordova. The Copper River Highway leads 48 miles east and north of Cordova, ending at the Million Dollar Bridge and Childs Glacier. (See "Copper River Highway" on page 642.)

Private Boats: Cordova has an 850-slip boat harbor serving recreational boaters as well as the commercial fishing fleet. Berth arrangements may be made by contacting the harbormaster's office at (907) 424-6400 or on VHF Channel 16.

Attractions

Take a walking tour. A one-hour audio-taped, self-guided walking tour of downtown Cordova is available for rent from the

---

CORDOVA AUTO RENTALS, INC.
907-424-5982
AT THE MAIN AIRPORT
www.ptialaska.net/~cars

Cordova Outboard, Inc.
SALES and SERVICE
MerCruiser and OMC Stern Drives
Johnson Outboards
Honda Power Equipment
CARQUEST AUTO PARTS
William T. Fisher — Phone (907) 424-3220
Box 960 — Cordova, Alaska 99574

POWDER HOUSE
Bar and Restaurant
Homemade Soup, Sandwiches and Sushi
Seasonal Seafood and Barbecues
Mile 2.1 Copper River Highway
On the Original Site of Copper River R.R. Powder House
Karaoke
Folk
Bluegrass and
Country Music
FOOD TO GO • (907) 424-3529
Join us on the deck overlooking Eyak Lake

The Northern Nights Inn

Offering you charm and comfort combined with value.

➤ Private Entrance, Bath, Phone
➤ Clean, Spacious, View Rooms
➤ Kitchens, TV/VCR, Laundry, Freezer

P.O. Box 1564, Cordova, AK 99574
(907) 424-5356 • Fax (907) 424-3291

northernnightsinn@hotmail.com

Warm, Friendly Alaskan Hospitality
Prince William Motel
16 Comfortable guest rooms equipped with phones, TV's, Microwave, fridge, and coffee makers • Kitchenettes available
Coin-op laundry • Store

Dan & Martha Nichols, Proprietors
2nd & Council • Box 908, Cordova, AK 99574
(907) 424-3201 • FAX (907) 424-2260 • e-mail: pwmotel@yahoo.com
Reservations only 1-888-PW MOTEL (796-6835)

CORDOVA
Alaska's Hidden Treasure

CORDOVA CHAMBER OF COMMERCE
Box 99, Cordova
Alaska 99574
Tel (907) 424-7260
Fax (907) 424-7259

CITY OF CORDOVA
Box 1210
Alaska 99574
Tel (907) 424-6200
Fax (907) 424-6000

www.cordovachamber.com   email: cchamber@ctcak.net

CORDOVA RESTAURANTS
- Homeport Gallery
- Powder House
- The Picnic Basket
- Cordova Light House Inn

ALASKA RIVER RAFTERS
www.alaskarafters.com
info@alaskarafters.com
907.424.7238
Toll free 800.776.1864
Box 2233, Cordova, AK 99574

Cordova Auto Rentals
907.424.5982
cars@ctcak.net
www.ptialaska.net/~cars
Box 1329, Cordova, AK 99574

CORDOVA TELEPHONE CO-OP
611 Second Street
www.ctcak.net
PO Box 459, Cordova, AK 99574

CORDOVA WIRELESS COMMUNICATIONS, INC.
(907) 424-2300
Toll Free (888) 240-7860
Your Local Cellular Service Provider
621 2nd Street, Cordova, AK
A subsidiary of Cordova Telephone Cooperative

CORDOVA COASTAL OUTFITTERS
www.cdvcoastal.com
cordovacoastal@ctcak.net
907.424.7424 or Toll free 800.357.5145
PO BOX 1834, CORDOVA, AK 99574

Cordova-Whittier-Valdez
1-800-642-0066
Alaska's Marine Highway
www.alaska.gov/ferry

ORCA ADVENTURE LODGE
907.424.7249
Toll free 1.866.424.6722
orca@ctcak.net
www.orcaadventurelodge.com
Box 2105, Cordova, AK 99574

CORDOVA AIR SERVICE
907.424.3289
Toll free in Alaska
800.424.7608
BOX 528, CORDOVA, AK 99574

CORDOVA ROSE LODGE Alaska
www.cordovarose.com
info@cordovarose.com
Box 1494, Cordova AK 99574

Bear's Den Cabins
* On Eyak River
* Boat rentals
* Awesome Fishing
Call 907-424-7168

Prince William Sound Science Center
907.424.5800
PO Box 705, Cordova, AK 99574

Alaskan HOTEL & BAR
- AND -
Alaskan LIQUOR STORE
907.424.3299
Box 484, Cordova, AK 99574

CORDOVA CHAMBER OF COMMERCE "SHOREBIRD FESTIVAL"
The 2003 Shorebird Festival
WILL BE HELD
May 9-11, 2003
www.cordovachamber.com
cchamber@ctcak.net
907.424.7260
P.O. Box 99, Cordova, AK 99574

Laura's
"Home-Style Comfort"
Fully furnished apartments
By the Day, Week or Month
~ Downtown Cordova ~
"Cordova's largest selection of spirits, wines & beers at the best prices!"
Espresso Bar ~ Ice Cream ~ Snacks
Internet Access
(907) 424-3144
email: cordovasales@gci.net

Prince William Motel
907.424.3201 or toll free 1.888.796.6835
pwmotel@yahoo.com
www.ak-biz.com/princewilliammotel
Box 908, Cordova, AK 99574

RELUCTANT FISHERMAN INN
907.424.3272
TOLL-FREE 1.800.770.3272
BOX 150, CORDOVA, AK 99574

www.cordovaak.com • reluctant@ctcak.net

Chamber of Commerce. A self-guided walking tour map of Cordova historic sites, prepared by the Cordova Historical Society, is also available. Although much of early Cordova was destroyed by fire, several picturesque old structures remain.

Cordova Fishermen's Memorial, *The Southeasterly,* is located on Nicholoff overlooking the "new harbor." Created by local sculptor Joan Bugbee Jackson, it was dedicated in 1985. The inscription (from Walt Whitman's "Song for All Seas, All Ships") reads: "Of sea-captains young or old, and the mates—and of all intrepid sailors ... Pick'd sparingly without noise, by thee, Old Ocean ... Indomitably untamed as thee."

Cordova Museum, located on First Street, offers an excellent overview of the area's history, tracing "the tracks of Cordova's past through industrial and cultural exhibits, displays and interpretation." The museum also displays original work by Alaskan artists Sydney Laurence, Eustace Ziegler and Jules Dahlager. Admission fee charged. Open 10 A.M. to 6 P.M. Monday through Saturday, and 2–4 P.M. Sundays, from Memorial Day to Labor Day. Winter hours are 1–5 P.M. Tuesday through Friday and 2–4 P.M. Saturday. Tours can be arranged. Write P.O. Box 391, phone (907) 424-6665 or visit www.cordovamuseum.org for more information. The Cordova Historical Society operates a small gift shop at the museum, featuring books of local interest and Alaskan crafts.

Visit the USCGC *Sycamore.* The USCGC *Sycamore* replaced the *Sweetbrier* in the fall of 2001. (The *Sweetbrier,* in service since 1944, was decommissioned and transferred to the Republic of Ghana). While there are no formal tours of the *Sycamore,* if the cutter is in port and the crew is not busy, you may be able to get on board. Inquire at the Quarterdeck shack on the North Fill Dock, just off of Seafood Lane or the "T" Pier.

Special Events: The major winter event is the Iceworm Festival, held the first full weekend of February, the highlight of which is the 100-foot-long "iceworm" that winds its way through the streets of Cordova.

In the spring, Cordova hosts the Copper River Delta Shorebird Festival (May 9–11, 2003), 5 days of birding along the tidal mudflats and wetlands of the Copper River Delta.

On June 7, 2003, the Cordova Running Club sponsors the Alaska Salmon Runs. This marathon starts at the Mile 27 Bridge on the Copper River Highway and ends in Cordova.

Watch Birds. The Copper River Delta is one of the most important stopover places in the Western Hemisphere for the largest shorebird migration in the world. Birders can view up to 31 different species. If you don't attend the Shorebird Festival in May, you can still see birds by visiting several bird-watching areas: Hartney Bay and Alaganik Slough are the most popular. Drive out Whitshed Road 5.5 miles to road end to reach Hartney Bay, part of the 300,000-acre Copper River Delta mudflats and a great place to see shorebirds.

The USFS recreation area at **Alaganik Slough** is a 20-mile drive from downtown, but worth the drive to see trumpeter swans up-close. There's a boardwalk with viewing blind at the slough for bird watchers. In addition, Orca Community Road and Odiak Slough offer excellent views of water birds.

Power Creek Road. This is a scenic drive out along the shore of Lake Eyak to the trailhead for the Power Creek USFS Trail. Check with the USFS office in town for trail status, (907) 424-7661.

Watch for seals and sea otters in Cordova harbor. (© Kris Graef, staff)

From 2nd Avenue in downtown Cordova, drive out Lake Street 0.6 mile to Nirvana Park on Lake Eyak. Built in 1930-35, you can see photographs at the museum in town of the whimsical sculptures that once graced this park. Continue out past the municipal airport. (The pavement ends and wide gravel road begins at Mile 1.3.) At Mile 1.8 is Crater Lake USFS Trail and Skaters Cabin. The 2.4-mile trail climbs to 1,500 feet. Excellent views, alpine lake with fishing for stocked rainbow trout. Watch for bears.

Past Mile 2.5 at Eyak Outlet, the road narrows as it winds toward the head of the lake at Mile 5.9. Power Creek Trail at Mile 6.9 accesses both the USFS public-use cabin in Power Creek Basin and a ridge that connects with the Crater Lake trail, creating a 12-mile loop. Power Creek Trail (4.2 miles long) offers spectacular scenery, with waterfalls, hanging glaciers and views of Power Creek Basin (called "surprise valley" by locals), the Chugach Range and Prince William Sound. Excellent berry picking. Watch for bears.

Drive the Copper River Highway to see the Million Dollar Bridge, Childs Glacier and the Copper River Delta. The 48-mile highway leads east from Cordova through the Delta to the historic Million Dollar Bridge. See "Copper River Highway" this section.

Take a hike. A popular family hike for local residents and visitors is the Haystack Trail at Mile 19.1 Copper River Highway. This easy 0.8-mile trail leads up stairs and along boardwalk through a lush spruce-hemlock forest to a spot overlooking the Copper River Delta. Wonderful view and a good chance of seeing moose.

The area's newest trail is Heney Ridge Trail at Mile 5.1 Whitshed Road. A 3.5-mile-long hike, the first 2 miles are rated easy and offer good views of Hartney Bay. The last mile is a steep climb up to the ridge, where you are treated to spectacular views of Prince William Sound on a clear day.

Stop by the USFS office on 2nd for current conditions and more details on area hiking trails.

Go Boating. Cordova is ideally situated for exploring Prince William Sound. Visit the harbor area, where you may rent a kayak or charter a jet boat for fishing or sightseeing.

Mount Eyak Ski Area. Ski Hill is usually open for skiing early December to the end of April, depending on weather. Winter schedule is Wednesday, Saturday, Sunday and holidays, 9 A.M. to dusk. Phone (907) 424-7766 for further information. To reach the chair lift from 4th Avenue, take Council Avenue 1 block, then follow Ski Hill Road to top (about 1 mile from Main Street).

The single chair lift rises 880 feet/268m up Mount Eyak and overlooks the town and harbor from 1,200 feet. Walk up, take a cab, take the tour bus or drive your own vehicle. A hiking trail from the base of the mountain to top of the chair lift and beyond connects with Forest Service Crater Lake trail.

AREA FISHING: According to the ADF&G, "Saltwater fishing in **Orca Inlet** and adjacent eastern Prince William Sound is accessible from Cordova. Species include halibut, rockfish and 5 species of salmon. Trolling for salmon is best for kings in the winter and spring, and silvers in the summer and fall. Boat charters are available locally. Road-accessible fishing opportunities exist for salmon in salt water at **Fleming Spit/ Lagoon,** near the ferry terminal off Orca Bay Road. Strong runs of hatchery-enhanced kings (in the spring) and silvers (August and September) return to this terminal fishery.

"Road-accessible freshwater fishing is also good in the Cordova Area. **Eyak River** supports strong returns of sockeye during June and July and silvers in August and September. The area at the outlet of the lake, where the road crosses, is fly-fishing only. Several streams along the **Copper River** Highway between Eyak Lake and the Million Dollar Bridge also support runs of sockeye and coho. These streams include **Clear Creek, Alaganik Slough, Eighteen-mile Creek** and **Twenty-mile Creek.** In addition, cutthroat trout and Dolly Varden are present in most of these streams. Lake fishing for sockeye salmon, Dolly Varden and cutthroat trout is available in **McKinley Lake** and the **Pipeline Lake** system. Fly-out fishing from Cordova is also popular for salmon, Dolly Varden and cutthroat trout. Charter operators are available locally." See also the Copper River Highway log for area fishing.

Cordova Air Service, Inc.
Charter Service
for
Prince William Sound

Wheels — Skis — Floats

Box 528
Cordova, Alaska 99574
(907) 424-3289

Copper River Highway

The Copper River Highway leads 48.8 miles northeast from Cordova across Million Dollar Bridge at the Copper River. This is a good gravel road with several U.S. Forest Service hiking trails and interpretive stops. Stop at the USFS office in Cordova for current trail conditions.

The highway is not maintained in winter beyond the airport. Snow may prevent access to many points along the highway well into spring.

Construction of the Copper River Highway began in 1945. Built along the abandoned railbed of the Copper River & Northwestern Railway, the highway was to extend to Chitina (on the Edgerton Highway), thereby linking Cordova to the Richardson Highway.

Construction was halted by the 1964 Good Friday earthquake, which severely damaged the highway's roadbed and bridges. The quake also knocked the north span of the Million Dollar Bridge into the Copper River and distorted the remaining spans. The 48 miles of existing highway have been repaired and upgraded since the earthquake, with temporary repairs to the Million Dollar Bridge. Road work between the Million Dollar Bridge and the Allen River is planned as part of the development of the proposed Copper River hiking and biking trail connecting Cordova, Chitina and Valdez.

The Million Dollar Bridge was a casualty of Alaska's 9.2 earthquake in 1964.
(© Rich Reid, Colors of Nature)

ALASKA ROUTE 10

Distance is measured from Cordova (C).

C 0 CORDOVA. See description beginning on page 638.

C 1.3 Turn south for **Whitshed Road.** At Mile 0.5 is Odiak municipal camper park (24 sites, tenting area; obtain shower tokens at City Hall). At Mile 5.1 is **Heney Ridge USFS Trail** (3.5 miles long); watch for bears. At Mile 5.5 (road end) is **Hartney Bay**, a popular birdwatching spot for the spring shore bird migration. Fishing from Hartney Bay bridge for Dolly Varden from May; pink and chum salmon, mid-July–August; closed for salmon upstream of bridge. Use small weighted spoons, spinners and eggs. Clam digging at low tide (license required).

C 2.1 Powder House Bar and Restaurant, a popular local spot overlooking **Eyak Lake.** Site of CR&NW railway powder house.

C 2.3 (3.7 km) Paved turnout to north by **Eyak Lake.** This Y-shaped lake has two 3-mile-long arms. Watch for trumpeter swans. Heney Range to the south. Mount Eccles (elev. 2,357 feet) is the first large peak. Pointed peak beyond is Heney Peak (elev. 3,151 feet).

C 3.6 Large paved turnout overlooking Eyak Lake.

C 4 Historical marker to north gives a brief history of the CR&NW railway. Also here is a monument erected by the railroad builder M.J. Heney in memory of those men who lost their lives during construction of the CR&NW. Begun in 1907 and completed in 1911, the CR&NW railway connected the port of Cordova with the Kennecott Copper Mines near Kennicott and McCarthy. The mine and railway ceased operation in 1938. Although the highway follows the CR&NW right-of-way, there is no evidence visible of the old railway line.

For the next 2 miles, watch for bears during early morning and late evening (most often seen in June).
CAUTION: Avalanche area.

C 5.6 Paved turnout at Eyak Lake to north.

C 5.7 Bridge over Eyak River; access to **Eyak River USFS Trail.** This is a good spot to see waterfowl feeding near the outlet of Eyak Lake. The 2.2-mile trail, much of which is boardwalk over muskeg, is popular with fishermen.

C 5.9 Eyak River USFS Boating Site. Toilet and boat launch. Dolly Varden; red salmon, June–July; silvers, August–September. Also pinks and chums. Use Vibrax spoon, spinner or salmon eggs. Fly-fishing only for salmon within 200 yards of weir.

C 6.4 *CAUTION: Road narrows eastbound, no shoulders.*

C 7.3 Paved turnout to south. *CAUTION: High winds for next 4 miles. In January and February, these winds sweep across this flat with such velocity it is safer to pull off and stop.*

C 7.4 Bridge over slough.

C 7.5 First bridge across Scott River.

C 8 Bridge over slough waters. Gravel turnout; access to slough.

C 8.3 Scott River bridge. Between here and **Milepost 10** there are several bridges across the Scott River and the slough. Sloughs along here are from the runoff of the Scott Glacier, visible to the northeast. Bear and moose are often seen, especially in July and August. In May and August, thousands of dusky Canada geese nest here. This is the only known nesting area of the dusky geese, which winter in Oregon's Willamette Valley. Also watch for swans.

Moose feed in the willow groves on either side of the highway. Moose are not native to Cordova; the mountains and glaciers prevent them from entering the delta country. Today's herd stems from a transplant of 26 animals made between 1949 and 1959.

C 10.5 (16.4 km) Beaver lodge. Watch for beaver dams and lodges beside the highway.

C 10.6 Large paved turnout with bear-proof litter barrel to south. U.S. Forest Service information pavilion (8 interpretive plaques about Copper River Delta/Chugach National Forest areas).

C 10.7 Bridge, beaver lodge.

C 11.1 Elsner River bridge.

C 11.7 State of Alaska Cordova highway maintenance station to northeast. U.S. Coast Guard station.

C 12.1 Cordova Airport to south; Alaska Airlines Terminal.

Access north 2.5 miles to **Lake Elsner USFS Trailhead**; toilet and bear-proof litter barrel at Cabin Lake; cutthroat fishing. *CAUTION: Narrow road, no directional signs.*

C 12.4 Pavement ends, gravel begins. No road maintenance after Nov. 1. Watch for potholes.

C 13.7 Access road leads 4 miles to the terminus of **Sheridan Glacier** and trailhead for **Sheridan Mountain USFS Trail** (2.9 miles long; difficult). *CAUTION: Narrow road, watch for other vehicles. Keep to right at fork.* The glacier was named by U.S. Army explorer Capt. Abercrombie for Gen. Philip H. Sheridan of Civil War fame. There is a partial view of the glacier at the end of the access road. It is about a 0.5-mile hike to the dirt-covered glacial moraine. Area also has picnic sites.

C 14.8 Bridge over Sheridan River. Large gravel turnout, raft takeout point. View of Sheridan Glacier. To the east of Sheridan Glacier is Sherman Glacier.

C 15.6 One Eye Pond unofficial picnic area.

C 16 Beautiful views of Sheridan Glacier to the northeast.

C 16.3 Second bridge over Sheridan River.

C 16.8 Turnoff for **Alaganik Slough Chugach National Forest Recreation Area.** Drive south 3.2 miles via narrow, maintained gravel road; picnic tables, firepits, wheelchair-accessible toilets, litter barrel, information kiosk and boat launch. Wheelchair-accessible interpretive boardwalk with viewing blind for watching birds and other wildlife. No water. Fishing for Dolly Varden,

sockeye (July) and silver salmon (Aug.–Sept.).
Bring mosquito repellent!

Trumpeter swans may be seen in ponds. One of the largest of all North American waterfowl (6- to 8-foot wingspan), it has been almost completely eliminated in the Lower 48 and Canada. Alaska harbors more than 80 percent of breeding trumpeters, and more than 7 percent of the world's trumpeter population breeds in the Copper River Delta.

Interpretive plaque on side road reads: "Why are Delta moose the largest and healthiest? This moose herd, first introduced in 1949, maintains its vitality primarily due to its abundant willow supply. As part of a normal cycle, accelerated by the 1964 earthquake, much of the willow is becoming unavailable to moose. As the willow grows tall, the moose can no longer reach the tender new shoots. In the future this could cause a decrease in the numbers of moose on the delta. To slow the cycle down, the Forest Service is experimenting in this area, cutting back the shrubs. This should increase the amount of available willow browse. Biologists will evaluate the response of moose to new willow growth."

C **18.8** Turnout to north access to **Muskeg Meander USFS Ski Trail**; length 3.1 miles. This trail offers a beautiful view of the Copper River Delta. Recommended for winter use only. This is the only cross-country ski trail in the district.

C **19.1 Haystack USFS Trail** and trailhead parking to south. Easy 0.8-mile boardwalk trail (lots of stairs) leads to delta overlook with interpretive signs. The overlook is an excellent place to see moose and bear. Popular family hike through lush spruce-hemlock forest; allow 45 minutes round-trip.

Several small turnouts next mile.

C **20** Large gravel turnout to south; beaver dam to north. Fishing. "Pay to park" area.

C **21.4 Pipeline Lakes USFS Trail** to north, trailhead parking to south. The 1.8-mile trail was originally built as a water pipeline route to supply locomotives on the CR&NW railway. Segments of the pipeline are still visible. Fishing for cutthroat, fly or bait. Trail joins McKinley Lake trail. Trail has been improved, and boardwalk is still under construction.

C **21.6 McKinley Lake USFS Trail** to north; easy 2.2-mile hike with excellent fishing for sockeye, Dolly Varden and cutthroat. Access to USFS public-use cabins: McKinley Trail cabin (100 yards from highway) and McKinley Lake cabin (45-minute walk in from highway; also accessible by boat via Alaganik Slough).

C **22 Alaganik Slough** boat ramp, picnic tables, firepits, toilets, litter barrel, wildflowers, interpretive signs on local cultural history and fishing access to south at west side of bridge. Sockeye (red) and coho (silver) salmon, July to September. Also boat access to McKinley Lake.

Alaganik Slough river bridge.

C **24.8** Channel to beaver pond for spawning salmon. Beaver dam at lake outlet to north. Plaque to south reads: "Pathway to salmon rearing grounds. Channel provides access to beaver pond (north side of road) for coho fry. Beaver pond can support up to 25,400 young salmon. Fallen trees and brush provide cover from predators."

Side road leads north 1 mile to **Saddlebag Glacier USFS Trail** and trailhead parking area. This is an easy 3-mile trail to Saddlebag Lake and the best trail in the district for mountain biking. View of Saddlebag Glacier and icebergs; look for goats on surrounding mountains. *CAUTION: Watch for bears.*

C **26.4 Flag Point.** Turnout with view of the Copper River which empties into the Gulf of Alaska. Downriver to the southwest is Castle Island Slough. Storey Slough is visible a little more to the south. Castle Island and a number of small islands lie at the mouth of the Copper River. Monument on the riverbank is dedicated to the men who built these bridges and "especially to the crane crew who lost their lives on July 21, 1971."

CAUTION: Extreme high winds next 10 miles in fall and winter. Stay in your vehicle.

C **26.7** Two bridges cross the Copper River to Round Island, a small island with sand dunes and a good place to picnic.

In midsummer, the Copper River has half a million or more red (sockeye) and king salmon migrating 300 miles upstream to spawn in the river's clear tributaries. There is no sportfishing in this stretch of the Copper River because of glacial silt.

Candlefish (eulachon) also spawn in the Copper River. Candlefish oil was once a significant trade item of the Coastal Indians. These fish are so oily that when dried they can be burned like candles.

C **27.5** Copper River Bridge No. 3 from Round Island to Long Island. There is a monument on the left honoring workers who died during the construction of the bridge. The 6.2 miles/10 km of road on Long Island pass through a sandy landscape dotted with dunes. Long Island is in the middle of the Copper River.

C **30.8** Watch for nesting swans, other birds and beaver in slough to south of road.
NOTE: Use extreme caution if you drive off road: sandy terrain.

C **31** Lakes to south.

C **33** View of 2 glaciers to the northwest; nearest is Goodwin, the other is Childs.

C **33.2** First bridge leaving Long Island. View to south down Hotcake Channel to Heart Island. Road built on top of a long dike which stretches across the Copper River Delta. From here to **Milepost C 37.7** there are 7 more bridges across the delta. The Copper River channels have changed and many bridges now cross almost dry gulches.
NOTE: Watch for large potholes before and after bridges through this section.

C **34.2** Large gravel turnout to north.

C **34.3** Copper River bridge.

C **35.7** Large gravel turnout to north.

C **36.8** Bridge crossing main flow of the Copper River (this is the 5th bridge after leaving Long Island eastbound). Access to river at east end of bridge.

C **37.4** Bridge, river access.

C **37.8** Bridge, river access, large gravel turnout to north.

C **38.8** Childs Glacier directly ahead.

C **39.7** Milky glacial waters of Sheep Creek pass through large culvert under road.

C **40.5 Clear Creek.** Dolly Varden, cutthroat, red salmon (July) and silvers (Aug.–Sept.). Use flies, lures, spinners or eggs. Watch for bears.

C **41.5** Park on old railroad grade to south for access to Clear Creek.

C **41.7** Goat Mountain (elev. 4,370 feet) rises to the east of the highway. To the west, parts of the Sherman and Goodwin glaciers flow down the sides of Mount Murchison (elev. 6,263 feet).

Caution is advised when approaching the face of Childs Glacier.
(© Rich Reid, Colors of Nature)

C **42.1** Side road to gravel pit, pond, informal camping and picnic site by Goat Mountain.

C **48** Access to **Childs Glacier Recreation Area** with 2 covered, wheelchair-accessible viewing areas, one at the bridge, the other 0.7 mile down access road. Picnic sites, covered tables, litter barrels, toilets and trails; no water. Limited RV parking. U.S. Forest Service hosts on site in summer. Childs Glacier was named by Capt. W.R. Abercrombie (1884 expedition) for George Washington Childs of Philadelphia. The glacier face is approximately 350 feet high and very active. In 1993 falling ice caused a 30-foot wave that crashed onto the viewing area. Car-sized icebergs were tossed onto the beach and viewing area. *CAUTION: Calving ice may cause waves to break over the beach and into the viewing area. Be prepared to run to higher ground!*

C **48.1 The Million Dollar Bridge.** Sign posted: Weight limit on bridge: 6,600 lbs. Viewing platform. Constructed from 1909 to 1910 for $1.4 million, the 1,550-foot-long steel truss bridge spans the Copper River. It was the longest steel bridge on the 196-mile-long Copper River and Northwestern Railway. The north span of the bridge collapsed during the 1964 earthquake. Temporary repairs were made and people have been driving across it, but driving across the bridge and beyond is definitely a "drive at your own risk" venture. The bridge was added to the National Register of Historic Places in 2000.

The road currently extends only about 10 miles/16 km beyond the bridge to the Allen River. Heavy snow blocks road in winter; road may not be open until June. Proposed extension of the Copper River Highway to Chitina is currently under debate.

From here there is a view of Miles Glacier to the east. This glacier was named by Lieutenant Allen (1885 expedition) for Maj. Gen. Nelson A. Miles.

C **48.2** End of bridge.

C **48.8** A 4X4 or 4-wheel-drive vehicle with very high clearance is a must to go any farther!

KODIAK

(See map, page 649)

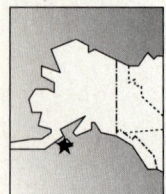

The Kodiak Island group lies in the Gulf of Alaska, southwest of Cook Inlet and the Kenai Peninsula. The city of Kodiak is located near the northeastern tip of Kodiak Island, at the north end of Chiniak Bay. By air it is 1 hour from Anchorage. By ferry from Homer it is 9½ hours. **Population:** 13,913 Kodiak Island Borough. **Emergency Services in Kodiak:** Dial 911 for emergencies. **Alaska State Troopers**, phone (907) 486-4121. **Police**, phone (907) 486-8000. **Fire Department**, phone (907) 486-8040. **Harbor:** phone (907) 486-8080. **Hospital**, Providence Kodiak Island Medical Center, Rezanof Drive, phone (907) 486-3281. **Coast Guard**, phone (907) 487-5760. **Crime Stoppers**, phone (907) 486-3113.

Visitor Information: Located at 100 Marine Way, Suite 200; open year-round. Hours in June, July and August are 8 A.M. to 5 P.M. weekdays, 10 A.M. to 4 P.M. Saturday, 10-4 P.M. Sunday (later for arriving ferries). Winter hours are 8 A.M. to 5 P.M. weekdays. Knowledgeable staff will answer questions and help arrange tours and charters. Free maps, brochures, hunting/fishing information. For information, contact the Kodiak Island Convention & Visitors Bureau, Dept. MP, 100 Marine Way, Suite 200, Kodiak 99615; (907) 486-4782 or 1-800-789-4782; www.kodiak.org/cvb.html.

Elevation: Sea level. **Climate:** Average daily temperature in July is 54°F; in January 30°F. September, October and January are the wettest months in Kodiak, with each month averaging more than 7 inches of precipitation. **Radio:** KVOK 560, KMXT-FM 100.1, KRXX-FM 101.1. **Television:** Via cable and satellite. **Newspapers:** *The Kodiak Daily Mirror* (daily except Saturday and Sunday).

Kodiak, known as the "Emerald Isle," is the largest island in Alaska.
(© W. Wright Diamond Photo)

Private Aircraft: Kodiak state airport, 4.8 miles southwest; elev. 73 feet; length 7,500 feet; asphalt; fuel 100LL, Jet A-1. Kodiak Municipal Airport, 2 miles northeast; elev. 139 feet; length 2,500 feet; paved; unattended. Trident Basin seaplane base, on east side of Near Island, unattended, floats for 14 aircraft; fuel. Trident Basin has AVgas, (credit card or prepay).

Gravel airstrips at Akhiok, length 3,320 feet; Karluk, length 2,000 feet; Larsen Bay, length 2,700 feet; Old Harbor, length 2,750 feet; Ouzinkie, length 2,085 feet; and Port Lions, length 2,200 feet.

Kodiak Island, home of the oldest permanent European settlement in Alaska, is known as Alaska's "Emerald Isle." It is the largest island in Alaska and the second largest island in the United States (after Hawaii), with an area of 3,588 square miles and about 87 miles of road (see logs this section). The Kodiak Island Borough includes some 200 islands, the largest being Kodiak (about 100 miles long), followed in size by Afognak, Sitkalidak, Sitkinak, Raspberry, Tugidak, Shuyak, Uganik, Chirikof, Marmot and Spruce islands. The borough has two unincorporated townsites, **KARLUK** (pop. 27), on the west coast of Kodiak Island, 75 air miles from Kodiak, and **ALENEVA** (pop. 68) on Afognak Island.

The 6 incorporated cities in the Kodiak Island Borough are: **KODIAK** (pop. 6,334) on Chiniak Bay, with all visitor services (see Visitor Services, Transportation and Attractions this section); **AKHIOK** (pop.80) at Alitak Bay on the south side of Kodiak Island, 80 miles southwest of Kodiak; **LARSEN BAY** (pop. 115) on the northwest coast of Kodiak Island, 62 miles southwest of Kodiak; **OLD HARBOR** (pop. 237) on the southeast side of Kodiak Island, 54 miles from Kodiak; **OUZINKIE** (pop. 225) on the west coast of Spruce Island; and **PORT LIONS** (pop. 256) on Settler Cove on the northeast coast of Kodiak Island.

Kodiak Island was originally inhabited by

Kodiak Bed and Breakfast
Comfortable, gracious hospitality in downtown Kodiak

(907) 486-5367

Mary A. Monroe • Fax (907) 486-6567
308 Cope Street, Kodiak, Alaska 99615
e-mail: monroe@ptialaska.net

Shelikof Lodge
LOCATED DOWNTOWN KODIAK

A Full Service Hotel with Restaurant, Lounge and 38 Comfortable Rooms

Free Local Calls • Full Cable TV • 24 Hour Desk
Hunting • Fishing • Brown Bear Viewing Information Available

Phone (907) 486-4141 • E-Mail: kyle@ptialaska.net • Fax (907) 486-4116
211 Thorsheim Ave. Kodiak, Alaska 99615 • www.ptialaska.net/~kyle

---

INLET GUEST ROOMS
Comfortable Private Rooms with Private Baths

Rooms from $55 to $85 plus tax
Phones, TV's, Free Coffee

AK- 907-486-4004
US- 800-423-4004
P.O. Box 89 Kodiak AK 99615

the Alutiiq people, who were maritime hunters and fishermen. More than 7,000 years later, the Alutiiq still call Kodiak home.

In 1763, the island was discovered by Stephen Glotov, a Russian explorer. The name Kodiak, of which there are several variations, was first used in English by Captain Cook in 1778. Kodiak was Russian Alaska's first capital city, until the capital was moved to Sitka in 1804.

Kodiak's turbulent past includes the 1912 eruption of Novarupta Volcano, on the nearby Alaska Peninsula, and the tidal wave of 1964. The Novarupta eruption covered the island with a black cloud of ash. When the cloud dissipated, Kodiak was buried under 18 inches of drifting pumice.

On Good Friday in 1964 the greatest earthquake ever recorded in North America (8.6 on the Richter scale, Mw 9.2) shook the Kodiak area. The tidal wave that followed virtually leveled downtown Kodiak, destroying the fishing fleet, processing plants, canneries and 158 homes.

Because of Kodiak's strategic location for defense, military facilities were constructed on the island in 1939. Fort Abercrombie, now a state park and a national historic landmark, was one of the first secret radar installations in Alaska. Cement bunkers still remain for exploration by the curious.

The Coast Guard occupies the old Kodiak Naval Station. Kodiak is the base for the Coast Guard's North Pacific operations; the U.S. Coast Guard cutters *Storis* and *Firebush* patrol from Kodiak to seize foreign vessels illegally fishing U.S. waters. (The 200-mile fishing limit went into effect in March 1977.) A 12-foot star, situated halfway up the side of Old Woman Mountain overlooking the base, was rebuilt and rededicated in 1981 in memory of military personnel who have lost their lives while engaged in operations from Kodiak. Originally erected in the 1950s, the star is lit every year between Thanksgiving and Christmas.

St. Paul and St. Herman harbors are home port to 800 local fishing boats and serve several hundred outside vessels each year.

Commercial fishing is the backbone of Kodiak's economy. Kodiak is one of the largest commercial fishing ports in the U.S. Some 1,000 commercial fishing vessels use the harbor each year, delivering salmon, shrimp, herring, halibut and whitefish, plus king, tanner and Dungeness crab to the 11 processing companies in Kodiak. Cannery

The Alaska Marine Highway vessel Tustumena *serves Kodiak from Homer and Seward.* (© Laurent Dick)

tours are not available. Kodiak's famous seafood is premarketed, with almost all the commercially caught seafood exported. Kodiak is also an important cargo port and transshipment center. Container ships stop twice weekly.

Lodging & Services

There are 6 hotels/motels in Kodiak and more than 30 bed and breakfasts. A variety of restaurants offers a wide range of menus and prices. Shopping is readily available for gifts, general merchandise and sporting goods. There is a movie theater and 750-seat performing arts center.

Dump stations are located at the Petro Express station on Mill Bay Road and St. Paul Harbor spit in front of Alaska Fresh Seafoods.

There are more than 30 remote fly-in hunting and fishing lodges in the Kodiak area; several roadhouses on the island road system; public-use cabins available within Kodiak National Wildlife Refuge, Shuyak Island and Afognak Island state parks; and private wilderness camps and cabin rentals available throughout the Kodiak area.

Camping

There are 3 state campgrounds: Fort Abercrombie, north of town (see Rezanof–Monashka Bay Road log); Buskin River state

KODIAK ADVERTISERS

Andrew Airways	Ph. (907) 487-2566
Baranov Museum	Ph. (907) 486-5920
Budget Rent-a-Car	Ph. (800) 527-0700
Cy's Sporting Goods & Outfitters	Ph. (907) 486-3900
Harvey Flying Service	Ph. (907) 487-2621
Inlet Guest Rooms	Ph. (800) 423-4004
Kodiak Bed and Breakfast	Ph. (907) 486-5367
Kodiak RV Adventures	Ph. (907) 486-8883
Northern Exposure Gallery	Ph. (907) 486-4956
Providence Alaska Medical Center	Ph. (907) 486-3281
Rent-A-Heap	Ph. (907) 487-4001
Sea Hawk Air	Ph. (800) 770-4295
Shelikof Lodge	Ph. (907) 486-4141
Statewide Ferry Reservations	Ph. 1-800-526-6731

Northern Exposure
Gallery and Frame Shop
est. 1977
Fine Art
Originals • Prints • Posters
Kodiak and Alaskan Artists
Gifts • Cards
Custom Framing
(907) 486-4956
1314 Mill Bay Rd.

Providence *is here...*

...helping you live life to the fullest.

(907) 486-3281

Providence | Kodiak Island Medical Center

417 1st Avenue • Seward, Alaska 99664
(907) 224-5205 • www.providence.org/alaska/seward

FERRY RESERVATIONS
1-800-526-6731
Ticketing & Information
for All Alaska Marine Highway Vessels
www.akferry.com
Kodiak Terminal - an Official Contract Agent for All Alaska Marine Highway Vessels for more than 30 years.
907-486-3800 • FAX: 907-486-6166

recreation site, south of town (see Chiniak Road log); and Pasagshak River state recreation site at the end of Pasagshak Bay Road (see log).

Transportation

Air: Scheduled service via Era Aviation and Alaska Airlines. Private commercial airlines serve Kodiak Island villages.

Ferry: The Alaska state ferry MV *Tustumena* serves Kodiak from Homer (9½-hour ferry ride) and Seward (13 hours). It also stops at Port Lions. Ferry terminal is downtown; phone (907) 486-3800 or toll free in the U.S. (800) 526-6731.

Highways: There are 4 roads on Kodiak Island (see logs this section). The 11.3-mile Rezanof–Monashka Bay Road leads from downtown Kodiak north to Fort Abercrombie and Monashka Bay. Chiniak Road leads 42.8 miles south from Kodiak along the island's eastern shore to Chiniak Point and Chiniak Creek. Anton Larsen Bay Road leads 11.8 miles from junction with Chiniak Road near Kodiak airport to Anton Larsen Bay. Pasagshak Bay Road branches off Chiniak Road and leads 16.5 miles to Fossil Beach at Pasagshak Point.

IMPORTANT: Using land owned by Leisnoi, Inc. requires a non-fee user permit, available at the Leisnoi office in Kodiak at 3248 Mill Bay Rd.; phone (907) 486-8191.

Car Rental and Taxi: Available.

Attractions

© Marion Owen

The Baranov Museum (Erskine House), maintained by the Kodiak Historical Society (101 Marine Way, Kodiak 99615; phone 907/486-5920), is open in summer, 10 A.M. to 4 P.M. Monday through Saturday; 12 noon to 4 P.M. Sunday. (Winter hours 10 A.M. to 3 P.M. weekdays, except Thursday and Sunday.) The building was originally a fur warehouse built in 1806-08 by Alexsandr Baranov. It is one of just 4 Russian-built structures in the United States today. Purchased by the Alaska Commercial Co. around 1867, the building was sold to W.J. Erskine in 1911, who converted it into a residence; it was then referred to as the Erskine House. In 1962 it was declared a national historic landmark. Many items from the Koniag and Russian era are on display. In the gift shop, Russian samovars, Russian Easter eggs, Alaska Native baskets and other items are for sale. Donations accepted, $2 per adult, children under 12 free; www.ptialaska.net/~baranov.

Kodiak Tribal Council's Barabara Sod House is an authentic Alutiiq dwelling that features presentations of Alutiiq dancing. The Kodiak Alutiiq Dancers form the only Alutiiq dance group in Alaska. The dances have been re-created from stories passed down through generations of the Alutiiq people, who have inhabited Kodiak Island for more than 7,000 years. Dance performances are held in the summer at 312 W. Marine Way. For more information about scheduled dances, call (907) 486-4449, or email tribe@ptialaska.net.

Diocesan Museum of the Russian Orthodox Church, St. Herman's Chapel, Mission Road. History of the first Christian church in Alaska (1784) and village religious art; hand-carved chandelier and votive lights; books dating back to 17th century. Call for more information, (907) 486-3524.

Go for a Hike. Hiking trails around the Kodiak area provide access to alpine areas, lakes, coastal rainforests and beaches. Trail guide available for $5 at the Visitors Center, (907) 486-4782. Pay attention to notes regarding footwear and clothing, tides, bears, trailhead access and weather conditions.

Picnic on the Beach. There are some outstandingly beautiful, unpopulated beaches along Chiniak Road (see log this section) excellent for beachcombing. Watch for Sitka black-tailed deer and foxes.

Kodiak Fisheries Research Center houses a variety of fisheries research and regulatory agencies, public informtion, "touch tank" and more. Phone (907) 481-1800.

Go Mountain Biking. Kodiak is fast becoming known for its premier mountain biking, attracting racers and enthusiasts from around the country. Biking guide available for $4 at Visitors Center.

Special Events. Kodiak has a full calendar of events throughout the year. Contact event coordinators directly for current information.

The irreverent and fun Pillar Mountain Golf Classic (March 28–30, 2003) starts off the year with a par-70, one-hole golf tournament up the side of 1,400-foot Pillar Mountain. For more information, phone (907) 486-2931, or visit http://chiniak.net/pillar.

The Kodiak Whale Festival (April 11–22, 2003) celebrates the return of migrating whales. Whale sightings are reported daily, with special art, literature and performances scheduled throughout the festival. Phone (907) 486-3737 or (907) 481-1719.

The Kodiak King Crab Festival (May 22–26, 2003) celebrate Kodiak's main industry with parades, carnival booths and midway, races and tournaments, blessing of the fleet and concerts. Contact Kodiak Chamber of Commerce (907) 486-5557.

The annual Kodiak Bear Country Music Festival takes place July 18–19, 2003. The festival features more than 50 bands from around the state performing bluegrass, folk, soft rock, country and Alaska music. Phone (907) 486-8766.

The Kodiak Kids' Pink Salmon Jamboree takes place August 9–10, 2003. Contact Kiwanis Everett Stone, phone (907) 486-5245.

Kodiak's State Fair and Rodeo are held Labor Day weekend at the fairgrounds in Womens Bay. (Stock car races are held at the fairgrounds on weekends during the summer.)

St. Herman's Day, Aug. 7–9, 2003, is of particular significance to the Kodiak community as Father Herman, the first saint of the Russian Orthodox Church in North America, was canonized in Kodiak in 1970. Father Herman arrived in Kodiak in 1794. An annual pilgrimage takes place to his home on Spruce Island. A schedule of services is available upon request; phone (907) 486-3854.

City Parks and Recreation Department maintains a swimming pool year-round, and the school gyms are available on a year-round basis for community use. The town has 8 parks and playgrounds including the 7-acre Baranof Park with 2 tennis courts, baseball field, track, playgrounds and picnic areas. North End Park on Near Island has a scenic 1-mile improved trail. For more information phone (907) 486-8665.

Bear Valley Golf Course. The 9-hole Bear Valley Golf Course is located on the Anton Larsen Bay Road. Owned and operated by the U.S. Coast Guard, the course has a driving range, putting green and pro shack. The course is open to the public from June until October, depending on weather. The pro shack carries golf clothing, items and rental equipment, and serves food and

---

Visit the
BARANOV MUSEUM
A National Historic Landmark
Summer Hours
Mon. - Sat. 10am to 4pm, Sun. 12-4pm
101 Marine Way (907) 486-5920

KODIAK RV ADVENTURES
Explore at your pace!
* Save money vs. hotel and car rental!
* www.kodiakrv.com   kodiakrv@ptialaska.net
(907) 486-8883

Cy's Sporting Goods & Outfitters
Over 34 years in Kodiak
Known for our friendly service and priceless advice
SPORTS & COMMERCIAL LICENSES
NEW EXPANDED STORE
HUNTING, FISHING, ARCHERY, CLOTHING & CAMPING SUPPLIES
Web Page: www.kodiak-outfitters.com
Open 7 days a week
Email: cykodiak@ptialaska.net
117 Lower Mill Bay Rd., Kodiak, Alaska 99615 • (907) 486-3900

The Smart Money is on Budget.®
Budget
CARS • TRUCKS • VANS
RESERVATIONS: TOLL FREE 800-527-0700
DOWNTOWN ON THE MALL
KODIAK STATE AIRPORT **487-2220**

Land of the Giants: Bear Viewing on Kodiak Island

Kodiak National Wildlife Refuge is home to at least 3,000 coastal brown bears.
(© Alaska Stock)

Our advice to visitors who hope to see a bear during their Alaska vacation is to head out to Kodiak Island.

Of the many mammal species that roam the state's vast wilderness, the Alaska brown bear or grizzly (*Ursus arctos*) undoubtedly creates more awed excitement among photographers, hunters and spectators than any other. It is common throughout most of the state.

Coastal brown bears rank as the largest living carnivorous land mammals in the world. These huge creatures, undisputed kings of their realms, are a subspecies (*Ursus arctos middendorffi*), with their greatest population density occurring in the grasslands of Kodiak Island and the Alaska Peninsula. Unusually large specimens may reach 8 to 9 feet in height, with weight approaching 1,500 pounds, although most are considerably smaller. The skull size of a coastal brown bear taken in 1952 on Kodiak still holds the record with a measurement of 30 $^{12}/_{16}$ inches, determined by combined width and length. Biologists credit the superior size of the Kodiak bears to their thousands of years of isolation from the mainland bear population and their nutrient-rich diet of salmon and other fish and food sources readily available on the islands.

Bear-viewing rates very high on visitors' wish-lists, and government agencies and private entrepreneurs have ensured that opportunities exist for these experiences. Carefully regulated and monitored venues include the Anan Creek Observatory in the Alexander Archipelago of Southeast Alaska, managed by the U.S. Forest Service and accessible by plane from Wrangell; contact the Forest Service office, (907) 874-2323; and the famous McNeil River State Game Sanctuary/Katmai National Park, where admission is by limited permit through the Alaska Department of Fish and Game, (907) 267-2100.

Two other bear-viewing sites in Southeast Alaska are the Stan Price Wildlife Sanctuary at Pack Creek on Admiralty Island; contact the Forest Service Information Center, (907) 586-8751; and the Fish Creek Wildlife Observation site near Hyder; contact the Forest Service field office, (907) 636-2367.

Then there is Kodiak. The Kodiak National Wildlife Refuge encompasses 2,812 square miles on Kodiak, Uganik, Afognak and Ban islands. Accessible only by air charter or boat, it is estimated to be home to at least 3,000 bears. Visitors go to the refuge to fish, camp, kayak, hunt and to observe and photograph bears and other abundant wildlife. Several flying services and lodges on and off the island offer tours to view the animals that have made the name of Kodiak Island virtually synonymous with "bears."

Despite many dramatic tales of bear attacks, it is reassuring to know there are few fatal attacks on humans in Alaska, seldom more than 1 per year throughout the entire state, and only a few incidents of maulings. Security is a high priority at the refuges where the bears abound, for human safety as well as the protection of the bears themselves. Changes affecting bear management in the Kodiak National Wildlife Refuge have been under consideration for the last few years and will result in more bear-related information for visitors to the island.

Visitors who hope to see the legendary bears in their natural habitat should contact the Kodiak Island Convention and Visitors Bureau, 100 Marine Way, Suite 200, Kodiak, AK 99615, phone (907) 486-4782 or 1-800-789-4782 for helpful suggestions and advice. Also visit the Visitors Bureau website at www.kodiak.org/cvb.html.

As it is rare to see a bear while driving the road system on Kodiak Island, you may want to visit one of the remote lodges in bear country. All feature bear viewing as a major attraction.

Some of the flying services on Kodiak Island providing transportation and tours include Andrew Airways, (907) 487-5266; Harvey Flying Service, (907) 487-2621; and Sea Hawk Air, (800) 770-4295. Homer-based air services offering bear viewing to Kodiak include Bald Mountain Air, (907) 235-7969, and Emerald Air Service, (907) 235-6993.

Applications to stay in the public-use cabins in the Kodiak National Wildlife Refuge must be submitted in advance to the refuge manager, 1390 Buskin River Road, Kodiak, AK 99615, phone (907) 487-2600. The U.S. Fish and Wildlife Service Visitor Center on Buskin River Road, near the state airport, features exhibits and films about Kodiak's wildlife and is open weekdays year-round and Saturdays June through September.

Bear Viewing Tours for Kodiak Island and the Katmai Coast.
Sea Hawk Air
1-800-770-4295
www.seahawkair.com

ANDREW AIRWAYS
FLOAT AND WHEEL PLANE CHARTERS
Flightseeing • Bear Viewing
Hunting • Fishing Trips
(907) 487-2566
Fax (907) 487-2578
P.O. Box 1037 • Kodiak, AK 99615
www.AndrewAirways.com
E-Mail: AndrewAir1@aol.com

KODIAK, ALASKA
HARVEY FLYING SERVICE
Pilot Steve Harvey - flying commercially in Alaska since 1966.
Located at the Kodiak State Airport
P.O. Box 3062
Kodiak, AK 99615
phone - (907) 487-2621
fax - (907) 487-1947
harveyfs@eagle.ptialaska.net
www.harveyflyingservice.com

Fly in a classic Grumman Widgeon!
Bear Viewing
Flightseeing
Remote Location Air transportation

beer. Hours of operation vary according to weather and daylight hours. Call (907) 486-9793.

Fort Abercrombie State Historic Park, located north of Kodiak on scenic Miller Point, offers picnicking and camping in a setting of lush rain forest, wildflowers, seabirds and eagles. The Kodiak Military History Museum is located inside the Ready Ammo bunker at Fort Abercrombie. The museum features displays of WWII memorabilia, including relics from the Aleutian campaign. The museum is open Monday, Wednesday and Saturday, 1–3 P.M.; and Sundays 2–4 P.M (Hours and dates of operation may vary).

Naturalist programs are offered Saturday evenings at 7 P.M. from late June through August at Fort Abercrombie State Historic Park. Programs include plant lore, outdoor photography, sea kayaking, tidepool exploration and more. For more information on park facilities and programs, phone the State Park office at (907) 486-6339.

Alutiiq Museum and Archaeological Repository in downtown Kodiak houses artifacts from coastal sites around Kodiak Island. The Alutiiq are descendants of the Pacific Eskimos, whom Russian explorers encountered and referred to as the Koniag people, many of whom lived in the Karluk area on Kodiak's west coast around 1200 A.D. However, some items found date to 3,000 and even 7,000 years ago. The Karluk area is billed as one of the most amazing archaeological finds in Alaska because of the abundance and the level of preservation of the artifacts. Located at 215 Mission Road; phone (907) 486-7004; www.alutiiqmuseum.com; alutiiq2@ptialaska.net. Summer hours (June–August): Monday-Friday, 9 A.M.–5 P.M.; Saturday, 10:30 A.M.–5 P.M.; Sunday by appointment; winter hours: Tuesday–Friday, 9 A.M.–5 P.M.; Saturday 10:30 A.M.–4:30 P.M.; closed Sunday and Monday. Admission fee: $2 per adult; museum members and children under 12 free.

Shuyak Island State Park encompasses 47,000 acres and is located 54 air miles north of Kodiak. Access by boat or float plane only. Hunting, fishing and kayaking are the major recreational activities. Four public-use cabins available at $50 per night. Cabins are 12 feet by 20 feet and sleep up to 8 people. Reservations accepted up to 6 months in advance with a full nonrefundable payment. Call (907) 486-6339 or (907) 269-8400; www.dnr.state.ak.us/parks/units/kodiak/shuyak.htm.

Holy Resurrection Russian Orthodox Church. The present church was built in 1945 and is listed on the National Register of Historic Places. The church and the Baranov Museum were spared in the earthquake and tsunami of 1964. The church interior provides a visual feast, and the public is invited to attend services. The public may visit Thursday and Saturday at 6:30 P.M.; Sunday service at 9 A.M. Phone (907) 486-3854. A $1 donation is encouraged.

A scale replica of the original (1796) church building is located on the grounds of St. Herman's Theological Seminary on Mission Road, just up the road from the original.

Arrange a Boat or air charter, or guide for fishing and hunting trips, adventure tours, sightseeing and photography. There are several charter services in Kodiak.

See Kodiak by Kayak. One of the best ways to experience Kodiak's beautiful coastline, and view marine mammals and seabirds, is from a kayak. Day tours around the nearby islands are available for all skill levels, or schedule an extended tour. Kayak rentals available.

Kodiak National Wildlife Refuge encompasses 2,812 square miles on Kodiak Island, Uganik Island, Afognak Island and Ban Island. The refuge was established in 1941 to preserve the natural habitat of the famed Kodiak bear and other wildlife. Biologists estimate that more than 3,000 bears inhabit Kodiak Island. Most bears enter dens by October and remain there until April. Bears are readily observable on the refuge in July and August when they congregate along streams to feed on salmon. At other times they feed on grasses or berries.

Visitors to the refuge typically go to fish, observe and photograph wildlife, backpack, kayak, camp and hunt.

NOTE: The refuge is accessible only by floatplane or boat. There are primitive public-use cabins available; applications must be made in advance to the refuge manager. For more information contact the Kodiak National Wildlife Refuge Manager, 1390 Buskin River Road, Kodiak, AK 99615; phone (907) 487-2600; www.r7.fws.gov/nwr/kodiak/kodnwr.html or www.kodiakisland.net; email kodiak@fws.gov. You may also stop by the **U.S. Fish and Wildlife Service Visitor Center** on Buskin River Road. The center features exhibits and films on Kodiak wildlife and is open weekdays year-round, and also Saturdays June through September; hours are variable.

AREA FISHING: Kodiak Island is in the center of a fine marine and freshwater fishery and possesses some excellent fishing for rainbow, halibut, Dolly Varden and 5 species of Pacific salmon. Visiting fishermen will have to charter a boat or aircraft to reach remote lakes, rivers and bays, but the island road system offers many good salmon streams in season. Roads access red salmon fisheries in the Buskin and Pasagshak rivers. Pink and silver salmon are also found in the **Buskin** and **Pasagshak rivers,** and **Monashka, Pillar, Russian, Salonie, American, Olds, Roslyn** and **Chiniak creeks.**

Afognak and Raspberry islands, both approximately 30 air miles northeast of Kodiak, offer excellent remote hunting and fishing. Both islands are brown bear country. Hikers and fishermen should make noise as they travel and carry a .30–06 or larger rifle. Stay clear of bears. If you take a dog, make sure it is under control. Dogs can create dangerous situations with bears.

CAUTION: A paralytic-shellfish-poisoning alert is in effect for all Kodiak Island beaches. This toxin is extremely poisonous. There are no approved beaches for clamming on Kodiak Island. For more current information, call the Dept. of Environmental Conservation in Anchorage at (907) 269-7500.

Sunrise on a peaceful morning on Kodiak Island.
(© W. Wright-Diamond Photo)

Rezanof–Monashka Bay Road Log

Distance is measured from the junction of Rezanof Drive and Marine Way in downtown Kodiak (K).

K 0.1 Mill Bay Road access to library, post office and Kodiak businesses.

K 0.4 Entrance to Near Island bridge and North End Park (trails, picnic areas); St. Herman Harbor (boat launch); Rotary Park. Access to Trident Basin seaplane base.

K 2 Benny Benson Drive. Turnoff left to Kodiak College and beginning of paved bicycle trail, which parallels main road to Fort Abercrombie State Historic Park. Excellent for walking, jogging and bicycling.

K 3.4 Turnout and gravel parking area for Mill Bay Park. Scenic picnic spot with picnic tables, barbecue grates. Good ocean fishing from beach.

K 3.8 Bayside Fire Department

K 3.9 Road right to **Fort Abercrombie State Historic Park**. Drive in 0.2 mile to campground; 13 campsites with 7-night limit at $10 per night, water, toilets, fishing, swimming and picnic shelter. Extensive system of scenic hiking trails. No off-road biking. View of bay and beach, WWII fortifications, "Ready Ammo" bunker at Miller Point, open Monday, Wednesday and Saturday, 1–3 P.M.; Sunday 2–4 P.M. for public viewing (Hours may vary.). Saturday evening naturalist programs June 1 to Aug. 30. Just beyond the campground entrance is the Alaska State Parks ranger station, open weekdays 8 A.M. to 5 P.M.; pay phone, public restrooms, park information.

K 4.6 Monashka Bay Park at junction with Otmeloi Way; playground, picnic area.

K 6.4 Kodiak Island Borough baler/landfill facility. Recycling center. *Pavement ends, gravel road begins.*

K 6.8 Gravel turnout.

K 6.9 Good view of Three Sisters mountains.

K 7.2 Turnoff for VFW RV park with camping facilities (including electrical hookups), scenic views, restaurant and lounge, (907) 486-3195; Sportsman Assoc. indoor shooting range, (907) 486-8566.

K 7.6 Pillar Creek bridge and Pillar Creek Hatchery.

K 8.3 Turnoff for Pillar Beach, a beautiful black-sand beach at mouth of creek. Scenic picnic area. Dolly Varden pink and silver salmon; fishing allowed only in mouth of creek.

K 8.5 Pullout.

K 9.3 Scenic overlook and panoramic views of Monashka Bay and Monashka Mountain.

K 10.1 Gravel pullout and parking; North Sister trailhead.

K 11.2 Bridge over Monashka Creek.

K 11.3 Road ends; large turnaround parking area. Paths lead through narrow band of trees to secluded **Monashka Bay** beach. Large, sweeping sandy beach. Excellent for picnics. Picnic tables, restrooms, improved beach access. Fishing off beach for Dolly Varden, pink salmon and silvers.

To the north of parking area is trailhead for **Termination Point Trail**, a beautiful 5-mile hike on a loop trail along meadows, ocean bluffs and dense Sitka spruce forest. *NOTE: Leisnoi user permit required to hike Termination Point Trail.*

Chiniak Road Log

Distance from Kodiak's U.S. post office building (K).

K 0 Kodiak U.S. post office building on Mill Bay Road.

K 2.4 Gibson Cove. Deadman's Curve provides panoramic view of Kodiak, Chiniak Bay and nearby islands.

K 3.8 **Boy Scout Lake**, stocked; gravel turnout and parking to left.

K 4.4 **U.S. Fish and Wildlife Service Visitor Center** and Kodiak National Wildlife Refuge headquarters. Exhibits and films on Kodiak wildlife.

Access to **Buskin River State Recreation Site**; 15 RV campsites with a 14-night limit at $10/night, picnic tables and shelter, water, trails and beach access. Fishing along Buskin River and on beach area at river's mouth for red, silver and pink salmon and trout. Parking; wheelchair-accessible fishing platform.

K 5 Unmarked turnoff for Anton Larsen Bay Road (see log this section).

K 5.1 Kodiak airport.

K 5.5 *CAUTION: Jet blast area at end of runway. Stop here and wait if you see a jet preparing for takeoff. Do not enter or stay in this area if you see a jet.*

K 5.6 Pullout with limited parking near trailhead to Barometer Mountain. Steep, straight, well-trodden trail to 2,500-foot peak. Beautiful panoramic views.

K 6.6 Entrance to U.S. Coast Guard station.

K 6.9 Women's Bay, USCG C-130 aircraft and helicopters may be seen on apron.

K 7.2 Road continues around Womens Bay. USCG cutters tie up at pier across the bay. The drive out to Chiniak affords excellent views of the extremely rugged coastline of the island.

K 9.3 Turnoff to Kodiak Island Fairgrounds and Kodiak Island Raceway. Excellent bird watching on tideflats to Salonie Creek.

K 10.1 **Sargent Creek** bridge. Good fishing for pink salmon in August.

K 10.3 Russian River and Bell's Flats Road.

K 10.7 Grocery and liquor store, diesel and unleaded gas. Fairwind Cafe.

K 10.9 Video store; tire repair.

K 11.7 Four-wheeler trail and trailhead

Kodiak Vicinity

to 2,300-foot Kachevaroff Mountain. Gradual incline, great views in alpine country, low-bush cranberries in fall. Watch for bear.

K 11.8 Small pullout.

K 12 Salonie Creek. Pinks (early August), chums, silvers, Dolly Varden.

K 12.4 Salonie Creek Rifle Range turnoff.

K 12.8 Begin climb up Marine Hill. Kashevaroff trailhead; wildflowers, cranberries in fall. *NOTE: Very hazardous road in winter when icy.*

Pavement ends, gravel begins. NOTE: Road can be dusty. Drive with headlights on at all times.

K 13.6 Turnout with panoramic view of Mary Island, Womens Bay, Bell's Flats, Kodiak. Mountain goats visible with binoculars in spring and fall in mountains behind Bell's Flats.

K 14.4 Pullout at **Heitman Lake** trailhead. Beautiful views. Lake is stocked with rainbow trout.

K 14.6 View of Long Island and Cliff Point.

K 15.2 Dirt road and trailhead to Horseshoe Lake. Trail continues past second grove of spruce trees down to lake.

K 17.0 USCG communication facility; emergency phone.

K 19 Undeveloped picnic area in grove of trees along beach of Middle Bay; easy access to beach. Watch for livestock.

K 19.6 Small Creek bridge.

K 20 Salt Creek bridge. Excellent bird watching on tideflats to left. Good fishing for pinks, chums and silver salmon.

K 20.8 American River bridge. River empties into Middle Bay.

K 20.9 Unimproved road on right to Saltery Cove. *NOTE: Road is barely passable even for 4-wheel-drive vehicles; not recommended.*

K 21 Felton Creek Bridge.

K 21.3 Eagle's nest in cottonwood tree, easily observed.

K 23.1 Foot access to gravel beach; nice picnic site.

K 24.1 *CAUTION: Steep switchbacks. Slow to 10 mph.*

K 24.5 Pullout and access to Mayflower

Lake; stocked with silver salmon.

K 24.6 Pullout for Mayflower Beach. Beachcombing, picnicking, hiking.

K 25.4 Pullout with view.

K 27.7 Turnout. Spectacular view of Kalsin Bay.

K 28.1 Improved pullout.

K 28.2 Improved pullout. Steep road drops down to head of Kalsin Bay; sheer cliff on one side of road. Road has been widened, and there is now a guard rail to the bottom of the hill.

K 28.5 Improved pullout.

K 28.9 Kalsin Bay Inn; food, bar, laundromat, showers, tire repair; open year-round. Goats often seen in hills in fall and spring.

K 29.2 Deadman Creek Bridge.

K 29.9 Improved pullout. Olds River. Excellent fishing for pinks, chums and silver salmon.

K 30.3 Kalsin River (creek) bridge.

K 30.6 Road forks: Turn left for Chiniak, right for Pasagshak Bay. See Pasagshak Bay Road log this section.

K 30.9 Kalsin Pond; excellent silver salmon fishing in fall.

K 31.1 Turnoff for access to mouth of Olds River and beach.

K 31.5 Highway maintenance station.

K 32 Picnic area beside Kalsin Bay. Nice beach.

K 32.4 Road to unimproved picnic area. Gravel beach. Fishing for pinks.

K 33.2 Turnoff. Myrtle Creek bridge just past turnoff; picnic site. Beach access.

K 34.9 Thumbs Up Cove. Unimproved boat launch ramp.

K 35.1 Chiniak post office. Window hours Tuesday and Thursday 4–6 P.M., Saturday noon to 2 P.M.

K 35.9 Brookers Lagoon. Access to gravel beach.

K 36.5 Chiniak Bakery.

K 36.7 Kodiak Island Winery.

K 36.9 Roslyn River. Access to Roslyn Bay beach and picnic area.

K 37.2 Roslyn River Bridge.

K 37.6 Access to mouth of Roslyn River.

K 39.5 Access to a beautiful point overlooking the sea; site of WWII installations. Good place for photos. Sea otters in kelp beds year-round.

K 39.9 Twin Creeks Beach, dark sand and rolling breakers. Park in pullout area. Do not drive onto soft beach sand.

K 40.4 Twin Creek.

K 40.7 Silver Beach.

K 40.8 Pony Lake (stocked).

K 41.3 Chiniak wayside, a borough park; benches, beautiful setting.

K 41.5 Chiniak school, public library, playground and ballfield. Baseball diamond, play area, picnic tables.

K 41.6 Turnoff onto King Crab Way. Location of Tsunami Evacuation Center.

K 42.4 Road's End lounge and restaurant. Excellent whalewatching for gray whales in April, across road from restaurant.

Beyond this point the cliff is eroded right to the edge of the road. Exercise extreme caution while driving this stretch.

K 42.5 **Chiniak Point**, also known as Cape Chiniak, is the south point of land at the entrance to Chiniak Bay. Capt. Cook named the point Cape Greville in 1778, but that name is now applied to the point of land 2 miles southeast of here. State road maintenance ends here. Unmaintained road continues as public easement across Leisnoi Native Corp. land. Public access discouraged beyond Chiniak Creek.

K 42.8 Public road ends at **Chiniak Creek**. Pink salmon fishing in mid-summer. View of Chiniak Point. Turnaround point.

Pasagshak Bay Road Log

Distance is measured from junction with Chiniak Road (J).

J 0 Turn at **Milepost K 30.6** Chiniak Road for Pasagshak Bay.

J 0.1 Northland Ranch Resort; lodging, food, lounge.

J 1.2 Turnout at access to Kalsin River; picnic area.

J 3.4 Turnout to picnic area by beautiful stream.

J 4.7 Top of Pasagshak Pass; scenic views.

J 5.3 Turnout.

J 6.8 Road crosses Lake Rose Tead on causeway. Good fishing in river from here to ocean. Good place to view spawning salmon and eagles late summer through fall.

J 7.1 Combined barn and single aircraft hangar to right. Remnant of Joe Zentner Ranch, established in the 1940s.

J 8.7 Entering **Pasagshak River State Recreation Site**.

J 8.8 Pasagshak River SRS campground; 12 campsites with a 14-night limit (no fee), toilets, water, picnic tables; fishing and beach access.

J 9.3 Mouth of Pasagshak River, view of Pasagshak Bay.

J 9.5 Turnout at Boat Bay, traditional gravel boat launch ramp and mooring area. Four-wheel-drive vehicles required to use launch ramp.

J 10.2 Turnoff to Pasagshak Point, 2 trout lakes, nice vistas.

J 10.7 *CAUTION: Watch for free-roaming cattle and bison beginning here. Free-ranging buffalo sometimes block the road. Stop and wait; they will eventually move. Sounding your horn is not advised. Do not approach free-ranging buffalo on foot. They can be dangerous.*

J 10.9 Cattle Guard crossing and beginning of Kodiak Cattle Co. grazing lease. Public land—hunting, fishing, hiking, but keep vehicle on road.

J 11.3 Turnout provides panoramas of Narrow Cape, Ugak Island, Pasagshak Point, Sitkalidik Island. Good beachcombing on sandy beaches.

J 11.7 Road to beach access.

J 12.0 Bear Paw Ranch Youth Camp.

J 12.1 Beach access.

J 13.6 Paved road begins and continues to **Milepost J 15.8**. Access to Kodiak Launch Complex facility and Fossil Beach.

J 14.4 Entrance to Kodiak Cattle Co. Ranch; guided horseback riding, fishing, camping, hunting.

J 14.8 Entrance at right to USCG Narrow Cape Loran Station. Emergency phone. No public access.

J 15.7 Kodiak Launch Complex, a 3,100-acre, low-earth-orbit launch complex of the Alaska Aerospace Development Corporation (AADC). Site includes support, payload and processing facilities and launch pad. Bear right on gravel road to Fossil Beach.

J 15.8 Paved road ends. *Minimal road maintenance from here to end of road. Drive with caution and have a good spare tire.*

J 16 Road on left leads to Twin Lakes. *NOTE: 4-wheel-drive accessible only beyond this point. Rental cars should park here and continue on foot.*

J 16.2 Twin Lakes; trout fishing.

J 16.4 Road ends at Fossil Cliffs. Fossils embedded in cliffs are visible along Fossil Beach to left and right (low tide only). Beautiful vistas and views of WWII observation bunkers on Narrow Cape to the left.

CAUTION: The road leading down to Fossil Beach is very steep and deeply rutted by rain and vehicle wear. Be certain of your ability to drive back up before descending the hill. Cliffs are extremely unstable. Do not approach cliff face, and watch for falling rocks at all times.

Anton Larsen Bay Road Log

Distance is measured from the turnoff (T) at Milepost K 5 Chiniak Road.

T 0 Unmarked turnoff for Anton Larsen Bay Road at **Milepost K 5** on Chiniak Road immediately before crossing the Buskin River bridge.

T 0.6 **Buskin River** bridge No. 6. Parking area accesses fishing along river. Side road leads to good fishing holes.

T 0.7 *Pavement ends, gravel begins.*

T 0.9 Enter posted restricted-access area in USCG antenna field. Do not leave road for approximately next 1.5 miles.

T 1.4 **Buskin River** bridge No. 7. Turnoff before crossing bridge to access river and outlet of Buskin Lake. Good fishing for Dolly Varden, salmon.

T 1.6 Paved road leads to USCG communications site. Gravel road leads to Anton Larsen Bay. Scenic drive, berry picking, mountain views, wildflowers, boat launch ramp. Excellent kayaking in bay and around outer islands.

T 2 Pyramid Mountain (elev. 2,420 feet).

T 2.3 End restricted access area.

© Marion Owen

T 2.9 **Bear Valley Golf Course** (USCG); driving range, 9-holes, open to the public April–Oct., weather permitting. Phone (907) 487-5323.

T 3.2 Turnout at unimproved trailhead to Buskin Lake. *Watch for bears.*

T 4.1 Steep switchback.

T 5.7 Buskin Valley Winter Recreation Area. Excellent spot for sledding, skiing, snowboarding; great for kids. Summer trailhead to top of 2,400-foot Pyramid Mountain. Trail follows ridgeline. Great vistas from top.

T 7.5 Red Cloud River bridge. Small, unimproved campsite adjacent river.

T 8 Red Cloud Ranch. Horseback riding.

T 9.3 Head of Anton Larsen Bay. Fox, land otters and deer can be seen in this area. Good bird watching along tidal flats.

T 10.3 Public small-boat launch adjacent to road.

T 10.4 Anton Larsen Bay public dock. Departure point for sea kayakers.

T 11.7 Road ends at turnaround; parking. A foot-path continues beyond this point.

INSIDE PASSAGE

Southeastern Alaska mainline ports from Ketchikan to Skagway

Commercial fishing boats are a common sight along the Inside Passage. *(© David Job)*

Alaska's Inside Passage, located in the southeastern section of the state, is known by many residents simply as "Southeast." It is a unique region where industry, transportation, recreation and community planning are dictated by spectacular topography.

Attractions in this region include Russian and Tlingit dance performances, museums, totem poles, colorful saloons and fine dining; sportfishing, hiking trails and wilderness adventure tours by kayak, canoe and raft; glaciers and icefield flightseeing. Sightseeing Glacier Bay National Park and Preserve, Misty Fiords and Admiralty Island national monuments, Mendenhall Glacier at Juneau, LeConte Glacier near Petersburg and the Stikine River near Wrangell are also some of Southeast's top attractions.

The region is accessible by air, land or sea. Jet service is available to Juneau, Ketchikan, Wrangell, Petersburg, Sitka and Gustavus. Smaller communities are served by local commuter aircraft. The port communities of Haines and Skagway offer road connections to the Alaska Highway system via the Haines Highway and Klondike Highway 2. The Alaska Marine Highway moves people and vehicles between ports and connects the Inside Passage with Prince Rupert, BC, and Bellingham, WA. Several cruise ship lines ply the waterways of the Inside Passage and offer a variety of cruising opportunities.

The region measures about 125 by 400 miles, with 60 percent consisting of thousands of islands covered with dense forests of spruce, hemlock and cedar, a result of the mild, moist coastal climate. These islands make up the Alexander Archipelago and include Prince of Wales Island, the third largest island in the United States (the Big Island of Hawaii is first, followed by Kodiak). The Coast Mountains form the mainland portion of southeastern Alaska.

Southeastern Alaska lies between 54°40' and 60° north latitude, the same as Scotland, Denmark and southern Sweden. The latitude of Scotland's Loch Ness is slightly north of the latitude at Wrangell Narrows. Stockholm and Skagway share the same latitude, and Ketchikan's latitude is a little south of Copenhagen's.

Warmed by ocean currents, this region experiences mild, warm summers, with July temperatures averaging around 60°F. An occasional heat wave may reach the high 80s. Winters are cool, alternating snow, rain and sunshine; January temperatures average 20° to 40°F. Sub-zero winter temperatures are uncommon. The region receives considerable annual rainfall, from 27 inches to more than 200 inches (heaviest in late fall, lightest in summer). Populated areas receive 30 to 200 inches of snow annually; the high mountains more than 400 inches a year.

The majority of southeastern Alaska lies within Tongass National Forest, the largest national forest in the United States. Southeastern Alaska has over 5.6 million acres of designated wilderness.

Numerous rivers and streams, mountains, valleys, melting glaciers and heavy rainfall create ideal spawning grounds for salmon. Local waters harbor abundant life, including crab, shrimp, halibut, herring and black cod.

About 72,000 people live along the Inside Passage, according to 1990 U.S. Census figures, with the majority living in the 5 major communities—Juneau (30,711), Ketchikan (14,070), Sitka (8,835), Petersburg (3,224) and Wrangell (2,308). More than 20 percent of the region's population is Native, mostly Tlingit (KLINK it) Indian, plus Haida (HI duh) and Tsimshian (SHIM shian).

Alaska's Natives, famous for their totem poles, weaving, beading, basketry and dancing, occupied the region long before Vitus Bering arrived in Alaska in 1741.

Russia controlled Alaska from the turn of the 19th century until 1867, centering its extensive fur-trading empire in Sitka, the Russian capital of Alaska. Sitka was a port of international trade, controlling trading posts from California to the Aleutians, and was considered cultured because of European influence. At a time when San Francisco was a crude new boom town, Sitka was called the "Paris of the Pacific."

Commercial interest in southeastern Alaska declined with the fur trade, following Alaska's purchase by the United States. Interest in Southeast was rekindled by the salmon industry as canneries were established, the first at Klawock in 1878. Salmon canning peaked in the late 1930s and then declined from overfishing.

But the first significant white populations arrived because of gold. By the time thousands of gold seekers traveled through the Inside Passage in 1898 to Skagway and on to Canada's Klondike (sparking interest in the rest of Alaska), the largest gold ore mine of its day, the Treadwell near Juneau, had been in operation since 1884.

Juneau became Alaska's capital in 1906, and Southeast remained Alaska's dominant region until WWII, when military activity and the Alaska Highway shifted emphasis to Anchorage and Fairbanks.

Additional population growth came to Southeast with new timber harvesting in the 1950s. Increased government activities, as a result of Alaska statehood in 1959, brought even more people.

The Inside Passage is the last stronghold of the American bald eagle. More than 20,000 eagles reside in the region, and sightings are frequent. Humpback and killer whales, porpoises, sea lions and seals are often observed from ferries, cruise ships and charter boats. Bear viewing opportunities are offered at Pack Creek on Admiralty Island and Anan Creek near Wrangell.

KETCHIKAN

Population: 7,922
(See map on page 654)

Ketchikan Special Events:

• **April**—Annual Alaska Hummingbird Festival. Phone (907) 228-6220 for dates.
• **July 4**—The Timber Carnival.
• **August 1, 2, 3**—Annual Blueberry Arts Festival and Gigglefest Dance Festival.

Ketchikan, first port of call in Alaska. (© Kris Graef, staff)

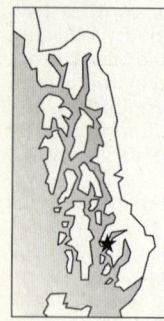

Located on the southwest coast of Revillagigedo Island, Ketchikan is 235 miles south of Juneau and 90 miles north of Prince Rupert, BC. Ketchikan and Saxman are the only communities on Revillagigedo Island. **Emergency Services: Alaska State Troopers,** phone (907) 225-5118. **City Police,** phone (907) 225-6631, or 911 for all emergency services. **Fire Department, Ambulance and Ketchikan Volunteer Rescue Squad,** phone (907) 225-9616. **Hospital,** Ketchikan General at 3100 Tongass Ave., phone (907) 225-5171. **Coast Guard,** phone (907) 228-0340.

Visitor Information: The **Ketchikan Visitor Information Center** is located downtown on the Cruise Ship Docks. Open during daily business hours and weekends May through September. Write them at 131 Front St., Ketchikan 99901; phone (907) 225-6166 or (800) 770-3300; fax (907) 225-4250; email kvb@ktn.net; www.visit-ketchikan.com.

Revillagigedo Island is located in Tongass National Forest. Maps, brochures, trip planning assistance and general information on recreational opportunities in Tongass National Forest and other federal lands in Alaska are available at the Alaska Public Lands Information Center in the **Southeast**

Alaska Discovery Center, 50 Main St., Ketchikan, AK 99901; phone (907) 228-6220, fax (907) 228-6234. Or visit the Tongass National Forest web site at www.fs.fed.us/r10/tongass.

The U.S. Forest Service office for **Ketchikan-Misty Fiords Ranger District** is located at 3031 Tongass Avenue; open 8 A.M. to 4:30 P.M. weekdays; phone (907) 225-2148. The Ketchikan-Misty Fiords Ranger District encompasses 3.2 million acres of Tongass National Forest land in Southeast, maintaining 60 miles of trails, 2 campgrounds, and 30 public-use cabins (most accessible by floatplane or boat). Cabins and campsites can by reserved; phone 1-877-444-6777 or visit www.reserveusa.com.

Elevation: Sea level. **Climate:** Rainy. Yearly average rainfall is 162 inches and snowfall is 32 inches. Average daily maximum temperature in July 65°F; daily minimum 50°F. Daily maximum in January 39°F; daily minimum 28°F. **Radio:** KTKN 930, KRBD-FM 105.9, KGTW-FM 106.7, KFMJ-FM 99.9. **Television:** CFTK (Prince Rupert, BC) and 27 cable channels. **Newspapers:** *Ketchikan Daily News* (daily); *New Alaskan* (monthly); *The Local Paper* (weekly), *Images* (weekly).

Private Aircraft: Ketchikan International Airport on Gravina Island; elev. 88 feet; length 7,500 feet; asphalt; fuel 100LL, A. Ketchikan Harbor seaplane base downtown; fuel 80, 100, A.

Ketchikan is located on the southwest side of Revillagigedo (ruh-vee-uh-guh-GAY-doh) Island, on Tongass Narrows opposite Gravina Island. The name Ketchikan is derived from a Tlingit name, Kitschk-Hin, meaning the creek of the "thundering wings of an eagle." The creek flows through the town, emptying into Tongass Narrows. Before Ketchikan was settled, the area at the mouth of Ketchikan Creek was a Tlingit Indian fish camp. Settlement began with interest in both mining and fishing. The first salmon cannery moved here in 1886, operating under the name of Tongass Packing Co. It burned down in August 1889. Gold was discovered nearby in 1898. Ketchikan was incorporated in 1900.

As mining waned, the fishing industry began to grow. By the 1930s, more than a dozen salmon canneries had been built; during the peak years of the canned salmon industry, Ketchikan earned the title of "Salmon Capital of the World." But overfishing caused a drastic decline in salmon by the 1940s. Today, Trident Seafoods shore-based pink salmon cannery operates from early July through September, producing up to 500,000 cases of canned salmon per year. Southeast accounts for slightly more than half the pink salmon harvested in Alaska.

As fishing reached a low point, the

KETCHIKAN Travel Directory

INSIDE PASSAGE • Ketchikan

ACCOMMODATIONS

KETCHIKAN PLUM TREE INN & CHARTER

CG Licensed & insured

Enjoy a family style atmosphere for your lodging and fishing in SE Alaska

JUNE-AUGUST
We cater to cruise ships

Call Fax or Email for details
Ph: 907-247-6500
Fax: 907-247-1179
email: jheart@kpunet.net
www.alaskasilvercat.com

Bed & Breakfast
Ketchikan, Alaska

Specialty Packages
* B&B's
* Outfitted Apts.
* Sportfishing
* Sightseeing
* Car Rentals

Book Online Enter to Win a Smoked Salmon Fillet!

www.Ketchikan-Lodging.com

Ketchikan Reservation Service
412 D-1 Loop Rd • Ketchikan, AK 99901
Phone/Fax 907.247.5337

Reservations 800.987.5337

TOURS

Experience Misty Fjords
Visit the grandeur of Misty Fjords National Monument. By air and by sea

GOLDBELT ALASKA CRUISES

(800) 228-1905 Toll Free • (907) 225-6044
PO Box 7815, Ketchikan, AK 99901 • www.mistyfjord.net
alaskacruises@goldbelt.com

ACTIVITIES

SOUTHEAST SEA KAYAKS ALASKA

Guided Trips
Misty Fjords • Prince of Wales
Instruction • Rentals & Sales

www.kayakketchikan.com
800•471•1262
907•225•1258
sekayak@aptalaska.net
1007 Water Street, Ketchikan, AK 99901

Southeast Alaska's Flightseeing Professionals

Southeast Aviation LLC

Misty Fjords & Glacier Tours • Fly Out Fishing & Hiking Trips
Bear Viewing Tours • Forest Service Cabin Trips

Visit our website at www.SoutheastAviation.com
email: info@southeastaviation.com
1249 Tongass Avenue, Ketchikan AK 99901
Phone: 907-225-2900 • Fax: 907-225-2902

timber industry expanded. The first sawmill was originally built in 1898 at Dolomi on Prince of Wales Island to cut timber for the Dolomi Mine. It was dismantled and moved to Ketchikan and rebuilt in 1903. A large pulp mill was constructed a few miles northwest of town in 1953 at Ward Cove. It closed in 1997.

Tourism is an extremely important industry here. Ketchikan is Alaska's first port of call for cruise ships and the Alaska state ferries. The Inter-Island Ferry Authority's MV *Prince of Wales* connects Ketchikan with Prince of Wales Island.

Ketchikan is Alaska's southernmost major city and the state's fourth largest (after Anchorage, Fairbanks and Juneau). The closest city in British Columbia is Prince Rupert.

Ketchikan is a linear waterfront city, with much of its 3-mile-long business district suspended above water on pilings driven into the bottom of Tongass Narrow. Its homes cling to the steep wooded hillside, many reached by "staircase streets"—lengths of wooden stairs rather than paved road. All of Ketchikan's original streets and walkways were built as wooden trestles because of the steep and rocky terrain.

The area supports 4 public grade schools, 4 parochial grade schools, a junior high school, 2 high schools and the University of Alaska Southeast campus.

Lodging & Services

Accommodations in Ketchikan include several motels/hotels and bed-and-breakfasts. Shopping and restaurants are located downtown and at Plaza Mall on Tongass Avenue (North Tongass Highway). Ketchikan also has a Walmarts.

Captain's Quarters Bed and Breakfast. Located in a historic hillside neighborhood within short walking distance of downtown. Private entrance. Spectacular view of the harbor and surrounding wilderness. Three rooms, each with queen-size bed, private bath, cable TV and phone. Continental breakfast. 325 Lund Street, Ketchikan. Phone (907) 225-4912. Email: captbnb@ptialaska.net. www.ptialaska.net/~captbnb.
[ADVERTISEMENT]

Ketchikan Eagle View Hostel is located in a private home overlooking Tongass Narrow at 2303 5th Ave., Ketchikan, AK 99901; phone (907) 225-5461; email info@eagleviewhostel.com; web site www.eagleviewhostel.com. The hostel is open April through October. Cost of $25/person/night includes use of kitchen, barbecue, decks and common area. Sheets and towels provided. Two upper floor rooms, one with double bed and one with bunk bed and twin, and; shared bathroom. Room on first level sleeps 6 and has its own bathroom.

HI-Ketchikan Youth Hostel is located downtown in the First United Methodist Church at Grant and Main Streets. The hostel accommodates 19 hostellers; separate male and female dorms for sleeping, floor mattresses provided (bring sleeping bags); showers and kitchen facillities. The Hostel is open from June 1 to August 31. Check-in time is 7–9 A.M. and 6–11 P.M. (will open for late ferry arrivals; phone from terminal). Cost is $12 per night for members (AYH membership passes may be purchased at the hostel), $15 for nonmembers. Reservations recommended. Write Box 8515, Ketchikan, AK 99901; phone (907) 225-3319 (summer only); email ktnyh@eagle.ptialaska.net.

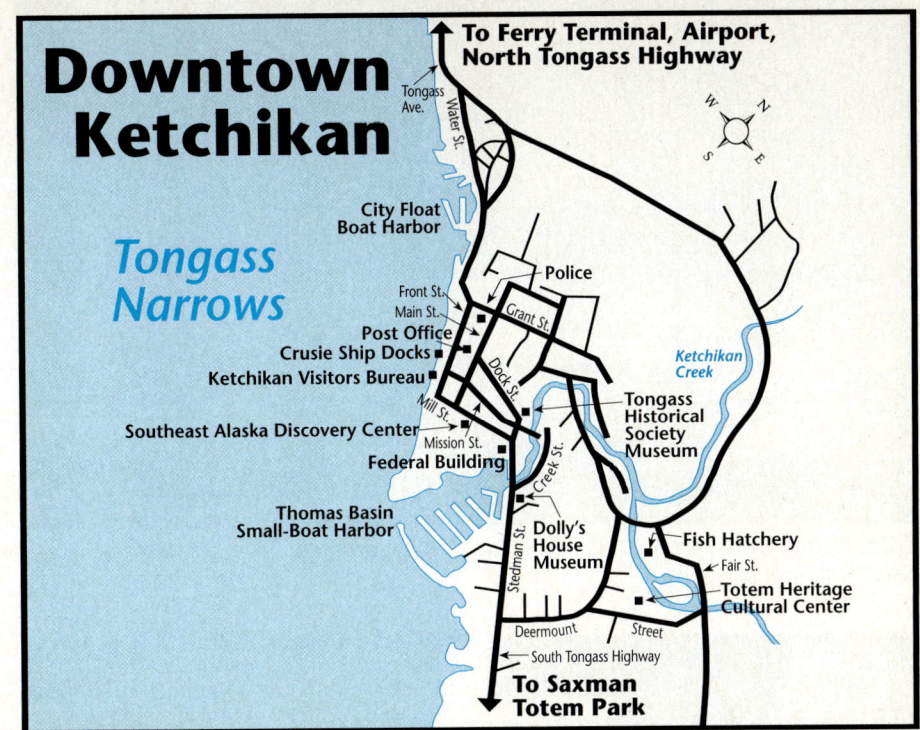

Camping

There are 2 campgrounds at the U.S. Forest Service's Ward Lake Recreation Area and a campground at Settlers Cove State Recreation Site; all are north of the city via North Tongass Highway (see highway log this section). Advance reservations can be made for designated sites at the Forest Service campgrounds through the National Recreation Reservation Service; phone toll-free 877-444-6777 or on the Internet at reserveusa.com.

Dump station located at Ketchikan Public Works office, 2 blocks north of state ferry terminal. Contact the visitors bureau for brochure on RV use and parking.

Transportation

Air: Daily scheduled jet service is provided from the Ketchikan International Airport by Alaska Airlines to other Southeast cities, Anchorage and Seattle, WA. Commuter and charter service is available to other Southeast communities via Pacific Airways, Taquan Air and Southeast Aviation.

Airport terminal, across Tongass Narrows on Gravina Island, is reached via shuttle ferry (10-minute ride one way) departing from the airport parking area on North Tongass Avenue at half-hour intervals. It is 2.7 miles from downtown to the airport shuttle ferry.

Ferry: Alaska Marine Highway vessels connect Ketchikan with all mainline southeastern Alaska port cities, Prince Rupert, BC, and Bellingham, WA. There are also daily state ferry connections between Ketchikan and Metlakatla (1 hr. 15 min.) via Alaska state ferry, and Ketchikan and Hollis on Prince of Wales Island (2 hrs. 45 min.) via the Inter-Island Ferry Authority.

The Alaska Marine Highway Terminal is located 2.3 miles north of downtown Ketchikan on Tongass Avenue (North Tongass Highway). The terminal building has a large waiting room, vending machines, restrooms, public phones and brochure racks; phone (907) 225-6182. Taxi cabs meet most ferry arrivals. Bus schedules are available in the terminal building and there is a bus stop on Tongass Avenue at the ferry terminal entrance. A post office, restaurant and grocery store are within walking distance of the terminal.

The Inter-Island Ferry Authority's MV *Prince of Wales*, providing daily passenger and vehicle service between Ketchikan and Prince of Wales Island, departs from a ferry dock adjacent the Alaska Marine Highway terminal. A reservation desk for the *Prince of Wales* is located inside the Alaska Marine Highway terminal building; phone (907) 225-4838. Or for information and reservations, phone toll-free (866) 308-4848 or visit interislandferry.com.

Bus: "The Bus" provides service between the ferry terminal and downtown every 15 minutes; to Walmart and Saxman every 30 minutes. Regular fares $1.25 to $2.25; 24-hour and 3-day unlimited use passes available. Contact Ketchikan Gateway Borough Transportation Services with questions; phone (907) 225-8726.

Car Rental: Available at airport and downtown locations from Alaska Car Rental (907) 225-5000 and Southeast Auto Rental (907) 225-8778.

Taxi: Sourdough Taxi Co. Taxi cabs meet ferry and airport arrivals.

Highways: North Tongass and South Tongass highways (see logs this section).

Cruise Ships: Ketchikan is the first port of call for many cruise ships to Alaska. Cruises depart from U.S. West Coast ports and Vancouver, BC.

Private Boats: Two public docks downtown, Thomas Basin and City Float, provide transient moorage. In the West End District, 1 mile from downtown, Bar Harbor has moorage, showers. No gas available. Permits required. Moorage space in Ketchikan is limited; all private boats should contact the harbormaster's office at (907) 228-5632 prior to arrival to secure a spot.

Attractions

Tour the city. Ketchikan is an easy town to explore on foot or by tour bus. For a view

Totem Bight State Historical Park is located approximately 10 miles north of Ketchikan. (© Kris Graef, staff)

of the city from the water, there are historical sightseeing cruises and amphibious boat tours. The waterfront is the center of the city, and most attractions are within walking distance of the cruise ship docks. Pick up an *Official Historic Ketchikan Walking Tour Map* at the Visitor Information Center on the cruise ship docks.

Highlights of the walking tour include: St. John's Episcopal Church and Seamen's Center, built in 1903; the Grant Street Trestle, on the National Register of Historic Places; the Ketchikan Creek Fish Ladder; and other landmarks, such as the Ketchikan Mural on Stedman Street, created by Don Barrie with the help of 25 Native youth in 1978. The commissioned work, 120-feet long, is collectively entitled *The Return of the Eagle*.

The city's public parks offer rest stops for walking tourists. City Park, located along Park Avenue near Deer Mountain Hatchery, has small ponds that were once used as holding ponds for Ketchikan's first hatchery. **Whale Park**, conveniently located betwee the cruise ship docks and Creek Street on Mill Street, is shaped like a whale. A very small park, it is a popular rest stop and has the Chief Kyan Totem Pole (carved by Israel Shotridge) and the historic Knox Brothers Clock.

Totem poles, a major attraction in Ketchikan, are scattered around the city. Major collections are found at the Totem Heritage Center, Saxman and Totem Bight (see detailed descriptions this section).

Southeast Alaska Discovery Center, located on Main Street, is 1 of 4 Alaska Public Lands Information Centers in the state (the others are located in Fairbanks, Anchorage and Tok). The Discovery Center, like the other APLCs, offers trip planning help for public lands and a well-stocked Alaska Natural History Assoc. store. In addition, the Discovery Center has interpretive exhibits on Native culture and Southeast Alaska history and resources. The 200-seat theatre presents the 14-minute multi-media program, *Mystical Southeast Alaska*, every half-hour during the summer.

Southeast Alaska Discovery Center is open 8 A.M to 5 P.M. daily, from May 9 to September 30; and 10 A.M. to 4:30 P.M., Tuesdays through Saturdays, between October 30 and May 8. Admission fee ; phone (907) 228-6220, fax 228-6234.

Cape Fox Hill–Creek Street Funicular. Constructed in 1990, this automated cable car traverses a 70 percent incline, rising 130 vertical feet from Creek Street to the top of Cape Fox Hill and the lobby of the West-Coast Cape Fox Lodge. (The hotel has an extensive collection of Native art. Cape Fox Lodge is also accessible by road.)

The funicular operates very much like an elevator. From Creek Street, press the call button for the funicular. When the doors open, get inside and push the Up button to go up or the Down button to go down.

Return to Creek Street by following **Married Man's Trail** (boardwalk and stairs) back down the hill through the trees. Great views and good photo ops of downtown from this trail.

Tongass Historical Museum, located in the Centennial Building on Dock Street. The museum features photos and artifacts of early-day Ketchikan and its development from Native fish camp to Alaska's "First City." The museum is open in summer (May 1 to Sept. 30) from 8 A.M. to 5 P.M. daily. Winter (October 1 to April 30) hours are 1–5 P.M. Wednesday–Friday, 10 A.M.–4 P.M. Saturday and 1–4 P.M. Sunday. The Raven Stealing the Sun totem stands at the entrance. Salmon viewing platforms. Admission fee is $2. Phone (907) 225-5600 for more information.

Ketchikan Public Library is also located in the Centennial Building, which was built to commemorate the purchase of Alaska from Russia in 1867.

Creek Street, a boardwalk street on pilings that spans Ketchikan Creek near the Stedman Street bridge, was once Ketchikan's "red-light district," where Black Mary, Dolly, Frenchie and others plied their trade for over half a century until 1954. At one time nearly 20 houses lined the far side of Ketchikan Creek. Today, the remaining old houses have been restored and along with newer structures house a variety of shops. Dolly's House, a former brothel, is open during the summer (admission charged).

In late August, watch for salmon in Ketchikan Creek. The viewpoint overlooking the creek also overlooks a metal sculpture that is a tribute to the salmon and a local landmark. Besides shopping and seeing the creek, visitors can take a ride on the Cape Fox Hill–Creek Street Funicular.

Totem Heritage Center, at 601 Deermount St., houses 33 totem poles and fragments retrieved from deserted Tlingit and Haida Indian villages. This national landmark collection comprises the largest exhibit of original totems in the United States. Facilities include craft exhibits, craft classes for children and reference library. Outside the center are 2 poles by Tlingit carver (and National Living Treasure), Nathan Jackson.

Gift shop, craft demonstrations and guided tours during summer months. General admission fee $4. Summer hours are 8 A.M. to 5 P.M. daily. Winter hours (October to mid-May) are 1–5 P.M. Monday through Friday. Phone (907) 225-5900.

Deer Mountain Hatchery and Eagle Center is located across Ketchikan Creek opposite the Totem Heritage Center, on the west side of the city park. The hatchery produces about 100,000 king, 150,000 coho, 30,000 rainbow trout and 6,500 steelhead

Metlakatla Side Trip

Metlakatla (population 1,375) is a Tsimshian Native village located on the west coast of Annette Island, 15 miles south of Ketchikan. The community is accessible by floatplane or by state ferry from Ketchikan.

Metlakatla was founded in 1887 by William Duncan, a Scottish-born lay minister, who moved here with several hundred Tsimshian Indians from a settlement in British Columbia after a falling-out with church authorities. Congress granted reservation status and title to the entire island in 1891, and the new settlement prospered under Duncan, who built a salmon cannery and sawmill.

Today, fishing and lumber continue to be the main economic base of Metlakatla. The community and island also retain the status of a federal Indian reservation, which is why Metlakatla has the only salmon fish traps in Alaska. (Floating fish traps were outlawed by the state shortly after statehood.)

There is a replica of the William Duncan Memorial Church here; the original was destroyed by fire in 1948. The Duncan Museum is located in the original cottage occupied by the Rev. William Duncan until his death in 1918.

Tours to Metlakatla depart daily from Ketchikan; reservations are required. Contact the Community Tour Office at (907) 886-8687 for scheduling information; or toll free 1-877-886-8687; fax (907) 886-7997; http://tours.metlakatla.net. The tour includes a Tshimshian dance performance, salmon bake, the Artists Village and Longhouse, the museum, fisheries plant and church. The tour operates from early-May to September.

fingerlings annually. Observation platforms and information signs provide education on the life cycles of salmon. Also an opportunity to photograph eagles up close at the Eagle Center. Open from 8 A.M. to 4:30 P.M. daily late May to late September.

Great Alaskan Lumberjack Show, featuring Alaska's frontier woodsmen as they compete in events such as buck sawing, axe throwing, power sawing, springboard chop, logrolling duels, and a 50-foot tree climb that ends in a free fall. Covered grandstand seating. Located 1 block off cruise ship docks at the historic spruce mill. Shows performed 3 times daily. Admission $30.60/adults; $15.30/children up to age 12; kids under 5 free. Phone 1-888-320-9049; email info@lumberjacksports.com; www.lumberjackshow.com.

Fish Pirate's Daughter, a well-done local musical-comedy melodrama, portrays Ketchikan's early fishing days, with some of the city's spicier history included. Performed at the Main Street Theatre at 338 Main Street. Shows at 7 P.M. and 8:45 P.M. Fridays in July. Contact First City Players box office at (907) 225-4792 or the Ketchikan Area Arts & Humanities Council hotline at (907) 225-2211 (online at www.Ketchikanarts.org).

Saxman Totem Park, located 2.5 miles south of downtown via South Tongass Highway, is included on the itineraries of most local sightseeing companies. The totem park, open year-round, has 30 totems and a clan house. There is no admission charge, but there is a fee for guided tours (offered May through September). This guided tour includes demonstrations at the Carving Center and performances by the Cape Fox Dancers at the Beaver Tribal House. For more information on hours, tours and events, phone the Cape Fox Tours office at (907) 225-4846, ext. 301; www.capefoxtours.com.

Totem Bight State Historical Park, located at **Milepost 9.9** North Tongass Highway, contains an excellent model of a Tlingit community house and 14 totems in a beautiful wooded setting. The park began as a Civilian Conservation Corps (CCC) project in 1938, when a U.S. Forest Service program aimed at salvaging abandoned totem poles by using older skilled Native carvers and young, unskilled apprentices to reconstruct or copy the poles. Alaskan architect Linn Forrest designed the model Native village, which was originally called Mud Bight. The name was changed to Totem Bight and title to the land transferred to the state in 1959. Totem Bight was added to the National Register of Historic Places in 1970.

The community house, or clanhouse, is representative of those found in many early 19th century Indian villages. The totems reflect Haida and Tlingit cultures.

Misty Fiords National Monument. Located east of Ketchikan, Misty Fiords National Monument encompasses 2.3 million acres of wilderness and is known for its spectacular scenery. Taking its name from the almost constant precipitation characteristic of the area, Misty Fiords is covered with thicks forests of Sitka spruce, western hemlock and cedar, which grow on nearly vertical slopes from sea level to mountain tops. Dramatic waterfalls cascade into glacially carved fjords. The monument is bisected by the 100-mile-long Behm Canal, extraordinary among natural canals for its length and depth. New Eddystone Rock, a 237-foot volcanic plug, rises straight out of Behm Canal

South Tongass Highway

The 12-mile-long South Tongass Highway provides access to Saxman Totem Park, Rotary Beach Park, Mountain Point and George Inlet.

Distance from downtown Ketchikan (K) is shown.

K 0 Junction of Stedman Street and Totem Way in downtown Ketchikan.

K 0.1 Ketchikan Creek and bridge.

K 0.9 U.S. Coast Guard Station Ketchiakn, established in 1989, provides search and rescue, maritime law enforcement and environmental protection.

K 2.5 SAXMAN (pop. 431) was founded in 1896 by Tlingit Alaska Natives and named

after a Presbyterian missionary who served the Tlingit people. The Native village of Saxman has a gas station and convenience store and is the site of **Saxman Totem Park**.

Developed by Cape Fox Corp., this popular attraction includes a carving center and tribal house. Guided tours available from Cape Fox Tours.

K 2.7 Petro Express gas station to west.

K 3.5 Rotary Beach Recreation Area; 2 parking areas, picnic shelters and tables.

K 5 Mountain Point, a point of land at the south coast of Revillagigedo Island, was named in 1883 by Lt. Comdr. H.E. Nichols, USN. Parking area and access to good salmon fishing from shore in July and August.

South Tongass Highway now heads northeast.

K 5.6 Public boat launch.

K 8.2 Herring Cove bridge. Private hatchery for chum, king and coho salmon.

K 8.4 *Pavement ends, gravel begins.*

K 8.7 Whitman Creek and bridge.

K 10.2 Scenic waterfall.

K 10.9 Another scenic waterfall.

K 11.8 George Inlet Lodge; a private fishing lodge

K 12.9 Road ends. View of power plant and abandoned George Inlet cannery. Two-mile walk up gravel road leads to Lower Silvis Lake picnic area. Trail continues to Upper Silvis Lake and joins Deer Mountain trail, which connects to John Mountain National Recreation trail. According to the U.S. Forest Service, the trail between Upper and Lower Silvis lakes is very difficult.

and is visible for miles.

The monument is readily accessible by boat or by floatplane from Ketchikan. Tours of Misty Fiords are available on charter boats out of Ketchikan. Some cruise ships include Behm Canal and Rudyerd Bay in their itineraries. Rudyerd Bay is also a popular destination for sea kayakers.

For more information on the monument stop by the Southeast Alaska Discovery Center on Main Street in Ketchikan (phone 907/228-6220), or the U.S. Forest Service office at 3031 Tongass Avenue (phone 907/ 225-2148). Or check the Tongass National Forest web site at www.fs.fed.us/r10/tongass.

Charter a boat. About 120 vessels operate out of Ketchikan for half-day, all-day or overnight sightseeing or fishing trips and transport to USFS public-use cabins and outlying communities. Stop by the Visitor Information Center on the cruise ship docks.

Go sea kayaking. Ketchikan is located on Revillagigedo Island. Circumnavigation of the island is about a 150-mile trip. The east coast of Revillagigedo Island lies within Misty Fiords National Monument Wilderness. Popular kayaking destinations within the monument include Rudyerd Bay, Punchbowl Cove and Walker Cove.

For trip planning help stop by the Southeast Alaska Discovery Center on Main Street (phone 907/228-6220), or the U.S. Forest Service office at 3031 Tongass Avenue (phone 907/ 225-2148). Or check the Tongass National Forest web site at www.fs.fed.us/r10/tongass. Sea kayaking information, guided trips and rentals are available locally.

Charter planes operate from the airport

and from the waterfront on floats and are available for fly-in fishing, flightseeing or service to lodges and smaller communities.

Picnic areas. Drive out to Settlers Cove State Recreation Site at **Milepost 18.2** North Tongass Highway. **Settlers Cove** has a day-use area with picnic tables. From the picnic area take the Lower Lunch Falls Loop, a 1/4-mile boardwalk trail through lush forest that also provides access to the gravel beach.

Other picnic areas accessible from the North Tongass Highway are Refuge Cove State Recreation Site at **Milepost 8.7**, and picnic facilities along Ward Lake, accessible from Mile 1.3 Revilla Road.

Rotary Beach Recreation Area is located south of downtown, at **Milepost 3.5** South Tongass Highway.

Hiking trails, from moderate nature walks to strenuous hikes, are accessible by road in the Ketchikan area.

Three U.S. Forest Service trails are accessible from Revilla Road north of Ketchikan (see Milepost 7 North Tongass Highway). **Ward Lake Nature Trail** is an easy 1.3-mile path around Ward Lake that connects facilities within Ward Lake Recreation Area and has interpretive signs on old-growth forests. The 2.3-mile **Perseverance Lake Trail** begins near Grassy Point picnic area in the Ward Lake Recreation Area providing access to fishing in Perseverance Lake. Past Ward Lake Recreation Area is the 2-mile **Connell Lake Trail**.

A strenuous hike but offering spectacular views as a reward is the **Deer Mountain Trail**, which begins at the corner of Fair and Deermount streets. The 3-mile, 3,001-foot ascent gives trekkers an excellent vantage of downtown Ketchikan and Tongass Narrows.

North Tongass Highway

Bridge across Lunch Creek at Settlers Cove SRS is the start of Lower Lunch Falls Loop trail. (© Kris Graef, staff)

From downtown Ketchikan, North Tongass Highway follows the shoreline of Revillagigedo Island northwest along Tongass Narrows, then north along Clover Passage to dead end at Settlers Cove State Recreation Site. The North Tongass Highway is 18.4 miles long with 15.4 miles paved.

Distance from downtown Ketchikan (K) is shown.

K 0 Ketchikan Visitor Information Center on the cruise ship docks at Front and Mission streets. Follow Front Street north.

K 0.3 Eagle Park to west with "Thundering Wings" totem, carved by Tlingit master Nathan Jackson.

Front Street becomes Tongass Avenue northbound after passing through the Tunnel (built in 1954).

K 0.5 City Float.

K 1.2 Plaza Mall to west; McDonald's. This is the West End commercial zone, much of which was built on fill in the late 1960s and early 1970s.

K 1.7 Bar Harbor boat basin to west.

K 2 Ketchikan General Hospital to east, Ketchikan Ranger Station/Misty Fiords National Monument to west.

K 2.3 Entrance to Ketchikan Ferry Terminal for the Alaska Marine Highway. Terminal building has seating area, restrooms, vending machines, brochure racks and Inter-Island Ferry Authority ticket desk for MV *Prince of Wales* service to Hollis.

K 2.4 Main branch U.S. post office.

K 2.6 Carlanna Creek and bridge.

K 2.7 Entrance to Ketchikan International Airport parking and airport ferry shuttle service.

K 3.2 Viewpoint to west. Airport terminal is visible across Tongass Narrows on Gravina Island.

K 4 Don King Road; access east to bank, Walmarts.

K 4.4 Alaska State Troopers and Dept. of Transportation (DOT) Highway Maintenance station.

K 5.5 Small viewpoint to west overlooking Tongass Narrows and floatplane dock.

K 6 Ward Cove Cannery, built in 1912 and purchased in 1928 by Wards Cove Packing Co.

Cannery Creek and bridge.

K 6.8 Ward Lake Road (open to hikers and bikers only); access to Ward Lake Recreation Area (see description at **Milepost 7**).

K 6.9 Ward Creek and bridge. Ketchikan sawmill, owned by Ketchikan Pulp Co

K 7 Junction with 6.7-mile **Revilla Road** to USFS **Ward Lake Recreation Area** and Harriet Hunt Road to Harriet Hunt Lake Recreation Area (descriptions follow).

Mile 1.3 Revilla Road: Turn off for paved access road to Ward Lake day-use area (0.6 mile) and Signal Creek campground (1 mile). **Ward Lake day-use area** has 3 picnic

shelters, paved parking and a nature trail. The Ward Lake Nature Trail loops around Ward Lake, and is an easy 1.3-mile walk on a well-graveled path. Single-vehicle picnic sites and access to the walk-in Grassy Point picnic area located along access road between day-use area and road end at Signal Creek USFS campground. Also on this stretch of road is parking for **Perseverance Lake Trail**; a 2.2 mile gravel and boardwalk trail to Perseverance Lake (elev. 518 feet).

Signal Creek Campground, at the end of the access road, has 24 gravel sites with tables and firepits; a campground host; water and pit toilets; and a $10 camping fee. (Three C's Campground, adjacent the Perseverance Lake Trail, is open only for overflow camping when other campgrounds are full.)

Mile 2.3 Revilla Road: Turn off for **Last Chance Campground**, with 19 gravel sites, tables, pit toilets, water, and a $10 camping fee.

Mile 2.4 Revilla Road: Pavement ends and gravel begins. Turn on Connell Lake Road for trailhead to 2-mile Connell Lake Trail.

Mile 6.5 Revilla Road: Turnoff for Harriet Hunt Road, which leads 2.4 miles to Harriet Hunt Lake Recreation Area; parking, pit toilets and fishing

Mile 6.6 Revilla Road: Road dead ends just past turnoff for Brown Mountain Logging Road

K 7.2 WARD COVE. Post office, gas station and grocery.

K 7.8 Ketchikan Pulp Co. pulp mill was built in 1953; it closed in 1997.

K 8.7 Refuge Cove State Recreation Site with 14 picnic sites.

K 9.3 Mud Bight; "float houses" rest on mud at low tide and float during high tide.

K 9.9 Totem Bight State Historical Park; parking area, restrooms, bookstore and phones. A short trail leads through the woods to Totem Bight community house and totem park. A striking setting. Don't miss this!

The park's totems are either restored originals or duplicates carved by Natives as part of a U.S. Forest Service program begun in 1938 using Civilian Conservation Corps (CCC) funds. The park's clan house or community house is representative of those found in many early 19th century Indian villages in Southeast.

K 10.8 Grocery store and Tesoro gas station.

K 12.9 Scenic viewpoint overlooking **Guard Islands Lighthouse**. This light marks the easterly entrance to Tongass Narrows/Clarence Strait. It was established in 1904; first lit in 1924; and automated in 1969. Present optic is solar powered. It is an active navigation aid.

K 14.2 Junction with Point Higgins Road; access to Knudson Cove Road, just west of highway, which leads 0.5 mile to Knudson Cove Marina and public boat launch ($5). Also access to Clover Pass Resort (0.6 mile west) via Point Higgins Road.

Knudson Cove Road rejoins North Tongass Highway at **Milepost K 14.7**.

K 14.7 Knudson Cove Road west to public boat launch (0.3 mile from highway).

K 15.4 *Pavement ends, gravel begins, northbound.*

K 16.6 Turnoff for Salmon Falls Resort.

K 18.2 Settlers Cove State Recreation Site has a 14-site campground ($10 camping fee) and picnicking; tables, water, picnic shelters, pit toilets. Good gravel beach. **Lower Lunch Falls Loop Trail** (1/4 mile); scenic boardwalk hike through forest with access to beach. Watch for pink samon in Lunch Creek in August.

18.4 Road ends.

PRINCE OF WALES ISLAND

(See map page 661)

	Coffman Cove	Craig	Hollis	Hydaburg	Kasaan	Klawock	Thorne Bay
Coffman Cove		60	75	88	64	52	53
Craig	60		31	44	52	8	41
Hollis	75	31		35	67	23	56
Hydaburg	88	44	35		80	36	69
Kasaan	64	52	67	80		44	23
Klawock	52	8	23	36	44		33
Thorne Bay	53	41	56	69	23	33	

Wildlife is plentiful on Prince of Wales Island. (© Ren Valencia)

Special Events:
- **April to July 4th**—Annual Craig–Klawock King Salmon Derby from April to July 3, followed by a big Fourth of July parade and celebration.
- **May**—Prince of Wales Island Hollis to Craig International Marathon (26.2 miles).
- **July 26-27**—POW Fair & Logging Show.

Visitor Information: Prince of Wales Island Chamber of Commerce, P.O. Box 497, Craig, AK 99921; phone (907) 826-3870, fax (907) 826-5467. email powcc@aptalaska.net; www.princeofwalescoc.org. U.S. Forest Service offices in Craig, phone (907) 826-3271, and Thorne Bay, (907) 828-3304).

Prince of Wales Island is the third largest island under the American flag (Kodiak is second, the Big Island of Hawaii is first), measuring roughly 135 miles north to south by 45 miles east to west. A mountainous, heavily forested island, the island is best known for its fishing and for having the most extensive road system in Southeast Alaska.

The island road system offers visitors a unique driving experience. Although narrow, winding and mostly gravel, the roads have good surfacing and very little traffic. And the scenery is anything but repetitive, as the roads travel through old-growth forest and clearcut areas, with mountain views and views of coastline and offshore islands.

There are good wildlife viewing opportunities on the island, from bald eagles to bears. It is not uncommon to have to brake for black bears or Sitka black-tailed deer crossing the road. The Forest Service has a bird checklist for the island that lists both resident and migratory species commonly found in various habitats on the island.

The road system also accesses hiking trails; roadside fishing streams (red, pink and silver salmon, cutthroat, rainbow trout and Dolly Varden); and some unique geological attractions.

The major geological attraction on the island is **El Capitan Cave**, located 75 miles from Craig via the North Prince of Wales Road. A steep staircase trail (more than 365 steps) leads up to the cave entrance. The Forest Service offers guided cave tours throughout the summer; phone the Thorne Bay ranger district for tour times and reservations. Because of prior damage to cave formations, there is now open visitation only to a locked gate a short distance within the cave; guided tours only beyond the gate.

Near El Capitan is the Beaver Falls Karst Trail. This 1-mile boardwalk trail crosses ancient muskegs and cathedral forests, and displays many karst features, such as sinkholes, deep vertical pits, lost rivers and collapsed channels.

Most of the island is within **Tongass National Forest** (www.fs.fed.us/r10/tongass). The Forest Service manages 5 designated wilderness areas on Prince of Wales Island, as well as public-use cabins, campgrounds, hiking trails and canoe trails.

Historically, salmon and timber have been the economic mainstays of Prince of Wales Island. One of Alaska's first canneries was built at Klawock in 1878, and some 25 more canneries were eventually built on the island to process salmon.

Many of the island's communities began as logging camps. Today, timber harvests on the island are only a fraction of what they once were. Motorists get a close-up look at the effects of logging as they drive the island's roads. Clear-cut areas, in various stages of regrowth, alternate with old-growth forest as you travel from one end of the island to the other.

A major attraction here is the world-class saltwater sportfishing that abounds immediately offshore and throughout the many smaller islands surrounding Prince of Wales Island. Most communities have boat ramps. Visiting fishermen may also charter out with a local operator at most communities. There are also several full-service fishing lodges on the island.

Ocean fishing for salmon is best in July and early August for kings (chinook), August and September for coho, July, August and September for pinks, and August and September for chum. Halibut to 100 lbs., 50-lb. king salmon and 15-lb. coho salmon are not considered uncommon in the sport season, usually May through August due to the weather and fish migration patterns. Abundant bottom fish, including lingcod, halibut and red snapper, reside throughout these waters year-round.

Communities

Of the 9 communities connected by the

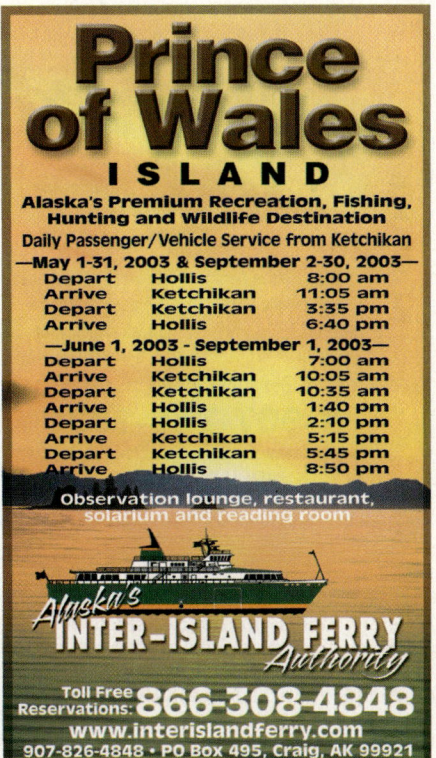

TRAVEL DIRECTORY
Prince of Wales Island

INSIDE PASSAGE • Prince of Wales Island

Prince of Wales Island
America's 3rd Largest Island & Alaska's Best Kept Secret
PO Box 497, Craig, AK 99921 • 907-826-3870 • Fax 907-826-5467
Email: powcc@aptalaska.net • Web: www.princeofwalescoc.org

COFFMAN COVE — OCEANVIEW RV PARK / CAMPGROUND
Located on the beach at Coffman Cove, Alaska.
2 1/2 Hour Scenic Drive from Hollis • 14 Full Hookups, Bunkhouse for Rent • Laundry, Showers & Restrooms
Email: djeffrey@coveconnect.com
www.coffmancove.org/rvpark.html
(907)329-2226

KLAWOCK — Custom Smoked Salmon & Fish Processing
KLAWOCK, ALASKA
Tel: 1-907-755-8870
Email: jodyss@hotmail.com
Jody's Seafood Specialties

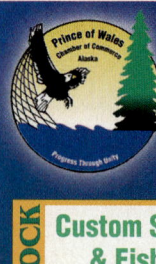

CRAIG — Wilderness Car Rental & Repair
Car & 4x4 Rentals PLUS ATVs
Toll Free 1-800-949-2205
Telephone 907-826-5200
Email: wcrr@aptalaska.net
www.wildernesscarrental.com
Barry & Terri Peratrovich • Craig, Alaska

CRAIG — Prince of Wales ISLAND REALTY
PO 89, Craig, Alaska 99921
Ph 907-826-2927 • Fax 907-826-2926
Email powir@aptalaska.net
Check our website at www.AlaskaIslandRealty.com

KLAWOCK — LOG CABIN RV PARK & RESORT
Full Hookups on Saltwater Beach
Cabins • Skiff & Outboards • Canoes
Charters • Full Fishing Packages
Klawock - Prince of Wales Island, AK
Call **1-800-544-2205**

KLAWOCK — DAVE'S DINER
755-2986 ✱ Klawock
"Best Burgers on the Island"

RED'S ROOST
Hollis Cabin Rental
Box 162 • Klawock AK 99925
(907) 530-7010

CRAIG — SHELTER COVE LODGE
The Finest Ocean Front Lodge & Fishing Service on Prince of Wales Island
• Year-round lodging
• Fine dining restaurant
• Charter fishing
For information & reservations contact:
Website: www.sheltercovelodge.com
Email: shelterc@aptalaska.net
Toll Free 1-888-826-3474 • Phone 1-907-826-2939
PO Box 798, Craig Alaska 99921

CRAIG — Haida Way Lodge
Located in Downtown Craig
• 25 Deluxe Rooms • Cable/HBO
• Private Phones • Jacuzzi Rooms
OPEN YEAR ROUND
Visa • Mastercard • American Express
Diners • Discover
501 Front St.,
P.O. Box 690, Craig AK 99921
1-800-347-4625
Fax (907) 826-3267

KLAWOCK — Fireweed Lodge
• Private Deluxe Rooms
• Super Family-Style Dining
• Hot Tub
• Color TV, Telephones
• Conference Rooms
• Steelhead, Salmon & Halibut Charters
PO Box 116, Klawock, AL 99925
1-907-755-2930
fireweedlo@aol.com ✱ www.fireweedlodge.com
Fax: 1-907-755-2936

CRAIG — SUNNAHAE LODGE
WE SPECIALIZE IN
Superior Charter Fishing Packages
P.O. Box 690 • Craig, Alaska 99921
Telephone (907) 826-4000

CRAIG — RAIN COUNTRY RV
■ Centrally Located
■ Close to All Services
Outback Convenience & Variety Store on site for your RV & personal needs • Full Hookups • New laundry • New showers & washroom
Ph: 907-826-3632 • Fax: 907-826-2988
510 JS Drive, Craig AK 99921

island road system, Craig, Klawock, Thorne Bay, Hydaburg, Coffman Cove and Kasaan have city status and are described in more detail in this section. The smaller communities of Hollis, Naukati and Whale Pass are described in the road logs in this section.

Lodging & Services

Rental cabins, lodges, bed and breakfasts and other forms of lodging are available in most communities on Prince of Wales Island, with Craig and Klawock—followed by Thorne Bay—offering the largest selection. See community descriptions this section for details.

If you are dining out, Craig has the widest selection of restaurants, from pizza places to hotel dining rooms. There are no dining out facilities on the north end of the island. Shopping and other services are also found mainly in Craig and in neighboring Klawock.

Camping

There are RV parks in Craig, Klawock and Coffman Cove. There are 2 developed USFS campgrounds on the island—Eagle's Nest on

660 ■ The MILEPOST® ■ 2003
www.themilepost.com

Craig–Klawock–Hollis Highway

Totem Park at Klawock. (© Kris Graef, staff)

This paved highway begins at the ferry landing at Hollis and leads 31 miles west through Klawock then south to Craig, taking motorists through the temperate rainforest environment typical of Southeast Alaska. It is a wide road. Posted speed is 50 mph with some 35 to 40 mph curves.

Distance from Craig (C) is followed by distance from ferry terminal at Hollis (H)). Physical mileposts reflect distance from Craig.

C 31 H 0 Entrance to **Inter-Island Ferry Authority Hollis terminal** at Clark Bay; phone (907) 530-4848.

C 29.6 H 1.4 Turnoff to south 0.3 mile to **HOLLIS** (pop. 139), a former Ketchikan Pulp Co. logging camp that served as the base for timber operations on Prince of Wales Island until 1962, when the camp was moved to Thorne Bay.

C 28.6 H 2.4 Gravel turnout at east end of **Maybeso Creek** bridge. Fish include cutthroat; Dolly Varden; pink and silver salmon; steelhead run begins in mid-April. Pools offer the best fishing. Walking good along streambed but poor along bank. Watch for bears.

C 26.8 H 4.2 Turnout with view of mouth of the Harris River.

C 24.6 H 6.4 Tongass National Forest boundary.

C 22.6 H 8.4 USFS hiking trail to **Harris River** fishing: cutthroat; steelhead run mid-April; salmon and Dolly Varden run beginning in mid-July. Easy walking on the gravel bars in the middle of 1.3-mile-long river.

C 20.5 H 10.5 Junction with Hydaburg Road (paved) which leads south 24 miles to the community of Hydaburg (see description this section).

C 20 H 11 USFS trailhead for 3-mile-long Twenty Mile Spur Trail to north.

C 19.7 H 11.3 Turnoff to southwest for **Harris River USFS Campground;** 14 sites on gravel loop road; firepits, tables, free firewood, campground host, outhouse, garbage and water. Camping fee $8. Muskeg nature trail.

C 19.6 H 11.4 Harris River bridge.

C 18.4 H 12.6 Tongass National Forest boundary.

C 16.4 H 14.6 Views of 7-mile-long Klawock Lake.

C 9 H 22 Prince of Wales Hatchery, operated by the Prince of Wales Hatchery Assoc., produces sockeye, coho and steelhead. Visitors welcome. Daily guided tours or by appointment, phone (907) 755-2231. Fresh coho for sale (August–Oct.).

C 8.1 H 22.9 Entering Klawock westbound (see description this section).

C 7.7 H 23.3 Klawock IGA supermarket, liquor store and post office at **junction** with Boundary Road (Big Salt Lake Road).

> **Junction** with Big Salt Lake Road; begins as Boundary Road and leads 16.2 miles to Control Lake Junction, where it intersects with Thorne Bay Road and North Prince of Wales Road. See Big Salt Lake Road log this section.

C 7.4 H 23.6 Junction with Old Big Salt Lake Road; access to Log Cabin Resort & RV Park.

C 7.3 H 23.7 Fireweed Lodge to east; church to west. **St. John's by the Sea Catholic Church** was designed and built with local lumber and materials by the local church community. The stained-glass were

designed and built by local artists. This is a "must-see" structure. Father Jean Paulin and Sister Zita welcome the opportunity to show the church. Good eagle viewing in Klawock River estuary during salmon season.

C 7 H 24 Turn west on Anchorage Street and follow continue on loop road to Bayview Blvd. and Church street to see **Klawock totem park**. Good collection of totems on hillside overlooking Klawock: good photo op. Also access via Klawock Street to city park, ballfields and boat launch.

C 6.7 H 24.3 Bayview Blvd. loops west totem park.

C 6.5 H 24.5 Klawock River bridge spans tidal estuary where river meets salt water; no fishing.

C 6.4 H 24.4 Alaska State Troopers and Alaska Dept. of Fish and Game.

C 4.1 H 26.9 Turnout with scenic view of Klawock Inlet and San Alberto Bay.

C 4 H 27 Craig city limits.

C 1.7 H 29.3 Craig High School.

C 1.5 H 29.5 Crab Creek. Begin bike path.

C 0.7 H 30.3 Easy Street. Prince of Wales Island Chamber of Commerce office adjacent Alaska Gifts shop to west.

C 0.5 H 30.5 Craig post office, Wells Fargo bank, restaurants and supermarket.

C 0.3 H 30.7 North and South Cove harbors, operated by the city of Craig. There is a good map of Craig at the entrance to the dock at North Cove Harbor.

Turn on 9th Street for access to USFS Craig Ranger District office.

C 0 H 31 Intersection of Third, Front and Water streets in Craig.

Thorne Bay Road and Harris River on the Craig–Klawock–Hollis Highway. Camping fee at both is $8. Campsites at Eagle's Nest campground may be reserved by phoning toll-free 877-444-6777 or online at reserveusa.com. Several undeveloped dispersed campsites are accessible via the island road system. See road logs this section.

There are also more than 20 USFS cabins (accessible by plane, boat or on foot) available for public use; reservations and a fee are required. Contact the USFS office in Ketchikan, Craig or Thorne Bay.

Transportation

Air: All communities on the island are served by floatplane, most daily. Wheel planes land at Klawock. Daily scheduled service from Ketchikan.

Ferry: Inter-Island Ferry Authority MV *Prince of Wales* from Ketchikan to Hollis; crossing time about 3 hours. (The ferry actually docks at Clark Bay, near Hollis.) Twice daily trips in summer. For vehicle or group reservations, phone 866-308-4848. In Craig, phone (907) 826-4848; for Hollis terminal, phone (907) 530-4848; online at www.interislandferry.com. In Ketchikan, stop by the IFA ticket counter in the Alaska Marine Highway terminal, or phone (907) 225-4838. TLC Hollis Shuttle connects with all IFA ferry arrivals and departures. One-way fare to Craig is $12. Phone (907) 826-2966 or 723-8311.

Car rentals: Available in Craig at Wilderness Car Rental, phone 800-949-2205; Shaub Ellison, phone (907) 826-3450); and at TLC, phone (907) 826-5388).

Highways: Four of the island's main roads are logged in this section: the Craig–Klawock–Hollis Highway; Big Salt Lake Road; Thorne Bay Road; and the North Prince of Wales Road. *NOTE: Most of the island's roads are narrow, 1-lane, winding gravel roads. Surfacing is generally good, but be alert for oncoming traffic on hills and corners, and watch for logging trucks.*

Taxi: TLC Taxi in Craig, phone (907) 826-2966.

Coffman Cove

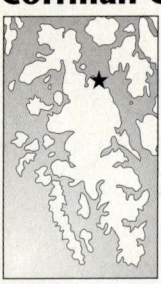

Located 52 miles north of Klawock, a 2½-hour drive from Hollis. **Population:** 199. **Emergency Services:** EMS, phone (907) 329-2209 or 329-2213. Formerly one of the largest independent logging camps in Southeast, Coffman Cove is now a small hamlet. Recreation includes hunting (deer and bear), good freshwater and saltwater fishing, boating, hiking. Charters for fishing and whalewatching available. Canoe Lagoon Oyster Co. here is the state's oldest and largest oyster producer; fresh oysters available locally.

Coffman Cove has a post office (open 1–3:30 P.M. weekdays); a liquor store; fishing tackle, ice, sundries and bait shop (Riggin Shack), open 1–5 P.M. Tuesday to Saturday; an RV park, which also offers bunkhouse accommodations (Oceanview RV Park); cabins and skiff rentals (Rain Country Cabins & B&B); a gas pump (limited hours; after hours inquire at Oceanview RV Park for key); a playground; and a public dock and a boat launch. Coffman Cove harbormaster, phone (907) 329-2922.

South Cove Harbor at Craig. (© Kris Graef, staff)

Craig

Located 31 miles from Hollis on the western shore of Prince of Wales Island. **Population:** 1,397. **Emergency Services:** Phone 911. **Police,** phone (907) 826-3330. **Clinic,** Craig Clinic, physician, public health nurses and the Craig Native health aide. Craig also has a chiropractic office and 2 dental clinics.

Visitor Information: Prince of Wales Island Chamber of Commerce; phone (907) 826-3870; www.princeofwalescoc.org. U.S. Forest Service office, open weekdays 8 A.M. to 5 P.M., phone (907) 826-3271. There is a good map of Craig at the North Cove Harbor dock entrance.

Named for founder Craig Millar, who established a saltery and cold storage facility here in the early 1900s, Craig was incorporated in 1922. Today, it is the largest city on the island and offers most services. There are 2 banks, a dozen restaurants and fast-food outlets; supermarket and liquor stores; an RV park (gravel pads) and dump station; gas stations, propane, towing and auto repair; and several gift shops.

Stone Arts of Alaska. We produce unique art and functional gift items from aphrodite and jupiter marble, fossil coral and other exceptionally colorful Prince of Wales stones. Local crystals and fossils. Jewelry. Raw stone for scupture and lapidary. Take home a piece of Alaska. 118 J.T. Brown Street, Craig, AK; (907) 826-3571; email boatstone@hotmail.com. [ADVERTISEMENT]

Craig has 2 modern boat harbors, North Cove and South Cove, located on either side of the causeway crossed by the Craig–Klawock–Hollis Highway. Bald eagles are common at the harbors and along the waterfront. Craig also has a seaplane float, fuel dock, city dock and float, 2 fish-buying docks and an old cannery dock. The Craig harbormaster's office, with public showers and restrooms, is located on the corner close to South Cove; phone (907) 826-3404, VHF Channel 16.

Craig is the home port of many commercial fishing and charter sportfishing boats. Halibut, coho and chinook salmon, lingcod and red snapper (yelloweye) are the primary target species.

Hydaburg

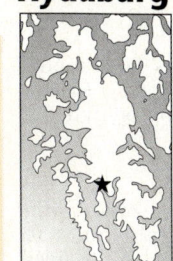

Located 36 miles from Hollis, 45 miles from Craig. **Population:** 382. **Emergency Services:** Village Public Safety Officer, phone (907) 285-3321. **Ambulance,** Hydaburg emergency response team, phone 911. **Health Clinic,** phone (907) 285-3462.

Hydaburg was founded in 1911, and combined the populations of 3 Haida villages: Sukkwan, Howkan and Klinkwan. President William Howard Taft established an Indian reservation on the surrounding land in 1912, but, at the residents' request, most of the land was restored to its former status as part of Tongass National Forest in 1926. Hydaburg was incorporated in 1927, 3 years after its people became citizens of the United States.

Most of the residents are commercial fishermen, although there are some jobs in construction and the timber industry. Subsistence is also a traditional and necessary part of life here. Hydaburg has an excellent collection of restored Haida totems. Native carvers restored and replicated totems brought in from the traditional Haida villages on southern Prince of Wales Island. The totem restoration project was founded in the late 1930s by the Civilian Conservation Corps and managed by the Tongass National Forest. There is also good salmon fishing here in the fall.

Four boardinghouses provide rooms and

Big Salt Lake Road

Big Salt Lake Road begins as Boundary Road at **Milepost C 7.7** on the Craig–Klawock–Hollis Highway and extends 16.2 miles to junction with Thorne Bay Road and North Prince of Wales Road at Control Lake Junction. It is an improved gravel road scheduled for paving.

Distance from junction with Craig–Klawock–Hollis Highway at Klawock (K) is followed by distance from Thorne Bay (T).

K 0 T 33.5 Boundary Road/Big Salt Lake Road junctions with Craig–Klawock–Hollis Highway at Klawock.

Junction with **Milepost C 7.7** Craig–Klawock–Hollis Highway; see highway log this section.

K 0.6 T 32.9 Junction with Old Big Salt lake Road and access to **Log Cabin R.V. Park & Resort**: tackle store, skiff rentals, lodging, campground. ▲

K 2.1 T 31.4 Klawock Airport Road. *Pavement ends, gravel begins, eastbound.*

K 3.6 T 29.9 Little Salt Creek. Big Salt Lake Road climbs eastbound. Beautiful views of coast, as well as views of clearcut areas.

K 4.7 T 28.8 *Begin major road construction eastbound (summer 2002). Driving distances may vary from log due to straightening of road.*

K 5.4 T 28.1 Duke Creek.

K 8 T 25.5 Big Salt Lake, actually a saltwater body protected by small islands but permitting tidal flow in and out, is visible from several spots along road. There is a boat ramp and canoe launching area on Big Salt Lake. If boating on this tidal lake, be aware of strong currents.

K 9.2 T 24.3 Turnout at west end of **Black Bear Creek** bridge. Fishing for cutthroat, Dolly Varden, red, pink, dog and silver salmon.

K 12 T 21.5 Steelhead Creek bridge. Fishing for cutthroat, Dolly Varden, steelhead, pink, dog and silver salmon.

K 13 T 20.5 *Gravel ends, pavement begins, norhbound. End road construction (summer 2002).*

K 16 T 17.5 Control Lake. Fishing for cutthroat, Dolly Varden, pink and silver salmon; good red salmon stream in August. USFS public-use cabin with skiff at lake.

K 16.2 T 17.3 Control Lake Junction.

Junction of Big Salt Lake Road (SR 929/FH 9) with Thorne Bay Road (FH 30) and North Prince of Wales Road (FH 20). See road logs this section.

Thorne Bay Road

Thorne Bay Road is a good gravel road with easy curves and no steep grades. It extends 17.3 miles from Control Lake Junction to the community of Thorne Bay. **Distance from Control Lake Junction (CJ) is followed by distance from Thorne Bay (T).**

CJ 0 T 17.3 Control Lake Junction.

> **Junction** with Big Salt Lake Road at Milepost K 16.2 from Klawock and Milepost CJ 0 of North Prince of Wales Road. See logs this section.

CJ 1.2 T 16.1 Control Creek.

CJ 1.7 T 15.6 Eagle's Nest USFS campground on a 0.6-mile road; 12 sites on level, gravel pads; $8 camping fee; walk-in tent sites; campground host; potable water, tables, firepits, garbage, outhouses. Advance reservations can be made for designated sites at the Forest Service campgrounds through the National Recreation Reservation Service;

phone toll-free 877-444-6777 or on the Internet at reserveusa.com.

Scenic trail down to **Balls Lake** connects with picnic area. Access to **Control Creek**. Area fishing for cutthroat; Dolly Varden; red, pink and silver salmon.

CJ 2 T 15.3 Balls Lake USFS picnic area; tables, outhouse, trail to Eagle's Nest campground.

CJ 4.6 T 12.7 Rio Roberts Creek bridge;, cutthroat, pink and silver salmon fishing. A 0.7-mile cedar-chip and double-plank boardwalk trail leads to a viewing deck overlooking falls and Rio Roberts Fish Pass.

CJ 5 T 12.3 Newlunberry Creek.

CJ 6.8 T 10.5 Rio Beaver Creek.

CJ 10.8 T 6.5 Goose Creek bridge; cutthroat; pink and silver salmon. Excellent spawning stream. Good run of pink salmon in mid-August.

Watch for turnoff to USFS Road 2030 which leads 4.5 miles south to **Lake No. 3 USFS campsite**; space to accommodate up to 2 RVs, pit toilet, 2 fire rings and 2 picnic tables. No water or garbage. Road continues beyond campsite to lake and hiking trail to Salt Chuck. Abandoned Salt Chuck Mine is located here.

CJ 10.9 T 6.4 Junction with Kasaan Highway. This narrow road runs southeast 17 miles to **KASAAN** (pop. 39). Located at the head of Kasaan Bay, Kasaan was connected to the road system in 1996. It has a post office, school and boat docks. There is also a totem park at Kasaan; inquire locally for permission to tour the park.

CJ 12.4 T 4.9 Thorne River bridge. Fishing in **Thorne River** for cutthroat, Dolly Varden, steelhead, rainbow, red, pink, dog and silver salmon.

CJ 13 T 4.3 Falls Creek bridge.

CJ 13.2 T 4.1 Gravelly Creek USFS picnic area; walk in to picnic area on the bank of Thorne River at the mouth of Gravelly Creek; 3 tables, fire rings, vault toilet and open-sided shelter. This site was logged in 1918. Note the large stumps with notches. Notches were used by old-time loggers for spring boards to stand on while sawing or chopping.

CJ 13.5 T 3.8 Gravelly Creek bridge.

CJ 16 T 1.7 KPC log sorting yard.

CJ 16.8 T 0.5 Welcome to Thorne Bay sign. *CAUTION: Slow to 15 mph.*

CJ 16.9 T 0.4 The Port; convenience store, gas and diesel, post office and floatplane terminal.

Junction with **Sandy Beach Road** to Coffman Cove. A very scenic drive with both mountain views and scenic views of Clarence Strait. *CAUTION: Road is 1-lane winding gravel with steep grades. There are no services or facilities along this road. Mileposts along Sandy Beach Road reflect distance from Control Lake Junction.*

Sandy Beach Road (FR 30) follows the east coast of Prince of Wales Island 28 miles north from Thorne Bay to Luck Lake Junction, where FR 3030 leads 9 miles north to Coffman Cove and FH 30 leads 10 miles to junction with FH 44 (see map this section). Driving distance from Thorne Bay to Coffman Cove via FH 30 and FR 3030 is 37 miles. Sandy Beach USFS picnic ground is located 6.6 miles north of Thorne Bay on Sandy Beach Road.

CJ 17.3 Junction with Shoreline Drive in Thorne Bay. Access to Pearl Nelson Community Park; playground, overlook with point of interest signs about logging.

Klawock

Located 23 miles from Hollis. **Population:** 854. **Emergency Services:** Phone 911 for all emergencies; **Alaska State Troopers**, phone (907) 755-2918. **Police**, phone (907) 755-2777; **Village Public Safety Officers**, phone (907) 755-2261. **Health Clinic**, phone (907) 755-4800.

Private Aircraft: Klawock airstrip, 2 miles northeast; elev. 50 feet; length 5,000 feet; lighted and paved.

Klawock originally was a Tlingit Indian summer fishing village; a trading post and salmon saltery were established here in 1868. Ten years later, a salmon cannery was built—the first cannery in Alaska and the first of several cannery operations in the area. Over the years the population of Klawock, like other Southeast communities, grew and then declined with the salmon harvest. The local economy is still dependent on fishing, along with timber cutting and sawmilling. A fish hatchery operated by Prince of Wales Hatchery Assoc. is located on Klawock Lake, very near the site of a salmon hatchery that operated from 1897 until 1917. Visitors are welcome. Klawock Lake offers good canoeing and boating.

Recreation here includes good fishing for salmon and steelhead in Klawock River, saltwater halibut fishing, and deer and bear hunting. Klawock's totem park contains 21 totems—both replicas and originals—from the abandoned Indian village of Tuxekan (developed by the Civilian Conservation Corps in 1938–40). A 5-year restoration project to restore and replace totems in the park was begun in 1995.

Groceries and gas are available in Klawock. Accommodations available at Columbine Inn (907/755-2287), Fireweed Lodge (907/755-2930), Log Cabin Resort (800/544-2205). Log Cabin Resort also offers full-hookup RV sites on the beach.

meals for visitors. Groceries, and sundry items available locally. There are a gas station, public telephones, video store and deli. Cable television is available.

Thorne Bay

Located 59 miles from Hollis; 36 miles from Klawock. **Population**: 557. **Emergency Services**: Phone 911. **Village Public Safety Officer**, phone (907) 828-3905.

Visitor Information: City web site is www.thornebayalaska.net.

Thorne Bay was incorporated in 1982, making it one of Alaska's newest cities. The settlement began as a logging camp in 1962, when Ketchikan Pulp Co. (KPC) moved its operations from Hollis. Thorne Bay was connected to the island road system in 1974. Camp residents created the community—and gained city status from the state—as private ownership of the land was made possible under the Alaska Statehood Act. The population fluctuates with the lumber industry. KPC is currently inactive here.

Thorne Bay has a grocery store and liquor store; general merchandise and boat fuel (Tackle Shack); convenience store, gas, diesel and post office (The Port); unleaded gas, propane, tire and auto repair (Bayview Fuel & Tire).

Lodging is available for both tourists and business travelers at: 4 bed and breakfasts; beachfront log cabins (McFarland's Floatel); and do-it-youself accommodations (Deer Creek Cottage). There are also several full-service fishing lodges in the area.

Thorne Bay is the site of the biggest annual event on the island: the POW Fair and Logging Show, held the last weekend in July. Competitions for working loggers include chain saw tossing, ax throwing, hand bucking, power saw bucking and speed climbing. Other events are firewood stacking, wheelbarrow races and a women's rolling-pin toss. The fair also has food and craft booths.

North Prince of Wales Road

El Capitan Cave is located on the north end of Prince of Wales Island. (© Kris Graef, staff)

The North Prince of Wales Road (FH 20), also referred to as the "island highway", leads north 79.5 miles from Control Lake Junction to Labouchere Bay on the northwest corner of the island. This road makes an interesting drive through old-growth forest and clear cut areas, with splendid mountain views and a good chance of seeing deer and black bear. *NOTE: This is a very narrow and winding gravel road with some steep grades. Slow down for approaching vehicles. Road conditions range from fair to excellent.*
Distance from Control Lake Junction (CJ) is followed by the physical milepost (MP). *Physical mileposts reflect distance from Hydaburg.*

CJ 0 MP 53.2 Control Lake Junction.
Improved wide road next 15 miles northbound.

Junction with Big Salt Lake Road and Thorne Bay Road; see logs this section.

CJ 10.8 MP 64.1 Junction with FR 2054 which leads west 5 miles to Staney Creek campsite, Staney Creek cabin and access to salt water.
CJ 15.3 MP 68.7 *CAUTION: Road narrows northbound. Slow for approaching vehicles.*
CJ 15.4 MP 68.8 Junction with **Coffman Cove Road** (FH 44, FRs 23, 30 and 3030), which leads northeast 20.5 miles to the community of Coffman Cove (see description on page 662). *Coffman Cove Road is a narrow, winding road; drive slowly and watch for approaching vehicles. Also watch for deer on road.* At Mile 9.5 Coffman Cove Road junctions with FR 30 to Luck Lake (13 miles) and Thorne Bay (38 miles) via Sandy Beach Road. Milepost marker 55 at that junction reflects distance from Control Lake Junction via FR 30. At Mile 13.2 Coffman Cove Road is Sweetwater Lake trailhead.
CJ 18.4 MP 71.8 Naukati Creek.
CJ 18.5 MP 71.9 Junction with FR 2057.
CJ 21 MP 74.5 Junction with FR 2058.
CJ 21.4 MP 74.9 Yatuk Creek.
CJ 23.3 MP 76.8 Junction with FR 2060 which leads 3 miles west to the coastal community of **NAUKATI** (pop. 135). Naukati was established as a mining camp and then a logging camp for Ketchikan Pulp Co. Naukati has a post office; liquor, groceries, gas, propane, diesel at the Naukati Connection; cabin rentals and charter skiffs from Naukati Cabins (907/629-4266) boat repair. The boat ramp at Naukati provides access to Tuxekan Narrows and Sea Otter Sound. There is a school and a floatplane dock.
Junction with FR 2059 to east.
CJ 25.9 MP 79.4 Clam Creek.
CJ 26.3 MP 79.8 Clam Creek No. 2.
CJ 26.4 MP 79.9 Sarkar Lake to east; parking, outhouses. This scenic lake is part

of the Sarkar Lake Canoe Loop. Fishing and boat launch. USFS public-use cabin at east end of lake. Skiff docked here is for registered cabin users only.
CJ 27 MP 80.5 Road forks; keep to right northbound on FH 20.
CJ 27.9 MP 81.6 Bridge over "Sarkar Rapids" (Sarkar Lake outlet to salt water).
CJ 28.3 MP 81.9 Deweyville Trail (signed).
CJ 29.4 MP 83 *NOTE: Watch for black bear.*
CJ 37.4 MP 91 Gravel pit turnout.
CJ 39.9 MP 93.6 Junction with FR 25 which leads east 8 miles to the community of Whale Pass and connects with FR 27, which loops back to the island highway at **Milepost CJ 48.8**. About 1 mile east of here, FR crossses **Neck Lake**. This beautiful 3-mile-long lake is also visible from the highway.

WHALE PASS (pop. 58) was the site of a floating logging camp on Whale Passage. The camp moved out in the early 1980s, but new residents moved in with a state land sale. The community has a small grocery store and gas pump; cabins and freezer space available. There is also a school, post office and floatplane dock.
CJ 41 MP 94.7 Junction with FR 2075.
CJ 41.8 MP 95.5 Junction with FR 207. The highway winds across the island's mountains with sweeping views.
CJ 46.9 MP 100.6 *Begin winding downgrade next 2 miles northbound.*
CJ 48.8 MP 102.6 Junction with FR 27 which leads east past **Twin Island Lake** to **Whale Pass** (7 miles) and **Exchange Cove** (16 miles). FR 27 junctions with FR 25, which loops back to the island highway at **Milepost CJ 39.9**. (See description of Whale Pass at CJ 39.9.)

There is a parking area and short trail down to **Cavern Lake Cave** overlook 3.4 miles east of here on FR 27. This unusual geological feature is at the lake outlet, where Cavern Lake drains first into a cave, then exits out of a cavern several hundred feet downstream.
CJ 51 MP 105 Junction with FR 15 which leads west 1 mile to **El Capitan Cave**. A steep staircase trail (more than 365 steps) leads up to the cave entrance. The Forest Service offers guided cave tours throughout the summer; phone the Thorne Bay ranger district (907/828-3304) for tour times, reservations and other information. Because of prior damage to cave formations, a gate was installed to regulate visitation and there is open visitation only to the locked gate a short distance within the cave; guided tours only beyond the gate.
Near El Capitan is the **Beaver Falls Karst Trail**. This 1-mile boardwalk trail crosses ancient muskegs and cathedral forests, and displays many karst features, such as sinkholes, deep vertical pits, lost rivers and collapsed channels.
Distance marker northbound shows Red Bay 8 miles, Labouchere 31 miles.
CJ 55.6 MP 109.6 Summit of the North Island Road (elev. 907 feet).
CJ 59.5 MP 113.5 Rough road, heavy truck traffic and 1-lane bridges north from here.
CJ 72.1 MP 126.1 Memorial Beach picnic area 1.7 miles north; follow signs to parking area. A short trail leads to picnic tables, pit toilet, memorial plaque and beach. Good view of Sumner Strait and Kupreanof Island. This site is a memorial to 12 victims of a 1978 air crash.
79.5 MP 133.5 Labouchere Bay. The road continues several miles and deadends at the base of Mount Calder.

WRANGELL

Population: 2,308

Brown bear at Anan Observatory near Wrangell. (© Ralph & Leonor Barrett)

Wrangell Special Events:
- **April 19-26**—The Garnet Festival. Marks the arrival of spring and the annual bald eagle migration on the Stikine River.
- **July 4**—Fourth of July celebration which begins with a salmon bake.
- **December**—A tree-lighting and Christmas celebration.

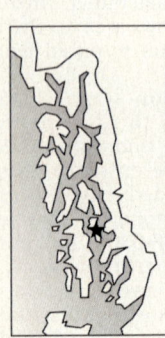

Located at northwest tip of Wrangell Island on Zimovia Strait; 6 miles southwest of the mouth of the Stikine River delta; 3 hours by ferry or 32 air miles southeast of Petersburg, the closest major community; and 6 hours by ferry or 85 air miles north of Ketchikan. **Emergency Services:** Phone 911 for all emergencies. **Police**, phone (907) 874-3304. **Fire Department** and **Ambulance**, phone (907) 874-2000. **Hospital**, Wrangell General, 310 Bennett St. just off Zimovia Highway, phone (907) 874-7000. **Maritime Search and Rescue**, contact the Coast Guard at (800) 478-5555.

Visitor Information: Center located in the Stikine Inn Building at 107 Stikine Ave., near the cruise ship dock; phone (800) 367-9745 or (907) 874-3901, fax (907) 874-3905, www.wrangell.com, email wrangell@wrangell.com. Write: Chamber of Commerce, Box 49MP, Wrangell, AK 99929. Information is also available at the Wrangell Museum, 318 Church St.; phone (907) 874-3770.

The U.S. Forest Service maintains several recreation sites and trails along the Wrangell Island road system, as well as remote cabins. Contact the USFS office in Wrangell, 525 Bennett St., phone (907) 874-2323.

Elevation: Sea level. **Climate:** Mild and moist with slightly less rain than other Southeast communities. Mean annual precipitation is 79.2 inches, with 63.9 inches of snow. Record monthly precipitation, 20.43 inches in October 1961. Average daily maximum temperature in June is 61°F; in July 64°F. Daily minimum in January is 23°F. **Radio:** KSTK-FM 101.7. **Television:** Cable and satellite. **Newspaper:** *Wrangell Sentinel* (weekly).

Private Aircraft: Wrangell airport, adjacent northeast; elev. 44 feet; length 6,000 feet; paved; fuel 100LL, A.

Wrangell is the only Alaskan city to have existed under 4 nations and 3 flags—the Stikine Tlingits, the Russians, Great Britain and the United States. Wrangell began in 1834 as a Russian stockade called Redoubt St. Dionysius, built to prevent the Hudson's Bay Co. from fur trading up the rich Stikine River to the northeast. The Russians leased the mainland of southeastern Alaska to Hudson's Bay Co. in 1840. Under the British the stockade was called Fort Stikine.

The post remained under the British flag until Alaska was purchased by the United States in 1867. A year later, the Americans established a military post here, naming it Fort Wrangell after the island, which was named by the Russians after Baron von Wrangel, a governor of the Russian–American Co.

Its strategic location near the mouth of the Stikine River made Wrangell an important supply point not only for fur traders but also for gold seekers following the river route to the goldfields. Today, Wrangell serves as a hub for goods, services and transportation for outlying fishing villages, and logging and mining camps. The town depended largely on fishing until Japanese interests arrived in the mid-1950s and established a mill now operated by Silver Bay Logging Inc. Fishing is one of Wrangell's largest industries, with salmon the major catch.

Lodging & Services

Wrangell has several motels and bed and breakfasts. The Wrangell Hostel is located in the Presbyterian church, about ¼ mile from the ferry terminal, next to the Wrangell Museum. Open from early June to Labor Day, 5 P.M. to 9 A.M.; $15/night; phone (907) 874-3534.

There are 4 restaurants downtown, as well as service stations, hardware and appliance stores, banks, drugstore, laundromat, grocery stores (1 with a bakery and deli), and gift shops. Bed-and-breakfasts are available. Lodges with restaurants are located on Peninsula Street and at **Milepost 4.3** Zimovia Highway.

Camping

RV camping at RV park on Berger street. Camping and picnic area at Shoemaker Bay, **Milepost 4.7** Zimovia Highway. Dump stations located at Shoemaker Bay and downtown. City Park, at **Milepost 1.9** Zimovia Highway, has campsites, picnic area with tables, flush toilets, shelters and playground. ▲

Transportation

Air: Daily scheduled jet service is provided by Alaska Airlines to other Southeast cities with through service to Seattle and Anchorage. Charter service available.

Airport terminal is 1.1 miles from ferry terminal or 1.1 miles from Zimovia Highway on Bennett Street. Hotel courtesy van is available from the airport to lodge on Peninsula Street. Taxi service is also available for about $5.

Ferry: Alaska Marine Highway vessels connect Wrangell with all Southeastern Alaska ports plus Prince Rupert, BC, and Bellingham, WA. Ferry terminal is at the north end of town at the end of Zimovia Highway (also named Church or 2nd Street at this point). Walk or take a taxi from terminal to town. Terminal facilities include ticket office, waiting room and vehicle waiting area. Phone (907) 874-3711.

Car Rental: Available from Practical Rent-A-Car (907) 874-3975.

Taxi: Available to/from airport and ferry terminal. Approximate cost is $5.

Highways: Zimovia Highway (see log this section). Logging roads have opened up most of Wrangell Island to motorists. Check with the USFS office at 525 Bennett St. for a copy of the Wrangell Island Road Guide map ($4). (Write USDA Forest Service, Wrangell Ranger District, Box 51, Wrangell, AK 99929; phone 907/874-2323.)

Cruise Ships: Wrangell is a regular port of call in summer for several cruise lines.

Petroglyphs are ancient designs carved into rock faces. (© Blake Hanna, staff)

Private Boats: Transient floats are located downtown and 4.5 miles south of Wrangell on Zimovia Highway at Shoemaker Bay Harbor. Reliance Float is located near Shakes Tribal House. If you are traveling to Wrangell by boat, radio ahead to the harbor master for tie-up space. Or phone (907) 874-3736 or 874-3051.

Attractions

Shakes Island and Tribal House, in Wrangell Harbor, is reached by boardwalk. It is the site of several excellent totem poles. The replica tribal house contains Indian working tools, an original Chilkat blanket design carved on a house panel and other cultural items. It is listed on the National Register of Historic Places. Open irregular hours when cruise ships are in port during summer (May to September) or by appointment; phone (907) 874-3747 or 874-2023. Admission $1.50.

Wrangell Museum, at 318 Church St., features local history and includes displays representing Tlingit, Russian, British, Chinese, Japanese and American influences in Wrangell. The oldest known Tlingit houseposts in Southeast Alaska are on exhibit, as is a rare "spruce canoe," and spruce root and cedar bark basket collection. Gold rush, trapping, logging, and fishing industry exhibits depict Wrangell's boom- and-bust economy. May to September hours are Monday through Friday 10–5; Saturdays and Sundays variable open 8–6 for cruise ships as staffing is available. October through April Tuesday through Friday 10–4; closed for lunch 11:30–12:30. Phone (907) 874-3770; Fax (907) 874-3785, Email: museum@wrangell.com. Admission $3; children 16 and under free.

Special events in Wrangell include a big Fourth of July celebration which begins with a salmon bake. The annual Tent City Festival, celebrated Feb. 7–9, 2003, commemorates Wrangell's gold rush days. The Garnet Festival, celebrated April 19–26, 2003, marks the arrival of spring and the annual bald eagle migration on the Stikine River. The festival celebrates the arts with family activities, and includes a golf tournament at Muskeg Meadows. A tree- lighting and Christmas celebration takes place in December.

Petroglyphs are ancient designs carved into rock faces, usually found between low and high tide marks on beaches. The Alaska State Park at Petroglyph Beach is located 0.7 mile from the ferry terminal; a fully accessible wooden boardwalk leads to the head of the beach from the left of the road. Turn right as you reach the beach and look for petroglyphs between there and a rock outcrop several hundred feet away. Newly made petroglyph reproductions are located on the wooden viewing platform. This beach has the largest number of petroglyphs found anywhere in southeastern Alaska; at times as many as 40 can be seen. Petroglyphs are also located on the library lawn and are on display in the museum.

Muskeg Meadows is a 9-hole, 36-acre regulation golf course and driving range. Contact the Wrangell Golf Assoc., Box 2199, Wrangell, AK 99929; phone (907) 874-4653; www.wrangellalaskagolf.com.

Anan Wildlife Observatory, managed by the U.S. Forest Service, is located 35 miles southeast of Wrangell; accessible by boat or plane only. During July and August, visitors can watch black and brown bears catch pink salmon headed for the salmon spawning grounds. Bald eagles, ravens, crows and seals are frequently seen feeding on the fish. Contact the visitor center. 1-800-367-9745, or the Forest Service office, (907) 874-2323, for list of guides permitted to transport visitors to Anan.

Wrangell Salmon Derby runs from May 10 to June 8, 2003. Kings weighing more than 50 lbs. are not unusual.

Garnet Ledge, a rocky outcrop on the right bank of the Stikine River delta at Garnet Creek, is 7.5 miles from Wrangell Harbor, reached at high tide by small boat. Garnet, a semiprecious stone, can be found embedded in the ledge here. The garnet ledge is on land deeded to the Southeast Council of the Boy Scouts of America and

Wrangell Harbor is the site of Shakes Island. (© Lynne Ledbetter)

the children of Wrangell by the late Fred Hanford (former mayor of Wrangell). The bequest states that the land shall be used for scouting purposes and the children of Wrangell may take garnets in reasonable quantities (garnets are sold by children at the docks when ships and ferries are in port). Permits are needed for non-Wrangell children to dig garnets. Contact the Boy Scout office in Juneau.

The Stikine River delta lies north of Wrangell within the Stikine–LeConte Wilderness and is accessible only by boat or plane. The Stikine River is the fastest free flowing, navigable river on North America, and can be rafted, canoed or run by skiff. Air or boat charters for drop-offs at put-in sites on the Stikine are available in Wrangell.

LeConte Glacier is at the head of LeConte Bay, just north of the Stikine River delta. It is the southernmost tidewater glacier in North America. Charter trips for sightseeing LeConte Glacier are available.

USFS trails, cabins and recreation sites on Wrangell Island and in the surrounding area are a major attraction here. Nemo Campsites, for example, only 14 miles south of Wrangell by road, provides spectacular views of Zimovia Strait and north Etolin Island. There are also 22 USFS public-use cabins scattered throughout the region that are accessible by air or by boat. For details on these sites and others, contact the Forest Service district office at (907) 874-2323; visit the Tongass web site at www.fs.fed.us/r10/tongass; or stop by the USFS office at 525 Bennett St. Or write Wrangell Ranger District, Box 51, Wrangell, AK 99929.

AREA FISHING: The Wrangell Island forest road system provides access to several recreation sites and trails with fishing. For more information, contact the USFS office in Wrangell at (907) 874-2323.

Fly in to **Thoms Lake, Long Lake, Marten Lake, Salmon Bay, Virginia Lake** and **Eagle Lake.** Thoms Lake and Long Lake are also accessible via road and trail. **Stikine River** near Wrangell (closed to king salmon fishing), Dolly Varden to 22 inches, and cutthroat to 18 inches, best in midsummer to fall; steelhead to 12 lbs., coho salmon 10 to 15 lbs., September and October. Saltwater fishing near Wrangell for king salmon, 20 to 40 lbs., best in May and June. There are bait, minimum size and other restrictions (see current sportfishing regulations). Stop by the Dept. of Fish and Game at 215 Front St. for details.

Zimovia Highway

Zimovia Highway leads 13.7 miles south from the ferry terminal to connect with the island's Forest Service road system.
Distance from ferry terminal is shown.

0 Alaska Marine Highway ferry terminal, ticket office and waiting area. There is a paved bike path to Mile 5.1.
0.3 St. Rose of Lima Catholic Church, the oldest Roman Catholic parish in Alaska, founded May 2, 1879.
0.4 First Presbyterian Church has a red neon cross, 1 of 2 in the world that serve as navigational aids. This was the first church in Wrangell and is one of the oldest Protestant churches in Alaska (founded in 1877 and built in 1879).
0.6 Bennett Street (Airport Road) loops north 2.2 miles to the airport and back to the ferry terminal.
0.7 Public Safety Bldg.
1.7 Private campground.
1.9 City park. Picnic area with shelters, firepits, restrooms, litter barrels. Tent camping only; 24-hour limit.
4.3 Lodge with restaurant and lounge.
4.4 Large turnout overlooking Zimovia Strait.
4.7 **Shoemaker Bay** small-boat harbor, boat launch, picnic, camping and parking area, phone and small convenience store. Camping area has tent sites, 16 RV sites with electricity ($10/night) and 10 sites without electricity ($6/night), water, dump station and restrooms; use of community pool with RV site rental. Tennis court, horseshoe pits and children's playground nearby. Rainbow Falls trailhead; 0.7-mile trail to scenic waterfall. Institute Creek trail intersects with Rainbow Falls trail at Mile 0.6 and leads 2.7 miles to viewpoint and shelter overlooking Shoemaker Bay and Zimovia Strait. North Wrangell Trail intersects with the Institute Creek Trail at Mile 1.7 and leads 2.3 miles over the highest peak on the north end of Wrangell Island and down to the Spur Road Extension southeast of town.
5.1 Bike path ends.
6.3 Sawmill.
7 Scenic turnout.
7.6 Turnout.
8.2 Turnout, beach access (8 Mile Beach undeveloped recreation area).
10.5 Access road west to Pat Creek Log Transfer Facility and small boat launch. Road east (Pat Creek Road) is a 1-lane, maintained gravel road with turnouts that leads 0.3 mile to Pat's Lake and continues approximately 6 miles northeast through both old and active logging areas.
10.7 Pat Creek camping area (unmaintained, no facilities); parking for self-contained vehicles.
12.9 McCormack Creek crossing on new concrete bridge. Trout and salmon fishing (in season) downstream at mouth of creek.
13.3 **Junction** with Nemo Road, single-lane gravel FS Road 6267, which leads to the **Nemo Campsites.** Views of Zimovia Strait and north Etolin Island; parking areas, picnic tables, fire grills and outhouses each site. Campground host during summer. No reservations, no fees.
13.7 Two-lane paved road ends at National Forest boundary; begin single-lane FS road with turnouts. Road 6265 connects with other FS roads. (A map showing island roads with recreation sites and trails is available from the USFS office in Wrangell.) Watch for log trucks and other heavy equipment.

PETERSBURG

Old shrimping vessel docked at Petersburg. (© Blake Hanna, staff)

Petersburg Special Events:
- **May**—Little Norway Festival, an annual event held the third weekend in May.

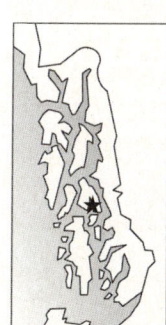

Located on the northwest tip of Mitkof Island at the northern end of Wrangell Narrows, midway between Juneau and Ketchikan. **Population:** 3,224. **Emergency Services: City Police, Poison Center, Fire Department** and **Ambulance,** phone 911. **Alaska State Troopers,** in Ketchikan, phone (907) 225-5111. **Hospital,** Petersburg Medical Center, 2nd and Fram St., phone (907) 772-4291. **Maritime Search and Rescue:** contact the Coast Guard at (800) 478-5555. Harbormaster, phone (907) 772-4688, CB Channel 9, or VHF Channel 16.

Visitor Information: Petersburg Visitor Information Center located at 1st and Fram streets; open Monday–Saturday from 9 A.M. to 5 P.M., noon to 4 P.M. Sundays, spring and summer; 10 A.M. to 2 P.M. Mon.-Fri. fall and winter. Write Petersburg Visitor Information Center, Box 649, Petersburg 99833; phone (866) 484-4700; www.petersburg.org. Clausen Memorial Museum, 2nd and Fram streets, open daily in summer, limited winter hours; phone (907) 772-INFO (4636). Alaska Dept. of Fish and Game, State Office Building, Sing Lee Alley; open 8 A.M. to 4:30 P.M., Monday through Friday, phone (907) 772-3801.

Elevation: Sea level. **Climate:** Average daily maximum temperature in July, 64°F; daily minimum in January, 20°F. All-time high, 84°F in 1933; record low, -19°F in 1947. Mean annual precipitation, 110 inches; mostly as rain. **Radio:** KRSA-AM 580, KFSK-FM 100.9. **Television:** Alaska Rural Communication Service, Channel 15; KTOO (PBS) Channel 9 and cable channels. **Newspaper:** *Petersburg Pilot* (weekly).

Private Aircraft: James A. Johnson Airport, 1 mile southeast; elev. 107 feet; length 6,000 feet; asphalt; fuel 100, A. Seaplane base 0.5 mile from downtown.

Petersburg was named for Peter Buschmann, who selected the present townsite for a salmon cannery and sawmill in 1897. The sawmill and dock were built in 1899, and the cannery was completed in 1900. He was followed by other Norwegian immigrants who came to fish and work in the cannery and sawmill. Since then the cannery has operated continuously (with rebuilding, expansion and different owners) and is now known as Petersburg Fisheries Inc., a division of Icicle Seafoods Inc. Petersburg Fisheries shares the waterfront with two other canneries, two other cold storage plants and several other fish processing facilities.

Today, Petersburg boasts the largest home-based halibut fleet in Alaska and is also well known for its shrimp, crab, salmon, herring and other fish products. Most families depend on the fishing industry for livelihood. Sportfishing questions should be directed to the Alaska Dept. of Fish and Game's Division of Sportfishing in Petersburg; phone (907) 772-3801.

Lodging & Services

Petersburg has 2 hotels, including Scandia House (1-800-722-5006) and Tides Inn (1-800-665-8433). There are also numerous bed and breakfasts and guest houses, and several restaurants located downtown.

The 5-block-long commercial area on Main Street (Nordic Drive) has a grocery store, marine and fishing supply stores, hardware, a drugstore, travel agency, banks, gift and variety stores specializing in both Alaskan and Scandinavian items, city hall, a liquor store, and a cocktail bar. A community gym with racquetball courts and a public swimming pool are located a couple of blocks off Nordic Drive. Petersburg has 13 churches. The post office is between Hammer, Witkan and the airport.

Feathered Nest Bed & Breakfast. Enjoy first class accommodations in a beautifully furnished 900-square-foot wheelchair-accessible suite. King-size bed, color TV, roll-in shower. Complete kitchen stocked to serve yourself breakfast. Private entrance. Close to Ferry Terminal. 20-minute walk to town. 609 Unimak St., Petersburg, AK. (907) 772-3090. www.featherednestbandb.com. [ADVERTISEMENT]

Camping

RV camping at Twin Creek RV Park. The city maintains an RV staging area downtown at 2nd & Haugen St. Parking $6 for up to 12 hours. The tent campground (known locally as Tent City) is on Haugen Drive with hot showers available. Public campgrounds (1 developed, several undeveloped) are located on Mitkof Highway some distance south of town. ▲

Transportation

Air: Twice daily scheduled jet service by Alaska Airlines to major Southeast cities and Seattle, WA, with connections to Anchorage and Fairbanks. A scheduled regional carrier and several local carrier and charter services also serve the area.

The airport is located 1 mile from the Federal Building on Haugen Drive. It has a ticket counter and waiting room. There is no shuttle service to town; hotel courtesy vans and taxis are available for a fee.

Ferry: Alaska Marine Highway vessels connect Petersburg with all Southeastern Alaska cities plus Prince Rupert, BC, and Bellingham, WA. Terminal at Milepost 0.8 Mitkof Highway, includes dock, ticket office with waiting room, and parking area. Phone (907) 772-3855.

Car Rental: Available.

Taxi: There are 2 taxi companies. Cab service to and from the airport and ferry terminal.

Highways: Mitkof Highway (see log this section).

Cruise Ships: Smaller cruise ships dock 1/4 mile from town. Vans take passengers to town.

Private Boats: Boaters must check with harbormaster for moorage assignment.

Attractions

Little Norway Festival, an annual event held the third weekend in May, is a celebration for Norwegian Independence Day. Pageantry, old-country dress, contests, Vikings, a Viking ship, dancing and a Norwegian "fish feed" for locals and visitors are featured.

Clausen Memorial Museum, 203 Fram St., features Petersburg area history. On display are artifacts representing the cannery and fisheries, a world-record 126.5-lb. king

PETERSBURG Travel Directory

ACCOMMODATIONS

TIDES INN
Overlooking Petersburg's Busy Harbor

- Best Rates in Town
- Harbor View Rooms Available
- Convenient Downtown Location
- Complimentary Continental Breakfast
- Free–Email Access
- Free Airport and Ferry Shuttle
- Fishing Licenses Available
- Avis Car Rentals

RESERVATIONS: 800-665-8433
P.O. Box 1048 ♦ Petersburg, Alaska 99833
Fax: 907-772-4286
Located at 1st & Dolphin Sts.
907-772-4288
tidesinn@alaska.net • www.tidesinnalaska.com

Scandia House
PETERSBURG'S NEWEST HOTEL

Central downtown location
Boat & car rentals
Conference room
Courtesy van
Complimentary continental breakfast
Barrier free

Reservations: 800-722-5006
P.O. Box 689 • Petersburg, AK 99833
Call: (907) 772-4281 • Fax: (907) 772-4301
E-mail: scandia@alaska.net

INFO

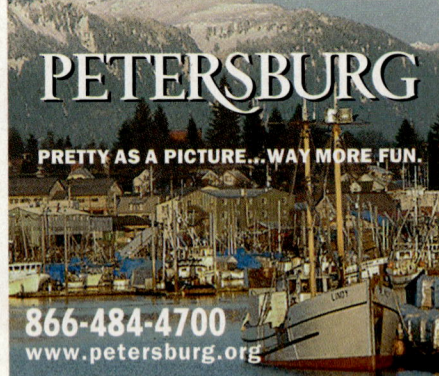

PETERSBURG
PRETTY AS A PICTURE...WAY MORE FUN.
866-484-4700
www.petersburg.org

RV PARKS

TWIN CREEK RV PARK
7.5 MILE MITKOF HIGHWAY
Spring Water • Level Spaces
Full & Partial Hookups
Grocery Store • TV • Laundromat
Rest Rooms • Showers • Dump Station
P.O. BOX 90-M, PETERSBURG, ALASKA 99833
PHONE   (907) 772-3244

SHOPPING

Lee's Clothing
(907) 772-4229
- Norwegian Sweaters
- Outdoor Gear: Boots & Shoes
- Alaska Caps, T-shirts & Sweatshirts

gear@leesclothing.com   Petersburg, AK

TRANSPORTATION

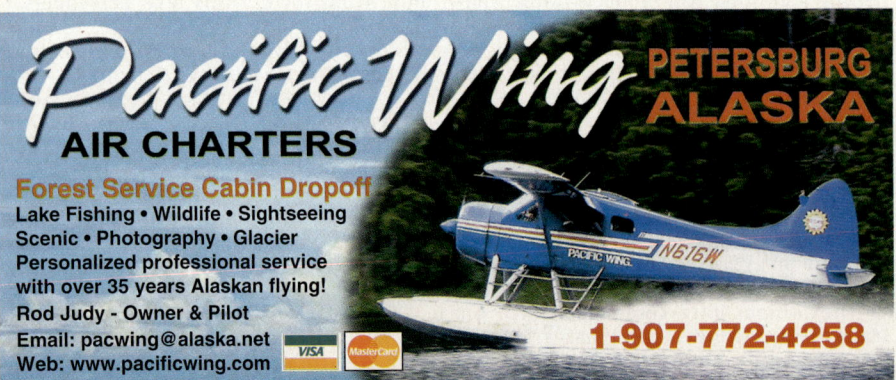

Pacific Wing AIR CHARTERS
PETERSBURG ALASKA

Forest Service Cabin Dropoff
Lake Fishing • Wildlife • Sightseeing
Scenic • Photography • Glacier
Personalized professional service
with over 35 years Alaskan flying!
Rod Judy - Owner & Pilot
Email: pacwing@alaska.net
Web: www.pacificwing.com

1-907-772-4258

PETERSBURG MOTORS, INC.
P.O. Box 767 * Petersburg, AK 99833
(907) 772-3223 / Fax (907) 772-3248
Auto - Marine Parts & Service
Towing Service - Gas - Diesel
Located at Corner of 2nd & Haugen

salmon, the Cape Decision light station lens, a Tlingit canoe and the wall piece "Land, Sea, Sky." Open two days a week and by appointment, 12:30–4:30 P.M., Oct. to third week in Dec. and Feb.-April. Open daily, 9:30 A.M. to 4:30 P.M., May 1 to mid-Sept. Phone (907) 772-3598 for programs, updated visitor information and to leave messages. Wheelchair accessible.

The Fisk (Norwegian for fish), a 10-foot bronze sculpture commemorating Petersburg's fishing tradition, stands in a working fountain in front of the museum. It was completed during the Alaska centennial year of 1967 by sculptor Carson Boysen.

Totem poles are displayed downtown. Petersburg has 2 totems poles, one commemorating the Eagle Clan and one the Raven Clan. They were carved by Sitka carver Tommy Joseph and raised in Oct. 2001 during the community celebration. The totems are on display in front of the Federal Building at Nordic and Haugen.

Sons of Norway Hall, on the National Register of Historic Places, was built in 1912. Situated on pilings over Hammer Slough (a favorite photography subject), its window shutters are decorated with rosemaling (Norwegian tole painting).

Fisherman's Memorial Park, next to the Sons of Norway Hall, commemorates those townspeople lost at sea.

LeConte Glacier, in LeConte Bay, 25 miles east of Petersburg, is the continent's southernmost tidewater glacier. Fast-moving, the glacier continually "calves," creating icefalls from its face into the bay. Seals and porpoises are common; whales are often seen. Helicopters, small aircraft and boats may be chartered in Petersburg or Wrangell to see LeConte Glacier.

Whale Research and Whale-Watching. Petersburg has become the center for humpback whale research in Southeast Alaska. Three feature documentaries have been filmed in adjacent waters in the past five years. The area attracts several researchers and professional photographers from around the world. The **Marine Mammal Center**, on Sing Lee Alley near Sons of Norway Hall, features displays and information on whale sightsing and ongoing whale research in Frederick Sound.

Kaleidoscope Cruises. This tour is a must! Specializing in glacier tours, whale watching and custom sightseeing. Professional biologist and naturalist Barry Bracken, skipper of the 28-foot *Island Dream*, has over 25 years experience in Southeast Alaskan waters, conducting research and exploring the area. Half-day, full-day, overnight tours. Phone (800) TO THE SEA. E-mail: bbsea@alaska.net. Internet: www.alaska.net/~bbsea. [ADVERTISEMENT]

Viking Travel, Inc. 101 N. Nordic, phone (800) 327-2571, (907) 772-3818. Great selection of tours and activities around Petersburg. Whale-watching, sea kayaking day trips, LeConte Glacier Bay, halibut and

Petersburg's scenic Hammer's Slough. (© Four Corners Imaging, Ralph & Leonor Barrett)

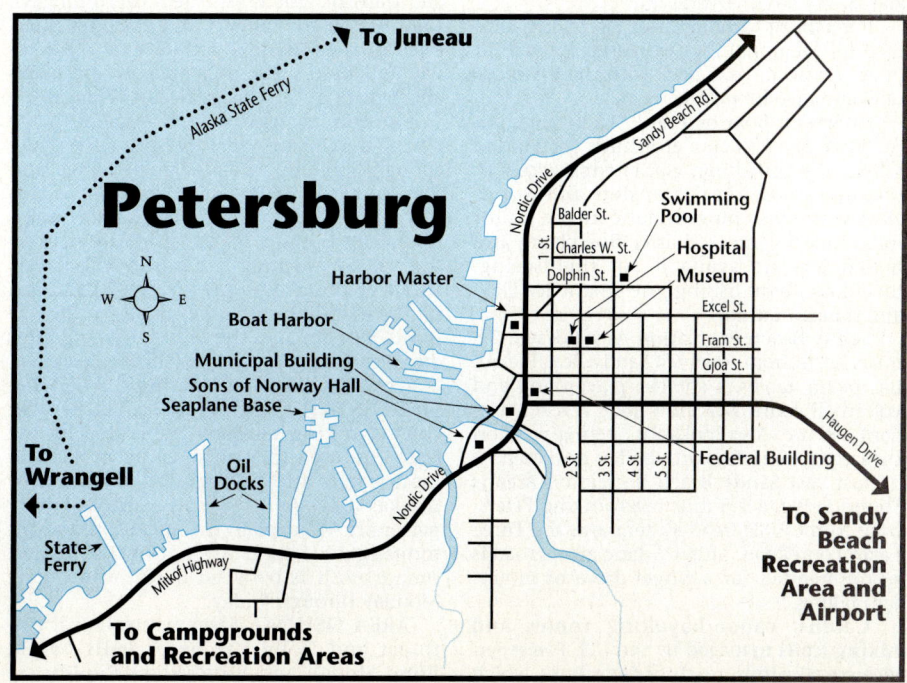

Mitkof Highway

The major road on Mitkof Island, Mitkof Highway leads 33.8 miles south from the downtown Petersburg to the Stikine River delta at the south end of the island. The highway is paved to **Milepost 17.5**; good wide gravel to road end.
Distance from downtown Petersburg is shown.

0 Federal Building and totem poles.
0.1 Bridge over Hammer Slough, an intertidal estuary.
0.5 Harbor parking.
0.6 Pier and floatplane base.
0.8 Alaska Marine Highway ferry terminal, office and waiting area on right.
2.9 **Scow Bay**, a wide portion of Wrangell Narrows with king salmon fishing in spring. Scow Bay Loop Road rejoins highway at **Milepost 3.1**.
7.5 **Twin Creek RV Park**, private campground, small store and phone.
10.7 **Junction** with **Three Lakes Loop Road**. This 21.4-mile-long, 1-lane road loops from **Milepost 10.7** to **Milepost 20.6** Mitkof Highway. (Locals use the entrance at Mile 20.6 to reach hiking trails on this side road.) There are no services available along the road, but there are several boardwalk hiking trails to lakes (rowboats available for public use at the lakes): Sand Lake trail at Mile 14.2; Hill Lake trail at Mile 14.7; and Crane Lake trail at Mile 15.1. There is also a boardwalk trail to Ideal Cove on the east side of Mitkof Island. LeConte Glacier Overlook, a picnic site with a spectacular view of the mainland, is located at Mile 12.8 from this junction.
10.8 **Falls Creek** and fish ladder. Steelhead, April and May; pink salmon below falls in August; coho, August and September; Dolly Varden and cutthroat late summer and fall. No fishing within 300 feet of fish ladder.
11 Road on right leads 0.5 mile to Papke's Landing; transient boat moorage and boat ramp. USFS Log Transfer Facility.
14.3 Entering Tongass National Forest.
14.5 **Blind River Rapids** parking area and trail; outhouse; 2,600-ft. wheelchair-accessible boardwalk loop added in 1999. 0.3-mile boardwalk trail through muskeg meadow to Blind River Rapids, hatchery steelhead, mid-April to mid-May; king salmon, June to late July; coho, mid-August to October. Also Dolly Varden and cutthroat trout.
14.8 Large paved pullout.
16.3 Blind Slough waterfowl viewing area on right. Covered platform with interpretive signs. Trumpeter swans winter in this area October through April.
17.5 Pavement ends; wide, hard-packed gravel to end of road. Short road leads to Crystal Lake Fish Hatchery and **Blind Slough Recreation Area** with picnic tables, shelter and pit toilets; no overnight camping. Hatchery is open for visiting, though no scheduled tours are available. Fishing for cutthroat and Dolly Varden in summer; coho salmon, mid-August to mid-September; king salmon in June and July. Fishing in this area may be regulated. Check with ADF&G, (907) 772-3801.
18.9 Turnout with outhouse.
20 **Manmade Hole** picnic area with tables, firepits, swimming and short trail. Fishing for cutthroat and Dolly Varden year-round; best in summer and fall. Ice skating in winter.
20.6 Three Lakes Loop Road begins on left leading to Three Lakes on other side of Mitkof Island, looping back to Mitkof Highway at **Milepost 10.7** near Falls Creek bridge.
21.4 Woodpecker Cove Road (1-lane) leads about 15 miles along south Mitkof Island to Woodpecker Cove and beyond. Good views of Sumner Strait. Watch for logging trucks.
21.5 **Ohmer Creek nature trail**, 1.5 mile loop; first 0.3 mile is barrier-free.
21.7 **Ohmer Creek Campground**, 10 sites (2 are wheelchair accessible), toilets, parking area, picnic tables, drinking water and firepits. Set in meadow area among trees. Open spring to fall; small fee; accommodates RVs to 32 feet.
24 Blind Slough USFS Log Transfer Facility. Fishing from skiff for coho salmon, mid-August to mid-September. Fishing from shore for kings.
26.1 Narrow 0.7-mile road on right to Sumner Strait Campground, locally called Green's Camp (undeveloped); must walk in, no facilities. May be inaccessible at high tide.
27 View of city of Wrangell.
28 Wilson Creek state recreation area (undeveloped); picnic tables, toilet, parking. Good view of Sumner Strait.
28.6 Banana Point; large turnaround for vehicles, boat ramp, outhouse.
31 Stikine River mud flats, visible on right at low tide. Part of the Stikine River delta, this is the area where Dry Strait meets Sumner Strait.
32.4 Boat launch.
33.8 Road ends with turnaround.

salmon fishing charters, bear viewing, river rafting, Glacier Bay tours. Independent travel planning for all Alaska. Instant ferry and airline reservations and ticketing. www.alaskaferry.com. [ADVERTISEMENT]

Petersburg King Salmon Derby is scheduled for Memorial Day weekend. $30,000 in prizes are awarded. Check with the Chamber of Commerce for details.

Charter a Boat or Plane. There are charter boat services in Petersburg for guided saltwater sportfishing, glacier trips, access to remote cabins, kayak transfers and world-class whale watching. Inquire at the visitor information center. Charter floatplanes and helicopters are available for flightseeing, including fly-in fishing, the Stikine Ice Field and transportation.

Sandy Beach Recreation Area, located 2.8 miles north from town via Sandy Beach Road, has picnic tables, a shelter, playground and volleyball court. Low tides here reveal abundant sea life. Also looks for petroglyphs on the large rock at the north end of the beach.

Just past Sandy Beach Recreation Area is Sound Drive, a 7.5-mile road linking Petersburg to the USFS road system and the Three Lakes Loop Road. This 1½-lane gravel road is recommended for 4-wheel drive or mountain biking.

Cabins, canoe/kayaking routes and hiking trails managed by the U.S. Forest Service are all within reach of Petersburg, which is the administrative center for the Stikine Area of Tongass National Forest. Stop by the USFS office in the Federal Building, or phone (907) 772-3871 for information on cabins and trails or visit www.fs.fed.us/r10/tongass. Information for canoers and kayakers interested in the Stikine River delta or Tebenkof Bay and Kuiu wilderness areas is also available here or at the USFS office in Wrangell.

Salmon migration and spawning are best observed in the Petersburg area July though September. Falls Creek bridge and fish ladder, at **Milepost 10.8** Mitkof Highway, is a good location. The ladder helps migrating salmon bypass difficult falls on the way to spawning grounds in Falls Creek. It can be observed from the creek bank just off the roadside. Other viewing areas include Blind Slough and the Blind River Rapids area, Petersburg Creek and Ohmer Creek.

Crystal Lake Fish Hatchery is at **Milepost 17.5** Mitkof Highway. This hatchery for coho and king salmon is operated by the state and used for fish-stocking projects in local waters and throughout southeastern Alaska. It is open for visits, and hatchery personnel will explain the operation, though formal guided tours are not available. Best time to visit is between 8 A.M. and 4 P.M., Monday through Friday.

AREA FISHING: Salmon, steelhead, cutthroat and Dolly Varden at **Falls Creek**, **Blind Slough** and **Blind River Rapids**; see log of Mitkof Highway this section. Salmon can be caught in the harbor area and **Scow**

Bay area. (Rapid tidal currents in front of the town necessitate the use of an outboard motor.) **Petersburg Creek**, directly across Wrangell Narrows from downtown within Petersburg Creek–Duncan Salt Chuck Wilderness Area, also offers good fishing. Blind Slough, located 15 miles south of the ferry terminal, offers good fishing for king salmon. Dolly Varden can be caught from the beach north of town and from downtown docks. Sportfishing opportunities for halibut, crab and shrimp. Harvest of mussels, clams and other shellfish is not recommended because of the possibility of paralytic shellfish poisoning. Contact the Sport Fish Division of the Alaska Dept. of Fish and Game (907) 772-3801 for more information.

SITKA

Sitka Special Events:
- June 7-29—Annual Sitka Summer Music Festival.
- Oct. 14-18—Alaska Day Celebration.

Sitka viewed from Japonski Island. (© Four Corners Imaging, Ralph & Leanor Barrett)

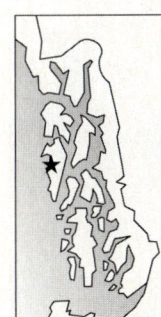

Located on west side of Baranof Island, 95 air miles southwest of Juneau, 185 air miles northwest of Ketchikan; 2 hours flying time from Seattle, WA. **Population:** City and Borough, 8,835. **Emergency Services: Alaska State Troopers, City Police, Fire Department,** and **Ambulance,** phone 911. **Hospital,** Sitka Community, 209 Moller Ave., phone (907) 747-3241; Mount Edgecumbe, 222 Tongass Dr., phone (907) 966-2411. **Maritime Search and Rescue,** phone the Coast Guard at (800) 478-5555.

Visitor Information: Contact the Sitka Convention and Visitors Bureau at Box 1226-MP, Sitka, AK 99835; phone (907) 747-5940; www.sitka.org. Information desk in Harrigan Centennial Hall, 330 Harbor Drive. For USDA Forest Service information write the Sitka Ranger District, 204 Siginaka Way, Sitka, AK 99835; phone (907) 747-4220. For information on Sitka National Historical Park, write 106 Metlakatla St., Sitka, AK 99835; phone (907) 747-6281.

Elevation: Sea level. **Climate:** Average daily temperature in July, 56°F; in January, 34°F. Annual precipitation, 95 inches. **Radio:** KIFW 1230, KAQU 88.1, KSBZ-FM 103.1, KCAW-FM 104.7. **Television:** Cable channels. **Newspaper:** *Daily Sitka Sentinel.*

Private Aircraft: Sitka airport on Japonski Island; elev. 21 feet; length 6,500 feet; asphalt; fuel 100, A1. Sitka seaplane base adjacent west; fuel 80, 100.

Sitka rests on the Pacific Ocean shore, protected by myriad small islands and Cape Edgecumbe. Dominating the horizon to the west is 3,201-foot Mount Edgecumbe, a dormant volcano.

The site was originally occupied by Tlingit Indians. Alexander Baranof, chief manager of the Russian–American Co. with headquarters in Kodiak, built a trading post and fort (St. Michael's Redoubt) north of Sitka in 1799. Indians burned down the fort and looted the warehouses. Baranof returned in 1804, and by 1808 Sitka was capital of Russian Alaska. Baranof was governor from 1790 to 1818.

Salmon was the mainstay of the economy from the late 1800s until the 1950s, when the salmon population decreased. A pulp mill operated at nearby Silver Bay from 1960 to 1993.

Today, tourism, commercial fishing, health care and government provide most jobs.

Lodging & Services

Services in Sitka's downtown area include restaurants, a laundromat, drugstore, clothing and grocery stores, and gift shops. Shopping and services are also available along Sawmill and Halibut Point roads. Dump stations are located at the Wastewater Treatment Plant on Japonski Island.

Sitka has several hotels/motels, most with adjacent restaurants, and bed-and-breakfasts. Contact the visitors bureau for more information; (907) 747-5940.

Sitka Hostel, open June 1–Aug. 31, is located in the United Methodist Church, 303 Kimsham St. Phone (907) 747-8661.

Alaska Ocean View Bed & Breakfast Inn. You'll enjoy casual elegance at affordable rates at this superior B&B, where guests experience exceptional personal comfort, privacy and friendly hosts. Open your day with the tantalizing aroma of fresh bread and fresh ground coffee; and a delicious breakfast. Close your day with a refreshing soak in the bubbling outdoors hot-tub spa. Open year-round, smoke- free. Central location, view. "Delighted beyond our expectations!" Brochure and reservations: 1101 Edgecumbe Drive, Sitka, AK 99835; (907) 747-8310. Email: alaskaoceanview@gci.net. See display ad this section. [ADVERTISEMENT]

Camping

There are 2 RV parks in the Sitka area. Sitka Sportsman's Assoc. RV Park, located 1 block south of the ferry terminal on Halibut Point Road, has 16 RV sites, water and electrical hookups; phone (907) 747-6033. The city-operated Sealing Cove, adjacent Sealing Cove Boat Harbor on Japonski Island, offers overnight parking for 26 RVs, water and electrical hookups; 15-night limit.

The U.S. Forest Service operates 2 campgrounds in the Sitka area. Starrigavan, at Mile 7.3 Halibut Point Road, has 17 campsites and picnic tables. Sawmill Creek Campground, at Mile 1.5 Blue Lake Road (accessible from **Milepost 5.4** Sawmill Creek Road), has 11 tent sites, vault toilet, no garbage service, no fee, and a 14-day limit. For more information contact the Forest Service office, phone (907) 747-4216; web site www.fs.fed.us/r10/tongass. ▲

Transportation

Air: Scheduled jet service by Alaska Airlines. Charter service also available. The airport is on Japonski Island, across O'Connell Bridge, 1.7 miles from downtown. Airport Shuttle (May–Sept.); van and taxi service available to downtown hotels and accommodations.

Ferry: Alaska Marine Highway ferry terminal is located at **Milepost 7** Halibut Point Road; phone (907) 747-8737 or toll free at 1-800-642-0066 for reservations. The Ferry Shuttle meets all ferries; taxi service also available.

Bus: Shuttle available to accommodations and downtown area. Visitor Transit to attractions 12:30–4:30 with extended hours on large tour ship days. Fee is $5–$7; phone (907) 747-7290.

Car Rental: Available.

Taxi: Available.

Highways: Area roads are Halibut Point Road (8 miles), Sawmill Creek Road (7.4 miles) and Blue Lake Road (2.2 miles).

Cruise Ships: Sitka is a popular port of call for several cruise lines.

Private Boats: Transient moorage available at Thomsen Harbor, Katlian Street, 0.6 mile from city center. Contact Harbor Master (907) 747-3439 or Channel 16 VHS.

Attractions

St. Michael's Cathedral, built in 1844–48, is the focal point of Sitka's history as the capital of Russian Alaska. St. Michael's is located in the center of Lincoln Street downtown. Open daily in summer; call to check winter hours, (907) 747-8120. Visitors are reminded that this is an active parish conducting weekly services.

Castle Hill (Baranof Castle Hill Historic Site) is where Alaska changed hands from Russia to the United States on Oct. 18, 1867. Walkway is located on south side by the bridge (look for sign) or on north side off of Lincoln Street.

Sitka Pioneers' Home, at Lincoln and Katlian streets, was built in 1934. Pioneers welcome visitors. **Totem Square,** across from the Pioneers' Home, contains items of historic interest.

Russian Blockhouse beside Pioneers' Home is a replica of the blockhouse that separated Russian and Tlingit sections of Sitka after the Tlingits moved back to the area 20 years after the 1804 battle.

New Archangel Dancers, a group of local women, perform authentic Russian dances in authentic costumes. For performances, check the schedule board at Harrigan Centennial Hall or call the Russian Dance Hotline at (907) 747-5516.

Sitka National Cemetery, Milepost 0.5 Sawmill Creek Road, is open 8 A.M. to 5 P.M. daily (maintained by the Veterans Administration).

Whale Watching is a popular pastime in Sitka. Whales congregate near Sitka's shores from mid-September to mid-January. Underwater microphones broadcast the humpback whales singing—live, 24 hours a day—over the local FM station, 88.1.

Whale Park, 3.8 miles from downtown on Sawmill Creek Road, has stationary binoculars for whale viewing at Silver Bay.

Alaska Day Celebration, Oct. 14–18, 2003, celebrates the transfer of Alaska from Russia to the United States with a reenactment of the event. Events ranging from pageant to costume ball and parade highlight the affair.

Annual Sitka Summer Music Festival (June 7–29, 2003). Concerts on Tuesday, Friday and some Saturday evenings in Harrigan Centennial Hall. An international group of professional musicians gives evening concerts of chamber music during the festival. Advance tickets are a good idea; the concerts are popular. Children under 6 years not admitted.

Sheet'ka Kwaan Naa Kahidi (Sitka's Tribal Community House) is a modern rendition of a northwest coast tribal clan house. Constructed in traditional Naa Kahidi design and aimed at preserving the Tlingit culture, the Community House offers Tlingit dance performances and Native culture exhibits. 200 Katlian St., Sitka, AK 99835; phone (907) 747-7290.

Harrigan Centennial Hall, by Crescent Harbor, is used for the New Archangel dance performances, music festivals, banquets and conventions. Its glass-fronted main hall overlooks Sitka Sound. Nearby is a large hand-carved Tlingit canoe made from a single log.

Isabel Miller Museum, in the Harrigan Centennial Hall, has permanent exhibits highlighting the history of Sitka and its people. Operated by the Sitka Historical Society; hosts available to answer questions. Open year-round; free admission. Hours are 8 A.M. to 5 P.M. daily in summer; 10 A.M. to 4 P.M. Tuesday through Saturday during the winter. Phone (907) 747-6455.

Sitka National Historical Park reflects

HELGA'S BED & BREAKFAST
Located on the beach — Fantastic View
• OPEN YEAR ROUND •
(907) 747-5497
2827 Halibut Point Road
P.O. Box 1885, Sitka, Alaska 99835

ALASKA OCEAN VIEW
Bed & Breakfast Inn
Delicious Complimentary Breakfast
• Microwave • Refrigerator • View
• Hot Tub Spa • King/Queen Beds
Toll Free 1-888-811-6870
e-mail: alaskaoceanview@gci.net
www.sitka-alaska-lodging.com
1101 Edgecumbe Dr. • Sitka, AK 99835
Local phone (907) 747-8310

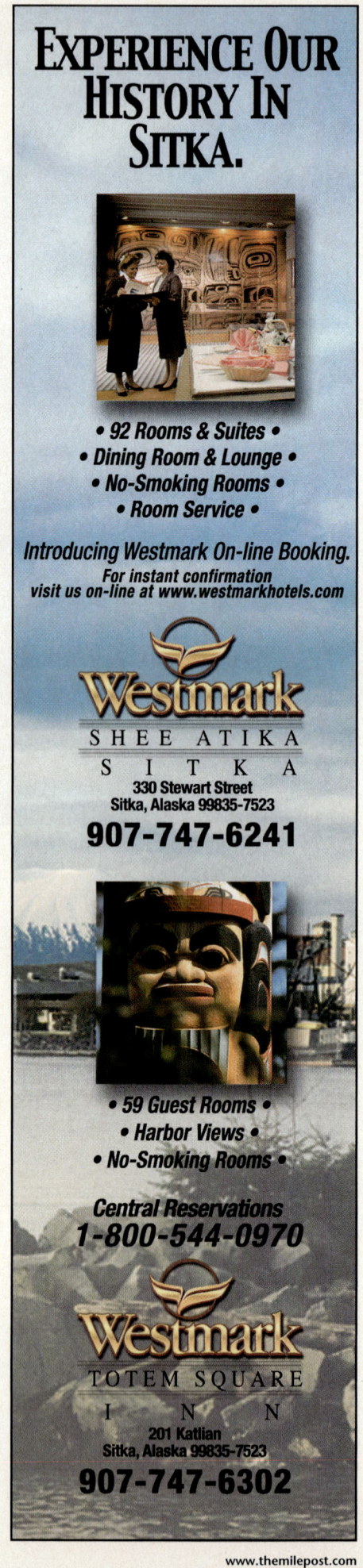

both the community's rich Tlingit Indian heritage and its Russian-ruled past. The park consists of 2 units—the Fort Site, located at the end of Lincoln Street, a half-mile from town, and the Russian Bishop's House, located on Lincoln Street near Crescent Harbor.

There is a self-guiding trail through the park to the fort site. The National Park Service conducts guided walks; check for schedule. The park's totem pole collection stands near the visitor center and along the trail. The collection includes original pieces collected in 1901–03, and copies of originals lost to time and the elements.

The Russian Bishop's House was built by the Russian–American Co. in 1842 for the first Russian Orthodox bishop to serve Alaska. It was occupied by the church until 1969, and was added to Sitka National Historical Park in 1972.

The park's visitor center is open daily, 8 A.M. to 5 P.M., June through September; by reservation in the fall. The park grounds and trails are open daily, 8 A.M. to 5 P.M. in summer; shorter hours in winter. Russian Bishop's House open 9 A.M. to 5 P.M. daily; other times by appointment. Admission fee $3 per person/$6 per immediate family. Tours $3 per person. Students under 18 free with student identification. Phone (907) 747-6281 for more information.

Sheldon Jackson Museum, 104 College Dr., on the Sheldon Jackson College campus, contains some of the finest Native arts and crafts found in Alaska. Museum shop specializes in Alaska Native arts and crafts. Admission $4. Open in summer 9 A.M. to 5 P.M. daily. Winter hours: Tuesday through Saturday, 10 A.M. to 4 P.M. Phone (907) 747-8981; www.museums.state.ak.us.

The Prospector is a 13½-foot clay and bronze statue in front of the Pioneers' Home. Sculpted by Alonzo Victor Lewis, the statue was dedicated on Alaska Day in 1949.

O'Connell Bridge, 1,225 feet long, connecting Sitka with Japonski Island, was the first cable-stayed, girder-span bridge in the United States. It was dedicated Aug. 19, 1972.

Old Sitka, at Milepost 7.5 Halibut Point Road, is a registered national historic landmark and the site of the first Russian settlement in the area in 1799, known then as Fort Archangel Michael. In 1802, in a surprise attack, the Tlingit Indians of the area destroyed the fort and killed most of its occupants, driving the Russians out until Baranof's successful return in 1804.

Visit the Alaska Raptor Center, located at 1000 Raptor Way (**Milepost 0.9**) just across Indian River, within walking distance of downtown Sitka. This unique facility treats injured eagles, hawks, owls and other birds. Tours and educational programs. Summer hours are 8 a.m.–4 p.m.; call for winter hours. Phone (907) 747-8662; email programs.alaskaraptor@alaska.com. Admission $10 for adults, $5 for children.

Old Sitka State Historical Site, at Milepost 6.9 Halibut Point Road, was the site of the Russian Fort Archangel Michael, established in 1799.

Mount Verstovia Hiking Trail. Mount Verstovia trail, accessible from Milepost 1.7 Sawmill Creek Road, is a strenuous 2.5-mile hike to the summit of Mount Verstovia; great views. The Sitka Ranger District office at 204 Siginaka Way has information sheets and maps for area trails.

AREA FISHING: Sitka holds an annual salmon derby Memorial Day weekend and the weekend following. Contact the Sitka Sportsmen's Association, P.O. Box 3030, Sitka, AK 99835 or phone (907) 747-8791. Saltwater fishing charters available locally. For a listing, contact Sitka Convention & Visitors Bureau at (907) 747-5940. There are also many lakes and rivers on Baranof Island with good fishing; these range from **Katlian River**, 11 miles northeast of Sitka by boat, to more remote waters such as **Rezanof Lake**, which is 40 air miles southeast of Sitka. USFS public-use cabins at some lakes. Stop by the Dept. of Fish and Game office at 304 Lake St. for details; phone (907) 747-5355.

The Russian Bishop's House was built in 1842. (© Blake Hanna, staff)

Halibut Point Road

Halibut Point Road (paved) leads northwest from the intersection of Harbor Drive and Lincoln Street past Old Sitka to Starrigavan Campground.

Distance from Harbor Drive and Lincoln Street.

0 Harbor Drive and Lincoln Street. Halibut Point Road begins as Lake Street.

0.3 Swan Lake Park, a lakeside picnic area, with rainbow trout fishing.

1.7 **Pioneer Park** picnic area; parking, beach access.

1.8 Paved turnout; picnic shelter.

1.9 Cascade Creek bridge.

2.2 **Sandy Beach**; good swimming beach, ample parking, view of Mount Edgecumbe, whale watching.

2.7 Gravel turnout.

3.2 Helga's Bed and Breakfast.

3.6 Viewpoint.

4 **Harbor Mountain Road**; steep, narrow, winding gravel (not suitable for low-clearance vehicles or RVs), currently accessible only to third gate (3 miles). From gate, walk 1 mile to first viewpoint; 1.5 miles to picnic area and second viewpoint; and 2.3 miles to Harbor Mountain Ridge Trailhead.

4.1 Turnout at **Magic Island** beach trail. This walk-in day-use area is accessible at low tide.

4.3 Granite Creek bridge. **Halibut Point State Recreation Site**; swimming beach, picnic shelters, tables, fireplaces and toilets.

4.8 Double-ended gravel turnout with view of Sitka Rocks and Anahootz Mountain.

5.4 Halibut Point commercial fishery marine.

6.5 Sportsman RV Park.

6.6 Alaska Marine Highway ferry terminal.

6.9 Boat launch, parking.

7 Starrigavan Creek bridge. Commemorative plaque marks **Old Sitka State Historic Site** and national historic landmark. Old Sitka was the site of the Russian Fort Archangel Michael, established in 1799. Picnic area.

7.1 Turnoff for narrow side road along bank of **Starrigavan Creek**; spawning pink salmon in August and September. Watch for herons.

7.3 USFS estuary life trail, Starrigavan Recreation Area; bird watching. Wheelchair access, vault toilets, parking, trails. Turnoff for **Starrigavan USFS campground** and picnic area; artesian well. Forest and muskeg nature trail, across from boat ramp, connects with Estuary life trail. Mosquito Cove trail (wheelchair-accessible). Access to beach. Fishing in **Starrigavan Bay** for Dolly Varden; pink and silver salmon, May to October.

7.4 Road ends.

JUNEAU

Population: 30,711

View of Juneau and Gastineau Channel from Mount Roberts. (© Kris Graef, staff)

Juneau Special Events:
- **May**—King Salmon Derby.
- **June**—Gold Rush Days.
- **August**—Golden North Salmon Derby.

History and Economy

In 1880, nearly 20 years before the great gold rushes to the Klondike and to Nome, 2 prospectors named Joe Juneau and Dick Harris found "color" in what is now called Gold Creek, a small, clear stream that runs through the center of present-day Juneau. (Local history states that a Tlingit, Chief Kowee, showed Joe Juneau where to find gold in Gold Creek.) . What the prospectors found led to the discovery of one of the largest lodes of gold quartz in the world. Juneau (called Harrisburg the first year) quickly boomed into a gold rush town as claims and mines sprang up in the area.

For a time the largest mine was the Treadwell, across Gastineau Channel south of Douglas (which was once a larger town than Juneau), but a cave-in and flood closed the mine in 1917. In 36 years of operation, Treadwell produced $66 million in gold. The Alaska–Gastineau Mine, operated by Bart Thane in 1911, had a 2-mile shaft through Mount Roberts to the Perseverance Mine near Gold Creek. The Alaska–Juneau (A–J) Mine was constructed on a mountain slope south of Juneau and back into the heart of Mount Roberts. It operated until 1944, when it was declared a nonessential wartime activity after producing over $80 million in gold. Post–WWII wage and price inflation and the fixed price of gold prevented its reopening.

In 1900, the decision to move Alaska's capital to Juneau was made because of the city's growth, mining activity and location on the water route to Skagway and the Klondike; the decline of post-Russian Sitka, as whale and fur trading slackened, secured Juneau's new status as Alaska's preeminent city.

Congress first provided civil government for Alaska in 1884. Until statehood in 1959 Alaska was governed by a succession of presidential appointees, first as the District of Alaska, then as the Territory of Alaska. Between 1867 (when the United States purchased Alaska from Russia) and 1884, the military had jurisdiction over the District of Alaska, except for a 3-year period (1877–79) when Alaska was put under control of the U.S. Treasury Dept. and governed by U.S. Collectors of Customs.

With the arrival of Alaska statehood in 1959, Juneau's governmental role increased even further. In 1974, Alaskans voted to move the capital from Juneau to a site between Anchorage and Fairbanks, closer to the state's population center. In 1976, Alaska voters selected a new capital site near Willow, 65 road miles north of Anchorage on the Parks Highway. However, in November 1982, voters defeated funding for the capital move.

Today, government (federal, state and local) comprises an estimated half of the total basic industry. Tourism is the largest employer in the private sector.

Description

Juneau, often called "a little San Francisco," is nestled at the foot of Mount Juneau (elev. 3,576 feet) with Mount Roberts (elev. 3,819 feet) rising immediately to the east on the approach up Gastineau Channel.

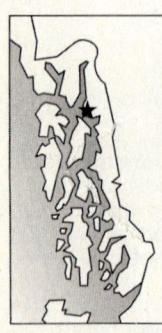

Located on Gastineau Channel, 95 miles north of Sitka. **Population:** Borough 30,790. **Emergency Services:** Phone 911 for all emergencies. **Police,** phone (907) 586-0600. **Fire Department,** phone (907) 586-5323. **Alaska State Troopers,** phone (907) 465-4000. **Hospital,** Bartlett Regional, 3260 Hospital Dr., phone (907) 796-8900. **Maritime Search and Rescue,** Coast Guard, phone (907) 463-2000 or (800) 478-5555.

Visitor Information: Juneau Convention & Visitors Bureau, Centennial Hall Visitor Center; 101 Egan Dr., phone (907) 586-2201 or (888) 581-2201; www.traveljuneau.com; Email: info@traveljuneau.com. Open year-round 8:30 A.M. to 5 P.M. Monday through Friday; additional hours during the summer, 9 A.M. to 5 P.M. Saturday and Sunday. Visitor information kiosk located in Marine Park on waterfront near Merchants Wharf, open when ships are docked at Marine Park from about mid-May to mid-September. Information booth at the airport terminal. Visitor information is also available at the cruise ship terminal on S. Franklin Street when cruise ships are in port, and at the Auke Bay ferry terminal. Large groups contact the Centennial Hall Visitor Center in advance for special assistance.

U.S. Forest Service information on camping, trails and cabins is available at Centennial Hall Visitor Center; 101 Egan Dr., phone (907) 586-2201 or (888) 581-2201. The Juneau Ranger District office at 8465 Old Dairy Rd., near the Nugget Mall in the airport area, issues permits for Pack Creek bear viewing on Admiralty Island. The office is open 8 A.M. to 5 P.M. weekdays; phone (907) 586-8800. For Tongass National Forest information online, visit www.fs.fed.us/r10/tongass.

Elevation: Sea level. **Climate:** Mild and wet. Juneau averages 222 days of rain a year, with September and October the wettest months and April through June the driest. The monthly rainfall record for July is 10.36 inches (1997). Average daily maximum temperature in July, 63°F; daily minimum in January, 19°F. Highest recorded temperature, 90°F in July 1975; the lowest -22°F in January 1968 and 1972. Average annual precipitation, 56.5 inches (airport), 92 inches (downtown); 103 inches of snow annually. Snow on ground intermittently from mid-November to mid-April. Prevailing winds are east-southeasterly. **Radio:** KBJZ 94.1, KJNO 630, KINY 800, KFMG 100.7, KSRJ 102.7, KTOO-FM 104.3, KTKU-FM 105.1, KSUP-FM 106.3. **Television:** KJUD Channel 8; JATV cable; KTOO (public television). **Newspapers:** *Juneau Empire* and *Capital City Weekly*.

Private Aircraft: Juneau International Airport, 9 miles northwest; elev. 18 feet; length 8,456 feet; asphalt; fuel 100LL, Jet A. Juneau harbor seaplane base, due east; restricted use, no fuel. International seaplane base, 7 miles northwest; 5,000 feet by 450 feet, avgas, Jet A. For more information, phone the Juneau Flight Service Station at (907) 586-7382.

JUNEAU Travel Directory

INSIDE PASSAGE • Juneau

ACCOMMODATIONS

FIDDLEHEAD & DI SOPRA (UPSTAIRS)
2 Great Restaurants! 1 Great Bakery! 1 Easy Location!
429 W. Willoughby Ave.
Juneau, Alaska
907-586-3150

The Driftwood Lodge
1-800-544-2239 Toll Free
Central Downtown Juneau Location • Courtesy Van Service
www.Driftwoodalaska.com • email: driftwood@gci.net
435 Willoughby Ave., Juneau, Alaska

AK Fireweed House Bed & Breakfast
Close to downtown with spectacular views of Thomas Glacier
Year Round * Large Secluded Cedar Guest House, Private Apartment or beautifully appointed rooms * King and Queen Beds * Jacuzzi's. The best personalized gourmet breakfast in town!
1-800-586-3885 • Ph. (907) 586-3885 • Fax 586-3385
8530 North Douglas Highway, Juneau 99801   www.fireweedhouse.com

JUNEAU'S STATELY ADDRESS.

- 196 Rooms & Suites
- No-Smoking Rooms
- Restaurant, Cafe & Lounge
- Alaska Airlines Miles
- Alaska Airlines Ticket Office
- Hair Salon
- Full Banquet & Meeting Facilities
- Gallagaskins Gift Shop

Introducing Westmark On-line Booking.
For instant confirmation visit us on-line at www.westmarkhotels.com

Central Reservations
1-800-544-0970

Westmark
BARANOF
JUNEAU
127 North Franklin Street
Juneau, Alaska 99801-1280
907-586-2660

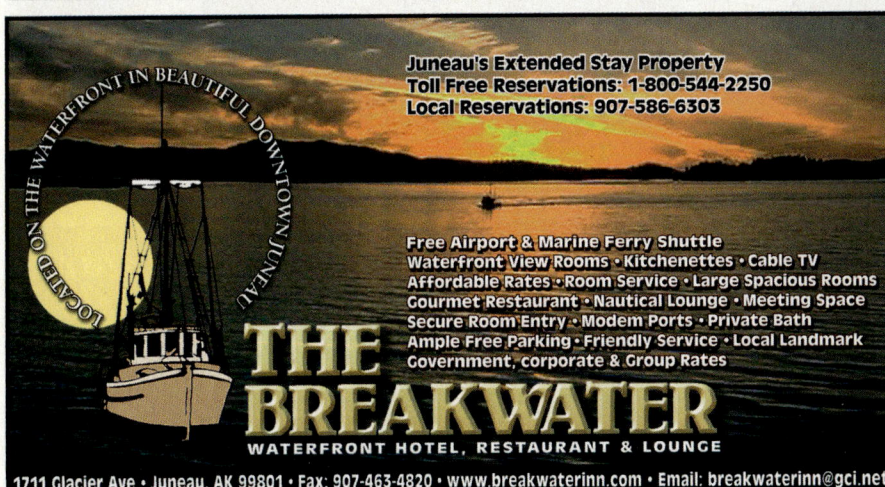

THE BREAKWATER
WATERFRONT HOTEL, RESTAURANT & LOUNGE
LOCATED ON THE WATERFRONT IN BEAUTIFUL DOWNTOWN JUNEAU
Juneau's Extended Stay Property
Toll Free Reservations: 1-800-544-2250
Local Reservations: 907-586-6303

- Free Airport & Marine Ferry Shuttle
- Waterfront View Rooms • Kitchenettes • Cable TV
- Affordable Rates • Room Service • Large Spacious Rooms
- Gourmet Restaurant • Nautical Lounge • Meeting Space
- Secure Room Entry • Modem Ports • Private Bath
- Ample Free Parking • Friendly Service • Local Landmark
- Government, corporate & Group Rates

1711 Glacier Ave • Juneau, AK 99801 • Fax: 907-463-4820 • www.breakwaterinn.com • Email: breakwaterinn@gci.net

Frontier Suites AIRPORT HOTEL
Juneau's Only All Suites Hotel

- Centrally Located near Airport, Shopping, Marine Ferry Terminal and Mendenhall Glacier
- Family Restaurant with Lounge
- Free Courtesy Van to Airport, Marine Terminal & Shopping Centers
- Fitness Facility, Playground, Public Laundry, RV & Bus Parking
- 1 bedroom Suites with Full Kitchens, Cable TV w/HBO
- Government, Corporate and Group Rates Available
- In Room Internet DSL
- Wheelchair Accessible

www.frontiersuites.com
Local Reservations: 907-790-6600   1-800-544-2250
9400 Glacier Highway • Juneau, Alaska 99801 • Email: frontiersuites@gci.net • Fax: 907-790-6612

AAA Approved • 3 DIAMOND RATING

www.themilepost.com   2003 ■ The MILEPOST® ■ 677

INSIDE PASSAGE • Juneau

ACCOMMODATIONS

JUNEAU ALASKA
A Beachside Luxury Inn

- Private Entrance
- Private Bath
- Jacuzzis In-room
- Two minutes to downtown
- Hi-speed cable modem access
- Kitchenettes

1-888-879-0858
or (907) 463-5531
www.abeachsideluxuryinn.com
e-mail: beachside@gci.net

Travelodge Hotel
Juneau Airport

- Full Service Hotel
- 24 Hour Courtesy Van

Direct Reservation 1-888-660-2327
Telephone 907-789-9700
9200 Glacier Highway,
Juneau, AK 99801

www.travelodge.com

DINING

AWARD WINNING FINE DINING
- Serving Fresh Alaskan Seafood, King Crab For 30 Years
- Certified Black Angus Steaks & Prime rib
- Catering For Meetings, Weddings and Groups
- WaterFront Views
- Full Service Lounge
- Outstanding Wine List
- Local Favorite For 30 Years

LOCATED ON THE WATERFRONT IN BEAUTIFUL DOWNTOWN JUNEAU

Reservations: 907-586-6303

THE BREAKWATER
RESTAURANT & LOUNGE

1711 Glacier Avenue • Fax: 907-463-4820 • www.breakwaterrestaurant.com • email: breakwaterinn@gci.net

Sally's B and B
HOME AWAY FROM HOME
- 5 minute walking distance to downtown
- Your own efficiency apartment w/continental breakfast

465 Whittier Street
Ph/Fax 907-780-4708
Email: sbb@alaska.net • Web: www.alaska.net/~sbb\
PO Box 22093, Juneau, AK 99802

ACTIVITIES AND ATTRACTIONS

FREE BROCHURE

Bears of Admiralty
- 1 & 3-day bear viewing at Pack Creek Sanctuary
- 1 to 12-day wilderness sea kayak and raft adventures
- Glacier Bay, Tatshenshini River, Arctic Refuge and more
- Whale viewing & sea kayaking at Pt. Adolphus

ALASKA DISCOVERY
800-586-1911
5310 Glacier Hwy. • Juneau, AK 99801 • http://www.akdiscovery.com

Adventures Afloat

Join us for personalized Inside Passage wilderness adventures aboard our elegant, classic 106' M/V VALKYRIE. Cruise or fly-in; multi-day trips for up to 12 guests

(800) 3AFLOAT   www.ptialaska.net/~valkyrie

An awesome Alaskan adventure awaits.

Temsco Helicopters will show you the best of Alaska in all of its glory. Our helicopter glacier tour options include:
- Glacier Landings
- Glacier Hiking
- Flightseeing
- Tour/Dog Sled Package

JUNEAU & SKAGWAY
1-877-789-9501
WWW.TEMSCOAIR.COM

TEMSCO HELICOPTERS, INC.

Macaulay SALMON HATCHERY
JUNEAU ALASKA

- Guided tours daily
- Features one of Alaska's largest aquarium displays with over 100 species
- Watch Pacific Salmon fight their way up a 450ft. fish ladder
- Famed Alaska Smoked Salmon on sale

Website: www.dipac.net   Toll Free: 1-877-463-2486
2697 Channel Drive, Juneau, Alaska

Mon to Sun 10am to 5pm
Open May 15 to September 15

The residential community of Douglas, on Douglas Island, is south of Juneau and connected by a bridge. Neighboring residential areas around the airport, Mendenhall Valley and Auke Bay lie north of Juneau on the mainland.

Shopping is in the downtown area and at suburban malls in the airport and Mendenhall Valley areas.

Juneau's skyline is dominated by several government buildings, including the Federal Building (1962), the massive State Office Building (1974), the State Court Building (1975) and the older brick, and marble-columned Capitol Building (1931). The modern Sealaska Plaza is headquarters for Sealaska Corp., 1 of the 13 regional Native corporations formed after congressional passage of the Alaska Native Claims Settlement Act in 1971.

The Juneau area supports 35 churches, 2 high schools, 6 middle schools, several elementary schools and a University of Alaska Southeast campus at Auke Lake. There are 3 municipal libraries and the state library.

The area is governed by the unified city and borough of Juneau, which encompasses 3,108 square miles. It is the first unified government in the state, combining the former separate and overlapping jurisdictions of the cities of Douglas and Juneau and the greater Juneau borough.

Sandy Beach on Douglas Island is a popular destination on sunny days.
(© Kris Graef, staff)

Lodging & Services

Juneau has several hotels and motels downtown and in the airport area. There are also numerous bed and breakfasts as well as wilderness lodges; see ads this section.

The Juneau International Hostel is located at 614 Harris St. (Juneau 99801), 4 blocks northeast of the Capitol Bldg. All ages are welcome. Check-in time is 7 to 9 A.M. and 5 P.M. to 11 P.M. during summer, 8 to 9 A.M. and 5 P.M. to 10:30 P.M. the rest of the year. Showers, cooking, laundry and storage facilities are available. Cost for members is $7, nonmembers $10, children accompanied by parent $5. Groups welcome. Open year-round. Phone (907) 586-9559; or email juneauhostel@gci.net; www.juneauhostel.org.

More than 60 restaurants offer a wide variety of dining. Also watch for sidewalk food vendors downtown in summer. Juneau also has 2 microbreweries. The Alaskan Brewing Co., located at 5429 Shaune Dr. in the Lemon Creek area, offers tours, phone (907) 780-5866.

AK Fireweed House Bed & Breakfast. If you are seeking the finest in private, plush accommodations and breakfast dining in the Juneau area, look no further than AK Fireweed House Bed & Breakfast. This fabulous 4-acre location on Douglas Island is just a few minutes from downtown Juneau; but when you are a guest at Fireweed House, you'll feel like you've stepped into a pampered world away from the vacation hustle and bustle. *What a find!* Although this is a destination by itself, a more ideal base for your Southeast Alaska experience would be difficult to locate. The accommodations are all first class and the breakfast dining experience is a *must!* The Thomas Glacier and the surrounding mountains are prominent from many of the windows. The 2-bedroom, cedar guest house on its own adjoining, 2-acre site is unsurpassed in its beauty, seclusion and spaciousness. In addition, the private Fireweed Apartment and guest rooms in the Main House are also extraordinarily appointed and comfortable. Many amenities. Several accommodations include King-size beds and Jacuzzi baths. Birds and other forms of wildlife grace the grounds surrounding this establishment. Complimentary arrangements for personalized tours and charters. Non-smoking. Children welcome. Toll free (800) 586-3885; phone (907) 586-3885; fax (907) 586-3385. 8530 North Douglas Highway, Juneau, AK 99801; website with e-mail: http://fireweedhouse.com. Reserve early to assure space at this B&B! [ADVERTISEMENT]

Camping

There are 2 full-service RV parks in Juneau. Spruce Meadow RV Park is located 2.2 miles east of the Glacier Highway via the Mendenhall Loop Road (turn off at **Milepost 12.1**). Phone (907) 789-1990.

There are 2 USFS campgrounds north of Juneau accessible from the Glacier Highway/Juneau Veterans' Memorial Highway (see log this section). Mendenhall Lake Campground, located off Mendenhall Loop Road (see **Milepost 9.3** or **12.1**), has 60 sites, tables, firepits, water, pit toilets and dump station. Some sites may be reserved through the National Recreation Reservation Service (NRRS); phone (877) 444-67777; or visit www.reserveusa.com. Auke Village Campground in the Auke Village Recreation Area (see **Milepost 14.7**) has 12 campsites, flush

Douglas Island

It is hard to ignore Douglas Island. Located across Gastineau Channel from Juneau, the island and city of Douglas are almost always in your viewfinder, whether you are taking photos of Juneau from Mount Roberts or snapping pics as you sail up the channel to the cruiseship terminal. But how many visitors drive across the Juneau–Douglas Bridge to explore the island?

'Explore the island' may be too grand a phrase, since there are less than 20 miles of highway on the 17-mile-long island. But there is quite a bit to see along those 2 highways.

Begin by taking the **Juneau–Douglas Bridge** across Gastineau Channel from Juneau. At the west end of the bridge, the **South Douglas Highway** leads 2.3 miles south through the city of **DOUGLAS** (pop. 2,000). Although the city has less than half the island's population (which is 5,100), this is where the services are concentrated: a post office, bank, stores, gas station, etc. Douglas is also the home of the **Perseverance Theatre**, one of Alaska's outstanding community theatres. Established in 1978, Perseverance Theatre presents classical and original works from September through May.

South Douglas Highway ends at Harbor Way (Savikko Road), which provides access to the Douglas boat harbor, Savikko Park ball fields and **Sandy Beach** (Lion's Club) recreation area. One of the few sandy beaches in southeastern Alaska, Sandy Beach is a popular place. The area has picnic shelters and tables, a playground, tennis courts, restrooms and parking.

Remnants from the **Treadwell Mine** may be seen from a marked trail that starts just south of Sandy Beach at the end of St. Ann's Avenue. Also look across the channel to see the impressive remains of the A–J Mine mill, on the hillside just south of downtown Juneau.

North Douglas Highway begins after crossing the Juneau–Douglas Bridge from Juneau and immediately turning right. The highway offers excellent views of Mendenhall Glacier, Favorite Channel and Lynn Canal. It also provides access to **Eaglecrest**, Juneau's downhill and cross-country ski area. Built and maintained by the city of Juneau, the area has 2 chair lifts; beginning to expert alpine runs; snowtubing area; snow terrain park for snowboarders and skiers; and 5 miles of cross-country trails. Ski season is from December to mid-April.

There are excellent views of Mendenhall Glacier from the North Douglas City Boat Launch at Mile 9.5; parking area, outhouse. And the scenic views continue from there as the North Douglas Highway follows the island's shoreline to **False Outer Point** at Mile 11.4. Follow the short False Outer Point Loop Trail to the beach. Situated near the northern tip of Douglas Island, this is an excellent spot to observe marine activity and eagles. The highway ends at Mile 13.

Nugget Falls at Mendenhall Glacier.
(© Ren Valencia)

and pit toilets, water, tables and fire rings. Phone the Juneau Ranger District office at (907) 586-8800 for more information.

The City and Borough of Juneau operates a dump station at Jackie Renninger park, 2400 Mendenhall Loop Road, next to the skateboard park. It is open 24 hours; phone (907) 586-5226. Dump stations are also located at Mendenhall Lake USFS campground, Valley Tesoro at Mendenhall Center shopping mall in the Mendenhall Valley, and Savikko Park at Douglas harbor.

Spruce Meadow RV Park. 49 level full-service sites in 12.5 acres of spruce and alder. 30-amp receptacles, cable TV, private showers and clean restrooms, handicap access, laundromat, gazebo, local tour information, public phone, modem, and located on city bus route. 4 miles to Mendenhall Glacier, 3.7 miles from ferry terminal. Big rigs and caravans welcome. Friendly service. MC/VISA. Reservations strongly recommended. 10200 Mendenhall Loop Rd, Juneau, AK 99801. Phone (907) 789-1990; email juneaurv@bci.net; web www.juneaurv.com. [ADVERTISEMENT] ▲

Transportation

Air: Juneau International Airport is northwest of downtown via Glacier Highway. Airport terminal contains ticket counters, waiting area, gift shop, rental cars, restaurant, lounge and information booth. Phone (907) 789-7821.

The city express bus stops at the airport weekdays from 8 A.M. to 5 P.M. Taxi van service to downtown is also available. Courtesy vans to some hotels.

Alaska Airlines serves Juneau daily from Anchorage (90-minute flight) and other Alaska cities, and from Seattle, WA (2-hour flight). Scheduled commuter service to Haines, Skagway, Sitka, Angoon and other points via various air services.

Charter air service (wheel and floatplanes and helicopters) is available for hunting, fishing, sightseeing and transportation to

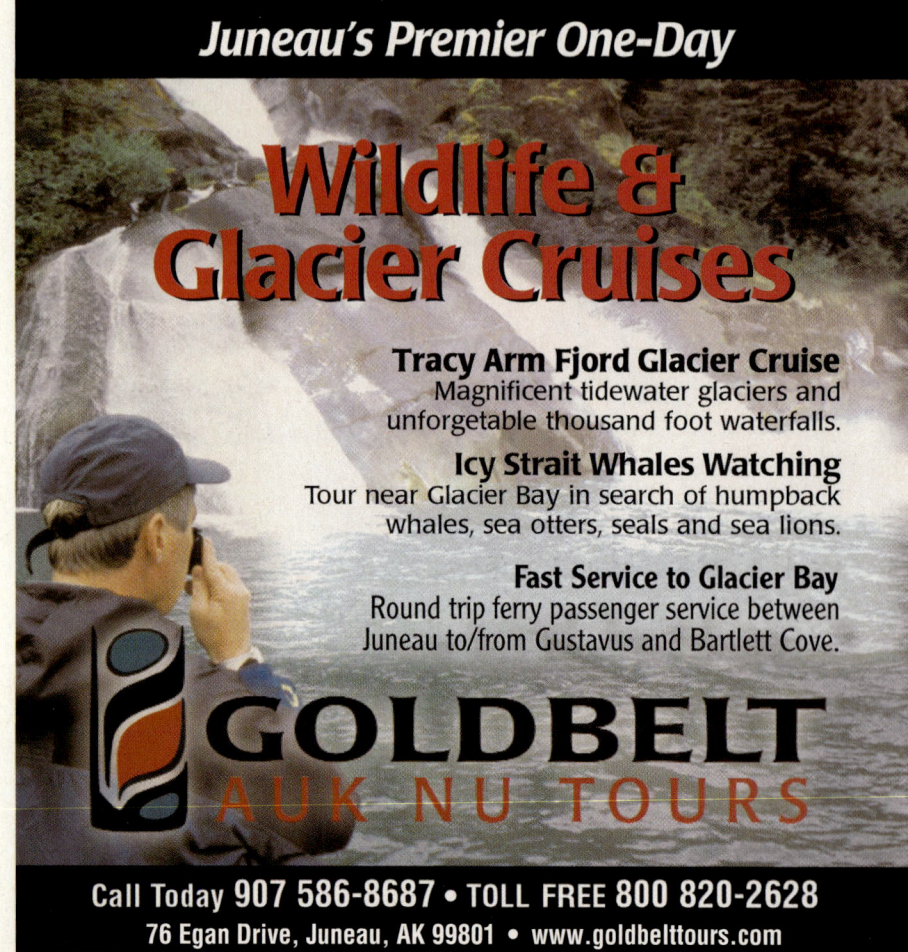

Captain Larry's **Professional Whale Watching**

Exhilarating close encounters

Fantastic photo opportunities

SIGHTINGS GUARANTEED!

PHOTOS BY CAPT. LARRY

Group Rates • Children's Rates

Adventures with Whales Orca Enterprises

495 S. Franklin Street
Be sure to visit our gift shop, across from the tram

TOLL FREE: 1-888-733-ORCA (6722)
(907) 789-6801

e-mail: whales@ptialaska.net
www.alaskawhalewatching.com

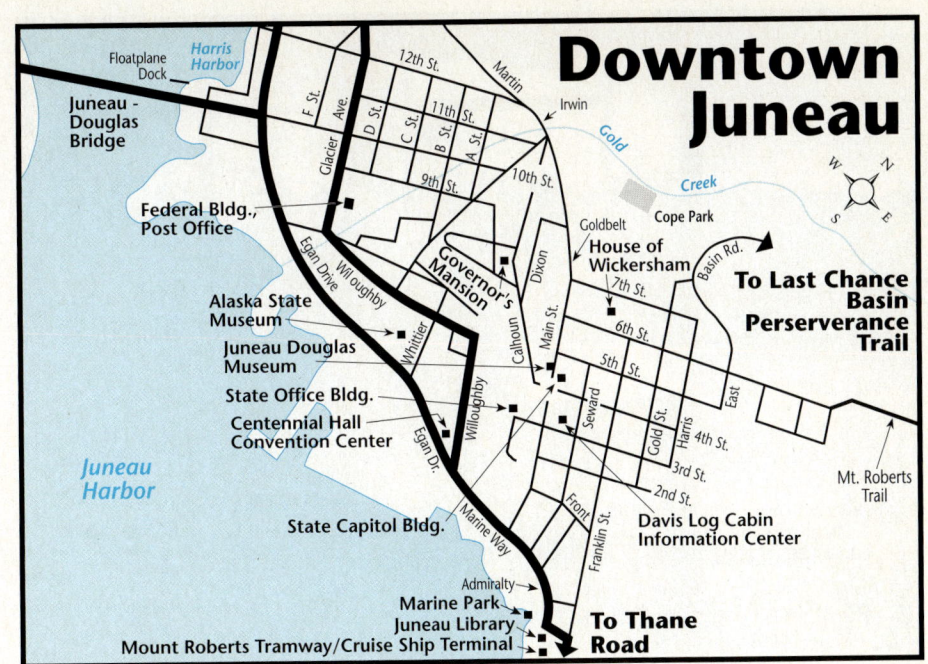

other communities (see ads in this section).

Ferry: Juneau is served by Alaska Marine Highway ferries. See ALASKA STATE FERRY SCHEDULES section. Alaska state ferries dock at the Auke Bay Terminal at **Milepost 13.8** Glacier Highway; phone (907) 789-7453. For recorded ferry schedule, phone (907) 465-3940; or www.alaska.gov/ferry.

Taxi service is available from Auke Bay terminal to downtown Juneau. There is also a bus stop 1.5 miles toward town from the ferry terminal (see following).

Bus: Capital Transit city bus system runs from the cruise ship terminal downtown and includes Juneau, Douglas, Lemon Creek, Mendenhall Valley and airport area, and Auke Bay. Hourly service Monday through Saturday, year-round; limited service on Sundays. Route map and schedule available at the visitor information center. Flag buses at any corner except in downtown Juneau, where bus uses marked stops only.

Highways: Longest road is Glacier Highway, which begins in downtown Juneau and leads 39.5 miles north to Echo Cove; see "Glacier Highway/Juneau Veterans' Memorial Highway" this section. Other major roads are Douglas and North Douglas highways; see "Douglas Island" this section.

Taxi: Available.

Cruise Ships: Juneau is southeastern Alaska's most frequent port of call. There are more than 500 port calls by cruise ships annually.

Car Rental: Car rental agencies are located at the airport and vicinity. Best to reserve ahead of time because of the great demand for cars. Hertz (800) 654-3131; Rent-A-Wreck (907) 780-4111; Evergreen Motors (888) 267-9300.

Boats: Charter boats are available for fishing, sightseeing and transportation. Kayak rentals available. The visitor information center can provide a list of charter operators; also see ads in this section.

Transient moorage is available downtown at Harris and Douglas floats and at Auke Bay. Most boaters use Auke Bay. For more information, call the Juneau harbormaster at (907) 586-5255.

Bikes. Bike rentals available downtown.

Designated bike routes to Douglas, Mendenhall Glacier and Auke Bay. The Mendenhall Glacier route starts at the intersection of 12th Street and Glacier Avenue; total biking distance is 15 miles. Bike-route map and information available at the Centennial Hall Visitor Center.

Attractions

Juneau walking tour. It is easy to explore downtown Juneau on foot, and preferable if you are driving. The streets are narrow and congested with pedestrians and traffic. On-street parking is scarce and limited to 15 minutes or 1 hour, with meters carefully monitored. Public parking is located at the corner of Main Street and Egan Drive and on Marine Way at the Juneau Library.

Walking tour maps of Juneau are available at the Centennial Hall Visitor Center at 101 Egan Drive, the Marine Park kiosk, and the cruise ship terminal. Free historical walking tour maps of Juneau are available at the Juneau–Douglas City Museum.

Downtown landmarks to look for include the Ed Way bronze sculpture, "**Hard Rock Miner,**" located at **Marine Park.** Marine Park is located at foot of Seward Street, and has tables, benches, an information kiosk and a small public dock. Free concerts on Friday evenings in summer.

Another bronze sculpture commemorates "**Patsy Ann,**" a bull terrier that during the 1930s and 40s would meet arriving vessels at Juneau's dock.

Located at the cruise ship dock on the waterfront is the **USS** *Juneau* Memorial, commemorating the sinking of the U.S.S. *Juneau* during WWII. Inscription on the plaque reads:

"Lest We Forget: The naval Battle of Guadalcanal was as ferocious and decisive as any battle of World War II. It was not won cheaply. The night action of Friday the 13th, November 1942 was the last day of life for 8 ships and hundreds of sailors, including the U.S.S. *Juneau* CL52. *Juneau* was in the thick of the battle until an enemy torpedo knocked her out of action. Retiring from the battle, an enemy submarine took *Juneau* in her sights and at 11:01 another torpedo found its mark. This cruiser disintegrated instantaneously and completely. All but 10 of her crew of 700 perished, including the 5 Sullivan brothers."

Observation platform on Mount Roberts is a brief tram ride from Juneau's waterfront. (© Kris Graef, staff)

Mount Roberts Tramway. One of Juneau's top attractions, the Mount Roberts Tramway brings spectacular views within easy reach of visitors. Two 60-passenger aerial trams transport visitors from Juneau's downtown waterfront to a modern mountain complex at the 1,800-foot level of Mount Roberts. Observation platform with panoramic view of the city, harbor and surrounding mountains. The mountaintop complex includes a theater, restaurant, bar, gift shop, and access to alpine walking trails. The tram ticket and a hand stamp allow you to ride the tram all day long if you wish. The tram operates daily, 9 A.M. to 9 P.M., from May through September.

Mount Roberts Trail. There is access from the mountaintop complex to trails on Mount Robert. Or hikers can start from the Mount Roberts trailhead at the top of Starr Hill (6th Street) and hike all the way to the 3,819-foot summit. For a less strenuous hike, there is an excellent observation point above Juneau reached by a 20-minute hike from the trailhead.

Mount Roberts hikers may purchase down-only tram tickets in the shop or bar at the Mount Roberts Tramway mountaintop complex at the 1,800 foot level. Or spend $5 or more in the restaurant or gift shop and use their receipt as a ticket.

Juneau Library. Built on top of the 4-story public parking garage in downtown Juneau, this award-winning library designed by Minch Ritter Voelckers Architects is well worth a visit. Take the elevator to the 5th floor and spend a morning or afternoon reading in this well-lit and comfortable space with a wonderful view of Juneau, Douglas and Gastineau Channel. The library also has a stained glass window representing the transfiguration of a salmon into Tlingit figures. The library is located at South Franklin and Admiralty Way, between Marine Park and the cruise ship terminal.

Juneau–Douglas City Museum, located in the Veterans Memorial Building across from the State Capitol Building at Fourth and Main streets, exhibits early gold-mining, Tlingit culture and life in the Juneau-Douglas area. Special exhibits on the greater Juneau area change yearly. A relief map of Juneau's topography and video, *Juneau: City Built on Gold*, are other attractions. Museum gift shop features gifts, books and hiking trail guides. Summer hours are 9 A.M. to 5 P.M. weekdays, 10 A.M. to 5 P.M. weekends. Admission $3, 18 and under free. Winter hours are noon to 4 P.M. Friday and Saturday or by appointment. Phone (907) 586-3572; web site www.juneau.lib.ak.us/parksrec/museum/museum.htm.

State Capitol Building, at 4th and Main streets, contains the legislative chambers and the governor's office. Free tours available from capitol lobby, most days in summer on the half-hour from 9 A.M. to 5 P.M. The **State Office Building**, one block west, houses the State Historical Library and Kimball theater organ.

Alaska State Museum is a major highlight of Juneau located downtown at 395 Whittier St. Exhibits include dioramas and contain materials from Alaska's Native groups, icons and other artifacts from Russian–America days, and a popular life-size eagle nesting tree surrounded by a mural of a Southeast Alaska scene. A replica of Capt. George Vancouver's ship, *Discovery*, is located in the children's room for kids to explore.

The museum store carries Alaska Native crafts and Alaska books and gifts for all ages. Summer hours are 8:30 A.M. to 5:30 P.M. daily mid-May to mid-Sept. Winter hours are 10 A.M. to 4 P.M. Tuesday through Saturday. Closed holidays. General admission is $5 in summer, $3 in winter. Visitors 18 and under and members of the Friends of the Alaska State Museum are admitted free. A $15 museum pass is also available. Phone (907) 465-2901; www.museums.state.ak.us.

St. Nicholas Orthodox Church, 5th and Gold streets, a tiny structure built in 1894, is now the oldest original Russian Orthodox church in southeastern Alaska. Visitors are welcome to Sunday services; open daily for summer tours. Phone (907) 586-1023.

Wickersham State Historic Site. A steep climb up to Seventh Street takes visitors to the historic home of Alaska's Judge James Wickersham. Wickersham was the first judge of the Third Judicial District of Alaska, arriving in Eagle, AK, from Tacoma, WA, in 1900. Wickersham House contains the judge's collection of Native artifacts and baskets, as well as many photographs and historical documents concerning Native culture, gathered during his extensive travels throughout his 300,000-square-mile district. Phone (907) 586-9001 for information and hours; www.dnr.state.ak.us.

The Alaskan Brewing Company. Be sure to enjoy our international award-winning beers on your travels throughout Alaska. In Juneau, visit Alaska's oldest and largest operating brewery for a fascinating tour. Learn about modern and turn-of-the-century brewing techniques. Sample our gold-rush recipe Alaskan Amber and other award-winning brews. Tours every half hour. Gift shop and hospitality bar. Guests 21 and over are welcome. Located in Lemon Creek area at 5429 Shaune Drive. Phone (907) 780-5866; Internet: www.alaskanbeer.com. [ADVERTISEMENT]

The Governor's Mansion at 716 Calhoun Ave. has been home to Alaska's chief executives since it was completed in 1913. The $2^{1}/_{2}$-story structure, containing 12,900 square feet of floor space, took nearly a year to build. Tours may be possible by advance arrangement. Phone (907) 465-3500.

Take a Drive. Glacier Highway/Juneau Veterans' Memorial Highway provides access to a number of attractions, including Mendenhall Glacier (description follows), Auke Village beachside picnicking, Eagle River and Eagle Beach picnic areas, the Shrine of St. Therese and numerous hiking trails. See "Glacier Highway/Juneau Veterans' Memorial Highway" log this section for details.

Thane Road begins just south of downtown Juneau and extends 5.5 miles along Gastineau Channel. Tours into the historic Alaska–Juneau Mine and Gastineau Mill are available daily from May 1 through September; phone (907) 463-3900.

Drive or walk to the end of Basin Road for the Last Chance Mining Museum, located in the Compressor Building of the historic Alaska–Juneau Mine. Tours available daily from mid-May to mid-September; phone (907) 586-5338. Basin Road also offers good views of Mount Juneau waterfall, a scenic but difficult to photograph falls that descends 3,576 feet from Mount Juneau to Gold Creek behind the city. (The waterfall is also visible from Marine Park.)

Douglas Island offers some fine scenery and sights for motorists. See "Douglas Island" feature this section.

Mendenhall Glacier is about 13 miles from downtown Juneau at the end of Mendenhall Glacier Spur Road. Turn right northbound at **Milepost 9.3** Glacier Highway/Egan Drive, and then drive straight for 3.4 miles to the glacier and visitor center. There is a large parking area, and trails lead down to the edge of the lake and glacier viewpoints. Or walk out to Nugget Falls along the shore of Mendenhall Lake. The waterfall—especially spectacular after a rain or recent snow melt—is fed by Nugget Creek. Trailheads for 2 longer trails—East Glacier and Nugget Creek—are a short walk from the visitor center.

The visitor center offers a hands-on exhibit hall, a theater, and an observatory. From May to September, the visitor center is open from 8 A.M. to 6:30 P.M. A Summer Visitor Use Fee of $3 per person is charged (12 and under are free). From October to April, the visitor center is open Thursday and Friday, 10 A.M. to 4 P.M. and weekends from 9 A.M. to 4 P.M. Kids' programs start every Saturday at 11 A.M. year-round; guided hikes are offered twice a day during summer; and a Fireside Lecture Series is offered Friday at 7 P.M. from January to March. Special programs and facility rental available. For more information phone (907) 789-0097.

Macaulay Salmon Hatchery, operated by Douglas Island Pink & Chum, Inc., is located on Channel Drive about 3 miles from downtown. The hatchery offers visitors a chance to see adult salmon, over 100 species of Southeast Alaska sea-life in saltwater aquariums, aquaculture displays and other seasonal activities. Visitor center open in summer; 10 A.M. to 6 P.M. weekdays, 10 A.M. to 5 P.M. weekends. Watch and feed salmon fry May 15 through June 30. Spawning salmon sites and hatchery operations tour July 1–Sept. 15. Tours by appointment rest of year. Educational tours provided; $3 adult; $1 child. Group: 5 adults, $12. Phone (907) 463-4810; www.dipac.net.

Tracy Arm. Located 50 miles southeast of Juneau, Tracy Arm and adjoining Endicott Arm are the major features of the Tracy Arm–Fords Terror Wilderness Area. Both Tracy and Endicott arms are long, deep and narrow fjords that extend more than 30 miles into the heavily glaciated Coast Mountain Range. Active tidewater glaciers at the head of these fjords calve icebergs into the fjords.

Fords Terror, off of Endicott Arm, is an area of sheer rock walls enclosing a narrow entrance into a small fjord. The fjord was named in 1889 for a crew member of a naval vessel who rowed into the narrow canyon at slack tide and was caught in turbulent icy currents for 6 terrifying hours when the tide changed.

Access to this wilderness area is primarily by boat or floatplane from Juneau. Large and small cruise ships and charter boats include Tracy Arm and Endicott Arm in their itineraries. It is also a popular destination for sea kayakers.

Tracy Arm Fjord–*Adventure Bound*, Alaska's greatest combination of mountains, wildlife, icebergs and tidewater glaciers. Tracy Arm could be called "cascade fjord" because of its many waterfalls or "icy fjord" because it is the home of Alaska's largest icebergs. Best viewed from the *Adventure Bound*. Juneau's favorite because the Weber family doesn't overcrowd and they take the time to enjoy it all. For comfort, viewing time, elbow room and personal attention, this is the quality cruise that you are looking for. The *Adventure Bound* office is located in the Marine View Center. It is the 9-story building that stands across from Juneau's Marine Park. Street address: 215 Ferry Way. Mailing address: P.O. Box 23013, Juneau, AK 99802. Reservations: Phone (907) 463-2509,

Observation trail at Mendenhall Glacier offers great views.
(© Kris Graef, staff)

(800) 228-3875; www.adventurebound alaska.com. [ADVERTISEMENT]

Orca Enterprises, Adventures with Whales—Juneau Alaska's professional whale watching and wildlife adventure tours. Exciting, intimate personalized viewing of whales, eagles, sealions, and porpoise. Professional whale watching captains and naturalist on board. Customized, handicap-accessible, "purple" jet boat. Juneau's most recommended whale watching tour. PO Box 35431, Juneau, AK, 99803 Toll free 1-888-733-ORCA (6722), Fax (907) 586-6929 Website: www.alaskawhalewatching.com E-mail whales@ptialaska.net. [ADVERTISEMENT]

Take a Tour. Tours of Juneau and area attractions—by boat, bus, plane and helicopter—can be arranged. These tours range from sightseeing trips out to Mendenhall Glacier to flightseeing trips of Mendenhall Glacier and Juneau Icefield.

Juneau Icefield, immediately to the east of Juneau, is a 1,500-square-mile expanse of glaciated mountains that is the source of all the glaciers in the area, including Mendenhall, Taku, Eagle and Herbert. Best way to experience and photograph it is via charter flightseeing. Flights usually take 30 to 60 minutes. Helicopter tours, which may land on the glacier, last from about 45 minutes to 1½ hours.

Era Helicopters. Visit the massive Juneau Icefield and see 4 unique glaciers in different stages on our fully narrated tours. Land on a glacier to explore with your pilot. Grab the reins and ride across the glacier on our Helicopter Dog Sled Adventure or go glacier hiking with a guide on our Glacier Outback Adventure. Local phone (907) 586-2030 or 1-800-843-1947. 6160 Carl Brady Dr., Anchorage, AK 99502. www.era aviation.com. fltsg@eraaviation.com. [ADVERTISEMENT]

Glacier Bay National Park contains some of the most impressive tidewater glaciers in the world. Juneau is located about 50 miles east of the bay and is the main jumping-off point for many Glacier Bay visitors. There are several local businesses offering 1- and 2-day or longer boat and air packages to the park. The state ferries do not service Glacier Bay. See GLACIER BAY NATIONAL PARK section for more information.

Hiking Trails. There are plenty of hiking trails in the Juneau area, from the easy 3-mile hike to the ruins of the old Perseverance Mine—the most popular hike in the Juneau area—to the demanding 12-mile Treadwell Ditch Trail on Douglas Island. Several trailheads for USFS trails are located along Glacier Highway/Juneau Veterans' Memorial Highway (see log this section). Hiking trail guidebooks can be purchased at the Mendenhall Glacier Visitor Center and at local bookstores. Information is available at the Centennial Hall Visitor Center. The USFS also offers maps and information.

Juneau Parks and Recreation Dept. offers free organized hikes Wednesday and Saturday, April through October; phone (907) 586-5226 for information.

Botanical Garden. Originally a nursery, Glacier Gardens Rainforest Adventure offers guided garden tours featuring motorized cart rides through a mountainside rainforest. Open 9 A.M. to 6 P.M. daily. Phone (907) 790-3377; www.glaciergardens.com.

AREA FISHING: (Several special sportfishing regulations are in effect in the Juneau area; consult current regulations booklet.) Good Dolly Varden fishing available along most saltwater shorelines in Juneau area; king salmon best from mid-May to mid-June, pink salmon available about mid-July through August, silver salmon best August to mid-September. Good fishing by boat from Juneau, Auke Bay or Tee Harbor in **Favorite** and **Saginaw channels**, **Chatham Strait** and near mouth of **Taku Inlet** for salmon, Dolly Varden and halibut. USFS public-use cabins available.

For up-to-date angling data in the Juneau area, phone (907) 465-4116 for recorded Alaska Dept. of Fish and Game message (April through Oct.). For specific angling information or for a copy of the local sportfishing guide, contact the ADF&G, Division of Sport Fish, Area Management Biologist, P.O. Box 240020, Douglas 99824; phone (907) 465-4320; www.state.ak.us/adfg. Fishing licenses are available on line at www.admin.adfg.state.ak.us/license/.

Glacier Highway/Juneau Veterans' Memorial Highway

Glacier Highway is a scenic drive along Favorite Channel. (© Kris Graef, staff)

From the cruiseship terminal on South Franklin Sreet in downtown Juneau, head northwest along the waterfront. South Franklin Street becomes Marine Way, then Egan Drive, named for William A. Egan (1914–84), first governor of the state of Alaska. Egan Drive becomes Glacier Highway at **Milepost 9.4**, then Juneau Veterans' Memorial Highway from **Milepost 12.1** to road end, 40 miles north of Juneau at Echo Cove on Berners Bay. This is a very scenic drive along Favorite Channel.

Distance from downtown Juneau cruiseship terminal is shown.

0 Cruise ship terminal, Mount Roberts Tramway terminal; South Franklin Street.

1.1 Stoplight. Tenth Street exit east. For access to Douglas Highway and North Douglas Highway, turn west across Juneau–Douglas bridge (see "Douglas Island" this section).

1.4 Turnoff for Harris boat harbor.

1.6 Turnoff for Aurora boat harbor.

3.8 Stoplight. Exit east for Bartlett Memorial Hospital and Alaska Native Health Center. Access via Old Glacier Highway to Twin Lakes picnic area to east. DOT/PF headquarters. Macaulay Salmon Hatchery to west.

6 Mendenhall Wetlands State Game Refuge observation platform on west side of divided highway. Great place to see eagles and waterfowl.

6.5 Exit east to Old Glacier Highway and Switzer Creek; gas station and K-Mart.

8 Fred Meyer shopping center. Access to Glacier Gardens Rainforest Adventure.

8.5 Stoplight. Access to McDonald's, Super 8, Nugget shopping mall and other major services via 0.3-mile loop road (Old Glacier Highway) to Juneau International Airport. Also access to Mendenhall Wetlands State Game Refuge dike trail (good bird watching). Old Glacier Highway Loop rejoins Egan Drive at **Milepost 9.3**.

9.3 Stoplight. **South junction** with **Mendenhall Loop Road**. Turn west for airport. Turn east for Mendenhall Mall and post office (just east of junction), and Mendenhall Glacier and visitor center (3.4 miles from junction).

Mendenhall Loop Road is a paved 6-mile loop that rejoins Glacier Highway at **Milepost 12.1**. To reach Mendenhall Glacier from here, drive east 3.4 miles. Mendenhall Glacier visitor center is open daily in summer; see description in Juneau Attractions.

From this junction it is 3.5 miles to Montana Creek Road and access to Mendenhall Lake USFS Campground and 3.8 miles to Spruce Meadow RV Park. ▲

9.5 Stoplight. Riverside Drive; access to Mendenhall Mall.

9.7 Begin 2-lane highway northbound. Begin 4-lane highway southbound.

9.8 Mendenhall River and Brotherhood Bridge. The bridge was named in honor of the Alaska Native Brotherhood; bronze plaques symbolize the Raven and Eagle clans.

10 Mendenhall Glacier viewpoint to east; parking area and trailhead for **Kaxdegoowu Heen Dei/Clear Water Creek Trail** (Mendenhall River Greenbelt). This popular paved trail extends 0.9 mile to Montana Creek, 2.1 miles to River Road parking lot. Wheelchair-accessible.

10.1 Industrial Blvd.; access to Mendenhall Golf Course; 9 holes, par 3; practice range; phone (907) 789-1221.

10.4 Alaska State Troopers and Fish & Wildlife office.

10.6 Engineer's Cutoff to west continues to Fritz Cove Road (2.1 miles). Mendenhall Peninsula Road branches off (south) of Engineer's Cutoff and has 2 trailhead markers to access the Mendenhall wetlands.

11.4 Auke Lake scenic wayside to east. Good view of Mendenhall Glacier reflected in the lake. This is one of the most photographed spots in Alaska. Red, pink and coho salmon spawn in Auke Lake system July to September.

11.5 Fritz Cove Road (paved) leads 2.6 miles west and dead-ends at Smuggler's Cove; excellent small-boat anchorage. Scenic viewpoint on Fritz Cove Road at Mile 1.2; Engineer's Cutoff at Mile 1.9 branches off to Mendenhall Peninsula Road and extends to Glacier Highway.

11.6 Turnoff to east for University of Alaska and **Chapel-by-the-Lake**. The Presbyterian Chapel-by-the-Lake is a log structure perched above Auke Lake. Its front, made entirely of glass, frames the scenic lake, Mendenhall Glacier and mountains. Popular marriage chapel.

11.8 Short road west to Alaska Fisheries Science Center's Auke Bay Laboratory. ABL conducts research programs on fishery management problems for the National Marine Fisheries Service.

12.1 **North junction** with **Mendenhall Loop Road**; gas station, liquor store, deli. Auke Bay small-boat harbor to west.

The 6-mile Mendenhall Loop Road rejoins Glacier Highway at Milepost 9.3. From this junction it is 2.2 miles to Spruce Meadow RV Park; 2.5 miles to Montana Creek Road and access to Mendenhall Lake USFS campground; and 5.4 miles to Mendenhall Glacier visitor center. ▲

Glacier Highway becomes Juneau Veterans' Memorial Highway northbound.

12.4 AUKE BAY; post office. RV park.

12.6 **Spaulding trailhead** to east; 3-mile hike through muskeg meadow (5 to 6 hours round trip). Popular cross-country ski route in winter. Also access to **Auke Nu Trail**, 3-mile hike to John Muir USFS cabin.

12.8 Waydelich Creek and bridge.

13.8 Alaska State Ferry Auke Bay Terminal. Follow signs for parking and loading lanes. Check-in at ticket counter. Restrooms and visitor information inside terminal.

NOTE: If you are arriving in Juneau by ferry, you will turn right on to the highway upon leaving the ferry terminal for Mendenhall Glacier or downtown Juneau (read this road log backwards from here.) You will turn left on the highway if you are headed for Auke Village recreation area or other destinations northwest of here along Juneau Veterans' Memorial Highway (continue with this road log).

14.7 Exit west for 2-mile loop road through **Auke Village Recreation Area**. Located along this side road are trails to beachside picnic shelters and Auke Village USFS campground, with 13 campsites, tables, firepits, water, flush and pit toilets; camping fee. ▲

16.3 South end of Point Lena Loop Road and access to north end of Auke Village Loop Road (0.1 mile west).

16.8 North end of Point Lena Loop Road.

17 Lena Beach picnic area.

18 Tee Harbor–Point Stevens turnoff. Paved road leads 0.3 mile west to public parking area and a private marina.

19.9 Inspiration Point. Turnouts to west

Auke Bay ferry terminal is at Milepost 13.8 Glacier Highway. (© Ren Valencia)

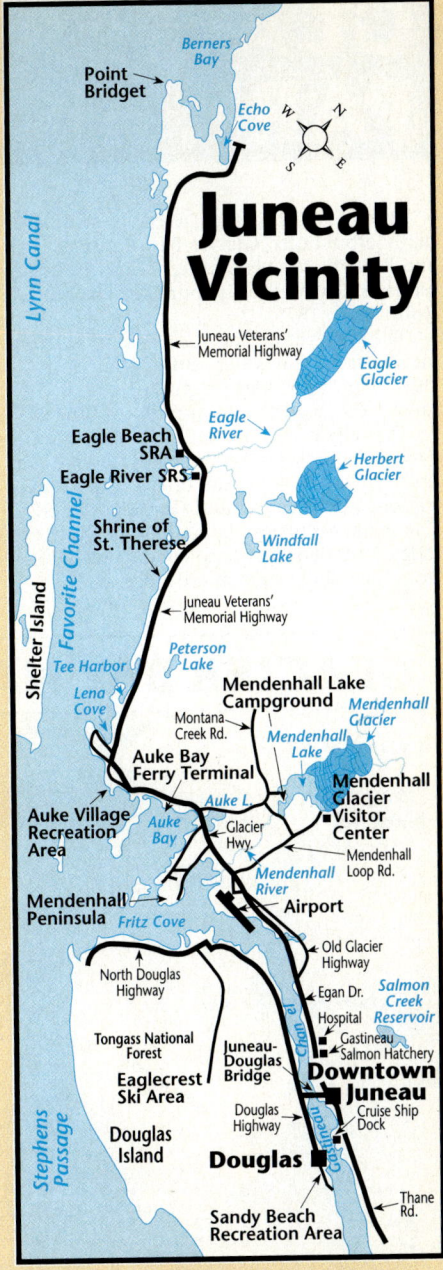

with view of the Chilkat Range, Tee Harbor and Shelter Island across Favorite Channel. Once a bread-and-butter commercial fishing area, hence the name "The Breadline" for this stretch of shoreline, it is now a popular sportfishing area.

22.5 Turnoff for **Shrine of St. Therese**, a complex that includes gardens, a labyrinth, lodge, cabins and the famous stone chapel. Park at first or "upper" lot and follow signs downhill to the complex. (There is handicap parking and passenger off-loading at the bottom of the hill for anyone with physical challenges.) Or park at lower lot overlooking channel and follow signed gravel path to the complex. Please keep pets on leash.

The Shrine of St. Therese, built in honor of St. Therese of Lisieux ("The Little Flower"), Patron Saint of Alaska, began with construction of a retreat house in 1933. It was to be followed by construction of a log chapel on Crow Island (later renamed Shrine Island), a tiny island located about 400 feet from the mainland shore. A causeway was built out to the island. The chapel—located in a quiet glade—was built in 1938 using natural stone.

The lodge and cabins can be rented by "groups or persons who respect the spirit of the shrine." Phone (907) 780-6112 for more information. The complex is open 8:30 A.M. to 10 P.M., April to September.

22.8 Turnout to west with view of channel. The island on which the Shrine of St. Therese is situated is in front of you.

23.5 Peterson Lake trailhead to east; 4-mile hike through muskeg (planked) and forest to Peterson Lake cabin. Estimated round-trip 5 to 7 hours.

23.8 Peterson Creek bridge. View spawning salmon here in late summer and early fall. Trout fishing. Bears in area.

26.6 Windfall Lake trailhead to east; 3.5-mile hike to lake, rated easy (4 hours round trip).

26.8 Herbert River bridge.

26.9 Herbert Glacier trailhead parking to east; 4.6-mile hike to views of glacier. Rated easy; allow 5 to 6 hours round trip.

27.2 Eagle River bridge.

27.3 Amalga (Eagle Glacier) trailhead parking to east at north end of bridge. Hike in 4 miles to old Amalga mine site and another 3.5 miles to Eagle Glacier. Rated difficult; round-trip 10 to 12 hours; rubber boots recommended.

27.6 Eagle River State Recreation Area (day-use only); wayside and trailhead parking; restrooms; picnic shelters; handicap accessible. Open all year; cross-country skiing in winter.

28 Watch for rough dirt roads to west providing access to **Eagle Beach State Recreation Area**; beachside picnic shelter, picnic tables, informal camping. View of Chilkat Range across Lynn Canal. Good bird watching, parasailing.

28.3 Scenic viewpoint to west.

28.8 Scenic viewpoint to west.

32.2 Turnout to west with view of Benjamin Island to southwest; just beyond it is Sentinel Island lighthouse. Visible to the northwest is North Island and northwest of it is **Vanderbilt Reef**, site of a great sea disaster. The SS *Princess Sophia*, carrying 288 passengers and 61 crew, ran aground on Vanderbilt Reef early in the morning of Oct. 24, 1918. All aboard perished when a combination of stormy seas and a high tide forced the *Princess Sophia* off the reef and she sank early in the evening of Oct. 25. Walter Harper, in 1913 the first person to stand on the summit of Mount McKinley, was among the *Princess Sophia*'s casualties. Vanderbilt Reef is now marked by a navigation light.

32.3 Turnout to east.

33.9 Scenic viewpoint to west.

34.7 Scenic viewpoints to west next 0.3 mile northbound.

35.1 Sunshine Cove public beach access; parking, toilets.

38 Point Bridget trailhead to west; 3.5-mile hike to Point Bridget (7 hours round-trip); panoramic view of Lynn Canal and Chilkat Mountains from point. The 2,850-acre **Point Bridget State Park** offers meadows, forests, rocky beaches, salmon streams and a trail system. Popular area for cross-country skiing in winter. Fires allowed on beach with fire ring.

38.8 Cowee Creek bridge. Large parking area to west at north end of bridge.

39.5 Road ends. Take left fork 0.3 mile for Echo Cove city boat launch on Berners Bay; outhouse, parking.

Berners Bay is a popular destination for Juneau paddlers. It is 3 miles across and 34 miles northwest of Juneau by water.

GLACIER BAY NATIONAL PARK AND PRESERVE

One of southeastern Alaska's most dramatic attractions, Glacier Bay National Park and Preserve has been called "a picture of icy wildness unspeakably pure and sublime" (John Muir, 1879).

The park's stunning scenery is most often viewed from the water, either from a cruise ship or by tour boat or charter out of Gustavus—the nearest community—or Juneau.

The only land route to Glacier Bay National Park is a 10-mile road connecting Gustavus airport to Bartlett Cove, site of the park's ranger station, visitor center and Glacier Bay Lodge. The park excursion boat departs from the lodge. Park naturalists also conduct daily hikes from the visitor center at the lodge.

Glacier Bay National Park, at the northwest end of Alexander Archipelago, includes not only tidewater glaciers but also Mount Fairweather in the Fairweather Range of the St. Elias Mountains, the highest peak in southeastern Alaska, and also the U.S. portion of the Alsek River.

With passage of the Alaska National Interest Lands Conservation Act in December 1980, Glacier Bay National Monument, established in 1925 by Pres. Calvin Coolidge, became a national park. Approximately 585,000 acres were added to the park/preserve to protect fish and wildlife habitat and migration routes in Dry Bay and along the lower Alsek River, and to include the northwest slope of Mount Fairweather. Total acreage is 3,328,000 (3,271,000 in park, 57,000 in preserve) with 2,770,000 acres designated wilderness.

When the English naval explorer Capt. George Vancouver sailed through the ice-choked waters of Icy Strait in 1794, Glacier Bay was little more than a dent in the coastline. Across the head of this seemingly minor inlet stood a towering wall of ice marking the seaward terminus of an immense glacier that completely filled the broad, deep basin of what is now Glacier Bay. To the north, ice extended more than 100 miles into the St. Elias Mountains, covering the intervening valleys with a 4,000-

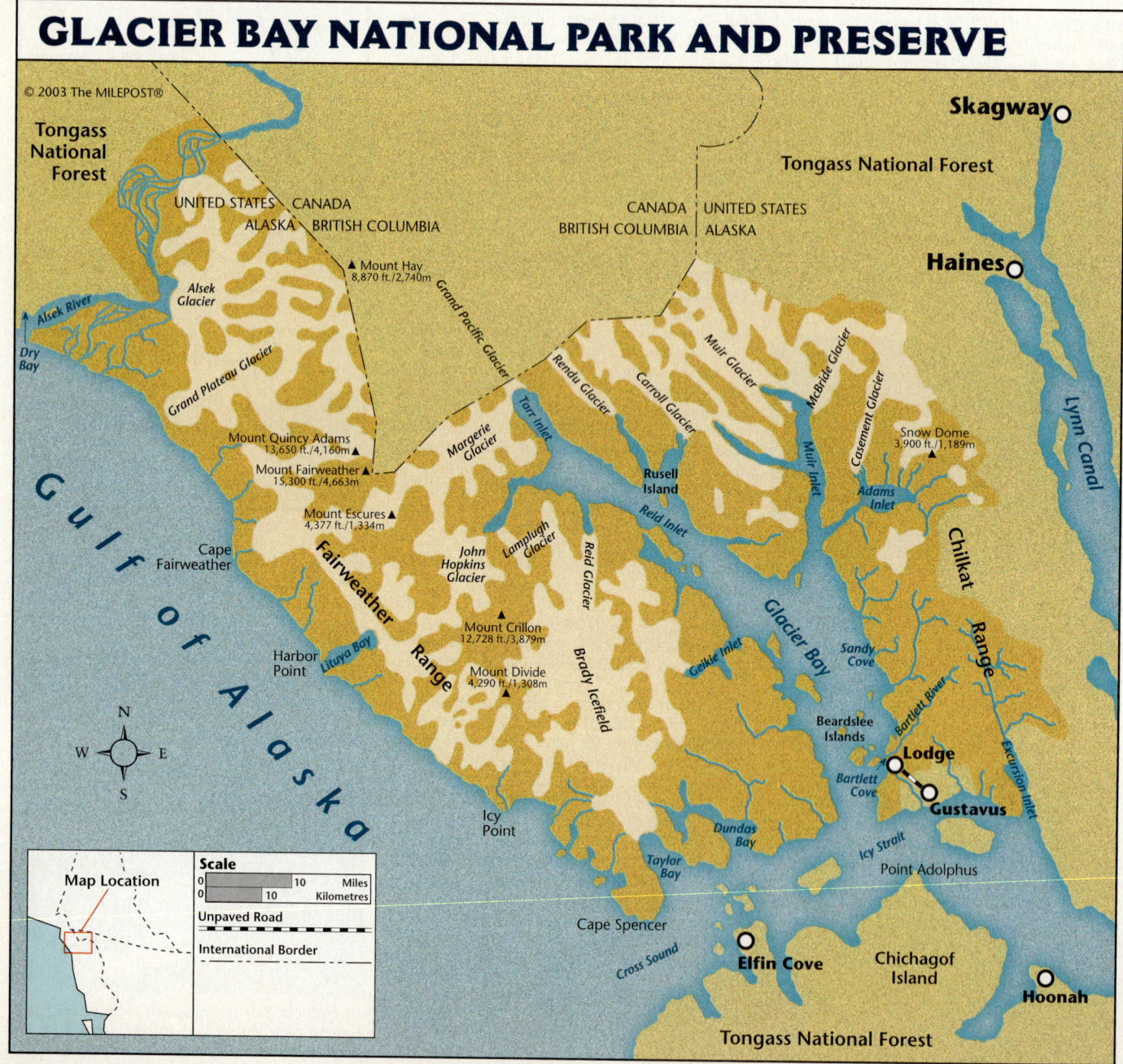

foot-deep mantle of ice.

During the century following Vancouver's explorations, the glacier retreated some 40 miles back into the bay, permitting a spruce–hemlock forest to gradually fill the land. By 1916, the Grand Pacific Glacier, which once occupied the entire bay, had receded some 65 miles from the position observed by Vancouver in 1794. Nowhere else in the world have glaciers been observed to recede at such a rapid pace.

Today, few of the many tributary glaciers that once supplied the huge ice sheet extend to the sea. Glacier Bay National Park encloses 12 active tidewater glaciers, including several on the remote and seldom-visited western edge of the park along the Gulf of Alaska and Lituya Bay. Icebergs, cracked off from near-vertical ice cliffs, dot the waters of Glacier Bay.

A decline in the number of humpback whales using Glacier Bay for feeding and calf-rearing led the National Park Service to limit the number of boats visiting Glacier Bay from June to August. These regulations affect all motorized vessels. Check with the National Park Service for current regulations.

Glacier Bay National Park is approximately 100 miles from Juneau by boat. Park rangers at Bartlett Cove are available to assist in advising visitors who wish to tour Glacier Bay in private boats or by kayak. Guided kayak trips are available through park concessionaire, Alaska Discovery. Permits are required for motorized pleasure boats between June 1 and Aug. 31. The permits are free. A limited number are available. Permits must be obtained prior to entry into Glacier Bay and Bartlett Cove. Request permits no more than 2 months in advance by writing the National Park Service, Box 140, Gustavus, AK 99826-0140. For more information, phone (907) 697-2627 (May 1–Sept. 7).

Glacier Bay Lodge is the only accommodation within the national park, although nearby Gustavus (see sidebar) has a number of lodges, inns, bed and breakfasts and rental cabins. Contact Glacier Cruiseline, (800) 451-5952 or (907) 687-2226, for more information on the concessionaire-operated Glacier Bay Lodge and excursion boat cruises offered from the lodge.

Gasoline and diesel fuel may be purchased at Bartlett Cove, where a good anchorage is available. There are no other public facilities for boats within park boundaries; Sandy Cove, about 20 miles from Bartlett Cove, is a popular anchorage. Gustavus has a dock and small-boat harbor.

CAUTION BOATERS: *No attempt should be made to navigate Glacier Bay without appropriate charts, tide tables and local knowledge. Floating ice is a special hazard. Because of the danger from waves caused by falling ice, small craft should not approach closer than 0.25 mile from tidewater glacier fronts.*

Wildlife in the national park area is protected and hunting is not allowed. Firearms are illegal.

CAUTION: *Brown and black bears are present.*

Fishing for silver and pink salmon, Dolly Varden and halibut is excellent. A valid Alaska fishing license is required. Charter fishing trips are available.

There is an established campground at Bartlett Cove with 25 sites. Wilderness camping is also available throughout the park. ▲

For more information on park facilities, contact Glacier Bay National Park and Preserve, Gustavus, AK 99826-0140; website www.nps.gov/glba. The Bartlett Cove visitor center is open mid-May to mid-September; phone (907) 697-2230.

Gustavus

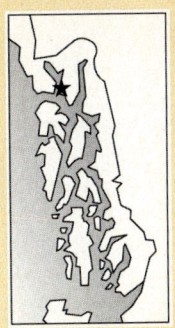

Gateway to Glacier Bay National Park and Preserve, the small community of Gustavus is located just outside the park boundary at the mouth of the Salmon River on the north shore of Icy Strait, 48 miles northwest of Juneau. It is 10 miles by road from Gustavus to Bartlett Cove within the park. **Population:** 429. **Emergency Services:** Phone 911. **Visitor Information:** Gustavus Visitors Assoc., Box 167, Gustavus 99826. Or visit www.gustavus.com.

Private Aircraft: Gustavus airport, adjacent northeast; elev. 36 feet; length 6,700 feet; asphalt. Landing within the park is restricted to salt water. All wilderness/non-motorized waters are closed to aircraft landing between May 1–Sept. 15.

Surrounded on 3 sides by Glacier Bay National Park, the Fairweather Mountains are about 60 miles from Gustavus. Gustavus offers miles of level land with expansive sandy beaches, open land and forest. Homesteaded in 1914 as a small agricultural community, the area was once named Strawberry Point because of its abundant wild strawberries. Today, most residents maintain gardens and make their living by fishing (commercial and subsistence), fish processing, tourism, arts and crafts, and working for the National Park Service and in various local trades. Charter fishing is very important to the industry.

Besides its proximity to the national park, Gustavus offers a number of attractions. Local charter boats—sometimes called "6 packs" because they carry about 6 passengers—are available for sportfishing (salmon, halibut), sightseeing Icy Strait and Glacier Bay, and whale watching. Whale sightings are almost guaranteed at Point Adolphus, where their food source is rich. A paved road in town is great for bike riding.

There are extensive beaches in Gustavus which are ideal for beachwalking. Flat land walking is possible in the fern wetland environment, which also offers good bird watching. Be sure to bring rubber boots.

Lodging & Services

Accommodations in Gustavus include several inns, lodges, bed and breakfasts, and self-sufficient cabins. There are 2 restaurants. The lodges and inns serve meals for guests; drop-in customers check for space-available meal reservations.

Businesses in Gustavus include a grocery store, 3 art galleries, cafe, gift shops, golf course, hardware/ building supply store, gas station, and fish-processing facilities. Fishing supplies and licenses may be purchased locally.

Mt. Fairweather Golf Course is a 9-hole, par 36, 3,000-yard facility in an amphitheater of mountains and inland waterways. Club and handcart rentals available. Box 51, Gustavus, AK 99826. (907) 697-3080; www.gustavus.com/golf.html.

Annie Mae Lodge. Old-fashioned good food and good company. Three meals using home-baked bread and pastries, fresh caught seafood, berries off the bush, and garden vegetables. We offer beautiful comfortable rooms, peace, quiet, abundant wildlife, wilderness, sportfishing, kayak trips, whale watching. Glacier Bay boat/plane tours. Box 55, Gustavus, AK 99826. Phone (800) 478-2346 or (907) 697-2346, fax (907) 697-2211. E-mail: anniemae@cheerful.com. www.anniemae.com. [ADVERTISEMENT]

Alaska's TRI Bed and Breakfast of Glacier Bay. Experience restful rainforest wilderness in a modern cottage with insuite bath. Centrally located from Glacier Bay National Park and restaurants/store. Full breakfast available. Whale watch, airflights, kayaking arranged. P.O. Box 214, Gustavus, AK 99826. (907) 697-2425, fax (907) 697-2450. Email: trigbay@pluto.he.net. Web site: www.glacierbaylodging.com. [ADVERTISEMENT]

Transportation

Ferry: Gustavus Ferry offers catamaran service between Auke Bay/Juneau and Gustavus from mid-May to early July; phone (800) 478-3610. *There is no state ferry service to Glacier Bay.* Closest port of call for state ferries is Hoonah. (Kayakers getting off at Hoonah can expect a 2-day paddle across Icy Strait.)

Air: Gustavus/Glacier Bay may be reached by Alaska Airlines daily jet flights from Juneau; summer service begins early June. Air taxi and charter service available from Juneau, Sitka, Haines and Skagway to Gustavus airport; there are many scheduled air taxi flights daily. Bus service between the airport and Bartlett Cove is available for arriving jet flights. Taxi service to local facilities and courtesy van service for some lodges are also available.

Many Gustavus bed and breakfasts will make transportation arrangements for guests from Juneau, Haines and Skagway.

Rental Cars: There is one car rental company in Gustavus.

Boat Service: Excursion boats operated by the park concession depart from Bartlett Cove. Charter boats are available in Gustavus for sightseeing or fishing. Overnight cruise tours are available from Juneau.

A Family Enterprise
The Annie Mae Lodge
Old fashioned comfort and hospitality
❄ *Relax with us, enjoy our lodge and gourmet meals. Experience the wilderness in the last frontier– Alaska.*
www.anniemae.com
anniemae@cheerful.com
P.O. Box 55, Gustavus, Alaska 99826
Telephone (907) 697-2346
1-800-478-2346 • Fax (907) 697-2211
Glacier Bay, Alaska

HAINES

Population: 2,800

The Chilkat Mountains provide a picturesque backdrop for Haines. (© Julie Collins)

Haines Special Events:

June 21— Kluane to Chilkat International Bike Relay. Starts in Haines Junction, YT, and finishes 150 miles later in Haines, AK. Summer Solstice Celebration takes place on the Saturday closest to the June 21 summer solstice and features bands, dances, games, a beer garden and special activities.

July—Fort Seward Day. Haines marks the 100th anniversary of the fort with games, activities and celebrations.

August 13–17—Southeast Alaska State Fair and Bald Eagle Music Festival.

November 12–16—Alaska Bald Eagle Festival.

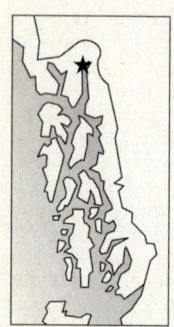

Located on Portage Cove, Chilkoot Inlet, on the upper arm of Lynn Canal, 80 air miles northwest of Juneau; 151 road miles southeast of Haines Junction, YT. Southern terminus of the Haines Highway. *NOTE: Haines is only 15 miles by water from Skagway, but it is 359 miles by road!* **Population:** 2,800. **Emergency Services:** Alaska State Troopers, phone (907) 766-2552. **City Police**, phone (907) 766-2121. **Fire Department and Ambulance**, emergency only phone 911; business phone: (907) 766-2115.. **Doctor**, phone (907) 766-2521. **Maritime Search and Rescue**, contact the Coast Guard at 1-800-478-5555.

Visitor Information Center: At 2nd Avenue South. There are free brochures for all of Alaska and the Yukon. Open daily, 8 A.M. to 8 P.M., June through August; 8 A.M. to 5 P.M. weekdays, September through May. Phone (907) 766-2234; toll free 1-800-458-3579; Internet: www.haines.ak.us; email hcvb@haines.ak.us. Write the Haines Convention and Visitors Bureau at Box 530, Haines, AK 99827. Phone the Alaska Dept. of Transportation at (907) 766-2340.

Elevation: Sea level. **Climate:** Average daily maximum temperature in July, 66°F; average daily minimum in January, 16°F. Extreme high summer temperature, 98°F; extreme winter low, -18°F; average annual precipitation, 59 inches. **Radio:** KHNS-FM 102.3. **Television:** 24 cable channels. **Newspaper:** *Chilkat Valley News* (weekly), *Eagle Eye* (weekly).

Private Aircraft: Haines airport, 4 miles west; elev. 16 feet; length 3,000 feet; asphalt; fuel 100; unattended.

History and Economy: The original Indian name for Haines was *Dei Shu,* meaning "end of the trail." It was an area near where Chilkat and Chilkoot Indians met and traded with Russian and American ships at the end of the peninsula It was also their portage route for transporting canoes from the Chilkat River to Portage Cove and Lynn Canal.

In 1879 missionary S. Hall Young and naturalist John Muir came to the village of Yen Dustucky (near today's airport) to determine the location of a Presbyterian mission and school. The site chosen, Dei Shu, was on the narrow portage between the Chilkat River and Lynn Canal. The following year, George Dickinson established a trading post for the Northwest Trading Company, next to the mission site. His wife Sarah began a school for Tlingit children. By 1881, Eugene and Caroline Willard arrived to establish Chilkat Mission. Later, the mission and eventually the town were named for Francina E. Haines, secretary of the Presbyterian Women's Executive Society of Home Missions, who raised funds for the new mission.

In 1882 the Haines post office was established. The Dalton Trail, which crossed the Chilkat mountain pass to the Klondike goldfields in the Yukon, started at Pyramid Harbor Cannery across the Chilkat River from Haines. The town became an important outlet for the Porcupine Mining District, producing thousands of dollars' worth of placer gold at the turn of the century.

Just to the south of Haines city center is Fort Seward on Portage Cove. Named Fort William H. Seward, in honor of the secretary of state who negotiated the purchase of Alaska from Russia in 1867, this was established as the first permanent Army post in the territory. The first troops arrived in 1904 from Camp Skagway. In 1922, the fort was renamed Chilkoot Barracks, after the mountain pass and the Indian tribe on the Chilkoot River. (There are 2 tribes in this area: the Chilkat and the Chilkoot.)

Until WWII this was the only permanent U.S. Army post in Alaska. Chilkoot Barracks was deactivated in 1946 and sold in 1947 to a group of enterprising U.S. veterans who had designs of creating a business cooperative on the site. Their original plans were never fully realized, but a few stayed on, creating the city of Port Chilkoot and converting some of the houses on Officers' Row into permanent homes.

In 1970, Port Chilkoot merged with Haines to become a single municipality, the City of Haines. Two years later, the post was designated a national historic site and became officially known, again, as Fort William H. Seward (although many people still call it Port Chilkoot).

Fishing and gold mining were the initial industries of the Haines area. Haines is also remembered for its famous strawberries, developed by Charles Anway about 1900. His Alaskan hybrid, *Burbank,* was a prize winner at the 1909 Alaska–Yukon–Pacific Exposition in Seattle, WA. A strawberry festival was held annually in Haines for many years, and this local event grew into the Southeast Alaska State Fair, which each summer draws thousands of visitors. Today, halibut and gill-net salmon fishing and tourism are the basis of the economy. Haines is an important port on the Alaska Marine Highway System as the southern terminus of the Haines Highway, 1 of the 2 year-round roads linking southeastern Alaska with the Interior.

Lodging & Services

Haines offers travelers accommodations at one hotel and 7 motels. There are also 10 bed and breakfasts and 2 apartment/condo rentals. See ads this section.

There is a youth hostel (families welcome) with cabin accommodations on Small Tracts Road.

Haines has all traveler facilities, including hardware and grocery stores, gift shops and art galleries, automotive repair, laundry, post office and bank. Gift shops and galleries feature the work of local artisans. There are several restaurants, cafes and taverns. First National Bank of Anchorage, Howser's Supermarket and Haines Quick Shop. FNBA and Howser's are both located on Main Street and have ATMs.

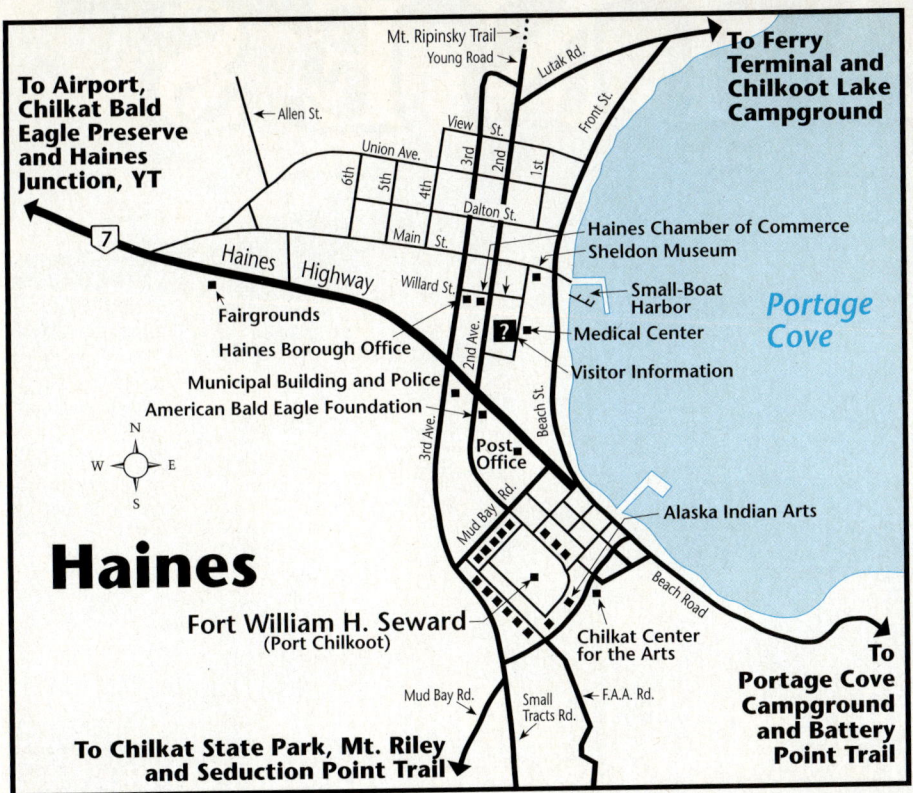

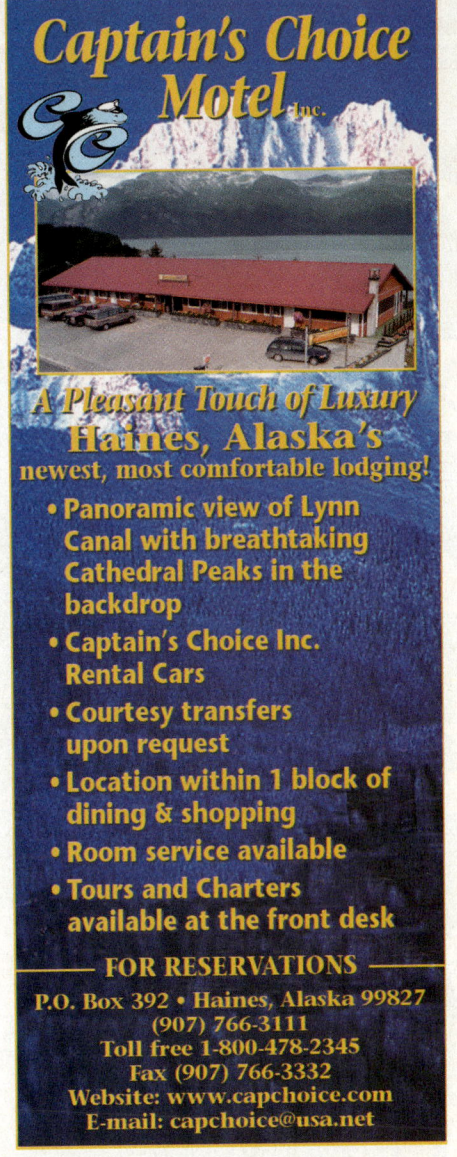

Camping

There are several private RV parks in Haines; see ads this section. There are 4 state campgrounds in the Haines area. Portage Cove State Recreation Site, located on the waterfront, offers 9 tent sites for walk-in and bicyclist camping only. Chilkat State Park, located 8 miles from downtown Haines via Mud Bay Road, has 32 tent/RV sites. Chilkoot Lake State Recreation Site, located 10 miles from downtown Haines via Lutak Road, has 32 sites. And Mosquito Lake State Recreation Site, 2 miles north of Haines on the Haines Highway, has 5 sites. ▲

Salmon Run Campground & Cabins. "Enjoy camping in Haines at the most beautiful natural campground in all of Alaska" (Dorothy Hook, *Water Colors of Alaska* Artist). Unique forested campground overlooking lovely Lutak Inlet with superb mountain and water vista. Watch for whales, porpoises, sea lions and eagles. Fish in ocean waters for salmon or book a charter. Sleep soundly in private sites near a bubbling stream. Sparkling clean restrooms and showers. Located on Lutak Road, 1.8 miles north of ferry terminal. P.O. Box 1582, Haines, AK 99827; (907) 766-3240. Email: salmonrun@wytbear.com. www.salmonrunadventures.com. [ADVERTISEMENT] ▲

Haines Hitch-Up RV Park offers easy access to 92 full hookups (50 amps available), spacious, grassy, level sites. 20 pull-throughs. Cable TV sites available. Immaculate restrooms and laundromat for registered guests only. Gift shop. Tour tickets and information. Located at the junction of Haines Highway and Main Street. See map in display ad this section. P.O. Box 383, Haines, AK 99827. Phone (907) 766-2882. www.hitchuprv.com HitchupRV@aol.com. See display ad this section. [ADVERTISEMENT] ▲

THE SUMMER INN
BED & BREAKFAST
— OPEN YEAR ROUND —
Full Breakfast • Convenient Location
*Excellent View of Lynn Canal * Built in 1912*
Recommended by Alaska Best Places Guide Book!
P.O. Box 1198, Haines, Alaska 99827
Tel/Fax: (907) 766-2970
email: summerinnb&b@wytbear.com
website: www.summerinn.wytbear.com

117 Second Avenue

Thunderbird Motel
Downtown ~ Haines, Alaska
2nd & Dalton St. (907) 766-2131
P.O. Box 589 Fax 766-2045
Haines, AK 99827 1-800-327-2556
14 Rooms & 6 Kitchenette Apartments
Cable TV - Phones - Private Baths
Fishing Charter - Tour Arrangements
All Major Credit Cards Accepted
Website: www.Thunderbird-Motel.com
Email: MBR@Thunderbird-Motel.com
"Come join the Warmth & Hospitality"

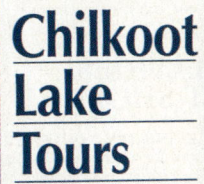

Chilkoot Lake Tours
• Fishing
• Sightseeing
• Photography trips

Eagle's Nest Motel

• Beautiful rooms • All non-smoking rooms • Queen beds
• Private bath • Phones • cable • Car rentals
• Complimentary Continental Breakfast

800-354-6009 (US) • (907) 766-2891 • Fax 766-2848 • Box 250, Haines, AK 99827
email: eaglesnestmotel@wytbear.com • website: www.alaskaeagletours.com

HAINES

THE ALASKA OF YOUR DREAMS
DRAMATIC MOUNTAIN SCENERY • HEART OF THE TLINGIT CULTURE
HISTORIC FORT WILLIAM H. SEWARD • VALLEY OF THE EAGLES

Sponsored by: Haines Chamber of Commerce 907-766-2202
www.haineschamber.org

ATTRACTIONS & TOURS

1. **ALASKA BALD EAGLE FESTIVAL** November 12-16, 2003. Celebrate the world's largest gathering of bald eagles. Speakers, Art Exhibits, Family Events, Eagle Release and more. PO Box 1449, Haines, AK 99827-1449 907-766-2202 907-766-2271 Fax E-mail: chamber@haineschamber.org www.baldeaglefest.org

2. **ALASKA FJORDLINES** Fjord Express to Juneau. Wildlife and day cruise package. See the Mendenhall Glacier, state capitol, governor's mansion and downtown Juneau. PO Box 246, Haines, AK 99827-0246 800-320-0146, 907-766-3395, 907-766-2393 Fax E-mail: alison@alaskafjordlines.com www.lynnncanal.com

3. **ALASKA MOUNTAIN GUIDES & CLIMBING SCHOOL** Sea kayaking trips and rentals, alpine and glacier hiking, mountaineering, ice climbing, backcountry skiing and climbing courses. No experience required. PO Box 1081, Haines, AK 99827-1081 800-766-3396, 907-766-3393 Fax E-mail: climb@alaskamountainguides.com www.alaskamountainguides.com

4. **ALASKA NATURE TOURS** Wildlife viewing in and around the Chilkat Bald Eagle Preserve by experienced local naturalists. Photography. Bus and walking tours & hiking adventures. 123 2nd Ave. S, PO Box 491, Haines, AK 99827-0491 907-766-2876 907-766-2844 Fax E-mail: aknature@kcd.com www.alaskanaturetours.net

5. **ALASKA'S GLACIER BAY TRAVEL** Local expertise for your vacation. Specializing in tours, cruises, lodging, sea-kayaking, whale watching, charter fishing, flight seeing packages. Family-owned. 4 Dungeness Way, PO Box 180, Gustavus, AK 99826 Phone/Fax 907-697-2475 E-mail: tours@glacierbaytravel.com www.glacierbaytravel.com

6. **CHILKAT GUIDES, LTD** Guided float trips through the Chilkat Valley Bald Eagle Preserve. Tatshenshini, Alsek and Kongakut multi-day river expeditions. 170 Sawmill Rd., PO Box 170, Haines, AK 99827-0170 907-766-2491 907-766-2409 Fax E-mail: raftalaska@chilkatguides.com www.raftalaska.com

7. **HAINES-SKAGWAY FAST FERRY** Only 35 minutes between ports, up to 26 crossings per day! Native owned & operated. 121 Beach Rd., PO Box 509, Haines, AK 99827-0509 888-766-2103 or 907-766-2100, 907-766-2101 Fax E-mail: fastferry@chilkatcruises.com www.chilkatcruises.com

8. **RIVER ADVENTURES** Breathtaking scenery and wildlife encounters abound as you explore the world famous Chilkat Bald Eagle Preserve by safe comfortable jetboat! 1.5 Mile Haines Hwy. PO Box 556, Haines, AK 99827-0556 800-478-9827 (US and Canada), 907-766-2050, 907-766-2051 Fax E-mail: KarenHess@wytbear.com www.AlaskaRiverTours.wytbear.com

9. **SHELDON MUSEUM & CULTURAL CENTER** Native Tlingit Art & Culture, Pioneer History, Fort William Seward, Haines Mission, lighthouse lens, and more. Store: Alaska books & gifts. 11 Main St., PO Box 269, Haines, AK 99827-0269 907-766-2366, 907-766-2368 Fax, E-mail: curator@sheldonmuseum.org www.sheldonmuseum.org

10. **SOCKEYE CYCLE CO.** Daily and multi-day guided on and off road bicycle tours. Two full-service shops in Haines & Skagway, Rentals. 24 Portage St., PO Box 829, Haines, AK 99827-0829 907-766-2869, 907-766-2851 Fax E-mail: sockeye@cyclealaska.com www.cyclealaska.com

11. **WEEPING TROUT SPORTS RESORT** Day tours & overnight accommodations for people seeking paradise. Trout & salmon fishing, Par 29 golf, fine food, spectacular scenery. Chilkat Lake, PO Box 129, Haines, AK 99827-0129 877-94-TROUT, 907-766-2827 907-766-2824 Fax E-mail: trout@weepingtrout.com www.weepingtrout.com

GALLERIES GIFT SHOPS

12. **ALASKA BACKCOUNTRY OUTFITTER** Quality adventure. Gear for all seasons. Camping, hiking, climbing, paddling, skiing, boarding hardwear, clothing & gifts. Sales service. Rentals. Tours with a smile. 210 Main St.(upstairs), PO Box 491, Haines, AK 99827-0491 907-766-2876, 907-766-2844 Fax E-mail: aknature@kcd.com   www.alaskanaturetours.net

13. **CAROLINE'S CLOSET** Gifts, Shoes, Women's Apparel, Music CD's, Tapes and Souvenir T-shirts. Birkenstock, Woolrich, Nike, ACG & more. Summer Hours: 10 a.m. - 6 p.m. daily. 209 Main Street, PO Box 1309, Haines, AK 99827-1309 907-766-3223 907-766-2787 Fax

14. **KING'S STORE** Photo Processing and Copy Center. Film, Camera Supplies, Nautical Charts, Frames, Office Supplies, Notary, Faxes and Gifts. 104 Main Street, PO Box 610, Haines, AK 99827-0610 907-766-2336, 907-2614 Fax

15. **OUTFITTER SPORTING GOODS** Fishing, Hunting, Camping & Hiking Products. Bait, Fishing & Hunting Licenses. Outdoor clothing including Nike, Woolrich, Helly Hansen, Xtratuff & Rocky Brand Boots. Open 8 a.m. - 8 p.m. daily. Mile 0 Haines Hwy., PO Box 1709, Haines, AK 99827-1709, 907-766-3221 907-766-2787 Fax

16. **THE WILD IRIS** Has a beautiful garden entrance and features exquisite handcrafted jewelry, local artist's prints, hand engraved silver, Eskimo art, tradebeads, hand-printed shirts, hats, cards, birch boxes. 22 Tower Rd., PO Box 77, Haines, AK 99827-0077   Phone/Fax 907-766-2300 E-mail: wildiris@wytbear.com

LODGING

17. **BEAR CREEK CABINS** Family Cabins ~ $42+. Clean, modern kitchen and bath facilities. Campsites, laundry, videos. 1.5 Mile Small Tracts Road, PO Box 908, Haines, AK 99827-0908 907-766-2259 907-766-3559 Fax E-mail: bearcreekcabin@yahoo.com www.kcd.com/hostel

18. **CABIN FEVER** Log cabins and cottage. Solar powered. Quiet beachfront location. Private baths & kitchenettes. 3 day/weekly rates. 907-766-2390, 8 Mile Mud Bay Rd., PO Box 541, Haines, AK 99827-0541 E-mail: jhill54@yahoo.com

19. **CHILKAT EAGLE BED & BREAKFAST** Lovely historic residence, waterfront & mountain views, walk to local services, full breakfast, kitchen facilities, TV lounge. Open year-round. 67 SoapSuds Alley, PO Box 387, Haines, AK 99827-0387 907-766-2763 907-766-3651 Fax E-mail: eaglebb@wytbear.com www.kcd.com/eaglebb

© Cynthia L. Jones (CI)

20. FORT SEWARD CONDOS Completely furnished 1 & 2 bedroom suites, full kitchen, bath & laundry. 2 day minimum – no pets. Reasonable. #3 Fort Seward Drive, PO Box 75, Haines, AK 99827-0075 Phone/Fax 907-766-2425
E-mail: fscondos@wytbear.com
www.haines.ak.us/condos

21. FORT SEWARD LODGE & RESTAURANT Affordable lodging, oceanview kitchenettes, restaurant, cocktail lounge. Full dinner menu, courtesy transfer, military & senior discounts. See our display ad. Mile 0 Haines Highway, PO Box 307, Haines, AK 99827-0307 800-478-7772, 907-766-2009, 907-766-2006 Fax
E-mail: ftsewardlodge@wytbear.com
http://www.ftsewardlodge.com

22. HAINES HITCH-UP RV PARK 92 Spacious Sites. 20 Pull Thrus. Cable TV. Sites Available. Gift Shop. Showers & Laundromat. Tour Information & Ticket Sales. 851 Main Street, PO Box 383, Haines, AK 99827-0383 907-766-2882, 907-766-2515 Fax
E-mail: hitchuprv@aol.com www.hitchuprv.com

23. HOTEL HALSINGLAND Haines only full service hotel. Restaurant & Lounge. Located in Historic Fort Seward. Lynn Canal view. Adjacent to downtown Haines. 13 Fort Seward Drive, PO Box 1649, Haines, AK 99827-1649 800-542-6363, 907-766-2000, 907-766-2060 Fax
E-mail: reservations@hotelhalsingland.com
www.hotelhalsingland.com

24. PORT CHILKOOT CAMPER/RV PARK Walking distance to downtown. Laundromat, Showers, Restrooms. Overlooking Lynn Canal. Full hookups available. Tenters welcomed. Weekly and monthly rates. 123 Mud Bay Road, PO Box 1649, Haines, AK 99827-1649 800-542-6363, 907-766-2000, 907-766-2060 Fax
E-mail: reservations@hotelhalsingland.com
www.hotelhalsingland.com

25. SUMMER INN BED & BREAKFAST Charming, historical house. Open year-round. Full homemade breakfast, centrally located, mountain & ocean views. Recommended by Alaska Best Places Guidebook. 117 Second Avenue, PO Box 1198, Haines, AK 99827-1198 Phone/Fax 907-766-2970
E-mail: summerinnb&b@wytbear.com
www.summerinn.wytbear.com

REAL ESTATE

26. HAINES REAL ESTATE "Expect the Best". Location downtown. Appointments recommended. 219 Main Street, Suite #14, PO Box 946, Haines, AK 99827-0946 907-766-3510 Phone/Fax
E-mail: jim@hainesrealestate.com
www.hainesrealestate.com

RESTAURANTS GROCERIES

27. ALASKAN LIQUOR STORE Specialty Liquor. Microbrew and Fine Wine Headquarters of Haines. Souvenirs, Phone Cards, Cigars and Local Information. Summer Hours: 9 a.m. - 10 p.m. 208 Main Street, PO Box 1309, Haines, AK 99827-1309 907-766-3131 907-766-2787 Fax

28. BAMBOO ROOM RESTAURANT Downtown Famous Halibut Fish & Chips. Breakfast, Lunch, Dinner, Espresso, Milkshakes. Seniors & Kid's Menu. Pool, Pull Tabs, Sports Bar. 11-13 Second Ave., PO Box 190, Haines, AK 99827-0190 907-766-2800, 907-766-3374 Fax
E-mail: bamboo@wytbear.com
www.bambooroom.net

29. DEJON DELIGHTS Smoked salmon & halibut, live crab in season, fresh/frozen sockeye, king salmon & halibut, custom processing of your catch. 37 Portage Street, PO Box 666, Haines, AK 99827-0666 Phone/Fax 907-766-2505
E-mail: dejon@alaskasmokery.com
www.alaskasmokery.com

30. HAINES QUICK SHOP Convenience Store, ATM, and Video Rentals. Ice, Cold Pop, Ice Cream and a Wide Variety of Snack Items. Open daily 7 a.m. - midnight. Mile 0 Haines Hwy., PO Box 1709, Haines, AK 99827-1709 907-766-2330 907-766-2787 Fax

31. HOWSERS IGA SUPERMARKET Shopping Center of Haines. Fast, Friendly Service. Fresh Meat, Produce & Dairy. ATM, Travelers needs, Ice & Western Union. Summer Hours: 7 a.m. - 9 p.m. daily. 209 Main Street, PO Box 1309, Haines, AK 99827-1309 907-766-2040, 907-766-2787 Fax

32. MOUNTAIN MARKET Natural foods, Espresso bar, Soups, Sandwiches, Tortilla wraps, Salads, Baked goods, Organic Coffee Roasted on the premises. Open year round. 151 3rd Ave. S., PO Box 1509, Haines, AK 99827-1509 907-766-3340 907-766-3339 Fax
E-mail: mountain_market@yahoo.com

33. OUTFITTER LIQUOR STORE Widest Variety & Best Selection in Haines. Coldest Beer and Best Deals. Local Information. Near Fort Seward. Open daily 8 a.m. - Midnight. Mile 0 Haines Hwy. PO Box 1709, Haines, AK 99827-1709 907-766-3220, 907-766-2052 Fax

SERVICES

34. BIGFOOT AUTO SERVICE INC Full service - cars, pick-ups, RVs, motorhomes - welding - 24 hour towing - Unleaded & Diesel - NAPA Parts - Tires. 987 Haines Hwy., PO Box 150, Haines, AK 99827-0150 800-766-5406, 907-766-2458 907-766-2460 Fax
E-mail: bigfootautoserv@wytbear.com

35. BUSHMASTER AUTO SERVICE Alignment/Brakes /Engines/Transmissions/Electronic Controls. Cars, Light Trucks, RVs. Factory Warranty Service. Professional Workmanship. 130 4th Avenue N., PO Box 1355, Haines, AK 99827-1355 907-766-3217, 907-766-2415 Fax
E-mail: Bushmaster@wytbear.com

36. HAINES QUICK LAUNDRY Convenient Hours 7 a.m. - midnight daily. Public Showers, Large Washers & Dryers. Located with Haines Quick Shop/Outfitters. Pay Phones. Mile 0 Haines Hwy., PO Box 170, Haines, AK 99827-1709 907-766-2330, 907-766-2052 Fax

37. PARTS PLACE Auto-RV-Marine. If you need it and we don't have it we will get it! 104 3rd Avenue S., PO Box 9, Haines, AK 99827-0009, 907-766-2940

38. TLC TAXI Full service transportation to/from airport, ferry terminal, Gustavus, Glacier Bay. Large vans able to carry people, gear and kayaks. Luggage included in fare. 4 Dungeness Way, PO Box 180, Gustavus, AK 99826 907-697-2239
E-mail: tlctaxi@glacierbaytravel.com
www.glacierbaytravel.com

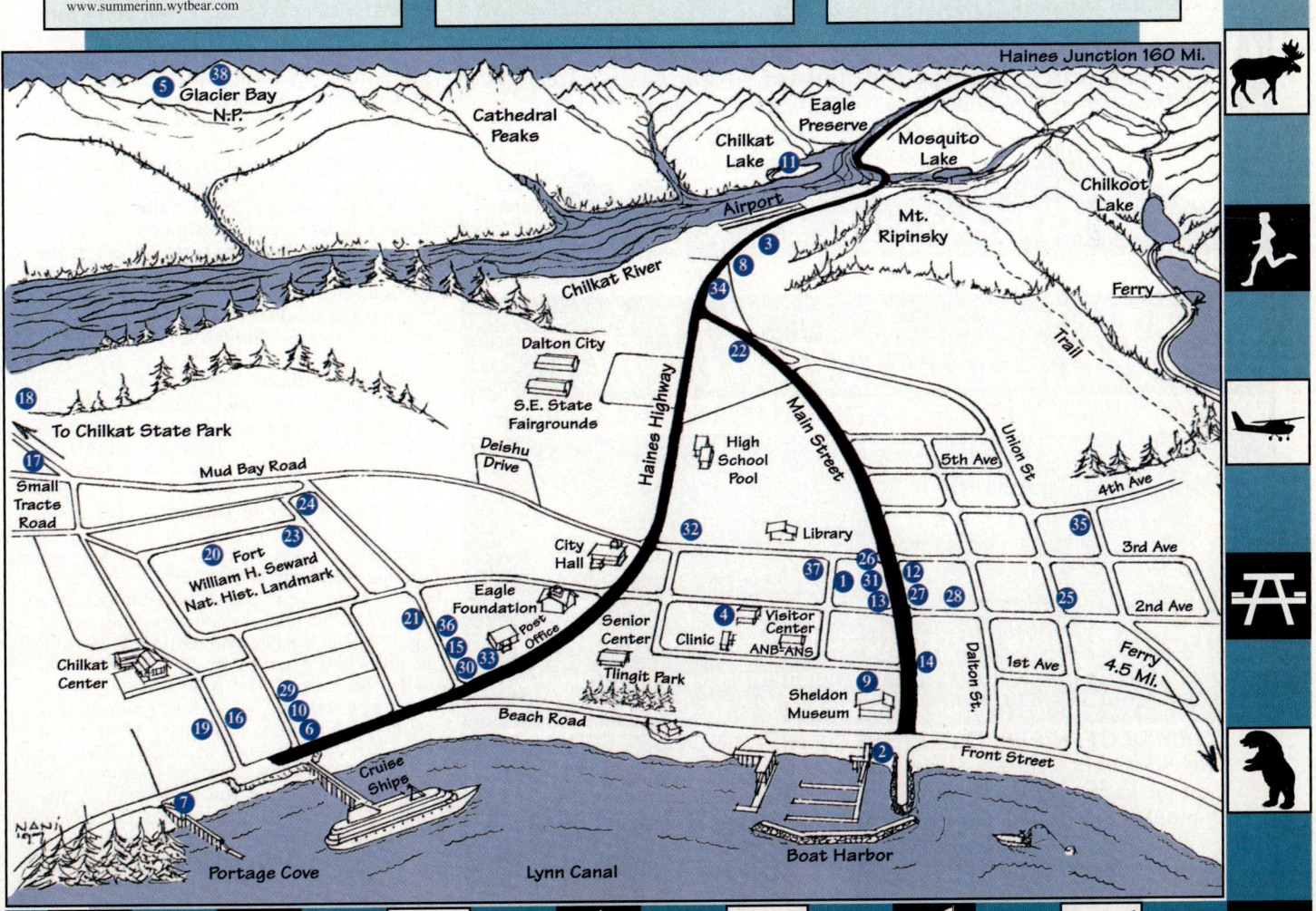

Transportation

Air: L.A.B. Flying Service, Wings of Alaska and Skagway Air offer several flights daily to and from Juneau, Skagway and other southeast Alaska communities. Haines airport is 3.5 miles from downtown. Commercial airlines provide shuttle service to and from motels, and some motels offer courtesy car pickup.

Bus: Local private bus service to ferry terminal and guided sightseeing tours are available. RC Shuttle connects Haines–Fairbanks and all points in between, (907) 479-0079.

Car Rental: At Captain's Choice Motel, phone (907) 766-3111; Eagle's Nest Motel, (907) 766-2891; and Avis Rent-A-Car summer only, (907) 766-2733.

Taxi: 24-hour service to ferry terminal and airport.

Highways: The Haines Highway connects Haines, AK, with Haines Junction, YT. It is maintained year-round. See HAINES HIGHWAY section. The 10-mile Lutak Road leads to the Alaska Marine Highway terminal and Chilkoot Lake SRS. The 8-mile Mud Bay Road accesses Chilkat State Park.

Ferries: Alaska Marine Highway vessels serve Haines from southeastern Alaska, Prince Rupert, BC, and Bellingham, WA. There's also daily Juneau–Haines–Skagway service in summer. Alaska state ferries run year-round; phone (907) 766-2111. Ferries unload at the terminal on Lutak Road, 4.5 miles from downtown Haines. Bus/van service meets all ferries in summer.

Chilkat Cruises MV *Fairweather Express* provides service to Skagway daily in summer; phone (907) 766-2100. Fjordlines offers a day cruise to Juneau in summer; phone (800) 320-0146.

Cruise Ships: Several cruise ships call in Haines.

Private Boats: Transient moorage is available at Letnikof Cove and at the small-boat harbor downtown. Contact the harbormaster, phone (907) 766-2448.

Attractions

Take the **walking tour** of historic Fort William H. Seward; details and map are available at the visitor information center and at other businesses. Historic buildings of the post include the former cable office; warehouses and barracks; "Soapsuds Alley," the housing for noncommissioned officers whose wives did washing for the soldiers; the former headquarters building, now a residence, fronted by a cannon and a totem depicting a bear and an eagle; Officers' Row at the "Top O' the Hill," restored homes and apartments; the commanding officers' quarters, now the Halsingland Hotel, where Elinor Dusenbury (who later wrote the music for "Alaska's Flag," which became the state song) once lived; the fire hall; the guard house (jail); the former contractor's office, the plumber's quarters; the post exchange (now a lodge), gymnasium, movie house and the mule stables. Look for historic and interpretive signs.

Visit Alaskan Indian Arts, located in historic Ft. Seward, to see local artists at work. Enjoy the gallery of Native art and a display of native dance costumes.

See the Chilkat Dancers perform at the Tribal House on the Fort Seward parade grounds. Ancient legends come to life as performers use masks, costuming and dialog to tell these stories. Phone (907) 766-2540 for schedule.

Totem Village, on the former post parade ground, includes a replica of a tribal ceremonial house. Haines Salmon Bake held on Wednesday and Thursday nights in summer next to the tribal house. Reservations recommended, phone (907) 766-2000.

See the Welcome Totems located at the Y on the Haines Highway. These poles were created by carvers of Alaska Indian Arts Inc. and are read from bottom to top. *The Raven* pole is symbolic of Raven, as founder of the world and all his great powers. The second figure is *The Whale*, representing Alaska and its great size. The bottom figure is the head of *The Bear*, which shows great strength. *The Eagle* pole tells of its feeding grounds (the Haines area is noted for eagles). The bottom figure is *The Brown Bear*, which feeds on salmon and is a symbol of strength. *The Eagle Chief*, head of the Eagle clan, is the third figure, and the top figure is *The Salmon Chief*, who provides the late run of salmon to the feeding grounds. Inquire at the visitor information center and museum about location of poles.

Sheldon Museum and Cultural Center is located on the old Haines Mission prop-

Haines Native heritage is reflected in its totems. *(© Kris Graef, staff)*

5 P.M. in summer. Located at the Haines Highway and 2nd Street, just across 2nd Street from the city/municipal building. Phone (907) 766-3094; http://baldeagles.org.

Alaska Chilkat Bald Eagle Preserve,

erty at the end of Main Street by the boat harbor. Exhibits present the pioneer history of the Chilkat Valley and the story and culture of the Tlingit Native people. Chilkat blankets, Russian trunks, the Eldred Rock Lighthouse lens, blue dishes, mounted eagles, Jack Dalton's sawed-off shotgun, photographs and videos on Haines and Haines Highway make a fascinating history lesson. Children's "discovery" sheet available. Open daily 1–5 P.M. in summer, plus most mornings and evenings; winter, 1–4 P.M Mon.-Fri.. Admission fee $3; children free. Phone (907) 766-2366; www.sheldonmuseum.org.

Hammer Museum. More than 900 hammers are on display at Haines' newest museum, some of them centuries old. The hammers are grouped by purpose and age, revealing the many uses of this familiar tool.

American Bald Eagle Foundation Interpretive Center shows visitors how the bald eagle interacts with its environment through exhibits; mounted eagles, a wide variety of mammals, and fish and undersea life. Admission fee charged. Open daily 9 A.M. to

HAINES-SKAGWAY FAST FERRY
M/V FAIRWEATHER EXPRESS
PASSENGER SERVICE MAY–SEPT.
- 35 min. between ports!
- Large comfortable vessels
- Smooth sailing–any weather!
- Native owned/operated
- Up to 28 crossings/day!

CHILKAT BALD EAGLE PRESERVE
DELUXE EXCURSION
- Daily trips into the heart of Haines' most notable attraction!
- Scheduled & custom departures!

CHILKAT CRUISES & TOURS
1-888-766-2103 TOLL FREE
P.O. Box 509 • Haines, AK 99827
(907) 766-2100 • Fax (907) 766-2101
www.chilkatcruises.com
e-mail: fastferry@chilkatcruises.com

HAINES HITCH-UP RV PARK

92 FULL SERVICE SPACES
CABLE TV SITES AVAILABLE
LAUNDROMAT • GIFT SHOP

TICKETS AVAILABLE FOR – GLACIER BAY TOURS, CRUISES & FLY OVERS. HAINES–SKAGWAY FAST FERRY, WHITE PASS & YUKON RAILWAY, MOUNTAIN FLYING SERVICE, FJORDLAND EXPRESS, AND JUNEAU EXCURSIONS.

1/2 MILE WEST ON MAIN STREET
P.O. BOX 383 HAINES, ALASKA 99827
HitchupRV@aol.com • www.hitchuprv.com

(907) 766-2882

INSIDE PASSAGE • Haines

Portage Cove SRS offers picnic tables, tent sites and scenic views. (© Kris Graef, staff)

State Recreation Site, about 10 miles from downtown Haines. Chilkoot Lake is a beautiful spot with a picnic area and camping. Just past the park entrance, the ADF&G operates a fish weir between June and September to count the sockeye salmon return to Chilkoot Lake.

Go Flightseeing. Local air charter operators offer flightseeing trips for spectacular close-up views of glaciers, ice fields, mountain peaks and bald eagles. The heart of Glacier Bay is just west of Haines.

Take a Tour: Charter boat operators in Haines offer fishing, sightseeing and photography trips. Local tour companies offer bicycle tours, guided hiking, bus tours and nature walks.

Watch totem carvers at the Alaska Indian Arts Inc. workshop, located in the restored hospital at Fort Seward. This nonprofit organization is dedicated to the revival of Tlingit Indian art. Craftsmen also work in silver and stone, and sew blankets. Visitor hours 9 A.M. to 5 P.M. weekdays year-round. Phone (907) 766-2160; email aia@wytbear.com; www.alaskaindianarts.com.

Hike Area Trails. Stop at the visitor information center for a free copy of the pamphlet *Haines is for Hikers*, which contains trail descriptions and maps.

Mount Ripinsky trail is a strenuous all-day hike—recommended for experienced hikers only—with spectacular views from the summit of mountains and tidal waters. Battery Point trail leads about 1.2 miles to Kelgaya Point overlooking Lynn Canal along relatively flat ground. Mount Riley (elev. 1,760 feet) has 3 routes to the summit. The steepest and most widely used trail starts at Mile 3 Mud Bay Road and climbs 2.8 miles to the summit.

AREA FISHING: Good fishing in the spring for king salmon in **Chilkat Inlet**. (Haines King Salmon Derby takes place May 25-27, June 1-2, 2003.) Halibut best in summer in **Chilkat**, **Lutak** and **Chilkoot inlets**. Dolly Varden fishing good in all lakes and rivers, and along marine shorelines from early spring to late fall. Great pink salmon fishing every other year in August along the marine shoreline of **Lutak Inlet** and in the **Chilkoot River**. Sockeye salmon in the **Chilkoot River**, late June through August. Coho salmon in the **Chilkoot** and **Chilkat rivers**, mid-September through October. Cutthroat trout year-round at **Chilkat** and **Mosquito lakes**. For more information, contact the Alaska Dept. of Fish and Game at (907) 766-2625.

where the world's greatest concentration of American bald eagles takes place late October through December on Chilkat River flats below Klukwan. The eagle viewing area begins at **Milepost H 17** on the Haines Highway. The 48,000-acre Alaska Chilkat Bald Eagle Preserve was established in 1982.

The Chilkat Valley at Haines is the annual gathering site of more than 3,500 bald eagles, which gather to feed on the late run of chum and coho salmon in the Chilkat River. For information contact Alaska State Parks, (907) 465-4563, or www.dnr.state.ak.us/parks/units/eagleprv.htm.

Dalton City is housed in the "White Fang" Disney film set. It is located at the fairgrounds. The former movie set houses a few businesses and a microbrewery. The Klondike restaurant is open in summer. Call (907) 766-2477 for schedule.

Drive out Mud Bay Road. From town, drive out Mud Bay Road 8 miles to Chilkat State Park. There are beautiful views along the way of Rainbow and Davidson glaciers across Chilkat Inlet. **Chilkat State Park** has picnic sites, beach access and a 6.9-mile hiking trail to Seduction Point at the southern tip of the Chilkat Peninsula.

Drive out Lutak Road. The Alaska Marine Highway terminal is located at Mile 3.6 Lutak Road. Continue north past the ferry terminal to road end at **Chilkoot Lake**

SHELDON MUSEUM AND CULTURAL CENTER

Visit
Daily Summer
M-F Winter

Discover
**Native Culture
Pioneer History**

Main and 1st, Haines AK, 907-766-2366
www.sheldonmuseum.org

Port Chilkoot CAMPER PARK

**FULL & PARTIAL HOOKUPS
LAUNDROMAT • SHOWERS • TENT SITES**

*In wooded setting on Mud Bay Road AT FORT SEWARD
Walking distance to Restaurants and Shops*

BOX 1649 ... HAINES, AK 99827 ... (907)766-2000
Call Toll Free 1-800-542-6363
www.HotelHalsingland.com
e-mail: Reservations@HotelHalsingland.com

L.A.B. FLYING SERVICE, INC.
Serving Juneau, Skagway, Haines, Hoonah, Gustavus, Glacier Bay, Kake, Petersburg, Ketchikan, Craig, Klawock, Excursion Inlet
www.labflying.com **1(907)766-2222**

Alaska Nature Tours
WILDLIFE VIEWING EYE-TO-EYE

**CHILKAT BALD EAGLE PRESERVE
Guided Wildlife Viewing,
Hiking Adventures, Birding**

(907) 766-2876 • P.O. Box 491 • Haines, AK 99827
E-mail: aknature@kcd.com • www.alaskanaturetours.net

SKAGWAY

Population: 862

Distinctive facade of the Arctic Brotherhood Hall is made up of driftwood sticks.
(© Blake Hanna, staff)

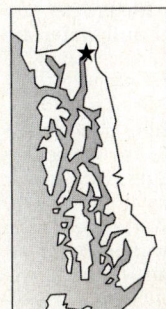

Located on the north end of Taiya Inlet on Lynn Canal, 90 air miles northwest of Juneau; 108 road miles south of Whitehorse, YT. The northern terminus of the Alaska Marine Highway Southeast ferry system and southern terminus of Klondike Highway 2 which connects with the Alaska Highway. **NOTE:** *Although Skagway is only 13 miles by water from Haines, it is 359 miles by road!* **Population:** 862. **Emergency Services: Skagway Police Department,** phone (907) 983-2232. **Fire Department** and **Ambulance,** phone 911. **Clinic,** phone (907) 983-2255. **Maritime Search and Rescue,** contact the Coast Guard at (800) 478-5555.

Visitor Information: Write the Skagway Convention and Visitors Bureau, Box 1029, Skagway, AK 99840. Phone (907) 983-2854, fax 983-3854. Klondike Gold Rush National Historical Park Visitor Center has exhibits and films on the history of the area and information on hiking the Chilkoot Trail; write Box 517, Skagway, AK 99840; phone (907) 983-2921, fax (907) 983-9249. Located in the restored railroad depot on 2nd Avenue and Broadway, it is open daily in summer.

Elevation: Sea level. **Climate:** Average daily temperature in summer, 57°F; in winter, 23°F. Average annual precipitation is 29.9 inches. **Radio:** KHNS-FM 91.9; KINY-AM 69.0. **Newspaper:** *Skagway News* (biweekly).

Private Aircraft: Skagway airport, adjacent west; elev. 44 feet; length 3,700 feet; asphalt; fuel 100LL; attended.

The name Skagway (originally spelled Skaguay) is said to mean "home of the north wind" in the local Tlingit dialect. It is the oldest incorporated city in Alaska (incorporated in 1900). Skagway is also a year-round port and 1 of the 2 gateway cities to the Alaska Highway in Southeast Alaska: Klondike Highway 2 connects Skagway with the Alaska Highway. (The other gateway city is Haines, connected to the Alaska Highway via the Haines Highway.)

The first white residents were Capt. William Moore and his son, J. Bernard, who settled in 1887 on the east side of the Skagway River valley. A small part of the Moore homesite was sold for construction of a Methodist college, now the city hall and the Trail of '98 Museum.

But Skagway owes its birth to the Klondike Gold Rush. Skagway, and the once-thriving town of Dyea, sprang up as thousands of gold seekers arrived to follow the White Pass and Chilkoot trails to the Yukon goldfields.

In July 1897, the first boatloads of stampeders bound for the Klondike landed at Skagway and Dyea. By October 1897, according to a North West Mounted Police report, Skagway had grown "from a concourse of tents to a fair-sized town, with well-laid-out streets and numerous frame buildings, stores, saloons, gambling houses, dance houses and a population of about 20,000." Less than a year later it was reported that "Skagway was little better than a hell on earth." Customs office records for 1898 show that in the month of February alone 5,000 people landed at Skagway and Dyea.

By the summer of 1899 the stampede was all but over. The newly built White Pass & Yukon Route railway reached Lake Bennett, supplanting the Chilkoot Trail from Dyea. Dyea became a ghost town. Its post office closed in 1902, and by 1903 its population consisted of 1 settler. Skagway's population dwindled to 500. But Skagway persisted, both as a port and as terminus of the White Pass & Yukon Route railway, which connected the town to Whitehorse, YT, in 1900. Cruise ships, and later the Alaska State Ferry System, brought tourism and business to Skagway. Scheduled state ferry service to southeastern Alaska began in 1963.

Today, tourism is Skagway's main economic base, with Klondike Gold Rush National Historical Park Skagway's major visitor attraction. Within Skagway's downtown historical district, false-fronted buildings and boardwalks dating from gold rush times line the streets. The National Park Service, the city of Skagway and local residents have succeeded in retaining Skagway's Klondike atmosphere.

Lodging & Services

Skagway offers a variety of accommodations; see ads this section. Reservations are advised in summer.

There are several restaurants, cafes and

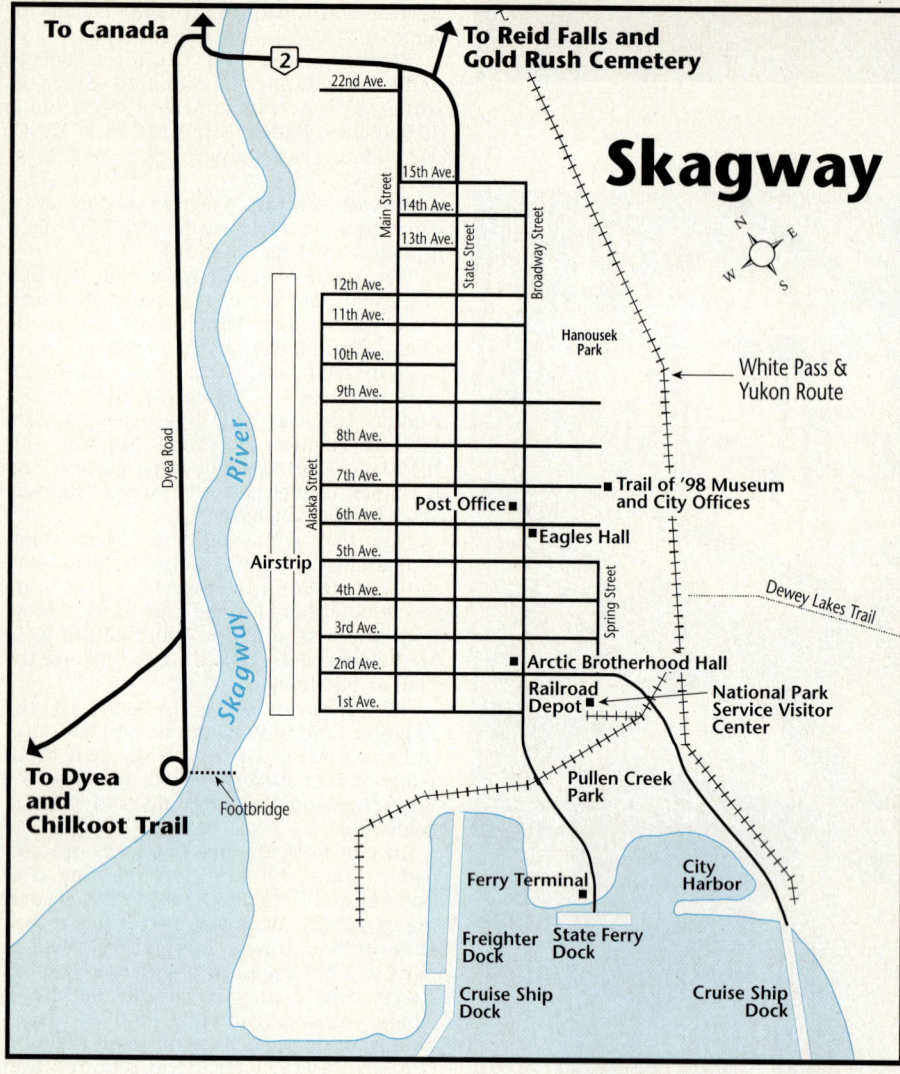

bars, grocery, hardware and clothing stores; many gift and novelty shops offering Alaska and gold rush souvenirs, photos, books, records, gold nugget jewelry, furs and ivory; a post office, gas station (with diesel); 2 hostels and several churches.

There is 1 bank in town (Wells Fargo), located at 6th and Broadway; open 9:30 A.M. to 5 P.M. Monday through Friday in summer. An ATM is located at the bank.

U.S. customs office is located at Mile 6.8 Klondike Highway 2; phone (907) 983-2325.

At The White House. You'll find historic accommodations reminiscent of days past with our family antiques, hardwood floors and restored woodwork. Clean comfortable

bedrooms feature many personal touches in addition to the private baths, handcrafted quilts, ceiling fans, telephones and TVs. Enjoy the breakfast buffet in the morning and complete your evening with tea and treats from our cookie jar. Year-round. 475 8th Avenue, Post Office Box 41-MP, Skagway, AK 99840-0041. Phone (907) 983-9000, Fax (907) 983-9010. www.atthewhitehouse.com. [ADVERTISEMENT]

Historic Skagway Inn, established 1897, located at 7th and Broadway in historic district. Once a gold rush brothel, now a 12-room, historic, frontier country inn filled with antiques. Includes breakfast served on premise at Gregis Bistro. Walking distance to all services and attractions. Travel desk for train and tour tickets. Courtesy van. Home of Alaska Garden Gourmet cooks–gardener tour of our 5,000-square-foot kitchen garden followed by an Alaska seafood cooking demonstration. Fully licensed. Espresso and box lunches. Ask about our Chilkoot Trail service. Phone (907) 9893-2289; 1-888-752-4929; stay@skagwayinn.com; www.skagwayinn.com. [ADVERTISEMENT]

Camping

There are 3 private campgrounds in Skagway offering hookups, tent sites, restrooms and showers, dump stations and laundromats; see ads this section. A campground is located at the Chilkoot Trail trailhead near Dyea. ▲

Transportation

Air: Daily scheduled service between Skagway and Haines and Juneau. Charter service also available between towns and for flightseeing via Skagway Air. Transportation to and from the airport is provided by the flight services and local hotels in the summer.

Bus: Bus/van service to Anchorage, Fairbanks, Haines and Whitehorse, YT.

Car Rental: Available.

Highway: Klondike Highway 2 was completed in 1978 and connects Skagway to the Alaska Highway. It is open year-round. See SOUTH KLONDIKE HIGHWAY section.

Railroad: White Pass & Yukon Route offers 3-hour excursions from Skagway to White Pass Summit and return. Phone 800-343-7373. Through rail/bus connections are also available daily between Skagway and Whitehorse.

Ferries: Skagway is the northern terminus of the Alaska Marine Highway Southeast ferry system. The ferry terminal is in the large building on the waterfront (see city map this section); restrooms and pay phone. Ferry terminal office hours vary: opening hours are usually posted at the front door. Phone (907) 983-2941 or 983-2229. It's an easy walk into town, but hotel and motel vans do meet ferries.

MV *Fairweather Express* service is available between Skagway and Haines; phone (888) 766-2103. *Fjord Express* service between Skagway and Juneau; phone (800) 320-0146.

Cruise Ships: Skagway is a regular port of call for cruise ships and the 17th most visited port in the world. Downtown is not far from the dock. Tours can be purchased dockside and at downtown offices.

Private Boats: Transient moorage is available at the Skagway small-boat harbor. Contact the harbormaster at (907) 983-2628. The boat harbor has space for cruisers up to 100 feet. Gas, diesel fuel and water are available.

Attractions

The Skagway Visitor Center is located in the Arctic Brotherhood Hall on Broadway between 2nd and 3rd avenues. The Arctic Brotherhood Hall's facade has almost 10,000 pieces of driftwood sticks arranged in a mosaic pattern, with the Brotherhood's AB letters and symbols, a gold pan with nuggets.

Skagway Museum is in the McCabe College Building (also City Hall) one block east of Broadway on 7th Avenue; The museum's primary interest is to help preserve Alaskan

historical material and to display Alaskan pioneer life. On display include a Tlingit canoe, a Portland Cutter sleigh, kayaks and an Alaska Native Heritage collection of baskets, beadwork and carvings. Also exhibited are tools, supplies and gambling equipment used in the Klondike Gold Rush of 1898. The museum is open daily May through the end of September: 9 A.M. to 5 P.M., Mon.–Fri.; 1 to 4 P.M., Sat.–Sun. Contact the museum for winter hours. Phone (907)983-2420; email skgmus@aptalaska.net; www.skagwaymuseum.org.

Klondike Gold Rush National Historical Park was authorized in 1976 to preserve and interpret the history of the Klondike Gold Rush of 1897–98. In 1998 this became the nation's only International Historical Park, with units in Seattle, Skagway, British Columbia and the Yukon. The park, managed by the National Park Service, consists of 4 units: a 6-block historic district in Skagway's business area; a 1-mile-wide, 17-mile-long corridor of land comprising the Chilkoot Trail; a 1-mile-wide, 5-mile-long corridor of land comprising the White Pass Trail; and a visitor center at 117 S. Main St. in Seattle, WA. The Skagway unit is the most-visited national park in Alaska. For more information, phone (907) 983-2921; fax: (907) 983-9249; www. nps.gov/klgo.

A variety of free programs are available in Skagway in the summer. There are daily guided walking tours of the downtown Skagway historic district and ranger talks on a variety of topics. Films are also shown. Check with the Park Service's visitor center in the restored railroad depot on 2nd Avenue and Broadway. Visitor center hours are 8 A.M. to 6 P.M. early May through September.

Hike the Chilkoot Trail. This 33-mile trail begins on Dyea Road and climbs Chilkoot Pass (elev. 3,739 feet) to Lake Bennett, following the historic route of the gold seekers of 1897–98. The original stampeders took an average of 3 months to transport the required "ton of goods" (a year's worth of supplies and equipment) over the Pass. Today's adventurers take 3 to 5 days to hike the Chilkoot.

Information on permits and fees, customs requirements, regulations, camping, weather, equipment and trail conditions are available from the Chilkoot Trail Center in Skagway. The center is open 7:30 A.M. to 4:30 P.M. daily, June to September; phone phone (907) 983-9234.

Dirce Ann's Fabric Shop. A quilter's paradise specializing in Alaskan wildlife prints and Northern quilt patterns. Locally-owned and operated, year-round supplier of fabrics, yarns, rubber stamps, crochet cotton and needlework supplies. Also featured are local handmade lap quilts, quillows and other gift itmes. Located across from the Library. 412 8th Avenue; (907) 983-2376, fax (907) 983-3114. [ADVERTISEMENT]

Fishfull Think-N. Located next to Pullen Pond. Fishing licenses and fishing tackle rentals. Sportfishing charters and wildlife excursions. Charter *The Spindrift*, a beautiful converted 34-foot gillnetter. Fish in comfort for king, pink, chum and silver salmon or Dolly Varden. Take our wildlife excursion and view our awesome fiord's sea and wildlife: Whales, eagles, goats, sea lions, seals and otters. (907) 983-2777, cell phone (907) 723-0315. Fishfull@aptalaska.net. www.fishfullthink-N-.com. [ADVERTISEMENT]

Picnic at Pullen Creek Park. This attractive waterfront park has a covered picnic shelter, 2 footbridges and 2 small docks. It is located between the cruise ship and ferry docks, behind the White Pass & Yukon Route depot. Watch for pink salmon in the intertidal waters in August, silver salmon in September.

Corrington Museum of Alaska History, located at 5th and Broadway, offers a unique record of events from prehistory to the present. Each of the 40 exhibits at the museum features a scene from Alaska history hand-engraved (scrimshawed) on a walrus tusk. The museum is open in summer. Free admission.

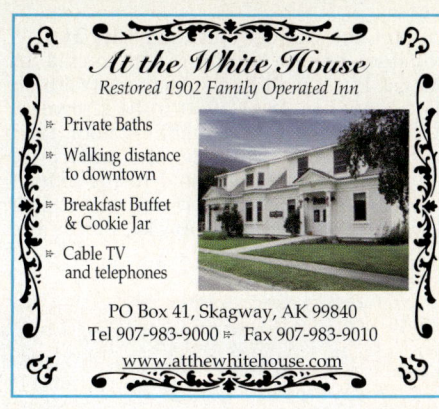

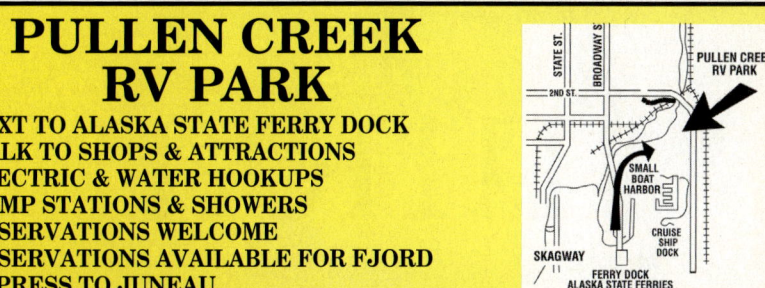

McCabe College Building/City Hall is the first granite building constructed in Alaska. It was built by the Methodist Church as a school in 1899–1900 to be known as McCabe College, but public-school laws were passed that made the enterprise impractical, and it was sold to the federal government. For decades it was used as U.S. District Court No. 1 of Alaska, but as the population of the town declined, the court was abandoned, and in 1956 the building was purchased by the city. From the waterfront, walk up Broadway and turn right on 7th Avenue.

Helicopter and airplane tours of Skagway and White Pass are available in summer.

Gold Rush Cemetery is 1.5 miles from downtown and makes a nice walk. Go north on State Street a short drive. Then follow posted direction signs to the cemetery. "Bad guy" Soapy Smith and "good guy" Frank Reid are buried here (both men died in a gunfight in July 1898). It is only a short hike from Frank Reid's grave to Reid Falls.

Drive Dyea Road. This narrow, winding, gravel road begins at **Milepost S 2.3** South Klondike Highway and leads southwest to Yakutania Point, then northwest past Long Bay and the Taiya River to the old Dyea townsite. There are fine views of Skagway, Taiya Inlet and the Skagway River from Dyea Road.

At Mile 1.9 is the Skyline trailhead. This trail leads to top of AB Mountain (elev. 5,000 feet). At Mile 5.1 there is a view of the old pilings in Taiya Inlet. The docks of Dyea used to stretch from the trees to beyond the pilings, which are still visible. These long docks were needed to reach deep water because of the great tidal range in this inlet.

Chilkoot Trail trailhead campground, parking area and ranger station are at Mile 6.7 Dyea Road. The Chilkoot Trail trailhead is at Mile 7.2.

At Mile 7.4, a primitive side road leads to Slide Cemetery (follow signs) and the old Dyea townsite (keep left at forks in road). The cemetery, reached by a short unmarked path through the woods, contains the graves of people killed in the Palm Sunday avalanche, April 3, 1898, on the Chilkoot Trail. At Dyea townsite, covered with fireweed and lupine in summer, hardly a trace remains of the buildings that housed 8,000

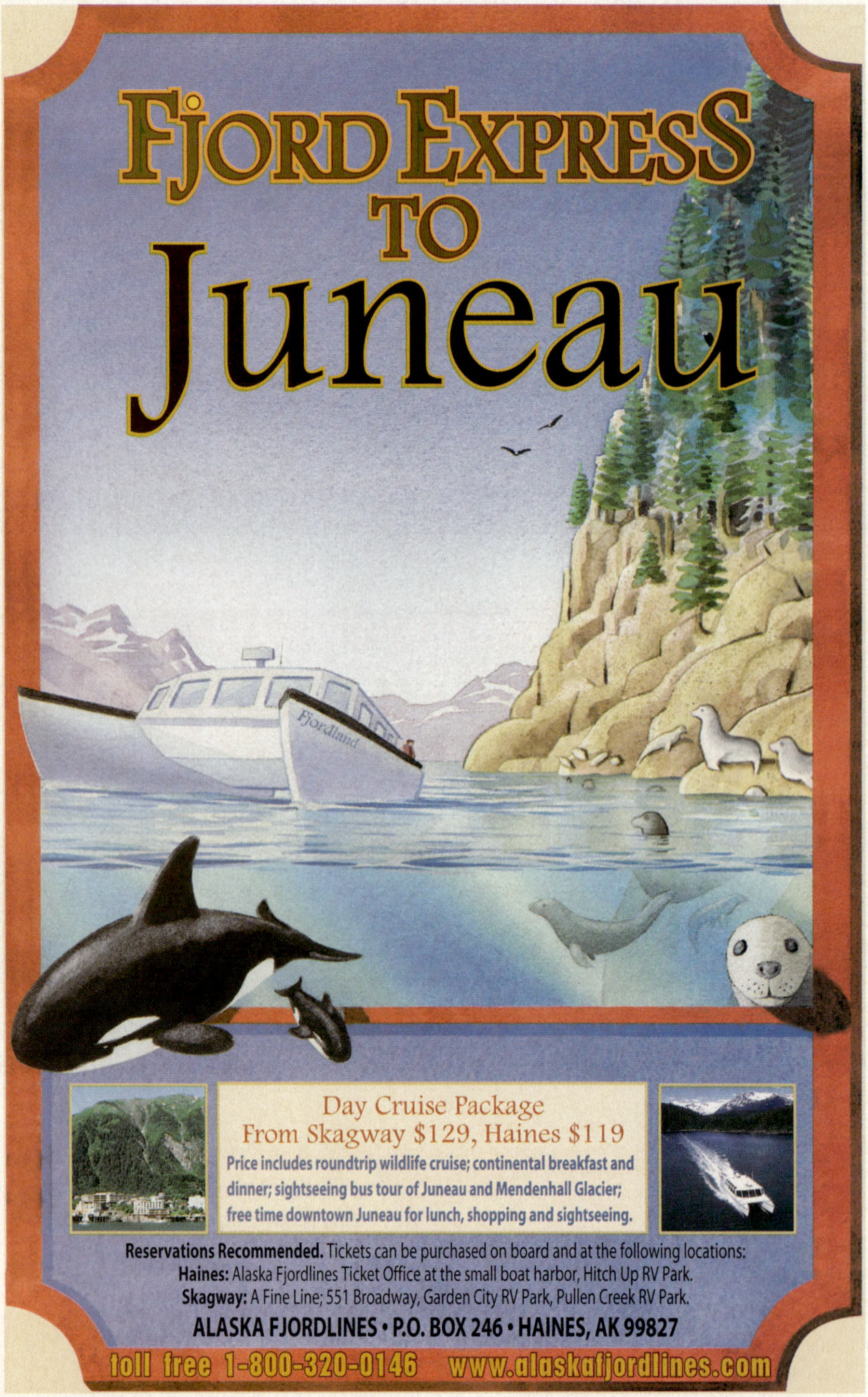

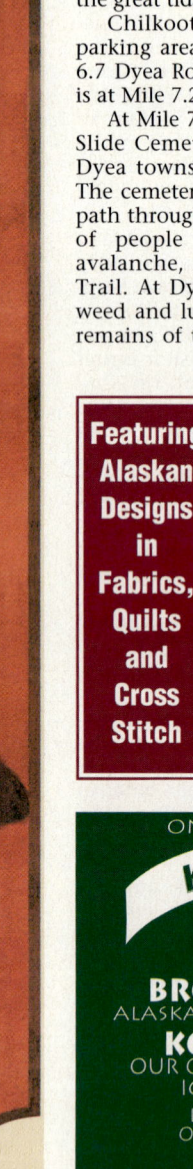

SKAGUAY NEWS DEPOT.

Historic Broadway's Bookstore and Newsstand

"Wonderful, stocked with local volumes, and the place to buy an out-of-town newspaper."
Old West

OPEN ALL YEAR

www.skagwaybooks.com
Box 498, Skaguay, AK 99840
Phone 907-983-3354

Visit us on Broadway near Third Ave.

FLIGHTSEE
Glaciers
Ice Fields
and Trail of '98
Gold Rush
Passes

SCHEDULED & CHARTER SERVICE

Alaska & Canada

SKAGWAY Air Service

BOX 357 MP SKAGWAY
(907) 983-2218

Stop by our office at 4th & Broadway for brochure and information.
...or contact our office in Juneau

www.skagwayair.com
Phone (907) 789-2006
Fax (907) 983-2948

VISIT SKAGUAY'S JEWELL GARDENS

www.jewellgardens.com
Phone: (907) 983-2111

GIANT VEGETABLES

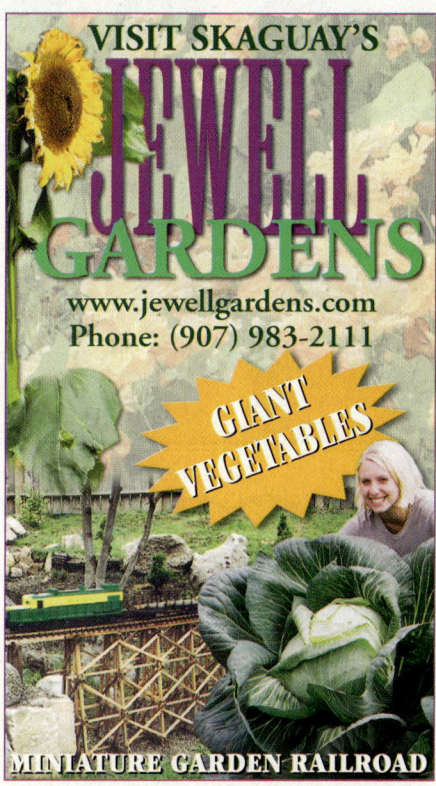

MINIATURE GARDEN RAILROAD

THE CHARM OF DAYS GONE BY.

- 195 Rooms -
- Dining Room & Lounge -
- Bonanza Bar & Grill -
- No-Smoking Rooms -
- Close to Shopping & Entertainment -
- Cable TV -

Introducing Westmark On-line Booking.

For instant confirmation visit us on-line at
www.westmarkhotels.com

Central Reservations
1-800-544-0970

Westmark INN SKAGWAY

Third & Spring Street
P.O. Box 515
Skagway, Alaska 99840
907-983-6000

Garden City RV Park

Tours & Tickets Available
Pull Through Sites Featuring
Full Hookups - 30 Amp, Water, Sewer
Laundromat • Modem Access

Located Between 15th & 17th on State St. in Skagway
1-866-983-2378 • 907-983-2378 • www.gardencityrv.com • gcrv@aptalaska.net

SKAGWAY True Value HARDWARE

Camping, Fishing, Hunting Supplies
Auto Supplies • Sporting Goods
Housewares & RV Supplies
Alaska & Canada Fishing Licenses
(907) 983-2233 • Fax (907) 983-2948
P.O. Box 357 • Skagway
E-mail: skagwayhardware@hotmail.com
www.skagwayhardware.com

Linger awhile

SKAGWAY

Visit Historic Skagway:

Gateway to the Klondike

Garden City of Alaska

Northern Terminus of the
Alaska Marine Highway System

Home of the Klondike Gold Rush
National Historic Park

SKAGWAY CONVENTION AND VISITORS BUREAU
Message Line: 888-762-1898 • (907) 983-2854 • Fax (907) 983-3854
P.O. Box 1029 • Skagway, AK 99840
http://www.skagway.org • E-mail: infoskag@aptalaska.net

people here during the gold rush. About 30 people live in the valley today. Ranger-led walking tours of the Dyea Townsite are offered daily in summer. Check with the National Park Service visitor center in Skagway for details.

The road ends at the steel bridge across West Creek at Mile 8.4.

AREA FISHING: Local charter boat operators offer fishing trips. The ADF&G Sport Fish Division recommends the following areas and species. Dolly Varden: Fish the shore of **Skagway Harbor**, **Long Bay** and **Taiya Inlet**, May through June. Try the **Taiya River** by the steel bridge in Dyea in early spring or fall; use red and white spoons or salmon eggs. Hatchery-produced king salmon have been returning to the area in good numbers in recent years. Try fishing in salt water during June and July and in **Pullen Creek** in August. Pink salmon are also plentiful at Pullen Creek in August. Coho and chum salmon near the steel bridge on the **Taiya River**, mid-September through October. Trolling in the marine areas is good but often dangerous for small boats. A steep trail near town will take you to Dewey lakes, which were stocked with Colorado brook trout in the 1920s. **Lower Dewey Lake**, ½-hour to 1-hour hike; heavily wooded shoreline, use raft. The brook trout are plentiful and grow to 16 inches but are well fed, so fishing can be frustrating. **Upper Dewey Lake**, a steep 2½-hour to 4-hour hike to above tree line, is full of hungry brook trout to 11 inches. Use salmon eggs or size #10 or #12 artificial flies. **Lost Lake** is reached via a rough trail near Dyea (ask locals for directions). The lake lies at about elev. 1,300 feet and has a good population of rainbow trout. Use small spinners or spoons.

For more information on area fishing, contact the Alaska Department of Fish and Game office in Haines; phone (907) 766-2625 (recorded message).

An **awesome** Alaskan adventure awaits.

Temsco Helicopters will show you the best of Alaska in all of its glory. Our helicopter glacier tour options include:
- Glacier Landings
- Glacier Hiking
- Flightseeing
- Tour/Dog Sled Package

JUNEAU & SKAGWAY
1-877-789-9501
WWW.TEMSCOAIR.COM

TEMSCO HELICOPTERS, INC.

SKAGWAY-HAINES FAST FERRY
M/V FAIRWEATHER EXPRESS
PASSENGER SERVICE MAY-SEPT.
- 35 min. between ports!
- Large comfortable vessels
- Smooth sailing– any weather!
- Native owned/operated
- Up to 28 crossings/day!

CHILKAT BALD EAGLE PRESERVE
DELUXE EXCURSION

- Daily trips into the heart of Haines' most notable attraction!
- Scheduled & custom departures!

CHILKAT CRUISES & TOURS
1-888-766-2103 TOLL FREE
P.O. Box 509 • Haines, AK 99827
(907) 766-2100 • Fax (907) 766-2101
www.chilkatcruises.com
e-mail: fastferry@chilkatcruises.com

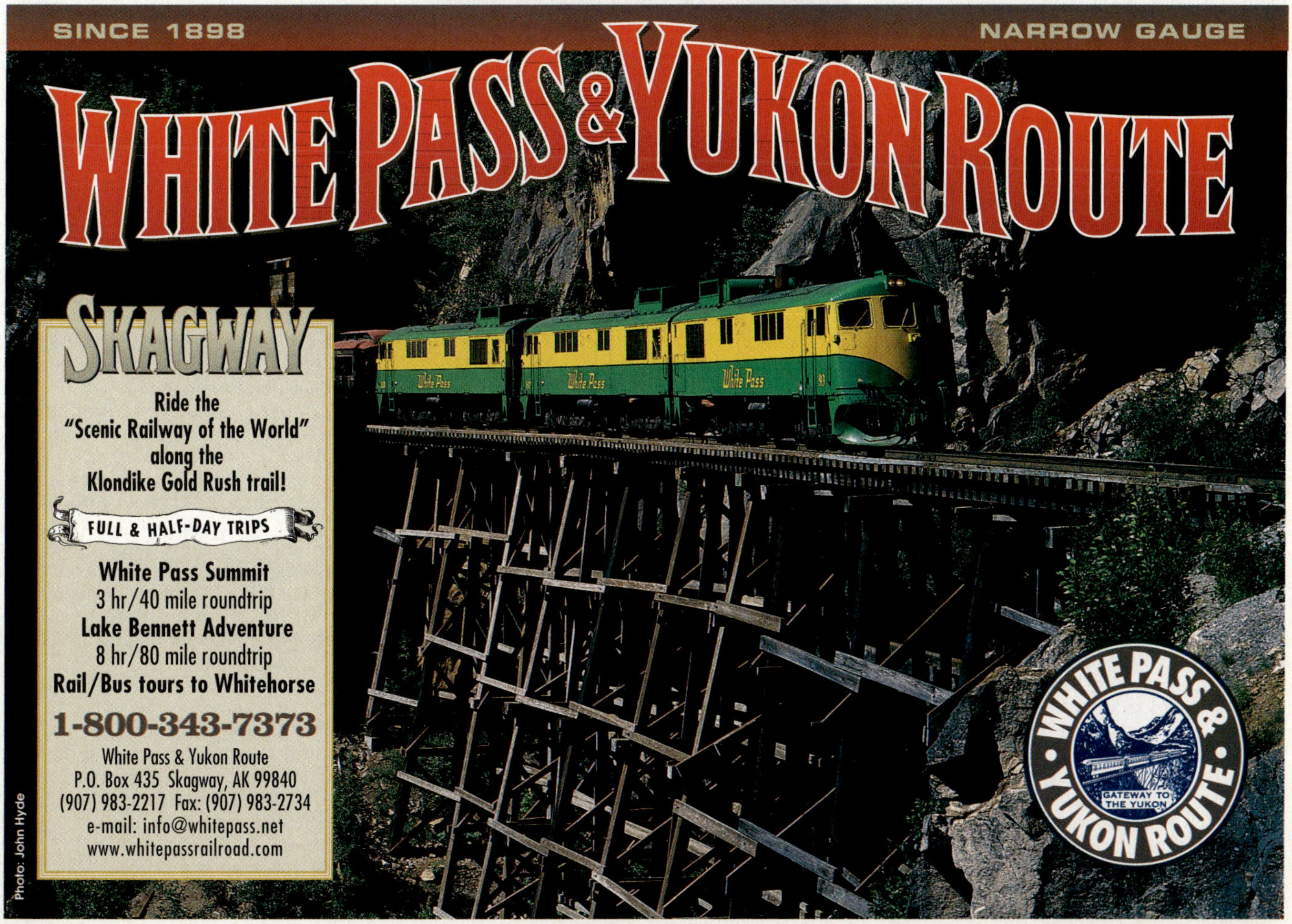

SINCE 1898   NARROW GAUGE

WHITE PASS & YUKON ROUTE

SKAGWAY
Ride the "Scenic Railway of the World" along the Klondike Gold Rush trail!

FULL & HALF-DAY TRIPS

White Pass Summit
3 hr/40 mile roundtrip
Lake Bennett Adventure
8 hr/80 mile roundtrip
Rail/Bus tours to Whitehorse

1-800-343-7373

White Pass & Yukon Route
P.O. Box 435 Skagway, AK 99840
(907) 983-2217 Fax: (907) 983-2734
e-mail: info@whitepass.net
www.whitepassrailroad.com

WHITE PASS & YUKON ROUTE
GATEWAY TO THE YUKON

HAINES HIGHWAY

Connects: Haines, AK, to Haines Junction, YT **Length:** 152 miles
Road Surface: Paved   **Season:** Open all year
Highest Summit: Chilkat Pass 3,493 feet
Major Attraction: Chilkat Bald Eagle Preserve

(7) (4) (3)

	Beaver Creek	Haines	Haines Jct.	Tok	Whitehorse
Beaver Creek		335	184	113	283
Haines	335		152	449	252
Haines Jct.	184	152		297	100
Tok	113	449	297		396
Whitehorse	283	252	100	396	

The Haines Highway starts in Alaska, passes through British Columbia and ends at Haines Junction, YT. (© Earl L. Brown, staff)

The paved 152 mile/244 km Haines Highway connects Haines, AK (on the state ferry route), at the head of Lynn Canal with the Alaska Highway at Haines Junction, YT. Allow about 4 hours driving time. The highway is open year-round. The road is usually snow-free by May.

Noted for the grandeur and variety of its alpine scenery, the Haines Highway leads from coastal forests near Haines through the Chilkat Eagle Preserve up over the backbone of the St. Elias Mountains, skirting Tatshenshini–Alsek Wilderness Provincial Park, and running along the eastern border of Kluane National Park Reserve. The park's visitor information centre is located in Haines Junction; open daily, May–Sept.

Part of what is now the Haines Highway was originally a "grease trail" used by the coastal Chilkat Indians trading eulachon oil for furs from the Interior. In the late 1880s, Jack Dalton developed a packhorse trail to the Klondike goldfields along the old trading route. The present road was built in 1943 as a military access highway during WWII to provide an alternative route from the Pacific tidewater into Yukon Territory.

U.S. customs is open from 7 A.M. to 11 P.M. (Alaska time); Canada customs is open from 8 A.M. to midnight (Pacific time). There are no facilities or accommodations at the border. All travelers must stop.

A valid Alaska fishing license is required for fishing along the highway between Haines and the international border at **Milepost H 40.7**. The highway then crosses the northern tip of British Columbia into Yukon Territory. You must have valid fishing licenses for both British Columbia and Yukon Territory if you fish these areas, and a national park fishing license if you fish waters in Kluane National Park.

In summer, gas is available along the highway only at 33 Mile Roadhouse and at Kathleen Lake Lodge, **Milepost H 135.2**.

If you plan to drive the Haines Highway in winter, check road conditions before starting out by phoning (867) 456-7623 for the daily recorded road condition report. Note that flashing lights at the Haines Junction weigh scales indicate hazardous winter road conditions; travel not recommended. In Haines Junction, the maintenance garage (867/634-2227) or weigh scale station (867/634-2228) may also have details on driving conditions.

Watch for bikes on the highway during the annual Kluane/Chilkat International Bike Race (June 21, 2003).

Emergency medical services: Between Haines and the U.S.–Canada border at **Milepost H 40.7**, phone 911. Between the U.S.–Canada border and Haines Junction, phone the RCMP at (867) 634-5555.

Haines Highway Log

Distance from Haines (H) is followed by distance from Haines Junction (HJ).

Driving distance is measured in miles from Haines, AK (mileposts are up along the Alaska portion of the highway). Kilometre figures given on the Canadian portion of the highway reflect the physical kilometreposts and are not an accurate metric conversion of the mileage figure.

ALASKA ROUTE 7

H 0 HJ 151.6 Junction of Front Street/Beach Street and Haines Highway in downtown Haines.

H 0.7 HJ 150.9 Haines Hitch-Up RV Park. ▲

H 0.9 HJ 150.7 Main Street Y.

H 1.3 HJ 150.3 Eagle's Nest Motel.

H 3 HJ 148.6 Sign indicates Customs 38 miles/61 km.

H 3.5 HJ 148.1 Private Aircraft: Haines airport; elev. 16 feet; length 4,000 feet; asphalt; fuel 100; unattended.

H 4 HJ 147.6 Takhinsha Mountains to the southwest form a backdrop to the Chilkat River. Haines Highway (2-lanes, 50 mph) winds through the Chilkat River Valley. The Chilkat River flows into Chilkat Inlet of Lynn Canal, a massive fjord about 60 miles/96.5 km long. Lynn Canal was named by English explorer Captain Vancouver for his birthplace (King's Lynn) in England.

H 4.3 HJ 147.3 Turnout along river.

H 6 HJ 145.6 Picnic spot next to Chilkat River.

H 6.6 HJ 145 Mount Ripinski trailhead (signed).

H 9 HJ 142.6 Watch for subsistence fish camps along the highway in June. Also watch for fish wheels on the river.

H 9.4 HJ 142.2 Entering **Alaska Chilkat Bald Eagle Preserve** northbound. *NOTE: Please use pullouts.* Established in 1982, the 48,000-acre preserve is the seasonal home to more than 3,500 bald eagles, which gather each year to feed on the late run of chum

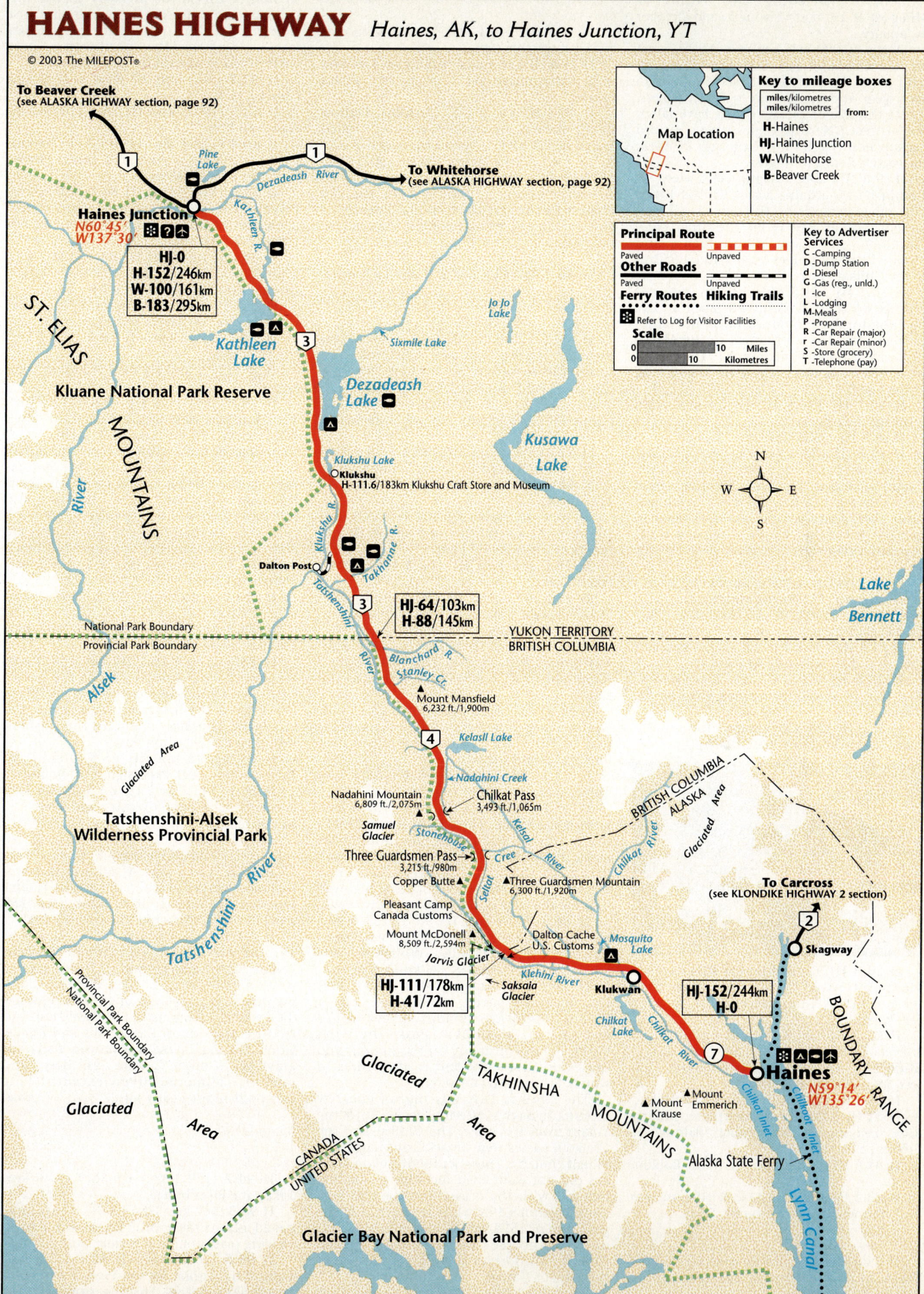

HAINES HIGHWAY

salmon. Eagle-viewing area begins at **Milepost H 19**; best viewing is mid-October to January.

Of the 40,000 bald eagles in Alaska, most are found in Southeast. Eagles build nests in trees along the shoreline. Nests are added to each year and can be up to 7 feet across. (Nests the size of pickup trucks have fallen out of trees.) Nesting eagles have a second backup nest. Eagles lay their eggs in April; the eaglets fledge in August.

H 9.6 HJ 142 Magnificent view of Takhinsha Mountains across Chilkat River. This range extends north from the Chilkat Range; Glacier Bay is on the other side. Prominent peaks are Mount Krause and Mount Emmerich (elev. 6,405 feet/1,952m) in the Chilkat Range.

H 10.1 HJ 141.5 Mile 12 sign indicates mileage on the U.S. Army oil pipeline. The pipeline formerly pumped oil from Haines over the St. Elias Mountains to the Alaska Highway at Haines Junction, YT. These signs were used for aerial checking and monitoring of the line.

H 14.7 HJ 136.9 Watch for mountain goats on the ridges.

H 18.8 HJ 132.8 Slide area.

H 19.2 HJ 132.4 Turnout with parking, interpretive panels and restrooms; Council Grounds Chilkat Bald Eagle Preserve. Begin eagle viewing area (northbound) on Chilkat River flats. Best viewing is mid-October to January. Paved and gravel biking and walking trail along river. *CAUTION: No stopping on highway; use turnouts!*

H 20.2 HJ 131.4 Paved turnout by river.

H 20.6 HJ 131 Paved parking area with interpretive panel. Council Grounds Chilkat Bald Eagle Preserve.

H 21.4 HJ 130.2 Turnoff via paved access road to Indian village of **KLUKWAN**.

H 23.8 HJ 127.8 Chilkat River bridge. Highway now follows Klehini River northbound. *CAUTION: Watch for moose.*

H 26.3 HJ 125.3 Porcupine Crossing; side road leads west across Klehini River.

H 26.8 HJ 124.8 Klehini River scenic viewpoint; paved parking area, picnic shelter and tables, interpretive signs, viewing telescopes.

H 27.3 HJ 124.3 Turnoff on Mosquito Lake Road for **Mosquito Lake State Recreation Site**; 13 campsites, tables, water, toilets, $8/night or resident pass.

H 28.9 HJ 122.7 Muncaster Creek bridge.

H 31 HJ 120.6 Scenic viewpoint; parking area. Leaving Alaska Chilkat Bald Eagle Preserve northbound.

H 31.6 HJ 120 Bridge over Little Boulder Creek.

H 33.2 HJ 118.4 33 Mile Roadhouse; gas and phone. RV campground. Store. *NOTE: Last available gas northbound until Kathleen Lake Lodge. Check your gas tank.*

H 33.8 HJ 117.8 Bridge over Big Boulder Creek. Watch for salmon during spawning season.

Begin improved highway northbound; 55 mph speed limit.

H 35.5 HJ 116.1 Paved turnout to east with interpretive signs.

H 35.6 HJ 116 Paved parking area to west with interpretive signs. View of Saksaia Glacier.

H 40.3 HJ 111.3 U.S. Customs, Dalton Cache station. All travelers entering United States MUST STOP. Open year-round 7 A.M. to 11 P.M., Alaska time. Phone (907) 767-5511. Restrooms, large parking area. Jarvis Glacier moraine is visible from the old **Dalton Cache** (on the National Register of Historic Places), located behind the customs building.

Begin improved highway southbound.

H 40.4 HJ 111.2 U.S.–Canada border. *TIME ZONE CHANGE: Alaska observes Alaska time, Canada observes Pacific time.*

BC HIGHWAY 4

H 40.6 (72 km) HJ 111 (178.6 km) Pleasant Camp Canada Customs and Immigration office. All travelers entering Canada MUST STOP. Office is open daily year-round, 8 A.M. to midnight, Pacific time. Phone (907) 767-5540. No public facilities. *NOTE: $500 fine for littering.*

H 43.4 (76.6 km) HJ 108.1 (174.1 km) Tatshenshini Alsek Park (northbound sign).

H 44.4 (78.5 km) HJ 106.2 (171 km) Five Mile Creek.

H 46.9 (82.3 km) HJ 104.7 (168.5 km) Distance marker northbound shows Haines Junction 108 miles/174 km.

H 48.5 (85 km) HJ 103.1 (165.9 km) Fuchs Creek.

H 49.9 (87.3 km) HJ 101.7 (163.7 km) Double-ended turnout to west with interpretive sign and historical milepost.

H 50 (87.4 km) HJ 101.9 (164 km) Highway crosses Seltat Creek. Three Guardsmen Mountain (elev. 6,300 feet/1,920m) to the east.

H 52.9 (92 km) HJ 98.7 (158.8 km) South end of Three Guardsmen Lake. Glave Peak, part of Three Guardsmen Mountain, rises directly behind the lake.

H 53.2 (92.5 km) HJ 98.4 (158.4 km) Three Guardsman Lake (sign).

H 55.1 (94.6 km) HJ 96.5 (155.3 km) Stonehouse Creek. Three Guardsmen Pass to the northeast, hidden by low hummocks along the road. To the north is the Kusawak Range. To the south is Three Guardsmen Mountain. The tall poles along the highway indicate the edge of the road for snowplows.

H 56.3 (97.6 km) HJ 95.3 (153.4 km) Distance marker northbound shows Haines Junction 149 km/93 miles, Whitehorse 308 km/191 miles, Fairbanks 981 km/610 miles.

H 59.1 (102 km) HJ 92.5 (148.8 km) Double-ended paved turnout to west at Haines Highway Summit (elev. 3,510 feet/1,070m) at **Chilkat Pass**. The wind blows almost constantly on the summit and causes drifting snow and road closures in winter. Snow until late May.

The Chilkat Pass was one of the few mountain passes offering access into the Yukon from the coast. The Chilkat and the Chilkoot passes were tenaciously guarded by Tlingit Indians. These southern Yukon Indians did not want their lucrative fur-trading business with the coastal Indians and Russians jeopardized by white strangers. But the gold rush of 1898, which brought thousands of white people inland, finally opened Chilkat Pass, forever altering the lifestyle of the Interior Natives.

From the Chilkat Pass over Glacier Flats to Stanley Creek, the highway crosses silt-laden streams flowing from the Crestline Glacier. Nadahini Mountain (elev. 6,809 feet/2,075m) to the northwest. Three Guardsmen Mountain to the southeast.

H 62.2 (107 km) HJ 89.4 (143.8 km) Chuck Creek.

H 63.5 (109.3 km) HJ 88.1 (141.8 km) Nadahini River.

H 66.4 (113.8 km) HJ 85.2 (137.a km) Distance marker northbound shows Haines Junction 142 km/88 miles.

H 67.5 (114.7 km) HJ 84.1 (135.3 km) Private Aircraft: Mule Creek airstrip; elev. 2,900 feet/884m; length 4,000 feet/1,219m; gravel. No services.

H 68.2 (116.4 km) HJ 83.4 (134.2 km) Mule Creek Highway Maintenance Station (no services) **Historical Mile 75**.

H 72.7 (124.2 km) HJ 78.9 (127 km) Goat Creek bridge. Watch for horses on road.

H 74.7 (127.3 km) HJ 76.9 (123.7 km) Holum Creek.

H 77 (130.5 km) HJ 74.6 (120 km) Twin Lakes.

H 78.8 (134 km) HJ 72.8 (117.2 km) Viewpoint to west for Tatshenshini–Alsek Wilderness Provincial Park. This park encompasses the northwest corner of British Columbia and is dominated by the St. Elias Mountains. It is also habitat for grizzly bears, Dall sheep, the rare "glacier" bear and also rare birds such as the king eider and Steller's eider. The Tatshenshini and Alsek rivers are famous for their river rafting opportunities.

H 79.3 (134.5 km) HJ 72.3 (116.3 km) Mansfield Creek.

H 80.4 (136.5 km) HJ 71.2 (114.5 km) Stanley Creek.

H 85.1 (143.9 km) HJ 66.5 (107 km) Turnout by pond.

H 85.6 (144.7 km) HJ 66 (106.2 km) Blanchard River bridge. This is the put-in point for whitewater rafting on the Blanchard River. The Blanchard River crosses the Yukon–BC boundary and joins the Tatshenshini River near Dalton Post.

H 85.8 (145 km) HJ 65.8 (105.9 km) Tatshenshini Alsek Park (sign southbound).

H 86.1 (145.5 km) HJ 65.5 (105.4 km) Welcome to Kluane Country and Welcome to Yukon signs.

BC–YT border.

YUKON HIGHWAY 3

H 86.8 (146.3 km) HJ 64.8 (104.2 km) Distance marker northbound shows Haines Junction 100 km/62 miles, Whitehorse 259 km/161 miles, Fairbanks 922 km/573 miles.

H 94.5 (159 km) HJ 57.1 (91.9 km) Turnoff for Yukon government **Million Dollar Falls Campground** (0.7 mile/1.1 km west); 33 campsites, kitchen shelters, camping permit ($12), playground, drinking water (boil water), hiking trails. Boardwalk trail and viewing platform of scenic falls and rapids. Good fishing below **Takhanne Falls** for grayling, Dolly Varden, rainbow and salmon. **Takhanne River**, excellent king salmon fishing in early July.

CAUTION: The Takhanne, Blanchard, Tatshenshini and Klukshu rivers are grizzly feeding areas. Exercise extreme caution when fishing or exploring in these areas.

H 94.7 (159.3 km) HJ 56.9 (91.6 km) Takhanne River bridge.

H 98.3 (162 km) HJ 53.3 (85.8 km) Large paved photo viewpoint of Kluane Range; viewing platform, litter barrels, outhouse.

H 99.5 (164.5 km) HJ 52.1 (83.8 km) Turnoff to historic **Dalton Post**, a way point on the Dalton Trail. Steep, narrow, winding access road; four-wheel drive recommended in wet weather. Road not recommended for large RVs or trailers at any time. Several old abandoned log cabins and buildings are located here. Indians once formed a human barricade at Dalton Post to harvest the Klukshu River's run of coho salmon. The river system here hosts seasonal runs of chinook, sockeye and coho salmon. Chinook are most visible in July, coho in late September and October, and sockeye from August to October. In fall, grizzly bears come here to feast on the fish.

Fishing for chinook, coho, sockeye salmon in **Village Creek**. Grayling, Dolly Varden and salmon in **Klukshu River**. Fishing restrictions posted. CAUTION: Watch for bears.

H 103.4 (169.7 km) HJ 48.2 (77.5 km) Viewpoint with information sign to west. Alsek Range and Tatshenshini River to southwest.

H 104 (171 km) HJ 47.6 (76.6 km) Motheral Creek.

H 105 (172 km) HJ 46.6 (75 km) Klukshu wetland overlook to west; watch for trumpeter swans.

H 106.1 (174 km) HJ 45.5 (73.2 km) Vand Creek.

H 110.8 (181.9 km) HJ 40.8 (65.6 km) Klukshu Creek. This area is frequented by grizzly bears.

H 111.6 (183 km) HJ 40 (64.4 km) **Historic Milepost 118** at turnoff for **KLUKSHU**, an Indian village, located 0.5 mile/0.8 km off the highway via a gravel road. This summer fish camp and village on the banks of the Klukshu River is a handful of log cabins, meat caches and traditional fish traps. Steelhead, king, sockeye and coho salmon are taken here. Each autumn, families return for the annual catch. The site is on the old Dalton Trail and offers good photo possibilities. Museum, picnic spot, souvenirs for sale. Information panels on First Nations heritage and traditional fishing techniques.

Klukshu Craft Store and Museum. A good selection of Native crafts—home-tanned moosehide beaded slippers, moose-hair tufting, beaded souvenirs, birchbark baskets. Homemade jams and jellies, local smoked salmon, soapberries. Cold pop and munchies. Our museum features area First Nation artifacts. Trading blankets, sheephorn potlatch spoons, traditional fishtrap and trapping displays, and lots more. [ADVERTISEMENT]

H 112.8 (185 km) HJ 38.8 (62.4 km) Gribbles Gulch.

H 114 (187 km) HJ 37.6 (60.5 km) Parking and outhouse at **St. Elias Lake trailhead** (Kluane National Park trail). Novice and intermediate hiking trail winds through subalpine meadow; 4.5 miles/7.2 km round-trip.

H 116.8 (191.5 km) HJ 34.8 (57.4 km) Hay Ranch to the east.

H 117.8 (193 km) HJ 33.8 (54.4 km) Old Dezadeash Lodge. Historically, this spot was known as Beloud Post. Mush Lake trail (13.4 miles/21.6 km long) begins behind lodge. It is an old mining road.

NOTE: Watch for horses on highway.

H 119.3 (195 km) HJ 32.3 (52 km) Turnout along **Dezadeash Lake**, one of the earliest known features in the Yukon, which parallels the highway for 9 miles/14.5 km northbound. Dezadeash (pronounced DEZ-dee-ash) is said to be the Indian word describing their fishing method. In the spring, the Indians built small fires around the bases of large birch trees, peeled the heat-loosened bark and placed it, shiny white side up, on the bottom of the lake near shore, weighted with stones. From log wharfs built over the white bark, Indians waited with spears for lake trout to cross the light area. Another interpretation of Dezadeash relates that Chilkat Indians referred to it as *Dasar-ee-ASH*, meaning "Lake of the Big Winds."

Dezadeash Lake offers good trolling, also fly-fishing along the shore where feeder streams flow into the lake. There are northern pike, lake trout and grayling in Dezadeash Lake. CAUTION: This is a mountain lake and storms come up quickly.

H 119.7 (195.7 km) HJ 31.9 (51.3 km) Entrance to Yukon government **Dezadeash Lake Campground**, a very scenic spot on the lake; 20 campsites, camping permit ($12), kitchen shelter, picnic area, boat launch, no drinking water, pit toilets. ▲

H 121.8 (199 km) HJ 29.8 (47.9 km) Distance marker northbound shows Haines Junction 47 km/29 miles, Whitehorse 206 km/128 miles, Fairbanks 819 km/509 miles.

H 123.9 (202.3 km) HJ 27.7 (44.6 km) **Rock Glacier Trail** to west; short 0.5-mile/0.8-km self-guiding trail, partially boardwalk. Interesting walk, some steep sections. Parking area and viewpoint.

Begin Haines Junction Highway Maintenance District northbound.

H 134.8 (219.6 km) HJ 16.8 (27 km) Turnoff for **Kathleen Lake Campground**, the only established campground within Kluane National Park; 39 campsites and a kitchen area; day-use area with picnic tables, restrooms; boat launch at lake; campfire programs by park staff. Camping fee charged. Campfire talks and backcountry registration. The 53-mile/85-km Cottonwood loop trail begins here.

Kathleen Lake is a glacier-fed turquoise-blue lake, nearly 400 feet/122m deep. The lake offers fishing for lake trout in June and July; kokanee, and grayling June to September. NOTE: National parks fishing license required.

H 135.2 (220.3 km) HJ 16.4 (26.4 km)

Viewpoint of Kathleen Lake at Milepost H 139.2 Haines Highway. (© Earl L. Brown, staff)

Kathleen Lake Lodge; food, gas and lodging.
NOTE: Last available gas southbound for next 102 miles. Check your gas tank.

H 135.8 (221 km) HJ 15.8 (25.4 km) **Kathleen River** bridge. Fishing for rainbow, June to September; grayling, July and August; lake trout in September. A rough turnout on the east side of the road provides access to the river. From here, you can canoe to Lower Kathleen Lake and Rainbow Lake. This is an easy half-day paddle, but do not attempt to go farther on Kathleen River, as there are many falls.

H 139.2 (226.5 km) HJ 12.4 (20 km) Turnout to west. Good view of Kathleen Lake. Information plaque on Kluane and Wrangell–St. Elias national parks (World Heritage Site).

H 143.4 (233.5 km) HJ 8.2 (13.2 km) Quill Creek. **Quill Creek trailhead**; 7-mile/11-km trail.

H 147.1 (239 km) HJ 4.5 (7.2 km) Parking area to west at **Auriol trailhead** (9.3-mile/15-km loop trail); skiing and hiking.

H 148.8 (242 km) HJ 2.8 (4.5 km) Rest area to southeast with litter barrels and pit toilets.

Welcome to Haine Junction (sign northbound). View of Haines Junction and Shakwak Valley.

H 151 (245 km) HJ 0.6 (1 km) Dezadeash River Bridge. **Dezadeash River Trail** (2.2 miles/3.5 km); easy walk along river's edge. This river is part of the headwaters system of the Alsek River, which flows into the Pacific near Yakutat, AK.

H 151.6 (246 km) HJ 0 **HAINES JUNCTION** (see description beginning on page 169); turn for Alaska, go straight for Whitehorse.

Junction of the Haines Highway (Yukon Highway 3) and Alaska Highway (Yukon Highway 1) at Haines Junction. Turn to **Milepost DC 985** on page 169 in the ALASKA HIGHWAY section for highway log. Whitehorse-bound travelers read log back to front, Alaska-bound travelers read log front to back.

SOUTH KLONDIKE HIGHWAY

Connects: Skagway, AK, to Alaska Hwy., YT **Length:** 99 miles
Road Surface: Paved   **Season:** Open all year
Highest Summit: White Pass 3,292 feet
Major Attraction: Klondike Gold Rush National Historical Park

	Alaska Hwy. Jct.	Atlin	Carcross	Skagway	Whitehorse
Alaska Hwy. Jct.		125	33	99	10
Atlin	125		92	158	81
Carcross	33	92		66	43
Skagway	99	158	66		109
Whitehorse	10	81	43	109	

The South Klondike Highway winds through the rocky valley of Summit Lake.
(© Earl L. Brown, staff)

The 98.9 mile/159 km South Klondike Highway (also known as the Skagway–Carcross Road) connects Skagway, AK, with the Alaska Highway at **Milepost 874.4**, south of Whitehorse. The highway between Skagway and Carcross (referred to locally as the Skagway Road) was built in 1978 and formally dedicated on May 23, 1981. The highway connecting Carcross with the Alaska Highway (referred to locally as the Carcross Road) was built by the U.S. Army in late 1942 to lay the gasoline pipeline from Skagway to Whitehorse.

The North Klondike Highway begins north of Whitehorse, turning off the Alaska Highway and leading to Dawson City. See KLONDIKE LOOP section for log of the North Klondike Highway between the Alaska Highway and Dawson City.

The South Klondike Highway is a 2-lane, asphalt-surfaced road, open year-round. For the daily recorded road condition report, phone (867) 456-7623, toll free from Yukon communities 1-877-456-7623 or the Skagway Dept. of Transportation at (907) 983-2333. The road has been improved in recent years and is fairly wide. There is a steep 11.5-mile/18.5-km grade between Skagway and White Pass.

IMPORTANT: If you plan to cross the border between midnight and 8 A.M., inquire locally regarding border stations' hours of operation or phone (907) 983-3144. For U.S. border information, phone (907) 983-2325. For Canada border information, phone (867) 821-4111.

The South Klondike Highway is 1 of 2 highways connecting ferry travelers with the Alaska Highway; the other is the Haines Highway out of Haines. South Klondike Highway offers some spectacular scenery and adds only an additional 55 miles/89 km to the trip for Alaska-bound motorists compared to the Haines Highway route. (The distance from Haines to Tok, AK, is approximately 445 miles/716 km; the distance from Skagway to Tok is 500 miles/805 km.) South Klondike Highway, like the Haines Highway, crosses from Alaska into British Columbia, then into Yukon Territory.

Emergency medical services: Between Skagway and Log Cabin at **Milepost S 27.3**, phone 911 or the Skagway Fire Department at (907) 983-2450. Between Log Cabin and Annie Lake Road at **Milepost S 87.5**, phone the RCMP at (867) 821-5555 or the Carcross Ambulance at (867) 821-4444. Between Annie Lake Road and the junction with the Alaska Highway, phone 911 for the Whitehorse ambulance.

South Klondike Highway Log

Distance from Skagway (S) is followed by distance from Alaska Highway (AH).

Mileposts in Alaska and kilometreposts in Canada reflect distance from Skagway. Kilometre distance from Skagway on the Canadian portion of the log reflects the physical kilometreposts and is not an accurate metric conversion of the mileage figure.

ALASKA ROUTE 98

S 0 AH 98.8 Ferry terminal in **SKAGWAY**. See description of Skagway beginning on page 695.

S 1.6 AH 97.2 Skagway River bridge.

S 2.3 AH 96.5 Junction with Dyea Road. This narrow, winding gravel side road leads 7.4 miles southwest from the highway to the old **Dyea Townsite** and **Slide Cemetery**. During the Klondike Gold Rush, some 8,000 people lived at Dyea. The cemetery contains the graves of men killed in the Palm Sunday avalanche (April 3, 1898) on the Chilkoot Trail.

S 2.6 AH 96.2 Highway maintenance camp.

S 2.8 AH 96 Plaque to east honoring men and women of the Klondike Gold Rush, and access to parklike area along Skagway River.

S 2.9 AH 95.9 Access road east to Skagway River.

Highway begins steep 11.5 mile/18.5-km ascent northbound from sea level to 3,290 feet/1,003m at White Pass.

S 4.7 AH 94.1 Turnout to west.

S 5 AH 93.8 Turnout to east with view across canyon of White Pass & Yukon Route railway tracks and bridge. The narrow-gauge WP&YR railway was completed in 1900.

S 5.5 AH 93.3 Turnout to west with historical information signs.

SOUTH KLONDIKE HIGHWAY
Skagway, AK, to Alaska Highway Jct. (includes Tagish and Atlin Roads)

SOUTH KLONDIKE HIGHWAY

WP&YR tracks wind around Bernard Lake on the South Klondike Highway.
(© Earl L. Brown, staff)

S 6 AH 92.8 Turnout to east.

S 6.8 AH 92 U.S. Border station; open 24 hours in summer (manned 8 A.M. to midnight, video camera reporting midnight to 8 A.M.). Phone (907) 983-3144 for border crossing (immigration); phone (907) 983-2325 for customs in Skagway. All travelers entering the United States must stop. Have identification ready. Residents of North America must present birth certificate, driver's license or voter registration. Permanent residents (not citizens) of the U.S. need their I-551 (green) card. All other foreign visitors must have a passport. ID is also required for children.

S 7.4 AH 91.4 View to east of WP&YR railway line.

S 7.7 AH 91.1 Good photo stop for **Pitchfork Falls**, visible across the canyon.

S 8.1 AH 90.7 Turnout to east.

S 9.1 AH 89.7 Paved turnout to east with historical interest signs about the Klondike Gold Rush trail. Viewpoint looks across the gorge to the WP&YR railway tracks.

S 9.9 AH 88.9 Truck emergency runout ramp to west for large transport units that may lose air brakes on steep descent southbound.

S 11.1 AH 87.7 Captain William Moore Bridge. This unique suspension bridge over Moore Creek spans a 110-foot-/34-m-wide gorge. Just north of the bridge to the west is a large waterfall. The bridge is named for Capt. William Moore, a riverboat captain and pilot, prospector, packer and trader, who played an important role in settling the town of Skagway. Moore helped pioneer this route over White Pass into the Yukon and was among the first to realize the potential of a railroad across the pass.

S 11.6 AH 87.2 Large paved turnouts to east with view of Skagway River gorge, Captain William Moore Bridge and waterfalls, next 0.1 mile/0.2 km northbound.

S 12 AH 86.8 Truck emergency runout ramp to west.

S 12.6 AH 86.2 Posts on east side of road mark highway shoulders and guide rails for snowplows.

S 14.4 AH 84.4 White Pass Summit (elev. 3,292 feet/1,003m). Turnout to west.
CAUTION: Southbound traffic begins steep 11.5-mile/18.5-km descent to Skagway.

Many stampeders on their way to the Klondike goldfields in 1898 chose the White Pass route because it was lower in elevation than the famous Chilkoot Pass trail, and the grade was not as steep. But the White Pass route was longer and the final ascent to the summit treacherous. Dead Horse Gulch (visible from the railway line) was named for the thousands of pack animals that died on this route during the gold rush.

Thousands of gold seekers poured into Canada over the Chilkoot and White passes on their way to Dawson City. An initial contingent of North West Mounted Police, led by Inspector Charles Constantine, had come over the Chilkoot Pass in 1894—well before the gold rush—to establish law among the miners at Dawson City. But in 1898, the Canadian government sent reinforcements, led by Superintendent Samuel Steele.

Upon his arrival at the foot of Chilkoot Pass in February of 1898, Steele found thousands of men waiting to pack their supplies over the pass. He immediately stationed permanent detachments at the summits of Chilkoot and White passes, both to maintain law and order and to assert Canadian sovereignty at these 2 international borders

After witnessing the desperate condition of many men arriving in the Klondike, Steele was also responsible for setting a minimum requirement of a year's supply of food and equipment for any miner entering Canada, which translated roughly into "one ton of goods."

S 14.5 AH 84.3 Paved turnout to west.

S 14.9 AH 84 U.S.–Canada (AK–BC) border. Turnout to west. Monument to east.
TIME ZONE CHANGE: Alaska observes Alaska time; British Columbia and Yukon Territory observe Pacific time.

BC HIGHWAY 2

S 16.2 (26.1 km) **AH 82.6** (133 km) Highway winds through rocky valley of Summit Lake (visible to east). Several small gravel turnouts next 6 miles/9.6 km northbound.

S 18.1 (29.1 km) **AH 80.7** (129.9 km) Summit Creek bridge.

S 18.4 (29.6 km) **AH 80.4** (129.4 km) Summit Lake to east.

S 19.3 (31.1 km) **AH 79.5** (128 km) North end of Summit Lake.

S 21.4 (34.4 km) **AH 77.4** (124.5 km) Creek and railroad bridge to east. Railroad parallels highway next 6 miles.

S 22.5 (36.2 km) **AH 76.3** (122.8 km) **Canada Customs** at **FRASER** (elev. 2,400 feet/732m). Open daily, 24 hours in summer. Phone (867) 667-3943 or 3944 for winter hours. Pay phone. All travelers entering Canada must stop. *Reminder: Have proper ID for all travellers, including children.*

Old railroad water tower to east, highway maintenance camp to west.

S 22.6 (36.4 km) **AH 76.2** (122.7 km) Beautiful deep-green Bernard Lake to east.

S 22.8 (36.7 km) **AH 76** (122.3 km) Large double-ended turnout with 2 interpretive panels on area attractions and the WP&YR.

S 24.2 (38.9 km) **AH 74.6** (120.1 km) Turnout to east.

S 25.1 (40.4 km) **AH 73.7** (118.6 km) Shallow Lake to east.

S 25.5 (41 km) **AH 73.3** (118 km) Old cabins and buildings to east.

S 26.6 (42.8 km) **AH 72.2** (116.2 km) Turnout to east. Beautiful view of Tormented Valley, a rocky desolate "moonscape" of stunted trees and small lakes east of the highway.

S 27.3 (43.9 km) **AH 71.5** (115 km) Highway crosses tracks of the White Pass & Yukon Route at **LOG CABIN**; Chilkoot Trail National Historic Site. With completion of the railway in 1900, the North West Mounted Police moved their customs checkpoint from the summit to Log Cabin. There is nothing here today.

There are numerous turnouts along the highway between here and Carcross. Turnouts may be designated for either commercial ore trucks or passenger vehicles.

S 30.7 (49.4 km) **AH 68.1** (109.6 km) Tutshi (too-shy) River visible to east.

S 31.1 (50 km) **AH 67.7** (108.9 km) Highway parallels **Tutshi Lake** for several miles northbound. Excellent fishing for lake trout and grayling early in season. Be sure you have a British Columbia fishing license.

S 40.1 (64.5 km) **AH 58.7** (94.5 km) Short, narrow gravel access road to picnic area with pit toilet on Tutshi Lake. Large vehicles check turnaround space before driving in.

S 40.7 (65.5 km) **AH 58.1** (93.5 km) Good views of Tutshi Lake along here.

S 43.7 (70.5 km) **AH 55.1** (88.7 km) Turnout to east with view of Tutshi Lake.

S 46.4 (75.1 km) **AH 52.4** (84.3 km) To the east is the **Venus Mines concentrator**, with a capacity of 150 tons per day. A drop in silver prices caused the Venus mill's closure in October 1981.

S 48.5 (78.1 km) **AH 50.3** (81 km) South end of Windy Arm, an extension of Tagish Lake.

S 49.2 (79.2 km) **AH 49.6** (79.9 km) Viewpoint to east.

S 49.9 (80.5 km) **AH 48.9** (78.7 km) Dall Creek.

S 50.2 (81 km) **AH 48.6** (78.2 km) **BC–YT border.** Turnout with picnic table and litter barrel to east overlooking Windy Arm.

Yukon Resources wildlife viewing guide suggests searching the slopes of Montana Mountain to the northwest and Racine Mountain to the southwest for signs of mountain goats and Dall sheep in the summer.

YUKON HIGHWAY 2

S 51.9 (83.5 km) **AH 46.9** (75.5 km) Large turnout to east with litter barrel, picnic table and historical information sign about Venus Mines.

The first claim on Montana Mountain was staked by W.R. Young in 1899. By 1904 all of the mountain's gold veins had been claimed. In 1905, New York financier Col. Joseph H. Conrad acquired most of the Montana Mountain claims, formed Conrad Consolidated Mines, and began exploration and mining. A town of about 300 people sprang up along Windy Arm and an aerial tramway was built from the Conrad townsite up the side of Montana Mountain to the Mountain Hero adit. (This tramline, visible from the highway, was completed in 1906 but was never used to ship ore because the Mountain Hero tunnel did not find a vein.) More tramways and a mill were constructed, but by 1911 Conrad was forced into bankruptcy: The ore was not as rich as estimated and only a small quantity of ore was milled before operations ceased.

Small mining operations continued over the years, with unsuccessful start-ups by various mining interests. United Keno Hill Mines (Venus Division) acquired the mining claims in 1979, constructed a 100-ton-per-day mill and rehabilitated the old mine workings in 1980.

S 52.9 (85.1 km) **AH 45.9** (73.8 km) Pooly Creek and canyon, named for J.M. Pooly, who staked the first Venus claims in 1901.

Access road east to Pooly Point and Venus Mines maintenance garage, trailers and security station. No services, facilities or admittance.

S 54.2 (87.2 km) **AH 44.6** (71.8 km) Venus Mines ore storage bin and foundation of old mill to east. The mill was built in the late 1960s, then disassembled and sold about 1970. A sign here warns of arsenic being present: Do not pick or eat berries.

S 55.7 (89.6 km) **AH 43.1** (69.4 km) Tramline support just east of highway.

S 59.5 (95.8 km) **AH 39.3** (63.3 km) Turnout with historic information sign. Lt. F. Schwatka, US Army, renamed Tagish Lake in 1883 after Lt. Bove of the Italian navy, who had served with the Austro-Hungarian Expedition of 1872-74. Dr. G.M. Dawson, GSC, gave Tagish Lake its original name in 1887 and left Bove's name on the island. Magnificent views along here of Windy Arm and its islands (Bove is the larger island). Windy Arm is an extension of Tagish Lake. Lime Mountain (elev. 5,225 feet/1,593m) rises to the east beyond Bove Island.

S 63.5 (102.2 km) **AH 35.3** (56.8 km) Sections of the old government wagon roads that once linked Carcross, Conrad and other mining claims, visible on either side of the highway.

S 66 (106.2 km) **AH 32.8** (52.7 km) Nares Bridge crosses the narrows between Lake Bennett to the west and Tagish Lake to the east. The larger lakes freeze to an ice depth of more than 3 feet/1m.

Nares Lake, on the east side of the highway at Carcross, remains open most winters, despite air temperatures that drop well below -40°F/-40°C. In spring and fall look for swans, teal, pintail, goldeneye and wigeon. This is one of the few areas in the Yukon where waterfowl may be seen in winter.

Carcross visitor centre is located in the old White Pass & Yukon Route train station.
(© Earl L. Brown, staff)

Caribou Mountain (elev. 5,645 feet/1,721m) is visible to the east.

S 66.2 (106.5 km) **AH 32.6** (52.4 km) Turnoff west for Carcross (description follows).

Carcross

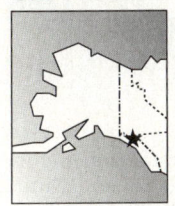

On the shore of Lake Bennett, 44 miles/71 km southeast of Whitehorse. **Population:** 400. **Emergency Services: RCMP**, phone (867) 821-5555. **Fire Department**, phone (867) 821-2222. **Ambulance**, phone (867) 821-4444. **Health Centre**, phone (867) 821-4444.

Visitor Information: Carcross Visitor Reception Centre, operated by Tourism Yukon, is located in the old White Pass & Yukon Route train station. Open daily from 8 A.M. to 8 P.M., mid-May to mid-September; phone (867) 821-4431. Yukon and Alaska travel information.

Elevation: 2,175 feet/663m. **Climate:** Average temperature in January, -4.2°F/-20.1°C; in July, 55.4°F/13°C. Annual rainfall 11 inches, snowfall 2 to 3 feet. Driest month is April, wettest month August. **Radio:** 590-AM, CHON-FM 90.5, CKRW. **Television:** CBC. **Transportation: Bus**—Scheduled bus service by Atlin Express Service, between Atlin and Whitehorse via Tagish and Carcross, 3 times weekly. Chilkoot Trail hikers should check with visitor centre for boat and bus connections.

Private Aircraft: Carcross airstrip, 0.3 mile/0.5 km north of town via highway; elev. 2,161 feet/659m; length 2,000 feet/610m.

Carcross has a bed and breakfast, a general store and a gift shop. Camping at Carcross government campground near the airstrip and at Montana Services and RV Park and Carcross government campground, which provides a gas station with gifts, groceries, laundromat, showers, RV park and cafe located on the highway. ▲

Carcross was formerly known as Caribou Crossing because of the large numbers of caribou that traversed the narrows here between Bennett and Nares lakes. In 1903 Bishop Bompas, who had established a school here for Native children in 1901, petitioned the government to change the name of the community to Carcross because of confusion in mail services due to duplicate names in Alaska, British Columbia and the Klondike. The post office made the change official the following year, but it took the WP&YR until 1916 to change the name of its station.

Carcross became a stopping place for gold stampeders on their way to the Klondike goldfields. It was a major stop on the White Pass & Yukon Route railroad from 1900 until 1982, when the railroad ceased operation. Passengers and freight transferred from rail to stern-wheelers at Carcross. One of these stern-wheelers, the SS *Tutshi* (too-shy), was a historic site here in town until it

---

MONTANA SERVICES & RV PARK
- SHELL GAS • LPG • LAUNDROMAT
- GROCERY STORE
- R.V. WASH • SHOWERS
- RESTAURANT • ICE CREAM

Box 75
Carcross, Yukon
Y0B-1B0
PH: 867-821-3708
FAX: 867-821-3503

FULL SERVICE PULL-THRU SITES (30 amp - 50 amp)
"Don't let the hills get you down - leave your RV while you drive around"

SOUTH KLONDIKE HIGHWAY • Carcross

burned down in July 1990. The WP&YR Boathouse (Koolseen Place) has been restored. Located behind the visitor centre, the boathouse contains historical photographs.

A cairn beside the railroad station marks the site where construction crews laying track for the White Pass & Yukon Route from Skagway met the crew from Whitehorse. The golden spike was set in place when the last rail was laid at Carcross on July 29, 1900. The construction project had begun May 27, 1898, during the height of the Klondike Gold Rush.

Other visitor attractions include St. Saviour's Anglican Church, built in 1902; the Royal Mail Carriage; and the little locomotive *Duchess*, which operated on the 2.5-mile portage between Lake Tagish and Lake Atlin until 1921. Caribou Crossing Trading Post, 2 miles/3.2 km north of town on the highway, is also a popular attraction.

On sunny days you may sunbathe and picnic at Sandy Beach on Lake Bennett. Or swim at Carcross Pool; for information call (867) 821-3211. Isabelle Pringle Public Library presents programs and displays; phone (867) 821-3801.

Behind the post office there is a footbridge across Natasaheenie River. This small body of water joins Lake Bennett and Nares Lake. Check locally for boat tours and boat service on Bennett Lake. Fishing in **Lake Bennett** for lake trout, northern pike, arctic grayling, whitefish and cisco.

Montana Services & RV Park. See display ad this section. ▲

South Klondike Highway Log
(continued)

S 66.4 (106.9 km) **AH 32.4** (52.1 km) Airstrip to east. Turn on access road directly north of airstrip for Yukon government **Carcross Campground**; 12 campsites, picnic tables, firewood, drinking water, outhouses, camping permit ($12). ▲

S 66.5 (107 km) **AH 32.3** (52 km)

Junction with Tagish Road (Yukon Highway 8), which leads east to Tagish, Atlin Road and the Alaska Highway at Jake's Corner. See TAGISH ROAD log on page 714.

Tagish Road junctions with the Alaska Highway at **Milepost DC 836.8**, 37.6 miles east of the South Klondike Highway junction with the Alaska Highway.

S 67.3 (108.3 km) **AH 31.5** (50.7 km) Turnout with point of interest sign about **Carcross Desert**. This unusual desert area of sand dunes, east of the highway between Kilometreposts 108 and 110, is the world's smallest desert and an International Biophysical Programme site for ecological studies. The desert is composed of sandy lake-bottom material left behind by a large glacial lake. Strong winds off Lake Bennett make it difficult for vegetation to take hold here; only lodgepole pine, spruce and kinnikinnick survive. (Kinnikinnick is a low trailing evergreen with small leathery leaves; used for tea.)

S 67.9 (108.6 km) **AH 30.9** (49.7 km) **Caribou Crossing Trading Post** near Carcross enroute to Skagway. Open mid-May to mid-September. The world's largest bear is displayed in the wildlife gallery along with Yukon and Ice Age mammals. The gift shop features Yukon made products and the coffee bar hosts a delightful array of baked

goods including our famous homemade "Mom's Donuts!" We have a convenient pull-through drive for RVs and caravans. Free parking for your RV with museum ticket when you unhitch to visit Skagway. Seating available for large groups with advance booking. Mention *The MILEPOST®* for 10% admission discount. Phone (867) 821-4055; cariboucrossing@yt.sympatico.ca; www.cariboucrossing.ca. [ADVERTISEMENT]

S 70.3 (112.3 km) **AH 28.5** (45.9 km) Dry Creek.

S 71.2 (113.8 km) **AH 27.6** (44.4 km) Carl's Creek.

S 71.9 (115.7 km) **AH 26.9** (43.3 km) Cinnamon Cache Bakery Coffee Shop.

S 72.1 (115 km) **AH 26.7** (43 km) **Spirit Lake Wilderness Resort**. All the right

reasons to visit. Licensed restaurant; try our world-famous Dutch apple pie and Dutch pancakes. Ice cream and off sales. New log-style motel, lakeside cabins. Rates starting at $59. Quiet and peaceful treed campground, breathtaking view, hiking trail, fishing, canoe rentals, horseback riding. RV sites with 30-amp power, dump station and water fill-up, showers. Phone/fax (867) 821-4337; www.spiritlakeyukon.com. [ADVERTISEMENT] ▲

S 73.2 (116.8 km) **AH 25.6** (41.2 km) Spirit Lake is visible to the east.

S 73.5 (117.3 km) **AH 25.3** (40.7 km) Large turnout with point of interest sign to west overlooking beautiful **Emerald Lake**, also called **Rainbow Lake** by Yukoners. (Good view of lake by climbing the hill across from the turnout.) The rainbow-like colors of the lake result from blue-green light waves reflecting off the white sediment of the lake bottom. This white sediment, called marl, consists of fragments of decomposed shell mixed with clay; it is usually found in shallow, freshwater lakes

that have low oxygen levels during the summer months.

S 75.4 (120.3 km) **AH 23.4** (37.7 km) Highway follows base of Caribou Mountain (elev. 5,645 feet/1,721m). View of Montana Mountain to south, Caribou Mountain to east and Gray Ridge Range to the west between Kilometreposts 122 and 128. Flora consists of jack and lodgepole pine.

S 79.8 (127.1 km) **AH 19** (30.6 km) Highway crosses Lewes Creek.

S 85.4 (136.3 km) **AH 13.4** (21.6 km) Access road west leads 1 mile/1.6 km to Lewes Lake.

S 85.6 (136.5 km) **AH 13.2** (21.2 km) Rat Lake to west.

S 86.7 (138.2 km) **AH 12.1** (19.4 km) Bear Creek.

S 87.3 (139.1 km) **AH 11.5** (18.5 km) Access road west to large gravel pull-through with historic information sign about Robinson and view of Robinson. In 1899, the White Pass & Yukon Route built a railroad siding at Robinson (named for Stikine Bill Robinson). Gold was discovered nearby in the early 1900s and a townsite was surveyed. A few buildings were constructed and a post office, manned by Charlie McConnell, operated from 1909 to 1915. Low mineral yields caused Robinson to be abandoned, but postmaster McConnell stayed and established one of the first ranches in the Yukon. Robinson is accessible from Annie Lake Road (see next milepost).

S 87.5 (139.4 km) **AH 11.3** (18.2 km) **Annie Lake Road** leads 0.8 mile/1.4 km to Annie Lake golf course, 1.9 miles/3.1 km to McConnell Lake and 11 miles/17.7 km to Annie Lake.

Yukon Resources wildlife viewing guide suggests a side trip on Annie Lake Road. Look for Dall sheep on cliffs on west side of road. There are many hiking routes along old mining roads into the interior of the coastal mountains. Birdwatching for gyrfalcons, golden eagles and ptarmigan (willow, rock and white-tailed). The Southern Lakes caribou herd resides here year-round; found in alpine terrain in summer.

Beyond Annie Lake this side road crosses the Wheaton River, entering the Wheaton Valley–Mount Skukum area. For the adventuresome, this is beautiful and interesting country. *CAUTION: Road can be very muddy during spring breakup or during rain.*

S 93 (148.5 km) **AH 5.8** (9.4 km) Turnoff west for Cowley and for access to Cowley Lake (1.6 miles/2.6 km).

S 95.5 (154.2 km) **AH 3.3** (5.3 km) Turnoff to east for Yukon government **Kookatsoon Lake Recreation Site** (day use only); picnic tables, firepits, pit toilets, canoe launch. Kookatsoon Lake is shallow and usually warm enough for swimming in summer. Look for Bonaparte's gulls and arctic terns nesting at the south end of the lake.

S 98.4 (156.5 km) **AH 0.4** (0.7 km) Rock shop on east side of road.

S 98.8 (157.1 km) **AH 0** Turn left (northwest) for Whitehorse, right (southeast) for Watson Lake.

Junction with the Alaska Highway. Turn to Milepost DC 874.4 on page 147 in the ALASKA HIGHWAY section: Whitehorse-bound travelers continue with that log; travelers heading south down the Alaska Highway read that log back to front.

ATLIN ROAD

Connects: Tagish Road Jct. to Atlin, BC
Road Surface: 60% gravel, 40% paved
Major Attraction: Atlin Lake
Length: 58 miles
Season: Open all year

(See map, page 707)

	Atlin	Carcross	Jake's Corner	Skagway	Whitehorse
Atlin		92	59	158	106
Carcross	92		35	66	43
Jake's Corner	59	35		101	47
Skagway	158	66	101		109
Whitehorse	106	43	47	109	

Mount Minto is reflected in the still waters of Atlin Lake. (© Ralph & Leonor Barrett)

This 58-mile/93.3-km all-weather road leads south to the pioneer gold mining town of Atlin. Built in 1949 by the Canadian Army Engineers, Atlin Road is a good road, usually in excellent condition, with some winding sections. The first 40 miles/64.4 km are gravel, with the remaining 18 miles/29 km into Atlin paved. Watch for slippery spots in wet weather.

To reach Atlin Road, turn south at Jake's Corner, **Milepost DC 836.8** on the Alaska Highway; drive 1.1 miles/1.8 km to the junction of Atlin Road (Highway 7) and Tagish Road (Highway 8); turn left (south) for Atlin.

It is about a 2½-hour drive to Atlin from Whitehorse, and the lake scenery from the village is well worth the trip. For more information contact the Atlin Visitors Assoc., Box 365, Atlin, BC V0W 1A0. Or phone the Atlin museum at (250) 651-7522 for visitor information.

Atlin Road Log

Distance from Tagish Road junction (J) is shown.
Physical kilometreposts in Yukon Territory and mileposts in British Columbia show distance from Tagish Road junction.

J 0 Junction of Tagish and Atlin roads.

J 1.4 (2.3 km) Fish Creek crossing. The road is bordered by many low-lying, boggy areas brilliant green with horsetail (*equisetium*).

J 1.8 (2.9 km) Side road west to Little Atlin Lake. Atlin Road descends along east shoreline of Little Atlin Lake approximately 7.6 miles/12.2 km southbound. During midsummer, the roadsides are ablaze with fireweed and wild roses.

J 2.4 (3.9 km) Large turnout to west on Little Atlin Lake; informal boat launch, dumpster, outhouse and camping area. Mount Minto (elev. 6,913 feet/2,107m) can be seen to the southwest. Road climbs southbound.

J 2.8 (4.5 km) Turnout to west. Watch for bald eagles.

J 3.8 (6 km) **Little Atlin Lodge.** (Watch for turnoff at Kilometrepost 6.) Discover our spacious comfortable lakefront guesthouses in a pristine peaceful setting. Enjoy the handsomely finished 2-story accommodations with fully equipped kitchens, separate bedrooms, comfortable bathrooms and relaxation decks (minimum stay 2 nights). An idyllic place to retreat. Photography and wildlife viewing opportunities, canoe and motorboat rentals, guided tours summer and winter. Call for reservations and information. Phone/fax (867) 393-1644; e-mail: lal@yukon.net; www.littleatlinlodge.com.
[ADVERTISEMENT]

J 5 (8 km) Information sign to east about 1983–84 mountain goat transplant. The 12 goats were brought from Kluane National Park. They may be observed on the mountainsides.

J 7.8 (12.6 km) Private campground, cabins and boat rentals.

J 8.1 (13 km) Greenhouse and farm, roadside vegetable stand in season. Haunka Creek. Turnout to west.

J 8.9 (14.3 km) Good view of Mount Minto ahead southbound.

J 13.8 (22.2 km) Unmarked side road leads 2.4 miles/3.9 km to **Lubbock River**, which connects Little Atlin Lake with Atlin Lake. Excellent for grayling from breakup to mid-September.

J 15.5 (24.9 km) Snafu Creek. Turnout to west, north of bridge. According to R. Coutts, author of "Yukon Places & Names," the creek name is an acronym bestowed by army crews who built the road. It stands for Situation Normal—All Fouled Up. (Mr. Coutts resides in Atlin.)

J 16.4 (26 km) Access road leads 0.7 mile/1.1 km to **Snafu Lake** Yukon government campground; 4 sites, camping permit ($12), pit toilets, tables, gravel boat ramp, good fishing.

J 18.6 (29.9 km) Tarfu Creek. Small turnout to east, north of bridge. Creek name is another army acronym. This one stands for Things Are Really Fouled Up.

J 18.7 (30 km) Abandoned cabin and turnout to west.

J 20.4 (32.8 km) Turnoff to east for **Tarfu Lake** Yukon government campground via 2.4-mile/3.8-km side road; 4 sites, camping permit ($12), pit toilets, fishing. Steep grade near campground; not recommended for large RVs or trailers.

J 20.5 (33 km) Short narrow side road leads east to Marcella Lake; good lake for canoeing.

J 21.8 (35.1 km) Turnout to west with view of Atlin Lake, which covers 307 square miles/798 square km and is the largest natural lake in British Columbia. Coast Mountains to the southwest.

J 25.8 (41.5 km) BC–YT border. Road follows east shoreline of Atlin Lake into Atlin.

J 27 (43.5 km) Mount Minto to west, Black Mountain to east, and Halcro Peak (elev. 5,856 feet/1,785m) to the southeast.

J 28.5 (45.8 km) Slow down for sharp curve.

J 32 (51.5 km) Excellent views of Coast Mountains, southwest across Atlin Lake, next 6 miles/9.7 km southbound.

J 32.7 (52.6 km) **Hitchcock Creek**, grayling to 2 lbs.

J 32.8 (52.7 km) Campground on Atlin Lake; 6 sites, pit toilets, tables, ramp for small boats.

J 36.3 (58.4 km) Turnout with litter barrel to west. Base Camp Creek.

J 36.8 (59.2 km) **Historic Milepost 38.**

J 40 (64.4 km) Indian River. Pull-through turnout south of creek. Highway is paved from here to Atlin.

J 40.2 (64.7 km) Big-game outfitter/guest ranch to east. Watch for horses.

J 45.3 (72.9 km) Turnout to west.

J 49.8 (80.1 km) Burnt Creek.

J 49.9 (80.3 km) Davie Hall Lake and turnout to west. Waterfowl are plentiful on lake.

J 51.6 (83 km) Ruffner Mine Road leads east 40 miles/64.4 km. Access to **MacDonald Lake**, 2 miles/3.2 km east; bird watching and lake trout fishing from spit.

J 52.8 (85 km) Fourth of July Creek.

J 53.4 (85.9 km) Spruce Mountain (elev. 5,141 feet/1,567m) to west.

J 55.1 (88.7 km) Road skirts east shore of Como Lake next 0.6 mile/1 km southbound.

J 55.2 (88.8 km) Turnout with litter barrel to west on **Como Lake**; good lake for canoeing, also used by floatplanes. Stocked with rainbow.

J 55.7 (89.6 km) South end of Como Lake; boat ramp.

J 57.1 (91.9 km) Atlin city limits.

J 58 (93.3 km) **Junction** of Atlin Road with Discovery Road. Turn right (west) on Discovery Avenue for town of Atlin; description follows. Turn left (east) for Discovery Road and Warm Bay Road (see description of these side roads in Atlin Attractions).

Atlin

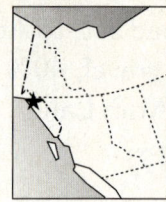

The most northwesterly town in British Columbia, located 112 miles/180 km southeast of Whitehorse, YT. **Population:** Approximately 500. **Emergency Services: Police**, phone (250) 651-7511. **Fire Department**, phone (250) 651-7666. **Ambulance**, phone (250) 651-7700. Red Cross outpost clinic, phone (250) 651-7677.

Visitor Information: Contact the Atlin Visitors Assoc., P.O. Box 365, Atlin, BC V0W 1A0; Toll free 1-877-399-2665; visitors@atlin.net; www.atlin.net. Information is also available at the Atlin Historical Museum.; phone (250) 651-7522.

Elevation: 2,240 feet/683m. **Radio:** CBC FM 90.1 (Whitehorse), CHON FM 96.1 (Whitehorse), CFMI FM 99.9 (Vancouver). **Television:** 3 channels (CBC, BCTV and the Knowledge Network).

Private Aircraft: Peterson Field, 1 mile/1.6 km northeast; elev. 2,348 feet/716m; length 3,950 feet/1,204m; gravel.

Transportation: Air—Charter service from Juneau. **Bus**—Service from Whitehorse 3 times a week.

Referred to by some visitors as Shangri-la, the village of Atlin overlooks the crystal clear water of 90-mile/145-km-long Atlin Lake and is surrounded by spectacular mountains. On Teresa Island in Atlin Lake is Birch Mountain (elev. 6,755 feet/2,060m), the highest point in fresh water in the world.

Atlin was founded in 1898. The name was taken from the Indian dialect and means Big Water. The Atlin Lake area was one of the richest gold strikes made during the great rush to the Klondike in 1897–98. The first claims were registered here on July 30, 1898, by Fritz Miller and Kenneth McLaren.

Lodging & Services

The village has a hotel, inns, cottages, bed and breakfasts, RV parking, laundromat (with showers), restaurants, gas station (propane, diesel and unleaded available), auto repair, grocery, government liquor store and general stores, and a post office. Boarding kennels are available. Bus tours are welcome, but phone ahead so this small community can accommodate you.

The Atlin branch of Bank of Montreal (250/651-7795) is located at Government Agents Office on 3rd Street; open weekdays 8:30 A.M.–noon and 1–3 P.M. There are ATMs at Atlin Inn and Pine Tree Rest.

The museum and several shops feature local gold nugget jewelry, arts and crafts, and other souvenirs. Air charter service for glacier tours and fly-in fishing trips are available. Charter boats and fishing charters are also available.

Camping

RV park with electric and water hookups; pay phone and boat moorage downtown on lake. Showers and laundromat in building at Atlin entrance on Discovery St. Dump station at Mile 2.3 Discovery Road. There are also several camping areas on Atlin Road, Discovery Road and Warm Bay Road. Atlin community operates the Pine Creek campground (18 sites) at Mile 1.6 Warm Bay Road; pay camping fee ($10) at any downtown business or at the museum.

Attractions

Atlin Historical Museum, home of the Atlin Visitor Centre, open weekends during June and September, daily July through August. Located in Atlin's original 1-room schoolhouse, the museum has mining artifacts and photo exhibits of the Atlin gold rush. Gift shop features northern and Atlin books and the work of local artisans. Admission fee; phone (250) 651-7522.

The **MV *Tarahne*** (Tah-ron) sits on the lakeshore in the middle of town. Built at Atlin in 1916 by White Pass & Yukon Route, she carried passengers and freight from Atlin to Scotia Bay until 1936. (Scotia Bay is across the lake from Atlin and slightly north.) A 2-mile/3.2-km railway connected Scotia Bay on Atlin Lake to Taku Landing on Tagish Lake, where passengers arrived by boat from Carcross, YT. The *Tarahne* was the first gas-driven boat in the White Pass fleet. After she was lengthened by 30 feet in 1927, she could carry up to 198 passengers. In recent years, Atlin residents have launched a drive to restore the boat; they hope to eventually refloat the vessel and offer tours of Atlin Lake.

ATLIN ADVERTISERS

Atlin Visitors Association	Ph. (877) 399-2665
Norseman Adventures R.V. Park	Ph. (250) 651-7535
Pine Tree Services	Ph. (250) 651-7636
Quilts & Comforts Bed & Breakfast	Ph. (250) 651-0007
Simply Gold	Ph. (250) 651-7708

R.V. PARK
POWER & WATER
➤ **On the Lake Shore**
Houseboats
Powerboats
Charters

(250) 651-7535
(604) 823-2259

NORSEMAN ADVENTURES LTD.
P.O. Box 184, Atlin, BC V0W 1A0
Email: vig@uniserve.com
vig@atlin.net

DISCOVER ATLIN
"Its a trip you won't forget"

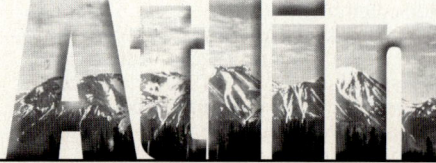

Full Services Include:

- Sporting Goods
- Air Craft Charters
- Canoes & Kayaks
- Fly in Salmon Fishing
- Glacier Flights
- Chartered House Boats
- Local Art
- Accommodations
- Restaurant & Lounges
- Entertainment
- Marina & Boat Launch
- Chartered Jet Boats
- Freight Deliveries
- Groceries & Bakery
- Weekly Bingo & Lottery
- Automotive Mechanic
- Hair Dresser
- Booking Agency

For reservations and information, call
Toll Free **1-877-399-BOOK** (2665)

Email: visitors@atlin.net
website: www.atlin.net
PO Box 365M, Atlin BC V0W 1A0

Globe Theatre and the Garrett Store in downtown Atlin. (© Earl L. Brown, staff)

ATLIN ROAD

Simply Gold (located on historic Pearl Avenue). Visit a workshop/showroom filled with award-winning handcrafted jewellry. Each piece is designed and fabricated on the premises by Kathryn Taylor/goldsmith. Nuggets are carefully selected from the best of Atlin's placer gold, then designed to enhance their individual character. Premier craftsmanship, enduring quality and unique designs set her work apart. Take this opportunity to visit Atlin and discover the treasures at Simply Gold. (250) 651-7708. [ADVERTISEMENT]

Participate in a Murder Mystery. Atlin residents hold a murder mystery theatre on Saturday evenings. For information, call toll free 1-877-399-BOOK. Reservations are strongly suggested as this is a very popular event.

The Globe Theatre, built in 1917, was restored by the Atlin Historical Society and re-opened in 1998. Information is available from the Atlin Museum, (250) 651-7522. A Coffee House is held at the Globe Theatre every month, featuring local talent doing skits, songs, readings, story telling, etc. The theatre also has weekly showings of old movies; call for details.

The Pioneer Cemetery, located at Mile 1.1 Discovery Road, contains the weathered grave markers of early gold seekers, including Fritz Miller and Kenneth McLaren, who made the first gold discovery in the Atlin area in July 1898. Also buried here is Walter Gladstone Sweet, reputed to have been a card dealer for Soapy Smith in Skagway.

Public Gold Panning Area has been set aside on Spruce Creek. Turn off Discovery Road at Mile 3.6. Check at the museum for details. Gold pans available locally for rent or purchase.

Take a Hike. At Mile 2.3 Warm Bay Road are 2 trails: the 3-mile/4.8-km Monarch trail and the short, easy Beach trail. The Monarch trail is a moderately strenuous hike with a steep climb at the end to a bird's-eye view of the area.

Tours and Rentals. Motorbike rentals; houseboat rentals; kayak, canoe and boat rentals; boat tours of Atlin and Tagish lakes, guided fishing trips and marine gas are available. Wilderness adventures from Atlin Quest Jet Boat Tours. Helicopter service, floatplanes for charter hunting and fishing trips and flight-seeing trips of Llewellyn Glacier and the Atlin area are also available.

Atlin Provincial Park, accessible by boat or plane only (charters available in Atlin). Spectacular wilderness area; varied topography; exceptional wildlife habitat.

Visit the mineral springs at the north end of town, where you may have a drink of sparkling cold mineral water. The gazebo-like structure over the springs was built by White Pass in 1922. Picnic area nearby. Other natural springs are found on Warm Bay Road (see description following).

Take a Drive. 13-mile/21-km Discovery Road and 16.5-mile/26.5-km Warm Bay Road are both suitable for passenger cars and RVs, and both offer sightseeing and recreation (mile-by-mile descriptions of both roads follow).

Discovery Road is a good, wide gravel road, bumpy in spots. At Mile 1.1, across from Atlin airport, is the pioneer cemetery, which contains grave markers and monuments to many of Atlin's historical figures. At Mile 3.5 is a turnout with view of Pine Creek and falls. At Mile 3.6 turnoff on to Spruce Creek Road, which leads south 0.9 mile/1.4 km to a designated public recreational gold panning area and 1.5 miles/2.4 km to active gold mining on Spruce Creek (no tours but operations can be photographed from the road). This side road is signed as rough and narrow; suitable for cars, vans and pickups.

Continue on Discovery Road to Mile 5.4 for former townsite of **Discovery**, originally called Pine Creek, now a ghost town. In its boom days, the town supplied miners working in the area.

Beyond Surprise Lake Dam bridge at Mile 11.8, Discovery Road become steep and winding for 1.2 miles/1.9 km until the road dead-ends along Boulder Creek. **Surprise Lake** recreation site has some campsites, pit toilets, picnic tables, firepits, and a boat launch for cartop boats and canoes. A gold mining operation is visible across the lake.

Warm Bay Road begins at Mile 0.3 on Discovery Road and leads south 16.5 miles/ 26.5 km to numerous points of interest and 5 camping areas. At Mile 1.6 is Pine Creek Campground and picnic area, and a short trail to Pine Creek. At Mile 2 is Atlin Art Centre. At Mile 2.3 is the trailhead for the easy Beach trail and for the more strenuous Monarch trail to the 4,723-foot/1,439-m summit of Monarch Mountain (scenic vista of Atlin area).

At Mile 7 on Warm Bay Road is a viewpoint of Llewellyn Glacier and Atlin Lake that is a good photo spot. At Mile 9.5 you'll cross McKee Creek 1-lane bridge. The McKee Creek area has been mined since the 1890s. In July 1981, 2 area miners found what has been dubbed the "Atlin nugget," a 36.86-troy-ounce, hand-sized piece of gold.

Continue on to Mile 11.9 for Palmer Lake recreation site (camping, fishing, picnicking) or Mile 13.9 for Warm Bay recreation site on Atlin Lake; camping, fishing, picnicking and boat launch for small boats. At Mile 14.4 is **Warm Spring**, a small and shallow spring, good for soaking road-weary bones. There's also a large grassy camping area and pit toilet. The meadow streams are lined with watercress.

At Mile 16.3 is Grotto recreation site (camping and picnicking). And just beyond is **"The Grotto"**, where water flows through a hole in the rocks from an underground stream. Locals report this is a good place to obtain drinking water.

AREA FISHING: The Atlin area is well known for its good fishing. Fly-in fishing for salmon, steelhead and rainbow, or troll locally for lake trout. Grayling can be caught at the mouths of most creeks and streams or off Atlin docks. Public boat launch on Atlin Lake, south of the MV *Tarahne*. Boat charters available. British Columbia fishing licenses are available from the government agent and local outlets. Fresh and smoked salmon may be available for purchase locally in the summer.

TAGISH ROAD

Connects: Alaska Hwy. to Carcross, YT
Road Surface: 40% gravel, 60% paved
Length: 34 miles
Season: Open all year

(See map, page 707)

This 33.8-mile/54.4-km road connects the Alaska Highway with South Klondike Highway. It leads south from the Alaska Highway junction at Jake's Corner (**Milepost DC 836.8**) through the settlement of Tagish to Carcross. It is good gravel road from the Alaska Highway junction to Tagish, asphalt-surfaced between Tagish and Carcross.

Tagish Road was built in 1942 to lay a gas pipeline during construction of the Alaska Highway.

If you are traveling South Klondike Highway between Skagway and Whitehorse, Tagish Road provides access to Atlin Road and also makes a pleasant side trip. This is also a very beautiful drive in the fall; good photo opportunities.

Emergency medical services: Phone the RCMP, (867) 667-5555; ambulance, phone (867) 667-3333.

Tagish Road Log

There's good fishing from the north side of Tagish River bridge. (© Lyn Hancock)

Kilometreposts measure east to west from Alaska Highway junction to Carcross turn-off. Posts are up about every 2 kilometres. Distance from the junction (J) is followed by distance from Carcross (C).

J 0 C 33.8 (54.4 km) Jake's Corner.

Junction with the Alaska Highway. Turn to **Milepost DC 836.8** on page 146 in the ALASKA HIGHWAY section.

Drive south 1.1 miles/1.8 km from the Alaska Highway to the junction of Tagish Road and Atlin Road (Highway 7).

J 1.1 (1.8 km) C 32.7 (52.6 km) Junction of Tagish and Atlin roads. Head west on Tagish Road.

Turn southeast for Atlin, BC. See ATLIN ROAD log on page 711.

J 8.8 (14.2 km) C 25 (40.2 km) For several miles, travelers may see the Northwes-Tel microwave tower on Jubilee Mountain (elev. 5,950 feet/ 1,814m) to the south between Little Atlin Lake and Tagish River. Jubilee Mountain was named by Dr. G.M. Dawson in 1887 in honor of Queen Victoria's Jubilee.

J 12.8 (20.6 km) C 21 (33.8 km) *Gravel ends, pavement begins, westbound.* Tagish Yukon government campground, on **Six Mile River** between Marsh Lake to the north and Tagish Lake to the south. Good fishing, boat launch, picnic area, playground, kitchen shelter, 28 campsites with firepits and tables, drinking water and toilets. Camping permit ($2). *CAUTION: Watch for black bears.*

J 13 (20.9 km) C 20.8 (33.5 km) Gas, oil, minor repairs, snacks and post office. Pay phone on road. Marina on north side of road at east end of Tagish bridge has bait, tackle, fishing licenses, boat rental.

J 13.1 (21 km) C 20.7 (33.3 km) **Tagish River Bridge.** Good fishing from north side of bridge on anglers' walkway for lake trout, arctic grayling, northern pike, whitefish and cisco.

West end of bridge has a day-use area with parking, 4 picnic sites and water pump.

J 13.5 (21.7 km) C 20.3 (32.6 km) Improved gravel road leads through parklike area to settlement of **TAGISH** (pop. about 160) on Tagish River between Marsh and Tagish lakes. Tagish means "fish trap" in the local Indian dialect. It was traditionally an Indian meeting place in the spring on the way to set up fish camps and again in the fall to celebrate the catch. Post office at Tagish Service at east end of Tagish bridge.

Two miles/3.2 km south of Tagish on the Tagish River is **TAGISH POST**, originally named Fort Sifton, the Canadian customs post established in 1897. Two of the original 5 buildings still stand. The North West Mounted Police and Canadian customs collected duties on thousands of tons of freight carried by stampeders on their way to the Klondike goldfields between September 1897 and February 1898.

J 16.3 (26.2 km) C 17.5 (28.1 km) Side road leads 1.2 miles/2 km to homes and **Tagish Lake**; fishing for trout, pike and grayling.

J 23 (37 km) C 10.8 (17.4 km) Bryden Creek.

J 23.8 (38.3 km) C 10 (16 km) Access to Tagish Lake Resort (8 miles to lake).

J 24.8 (39.9 km) C 9 (14.4 km) Crag Lake. Road now enters more mountainous region westbound. Caribou Mountain (elev. 5,645 feet/1,721m) on right.

J 27.2 (43.8 km) C 6.6 (10.6 km) Porcupine Creek.

J 27.5 (44.3 km) C 6.3 (10.1 km) **Historic Milepost 7.**

J 28.4 (45.7 km) C 5.4 (8.7 km) Pain Creek.

J 30.2 (48.6 km) C 3.6 (5.8 km) Side road to Chooutla Lake.

J 31 (49.9 km) C 2.8 (4.5 km) First glimpse westbound of Montana Mountain (elev. 7,230 feet/2,204m) across narrows at Carcross.

J 33.8 (54.4 km) C 0 Tagish Road ends westbound; turn left for Carcross, right for Whitehorse.

Junction with South Klondike Highway. See **Milepost S 66.5** on page 710 in the SOUTH KLONDIKE HIGHWAY section for log.

CAMPBELL HIGHWAY

	Carmacks	Dawson City	Faro	Ross River	Watson Lake
Carmacks		225	115	150	375
Dawson City	225		338	373	598
Faro	115	338		32	271
Ross River	150	373	32		239
Watson Lake	375	598	271	239	

Connects: Watson Lake, YT, to Klondike Hwy. **Length:** 362 miles
Road Surface: 85% gravel, 15% paved **Season:** Open all year
Major Attraction: Pelly River, Campbell Region Interpretive Centre

(See maps, page 716)

A sunny day brightens fall colors at Finlayson Lake on the Campbell Highway.
(© Earl L. Brown, staff)

Named for Robert Campbell, the first white man to penetrate what is now known as Yukon Territory, this all-weather, mostly gravel road leads 362 miles/583 km northwest from the Alaska Highway at Watson Lake, to junction with the Klondike Highway just north of Carmacks (see the KLONDIKE LOOP section). Gas is available at Watson Lake, Ross River, Faro and Carmacks.

The highway is gravel with the exception of stretches of pavement at Watson Lake, Ross River and the Klondike Highway junction (see map). *NOTE: Drive with your headlights on at all times.*

The Campbell Highway is an alternative route to Dawson City. It is about 20 miles/32 km shorter than driving the Alaska Highway through to Whitehorse, then driving up the Klondike Highway to Dawson City.

The Robert Campbell Highway was completed in 1968 and closely follows sections of the fur trade route established by Robert Campbell. Campbell was a Hudson's Bay Co. trader who was sent into the region in the 1840s to find a route west into the unexplored regions of central Yukon. Traveling from the southeast, he followed the Liard and Frances rivers, building a chain of posts along the way. His major discovery came in 1843, when he reached the Yukon River, which was to become the major transportation route within the Yukon.

Emergency medical services: Phone the RCMP or ambulance in Watson Lake, Ross River or Carmacks. Or phone toll free, Yukon-wide, the RCMP at (867) 667-5555, or the ambulance at (867) 667-3333.

Campbell Highway Log

Distance from Watson Lake (WL) is followed by distance from junction with the Klondike Highway just north of Carmacks (J).

YUKON HIGHWAY 4
WL 0 J 362.2 (582.9km) **WATSON LAKE.**

Junction of the Campbell Highway with the Alaska Highway. Turn to description of Watson Lake beginning on page 133 in the ALASKA HIGHWAY section.

WL 4.3 (6.9 km) **J 357.9** (576 km) Access road on right northbound to Mount Maichen ski hill.

WL 6.3 (10.1 km) **J 355.9** (572.7 km) Airport Road left to Watson Lake airport.

WL 6.4 (103. km) **J 355.8** (572.6 km) Sign advises no gas next 383 km (238 miles).

WL 6.7 (10.8 km) **J 355.5** (572.1 km) Watson Creek. The highway begins to climb to a heavily timbered plateau and then heads north following the east bank of the Frances River. Tamarack is rare in Yukon, but this northern type of larch can be seen along here. Although a member of the pine family, it sheds its needles in the fall.

WL 10.4 (16.7 km) **J 351.8** (566.2 km) MacDonald Creek.

WL 22.3 (35.9 km) **J 339.9** (547 km) Tom Creek, named after an Indian trapper whose cabin is at the mouth of the stream.

WL 29.1 (46.9 km) **J 333.1** (536.1 km) Sa Dena Hes Mine access.

WL 35.5 (57.1 km) **J 326.7** (525.8 km) **Frances River** bridge. Turnout at north end of bridge; picnic spot. Named by Robert Campbell for the wife of Sir George Simpson, governor of the Hudson's Bay Co. for 40 years, the Frances River is a tributary of the Liard River. The Frances River was part of Hudson's Bay Co.'s route into central Yukon for many years before being abandoned because of its dangerous rapids and canyons.

WL 46.1 (74.2 km) **J 316.1** (508.7 km) Lucky Creek.

WL 48.3 (77.8 km) **J 313.9** (505.2 km) Simpson Creek.

WL 50.5 (81.3 km) **J 311.7** (501.6 km) Access road leads west 1 mile/1.6 km to **Simpson Lake** Yukon government campground: 10 campsites, camping permit ($12), boat launch, dock, swimming beach, playground, kitchen shelter and drinking water (boil water). Excellent fishing for lake trout, arctic grayling and northern pike; wheelchair accessible.

WL 57.2 (92 km) **J 305** (490.8 km) Large turnout with litter barrels.

WL 57.4 (92.3 km) **J 304.8** (490.5 km) Access road west to Simpson Lake.

WL 67 (107.8 km) **J 295.2** (475.1 km) **Miner's Junction**, formerly known as Cantung Junction; no services. **Junction** with Nahanni Range Road to Tungsten (description follows).

The **Nahanni Range Road** leads 125 miles/201 km northeast to the former mining town of Tungsten, NWT. Construction of the Nahanni Range Road was begun in 1961 and completed in 1963, providing access to the mining property. The road is gravel surfaced with some washouts and soft steep shoulders. *NOTE: The Yukon government does not recommend Nahanni Range Road for*

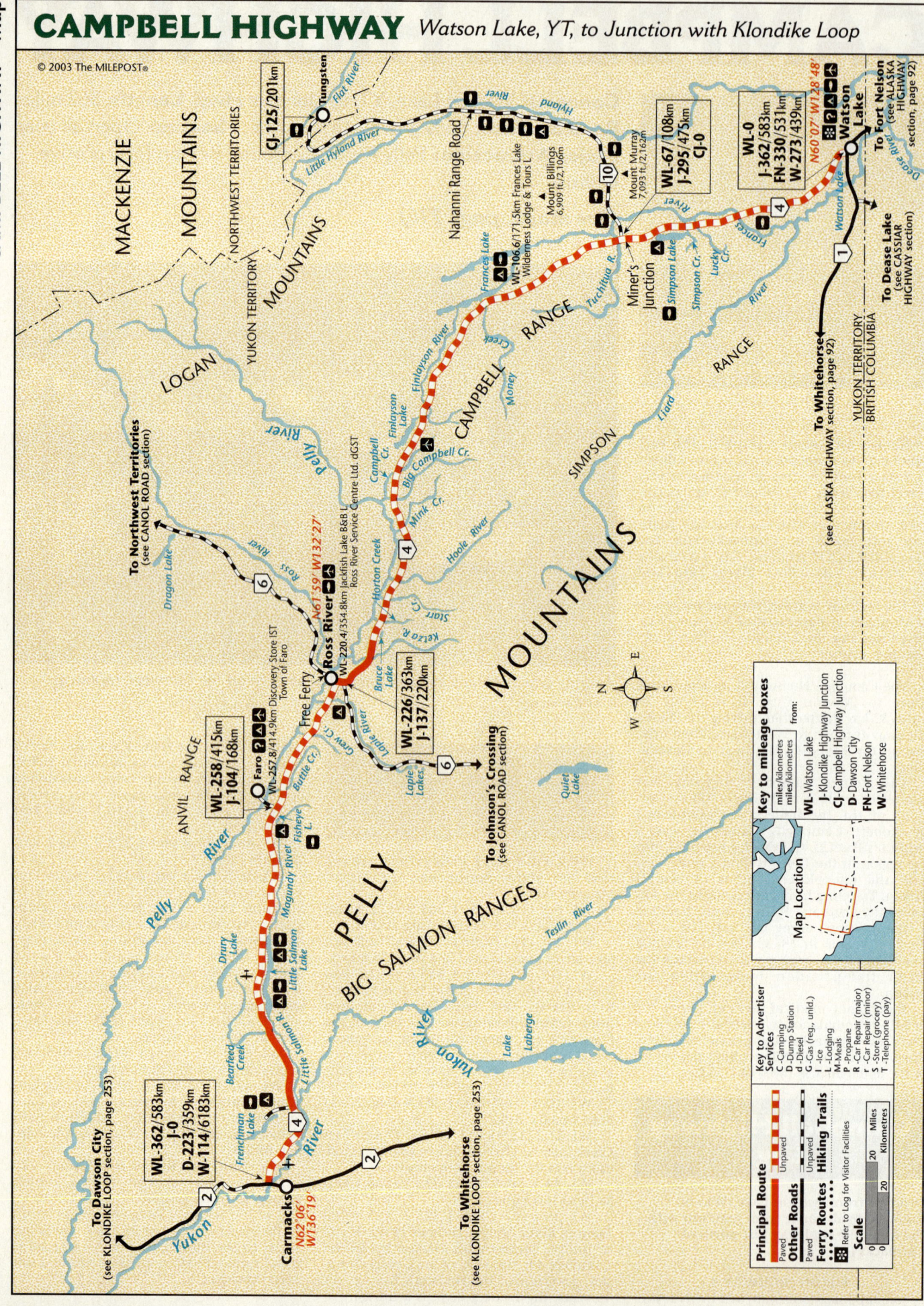

tourist travel due to lack of services. The NWT portion of the road is maintained by the mining company. Tungsten mine reopened in 2002. No visitor services.

TUNGSTEN, Canada's only tungsten producer, was originally called Cantung (Canada Tungsten Mining Corp. Ltd.). Open-pit mining began here in the early 1960s with the discovery of scheelite in the Flat River area. Scheelite is an ore of tungsten, an oxide used for hardening steel and making white gold.

WL 68.7 (110.5 km) J 293.5 (472.3 km) Yukon government Tuchitua River maintenance camp to east.

WL 68.8 (110.7 km) J 293.4 (472.2 km) One-lane bridge over Tuchitua River.

WL 98.8 (159 km) J 263.4 (423.9 km) 99 Mile Creek.

WL 104.6 (168.3 km) J 257.6 (414.6 km) Caesar Creek.

WL 106.6 (171.5 km) J 255.4 (411 km) Access road east leads 0.6 mile/1 km to Frances Lake Yukon government campground: 24 campsites, camping permit ($12), boat launch, kitchen shelter, drinking water (boil water). The solitary peak between the 2 arms of Frances Lake is Simpson Tower (elev. 5,500 feet/1,676m). It was named by Robert Campbell for Hudson's Bay Co. Governor Sir George Simpson. Fishing for lake trout, grayling and northern pike.

Frances Lake Wilderness Lodge & Tours. See display ad this section.

WL 106.6 (171.6 km) J 255.4 (410.9 km) Money Creek, named for Anton Money, a mining engineer and prospector who mined placer gold in this area between 1929 and 1946. Money later operated "The Village" service station at Mile 442 on the Alaska Highway.

WL 106.9 (172.1 km) J 255.1 (410.5 km) Gravel turnout. View southbound of Frances Lake.

WL 111.1 (178.8 km) J 250.9 (403.8 km) Dick Creek.

WL 120.9 (194.6 km) J 241.1 (388 km) Highway descends Finlayson River valley northbound. Mountains to the west are part of the Campbell Range.

WL 123.6 (198.9 km) J 238.4 (383.7 km) Light Creek.

WL 126.2 (203.1 km) J 235.8 (379.5 km) Van Bibber Creek.

WL 143 (230.1 km) J 219 (352.4 km) Finlayson Creek. Named by Robert Campbell in 1840 for Chief Factor Duncan Finlayson, who later became director of the Hudson's Bay Co. Placer gold mined at the mouth of Finlayson River in 1875 is believed to be some of the first gold mined in the territory. Finlayson Lake (elev. 3,100 feet/ 945m), on the Continental Divide, separates watersheds of Mackenzie and Yukon rivers.

WL 144 (231.7 km) J 218 (350.8 km) Access road north to Finlayson Lake picnic area; litter barrels. To the southwest are the Pelly Mountains.

WL 144.8 (233.1 km) J 217.2 (349.5 km) Turnout with observation platform and information panel on Finlayson caribou herd.

WL 153 (246.2 km) J 209 (336.3 km) Private Aircraft: Finlayson Lake airstrip to south; elev. 3,300 feet/1,006m; length 2,100 feet/640m; gravel. No services.

WL 160.4 (258.0 km) J 201.6 (324.4 km) Little Campbell Creek. Robert Campbell followed this creek to the Pelly River in 1840.

WL 166.2 (267.7 km) J 195.7 (314.9 km) Bridge over Big Campbell Creek, which flows into Pelly River at Pelly Banks. The highway follows the Pelly River for the next 90 miles/145 km.

Robert Campbell named the river and banks after Hudson's Bay Co. Governor Sir John Henry Pelly. Campbell built a trading post here in 1846; never successful, it burned down in 1849. Isaac Taylor and William S. Drury later operated a trading post at Pelly Banks, one of a string of successful posts established by their firm in remote spots throughout the Yukon from 1899 on.

WL 174 (280 km) J 188 (302.5 km) Mink Creek culvert.

WL 188.3 (303 km) J 173.7 (279.5 km) Bridge over **Hoole Canyon**; turnout to north. Confluence of the Hoole and Pelly rivers. Dig out your gold pan—this river once yielded gold.

Hoole Canyon has interesting volcanic rock formations and a walking trail that leads into the canyon.

WL 194.2 (312.5 km) J 167.8 (270 km) Starr Creek culvert.

WL 200.9 (323.3 km) J 161.1 (259.3 km) Horton Creek.

WL 205.7 (331 km) J 156.3 (251.5 km) Bruce Creek.

WL 209.2 (336.7 km) J 152.8 (245.9 km) Private side road (not maintained) leads south 27 miles/44 km through the Ketza River Valley to Ketza River Project. The first gold bar was poured at Ketza River mine in 1988. The Ketza River hard-rock gold deposit was first discovered in 1947. No visitor facilities.

The Ketza is a scenic river/mountain valley and a good area for canoeing, kayaking, hiking, climbing, mountain biking and gold panning. The valley has 3 old gold mines and an old silver mine.

WL 211.7 (340.7 km) J 150.3 (241.9 km) Ketza River. St. Cyr Range to southwest.

WL 212.9 (342.7 km) J 149.1 (239.9 km) Little Ketza Creek.

WL 215 (346.1 km) J 147 (236.6 km) Beautiful Creek culvert.

WL 218.4 (351.5 km) J 143.6 (231.1 km) **Coffee Lake** to south; local swimming hole, picnic tables, trout fishing (stocked).

WL 220.4 (354.8 km) J 141.6 (227.9 km) Ross River Flying Service; floatplane base on Jackfish Lake here.

Jackfish Lake Bed and Breakfast. See display ad this section.

Junction with South Canol Road, which leads south 129 miles/207 km to Johnson's Crossing and the Alaska Highway. See **Milepost J 136.8** in the CANOL ROAD section on page 722.

WL 220.6 (355.1 km) J 141.4 (227.6 km) Unmaintained side road on right westbound is continuation of Canol Road to Ross River. Use the main Ross River access road next milepost.

WL 225.5 (362.9 km) J 136.5 (219.7 km) Access road leads 7 miles/11.2 km to Ross River (description follows). Rest area with toilets on highway just north of this turnoff.

Ross River

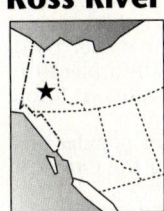

Located on the Pelly River. **Population:** about 364. **Emergency Services:** RCMP, phone (867) 969-5555. **Nursing Station**, phone (867) 969-2222. **Radio:** CBC 990 (local FM station), CHON 90.5 FM (road reports and weather). **Transportation:** Scheduled air service via Trans North Air. **Visitor Information:** www.rossriver.yk.net; www.rossriveryukon.info/; Box 115, Ross River, YT Y0B 1S0, phone (8670 969-2331, fax (867) 969-2325, email rossriverenterprises@yahoo.com.

Private Aircraft: Ross River airstrip; elev. 2,408 feet/734m; length 5,500 feet/1,676m; gravel; fuel 40.

Ross River is a supply and communication base for prospectors testing and mining mineral bodies in this region. It was named by Robert Campbell in 1843 for Chief Trader Donald Ross of the Hudson's Bay Co.

With the building of the Canol pipeline service road in WWII and the completion of the Robert Campbell Highway in 1968, Ross River was linked to the rest of the territory by road. Originally situated on the north side of the Pelly River, the town has been in its present location on the southwest bank of the river since 1964.

Ross River has hotel and bed-and-breakfast accommodations; a cultural retreat; a restaurant; a pub; a gas station with diesel, mechanical and tire repair; hardware store; guides and outfitters; grocery stores and a post office.

GET OFF THE ROAD

FRANCES LAKE WILDERNESS LODGE & TOURS

Remote location off the beaten track, no road access, pickup by boat from Frances Lake campground (175km from Watson Lake), minimum stay 2 nights in cozy lakeshore log cabins with great view. Enjoy family style hosting, full board, canoeing, daytrips, wildlife watching.

Please call collect.
Summer by radiophone:
2M3180 ON MURRAY CHANNEL
Winter by telephone or fax:
867.393.3394
online: www.franceslake.com
email: frances@internorth.com

Jackfish lake
BED AND BREAKFAST
(km 365.8 Campbell Hwy.) • Located 15 kms from Ross River
Phone: (867) 969-2212 or (867) 994-2751
For information or to leave a message
YOUR HOSTS BRIAN & COLLEEN HEMSLEY

ROSS RIVER SERVICE CENTRE LTD.

Gas & Diesel
Grocery & Hardware
Supplies

EXPEDITING SERVICES • Ask us about area fishing!

General Delivery
Ross River   Phone (867) 969-2212
Yukon Y0B 1S0   FAX (867) 969-2108

The nearest campground is Lapie Canyon (see **Milepost WL 226.5**). Self-contained RVs may overnight at the gravel parking lot at the end of the pedestrian suspension bridge on the Ross River side.

Ross River, located in the heart of the Tintina Trench, is a jumping-off point for big game hunters and canoeists. Guides and outfitters are available locally. Canoeists traveling the Pelly River can launch just downriver from the ferry crossing. Experienced canoeists recommend camping on the Pelly's many gravel bars and islets to avoid bears, bugs and the danger of accidentally setting tundra fires. The Pelly has many sweepers, sleepers and gravel shallows, some gravel shoals, and extensive channeling. There are 2 sets of rapids between Ross River and the mouth of the Pelly: Fish Hook and Granite Canyon. Water is potable (boil), firewood available and wildlife plentiful. Inquire locally about river conditions before setting out.

Wildlife viewing is a very popular area around Ross River and along the Campbell Highway. Because of its variety of terrain and geographic features, this area is said to have one of the highest concentrations of wildlife in the Yukon, including the moose, black and grizzly bears, wolves, lynx, Fannin sheep, Finlayson wooldland caribou and a variety of waterfowl and migratory birds. There are at least 160 species of birds in the Ross River area and 284 in the Yukon Territory.

Rock hounds check Pelly River gravels for jaspers and the occasional agate, and plant lovers keep your eye out for the numerous Yukon endemic plants in the area.

Other popular activities in the area include camping, biking, canoeing, fishing, kayaking and hiking in and around the many lakes and rivers in the area; photography (spectacular autumn colors); gold panning and winter activities such as snowmobiling, skiing, ice fishing and snowshoeing.

The Dena Cho Trail, scheduled to be completed in 2003, is a 49.7-mile/80-km trail that follows the original gold prospecting route between Ross River and Faro. The trail has spectacular views and will feature 5 recreation cabins and footbridge over the Orchay River when completed. For more information, contact the Ross River Dena Council at (867) 969-2277 or the Town of Faro at (867) 994-2728.

The suspension footbridge at Ross River leads across the Pelly River to the site of an abandoned Indian village 1 mile/1.6 km upstream at the mouth of the Ross River.

A government ferry crosses the Pelly River daily in summer, from 8 A.M. to noon and 1–5 P.M. Across the river, the North Canol Road leads 144 miles/232 km to Macmillan Pass at the Northwest Territories border. See the CANOL ROAD section for details.

Ross River Service Centre Ltd. See display ad this section.

Campbell Highway Log
(continued)

WL 225.5 (362.9 km) **J 136.5** (219.7 km) Access road leads 7 miles/11 km to Ross River (see preceding description).

WL 225.7 (363.3 km) **J 136.3** (219.3 km) Rest area with toilets.

WL 226.4 (364.4 km) **J 135.6** (218.2 km) **Lapie River** bridge crosses deep gorge of Lapie River, which flows into the Pelly River from Lapie Lakes on the South Canol Road. Highway continues to follow the Pelly River and Pelly Mountains.

WL 226.5 (364.5 km) **J 135.5** (218.1 km) Turnoff to left (south) to **Lapie Canyon** Yukon government campground adjacent Lapie River: short scenic trails, viewpoint, picturesque canyon; kitchen shelters, firewood, group picnic area; walk-in tent sites, 18 campsites, camping permit ($12), drinking water (boil water); boat launch; fishing for lake trout; mountain biking; access to other lakes and streams with grayling fishing.

WL 229.1 (368.8 km) **J 132.9** (213.9 km) Danger Creek.

WL 232.7 (374.5 km) **J 129.3** (208.1 km) Panoramic view of the Pelly River valley just ahead westbound.

WL 236.5 (380.6 km) **J 125.5** (202 km) Highway narrows over Grew Creek, no guide rails. This creek was named for Hudson's Bay Co. trader Jim Grew, who trapped this area for many years before his death in 1906.

WL 243.2 (391.5 km) **J 118.8** (191.2 km) Turnout to north.

WL 252.6 (406.5 km) **J 109.4** (176.1 km) Buttle Creek, named for Roy Buttle, a trapper, prospector and trader who lived here in the early 1900s and at one time owned a trading post at Ross River.

WL 257.2 (413.9 km) **J 104.8** (168.7 km) Across the wide Pelly River valley to the north is a view of the mining community of Faro.

WL 257.8 (414.9 km) **J 104.2** (167.7 km) Access road on right westbound leads 5.6 miles/9 km to Faro. Point of interest sign about Faro at intersection. Rest area with toilets and litter barrels to south just west of this junction.

Faro

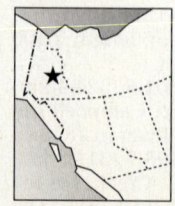

Located in east-central Yukon Territory, 220 road miles/354 km from Whitehorse. **Population:** 384. **Emergency Services:** RCMP, phone (867) 994-5555. **Fire Department**, phone (867) 994-2222. **Hospital**, phone

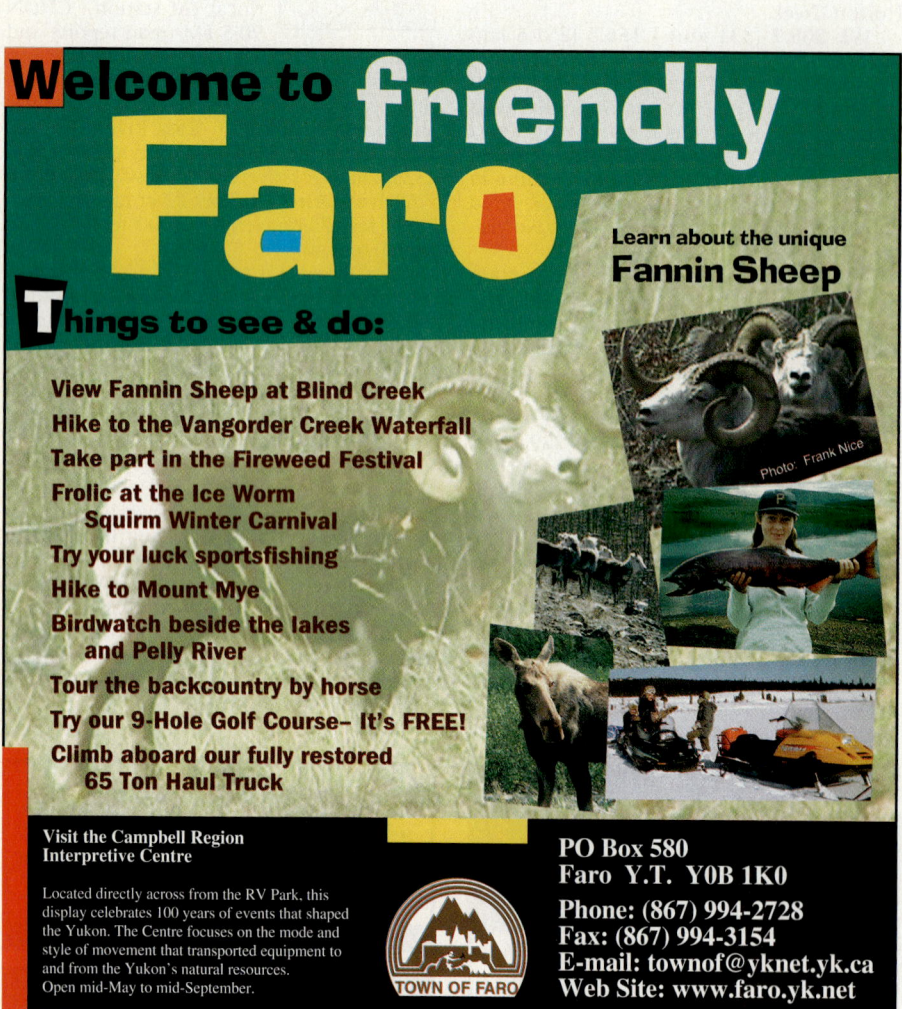

(867) 994-4444.

Visitor Information: At the **Campbell Region Interpretive Tourist Information Centre**, located across from John Connelly RV Park; phone (867) 994-2728. The interpretive centre, a popular attraction, has historical displays and information on local artisans. They even loan golf clubs so visitors can play Faro's 9-hole golf course. Get your Yukon Gold Explorers Pass stamped here. Or contact the Faro Town Office, phone (867) 994-2728, fax (867) 994-3154; www.faro.yk.net; email townof@yknet.yk.ca.

Climate: Temperatures range from -51°F/-46°C in winter to a summer maximum of 84°F/29°C. **Radio:** CBC-FM 105.1, CKRW-FM 98.7, CHON-FM 90.5 (road reports and weather). **Television:** CBC and 7 cable channels. **Transportation:** Floatplane service from Horizons North.

Private Aircraft: Faro airstrip; 1.5 miles/2.4 km south; elev. 2,351 feet/717m; length 3,000 feet/914m; gravel; fuel 100.

A former mining town, named after a card game, Faro lies on the northern escarpment of the Tintina Trench. Many places in town offer a commanding view of the Pelly River. The Anvil lead-silver and zinc mine, one of the largest open-pit mines in the world operated off and on from 1969 until 1998.

There are 2 restaurants in town and motel and bed and breakfast accommodations. RV camping and dump station at municipal and private campgrounds. The service station has gas, diesel, propane and full garage services. The area offers excellent fly-in fishing. Other services in town include a large grocery, liquor store, video rental, post office, public library, movie theatre and recreation centre with indoor swimming pool, squash courts and outdoor tennis courts. Catholic and Protestant Sunday services are available.

Attractions include an all-season observation cabin and isolated photographer's blind for wildlife viewing. Viewing areas are accessible via a gravel road skirting the Fannin sheep grazing area and are within 4 miles/6.4 km of town. A public boat ramp and canoe rentals are available for exploring the Pelly River.

Faro has a unique, "urban," 9-hole golf course that plays through the town's "green spaces." It offers great views along the valley.

Farrango is Faro's annual summer music festival. It will be held the last weekend in June, 2003 (over the Canada Day long weekend). Phone (867) 994-2728 for details.

Discovery Store. See display ad this section.

Town of Faro. See display ad this section.

Campbell Highway Log
(continued)

WL 260.6 (419.5 km) **J 101.4** (163.2 km) **Johnson Lake** Yukon government campground; 15 sites (7 pull-throughs), $12 fee, toilets, water pump, firewood, picnic shelter, boat launch.

Westbound, the Campbell Highway follows the Magundy River. There are several turnouts.

WL 277.5 (446.6 km) **J 84.5** (136 km) Magundy River airstrip to north; summer use only. Watch for livestock.

WL 279.7 (450.2 km) **J 82.3** (132.4 km) First glimpse of 22-mile-/35-km-long Little Salmon Lake westbound.

WL 290.3 (467.3 km) **J 71.7** (115.4 km) East end of **Little Salmon Lake**. Highway follows north shore of this large, deep, fjord-like lake. Lodge with meals, groceries, fishing licenses, guided fishing charters and boat rentals. Fishing for northern pike, grayling, lake trout.

WL 291.1 (468.6 km) **J 70.9** (114.1 km) Short access road south to **Drury Creek** Yukon government campground, situated on the creek at the east end of **Little Salmon Lake**: boat launch, fish filleting table, kitchen shelter, group firepit, 10 campsites, $12 fee, drinking water. Good fishing for northern pike, grayling, whitefish, lake trout 2 to 5 lbs., June 15 through July.

WL 291.4 (469 km) **J 70.6** (113.6 km) Turnout at east end Drury Creek bridge. Yukon government maintenance camp to north.

WL 299.2 (481.5 km) **J 62.8** (101.1 km) Turnout overlooking lake.

WL 302.2 (486.5 km) **J 59.8** (96.2 km) *CAUTION: Slow down for curves.* Highway follows lakeshore; no guide rails. Turnouts overlooking Little Salmon Lake next 8.5 miles/13.6 km westbound.

WL 307.9 (495.5 km) **J 54.1** (87.1 km) **Private Aircraft**: Little Salmon airstrip; elev. 2,200 feet/671m; length 1,800 feet/549m; sand and silt.

WL 311.8 (501.9 km) **J 50.2** (80.8 km) Steep, narrow, winding road south leads to Yukon government **Little Salmon Lake** campground; boat launch, fishing, 15 campsites, $12 fee, drinking water, picnic tables, outhouses, firepits and kitchen shelter.

WL 315.2 (507.3 km) **J 46.8** (75.3 km) **Bearfeed Creek**, a tributary of Little Salmon River, named because of the abundance of bears attracted to the berry patches in this area. Access to creek to north at west end of bridge.

Highway follows Little Salmon River (seen to south) for about 25 miles/40 km westbound.

WL 331.2 (533 km) **J 30.8** (49.6 km) *CAUTION: Slow down for hill.*

WL 333.9 (537.5 km) **J 28.1** (45.2 km) Picnic spot on Little Salmon River, which flows into the Yukon River.

WL 337.6 (543.3 km) **J 24.4** (39.3 km) Access road leads 4.9 miles/8 km north to **Frenchman Lake** Yukon government campground (10 sites, $12 fee, boat launch), 5.6 miles/9 km to photo viewpoint of lake, and 9.3 miles/15 km to Nunatak Yukon government campground (10 sites, $12 fee, boat launch). Access road narrows and surface deteriorates beyond Frenchman Lake Campground. South end of this 12-mile/19-km-long lake offers good fishing for trout, pike and grayling.

WL 339.7 (546.7 km) **J 22.3** (35.9 km) Turnoff to south for 0.9-mile/1.4-km gravel road to Little Salmon Indian village near confluence of Little Salmon River and Yukon River. There are some inhabited cabins in the area and some subsistence fishing. Private lands, no trespassing.

WL 345.6 (556.2 km) **J 16.4** (26.4 km) Turnout with point of interest sign overlooking **Eagles Nest Bluff** (formerly called Eagle Rock), well-known marker for river travelers. One of the worst steamboat disasters on the Yukon River occurred near here when the paddle-wheeler *Columbian* blew up and burned after a crew member accidentally fired a shot into a cargo of gunpowder. The accident, in which 6 men died, took place Sept. 25, 1906.

WL 346.1 (557 km) **J 15.9** (25.6 km) View of the Yukon River.

WL 349.8 (563 km) **J 12.2** (19.6 km) Northern Canada Power Commission's transmission poles and lines can be seen along highway. Power is transmitted from Aishihik dam site via Whitehorse dam and on to Cyprus Anvil mine and Faro. Orange balls mark lines where they cross river as a hazard to aircraft.

WL 359.3 (578.3 km) **J 2.7** (4.3 km) **Private Aircraft**: Carmacks airstrip to south; elev. 1,770 feet/539m; length 5,200 feet/1,585m; gravel.

WL 360 (579.4 km) **J 2** (3.2 km) Tantalus Butte coal mine on hill to north overlooking junction of Campbell and Klondike highways. The butte was named by U.S. Army Lt. Frederick Schwatka in 1883 because of the tantalizing appearance of the formation around many bends of the river before it is reached.

WL 362.2 (582.9 km) **J 0** Turn south on the Klondike Highway for Carmacks (2 miles/3.2 km) and Whitehorse (115 miles/184 km); turn north for Dawson City (220 miles/353 km).

Junction with the North Klondike Highway (Yukon Highway 2). Turn to **Milepost J 103.9** on page 258 in the KLONDIKE LOOP section for highway log.

Canoeists paddle the Yukon River near its confluence with the Little Salmon River.
(© Rollo Pool)

CANOL ROAD

Connects: Alaska Hwy. to NWT Border **Length:** 286 miles
Road Surface: Gravel **Season:** Closed in winter
Highest Summit: Macmillan Pass 4,480 feet
Major Attraction: Canol Heritage Trail

	Alaska Hwy. Jct.	Ross River	NWT Border
Alaska Hwy. Jct.		142	286
Ross River	142		144
NWT Border	286	144	

The winding South Canol Road turns off the Alaska Highway at Johnson's Crossing. (© Earl L. Brown, staff)

The 513-mile-/825-km-long Canol Road (Yukon Highway 6) was built to provide access to oil fields at Norman Wells, NWT, on the Mackenzie River. Conceived by the U.S. War Dept. to help fuel Alaska and protect it from a Japanese invasion, the Canol (Canadian Oil) Road and a 4-inch-diameter pipeline were constructed from Norman Wells, NWT, through Macmillan Pass, past Ross River, to Johnson's Crossing on the Alaska Highway. From there the pipeline carried oil to a refinery at Whitehorse.

Begun in 1942 and completed in 1944, the Canol Project included the road, pipeline, a telephone line, the refinery, airfields, pumping stations, tank farms, wells and camps. Only about 1 million barrels of oil were pumped to Whitehorse before the war ended in 1945 and the $134 million Canol Project was abandoned. (Today, Norman Wells is still a major supplier of oil with a pipeline to Zama, AB, built in 1985.) The Canol Road was declared a National Historic Site in 1990.

Since 1958, the Canol Road between Johnson's Crossing on the Alaska Highway and Ross River on the Campbell Highway (referred to as the South Canol Road) and between Ross River and the YT–NWT border (referred to as the North Canol Road) has been rebuilt and is open to summer traffic. It is maintained to minimum standards. Services are available only at Johnson's Crossing and Ross River.

The scenic Canol Road is accessible by foot, bike, car or plane; the rivers along the road are popular for canoers and kayakers; and the numerous fish-filled lakes in the area are accessible by road or float plane. There are also many opportunities for camping.

The 137-mile/220-km South Canol Road is a narrow winding road which crests the Big Salmon Range and threads its way above Lapie Canyon via a difficult but scenic stretch of road. Reconstruction on the South Canol has replaced many old bridges with culverts, but there are still a few 1-lane wooden bridges. Driving time is about 4 hours one way. Watch for steep hills and bad corners. There are no facilities along the South Canol Road, and it is definitely not recommended for large RVs or trailers. Not recommended for any size vehicle in wet weather. Inquiries on current road conditions should be made locally, with the Yukon Dept. of Highways in Whitehorse or at (867) 456-7623, toll free from Yukon communities 1-877-456-7623, before driving this road.

The 144-mile/232-km North Canol Road is also a narrow, winding road which some motorists have compared to a roller coaster. The North Canol area offers many opportunities for biking and wilderness camping. All bridges on the North Canol are 1-lane, and the road surface can be very slippery when wet. Not recommended during wet weather and not recommended for large RVs or trailers. If mining is under way along the North Canol, watch for large transport trucks. *NOTE: Drive with headlights on at all times!*

Our log of the North Canol ends at the YT–NWT border, where vehicles may turn around. Road washouts prohibit travel beyond this point. From the border to Norman Wells it is 230 miles/372 km of unusable road that has been designated the Canol Heritage Trail by the NWT government. Northwest Territories Tourism recommends contacting the Norman Wells Historical Centre (phone 867/587-2415, fax 867/587-2469) for current description of trail conditions and recommended precautions.

WARNING: The only facilities on the Canol Road are at Ross River and at Johnson's Crossing on the Alaska Highway.

Emergency medical services: In Ross River, phone (867) 969-2222; or phone the RCMP, (867) 969-5555, or (867) 667-5555.

South Canol Road

Distance from the junction with the Alaska Highway (J) is followed by distance from the Campbell Highway junction (C). *Kilometre figures in the log from the Alaska Highway junction reflect the location of physical kilometreposts when they occur.*

YUKON HIGHWAY 6

J 0 C 136.8 (220.2 km) Johnson's Crossing, 0.7 mile/1.1 km from Canol Road turnoff, has food, gas and camping.

Junction of the Canol Road (Yukon Highway 6) with the Alaska Highway (Yukon Highway 1). Turn to **Milepost DC 808.2** on page 145 in the ALASKA HIGHWAY section for log.

J 0.2 (0.3 km) **C 136.6** (219.8 km) Information panel on the history and construction of Canol Road.

Short, dirt road west to auto "boneyard" that includes several WWII Canol Project trucks (all have been significantly cannibalized). Limited turnaround area, not suitable for trailers. Not recommended for any vehicle in wet weather.

J 3.9 (6.2 km) **C 132.9** (213.8 km) Fourmile Creek. Road begins ascent across the

CANOL ROAD
Alaska Highway Junction, YT, to NWT Border

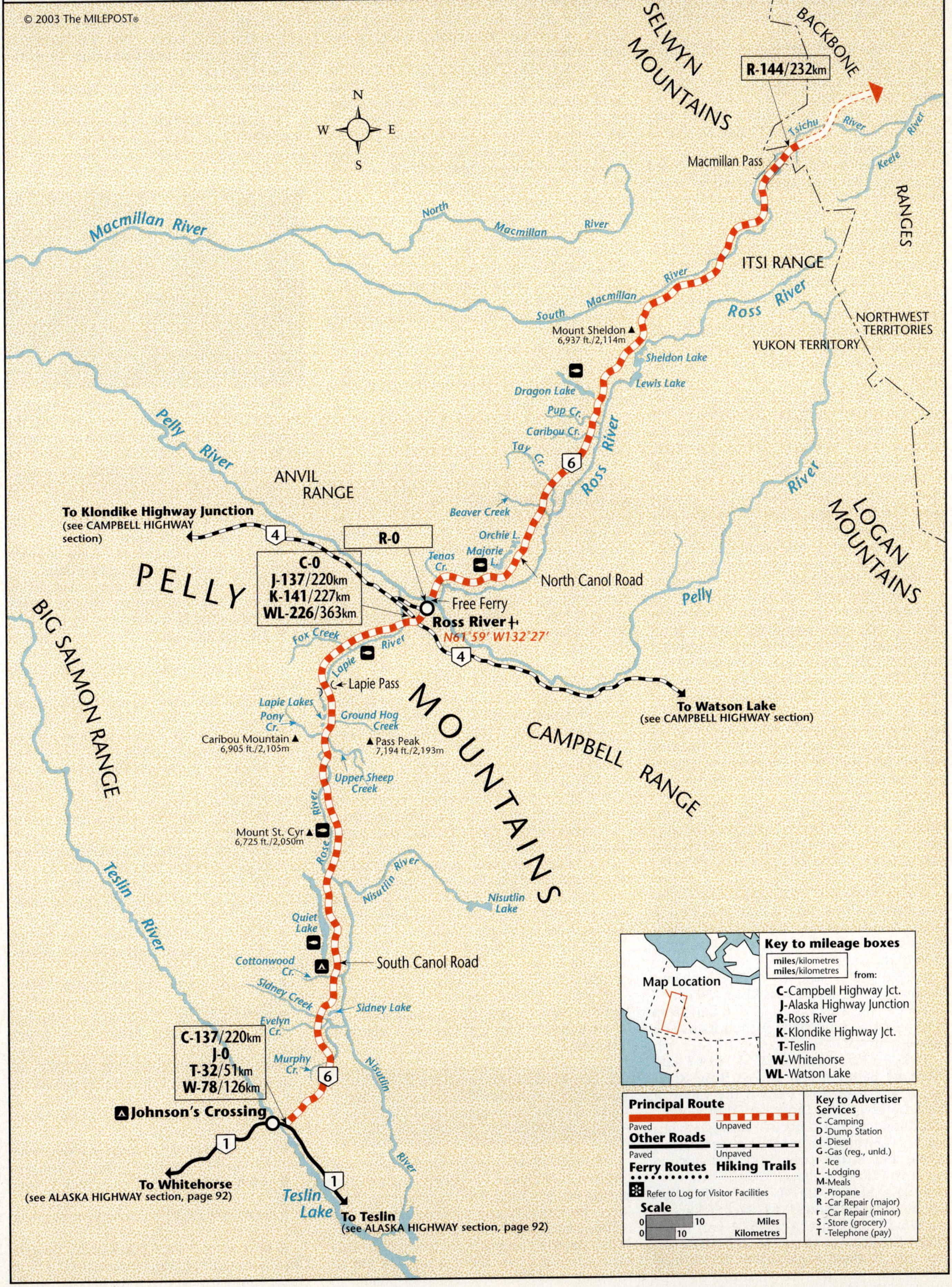

© 2003 The MILEPOST®

Big Salmon Range to the summit (elev. about 4,000 feet/1,219m). Snow possible at summit early October to late spring.

J 13.9 (22.4 km) C 122.9 (197.8 km) Moose Creek. Small gravel turnout with litter barrels.

J 27 (43.4 km) C 109.8 (176.7 km) Evelyn Creek 1-lane wooden bridge.

J 28.7 (46.2 km) C 108.1 (174 km) Sidney Creek 2-lane bridge.

J 30.6 (49.2 km) C 106.2 (170.9 km) Access road east to **Sidney Lake**. Nice little lake and good place to camp.

From here northbound the South Canol follows the Nisutlin River, which is to the east and can be seen from the road the next 30 miles/48 km until the road crosses the Rose River beyond Quiet Lake.

J 30.9 (49.7 km) C 105.9 (170.4 km) Turnout with litter barrel to east.

J 39.1 (62.9 km) C 97.7 (157.2 km) Good view of Pelly Mountains ahead. Road crosses Cottonwood Creek.

J 42 (67.6 km) C 94.8 (152.5 km) Access road east 0.4 mile/0.6 km to **Nisutlin River**. Good place to camp with tables and outhouse. ▲

J 47.8 (76.9 km) C 89 (143.2 km) Quiet Lake Yukon government campground; 20 sites, camping permit ($12), boat launch, picnic tables, kitchen shelter, firewood. Steep hills northbound to Quiet Lake. ▲

J 54.7 (88 km) C 82.1 (132.1 km) Lake Creek. Road now follows Quiet Lake to west; good fishing for lake trout, northern pike and arctic grayling. ⌕

J 56 (90.1 km) C 80.8 (130 km) Turnout with litter barrels and point of interest sign overlooking **Quiet Lake**. This is the largest of 3 lakes that form the headwaters of the Big Salmon River system. The 17-mile-/28-km-long lake was named in 1887 by John McCormack, 1 of 4 miners who prospected the Big Salmon River from its mouth on the Yukon River to its source. Although they did find some gold, the river and lakes have become better known for their good fishing and fine scenery. Until the completion of the South Canol Road in the 1940s, this area was reached mainly by boating and portaging hundreds of miles up the Teslin and Nisutlin rivers.

J 61.2 (98.5 km) C 75.6 (121.6 km) Turnoff west for Quiet Lake, day-use area with picnic sites, water, boat launch and fishing. Entry point for canoeists on the Big Salmon River. ⌕

J 61.5 (99 km) C 75.3 (121.2 km) Yukon government Quiet Lake maintenance camp on left northbound. A vintage Canol Project dump truck and pull grader is on display in front of the camp.

J 62.6 (100.7 km) C 74.2 (119.4 km) Distance marker shows Ross River 126 km.

J 63.7 (102 km) C 73.1 (117.6 km) Steep hill and panoramic view of mountains and valley.

J 65.5 (105.4 km) C 71.3 (114.7 km) One-lane Bailey bridge across **Rose River No. 1**. The road now follows the valley of the Rose River into Lapie Pass northbound. According to R.C. Coutts in *Yukon Places and Names*, Oliver Rose prospected extensively in this area in the early 1900s. He came to the Yukon from Quebec.

J 94.1 (151.4 km) C 42.7 (68.7 km) Distance marker shows Ross River 76 km.

J 95.1 (153 km) C 41.7 (67.1 km) Upper Sheep Creek joins the Rose River here. To the east is **Pass Peak** (elev. 7,194 feet/2,193m).

J 96.4 (155.1 km) C 40.4 (65 km) Rose River No. 6.

J 97.1 (156.2 km) C 39.7 (63.9 km) Rose Lake to east.

J 97.5 (156.9 km) C 39.3 (63.2 km) Pony Creek. **Caribou Mountain** (elev. 6,905 feet/2,105m) to west.

J 101.1 (162.7 km) C 35.7 (57.4 km) Lakes to west are part of **Lapie Lakes** chain, headwaters of the Lapie River. These features were named by Dr. George M. Dawson of the Geological Survey of Canada in 1887 for Lapie, an Iroquois Indian companion and canoeman of Robert Campbell, who was the first to explore the Pelly River area in 1843 for the Hudson's Bay Co.

A short new walking trail takes you to Ian H. Thomson Falls. Old gold exploration trails in the area are great for hiking and mountain biking. There is also a gravel road between the lakes that leads east to the Groundhog Creek area. The creek leads to Seagull Lakes, which have excellent grayling fishing.

A short dirt road provides access to the lake shore. Watch for grazing moose and nesting waterfowl. Unmaintained camping area and boat launch. ▲

J 102.5 (165 km) C 34.3 (55.2 km) Access road west to Lapie Lakes. Good place to camp; excellent lake trout fishing.

J 107.4 (172.8 km) C 29.4 (47.3 km) Lapie River No. 1 culverts. Ponds reported good for grayling fishing. *NOTE: Watch for horses on the road.*

J 107.5 (173 km) C 29.3 (47.1 km) Ahead northbound is Barite Mountain (elevation approximately 6,500 feet/1,981m).

J 120.7 (194.2 km) C 16.1 (25.9 km) The road follows the Lapie River Canyon for about the next 11 miles/18 km, climbing to an elevation of about 500 feet/152m above the river. *CAUTION: Narrow road, watch for rocks.*

J 123.3 (198.4 km) C 13.5 (21.7 km) Kilometrepost 200. Distance marker shows Ross River 26 km. Lapie River runs to east.

J 126.3 (203.2 km) C 10.5 (16.9 km) Turnouts on right side of road northbound overlooking Lapie River Canyon.

J 132.3 (212.9 km) C 4.5 (7.2 km) Narrow 1-lane bridge over **Lapie River No. 2**. Point of interest sign on north end of bridge about the **Lapie River Canyon**. The old Lapie Canyon walking trail (south of the west side of the bridge) has been restored and maintained and is a great place for a short hike.

J 133 (214 km) C 3.8 (6.1 km) Erosional features called hoodoos can be seen in the clay banks rising above the road.

J 133.3 (214.5 km) C 3.5 (5.6 km) Ash layer can be seen in clay bank on right side of road.

J 135.6 (218.2 km) C 1.2 (1.9 km) **Jackfish Lake** to west; floatplane dock.

J 136.8 (220 km) C 0 Campbell Highway **junction**.

Junction of South Canol Road with the Campbell Highway. Turn to Milepost WL 220.4 on page 717 in the CAMPBELL HIGHWAY section for log.

Straight ahead northbound, across the Campbell Highway, a poorly maintained section of the Canol Road continues to Ross River. Motorists bound for Ross River or the North Canol Road are advised to turn left (west) on the Campbell Highway from this junction and drive about 5 miles/8 km to the main Ross River access road (see map).

North Canol Road

The North Canol Road leads 144 miles/232 km to the NWT border. Physical kilometreposts along road reflect distance from the Alaska Highway junction.

Distance from Ross River (R) is shown.

R 0 ROSS RIVER. Yukon government Ross River ferry (free) crosses the Pelly River. Ferry operates from 8 A.M. to noon and 1–5 P.M. daily from late May to mid-October.

Those who miss the last ferry crossing of the day may leave their vehicles on the opposite side of the river and use the footbridge to walk into Ross River; vehicles can be brought over in the morning.

WARNING: There are no services along the North Canol Road.

R 0.4 (0.6 km) Stockpile to west is barite from the Yukon Barite Mine.

R 0.6 (1 km) Road to east leads to original site of Ross River and Indian village.

R 0.9 (1.4 km) Second access road east to old Ross River and Indian village. Canol Road follows the Ross River.

R 2.1 (3.4 km) *CAUTION: Slide area, watch for falling rocks.*

R 4.7 (7.6 km) Raspberry patch. Good pickings.

R 6.8 (10.9 km) Tenas Creek 1-lane bridge.

R 20.9 (33.6 km) **Marjorie Creek**. Locals report good grayling fishing. ⌕

R 21 (33.8 km) Access road to west leads to Marjorie Lake. Access road not recommended for large RVs.

R 28.1 (45.2 km) Boat launch on Orchie Lake to west.

R 29.8 (48 km) Distance marker indicates NWT border 195 km, Ross River 50 km.

R 31.9 (51.3 km) Gravel Creek 1-lane bridge. The next 15 miles/24 km are excellent moose country.

R 33.4 (53.7 km) Flat Creek 1-lane bridge.

R 37 (59.5 km) Beaver Creek 1-lane bridge.

R 41.8 (67.2 km) 180 Mile Creek 1-lane bridge.

R 43.9 (70.6 km) Tay Creek 1-lane bridge.

R 46.3 (74.5 km) Blue Creek 1-lane bridge.

R 48.1 (77.4 km) Kilometrepost 306.

R 57.6 (92.7 km) Clifford's Slough to the east.

R 58.6 (94.3 km) Steep hill to 1-lane bridge over Caribou Creek.

R 61.1 (98.3 km) Distance marker shows NWT border 145 km, Ross River 100 km.

R 61.8 (99.4 km) Pup Creek 1-lane bridge.

R 64.8 (104.3 km) Turnout to west. Steep hill.

R 65.1 (104.7 km) Turnout to **Dragon Lake**; overnight parking, litter barrels. Locals report that early spring is an excellent time for pike and trout in the inlet. Rock hounds check roadsides and borrow pits for colorful chert, which can be worked into jewelry.

R 65.4 (105.2 km) Kilometrepost 334. Large, level gravel turnout to west overlooking Dragon Lake; boat launch.

R 69.6 (112 km) Wreckage of Twin Pioneer aircraft to west. WWII remnants can be found in this area.

R 69.9 (112.5 km) Road to Twin Creek.

R 70.8 (113.9 km) Airstrip.

R 71 (114.2 km) One-lane bridge over Twin Creek No. 1. Yukon government maintenance camp.

R 71.1 (114.4 km) One-lane bridge over Twin Creek No. 2. Good views of Mount Sheldon.

R 75.1 (120.8 km) Kilometrepost 350. **Mount Sheldon** (elev. 6,937 feet/2,114m) ahead northbound, located 3 miles/4.8 km north of Sheldon Lake; a very beautiful and distinguishable feature on the Canol Road. In 1900, Poole Field and Clement Lewis, who were fans of writer Rudyard Kipling, named this peak Kipling Mountain and the lake at its base Rudyard. In 1907, Joseph Keele of the Geological Survey of Canada renamed them after Charles Sheldon, a well-known sheep hunter and naturalist who came to the area to collect Stone sheep specimens for the Chicago Natural History Museum in 1905.

Sheldon Lake has a sandy beach that is great for camping; popular float plane lake.

R 76.4 (123 km) Kilometrepost 352. Of the 3-lake chain, Sheldon Lake is farthest north, then Field Lake and Lewis Lake, which is just visible from here. Lewis Lake is closest to the confluence of the Ross and Prevost rivers.

Field Lake and Lewis Lake were named in 1907 by Joseph Keele of the Geological Survey of Canada after Poole Field and Clement Lewis. The 2 partners, who had prospected this country, ran a trading post called Nahanni House at the mouth of the Ross River in 1905.

R 77.6 (124.9 km) Kilometrepost 354. Riddell Creek 1-lane bridge. Tip of **Mount Riddell** (elev. 6,101 feet/1,859m) can be seen to the west.

R 78.8 (126.8 km) View of Sheldon Lake ahead, Field Lake to east.

R 79.8 (128.4 km) Access road east to Sheldon Lake.

R 82.7 (133.1 km) Sheldon Creek 1-lane bridge. Road climbs, leaving Ross River valley and entering Macmillan Valley northbound.

R 89.3 (143.7 km) Height of land before starting descent northbound into South Macmillan River system.

R 89.7 (144.3 km) *Steep hill*. Road may wash out during heavy rains. Deep ditches along roadside help channel water.

R 91.4 (147.1 km) Moose Creek 1-lane bridge.

R 91.6 (147.4 km) **B 52.6** (84.6 km) Milepost 230.

R 92.3 (148.5 km) Kilometrepost 378. Peaks of the Itsi Range ahead. Rugged, spectacular scenery northbound.

R 92.7 (149.1 km) Distance marker shows NWT border 95 km, Ross River 150 km.

R 93.8 (151 km) First of several WWII vehicle dumps to west. To the east is a wannigan, or skid shack, used as living quarters by Canol Road workers during construction of the road. It was too far to return to base camp; these small buildings were strategically located along the route so the workers had a place to eat and sleep at night.

The remote North Canol Road ends at the YT–NWT border. (© Earl L. Brown, staff)

R 94 (151.3 km) To east are remains of a maintenance depot where heavy equipment was repaired. Concrete foundations to west. First glimpse of the South Macmillan River northbound.

R 94.7 (152.4 km) Kilometrepost 382. Another Canol project equipment dump to explore. Watch ditches for old pieces of pipeline.

R 97.8 (157.4 km) Boulder Creek 1-lane bridge.

R 98.5 (158.5 km) Access road west to **South Macmillan River** where boats can be launched. Locals advise launching boats here rather than from the bridge at Milepost **R 113.6**, which washes out periodically and leaves dangerous debris in the river. Popular but challenging canoe trip.

R 100.8 (162.5 km) Kilometrepost 392. **Itsi Range** comes into view ahead northbound. Itsi is said to be an Indian word meaning "wind" and was first given as a name to Itsi Lakes, headwaters of the Ross River. The road dips down and crosses an unnamed creek.

R 104.5 (168.2 km) Kilometrepost 398. View of the South Macmillan River from here.

R 105.3 (169.4 km) View of **Selwyn Mountains**, named in 1901 by Joseph Keele of the Geological Survey of Canada for Dr. Alfred Richard Selwyn (1824–1902), a distinguished geologist in England. Dr. Selwyn later became director of the Geological Survey of Australia and then director of the Geological Survey of Canada from 1869 until his retirement in 1895.

R 111 (178.6 km) Itsi Creek 1-lane bridge.

R 112.2 (180.5 km) Wagon Creek 1-lane bridge.

R 113.6 (182.8 km) Turnout to east on South Macmillan River. Good place for a picnic but not recommended as a boat launch. One-lane Bailey bridge over South Macmillan River No. 1.

Robert Campbell, a Hudson's Bay Co. explorer on a journey down the Pelly River in 1843, named this major tributary of the Pelly after Chief Factor James McMillan, who had sponsored Campbell's employment with the company.

R 115.1 (185.2 km) Access road on left northbound leads about 7 miles/11 km to Yukon Barite Mine. Barite is a soft mineral that requires only crushing and bagging before being shipped over the Dempster Highway to the Beaufort Sea oil and gas wells, where it is used as a lubricant known as drilling mud.

R 118.9 (191.3 km) Jeff Creek 1-lane bridge.

R 121.2 (195 km) Hess Creek 1-lane bridge. Bears in area.

R 123.2 (198.3 km) Gravel turnout to west. Distance marker indicates NWT border 45 km, Ross River 200 km. One-lane bridge over Dewhurst Creek.

R 127.5 (205.2 km) Entering **Macmillan Pass**, "Mac Pass" (elev. 4,480 feet/1,366m). This area is very scenic in late summer and fall; good places to hike and camp, but no developed trails or campgrounds.

R 129.4 (208.2 km) One-lane bridge over Macmillan River No. 2.

R 129.5 (208.4 km) Abandoned Army vehicles from the Canol Project to west and east.

R 133.6 (215 km) To the west is Cordilleran Engineering camp, managers of the mining development of Ogilvie Joint Venture's Jason Project. The Jason deposit is a zinc, lead, silver, barite property.

One-lane bridge over Sekie Creek No. 1.

R 136.4 (219.5 km) Access to Macmillan airstrip on left northbound. Access road east to Hudson Bay Mining & Smelting's Tom lead–zinc mineral claims.

R 137.7 (221.6 km) One-lane bridge over Macmillan River No. 3.

R 141.8 (228.2 km) One-lane bridge over Macmillan River No. 4.

R 142.9 (230 km) One-lane bridge over Macmillan River No. 5.

R 144.1 (231.9 km) One-lane bridge over Macmillan River No. 6.

R 144.2 (232 km) **YT–NWT Border**. Sign cautions motorists to proceed at their own risk. The road is not maintained and bridges are not safe beyond this point. Vehicles turn around here.

Ahead is the Tsichu River valley and the Selwyn Mountains. The abandoned North Canol Road continues another 230 miles/372 km from the YT–NWT border to Norman Wells, NWT. Designated the Canol Heritage Trail, and set aside as a territorial park reserve, the trail is under development. Some river crossings required; large stretches deemed dangerous and arduous. It passes through mountains, tundra and forest, and past many relics of the Canol Project. The Historical Centre museum in Norman Wells features the history of the Canol Project and has outdoor displays of Canol vehicles. Phone (867) 587-2415; fax (867) 587-2469.

DEMPSTER HIGHWAY

Connects: Klondike Hwy. to Inuvik, NWT **Length:** 456 miles
Road Surface: Gravel   **Season:** Open all year
Highest Summit: North Fork Pass 4,265 feet
Major Attractions: Lost Patrol Gravesite, Mackenzie River Delta, Arctic Circle Crossing

	Dawson City	Ft. McPherson	Inuvik	Klondike Hwy.
Dawson City		367	481	25
Ft. McPherson	367		114	342
Inuvik	481	114		456
Klondike Hwy.	25	342	456	

The Dempster Highway snakes across a fall landscape. (© Earl L. Brown, staff)

The Dempster Highway (Yukon Highway 5, NWT Highway 8) begins about 25 miles/40. km east of Dawson City, YT, at its junction with the South Klondike Highway and leads 456.3 miles/734.3 km northeast to Inuvik, NWT. The highway can be driven in 12 to 16 hours, but allow extra time to enjoy the wilderness. The Dempster offers hiking, camping, fishing and spectacular photo opportunities. It also has a reputation as a birder's paradise.

Construction of the Dempster Highway began in 1959, under the Road to Resources program. It was completed in 1978. A 5-year major reconstruction program on the highway was completed in 1988.

The Dempster is a mostly gravel road. The first 5 miles/8 km are seal-coated, and the last 6 miles/10 km are paved. There are stretches of clay surface that can be slippery in wet weather. Summer driving conditions on the Dempster vary depending on weather and maintenance. Generally, road conditions range from fair to excellent, with highway speeds attainable on some sections. But freezing winter weather and heavy truck traffic can erode both road base and surfacing, resulting in areas of rough road. Calcium chloride is used to reduce dust and as a bonding agent; wash your vehicle as soon as practical.

It is strongly recommended motorists carry at least 2 spare tires while traveling the Dempster. *Drive with your headlights on.*

Facilities are still few and far between on the Dempster. Full auto services are available at Klondike River Lodge at the Dempster Highway turnoff on South Klondike Highway. Gas, propane, food and lodging, and car repair are also available at Eagle Plains Hotel, located at about the halfway point on the Dempster. Gas, food and lodging are also available in Fort McPherson. Gas up whenever possible.

The Dempster is open year-round, but summer travel gives visitors long hours of daylight for recreation. The highway is fairly well-traveled in summer: A driver may not see another car for an hour, and then pass 4 cars in a row. Locals say the highway is smoother and easier to drive in winter, but precautions should be taken against cold weather, high winds and poor visibility; check road conditions before proceeding in winter. Watch for herds of caribou mid-September to late October and in March and April.

There are 2 ferry crossings on the Dempster, at **Milepost J 334.9** (Peel River crossing) and **J 377.9** (Mackenzie River and Arctic Red River crossings). Free government ferry service is available 15 hours a day (9 A.M. to 12:45 A.M. Northwest Territories time) during summer (June to mid-October). Cross by ice bridge in winter. For recorded messages on ferry service, road and weather conditions, phone (800) 661-0752.

General information on Northwest Territories is available by calling the Arctic Hotline at (800) 661-0788. If you are in Dawson City, we recommend visiting the Western Arctic Visitor Centre for information on Northwest Territories and the Dempster Highway. Located in the B.Y.N. Building on Front Street, across from the Yukon Visitor Centre, it is open daily 9 A.M. to 8 P.M., May 15 to Sept. 15; phone (867) 777-7237 or 4727; fax (867) 777-7321; email travel_westernarctic@gov.nt.ca. Or write Western Arctic Trade & Tourism, Box 2600, Inuvik, NT X0E 0T0; phone (867) 777-8600, fax (867) 777-8601 for more information.

The MILEPOST® expresses its appreciation to the Yukon Dept. of Renewable Resources, Parks and Recreation for its assistance with information in this highway log.

Dempster Highway Log

Distance from junction with Klondike Highway 2 (J) is followed by distance from Inuvik (I).

Driving distance is measured in miles. The kilometre figure on the Yukon portion of the highway reflects the physical kilometreposts and is not necessarily an accurate metric conversion of the mileage figure. Kilometreposts are green with white lettering and are located on the right-hand side of the highway, northbound.

YUKON HIGHWAY 5

J 0 I 456.3 (734.3 km) Dempster Corner, 25 miles/40. km east of Dawson City. Klondike River Lodge with food, gas, propane, lodging, camping, and tire repair.

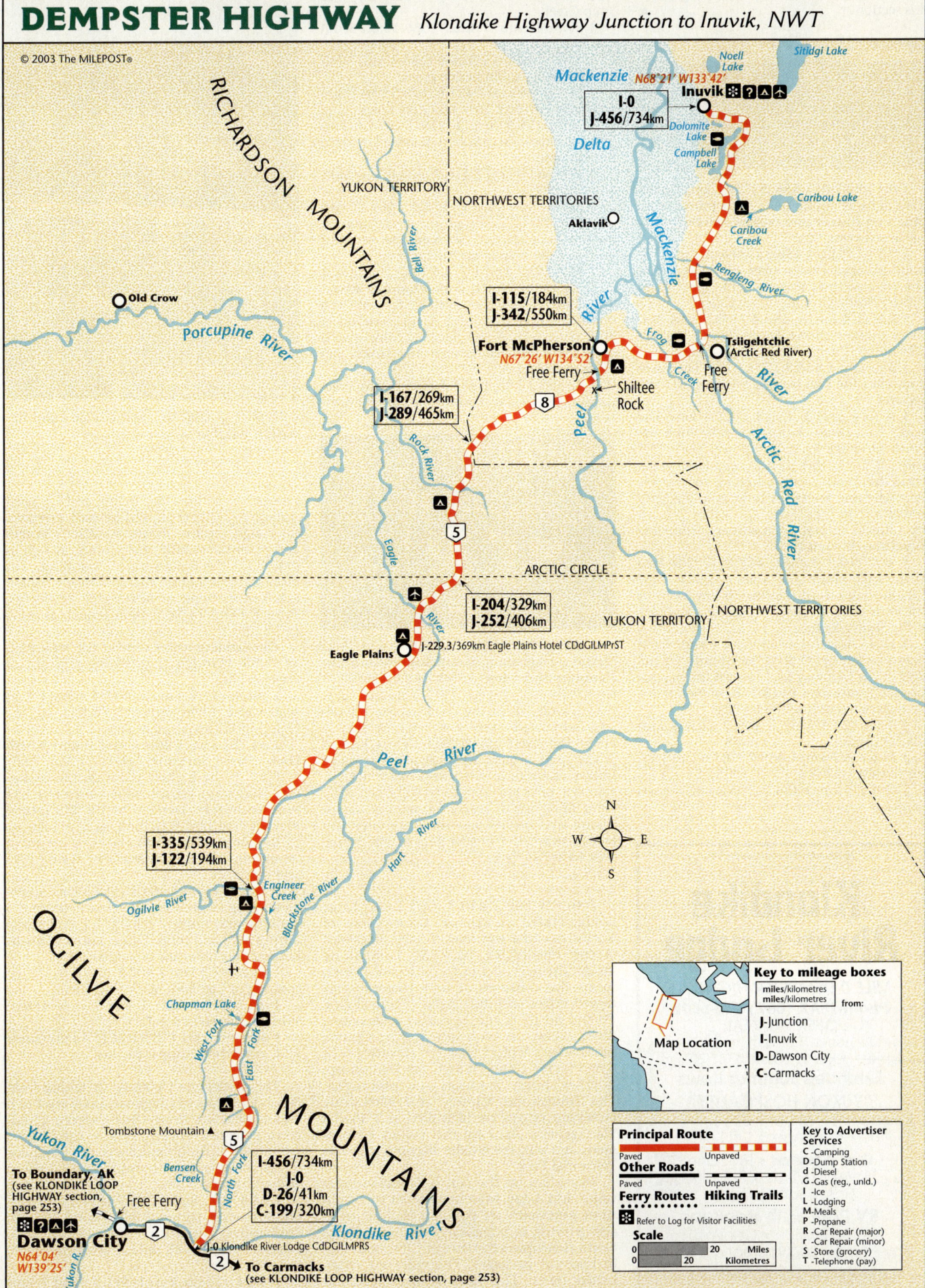

Klondike River Lodge. See display ad this section. ▲

NOTE: Next available gas northbound is at Eagle Plains, 229 miles/369 km from here.

Junction of Klondike Highway (Yukon Highway 2) and Dempster Highway (Yukon Highway 5). Turn to Milepost J 297.9 on page 264 in the KLONDIKE LOOP section for log of Klondike Highway to Dawson City.

J 0.1 (0.2 km) I 456.2 (734.2 km) Dempster Highway monument with information panels on history and culture, wildlife, ecology and driving tips.

J 0.2 (0.3 km) I 456.1 (734 km) One-lane wood-planked bridge over Klondike River. The road follows the wooded (spruce and poplar) North Klondike River valley.

J 0.9 (1.4 km) I 455.4 (732.9 km) Distance marker shows Eagle Plains 363 km (226 miles), Inuvik 735 km (457 miles).

J 3 (5 km) I 453.3 (729.5 km) Burn area from 1991 fire that burned 5,189 acres/2,100 hectares.

J 4 (6.4 km) I 452.3 (727.9 km) The North Fork Ditch channeled water from the North Klondike River to a power plant 15.5 miles/25 km farther west for nearly 60 years, until the 1960s, and it helped to provide electricity and water for huge gold-dredging operations farther down the valley. Watch for salmon migrating upstream from late July through August.

J 6.5 (10.5 km) I 449.8 (723.9 km) Antimony Mountain (elev. 6,693 feet/2,040m), about 18.5 miles/30 km away, is one peak of the Ogilvie Mountains and part of the Snowy Range.

J 12.4 (20 km) I 443.9 (714.4 km) North Klondike Range, Ogilvie Mountains to the west of the highway lead toward the rugged, interior Tombstone Range. These mountains were glaciated during the Ice Age.

J 15.4 (24.5 km) I 440.9 (709.5 km) Glacier Creek.

J 16.6 (26.7 km) I 439.7 (707.6 km) Pullout to west.

J 18.1 (29 km) I 438.2 (705.2 km) Bensen Creek.

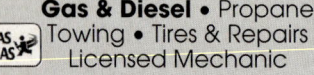

Klondike River Lodge

25 Miles South of Dawson City
At Dempster Corner

MILE 0 DEMPSTER HIGHWAY
Phone/FAX (867) 993-6892
OPEN ALL YEAR
WINTER HOURS 7:30 a.m. to 8:30 p.m.
SUMMER HOURS 7:00 a.m. to 10:30 p.m.
Extended Summer Hours
"YUKON HOSPITALITY"
Restaurant • Motel • Grocery Store
Ice • Lounge & Off Sales
Gas & Diesel • Propane VISA
Towing • Tires & Repairs MasterCard
Licensed Mechanic
RV Park With Hookups
Dump Station • Car Wash
Pay Phone • Laundromat & Showers

"Stop Here For Dempster Highway Information"

J 25.6 (41 km) I 430.7 (693.1 km) Pea Soup Creek.

J 29.8 (48 km) I 426.5 (686.4 km) Scout Car Creek.

J 31.7 (51 km) I 424.6 (683.3 km) Wolf Creek. Private cabin beside creek.

J 34.7 (55.8 km) I 421.6 (678.5 km) Highway follows North Fork Klondike River.

J 36.6 (58.9 km) I 419.7 (675.4 km) Grizzly Creek. Mt. Robert Service on right northbound.

J 39.6 (63.7 km) I 416.7 (670.6 km) Mike and Art Creek.

J 40.4 (65 km) I 415.9 (669.3 km) Klondike Camp Yukon government highway maintenance station. No visitor services but may provide help in an emergency.

J 41.8 (67.3 km) I 414.5 (667.1 km) First crossing of the North Fork Klondike River. The highway now moves above tree line and on to tundra northbound. At an elevation of approximately 4,003 feet/1,220m, you'll cross the watershed between the Yukon and Mackenzie basins.

J 43 (69.2 km) I 413.3 (665.2 km) Spectacular first view of Tombstone Range northbound.

J 44.4 (71.5 km) I 411.9 (662.9 km) Yukon government Tombstone Mountain Campground (elev. 3,392 feet/1,034m); 36 sites, camping permit ($12), shelter, fireplaces, water from the river, tables, pit toilets. Designated cyclist camping area. Stop in at the Dempster Interpretive Centre located at the campground; fossil displays, resource library, handouts with area information, campfire talks and nature walks. Open daily from mid-June to early September. Good hiking trail begins past the outhouses and leads toward the headwaters of the North Fork Klondike River. CAUTION: Hikers should inquire about recent bear activity in the area before setting off. ▲

J 46 (74 km) I 410.3 (660.3 km) Large double-ended viewpoint. Good views of North Fork Pass and river. To the southwest is the needle-like peak of Tombstone Mountain (elev. 7,195 feet/2,193m), which forms the centrepoint in a panorama of ragged ridges and lush green tundra slopes. To the north is the East Fork Blackstone River valley; on each side are the Ogilvie Mountains, which rise to elevations of 6,890 feet/2,100m. Watch for Dall sheep, grizzlies, hoary marmots and ptarmigan. The Tombstone, Cloudy and Blackstone mountain ranges are identified as a Special Management Area by the Yukon government and will eventually become a Yukon Territorial Park.

Day hikes up the North Klondike River valley and 4-day wilderness hikes to Tombstone Mountain are popular. Heli-hiking is also growing in popularity; inquire at Trans North Helicopters in Dawson City about fly-in/hike-out packages. There are no established trails. The staff at the Dempster Interpretive Centre at Tombstone Campground can provide maps and suggest itineraries. Hikers should be well prepared for rough terrain, drastic weather changes and potential wildlife encounters, as well as practicing "leave-no-trace" camping. For more information on the Tombstone region, call Yukon Dept. of Renewable Resources, Parks & Outdoor Recreation Branch at (867) 667-8299.

Outstanding aerial view of the mountain available through flightseeing trip out of Dawson City.

J 48.4 (77.9 km) I 407.9 (656.4 km) Blackstone River culvert. Tundra in the region indicates permafrost.

J 51 (82 km) I 405.3 (652.2 km) North Fork Pass Summit, elev. 4,265 feet/1,300m, is the highest point on the Dempster Highway. Wildflowers abundant late June–early July. Descent to the Blackstone River. Good bird-watching area. A hike up to the lower knoll to the right of the main mountain increases chances of seeing pika and marmots.

J 52.2 (84 km) I 404.1 (650.3 km) Anglecomb Peak (also called Sheep Mountain) is a lambing and nursery habitat for Dall sheep during May and June. This is also a frequent nesting area for a pair of golden eagles.

J 54.2 (87.2 km) I 402.1 (647.1 km) First crossing of East Fork Blackstone River.

J 54.6 (87.9 km) I 401.7 (646.4 km) White fireweed in summer.

J 56.5 (91 km) I 399.8 (643.4 km) Guide and outfitters camp to east. CAUTION: Watch for horses on road.

The Blackstone Uplands, stretching from North Fork Pass to Chapman Lake, are a rich area for birdlife (long-tailed jaegers, gyrfalcons, peregrine falcons, red-throated loons, whimbrels, upland sandpipers and oldsquaw ducks) and big game hunting for Dall sheep and grizzly bear.

J 63.4 (102 km) I 392.9 (632.3 km) Distance marker shows Eagle Plains 261 km (162 miles), Inuvik 633 km (393 miles), Dawson 142 km (88 miles), Whitehorse 600 km (373 miles).

J 64.4 (103.6 km) I 391.9 (630.7 km) Two Moose Lake; turnout with information

Campers gather at Two Moose Lake to watch wildlife. (© Earl L. Brown, staff)

panels and viewing platform.

J 66.9 (107.6 km) I 389.4 (626.7 km) Large gravel pullout with dumpster. Access to Blackstone River.

J 71.5 (115 km) I 384.8 (619.3 km) First crossing of **West Fork Blackstone River**. Watch for arctic terns. Good fishing for Dolly Varden and grayling a short distance downstream where the west and east forks of the Blackstone join to form the Blackstone River, which the road now follows. After the river crossing, 2 low, cone-shaped mounds called pingos are visible upriver about 5 miles/8 km.

J 72.1 (116 km) I 384.2 (618.3 km) Turnout to west. View over **Chapman Lake**, one of the few lakes close to the highway that is large enough to permit floatplane operations. Common loons nest on island. Commemorative road sign about sled dog patrols of the Royal North West Mounted Police.

Porcupine caribou herd sometimes crosses the highway in this area in mid-October.

J 77.3 (124.4 km) I 379 (609.9 km) **Private Aircraft:** Government airstrip (road is part of the strip); elev. 3,100 feet/945m; length 3,000 feet/914m.

J 96 (154.5 km) I 360.3 (579.8 km) Northbound, highway passes through barren gray hills of Windy Pass. The mountain ridges are the breeding habitat for some species of butterflies and moths not known to exist anywhere else.

J 98.2 (158 km) I 358.1 (576.3 km) Gyrfalcon nest on ledge on side of cliff.

J 106 (169.7 km) I 350.3 (563.7 km) Creek culvert is red from iron oxide. Sulfurous smell is from nearby sulfur springs. Watch for interesting geological features in hills along road.

J 108.1 (173 km) I 348.2 (560.4 km) Views of red-coloured **Engineer Creek**, and also erosion pillars and red rock of nearby hills between here and Kilometrepost 182.

J 121.7 (194 km) I 334.6 (538.5 km) **Sapper Hill**, named in 1971 in honour of the 3rd Royal Canadian Engineers who built the Ogilvie River bridge. "Sapper" is a nickname for an army engineer. Yukon government **Engineer Creek Campground**; 15 sites, camping permit $12, fireplaces, water, tables, pit toilets. Grayling fishing.

J 122.9 (195.7 km) I 333.4 (536.5 km) The 360-foot/110-m Jeckell Bridge spans the **Ogilvie River** here. Built by the Canadian Armed Forces Engineers as a training exercise, it is named in honour of Allan Jeckell, controller of the Yukon from 1932 to 1946. Fossil coral may be visible in limestone outcrops to the northeast of the bridge.

The Ogilvie River and Ogilvie Mountains were named in honour of William Ogilvie, a highly respected Dominion land surveyor and commissioner of the Yukon during the Klondike Gold Rush.

J 123 (195.8 km) I 333.3 (536.4 km) Ogilvie grader station, Yukon government maintenance camp is on north side of the river.

For the next 25 miles/40 km, the highway follows the narrow valley of the Ogilvie River. For the first 12 miles/20 km, talus slopes edge the road, and game trails are evident along their precipitous sides.

J 124.3 (197.7 km) I 332 (534.3 km) View of castlelike outcroppings of rock, known as **tors**, on mountaintops to north.

J 131.9 (209.5 km) I 324.4 (522.1 km) Between here and Kilometrepost 216, watch

Homemade sign warns of slippery road north of Eagle Plains. (© Earl L. Brown, staff)

for bird nests in the shale embankments along the highway and unusual rock outcroppings and erosion pillars in surrounding hills. Highway crosses rolling plateau country near Kilometrepost 218.

J 137.5 (221.2 km) I 318.8 (513 km) Small turnout with litter barrels. Easy access to **Ogilvie River**. Good grayling fishing. Elephant Rock may be viewed from right side of road northbound. Fascinating mountain of broken rock and shale near Kilometrepost 224.

J 137.6 (221.5 km) I 318.7 (512.9 km) Davies Creek.

J 149.1 (235.8 km) I 307.2 (494.4 km) Ogilvie airstrip. The great gray owl, one of Canada's largest, is known to nest as far north as this area.

J 154.4 (244 km) I 301.9 (485.8 km) Highway climbs away from the Ogilvie River, following a high ridge to the Eagle Plains plateau. One of the few unglaciated areas in Canada, this country is shaped by wind and water erosion rather than by ice. Views of Mount Cronkhite and Mount McCullum to the east.

Overgrown seismic lines next 62 miles/100 km are a reminder that this was the major area of oil and gas exploration activity for which the road was originally built. In season, fields of cotton grass and varieties of tundra plants make good photo subjects. The road continues to follow a high ridge (elev. 1,969 feet/600m) with broad sweeps and easy grades.

J 160.9 (259 km) I 295.4 (475.4 km) Panoramic **Ogilvie Ridge** viewpoint is a large double-ended turnout with interpretive panels on the geology of the area; outhouse, litter barrels. Lowbush cranberries in August.

J 169.4 (272.6 km) I 286.9 (461.7 km) Highway begins descent northbound and crosses fabulous high rolling country above tree line.

J 202 (325 km) I 254.3 (409.2 km) Road widens to become part of an airstrip.

J 206.9 (325 km) I 249.4 (401.3 km) Double-ended turnout with litter barrels.

J 215.6 (347 km) I 240.7 (387.4 km) Richardson Mountains to the northeast. The thick blanket of rock and gravel that makes up the roadbed ahead is designed to prevent the underlying permafrost from melting. The roadbed conducts heat more than the surrounding vegetation does and must be extra thick to compensate. Much of the highway was built in winter.

J 229.3 (369 km) I 227 (365.3 km) Milepost 231. **EAGLE PLAINS**; hotel, phone (867) 993-2453; food, gas, propane, aviation fuel, diesel, tire repair, lodging and camping. Open year-round.

Built in 1978, just before completion of the Dempster Highway, the hotel here was an engineering challenge. Engineers considered the permafrost in the area and found a place where the bedrock was at the surface. The hotel was built on this natural pad, thus avoiding the costly process of building on pilings as was done at Inuvik.

Mile 231. Eagle Plains Hotel. Located midway on the Dempster, this year-round facility is an oasis in the wilderness. Modern hotel rooms, plus restaurant and lounge. Full camper services including electrical hookups, laundry, store, dump station, minor repairs, tires, propane and road and area information. Check out our historical photos. See display ad this section. [ADVERTISEMENT]

J 234.8 (377.8 km) I 221.5 (356.5 km)

Eagle Plains Hotel
MIDWAY ON THE DEMPSTER
MILE 231
Explore the Land of Legend

MODERN HOTEL • RESTAURANT • LOUNGE
GIFT SHOP
CAMPGROUND • LAUNDRY
SHOWERS
SERVICE STATION
UNLEADED • DIESEL • PROPANE
AVIATION GAS & JP4

Bag Service 2735
Whitehorse, Yukon Y1A 3V5

**Phone/Fax
(867) 993-2453**

Arctic Circle sign at Milepost J 252 is a popular photo stop on the Dempster Highway. (© Earl L. Brown, staff)

Short side road to picnic site with information sign about Albert Johnson, "The Mad Trapper of Rat River." Something of a mystery man, Johnson killed one mounted policeman and wounded another in 2 separate incidents involving complaints that Johnson was tampering with Native trap lines. The ensuing manhunt became famous in the North, as Johnson eluded Mounties for 48 days during the winter of 1931–32. Johnson was killed in a shoot-out on Feb. 17, 1932. He was buried at Aklavik, a community located 36 miles/58 km west of Inuvik by air.

Dick North, author of 2 books on Johnson (and also author of *The Lost Patrol*), was quoted in the *New York Times* (June 3, 1990) as being 95 percent certain that Johnson, whose true identity has not been known, was a Norwegian–American bank robber named Johnny Johnson.

J **234.9** (378 km) I **221.4** (356.3 km) **Eagle River Bridge**. Like the Ogilvie bridge, it was built by the Dept. of National Defense as a training exercise. In contrast to the other rivers seen from the Dempster, the Eagle is a more sluggish, silt-laden stream with unstable banks. It is the main drainage channel for the western slopes of the Richardson Mountains. It and its tributaries provide good grayling fishing. Canoeists leave here bound for Alaska via the Porcupine and Yukon rivers.

J **239.4** (385.3 km) I **216.9** (349.1 km) Views of the Richardson Mountains (elev. 3,937 feet/1,200m) ahead. Named for Sir John Richardson, surgeon and naturalist on both of Sir John Franklin's overland expeditions to the Arctic Ocean.

J **241.7** (389 km) I **214.6** (345.4 km) **Private Aircraft**: Emergency airstrip; elev. 2,365 feet/721m; length 2,500 feet/762m; gravel. Used regularly by aircraft hauling freight to Old Crow, a Kutchin Indian settlement on the Porcupine River and Yukon's most northerly community.

J **252** (405.5 km) I **204.3** (328.8 km) Large double-ended turnout at **Arctic Circle Crossing**, 66°33′N; picnic tables, litter barrels, outhouses. On June 21, the sun does not fall below the horizon for 24 hours at this latitude.

Highway crosses arctic tundra on an elevated berm beside the Richardson Mountains; sweeping views.

J **269** (432.9 km) I **187.3** (301.4 km) Rock River.

J **277** (445.8 km) I **179.3** (288.5 km) Yukon government **Cornwall River Campground**; 18 sites, camping permit ($12), tables, kitchen shelter, water, firepits, outhouses. Black flies; bring repellent.

J **280.1** (450.8 km) I **176.2** (283.6 km) Turnout. Northbound, the highway winds toward the Richardson Mountains, crossing them at George's Gap near the YT–NWT border. Good hiking area and excellent photo possibilities.

J **288** (463.5 km) I **168.3** (270.8 km) Turnout; good overnight spot for self-contained vehicles.

J **288.5** (464.3 km) I **167.8** (270 km) Plaque about Wright Pass, named for Al Wright, a highway engineer with Public Works Canada who was responsible for the routing of the Dempster Highway.

J **288.9** (465 km) I **167.4** (269.4 km) **YT-NWT Border**. Historical marker. *TIME ZONE CHANGE: Yukon Territory observes Pacific standard time; Northwest Territories is on Mountain time.* Continental Divide in the Richardson Mountains: West of here, water flows to the Pacific Ocean. East of here, water flows to the Arctic Ocean. Good photo spot.

NWT HIGHWAY 8

IMPORTANT: Kilometreposts northbound (with white letters on a blue background) indicate distance from YT–NWT border and are indicated at intervals in our log. Highway descends, road narrows, northbound.

J **297.6** (479 km) I **158.7** (255.4 km) Kilometrepost 14. **James Creek**; good grayling fishing. Highway maintenance camp. Good spot to park overnight.

J **299** (481.2 km) I **157.3** (253.1 km) Sign advises no passing next 4.3 miles/7 km; climb to Wright Pass summit.

J **303.7** (488.7 km) I **152.6** (245.6 km) **Wright Pass Summit**. From here northbound, the Dempster Highway descends 2,300 feet/853m to the Peel River crossing, 32 miles/51 km away.

J **316.3** (509 km) I **140** (225.3 km) Kilometrepost 44. Side road leads down to **Midway Lake**.

J **319.4** (514 km) I **136.9** (220.3 km) **Private Aircraft**: Highway widens to form Midway airstrip; length 3,000 feet/914m.

J **329.3** (530 km) I **127** (204.4 km) View of Peel River Valley and Fort McPherson to north. Litter barrels.

J **332.4** (535 km) I **123.9** (199.4 km) Kilometrepost 70. Highway begins descent northbound to Peel River.

J **334.9** (539 km) I **121.4** (195.4 km) **Peel River Crossing**, locally called Eightmile because it is situated 8 miles/12.8 km south of Fort McPherson. Free government ferry (CF *Abraham Francis*) operates 15 hours a day during summer from early June to late October. Double-ended cable ferry: Drive on, drive off. Light vehicles cross by ice bridge in late November; heavier vehicles cross as ice thickens. *No crossing possible during freezeup or breakup*. Phone toll free (800) 661-0752 for information on ferry crossings, road conditions and weather.

The level of the Peel River changes rapidly in spring and summer in response to meltwater from the mountains and ice jams on the Mackenzie River. Extreme high and low water level fluctuations may cause delays in ferry service. The alluvial flood plain is covered by muskeg on the flats, and scrubby alder and stunted black spruce on the valley sides.

Natives from Fort McPherson have summer tent camps on the Peel River. The Indians net whitefish and sheefish (inconnu) then dry them on racks or in smokehouses for the winter.

About 4 miles/6.4 km south upstream is a trail leading to Shiltee Rock, which gives excellent views of the Peel River and the southern end of the Mackenzie.

J **335.9** (540.6 km) I **120.4** (193.8 km) Nitainilaii territorial campground with 20 sites. (Campground name is from the Gwich'in term *Noo-til-ee*, meaning "fast flowing waters.") Information centre open daily June to September. Camping permits, potable water, firewood, pit toilets and kitchen shelter available.

J **337.4** (543 km) I **118.9** (191.3 km) Kilometrepost 78.

J **340.4** (547.8 km) I **115.9** (186.5 km) Access road right to Fort McPherson airport.

J **341.8** (550 km) I **114.5** (184.3 km) Side road on left to Fort McPherson (Tetlin Zheh); description follows.

Fort McPherson

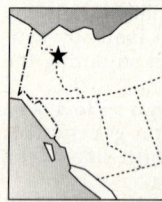

Located on a flat-topped hill about 100 feet/30m above the Peel River, 24 miles/38 km from its junction with the Mackenzie River; 100 miles/160 km southwest of Aklavik by boat along Peel Channel, 31 miles/50 km directly east of the Richardson Mountains. **Population**: 952. **Emergency Services**: RCMP, phone (867) 952-2551. **Health Center**, phone (867) 952-2586.

Visitor Information: Located in a restored log house, the former home of elder Annie G. Robert; open daily, early June through mid-September, 9 A.M. to 9 P.M. Or contact Hamlet of Fort McPherson at Box

Arctic Red River (Tsiigehtchic) is accessible by ferry. (© Lyn Hancock)

57, Fort McPherson, NT Canada X0E 0J0; phone (867) 952-2428; fax (867) 952-2725. Or visit www.yukoninfo.com/inuvik/fortmcpherson.htm. **Radio**: CBC 680.

Transportation: Air—Aklak Air provides scheduled air service from Inuvik.

Private Aircraft: Fort McPherson airstrip; 67°24'N 134°51'W; elev. 142 feet/43m; length 3,500 feet/1,067m; gravel.

This Déné Indian settlement has a public phone, cafe, bed and breakfast, 2 general stores and 2 service stations (1 with tire repair). A co-op hotel here offers 8 rooms. Arts and crafts include beadwork and hide garments. Wildlife watching, adventure tours and canoe trips are popular along the Peel River.

Fort McPherson was named in 1848 for Murdoch McPherson, chief trader of the Hudson's Bay Co., which had established its first posts in the area 8 years before. Between 1849 and 1859 there were frequent feuds with neighboring Inuit, who later moved farther north to the Aklavik area, where they established a fur-trading post.

In addition to subsistence fishing and hunting, income is earned from trapping (mostly muskrat and mink), handicrafts, government employment, and commercial enterprises.

Photos and artifacts depicting the history and way of life of the community are displayed in the Chief Julius School. Buried in the cemetery outside the Anglican church are Inspector Francis J. Fitzgerald and 3 men from the ill-fated North West Mounted Police patrol of 1910–1911 between Fort McPherson and Dawson.

Inspector Fitzgerald and the men had left Fort McPherson on Dec. 21, 1910, carrying mail and dispatches to Dawson City. By Feb. 20, 1911, the men had not yet arrived in Dawson, nearly a month overdue. A search party led by Corporal W.J.D. Dempster was sent to look for the missing patrol. On March 22, 1911, Dempster discovered their frozen bodies only 26 miles from where they had started. Lack of knowledge of the trail, coupled with too few rations, had doomed the 4-man patrol. One of the last entries in Fitzgerald's diary, quoted in Dick North's *The Lost Patrol*, an account of their journey, read: "We have now only 10 pounds of flour and 8 pounds of bacon and some dried fish. My last hope is gone. ... We have been a week looking for a river to take us over the divide, but there are dozens of rivers, and I am at a loss."

Dempster Highway Log
(continued)

J 342.4 (551 km) **I 113.9** (183.3 km) Kilometrepost 86.

J 365.1 (587.6 km) **I 91.2** (146.8 km) **Frog Creek**. Grayling and pike. Road on right northbound leads to picnic area.

J 377.1 (606.8 km) **I 79.2** (127.5 km) Mackenzie River wayside area.

J 377.9 (608.2 km) **I 78.4** (126.2 km) **Mackenzie River Crossing**. Free government ferry (MV *Louis Cardinal*) operates 15 hours a day during summer from early June to late October. Double-ended ferry: Drive on, drive off. Light vehicles may cross by ice bridge in late November; heavier vehicles can cross as ice thickens. *No crossing possible during freezeup and breakup.*

The ferry travels between landings on either side of the Mackenzie River and also provides access to **TSIIGEHTCHIC** (formerly **ARCTIC RED RIVER**), a small Gwichya Gwich'in community (pop. 195) located at the confluence of the Mackenzie and Arctic Red rivers. Tsiigehtchic has a community-owned grocery store and cafe. The Sunshine Inn provides accommodations for up to 8 people. Boat tours are available through the Band Store or local operators. For more information on lodging or tours call (867) 953-3003 or fax (867) 953-3906.

The Arctic Red River (Tsiigehnjik) was declared a Canadian Heritage River in 1993. Tsiigehnjik, the Gwich'in name for the river, winds its way out of the Mackenzie Mountains and flows into the Mackenzie River at Tsiigehtchic. The Gwichya Gwich'in have long used and traveled the river for fishing, hunting and trapping.

J 399.6 (643 km) **I 56.7** (91.2 km) **Rengling River**, grayling fishing.

J 404.4 (650.8 km) **I 51.9** (83.5 km) Beginning of 13-mile/21-km straight stretch.

J 409.7 (659.3 km) **I 46.6** (75 km) Distance marker shows Inuvik 75 km.

J 426.3 (686 km) **I 30** (48.3 km) Vadzaih Van Tshik picnic and camping area.

J 431.4 (694.3 km) **I 24.9** (40.1 km) Campbell Lake and Campbell escarpment ahead northbound. Good place to glass for peregrine falcons.

J 440.6 (709 km) **I 15.7** (25.3 km) Ehjuu Njik picnic spot; pit toilets.

J 442.4 (712 km) **I 13.9** (22.4 km) Nihtak picnic and camping area; pit toilets. Good fishing for pike and whitefish, some sheefish (inconnu). Creek leads a short distance to Campbell Lake. Boat launch. Bring mosquito repellent.

J 449.9 (724 km) **I 6.4** (10.3 km) Airport Road turnoff; pavement begins.

J 451.7 (727 km) **I 4.6** (7.4 km) Kilometrepost 262.

J 454 (730.6 km) **I 2.3** (3.7 km) Chuk Park territorial campground; 38 campsites, 14 pull-through, electric hookups, firewood, water, showers, $12–$15 fee. Lookout tower. Interpretive information available.

J 456.3 (734.3 km) **I 0** Turn left northbound for Inuvik town centre (description follows).

Inuvik

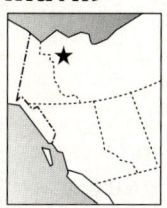

Situated on a flat wooded plateau on the east channel of the Mackenzie River, some 60 air miles/96 km south of the Beaufort Sea, 36 air miles/58 km and 70 water miles/113 km from Aklavik on the western edge of the delta. **Population**: 3,451, Déné, White and Inuvialuit.

Emergency Services: RCMP, phone (867) 777-2935. **Hospital**, Inuvik General, phone (867) 777-2955.

Visitor Information: Western Arctic Regional Visitors Centre is located on Mackenzie Road across from the hospital.

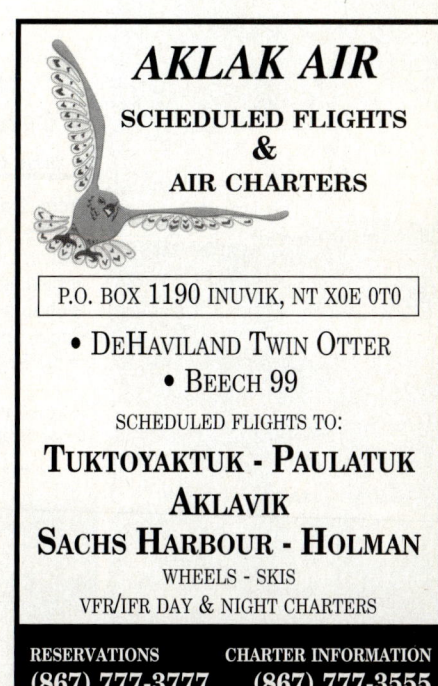

Drive with headlights on at all times.

The centre is open mid-May to mid-September and features interactive displays, excellent wildlife displays, clean restrooms and knowledgeable staff. A must visit in Inuvik. A green and white Cessna 170 is mounted as a weather vane at the centre and rotates to face into the wind. Contact Town of Inuvik, Box 1160, Inuvik, NT X0E 0T0; phone (867) 777-8618; fax (867) 777-8619. Or visit www.town.inuvik.nt.ca or www.yukoninfo..com/inuvik. Visitors are also welcome to stop by the Ingamo Hall Friendship Centre.

Visitors are encouraged to stop by the town office (2 First St.) to sign the guest book and pick up an "Order of the Arctic" adventures certificate. Phone (867) 777-8600 for more information.

Elevation: 224 feet/68m. **Climate:** May 24 marks 57 days of midnight sun. The sun begins to set on July 19; on Dec. 6, the sun sets and does not rise until Jan. 6. Average annual precipitation 4 inches rainfall, 69 inches snowfall. July mean high 67°F/19°C, mean low 45°F/7°C. January mean high is -11°F/-24°C, mean low is -30°F/-35°C. **Radio** and **Television:** CBC and local. **Newspaper:** *The Drum* (weekly).

Private Aircraft: Tom Zubko Airport (daily jet service); elev. 224 feet/68m; length 6,000 feet/1,829m; asphalt; fuel 80, 100.

Inuvik, meaning "The Place of Man," is the largest Canadian community north of the Arctic Circle, and the major government, transportation and communication centre for Canada's western Arctic. Construction of the town began in 1955 and was completed in 1961. It was the main supply base for the petrochemical exploration of the delta until Tuktoyaktuk took over that role as activity centered in the Beaufort Sea. In Inuvik some hunting, fishing and trapping is done, but most people earn wages in government and private enterprises, particularly in transportation, tourism and construction. As the delta is one of the richest muskrat areas in the world, Inuvik is the western centre for shipping furs south.

The town's official monument says, in part, that Inuvik was "the first community north of the Arctic Circle built to provide the normal facilities of a Canadian town."

Transportation

Air: Aklak Air provides scheduled service between Inuvik and Tuktoyaktuk, Sachs Harbour, Holman and Paulatuk. Scheduled service is also available to Aklavik; Whitehorse and Old Crow, YT; Edmonton, AB; and Yellowknife, NWT. Several air charter services operate out of Inuvik, offering flights to delta communities and charter service for hunting, fishing and camping trips.

Highways: Dempster Highway from Dawson City. Winter roads (December into April) to Aklavik (73 miles/117 km) and Tuktoyaktuk (121 miles/194 km).

Bus: Service from Tuktoyaktuk to Inuvik by charter service via Arctic Tour Co. Or service from Dawson City via Dawson City Courier, phone (867) 993-6688.

Taxi and **rental cars:** Available.

Lodging & Services

Visitors will find most facilities available, although accommodations should be reserved in advance. Inuvik has 5 hotels, all with dining lounges, and bed and breakfasts. There are also a laundry, post office, territorial liquor store, banks and churches. There are 3 gas stations and a car wash; propane, auto repair and towing are available. Hardware, grocery and general stores, and gift shops are here.

Arctic Chalet. Lakeside country setting on edge of town. Seven cabin units, homey and comfortable, with private or shared bath. Clean, comfortable, non-smoking rooms with single, double and queen beds. Laundry facility. Complimentary canoes. $96 single, $110 double, twin rooms $130. Courtesy cars and rental vehicles available. Winter dogsledding at its best. Visa, MasterCard & Diners accepted. Phone (867) 777-3535, fax (867) 777-4443; www.arcticchalet.com; email judi@arcticchalet.com.
[ADVERTISEMENT]

Camping

Happy Valley territorial campground; 38 RV sites, electrical hookups, 10 tent pads,

---

TOP of the world adventure! From Inuvik, NWT

ARCTIC NATURE TOURS

to Tuktoyaktuk, Herschel Island, Delta cruises & more...
1-867-777-3300
www.arcticnaturetours.com
arcticnt@idc.inuvialuit.com

INUVIK ADVERTISERS

Aklak Air	Ph. (867) 777-3777
Arctic Chalet	Ph. (867) 777-3535
Arctic Esso Service	Ph. (867) 777-3974
Arctic Nature Tours	Ph. (867) 777-3300
Great Northern Arts Festival, The	Ph. (867) 777-3536
Town of Inuvik Tourism	Ph. (867) 777-8618

INUVIK
www.town.inuvik.nt.ca
Northwest Territories, Canada
"Gateway to the Beaufort - Delta"

Drive Our Northernmost ROAD
From Dawson City Yukon, drive the world's most spectacular wilderness routes. Dempster Highway - Watch for wildlife as you skirt the peaks of the Richardson range, cross the Arctic Circle, and head for **Inuvik**, in the heart of the Beaufort/Mackenzie Delta.

For information on the Dempster Highway:
Resources, Wildlife & Economic Development.
E-mail: travel_westernarctic@gov.nt.ca

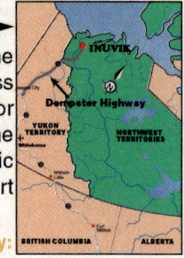

Visit Our Northernmost TOWN
Inuvik means the "Place of People". Inuvik offers all modern amenities with northern hospitality that will ensure any visitor a pleasant stay and an adventure of a lifetime!

For information on Inuvik:
Town of Inuvik
Box 1160
Inuvik, NT X0E 0T0
Phone: 867-777-8618 Fax: 867-777-8619
E-mail: cmitchell@town.inuvik.nt.ca

ARCTIC ESSO SERVICE (Esso)

Box 2508, 17 Distributor St., Inuvik, NWT X0E 0T0
Gas • Diesel & Oil • Automotive Lubes
Hankook Tires & Repair
Coin-operated Car Wash, Ice, Misc. Merch.
Phone (867) 777-3974
Fax (867) 777-3174
24 Hour Credit Card Pumps
Most Major Credit Cards Accepted

hot showers, laundromat, firewood, water, dump station, fee. Chuk Park territorial campground; 38 sites, electrical hookups, firewood, water, showers, $12–$15 fee. ▲

Attractions

Igloo Church, painted white with lines to simulate snow blocks, is on Mackenzie Road as you drive into Inuvik. Inside the church is Inuit painter Mona Thrasher's interpretation of the Stations of the Cross. Visitors are welcome.

Ingamo Hall is a 2-story log community hall that serves the social and recreational needs of Native families. Visitors are welcome. The hall was built by Allan Crich over a 3-year period, using some 1,020 logs that were cut from white spruce trees in the southern part of the Mackenzie River valley and floated down the river to Inuvik.

Tour Western Arctic Communities: Air charter service is available to **AKLAVIK** (pop. 735), an important centre for muskrat harvesting; **TUKTOYAKTUK** (pop. 930), an Inuit village on the Arctic coast and site of oil development; **SACHS HARBOUR** (pop. 114) on Banks Island, an Inuit settlement supported by trapping and some big game outfitters; **PAULATUK** (pop. 300), an Inuit settlement supported by hunting, fishing, sealing and trapping; and **HOLMAN** (pop. 450), an Inuit community on the west coast of Victoria Island, famous for its printmaking. Scheduled air service is also available to **OLD CROW** (pop. 267), an Indian settlement on the Porcupine River in Yukon Territory.

The **Mackenzie River delta**, one of the largest deltas in North America (one of the tenth largest in the world) and an important wildlife corridor to the Arctic, is 40 miles/64 km wide and 60 miles/97 km long. A maze of lakes, channels and islands, the delta supports a variety of bird life, fish and muskrats. Boat tours of the Mackenzie River are available.

Go for a hike on one of the areas walking trails. Jimmy Adams Peace Trail follows a loop around Boot Lake. There is also a trail in Chief Jim Vide Park.

Other attractions include the community greenhouse, Inuvik Centennial Library and the Dick Hill Collection, ice roads on and around the delta and permafrost and Utilidor System exhibits.

Special Events. The annual Northern Games are held in Inuvik or other western Arctic communities in summer. Visitors are welcome to watch participants compete in traditional Inuit and Déné sports; dances, and crafts are also part of the festival. For information, write Northern Games Assoc., Box 1184, Inuvik, NT X0E 0T0.

The 14th annual **Great Northern Arts Festival** is scheduled for July 11–20, 2003. Over 80 artists and 40 performers from across the North—Inuit, Inuvialuit, Gwich'in, Dene, Metis and non-Native—gather for 10 days every summer for a festival under the midnight sun. Soapstone carvers, print-makers, painters, jewellers and sewers create works of art as visitors look on. Meet the artists, take art workshops or choose from more than 1,500 works of art in the gallery. Evenings are full of music, dance, story-telling and fashion shows showcasing the diverse cultures of the North. A remarkable cultural event. For more information contact the Great Northern Arts Festival, Box 2921, Inuvik, NT X0E 0T0; phone (867) 777-3536, fax (867) 777-4445; email info@gnaf.ca web site www.greatart.nt.ca or www.gnaf.ca.

The **Sunrise Festival**, held the first week in January, is an annual celebration to welcome the sun back after 30 days of darkness. The festival is held at the old airstrip and includes bonfires, concessions and a fireworks display.

Other special events include Delta Daze in October and the Muskrat Jamboree in April. For more information, phone (867) 777-8600, or visit www.town.inuvik.nt.ca.

Exterior of Inuvik's Igloo Church is painted to simulate snow blocks. (© Lyn Hancock)

Inuit, Inuvialuit, Gwich'in, Dene, Metis and non-Natives participate in the Great Northern Arts Festival In Inuvik in July.

LIARD HIGHWAY

Connects: Alaska Hwy. to Mackenzie Hwy. **Length:** 244 miles
Road Surface: Paved and gravel **Season:** Open all year
Steepest Grade: 10 percent
Major Attraction: Nahanni National Park

	Fort Liard	Fort Nelson	Simpson
Fort Liard		126	176
Fort Nelson	126		302
Fort Simpson	176	302	

Paving is planned for the BC portion of the Liard Highway. (© Ernest Manewal)

The Liard Highway begins about 17 miles/27 km north of Fort Nelson on the Alaska Highway and leads northeast through British Columbia and Northwest Territories for 243 miles/391 km to junction with the Mackenzie Highway (NWT Highway 1).

The Liard Highway, also called the Liard Trail or "Moose Highway" (after the road sign logo), is named for the Liard River Valley through which it runs for most of its length. In French, Liard means "black poplar," and this wilderness highway (officially opened in June 1984) is a corridor through a forest of white and black spruce, trembling aspen and balsam poplar.

The Liard is a relatively straight 2-lane road. The NWT portion of the highway is well-maintained. Road reconstruction and paving are planned for the 85-mile BC portion of the Liard Highway. The gravel portion of the road can be dusty when dry and very muddy when wet. "Dust-free zones" are treated with calcium chloride .For current road conditions, check with the Visitor Infocentre in Fort Nelson, BC. Travel information for the Northwest Territories is available from Northwest Territories Tourism; phone toll free weekdays (800) 661-0788.

Food, lodging, gas and diesel are available at Fort Liard. Gas, food and lodging are also available at the Mackenzie Highway junction. It is a good idea to fill up your gas tank in Fort Nelson.

Although the Northwest Territories portion of the Liard Highway parallels the Liard River, there is limited access to the river. The Liard Highway does offer good views of the Liard River Valley and the Mackenzie Mountain Range. Travelers may enhance their trip by visiting Blackstone Territorial Park (accessible by road) and exploring Nahanni National Park by air charter out of Fort Liard, Fort Simpson or Fort Nelson.

Fishing the highway streams is only fair, but watch for wildlife such as moose, black bear, wood bison and grouse. Remember to bring along lots of insect repellent!

Liard Highway Log

Distance from the junction with the Alaska Highway (A) is followed by distance from the Mackenzie Highway junction (M).

NOTE: Physical kilometreposts are up on the British Columbia portion of the highway about every 5 kilometres, starting here with Km 0 at the Alaska Highway junction and ending at the BC–NWT border.

BC HIGHWAY 77

A 0 M 243 (391.3 km) *Watch for road construction to Fort Liard in summer 2003. Paving/chip sealing underway. Speed limit is 60 kmph. Speeding fines double in construction areas.*

Junction with the Alaska Highway. Turn to **Milepost DC 301** on page 122 in the ALASKA HIGHWAY section for log.

A 6.2 (10.1 km) **M 236.8** (381.2 km) Beaver Creek.

A 6.4 (10.3 km) **M 236.6** (381 km) Short side road east to Beaver Lake recreation site; 7 picnic tables, litter barrels, pit toilet, firewood, boat launch, turnaround space. Short hike downhill through brush to floating dock; limited lake access.

A 14.3 (23.1 km) **M 228.7** (368.2 km) Stanolind Creek. Beaver dams to west.

A 17.5 (28.2 km) **M 225.5** (363.1 km) Pond to west and cut line through trees shows Cat access in summer, ice road in winter.

A 21.1 (34 km) **M 221.9** (357.3 km) Westcoast Transmission Pipeline crossing. Pipeline transports natural gas from Pointed Mountain near Fort Liard to the company's gas plant on the Alaska Highway just south of Fort Nelson.

A 24.2 (38.9 km) **M 218.8** (352.4 km) Road begins descent northbound to Fort Nelson River.

A 26.4 (42.5 km) **M 216.6** (348.8 km) **Fort Nelson River bridge** (elev. 978 feet/298m), single lane, reduce speed. The Nelson bridge is the longest Acrow bridge in the world at 1,410 feet/430m. It is 14 feet/4m wide, with a span of 230 feet/70m from pier to pier. The Acrow bridge, formerly called the Bailey bridge after its designer Sir Donald Bailey, is designed of interchangeable steel panels coupled with pins for rapid construction.

A 26.6 (42.9 km) **M 216.4** (348.4 km) Turnout at north end of bridge with pit toilet, table and garbage container.

A 39.7 (63.9 km) **M 203.3** (327.4 km) Tsinhia Creek, grayling run for about 2 weeks in spring.

A 43.4 (69.8 km) **M 199.6** (321.5 km) Trapper's cabin to east.

A 51.8 (83.3 km) **M 191.2** (308 km) Side road leads west 1.9 miles/3 km to Tsinhia Lake and dead-ends in soft sandy track. A recreation site is planned at Tsinhia Lake.

A 59.2 (95.3 km) **M 183.8** (296 km) There are several winter roads in this area used by the forest, oil and gas industries. To most summer travelers these roads look like long cut lines or corridors through the Bush.

The Liard Highway replaced the old Fort Simpson winter road that joined Fort Nelson and Fort Simpson. The original Simpson Trail was first blazed in November 1942 by Alaska Highway engineers, including the 648th, Company A detachment.

A 69.4 (111.7 km) **M 173.6** (279.6 km) Bridge over d'Easum Creek (elev. 1,608 feet/490m). Good bird-watching area.

A 71.4 (115 km) **M 171.6** (276.3 km) Access to Maxhamish Lake via 8-mile/13-km winter road accessible in summer by all-terrain vehicles only. A recreation site is planned for Maxhamish Lake.

A 74 (119.1 km) **M 169** (272.2 km) Wide unnamed creek flows into Emile Creek to east. Good bird-watching area, beaver pond.

A 75.4 (121.4 km) **M 167.6** (269.9 km) Highway emerges from trees northbound; view west of Mount Martin (elev. 4,460 feet/1,360m) and the Kotaneelee Range.

A 80.6 (129.7 km) **M 162.4** (261.6 km) View northwest of mountain ranges in Northwest Territories.

A 81.2 (130.7 km) **M 161.8** (260.6 km) *Highway begins 7 percent downgrade northbound to Petitot River.*

A 82.8 (133.2 km) **M 160.2** (258.1 km) Petitot River bridge. The **Petitot River** is reputed to have the warmest swimming water in British Columbia (70°F/21°C). A 9-hour canoe trip to Fort Liard is possible from here (some sheer rock canyons and rapids en route). Good bird-watching area. Also freshwater clams, pike and pickerel; short grayling run in spring.

The Petitot River was named for Father Petitot, an Oblate missionary who came to this area from France in the 1860s.

The Petitot River bridge was the site of the official opening of the Liard Highway on June 23, 1984. The ceremony was marked by an unusual ribbon-cutting: A 1926 Model T Ford, carrying dignitaries, was driven through the ribbon (which stretched for about 20 feet before snapping) while a guard of kilted pipers from Yellowknife played. The Model T, driven by Marl Brown of Fort Nelson, had been across this route in March 1975 just weeks after the bush road had been punched through by Cats and seismic equipment. This earlier trip, in which Mr. Brown was accompanied by Mickey Hempler, took 44 hours from Fort Nelson to Fort Simpson.

A 84.1 (135.4 km) **M 158.9** (255.9 km) Crest of Petitot River hill. *Highway begins 10 percent downgrade northbound.*

NWT HIGHWAY 7

NOTE: Kilometreposts are up about every 2 kilometres on the Northwest Territories portion of the highway, starting here with Km 0 at the BC–NWT border and ending at the junction with the Mackenzie Highway.

A 85 (136.8 km) **M 158** (254.5 km) **BC–NWT border**. TIME ZONE CHANGE: British Columbia observes Pacific time, Northwest Territories observes Mountain time.

Northwest Territories communities impose their own restrictions on alcohol. Possession of alcohol is prohibited in some communities and restricted in others. Trading of alcohol for other items is illegal. Do not leave behind any left-over alcohol. For current information on restrictions, contact the local RCMP, or inquire at your hotel or

www.themilepost.com

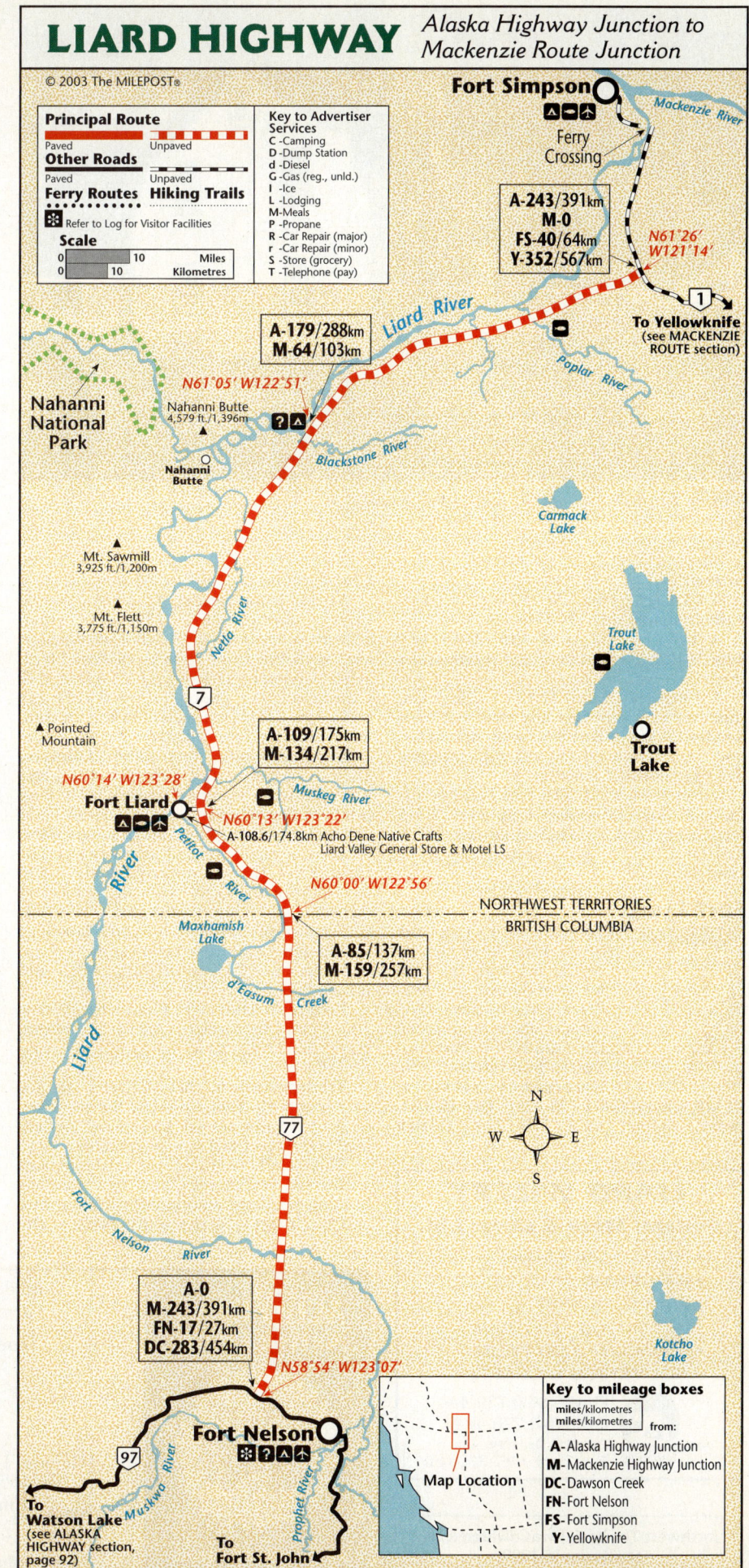

LIARD HIGHWAY • Fort Liard

Roman Catholic mission in Fort Liard. (© Lyn Hancock)

outfitter's.

A 85.2 (137.1 km) **M 157.8** (254.2 km) Turnout to east with litter barrels.

A 107 (172.2 km) **M 136** (219.1 km) Vehicle inspection station and weigh scales to east.

A 108.6 (174.8 km) **M 134.4** (216.5 km) Junction with dust-free side road that leads 4 miles/6.4 km to Fort Liard (description follows). Double-ended turnout with interpretive signs north of junction.

Views from road into Fort Liard across the Liard River of Mount Coty (elev. 2,715 feet/830m) and Pointed Mountain (elev. 4,610 feet/1,405m) at the southern tip of the Liard Range.

Fort Liard

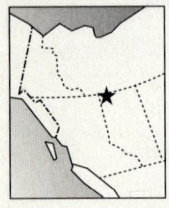

Located on the south bank of the Liard River near its confluence with the Petitot River (known locally as Black River because of its colour), about 50 miles/80 km south of Nahanni Butte. **Population:** 530. **Emergency Services:** RCMP, phone (867) 770-4221. **Fire Department,** phone (867) 770-2222. Health Centre, phone (867) 770-4301.

Visitor Information: Acho Dene Native Crafts, phone (867) 770-4161; email achoart@internorth.com. Visitor information also available from Hamlet of Fort Liard. Write: Generaly Delivery, Fort Liard, NT Canada X0E 0A0; phone (867) 770-4104; Fax (867) 770-4004; emai ftliard@ssimicro.com; www.ssimicro.com/~ftliard.

Elevation: 686 feet/209m. **Climate:** There is no permafrost here. Good soil and water, a long summer season with long hours of daylight, and comparatively mild climate considering Fort Liard's geographical location. Several luxuriant local gardens. The Liard River here is approximately 1,500 feet/450m wide, fairly swift and subject to occasional flooding. **Radio** and **Television:** CBC radio (microwave), a Native language station and CKLB from Yellowknife; 4 channels plus CBC Television (Anik), APTN and private satellite receivers. .

Private Aircraft: Fort Liard airstrip; elev. 700 feet/213m; length 2,950 feet/899m; gravel; fuel 100/130 (obtain from Deh Cho Air Ltd.).

Transportation: Air—Charter service year-round via Deh Cho Air. **Barge—**Non-scheduled barge service in summer. Scheduled and charter taxi service available.

This small, well-laid-out settlement of traditional log homes and new modern housing is located among tall poplar, spruce and birch trees on the south bank of the Liard River. Many residents live a comparatively traditional life of hunting, trapping, fishing and making handicrafts. Recently, oil, gas and forestry have created a rise in the local economy. Construction and highway maintenance also provide employment opportunities.

Recreation and sightseeing in the area include fishing (for pike, pickerel, goldeye and spring grayling) at the confluence of the Liard and Petitot rivers and Liard River interpretive boat tours (Hope's Adventures). Air charters and self-guided canoe trips to Trout Lake, Virginia Falls in Nahanni National Park, Nahanni Butte and other destinations are available from Deh Cho Air Ltd. The traditional Dene settlement of **TROUT LAKE** (pop. 70) is also accessible by air from Fort Liard.

The North West Co. established a trading post near here at the confluence of the Liard and Petitot rivers called Riviere aux Liards in 1805. The post was abandoned after the massacre of more than a dozen residents by Indians. It was re-established in 1820, then taken over by the Hudson's Bay Co. in 1821 when the 2 companies merged. The well-known geologist Charles Camsell was born at Fort Liard in 1876.

Food and lodging are available at Liard Valley General Store and Motel and Riverside Inn. Gas, diesel and propane fuel available. Food and general merchandise at the Northern Store, which also houses the Canada Post outlet. There are also a cafe/take-out, the modern Acho Dene School and a Roman Catholic mission. There is no bank in Fort Liard. There is a direct cash ATM in the Liard Fuel Centre. ATM accepts Interac, Amex, Maestro, Mastercard, Cirrus.

Fort Liard residents are well known for the high quality of their birch-bark baskets and porcupine quill workmanship. Local arts and crafts are featured at Echo Dene Native Crafts shop.

Community-run Hay Lake Campground located just off the access road into Fort Liard; 12 campsites, picnic tables, cooking shelter, toilets and a hiking trail around the lake. Bring insect repellent. Campground

---

LIARD VALLEY
General Store & Motel Ltd.

- MOTEL • GROCERIES
- ICE CREAM
- CONFECTIONARY
- DRY GOODS • PRODUCE
- TOBACCO • FAST FOOD
- SOUVENIRS & CRAFTS

Northwest Territories

Phone (867) 770-4441
FAX (867) 770-4442
General Delivery,
Fort Liard, NWT X0G 0A0

Northwest Territories was divided into 2 territories in 1999.

ACHO DENE
Native Crafts

Fort Liard, NT Canada

Quill decorated birch-bark baskets, plus a variety of moosehide products.

Traditional Native Handicrafts

Ms. Eva Hope
General Manager

General Delivery, Fort Liard, NWT X0G 0A0
Tel (867) 770-4161   Fax (867) 770-4160
Email: Achoart@internorth.com

VISA

Open Mon.-Fri. Additional summer hours.

Northwest Territories

road may be slippery when wet.

Acho Dene Native Crafts. See display ad this section.

Liard Valley General Store & Motel Ltd. See display ad this section.

Liard Highway Log
(continued)

A **108.6** (174.8 km) M **134.4** (216.5 km) **Fort Liard junction**. Dust-free zone next 12 miles/20 km northbound.

A **114.2** (183.8 km) M **128.8** (207.5 km) **Muskeg River** bridge (elev. 814 feet/248m); turnout with interpretive sign at north end. Gravel bars on the river make a good rest area. Trapper's cabin. Fishing for pike, pickerel and freshwater clams. The Muskeg River is the local swimming hole for Fort Liard residents.

A **122.5** (197.2 km) M **120.5** (194.1 km) Rabbit Creek.

A **123.4** (198.6 km) M **119.6** (192.7 km) Kilometrepost 62.

A **125.4** (201.9 km) M **117.6** (189.4 km) Big Island Creek bridge (elev. 827 feet/252m). Highway now runs close to the Liard River with good views of Liard Range to the west and northwest for the next 13 miles/21 km northbound.

A **125.8** (202.5 km) M **117.2** (188.8 km) Kilometrepost 66.

A **126.2** (203.2 km) M **116.8** (188.1 km) Views of Mackenzie Mountains to northwest.

A **126.8** (204.1 km) M **116.2** (187.2 km) Highway maintenance site to west with gravel stockpile.

A **127** (204.4 km) M **116** (186.9 km) Kilometrepost 68. Views of Mackenzie Mountains next mile northbound.

A **128.3** (206.6 km) M **114.7** (184.7 km) Kilometrepost 70.

A **131.5** (211.8 km) M **111.5** (179.5 km) Microwave tower to west.

A **132** (212.4 km) M **111** (178.9 km) Kilometrepost 76.

A **133.2** (214.5 km) M**109.8** (176.8 km) Double-ended turnout to west with litter barrels and interpretive signs.

A **137.3** (221.1 km) M **105.7** (170.2 km) Kilometrepost 84.

A **142.5** (229.4 km) M **100.5** (161.9 km) Kilometrepost 92.

A **146.8** (236.3 km) M **96.2** (155 km) Short road west to locally named Whissel Landing on the Liard River, where road construction materials were brought in by barge during construction of the Liard Highway. This Liard River access site is a fall hunting camp for Fort Liard residents. *Please respect private property.*

A **147.3** (237.1 km) M **95.7** (154.2 km) Road widens for an emergency airstrip; elev. 981 feet/299m.

A **155.3** (250 km) M **87.7** (141.3 km) Views of Mackenzie Mountains next 11 miles/17 km southbound .

A **157.4** (253.4 km) M **85.6** (137.9 km) Netla River bridge. The Netla River Delta is an important waterfowl breeding habitat, and Indian fishing and hunting area.

A **157.5** (253.5 km) M **85.5** (137.8 km) Kilometrepost 116.

A **162.8** (262 km) M **80.2** (129.3 km) Road widens for an emergency airstrip; elev. 512 feet/156m.

A **165** (265.5 km) M **78** (125.8 km) Kilometrepost 128.

A **165.8** (266.9 km) M **77.2** (124.4 km) Turnoff to west for winter ice road that leads 13.8 miles/22.3 km to the Dene settlement

Paddlers explore near Lindberg Landing. (© Lyn Hancock)

of **NAHANNI BUTTE** (pop. 107), at the confluence of the South Nahanni and Liard rivers. Summer access by boat or floatplane.

A **168.6** (271.4 km) M **74.4** (119.9 km) Kilometrepost 134.

A **171.7** (276.3 km) M **71.3** (115 km) Creek Bridge, once called Scotty's Creek after an old trapper who had a cabin upstream. There are many such cabins in this area that once belonged (and still belong) to prospectors and trappers, but they are not visible to the motorist. Stands of white spruce, white birch and balsam poplar along highway.

A **174.6** (281 km) M **68.4** (110.3 km) Highway passes through stands of mature aspen next mile northbound.

A **175** (281.7 km) M **68** (109.6 km) Microwave tower.

A **176** (283.2 km) M **67** (108.1 km) Bridge over Upper Blackstone River (elev. 666 feet/203m). Picnic day-use area on riverbank with tables, firewood, firepits and garbage containers.

A **176.1** (283.4 km) M **66.9** (107.9 km) Kilometrepost 146.

A **176.2** (283.7 km) M **66.8** (107.6 km) Blackstone River bridge.

A **178.5** (287.4 km) M **64.5** (103.9 km) Kilometrepost 150.

A **179** (287.9 km) M **64** (103.4 km) Entrance to **Blackstone Territorial Park**; 19 campsites ($12) with tables and firepits; firewood, water and garbage containers, boat dock and state-of-the-art restroom and shower facility. The boat launch is usable only in high water early in the season; use boat launch at Cadillac Landing, **Milepost** A **182.9**, during low water. The visitor information building, built with local logs, is located on the bank of the Liard River with superb views of Nahanni Butte (elev. 4,579 feet/1,396m). The centre is open mid-May to mid-September.

A **180.6** (290.7 km) M **62.4** (100.6 km) Entrance to Lindberg Landing, the homestead of Liard River pioneers Edwin and Sue Lindberg. The Lindbergs offer a bed and breakfast; rustic accommodations, bring your own sleeping bag. By appointment only. Contact Mobile Telephone JR36644 Arrowhead Channel, or write Sue and Edwin Lindberg, Box 28, Fort Simpson, NWT X0E 0N0.

A **182.5** (293.7 km) M **60.5** (97.6 km) Barge landing once used to service Cadillac Mine and bring in construction materials. Access to river via 0.6-mile/0.9-km road (muddy when wet).

A **192.4** (309.7 km) M **50.6** (81.6 km) Road widens northbound (old emergency airstrip).

A **195.6** (314.9 km) M **47.4** (76.4 km) Kilometrepost 178.

A **198.4** (319.3 km) M **44.6** (72 km) Kilometrepost 182.

A **208.9** (336.2 km) M **34.1** (55.1 km) Doubled-ended turnout with interpretive signs. Hike up gravel pile for view of mountains and Liard River valley.

A **211.3** (340 km) M **31.7** (51.3 km) Bridge over Birch River (elev. 840 feet/256m).

A **220.5** (355 km) M **22.5** (36.3 km) Kilometrepost 218.

A **221.5** (356.5 km) M **21.5** (34.8 km) Good grayling and pike fishing in **Poplar River** culverts.

A **221.7** (356.8 km) M **21.3** (34.5 km) Dirt road on left northbound leads 4 miles/ 6.4 km to Liard River; 4-wheel drive recommended. Wide beach, good spot for viewing wildlife.

A **225.5** (362.9 km) M **17.5** (28.4 km) Kilometrepost 226.

A **226.7** (364.9 km) M **16.3** (26.4 km) Microwave tower to east. Vegetation changes northbound to muskeg with black spruce, tamarack and jackpine.

A **230.4** (370.8 km) M **12.6** (20.5 km) Kilometrepost 234.

A **240.2** (386.7 km) M **2.8** (4.6 km) Kilometrepost 250.

A **242.2** (389.9 km) M **0.8** (1.4 km) Double-ended turnout with interpretive signs about the Liard Highway.

A **243** (391.3 km) M **0** "Checkpoint." Gas, diesel, propane, licensed restaurant and motel; phone (867) 695-2953. Turn right (south) for Hay River and Yellowknife; turn left (north) for Fort Simpson.

Junction with the Mackenzie Highway (NWT 1). Turn to **Milepost B 255.3** on page 742 in the MACKENZIE ROUTE section following for log.

MACKENZIE ROUTE

Connects: Grimshaw, AB to Western NWT
Road Surface: 60% paved, 40% gravel
Major Attractions: Nahanni National Park; Wood Buffalo National Park
Length: 1,225 miles
Season: Open all year

(See maps, pages 737-738)

(35) (1) (2) (3) (4) (5) (6)

	Ft. Resolution	Ft. Simpson	Ft. Smith	Grimshaw	Yellowknife
Ft. Resolution		358	185	459	391
Ft. Simpson	358		431	588	393
Ft. Smith	185	431		531	464
Grimshaw	459	588	531		620
Yellowknife	391	393	464	620	

Summer ferry crossing of the Liard River becomes an ice road in winter. (© Lyn Hancock)

Named for explorer Alexander Mackenzie, who in 1779 navigated Great Slave Lake and sailed to the mouth of the Mackenzie River seeking a trade route for the Hudson's Bay Co., the Mackenzie Route is an adventure for modern explorers. It is not a trip for the impulsive. While there are accommodations, gas stations and other services in cities and settlements along the highways, long distances require that motorists plan in advance.

The Mackenzie Route covers the following highways: Alberta Highway 35 and NWT Highway 1 to Fort Simpson (Mackenzie Highway) and the extension to Wrigley; Highway 2 to Hay River; Highway 3 to Yellowknife; Highway 4 (Ingraham Trail); Highway 5 to Fort Smith; and Highway 6 to Fort Resolution. NWT Highway 7, the Liard Highway, connecting the Mackenzie Highway with the Alaska Highway north of Fort Nelson, is covered in the LIARD HIGHWAY section. The Dempster Highway (NWT Highway 8) to Inuvik is covered in the DEMPSTER HIGHWAY section.

Allow at least 2 weeks to travel the entire route. For visitor information on travel in the Northwest Territories, phone (800) 661-0788 or visit www.nwttravel.nt.ca.

Northwest Territories highways are both paved and gravel. Asphalt chip seal surfacing is under way on the remaining gravel portions of Highways 1 (Mackenzie Highway) and 3 (Yellowknife Highway). Gravel road is treated with calcium chloride to control the dust; wash your vehicle when possible. For road conditions, phone (800) 661-0750.

In summer, the Northwest Territories government provides free ferry service for cars and passengers across the Mackenzie River to Fort Providence, across the Liard River to Fort Simpson and across the Mackenzie River to Wrigley. In winter, traffic crosses on the ice. For current ferry information call (800) 661-0751.

The Mackenzie Highway begins at Grimshaw, AB. There are several routes to Grimshaw to choose from (see map). The Valleyview–Peace River route to the Mackenzie Highway via Highways 49 and 2 is a popular choice, with a driving distance of 101 miles/162 kms.

Mackenzie Highway

Distance from Grimshaw (G) is followed by distance from Alberta–NWT border (B).

ALBERTA HIGHWAY 35

Grimshaw

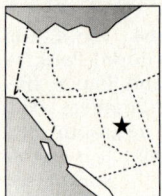

G 0 B 293.7 (472.7 km) Mile 0 of the Mackenzie Highway (Alberta Highway 35). **Population:** about 1,100. **Town office,** phone (780) 332-4626. **Emergency Services: Fire/Ambulance/Police,** phone 911. RCMP, phone (780) 3324666. **Hospital** phone (780) 332-6500. **Fire Department,** phone (780) 332-4586.

Visitor Information: In the Rail Link railway car located adjacent the centennial monument marking Mile 0 of the Mackenzie Highway. The Mile Zero Antique Truck Museum is opposite Visitor Information Centre and operates a visitor centre in winter; phone (780) 332-2969.

Private Aircraft: Airstrip 0.2 mile/0.4 km north; elev. 2,050 feet/625m; length, 3,000 feet/914m; turf.

Named for pioneer doctor M.E. Grimshaw, who established a practice at Peace River Crossing in 1914, Grimshaw developed as a community centre for area farmers and as a shipping point with the arrival of the railroad in 1921. Scheduled air service from Edmonton, High Level and Grande Prairie to Peace River airport, 8 miles/12.8 km east.

Grimshaw became a town in February 1953. Local resources are wheat and grains, livestock, gravel, lumber, gas and oil.

Grimshaw has 2 motels (1 with restaurant, Mile 0 Motor Inn), 1 hotel, 4 service stations, 2 car washes, a laundromat, 2 RV/campsites in town, 2 golf courses, tennis courts, outdoor swimming pool and arena and all other visitor facilities. RV dump station and drinking water located 3 blocks south and 1 block east of Tourist Information Centre.

Mackenzie Highway Log
(continued)

Queen Elizabeth Provincial Park, 3 miles/5 km west on Lac Cardinal; 56 campsites, picnic shelter, firewood, firepits, toilets, playground and swimming. Also Lac Cardinal Regional Pioneer Village Museum. ▲

G 2.8 (4.6 km) **B 290.9** (468.1 km) **Junction** of Highways 35 and 2 East.

G 3.4 (5.5 km) **B 290.3** (467.2 km) Signs about construction of the Mackenzie Highway and historic Pine Bluff post office.

G 4.1 (6.6 km) **B 289.6** (466.1 km) Turnout to east with litter barrels.

G 7.8 (12.5 km) **B 285.9** (460.1 km) Bear

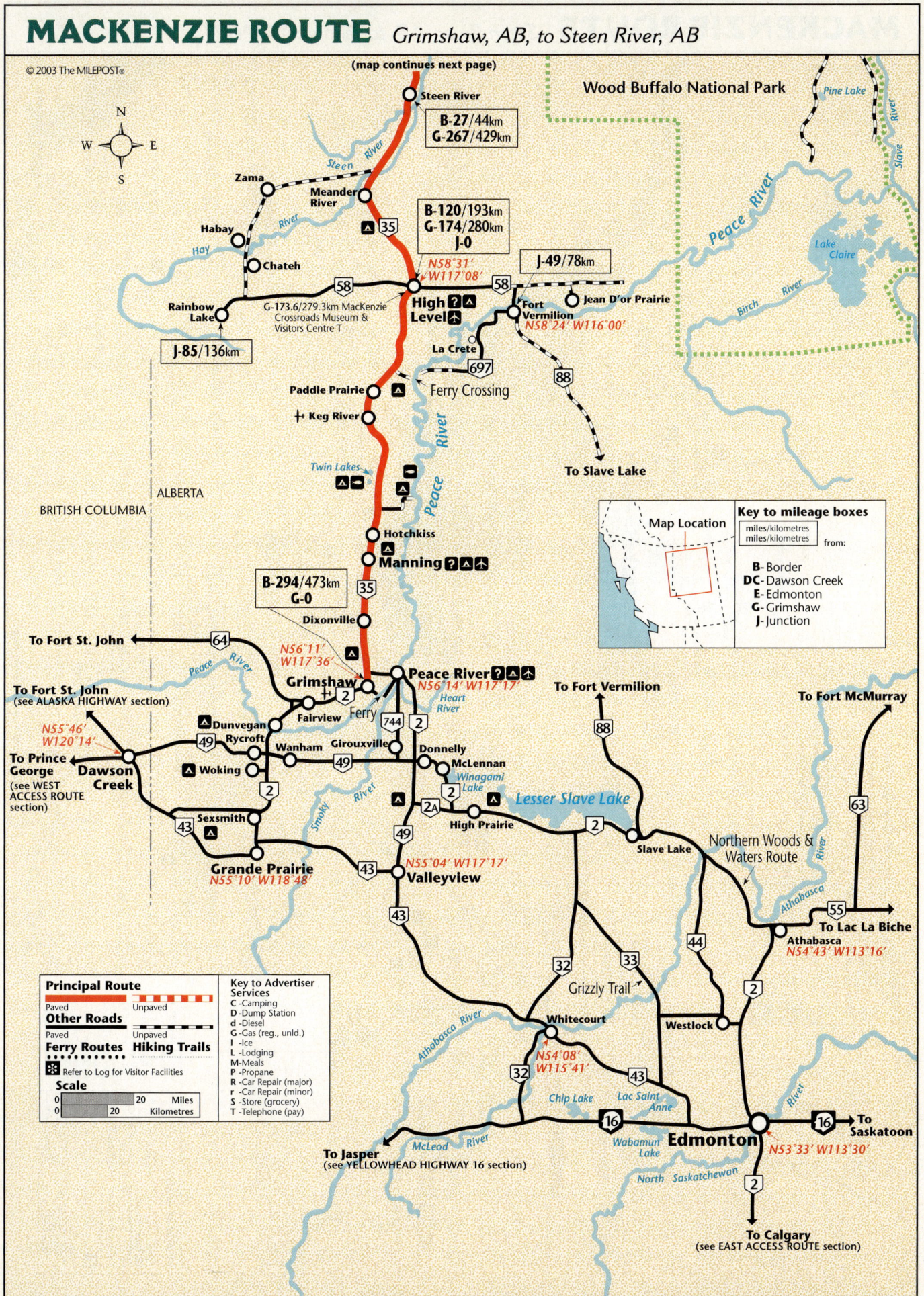

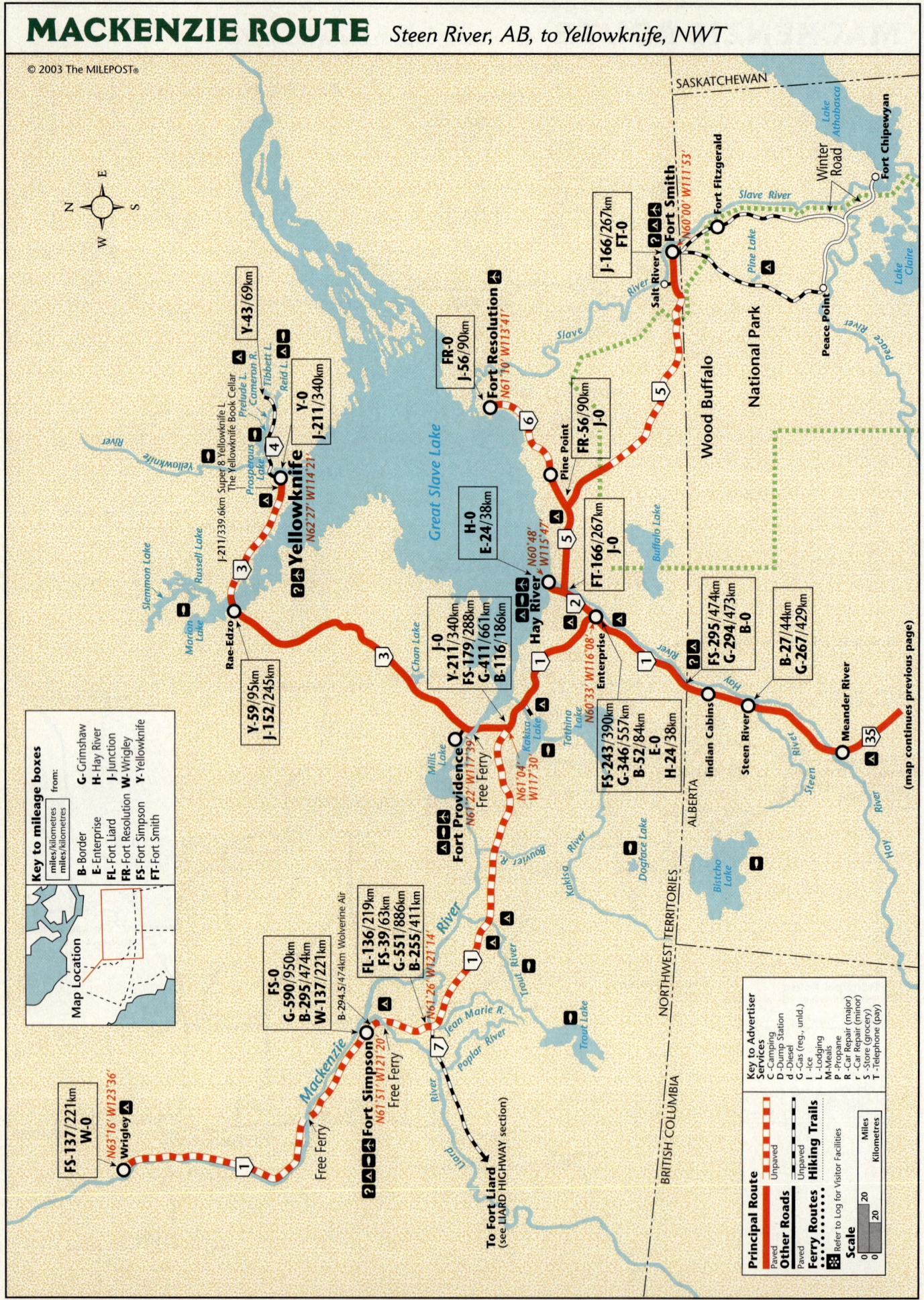

Creek Drive and the Creek Golf Course & Campground, 1 mile to west; 9 holes, grass greens, clubhouse, lounge and restaurant and campground with 30 sites, water and power. ▲

G 8.6 (13.8 km) **B 285.1** (458.8 km) **Junction** with SR 737 (Warrensville). To west 12.4 miles/20 km is Figure 8 Lake Provincial Recreation Area with 19 campsites, firepits, water, tables, outhouses and boat launch. Lake is stocked with rainbow trout; no gas motors. Fees include firewood. Groomed hiking trails.

G 12.3 (19.8 km) **B 281.4** (452.9 km) Road widens to 4 lanes northbound.

G 12.6 (20.3 km) **B 281.1** (452.4 km) **Junction** with SR 986 to east, leads to Daishowa-Maruberi Pulp Mill on Peace River.

G 13 (20.9 km) **B 280.7** (451.7 km) Road narrows to 2 lanes northbound.

G 19 (30.6 km) **B 274.7** (442.1 km) Entering Manning Ranger District northbound.

G 23 (37 km) **B 270.7** (435.6 km) Whitemud River bridge.

G 25.1 (40.4 km) **B 268.6** (432.3 km) Hamlet of **DIXONVILLE** (pop. 200) has a postal service, souvenir shop, museum, gas station and store. Shady Lane campground in the southwest corner of the hamlet has 24 sites, 17 with power, washrooms with showers, picnic tables, firepits, water and a dumping station

G 26.9 (43.3 km) **B 266.8** (429.4 km) Sulphur Lake Road leads west to junction with Highway 689 from Dixonville. Sulphur Lake Provincial Campground is located 34 miles (55km) west via 689; the first 14 miles (22.5km) is paved with remainder gravel to the campground. Has 11 campsites, water, outhouses, firepits, tables, firewood, garbage bins, fishing, pier and boat launch. Group rate reservations available, phone (780) 624-6405.

G 38.4 (61.8 km) **B 255.3** (410.9 km) **Junction** with SR 690 east to hamlet of Deadwood (7 miles/11 km). The Bradshaw family operates a private exotic bird farm located 2 miles/3.2 km east then 1 mile/1.6 km south. The Bradshaws have geese, peacocks, turkeys, pheasants and other birds. Visitors welcome.

G 46.8 (75.4 km) **B 246.9** (397.3 km) Hamlet of **NORTH STAR** (pop. 35) to east has roadside postal service (spot historically known as "Little Prairie"). Private lodge 13.7 miles/22 km to east offers hunting, ecotours and overnight camping.

Manning

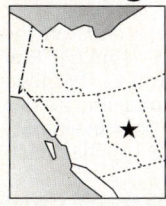

G 50.7 (81.6 km) **B 243** (391.1 km) Located on the Notikewin River at the junction of Highways 35 and 691. **Population**: 1,295. **Emergency Services**: 911; **RCMP**, phone (780) 836-3007. **Hospital** and **Ambulance**, phone (780) 836-3391. **Fire Department**, phone (780) 836-3000.

Visitor Information: In the information centre. There is a playground adjacent the centre and a dump station across the street.

Named for an Alberta premier, Manning was established in 1947. The railway line from Roma, AB, to Pine Point, NWT, reached Manning in September 1962. Today, Manning is a service centre and jumping-off point for hunters and fishers.

Manning has 5 restaurants, 3 hotel/motels, a pharmacy, food market, golf course, swimming pool and ice rink. Attractions here include the Battle River Pioneer Museum, located on the grounds of the Battle River Agricultural Society, 0.6 mile/1 km east via Highway 691. The museum, which features tools and machinery from the pioneer days, is open daily 1–5 P.M., from June 1 to mid-September.

Turn east at the information centre for Manning municipal campground; 9 sites on the banks of the Notikewin River, fireplaces, tables, water and flush toilets. ▲

Mackenzie Highway Log
(continued)

G 50.9 (81.9km) **B 242.8** (390.7km) Notikewin River Bridge (historically known by travelers as the "First Battle").

G 52 (83.7km) **B 239.3** (385.1km) Manning airport to west. Elevation 1612ft/491m; paved strip; fuel 100 Jet B, navigational aids, tie-down parking, terminal, year-round maintenance, runway 07/25. Private/charter/commercial/fire tanker aircraft.

G 53.2 (85.6 km) **B 240.5** (387 km) Truck stop with 24-hour food, gas and lodging.

G 54.6 (87.8 km) **B 239.1** (384.8 km) Community of Notikewin to west. Historically known as "Big Prairie."

G 60.6 (97.6 km) **B 233.1** (375.1 km) Hotchkiss River bridge. Historically known as the "Second Battle."

G 60.8 (97.8 km) **B 232.9** (374.8 km) Hotchkiss Community Club Park to east in the river valley; 10 sites, picnic shelter, tables, firepits, fishing, outhouses and water pump. ◄▲

G 61.3 (98.6 km) **B 232.4** (374 km) Community of **HOTCHKISS** to east, 9-hole golf course and campground to east; 25 campsites, 15 with power and water, restaurant/lounge and pro shop; grass greens and power carts for rent. Hotchkiss has a post office, service station, pay phone, coffee bar, grocery, and fuel and propane available.

G 66.9 (107.6 km) **B 226.8** (365 km) Meikle River bridge. Historically known as the "Third Battle."

G 71.2 (114.6 km) **B 222.5** (358.1 km) Turnout with litter barrel to west.

G 74.3 (119.5 km) **B 219.4** (353.1 km) **Junction** with Highway 692 and access to **Notikewin Provincial Park** (18.6 miles/30 km) on the Notikewin and Peace rivers. Highway 692 is fairly straight with pavement for the first 8 miles/13 km followed by good gravel surface to the park, although the road narrows, and the surfacing may be muddy in wet weather as you approach the park. At the top of the valley, just past the entrance to the park, is a parking area with picnic tables, firepis, outhouses and garbage containers. From here, there is a hiking trail to a lookout point. The park road then winds down a steep hill for 1.4 miles/2.2 km (not recommended for trailers, slippery when wet) to the riverside campground and day-use area; 19 campsites on the **Notikewin River** and 6 picnic sites on the **Peace River**; facilities include tables, water pump, pit toilets, garbage containers, firepits and fishing. Fees include firewood. *CAUTION: Bears in area.* ◄▲

G 88.4 (142.3 km) **B 205.3** (330.4 km) Twin Lakes Lodge to east; gas, food, lodging, pay phone and fishing supplies.

G 88.9 (143 km) **B 204.8** (329.6 km) Twin Lakes Campground 1/2 mile to west; 48 shaded campsites, picnic shelter, firepits, firewood, tables, outhouses, water pump,

Sign promotes circle route using Northwest Territories highways.
(© Roger Pickenpaugh)

beach, boat launch (no gas motors). Lakes are stocked with rainbow trout; good fishing June to September. ◄▲

G 95.8 (154.1 km) **B 197.9** (318.5 km) Turnout to west with litter barrels.

G 111.2 (179 km) **B 182.5** (293.7 km) **Junction** with Highway 695 East which leads 24 miles/38 km to community of **CARCAJOU** (pop. about 20).

G 111.5 (179.4km) **B 182.2** (293.2km) Access to Keg River airstrip 0.4 mile/0.6 km east.

Private Aircraft: Keg River airstrip; elev. 1,350 feet/410m; approximate length 2,700 feet/832m; turf; emergency only.

G 112.3 (180.8 km) **B 181.4** (291.9 km) Keg River bridge. The community of **KEG RIVER** (area pop. 400) just north of the bridge has a gas station, post office, grocery, cafe, motel, confectionery, pay phone and airstrip. South of bridge is school, teacherages and medical clinic.

G 115.6 (186 km) **B 178.1** (286.6 km) **Junction** with Secondary Road 695 West. This paved road leads 9 miles/14.5 km to Keg River Post (area pop. about 200) with library, community hall, church and baseball diamond. A spot once rich in fur trade history, the post has Peace River Constituency's first MLA, "Allie" Brick, buried in its cemetery.

G 124 (199.6 km) **B 169.7** (273.1 km) Boyer River bridge.

G 129.5 (208.4 km) **B 164.2** (264.2 km) **PADDLE PRAIRIE** (pop. 164) has a gas station, grocery store and cafe. Paddle Prairie is a Metis settlement. The Metis culture, a combination of French and Amerindian, played a key role in the fur trade and development of northwestern Canada.

G 134.2 (216 km) **B 159.5** (256.7 km) Turnout to west with litter barrels.

G 136.2 (219.2 km) **B 157.5** (253.5 km) **Junction** with SR 697, which leads northeast 75 miles/121 km to junction with Highway 88 near Fort Vermilion. This is a 2-lane, paved road with a free ferry crossing on the Peace River at Tompkin's Landing, 11 miles/18 km east from here. The ferry operates 24 hours a day, except in heavy fog, and carries 6 cars or 4 trucks.

Highway 697 provides access to **BUFFALO HEAD PRAIRIE** (pop. 453), 44 miles/70 km east, which has a small store and gas. Highway 697 also accesses **LA CRETE** (pop. 902), 54 miles/87 km east and north. Established in the early 1900s by Mennonite settlers, it celebrates Farmer's Day in August with pioneer demonstrations and traditional Mennonite food. La Crete Mennonite Heritage Village is 1.2 miles/2km south of town. La Crete has a motel, 3 restaurants, service stations with repair facilities, car wash, grocery, hardware and retail stores, a laundromat and bank.

G 141 (226.9 km) **B** 152.7 (245.7 km) Entering High Level Ranger District northbound.

G 153.5 (247 km) **B** 140.2 (225.6 km) Turnout with litter barrel to west. Watch for waterfowl in small lakes along highway.

G 161.2 (259.4 km) **B** 132.5 (213.2 km) Bede Creek.

G 161.9 (260.5 km) **B** 131.8 (212.1 km) Parma Creek.

G 165.5 (266.3 km) **B** 128.2 (206.3 km) Melito Creek.

G 170.6 (274.6 km) **B** 123.1 (198.1 km) Turnout with litter barrel to west.

G 171.9 (276.7 km) **B** 121.8 (196 km) Private campground. ▲

G 173.3 (278.9 km) **B** 120.4 (193.8 km) **Junction** with Highway 58 West, which leads 85 miles/136 km to **RAINBOW LAKE** (pop. 1,146), a service community for oil and natural gas development in the region. Food, gas and lodging available.

High Level

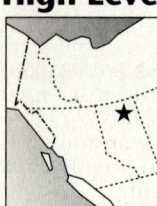

G 173.6 (279.3 km) **B** 120.1 (193.3 km) Located at the junction of Highways 35 and 58. **Population:** 3,639. **Emergency Services:** Phone 911. **RCMP**, phone (780) 926-2226. **Hospital**, phone (780) 926-3791. **Ambulance**, phone 911. **Fire Department**, phone 911.

Visitor Information: South end of town at Mackenzie Crossroads Museum & Visitor Centre; includes local and regional information for Alberta and the Northwest Territories; museum displays, local native crafts and rest area. Open in summer 9 A.M. to 4:30 P.M. Monday–Friday, 10 A.M. to 6 P.M. weekends and holidays. Hours are extended May–Sept. www.town.highlevel.ab.ca.

Private Aircraft: High Level airport, 7.5 miles/12 km north; elev. 1,110 feet/338m; length 5,000 feet/1,524m; asphalt; fuel 80, 100, Jet B. Floatplane base at Footner Lake, 0.6 mile/1 km west.

Begun as a small settlement on the Mackenzie Highway after WWII, High Level grew with the oil boom of the 1960s and completion of the railroad to Pine Point. The town is still growing rapidly. High Level has a strong agricultural economy and boasts the most northerly grain elevators in North America. The community is also supported by two major forestry companies and serves as a transportation centre for the northwestern Peace River region. Tolko Industries gives sawmill tours with advance notice, phone (780) 926-3781. There is scheduled air service to Edmonton daily.

Visitor facilities include 9 motels, bed and breakfasts, 3 grocery stores, restaurants and service stations providing major repairs. RV dump located at the Shell station. Construction of 2 additional hotels began in 2002. There are also an ice arena and curling rink, golf course, indoor swimming pool, playgrounds, tennis courts, ball diamonds, bowling, hiking trails, cycling, cross-country skiing, banks, schools and churches. Recreation includes hunting (moose, caribou, deer, bear) and fishing for northern pike, perch, walleye, whitefish, goldeye and grayling.

There is a private campground at the south edge of town. ▲

Mackenzie Crossroads Museum & Visitors Centre. See display ad this section.

Mackenzie Highway Log
(continued)

G 174 (280 km) **B** 119.7 (192.6 km) **Junction** with Highway 58 East to Jean D'Or Prairie and **junction** with Highway 35 (77 miles/125 km, gravel). Highway 58 leads 49 miles/78 km east (paved) to **FORT VERMILION** (pop. 850). The community calls itself "Where Alberta Began," as in 1788, it was one of the first two forts (trading posts) established in Alberta by the North West Co. The last of the historic mission log buildings, a grain-handling facility, now serves as the clubhouse for a golf course. An all-service RV park, a 9-hole golf course, a mini-golf park and driving range now stand on the old mission hospital site and adjacent mission farm site. Visit the Museum, Archives and Information Centre for other historic sites of the area. Fort Vermilion is the northern limit of the Peace River grainfields. Visitor services in Fort Vermilion include food, gas and lodging. Highway 88 Bicentennial Highway continues south 255 miles/410 km to Slave Lake (unpaved); no services on highway south of Fort Vermilion.

G 176.2 (283.5 km) **B** 117.5 (189.1 km) High Level golf and country club north of High Level on east side of highway; clubhouse, grass greens 9 holes, pro shop, power carts and camping facilities. ▲

G 193.4 (311.2 km) **B** 100.3 (161.4 km) Turnoff to west for Hutch Lake Recreation Area; parking, 8 picnic sites with tables and firepits, toilets. Short path leads down to lake. Bring mosquito repellent.

G 196 (315.5 km) **B** 97.7 (157.2 km) Hutch Lake municipal campground, 3 miles/4.6 km west; 12 sites, firepits, firewood, tables, toilets. Beach and boat launch on Hutch Lake. Hiking trails. Good spot for bird watchers. Camping fee $9. Fishing July and August for walleye, perch and northern pike (catch-and-release). ▲

G 196.8 (316.7 km) **B** 96.9 (155.9 km) Turnouts with litter barrels both sides of highway.

G 207.3 (333.6 km) **B** 86.4 (139 km) Wooden railway bridge to east.

G 219.3 (352.9 km) **B** 74.4 (119.7 km) **MEANDER RIVER** (pop. 340) has a post office, gas, grocery store and confectionery with pay phone.

G 221.5 (356.4 km) **B** 72.2 (116.2 km) Mission Creek.

G 223.8 (360.1 km) **B** 69.9 (112.5 km) The Mackenzie Highway crosses the Hay River here and follows it north into Northwest Territories.

G 227.5 (366.2 km) **B** 66.2 (106.5 km) Railway bridge over Hay River to east. Construction of the Great Slave Lake Railway was one of the largest railway construction projects since the boom of the first transcontinental railway lines in the late 1800s and early 1900s in Canada. The line extends 377 miles/607 km from Roma Junction near Peace River, AB, to Hay River, NWT, on the shore of Great Slave Lake. (A 54-mile/87-km branch line extended the line to the now-defunct lead–zinc mine at Pine Point, NWT.) Opened for traffic in 1964, the line carries mining shipments south and supplies (fuel) north to Hay River.

G 228.1 (367.1 km) **B** 65.6 (105.6 km) Gravel road leads west 39 miles/63 km to **ZAMA** (pop. 200), an oilfield community. Drilling and related operations take place at Zama in winter. Zama is the southern terminal of the interprovincial pipeline, carrying Norman Wells crude to Edmonton refineries.

G 231.5 (372.5 km) **B** 62.2 (100.1 km) Slavey Creek.

G 243.5 (391.9 km) **B** 50.2 (80.8 km) Paved turnout with litter barrels to west.

G 250.2 (402.6 km) **B** 43.5 (70 km) Lutose Creek.

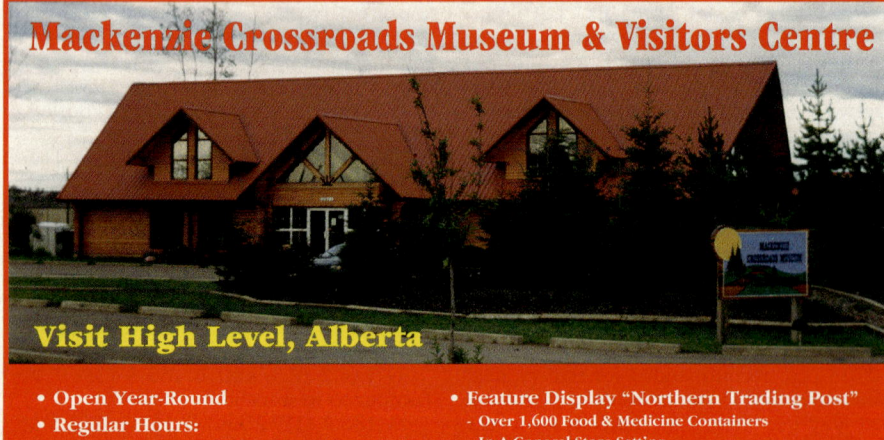

Mackenzie Crossroads Museum & Visitors Centre

Visit High Level, Alberta

- Open Year-Round
- Regular Hours:
  9 a.m.-4:30 p.m. (hours are extended from May to September)
- Visitor Information for Northern Alberta & NWT
- Outdoor Picnic Area
- Large Parking Area
- $2 admission for adults, $1 for children
- Feature Display "Northern Trading Post"
  - Over 1,600 Food & Medicine Containers In A General Store Setting
- Mile 180 of the Mackenzie Highway
  (#35) Midway Between Edmonton, AB & Yellowknife, NWT
- All Services Available
- Visit Our Website:
  http://www.highlevelchamber.com

10803 96 Street, High Level, AB, Canada T0H 1Z0
Phone (780) 926-4811 • Fax (780) 926-4017 • email: hlchambr@incentre.net

G 263.3 (423.7 km) B 30.4 (48.9 km) Steen River bridge.

G 266.7 (429.2 km) B 27 (43.5 km) STEEN RIVER (pop. 25) to east; no services.

G 266.9 (429.5 km) B 26.8 (43.1 km) Steen River Forestry Tanker Base to west. Grass airstrip.

G 268.1 (431.5 km) B 25.6 (41.2 km) Sam's Creek.

G 270.1 (434.5 km) B 23.6 (38 km) Jackpot Creek.

G 276.2 (444.5 km) B 17.5 (28.2 km) Bannock Creek.

G 283.3 (455.9 km) B 10.4 (16.7 km) Indian Cabins Creek.

G 284 (457 km) B 9.7 (15.6 km) **INDIAN CABINS** (pop. 10); gas, diesel, cafe and native crafts. The old Indian cabins that gave this settlement its name are gone, but nearby is an Indian cemetery with spirit houses. Historic log church.

G 285.3 (459.1 km) B 8.4 (13.5 km) Delphin Creek.

G 293.7 (472.7 km) B 0 60th parallel. Border between Alberta and Northwest Territories. The Mackenzie Highway now changes from Alberta Highway 35 to NWT Highway 1.

Distance from AB–NWT border (B) is followed by distance from Fort Simpson (FS).

Highway 1 begins its own series of kilometre markers, starting with Kilometre 0 at the border, which appear about every 2 kilometres.

NWT HIGHWAY 1

B 0 FS 294.5 (474 km) **AB–NWT border, 60th Parallel.** Visitor information centre with brochures, maps, fishing licenses, camping permits, a dump station, pay phone, drinking water and free coffee. Dene (Indian) arts and crafts are on display. Check here on road and ferry conditions before proceeding. The visitor centre is open May 15 to September 15 from 8:30 A.M. to 8:30 P.M.

A short walking trail around a pond leads to the 60th Parallel Monument. A mock trapper's cabin and a commemorative monument for the railway into the north can also be found along this trail.

60th Parallel Campground and picnic area adjacent visitor centre. Facilities include 10 campsites, 2 picnic sites and kitchen shelter. The park overlooks the Hay River and canoeists may launch here though the boat launch is not maintained. Obtain information on canoeing at Hay River at the visitor centre. ▲

Driving distances from the border to destinations in Northwest Territories are as follows (see highway logs this section for details): Hay River 75 miles/121 km; Fort Simpson 295 miles/474 km; Wrigley 432 miles/695 km; Fort Providence 138 miles/222 km; Yellowknife 326 miles/525 km; Fort Smith 238 miles/382 km.

B 1.8 (2.9 km) FS 292.7 (471.1 km) Reindeer Creek; pike and pickerel fishing.

B 24.8 (39.9 km) FS 269.7 (434.1 km) Swede Creek.

B 25.1 (40.4 km) FS 269.4 (433.6 km) Grumbler Rapids, just off highway, is audible during low water in late summer.

B 26.1 (42 km) FS 268.4 (432 km) Large turnout and gravel stockpile to west.

B 40.5 (65.1 km) FS 254.1 (408.9 km) Mink Creek.

B 45 (72.4 km) FS 249.5 (401.6 km) Turnoff to east for **Twin Falls Gorge Territorial Park**, **Alexandra Falls** picnic area; toilets, picnic shelters and interpretive program. Paved parking area and gravel walkway to falls viewpoint, overlooking the Hay River, which plunges 109 feet/33m to form **Alexandra Falls**. Excellent photo opportunities; walk down stairs to top of falls. A 1.9-mile/3-km trail through mixed boreal forest (with good canyon views) connects with Louise Falls.

B 46.4 (74.6 km) FS 248.2 (399.4 km) Turnoff to east for **Twin Falls Gorge Territorial Park**, **Louise Falls** picnic area and campground; 18 campsites, 6 picnic sites, kitchen shelter, playground, electric hookups, tables, toilets, firepits, firewood, water. Hiking trails to viewpoint overlooking 3-tiered Louise Falls, which drops 50 feet/15m. Walk down spiral stairs to top of falls. Look for fossils at edge of falls. A 1.9-mile/3-km aboriginal interpretive hiking trails connects with Alexandra Falls. ▲

B 47.9 (77.1 km) FS 246.6 (396.9 km) **Escarpment Creek** picnic and group camping area; tables, shelter, toilets, firepits, garbage container, water. Spectacular series of waterfalls on Escarpment Creek; access from north side of creek. A 2.6-mile (4.4km) hiking trail connects to Louise Falls.

B 48.1 (77.4 km) FS 246.4 (396.6 km) Highway crosses Escarpment Creek.

B 51.4 (82.8 km) FS 243.1 (391.2 km) Service station, restaurant (Winnie's Kitchen) and craft shop to west. Entering Enterprise northbound.

B 51.7 (83.3 km) FS 242.8 (390.1 km) Old weigh station. Now Enterprise Visitor Centre.

Junction of Highway 1 with Highway 2 to Hay River. See Hay River Highway log on page 744.

Continue on Highway 1 for Enterprise (description follows) and Fort Simpson.

ENTERPRISE (pop. 80), a highway community with food, gas, diesel, lodging, grocery store, pay phone. Excellent native craft shop. View of Hay River Gorge just east of the highway. View of historic transportation equipment from road just behind Winnie's Restaurant (private property, but the glimpses from the road are worthwhile).

B 74.4 (119.8 km) FS 220.1 (354.2 km) Large paved double-ended turnout north to McNally Creek Day Use Site with outhouses, picnic area, viewing platform and trail with bridge to view falls from north side of canyon. Plaque explains origin of name.

Highway crosses McNally Creek northbound.

B 76.4 (122.9 km) FS 218.2 (351.1 km) Large paved turnout to north with picnic site, litter barrels and scenic view from escarpment.

B 80.5 (129.5 km) FS 214 (344.5 km) Easy-to-miss **Hart Lake Fire Tower** access road turnoff leads 0.6 mile/1 km to forest fire lookout tower. Panoramic view over more than 100 square miles/259 square km of forest to Great Slave Lake and Mackenzie River. (On a clear day, sharp eyes can spot Yellowknife high-rises on the skyline.) Path to ancient coral reef. *CAUTION: Keep the fly repellent handy and stay away from the edge of escarpment.*

B 84.5 (136 km) FS 210 (338 km) Crooked Creek.

B 85 (136.8 km) FS 209.5 (337.2 km) Trapper's cabin to north.

B 92.2 (148.3 km) FS 202.4 (325.7 km) Side road to gravel pits.

View of Louise Falls from Twin Falls Gorge Territorial Park.
(© Lyn Hancock)

B 103.8 (167.1 km) FS 190.7 (306.9 km) Access road leads south 4.2 miles/6.8 km to **Lady Evelyn Falls Territorial Campground** where the Kakisa River drops 49 feet/15m over an escarpment. Staircase down to viewing platform. Hiking trail to base of falls; swimming and wading. Ample parking, interpretive display, territorial campground with 13 campsites, 7 picnic sites; a group picnic site, showers, toilets, tables, firepits, firewood, garbage containers, water pump, kitchen shelters, visitor centre. At end of road, 3 miles/5 km past campground, is Slavey Indian village and **Kakisa Lake**; fair fishing for walleye, pike and grayling. ◀▲

B 104.7 (168.8 km) FS 190.8 (305.5 km) Kakisa River bridge.

B 106.1 (170.7 km) FS 190.6 (306.8 km) Kakisa River Day Use Site and picnic area with 10 sites, tables, fireplaces and firewood. Hiking trails along river lead upstream to Lady Evelyn Falls and a short distance downstream. Fair fishing in **Kakisa River** for grayling. ◀

B 115.4 (185.7 km) FS 179.1 (288.3 km) Turnout with litter barrels, log cabin (temporary shelter), outhouse, picnic tables and map display on Highways 1 and 3.

B 115.5 (185.8 km) FS 179.1 (288.2 km)

Junction of Highway 1 and Highway 3. See Yellowknife Highway log beginning on page 745.

Highway 3 (paved and gravel) leads 211 miles/340 km north to Yellowknife.

B 143.5 (230.9 km) FS 151 (243.1 km) Emergency survival cabin and turnout with litter barrels and outhouse to south.

B 157.9 (254.1 km) FS 136.6 (219.9 km) Turnout to north with parking and scenic view.

B 161.3 (260.8 km) FS 133.2 (214.4 km) Axehandle Creek (no sign); good fishing. ◀

B 169.4 (272.7 km) FS 125.1 (201.3 km) Turnout to south.

Resident of Jean Marie River scrapes moosehide. (© Lyn Hancock)

B 171.7 (276.3 km) FS 122.8 (197.7 km) Bouvier River.

B 172.6 (277.8 km) FS 121.9 (196.2 km) Emergency survival cabin and turnout with litter barrels to south.

B 178.5 (287.3 km) FS 116 (186.7 km) Turnout to north.

B 179.2 (288.4 km) FS 115.3 (185.6 km) Wallace Creek. Scenic canyon to north; trail access on west side of creek; 15-minute walk to canyon and waterfall.

B 182.9 (294.3 km) FS 111.7 (179.7 km) Redknife River.

B 194 (312.2 km) FS 100.5 (161.8 km) Morrissey Creek.

B 199.2 (320.5 km) FS 95.4 (153.5 km) Winter ice road leads south 78 miles/126 km to **TROUT LAKE** (pop. 80), a Dene settlement known for its big fish (lake trout), sandy beaches and traditional lifestyles.

B 201 (323.5 km) FS 93.5 (150.5 km) Trout River bridge just east of turnoff to **Sambaa Deh (Whittaker Falls) Territorial Park**; 5 picnic sites, 13 campsites, tables, litter barrels, showers, kitchen shelter, firepits, firewood, water, emergency phone, visitor centre.

Whittaker Falls is under highway bridge. From the campground, hike 0.6 mile/1 km south to **Coral Falls**. Hike 0.6 mile/1 km north on west side of river to third falls and access to **Trout River Canyon**. Fossils are embedded in the rocks along the Trout River.

B 202.2 (325.4 km) FS 92.3 (148.6 km) Turnout with litter barrels to south.

B 205.5 (330.7 km) FS 89 (143.3 km) Emergency survival cabin and turnout with litter barrels to north.

B 229.9 (370 km) FS 64.6 (104 km) **Ekali Lake** access; pike and pickerel.

B 233 (374.9 km) FS 61.5 (99.1 km) **Junction** with an all-weather, gravel road leading 17 miles/27 km to community of **JEAN MARIE RIVER** (pop. 53), located on the south shore of the Mackenzie River at the confluence with the Jean Marie River. A very traditional community well known for its native crafts. Visitors are welcome to visit traditional camps along the road. Please respect private property while visiting. Check local road conditions after rain and watch for sharp stones in road. Bailey Bridge over creek at 12 miles (21.6km), fair bird watching.

Visitor Information: Available from friendly staff at the Band Office in the large brown building in front of the central playground. If the office is closed, ask anyone you see in the community. Residents are happy to help.

Services here include a campground (located near airport); picnic site on the river; general store, open 10 A.M. to noon and 5–7 P.M.; and gas, available 9 A.M. to 5 P.M. and by call-out after hours. Community known for beaded moose skin and local craftspeople. Arts and crafts available; inquire at the Band Office. Boat tours and fishing on the Mackenzie River. The historic tugboat *Jean Marie River* rests up shore, retired from shipping lumber down the Mackenzie to Arctic communities. Good photo opportunity.

B 235.5 (379 km) FS 59 (95 km) Emergency survival cabin and turnout to north with outhouse and litter barrels.

B 240.5 (387.1 km) FS 54 (86.9 km) I.P.L. pipeline camp and pump station to north. Highway crosses pipeline.

B 241.2 (388.2 km) FS 53.3 (85.8 km) Microwave tower to south.

B 255.2 (410.7 km) FS 39.3 (63.3 km) Jean Marie Creek bridge.

B 255.3 (410.8 km) FS 39.2 (63.2 km) "Checkpoint" at junction with the Liard Highway; open 8 A.M. to midnight. A popular stopping point with gas, diesel, propane, emergency repairs, crafts, licensed restaurant and accommodations. Phone (403) 695-2953. Open year-round.

The Liard Highway leads south to Fort Liard and junctions with the Alaska Highway near Fort Nelson.

Junction with the Liard Highway (NWT Highway 7). See the LIARD HIGHWAY section on page 732 for details.

B 256.4 (412.6km) FS 38.2 (61.4 km) Turnout to east.

B 268.2 (431.6 km) FS 26.3 (42.4 km) Emergency survival cabin and turnout with litter barrels and outhouse to west.

B 282.6 (454.8 km) FS 11.9 (19.2 km) Highway crests hill; view of Liard River ahead. Ferry landing 3,280 feet/1,000m.

B 283 (455.5 km) FS 11.5 (18.5 km) Liard River Campground, to accommodate travelers who miss the last ferry at night, has 5 sites, tables, firepits, water, outhouse and garbage container.

B 283.2 (455.8 km) FS 11.3 (18.2 km) Free government-operated Liard River (South Mackenzie) ferry service operates daily late May through October from 8 A.M. to 11:45 P.M., 7 days a week; once an hour on the half-hour for westbound traffic, on the hour for eastbound traffic. Crossing time is 6 minutes. Capacity is 8 cars or 2 trucks, with a maximum total weight of 130,000 lbs./59,090 kg. An ice bridge opens for light vehicles in late November and heavier vehicles as ice thickens. *NOTE: This crossing is subject to extreme high and low water level fluctuations which may cause delays. No crossing possible during breakup (about mid-April to mid-May) and freezeup (mid-October to mid-November).* For ferry information phone (867) 695-2018 or (800) 661-0751.

B 284.6 (458 km) FS 9.9 (15.9 km) Fort Simpson airport. See Private Aircraft information in Fort Simpson.

B 289.1 (465.2 km) FS 5.5 (8.8 km) Kilometrepost 466.

B 290.5 (468.4 km) FS 4 (6.4 km) Gravel ends, pavement begins northbound.

B 292.4 (470.5 km) FS 2.2 (3.5 km) **Junction** with Fort Simpson access road which leads 2.3 miles/3.8 km to Fort Simpson (description follows). The extension of NWT Highway 1 to Wrigley was completed in 1994; see log following Fort Simpson description.

B 294 (473.2 km) FS 0.5 (0.8 km) Causeway to Fort Simpson Island.

B 294.4 (473.9 km) FS 0.1 (0.1 km) Turnoff for village campground; 30 campsites, 4 picnic sites, kitchen shelter; shower planned.

Fort Simpson

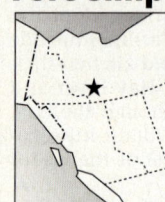

B 294.5 (474 km) FS 0 Located on an island at the confluence of the Mackenzie and Liard rivers. **Population:** 1,200. **Emergency Services: RCMP**, phone (867) 695-3111. **Health Centre** with 1 doctor, daytime phone (867) 695-7000 or (867) 695-3232 foor after hours emergencies. **Fire Department** (volunteer), phone (867) 695-2222.

Visitor Information: Village office operates an information centre May through October and has a photo exhibit and films. The visitor information centre is open 10 A.M. to 8 P.M. Mon.-Fri. and 11 A.M. to 7 P.M. Saturdays, Sundays and holidays. Ask for Historical Walking Tours booklet and guide. Nahanni National Park office is open 8:30 A.M. to 5 P.M., 7 days a week in July and August, weekdays the rest of the year.

Transportation: Scheduled service to Yellowknife and Whitehorse, YT. Fixed wing and helicopter charters available. **Rental cars**—Available. **Taxi service**—Available.

Private Aircraft: Fort Simpson airport; elev. 554 feet/169m; length 6,000 feet/1,829m; asphalt; fuel 100, Jet B. Fort Simpson Island; elev. 405 feet/123m; length 3,000

Porcupine quill roses by master quiller Louise Moreau.
(© Lyn Hancock)

feet/914m; gravel; fuel 100, Jet B.

Fort Simpson is a full-service community. There is a motel with kitchenettes, a hotel with licensed dining and a bed and breakfast on the Liard River on the outskirts of town; 2 gas stations with repair service (unleaded, diesel and propane available); 2 grocery stores, department store, hardware store, a bank, laundromat, post office, 1 craft shop and a sports shop. Small engine repair shop and mechanics available. Recreational facilities include an arena, curling rink, gym, ball diamond, tennis, small indoor pool, a 6-hole golf course with clubhouse and gear rental ($10 day pass) and a boat launch at government wharf. Public campground with showers at edge of town.

Fort Simpson or Liidlii Kue (Slavey for "the place where the rivers come together") is the administrative headquarters for the Deh Cho (Big River) region. It is the oldest continuously occupied site on the Mackenzie River, dating from 1804 when the North West Co. established its Fort of the Forks. There is a historical marker on the bank of the Mackenzie. The Hudson's Bay Co. began its post here in 1822. At that time the fort was renamed after Sir George Simpson, one of the first governors of the combined North West Co. and Hudson's Bay Co. Fort Simpson served as the Mackenzie District headquarters for the Hudson's Bay Co. fur-trading operation. Its key location on the Mackenzie River also made Fort Simpson an important transportation centre. Anglican and Catholic missions were established here in 1858 and 1894.

Fort Simpson continues to be an important centre for the Northwest Territories water transport system. Visitors may walk along the high banks of the Mackenzie River and watch the boat traffic and floatplanes.

One of the easiest places to get down to the water is by Alfred Faille's cabin on Mackenzie Drive. Faille was a well-known Fort Simpson pioneer and prospector. Fort Simpson Heritage Park, overlooking the Papal Grounds where Pope John Paul II landed in 1987, features the McPherson House, built in 1936 and home to local pioneers George and Lucy McPherson and "Doc" Marion. Contact the Historical Society, phone (867) 695-2176 for tours.

For visitors, Fort Simpson features Dene crafts, such as birch-bark baskets and beadwork. Nats'enelu, an aboriginal-style house, offers finely crafted clothing trimmed with local beadwork, Dene dolls and other native crafts. Check Visitor Information Centre for hours.

Fort Simpson is also a jumping-off point for jet boat trips on the North Nahanni River; Cli Lake Lodge; Mackenzie River traffic; and fly-in trips to Nahanni National Park. Flightseeing trips to Little Doctor and Glacier lakes, Ram Plateau, Cirque of the Unclimbables, the Ragged Range and Virginia Falls on the South Nahanni River in Nahanni National Park are recommended. Virginia Falls are 300 feet/90m high, twice as high as Niagara Falls.

Nahanni National Park, listed as a unique geological area on the UNESCO world heritage site list, is accessible only by nonpowered boat or aircraft. Located southwest of Fort Simpson near the Yukon border, charter companies operate day-trip flightseeing tours that may be arranged in Fort Simpson, Fort Liard and Yellowknife, and from Fort Nelson, BC, and Watson Lake, YT.

One of the most popular attractions in the park is running the South Nahanni River or its tributary, the Flat River. Charter air service for canoe drop-offs is available in Fort Simpson.

The park has a mandatory reservation and registration system for overnight use and charges user fees. For details contact Nahanni National Park Reserve, Box 348, Fort Simpson, NT X0E 0N0; phone (867) 695-3151; email nahanni.info@pch.gc.ca; www.parkscanada.gc.ca/nahan.

Willow, Dogface and Trout lakes are accessible by air. Good fishing for trout and grayling. Inquire locally.

Wolverine Air. See display ad this section.

Mackenzie Highway Log
(continued)

Distance from Fort Simpson (FS) is shown. *Physical kilometreposts reflect distance from Alberta border.* Distance to Wrigley is 137 miles/220.5 km; driving time is approximately 3 hours. Allow at least 2 hours from Wrigley to the Camsell ferry crossing.

WRIGLEY EXTENSION

FS 0 Junction with Fort Simpson access road.

FS 10.9 (17.5 km) Single-lane bridge over **Martin River**. Turnout at north end of bridge. Good fishing. *CAUTION: Slow down for steep descent to bridge.*

FS 17.9 (28.8 km) Creek crossing. *CAUTION: Slow down, steep drop-offs and no*

guardrails.

FS 35.5 (57.1 km) Single-lane bridge over Shale Creek.

FS 36 (58 km) Turnout to east.

FS 47.8 (76.9 km) Northbound vista of Mackenzie River from crest of hill.

© Lyn Hancock

FS 48.3 (77.8 km) Ferry crossing of the Mackenzie River at Camsell Bend (Ndulee Crossing). Ferry operates daily, late May through October, 9 to 11 A.M. and 2 to 8 P.M.. Capacity is 6 cars or 4 trucks. NOTE: There are no overnight facilities for anyone missing the ferry. Ferry does not operate in fog. Be prepared to wait.

FS 75.1 (120.9 km) Highway maintenance camp to east.

FS 96.2 (154.8 km) Willowlake River bridge, longest bridge in the Northwest Territories.

FS 96.5 (155.3 km) Kilometrepost 626. Road east and up to Wrigley.

FS 97.2 (157 km) Highway climbs steep hill northbound; views to west.

FS 99.8 (160.7 km) Turnout to west at top of hill with litter barrels and scenic view of the Mackenzie River and Mackenzie Mountains.

FS 112.8 (181.6 km) Single-lane wooden bridge over the "River Between Two Mountains."

FS 123.9 (199.4 km) Wrigley interprovincial pipeline pump station and radio tower to east.

FS 130.7 (210.4 km) Road east to gravel yard; great views of Pine Phen Mountain and other peaks.

FS 131.2 (211.1 km) Single-lane bridge over Smith's Creek.

FS 133 (214.1 km) Southbound views of Cap Mountains to east.

FS 133.3 (214.5 km) Highway maintenance camp to west.

FS 134.4 (216.3 km) Airport Lake, Pehdzeh Ki campground; 12 sites, firepits and outhouses. Suitable for RVs; located on high, dry ground in mostly birch and white spruce trees. ▲

FS 134.6 (216.6 km) Junction with winter ice road to east which leads north to Fort Norman, Norman Wells, Fort Franklin and Fort Good Hope. Winter road mileages are as follows: Wrigley to Fort Norman, 148 miles/238 km; Fort Norman to Norman Wells, 50 miles/80 km; Norman Wells to Fort Good Hope, 91 miles/147 km; Norman Wells to Franklin, 68 miles/110 km.

FS 134.8 (216.9 km) Turnoff to west for Wrigley airport. Private Aircraft: Wrigley airport, 4 miles/7 km south of town; elev. 493 feet/142m; length 3,500 feet/1,148m; gravel; fuel 80.

FS 137 (220.5 km) W 0 WRIGLEY (pop. 200; 90 percent Dene ancestry). Emergency Services: RCMP, station manned intermittently. Nursing Station, with full-time nurse, phone (867) 587-3441.

Visitor Information: Available at the Youth Centre (open daily in summer). The Pehdzeh Ki Dene Band Complex can also be a source of information.

The Hudson's Bay Co. built a trading post here in 1870 called Fort Wrigley. The fort was abandoned in 1910 due to disease and famine, and the inhabitants moved downriver to Old Fort Wrigley near Roche-qui-trempe-a'-l'eau (the rock that plunges into the water), a well-known land form. Although a church and school were built at that site in 1957, the community decided to move to higher ground in 1965. 15 homes were built at the "new" townsite of present-day Wrigley. The church, school and other buildings were moved from the old townsite by boat. Wrigley is the home of the Pehdzeh Ki First Nation. Log-cabin-style homes often have teepees to dry and store fish and game in traditional ways. An all-weather road opened to the communiy in 1994. Wrigley is now the northernmost all-year access point on the Mackenzie Highway.

Visitor facilities here include the Petanea Hotel and restaurant; co-op store; Ed's Mobile Mechanical Service; a convenience store; and a government gas station operating 9 A.M. to 6 P.M. weekdays and 1 to 6 P.M. weekends. Local native crafts are available.

There are hiking trails into the mountains to the east of the community. Inquire locally.

A community-built, walk-in campground with washrooms and fireplaces along the bank of the Mackenzie River, with picturesque, bug-free views of the Mackenzie Mountains. ▲

Hay River Highway

Distance from Enterprise (E) is followed by distance from hay River.

Highway 2 is paved from Enterprise to Hay River. Kilometreposts along the highway reflect distance from Enterprise.

NWT HIGHWAY 2

E 0 H 23.6 (38 km) Junction with Highways 1 at Enterprise, Milepost B 51.7 Mackenzie River.

E 8.5 (13.7 km) H 15.1 (24.3 km) Private campground, 0.7 mile/1.1 km east, with large organic gardens. ▲

E 11.3 (18.2 km) H 12.3 (19.8 km) Sawmill Road to east.

E 15.7 (25.3 km) H 7.9 (12.7 km) Gravel road leads east 0.6 mile/1 km to Hay River golf course and ski club; large log clubhouse, driving range, 9 holes (par 36), artificial greens.

E 19.8 (31.9 km) H 3.8 (6.1 km) Junction with Highway 5 to Fort Smith. See Fort Smith Highway log on page 747 this section.

E 20.4 (32.8 km) H 3.2 (5.1 km) Motel and restaurant north of junction.

E 22 (35.4 km) H 1.6 (2.6 km) Chamber of Commerce Welcome to Hay River sign and detailed town map. Parking area to east.

E 22.1 (35.6 km) H 1.5 (2.4 km) Turnoff to east for parking area and Kiwanis Club picnic site.

E 22.7 (36.6 km) H 0.9 (1.4 km) Gas, motel, groceries to east.

E 23.2 (37.4 km) H 0.4 (0.6 km) Chamber of Commerce tourist information booth, payphone, water and sewer dumping station.

A sunny day at Hay River's Beach Park on Great Slave Lake.
(© Roger Pickenpaugh)

Hay River

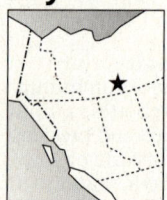

E 23.6 (38 km) H 0 Located on the south shore of Great Slave Lake at the mouth of the Hay River, on both the mainland and Vale Island. Population: 3,600 Emergency Services: RCMP, phone (867) 874-6555. Fire Department, phone (867) 874-2222. Ambulance, phone (867) 874-9333. Hospital, phone (867) 874-7100.

Visitor Information: Visitor information centre, just east of the highway, is housed in a 2-story brown structure; phone (867) 874-3180. The centre is open daily, 9 A.M. to 9 P.M., late May to early September. There is a dump station located here. Write the Town of Hay River, 73 Woodland Dr., Hay River, NWT X0E 1G1. Or the Chamber of Commerce at 10K Gagnier St., Hay River, NWT X0E 1G1; phone (867) 874-2565, fax (867) 874-3255.

Transportation: Air—Scheduled service. Bus—Frontier Coachlines. Rental cars—Renta Relic (867/874-3485) and Budget (867/874-7777).

Private Aircraft: Hay River airport; elev. 543 feet/165m; length 6,000 feet/1,830m, paved; 4,000 feet/1,219m, gravel; fuel 100, Jet B.

Hay River was established in 1868 with the building of a Hudson's Bay Co. post. Today's economy combines transportation, communications, commercial fishing and service industries. Hay River also has Paradise Gardens, the largest market-gardening operation in Northwest Territories.

The community is the transfer point from highway and rail to barges on Great Slave Lake bound for arctic and subarctic communities. Hay River harbour is also home port of the Mackenzie River barge fleet that plies the river in summer.

The airstrip was built in 1942 on Vale Island by the U.S. Army Corps of Engineers. Vale Island was the townsite until floods in 1951 and 1963 forced evacuation of the population to the mainland townsite, where

ALASKA STATE FERRY SCHEDULES

On the following pages are summer schedules and fares—effective May 1 through September 30, 2003—provided by the Alaska Marine Highway office, as well as information on reservations, fare payment, stopovers, etc. For more detailed information on any aspect of Alaska Marine Highway travel, contact the main office of the Alaska Marine Highway System, 6858 Glacier Highway, Juneau, AK 99801-7909; phone toll free 1-800-642-0066; fax (907) 277-4829; or consult the web site at www.alaska.gov/ferry. On-line updates on the Alaska state ferry system are also available on the Internet. *NOTE: The state reserves the right to revise or cancel schedules and rates without prior notice and assumes no responsibility for delays and/or expenses due to such modifications.* The Alaska Marine Highway is also covered in the TRAVEL PLANNING section under "Ferry Travel."

Reservations: Walk-on traffic is usually accommodated, but reservations are advised, especially for those traveling with a vehicle or wanting a cabin. For reservations write the Alaska Marine Highway, 6858 Glacier Highway, Juneau, AK 99801-7909; phone toll free 1-800-642-0066; fax (907) 277-4829; TDD 1-800-764-3779; web site www.alaska.gov/ferry. Local ferry reservation numbers in Alaska are: Juneau (907) 465-3941; and Anchorage (907) 272-7116.

The Alaska state ferries are very popular in summer. Reservations should be made as far in advance as possible to get the sailing dates you wish. Cabin space on summer sailings is often sold out quickly on the Bellingham sailings. Requests for space are accepted year-round and held until reservations open.

In order to guarantee your reservation, payment must be received by the payment due date on your reservation confirmation. Reservations not paid for by this date are automatically cancelled. Tickets may be picked up at any ferry office or terminal, or if there is time before your departure date they will be mailed to you.

Cancellation charges apply for changes made within 14 days of sailing.

Deck Passage: If cabin space is filled, or you do not want a cabin, you may go deck passage. This means you'll be sleeping in one of the reclining lounge chairs or rolling out your sleeping bag in an empty corner or even out on deck. There is a limited number of recliner chairs and spaces to roll out sleeping bags. Small, free-standing tents are permitted on the solarium deck (but not under the heated covered area) and on the stern of the cabin deck if space allows (except on the *Kennicott*). Beware of wind; some campers duct-tape their tents to the deck. Pillows and blankets are available for rent from the purser on most sailings. Public showers are available on all vessels.

Waitlisted and Standby Travel: If the desired space is not available, reservation personnel may offer to place your request on a waitlist. If cancellations occur, you will be notified of confirmation of space, at which time payment will be due.

If your cabin request has not been confirmed by the time of sailing, you may sign up on the purser's standby list on board. Once the sailing is underway, the purser assigns available cabins to those on the standby list.

If you arrive at a ferry terminal without confirmed vehicle space, you must sign up on the standby list at the terminal.

Fares and fare payment: For Inside Passage/Cross-Gulf fares and cabin rates, see pages 761-762. For Southcentral/Southwest rates, see pages 765-766.

Payment for reserved space may be made by phone or online with a credit card or by
(Continues on page 751)

ALASKA STATE FERRIES

Homer Ferry Terminal
Contract Agent • Alaska Marine Highway

Information, Reservations & Ticketing
1-800-382-9229

Open All Year • Major Credit Cards • (907) 235-8449 • Fax (907) 235-6907
www.akmhs.com

ALASKA MARINE HIGHWAY 800-642-0066
MAY 2003 Northbound Schedule - REV. 1-8-03

ALASKA STATE FERRY SCHEDULES

AUR-AURORA MAL-MALASPINA
COL-COLUMBIA MAT-MATANUSKA
LEC-LE CONTE TAK-TAKU
KEN-KENNICOTT

Ship	LEAVE BELLINGHAM	LEAVE PRINCE RUPERT	METLAKATLA	KETCHIKAN	HOLLIS	WRANGELL	PETERSBURG	KAKE	ARRIVE SITKA	ANGOON	TENAKEE	HOONAH	JUNEAU AUKE BAY	HAINES	ARRIVE SKAGWAY
LEC			W30 8:30A	W30 10:00A											
LEC			W30 4:10P	W30 7:30P		TH1 2:15A	TH1 6:00A		TH1 11:00A	TH1 8:00P	F2 4:30A		F2 9:30A	F2 12:45P		
TAK		TH1 10:45A		TH1 6:15P	SEE INTER-ISLAND FERRY AUTHORITY SCHEDULE BELOW	F2 1:00A	F2 4:45A						F2 3:45P	F2 9:15P	F2 10:15P
KEN									Lv.Sitka S3 5:15P	S3 10:45P		SU4 3:45A	SU4 7:00A			
LEC										Lv.Pelican SU4 4:30P			SU4 11:00A			
COL	F2 6:00P			SU4 9:00A		SU4 3:30P	SU4 7:30P						M5 7:00A	M5 12:45P	M5 1:45P	
TAK		SU4 1:00P		SU4 7:00P		M5 1:45A	M5 5:15A	M5 4:00P					T6 6:30A	T6 11:55A	T6 1:00P	
KEN		M5 2:15P		M5 8:45P		T6 3:45A	T6 8:00A						T6 5:30P	T6 11:00P	W7 12:15A	
LEC			W7 8:30A	W7 10:00A												
LEC			W7 4:10P	TH8 2:00A		W7 8:45P	TH8 1:45P	TH8 6:45P		TH8 11:45P	F9 3:00A	F9 7:15A	F9 10:30A			
TAK		TH8 9:00A		TH8 3:00P		TH8 11:45P	F9 3:30A						F9 12:15P	F9 5:45P	F9 6:45P	
KEN		F9 11:45A		F9 5:45P									S10 11:15A	S10 4:45P	S10 6:00P	
LEC									Lv.Sitka S10 5:30P	S10 11:30P	SU11 2:15A	SU11 6:30A	SU11 9:45A			
COL	F9 6:00P			SU11 10:00A		SU11 4:30P	SU11 8:30P						M12 7:00A	M12 12:45P	M12 1:45P	
TAK		SU11 10:30A		SU11 4:30P		SU11 11:15P	M12 3:00A						M12 11:45A	M12 5:15P	M12 6:15P	
KEN		M12 11:30A		M12 6:00P									T13 2:30P	***To Cross-Gulf		
LEC			T13 9:10P	T13 10:40P												
TAK		W14 8:00A		W14 2:00P		W14 10:15P							TH15 7:00A	TH15 12:45P	TH15 1:45P	
LEC			W14 8:30A	W14 10:00A												
LEC			W14 4:10	TH15 3:30A		W15 10:15A	TH15 2:00P	TH15 7:00P		TH15 11:55P		F16 7:30A	F16 10:45A			
TAK													F16 7:00A	F16 12:45P	F16 1:45P	
TAK													S17 7:00A	S17 12:45P	S17 1:45P	
KEN									Lv.Sitka S17 5:00P	S17 10:45P		SU18 3:45A	SU18 7:00A			
TAK													SU18 7:00A			
LEC										Lv.Pelican SU18 4:30P			SU18 11:00P			
COL	F16 6:00P			SU18 9:00A		SU18 3:30P	SU18 7:30P						M19 7:00A	M19 12:45P	M19 1:45P	
KEN		M19 12:30P		M19 6:30P		T20 1:15A	T20 5:15A						T20 2:30P	T20 8:00P	T20 9:15P	
LEC			T20 9:10P	T20 10:40P												
TAK		W21 5:00A		W21 11:30A		W21 6:15P	W21 10:00P						TH22 7:00A	TH22 12:45P	TH22 1:45P	
TAK													F23 7:00A	F23 12:45P	F23 1:45P	
LEC			W21 8:30A	W21 10:00A												
LEC			W21 4:10P	TH22 2:15A		TH22 9:00A	TH22 2:45P	TH22 7:45P		F23 12:45A	F23 4:00A	F23 8:15A	F23 11:30A			
TAK													S24 7:00A	S24 12:45P	S24 1:45P	
KEN		F23 9:00A		F23 3:30P									S24 9:00A	S24 3:00P	S24 4:15P	
TAK													SU25 7:00A	SU25 12:45P	SU25 1:45P	
LEC									Lv.Sitka S24 5:45P	S24 11:45P	SU25 2:30A	SU25 6:45A	SU25 10:00A			
COL	F23 6:00P			SU25 9:45A		SU25 4:00P	SU25 8:15P						M26 7:00A	M26 12:45P	M26 1:45P	
KEN		M26 10:30A		M26 6:00P									T27 2:30P	***To Cross-Gulf		
LEC			T27 9:10P	T27 10:40P												
TAK		W28 5:00A		W28 11:30A		W28 6:15P	W28 10:00P						TH29 7:00A	TH29 12:45P	TH29 1:45P	
TAK													F30 7:00A	F30 12:45P	F30 1:45P	
LEC			W28 8:30A	W28 10:00A												
LEC			W28 4:10P	TH29 3:30A		TH29 10:15A	TH29 2:00P	TH29 7:00P		TH29 11:55P		F30 7:30A	F30 10:45A			
TAK													S31 7:00A	S31 12:45P	S31 1:45P	
LEC									Lv.Sitka S31 4:30P	S31 10:15P	SU1 1:00A	SU1 5:00A	SU1 8:15A			
COL	F30 6:00P			SU1 9:00A		SU1 3:30P	SU1 7:30P						M2 7:00A	M2 12:45P	M2 1:45P	

ALL TIMES ARE LOCAL TIMES

SOUTHEAST/SOUTHWEST CROSS-GULF TRIPS

Lv. Juneau	Ar. Valdez	Lv. Valdez	Ar. Seward	Lv. Seward	Ar. Valdez	Lv. Valdez	Ar. Juneau
				TH1 11:30P	F2 9:00A	F2 12:30P	SU4 1:30A
T13 2:30P	TH15 2:00A	TH15 6:00A	TH15 3:30P	TH15 11:30P	F16 9:00A	F16 12:30P	SU18 1:30A
T27 2:30P	TH29 2:00A	TH29 6:00A	TH29 3:30P	TH29 11:30P	F30 9:00A	F30 12:30P	SU1 1:30A

Whistle Stop service is provided to Yakutat on Cross-Gulf trips in both directions between Juneau and Valdez. The vessel will stop ONLY if there are vehicle reservations.

JUNEAU ~ HAINES ~ SKAGWAY DAILY SCHEDULE - EFFECTIVE JUNE 3 THROUGH SEPTEMBER 11, 2003

Lv. Juneau	Ar. Haines	Lv. Haines	Ar. Skagway	Lv. Skagway	Ar. Haines	Lv. Haines	Ar. Juneau
7:00A	11:30A	12:45P	1:45P	4:15P	5:15P	6:30P	11:00P

ALASKA MARINE HIGHWAY 800-642-0066
MAY 2003 Southbound Schedule - REV. REV. 1-8-03

AUR-AURORA MAL-MALASPINA
COL-COLUMBIA MAT-MATANUSKA
LEC-LE CONTE TAK-TAKU
KEN-KENNICOTT

ALASKA STATE FERRY SCHEDULES

	LEAVE SKAGWAY	HAINES	JUNEAU AUKE BAY	HOONAH	TENAKEE	ANGOON	ARRIVE SITKA	KAKE	PETERSBURG	WRANGELL	HOLLIS	KETCHIKAN	METLAKATLA	ARRIVE PRINCE RUPERT	ARRIVE BELLINGHAM
LEC												W30 6:30A	W30 8:00A		
LEC												W30 2:10P	W30 3:40P		
LEC									S3 5:15P	S3 9:00P		SU4 4:00A		SU4 11:00A	
TAK	S3 1:15A	S3 3:15A	S3 8:45A						SU$ 2:00P	SU4 6:15P		M5 3:30A		M5 10:45A	
KEN	***FromCross-Gulf		SU4 5:00A												
LEC			SU4 8:00A	Ar.Pelican	SU4 2:30P										
LEC			M5 2:00A	M5 6:15A		M5 11:15A	M5 4:15P	T6 3:45A	T6 12:15P	T6 4:00P		W7 6:30A	W7 8:00A		
COL	M5 4:15P	M5 6:30P	T6 2:00A				T6 10:45A		T6 11:30P	W7 3:30A		W7 5:00P			F9 8:00A
TAK	T6 4:00P	T6 6:00P	W7 12:30A						W7 9:00A	W7 12:45P		W7 11:00P		TH8 6:00A	
KEN	W7 5:15A	W7 7:15A	W7 2:30P				W7 11:30P	TH8 4:45P				F9 2:00A		F9 9:15A	
LEC												W7 2:10P	W7 3:40P		
LEC			F9 3:45P	F9 8:00P	F9 11:55P	S10 3:15A	S10 8:15A								
TAK	F9 8:45P	F9 10:45P	S10 4:15A						S10 12:45P	S10 4:30P		SU11 1:30A		SU11 8:30A	
KEN	S10 10:00P	S10 11:55P	SU11 5:45A									M12 1:15A		M12 8:30A	
LEC			SU11 6:15P	SU11 10:30P	M12 2:30A	M12 6:00A	M12 11:00A	M12 10:30P	T13 7:00A	T13 10:45A		T13 6:15P	T13 7:45P		
COL	M12 4:15P	M12 6:30P	T13 3:00A				T13 11:45A		W14 12:30A	W14 4:30A		W14 1:00P			F16 8:00A
TAK	M12 8:15P	M12 10:15P	T13 3:45A						T13 12:15P	T13 4:00P		T13 11:00P		W14 6:00A	
LEC												W14 6:30A	W14 8:00A		
TAK	TH15 4:15P	TH15 6:30P	TH15 11:00P												
LEC												W14 2:10P	W14 3:40P		
LEC			F16 4:00P	F16 8:15P	S17 12:15A	S17 3:30A	S17 8:30A								
TAK	F16 4:15P	F16 6:30P	F16 11:00P												
TAK	S17 4:15P	S17 6:30P	S17 11:00P						SU18 2:15P	SU18 6:15P		M19 2:15A		M19 9:30A	
KEN	***FromCross-Gulf		SU18 5:30A												
LEC			SU18 8:00A	Ar.Pelican	SU18 2:30P										
TAK	SU18 4:15P	SU18 6:30P	M19 12:30A				M19 10:15A		T20 12:15A	T20 4:00A		T20 11:00A		T20 6:00P	
LEC			M19 1:45A	M19 6:00A		M19 11:00A	M19 4:00P	T20 3:00A	T20 7:30A	T20 11:15A		T20 6:15P	T20 7:45P		
COL	M19 4:15P	M19 6:30P	T20 2:30A				T20 11:15A		W21 1:00A	W21 5:00A		W21 3:00P			F23 8:00A
KEN	W21 1:15A	W21 3:15A	W21 9:15A				W21 6:15P		TH22 7:30A	TH22 11:30A		TH22 10:45P		F23 6:00A	
LEC												W21 6:30A	W21 8:00A		
TAK	TH22 4:15P	TH22 6:30P	TH22 11:00P												
TAK	F23 4:15P	F23 6:30P	F23 11:00P												
LEC												W21 2:10P	W21 3:40P		
LEC			F23 4:45P	F23 9:00P	S24 1:00A	S24 4:15A	S24 9:15A								
TAK	S24 4:15P	S24 6:30P	S24 11:00P												
KEN	S24 7:30P	S24 10:00P	SU25 4:00A						SU25 12:45P	SU25 4:45P		M26 12:15A		M26 7:30A	
TAK	SU25 4:15P	SU25 6:30P	M26 1:00A				M26 10:45A		T27 12:45A	T27 4:30A		T27 11:30A		T27 6:30P	
LEC			SU25 6:15P	SU25 10:30P	M26 2:30A	M26 6:00A	M26 11:00A	M26 10:30P	T27 6:30A	T27 10:15A		T27 6:15P	T27 7:45P		
COL	M26 4:15P	M26 6:30P	T27 3:15A				T27 11:55A		W28 1:00A	W28 5:00A		W28 4:00P			F30 8:00A
LEC												W28 6:30A	W28 8:00A		
TAK	TH29 4:15P	TH29 6:30P	TH29 11:00P												
TAK	F30 4:15P	F30 6:30P	F30 11:00P												
LEC												W28 2:10P	W28 3:40P		
LEC			F30 3:30P	F30 7:45P	F30 11:45P	S31 3:00A	S31 8:00A								
TAK	S31 4:15P	S31 6:30P	S31 11:00P												

SEE INTER-ISLAND FERRY AUTHORITY SCHEDULE BELOW

INTER-ISLAND FERRY AUTHORITY - DAILY SCHEDULE - EFFECTIVE JUNE 1 - AUGUST 31, 2002

Lv. Hollis	Ar. Ketchikan	Lv. Ketchikan	Ar. Hollis	Lv. Hollis	Ar. Ketchikan	Lv. Ketchikan	Ar. Hollis
7:00A	10:05A	10:35A	1:40P	2:10P	5:15P	5:45P	8:50P

mail with a cashier's check, money order or personal check drawn on an Alaska bank.

Vehicle tariffs depend on the size of vehicle. You are charged by how much space you take up, so a car with trailer is measured from the front of the car to the end of the trailer, including hitch space. Bicycles, kayaks and inflatables are charged a surcharge.

Passenger tariffs are charged as follows: adults and children 12 and over, full fare; children 2 to 11, approximately half fare; children under 2, free. Passenger fares do not include cabins or meals. Seasonal senior citizen (over 65) discount of 50 percent off the passenger fare between Alaskan ports only; restrictions may apply. Special passes and travel rates are also available to persons with disabilities. Contact the Alaska Marine Highway System for more on these fares and restrictions.

Surcharges are assessed on pets ($25 to/from Bellingham, $10 to/from Prince Rupert) and unattended vehicles ($50 to/from Bellingham, $20 to/from Prince Rupert, and $10 to/from other ports).

Check-in times: Summer check-in times for reserved vehicles prior to departure are: Bellingham and Prince Rupert, 3 hours; Ketchikan, Juneau, Haines, Skagway, Homer, Seward, Kodiak, 2 hours; Petersburg, 1½ hours; all other ports, 1 hour except for Sitka. Call the Sitka terminal for check-in time (907) 747-3300. Passengers without vehicles must check in 1 hour prior to departure at all ports except Bellingham, where check-in is 2 hours prior to departure.

To arrive at the terminal on time, Whittier passengers are advised to call ahead to the Whittier Tunnel for a vehicle traffic schedule; phone 1-877-611-2586.

Cabins: Most cabins on the Southeast system ferries have a toilet and shower. Linens (towels, sheets, blankets) are provided. Pick up cabin keys from the purser's office when you board. Cabins are sold as a unit, not on a per berth basis. In other words, the cost of the cabin is the same whether 1 or more passengers occupy it. You can get on a waitlist for a cabin at the purser's office.

Restrooms are available for deck-passage (walk-on) passengers on all vessels. Public showers are available on all vessels.

Vehicles: Reservations are strongly recommended. Any vehicle that may be driven legally on the highway is acceptable for transport on the 4 larger vessels. Most *(Continues on page 760)*

ALASKA MARINE HIGHWAY 800-642-0066
JUNE 2003 Northbound Schedule - REV. REV. 1-8-03

ALASKA STATE FERRY SCHEDULES

AUR-AURORA MAL-MALASPINA
COL-COLUMBIA MAT-MATANUSKA
LEC-LE CONTE TAK-TAKU
KEN-KENNICOTT

Ship	Leave Bellingham	Leave Prince Rupert	Metlakatla	Ketchikan	Hollis	Wrangell	Petersburg	Kake	Arrive Sitka	Angoon	Tenakee	Hoonah	Juneau Auke Bay	Haines	Arrive Skagway
KEN															
LEC									Lv.Sitka S31 4:30P	S31 10:15P	SU1 1:00A	SU1 5:00A	SU1 8:15A		
MAT															
TAK													SU1 7:00A	SU1 12:45P	SU1 1:45P
LEC									Lv.Pelican SU1 5:15P				SU1 11:45P		
COL	F30 6:00P			SU1 9:00A		SU1 3:30P	SU1 7:30P						M2 7:00A	M2 12:45P	M2 1:45P
MAT		SU1 11:00A		SU1 5:15P		SU1 11:55P	M2 3:45A						M2 2:00P	M2 7:30P	M2 8:30P
AUR				M2 8:30A		M2 3:15P	M2 7:00P						T3 7:00A	T3 12:45P	T3 1:45P
KEN		M2 12:30P		M2 7:00P		T3 2:00A	T3 6:00A						T3 3:30P	T3 9:15P	T3 10:30P
AUR													W4 7:00A	W4 12:45P	W4 1:45P
LEC						T3 7:45A	T3 12:45P	T3 9:30P	W4 6:00A			W4 1:30P	W4 4:45P		
TAK		W4 5:00A		W4 11:30A		W4 6:15P	W4 10:00P						TH5 7:00A	TH5 12:45P	TH5 1:45P
MAT		W4 12:15P		W4 7:30P		TH5 2:15A	TH5 6:00A		TH5 5:15P				F6 9:45A	F6 3:15P	F6 4:15P
LEC							TH5 2:30P	TH5 7:30P		F6 12:30A	F6 4:00A	F6 8:15A	F6 11:30A		
KEN		F6 12:30P		F6 6:30P									S7 11:30A	S7 5:15P	S7 6:30P
LEC									Lv.Sitka S7 3:30P	S7 9:30P	SU8 12:15A	SU8 4:30A	SU8 7:45A		
MAL															
TAK													SU8 7:00A	SU8 12:45P	SU8 1:45P
COL	F6 6:00P			SU8 9:00A		SU8 3:30P	SU8 7:30P						M9 7:00A	M9 12:45P	M9 1:45P
MAT		SU8 11:30A		SU8 5:45P		M9 12:30A	M9 4:15A						M9 2:00P	M9 7:30P	M9 8:30P
AUR				M9 8:30A		M9 3:15P	M9 7:00P						T10 7:00A	T10 12:45P	T10 1:45P
KEN		M9 11:55A		M9 6:00P									T10 2:30P	***To Cross-Gulf Trip	
AUR													W11 7:00A	W11 12:45P	W11 1:45P
LEC						W11 6:15P	T10 2:45P	T10 7:45A	T10 4:15P	W11 1:15A	W11 4:30A	W11 8:45A	W11 11:55A		
TAK		W11 5:00A		W11 11:30A			W11 10:00P						TH12 7:00A	TH12 12:45P	TH12 1:45P
LEC							TH12 12:45P	TH12 5:45P		TH12 10:45P		F13 6:15A	F13 9:30A		
MAT		W11 12:45P		W11 7:00P		TH12 3:15A	TH12 6:00P		F13 6:45A				F13 9:45A	F13 3:15P	F13 4:15P
MAL	T10 6:00P			TH12 9:30A		TH12 4:15P	TH12 8:00P						F13 9:00P	S14 3:00A	S14 4:00A
KEN															
LEC									Lv.Sitka S14 4:00P	S14 9:45P	SU15 12:30A	SU15 4:30A	SU15 7:45A		
TAK													SU15 7:00A	SU15 12:45P	SU15 1:45P
LEC									Lv.Pelican SU15 4:45P				SU15 11:15P		
COL	F13 6:00P			SU15 8:30A		SU15 3:00P	SU15 7:00P						M16 7:00A	M16 12:45P	M16 1:45P
MAT		SU15 9:15A		SU15 3:30P		SU15 10:15P	M16 2:00A						M16 11:45A	M16 5:15P	M16 6:15P
AUR				M16 8:30A		M16 3:15P	M16 7:00P						T17 7:00A	T17 12:45P	T17 1:45P
KEN		M16 12:30P		M16 7:00P		T17 2:00A	T17 6:00A						T17 3:00P	T17 8:30P	T17 9:45P
AUR													W18 7:00A	W18 12:45P	W18 1:45P
LEC							T17 7:30A	T17 12:30P	T17 10:00P	W18 6:30A		W18 11:30A	W18 2:45P		
TAK		W18 5:00A		W18 11:30A		W18 6:15P	W18 10:00P						TH19 7:00A	TH19 12:45P	TH19 1:45P
MAT		W18 11:55A		W18 7:00P		TH19 1:45A	TH19 5:30A		TH19 5:45P				F20 9:45A	F20 3:15P	F20 4:15P
LEC							TH19 2:45P	TH19 7:45P		F20 12:45A	F20 4:00A	F20 8:15A	F20 11:30A		
MAL	T17 6:00P			TH19 9:00A		TH19 3:45P	TH19 7:30P		F20 6:15A				F20 9:00P	S21 3:00A	S21 4:00A
KEN		F20 4:00A		F20 10:00A		F20 4:45P	F20 8:45P						S21 6:00A	S21 11:30A	S21 12:45P
TAK													SU22 12:45P	SU22 12:45P	SU22 1:45P
LEC									Lv.Sitka S21 3:45P	S21 9:45P	SU22 12:30A	SU22 4:45A	SU22 9:45A	SU22 2:15P	
COL	F20 6:00P			SU22 9:00A		SU22 3:30P	SU22 7:30P						M23 7:00A	M23 12:45P	M23 1:45P
MAT		SU22 10:45A		SU22 6:00P		M23 12:45A	M23 4:30A						M23 2:30P	M23 8:00P	M23 9:00P
AUR				M23 8:30A		M23 3:15P	M23 7:00P						T24 7:00A	T24 12:45P	T24 1:45P
KEN		M23 10:30A		M23 6:30P									T24 2:30P	***To Cross-Gulf Trip	
AUR													W25 7:00A	W25 12:45P	W25 1:45P
LEC							T24 8:45A	T24 1:45P	T24 10:15P	W25 6:45A		W25 11:45A	W25 3:00P		
TAK		W25 5:00A		W25 11:30A		W25 6:15P	W25 10:00P						TH26 7:00A	TH26 12:45P	TH26 1:45P
LEC							TH26 12:45P	TH26 5:45P		TH26 10:45P		F27 6:15A	F27 9:30A		
MAT		W25 1:45P		W25 8:00P		TH26 4:15A	TH26 5:45P		TH26 5:45P				F27 9:45A	F27 3:15P	F27 4:15P
MAL	T24 6:00P			TH26 9:00A		TH26 3:45P	TH26 7:30P		F27 6:15A				F27 9:00P	S28 3:00A	S28 4:00A
KEN															
LEC									Lv.Sitka S28 3:45P	S28 9:45P	SU29 12:30A	SU29 4:30A	SU29 7:45A		
TAK													SU29 7:00A	SU29 12:45P	SU29 1:45P
LEC									Lv.Pelican SU29 4:30P				SU29 11:00P		
COL	F27 6:00P			SU29 9:00A		SU29 3:30P	SU29 7:30P						M30 7:00A	M30 12:45P	M30 1:45P
MAT		SU29 9:30A		SU29 3:45P		SU29 10:30P	M30 2:15A						M30 11:45A	M30 5:15P	M30 6:15P
AUR			SU29 4:10P	M30 8:30A		M30 3:15P	M30 7:00P						T1 7:00A	T1 12:45P	T1 1:45P
KEN		M30 12:30P		M30 7:00P		T1 1:45A	T1 5:45A						T1 3:15P	T1 9:15P	T1 10:30P

ALL TIMES ARE LOCAL TIMES

SOUTHEAST/SOUTHWEST CROSS-GULF TRIPS

Lv. Juneau	Ar. Valdez	Lv. Valdez	Ar. Seward	Lv. Seward	Ar. Valdez	Lv. Valdez	Ar. Juneau
T10 2:30P	TH12 2:00A	TH12 6:00A	TH12 3:30P	TH12 11:30P	F13 9:00A	F13 12:30P	SU15 1:30A
T24 2:30P	TH26 2:00A	TH26 6:00A	TH26 3:30P	TH26 11:30P	F27 9:00A	F27 12:30P	SU29 1:30A

Whistle Stop service is provided to Yakutat on Cross-Gulf trips in both directions between Juneau and Valdez. The vessel will stop ONLY if there are vehicle reservations.

JUNEAU ~ HAINES ~ SKAGWAY DAILY SCHEDULE - EFFECTIVE JUNE 3 THROUGH SEPTEMBER 11, 2003

Lv. Juneau	Ar. Haines	Lv. Haines	Ar. Skagway	Lv. Skagway	Ar. Haines	Lv. Haines	Ar. Juneau
7:00A	11:30A	12:45P	1:45P	4:15P	5:15P	6:30P	11:00P

ALASKA MARINE HIGHWAY 800-642-0066
JUNE 2003 Southbound Schedule - REV. REV. 1-8-03

AUR-AURORA MAL-MALASPINA
COL-COLUMBIA MAT-MATANUSKA
LEC-LE CONTE TAK-TAKU
KEN-KENNICOTT

ALASKA STATE FERRY SCHEDULES

	LEAVE SKAGWAY	HAINES	JUNEAU AUKE BAY	HOONAH	TENAKEE	ANGOON	ARRIVE SITKA	KAKE	PETERSBURG	WRANGELL	HOLLIS	KETCHIKAN	METLAKATLA	ARRIVE PRINCE RUPERT	ARRIVE BELLINGHAM
KEN	***FromCross-Gulf		SU1 5:30A						SU1 2:15P	SU1 6:15P		M2 2:15A		M2 9:30A	
LEC			SU1 9:00A	Ar.Pelican	SU1 3:30P							SU1 12:30A		SU1 8:00A	
MAT												T3 4:00P		T3 11:00P	
TAK	SU1 4:15P	SU1 6:30P	M2 5:30A				M2 3:15P		T3 5:15A	T3 9:00A					
LEC			M2 12:45A	M2 5:00A		M2 10:00A	M2 3:00P	T3 2:30A	T3 6:30A			W4 5:00P			F6 8:00A
COL	M2 4:15P	M2 6:30P	T3 1:00A				T3 9:45A		W4 12:30A	W4 5:00A		W4 1:45A		W4 9:15A	
MAT	M2 10:15P	T3 12:15A	T3 5:45A						T3 2:45P	T3 6:45P					
AUR	T3 4:15P	T3 6:30P	T3 11:00P									F6 2:15A		F6 9:30A	
KEN	W4 3:30A	W4 6:00A	W4 1:30P				W4 10:30P		TH5 3:15P	TH5 7:15P		TH5 10:15P			
AUR	W4 4:15P	W4 6:30P	TH5 1:45A												
LEC			W4 7:15P	W4 11:30P		TH5 4:30A		TH5 9:30A	TH5 1:30P						
TAK	TH5 4:15P	TH5 6:30P	TH5 11:00P									SU8 1:15A		SU8 8:45A	
MAT	F6 7:15P	F6 9:15P	S7 3:45A						S7 2:15P	S7 6:15P					
LEC			F6 2:00P	F6 6:15P	F6 10:15P	S7 1:30A	S7 6:30A					M9 1:45A		M9 9:00A	
KEN	S7 11:15P	SU8 1:45A	SU8 8:45A												
LEC			SU8 4:30P	SU8 8:45P	M9 12:45A	M9 4:15A	M9 9:15A	M9 8:45P	T10 12:45A			SU8 5:00P		T10 8:00A	
MAL												T10 5:00P		T10 11:55P	
TAK	SU8 4:15P	SU8 6:30P	M9 5:30A				M9 3:15P		T10 6:15A	T10 10:00A		W11 3:00P		F13 8:00A	
COL	M9 4:15P	M9 6:30P	T10 1:15A				T10 10:30A		W11 1:00A	W11 5:00A		W11 2:15A		W11 9:45A	
MAT	M9 10:45P	T10 12:45A	T10 6:15A						T10 3:15P	T10 7:15P					
AUR	T10 4:15P	T10 6:30P	T10 11:00P												
KEN															
AUR	W11 4:15P	W11 6:30P	TH12 1:00A						TH12 10:00A	TH12 1:45P		TH12 7:45P			
LEC			W11 4:30P	W11 8:45P		TH12 1:45A		TH12 6:45A	TH12 10:45A						
TAK	TH12 4:15P	TH12 6:30P	TH12 11:00P												
LEC			F13 3:00P	F13 7:15P	F13 11:15P	S14 2:30A	S14 7:30A								
MAT	F13 7:15P	F13 9:15P	S14 2:45A						S14 11:45A	S14 3:45P		S14 10:45P		SU15 6:15A	
MAL	S14 7:00A	S14 9:30A	S14 6:30P						SU15 3:00A	SU15 6:45A		SU15 2:30P			T17 8:00A
KEN	***FromCross-Gulf		SU15 5:30A						SU15 2:15P	SU15 6:15P		M16 2:15A		M16 9:30A	
LEC			SU15 8:30A	Ar.Pelican	SU15 3:00P										
TAK	SU15 4:15P	SU15 6:30P	M16 5:30A				M16 3:15P		T17 5:15A	T17 9:00A		T17 4:00P		T17 11:00P	
LEC			M16 12:45A	M16 5:00A		M16 10:00A	M16 3:00P	T17 2:30A	T17 6:30A			W18 4:00P			F20 8:00A
COL	M16 4:15P	M16 6:30P	T17 1:15A				T17 10:00A		W18 1:00A	W18 5:00A		W18 1:30A		W18 9:00A	
MAT	M16 9:30P	M16 11:30P	T17 5:30A						T17 2:30P	T17 6:30P					
AUR	T17 4:15P	T17 6:30P	T17 11:00P												
KEN	W18 12:30A	W18 2:30A	W18 8:00A				W18 5:00P		TH19 6:15A	TH19 10:15A		TH19 5:45P		F20 1:00A	
AUR	W18 4:15P	W18 6:30P	TH19 1:45A									TH19 10:45P			
LEC			W18 7:30P	W18 11:45P		TH19 4:45A		TH19 9:45A	TH19 1:45P						
TAK	TH19 4:15P	TH19 6:30P	TH19 11:00P												
MAT	F20 7:15P	F20 9:15P	S21 3:45A						S21 12:45P	S21 4:45P		SU22 12:15A		SU22 7:45A	
LEC			F20 2:45P	F20 7:00P	F20 11:00P	S21 2:15A	S21 7:15A								
MAL	S21 7:00A	S21 9:30A	S21 6:30P						SU22 3:00A	SU22 6:45A		SU22 2:30P			T24 8:00A
KEN	S21 1:45P	S21 4:15P	SU22 2:00A						SU22 10:45A	SU22 2:45P		M23 12:15A		M23 7:30A	
TAK	SU22 4:15P	SU22 6:30P	M23 5:45A				M23 3:30P		T24 5:30A	T24 9:15A		T24 4:15P		T24 11:15P	
LEC			SU22 4:15P	SU22 10:30P	M23 2:45A	M23 6:45A	M23 10:15A	M23 3:15P	T24 2:45A	T24 6:45A					
COL	M23 4:15P	M23 6:30P	T24 1:45A				T24 10:30A		W25 1:00A	W25 5:00A		W25 5:00P			F27 8:00A
MAT	M23 11:55P	T24 2:00A	T24 7:30A						T24 4:30P	T24 8:30P		W25 3:30A		W25 11:00A	
AUR	T24 4:15P	T24 6:30P	T24 11:00P												
KEN															
AUR	W25 4:15P	W25 6:30P	TH26 1:00A						TH26 10:00A	TH26 1:45P		TH26 7:45P			
LEC			W25 4:30P	W25 8:45P		TH26 1:45A		TH26 6:45A	TH26 10:45A						
TAK	TH26 4:15P	TH26 6:30P	TH26 11:00P												
LEC			F27 2:45P	F27 7:00P	F27 11:00P	S28 2:15A	S28 7:15A								
MAT	F27 7:15P	F27 9:15P	S28 2:45A						S28 11:45A	S28 3:45P		S28 11:00P		SU29 6:30A	
MAL	S28 7:00A	S28 9:30A	S28 6:30P						SU29 3:00A	SU29 6:45A		SU29 2:45P			T1 8:00A
KEN	***FromCross-Gulf		SU29 5:30A						SU29 2:15P	SU29 6:15P		M30 2:15A		M30 9:30A	
LEC			SU29 8:30A	Ar.Pelican	SU29 3:00P										
TAK	SU29 4:15P	SU29 6:30P	M30 4:30A				M30 2:15P		T1 4:15P	T1 8:00A		T1 3:00P		T1 10:00P	
LEC			SU29 11:55P	M30 4:15P		M30 9:15A	M30 2:15P	T1 1:45A	T1 5:45A						
COL	M30 4:15P	M30 6:30P	T1 6:30A				T1 3:15P		W2 4:00A	W2 8:00A		W2 4:45P			F4 8:00A
MAT	M30 9:15P	M30 11:15P	T1 4:45A						T1 1:45P	T1 5:45P		W2 1:00A		W2 8:30A	

ALL TIMES ARE LOCAL TIMES

M/V AURORA - FRI-SAT-SUN SCHEDULE EFFECTIVE JUNE 1 THROUGH SEPTEMBER 28, 2003

Lv. Ketchikan	Ar. Metlakatla	Lv. Metlakatla	Ar. Ketchikan	Lv. Ketchikan	Ar. Metlakatla	Lv. Metlakatla	Ar. Ketchikan
6:30A	8:00A	8:30A	10:00A	2:10P	3:40P	4:10P	5:10P

INTER-ISLAND FERRY AUTHORITY - DAILY SCHEDULE - EFFECTIVE JUNE 1 - AUGUST 31, 2002

Lv. Hollis	Ar. Ketchikan	Lv. Ketchikan	Ar. Hollis	Lv. Hollis	Ar. Ketchikan	Lv. Ketchikan	Ar. Hollis
7:00A	10:05A	10:35A	1:40P	2:10P	5:15P	5:45P	8:50P

ALASKA MARINE HIGHWAY 800-642-0066
JULY 2003 Northbound Schedule - REV. REV. 1-8-03

AUR-AURORA MAL-MALASPINA
COL-COLUMBIA MAT-MATANUSKA
LEC-LE CONTE TAK-TAKU
KEN-KENNICOTT

ALASKA STATE FERRY SCHEDULES

Ship	LEAVE BELLINGHAM	LEAVE PRINCE RUPERT	METLAKATLA	KETCHIKAN	HOLLIS	WRANGELL	PETERSBURG	KAKE	ARRIVE SITKA	ANGOON	TENAKEE	HOONAH	JUNEAU AUKE BAY	HAINES	ARRIVE SKAGWAY
AUR		M30 12:30P		M30 8:30A		M30 3:15P	M30 7:00P						T1 7:00A	T1 12:45P	T1 1:45P
KEN		M30 12:30P		M30 7:00P		T1 1:45P	T1 5:45A						T1 3:15P	T1 9:15P	T1 10:30P
AUR													W2 7:00A	W2 12:45P	W2 1:45P
LEC						T1 6:45A	T1 11:45A	T1 8:45P	W2 5:15A			W2 10:15A	W2 1:30P		
TAK		W2 5:00A		W2 11:30A		W2 6:15P	W2 10:00P						TH3 12:45P	TH3 12:45P	TH3 1:45P
MAT		W2 11:30A		W2 5:45P		TH3 12:30A	TH3 4:30A		TH3 4:15P				F4 9:45A	F4 3:15P	F4 4:15P
LEC						TH3 1:30P	TH3 6:30P		TH3 11:30P	F4 2:45A	F4 7:00A		F4 10:15A		
MAL	T1 6:00P			TH3 1:30P		TH3 8:15P	TH3 11:55P		F4 10:45A				S5 12:30A	S5 6:00A	S5 7:00A
KEN		F4 11:45A		F4 6:15P									S5 11:45A	S5 5:15P	S5 6:30P
TAK													SU6 7:00A	SU6 12:45P	SU6 1:45P
LEC									Lv.Sitka S5 8:30P	SU6 2:30A	SU6 5:15A	SU6 9:30A	SU6 12:45P		
COL	F4 6:00P			SU6 9:00A		SU6 3:30P	SU6 7:30P						M7 7:00A	M7 12:45P	M7 1:45P
MAT		SU6 11:55A		SU6 6:15P		M7 1:00A	M7 4:45A						M7 2:00P	M7 7:30P	M7 8:30P
AUR				M7 8:30A		M7 3:15P	M7 7:00P						T8 7:00A	T8 12:45P	T8 1:45P
KEN		M7 10:45A		M7 5:15P									T8 2:30P	***To Cross-Gulf	
AUR													W9 7:00A	W9 12:45P	W9 1:45P
LEC						T8 1:00A	T8 6:00A	T8 2:45P	T8 11:45P	W9 3:00A	W9 7:15A		W9 10:30A		
TAK		W9 5:00A		W9 11:30A		W9 6:15P	W9 10:00P						TH10 7:00A	TH10 12:45P	TH10 1:45P
LEC						TH10 11:15A	TH10 4:15P		TH10 9:15P			F11 4:45A	F11 8:00A		
MAT		W9 12:30P		W9 6:45P		TH10 2:45P	TH10 4:45P						F11 9:45A	F11 3:15P	F11 4:15P
MAL	T8 6:00P			TH10 10:30P		TH10 6:45P	F11 5:30A						F11 9:00P	S12 3:00A	S12 4:00A
KEN															
LEC									Lv.Sitka S12 3:00P	S12 9:00P	S12 11:45P	SU13 3:45A	SU13 7:00A		
TAK													SU13 7:00A	SU13 12:45P	SU13 1:45P
LEC									Lv.Pelican SU13 4:15P				SU13 10:45P		
COL	F11 6:00P			SU13 8:00A		SU13 2:15P	SU13 6:00P						M14 7:00A	M14 12:45P	M14 1:45P
MAT		SU13 11:00A		SU13 5:45P		M14 12:30A	M14 4:15A						M14 2:00P	M14 7:30P	M14 8:30P
AUR				M14 8:30A		M14 3:15P	M14 7:00P						T15 7:00A	T15 12:45P	T15 1:45P
KEN		M14 12:30P		M14 7:00P		T15 1:45A	T15 5:45A						T15 3:15P	T15 9:15P	T15 10:30P
LEC						T15 6:30A	T15 11:30A	T15 9:00P	W16 5:30A			W16 10:30A	W16 1:45P		
AUR													W16 7:00A	W16 12:45P	W16 1:45P
TAK		W16 5:00A		W16 11:30A		W16 6:15P	W16 10:00P						TH17 7:00A	TH17 12:45P	TH17 1:45P
MAT		W16 12:30P		W16 6:45P		TH17 1:30A	TH17 5:15A		TH17 4:30P				F18 9:45A	F18 3:15P	F18 4:15P
LEC						TH17 1:30P	TH17 6:45P		TH17 11:45P	F18 3:00A	F18 7:15A		F18 10:30A		
MAL	T15 6:00P			TH17 1:45P		TH17 8:30P	F18 12:15A		F18 11:00A				S19 1:15A	S19 7:15A	S19 8:15A
KEN		F18 11:55A		F18 6:30P									S19 11:45A	S19 5:15P	S19 6:30P
TAK													SU20 7:00A	SU20 12:45P	SU20 1:45P
LEC									Lv.Sitka S19 8:30P	SU20 2:30A	SU20 5:15A	SU20 9:30A	SU20 12:45P		
COL	F18 6:00P			SU20 9:00A		SU20 3:30P	SU20 7:30P						M21 7:00A	M21 12:45P	M21 1:45P
MAT		SU20 10:15A		SU20 4:30P		SU20 11:00P	M21 2:45A						M21 11:45A	M21 5:15P	M21 6:15P
AUR				M21 8:30A		M21 3:15P	M21 7:00P						T22 7:00A	T22 12:45P	T22 1:45P
KEN		M21 11:00A		M21 6:00P									T22 2:30P	***To Cross-Gulf	
LEC						T22 1:00A	T22 6:00A	T22 2:45P	T22 11:30P	W23 2:45A	W23 7:00A		W23 10:15A		
AUR													W23 7:00A	W23 12:45P	W23 1:45P
TAK		W23 5:00A		W23 11:30A		W23 6:15P	W23 10:00P						TH24 7:00A	TH24 12:45P	TH24 1:45P
MAT		W23 11:15A		W23 5:45P		TH24 12:30A	TH24 4:15A		TH24 4:30P				F25 9:45A	F25 3:15P	F25 4:15P
LEC						TH24 11:00A	TH24 4:00P		TH24 9:00P			F25 4:30A	F25 7:45A		
MAL	T22 6:00P			TH24 2:00P		TH24 8:45P	F25 12:30A		F25 11:15A				S26 1:00A	S26 6:30A	S26 7:30A
KEN															
LEC									Lv.Sitka S26 2:30P	S26 8:30P	S26 11:15P	SU27 3:15A	SU27 6:30A		
TAK													SU27 7:00A	SU27 12:45P	SU27 1:45P
LEC									Lv.Pelican SU27 3:30P				SU27 10:00P		
COL	F25 6:00P			SU27 9:00A		SU27 3:30P	SU27 7:30P						M28 7:00A	M28 12:45P	M28 1:45P
MAT		SU27 9:45A		SU27 4:00P		SU27 10:45P	M28 2:30A						M28 11:45A	M28 5:15P	M28 6:15P
AUR				M28 8:30A		M28 3:15P	M28 7:00P						T29 7:00A	T29 12:45P	T29 1:45P
KEN		M28 11:55A		M28 6:15P		T29 1:00A	T29 5:00A						T29 2:30P	T29 8:30P	T29 9:45P
AUR													W30 7:00A	W30 12:45P	W30 1:45P
LEC						T29 5:45A	T29 10:45A	T29 8:15P	W30 4:45A			W30 9:45A	W30 1:00P		
TAK		W30 5:00A		W30 11:30A		W30 6:15P	W30 10:00P						TH31 7:00A	TH31 12:45P	TH31 1:45P
MAT		W30 11:00A		W30 5:30P		TH31 12:15A	TH31 4:00A		TH31 3:15P				F1 9:45A	F1 3:15P	F1 4:15P
LEC						TH31 12:30P	TH31 5:30P		TH31 10:30P	F1 1:45A	F1 6:00A		F1 9:15A		
MAL	T29 6:00P			TH31 12:30P		TH31 7:15P	TH31 11:00P		F1 9:45A				F1 11:55P	S2 5:30A	S2 6:30A

SEE M/V AURORA SCHEDULE BELOW

SEE INTER-ISLAND FERRY AUTHORITY SCHEDULE BELOW

ALL TIMES ARE LOCAL TIMES

SOUTHEAST/SOUTHWEST CROSS-GULF TRIPS

Lv. Juneau	Ar. Valdez	Lv. Valdez	Ar. Seward	Lv. Seward	Ar. Valdez	Lv. Valdez	Ar. Juneau
T8 2:30P	TH10 2:00A	TH10 6:00A	TH10 3:30P	TH10 11:30P	F11 9:00A	F11 12:30P	SU13 1:30A
T22 2:30P	TH24 2:00A	TH24 6:00A	TH24 3:30P	TH24 11:30P	F25 9:00A	F25 12:30P	SU27 1:30A

Whistle Stop service is provided to Yakutat on Cross-Gulf trips in both directions between Juneau and Valdez. The vessel will stop ONLY if there are vehicle reservations.

JUNEAU ~ HAINES ~ SKAGWAY DAILY SCHEDULE - EFFECTIVE JUNE 3 THROUGH SEPTEMBER 11, 2003

Lv. Juneau	Ar. Haines	Lv. Haines	Ar. Skagway	Lv. Skagway	Ar. Haines	Lv. Haines	Ar. Juneau
7:00A	11:30A	12:45P	1:45P	4:15P	5:15P	6:30P	11:00P

ALASKA MARINE HIGHWAY 800-642-0066
JULY 2003 Southbound Schedule - REV. REV. 1-8-03

AUR-AURORA MAL-MALASPINA
COL-COLUMBIA MAT-MATANUSKA
LEC-LE CONTE TAK-TAKU
KEN-KENNICOTT

ALASKA STATE FERRY SCHEDULES

	LEAVE SKAGWAY	HAINES	JUNEAU AUKE BAY	HOONAH	TENAKEE	ANGOON	ARRIVE SITKA	KAKE	PETERSBURG	WRANGELL	HOLLIS	KETCHIKAN	METLAKATLA	ARRIVE PRINCE RUPERT	ARRIVE BELLINGHAM
LEC			SU29 11:55P	M30 4:15A		M30 9:15A	M30 2:15P	T1 1:45A	T1 5:45A						
TAK	SU29 4:15P	SU29 6:30P	M30 4:30A				M30 2:15P		T1 4:15A	T1 8:00A		T1 3:00P		T1 10:00P	
COL	M30 4:15P	M30 6:30P	T1 6:30A				T1 3:15P		W2 4:00A	W2 8:00A		W2 4:45P			F4 8:00A
MAT	M30 9:15P	M30 11:15P	T1 4:45A						T1 1:45P	T1 5:45P		W2 1:00A		W2 8:30A	
AUR	T1 4:15P	T1 6:30P	T1 11:00P												
KEN	W2 3:30A	W2 6:00A	W2 12:30P				W2 9:30P		TH3 2:15P	TH3 6:15P		F4 1:30A		F4 8:45A	
AUR	W2 4:15P	W2 6:30P	TH3 12:15A									TH3 9:45P			
LEC			W2 6:30P	W2 10:45P		TH3 3:45A		TH3 8:45A	TH3 12:45P						
TAK	TH3 4:15P	TH3 6:30P	TH3 11:00P												
MAT	F4 7:15P	F4 9:15P	S5 5:30A						S5 2:30P	S5 6:30P		SU6 1:30A		SU6 9:00A	
LEC			F4 7:00P	F4 11:15P	S5 3:15A	S5 6:30A	S5 11:30A								
MAL	S5 9:30A	S5 11:30A	S5 8:00P						SU6 4:30A	SU6 8:15A		SU6 3:30P			T8 8:00A
KEN	S5 10:45P	SU6 1:15A	SU6 7:30A									M7 12:30A		M7 7:45A	
TAK	SU6 4:15P	SU6 6:30P	M7 4:00A			M7 1:45P			T8 3:45A	T8 7:30A		T8 2:30P		T8 9:30P	
LEC			SU6 2:45P	SU6 7:00P	SU6 11:00P	M7 2:30A	M7 7:30A	M7 7:00P	M7 11:00P						
COL	M7 4:15P	M7 6:30P	T8 5:15A				T8 3:00P		W9 6:15A	W9 10:00A		W9 5:00P			F11 8:00A
MAT	M7 11:00P	T8 1:00A	T8 6:30A						T8 3:30P	T8 7:15P		W9 2:15A		W9 9:45A	
AUR	T8 4:15P	T8 6:30P	T8 11:00P												
AUR	W9 4:15P	W9 6:30P	TH10 1:00A						TH10 10:00A	TH10 1:45P		TH10 7:45P			
LEC			W9 3:00P	W9 7:15P		TH10 12:15A		TH10 5:45A	TH10 10:15A						
TAK	TH10 4:15P	TH10 6:30P	TH10 11:00P												
LEC			F11 2:00P	F11 6:15P	F11 10:15P	S12 1:30A	S12 6:30A								
MAT	F11 7:15P	F11 9:15P	S12 4:00A						S12 1:00P	S12 5:00P		SU13 12:30A		SU13 8:00A	
MAL	S12 7:00A	S12 9:30A	S12 7:00P						SU13 3:30A	SU13 7:15A		SU13 3:30P			T15 8:00A
KEN	***FromCross-Gulf		SU13 5:30A						SU13 2:15P	SU13 5:30P		M14 2:15A		M14 9:30A	
LEC			SU13 7:45A	Ar.Pelican SU13 2:15P											
TAK	SU13 4:15P	SU13 6:30P	M14 4:30A						M14 4:15A	T15 8:00A		T15 3:00P		T15 10:00P	
LEC			SU13 11:55P	M14 4:15A		M14 9:15A	M14 2:15P	T15 1:45A	T15 5:45A						
COL	M14 4:15P	M14 6:30P	T15 5:15A				T15 3:15P		W16 3:45A	W16 7:30A		W16 5:00P			F18 8:00A
MAT	M14 10:45P	T15 12:45A	T15 6:15A						T15 3:15P	T15 7:15P		W16 2:15A		W16 9:45A	
AUR	T15 4:15P	T15 6:30P	T15 11:00P												
KEN	W16 3:30A	W16 6:00A	W16 1:00P				W16 10:00P		TH17 2:45P	TH17 6:45P		F18 1:45A		F18 9:00A	
LEC			W16 6:30P	W16 10:45P		TH17 3:45A		TH17 8:45A	TH17 12:45P						
AUR	W16 4:15P	W16 6:30P	TH17 12:15A									TH17 9:45P			
TAK	TH17 4:15P	TH17 6:30P	TH17 11:00P												
MAT	F18 6:45P	F18 8:45P	S19 2:15A						S19 12:45P	S19 4:45P		S19 11:45P		SU20 7:15A	
LEC			F18 7:30P	F18 11:45P	S19 3:45A	S19 7:00A	S19 11:55A								
MAL	S19 11:55A	S19 2:30P	S19 9:00P						SU20 5:30A	SU20 9:30A		SU20 5:30P			T22 8:00A
KEN	S19 11:15P	SU20 1:15A	SU20 7:15A									M21 12:45A		M21 8:00A	
TAK	SU20 4:15P	SU20 6:30P	M21 4:00A				M21 1:45P		T22 3:45A	T22 7:30A		T22 2:30P		T22 9:30P	
LEC			SU20 2:45P	SU20 7:00P	SU20 11:00P	M21 2:30A	M21 7:30A	M21 7:00P	M21 11:00P						
COL	M21 4:15P	M21 6:30P	T22 6:00A				T22 2:45P		W23 6:00A	W23 9:45A		W23 4:30P			F25 8:00A
MAT	M21 9:15P	M21 11:15P	T22 4:45A						T22 1:45P	T22 5:45P		W23 12:45A		W23 8:15A	
AUR	T22 4:15P	T22 6:30P	T22 11:00P												
KEN															
LEC			W23 2:45P	W23 7:00P		W23 11:55P		TH24 5:30A	TH24 10:00A						
AUR	W23 4:15P	W23 6:30P	TH24 1:00A						TH24 10:00A	TH24 1:45P		TH24 7:45P			
TAK	TH24 4:15P	TH24 6:30P	TH24 11:00P												
MAT	F25 7:15P	F25 9:15P	S26 2:45A						S26 11:45A	S26 3:45P		S26 11:15P		SU27 6:45A	
LEC			F25 1:30P	F25 5:45P	F25 9:45P	S26 1:00A	S26 6:00A								
MAL	S26 9:30A	S26 11:30A	S26 7:00P						SU27 3:30A	SU27 7:15A		SU27 3:00P			T29 8:00A
KEN	***FromCross-Gulf		SU27 5:30A						SU27 2:15A	SU27 6:15P		M28 1:45A		M28 9:00A	
LEC			SU27 7:15A	Ar.Pelican SU27 1:45P											
TAK	SU27 4:15P	SU27 6:30P	M28 3:45A				M28 1:30P		T29 3:30A	T29 7:15A		T29 2:15P		T29 9:15P	
LEC			SU27 11:00P	M28 3:15A		M28 8:15A	M28 1:15P	T29 12:45A	T29 5:00A						
COL	M28 4:15P	M28 6:30P	T29 5:30A				T29 2:15P		W30 2:45A	W30 6:30A		W30 4:45P			F1 8:00A
MAT	M28 9:30P	M28 11:30P	T29 5:00A						T29 2:00P	T29 6:00P		W30 1:00A		W30 8:30A	
AUR	T29 4:15P	T29 6:30P	T29 11:00P												
KEN	W30 2:45A	W30 5:15A	W30 11:45A				W30 8:45P		TH31 1:15P	TH31 5:15P		F1 12:45A		F1 8:00A	
AUR	W30 4:15P	W30 6:30P	TH31 3:45A									TH31 10:30P			
LEC			W30 5:30P	W30 9:45P		TH31 2:45A		TH31 7:45A	TH31 11:45A						
TAK	TH31 4:15P	TH31 6:30P	TH31 11:00P												

M/V AURORA - FRI-SAT-SUN SCHEDULE - EFFECTIVE JUNE 1 THROUGH SEPTEMBER 28, 2003
ALL TIMES ARE LOCAL TIMES

Lv. Ketchikan	Ar. Metlakatla	Lv. Metlakatla	Ar. Ketchikan	Lv. Ketchikan	Ar. Metlakatla	Lv. Metlakatla	Ar. Ketchikan
6:30A	8:00A	8:30A	10:00A	2:10P	3:40P	4:10P	5:10P

INTER-ISLAND FERRY AUTHORITY - DAILY SCHEDULE - EFFECTIVE JUNE 1 - AUGUST 31, 2002

Lv. Hollis	Ar. Ketchikan	Lv. Ketchikan	Ar. Hollis	Lv. Hollis	Ar. Ketchikan	Lv. Ketchikan	Ar. Hollis
7:00A	10:05A	10:35A	1:40P	2:10P	5:15P	5:45P	8:50P

www.themilepost.com

ALASKA MARINE HIGHWAY 800-642-0066
AUGUST 2003 Northbound Schedule - REV. REV. 1-8-03

AUR-AURORA MAL-MALASPINA
COL-COLUMBIA MAT-MATANUSKA
LEC-LE CONTE TAK-TAKU
KEN-KENNICOTT

ALASKA STATE FERRY SCHEDULES

Ship	LEAVE BELLINGHAM	LEAVE PRINCE RUPERT	METLAKATLA	KETCHIKAN	HOLLIS	WRANGELL	PETERSBURG	KAKE	ARRIVE SITKA	ANGOON	TENAKEE	HOONAH	JUNEAU AUKE BAY	HAINES	ARRIVE SKAGWAY
KEN															
LEC							TH31 12:30P	TH31 5:30P		TH31 10:30P	F1 1:45A	F1 6:00A	F1 9:15A		
MAT		W30 11:00A		W30 5:30P		TH31 12:15A	TH31 4:00A		TH31 3:15P				F1 9:45A	F1 3:15P	F1 4:15P
MAL	T29 6:00P			TH31 12:30P		TH31 7:15P	TH31 11:00P	F1 9:45A					F1 11:55P	S2 5:30A	S2 6:30A
KEN		F1 11:00A		F1 5:30P		S2 12:15A	S2 4:15A						S2 2:00P	S2 7:30P	S2 8:45P
TAK													SU3 7:00A	SU3 12:45P	SU3 1:45P
LEC							Lv.Sitka S2 7:15P		SU3 1:15A	SU3 4:00A	SU3 8:15A	SU3 11:30A			
COL	F1 6:00P			SU3 9:00A		SU3 3:30P	SU3 7:30P						M4 7:00A	M4 12:45P	M4 1:45P
MAT		SU3 11:00A		SU3 5:15P		SU3 11:55P	M4 3:45A						M4 2:00P	M4 7:30P	M4 8:30P
AUR				M4 8:30A		M4 3:15P	M4 7:00P						T5 7:00A	T5 12:45P	T5 1:45P
KEN		M4 11:30A		M4 6:00P									T5 2:30P	***To Cross-Gulf	
AUR													W6 7:00A	W6 12:45P	W6 1:45P
LEC						M4 11:30P	T5 4:30A	T5 1:00P	T5 10:00P	W6 1:15A	W6 5:30A	W6 8:45A			
TAK		W6 5:00A		W6 11:30A		W6 6:15P							TH7 7:00A	TH7 12:45P	TH7 1:45P
LEC							TH7 9:30A	TH7 2:30P	TH7 7:30P			F8 3:00A	F8 6:15A		
MAT		W6 2:30P		W6 11:45P		TH7 6:30A	TH7 10:15A		TH7 9:30P				F8 11:45A	F8 5:15P	F8 6:15P
MAL	T5 6:00P			TH7 1:15P		TH7 8:00P	TH7 11:45P	F8 10:30A					S9 12:15A	S9 5:45A	S9 6:45A
KEN															
LEC							Lv.Sitka S9 2:00P		S9 8:00P	S9 10:45P	SU10 2:45A	SU10 6:00A			
TAK													SU10 12:45P	SU10 1:45P	
LEC									Lv.Pelican SU10 3:30P				SU10 10:00P		
COL	F8 6:00P			SU10 8:00A		SU10 2:30P	SU10 7:45P						M11 7:00A	M11 12:45P	M11 1:45P
MAT		SU10 11:45A		SU10 6:15P		M11 1:00A	M11 4:45A						M11 2:15P	M11 7:45P	M11 8:45P
AUR				M11 8:30A		M11 3:15P	M11 7:00P						T12 7:00A	T12 12:45P	T12 1:45P
KEN		M11 11:55A		M11 6:00P		T12 12:45A	T12 4:45A						T12 2:00P	T12 8:15P	T12 9:30P
AUR													W13 7:00A	W13 12:45P	W13 1:45P
LEC						T12 5:30A	T12 10:30A	T12 8:00P	W13 4:30A		W13 9:30A	W13 12:45P			
TAK		W13 5:00A		W13 11:30A			W13 7:45P						TH14 7:00A	TH14 12:45P	TH14 1:45P
LEC						TH14 3:15A	TH14 12:15P	TH14 5:45P	TH14 10:45P	F15 2:00A	F15 6:15A	F15 9:30A			
MAT		W13 2:15P		W13 8:30P		TH14 3:15A	TH14 7:00A		TH14 9:30P				F15 11:15A	F15 4:45P	F15 5:45P
MAL	T12 6:00P			TH14 9:30A		TH14 4:15P	TH14 8:00P	F15 9:45A					F15 11:55P	S16 6:00A	S16 7:00A
KEN		F15 11:15A		F15 6:15P									S16 11:45A	S16 5:15P	S16 6:30P
LEC							Lv.Sitka S16 12:45P		S16 6:30P	S16 9:15P	SU17 1:15A	SU17 5:30A	SU17 10:00A		
TAK													SU17 7:00A	SU17 12:45P	SU17 1:45P
COL	F15 6:00P			SU17 9:00A		SU17 3:30P	SU17 7:30P						M18 7:00A	M18 12:45P	M18 1:45P
MAT		SU17 11:45A		SU17 7:00P		M18 1:45A	M18 5:30A						M18 3:30P	M18 9:00P	M18 10:00P
AUR				M18 8:30A		M18 3:15P	M18 7:00P						T19 7:00A	T19 12:45P	T19 1:45P
KEN		M18 10:15A		M18 4:45P									T19 2:30P	***To Cross-Gulf	
AUR													W20 7:00A	W20 12:45P	W20 1:45P
LEC						T19 4:45A	T19 9:45A	T19 6:15P	W20 3:15A		W20 8:15A	W20 11:30A			
TAK		W20 5:00A		W20 11:30A		W20 6:15P	W20 10:00P						TH21 7:00A	TH21 12:45P	TH21 1:45P
LEC						TH21 8:30A	TH21 1:45P		TH21 6:45P		F22 2:15A	F22 5:30A			
MAT		W20 3:30P		W20 10:45P		TH21 5:30A	TH21 9:15A		TH21 8:30P				F22 11:15A	F22 4:45P	F22 5:45P
MAL	T19 6:00P			TH21 12:30P		TH21 7:15P	TH21 11:00P	F22 9:45A					F22 11:00P	S23 5:00A	S23 6:00A
KEN															
LEC							Lv.Sitka S23 1:15P		S23 7:15P	S23 10:00P	SU24 2:00A	SU24 5:15A			
TAK													SU24 7:00A	SU24 12:45P	SU24 1:45P
LEC									Lv.Pelican SU24 2:30P				SU24 9:00P		
COL	F22 6:00P			SU24 9:00A		SU24 3:30P	SU24 7:30P						M25 7:00A	M25 12:45P	M25 1:45P
MAT		SU24 11:15A		SU24 5:30P		M25 12:15A	M25 4:00A						M25 2:00P	M25 7:30P	M25 8:30P
AUR				M25 8:30A		M25 3:15P	M25 7:00P						T26 7:00A	T26 12:45P	T26 1:45P
KEN		M25 11:00A		M25 5:15P		M25 11:55P	T26 4:00A						T26 2:00P	T26 8:00P	T26 9:15P
AUR													W27 7:00A	W27 12:45P	W27 1:45P
LEC						T26 4:45A	T26 9:45A	T26 7:15P	W27 3:45A		W27 8:45A	W27 11:55A			
TAK		W27 5:00A		W27 12:15P		W27 7:00P	W27 10:30P						TH28 7:15A	TH28 1:00P	TH28 2:00P
LEC						TH28 11:15A	TH28 4:45P		TH28 9:45P	F29 1:00A	F29 5:15A		F29 8:30A		
MAT		W27 1:15P		W27 7:30P		TH28 2:15A	TH28 6:00A		TH28 8:15P				F29 11:30A	F29 5:00P	F29 6:00P
MAL	T26 6:00P			TH28 8:15A		TH28 3:00P	TH28 7:45P	F29 8:45A					F29 11:00P	S30 5:00A	S30 6:00A
KEN		F29 9:45A		F29 4:15P		F29 11:00P	S30 3:00A						S30 2:00P	S30 7:30P	S30 8:45P
TAK													S31 7:00A	S31 12:45P	S31 1:45P
LEC									S30 6:00P	S30 11:55P	SU31 2:45A	SU31 7:00A	SU31 10:15A		
COL	F29 6:00P			SU31 9:00A		SU31 3:30P	SU31 7:30P						M1 7:00A	M1 12:45P	M1 1:45P
MAT		SU31 1:30P		SU31 8:45P		M1 3:30A	M1 7:15A						M1 4:45P	M1 10:15P	M1 11:15P
AUR				M1 8:30A		M1 3:15P	M1 7:00P						T2 7:00A	T2 12:45P	T2 1:45P

ALL TIMES ARE LOCAL TIMES

SOUTHEAST/SOUTHWEST CROSS-GULF TRIPS

Lv. Juneau	Ar. Valdez	Lv. Valdez	Ar. Seward	Lv. Seward	Ar. Valdez	Lv. Valdez	Ar. Juneau
T5 2:30P	TH7 2:00A	TH7 6:00A	TH7 3:30P	TH7 11:30P	F8 9:00A	F8 12:30P	SU11 1:30A
T19 2:30P	TH21 2:00A	TH21 6:00A	TH21 3:30P	TH21 11:30P	F22 9:00A	F22 12:30P	SU24 1:30A

Whistle Stop service is provided to Yakutat on Cross-Gulf trips in both directions between Juneau and Valdez. The vessel will stop ONLY if there are vehicle reservations.

JUNEAU ~ HAINES ~ SKAGWAY DAILY SCHEDULE - EFFECTIVE JUNE 3 THROUGH SEPTEMBER 11, 2003

Lv. Juneau	Ar. Haines	Lv. Haines	Ar. Skagway	Lv. Skagway	Ar. Haines	Lv. Haines	Ar. Juneau
7:00A	11:30A	12:45P	1:45P	4:15P	5:15P	6:30P	11:00P

Note: Center of schedule indicates "SEE M/V AURORA SCHEDULE BELOW" and "SEE INTER-ISLAND FERRY AUTHORITY SCHEDULE BELOW"

ALASKA MARINE HIGHWAY 800-642-0066
AUGUST 2003 Southbound Schedule - REV. REV. 1-8-03

AUR-AURORA, COL-COLUMBIA, LEC-LE CONTE, KEN-KENNICOTT, MAL-MALASPINA, MAT-MATANUSKA, TAK-TAKU

ALASKA STATE FERRY SCHEDULES

Ship	LEAVE SKAGWAY	HAINES	JUNEAU AUKE BAY	HOONAH	TENAKEE	ANGOON	ARRIVE SITKA	KAKE	PETERSBURG	WRANGELL	HOLLIS	KETCHIKAN	METLAKATLA	ARRIVE PRINCE RUPERT	ARRIVE BELLINGHAM
KEN	W30 2:45A	W30 5:15A	W30 11:45A				W30 8:45P		TH31 1:15P	TH31 5:15P		F1 12:45A		F1 8:00A	
LEC			F1 5:45P	F1 10:00P	S2 2:00A	S2 5:15A	S2 10:15A								
MAT	F1 7:15P	F1 9:15P	S2 4:30A						S2 1:30P	S2 5:30P		SU3 12:30A		SU3 8:00A	
MAL	S2 9:30A	S2 11:30A	S2 8:00P						SU3 4:30A	SU3 8:15A		SU3 3:30P			T5 8:00A
KEN	S2 11:55P	SU3 2:00A	SU3 8:00A									M4 1:15A		M4 8:30A	
TAK	SU3 4:15P	SU3 6:30P	M4 2:15A				M4 11:55A		T5 3:00A	T5 6:45A		T5 1:45P		T5 8:45P	
LEC			SU3 1:15P	SU3 5:30P	SU3 9:30P	M4 1:00A	M4 6:00A	M4 5:30P	M4 9:30P						
COL	M4 4:15P	M4 6:30P	T5 4:30A					T5 1:15P	W6 5:00A	W6 9:00A		W6 5:00P			F8 8:00A
MAT	M4 11:30P	T5 1:30A	T5 8:00A					T5 5:00P	T5 9:00P			W6 4:00A		W6 11:30A	
AUR	T5 4:15P	T5 6:30P	T5 11:00P												
KEN															
AUR	W6 4:15P	W6 6:30P	TH7 2:00A						TH7 11:00A	TH7 2:45P		TH7 8:45P			
LEC			W6 1:15P	W6 5:30P		W6 10:30P		TH7 3:30A	TH7 7:30A						
TAK	TH7 4:15P	TH7 6:30P	TH7 11:00P												
LEC			F8 1:00P	F8 5:15P	F8 9:15P	S9 12:30A	S9 5:30A								
MAT	F8 9:15P	F8 11:15P	S9 5:15A						S9 2:15P	S9 6:15P		SU10 1:15A		SU10 8:45A	
MAL	S9 9:30A	S9 11:30A	S9 6:15P						SU10 2:45A	SU10 6:30A		SU10 3:30P			T12 8:00A
KEN	***FromCross-Gulf		SU10 5:30A						SU10 2:15P	SU10 6:15P		M11 2:15A		M11 9:30A	
LEC			SU10 7:00A	Ar.Pelican SU10 1:30P					M11 1:15P	T12 3:15P	T12 7:00A		T12 2:00P		T12 9:00P	
TAK	SU10 4:15P	SU10 6:30P	M11 3:30A												
LEC			SU10 11:00P	M11 3:15A		M11 8:15A	M11 1:15P	T12 12:45A	T12 4:45A						
COL	M11 4:15P	M11 6:30P	T12 5:30A					T12 2:15P	W13 2:45A	W13 6:30A		W13 5:00P			F15 8:00A
MAT	M11 11:45P	T12 1:45A	T12 7:15A						T12 4:15P	T12 8:15P		W13 3:45A		W13 11:15A	
AUR	T12 4:15P	T12 6:30P	T12 11:00P												
KEN	W13 2:30A	W13 5:00A	W13 11:45A						TH14 1:00P	TH14 5:00P		F15 1:00A		F15 8:15A	
AUR	W13 4:15P	W13 6:30P	TH14 3:45A									TH14 10:30P			
LEC			W13 5:30P	W13 9:45P		TH14 2:45A	TH14 7:45A	TH14 11:45A							
TAK	TH14 4:15P	TH14 6:30P	TH14 11:00P												
LEC			F15 11:45A	F15 4:00P	F15 8:00P	F15 11:15P	S16 4:15A								
MAT	F15 8:45P	F15 10:45P	S16 4:45A						S16 1:45P	S16 5:45P		SU17 1:15A		SU17 8:45A	
MAL	S16 11:45A	S16 1:45P	S16 8:00P						SU17 4:30A	SU17 8:15A		SU17 3:30P			T19 8:00A
KEN	S16 10:00P	SU17 12:30A	SU17 6:30A									SU17 11:55P		M18 7:15A	
LEC			SU17 11:30A	SU17 6:30P	SU17 10:45P	M18 2:45A	M18 6:15A	M18 11:15A	M18 10:45P	T19 2:45A		T19 12:30P		T19 7:30P	
TAK	SU17 4:15P	SU17 6:30P	M18 2:00A				M18 11:45A		T19 1:45A	T19 5:30A		T19 5:00P			F22 8:00A
COL	M18 4:15P	M18 6:30P	T19 4:00A				T19 12:45P		W20 3:15A	W20 7:15A		W20 5:00P			
MAT	T19 1:00A	T19 3:00A	T19 8:30A						T19 5:30P	T19 9:30P		W20 5:00A		W20 12:30P	
AUR	T19 4:15P	T19 6:30P	T19 11:00P												
AUR	W20 4:15P	W20 6:30P	TH21 1:00A						TH21 10:00A	TH21 1:45P		TH21 7:45P			
LEC			W20 12:45P	W20 4:45P		W20 9:45P		TH21 2:45A	TH21 6:45A						
TAK	TH21 4:15P	TH21 6:30P	TH21 11:00P												
LEC			F22 12:15P	F22 4:30P	F22 8:30P	F22 11:45P	S23 4:45A								
MAT	F22 8:45P	F22 10:45P	S23 4:45A						S23 1:45P	S23 5:45P		SU24 12:45A		SU24 8:15A	
MAL	S23 9:00A	S23 11:30A	S23 6:00P						SU24 2:30A	SU24 6:15A		SU24 3:30P			T26 8:00A
KEN	***FromCross-Gulf		SU24 4:00A						SU24 12:45P	SU24 5:45P		M25 12:45A		M25 8:00A	
LEC			SU24 6:00A	Ar.Pelican SU24 12:30P											
TAK	SU24 4:15P	SU24 6:30P	M25 2:45A				M25 12:30P		T26 2:30A	T26 6:15A		T26 1:15P		T26 8:15P	
LEC			SU24 10:00P	M25 2:15A		M25 7:15A	M25 12:15P	M25 11:45P	T26 4:00A						
COL	M25 4:15P	M25 6:30P	T26 4:30A					T26 1:15P	W27 2:00A	W27 6:00A		W27 5:00P			F29 8:00A
MAT	M25 9:30P	T26 1:30A	T26 7:00A						T26 4:00P	T26 8:00P		W27 3:00A		W27 10:30A	
AUR	T26 4:15P	T26 6:30P	T26 11:00P												
KEN	W27 1:45A	W27 4:15A	W27 10:45A				W27 7:45P		TH28 11:55A	TH28 4:00P		TH28 11:30P		F29 6:45A	
AUR	W27 4:15P	W27 6:30P	TH28 2:45A									TH28 9:30P			
LEC			W27 4:45P	W27 9:00P		TH28 1:45A		TH28 6:45A	TH28 10:45A						
TAK	TH28 4:15P	TH28 6:30P	TH28 11:00P												
LEC			F29 4:30P	F29 8:45P	S30 12:45A	S30 4:00A	S30 9:00A								
MAT	F29 9:00P	F29 11:30P	S30 6:30A						S30 3:30P	S30 7:30P		SU31 3:00A		SU31 10:30A	
MAL	S30 9:00A	S30 11:30A	S30 9:00P						SU31 5:30A	SU31 9:15A		SU31 5:30P			T2 8:00A
KEN	S30 11:45P	SU31 1:45A	SU31 7:15A						SU31 4:00P	SU31 8:00P		M1 3:00A		M1 10:15A	
TAK	SU31 4:15P	SU31 6:30P	M1 1:00A				M1 10:45A		T2 2:15A	T2 6:00A		T2 1:00P		T2 8:00P	
LEC			SU31 11:55A	SU31 4:15P	SU31 8:15P	SU31 11:45P	M1 4:45A	M1 4:15P	M1 8:15P						

See INTER-ISLAND FERRY AUTHORITY SCHEDULE BELOW
See M/V AURORA SCHEDULE BELOW

ALL TIMES ARE LOCAL TIMES

M/V AURORA - FRI-SAT-SUN SCHEDULE - EFFECTIVE JUNE 1 THROUGH SEPTEMBER 28, 2003

Lv. Ketchikan	Ar. Metlakatla	Lv. Metlakatla	Ar. Ketchikan	Lv. Ketchikan	Ar. Metlakatla	Lv. Metlakatla	Ar. Ketchikan
6:30A	8:00A	8:30A	10:00A	2:10P	3:40P	4:10P	5:10P

INTER-ISLAND FERRY AUTHORITY - DAILY SCHEDULE - EFFECTIVE JUNE 1 - AUGUST 31, 2002

Lv. Hollis	Ar. Ketchikan	Lv. Ketchikan	Ar. Hollis	Lv. Hollis	Ar. Ketchikan	Lv. Ketchikan	Ar. Hollis
7:00A	10:05A	10:35A	1:40P	2:10P	5:15P	5:45P	8:50P

ALASKA MARINE HIGHWAY 800-642-0066
SEPTEMBER 2003 Northbound Schedule - REV. REV. 1-8-03

AUR-AURORA MAL-MALASPINA
COL-COLUMBIA MAT-MATANUSKA
LEC-LE CONTE TAK-TAKU
KEN-KENNICOTT

ALASKA STATE FERRY SCHEDULES

	LEAVE BELLINGHAM	LEAVE PRINCE RUPERT	METLAKATLA	KETCHIKAN	HOLLIS	WRANGELL	PETERSBURG	KAKE	ARRIVE SITKA	ANGOON	TENAKEE	HOONAH	JUNEAU AUKE BAY	HAINES	ARRIVE SKAGWAY
TAK													SU31 7:00A	SU31 12:45P	SU31 1:45P
COL	F29 6:00P			SU31 9:00A		SU31 3:30P	SU31 7:30P						MI 7:00A	MI 12:45P	MI 1:45P
MAT		SU31 1:30P		SU31 8:45P		MI 3:30A	MI 7:15A						MI 4:45P	MI 10:15P	MI 11:15P
AUR				MI 8:30A		MI 3:15P	MI 7:00P						T2 7:00A	T2 12:45P	T2 1:45P
KEN		MI 1:15P		MI 8:00P									T2 2:30P	***ToCross-Gulf	
LEC						MI 9:45P	T2 2:45A	T2 11:15A	T2 8:15P	T2 11:30P		W3 3:45A	W3 7:00A		
AUR													W3 7:00A	W3 12:45P	W3 1:45P
TAK		W3 5:00A		W3 11:30A		W3 6:15P	W3 10:00P						TH4 7:00A	TH4 12:45P	TH4 1:45P
MAT		W3 4:15P		W3 10:30P		TH4 5:15A	TH4 9:00A		TH4 8:15P				F5 10:30A	F5 4:00P	F5 5:00P
MAL	T2 6:00P			TH4 11:55A		TH4 6:45P	TH4 10:30P		F5 9:15A				F5 11:30P	S6 5:30A	S6 6:30A
LEC						TH4 7:45A	TH4 12:45P		TH4 5:45P			F5 1:15A	F5 4:30A		
KEN															
LEC								Lv.Sitka S6 12:45P	S6 6:45P	S6 9:30P		SU7 1:30A	SU7 5:45A		SU7 10:45A
TAK													SU7 7:00A	SU7 12:45P	SU7 1:45P
COL	F5 6:00P			SU7 10:45A		SU7 5:00P	SU7 9:00P						M8 7:00A	M8 12:45P	M8 1:45P
MAT		SU7 10:30A		SU7 5:30P		M8 12:15A	M8 4:00A						M8 2:00P	M8 7:30P	M8 8:30P
AUR				M8 8:30A		M8 3:15P	M8 7:00P						T9 7:00A	T9 12:45P	T9 1:45P
KEN		M8 10:30A		M8 5:00P		M8 11:45P	T9 3:45A						T9 2:00P	T9 7:30P	T9 8:45P
AUR													W10 7:00A	W10 12:45P	W10 1:45P
LEC						T9 4:45A	T9 9:45A	T9 6:45P	W10 3:15A		W10 8:15A	W10 11:30A			
TAK		W10 4:30A		W10 11:00A			W10 9:15P						TH11 7:00A	TH11 12:45P	TH11 1:45P
MAL	T9 6:00P			TH11 1:30P		TH11 8:15P	TH11 11:55P						F12 9:15A	F12 3:00P	F12 4:00P
LEC							TH11 1:30P	TH11 7:00P	TH11 11:55P	F12 3:15A	F12 7:30A		F12 10:45A		
MAT		W10 1:00P		W10 7:30P		TH11 2:15A	TH11 6:00A		TH11 8:15P				F12 11:30A	F12 5:00P	F12 6:00P
KEN		F12 9:15A		F12 3:30P									S13 11:00A	S13 4:30P	S13 5:45P
LEC								Lv.Sitka S13 6:00P	S13 11:55P	SU14 2:45A	SU14 7:00A		SU14 10:15A		
COL	F12 6:00P			SU14 7:30A											
MAL				SU14 10:00A									MI15 7:00A	MI15 12:45P	MI15 1:45P
MAT		SU14 1:30P		SU14 8:45P		MI15 3:30A	MI15 7:15A						MI15 5:15P	MI15 10:45P	MI15 11:45P
AUR				MI15 8:30A		MI15 3:15P	MI15 7:00P						TI16 7:00A	TI16 12:45P	TI16 1:45P
KEN		MI15 10:45A		MI15 5:00P		MI15 11:45P	TI16 3:45A						TI16 2:00P	TI16 7:30P	TI16 8:45P
AUR													W17 7:00A	W17 12:45P	W17 1:45P
LEC						MI15 9:00P	TI16 2:30A	TI16 10:30A	TI16 7:30P	TI16 10:45P		W17 4:15A	W17 7:30A		
MAT		W17 5:15P		W17 10:30P											
LEC						TH18 7:00A	TH18 11:55A		TH18 5:00P			F19 12:30A	F19 3:45A		
KEN		TH18 1:30P		TH18 7:30P		F19 2:15A	F19 6:15A						F19 3:45P	F19 9:45P	F19 11:00P
LEC								Lv.Sitka S20 11:30A	S20 5:30P	S20 8:15P	S21 12:15A	SU21 3:30A			
LEC								Lv.Pelican SU21 12:45P				SU21 7:15P			
MAL	F19 6:00P			SU21 8:00A		SU21 2:45P	SU21 6:30P						M22 7:00A	M22 12:45P	M22 1:45P
AUR				M22 8:30A		M22 3:15P	M22 7:00P						T23 7:00A	T23 12:45P	T23 1:45P
KEN		SU21 5:00P		SU21 11:30P		M22 6:15A	M22 10:15A		M22 11:30P				T23 2:00P	T23 7:30P	T23 8:45P
AUR													W24 7:00A	W24 12:45P	W24 1:45P
LEC						T23 4:00A	T23 9:00A	T23 6:00P	W24 2:30A		W24 7:30A		W24 10:45A		
LEC						TH25 11:15A	TH25 4:15P		TH25 9:15P	F26 12:30A	F26 4:45A		F26 8:00A		
KEN		TH25 11:55A		TH25 6:15P		F26 1:00A	F26 5:00A						F26 2:15P	F26 7:45P	F26 9:00P
LEC								Lv.Sitka S27 10:45A	S27 4:45P	S27 7:30P	S27 11:45P	SU28 3:00A			
MAL	F26 6:00P			SU28 8:45A		SU28 3:30P	SU28 7:15P						M29 7:00A	M29 12:45P	M29 1:45P
AUR				M29 8:30A		M29 3:15P	M29 7:00P						T30 7:00A	T30 12:45P	T30 1:45P
KEN		SU28 2:00P		SU28 8:30P		M29 3:15A	M29 7:15A		M29 10:00P				T30 11:00A	T30 5:00P	T30 6:15P
LEC						T30 3:00A	T30 8:00A	T30 4:00P	W1 1:00A		W1 6:00A		W1 9:15A		

ALL TIMES ARE LOCAL TIMES

SOUTHEAST/SOUTHWEST CROSS-GULF TRIPS

Lv. Juneau	Ar. Valdez	Lv. Valdez	Ar. Seward	Lv. Seward	Ar. Valdez	Lv. Valdez	Ar. Juneau
T2 2:30P	TH4 2:00A	TH4 6:00A	TH4 3:30P	TH4 11:30P	F5 9:00A	F5 12:30P	SU7 1:30A

Whistle Stop service is provided to Yakutat on Cross-Gulf trips in both directions between Juneau and Valdez. The vessel will stop ONLY if there are vehicle reservations.

JUNEAU ~ HAINES ~ SKAGWAY DAILY SCHEDULE - EFFECTIVE JUNE 3 THROUGH SEPTEMBER 11, 2003

Lv. Juneau	Ar. Haines	Lv. Haines	Ar. Skagway	Lv. Skagway	Ar. Haines	Lv. Haines	Ar. Juneau
7:00A	11:30A	12:45P	1:45P	4:15P	5:15P	6:30P	11:00P

ALASKA MARINE HIGHWAY 800-642-0066
SEPTEMBER 2003 Southbound Schedule - REV. REV. 1-8-03

AUR-AURORA, COL-COLUMBIA, LEC-LE CONTE, KEN-KENNICOTT, MAL-MALASPINA, MAT-MATANUSKA, TAK-TAKU

ALASKA STATE FERRY SCHEDULES

	LEAVE SKAGWAY	HAINES	JUNEAU AUKE BAY	HOONAH	TENAKEE	ANGOON	ARRIVE SITKA	KAKE	PETERSBURG	WRANGELL	HOLLIS	KETCHIKAN	METLAKATLA	ARRIVE PRINCE RUPERT	ARRIVE BELLINGHAM
KEN	S30 11:45P	SU31 1:45A	SU31 7:15A						SU31 4:00P	SU31 8:00P		M1 3:00A		M1 10:15A	
LEC			SU31 11:55A	SU31 4:15P	SU31 8:15P	SU31 11:45P	M1 4:45A	M1 4:15P	M1 8:15P						
TAK	SU31 4:15P	SU31 6:30P	M1 1:00A				M1 10:45A		T2 2:15A	T2 6:00A		T2 1:00P		T2 8:00P	
COL	M1 4:15P	M1 6:30P	T2 3:00A				T2 11:45A		W3 3:30A	W3 7:30A		W3 5:00P			F5 8:00A
MAT	T2 2:15A	T2 4:15A	T2 9:45A						T2 6:45P	T2 10:45P		W3 5:45A		W3 1:15P	
AUR	T2 4:15P	T2 6:30P	T2 11:00P												
KEN															
LEC			W3 11:30A	W3 3:45P		W3 8:45P		TH4 1:45A	TH4 5:45A			TH4 7:45A			
AUR	W3 4:15P	W3 6:30P	TH4 1:00A						TH4 10:00A	TH4 1:45P					
TAK	TH4 4:15P	TH4 6:30P	TH4 11:00P												
MAT	F5 8:00P	F5 10:00P	S6 4:00A						S6 1:00P	S6 5:00P		S6 11:55P		SU7 7:30A	
MAL	S6 9:30A	S6 11:30A	S6 5:45P						SU7 2:15A	SU7 6:00A		SU7 3:30P			T9 8:00A
LEC			F5 11:45A	F5 4:00P	F5 8:00P	F5 11:15P	S6 4:15A								
KEN	***FromCross-Gulf		SU7 3:30A						SU7 12:15P	SU7 4:15P		M8 12:15A		M8 7:30A	
LEC	SU7 12:15P	SU7 2:15P	SU7 10:00P	M8 2:15A		M8 7:15A	M8 12:15P	M8 11:45P	T9 3:45A						
TAK	SU7 4:15P	SU7 6:30P	M8 2:30A				M8 12:15P		T9 2:15A	T9 6:00A		T9 1:00P		T9 8:00P	
COL	M8 4:15P	M8 6:30P	T9 4:30A				T9 1:15P		W10 2:00A	W10 6:00A		W10 5:00P			F12 8:00A
MAT	M8 11:00P	T9 1:00A	T9 6:30A						T9 3:30P	T9 7:30P		W10 2:30A		W10 10:00A	
AUR	T9 4:15P	T9 6:30P	T9 11:00P												
KEN	W10 1:45A	W10 3:45A	W10 10:45A				W10 7:45P		TH11 11:55A	TH11 4:00P		TH11 11:00P		F12 6:15A	
AUR	W10 4:15P	W10 6:30P	TH11 2:30A						TH11 11:15A	TH11 3:00P		TH11 9:00P			
LEC			W10 6:15P	W10 10:30P		TH11 3:30A		TH11 8:30A	TH11 12:30P						
TAK	TH11 4:15P	TH11 6:30P	F12 1:00A									F12 7:00P			
MAL	F12 7:00P	F12 9:15P	S13 4:45A						S13 1:15P	S13 5:00P		S13 11:00P			
LEC			F12 4:30P	F12 8:45P	S13 12:45A	S13 4:00A	S13 9:00A								
MAT	F12 9:00P	F12 11:30P	S13 6:30A						S13 3:30P	S13 7:30P		SU14 3:00A		SU14 10:30A	
KEN	S13 8:45P	S13 10:45P	SU14 4:45A						SU14 1:30P	SU14 5:30P		M15 12:30A		M15 7:45A	
LEC			SU14 11:15A	SU14 3:30P	SU14 7:30P	SU14 11:00P	M15 4:00A	M15 3:30A	M15 7:30P						
MAL	M15 4:15P	M15 6:30P	T16 1:00A				T16 10:45A		W17 12:45A	W17 4:30A		W17 3:30P			F19 8:00A
MAT	T16 2:45A	T16 4:45A	T16 10:15A						T16 7:15P	T16 11:15P		W17 6:45A		W17 2:15P	
AUR	T16 4:15P	T16 6:30P	T16 11:00P												
KEN	T16 11:45P	W17 1:45A	W17 7:30A						W17 4:15P	W17 8:15P		TH18 3:15A		TH18 10:30A	
AUR	W17 4:15P	W17 6:30P	TH18 1:00A						TH18 10:00A	TH18 1:45P		TH18 7:45P			
LEC			W17 10:45A	W17 3:00P		W17 8:00P		TH18 1:00A	TH18 5:00A						
MAT															
LEC			F19 10:30A	F19 2:45P	F19 6:45P	F19 10:00P	S20 3:00A								
KEN	S20 2:00A	S20 4:30A	S20 10:30A						S20 7:15P	S20 11:15P		SU21 6:45A		SU21 2:00P	
LEC			SU21 4:15A	Ar.Pelican SU21 10:45 A											
LEC			SU21 8:45P	M22 1:00A		M22 6:00A	M22 11:00A	M22 10:30P	T23 2:30A						
MAL	M22 4:15P	M22 6:30P	T23 2:15A				T23 11:55A		W24 2:00A	W24 5:45A		W24 3:30P			F26 8:00A
AUR	T23 4:15P	T23 6:30P	T23 11:00P												
KEN	T23 10:30P	W24 12:30A	W24 6:00A						W24 2:45P	W24 6:45P		TH25 1:45A		TH25 9:00A	
AUR	W24 4:15P	W24 6:30P	TH25 1:15A						TH25 10:15A	TH25 2:00P		TH25 8:00P			
LEC			W24 4:00P	W24 8:15P		TH25 1:15A		TH25 6:15A	TH25 10:15A						
LEC			F26 9:45A	F26 2:00P	F26 6:00P	F26 9:15P	S27 2:15A								
KEN	F26 11:55P	S27 2:00A	S27 7:45A						S27 4:30P	S27 8:30P		SU28 3:45A		SU28 11:00A	
LEC			SU28 4:45P	SU28 9:00P	M29 1:00A	M29 4:30A	M29 9:30A	M29 9:00P	T30 1:00A						
MAL	M29 4:15P	M29 6:30P	T30 12:45A				T30 10:30A		W1 2:30A	W1 6:15A		W1 3:30P			F3 8:00A
AUR	T30 4:15P	T30 6:30P	T30 11:00P												

ALL TIMES ARE LOCAL TIMES

SEE INTER-ISLAND FERRY AUTHORITY SCHEDULE BELOW
SEE M/V AURORA SCHEDULE BELOW

M/V AURORA - FRI-SAT-SUN SCHEDULE - EFFECTIVE JUNE 1 THROUGH SEPTEMBER 28, 2003

Lv. Ketchikan	Ar. Metlakatla	Lv. Metlakatla	Ar. Ketchikan	Lv. Ketchikan	Ar. Metlakatla	Lv. Metlakatla	Ar. Ketchikan
6:30A	8:00A	8:30A	10:00A	2:10P	3:40P	4:10P	5:10P

INTER-ISLAND FERRY AUTHORITY - DAILY SCHEDULE - EFFECTIVE JUNE 1 - AUGUST 31, 2002

Lv. Hollis	Ar. Ketchikan	Lv. Ketchikan	Ar. Hollis	Lv. Hollis	Ar. Ketchikan	Lv. Ketchikan	Ar. Hollis
7:00A	10:05A	10:35A	1:40P	2:10P	5:15P	5:45P	8:50P

ALASKA STATE FERRY SCHEDULES

(Continued from page 751)
vessels on the Southeast system can load vehicles up to 70 feet long with special arrangements. Maximum length on the *Tustumena* is 40 feet. Vehicle fares are determined by the overall length and width of the vehicle. Vehicles from $8^1/_2$ to 9 feet wide are charged 125 percent of the fare listed for the vehicle length. Vehicles over 9 feet in width are charged 150 percent of the fare listed for vehicle length.

On the vehicle deck, a crew member will direct you to your parking location. Park, set your hand brake, lock your vehicle, take the personal possessions you will need and proceed to a passageway leading to the passenger areas. If the vehicle you are putting on board will not be accompanied, lock the vehicle and leave the keys with the loading officer. RVs cannot be used as dining or sleeping facilities while on the ferries.

Hazardous materials may not be transported on the ferries. The valves on propane or similar type tanks must be turned off and sealed by a ferry system employee. If this has not been done by the time you board, notify the purser when surrendering your ticket for boarding. Portable containers of fuel are permitted but must be stored with vessel personnel while en route.

The state assumes no responsibility for the loading and unloading of unattended vehicles.

Food Service: Food service varies from vessel to vessel. There's dining room service on the *Columbia* and *Tustumena*. Cafeteria service is available on all ferries except the *Bartlett*. Alcoholic beverages are available on some vessels. The cost of meals is not included in passenger, cabin or vehicle fares. Tipping is prohibited.

Luggage: You are responsible for your own luggage! Foot passengers may bring hand luggage only (not to exceed 100 lbs.). There is no limit on luggage carried in a vehicle. Coin-operated storage lockers are available aboard most ships, and baggage carts are furnished on the car deck. Baggage handling is NOT provided by the Marine Highway.

Vehicle deck restrictions: Periodic "car-deck calls" are made 3 times a day between Bellingham and Ketchikan. These are announced over the loudspeaker and allow passengers approximately 15 minutes to visit the car deck and walk pets, retrieve items from cars, etc. North of Ketchikan, car deck visits are allowed only when the ferry is in port.

Pet policy: Dogs and other pets are not allowed in cabins and must be transported on the vehicle deck only—*NO EXCEPTIONS*. (There are special accommodations for animals aiding disabled passengers. Proper paperwork is required.) Animals and pets are to be transported inside a vehicle or in suitable containers furnished by the passenger. Animals and pets must be cared for by the owner. Passengers who must visit pets or animals en route should apply to the purser's office for an escort to the vehicle deck. (On long sailings the purser periodi-
(Continues on page 766)

INSIDE PASSAGE/SOUTHEAST ALASKA PASSENGER & VEHICLE FARES

ALASKA STATE FERRY SCHEDULES

ADULT 12 YEARS OR OVER (Meals and berth not included)
(Children under 2 travel free. Children 2 through 11 years—1/2 adult fare rounded to nearest dollar.)

BETWEEN AND	Bellingham	Prince Rupert	Ketchikan	Metlakatla	Wrangell	Petersburg	Kake	Sitka	Angoon	Hoonah	Juneau	Haines	Skagway
Prince Rupert	172												
Ketchikan	193	45											
Metlakatla	197	49	16										
Wrangell	211	66	34										
Petersburg	226	80	45	49	22								
Kake	237	93	57	61	39	25							
Sitka	245	102	64	68	45	32	27						
Angoon	261	118	80	84	61	47	34	25					
Hoonah	266	125	87	92	66	50	45	27	23				
Juneau	266	125	87	92	66	50	32	27	23	23			
Haines	287	143	107	113	87	72	72	50	49	45	27		
Skagway	296	152	116	120	96	82	82	59	57	55	37	21	
Pelican	292	149	113	118	92	79	61	47	45	25	37	59	70
Tenakee	266	125	87	92	66	50	37	25	20	20	25	45	55	37

BICYCLES (without trailer)

BETWEEN AND	Bellingham	Prince Rupert	Ketchikan	Metlakatla	Wrangell	Petersburg	Kake	Sitka	Angoon	Hoonah	Juneau	Haines	Skagway
Prince Rupert	25												
Ketchikan	30	12											
Metlakatla	32	13	8										
Wrangell	34	15	11	12									
Petersburg	35	16	13	14	9								
Kake	37	17	14	15	12	9							
Sitka	38	18	15	16	13	11	9						
Angoon	40	20	17	17	15	13	11	8					
Hoonah	41	23	17	18	16	14	13	9	9				
Juneau	41	23	17	18	16	14	11	11	9				
Haines	45	26	21	23	19	17	17	15	14	14	12		
Skagway	46	23	24	20	18	18	16	15	15	13	9		
Pelican	45	25	20	21	18	17	15	13	12	9	12	16	17
Tenakee	41	23	17	18	16	14	12	9	8	8	11	14	15	12

KAYAKS AND INFLATABLES

BETWEEN AND	Bellingham	Prince Rupert	Ketchikan	Metlakatla	Wrangell	Petersburg	Kake	Sitka	Angoon	Hoonah	Juneau	Haines	Skagway
Prince Rupert	38												
Ketchikan	45	18											
Metlakatla	48	20	12										
Wrangell	51	23	17	18									
Petersburg	53	24	20	21	14								
Kake	56	26	21	23	18	14							
Sitka	57	27	23	24	20	17	14						
Angoon	60	30	26	26	23	20	17	12					
Hoonah	62	35	26	27	24	21	20	14	14				
Juneau	62	35	26	27	24	21	17	17	14				
Haines	68	39	32	35	29	26	26	23	21	21	18		
Skagway	69	41	35	36	30	27	27	24	23	23	20	14	
Pelican	68	38	30	32	27	26	23	20	18	14	18	24	26
Tenakee	62	35	26	27	24	21	18	14	12	12	17	21	23	18

VEHICLES UP TO 10 FEET (Driver not included)

BETWEEN AND	Bellingham	Prince Rupert	Ketchikan	Metlakatla	Wrangell	Petersburg	Kake	Sitka	Angoon	Hoonah	Juneau	Haines	Skagway
Prince Rupert	202												
Ketchikan	233	49											
Metlakatla	239	57	16										
Wrangell	260	79	34	41									
Petersburg	277	96	53	58	25								
Kake	294	113	70	77	47	30							
Sitka	305	122	79	84	53	36	33						
Angoon	324	143	98	105	75	57	39	28					
Hoonah	332	151	106	113	81	63	53	33	27				
Juneau	332	151	106	113	81	63	63	36	33	26			
Haines	359	179	133	140	107	88	88	61	59	53	34		
Skagway	371	188	143	148	117	100	100	72	69	63	45	19	
Pelican	365	183	139	144	112	92	74	57	53	32	47	75	84
Tenakee	332	151	106	113	81	63	45	30	21	21	30	55	66	47

VEHICLES UP TO 15 FEET (Driver not included)

BETWEEN AND	Bellingham	Prince Rupert	Ketchikan	Metlakatla	Wrangell	Petersburg	Kake	Sitka	Angoon	Hoonah	Juneau	Haines	Skagway
Prince Rupert	347												
Ketchikan	400	81											
Metlakatla	398	90	23										
Wrangell	434	125	55	66									
Petersburg	463	155	85	97	38								
Kake	491	186	117	127	76	48							
Sitka	506	201	131	142	85	56	53						
Angoon	541	235	166	176	124	92	64	45					
Hoonah	571	258	181	189	135	105	88	53	42				
Juneau	571	258	181	189	135	105	105	56	50	41			
Haines	617	303	225	235	181	148	148	102	97	87	53		
Skagway	635	319	243	253	198	167	167	120	114	105	71	28	
Pelican	609	306	235	245	188	158	122	92	85	50	76	122	142

VEHICLES UP TO 19 FEET (Driver not included)

BETWEEN AND	Bellingham	Prince Rupert	Ketchikan	Metlakatla	Wrangell	Petersburg	Kake	Sitka	Angoon	Hoonah	Juneau	Haines	Skagway	Pelican
Prince Rupert	412													
Ketchikan	476	97												
Metlakatla	475	107	27											
Wrangell	516	148	66	79										
Petersburg	550	184	102	114	46									
Kake	586	222	140	151	89	56								
Sitka	603	239	155	168	103	68	62							
Angoon	644	279	197	210	148	111	77	53						
Hoonah	679	308	213	226	161	125	104	62	50					
Juneau	679	308	213	226	161	125	125	67	60	49				
Haines	735	359	267	279	213	177	177	120	114	102	61			
Skagway	756	380	288	302	235	200	200	142	137	124	83	34		
Pelican	726	362	279	290	225	187	146	111	102	60	89	145	167	

VEHICLES UP TO 21 FEET (Driver not included)

BETWEEN AND	Bellingham	Prince Rupert	Ketchikan	Metlakatla	Wrangell	Petersburg	Kake	Sitka	Angoon	Hoonah	Juneau	Haines	Skagway	Pelican
Prince Rupert	531													
Ketchikan	595	120												
Metlakatla	611	139	34											
Wrangell	666	191	83	100										
Petersburg	711	238	131	147	57									
Kake	756	286	180	195	114	72								
Sitka	777	308	201	216	132	85	80							
Angoon	831	360	253	270	189	142	98	68						
Hoonah	878	395	275	291	207	161	134	80	64					
Juneau	878	395	275	291	207	161	161	84	78	61				
Haines	948	464	344	360	275	228	228	155	147	132	80			
Skagway	975	491	372	390	305	256	256	183	176	161	109	42		
Pelican	937	467	360	375	289	242	187	142	131	77	114	186	216	

VEHICLES UP TO 23 FEET (Driver not included)

BETWEEN AND	Bellingham	Prince Rupert	Ketchikan	Metlakatla	Wrangell	Petersburg	Kake	Sitka	Angoon	Hoonah	Juneau	Haines	Skagway	Pelican
Prince Rupert	666													
Ketchikan	746	149												
Metlakatla	765	174	42											
Wrangell	833	242	104	125										
Petersburg	890	297	163	184	71									
Kake	947	358	225	245	144	90								
Sitka	972	384	250	271	165	107	100							
Angoon	1040	452	317	337	237	177	121	84						
Hoonah	1099	492	344	363	259	202	168	100	81					
Juneau	1099	492	344	363	259	202	202	106	97	77				
Haines	1187	581	431	450	344	285	285	194	182	164	98			
Skagway	1224	616	465	488	380	322	322	230	221	203	138	53		
Pelican	1173	586	452	468	361	302	234	177	163	96	144	232	272	

VEHICLES OVER 23 FEET (Driver not included)

BETWEEN AND	Bellingham	Prince Rupert	Ketchikan	Metlakatla	Wrangell	Petersburg	Kake	Sitka	Angoon	Hoonah	Juneau	Haines	Skagway	Pelican
Prince Rupert	33.80													
Ketchikan	37.90	7.60												
Metlakatla	39.00	8.70	2.10											
Wrangell	42.30	12.20	5.30	6.30										
Petersburg	45.30	15.10	8.30	9.30	3.60									
Kake	48.20	18.20	11.30	12.40	7.20	4.50								
Sitka	49.60	19.50	12.70	13.80	8.40	5.50	5.00							
Angoon	52.90	23.00	16.20	17.20	12.10	9.00	6.20	4.30						
Hoonah	54.30	24.40	17.50	18.60	13.10	10.20	8.50	5.00	4.10					
Juneau	54.30	24.40	17.50	18.60	13.10	10.20	10.20	5.40	4.90	3.90				
Haines	58.70	28.80	21.80	22.90	17.40	14.50	14.50	9.80	9.30	8.30	5.00			
Skagway	60.40	30.50	23.60	24.80	19.30	16.30	16.30	11.70	11.10	10.20	6.80	2.80		
Pelican	59.70	29.80	22.90	23.80	18.40	15.30	11.90	9.00	8.30	4.80	7.20	11.80	13.80	

To calculate rates for vehicles 24 to 70 feet, multiply the per foot rate in the chart above times the number of feet. Round the result up to the nearest dollar.

TARIFFS—One-way fares for passengers, vehicles, bicycles and small boats are charged from the port of embarkation to the port of debarkation. Cabin fares are calculated according to the route taken, and may vary depending on the ship and schedules.

VEHICLES—Vehicles may be measured at check-in prior to boarding and adjustments will be made to quoted fares based on actual length.

ALASKA STATE FERRY SCHEDULES

INSIDE PASSAGE/SOUTHEAST ALASKA CABIN RATES

FOUR BERTH CABIN/SITTING ROOM–OUTSIDE/COMPLETE FACILITIES
M/V Columbia, M/V Malaspina

BETWEEN AND	Bellingham	Prince Rupert	Ketchikan	Wrangell	Petersburg	Sitka	Juneau	Haines
Prince Rupert	292							
Ketchikan	321	76						
Wrangell	353	105	68					
Petersburg	374	122	84	56				
Sitka	414	150	107	84	70			
Juneau	437	171	126	107	92	65		
Haines	477	208	168	143	129	103	77	
Skagway	477	208	168	143	129	103	77	58

FOUR BERTH CABIN–OUTSIDE/COMPLETE FACILITIES
M/V Columbia, M/V Kennicott, M/V Malaspina, M/V Matanuska, M/V Taku

BETWEEN AND	Bellingham	Prince Rupert	Ketchikan	Wrangell	Petersburg	Sitka	Juneau	Haines
Prince Rupert	266							
Ketchikan	292	68						
Wrangell	322	93	64					
Petersburg	339	108	78	49				
Sitka	376	135	100	77	65			
Juneau	396	159	118	93	81	57		
Haines	439	193	156	131	120	92	66	
Skagway	439	193	156	131	120	92	66	53

FOUR BERTH CABIN–INSIDE/COMPLETE FACILITIES
M/V Columbia, M/V Malaspina, M/V Kennicott

BETWEEN AND	Bellingham	Prince Rupert	Ketchikan	Wrangell	Petersburg	Sitka	Juneau	Haines
Prince Rupert	226							
Ketchikan	247	59						
Wrangell	275	81	57					
Petersburg	293	93	67	46				
Sitka	323	118	89	66	57			
Juneau	344	139	104	81	70	49		
Haines	378	166	137	116	105	81	58	
Skagway	378	166	137	116	105	81	58	46

TWO BERTH CABIN–OUTSIDE/NO FACILITIES
M/V Kennicott

BETWEEN AND	Bellingham	Prince Rupert	Ketchikan	Wrangell	Petersburg	Sitka	Juneau	Haines
Ketchikan	168	39						
Wrangell	185	55	36					
Petersburg	194	64	44	27				
Sitka	215	78	57	44	37			
Juneau	228	92	67	55	46	33		
Haines	251	110	89	76	67	53	37	
Skagway	251	110	89	76	67	53	37	30

TWO BERTH CABIN–INSIDE/NO FACILITIES
M/V Kennicott

BETWEEN AND	Bellingham	Prince Rupert	Ketchikan	Wrangell	Petersburg	Sitka	Juneau	Haines
Ketchikan	150	36						
Wrangell	166	49	33					
Petersburg	175	56	39	25				
Sitka	193	69	50	39	34			
Juneau	205	83	61	49	42	30		
Haines	227	100	80	67	62	47	35	
Skagway	227	100	80	67	62	47	35	27

THREE BERTH CABIN–OUTSIDE/COMPLETE FACILITIES
M/V Matanuska

BETWEEN AND	Bellingham	Prince Rupert	Ketchikan	Wrangell	Petersburg	Sitka	Juneau	Haines
Prince Rupert	221							
Ketchikan	238	54						
Wrangell	263	76	53					
Petersburg	274	85	62	42				
Sitka	299	106	79	62	54			
Juneau	320	122	91	74	65	47		
Haines	358	151	120	100	91	76	56	
Skagway	358	151	120	100	91	76	56	45

TWO BERTH CABIN–OUTSIDE/COMPLETE FACILITIES
M/V Columbia, M/V Malaspina, M/V Matanuska, M/V Taku

BETWEEN AND	Bellingham	Prince Rupert	Ketchikan	Wrangell	Petersburg	Sitka	Juneau	Haines
Prince Rupert	192							
Ketchikan	208	50						
Wrangell	228	68	44					
Petersburg	240	79	55	39				
Sitka	267	100	72	56	47			
Juneau	287	114	85	68	59	44		
Haines	320	143	108	91	82	66	49	
Skagway	320	143	108	91	82	66	49	39

TWO BERTH CABIN–INSIDE/COMPLETE FACILITIES
M/V Columbia, M/V Malaspina, M/V Matanuska, M/V Taku

BETWEEN AND	Bellingham	Prince Rupert	Ketchikan	Wrangell	Petersburg	Sitka	Juneau	Haines
Prince Rupert	168							
Ketchikan	184	45						
Wrangell	206	64	41					
Petersburg	211	70	49	35				
Sitka	234	88	64	49	42			
Juneau	250	99	76	61	53	39		
Haines	276	124	99	82	77	61	45	
Skagway	276	124	99	82	77	61	45	37

TWO BERTH ROOMETTE–OUTSIDE/NO FACILITIES (Linen rented separately)
M/V Kennicott

BETWEEN AND	Bellingham	Prince Rupert	Ketchikan	Wrangell	Petersburg	Sitka	Juneau	Haines
Ketchikan	50	12						
Wrangell	56	17	12					
Petersburg	59	19	14	10				
Sitka	64	23	18	14	12			
Juneau	68	28	21	17	15	11		
Haines	76	34	27	23	21	17	12	
Skagway	76	34	27	23	21	17	12	10

TWO BERTH ROOMETTE–INSIDE/NO FACILITIES (Linen rented separately)
M/V Kennicott

BETWEEN AND	Bellingham	Prince Rupert	Ketchikan	Wrangell	Petersburg	Sitka	Juneau	Haines
Ketchikan	42	11						
Wrangell	46	14	10					
Petersburg	49	16	12	8				
Sitka	54	20	15	12	11			
Juneau	57	24	18	14	12	10		
Haines	63	27	23	19	18	14	11	
Skagway	63	27	23	19	18	14	11	9

CROSS-GULF FARES AND CABIN RATES

Between and	Pr. Rupert Valdez	Ketchikan Valdez	Juneau Valdez	Pr. Rupert Yakutat	Ketchikan Yakutat	Juneau Yakutat	Pr. Rupert Seward	Ketchikan Seward	Juneau Seward
Passengers-Adult Fare	237	193	108	195	150	65	302	261	177
Children (2 through 11 years)	119	97	54	98	75	33	151	131	89
Bicycles	41	30	16	36	25	11	49	41	26
Kayaks	62	45	24	54	38	17	74	62	39
Vehicles up to 10 feet	281	233	129	230	182	79	352	307	203
Vehicles up to 15 feet	480	400	223	393	312	134	599	520	342
Vehicles up to 19 feet	572	476	265	467	372	159	714	618	407
Vehicles up to 21 feet	715	595	321	587	467	193	900	779	506
Vehicles up to 23 feet	896	746	403	736	586	243	1127	977	634
Per foot rate 23 to 50 feet	45.60	37.90	20.50	37.40	29.70	12.30	56.90	49.40	31.80
Cabins									
4-berth–Outside/complete facilities	360	292	182	291	222	111	457	399	289
4-berth–Inside/complete facilities	307	247	150	250	191	92	391	336	240
2-berth–Outside/no facilities	207	168	106	166	127	65	263	231	170
2-berth–Inside/no facilities	186	150	93	150	114	58	235	207	152
2-berth roomette–outside/no facilities*	62	50	33	50	39	20	79	69	51
2-berth roomette–inside/no facilities*	53	42	26	42	33	17	66	58	42

*No linen-may be rented separately

KENNICOTT–Limited to 50 foot vehicle length in Southcentral/Southwest ports.

Southcentral Alaska & Prince William Sound
May 1 - September 30, 2003 -- M/V Bartlett

ALASKA STATE FERRY SCHEDULES

May 1 ~ June 9, 2003

Leave Cordova	Leave Valdez	Arrive Whittier	Leave Whittier	Arrive Valdez	Arrive Cordova	Leave Cordova	Leave Valdez	Arrive Whittier	Leave Whittier	Arrive Valdez	Arrive Cordova
TH1 12:15A				TH1 6:00A			TH1 7:15A	TH1 2:00P	TH1 2:45P	TH1 9:30P	
	F2 7:15A	F2 2:00P	F2 2:45P		F2 9:45P						
F2 11:45P	S3 7:15A	S3 2:00P	S3 2:45P	S3 9:30P			SU4 8:00A**				SU4 3:00P
M5 7:00A		M5 2:00P	M5 2:45P		M5 9:45P						
M5 11:00P**	T6 7:15A	T6 2:00P	T6 2:45P	T6 9:30P			T6 11:00P**				W7 6:00A
W7 7:00A		W7 2:00P	W7 2:45P		W7 9:45P						
W7 11:00P**	TH8 7:15P	TH8 2:00P	TH8 2:45P	TH8 9:30P			F9 12:30A	F9 7:15A	F9 8:00A		F9 3:00P
F9 4:00P				S10 9:45P			S10 8:45A				S10 2:30P
SU11 3:30P				SU11 9:00P			SU11 11:30P				M12 5:00A
M12 6:00A								M12 12:30P	M12 2:45P		M12 9:45P
T13 6:00A	Ar. C.B. 12:15P	T13 5:15P	T13 6:00P	W14 1:15A	W14 10:00A					W14 4:00P	
	TH15 7:15A	TH15 2:00P	TH15 2:45P	TH15 9:30P			F16 7:15A	F16 2:00P	F16 2:45P		F16 9:45P
				S17 5:30A			S17 7:15A	S17 2:00P	S17 2:45P	S17 9:30P	
F16 11:45P**				SU18 3:00P	SU18 5:00P					SU18 10:45P	
	SU18 8:00A**						M19 9:00A				M19 2:45P
T20 7:00A		T20 2:00P	T20 2:45P*		W21 2:00A						
W21 10:00A				W21 4:00P			TH22 7:15A	TH22 2:00P	TH22 2:45P	TH22 9:30P	
	F23 7:15A	F23 2:00P	F23 2:45P		F23 9:45P						
F23 11:45P**	S24 7:15A	S24 2:00P	S24 2:45P	S24 9:30P			SU25 8:00A**				SU25 3:00P
SU25 5:00P				SU25 10:45P							
	M26 9:00A				M26 2:45P	T27 6:00A	Ar. C.B.*12:15P	T27 5:15P	T27 6:00P		W28 1:15A
W28 10:00A				W28 4:00P			TH29 7:15A	TH29 2:00P	TH29 2:45P	TH29 9:30P	
	F30 7:15A	F30 2:00P	F30 2:45P		F20 9:45P						
F30 11:45P**	S31 7:15A	S31 2:00P	S31 2:45P	S31 9:30P			SU1 8:00A**				SU1 3:00P
SU1 5:00P				SU1 10:45P							
	M2 7:15A	M2 2:00P	M2 2:45P		M2 9:45P	M2 10:45P**				T3 6:15A	
	T3 7:15A	T3 2:00P	T3 2:45P	T3 9:30P			T3 11:45P				W4 5:30A
W4 7:00A							TH5 7:15A	TH5 2:00P	TH5 2:45P	TH5 9:30P	
	F6 7:15A	F6 2:00P	F6 2:45P		F6 9:45P						
F6 10:45P**	S7 7:15A	S7 2:00P	S7 2:45P	S7 9:30P			SU8 7:15A				SU8 12:45P
SU8 1:45P		SU8 8:45P	SU8 9:30P	M9 4:15A							

June 9 ~ September 7, 2003

Leave Cordova	Leave Valdez	Arrive Whittier	Leave Whittier	Arrive Valdez	Arrive Cordova	Leave Cordova	Leave Valdez	Arrive Whittier	Leave Whittier	Arrive Valdez	Arrive Cordova
	MON 7:15A	MON 2:00P	MON 2:45P		MON 9:45P						
MON 10:45P**				TUE 6:15A			TUE 7:15A	TUE 2:00P			
			TUE 2:45P	TUE 9:30P			TUE 11:45P				WED 5:30A
WED 7:00A		WED 2:00P	WED 2:45P	WED 9:30P							
	THU 7:15A	THU 2:00P	THU 2:45P	THU 9:30P							
	FRI 5:00A**				FRI 12:45P	FRI 6:30P				SAT 12:15A	
	SAT 7:15A	SAT 2:00P	SAT 2:45P	SAT 9:30P							
	SUN 7:15A	SUN 2:00P	SUN 2:45P	SUN 9:30P							

September 8 ~ 30, 2003

Leave Cordova	Leave Valdez	Arrive Whittier	Leave Whittier	Arrive Valdez	Arrive Cordova	Leave Cordova	Leave Valdez	Arrive Whittier	Leave Whittier	Arrive Valdez	Arrive Cordova
	M8 9:00A				M8 2:45P	T9 7:00A		T9 2:00P	T9 2:45P*		W10 2:00A
	W10 10:00A			W10 4:00P			TH11 7:15A	TH11 2:00P	TH11 2:45P	TH11 9:30P	
	F12 7:15A	F12 2:00P	F12 2:45P		F12 9:45P						
F12 11:45P**	S13 7:15A	S13 2:00P	S13 2:45P	S13 9:30P			SU14 8:00A**				SU14 3:00P
SU14 5:00P				SU14 10:45P							
	M15 9:00A				M15 2:45P	T16 6:00A*		T16 6:15P	T16 7:00P		W17 2:15A
W17 10:00A				W17 4:00P			TH18 7:15A	TH18 2:00P	TH18 2:45P	TH18 9:30P	
	F19 7:15A	F19 2:00P	F19 2:45P		F19 9:45P						
F19 11:45P**	S20 7:15A	S20 2:00P	S20 2:45P	S20 9:30P			SU21 8:00A**				SU21 3:00P
SU21 5:00P				SU21 10:45P			M22 9:00A				M22 2:45P
T23 7:00A		T23 2:00P	T23 2:45P*		W24 2:00A	W24 10:00A				W24 4:00P	
	TH25 7:15A	TH25 2:00P	TH25 2:45P	TH25 9:30P			F26 7:15A	F26 2:00P	F26 2:45P		F26 9:45P
F26 11:45P**	S27 7:15A	S27 2:00P	S27 2:45P	S27 9:30P							
	SU28 8:00A**				SU28 3:00P	SU28 5:00P				SU28 10:45P	
	M29 9:00A			M29 2:45P		T30 7:00A		T30 2:00P	T30 2:45P		T30 9:30P

*Chenega Bay whistle stops available by contacting the Valdez Terminal
** Tatitlek whistle stops available by notifying the Cordova Terminal

ALASKA STATE FERRY SCHEDULES

Kenai Peninsula, Kodiak & Aleutian Chain Schedule
April 29 - September 16, 2003 -- M/V Tustumena

Apr 29 - Jun 10 / Aug 26 - Sep 30			Jun 17 - Aug 26			May 6 - May 13 / Jun 10 - Jun 17 / Jul 15 - Jul 22 / Aug 12 - Aug 19 / Sep 9 - Sep 16		
Leave Seldovia	TU	4:00P	Leave Seldovia	TU	4:00P	Leave Seldovia	TU	4:00P
Arrive Homer	TU	5:30P	Arrive Homer	TU	5:30P	Arrive Homer	TU	5:30P
*Leave Homer	TU	7:55P	Leave Homer	TU	7:55P	Leave Homer	TU	9:00P
*Arrive Port Lions	WE	6:00A	Arrive Port Lions	WE	6:00A	Arrive Kodiak	WE	6:30A
*Leave Port Lions	WE	6:30A	Leave Port Lions	WE	6:30A	Leave Kodiak	WE	4:55P
*Arrive Kodiak	WE	9:00A	Arrive Kodiak	WE	9:00A	Arrive Chignik	TH	11:30A
Leave Kodiak	WE	4:55P	Leave Kodiak	WE	4:55P	Leave Chignik	TH	1:00P
Arrive Seward	TH	6:45A	Arrive Seward	TH	6:45A	Arrive Sand Point	TH	10:15P
			Leave Seward	TH	10:45A	Leave Sand Point	FR	12:30A
Leave Seward	TH	5:00P	Arrive Chenega Bay	TH	3:45P	Arrive King Cove	FR	7:00A
Arrive Kodiak	FR	6:15A	Leave Chenega Bay	TH	4:15P	Leave King Cove	FR	8:30A
Leave Kodiak	FR	7:45A	Arrive Valdez	TH	11:00P	Arrive Cold Bay	FR	10:30A
Arrive Homer	FR	5:15P				Leave Cold Bay	FR	11:55A
Leave Homer	FR	6:45P	Leave Valdez	FR	6:00A	Arrive False Pass	FR	4:15P
Arrive Seldovia	FR	8:15P	Arrive Seward	FR	5:00P	Leave False Pass	FR	5:30P
			Leave Seward	FR	9:30P	Arrive Unalaska	SA	6:30A
Leave Seldovia	FR	9:45P	Arrive Kodiak	SA	10:45A			
Arrive Homer	FR	11:15P	Leave Kodiak	SA	12:45P	Leave Unalaska	SA	11:45A
Leave Homer	SA	1:15A	Arrive Port Lions	SA	3:15P	Arrive Akutan	SA	3:15P
Arrive Kodiak	SA	10:45A	Leave Port Lions	SA	3:45P	Leave Akutan	SA	4:00P
			Arrive Homer	SU	1:45A	Arrive Cold Bay	SU	4:00A
Leave Kodiak	SA	12:45P	Leave Homer	SU	3:30A	Leave Cold Bay	SU	4:45A
Arrive Port Lions	SA	3:15P	Arrive Seldovia	SU	5:00A	Arrive King Cove	SU	6:45A
Leave Port Lions	SA	3:45P				Leave King Cove	SU	7:15A
Arrive Homer	SU	1:45A	Leave Seldovia	SU	6:00A	Arrive Sand Point	SU	1:45P
Leave Homer	SU	3:30A	Arrive Homer	SU	7:30A	Leave Sand Point	SU	3:00P
Arrive Seldovia	SU	5:00A	Leave Homer	SU	10:30A	Arrive Chignik	MO	12:15A
			Arrive Kodiak	SU	8:00P	Leave Chignik	MO	1:00A
Leave Seldovia	SU	6:00A				Arrive Kodiak	MO	7:30P
Arrive Homer	SU	7:30A	Leave Kodiak	SU	10:30P	Leave Kodiak	MO	10:30P
Leave Homer	SU	10:30A	Arrive Homer	MO	8:00A	Arrive Homer	TU	8:00A
Arrive Kodiak	SU	8:00P				Leave Homer	TU	10:30A
			Leave Homer	MO	10:30A	Arrive Seldovia	TU	11:55A
Leave Kodiak	SU	10:30P	Arrive Kodiak	MO	8:00P			
Arrive Homer	MO	8:00A						
			Leave Kodiak	MO	10:30P			
Leave Homer	MO	10:30A	Arrive Homer	TU	8:00A			
Arrive Kodiak	MO	8:00P	Leave Homer	TU	10:30A			
			Arrive Seldovia	TU	11:55A			
Leave Kodiak	MO	10:30P				**May 21, 2003 only**		
Arrive Homer	TU	8:00A	==> ==>			Leave Homer	WE	12:30A
Leave Homer	TU	10:30A				Arrive Kodiak	WE	10:00A
Arrive Seldovia	TU	11:55A	* See schedule at right for May 21 variation due to Crab Festival in Kodiak			Leave Kodiak	WE	4:55P

SOUTHCENTRAL/SOUTHWEST ALASKA PASSENGER & VEHICLE RATES

ADULT 12 YEARS AND OLDER (Meals and berth not included)
(Children under 2 travel free. Children 2 through 11 years–1/2 adult price rounded up to nearest dollar.)

BETWEEN AND	Unalaska	Akutan	False Pass	Cold Bay	King Cove	Sand Point	Chignik	Kodiak	Port Lions	Seldovia	Homer	Seward	Chenega Bay	Whittier	Valdez	Tatitlek
Akutan	20															
False Pass	55	39														
Cold Bay	72	59	22													
King Cove	87	79	39	22												
Sand Point	116	106	68	49	37											
Chignik	154	146	107	90	79	49										
Kodiak	237	228	191	172	161	131	90									
Port Lions	237	228	191	172	161	131	90	23								
Seldovia	290	281	245	226	211	184	143	61	61							
Homer	285	278	239	221	207	177	139	57	57	22						
Seward	293	285	247	228	216	188	146	64	64	118	113					
Chenega Bay													68			
Whittier	372	362	324	307	293	266	223	141	141	195	191		68			
Valdez	343	336	298	279	266	237	197	116	116	166	163	68	68	68		
Tatitlek	343	336	298	279	266	237	197	116	116	166	163	68	68	68	36	
Cordova	343	336	298	279	266	237	197	116	116	166	163	68	68	68	36	36

BICYCLES (without trailer)

BETWEEN AND	Unalaska	Akutan	False Pass	Cold Bay	King Cove	Sand Point	Chignik	Kodiak	Port Lions	Seldovia	Homer	Seward	Chenega Bay	Whittier	Valdez	Tatitlek
Akutan	7															
False Pass	12	9														
Cold Bay	14	12	9													
King Cove	16	14	12	7												
Sand Point	19	17	14	11	9											
Chignik	25	19	16	17	15	11										
Kodiak	36	25	19	27	25	21	17									
Port Lions	36	36	25	27	25	21	17	7								
Seldovia	43	36	36	35	33	28	23	13	13							
Homer	42	43	36	34	32	28	23	12	12	6						
Seward	43	42	43	35	33	29	24	13	13	19	18					
Chenega Bay													12			
Whittier	54	43	42	46	43	40	34	23	23	30	29		12			
Valdez	50	50	54	41	40	36	30	19	19	26	26	12	12	9		
Tatitlek	50	50	54	41	40	36	30	19	19	26	26	12	12	9	9	
Cordova	50	50	54	41	40	36	30	19	19	26	26	12	12	9	9	9

KAYAKS AND INFLATABLES

BETWEEN AND	Unalaska	Akutan	False Pass	Cold Bay	King Cove	Sand Point	Chignik	Kodiak	Port Lions	Seldovia	Homer	Seward	Chenega Bay	Whittier	Valdez	Tatitlek
Akutan	11															
False Pass	18	14														
Cold Bay	21	18	14													
King Cove	24	21	18	11												
Sand Point	29	26	21	17	14											
Chignik	38	29	24	26	23	17										
Kodiak	54	38	29	41	38	32	26									
Port Lions	54	54	38	41	38	32	26	11								
Seldovia	65	54	54	53	50	42	35	20	20							
Homer	63	65	54	51	48	42	35	18	18	9						
Seward	65	63	65	53	50	44	36	20	20	29	27					
Chenega Bay													18			
Whittier	81	65	63	69	65	60	51	35	35	45	44		18			
Valdez	75	75	81	62	60	54	45	29	29	39	39	18	18	14		
Tatitlek	75	75	81	62	60	54	45	29	29	39	39	18	18	14	14	
Cordova	75	75	81	62	60	54	45	29	29	39	39	18	18	14	14	14

VEHICLES UP TO 10 FEET (Driver not included)

BETWEEN AND	Unalaska	Akutan	False Pass	Cold Bay	King Cove	Sand Point	Chignik	Kodiak	Port Lions	Seldovia	Homer	Seward	Chenega Bay	Whittier	Valdez	Tatitlek
False Pass	66															
Cold Bay	90	25														
King Cove	106	49	25													
Sand Point	143	84	60	45												
Chignik	194	138	113	97	60											
Kodiak	298	242	217	202	165	113										
Port Lions	298	242	217	202	165	113	27									
Seldovia	365	307	282	267	230	179	75	75								
Homer	358	301	277	261	225	173	69	69	20							
Seward	370	311	287	271	234	182	79	79	146	141						
Chenega Bay													74			
Whittier	466	411	384	370	333	281	177	177	246	239		74				
Valdez	434	375	351	335	298	246	143	143	210	205	74	74	53			
Tatitlek	434	375	351	335	298	246	143	143	210	205	74	74	53	42		
Cordova	434	375	351	335	298	246	143	143	210	205	74	74	53	42	42	

To calculate rates for vehicles 24 to 70 feet, multiply the per foot rate in the chart at right times the number of feet. Round the result up to the nearest dollar.

TARIFFS–One-way fares for passengers, vehicles, bicycles and kayaks are charged from the port of embarkation to the port of debarkation. Cabin fares are calculated according to the route taken, and may vary depending on the ship and schedules.

VEHICLES–Vehicles may be measured at check-in prior to boarding and adjustments will be made to quoted fares based on actual length.

TUSTUMENA–Limited to 40 foot vehicle length

KENNICOTT–Limited to 50 foot behicle length in Southcentral/Southwest ports.

VEHICLES UP TO 15 FEET (Driver not included)

BETWEEN AND	Unalaska	Akutan	False Pass	Cold Bay	King Cove	Sand Point	Chignik	Kodiak	Port Lions	Seldovia	Homer	Seward	Chenega Bay	Whittier	Valdez	Tatitlek
False Pass	112															
Cold Bay	152	41														
King Cove	181	78	37													
Sand Point	243	141	100	72												
Chignik	333	230	189	162	100											
Kodiak	512	411	371	342	280	189										
Port Lions	512	411	371	342	280	189	42									
Seldovia	628	526	485	458	395	306	124	124								
Homer	616	516	476	446	383	294	114	114	32							
Seward	634	532	491	464	402	312	131	131	249	239						
Chenega Bay													120			
Whittier	804	702	662	634	572	481	301	301	419	410		120				
Valdez	744	644	604	574	512	422	243	243	360	350	120	120	78			
Tatitlek	744	644	604	574	512	422	243	243	360	350	120	120	78	69		
Cordova	744	644	604	574	512	422	243	243	360	350	120	120	78	69	69	

VEHICLES UP TO 19 FEET (Driver not included)

BETWEEN AND	Unalaska	Akutan	False Pass	Cold Bay	King Cove	Sand Point	Chignik	Kodiak	Port Lions	Seldovia	Homer	Seward	Chenega Bay	Whittier	Valdez	Tatitlek
False Pass	132															
Cold Bay	181	49														
King Cove	213	93	45													
Sand Point	288	167	118	85												
Chignik	396	275	226	192	118											
Kodiak	610	489	441	408	334	226										
Port Lions	610	489	441	408	334	226	49									
Seldovia	747	627	576	544	469	362	148	148								
Homer	735	613	565	531	458	350	135	135	38							
Seward	755	635	586	552	478	372	155	155	296	284						
Chenega Bay													144			
Whittier	958	837	788	755	680	573	358	358	500	486		144				
Valdez	887	768	718	686	610	503	288	288	429	416	144	144	91			
Tatitlek	887	768	718	686	610	503	288	288	429	416	144	144	91	82		
Cordova	887	768	718	686	610	503	288	288	429	416	144	144	91	82	82	

VEHICLES UP TO 21 FEET (Driver not included)

BETWEEN AND	Unalaska	Akutan	False Pass	Cold Bay	King Cove	Sand Point	Chignik	Kodiak	Port Lions	Seldovia	Homer	Seward	Chenega Bay	Whittier	Valdez	Tatitlek
False Pass	169															
Cold Bay	232	63														
King Cove	275	119	56													
Sand Point	372	215	152	110												
Chignik	509	354	291	248	152											
Kodiak	788	632	569	526	431	291										
Port Lions	788	632	569	526	431	291	63									
Seldovia	965	807	744	702	607	467	189	189								
Homer	948	793	730	687	590	452	174	174	48							
Seward	974	819	756	713	616	478	201	201	381	366						
Chenega Bay													184			
Whittier	1236	1080	1017	974	879	739	462	462	644	628		184				
Valdez	1146	990	927	884	788	649	372	372	552	538	184	184	118			
Tatitlek	1146	990	927	884	788	649	372	372	552	538	184	184	118	104		
Cordova	1146	990	927	884	788	649	372	372	552	538	184	184	118	104	104	

VEHICLES UP TO 23 FEET (Driver not included)

BETWEEN AND	Unalaska	Akutan	False Pass	Cold Bay	King Cove	Sand Point	Chignik	Kodiak	Port Lions	Seldovia	Homer	Seward	Chenega Bay	Whittier	Valdez	Tatitlek
False Pass	213															
Cold Bay	291	79														
King Cove	344	148	70													
Sand Point	464	270	190	137												
Chignik	638	443	363	312	190											
Kodiak	987	791	712	659	539	363										
Port Lions	987	791	712	659	539	363	79									
Seldovia	1208	1011	933	880	760	586	237	237								
Homer	1188	992	912	861	738	565	217	217	59							
Seward	1222	1025	947	894	773	597	250	250	478	459						
Chenega Bay													231			
Whittier	1549	1353	1274	1222	1099	927	579	579	805	785		231				
Valdez	1434	1239	1161	1107	987	812	464	464	693	673	231	231	148			
Tatitlek	1434	1239	1161	1107	987	812	464	464	693	673	231	231	148	130		
Cordova	1434	1239	1161	1107	987	812	464	464	693	673	231	231	148	130	130	

RATE PER FOOT FOR VEHICLES OVER 23 FEET (Driver not included)

BETWEEN AND	Unalaska	Akutan	False Pass	Cold Bay	King Cove	Sand Point	Chignik	Kodiak	Port Lions	Seldovia	Homer	Seward	Chenega Bay	Whittier	Valdez	Tatitlek
False Pass	10.80															
Cold Bay	14.70	4.00														
King Cove	17.40	7.50	3.50													
Sand Point	23.70	13.50	9.70	6.90												
Chignik	32.60	22.50	18.60	15.80	9.70											
Kodiak	50.20	40.20	36.20	33.50	27.40	18.60										
Port Lions	50.20	40.20	36.20	33.50	27.40	18.60	4.00									
Seldovia	61.50	51.50	47.50	44.70	38.60	29.40	12.10	12.10								
Homer	60.50	50.40	46.40	43.70	37.60	28.80	11.00	11.00	2.90							
Seward	62.20	52.10	48.20	45.40	39.30	30.50	12.70	12.70	24.40	23.30						
Chenega Bay													11.30			
Whittier	78.90	68.80	64.90	62.20	56.10	47.10	29.40	29.40	41.10	40.00		11.30				
Valdez	73.10	63.00	59.10	56.40	50.20	41.40	23.60	23.60	35.20	34.20	11.30	11.30	7.20			
Tatitlek	73.10	63.00	59.10	56.40	50.20	41.40	23.60	23.60	35.20	34.20	11.30	11.30	7.20	6.60		
Cordova	73.10	63.00	59.10	56.40	50.20	41.40	23.60	23.60	35.20	34.20	11.30	11.30	7.20	6.60	6.60	

SOUTHCENTRAL/SOUTHWEST ALASKA CABIN RATES

ALASKA STATE FERRY SCHEDULES

FOUR BERTH CABIN–OUTSIDE/COMPLETE FACILITIES
M/V Tustumena, M/V Kennicott

BETWEEN AND	Unalaska	Akutan	False Pass	Cold Bay	King Cove	Sand Point	Chignik	Kodiak	Port Lions	Seldovia	Homer	Seward	Chenega Bay	Whittier	Valdez	Tatitlek
Akutan	27															
False Pass	93	67														
Cold Bay	128	102	35													
King Cove	145	151	85	50												
Sand Point	180	194	127	92	80											
Chignik	229	247	181	147	134	93										
Kodiak	333	348	279	246	229	195	147									
Port Lions	333	348	279	246	229	195	147	50								
Seldovia	396	412	345	311	293	254	215	113	113							
Homer	385	403	335	301	286	246	207	104	104	50						
Seward							229	116	116	193	183					
Chenega Bay												107				
Whittier													107			
Valdez					193	193	254	246	107	107						
Tatitlek													69			
Cordova					193	193	254	246	107	107			69		69	
Yakutat								211			111					

FOUR BERTH CABIN–OUTSIDE/NO FACILITIES
M/V Tustumena

BETWEEN AND	Unalaska	Akutan	False Pass	Cold Bay	King Cove	Sand Point	Chignik	Kodiak	Port Lions	Seldovia	Homer	Seward	Chenega Bay	Whittier	Valdez	Tatitlek
Akutan	22															
False Pass	79	56														
Cold Bay	107	85	30													
King Cove	122	127	72	43												
Sand Point	150	163	107	79	67											
Chignik	192	207	150	122	111	79										
Kodiak	277	290	234	206	192	163	122									
Port Lions	277	290	234	206	192	163	122	43								
Seldovia	332	344	289	258	245	211	180	93	93							
Homer	322	335	279	251	238	206	172	87	87	43						
Seward							192	97	97	161	151					
Chenega Bay												90				
Whittier													90			
Valdez								162	162	211	206	90	90			
Cordova								162	162	211	206	90			58	

TWO BERTH CABIN–OUTSIDE/COMPLETE FACILITIES
M/V Tustumena (Wheelchair only)

BETWEEN AND	Unalaska	Akutan	False Pass	Cold Bay	King Cove	Sand Point	Chignik	Kodiak	Port Lions	Seldovia	Homer	Seward	Chenega Bay	Whittier	Valdez	Tatitlek
Akutan	20															
False Pass	65	46														
Cold Bay	89	69	23													
King Cove	102	107	62	38												
Sand Point	129	137	91	67	56											
Chignik	164	175	129	106	93	65										
Kodiak	228	247	203	177	166	140	102									
Port Lions	228	247	203	177	166	140	102	38								
Seldovia	270	288	242	218	206	175	148	79	79							
Homer	264	279	234	210	197	169	141	74	74	38						
Seward							151	85	85	128	122					
Chenega Bay												79				
Whittier													79			
Valdez								134	134	177	172	79	79			
Tatitlek													54			
Cordova								134	134	177	172	77	79		54	54
Yakutat												152			76	

TWO BERTH CABIN–OUTSIDE/NO FACILITIES
M/V Tustumena, M/V Kennicott

BETWEEN AND	Unalaska	Akutan	False Pass	Cold Bay	King Cove	Sand Point	Chignik	Kodiak	Port Lions	Seldovia	Homer	Seward	Chenega Bay	Whittier	Valdez	Tatitlek
Akutan	16															
False Pass	56	39														
Cold Bay	77	61	21													
King Cove	89	92	54	34												
Sand Point	118	114	76	55	47											
Chignik	151	151	112	92	80	50										
Kodiak	210	227	186	166	152	129	90									
Port Lions	210	227	186	166	152	129	90	34								
Seldovia	251	266	227	207	193	164	135	66	66							
Homer	245	261	221	200	187	161	131	62	62	34						
Seward							140	70	70	120	113					
Chenega Bay												65				
Whittier													65			
Valdez								122	122	170	164	65	65			
Tatitlek															45	
Cordova								122	122	170	164	65	65		45	45
Yakutat												124			65	

FOUR BERTH CABIN–INSIDE/COMPLETE FACILITIES
M/V Kennicott

BETWEEN AND	Unalaska	Akutan	False Pass	Cold Bay	King Cove	Sand Point	Chignik	Kodiak	Port Lions	Seldovia	Homer	Seward	Chenega Bay	Whittier	Valdez	Tatitlek
Seldovia										103						
Homer										88	45					
Seward										97	170	152				
Chenega Bay													90			
Whittier														90		
Valdez										162	226	207	90	90		
Tatitlek															58	
Cordova											226	207	90	90	58	58
Yakutat											175			92		

TWO BERTH ROOMETTE–OUTSIDE/NO FACILITIES
M/V Kennicott

BETWEEN AND	Unalaska	Akutan	False Pass	Cold Bay	King Cove	Sand Point	Chignik	Kodiak	Port Lions	Seldovia	Homer	Seward	Chenega Bay	Whittier	Valdez	Tatitlek
Seldovia										21						
Homer										19	11					
Seward										21	37	33				
Chenega Bay													19			
Whittier														19		
Valdez										35	51	44	19	19		
Tatitlek															13	
Cordova										35	51	44	19	19	13	13
Yakutat											38			20		

TWO BERTH CABIN–INSIDE/NO FACILITIES
M/V Kennicott

BETWEEN AND	Unalaska	Akutan	False Pass	Cold Bay	King Cove	Sand Point	Chignik	Kodiak	Port Lions	Seldovia	Homer	Seward	Chenega Bay	Whittier	Valdez	Tatitlek
Seldovia										59						
Homer										56	30					
Seward										62	107	99				
Chenega Bay													58			
Whittier														58		
Valdez										104	152	133	58	58		
Tatitlek															38	
Cordova										104	152	133	58	58	38	38
Yakutat											111			58		

TWO BERTH ROOMETTE–INSIDE/NO FACILITIES
M/V Kennicott

BETWEEN AND	Unalaska	Akutan	False Pass	Cold Bay	King Cove	Sand Point	Chignik	Kodiak	Port Lions	Seldovia	Homer	Seward	Chenega Bay	Whittier	Valdez	Tatitlek
Seldovia										17						
Homer										16	10					
Seward										18	30	27				
Chenega Bay													17			
Whittier														17		
Valdez										29	43	37	17	17		
Tatitlek															12	
Cordova										29	43	37	17	17	12	12
Yakutat											32			17		

THE STATE OF ALASKA RESERVES THE RIGHT TO ALTER, REVISE OR CANCEL SCHEDULES AND RATES WITHOUT PRIOR NOTICE AND ASSUMES NO RESPONSIBILITY FOR DELAYS AND/OR EXPENSES DUE TO SUCH MODIFICATIONS.

(Continued from page 760) cally announces "car-deck calls.") You may walk your pet at port stops. Keep in mind that some port stops are very brief and that sailing time between some ports will be as long as 36 hours (Bellingham to Ketchikan).

In-port time: In-port time on all vessels is only long enough to unload and load. You may go ashore while the ferry is in port, but you must have your ticket receipt with you to reboard. Keep in mind that ferry terminals are often some distance from city center, and you may not have enough time to see much of anything, depending on how long and at what hour you are in port. You may want to make a "stopover." If you don't have time for a stopover, you still may be able to take a quick tour. In Ketchikan, for example, the city bus stops in front of the ferry terminal and you may be able to hop on the bus, ride it around town, and get back to the terminal in time for your departure.

Ferry terminals in the Southcentral/Southwest system are located within a half-mile of city centers. In Southeast, ferry terminals close to city center include Wrangell and Skagway. Terminals more distant from city center (from nearest to farthest) are: Petersburg (0.9 mile); Ketchikan (2.5 miles); Haines (5 miles); Sitka (7.1 miles); and Juneau (14 miles).

Stopovers: A stopover is getting off at any port between your point of origin and final destination and taking another vessel at a later time. For travelers with vehicles and/or cabins this can be done as long as reservations to do so have been made in advance. Passenger, vehicle and cabin fares are charged on a point-to-point basis, and stopovers will increase the total ticket cost.

NOTE: Check the schedules carefully. Ferries do *NOT* stop at all ports daily, and northbound and southbound routes vary.

INDEX

Abbotsford, BC, 64
Airdrie, AB, 40
Aishihik Road, 168
Akhiok, AK, 644
Aklavik, NT, 731
Alaganik Slough Rec.Area, 642
Alaska Chilkat Bald Eagle
  Preserve, 693, 702
Alaska Highway, 92
Alaska Railroad, 28
Aleneva, AK, 644
Alexis Creek, BC, 73
Alyeska Highway, 511
Anacortes, WA, 61
Anahim Lake, BC, 74
Anchor Point, AK, 603
Anchor River Road, 605
Anchor River SRA, 605
Anchorage, AK, 317
Anderson, AK, 394
Anton Larsen Bay Road, 650
Arctic Circle, 497, 728
Arctic Red River, NT, 729
Ashcroft, BC, 69
Athabasca, AB, 48
Athabasca Route, 48
Atlin, BC, 712
Atlin Road, 711
Auke Bay, AK, 684
Balzac, AB, 40
Barkerville, BC, 81
Bear Lake, BC, 86
Beaver Creek, YT, 182
Beaverlodge, AB, 60
Beiseker, AB, 41
Bella Coola, BC, 75
Bellingham, WA, 64
Bezanson, AB, 57
Big Delta, AK, 464
Big Delta SHP, 205, 465
Big Lake, AK, 370
Big Lake Road, 370
Big Salt Lake Road, 663
Bighorn Route, 213
Bing's Landing SRS, 564
Birch Lake SRS, 466
Bird Creek SRS, 508
Blackstone Territorial Park, 179
Blueberry Lake SRS, 456
Bodenburg Butte, 308
Boston Bar, BC, 67
Boundary, AK, 275
Bowden, AB, 42
Broad Pass, 386
Brule, AB, 213
Buffalo Head Prairie, AB, 739
Burlington, WA, 61
Burns Lake, BC, 221
Burwash Landing, YT, 178
Buskin River SRS, 649
Butte, AK, 308
Cache Creek, BC, 69
Calais, AB, 57
Calgary, AB, 40
Campbell Highway, 715
Canol Road, 720
Cantwell, AK, 387
Canyon City, YT, 148
Canyon Creek, AB, 50
Captain Cook SRA, 589
Carcajou, AB, 739
Carcross, YT, 709
Carcross Desert, 710
Cardston, AB, 36
Carmacks, YT, 257
Carrot Creek, AB, 211
Carstairs, AB, 140

Cassiar, BC, 257
Cassiar Highway, 238
Central, AK, 486
Centreville, BC, 252
Champagne, YT, 167
Charlie Lake, BC, 111
Chatanika, AK, 484
Chena Hot Springs, AK, 447
Chena Hot Springs Road, 446
Chena Lake Rec. Area, 469
Chena River SRA, 446
Chetwynd, BC, 88
Chickaloon, AK, 303
Chicken, AK, 278
Chilcotin Highway, 73
Childs Glacier Rec. Area, 643
Chilkat SP, 694
Chilkoot Lake SRS, 694
Chilkoot Trail, 697
Chilliwak, BC, 65
Chiniak Road, 649
Chistochina, AK, 290
Chitina, AK, 472
Chugach SP, 354
Chugiak, AK, 315
Ciechanski SRS, 590
Circle, AK, 487
Circle Hot Springs, AK, 487
Circle Hot Springs Road, 487
Clam Gulch, AK, 595
Clam Gulch SRA, 595
Claresholm, AB, 39
Clearwater SRS, 201
Clinton, BC, 70
Coal River, BC, 130
Coalhurst, AB, 38
Coffman Cove, AK, 662
Cohoe, AK, 594
Cohoe Loop Road, 594
Coldfoot, AK, 498
Columbia Glacier, 626
Conrad, MT, 33
Contact Creek, BC, 131
Cooper Landing, AK, 556
Cooper Landing SRS, 555
Copper Center, AK, 458
Copper Center Loop, 458
Copper River Highway, 642
Cordova, AK, 638
Coutts, AB, 36
Craig, AK, 663
Craig-Klawock-Hollis
  Highway, 662
Crooked Creek, AB, 57
Crooked Creek SRS, 594
Crossfield, AB, 40
Crow Creek Mine NHS, 511
Dalton Cache, 704
Dalton Highway, 493
Davidson Ditch Historical
  Site, 485
Dawson City, YT, 266
Dawson Creek, BC, 100
Deadhorse, AK, 501
Dease Lake, BC, 247
DeBolt, AB, 57
Decker Lake, BC, 221
Deep Creek SRA, 601
Delta Junction, AK, 201, 464
Demmitt, AB, 60
Dempster Highway, 724
Denali Highway, 477
Denali NP, 399
Denali SP, 384
Destruction Bay, YT, 177
Devon, AB, 44
Devonian Way Bypass, 43

Discovery Claim, 265
Dixonville, AB, 739
Donnelly, AB, 52
Donnelly Creek SRS, 463
Dot Lake, AK, 200
Douglas, AK, 680
Douglas Island, 680
Drumheller, AB, 41
Dry Creek SRS, 291, 459
Dyea Road, 698
Eagle, AK, 282
Eagle Plains, YT, 727
Eagle River, AK, 315
Eagle River Road, 314
Eagle Trail SRS, 287
Eagle Village, AK 283
Eaglesham, AB, 52
Edgerton Highway, 470
Edmonds, WA, 61
Edmonton, AB, 44, 206
Edson, AB, 211
Eielson AFB, AK, 425, 466
83 Mile House, BC, 71
Eklutna, AK, 313
Eklutna Lake SRA, 313
Elliott Highway, 488
Elmendorf AFB, AK, 316
Elsa, YT, 263
Emerald Lake, 710
Endako, BC, 221
Enilda, AB, 51
Enterprise, NT, 741
Entrance, AB, 213
Entwistle, AB, 211
Ester, AK, 397
Everett, WA, 61
Exit Glacier Road, 528
Fairbanks, AK, 418
Falher, AB, 52
Fallis, AB, 211
Faro, YT, 718
Faust, AB, 51
Finger Lake SRS, 311, 362
Fireside, BC, 130
Fort Abercrombie SHP, 648
Fort Egbert, AK, 283
Fort Fraser, BC, 219
Fort Greely, AK, 463
Fort Liard, NT, 734
Fort MacLeod, AB, 38
Fort Mcleod, BC, 87
Fort McPherson, NT, 728
Fort Nelson, BC, 116
Fort Providence, NT, 745
Fort Resolution, NT, 748
Fort Resolution Highway, 748
Fort Richardson, AK, 316
Fort St. James, BC, 220
Fort St. James National
  Historic Site, 220
Fort St. John, BC, 108
Fort Simpson, NT, 742
Fort Selkirk, YT, 259
Fort Smith, NT, 748
Fort Smith Highway, 747
Fort Vermilion, AB, 740
Fox, AK, 484, 488
Fox Creek, AB, 55
Fraser, BC, 708
Fraser Lake, BC, 220
Funny River Road, 581
Funny River SRS, 581
Gainford, AB, 211
Gakona, AK, 290
Gakona Junction, AK, 291, 460
Galbraith Camp, AK, 500
Girdwood, AK, 511

Girouxville, AB, 52
Gitanyow, BC, 240
Gitwangak, BC, 229, 238
Glacier Bay NP, 686
Glenn Highway, 284
Glennallen, AK, 292, 459
Good Hope Lake, BC, 252
Grande Cache, AB 214
Grande Prairie, AB, 58
Granisle, BC, 222
Granum, AB, 39
Great Falls, MT, 33
Grimshaw, AB, 736
Grouard, AB, 51
Gulkana, AK, 291, 460
Gustavus, AK, 687
Hagensborg, BC, 75
Haines, AK, 688
Haines Highway, 702
Haines Junction, YT, 169
Halibut Cove, AK, 623
Halibut Point Road, 675
Harding Lake SRA, 466
Hat Creek Heritage Ranch, 70
Hatcher Pass Road, 305
Hay River, NT, 744
Hay River Highway, 744
Hazelton, BC, 228
Head-Smashed-In Buffalo
  Jump, 39
Healy, AK, 392
Hells Gate, BC, 67
Herman Leirer Road, 528
High Level, AB, 740
High Prairie, AB, 51
High River, AB, 40
Highway 26, 81
Hinton, AB, 212
Hixon, BC, 81
Hollis, AK, 662
Holman, NT, 731
Homer, AK, 607
Hope, AK, 523
Hope, BC, 66
Hope Highway, 521
Hotchkiss, AB, 739
Houston, AK, 371
Houston, BC, 222
Hudson's Hope, BC, 90
Hudson's Hope Loop, 90
Hydaburg, AK, 663
Hyder, AK, 242
Hythe, AB, 60
Independence Mine SHP, 306
Indian, AK, 508
Indian Cabins, AB, 741
Ingraham Trail, 747
Innisfail, AB, 42
Inuvik, NT, 729
Iskut, BC, 246
Island Lake, AB, 49
Izaak Walton SRS, 565
Jade City, BC, 251
Jake's Corner, YT, 146
Jasper, AB, 215
Jasper NP, 213
Jean Marie River, NT, 742
Johnson's Crossing, YT, 145
Johnson Lake SRA, 594
Joussard, AB, 51
Juneau, AK, 676
Juneau Veteran's Memorial
  Highway, 684
Kachemak Bay State Park, 620
Kalifornsky Beach Road, 590
Kantishna, AK, 417
Karluk, AK, 644

INDEX

Kasaan, AK, 664
Kasilof, AK, 591
Kasilof River SRS, 593
Keg River, AB, 739
Kenai, AK, 582
Kenai Fjords NP, 548
Kenai NWR, 562
Kenai River, 562, 571
Kenai Spur Highway, 582
Kennicott, AK, 474
Kenny Lake, AK, 470
Keno City, YT, 263
Kepler–Bradley Lakes SRA, 312
Ketchikan, AK, 652
King Mountain SRS, 304
Kinuso, AB, 51
Kispiox, BC, 228
Kitimat, BC, 229
Kitseguecla, BC, 229
Kitsumkalum, BC, 231
Kitwanga, BC, 240
Klawock, AK, 664
Klondike Gold Rush NP, 697
Klondike Highway, 253
Kluane NP, YT, 172
Klukshu, YT, 705
Klukwan, AK, 704
Knik, AK, 366
Knik-Goose Bay Road, AK, 366
Kodiak, AK, 644
Kodiak NWR, 648
Ksan Historical Village, 228
La Conner, WA, 61
La Crete, AB, 739
Lac La Hache, BC, 72
Lacombe, AB, 42
Lake Forest Park, WA, 61
Lake Louise Road, 297
Lake Louise SRA, 297
Larsen Bay, AK, 644
Lazy Mountain Rec. Area, 308
Leduc, AB, 43
Lethbridge, AB, 36
Liard Highway, 732
Liard River, BC, 129
Liard River Hotsprings Provincial Park, 129
Liberty Falls SRS, 472
Likely, BC, 72
Lillooet, BC, 70
Little Nelchina SRS, 298
Little Smoky, AB, 55
Little Tonsina River SRS, 457
Livengood, AK, 491
Log Cabin, BC, 708
Long Lake SRS, 303
Lower Chatanika River SRA, 488
Lower Troublesome Creek SRS, 385
Lytton, BC, 68
Mackenzie, BC, 87
Mackenzie Route, BC, 736
Mackenzie Highway, 736
Manley Hot Springs, AK, 492
Manning, AB, 739
Marysville, WA, 61
Matanuska Glacier, 302
Matanuska Glacier SRS, 302
Mayerthorpe, AB, 53
Mayo, YT, 262
McBride, BC, 217
McCarthy, AK, 474
McCarthy Road, 470
McKinley Park, AK, 390
McLeese Lake, BC, 77
McLennan, AB, 51
McLeod Lake, BC, 87
Meander River, AB, 740
Mendeltna, AK, 298
Mendenhall Glacier, 682
Mentasta Lake, AK, 287
Metlakatla, AK, 656
Miles Canyon, 148
Milk River, AB, 36
Million Dollar Bridge, 643
Minto, AK, 491
Minto, YT, 259
Misty Fiords NM, 657
Mitkof Highway, 672
Moberly Lake, BC, 90
Montana Creek, AK, 374
Moon Lake SRS, 199
Moose Pass, AK, 525
Morgan's Landing SRA, 567
Moricetown, BC, 226
Mosquito Lake SRS, 704
Mount McKinley, 399
Mount Vernon, WA, 61
Muncho Lake, BC, 125
Muskeg River, AB, 213
Nabesna, AK, 288
Nabesna Road, 288
Nahanni Butte, NT, 735
Nahanni NP, 743
Nahanni Range Road, 715
Nancy Lake SRA, 371
Nanton, AB, 39
Naukati, AK, 665
Nelchina, AK, 298
Nenana, AK, 395
New Hazelton, BC, 226
Nikiski, AK, 588
Nimpo Lake, BC, 74
Ninilchik, AK, 596
Ninilchik SRA, 596
Ninilchik Village, AK, 596
Niton Junction, AB, 211
Nojack, AB, 211
Nolan, AK, 499
North Canol Road, 722
North Island Road, 665
North Pole, AK, 467
North Star, AB, 739
North Tongass Highway, 658
Northway, AK, 187
Okotoks, AB, 40
Old Crow, NT, 731
Old Glenn Highway, 308
Old Harbor, AK, 644
Olds, AB, 40
100 Mile House, BC, 71
108 Heritage Site, 71
150 Mile House, BC, 72
Onoway, AB, 47
Ouzinkie, AK, 644
Paddle Prairie, AB, 739
Palmer, AK, 309
Palmer–Wasilla Highway, 311, 362
Parks Highway, 357
Pasagshak Bay Road, 650
Pasagshak River SRS, 650
Paulatuk, NT, 731
Paxson, AK, 461, 477
Pelly Crossing, YT, 259
Peters Creek, AK, 314
Petersburg, AK, 669
Petersville Road, 383
Pine Point, NT, 748
Pink Mountain, BC, 113
Pioneer Park, 442
Pleasant Camp, BC, 704
Pocahontas, AB, 213
Ponoka, AB, 42
Porcupine Creek SRS, 287
Port Alcan, AK, 184
Port Edward, BC, 232
Port Lions, AK, 644
Portage, AK, 515
Portage Glacier Road, 517
Pouce Coupe, BC, 60
Prince George, BC, 82
Prince of Wales Island, AK, 659
Prince Rupert, BC, 232
Prince William Sound, 626
Prophet River, BC, 115
Prudhoe Bay, AK, 501
Quartz Creek Recreation Area, 553
Quartz Creek Road, 553
Quartz Lake SRA, 465
Quesnel, BC, 78
Rae–Edzo, NT, 746
Rainbow Lake, 710
Rainbow Lake, AB, 740
Red Deer, AB, 42
Rezanof–Monashka Road, 648
Richardson Highway, 452
Rika's Roadhouse SHP, 465
Rochfort Bridge, AB, 53
Rocky Lake SRS, 370
Ross River, YT, 717
Rycroft, AB, 52
Sachs Harbour, NT, 731
Salcha, AK, 466
Salcha River SRS, 466
Salt River, NT, 748
Sangudo, AB, 47
Saxman, AK, 657
Scout Lake SRS, 567
Seattle, WA, 61
Seldovia, AK, 624
70 Mile House, BC, 71
Seward, AK, 531
Seward Highway, 504
Sheep Mountain, YT, 176
Sheep Mountain, AK, 300
Shelby, MT, 33
Shuyak Island SP, 648
Sikanni Chief, BC, 114
Silver Trail, 261
Sitka, AK, 673
Sitka National Historic Park, 674
Skagway, AK, 695
Skilak Lake Loop Road, 563
Slana, AK, 288
Slave Lake, AB, 50
Smith, AB, 49
Smithers, BC, 224
Soda Creek, BC, 77
Soldotna, AK, 569
South Canol Road, 720
South Hazelton, BC, 228
South Klondike Highway, 706
South Tongass Highway, 657
Southeastern Alaska, 651
Spences Bridge, BC, 69
Spirit River, AB, 52
Spruce Grove, AB, 47, 206
Squirrel Creek SRS, 457
St. Albert, AB, 48
Stariski SRS, 602
Steamboat, BC, 122
Steen River, AB, 741
Steese Highway, 482
Sterling, AK, 564
Sterling Highway, 550
Stewart, BC, 242
Stewart Crossing, YT, 260
Stewart, BC–Hyder, AK Access Road, 242
Stone Mountain Provincial Park, 122
Stony Plain, AB, 47, 211
Sumas, WA, 64
Summit Lake, AK, 461
Summit Lake, BC, 123
Summit Lake SRS, 306
Sunburst, AB, 36
Sutton, AK, 304
Swanson River Road, 567
Sweetgrass, MT, 36
Swift River, YT, 141
Tagish, YT, 714
Tagish Post, YT, 714
Tagish Road, 714
Takhini Hot Springs, 255
Talkeetna, AK, 376
Talkeetna Spur Road, 375
Tanacross, AK, 199
Taylor, BC, 107
Taylor Highway, 276
Telegraph Creek, BC, 249
Telegraph Creek Road, 248
Telkwa, BC, 223
Terrace, BC, 230
Teslin, YT, 142
Tete Jaune Cache, BC, 216
Tetlin NWR, 184
Thorne Bay, AK, 664
Thorne Bay Road, 664
Toad River, BC, 124
Tok, AK, 189
Tok Cutoff, 284
Tok River SRS, 188
Tolsona, AK, 296
Tomslake, BC, 60
Top of the World Hwy., 274
Topley, BC, 222
Totem Bight SHP, 657, 658
Tracy Arm, AK, 683
Trapper Creek, AK, 382
Trout Lake, NT, 742
Tsiigehtchic, NT, 729
Tuktoyaktuk, NT, 731
Tumbler Ridge, BC, 89
Tungsten, NT, 717
Tupper, BC, 60
Turnagain Pass Rec. Area, 516
Two Rivers, AK, 446
Upper Chatanika River SRA, 485
Upper Liard Village, YT, 138
Usk, BC, 229
Valdez, AK, 627
Valemount, BC, 216
Valleyview, AB, 56
Vanderhoof, BC, 219
Wabamun, AB, 211
Wanham, AB, 52
Ward Cove, AK, 658
Warner, AB, 36
Wasilla, AK, 363
Waterton Lakes NP, 36
Watson Lake, YT, 133
Wells, BC, 81
Wembley, AB, 60
Wetaskiwin, AB, 42
Whale Pass, AK, 665
White Mountains NRA, 485
White Pass & Yukon Route, 29
Whitecourt, AB, 53
Whitehorse, YT, 151
Whittier, AK, 518
Whittier Access Road, 517
Widewater, AB, 50
Wildwood, AB, 211
Williams Lake, BC, 76
Willow, AK, 372
Willow Creek SRA, 372
Wiseman, AK, 499
Wonowon, BC, 113
Wood Buffalo NP, 747
Worthington Glacier SRS, 456
Wrangell, AK, 666
Wrangell-St. Elias NP, 475
Wrigley, NT, 744
Yale, BC, 66
Yellowhead Highway 206
Yellowknife, NT, 746
Yellowknife Highway, 745
Yukon-Charley Rivers NP, 283
Yukon River Bridge, 496
Zama, AB, 740
Zimovia Highway, 668